VISITING

South

WORLDWIDE.

<u>READ THIS!</u>
The advice below is designed to help you if you are travelling to South Asia.

The US Dollar is the principally accepted foreign currency.
Other currencies will offer you less attractive exchange rates and may
not even be accepted in certain places.
Be smart. Shop around for rates. Hotel exchange rates, for example,
may offer better than official rates, but they are rarely the best.
Only certain Bank branches are authorised to deal in foreign exchange;
so do take a supply of local currency when travelling outside large cities.
In some countries it is necessary to have an encashment certificate
for reconversion of unspent local currency at the time of
departure from the country.
Take the bulk of your money in Thomas Cook US Dollar travellers cheques;
you will find them convenient, safe and easy to use. With Thomas Cook
travellers cheques, you are carrying with you over a century of experience
and reliable service. Plus, you have the confidence of knowing that our
travellers cheques are fully backed by the MasterCard® and euro travellers
cheque International organisations. If your travellers cheques are lost,
stolen or destroyed, we have an extensive network of refund locations
worldwide to ensure that your problem will be resolved quickly.
So, insist on Thomas Cook travellers cheques today!

*See the lists at the end of this book
for Refund locations.*

**Thomas
Cook**

1992 SOUTH ASIAN HANDBOOK

Editor
Robert Bradnock

Associate Editors
William Whittaker, Roma Bradnock
Cartographer
Sebastian Ballard

"Send thy welcome signal across the dark,
O Rising Sun!
Open the golden gate at the ancient shrine of the East,
where dwells the spirit of Man,
Great as the grass that blesses the lowly dust,
meek as the mountain under the stars."

Rabindranath Tagore 'A Weary Pilgrim'

TRADE & TRAVEL PUBLICATIONS

TRADE & TRAVEL PUBLICATIONS LTD
6 RIVERSIDE COURT
RIVERSIDE ROAD
BATH BA2 3DZ
ENGLAND
TEL 0225 469141
FAX 0225 462921

©Trade & Travel Publications Ltd., 1991

ISBN 0 900751 36 3

CIP DATA: A catalogue record for this book is available from the British Library

Published in the United States of America and Canada by
Prentice Hall Travel
A division of Simon & Schuster Inc.
15 Columbus Circle
New York, NY 10023-7780

In North America, ISBN 0-13-457359-5

The Bengal Tiger

Once hunted for sport and for its fur, particularly during the last two centuries, the Bengal tiger (once named 'Royal' by the British) is now protected all across the region. Less than 2,000 remain in India and about 600 in Nepal, Bhutan, and Bangladesh. The conservation programme 'Project Tiger' was initiated in India in 1973.

The majestic animal with its warm tan coat and narrow, almost black stripes, has whitish underparts, insides of legs, cheeks and spots over each eye. The male tiger, about 1 m high at the shoulder and 3 m long, nose to tail, often weighs over 200 kg. More powerful than a lion, it hunts by night, lying in wait at a water hole or at the end of a jungle trail, and then attacks by leaping on its prey. Only when injured, old or sick may a tiger turn into a 'man-eater'.

The Taj Mahal

To the Nobel prize winning Indian poet, Rabindranath Tagore the Taj Mahal was 'a tear on the face of eternity', a building to echo the cry, 'I have not forgotton, O beloved'. An enduring monument to love, with a continually fulfilling beauty, it was built by the Mughal Emperor **Shah Jahan** between 1631-52, as a tomb and memorial for his wife **Mumtaz Mahal** (Jewel of the Palace).

Cover illustration by Jeremy Pyke
Printed and bound in Great Britain by Clays Ltd., Bungay, Suffolk.

CONTENTS

NEPAL   1265

BHUTAN   1344

BANGLADESH   1355

SRI LANKA   1399

MALDIVES   1463

PREFACE

India and its neighbours in South Asia have long been a favourite destination for travellers. For a region that is less than half the size of the United States, it is astonishingly varied. Its cultural life has developed with remarkable strands of continuity over at least 10,000 years, yet visitors are continuously struck by its extremes and its contrasts. South Asian landscapes include the world's most recently formed, and still rising mountains, the Himalayas, as well as the most ancient of the world's rocks in the Peninsula. It has the wettest places on earth and some of the hottest deserts, and stretches from the permanent snows of the Himalayas and Karakoram to the tropical rainforest of Kerala and Sri Lanka. Great wealth and extreme poverty exist side by side.

Despite the physical contrasts within the region, and the political developments that have seen the formation of seven independent states in the last fifty years, geographically, culturally and socially South Asia still forms a remarkably integrated region. Thus, for example, it is impossible to understand northern India without knowing something of Islam. At the same time Islam in Bangladesh has been strongly affected by Hindu social customs. While Buddhism has been reduced to a tiny minority religion in its homeland, India, it plays an important part in the life of both Nepal and Sri Lanka. Constant population movement over millenia has ensured a physical as well as a cultural mixing. Art, architecture, music, language – common roots lie underneath many regional variations, often crossing modern national frontiers.

Such interweaving adds to South Asia's interest, but also makes it difficult for many visitors from outside to come to terms with and understand its complexity. Furthermore, today it is not always easy to go from one South Asian country to another. However, this Handbook tries to provide the practical information and the description of places and peoples which will make it easier to travel enjoyably and intelligently. It is intended above all as a practical guide. The information is updated every year with the most recent official information supplemented by reports from travellers. Like the other titles in the series, it is travellers who provide the most important material – facts, comments, advice – which will provide an essential element in the annual revision.

Samuel Johnson said that "in travelling, a man must carry knowledge with him if he would bring home knowledge". We hope that this Handbook will help to increase both knowledge and understanding by providing reliable and authoritative information for people with independent minds who want to travel in their own way and form their own judgements. We would be delighted to hear from you if you have any comments, suggestions, or information to include for next year's edition.

The Editor

ACKNOWLEDGEMENTS

Original text for this Handbook was written by: East India, South India, Pakistan (Punjab, Sind, Baluchistan), Bangladesh, Sri Lanka and the Maldives – Robert Bradnock; North India, West India, Nepal, Sikkim and Bhutan – William Whittaker; The North West and Northern Areas of Pakistan – Ivan Mannheim.

This book is the result of many years spent living, working and travelling in South Asia. It could not have been written without the help of many more people than can be acknowledged by name.

In particular I must thank the many friends who provided much generous hospitality as well as practical help with the book: Kanwal and G.B. Singh in Delhi, Romola Banerjee in Calcutta, and Mandira and Akkhoy Mukherjee and their family in Madras. Paul and Donna Wiebe added to years of friendship with further hospitality and comment while this book has been in preparation. In Pakistan Dr. Gul Mohammad of Islamabad and Dr. M.K. Malik of Bahawalpur have shared their knowledge and experience of Pakistan over many years. Dr. Gul gave invaluable guidance in Islamabad and the North West Frontier, and Dr. Malik in Punjab, while in Sri Lanka Chandra Schaffter has repeatedly been a source of help and advice. Dr. F.R.M. Hasan helped me to explore southern Bangladesh, and Professor Aminul Islam taught me much about Bangladesh.

Inevitably proof reading and advising on such a large text has been a huge task. I am deeply grateful to John Marr and Kasturi Gupta Menon, who commented on much of the text, and to Rachel and Michael Dwyer, who paid particular attention to the West India section. Binna Gupta Kapur, Sanjib Basu, Kanwal Singh and Keith Wiebe made some very helpful comments at various stages of writing. Simon Wilson also contributed valuable material from South India.

I am also extremely grateful to Dr. S. Dandapani of SDEL Ltd, Wembley, who proof read the railway timetable information, and made valuable suggestions from his own wealth of practical knowledge.

The help given by official bodies in South Asia is often extremely generous. The Indian Tourist Development Corporation offered very generous assistance and advice, and accommodation in Kerala and Orissa. I am grateful to Mrs. Chandini Luthra who facilitated arrangements.

This handbook could not have been completed in time if William Whittaker had not written the original material for North India, West India, Nepal, and Bhutan. His long experience of leading treks to various parts of the Himalayas and of research in North India made him ideally qualified. He particularly wants to thank Helen Sayer for compiling rail information, Cat McBean for compiling practical information on the major centres of North and West India, and J.C. Pandey for assistance on Nainital and the UP Hill region. His thanks also go to Kerry Lee Howell for reports from various parts of India, to Kristal Prestidge for assistance on ordering material on Maharashtra and to Christina Rush for similar on Goa. In Nepal he received help from Cat McBean, compiling practical information on the country introduction and Kathmandu, and from Stan Walker on the Annapurna region. William Whittaker also received help from Michael Edgington of the Department of Conservation, NZ Government, for help with the Bhutan section.

As Editor I am also indebted to Ivan Mannheim, who wrote on Pakistan's North West Frontier and Northern Areas, to Dr. David Snashall for his authoritative piece on health for travellers in South Asia and to Janet Krengal of Lloyds Bank for the table of economic indicators.

Computer technology offers exciting new possibilities in map design. The outstanding cartographic work of Sebastian Ballard in applying that technology speaks for itself. He has created a remarkable collection of maps, whose unique clarity should prove immensely valuable.

No Handbook such as this could be produced except through work as a team. The concept of the South Asian Handbook originated with Trade and Travel, and working with James, Patrick and Rosemary Dawson has been a tremendous pleasure. Debbie Wylde helped enormously by compiling the railway timetable for East and South India, as well as much of the airline and foreign representation information.

Finally, I owe the greatest debt to my family. Catherine Lewis helped in the preparation of a number of maps. She and Nicola Lewis who helped enormously with the typing, and Clare and Helen Bradnock, all contributed directly, and put up with the pressures of meeting deadlines. However, the Handbook would not have been completed without the tremendous work and support of my wife Roma, and her advice and help has been invaluable.

We would like to acknowledge the written contributions of a number of travellers, over the last year and thank them for the interest they have taken.

From England: Kalpana Basu, Woburn Green; Hilary Bowker, Hughenden; Anne Bowyer, Kingston upon Thames; Julie Brooks, Prestwood; Suzanna Chambers, Wimborne; Madeleine Durie, Richmond; Michael, Anne, Katherine, Sian and Jonathan Floyd, Jordans; Mark and Ros Flinn, Seer Green; Tracey German, Great Missenden; Henry and Joanna Greenfield, Little Kingshill; Dr. Robin Holmes, Brentwood; Catherine Lewis, Prestwood; Dr. Christopher Mitchell, Hampshire, England; David Kerr, Great Missenden; Tom Killick, London; Liz McGill, High Wycombe; Jim and Margaret Osbond, Prestwood; Sara Perraton, Devon; Andy Perrett, Great Missenden; Michael Reupke, Stokenchurch.

From India: S.D. Ahuja, Sanjib Basu, Prosenjit Das Gupta and Kasturi Gupta Menon from Calcutta, Mandira Mukerjee, Madras and Simon Wilson, Ooty; Emma Ko, Hong Kong; Keith Wiebe, Madison USA. I am also very grateful to Shahnaz Hussain for enlisting the help of a number of students in Bangladesh.

Copyright citations

Dear Editor

WILL YOU HELP US?

We do all we can to get our facts right in **THE SOUTH ASIAN HANDBOOK.** Each section is thoroughly revised each year, but the territory covered is vast and our eyes cannot be everywhere.

Your information may be more up to date than ours and if you have enjoyed a tour, trek, train trip, beach, museum, temple, fort or any other activity and would like others to share it, please write with the details. We are always pleased to hear about any restaurants, bars or hotels you have enjoyed.

When writing, it will be very helpful if you can give the year on the cover of your Handbook and the page number referred to.

If your letter reaches us early enough in the year, it will be used in the next annual edition, but write whenever you want to, for all your information will be used.

Thank you very much indeed for your help.

Write to: The Editor,
South Asian Handbook
Trade & Travel Publications
6 Riverside Court, Lower Bristol Road,
Bath BA2 3DZ. England

HOW TO USE THIS HANDBOOK

The South Asian Handbook is a unique source of information for independent travellers to the 7 countries of South Asia: India, Pakistan, Nepal, Bangladesh, Bhutan, Sri Lanka and the Maldives. The text will be throughly revised every year: a new edition which will be published annually on 1 September. It is based on extensive personal travel, information from official tourist authorities, notes from correspondents and visitors and the wide range of statistical and other material available in South Asia and Europe.

Editorial logic The countries of South Asia share a great deal of common geography and history. The Handbook therefore starts with practical advice on travel and health, and an introduction to the land and people of the region as a whole. Thereafter the handbook is organised on a national and regional basis. India and Pakistan are divided into major regions, the other countries are treated as single units. The capital city or regional centre is the first place covered. The places of interest are then described as they lie along major routes radiating from the regional centre, which are described in clockwise order, starting with routes running north. The routes link the most interesting places and are not necessarily the shortest.

Air, rail and road are all widely used means of travel in many parts of South Asia. The routes described are by road. While rail still offers a unique experience, and is often an excellent way of travelling long distances, buses now reach virtually every part of the sub-continent, offering a cheap, if often uncomfortable, means of visiting places off the rail network. It is also possible to hire cars in many places, though self drive is still difficult and in many areas not advised. None the less, road is the best choice for visiting many of the places of outstanding interest in which South Asia is so rich. Supplementary information with respect to rail and air travel for major towns is provided.

Cross referencing, indexing and glossaries There is a complete index of place names at the end of the book. This is supplemented by separate indexes for categories such as Names, Historical sites, Nature and Culture. Entries are extensively cross-referenced. For ease of use the "see page" entry has been highlighted in heavier type. On the page referred to you will find the entry again emphasised in some form of heavier type. In addition, there are 3 glossaries listing General terms, Architectural terms and Names.

Maps Good maps and reliable street plans are often very hard to find in South Asia. This Handbook has drawn on extensive field visits and a wide range of authoritative sources to compile a series of original maps, all drawn with the most up to date information available.

A. Relief maps The Bartholomew maps in the centre pages are the most authoritative and clearest small scale maps of South Asia published. In addition to the main physical features of South Asia they show the major surface transport networks and a wide range of towns and cities.

B. Regional maps Each of the major regions is introduced by a detailed map,

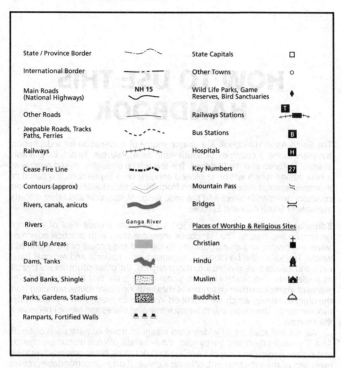

State / Province Border		State Capitals	□
International Border		Other Towns	o
Main Roads (National Highways)	NH 15	Wild Life Parks, Game Reserves, Bird Sanctuaries	♦
Other Roads		Railways Stations	T
Jeepable Roads, Tracks Paths, Ferries		Bus Stations	B
Railways		Hospitals	H
Cease Fire Line		Key Numbers	27
Contours (approx)		Mountain Pass	⤳
Rivers, canals, anicuts		Bridges	⤨
Rivers	Ganga River	Places of Worship & Religious Sites	
Built Up Areas		Christian	†
Dams, Tanks		Hindu	🛕
Sand Banks, Shingle		Muslim	🕌
Parks, Gardens, Stadiums		Buddhist	⌂
Ramparts, Fortified Walls			

showing all the places of interest referred to in the text.

C. Town plans Detailed maps of town centres and site plans of many places of interest, with numbered keys.

Introduction and Hints This first section gives information which applies to all the countries of the region

- travel to and in South Asia
- money
- law enforcement
- security
- travelling with children
- Accommodation including camping
- language
- photography
- surface transport
- travelling by train and air
- Hitch-hiking
- motor and motor-cycling
- cycling
- what to take

Health information This section has been written specially by Dr. David Snashall of St. Thomas' Hospital Medical School, London, and Chief Adivsor on Health to the the British Foreign and Commonwealth Office. It gives details of the health risks common in South Asia, and the sensible precautions travellers should take to combat them.

Climatic Charts are provided for regions and the main towns, showing rainfall and temperatures. Months are shaded to indicate the best time for a visit.

Country sections India is divided into four regions, North, East, South and West. Pakistan is divided into four Provinces and the Northern Areas. The other countries are treated as single regions. Information is set out in a constant sequence as follows:

- List of contents
- Introduction: Geography

Climate	People and Language
Economy	Handicrafts
Religion	Art and Architecture
Music and dance	Cuisine
History	

- Description of the national or regional capital city:

Introduction	places of interest
hotels and restaurants	services for visitors
travel information	

- Excursions close to cities
- Routes covering states or regions
- Information for Visitors

  Documents
  Travel, including customs, arrival and departure regulations

Internal travel	Money
Other essential information	National holidays and festivals

Hotels and restaurants Throughout the Handbook an attempt is made to keep the information on hotels and restaurants up to date and acurate both in terms of prices and comments. While much greater emphasis is placed on positive recommendations, where appropriate unfavourable coments are also reported.

Prices The hotel price ranges are for the best quality double rooms available, exclusive of local taxes. are as follows:

AL—Over US$90	**A**—US$60-90	**B**—US$45-60
C—US$25-45	**D**—US$10-25	**E**—US$3-10
F—up to US$3		

Details of facilities offered in each category are given on **page 13**. Local prices are given in the relevant country sections under **Information for Visitors**.

Other abbreviations used in the book (a/c = air conditioned; T = telephone; nr =near; opp = opposite; under Hotels bath = WC, shower or bath) should be self-explanatory.

Maps: Publisher's note: The Government of India state that "The external boundaries of India are neither correct nor authenticated". Neither the coloured nor the black and white text maps are intended to have any political significance.

WARNING: Whilst every endeavour is made to ensure that the facts printed in this book are correct at the time of going to press, travellers are cautioned to obtain authoritative advice from consulates, airlines, etc. concerning current travel and visa requirements and conditions before embarkation. The publishers cannot accept legal responsibility for errors, however caused, which are printed in this book.

INTRODUCTION AND HINTS

TRAVEL TO AND WITHIN SOUTH ASIA

By air It is possible to fly direct to several South Asian destinations from Europe and Australasia, and via Europe from the United States, as well as from East Africa, the Gulf and from South East Asia and Japan. The major destinations are New Delhi and Bombay in India, Karachi in Pakistan, Dhaka in Bangladesh and Colombo in Sri Lanka. Several airlines offer non-stop flights from European cities. The scheduled flying time from London to Delhi or Bombay is 9 hr on direct flights, but may be up to 15 hours on flights with more than one stop. Overbooking on some flights to South Asia can be a problem, especially during the peak season of November to March. It is always best to confirm your ticket 24 hours before departure and to check in early. Onward reservations should be reconfirmed at every stage. Within South Asia there is a wide range of flight connections on internal airlines.

Discounts It is possible to obtain significant discounts, especially from Apr-Jun, from some European and American cities, most notably London, even on non-stop flights. It is therefore well worth shopping around, and booking as early as possible. It is also possible to get discounts from Australasia, SE Asia and Japan. Mid-July to mid-August is the peak season and most expensive.

Non-stop flights to Delhi from London are currently offered by Air India, British Airways, and Thai International. Air India and British Airways fly non-stop to Bombay. The cheapest tickets can still usually be obtained on Middle Eastern airlines. PIA and British Airways fly direct to Karachi; Bangladesh Biman and British Airways fly direct to Dhaka; Air Lanka and British Airways fly direct to Colombo; Royal Nepal Airlines to Kathmandu.

Group tickets With increasing movement between the countries of South Asia new travel opportunities are opening up. It is now possible for groups of 10 or more to obtain tickets to visit the member countries of the South Asian Association of Regional Co-operation (SAARC). Therefore if you plan to visit 2 or more South Asian countries in 3 weeks or less you may obtain discounts of 30% on your full-fare international tickets. Information is available through the National Tourist offices.

Stop-overs and round the world tickets You can arrange several stop-overs in South Asia on round the world and other longer distance tickets. RTW tickets allow you to fly in to Delhi and out from another international airport such as Bombay, Madras, Calcutta or Kathmandu. Different travel agents organise different deals. Trailfinders of London, one of the world's biggest agencies, has a range of discounted deals. Contact at 194 Kensington High St, London

W8 7RG T 071 938 3939.

Airline security International airlines vary in their arrangements and requirements for security. In particular, it is impossible to lay down general rules about the carrying of equipment like radios, tape-recorders and lap top computers as airlines vary in the way in which they handle battery-powered equipment. Some insist on all batteries being removed from equipment going into the baggage hold, some do not allow any battery operated equipment in the passenger compartment. Furthermore, the position changes from time to time. If you have any doubts about how best to pack your luggage to avoid the inconvenience of unpacking and repacking in the airport check-in, ring the airline in advance to confirm what their current regulations are. **Note that internal airlines often have different rules from the international carriers.** Some do not allow knives and scissors in the cabin.

Internal flights within South Asia are operated by national airlines in each of the main South Asian countries. India is the hub of such international connections within South Asia, routes radiating to each of India's neighbours. **Indian Airlines** fly to Pakistan, Nepal, Bangladesh, Sri Lanka and the Maldives.

Warning Tickets can be bought in India but must be paid for in foreign exchange. Major credit cards are accepted, but it may cost as much as one third extra to use credit cards. Travellers' cheques are therefore the best form of payment. Indian Airlines only accept American Express, Thomas Cook, Bank of America, Citibank and Bank of Tokyo Travellers cheques. If you wish to use Indian Rupees it is essential to produce the exchange certificate to prove that you obtained the Rupees from a hard currency. Discount tickets cannot be bought with Rupees.

Flights operated by **PIA**, **Royal Nepal Airlines**, **Druk Air**, Bangladesh **Biman** and **Air Lanka** link India with Pakistan, Nepal, Bhutan, Bangladesh and Sri Lanka and the Maldives respectively. There are much more limited direct connections between the non-Indian South Asian states. **PIA** operates from Pakistan to the Maldives, Nepal, Colombo and Dhaka. **Air Druk** links Dhaka with Bhutan. **Royal Nepal Airlines** links Nepal with Pakistan, and Bangladesh. Life can be made very much simpler by using a good local travel agent. Good agencies are listed in the country sections.
It is also possible to get good air travel arrangements for some internal flights using international carriers. On Air India flights to Delhi or Bombay can be extended to include Madras, Goa and Calcutta for example for considerably less than the tickets bought individually on Indian Airlines. Such arrangements must be made in advance.
International air tickets can be bought in South Asia. Payment must be made in foreign exchange. Check to see if you are eligible for a discount, which are available on some routes.

Note See India Introduction for details of internal travel pass, **page 124.**

In this Handbook arrival and departure regulations, airport taxes, customs regulations and security arrangments for air travel are outlined in the relevant country sections as they vary from country.

Sea travel

No regular passenger liners operate to South Asia. Round the world cruise ships do stop at some South Asian ports like Bombay, Marmagao, Cochin, Madras, and Colombo. The main shipping lines operating such cruises are American President Lines, British India, Cunard, Holland Line of America, McKinnon & McKenzie, Salen Linblad Cruising, Costa Cruises, Hapag Lloyd, the Royal Cruise Line, Mitsui O.S.K. Line, Royal Viking Line, Black Sea Shipping Co. and Far Eastern Shipping Co.

Warning Shipping in the Gulf was disrupted by the Iran-Iraq War, and has subsequently been further disrupted by the war in Iraq and Kuwait. It is too early to say whether the routes to Karachi and Bombay from ports in the Gulf, notably Kuwait and Muscat, will be re-opened in 1991-92.

DOCUMENTS AND SECURITY

Documents It is essential for all foreign tourists to have a passport that is valid for the whole period of stay in South Asia. It is also essential for nearly all foreigners to have a visa to visit any South Asian country for periods of more than a month. Details are given in the country sections, but the broad variations are as follows:

India: All foreigners must have a visa. Tourist visas last 4 months, extendable to 6 months. Obtainable from Indian representations abroad.

Pakistan: A valid passport is required by all visitors. All nationals of India, Afghanistan, South Africa, Bangladesh, Iran, and any country not recognised by Pakistan must have a visa. Israeli passport holders are not permitted entry. Bona fide tourists from most other countries need a visa only if they wish to stay for more than 30 days. Nationals of a few countries may stay up to 90 days without a visa. Check with the Pakistan Embassy or consulate in your own country. Visas are usually for three months.

Sri Lanka: Tourists visiting for less than 30 days do not require a visa.

Bangladesh: Apart from UK nationals most tourists are allowed to visit for up to 15 days without a visa. UK nationals visiting Bangladesh from India should try to obtain their visa in London rather than from Bangladesh consulates in India, which may refuse to issue them without reason.

Nepal: It is possible to obtain a 7 day visa for Nepal at Kathmandu airport. This may be extended for a full 30 day period at no extra cost. 30 day visas can be obtained from Nepali consulates abroad. Trekkers must obtain a special permit.

Bhutan: It takes 15 days to process a tourist visa application, which needs to be sent to Bhutan Tourism Corporation, Box 159, Thimpu, Bhutan. Visas are paid for on arrival.

The Maldives: All tourists, except those from Sri Lanka, are permitted to enter the Maldives for 30 days; those from India, Pakistan, Bangladesh and Italy are permitted to stay for 90 days. The stay can be extended for a nominal fee. Sri Lankans must obtain a visa before entering the country and Israeli passport holders are not allowed to enter. A valid passport is necessary.

Sensitive areas in South Asia All the countries of South Asia define particular regions as "sensitive" and restrict travel to them. Border regions, tribal areas and some of the Himalayan zones are subject to restrictions and special permits may be needed to visit them. Details of these are given in the country sections. Pakistan and Nepal require permits for most trekking and mountaineering.

Personal security In general the threats to personal security for travellers in South Asia are remarkably small. In most parts of the region it is possible to travel either individually or in groups without any risk of personal violence. However, care is necessary in some places, and basic common sense needs to be used with respect to looking after valuables.

Some parts of South Asia are subject to political violence. Punjab, Kashmir and Assam in India, various parts of Sri Lanka, and Sind in Pakistan, are just five regions where politically motivated violence occurred sporadically in the early 1990s. This violence has nearly always been directed at specific political targets, and tourists have very rarely been directly affected. Access to such regions can however be restricted from time to time.

Some areas in India and Pakistan have long been noted for banditry. The word **thug** comes from an Indian group of violent robbers. Again, these are not in areas usually visited by tourists. Details are given in the relevant country sections. In the great majority of areas visited by tourists, however, violent crime and personal attacks are extremely rare. Goa is becoming an exception to this rule, where incidents of petty theft and violence directed specifically at tourists has been on the increase.

Theft is not uncommon. It is essential to take good care of personal valuables both when you are carrying them, and when you have to leave them in hotels or other places. **You cannot regard hotel rooms as automatically safe.** It is wise to use hotel safes for valuable items, including travellers cheques and passports when you don't need them. It can be difficult to protect your valuables if travelling alone by train. 1st class a/c and 1st class compartments are self-contained and normally completely secure, although nothing of value should be left close to open train windows. 2nd class a/c compartments in India, which have much to recommend them, are larger, allowing more movement of passengers. Attendants are always present in each carriage, and personal security is not at risk, but it is necessary to keep close care of personal possessions.

Warning Travelling bags and cases should be made of tough material, if possible not easily cut, and external pockets (both on bags and on clothing) should never be used for carrying either money or important documents. Strong locks for travelling cases are invaluable. Extra security can be obtained from surrounding conventional cases with a leather strap. Pickpockets and other thieves do operate in the big cities. Crowded areas are particularly high risk, and it's impossible to travel far on railways in South Asia without being in crowded areas from time to time. Keep valuables as close to the body as possible. Women may prefer to make use of compartments which are reserved for women on South Asian trains.

Confidence tricksters The risk of being approached by confidence tricksters is far greater than that of personal attack. They are particularly common in places where people are on the move, notably around railway stations, but you may be approached almost anywhere in the larger cities. Although they appear in a variety of forms, a common plea is some sudden and desperate calamity which has overtaken their family, usually some hundreds of miles away. Sometimes a letter will be produced in English to back up the claim. All they ask is "for the money for a ticket" or for "sending a telegram", but if the person approached shows signs of being sympathetic the demands are likely to increase sharply. These appeals to common humanity are often couched in very convincing terms – they only succeed because it is all too easy not to realise what is happening until too late. Forewarned may be fore-armed.

The Police Even after taking all reasonable precautions people do have valuables stolen. This can cause great inconvenience. You can minimise this by keeping a record of vital documents, including your passport number and travellers cheque numbers in a completely separate place from the documents themselves. If you have items stolen, they should be reported to the police as soon as possible. Larger hotels will be able to assist in contacting and dealing with the police.

Warning Dealings with the police are not always easy. The paper work involved in reporting losses can be time consuming, and your own documentation (e.g. passport and visas) may be demanded. In some states the police themselves are not highly regarded, often demanding bribes. Tourists should not assume, however, that if procedures move slowly they are automatically being expected to offer a bribe.

If you face really serious problems, for example in connection with driving accidents, you should contact your consular offices as quickly as possible.

ETIQUETTE AND LANGUAGE

Courtesy and Appearance Cleanliness and modesty are appreciated even in informal situations. Officially nudity is not permitted on beaches in S. Asia. Although there are some places where this is ignored, it causes widespread offence. Displays of intimacy are not considered suitable in public and may draw undue attention. Although unaccompanied women are perfectly safe in most places, in Pakistan this may be frowned upon.

Warmth and hospitality will be experienced by most travellers, however, with it comes an open curiosity about personal matters and one should not be surprised by total strangers on a train, for example, asking details of one's job, income and family circumstances.

Outside Westernized circles, Asian women are shy and may appear to be ignored even though they, in reality, perform an important role in the social structure.

It is almost universally expected that visitors to temples and mosques will be asked to remove their shoes and sometimes leave leather obects (handbags, camera cases) outside with an attendant. Sikh gurdwaras and mosques (?) also expect heads to be covered and a scarf or handkerchief suffice. Non-Hindus are usually not permitted into the inner sanctum and occasionally even into the temple itself. Donations if desired should not be handed to priests or monks since they may be forbidden to touch money but should be left in a bowl or plate provided. It is also not customary to shake hands with a priest or monk. Separate rules apply to Buddhist gompas, which are given in the appropriate sections.

Drugs It is illegal to carry drugs into or out of any of the South Asian countries. Drugs are being circulated in some areas by powerful syndicates, and despite some efforts to limit their spread are still being offered in places.

Firearms It is illegal to import firearms into South Asia without special permission. Enquire at Consular offices abroad for details.

Language English is a common lingua franca in all the countries of South Asia. National and regional languages are outlined in the appropriate country sections.

ACCOMMODATION

There is a very wide range of accommodation in South Asia, both in terms of facilities offered and in terms of quality. In all the major cities of India, Pakistan, Nepal and Sri Lanka there are top quality hotels. Overall, the quality of hotel accommodation has improved enormously in the last five years. Some hotels are among the best in the world. In small centres even the best hotels are far more variable. If you travel just to the major centres, therefore, it is possible to stay in top class accommodation with a full range of personal and business facilities. In the peak season (Oct to Apr for most of South Asia) bookings can be extremely heavy. It is therefore necessary to reserve bookings well in advance if you are making your own arrangements. If you travel out from the major centres it will often be necessary to accept much more modest accommodation.

Prices for top class hotels are sometimes comparable with the West, although some of the most outstanding hotels are considerably less expensive than their western counterparts. However, moderately priced hotels are almost always much cheaper than in the west. There are also some excellent value hotels in the cheapest categories, though quality and cleanliness varies very much more.

The 6 categories used in this Handbook are based on the dollar equivalent prices of the best double rooms, as at mid-1991. Only exceptional services and facilities are listed for the top three categories, as a full range is standard. Price guides in local currencies are quoted in the individual country sections.

AL More than US$90 International class luxury hotels, usually found only in the regional capitals and the largest cities. All facilities for business and leisure travellers to the highest international standard.

A US$60-US$90 Usually international class hotels, with a choice of restaurants, coffee shop, shops, business services, pool, and all expected facilities, including sports. Some palace conversions fall into this category.

B US$45-60 Central a/c and offering most of the facilities of A class but without the luxury. Many have only one restaurant, though still a choice of cuisine, and a more limited range of shopping, business services, and sports facilities, and may not be in top locations.

C US$25-US$45 Often the best hotels available in medium and small towns. Usually central a/c, comfortable, with restaurant, exchange facilities, travel agent, shops and swimming pool.

D US$10-US$25 Sometimes a/c rooms with bath attached. Restaurant and rm service normally available. Most medium to large towns will have at least one hotel in this category.

E US$3-US$10 Simple rm with fan (occasionally a/c), shower or bucket 'bath'. May have shared toilet facilities. Limited rm service may include meals broiught in when no restaurant available. At the lower end of this scale, some may not provide sheets, pillow cases and towels.

F Less than US$3 Very basic, with shared toilet facilities. May be in noisy or remote locations. Very variable cleanliness and hygiene. There are some real bargains in this class, but there are also some appallingly squalid 'hotels'. Care essential.

Indian style hotels In India a big expansion is taking place in what travel agents often call "Indian style hotels". These are generally medium and small sized hotels. Although they generally have a much more limited range of facilities than the western style hotels, they will often have individual air-conditioning, showers rather than baths and "squat" toilets. Although medium sized and small hotels are much more variable in quality than the big hotels run by the major hotel chains it is possible to find excellent value accommodation even in remote areas. However, you have to be prepared for difficulties which are uncommon in Europe, America or Australasia. In some states power cuts are common, or tap water may be restricted to certain times of day. You are unlikely to be affected in the largest hotels, which have their own generators, but it is always as well to have a good torch.

Unmarried people sharing hotel rooms usually causes no difficulties. However, some visitors have encountered hostility when booking in with a South Asian in smaller hotels.

Airconditioning Only the largest hotels have central airconditioning. Elsewhere airconditioned rooms are widely available, but are cooled by individual airconditioning units. These can be noisy and unreliable. When they fail to operate it is usually well worthwhile telling the management immediately, as it is often possible to get a rapid repair, or to arrange a transfer to a room where the unit is working. Fans are provided in all but the cheapest of hotels, and can greatly increase comfort.

Toiletries Even medium sized hotels which are clean and pleasant do not always have towels, soap and toilet paper. It is common to find that only showers, or a tap and a bucket, are available rather than baths, and in some cases Indian style (squat) toilets are all that are available in some rooms.

Water supply In many Indian towns the water supply is rationed periodically. Water from the taps should never be regarded as safe to drink. The biggest hotels will supply boiled water. Bottled mineral water is now widely available. See the section on health for further details. **See page 25**.

Youth hostels and camping Camping is almost unheard of in South Asia other than by tourists. There is a very limited number of youth hostels and camp sites available, offering very basic facilities. Trekking is discussed in the Nepal section. Other facilities are listed in the appropriate country sections of the Handbook. Some cities have YHA hostels. Many cities have inexpensive YMCA, YWCA or Salvation Army hostels.

Short term stays For people who are travelling off the beaten track there are several cheap options for short stay or temporary accommodation. Railway stations often have "Retiring Rooms" or "Rest Rooms'. These may be hired for periods of between 1 and 24 hours. They are cheap, usually provide a bed and a fan, and some have a couple of a/c rooms, but they are often very heavily booked. They can be extremely convenient for short stops if travelling extensively by train.

In many areas outside the biggest cities there are government guest houses, ranging from *dak bungalows* to *circuit houses*. The latter are now reserved almost exclusively for travelling government officers, but dak and travellers' bungalows are often available for overnight stays. Although they are usually extremely basic, for example rarely having a cook or kitchen facilities, they can be attractive places to stay. There is little point in making advance reservations for dak bungalows as travelling officials always take precedence, even over booked guests.

In some parts of South Asia travellers may also stay in religious hostels of various kinds, sometimes free of charge or in exchange for voluntary offerings. Usually only vegetarian food is permitted; smoking and alcohol are not.

Insects The odd mosquito may penetrate even the best hotels. In cheap hotels you need to be prepared for a wider range of insect life, including flies, cockroaches, spiders, ants, and harmless house lizards. Poisonous insects, including scorpions, are extremely rare in towns. Hotel managements are nearly always prepared with insecticide sprays, and will come and spray rooms if asked. The sprays used often smell extremely unpleasant, and it can be well worthwhile taking your own repellent creams if you are travelling to places off the main hotel routes. Remember to shut windows and doors after dark. Many non a/c rooms have wire mesh windows to keep out insects while allowing air to circulate. Electrical devices, used with insecticide pellets, are now widely available. Many small hotels in mosquito-prone areas have mosquito nets.

Food South Asian food is now so widely available outside South Asia that it is worth experimenting with at least one or two of the dishes prepared in the region you will be visiting before you go if you have the chance. First class food – Indian and Western, and to a more limited extent Chinese – is available in the biggest hotels. It is perfectly possible to stay in all the major cities of India and not eat an Indian meal. It is equally possible to eat – deliciously – a wide range of regional cuisines.

Unlike Europe and America, in South Asia many of the good restaurants are in the large hotels, the best of which may have four or five specialist restaurants. In the big cities there are also good restaurants outside the hotels. However, particularly for the short term visitor, it is necessary to be careful in eating food prepared outside the best hotels or private homes. Raw food such as salads and unpeeled fruit are best avoided, and highly spiced food may be difficult for both the palate and the stomach to adjust to quickly.

There are many South Asian foods that are not widely available outside the region, even in South Asian restaurants abroad. There is an enormous variety of sweet dishes, for example, that are largely unkown outside their countries of origin. They are well worth trying, but care should be taken in where they are bought. The hygiene of many small sweet stalls often leaves something to be desired.

In contrast some foods that are common in Europe are both less readily available and of much lower quality in South Asian countries. Cheese and chocolates are two. Bringing small quantities of such foods can help. They can also be very acceptable as small presents for Indian hosts, but naturally you need to be certain of being able to keep them cool.

Drink Alcoholic drinks are generally either imported and extremely expensive, or local and of poor quality. This applies particularly to wines and spirits. Some local brands of beer, specified in the country sections, are an exception to this rule. There is a wide range of bottled soft drinks. International brands like Pepsi Cola and Coca Cola are just coming back into India after being banned in 1977, but there are plenty of locally produced carbonated drinks that are completely safe, if often rather sickly. Branded mineral water and cartons of fruit juice are now widely available at reasonable prices. Do not add ice cubes to drink as the ater from which the ice is made is very unlikely to be pure. Tea and coffee are almost universally available and are generally safe.

Tipping Hotels and restaurants frequently add a service charge to the bill but the amount paid may be rounded off. Otherwise 10% is the usual amount to leave. Taxi drivers do not expect to be tipped but a small extra amount over the fare is welcomed and particularly if a large amount of luggage is being carried. Porters at airports and railway stations often have a fixed rate displayed but here too a small extra amount is appreciated

INTERNAL SURFACE TRANSPORT

Road travel As a result of the Iranian revolution in 1979 and the continuing Afghan war it has become virtually impossible to travel from Europe overland to South Asia by private vehicle. Some people do still travel by public transport through Turkey and Iran to Pakistan, entering South Asia through the Baluchistan region of Pakistan. Some companies offer organised trips by bus or four wheel drive vehicle, and it is still possible for individuals of some nationalities to travel that route by train, bus or car.

Tourists may import their own vehicles into South Asian countries as long as they hold a Carnet de Passage (Triptyques) issued by any recognised automobile association or club affiliated to the Alliance Internationale de Tourisme in Geneva. Cars may be imported free of duty for up to six months. The vehicle must be re-exported at the end of six months **even where the Carnet has a validity of one year.** In India it is also advisable to obtain an International Certificate for Motor Vehicles (ICMW) and an International Driving Permit(IDP). An IDP should be obtained from the tourists own licensing authority. IDPs obtained through an automobile association must be endorsed by the regional licensing authority in which the tourist arrives in India.

Road Standards

● All the countries of South Asia drive on the left. Speed limits vary, and are rarely clearly signposted. See practical information under each country heading.

● Roads are generally of far lower standards than in Europe or the United States. Even some National Highways are single lane.

● Driving yourself is perfectly possible, but it is essential to be cautious. Oncoming trucks and buses very rarely give way. You always have to be ready to get off the road. Outside the largest towns there are usually no road markings. While many roads are little used and are very attractive, some of the main roads, especially in India and Pakistan, now have a great deal of heavy traffic. In Pakistan it moves comparatively fast. Everywhere in South Asia there is a mixture of traffic. Bullock carts, animals and pedestrians often give a sense of total confusion. It is particularly difficult to drive after dark. Many vehicles have no lights, and there are often almost invisible obstacles on the road. It is much better only to drive in the daylight.

● You need an international driving licence

● In case of breakdowns there is nearly always somebody to help. Every small town has mechanics who are normally able to cope with even the most severe problems with Indian made cars. Foreign cars can be more difficult. You have to be careful of any luggage you may have in the car. Be particularly careful if you have any good tools in the car. They are very likely to disappear.

● If you are involved in an accident you should be very careful to avoid any crowd that may gather. If necessary you may have to drive on before reporting any incident to the police.

● On main roads across South Asia petrol stations are reasonably frequent, but there are areas which are poorly served. Always carry a spare can.

● Diesel is widely available and normally much cheaper than petrol. Petrol is rarely above 92 octane.

● Each of the major countries in South Asia has an Automobile Association. Addresses are given in the individual country sections. If you are driving yourself it is well worth consulting the local Association for up to date information.

● All countries require drivers to have third party insurance. This may have to be with a national insurer, or with a foreign insurer which has a national guarantor.

● You need a carnet de passage if you want to import a car (max 6 months).

Car Hire In most countries of South Asia self drive car hire is a recent and unusual practice. It is far more common to hire a car with a driver, and it is often cheaper. You may also feel it is safer and easier. See the individual country sections for details.

Bus Travel It is now possible to go almost anywhere by bus. For long distance travel they are usually uncomfortable. Video coaches dominate long distance routes. Despite the word 'luxury' which is used to describe them, they are normally noisy and bumpy. Most are not airconditioned, and very few serve drinks or have toilets on board. They would usually stop approximately every 2 hours. If travelling by bus, avoid the back if possible as the bumps are far worse than in the front or middle. For shorter journeys buses do make it possible to get to many places which the railways do not reach. Details of companies and routes are given in the individual country sections. It is often advisable to book in advance for longer distance journeys.

Train Travel For long distance travel in India and Pakistan trains still offer an attractive means of travel. Very cheap by Western standards, the Indian 2nd class a/c sleeper and chair car trains are very comfortable and economical. They all have toilets (not always very clean); if there is a choice of western or Indian style it is nearly always better to use the Indian style as they are better maintained. Meals and drinks are available on long distance trains. It is usually necessary to book train tickets in advance. Indian and Pakistani railways offer discounts and special passes for foreign tourists. These can offer excellent value, and are described in the individual country sections.

Hitch Hiking Hitch hiking is almost unheard of in South Asia, partly because public transport is so cheap. If you try you are likely to spend a very long time on the roadside. Trucks do sometimes give lifts, especially in emergencies, but they rarely average more than 40 kph.

Motor Cycling Motor cycling is increasingly common across South Asia. It is easy to buy new Indian made or assembled motorcycles in India and imported ones elsewhere if you pay direct with foreign exchange. Among the Indian models available are the 350 cc Enfield Bullet and several 100 cc models, including Suzuki and Hondas, made in collaboration with Indian firms. Buying second hand in Rupees takes more time but is quite possible. Repairs are usually easy to arrange and quite cheap. Carry appropriate tools with you.

Cycling A growing number of people are taking to bikes for at least part of a visit to South Asia. It is easy to hire bikes in most small towns. Although Indian made bikes are heavy and without gears, they can be an excellent means of exploring comparatively short distances outside towns and to special places of interest. It is also quite possible to tour more extensively. Imported bikes have the advantage of greater sophistication – lighter weight and gears – but the disadvantage of greater difficulty of maintenance and repair, and the much greater risk of being stolen or damaged.

Travelling with children Many visitors report on both the ease and enjoyment of travelling with children of all ages in many parts of South Asia. They are widely welcomed, being greeted with a warmth in their own right which is often then extended to those accompanying them. In the big hotels there is no difficulty with obtaining safe baby foods, though disposable nappies are not readily available in many areas. Packets and jars may be carried if the child is used to them before starting the journey. It doesn't harm a child to eat an unvaried and limited diet of familiar food for a few weeks if the local dishes are not acceptable but it may be an idea to give vitamin and mineral supplements.

Extra care must be taken to protect children from the heat by creams, hats, umbrellas etc. and by avoiding being out in the hottest part of the day. Cool showers or baths help if children get too hot. Dehydration may be counteracted with plenty of drinking water – bottled, boiled (furiously for 5 minutes) or purified with tablets. Preparations such as 'Diarolyte" may be given if the child suffers from diarrhoea. Moisturiser, zinc and castor oil (for sore bottoms due to change of diet) are worth taking. Mosquito nets or electric insect repellents at night may be provided in hotel rooms which are not airconditioned, but insect repellent creams are a must.

It is best to visit S. Asia in the cooler months, especially when travelling with young children. The biggest hotels provide babysitting facilities.

Hiking and Trekking Many of the Himalayan regions of India, Pakistan and Nepal are magnificent trekking country. Details are given in the relevant country sections. Be particularly careful of pickpockets at the start of a trek. Thieves sometimes hang around groups of trekkers knowing that many will be carrying all their money for the trek in cash.

Maps Sources of maps outside S. Asia *Stanford International Map Centre*, 12-14 Long Acre, London WC2E 9LP; *Zumsteins Landkartenhaus*, Leibkerrstrasse 5, 8 Munchen 22, Germany; *Geo Buch Verlag*, Rosenthal 6, D-6000 Munchen 2, Germany; *Geo Center GmbH*,Honigwiessenstrasse 25, Postfach 800830, D-7000 Stuttgart 80, Germany;*Libreria Alpina,* Via C. Coroned-Berti, 4 40137 Bologna, Zona 370-5, Italy; *Library of Congress*, 101 Independence Ave, Washington, DC 20540 USA; *Michael Chessler Books*, PO Box 2436, Evergreen, CO 80439, USA T 800 654 8502; 303 670 0093; NOAA Distribution Branch (N/CG33), National Ocean Service, Riverdale MD 20737

GENERAL ADVICE

Begging The number of beggars on the streets of the larger cities of South Asia, some of whom may be badly physically handicapped, can be very distressing. The great poverty of the many in contrast to the affluence of the few is equally striking. It is best to give any donations to an organisation rather than to individuals. A coin to one child or a destitute woman on the street will make you the focus of demanding attention from a vast number before long. There are also networks of beggar rings that operate in various cities which are run on a business scale.

It is common to find young children who will offer to do 'jobs' such as call a taxi, carry shopping, clean your shoes (apart from shoe-shine boys), or pose for a photo. You may want to give a small coin in exchange.

Shopping It is best to buy souvenirs from Government Fixed Price Emporia which are found widely across the countries of South Asia. Bazaars, the local markets, are worth exploring but one must be prepared to bargain, which is an acceptable method of arriving at a fair price. However, it would pay to first look around to get an idea of the range and quality of goods on offer. It is possible to be offered good 'bargains' by street hawkers for what may be passed off as marble, ivory, silver, semi-precious stones, coral etc. but are imitations. Taxi drivers and couriers may sometimes insist on recommending certain shops where they expect a commission and prices are likely to be inflated. Individual countries have their own laws regarding export of certain items such as antiquities, ivory, furs and skins so it is essential to get a certificate of legitimate sale and permission for export.

Postal services. The post is safe and reliable as a general rule in most countries. However, delays are not unheard of and it is advisable to use the hotel's letter box or a post office where it is possible to hand over mail for franking across the counter. Valuable items should only be sent by Registered Mail and it is possible to use the Government Emporia or shops in the larger hotels, to parcel purchases home if the items are difficult to carry. Poste restante facilities are widely available in even quite small towns. DHL and similar courier services are available in the larger towns. All the countries of South Asia have international direct dialling. Collect (reverse charge) calls can be made. In India public direct dialling is increasingly widely avaiable from telegraph offices, the cheapest way of dialling abroad. Hotels often add up to a third of the cost of the call.

Time + GMT and US (East) is given in separate sections. Conception of "time" is different in S. Asia, being rather vague. Unpunctuality can therefore be frustrating so patience is needed.

Photography It is advisable to take rolls of films and batteries although they are available at major tourist centres. There are strict restrictions on photography of airports, bridges and 'sensitive border areas' and it is often necessary to obtain permits at sites on payment of a fee in addition to the entrance charge. Bhutan is especially strict – no 16mm film is allowed and tourist permits are needed to enter and visit temples etc. Many monuments now charge a camera fee, with higher fees for video use. Charges range from approximately Rs 1 to Rs 10 for still cameras, and may be as high as Rs50 for video cameras. A much higher charge may be levied at wildlife sanctuaries.

Low impact travel Travellers can put new strains on the environment and on local communities. Litter and the use of scarce resources such as firewood, are problems associated with some trekking areas. Over recent years the illegal removal of antiquities has also been a major problem. More detailed comments are made in the appropriate country and regional sections of this handbook.

Recommended reading
The literature on South Asia is as huge and varied as the subcontinent itself. Below are a few suggestions:

Academic and reference books Allchin, B. & R *The Rise of cilvilisation in India and Pakistan* Cambridge, CUP, 1982. The most authoritative survey of the origins of South Asian civilisations. **Basham, A.L.** (ed.) *A Cutural history of India* Oxford, OUP, 1975. A collection of excellent academic essays, which wear their learning lightly. **Basham, A.L.** *The Wonder that was India* London, Sidgwick & Jackson, 1985. Still one of the most comprehensive and readable accounts of the development of India's culture. **Bock, K.R.** *A Guide to the common reef fish of W Indian Oceans* London, Macmillan, 1987. **Brown, P.** *Indian Architecture* 2 vols. Bombay, Taraporevala, 1976. A classic, dated but still an invaluable reference. **Chauduri, N.C.** Four books give vivid, witty and often sharply critical accounts of India across the 20th century. *The autobiography of an unknown Indian* MacMIllan, London and *Thy hand Great Anarch!* London, Chatto & Windus, 1987. *The continent of Circe* and *Hinduism: A religion to live by* New Delhi, B.I. Publications, 1979. **Farmer B.H.** *An introduction to South Asia* Methuen Perhaps the best and most balanced short introduction to modern South Asia. **Fleming, R.L.**& others *Birds of Nepal* Kathmandu, Avalok, 1979. Excellent reference. **Gandhi, M.K.** *An Autobiography* London, 1982. **Ghosh A.** 1990 An Encyclopaedia of Indian archaeology E.J. Brill Excellent 2 volume reference work. **O'Flaherty, W.** *Hindu Myths* A sourcebook translated from the Sanskrit. London, Penguin, 1974. **Rajagopalachari, C.**

The Mahabharata. Bombay, Bharatiya Vidya Bhavan, 1979. *Ramayana*. Bombay, Bharatiya Vidya Bhavan, 1978. **Robinson F.** ed. *Cambridge Encyclopedia of India, Pakistan* 1989 ed. Cambridge. Excellent and readable introduction to many aspects of S. Asian society. **Sen, K.M.** *Hinduism* London, Penguin, 1961. **Shackle, C.** *South Asian languages* London, SOAS, 1985. **Snellgrove, D.L.** *Buddhist Himalaya* Oxford, Bruno Cassirer, 1957. **Welch, S.C.** *India: Art and Culture 1300-1900*. New York, Metropolitan Museum of Modern Art, 1985. Magnificent and authoritative illustrated review. Superbly illustrated.

People and place Furer-Haimendorf, C. von A world authority on tribal people of S. Asia, *The Sherpas of Nepal* Berkeley, Univ of California, 1964 and *The Naked Nagas* are two sensitively written anthropologies. **Heyerdahl, T.** *The Maldive mystery* London, Allen & Unwin, 1986. **Maloney, C.** *Peoples of South Asia* New York, Holt, Rheinhart & Winston, 1974. A wide ranging and authoritatve review. **Messerli, B. & Ives J.D.** *Himalayan crisis: reconciling development and conservation* London, Routledge & K Paul, 1989. Excellent review of the debate over environmental change in the Himalayas. **S. Mutthiah** *Madras discovered* 1987. East West Press Pvt Ltd; **Johnson B.L.C.** has written books on the geography of each of the larger South Asia countries which contain much helpful factual material. *India:resources and development*; *Pakistan*; *Bangladesh*; and *Sri Lanka* (written with M. Le M. Scrivenor) are all published by Heinemann and Barnes and Noble. **Stainton, J.D.A.** *Forests of Nepal* London, Murray, 1972.

Mountaineering Bonnington, C. *Annapurna South face* London, Cassell, 1971. *Everest the hard way*. London, Hodder & Stoughton, 1979 **Hillary, E.** *High adventure* New York, Dutton, 1955 **Tilman, H.M.** *Two mountains and a river* Cambridge University P., 1948. (Pakistan) They are all classic accounts of Himalayan mountaineering.

Political commentaries Burki, S.J. *Pakistan under Bhutto, 1971-77*. London, Macmillan, 1988. Outstanding review of Pakistan's political system. **Fishlock, T.** *India file*. London, 1983. Readable collection of journalist's impressions of India. **Tully M. & Jacob S.** 1986 *Amritsar: Mrs. Gandhi's last battle* Jonathan Cape A vivid account from the best foreign correspondent in India during the 1980s. **Ziring, L.** *Pakistan: The Enigma of political development*. Sawson Westview, 1980.

Travel Anderson, M.M. *Festivals of Nepal* London, Allen & Unwin, 1971. **Cameron, J.** *An Indian summer* London, 1974. Beautifully written and perceptive view. **Mohd Farook** The *Fascinating Maldives*. Male, Novelty Printers, 1985. **Frater, A.** *Chasing the monsoon* London, Viking, 1990. (India) **Godden R. & J.** *Two under the Indian Sun* A beautifully painted account of the two sisters' childhood in Bengal. **Insight Guides** Beautifully illustrated guides to each of the major countries of South Asia. Recent editions cary much improved brief text. *India*. *Nepal*. *Pakistan*. *Sri Lanka*. **Keay J.** *Into India*. 1973. Now out of print, but well worth getting if you can find a copy. London, Murray. **Naipaul, V.S.** *An area of darkness* London, 1977. (India) **Newby, E.** *A short walk in the Hindu Kush*. London, Pan, 1981. *Slowly down the Ganges*. London, Pan, 1983. Both good humoured and often very funny. **Rushbrook Williams** L.F. (Ed.) *A Handbook for travellers in India, Pakistan, Nepal, Bangladesh and Sri Lanka* John Murray 1982 (22nd edition). **Swift, H.** *Trekking in Pakistan and India*. London, Hodder & Stoughton, 1990. Detailed practical guide, based on first hand experience. **Theroux, P.** *Great Railway Bazaar*. London, Penguin, 1977.

Novels Desai A. *The village by the sea* Penguin **Farrell, J.G.** *The siege of Krishnapur.* **Forster, E.M.** *A Passage to India* London **Fraser, G.M.** *Flashman* London, Pan. (Pakistan) *Flashman in the Great Game* London, Pan, 1976. (The 1857 Mutiny) **Godden R.** 1955 *Kingfishers catch fire* **Narayan, R.K.** Has written many gentle and humourous novels and short stories of South India. *The Man eater of malgudi* and *Under the Banyan tree and other stories* are two examples. London, Penguin, 1985. (India) **Rushdie, S.** *Midnight's children* London, 1981. A novel of India since Independence, while his later *Shame* focuses on Pakistan. At the same time funny and bitterly sharp critiques of contemporary South Asian life. **Scott, P.** *The Raj Quartet*. London, Panther, 1973. *Staying on*. London, Longmans, 1985. Outstandingly perceptive novels of the end of the Raj.

Architecture Mitra, D. *Buddhist monuments*. Calcutta, Sahitya Samsad, 1971. **Morris, J. & Winchester S.** *Stones of Empire* Oxford, OUP, 1983. **Mumtaz, K.K.** *Architecture in Pakistan* Singpore, Concept Media, 1985. **Tillotson G. H.R.** *The Rajput Palaces* Yale, 1987. *Mughal architecture* London, Viking,1990. *The tradition of Indian architecture* Yale 1989. Superbly clear writing on development of Indian architecture under Rajputs, Mughals and the British.

Popular history Allen, C. & Dwivedi, S. *Lives of the Indian Princes* London, Century

Publications, 1984. Colourful view of an often romanticised past. Gascoigne, B.*The Great Moghuls* London, Cape, 1987. **Hopkirk** P. 1990 *The Great Game: on secret service in High Asia* John Murray **Keay, J.** *When men and mountains meet* 1973. *The Gilgit game.* 1979. John Murray. **Mason, P.** *Men who ruled India.* and *The Guardians* London, Cape, 1985. **Nehru, J.** *The discovery of India* New Delhi, ICCR, 1976. **Russell, R. &** *Khurshidul Islam Ghalib: Life and letters.* London, Allen & Unwin, 1969. **Spear, P. & Thapar, R.** *A history of India.* 2 vols. London, Penguin, 1978.

A checklist Clothing – light cottons and cotton/poyester most suitable although some regions get cool or cold even on the plains and light woollens are needed in the evenings. (Trekkers need special gear.) Women should dress modestly and avoid exposing too much of themselves. It is worth shopping locally for cotton items which are very good value.

Headcovering – sun hat and for women a scarf if useful to keep off dust and wind.
Footwear – light walking shoes (trainers), comfortable sandals, rubber 'flip flops' (available locally). Socks are indispensable to wear for visits to temples and mosques where shoes must be removed.
sunglasses
spectacle prescription, soft contact lens cleaning tablets (**not readily available in S Asia**)
sun protection cream/lotion (Factor 10+)
moisturising cream
insect repellant cream
'Baby Wipes'
Torch and spare batteries
Swiss Army type knife
water purifying tablets
Films
Zipped bag to keep posessions out of dust and dirt
Toilet paper (often not available or supplied)
For cheaper hotel stays – soap, towel, cotton sheet sleeping bag, universal rubber plug, rubber window wedges, earplugs, eye mask, padlock
For women – sanitary tampons/towels
For backpackers – money belt, water bottle, and lock and chain to attach luggage to seat or bunk when travelling.
Bin liners on a roll (for dirty clothes, damp things)
Long plastic sheet to protect against bedbugs
Spare passport photos and photocopies of essential documents
Umbrella

HEALTH INFORMATION

The following information has been very kindly compiled for us by Dr. David Snashall Senior Lecturer Occupational Health, United Medical Schools of Guy's and St Thomas' Hospitals and Chief Medical Adviser, Foreign and Commonwealth Office, London. The publishers have evry confidence that the following information is correct, but cannot assume any direct responsibility in this connection.

The traveller to South Asia is inevitably exposed to health risks not encountered in North America or Western Europe. Despite the fact that most of the area lies geographically within the Tropics, the climate is far from tropical in, for example, the Himalayas and so tropical diseases are often not a major problem for visitors. Because much of the area is economically underdeveloped, infectious diseases still predominate in a way in which they used to predominate in the West some decades ago. There is an obvious difference in health risks between the business traveller who tends to stay in international class hotels in large cities, and the back-packer trekking through the rural areas. There are no hard and fast rules to follow; you will often have to make your own judgements on the healthiness or otherwise of your surroundings.

There are many well qualified doctors in the area, a large proportion of whom speak English but the quality and range of medical care diminishes very rapidly as you move away from big cities. In some of the countries such as India, there are systems and traditions of medicine wholly different from the Western model and you may be confronted with unusual modes of treatment such as herbal medicine and acupuncture. At least you can be sure that local Practitioners have a lot of experience with the particular diseases of their region. If you are in a City, it may be worthwhile calling on your Embassy to provide a list of recommended Doctors.

If you are a long way away from medical help, a certain amount of self medication may be necessary and you will find many of the drugs available have familiar names. However, always check the date stamping and buy from reputable pharmacies because the shelf life of some items, especially vaccines and antibiotics, is markedly reduced in hot conditions. Unfortunately, many locally produced drugs are not subjected to quality control procedures and so can be unreliable. There have, in addition, been cases of substitution of inert materials for active drugs.

With the following precautions and advice, you should keep as healthy as usual. Make local enquiries about health risks if you are apprehensive and take the general advice of European and North American families who have lived or are living in the Area.

Before You Go Take out Medical Insurance. You should have a dental check up, obtain a spare glasses prescription and, if you suffer from a longstanding condition such as diabetes, high blood pressure, heart/lung disease or a nervous disorder, arrange for a check up with your doctor who can at the same time provide you with a letter explaining details of your disability. Check the current practice for malaria prophylaxis (prevention) for the countries you intend to visit.

Inoculations Small-pox vaccination is no longer required. Neither is cholera vaccination, despite the fact that the disease is endemic in Bangladesh and can occur in the other countries of South Asia. Yellow fever vaccination is not required either, although you may be asked for a certificate if you have been in a country affected by yellow fever immediately before travelling to India. The following vaccinations are recommended:

Typhoid (monovalent): 1 dose followed by a booster in 1 month's time. Immunity from this course lasts 2-3 years. An oral preparation is currently being marketed in some countries.

Polio-myelitis: This is a live vaccine generally given orally and a full course consists of 3 doses with a booster in tropical regions every 3-5 years.

Tetanus: 1 dose should be given with a booster at 6 weeks and another at 6 months and 10 yearly boosters thereafter are recommended. Children should, in addition, be properly protected against diphtheria, whooping cough, mumps and measles. Teenage girls, if they have not had the disease, should be given rubella (German measles) vaccination. Consult your doctor for advice on BCG innoculation against tuberculosis; the disease is still common in the region.

Meningitis and Japanese B Encephalitis (JBE) There is an extremely small risk, though it varies seasonally and from region to region. Consult a Travel Clinic such as British Airways or Thomas Cook, or MASTA (see below for details).

Infectious Hepatitis (jaundice) is common throughout South Asia. It seems to be frequently caught by travellers. The main symptoms are stomach pains, lack of appetite, nausea, lassitude and yellowness of the eyes and skin. Medically speaking, there are two types: the less serious but more common is hepatitis A for which the best protection is careful preparation of food, the avoidance of contaminated drinking water and scrupulous attention to toilet hygiene. Human normal immuno-globulin (gamma globulin) confers considerable protection against the disease and is particularly useful in epidemics. It should be obtained from a reputable source and is certainly recommended for travellers who intend to live rough. The injection should be given as close as possible to your departure and, as the dose depends on the likely time you are to spend in potentially infected areas, the manufacturer's instructions should be followed.

The other, more serious, version is hepatitis B, which is acquired as a sexually transmitted disease, from a blood transfusion or an injection with an unclean needle or possibly by insect bites. The symptoms are the same as hepatitis A but the incubation period is much longer.

You may have had jaundice before or you may have had hepatitis of either type before without becoming jaundiced, in which case it is possible that you could be immune to either hepatitis A or B. This immunity can be tested for before you travel. If you are not immune to hepatitis B already, a vaccine is available (3 shots over 6 months) and if you are not immune to hepatitis A already, then you should consider having gamma globulin.

AIDS in South Asia is increasing in its prevalence as in most countries but with a pattern closer to that of developing societies. Thus, it is not wholly confined to the well known high risk sections of the population i.e., homosexual men, intravenous drug abusers, prostitutes and the children of infected mothers. Heterosexual transmission is probably now the dominant mode and so the main risk to travellers is from casual sex. The same precautions should be taken as when encountering any sexually transmitted disease. In some of the countries, almost the whole of the female prostitute population is HIV positive and in other parts, intravenous drug abuse is common. The AIDS virus (HIV) can be passed via unsterile needles which have been previously used to inject a HIV positive patient but the risk of this is very small indeed. It would, however, be sensible to check that needles have been properly sterilised or disposable needles used. The chance of picking up hepatitis B in this way is much more of a danger. Be wary of carrying disposable needles yourself; Custom officials may find them suspicious. The risk of receiving a blood transfusion with blood infected with the HIV virus is greater than from dirty needles because of the amount of fluid exchanged. Supplies of blood for transfusion are now largely screened for HIV in all reputable hospitals, so the risk must be very small indeed. Catching the AIDS virus does not necessarily produce an illness in itself; the only way to be sure if you feel you have been put at risk is to have a blood test for HIV antibodies on your return to a place where there are reliable laboratory facilities. The test does not become positive for many weeks.

Common Problems

Heat And Cold Full acclimatization to high temperatures takes about 2 weeks and during this period, it is normal to feel relatively apathetic, especially if the relative humidity is high. Drink plenty of water (up to 15 litres a day are required when working physically hard in the tropics), use salt on your food and avoid extreme exertion. Tepid showers are more cooling than hot or cold ones. Large hats do not cool you down but prevent sunburn. Remember that, especially in the mountains, there can be a large and sudden drop in temperature between sun and shade and between night and day, so dress accordingly. Loose fitting cotton clothes are still the best for hot weather. Warm jackets and woollens are essential after dark at high altitude.

Altitude Acute mountain sickness can strike from about 3,000 metres upwards. It is more likely to affect those who ascend rapidly (e.g. by plane) and those who over-exert themselves. Teenagers seem to be particularly prone. Past experience is not always a good guide: the Author, having spent years in Peru travelling constantly between sea level and very high altitude never suffered the slightest symptoms, then was severely affected climbing Kilimanjaro in Tanzania.

On reaching heights above 3,000 metres, heart pounding and shortness of breath, especially on exertion are almost universal and a normal response to the lack of oxygen in the air. Acute mountain sickness takes a few hours or days to come on and presents with headache, lassitude, dizziness, loss of appetite, nausea and vomiting. Insomnia is common and often associated with a suffocating feeling when lying down in bed. Keen observers may note that their breathing tends to wax and wane at night and their face tends to be puffy in the mornings – this is all part of the syndrome. If the symptoms are mild, the treatment is rest, painkillers (preferably not Aspirin based) for the headache and anti-sickness pills for vomiting. Oxygen may help at very high altitudes but is unlikely to be available.

The best way of preventing acute mountain sickness is a relatively slow ascent and, when trekking through the Himalayas to high altitude, some time spent in the foothills getting fit and adapting to moderate altitude is beneficial. On arrival at places over 3,000 metres, a few hours rest in a chair and the avoidance of alcohol, cigarettes and heavy food will go a long way towards preventing acute mountain sickness. Should the symptoms be severe and prolonged, it is best to descend to a lower altitude and to re-ascend slowly or in stages. The symptoms disappear very quickly with even a few hundred metres of descent. If a slow staged attempt is impossible because of shortage of time, then the drug Acetazolamide (Diamox) can be used as a preventative and continued during the ascent. There is good evidence of the value of this drug in the prevention of acute mountain sickness but some people do experience funny side effects. The usual dose is 500 mgs of the slow release preparation each night, starting the night before ascending above 3,000 metres.

Other problems experienced at high altitude are sunburn, excessively dry air causing skin cracking, sore eyes (it may be wise to leave your contact lenses out) and stuffy noses. It is unwise to ascend to high altitude if you are pregnant, especially in the first 3 months, or if you have any history of heart, lung or blood disease, including sickle cell.

There is a further, albeit rare, hazard due to rapid ascent to high altitude – a kind of complicated mountain sickness presenting as acute pulmonary oedema or acute cerebral oedema. Both conditions are more common the higher you go. Pulmonary oedema comes on quite rapidly with breathlessness, noisy breathing, cough, blueness of the lips and frothing at the mouth. Cerebral oedema usually presents with confusion, going on to unconsciousness. Anybody developing these serious conditions must be bought down to low altitude as soon as possible and taken to hospital.

Rapid descent from high places will aggrevate sinus and middle ear infections and make bad teeth ache. The same problems are sometimes experienced during descent at the end of an aeroplane flight. Do not ascend to high altitude in the 24 hours following scuba-diving. Remember that the Himalayas and other South Asian mountain ranges are very high, very cold, very remote and potentially very dangerous. Do not travel in them alone, when you are ill or if you are poorly equipped. As telephone communication can be non-existent, mountain rescue is extremely difficult and medical services may not be up to much.

Despite these various hazards (mostly preventable) of high altitude travel, many people find the environment healthier and more invigorating than at sea level.

Intestinal Upsets Practically nobody escapes this one, so be prepared for it. Some of these countries lead the world in their prevalence of diarrhoea. Most of the time, intestinal upsets are due to the insanitary preparation of food. Do not eat uncooked fish or vegetables or meat (especially pork), fruit with the skin on (always peel your fruit yourself) or food that is exposed to flies (especially salads). Tap water may be unsafe, especially in the monsoon and the same goes for stream water or well water. Filtered or bottled water is usually available and safe. If your hotel has a central hot water supply, this is safe to drink after cooling. Ice for drinks should be made from boiled water but rarely is, so stand your glass on the ice cubes, instead of putting them in the drink. Dirty water should first be strained through a filter bag (available from camping shops) and then boiled or treated. Bringing the water to a rolling boil at sea level is sufficient but at high altitude you have to boil the water for longer to ensure that all the microbes are killed. Various sterilising methods can be used and there are proprietary preparations containing chlorine or iodine compounds. Pasteurised or heat treated milk is now widely available, as is ice cream and yogurt produced by the same methods. Unpasteurised milk products, including cheese, are sources of tuberculosis, brucellosis, listeria and food poisoning germs. You can render fresh milk safe by heating it to 62°C for 30 minutes, followed by rapid cooling or by boiling it. Matured or processed cheeses are safer than fresh varieties.

Diarrhoea is usually the result of food poisoning, occasionally from contaminated water. There are various causes – viruses, bacteria, protozoa (like amoeba), salmonella and cholera organisms. It may take one of several forms, coming on suddenly, or rather slowly. It may be accompanied by vomiting or by severe abdominal pain and the passage of blood or mucus when it is called dysentery. How do you know which type you have and how do you treat them? All kinds of diarrhoea, whether or not accompanied by vomiting respond favourably to the replacement of water and salts taken as frequent small sips of some kind of rehydration solution. There are proprietary preparations, consisting of sachets of powder which you dissolve in water, or you can make your own by adding half a teaspoonful of salt (3.5 grams) and 4 tablespoonfuls of sugar (40 grams) to a litre of boiled water.

● If you can time the onset of diarrhoea to the minute, then it is probably viral or bacterial and/or the onset of dysentery. The treatment, in addition to rehydration, is Ciprofloxacin 500 mgs every 12 hours. The drug is now widely available.

● If the diarrhoea has come on slowly or intermittently, then it is more likely to be protozoal, i.e. caused by amoeba or giardia and antibiotics will have no effect. These cases are best treated by a doctor as should any diarrhoea continuing for more than 3 days. If there are severe stomach cramps, the following drugs may help: Loperamide (Imodium, Arret) and Diphenoxylate with Atropine (Lomotil).

Thus, the lynch pins of treatment for diarrhoea are rest, fluid and salt replacement, antibiotics such as Ciprofloxacin for the bacterial types and special diagnostic tests and medical treatment for amoeba and giardia infections. Salmonella infections and cholera can be devastating diseases and it would be wise to get to a hospital as soon as possible if these were suspected. Fasting, peculiar diets and the consumption of large quantities of yogurt have not been found useful in calming traveller's diarrhoea or in rehabilitating inflamed bowels. Oral rehydration has, especially in children, been a lifesaving technique and as there is some evidence that alcohol and milk might prolong diarrhoea, they should probably be avoided during and immediately after an attack. There are ways of preventing traveller's diarrhoea for short periods of time when visiting these countries by taking antibiotics but these are ineffective against viruses and, to some extent, against protozoa, so this technique should not be used, other than in exceptional circumstances. Some preventives such as Entero-vioform can have serious side effects if taken for long periods.

Insects These can be a great nuisance. Some of course are carriers of serious diseases such as malaria, dengue fever or filariasis and various worm infections. The best way of keeping mosquitoes away at night is to sleep off the ground with a mosquito net and to burn mosquito coils containing Pyrethrum. Aerosol sprays or a "flit" gun may be effective as are insecticidal tablets which are heated on a mat which is plugged into the wall socket (if taking your own, check the voltage of the area you are visiting so that you can take an appliance that will work. Similarly, check that your electrical adaptor is suitable for the repellent plug).

Or you can use personal insect repellent of which the best contain a high concentration of Diethyltoluamide. Liquid is best for arms and face (take care around eyes and make sure you do not dissolve the plastic of your spectacles). Aerosol spray on clothes and ankles deter mites and ticks. Liquid DET suspended in water can be used to impregnate cotton clothes and mosquito nets. If you are bitten, itching may be relieved by cool baths and anti-histamine tablets (care with alcohol or driving), corticosteroid creams (great care – never use if any hint of sepsis) or by judicious scratching. Calamine lotion and cream have limited effectiveness and anti-histamine creams have a tendency to cause skin allergies and are, therefore, not generally recommended. Bites which become infected (commonly in the tropics) should be treated with a local antiseptic or antibiotic cream such as Cetrimide as should infected scratches. Skin infestations with body lice, crabs and scabies are unfortunately easy to pick up. Use Gamma benzene hexachloride for lice and Benzyl benzoate for scabies. Crotamiton cream alleviates itching and also kills a number of skin parasites. Malathion lotion 5% is good for lice but avoid the highly toxic full strength Malathion used as an agricultural insecticide.

Malaria is prevalent in South Asia. It remains a serious disease and you are advised to protect yourself against mosquito bites as above and to take prophylactic (preventive) drugs. Start taking the tablets a few days before exposure and continue to take them 6 weeks after leaving the malarial zone. Remember to give the drugs to babies and children and pregnant women also. The subject of malaria prevention is becoming more complex as the malaria parasite becomes immune to some of the older drugs. In particular, there has been an increase in the proportion of cases of falciparum malaria which is particularly dangerous. Some of the preventive drugs can cause side effects, especially if taken for long periods of time, so before you travel you must check with a reputable agency the likelihood and type of malaria in the countries which you intend to visit and take their advice on prophylaxis and be prepared to receive conflicting advice. Because of the rapidly changing situation in the area I have not included the names and dosage of the drugs. You can catch malaria even when taking prophylactic drugs, although it is unlikely. If you do develop symptoms (high fever, shivering, severe headache, sometimes diarrhoea) seek medical advice immediately. The risk of the disease is obviously greater the further you move from the cities into rural areas with primitive facilities and standing water.

Sunburn The burning power of the tropical sun is phenomenal, especially at high altitude. Always wear a wide brimmed hat and use some form of sun cream or lotion on untanned skin. Normal temperate zone suntan lotions (protection factor up to 7) are not much good. You need to use the types designed specifically for the tropics or for mountaineers or skiers with a protection factor between 7 and 15. Glare from the sun can cause conjunctivitis so wear sunglasses, especially on tropical beaches.

Heat stroke There are several varieties of 'heat stroke'. The most common cause is severe dehydration. Avoid dehydration by drinking lots of non-alcoholic fluid.

Snake Bite If you are unlucky enough to be bitten by a venomous snake, spider, scorpion, centipede or sea creature try (within limits) to catch the animal for identification. The reactions to be expected are fright, swelling, pain and bruising around the bite, soreness of the regional lymph glands, nausea, vomiting and fever. If, in addition, any of the following symptoms supervene get the victim to a doctor without delay: numbness, tingling of the face, muscular spasm, convulsions, shortness of breath or haemorrhage. Commercial snake bite or scorpion sting kits may be available but are only useful for the specific type of snake or scorpion for which they are designed. The serum has to be given intravenously, so is not much good unless you have had some practice in making injections into veins. If the bite is on a limb, immobilise the limb and apply a tight bandage between the bite and the body, releasing it for 90 seconds every 15 minutes. Reassurance of the bitten person is very important because death from snake bite is, in fact, very rare. Do not slash the bite area and try to suck out the poison because this sort of heroism does more harm than good. Hospitals usually hold stocks of snake bite serum. Best precaution: do not walk in snake territory with bare feet, sandals or shorts. If swimming in an area where there are poisonous fish such as stone or scorpion fish (also called by a variety of local names) or sea urchins on rocky coasts, tread carefully or wear plimsolls.

The sting of such fish is intensely painful and this can be helped by immersing the stung part in water as hot as you can bear for as long as it remains painful. This is not always very practical and you must take care not to scald yourself, but it does work. Avoid spiders and scorpions by keeping your bed away from the wall, look under lavatory seats and inside your shoes in the morning. In the rare event of being bitten, consult a doctor.

OTHER AFFLICTIONS Remember that **rabies** is endemic in many South Asian countries. If you are bitten by a domestic animal, try to have it captured for observation and see a doctor at once. Treatment with human diploid vaccine is now extremely effective and worth seeking out if the likelihood of having contracted rabies is high. A course of anti-rabies vaccine might be a good idea before you go.

Dengue fever is present in most of the countries of South Asia. It is a virus disease, transmitted by mosquito bites, presenting with severe headache and body pains. Complicated types of dengue known as haemorrhagic fevers occur throughout Asia but usually in persons who have caught the disease a second time. Thus, although it is a very serious type, it is rarely caught by visitors. There is no treatment, you must just avoid mosquito bites.

Intestinal Worms are common and the more serious ones, such as hook worm can be contracted by walking barefoot on infested earth or beaches.

Leishmaniasis – this can be a serious disease taking several forms and transmitted by sand flies. These should be avoided in the same way as mosquitoes.

Influenza and Respiratory Diseases is common, perhaps made worse by polluted cities and rapid temperature and climatic changes.

Prickly Heat A very common itchy rash is avoided by frequent washing and by wearing loose clothing. It is helped by the use of talcum powder to allow the skin to dry thoroughly after washing.

Athlete's foot and other fungal infections are best treated by sunshine and a proprietary preparation such as Tolnaftate.

When You Return Home Remember to take your anti-malaria tablets for 6 weeks. If you have had attacks of diarrhoea, it is worth having a stool specimen tested in case you have picked up amoebic dysentery. If you have been living rough, a blood test may be worthwhile to detect worms and other parasites.

Basic Supplies The following items you may find useful to take with you from home:
sunglasses, ear plugs, suntan cream, insect repellent, flea powder, mosquito net, coils or tablets, tampons, condoms, contraceptives, water sterilising tablets, anti-malaria tablets, anti-infective ointment, dusting powder for feet, travel sickness pills, antacid tablets, anti-diarrhoea tablets, sachets of rehydration salts, first aid kit.

The following organisations give information regarding well trained English speaking Physicians throughout the world:
International Association for Medical Assistance to Travellers, 745 5th Avenue, New York, 10022.
   Intermedic 777, Third Avenue, New York, 10017.
Information regarding country by country malaria risk can be obtained from the World Health Organisation (WHO) or the Ross Institute, The London School of Hygiene and Tropical Medicine, Kepple Street, London WClE 7HT, which publishes a strongly recommended book entitled: *The Preservation of Personal Health in Warm Climates*.
   The organisation MASTA (Medical Advisory Service for Travellers Abroad) also based at the London School of Hygiene and Tropical Medicine, Telephone 071 631-4408 – Telex 895 3474) will provide country by country information on up to date health risks.

Further information-on medical problems overseas can be obtained from the new edition of *Travellers' Health: How to Stay Healthy Abroad*, edited by Richard Dawood (Oxford University Press,1989, £5.95). We strongly recommend this revised and updated edition, especially to the intrepid travellers who go to the more out-of-the-way places.

SOUTH ASIA – THE LAND AND PEOPLE

INTRODUCTION

For most visitors the first point of contact with any of the South Asian countries today is one of the region's major cities – Delhi, Bombay, Calcutta or Madras in India, Karachi in Pakistan, Colombo in Sri Lanka. None of them is in any sense "typical", either of their own countries or of the region as a whole. They are some of the world's largest cities. According to the 1991 Census, Bombay now has a population of 12.57 million, Calcutta 10.86 m, and Delhi 8.38 m. Yet despite their size, most people in India, and all the countries of South Asia, live in villages. Equally, all these cities except Delhi, are comparatively new. Madras, the oldest of them, was founded less than 400 years ago. Again, all of them owe their origins to foreigners, although South Asia was the home of one of the world's oldest urban civilisations centred on the cities of Moenjo Daro and Harappa.

Tradition and change It is not necessary to travel far from any one of these metropolitan cities to begin to see something more representative of both traditional and modern South Asia. Even within them it's impossible not to be struck by the variety of peoples as well as of ways of life. The past and the present often seem to be bound up together, even in the faces and dress of the people who crowd around the airport terminals, the railway stations and the hotels of all the major cities. Whichever point you touch down at, you quickly see something of the great variety which is South Asia, and yet also something of the common heritage – of ethnic backgrounds, of culture and of tradition – which give South Asia such a distinctive place in the world.

Although they are now politically independent, the countries which make up South Asia today have a great deal in common. They share a land which, despite its great diversity, forms a remarkably self-contained geographical region. The nation states which make up modern South Asia – **India** at the centre, surrounded clockwise by **Pakistan, Nepal, Bhutan, Bangladesh, Sri Lanka** and the **Maldives** – do have their distinct social and political histories, just as they have contrasting physical environments. But these histories are tightly intertwined, making it impossible to understand many features of their present societies without reference to their links with the wider region.

South Asia's diversity Despite its fascinating complexity, great size and often daunting diversity, a great deal can be gained even by a short visit to just one part of South Asia. It is easy to be overwhelmed, and you can be certain that however long you spend there, there will be plenty left to discover.

Throughout the countries of South Asia there are very close links between the people and their environment. Since the early Stone Age, people have developed remarkable adjustments to the soils, climate, and relief of their own locality. Thus if you drive out from Delhi to Agra, for example, you pass through a region which has witnessed successive agricultural developments to its traditional farming practices. Green revolution practices of today have been married to 19th century irrigation schemes. In turn these enhanced the productivity of already well-established wheat farming based on the fertile alluvial soils of the Ganga valley.

In this handbook short introductory sections will describe the most important features of the landscapes which can be seen today as you travel across the countries of the region. South Asia has some of the most beautiful scenery in the world. But these are landscapes which have played a vital part in the evolution of South Asian societies.

GEOGRAPHY

South Asia falls into three major geological regions, each of which has quite different origins. The N is enclosed by the great arc of the Himalayas. To the S of these ranges lie the alluvial plains of the Indus and the Ganga. To the S again is the Peninsula, marked roughly by a line from Bombay NE towards Agra, then ESE to Calcutta and beyond. Geologically, Sri Lanka is a continuation of the Indian Peninsula, separated by the 30 km wide shallows known as Adam's Bridge. In contrast, the island chains of the Laccadives and Minicoy off the W coast of India, and the Maldives to the SW, are coral atolls. These developed on the easternmost of three submarine ridges formed beneath the Arabian Sea which were pushed up during the last 50 million years as the ocean floor spread.

The Himalayas

Dominating the entire northern borders of South Asia, the *Himalayas* stretch 2500 kilometres from NW to SE. They are between 150 and 400 kilometres wide from N to S. The mountains that extend W from the Himalayas proper into the Hindu Kush enclose the lowlands of Pakistan, while those in the E curve abruptly southwards into Burma. The Himalayas provide a dramatic barrier between South Asia and China, but they also enclose the two Himalayan states of Nepal and Bhutan.

The Himalayas are of very recent origin, and they are still being actively pushed upwards as the plate which bears the Peninsula continues to move N under the Tibetan Plateau. The Himalayan Mountains proper, stretching from the **Pamirs** in Pakistan to the easternmost bend of the Brahmaputra in **Assam**, can be divided into three broad zones.

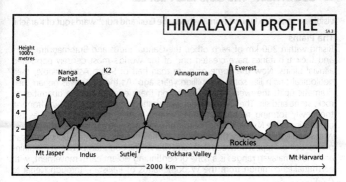

On the S flank are the Siwaliks, or Outer Ranges. **To their immediate N**
run the parallel Middle Ranges of **Panjal** and **Dhauladhar**, and to the N again
is **the third zone**, the **Inner Himalaya**, which has the highest peaks.

The scale of the Himalayas is unparalleled anywhere in the world. Of the 94
mountains in Asia above 7,300 m, all but two are in the Himalayas (including the
Karakoram). Nowhere else in the world are there mountains as high. Although
the ranges themselves are recently formed, they include rocks from all the major
geological periods. In the E Himalayas, for example, there are examples of ancient
gneissic rocks, more than 3000 million years old.

The **Siwalik Ranges**, in contrast, which run along the southern flank from
Pakistan eastwards to the Kosi River, are made up of a set of sedimentary deposits
less than 5 million years old. The speed with which the Himalayas were raised
meant that there have been colossal amounts of debris washed down onto the
plains at their foot. Thus the sediments are between 5,000 m and 6,000 m thick,
although the Siwaliks rarely rise to more than 1,000 m in height. They have been
raised to their present height in the most recent phase of mountain building,
which is still going on.

The first ranges to begin the mountain building process were probably the
Karakoram, which may have begun their ascent more than 100 million years
ago. The central core of the Himalayan Ranges did not begin to rise until about
35 million years ago, followed by further major movements between 25 and 5
million years ago. The latest mountain building period, responsible for the
Siwaliks, began less than 5 million years ago and is still continuing.

    The rocks of the central core of the Himalayas were formed under the intense
pressure and heat of the mountain building process. Largely crystalline, they
comprise granites, gneisses, schists and non-fossil bearing sedimentary rocks,
formed as the main mountain building period began. Before that the present
Himalayan region and what is now the Tibetan Plateau had lain under the sea.

The Hindu Kush The extensions of the W end of the Himalayas run almost due
S of the Pamirs through the W borderlands of Pakistan and Afghanistan. The
Hindu Kush is dominated by Permo-Carboniferous rocks, and to the S of the
Khyber Pass are the sandstone ranges and the Safed Koh. Still further S, the
borderlands of Baluchistan fall into two distinct parts. To the W of a line running
due S from **Nushki**, weak sandstones predominate in an extension of the Iranian
plateau. To the E of this line are successive crests of N-S running limestone hills.
These parallel ridges and valleys give dramatic views from the air, often clearly

visible on routes to Europe from Delhi via the Gulf and northwards out of Karachi.

The Plains

Rising within 200 km of each other, the Ganga, Indus and Brahmaputra rivers and their tributaries have created one of the world's most densely populated alluvial plains. Now the home of more than half of South Asia's people, their geological origin lies some 40 million years ago. As the Himalayas began their dramatic uplift the rivers which formed on them eroded massive quantities of rock, stone and silt. The finer material was washed down onto the plains fronting the newly forming mountain ranges, which were themselves sinking as the mountains to the N were rising. The trough which formed as a result of this process was steadily filled. Today the alluvium reaches depths of over 5,000 metres in places, being deepest between Delhi and Orissa. The boundary between the plains and the Himalayan ranges is a zone of continuing violent earth movement, with earthquakes common from the W borderlands of Pakistan, through Nepal to Assam.

Silt and mud Just as the Himalayas are still rising so the *Indo-Gangetic plains* are also being extended and modified. The S part of Bangladesh and of W Bengal only emerged from the sea during the last 5,000 years. The Ganga and the Indus have each been estimated to carry over a million tonnes of suspended material every year – considerably more than the Mississippi, though much less than the Yellow River in China.

Such loads have brought great rewards for farmers in the eastern deltas, for the silts are very rich in plant foods, and have made it possible for intensive rice cultivation to be practised continuously for hundreds of years. However, they also bring enormous problems, especially where large scale irrigation is undertaken. Thus dams such as the **Mangla Dam** on the **Jhelum River** in Pakistan, and the **Bhakra Dam** on the **Sutlej River** in India are being rapidly filled by silt. Over 33 million tonnes of silt a year are being deposited behind the Bhakra Dam alone.

Underground water The plains have some of the largest reserves of underground water in the world. These reserves have been put to use on an unparalleled scale during the last 40 years. They have made possible extensive well irrigation, especially in Pakistan and the NW plains of India, thereby contributing to the rapid agricultural changes which have taken place. The resources in Bangladesh offer promise of a great extension of dry season farming.

The plains of the **Indus** and the **Ganga** stretch apparently endlessly and unchangingly from E to W. Yet there are extremely important differences in soil and local relief which have a great effect on agriculture. This is particularly striking in Bangladesh, where differences of height of one or two metres above sea level determine the levels of annual flooding. In turn that gives farmers the challenge of selecting crops to suit the differing conditions. Generations of farmers have practised agriculture with enormous subtlety and sensitivity to their environment.

The Peninsula

As recently as 50 million years ago the land mass S of the line Karachi – Delhi – Calcutta lay in the S hemisphere. Many of the rocks which form the peninsula and the related structures of Sri Lanka were formed alongside their then neighbours in S Africa, S America, Australia and Antarctica.

Early origins A major part of the Peninsula is made up of *Archaean* rocks, some of the oldest in the world. They are generally crystalline, contorted and faulted. The oldest series are the *Charnockites*, named after the servant of the E India Company and enthusiastic amateur geologist, **Job Charnock**, see page 516. Along with the *Khondalite* rocks, these are over 3,100 million years old. Some of the most striking examples are found in the **Nilgiri** and **Palani Hills** in Tamil Nadu. Other major areas of gneissic rocks are found in the **Eastern Ghats**, in **Rajasthan**

and the **Aravalli-Delhi** belt, and in **Bihar** and **Orissa**. The Charnockites themselves extend into the Highlands of Sri Lanka.

Economic minerals Economically there are several important geological series. One is the greenstone belt, commonest in S India. Formed between 2,700 and 3,000 m years ago, these rocks contain gold, silver and copper. South Asia's main gold mining area is at **Kolar**, just E of Bangalore. Further N, around **Jabalpur** and **Nagpur**, these rocks contain some of India's most famous marble, as well as important deposits of manganese. However, it is their deposits of very high grade **iron ore** which make these geological formations particularly significant.

Diamonds The Peninsula also has very extensive areas of ancient sedimentary rocks. The oldest is the **Vindhyan series** which are found in the Vindhyan Mountains of W central India. Sandstones, limestones and shales, these comprise beds that are often 4000 m thick and cover over 100,000 square kilometres. They stretch from W Bihar to the gneissic rocks of the **Aravallis** and **Mount Abu**, and they form particularly dramatic ridges just N of the **Narmada River**, where they are strikingly visible in the sharp-fronted scarp overlooking the **Son**. Their upper beds have two diamond bearing layers from which the famous diamonds of **Panna** and **Golconda** have been mined. Of the latter the **Koh-i-noor** is perhaps the most famous single diamond in the world.

Red sandstones The sandstones have also made an enormous contribution to Indian architecture as the source of the red sandstone of which the Mughals made such extensive use in their city building through northern India and Pakistan.

Coal In addition to the iron ore and gemstone bearing rocks, the Peninsula also has South Asia's most extensive deposits of coal. These were laid down in what are known as the Lower Gondwana Series which form three main belts in India: a linear tract along the Damodar Valley in W Bengal; an extensive outcrop along the upper reaches of the Mahanadi River in Madhya Pradesh; and a series of troughs along the upper Godavari River from Nagpur to the river's delta.

Deccan lavas Some 60 million years ago great cracks developed in the earth's surface, allowing a mass of **volcanic lava** to well up from the deep, covering some 500,000 square km of underlying Vindhyan sedimentaries and Archaean rocks – N Karnataka, Maharashtra, N into Gujarat and Madhya Pradesh. The deepest lava was near the fissures themselves, just inland of Bombay, where today they have depths of more than 3000 m. They thin rapidly E. The opening up of these volcanic cracks was directly related to the separation of the Indian Peninsula from the African coastline, and the subsequent NE movement of the Indian plate to its present location.

The Western Ghats
Although the Peninsula has none of the dramatic scenery of the Himalayas it is an area of great variety. Running N-S down its W flank are the **Western Ghats**. Formed by the subsidence of the Arabian Sea as the Indian plate moved NE away from Africa, the Ghats today are set back from the sea by a coastal plain which varies from ten to over 80 km wide. In the S, the Nilgiris and Palanis are over 2,500 metres high.

From the crest line of the Western Ghats, the Peninsula slopes generally E, interrupted on its E edge by the much more broken groups of hills sometimes referred to as the Eastern Ghats. Most of the peninsular rivers rise within 80 km to 100 km from the W coast, but actually flow into the Bay of Bengal. Their flat alluvial deltas have been the basis of successive peninsular kingdoms and empires from the **Pallavas**, **Pandiyans** and **Cholas** in the far S to the **Kalingans** in Orissa.

Sri Lanka
Except for the limestone outcrops of the Jaffna Peninsula and the NW coast, the

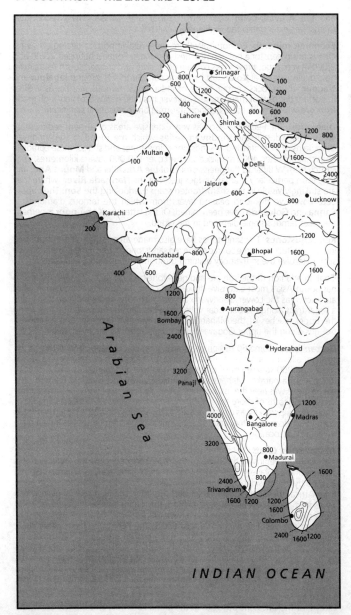

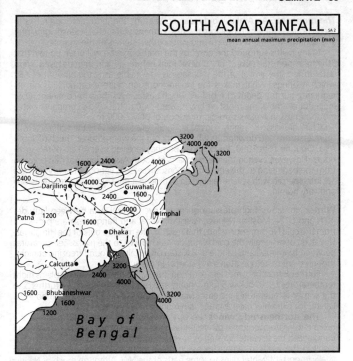

SOUTH ASIA RAINFALL SA2
mean annual maximum precipitation (mm)

MAPS: Publisher's note.
The Government of India state that "The external boundaries of India are neither correct or authenticated." The maps in the Handbook are not intended to have any political significance.

whole of Sri Lanka is composed of the same pre-Cambrian rocks characteristic of S India, many of them more than 3,000 million years old. They have been raised in three tiers from sea level, each separated from the next by a dramatic scarp front. These steep scarps have themselves been deeply eroded. The alternation of steep slopes and deep cut valleys contributes to Sri Lanka's often stunningly beautiful scenery, but in the past it often made it very difficult to get in to many parts of the central highlands.

CLIMATE

South Asia is divided almost exactly by the Tropic of Cancer, stretching from the Equatorial Maldives to the Mediterranean latitudes of Kashmir – roughly the same as from the Amazon to San Francisco or from Lagos to Madrid. Not surprisingly, climate varies considerably. High altitudes both in the N and in the Western Ghats modify local climates, often dramatically.

The monsoon An Arabic word meaning 'season', the term monsoon refers to the wind reversal which replaces the dry northeasterlies, characteristic of winter and spring, with the very warm and wet southwesterlies of the summer.

Many myths surround the onset of the monsoon. You will often be told that "the monsoon starts on..." or "it never rains before...." and then be given a firm date. In fact the arrival of the monsoon is as variable as is the amount of rain which it brings. What makes the Indian monsoon quite exceptional is not its regularity but the depth of moist air which passes over the sub-continent. Over India, for example, the moist airflow is over 6,000 m thick. This compares with a moist airmass in Japan's summer monsoon of only 2,000 m.

This airmass is highly unstable, and gives rise to the characteristic thunderstorms and downpours which mark out the wet season in much of South Asia. On June 16th 1990, for example, Bombay received over 40 cm of rain in 16 hours. However, even in the wettest parts of South Asia it does not rain nonstop from the beginning to the end of the monsoon season. Periods of heavy showers are interspersed with several rainless days, though it usually remains cloudy, windy and very humid.

Winter In winter high pressure builds up over central Asia between latitudes 40°N and 60°N. Most of N India, Pakistan, Nepal and Bangladesh are protected from the cold NE monsoon winds that result from the massive bulk of the Himalayas. However, occasionally the cold winds do reach down to the plains. Temperatures between Islamabad and Lahore in Pakistan often fall to around freezing at night, though daytime temperatures rise sharply in the sun.

Further E frost becomes less common, but right across the Ganga plains night temperatures fall to below 5°C in January and February. As you move further S so the winter temperatures increase. Madras in the S of India and Colombo in Sri Lanka, for example, have average minimum temperatures of 20°C.

The northeasterly winds are very shallow, and from 3000 m above the ground they are overridden by westerlies. In Pakistan, N India, Nepal, Bhutan and Bangladesh these winter westerlies are often found at ground level as well. They result in the western regions receiving Mediterranean depressions which bring vitally important winter rains to some parts of the NW. Although much of N India and Pakistan often has beautiful weather from November through to March, there are sometimes periods of four or five days when it is cool and overcast. Elsewhere, however, the winter is a dry season through nearly all of South Asia, except for the near-Equatorial islands of Sri Lanka and the Maldives, which receive some rain through most of the year.

Summer From May onwards much of South Asia becomes almost unbearably hot. In the six weeks or so before the SW monsoon sets in, heat builds up over the land mass of both South Asia and continental Asia to the N. Temperatures in the plains of Pakistan, India and Bangladesh are generally over 40°C, and temperatures of over 50°C are not unknown. It is a time of year to be avoided.

At the end of May the upper air westerly jet stream, which controls the atmospheric system over the Indo-Gangetic plains through the winter, suddenly breaks down. It then re-forms to the N of Tibet. This allows very moist southwesterlies to sweep across the Maldives, Sri Lanka and then the S part of India and up across the **Bay of Bengal**. They then double back northwestwards, bringing rain across the Indo-Gangetic Plains to NW India and Pakistan.

The wet season From a visitor's point of view the monsoon season can be even worse in many parts of South Asia than the greater heat that precedes it, for it brings an enveloping dampness which makes cooling down impossible. It also makes it very difficult to keep things dry – particularly important for photographic equipment and films. The rainy season lasts from between three to six months before the northeasterlies reassert themselves.

The total amount of rain received varies enormously across the sub-continent. The crest of the Western Ghats and some of the wetter parts of the W coast receive over 2500 mm of rain a year. Parts of Assam and NE India receive more than 5000 mm in a year. Yet in the central Indian peninsula and in NW India and Pakistan, rainfall is as low as 100 mm, giving rise to desert conditions in Rajasthan and S Pakistan.

VEGETATION

Today, wherever you arrive in South Asia your first impression is not of forests, jungle or even open woodland but of intensively cultivated fields (as around Calcutta, Madras or Dhaka) or arid rocky hills or even desert (Karachi and Delhi), a reminder that there is virtually no strictly natural vegetation left in South Asia. Forest cover in India has been reduced since the early 1970s from around 18% of the total area to 13%. Most of that loss is accounted for by peasant cultivators trying to bring new land into cultivation.

From the northernmost point of Pakistan to southern Sri Lanka, people have had a major effect on the original vegetation. Everything you see travelling round South Asia is the result of that interaction between people and their environment. Travel even a short distance from any of the major cities and the point is visibly reinforced. Roadsides right across South Asia are commonly lined with trees, frequently numbered so that use of the leaves and branches can be monitored and paid for.

Forest cover Both its tropical location and its position astride the wet monsoonal winds ensured that the original vegetation cover of most parts of South Asia just under one million years ago was tropical deciduous forest. Perhaps as much as 90% of South Asia has a climate suitable for such forest cover, although there was great variety within it. Areas with around 1700 mm of rainfall had forests ranging from tropical semi-evergreen types to moist tropical deciduous. In contrast, areas with around 1000 mm had dry tropical deciduous woodland.

Teak and sal Two types of deciduous tree were particularly common then and even today they remain important. **Sal** (*Shorea robusta*) and **teak** (*Tectona grandis*) are still found extensively, though in the case of teak the great majority has been planted. Both are resistant to burning, which helped to protect them where man used fire as a chief means of clearing the forest. While most tropical deciduous forest is highly varied both teak and sal are commonly found in extensive stands.

Sal, which used to dominate on the S slopes of **Nepal**, is now largely restricted to the E region, and to E India. Teak, which is highly valued as a building timber because of its resistance to termites, used to be concentrated in W regions of India, but is now much more widely spread. You can get the best views of teak forests in central Madhya Pradesh and Orissa in India, and the main railway S from Nagpur passes through some of the few remaining areas of dense forest.

Tropical rain forest In wetter areas, particularly along the Western Ghats to the S of Bombay, you can still find *tropical evergreen forest*, but even these forests are now extensively managed. In contrast, across the drier areas of the peninsula and Pakistan, the forest cover thins out. In many areas it has also been heavily grazed and has often been reduced to little more than thorn scrub.

In areas like W Rajasthan and Sind, drought-tolerant shrubs become common. In these marginal lands small changes in climate since people first settled have been very significant. Much of Pakistan and parts of Rajasthan are now known to have been significantly wetter as little as 8,000 years ago, when the pastoral settlements of the NW were beginning to develop into settled agricultural communities. It is still not clear what caused the reduction in rainfall.

Sandalwood   The demand for forest resources is threatening a number of India's well known species. Commercial pressures are also taking their toll. Indian rose wood, much favoured for its use in high quality furniture making, is now restricted to very limited areas in S India. The fragrant sandalwood, still a favourite medium for carving small images of Hindu deities, is so valuable that its exploitation is totally controlled by the government. In practice there are organised smuggling rings, and vast sums of money are said to be at stake in the illegal trade in sandalwood.

Palm trees   A far more visible feature of the peninsular landscape are the different varieties of **palm** tree. Two in particular make a very important economic contribution. **Coconut** palms (*Cocos nucifera*) dominate the entire W coast of India and are also common in S and E India. The large green fruit of the tender coconut, which looks so different from the small hairy brown inner nut which is seen in markets and on coconut shies in Europe, is widely available on street corners in towns and villages. It gives one of the most refreshing – and healthy – drinks available.

   The other palm tree, the *palmyra* palm (*Borassus flabellifer*), is more common in SE and E India. When cut off, its palm fronds pour profuse quantities of sap. This is widely collected and then boiled to produce sugar. Alternatively, if left to ferment for a few hours the juice makes the highly alcoholic local drink, arrack.

Sri Lanka has both **dry deciduous forest** and **wet semi-evergreen tropical forests** with as many as 1300 species of flowering plants. Little of the original cover in either the dry or the wet zone remains.

Mountain forests   Altitude has important local effects on modifying the natural forest cover. At between 1000 m and 2000 m in the E hill ranges of India, and in Bhutan and Nepal, for example, wet hill forest include **evergreen oaks** and **chestnuts**. Further W in the foothills of the Himalayas are belts of **subtropical pine** at roughly the same altitudes. From the W regions of Nepal through to Pakistan, **deodars** (*Cedrus deodarus*) form large stands, and **moist temperate forest**, with pines, cedars, firs and spruce, is dominant, giving many of the valleys a beautifully fresh, Alpine feel.

Rhododendrons   Between 3000 m and 4000 m alpine forest predominates. The famous belts of **rhododendron** are often mixed with other forest types. In **Nepal** rhododendrons are most common in areas of very heavy rainfall, and at altitudes of more than 2500 m on the upper stretches of the **River Arun** and **Tamur** is a zone of almost pure rhododendron. Birch, juniper and pine are widespread, and poplars are found from Kashmir in the W to Bhutan in the east.

Grasslands   Forest is the most extensive natural vegetation of South Asia, but there are also areas of **savanna grassland**, produced as a result of man's action. There are several varieties of coarse grassland along the S edge of the **Terai**. Alpine grasses are important for grazing above altitudes of 2000 m. A totally distinctive grassland is the **bamboo region** of the E Himalayas. **Bamboo** (*Dendocalamus*) is widespread throughout India, and there are some magnificent specimens in urban zoos and parks as in Bangalore, Calcutta and Trivandrum. It is now widely used in the NE for the paper making industry.

Pakistan and Bangladesh   Natural vegetation is very sparse in both Bangladesh and Pakistan. In the latter the flooded delta landscape, coupled with intensive cultivation, has left only the salty marshes of the **Sundarbans** free from intensive human use. These have some 600 sq km of mangrove forest, but even here there are six or seven species which are economically important. The SE region, inland of Chittagong, still has around 150,000 sq km of semi-evergreen forest and bamboo jungle. Pakistan's arid climate restricts natural vegetation to drought-tolerant shrubs in all except the N mountain belt.

SOILS

The most fertile are the **alluvial soils** of the Indo-Gangetic plains and the deltas of the E coast of India. In practice these vary greatly. Many deteriorate rapidly if green manure and fertiliser are not applied. Others are often at risk of becoming encrusted with salts if irrigated without proper drainage. Yet the whole of **Bangladesh**, large parts of **Pakistan** and the heartland of N India are dependent on them.

The largest broad category of soils in peninsular India (with extensions into Sri Lanka) are the **red soils** which have developed on the ancient archaean rocks. These are mainly light, sandy and often gravelly, and although they are easily worked they are usually poor in plant nutrients and dry out very quickly. There are limited areas of genuine tropical **laterites**, as in **Orissa** and **Kerala** for example, but true laterites are not nearly as extensive as was once believed.

The most important exception to these broad regional soil types are the **black cotton soils** of the Deccan plateau. On the 500,000 sq km of the so-called **Deccan Trap** the volcanic lavas have given rise to heavy black soils, often referred to as cotton soils, as they have proved extremely well suited to cotton growing. The great cotton industries of Bombay, Maharashtra and Gujarat owe their pre-eminence in part to the quality of these soils. Their naturally high fertility is offset to some extent by the fact that they are often too heavy to irrigate successfully.

WILDLIFE

South Asia has enormous diversity of wildlife, yet today many species are at risk, and many more owe their continued existence to the development of reserves. There are over 2,000 species of birds, over 500 species of mammals and several hundred species of reptiles and amphibians. Most of India's species were adapted to forest conditions, and thus are particularly at risk from the destruction of their natural habitat. South Asia has four times as many species of bird, for example, as does Europe, but they too are threatened, along with the more widely publicised animals at risk such as tigers and lions.

Tigers were reduced to the verge of extinction by the early 1970s, but now they are reported to be increasing steadily in several of the game reserves. The same is true of other, less well known species. Their natural habitat has been destroyed not just by the direct activities of people but also by the domesticated animals. In addition to the 1.1 billion people now living in South Asia, India alone has some 250 million cattle and 50 million sheep and goats.

National parks All the countries are taking steps to preserve their wildlife heritage. All the larger countries have created national parks. Even the tiny state of Bhutan has declared approximately one fifth of its total area to be a natural reserve. In India, 25,000 sq km were set aside in 1973 for Project Tiger, just part of a much wider programme covering 250 reserves in total. There are big reserves in Pakistan, Nepal, Bangladesh and Sri Lanka, and even the Maldives is taking a strict line on exploitation of its precious species of coral.

Mammals

Even the comparatively small island of Sri Lanka has one hundred species of mammal, Bangladesh twice as many, and India twice as many again. *Elephants* are both the most striking of the mammals and the most economically important, for there are many areas where they are put to work. One of the distinctive features of Indian elephants is that only the male bears tusks. Much of the elephants' natural habitat has been destroyed, but there are approximately 6,500 elephants living in the wild in northern W Bengal, Assam and Bhutan. There are a further 200 in the Chittagong Hill Tracts of Bangladesh, 2,000 in central India and 6,000 in the three S Indian States of Kerala, Tamil Nadu and Karnataka, as well as further herds in Sri Lanka. There are plans for a new elephant reserve on the borders of Bhutan and India.

Elephants are not yet an endangered species, but other large South Asian mammals are very much under threat. The sub-continent's second largest mammal, the **one-horned** *rhinoceros*, was once found right across the Indo-Gangetic plains. Now there are only 1,500 left, in three locations of Assam, northern W Bengal and Nepal. Occasionally the smaller **Sumatran rhinoceros** is seen in the Chittagong Hill Tracts.

The numbers of the **cat family** have also been drastically reduced. **Tiger** numbers fell to around 2,000 in India, with a further 600-700 scattered among the sub-Himalayan regions and Bangladesh. **Cheetahs** are already extinct, and the only lion species, the **Gir**, was down to fewer than 200 until a successful breeding programme in the Gir sanctuary in Gujarat has brought some recovery in their numbers.

South Asia has three varieties of **leopard**. In the far N of Pakistan there are snow leopards in the Khunjerab National Park and in the high Himalayas of Bhutan. The arboreal **clouded leopard** is still found in northern Assam, Nepal, Bhutan and the Chittagong Hill Tracts of Bangladesh, while India's most famous leopard, the **black panther** is still found virtually throughout its original territory.

Desert and jungle cats are found in Pakistan and NW India, as are the **Caracal**, which hunt birds as their prey. **Lynx** live up to altitudes of 3,000 m in the ranges of Gilgit,Ladakh and Tibet, and the Himalayas remain a vitally important region for other species of wildlife such as **Brown**, **Black** and **Sloth Bears**. Black bears are fairly common up to heights of 3,700 m, and Sloth bears, which live on fruit, insects and wild bees, are still found in Nepal, and in two reserves in India.

Wild cattle Both in the Himalayan region and in game reserves in the Peninsula there is a wide range of wild species of cattle, sheep and goats. One of the most impressive is the huge **Gaur**, or Jungle Bison, which is found in the S Indian game reserves of Madumalai and Bandipur, and in parts of Nepal. **Wild buffalo** live in the forests of Assam and central India, and in addition to the domesticated varieties there are wild **yaks** on Nepal and Ladakh. There are four South Asian species of wild sheep and five species of wild goat. The **Nilgiri Tahrs**, found as their name implies in the southern hills of India up to altitudes of 1,800 m, are also found at much higher altitudes in the Himalayas.

Deer used to roam across the whole region. Some herds can still be seen even in densely populated areas, such as **Haus Khas** on the outskirts of New Delhi. Reserves have made it possible for the large **Barasingha**,or **swamp deer**, to survive in W Nepal, Assam and Madhya Pradesh. The smaller **Muntjac**, or barking deer, are found extensively on the lower wooded slopes of the Himalayas, and in forests of S India, and **Musk deer** live in the birch woods and higher forests of the Himalayas.

Monkeys In any city of South Asia both the **Rhesus Macaque** and the **Common Langur**, the two commonest species, are widely evident. They have many related species, some of which are now extremely rare. In the extreme S of India, for example, the are about 800 **lion-tailed Macaque** monkeys left in the rain forests of Kerala, while the **Assamese Macaque**, the **Pig-Tailed Macaque** of the Naga Hills and the **Bonnet Macaque** all live in the northern regions of South Asia. The Common Langur, which is found in most South Asian forests, also has several variants: the **Nilgiri Langur**, the **Capped Langur** of Assam and the Chittagong Hill Tracts, and the **Golden Langur** of Bhutan. Sri Lanka has its own varieties of Macaque and Langur monkeys, such as the **Ceylon Grey Langur** and the **Bear Monkey**.

Carnivores Rudyard Kipling made the **mongoose** famous in his story of Rikki-Tikki-Tavi, the mongoose that killed a giant cobra. Various species of mongoose (Herpestinae) are found across both the South Asian mainland and in Sri Lanka. The three commonest species are small: the **Grey Mongoose**, the **Small Indian Mongoose** and the **Desert Mongoose**. There are also three larger but rare species. They are valued (and sometimes tamed) for their ability to fight effectively even the most deadly of snakes such as the cobra and the krait, although one of the mongoose species in Assam and Nepal has made freshwater crab the chief element of its diet. Snake charmers who gather round the tourist centres of India will often offer the visitor the spectacle of a mongoose fighting a cobra – all carefully controlled so that neither gets hurt.

There is an enormous range of small mammals, some of which are omnivorous. **Civet cats** are widespread from Sri Lanka northwards, for example. In the Himalayas and in S India otters are found, and in the Sundarbans of W Bengal and Bangladesh have been trained to catch fish. There are over two dozen species of weasels, ferrets and badgers.

Insectivores such as **shrews**, **hedgehogs** and **moles** are common, and if you visit any caves you will come across **bats**. In many parts of the region, including Sri Lanka, the **Flying Fox** is common, and rodents and squirrels are ubiquitous. The small striped Indian **squirrel** is one of the commonest sights right across South Asia, treating humans with scant regard and scurrying in and out of buildings as well as trees and bushes.

Dolphins and porpoises Mammalian life is not restricted to the land. In the rivers of the Ganga-Brahmaputra delta are dolphins and porpoises, also be found in the Indus. **Gangetic dolphins** often move far inland as they tolerate fresh as well as salt water.

Reptiles and Birds

Visitors to South Asia very rarely see snakes, although they remain very common in the countryside. There are over 200 different species or subspecies of snakes alone, many of which are non-poisonous.

Cobras and Kraits are the most feared species. The **King Cobras**, which live in the tropical rain forests and may reach lengths of over 5 m, are by far the largest poisonous snakes, though both the **Rock Python** and the **Reticulated Python**, which have recorded lengths of over 7 m and weights of over 115 kg, are even bigger. **Kraits** are less than 0.5 m long, but they move exceptionally fast and have one of the most deadly venoms. **Vipers**, such as the **Himalayan Pit Viper** and the **Bamboo Viper**, and several species of **sea snake**, are further examples of poisonous snakes. By and large fresh water snakes, some of which look impressive if you come across them while bathing in hill rivers, are generally not poisonous.

Crocodiles and turtles The **Blunt Nosed** or **Marsh Crocodile** (the **Magar**) is still found in the Terai of Nepal, but the **Gharial** has only just survived as a result of government efforts to protect it. The big Estuarine crocodile in still found from the Ganga in Bangladesh to the Mahanadi in Orissa. All five species of **Monitor Lizard**, found in both deserts and forests, are endangered, but both India and Pakistan retain important breeding beaches for a number of species of turtle. In Orissa there are about 300,000 **Olive Ridley Turtles** breeding; others live in the Sundarbans of Bengal. **Green Turtles** and Olive Ridley turtles breed on the beaches immediately to the W of Karachi, and **Hawksbill turtles** breed in S Tamil Nadu.

Birds There are over 2000 species of birds in South Asia, reflecting its tropical location and traditionally forested environment. Most species originated in the tropical oriental region, although some undoubtedly have African origins. There are also large numbers of migratory birds such as ducks, cranes, swallows and fly-catchers which come annually from Central Asia over the Himalayas.

Birds of prey Pakistan and N India are the home of some of the world's finest birds of prey. **Eagles** and **falcons** used to be very common. Although there are still over 20 species their survival is seriously threatened by systematic hunting. In contrast there are several common species of vulture and of kite which remain highly visible in many parts of South Asia. Equally, fishing birds such as egrets are a common sight along any stretch of water or in irrigated fields.

But while all of the countries of South Asia have splendid examples of the largest birds of prey, they also have an enormous variety of small and colourful birds. Parakeets, woodpeckers and kingfishers abound, while various songbirds such as the Indian shama and the famous Indian mynah bird complement the range. The latter is not to be confused with its much more common but untuneful relative, seen very widely throughout South Asia. The wealth and colour of South Asia's bird life is symbolised most effectively perhaps in the dramatic plumage of India's national bird, the peacock.

THE PEOPLES OF SOUTH ASIA

There are more than one billion people now living in South Asia. India, with 844 million in 1991, is the second most populated country in the world after China, and Pakistan and Bangladesh, each with more than 100 million, are also in the top ten. That population size reflects both the suitability of much of South Asia for permanent settlement, and the long history of human occupation of nearly every part of the sub-continent.

Ethnic origins Until recently it was thought that the skeletons of two hominoids (the term used to describe the common ancestors of apes and humans), Ramapithecus and Sivapithecus, found in what is now N Pakistan and N central India, were some of the earliest direct ancestors of man in the world. Estimated to have lived between 11 million and 13 million years ago, we now know that they were apes rather than early men.

There is no such thing as a pure racial type, and intermixture has clearly been characteristic of South Asia through most of its history. Indeed, in detail the racial and ethnic origins of the present peoples of South Asia are obscure. Its first inhabitants came, like so many of their successors, from the NW.

The overwhelming majority of South Asians today are of **Mediterranean** stock. Generally brown skinned, with dark and usually straight hair, and brown eyes, there are recognisable differences in physical type across the regions of the subcontinent. People in the S tend to have darker complexions, a lighter build and to be shorter than those in the N. In the NE many people have the higher cheekbones characteristic of **Mongoloid** features. Numerically tiny groups of tribal people such as the **Veddas** in Sri Lanka, or the **Andaman Island tribals**, form exceptions.

Early Mediterranean groups form the main component of the Dravidian speakers of the four S Indian states and N Sri Lanka. **Later Mediterranean** types also seem to have come from the NW and down the Indus Valley, but more important were the Indo-Aryans, who migrated from the steppes of Central Asia from around 2000 BC.

SOUTH ASIAN LANGUAGES

The graffiti written on the walls of any Indian city bear witness to the number of major languages spoken across the country, many with their own distinct scripts. In all the capital cities of the South Asia an Indo-Aryan language – the easternmost group of the Indo-European family – is predominant; Hindi in Delhi, Urdu and Punjabi in Islamabad, Bengali in Dhaka, Sinhalese in Colombo and Nepali in Kathmandu. Even Divehi in the Maldives is an Indo-European language.

Sir William Jones, the great 19th century scholar, discovered the close links between German, Greek and Sanskrit. He showed that all these languages must have originated in the common heartland of Central Asia, being carried W, S and E by the nomadic tribes who shaped so much of the subsequent history of both Europe and Asia.

Sanskrit As the pastoralists from Central Asia moved into South Asia from 2000 BC onwards, the Indo-Aryan languages they spoke were gradually modified. **Sanskrit** developed from this process, emerging as the dominant classical language of India by the 6th century BC, when it was classified in the grammar of **Panini**. It remained the language of the educated right across South Asia until about AD 1000, though it had ceased to be in common use several centuries earlier. The Muslims brought Persian into South Asia as the language of the rulers. Like Sanskrit before it, and English from the 18th century onwards, Persian became the language of the numerically tiny but politically powerful elite across South Asia.

Hindi and Urdu All the modern languages of N India, Pakistan, Bangladesh and Nepal owe their origins to the blending of the earlier **Indo-Aryan** languages, with the later additions coming from Muslim influence. The most striking example of that influence is that of the two most important languages of India and Pakistan, **Hindi** and **Urdu** respectively. Most of the other modern N Indian languages were not written until the 16th century or after.

Hindi and Urdu developed as a common language in the Delhi region out of the fusion of the local language with the import of many words of **Persian** origin, brought by the Muslim rulers and their camp followers. During the 19th century **Hindustani**, as it was known by the British, divided along religious lines. Hindi moved towards its Sanskrit Hindu roots. It used the script known as **Devanagari**, now common across the N states of India from Haryana to Bihar. Urdu, on the other hand, with its script derived from Persian and Arabic, was taken up particularly by the Muslim community. It consciously incorporated Persian words, and thus while the common spoken languages of Hindi and Urdu were – and are – quite easily understood by speakers of the other language, the higher literary forms of both languages became mutually unintelligible.

Bengali While Hindi developed into the language of the heartland of Hindu culture, stretching from Punjab in the W to Bihar in the East, and from the foothills of the Himalayas in the N to the marchlands of Central India to the South, the Indo-Aryan languages of the early invaders developed into quite different languages on the margins of that NW core region. At the E end of the Ganga plains Hindi gives way to **Bengali**. Bengali (known officially in Bangladesh today as **Bangla**) is the national language today of over 100 million people in Bangladesh, as well as more than 50 million in India. It is close to both **Assamese** to the N and **Oriya** to the S, though they are sufficiently different to be mutually almost unintelligible.

Gujarati and Marathi Travelling S or SW of the main Hindi and Urdu belt of India and Pakistan you meet a series of quite different Indo-Aryan languages. **Sindhi** in Pakistan, and **Panjabi** in both Pakistan and India (on the Indian side of the border written in the **Gurumukhi** script), and further S in India, **Gujarati** and **Marathi**, all have common features with Urdu or Hindi, but are major languages in their own right. There are also two "outliers" of Indo-Aryan languages in the form of **Sinhala** in Sri Lanka and **Divehi** in the Maldives. Both owe their origins to the southwards movement of Buddhist missionaries. They took with them the language of **Pali**, which originated in the 4th century BC. This is still used in the Buddhist scriptures and was a major influence on the development of Sinhala, which developed its own character, separated by nearly 1500 km from its Indo-Aryan heartland.

The Dravidian languages The invading Indo-Aryan speakers who came into South Asia over 3,500 years ago encountered people who spoke languages belonging to the other major language family of South Asia today, **Dravidian**. Four of South Asia's major living languages belong to this family group – **Tamil**, **Telugu**, **Kannada** and **Malayalam**, spoken in Tamil Nadu (and northern Sri Lanka), Andhra Pradesh, Karnataka and Kerala respectively.

Each has its own script, just as Hindi, Urdu, Bengali and the other Indo-Aryan languages have their distinct scripts. All the Dravidian languages were influenced by the prevalence of Sanskrit as the language of the ruling and educated elite.

Although there have been recent politically-inspired attempts to rid **Tamil** of its Sanskrit elements, and to recapture the supposed purity of a literature that stretches back to the early centuries BC, all the Dravidian languages retain evidence of their close contact with Indo-Aryan languages. **Kannada** and **Telugu** were clearly established by AD 1000, and **Malayalam**, which started as a dialect of Tamil, did not develop its fully distinct form until the 13th century. Today the four main Dravidian languages are spoken by over 180 million people.

Scripts

It is impossible to spend even a short time in India or the other countries of South Asia without coming across several of the different scripts that are used. The earliest ancestor of scripts in use today was the **Brahmi** script, in which the great Emperor Asoka's famous inscriptions were written in the 3rd century BC. It was written from left to right, and was based on the principle of having a separate symbol to represent each different sound.

Devanagari For about a thousand years the major script of N India has been the **Nagari** or **Devanagari**, which means literally "the script of the city of the gods". **Hindi**, **Nepali** and **Marathi** join the classical and religious language of **Sanskrit** in their use of Devanagari. The Muslim rulers developed a right to left script based on Persian and Arabic. In New Delhi you can see three scripts used extensively in the N, the road names being written in Devanagari, Gurumukhi (the script used for Panjabi) and Urdu, as well as English.

Dravidian scripts The Dravidian languages were written originally on leaves of the *palmyra* palm. Some very early examples of such writing can still be seen in museums such as the palace in Jaipur. Cutting the letters on the hard palm leaf made particular demands which had their impact on the forms of the letters adopted. The letters became rounded because they were carved with a stylus. This was held stationary while the leaf was turned. The southern scripts were carried overseas, contributing to the form of **Thai**, **Burmese** and **Cambodian**, even though those languages are not Dravidian and they are representative of Buddhist rather than Hindu cultures.

If you want to remind yourself what the major scripts look like, Indian banknotes carry their denomination (one Rupee, five Rupees, etc.) listed in the major regional languages on one side. From the top they are Assamese, Bengali, Gujarati, Kannada, Kashmiri, Malayalam, Hindi, Oriya, Panjabi, Rajasthani, Tamil, Telugu and Urdu.

Many of the Indian alphabets have their own notation for numerals. However, this is not without irony, for what in the western world are called 'Arabic' numerals are in fact of Indian origin. In some parts of South Asia local numerical symbols are still in use (Bengali on road signs and currency notes in Bangladesh, Marathi for the bus numbers in Bombay, and Persian-Arabic in Pakistan, for example), but by and large you will find that the Arabic number symbols familiar in Europe and the W are extremely common.

The role of English English now plays an important role in all the countries of South Asia. It is widely spoken in towns and cities, and even in quite remote villages it is usually not difficult to find someone who speaks at least a little English. Other European languages are almost completely unknown. English has undergone some important modifications during nearly four centuries of use in South Asia. The accent in which it is spoken is often affected strongly by the mother tongue of the speaker, and there have been changes in common grammar which sometimes make it sound unusual. Many of these changes are not mere quirks but have become standard Indian English usage, as valid as any other varieties of English used around the world. Oxford University Press in India have published a grammar of Indian English if you want to read more about common English use in South Asia.

Some of the major scripts of South Asia

Script	Language	Where used
تُبِ مِيوَتَّ	Urdu	Pakistan & North India
ਸਤਯਮੇਵ ਜਯਤੇ	Panjabi/Gurumukhi	North West India
सत्यमेव जयते	Devanagari	North India
সত্যমেব জয়তে	Bengali	East India & Bangladesh
ସତ୍ୟମେବ ଜୟତେ	Oriya	East India
સત્યમેવ જયતે	Gujarati	West India
సత్య మేవ జయతే	Telugu	South East India
ಸತ್ಯಮೇವ ಜಯತೇ	Kannada	South West India
சத்தியமேவ ஜயதே	Tamil	South/East India
സത്യമേവ ജയതേ	Malayam	South West India
සත්‍යයමේව ජයති	Sinhala	Sri Lanka

Roughly translated, these words mean 'truth alone triumphs'. The Government of India prints an everyday example of the scripts on its bank notes.

LITERATURE

Sanskrit was the first all-India language. Its literature had a fundamental influence on the religious, social and political life of the entire region. Beginning with the development of texts which were not written down but memorised and recited, it is still impossible to date with any accuracy the earliest Sanskrit hymns. They are in the collection now known as the Rig Veda, which probably didn't reach its final form until about the 6th century BC, but the earliest parts of which may go back as far as 1200 BC – approximately the period of the fall of Mycenean Greece in Europe.

The Vedas The **Rig Veda** is a collection of 1028 hymns, not all directly religious. However, the main function of the Rig Veda was to provide orders of worship for priests responsible for the sacrifices which were central to the religion of the Indo-Aryans. This is also true of two further texts that began to be created towards the end of the period in which the Rig Veda was being written down, the **Yajurveda** and the **Samaveda**. A fourth collection, the **Atharvaveda**, is made up largely of magic spells.

The Brahmanas Central to the Vedic literature was a belief in the importance of sacrifice. At some time after 1000 BC a second category of Vedic literature, the **Brahmanas**, began to take shape. Story telling developed as a means to interpret the significance of sacrifice. The most famous of these, and the most important for the much later development of some strands of Hindu philosophy, were the **Upanishads**, probably written at some time between the 7th and 5th centuries BC. The origin, composition and ultimately writing of the Sanskrit classics was thus taking place at approximately the same time as the epics of Homer were taking shape, being recited and ultimately written down on the W coast of what is now Turkey.

The Mahabharata

The Brahmanas gave their name to the religion emerging between the 8th and 6th centuries BC, Brahmanism, the still distant ancestor of Hinduism. Two texts from about this period remain the best known and most widely revered compositions in South Asia, the epics known as the Mahabharata and the Ramayana. In the late 1980s both were serialised for Indian television and commanded enormous audiences from every class of Indian society and in every region of the country, for their stories of the gods which are still revered by Hindus today are known in every town and village, irrespective of the particular language of the region.

Dating the Mahabharata The epic is believed to have a basis in history, although details of the great battle recounted in the **Mahabharata** are unclear. Tradition puts its date at precisely 3102 BC, the start of the present era, and also suggests that the author of the poem was a sage named **Vyasa**. Evidence suggests however that the battle was fought around 800 BC, at **Kurukshetra, see page 420**. It was another 400 years before priests began to write the stories down, a process which was not complete until 400 AD. The Mahabharata was probably an attempt by the warrior class, the **Kshatriyas**, to merge their brand of popular religion with the ideas of **Brahmanism**. It was an uneasy process that took hundreds of years to complete. The original version of the Mahabharata was probably about 3,000 stanzas long, but now contains over 100,000 – eight times as long as Homer's Iliad and the Odyssey put together.

The story Dhrtarastra captured the throne of the **Kurus**. Being blind, however, he was not eligible to rule. His younger brother **Pandu** became king, but having been cursed, was forced to become a hermit in the Himalayas with his two wives, and Dhrtarastra resumed the throne. Pandu's five sons, **Yudhisthira, Bhima, Arjuna, Nakula** and **Sahadeva** (the **Pandavas**) were brought up after his death with Dhrtarastra's own children in the capital of **Hastinapur**.

Duryodhana, Dhrtarastra's eldest son, and the other brothers, resented the Pandavas, and planned to prevent them assuming the throne. The five Pandava brothers foiled several assassination attempts before deciding to flee, travelling through neighbouring countries as mercenaries. **Arjuna**, one of the sons, won the Princess **Draupadi** to be his bride in a *svayamvara*, a contest in which Draupadi's father challenged those contesting for his daughter to string a steel bow, then shoot an arrow through a slit in a revolving target. Arjuna was the only successful contestant. However, Draupadi wanted to avoid jealousy among the brothers, and agreed to become their joint wife.

At court the Pandavas met **Krishna**, chief of the **Yadavas**, who was to become their main ally. They returned to Hastinapur when Dhrtarastra recalled them, sharing out his kingdom between them and his own sons. The Pandavas then built a new capital at **Indraprastha** (now in modern Delhi), **see page 151**.

Dhrtarastra's sons were deeply unhappy with the arrangement. **Yudhisthira**, the eldest of the Pandava sons, accepted an invitation from **Duryodhana** to a great gambling match, not realising that the result was fixed. He lost his whole kingdom, his brothers and their joint wife, but Duryodhana accepted a compromise in which the Pandavas and Draupadi would be banished for thirteen years, after which he would give them back their kingdom.

At the end of the period, **Duryodhana** went back on his promise, so the brothers got ready to fight. They gathered an enormous army, while the **Kauravas** (Duryodhana and his brothers) also made preparations, and the armies met on the plain of Kurukshetra. Greeks, Bactrians and Chinese were all reputed to back one side or the other.

The battle lasted 18 days, after which the only chiefs left alive were the five brothers and Krishna. **Yudhisthira** was crowned king, ruling peacefully for many years. Eventually he enthroned Arjuna's grandson **Pariksit**, as king, walking into voluntary exile with Draupadi and his brothers to the summit of **Mount Meru**, where they entered the city of the Gods.

The Mahabharata introduced the new God, *Krishna*, to the Vedic pantheon. Krishna's role in the battle was to serve as one of the charioteers of Arjuna. On the battlefield, Arjuna hesitated, for he could not reconcile himself to slaughtering his own family. He asked Krishna's advice, which was given in what came to known as the **Bhagavad Gita**. Krishna advised him that he should obey his dharmic duty and fight, which he was finally persuaded to do with the result outlined above. The story tells how Krishna himself was accidentally killed some 36 years later by a hunter's arrow which hit his only vulnerable spot – his left heel.

Good and evil The battle was seen as a war of the forces of good and evil, the **Pandavas** being interpreted as gods and the **Kauravas** as devils. The arguments were elaborated and expanded until about the 4th century AD by which time, as Shackle says "Brahmanism had absorbed and set its own mark on the religious ideas of the epic, and Hinduism had come into being". A comparatively late addition to the Mahabharata, the Bhagavad-Gita is the most widely read and revered text among Hindus in South Asia today.

The Ramayana
Valmiki, is thought of in India as the author of the second great Indian epic, the **Ramayana**, though no more is known of his identity than is known of Homer's. Like the Mahabharata, the Ramayana underwent several stages of development before it reached it final version of 48,000 lines.

Ravana, villanous king of Lanka

The story of Rama Under Brahmin influence, **Rama** was transformed from the human prince of the early versions into the divine figure of the final story. Rama, the "jewel of the solar kings", became deified as an incarnation of Vishnu. The story tells how Rama was banished from his father's kingdom. In a journey that took him as far as **Sri Lanka**, accompanied by his wife **Sita** and helper and friend **Hanuman** (the monkey-faced God depicted in many Indian temples, shrines and posters), Rama finally fought the king **Ravana**, again changed in late versions into a demon. Rama's rescue of Sita was interpreted as the Aryan triumph over the barbarians. The epic is widely seen as South Asia's first literary poem, and like the Mahabharata is known and recited in all Hindu communities.

Sanskrit literature Sanskrit was always the language of the court and the elite. Other languages replaced it in common speech by the 3rd century BC, but it remained in restricted use for over 1000 years after that period, essentially as a medium for writing. The remarkable Sanskrit grammar of **Panini** (see page 642) helped to establish grammar as one of the six disciplines essential to pronouncing and understanding the texts of the Vedas properly, and to conducting Vedic rituals. The other five were phonetics, etymology, meter, ritual practice and astronomy. Sanskrit literature continued to be written long after it had ceased to be a language of spoken communication. Thus perhaps the greatest Sanskrit poet, **Kalidasa**, wrote in the 5th century AD, and the tradition of writing in Sanskrit in the courts continued until the Muslims replaced it with Persian.

Literally, stories of ancient times, the Puranas are stories of the 3 major deities, Brahma, Vishnu and Siva. Although some of the stories may relate back to real events that occured as early as 1500 BC, they were not compiled until the Gupta period in the 5th century AD. Margaret and James Stutley record the belief that "during the destruction of the world at the end of the age, Hayagriva is said to have saved the Puranas. A summary of the original work is now preserved in Heaven!"

The stories are often the only source of information about the period immediately following the early Vedas. The Stutleys go on to say that each Purana was intended to deal with five themes: "the creation of the world (sarga); its destruction and re-creation (pratisarga); the genealogy of gods and patriarchs (vamsa); the reigns and periods of the Manus (manvantaras); and the history of the solar and lunar dynasties".

The Muslim influence

Persian In the first three decades of the 10th century AD, just before the Norman conquest of England, the Turk **Mahmud of Ghazni** carried Muslim power across the plains of the Punjab into India. For considerable periods until the 18th century, **Persian** became the language of the courts. Classical Persian literature was the dominant influence, with Iran as its country of origin and Shiraz its main cultural centre, but India developed its own Persian-based style. Two writers stood out at the end of the 12th century AD, when Muslim rulers had established a sultanate in Delhi, the Indian-born poet **Amir Khusrau**, who lived from 1253 to 1325, and the mystic poet **Amir Hasan**, who died about AD 1328.

Turki Muslim power was both confirmed and extended by the Mughals, the most notable of whom as a sponsor of literature was **Akbar** (1556-1605), himself illiterate. Babur left one of the most remarkable political autobiographies of any generation, the **Babur-nama** (History of Babur), written in Turki and translated into Persian. His son Akbar commissioned a biography, the **Akbar-nama**, which reflected his interest in all the world's religions. His son **Jahangir** left his memoirs, the **Tuzuk-i Jahangiri**, in Persian. They have been described as intimate and spontaneous, and an insatiable interest in things, events and people. Iranians continued to be drawn into the Indian courts of Delhi and the region of the Deccan around Hyderabad, and poetry flourished.

The colonial period

English Persian was already in decline during the reign of the last great Muslim Emperor, **Aurangzeb**, and as the British extended their political power so the role of English grew. There is now a very wide Indian literature accessible in English, which has thus become the latest of the languages to be used across the whole of South Asia.

In the 19th century English became a vehicle for developing nationalist ideals. However, notably in the work of *Rabindranath Tagore*, it became a medium for religious and philosophical prose and for a developing poetry. Tagore himself won the Nobel Prize for Literature in 1913 for his translation into English of his own work, **Gitanjali**. Leading South Asian philosophers and thinkers of the 20th century have written major works in English, including not only **M.K. Gandhi** and **Jawaharlal Nehru**, the two leading figures in India's independence movement, but **S. Radhakrishnan**, **Aurobindo Ghose** and **Sarojini Naidu**, who all added to the depth of Indian literature in English.

Naturally Indian writing in English often reflects the contact of South Asian and western cultures. Perhaps the most famous contemporary Indian writer is **Nirad Chaudhuri**, whose *Autobiography of an Unknown Indian*, published in 1951, has recently been supplemented by his second autobiographical volume *Thy Hand, Great Anarch!: India 1921-1952*. Together these volumes give a remarkable insight into the development of modern South Asia. In totally different vein are the short stories and novels of **R.K. Narayan**, full of light touches and sharp observations about village communities in S India.

Some suggestions for reading are listed in the **Introduction and Hints**. However, several South Asian regional languages have their own long traditions of both religious and secular literature which are discussed in the relevant regional sections of this handbook.

THE RELIGIONS OF SOUTH ASIA

It is impossible to write briefly about the religions of South Asia without greatly oversimplifying. There are approximately 680 million Hindus in South Asia today, making them the largest single group. It has always been easier to define Hinduism by what it is not than by what it is. Indeed, the name Hinduism was given by foreigners to the peoples of the sub-continent who did not profess the other major faiths, such as Muslims or Christians.

The first Christians arrived within 60 years of the birth of Christ, and were influential in S India, particularly Kerala, for 1500 years before the European missionary movement brought a renewed increase in the numbers of Christians, particularly in S India and in the tribal belts of E and NE India. Today there are about 18 million Christians in India and far smaller numbers in the other countries of South Asia.

Religious development didn't stop with the arrival of the Muslims. The most recent of the religious reform movements of India to make a significant impact was that of the **Sikhs** (the Panjabi word for "disciples"), whose founder **Guru Nanak** lived from 1469 to 1539. Although numerically smaller than the Christian population, the Sikhs greatly outnumber both Jains and Buddhists. They play a much more prominent role in national life than any of the other minor religious groups.

HINDUISM

The beliefs and practices of modern *Hinduism* began to take shape in the centuries on either side of the birth of Christ. But while some aspects of modern Hinduism can be traced back more than 2000 years before that, other features are recent. Hinduism has undergone major changes both in belief and practice. Such changes came from outside as well as from within. As early as the 6th century BC the Buddhists and Jains had tried to reform the religion of **Vedism** (or **Brahmanism**) which had been dominant in some parts of South Asia for five hundred years. Great philosophers such as **Shankaracharya** (in the 7th and early 8th centuries A.D.) and **Ramanuja** (in the 12th century AD) transformed major aspects of previous Hindu thought.

Modern Hinduism has many different strands. Some Hindu scholars and philosophers talk of Hinduism as one religious and cultural tradition, in which the enormous variety of belief and practice can ultimately be interpreted as interwoven in a common view of the world. Guides to Hindu temples will also often talk in terms of "Hindus believe that…" and then go on to describe concepts such as *maya*, *dharma* or *karma* in terms of a universal faith.

Yet there is no Hindu organisation, like a church, with the authority to define belief or establish official practice. Hinduism has no universally recognised leaders. There is no universally agreed set of scriptures. There are spiritual leaders and philosophers who are widely revered, and there is an enormous range of literature that is treated as sacred.

That reverence does not necessarily carry with it belief in the doctrines enshrined in the text. Thus the Vedas of the much earlier religion, Brahmanism, are still regarded as sacred by most Hindus, but virtually no modern Hindu either shares the beliefs of the Vedic writers or the practices, such as sacrifice, enjoined on worshippers. Not all Hindu groups believe in a single supreme God; and even today there are adherents of several of the major systems of philosophy which developed in the course of Hinduism's most formative period from the early centuries BC to the 13th or 14th century AD. In view of these characteristics, many authorities argue that it is misleading to think of Hinduism as a religion at all.

Be that as it may, the evidence of the living importance of Hinduism, in activities ranging from everyday family life to great temple rituals, is visible across India, Nepal and N Sri Lanka. Hindu philosophy and practice has also touched many of those who belong to other religious traditions, particularly in terms of social institutions such as caste.

Hindu beliefs

Although it is impossible to tie down Hindu belief to a universally accepted creed, a number of ideas do run like a thread through intellectual and popular Hinduism. According to the great Indian philosopher and former President of India, **S. Radhakrishnan**, religion for the Hindu "is not an idea but a power, not an intellectual proposition but a life conviction. Religion is consciousness of ultimate reality, not a theory about God."

One of the recurring themes associated with that 'life conviction' is that of 'vision', 'sight' or 'view' – **darshana**. Applied to the different philosophical systems themselves, such as *yoga* or *vedanta*, 'darshana' is also used to describe the sight of the deity that worshippers hope to gain when they visit a temple or shrine. Equally it may apply to the religious insight gained through meditation or prayer.

The four stages of life It is widely believed that an ideal life has four stages: that of the **student**, the **householder**, the **forest dweller** and the **wandering dependent** or beggar (**sannyasi**). These stages represent the phases through which an individual learns of life's goals and of the means of achieving them, in which he "carries out his duties and raises sons", and then retires to meditate alone; and then finally when he gives up all possessions and depends on the gifts of others. It is an ideal pattern which some still try to follow.

The age in which we live is seen by Hindu philosophers as a dark age, the **kaliyuga**, and the most important behaviour enjoined on Hindus for this period was that of fulfilling the obligations of the householder. However, each of the stages is still recognised as a valid pattern for individuals.

One of the most striking sights is that of the saffron clad **sadhu**, or wandering beggar, living out his last years seeking gifts of food and money to support himself in the final stage of his life. There may have been sadhus even before the Aryans arrived. Today, most of these wanderers, who have cast off all the moral requirements of their surrounding cultures, are devotees of popular Hindu beliefs. Most give up material possessions, carrying only a strip of cloth, a staff (*danda*), a crutch to support the chin during meditation (*achal*), prayer beads, a fan to ward off evil spirits, a water pot, a drinking vessel, which may be a human skull, and a begging bowl. You may well see one, almost naked, covered only in ashes, on a city street.

The four human goals Many Hindus also accept that there are four major human goals; material prosperity (**artha**), the satisfaction of desires (**kama**), and performing the duties laid down according to your position in life (**dharma**). Beyond those is the goal of achieving liberation from the endless cycle of re-births into which everyone is locked (**moksha**). It is to the last – the search for liberation – that the major schools of Indian philosophy have devoted most attention. Together with dharma, it is basic to Hindu thought.

Dharma represents the order inherent in human life. It is essentially secular rather than religious, for it doesn't depend on any revelation or command of God. The Mahabharata talks of ten embodiments of dharma: good name, truth, self-control, cleanness of mind and body, simplicity, endurance, resoluteness of character, giving and sharing, austerities and continence. In Dharmic thinking these are inseparable from five patterns of behaviour: non-violence, an attitude of equality, peace and tranquillity, lack of aggression and cruelty, and absence of envy.

Karma Central to achieving liberation is the idea of **karma** (not to be confused with kama). This is often misleadingly talked of in terms of 'fate'. More accurately it can be thought of as the effect of former actions. As C. Rajagopalachari, a leading Tamil philosopher, has put it: "Every act has its appointed effect, whether the act be thought, word or deed. If water is exposed to the sun, it cannot avoid being dried up. The effect automatically follows. It is the same with everything. The cause holds the effect, so to say, in its womb. If we reflect deeply and objectively, the entire world will be found to obey unalterable laws. That is the doctrine of karma."

According to this doctrine, every person, animal or god has a being or self which has existed without beginning. Every action, except those that are done without any consideration of the results, leaves an indelible mark on that self. This is carried forward into the next life, and the overall character of the imprint on each person's 'self' determines three features of the next life. It controls the **nature** of his next birth (animal, human or god) and the kind of family a person will be born into if human. It determines the **length** of the next life. Finally, it controls the **good or bad experiences** that the self will experience. However, it does not imply a fatalistic belief that the nature of action in this life is unimportant. Rather, it suggests that the path followed by the individual in the present life is vital to the nature of its next life, and ultimately to the chance of gaining release from this world.

Rebirth The belief in the transmigration of souls (**samsara**) in a never-ending cycle of re-birth has been Hinduism's most distinctive and important contribution to Indian culture. It also marks it sharply apart from Judaism, Christianity and Islam. The earliest reference to the belief is found in one of the Upanishad's, around the 7th century BC, at about the same time as the doctrine of karma made its first appearance. By the late **Upanishads** it was universally accepted, and in Buddhism and Jainism there is never any questioning of the belief.

A.L Basham pointed out that belief in transmigration must have encouraged a further distinctive doctrine, that of non-violence or non-injury – **ahimsa**. Buddhism and Jainism campaigned particularly vigorously against the existing practice of animal sacrifice. The belief in re-birth meant that all living things and creatures of the spirit – people, devils, gods, animals, even worms – possessed the same essential soul. One inscription which has been found in several places threatens that anyone who interferes with the rights of Brahmins to land given to them by the king will "suffer re-birth for eighty thousand years as a worm in dung". Belief in the cycle of rebirth was essential to give such a threat any weight!

Hindu philosophy

It is common now to talk of six major schools of Hindu philosophy. The best known are **yoga** and **vedanta**. **Yoga** can be traced back as a system of thought to the 3rd century AD and possibly further. It is concerned with systems of meditation that can lead ultimately to release from the cycle of rebirth. In some senses it is just one part of the wider system known as Vedanta. Literally the term Vedanta refers to the final parts of the Vedantic literature, the **Upanishads**. The basic texts also include the **Brahmasutra** of Badrayana, written about the 1st century AD, and the most important of all, the **Bhagavad-gita,** which is a part of the epic the Mahabharata.

Vedanta There are many interpretations of these basic texts. The Madras daily newspaper, The Hindu, carries an exposition of points of philosophy every day. Three major schools of vedanta are particularly important:

Advaita Vedanta According to this school there is no division between the cosmic force or principle, **Brahman**, and the individual self, **atman**, (which is also sometimes referred to as soul). The fact that we appear to see different and separate individuals is simply a result of ignorance. This is termed **maya**, sometimes translated as illusion. This is not to say that Vedanta philosophy argues that the world in which we live is an illusion. Rather it argues that it is only our limited understanding which prevents us seeing the full and real unity of self and Brahman. **Shankaracharya**, who lived in the 7th century AD, and is the best known **Advaitin** Hindu philosopher, argued that there was no individual self or soul separate from the creative force of the universe, or Brahman. He also argued that it was impossible to achieve liberation, or **moksha**, through any kind of action, including meditation and devotional worship. He saw these as signs of remaining on a lower level, and of being unprepared for true liberation.

Vishishtadvaita Shankaracharya'sbeliefs were directly contrary to the school of Vedanta associated with the 12th century philosopher, **Ramanuja**. He transformed the idea of God from an impersonal force to a personal God. His school of philosophy, known as **Vishishtadvaita**, views both the self and the world as real but only as part of the whole. In contrast to Shankaracharya's view, devotion is of central importance to achieving liberation, and service to the Lord becomes the highest goal of life.

Dvaita Vedanta originated with a third renowned philosopher, **Madhva**, in the 14th century. According to this school, **Brahman**, **the self** and **the world** are completely distinct. Worship of God is a key means of achieving liberation.

One of the reasons why Hindu faith is often confusing to those approaching it from outside is that as a whole it has many elements which appear mutually self-contradictory but which are reconciled by Hindus as different facets of the ultimate truth. S. Radhakrishnan suggests that for a Hindu "tolerance is a duty, not a mere concession. In pursuance of this duty Hinduism has accepted within its fold almost all varieties of belief and doctrine and accepted them as authentic expressions of the spiritual endeavour." Such a tolerance is particularly evident in the attitude of Hindus to the nature of God and of divinity. C. Rajagopalachari writes that there is a distinction that marks Hinduism sharply from the other monotheistic faiths such as Christianity or Islam. This is "its reconciliation of monotheism with the polytheistic approach of traditional Hinduism. All the gods and goddesses worshipped by Hindus are aspects of the Supreme Being governing the Universe and well recognised as such, both by the learned and by the least learned."

He goes on to argue that "the philosophy of Hinduism has taught and trained the Hindu devotee to see and worship the Supreme Being in all the idols that are worshipped, with a clarity of understanding and an intensity of vision that would surprise the people of other faiths. The Divine Mind governing the Universe, be it as Mother or Father, has infinite aspects, and the devotee approaches him or Her, or both, in any of the many aspects as he may be led to do according to the mood and the psychological need of the hour."

Diversity of worship This is perhaps the most helpful light in which to look at enormous variety of Hindu worship and the different sects of Hinduism which have grown up. The complexities of the different schools of philosophy continue to exercise the minds of intellectual Hindus. But the abstractions of philosophy don't mean much for the millions of Hindus living across South Asia today, nor have they in the past. S. Radhakrishnan puts a common Hindu view very briefly: "It does not matter what conception of God we adopt so long as we keep up a perpetual search after truth."

The sacred in nature Some Hindus believe in one all powerful God who created all the lesser gods and the universe. The Hindu gods include many whose origins lie in the Vedic deities of the early Aryans. These were often associated with the forces of nature, and Hindus have revered many natural objects. Mountain tops and hills, trees, rocks and above all rivers, are all regarded as sites of special religious significance. They all have their own guardian spirits. You can see the signs of the continuing lively belief in these gods and demons wherever you travel in India. In S India, for example, trees are often painted with vertical red and white stripes and will have a small shrine at their base. Hill tops will frequently have a shrine of some kind at the highest point, dedicated to a particularly powerful god.

Those gods have constantly undergone changes. **Rudra** (the Roarer), the great Vedic god of destruction, became **Siva**, one of the two most worshipped deities of Hinduism. Other gods disappeared. All the time the creative spirit of Hindus gave new names to forces to be worshipped, because, as Basham says, "the universe for the simple Hindu, despite its vastness, is not cold and impersonal, and though it is subject to rigid laws, these laws find room for the soul of man. The world is the expression of ultimate divinity; it is eternally informed by God, who can be met face to face in all things."

Worship For most Hindus today worship (often referred to as "performing *puja*") is an integral part of their faith. The great majority of Hindu homes will have a shrine to one of the gods of the Hindu pantheon. Individuals and families will often visit shrines or temples, and on special occasions will travel long distances to particularly holy places such as Benaras or Puri. Such sites may have temples dedicated to a major deity but will always have numerous other shrines in the vicinity dedicated to other favourite gods.

Acts of devotion are often aimed not so much at the relatively abstract goal of liberation from re-birth as at the granting of favours and the meeting of urgent needs for this life – good health, finding a suitable wife or husband, the birth of a son, prosperity and good fortune. In this respect there is a remarkable similarity in the popular devotion of simple pilgrims of all faiths in South Asia when they visit shrines, whether Hindu, Buddhist or Jain temples, the tombs of Muslim saints or even churches such as Bom Jesus in Goa, where St Francis Xavier lies entombed.

Whether at the domestic shrine or in a great temple, performing puja involves making an offering to God and darshana – having a view of the deity. Although there are devotional movements among Hindus in which singing and praying is practised in groups, more generally Hindu worship is an act performed by individuals. Thus Hindu temples may be little more than a shrine in the middle of the street, housing an image of the deity which will be tended by a priest and visited at special times when a darshan of the resident God can be obtained. When it has been consecrated, the image, if exactly made, becomes the channel for the godhead to work.

Pilgrimage Most Hindus regard as particularly beneficial to worship at places where God has been revealed. They will go great distances on pilgrimage, not just to the most famous sites such as those like Varanasi, on the banks of the Ganga, but to temples, hill tops and rivers across India.

Holy sites Certain rivers and towns are particularly sacred. Thus there are seven holy rivers – the **Ganga**, **Yamuna**, **Indus** and mythical **Sarasvati** in the N, and the **Narmada**, **Godavari** and **Kaveri** in the Peninsula. There are also **7 holy places** – **Haridwar**, **Mathura**, **Ayodhya**, and **Varanasi**, again in the N, **Ujjain**, **Dwarka** and **Kanchipuram** to the S. In addition to these 7 holy places there are four **Holy Abodes**; **Badrinath**, **Puri** and **Ramesvaram**, with **Dwarka** in modern Gujarat having the unique distinction of being both a Holy Abode and a Holy Place.

Festivals Every temple has its special festivals. Some, like the **Jagannath temple** in **Puri**, have festivals that draw Hindus from all over India. Others are village and family events. At festival times you can see villagers walking in small groups, brightly dressed and often high spirited, sometimes as far as eighty to a hundred kilometres.

For the celebration of the **Kumbh Mela** in January 1989 whole new temporary towns were built in order to house the estimated 13 million worshippers who gathered to bathe where two of India's most holy rivers, the Ganga and Yamuna, are believed to be joined by the third, invisible, stream, the Saraswati.

Images The image of the deity may be in one of many forms. Temples may be dedicated to **Vishnu** or **Siva**, for example, or to any one of their other representations. **Parvati**, the wife of Siva, and **Lakshmi**, the wife of Vishnu, are the focus of many temple shrines. The image of the deity becomes the object of worship and the centre of the temple's rituals. These often follow through the cycle of day and night, as well as yearly lifecycles. The priests may wake the deity from sleep, bathe, clothe and feed it. Worshippers will be invited to share in this process by bringing offerings of clothes and food. Gifts of money will usually be made, and in some temples there is a charge levied for taking up positions in front of the deity in order to obtain a darshan at the appropriate times.

Vishnu, preserver of the Universe

Hindu sects

Three Gods are widely seen as all-powerful; **Brahma**, **Vishnu** and **Siva.** Their functions and character are not readily separated. While Brahma is regarded as the ultimate source of creation, Siva also has a creative role alongside his function as destroyer. Vishnu in contrast is seen as the preserver or protector of the universe. Although there are images and sculptures of Brahma, Vishnu and Siva have come to be seen as the most powerful and important. Their followers are referred to as **Vaishnavites** and **Shaivites** respectively, and numerically they form the two largest sects in India.

Vishnu is seen much more as the God with the human face. From the 2nd century a new and passionate devotional worship of Vishnu's incarnation as **Krishna** developed in the S. By 1000 AD Vaishnavism had spread across S India, and it became closely associated with the devotional form of Hinduism preached by **Ramanuja**. Re-birth and reincarnation were already long-established by the time Ramanuja's followers spread the worship of Vishnu and his ten successive incarnations in animal and human form. For Vaishnavites, God took these different forms in order to save the world from impending disaster. A.L. Basham has summarised the ten incarnations as follows:

Name	Form	Story
1. *Matsya*	Fish	The earth was covered in a flood. Vishnu took the form of a fish to rescue Manu (the first man), his family and the Vedas. The story is similar to that of Noah's ark.
2. *Kurma*	Tortoise	Vishnu became a tortoise to rescue all the treasures that were lost in the flood. These included the divine nectar (ambrosia or Amrita) with which the gods preserved their youth. The gods put a mountain (**Mount Kailasa**) on the tortoise's back, and when he reached the bottom of the ocean they twisted the divine snake round the mountain. They then churned the ocean with the mountain by pulling the snake. The ambrosia rose to the top of the churning waters along with other treasures, and the Goddess *Lakshmi*, Vishnu's consort.
3. *Varaha*	Boar	Vishnu appeared again to raise the earth from the ocean's floor where it had been thrown by a demon, Hiranyaksa. The story probably developed from a non-Aryan cult of a sacred pig, incorporated into the Vishnu myth. The boar incarnation was an important focus of worship in the 4th century AD.
4. *Narasimha*	Half man/half lion	The demon *Hiranyakasipu* had persuaded Brahma to guarantee that he could not be killed either by day or night, by god, man or beast. He then terrorised everybody. When the gods pleaded for help, Vishnu burst out from a pillar in the demon's palace at sunset, when it was neither day nor night, in the form of a half man and half lion and killed Hiranyakasipu.
5. Vamana	A dwarf	*Bali*, another demon, achieved enormous supernatural power by following a course of asceticism. To protect the world Vishnu appeared before him in the form of a dwarf and asked him a favour. Bali agreed, and Vishnu asked for as much land as he could cover in three strides. Once granted, Vishnu became a giant, covering the earth in three strides. He left only hell to the demon.
6. *Parasurama*	Rama with the axe	Vishnu took human form as the son of a brahman, Jamadagni. *Parasurama*, killed the wicked king for robbing his father. The king's sons then killed Jamadagni, and in revenge Parasurama destroyed all male *kshatriyas*, twenty one times in succession.
7. *Rama*	The Prince of Ayodhya	In this form he came to the world to rescue it from the dark demon, *Ravana*. His story, told in the *Ramayana*, is seen by his devotees as one of longsuffering and patience, shown particularly by his faithful wife Sita. This epic also saw the creation of Hanuman, the monkey-faced god who is the model of a strong and faithful servant, and who remains one of the most widely worshipped minor deities across India.

Name	Form	Story
8. *Krishna*	The charioteer for Arjuna. Many forms	The stories of his incarnations, childhood and youth, in the words of A.L. Basham "meet almost every human need. As the divine child he satisfies the warm maternal drives of Indian womanhood. As the divine lover, he provides romantic wish-fulfilment in a society still tightly controlled by ancient norms of behaviour which give little scope for freedom of expression in sexual relations. As charioteer of the hero Arjuna on the battlefield of Kurukshetra, he is the helper of all those who turn to him, even saving them from evil rebirths, if he has sufficient faith in the Lord."
9. *The Buddha*		Probably incorporated into the Hindu pantheon in order to discredit the Buddhists, the dominant religious group in some parts of India until the 6th century AD. One of the earliest Hindu interpretations however suggests that Vishnu took incarnation as Buddha in order to show compassion for animals and to end sacrifice.
10. *Kalki*	Riding on a horse	Vishnu's arrival will accompany the final destruction of this present world, judging the wicked and rewarding the good.

Rama By far the most influential incarnations of Vishnu are those in which he was believed to take recognisable human form, especially as **Rama** (twice) and **Krishna**. As the Prince of Ayodhya, history and myth blend, for Rama was probably a chief who lived in the 8th or 7th century BC – perhaps 300 years after King David ruled in Israel and the start of the Iron Age in central Europe, or at about the same time as the Greeks began to develop city states.

In the earliest stories about Rama he wasn't regarded as divine. Although he is now seen as an earlier incarnation of Vishnu than Krishna, he was added to the pantheon very late, probably after the Muslim invasions of the 12th century AD. The story has become part of the cultures of SE Asia.

Rama is a powerful figure in contemporary India. His supposed birthplace at Ayodhya has become the focus of fierce disputes between Hindus and Muslims. Hindus have identified Ram's birthplace as a site currently occupied by a mosque. One of India's leading historians, Romila Thapar, argues that there

Krishna, eighth and most popular incarnation of Vishnu

is no historical evidence for this view, but it has taken widespread hold. Demands for the building of a special temple on the site caused major political disturbances in 1989-91.

Krishna is worshipped extremely widely as perhaps the most human of the gods. His advice on the battlefield of the Mahabharata is one of the major sources of guidance for the rules of daily living for many Hindus today.

Siva is interpreted as both creator and destroyer, the power through whom the universe evolves, while Vishnu is seen as its preserver. Siva lives on Mount Kailasa with his

Ardhanarishvara, the male/female form of Siva

Siva as Nataraj, Lord of the Dance

wife Parvati and two sons, the elephant-headed Ganes and the six-headed Kartikkeya, known in S India as Subrahmanyam. Siva is always accompanied by his 'vehicle', the bull (*nandi*). They form a model of sorts for family life.

Although Siva is often seen as rather more remote, he is also widely portrayed in sculpture and art, most famously as the dancing **Natarajan** of S Indian bronzes, the Lord of the Cosmic Dance. He is also shown as an **ascetic**, sitting among the mountain peaks around **Mount Kailasa**, accompanied by his wife **Parvati** and meditating on the nature of the universe.

More widely than either of these forms, **Siva** is also represented in Shaivite temples throughout South Asia by the *lingam*, or phallic symbol, a symbol of energy, fertility and potency. This has become the most important form of the cult of Siva. Professor Wendy O'Flaherty suggests that the worship of the linga of Siva can be traced back to the pre-Vedic societies of the Indus Valley civilisation (c.2000 BC), but that it first appears in Hindu iconography in the 2nd century BC.

Parvati, daughter of Parvata (Himalaya), wife of Siva

From that time a wide variety of myths appeared to explain the origin of linga worship. The myths surrounding the twelve **jyoti linga** (linga of light) found at centres like **Ujjain** go back to the 2nd century BC, and were clearly developed in order to explain and justify linga worship. O'Flaherty has translated this story of competition between the gods, in which Siva (in the form of **Rudra**) terrorizes the other gods into worshipping him with a devotion to the linga. Her translation of the Puranic myth is summarised below. Note that the gods appear in several forms; **Siva** as Rudra, Sambha and Sankara, **Vishnu** as Hari, **Brahma** as Ka.

The story of linga worship

"Once in the past, when all the universe had become a single ocean, Brahma, Vishnu and Rudra arose from the water. Their arrival was unwitnessed, and even wise men do not know it. The earth, which had been the domain of former beings, had been destroyed for a piercing wind had arisen and dried up the seven oceans. A single sun appeared, rising in the east, and then a second in the south, just like the first, drying up all the water with its rays and burning all that moved and was still. Then in the W a third sun arose, and in the N there arose a fourth, burning all that moved or was still; later on eight more arose, and there were twelve.

Rudra, the Fire of Doomsday, arose from the subterranean hell and filled all the regions out of the sky. The exalted one, as he is known everywhere, burnt all of the underworld above and sideways, without exception, and then he went to his own dwellingplace which he had made before. Then clouds arose and rained in all directions, flooding the whole earth and all the regions of the sky with waters; afterwards they plunged into the single ocean which the universe had become. There was no earth, nor any regions of the sky, no space, no heaven; everything was like a giant cask filled to the brim.

Then the three eternal gods arose from the midst of the water – Brahma, Vishnu and Rudra, whose arrivals were unwitnessed. The two – Ka and Vishnu – bowed and said to Sarva, who blazed with sharp energy and embraced the sakti of Rudra, 'You are the lord of everything, our lord. Perform creation as you wish.' 'I will perform it' he said to them, and then he plunged into the waters and remained immersed for a thousand celestial years. Then they said to one another, ' What will we do without him? How will creation take place?' Hari said to the creator. ' Do as I tell you Grandfather: let no more time elapse, but make an effort to create progeny. For you are capable of creating various creatures in the worlds; I will give you your own sakti, so that you will be the creator.' Thus encouraged by the words that Vishnu had spoken to him, he thought about creating, and then he created everything conducive to happiness – gods, demons, Gandharvs, Yaksas, serpents, Raksasas. When that creation had been performed, Sambhu emerged from the water, desirous of creating and thinking about it in his mind. But when he saw the whole universe stretching above and below with the gods, demons, Gandharvs, Yaksas, serpents, Raksasas and men, the great god's heart was filled with anger, and he thought, 'What shall I do? Since creation has been performed by Brahma, I will therefore destroy, cutting off my own seed.' When he said this, he released from his mouth a flame which burnt everything.

When Brahma saw that everything was on fire, he bowed to the great lord with devotion and praised the lord...Sankara was pleased by Brahma's praise and told him, 'I am Sankara. I will always accomplish everything that is to be done for anyone who seeks refuge with me, devotedly. I am pleased with you; tell me what you desire in your heart.' When Brahma heard this he said, 'I created an extensive range of progeny; let that be as it was, O Lord, if you are pleased with me.' When Rudra heard this he said to Ka, 'That energy which I gathered in excess in order to destroy your creation – tell me, what shall I do with it for you?' Brahma thought carefully for the sake of the world, and then he said to Sankara, 'Cause your own energy to enter the sun, since you are lord over the sun; for you are the creator, protector and destroyer. Let us live together with all the immortals in the energy of the sun, and we will receive with devotion the sacred image of the three times (past, present and future) that was given by mankind. Then great god, at the end of the aeon you will take the form of the sun and burn this universe, moving and still, at that moment.'

He agreed to this and laughed, for he was secretly amused, and he said to Brahma, 'There is no good use for this linga except for the creation of progeny.' And as he said this he broke it off and threw it upon the surface of the earth. The linga broke through the earth and went to the very sky. Vishnu sought the end of it below, and Brahma flew upwards, but they did not find the end of it, for all their vital effort. Then a voice arose out of the sky as the two of them sat there, and it said. 'If the linga of the god with braided hair is worshipped, it will certainly grant all desires that are longed for in the heart.' When Brahma and Vishnu heard this, they and all the divinities worshipped the linga with devotion, with their hearts set upon Rudra. "

Ganes is one of Hinduism's most popular gods. He is seen as the great clearer of obstacles. Shown at gateways and on door lintels with his elephant head and pot belly, his image is revered across India. Meetings, functions and special family

Ganes, bringer of prosperity

Kali, the bloodthirsty consort of Siva

gatherings will often start with prayers to Ganes, and any new venture, from the opening of a building or inaugurating a company to the commissioning by Air India of a Jumbo Jet (seen in India as a highly auspicious name), will often not be deemed complete without a Ganes puja.

The Mother Goddess One of the best known cults is that of **Shakti**, a female divinity often worshipped in the form of **Durga**. The worship of female goddesses developed into the widely practised form of devotional worship called **Tantrism**.

Goddesses such as **Kali** became the focus of worship which often involved practices that flew in the face of wider Hindu moral and legal codes. Animal and even human sacrifices, and ritual sexual intercourse were part of Tantric belief and practice, the evidence for which may still be seen in the art and sculpture of some major temples. Tantric practice affected both Hinduism and Buddhism from the 8th century AD, its influence is shown vividly in the sculptures of Khajuraho and Konarak and in the distinctive Hindu and Buddhist practices of the Kathmandu Valley in Nepal.

Durga, Mother-goddess, destroyer of demons

Hindu society

Dharma is seen as the most important of the objectives of individual and social life. But what were the obligations imposed by dharma? Hindu law givers, such as those who compiled the code of **Manu** (AD 100-300), laid down rules of family conduct and social obligations related to the institutions of **caste** and **jati** which were beginning to take shape at the same time.

As with the word Hinduism itself, caste was a not an indigenous term. It was applied by the Portuguese to the dominant social institution which they found practised on their arrival in India. Two terms – **varna** and **jati** – are used in India itself, and have come to be used interchangeably and confusingly with the word caste.

Varna, which literally means colour, had a fourfold division. The priestly varna, the **Brahmins**, were seen as coming from the mouth of Brahma; the **Kshatriyas** (or **Rajputs** as they are commonly called in NW India) were a warrior varna, coming from Brahma's arms; the **Vaishyas**, a trading community, came from Brahma's thighs, and the **Sudras**, classified as agriculturalists, from his feet. These groups were ranked in a hierarchy of ritual purity, with the Brahmins at the top. Relegated beyond the pale of civilised Hindu society were the **untouchables** or outcastes, who were left with the jobs which were regarded as impure, usually associated with dealing with the dead (either human or animal) or with excrement.

The highest three groups were classified as "**twice born**", and could wear the **sacred thread** symbolising their status. The age at which the initiation ceremony (**upanayana**) for the upper caste child was carried out, varied according to class – 8 for a **brahman**, 11 for a **kshatriya** and 12 for a **vaishya**.

The boy, dressed like an ascetic and holding a staff in his hand, would have the sacred thread (**yajnopavita**) placed over his right shoulder and under his left arm. A cord of three threads, each of nine twisted strands, it was made of cotton for brahmans, hemp for kshatriyas or wool for vaishyas. It was – and is – regarded as a great sin to remove it.

The Brahmin who officiated would whisper a verse from the Rig Veda in the boy's ear, the *Gayatri mantra*. Addressed to the old solar god **Savitr**, the holiest of holy passages, the Gayatri can only be spoken by the three higher classes. A.L. Basham translated it as: "Let us think on the lovely splendour of the god Savitr, that he may inspire our minds."

Jati Important elements of the fourfold classification are still found. Many Brahmins and Rajputs are conscious of their status, but the great majority of Indians do not put themselves into one of the four varna categories, but into a **jati** group.

There are thousands of different jatis across the country. None of the groups regard themselves as equal in status to any other, but all are part of local or regional hierarchies. These are not organised in any institutional sense, and traditionally there was no formal record of caste status. While individuals found it impossible to change caste or to move up the social scale, groups would sometimes try to gain recognition as higher caste by adopting practices of the Brahmins such as becoming vegetarians. Many used to be identified with particular activities, and occupations used to be hereditary. Caste membership is decided simply by birth. Although you can be evicted from your caste by your fellow members, usually for disobedience to caste rules such as over marriage, you can't join another caste, and technically you become an outcaste.

The Harijans Right up until Independence in 1947 such punishment was a drastic penalty for disobeying one's dharmic duty. In many areas all avenues into normal life could be blocked, families would disregard outcaste members, and it could even be impossible for the outcaste to continue to work within the locality. Similarly members of the lower castes and outcaste groups were severely discriminated against.

Gandhi spearheaded his campaign for Independence from British colonial rule with a powerful campaign to abolish the disabilities imposed by the caste system. Coining the term **Harijan**, (meaning "person of God"), which he gave to all former outcastes, Gandhi demanded that discrimination on the grounds of caste be outlawed. Lists – or "schedules" – of backward castes were drawn up during the early part of this century in order to provide positive help to such groups.

Job reservations Since 1947 the Indian government has extended its positive discrimination to scheduled castes and scheduled tribes, particularly through reserving up to 30% of jobs in government-run institutions and in further education leading to professional qualifications for these groups, and members of the scheduled castes are now found in important positions throughout the economy. Furthermore, most of the obvious forms of social discrimination, particularly rules which prohibit eating or drinking with members of lower castes, or from plates and cups that have been touched by them, have disappeared.

Yet caste remains an extremely important aspect of India's social structures. **Marriage**, which is still generally arranged, continues to be dictated almost entirely by caste rules. Even in cities, where traditional means of arranging marriages have often broken down, and where many people resort to advertising for marriage partners in the columns of the Sunday newspapers, caste is frequently stated as a requirement. Marriage is generally seen as an alliance between two families. Great efforts are made to match caste, social status and economic position, although the rules which govern eligibility vary from region to region. In some groups marriage between even first cousins is common, while among others marriage between any branch of the same clan is strictly prohibited.

Caste also remains an explosive political issue. Attempts to improve the social and economic position of **outcastes** (re-named "**harijans**" – people of god – by Gandhi) and what are termed "**other backward castes**" (OBCs) by increasing the number of Government jobs reserved for them produced an enormous backlash of opposition in late 1990, with widespread rioting and a number of highly publicised suicides.

Hindu reform movements

Hinduism today is more self-conscious a religious and political force than it was even at Independence in 1947. The signs of renewed Hindu awareness take several forms. The building of new temples, notably by the Birla foundation, such as those in Delhi and Calcutta, are matched by political movements like the Bharatiya Janata Party (the BJP), which suggests that Hinduism is an increasingly important focus of political identity. However, reform movements of modern Hinduism can be traced back at least to the early years of the 19th century. These movements were unique in Hinduism's history in putting the importance of political ideas on the same level as strictly religious thinking, and on attempting to interrelate the two.

In the 19th century the extension of British political power, English education and European literature, and modern scientific thought, alongside the religious ideas of Christian missionaries, all became powerful influences on the newly emerging western educated Hindu opinion. That opinion was challenged to re-examine inherited Hindu beliefs and practice.

The first major reform movement was launched by the Bengali Brahmin, **Ram Mohan Roy** (1772-1833). A close study of Christian teaching, as well as of Arabic, Persian and Classical Sanskrit texts, led him to challenge traditional Hindu practices such as untouchability, widow burning, female infanticide and child marriage, without leading him to accept Christian doctrine. He founded the **Brahmo Samaj**, the Society of God, in 1828, 'to teach and to practise the worship of the one God'. Services were modelled closely on those of the Unitarian Church, but he never broke with orthodox Hinduism.

The Brahmo Samaj became very influential, particularly in Bengal, even though it divided, and its numbers remained tiny. In N India reform was carried out under the leadership of what one writer has called "the Luther of modern Hinduism", **Dayananda Saraswati** (1824-83). Rejecting idolatry and many of the social evils associated with mid-19th century Hinduism, Dayananda Saraswati established the **Arya Samaj** (the Aryan Society). In the early 19th century the Arya Samaj launched a major attack on the caste system, through recruiting low caste Hindus and investing them with high caste status. At the same time they encouraged a movement for the re-conversion of Christians and Muslims (the *suddhi* movement). By 1931 the Arya Samaj claimed about one million members. With a strongly Hindu nationalist political line, its programme underlay the rise in post-Independence India of the **Jana Sangh Party** and the present day **BJP**.

Other reform movements have had regional importance. Two of these originated, like the Brahmo Samaj, in Bengal. The **Ramakrishna Mission**, named after a temple priest in the **Kali** temple in S Calcutta, **Ramakrishna** (1834-1886). He achieved all-India fame as a mystic, preaching the basic doctrine that "all religions are true." He believed that the best religion for any individual was that into which he or she was born. One of his followers, **Vivekenanda**, became the founder of the Ramakrishna Mission, which has been an important vehicle of social and religious reform, notably in Bengal. **See page 527.**

Aurobindo Ghose (1872-1950) links the great reformers from the 19th century with the post-Independence period. Educated in English – and for fourteen years in England itself – he developed the idea of India as "the Mother", a concept linked with the pre-Hindu idea of **Sakti**, or the Mother Goddess. For him 'nationalism was religion'. After imprisonment in 1908 he retired to **Pondicherry**, where his ashram became a focus of an Indian and international movement. **See page 733.**

ISLAM

Islam is a highly visible presence in all the countries of South Asia today. In Pakistan and Bangladesh it is the faith of the overwhelming majority of the people, and it is also the national religion of the tiny island nation of the Maldives. But its influence stretches far beyond the present distribution of "Muslim states". India alone has over 100 million Muslims, giving it one of the largest Muslim populations in the world, and even Nepal, the only Hindu State in the world, and Sri Lanka, with its Buddhist majority, have significant Muslim communities.

It is the most recent of imported religions. Islamic contact with India was first established by the navies of the Arab **Muhammad bin Qasim**. These conquerors of Sind made very few converts, although they did have to develop a legal recognition for the status of non-Muslims in a Muslim ruled state. From the creation of the **Delhi Sultanate** in 1206, by Turkish rather than Arab power, Islam became a permanent living religion in South Asia.

Across **N India** and **Pakistan** the imprint of Muslim political power forms a major part of the modern legacy. Some of the most striking architectural achievements of the N were designed and built by the Muslims. However, they were not simply imported from elsewhere in the Muslim world. They developed out of the skills cultivated in Muslim India, many of which reflected the contact between Hindu and Muslim cultures through successive generations. This pattern of artistic development would not have been predicted either from the history of Muslim conquest or from the nature of Islamic and Hindu faiths.

The victory of the Turkish ruler of **Ghazni** over the **Rajputs** in AD 1192 established a 500 year period of Muslim power in South Asia. Within only eight years of that victory the **Turkish sultans** had annexed Bihar in the E, in the process wiping out the last traces of Buddhism with the massacre of a Buddhist monastic order, sacked Benaras and captured Gwalior to the S. Within 30 years Bengal had been added to the Turkish empire, and by AD 1311 a new Turkish dynasty, the **Khaljis**, had extended the power of the Delhi Sultanate to the doors of **Madurai** in the extreme S.

The extension of Muslim political power provided the conditions for transforming many features of the cultural and political life of South Asia. The contact between the courts of the new rulers and the indigenous Hindu populations produced innovative developments in art and architecture, language and literature. This blending and development is evident in an enormous variety of ways. Hindus and Hindu culture were profoundly affected by the spread and exercise of Muslim political power, but Islam too underwent major modifications in response to the new social and religious context in which the Muslim rulers found themselves.

Islamic patronage In South Asia **Islam** and **Hinduism** have often been seen as fundamentally opposed to each other. The contrasts in basic beliefs and practice are certainly sharp. Yet during many periods of Muslim government, Muslim and Hindu lived and worked side by side. The intermingling of people of the different faiths is still evident in the cities of many parts of India. The spread of Islam across India was achieved not so much by forcible conversion, though that happened in places, as by the patronage offered by the new rulers to Muslim saints and teachers. These were particularly influential in achieving mass conversions among the lower castes of Hindus. As Welch has suggested, in the courts there was also the subtle influence of the demonstration effect on Hindus who saw the advantages in terms of jobs and power of being a Muslim.

But Islam also underwent important modifications as it became entrenched in India. From the outset the Arab invaders had to come to terms with the Hindu majority population. If they had treated them as idolators they would have been forced, under Qu'ranic law, to give them the choice of conversion or death. The political impossibility of governing as a tiny minority on those terms encouraged them to give Indian subjects the status of '**protected peoples**'.

The early Muslim rulers looked to the **Turkish** ruling class and to the **Arab** caliphs for their legitimacy, and to the Turkish elite for their cultural authority. From the middle of the 13th century, when the Mongols crushed the Arab caliphate, the Delhi sultans were left on their own to exercise Islamic authority in India. From then onwards the main external influences were from Persia. Small numbers of migrants, mainly the skilled and the educated, continued to flow into the Indian courts. Periodically their numbers were augmented by refugees from Mongol repression in the regions to India's NW. Thus the Delhi Sultanate not only kept the Mongols at bay in the 14th century, but provided a refuge for craftsmen and artists from the territories the Mongols had conquered from Lahore westwards.

Muslim populations Muslims only became a majority of the South Asian population in two areas, the plains of the Indus and W Panjab, and in parts of Bengal. Elsewhere across N India they formed important minorities, notably in the towns of the central heartland such as Lucknow. The concentration at the E and W ends of the Ganga valley reflected the policies pursued by successive Muslim rulers of colonising forested and previously uncultivated land. In the central plains there was already a densely populated, Hindu region, where little attempt was made to achieve converts.

The Mughals wanted to expand their territory and their economic base. To pursue this they made enormous grants of land to those who had served the empire. Both in Sind and Punjab in the W, and in Bengal in the E, new land was brought into cultivation. At the same time, shrines were established to Sufi saints who attracted peasant farmers, see page 1090. The mosques built in E Bengal were the centres of devotional worship where saints were venerated. By the 18th century many Muslims had joined the **Sunni** sect of Islam. The characteristics of

Islamic practice in both these regions continues to reflect this background.

Islam in South India The most important route for Muslim influence in India was from the NW. However, not all Muslim contact was by land through the passes of Afghanistan or Baluchistan. In the Deccan of S India, where the power of the Delhi-based empires was always much weaker than in the N plains, a succession of Muslim-ruled states maintained strong contact with Arab communities through trade.

From the 15th century to the 18th century much of S India was ruled under independent Muslim kings. *Hyderabad*, for example, developed a distinctive cultural and artistic life, drawing on a mixed population of Indian Muslims and Hindus, Turks, Persians, Arabs and Africans, see page 897 Until the Mughals conquered the Deccan kingdoms in 1687, Hyderabad was one of the great centres of Arab learning outside the Middle East, a link maintained through trade across the Arabian Sea with Egypt, Yemen and Iraq.

In some areas Muslim society shared many of the characteristic features of the Hindu society from which the majority of them came. Many of the Muslim migrants from Iran or Turkey, the elite **ashraf** communities, continued to identify with the Islamic elites from which they traced their descent. They held high military and civil posts in imperial service. In sharp contrast, many of the non-ashraf Muslim communities in the towns and cities were organised in social groups very like the **jatis** of their neighbouring Hindu communities. While the elites followed Islamic practices close to those based on the Qu'ran as interpreted by scholars, the poorer, less literate communities followed devotional and pietistic forms of Islam. The distinction is still very clear today, and the importance of veneration of the saints can be seen at tombs and shrines across Pakistan, India and Bangladesh.

Muslim beliefs
In the Semitic tradition, the beliefs of Islam (which means "submission to God") could apparently scarcely be more different from those of Hinduism. Unlike Hinduism, Islam has a fundamental **creed**; "There is no God but God; and Mohammad is the Prophet of God" (*La Illaha illa 'llah Mohammad Rasulu 'llah*). One book, **the Qu'ran**, is the supreme authority on Islamic teaching and faith. Islam preaches the belief in bodily **resurrection** after death, and in the reality of **heaven** and **hell**.

The idea of heaven as **paradise** is clearly pre-Islamic. **Alexander the Great** is believed to have brought the word into Greek from Persia, where he used it to describe the walled Persian gardens that were found even three centuries before the birth of Christ. For Muslims, Paradise is believed to be filled with sensuous delights and pleasures, while hell is a place of eternal terror and torture, which is the certain fate of all who deny the unity of God.

There are **four obligatory requirements** imposed on Muslims. **Daily prayers** are prescribed at daybreak, noon, afternoon, sunset and nightfall. In Pakistan these are now marked by official breaks from work, though there is some flexibility in the timing. Muslims must **give alms** to the poor. They must observe a **strict fast** during the month of **Ramadan**. They must not eat or drink between sunrise and sunset. Lastly, they should attempt the **pilgrimage to the Ka'aba in Mecca**, known as the **Hajj**. Those who have done so are entitled to the prefix Hajji before their name.

Islamic rules differ from Hindu practice in several other aspects of daily life. Muslims are strictly forbidden to drink **alcohol** (though some suggest that this prohibition is restricted to the use of fermented grape juice, that is wine, it is commonly accepted to apply to all alcohol). **Eating pork**, or any meat from an animal not killed by draining its blood while alive, is also prohibited. Meat prepared in the appropriate way is called **Halal**. Finally **usury** (charging interest on loans) and **games of chance** are forbidden. The government of Pakistan, under the late President Zia ul Haq, took several steps in the direction of basing Pakistan's legal system on the **Sharia**, or Islamic law.

Islam has no priesthood. The authority of **Imams** derives from social custom, and from their authority to interpret the scriptures, rather than from a defined status within the Islamic community. Islam also prohibits any distinction on the basis of race or colour, and there is a strong antipathy to the representation of the human figure. It is often thought, inaccurately, that this ban stems from the Qu'ran itself. In fact it probably has its origins in the belief of Mohammad that images were likely to be turned into idols.

Muslim Sects
During the first century of its existence Islam split in two sects which were divided on political and religious grounds, the **Shi'is** and **Sunni's**. The religious basis for the division lay in the interpretation of verses in the Qur'an and of traditional sayings of Mohammad, the **Hadis**. Both sects venerate the Qur'an but have different *Hadis*. They also have different views as to Muhammad's successor.

The Sunnis – always the majority in South Asia – believe that Muhammad did not appoint a successor, and that **Abu Bak'r**, **Omar** and **Othman** were the first three **caliphs** (or viceregents) after Mohammad's death. **Ali**, whom the Sunni's count as the fourth caliph, is regarded as the first legitimate caliph by the **Shi'is**, who consider Abu Bak'r and Omar to be usurpers. While the Sunni's believe in the **principle of election** of caliphs, Shi'is believe that although Muhammad is the last prophet there is a continuing need for intermediaries between God and man. Such intermediaries are termed **Imams**, and they base both their law and religious practice on the teaching of the **Imams**.

The two major divisions are marked by further sub-divisions. The **Sunni Muslims** in India have followers of the **Hanafi**, **Shafei**, **Maliki** and **Hanbali** groups, named after their leaders. Numerically one of the smallest groups in South Asia is that of the **Ismailis**, who regard their leader, the **Aga Khan**, as their spiritual head.
   In practice Islam in India has been very diverse. In part this diversity has been conditioned by attitudes to the Hinduism of the majority of the population. From the Mughal emperors, who enjoyed an unparalleled degree of political power, down to the poorest peasant farmers of Bengal, Muslims in India have found different ways of adjusting to their Hindu environment. Some have reacted by accepting or even incorporating features of Hindu belief and practice in their own. **Akbar**, the most eclectic of Mughal emperors, went as far as banning activities like cow slaughter which were offensive to Hindus and celebrating Hindu festivals in court.
   Eaton has pointed out that the Mughal prince **Dara Shikoh**, who died in 1659, even argued that the study of Hindu scriptures was necessary to obtain a complete understanding of the Qu'ran. The 16th century Bengali poet **Sayyed Sultan** wrote an epic in which the main Hindu gods were shown as prophets who preceded Adam, Noah, Abraham, Moses, Jesus and Mohammad, and the idea of prophet was matched to the Hindu concept of *avatar*, or incarnation.

In contrast, the later Mughal Emperor, **Aurangzeb**, pursued a far more hostile approach to Hindus and Hinduism, trying to point up the distinctiveness of Islam and denying the validity of Hindu religious beliefs. That attitude generally became stronger in the twentieth century, related to the growing sense of the Muslim's minority position within South Asia, and the fear of being subjected to Hindu rule. It was a fear that led to the creation of the separate Muslim majority state of Pakistan in 1947 and which still permeates political as well as religious attitudes across South Asia.

The Muslim year
The first day of the *Muslim calendar* is July 16th 622 AD. This was the date of the Prophet's migration from Mecca to Medina, the **Hijra**, from which the date's name is taken (AH = Anno Hijrae).

The Muslim year is divided into twelve lunar months, alternating between 29 and 30 days. The first month of the year is *Moharram*, followed by *Safar, Rabi-ul-Awwal, Rabi-ul-Sani, Jumada-ul-Awwal, Jumada-ul-Sani, Rajab, Shaban, Ramadan, Shawwal, Ziquad* and *Zilhaj*.

Calculating the Hijra year Murray's Handbook for travellers in India gave a wonderfully precise method of calculating the current date in the Christian year from the AH date: "To correlate the Hijra year with the Christian year, express the former in years and decimals of a year, multiply by .970225, add 621.54, and the total will correspond exactly with the Christian year."

Significant dates 1st day of *Moharram* – New Year's Day; 9th and 10th of *Moharram* – Anniversary of the killing of the Prophet's grandson Hussain, commemorated by Shi'i Muslims; 12th of *Rabi-ul-Awwal* – Birthday of the Prophet (Milad-ul-Nabi); 1st of *Ramadan* – Start of the fasting month; 21st of *Ramadan* – Night of prayer (Shab-e-Qadr); 1st of *Shawwal: Eid-ul-Fitr* – Three day festival to mark the end of Ramadan; 10th of *Zilhaj: Eid-ul-Ajha* – Two day festival commemorating the sacrifice of Ismail. The main time of pilgrimage to Mecca (the Haj).

Warning From the point of view of the tourist it is very important to note that many aspects of life are significantly altered during Ramadan. Muslims do not eat between sunrise and sunset, and food and drink are not publicly available. In Pakistan travel can become difficult, particularly when Ramadan falls during the hot season. For the next ten years Ramadan falls in the winter. The date for 1992 is approximately March 4th – April 3rd, and for 1993 February 22nd – March 21st. The exact date is determined by the appearance of the new moon.

BUDDHISM

India was the home of ***Buddhism***, but today it is practised only on the margins of the sub-continent, from Leh, Ladakh, Nepal and Bhutan in the N to Sri Lanka in the S, where it is the religion of the majority Sinhalese community. Although there are approximately 5 million Buddhists in India, most are very recent converts, the last adherents of the early schools of Buddhism having been killed or converted by the Muslim invaders of the 13th century.

The 1951 Census of India recorded only 181,000 Buddhists. However, in October 1956 a Hindu leader of the outcaste community, ***Dr. B.R. Ambedkar***, embraced Buddhism, and was joined by 200,000 other outcastes. The movement has continued, particularly in W India, and there are now approximately 5 million Buddhists. However, the home of what became one of Asia's major religions is now mainly the setting for important and sometimes extraordinarily beautiful artistic and architectural remnants of what was for several centuries the region's dominant religion.

South Asia has sites of great significance for Buddhists around the world. Some say that the Buddha himself spoke of the four places his followers should visit. **Lumbini**, the Buddha's birthplace, is in the Nepali foothills, near the present border with India. **Bodh Gaya**, where he attained what Buddhists term his "supreme enlightenment", is about 80 km S of the modern Indian city of Patna; the deer park at **Sarnath**, where he preached his first sermon and set in motion the Wheel of the Law, is just outside Varanasi; and **Kushinagara**, where he died at the age of 80, is 50 km E of Gorakhpur. In addition there are remarkable monuments, sculptures and works of art, from **Gandhara** in modern Pakistan to **Sanchi** and **Ajanta** in central India, where it is still possible to see the vivid evidence of the flowering of Buddhist culture in South Asia. In Sri Lanka, Bhutan

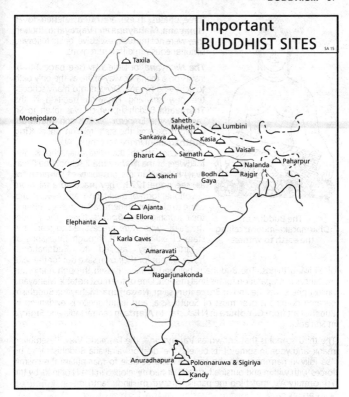

Important BUDDHIST SITES SA 15

Taxila

Moenjodaro

Saheth Maheth
Lumbini
Sankasya
Kasia
Bharut
Sarnath
Vaisali
Sanchi
Bodh Gaya
Nalanda
Paharpur
Rajgir

Ajanta
Ellora
Elephanta
Karla Caves
Amaravati
Nagarjunakonda

Anuradhapura
Polonnaruwa & Sigiriya
Kandy

and Nepal the traditions remain alive.

The Buddha's life

Siddharta Gautama, who came to be given the title of the *Buddha* – the Enlightened One – was born a prince into the warrior caste in about 563 B.C. He was married at the age of 16 and his wife had a son. When he reached the age of 29 he left home and wandered as a beggar and ascetic. After about six years he spent some time in **Bodh Gaya**. Sitting under the Bo tree, meditating, he was tempted by the demon **Mara**, with all the desires of the world. Resisting these temptations, he received enlightenment.

These scenes are common motifs of Buddhist art. The next landmark was the preaching of his first sermon on "**The Foundation of Righteousness**" in the deer park near **Benaras**. By the time he died the Buddha had established a small band of monks and nuns known as the **Sangha**, and had followers across N India. His body was cremated, and the ashes, regarded as precious relics, were divided up among the peoples to whom he had preached. Some have been discovered as far W as Peshawar, in the NW frontier of Pakistan, and at **Piprawa**, close to his birthplace.

From the Buddha's death – or **parinirvana** – to the destruction of **Nalanda** (the last Buddhist stronghold in India) in 1197 AD, Buddhism in India went through

The Buddha in
Dharmacaka-mudra: calling
the earth to witness

three phases. These are often referred to as **Hinayana**, **Mahayana** and **Vajrayana**, though they were not mutually exclusive, being followed simultaneously in different regions.

The Hinayana, or Little Way (**see page 1404**), insists on a monastic way of life as the only path to achieving nirvana. Divided into many schools, the only surviving Hinayana tradition is the **Theravada** Buddhism, which was taken to Sri Lanka by the Emperor Asoka's son **Mahinda**, where it became the state religion under **King Dutthagamini** in the 1st century AD.

In contrast to the Hinayana schools, the followers of the *Mahayana* 2 school (the Great Way) believed in the possibility of salvation for all, **see page 1273**. They practised a far more devotional form of meditation, and new figures came to play a prominent part in their beliefs and their worship – the *Bodhisattvas*. These were the saints who were predestined to reach the state of enlightenment through thousands of re-births. They aspired to Buddhahood, however, not for their own sake but for the sake of all living things. The Buddha is believed to have passed through numerous existences in preparation for his final mission. One of the most notable Mahayana philosophers was the 2nd or 3rd century saint, **Nagarjuna**. Mahayana Buddhism became dominant over most of South Asia, and its influence is evidenced in Buddhist art from **Gandhara** in N Pakistan to **Ajanta** in central India and **Sigirya** in Sri Lanka.

The third school is that known as *Vajrayana* – the Diamond Way. Resembling magic and yoga in some of its beliefs, the ideal of Vajrayana Buddhists is to be "so fully in harmony with the cosmos as to be able to manipulate the cosmic forces with within and outside himself". It had developed in the N of India by the 7th century AD, matching the parallel growth of Hindu Tantrism.

Buddhist Beliefs

Buddhism is based on the Buddha's own preaching. However, when he died none of those teachings had been written down. He developed his beliefs in reaction to the Brahmanism of his time, rejecting several of the doctrines of Vedic religion which were widely held in his lifetime; the Vedic gods, scriptures and priesthood, and all social distinctions based on caste. However, he did accept the belief in the cyclical nature of life, and that the nature of an individual's existence is determined by a natural process of reward and punishment for deeds in previous lives – the Hindu doctrine of **karma** (see above). In the Buddha's view, though, there is no eternal soul.

The Buddha preached **Four Noble Truths**: that life is painful; that suffering is caused by ignorance and desire; that beyond the suffering of life there is a state which cannot be described but which he termed **nirvana**; and that nirvana can be reached by following an eightfold path.

The concept of nirvana is often understood in the W in an entirely negative sense – that of "non-being". The word has the rough meaning of "blow out" or "extinguish", meaning to blow out the fires of greed, lust and desire. In a more positive sense it has been described by one Buddhist scholar as "the state of absolute illumination, supreme bliss, infinite love and compassion, unshakeable serenity, and unrestricted spiritual freedom." The essential elements of the eightfold path are the perfection of **wisdom**, **morality** and **meditation**.

Following the Buddha's death a succession of councils was called to try and reach agreement on doctrine. The first three were held within 140 years of the Buddha's death, the fourth being held at **Pataliputra** (modern Patna) during the reign of the **Emperor Asoka** (272-232 B.C.), who had recently been converted to Buddhism. Under his reign Buddhism spread throughout South Asia and opened the routes through NW India for Buddhism to travel into China, where it had become a force by the 1st century AD.

The decline of Buddhism in India probably stemmed as much from the growing similarity in the practice of Hinduism and Buddhism as from direct attacks. **Mahayana Buddhism**, with its reverence for Bodhisattvas and its devotional character, was more and more difficult to distinguish from the revivalist Hinduism characteristic of several parts of N India from the 7th to the 12th centuries AD. The Muslim conquest dealt the final death blow, being accompanied by the large scale slaughter of monks and the destruction of monasteries. Without their institutional support Buddhism faded away.

JAINISM

Like Buddhism, **Jainism** started as a reform movement of the **Brahmanic** religious beliefs of the 6th century BC. Its founder was a widely revered saint and ascetic, **Vardhamma**, who became known as **Mahavir** – "great hero". Mahavir was born in the same border region of India and Nepal as the Buddha, just 50 km to the N of modern Patna, probably in 599 BC. Thus he was about 35 years older than the Buddha. His family, also royal, were followers of an ascetic saint, Parvanatha, who according to Jain tradition had lived two hundred years previously.

Mahavir's life story is embellished with legends, but there is no doubt that he left his royal home for a life of the strict ascetic. He is believed to have received enlightenment after 12 years of rigorous hardship, penance and meditation. Afterwards he travelled and preached for 30 years, stopping only in the rainy season. He died aged 72 in 527 BC. His death was commemorated by a special lamp festival in the region of Bihar, which Jains claim is the basis of the now-common Hindu festival of lights, **Deepavali**.

Unlike Buddhism, however, Jainism never spread beyond India, but it has survived continuously into modern India, claiming 3.2 million adherents in 1981. In part this may be because Jain beliefs have much in common with puritanical forms of Hinduism, and are greatly respected and admired. Some Jain ideas, such as vegetarianism and reverence for all life, are widely recognised by Hindus as highly commendable, even by those who don't share other Jain beliefs. The value Jains place on non-violence has contributed to their importance in business and commerce, as they regard nearly all occupations except banking and commerce as violent.

From the time of the Emperor **Chandragupta Maurya** in the 3rd century BC, Jains have enjoyed official patronage in various parts of India at different times, though Jainism became strongest in the W and parts of the S. Remarkable Jain temples can be found from **Jaisalmer** in **W Rajasthan** to **Orissa** in the E, and as far S as southern Karnataka. The 18 m high free standing statue of **Gommateshvara** at **Sravana Belgola** near Mysore (built about 983 AD) is just one outstanding example of the contribution of Jain art to India's heritage.

Jain Beliefs

Jains (from the word **Jina**, literally meaning "descendants of conquerors") believe that there are two fundamental principles, the **living** (*jiva*) and the **non-living** (*ajiva*). The essence of Jain belief is that **all life is sacred**, and that every living entity, even the smallest insect, has within it an indestructible and immortal soul. Jains developed the view of *ahimsa* – often translated as "non-violence", but better perhaps as "**non-harming**". Ahimsa was the basis for the entire scheme of Jain values and ethics, and alternative codes of practice were defined for householders and for ascetics.

The five vows may be taken both by monks and by lay people: **Not to harm any living beings**. Jains must practise strict vegetarianism – and even some vegetables, such as potatoes and onions, are believed to have microscopic souls; **To speak the truth**; **Not to steal**; **To give up sexual relations** and practice complete chastity; **To give up all possessions**. For the **Digambara** sect that includes clothes.

Celibacy is necessary to combat physical desire. Jains also regard the manner of dying as extremely important. Although suicide is deeply opposed, vows of fasting to death voluntarily may be regarded as earning merit in the proper context. **Mahavir** himself is believed to have died of self-starvation, near **Rajgir** in modern Bihar.

In principle the objectives for both lay and ascetic Jains is the same, and many lay Jains pass through the stage of being a householder, and then accept the stricter practices of the monks. The essence of all the rules is to avoid intentional injury, which is the worst of all sins. Like Hindus, the Jains believe in **karma**, by which the evil effects of earlier deeds leave an indelible impurity on the soul. This impurity will remain through endless rebirths unless burned off by extreme penances.

Jain Sects

Jains have long been divided by factionalism. There are two main sects, whose origins can be traced back to the 4th century BC. The more numerous *Svetambaras* – the 'white clad' – concentrated more in E and W India, separated from the *Digambaras* – or 'sky-clad'– who often go naked. The Digambaras may well have been forced to move S by drought and famine in the N region of the Deccan, and they are now concentrated in the S of India.

The two sects differ chiefly on the nature of proper ascetic practices. The **Svetambara** monks wear white robes, and carry a staff, some wooden pots, and a woollen mop for sweeping the path in front of them, wool being the softest material available and the least likely to hurt any living thing swept away. The highest level of **Digambara** monks will go completely naked, although the lower levels will wear a covering over their genitalia. They carry a waterpot made of a gourd, and peacock feathers to sweep the ground before they sit down.

Jains believe that the spiritual journey of the soul is divided into fourteen stages, moving from bondage and ignorance to the final destruction of all karma and the complete fulfilment of the soul. The object throughout is to prevent the addition of new karma to the soul, which comes mainly through passion and attachment to the world. Bearing the pains of the world cheerfully contributes to the destruction of karma.

Unlike Buddhists, Jains accept the idea of God, but not as a creator of the universe. They see him in the lives of the twenty four *Tirthankaras* (prophets, or literally "makers of fords" – a reference to their role in building crossing points for the spiritual journey over the river of life), or leaders of Jainism. Their lives are recounted in the **Kalpsutra** – the 3rd century BC book of ritual for the Svetambaras. Mahavir is regarded as the last of these great spiritual leaders. Much Jain art details stories from these accounts, and the Tirthankaras play a similar role for Jains as the Bodhisattvas do for Mahayana Buddhists.

SIKHISM

Guru	Teachings	External powers	Events
1. *Nanak* 1469-1539	Born just W of Lahore, grew up in what is now the Pakistani town of Sultanpur. The life stories (**janam-sakhis**) of Guru Nanak, written between 50 and 80 years after his death, recorded wide travels, including Bengal in the E and Mecca in the W, studying different faiths before returning to Panjab. One of the many stories about his travels tells of how he was rebuked on his visit to Mecca for sleeping with his feet pointing towards the Qa'aba, an act Muslims would consider sacrilegious. Apologising profusely, he is said to have replied "If you can show me in which direction I may lie so that my feet do not point towards God I will do so."	Devotional and mystic tradition established by Guru Nanak, similar to that of Kabir. Guru Nanak had contact with Muslim families, and while he was still young organised community hymn singing when both Hindus and Muslims were welcomed. Along with a Muslim servant in the home in which he was working he also organised a common kitchen where Hindus of all castes and Muslims could eat together, thereby deliberately breaking one of the strictest of caste rules.	Delhi sultanates
2. **Angad** 1504-1538		Developments took place in Sikh worship, moving from purely individual acts of inner devotion to the introduction of special ceremonies and festivals.,	
3. **Amar Das** 1509-1574	Introduction of worship in Gurudwaras.	Continued development of the Sikh community.	Mughal Empire
4. **Ram Das** 1534-1581	Built first lake temple in Amritsar; the first hereditary guru	Widening of congregational worship	Akbar Tolerance for Religious experiment
5. *Arjan* 1563-1606	Collected the hymns and sayings of the first three Gurus, as well as of other Sikh saints and mystics. He brought these together with many of his father's and his own in a single volume in 1603-4 which became known as the **Adi Granth** (the "original scripture"). Started the Golden Temple at Amritsar.	The **Adi Granth** comprises nearly 6,,000 hymns composed by the first five gurus, 974 attributed to Guru Nanak himself. Written in the **Gurumukhi** script, which was developed from Panjabi by the second Guru, this later became known as the Guru Granth Sahib.	Akbar and Jahangir. Arjan Singh executed by Jahangir at Lahore.
6. **Har Gobind** 1595-1645	Jat caste becomes dominant influence. Sikhs began to take up arms, largely to protect themselves against Mughal attacks. Hargobind decided to withdraw to the Siwalik Hills.	McLeod, the British historian of the Sikhs, believes that the Sikh's martial traditions stemmed from the fact that the next four Gurus all spent much of their time as Gurus outside Punjab in the Siwalik Hills, where they developed such martial traditions as honouring the sword.	Mughal Emperors Jahangir and Shah Jahan.
7. **Har Rai** 1630-1661			Shah Jahan

Guru	Teachings	External powers	Events
8. **Har Krishna** 1656-1664	Died at Delhi.		Aurangzeb
9. **Tegh Bahadur** 1622-1675	Executed by Aurangzeb.		Aurangzeb
10. *Gobind Singh* 1666-1708	Reformed Sikh government. It is widely believed among Sikhs that **Guru Gobind Singh** introduced the features now universally associated with Sikhism. On April 15th 1699, he started the new brotherhood called the **Khalsa** (meaning "the pure", from the Persian word *khales*). An inner core of the faithful, accepted by baptism (**amrit**). The "five k's" date from this period: **kesh** (uncut hair), **kangha** (comb), **kirpan** (dagger or short sword), **kara** (steel bangle) and **kachh** ("boxer" shorts). The most important is the uncut hair, adopted before the other four. The comb is sometimes designated specifically as wooden. The dagger and the shorts reflect military influence, while the bangle may be a form of charm like the thread Hindu girls may tie on their brothers' arms, **see page 209**. Assassinated at Nanded in Maharashtra.	The **Khalsa** was open to both men and women, who on admission were to replace their caste names with the names **Singh** (lion) and **Kaur** ("lioness" or "princess") respectively (the reason why the great majority of Sikh men have the surname Singh, though there are many other non-Sikhs who are also called Singh). In addition to the compulsory 'five k's', the new code prohibited smoking, eating halal meat, and sexual intercourse with Muslim women. These date from the 18th century , when the Sikhs were often in conflict with the Muslims. Other strict prohibitions include: idolatry, caste discrimination, hypocrisy, and pilgrimage to Hindu sacred places. The khalsa also explicitly forbade the seclusion of women, one of the common practices of Islam. It was only under the warrior king **Maharaja Ranjit Singh** (1799-1838) that the idea of the Guru's presence in meetings of the Sikh community (**the Panth**) gave way to the now universally held belief in the total authority of the **Guru Granth** – the recorded words of the Guru in the scripture.	Auurangseb

The Sikhs (derived from the Sanskrit word for "disciples") are perhaps one of India's most recognisable groups. Beards and turbans give them a very distinctive presence, and although they represent less than 2% of the population they are both politically and economically significant. There are Sikhs living in all the major cities of India and playing an important role in all India's major institutions.

Distribution Before the partition of India and Pakistan in 1947 the Sikh community was spread evenly across the Punjab, but the region was divided in two by the international boundary created between India and Pakistan. Partition was preceded by savage Muslim-Sikh riots, and although some of their most sacred places were in Pakistan, Sikhs opted to become part of India, where the secular constitution seemed to offer better guarantees of long term security.

Over 2.5 million Sikhs left Pakistan for India. However, their loss of rich agricultural land, and the reduced opportunities in military and other services, led to a sense of resentment and demands for fuller political autonomy within India. Although in 1965 they won the demand for a Panjabi speaking state, Punjab has remained a centre of political unrest. Today over 90% of the 15 million Sikhs in India live in the Punjab, Haryana and Delhi. There are also significant emigrant communities abroad.

Sikh Beliefs

From Hinduism came an acceptance of the ideas of **samsara** – the cycle of re-births – and **karma**. However, Sikhism is unequivocal in its belief in the oneness of God, rejecting idolatry and any worship of objects or images. Possibly reflecting the influence of Islamic beliefs, Guru Nanak also fiercely opposed discrimination on the grounds of caste.

Some of Guru Nanak's teachings are close to the ideas of the Banaras mystic **Kabir**, who, in common with the Muslim mystic **sufis**, believed in mystical union with God. Guru Nanak believed that God is One, formless, eternal and beyond description. However, he also saw God as present everywhere, visible to anyone who cared to look, and essentially full of grace and compassion.

His belief in the nature of God was matched by his view that man was deliberately blind and unwilling to recognise God's nature. He transformed the Hindu concept of **maya** into meaning the unreality of the values commonly held by the world. Guru Nanak held that **salvation** depended on accepting the nature of God. If man recognised the true harmony of the divine order (**hukam**) and brought himself into line with that harmony he would be saved. However, Guru Nanak rejected the prevailing Hindu belief that such harmony could be achieved by ascetic practices. In their place he emphasised **three actions**; meditating on and repeating God's name (**nam**), giving or charity (**dan**) and bathing (**isnan**).

Sikh Worship

The meditative worship he commended is a part of the life of every devout Sikh today. Many Sikh homes will have a room set aside which houses a copy of the **Guru Granth**, and members of the house will start each day with private meditation and a recitation of the meditative verses of Guru Nanak himself, the **Japji**. However, from the time of the 3rd Guru, Sikhs have also worshipped as congregations in temples known as Gurudwara ("gateway to the Guru"). The Golden Temple in Amritsar, built by Guru Arjan at the end of the 16th century, is the holiest site of Sikhism.

The present institutions of Sikhism owe their origins to reform movements of the 19th century. Under the **Sikh Gurudwaras Act** of 1925 all temples were restored to the management of a Central Gurudwara Management Committee, thereby removing them from the administrative control of the Hindus under which many had come. This body has acted as the religion's controlling body ever since.

CHRISTIANITY

There are more Christians in South Asia than there are Sikhs, Buddhists or Jains, and Christianity ranks third in terms of religious affiliation after Hinduism and Islam. There are churches in all the major towns of South Asia today, and there are about 20 million Christians in India alone, with smaller but significant numbers in the other South Asian countries.

The great majority of the *Protestant* Christians in India are now members of two broad groups of united denominations. The **Church of S India** was formed from the major Protestant denominations in 1947, and the **Church of N India** followed suit in 1970. Together they account for approximately half the total number of Christians, **Roman Catholics** making up the majority of the other 50%. Many of the church congregations, both in towns and villages, are active centres of Christian worship, the great majority using the local regional language rather than English, which is typical of some of the larger city-based churches.

Origins Some of the churches owe their origin either to the modern missionary movement of the late 18th century onwards, or to the colonial presence of the European powers. However, Christians probably arrived in India during the 1st century after the birth of Christ. There is evidence that one of Christ's Apostles, **Thomas**, reached India in 52 AD, only twenty years after Christ was crucified. He settled in **Malabar** and then expanded his missionary work to China. It is widely believed that he was martyred in Tamil Nadu on his return to India in 72 AD, and is buried in Mylapore, in the suburbs of modern Madras. **St. Thomas' Mount**, a small rocky hill just N of Madras airport, takes its name from him. Today there is still a church of Thomas Christians in Kerala.

The Syrian Church Kerala was linked directly with the Middle East, when **Syrian Christians** embarked on a major missionary movement in the 6th century AD. The Thomas Christians have forms of worship that show very strong influence of the Syrian Church, and they still retain a Syriac order of service. They remained a close knit community, coming to terms with the prevailing caste system by maintaining strict social rules very similar to those of the surrounding upper caste Hindus. They lived in an area restricted to what is now Kerala, where trade with the Middle East, which some centuries later was to bring Muslims to the same region, remained active.

Roman Catholicism The third major development took place with the arrival of the **Portuguese**. The Jesuit **St Francis Xavier** landed in Goa in 1542, and in 1557 Goa was made an Archbishopric, **see page 1023**. Goa today bears rich testimony to the Portuguese influence on community life and on church building. They set up the first printing press in India in 1566 and began to print books in Tamil and other Dravidian languages by the end of the sixteenth century. The spread of **Roman Catholicism** was uneven, but was much stronger in the south. Jesuits concentrated their missionary efforts on work among the high caste Hindus, the most striking example of which was that of Robert de Nobili, who followed a Brahmin way of life in Madurai for many years.

Both the Roman Catholic and subsequently the Protestant denominations struggled to come to terms with the caste system. By the late 18th century the Roman Catholic church had moved substantially to abolishing discrimination on grounds of caste, a pattern which the main Protestant communities tried to follow. The American Mission in Madurai, for example, instituted "agapé meals", or "love feasts", to which Christians of all castes were invited to eat meals together cooked by members of low castes.

The nature and the influence of Christian missionary activity in **N India** were different. There are far fewer Christians in N India than in the S, but Protestant missions in Bengal from the end of the eighteenth century had a profound influence on cultural and religious development. On November 9th 1793 the Baptist missionary *William Carey* reached the Hugli River. Although he went to India to preach, he had wide-ranging interests, notably in languages and education, and the work of 19th century missions rapidly widened to cover educational and medical work as well.

Converts were made most readily among the backward castes and in the tribal areas. The Christian populations of the tribal hill areas of **Nagaland** and **Assam** stem from such late 19th century and 20th century movements. But the influence of Christian missions in education and medical work was greater than as a proselytizing force. Education in Christian schools stimulated reformist movements in Hinduism itself, and mission hospitals supplemented government run hospitals, particularly in remote rural areas, where they often offered the only medical care available. Some of these Christian-run hospitals, such as that at **Vellore**, continue to provide high class medical care alongside Government run medical services.

Christian Beliefs

Christian theology had its roots in **Judaism**, with its belief in one God, the eternal Creator of the universe. Judaism saw the Jewish people as the vehicle for God's salvation, the "chosen people of God", and pointed to a time when God would send his Saviour, or Messiah. **Jesus**, whom Christians believe was **"the Christ"** or Messiah, was born in the village of Bethlehem, some 20 kilometres S of Jerusalem. Very little is known of his early life except that he was brought up in a devout Jewish family. At the age of 29 or 30 he gathered a small group of followers and began to preach in the region between the Dead Sea and the Sea of Galilee. Two years later he was crucified in Jerusalem by the authorities on the charge of blasphemy – that he claimed to be the Son of God.

Christians believe that all people live in a state of sin, in the sense that they are separated from God and fail to do his will. They believe that God is personal, "like a father". As God's son, Jesus accepted the cost of that separation and sinfulness himself through his death on the cross. Christians believe that Jesus was raised from the dead on the third day after he was crucified, and that he appeared to his closest followers. They believe that his spirit continues to live today, and that he makes it possible for people to come back to God.

The **New Testament** of the Bible, which, alongside the **Old Testament**, is the text to which Christians refer as the ultimate scriptural authority, consists of four "Gospels" (meaning "good news"), and a series of letters by several early Christians referring to the nature of the Christian life.

Denominations Between the 2nd and the 4th centuries AD there were numerous debates about the interpretation of Christian doctrine, sometimes resulting in the formation of specific groups focussing on particular interpretations of faith. One such group was that of the **Nestorian Christians**, who played a major part in the theology of the Syrian Church in Kerala. They regarded the Syrian patriarch of the East their spiritual head, and followed the Nestorian tradition that there were two distinct natures in Christ, the divine and human. The **Roman Catholic Church** believes that Christ declared that his disciple **Peter** should be the first spiritual head of the Church, and that his successors should lead the Church on earth. Modern Catholic churches still recognise the spiritual authority of the **Pope** and **Cardinals**.

The **reformation** which took place in Europe from the 16th century onwards resulted in the creation of the **Protestant churches**, which became dominant in several European countries. They reasserted the authority of the Bible over that of the Church. A number of new denominations were created. This process of division left a profound mark on the nature of the Christian church as it spread into South Asia. The re-unification of the Church which has taken significant steps since 1947 has progressed faster in South Asia than in most other parts of the world. Most main Protestant denominations in India are now part either of the *Church of S India* or the *Church of N India*, and relations with both the Roman Catholic and Protestant churches are much closer than at any time in the past.

ZOROASTRIANISM

The first Zoroastrians arrived on the W coast of India in 936 AD, forced out from their native Iran by persecution of the invading Islamic Arabs. Until 1477 they lost all contact with Iran, and then for nearly 300 years maintained contact with **Persian Zoroastrians** through a continuous exchange of letters. They became known by their now much more familiar name, the **Parsis** (or Persians).

Although in terms of numbers (approximately 100,000) they are a tiny minority, even in the cities where they are concentrated, they have been a prominent economic and social influence, especially in W India. They adopted westernised customs and dress, and took to the new economic opportunities that came with colonial industrialisation. Families in W India such as the Tatas continue to be among India's leading industrialists, just part of a community that in recent generations has spread to Europe and N America.

Origins Zoroastrians trace their beliefs to the prophet *Zarathustra*, who lived in NE Iran around 7th or 6th century BC. His place and even date of birth are uncertain, but he almost certainly enjoyed the patronage of the father of **Darius the Great**. The passage of **Alexander the Great** through Iran severely weakened support for Zoroastrianism, but between the 6th century BC and the 7th century AD it was the major religion of peoples living from N India to central Turkey. The spread of Islam reduced the number of Zoroastrians dramatically and forced those who did not retreat to the desert to emigrate altogether.

Parsi Beliefs

The early development of Zoroastrianism marked a movement towards belief in a single God. **Ahura Mazda**, the Good Religion of God, was shown in rejecting evil and in purifying thought word and action. Fire plays a central and symbolic part in Zoroastrian worship, representing the presence of God. There are eight **Atash Bahram** – major fire temples– in India; four are in **Bombay**, two in **Surat** and one each in **Navsari** and **Udwada**. There are many more minor temples, where the rituals are far less complex – perhaps forty in Bombay alone.

Earth, **fire** and **air** are all regarded as sacred, while death is the result of evil. Dead matter pollutes all it touches. Where there is a suitable space therefore dead bodies are simply placed in the open to be consumed by vultures, as at the towers of silence in Bombay. However, burial and cremation are also common.

THE HISTORY OF SOUTH ASIA

Settled agriculture in South Asia goes back at least 10,000 years before the present day, when the first village communities of what became the great Indus Valley civilisation grew up on the arid western fringes of the Indus plains in modern Pakistan. Over the following generations successive waves of settlers – sometimes bringing goods for trade, sometimes armies to conquer territory, and sometimes nothing more than domesticated animals and families in search of land to cultivate and peace to live – moved across the Indus and into India. They left an indelible mark on the landscape and culture of all the countries of modern South Asia.

EARLY SETTLEMENTS

Recent research suggests ever earlier dates for the earliest settlements. A site at Mehrgarh, where the Indus Plains meet the dry Baluchistan Hills, has revealed evidence of agricultural settlement as early as 8500 BC. By 3500 BC agriculture had spread throughout the Indus plains, and in the thousand years following it there were independent settled villages well to the E of the Indus. See page 1197 Between 3000 BC and 2500 BC many new settlements sprang up in the heartland of what became the Indus Valley civilisation, but development also took place rapidly in many other parts of South Asia.

Despite the effects of repeated migrations, most cultural, religious and political developments in South Asia over that period owed more to local development than to external control. From the earliest evidence of the magnificent remains of **Moenjo Daro** and many other sites in Pakistan and India, going back to before

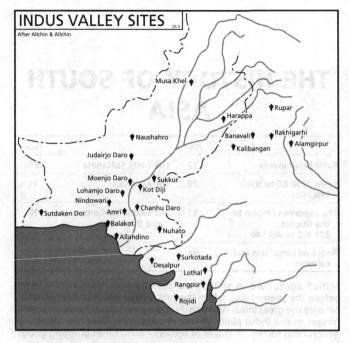

INDUS VALLEY SITES SA 5

After Allchin & Allchin

Musa Khel

Rupar

Harappa

Banavali
Naushahro

Rakhigarhi

Alamgirpur

Kalibangan

Judairjo Daro

Moenjo Daro

Sukkur

Lohamjo Daro

Kot Diji

Nindowari

Chanhu Daro

Amri

Sutdaken Dor

Balakot

Nuhato

Allahdino

Surkotada

Desalpur

Lothal

Rangpur

Rojidi

3000 BC, we can see that South Asia had extensive contacts with other regions, notably with **Mesopotamia**. At its height the **Indus Valley** civilisation covered as great an area as Egypt or Mesopotamia. **See pages 1184.** However, the culture that developed was distinctively South Asian. The language, which is still untranslated, may well have been an early form of the Dravidian languages which today are found largely in S India. The only written forms of the Indus Valley language are found on seals in the form of short inscriptions. Aside from linguistic evidence, a clue to the possibility of Dravidian origins, however, may be the presence of the Dravidian **Brahui** language in the region today. 250,000 Brahui speaking people live on the Pakistan-Afghan border.

BC	Northern S.Asia	Peninsular India	External events	BC
900,000	Earliest hominids in W. Asia		First occupation of N China	450,000
500,000	Lower Paleolithic sites from NW to the Peninsula; Pre-Soan and Soan stone industries in NW	Earliest Palaeolithic sites – Narmada Valley; Karnataka; Tamil Nadu and Andhra	First Homo sapiens in E Asia	120,000
			First human settlement in Americas (Brazil)	30,000
10,000	Beginning of Mesolithic period	Continuous occupation of caves and riverside sites	Earliest known pottery – Kukui, Japan	10,500
			Ice Age retreats – Hunter gatherers in Europe	8,300

BC	Northern S.Asia	Peninsular India	External events	BC
8000	First Wheat and barley grown in Indus Plains	Mesolithic	First domesticated wheat, barley in fertile crescent; first burials in N America	8000
7500	Pottery at Mehrgarh; development of villages	Increase in range of cereals in Rajasthan	Agriculture begins in New Guinea	7000
6500	Humped Indian cattle domesticated	Cultivation extends S	Britain separated from Continental Europe by rising sea level	6500
6000	Farming widespread on margins of Indus plains		High altitude grain in Peru; potato cultivation; pigs and dogs domesticated in China	6300
5000	Origins of Indus Valley civilisation, settled agriculture and trade with Middle East		Wet rice cultivation in China; rising sea level separates New Guinea and Tasmania from mainland Australia	5000
4000	Agriculture continues to develop		Guyana: first pottery in Americas	4000
3500	Potter's wheel in use. Long distance trade. Indus sees expansion of agricultural settlements		Sumeria, Southern Mesopotamia: first urban civilisation	3500
3000	Incipient urbanisation in the Indus plains	First Neolithic settlements in S Deccan (Karnataka). Ash mounds, cattle herding	First Egyptian state; Egyptian hieroglyphics; walled citadels in Mediterranean Europe	3100
2500	Indus Valley Civilisation Cities of Moenjo Daro, Harappa and many others.	Chalcolithic ("Copper" age) in Rajasthan; Neolithic continues in S.	Great Pyramid of Khufu China: walled settlements; European Bronze Age begins; hybridization of maize in S. America	2530 / 2500
2000	Occupation of Moenjo Daro ends	Chalcolithic in Malwa Plateau, Maharashtra Utnur and Piklihal – Neolithic ends in S: in Karnataka and Andhra – rock paintings	Earliest ceramics in Peruvian Andes Collapse of Old Kingdom in Egypt Stonehenge in Britain; Minoan Crete	2300 / 2150 / 2000
1750	Indus Valley civilisation ends	Hill-top sites in S. India	Joseph sold into Egypt – Genesis	1750

SOUTH ASIA FROM 1750 BC TO THE MAURYAS

In about 2000 BC **Moenjo Daro** became deserted, and within the next 250 years the entire Indus Valley civilisation disintegrated. The causes may have been related to the violent arrival of new waves of Aryan immigrants, to increasing desertification of the already semi-arid landscape, to a shift in the course of the Indus, or to internal political decay. Whatever the cause of the decline, it is becoming increasingly clear that some features of Indus Valley culture were carried on by succeeding generations. See page 1184.

From 1500 BC the N region of South Asia entered what has been called the **Vedic period**. Aryan settlers from the NW moved further and further E towards the Ganga valley. Grouped into tribes, conflict was common. Even at this stage it is possible to see the development of classes of rulers – *rajas* – and priests – *brahmins*. In one battle of this period a confederacy of tribes known as the Bharatas defeated another grouping of ten tribes. They gave their name to the region to the E of the Indus which has become the official name for India today – Bharat.

BC	Northern S.Asia	Peninsular India	External events	BC
1750	Successors to Indus Valley	Copper age begins, but neolithic continues; cattle raising, gram and millet cultivation. Hill terracing for cultivation. Cattle, goats and sheep.	Anatolia: Hittite empire New Kingdom in Egypt First metal working in Peru First inscriptions in China; Linear B script in Greece	1650
1500	Aryans invade in successive waves. Cemetery H at Harappa. Development of Indo-Aryan language			1570
				1500
				1400
1400	Indo-Aryan settlement spreads E and S onto Ganga – Yamuna doab	Horses introduced into S. Cave paintings, burials	Tutankhamun buried in Valley of Kings	1337
1200	Composition of Rig Veda begins?	Iron age sites at Hallur, Karnataka	Middle America: first urban civilisation in Olmec; collapse of Hittite empire	1200
1000	Earliest Painted Grey Ware in Upper Ganga Valley; Brahmanas begin to be written, see page 263.	Iron Age becomes more widespread across Peninsula	Australia: large stone-built villages; David King of Israel Kingdom of Kush in Africa	
800	Mahabharata war – origin of Bhagavad Gita; Aryan invaders reach Bengal Rise of city states in Ganga plains, based on rice cultivation.		First settlement at Rome Celtic iron age begins in N & E of Alps	850
				800
		Megalithic grave sites	Greek city states	750
700	Upanishads begin to be written; concept of transmigration of souls develops; Pannini's Sanskrit grammar		Iliad composed	700
600	Northern Black Pottery Ware		First Latin script; first Greek coins	600
599	Mahavir born – founder of Jainism		First iron production in China; Zoroastrianism becomes official religion in Persia	550
563	Gautama Buddha born			
500	Upanishads finished; Taxila and Charsadda become important towns and trade centres	Aryans colonise Sri Lanka. Irrigation practised in Sri Lanka	Wet rice cultivation introduced to Japan	500

The centre of population and of culture shifted E from the banks of the Indus to the land between the rivers **Yamuna** and **Ganga**. This region, known as the *doab* (pronounced *doe-ab*, literally "two waters"), became the heart of emerging Aryan culture, which, from 1500 BC onwards, laid the literary and religious foundations of what ultimately became Hinduism.

The Vedas The first fruit of this development was the **Rig Veda**, the first of four **Vedas**, composed, collected and passed on orally by Brahmin priests from 1300 BC to about 1000 BC. In the later Vedic period, from about 1000 BC to 600 BC, the **Sama**, **Yajur** and **Artha Vedas** show that the Indo-Aryans developed a clear sense of the *doab* as "their" territory. Modern Delhi lies just to the S of this region, central both to the development of history and myth in South Asia. Later texts extended the core region from the Himalayas in the N to the Vindhyans in the S, and to the Bay of Bengal in the E. Beyond this core region lay the land of mixed peoples and then of barbarians, beyond the pale of Aryan society.

The Mahabharata Details of the great battle recounted in the Mahabharata are unclear. Tradition puts its date at precisely **3102 BC**, the start of the present era. Evidence suggests however that it was fought around 800 BC, about 100 kilometres N of modern **Delhi**. Delhi itself is on the site of **Indraprastha**, clearly identifiable from the Mahabharata, along with **Kurukshetra**, the site of the battle.

Caste Although the word **caste** was given by the Portuguese in the 15th century AD, the main feature of the system emerged at the end of the Vedic period. This was **varna** – a word meaning "colour" – and by 600 BC this had become a standard means of classifying the population. The fair-skinned Aryans distinguished themselves from the darker skinned earlier inhabitants. They saw themselves as falling into three groups, the priests, soldiers or rulers, and ordinary people like merchants – **Brahmins**, **Kshatriyas**, and **Vaishyas**. All of these were given high status, a position which was reinforced by calling them "twice-born". A fourth category was added at the bottom of the hierarchy, the low born people – **Sudras**.

From the 6th to the 3rd centuries BC the region from the foothills of the Himalayas across the Ganga plains to the edge of the Peninsula was governed under a variety of kingdoms or **Mahajanapadhas** – "great states". Trade gave rise to the birth of towns in the Ganga plains themselves, many of which have remained occupied to the present. **Varanasi** (Benaras) is perhaps the most famous example, but a trade route was established that ran from **Taxila** (just 20 kilometres from modern Islamabad in Pakistan) to **Rajagriha** 1500 km away in what is now Bihar. It was into these kingdoms of the Himalayan foothills and northern plains that both Mahavir, founder of Jainism, and the Buddha, were born.

THE MAURYAN EMPIRE TO THE GUPTAS – 321 BC-AD 540

Within a year of the retreat of **Alexander the Great** from his great march to the Indus, *Chandragupta Maurya* established the first indigenous empire since the Indus Valley Civilisation to exercise control over a major region of the sub-continent. Under his successors that control was extended to all but the extreme S of peninsular India.

The centre of political power had shifted steadily eastwards into wetter, more densely forested but also more fertile regions. The Mauryans had their base in the region known as Magadh, in what is now Bihar, and their capital was at Pataliputra, near modern Patna. Their power was based on massive military force and a highly efficient, centralised administration. Chandragupta's army may have had as many as 9,000 elephants, 30,000 cavalry and 600,000 infantry. Bindusara, his successor, extended the empire southwards as far as Mysore.

BC	Northern S.Asia	Peninsular India	External events	BC
326 321	Alexander at Indus Chandragupta establishes Mauryan Dynasty	Megalithic cultures	Crossbow invented in China	350
300 297	Bindusara extends Mauryan power as far as Mysore	First Ajanta caves; Sarnath stupa in original form	Mayan writing and ceremonial centres established	300
272-232 250	Asoka's empire Death of Asoka Brahmi script	Chola, Pandiya, Chera kingdoms: Earliest Tamil inscriptions	Ptolemy First towns in SE Asia Rome captures Spain	285 250 206
185	Shunga dynasty, centred on Ujjain	Megalithic cultures in hills of South	Romans destroy Greek states	146
100	Kharavela King of Kalingans in Orissa Final composition of Ramayana	South Indian trade with Indonesia and Rome. Roman pottery and coins in S. India	Indian religions spread to South East Asia Introduction of Julian calendar	100 46
AD 100 50	Vaishnavism spreads in N and NW	Satavahanas control much of Peninsula Discovery of monsoon winds Irrigation in Sri Lanka Thomas brings Christianity to S India Tamil Sangam poems	Rome population of 1 million; Pyramid of the sun at City of Teotihuacan, Mexico	**AD** 50
78 120?	Kushan rulers in NW followed by Scythians; Taxila a major centre; strong links with Roman empire. Kanishka accedes to throne (date strongly disputed); capital at Peshawar	Arikamedu – trade with Rome	Buddhism reaches China. Paper introduced in China; first metal work in SE Asia	68 100
125 200	Lawbook of Manu Gandharan art Hinayana/Mahayana Buddhist split	Mahayana Buddhism spreads; Nagarjunakomda major centre in Andhra Pradesh First cities on Deccan plateau	Hadrian's wall in Britain	125
300 319	Chandra Gupta founds Gupta dynasty: Classical age of Indian art and sculpture; Samadragupta (335), Chandragupta II (376), Kumara Gupta (415)	Rise of Pallavas	Classic period of Mayan civilisation; wet rice agriculture through Japan Edict of Milan – Christianity tolerated in Roman Empire Constantinople founded	300 313 330
454	Skanda Gupta, the last imperial Gupta, takes power. Dies 467.		End of Roman Empire Teotihuacan, Mexico, pop. 200,000	476 500
540 578	Gupta rule ends	Bhakti movement Chalukya dynasty, Badami cave temple; Last Ajanta paintings	Saint Sophia, Constantinople Buddhism arrives in Japan	532 550

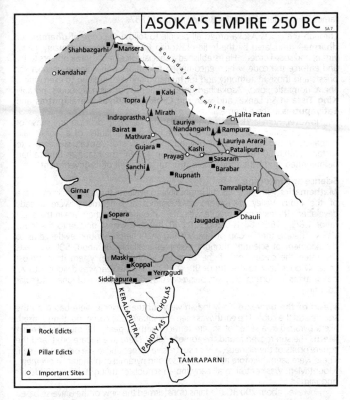

ASOKA'S EMPIRE 250 BC SA 7

Boundary of Empire

- Shahbazgarhi
- Mansera
- Kandahar
- Kalsi
- Topra
- Mirath
- Indraprastha
- Lauriya Nandangarh
- Lalita Patan
- Bairat
- Rampura
- Mathura
- Lauriya Araraj
- Gujara
- Kashi
- Pataliputra
- Sanchi
- Prayag
- Sasaram
- Barabar
- Rupnath
- Girnar
- Tamralipta
- Sopara
- Jaugada
- Dhauli
- Maski
- Koppal
- Yerragudi
- Siddhapura
- KERALAPUTRA
- CHOLAS
- PANDIYAS
- TAMRAPARNI

- ■ Rock Edicts
- ▲ Pillar Edicts
- ○ Important Sites

Asoka, the greatest of the Mauryan emperors, took power in 272 BC. He inherited a full blown empire, but extended it further by defeating the **Kalingans** in modern **Orissa**, before turning his back on war and preaching the virtues of Buddhist pacifism. Asoka's empire stretched from Afghanistan to Assam, and from the Himalayas to Mysore. He inherited a structure of government set out by Chandragupta's Prime Minister, *Kautilya*, in a book on the principles of government, the **Arthashastra**. The state maintained itself by raising revenue from taxation – on everything, from agriculture, to gambling and prostitution. He decreed that "no waste land should be occupied and not a tree cut down" without permission, not out of a modern "green" concern for protecting the forests, but because all were potential sources of revenue for the state. The **sudras** were used as free labour for clearing forest and cultivating new land.

Asoka (described on the edicts as "the Beloved of the Gods, of Gracious Countenance") left a series of inscriptions on pillars and rocks across the sub-continent. One of the most accessible for modern visitors is now in the Indraprastha fort in Delhi, where **Feroz Shah Tughluq** had it taken in the 14th century. Over most of India these inscriptions were written in **Prakrit**, using the **Brahmi** script, although in the NW they were in Greek using the **Kharoshti** script. They were unintelligible for over 2000 years after the decline of the empire until

James Prinsep deciphered the Brahmi script in 1837.

Through the edicts Asoka urged all people to follow the code of *dhamma* or *dharma*– translated by the Indian historian Romila Thapar as 'morality, piety, virtue, and social order'. He established a special force of dhamma officers to try and enforce the code, which encouraged toleration, non-violence, respect for priests and those in authority and for human dignity. In addition to exercising a liberal domestic policy, Asoka had good relations with his neighbours, notably **King Tissa** in Sri Lanka, and with the **Cholas**, **Pandiyas**, **Keralaputras** and **Satiyaputras** in the extreme S.

However, Romila Thapar suggests that the failure to develop any sense of national consciousness, coupled with the massive demands of a highly paid bureaucracy and army, proved beyond the abilities of Asoka's successors to sustain. Within 50 years of Asoka's death in 232 BC the Mauryan Empire had disintegrated, and with it the whole structure and spirit of its government.

Science and medicine

Mathematics Although it is still impossible to evaluate the scientific knowledge of the Indus Valley civilisation, mathematics and geometry were already developed. The extremely precise weights, cut out of grey chert, are in the exact ratios 1:8/3:4:16:32:64:160:200:320:640. It was a system unique to the Indus Valley. There is then a gap of nearly 1500 years before written evidence as to development of scientific thought becomes available. By about 500 BC texts illustrated the calculation of the calendar, although the system itself almost certainly goes back to the 8th or 9th century BC. The year was divided into 27 **nakshatras**, or fortnights, years being calculated on a mixture of lunar and solar counting.

Views of the universe Early Indian views of the universe were based on the square and the cube. The earth was seen as a square, one corner pointing S, rising like a pyramid in a series of square terraces with its peak, the mythical **Mount Meru**. The sun moved round the top of Mount Meru in a square orbit, and the square orbits of the planets were at successive planes above the orbit of the sun. These were seen therefore as forming a second pyramid of planetary movement. Mount Meru was central to all early Indian schools of thought, Hindu, Buddhist and Jain.

However, about 200 BC the Jains transformed the view of the universe based on squares by replacing the idea of square orbits with that of the circle. The earth was shown as a circular disc, with Mount Meru rising from its centre and the Pole Star directly above it. The mathematics that was derived from the interpretations of the universe was put to use in the rules developed for building altars.

Conceptions of the universe and the mathematical and geometrical ideas that accompanied them were comparatively advanced in South Asia by the time of the Mauryan Empire. So also was technology. The only copy of **Kautiliya**'s treatise on government (which was only discovered in 1909) dates from about 100 BC. It describes the weapons technology of catapults, incendiary missiles, and the use of elephants, but it is also evident that gunpowder was unknown. Large scale irrigation works were developed, though the earliest examples of large tanks may be those of the Sri Lankan King Panduwasa at Anuradhapura, built in 504 BC.

A period of fragmentation: 185 BC to AD 300

Beyond the Mauryan Empire other kingdoms had survived in S India. The early kingdoms of the **Cholas** and the **Pandiyas,** in what is now **Tamil Nadu**, gave a glimpse of both power and cultural development that was to flower over a thousand years later. In the centuries following the break up of the Mauryan Empire these kingdoms were in the forefront of developing overseas trade, especially with Greece and Rome. Internal trade also flourished, and Indian traders carried goods to China and SE Asia.

Although Asoka had given patronage to Buddhist religious orders it was the development of strong trading and merchant guilds that extended patronage beyond individual royal households. Buddhist stupas at **Sanchi**, **Barhaut** and **Amaravati** could not have been built without the financial backing of such groups. Art and sculpture were also influenced by the new contacts. **Gandharan** art, of which there are superb examples in the Lahore museum and in the National Museum in Delhi, shows strong Greek influence.

The Classical Period – the *Gupta Empire* AD 319-467

Although the political power of **Chandra Gupta** and his successors never approached that of his unrelated namesake nearly 650 years before him, the Gupta Empire which was established with his coronation in AD 319 produced developments in every field of Indian culture. Their influence has been felt profoundly across South Asia to the present.

Geographically the Guptas originated in the same Magadhan region that had given rise to the Mauryan Empire. Extending their power by strategic marriage alliances, **Chandra Gupta**'s empire of **Magadh** was extended by his son, **Samudra Gupta**, who took power in AD 335, across N India. He also marched as far S as **Kanchipuram** in modern Tamil Nadu, but the heartland of the Gupta Empire remained the plains of the Ganga.

Patronage of the arts and religion was particularly far-reaching under **Chandra Gupta II**, who reigned for 39 years from AD 376. Political power was much less centralised than under the Mauryans, and as Thapar points out, collection of land revenue was deputed to officers who were entitled to keep a share of the revenue rather than to highly paid bureaucrats. Trade – with SE Asia, Arabia and China – all added to royal wealth.

That wealth was distributed to **the arts** on a previously unheard of scale. Some went to religious foundations, such as the Buddhist monastery at **Ajanta**, which produced some of its finest murals during the Gupta period. But Hindu institutions also benefitted, and some of the most important features of modern Hinduism date from this time. The sacrifices of Vedic worship were given up in favour of personal devotional worship, known as *bhakti*. *Tantrism*, both in its Buddhist and Hindu forms, with its emphasis on the female life force and worship of the Mother Goddess, developed. The focus of worship was increasingly towards a personalized and monotheistic deity, represented in the form of either **Siva** or **Vishnu**. The myths of Vishnu's incarnations also arose at this period.

The Brahmans, in the key position to shape and mediate change, re-focused earlier literature to give shape to the emerging religious philosophy. In their hands the Mahabharata and the Ramayana were transformed from secular epics to religious stories. At an individual level the excellence of sculpture both reflected and contributed to an increase in image worship and the growing role of temples as centres of devotion.

Romila Thapar has recounted the remarkable developments in science made during the Gupta period. **Metallurgy** made dramatic progress, evidenced in the extraordinarily pure **iron pillar** which can be seen in the **Qutb Minar** complex in Delhi. In mathematics, Indians were using the concept of **zero** and decimal points. Furthermore in AD 499, just after the demise of the Gupta Empire, the astronomer **Aryabhata** "calculated Pi as 3.1416 and the length of the solar year as 365.358 days. He also postulated that the earth was a sphere rotating on its own axis and revolving around the sun, and that the shadow of the earth falling on the moon caused eclipses. " All this almost exactly 1000 years before the birth of Copernicus and more than 1000 years before Galileo was threatened with torture by the Inquisition in Europe for contemplating such a reality.

Science in South India The development of science in South Asia was not restricted to the Gupta court. In S India, Tamil kings developed extensive contact with Roman and Greek thinkers during the first four centuries of the Christian era. Babylonian methods used for astronomy in Greece remained current in Tamil Nadu until very recent times. The basic texts of astronomy which influenced Indian development were completed by AD 400, when the **Surya Siddhanta** was completed.

This was also an age of great literature. **Kalidasa**, one of the "nine gems" of Chandragupta II's court, and one of South Asia's greatest poets, contributed to the development of Sanskrit as the language of learning and the arts. **Vatsyana's Kamasutra** not only explores the diversity of physical love but sheds light on social customs. In architecture the **Nagara** and **Dravida** styles were first developed. The Brahmins also produced theses on philosophy and on the structure of society, but these had the negative effect of contributing to the extreme rigidity of the caste system which became apparent from this period onwards.

Eventually the Gupta Empire crumbled in the face of repeated attacks from the NW, this time by the Huns. By the end of the 6th century Punjab and Kashmir had been prised from Gupta control, and the last great Hindu Empire to embrace the whole of northern India and part of the Peninsula was at an end.

REGIONAL KINGDOMS AND REGIONAL CULTURES

The collapse of Gupta power in the N opened the way for successive smaller kingdoms to assert themselves. In doing so the main outlines of the modern regional geography of South Asia began to take clear shape. After the comparatively brief reign of **Harsha** in the mid 7th century, which recaptured something both of the territory and the glory of the Guptas, the Gangetic plains were constantly fought over by rival groups, none of whom were able to establish unchallenged authority.

Regional kingdoms developed, often around comparatively small natural regions. Thus in Orissa, the delta of the Mahanadi and Brahmani rivers was the focus of several small kingdoms which only united, along with tracts of central Orissa, in the 10th and 11th centuries. This fusion of power culminated in the 12th century, when **Kalinga** was united with central and N Orissa. Today's **Jagannath** festival in Puri dates back to this period, and was an attempt to provide a focus of cultural integration through the worship of Vishnu.

The central Peninsula of India, was under the control of the **Rashtrakutas**. To their S the **Pandiyas**, **Cholas** and **Pallavas** controlled the Dravidian lands of what is now Kerala, Tamil Nadu and coastal Andhra Pradesh. The Pallavas, responsible for building the temples at Mamallapuram, just S of modern Madras, had come to power in the 7th century, centred on the Palar River valley around Kanchipuram. They warded off attacks both from the Rashtrakutas to their N and from the Pandiyans, who controlled the S deltas of the Vaigai and Tamraparni Rivers, with Madurai as their capital.

In the 8th century Kerala began to develop its own regional identity with the rise of the Kulashekharas in the Periyar Valley, now well known for its game reserve. Caste was a dominating feature of the kingdom's social organisation, but with the distinctive twist that the Nayars, the most aristocratic of castes, developed a matrilineal system of descent.

AD	Northern S.Asia	Peninsular India	External events	AD
600	Period of small Indian states	Chalukyan dynasty in W and C Deccan		
629	Hiuen Tsang travels round India		Death of Mohammad	632
630		Pallavas in Tamil Nadu: Narasimhavarman	Buddhism reaches Tibet	645
670		Mamallapuram shore temples		
712	Arabs arrive in Sind	Nandivarman II in Tamil Nadu. Pandiyas in Madurai	Muslim invasions of Spain	711
750	Rajputs become powerful force in NW	Pala dynasty in Bengal and E India		
775		Rashtrakutas dominate central peninsula Kailasanath Temple, Ellora	Charlemagne crowned	800
850		Cholas overthrow Pallavas in Tamil Nadu	Settlement of New Zealand	850
		Tamil philosopher Shankaracharya	Cyrillic script developed	863
950	Khajuraho temples started			
984		Rajaraja I	Sung dynasty in China	979
1001	Mahmud of Ghazni raids Indus plains Rajput dynasties grow		Easter Island stone carvings	1000
1014	Sufism in N India	Rajendra Chola		
1050	Rajput dynasties in NW Senas in Bengal	Chola kings – navies sent to SE Asia: Chola bronzes	Norman conquest of England	1066
		Kalinga becomes united kingdom in Eastern Peninsula		
1100		Polonnaruwa becomes capital of Sri Lanka in place of Anuradhapura	First European universities	1100
1192	Rajputs defeated at Battle of Tarain by Mu'izzu'd Din		Angkor Wat, Cambodia; paper making spreads from Muslim world	1137 1150
1198	First mosque built in Delhi; Qutb Minar, Delhi	Konarak Sun Temple, Orissa	Rise of Hausa city states in West Africa	1200
1206	Delhi Sultanate established :Khalji Sultans		Mongols begin conquest of Asia under Gengis Khan	1206

However, it was the **Cholas** who came to dominate the S from the 8th century. Overthrowing the Pallavas, they controlled most of Tamil Nadu, S Karnataka and S Andhra Pradesh from 850 AD to 1278 AD. They often held the Kerala kings under their control. Under their kings **Rajaraja I** (984-1014) and **Rajendra** (1014-1044) the Cholas also controlled northern Sri Lanka, sent naval expeditions to SE Asia, and successful military campaigns N to the Ganga plains. They lavished endowments on temples, dedicated to their personal deities, and also extended the gifts of land to Brahmins instituted by the Pallavas and Pandiyans. Many thousands of Brahmin priests were brought S to serve in major temples such as those in Chidambaram, and Rajendra wished to be remembered above all as the king who brought water from the holy Ganga all the way to his kingdom.

The Rajputs The political instability and rivalry that resulted from the ending of Gupta power in the N opened the way for new waves of immigrants from the N west, and for new groups and clans to seize power. Among these were the **Rajputs** (a name meaning "*sons of kings*"). Claiming to be descended from a mythical figure who rose out of a sacrificial pit near **Mount Abu**, the Rajput clans probably originated from outside India.

From the seventh century AD Rajputs were always a force to be reckoned with in the NW. Independent Rajput dynasties became vital centres of power, albeit at a comparatively local level. The temples at Khajuraho in central India, one of contemporary India's most remarkable sites, were built during the Rajput dynasty of the Chandelas (916-1203). However, the Rajputs never succeeded in forging a united front strong enough to establish either effective central government control internally or protection from external attack.

THE DELHI SULTANATE

AD	Northern S.Asia	Peninsular India	External events	AD
1206	Turkish "slave dynasty"	Pandiyas rise	Srivijaya Kingdom at its height in Java; Angkor empire at greatest	1170
1229	Iltutmish Sultan of Delhi		First Thai kingdom	1220
1290	Khaljis in Delhi; Jalal ud Din Khalji		Marco Polo reaches China	1275
1320-24 1324-51	Ghiyas ud Din Tughluq Mohammad bin Tughluq		Black death spreads from Asia to Europe	1348
1336 1347 1351-88	 Firuz Shah	Vijayanagar empire established, Harihara I Ala'ud Din sets up Bahmani dynasty, independent of Delhi, in Gulbarga	Ming dynasty in China established Peking the largest city in the world; Collapse of Khmer kingdom	1368 1400
1398 1412 1414 1440 1451 1469 1482	Timur sacks Delhi End of Tughlaq dynasty Sayyid Dynasty Mystic Kabir born in Banaras Afghan Lodi dynasty established under Bahlul Guru Nanak born in Punjab	 Bidar/Bahmani kingdom in Deccan Fall of Bahmanis	Ming sea going expeditions to Africa Aztecs defeat Atzcapatzalco Incas centralise power Byzantine Empire falls to Ottomans Columbus reaches the Americas; Spanish begin conquest of N. African coast; Arabs and Jews expelled from Spain	1405 1428 1438 1453 1492
1500 1506	 Sikander Lodi founds Agra	Vasco da Gama reaches India Vijayanagar dominates S. India; Krishnadevraya rules 1509-30	Inca Empire at its height Spanish claim Brazil; Safavid empire founded in Persia	1498 1500
1526	Babur defeats Ibrahim Lodi to establish Mughal power	Albuquerque seizes Goa; Nizamshahis establish independent Ahmadnagar sultanate		1510

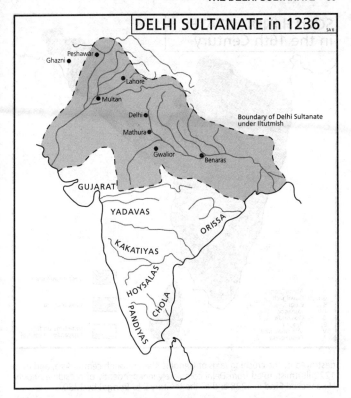

DELHI SULTANATE in 1236 SA 6

Ghazni
Peshawar
Lahore
Multan
Delhi
Mathura
Gwalior
Benaras

Boundary of Delhi Sultanate
under Iltutmish

GUJARAT
YADAVAS
ORISSA
KAKATIYAS
HOYSALAS
CHOLA
PANDIYAS

From about 1000 AD those attacks came increasingly from the **Arabs** and **Turks**. *Mahmud of Ghazni* raided the **Punjab** virtually every year between 1000 and 1026, attracted both by the agricultural surpluses and the wealth of India's temples. Such raids were never taken seriously as a long term threat by kings further E, and as the **Rajputs** continually feuded among themselves the NW plains became an increasingly attractive prey.

Those early Muslim raids were the first hint of Muslim political power to come. It was heralded by the raids of *Mu'izzu'd Din* and his defeat of massive Rajput forces at the **Second Battle of Tarain** in **1192**. Mu'izzu'd Din left his deputy, **Qutb ud Din Aibak**, to hold the territorial gains from his base at **Indraprastha** with his army of occupation. Mu'izzu'd Din made further successful raids in the 1190s, inflicting crushing defeats on Hindu opponents from **Gwalior** to **Benaras**. The foundations were then laid for the first extended period of such power, which came under the Delhi Sultans.

Qutb ud Din Aibak took Lahore in 1206, although it was his lieutenant *Iltutmish* who really established control from Delhi in 1211. He was a Turkish slave – a **Mamluk** – and the Sultanate continued to look W for its leadership and inspiration. However, the possibility of continuing control from outside India was

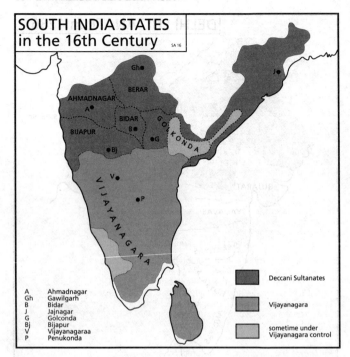

SOUTH INDIA STATES in the 16th Century SA 16

A	Ahmadnagar
Gh	Gawilgarh
B	Bidar
J	Jajnagar
G	Golconda
Bj	Bijapur
V	Vijayanagaraa
P	Penukonda

Deccani Sultanates

Vijayanagara

sometime under Vijayanagara control

destroyed by the crushing raids of Genghis Khan through central Asia, and from 1222 Iltutmish ruled from Delhi completely independently of outside authority. He annexed **Sind** in 1228 and all the territory E to **Bengal** by 1230.

A succession of dynasties followed, drawing on refugees from Genghis Khan's raids and from still further to the W to strengthen the leadership. In 1290 the first dynasty was succeeded by the Khaljis, which in turn gave way to the Tughluqs in 1320. Their ruined city of Tughluquabad is still a memorable site on the southern outskirts of Delhi. Their power was usurped by the Sayyids in 1414, who in turn lost power to the Lodis, the last of the Delhi Sultans.

The Delhi Sultanate never achieved the dominating power of earlier empires or of its successor, the Mughal Empire. It exercised political control through crushing military raids and the exaction of tribute from defeated kings, but there was no real attempt to impose central administration. Power depended on maintaining vital lines of communication and trade routes, and keeping fortified strongholds. There remain today many examples of such massive fortifications.

The Vijayanagar Empire

Across W and S India today are the remains of the only major medieval Hindu empire to resist effectively the Muslim advance. The ruins at **Hampi** demonstrate the power of a Hindu coalition that rose to power in the S Deccan in the first half of the fourteenth century, only to be defeated by its Muslim neighbours in 1565, see page 879.

For over two hundred years **Vijayanagar** (*"city of victory"*) kings fought to establish supremacy. It was an Empire that, in the words of one Indian historian, made it "the nearest approach to a war state ever made by a Hindu kingdom". At times its power reached from Orissa in the NE to Sri Lanka. In 1390 the king Harihara II claimed to have planted a victory pillar in Sri Lanka. Much of modern Tamil Nadu and Andhra Pradesh were added to the core region of Karnataka in the area under Vijayanagar control.

THE MUGHALS

Within 150 years of taking power in Delhi the Delhi Sultans had lost control of both Bengal and Kashmir. These came under the rule of independent Muslim Sultans until nearly the end of the 16th century, when the Mughals brought them firmly back under central authority.

In N India and Pakistan it is the impact of the Mughal rule that is most strikingly evident today. The descendants of conquerors, with the blood of both **Tamerlane** (Timur) and **Gengis Khan** in their veins, they dominated Indian politics from Babur's victory near Delhi in 1526 to Aurangzeb's death in 1707. Their legacy was not only some of the most magnificent architecture in the world, but a profound impact on the culture, society and future politics of much of N South Asia.

Babur (*the tiger*), founder of the Mughal dynasty, was born in Russian Turkestan in 1482. He established the Mughal Empire by leading his cavalry and artillery forces to a stupendous victory over the combined armies of Ibrahim Lodi, last ruler of the Delhi Sultanate, and the Hindu Raja of Gwalior, at **Panipat**, 80 km N of Delhi, in 1526. When he died four years later, the Empire was still far from secured, but he had not only laid the foundations of political and military power but also begun to establish courtly traditions of poetry, literature and art which became the hallmark of subsequent Mughal rulers.

The hunt The American art historian Stuart Cary Welsh quotes Babur's vivid description of a hunting incident: "A hunting circle was formed on the plain of Kattawaz where deer and wild-ass are always plentiful and always fat. Masses went into the ring; masses were killed. During the hunt I galloped after a wild-ass, on getting near shot one arrow, shot another, but did not bring it down, it only running more slowly for the two wounds. Spurring forward and getting into position quite close to it, I chopped at the nape of its neck behind the ears, and cut through the windpipe; it stopped, turned over and died. My sword cut well! The wild-ass was surprisingly fat. Its rib may have been a little under one yard in length."

AD	Northern S.Asia	Peninsular India	External events	AD
			Ottomans capture Syria, Egypt and Arabia	1516
		Dutch, French, Portuguese and Danish traders	Spaniards overthrow Aztecs in Mexico	1519
1526	**Babur** founds Mughal empire in Delhi		Potato introduced to Europe from S. America	1525
1538	Sher Shah forces **Humayun** into exile			
1542 1555	Humayun re-conquers Delhi,	St. Francis Xavier reaches Goa		
1556	**Akbar** Emperor			

AD	Northern S.Asia	Peninsular India	External events	AD
1565		Vijayanagar defeated	Wm. Shakespeare born	1564
		First printing press in India		1566
			Dutch E India Co. set up	1602
1603	Guru Granth Sahib compiled		Tokugawa Shogunate in Japan	1603
1605	**Jahangir** Emperor		First permanent English settlement in America	1607
1608	East India Company base at Surat		Telescope invented in Holland	1609
1628	**Shah Jahan** Emperor		Masjid -i-Shah Mosque in Isfahan	1616
			First Europeans land in Australia	1629
1632-53	Taj Mahal built			
1639		Fort St. George, Madras, founded by E.India Company	Manchus found Ch'ing dynasty	1644
1658	**Aurangzeb** Emperor		Tasman 'discovers' New Zealand	1645
			The Fire of London	1666
1677		**Shivaji** and Marathas		
1690	Calcutta founded			
1699	Guru Gobind Singh forms Sikh Khalsa	Regional powers dominate through 18th century: Nawabs of Bengal (1703); Nawabs of Arcot (1707); Nizams of Hyderabad (1724); Maratha Peshwas (1714)	Chinese occupy Outer Mongolia	1697
1703			Foundation of St. Petersburg, capital of Russian Empire	1703
1707	Death of Aurangzeb; Mughal rulers continue to rule from Delhi until 1858			
1724	Nawabs of Avadh			
1739	The Persian Nadir Shah captures Delhi and massacres thousands			
1757	Battle of Plassey; British power extended from E India.	E India Company strengthens trade and political power through 18th century		

First impressions Babur, used to the delights of Persian gardens and the cool of the Afghan hills, was not impressed initially by what he saw of India. In his autobiography he wrote: "Hindustan is a country that has few pleasures to recommend it. The people are not handsome. They have no idea of the charms of friendly society, of frankly mixing together, or of familiar intercourse. They have no genius, no comprehension of mind, no politeness of manner, no kindness or fellow-feeling, no ingenuity or mechanical invention in planning or executing their handicraft works, no skill or knowledge in design or architecture; they have no horses, no good flesh, no grapes or musk melons, no good fruits, no ice or cold water, no good food or bread in their bazaars, no baths or colleges, no candles, no torches, not a candlestick."

Sher Shah That depressing catalogue was the view of a disenchanted outsider. Within two generations the Mughals had become fully at home in their Indian environment, and brought some radical changes. Babur had a charismatic appeal to his followers. He ruled by keeping the loyalty of his military chiefs, giving them control of large areas of territory, see page 666 .

However, their strength posed a problem for Humayun, his successor. Almost immediately after Babur's death Humayun was forced to retreat from Delhi by two of his brothers and one of his father's lieutenants, **Sher Shah Suri**, who had administered Babur's Bengal territory. Humayun fled through Sind with his pregnant wife and a few servants before being given refuge by Shah Tahmasp, the Safavid ruler of Iran. His son Akbar, who was to become the greatest of the Mughal emperors, was born at Umarkot in Sind, modern Pakistan, during this period of exile on November 23rd 1542.

Humayun found the artistic skills of the Iranian court stunningly beautiful, and he surrounded himself with his own group of Iranian artists and scholars. In 1545 he was given Iranian help to recapture Kandahar and Kabul from his brother, Kamran. Initially he forgave his brother repeated acts of treachery, but ultimately was forced by his nobles to have him blinded – reminiscent of the fate of Shakespeare's King Lear, written some fifty years later. Planning his move back into India proper, Humayun urged his group of artists to join him, and between 1548 and his return to power in Delhi in 1555 he was surrounded by this highly influential entourage, **see page 163**.

Akbar One year after his final return to Delhi, Humayun died from the effects of a fall on the stairs of his library in the Purana Qila. **Akbar** was therefore only thirteen when he took the throne in 1556. The next 44 years were one of the most remarkable periods of South Asian history, paralleled by the Elizabethan period in England, where Queen Elizabeth 1st ruled from 1558 to 1603. Although Akbar inherited the throne, it was he who really created the empire. He also gave it many of its distinguishing features.

Through his marriage to a Hindu princess he ensured that Hindus were given honoured positions in government, as well as respect for their religious beliefs and practices. He sustained a passionate interest in art and literature, matched by a determination to create monuments to his empire's political power, and he laid the foundations for an artistic and architectural tradition which developed a totally distinctive Indian style. This emerged from the separate elements of Iranian and Indian traditions by a constant process of blending and originality of which he was the chief patron.

But these achievements were only possible because of his political and military gifts. From 1556 until his 18th birthday in 1560 Akbar was served by a prince regent, **Bairam Khan**. However, already at the age of fifteen he conquered Ajmer and large areas of central India. Chittor and Ranthambor (now famous for its game reserve) fell to him in 1567-68, bringing most of what is now Rajasthan under his control.

This opened the door S to Gujarat, which he took in 1573 in an astonishing military feat. He marched the 1000 km from his new capital city, Fatehpur Sikri, to Ahmadabad, with 3,000 horsemen in 9 days travelling. On the 11th day after his departure he defeated the massed armies of Gujarat, and 32 days later was back in Fatehpur Sikri. He celebrated his victory by building the massive Buland Darvaza gate in his new capital city.

Afghans continued to cause his empire difficulties, including **Daud Karrani**, who declared independence in E India in 1574. That threat to Mughal power was finally crushed with Karrani's death in 1576. Bengal was far from the last of his conquests. He brought Kabul back under Mughal control in the 1580s and established a presence from Kashmir, Sind and Baluchistan in the N and W to the Godavari River on the northern edge of modern Andhra Pradesh in the South.

It was Akbar who created the administrative structure employed by successive Mughal emperors to sustain their power. Revenue was raised using detailed surveying methods. Rents were fixed according to the quality of the soil in a move which was carried through into British revenue raising systems. The basis of the system had already been fixed by Sher Shah. Akbar modified it, introducing a new standard measure of length and calculating the assessment of tax due on the basis of a ten year average of production. Each year the oldest record was

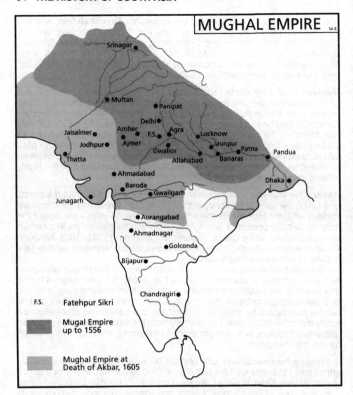

MUGHAL EMPIRE SA 8

F.S.   **Fatehpur Sikri**

Mugal Empire
up to 1556

Mughal Empire at
Death of Akbar, 1605

dropped out of the calculation, while the average produce for the current year was added. The government's share of the produce was fixed at one quarter.

Akbar deliberately widened his power base by incorporating Rajput princes into the administrative structure and giving them extensive rights in the revenue from land. He abolished the hated tax on non-Muslims (**jizya**), ultimately re-instated by his far more orthodox great grandson Aurangzeb, ceased levying taxes on Hindus who went on pilgrimage and ended the practice of forcible conversion to Islam.

Art and literature The Mughals followed in a tradition of Indian Muslim princes in their appreciation of art and literature. For an Indian king, presiding over a poetry festival was like attending Royal Ascot or the final of the Superbowl. Like his grandfather Babur, Akbar commanded deep respect and admiration for his extraordinary gifts. Like Babur, he loved hunting, scenes shown in some of the finest miniatures of the period.

Again, Stuart Cary Welch quotes a stunning description of the physical strength and presence of the Emperor given by Akbar's close friend and biographer, **Abu'l Fazl**. "When Akbar's crescent standards cast their rays on the territory appertaining to the fort of Narwar, a tiger such as might terrify the leopard of heaven came out of the forest with five cubs and onto the track by which the cavalcade was proceeding. His majesty, the Shahinshah who had the strength of the lion of God in his arms and the coat of mail of the Divine protection on his breast, went alone and without hesitation in front of that lion-clawed, fiery-natured wild animal. When the spectators beheld this the hair on their bodies stood erect and sweat distilled from their pores. His Majesty, with swift foot and alert arm attacked the brute and killed it by one stroke of his sword."

What Cary Welch calls Akbar's "fearlessness and electric energy" are shown in some of the episodes recalled in famous miniature paintings, some of them marvels in their own right. But he was patron not just of art but of an extraordinary range of literature. His library contained books on "biography, theology, comparative religion, science, mathematics, history, astrology, medicine, zoology, and anthropology". Almost hyper-active throughout his life, he is said to have required very little sleep, using moments of rest to commission books and works of art.

The influence of his father Humayun's Iranian artists is still clearly evident in the earlier of these works, but the works were not just those of unidentified "schools" of artists, but of brilliant individuals such as **Basawan** and **Miskin**, unparalleled in their ability to capture animal life. Examples of their work can be seen not just in India, but at major museums in Europe and the United States.

Artistic treasures abound from Akbar's court – paintings, jewellery, weapons – often bringing together material and skills from across the known world. Emeralds were particularly popular, with the religious significance which attaches to the colour green in mystic Islam adding to their attraction. Some came from as far afield as Colombia. Akbar's intellectual interests were extraordinarily catholic. He met the Portuguese Jesuits in 1572, and welcomed them to his court in Fatehpur Sikri, along with Buddhists, Hindus and Zoroastrians, every year between 1575 and 1582.

This eclecticism had a purpose, for Akbar was trying to build a focus of loyalty beyond that of caste, social group, region or religion. Like Roman Emperors before him, he deliberately cultivated a new religion in which the emperor himself attained divinity, hoping thereby to give the Empire a legitimacy which would last. While his religion disappeared with his death, the legitimacy of the Mughals survived another two hundred years, long after their real power had almost disappeared.

Despite their artistic achievements, Mughal politics could also be cruel and violent. Akbar himself ordered that the beautiful *Anarkali*, a member of his harem, should be buried alive when he suspected that she was having an affair with his son Jahangir. While Akbar sometimes used great violence himself, Jahangir left his special guards to murder and maim suspects on his behalf, see page 1133.

Jahangir Akbar died of a stomach illness in 1605. He was succeeded by his son, **Prince Salim**, who inherited the throne as Emperor **Jahangir** ("*world seizer*"). He added little to the territory of the empire, consolidating the Mughals hold on the Himalayan foothills and parts of central India but restricting his innovative energies to pushing back frontiers of art rather than of land. He commissioned works of art and literature, many of which directly recorded life in the Mughal court. Hunting scenes were not just romanticised accounts of rural life, but conveyed the real dangers of hunting lions or tigers; implements, furniture, tools and weapons were made with lavish care and often exquisite design.

From early youth Jahangir had shown an artistic temperament, but he also became addicted to alcohol and then to opium. The drinking cups and vessels such as the opium cup now in the Bharat Kala Bhavan in Benaras Hindu University were in regular use.

Stuart Cary Welch records how, in his autobiography, Jahangir described his addiction: "I had not drunk until I was eighteen, except in the time of my infancy two or three times my mother and wet nurses gave it by way of infantile remedy, mixed with water and rose water to take away a cough...years later a gunner said that if I would take a glass of wine it would drive away the feeling of being tired and heavy. It was the time of my youth, and as I felt disposed towards it ordered an intoxicating draught.... After that I took to drinking wine, and increased from day to day until wine made from grapes ceased to intoxicate me, and I took to drinking arrack (local spirits). By degrees my potions rose to twenty cups of doubly distilled spirits, fourteen during the daytime and the remainder at night."

Although Jahangir cut back on that perilously high level of alcohol intake on the advice of his doctors, he subsequently became addicted to eating opium. Yet his greatest pleasures came from the works of art that his outstandingly gifted artists continued to produce for him. Paintings, carpets, daggers, jewels– all embellished the court. His favourite wife, **Nur Jahan**, brought her own artistic gifts to the Mughal court. Born the daughter of an Iranian nobleman, she had been brought to the Mughal court along with her family as a child, and moved to Bengal as the wife of Sher Afgan, **see page 274**. She made rapid progress after her first husband's accidental death in 1607, which caused her to move from Bengal to be a lady in waiting for one of Akbar's widows.

Early in 1611, she was playing with her ladies-in-waiting at being a shopkeeper in the bazaar. There she met Jahangir. Mutually enraptured, they were married in May. **Jahangir** gave her the title **Nur-Mahal** (Light of the Palace), soon increased to **Nur-Jahan** (Light of the World). Aged 34, she was strikingly beautiful, and had an astonishing reputation for physical skill and intellectual wit. She was a crack shot with a gun, highly artistic, determined yet philanthropic. Throughout her life Jahangir was captivated by her, so much so that he flouted Muslim convention by minting coins bearing her image.

By 1622 Nur-Jahan effectively controlled the empire. She commissioned and supervised the building in Agra of one of the Mughal world's most beautiful buildings, the **I'timad ud-Daula** (meaning "Pillar of government"), as a tomb for her father and mother. Her father, **Ghiyas Beg**, an Iranian nobleman, had risen to become one of Jahangir's most trusted advisers, and Nur Jahan was determined to ensure that their memory was adequately honoured. She was less successful in her wish to deny the succession after Jahangir's death at the age of 58 to **Prince Khurram**. Acceding to the throne in 1628, he took the title of Shah Jahan (*Ruler of the World*), and in the following 30 years his reign represented the height of Mughal power.

Shah Jahan The Mughal Empire was under attack in the Deccan and the NW when **Shah Jahan** became Emperor. He tried to re-establish and extend Mughal authority in both regions by a combination of military campaigns and skilled diplomacy. He was much more successful in pushing S than he was in consolidating the Mughal hold in Afghanistan, and most of the Deccan was brought firmly under Mughal control.

But he too commissioned art, literature, and above all architectural monuments, on an unparalleled scale. The **Taj Mahal** may be the most famous of these, but a succession of brilliant achievements can be attributed to his reign. From miniature paintings and manuscripts, which had been central features of Mughal artistic development from Babur onwards, to massive fortifications such as the Red Fort in Delhi, Shah Jahan added to the already great body of outstanding Mughal art, **see page 276**.

Buildings such as the fort and mosque complexes in Delhi, Agra and Lahore were magnificent, not only in the scale but in their detail. Wonderful examples of the superbly executed carved marble screens (known as *jalis*), perforated both for decoration and to allow cooling breezes to penetrate the buildings, illustrate the attention paid to minute details by Mughal artists and craftsmen.

Akbar's craftsmen had already carved outstandingly beautiful jalis for the tomb of **Salim Chisti** in Fatehpur Sikri, but Shah Jahan developed the form further. Undoubtedly the finest tribute to these skills is found in the Taj Mahal, the tribute to his beloved wife Mumtaz-Mahal, who died giving birth to her fourteenth child in 1631.

A monument to grief The grief that her death caused may have been the chief motivating force behind his determination to build a monument not just to his love for her but also to the supremacy of Mughal refinement and power. However, that power had to be paid for, and the costs were escalating. Shah Jahan himself had inherited an almost bankrupt state from his father. Expenditure on the army had outstripped the revenue collected from tribute kings and from the chiefs given the rights and responsibility over territories often larger than European countries. Financial deficits forced Shah Jahan onto the offensive in order to guarantee greater and more reliable revenue.

Despite major reforms which helped to reduce the costs of his standing army, maintaining the force necessary to control the huge territories owing allegiance to the Emperor continued to stretch his resources to the full. By 1648, when he moved his capital to Delhi, the Empire was already in financial difficulties, and in 1657 the rumour that Shah Jahan was terminally ill immediately caused a series of battles for the succession between his four sons.

Aurangzeb, the second son and sixth child of Shah Jahan and Mumtaz-Mahal – tough, intriguing and sometimes cruel, but also a highly intelligent strategist – emerged the winner, only to find that Shah Jahan had recovered his health. Rather than run the risk of being deposed, Aurangzeb kept his father imprisoned in Agra Fort, where he had been taken ill, from June 1658 until his death in February 1666.

Aurangzeb The need to expand the area under Mughal control was felt even more strongly by Aurangzeb ('*The jewel in the throne*") than by his predecessors, **see page 983**. He had grown up in his grandfather's imperial court as a hostage to guarantee his father, Shah Jahan's, good behaviour after a rebellion in 1626. There he had shown his intellectual gifts, learning Arabic, Persian, Turkish and Hindi. When he seized power at the age of forty, he needed all his political and military skills to hold on to an unwieldy empire that was in permanent danger of collapse from its own size.

If the Empire was to survive Aurangzeb realised that it could not remain static. The demand for revenue was still beyond the resources of the territory he inherited from his father, and thus through a series of campaigns he pushed S, while maintaining his hold on the E and N. Initially Aurangzeb maintained his alliances with the Rajputs in the west, which had been a crucial element in Mughal strategy. However, in 1678 he claimed absolute rights over Jodhpur and went to war with the Rajput clans.

The decline of the Mughals Some of the Muslim kingdoms of the Deccan refused to pay the tribute to the Mughal Empire that had been forced on them after defeats in 1656. This refusal, and their alliance with the rising power of **Sivaji** and his **Marathas**, forced Aurangzeb to attack the Shi'i-ruled states of Bijapur (1686) and Golconda (1687), and to re-impose Mughal supremacy.

Sivaji was the son of a Hindu who had served as a small-scale chief in the Muslim ruled state of Bijapur. The weakness of the Bijapur state encouraged Sivaji to extend his father's area of control, and he led a rebellion. The Bijapur general Afzal Khan was sent to put it down, but agreed to meet Sivaji in private to reach a settlement. In an act which Spear records is still remembered by both Muslims and Marathas, Sivaji killed him by embracing him with steel claws attached to his fingers and tearing him apart. It was the start of a campaign which took Maratha power across the Deccan as far S as Madurai and to the doors of Delhi and Calcutta, **see page 937**.

Sivaji had taken the fratricidal struggle for the succession which brought Aurangzeb to power as the signal and the opportunity for launching a series of attacks against the Mughals. This in turn brought a riposte from Aurangzeb, once his hold on the centre was secure. However, despite the apparent expansion of his power the seeds of decay were already germinating. Although Sivaji himself died in 1680 Aurangzeb never fully came to terms with the rising power of the Marathas, though he did end their ambitions to form an empire of their own.

Nor was Aurangzeb able to create any wide sense of identity with the Mughals as a legitimate popular power. Instead, under the influence of Sunni Muslim theologians, he retreated into insistence on Islamic purity. He imposed Islamic law, the *sharia*, promoted only Muslims to positions of power and authority, and tried to replace Hindus administrators and revenue collectors with Muslims. In addition he re-imposed the *jizya* tax on all non-Muslims. By the time of his death in 1707 the empire no longer had either the broadness of spirit or the physical means to survive.

The decline was postponed briefly by the five year reign of Aurangzeb's son, Bahadur Shah. Sixty three when he acceded to the throne, Bahadur Shah restored some of the faded fortunes of his father's extended empire. He made agreements with the Marathas and the Rajputs and defeated the Sikhs in Punjab, before taking the last Sikh guru into his service.

The decay of the Mughal Empire has been likened to "a magnificent flower slowly wilting and occasionally dropping a petal, its brilliance fading, its stalk bending ever lower". Nine emperors succeeded Aurangzeb between his death and the exile of the last Mughal ruler in 1858. It was no accident that it was in that year that the British ended the rule of its East India Company and decreed India to be its Indian Empire.

Successive Mughal rulers saw their political control diminish and their territory shrink. Ten emperors followed in as many years. Then **Nasir ud Din Muhammad Shah**, known as Rangila ("*the pleasure loving*"), who reigned between 1719 and 1748, presided over a continued flowering of art and music, but a disintegration of political power. Hyderabad, Bengal and Oudh (the region to the E of Delhi) became effectively independent states; the Marathas dominated large tracts of central India, the Jats captured Agra, the Sikhs controlled Punjab.

Muhammad Shah remained in his capital of Delhi, resigning himself to enjoying what Carey Welch has called "the conventional triad of joys: the wine was excellent, as were the women, and for him the song was especially rewarding." The idyll was rudely shattered by the invasion of **Nadir Shah** in 1739, an Iranian marauder who slaughtered thousands in Delhi and carried off priceless Mughal treasures, including the Peacock Throne, see page 173.

Nadir Shah's invasion was a flash in the pan. Of far greater substance was the development through the 18th century of the power of the **Maratha confederacy**. They were unique in India in uniting different castes and classes in a nationalist fervour for the region of Maharashtra. As Spear has pointed out, when the Mughals ceded the central district of Malwa the Marathas were able to pour through the gap created between the Nizam of Hyderabad's territories in the S and the area remaining under Mughal control in the N. They rapidly occupied Orissa in the E and raided Bengal.

By 1750 they had reached the gates of Delhi. When Delhi collapsed to Afghan invaders in 1756-57 the Mughal minister called on the Marathas for help. Yet again Panipat proved to be a decisive battlefield, the Marathas being heavily defeated by the Afghan forces on 13 January 1761. What followed, however, was a power vacuum in the whole of northern India, for Ahmad Shah was forced to retreat to Afghanistan by his own rebellious troops, demanding two years arrears of pay.

The Maratha confederacy dissolved into five independent powers, with whom the incoming British were able to deal separately. The door to the N was now open.

THE EAST INDIA COMPANY AND THE RISE OF BRITISH POWER

The British were unique among the foreign rulers of India in coming by sea rather than through the NW, and in coming first for trade rather than for military conquest. The ports that they established – Madras, Bombay and Calcutta – became completely new centres of political, economic and social activity. Before them Indian empires had controlled their territories from the land. The British dictated the emerging shape of the economy by controlling sea-borne trade. From the middle of the 19th century railways transformed the economic and political structure of South Asia, and it was those three centres of British political control, along with the late addition of Delhi, which became the foci of economic development and political change.

The East India Company In the century and a half that followed the death of Aurangzeb the **British East India Company** extended its economic and political influence into the heart of South Asia. In its first 90 years of contact with South Asia after the Company set up its first trading post at **Masulipatnam**, on the E coast of India, it had depended almost entirely on trade for its profits. However, in 1701, only 11 years after a British settlement was first established at Calcutta, the Company was given rights to land revenue in Bengal.

The Company was accepted, and sometimes welcomed, partly because it offered to bolster the inadequate revenues of the Mughals by exchanging silver bullion for the cloth it bought. However, in the S the Company moved further and faster towards consolidating its political base. Wars between S India's regional factions gave the East India Company's servants the opportunity to extend their influence by making alliances, and offering support to some of these factions in their struggles, which were complicated by the extension to Indian soil of the European contest for power between the French and the British.

Robert Clive The British established effective control over both Bengal and SE India in the middle of the 17th century. **Robert Clive**, in alliance with a collection of disaffected Hindu landowners and Muslim soldiers, defeated the new Nawab of Bengal, the twenty year old *Siraj -ud- Daula*, in June 1757. The battlefield was at **Plassey**, about 100 km N of Calcutta, though the battle itself was little more than a skirmish, **see page 555**. Eight years later Clive took over the management of the revenues of the whole of Bengal. By 1788 Calcutta, which one hundred years earlier had been nothing more than a collection of small villages, had become the chief city of E India, with a population of a quarter of a million.

In 1773 Calcutta had already been put in charge of Bombay and Madras. The essential features of British control were mapped out in the next quarter of a century through the work of *Warren Hastings*<$lNames;Hastings, W.+, Governor-General from 1774 until 1785, and Lord Cornwallis who took over in 1786 and remained in charge until 1793. Cornwallis was responsible for putting Europeans in charge of all the higher levels of revenue collection and administration, and for introducing government by the rule of law, making even government officers subject to the courts.

Alliances As the Mughal Empire lost its power India fell into many smaller states. The Company undertook to protect the rulers of several of these states from external attack by stationing British troops in their territory. In exchange for this service the rulers paid subsidies to the Company. As the British historian Christopher Bayly has pointed out, the cure was usually worse than the disease, and the cost of the payments to the Company crippled the local ruler. The British extended their territory through the 18th century as successive regional powers were annexed and brought under direct Company rule.

Progress to direct British control was uneven and often opposed. The Sikhs in Punjab, the Marathas in the W, and the Mysore Sultans in the S, fiercely contested British advances. **Haidar Ali** and **Tipu Sultan**, who had built a wealthy kingdom in the Mysore region, resisted attempts to incorporate them. Tipu was finally killed in 1799 at the battle of Srirangapatnam, an island fort in the Kaveri River just N of Mysore, where Arthur Wellesley, later the Duke of Wellington, began to make his military reputation.

The Marathas were not defeated until the war of 1816-18, a defeat which had to wait until Napoleon was defeated in Europe and the British could turn their wholehearted attention once again to the Indian scene. Even then the defeat owed as much to internal faction fighting as to the power of the British-led army. Only the NW of the sub-continent remained beyond British control until well into the 19th century. The Punjab and the NW frontier were the remotest regions from the ports through which the British had asserted and extended their power. In 1799 **Ranjit Singh** set up a Sikh state in Punjab which survived until the late 1830s.

In 1818 India's economy was in ruins and its political structures destroyed. Irrigation works and road systems had fallen into decay, and gangs terrorised the countryside. Many of these claimed to have a religious basis. **Thugs** and **dacoits** controlled much of the open countryside in central India and often robbed and murdered even on the outskirts of towns. The peace and stability of the Mughal period had long since passed. Between 1818 and 1857 there was a succession of local and uncoordinated revolts in different parts of India. Some were bought off, some put down by military force.

A period of reforms The first half of the 19th century was also a period of radical social change. Lord William Bentinck became Governor-General at a time when England was also entering a period of major reform. In 1828 he banned the burning of widows on the funeral pyres of their husbands (**sati**), and then moved to suppress **thuggee** (the ritual murder and robbery carried out in central India in the name of the goddess Kali). But his most far reaching change was to introduce education in English.

The resolution of March 7 1835 stated that 'the great objects of the British government ought to be the promotion of European literature and science'. It went on to promise that funds 'should henceforth be employed in imparting to the native population the knowledge of English literature and science through the medium of the English language'. Out of this concern were born new educational institutions such as the Calcutta Medical College, but from the late 1830s massive new engineering projects began to be taken up; first canals, then railways.

The innovations stimulated change, and change contributed to the growing unease with the British presence. The greatest of these changes were encouraged by the Governor-General of India between 1848-56, the Marquess of Dalhousie. A series of innovations was brought to India: the telegraph, the railway and new roads; three universities, and the extension of massive new canal irrigation projects in northern India. To many in India these developments threatened traditional society, but were made more threatening by the annexation of Indian states to bring them under direct British rule. The most important of these was Oudh.

The Mutiny Out of the growing discontent and widespread economic difficulties, came the mutiny of 1857. In May and June the atmosphere in the Bengal army, which had a large component of Brahmins, reached an explosive peak. At that moment the army issued new Lee Enfield rifles to its troops, whose cartridges were smeared with a mixture of cow and pig fat. It was taken as a direct affront to both Muslim and Hindu feeling. On 10 May 1857 troops in Meerut, just under 70 km NE of Delhi, mutinied. They reached Delhi the next day, where **Bahadur Shah**, the last Mughal Emperor, took sides with the mutineers. Troops in Lucknow joined the rebellion and Gwalior was captured on 20 June. For three months Lucknow and other cities in the N were under siege. Appalling scenes of butchery and reprisals marked the struggle, only put down after troops were brought in from outside.

The period of Empire   The 1857 rebellion marked the end not only of the Mughal Empire but also of the East India Company. From that moment the British Government in London took overall control. And yet within thirty years a movement for self-government had begun to take root, and there were the first signs of a demand among the new western educated elite that political rights be awarded to match the sense of Indian national identity.

The movement for independence went through a series of steps. The creation of the *Indian National Congress* in 1885 was the first all-India political institution, and in the 20th century was to become the key vehicle of demands for independence. However, Muslims remained at a distance from the new political process. The educated Muslim elite of what is now Uttar Pradesh saw a threat to Muslim rights, power and identity in the emergence of democratic institutions which gave Hindus, with their built in natural majority, significant advantages. Thus Sir Sayyid Ahmad Khan, who had founded a Muslim University at Aligarh in 1877, advised Muslims against joining the Congress, seeing it as a vehicle for Hindu, and especially Bengali, nationalism.

The Muslim League   In the early 20th century the educated Muslim community of N India remained deeply suspicious of the Congress, making up less than 8% of those attending its conferences in the two decades around the turn of the century. Muslims from UP were responsible for creating the All-India Muslim League in 1906. However, the demands of the Muslim League were not always opposed to those of the Congress. In 1916 they concluded the Lucknow Pact with the Congress, in which the Congress won Muslim support for self-government, in exchange for the recognition that there would be separate constituencies for Muslims.
The nature of the future Independent India was still far from clear, however. The principle of self-government was conceded in 1918 in a report which laid the foundations for a future federal state. However radical the reforms would have seemed five years earlier they already fell far short of heightened Indian expectations.

Mahatma Gandhi   Into a tense and fragile atmosphere *Mohandas Karamchand Gandhi* returned to India in 1915 after twenty years practising as a lawyer in S Africa. On his return the Bengali Nobel Laureate poet, **Rabindranath Tagore**, had dubbed him "**Mahatma**" – Great Soul. The name became his. He arrived as the Government of India was being given new powers by the British Parliament to try political cases without a jury and to give provincial governments the right to imprison politicians without trial. In opposition to this legislation Gandhi proposed to call a *hartal*, when all activity would cease for a day. It is a form of protest still in widespread use in India today. Such protests took place across India.

The protests were often accompanied by riots. On 13 April 1919 a huge gathering took place in the enclosed space of *Jallianwala Bagh* in Amritsar, **see page 415**. It had been prohibited by the government, and General Dyer ordered troops to fire on the people without warning, killing 379 and injuring at least further 1,200. It marked the turning point in relations with Britain and the rise of Mahatma Gandhi to the key position of leadership in the struggle for complete Independence that followed.

Mahatma Gandhi was an extraordinarily complex figure. A westernised, English educated lawyer, who had lived outside India from his youth to middle age, he preached the general acceptance of some of the doctrines he had grown to respect in his childhood stemming from deep Indian traditions – notably **ahimsa**,

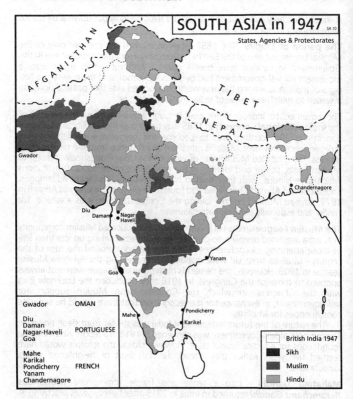

or non-violence. From 1921 he gave up his western style of dress and adopted the hand spun dhoti worn by poor Indian villagers, but he preached against the iniquities of the traditional caste system which still dominated life for the overwhelming majority of Hindus.

Through the 1920s much of his work was based on writing for the weekly newspaper *Young India*, which changed its name in 1932 to **The Harijan**. The change symbolised his commitment to helping change the status of the outcastes of India, for Harijan (*person of God*) is the name he coined to replace the term outcaste.

The thrust for Independence In 1930 the Congress declared that January 26 would be Independence day – still celebrated as such in India today. The Leader of the Muslim League, Mohammad Iqbal, took the opportunity of his address to the League in the same year to suggest the formation of a Muslim state within an Indian Federation. Also in 1930 a Muslim student in Cambridge, **Chaudhuri Rahmat Ali**, coined a name for the new Muslim state – Pakistan. The letters were to stand P for Punjab, A for Afghania, K for Kashmir, S for Sind with the suffix *stan*, Persian for country. The idea still had little real shape however, and waited on developments of the late 1930s and 1940s to bear fruit.

By the end of the Second World War the positions of the Muslim League, now under the leadership of **Mohammad Ali Jinnah**, and the Congress led by Jawaharlal Nehru, were irreconcilable. While major questions of the definition of separate territories for a Muslim and non-Muslim state remained to be answered, it was clear to General Wavell, the British Viceroy through the last years of the War, that there was no alternative but to accept that Independence would have to be given on the basis of separate states.

Independence and Partition One of the main difficulties for the Muslims was that they made up only a fifth of the total population. Although there were regions both in the NW and the E where they formed the majority, Muslims were also scattered throughout India. It was therefore impossible to define a simple territorial division which would provide a state to match Jinnah's claim of a "*two-nation theory*". On February 20 1947, the Labour Government announced its decision to replace **Lord Wavell** as Viceroy with **Lord Mountbatten**, giving him the responsibility of overseeing the transfer of power to new independent governments. It set a deadline of June 1948 for British withdrawal. The announcement of a firm date made the Indian politicians even less willing to compromise, and the resulting division satisfied no-one.

When Independence arrived – on August 14th for Pakistan and August 15th for India, because Indian astrologers deemed the 15th to be the most auspicious moment – many questions remained unanswered. Several key Princely States had still not decided firmly to which country they would accede. Kashmir was the most important of these, with results that have lasted to the present day.

The newly created state of Pakistan was divided into two wings separated by over 1500 km of Indian territory. Nor did it have anything like the extent of territory in Punjab it had expected, and it ended up, in Jinnah's words, a "truncated" and "moth-eaten" state. Worst of all, the process resulted in the mass migration of Muslims from India to Pakistan and of Hindus and Sikhs from Pakistan to India. Perhaps 13 million people moved their homes, and nearly a million were slaughtered in the violence. The bitterness of the partition process has coloured relations between India and Pakistan to this day.

INDIA

Official name The Republic of India

National flag A horizontal tricolour with equal bands of saffron, white and green from top to bottom. At the centre is an Asoka wheel in navy blue.

National anthem *Jana Gana Mana*

Basic indicators *Population* 844 m 1991 *Annual increase* 18 m *Area* 3,287,000 sq km *Literacy* 52% (Male 64%, Female 39%) *Birth rate per '000* Urban 27 Rural 34 *Death rate per '000* Urban 7 Rural 12 *Infant mortality rate* Urban 62 Rural 105 *Religion* Hindu 700 m Muslim 97 m Christian 21 m Sikh 17 m Buddhist 6 m Jain 4 m Scheduled castes 134 m Scheduled tribes 66 m *Per capita Income* Rs 3,760 *Registered job seekers* 33 m.

GENERAL INTRODUCTION

India lies between 8°N-36°N and 68°E-97°E. It is surrounded by the Arabian Sea, the Indian Ocean and the Bay of Bengal to its SW, S, and SE respectively, and it has land borders with Pakistan, China, Nepal, Bhutan, Bangladesh and Burma.

GEOGRAPHY

The land India falls into 3 major natural regions, the Himalayas in the N, the Ganga plains, and the Peninsula. However, there is great local variety even within these regions. The Himalayas, for example include some of the wettest, jungle clad regions in the world in the foothills at the E, while they also include high altitude deserts in Ladakh. Similarly the Ganga plains stretch from the fertile and wet delta of Bengal to the deserts of N Rajasthan. Even the Peninsula ranges from the tropical humid climate of the W coast to the dry plateaus of N Maharashtra. The origins of this diversity are outlined in the Introduction to S. Asia, see page 30.

Rivers and lakes India's most holy river, the Ganga, runs not just across the strategically vital heartland of the country but through the mythology of Hinduism. Joined by other holy rivers along its route, such as the **Yamuna** (Jumna), its waters are also a vital source of irrigation for the plains along its route. Its path is dotted with towns and settlements of great sanctity. It has by far the largest catchment area in India, and is a vital economic asset as well as the focus of

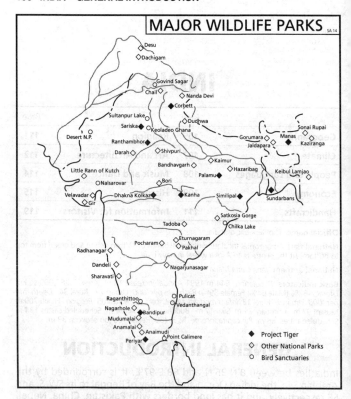

MAJOR WILDLIFE PARKS

SA 14

Desu
◇Dachigam

◇Govind Sagar
Chail◇ ◇Nanda Devi
◆Corbett
Sultanpur Lake◇ ◇Dudhwa
Sariska◇ ◇Keoladeo Ghana
Desert N.P.◇ Gorumara Manas ◇Sonai Rupai
Ranthambhor◇ Jaldapara Kaziranga
Darah◇ ◇Shivpuri
Little Rann of Kutch Bandhavgarh◇ ◇Kaimur ◇Hazaribag Keibul Lamjao
◇Nalsarovar Palamu◆
Bori Keibul Lamjao
Velavadar◇ Dhakna Kolkaz◆ ◆Kanha Similipal ◆Sundarbans
◇Gir
Satkosia Gorge
Tadoba◇ Chilka Lake
Pocharam◇ Eturnagaram
Radhanagar◇ ◇Pakhal
Dandeli◇
Sharavati◇ Nagarjunasagar
Raganthittoo◇ ◇Pulicat
Nagarhole◆ ◇Vedanthangal
Mudumalai◆ Bandipur
Anamalai◇ ◇Anaimudi
Periyar◆ ◇Point Calimere

◆ Project Tiger
◇ Other National Parks
○ Bird Sanctuaries

devotion for hundreds of millions.

To the S are other important rivers, many of which have their own religious connotations. There are only 2 major W flowing rivers on the Peninsula, the Narmada and the Tapti, the former of which is subject to fierce dispute as the Government of India plans to implement a massive scheme for controlling its water for irrigation and power development. All the other main rivers of the Peninsula rise within 50 km or so of the W coast and flow E, entering the Bay of Bengal across often fertile deltas.

Vegetation Much of India's natural forest has now been replaced by cultivated fields (see S. Asia Introduction **page 37**), or been degraded by heavy grazing, the collection of firewood and other uses. Until quite recent times much of India was covered by forest, ranging from dense tropical forests, as on the wet slopes of the W. Ghats, or much more open dry deciduous forest in the drier interior. India still has evidence of the great diversity of species which were found across the country, and the wildlife reserves also help to preserve natural habitat. A detailed description is given in the regional sections.

Wildlife The diversity of India's land features and natural vegetation has provided it with a rich variety of fauna. Ancient traditions have forged a deep link between the people and the natural environment and conservation and protection of wildlife is a part of life. Animals and birds enjoy an important position in myths and legends and many are associated with the Hindu pantheon. Even in civic life the Asokan edicts of the 3rd century BC lists protected animals. It is interesting to note that the country's national animal the tiger was chosen by the Moenjodaro civilization as their national emblem as far back as 4,000 years ago.

However, the wilderness under forest cover has been depleted to less than 12% of the land mass with a consequent threat to wildlife. The threat has come from encroachment into forests and jungles with man's increasing need to exploit natural resources, to bring more land under cultivation. The previously unchecked trade in precious products such as skins and ivory had also depleted numbers of certain species.

Preventive measures have been taken and there are now over 20 National Parks and more than 200 sanctuaries spread across the vast subcontinent which harbour over 500 species of mammals and hundreds of species of birds and reptiles. Certain sanctuaries have become associated with one or more particular species. Gujarat's Gir Forest for the Asiatic lion, Periyar in Kerala for the elephant, Manas and Kaziranga for the one-horned rhino; Manipur's Keibul Lamjao Park for Thiamin deer, Srinagar's Dachigam Park for the Kashmir stag and Velvadhar in Gujarat as the home of the blackbuck. The Bengal tiger is now protected in Parks as a part of the Project Tiger scheme started in 1973 with the Corbett Park in UP, which also has Dudhwa. Bandhavgarh and Kanha in MP and Sariska and Ranthambore in Rajasthan also have a significant number of tigers. The largest bird sanctuary is only 5 hours' drive from Delhi and attracts vast numbers of migratory water birds, some travelling long distances across a continent.

CLIMATE

Climate in India varies greatly according to latitude, altitude and season. The broad patterns of S. Asia's climate are discussed in the Introduction to S. Asia, **see page 35**.

Temperatures Average maximum winter temperatures range from the high 20°C in the S to below freezing in parts of Kashmir, Leh and Ladakh, and the low 20s on the northern plains. The range of minimum winter temperatures between N and S is greater. In many parts of the N plains, especially in the NW, close to the foothills of the Himalayas, night temperatures fall close to freezing. In contrast, in the far S, minimum temperatures never fall below 20°C except in the hills.

In summer the N is generally hotter than the S, with daytime temperatures usually over 40°C and in parts of the NW up to nearly 50°C from time to time. Night time temperatures also remain high. The end of Apr-May is the hottest time. Once the clouds of the monsoon season arrive temperatures fall a few degrees, but the air gets much more humid, often making it intensely uncomfortable. In the S max temperatures never reach those experienced in the N, rarely rising above 40° for more than a day or two at a time. May is also generally the hottest month.

Rainfall India's seasonal rainfall pattern is dominated by the monsoon, which generally arrives at the SW coast in late May or June, covering most of the country by the beginning of July, and retreating in October. However, the popular image of the monsoon is misplaced. Even in the wettest areas – the West coast or the NE hills of the Shillong plateau – there are periods of days at a time when it does not rain. Elsewhere the rainy season is marked by prolonged very heavy showers, interspersed with cloudy, humid weather and occasional bright patches.

Rainfall totals vary enormously. Many parts of the W coast receive over 2,500 mm a year, and the Shillong plateau has received as much as 26 metres in one year! If you are travelling in the wetter parts of India during the monsoon you need to be prepared for extended periods of torrential rain. This often disrupts travel arrangements. However, many parts of India receive a total of under 1,000 mm a year, and although much of this comes in the monsoon season it is mainly in the form of heavy isolated showers. Rainfall generally decreases towards the NW, Rajasthan and N Gujarat merging imperceptibly into genuine desert. Tamil Nadu in the SE has an exceptional rainfall pattern. It receives most of its rain in the period of the retreating monsoon, Oct-Dec.

Storms Some regions of India experience quite regular and major climatic disturbances. Cyclones may hit the E coast of India anywhere between S Tamil Nadu and Bengal. They can cause enormous damage and loss of life. A cyclone in coastal Andhra Pradesh in December 1977 for example killed many thousands and devastated hundreds of sq km of agricultural land. A similar cyclone in Nov 1990 caused much less loss of life, because protected buildings had been constructed for such an emergency, but still caused massive damage to crops and property. Risk of cyclones along the E coast is greatest between the end of Oct and early Dec.

The NW of India experiences occasional dust storms and very hot winds, known locally as *the Loo*, between Apr-Jun. In Bengal Nor'westers can cause enormous damage in Apr-May, but are widely welcomed as bringing some relief from the heat.

Humidity The coastal regions have humidity levels above 70% for most of the year. In the S it is rare for levels to fall below 80%, which can be very uncomfortable. However, sea breezes often bring some relief on the coast itself. Moving N and inland, between Dec-May humidity drops sharply, often falling as low as 20% in the NW during the daytime. These exceptionally dry conditions are dessicating for the skin – most people travelling across the N between Mar-May find that they need plenty of skin cream.

Fog The low winter night temperatures across N India, coupled with high atmospheric pressure and increasing pollution in the larger cities, notably Delhi, contribute to the growing problem of early morning fog in Dec-Jan. Occasionally this may last all day. It can have a severely disrupting effect on air travel, as Delhi is the hub of India's internal air network, as well as of its main international connections.

Warning During the monsoon travelling by road, especially off the National Highways, can be hazardous. Many river causeways become unpassable and occasionally bridges are washed away. Railway timetables can also be unpredictably disrupted.

PEOPLE AND LANGUAGE

Ethnic origins The ethnic and linguistic origins and character of India are outlined in the South Asia introduction and the introductions to the regions. India has elements of Negrito, Australoid, Mongoloid and Caucasoid stocks, though the last are overwhelmingly the most important in numerical terms. The Mediterranean type is the largest Caucasoid group, one section referred to as *Paleo-Mediterraneans* being represented by the Dravidians in the S, and another, generally with paler complexions and coming into India much later, being common in the N. They are mixed in the N with a number of Indo-Aryan groups who entered India from the NW.

Population growth The 1991 Census showed the total Indian population to have reached 843 m by early 1991. It is increasing at approximately 18 m each year. Although the birth rate has fallen steadily over the last 40 years, death rates have fallen just as fast, so the rate of population increase has continued to be above 2% a year. There has been a slow but steady growth in the proportion of

India's population living in towns since 1901, when 10% were classified as urban. Today approximately 28% are urban. However, the absolute growth of India's urban population is far more striking than the relative growth. In 1971, 109 m people lived in towns and cities. The figure grew to 159 m in 1981 and to approximately 240 m in 1991. The largest cities were Bombay (12.57 m), Calcutta (10.86 m), Delhi (8.38 m), Madras (5.36 m), Hyderabad (4.27 m) and Bangalore (4.11 m).

Languages Soon after Independence the 1951 Census of India listed 720 languages or dialects with less than 100,000 speakers. Yet the top 10 languages account for about 90% of the population. In the N, Hindi is the most widely spoken (324 m), followed by the related languages of Bengali (63 m), Marathi (61 m), Urdu (43 m), Gujarati (40 m), Oriya (28 m), Punjabi (22 m), Assamese (18 m) and Kashmiri (4 m). The four main Dravidian languages, spoken in the S, are Telugu (66 m), Tamil (55 m), Kannada (32 m) and Malayalam (30 m). Most of the languages have their own scripts. See S. Asia Introduction, **page 42** for details.

ECONOMY

Agriculture and fishing Although agriculture now accounts for less than 30% of India's GDP, compared with over 60% at Independence, it remains the most important single sector of the economy. More than half India's people depend directly on agriculture, and the success of the annual harvest has a crucial effect on the remainder of the economy.

Indian agriculture is enormously varied, reflecting the widely different conditions of climate, soil and relief which prevail in different regions. Cereal farming dominates most areas. Wheat, grown as a winter crop, is most important in the NW, from W Uttar Pradesh through Haryana to Punjab. Output has grown dramatically since 1947, total wheat production in 1990 rising towards 50 m tonnes, double the figure twenty years earlier. Rice, the most important single foodgrain, has seen a much slower growth in output. Concentrated in the wetter regions of the E and S, output rose from 40 m tonnes to just over 60 m tonnes between 1971 and 1990.

Other cereal crops – sorghum and the millets – predominate in central India and unirrigated parts of the N. In addition to its cereals, and a range of pulses, India produces some vital cash crops. The most important are tea, cotton and sugar cane. All have seen significant growth, tea and cotton being particularly important contributors to export earnings (cotton in manufactured form).

Between Independence and the late 1960s most of the increase in India's agricultural output came from extending the cultivated area. Over 50% of the total area is now cultivated, a very high figure compared with States such as China with under 12%. With little opportunity for further expansion, increased production since then has been the result of increasingly intensive use of land through greater irrigation and use of fertiliser, pesticides and high yielding varieties of seeds (hyvs). The area under irrigation has risen from 18% of the cultivated area in 1960 to over 33% in 1991, while fertiliser use has increased 25 times in the same period. Indian agriculture is dominated by small holdings. Only 20% of the land is farmed in units of more than 10 ha, compared with 31% 20 years ago, while nearly 60% of farms are less than 1 ha.

Despite its long coastline the fishing industry remains generally only of local importance.

Resources and industry India has extensive resources of iron ore, coal, bauxite and some other minerals. Exploitation has speeded up with the programme of industrial development launched at Independence. Reserves of coal at likely rates of use are estimated at well over 100 years (at least 30 bn tonnes, plus 6 bn tonnes of coking coal). Medium and high grade iron ore reserves (5 bn tonnes) will last over over 200 years at present extraction rates. Although iron ore is found widely across peninsular India, coal is largely restricted to the West Bengal, Bihar, and Orissa. India's coal output reached 200 m tonnes in 1991, and iron ore 52 m tonnes, much of which was exported to Japan.

The search for oil has intensified after the oil price rises of the 1970s and late 1980s. Discoveries have still not matched early expectations, but development of the Bombay High, off the coast of Gujarat, have contributed to the total output of over 30 m tonnes. Oil, coal and gas provide the energy for just over half India's 65 m kw electric generation capacity, 18 m kw being hydro and 1.3 m mw nuclear.

In 1951 India produced just 5.3 bn kwh of electricity. By 1990 it had grown to over 240 bn kwh, but demand has risen so fast that nearly every state continues to have power blackouts or 'loadshedding'. Traditional sources of energy continue to be important, especially in rural areas. Firewood is estimated to provide nearly 30% of the total energy requirement, agricultural waste 9% and cow dung, a universal fuel in some poorer areas and households, 7%.

In the early 1950s India embarked on a programme of planned industrial development. Borrowing planning concepts from the Soviet Union, the government tried to stimulate development through massive investment in the public sector, imposing a system of tight controls on foreign ownership of capital in India, and playing a highly interventionist role in all aspects of economic policy. The private sector was allowed to continue to operate in agriculture, and in a wide range of 'non-essential' industrial sectors.

Although significant achievements were made in the first two Five Year Plans (1951-56, 1956-61), the Third Five Year Plan failed catastrophically to reach any of the targets set. Agriculture was particularly hard hit by three poor monsoons. After a period of dependence on foreign aid at the end of the 1960s, especially imported food grains, the economy started moving forward again. The 'Green Revolution', a package of practices designed to increase farm output, enabled Indian agriculture to increase production faster than demand, and through the 1980s it was producing surplus foodgrains, enabling it to building up reserves.

Industrial development continued to lag behind expectations, however. Although India returned to the programme of Five Year Plans (in 1991 it begins its Eighth Plan), central control has been progressively loosened. Indira Gandhi began to move towards liberalising imports and foreign investment. Rajiv Gandhi pursued this policy much more strongly in the first two years of his government, before slowing down in the face of increasing opposition from the many vested interests that saw their protected status at risk. However, there was growing support for liberalising India's economic strategy further and faster, a programme that seemed to have the support of several parties and political leaders campaigning in the May-June 1991 election.

Achievements and problems As a result of four decades of planned development India has a far more diversified industrial base than seemed imaginable at Independence. It produces goods from aeroplanes and rockets to watches and computers, from industrial and transport machinery to textiles and consumer goods. The influence of India's manufacturing industry reaches every village. Yet despite the successes, many in India claim that the weaknesses remain profound. Perhaps half of the population continues to live in absolute poverty, and despite surplus grain production many still lack an adequate diet.

While India's industrial economy is producing a range of modern products, most are uncompetitive on world markets. Furthermore, critics within India increasingly argue that goods are made in factories that often fail to observe basic safety and health rules, and that emit enormous pollution into the environment. On top of that, the industrial expansion barely seems to have touched the problems of unemployment which grow by the day. Employment in India's organised industry has risen from 12 m in 1961 to over 25 m in 1991, yet during the same period the number of registered unemployed rose from 1.6 m to 32 m.

Recent developments The 1980s saw very considerable expansion in India's industrial output, and a widening of its economic base. Ranking 16th in the world in terms of the value of its output from industry (but of course very much lower in per capita terms) industrial output through the last half of the 1980s was growing at about 10% a year, achieved with relatively modest rates of inflation.

In 1990 the situation had already taken a turn for the worse. By early 1991 India was facing a severe balance of payments crisis, worsened by the Gulf War, which interrupted India's concessional terms for oil imports with Kuwait and Iraq. Some of India's biggest public sector enterprises were suffering major losses, food prices rose steeply and India's foreign debt worsened alarmingly. The Rupee has been progressively devalued over the last two years, but the government has not taken the measures necessary to lessen the foreign or domestic debt. In Feb 1991 India took a loan from the IMF, and was set to approach them again in June after the elections. Strong action seemed likely to tackle a mounting crisis in economic management.

HANDICRAFTS

The richness of India's traditional handicrafts is known across the world. The traditions are still alive, not in some purely commercialised and tourist-oriented recreation of lost skills, but in the living traditions handed on through families that have practised them for generations. The variety and the often outstandingly high quality of the work is still astonishing. Each region has its own specialities.

Fabrics Textiles, especially cottons and silks, range from the simplest of handmade garments to stunningly beautiful and ornate saris. Silk brocades from Varanasi and Kanchipuram, Patna, Murshidabad and Surat, are sought after all over India. Rajasthan specialises in brightly coloured tie and dye cottons, while Kashmir specialises in woollens, especially the finest of goats' wool *pashmina**.

Carpets Kashmir has long had links with Persian carpet makers. Pure wool, woven wool and silk are superbly made in N India. Tibetan rugs are also widely available, many made by Tibetan refugees living in India.

Jewellery Gems have become India's leading export by value, reflecting the importance both of the gemstones and the finished jewellery. Rajasthani silverwork, and diamonds, lapis lazuli, moonstones and aquamarine are among the precious stones, and Hyderabad is famous for its pearls.

Wood carving and metalwork Sandalwood and rose wood from the South, and walnut in Kashmir, are the raw materials for some beautiful carving and marquetry. Metalwork, especially brass in the North, bidri ware in Andhra, and bronzes in the South, are also famous.

Other crafts Stone carving, in alabaster, marble and granite in both N and S, papier mâché in Kashmir, canework, pottery and leather work: all offer a tremendous range of excellent goods from the smallest mementos to life size statuary.

RELIGION

India has been home to all the world's major religions. Today over 80% of Indians are Hindu, but there are significant minorities. Muslims number about 100 m, and there are over 20 m Christians, 18 m Sikhs, 6 m Buddhists and a number of other religious groups. The origins and beliefs of India's major religious communities are outlined in the Introduction to S. Asia, **page 49**. One of the most persistent features of Indian religious and social life is the caste system. This has undergone substantial changes since Independence, especially in towns and cities, but most people in India are still clearly identified as a member of a particular caste group. The Government has introduced measures to help the backward, or 'scheduled' castes, though in recent years this has produced a major political backlash. See Introduction to South Asia, **page 60**.

ART AND ARCHITECTURE

India lies at the heart of a region in which art and architecture have developed with a remarkable continuity in the developing of traditions, a continuity which runs through successive regional and religious influences and styles. Over the 4,000 years since the Indus Valley civilisation was at its height Hinduism and Buddhism inherited, developed and transformed features of a culture whose origins may now be held to have lain in the period of the emerging Indus Valley Civilisation.

The Buddhist art and architecture of the 3rd century BC left few remains, but the stylistic influence on early Hindu architecture was profound. From the 6th century AD the first Hindu religious buildings to have survived into the modern period were constructed in S and E India, alongside a continuing development of the Buddhist tradition in India and elsewhere in S. Asia. Although there were many features in common in Hindu buildings across India, regional styles began to develop. These are outlined in the relevant regional sections below.

The continuity of development underwent its severest challenge in the 12th century with the arrival of the Muslims. Coming into India as vanquishing hordes, the early Muslims destroyed much that was in their path. Temples that had been encrusted with jewels were left bare. Mosques were built out of the stones of destroyed temples, often with bizarre results, as in the Qutb complex in Delhi. To the E, the Muslims finally completed the decline of Buddhism in India by destroying the last remaining Buddhist monasteries, notably the great monastery at Nalanda.

Out of the destruction of Hindu and Buddhist religious buildings it might have seemed that a wholly new art and architecture would inevitably emerge. Developing concepts of religious buildings from a faith completely different from that of the Hinduism into which it was transplanted, the new Islamic rulers also brought alien cultural concepts – notably from Turkey and Persia. Yet the greatest flowering of Islamic architecture India ever saw, under the Mughals, was not simply a transplant from another country or region. It developed out of India's own traditions as a new and distinctive architecture, yet with recognisable links to the culture which surrounded it. That continuity reflected many forces, not least the use made by the great Mughal Emperors of local skilled craftsmen and builders at every stage of their work. Constantly in contact not just with Hindu religious buildings, but with the secular buildings of the Rajputs to their S and W, the Mughal Emperors set their seal on developments which took up themes present in the Hindu traditions of their time, and bent them to a new and developing purpose.

Painting – the Mughal miniatures are a wonderful example – sculpture, inlay work, all blended skills from a variety of sources, and craftsmen – even occasionally from Europe – were sometimes employed to embellish the great works. What emerged was another stepping stone in a tradition of Indian architecture, which, far from breaking the threads of Hindu tradition actually wove them into new forms. The Taj Mahal was the ultimate product of this extraordinary process.

Yet great contrasts do of course exist. Regional styles developed their own special features, and the main thrust of Hindu and Muslim religious buildings remains fundamentally different.

The principles of Hindu temple building The principles of religious building was laid down in the *Sastras**, sets of rules compiled by priests. Every aspect of Hindu, Jain and Buddhist religious building is identified with conceptions of the structure of the universe. This applies as much to the process of building – the timing of which must be undertaken at astrologically propitious times – as to the formal layout of the buildings. The cardinal directions of N,S,E, and W, derived from our position with respect to the stars, are the basic fix on which buildings are planned. The E-W axis is nearly always a fundamental building axis. The noted writer on Indian architecture, George Michell, suggests that in addition to the cardinal directions, number is also critical to the design of the religious building. The Sastras devote great space to the significance of number, the key to the ultimate scale of the building being derived from the measurements of the sanctuary at its heart.

Indian temples were nearly always built to a clear and universal design, which had built into it philosophical understandings of the universe. This cosmology, of an infinite number of universes, isolated from each other in space, proceeds by imagining various possibilities as to its nature. Its centre is seen as dominated by *Mt Meru* which keeps earth and heaven apart. Continents, rivers, and oceans occupy concentric rings around the mountain, while the stars encircle the mountain in another plane. Humans live on the continent of *Jambudvipa*, characterised by the rose apple tree (*jambu*).

The Sastras show plans of this continent, organised in concentric rings and entered at the cardinal points. Such a diagram was known as a *mandala*. Such a geometric scheme could then be subdivided into almost limitless small compartments, each of which could be designated as having special properties or be devoted to a particular deity. The centre of the mandala would be the seat of the major god. Such a mandala provided the ground rules for the building of stupas and temples across India, and provided the key to the symbolic meaning attached to every aspect of religious buildings.

Temple design Hindu temples developed characteristic plans and elevations. The focal point of the temple lay in its sanctuary, the home of the presiding deity, known as the womb-chamber (*garbhagriha**). A series of doorways, in large temples leading through a succession of buildings, allowed the worshipper to move towards the final encounter with the deity himself and to obtain *darshan* – a sight of the god. Both Buddhist and Hindu worship encourages the worshipper to walk clockwise around the shrine, performing *pradakshina*.

The elevations are designed to be symbolic representations of the home of the gods. Mountain peaks such as Kailasa are common names for the most prominent of the towers. In N and E Indian temples the tallest of these towers rises above the garbagriha itself, symbolising the meeting of earth and heaven in the person of the enshrined deity. In later S Indian temples the gateways to the temple come to overpower the central tower. In both, the basic structure is usually richly embellished with sculpture. When first built this would usually have been plastered and painted, and often covered in gems. In contrast to the extraordinary profusion of colour and life on the outside, the interior is dark and cramped. Here is the true centre of power.

Temple development Buddhist and Hindu architecture probably began with wooden building, for the rock carving and cave excavated temples show clear evidence of copying styles which must have been developed first in wooden buildings. The 3rd-2nd century BC caves of the Buddhists were followed in the 7th and 8th centuries AD by free standing but rock-cut temples such as those at Mamallapuram, **see page 727**. They were subsequently replaced by temples built entirely out of assembled material, usually stone. By the 13th century AD most of India's most remarkable Hindu temples had been built, from the Chola temples of the S to the Khajuraho temples of the N Peninsula. Only the flowering of Vijayanagar architecture in S India produced continuing development, culminating in the Meenakshi Temple in Madurai, **see page 780**.

Muslim religious architecture Although the Muslims adapted many Hindu forms in their subsequent architectural development, they also brought totally new forms. Their most outstanding contribution, dominating the inherited architecture of many N Indian cities, are the mosques and tomb complexes (*dargah*). The use of brickwork was widespread, and they brought with them from Persia the principle of constructing the true arch. Muslim architects succeeded in producing a variety of domed structures, often incorporating distinctively Hindu features such as the surmounting finial. At the end of the great period of Muslim building, which terminated with the reign of Aurangzeb in 1707, the Muslims had added magnificent forts and palaces to their religious structures. Both – mosques such as the Jami Masjid in Delhi and tombs such as the Taj Mahal itself – were testaments to imperial splendour, a statement of power as well as of aesthetic taste.

European buildings Nearly two centuries of architectural stagnation and decline followed the demise of Mughal power. The Portuguese built a series of churches in Goa that owed nothing to local traditions and everything to baroque developments in Europe. Despite their apparently decaying exteriors many of these remain extraordinary buildings. It was not until the end of the Victorian period, when British imperial ambitions were at their height, that the British colonial impact began to be felt. Great arguments divided British architects as to the merits of indigenous design and skills. The ultimate design for New Delhi (**see page 152**) was carried out by men who had little time for Hindu architecture and believed themselves to be on a civilising mission. Others at the end of the 19th century wanted to recapture and enhance a tradition for which they had great respect. They have left a series of buildings, both in formerly British ruled territory and in the Princely States, which illustrates this concern through the development of what became known as the Indo-Saracenic style.

In the immediate aftermath of the colonial period, Independent India set about trying to establish a break from the immediately imperial past, but was uncertain how to achieve it. In the event foreign architects were commissioned for major developments, such as Le Corbusier's design for Chandigarh. Ahmadabad has become a centre for training and experiment, and contains a number of new buildings such as those of the Indian architect Charles Correa.

MUSIC AND DANCE

Music Indian music can trace its origins to the metrical hymns and chants of the Vedas, in which the production of sound according to strict rules was understood to be of vital importance to the continuing order of the Universe. Over more than 3,000 years of development, through a range of regional schools, India's musical tradition has been handed on almost entirely by ear. The chants of the Rig Veda developed into songs in the Sama Veda and music found expression in every sphere of life, closely reflecting the cycle of seasons and the rhythm of work.

Over the centuries the original 3 notes, which were sung strictly in descending order, were extended to 5 and then 7 and developed to allow freedom to move up and down the scale. The scale increased to 12 with the addition of flats and sharps and finally to 22 with the further sudivision of semitones. Books of musical rules go back at least as far as the 3rd century AD. Classical music was totally intertwined with dance and drama, an interweaving reflected in the term *sangita*.

At some point after the Muslim influence made itself felt in the N, North and South Indian styles diverged, to become Karnatak music in the S and Hindustani music in the N. However, they still share important common features: *svara* (pitch), *raga* (the melodic structure), and *tala* or *talam* (metre).

Hindustani music is believed to have originated in the Delhi Sultanate during the 13th century, when the most widely known of North Indian musical instruments, the *sitar*, was believed to have been invented. Amir Khusrau is also believed to have invented the small drums, the *tabla*. Hindustani music is held to have reached its peak under *Tansen*, a court musician of Akbar. The other important northern instruments are the stringed **sarod**, the reed instrument **shahnai** and the wooden flute. Most Hindustani compositions have devotional texts, though they encompass a great emotional and thematic range. A common classical form of vocal performance is the *dhrupad*, a four part composition.

The essential structure of a melody is known as a *raga* which usually has 5 to 7 notes, and can have as many as 9 (or even 12 in mixed ragas). The music is improvised by the performer within certain governing rules and although theoretically thousands of ragas are possible, because of the need to be aesthetically pleasing only a few hundred exist of which around a hundred are commonly performed. Ragas have become associated with particular moods and specific times of the day. Music festivals often include all night sessions to allow performers a wider choice of repertoire.

Karnatak music Contemporary S Indian music is traced back to *Tyagaraja* (1759-1847), *Svami Shastri* (1763-1827) and *Dikshitar* (1775-1835), three musicians who lived and worked in Thanjavur, and who are still referred to as 'the Trinity'. Their music placed more emphasis on extended compositions than Hindustani music. Perhaps the best known S Indian instrument is the stringed *vina*, the flute being commonly used for accompaniment along with the violin (played rather differently to the European original), an oboe-like instrument called the *nagasvaram* and the drums, *tavil*.

Music festivals Many cities hold annual festivals, particularly during winter months. Some important ones are listed here. **Jan** Sangeet Natak Akademi's Festival, New Delhi; Tyagaraja Festival, Tiruvayyaru, nr Thanjavur. **Feb** ITC Sangeet Sammelan, New Delhi. **Mar** Shankar Lal Festival, New Delhi. **Aug** Vishnu Digambar Festival, New Delhi. **Sep** Bhatkhande Festival, Lucknow. **Oct** Shanmukhananda, Bombay. **Nov** Sur-Singar Festival, Bombay. **Dec** Tansen Festival, Gwalior; Music Academy Festival, Madras; Music and Dance Festival, Madras.

Dance India is rich with folk dance traditions. The rules for classical dance were laid down in the *Natya shastra* in the 2nd century BC. It is still one of the bases for modern dance forms, although there are many regional variations, described in the appropriate regional sections of the Handbook. The most common sources for Indian dance are the epics, but there are three essential aspects of the dance itself, *Nritta* (pure dance), *Nrittya* (emotional expression) and *natya* (drama). Like the music with which it is so closely intertwined, dance has expressed religious belief and deep emotion. The importance of religion in dance was exemplified by the tradition of temple dancers, *devadasis*, girls and women who were dedicated to the deity in major temples to perform before them. In S and E India there were thousands of *devadasis* associated with temple worship, though the practice fell into widespread disrepute and was banned in Independent India.

HISTORY

India's pre-modern history is outlined in the Introduction to South Asia, **see page 77.**

When India became Independent on 15 Aug 1947 it faced three immediate political crises. Partition left it with a bitter struggle between Hindus, Muslims and Sikhs which threatened to tear the new country into pieces at birth. 11 m people migrated between the two new countries, and perhaps 1 m were killed in the slaughter that accompanied the migration. Almost immediately it was plunged into a war with Pakistan over Kashmir, which only ended in an inconclusive ceasefire more than 12 months later, in January 1949. Finally it had the task of developing a constitution which would allow the diverse and often conflicting interest groups which made up Indian society to cement their allegiance to the new State. Without the binding force of opposition to the colonial power, a new raison d'etre had to be found for the Congress party and for the country it led.

In the 45 years since Independence, striking political achievements have been made. With the two year exception of 1975-77, when Indira Gandhi imposed a state of emergency in which all political activity was banned, India has sustained a democratic system in the face of tensions and pressures which many outside observers thought would bring it down within months. The General elections of May-June 1991 were the country's tenth. Deeply scarred by the assassination of Rajiv Gandhi, the electoral process none the less continued.

The constitution Establishing itself as a sovereign and democratic republic, the Indian Parliament accepted Nehru's leadership in his advocacy of a secular constitution. The President is formally vested with all executive powers, always understood to be exercised under the authority of the Prime Minister. That assumption has been challenged from time to time, but never seriously been put to the test, although the President has been able to use very limited discretionary power.

Effective power under the Constitution lies with the Prime Minister and Cabinet, following the British model. In practice there have been long periods, ever since the Prime Ministership of Lal Bahadur Shastri, when the role of the Cabinet has been much reduced compared to that of the Prime Minister's secretariat. In principle Parliament chooses the Prime Minister. The Parliament has a lower house (the *Lok Sabha*, or 'house of the people') and an upper house (the *Rajya Sabha* – Council of States). The former is made up of directly elected representatives from the 543 parliamentary constituencies (plus 2 nominated members from the Anglo-Indian community), the latter of a mixture of members elected by an electoral college and of nominated members. Constitutional amendments require a two thirds majority in both houses.

India's constitution is federal, devolving certain powers to elected state assemblies. Each state has a Governor who acts as its official head. Many states also have two chambers, the upper generally called the Rajya Sabha and the lower (often called the Vidhan Sabha) being of directly elected representatives. In practice many of the state assemblies have had a totally different political complexion from that of the Lok Sabha. Regional parties have played a far more prominent role, while in many states under Mrs Gandhi and Rajiv Gandhi central government has effectively dictated both leadership and policy of state assemblies.

One of the key features of India's constitution is its secular principle. This is not based on the absence of religious belief, but on the commitment to guarantee freedom of religious belief and practice to all groups in Indian society. There were signs in the period leading up to the 1991 election campaign that the commitment to a secular constitution was under increasing challenge, especially from the Hindu nationalism of the **Bharatiya Janata Party**, the BJP and the Sikh fundamentalist **Akali Dal** party.

The judiciary India's Supreme Court has similar but somewhat weaker powers to those of the United States. The judiciary has remained effectively independent of the government except under the Emergency between 1975-77.

The civil service India continued to use the small but highly professional administrative service inherited from the British period. Re-named the Indian Administrative Service (IAS), it continues to exercise remarkable influence across the country. The administration of many aspects of central and regional government is in the hands of a highly educated and trained elite body, who continue to act largely by the constitutional rules which bind them as servants of the state. Many Indians accept the continuing efficiency and high calibre of the top ranking officers in the administration while believing that the bureaucratic system as a whole has been overtaken by widespread corruption.

The police India's police is divided into a series of groups, numbering nearly 1 million. While the top ranks of the Indian Police Service are comparable to the IAS, lower levels are extremely poorly trained and very low paid. In addition to the domestic police force there are special groups: the Border Security Force, Central Reserve Police, Central Reserve Police and others. They may be armed with modern weapons, and are called in for special duties.

The armed forces Unlike its immediate neighbours India has never had military rule. With over 1.25 m men in the army, India has one of the largest armed forces in the world. Although they have remained out of politics, and there is little likelihood of their direct involvement, the armed services have been used increasingly frequently to put down civil unrest.

The Congress Party Indian national electoral politics has been dominated by the Congress Party. Its strength in the Lok Sabha has often overstated the volume of its support in the country, however, and state governments have frequently been dominated by parties – and interests – only weakly represented at the centre.

The Congress won overall majorities in 7 of the 9 general elections held before the 1991 election. However, those victories often reflected the fragmented nature of the opposition rather than the underlying strength of the Congress. In no election did the Congress obtain more than 50% of the popular vote, yet it has won huge majorities on the basis of the lack of a united opposition. It has been defeated only when the opposition has agreed to field only one candidate against the Congress candidate, in 1977 and in 1989. In the latter election it still gained the largest number of seats, though not enough to form a government on its own, and it was unable to find allies.

Within the Congress Party the Nehru family played the pivotal role from 1947 until Rajiv Gandhi's assassination in 1991. From 1950 until his death in 1964 Jawaharlal Nehru was the Party's undisputed leader, His daughter Indira Gandhi took up the leadership after the unexpected death of his immediate successor, Lal Bahadur Shastri. She set about radically transforming the party into a vehicle of her own power, centralising the structure of the party and of the government. Her assassination in 1984 at the hands of her Sikh bodyguard followed the months of turmoil surrounding rising Sikh demands for the creation of a separate state.

The Congress had built its platform of broad based support partly by championing the causes of the backward castes and the minorities. Rajiv Gandhi began to place an emphasis on a new image for the Congress, that of a party committed to modernisation and change. He pushed hard for economic reform, but lost the support of key members of his Cabinet, notably V.P. Singh, who left the Congress to become a leading figure in the Opposition. In November 1989 the Congress was defeated for only the second time in its history, deeply wounded by charges of corruption at the highest levels.

The Non-Congress Parties Political activity outside the Congress can seem bewilderingly complex. There are no genuinely national parties. The only alternative governments to the Congress have been formed by coalitions of regional and ideologically based parties. Parties of the left – Communist and Socialist – have never broken out of their narrow regional bases. The Communist Party of India split into two factions in 1964, with the **Communist Party of India Marxist** (the CPM) ultimately taking power in West Bengal and Kerala. In the 1960s the Swatantra Party (a liberal party) made some ground nationally, opposing the economic centralisation and state control supported by the Congress. In the North a peasants' party, the *Lok Dal* also made some headway under the leadership of a powerful Jat leader, Charan Singh.

At the right of the political spectrum, the Jan Sangh has been seen as a party of right wing Hindu nationalism with a concentrated but significant base in parts of the N, especially among higher castes and merchant communities. The most organised political force outside the Congress, the Jan Sangh merged with the Janata Party for the elections of 1977. After the collapse of that government it reformed itself as the *Bharatiya Janata Party*, (BJP). In the 1989 elections it established a bridgehead in N India, and in 1990-91 developed a powerful campaign focusing on reviving Hindu identity against the minorities. The elections of 1991 showed it to be the most powerful single challenger to the Congress.

The power of the BJP remained confined largely to N India. Elsewhere a succession of regional parties dominated politics in several key states. The most important were Tamil Nadu and Andhra Pradesh in the S. In Tamil Nadu power has alternated since 1967 between the Dravida Munnetra Kazhagam (the DMK) and a faction which split from it, the All India Anna

DMK, named after one of the earliest leaders of the Dravidian political movement, C. N. Annadurai. In Andhra Pradesh, The Telugu Desam offered a similar regional alternative to Congress rule.

Recent developments The failure of the new National Front Government to live up to its expectations led to growing disenchantment. The new Prime Minister, V.P. Singh, had to balance a wide spectrum of support from within his government and from outside it, as he was dependent on the Communist Party Marxist and the BJP to stay in power. The unlikely coalition held together until V.P. Singh announced that he would introduce measures to implement the Mandal Commission report, which recommended increasing the number of government jobs reserved for what are termed the 'other backward castes' – the OBCs. This led to extraordinary violence on the streets in the summer of 1990, several young people committing suicide by self-immolation. V.P. Singh's resignation led to the collapse of the Janata led Government and its replacement by the fraction of the Janata Party, led by S. Chandrasekhar. He was only able to remain in power by courtesy of the Congress, with Rajiv Gandhi as its leader effectively in control. In March 1991 Chandrasekhar announced his determination to call a General Election. In the course of the campaign Rajiv Gandhi was assassinated at Sriperumbudur, just outside Madras, on 21 May 1991. The election was completed after a two week delay and gave the Congress Party at least 233 seats against 111 seats for the BJP and 61 seats for the National Front. At the end of June 32 seats remained to be declared. The Congress Party chose P.V. Narasimha Rao as their President. He was sworn in as Prime Minister on June 21st 1991.

Date	Prime Minister	President
1947-64	Jawaharlal Nehru	
1948-50		C. Rajagopalachari
1950-62		Rajendra Prasad
1962-67		S. Radhakrishnan
1964-66	Lal Bahadur Shastri	
1966-77	Indira Gandhi	
1967-69		Zakir Hussain
1969-74		V.V. Giri
1974-77		Fakhruddin Ali Ahmed
1977-79	Morarji Desai	
1977-82		Neelam Sanjiva Reddy
1979-80	Charan Singh	
1980-84	Indira Gandhi	
1982-87		Giani Zail Singh
1984-89	Rajiv Gandhi	
1987-		R. Venkataraman
1989-90	V.P.Singh	
1990-91	S. Chandrasekhar	
1991-	P.V. Narasimha Rao	

INFORMATION FOR VISITORS

DOCUMENTS

Passports and visas Tourist Visas are issued for an initial period of 4 months extendible for a further period of 2 months. Tourists must enter India within 6 months of the date of issue. Applications must be made on the prescribed form and be accompanied by 3 passport size photographs, a passport valid to cover the period of visit, and the visa fee (either by cheque if sent by post or in cash if calling in person). Entry Visas are issued to persons who wish to visit on business, employment or for residence, while Transit Visas are issued to those passing through India en route to another country. Nationals of Bhutan and Nepal do not require a Visa – they only require a suitable means of identification.

The cost of visas is variable according to the nationality of the applicant and the type of visa applied for. Arrangements for visa application and collection vary from office to office, and should be confirmed by phone with the relevant office. Tourists from countries which do not have Indian representatives may apply to resident British representatives, or enquire at the Air India Office.

Extensions Applications should be made to the Foreigners' Regional Registration Offices at New Delhi, Bombay, Calcutta or Madras, or an office of the Superintendent of Police in the District Headquarters.

Restricted and Protected Areas Parts of the country require special permits - *Arunachal Pradesh, Manipur, Mizoram, Nagaland* and *Sikkim*. For Sikkim, 7 day permits are issued to individuals wishing to visit Gangtok, Rumtak and Phodong and organized groups trekking in Dzongri may enter for 15 days if sponsored by a recognized Indian travel agency. Applications to Under Secretary, Ministry of Home Affairs, Foreigners Division, Lok Nayak Bhavan, Khan Market, New Delhi 110003 at least 4 weeks in advance. Foreign visitors may apply to visit Imphal town in Manipur if they travel to and from Imphal by air.

Special permission is needed for *Assam, Meghalaya* and *Tripura* as well as some northern districts of *West Bengal* although those travelling by air to and from Bagdogra do not need prior permission to visit Darjiling for up to 15 days.

Andaman and Nicobar Islands Individuals may visit Port Blair, Jolly Buoy and Cinque Islands for up to 15 days, permission for which is available on arrival at Port Blair. Organised groups may also visit Snob, Red Skin, Grub and Boat Islands.

Lakshadweep Islands Individuals may visit Bangaram and Suheli Islands after obtaining a permit from the Lakshadweep Administration. Wellington Island, Harbour Rd, Cochin 3.

Registration Foreigners do not need to register within the 120 day period of their visa (Bangladeshis are only required to do so after 6 months).

Income Tax Clearance All foreign visitors who stay in India for more than 90 days are required to get an income tax clearance exemption certificate from the Foreign Section of the Income Tax Dept in Delhi, Bombay, Calcutta or Madras.

Work permits All foreigners require work permits. Apply to the Indian representative in your country of origin.

Representations overseas *Bangladesh*, House 120, Road 2, Dhanmondi RA, Dhaka-2, T

507670, Tlx 642336. Consulate; Chittagong T 210291, Rajshahi T 3641; *Bhutan*, India House Estate, Thimphu, T 2162, Tlx 211 INDEMB; *Maldives*, Mafabbu Aage 37, Orchid Magu, Male 20-02, T 323015, Tlx 66044 HICOMIND MF; *Nepal*, Lainchour, P.O. Box No. 292, Kathmandu, T 410900, Tlx 2449 INDEM NP; *Pakistan*, 482-, Sector G-6/4, Islamabad, T 826718, Tlx 5849 INDEM. Consulate: Karachi T 522275; *Sri Lanka*, 36-38 Galle Road, Colombo 3, T 21605, Tlx 21132 HICOMIN. Consulate: Kandy T 22430.

Australia, 3-5 Moonah Place, Yarralumla, Canberra, T 733999, Tlx AA-62362. Consulates: Sydney T 927055, Melbourne T 3503351; *Austria*, Kärntner Ring 2, A-1015 Vienna, T 50 58 666-669, Fax: 50 59 219, Telex: 113 721; *Belgium*, 217-Chaussée de Vleurgat, 1050 Brussels, T 640 93 73, Fax 648 9638. Consulates: Ghent T 091/263423, Antwerp (03) 234 1122; *Canada*, 10 Springfield Rd., Ottawa, ON K1M 1C9, T (613) 744-3751, Tlx: 053-4172. Consulates: Toronto T (416) 960-0751, Vancouver T (926-6080; *Denmark*, Vangehusvej 15, 2100 Copenhagen, T (01) 18288, Tlx 15964 INDEB-DK; *Finland*, Satamakatu 2 A8, 00160 Helsinki-16, T 60 89 27, Tlx 125202 INDEM SF; *France*, 15 Rue Alfred Dehodencq, Paris, T 4520-3930, Tlx 610621 F; *Germany*, Adenauerallee, 262/264, 5300 Bonn-1, T 54050, Tlx 8869301 INDM D. Consulates: Berlin T 881-7068, Frankfurt T 069-271040, Hamburg T 338036, Munich T089 -92562067, Stuttgart T0711-297078; *Ireland*, 6 Lesson Park, Dublin 6, T 0001-970843, Tlx 30670 DTLX; *Italy*, Via XX Settembre 5, – 00187 Rome, T 464642, Tlx 611274 INDEMB I. Consulates: Milan, T 02 869 0314, Genoa T 54891; *Japan*, 2-11, Kudan Minami 2-Chome, Chiyoda-ku, Tokyo 102, T (03) 262-2391, Fax (03) 234-4866, Tlx 2324886 INDEMB J. Consulate: Kobe T 078-241 8116; *Korea*, 37-3, Hannam-dong, Yongsan-Ku, Seoul, T 998-4257, Fax 796-9534, Tlx 24461 INDEMB K; *Malaysia*, 20th Floor Wisma Selangor Dredging, West Block, 142-C, Jalan Apang, 50450 Kuala Lumpur, T 03-261 7000, Tlx 30317; *Netherlands* (Consul), Buitenrustweg 2, The Hague (2517KD), T 070-46 97 71, Tlx 33543 INDEM NL; *New Zealand*, 10th floor, Princess Tower, 180 Molesworth Street, (PO Box 4045) Wellington, T 736 390/1, Tlx: NZ 31676 (HICOIND); *Norway*, 30 Niels Jules Gate, 0272 Oslo-2, T 443194, Tlx 78510 INDEM N; *Singapore*, India House, 31 Grange Road, Singapore 0923, T 7376777, Tlx 25526 BHARAT RS; *Spain*, Avenida Pio XII 30-32, 28016 Madrid, T 457-02-09, Tlx 22605 EOIME. Consulate: Barcelona T 93/2120422; *Sweden*, Adolf Fredriks Kyrkogata 12, Box 1340, 11183 Stockholm, T 08-10 70 08, Tlx 11598 INDIATEL S, Fax: 08-24 85 05; *Switzerland*, 17 Weltpoststrasse 17, 3015 Berne, T 031-44 01 9, Tlx 911829 INDE CH, Fax: 26 26 87; *Thailand*, 46, Soi 23 (Prasarn Mitr) Sukhumvit 23, Bangkok 10110, T 2580300-6, Tlx 82793 TH; *United Kingdom*, India House, Aldwych, London WC2B 4NA, T 071-836 8484, Tlx 267166 HICOMIND. Consulate: Birmingham T 021-643 0366; *USA*, 2107 Massachusetts Ave., Washington DC 20008, T (202) 939-7000, Tlx 64333 INSUMIS, Fax (202) 939-7027. Consulates: New Orleans T (504) 582 8105, New York (212) 879-7800, San Francisco T (415) 668-0662, Chicago T (312) 781680; Cleveland T 216/696.

Tourist Board offices   Indian Tourism Ministry of Tourism, Transport Bhavan, Parliament Street, T (11) 384111. Tlx: 312827, New Delhi 110001 India.

Overseas *Australia* Level 5, 65 Elizabeth St, Sydney, NSW 2000, T (02) 232-1600, Fax: (02) 223-3003. *Canada* 60 Bloor Street, West Suite No. 1003, Toronto, Ontario, T 416-962 3787, Fax: 416-962 6279. *France* 8 Boulevard de la Madeleine, 75009 Paris, T 42-65-83-86. *Germany* 77 (III) Kaiserstrasse, D-6000 Frankfurt am Main 1, T 235423, Fax: 069-234724. *Italy* Via Albricci 9, Milan 20122, T 804952. *Japan* Pearl Building, 9-18 Chome Ginza, Chuo Ku, Tokyo 104, T (03) 571-5062. *The Netherlands* Rokin 9-15, 1012 Amsterdam, T 020-208891. *UK* 7 Cork Street, T 071-437 3677/8, Fax: 071-494 1048, London W1X 2AB, United Kingdom. *USA* 30 Rockefeller Plaza, Room 15, North Mezzanine, T (212) 586 4901/2/3, Fax: (212) 582 3274, New York NY 10020, USA.

TRAVEL

By air Access to India by air is highly developed. Most international flights arrive at Delhi, but there are also international airports at Bombay, Madras and Calcutta.

To Delhi

From Europe Approx Time From London To Delhi (non-stop): **9 Hours**. The best flights are from London, Paris, Frankfurt, Rome and Geneva or Zurich. There are connections from all other European capitals. From Paris Air France has 4 flights a week and Air India 5. From London Heathrow Air India has daily flights and Thai International 3 a week. From London Gatwick British Airways flies daily. From Frankfurt there 4 flights a week with PIA, Lufthansa 5 and Air India 6. You can fly from Rome with Alitalia and Air India both twice a week. Swissair flights leave Zurich 3 times a week and there are 2 from Geneva with Air India. From Moscow, Air India flies 3 times a week and Aeroflot 4 times.

From the USA and Canada Approx Time From JFK (New York): 17 Hours. Air India and PIA both fly 4 times a week from New York (JFK). Air India has 2 flights a week from Toronto.

From Australasia you can fly to Delhi from Sydney via Singapore with Singapore Airlines then KLM once a week or Air India twice.

From the Far East there are Air India flights from Tokyo 3 times a week, Alitalia twice and Japan Airlines once. From Singapore (approx 5 hours), Singapore Airlines has 3 flights a week, Aeroflot and Air India 2 and Turkish Airlines one. KLM flies twice a week from Jakarta and there are 2 flights a week each from Kuala Lumpur with Malaysian Airlines and Air India. Hong Kong has Air India flights twice a week, British Airways 5 times, Air France twice and Alitalia once.You can fly from Bangkok (approx 4 hrs.) with Thai International 5 times a week, Air India 4 times, Air France twice and Japan Airlines once.

From the Middle East Gulf Air has 5 flights a week from Bahrain.

To Bombay
From Europe there is a very wide choice of flights.
Paris with Air India 4 times and Air France 3 times a week. Amsterdam with Biman Bangladesh Airlines weekly and KLM twice a week. London Heathrow with British Airways 5 times a week, Singapore Airlines twice and Air India daily. Frankfurt (with connections from San Francisco) with PIA three times a week, Lufthansa 5 times, Air India 6 times. Rome with Alitalia and Air India both twice a week. Geneva with Air India twice a week and Zurich with Swissair, 4 flights a week.

From USA and Canada. From New York (JFK) there are daily flights with Air India and 3 with PIA. PIA also has 6 flights a week from LA via JFK and 3 from San Francisco via Frankfurt. Air India has twice weekly flights from Toronto.

From Australasia there is a weekly flight from Sydney via Kuala Lumpur with Quantas: connecting flight to Bombay with Air Nova.

From the Far East there are plenty of flights on all the main routes. From Tokyo Air India flies 4 times a week. From Singapore, Singapore Airlines has 3 flights a week, Air India 6 and Turkish Airlines one. There are weekly flights from Jakarta with Swissair and from Kuala Lumpur with Air India and CSA. From Hong Kong, Cathay Pacific flies 4 times a week, Air India, Air France and British Airways twice, and Swissair 3 times. From Bangkok, Air India and Cathay Pacific have 4 flights a week, and Air France 3.

From the Middle East Gulf Air has daily flights from Bahrain, Air India 2 a week and Kuwait Airways 3.

To Calcutta
From Europe there are connections via Bombay, Amman, Delhi, Frankfurt and Dhaka. There is a weekly Aeroflot flight from Moscow.

From USA and Canada passengers should travel via Europe.

From Australasia and the Far East Thai International flies via Bangkok to Calcutta on several routes: Sydney twice a week, Jakarta, Kuala Lumpur and Hong Kong 3 times. Also from Hong Kong, Cathay Pacific has 6 flights a week via Bangkok. From Bangkok there are direct flights with Indian Airlines and Alisarda 3 times a week and Air India once. Singapore has a twice weekly connection with Singapore Airlines and there is a weekly Air India flight from Tokyo.

From the Middle East there is a weekly flight from Bahrain via Dhaka with Biman Bangladesh Airlines.

To Madras
From Europe various flights are available. From Paris with Air India once a week. London Heathrow has a weekly direct flight with Air India and 2 a week with British Airways with connections from Oslo, Helsinki, San Francisco and New York (JFK).

From USA and Canada travel via Europe.

From Australasia travel via Singapore or Bangkok or with Malaysian Airlines have a twice weekly connection from Sydney via Kuala Lumpur.

From the Far East there are flights from Singapore with Air India 6 times a week and with Singapore Airlines 3 times. From Kuala Lumpur there are flights with Air India twice a week, Malaysian Airlines 6 times and British Airways twice. Malaysian Airlines have flights which connect with their Kuala Lumpur-Madras route from Jakarta twice a week and from Bangkok 5 times.

Note Airline schedules change frequently, so be sure to check with a travel agent before making travel arrangements.

Customs regulations   Foreign currency There are no restrictions on the amount of foreign currency or travellers cheques a tourist may bring into India. If you are carrying more than US$ 1,000 or its equivalent in cash or traveller's cheques you should fill in a currency declaration form. However, loss of such forms is rarely crucial; it is now exceptional for them to be asked for or looked at on departure.

Duty Free Allowances Tourists are allowed to bring in all personal effects "which may reasonably be required" without charge. The official customs allowance includes, for example, 200 cigarettes or 50 cigars, 0.95 litres of alcohol, a camera with five rolls of film, a pair of binoculars. However, valuable personal effects or professional equipment must be registered on a Tourist Baggage Re-Export Form (TBRE). This applies for example to jewellery, special camera equipment and lenses, lap top computers, sound and video recorders. These forms require the serial numbers of such equipment and it saves considerable frustration if you know the numbers in advance and are ready to show the serial numbers on the equipment. In addition to the forms, details of imported equipment will be entered into your passport. **It is essential to keep these forms** for showing to the customs when leaving India, otherwise considerable delays are very likely at the time of departure.

Prohibited and restricted items The import of dangerous drugs, live plants, gold coins, gold and silver bullion and silver coins not in current use are either banned or subject to strict regulation. Export of gold jewellery purchased in India is allowed up to a value of Rs 2,000 and other jewellery (including settings with precious stones) up to a value of Rs 10,000. **Warning** Export of antiquities and art objects over 100 years old is restricted. Skins of all animals, snakes and articles made from them are banned. You may, however, take out a an article made of a reasonable quantity of peacock feathers.

Arrival The formalities on arrival in India have been increasingly streamlined during the last five years and the physical facilities at Delhi, Bombay and Madras greatly improved. However, arrival can still be a slow and confusing process. The procedure conforms to normal international procedures, with immigration first, followed by luggage collection and customs. Disembarkation cards, with an attached customs declaration, are handed out to passengers during the inward flight. The immigration form should be handed in at the immigration counter on arrival. The customs slip will be returned, for handing over to the customs on leaving the baggage collection hall.

Departure Tax Rs 300 is payable for all international departures. This must be paid in Rupees and a receipt obtained at a special counter at the airport, so make sure that you keep this available for when you leave.

INTERNAL TRAVEL

Planning a route

The opportunities for independent travellers are now so wide that it may be difficult to know where to begin. Delhi, Bombay and Madras are all easy starting or finishing points for a tour. Several airlines make it possible to enter India from one of these cities and leave from another, so you are not bound to a circular route. A number of options for tours lasting between 10 days and 3 weeks are published by the Indian Tourist Development Corporation. Below we list a few outline suggestions. The suggested length of the tour allows for some sectors being flown. Allow a little more as the minimum time if you are planning to travel entirely by road and rail. However, the use of overnight trains for longer journeys can allow you to cover almost as much ground in the same time as flying. Some of the tours can easily be shortened by cutting out some centres.

1. **The Himalayan foothills** Delhi – Corbett – Shimla -Kulu – Manali – Leh – Delhi 18 days. Delhi gives access to some of the most beautiful sights in the Himalayan foothills, and up to the high plateaus of Leh and Ladakh. This route

goes to the Corbett National Park, India's first and possibly most magnificent reserve. It then goes West via Shimla, the British summer capital and summer hill resort to Manali and Kulu, then up to the high altitude Tibetan-Buddhist area of Leh. Even if Kashmir is closed to visitors access is still possible.

2. **Delhi and Rajasthan to Bombay** Delhi – Agra – Jaipur – Bikaner – Jaisalmer – Jodhpur – Udaipur – Mt. Abu – Ahmadabad -Bombay. If you fly on some sectors this tour can be done in 18 days. The most interesting sites of Mughal and Rajput India, the Jain and Hindu shrines at Mt. Abu and the distinctive Gujarat architectural style of Ahmadabad, culminating in the colonial hub of Bombay.

3. **Delhi, East India and Khajuraho** Delhi – Gangtok – Darjiling – Calcutta – Bhubaneshwar – Konarak – Puri – Varanasi – Khajuraho – Agra – Delhi. 21 days. Some flights desirable. Considerably longer by land. A chance to see some of India's most sacred Hindu sites such as Puri and Varanasi, and some of the most magnificent temples at Konarak and Khajuraho. The tour would start by visiting the foothills of the Himalayas in Sikkim, with its distinctive Buddhist influences, and Darjiling, famous for its tea estates and magnificent views of Kanchengdzonga, then passes S through Calcutta, early capital of the British in India, to Orissa. It concludes with the return to Delhi, stopping at Agra to see the finest Mughal buildings, including the Taj Mahal.

4. **Central India tour** Delhi – Agra – Gwalior – Jhansi – Orchcha – Bhopal – Sanchi – Indore – Mandu – Bombay – Belgaum – Badami – Hampi – Goa – Bombay. 21 days. This tour starts in the centre of Muslim influence, and goes S through some of the great Rajput cities and forts (Gwalior, Jhansi and Orchcha) to Bhopal. Around Bhopal are some of the finest prehistoric rock paintings in the world, and early Buddhist remains. Continuing through Bombay you can visit Badami, with its 6th century *Chalukya* temples, and Hampi, capital of the medieval Hindu Vijayanagar Empire. Return via the former Portuguese colony of Goa, with its churches and beaches, to Bombay.

5. **From North to South** Delhi – Agra – Jaipur – Ajanta – Ellora – Bombay – Goa – Cochin – Madurai – Madras. 18 days if flying some sectors. Starting with the Mughal and Rajput North, the tour goes on to the magnificent Buddhist and Hindu cave temples of Ajanta and Ellora, passes through Bombay to Goa, and then samples the completely different world of the South. The great temple city of Madurai gives an excellent view of the temple life and architecture of the Tamil cultural heartland, returning to the colonial city of Madras.

6. **Tamil Nadu and Southern Karnataka** Bombay – Cochin – Periyar – Madurai – Trichy – Thanjavur – Madras – Bangalore – Belur – Halebid – Bangalore – Bombay. 18 days. A quite brief Southern tour, with so much to see that it can easily be extended. From Bombay down the W coast to Cochin, a fascinating meeting point of cultures – Hindu, Christian, Jew and Muslim, Indian, European and even a touch of Chinese – then South to one of India's game reserves at Periyar, high in the Western Ghats. From Periyar down to the Tamil plains, visiting Madurai, Trichy and Thanjavur, centres of successive Tamil kingdoms, then on to Madras and Bangalore. There are several fascinating excursions possible if you have time to extend the tour. The route then goes on to Mysore, Belur and Halebid, with remarkable Hindu and Jain monuments, returning to Bangalore and then Bombay.

7. **A South Indian circuit** Bombay – Ajanta and Ellora – Hyderabad – Madras – Trichy – Madurai – Bangalore – Mysore – Belur – Halebid – Goa – Bombay. 14 days. In two weeks it is possible to see major sites of interest in southern India, including the Hindu and Buddhist caves of Ajanta and Ellora, the city of Hyderabad, former capital of the Muslim Nizam, reputedly one of the wealthiest men in the world, then South to the centres of Tamil culture. The tour returns through southern Karnataka via Bangalore, Mysore and the religious sites of Belur and Halebid.

8. **Bombay to Delhi, across central India** Bombay – Aurangabad – Udaipur – Jaipur – Agra – Khajuraho – Varanasi – Delhi. 14 days. Across the heart of central India, in 14 days it is possible to see some of the best examples of Buddhist, Hindu and Muslim art and architecture. Travelling by road or rail, you also see a range of India's varied scenery and agriculture, going first across the Deccan plateau, with its rich black lava soils, then over the northern edge of the Peninsula to the centre of the Ganga plains at Varanasi, possibly India's holiest site.

9. **Special wildlife tour** Bombay – Gir – Bombay – Bangalore – Mysore – Ranganathittoo – Bandipur – Mudumalai – Cochin – Periyar – Bombay; Bombay – Bhopal – Jabalpur – Kanha – Nagpur – Calcutta – Kaziranga – Delhi – Corbett – Bharatpur – Sariska – Delhi. 30 days. The suggested tour falls into two halves, the first being mainly the South, with a brief excursion to the lion sanctuary at Gir in Gujarat, the second the centre and north. If you have time to do the whole tour you have the chance to see nearly the full range of Indian wildlife habitats. Much of the route has to be covered by land.

Air travel

India has by far the largest route mileage. **Indian Airlines** (the nationalised carrier) and **Vayudoot** (a small private carrier which started operating in 1981) serve over 80 airports. In 1991 Indian Airlines has a fleet of Airbuses, Boeing 737s and Avro HS 748s. All major routes are now served by Airbuses or Boeings. Recent expansion has helped to relieve a chronic lack of space which made booking a nightmare. However, it is still necessary to book as early as possible. Computerised booking is now fully in place, and all the major airline offices are connected to the central system. However, the more you can get done before you leave home, the better, as buying tickets anywhere in South Asia can be a very time consuming and frustrating job. Vayudoot has undergone major restructuring with wide ranging reductions in its route mileage in 1991. Timetables are frequently altered. Vayudoot have 19-seater Dornier-228, 48-seater Avro HS-748 and 44-seater Fokker F 27 aircraft. The reliability of their timekeeping is even less than that of Indian Airlines. New airlines are just beginning to operate. Enquire at a local travel agent for details of new routes.

Air ticket pricing Ticket pricing can seem bewildering and frustrating. The rules are quite straightforward, though they don't always seem it in airline booking offices. In India and Pakistan internal flights are priced differently according to the form of payment. Tickets bought outside India for Indian Airlines flights are charged at what is called the "dollar rate". This is 40% higher than the Rupee rate, which is payable if tickets are paid for within India or Pakistan. However, the "Rupee rate" is only available if the tickets are paid for in foreign exchange (i.e. Travellers' cheques, cash or Rupees for which an encashment certificate can be shown). **Warning** This does not include credit cards. As the payment for these is collected from outside India, the tickets are deemed to have been bought abroad.

When foreigners buy internal air tickets within India, and with foreign exchange, they qualify for the Rupee rate plus a 10% discount, as they are not liable to pay the air travel tax that local people have to pay. It therefore pays to come prepared with adequate travellers cheques or cash to pay for any likely internal air flights within India, and you save 40% by waiting to buy until you arrive rather than buying in Europe, America or Australasia. All these matters will be taken care of by a good travel agent. These rules also apply in Pakistan.

Special fares Indian Airlines offers special fares for tourists which can be bought abroad. Trailfinders (in London) will confirm reservations if main ticket is with Air India or BA. If flying with other airlines, confirmation can take weeks. At the time of going to press they include: **Discover India** Unlimited travel within India for 21 days. US$ 400.
India Wonderfares Unlimited travel in ONE Indian region (N,S,E or W) for 7 days. US$ 200.

South India excursion 30% discount on US dollar fare on selected sectors in S. India.
Youth fare 25% of US$ fare for tourists between ages of 12 and 30.

Note that in view of the comments made above, the discounts on US$ rates are not always as generous as they look.

Delays As with all forms of travel in South Asia it is essential to be prepared for delays. For long journeys flying will undoubtedly save time – but often not as much as you may hope! Unfortunately the worst time for air travel, especially in northern India, is also climatically the best time of year to visit. The problems stem from the fact that Indian Airlines' northern routes all originate in New Delhi. From early Dec through to Feb, fog has become an increasingly common morning hazard at Delhi airport, sometimes delaying departures of all flights by several hours. These delays then affect the whole northern system for the rest of that day.

Air travel tips

● Waiting lists for Indian Airlines flights are often very long. It pays to arrive early at the airport and to be persistent in enquiring about your position in the queue.

● Indian Airlines have been insisting that all batteries are packed in luggage to be carried in the hold. No batteries are allowed in hand luggage or on your person. Check beforehand.

● If your flight is delayed Indian Airlines may issue a ticket for refreshments if you ask for it.

Rail

Indian Railways has the world's second largest network. For covering long distances, rail travel provides a good option. Computerised booking has brought some major changes to rail travel in India since 1988. In theory it is now very straightforward to get your own rail tickets from any sales window in any of the major cities, and an increasing number of minor ones. In practice there remain some complications. There are special quotas for tourists on many trains. Thus when tickets are not available over the general sales counter, it may still be possible to travel on a tourist quota ticket. Again, payment must be in foreign exchange. Although these schemes are designed to help tourists they do have disadvantages. In some booking offices in some cities, notably Calcutta, the booking process itself much slower in the tourist section than in the open booking hall. If you are buying tickets for a single journey, it may be advisable to check first whether places are available under the general quota.

There are the following classes of travel: *A/c 1st Cl* (Bed rolls provided); *A/c Sleeper* which are clean and comfortable (Bed rolls can be ordered); *A/c Chair Car* (reclining for long inter-city journeys and tickets include meals); *1st Cl non a/c* (cheaper than 2nd Cl a/c) can be hot and dusty during the warm weather; *2nd Cl (non a/c) 2-tier and 3-tier* provide exceptionally cheap travel. Remember that a/c compartments can get very cold, so have a thick jumper easily accessible. For security, carry a good lock to attach your luggage to the chains provided on trains with large carriages.

There are special high-speed Tourist Trains like the *Rajdhani Express* (Delhi-Calcutta, Delhi-Bombay), *Shatabdi Express* (Delhi to Agra, Gwalior, Jhansi and Bhopal) or the convenient *Taj Express* to Agra and *Pink City Express* to Jaipur. For a special experience of travelling in 'royal style' the *Palace on Wheels* gives visitors an opportunity to see some of the 'royal' cities in Rajasthan during the winter months. **See under Rajasthan for details, page 350.**

Tourists (foreigners and Indians resident abroad) may buy **Indrail Passes** which allow travel across the network, without route restrictions, and without incurring reservation fees, sleeper charges and supplementary fees. Reservations however must be made, which can be done well in advance when purchasing your Pass. They may be obtained from the tourist sections of railway booking offices at the major centres, for periods ranging from 7 to 90 days, but payment must be in

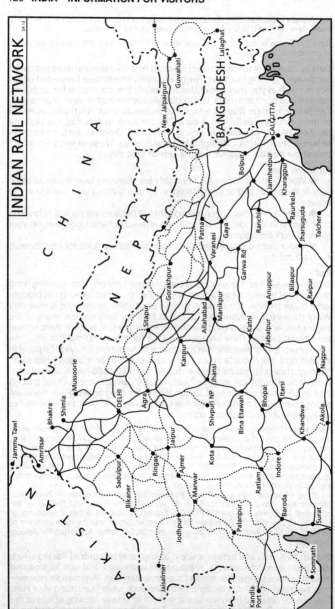

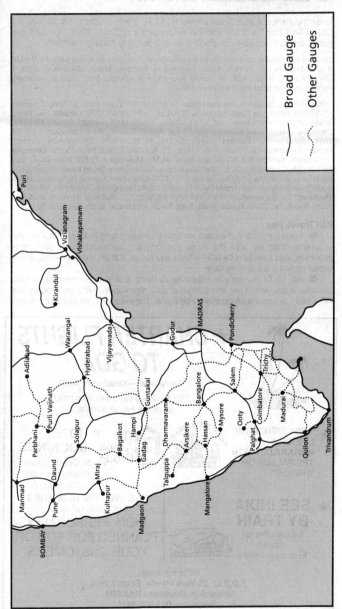

foreign currency. A Blue ticket allows 1st Cl a/c travel, a Green, A/c Sleeper, 1st Cl and A/c Chair Car travel and the Yellow card only 2nd Cl travel. Special 1 day passes are also available, for single journeys, but only if bought abroad.

Indrail passes can also conveniently be bought abroad. The agent for Indrail passes in the **UK** is SD Enterprises Ltd, 21 York House, Empire Way, Wembley, Middx HA9 0PA, England, T 081-903 3411. If you wish to choose your route in advance they make all necessary reservations, and offer much excellent advice.

Other international agents are: **Australia** Adventure World, 8th Floor, 37 York St, Sydney NSW 2000; Penthouse Travel, 5th Level, 72 Pitt St., Sydney NSW 2000. **Canada** Hari World Travels Inc., Royal York Hotel, 106 Front St West, Arcade Level, Toronto, Ontario M5J 1E3. **Denmark** Danish State Railways, DSW Travel Agency Division, Reventlowsgade – 10, DK 1651 Kobenhaven V. **Finland** Intia-Keskus Ltd., Yrjonkatu 8-10, 00120 Helsinki, Finland. **France** Le Monde de L'Inde et de L'Asie, 15 Rue Des Ecoles, Paris 75005. **Germany** Asra-Orient, Kaiserstrasse 50, D-6000 Frankfurt/M.I. **Malaysia** City East West Travels Sdn, BhD, No 28-A, Loreng Bunus, 6, Jalan Masjid India, Kuala Lumpur. **Hong Kong** Thomas Cook Travel Services (HK) Ltd, 6/F D'Aguilar Place, 1-13 D'Aguilar Street, Central, Hong Kong. **Japan** Japan Travel Bureau Inc., Overseas Travel Division, 1-6-4 Marunouchi, Chiyoda-ku, Tokyo-100. **Thailand** S.S. Travel Service, 10/12-13 Convent Road, S.S. Building, Bangkok. **USA** Hari World Travels Inc. 30 Rockefeller Plaza, Shop No 21, Mezzanine North, New York 10112.

Rail Travel Tips
● Trains are still the cheapest means of travelling long distances. In 2 tier A/c or above, they are also the most comfortable. Overnight trains save hotel expenses, and travelling by train allows you to use station retiring rooms, a very useful facility from time to time.

● A/c 1st Cl is nearly as expensive as flying, but is recommended for long journeys if you would like arrive fresh at your destination. A/c 2 tier Sleeper and A/c Chair Car provide an excellent alternative (these are very popular so book well in advance if you have an itinerary planned). 2nd Cl non a/c is not recommended unless you are on a shoe-string as it can be very uncomfortable and toilet facilities can be unpleasant.

● It is well worth buying a Blue or Green Indrail Pass if you plan to make more than one journey and wish to travel in air-conditioned comfort. Although there is little financial saving buying a Green Ticket, preferential bookings and freedom from restrictions makes for easier travel. Also consider single day passes, before setting off. There is little advantage however in buying a Yellow Ticket.

● Always allow time for booking and for making connections. Delays are common on all means of transport.

● If you do not have a reservation for a particular train, it may be possible to get one with your Indrail Pass by arriving about 3 hr early at the station or asking if the Superintendent on duty can help.

● A woman travelling alone overnight can ask to be put in a compartment with other women.

● Make sure you keep valuables close to you and away from windows. Lock your luggage securely.

● If you are travelling extensively, allow free time to recover.

● Always carry plenty of liquid. Bottled water and/or juice and other soft drinks are the safest options. Tea and coffee are also widely available. Although you can order meals in 1st class and 2nd class a/c, a supply of fruit and biscuits can be useful.

● Take a good supply of toilet paper.

Road

Vehicles drive on the left – in theory. India has a very extensive road network, and roads offer the only way of reaching many sites of great interest. Routes around the major cities are usually crowded with lorry traffic, and the main roads are often poor and slow in comparison with those in Europe or the United States. There are no motorways, and many main roads are single track. Many District roads are very quiet, and although they are not fast they can be an excellent way of seeing the country and village life. Even near the big cities traffic is very mixed.

Bus Very few villages, even in the remotest areas, are now more than 2 or 3 km from a bus stop. Buses fall into 3 categories. Special tourist *"luxury" coaches* can be hired, either for day trips or for longer journeys. They may be airconditioned. It is increasingly common for groups to use hired buses for at least some sections of the tour. However, apart from the very best buses they are often not very comfortable for really long journeys.

Express buses, are run both by private companies and state enterprises, on long distance routes. These are often called "video coaches", and frequently run overnight. The video coach can be an appalling experience, unless you appreciate very loud film music blasting through the night. However, they are often the quickest way of covering medium to long distances. Take ear plugs.

Local buses. These can be very crowded and quite slow. However, on many routes they can be a friendly and easy way of getting about, especially for quite short distances. Even where signboards are not in English it is usually possible to find someone who will give you directions.

Mini buses Many towns have minibus services. These pick up and drop passengers on request. Often very crowded, and with restricted headroom, they are the fastest way of getting about many of the larger towns.

Bus travel tips

● Avoid the back half of the bus if possible, as the ride is often very bumpy.

● Note that many towns have different bus stations for different destinations.

Car At the end of 1989 India opened its doors to the first official self-drive hire. It remains a service that is in its infancy. It is possible to hire a car with a driver (which in India is less expensive than hiring it without) very widely, and tours can be arranged entirely to suit individual requirements. However, Indian roads are often in poor condition and driving conditions are extremely slow by European and American standards. Furthermore standards of comfort are low in the most widely used hire car, the Hindustan Ambassador. Drivers usually have only a limited amount of English. The cost of a non-airconditioned Ambassador for a week is approximately Rs 6000 (i.e. just over £220). They can be hired either through the ITDC or through private companies, but the ITDC fleet of cars is generally inferior to those available privately. It is also possible to hire airconditioned Indian cars and there is a limited number of imported cars such as Mercedes available for hire. The price of the top of the range cars is approximately three times that of the Ambassador. **Note** Drivers stay in the car overnight. They are responsible for all their expenses (including petrol). A tip of up Rs 40 per day is perfectly acceptable.

It can be best to plan using hire cars on a daily basis, driving out from major centres, rather than for extended tours. However, longer tours do provide opportunities for travelling off the beaten track, and give unrivalled opportunities for seeing something of India's great variety of villages and small towns. That freedom can more than compensate for the other inconveniences of hired cars.

The situation is changing rapidly, and apart from local car hire firms, international companies such as Hertz have begun operating much more widely than in Delhi alone, and that may transform the hiring options.

Car travel tips

● If you drive yourself it is essential to take great care. Pedestrians, cattle and a wide range of other animals roam at will. This can be particularly dangerous when driving after dark especially as even other vehicles often carry no lights. Accidents often produce large and angry crowds very quickly. It is best to leave the scene of the accident and report it to the police as quickly as possible thereafter.

● Ensure that you have adequate food and drink, and a basic tool set, in the car.

● An umbrella can be very useful for shade as well as rain.

● The Automobile Association offers a range of services to members. **Delhi** AA of Upper India Lilaram Building, 14F Connaught Place, New Delhi; **Bombay** Western India AA, Lalji Narainji Memorial Building, 76, Vir Nariman Rd, Bombay; **Calcutta** AA of Eastern India, 13 Promothesh Barua Sarani, Calcutta; AA of Southern India, 187 Anna Salai, Madras; **UP** AA, 32A, Mahatma Gandhi Marg, Allahabad.

Taxis Yellow-top taxis in cities and large towns are metred, although tariffs change frequently. These changes are shown on a fare chart which should be read in conjunction with the meter reading. Increased night time rates apply in some cities, and a surcharge may be levied for luggage. In some cities taxis refuse to use the metre. Official advice is to call the police. This also may not work, but it is worth trying. Other taxis and auto-rickshaws do not always have a metre so a fare should be negotiated before starting the journey. You always need to negotiate with drivers of cycle rickshaws and *tongas**.

Tips

● Always insist on the taxi metre being 'flagged' in your presence. Do not assume that the price asked by an unmetred vehicle driver is the fair rate, so try to bargain down to a reasonable fare by first asking at the hotel desk for a guide price, if you have not already undertaken a similar journey before.

● At stations and airports it is often possible to share taxis to a central point. It is worth looking for fellow passengers who may be travelling in your direction.

MONEY

Currency Indian currency is the Rupee. New notes are printed in denominations of Rs 1000, 100, 50, 20, 10, 5, 2, though some Rs 1 notes are still in circulation. The Rupee is divided into 100 Paise. Coins are minted in denominations of Rs 2, 1, 50, 25, 20, 10 and 5 Paise. Periodically coins are in short supply, though currently they seem to be widely available. It can be useful to keep a supply of change.

Money changing When changing money anywhere in India it is important to retain the **encashment certificate**. This gives proof of exchange through an authorized dealer. It allows you to change Indian Rupees back to your own currency on leaving India (you are not allowed to take any Rupees out of India). It also enables you to use Rupees to pay hotel and other bills for which payment in foreign exchange is compulsory.

If you are staying in a major hotel you will be able to change money there 24 hours a day. However, if you want cash on arrival it is best to get it at the airport bank. Many international flights arrive during night hours, and it is generally far easier and less time consuming to change money at the airport than at banks in the city. Banks often give a substantially better rate of exchange than hotels.

Black market The currency black market in India was severely curtailed by the Indian Government's decision to partially float the Rupee. None the less the laws prohibiting the export of Rupees do create a demand for exchangeable foreign currency, and from time to time a premium may be offered for hard currencies by street corner dealers in the big cities. In 1991 such premiums in most places were small. **Warning** Changing money through unauthorised dealers is illegal and may be risky.

Travellers cheques Most travellers cheques are accepted without difficulty, but some organisations, like Indian Airlines, only accept travellers cheques from the biggest companies. They nearly always have to be exchanged in banks or hotels, and can only very rarely be used directly for payment. Identification documents, usually a passport, need to be shown. Except in hotels, encashing travellers cheques nearly always takes up to half an hour and may take longer, so it is worth taking larger denomination travellers cheques and changing enough money to last for some days. Hotels will normally only cash travellers for resident guests, but the rate is often poorer than in banks. **Note** If you are travelling to remote areas it can be worth buying Indian Rupee travellers cheques from a major bank. These are more widely accepted than foreign exchange travellers cheques.

Credit cards Major credit cards are increasingly widely acceptable in the major centres, though in smaller cities and towns it is still rare to be able to pay by credit card. Payment by credit card can be significantly more expensive than payment by cash. However shopping by credit card for items such as handicrafts, clothing, and carpets from larger dealers, does not mean that you have to accept the first price asked. Bargaining is still expected and essential. American Express cardholders can use their cards to obtain either cash or travellers cheques in the major cities. Diners, Master Card and Visa are widely used.

Cost of Living Indian costs of living remain well below those in the industrialised world. Most food, accommodation, and public transport, especially rail and bus, are exceptionally cheap. Even the most expensive hotels and restaurants in the major cities are much less expensive than their counterparts in Europe, Japan or the United States. There is a widening range of moderately priced but clean hotels and restaurants outside the big cities, making it possible to get a great deal for your money.

Tipping and bargaining In the largest hotels a tip of Rs 5 per piece of luggage carried would be appropriate. In restaurants 10% is regarded as extremely generous. In most places 5% or rounding off with small change is completely acceptable, including taxis. Indians do not tip taxi drivers. Tour companies sometimes make recommendations for 'suitable tips' for coach drivers and guides.

Some of the figures may seem modest by non-Indian standards but are very inflated if compared with normal Indian earnings. Some companies currently recommend a tip of Rs 50 per day for drivers and guides. This can safely be regarded as generous, though some will try hard to persuade you to give more.

When shopping outside Government emporia and the biggest hotels, expect to bargain hard.

Liquor Permits   Periodically some Indian states have tried to enforce prohibition. Only Gujarat is now a "dry"state, but in mid 1991 other states were talking of re-imposing prohibition, and the situation can change. Permits are obtainable for foreigners.

Shopping and best buys

If your time or travelling are limited, you can get excellent examples of the handicrafts of different states from the government handicrafts emporia in the major cities. These are listed under the shopping sections. As a general rule the official emporiums are the safest bet for guaranteed quality at reasonable prices. There is no bargaining. In private shops and markets bargaining is normally essential and you can get excellent material at bargain prices.

Some shops offer to pack and post your purchases. Many small private shops cannot be trusted. Unless you have a specific recommendation from a person you know well, only make such arrangements in Government emporia.

Note   See departure regulations above for items that are prohibited for export.

OTHER ESSENTIAL INFORMATION

Official time   GMT + 5 hr 30 min.

Weights and measures   India now uses the metric system for weights and measures. It has come into universal use in the cities. In remote rural areas local measures are sometimes used. The more common are listed in the glossary at the end of the Handbook, where a conversion table is also provided.

Postal services

This is reliable and Poste Restante is available in most towns at the GPO. Ask for mail to be addressed to you with you surname in capitals and underlined. When asking for mail at Poste Restante check under surname as well as Christian name. Airmail service to Europe, Africa and Australia takes at least a week and a little longer for the Americas.

Telephone and telegraph services

International Direct Dialling is available 24 hr from Telegraph Offices and major hotels in larger cities. Most calls within India can be dialled direct with a few exceptions which have to be connected by the operator. Collect calls can also be made from telegraph offices. However, the queue for calls connected by the operator is often very long. Telephone calls from hotels are usually more expensive. Check before calling.

Business hours Banks 1000-1400, Mon-Fri; 1000-1230, Sat. Top hotels sometimes have 24 hr service. **Post Offices** 1000-1700, Mon-Fri; Sat mornings. **Government offices** 0930-1700, Mon-Fri; 0930-1300, Sat (some open on alternate Sat only). **Shops** 0930-1800, Mon-Sat. Bazaars keep longer hours. **Note** There are regional variations.

Electricity   220-240 volts AC. Some top hotels have transformers to enable visitors to use their appliances. There may be pronounced variations in the voltage, and power cuts are common. Socket sizes vary so you are advised to take a universal adaptor (available at airports).

Media

Broadcasting   *Doordarshan* is the official broadcasting agency. Government controlled, its TV and radio broadcasts continue to reflect the Government interest. Hotels often have TV in the rooms, the top hotels showing live Indian TV and video films. News is broadcast in English during the evening. Check the local paper for the timing.

The press India has a large English language press. National English language newspapers are printed in all the major cities. The best known are the The Hindu, The Hindustan Times, The Independent, The Indian Express, The Times of India, and The Statesman. The Indian Express has stood out as being consistently critical of the Congress Party and Government. All these papers have extensive analysis and discussion of contemporary Indian and international issues. There is a wide range of weekly and fortnightly magazines, available across the country. Some of the most widely read are The Illustrated Weekly (generally an entertainment weekly, with some political and social content), Sunday, India Today and Frontline, all of which are current affairs journals on the model of Time or Newsweek. In all the major cities it is possible to buy international newspapers. These are often stocked by bookshops in the top hotels, and occasionally by booksellers elsewhere. There is a flourishing local press.

Maps The Bartholomew 1:4 m map sheet South Asia is the most authoritative, detailed and easy to use map available. It can be bought worldwide, or from John Bartholomew & Son Ltd., 12 Duncan Street, Edinburgh EH9 1TA, Scotland. Nelles' regional maps of S. Asia at the scale of 1:1.5 m, published by Nelles Verlag BmbH, D 8000 Munchen 45, Germany offer generally good and extremely clear route maps. Though they are not always entirely reliable, they are the best maps of their kind. State maps and town plans are published by the TT Company , PO Box 21, 328 GST Rd Chromepet Madras 600044. These are constantly being updated and improved and are the best available. For the larger cities they provide the most compact yet clear map sheets (generally 50 mm x 75 mm format).

The US Army Series (AMS) U502 at the scale of 1:250,000 are available from selected booksellers in the United States and Europe. Showing contours at 250 or 500 feet, the series was completed before 1960, so some features, notably roads, are out of date. However, they provide good topographic information. Available from: Michael Chessler Books, PO Box 2436, Evergreen, CO 80439, USA; Stanfords International Map Centre, 12-14 Long Acre, London WC2E 9LP; Geo Buch Verlag, Rosenthal 6, D-8000 Munchen 2, Germany; Geo Center GmbH, Honigwiessenstrasse 25, Postfach 80 08 30, D-7000 Stuttgart 80, Germany.

The Survey of India publishes large scale 1:10,000 town plans of approximately 30 cities. These detailed plans are the only surveyed town maps in India and are therefore the most reliable, though some are 20 years old. The Survey of India also has topographic maps at the scale of 1:50,000, but these are only available for some areas. It is illegal to sell maps of this scale which show any restricted area. That includes all areas within 80 km of the coast. The export of maps from India is prohibited.

Hints on social behaviour Use your right hand for giving, taking, eating or shaking hands as the left is considered to be unclean. Women do not shake hands with men as this form of contact is not traditionally acceptable between acquaintances. Do not photograph women without permission.

The greeting when meeting or parting used universally among the Hindus across India is the palms joined together as in prayer, sometimes accompanied with the word *Namaste* (N and W) *Namoshkar* (E) and *Vanakkam* (S), translated as 'I salute all divine qualities in you.' "Thank you" is often expressed by a smile and occasionally with somewhat formal *Dhannyabad* or *Shukriya* in the N and W and *Dhonnyobad* in the E and *nandri* in the S.

Accommodation
The range on offer starts with luxury hotels, often owned by a well-known national chain such as the Taj, Oberoi or Welcome Group, and occasionally by a multi-national group. In Rajasthan, old maharajas' palaces have been privately converted into comfortable, unusual hotels. Hotels in beach resorts and

hill-stations, because of their location and special appeal, often deviate from the description of the different categories given below. The Indian Tourism Development Corporation (ITDC) with the 'Ashoka' chain, and State Tourism Development Corporations, also run a number of hotels throughout the country which are often located in places of special interest. These are quite often reasonably priced, though the standard of restaurant service may be somewhat limited in the modest ones. At the other end of the scale are Youth Hostels, YMCAs, YWCAs and Guest Houses with the occasional possibility of camping.

Railway Retiring rooms are available at many stations for passengers in transit for a short stay only. The few inexpensive a/c rooms are good value although you will have to be prepared for noise. Houseboats in Kashmir on the Dal and Nagin lakes are 2 and 3-bedroomed wooden 'hotels', afloat with chintz upholstery and modern conveniences in the deluxe class. Government Rest Houses, *Dak Bungalows* and Circuit Houses offer another alternative in India, as well as in Pakistan, Sri Lanka and Bangladesh. These are usually only available to visitors when not required by government officials who have priority (even if you make a provisional reservation).

Price categories in the Handbook Hotels have been graded from A down to F (with a few exceptional ALs) and the price for each category is a guide to what you would pay for the best room (double) remembering that taxes vary widely from state to state and can sometimes add considerably to the basic price: see surcharges below. **Note** Hotels in categories AL to B all have the main facilities. They are not listed separately for each hotel.

AL Rs 1,750+. In the regional capitals there are luxury hotels which are comparable to the best anywhere in the world.
A Rs 1,200+ International class. Central a/c, rooms with attached baths, telephone and TV with video channel, a business centre, multicuisine restaurants, bar, and all the usual facilities including 24 hr room service, shopping arcade, exchange, laundry, travel counter, swimming pool and often other sports such as tennis and squash. Accept credit cards. They often have hairdresser, beauty parlour and a health club.
B Rs 800-1,200 Most of the facilities of **A** but perhaps not business centre, swimming pool and sports and lacking the feeling of luxury.
C Rs 400-800. A/c rooms. Restaurant, rooms with attached baths and TV, and most have a shopping arcade, exchange, travel counter and accept credit cards. If a hotel has central a/c or does not accept credit cards this is mentioned.
D Rs 200-400. Reasonably comfortable, probably with some a/c rooms, attached baths and a restaurant.
E Rs 75-200. Simple. Usually shared bath. May have a dining room.
F Rs 75. Very basic.

Note Apart from the AL and A categories, 'baths' do not necessarily refer to bathrooms with western bathtubs. Other hotels may provide a bathroom with a toilet, basin and a shower. In the lower priced hotels and outside large towns, a bucket and tap may replace the shower, and an Indian 'squat' toilet instead of a western WC. During the cold weather and in hill stations, hot water will be available at certain times during the day.

Owing to the erratic electricity supply in some cities, larger hotels have been forced to have their own generators, but if you stay in a modest establishment you may find yourself without electricity from time to time. Water supply too can be a problem during the dry season in some parts of the country, although you will not be affected in the top hotels.

Prices away from large cities tend to be lower for the comparable standard of hotel and you will notice that, particularly in S India, you will often find a comfortable hotel in the D category and certainly clean, adequate rooms in the E. Restaurants in modest (D,E,F) hotels in certain parts of the country, especially in the S and W, may only offer vegetarian food.

Off season rates Large reductions are made by hotels in all categories during the offseason in many resort centres. Always ask if a discount is available.

Warning Many visitors complain of incorrect hotel bills, even in the most expensive hotels. The problem particularly afflicts visitors who are part of groups, when last minute extras sometimes appear mysteriously on some guests' bills. Check the evening before departure, and keep all receipts. It is essential to check carefully again when paying your bill.

Surcharges Hotels in the 'luxury' category charge an extra 20% *expenditure tax* on accommodation and meals. However, visitors paying with foreign exchange (cash, credit cards or travellers' cheques) are exempt. This sum often appears on the bill automatically. Check that it has also been removed. However, *sales tax* and *luxury tax* are applicable, though they vary from state to state.

Camping For information contact: **YMCA** The National General Secretary, National Council of YMCAs of India, PB No 14, Massey Hall, Jai Singh Rd, New Delhi 1.

Boy Scouts Association The General Secretary for All India, Boy Scouts Association, 7 Jangpura-B, Mathura Rd, New Delhi 14. The National Secretary, Bharat Scouts and Guides, 16 Ring Rd, Indraprastha Estate, New Delhi 1.

Youth hostels The Department of Tourism runs 16 hostels, each with about 40 beds, usually organised into dormitory accommodation. Details are included in the appropriate sections.

Noise in cities is difficult to avoid, so if you are in a non a/c room, be prepared for it. People wake up early in India, and temple and bazaar loudspeakers often play very loud music!

Security See note in S Asia Introduction. Do not leave valuables and documents in your room.

Clothing Light cotton clothes are useful almost anywhere in India at any time of year. It is a good idea to have some very lightweight long sleeve cottons and trousers for evenings, preferably light in colour, as they also give some protection against mosquitoes. Between Dec-Feb it can be cool at night even on the plains in N and E India, and at altitudes above 1,500 m right across India some woollens are essential. Dress is rarely formal. In the large cities shortsleeve shirts and ties are often worn for business. For travelling loose clothes are most comfortable.

Food and drink Indian food is now so widely available across the world that it may need little introduction. Yet most visitors are surprised – and often delighted – at the enormous variety of delicious food, some bearing little relation to the various 'curries' available outside India. You find just as much variety in dishes and presentation crossing India as you would on an equivalent journey across Europe. Furthermore, on top of the variety of main meals is a remarkable range of delicious savoury snacks (for example, *chaat* in N India) and sweets.

Given the limited basic ingredients, the diversity is surprising. Rice is the almost universal basis of meals in the South and East, while wheat is more common in the North. But accompanying these essential grains is a huge variety of dishes, many of them spiced, but not always with the kind of hot spices usually associated with Indian food abroad. Chilli, it should be remembered, was only introduced to India by the Portuguese, adding just one more ingredient to the already richly flavoured and spiced diet. Whole or ground, spices are essential to giving each region its distinctive combination of flavours. The cooking medium is generally oil. Clarified butter – the ubiquitous *ghee* – is now both too expensive and too rich in fat to be as lavishly used as it once was, but mustard oil in the North and East, sesame in the South and East, and coconut oil in the West are widely used substitutes.

If it is possible to talk of a typical meal it is the '*thali*'. Served on a banana leaf or metal tray, several preparations, placed in small bowls, surround the central serving of wholewheat puris and rice. In a private home you might well find that the dishes were placed in large bowls on the table and you would serve yourself to fill the small dishes which would surround your plate. Fish, mutton or chicken are popular non-vegetarian dishes. Vegetable dishes depend on seasonal availability, but there would always be *dal* (lentils) and usually some kind of yoghurt. In the North this is often served as a marinade for a salad vegetable such as cucumber. In the S it is usually served plain. It is widely regarded as offering an essentially bland cooling dish to accompany any highly spiced food, and as an excellent aid to digestion. Surrounding the thali on the banana leaf or tray would be placed a variety of sweet and hot pickles – mango and lime are two of the most popular, but there are many others. These can be exceptionally hot, and are designed to be taken in minute quantities alongside the main dishes.

Vegetarians are particularly well provided for in India, as some groups, notably the Brahmins in the South for example, are strictly vegetarian. South Indian Brahmin food is a wholly distinctive diet. Tamarind and coconut provide distinctive S Indian ingredients, but clear peppery soups such as *rasam* add a unique touch. Boiled rice provides the basis of the main meal in South India, with several vegetable dishes (not cooked with hot spices), *sambhar*, another soup-like preparation but much thicker than rasam, and coconut chutney and pickles as side dishes.

The South is also particularly known for three of its snacks – *dosai*, *idli* and *vadai*. North Indians sometimes talk of Southerners disparagingly as "idli-dosai" after their best known dishes, but their popularity has swept the country. The dosai is a pancake made of a mixture of fermented rice and lentil flour, and may be served with a savoury filling (*masala dosai*) or without (*ravai* or *plain dosai*). Idlis are steamed rice cakes, a bland breakfast food given flavour by its spiced accompaniment, while vadai are deep fried.

North Indian cooking is often called *Mughlai*, hinting at the Muslim influence on North Indian diet over the last six centuries. Cream and ghee are favourite cooking mediums, and spices, herbs, nuts and fruit are all added ingredients to dishes which usually have meat as the main focus of the meal. Several different kinds of kebab, meat balls (*kofta*) and minced meat preparations (*keema*) are served alongside *biriyani* (fried rice, saffron, vegetables and marinated lamb) and *pulao*, similar to biriyani but usually served as a vegetarian dish. *Tandoori* dishes, marinated meat cooked in a special earthen oven, come from the far North West, but are widely popular.

East India has long specialised in fish. River fish from the Ganga and freshwater fish from ponds and streams are favourite, *hilsa* and *bekti* being the best known. Bekti is often served as fried fish, while hilsa tends to be the centrepiece of a curried stew, though the smoked hilsa is a real delicacy – if exceptionally bony. However, if the Indian regions achieve national fame for a particular contribution to the nation's diet, Bengal's is that of its sweets. *Sandesh* and *rasgollah* are made from curds (though most people would never guess), steeped in syrup. In place of plain yoghurt, which is not part of the Bengali diet, there is the exceptional *mishti doi*, a sweet yoghurt.

The West also has its distinctive cuisine. Maharashtrian vegetarian cooking, which uses both wheat and rice, specialises in sprouted lentils, relatively lightly spiced, but with a number of sweet and sour dishes. The Parsis of Bombay and the West coast have introduced *dhansak*, chicken or lamb cooked with lentils. To India's seemingly never ending array of sweets the West has contributed *gulab jamun* and *barfi*, and *jelabis*, *laddus* and *halvas*.

One of the best known features of Indian diets right across the country is the paan with which all main meals would be expected to end. The betel leaf is the vehicle for a succession of pastes and spices, the making of which is regarded as an art. Areca nuts, cardomom, cloves, lime for the digestion, tobacco and a number of other ingredients will go into the bright green leaf, to be carefully folded and then chewed, seemingly endlessly.

It is still very exceptional for Indians to accompany meals with alcohol, water being on hand but not usually drunk until the end of the meal.

Fruit India has many delicious tropical and semi tropical fruit. Some are highly seasonal – mangos in the hot season, for example, while others are available throughout the year, such as bananas. Regional specialties are described in the appropriate sections of the Handbook.

Drink Many states have Dry days. Prohibition also operates in some states, details of which are available from the Indian Mission/ Tourist Office abroad. When applying for your visa you can ask for an All India Liquor Permit which will enable you to buy a certain specified quantity of alcoholic drinks in a specified time provided the State laws allow the use of the Liquor Permit. You can also get the Permit from any Govt of India Tourist Office in Bombay, Calcutta, Delhi or Madras on arrival.

Note Taxes are added to the listed price and can be high in some states especially if there is music (whether live or otherwise).

Visiting religious sites Many Hindu temples are now open to non Hindus. In all temples and mosques visitors should observe customary courtesy especially in clothing. Shoes must always be removed outside (take thick socks for protection when walking on areas exposed to the sun). In Jain temples all leather goods must be left outside. Heads should be covered before entering Sikh gurdwaras.

Mosques may be closed to non-Muslims shortly before prayers. Women should be covered from head to ankle when entering a mosque. Special rules apply to visiting Buddhist shrines, detailed under Nepal – Information for Visitors, **page 1200**.

Visiting Wildlife Parks The best time to visit is Oct-Mar when it is cool (except Dachigam, which is best in summer), although it is easier to see wildlife from Mar-Jun when the heat dries the vegetation and exposes the animals. The Parks and Sanctuaries are accessible by car and there is usually simple accommodation available in the park or nearby.

Visits to most wildlife parks are only possible in the company of a forest ranger. Booking in advance is normally essential, and it may also be necessary to hire a jeep or other transport provided with a Ranger, who has an intimate knowledge of the forest and of animal habits and can help with spotting them more easily. In some cases, specified in the appropriate places in the Handbook, it is possible to visit parks for just a day, and to go on elephant back into the forest. A few rules to observe are: wear clothes that blend with the colours in the forest. Do not wear strong perfume or smoke, since animals have a very keen sense of smell. Never approach a potentially dangerous animal on foot.

Photography Warning Photography is not permitted at airports, military installations or of bridges and in 'sensitive' tribal areas. Special permits are needed from the Archaeological Survey of India for photographing monuments with the use of tripods and artificial lights.

Wildlife Sanctuaries individually levy fees for photography, depending on the type of equipment, which can vary between sanctuaries. Many have hides, usually near water-holes. Lenses with a focal length of less than 300 mm are not useful; it is best to have 600-1,200mm.

Best time for a visit Across much of India the most comfortable time to visit is the winter, from Nov-Mar. The Handbook gives temperatures and rainfall details for all regions and some cities, indicating the best times to visit.

NATIONAL HOLIDAYS AND FESTIVALS

There are numerous religious festivals and special celebrations throughout the country which may vary from state to state – only a few count as full public holidays. **26 Jan** Republic Day. **15 August** Independence Day. **2 October** Mahatma Gandhi's Birthday. **25 December**

Christmas Day.
Religious and folk festivals fall on different dates each year, depending on the lunar calendar, so check with the Tourist Office. The major religious festivals are detailed under New Delhi. Certain festivals are associated with a particular state or town, others are celebrated throughout the country. Some are listed below, while others appear under the particular state or town.

Jan *Desert Festival* – Jaisalmer, Rajasthan. *International Kite Festival* – Ahmadabad, Gujarat. *Elephant March* – Kerala. *Ganga Sagar Mela*- West Bengal. 26 *Republic Day Parade* -New Delhi.

Feb *Surajkund Crafts Mela* – Surajkund, Haryana. *Nagaur Camel Fair* – Nagaur, Rajasthan. *International Yoga Festival*- Rishikesh, UP. *Elephanta Festival* – Elephanta, Rajasthan. *Konarak Festival* – Konarak, Orissa. Feb/Mar *Sivaratri*.

Mar *Ellora Festival of Classical Dance and Music* – Ellora Caves, Maharashtra. *Khajuraho Dance Festival* – Khajuraho, MP. *Holi*. Gangaur – Jaipur, Rajasthan.

Apr *Mahavir Jayanti. Baisakhi* – N India. *Carnival* – Goa. Apr/May *Sikkim Flower Festival* – Gangtok, Sikkim. *Bihu* – Assam. *International Spice Festival* – Cochin, Kerala.

May *Buddha Purnima* – N India. *Pooram* – Kerala.

Jun/Jul *Rath Yatra* – Puri, Orissa.

Jul *Hemis Festival* – Leh, Ladakh. *Teej* – Jaipur, Rajasthan. *International Mango Festival* – Saharanpur, UP.

Aug *Ganesh Chaturthi. Rakhi. Tarnetar Mela* – Gujarat.

Sep *Onam* – Kerala.

Oct/Nov *Pushkar Fair* – Ajmer, Rajasthan.

Nov *Sonepur Fair* – Sonepur, Bihar.

Dec *Shekhavati Festival* – Shekhavati, Rajasthan. *Hampi-Vijaynagar Festival* – Karnataka.

SPECIAL INTEREST HOLIDAYS

Opportunities are now being developed to visit the country with a specific interest or sport in mind.

Adventure holidays Trekking is becoming increasingly popular in the Himalayas, many trails falling within 'Inner Line' areas for which permits are required. Details of Indian treks appear under Uttar Pradesh, Himachal Pradesh, Kashmir, Ladakh, Darjiling and Sikkim. Practical advice is given in the Nepal section, **see page 1302**.

Two recommended trekking companies are: *Arventures Adventure Holidays* (P) Ltd, Post Bag 7, Dehra Dun, 248001, India T 29172; *Tiger Mountain Pvt Ltd* 1/1 Rani Jhansi Rd, New Delhi 110055, New Delhi T 522004.

Other **sports** are now being offered including River Running, White-water rafting, Fishing, Skiing, Heli-skiing, Water Sports (wind surfing, yachting, scuba diving etc) and camel and horse safaris. Ask for details at the Tourist Office.

Golf India has a number of beautiful and challenging golf courses. Mountain courses, as at Gulmarg in Kashmir or Ootacamund in Tamil Nadu, offer very attractive scenery and are well laid out, but there are long established clubs in all the major cities. Details are given in the regional sections.

Buddhist sites When he entered the state of Parinirvana, the Buddha named 4 places that a devout believer should visit – Lumbini grove in Nepal, his birthplace, Bodhgaya the place of Enlightenment, the Deer Park in Sarnath where he pronounced the Wheel of Law and Kushinagar where he entered the state of Parinirvana. There are 4 other sacred places of pilgrimage where the Buddha performed miracles – Sravasti, Sankasya, Rajagriha and Vaisali. The pilgrimage or *Dhammayatra* of old, undertaken by Emperor Asoka in the 3rd century BC, has been extended today to include great centres of Buddhist art and sculpture – Sanchi, Bharaut, Amaravati, Nagarjunakonda, Ajanta and Ellora, Karla and Bhaja.

NORTH INDIA

North India forms the largest region in India. From the high peaks of the Himalaya it embraces the great flat plains of the Ganga valley and the upland plateaus of the northern Peninsula. This enormously diverse landscape is home to an equally wide range of peoples, from those of Mongolian and Tibetan stock in Leh and Ladakh to some of the earliest of India's settlers, the tribal peoples in Madhya Pradesh. At the same time it has what is rapidly becoming the country's fastest growing and most important metropolitan city, Delhi. Delhi has become the starting point for most travellers. Centrally located to the northern region and well connected with all parts of the country, it has developed the style and facilities of a modern and sophisticated capital. However, many of its densely populated quarters still show all the signs of urban poverty and deprivation which successive governments have been unable to remove.

GEOGRAPHY

North India has two Union territories – Delhi and Chandigarh – and seven states: Haryana, Punjab, Uttar Pradesh, Rajasthan, Madhya Pradesh, Jammu & Kashmir and Himachal Pradesh. Together they cover 1,452,602 sq km, 44% of the country's land area. The two Union Territories are small (Delhi – 1,488 sq km,

Chandigarh 114 sq km) and the states fall into 2 categories. The large states are Madhya Pradesh (443,000 sq km), Rajasthan (342,000 sq km), Uttar Pradesh (294,000 sq km) and Jammu & Kashmir (222,000 sq km). In all-India ranking they are the largest, second, fourth and sixth respectively. The smaller states are all more or less the same size – Haryana (44,000 sq km), Punjab (50,000 sq km) and Himachal Pradesh (56,000 sq km).

In 1981 Delhi's population was just over 6 million. Today it is over 8 million. Uttar Pradesh is the most populous state with 140 million, 16% of the nation's total. Throughout most of the state the population density is high. The populations of Haryana (13 million) and Punjab (17 million) are, of course smaller but because of their smaller size the population densities are similar. These 3 states, along with Delhi and Chandigarh, form a heavily populated belt stretching from the NW to SE. This corresponds to the distribution of fertile alluvial soils on the Gangetic plain, along the Yamuna and the Punjab river system. This pattern is continued in the neighbouring states of Bihar and West Bengal in Eastern India.

Approximately 75% of the population of the region lives in rural areas and most people depend on agriculture for a livelihood. The mountain regions of Jammu & Kashmir, Himachal Pradesh and the hill region of Uttar Pradesh are sparsely populated, but the cultivated area is relatively limited because of the mountainous terrain and its altitude. In terms of the land available for agriculture the densities are as high as those on the plains.

Rajasthan and Madhya Pradesh are both large in area and have medium sized populations – 34 million and 52 million. Rajasthan, however, has extensive deserts and semi-arid regions which produce low agricultural returns. Madhya Pradesh is still in the fortunate position of having extensive forests. Both, then have large areas with very few people, meaning that the majority of their populations are concentrated into specific areas. The densities here are reasonably high. So, unless you go trekking in the remoter regions of the Himalaya, there will always be people about.

The Himalayas Nearly all the Indian Himalaya lies in the northern region. Himachal Pradesh and Jammu & Kashmir are almost wholly Himalayan, and in Uttar Pradesh the Himalayan region of Garhwal and Kumaon make up about a quarter of the state. The mountain region is magnificent, containing numerous strikingly beautiful and contrasting sub-regions. The Himalaya (Abode of Snow) stretches from the disputed border with Pakistan in Kashmir to the Western border of Nepal. To the N is Tibet. Over 1,000 km long, it varies in width from 160 km in Garhwal and Kumaon to 400 km in Kashmir and Ladakh. In places the mountains tower to almost 8,000 m.

The Himalaya itself forms the backbone of the mountain region. To the S, bordering the plains are the **Siwaliks**, a range of foothills, sometimes separated from the **Lesser Himalaya** by valleys (duns), e.g Dehra Dun. In the Kashmir section there is also the **Pir Panjal** range, which rises to nearly 5,000 m in places. This forms the southern wall to the **Vale of Kashmir**. There are other lesser ranges, such as the **Zanskar** and **Ladakh** ranges, both reaching 6,000 m. These two are often referred to as the **Trans-Himalaya,** as the area is transitional between the Himalaya proper and the Tibetan plateau. Because of the influence of the High Himalaya over rainfall distribution, the Ladakh region is arid and receives only 100 mm of rain per year, which makes agriculture difficult. This rain deficit region extends into Lahul and Spiti in Himachal Pradesh.

The mountains to the south of the **Great Himalayan axis** receive enough rain to allow 2 crops a year to be grown up to an altitude of approximately 3,000 m. The N presents a bleak contrast, alpine desert with a stark, stony beauty. Only one hardy crop of wheat or barley can be grown each year. Irrigation is difficult because of the wildly fluctuating river levels and the deep gorges many of them have cut. The **Indus River** runs through Ladakh before entering Baltistan in Pakistan and turning S towards the plains in Gilgit. Within Kashmir there is immense diversity. **Ladakh** is strongly Buddhist in character, a religion of asceticism that seems at home in this austere environment. The **Vale of Kashmir** is well wooded, lush, moist and predominantly Muslim. There are a number of large lakes, of which Lake Dal is the most famous. If there is a Switzerland of Asia, this is it. Further S and bordering the plains is Jammu, different again in religious character. The Dogras who once governed Kashmir and Ladakh and also attempted to conquer Tibet are Hindu and have more affinities with the Punjab than the regions to the N.

Himachal Pradesh is also a beautiful region of lovely mountains, ridges and valleys. Of these the **Kulu Valley** is the best known. The others are Kangra and Chamba. Garhwal and Kumaon in the Uttar Pradesh Himalaya can claim to be the home of the gods. The sacred **Ganga** and almost equally sacred **Yamuna** both have their sources here at **Gangotri** and **Yamunotri**. **Nanda Devi** (7816 m) is the highest mountain in the region, and one of the most beautiful and mysterious in the entire range. **Garhwal** and **Kumaon** are Himalayan trekking's best kept secret – see page 225.

Punjab and the Gangetic Plain When Indians speak of 'the North', they are usually referring not to the Himalayas or Kashmir but to a broad belt of land that includes the Ganga Basin and the **Haryana** and the **Punjab** region NW of Delhi. In this wedge lives a very large proportion of the country's population. The reason is that the soils are generally very fertile, the product of silt brought down by the rivers of the Himalayas and deposited in a great trench formed by the pressure of the N-moving Peninsula against the Tibetan Plateau – see page 32. Over the past 20 million years, this 3,000 m deep trough has been filled with alluvium, creating an ideal farming environment that is flat and therefore suited to large scale irrigation. Because of the high density of population there is now hardly any natural forest cover left.

Across the unrelentingly flat plain that comprises nearly three quarters of Uttar Pradesh flows the **Ganga**, the physical as well as spiritual life force of northern India. At **Haridwar**, the Gateway to the hills, it is nearly 300 m above sea level. When it leaves the northern Region at the border of Uttar Pradesh and Bihar near Patna, it has fallen only 220 m over more than 1,000 km. The Ganga and Yamuna join at Allahabad.

Central Plateau and Uplands Along the southern edge of the Gangetic plain is the peninsular block of India. **Madhya Pradesh** and the southern part of **Rajasthan** belong to this region of gently undulating plateau and hill ranges. Running diagonally across Rajasthan from **Mount Abu** (1,300 m) to the **Delhi Ridge**, effectively dividing the state in two, are the **Aravalli Hills**. To the S is a region of hill and plateaus of varying height (330 m to 1,150 m), while to the N is the Thar Desert. Delhi is strategically sited at the narrowest point between the Aravallis and the Himalayas, the natural gateway to the Gangetic plain. In Madhya Pradesh the topography is similar except in the SW where the **Malwa plateau** belongs to outliers of the **Western Ghats**. The old erosion front in the N of the state is strikingly beautiful, presenting bare cliffs and densely forested ravines. The state has excellent forests, yet for all its varied beauty, cultural heritage and stable political climate, it is surprisingly little visited.

Thar Desert The Great Indian or Thar desert lies N of the Aravallis and the Luni river. There are Sahara type shifting sand dunes W of **Jaisalmer** but as you move E the desert becomes gently undulating, stony and relatively uninteresting. **Jodhpur** dominates the central part.

CLIMATE

There are wide variations in climate over the region both within the hills and plains as between them. The standard seasons of winter, spring, summer, monsoon and autumn are experienced by all regions except Ladakh and the Lahul/Spiti region of Himachal Pradesh which lie beyond the Great Himalayan Axis and therefore do not receive the monsoon.

Temperature Winter is long in Ladakh lasting from Nov to Mar. Elsewhere it is of shorter duration. Generally **December** and **January** are cold with maximum daily temperatures on the plains reaching the 20°C and the minimum around 7°C though as you move S both increase. After dark, though, it can get quite cold. Freezing on the plains is uncommon, but winter showers occur sporadically and mist or morning fog is relatively common especially around Agra. In the hills there is snow down to around 2,000 m and temperatures are correspondingly low. In **Nainital**, **Shimla** and **Srinagar** the daily minimum is 2°C and the maximum 10°C in **Nainital** and 4°C in **Srinagar** in Jan. In Leh it can reach as low as -35°C though this is extreme. In summer it can reach over 30°C. Sunstroke and frostbite are unlikely bedfellows in Ladakh. Unsettled weather originating from the Tibetan plateau is not uncommon, resulting in cold wind and snow or rain.

In the hills **Feb** and **Mar** are very pleasant months. The rhododendrons are in bloom and with snow melt the meadows are carpeted with spring flowers. There is snow above 3,500 m and Ladakh is still snow bound. Daytime temperatures are pleasantly warm and reach around 19°C. At night, whilst it is cool, the temperatures do not drop below freezing. Srinagar has relatively heavy precipitation at this time. On the plains, its is gradually hotting up and around Bhopal can reach 34°C. Delhi is a few degrees cooler. At night, air conditioning is not really necessary. Because of low rainfall the landscape is rather dusty looking. Humidity levels are low.

The hot weather lasts from **Apr** and until the middle of **Jun** temperatures rise inexorably. Delhi and Agra become very hot in **May** with daytime temperatures consistently over 40°C whilst at night they fall to around 27°C. It is hot but because of low humidity bearable. However, air-conditioning becomes a necessity. This is the time when the British migrated to the hills. Indians who can afford it do likewise. During **the monsoon** maximum daytime temperatures fall to around 35°C on the plains and 21°C in the hills. Humidity levels are high and the atmosphere is enervating. Clothes always seem damp and insects, particularly mosquitoes, are more active.

When the monsoon finishes the weather pattern is invariably very stable. From Oct to Dec the skies clear, temperatures are pleasantly warm and the countryside looks delightful. As winter approaches, night time temperatures will fall and the mornings can be quite cool. Throughout the region conditions are normally excellent for travel.

Rain and snow fall Some areas of the hills and the northern plains receive rain from depressions through the winter. However, most of the region receives its precipitation largely in the Jun to Oct monsoon. The onset of the rainy season is traditionally celebrated in rural areas because of its importance to crop growth. All areas except **Ladakh** and **Lahul/Spiti** receive 75% of their annual rainfall over this 5 month period. Flooding is still common over much of the Gangetic Plain and communications can be disrupted. This is a difficult and unpleasant time for travelling, even though some places such as **Mandu** in Madhya Pradesh look their best. Vegetation growth is rapid and the landscape looks green and lush. **Kashmir** is one of the few places that receive comparatively little rain over this period, and its relatively high altitude make it the perfect time to visit.

ECONOMY

Agriculture In most states agriculture employs over two-thirds of the population.

However, there is considerable regional variation. The Punjab is by far the most productive area with ⅘ of the cultivated area under irrigation and impressive yields per hectare. Large parts of western Uttar Pradesh and Haryana are not far behind. In these 3 states production of the wheat and rice are grown as commercial crops, sold in the large cities of Delhi and the Gangetic Plain. In the peripheral regions such as Ladakh, the hill region of Uttar Pradesh, Himachal Pradesh, and extensive areas of Rajasthan and Madhya Pradesh, farmers produce for their own families consumption. When they do not produce enough to survive, as in the hill region of Uttar Pradesh, for example, they have to import grain from the plains.

Up to an altitude of about 3,000 m, there are two cropping seasons. The *rabi** season runs from Oct to Mar/Apr. The *kharif** is the monsoon growing season, in which as much arable land as possible is sown. Wheat is the major rabi crop throughout the region and on poorer soils such as those in Ladakh is replaced with barley. The northern region produces the bulk of the nation's wheat and all its surplus. This is in contrast to E and S India which are rice growing regions. Rice is the important kharif crop and is favoured at this time because of the monsoon and the opportunities the abundant rainfall creates for irrigation.

The green revolution The supply of uncultivated land in the northern Region has virtually run out. Increasing agricultural returns rests on improving the efficiency with which the land is farmed. This can be achieved by introducing higher yielding varieties of seeds, irrigating more land and using crop enhancing fertilisers and pesticides. Farmers in Punjab, Haryana and Uttar Pradesh have increased their yields 4 or 5 times since Independence. The other regions either side have a long way to go, mainly because their soils are poorer, they have less irrigation water, their cultivation techniques are more primitive and because scientific research has tended to favour the areas well endowed with physical resources. This has been justified on the grounds that in places like the Punjab yields can be increased more dramatically, producing a grain surplus quicker. Slowly, more attention is being paid to other less fortunate regions. Commercial crops are sugar cane along the Indo-Gangetic belt and cotton in southern Rajasthan and Madhya Pradesh. Market gardening is important around the urban centres such as Delhi.

The huge livestock populations places additional burdens on the farmed area. In the alpine regions and semi arid areas of Rajasthan, where there is often only one cropping season, animal husbandry complements arable farming. Goats and sheep are popular for their wool production and, to a lesser extent, for their meat, which is acceptable to Muslims and less orthodox Hindus. Cattle are kept for their services as draught animals and their milk production.

Forests Pressure of population has caused a drastic reduction in the region's forests. Good reserves exist in the less accessible areas in the hills and over eastern Madhya Pradesh. Wood is still a vital cooking fuel, and as the population increases the remaining forest resources are in jeopardy. In the towns kerosene and electricity are the main sources of energy for cooking for middle class households, but for the poor cow dung, leaves, charcoal and wood remain essential cooking fuels.

Manufacturing Various types of industry are distributed over the lowland areas. **Kanpur** was one of the first textile factory cities in India and maintains its importance within the region as a processing centre for agricultural products and chemicals. Textiles play an important part in the industrial economies of **Rajasthan** and **Madhya Pradesh** as well. Madhya Pradesh and Rajasthan are well endowed with minerals ranging from diamonds from Panna to high grade iron and tin ore. There are steel plants at **Bhilai**, heavy electrical enterprises at **Bhopal** and an aluminium plant at **Korba**. Heavy industry includes the construction of railway rolling stock in Rajasthan along with zinc and copper smelting. Punjab on the other hand has practically no mineral resources and its industries are concerned with the textiles and the manufacture of consumer goods such as bicycles. **Haryana** is the largest producer of automobile spare parts in India. Light industrial zones have been established in Central and southern Rajasthan around **Kota**, **Jaipur**, **Udaipur** and **Bhilwara**.

Traditional handicrafts provide a source of additional income for many villagers. **Kashmir** has traditionally been reliant on its high quality handicrafts such as carpets, papier mâché goods and shawls. In terms of its contribution to the regional economy tourism is relatively insignificant. However, in the popular areas such as **Delhi, Agra, Rajasthan,** the hill stations, and **Kashmir** and **Ladakh** tourism has generated employment and income.

Communications throughout the northern region are generally good. The plains have an extensive road and rail network though the quality of roads is often poor and they are increasingly heavily used. Roads have been built into remote hill areas of the north because of their strategic importance. If anything it has increased their reliance on the more productive regions rather than aided local economic development.

HISTORY AND RELIGION

The Indus Valley Civilization and the Aryans Punjab was part of the Indus Valley civilization which then spread southwards along the western seaboard and eastwards to the Ganga – see page 78. Some of the **Harappan** cities in N India had trade links with Egypt and Mesopotamia. A Harappan dry dock has been excavated at the Harappan port of Lothal in Gujarat, for example. The Harappan people were followed – perhaps even swept away – by the invading Aryans, 'their onslaught like a hurricane: a people who had never known a city' according to a Mesopotamian chronicler. As the Aryans settled to an agricultural way of life new religious ideas and practices began to take shape. Indigenous tribes were displaced and retreated to the remoteness of hills and forests. Well-wooded Madhya Pradesh still has a significant tribal population of which the Gonds are the most numerous. **Kausambi** in Uttar Pradesh dates from the 8th century BC, when the Aryans had taken up farming. By this period the early **Vedas** were already written down, and the upper plains of the Ganga had become the hearth of what was to become modern Hindu civilisation.

This was the setting for the classics of Sanskrit literature. Today the country immediately to the N of Delhi in Haryana is revered as the home of the **Mahabharata**. **Mathura** to the S is equally surrounded by sites associated with one of contemporary Hinduism's most popular gods, **Krishna**, and holy centres such as **Varanasi** and **Haridwar** are associated with the great river Ganga. As the faith developed, so did the number and importance of pilgrimage centres. **Ujjain**, one of the 4 cities in the triennial **Kumbh Mela** cycle, traces its origins to the age of the great Hindu epics. Asoka's sons were born here. Rama is believed by many Hindus to have been born in **Ayodhya**, E of Lucknow, is the surrounding countryside is alive with stories from the Rama myth.

Pilgrimage (yatra) also became popular and many centres emerged in the mountains and along the great rivers. Rishikesh and Haridwar became the gateways to the hills whilst in the Great Himalaya Badrinath, Kedarnath, Yamunotri and Gangotri all achieved prominence. All these are in Uttar Pradesh. The cave at Amarnath in Kashmir was also revered whilst the Kulu Valley in Himachal Pradesh became known as the Valley of the Gods.

Buddhism emerged as an alternative to the Brahminism of the 6th century BC. The crucible of Buddhism was **Bihar** but the Deer Park at **Sarnath,** where the Buddha delivered his first sermon, and **Kushinagar**, where he died, are both in eastern **Uttar Pradesh**. Buddhism was espoused by the Emperor Asoka who erected pillars around the country entreating the population to be virtuous and clean living. One is at **Sanchi** in S **Madhya Pradesh**. Whilst the magnificent Stupa has no direct connection with the Buddha, it is one of the finest Buddhist monuments in the country, and is revered by Buddhists from all over the world. In the 3rd century BC Asoka's missionaries carried Buddhism to Sri Lanka and along the Silk Road to E Asia. **Ladakh's** spectacular mountain scenery provides a stunning backcloth to the visible features of its Tibetan Buddhist religion, incorporating elements of the Bon religion which had been practised there before Buddhism arrived.

The difficulties of practising **Jainism**, with its austere injunctions against harming any form of life, probably prevented it from achieving lasting popularity, but in its prime it spread to Maharashtra (Ajanta and Ellora) and was represented over most of the country. Jains often became traders, an occupation regarded as the least physically harmful, open to them. In the orthodox Hindu hierarchy trade was a lower occupation than that of the priest or warriors, activities performed by the Brahmins and Kshatriyas, and later many of the Rajput states and capitals had influential Jain merchants who were allowed to construct temples – see Gwalior (Madhya Pradesh), Osian near Jodhpur, Jaisalmer, Mount Abu, Ranakpur and Kumbhalgarh near Udaipur in Rajasthan.

Alexander the Great Small communities of Greek origin settled in the Punjab and Northwest Frontier following Alexander's invasion of 326 BC. Owing to his untimely death in 323 BC, arrangements to annex the Indian provinces proved fruitless. At Vidisha (MP) there is the 2nd century Heliodorus votive pillar named after the Greek who had settled in India and become a Hindu. At this time many of the cities of N India were already long-established.

The Gupta period (4th-6th centuries AD), was the golden age of Hindu culture in N India. The Guptas created an empire that stretched across northern India from the Punjab to the Bay of Bengal and S to a line running from the Gulf of Cambay in Gujarat to N Orissa. The Gupta emperors were all Hindu rulers but there was no religious fanaticism. The Chinese traveller and Buddhist pilgrim Fa Hien visited India at the beginning of the 5th century and his account gives a picture of Gupta India as a prosperous and peaceful country. It traded with Egypt and was ruled by an efficient government with a very high standard of justice and a high level of technology for the period. However, Hun invasions from the NW contributed to the collapse of the Gupta Empire which finally ended in 535 AD. Eighty years later a new king, Harsha, inherited his father's small kingdom at Thanesar (Haryana) on the Upper Yamuna. This he expanded into an empire slightly smaller in extent but similar in administration to that of the Gupta's. The capital was at Kannauj in E Uttar Pradesh.

The Rajputs By this time Buddhism was already in decline. After **Harsha's** death the region lapsed into a state of political anarchy. Kashmir developed into a fairly strong kingdom whilst in Rajasthan there arose a number of Hindu principalities. Until the end of the 12th century, control of the region was concentrated in the hands of the Hindu ruling classes, of which the **Rajputs** are the best example. They rose to political supremacy in the 9th and 10th centuries and many of the Rajasthan dynasties trace their origins to this period. Most authorities now accept that the Rajput clans were descended either from the Huns who settled in North and West India during the 6th century AD, or from other Central Asian tribes who accompanied the Huns. Though the Rajputs spanned a wide range of social groups, they boasted a proud warrior heritage and raised the concepts of loyalty, honour in battle and bravery to the highest moral plane.

Internal squabbling, jostling for power, the disintegration of larger territories and the emergence of new petty principalities marked the period up until the

12th century when the first impact of Muslim rule began to be felt across the region. Until that time, N India had a long respite from foreign aggression. The Huns had been assimilated, and the **Arab conquest of Sind** in 712 AD only touched the S plains of the Indus. For many centuries W India had enjoyed a lively trade with the Middle East and Arab seamen and merchants were familiar faces in the ports along India's western seaboard. Over the whole region, the political scene was quite introverted. Minor disputes were magnified into major causes for endless campaigns which devoured funds and sapped the energies of their protagonists. Trade with the west diminished and India became quite isolated. As Romila Thapar suggests, there was a period of self-satisfaction across the country. The **Chandelas** emerged as a strong regional power in N Madhya Pradesh and their fine temples at Khajuraho are evidence of a period of enormous wealth.

The arrival of Islam The calm was shattered by incursions over the northwest passes of the Hindu Kush. **Mahmud of Ghazni**, a local ruler from Afghanistan, was attracted to India by its proverbial wealth and the fertility of its lands. By launching regular raids rather than full-scale invasions, Mahmud financed his struggles in Central Asia, at that time a far more lucrative prospect because of the profitable trade conducted along the Silk Road between China and the Mediterranean. Mahmud's Indian forays became an annual occurrence. Careful planning of the campaigns saw the arrival of the Afghans in India during the harvest season. The plentiful crops in the fields cut out the need for elaborate provisioning and baggage trains, and thus enhanced his army's mobility. The temples of N India, with their enormous wealth in cash, golden images and jewellery, made them natural targets for a non-Hindu. Mahmud's insatiable greed for gold was complemented by his religious motivation as an image-breaker. He sacked the wealthy centres of **Mathura** (UP) in 1017, **Thanesar** (Haryana) in 1011, **Somnath** (Gujarat) in 1024 and **Kanauj** (UP). Mahmud died in 1030 but in spite of him, India did not become more aware of the world to the NW. Defence remained purely local, its purpose to defend one king against another. Mahmud was just another *mlechchha*** ('impure' or sullied one), as had been the Huns and the Sakas before him, soon to be forgotten.

The Rajput clans returned to their battles against each other in the 11th and 12th centuries. The possession of kingdoms was often precarious and competition for territory intense. War became a part of the general chivalric code, but confederation of forces against Muslim a common foreign enemy was uncommon. When the second wave surged over the NW passes, the country was no better prepared.

The Muslim conquests In the late 12th century **Muhammad Ghuri** attacked the plains. Entering India by the Gomal Pass near **Bannu** in Pakistan (**see page 1219**), by 1191 he had overrun the former **Ghaznavid** (after Mahmud of Ghazni) dependencies in the Punjab and acquired the suzerainty of Arab **Sind**. Muhammad was thinking in terms of establishing a kingdom rather than indulging in periodic raids and this brought Rajput chivalry a fresh challenge. At **Taraori** on the **Panipat** plain N of Delhi, the Rajputs gathered together as best they could, won a first battle, but were only able to hold off the Muslim threat for a year. In 1192 a second battle was fought in the same place, the Hindu commander **Prithviraj** was defeated and the kingdom of Delhi fell to the invaders. Muhammad pressed on and took **Ajmer** in Rajasthan. In 1206 he was assassinated, but this did not herald a general withdrawal. Muhammad had been determined to retain his Indian acquisitions and this policy was followed to by his successors.

The Delhi sultanate The early rulers of what came to be called the Delhi Sultanate and a large number of their followers were Turks, mainly from Central Asia, who had settled in Afghanistan. The armies with which they invaded India consisted of Turkish, Afghan and Persian mercenaries. The majority were probably Afghan. These Afghans, brought up in the harsh environment of the mountains and burning plains of Afghanistan, were tough and eager fighters who also saw plunder as an added attraction. The Ghuri (after Muhammad of Ghur) kingdom in Afghanistan did not last long after Muhammad's death but the Indian part of his kingdom became the nucleus of a new political entity – the Delhi Sultanate. Control passed to his slave governor, Qutb-ud-din-Aibak who made no new conquests but consolidated Muslim dominion by an even-handed policy of conciliation and patronage. In Delhi he converted the old Hindu stronghold of Qila Rai Pithora into his Muslim capital and commenced a number of magnificent building projects, the Quwwat-ul-Islam mosque and the Qutb Minar, a victory tower.

Under the **Slave Dynasty** (1206-1290) as it is known, the Muslim hold on N India was still relatively insecure, and a determined attempt to dislodge it could well have been successful. However, it was an opportunity that the former Indian rulers neglected. All N India including Delhi, present day Rajasthan and Gujarat in the W, Bengal and Bihar in the E, and eventually the Deccan, fell to the invaders who, with few exceptions, mercilessly advanced not only their authority but also their faith. Temples were reduced to rubble, thousands were put to the sword or forcibly converted. Many of the Sultans were themselves assassinated by rivals, favourites and impatient heirs. One, **Muhammad bin Tughluq** (r1325-51), was described by the Moorish traveller **Ibn Batuta** as 'a man who above all others is fond of making presents and shedding blood'. returning from a victorious campaign to his capital **Tughluqabad** in Delhi, he had erected a splendid pavilion, secretly and successfully designed by his engineer to collapse fatally upon the Sultan at the first tread of his elephant, **see page 167.**

Timur and Genghis Khan The Delhi sultans ruled by military power, but they were open to local influences – they employed Hindus in their administration. They settled and, according to Ibn Batuta, their capital city of Delhi in the mid 14th century was one of the leading cities of the contemporary world. In 1398 this came to an abrupt end with the arrival of the Mongol **Timur**, whose limp caused him to be called Timur-i-leng (Timur the Lame or Tamburlaine). This self-styled 'Scourge of God' was illiterate, a devout Muslim, an outstanding chess player and a patron of the arts. Five years before his arrival in India he had taken Baghdad and 3 years before that he had ravaged Russia, devastating land and pillaging villages to within 300 km of Moscow. India had not been in such danger from Mongols since **Genghis Khan** had arrived on the same stretch of the Indus 200 years before in pursuit of one of his foes. Fortunately, he had had business elsewhere and vanished again.

Timur cut a bloody swathe through to Delhi. In a medieval army so far from home (Samarkand), the troops' loyalty depended on whether their leader could find enough for them to pillage. It would appear that they were able to do this to their heart's content. When a reconnaissance party led by Timur himself was attacked and beaten off by Indian troops, 50,000 prisoners in his camp failed to conceal their excitement that his campaign might fail. Within the space of an hour all were butchered. Timur did not stay long in India. With captured elephants, rhinos, booty which needed 20,000 pack animals for its transport, craftsmen and slaves, he returned home. He had been in the country for less than 6 months but left behind a carnage, unprecedented in India's long history. He is believed to have been responsible for 5 million deaths. Famine followed the destruction caused by his troops and plague resulted from the corpses left behind.

The Mughals After Timur, it took nearly 50 years for the Delhi kingdom to become more than a local headquarters. Even then the revival was slow and fitful. There were the last **Tughluqs**, an undistinguished line of **Sayyids,** who began as Timur's deputies but later called themselves Sultans, and three **Lodi** kings

(1451-1526), who were essentially Afghan soldier/administrators. They moved their capital to **Agra**, but left their tombs in Delhi. Nominally they controlled an area from the upper Punjab to Bihar but they were, in fact, in the hands of a group of factious nobles. Their wrangling let in **Babur**, the man who was to establish India's greatest dynasty, in 1526.

The forces of the Delhi Sultanate were patently in disarray. The Hindus were not in much better shape. All over the N they had lost power. Many were forced into the Himalayas, where they formed 'Pahari' (Hill) kingdoms, for example in **Garhwal**, **Chamba** and **Kangra**. Only in **Rajasthan** had they held out, but here they were deeply divided by clan rivalry. In the Deccan they had given way to the **Bahmanis**, whilst in the S the hold of the Vijayanagar empire was more precarious than it seemed. Everywhere division met the eye and India was ripe for the picking, just as it had been before the first Muslim onslaught.

Timur had died in 1405, 6 years after he had wrecked N India. His departure proved to be the last that Delhi would see of his family for over a century. When they returned they came to stay. The Timurid heartland comprised the golden city states of Samarkand, Bukhara, Ferghana and Herat in Central Asia. All the rulers were descended from Timur in the late 15th century and there were too many princes for thrones. Babur turned his attention to S of the Hindu Kush, took Kabul, and from there launched his military expedition into India.

A new tradition The family character had changed since Timur's day. As Bamber Gascoigne has noted apart from the ability to win battles, they also inherited from their gruesome ancestor a liking for learned men and a passion for beautifying their capital cities. Where his ambition was to terrify the world, theirs seemed more to impress it. Where he brought destruction to Delhi, they gave Muslim India one of its periods of greatest splendour. With magnificent buildings such as the Red Forts at Agra and Delhi, Humayun's Tomb in Delhi, the Itimad-ud-daula and Taj Mahal tombs at Agra, Akbar's beautiful new capital at Fatehpur Sikri, Jahangir's pleasure gardens in Kashmir, the pavilions and mosques at Ajmer in Rajasthan, who could deny this.

Aurangzeb There was a price to pay for this opulence and extravagance. After **Shah Jahan's** aesthetically stunning but economically crippling reign, **Aurangzeb** tried to restore a sound financial an political basis to the Mughal empire. Able, but in many contemporary Indian eyes bigoted and mean-minded, he succeeded in extending the Mughal Empire. However, in the process he severed the remaining threads of loyalty from Hindu nobles that his great grandfather Akbar had so skilfully spun. The Maratha Shivaji exploited a groundswell of resentment by introducing the concept of Swaraj (Home Rule) for the Hindu masses. Maratha victories across the centre of the sub continent seemed to assure this. However, on the battlefield at Panipat in Haryana the opportunity for seizing the imperial sceptre was lost by the Maratha confederacy. A political vacuum was created which the British exploited as they advanced up the Ganga from their Calcutta base.

The Gurkha Wars of the early 19th century saw the inclusion of **Garhwal** and **Kumaon** in Uttar Pradesh and what is now Himachal Pradesh, into the territory of the East India Company. **The Sikhs** had developed as a strong regional power with a vigorous new religion in the Punjab and during the 18th century, tore free of the Mughals and established their own empire under Ranjit Singh. Ultimately they came into conflict with the British but, once beaten, proved loyal subjects.

The British in North India The British advance up the Ganga saw the formal absorption of princely states into the Company's territories or the indirect control of those who remained independent. Oudh was annexed under dubious circumstances and its capital Lucknow was one of the centres in which the flames of Indian discontent were fanned when the **Mutiny** broke in 1857. Kanpur and

Lucknow in Oudh, Meerut, Delhi and Jhansi were the scenes of desperate struggles. Afterwards, the British, shaken by the experience, adopted a more conciliatory attitude towards Indians. The railway system was rapidly expanded during this period, linking regions together economically, enabling the rapid movement of vital supplies during famines and other times of crisis. It also gave Indians an hitherto unknown mobility. Canals permitted the irrigation of larger areas of the Gangetic plain and the Punjab.

Hill stations Hill stations developed as a means by which the overheated Europeans could cool off during the stiflingly hot summer months. Along the length of the Himalaya, at an average altitude of around 2,000 m, summer resorts emerged. The Himalayan stations include Nainital, Mussoorie and Ranikhet in Uttar Pradesh and Shimla, Dalhousie and Dharamshala in Himachal Pradesh. The Mughals had already developed Kashmir but Pahalgam and Gulmarg were also popularised. Mount Abu catered to residents of S Rajasthan and Pachmarhi to those in S Madhya Pradesh.

Government escaped from hot and sticky cities of Calcutta or Delhi (before and after 1911 respectively) to the cool breezes of **Shimla**, over 1,500 km away. In May government officers, wives and servants went up to the summer capital. In Sep they all came down again. In 1911 the capital was transferred to Delhi, which naturally meant that the N became the focal region of India. To mark the change another new city was built. New Delhi is the extravagant work of Britain's empire builders who were no doubt in agreement with Lord Curzon's view that 'there has never been anything so great in the world's history as the British Empire, so great an instrument for the good of humanity. We must devote all our energies and our lives to maintaining it'. In fact, within 15 years of the new city's completion the British Indian Empire came to an end.

Independence came after a remarkable struggle initially orchestrated by Mahatma Gandhi and waged in the best principles of Jainism and Buddhism, through non-violence. The Partition of India along religious lines, however, let loose a violence which was often uncontrollable. The transfer of power and boundary delineation resulted in a broken Punjab and a horrible episode of fear and brutality as millions attempted to relocate to their chosen country. Independence saw the redrawing of state boundaries along linguistic grounds, the extension of the *panchayat raj** over village administration and the emphasis in the first Five Year Plans on industrialization.

Recent developments Political troubles have dogged the Punjab with the demands of a minority of Sikhs for greater autonomy hardening into a violent campaign for the creation of a Sikh state, Khalistan. Kashmir is claimed by India and Pakistan, who have twice gone to war over it. Recent unrest has seen the Vale of Kashmir effectively closed to foreign visitors, a tragedy for all concerned.

Urban growth has proceeded at an unprecedented rate as the country strives to diversify economically and as the population in rural areas continues to increase almost as fast as that of the cities. New Delhi has witnessed tremendous building activity as the government bureaucratic machine has multiplied. The planned city of Chandigarh exemplifies the building style. The Hill stations today receive fewer European visitors but their popularity is strong among the mobile Indian middle classes. The range and coverage of the communications and transport systems has been steadily improved but pressure on both is enormous.

NEW DELHI

New Delhi is the capital of India and a Union Territory. Altitude 216 m. Area 483 sq km. The monsoon lasts from mid-June to mid-September. May and June are very hot and dry. Best season October to March. December and January can be colder than most people realise, particularly at night, so woollens are recommended.

Social indicators Population 8.38m (1991); *Literacy* M 68% F 53%; **Newspaper circulation** 1.3 million; **Birth rate** *Rural* 33:1000 *Urban* 27:1000; **Death rate** *Rural* 8:1000 *Urban* 7:1000; **Registered graduate job seekers** 64,000; **Average annual income per head**: Rs 2,900;**Inflation** *1981-87* 77%; **Religion** *Hindu* 84% *Muslim* 8% *Sikh* 6% *Christian* 1%.

	Jan	Feb	Mar	Apr	May	Jun	Jul	Aug	Sep	Oct	Nov	Dec	Av/Tot
Max (°C)	21	24	30	36	41	40	35	34	34	35	29	23	32
Min (°C)	7	10	15	21	27	29	27	26	25	19	12	8	19
Rain (mm)	25	22	17	7	8	65	211	173	150	31	1	5	715

Main languages: Hindi, Urdu, Punjabi and English.

Distance of Connaught Circus to airport 23 km (Indira Gandhi International) 15 km (Palam Domestic).

INTRODUCTION

Modern Delhi is the fastest growing large city in India, rapidly overtaking the colonial cities of Bombay and Calcutta in sheer size, and long since eclipsing them in political importance. The first impressions for any first time visitor travelling in from the airport are of a spacious, garden city, tree-lined and with a number of beautiful parks, which in the winter are packed with colour. Many different regional and religious sub-groups make up the rapidly growing population. The turbaned Sikhs, colourfully dressed Rajasthani and Gujarati women working as manual labourers on building sites, Muslim shopkeepers along Chandni Chowk in Old Delhi, Tibetans and Ladakhis in the street stalls along Janpath, and Kashmiris in the handicraft emporia around Connaught Place, all add to the cosmopolitan feel of the city, a microcosm of India itself. Khushwant Singh, one of India's foremost journalists and novelists, has noted that Delhi's charm depends on a suitable combination of season, time of day, weather and mood, which can transform a casual street scene or an inconspicuous tomb.

Old Delhi   Yet first impressions do not tell the whole story. Delhi today is essentially 4 cities, spreading over the remains of nearly a dozen earlier centres which once occupied this vital strategic site.

The oldest surviving city is what is now known as "Old Delhi", or **Shah Jahanabad**, built by the Mughal Emperor Shah Jahan in the first half of the 17th century. Focusing on the great imperial buildings of the Red Fort and the Jama Masjid, this old city is a dense network of narrow alleys and tightly packed houses,

Muslims, Sikhs and Hindus living side by side, but separated in their own defined community quarters, with packed bazars, specialist markets and narrow lanes.

The new cities Immediately to the S of the old city is the British-built capital of New Delhi. A self conscious attempt to match the imperial grandeur of the Mughal capital, New Delhi retains the monumental buildings and street layout of its imperial builders. However, it has already been engulfed by the dramatic sprawl of the contemporary city. Spreading in all directions from the twin centres of Old and New Delhi, the post-Independence city has accelerated its suburban expansion with government built and privately-owned flats and houses. Together they have produvced a third city that already dwarfs the earlier two centres.

But there is also a fourth city, often scarcely seen. For unlike Bombay and Calcutta, notorious for the desperate housing problems of the poor, Delhi has confined much of its worst housing to the areas distant from the main commercial and administration centres. Yet squatter settlements provide the only shelter for at least ⅓ of Delhi's 9 million people, and their growth continues remorselessly.

Arrival If you are arriving at Indira Gandhi International Airport, you will drive along the broad tree-lined boulevards of New Delhi towards the city centre. This British city stands in marked contrast to Old Delhi. There your senses will be bombarded by the noise, bustle and smells of a more traditional world. The station in Old Delhi sometimes seems more like a refugee camp, with people camped out on the platform, waiting for a train which may be scheduled to depart in 2 or 3 day's time! Outside, taxi rivers, rickshaw wallahs and hotel touts will be jostling for attention, and out on the street the impression will be one of unrelieved chaos.

These various elements combine to make Delhi a city of stark contrasts. It can also be exciting and rewarding. East and west, old and new, traditional and modern, simple and sophisticated, are all juxtaposed. It is at the forefront of India's social and economic development. Unrepresentative of much of the rest of India, Delhi and its inhabitants nevertheless suggest great confidence and vitality.

The site Delhi owes its historic importance to the influence of geography. Sited at the narrowest point between the Aravalli hills and the Himalayas, it has commanded the route from the vital NW frontier into the rich agricultural hinterland of the Ganga plains. From Tughluqabad in S Delhi you can appreciate the strategic significance of the Delhi ridge, controlling the western approaches to the Gangetic plain across the River Yamuna. So great was the impact of the arrival of Islam in NW India that from viewing the monuments alone, you might think that Delhi was the centre of a Muslim state.

A brief chronology illustrates Delhi's complex past.

The Cities of Delhi

City	Date	Site	Remains
1 Indraprastha	4th century BC- 4th centuryIndraprasthaIndraprastha AD	In Purana Qila, Nr. Pragati Maidan	Recent archaeological finds at Shergarh support the view that this was the site of Delhi's earliest city. Nothing remains
2 Lal Kot	850 AD. Built by the Rajput Tomar kings	Qutb Minar complex	Recent archaeological finds: nothing is standing

City	Date	Site	Remains
3 Lal Kot enlarged	1180 AD Built by the Rajput king Prithviraj	Qutb minar complex	Some walls of the fort
4 **Qutb Minar** area	1193 AD	Qutb Minar	Mosques, Qutb Minar, walls
5 **Siri**	1304 AD Built by Ala ud Din Khalji, developed into prosperous trading and commercial centre through 14th century	Nr Hauz Khas	Walls remain
6 Tughluqabad	Early 14th century. Built by Ghiyas ud Din Tughluq, only occupied for 5 years	Rocky outcrop 8 km E of Qutb	Walls and some ruined buldings
7 Jahanapanah	Mid 14th century. Built by Ghiyas ud Din's son Mohammad Tughluq. Abandoned soon after completion	Between Siri and Qutb Minar	A few remnants of defensive walls
8 **Firozabad**	1354. Firoz Tughluq built his capital here, repaired Qutb Minar and built new roads and houses. Capital until Sikander Lodi moved it to Agra	7 km NE of Siri – Feroze Shah Kotla	Only the Asoka pillar rising from the ruins remains
9 Purana Qila (Old Fort)	1534 Humayun, the 2nd Mughal Emperor, built the Purana Qila	ESE of India Gate	High gates, walls, mosque, and a great baoli (well)
10 **Shergarh**	Mid 16th century. Built by Sher Shah during Humayun's enforced exile	Around the Purana Quila	Kabuli and Lal Darwaza gates and the Sher Mandal
11 **Shah Jahanabad**	Mid 17th century. Built by Shah Jahan as his capital when he moved from Agra	The existing Old Delhi	The Red Fort, Jama Masjid and the main streets of Old Delhi such as Chandni Chowk, long sections of the walls and several of the city gates
12 New Delhi	1920s. King George V announced that the capital would be moved from Calcutta to Delhi in 1911. Main buildings were completed 20 years later	Centred on Connaught Circus and Raj Path	All the main British buildings

New Delhi: the origins

New Delhi has become the centre of modern India's political life and is a dynamic hub of economic and social change. Its present position as capital was only confirmed on 12 December 1911, when the King Emperor George V announced at the Delhi Durbar that the capital of India was to move from Calcutta to Delhi. In keeping with the grand designs that other rulers had imposed on India, New Delhi was to be an emphatic statement of the magnificence and permanence of British rule in India. The planning of New Delhi began as soon as the 1911 Durbar was over, and a team of planners and architects under the leadership of Edwin Lutyens was set up. The new city was inaugurated on 9 February 1931.

Lutyens and Baker For an architect, the project was a dream. The new city was to cover 26 sq km and include the boldest expressions anywhere in the world of British imperial ambitions. Lutyens decided that he would design the palatial Viceroy's House and its surroundings and his old friend, Herbert Baker would design the nearby Government Secretariat and Imperial Legislative Assembly. Between them they would style the symbolically important approach to these magnificent structures. The other architects would work on other buildings in the new city which was destined to be the last of the great Imperial cities of the world.

The King Emperor favoured something in form and flavour similar to the Mughal masterpieces but fretted over the horrendous expense that this would incur. A petition signed by eminent public figures such as Bernard Shaw and Thomas Hardy advocated an Indian style and an Indian master builder. Herbert Baker had made known his own views even before his appointment when he wrote "first and foremost it is the spirit of British sovereignty which must be imprisoned in its stone and bronze". Lord Hardinge, the Viceroy suggested 'Western architecture with an Oriental motif'. As Tillotson has shown, Lutyens himself was appalled by the political pressure to adopt any Indian styles. For one thing, he despised Indian architecture. "Even before he had seen any examples of it," writes Tillotson, "he pronounced Mughal architecture to be 'piffle', and seeing it did not disturb that conviction. " Yet in the end the compromise was what Lutyens was forced to settle for.

The choice of site The city would accommodate 70,000 people and have boundless possibilities for future expansion. A foundation stone was hastily cut and laid in New Delhi by King George V and Queen Mary at the Durbar, but when Lutyens and his team arrived and toured the site on elephant back they decided that this was unsuitable. The Viceroy decided on an another site in S Delhi. So in 1913 the foundation stone was uplifted and moved on a bullock cart to **Raisina Hill.**

Land was levelled, roads were built, water and electricity connected to the site, and the same red sandstone employed that Akbar and Shah Jahan had used in their magnificent forts and tombs. It was transported from Dholpur to the site and an impressive range of marble lavished on the interiors. In the busiest year 29,000 people were working on the site. Slowly the work advanced and the buildings took shape. The Viceroy's house, the centre-piece, was of imperial proportions; it was one km round the foundations, bigger than Louis XIV's palace at Versailles, had a colossal dome surmounting a long colonnade and 340 rooms in all. It took nearly two decades to carry out the plans, a similar period of time to that of the building of the Taj Mahal.

Indian touches to a classical style The project was surrounded by controversy from beginning to end. Opting for a fundamentally classical structure, both Baker and Lutyens sought to incorporate Indian motifs. Many were entirely superficial. While some claim that Luytens in particular achieved a unique synthesis of the two traditions, Tillotson queries whether "the sprinkling of a few simplified and classicised Indian details (especially *chattris*) over a classical palace" could be called a synthesis. The chief exception was the dome of the Viceroy's house itself, which made strong allusions to the Buddhist stupa at Sanchi while marrying it to an essentially classical form, **see page 317.** A striking irony in the overall design came as a result of the late necessity of building a council chamber for the representative assembly which was created by political reforms in 1919. This now houses the Lok Sabha, but its centrality to the current Indian constitution is belied by Baker's design which tucks it away almost invisibly to the north of the northern Secretariat.

The Raisina crossing The grand design was for an approach to all the Government buildings along the King's Way (Raj Path). This was to be 2.4 km long, would lead onto the Great Palace where ceremonial parades could be held, then on up Raisina Hill between the Secretariat buildings to the entrance to the Viceroy's House. The palace was intended to be in view at all times, gradually increasing in stature as one got nearer. There was much debate over the gradient of Raisina Hill and eventually 1 in 22 was agreed upon.

In the event the effect was not what was intended. Only when the Viceroy's House was nearing completion was it realised that as you progress from the bottom of the Kings Way up Raisina Hill, the Viceroy's House sinks down over the horizon like the setting sun so that only the top part of the palace is visible. Lutyens recognised the mistake too late to make any change, and called this effect his 'Bakerloo'. Baker and Lutyens blamed each other and did not speak to one another for the next 5 years.

Delhi post-Independence Since 1947 the population of Delhi has increased dramatically and now stands at over 8 million. New satellite towns such as Ghaziabad on the East bank of the River Yamuna have sprung up to accommodate the capital's rapidly growing population as have numerous housing colonies, such as Greater Kailash I and II, Ashok Vihar, and R. K. Puram. Government Ministries and Departments have spread across S Delhi and there is a wide range of first class hotels. But, for all this building over the centuries, Delhi is also one of the world's greenest cities, with many trees and attractive parks. However, beyond the range of New Delhi's broad avenues is another city. At least ⅓ of the city's population continue to live in squatter huts, or "jhuggies", often in squalor, but attracted to the city by its prospects of work. In the 1970s **Sanjay Gandhi**, Mrs. Gandhi's younger son, pushed through a programme of bulldozing squatter settlements from the more public places, but some argue that the housing problem has simply been pushed a little further from sight.

One attempt to meet the most basic problems of shelter has been the provision of night shelters for homeless workers. By 1991 17 centres had been opened, catering for 125,000 people every night. The largest of these is near Old Delhi Railway Station. Each centre has fans and air coolers; cleaners go through every day, and 100,000 blankets are washed every day. They are open from 1900 to 0700, the charge is Rs1. 50 a night.

Local festivals

Consult the weekly Delhi Diary (available at hotels and many shops and offices around town) for exact dates. The following list gives an approximate indication of the dates.

Jan 13 *Lohri*, the climax of winter is celebrated with bonfires and singing. **26** *Republic Day* Parade, Raj Path. A spectacular fly past and military march past, with colourful pageants and tableaux from every state, dances and music. Tickets available through travel agents and most hotels. Cost approx. Rs 100. It is possible to see the full dress preview free, usually two days in advance. Week long celebrations during which government buildings are illuminated. **29** *Beating the Retreat*, Vijay Chowk, a stirring display by the armed forces bands marks the end of the Republic Day Celebrations. **30** *Martyr's Day* marks the anniversary of Mahatma Gandhi's death; devotional **bhajans*** and Guard of Honour at Raj Ghat. Jan (end) *Delhi Rose Show*, Safdarjang Tomb. Jan (end) *Shankarlal Sangeet Sammelan*, North Indian music festival.

Feb 2 *Basant Panchami* celebrates the first day of spring. The Mughal Gardens are opened to the public for a month. *Delhi Flower Show*, Purana Qila. *Horse Show*, Lal Qila. *Thyagaraja Festival* Homage, S Indian music and dance, Vaikunthnath temple, opposite Jawaharlal Nehru University.

Mar *Holi*, the festival of colours, marks the climax of spring. People throw coloured powder and water at each other and in the evening gamble with friends. If you don't mind getting covered in colours then you can risk going out and about, but it can get very vigorous. *Basant Ritu Sammelan*, N Indian music festival.

Apr *Amir Khusraw* 's Birth Anniversary, a fair in Nizamuddin celebrates this with prayers and *qawwali** singing at his tomb. National Drama Festival, Rabindra Bhavan.

May *Buddha Jayanti*. The first full moon night in May marks the birth of the Buddha and prayer meetings are held at Ladakh Buddha Vihara, Ring Rd and Buddha Vihara, Mandir Marg.

Aug 4 *Raksha Bandhan* (literally 'protection bond') is celebrated symbolizing the bond between brother and sister. Sisters say special prayers for the long life of their brothers and tie ornamental strings around their brothers' wrist to remind them of the special bond and obligation to protect and care for their sisters. *Janmash-tami* observed as the birth anniversary of the Hindu god Krishna. Special *puja**, Lakshmi Narayan Mandir. **15** *Independence Day* Impressive flag hoisting ceremony at the Red Fort. *Teej*, the rural festival of swings, celebrates the coming of the rains. It is also a great kite flying season. *Vishnu Digamber Sammelan*, N Indian music and dance festival.

Sept 30 *Phoolwalon ki Sair*, Festival of Flower Vendors, dating back to Mughal times symbolizes communal harmony.

Oct 2 *Gandhi Jayanti*, the birth anniversary of Mahatma Gandhi; devotional singing at Raj Ghat. *Dasara* celebrations for 10 nights; over 200 Ramlila performance all over the city. These recount the Ramayana story (**See Introduction on Hinduism, page 461**). The Ramlila Ballet at Delhi Gate is performed for a month and is the most spectacular rendering. The effigy of the demon king Ravana is burnt on the 9th night of Dasara on every large public open space and is a noisy and flamboyant affair signifying the triumph of good over evil. Special *dasara* discounts at State Government Emporia and Khadi Gram Udyog Bhavan, Connaught Place. National Drama Festival, Shri Ram Centre.

Nov 14 *Children's Day*, Jawaharlal Nehru's birth anniversary; Bal Mela (Children's Fair), India Gate; special programmes at the Dolls Museum, Bal Bhavan and Teen Murti Bhavan.
    Diwali, the festival of lights and fireworks; a pretty and noisy affair similar to Christmas with the lighting of earthen lamps, candles and firework displays. People usually send one another Diwali cards. Innumerable Diwali melas (fairs). National Drama Festival, Rabindra Bhavan.

Dec 10 *Chrysanthemum Show*, YMCA. **25** *Christmas*. Privately a low key affair, but with special Christmas Eve entertainments at all major hotels and restaurants; midnight mass and services at all churches. *Ayyappa Temple Festival*, Ayyappa Swami temple, Ramakrishnapuram; S Indian music. **31** New Year's Eve Widely celebrated in all hotels and restaurants offering special fare and entertainment with prices ranging from expensive to exorbitant.

PLACES OF INTEREST

The sites of interest are grouped in 3 main areas. The Old city of **Shah Jahanabad** is about 7 km to the N of present day New Delhi. 10 km to the S is the Qutb Minar complex, with the old fortress city of Tughluqabad 8 km to its E. In the centre is the British built capital of New Delhi, with its government buildings and wide avenues. Each can be visited separately, but it is quite possible to link routes together into a day tour which takes in several of the most interesting sites. This description starts near the centre of the modern political and administrative centre of Indian government. The second section describes sites in the S and the third the city of Shahajahanabad.

CENTRAL DELHI

India Gate A tour of New Delhi will usually start with a visit first to India Gate. This war memorial is situated at the E end of *Rajpath*. Designed by Lutyens, it commemorates more than 70,000 Indian soldiers who died in the First World War. An additional 13,516 names are engraved on the arch and foundations and are those of British and Indian soldiers killed on the NW Frontier and in the Afghan

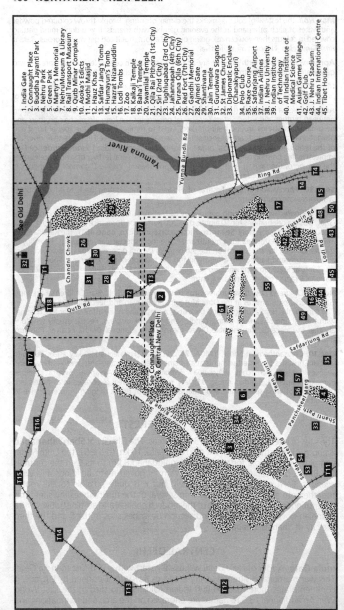

1. India Gate
2. Connaught Place
3. Buddha Jayanti Park
4. Nehru Park
5. Green Park
6. Martyr's Memorial
7. Nehru Museum & Library
8. Rail Transport Museum
9. Qutb Minar Complex
10. Aoka's Edicts
11. Moti Masjid
12. Hauz Khas
13. Safdar Jang's Tomb
14. Humayun's Tomb
15. Hazrat Nizamuddin
16. Lodi Tombs
17. Zoo
18. Kalkaji Temple
19. Baha'i Temple
20. Swaminal Temple
21. Qila Rai Pithora (1st City)
22. Siri (2nd City)
23. Tughluqabad (3rd City)
24. Jahanpanah (4th City)
25. Purana Qila (6th City)
26. Red Fort (7th City)
27. Gandhi Memorial
28. Ajmeri Gate
29. Shantivana
30. Jain Temple
31. Gurudwara Sisgans
32. St James Church
33. Diplomatic Enclave (Chanakyapuri)
34. Race Course
35. Safdarjang Airport
36. Indian Airlines
37. J. Nehru University
38. Indian Institute of Technology
39. All Indian Institute of Medical Science
40. Asian Games Village
41. Golf Club
42. Hauz Stadium
43. Indian International Centre
44. Tibet House

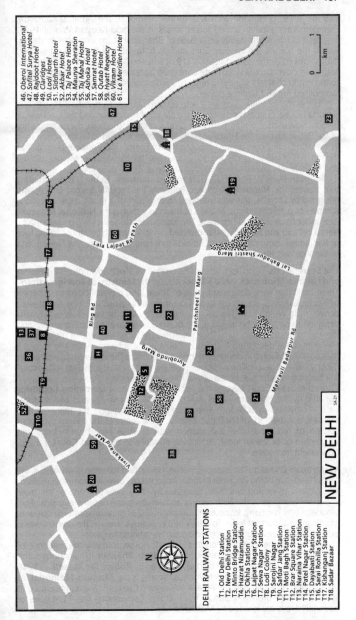

46. Oberoi International
47. Sofitel Surya Hotel
48. Rajdoot Hotel
49. Claridges
50. Lodi Hotel
51. Siddharth Hotel
52. Akbar Hotel
53. Taj Palace Hotel
54. Maurya Sheraton
55. Taj Mahal Hotel
56. Ashoka Hotel
57. Samrat Hotel
58. Hyatt Regency
59. Qutab Hotel
60. Vikram Hotel
61. Le Meridien Hotel

NEW DELHI

DELHI RAILWAY STATIONS

T1. Old Delhi Station
T2. New Delhi Station
T3. Minto Bridge Station
T4. Hazrat Nizamuddin
T5. Okhla Station
T6. Lajpat Nagar Station
T7. Sewa Nagar Station
T8. Lodi Colony
T9. Sarojini Nagar
T10. Sadar Bazar Station
T11. Moti Bagh Station
T12. Brar Square Station
T13. Naraina Vihar Station
T14. Patel Nagar Station
T15. Dayabasti Station
T16. Sarai Rohilla Station
T17. Kishanganj Station
T18. Sadar Bazaar

War of 1919. Under the arch is a further memorial, the Amar Jawan Jyoti, commemorating Indian armed forces' losses in the Indo-Pakistan War of 1971. The arch (43 m high) stands on a base of Bharatpur stone and rises in stages. Below the cornice are Imperial Suns and on both sides of the arch is inscribed INDIA flanked by the dates MCMXIV (1914 left) and MCMXIX (1919). Facing the arch is an open cupola which one contained a statue of King George V. Similar to the Hindu *chattri** signifying regality, it is decorated with nautilus shells which symbolized British Maritime power.

To the NW of India Gate are 2 impressive buildings, **Hyderabad House** and **Baroda House**, built as residences for the Nizam of Hyderabad and the Gaekwar of Baroda. Now used as offices, both were carefully placed to indicate the paramountcy of the British Raj over the Princely States. The Nizam, reputed to be the richest man in the world, ruled over an area equal to that of France. The Gaekwar belonged to the top level of Indian Princes and both, along with the Maharajas of Mysore, Jammu and Kashmir and Gwalior were entitled to receive 21 gun salutes.

Rajpath leads W from India Gate towards **Janpath**. To the N is the building that houses the **National Archives**. Formerly the Imperial Record Office, and designed by Lutyens, this was intended to be a part of a much more ambitious complex of public buildings. To the S of the intersection is the **National Museum** (see under Museums and Libraries). The foundation stone was laid by Jawarharlal Nehru in 1955 and the building completed in 1960. Rajpath continues to the foot of Raisina Hill, now called Vijay Chowk. From here you can see the flawed vista of the Viceroy's House.

The Secretariats lie on both sides of Raisina Hill. **N Block** now houses the **Home and Finance Ministries**, while **S Block** houses the **Ministry of Foreign Affairs**. These buildings were designed by Baker. These long classical buildings, topped by Baroque domes, are similar to his Government Buildings of Pretoria, and were derived from Wren's Royal Naval College at Greenwich. The towers were originally designed to be twice the height of the buildings, and to act as beacons guarding the way to the inner sanctum. Their height was reduced, and with it their impact. The domes are decorated with lotus motifs and elephants, while the N and S gateways are Mughal in design. On the N Secretariat is the imperialistic inscription 'Liberty will not descend to a people: a people must raise themselves to liberty. It is a blessing which must be earned before it can be enjoyed'.

In the Great Court beyond the Secretariats are the 4 **Dominion Columns**, donated by the governments of Australia, Canada, New Zealand and S Africa. Each is crowned by a bronze ship sailing east, symbolizing the maritime and mercantile supremacy of the British Empire. In the centre of the court is the Jaipur column of red sandstone and topped with a white egg, bronze lotus and six-pointed glass star of India. Across the entrance to the **Great Court** is a 205 m wrought iron screen.

Rashtrapati Bhavan The Viceroy's House, now called Rashtrapati Bhavan, is the official residence of the President of India. Designed by Lutyens, it combines western and eastern styles and has been described by Philip Davies as one of the most important buildings of the 20th century and a masterpiece of symmetry, discipline, silhouette and harmony. Inside is the Durbar Hall, 23 m in diameter with coloured marble from all parts of India. To the W of the Viceroy's House is the garden, which extends the principles of hierarchy and order from house to garden.

To the S of the Viceroy's House is Flagstaff House, formerly the residence of the Commander-in-Chief. Renamed *Teen Murti Bhawan* it now houses the Nehru Memorial Museum (See below). Designed by *Robert Tor Russell*, in 1948 it became the Prime Minister's residence. Nearby is the **Martyr's Memorial**, at the junction of Sardar Patel Marg and Willingdon Crescent. A magnificent 26 m long, 3 m high bronze sculpture by D. P. Roy Chowdhury. The 11 statues of national heroes are headed by Mahatma Gandhi.

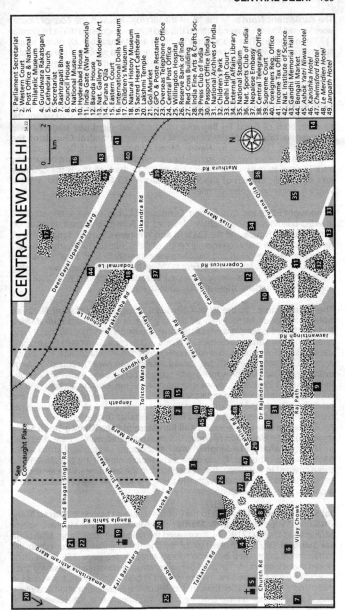

CENTRAL NEW DELHI

1. Parliament Secretariat
2. Western Court
3. Post Office & National Philatelic Museum
4. Gurudwara Rakatsganj
5. Cathedral Church
6. Secretariat
7. Rashtrapati Bhavan
8. Council House
9. National Museum
10. Hyderabad House
11. India Gate (War Memorial)
12. Baroda House
13. Nat. Gallery of Modern Art
14. Purana Qila
15. Eastern Court
16. International Dolls Museum
17. Children's Museum
18. Natural History Museum
19. Sacred Heart Cathedral
20. Lakshmi Temple
21. GPO Market
22. Poste Restante
23. Overseas Telephone Office
24. Central Post Office
25. Willingdon Hospital
26. Reserve Bank of India
27. Red Cross Building
28. India Fine Arts & Crafts Soc.
29. Press Club of India
30. Passport Office (India)
31. National Archives of India
32. Children's Park
33. Delhi High Court
34. External Affairs Library
35. National Stadium
36. Nat. Sports Club of India
37. Nepalese Embassy
38. Central Telegraph Office
39. Supreme Court
40. Foreigners Reg. Office
41. Income Tax Office
42. Nat. Institute of Science
43. Gandhi Memorial Hall
44. Bengali Market
45. Ashok Yatri Niwas Hotel
46. Janpath Hotel
47. Chelmsford Hotel
48. Le Meridien Hotel
49. Janpath Hotel

The **Parliament House** To the NE of the Viceroy's House is the *Council House*, now *Sansad Bhavan*. Baker designed this and Lutyens suggested that it be circular (173 m diameter). This shape came to be an architectural parody of the simple spinning wheel which had been adopted by Gandhi as a symbol of the nationalist movement. Originally, it was intended to have a dome but this plan was dropped. Inside is the library and chambers for the Council of State, Chamber of Princes and Legislative Assembly – the *Lok Sabha*.

Just opposite the Council House is the **Rakabganj Gurudwara** in **Pandit Pant Marg**. This 20th century white marble shrine in a style that is a subtle integration of the late Mughal and Rajasthani styles marks the spot where the headless body of **Guru Tej Bahadur**, the ninth Sikh Guru (**see page 72**) was cremated in 1657. W of the Council House is the **Cathedral Church of the Redemption** (1927-35) by **Henry Medd**, whose design (after Palladio's Il Redentore in Venice) won an architectural competition. The altar was donated by York Minster to mark its thirteenth centenary. To the N of this is the Italianate Roman Catholic **Church of the Sacred Heart** (1930-4), also by Medd, and the winning design in another competition.

Connaught Place and its outer ring, **Connaught Circus**, comprise two-storeyed arcaded buildings, ranged radially. Designed by Robert Tor Russell (in common with **Flagstaff House** and the **Eastern and Western Courts** in **Janpath**), they have become the main commercial centre of Delhi. Architecturally, they are very distinctive, very un-Indian and the complete antithesis to Shah Jahan's **Chandni Chowk**. To the S in Jan Path (*the People's Way*) the E and W Courts were hostels for the members of the newly convened Legislative Assembly. With their long colonnaded verandahs, these are Tuscan in character.

The Birla Temple To the W of Connaught Circus is the **Lakshmi Narayan Mandir** in Mandir Marg. Financed by the prominent industrialist **Raja Baldeo Birla** in 1938, this temple is one of the most popular Hindu shrines in the city and one of the few striking examples of Hindu architecture. Dedicated to Lakshmi, the goddess of well-being, it is commonly referred to as Birla Mandir. The design is in the Orissan style with tall curved towers (*shikhara**) capped by large *amalakas**. The exterior is faced with red and ochre stone and white marble. Built around a central courtyard, the main shrine has idols of Narayan and his consort Lakshmi while two separate cells have icons of Siva (the Destroyer) and his consort Durga (the ten-armed destroyer of demons). The temple is flanked by a *dharamshala** (rest house) and a Buddhist *vihara** (monastery).

E from the Birla temple, down **Kali Bari Marg** to **Baba Kharag Singh Marg** (Irwin Rd), is the **Hanuman Mandir**. This small temple appears to have been built in 1724 by **Maharaja Jai Singh** of Jaipur at about the same time that the Jantar Mantar was constructed. Of no great architectural interest, it is popular among those devoted to Hanuman, the monkey god. In the last 10 years the temple has become increasingly popular with devotees. The **Mangal haat** (Tuesday Fair) is a popular market for local people.

Jai Singh's observatory Just to the E of the Hanuman Mandir in **Sansad Marg** (Parliament Street) is the **Jantar Mantar** or old observatory. The Mughal Emperor Muhammad Shah (r1719-1748) entrusted the renowned astronomer **Maharaja Jai Singh** of Jaipur with the task of revising the calendar and correcting the astronomical tables used by contemporary priests – **see page 355**. Daily astral observations were made for years before construction began and plastered brick structures were favoured for the site instead of brass instruments. It was built in 1725 and is slightly smaller than that at Jaipur. There are explanation boards on site. A small Bhairev temple E of the instruments appears to have been built at the same time. Guide books available.

The road to Raj Ghat

There are several interesting and important sites immediately to the E and SE of Connaught Circus. The best way to visit them is to t ravel NE from Connaught Circus under the Minto Bridge, which carries the railway line to New Delhi Railway Station, you reach the open space of the Ram Lila grounds, part of which still serves as a camp site. Along its N side runs Asaf Ali Road, along which a line of shops conceals what used to be the wall of Shah Jahanabad. To the left is the old Ajmeri Gate. To the right the road runs to the banks of the old Delhi Gate, still clearly visible, where the main road N into the city turns sharp left – the often chaotically noisy, fume-ridden bedlam of Darya Ganj.

The *memorial ghats* Beyond Delhi Gate at the end of **Jawaharlal Nehru Marg**, lie the banks of the Yamuna, marked by a series of memorials to India's leaders. The river itself is now more than a km away and is invisible from the road, protected by a low rise and banks of trees. The most prominent memorial, immediately opposite the end of Jawaharlal Nehru Rd is that of **Mahatma Gandhi** at **Raj Ghat**. To its N is **Shanti Vana** ("forest of peace"), landscaped gardens where Prime Minister **Jawaharlal Nehru** was cremated in 1964, his grandson **Sanjay Gandhi** in 1980, daughter **Indira Gandhi** in 1984 and elder grandson, Rajiv, in 1991. To the N again is **Vijay Ghat** ("Victory bank") where Prime Minister **Lal Bahadur Shastri** was cremated in 1965.

Kotla Firoz Shah Moving S down the Mathura Rd is a succession of sites illustrating Delhi at its most modern and its most ancient. Immediately to the S of Rajghat is the Yamuna Velodrome and the Indraprastha Stadium, one of India's biggest sports stadiums. Between that and the Mathura Rd is **Kotla Firoz Shah**. This was the citadel of Firozabad, the 5th capital city of Delhi, built by *Firoz Shah Tughluq* (1351-1388) in 1351. Little remains as the ruins of Firozabad were extensively used for the later cities of *Sher Shah* (Shergarh) and *Shah Jahan* (Shajahanabad). At its height it stretched from **Hauz Khas** in the S to N of the Delhi ridge, and E to the Yamuna river.

From **Bahadurshah Zafar Marg** you enter the central enclosure, the largest of the three original ones (covered for the most part by modern buildings). The most striking feature is the tapering 14m high monolithic polished sandstone *Asoka pillar* which dates to the 3rd century BC. **Firoz Shah** was deeply interested in antiquities and had it brought from **Topra** (Haryana), 100 km away, wrapped in silk and muslin, on a 42 wheeled carriage drawn apparently by 200 men at each wheel. The Brahmi inscription carries the Emperor Asoka's message of goodwill to his subjects – see page 83. Nearby is a a circular *baoli** (well) and a ruined mosque. In its original state it is said to have accommodated over 10,000 worshippers and was where the Mongol Timur prayed during his sacking of Delhi in 1398. Apparently, he was so impressed by it that the Samarkand mosque was modelled on it. If popular legends are to be believed S Asia is riddled with secret **underground tunnels**! It is said that 3 secret passages lead from the *Kush-ki-Firoz* (Palace of Firoz) to the river, his hunting lodge on the Ridge and to Jahanpanah near the Qutb Minar.

The *Purana Qila* (Old Fort) To the S of Kotla Firoz Shah is the **Pragati Maidan**, a permanent exhibition centre for trade fairs and other public exhibitions. Immediately to its S, in another step back in time, is the **Purana Qila**. The ruins here witnessed the crucial struggle in the 16th century between the Mughal Emperor **Humayun** and his formidable Afghan rival **Sher Shah Sur**. The massive gateways and walls were probably built by Humayun, who laid the first brick of his new capital **Dinapanah** in 1534. The few surviving buildings within this roughly octagonal fort were the work of Sher Shah, who defeated Humayun in 1540, razed Dinapanah to the ground and started to build his own capital **Shergarh** on the same site. Humayun regained his throne in 1555 and destroyed

Shergarh, but he died a year later.

The massive double storeyed **Bara Darwaza** (Great Gate) is the main entrance to the fort. The two-bay deep cells on the inside of the enclosure were used after the Partition of India in 1947 to provide shelter for refugees from Pakistan. The S gate, the **Humayun Darwaza**, bears an ink inscription mentioning **Sher Shah** and the date 950 AH (1543-4), while the N gate is known as the **Talaqi Darwaza** (Forbidden Gate). The **Qila-i-Kuhna Masjid** (mosque of the Old fort) was built by Sher Shah and is considered one of the finest examples of Indo-Afghan architecture. The arches, tessellations and rich ornamentation in black and white marble against red sandstone became very popular during the Mughal period. Though the Fort is in ruins, the mosque is in good condition. Guide books and postcards available. Clean toilets.

Sher Mandal, a small octagonal tower S of the mosque was probably built by Sher Shah as a pleasure pavilion from which to view the river. Humayun later used it as a library spending hours poring over his cherished collection of miniatures and manuscripts. It is said that when he heard the *muezzin's** call to prayer he hurried down the steps of the building and slipped. The fall proved fatal. Trenches dug south of **Sher Mandal** in 1955 revealed pieces of **Grey Ware**, also discovered at other sites and associated with the Mahabharata (c 1100 BC), reinforcing the tradition that this was also the site of the legendary Indraprasta.

Outside the Purana Qila and across **Mathura Rd** is **Khairul Manzil Masjid** (*Most Auspicious of houses*), built in 1561 by **Maham Anga**, a wet-nurse to Akbar, who is said to have held considerable influence over him. Alongside this is Sher Shah Darwaza, the S gate to Shergarh.

SOUTH DELHI

The route now enters S Delhi. The southern part of the city can conveniently be seen separately from those described above, though it is perfectly possible to continue on the route as follows. The spacious layout of New Delhi has been preserved despite the building on empty sites and the sub-division of previously large gardens. Still close to the centre, there are several attractive high class residential areas, such as Jor Bagh near the Lodi Gardens, while beyond the Ring Road sprawling estates of flats and larger apartments, and huge shopping and commercial centres such as Nehru Place, have pushed the limits of Delhi to Tughluqubad and the Qutb Minar.

The Lodi Gardens A further km to the S of the **Purana Qila**, the **Mathura Rd** is joined on the right by Lodi Rd, leading to the *Lodi Gardens* and the *Lodi Tombs*. The gardens now are beautiful parks. Set in the heart of one of the best residential districts of Delhi, they are much used by anyone from joggers to those out for a gentle stroll. The mellow stone tombs of the 15th and 16th century Lodi rulers are situated in the gardens. In the middle of the garden facing the E entrance from Max Mueller Rd is *Bara Gumbad** (Big Dome), a mosque built in 1494. The raised courtyard, ascended by steps from the N is provided with an imposing gateway and mehman khana (guest rooms). The platform in the centre appears to have been a tank for ritual ablutions.

The **Sheesh Gumbad** (Glass Dome, late 15th century) is built on a raised incline a few metres N of the Bara Gumbad and was once decorated with glazed blue tiles, painted floral designs and Koranic inscriptions. The façade gives the impression of a two storeyed building, typical of Lodi architecture. **Mohammad Shah's Tomb** (1450) is that of the third Sayyid ruler. It has sloping buttresses, an octagonal plan, projecting eaves and lotus patterns on the ceiling. *Sikander Lodi's tomb*, built by his son in 1517 is also an octagonal structure decorated with Hindu motifs. A structural innovation is the double dome which was later refined under the Mughals. **Athpula** (*Bridge of Eight Piers*) is nearby and was used to enter the garden from the NE. It is believed to have been built in the 16th century by **Nawab Bahadur**, a nobleman at Akbar's court.

Safdarjang's Tomb At the E end of Lodi Road is *Safdarjang's Tomb*. Open sunrise to sunset. Entry Re 0.50. This tomb was built by Nawab Shuja-ud-Daulah for his father Mirza Mukhim Abdul Khan, entitled **Safdarjang**, who was Governor of Oudh during the reign of **Muhammad Shah** (1719-1748), and Wazir of his successor **Ahmad Shah** (1748-1754). Safdarjang died in 1754. With its high enclosure walls, *char bagh** layout of gardens, fountain and central domed mausoleum, it follows the tradition of Humayun's tomb but despite its attractiveness and the elements reminiscent of the Taj Mahal, it shows a weakening of form typical of a late architectural style. It has the advantage of not being full of tourists. Typically, the real tomb is just below ground level. Flanking the mausoleum are pavilions used by Shuja-ud-Daulah and his family as their Delhi residence. Immediately to its S is the battlefield where Timur and his Mongol horde crushed Mahmud Shah Tughluq on 12 December 1398.

At the W end of the **Lodi Road** is **Hazrat *Nizamuddin Dargah***. Nizamuddin *basti** (village), now tucked away behind the residential suburb of Nizamuddin West, off Mathura Rd, grew up around the tomb and shrine of **Sheikh Nizamuddin Aulia** (1236-1325), the fourth Chishti saint. The original tomb no longer exists and the present structure was built in 1526 and subsequently extensively renovated. Legend states that the then emperor Ghiyas-ud-din Tughluq tried to prevent workmen from building the shrine as his own city **Tughluqabad** was then being constructed. The craftsmen worked at night and when the emperor forbade the sale of oil, they used water from the sacred baoli (well) near the N gate, to fuel the lamps. West of the central shrine is the **Jama-at-khana** mosque built in 1325. Its decorated arches are typical of the Khalji design also seen at the **Alai Darwaza** at the **Qutb Minar**. S of the main tomb and behind finely crafted screens is the grave of princess Jahanara, Shah Jahan's eldest and favourite daughter. She shared the emperor's last years when he was imprisoned at Agra fort – see page 273. The grave, open to the sky is in accordance with the epitaph written by her ' Let naught cover my grave save the green grass, for grass suffices as the covering of the lowly'.

Pilgrims congregate at the shrine twice a year for the *Urs** (fair) held to mark the anniversaries of **Hazrat Nizamuddin Aulia** and his disciple **Amir Khusrau**, whose tomb is nearby. A visit at about 1900 is rewarding as *qawwalis** are sung after *namaaz** (the evening prayer).

Humayun's Tomb

Open daily, sunrise to sunset. Entry Re 0.50 Fridays free. Located in Nizamuddin, 15 min by taxi from Connaught Circus. Allow 45 minutes to see. It is a popular place because it is the most interesting and best preserved tomb in Delhi and is therefore included in organised sightseeing tours. Proximity to Rly Stations means peace is destroyed by constant train noise. You can buy soft drinks, guide books and postcards at the entrance.

Warning Reports in 1991 say that video cameras are not allowed. These rules sometimes change unpredictably, but be prepared.

In most other countries Humayun's tomb would be considered a great monument. Eclipsed later by the Taj Mahal and the Jama Masjid, it is the best example in Delhi of the early Mughal style of tomb and is well worth a visit, preferably before visiting the Taj Mahal in Agra.

Humayun, the second Mughal Emperor, was forced into exile in Persia after being heavily defeated by the Afghan Sher Shah in 1540. He returned to India in 1545, finally re-capturing Delhi in 1555. For the remaining year of his life the emperor spent much of his time in the octagonal **Sher Mandal** at Sher Shah's fort (now the Purana Qila), poring over his cherished collection of miniatures and manuscripts. He is reputed to have died from the effects of a fall on the stairs of his library.

Haji Begum Humayun's tomb was built by his senior widow and mother of his son Akbar, **Hamida Begum**. A Persian from Khurasan, after her pilgrimage to Mecca she was known as **Haji Begum**. She supervised the construction of the tomb, which was begun in 1564 and completed in 1573, camping on the site. Her design was before its time, though it was used immediately afterwards in the much smaller tomb of **Atkah Khan.**

The tomb's plan Humayun's tomb is the first substantial example of Mughal architecture in India with its octagonal plan, lofty arches, pillared kiosks and the double dome, of Central Asia origin, which appears here for the first time in India. Hindu temples make no use of the dome, but the Indian Muslim dome had until now been of a flatter shape, much like a half grapefruit as opposed to the tall Persian dome rising on a more slender neck. Here also is the first standard example in India of the garden tomb concept: the **char bagh*** (garden divided into quadrants), water channels and fountains. This form culminated in the gardens of the Taj Mahal. However, the tomb also shows a number of distinctively Hindu motifs. Tillotson has pointed out that in Humayun's tomb, Hindu **chattris** (small domed kiosks), complete with temple columns and **chajjas** (broad eaves), surround the central dome. The **bulbous finial** on top of the dome and the **star motif** in the spandrels of the main arches are also Hindu, the latter being a solar symbol.

The approach From the car park you enter the Bu Halima garden before reaching the admission kiosk. The tomb enclosure has 2 high double-storeyed gateways, one on the W (through which visitors enter the tomb garden) and the other to the S. A **baradari*** pavilion occupies the centre of the E wall, and a bath chamber that of the N wall. Several Moghul princes, princesses and Haji Begum herself lie buried here. During the Mutiny of 1857 **Bahadur Shah II**, the last Moghul Emperor of Delhi, took shelter here with his 3 sons. In his eighties, he was seen as a figurehead by Muslims opposing the British. When captured he was transported to Rangoon for the remaining 4 years of his life.

   The platform on which the tomb is stands measures 47. 5 m square. The corners of the octagonal tomb are similarly large. **The dome** (38 m high) does not have the swell of the Taj Mahal and the decoration of the whole edifice is much simpler. It is of red sandstone with some white marble to highlight the lines of the building. There is some attractive inlay work, though far simpler than in the Taj. There are also some **jalis** (carved stone or marble screens) in the balcony fence, and on some of the recessed keel arch windows.

The interior is quite austere and consists of 3 storeys of arches rising up to the dome. The Emperor's tomb is of white marble and quite plain without any inscription. The overall impression is that of a much bulkier, more squat building than the Taj Mahal or Safdarjang's tomb. The cavernous space under the main tombs is an ideal home for great colonies of bats.

Minor sites S of the tomb To the S of Humayun's tomb, a further 3 km down the **Mathura Road** and 500 m to the W of the road itself is an **Asokan Rock Edict**, at **Okhla**. Discovered in 1966, this is one of Asoka's (272-232BC) minor Rock Edicts. It confirms that ancient Delhi was an important town on a trunk route connecting commercial centres with provincial capitals. The 18th century **Kalkaji temple** is close by and is dedicated to the goddess Kali (see Calcutta) who having killed all the demons who terrorized the neighbourhood installed herself on the hill nearby to be worshipped.

   From here it is possible either to continue on an outer circuit of Delhi by continuing S to **Tughluqabad** or travelling W on a shorter inner circuit of the southern city. The **Begumpuri Masjid**, lies just off Aurobindo Marg, to the S of its junction with Panscheel Marg. A 14th century mosque built by Khan-i-Jahan. The 94 m by 88 m courtyard of this imposing rubble-built mosque is enclosed by arched cloisters and contains a prayer hall to the W.

   About 1 km to the N is **Bijai Mandal** (Victory Palace), an unusual octagonal building with sloping sides and a doorway at each cardinal point. It is not clear whether it was the bastion of Muhammad-bin Tughluq's **Jahanpanah** or a tower to review his troops from. It is said that an **underground passage** links it with **Tughluqabad** (S) and **Firoz Shah Kotla** (N). 1 km to the SE is the **Khirki Masjid** (the Mosque of Windows), built in 1380 by the **Wazir*** of Firoz Shah Tughluq. It is a covered mosque with 4 open courts. The upper storey is broken with **khirki** (windows), hence its name.

Hauz Khas Immediately to the N again, and entered off either Aurobindo Marg on the E side or Africa Ave on the W side is **Hauz Khas. Ala-ud-din Khalji** (r1296-1313) created a large tank here for the use of the inhabitants of the Siri, the capital city of medieval Delhi founded by him. It was originally known as Hauz ul Alai after his name. 50 years later **Firoz Shah Tughluq** cleaned up the silted tank and raised several buildings on its E and S banks which are known as Hauz Khas or Royal Tank.

Firoz Shah' s austere tomb is found here. The multi storeyed wings, consisting of a series of halls on the N and W of Firoz Shah's tomb, were built by him in 1354 as a madrasa (college). The octagonal and square chattris were built as tombs, possibly to the teachers at the college. Nearby is the **Idgah mosque** built in 1405. Allow 20 min visiting time.

Hauz Khas is now widely used as a park for early morning recreation by the rapidly growing population of S Delhi – walking, running and yoga exercises. The courts of the Delhi Lawn Tennis Association, where Indian Davis Cup matches are played when held in Delhi, are just to the N of the gardens on Africa Ave. To the NE of Hauz Khas between **Aurobindo Marg** and the **Ring Rd** in New Delhi S Extension is the *Moth ki Masjid*. Sikander Lodi (r1488-1517) is said to have picked up a grain of lentil *(moth)* from a mosque and given it to his Prime Minister *(Wazir)* Miyan Bhuwa. The grain was sown and it multiplied until enough had been earned to build this mosque. Possibly the finest example of Lodi architecture, the design shows innovation in the decoration of its *mihrab** and arches, special treatment of the central arch and the construction of domes over the prayer hall. In these it anticipates several features of later Mughal architecture.

Qutb Minar Open sunrise to sunset. Entry Re 0.50
Muhammad Ghuri conquered NW India at the very end of the 12th century. The conquest of the Gangetic plain down to Benares was undertaken by Muhammad's Turki slave and chief general, Qutb-ud-din-Aibak, whilst another general took Bihar and Bengal. In the process, temples were reduced to rubble, the remaining Buddhist centres were dealt their death blow and their monks slaughtered. When Muhammad was assassinated in 1206, his gains passed to the loyal Qutb-ud-din-Aibak. Thus the first sultans or Muslim kings of Delhi became known as the Slave Dynasty (1026-1290).

For the next 3 centuries the **Slave Dynasty** and the succeeding **Khalji** (1290-1320), **Tughluq** (1320-1414), **Sayyid** (1414-45) and **Lodi** dynasties (1451-1526) provided Delhi with fluctuating authority. The legacy of their ambitions survives in the tombs, forts, palaces that litter Delhi Ridge and the surrounding plain.

Qutb-ud-din-Aibak died after only 4 years in power, but he left his mark with the **Qutb Minar** and his **citadel**. The Qutb Minar dominates the countryside for miles around, thereby fulfilling its purpose as a tower to proclaim the victory of Islam over the infidel (unbeliever). Qutb-ud-din-Aibak's city centred on the ruins of Lal Kot, the monuments being built with the materials from the 27 Hindu and Jain temples. The Qutb Minar should be visited first.

The construction Occasionally local guides will say that the tower was originally a Rajput building. There is absolutely no truth in this story. In 1199 work began on what was intended to be the most glorious tower of victory in the world and was to be the prototype of all minars (towers) in India. **Qutb-ud-din-Aibak** had probably seen and been influenced by the brick victory pillars in Ghazni in Afghanistan, but this one was to also serve as the minaret attached to the Might of Islam Mosque. From here the muezzin could call the faithful to prayer, though without the aid of modern speakers he would have had great difficulty in making himself heard. Later every mosque would incorporate its minarets.

As a mighty reminder of the importance of the ruler as Allah's representative on earth, the **Qutb Minar** (literally "axis minaret") stood at the centre of the community and the world revolved around it. A pivot of Faith, Justice and Righteousness, its name also also carried the message of Qutb-ud-din's ("Axis of the Faith") own achievements. The inscriptions carved in kufi script tell that the tower was erected' to cast the shadow of God over both East and

West'. For Qutb-ud-din-Aibak it marked the eastern limit of the empire of the One God. Its western counterpart is the **Giralda tower** built by **Yusuf I** in Seville, now attached to Seville's Cathedral.

The decoration The Qutb Minar is 73 m high and consists of five storeys. The diameter of the base is 14.4 m and 2.7 m at the top. Qutb-ud-din built the first three and his son-in-law Iltutmish embellished these and added a fourth. This is indicated in some of the Persian and Nagara (North Indian) inscriptions which also record that it was twice damaged by lightning in 1326 and 1368. While repairing the damage caused by the second, **Firuz Tughluq** (see above) added a 5th storey and used marble to face the red and buff sandstone. This was the first time contrasting colours were made a deliberate decorative feature. The later Mughals used this effect to its fullest. Firuz's fifth storey was topped by a graceful cupola but this fell down during an earthquake in 1803. A new one was added by a Major Robert Smith in 1829 but was so out of keeping that it was removed in 1848. Smith's cupola now stands in the gardens.

The original storeys are heavily indented with different styles of fluting, alternately round and angular on the bottom, round on the second and angular on the third. The beautifully carved honeycomb detail beneath the balconies are reminiscent of the Alhambra Palace in Spain. The calligraphy bands are verses from the Koran and praises to its patron builder. The staircase inside the tower to the balconies has been closed following an accident in 1979 when a party of schoolgirls panicked when the lights failed. Some were crushed to death in the resultant scramble to reach the exit.

The Might of Islam Mosque (Quwwat-ul-Islam) is to the right of the Qutb Minar. This is the earliest surviving mosque in India. It was begun in 1192, immediately after Qutb-ud-din's conquest of Delhi, and completed in 1198. The remains of no fewer than 27 local Hindu and Jain temples were used in its construction.

The architectural style that the Muslims brought with them contained elements that Islam had encountered on its passage east from Arabia. This included buildings made of mud and brick and decorated with glazed tiles, *squinches** (arches set diagonally across the corners of a square chamber to facilitate the raising of a dome and to effect a transition from a square to a round structure), the pointed arch and the true dome. Finally, Muslim buildings came alive through ornamental calligraphy and geometric patterning. This was in marked contrast to indigenous Indian styles of architecture. Hindu, Buddhist and Jain buildings relied on the post-and-beam system in which spaces were traversed by corbelling, i.e. shaping flat-laid stones to create an arch. The arched screen that runs along the W end of the courtyard beautifully illustrates the fact that it was Hindu methods that still prevailed at this stage, for the 16 m high arch uses Indian corbelling, the corners being smoothed off to form the curved line.

The screen The idea of a screen may have been borrowed from the sanctuary in the courtyard of the Prophet's mosque at Medina in Arabia. Whatever the influence, Qutb-ud-din's screen formed the facade of mosque and, facing in the direction of Mecca, became the focal point. The sandstone screen is carved in the Indo-Islamic style, lotuses mingling with Koranic calligraphy. The later screenwork and other extensions (1230) are fundamentally Islamic in style, the flowers and leaves having been replaced by more arabesque patterns.

Indian builders mainly used stone, which from the 4th century AD had been intricately carved with representations of the gods. In their first buildings in India the Muslim architects designed the buildings and local Indian craftsmen built them and decorated them with typical motifs such as the vase and foliage, tasselled ropes, bells, cows and leaves.

The Gupta pillar In the courtyard is the **iron pillar**. This dates from the 4th century AD and bears a Sanskrit inscription in the Gupta style of the period, telling that it was erected as a flagstaff in honour of Vishnu and in memory of the Gupta King Chandragupta II (375-413). Originally the pillar was topped by an image of Garuda, Vishnu's charge or vehicle and it probably stood facing a Vishnu temple. The purity of its wrought iron (98%) is extraordinary, and it has survived 1600 years virtually without blemish. A local tradition regards the pillar as having magical qualities. Anyone who can encircle it with their hands behind their back will have good fortune. Plenty seem to manage it.

Iltutmish's extension The mosque was enlarged twice. In 1230 Qutb-ud-din's son-in-law and successor **Shamsuddin Iltutmish** doubled its size by extending the colonnades and prayer hall – "Iltutmish's extension". This accommodated a larger congregation, and in the more stable conditions of Iltutmish's reign Islam was obviously gaining ground. The arches of the extension are nearer to the true arch and are similar to the Gothic arch that appeared in Europe at this time. The decoration is Islamic.

Ala-ud-din Khalji Almost 100 years after Iltutmish's death, the mosque was enlarged again, this time by **Ala-ud-din Khalji**. The conductor of tireless and bloody military campaigns, Ala-ud-din proclaimed himself 'God's representative on earth'. His architectural ambitions, however, were not fully realised, because on his death in 1316 only part of the N and E extensions were completed.

He did complete the S gateway to the building, the **Alai Darwaza**. Inscriptions on its surface testify that it was built in 1311 (the Muslim year 710 AH). Ala-ud-din benefited from events in Central Asia. Since the beginning of the 13th century Mongol hordes had been sweeping down from Central Asia and fanning out E and W. These invasions destroyed the civilisation of the Seljuk Turks in W Asia, and refugee artists, architects, craftsmen and poets fled E. Received and employed by Ala-ud-din they brought to India features and techniques that had developed in Byzantine Turkey. Some of these can be seen in the **Alai Darwaza**. The gate-house is a large sandstone cube 17 m square and 18 m high, into which are set small cusped arches with carved jali screens. The lavish ornamentation of geometric and floral designs in red sandstone and white marble produced a dramatic effect when viewed against the surrounding buildings.

The inner chamber, 11 m square, has a doorway in each side and, for the first time in India, true arches. Above each of these doorways is an Arabic inscription with its creators name and one of his self-assumed titles – 'The Second Alexander'. The N doorway, which is the main entrance, is the most elaborately carved. The dome, raised on squinched arches is flat and shallow, and topped with a button finial. Of the effects employed, the arches with their 'lotus-bud' fringes are Seljuk, as is the dome and rounded finial, and the general treatment of the facade. These now became trademarks of the **Khalji style**, remaining virtually unchanged until their further development in Humayun's tomb.

The Tomb of Iltutmish There are 3 tombs, all round the perimeter of the extended Might of Islam Mosque and in chronological order are: **The Tomb of Iltutmish** Built in 1235 this lies in the NW of the compound midway along the W wall of the mosque. It is the first surviving tomb of an Muslim ruler in India. The idea of a tomb was, of course, quite alien to Hindus, who had been practising cremation since around 400 BC. Blending Hindu and Muslim styles the outside is relatively plain, with three arched and decorated doorways. The interior carries reminders of the nomadic origins of the first Muslim rulers of India. It is like a Central Asian **yurt** (tent) in its decoration, combining the familiar Indian motifs of the wheel, bell, chain and lotus with the equally familiar geometric arabesque patterning. The W wall is inset with three mihrabs (arched alcoves) that indicate the direction of Mecca in any Muslim shrine.

The tomb originally supported a dome resting on *squinches**. If you look up these can be seen. The dome collapsed, as can be seen from the slabs of stone lying around, suggesting that the technique was as yet unrefined. The blocks of masonry were fixed together using the Indian technology of iron dowels. In later Indo-Islamic buildings lime plaster was used for bonding. To the SW of his uncompleted mosque an L-shaped ruin marks the site of the tomb within the confines of a *madrasa** where **Ala-ud-din Khalji** was buried. This is the first time in India that a tomb and madrasa are found together, another custom inherited from the Seljuks.

Immediately to the E of the **Alai Darwaza** stands the tomb of **Imam Zamin**, a sufi 'saint' from Turkestan who arrived in India at the beginning of the 16th century. It is an octagonal structure with a plastered sandstone dome and has *jali** screens, a characteristic of the Lodi style of decoration.

The Qutb Minar is less than 8 km W of the medieval Muslim fort of *Tughluqabad*, open sunrise 1700. Entry free. Despite its desolate and ruined appearance, Tughluqabad retains a sense of the power and energy of the newly arrived Muslims in India. **Ghiyas-ud-din Tughluq** (r1321-1325), after ascending the throne of Delhi, selected this site for his capital, see page 147. For strategic reasons he built a massive fort around his capital city which stands high on rocky outcrop of Delhi Ridge. The fort is roughly octagonal in plan with a circumference of 6.5 km. Its 10-15 m high rubble walls are provided with bastions and gates and are pierced with loopholes and are crowned with a line of battlements of solid stone. Presently the fort has 13 gates and there are 3 inner gates to the citadel. The vast size, strength and obvious solidity of the whole give it an air of massive grandeur.

The plan Tughluqabad was divided into 3 parts. To the E of the main entrance is a rectangular area, **the citadel**. A wider area immediately to the W and bounded by walls contained **the palaces**. Beyond this to the N lay **the city**. Now marked by the ruins of houses, the streets were laid out in a grid fashion. Inside the citadel enclosure is a tower known as **Vijay Mandal** and the remains of several halls including a long underground passage. The fort also contained 7 tanks. To the S of the fort outside was a vast reservoir created by erecting bunds between the hills. A causeway connects the fort with the tomb of **Ghiyas'ud-Din Tughluq** while a wide embankment near its SE corner gave access to the fortresses of **Adilabad** about 1 km away on another hill and built a little later by Ghiyas'ud-Din's son Muhammad. The tomb is in a state of excellent preservation, has red sandstone walls with a pronounced slope (the first Muslim building in India to have sloping walls) crowned with a white marble dome. According to Percy Brown this distinctive slope reflects the fact that Ghiyas'ud-Din modelled the design on a mausoleum he was building over 300 km away at **Multan**, in modern Pakistan. Lack of building stone in the Indus plains meant that they had to be built of brick, subsequently covered in plaster, and sloping walls dominate their design. It is one of the tragedies of the present political relationship between India and Pakistan that it is difficult to make the direct comparison. Inside are three cenotaphs belonging to Ghiyas'ud-Din, his wife and son Muhammad.

Ghiyas'ud-Din Tughluq quickly found that military victories were no guarantee of lengthy rule. When he returned home after a victorious campaign the welcoming pavilion erected by his son and successor, **Muhammad-bin Tughluq**, was deliberately collapsed over him. Tughluqabad was abandoned by Muhammad shortly afterwards and was thus only inhabited for 5 years. From the walls you get a magnificent impression of the strategic advantages of the site. It is worth visiting Tughluqabad to see the style of fort construction and to compare it with the later Red Fort in Old Delhi. You can see how the various functions of the capital were combined in the garrison, palace and city. It was not until Babur (r1526-1530) that dynamite was used in warfare, so this is a very defensible site. Allow 45-60 min for a tour of the site. Free.

To the N of Tughluqabad on the way back into Delhi is the *Baha'i Temple* in Bahapur. Visiting hours 1 Apr-30 Sep 0900-1900, 1 Oct-31 Mar 0930-1730. Closed Mon. Audio visual shows in English at 1100, 1200, 1400 and 1530. There is a library on the Left of the main entrance. Shoes must be left at the entrance. There is a very friendly and helpful staff of volunteers. Very peaceful atmosphere.

Constructed in 1980-1, the latest of 7 Baha'i temples in different parts of the world, it is built out of white marble and in the characteristic Baha'i temple shape of a lotus flower. In appearance it is reminiscent of the Sydney Opera House. The temple is 34 m from floor to apex, 70 m in diameter and with a seating capacity for 1300 worshippers. 45 lotus petals form the walls and surrounding the building are 9 pools. It is a simple design, brilliantly executed and very elegant in form.

The structure All Baha'i temples are 9 sided, symbolising "comprehensiveness, oneness and unity". The Delhi temple surrounded by 9 pools, not only making an attractive feature but helping to keep the building cool. Architecturally it is a remarkably striking building. Externally is has the form of the opening lotus flower. Internally it creates a feeling of light and space. Baha'i Houses of worship everywhere are "dedicated to the worship of God, for peoples of all races, religions or castes. Within their portals only the Holy Scriptures of the Baha'i Faith and earlier revelations are read or recited, according to arranged programmes". Visitors are welcome to such services, and at other times the temple is open for silent meditation and prayer.

The Baha'i faith was founded by a Persian, *Baha'u'llah* (meaning "glory of God": 1817-1892). It preaches that "all revelations are from the same divine source, brought to mankind progressively in different ages, through manifestations of the supreme creator, for the sole purpose of the spiritual and social upliftment of the entire human race, for carrying forward an ever-advancing civilisation. Baha'i's believe that *Baha'u'llah* is the manifestation of God for this age. His teachings were directed towards the "unification of the human race, the establishment of a permanent universal peace, the bringing into existence of a world commonwealth of nations. "The earth is but one country, and mankind its citizens". Baha'i's claim 1. 8 million adherents, though it is not clear what such adherence means.

NORTH OF CONNAUGHT CIRCUS

Shah Jahanabad (Old Delhi) Today, Shah Jahan (r1628-1658) is chiefly remembered for the astonishing achievement of the Taj Mahal. However, the Red Fort and the Jama Masjid in Delhi, both part of Shah Jahan's city, are also remarkable examples of the mature Mughal style that developed under his patronage. Both are well worth visiting, though the Red Fort in Delhi could be sacrificed for the Red Fort in Agra if time is at a premium. **Old Delhi: 10 Easy Walks** by Gaynor Barton and Lauraine Malone published by Rupa and Co, is an excellent short guide.

The city It was not until 1638 that Shah Jahan decided to move back from Agra to Delhi. Within ten years the huge city of Shah Jahanabad, now known as Old Delhi, was built. Much of the building material was taken from the ruins of Firozabad and Shergarh. The city was laid out in blocks with wide roads, residential quarters, bazaars and mosques. Its principal street was **Chandni Chowk** (Silver Street) which had a tree-lined canal flowing down its centre and which quickly became renowned throughout Asia. Today, Chandni Chowk retains some of its former magic, though now it is a bustling jumble of shops, of labyrinthine alleys running off a main thoroughfare with craftsmen's workshops, hotels, mosques and temples. Here goldsmiths, silversmiths, ivory workers, silk traders and embroiderers can all be found.

The city of Shajahanabad was protected by rubble-built walls, some of which still survive. These walls were pierced by 14 main gates. The most important of these still in existence are **Ajmeri Gate**, **Turkman Gate** (often referred to by auto-rickshaw *wallahs** as 'Truckman Gate'!), **Kashmiri Gate** and **Delhi Gate**. Between this new city and the River Yamuna Shah Jahan built a fort. Most of it was built out of red sandstone, hence the name **Lal Qila** (Red Fort), the same as that at Agra on which the Delhi fort is modelled. Begun in 1639 and completed in 1648, it is said to have cost Rs 10 million, much of which was spent on the opulent marble palaces within.

The Red Fort (Lal Qila) Open daily sunrise to sunset. Entry Re 0.50, free on Fridays. Allow 1 hour. The entrance is through the Lahore Gate, which is nearest the car park. The admission kiosk is opposite the Gate. Keep your ticket as you will need to show it at the entrance to the Drum House.

Even from a distance the walls of the fort towered massively above the flat banks of the Yamuna on which it was built. Despite the modern development of roads and shops and the never ending traffic, that dominating impression is still immensely powerful. The Fort is built as an octagon measuring 900 m by 550 m It was surrounded by a 9 m deep moat, now empty, fed by the Yamuna river. The river itself has now shifted more than 1 km to the E and is invisible beyond its high levee and the trees along it. In front of the fort is a massive *maidan** (open space) which has been used for political rallies ever since the time of the Independence Movement. From the **Lahore Gate** overlooking **the Maidan**, leaders such as Jawaharlal Nehru and Indira Gandhi have addressed enormous crowds on auspicious occasions such as the celebration of Independence and Prime Ministers still speak there on 15 August, Independence Day.

What is not obvious today on the ground is the symbolism of the plan of Shah Jahan's new city. If you look back from the gateway you can still make out the axis which Chandni Chowk represents between the seat of religious authority enshrined in the Jam Masjid to the W and the centre of political authority represented by the Diwan i Am in the heart of the Fort. This was the route used by the Emperor to go from his palace to the mosque, and it was designed to reinforce the popular awareness of the divine authority of the Mughal's political power. Entering the fort you now follow the same path.

The approach As you can see from the map, it is best to visit the places inside in a clock-wise

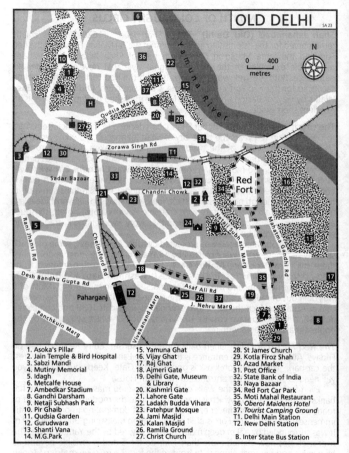

OLD DELHI SA 23

0   400
metres

N

Yamuna River

Red Fort

Sadar Bazaar

Qudsia Marg

Zorawa Singh Rd

Chandni Chowk

Rani Jhansi Rd

Chelmsford Rd

Desh Bandhu Gupta Rd

Paharganj

Panchkuin Marg

Vivekanand Marg

Asaf Ali Rd

J. Nehru Marg

Netaji Subhash Marg

Mahatma Gandhi Rd

1. Asoka's Pillar	15. Yamuna Ghat	28. St James Church
2. Jain Temple & Bird Hospital	16. Vijay Ghat	29. Kotla Firoz Shah
3. Sabzi Mandi	17. Raj Ghat	30. Azad Market
4. Mutiny Memorial	18. Ajmeri Gate	31. Post Office
5. Idagh	19. Delhi Gate, Museum	32. State Bank of India
6. Metcalfe House	& Library	33. Naya Bazaar
7. Ambedkar Stadium	20. Kashmiri Gate	34. Red Fort Car Park
8. Gandhi Darsham	21. Lahore Gate	35. Moti Mahal Restaurant
9. Netaji Subhash Park	22. Ladakh Budda Vihara	36. Oberoi Maidens Hotel
10. Pir Ghaib	23. Fatehpur Mosque	37. Tourist Camping Ground
11. Qudsia Garden	24. Jami Masjid	T1. Delhi Main Station
12. Gurudwara	25. Kalan Masjid	T2. New Delhi Station
13. Shanti Vana	26. Ramlila Ground	
14. M.G.Park	27. Christ Church	B. Inter State Bus Station

manner. You enter through the **Lahore Gate.** The defensive barbican that juts out in front of the gate was built by Aurangzeb who, impatient to rule, imprisoned his father in the Red Fort at Agra. The additions were in order to make it more difficult for an attacking army which, on passing through the outer gateway would then have to do a right angle turn before reaching the next, making it vulnerable to the defenders on the walls.

Inside is the **Covered Bazaar (Chatta Chowk).** Bazaars in the 17th century were usually open air, so a covered one such as this was quite exceptional. Above the signboard of shop no. 19 you can see the top of the original cusped arch of one of Shah Jahan's shops. Each shop on the lower arcade must have had an arch like this and in Shah Jahan's time there were shops on both upper and lower levels. Today the upper levels are the dwellings of Indian Army families and today the shops specialize in souvenirs. Originally they catered to the luxury trade of the Imperial household and carried stocks of silks, brocades, velvets, gold and silver ware, jewellery and gems. There were coffee shops too where nobles and courtiers sat discussing the latest campaigns, successes and defeats of the Mughal army. There are toilets near the Art Corner shop. Walk through the left-hand archway and you will see a small building on your right. These are the only visitor's toilets in the Red Fort.

The Naubat khana (or Nakkar Khana: drum house) is immediately beyond the bazar. This marked the entrance to the inner apartments of the fort. Here everyone except the princes of the royal family had to dismount and leave their own horses or elephants (*hathi*), hence its other name of **Hathi Pol** (Elephant Gate). But as well as a gate-house, the Drum House was a music gallery. Five times a day ceremonial music was played to the glory of the Emperor. Also, various princes are believed to have had their own special signature tunes which were played on their arrival at the court to notify those inside who was approaching. The instruments played were the **kettle drum**, **shenais** (a kind of oboe) and **cymbals**.

The Drum house has 4 floors and is very attractively decorated, the herbal or floral designs being especially noteworthy. Originally panels such as these were painted in gold or other colours, traces of which are still visible on the interior of the gateway. In Shah Jahan's day, the Drum House gave onto an inner courtyard 165 m wide and 128 m long, around which ran galleries. Here the palace guards were stationed. During the British period, the fort underwent a number of changes when it became the Army H. Q. and now the courtyard is a lawn bordered by shrubs.

The Diwan i Am Between the first inner court and the royal palaces at the heart of the fort, stood the Diwan-i-am (Hall of Public Audience). This was the farthest point the normal visitor would reach. Designed to be a functional building in which much of the administrative work of the empire could be conducted, it also acts as a showpiece intended to impress and hint at the even greater riches and opulence of the palace itself. The hall is well proportioned with a façade of 9 cusped arches standing 3 bays deep.

Now the hall has an elegant bare beauty, as do most of the Mughal monuments. However, it used to be very different. In Shah Jahan's time all the sandstone was hidden behind a very thin layer of white plaster, chunam, polished to shine like white marble. This was then decorated with floral motifs in many colours, especially gilt. There used to be silk carpets and heavy curtains hung from the outside of the building – you can see the canopy rings above the pillars. These could be raised and lowered by a system of ropes.

The throne surround At the back of the hall is a platform for the emperor's throne. Around this was a gold railing, within which stood the princes and great nobles. At the edges of the hall there was another railing, this time of silver, to separate the lesser nobles (inside the hall) from the rest. A third railing of sandstone stood in the courtyard (now the lawn) to separate minor officials from the general public. A canopy was erected above the minor officials' enclosure, supported by massive silver-plated poles and capable of shading 1000 people. The white marble dais at the rear of the hall throne and on which the throne itself was placed marries Persian with Bengali influences. The Persian input is in the inlaid floral decoration. The roof is in the Bengali style – modelled on the bamboo roofs of eastern India which were curved to facilitate the draining of the heavy monsoon rains and this represents the archaic convention of the sacred tree umbrella. Canopies such as this had been protecting sovereigns and teachers since at least the time of the Buddha (6th century BC).

The contact with Italy The throne was known as 'The Seat of the Shadow of God', giving a clear indication of the emperor's self-perceived role in the world. Wherever you stand in the hall (everyone except the emperor's favourite son had to stand), there is an uninterrupted view of the throne – a powerful psychological effect. The low marble bench was the platform of the **Wazir*** (Chief Minister). Behind the throne canopy are twelve marble inlaid panels. Figurative workmanship is very unusual in Islamic buildings, and this one panel is the only example in the Red Fort. Ebba Koch suggests that in all there are 318 ***Florentine pietre dure*** plaques in the niche behind the throne, showing flowers, birds, and lions as well as the central figure of Orpheus, playing to the beasts. In between these Italian panels are Mughal pietre dure works with flowery arabesques in the lower area, and birds, fashioned like those in the Italian plaques, in the lunette-shaped sections of the wall. Ebba Koch argues that the technique employed by the Mughal artisans are exactly the same as the Italian ones, so there must have been a direct connection.

This is not to say that there was no independent development of Mughal inlay craftsmanship. Such a view has been described by Tillotson as the result of wishful thinking by Europeans, eager to claim a stake in the superb work. In fact the Mughals had an equally fine tradition of stone carving and of inlay work on which to draw as had the Florentine princes, as can be seen from the work in the **Jami Masjid** in Ahmadabad, built in 1414. **see page 1041**. The development in technique under Shah Jahan paralleled that in Italy, but the view that this resulted from the presence of European lapidaries in the Mughal court needs careful scrutiny. As Ebba Koch concludes, the similar tastes and interests of the Mughal patrons and artists, (scientific naturalism and involvement in precious stones and their courtly uses) led to similar artistic expressions even if some of the lessons came from European

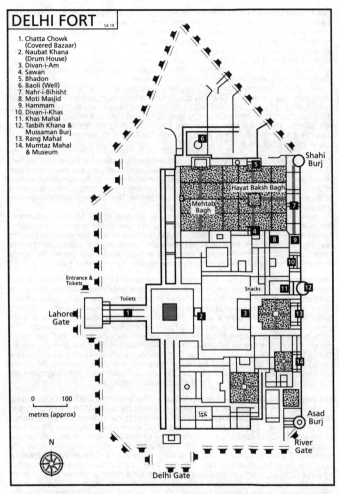

DELHI FORT SA 19

1. Chatta Chowk
   (Covered Bazaar)
2. Naubat Khana
   (Drum House)
3. Divan-i-Am
4. Sawan
5. Bhadon
6. Baoli (Well)
7. Nahr-i-Bihisht
8. Moti Masjid
9. Hammam
10. Divan-i-Khas
11. Khas Mahal
12. Tasbih Khana &
    Mussaman Burj
13. Rang Mahal
14. Mumtaz Mahal
    & Museum

teachers. He argues that the Mughals were quick to realise the potential of the European form for their own needs, and in the end similar solutions might have been produced by an artistic development that had become quite independent from its initial impetus. "

Shah Jahan's day Shah Jahan used to spend about 2 hours a day in the **Diwan-i-Am**. According to Bernier, the French traveller, the subjects waited patiently, their eyes downcast and their hands crossed. The emperor would enter to a fanfare and mounted the throne by a flight of moveable steps. The business conducted was a mixture of official and domestic administration. There would be reports from the provinces, tax and revenue matters and official appointments. On the personal side, Shah Jahan would listen to accounts of illness, dream interpretations and anecdotes from his ministers and nobles. Also, many animals would be paraded across the courtyard for inspection. Wed was the day of judgment. Sentences were often brutal but swift and sometimes the punishment of dismemberment, beating or death was carried out on the spot. The hangmen were always close at hand with their axes and whips to mete out this rough justice. On Fri, the Muslim holy day, there would be no business.

The inner palace buildings The Diwan-i-am has seen many dramatic events – the destructive whirlwind of the Persian **Nadir Shah** in 1739 and of Ahmad Shah the Afghan in 1756, and the trial of the last 'King of Delhi' – **Bahadur Shah II** in 1858. Behind the Hall of Public Audience is the private enclosure of the fort in which Shah Jahan set 6 small palaces (5 survive). These are along the E wall of the fort overlooking the river Yamuna. Also within this compound are the harem, the Life-Bestowing Garden and the Nahr-i-Bihisht (Stream of Paradise). Leave the throne canopy area by the steps to your left, follow the path and carry on until you reach the white marble garden pavilion (See Map).

Like all Islamic formal gardens the **Life-Bestowing Gardens** (*Hayat Baksh Bagh*) were designed to imitate the heavenly gardens of paradise. Though the present layout is new, the original was landscaped according to the Persian *char bagh** with pavilions, fountains and water courses dividing the garden into various but regular beds. The pavilion you are now standing in is one of two. The other is directly opposite, and they are known as **Sawon** and **Bhadon**. Their names reveal something of the character of the garden. **Sawon** is the first month of the rainy season (Jul) and **Bhadon** the second (Aug). The garden used to be so alive with water as to create the effect of the monsoon and contemporary accounts tell us that in the pavilions, and some were especially erected for the Hindu festival of Teej which marks the arrival of the monsoon, the royal ladies would sit in silver swings and watch the rains.

Water flowed from the back wall of the pavilion through a slit above the marble shelf and over the niches in the wall. Gold and silver pots of flowers were placed in these alcoves during the day whilst at night candles were lit to create a glistening and colourful effect. The water then flowed from along a channel to a square pool in the centre of the garden. The pool area is now filled with grass and there is a sandstone pavilion in the centre of it, built in the 19th century. During Shah Jahan's reign apparently there was also a pavilion hidden by the jets of water from the 281 fountains surrounding it. To the W is Mehtab Bagh which has a *Baoli** (well) to its NW.

The *Shahi Burj* From here you can walk to the next pavilion which is opposite and then to the tower at the right hand side. The latter is the **Shahi Burj**. It was from the pavilion next to the tower that the canal known as the **Nahr-i-Bihisht** (Stream of Paradise) began its journey along the Royal Terrace. The octagonal Royal Tower is closed to the public as it was seriously damaged in 1857 and is still unsafe! It has 3 storeys. The lower one contained a tank from which water was raised to flow into the garden. The view from the wall by the tower shows that there is some distance to the River Yamuna. In Shah Jahan's time it lapped the walls and in 1784 a Prince, concerned that he might be about to lose his life, jumped from the Royal Tower into the river, swam across it and fled to Lucknow. Shah Jahan used the tower as his most private working place and only his sons and 3 or 4 senior ministers were allowed with him. Looking along the length of the Royal Terrace you can see the Stream of Paradise flowing south to the next building along the walls. These are the Royal baths.

To the right are the 3 marble domes of the ***Moti Masjid*** (Pearl Mosque) To enter you must take off your shoes. Built in 1662 by Aurangzeb for his personal use, it is a small building and, except for the cupolas, completely hidden behind a wall of red sandstone. It is of polished marble and like a pearl it is small, white and with some exquisite decoration. Aurangzeb's style is more ornate than Shah Jahan's. All the surfaces are highly decorated in a fashion similar to rococo, which was developed at the same time in Europe. The prayer hall is on a raised platform which is unusual in a mosque and the hall is inlaid with the outlines of individual prayer mats (musallas) in black marble. Interestingly the interior and exterior walls are not aligned with each other. The outer walls are aligned to the cardinal points, for this was the layout of all the buildings in the fort (See Map). But, in order for the Mosque to be correctly facing Mecca the inner walls were positioned so that in fact they are out of true with the rest of the buildings.

The baths and the Diwan-i-Khas Move back towards the wall to the first of a line of buildings, the **Hammam** (Royal Baths), three apartments separated by corridors with canals to carry water to each room. The 2 rooms flanking the entrance had hot and cold baths were for the royal children. The room furthest away from the door has 3 fountain basins which emitted rose water. It is reputed that 4 tonnes of wood were required to heat the water. Beyond is the **Diwan-i-Khas** (Hall of Private Audience), the hub of the court, a one-storeyed building topped by 4 Hindu-style *chhatris* (cupolas) and built completely of white marble. The *dado** (lower part of the wall) on the interior was richly decorated with inlaid precious and semi-precious stones. The ceiling was silver but was removed by the Marathas in 1760 – **see page 97**. Outside, the hall used to have a marble pavement and an arcaded court. Both have gone.

The **Peacock Throne** In the centre of the hall is a marble pedestal on which stood the Peacock Throne. This was designed with the form of two peacocks standing behind it and was 2 m long by 1.3 m broad. It was inlaid with an extraordinary range of precious stones – sapphires, rubies, emeralds, pearls and other precious stones. Even the 6 huge feet were made of solid gold inlaid with rubies, emeralds and diamonds. Over the top was a canopy of gold, supported by 12 pillars, all gem encrusted. The figure of a parrot, said to have been carved out of a single emerald, gave the final touch. Shah Jahan commissioned it on his accession to the throne in 1627.

Nadir Shah The throne was taken off and dismantled when Nadir Shah, a Turk who had overthrown the **Safavid Dynasty** in Persia sacked Delhi in 1739. The first two days of his occupation of Delhi were quiet enough, then a riot broke out which resulted in the death of 900 of his soldiers. Nadir Shah himself rode through the streets of Delhi to assess the situation and some residents were rash enough to throw stones at him. Enraged, Nadir Shah ordered the entire population of Delhi to be massacred, and by the end of the day 30,000 corpses littered the streets. In the evening the 'Great' Mughal (Mohammad Shah) begged for mercy, and such was Nadir Shah's control over his troops that he was able immediately to halt the carnage. The invaders packed up to go, taking with them as much as they could extort from all the nobles and rich citizens, never hesitating to use torture when verbal encouragement failed. The Mughal Emperor was forced to hand over the keys of the treasury, jewels, and the Peacock Throne. The haul was so large that Nadir Shah was able to suspend taxes in Persia for the next 3 years! The throne was later broken up by the assassins of Nadir Shah in 1747, and some of the jewels found their way into the possession of the late Shah of Iran's family. Shah Jahan's Peacock Throne bears no relation to the Persian one.

The office of state It was in **the Diwan-i-Khas** that all the important affairs of state and policies were decided. It was the Mughal 'Oval Office' or 10 Downing Street. Here also, the emperor would also inspect paintings and miniatures or review select animals and birds such as cheetahs and hawks that would be presented in the forecourt. Shah Jahan spent 2 hours (1000-1200) in the Diwan-i-Khas before retiring for a meal, siesta and prayers. In the evening he would return to the Hall for more work before going to the harem and his women. He usually retired to bed at around 2200 and liked to be read to, his particular favourite being the **Babur-i-nama**, the autobiography of his great-great-grandfather. Such was the splendour of the hall that in the eyes of many there was little reason to doubt the words of the 14th century poet **Amir Khusrau** inscribed above the corner arches of the N and S walls: *Agar Firdaus bar rue Zamin-ast/ Hamin asto Hamin asto Hamin ast*. (If there be a paradise on earth, it is here, it is here, it is here.)

Next to the Diwan-i-Khas is the **Khas Mahal** (The Private Palace). This is consists of three rooms. To the N, nearest the Diwan-i-Khas, is the **Tasbih Khana** (Chamber for the Telling of Rosaries). Here the Emperor would worship privately with his rosary of 99 beads, one for each of the mystical names of Allah. After the death of his beloved wife Mumtaz, for whom the Taj Mahal was constructed, Shah Jahan became quite devout. In the centre is the **Khwabgah** *(The Royal Sleeping Chamber)* which gives on to the octagonal tower. Here Shah Jahan would be seen each morning. A balcony was added to the tower in 1809 and here George V and Queen Mary appeared in the Durbar of 1911. The Durbar celebrated their coronation and coincided with the announcement of the decision to move the capital from Calcutta to Delhi.

To the S is a long hall with painted walls and ceiling, the **Tosh Khana** *(Robe Room)*. At the N end is a beautiful marble screen. This is carved with the scales of justice – above the filigree grille. If you are standing with your back to the Diwan-i-Khas you will see a host of circulating suns but if your back is to the next building, i.e. the Rang Mahal, you will see moons surrounding the scales. The sun was widely used to symbolize royalty, e.g. Louis XIV of France (Le Roi Soleil). It is most appropriate for the suns to be there as that particular side faced the throne of the 'Sun' himself, Shah Jahan. All these rooms were sumptuously decorated with fine silk carpets, rich silk brocade curtains and lavishly decorated walls. Beneath the Khas Mahal is the **Khirzi Gate**. This is neglected now, but was an important and convenient private entrance for the Emperor and his most senior nobles. After 1857 the British used the Khas Mahal as an officer's mess and sadly it was defaced.

The Palace of Colours Next again to the S is the **Rang Mahal** *(Palace of Colours)*, the residence of the chief **sultana***. It was also the place where the emperor ate most of his meals. To protect the rich carpets, calico-covered leather sheets were spread out. It was divided into six apartments. Privacy and coolness was ensured by the use of marble *jali** screens. Like the other palaces it was beautifully decorated with a silver ceiling ornamented with golden flowers to reflect the water in the channel running through the building. The N and S apartments were both known as **Shish Mahal** (Palace of Mirrors) since into the ceiling were set hundreds of small mirrors. In the evening when candles were lit a starlit effect would be produced. This type of decoration was a favourite in Rajasthan before the Mughals arrived (**see page 616** – Amber Fort).

Through the palace ran the Life-bestowing Stream and at its centre is a lotus shaped marble basin which had an ivory fountain. As might be expected in such a cloistered and cossetted environment, the ladies sometimes got bored. In the 18th century the Empress of Jahandar Shah sat gazing out at the river and remarked that she had never seen a boat sink. Shortly afterwards a boat was deliberately capsized so that she could be entertained by the sight of people bobbing up and down in the water crying for help. In the summer the ladies went underground. Access is not permitted but the rooms would have been cool because they were cellars and had water running above them.

Museum The southernmost of the palaces is the **Mumtaz Mahal** (*Palace of Jewels*) which was also used by the harem. The lower half of its walls are of marble and it contains six apartments. After the Mutiny of 1857 it was used as a guardroom and since 1912 it has been a **museum** with exhibits of textiles, weapons, carpets, jade and metalwork as well as works depicting life in the court. It should not be missed. Open daily except Fri, 0900-1700.

Between the Mumtaz Mahal and Rang Mahal was a small palace known as **Choti Baithak** (Little Sitting Room) but this has disappeared. The other parts of the Red Fort are inaccessible. You leave the same way as you entered.

One km to the W of the Red Fort is the magnificent *Jama Masjid* (The Friday Mosque), the largest mosque in India and the last great architectural work of Shah Jahan, intended to dwarf all mosques that had gone before it. In this way, it is quite in keeping with most of Delhi's other monuments. It also has the distinction of being one of the few mosques, either in India or elsewhere that was designed to produce a pleasing external effect. Though large it is also elegant.

With the Fort it dominates Old Delhi. Both symbolize the mighty aspirations of their maker and demonstrate the gulf that existed between monarch and subject. Each Friday the emperor and his male retinue would travel the short distance from the fort to participate in the midday prayers, the foremost service of the Muslim week.

The gateways The Mosque has 3 huge gateways, the largest being on the E. This was reserved for the royal family, who gathered in a private gallery in its upper storey. Today, the faithful enter through the E gate on Fri and on the occasion of the two annual **Id** festivals to mark the end of Ramadan, **Id-ul-Fitr**, and **Id-ul-Adha**, which commemorates Abraham's sacrificial offering of his son Ishmael. (Islamic traditions varies from the Jewish and Christian tradition that Abraham offered to sacrifice Isaac, Ishmael's brother.) The general public enter by the N gate.

The purpose of gateways is symbolic as well as practical for they separate the sacred and secular worlds (See also The Taj Mahal). So, the threshold is a place of great importance where one steps to a higher plane. Shoes must be removed. Visitors should cover their heads.

The courtyard (*sahn*) acts as an extended prayer hall and here is nearly 900 m square. It can accommodate over 20,000 worshippers. The mosque itself comprises a facade which includes the main arch (*iwan*) 5 smaller arches on each side and 2 flanking minarets. Behind sit 3 bulbous domes, a large central one flanked by two smaller ones, all perfectly proportioned and placed in relation to one another. The effect of the *iwan* is to draw the worshippers attention into the building.

The Jama Masjid is much simpler in its ornamentation than Shah Jahan's secular buildings, a judicious blend of red sandstone and white marble. Marble and sandstone are interspersed in the domes, minarets and cusped arches. All these features are intended to emphasize the architectural merits of the building rather than to merely act as decoration. In the centre of the courtyard is a tank. Water plays an important role is Islam just as it does in Hinduism. It is used as a means of initiation. The ablution tank (*hauz*) is placed between the inner and outer parts of a building to remind the worshipper that it is through the ritual of baptism that one first enters the community of believers.

In front of the ablution tank stands a raised platform about 3 m high. This is a **dikka**. Muslim communities grew so rapidly that by the 8th century it became necessary in many places to introduce a second prayer leader (*muballigh**). This was his platform, and his role was to copy the postures and chants of the *imam** who was inside the building and thus relay them to a much larger congregation. With the introduction of the loudspeaker and amplification, the dikka and the muballigh became redundant.

The Kawthar Inscription Set up in 1766, the inscription commemorates the place where a worshipper had a vision of the Prophet standing by the celestial tank in paradise. It is here that the Prophet will stand on Judgment Day. In most Islamic buildings, the inscriptions are passages from the Koran or Sayings of the Prophet. Shah Jahan, however, preferred to have sayings extolling the virtues of the builder and architect as well. The 10 detailed panels on the façade indicate the date of construction (1650-1656), the cost (10 lakhs – one million rupees), the history of the building, the architect (Ustad Khalil) and the builder (Nur Allah Ahmed, probably the son of the man who did most of the work on the Taj Mahal).

North of The Red Fort

The centre of gravity of the city has shifted steadily S since 1947. The old civil lines area to the N of Kashmiri Gate and the Red Fort, is now often by-passed. However, there are several sites of interest.

Going N past the Old Delhi Post Office, just before Kashmere Gate (now by-passed by the main road), is **St James Church**, completed in 1836. It was bult by Colonel James Skinner, who had a great military reputation in the Punjab. **See page 702.**

Kashmere Gate was built by the British, along with other bastions in Shah Jahan's original city walls, in 1835. It was blown up in the Mutiny of 1857. Immediately to the N of the gate today is the main inter-state Bus terminal. On the opposite side of the road are the Qudsia Gardens, named after the wife of the Mughal Emperor Muhammad Shah, who laid out the gardens in 1748.

The **Oberoi Maiden's Hotel** is 1 km further N, in the heart of the Civil Lines, and just to the N again a mound on which Tamerlane camped when he attacked Delhi. The Civil Lines were the centre of British Administration until New Delhi was completed. Running N to S is the Delhi Ridge. At the S end of the Ridge is the President's Estate in New Delhi. However, it was on the N end that the major monuments of British India, before New Delhi itself, was thought of were built.

To reach the crest of the ridge, still covered in low scrub, go down Raj Niwas Rd, just S of the Oberoi Maidens Hotel. At the end of Raj Niwas Marg turn left and then right into Hindu Rao Marg, named after Hindu Rao, whose house (now a hospital on the W facing the Ridge) played a vital role in the British troops defence after the Mutiny. The road makes the short but quite steep climb up the Ridge. Turning left at the top of the ridge, and Asokan pillar is just off to the left. Further down the road is the Gothic **Mutiny Memorial**. There are excellent views over the old city. To the SW is Sabzi Mandi, the old city's vegetable market, to the SE the Jama Masjid. Running N from the Mutiny Memorial, the Ridge Road (re-named *Rani Jhansi Marg*) goes to the University.

SERVICES

Hotels Note: 10% Luxury Tax, 10% Service Charge and 20% Expenditure Tax (on hotels with room rates over Rs 450 per night) are charged by most hotels in addition to the basic rate. Payment in foreign exchange (which is compulsory), either by cash, travellers cheque, credit card, or on production of Foreign Exchange Encashment Certificate (received every time money is changed) enables Expenditure Tax to be refunded (by the hotel at time of settlement of bill). Children under 12 years are generally free if sharing a room with parents. If 3 persons travelling together wish to share a room and extra beds are available, savings can be made. Some hotels offer large discounts out of season, generally Apr to Sep.

Delhi has a wide range of hotels covering all categories. The following category **AL** establishments are International Luxury class hotels and have a full range of facilities including Business Centres, Conference and Banquet facilities and comprehensive in-house services.

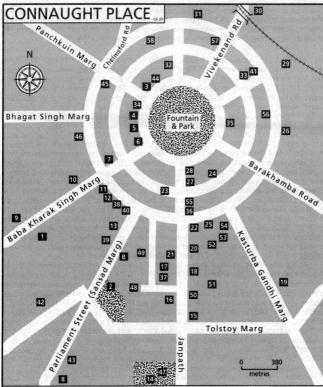

CONNAUGHT PLACE SA 20

Panchkuin Marg
Chelmsford Rd
Vivekenand Rd
Bhagat Singh Marg
Fountain & Park
Barakhamba Road
Baba Kharak Singh Marg
Parliament Street (Sansad Marg)
Kasturba Gandhi Marg
Tolstoy Marg
Janpath

0 — 380 metres

1. Hanuman Mandir
2. Jantar Mantar
3. Bata
4. Thai International
5. Post Office
6. British Airways
7. American Express
8. Grindlays Bank
9. State Emporia
10. Benetton
11. Khadi Gramodyog Bhavan
12. Regal Cinema
13. The Shop
14. Thomas Cook
15. Nepal Airlines
16. Tibetan Market
17. Central Cottage Industries Emporium
18. Tourist Office
19. Hindustan Times
20. Air India
21. Clothes Market
22. Air France
23. Palika Underground Bazaar
24. Automobile Association
25. Delhi Transport Corporation (DTC)
26. Super Bazaar
27. Vayudoot (Airline)
28. Airport Bus
29. Shankar Market
30. Minto Bridge

31. First Class Railway Reservation Office
32. The Bookworm
33. ITDC Transport Office
34. Wenger's Restaurant
35. United Coffee House
36. Wimpey & Pizza King
37. Bankura Coffee House & Map Sales Office
38. Gaylord Restaurant
39. El Arab Restaurant
40. Kwality Restaurant
41. *Nirula's Hotel & Restaurant*
42. *YMCA Tourist Hostel*
43. *YWCA International Guest House*
44. Volga Restaurant
45. *Marina Hotel*
46. *Alka Hotel*
47. *Imperial Hotel*
48. *SC Jain Guest House*
49. *Mrs Colack's Guest House*
50. *Janpath Guest House*
51. *Gandhi Guest House*
52. *Ringo Guest House*
53. *Sunny Guest House*
54. *Asia Guest House*
55. *Metro Hotel*
56. *Hotels Blue & Bright*
57. *York Hotel*
58. *Hotel 55*
B. DTC Bus Stand

The Govt of India classes them as 5 Star Deluxe. They cater just as much to the tourist as to the business traveller, and all have central a/c, pools, shopping arcades and a wide array of services. **Note** The symbols shown represent the distance from the international airport (✈), domestic airport (⚑), New Delhi railway station (®) and the city centre (©).

AL *Ashok*, 50-B Chanakyapuri. T 600412, Cable: Ashokahotel, Telex 031-65207. 571 rm. ✈ 15 km, ⚑ 10 km, ® 9 km. ITDC's flagship hotel, recently renovated, fresh looking garden bar and sunny coffee shop. Big rooms and quiet location. Not in the heart of town. Restaurants: *Durbar* and *Frontier* (NW Frontier), Ashok, T 600121: Similar to Bukhara. Good, especially murg daranpur, a chicken stuffed with minced chicken, cheese and spices. *China Town* serves both Szechuan and Cantonese dishes in a room with foods displayed on colourful carts. Special restaurants offering Japanese (Tokyo) and Greek food, in addition to multi cuisine restaurants. French *Burgundy*. **AL** *Holiday Inn Crowne Plaza*. Barakhamba Ave., Connaught Place. T 3320101, Telex: 031-61186 Hind in, Fax: 3325335. 500 rm. ✈ 20 km, ® 2 km, © 0.5 km. Delhi's most recent and most centrally located luxury hotel. 25-storey 'standard' hotel and the exclusive 11-storey Presidential Tower with even more superior rooms and suites and access to 'Club Privee', the hotel's business facility that offers a private business centre, board rooms, dining lounge and bar. 'Club Select' for business traveller's – 2 floors of executive accommodation with its own manager, lounge, bar, business library and express check-in. No Smoking floor, wheelchair accommodation and underground car parking for all guests. Good views. Special Indian restaurant: *Baluchi*; Chinese: *Noble House*. **AL** *Hyatt Regency,* Bhikaiji Cama Pl, Ring Rd. T 609911, Telex: 031 61512 Hyt In, Fax: 678833 535. 535 rm. ✈ 12 km, © 8 km. Exclusive 'Regency Club' floor, modern Business Centre, good pool plus discotheque, health club and tennis, geared to the business traveller. Excellent restaurants. Indian *Aangan* ; excels in Peshawari foods such as fruit filled nan (tandoori bread) and tangri kebab (chicken legs stuffed with minced chicken and laced with yoghurt and spices). Also Hyderabadi dishes. Chinese *Pearls* Italian *Valentino's*.

AL *Le Meridien*, Windsor Place, Janpath. T 383960, Telex: 63076 Home in, Cable: Meridhotel, Fax: 384220. 373 rm. ✈ 23 km, ® 2 km, © 0.5 km. Ideally located just to the S of Connaught Place, a stunning hotel both externally and internally. Good views, impressive elevated pool. Suffered major problems with New Delhi authorities in 1990 over tax claims, and in 1990-91 was not always fully operational. **AL** *The Oberoi*, Dr Zakir Hussain Marg. T 363030, Telex: 74019, Obdl in, Cable: Obhotel, Fax: 360484. 288 rm. ✈ 20 km, ⚑ 16 km, ® 9 km, © 8 km. Recently refurbished at great expense and with considerable flair, this is one of the prestigious 'Leading Hotels of the World' and probably ranks as the city's best hotel for its quiet efficiency and dignity'. Overlooks Golf Course and has fine views of Humayun's Tomb. Exclusive butler service throughout. Full business facilities the Executive Centre has a 24-hr secretarial service, and a global courier network. Excellent restaurants, including *Esmeralda* (Mediterranean) and *La Rochelle* (French). *Orient Express* (Taj Palace), T 3010404; a replica of the famous Belle Epoque dining car provides the setting. Fixed menu inspired by the cities the train passes through. **AL** *The Taj Mahal*, 1 Mansingh Rd. T 3016162, Telex: 66874/61898 Tajd in, Cable: Tajdel, Fax: 3017299. 300 rm. ✈ 18 km, ® 5 km, © 5 km. Often referred to as Taj Man Singh to distinguish it from the Taj Palace. An excellent, lavishly finished and very well run hotel with good views over the city, especially from higher floors. Excellent restaurants: Indian – *Haveli* and Chinese *House of Ming* Expensive and exquisite. *Captain's Cabin* Seafood. *Casa Medici* Italian. Good pool, a Disco and an exclusive patisserie.

AL *Taj Palace Inter-Continental*, 2 Sardar Patel Marg, Diplomatic Enclave. T 3010404, Telex: 61673, Tajs in, Fax: 301-1252. 504 rm. ✈ 12 km, ® 9 km, © 10 km. Younger brother to the Taj Mahal and purpose built for convention business, tour groups and business travellers. Restaurants include: *Handi* Excellent dishes from N and W India, again cooked in handis. Comfortable Gujarati surroundings of carved wood and *patola** canopies. Central Asian specialty and *Orient Express* restaurants, with authentic coaches. *Tea House of the August Moon* with a bridge, pond and bamboo grove adorn this restaurant which also serves a typical Chinese lunch. Location good for airport but away from centre. **AL** *Welcomgroup Maurya Sheraton Hotel and Towers*, Sardar Patel Marg, Diplomatic Enclave. T 3010101, Telex: 61447 Welc in, Cable: Welcotel, Fax: 3010908. 500 rm. ✈ 12 km, ® 8 km, © 10 km. Excellent hotel in all respects. Executive Club rooms designed for business travellers, Towers Club, a separate hotel-within-a-hotel for even more luxurious rooms and service, splendid pool (solar heated in winter), and tennis. It is almost equidistant from the airport and centre. Restaurants: *Bukhara* (NW Frontier, Maurya Sheraton) Very popular and very good. Frontier cuisine, e.g. kebabs and delicious breads, served on low tables with tree stumps as chairs. Diners are issued with bibs! Recommended but worth going early. *Dum Phukt* Excellent N Indian fare cooked in *handis** (sealed brass vessels so that the food cooks in its own steam. *Bali Hi* Chinese and Polynesian, European band.

The following **A** category hotels (Govt. classification is 5 Star) are all very comfortable and good but do not meet the exceptionally high standards set by the AL group in terms of rooms, facilities and service. **A** *Centaur,* Indira Gandhi International Airport. T 5481411, Telex: 62744 Chda in, Cable: Centaur. 376 rm. ✈ 2 km, ⊛ 16 km, © 16 km. Floodlit tennis court and putting green, secretarial service. Service unreliable – can be lamentably bad, but free bus service to airport and centre. **A** *Claridges,* 12 Aurangzeb Rd. T 3010211, Telex: 65526, Clar in, Cable: Claridges, Fax: 3010625. 167 rm. ✈ 20 km, ⊛ 16 km, ⊛ 6 km, © 4 km. Colonial atmosphere and attractive restaurants: *Corbett's* (Tandoori) and *Dhaba.* The first is inspired by Jim Corbett National Park and has a jungle 'feel', the second, though indoors, is decorated with a realistic replica of a brightly painted truck (dhaba means *truck stop*) pulled into a village. Both have very good food and are extremely popular. Chinese *Jade Garden.* **A** *Imperial,* Janpath. T 3325332, Telex: 62603, Cable: Comfort, Fax: 3314542. 175 rm. ✈ 20 km, ⊛ 17 km, ⊛ 2 km, central. Attractive colonial feel, especially in the bedrooms and well tended gardens, a haven in the heart of town. Good for breakfasts and lunch even if you are not staying. Given the hotel's central location the swimming pool is an added attraction. **A** *Kanishka,* 19 Ashoka Rd. T 3324422, Telex: 62788, Cable: Kanishotel. 317 rm. ✈ 20 km, ⊛ 17 km, ⊛ 2.5 km, © 0.5 km. Secretarial service. Excellent views from upper floors, but otherwise a rather characterless hotel run by ITDC. Service can be slow. Restaurants: *Dilkusha* (Kanishka), T 3324422; Lucknowi and Hyderabadi dishes featured.

A *Oberoi Maidens,* 7 Sham Nath Marg. T 252564, Telex: 66303, Cable: Obmaidens 53 rm. ✈ 30 km, ⊛ 10 km (Old Delhi) 2 km. Many large rm (especially suites), verandahs, though some rm are enclosed and windowless. A very attractive colonial style hotel (one of the oldest) in quiet area of Old Delhi set in spacious gardens. Poor location for New Delhi, but reasonably priced. More personal attention than in the larger top class hotels. Lacks arcade shops but has a disco. Restaurants include continental *Auberge* **A** *Park,* 15 Parliament St. T 352447, Telex: 65231, Cable: Parkotel, Fax: 352025. 234 rm. ✈ 20 km, ⊛ 2 km, central. Small pool. Very central. 50% discount April – September. Rooms modern and comfortable, but walls much too thin! Friendly service. Exclusive Bengali cuisine in special restaurant. **A** *Qutab,* Off Sri Aurobindo Marg. T 660060, Telex: 62537, Cable: Qutabotel 64 rm. ✈ 15 km, ⊛ 12 km, ⊛ 15 km, © 15 km. Pool, tennis, bowling alley. Also apartments (12S, 18D) have kitchens equipped with refrigerator and cooking range (no room service in apartments). **A** *Samrat,* Chanakyapuri. T 603030, Telex: 72122, Cable: Hotelsmrat. 268 rm. ✈ 15 km, ⊛ 12 km, ⊛ 9 km. Secretarial service. **A** *Siddharth,* 3 Rajendra Place. T 5712501, Telex: 77125, Cable: Ironhotel. 100 rm. ✈ 15 km, ⊛ 4 km, © 4 km. **A** *Sofitel Surya,* New Friends Colony. T 6835070, Telex: 66700, Sura in, Cable: Surotel. 230 rm. ✈ 18 km, ⊛ 12 km, © 10 km. Courtesy coach. **A** *Vasant Continental,* Vasant Vihar. T 678800, Telex: 72263, Cable: Contihotel, Fax: 678899. 110 rm. ✈ 10 km, ⊛ 6 km, ⊛ 13 km, © 10 km. Convenient for the airports, smaller than the others and with a more Indian atmosphere. Commercial centre next door. All facilities. Courtesy coach. **A** *The Ambassador,* Sujan Singh Park. T 690391, Telex: 3277, Cable: Hotel Ambassador 69 rm. ✈ 12 km, ⊛ 6 km, © 5 km. No pool but Discotheque, garden. Restaurant: *Dasaprakash* (south Indian) Wide menu including fresh grape-juice, butter dosa and fig ice-cream. Surroundings have been described as 'a cross between a church and a film set'.

B *The Connaught Palace,* 37 Shaheed Bhagat Singh Marg. No pool. **B** *Diplomat,* 9 Sardar Patel Marg. T 3010204, Telex: 3161042 Dipin, Cable: Diplomatic. 25 rm. ✈ 10 km, ⊛ 10 km, © 10 km. No pool. Quietly located in the Diplomatic section of town. **B** *Hans Plaza,* 15 Barakhamba Rd. T 3316868, Telex: 63126 Hans in, Cable: Hanstel 67 rm. ✈ 20 km,⊛ 2 km, © 1 km, excellent location. No pool. Business centre, health club. Good views. **B** *Janpath,* Janpath. T 3320070, Telex: 61546, Cable: Restwell. 213 rm. ✈ 20 km, ⊛ 17 km, ⊛ 2 km, © 0.5 km. No pool. TV. Good location but poor rooms and service. Restaurants Indian, Continental, and Chinese – *Mandarin Room.*

C Marina, G-59 Connaught Circus. T 3324658, Telex: 62969, Cable: Marina. 93 rm. ✈ 20 km, ⊛ 1 km, central. **C** *Nirula's,* L-Block, Connaught Circus. T 3322419, Telex: 66224 Nchs in, Cable: Nirulabros. 29 rm. ✈ 22 km, ⊛ 1 km. No pool. Central location right at the heart of things. TV and Video. Good "fast-food" style restaurant and own ice cream parlour – a focus for Delhi social life! **C** *Jukaso Inn,* 50 Sunder Nagar. T 690308/9. 50 rm. ✈ 21 km, ⊛ 9 km, ⊛ 8 km. Central a/c. Restaurant, credit cards, lawns. Pleasant hotel in quiet location, friendly staff. **C** *Rajdoot,* Mathura Rd. T 699583, Telex: 74129, Cable: Riverview. 55 rm. ✈ 16 km, ⊛ 7 km (close to Hazrat Nizammudin rly), © 6 km. Pool. TV, car hire, dubious nightclub! **C** *Alka,* 16/90 Connaught Circus. T 344328, Cable: Hotel Alka. 23 rm. ✈ 20 km, ⊛ 1.5 km, central. Central a/c. Credit cards. **C** *Asian International,* Janpath Lane. T 3321636, Telex: 61258 Hai-in, Cable: Haihotels. 33 rm. ✈ 20 km, ⊛ 3 km, © 1 km. A/c. Restaurant, 24 hr rm service, coffee shop, exchange, car hire, credit cards, TV and Video. **C** *Broadway,* 4/15A Asaf

Ali Rd. T 273821, Telex: 66299 Bway in, Cable: Luxury. 32 rm. ✈ 15 km, ⑬ 2 km, © 2 km. Central a/c. Restaurant, bar, TV and Video, 24 hr coffee shop, car hire, exchange, credit cards.

C *Jukaso Inn*, L-1 Connaught Circus. T 3324977. 28 rm. ✈ 20 km, ⑬ I km, central. Travel desk, exchange, video, credit cards. **C** *Lodi*, Lala Lajpat Rai Marg. T 362422, Telex: 74068, Cable: Livwell. 207 rm. ✈ 22 km, ⑬ 8 km (1 km Nizamuddin rly), © 7 km. Central a/c. Restaurant *Woodlands* Highly recommended **S** Indian food, bar, car hire, shopping arcade, pool, TV and Video. **C** *President*, 4/23B Asaf Ali Rd. T 277836-8, Telex: 62422, Cable: Bhaisons. 20 rm. ✈ 17 km, ⑬ 3 km, © 2 km. Central a/c. Restaurant *Tandoor* Good quality tandoori food. Indian music. Coffee shop, bar, travel, TV, credit cards. **C** *Ranjit*, Maharaja Ranjit Singh Rd. T 3311256, Telex: 66001, Cable: Staywell. 186 rm, about half a/c. ✈ 26 km, ⑬ 2 km, © 3 km. Restaurant (pure vegetarian cuisine), car hire, TV, exchange, coffee shop, bar, credit cards, pool. **C** *Sartaj*, A-3 Green Park Main. T 667759, Telex: 73009 Srtj in, Cable: Daawat. 45 rm. ✈ 10 km, ⑬ 11 km, © 10 km. Central a/c. Restaurant, bar, TV, travel, credit cards. **C** *Sobti*, 2397-98 Hardian Singh Rd, Karolbagh. T 5729065, Cable: Stayfine. 27 rm. ✈ 21 km, ⑬ 4 km, © 5 km. Central a/c. Restaurant, refrigerator, 24 hr rm service, garden, credit cards, TV. **C** *Vikram*, Ring Rd, Lajpatnagar. T 6436451, Telex: 71161, Cable: Hotelvikram. 72 rm. ✈ 12 km, ⑬ 13 km, © 12 km. Central a/c. Restaurant, bar, travel, exchange, credit cards, pool, TV. **C** *York*, K-Block, Connaught Circus. T 3323769, Telex: 63031 York in, Cable: Yorkhotel. 28 rm. ✈ 20 km, ⑬ 1 km, central. Central a/c. Restaurant, pool, TV.

D *La Sagrita Tourist Home*, 14 Sunder Nagar. T 694541, Cable: LASAGRITA,Telex: 031 74040 LASG IN. 25 rm with phone. Close to Supreme Court, Pragati Maidan, quiet location. ✈ 16 km, © 4 km. Central a/c. Restaurant, travel, lawns, TV and video. Very helpful staff, strict hygiene. Room service and food very good. Excellent value for money for Delhi. **D** *YMCA Tourist Hostel*, (Postal address Box 612) Jai Singh Rd. T311915, Telex: 62547 YMCA in, Cable: Manhood. 123 rm. ✈ 19 km, ⑬ 3 km, © 1 km. Open to both sexes. A/c rooms with baths and telephone; B block is non a/c. Small membership charge, max stay 15 days. "Luxury" rooms available with thicker mattresses. Restaurant, pool, exchange, travel, roller-skating, Amex, Diners and Visa cards. Good value. **D** *YWCA International Guest House*, Sansad Marg, T 311561. 24 a/c rm. ✈ 20 km, © 1 km. Open to both sexes, restaurant serving largely western style food. Convenient location. **D** *Ashok Yatri Niwas*, 19 Ashok Rd. T 3324511, Cable: Yatriniwas. 547 rm. ✈ 20 km, ⑬ 3 km, © 1 km. 547 rm. ITDC run. Good self-service restaurant, bar, exchange, car hire. Magnificent views from higher floors, but rooms up to floor 14 not very clean, poorly lit. Lifts inadequate. Service at main desk can be very slow, and sometimes demand full payment in advance. Restaurant: *Coconut Grove* (South Indian) Pleasant atmosphere, good value.

D *Maharani Guest House*, 3 Sunder Nagar. ✈ 16 km, © 4 km. Quiet location. Restaurant (Indian), roof terrace. Good value. **D** *Woodstock Motel*, 11 Golf Links, T 619571. 16 a/c rm. ✈ 14 km, © 4 km. Restaurant. A guest house which is recommended for its friendly attention and quiet location with a pleasant garden. Recommended. **D** *Bright*, M-85 Connaught Place. T 3320444, Telex: 61815 lita in Cable: Hotel Bright. 18 rm. ✈ 20 km, ⑬ 2 km, central. Exchange, credit cards. **D** *Central Court*, N Block Connaught Circus. T 3315013, Cable: Central Court. 36 a/c rm. ✈ 20 km, ⑬ 1 km, centre location. Restaurant, coffee shop, exchange, credit cards, TV and refrigerator. **D** *Flora*, Dayanand Rd, Darya Ganj. T273634-6, Cable: Fusee. 24 a/c rm. ✈ 21 km, ⑬ 3 km, © 2 km. Restaurant, room service, car hire. **D** *Gautam Deluxe*, D. B. Gupta Rd, Karol Bagh. T 5729162, Cable: Gaut delux. 63 rm. ✈ 22 km, ⑬ 2 km (4 km Old Delhi rly), © 3 km. A/c (29 rm). Restaurant, 24 hr rm service, credit cards. **D** *Manor*, 77 Friends Colony. T 632171, Telex: 4815 Manr, Cable: Count hotel. 24 a/c rm. ✈ 16 km, ⑬ 10 km, © 8 km. Restaurant, car hire, travel, pool, tennis. **D** *Metro*, N-49 Connaught Circus. T 3313856, Cable: Metro. 10 rm, half a/c. ✈ 20 km, ⑬ 2 km, central. Credit cards. **D** *Rajdeep*, 2632-4 Bank Street, Karol Bagh. Central a/c. Restaurant, 24 hr rm service, travel, TV. **D** *Regal*, S. P. Mukherjee Marg. T 2526197. 37 rm, some a/c with TV. ✈ 22 km, ⑬ 6 km (2 km Old Delhi rly), © 6 km. **D** *Sodhi Lodge*, E-2 East of Kailash. T 6432381. 9 a/c rm. ✈ 14 km, ⑬ 10 km, © 8 km. Restaurant, TV lounge, car hire, Diners Club Cards. **D** *S Indian*, Ajmal Khan Rd, Karol Bagh. T 5717126, 25 rm, some a/c. ✈ 20 km, ⑬ 2 km, © 2 km. Restaurant, travel, credit cards. **D** *Tera Hotel* and Restaurants, 2802 Bara Bazar, Kashmir Gate. T 239660-1, Cable: Terejoga. 42 rm, some a/c. ✈ 24 km, ⑬ 4 km (0.5 km Old Delhi rly), © 4 km. Restaurant, 24 hr coffee shop, TV and Video, Diners Club Cards. **D** *Tourist*, Ram Nagar. T 510334-40, Telex: 61210 Sccl, Cable: Hotel Tourist. 65 rm, some a/c. ✈ 22 km, nr New Delhi rly, © 1 km. Restaurant, car hire, safe deposit, travel, Diners Club Cards, TV. **D** *Tourist Holiday Home*, 7 link Rd, Jangpura. T 618797. 16 rm, some a/c. ✈ 16 km, ⑬ 6 km, © 6 km.

E *Asian Guest House*, 14 Scindia House, Kasturba Gandhi Marg. Single and double rm with bath, some a/c, a bit spartan but clean. Good services, friendly, helpful management. Phone (local/international available). **E** *Bhagirath Palace*, Opposite Red Fort, Chandni Chowk. T

236223, Cable: Hotbha. 18 rm. ✈ 26 km, ® 5 km (1 km Old Delhi rly), © 5 km. A/c and non a/c. Bar, TV, rental car. **E** *Hotel Fifty Five*, H-55 Connaught Circus. T 3321244. 15 rm. ✈ 20 km, ⊕ 1 km, central. Central a/c. 24 hr room service, travel, car hire, safe deposit, Diners Card. **E** *Host Inn*, F-33 Connaught Place. T 3310431. 10 rm. ✈ 20 km, ® 1 km, central. Central a/c. TV and Video, Amex cards. **E** *Neeru*, 10 Netaji Subhash Marg, Darya Ganj. T 278522, Cable: Feelhome. 24 rm. ✈ 23 km, ® 2 km, © 2 km. A/c and non a/c, restaurant. **E** *Palace Heights*, D-Block Connaught Circus. T 3321369. 18 rm. ✈ 20 km, ® 2 km, central. Non a/c, breakfast and beverages only. **E** *Satkar*, Green Park. T 664572. 9 rm. ✈ 12 km, ® 12 km, © 10 km. A/c and non a/c. Restaurant (veg). **E** *Shiela*, Pawha House, 9 Qutab Rd. T 525603. 44 rm. ✈ 20 km, ® 1 km, © 1 km. A/c and non a/c. Car hire, travel, safe deposit, Diners Club Cards. **E** *The Nest*, Corner House, 11 Qutab Rd. T526614, Telex: 62416, Cable: Nest. 18 rm. ✈ 20 km, ® 1 km, © 1 km. A/c and non a/c. Car hire, exchange, safe deposit, room service.

Very cheap accommodation There are a number of inexpensive hotels around Janpath and Paharganj – all are in the **F** category. Well patronised but basic and, usually cramped, they are good places for meeting fellow budget travellers. The Government of India Tourist Office on Janpath keep an update on these, as does the Student Travel Information Centre at the Imperial Hotel, also on Janpath.

Some of the Janpath establishments are: *Ringo Guest House*, 17 Scindia House. Some rm with bath and dormitory; *Sunny Guest House*, 152 Scindia House. Single and double rm; *Gandhi Guest House*, 80 Tolstoy Marg. Single and double rm; *Royal Guest House*, 44 Janpath, nr Nepal Airlines. Some rm with bath; *R. C. Mehta*, 3rd floor 52 Janpath; Mr S. C. *Jain's Guest House*, 7 Pratap Singh Building, Janpath Lane, rm without bath; *Soni Guest House*, Janpath Lane; Hotel Blue, M-85 Connaught Circus, opp Super Bazar, cheap.

Along the main bazaar leading up to New Delhi Rly station in the Paharganj area there are numerous establishments, all fairly cheap, pretty noisy and basic. Some of the places are: *Hotel Kiran*, 4473 Main Bazaar; *Hotel Navrang*, some rm with bath, friendly; *Hotel Vishal*, some rm bath and dormitories; *Hotel Sapna*, rm with baths, clean; *Hotel Chanakya*, rm and dormitory, pleasant; *Venus Hotel*, 1566 Main Bazaar. Some rm with bath; *White House Tourist Lodge*, 8177 Main Bazaar. More expensive; *Apsara Tourist Lodge*, 8501/1 Main Bazaar, similar; Hotel Crystal; *Hotel Airlines*, opp Rly Station; *Hotel Little Star*, between Main Bazaar and Desh Bandhu Gupta Rd. Cheap.

Paying Guest Accommodation. A number of Delhi families welcome tourists as paying guests. Consult the Government of India Tourist Office, 88 Janpath for full details.

Airport Retiring Rooms, T 391351. Rooms at Rs 200 (D) and Rs 100 (S). Contact Airport Manager. Room allocation on first-come, first served basis for confirmed ticket holders only. Basic. *Rly Retiring Rooms*, Old and New Delhi Rly Stations are available for 12 and 24 hours periods. Do rm beds and a/c and non a/c rooms. Users must have a train ticket. Basic, noisy but convenient.

Youth Hostels and camping **F** Vishwa Yuvak Kendra (International Youth Centre), Circular Rd, Chanakyapuri, T 3013631. 8 km Connaught Place. 36 rm, some with bath and Dormitory.,12 km airport. Open to all ages. Modestly priced cafeteria. On 620 bus route to Connaught Place. Reservations: The Manager. **F** *Youth Hostel*, 5 Nyaya Marg, Chanakyapuri, T 3016285. Dormitories. Breakfast available. Preference given to International YHA members. Often full. **F** *New Delhi Tourist Camp*, Nehru Marg, opp Jai Prakash Hospital, T 272898. Restaurant, gardens. Near Connaught Place and New Delhi rly. **F** *Tourist Camp*, Qudsia Gardens, opp Inter-State Bus Terminal, T 2523121. Camping and huts. Food available. Handy for bus station.

Restaurants For the foreign visitor, the larger hotels have many of the best restaurants, some of which are excellent not only for the food but also for the decor and ambience. These are described in the hotel section. All hotels take non-residents. There are also a number of fine restaurants outside hotels. Establishments are categorised by the type of food served. Eating out is very popular in Delhi and restaurants do not usually open until 1930-2000. Indian families sometimes eat very late, eg 2300 so if you do not have a reservation, you will probably have more success eating early. The very popular establishments, e.g. *Bukhara* (Maurya Sheraton) do not take reservations from non-residents. It is worth telephoning beforehand to check. If you wish to drink alcohol with your meal, then go to a hotel. Alcohol is not served in restaurants outside hotels.

24-Hour Coffee shops Usually pleasantly situated by garden or poolside, often serving substantial snacks and quicker than restaurant service. The best are in the **AL** category. E.g. *Cafe Promenade* (Hyatt Regency), T 609911; very pleasant for breakfast, English and Indian style. *Machan* (Taj Mahal), T 3016162 the name means 'jungle lookout'. *Samovar* (Ashok), T 600121; good cappuccino. *Verandah* (Imperial), T 3325332. Very pleasant setting.

Indian The emphasis is more on authentic cooking for Indian palates than on elegant or imaginative surroundings. *Angeethi* (barbecue), The Village, T 6447320. *Ankur*, The Village, T 6441945. *Bankura*, (Central Cottage Industries Emporium), Janpath, T 3322371. A cafe, not restaurant, serving snacks only. *Degchi*, 13 Regal Building, Connaught Place, T 3321444: Unremarkable surroundings but very good food. *Dum Pukht* (Maurya Sheraton) A genuinely unique restaurant. Exceptional cuisine, superb ambience. *Kaka's*, Plaza Building, Connaught Place; Handi dishes and delicious green masala fish. *Flora*, opp the Jama Masjid, T 264593; very popular with locals. *Karim's*, Jama Masjid, T 269880: Some of the best Mughlai food in Delhi, e.g. kalmi chicken kebab, biryani and breads. Unpretentious surroundings but extremely popular with locals. *Karim's Nemat Kada*, Nizamuddin West, T 698300. Same as Karim's. *Khyber*, Kashmere Gate, T 2520867: Peshawari dishes, often cooked in a kadhai (Indian wok). *Mini Mahal*, C-25A Vasant Vihar, T 674620. *Moti Mahal Delux*, NDSE II, T 6410480. *Moti Mahal*, Darya Ganj, T 273661: The original Moti Mahal, serving tandoori food. Pleasant, but not as good as it used to be. Open air. Closed Tues. *Moti Mahal*, M-13 Greater Kailash I, T 6412467. *Mughlai*, M-17 Connaught Place, T 3321101. *Moets*, Defence Colony Market, T 626814. Peshawari, 3707 *Subhash Marg*, Daryaganj, T 262168; tiny restaurant with tiled walls serves delicious buttered chicken. Closed Tues. *Sona Rupa*, Janpath: south Indian and Bengali. *S Indian Boarding House*, opp Shankar Market. Very popular with S Indians.

Chinese *Aka Saka*, Defence Colony Market, T 626640. *Berco's*, L-Block Connaught Place, T 3323757. *Chopsticks*, The Village, T 6442348. *Chungwa*, D-13 Defence Colony Flyover Market, T 623612. *Daitchi*, E-19A NDSE II, T 6447511. *Dynasty*, M-17 Connaught Place, T 3321102. *Faley's*, Defence Colony Market, T 623612. *Fujiya*, 12/48 Malcha Marg, T 3016059; has Japanese dishes too. *Ginza*, K-Block Connaught Place, T 3323481. *Golden Dragon*, C-2 Vasant Vihar, T 670426, also Khel Gaon Marg, T 660582; popular with diplomats as a take-out and eat-in place. *Hong Kong*, M-31 Greater Kailash I, T 6412721. *Nirula's Chinese Room*, L-Block Connaught Place, T 3322419.

Continental *El Arab*, 13 Regal Building, Connaught Place, T 3321444; Lebanese. *Fisherman's Wharf*, A-1 Moolchand Shopping Complex, T 698123. *Potpourri*, Nirula's, L-Block Connaught Place, T 3322419. Popular for lunch and evening meals. Good value self service restaurant, very central. *A Touch of Class*, Hauz Khas Village.

Multi-Cuisine *Embassy*, 11-D Connaught Place, T 351191. *Gaylord*, Regal Building, Connaught Place, T 352755. *Host*, F-8 Connaught Place, T 3316576. *Kwality*, Regal Building, Connaught Place, T 311752. *Minar*, L-11 Connaught Place, T 311778. *Shivaji*, Shivaji Stadium, T 343607. *United Coffee House*, E-15 Connaught Place, T 3322075. *Volga*, B-19 Connaught Place, T 3321473. *Yorks*, K-Block Connaught Place, T 3323769.

Tea Lounges The old fashioned 'tea on the lawns' still served at the *Imperial* and in the *Claridges'* courtyard, though you can go inside to the airconditioning if you prefer. Some other hotels offer tea, coffee and cold drinks with light snacks, e.g. sandwiches and cakes. *Chaitya Hall* (Maurya Sheraton). *Emperor's Tea Lounge* (Taj Mahal). *La Plaza* (Le Meridien). *The Tea Lounge* (Ashok). *The Tea Lounge* (Kanishka).

Fast Food *American Pie*, Asian Games Village Complex (1100-2400). *Laziz*, 1 Jor Bagh for S Indian coffee and snacks; *Nizam's Kathi Kebabs*, H-5 Plaza Connaught Place. *Nirula's*, L-Block Connaught Place for snacks, pastries and ice creams in a cluster of shops (1100-2230); Also at 13/30 Ajmal Khan Rd, Chanakya Theatre , Defence Colony Flyover, NOIDA Phase IV, Vasant Vihar; and New Friends Colony. *Tej's*, N-Block Connaught Place; *The Treat*, Palika Parking Complex, Connaught Place. *The Regency Midtown*, B-29 Connaught Place. *Wimpy's*, N-5 Connaught Place. *Pantry*, M-15 Connaught Place. *Sona Rupa*, 46 Janpath for vegetarian snacks (0900-2200). When shopping in the State Emporia, walk across to Mohan Singh Place Building on Baba Kharak Singh Marg for excellent coffee and snacks on top floor.

Confectioners and Pastry Shops **Outside hotels**: *Chocolate Wheel*, 55 Jorbagh. *Nirula's Pastry Shop*, L-Block Connaught Place. *Wengers*, A-Block Connaught Place.

Bars The first and seventh day of each month and national holidays are 'dry'. On these days, liquor stores and hotel bars are closed but you can get a drink through room service. Normally, hotel restaurants, coffee shops, tea lounges and bars and, of course, clubs serve alcohol,

restaurants outside hotels do not. All the more expensive hotels have bars.

Clubs *Chelmsford Club*, Raisina Rd. T 384693. *Delhi Gymkhana Club*, Safdarjang Rd. T 375531. Membership mostly for government and defence personnel. Long waiting list. Squash, tennis, swimming, bar and restaurant. *Roshanara Club*, Roshanara Rd. T 712715. Cricket club and ground, used in the film 'Gandhi'.

Banks Banking hours – Mon-Fri 1000-1400, Sat 1000-1200. **NB** Localities in Delhi, including banks, close in rotation on different days of the week. See tips for shopping to get an idea of closing days. It is usually quicker to change foreign cash and travellers cheques at hotel exchange counters, though the exchange rate may be slightly poorer.
    Foreign Banks: *American Express*, A-Block Connaught Place, T 3324119. One of the best places to change money. Hours are longer than normal banking hours. *Bank of America*, 15 Barakhamba Rd, T 3315101. *Bank of Tokyo*, Jeevan Vihar, Sansad Marg, T 310033. *Banque Nationale de Paris*, 2nd Floor, Suryakiran Bldg, Kasturba Gandhi Marg, T 3313883. *Citibank*, Jeevan Vihar Bldg, Parliament St. T 3315367. *Grindlays Bank*, Sansad Marg, T 3323735. *Mercantile Bank*, ECE House, 28 Kasturba Gandhi Marg, T 3314355.
    Indian Banks dealing in foreign exchange: Open 24 hours: *Central Bank of India*, Ashok Hotel, T 601848. *State Bank of India*, Palam Airport, T 392807. Normal hours: *Bank of Baroda*, 16 Parliament St., T 332557. *Bank of India*, Bahadur Shah Zafar Marg, T 3312654. *Canara Bank*, 7 Tolstoy Marg, T 3317066. *Federal Bank Ltd.*, M-73 Connaught Circus, T 3326494. *Indian Overseas Bank*, Rachna Building, Rajendra Place, T 5718580. *New Bank of India*, 1 Tolstoy Marg, T 3314402. *Punjab National Bank*, 28 Kasturba Gandhi Marg, T 3316183. *Punjab National Bank*, 5 Sansad Marg, T 383626. *State Bank of India*, SBI Bldg, Sansad Marg, T 310635. *The Chartered Bank*, 17 Sansad Marg, T 310195.

Shopping Shops generally open from 1000 to 1930 Winter timings 1000 to 1900. Food stores, chemists stay open later. Most shopping areas close on Sun including Connaught Circus, Khan Market, Jor Bagh and Sundernagar. However, S Extension and Greater Kailash are closed on Mon and Green Park, Haus Khaz and Sarojini Nagar Markets are closed on Tues. Banks tend to follow the same pattern.

Handicrafts The *Central Cottage Industries Emporium*, Janpath, is Govt. run and has fixed prices. The range and quality of goods is generally excellent and there is the bonus of hassle-free shopping under one roof if you are in a hurry. They will also pack and post your purchases overseas. Exchange counter and gift wrapping service. Other Govt emporia like *Khadi Gramodyog Bhawan*, for homespun cotton kurta (loose shirts), pyjamas and cotton/silk waistcoats. Usually there are further discounts to the already low prices. Very popular with locals. *Handicrafts and Handloom Export Corporation*, Lok Kalyan Bhawan, 11A Rouse Avenue Lane. *Kashmir Govt. Arts Emporium*, 5 Prithviraj Rd. Each state has its own emporium and all these are conveniently located on Baba Kharak Singh Marg which runs off Connaught Place.
    The *Tibetan Market* of streetside shops and stalls along Janpath has plenty of trinkets, curios and knick-knacks. Nearly all the items have been made recently and are rapidly aged so don't be fooled into thinking that they are old or authentic. There are carpet shops to be found in most hotels and there are a number round Connaught Place. If you are making a trip to Agra, check out the prices there before committing yourself to a purchase.
    Craftsmen carving ivory can be seen at *Ivory Mart* in Chawri Bazaar behind the Jama Masjid. Finished works can be purchased. If you want to see marble inlay, Agra is the place for that (though much of it is soapstone, not marble). Unglazed earthenware khumba matkas (water pots) can be bought round New Delhi Rly Station. The workshops are behind the main road.

Leather Goods Khan Market and **S Extension** are good for leather goods and shoes, as are the shops at the Taj Mahal, Taj Palace and Maurya Sheraton hotels. *Bharat Leather Shop*, opp Nirula's on Connaught Place and the *Central Cottage Industries Emporium*, Janpath have good selections whilst *Bata* and *Baluja*, both on Connaught Place have good selections of readymade shoes (except for men and women with large feet). *Bata* is very popular with Delhi-ites and also has a selection of leather bags and cases.
    Tailoring is not as cheap as it used to be – Bangkok for example is much cheaper – and styles tend to be somewhat dated. Nearly all hotels will have a fabric/tailor's shop and these all more likely to be able to reproduce your preferences than tailors patronised almost exclusively by locals. Allow 24-hours or so for stitching. It is usually quite permissible to take in fabric purchased elsewhere but your bargaining power over the cost will be reduced. Readymade clothes (Western style) can be found in the small shops along Janpath before the Tibetan Market and between Parliament Street and Janpath and also at the underground

Palika bazaar where Janpath joins Connaught Circus. Top quality clothes in the latest styles and fashionable fabrics are virtually unobtainable – it seems that India exports all this, but a modest selection can be found at *The Shop*, in the parade of shops just round from the Regal Cinema on Connaught Place. They also have a good selection of table linen and printed bed covers. Indian style clothing is readily available from the *Khadi shop*, near the Regal building, and more regional styles of dress at the state emporia on Baba Kharak Singh Marg. Sari shops abound. *Fab India*, 14 N Greater Kailash, has unusual household linen and some ready-made garments.

The shopping centres at Chandni Chowk, catering to Indian taste and demand and at Sunder Nagar which is more western oriented are also worth visiting. Some designer wear in European styles can be bought from the *Hauz Khas village* – a series of authentic, old village houses converted into designer shops selling a whole range of handicrafts, ceramics, antiques, furniture in addition to luxury wear. Private entrepreneurs have their small boutiques, *Dastakaar*, in an excellent, moderately priced cooperative outlet. Art galleries, restaurants also found here. *Archana* in Gt Kailash I has several boutiques.

Food Pre-packaged **namkeen** (savoury snacks) can be bought from the grocery shops along Janpath and also at *Super Bazaar* on the outer circle of Connaught Circus, and at many other places besides. Excellent Indian teas can be purchased from the *Cottage industries Emporium*, *Modern Bazaar* and from *Tea City* outlets – they are widely advertised. Also at the charming shop in the small Kaka Nagar Market on Zakir Hussain Marg, opp the Golf Course. Well worth a visit. Some of the best, freshest and, therefore, safest Indian sweets are at *Bhim Sen's* at the Bengali Market at the end of Tansen Marg not far from Connaught Place. Delicatessen products like cold meats, cheeses, yoghurts can be bought at the *Steakhouse, Jorbagh Market, Modern Bazar* in Vasant Vihar market. Fresh fruit and vegetables at INA Market, Bengali Market and Khan Market among others.

Maps *The Survey of India Map Sales Office* above the Bankura cafe next door to the Central Cottage Industries Emporium on Janpath has a selection of guide maps of different Indian cities and states. This is a typically bureaucratic Indian government office. Maps are regarded as highly sensitive information and it is difficult to obtain good maps at any scale. It is illegal to sell large scale maps of any area within 50 miles of the coast and there are other restricted areas. However, the sales office does have a number of 1:20,000 maps of major Indian cities, though some have not been revised for over ten years. There is also a range of other maps available. For anyone interested in the geography of India, however, trying to buy good maps is a depressing experience. Open 1000-1700.

Photography *Delhi Photo Company*, 78 Janpath, T 3320577. *Fotofare*, N-54 Connaught Place, T 3318586. *Goyal Colour Photo Labs*, C-24 Connaught Place, T 3324738. *Imperial Photo Stores*, opp State Bank of India, Chandni Chowk, T 264266. *Kodak*, A-22 Janpath, T 387215. *Quick Colour Lab*, Kanishka Shopping Plaza, T 3325353. *Simla Studio*, 4 Regal Building, Connaught Place, T 310383.

Books *Jains Bookshop* in F block, Connaught Circus, is the Govt book agency. Excellent range. *Oxford Book and Stationery Co.* , Scindia House, and The Bookworm, B-Block, are both on Connaught Place and have good selections of fiction and books on India. Moti Lal Benarsi Das, Nai Sarak, Chandni Chowk, has books on Indology. *The Bookshop*, Khan Market, has a wide choice of new books. All around Connaught Place there are street booksellers and a wide range of foreign authors' works have been printed in India at a fraction of the book price elsewhere. *Rupa and Co* is foremost among these. In many hotels there are booksellers but often they charge inflated prices. *Prabhu Service* at Gurgaon village beyond the airport is an excellent second-hand bookshop. If you don't want to carry your books home, you can have them sent. Many booksellers offer this service, taking the books to be weighed at the P.O. and notifying you of the postal charge. You will have to make a return visit though.

Local Transport

Transport to and from the airport There are taxis available from the airport into the city. **Note** At both the International and Domestic terminals there are pre-paid taxi counters. By using these, you know that you are paying the right amount. Keep your receipt as the driver will want this at the end of the journey. Often, the taxi driver will ask for more. Further payment is not required, nor is a tip. If you take a taxi without buying your ticket first the driver will usually demand an inflated fare. During the day Rs 80-100 is reasonable for travel to hotels and the centre of town. At night, add another 15-20%.

There is also a **bus service** run by the Ex-Airmens Transport Association (EATS) which runs from the airport via some hotels to **F-Block Connaught Place**. It leaves from IA office in Connaught Place at regular intervals up to 2300 and connects with most flights. The fare is Rs 20 per person. There is a booth just outside the arrival terminals at the International and Domestic airports.

Taxis Private taxis/cars are usually hired on a half or full day basis. A/c and non a/c are available. Full day local running (non a/c) is Rs 300 approx, Half day Rs 200. Check on the charge beforehand. **Adarsh Tourist Transport Service**, 38 Yashwant Place. **Auto Rental Service**, YMCA Hostel, Jai Singh Rd. **Delhi Transport Service**, Arambagh, Panchkuin Rd. **Hindustan Tourist Taxi Service**, 36 Janpath. **I.S. Goel and Co**, 16 Sunder Nagar Market. **Karachi Taxi Service**, 36 Janpath. **All India Road Tourist Taxi Service**, Hotel Imperial. **Venus Travels**, 16-1708, Arya Samaj Rd, Karol Bagh. **Western Court Tourist Taxi Service**, 36 Janpath. **American Express Taxi Co.**, 36 Janpath. **Ex-Soldiers Tourist Taxi Service**, opp 16 Dr. Rajendra Prasad Marg.

Yellow top taxis are easily available. Most of the large hotels have stands outside and the doorman will call one for you. There are also numerous taxi stands around town. Taxis can also be hailed on the roads. Before the Gulf War prices were Rs 3.50 for the first l km and Rs 2.50 for every subsequent km. The Gulf War resulted in severe fuel shortages and an increase in price. Many meters will not have been changed, so you should ask to see the conversion card. Night charges (20% extra) apply after 2300. There may also be a charge for heavy luggage or more than 4 persons travelling.

Scooter-rickshaws are widely available. Rs 2.60 for the first km, Re 1.30 for every subsequent km. Normal capacity for foreigners is two persons. More can be taken but this is negotiable with the driver who may charge more. Night charges apply.

Motor Cycle rickshaws Matador Taxis (4 seater plus). For point-to-point travel only, e.g. between the railway station and a residential area.

Cycle rickshaws are available in the Old city. They are not allowed into Connaught Place. Rates negotiable. Be prepared to haggle over the price, remembering that it should be cheaper than motorised transport. **Tongas** (Horse drawn traps) are also available in Old Delhi. Fares negotiable.

Bike rentals Shops are near Minto Bridge, just off Connaught Place and on Mohan Singh Place near the Rivoli cinema. Rentals cost Rs 4 to 5 per hour to Rs 15 per day plus a refundable deposit. Shops in Paharganj also rent bikes for similar rates.

Bus The city bus service run by the Delhi Transport Corporation connects all important points in the city. There are over 300 routes. Information is available at DTC assistance booths and at all major bus stops. Don't be afraid to ask fellow passengers. Indians are usually very helpful if they understand what you are saying. **Directional Route Classification**: The first digit of the bus route numbers (1-9) determines the direction in which it travels and also indicates the terminal depot: 1 Azadpur (NW), 2 Kashmiri Gate (NE), 3 ITO (Income Tax Office) and Indraprastha (Central), 4 Lajpat Nagar (SE), 5 All-India Medical School (S), 6 Sarojini Nagar (SW), 7,8,9 Dhaula Khan, Raja Garden and Punjabi Bagh respectively (W). Night services: A skeletal service 2300-0130. This can also take extremely roundabout routes, double backing on themselves frequently. Tickets are Re 0.50, Re 1 and Rs 2. Delhi Transport Corporation Head Office, T 3315085. Local enquiries T 3319847, 3316745. ISBT Office T 2518836. The bus system is often hopelessly overcrowded.

Private buses and mini buses also operate a large number of the same DTC routes. Tickets are Re 1 and Rs 2.

Trains The Delhi suburban railway is neither very popular nor convenient. A ring route operates 3 times a day – 0755, 1625, 1725, starting from the main suburban terminal station Hazrat Nizamuddin.

Travel Tips Check that scooter and taxi metres are cleared and try and insist on the metre being used. If you are wishing to travel a short distance, e.g. from Jan Path to the New Delhi Rly Station, often *rickshaw wallahs** may ask Rs 30 or more, 4 or 5 times the proper rate. Similarly, if you are staying away from the centre, it may be difficult to get a scooter or taxi late at night. If this is the case, go to a hotel and get the doorman to call you one. For this service, a small tip should be given. Carry plenty of coins and small notes. As a last resort you can threaten drivers with police action if they prove to be particularly difficult. Whilst you do not want the trouble that this entails, drivers can lose their permits if they attempt to cheat. However, it is common that with fare revisions, the meter is not always changed. Drivers must carry a card with the revised fares, so if a driver asks for more than is on the meter, ask to see the card to check. Most will oblige. Official night rates for taxis apply after 2200.

Warning If travelling on a crowded bus, take care of your belongings as pickpockets are often at work. The row of seats along the kerb side of the bus are for women, who are entitled to ask any male to vacate it. Women should be aware of what is known as "Eve teasing" (bottom pinching). There are often signs up saying "No Eve teasing".

Entertainment The weekly Delhi Diary, free from hotels and many other outlets round the city gives information on what is on.

Son et Lumière *Red Fort*: 1800-1900 (Hindi), 1930-2030 (English). Entry Rs 4 and Rs 8. Tickets available at the Red Fort. Enquiries T 600121 ext. 2156 and 274580 (after 1700). Teen Murti House 'A Tryst with Destiny': 1800-1900 (Hindi), 1915-2015 (English). Entry Rs 2 and Rs 5. Tickets available at Teen Murti house. Enquiries T 3015026. Both Son et Lumière shows do not usually operate over the monsoon period. Check in Delhi Diary.

Discotheques. *Oasis*, Hyatt Regency, T 609911. *Ghungroo*, Maurya Sheraton, T 3010101. *No. 1*, Taj Mahal, T 3016162. All popular (2200 until early hr).

Cultural Centres Foreign: *Alliance Francaise de Delhi*, M-5 NDSE Part II, T 6440128. French classes, library of French literature, theatre activities and active film club. Open 1000-1700, Closed Sun. *American Centre* (United States Information Service), 24 Kasturba Gandhi Marg, T 3316841. Large library (20,000 books). American fine arts and performing arts are energetically promoted. Also houses US information offices. Open 0930-1800, Closed Sun. *British Council*, Rafi Marg, T 381401. Extensive library with an excellent reference section for the sciences. Special facilities include large print and audio visual sections and a postal loan service. Membership now essential. Open 0900-1800, Closed Sun. *French Cultural Centre*, 2 Aurangzeb Rd, T 3014682. *Italian Cultural Centre*, 38 Ring Rd, T 623441. *Japan Cultural Centre*, 32 Feroze Shah Rd, T 329803. Language classes, films, exhibitions and lectures. Open 0900-1300 and Tues-Fri 1400-1700. Closed Sun. *Max Mueller Bhawan*, 3 Kasturba Gandhi Marg, T 3329506. Houses the Goethe Institute of German. Language classes, cultural programmes, lectures, discussions, seminars and films. Good library for sociology and art. Open 0900-1400, 1500-1800, Closed Sun. *House of Soviet Culture*, 24 Feroze Shah Rd, T 386629. Regular exhibitions and films promoting both Indian and Soviet culture. Open 1000-1700, Closed Sun.

Sports **Boating**: Paddle and row boats are available for hire at Purana Qila lake, Mathura Rd. Open 0600-1800. *Bal Sahyog Boat Club*, Connaught Place, T 3310995. Also at Surajkund (see under Excursions). **Bowling**: The Qutab Hotel has a 4 lane semi-automatic bowling alley, T 62537. **Flying**: *Delhi Flying and Gliding Clubs*, Safdarjang Airport, T 618271. Temporary membership available. Open 1300-1800. Gliding season Mar-Jun and Sept-Nov. It was from Safdarjang that Indira Gandhi's younger son, Sanjay, flew. He died in a light aircraft crash in 1980.

   Golf: *Delhi Golf Club*, Dr Zakir Hussein Marg, T 699236. Country's busiest with 500 attending daily. A sanctuary attracting over 300 species of birds! Temporary membership available with clubs for hire. 6,972 yard, par 72, 18-hole course and 9 hole beginners' course. Open all year. Another at Suraj Kund (see under excursions). **Polo**: *Delhi Polo Club*, President's Estate, Rashtrapati Bhawan, T 375604). Temporary membership available. Apply to The Secretary, c/o The President's Body Guard. **Riding**: *Delhi Riding Club*, Safdarjang Rd. T 3011891. Open to all. Information from the Club Secretary and to book the day before.. Rides 0630-0930 and 1400-1900. *Children's Riding Club*, T 3012265. **Skating** rink at Pragati maidan. **Swimming**: Many hotels empty their pools over the winter (Dec-Feb). The *Maurya Sheraton's* is solar heated and open all year round. When open, the *Taj Mahal*, *Oberoi* and *Imperial* pools are very good. The *Maurya, Ashok, Claridges* and *Imperial* allow non residents to use their pools at daily charges of Rs 50-150. *NMDC Pools* at Nehru Park near Hotel Ashok and Block Sarojini Nagar. **Tennis**: *Delhi Lawn Tennis Association*, Africa Ave, T 653955.

Museums

The National Museum is one of the best museums in the country, Janpath, T 3019538. Open 1000-1700, closed Mon. Entry free. It gives an excellent overview of the cultural development of S Asia. The collection was formed form the nucleus of the Exhibition of Indian Art, London (1947) which brought together selected works from state museums and private collections. Now merged with the Asian Antiquities Museum it displays a rich collection of the artistic treasure of Central Asia and India. The museum provides a comprehensive review of ethnological objects from prehistoric archaeological finds to the late Medieval period. Research is facilitated by a library. Films are screened every day (1430). Replicas of exhibits on display and books on Indian culture and art are on sale at the entrance. The galleries are: *Prehistoric* (Ground). Included are seals, figurines, toy animals and jewellery from the Harappan civilization (2400-1500 BC). *Maurya Period* (Ground). Terracottas and stone heads from the Sunga period (3rd century BC) include the *chaturmukha lingam**, a four faced phallic symbol connected with the worship of Siva (1st century BC). *Gandhara School* (Ground), a series of stucco heads showing the Graeco Roman influence. *Gupta terracottas* c 400 AD (Ground) include two life size images of the river goddesses Ganga and Yamuna and the four-armed bust of Vishnu from a temple near Lal Kot. *S Indian sculpture* from Pallava and early Chola temples and relief panels from Mysore are presented. 10th century AD sculptures (Ground). Bronzes from the Buddhist monastery at Nalanda.

Illustrated manuscripts (First Floor) includes the **Babur-i-nama** in the emperor's own handwriting and an autographed copy of Jahangir's memoirs. *Miniature paintings* (First)includes the 16th century Jain School, the 18th century Rajasthani School and the Pahari (Hill) Schools of Garhwal, Basoli and Kangra. *Aurel Stein Collection* (First) consists of antiquities recovered by him during his explorations of Central Asia and the western borders of China at the turn of the century. *Pre-Columbian and Mayan artefacts* (Second Floor). Anthropological Section (Second) devoted to Indian tribal artifacts and folk arts. Sharan Rani Bakkiwal Gallery of Musical Instruments (Second) displays over 300 instruments collected by the famous *sarod** player Sharad Rani and donated to the museum in 1980.

Airforce Museum, Palam Marg, T 393461. Open 1000-1330, Closed Mon. Guns, bullets, uniforms and photographs record the history of the Indian Air Force. Excellent aircraft.

Crafts Museum, Pragati Maidan, Bhairon Rd, T 3317641,3319817. Open 1000-1800, Sun and Public Holidays 1000-2000. Contains over 20,000 pieces of traditional Indian crafts from all parts of the country. A rich collection of 18th-20th century objects including terracottas, bronzes, enamel work, wood painting and carving, brocades and jewellery. Library.

Dolls Museum, Nehru House, Bahadur Shah Zafar Marg. Open 1000-1800, Closed Mon. Entry Re 1 Adults, Re 0.25 Children. Something of a miniature United Nations. Started in 1954 by the well known journalist Shankar. Over 6,000 dolls. The BC Roy Children's Library offers a wide selection of books and a play corner for those below reading age. Membership restricted to under 16s. Films are screened for members on 2nd Saturdays.

Field Museum, Purana Qila, Mathura Rd. Open 1000-1700, Closed Mon. Displays archaeological finds of excavations at this site, below which lies the legendary city of Indraprashta described in the Mahabharata. Coins from the early Sunga period (200-100 BC), red earthenware from the Kushan period (100 BC-300 AD), seals and figurines from the Gupta period (200-600 AD) and stone sculptures (700-800 AD). Later artefacts include coins from the Rajput period (900-1200 AD), glazed ware and coins from the Sultanate period (1206-1526).

Gandhi Darshan, Raj Ghat. Open 1000-1700, Closed Mon. Five pavilions bring together in sculpture, photographs and paintings the life of Gandhi, the history of the *Satyagraha** movement, the philosophy of non-violence and the Constructive Programme formulated by Gandhi. A children's section recreates the history of the freedom movement from 1857 to 1948 when Gandhi was assassinated.

Gandhi Smarak Sangrahalaya, Raj Ghat. Open 0930-1730, Closed Th. Displays some of Gandhi's personal belongings: walking stick, spinning wheel, sandals, watch and spectacles. Small library and collection of tape recordings of speeches. Films on the *Sarvodaya** Movement and allied subjects are screened on Sundays: 1600 Hindi, 1700 English.

National Gallery of Modern Art, Jaipur House, nr India Gate, T 382835. Open 1000-1700, Closed Mon. Housed in the former Delhi residence of the Maharaja of Jaipur. Excellent collection of Indian modern art. Some of the best exhibits are on the ground floor which is devoted to post 1930 works. Visitors who would like to view the collections chronologically are advised to begin their tour on the first floor. Some of the collections displayed: *Amrita Shergil* (Ground), contains over 100 examples of her work, including one self portrait. Her style was a synthesis of the flat treatment of Indian painting with a realistic tone. **Rabindranath Tagore** (Ground). An invaluable collection by the poet who for a brief but intense spell in the 1930s expressed himself through painting as well as poetry. **The Bombay School** (or Company School)(First). This includes Western painters who documented their visits to India. Foremost among them is the British painter **Thomas Daniell**. With a style that seems to anticipate the camera, the realism characteristic of this school is reflected in Indian painting of the early 19th century represented by the schools of Avadh, Patna, Sikkim and Tanjore. **The Bengal School** (The Late 19th century Revivalist Movement). Artists such as Abanindranath Tagore and **Nandalal Bose** have their works exhibited here. Western influence was discarded in response to the nationalist movement. Inspiration derived from Indian folk art is evident in the works of *Jamini Roy*, and in the works of *Y.D. Shukla* the Japanese influence can be seen in the use of wash techniques and a miniature style. Some of the works would benefit from better labelling. Postcards, booklets and prints are available at the reception.

Natural History Museum, FICCI Building, Barakhamba Rd. Open 1000-1700, Closed Mon. A small but well assembled introduction to India's natural heritage. A Discovery Room offers children the opportunity to handle specimens and take part in creative activities such as animal modelling. Daily filmshow (1130-1530), regular lectures and exhibitions organized in conjunction with other natural history organizations.

Nehru Memorial Museum and Library, *Teen Murti Bhavan*, T 3016734. Museum Open 1000-1700, Closed Mon. Library Open 0900-1900, Closed Sun. The official residence of India's first Prime Minister, Jawaharlal Nehru, was converted after his death (1964) into a national memorial consisting of a museum and research library. The reception, study and bedroom have been preserved as they were. Note his extensive reading and wide interests. A Jyoti Jawahar, kept burning day and night in the garden, is a symbol of the eternal values he inspired, and a granite rock is carved with extracts from his historic speech at midnight 14-15 August 1947. Library resources include unpublished records, private correspondence and micro-film facilities. Films are screened in the auditorium and a son et Lumière is held after sunset. Very informative and vivid history of the Independence Movement.

Philatelic Museum, Dak Tar Bhavan, Parliament St. Open 1030-1230 and 1430-1630, Closed Mon. Entry passes are available from the basement of the Parliament St Head Post Office. Extensive stamp collection including the first stamp issued in India by the Sindh Dak (1854) and stamps issued before Independence by the ruler of the Princely States. A record is maintained of contemporary stamps issued by the Government. Library.

Pragati Maidan, Mathura Rd. Open 0930-1730, Sun and Public Holidays 0930-2000. A sprawling exhibition ground containing a restaurant, children's park, shopping centre and cinema theatres where Indian and foreign films are screened daily. The 5 permanent exhibitions include The Nehru Pavilion displaying a small but comprehensive exhibition on Jawaharlal Nehru, easier to take in than the Nehru Memorial Museum. The Son of India Pavilion features the life of Sanjay Gandhi and the Atomic Energy and Defence Pavilions demonstrate through models, photographs and statistics the country's technological and industrial achievements. The 7 acre Village Complex recreates a village scene with about 10 kinds of rural dwellings. Musical instruments, deities, folk arts and crafts and items of everyday use are displayed inside.

Rabindra Bhavan, Copernicus Marg. Housing the national academies of literature (Sahitya Akademi), fine arts and sculpture (Lalit Kala Akademi) and the performing arts (Sangeet Natak Akademi) in separate wings. Founded in 1954 at the inspiration of Maulana Abul Kalam Azad. All have libraries and display galleries which also have post cards and reproductions on sale.

Rail Transport Museum, Chanakyapuri, T 601816. Open 0930-1730, Closed Mon. Entry Re 1 Adults, Re 0.50 Children. Opened in 1977, the museum preserves a memorable account of 125 years of the history of Indian Railways. The collection includes 26 vintage locomotives, 17 carriages and saloons including the 4-wheeled saloon used by the Prince of Wales (Edward VII) in 1876 and the Maharaja of Mysore's saloon made of seasoned teak and laced with gold and ivory. The open display recreates a yard and facilitates the movement of stock. Guidebooks on sale.

Red Fort Museum, Mumtaz Mahal, Lal Qila, T T267961. Open 1000-1700, Closed Mon. On display are the swords, hookahs, chess sets, armoury, carpets etc of the Mughal emperors from Babur to Bahadurshah Zafar. Miniatures depict life at the court, maps and monuments of Delhi and portraits.

Tibet House, Institutional Area, Lodi Rd, T 611515. Open 1000-1300 and 1400-1700, Closed Sun. Tibetan Art.

Libraries Central Secretariat Library, Shastri Bhavan. Open 0900-1800, Closed Sun. Suitable for the social sciences with a strong political science and economics section. A Student Information Service provides a very useful research service for scholars. **Delhi Public Library**, S.P. Mukherjee Marg. Open 1400-1945, Closed Sun. The biggest public library in Delhi with branches at Karol Bagh, Patel Nagar and Shahdara. **National Archives**, Janpath. Open 0900-1630, Closed Sun. Probably the single most important reference library in Delhi. The archives contain 75,000 bound volumes and 4 million unbound documents and government materials published since 1947. **Parliament House Library**, Sansad Bhavan. Open 1000-1700, Closed Sun and the Second Sat. in the month. Was once the meeting hall of the Chamber of Princes. Panelled in dark wood, the walls are lined with the insignia of the former princely states of India. The library is especially good for political science and modern history.

Parks and Zoos Delhi has an abundance of parks, especially New Delhi. Many are very well kept and ideal places to rest, relax and watch the world go by. They are also good places for casual birdwatching. Delhi's Birdwatching Society has listed over 350 species of birds seen in the city. Peacocks, weaver-birds, spotted owlets, kingfishers and the koel are relatively common. The arrival of the pied-crested cuckoo heralds the monsoon. Visit Sultanpur if you are a serious birdwatcher. Parks open 0600-2000.

Warning Although Delhi is safe by the standards of many cities, after dark visitors should be careful as muggings and theft are not unknown.

Buddha Jayanti Park, Sardar Patel Marg, opp. Assam House. Laid out to commemorate the 2500th anniversary of Gautama Buddha's attainment of nirvana. A sapling of the original bodhi tree taken to Sri Lanka by Emperor Asoka's daughter in the 3rd century BC is planted here. Rockeries, streams, bridges and the sloping terrain create an atmosphere of peace and tranquillity. **Central Fountain Park**, Connaught Place. A well used park in the heart of the city in the centre of which is a hideous coloured fibre glass 'statue'. **Children's Park**, India Gate. A small children's recreation complex. **District Park, Hauz Khas**. Deer in the Chinkara complex near to Hauz Khas. Heavily used for early morning yoga exercises jogging and walking. **Lodi Gardens**, Lodi Estate. Officially named Lady Willingdon Park, a very popular and pleasant park set around the 14th and 15th century Lodi and Sayyid tombs. **Mughal Gardens**, Rashtrapati Bhavan Estate. A carefully tended Mughal style garden laid out in the classic char bagh (four gardens or quarters) style. This exclusive garden is thrown open to the public once a year in February when the flowers are in full bloom. For an entry permit at other times contact the India Tourist Office. **National Rose Garden**, Safdarjang's Tomb. Worth a visit during the winter months. For bird-watchers, the ornamental pool behind the tomb is likely to have white-fronted and common kingfishers. **Nehru Park**, Chanakyapuri. An 85 acre landscaped garden. Sayings of the late Jawaharlal Nehru are inscribed on the rocks. Swimming pool and snack bar at the S end. **Qudsia Bagh**, Near Kashmiri Gate. Originally laid out in 1748 by Qudsia Begum, a slave who became the favourite mistress of the Mughal Emperor Mohammad Shah and mother of his successor. It was from here that the British opened fire on Kashmiri Gate during the Mutiny of 1857. The imposing gateway with pavilions at each end overlooks the river. Peacocks are common.

    Roshanara Gardens, Gulabi Bagh. Laid out in 1640 by Princess Roshanara, Shah Jahan's younger daughter, shortly after the completion of Shah Jahanabad. In recent years the garden has been landscaped in Japanese style. **Talkatora Gardens**, Talkatora Stadium. Small Japanese garden with mini lake and fountains. **Yamuna Waterfront**, near Inter-State Bus Terminal. River bank developed with Mughal style gardens. **Zoological Gardens**, Purana Qila. Open 0900-1700 Winter, 0800-1800 Summer. Entry Re 0.50. The enclosures house over 1,000 animals, reptiles and birds. The most popular attractions are the white tiger from Rewa and the elephant who plays the harmonica!

Useful Addresses/ Emergency Numbers Ambulance (24 hr) T 102. Police T 100. Traffic police are identified by their blue and white uniforms and white helmets. Women officers wear green saris and white blouses. The Central Reserve Police Force (CRPF) in khaki uniforms and berets are mainly concerned with assisting in traffic operations, patrolling and riot control. All police stations register complaints. This can be a very lengthy process. *Foreigners' Registration Office,* 1st Floor, Hans Bhawan, Tilak Bridge.

High Commissions, Embassies and Consulates Afghanistan, Shantipath, Chanakyapuri, T 606625 **Algeria**, 15 Anand Lok, T 6445216. **Argentina**, B8/9 Vasant Vihar, T 671345 **Australia**, 1/50G Shantipath, Chanakyapuri, T 601336 **Austria**, EP 13 Chandra Gupta Marg, Chanakyapuri, T 601112 **Bangladesh**, 56 MG Rd, Lajpat Nagar III, T 6934668 **Belgium**, 50 Chanakyapuri, T 607957 **Bhutan**, Chandra Gupta Marg, Chanakyapuri, T 604076 **Burma**, 3/50-F Nyaya Marg, Chanakyapuri, T 600251/2. **Canada**, 7-8 Shantipath, T 608161 **China**, 50-D Shantipath, Chanakyapuri, T 600238 **Denmark**, 2 Golf Links, T 616273 **Finland**, Nyaya Marg, T 605409 **France**, 2/50E Shantipath, T 604004 **Germany**, 6/50 Shantipath, T 604861 **Greece**, 16 Sunder Nagar, T 617800 **Indonesia**, 50-A Chanakyapuri, T 602352 **Ireland**, 13 Jor Bagh, T 617435 **Italy**, 13 Golf Links, T 618311

    Japan, 4/50G Chanakyapuri, T 604071 **Korea** (Republic) 9 Chandragupta Marg, T 601601 **Laos**, 20 Jor Bagh, T 615865 **Malaysia**, 50 M Satya Marg, T 601291 **Mauritius**, 5 Kautilya Marg, T 3011112 **Monaco**, D-1 Defence Colony. T 623193 **Nepal**, Barakhamba Rd, T 3329969 **Netherlands**, 6/50 Shantipath, Chanakyapuri, T 609571 **New Zealand**, 25 Golf Links, T 697296 **Norway**, Shantipath, T 605982 **Pakistan**, 2/50 G Shantipath, Chanakyapuri, T 600601 **Poland**, 50 M Shantipath, Chanakyapuri, T 608596 **Portugal**, A-24 West End

Colony, T 674596 **Singapore,** E 6 Chandragupta Marg, T 608149 **Somalia,** 12-A Golf Links, T 619559

Spain, 12 Prithviraj Rd, T 3015892 **Sri Lanka,** 27 Kautilya Marg, T 3010201 **Sweden,** Nyaya Marg, T 604961 **Switzerland,** Nyaya Marg, T 604225/6 **Thailand,** 56 NNyaya Marg, T 607807 **UK,** Shantipath, Chanakyapuri T 601371 **USA,** Shantipath, T 600651 **USSR,** Shantipath, T 605875.

Hospitals and Medical Services High Commissions, Embassies and Consulates maintain lists of recommended doctors and dentists. Most hotels (Category C upwards) have doctors on call. There is also a Directory of hospitals and nursing homes of which several have doctors approved by IAMAT (International Association for Medical Assistance to Travellers). Casualty and emergency wards in both private and government hospitals are open 24 hours. *All India Institute of Medical Sciences*, Sri Aurobindo Marg, T 661123. *Dr Ram Manohar Lohla Hospital*, Willingdon Crescent, T 345525. *Freemasons Poly Clinic*, Tolstoy Marg, T 3327935. *Hindu Rao Hospital*, Sabzi Mandi, T 2522362. *Holy Family Hospital*, Okhla, T 631626. *Lok Nayak Jai Prakash Narain Hospital*. Jawaharlal Nehru Marg., T 3316271. *Safdarjang General Hospital*, Sri Aurobindo Marg, T 665060. *Sucheta Kripalani Hospital*, Panchkuin Rd, T 344037.

Chemists (24 hr) *All India Institute of Medical Sciences*, Sri Aurobindo Marg, T 661123. *Hindu Rao Hospital*, Sabzi Mandi, T 2522060. *Super Bazar*, Connaught Place, T 3310166. *Dr Ram Manohar Lohia Hospital*, Willingdon Crescent, T 345525.

Post and Telegraph There are numerous post offices throughout the city. Stamps can often be obtained from the Bell Captain in the larger hotels. Head Post Office, Parliament St, T 385605, Open 1000-1830 Mon-Sat. Eastern Court P.O., Janpath, T 3322681, Open 1000-1830 Mon-Sat. Connaught Place P.O., A-Block, T 3324214, Open 1000-1700 Mon-Sat. G.P.O. Ashoka Place, T 344111, Open 1000-1700 Mon-Fri, 1000-1300 Sat. G.P.O. Kashmere Gate, T 2524369, Open 1000-1900 Mon-Fri, 1000-1230 Sat. Central Telegraph Office, Eastern Court, Janpath, T 3324010, Open 24 hours. Overseas Communication Service (Telex, Telephone), Bangla Sahib Rd, T 186,187, Open 24 hr.

Mail can be received at: Post Restante, G.P.O. (care of the Postmaster), Baba Kharak Singh Marg, New Delhi 110001 (make sure senders specify New Delhi and the Pin Code) from 0800-1900; c/o The Tourist Office, 88 Janpath, New Delhi 10001; c/o American Express, Hamilton House, A-Block, Connaught Place, New Delhi 11001. If you are staying at a hotel and intend returning, mail can also be directed there. When asking if there is any mail, it pays to be quite persistent as some hotels are not as well organized in their mail storage as you would expect.

International telephone calls from hotels usually attract a heavy surcharge, even when it is a collect call. If in doubt, ask first. There are now international STD public telephones at a number of telegraph offices across the city. The most central is at the Central Telegraph Office, Janpath, opp the Imperial Hotel.

Places of Worship *Hindu*: Gauri Shanker Temple, Chandni Chowk. Hanuman Temple, Baba Kharak Singh Marg. Kali Bari Temple, Mandir Marg. Lakshmi Narayan Temple, Mandir Marg. Swami Malai Temple, R. K. Puram. Devi Katyayani Mandir, Chattarpur. *Muslim*: Fatehpuri Mosque, Chandni Chowk. Jama Masjid, opp. Red Fort. Sonchri Mosque, Chandni Chowk. *Christian*: Cathedral Church of The Redemption, Church Rd. Cathedral of the Sacred Heart, Ashok Place. Catholic Church, near Holy Family Hospital, Okhla. Centenary Methodist Church, Lajpat Rai Marg. Free Church, Parliament St. Religious Society of Friends (Quakers), C4/24 Safdarjang Development Area, 224 Jor Bagh. Seventh Day Adventists, 11 Hailey Rd. St. Anthony's Church, Paharganj. St. James' Church, Kashmere Gate. St. Mary's Church, S.P. Mukherjee Marg. St. Stephen's Church, New Delhi Rly Station. St. Thomas' Church, 59 Mandir Marg. Union Church (Inter-denominational), 5 Amrita Shergil Marg. Vatican Embassy Chapel, Chanakyapuri. *Sikh*: Gurudwara Bangla Sahib, Ashoka Rd. Gurudwara Rakabganj, Rakabganj Marg. Gurudwara Siganj, Chandni Chowk. Baha'i: Baha'i Temple, Kalkaji. *Buddhist*: Buddha Vihar, Mandir Marg. Ladakh Buddha Vihar, Bela Rd. *Jain*: Digamber Jain Temple, Chandni Chowk. *Jewish*: Judah Hyam Hall, 2 Humayun Rd. *Parsi*: Parsi Fire Temple, Mathura Rd.

Chambers of Commerce International Trade Fairs are held in Delhi from time to time. The *Trade Fair Authority of India*, Pragati Maidan, T 3318374 have details. *Federation of Indian Chambers of Commerce and Industry*, Federation House, Tansen Marg, T 3319251. *Punjab Haryana and Delhi Chambers of Commerce and Industry*, T 665425; *Indo-American Chamber of Commerce*, T 669021; *Indo-Italian Chamber of Commerce*, T 665425 all at PHD House, 4-2 Siri Institutional Area. *Indo-German Chamber of Commerce*, 86 FG Himalaya House, Kasturba Gandhi Marg, T 3314151. *Indo-French Chamber of Commerce* and *Indo-Polish*

Chamber of Commerce, Philips Building, 9A Connaught Pl, T 3327421. *World Bank,* 55 Lodi Estate, T 619496.

Travel Agents and Tour Operators Agents can be found in all the major hotels and clustered in several different centres of Delhi. The most important are Connaught Circus (especially F to H blocks), Pahar Ganj, Rajendra Place and Nehru Place. Most belong to national and international associations foremost among which are the International Air Transport Association (IATA), the Pacific Area Travel Association (PATA) and the Travel Agents' Association of India (TAAI). Complaints can be addressed to the association if the agency's service is not satisfactory. Many of these agencies will send their representative to your hotel to discuss your plans. The following is a short list of some of the best.

American Express, A-Block, Connaught Place, T 3327617. **Ashok Tours and Travels,** Kanishka Shopping Plaza, 19 Ashok Rd., T 3324422 **Balmer and Lawrie,** 32-33 Nehru Place, T 6419222 **Cox and Kings,** Connaught Circus, T 3321028 **Everett Travel Service,** C-11 Connaught Place, T 3321117 **Hans Travel Service** Vishal Hotel Main Bazar Pahar Ganj T 527629 **Indtravels,** Hotel imperial, Janpath, T 3322887 **Mackinnon Travel Service,** 16 Parliament St, T 3323741. **Mercury Travels,** Jeevan Tara Building, Parliament St, T 312008 **Sita World Travels,** F-12 Connaught Place, T 3313103 **Students Travel Information Service,** Hotel Imperial, Janpath, T 3328512. **Sunshine Travels,** M-13 Connaught Circus, T 3323122. **Swagatam Tours and Travels,** 55 Ram Nagar, T 772177, **Thomas Cook,** Hotel Imperial, Janpath, T 3328468 **Trade Wings,** 60 Janpath, T 351637. **Travel Corporation of India (TCI),** N-49 Connaught Circus, T 3327468. **Travel House,** 102 AVG Bhavan, M-3 Connaught Place, T 3329609

Tourist Offices and Information Information Offices: *Govt. of India Tourist Office,* 88 Janpath, T 3320008. Helpful assistance. Issues permits for visits to Rashtrapati Bhavan and gardens. Open 0900-1800, Closed Sun. Also at Indira Gandhi International Airport, T 39117. *Delhi Tourism Development Corporation* (DTDC), N-Block Connaught Place, T 3313637,3314229. Counters at: 18,DDA Office Complex, Moolchand, T 618374; Indira Gandhi International Airport, T 392297; New Delhi Rly Station, T 350574; Inter State Bus Terminal (ISBT), T 2512181; Delhi Rly Station, T 2511083. *India Tourism Development Corporation* (ITDC), L-Block Connaught Place, T 3320331. Counters at ITDC Hotels (Ashok Group): Ashok, T 600121 Ext. 2155. Ashok Yatri Niwas, T 3324511 Ext. 15. Janpath, T 3320070 Ext. 814. Kanishka, T 3324422 Ext. 2336. Lodi, T 362422 Ext. 207. Ranjit, T 3311256 Ext. 630. Indira Gandhi International Airport; (Domestic), T 392825; (International) T 394410.

State Tourist Offices Each state has a tourist office in Delhi. Plenty of useful information available and, often, tourist maps. Most are open 1000-1800, Mon-Fri.

A number are on **Kharak Singh Marg:** Assam, B-1,T 345897; **Bihar,** A-5, T 311087; **Gujarat,** A-6, T 343173; **Karnataka,** T 343862; **Maharashtra,** T 343281; **Manipur,** T 343497; **Orissa,** T 344580; **Tamil Nadu,** T 343913. Several others in the **Chandralok Building, 36 Janpath Rd:** Haryana, T 3324911; **Himachal Pradesh,** T 3324764; **Rajasthan,** T 3322332; **Uttar Pradesh,** T 3322251; **West Bengal,** T 343775. A few others are in the **Kaniksha Shopping Plaza,** 19 Ashok Rd: **Jammu and Kashmir,** T 3325373; **Madhya Pradesh,** T 3015545; **Punjab,** T 385431.

Others are: **Andaman and Nicobar Islands,** F-105, Curzon Rd Hostel, Kasturba Gandhi Marg, T 387015. **Andhra Pradesh,** Andhra Bhavan, 1 Ashok Rd, T 389182; **Kerala,** 3 Jantar Mantar Rd, T 353424; **Nagaland,** 4 Rao Tula Ram Marg, T 679177; **Sikkim,** Chanakyapuri, T 3014981; and **Tripura,** Kautliya Marg, T 3014607.

Conducted Tours Guided sightseeing tours can be arranged through approved travel agents (see Travel Agents section) and tour operators. There are numerous small establishments clustered together in commercial areas, e.g. opposite New Delhi Rly Station, and although they offer seemingly unusual itineraries their standards cannot be guaranteed and their rates are not significantly lower. ITDC and DTDC both run city sightseeing tours. Special concessional fares are offered by both for those who elect to combine Old Delhi and New Delhi tours on the same day. This can be very tiring. Air conditioned services are particularly recommended during the summer months. The tour price includes transport, entry fees to monuments and museums and guide services. Of these, the transport cost is the highest. All tend to be whistle stop tours. **N.B.** As transport costs tend to be high, a group of three or four people should consider hiring a car and doing the tour at their own pace. Approved tourist guides may be engaged through the India Tourist Office and travel agents for local and outstation sightseeing. Rates: Delhi only, Half day Rs 60 approx, Full day Rs 100 approx.

DTDC Tours Departure point, Bombay Life Building, N-Block, Connaught Place. **New Delhi Tour** (0900-1400): Jantar Mantar, Qutb Minar, Lakshmi Narayan temple, Safdarjang's Tomb,

Diplomatic Enclave, India Gate. Old **Delhi Tour** (1415-1715): Jama Masjid, Red Fort (Lal Qila), Shanitvana, Raj Ghat, Kotla Firoz Shah. **Evening Tour** (1800-2200): Lakshmi Narayan Temple (evening prayer), India Gate, Purana Qila (floodlit monument), Son et Lumière (Red Fort), Jama Masjid (Dinner at a Mughlai and tandoori restaurant included in the tour price). **Museum Tour,** Sunday only, check time: Air Force, Rail and Transport, and National Museums, Indira Gandhi Memorial, Nehru Planetarium, Museum of Natural History and Dolls Museum.

ITDC Tours Departure point: L-Block Connaught Place. **New Delhi Tour** (0900-1400): Jantar Mantar, Lakshmi Narayan temple, India Gate, Nehru Pavilion, Pragati Maidan (closed Mon), Humayun's tomb, Qutb Minar. **Old Delhi Tour** (1400-1700): Kotla Firoz Shah, Raj Ghat, Shantivana, Jama Masjid and Red Fort. Good value, entry fees included.

Airlines Domestic: *Indian Airlines*, 18 Barakhamba Rd, T 3310071. Airport 5452433-6. Enquiries, T 3014433. Newly opened office on Safdarjang Rd. The service here is generally very good. To avoid delays be there at 0830. *Vayudoot*, Malhotra Building, F-Block, Janpath, T 3312779. *Palam Airport* (Domestic), T 391361, Ext. 2268

International: Aeroflot, BMC House, N-1 Connaught Place, T 3312843. **Air Canada**, Ashok Hotel, T 604755. **Air France**, Scindia House, Connaught Place, T 3310407. Airport T 394308. **Air India**, Jeevan Bharati Building, 124 Connaught Circus, 3311225. Airport, T 5452050. **Alitalia**, 19 Kasturba Gandhi Marg, T 3311019-21. Airport, T 393140. **Ariana Afghan Airlines**, 19 Kasturba Gandhi Marg, T 3311432. **Bangladesh Biman**, City Office, T 3325888. **British Airways**, 1A Connaught Place, T 3327428. Airport, T 5452077-8. **Cathay Pacific**, Tolstoy House, Tolstoy Marg, T 3325789. **Druk Air** (Royal Bhutan), Malbro Travels, 403 Nirmal Towers, 26 Barakhamba Rd, T 3322859. **Gulf Air**, Marina Arcade, G-12 Connaught Circus, T 3324293. Airport, T 5952065. **Japan Airlines**, Chandralok Building, Janpath, T 3327104-8. Airport, T 5452082.

KLM Royal Dutch Airlines, Prakash Deep, Tolstoy Marg, T 3315841. Airport, T 392192, Ext. 2219. **Lufthansa**, 56 Janpath, T 3323310. Airport, T 5452063. **Malaysian Airlines**, G-55 Connaught Circus, T 3326302. **Pakistan International Airlines**, 26 Kasturba Gandhi Marg, T 3313161-2. Airport, T 5452093-4. **Philippine Airlines**, City Office, T 3325888. **Qantas Airways**, Mohandev, 13 Tolstoy Marg, T 3321434. **Royal Nepal Airlines**, 44 Janpath, T 3320817. Airport, T 393876. **Sabena (Belgian) Airlines**, Himalaya House, Kasturba Gandhi Marg, T 3312701. **Saudi Arabian Airlines**, Hansalaya, 15 Barakhamba Rd, T 3310466-7. Airport, T 391357. **SAS (Scandinavian Airline)**, City Office, T 3327668. **Singapore Airlines**, G-11 Connaught Circus, T 3320145. Airport, 394200. **Swissair**, 56 Janpath, T 3325511. **Thai Airways International**, 12A Connaught Place, T 3323608. Airport, T 392526. **Trans World Airlines (TWA)**, City Office, T 3327418. **United Airlines**, City Office, T 3315014.

Air Services Indian Airlines connects Delhi with the following Indian cities (Times given are journey time): Agra (30 min), Ahmedabad (1 hr 15 min), Allahabad (1 hr 15 min), Amritsar (50 min), Aurangabad (4 hr 15 min: 3 stops), Bagdogra for Darjiling (1 hr 55 min), Bangalore (2 hr 35 min), Bhopal (1 hr 55 min: 1 stop), Bhubaneshwar (4 hr: 2 stops), Bombay (1 hr 50 min), Calcutta (1,hr 55 min), Chandigarh, Cochin (4 hr: 1 stop), Dabolim (Goa; 2 hr 25 min), Gorakhpur, Guwahati (3 hr 10 min: 1 stop), Gwalior, Hyderabad (1 hr 55 min), Imphal, Indore (2 hr 50 min: 2 stops), Jabalpur (2 hr 10 min), Jaipur (35 min), Jammu, Jodhpur (1 hr 45 min: 1 stop), Kanpur, Khajuraho (1 hr 40 min: 1 stop), Leh (2 hr: 1 stop), Lucknow (55 min), Madras (2 hr 35 min: 1 stop), Nagpur, Patna (1 hr 25 min), Pune (1 hr 55 min), Raipur, Ranchi, Srinagar (1 hr 15 min), Trivandrum (5 hr: 2 stops), Udaipur (2 hr 45 min: 2 stops), Vadodara and Varanasi (1 hr 15 min). **Indian Airlines** international services also connect Delhi to Dhaka, Kabul, Kathmandu, Lahore and Karachi. **Vayudoot** connects Delhi with Chandigarh, Dehra Dun, Jaipur, Kanpur, Kota, Ludhiana, Pantnagar and Shimla.

Rail New Delhi Rly Station (ND) is the focus of the Broad gauge network and connects Delhi with all major destinations in India. **Old Delhi Rly Station (OD)** is on the metre gauge network of the Western Railways and connects Delhi with Jaipur, Ajmer, Jodhpur, Bikaner, Udaipur and Ahmedabad and many more. Some of the principal services to major destinations are: **Amritsar**: *Dadar-Amritsar Exp*, 1057, daily, 0805, 10 hr 25 min; *New Delhi-Amritsar Exp*, 2459, daily, 1420, 7 hr 10 min; *Flying Mail*, 4647, daily, 1215, 8 hr 45 min; *Shane Punjab Exp*, 2497, daily, 0645, 6 hr 50 min. **Bombay** (Central): *Rajdhani Exp*, 2952, daily except Tues, ND, 1605, 16 hr 30 min; *Paschim Exp*, 2926, daily, ND, 1700, 22 hr; *Frontier Mail*, 2904, daily, ND, 0825, 22 hr 35 min; *Jammu Tawi-Bombay Exp*, 2972, Tues, Wed, Fri, Sat, ND 2145, 20 hr 25 min; *Bombay Exp*, 9020, daily, ND, 2210, 30 hr 20 min. **Calcutta**: *Rajdhani Exp*, 2302, daily except Th and Sun, ND, 1715, Mon-Wed, Fri, Sat 17 hr 30 min; *Howrah Exp*, 3012, daily, OD, 2210, 32 hr; *A. C. Exp*, 2382, Tues, Th, Sat, ND, 1600, 26 hr. **Jabalpur**: *Mahakoshal Exp*, 1450, daily, 1620, 18 hr 10 min. **Madras**: *G. T. Exp*, 2304, Mon, Wed, Fri, Sun, ND 1840

(36 hr 20 min); *Tamil Nadu Exp,* 2622, daily, ND, 2230, 33 hr 20 min; *6068/6032 Exp,* Mon, Wed, Fri, Sun, N. Del. (Originates OD, 1435) 1500, 45 hr 35 min.

Agra: *Shatabdi Exp,* 2002, daily, ND 0615, 1 hr 50 min; *Taj Exp,* 2180, daily, ND, 0705, 2 hr 45 min. **Mathura:** *Taj Exp,* 2180, daily, 0705, 1 hr 55 min. **Lucknow:** *Neelachal Exp,* 8476, Tues, Th, Sun, ND, 0540, 8 hr 5 min; *Lucknow Mail,* 4230, daily, ND 2130, 9 hr 45 min; *Gomti Exp,* 2420, daily except Tue, ND, 1440, 8 hr 10 min. **Kanpur** *Shatabdi Exp,* 2004, Mon-Fri, ND, 0620, 4 hr 50 min; *Prayag Raj Exp,* 2418, daily, 2200, 6 hr 45 min; *Vaishali Exp,* 2554, daily, 1930, 6 hr 25 min. **Varanasi:** *A. C. Exp,* 2382, Tues, Th, Sat, ND, 1600, 13 hr 15 min; *Neelachal Exp,* 8476, Tues, Th, Sun, ND, 0540, 13 hr 10 min; *Ganga-Yamuna Exp,* 3284 on Tues, Wed, Fri, Sun, 3214 on Mon, Th, Sat, OD, 2145, 17 hr; *Saryu Yamuna Exp,* 2450, Mon, Th, Sat, ND, 2105, 15 hr 10 min. **Bhopal:** *Shatabdi Exp,* 2002, daily, ND, 0615, 7 hr 45 min. **Gwalior:** *Shatabdi Exp,* 2002, daily, N. Del 0615, 3 hr 15 min.

Jhansi: *Shatabdi Exp,* 2002, daily, 4 hr 25 min; *Jhelum Exp,* 4678, daily, 1050, 7 hr 30 min; *Karnataka Exp,* 2628, daily, 2320, 5 hr 32 min; *Tamil Nadu Exp,* 2622, daily, 5 hr 25 min; *A. P. Exp,* 2724, daily, 1430, 5 hr 25 min. **Jaipur:** *Pink City Exp,* 2901, daily, OD 0600, 5 hr 5 min. **Jodhpur:** Jodhpur Mail, 4893, daily, dep. OD, 2030, 14 hr 15 min; *Mandore Exp,* 2461, daily, OD, 1810, 11 hr 35 min. **Bikaner:** *Bikaner Exp,* 4789, daily, OD, 0830, 11 hr 45 min; Bikaner Mail, 4791, daily, OD, 2100, 11 hr 30 min. **Udaipur:** *Chetak Exp,* 9615, daily, OD, 1300, 20 hr 15 min. **Jammu:** (for Kashmir): *Jhelum Exp,* 4677, daily, ND, 2140, 13 hr 25 min. **Chandigarh** Dep ND, *Himalayan Queen,* 4095, daily, 0600, 4 hr 10 min. *Shatabdi Exp,* 2005, Daily, 1625, 3 hr 20 min. From OD: Howrah-Kalka Mail, 2311, daily, 2245, 14 hr 55 min. **Shimla:** Dep OD: *Howrah-Kalka Mail,* 2311 (change at Kalka to 253 Mail), daily, 1955, 16 hr 30 min. ND *Himalayan Queen,* 4095 (change at Kalka to 251), daily, 0521, 5 hr 19 min. **Haridwar:** *Bombay-Dehradun Exp,* 9019, daily, 0735, 6 hr 55 min; *Mussoorie Exp,* 4041, daily, 2225, 7 hr 55 min.

Road Delhi is well connected by road with major cities: by NH2 (National Highway) to Agra (200 km), Ajmer (399 km), by NH1 to Amritsar (446 km), Bhopal (741 km), Chandigarh (249 km), Gwalior (319 km), by NH8 to Jaipur (261 km), Jammu (586 km), Jodhpur (604 km), Kanpur (490 km), Kota (505 km), by NH24 to Lucknow (569 km), Pathankot (478 km), Simla (368 km), Srinagar (876 km), Udaipur (635 km) and Varanasi (765 km). However, all road journeys in India are much slower than their western equivalents. Main roads out of Delhi are very heavily congested with slow moving traffic, particularly lorries. The best time to leave Delhi is very early morning.

Bus Delhi is linked to most major centres in northern India and services are provided by Delhi Transport Corporation and the State Roadways of neighbouring states. Most inter-state buses leave from the Inter-State Bus Terminal (ISBT) Kashmiri Gate. It is best to allow at least 30 mins for buying a ticket and finding the right bus. Enquiries: **ISBT** General Enquiries, T 2519083. **Haryana Roadways,** ISBT, T 2521262. **Himachal Pradesh** Road Transport Corporation, ISBT, T 2516725 **Jammu and Kashmir** Road Transport Corporation, Hotel Kanishka, T 3324422 Ext. 2243. **Punjab Roadways,** ISBT, T 2517842. **Rajasthan** State Road Transport Corporation, ISBT, T 2514417. Deluxe services, Bikaner House, Pandara Rd, T 383469. **Uttar Pradesh** Road Transport Corporation, Ajmeri Darwaza (Gate), T 2518709.

EXCURSIONS SOUTH FROM DELHI

The route along NH 2 from **Delhi** to **Agra** via **Mathura** is described in the Uttar Pradesh section. It is possible to take a day trip south west of Delhi into Haryana following the Jaipur road.

Surajkund (Sun pool), 11 km from the **Qutb Minar** (Delhi), on the Badarpur-Mehrauli road is a perennial lake surround by rock cut steps. This was built by the Rajput king **Surajpal Tomar,** and according to tradition this is where the Rajputs first settled before **Anangpal Tomar** built Lal Kot in Delhi in the 11th century AD. At the head of the reservoir, to the E, are the ruins of what is believed to have been a sun temple (the Rajput dynasties often associated themselves with the Sun or Moon). A little S is **Siddha Kund,** a pool of fresh water trickling from a rock crevice. This is said to have healing properties. About 2 km west is the **Anangpur dam,** made by depositing local quartzite rocks across the mouth of a narrow ravine. The whole area has become something of a picnic spot for Delhi-ites. The tourist hotel/resort run by Haryana Tourism provides facilities for comfortable one-day or weekend trips out of Delhi.

Hotels D *Raj Hans* (Haryana Tourism), T 630766. Less expensive, **D** *Suraj Kund Motel* and *Tourist Huts,* (Haryana Tourism), T 825367. Restaurant, bar. Set in landscaped lawns, deer park, golf. Boating on the pool. Facilities open to residents and visitors.

The annual **Craft Mela** is the fair held in Feb in the Village complex draws crafts people from all over India. You will see potters, weavers, metal and stone workers, painters, printers, wood carvers, embroiderers and many more. In addition, folk singers, dancers, magicians and acrobats perform for the crowds. It is a unique opportunity to see the traditional handicrafts being produced, buy direct from the craftsmen, as well as sample village food in a rural atmosphere, served on banana leaves and in clay pots.

Surajkund is something of a diversion because you reach it by driving S on NH2 then turning right halfway to Faridabad. This road will bring you back to **NH8** at **Gurgaon** (37 km from Delhi Population 89,000). For accommodation try the **D** *Shama* (Haryana Tourism), T 20683. Tourist Guest house. Non a/c rm. Restaurant.

Sultanpur Jheel is a small wildlife sanctuary 46 km from Delhi and just beyond Gurgaon. There are a number of birds here, including flamingos and, as with the better known Bharatpur Bird Sanctuary, the best time is from November to February, the reason being that it too attracts northern migratory birds. A jheel is a shallow expansive lake. Reeds and other waterside plants grow round the rim and there are some small mud-spits in the water. Sarus cranes, the only indigenous Indian crane, breed in the reed beds. The migratory demoiselle is found here in large numbers over the winter, coming to the lakeside in huge flights late in the evening. Surus are large and handsome. Demoiselle are the smallest members of the ancient crane family and are graceful and pretty, especially in flight. The other migratory birds are geese and ducks. The greylag and bar-headed goose and most of the migratory duck species that visit India, e.g. the ruddy shelduck, mallard, teal, gadwall. Coots are common as are white (rosy) pelicans, flamingoes and a variety of waders. Of the indigenous birds visiting Sultanpur, the grey pelican, cormorant, painted stork, grey heron and pond heron, egret, are all to be seen plus a few white ibis and the blacknecked stork. Sultanpur is administered by the Tourism Department of Haryana. For further information contact the Project Officer, Haryana Tourism, Chanderlok Buildings, Delhi.

Hotels D *Rosy Pelican Complex* (Haryana Tourism), Sultanpur Bird Sanctuary. Restaurant, A/C rooms, camper huts, camping site, birdwatching facilities. Facilities open to residents and visitors.

Travel Bus: Take a blue Haryana bus to Gurgaon from Delhi. Departures every 10 min from Dhaula Khan. At Gurgaon take a Chandu bus (get off at Sultanpur) – 3-4 times a day.

Rewari (83 km from Delhi) was founded in 1000 AD by Raja Rawat and reputedly named after his daughter. There are the ruins of a still older town east of the 'modern' walls. The Rajas of Rewari were partially independent, even under the Mughals, coined their own currency called 'Gokal Sikka' and built the mud fort of Gokalgarh near the town. Rewari fell first to the Marathas and then to the Jat Rajas of Bharatpur. In 1805 it came under direct British rule. It has been a prosperous centre for the manufacture of iron and brass vessels. To the southwest of the town is an attractive tank with ghats built by Tej Singh and also Jain temples.

Jahazgarh 20 km N of Rewari, is a corruption of Georgegarh (George's fort) and the place was supposedly built by George Thomas, the military adventurer in the late 18th century. With the erosion of central authority in the 18th century, local resources were denied the centre and used by local chiefs for local wars of supremacy. The Marathas used the method of levying one fourth of the revenue (*chauth*) to subjugate areas and this process had proceeded so far by the last years of the century in the old Punjab that any adventurer who could gather some followers might seize a fort and terrorise the countryside. George Thomas was one of these. In 1801 the Marathas ousted him and, abandoning his conquests, he retired to Berhampur which was in British territory and, therefore, safe.

UTTAR PRADESH

Uttar Pradesh ("Northern Province") is India's most populous state with about one seventh of the nation's population. If it were a nation it would be the seventh largest country in the world. In terms of area it is the fourth largest (294,413 sq km). The region of today's Uttar Pradesh has been the hearth of much of India's contemporary religious and cultural life. It contains the source of the sacred river Ganga – "Ganga Ma" or Mother Ganga – regarded by Hindus as the physical and spiritual life source of the country. To bathe in it is to wash away guilt. To drink the water is meritorious. To be cremated on its banks at Varanasi, India's holiest city, and to have one's ashes cast on its waters, holds the promise of removing all the stains of one's karma and finding release from the endless cycle of re-births. Along it are a number of towns of religious significance; where it leaves the hills at Rishikesh and Haridwar, one of the scenes of the great Kumbh Mela festival; Allahabad, at its confluence with its principal tributary the Yamuna and with the mystical Saraswati river flowing from heaven, is another. Mathura, S of Delhi and on the banks of the Yamuna river, is regarded as the birthplace of Lord Krishna. The state has three of Hinduism's seven holy cities in Haridwar, Mathura and Varanasi and each year vast numbers of pilgrims travel through the state.

Home of the Buddha While the region is of special significance to Hindus it has also shaped both **Buddhism** and **Islam**. The Buddha was born on the borders of eastern UP and Bihar. He gave his first sermon at **Sarnath**, a few km from Varanasi, and at other places such as **Kusinagara** and **Srivasti** there were important monasteries. Today these holy places draw pilgrims from the countries to which Buddhism later spread. 2,000 years after the Buddha's birth, UP became the heartland of various Muslim dynasties, especially the Mughals. Akbar briefly had his capital at **Fatehpur Sikri**, 40 km W of Agra, and **Agra** itself was a long serving capital. In it are the Red Fort, the Itimad-ud-Daula tomb and the legendary Taj Mahal, one of the most popular sites in the world. The Muslim influence is not restricted to historic monuments. There is a large Muslim minority in many parts of the State.

While the plains of UP are a vital part of the hearth of Hindu and Muslim cultures in India, the State also has some beautiful hill stations such as Mussoorie and Nainital. Although UP contains some of the poorest parts of India, the W of the state has shared in the dynamic growth of the entire Delhi region. Literacy levels are low, especially among women, and this makes development efforts such as family planning more difficult.

Social indicators   Area 294,000 sq km; **Population** 135 million – *Urban* 18%; **Literacy**

M 39%; F 14%; **Birth rate** – *Rural* 33:1000, *Urban* 29:1000; **Death rate** – *Rural* 16:1000, *Urban* 10:1000; **Infant mortality** – *Rural* 156:1000, *Urban* 99:1000; **Registered graduate job seekers** 355,000; **Average annual income per head**: Rs 1280; **Inflation** (1981-87) 72%; **Religion** *Hindu* 83%, *Muslim* 16%, *Christian* 0.2%, *Sikh* 0.1%.

INTRODUCTION

The land
UP is one of India's border states, sharing one third of its northern boundary with **Tibet** and two-thirds with **Nepal**. In the mountains it adjoins Himachal Pradesh in the NW whilst on the plains its neighbours are: Haryana and Delhi (W) Rajasthan (SW), Madhya Pradesh (S) and Bihar (E). Approximately three quarters of UP comprises plain, the rest being the Siwalik hills and the Himalaya in the N and the Vindhya Hills and central plateau in the S.

There are four physical regions. In the N are the **Himalaya** (from the Sanskrit meaning *The Abode of Snow*), created by the crushing together of continental plates which is still causing dramatic uplifting and folding. The rocks are a mixture of Tertiary marine sediments, granite and metamorphosed material. Uplift still continues at the rate of between 1 cm and 6 cm per year. There are many snow capped peaks, e.g. **Nanda Devi** (7,816 m) and other peaks such as **Kamet**, **Trisul**, **Badrinath**, **Dunagiri** and **Shivling**, all over 6,400 m and many associated with the Hindu gods. This part of the Himalaya more than any other can justly claim to be the throne room of the Gods. The **Ganga** also has its source here. Soils tend to be easily drained but thin, stony, and poor.

Moving S into the **Siwaliks** the elevation of hills and the depth of valleys decreases. The **Siwaliks** form a low range of hills running parallel with the the Himalaya. To the S is the **Bhabar** and **Terai**. Formed of coarse and loose gravels, many mountain streams disappear below the quite steep loose slopes of the Bhabar during the dry season. On the plains side of this is the *terai*, a belt of jungle approximately 65 km wide, originally running from the Ganga gorge at Haridwar to Bihar. Here the streams that vanish in the *Bhabar* resurface.

The Gangetic Plain occupies the largest part of the state. When the Himalaya were created this region was a trough in between the two landmasses of peninsular India and Central Asia. Erosion in the hills and silt deposition downstream have formed beds of alluvium of up to 2,000 metres deep. The elevation of the plain gradually decreases from 365 metres in the NW at **Haridwar** to 80 metres in the E at **Varanasi**. This featureless and flat plain, stiflingly hot, dry and dusty in summer, is drained by the Ganga and its many tributaries.

The final region comprises the N margins of the Peninsula. This runs along the S edge of the state and includes the Vindhya hills in the SE which rise to more than 600 metres in places. They back onto the central Indian plateau.

Rivers and Lakes The major river of UP and N India is the **Ganga**. It is not only sacred to the Hindu population but invaluable for irrigating large areas. Nearly all the other rivers are part of the Ganga system. Second most important is the **Yamuna** which has its source in the **Garhwal Himalaya** at **Yamunotri**, flows through Delhi and Agra and joins the Ganga at **Allahabad**. The **Ghaghra**, **Gomti**, **Ramganga** and **Kosi** are other major rivers. There are no lakes on the plains and only a few in the mountains. Of these, **Nainital** is the biggest. It situated at 1830 metres above sea level is 1.5 km long and 300 metres wide. In the region round Nainital there are a number of smaller lakes.

Climate
Except for the mountain region, the whole state experiences a tropical monsoon

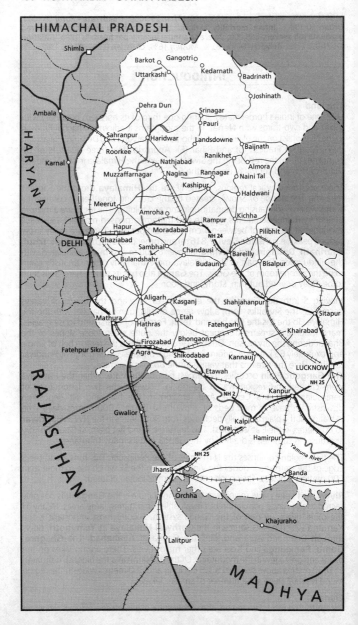

HIMACHAL PRADESH

Shimla

Barkot Gangotri
Uttarkashi Kedarnath Badrinath
Joshinath

Dehra Dun
Srinagar
Ambala Pauri
Sahranpur Haridwar Landsdowne Baijnath
Roorkee Ranikhet Almora
Karnal Nathjabad Rannagar Naini Tal
Muzzaffarnagar Nagina Kashipur Haldwani
Meerut Amroha Kichha
Hapur Moradabad Rampur Pilibhit
DELHI NH 24
Ghaziabad Sambhal Chandausi Bareilly
Bulandshahr Budaun Bisalpur
Khurja
Aligarh Kasganj Shahjahanpur
Mathura Hathras Etah Sitapur
Firozabad Bhongaon Fatehgarh Khairabad
Fatehpur Sikri Agra Shikodabad Kannauj LUCKNOW
Etawah NH 25
NH 2 Kanpur
Gwalior Kalpi
Orai Hamirpur
NH 25 Yamuna River
Jhansi Banda
Orchha
Khajuraho
Lalitpur

HARYANA

RAJASTHAN

MADHYA

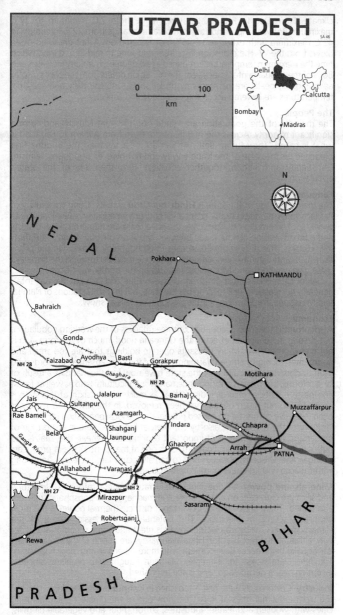

UTTAR PRADESH

SA 46

0   100
km

Delhi
Calcutta
Bombay
Madras

N

NEPAL

Pokhara

☐ KATHMANDU

Bahraich

Gonda

Faizabad   Ayodhya   Basti   Gorakpur

NH 28

Ghaghara River

NH 29

Jalalpur   Barhaj

Jais

Sultanpur

Azamgarh

Indara

Rae Bameli

Shahganj

Bela

Jaunpur

Ghazipur

Motihara

Muzzaffarpur

Chhapra

Ganga River

Allahabad   Varanasi

Arrah

☐ PATNA

NH 27   NH 2

Mirazpur

Sasaram

Robertsganj

Rewa

BIHAR

PRADESH

climate. From Dec to Feb temperatures range from 7°C minimum to 27°C maximum. Between April and June temperatures range from 22°C minimum to 42°C maximum with extremes of 45°C not uncommon. A hot dry wind often blows from the W. The monsoon lasts from mid-June to mid-Sep, during which time the maximum temperature is reduced a few degrees, humidity increases and 80% of the annual rainfall is received. The hill region differs from the plains insofar as its highest peaks are permanently under snow, and the daily and seasonal temperatures are lowered according to altitude and aspect.

The People

The majority of the population are Hindu but 15% are Muslim and form a significant minority. Across the middle of the state from Aligarh to Faizabad is what is called 'The Muslim Belt'. At Sarnath near Varanasi the Buddha first preached his message of the Middle Way. Today, however, Buddhism, Jainism, Christianity and Sikhism together constitute less than 3% of the state's population.

Language

The main language of the state is **Hindi**, but **Urdu** with its strong vocabulary of Persian words, modified Arabic script and Hindi grammatical structure is still quite widely spoken among Muslims. Over the state there are numerous local dialects and a broad division can be made between those on the plains and the *Pahari* (hill) dialects. This distinction also applies to ethnographic origins. On the plains the inhabitants exhibit Aryan features and as one moves N through the Himalaya these give way to strong Mongoloid features on the border with Tibet.

All of UP receives most of its rain between June and October. Rainfall totals generally decreases from E to W across the state, but in the hill stations of Nainital and Mussoorie, for example, winter precipitation falls as snow.

Economy

Agriculture is the main occupation of three quarters of the working population, but despite the enriching effect of the Ganga in flood, much of the farm land is not highly productive. Many peasants operate holdings that are too small and fragmented for highly efficient farming. Most of the large absentee landlords who used to dominate agriculture of the state have now lost their land as a result of land reforms, but there is enormous demand for agricultural land as well as forest and pasture. Official records indicate that as much as one sixth of the state is under forest, but much of that has been removed. In the **Himalaya** there has been extensive deforestation caused not only by the local population taking more land under the plough but also by commercial logging. There is a shortage of timber and firewood, the most important cooking fuel. Wheat, rice, maize and pulses dominate the cropping pattern. UP is one of the country's major producers of sugarcane. Oilseeds, potatoes and cotton all occupy large acreages and along with tobacco and jute have good commercial returns.

Minerals and power   UP does not have lucrative mineral resources. Limestone and silica are extracted on a large scale and magnesite and phosphatic shale are also mined. There are coalfields in Mirzapur district. Thermal power is the most important source of electricity. The potential for harnessing some of the Himalayan rivers for hydro-electric power is great and some schemes are under way, although the fact that the Himalayan valleys are in one of the world's great earthquake belts makes development both more expensive and more hazardous. The Tehri Dam Project, for example, has been fraught with problems since its inception over a decade ago, and is still unfinished.

Industry   Cotton mills were first established in **Kanpur** in 1869 making it one of the older industrial cities of India. It is now one of the greatest manufacturing cities with woollen and leather industries, cotton, flour and vegetable oil mills, sugar refineries and chemical works. The state government has established cement factories near **Mirzapur**, precision instrument factories around Lucknow and a chemical plant at **Bareilly** to diversify the industrial base. The severely damaging effects on the pollution of the Ganga are only now beginning to be recognised and tackled. Despite the presence of some very large factories small-scale enterprises dominate industry. Cottage and village-based industries such as weaving, leather and woodwork, ceramics, silk weaving and perfumery are all important.

Communications Travel across UP is comparatively easy. There is an extensive road and rail network over the state which because of the size of its population is constantly under pressure. The main railway junctions are Agra, Allahabad, Jhansi, Kanpur, Lucknow, Mathura, Moradabad and Varanasi. The major defect of the rail system is that there are two different gauges. Railways do not extend into the hills. The railheads are Kathgodam, Ramnagar, Kotdwara, Haridwar and Dehra Dun. River transport has declined to relative insignificance. There is a surprisingly good road network which has been extended to the border with Tibet/China to facilitate troop movements. It has undoubtedly benefitted the local population and the annual 300,000 pilgrims travelling from all parts of India to worship at the mountain shrines. However, because of the inherent fragility of the hillsides and the widespread removal of natural vegetation for cultivation and fuel and commercial forest products, landslips are common and disrupt traffic flows, especially during the monsoon.

History
The rise of Hinduism UP is regarded by many Hindus as the birthplace of the legendary Rama and Krishna, the heroes of the epic and immensely popular poems the *Ramayana* and *Mahabharata*. It was the home first of the Vedic religion developed by the earliest Ind-Aryan immigrants from around 1500 BC, then of Brahmanisim and, from the 4th century BC to the 4th century AD, the development of Hinduism in something close to its present form. In the Vedic period (c.1500-600 BC) it formed part of *Madhyadesa* (Middle Country).

The Buddha preached his first sermon in the deer park at Sarnath and attained *parinirvana* (spiritual release from the body) at Kusinagara. Varanasi, one of UP's ancient cities, can be traced back at least a century before the Buddha came to it in 500 BC. It became a great centre of culture, education, commerce and craftsmanship, drawing students and pilgrims from all over the country. Its fame also drew the attention of the rich and powerful and its temples and mansions were ransacked on many occasions from the 11th to the 18th centuries. Over two millennia ago, UP was part of Asoka's great Mauryan empire.

Mughal influence and the British Later most of UP was controlled by various Hindu dynasties until the arrival of the Muslims in the 12th century. **Agra** was one of the capitals of the Mughal Empire which stretched from the Bay of Bengal to Kabul in Afghanistan. **Shah Jahan** more than any other Mughal Emperor, was responsible for encouraging the development of a fully distinct and uniquely beautiful Mughal architecture, the foremost example of which is the **Taj Mahal**.

The arrival of the British in India was followed by their gradual advance up the river Ganga. In 1836 East India Company possessions in UP and Delhi were combined and renamed the North-Western Provinces. The annexation of the independent province of Oudh in 1856 undoubtedly contributed to the outbreak of the 1857 Indian Mutiny. The first revolt occurred in Meerut and quickly spread to Lucknow, Kanpur, Agra, Allahabad and Jhansi. Some of its most dramatic incidents occurred at Lucknow and Kanpur (Cawnpore).

After the Mutiny control of East India Company territories passed to the British crown. In 1877 the North-Western Provinces and Oudh were combined to form the United Provinces of Agra and Oudh. UP was in the forefront of the national movement for independence with many incidents associated with the *Swaraj* (Home Rule) struggle occurring within its boundaries.

Recent political developments UP has the same administrative structure as other Indian States. The head of state is the governor who is appointed by the President for a five year term. The 425 seat legislative assembly is at Lucknow, the state capital. UP has 85 seats in the Lok Sabha (Lower House) and 34 seats in the Rajya Sabha (Upper House), more than any other. It is regarded as the political heartland and has produced most of India's prime ministers since Independence, including Jawaharlal Nehru, his daughter Indira Gandhi and grandson Rajiv Gandhi. In only two of the elections to the State Assembly since Independence has the Congress Party failed to win an overall majority in the state. The first occasion was in 1977, immediately following Mrs. Gandhi's emergency, and the second the Dec 1989 election. The Congress has also dominated representation to the Lok Sabha in most elections. Again 1977 was an exception, when it won none of the 85 seats despite polling 25% of the vote. The position was dramatically reversed in 1984 when Rajiv Gandhi won a landslide across the state capturing 83 of the 85 seats with 51% of the poll. In the 1989 elections a combination of the Janata Dal, under V.P. Singh, and the right wing Hindu party the BJP, captured the majority of the state's seats.

DELHI TO DEHRA DUN AND MUSSOORIE VIA MEERUT & RISHIKESH

Between Delhi and Dehra Dun the road runs across the flat but fertile plais between the Ganga and the Yamuna Rivers. Irrigated by canals for over 150 years, the land is intensively cultivated. The journey from **Haridwar** along the Pilgrim Rd that follows the Ganga to **Badrinath** and **Kedarnath** and finally to its source at **Gangotri** is one of Hinduism's great pilgrimages. Every devout Hindu tries to make the journey at least once in their lifetime.

From **Delhi** the main road N crosses the Yamuna bridge and continues E as the NH24 towards **Ghaziabad** (19 km). The road crosses the railway at **Shahdara** (6 km). After a further 11 km, on the outskirts of Ghaziabad, the road crosses the River Hindon. Take the left turn for Meerut. After 17 km the road passes through Muradnagar and reaches *Modinagar* (11 km). Modinagar is what its name suggests – the town of the Modis which has developed around the Modi family conglomerate's industries. Every lamp-post and, seemingly, every blank wall carries hoardings advertising the diverse range of Modi products from thread and material to pipes and tyres. To the N of Modinagar you cross the Upper Ganga Canal. The goes goes through Partapur (9 km) to Meerut (9 km).

Meerut is an important commercial and administrative town, with a number of attractive broad streets. It is a major agricultural market. However, it is better known as the place where the Indian Mutiny started on 10 May 1857. The extensive British cantonment has a particularly fine **Mall,** a Club and churches. The cemetery contains the graves of Sir Rollo Gillespie who subdued the uprising at **Vellore** in 1806 (**see page 772**) and of Sir David Ochterlony – **see page 525**. **St John's Church** (1821) contains many memorials to British officers.

Meerut was a settlement in Asoka's time and contains various Hindu and Muslim buildings from the 11th century onwards. The **Jama Masjid** (1019) was built by Hasan Mahdi, Mahmud of Ghazni's *wazir** (chief minister)and although it was restored by Humayun it is one of the oldest Muslim mosques in India. The **Tomb of Shah Pir** (1628) was erected by the empress Nur Jahan in honour of a local Muslim saint. Qutd-ud-din Aibak is believed to have built the **Maqbara of Salar**

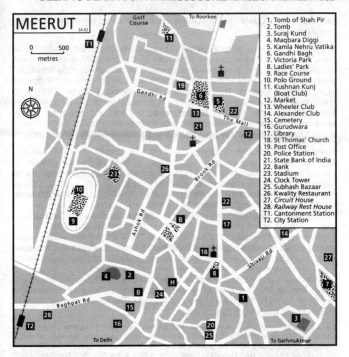

MEERUT SA 62

0   500
metres

N

Golf Course

To Roorkee

Gandhi Rd

The Mall

Brook Rd

Ashok Rd

Shivaji Rd

Baghpat Rd

To Delhi

To Garhmuktesar

1. Tomb of Shah Pir
2. Tomb
3. Suraj Kund
4. Maqbara Diggi
5. Kamla Nehru Vatika
6. Gandhi Bagh
7. Victoria Park
8. Ladies' Park
9. Race Course
10. Polo Ground
11. Kushnan Kunj (Boat Club)
12. Market
13. Wheeler Club
14. Alexander Club
15. Cemetery
16. Gurudwara
17. Library
18. St Thomas' Church
19. Post Office
20. Police Station
21. State Bank of India
22. Bank
23. Stadium
24. Clock Tower
25. Subhash Bazaar
26. Kwality Restaurant
27. *Circuit House*
28. *Railway Rest House*
T1. Cantonment Station
T2. City Station

Masa-ud Ghazi (1194). There are other mausolea and mosques indicating the strong Muslim presence in Meerut.

Meerut lies in what has been termed the Muslim belt – others are **Moradabad** and **Aligarh** – and tension between Muslims and Hindus has periodically erupted into violent conflict. There are as many Hindu temples as mosques. The **Baleshwar Nath Temple** pre-dates the arrival of Islam in India. The **Suraj Kund** (also called "Monkey Tank") is to the W of Victoria Park and is lined with shrines and small temples. It was built in 1714 by the merchant Jowahir Mal.

Continue N from Meerut. Just over half way between **Meerut** and **Muzaffarnagar** you cross the **Upper Ganga Canal** at **Khatauli**. On the N bank of the canal on the N edge of town is a very pleasant fast food cafe in Forest Department grounds with open air seating and a small zoo. Highly recommended as a refreshment stop, and very popular with Indian travellers. Continue to *Muzaffarnagar* (51 km) and then direct to **Saharanpur** and **Dehra Dun** (67 km).

Saharanpur (54 km *Population* 320,000) was founded in 1340 and was named after the Muslim saint Shah Haran Chisti. The shrine is visited by Hindus and Muslims, and was a summer retreat for the Mughals. During the British period it became an important military base, especially for operations in the Gurka War, but the government also set out botanical gardens in 1817. It has become a particularly important source of fruit trees for the whole of India. The town is close enough to the mountain to have superb views of the Himalayas. Nearby is the small town of **Nolji** from which the trigonometrical survey of the Himalayas was extended.

Alternatively continue on to **Roorkee** (52 km), developed as India's first "canal town", near the headworks on what was at the time N India's first great experiment with really large scale river diversion. It has subsequently developed a very high reputation as an engineering centre, not only for canal equipment but also for army sappers. The **Thomason Engineering College** (1847) was transformed into a university specialising in technical sciences. The road leaves Roorkee and passes through **Bahadurabad** (17 km) and **Jawalpur** before reaching **Haridwar** (7 km). By car and with a reasonable stop for food en route, e.g at **Khatauli**, the journey from Delhi will take about 4 hr 30 min.

Haridwar (*Altitude* 294 m) One of the seven holy cities of Hinduism – see also Mathura, Varanasi and Ayodhya in UP, Ujjain in Madhya Pradesh, Dwarka in Gujarat and Kanchipuram in Tamil Nadu. Haridwar is where legend has placed Vishnu's footprint on the bank of the holy river giving it its sanctity. Various episodes from the *Mahabharata* are set here. Every twelfth year the **Kumbh Mela** is held here – see Allahabad, page **247**.

Situated at the base of the Siwalik Hills, Haridwar is where the **River Ganga** passes through its last gorge and begins a 2,000 km journey across the plains of UP, Bihar and W Bengal to the Bay of Bengal. These three states alone contain almost a third of India's population. From here it begins to irrigate vast expanses of land with the aid of canals and wells. Water is drawn off for the Upper Ganga Canal system and there is also a hydro-electric power station.

Haridwar is a very old town and was mentioned by the Chinese traveller Hiuen Tsang. The wealth of Haridwar attracted the attention of **Timur** who sacked it in Jan 1399 during his bloodthirsty foray into N India. The name Haridwar 'Door of Vishnu (Hari)' dates from about 1400.

Local Festivals Haridwar receives thousands of pilgrims every year, the numbers increasing to almost 100,000 when the birth of the river (*Dikhanti*) is celebrated in spring. Numbers attending the *Kumbh Mela* (usually April) are growing all the time. Now over 2 million devotees throng to the confined area near **Hari-ki-pairi** to bathe in the waters. In the past there have been a high number of fatalities due to the great congestion and violence, e.g. in 1760 when rival gangs of the Gosain and Bairagi sects set upon one another. Elaborate security preparations and extraordinary efforts to provide basic sanitation have helped to minimise the risk.

Places of interest The town is situated on the W bank of the river and centres on **Hari-ki-Pairi**, the place where **Vishnu** is believed to have left his *charan*** (footprint). Part of the Ganga has been diverted here and this later becomes the canal. Bathing here is believed to cleanse all sins. Surrounding the steps are a modern clocktower and some temples, none particularly old. Further down along the waterfront are more bathing ghats, numerous sheds where *pandas*** of various castes and sects dispense wisdom to the willing, and food stalls, shrines and alleyways leading off into the bazaar. There are five bridges across the river – it is pleasant to go over to the other side, which is much quieter. Along the banks are various *sadhus*** who have made make-shift homes under trees.

The **bazaar** is interesting, always colourful, invariably crowded and surprisingly clean and tidy. There are stalls with piles of coloured powder piled high in carefully made cones (this is used to make the tikka and sect marks), stalls selling saris, jewellery, brass and aluminium pots and, of course, sweets and snacks.

The *railway station* is beyond the bazaar along the Jahawalapur Haridwar Rd. The **Mansa Devi Temple** is worth visiting for the view. Set on the southernmost hill of the Siwaliks it can be reached by chairlift (About Rs 10 return). The *Tourist Office* is near bottom of chairlift.

Kankhal, 3 km downstream, is where **Siva's** wife **Sati** is believed to have burnt herself to death because her father **Daksa's** failed to invite Siva to a *yagna*.

Prof Wendy O'Flaherty vividly summarises the story as told in the Puranas; "**Daksa**, a son of

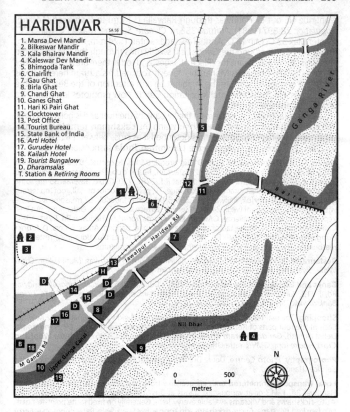

HARIDWAR SA 56

1. Mansa Devi Mandir
2. Bilkeswar Mandir
3. Kala Bhairav Mandir
4. Kaleswar Dev Mandir
5. Bhimgoda Tank
6. Chairlift
7. Gau Ghat
8. Birla Ghat
9. Chandi Ghat
10. Ganes Ghat
11. Hari Ki Pairi Ghat
12. Clocktower
13. Post Office
14. Tourist Bureau
15. State Bank of India
16. Arti Hotel
17. Gurudev Hotel
18. Kailash Hotel
19. Tourist Bungalow
D. *Dharamsalas*
T. Station & *Retiring Rooms*

Brahma, gave his daughter Sati in marriage to Siva, but he did not invite Siva to his sacrifice. Sati, in anger, burnt herself to death. Siva destroyed Daksa's sacrifice and beheaded Daksa, but when the gods praised Siva he restored the sacrifice and gave Daksa the head of a goat. When Siva learned that Sati had killed herself, he took up her body and danced in grief, troubling the world with his dance and his tears until the gods cut the corpse into pieces. When the *yoni* fell, Siva took the form of a *linga*, and peace was re-established in the universe." At Kankhal there is the **Temple of Daksehwara.**

Hotels C *Hotel Surprise*, Haridwar- Delhi Rd, Jawala Pur, T 1146. 55 a/c rm. On outskirts. Restaurant, coffee shop, rm service, shops, pool. Most modern in the area, one of few non-veg restaurants. **D** *U.P. Tourist Bungalow*, on the E bank of the Ganga. T 379 22 rm, some air cooled with bath plus dormitory. Restaurant (simple veg), TV lounge. **D** *Gurudev*, between rly station and Tourist Office on Jahawalpur-Haridwar Rd, T 101. 30 rm, some with balcony overlooking st others on court yard. Some a/c or air cooled. Veg food, rm service. **E** *Vikrant* is nr the river. There are other **E** and **F** hotels in the bazaar area and round the rly station. **E** *Railway Retiring Rooms* Rm (D) and dormitory beds.

Rail Old Delhi: *Dehradun Exp* 9020, daily, 1250, 9 hr 55 min; *Mussoorie Exp* 4042, daily, 2250, 7 hr 5 min. **Dehra Dun:** *Dehra Dun Exp* 9019, daily, 1455, 1 hr 55 min; *Mussoorie Exp* 4041, daily, 0650, 1 hr 40 min. **Bus** There are regular bus services to Haridwar from Delhi and other centres in the part of the state. The bus stand is a short walk from the station. Cycle rickshaws are available for hire – fares negotiable.

Continue NE out of Haridwar through Raiwalla (11 km) to **Rishikesh** (14 km). *Population* 28,897 (1981) *Altitude* 356 m *Climate*. Summer Max 41˚C, Min 37˚C. Winter Max 32˚C, Min 18˚C. Annual average rainfall 1524 mm, mostly Jun to Sep. The town nestles around the Ganga as it swiftly runs through the last hills of the Himalaya. Rishikesh means the 'Place of Sages' and today there are a large number of ashrams. The notorious Maharishi Mahesh Yogi had his ashram here and was fortunate enough to capture the imagination and attention of the Beatles in the early sixties. His Transcendental Meditation Centre now promotes levitation as a product of enlightenment.

The secular business centre is on the W bank of the river and is noisy and dirty. The spiritual haven of the various ashrams and the **Lakshman Temple** are on the other side. Geoffrey Moorhouse has described it as cross between Blackpool and Lourdes. You cross the Ganga by the **Lakshman Jhula** suspension bridge.

Hotels Mostly 15 km from Jolly Grant D'Dun airport, 0.5 km rly, central. **B** *Natraj*, Dehradun Rd. T 1099, 1272, Cable: Natraj. 75 rm. Restaurant, health club, TV, exchange, parking and 'drivers' dormitory'. Modern. **C** *Basera*, 1 Ghat Rd. T 767, 720, Cable: Baseraa. 33 rm, some a/c, others air cooled. Restaurant (veg), exchange, TV, parking, doctor on call, roof top terrace garden, Diners. **C** *Inderlok*, Railway Rd. T 555-6, 99, Cable: Inderlok. 52 rm, some a/c, some with balconies. Restaurant (veg), 24 hr rm service, terrace lawn, Diners. Older hotel, but well kept and with pleasant ambience. **C** *Mandakini International*, 63 Haridwar Rd. T 781, 1081, Cable: Mandakini. 31 rm. Restaurant (veg), travel, car hire, parking. Amex, Diners. **D** *Tourist Bungalow (GMVN)*, Badrinath Rd. Non a/c rooms with baths plus dormitory, restaurant, reasonable. There are also a number of *dharamshalas** for pilgrims.

Restaurants Indian vegetarian: *Darpan*, Railway Rd, T 405. *Vishwas*, Muni-ki-Ret. *Choti Wala*, Sivananda Jhula (Ram Jhula), Swarg Ashram.

Banks and Exchanges *New Bank of India*, Dehra Dun Rd, T 561. *Punjab National*, Haridwar Rd, T 213. *Punjab and Sind*, Ghat Rd, T 449. *State Bank of India*, Railway Rd, T 114. *Union Bank of India*, Haridwar Rd, T 73.

Shopping The main shopping areas are Dehra Dun Rd, Haridwar Rd, Ghat Rd, Railway Rd. Each of the four parts of Rishikesh has markets for daily needs and curios. *UP Handlooms*, Dehra Dun Rd. *Gandhi Ashram Khadi Bhandar*, Haridwar Rd, T 367. *Garhwal Wool and Craft House* (opp GMVN Yatra Office), Muni-ki-Reti.

Photography *Photo Centre*, Dehra Dun Rd. *Agarwal Photo Co*, Ghat Rd. *Yatrik Photo Service*, Haridwar Rd.

Local Transport Unmetered taxis are available from Garhwal Mandal Taxi Chalak Sangh, Haridwar Rd, T 413 or at various taxi stands at Bus Stands, Railway Stn. Rates negotiable. Auto-rickshaws and Vikrams available everywhere. Generally on fixed route point-to-point. Min fare Re 1 per stage. Cycle-rickshaws and Tongas freely available. Rates negotiable. Ferry Service available at Ghat near Sivananda Jhula (Ram Jhula) for river crossing. Re 1.50.

Sports Swimming at Hotel Natraj's pool. Open to non-residents on temporary membership. Boat rides on the Ganga from Swarg Ashram Ghat. Rates negotiable with local boatmen.

Trekking and Mountaineering Garhwal Mandal Vikas Nigram organises trekking, mountaineering and allied sports activities from Rishikesh. GMVN Ltd, Muni-ki-Reti, T 372.

Useful Numbers Police: T 100. Fire: T 101, 140.

Hospitals and Medical Services G.D. Hospital, Dehra Dun Rd, T 96. Rajkiya Mahila Chikitsalaya, D\ehra Dun Rd. Govt. Ayurvedic, Sivananda Ashram, Muni-ki-Reti.

Post and Telegraphs GPO and Telegraph Office, Ghat Rd, T 340. Post Offices at Hiralal Marg, T 645, Lakshman Jhula, T 292 and Muni-ki-Reti. Telegraph Office, Hiralal Marg, T 645. Open 0700-2200.

Places of Worship *Hindu*: Bharat Mandir, Rishikesh; Lakshman Temple, Lakshman Jhula; Sri Venkateswara Temple, Muni-ki-Reti. *Jain*: Shwetambara Jain Temple, Hiralal Marg. *Sikh*: Gurudwara, Dehra Dun Rd; Hemkund Gurudwara, Muni-ki-Reti.

Travel Agents and Tour Operators *Garhwal Mandal Vikas Nigram Ltd*, Muni-ki-Reti, T 372. Maintains tourist accommodation at many places in Garhwal.

Tourist Offices and Information Govt. of UP Tourist Office, Railway Rd, T 209. Govt. of

RISHIKESH SA 57

To Badrinath & Srinagar

To Tehri

Ferry

Chandrabhaga River

Dehra Dun Rd

Lakshman-jhula Rd

Nehru Rd

N

0   500
metres

Ganga River

Landsdowne

Gohri
Reserve
Forest

Haridwar Rd

1. Lakshman Temple
2. Parmarth Temple
3. Lakshman Jhula
4. Swarg Niwas Mandir
5. Raghunath Mandir
6. Shankacharya Ashram
7. Maharishi Mahesh Yogi Ashram
8. Dayanand Ashram
9. Kailash Ashram
10. Shivanand Ashram
11. State Bank of India
12. Railway Booking Agency
13. Post Office & Hotel Basera
14. Tourist Office
15. Hotel Menka
16. Neelam Hotel
17. Hotel Inderlok
18. GMVN Tourist Bungalow
19. Hotel Green
20. Viswas Hotel
21. Forest Rest House
22. Triveni Ghat

UP Tourist Office (during Yatra season only), Samyukt Yatra Bus Stand. Garhwal Mandal Vikas Nigram Ltd, Muni-ki-Reti, T 372.

Travel N.B. Registration of *Yatra** tourists is essential with State Government Yatra Office at Yatra Bus Stand, T 383. Open 0600-2200. Buses to Northern Hill regions, serviced by Garhwal Mandal Motor Operators Union, Tehri Garhwal MOU and Yatayat Ltd, operate from Samyukt Yatra Bus Stand, Dehra Dun Rd.

Air Nearest airport is Jolly Grant (16 km). **Vayudoot** (Handling and Booking Agents) offices are available only at Dehra Dun, 42 km away by road. Vayudoot flies from Delhi and Lucknow.

Rail There is a branch line from Haridwar to Rishikesh. The bus is quicker.

Bus Rishikesh is serviced by various States' Government bus services, like DTC, Haryana Roadways, Himachal RTC, UP Roadways. Major destinations are: Delhi, Agra, Dehra Dun, Mussoorie, Haridwar, Chandigarh, Patiala, Saharanpur, Shimla, Sarkaghat. Roadways Bus Stand, Haridwar Rd, T 66. No reservations. During Yatra season (May-Nov), reservations are made on these bus services one day prior to journey. Reservations open 0400-1900.

Road Rishikesh is connected by road via Haridwar and Dehra Dun to various parts of the country. It is also the base for travel to the hill regions of Garhwal and the four holy shrines of Badrinath, Kedarnath, Gangotri and Yamunotri, and also the Sikh shrine at Hemkund Sahib. From: **Delhi** (238 km); **Dehra Dun** (42 km); **Haridwar** (24 km); **Mussoorie** (77 km); **Yamunotri** (288 km); **Gangotri** (258 km); **Uttarkashi** (154 km); **Kedarnath** (228 km); **Badrinath** (301 km); **Chandigarh** (252 km).

The Pilgrimage (Yatra) From Haridwar to Badrinath

Purification After a ritual purificatory bathe in the Ganga at Haridwar and, preferably, Rishikesh as well, the pilgrim then begins the 301 km journey from Haridwar to Badrinath, one of the four holiest places in India for Hindus. The purpose is to worship, purify and acquire merit. There are two types of pilgrimage aim: purification from bad *karma** (impurity as a consequence of bad actions) or the performance of specific rituals usually associated with death. This rational belief is connected with the belief in the purifying power of certain precisely performed rituals. These rituals of purification, since they are very often based on the simple analogy between physical and moral impurity, use water as a medium. The purifying power of a sacred river is stronger at the source, at the confluence of rivers and at the mouth. There are five *prayags** (confluences) in the Himalayan section of the Ganga. From Rishikesh they are **Deoprayag**, **Rudraprayag**, **Karnaprayag**, **Nandaprayag** and **Vishnuprayag**. On the plains, Allahabad is the most important confluence of all, where the Yamuna the Ganga and the mythical underground river the Sarasvati all meet.

Piety Hardship enhances the rewards. It is common to see *sadhus** dressed in the characteristic saffron robes, staff in one hand, brass pitcher in the other walking along this road. The really devout prostrate themselves for the whole distance, lying face down on the road, reaching arms stretched above their heads, standing up, moving forwards to where their fingertips reached and then repeating the exercise, each one accompanied by a chant to the gods. This act of extreme piousness is rarely seen nowadays and most pilgrims prefer to make the journey by bus or, if they are fortunate enough, by car. The regional tourism organization *Garhwal Mandal Vikas Nigam* (Garhwal Tourism Development Corporation) has established a string of moderately priced basic lodges for travellers all along this route.

From **Rishikesh** the road follows the right (W) bank of the river and quickly enters forest. The section up to **Deoprayag** (68 km) is one of astounding beauty. The folding and erosion of the hills can be clearly seen on scarps on the opposite bank which for the most part is uninhabited due to the steepness of the valley sides. Luxuriant forest runs down to the waters edge which in many places is fringed with silver sand beaches. In places the river, visibly fast flowing, rushes over gentle rapids. After the truck stop village of **Vayasi** the road makes a gradual ascent to round an important bluff. At the top, there are fine views down to the river. Villages now become more common and noticeable. The way that small pocket handkerchief-sized fields have been created by terracing is marvellous.

Warning It is an offence to photograph sensitive installations, troop movements and bridges on this route. Offenders can be treated very severely.

Deoprayag is the most important of the hill *prayags* because it is at the junction of the **Bhagirathi** and **Alaknanda** rivers. Gangotri is the source of the Bhagirathi and Badrinath is near the source of the Alaknanda. Below Deoprayag, the river becomes the Ganga proper. The town is mostly confined and squashed into the deeply cut V between the junction of the two rivers and tumbles down the hillside, houses almost on top of one another. Where the rivers meet is a bathing ghat, artificially made into the shape of India. Here pilgrims bathe and to prevent them being swept downstream there are chains for them to cling to.

From Deoprayag, the road is relatively flat as far as *Srinagar* (35 km) and for much of the way you pass through well cultivated village lands. At Kirtinagar the road crosses the river to the E bank. The valley is quite wide here and is known as the **Panai pasture**. **Srinagar** (not to be confused with its better known Kashmiri namesake) is the old capital of **Garhwal** (Land of the Forts). Up until the 14th century Garhwal comprised a number of petty principalities, each no larger than a valley. Ajai Pal (1358-70) consolidated these and became the Raja of **Garhwal**. The Mughals showed little interest in acquiring the region but it was a popular plundering ground for Sikh brigands from the Punjab and the Rohillas – see Rampur (**page 216**). The **Gurkhas** overran it in 1803 and treated the population harshly, taking men, women and children into slavery and conscripting males into their army. Compelled to action by Gurkha encroachments on the territory around **Gorakhpur**, the British expelled the Gurkhas from Garhwal and Kumaon in 1814, took the eastern part of Garhwal as British Garhwal and returned the western part, Tehri Garhwal to the deposed Raja.

Srinagar was devastated by a great earthquake in the mid 19th century. Consequently, there is little of antiquity. The most attractive part of Srinagar, which is a development centre and University town, is down from the square towards the river. There are some typical Hill houses with elaborate carved door jambs.

Hotels As you approach the central square where northbound buses halt for the night, on your right is the **E** *Tourist Reception Centre (GMVN)* with approx. 40 non a/c rms with bath plus a dormitory and restaurant. Recommended. Opp is the **E** *Alka*.

The next stretch is from Srinagar to **Rudraprayag** (700 m, 35 km), again mostly through cultivated areas. Roughly half way there is an enormous landslip indicating the fragility of the mountains. Approx 5 km before reaching **Rudrapayag** in a grove of trees by a village is a tablet marking the spot where the Man-eating Leopard of Rudraprayag was finally killed by Jim Corbett – see Corbett National Park (**page 222**). Rudraprayag is a linear town strung out along a fairly narrow part of the Alaknanda valley. The Mandakini is the affluent and if upstream in Kedarnath. At Rudraprayag you turn left, cross the river for Kedarnath – **see page 210**.

Gauchar, famous locally for its annual cattle fair, is about midway between Rudraprayag and Karnaprayag. The valley is wider here providing the local population with very good agricultural land. **Karnaprayag** (788 m, 17 km) is where the beautiful Pindar River joins the Alaknanda. At **Nandaprayag** is the confluence of the Nandakini River. All these places have GMVN accommodation.

Chamoli (960 m, 40 km) is the principal market for the district of the same name though the HQ is Gopeshwar on the hillside opposite. The valley walls are now much higher and steeper and the road twists and turns more. There is constant troop movement up to the border with Tibet/China and military establishments are a frequent site on the Pilgrim Road.

From Chamoli onwards the road is particularly impressive from an engineering standpoint. **Joshimath** (1,875 m, 243 km) is at the junction of 2 formerly important Trans-Himalayan trading routes. Beyond Badrinath is the Mana Pass. To your right along the valley of the **Dhauliganga** is the **Niti Pass**. **NB** Both are now off-limits to foreigners. The route over the Niti Pass (5,067 m) into W Tibet leads to the **Mount Kailas**, sacred to Hindus and Buddhists, and **Lake Mansarovar**.

Over these passes are the **Bhutias**, a border people with Mongoloid features and strong ties with Tibet – **see page 572**. The women with their distinctive Arab-like headdress are quite noticeable. Like their counterparts in the E Himalaya they combined cultivation in high places with animal husbandry and trading, taking manufactured goods from India to Tibet and returning with salt and borax. With the closure of the border following the 1962 Indo-Chinese War, they were forced to seek alternative supplements to their income and some were resettled by the government. **Vishnuprayag** and Joshimath are virtually the same place. This is the winter headquarters of the Rawal of Badrinath.

At **Govindghat** is the valley leading up to **The** *Valley of Flowers* and **Hemkund Sahib**. Mules can be hired here for the two day journey. The first day is a 10 km walk to **Ghangaria** (12 km) where there is a Sikh gurdwara offering free accommodation and food to all travellers. To the right a track leads up to **Hemkund** (4 km). This is where **Guru Gobind Singh** – **see page 72** – is believed to have sat in meditation during a previous incarnation. It is an important Sikh pilgrimage site. On the shore of the lake (4,340 m) is a modern gurudwara. Pilgrims take a bath in the icy cold waters of the pool. Hemkund is also a Hindu pilgrimage site, Hindus referring to it as as *Lokpal*. Here Lakshman, the younger brother of Rama, meditated. A small temple dedicated to him stands near the Gurudwara. Despite its ancient connections, Hemkund/Lokpal only became a major pilgrimage place from 1930 onwards. It was 'discovered' by a Sikh *Havildar**, Solan Singh.

The **Valley of Flowers** (4 km from **Ghangariya**) was popularised by the Frank Smythe, the well known mountainee,r in 1931. Popular because of its accessibility (primarily due to Sikh enterprise) the valley floor is carpeted with alpine flowers during the monsoon and is highly colourful and attractive. Camping is not permitted.

The final 20 km of the journey to Badrinath passes through the occasional Bhotia settlement.

Badrinath (3,150 m) 301 km from Haridwar, 502 km from Delhi. The Hindu *Shastras** enjoin that no pilgrimage would be complete unless a pilgrim paid a visit to Badrinath, the abode of Vishnu. Along with **Ramesvaram**, **Dwarka** and **Puri** it is one of the four holiest places in India and it is a living faith with every Hindu to visit the shrine of Badrinath once in a lifetime. See page 58. According to the *Skanda Purana* 'There are many shrines on earth, heaven and hell but none has been, nor will be, like Badrinath'. Guarding it are the Nar and Narayan ranges and in the distance towers the magnificent Neelkanth peak. The word Badri is derived from a wild fruit that Vishnu was said to have lived on when he did penance at Badrivan, the area which covers all five important temples including Kedarnath. **Shankaracharya**, the monist philosopher from S India, is credited with establishing the four great pilgrimage centres mentioned above in the early 9th century AD. See page 52.

The main **Badrinath Temple** is small and brightly painted in green, blue, pink, yellow, white, silver and red. Worship at the shrine is always a crowded affair. The **Rawal** (Head Priest) hails from the Namboodri village in Kerala, the birthplace of Shankacharya. Badrinath is snowbound over winter and open from late Apr to Nov. After worshipping in the temple and dispensing alms to the official (and wealthy) temple beggars outside it is customary to bathe in **Tapt Kund**, a cistern of hot water a short distance below the temple. This is fed by a hot sulphurous spring in which **Agni** (The god of fire) resides by kind permission of Vishnu. The temperature is around 45C. There are numerous resthouses and *dharamshalas* in Badrinath to cater in a basic way for pilgrims and travellers. As one would expect in such a holy place, meat is prohibited. Near the village of **Mana**, 6 km N of Badrinath, is the cave where **Vyasa** is said to have written commentaries on the epic poems of Hinduism.

Kedarnath (*Altitude* 3,584 m), 77 km from **Rudrapayag**, 241 km from **Haridwar**, 442 km from **Delhi**. The area around Kedarnath in the Garhwal Himalaya is known as Kedarkhand, the *Abode of Siva*. **Kedarnath** is one of the twelve *jyotirlingas** – see page 58. Legend has it that it was built by the **Pandavas** to atone for their sins after the battle at Kurukshetra – see Haryana (see page 420), but there is no archaeological evidence to support the claim.

To reach Kedarnath you have to leave the Pilgrim Road at Rudraprayag and travel by bus up the **Mandakini Valley** to **Gaurikund**. Here there are numerous *dharamshalas** and rest houses. From here you have to either walk or ride a mule to Kedarnath (15 km). The ascent is reasonably steep and over 1,500 m. There are *chattis** (rest-houses) en route. The Temple at Kedarnath is older and more impressive than that at Badrinath. Built of stone and unpainted it comprises a simple, squat, curved tower and a wooden roofed *mandapa** (hall). Set against an impressive backdrop of snow capped peaks, the view from the forecourt is ruined by ugly 'tube' lights. At the entrance to the temple is a large statue of Nandi the bull.

In what is known as the *Panch Kedar* there are five temples that the pilgrim should visit: **Kedarnath**, **Madmaheshwar**, **Tungnath**, **Rudranath** and **Kalpeshwar**. This is quite an arduous circuit and now the majority only visit Kedarnath. Kedarnath and Badrinath are only 41 km apart and there is an tiring *yatra** (pilgrim route) between the two. Nowadays most will take the longer but easier way round by bus or car.

Yamunotri (*Altitude* 3,291 m), the westernmost shrine in the region, is dominated by **Banderpunch** (*Altitude* 6,316 m). Yamunotri is the source of the river, the twin sister of **Yama**, the Lord of Death. Anyone who bathes in her waters will be spared a tortuous death. Yamuna is also the daughter of Surya the Sun. To reach the temple you must trek from **Hanuman Chatti** (13 km), the roadhead.

The trek along the riverbank is exhilarating with the mountains rising up on each side. According to legend the temple must be rebuilt every few years. Floods and snow seem to ensure that it is. There is a hot spring nearby in which pilgrims immerse potatoes and rice tied in a piece of cloth. The meal, which takes only a few minutes to cook is then offered to the deity and later distributed as *prasad*. On the return to Hanuman Chatti, you can visit the Temple of Someshwar at Kharsali, 1 km across the river from Janki-Chatti. This is one of the oldest and finest in the region and worth a visit. **Accommodation** There are *dharamshalas* and other resthouses in Hanuman Chatti, Janki-Chatti and Yamunotri.

Yamunotri can be reached from **Dehra Dun** via Yamuna Bridge and Barkot or from Rishikesh. The latter is the most popular. It is 83 km to Tehri direct or 165 km via Deoprayag. *Tehri*, the capital of the Princely State will eventually be submerged by the waters behind the controversial and still unfinished **Tehri Dam**. From here drive to **Dharasu** (37 km). Here the road divides. To the left leads to **Barkot** and **Hanuman Chatti**, to the right to **Uttarkashi** (26 km), **Lanka** (87 km) and **Gangotri** (13 km). It is 102 km from **Dharasu** to **Yamunotri**.

Gangotri (*Altitude* 3,140 m) 248 km from Rishikesh, is the fourth of the major shrines in the Garhwal Himalaya. The Temple of Gangotri is dedicated to the Goddess Ganga and is erected where she is believed to have descended to earth. According to Hindu belief, this daughter of heaven came down to earth as a reward for **King Bhagirathi's** penance of several centuries. Here the river is worshipped as a deity. The temple was built by a Gurkha commander, Amar Singh Thapa in the early 18th century and later rebuilt by the Maharaja of Jaipur. The *Gaurikund waterfall*, one of the most beautiful in the Himalaya, the rocks resembling giant stone chip tools, is nearby. *Gaumukh* (Cow's Mouth) is 18 km away and a gradual but nevertheless scenically stunning trek. There are many *ashrams** and a sizeable permanent population of *sadhus** who brave the elements throughout the year. Like the other shrines, Gangotri is effectively closed over winter. But still the sadhus remain. **Accommodation** is in the form of *dharamshalas* and *resthouses*.

Dehra Dun From Rishikesh a road runs N W to Dehra Dun (42 km; *dun** – valley, *Altitude* 695 m). The town lies in the **Siwalik Hills,** and because of its equable climate (by plain's standards) is a popular retirement town, particularly among army officers. In Hindu legend it formed part of **Kedarkhand** – see Kedarnath above, and was Siva's stamping ground, hence the name **Siwaliks**. Rama and his brother are said to have done penance for killing **Ravana** and the five Pandavas stopped here on their way to the high, snowy mountains. In the 17th and 18th century it changed hands a number of times. **Guru Ram Rai** retreated here from the Punjab after failing to succeed his father. **Najib-ud-daula**, Mughal Governor of Sahranpur, occupied it in 1757 and held it until his death in 1770. The Gurkhas also overran it on the westward expansion from Kumaon to Kangra. They ceded it to the British in 1815.

Dehra Dun appealed to the British, who developed it as a centre of education and research. The **Forest Research Institute** was established in 1914. In 1922 the **Royal Indian Military College** for boys intent on an army career was established along the lines of Welbeck. Ten years later the **Indian Military Academy** was opened to provide officer training. Modelled on Sandhurst, all officers in the Indian army undergo their initial training here. The country's most prestigious public school, **The Doon School**, is here. Rajiv Gandhi was one of its old boys. The **Survey of India** (founded 1767, whose Surveyor Generals included Sir George Everest after whom the mountain was named) has its headquarters here too. It is pleasant place to relax in or stop en route to Mussoorie. The bazaar area is typically chaotic-looking but the cantonment across the Bindal *nallah** is spacious and well wooded. The Mussoorie road is lined with very attractive houses.

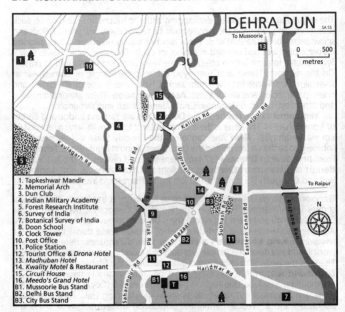

```
                                                    DEHRA DUN  SA 55
                                                    To Mussoorie
```

1. Tapkeshwar Mandir
2. Memorial Arch
3. Dun Club
4. Indian Military Academy
5. Forest Research Institute
6. Survey of India
7. Botanical Survey of India
8. Doon School
9. Clock Tower
10. Post Office
11. Police Station
12. Tourist Office & Drona Hotel
13. Madhuban Hotel
14. Kwality Motel & Restaurant
15. Circuit House
16. Meedo's Grand Hotel
B1. Mussoorie Bus Stand
B2. Delhi Bus Stand
B3. City Bus Stand

Hotels Most 2-4 km rly and 1 km or less from centre. **B** *Madhuban*, 97 Rajpur Rd. T 24094, Cable: Madhuban, Telex: 585-268 Hmb in. 42 rm. Restaurant, exchange, car hire, credit cards. **C** *Ajanta Continental*, Rajpur Rd. T 29595, Telex: 0585-330 AC IN. 30 rm. Restaurant, pool, TV, Diners, Visa. **C** *Kwality*, 19 Rajpur Rd. T 27001, Cable: Kwality. 20 rm. Restaurant, bar, Diners. **C** *President*, 6 Astley Hall, Rajpur Rd. T 28883, Cable: Prestravel, Telex: 0595-238 Pres in. 18 rm. Restaurant, bar, coffee shop, exchange, car hire, travel and tourist information, doctor on call. **C** *Relax*, 7 Court Rd. T 27776, Cable: Hotel Relax, Telex: 585-311 Nis in. 30 rm. Restaurant, bar permit, 24 hr coffee shop, sightseeing bus. **D** *Meedo's Grand*, 28 Rajpur Rd. T 27171, Cable: Medgran/ Clasotel. 35 rm. Restaurant, bar, coffee shop, TV, exchange, travel, parking, Diners, Visa, Mastercard. **D** *Nidhi*, 74-c Rajpur Rd. T 24611, Cable: Nidhi, Telex: 0585-312 Nidi in. 24 rm. Restaurant, Amex, Diners. **E** *Prince*, 1 Haridwar Rd. T 7070. 21 rm. Restaurant (Indian).

Train Lucknow: *Doon Exp* 3010, daily, 1945,12 hr 35 min; *Dehra Dun-Varanasi Exp* 4266, daily, 1830, 13 hr 40 min.

The drive to from **Dehra Dun to Mussoorie** is in stark contrast to the similar uphill climb from Haldwani to Nainital. Whereas much of the latter is through rich forest with splendid vistas of similarly forested hills, here the hillsides are virtually bare of trees. It has been suggested that this is due to exposure to prevailing winds but deforestation by humans is a prime cause.

Mussoorie *Population* 19,000 *Altitude* 1970 m *Climate*. Summer Max 32°C, Min 7°C. Winter Max 7°C Min 1°C. Monsoons end Jun/end Jul to Sep. Winter showers and snowfalls in Dec/Jan.

Places of Interest Another self-styled Queen of the Hills, Mussoorie is spread out over 16 km along a horseshoe shaped ridge. Off this runs a series of buttress-like subsidiaries. In this respect it is like Shimla. In terms of its buildings it is a poor relation. Nevertheless it is an extremely popular destination among Indian tourists who have enthusiastically taken up what the British left. It is the nearest hill station to Delhi. The credit for its establishment goes to a Captain Young who built the first British building in 1829. The early visitors came by road to Raipur, about 10 km E of Dehra Dun, and were then carried up via **Barlowganj**. There is the usual miscellany of British creations, e.g. a Mall, club, Anglican Church (1837), library and of course houses.

At the E end of town, a narrow spur leads to **Landaur** (2270 m) and the old barracks area. **Woodstock School,** an international school which has a sister school in S India at Kodaikkanal is located here. To the W is Convent Hill and **Happy Valley** where Tibetan refugees have settled. **Mall road** connects the two bazaars, **Kulri** and **Library**. Two other roads, the Camel's Back Rd and the Cart Rd also connect the two but more circuitously. Like other hill stations, Mussoorie is best for walks. **Lal Tibba** is the highest hill and there is a cable car to **Gun Hill.** The view to the N and the snow capped peaks is stunning and best at sunrise. The **Camel's Back Rd** starts from Kulri and ends at Library and is a pleasant 3 km walk. En route you will see the **Camel's Rock**.

Hotels Many of these centrally located hotels will offer off-season discounts. Dehra Dun airport 2.5 km. Restaurants may be closed in some hotels in the off-season.

B *Savoy*, The Mall, Library. T 2510 PBX, 2620, Cable: Savoy, Telex: 585 302 Savy in. 121 rm. Restaurant (Continental, Vegetarian, Gujarati), bar, beer garden, coffee shop, exchange, travel, doctor on call, parking, post, car hire, lawns, tennis. credits cards. Good views and setting, spacious and with character, ballroom in use in season. Restaurant recommended. **C** *Carlton's Plaisance*, nr the L.B.S. Academy, The Mall. T 2800, Cable: Plaisance. 10 rm. Restaurant (incl Tibetan). Very Victorian with period furniture. Lacks views but peaceful, spacious and charming. **C** *Mussoorie International*, Kulri, The Mall. T 2943, Cable: Hotmuss. 22 rm. Restaurant, rm service, doctor on call, car hire, TV. **C** *Roselynn Estate*, Mall, Library. T 2201. 20 rm. Restaurant, bar, car hire, TV, indoor games. Older hotel. **C** *Shilton*, Library Bazaar, Club Chowk. T 2842, Cable: Shilton. 50 rm. Central. Restaurant and bar-be-que, coffee shop, ice cream parlour, TV, exchange, guide, travel, car hires, outdoor sports, doctor on call, recreation centre, credit cards. Modern.

D *Connaught Castle*, The Mall. T 2538. 27 rm. Indoor and outdoor games, play ground, parking. **D** *Hakman's Grand*, The Mall. T 2559, Cable: Hakman's. 24 rm. Restaurant, bar, coffee bar, parking, exchange, car hire, doctor, shops, Cinema, Amex, Diners. Very much a Raj hotel with good views. **D** *Roanoke*, Kulri. T 2215, 2874, Cable: Roanoke. 20 rm. Open air garden, restaurant (Indian, Continental), doctor on call. **D** *Valley View*, The Mall (Kulri). T 2324, Cable: NINA. 13 rm. Bakery and confectionary, parking, coffee shop, restaurant (Indian, Continental). **D** *Padmini Nivas*, Library, The Mall, T 2793. 24 rm in former palace. Also cottages. Not grand but pleasant ambience. Restaurant (veg) open in season. **D** *YWCA Holiday Home*, The Mall, T 2513. Meals on order. **E** *GMVN Tourist Complex*, The Mall, T 2984. 24 rm, Dormitory. Restaurant, rm service. Clean, good views, basic.

Restaurants Library Area: *Whispering Windows*, T 2256. *Jeet Restaurant. Jungli Murghi Restaurant*, Roselynn Estate Hotel, T 2201 has superb views. *Laxmi Mishtaan Bhandar*. Indian sweets, samosas and snacks. Caravan Corner. *Chow Chow* and *Momos*. Between Library and Ropeway: *Garhwal Ashok Terrace Restaurant*. Fast foods like bhelpuri, chaat, kababs, ice cream, also chicken curry with pulao, kulchas, dosas. Kulri Bazar: *Kwality*, T 2617. *Apsara*, T 2480. *Tavern*, T 2829. *Neelam International*, T 2495. Indian and Chinese. *Madras Cafe*. S Indian. *Shakahari Kutir*. S Indian and some N Indian.

Shopping Four main shopping areas; Library Bazaar, Kulri Bazaar, Landaur Bazaar, and Shawfield Rd near Padmini Niwas. *K.Main and Co*, Chinese shoe maker. *Inder Singh* for sticks and carved wooden curios. *Nirankari Cottage* Industries for curios and antiques. *Jagjeet Eng. Works* especially good for roller skates. *Natraj Wool and Knitwears*, woollen clothes. *Anand Gift Emporium*, woollen item and woven jute bags. *Garwhal Wool House*, near GPO, for pre wool and sweaters. *Star Walking Stick Mfg. Co.*, walking sticks and batons. *Baru Mal Janki Dass*, jewellers, silver jewellery worn by the hill women. *Tibetan outdoor market* selling woollens, clothes and various knick-knacks.

Photography *Computerised Colour Lab*, Mela Ram and Sons, The Mall, T 2422.

Local Transport Private Taxi Operators in Mussoorie Kulwant Travels, Masonic Lodge Bus Stand, T 2717. To Dehra-Dun, approx Rs 25 to 35.

Entertainment *Mussoorie Library*, Gandhi Chowk. Membership available Rs 10 per month.

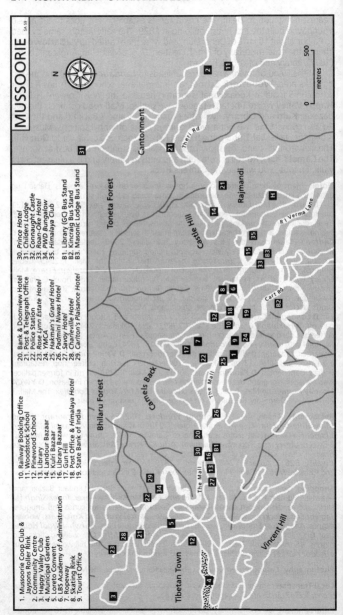

MUSSOORIE

1. Mussoorie Coop Club & Jaysons Roller Rink
2. Community Centre
3. Happy Valley Club
4. Municipal Gardens
5. Loreto Convent
6. LBS Academy of Administration
7. Gun Hill
8. Ropeway
9. Tourist Office
10. Railway Booking Office
11. Woodstock School
12. Pinewood School
13. Library
14. Landour Bazaar
15. YWCA
16. Kulri Bazaar
17. Libra Bazaar
18. Post Office & Himalaya Hotel
19. State Bank of India
20. Bank & Doonview Hotel
21. Post & Telegraph Office
22. Police Station
23. Rose Lynn Estate Hotel
24. Hakman's Grand Hotel
25. Padmini Niwas Hotel
26. Savoy Hotel
27. Charleville Hotel
28. Carlton's Plaisance Hotel
29. Skating Rink
30. Prince Hotel
31. Childers Lodge
32. Ronnaugh Castle
33. Roanoke Hotel
34. PWD Bungalow
35. Himalaya Club
B1. Library (GC) Bus Stand
B2. Kincraig Bus Stand
B3. Masonic Lodge Bus Stand

Sports Tennis, at the Savoy Hotel. **Fishing** in the Aglar and Yamuna Rivers for mahaseer and hill trout. Permit from Divisional Forest Officer, Yamuna Division is required. **Roller Skating** at The Rink, Kulri Bazaar and Disco Skating Rink behind Tourist Office.

Useful Numbers Police: T 2682, 2683, 2713.

Hospitals and Medical Services St Mary's Hospital, The Mall, Mussoorie, T 2845. Community Hospital, Landour Cantt, T 2653. Civil Hospital, Landour, T 2589.

Post and Telegraph General Post Office, Kulri, T 2802.

Places of Worship *Hindu*: Arya Samaj Mandir, Landaur Bazaar; Laxmi Narain Mandir, Library; Sanatan Dharam Mandir, Landur Bazaar; Jan Mandir, Landaur Bazaar. *Buddhist*: Tibetan Temple, The Mall, Happy Valley. *Muslim*: Mosques at Library Bazaar, Kulri Bazaar, Landaur Bazaar. *Sikh*: Gurudwaras at Library Bazar; Landaur Bazaar. *Christian*: Christ Church, The Mall, Near Library Bazaar; St Emilian's Church, Landur Bazaar; Methodist Church, Kulri Bazaar; Union Church, near Picture Palace.

Tourist Offices and Information Foreigner's Registration at Katwali adjacent to the Courts, opp Hakmans, T 2205. Tourist Bureau, UP Tourism, The Mall, T 2863.

Conducted Tours Operated by Garhwal Mandal Vikas Nigam. Reservations at the Tourist Bureau, The Mall, T 2863; Library Bus Stand and Tourist Bungalow, Garhwal Mandal Vikas Nigam, The Mall, Mussoorie, T 2948. Kempty Falls, half day (1100 and 1400). Rs 16 per adult, Rs 8 per child. Dhanolti-Surkhanda Devi Temple, full day (0900). Rs 33 per person. Kempty Falls, Yamuna Valley and Lakhamandal. Sun full day (0730). Rs 60 per adult, Rs 45 per child. Run only when coach is full.

Air Jolly Grant on the outskirts of Dehra is the nearest airport, 60 km. Daily Vayudoot flight from Delhi. Transport, coach to Dehra Dun Rs 18. Taxi to Mussoorie Rs 250. Booking agent in Mussoorie, Savoy Hotel, T 2510.

Rail **Varanasi**: *Doon Exp* 3010, daily, 1945, 20 hr 25 min; *Dehra Dun-Varanasi Exp* 4266, daily, 1830, 24 hr.

Bus Bus service enquiries at Mussoorie; Kincraig, T 2691; Library, T 2258; Masonic Lodge, T 2259. Four buses run by the Himachal Pradesh Roadways from Shimla to Dehra Dun. 2 delux buses, departing 0700 and 0900. Rs 75. 2 ordinary buses, last departing 1030, journey time 10 hr. Rs 45. From Delhi UP Roadways operate 2 buses, departing 0515 and 2230, 8 hr. Rs 67.50, video coach additional Rs 5.

Road Accessible via Dehra-Dun from State Highways to Nahan, and Meerut off **NH22** and **NH24**. **Delhi** (263 km); **Shimla** (322 km); **Dehra Dun** (34 km); **Haridwar** (100 km).

Excursions *Kempty Falls* 15 km on the Chakrata road, is pretty and a popular picnic spot.

DELHI TO NAINITAL, ALMORA AND RANIKHET

If you travel E from Delhi you can visit the the hill stations of **Nainital**, **Almora** and **Ranikhet** and the Kumaon region of the UP Himalaya. The road passes through some of N India's most important modern industrial estates and then the fertile irrigated agricultural lands of NW UP before ascending to the hills and lakes. Roads are often very busy with slow moving traffic.

Leaving **Delhi** on NH24, you cross the Yamuna river to *Ghaziabad* (19 km), a modern satellite town for Delhi of tall blocks and low-rise buildings – low-cost housing, all made of brick or reinforced concrete. Ghaziabad illustrates the contemporary emphasis on the provision of living quarters with little or no aesthetic appeal. Even the most modest houses now have TVs. Beyond Ghaziabad is countryside, an area where two crops are cultivated each year, mostly rice and wheat but also substantial quantities of sugar cane. Countless bullock carts will be trundling along the highway and lining up outside the refineries, their drivers waiting patiently.

Hapur (34 km) is a market centre, typical of those scattered evenly across the Gangetic plain. The main streets are lined with small shops, the roadsides containing street artisans, fruit sellers and vegetable stalls. The road crosses the Ganga just after passing *Garmukhteswar* (34 km) the W bank containing some ghats and the small town some typical N Indian temples. According to the *Mahabharata**, this is where King Santanu met the Goddess Ganga in human form. Each year at the full moon in Oct/Nov, thousands of pilgrims converge to bathe in the holy waters. If you stand on the road bridge, you may see turtles swimming around in the green-brown waters below.

Just beyond the river is *Gajraula*, a popular truck stop. The centre of this one street town has a number of restaurants. The best is the **Hi-Way Cafe** on the right by the petrol pumps. There is a respectable toilet behind the filling station building.

Carry on through **Gajrola** (24 km) and **Joya** (23 km) to *Moradabad* (29 km), a large provincial town, railway junction and traffic bottleneck, especially around the bus stand which is near the station. It was founded in 1625 by Rustam Khan, Mughal general, who named it after Prince Murad Baksh, one of Shah Jahan's four sons. The **Jama Masjid** (1634) lies N of the ruined fort which is by the **River Ramganga**. There is also the **Tomb of Nawab Azmat-ulla Khan**, a former governor, and the **American Church** (mid 19th century). Moradabad is a bustling centre noted for its inlaid tin, brass and bellmetal. The **Loveena Restaurant** is about 500 m beyond the bus stand and is a suitable refreshment stop.

Hotels D Maharaja Station Rd. T 24283. 20 rm. Central, restaurant, car hire, British Airways booking office, exchange, Diners.

Leaving Moradabad, you have the choice of continuing on **NH24** to **Haldwani** (and **Kathgodam** and then up to **Nainital**, or turning left and driving N via **Kashipur** to **Ramnagar** and the **Corbett National Park**. From Corbett there is a direct road to **Ranikhet**, and if you backtrack to Ramnagar you can reach Nainital via **Kaladhungi** by an attractive metalled forest road.

Continuing along the **NH24** the road passes through *Rampur* (26 km) a town founded in the 1623 by Shah Alam and Hussain Khan, two Afghan Rohillas who had sought service with the Mughals. Under Shah Alam's grandson, Ali Muhammad Khan, the Rohillas were united in what was to become known as *Rohilkhand* and later expanded their empire to Almora in the N and Etawah in the S. On the death of Najib-ud-daula in 1772 the region was invaded by the Marathas. With the Nawab of Oudh's and British support the Marathas were beaten off but afterwards the Rohillas fell foul of Oudh and in the ensuing Rohilla War (1773-4) the empire was lost and later dismantled. Rampur, however remained a Rohilla centre. The Nawab of Rampur remained loyal to the British during the Mutiny and supported them in the Second Afghan War and was rewarded with a grant of new territory. There is an extensive palace and fort.

Library The State library has oriental manuscripts and an excellent collection of portraits from the 16th to the 18th centuries, including a contemporary painting of *Babur* and a small book of Turki verse with notes by both Babur and *Shah Jahan*.

Hotels D *Modipur*, Modipur. T 4047, Telex: 0577-213. 22 rm. 5 km rly. Restaurant (Indian, Continental, Chinese), TV, tennis. **E** *Tourist and Restaurant*, Tourist Bldg, Railway Station Rd. T 4644, Cable: Tourist. 34 rm. Close to rly, 3.5 km centre. Restaurant (Indian, Continental)., parking, shops, general store.

In **Rampur** take the left fork to *Bilaspur* (30 km), one of many sites in the upper Ganga valley which have revealed a style of pre-historic pottery known as *Painted Grey Ware*, see page 263. Chakrabarti has suggested that the basic importance of painted grey ware levels is that it provided the immediate background to the early historic period – see page 80. It was an essentially Iron Age culture. Continue to **Kichha** (22 km) where the main road turns N to *Haldwani* (32 km), an important market town and transhipment centre at the foot of the hills.

The land between Rampur and Haldwani used to be covered in jungle known as the *terai**. This once extended unbroken from the gorge below **Haridwar** to the NE corner of Bihar and was approximately 50 km wide. Under natural conditions it consisted of tall elephant grass and thick *sal** (*Shorea robusta*) forest and was both malarial and tiger infested. It was largely impenetrable and provided an effective natural barrier to communication between the hills and plain and was only extensively cleared and colonised after Independence in 1947. Large numbers of refugees – especially Sikhs – settled here following Partition and converted the forest into good agricultural land. The Corbett National Park and Dudhwa Sanctuary are the last extensive tracts of terai in India. As you drive across this belt the Himalayan foothills appear out of the characteristic haze.

Hotels D *Saurabh Mountview*, Haldwani. T 519, Cable: Saurabh, Telex: 0576-209 KSS IN. 49 rm. 2 km rly, centrally located. Restaurant, bar, sight seeing, Diners, Visa.

Kathgodam (4 km further on from **Haldwani**) is the railhead for Nainital (34 km). See Nainital, below, for timings. The climb from Kathgodam to Nainital is dramatic, rising 1300 m over 30 km. The road follows the valley of the Balaya stream then winds up the hillsides. Forest and small villages are interspersed. After the long drive the town appears suddenly. It is situated round the lake (*tal*), the land S and on the plains side falling away quite steeply. Thus, you only see the lake when you are at its edge.

Nainital

Population 24,667 *Altitude* 1,938 m *Best time for a visit* Apr-May (May and Jun are very busy) and Oct-Nov. Nainital is 306 km NE of Delhi. The nearest airport is *Pantnagar* (71 km) on the plains. Vayudoot connects Delhi with Pantnagar.

	Jan	Feb	Mar	Apr	May	Jun	Jul	Aug	Sep	Oct	Nov	Dec	Av/Tot
Max (°C)	10	13	17	21	24	24	21	21	21	19	16	13	18
Min (°C)	2	4	8	12	15	17	17	16	15	10	6	3	10
Rain (mm)	117	44	54	25	75	273	769	561	331	305	7	35	2496

Set around the 1.5 km long and 500 m wide Naini Lake is the charming Hill Station of Nainital. Graceful weeping willows encircle the lake, villas, bungalows and larger buildings occupy the tree covered hillsides. 150 years ago there was a small hamlet which was 'discovered' in 1841 by a P. Barron, a sugar manufacturer from Saharanpur. He was impressed by the lake and decided to return with a sailing boat. This occurred a year later, the boat being carried up in sections from the plains. Barron got his sail and the spot was developed as a Hill Station, in due course becoming the Summer Capital of the then United Provinces (see also Shimla **page 263**).

On 18th Sep 1880, disaster struck the township. At the N end of the Lake, known now as Mallital (the S part is Tallital) stood the Victoria Hotel. Two days before it had started raining heavily and in the next two days nearly 1000 mm fell. On the 18th at 1000 a landslip crushed some outhouses burying several people. At 1330 the cliff overhanging the hotel collapsed burying the soldiers and civilians who had been working to clear the rubble and extricate the victims of the previous damage. The fall was so extensive that any hope of freeing the buried, numbered at over 150, was impossible. Later the area was levelled, became known as The Flats and is now a popular ground for public meetings, impromptu games of football and cricket and festive occasions.

Today Nainital is very popular with affluent Indians especially in May and Jun. It is best avoided at this time as accommodation is difficult to obtain and room rates soar. Out of season Nainital is a delightful place to stay in: the town is clean, there are some attractive walks and there are only a handful of foreign tourists .

Local Festivals Naini Devi (Oct/Nov), annual festival of performing arts and crafts of Kumaon.

Places of Interest There is little of great architectural interest in Nainital other than the colonial style villas overlooking the lake. The **Church of St John-in-the-Wilderness** (1846) was one of the earliest buildings, situated beyond Sukhatal (Mallital) below the Nainital Club. (It is as though the English found this biblical episode aptly suited their circumstances in the hills because there is also a church of the same name in Dharamshala.) The most distinctive building is **Government House** (1899, now the Secretariat) which was designed by F.W. Stephens who also left his mark on the Bombay skyline with the VT and Churchgate Stations. Built of stone it would look more at home on the banks of a Scottish loch.

There are other examples of colonial hill architecture dotted around the town. The other places of interest are views on walks. **Naina (Cheena) Peak** (2,610 m) is a 5 km walk from the lake. From the top, there are stunning views of the Himalaya including *Nanda Devi* (7,816 m) and the mountains on the Tibetan border. In season there is a gondola which runs from the Mallital end of the lake to **Snow View** (2,270 m) another good vantage point for viewing the snow-capped peaks. **Hanumangarh** and the **Observatory** are 3.2 km from the lake and are places for watching the sun set over the plains. Hanumangarh is a small temple to the Monkey God.

It is also very pleasant to walk round the lake. Cycle rickshaws run the length of the Mall for a fixed charge. The opposite side of the lake has hardly been built on. There are one or two cottages and much higher up near the ridge are two private boys' schools – Sherwood College and St Joseph's. You can also be rowed across the lake.

Hotels C *Alka* and *Alka Annexe*, The Mall, Tallital. T 2220. 72 rm. Restaurant, shops, travel, floating restaurant on lake. **C** *Arif Castles*, Mallital. T 2231, Cable: Castles. 66 rm. 60 km airport, 38 km rly, 1.5 km centre. Centrally heated. Restaurant, 24 hr coffee shop, bar, shops, health club, dance hall, travel, exchange, jeep transfers centre, TV, credit cards. **C** *Armadale*, Waverly Rd, Mallital. T 2855, Cable: Armadale. 20 rm. 24 hr rm service, TV, car hire. **C** *Everest*, The Mall, Tallital. T 2453. 47 rm. Dining hall. **C** *Royal*, Mallital. T 2007, Cable: Royal. 46 rm. 1 km centre. Restaurant, bar, travel, lounge, parking, library, sports, credit cards. **C** *Shervani Hilltop Inn*, Mallital. T 2504. 20 rm. Restaurant, bar, TV, parking, travel, heating, indoor sports, children's park. **C** *Swiss*, Mallital. T 2603. 18 rm. Dining hall, TV, travel, guides for wildlife viewing. **C** *Vikram Vintage Inn*, Mallital. T 2877. Reservations: Hotel Vikram, New Delhi, T 643 6451. 34 rm. 2 km centre. Restaurant, exchange, rm service, doctor on call, parking, health club, sports, Diners, Visa. **D** *Silverton*, Sher-Ka-Danda, Nainital. T 2249. 27 rm. 2.5 km centre. Restaurant. Kumaon TDC **F** *Tourist Reception Centre* at Tallital, T 2570 with dormitories and the **D** *Tourist Reception Centre* at Mallital, T 2374. 20 doubles with bath, some with TV. Restaurant, car parking, table tennis and gardens. Good value.

Restaurants All on the Mall. Indian and Continental: *Capri*, Mallital, T 2690; *Embassy*, Mallital, T 2597; *Flatties*, T 2567; *Kwality*, T 2506. Indian: *New Sher-e-Punjab*, T 2634; *Tandoor*, Tallital; *Kumaon Farm Products*, T 2172. *Sher-e-Punja*. Indian Vegetarian: *Apar Vihar*, T 2446; *Paradise*, Mallital; *Purohit Thal*. *Heritage* is Chinese.

Banks and Exchanges *State Bank of India*, Mallital, T 2186; *Nainital*, The Mall, T 2403; *Allahabad*, Mallital, T 2019; *Bank of Baroda*, Mallital, T 2385; *Central Bank of India*, The Mall, T 2495; *Punjab National*, The Mall, T 2604.

Shopping There are two bazaars, at Tallital and Mallital, the latter being more extensive. Here household provisions can be purchased. Along the Mall there are some souvenir shops: *UP Brassware*, Mallital; *Garud Woollens*, Mallital; *UP Handlooms*, The Mall; *Gandhi Ashram*, Mallital. Along the far edges of the Flats are stalls run by Tibetan refugees. Woollen and acrylic shawls are a good buy. *Kumaon Woollens* in the Mallital Bazaar has a good selection of shawls as well as lengths of locally made tweed – see also Almora, below.

Photography *Kala Mandir*, The Mall.

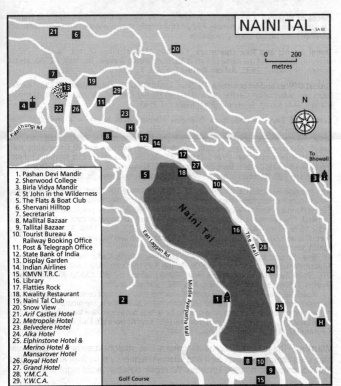

NAINI TAL SA 60

0   200
metres

N

To
Bhowali

Naini Tal

Kaladhungi Rd

East Laggan Rd

Middle Ayarpatha Mall

The Mall

Golf Course

1. Pashan Devi Mandir
2. Sherwood College
3. Birla Vidya Mandir
4. St John in the Wilderness
5. The Flats & Boat Club
6. Shervani Hilltop
7. Secretariat
8. Mallital Bazaar
9. Tallital Bazaar
10. Tourist Bureau &
    Railway Booking Office
11. Post & Telegraph Office
12. State Bank of India
13. Display Garden
14. Indian Airlines
15. KMVN T.R.C.
16. Library
17. Flatties Rock
18. Kwality Restaurant
19. Naini Tal Club
20. Snow View
21. Arif Castles Hotel
22. Metropole Hotel
23. Belvedere Hotel
24. Alka Hotel
25. Elphinstone Hotel &
    Merino Hotel &
    Mansarover Hotel
26. Royal Hotel
27. Grand Hotel
28. Y.M.C.A.
29. Y.W.C.A.

Local Transport Ropeway carriages run by KMVN from Mallital (Near GB Pant Statue) to Snow View. Summer 0800-1800, Winter 0930-1600. Fare Rs 16 adult, Rs 12 child. **Cycle-rickshaws, horses, boats and dandis** – rates negotiable. **Coaches and taxis** are available from Parvat Tours, Tallital, T 2656. Coach full day Rs 900 (120 km); basic rates Rs 5.65 per km in hills and Rs 4.40 per km in plains. **Taxis** full day Rs 300 (120 km), basic rate Rs 2.50 per km.

Entertainment For information on cultural programmes, contact the UP Govt Tourist Office, The Mall, T 2337.

Sports Fishing permits for Nainital Lake from Executive Officer, Nagar Palika. For other lakes Fisheries Officer, Bhimtal. Boat hire from Boat Club, Mallital. **Yacht hire** from Yacht Club.

Mountaineering and Trekking Equipment can be hired from the Nainital Mountaineering Club and Kumaon Mandal Vikas Nigam (Kumaon Tourism Development Corporation), Tourist Reception Centre, Mallital.

Parks and Zoos *Children's Park*, Mallital. *Municipal Garden*, Mallital. *Horticultural Department Park*, Mallital.

Useful Numbers Police: T 2424; Fire: T 2626; Ambulance: T 2012.

Hospitals and Medical Services Badri Dutt Pande Govt. Hospital, Mallital, T 2012; GB Pant Hospital, Tallital, T 2388; Sitapur Eye Hospital, The Mall, T 2507.

Post and Telegraph Head Post Office, Mallital; Branch Post Office, Tallital.

Places of Worship   *Christian*: Church of St Mary; Central Methodist Church; St Francis Church. *Hindu*: Naina Devi Temple; Pashan Devi Temple; Hanumangarhi; Arya Samaj Mandir. *Muslim*: Jama Masjid. *Sikh*: Gurudwara.

Travel Agents and Tour Operators   *Kumaon Mandal Vikas Nigam*, Tallital, T 2656. Operates tours under the name of Parvat Tours; *Anamika Travels*, The Mall, T 2186; *Jeetu Travels*, The Mall, T 2633; *Ashola Travels*,The Mall, T 2180.

Tourist Offices and Information   UP Govt. Tourist Office, The Mall, Mallital, T 2337; Parvat Tours and Information Centre, (KMVN), Dandi House, The Mall, Tallital, T 2656; Kumaon Mandal Vikas Nigam, Secretariat Bldg, Mallital, T 2543.

Conducted Tours   Parvat Tours (Kumaon Mandal Vikas Nigam – Kumaon Tourism Development Corporation), The Mall, Tallital, T 2656, Cable: Parvat; Bhimtal, half day Rs 25; Sattal, full day, Rs 50; Ranikhet, full day, Rs 75; Mukteshwar, full day, Rs 50; Kaladhungi, full day Rs 50; Kausani, two days, Rs 120; Ranikhet/Almora, two days Rs 100; Observatory, half day Rs 15; Kumaon Darshan, three days Rs 300; Chaukori, three days Rs 250; Kausani/Corbett, three days Rs 325; Corbett Park, two days Rs 175; Nanakmatta, full day Rs 75; Jageshwar, two days Rs 100; Badrinath, four days Rs 300; Purnagiri, two days, Rs 135.

Air   The nearest airport is Pantnagar, 71 km, from where Vayudoot connects with Delhi. Parvat Tours run coaches for transfer from and to Nainital. Reservations: Tourist Reception Centre (Kumaon Mandal Vikas Nigam), Tallital, The Mall, T 2570. Open 1000-1600
   Rail   The nearest railhead is **Kathgodam** (34 km) Lucknow *Nainital Exp* 5307, daily, 1935, 10 hr 50 min. **Bareilly Junction**: *Kumaon Exp* 5312, daily, 1750, 3 hr 20 min. **Agra Fort**: *Kumaon Exp* 5312, daily, 1750, 12 hr 40 min. From and to Delhi you have to travel to Bareilly Junction.
   Bus   Regular bus services operate to Lucknow, Bareilly, Delhi, Haridwar, Dehra-Dun, Almora, Ranikhet and Ramnagar UPSTRC Tallital, T 2518. Open 0930-1200 and 1230-1700; DTC (Delhi Transport Corporation), Hotel Ashok, Tallital, T 2180. KMOU (Kumaon Motor Owners' Union) Ltd, KMO Bus Stand, near TRC, Sukhatal, Mallital.
   Road   Nainital is connected by good all-weather roads to major centres in N India. During the monsoon (Jun-Sep) landslips are fairly common. Usually these are promptly cleared but in the case of severe slips requiring days to clear, bus passengers are trans-shipped. From: **Delhi** (322 km); **Bareilly** (141 km); **Lucknow** (401 km); **Almora** (66 km); **Ranikhet** (60 km); **Kausani** (120 km); **Corbett** (Dhikala; 128 km).

Warning   The hill roads can be dangerous. Flat, straight stretches are extremely rare, road lighting does not exist and villagers frequently drive their animals along them or graze them at the kerbside. Wherever possible, avoid night driving.

Excursions   Because of the presence of some lakes in the Nainital region, some have called it "the Switzerland of Asia". **Sat Tal** (21 km) is what its name suggests, seven lakes. The most important is the jade green **Garud Tal**, after Vishnu's vehicle, followed by the olive green Rama Tal and Sita Tal. On the banks of **Sita Tal** is a four roomed **E** *Tourist Bungalow* (KMVN). **Bhim Tal** (22.5 km) is a large lake in an amphitheatre of hills. Boating and fishing are available and in the middle of the lake is a tree-covered island that is a popular picnic spot with visitors. **Naukuchiya** (26 km) is another lake, this time with nine corners, hence the name. Row and paddle boats available.

From Nainital it is an attractive 66 km drive to Almora passing through **Bhowali** (12 km W of Nainital). The road winds through attractive pine mixed forest with good views down towards Kathgodam and the plains. Bhowali, is a small subsidiary market well known in the past for its sanatorium and apple orchards. There is a direct road from Haldwani to Bhowali which bypasses Nainital. This is convenient for travellers bound for Almora. Below Bhowali in the valley of the Kosi River is **Gharampani**, a popular refreshment stop. The road then runs along the the Kosi passing refreshing looking rock pools, riverside terraced fields and small meadows, before beginning the long gradual climb to **Almora**. About 5 km before you reach the town 'proper' there is a toll barrier and just beyond this is the Almora by-pass forking off to the left. This is worth taking if you intend driving straight through the town as the main street is invariably congested.

Almora (*Altitude* 1,646 m) 66 km from Nainital, was founded by the Chand dynasty in 1560. The Chands ruled over most of Kumaon which comprises the present districts of Nainital, Almora and Pithoragarh, and Almora still claims to be the cultural capital of the area. Traces of the old Chand fort, paved roads, wooden houses with beautifully carved facades and homes decorated with traditional murals reflect its heritage. Along with the rest of the UP Himalaya it was overrun by the Gurkhas in 1798. In the Gurkha Wars of 1814-15 it suffered heavy bombardment by the British as they endeavoured to expel the Gurkhas. Now it is an important market town and administrative centre with an agricultural research station. The picturesque old part of the town is along the ridge. The main thoroughfare runs around the horse-shoe shaped ridges about 100 m below the ridgeline. *Swami Vivekenanda* came to Almora and in a small cave at **Kasar Devi**, 6 km outside the town, he reputedly gained enlightenment and dreamt that he should share his message with the world.

Almora's Tamta artisans still use traditional methods to work with brass and copper and just above the *Holi-day Home* there is the factory for Kumaon Woollens which produces tweed in the Harris Tweed style. This is worth a visit. Door sales.

Hotels E *Tourist Bungalow/Holi-day Home* (KMVN), T 2250. 7 cotttages and 18 non a/c rm with bath. Restaurant. Overlooking the Kosi valley, good mountain views. 1 km from bus stand. Also near the Kumaon Woollens factory. Recommended. **F** *Tourist Cottage*, T 12 and **F** *Neelkanth*.

Leaving Almora, the road descends to cross the **Kosi river** where there is a turnoff for **Ranikhet**. If you are proceeding N and further into the hills, the road follows the river, crosses the broad open valley at **Someswar**, regarded as one of the most fertile in Kumaon, then climbs to *Kausani* (1,890 m, 51 km from Almora). From here there are good views of the *Nanda Devi* group of mountains. You need to be there early, otherwise it is hazy. *Mahatma Gandhi* spent twelve days here in 1929 during which time he wrote his commentary on the *Gita-Anashakti Yoga*. The guesthouse where he stayed is now known as the Anashakti Ashram. Hindi poet-laureate **Sumitra Nandan Pant** was born at Kausani. There is a *PWD Guesthouse* and **E** *Tourist Bungalow* (KMVN), T 26 with 6 cottages and a dormitory.

From **Kausani**, the road descends to *Baijnath* with its distinctive Nagara temples by the Gomati River – see also Kulu Valley (**page 450**) and **Garur**. Just out of Garur there is the turning (right) for *Bageshwar* (**E** *KMVN Tourist Bungalow*, 20 doubles) and **Bharari** – see **Gwaldam** Trekking in the Garhwal Himalaya, below. If you carry on, after 30 km you will cross into Garhwal and reach *Gwaldam* (1,950 m), a small market where the British established tea plantations. These have since been abandoned. Stay at the Garhwal Mandal Vikas Nigam **E** *Tourist Bungalow* (GMVN-Garhwal Tourism Development Corporation). From the garden there are splendid views, especially at dawn and dusk, of **Trisul** (7,120 m) and **Nanda Ghunti** (6,310 m). Gwaldam is one of the starting points for the trek to Roopkund. It overlooks the beautiful **Pindar River** which the road follows down to its confluence with the Alaknanda River at **Karnaprayag**. You are now on the Pilgrim Road which runs from **Rishikesh** and **Haridwar** to **Badrinath**.

DELHI TO MORADABAD AND CORBETT NATIONAL PARK

The road gives an excellent view of the almost flat, fertile and densely populated Ganga-Yamuna doab, one of the most prosperous agricultural regions of UP and of N India. The Corbett National Park with its abundant wildlife is one of the finest in India.

Leave Delhi over the Yamuna Bridge and follow the NH24 through **Ghaziabad** (19 km) to **Hapur** (35 km) and **Garh Mukteshwar** (34 km). NH24 continues through **Gajrola** (24 km) and **Joya** (23 km) to **Moradabad** (29 km). Only 1-2 km out of Moradabad travelling east turn left for **Kashipur** (54 km) and **Ramnagar** (80 km). Much of the way is across farmed land but the final stretch is through remnants of the terai. Ramnagar has little to commend it other than there being a branch railway line to Moradabad, the Project Tiger Office for Corbett National Park reservations and a night halt. If you are travelling to the Park without reserved accommodation, you must call here first to make a booking, otherwise you will not be admitted to the Park. The very good **E** *Tourist Reception Centre* (Kumaon Mandal Vikas Nigam), a/c and non a/c rooms with attached bath is ideal overnight accommodation. Restaurant. Recommended.

From Ramnagar it is 50 km to **Dhikala**, 32 km of which is inside the Park. Night driving is not allowed in the park.

Corbett National Park

The **Corbett National Park** is India's first national park and one of its finest. It is notable not only for its rich and varied wildlife and birdlife but also for its scenic charm and magnificent sub-montane and riverain views. Set up in 1936, in large part due to the efforts of Jim Corbett, this 350 sq km wildlife reserve was named Hailey National Park after the Governor of the United Provinces. On Independence it was renamed the Ramganga National Park and later still the Corbett National Park. **Jim Corbett** was born in 1875 into the large family of Christopher Corbett, the postmaster at Nainital. Jim was the eighth child and was a 'domiciled' European. From childhood Corbett had a great fascination with the jungles around Nainital and their inhabitants. This developed into a considerable knowledge of the ecosystem's workings. Like most *pukka sahibs*** (proper gentlemen) he learnt to shoot and became an superb shot, killing his first leopard when he was eight. Tigers were his most sought after prey, followed by leopards which were very difficult to sight let alone shoot.

This interest was sustained during his working life in the Bengal and North Western Railway and later the army. But, from the mid-1920's he ceased to shoot tigers for sport and instead photographed them. The exception to this rule was that he was prepared to track and kill the man-eating leopards and tigers that terrorised the Kumaon hills from time to time. Later in life he recounted his exploits in a series of books about maneaters and the jungle: *The Man Eating Leopard of Rudrapayag, The Man-eaters of Kumaon* and *Jungle Lore*. For a biography of Corbett see *Carpet Sahib: A life of Jim Corbett* by Martin Booth.

Project Tiger On April 1 1973 and with World Wildlife Fund backing, Project Tiger was inaugurated, the aim being to preserve the rapidly dwindling population of tigers in India. The scheme was later extended to over a dozen reserves. The results have been encouraging and the Indian tiger population has stabilised at around 3,000 individuals. Corbett has over 100.

The park covers 500 sq km, of which 350 sq km is core reserve, and comprises the broad valley of the **Ramganga River** backing onto the forest covered slopes of the Himalayan foothills which rise to 1,210 m at Kand Peak. A dam at Kalagarh has created a large reservoir at the W end of the park. The valley floor is covered with tall elephant grass, lantana bushes and patches of *sal* and **sheesham*** (Dalbergia sissoo) forest whilst the enclosing hills on both sides are completely forest covered comprising *sal, bakli* (Anogeissus latifolia), *khair* (Acacia catechu), *jhingan* (Lannea coromandelica), *tendu* (Diospyros tomentosa), *pula* (Kydia calycina) and *sain* (Terminalia tomentosa). Nullahs and ravines running deep into the forests are dry for much of the year, but swift torrents during the monsoon. These hold brakes of bamboo and thick scrub growth. Rainfall varies, being heavier in the higher hills: on average the valley receives 1550 mm, the bulk of this from July to the middle of Sep. Summer days are hot but the nights quite pleasant. Winter nights can get very cold and there is often a frost and freezing fog in the low lying tracts.

Wild life The park has always been noted for its **tigers** which are seen quite frequently. There are **leopards** too but they are seldom seen. **Sambar, chital, para** (Hog Deer) and **muntjac** (Barking Deer) are the main prey of the big cats and their population fluctuates around 20,000. Some like the chital are highly gregarious whilst the large sambar, visually very impressive with its antlers, is invariably solitary. The two monkeys of N India, the rhesus (a macaque – reddish face and red brown body) and the common langur (black face, hands and feet and silvery coat) are common. Elephants are now permanent inhabitants following the building of the dam and the inundation of their old trekking routes. There are now a few hundred and they are seen quite often. Other animals include **porcupine, wild pigs** (often seen around Dhikala) and **fox**.

In certain stretches of the river and in the lake are the common **mugger crocodile** (*Crocodylus palustris*), the fish eating **gharial** (*Gavialis gangeticus*), soft shelled **tortoises** in the streams and otters. The python is quite common.

Birds The birdlife is especially impressive with over 600 species and this includes a wide range of water birds, birds of prey such as the crested serpent eagle, Pallas' fishing eagle, osprey, buzzards and harriers. Vultures (the solitary black or king, the white scavenger and the Himalayan long-billed) are present. Woodland birds include: Indian and **Great Pied Hornbills**, parakeets, **woodpeckers, drongos,** pies, flycatchers and cuckoos. Doves, **bee-eaters,** rollers, **mynas,** bulbuls, warblers, finches, robins and chats are to be seen in the open scrub.

Dhikala is the park centre and offers accommodation for the visitor. There are forest resthouses dotted around but these are only suitable for visitors with their own transport and provisions. Elephant rides are available at low cost from Dhikala and this is the best way to see the jungle and its inhabitants.

Note During the rainy season, when the park is closed, the road to **Dhikala** from the gate at *Dhangarhi*, a distance of 32 km, is almost impassable. Jan to Jun are the best months for a visit and one's particular interest in what Corbett has to offer will determine the month chosen. Summer is the best time for seeing the larger mammals which are bolder in forsaking the forest cover and protection and coming to the river and water holes, early summer for scenic charm and floral interest. If you are interested in birdwatching, Jan is best. Whatever the time of year, the park is a delightful place to visit.

Hotels If at all possible, stay in the park at Dhikala. A range of accommodation is available from *Cabins* and the *New Forest Rest House* (Rs 150 foreigners, Rs 90 Indians), *Tourist Hutments* (Rs 60 foreigners, Rs 40 Indians). Both have attached bath. Independently run Restaurant (Indian and Continental). Reasonably priced but limited choice.

Booking accommodation can be a problem as there are only three places and each has a quota. Book as early as possible from: **Chief Wildlife Warden**, 17 Rana Pratap Marg, Lucknow, T 46140, Cable: Wildlife. Other information from: **Tourist Officer**, UP Tourist Office, Chandralok Building, 36 Janpath, New Delhi, T 3322251, 3326620. Field director or Wildlife Warden, Project Tiger, Corbett National Park, Ramnagar, T 853189, 85332, Cable: Pro-tiger.

The **B** *Corbett Jungle Resort* (Quality Inns), is about 10 km from the Dhangarh entrance. The rooms are in small purpose built cottages in pleasant surroundings on the edge of the Ramganga River. Full board only. The charge made for arranging elephant rides is high at Rs 200 per person. Very pleasant but expensive.

There are other hotel/resorts also coming up outside the park.

Local Transport The main gate is at Dhangarhi, approximately 16 km N of Ramnagar on the Ranikhet road. Foreigners Rs 35 for first three days, Rs 12 per day thereafter, Indians Rs 10 and Rs 5. Students Rs 2 for both. Vehicle charge: light (Car, jeep) Rs 10, heavy (coach) Rs 50. Cine camera fee Rs 50.

Elephant rides, morning and evening, 2 hr duration, Rs 25 (foreigners), Rs 10 (Indians). Book at reception desk at Dhikala. Cars and jeeps may drive round part of the park. Check with reception at Dhikala.

Apart from the immediate area around Dhikala, **do not go walking in the park**. A British photographer was mauled to death by a tiger a few years ago. To enjoy the park and its wildlife, talk quietly and try to dress soberly, 'leave only footprints, take only photographs' to use the Sierra Club motto.

Conducted Tours Garhwal Mandal Vikas Nigam run 3-day tours from Delhi departing every Fri in season. For reservations, contact UP Tourist Office, Chandralok Building, 36 Janpath, New Delhi. T 3322251.

Air The nearest airport is at **Pantnagar** (130 km). **Vayudoot** connects it with Delhi. Transport from there to Corbett is difficult and lengthy. **Avoid this route**. **Rail** The nearest railway station is at **Ramnagar** (50 km from Dhikala). A metre gauge line connects Ramnagar with Moradabad and Lucknow. **Bus** Dhikala is connected with Ramnagar by a daily bus. Contact KMOU or UP Roadways Bus Stands at Ramnagar. **Road** Ramnagar is well connected with Moradabad and Ranikhet by metalled roads, Dhikala with Ramnagar by unmetalled road.

CORBETT TO NAINITAL AND RANIKHET

It is possible to reach **Nainital** from Corbett via **Ramnagar** and **Kaladhungi** on a picturesque road.

Drive from Dhikala to Dhangarhi gate, on to Ramnagar and turn left. The road crosses the river which has a barrage and skirts along the edge of the hills. At **Kaladhungi** visit **Jim Corbett's house**, now a small museum. Turn up the road opposite and continue up into the hills, travelling along a delightful and well engineered metalled road that winds its way up the hillsides through *chir** pine (*Pinus longifolia*) forest and the occasional village. There are impressive views of the plains. You enter Nainital at the N (Mallital) end of the lake.

If **Ranikhet** is your destination, go from **Dhikala** to **Dhangarhi** and turn left. Buses will pick up passengers for Ranikhet and intermediate points without you having to return to Ramnagar. This drive is very attractive as the road gradually climbs up to the first ridges of the Himalaya. The forest jungle looks drier and more open here than nearer Nainital but just a impressive.

Ranikhet (1,800 m), 72 km from Nainital. No one quite knows the name of the queen whose field gave Ranikhet (The Queen's Field) its title. In 1869 the land was bought from local villagers and the British established a summer rest and recreation settlement for their troops, made it a cantonment town governed by the military authorities and developed it as a quiet hill station. Set along a 1,800 m high ride, Ranikhet sprawls out through the surrounding forest giving very little indication of where its centre is. This is one of its attractions in that there are many enjoyable walks.

At one time, Lord Mayo, Viceroy of India, was so enchanted with the place that he wanted to move the Summer Headquarters of the army away from Shimla. That did not happen but Rankhet became and still is the Regimental Centre for the Kumaon Regiment. The views from the ridge are magnificent and the twin peaks of Nanda Devi (7.816 m) can be clearly seen. At *Upat* (6 km) there is a golf course, and at *Chaubatia* (10 km) there is a government Fruit Garden and Research Station.

Hotels D *West View*, Mahatma Gandhi Rd. T 61, 196, Cable: Westview Hotel. 19 rm. 5 km centre. Restaurant, car hire, exchange, indoor sports and games, parking, golf course. The **E** *Tourist Bungalow* (KMVN), T 97, is the best available and has very pleasant doubles with bath. The restaurant serves mostly Indian cuisine. Attractive location in the upper, cantonment part of town, with good views. A short walk from here is a pretty temple festooned with hundreds of bells. Other hotels include the **E** *Alka, Moon* and *Natraj*, all of which are in Sadar Bazaar plus the **E** *Norton's* in Mall Rd.

Travel Bus There are regular buses to Ramnagar, Almora and Nainital operated by KMOU and UP roadways. **Road** Ranikhet is well connected with these places by all-weather roads.

TREKKING IN THE GARHWAL AND THE KUMAON HIMALAYA

This region contains some of the finest mountains in the Himalaya and is highly accessible. Yet surprisingly very few western visitors go trekking there, many prefering to visit Nepal. Of the many treks available, 8 routes are included here which offer some of the most spectacular walking and scenery.

The historical explanation behind this goes back to the beginning of the 19th century. When the Gurkhas were expelled from Kumaon, Garhwal and Himachal Pradesh after the 1814-15 Gurkha War, Nepal and Britain signed a non-aggression pact which neither side violated. However, Nepal adopted an isolationist policy, closing its doors to the rest of the world. Like Tibet, then, it became a forbidden land and, as is always the case, this stimulated a curious fascination among outsiders. The discovery that Everest was the highest mountain in the world added to the mystique.

When Nepal opened its doors again in 1950, the first visitors were captivated by this medieval kingdom that was seemingly unaffected by the 20th century. Members of the first expeditions to Everest marvelled at the beauty of Nepal and widely advertised this. Then came the trekkers and tourism gathered a momentum which inertia has sustained despite the fact that large areas are 'trekked out', some of the trails filthy, e.g. to Everest, most of the forest gone and the local population far more commercialised than their Himalayan neighbours.

Exploration in Garhwal and Kumaon This region had been open since the British took over in 1815 but it was abandoned by explorers in favour of the more mysterious Nepal. Much of the early Himalayan exploration was undertaken here. **Trisul** (*Altitude* 7,100 m), after it had been climbed by Dr Tom Longstaff in 1906 remained the highest mountain climbed for the next 30 years. Famous mountaineers of the 1930s like Bill Tilman, Eric Shipton and Frank Smythe all marvelled at the beauty of the region and Edmund Hillary cut his Himalayan teeth on Mukut Parbat in Garhwal. Later climbers like Chris Bonington, Peter Boardman and Mick Tasker used alpine techniques to conquer Changabang and Dunagiri.

The scenic splendour of these mountains lies partly in the fact that the forests around the big peaks are still in marvellous condition and the local population unaffected by the ravages of mass tourism. Also in Garhwal and Kumaon there are ranges that you can easily get among, enabling a greater feeling of intimacy with the alpine giants. The mountains have been described as 'a series of rugged ranges tossed about in the most intricate confusion' (Walton, 1910).

Trekking in this region is not highly organised. There are no local operators who fully understand and cater for western requirements. There is no government regulation of porter's rates and a network of traveller's accommodation that is still in its infancy. Therefore, you need to be well prepared. It is possible to do some treks, e.g. The Pindar Glacier trek without a tent, but on other routes this will be very limiting. If you are travelling in small groups of 3-4 persons, it is often possible to get overnight accommodation in villagers' houses but despite their hospitality, this is uncomfortable. Furthermore, communication is a problem as very few villagers speak English. Porters can usually be obtained by asking around at the place where you intend starting your trek. You will need to allow for the time spent in carefully negotiating rates. Nevertheless, the rewards for the well-equipped trekker who has planned carefully are great, especially the feeling of being far from the madding crowd.

Best season The best seasons for trekking are **Feb/Mar** at lower altitudes for the spectacular rhododendrons; **Apr/May** at higher altitudes, though it can get very hot; and **Oct/Nov,** when temperatures are lower, the skies clearer and the vegetation greener following the monsoon. The monsoon is good for alpine flowers but wet, humid and cloudy for much, though not all, of the time.

There are 2 general trekking areas. Around **Gangotri and Yamunotri** in Garhwal there are a number very good treks, some suitable for the independent or 'go it alone' trekker. **Nanda Devi** is the other area and this is mostly in Kumaon. There are far more treks than those indicated which are intended as a representative sample only. You will not be allowed to go beyond Badrinath or N of the

Dhauliganga towards the Niti Pass as this is a sensitive border zone, usually referred to as the Inner Line.

Gangotri To Gaumukh

The best known trek here is to *Gaumukh* (The Cow's Mouth) and, if desired, beyond onto the Gangotri Glacier. To Gaumukh can easily be undertaken with minimal equipment. From Gangotri 3,046 m) follow the well-defined, gradually ascending path *Bhujbasa* (3,800 m, 11 km, 4-5 hr). There is a Forest Rest House at Chirbasa, 4 km before Bhujbasa. At Bhujbasa there is a *Tourist Bungalow* and ashram where trekkers and pilgrims can stay. It is 5 km to Gaumukh across boulder scree and moraine and should take about 3 hr so it is quite feasible to go from Bhujbasa to Gaumukh, spend some time there then return to Bhujbasa or Chirbasa in the same day.

Beyond Gaumukh (3,969 m) more care and camping equipment is required. The Gangotri Glacier is situated in an amphitheatre of 6,500-7,000 m peaks which include Mana Parbat, Satopanth (7,084 m), Vasuki (6,792 m), Bhagirathi (6,556 m), Kedar Dome and Shivling (6,543 m).

Tapovan (4463 m, 5 km) a grassy meadow on the east bank of the Gangotri glacier is the base camp for climbing expeditions to the stunningly beautiful *Shivling* (6,543 m), Siva's lingam and the 'Matterhorn of the Himalaya'. You can either return the same way or make a round trip by crossing over the glacier to *Nandanvan* (4,400 m, 3 km) and going up to **Vasuki Tal** (6 km) beneath *Vasuki* peak (6,792 m). The return is via Nandanvan the W bank of the Gangotri glacier crossing the Raktwan Glacier to Gaumukh.

Gangotri To Kedartal

This trek requires a tent, stove and, of course, food. It is 17 km to **Kedar Tal** (5,000 m), a small glacial lake surrounded by **Meru** (6,672 m), **Pithwara** (6,904 m) and **Bhrigupanth** (6,772 m). Leaving Gangotri you proceed up the gorge of the Kedar Ganga, Lord Siva's contribution to the Bhagirathi river, for 8 km to **Bhoj Kharak** and then a further 4 km to **Kedar Kharak** passing through some beautiful Himalayan Birch forest (*Betula Utiles*) en route. The bark from the trees (*bhoj* in Garhwali) was used by sages and hermits for manuscripts. From Kedar Kharak, where you can camp, it is a laborious 5 km ascent to **Kedar Tal**. Besides the peaks surrounding the lake you can also see the Bandarpunch range.

The return to Gangotri can be the same way or over the ridge separating the Kedar Tal from the Rudragaira Gad (river). This ridge is 700 m above Kedar Tal and at least 5 hr should be allowed for the crossing. **Rudragaira Kharak** is the base camp for the peaks at the head of this valley. Coming down towards Gangotri you must cross to the opposite bank to avoid the cliffs on the W bank. Nearer Gangotri cross back to the W bank.

This is an excellent trek with scenic variety and spectacular views but you must be aware of the problems associated with altitude and allow time for acclimatisation.

Gangori To Yamunotri Via Dodital

This is a trek of great beauty between **Kalyani** and *Hanuman Chatti*, a distance of 49 km. You can do a round trip from either end.

From **Uttarkashi** take a local bus to **Gangotri** and get off at the confusingly named *Gangori* (3 km) or walk it. Here take the track to your left up to **Kalyani** (1,829 m), the recognised starting point of the trek. From here it gets steeper as the path climbs through forest to **Agoda** (2,280 m, 5 km), a suitable camping or halting place. The next day carry on to **Dodital** (3,024 m), picturesquely set in a forest of pine (*Pinus Wallichiana*), deodar (*Cedrus deodara*) and oak (*Quercus* *dilatata* and *Q. semecarpifolia*). This is the source of the Asi Ganga and is stocked with trout. There is a *Forest Rest House*. Above the lake there are fine views of Bandar Punch (6,387 m, Monkey's Tail). To reach **Hanuman Chatti** (2,400 m) walk up to the Aineha Pass (3,667 m, 6 km) which also has splendid views. Then it is a 22 km walk down to Hanuman Chatti, the roadhead for Yamunotri.

The Har-ki-dun Trek

Har-ki-Dun (God's Valley) nestles in the NW corner of Garhwal near the Sutlej-Yamuna watershed. The valley is dominated by **Swargarohini** (6,096 m). From **Nowgaon**, 9 km S of Barkot, take a bus to the roadhead of **Netwar** (1,401 m) at the confluence of the Rupin and Supin streams which become the Tons.. From here is is a gradual ascent over 12 km to **Saur** then a further 11 km to **Taluka**. There is a *Forest Rest House* at **Osla** (2,559 m) which is 11 km from Taluka. There is a second *Forest Rest House*, 8 km and 1,000 m higher, in **Har-ki-Dun** (3,565 m). This is an ideal base for exploring the valley.

You can return to Nowgaon or, if properly equipped and provisioned, trek on to **Yamunotri** (29 km) via the **Yamunotri Pass** (5,172 m). You will need to allow time for acclimatisation. The views from the pass are well worth the effort.

The Nanda Devi Area

Dominating the Garhwal and Kumaon Himalaya is the Nanda Devi Group of mountains with *Nanda Devi* (7,816 m), named after the all-encompassing form of the female deity, at its centre. *Nanda Devi* is the highest mountain in India (excluding Sikkim) and was once the highest in the British Empire. It is an incredibly beautiful mountain of two peaks separated by a 4 km long ridge.

The legend Legend has it that the hand of Nanda Devi ("She who Gives Bliss"), daughter of a local king, was demanded in marriage by a marauding prince. War ensued, her father was killed and she fled, eventually finding refuge on top of the mountain now bearing her name. She is protected by a ring of mountains 112 km in circumference containing 12 peaks over 6,400 m in height and in only one place is this defensive ring lower than 5,500 m, at the Rishi Gorge, one of the deepest in the world. It is the place of sages (*rishi**).

Early exploration For half a century the problems which engaged the attention of many experienced explorers and mountaineers was not so much how to climb the mountain but how to get to it. Various attempts were made from a number of places to gain entry into what became known as the Nanda Devi Sanctuary. The riddle was finally solved by the 'Terrible Twins', Bill Tilman and Eric Shipton, in a characteristically lightweight expedition (these two great mountaineers would agonise over whether to take one shirt or two on an expedition lasting a few months!). The way they discovered was up the Rishiganga and through the difficult Rishi Gorge. They made two trips into the Sanctuary during their five month expedition in the Garhwal Himalaya in 1934 (which incidentally cost them UK £143 each for everything, including passage!). Bill Tilman returned in 1936 (Shipton was on Hugh Ruttledge's Everest Expedition) with a small climbing party and climbed the mountain with little real difficulty.

Tilman, a purist, wrote 'We live in an age of mechanisation and in recent years it has become apparent that even mountaineering is in danger of becoming mechanised. It is therefore pleasing to record that in climbing Nanda Devi no climbing aids were used, apart, that is from the apricot brandy we took. Our solitary oxygen apparatus was fortunately drowned, pitons were forgotten at base camp and crampons were solemnly carried up only to be abandoned.' (W.H. Tilman, *The Ascent of Nanda Devi*).

In 1936 the monsoon was particularly heavy. The Pindar River,which is fed by the glaciers of Nanda Kot ("The Stronghold of Nanda") and Trisul ("Siva's Trident"), both mountains in the protective ring, rose dramatically. In the village of Tharali 40 lives were lost. This was on 29 Aug, the day that Tilman's party reached the summit. Some say the anger of the Goddess was provoked by the violation of her sanctuary.

The Pindari Glacier Trek

This is along the S edge of the **Nanda Devi Sanctuary** and is an 'out and back' trek, i.e. you return by the same route.

From **Bageshwar** – page 221, get a local bus to **Bharari** (1,524 m) which has a PWD Resthouse and a cheap hotel. From here you can walk 16 km along the Sarju valley to **Song** or take another bus. From here it is just over 1 km and 200 m to **Loharkhet** (1,829 m) which also has a PWD Bungalow in the village and a basic KMVN Travellers Lodge overlooking it. Good views of the hillside opposite and the head of the Sarju Valley. It is 11 km from Loharkhet to **Dhakuri** via the **Dhakuri Pass** (2,835 m) which has a wonderful view of the S of the Nanda Devi Sanctuary including Panwali Dhar (6,683 m) and Maiktoli (6,803 m). The walk to the pass is mostly through forest on a well graded path. About 100 m below the pass on the N side is a clearing with a PWD Bungalow and a KMVN Travellers Lodge. Great views, especially at sunrise and sunset.

You are now in the valley of the River Pindar and descend to the village of **Khati** (2,194 m, 8 km) first through rhododendron, then mixed forests dominated by stunted oak. Khati is a large village of over 50 households and situated on a spur that runs down to the river, some 200 m below. There is a PWD Bungalow, KMVN Travellers Lodge and a village hotel run by the local shopkeeper. You can buy delicacies (biscuits, eggs and chocolate), brought in by mule from Bharari.

From Khati follow the Pindar to **Dwali** (8 km) which is at the confluence of the Pindar and the Kaphini Rivers. Here there is a run down and grubby PWD Bungalow. If you have a tent, camp in front. The next halt is Phurkiya (6 km) which also has a run-down PWD Bungalow. this can be used as a base for going up to **Zero Point** (4,000 m) and the snout of the glacier. On either side there are impressive peaks, including Panwali Dhar (6,683 m), Nanda Kot (6,876 m). You return to Bharari the same way. From Dwali, however, a side trip to the **Kaphini Glacier** is worthwhile. Including this the trek can be accomplished in a week but for comfort allow 9 days. As there is accommodation in every place, this trek can obviously be done with little equipment although a sleeping bag is essential.

Roopkund Trek

Roopkund (4,800 m, kund* is lake in Garhwali), nestles in the lap of Trisul (7,100 m) and **Nanda Ghunti** (6,310 m). Thirty years ago the respected Indian anthropologist D.N. Majumdar discovered hundreds of skeletons around this small mountain tarn. There are two explanations behind their presence. The first is that are the remains of a party of pilgrims on a **yatra*** to the base of Trisul (The Lord Siva's Trident) who died when bad weather closed in. Alternatively they may have been the remains of the Dogra General **Zorawar Singh's** army from Jammu, which tried to invade Tibet in 1841, was beaten off and forced to find its way back home over the Himalaya. To this day, the mystery remains unsolved. This is a highly varied and scenic trek which can be undertaken by a suitably equipped party. A week is sufficient to do this trek, nine days if you want to take it more comfortably and have a rest day to allow for acclimatisation. Porters can usually be obtained at **Gwaldam** or **Debal**.

From **Gwaldam** (1,950 m) (See Almora above) walk down through attractive pine forest, cross the River Pindar and continue to **Debal** (1,350 m, 8 km) where there is a KMVN Travellers Lodge and Forest Resthouse. From here you can either walk 12 km along a dirt road through villages with views of Mrigthuni (6,855 m), or go by cramped jeep taxi to Bagrigadh which is 500 m below the **Lohajung Pass** (2,350 m) where there is an attractive KMVN Travellers Lodge right on the ridge beside a pretty shrine. Good views here of Nanda Ghunti. If time is at a premium, you can save a day by going by bus from Gwaldam to **Tharali,** taking another bus to **Debal**, catching the jeep taxi to Bagrigadh and walking up to Lohajung in one long day.

From **Lohajung** you walk down through stunted oak forest and along the *Wan Gad** (river) to the village of **Wan** (2,500 m, 10 km) which has a *Forest Resthouse* and *KMVN Travellers Lodge*. From Wan it is essentially wilderness travel as you make the ascent to Roopkund, first walking through thick forest to Bedni Bugyal (*bugyal** – meadow) which is used a summer pasture. This is at 3,550 m and has good views of Trisul and the Badrinath range to the N. There are some stone shepherds huts which you may be able to use but it is advisable to take a tent. From Bedni it is a gradual 7 km climb along a well defined path over the 4,500m **Kovali Pass** to more shepherds huts at **Bakwa Basa** (4,400 m), the base for the final walk up to **Roopkund**. This is not a good camp site as water is some way off. A stove is necessary for cooking. From here, it is 2-3 hr up to Roopkund. Care must be taken on the final steep part because the ground can be icy. From the 4,900 m ridge approximately 50 m above Roopkund is a magnificent view of the W face of Trisul rising over 3,500 m from the floor of the intervening hanging valley to the summit which Longstaff reached dressed only in tweeds. 'The tent was not windproof ' he wrote, 'those were primitive days'. Return to **Gwaldam** by the same route or via **Ali Bugyal** which bypasses the village of Wan.

The Curzon/Nehru Trail

The Curzon/Nehru trail is a trek of unrivalled beauty. It was the route followed by Tilman and Shipton on their way to the Rishi Gorge, and by other mountaineers en route to the peaks on the Indo-Tibetan border. The crossing of the Kuari (Virgin) Pass is a fitting conclusion to a trek that takes in three lesser passes and five major rivers – the Pindar, Kaliganga, Nandakini, Birehiganga and Dhauliganga. The trail was named after Lord Curzon, who was a keen trekker, and it is said that the path was specially improved so that he could do the trek. With Independence it was renamed the Nehru Trail.

This trek begins at **Gwaldam** and ends at **Tapoban** in the **Dhauliganga Valley** on the **Joshimath Niti Pass** road, after crossing the **Kuari Pass** (3,500 m), one of the finest vantage points in the Himalaya.

From **Gwaldam** proceed to **Wan** as in the previous itinerary. Then, go over the **Kanol Pass** (2,900 m) through thick mixed forest to **Sutol** (2,100 m, 10 km) in the **Nandakini** valley. There is a good camp site by the river. The next two stages follow the Nandakini downstream to Ramni (2,500 m, 20 km) where the path leads up over the rhododendron forest clad *Ramni Pass* (3,100 m). From here there is a good view of the Kuari Pass. To reach it, however, is a good three day walk, down through lush forest to cross the Birehiganga River by an impressive suspension bridge, up around the horseshoe-shaped hanging valley around **Pana** village, over an intervening spur and into the forested tributary valley of the Kuari nallah. There is no settlement here and **bharal** (mountain goats) and **Himalayan black bear** inhabit the rich forest, though they are rarely seen. Waterfalls tumble down over steep crags. There is a good camp about an hour below the pass at *Dhakwani* (3,200 m).

Leave as early as possible to get the full effect of sunrise over the peaks on the Indo-Tibetan border. Frank Smythe who came this way in 1931 en route to Kamet (7,755 m), the second highest mountain in this region summed it up beautifully: 'We breasted the slope and halted, silent on the pass. No words would express our delight. The Himalaya were arrayed before us in a stupendous arc' (*Kamet Conquered*, 1931). Some of the mountains seen are **Kamet**, **Badrinath** (7,140 m), **Dunagiri** (7,066 m), **Changabang** (6,863 m) and **Nanda Devi** herself (7,816 m). There is a wonderful wooded camp site with marvellous views about 300 m below the pass. From here it is down to **Tapoban** and the Joshimath – Niti road. There is a hot spring here and a bus service to *Joshimath*. Allow ten days for the trek.

DELHI TO KATHMANDU VIA LUCKNOW AND GORAKHPUR

There are several possible routes across the plains of the Ganga. The more northerly route via Moradabad and Bareilly follows the **NH24**, and passes through Lucknow, scene of some of the bloodiest fighting during the 1857 mutiny.

Details of the route from Delhi to Moradabad are given in the description of the route from Delhi to Nainital – **see page 215**. In Moradabad keep on **NH24** due E to Rampur. The road turns SE in **Rampur** (30 km) to **Bareilly** (66 km). Bareilly was the capital of Rohilkhand and was founded in 1537 by the Bas Deo and Barel (hence Bareilly) Deo brothers. Traces of their fortress remain. It was ceded to the British in 1801 and also contributed to the drama of the Mutiny. The important mosques are **Mirza Masjid** (1600), **Jami Masjid** (1657) and the Mosque of Ahmad Khandar, and two churches, Christ Church and St Stephens. **Bareilly** is a transfer point for rail travel to Haldwani and Nainital as well as a suitable overnight halt.

Hotels **D** *Oberoi Anand*, 46 Civil Lines. T 77448, Cable: Obi Hotel. 78 rm. 3 km rly, central. Restaurant, exchange, shops, TV, 24 hr rm service, parking, doctor on call, car hire.
E *Civil and Military Hotel*, Station Rd. T 75879. 22 rm. 10 km airport, close to rly, centrally located. Bar permit, restaurant (Indian, English, Mughlai), coffee shop, car hire, TV.

Rail Kathgodam and Nainital: *Kumaon Exp* 5311, daily, 0600, 3 hr 50 min. **Bus** Extensive local bus routes and connections with all major cities on the plains.

The road continues out of **Bareilly** through **Faridpur** (20 km), **Miran Katra** (23 km) and **Tilhar** (11 km) to **Shajahanpur**, (21 km). Named after the Mughal Emperor by its founder, Nawab Bahadur Khan in 1647. It came under British control and experienced the Mutiny when residents were attacked in the church.
    The main road to the right out of Shahjahanpur goes to Jajalabad (34 km), Fatehgarh (73 km) Etawah and Gwalior. Continue straight on for the main road to Lucknow. Through **Chapartala** (41 km), **Maholi** (19 km) and **Sitapur** (25 km). The succession of small towns and villages continues, through **Kamalpur** (23 km) **Sidhauli** (30 km) and **Arjunpur** (27 km) to **Lucknow** (21 km.

Lucknow

Population 1.14 million (1981) *Altitude* 123 m. Area 79 sq km. Best Season Oct-Mar. Languages Hindi, Urdu and English. Lucknow has daily Indian Airlines services with Delhi (369 km, 55 min). Amousi airport is 14 km from the city centre.

	Jan	Feb	Mar	Apr	May	Jun	Jul	Aug	Sep	Oct	Nov	Dec	Av/Tot
Max (°C)	23	26	33	38	41	39	34	33	33	33	29	25	32
Min (°C)	9	11	16	22	27	28	27	26	23	20	13	9	19
Rain (mm)	24	17	9	6	12	94	299	302	182	40	1	6	992

Early settlement Lucknow, the capital of UP is not a very attractive city. It sprawls along the banks of the **Gomti** river in the heart of eastern U.P. surrounded by the unrelentingly flat Gangetic plain. Although the discovery of Painted Grey Ware and Northern Black Polished Ware pottery demonstrates the long period over which the site has been occupied, its main claim to fame is as the capital of the Nawabs of **Oudh** (*Avadh*), and later the scene of one of the most remarkable episodes in the Mutiny of 1857. Now it is a bustling administrative centre and market city.

It is not clear when **Lucknow** was first populated or who its founder may have been. When the Mughals conquered N India in the 16th century it was absorbed into their empire and rapidly developed under Akbar's patronage. In the 18th century, **Nawab Sadat Ali Khan** founded the Oudh dynasty. The builder of 'modern' Lucknow was **Nawab Asaf-ud-Daula** who shifted his capital here from Faizabad in 1775. He intended to build a city of wonderful buildings. Certainly some are remarkable, like the **Great Imambara** with the largest vaulted apartment in the world. However, he also emptied the regal coffers with his ambitious building and personal extravagance. In Kipling's Kim 'no city -except Bombay, the queen of all – was more beautiful in her garish style than Lucknow', famous for its silks, perfumes and jewellery. In the event the resulting buildings were themselves a disappointment. As Tillotson has said, the style of most of the major buildings constructed by the nawabs of Lucknow is debased Mughal.

The British takeover In the mid 1850s under **Lord *Dalhousie***, the British annexed a number of Indian states. Percival Spear suggested that Dalhousie considered British rule so superior to Indian that the more territory directly administered by the British the better it would be for the Indian people. He therefore evolved a policy of lapse whereby the states of Indian princes without direct heirs could be taken over on the ruler's death. Chronic mismanagement was also deemed just cause for takeover. The great Muslim state of Oudh was annexed for this second reason.

The famous Indian novelist ***Premchand*** in the Chess Players recounts the fall of Oudh because the population of Lucknow 'small and big, rich and poor, were alike dedicated to sensual joys. One would be devoted to song and dance; another would be enjoying the fumes of opium'. History suggests that Nawab Wajid Ali Shah was so engrossed in his game of chess that he remained unheeding to his tasks even as British soldiers occupied his capital. Whatever the justification, there was considerable resentment against the British because it was generally regarded as a breach of faith. Needless to say, a strong British presence was established in the city as it became a key administrative and military centre. **Satyajit Ray's** film adaptation is excellent.

The mutiny In 1857, when the mutiny broke, Sir Henry Lawrence gathered the British community into the Residency which was turned into a fortress as quickly as possible. The ensuing siege lasted for 87 days. When the relieving force under Sir Colin Campbell finally broke through, the once splendid Residency was a blackened ruin, its walls pockmarked and gaping with cannon ball holes. Today it is a mute witness to a desperate struggle.

Culture Under the Nawabs, Lucknow evolved specialised levels of dance, poetry, music and calligraphy. Formal mannerisms, the rendering of poetry, the Lucknowi gharana (house) of music and the shadow-worked embroidery are reminders of its splendid past. It is a regional cultural capital though according to Muzaffar Ali 'its streets are thronged with cycles and rickshaws. A number of garden roads such as the Kaiser Bagh quadrangle which were at one time pleasant walks are now thoroughfares for Tata trucks belching diesel. In the 1920s the city had seen some of the most outstanding cars the world had known. Today of the vintage modes of travel, only the *ekka** (one-horse carriage) has survived'.

Local Festivals The major Hindu and Muslim festivals are celebrated. There are also several festivals celebrated distinctively in Lucknow. The day after Diwali in Oct-Nov is celebrated with a great fair and national kite flying competition at the Patang Park, M.G. Rd. Each Feb the UP Government organises a special festival. Song, drama and dance, processions, boating, ekka races are features of the ten day festival with special emphasis on the performance of Indian classical music.

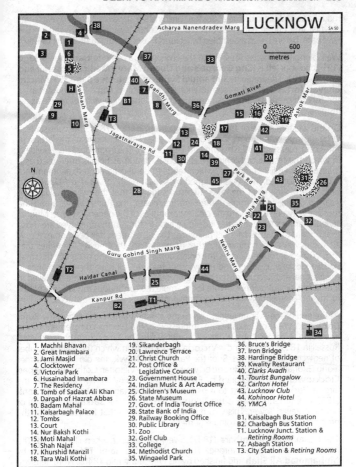

LUCKNOW

Acharya Nanendradev Marg

SA 50

0   600
metres

1. Machhi Bhavan
2. Great Imambara
3. Jami Masjid
4. Clocktower
5. Victoria Park
6. Husainabad Imambara
7. The Residency
8. Tomb of Sadaat Ali Khan
9. Dargah of Hazrat Abbas
10. Badam Mahal
11. Kaisarbagh Palace
12. Tombs
13. Court
14. Nur Baksh Kothi
15. Moti Mahal
16. Shah Najaf
17. Khurshid Manzil
18. Tara Wali Kothi

19. Sikanderbagh
20. Lawrence Terrace
21. Christ Church
22. Post Office &
    Legislative Council
23. Government House
24. Indian Music & Art Academy
25. Children's Museum
26. State Museum
27. Govt. of India Tourist Office
28. State Bank of India
29. Railway Booking Office
30. Public Library
31. Zoo
32. Golf Club
33. College
34. Methodist Church
35. Wingaeld Park

36. Bruce's Bridge
37. Iron Bridge
38. Hardinge Bridge
39. Kwality Restaurant
40. Clarks Avadh
41. Tourist Bungalow
42. Carlton Hotel
43. Lucknow Club
44. Kohinoor Hotel
45. YMCA

B1. Kaisalbagh Bus Station
B2. Charbagh Bus Station
T1. Lucknow Junct. Station &
    Retiring Rooms
T2. Asbagh Station
T3. City Station & Retiring Rooms

Places of Interest The original centre of the city is believed to be the high ground crowned by the Mosque of Aurangzeb on the right bank of the Gomti. Here at Lakshman Tila a family from Bijnor built a fort at the end of the 13th century. It then passed through a number of hands, including the Sharqi kings of Jaunpur (1394-1476), Sher Shah of Delhi (1540-5). The first Nawab, Sadat Khan Burhan-ul-mulk (1724-9) was made governor of Oudh in 1732 by Aurangzeb. His successor, Safdarjang (1739-53) was buried at Delhi, **see page 163**. The monuments in Lucknow (often open between 0600 and 1700 hr) have been divided into three main groups:

W and NW of the City station

This is a circular walk, conducted anti-clockwise from the City Station. First walk N along Nabiullah Rd. The Iron Bridge (1798) was designed by Sir John Rennie modelled on Witham bridge at Boston, Lincolnshire. It was cast only 20 years after the first iron bridge had been erected in India but lay for over 40 years on the river bank before it was assembled by Colonel Fraser for Amjad Ali Shah (1842-7).

Walk along Husainabad Trust Rd to the NW and you come to **Hardinge Bridge** (1914). To your left is **King George's and Queen Mary's Medical Hospital and College** (1912) designed by **Sir Samuel Swinton Jacob** – see page 355. **Macchi Bhavan fort** is across the road to your left and got its name 'Fish house' after the fish which Safdarjang was permitted by Mughal Imperial edict to use as his insignia.

On the western slope of this is the **Great Imambara** (1784). This consists of a large mosque with two minarets on the W side. The hall is one of the largest in the world, measuring 49.6 m long and 14.9 m high. The *imambara* is a building in which the festival of Mohurram is celebrated, and as here is often used as a mausoleum. Unlike a mosque, which tends to be unornamented, an imambara is often decorated. This was designed by Kifayat-ullah for **Asaf-ud-Daula** and built as a famine relief measure. Tillotson suggests that the major buildings of Asaf-ud Daula, for example – the Bara Imambara, the Rumi Darwaza and the mosque between them – are the clearest examples of the degeneration of Mughal style. He argues that while the individual architectural forms employed are those that appear in mature Mughal buildings, their treatment has been dramatically altered in ways which diminish rather than enhance their power. He writes that "the cusped or foliated arches, the onion domes, the tapering minarets, the small domed kiosks or chattris, and many other features, all have their prototypes in the Mughal architecture of the preceding century; but here they are deployed in a new, less skillful manner." Note for example the continuous row of tiny chattris or the replacement of Mughal decorative inlay work with crude stucco.

At the end of the avenue leading up to the Imambara from the river is the **Rumi Darwaza** (1784) or Turkish Gate. Impressive and a worthy complement to the Imambara, it 'recalls Kublai Khan's Xanadu' wrote The Times correspondent W.H. Russell in 1857. Just beyond is **Victoria Park** (1890) in which there are a number of neglected British tombs. S of the Park is the **Chowk**, the old bazaar. Further along Girdharilal Mathur Rd and on your right is the Victorian Gothic **Husainabad Clocktower** (1881) designed by Roskell Payne. It is 67 m high and carries the largest clock in India. Next to it is the attractive octagonal **Husainabad Tank** (1837-42), around which is the **Taluqdar's Hall** and the **Satkhanda** (1840) or Seven-Storeyed Tower. This was built for **Ali Shah** so that he could survey the progress of his various building schemes.

The **Husainabad Imambara** (1837) is very picturesque when illuminated. The hall contained a silver throne. Further W is the **Jami Masjid** begun by **Muhammad Ali Shah** and finished by his wife in the mid 1840s. From here you can return to the city station by walking down Napier St into Khunkhunji Marg. Alternatively if you turn right down Dargah Hazrat Abbas Rd you will come to the **Dargah of Hazrat Abbas**. Mohurram banners are hung around this shrine on the fifth day of that festival. Down Hakim Abdul Aziz Rd, across Tulsidas Marg and down Nadan Mahal Rd is the **Badam Mahal** (c.1600), the tomb of **Shaikh Abdur Rahim**, Akbar's Governor of Oudh. This is a fine building, built in the Mughal style and faced with red sandstone from Agra. Abdur Rahim's father's tomb, Ibrahim Chishti (c.1545) is nearby to the E. Allow 2-3 hr for this tour.

The Residency and Hazratganj area
The Residency and its 3,000 mostly European occupants, hastily brought there by **Sir Henry Lawrence**, came under siege on the evening of June 30 1857. Two days later Lawrence was fatally hit. After 90 days Generals Sir Henry Havelock and Sir James Outram appeared through the battered walls with a column of

Highlanders. The occupants no doubt felt relieved that it was all over. However, the siege was intensified and sepoy sappers (engineers) began tunnelling to lay mines to blow the place up.

From quite early on the beleaguered community of Britons and Indians loyal to the crown ran into considerable difficulties with food supplies, sickness and disease. Small birds were captured and consumed. Sir Henry Lawrence's belongings were auctioned off almost as soon as he was buried. As rations dwindled and prices rose, smallpox, cholera and scurvy set in. Surgeons amputated limbs without chloroform. Havelock was slowly dying of dysentery.

The heroic Irishman, Henry Kavanagh had sat in the tunnels and shot mutineers as they wriggled forward to lay more mines. Now he volunteered to run the gauntlet through the enemy lines to find Sir Colin Campbell's relieving force. This he did and after swimming the Gomti made contact. On 17 November, Lucknow was finally relieved. Of the 3,000 Indians and British who had sought refuge in the Residency, only 1,000 marched out.

This was one of the great heroic struggles of the Mutiny which was to drag on elsewhere for a few months more. It seemed to bring out all the extremes of human nature – courage, daring, heroism, stupidity, loyalty, bewilderment and if the records are to be believed, only very rarely cowardice. Two books are recommended if you have an interest in the Mutiny, particularly at Lucknow: The Great Mutiny: India 1857 by Christopher Hibbert (Penguin) for a factual history and The Siege of Krishnapur by J.G. Farrell for a novel.

The Residency Compound is across the road from the City Station. Originally the British left the compound in its ruined state. The site is now a national monument and has been landscaped. You enter by the Baillie Guard gateway. The Treasury on the right was used as an arsenal whilst the adjacent Banquet Hall served as the hospital. On the lawn of **Dr Fayrer's House** is a stone cross to Sir Henry Lawrence. The **Begum Kothi** behind was the house of Mrs Walters who was married to the king of Oudh.

The Residency (1800) designed by Saadat Ali stands on the NE side of the compound. Women and children stayed in the *tykhanas** (cool underground rooms used in the hot weather). The ground floor houses a small museum in which there is a model showing the layout of the whole area in 1857. The graves of Lawrence, Neill and others are in the Cemetery. To balance the scene, just outside the Residency on the banks of the Gomti river is a white obelisk erected to commemorate 'The Nationalist Insurgents' who lost their lives in 1857. Next door to the Residency is the **Tomb of Saadat Ali Khan** (1814). Here there are two almost identical tombs, that of the king and his queen. His is the larger and is paved with black and white marble. Immediately to the S is the **Kaisarbagh Palace** (1848-50). Wajid Ali Shah intended this to be the eighth wonder of the world. It scarcely qualifies. In front of the NE gate is a small memorial to two groups of Europeans who were massacred after being held in the palace during the Mutiny. The **State Museum**, just to the E, is housed in the **Lal Baradari** a red sandstone building which was formerly the throne room of the Nawabs of Oudh.

To the E again is the **Nur Bakhsh Kothi** (Light Giving Palace). From the roof Havelock planned his assault to relieve the Residency. **Tara Wali Kothi** (1820s) was the bungalow of Colonel Wilcox, the astronomer of Nasir-ud-din Haidar, the seventh Nawab of Oudh (1827-37). To the N is the **Khurshid Manzil** (House of the Sun, 1800-1810), begun by Saadat Ali Khan and finished by his son. It is now La Martinière Girls' School. Generals Outram, Campbell and Havelock met here in Nov 1857 to discuss the relief of the Residency. To the NE, near the banks of the Gumti River, is the **Moti Mahal** (Pearl Palace), so named because the original dome, now destroyed, resembled a pearl. It was built by Saadat Ali Khan and was later complemented with two additional buildings constructed during his son Ghazi-ud-din Haidar's (1814-27) reign. The royal fish of the Nawabs can be seen on the wrought iron gates.

Due W, the **Chattar Manzil** (Umbrella Palaces, 1820s) were royal pavilions which Davies considers 'impressive if ill-disciplined architectural hybrids'.

The southern group

Near the Gomti lies the **Shah Najaf**, the tomb of Ghazi-ud-Din Haidar (r.1814-27), a pleasant white domed building with elaborate interior decorations. During Mohurram it is illuminated. The Nawab's tomb is flanked by those of his two wives. Wajid Ali Shah's (r 1847-56) pleasure garden Sikanderbagh is a short distance to the W.

To the S of these two are **Wingfield Park**, laid out by Sir Charles Wingfield, Chief commissioner of Oudh (1859-66), which contains a marble pavilion and statues that were once housed in the **Kaisarbagh Palace**. **Christchurch** (1860), a memorial to the Europeans killed during the Mutiny is nearby, along with the large Legislative Council Chamber (1928) and **Raj Bhawan** or Government House (1907), the former residence of the Commissioner of Lucknow and reputedly haunted by Major Hodson who was brought here to die in Mar 1858.

Some distance further to the W are the **Dilkusha** (Heart's Delight), a Shooting Bax located in what was a well stocked game park. The scene of some fierce fighting, Major-General Sir Henry Havelock died here on 18 Nov 1857. There are a number of European graves. To the E is the abandoned **Wilaiti Bagh** which was laid out by Nasir-ud-Din Haidar (r.1827-37). Finally, there is **Constantia**, now La Martinière's School, the former country residence of Major-General Claude Martin (1735-1800) who acted as an intermediary between the Nawab and the British. The main building has five storeys and extensive wings. The façade is bastioned and loopholed. In the central room there is a bust of Martinière and he is buried in the crypt. It is now a school endowed by funds set aside by Martin and there are similar at Calcutta and Lyons, his birthplace. This is not an open monument but permission may be sought at the school to look around.

Hotels **B** *Clarks Avadh*, 8 Mahatma Gandhi Marg. T 40131-3, Cable: Avadh, Telex: 0535-243 Htlc in. 98rm. 15 km airport, 5 km rly, 1 km centre. Very good restaurant, exchange, hairdresser, secretarial services, car hire, credit cards,TV. The best hotel in town, and very good shops. **D** *Capoor's Hotel and Restaurant*, 52 Hazratganj. T 43958. 24 a/c rm. 14 km airport, 4 km rly, centre location. Restaurant, laundry, travel, TV,. Old world and a little neglected. **D** *Carlton*, Shahnajaf Rd. T 44021-4, Cable: Carlton, Telex: 0535-217. 66 a/c rm, some with TV. 15 km airport, 4 km rly, 1 km centre. Restaurant, bar, exchange, laundry, beauty parlour, secretarial services, house doctor, car hire, Amex, Diners. Palatial exterior and lawns but neglected inside. Large rooms and close to market. **D** *Gomti* (UPSTDC), 6 Sapru Marg. T 34282. 30 rm, some a/c. Restaurant, bar. Clean, attentive service. Good value. **D** *Kohinoor*, 6 Station Rd. T 35421-5, Cable: Dapna, Telex: 0535-227. 52 rm, central a/c. 12 km airport, 1 km rly, central. Restaurant. Clean and good service.

D *Mohan*, Char Bagh. T 52251. 80 rm, some a/c. 10 km airport, near rly, 2 km centre. Daytime rm service, laundry, car hire, travel, Diners. **D** *Charan International*, 16 Vidhan Sabha Marg, T 47221, 47219. 52 rm, some a/c with TV. Restaurant, 24 hr rm service, car hire, travel. **D** *Ellora*, 3 Lalbagh, T 31307-8, Cable: Ellora. 22 a/c rm. Restaurant. Overpriced in its category. **D** *Deep Avadh*, Naka Hindola Aminabad Rd. T 36521-6, 36 rm, some a/c with TV. 24 hr rm service, laundry. **D** *Gulmarg*, Dr B.N. Verma Rd, Aminabad. T 321227-9, Cable: Hotel Gul. 53 rm, some a/c. Restaurant, 24 hr rm service, TV in restaurant, travel. **D** *Deep*, 5 Vidhan Sabha Marg, T 48814, Cable: Deep. 52 rm, some a/c. TV in some rooms, restaurant, bar, 24 hr rm service, laundry. **D** *Raj*, 9 Vidhan Sabha Marg, T 44232. 40 rm, some a/c. 18 hr rm service.

E *Central*, Jhandewala Park, Aminabad. T 42525, 44558. 54 non a/c rm, some with bath. **E** *Mayur*, opp rly station, Charbagh, T 50464. 16 rm, some a/c. 24 hr rm service. **E** *Mohan*, Charbagh. T 52251. 80 non a/c rm. Restaurant, TV lounge. **E** *Ram Krishna*, opp Jawahar Bhawan, Ashok Marg. T 49827. 25 non a/c rm. 18 hr rm service. **F** *Railway Retiring Rooms*, Charbagh station. **F** *YMCA*, Rana Pratap Marg, T 47227.

Restaurants *Falaknuma*, Clarks Avadh, T 40131. Specialises in regional dishes. Indian classical music during meals and some tables with a good view. *Gulfam* there serves continental and it also has a *Kebab corner*. *Continental Mashal*, Carlton, T 44021. *Sapna*, Kohinoor, T 35421. *Mehfil*, Charan International, T 47221. *Seema*, Ellora, T 31307. *Gulmohar* Restaurant and *Gulstan* for snacks in Hotel Gulmarg, T 31227. Indian and Continental: *Gazal*, Deep, T 36441. Indian *Satkar*, Mohan, T 52251. Indian *Royal Cafe*, Hazratganj. Good. *Indian Coffee House*, Hazratganj. Indian: *Mayuram* Hussunganj. *Ritz*

Continental, Ashok Marg, opp Jawahar Bhavan and *Kwality*, Haratganj for meals and fast food. *Simon*, Vidhan Sabha Marg. Chinese.

Note Certain days, the first and seventh day of the month and public holidays, are declared "dry" i.e. no alcohol is served.

Banks Weekdays 1000-1400, Sat 1000-1200. *Allahabad*, GPO Crossing, Hazratganj, T 42187; *Andhra*, Aminabad, T 46668; *Bank of Baroda*, Hazratganj, T 44417 *Bank of India*, Hazratganj, T 33060; *Bank of Maharashtra*, 21 Vidhan Sabha Marg, T 46101; *Canara*, 31-32 Halwasia Complex, Hazratganj, T 47743; *Central Bank of India*, Vidhan Sabha Marg, T 44019; *Dena*, Hazratganj, T 32584. *State Bank of India*, Hazratganj, T 34463.

Shopping Usually open 1000-1930. Lucknow is famous for *chikan** work, embroidery of fabrics, silversmiths, gold zari and sequin work. Available from *Lal Behari Tandon* Chowk. Main shopping areas are Hazratganj, Aminabad and Chowk. *Gangotri*, UP Handicrafts, Hazratganj *UPICA*, Hazratganj *Khadi Gram Udyog Bhawan*, Hazratganj *Black Partridge*, Haryana Emporium, Hazratganj *Maharashtra Handlooms*, Hazratganj *Co-optex*, Tamil Nadu Handlooms, Hazratganj *Kashmir Government Arts Emporium*, Hazratganj. *Kannauj* and *Asghar Ali* Nr Chowk for Indian perfumes and *attar*. In Nakhas, one of the old areas of Lucknow, many thousands of birdsellers live and do business.

Photography *C. Mull and Co.*, Ashok Rd, T 42641.

Local Transport There are no metered yellow-top taxis. **Private taxis** are available from Lucknow Car Taxi Owners Association, Station Rd, and hotels and agencies. Tariff: Full day (8 hr, 80 km) Rs 140. Half day (4 hr, 40 km) Rs 80. **Tempo-rickshaws** run on fixed routes and are a convenient mode of transport with an extensive network. Tariff: per stage Re 0.75-1. **Cycle-rickshaws** and **Horse Tongas** are widely available, rates negotiable. **City Bus Service**, extensive network. Min fare Re 0.50. UPSRTC Bus stand – Local, Char Bagh, T 50988; **Long distance**, Kaiser Bagh, T 42503.

Sports **Golf Course**, Kalidas Marg; **Watersports Club**, New Hyderabad. **Race Course**, Cantt. **Swimming** Pools at KD Singh Baba Stadium and Hotel Clarks Avadh.

Museums **State Museum** Banarsi Bagh T 35542 Open 1030-1730 Closed Mon. The oldest museum in UP and one of the richest in India. The collection contains pieces from the 1st-11th centuries and includes stone sculptures from Mathura, busts and friezes from Allahabad and Garhwa, Hindu, Buddhist and Jain works. Relics of the British Raj have been unceremoniously dumped in the back yard of the museum by the scooter stand, where you can see a range of marble sculptures of former British citizens, removed at the time of Independence when they were replaced by statues deemed to be more appropriate. **Motilal Nehru Children's Museum** Station Rd Charbagh Open 1030-1730. Closed Mon. Special collection of dolls. **Geological Survey of India Museum** Mahatma Gandhi Marg Open 1000-1600. **Picture gallery** Hussainabad Open 1000-1630 Closed Sun and public holidays. **Lalit Kala Academy** Lal Baradari Kaiser Bagh Open 1000-1700

Parks and Zoos *Botanical Gardens of National Botanical Research Institute* Shahnajaf Imambara.

Useful Numbers Police: T 100, 49999 Fire: T 101 Ambulance: T 102 *Foreigners' Regional Registration Office* 5th floor Jawahar Bhavan Ashok Marg

Hospitals and Medical Services *KG Medical College Hospital*, Chowk, T 82303 *Dufferin Hospital (Women)*, Golaganj, T 44050.

Post and Telegraph Open 0930-1730. *General Post Office*, GPO Square, Vidhan Sabha Marg T 42887 *Head Post Office*, New Hyderabad, T 40061 *Head Post Office*, Mahanagar, T 47771. Post Office Chowk T 82502

Places of Worship *Hindu*: Hanuman Mandir, Aliganj. *Muslim*: Jama Masjid, Hussainabad *Christian*: Cathedral Church, Hazratganj; Methodist Church, Lalbagh *Sikh*: Gurudwara, Guru Gobind Singh Marg *Buddhist*: Budh Vihar, Latouche Rd.

Travel Agents and Tour Operators *Travel Corporation of India*, 3 Shahnajaf Marg, T 33212 *Swan Travels* (P) Ltd, 50 Hazratganj, T 44150, 43859 *Janta Travels*, Hotel Clarks Avadh, M.G. Rd, T 46171 *Civica Travel Consultants*, Hotel Charan International, Vidhan Sabha Marg, T 35409 *Iyer and Sons*, Halwasia Market, Hazratganj.

Tour Operators *UP State Tourism Development Corporation*, 3 Naval Kishore Rd, T 48349, *Garhwal Mandal Vikas Nigam*, 2A/1 Rana Pratap Marg, T 47270 *Holiday Nepal*, Hotel Carlton, Shahnajaf Marg *Hollywood (India) Travel*, Mayfair Bldg, 29 Hazratganj, T 46559.

Tourist Office and Information *UP Govt. Tourist Office*, Hotel Gomti Complex, 6 Sapru Marg, T 46205. Open 1000-1700. *UP Govt. Tourist Reception Centre*, Railway Station (Northern Railway), Charbagh, T 52533. Open 1000-1700.

Air Indian Airlines flies daily from Delhi, Bombay, Calcutta, Allahabad, Gorakhpur, Patna, and Ranchi. Five times a week from Kanpur, and three times a week from Ahmedabad. Amousi airport is 14 km from the city centre. Offices: Indian Airlines, Hotel Clarks Azadh, 8 Mahatma Gandhi Marg. Booking and Reservations T 44030. Open 1000-1300 and 1400-1630. Airport, T 51030. **Vayudoot**, Civica Travel Consultants, Hotel Charan, Vidhan Sabha Marg, T 35409. Telex: 0535-436 Fast In.

Rail Lucknow is serviced by the the Northern and North-Eastern railway networks. **Old Delhi:** *Avadh-Assam Express* 5609, daily, 0540, 9 hr 5 min. From Old Delhi: *Avadh-Assam Express* 5610, daily, 0850, 8 hr 50 min. **New Delhi:** *Lucknow Mail* 4229, daily, 2200, 8 hr 45 min; *Gomti Express* 2419, daily except Tue, 0515, 8 hr 10 min. **Bombay (VT):** *Kushi Nagar Express* 1016, daily, 1125, 28 hr 35 min. **Calcutta** (Howrah): *Amritsar-Howrah Express* 3050, daily, 1155, 27 hr 50 min; *Amritsar-Howrah Mail* 3006, daily, 1120, 21 hr 45 min; *Doon Express* 3010, daily, 0850, 23 hr 30 min. **Agra Fort** *Avadh Express* 5063, daily, 2150, 7 hr 40 min. From Agra Fort: *Avadh Express* 5064, daily, 2202, 8 hr 30 min. **Agra Cantt** *Ganga-Yamuna Express* 4283/4213/1187, daily, 2035, 8 hr 5 min. **Jhansi** *Pushpak Express* 2134, daily, 2010, 6 hr 20 min; *Chhapra-Gwalior Mail* 1144, daily, 070, 7 hr 5 min; *Kushi Nagar Exp* 1016, daily, 1125, 5 hr 35 min. **Allahabad** *Nauchandi Exp* 4012, daily, 0610, 4 hr 45 min; *Ganga-Gomti Exp* 2416, daily, 1800, 3 hr 55 min. **Dehra Dun** *Doon Exp* 3009, daily, 1915, 12 hr 45 min; *Varanasi-Dehra Dun Exp* 4265, daily, 1955, 13 hr 50 min.

Bhopal *Pushpak Exp* 2134, daily, 2010, 11 hr 10 min; *Kushi Nagar Exp* 1016, daily 1125, 12 hr. **Varanasi** *Kashi Vishwanath Exp* 4058, daily, 2320, 7 hr 40 min; *Lucknow-Varanasi Varuna Exp* 2428, daily, 1815, 4 hr 45 min. **Kanpur** *Sabarmati Exp* 9166, daily, 2150, 2 hr 50 min; *Ganga-Yamuna Exp* 4283, Mon,Wed,Th,Sat, 1950, 3 hr 30 min; *Ganga-Yamuna Exp* 4213, Tue,Fri,Sat, 0110, 1 hr 35 min. **Jabalpur** (for Kanha): *Chitrakot Exp* 5010, daily, 1625, 16 hr 50 min. **Kathgodam** (from Nainital): *Nainital Exp* 5308, daily, 2135, 11 hr. **Gorakhpur** (for Nepal): *Vaishali Exp* 2554, daily, 0350, 4 hr 55 min; *Sabarmati Exp* 9165, daily, 0550, 5 hr; *Kushi Nagar*, 1115, daily, 1550, 5 hr 10 min. Charbagh railway station is 3 km from the centre of town. **Northern Railway Enquiries** T 51234; Reservations 1st Class T 57833, 2 nd Class T 51488. **North-Eastern Railways Enquiries** T 51433; **Reservations** T 51383. Reservations open: weekdays 0830-1530 and 1600-1930, Sundays 0830-1530.

Road Lucknow is at an important intersection of NH24, NH25 and NH28. From: **Delhi** (569 km); **Agra** (369 km); **Calcutta** (963 km); **Allahabad** (237 km); **Kanpur** (79 km); **Khajuraho** (320 km); **Varanasi** (286 km).

Bus Lucknow is connected to major tourist centres in the region by regular bus services. UPSRTC Bus Stand at Charbagh, opp Railway Station. Travel Reservations: UPSRTC Bus Stand, Charbagh; UPSRTC Bus Stand, Kaiserbagh, T 42503.

Excursions *Dudhwa National Park* (150-182 m), 238 km N of Lucknow, is very similar to its better known neighbour, the Corbett National Park. The terrain and vegetation is that of the terai. With an area of 613 sq km and bordering the Sarda River, Dudhwa has tigers, leopards, sambar, swamp deer and nilgai. It is famous for its sloth bears (Melursus ursinus). Like Corbett, it has a rich birdlife. The park is open from 15 Nov to 15 Jun and the best season for viewing the large game is Mar to Jun. The main tourist centre and entry point is **Dudhwa**.

Hotels There is a range of fairly basic accommodation, all run by the Forest Department. At Dudhwa there is a *Forest Rest House, Swiss Cottage Tent, Huts and Dormitory*. At other places in the park, i.e. Sathiana, Bankatti, Sonaripur and Kila, there is a *Forest Rest House*. A/c is available in some of the rooms at a small extra charge. **Reservations:** Chief wildlife Warden, U.P., 17 Rana Pratap Marg, Lucknow. T 46140, Cable: Wildlife; Director Dudhwa National Park, Lakhimpur Kheri, U.P. T 2106. If a reservation is to be made, 15 days prior notice is required and 30% of the accommodation charge as a deposit.

Restaurants Only *Dudhwa* has a restaurant. At the other places there are cooking facilities (crockery and utensils). Provisions must be brought in. At Palia (5 km) there are restaurants.

Local Transport Jeeps can be hired from the National Park Office at Dudhwa at Rs 4 per km plus 15% passenger tax. **Elephants** are available at Dudhwa only. Rs 25 per person for trip lasting approximately 2 hr. Each elephant carries 4 persons. Minimum charge Rs 50 (i.e. 2 people must ride or one person must pay double). On arrival at the park, it is advisable to make a elephant ride booking.

Tourist Office and Information Reception Centre, Dudhwa National Park, Lakhimpur Kheri, U.P. T 2106. Near District Magistrate's residence. Wildlife Warden, Dudhwa National Park, Palia. T 185. Reception Centre, Dudhwa. T 182. Tours available in season. **Entrance fees** For first three days Indians Rs 10, foreigners Rs 35. Subsequently Indians Rs 5 per day, foreigners Rs 12. Students Rs 2 per day. **Movie camera charge** Rs 50 per visit. **Vehicle charge**: Heavy (truck, bus) Rs 20, light (car, van) Rs 5 per visit.

Bank There is a *State Bank of India* at **Palia**, medical facilities at Dudhwa and Palia, a Post and Telegraph office at Palia and a **Post Office** at Dudhwa.

Air The nearest airports are Lucknow (238 km) and Bareilly (260 km).

Rail Dudhwa is on the NE Railway metre gauge line and is connected with Lucknow and Nainital from Mailani (approx. 45 km from the park). A branch line from Mailani links places in the park.

Bus UPSTRC buses connect Palia (5 km from the Park) with Lakhimpur Kheri, the local centre, and Lucknow.

170 km NE from Lucknow, **Srivasti** was an important city during the time of Buddha who lived and preached at the monastery of **Jetavana**. After his death the monastery enjoyed royal patronage, particularly from **Asoka** and it remained active until the 11th century. Remains of the city and monastery are around the current villages of Maheth and Seth which are no more than half a kilometre apart. **Maheth** on the banks of the **Achiravati River** consists of an earthen embankment and the ruins of two stupas and temples. Seth contains the remains of the Jetavana monastery. The nearest centres for rail travel and accommodation are Bahraich to the W and Balrampur to the E.

Hotels E *Hotel Maya*, a TCI hotel, and a *Tourist Bungalow* at Balrampur. At **Sravasti** itself there are several pilgrim guesthouses (all **F**) *PWD Inspection Bungalow, Burmese Temple Rest House, Chinese Temple Rest House, Jain Dharamsala*.

To continue the route from Lucknow take the **NH28** E through **Barabanki** (7 km) and continue to Ramsanchi Ghat (33 km), where the road crosses the River Kalyani. Head straight on to **Mohammadpur** (35 km) and **Faizabad** (32 km) which was once the capital of Oudh and was also called Bungle. Shuja-ud-Daula (1754-75), the third Nawab of Oudh lived here and built Fort Calcutta here after his defeat by the British as Buxar in 1764. His widow Bahu Begum remained in Faizabad while his successor Asaf-ud-Daula moved to Lucknow.

The town is situated of the S bank of the Ghaghara River. **Bahu Begum's Mausoleum** (c.1816) is 'the finest mausoleum in UP' according to Rushbrook Williams. He was obviously forgetting Agra! The tomb is 42 m high and in white marble. There are no inscriptions. The **Gulab Bari** (Mausoleum of Shuja-ud-Daula, c.1775) is nearby, and probably influenced the design of Bahu Begum's. It also contains the tombs of his mother and father.

A region of myths The whole region is rich with myth, and many of the stories in the Ramayana are supposed to have taken place here. Guptar Park, for example, is where **Rama** is believed to have disappeared. The story of his birth illustrates how his origins have been traced back to **Vishnu**. Rajagopalachari summarises the account of how Rama's father, **Dasaratha**, unable to have children by any of his wives, was instructed to perform a great sacrifice in order that his wives might conceive. At the same time there was great trouble in the home of the gods, for **Ravana**, the king of the demons, had been assured by Brahma that he could never be harmed by a human, or by "devas and other supernatural beings". As a result he was causing havoc on earth. When the gods learned of this promise they turned to Vishnu and begged him to be born as a man so that he could put an end to Ravana and his trouble-making. Vishnu agreed that he would be born as four sons of Dasaratha, who was then performing his sacrifice.

Rajagopalachari goes on: "As the ghee was poured into the fire and the flames shot up to meet it, from out of the flames came a majestic figure, resplendent like the noonday sun, holding a bowl of gold. Calling King Dasaratha by name, the figure said: 'The Devas are pleased with you and are answering your prayer. Here is payasam sent by the gods for your wives. You will be blessed with sons if they drink of this divine beverage.' With joy unbounded, Dasaratha received the bowl as he would receive a child and distributed the payasam to his three wives, Kausalya, Sumitra, and Kakeyi. He asked Kausalya to drink a half of the payasam and he gave half of what remained to Sumitra. Half of what was then left was drunk by Kaikeyi, and what remained was given to Sumitra again. Dasaratha's wives were happy, even as a beggar suddenly coming upon buried treasure. And in due course all of them were expectant mothers. In course of time" the story goes on "Dasaratha's sons were born. Rama, of Kausalya and Bharata of Kaikeyi. Sumitra gave birth to twins, Lakshmana and Satrughna, she having drunk the divine payasam. In proportion to the quantity of payasam drunk by the respective mothers, the sons are traditionally considered to be parts of Visnu. Rama was thus half Vishnu."

The road continues E from Faizabad to **Ayodhya** (6 km), now regarded by many Hindus as the birthplace of Rama. The historian Romila Thapar stresses that there is no evidence for such a belief. Jains believe that it is the birth place of the first and fourth Tirthankaras, and the Buddha is also believed to have stayed in the town for some time. The town's name means "that which cannot be subdued by war". Situated on the banks of the **Gaghara River**, Ayodhya is one of the seven holy Hindu cities – see also Mathura, Haridwar, Varanasi, Ujjain (Madhya Pradesh), Dwarka (Gujarat) and Kanchipuram (Tamil Nadu). According to Hindu belief, **Ram Chandra** once reigned here as the capital of Rama. In view of the special significance of the site to Hindus, the Archaeological Survey of India and the Indian Institute of Advanced Study started on a project in 1978 to explore the town's origins which is still continuing.

The ancient site Little remains of the ancient settlement. The ruins have a circumference of between 4 and 5 km, rising at some places to 10 metres above the ground. The excavations carried out so far, according to the project's director Professor B.B. Lal suggest that "the site came under occupation at a time when the **Northern Black Polished Ware** of a very high quality and in a variety of shades – steel grey, blue, silvery and golden – was in use. It is now possible to distinguish at least two stages in the history of this ware, and the first occupation at Ayodhya would belong to the earlier stage...The houses were made of wattle and daub or of mud. The use of kiln-burnt brick for house construction was not in evidence. Both iron and copper were in use. Although no Carbon 14 dates for the earliest levels at Ayodhya are yet available those available from other sites suggest that...the beginning of the Northern Black Polished Ware may go back to circa 7th century BC if not earlier."

At later levels of the site some interesting finds have been made, including a Jain figure from the 4th-3rd century B.C., possibly the earliest Jain figure found in India. Houses during this period were built in kiln baked brick, and various coins have been found from periods up to the 4th century AD. Some of the finds in this latter period suggest extensive trade with eastern India. The trenches excavated to date have not revealed any evidence of occupation between the 5th and 10th centuries AD, although both Fa-Hien and Hiuen Tsang are said to have visited it in the 5th and 7th centuries respectively. B.B. Lal goes on: "within a couple of centuries after the re-occupation of the site around the 11th century the usual medieval glazed wares appear on the scene. Since the medieval times the site has struggled on in one way or another, many of the now standing temples having been erected during the past two centuries only."

In accordance with Muslim practice elsewhere, a number of temples were razed and mosques were built on the site, often using the same building material. In recent years Ayodhya has become the focus of intense political activity by the **Vishwa Hindu Parishad**, an organisation which wants to assert a form of militant Hinduism. Violence between Muslims and Hindus flared in Ayodhya in 1990 because the VHP and the Bharatiya Janata Party, its leading party political ally, claimed that Ayodhya was "Ramajanambhumi" – Rama's birthplace. This is beneath the **Babri Mosque mosque** built by Babur, though deserted now for many years. The demands that a temple should be built on the spot caused widespread tension between the Hindu and Muslim communities in 1990-1991. Other sites associated with Rama are **Janam Sthana** where the god was raised and **Lakshmana Ghat** where Rama's brother committed suicide. Hanuman's Fortress takes its name from the Hanuman and Sita temple and the massive walls surrounding it. Other temples are Kala Rama and Kanak Bhavan.

Warning In Aug 1991 there was still fierce dispute over the building of a temple, sometimes accompanied by riots and extensive violence. Check on the situation if you plan to visit.

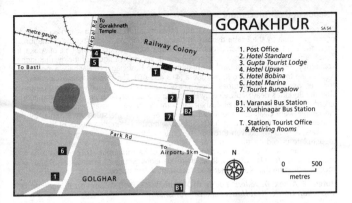

GORAKHPUR SA 54

1. Post Office
2. Hotel Standard
3. Gupta Tourist Lodge
4. Hotel Upvan
5. Hotel Bobina
6. Hotel Marina
7. Tourist Bungalow

B1. Varanasi Bus Station
B2. Kushinagar Bus Station

T. Station, Tourist Office & Retiring Rooms

0   500
metres

Hotels E *Tourist Bungalow*, Nr. Railway station; F *Saket*, near the railway station. Rooms and dormitory. Cheap. F *Railway retiring room*. There is a *Circuit House* at Faizabad (nr the Bus Stand), which may be available if government officers are not using it.

Rail Varanasi: *Ganga-Yamuna Exp* 4284, Tue,Wed,Fri, Sun, 1055, 3 hr 50 min; New Delhi-Varanasi Exp 2450, Mon,Th,Sat, 0910, 3 hr 5 min.

From **Ayodhya** the road crosses the **Ghaghara River** (2 km) and passes through **Katragundu** (4 km), **Basti** (55 km), **Munderwa** (26 km), **Khalilabad** (13 km), to **Sarjanwa** (15 km). It then crosses the **Rapti River** (13 km) before reaching **Gorakhpur** (4 km).

Gorakhpur (Population 390,000) is the last major Indian town travellers bound for Nepal pass through. The British and the Gurkha armies clashed in the region around the town in the early 18th century. Later it became the recruitment centre for Gurkha soldiers enlisting into the British and Indian armies. It is a delightful centre and a major railway maintenance town. It is also a pilgrimage centre for certain Hindu *sannyasis* and for the Gorakhnath Temple.

Hotels The hotels here cater for the budget traveller. The **E** *Modern* near the bus and railway stations is good as is the **E** *Standard* Opposite the bus station. The **F** *Gupta Tourist Lodge* opp the bus station is cheaper. The **E** *York* is in the city centre. There are also *Railway Retiring Rooms* and Government *inspection Bungalows* and *Dak Bungalows*.

Air Indian Airlines and Vayudoot connect Lucknow with Gorakhpur. The airport is 7 km from the town centre.
   Rail Lucknow: *Vaishali Exp* 2553, daily, 1735, 4 hr 50 min; *Sabarmati Exp* 9166A, daily, 1525, 6 hr; *Kushi Nagar Exp* 1016, daily, 0600, 5 hr. Varanasi: *Exp* 3020/5449, daily, 1515, 6 hr 20 min; *Triveni Exp* 5206/5405, daily, 1920, 6 hr 45 min; *Fast Passenger*, 1143/81, daily, 0305, 8 hr 35 min. **Bombay (to VT)**: *Kushi Nagar Exp* 1016, daily, 0600, 34 hr 20 min
   Bus There are buses to Lucknow, Varanasi (205 km, 5-6 hr), Patna and other towns in the region. Buses for **Nautanwa** (95 km, 3-4 hr) start from the bus stand near the railway station. At **Nautanwa** you can hire a **rickshaw** to take you through customs and to **Bhairawa** (6 km), the first town in Nepal. There are buses to **Pokhara** from **Sunail** which is just over the border.

Excursion *Kushinagar*, 55 km E of Gorakhpur on NH28 is celebrated as the place where the Buddha died and was cremated and passed away into *Parinirvana**. It was known in ancient times as Kushinara and was a small town of no great significance in the Malla Kingdom. The actual site of the original town has not been established, but the site of the Buddha's death was one of the four major sites of Buddhist pilgrimage. On the Buddha's death monasteries were established which flourished until the last Buddhist monastery was destroyed at

Nalanda in the 13th century.

The most interesting of the structures is the **Mukutabandhana Stupa** which according to legend was built by the **Malla** dynasty to house the Buddha's relics after the cremation. 1 km to the W the core of the smaller **Nirvana stupa** could go back to the time of Asoka. In front is a renovated shrine in which there is a large recumbent figure of the dying Buddha. Apparently, this was made in Mathura and brought to Kushinagar by Haribala, a monk who lived during the reign of King Kumargupta (413-455 AD). The *stupas, chaityas* and *viharas,* however, were 'lost' for centuries. The Chinese pilgrim Fa Hien, visited the town 9 centuries after the Buddha's death, followed by Hiuen Tsang, a century later and then I Tsing and all recorded the decay and ruins of Kushinagar. A thousand years passed before the *stupa* and the temple were cleared in the 1880s and excavations of the stupa were begun by the Archaeological Survey of India in 1904-5, following clues left in the writings of the Chinese travellers. A shaft was driven through the centre of the stupa "which brought to light a copper-plate placed on the mouth of a relic casket in the form of a copper vessel with charcoal, cowries, precious stones and a gold coin of Kamaragupta I." The whole area was occupied until the 11th century. In all there are eight groups of monasteries, stupas and images, indicating that Kushinagar was a substantial community.

Hotels E *Ashok Travellers' Lodge* (ITDC run), T 38. PWD *Inspection Bungalow*, LRP *Inspection House*, *Rest Houses* and *Dharamshalas*.

Bus There are **buses** and taxis from Gorakhpur (2 hr).

From Gorakhpur the shortest route into Nepal is to go N to Pharenda crossing the Nepalese border by the much less-used route across the Nepalese border at **Sonauli.** 5 km out of **Gorakhpur** the road passes the Gorakhanath Temple on the left. Keep straight on to **Campierganj** (29 km). 7 km out of Campierganj is the left turn to **Nowgarh** (32 km) and **Lumbini** (65 km) just across the Nepalese border, and the birthplace of the Buddha. However, this border crossing is not open at the moment and you have to continue to **Pharenda** (9 km) and **Sonauli** (50 km). It is easy to travel this route by bus to the border and across into Nepal and to Pokhara – see page 1335.

DELHI TO VARANASI VIA ALIGARH, KANPUR AND ALLAHABAD

This route runs along the historic **Grand Trunk Rd (NH2)** through the heart of the Ganga-Yamuna doab. It is relentlessly flat, but passes through Kanpur and other interesting places on its way to Varanasi, India's most sacred city, on the bank of the Ganga.

The United Provinces Gazetteer of 1908 summed up the landscape with great clarity: "a level plain, the monotony of which is broken only by the numerous village sites and groves of dark olive mango trees which meet the eye in every direction. The great plain is, however, highly cultivated, and the fields are never bare except in the hot months, after the spring harvest has been gathered, and before the rainy season has sufficiently advanced for the autumn crops to have appeared above the ground. The countryside then puts on its most desolate appearance; even the grass withers, and hardly a green thing is visible except a few patches of garden crops near the village sites, and the carefully watered fields of sugar cane. At this time the dhak trees burst forth with brilliant scarlet flowers.... With the breaking of the monsoon in the middle or end of June the scene changes as if by magic; the turf is renewed, and tall grasses begin to shoot in the small patches of jungle. Even the salt plains put on a green mantle, which lasts for a very short time at the close of the rains. A month later, the autumn crops – rice, the millets and maize – have begun to clothe the naked fields. These continue to clothe the ground till late in the year, and are succeeded by the spring crops – wheat, barley, and gram. In March they ripen and the great plain is then a rolling sea of golden corn, in which appear islands of trees and villages."

There are two main routes to Kanpur by road. Although slightly further it is probably quicker to take the **NH2** to Agra. The Grand Trunk Rd crosses the Yamuna and goes through **Firozabad** and **Etawah** and then across the doab to **Kanpur**. The alternative is to cross the Yamuna in Delhi and travel S from **Ghaziabad** to **Aligarh**. The road crosses the *doab* to the Ganga, which you finally see a few km beyond **Kannauj** (356 km).

Cross the Yamuna bridge and follow the road through **Shahdara** to **Ghaziabad**. Take a right turn on leaving Ghaziabad for **Dadri** (17 km) and **Sikandrabad** (17 km). At the small town of **Bhur** (17 km) there is a road to the left to the important market town of **Bulandshahr** (3 km from the turning). Go straight on to **Khurja** (16 km), **Somna** (23 km) and **Aligarh** (23 km).

Aligarh Population 370,000 Altitude 200 m. The name means "the high fort". Before the first Muslim invasion Aligarh was a Rajput stronghold. From 1194 it was administered by Muslim Governors appointed by the King of Delhi. The Fort was built in 1524 and subsequently reinforced by French and then British engineers. With the decline of the Mughal Empire, it fell into Jat, Maratha and Rohilla hands before being taken by the British under Lord Lake in 1803. The Mutiny of 1857 quickly spread from Meerut when the 9th Native Infantry went off to join the rebels at Delhi. The British regained control five months later.

There are a number of mosques and also the **Aligarh Muslim University** which was founded by Sir Saiyad Ahmad Khan in 1875 under the name of the **Anglo-Oriental College** and modelled on the Oxford and Cambridge collegiate system.

Hotels D *Ruby*, opp Roadways Bus Stand, G.T. Rd. T 5713, Cable: Hotel Ruby. 16 rm. Close to rly and centre. Restaurant, bank, Diners card.

From Aligarh the road continues through **Nanu** (19 km) and **Sikandrarao** (18 km) to **Etah** (32 km), a district headquarters. Then across the flat plains through a series of small towns: **Malawan** (18 km), **Kurauli** (17 km) to **Bongaon** (27 km); **Bewar** (13 km), **Nabiganj** (10 km), **Chhibramau** (10 km) to **Gursahaiganj** (18 km). 17 km past Gursahaiganj is a turn on the left to *Kannauj* (3 km from turning). Kannauj was **Harsha's** capital in the 7th century and later that of the Tomar and Rathor Rajputs. **Mahmud of Ghazni** left his devastating mark in 1018 when he sacked it. **Qutb-ud-din-Aibak** took it in 1194 forcing the Rathors to flee to Rajasthan. There is little of interest however, except the Archaeological Museum with its collection of sculptures from the area, some dating from the 1st and 2nd centuries AD, the Shrine of Raja Ajaipal (1021) and the Jama Masjid which was converted from a Hindu temple by Ibrahim Shah of Jaunpur at the turn of the 15th century.

Kannauj used to be on the banks of the Ganga. Now it is several km to its S. From Kannauj the road goes SE through **Manimau** (6 km), **Bilhaur** (19 km), **Sheorajpur** (19 km) and **Kalyanpur** (24 km) to **Kanpur**.

Kanpur

Population 1.6 million (1981 census) Best season October to March. The largest city of Uttar Pradesh, Kanpur is its most important industrial centre. Cotton mills were first established there in 1869 making it one of the older factory cities of India. It is now one of the greatest industrial cities with woollen and leather industries, cotton, flour and vegetable oil mills, sugar refineries and chemical works.

	Jan	Feb	Mar	Apr	May	Jun	Jul	Aug	Sep	Oct	Nov	Dec	Av/Tot
Max (°C)	23	26	33	38	42	40	34	32	33	33	29	24	32
Min (°C)	9	11	16	22	27	29	27	26	25	20	12	9	19
Rain (mm)	23	16	9	5	6	68	208	286	202	43	7	8	881

Under the British it was one of the most important garrisons on the Ganga. During the Mutiny in Delhi, the insurgents turned towards Cawnpore as the British called it. Here they rallied under a princeling called **Nana Sahib** who bore a grievance against the British because they had not pensioned him off as handsomely as his father. He laid siege to the British community of around 1,000 people under Sir James Wheeler. After a few weeks the defenders were reduced to a few hundred through gunshot wounds, starvation and disease. Nana Sahib then offered a truce and arranged for boats to take the survivors downstream to Allahabad. When they were boarding these at Satichura Ghat, they were raked with fire and hacked down by horsemen. One boat escaped. The survivors were either butchered and thrown down a well or died of cholera and dysentery.

The reprisals were as horrible. General Sir James Neill 'was seized with an Old Testamental vision of revenge when he saw the mangled bodies down the well' (Moorhouse). Captured mutineers had to lick clean a portion of the bloody ground, and were then hanged. To break a man's caste, pork and beef were stuffed down his throat, thus condemning him to eternal damnation. More often than not, persons suspected of belonging to the Mutineer army were bayoneted on sight, regardless of whether they were armed or not. Nana Sahib escaped after pretending to commit suicide in the Ganga and is believed to have died of fever in Nepal in 1859.

Places of Interest The principal British monuments are located at the site of Wheeler's entrenchment in the SE of the city. This was the old cantonment area. The lines of the trenches are marked by inscribed stone posts. At the centre stands All Soul's Memorial Church (1862-75), a handsome Gothic style building with a campanile and spire designed by Walter Granville. The interior is cool and spacious and has an attractive stained glass window. Outside there is an enclosed pavement marking the graves of over 70 officers and men captured and executed on 1 July 1857, four days after the Satichaura ghat* massacre. In a separate Memorial Garden there is a statue by **Marochetti** and a screen designed by **Sir Henry Yule**. Originally these stood over the Bibighar well where the dismembered bodies of European women and children had been thrown. They were relocated here in 1948.

The **Satichaura Ghat** is just over 1 km NE of the church and apparently is little changed. A dusty track leads down to the river Ganga and a small Siva temple stands by it. There is a small plaque in the wall at the head of the track. In the city centre there is the **King Edward VII Memorial Hall** and **Christ Church** (1848).

Hotels B *Meghdoot*, The Mall. T 211999, Cable: Meghotel, Telex: 0325-282 A/B Mgdt In. 99 rm. 9 km airport, 3 km rly, 1 km centre. Central a/c. Restaurants, coffee shop, exchange, shops, laundry, health club and sauna, doctor on call, car hire, Amex, Diners, TV, pool, snooker. **C** *Grand Trunk*, 84/79 Grand Trunk Rd. T 245435, 249595, Cable: Pigments. 30 rm. Central a/c. Restaurant, bar, 24 hr rm service, beauty parlour, travel, pool. **D** *Atithi*, 17/11 The Mall. T 63662. A/c and non a/c rm. Restaurant, TV, 24 hr rm service, travel. **D** *Attic*, 15/198 Civil Lines, 7 a/c rm. TV in suites, room service. **D** *Gaurav*, 18/54 The Mall. T 61580, Cable: Kings, Telex: 0325-432 Ptku in, 0325-285 Fran in. 33 a/c rm. 6 km airport, 1 km rly, near centre. Restaurant , TV, laundry, doctor on call, car hire, secretarial service, Diners. Garden. **D** *Geet*, 18/174-5 The Mall. T 53647, Cable: Geetinn. 32 rm. Restaurant, TV, 24 hr rm service, travel. **D** *Meera Inn*, 37/19H The Mall. T 66821-2, Telex: 0325-328. A/c and non a/c rm. TV in

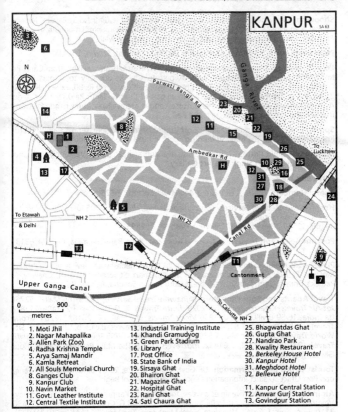

KANPUR SA 63

1. Moti Jhil
2. Nagar Mahapalika
3. Allen Park (Zoo)
4. Radha Krishna Temple
5. Arya Samaj Mandir
6. Kamla Retreat
7. All Souls Memorial Church
8. Ganges Club
9. Kanpur Club
10. Navin Market
11. Govt. Leather Institute
12. Central Textile Institute
13. Industrial Training Institute
14. Khandi Gramudyog
15. Green Park Stadium
16. Library
17. Post Office
18. State Bank of India
19. Sirsaya Ghat
20. Bhairon Ghat
21. Magazine Ghat
22. Hospital Ghat
23. Rani Ghat
24. Sati Chaura Ghat
25. Bhagwatdas Ghat
26. Gupta Ghat
27. Nandrao Park
28. Kwality Restaurant
29. Berkeley House Hotel
30. Kanpur Hotel
31. Meghdoot Hotel
32. Bellevue Hotel

T1. Kanpur Central Station
T2. Anwar Gurj Station
T3. Govindpur Station

some rooms, 24 hr rm service. **D** *Saurabh*, 24/54 Birhana Rd. T 53165, Cable: Tewaribros, Telex: 0325-317. 22 a/c rm. 8 km airport, 2 km rly. Restaurant (Indian Vegetarian, Continental), TV, exchange, car hire, travel. **D** *Swagat*, 80 Feet Rd. T 241923-7, Cable: Swagat. 19 rm, some a/c. 12 km airport, 4 km rly, centre location. Restaurant (S Indian, Mughlai, Chinese), TV, laundry, beauty parlour, travel, Diners. **D** *Yatrik*, 65/58A Circular Rd. T 60373. 15 rm, some a/c with TV. Near rly. Restaurant, doctor on call, travel, Diners **E** *Ganges*, 51/50 Nayaganj. T 69185-8. 80 non a/c rm. 12 km airport, near rly. TV in hall **E** *Godavari*, 3A Sarvodaya Nagar. T 217126-8, Cable: Wasul. 9 a/c rm. Restaurant, bar, car hire. **E** *Pandit*, 49/7 General Ganj. T 67166-8, Cable: Pandit. 45 rm a/c and non a/c rm. Restaurant (Indian veg, Chinese), doctor on call, car hire. **E** *Shivoy*, Shivoy Tower, The Mall. T 212664, Cable: Shivoy. A/c rm. Restaurant, travel.

Restaurants *Shalaka* (Hotel Maghdoot), fast food; *Gagan* (Hotel Meghdoot), Indian and Continental; *Suruchi* (Hotel Meghdoot), Chinese; *Pandal* (Hotel Grand Trunk); *Tewari* (Hotel Surabh), Indian, Continental and Vegetarian; *Sapna*, (Hotel Shivoy). *Angithi* (Hotel Atithi); *Saumya* (Hotel Geet). *Kwality*, The Mall; *Hamso*, Arya Nagar, 7/110 Swaroop Nagar; *Fu-Tu*, The Mall. Chinese. Upvan, Cantt. *Shang-hai*, The Mall, Chinese.

Banks and Exchanges *Allahabad*, Bara Chauraha, The Mall; *Dena*, Birhana Rd. *Grindlays*, Bara Chauraha, The Mall; *Indian Overseas Bank*, The Mall *Standard and Chartered*, The Mall; *State Bank of India*, The Mall.

Shopping Main shopping areas are The Mall, Birhara Rd, Gumti No.5, Parade, Naveen Market. Kanpur is famous for leather products. *UPICA*, UP Handlooms Emporium, The Mall; *Phulkari*, Punjab Emporium; *Tantuja*, Bengal Emporium, The Mall.

Photography *Chitra Studio*, Meston Rd, T 63954. *Chetan's Studio*, The Mall.

Local Transport There are no yellow-top taxis. **Private taxis** are available from Canal Rd taxi stand, hotels and agencies. Tariff: Airport to City Rs 80. City to Airport Rs 60. City/Airport/City (RT) Rs 100. Full day (8 hr) Rs 140. Half day (4 hr) Rs 80. Extra mileage Rs 2.25 per km. **Tempo-rickshaws** operate to all part of the city. Tariff: Re 0.75-1 per stage. **Auto-rickshaws, cycle-rickshaws** and **horse tongas** are available, rates negotiable. **City Bus Service**, extensive network, min fare Re 1.

Sports Green Park **Cricket** Stadium. **Golf** Course, Jajmau. Kanpur **Tennis** Club. **Billiards** Room, Hotel Orient, The Mall. **Swimming** Pools, in hotels Meghdoot and Grand Trunk.

Museums Kamla Retreat Museum, historical and archaeological. Visits only with prior approval. Shyam Hari Singhania Art Gallery.

Parks and Zoos Zoo.

Useful Numbers *Police*: T 100 *Fire*: T 44444 *Ambulance*: T 62500.

Hospital and Medical Services *Cantonment General Hospital*, T 60540 *Dufferin Hospital*, T 62500 *KPM Hospital*, T 60351 *Guru Nanak Hospital*, T 20156 *Cardiology Institute*, T 44166, 40159 *Chacha Nehru Children's Hospital*, T 62895.

Post and Telegraph Head Post Office and Telegraph Office, Bara Chauraha, T 60324, 63131 (open 24 hr).

Places of Worship *Hindu*: JK Temple, Pandu Nagar; Tapeshwari Devi Temple. *Muslim*: Mosque, Patkapur. Sikh: Gurudwara, G.T. Rd.*Christian*: St Joseph's Church, Chakery; St Patrick's Church. *Jain*: Jain Shwetambre, Maurti Poojan Sangha, Birhana Rd.

Travel Agents and Tour Operators *Nijhawan Travel Service*, 18/25 The Mall, T 52768 *Jet Air Travels*, Karachi Khana, T 212029 *Janta Travels*, 25/3 The Mall, T 212409, 212874 *Italindia*, 16/59 Civil Lines, T 211836 *Vicky Travels*, The Mall, T 212616, 212204 *Group Travels*, 17/13 The Mall, T 61642, 52788 *Pan Express Travels*, Bic Club, Chunnyganj *Sita World Travels*, 18/53 The Mall, T 52980; *Iyer and Sons*, 18/55 The Mall, T 53678 *Pacific Travels*, 37/19B The Mall, T 61432. *Indtravels*, 24/18 The Mall. *Pioneer Travels*, Hotel Gaurav, The Mall.

Tourist Office and Information UP Govt. Tourist Centre, 26/51 Birhana Rd (Back Lane), opp Post Office. District Information Office, KEM Hall, Phool Bagh.

Air Indian Airlines flies five times a week form Delhi to Kanpur, and returns via Lucknow. **Vayudoot** connects Kanpur to Delhi. Indian Airlines, opp M.G. College, Civil Lines, T 211430, 211095 Airport, T 43042. Vayudoot, Hotel Meghdoot, The Mall, T 51141 Ex 29, 211037

Rail Kanpur is on the main Broad Gauge Delhi-Calcutta line and also has lines from Lucknow, Agra and Central India. **Agra Fort**: *Avadh Exp* 5063, daily, 2335, 6 hr; *Udyan Abha Toofan Exp* 3007, daily, 0835, 5 hr 30 min. **New Delhi**: *Shatabdi Exp* 2003, Mon-Fri, 1700, 4 hr 50 min; *Howrah-Danapur Exp* 3031, daily, 0015, 6 hr 35 min; *Gomti Exp* 2419, daily except Tue, 0705, 6 hr 20 min. **Calcutta (Howrah)**: *Rajdhani Exp* 2302, daily except Th and Sun, 2215, 12 hr 30 min; *Kalka-Howrah Mail* 2312, daily, 1505, 17 hr 25 min; *Howrah Exp* 3012, daily, 0635, 23 hr 45 min. **Patna**: *Northeast Exp* 2522, daily, 1240, 8 hr 30 min; *Tinsukia Mail* 2456, daily, 0130, 9 hr. **Varanasi**: *Neelachal Exp* 8476, Tue,Th, Sun, 1220, 6 hr 30 min; *Ganga-Yamuna Exp* 4284, Tue, Wed,Fri,Sun, 0605, 8 hr 40 min; *Ganga-Yamuna Exp* 4214, Mon,Tue,Sat, 0605, 8 hr 10 min. **Lucknow**: *Ganga-Yamuna Exp* 4284, Tue,Wed,Fri,Sun, 0540, 2 hr 10 min; *Ganga-Yamuna Exp* 4214, Mon,Th,Sat, 0540, 2 hr 10 min; *Gomti Exp* 2420, daily except Tue, 2050, 2 hr; *Sabarmati Exp* 9165, daily, 0240, 2 hr 25 min.

Road On NH2 and NH25, Kanpur is connected to all parts of the country on good roads. To: **Lucknow** (79 km); **Allahabad** (193 km); **Varanasi** (329 km); **Khajuraho** (389 km); **Agra** (296 km); **Jhansi** (222 km); **Bhopal** (369 km); **Delhi** (438 km); **Calcutta** (1007 km); **Bombay** (1345 km); **Madras** (1998 km).
  Bus Buses of the UP State Road Transport Corporation (UPSRTC) and the SRTCs of neighbouring states connect Kanpur to various centres in the region, such as Lucknow, Allahabad, Varanasi, Agra, Unnao, Rae Bareli, Kannauj and Jhansi. UPSRTC Bus Stand, Collectorganj, T 63259; Chunnyganj, T 63603.

Leaving Kanpur on the **NH2** continue through **Asapur** (37 km) and cross the Pandu River. It is then 21 km to Daulatpur and 19 km to **Fatehpur** (not be confused with Fatehpur Sikri). At the end of the 18th century Fatehpur was waste land. Land revenue settlements in 1814 encouraged its further growth from a Mughal market town. The Islamic monuments are the **Tomb of Nawab Ali Khan** (late 18th century), a minister at the court of the Nawabs of Oudh, the **Jami Masjid** and **Mosque of Hakim Abdul Hasan of Kara**. Four pillars erected by a Mr Tucker who was later killed in the Mutiny stand by the road. They have the Ten Commandments and quotations from St John's Gospel carved on them in Urdu and Hindi.

From Fatehpur continue down the **NH2** through **Khaga** (35 km), **Muratganj** (51 km) and **Bamrauli** (22 km) to **Allahabad** (10 km).

Allahabad

Population 1 million *Altitude* 98 m. Area 3 sq km. Best Season Oct-Mar. Allahabad has regular flights to Delhi (643 km, 1 hr 5 min). Bamrauli airport is 10 km from the city centre.

	Jan	Feb	Mar	Apr	May	Jun	Jul	Aug	Sep	Oct	Nov	Dec	Av/Tot
Max (°C)	24	26	33	40	42	40	33	32	33	32	28	24	32
Min (°C)	8	11	16	22	27	28	27	26	25	19	12	8	19
Rain (mm)	23	15	15	5	15	127	620	254	213	58	8	8	1361

Early settlement There are several early historical sites in the city. **Draupadi Ghat**, for example, has revealed signs of extensive habitation and considerable quantities of **Northern Black Pottery Ware** of the type found across northern India to Taxila and beyond. It has been dated from between 1100 and 800 BC. Two other sites in the city have revealed similar finds. On the present site of the **Bharadwaj ashram** remains of the **Kushan period** have also been found. Allahabad was visited 500 years after that period ended by Hiuen Tsang, the Chinese traveller, in 643 AD. The Muslims first conquered it in 1194 and it received its current name in 1584. **Akbar** built the fort and Khusrau, Jahangir's eldest son, is buried in the city. The Mahrattas took the town in 1739 but held it only until 1750 when it was sacked by the Pathans. Later, it was the HQ of the British Government of the NW Provinces and Oudh and here the transfer of government from the East India Co. to the crown was announced by Lord Canning in 1858. The first Indian National Congress was held in Allahabad in 1885 with one of its founders, Allan Octavian Hulme, presiding. The Nehru family home is also here. Today Allahabad is a rapidly growing commercial and administrative city.

The confluence For Hindus Allahabad is particularly sacred because it is at the junction of the Ganga and the Jamuna – hence its other name, **Prayag** ("confluence"). Rituals of purification, based as they very often are on the simple analogy between physical and moral impurity, use water as a medium of ritual purification. The purifying power of a sacred river is thus strengthened at a confluence just as the physical power is. In addition the mythical underground river of enlightenment, the *Sarasvati*, also surfaces here. Bathing in the rivers at the prayag is auspicious at all times of the year, more so at **Magh Mela** which occurs every year for 15 days (Jan/Feb) and even more at the **Kumbh Mela**,. This festival moves every 3 years from **Allahabad**, to **Haridwar (UP)**, to **Ujjain** (MP) and **Nasik** (Maharashtra), returning to **Allahabad** every twelfth year. This *mela** (fair) is what Eric Newby has described as 'almost certainly the greatest assemblage

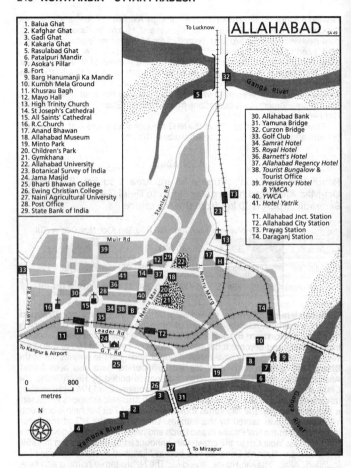

ALLAHABAD

1. Balua Ghat
2. Kafghar Ghat
3. Gadi Ghat
4. Kakaria Ghat
5. Rasulabad Ghat
6. Patalpuri Mandir
7. Asoka's Pillar
8. Fort
9. Barg Hanumanji Ka Mandir
10. Kumbh Mela Ground
11. Khusrau Bagh
12. Mayo Hall
13. High Trinity Church
14. St Joseph's Cathedral
15. All Saints' Cathedral
16. R.C.Church
17. Anand Bhawan
18. Allahabad Museum
19. Minto Park
20. Children's Park
21. Gymkhana
22. Allahabad University
23. Botanical Survey of India
24. Jama Masjid
25. Bharti Bhawan College
26. Ewing Christian College
27. Naini Agricultural University
28. Post Office
29. State Bank of India

30. Allahabad Bank
31. Yamuna Bridge
32. Curzon Bridge
33. Golf Club
34. Samrat Hotel
35. Royal Hotel
36. Barnett's Hotel
37. Allahabad Regency Hotel
38. Tourist Bungalow & Tourist Office
39. Presidency Hotel & YMCA
40. YWCA
41. Hotel Yatrik

T1. Allahabad Jnct. Station
T2. Allahabad City Station
T3. Prayag Station
T4. Daraganj Station

To Lucknow

Ganga River

Yamuna River

To Kanpur & Airport

To Mirzapur

0   800
metres

N

of people gathered together in a confined space for a single purpose anywhere on earth'. On 3 Feb 1954, it was estimated that 5 million people were present. In 1989 the *Kumbhayog**, or most auspicious time for bathing and washing away of a lifetime's sins, was 4 Feb. It is estimated that 13 million bathed in the rivers at that time. At any time of day or year you will find people bathing where the muddy waters of the Ganga meet the much clearer water of the Yamuna and the invisible water of the Sarasvati.

The story behind the Kumbh Mela is that Hindu gods and demons vied for the pot (*kumbha**) that held the nectar of immortality (*amrit**). During the fight for possession, which lasted 12 days, Vishnu was running with the pot and four drops of *amrit** fell to earth, making four sacred places. Holiest of all is Allahabad, the site of the Maha (Great) Kumbh Mela. The sangam itself is a narrow spit of land where the rivers gently mingle and is quite shallow and muddy.

Local Festivals Kumbh Mela – see Introduction.

Places of Interest For a town of such antiquity, Allahabad has few monuments pre-dating the Muslim period.

The Mughal Period The Fort was built by **Akbar** from 1583 onwards and is near Sangam. It was the largest of his forts, has three massive gateways, high (7 m) brick walls and is most impressive when viewed from across the river. Most of the fort is not accessible to tourists so the Asoka pillar (3rd century BC and, like the others, bearing the Mauryan Emperor Asoka's edicts, it was moved inside the fort under Akbar's orders) cannot be seen, nor too the Zenana (Harem) Palace. A small door in the E wall of the fort leads to the Undying Banyan Tree (Akshai Vata). Hiuen Tsang mentioned it saying that pilgrims would throw themselves from it to their death. An object of veneration, it is in a basement and little of it can be seen.

Khusrau Bagh Prince **Khusrau** was murdered in 1615 by his own brother, later the emperor **Shah Jahan** (r1627-1658). After staging an unsuccessful rebellion against his father **Jahangir** (r1605-1627) in 1607, Khusrau spent the next year in chains. Two of his closest associates were less fortunate. They were sewn into the skins of a freshly slaughtered ox and ass, mounted the wrong way round on donkeys and paraded through the streets of Lahore. The hot sun dried the skins and one died from suffocation. Khusrau himself was forced to ride an elephant down a street lined with the heads of his supporters. When freed, Khusrau undeterred encouraged a plot to assassinate his father but was discovered. Khusrau was blinded, though he did regain partial sight and spent the rest of his life as a captive. The garden is a typical Mughal garden enclosure, entered through a 18m high archway, houses the large, handsome tomb. The burial chamber is undergound and the decoration is plasterwork painted with birds, flowers and Persian inscriptions. W of the tomb is another, believed to be that of Khusrau's sister. Further W is a two-storey tomb, that of his Rajput mother.

Buildings from the British Period Canning Town, opp the Junction Railway Station, was laid out on a grid in the 1860s. Within it are the Old High Court and Public Offices, classical style buildings built in 1870 and the 13th century Gothic style All Saint's Cathedral started in 1877. At the E end of the Civil Lines is Alfred Park, founded to commemorate the visit of the Duke of Edinburgh in 1870. N of the park is **Muir College**, built 1874-1886 and regarded as a fine example of Indo-Saracenic architecture. It was later established as the University of Allahabad. W of the college is the poorly designed Mayo Memorial College (1879) and W of the park is **St Joseph's Roman Catholic Cathedral** (1879) and accompanying schools, all in the Italian style. The Holy Trinity Church (early 19th century) contains memorials from the Gwalior Campaign (1843) and the Mutiny (1857). **The New High Court** (1916) is Edwardian Baroque. W of the fort is **Minto Park** where the Royal Proclamation of the Assumption of Rule by the Crown ('the Magna Carta of India' according to Curzon) was made in 1858.

Hotels **C** *Allahabad Regency*, 16 Tashkent Marg. T 56043, Telex: 0540-216. 13 rm a/c. Restaurant (Indian, Continental, Chinese), coffee shop, TV, pool, laundry, car hire. Pleasant garden. **C** *Presidency*, 19D Sarojini Naidu Marg. T 4460. 10 rm a/c. 8 km airport, 2 km rly, 2 km centre. Restaurant (Indian, Continental, Chinese), TV, pool, 24 hr rm service, exchange, laundry, doctor on call, Diners Club, Visa. **D** *Yatrik*, 33 S.P. Marg, Civil Lines. T 56920, Cable: Yatrik. 37 rm, 30 a/c. 12 km airport, 1 km rly, 1 km centre. Restaurant (Indian, Continental, Chinese), TV, pool, car hire, travel. Really excellent value. Clean and comfortable rooms, first class, lovely pool, good service. **D** *Samrat*, 49A Mahatma Gandhi Marg. T 4854, Cable: Samrat. 30 rm, 16 a/c. 8 km airport, close rly, centre location. Restaurant (Indian, Continental, Chinese), TV, 24 hr rm service, exchange, laundry, Diners Club. **D** *Tourist Bungalow* (UPSTDC), 35 M.G, Rd, T 53640. A/c and non a/c rm. Restaurant, bar , coffee shop. **E** *Sri Gulab Mansion*, Leader Rd. T 56322. Non a/c rm. **F** *Greenwood*, Tashkent Rd, T 56274. **F** *Taossi*, 31A Stanley Rd, T 56273. **F** *Tepso*, Civil Lines, T 3635. **F** *N.C. Continental*, Katju Rd, T 5642/3. **F** *Harsh*, Civil Lines, T 4171. **F** *Central*, Chowk. Very Cheap. **F** *Milan*, Leader Rd, T 56021. **F** *Royal*, S Rd, T 2520. Large house with big rooms. **F** *Satyam*, Vivekenand Marg, T 55436. **F** Finaro, Nyaya Marg, T 2452. Also *Circuit House*, Hastings Rd. *Jal Nigam Rest House*, Sangam area. *Railway Retiring Rooms*. Doubles and dormitories.

Restaurants UPSTDC *Tourist Bungalow*, 35 M.G. Rd, T 53640. Bar and restaurant. There are a number of restaurants in the Civil Lines: *Jade Garden*, Tepso Hotel. Indian, Chinese and Continental; *Tandoor* Indian and Continental; El Chico. *Kwality* Hot Stuff, fast foods and ice-cream; *Tripti*, Katju Rd *Pallav*, Ashok Vihar.

Bar UPSTDC Tourist Bungalow, 35 M.G. Rd.

Banks *Punjab National*, Mahatma Gandhi Rd, Chowk. T 51277; Civil Lines, T 2794; Darbanga Castle, T 51658 *State Bank* of India, KYT Rd, T 53250 *Union Bank of India*, Couper Rd, T 51417 *United Bank of India*, 80-A Tagore Nagar, T 53216; *United Commercial*, 4-A Sardar Patel Marg, T 52407.

Shopping The main shopping areas are Civil Lines, Chowk and Katra.

Photography *B.R. Tandon and Co*, Flashlight and Kohli are all in the Civil Lines.

Local Transport Yellow top taxis, auto-rickshaws and cycle rickshaws are all widely available. Fares negotiable.

Entertainment Prayag Sangeet Samiti is an important music and dance training institution with indoor and outdoor auditoria.
   Cultural and musical programmes are held in the evenings.

Sports Mayo Hall Sports Complex is one of the largest sports training centres in India. Facilities available are: table tennis, basketball, badminton and volleyball.

Museums Chandra Sekhar Azad Park and **The Allahabad Museum**, Kamla Nehru Rd. Open 1100-1630. Closed Mondays. Entrance Re 0.50. This park was originally the Prince Albert Park but later renamed after the famous freedom fighter. Contains a wide range of stone sculptures (2nd century BC from Bharhut and Kausambi, 1st century AD Kushana pieces from Mathura, 4th-6th century Gupta carvings and 11th century carvings from Khajuraho). Also, a fine collection of Rajasthani miniatures, terracotta figurines and paintings by Nicholas Roerich.
   Anand Bhawan Open 1000-1700 Closed Mondays. Small charge for upstairs. The Nehru family home, given to the state by Indira Gandhi in 1970. Containing many items belonging to the family – Motilal Nehru (1861-1931), a principal player in the Independence movement, Jawaharlal Nehru (1889-1964), Independent India's first Prime Minister, **Indira Gandhi** (1917-84) and Prime Minister (1966-77, 1980-4) and her sons **Sanjay Gandhi** (died 1980) and **Rajiv Gandhi** died (1991). Next to Anand Bhawan stands Swaraj Bhawan which was given to the nation by Motilal Nehru.
   Kausambi Museum, University of Allahabad. Various artifacts from Kausambi (see Excursions) including pottery, terracotta figurines, coins, beads and bangles.

Parks and Zoos Childrens' Park; Botanical Gardens.

Useful Addresses Regional Tourist Office, 35 Mahatma Gandhi Rd, Civil Lines, T 53883 *Foreigners' Regional Registration Office*, 2A Mission Rd, Katra *U.P. Automobile Association*, 32A Mahatma Gandhi Rd, Civil Lines, T 51543.

Hospitals and Medical Services *Kamla Nehru Medical College*, Medical College Area. *Bailey Hospital*, Civil Lines *Dufferin Hospital*, Chowk.

Post and Telegraph Sarojini Naidu Marg in the cantonment, just N of All Saints Cathedral.

Places of Worship *Christian* All Saints Cathedral, CNI, Mahatma Gandhi Rd.

Travel Agents and Tour Operators *Krishna Travel Agency*, 936 Daraganj, T 51536 *Laxmi Travels*, 35 Zero Rd, T 50212. *Kant Travels*, 917 Daraganj, T 52699. *Gupta Motels (P) Ltd Travels*, 25 Muthiganj, 52577.

Tourist Offices and Information (incl Conducted Tours and Excursions) Regional Tourist Office, 35 Mahatma Gandhi Rd, Civil Lines, T 53883.

Air Indian Airlines operates a service from Delhi to Patna via Allahabad and Varanasi five days a week. This returns via Allahabad. On the other two days there is a fight from Delhi to Gorakhpur via Allahabad. The return is non-stop. Reservations: Indian Airlines, Tashkent Rd, T 2832. **Vayudoot** also connects Allahabad with Lucknow. Reservations: Vayudoot, Yatrik Hotel, Patel Rd, T 55707

Rail Allahabad is on the major broad gauge route from Delhi to Calcutta. It is also linked to other cities in N, E and central India by broad and metre gauge lines. Enquiries: Allahabad Junction, T 50815, 54057; Prayag (Broad gauge for trains for Kanpur and Lucknow); Allahabad City (for most trains to and from Varanasi), T 52202; Daraganj (Metre Gauge). **New Delhi:** *A.C. Exp* 2381, Tue,Th,Sat, 0030, 10 hr 10 min; *A.C. Exp* 2303, Mon,Wed,Fri,Sun, 0030, 10 hr 10 min; *Prayag Raj Exp* 2417, daily, 2100, 9 hr 50 min. **Bombay (VT):** *Mahanagri Exp* 1094, daily, 1510, 23 hr 40 min; *Bombay Mail* 3003, daily, 1110, 24 hr 15 min; *Varanasi-Bombay Ratnagiri Exp* 2166, Tue,Th,Fri, 2105, 26 hr 30 min. *Bhagalpur Exp* 3417, Mon,Wed,Th,Sun, 0820, 28 hr 20 min. **Calcutta (Howrah):** *Kalka-Howrah Mail* 2312, daily, 1800, 16 hr 30 min; *Udyan Abha-Toofan Exp* 3008, daily, 2245, 19 hr 30 min; *Howrah-Janata Exp* 3040, daily, 0700, 27 hr 30 min. **Jhansi:** *Bundelkhand Exp* 1108, daily, 1825, 14 hr 35 min.

Lucknow: *Nauchandi Exp* 4011, daily, 1730, 4 hr 45 min; *Ganga-Gomti Exp* 2415, daily, 0600, 3 hr 30 min. **Patna:** *Udyan Abha-Toofan Exp* 3008, daily, 2245, 6 hr 52 min; *Howrah Exp* 3012, daily, 1055, 7 hr 35 min; *Tisukia Mail* 2456, daily, 0420, 6 hr 12 min. **Varanasi:** *A.C. Exp* 2382, Tue,Th,Sat, 0230, 2 hr 45 min; *Mahanagri Exp* 1093, daily, 0035, 3 hr 25 min; *Varanasi Exp* 1027, daily, 0845, 3 hr 35 min. *Sarnath Exp* 4259, daily, 1310, 2 hr 55 min; *Bundelkhand Exp* 1107, daily, 0625, 3 hr 50 min. **Jabalpur** *Varanasi-Tirupati/Cochin Exp* 7492,7490, Tues,Fri,Sat, 1030, 5 hr 45 min – from Varanasi and via Allahabad, Lucknow, Kanpur and Satna; *Ganga-Kaveri Exp* 6040, Mon,Wed, 2105, 6 hr 20 min.

Road Allahabad is on **NH27** to Mangawan and **NH2** (The Grand Trunk Rd) from Delhi to Calcutta. It is also near NH7 which runs from Varanasi to Kanyakumari. The distances to important and neighbouring centres are: **Varanasi** (122 km), **Patna** (368 km), **Lucknow** (237 km), **Agra** (433 km), **Jhansi** (375 km), **Nagpur** (618 km), **Bhopal** (680 km), **Delhi** (643 km), **Calcutta** (799 km), **Hyderabad** (1,086 km).

Bus UPSRTC and those of neighbouring states link Allahabad with various centres in the region: Lucknow, Varanasi, Meerut, Delhi, Patna, Muzaffarpur, Rewa, Sasaram, Kanpur, Gwalior and Jhansi. There are also services operated by private companies. Roadways Bus Stations: Civil Lines, T 53443; Zero Rd, T 50192; Leader Rd, 2718. **Private bus** stands are at Ram Bagh and Leader Rd.

Excursions *Bhita*, 2 km S of the Yamuna 22 km SW of Allahabad, was the site of a trading community well before 350 B.C., the start of the Mauryan period. A series of mounds were excavated by Marshall in 1910-11. Brick structures belonging to five periods were identified but below these lie a series of occupational deposits which include Northern Black Polished Ware, proving its very early historical origins.

Kausambi

Take the **NH2** W out of Allahabad to **Bamrauli** (10 km), then the left turn which leads past the airport to **Kausambi** (35 km) on the **Chitrakoot Rd**. The enormous ruins of Kausambi are spread through several villages. Two of them – **Kosam-Inam** and **Kosam-Khiraj** – carry names that still suggest their links with the ruins of the city of Kausam. According to the epics, Kausam was founded by a descendant of the **Pandavas** who left Hastinapur when it was destroyed by floods from the Ganga. In the Buddha's time it was the capital of the Vatsa king **Udayana**. It is one of the earliest historical cities of the region. According to Hiuen Tsang the Buddha preached here and in commemoration of his visit there are two *viharas** (monasteries).

The site The site is demarcated by the remains of a wall with bastions at regular intervals. The ramparts, which form an approximate rectangle over 6 km in perimeter, still average more than 10 metres above field level, while the bastions tower up to nearly 23 metres. Originally made of mud they were later surfaced with bricks. There was also a moat which was filled with water from the Yamuna river. Excavations have revealed that the town was occupied continuously from around the 8th century BC to the 6th century AD. In the SW corner are the remains of what is thought to be a palace. The main **stupa** measured 25 m diameter and 25 m high and was built in the 5th century BC. There is also the damaged shaft of a sandstone column. This was probably erected during the rule of the Mauryan Emperor Asoka. There was another column but this was removed to Allahabad by the Mughals. When it was first discovered by Cunningham coins and terracotta figurines were scattered over the surface.

Recent discoveries Excavations have now been made by G.R. Sharma of the University of Allahabad at four main areas on the site. The earliest excavations were made near the Asokan pillar, and suggested that the first of the three periods of settlement of the site came immediately before the **Northern Black Polished Ware** period. The second period at this excavation dated back to 300 BC and included the first brick building, a road and finds of coins with the typical Kausambi "lanky bull" motifs. In the third period of occupation, dating from 175 BC to 325 AD the coins found testify to a succession of rulers; Mitras, followed by Kushan kings and then by Maghas. The road evidently continued in use up to about 300 AD and the site itself was occupied until about 400 AD. Sharma suggests that excavations in the defence area have pushed back the dates of earliest settlement as far as 1165 BC while the site appears to have been occupied as late as 580 AD. Ghosh argues that these early dates are probably unreliable and that there is no hard evidence to support them. While the dating may thus be open to question, the importance of the site itself and the remarkable evidence of enormous defensive structures is not.

Many of the coins and terracottas discovered here are now on display in the Allahabad City Museum and Kausambi Museum at the University of Allahabad. Ghosh writes that "The terracottas of Kausambi have a special place in the history of clay art of India. On the basis of manufacturing technique they can be grouped into 1. early handmade, 2. moulded and 3. later partly hand-modelled and partly moulded. The first group has grey and dull-red pieces, sometimes with applied decorations. The second group, of the 2nd – 1st century BC represents conceptional rather than realistic portrayal of figures and reflects the traits of contemporary art in dress, ornamentation etc. The third group, in the round, recalls the features of contemporary Kushan art, particularly in facial features. Important are those with elaborate decorations, mother goddesses, reclining women, dancers and drummers with peaked caps indicating Saka-Parthian influence...The handmade-cum-moulded plaques as usual belong to the early centuries of the Christian era."

From Allahabad there are two routes to **Varanasi**. The **NH2** goes straight to the N of the Ganga via Handia and Gopiganj. The more southerly route crosses the Yamuna over the Yamuna Bridge (**NH27** to **Rewa**) then turns left immediately after the bridge and runs along the S bank of the Ganga, crossing and re-crossing the railway line. The bridge over the **Tons River** (30 km) is 363 m long and was constructed in 1864. A road on the left after 7 km leads down to **Sirsa Ghat**, on the S bank of the Ganga. **Mirzapur** (58 km) was the largest grain and cotton market on the Ganga before the opening of the E Indian Railway. Good quality sandstone is quarried nearby and it has an attractive river front with ghats and temples. The town is noted for is brass industry and manufacture of woollen carpets. Approximately 7 km from Mirzapur is a Kali temple used as a rendezvous for *Thugs**.

Continue E through *Chunar* (35 km), noted for its fort built on a spur of the **Kaimur Hills**. It stands 53 m above the surrounding plain, was of obvious strategic importance, and changed hands a number of times. **Humayun** took it in 1537, **Sher Shah** relieved him of it shortly afterwards. **Akbar** recovered it for the Mughals in 1575 in whose hands it stayed until 1750 when it passed to the Nawabs of Oudh. The British stormed it in 1764 and Warren Hastings retreated to it after Raja Chait Singh's rebellion in 1781.

From Chunar it is about 30 km to **Ramnagar** which also has a fort, then 7 km to **Varanasi**, entering it from the S.

Varanasi

Population 793,542 (1981) *Altitude* 81 m *Best time for a visit* Avoid May and Jun when it is very hot and Jul-Sep when it is the monsoon. Indian Airlines connects Varanasi with Delhi (765 km, 1 hr 15 min). The airport is 22 km from the centre.

	Jan	Feb	Mar	Apr	May	Jun	Jul	Aug	Sep	Oct	Nov	Dec	Av/Tot
Max (°C)	23	37	33	39	41	39	33	32	32	32	29	25	32
Min (°C)	9	11	17	22	27	28	26	26	25	21	13	9	204
Rain (mm)	23	8	14	1	8	102	346	240	261	38	15	2	1058

Varanasi is situated on the W bank of the Ganga at a point where , seemingly perversely, it sweeps in a great bend to run due N before resuming its SE course to the sea. Without question it is India's most sacred city. It is impossible to date its origins precisely. It was probably already an important town by the 7th century BC when Babylon and Nineveh were at the peak of their power. The Buddha came to it in 500 BC and it was mentioned in both the Mahabharata and the Ramayana. Its name is a derivation of the names of two streams, the Varuna on the N side of the city and the Asi, a small trickle on the S. The name Benares is a corruption of Varanasi. It is also called Kashi, 'The City of Light', by Hindus who as a mark of respect add the suffix *-ji** to it. It is one of the Seven Sacred Cities of Hinduism (the others being, Haridwar, Mathura and Ayodhya, all of which are also in U.P., Ujjain (M.P.), Dwarka (Gujarat) and Kanchipuram in Tamil Nadu. Each year well over one million pilgrims visit it and the number of Brahmins living there is approximately 50,000.

Early settlement The earliest inhabitants of Varanasi were the Aryans who contributed to its growth as a great centre of culture, education, commerce and craftsmanship. Students from all over the country came to visit the city and its fame drew the attention of the rich and powerful. Its temples and mansions were ransacked on many occasions from the 11th to the 18th centuries. It was raided by **Muhammad of Ghazni's** army in 1033. In 1194 Qutb-ud-din Ghori defeated the local Raja's army and **Ala-ud-din Khalji**, the King of Delhi (l294-1316) destroyed temples and built mosques on their sites, and for a brief period in the 18th century it was known as Mohammadabad. Despite its early foundation hardly any building dates before the 17th century and few are more than 200 years old. Strikingly there have been no archaeological finds of any antiquity at the site.

A centre of learning Varanasi stands as the centre of Sanskrit learning in northern India. Sanskrit, the oldest of the Indo-European languages, is one of learning and religious ritual and has been sustained here long after it stopped being used as a living language elsewhere. The Sanskrit University, for example, has over 150,000 rare manuscripts. Hindu devotional movements flourished here, especially in the 15th century under Ramananda and **Kabir**, one of India's greatest poets lived in the city. *Tulsi Das* translated the Ramayana from Sanskrit into Hindi.

Handicrafts Today Varanasi is famous for ornamental brasswork, silks and embroideries and for the manufacture of glass beads, which are exported all over the world. The significance of *silk* in India's traditional life is deep-rooted. Silk was considered a pure fabric, most appropriate for use on ceremonial and religious occasions. Its lustre, softness and richness of its natural colour gave it precedence over all other fabrics. White or natural coloured silk was worn by the Brahmins and 'twice born'. Women wore bright colours and the darker hues were reserved for the Sudras or lowest caste in the hierarchy, not that many, if any, could afford it. Silk garments were worn for rites of passage like births and marriages, and offerings of finely woven silks were made to deities in temples. It has been suggested that this concept of purity may have given impetus to the growth of silk-weaving centres around ancient towns like Kanchipuram, Varanasi, Bhubaneshwar and Ujjain, a tradition that is kept alive today.

Local Festivals The city celebrates a number of special festivals. **April**. During the first month of the calendar, pilgrims perform the circumambulation of Kasi Dharmakshetra, as laid down in the scriptures. **May**. *Ganga Dasara* celebrates the day when the waters of the Ganga reached Haridwar. **Nov**. *Nagnathaiya* at Tulsi Ghat enacts the story of Krishna jumping into the Jamuna to overcome *Kalia*, the king of the Serpents. Also a fair at Chetganj to remember the occasion when Rama's brother Laksham, cut off Ravana's sister's nose when she attempted to force him into a marriage – *Nakkataiya*! At Nati Imli, *Bharat Milap*, the meeting of Rama and Bharat after a separation of 14 years is celebrated with great ceremony with the Maharaja of Varanasi attending in full regalia, on elephant back. Music festivals are mainly held in the winter months between **Dec** and **Feb**.

Places of Interest The city stands on the W bank of the Ganga and stretches back from its impressive waterfront in a confusion of narrow alleys (*gali**),

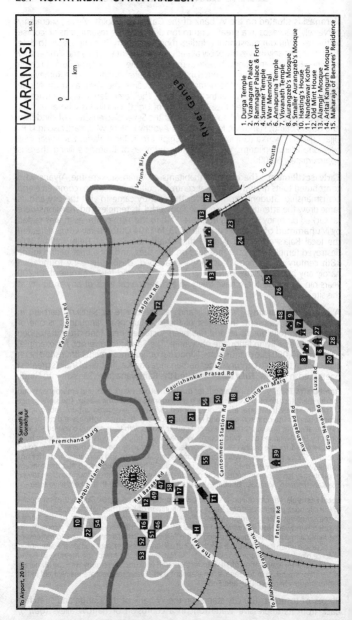

VARANASI

SA.52

0   1
km

River Ganga

Varuna River

To Calcutta

To Samath &
Gorakhpur

Panch Koshi Rd

Premchand Marg

To Airport, 20 km

Maqbul Alam Rd

Rajghat Rd

Kabir Rd

Gaurishankar Prasad Rd

Chattgani Marg

Cantonment Station Rd

Aurangabad Rd

Luxa Rd

Guru Nanak Rd

Raj Bazar Rd

The Mal

Fatman Rd

Grand Trunk Rd

To Allahabad

1. Durga Temple
2. Vizianagram Palace
3. Ramnagar Palace & Fort
4. Summer Temple
5. War Memorial
6. Annapurna Temple
7. Visvanath Temple
8. Aurangzeb's Mosque
9. Smaller Aurangzeb's Mosque
10. Hasting's House
11. Nandeswar Kothi
12. Old Mint House
13. Lesser Mosque
14. Aurangzeb Mosque
15. Maharaja of Benares' Residence

16. St. Mary's Church &
    Tourist DAK Bungalow
17. Catholic Church
18. Zenana Mission
19. Victoria Park
20. Observatory
21. Queen's College
22. Civil Court
23. Raj Ghat
24. Prahlad Ghat
25. Trilochan Ghat
26. Gai Ghat
27. Panchganga Ghat
28. Ram Ghat
29. Manikarnika Ghat
30. Lalita Ghat
31. Mir Ghat
32. Dasashwameda Ghat &
    Rana Ghat
33. Kedar Ghat
34. Harishchandra Ghat
35. Hanuman Ghat & Shivala Ghat
36. Tulsidas Ghat & Asi Ghat
37. Nagwa Ghat
38. Bharat Kala Bhawan
39. Bharat Mata Temple
40. Gaekwar Library
41. Benares Hindu University
42. Sanskrit Institute of Studies
43. Sanskrit University of
44. Indian Institute of
    Handloom Technology
45. Foreigners' Registration Office
46. Tourist Office
47. Indian Airlines
48. Post Office
49. Telegraph Office
50. Kwality Restaurant
51. Hotel de Paris
52. Clark's Hotel
53. Benares Ashok Hotel
54. Benares Club
55. UP Tourism Dept. Bungalow
56. Pradeep Hotel
57. International Hotel
58. Hotel India
T1. Varanasi Jnct. Station
T2. City Station & Retiring Rooms
T3. Kashi Station

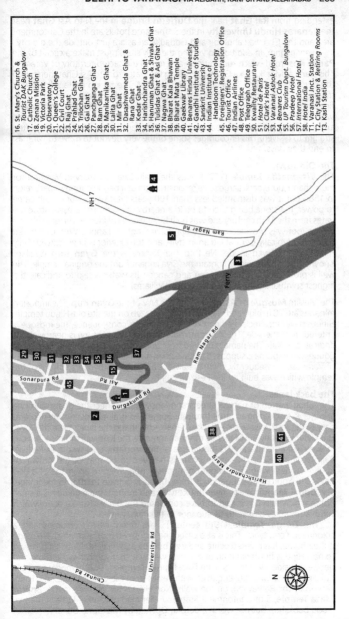

N

extending from **Raj Ghat** near the **Dufferin Bridge** in the N to **Asi Ghat** near the **Banaras Hindu University** in the S. The large hotels are in the Cantonment area and the Chowk, Lahurabir and Godaulia areas are just outside the old city.

Every pilgrim, in addition to visiting the holy sites, must make a circuit of the **Panch Kosi** road which runs outside and round the sacred territory of Varanasi. This starts at Manikarnika Ghat, runs along the waterfront to Asi Ghat then round the outskirts in a large semi-circle to Barna Ghat. The 58 km route is lined with trees and shrines and the pilgrimage is supposed to take 6 days, each day's walk finishing in a small village, suitably equipped with temples and *dharamshalas**. Varanasi is said to combine all the virtues of all other places of pilgrimage and anyone dying within the area marked by the Panch Kosi road is transported straight to heaven. This encourages some of the very devout to move to Varanasi to end their days.

The Old Town
The *Visvanatha Temple* (1777) was the main Siva sanctuary in Varanasi for more than 1,000 years. Large scale reconstruction of it began during Akbar's reign in 1585 but it was dismantled less than 100 years later when Aurangzeb came to power, the stone being used to build a nearby mosque. The present structure dates from the 18th century and was built by Ahilya Bai of Indore. The gold plating on the roof was provided by Maharaja Ranjit Singh of Lahore. With its pointed spires, it is typically Central Indian in style, and the exterior is finely carved. Only Hindus are allowed inside. Next to the Temple is the **Gyan Kup** (Well of Knowledge). This is said to contain the Siva lingam from the original temple. The well is protected by a stone screen and canopy. Its water is said to 'indicate the highest spiritual illumination' (Rushbrook Williams).

The Muslim *Mosque of Alamgir* lies to the NW of the **Gyan Kup**. The imposing minarets are 70 m high and was built by Aurangzeb on the site of a Hindu temple. Hindus have since reclaimed part of the land and in consequence, the mosque is entered from the side. The **Annapurna Temple** (18th century) is nearby and is dedicated to Kali. The name is derived from *anna* (food) *purna* (who is filled). The goddess Annapurna is supposed to have been given orders to feed the inhabitants of Varanasi. Consequently, there are always a number of beggars in front of the temple which was built by the Peshwa Baji Rao I.

The back lanes
The rabbit warren of narrow streets and lanes that connect the ghats with one another is fascinating to stroll through. Some find it all too over-powering and easy to get lost! Tall houses – *Pakku Mahals* – overhang the lanes. Near the Town Hall (1845) built by the Maharaja of Vizianagram, is the **Kotwali** or Police Station, looking like a fort. Nearby is the Temple of **Bhaironath**, built by the ex-Peshwa Baji Rao II in 1825. The image inside is believed to be that of the Kotwal or Superintendent who rides about on a ghostly dog. There is an image of a dog next to it. You can buy sugar dogs from the stalls outside to offer to the image. The **Gopal Mandir** is also near the Kotwali and in the temple garden is a small hut in which Tulsi Das is said to have composed the Binaya Patrika poem which some authorities believe to be superior to the Ramayana.

The *Durga Temple* (19th century) has finely carved columns and a colonnaded courtyard. This is also called the monkey temple as many have made it their home. It is painted ochre and was built by a Bengali Maharani. It is closed to non-Hindus but there is an upper level walkway that you can walk round and get views inside. Next to this is the **Tulsi Manas Temple** (1964), a modern marble building whose walls are engraved with verses from the Charit Manas, the Hindi version of the Ramayana, on the walls. Non-Hindus are allowed inside. **Bharat Mata Temple**, S of Cantonment Station. Relief map of Mother India in marble. Good bookshop but not worth a detour. Opened by Mahatma Gandhi.

The River Front

The ghats and the human activity on them are the principal attraction for visitors to Varanasi. There are over a hundred of these flights of steps (ghats), their functions varying. Dawn is the best time to visit them, observe and try and unravel some of the mysteries of Hinduism. Start near the southern end of the ghats at *Dasasvamedh Ghat* where you can hire a boat quite cheaply. You may want to go either upstream (S) to Harishchandra Ghat or downstream to Marnikarnika Ghat.

Dashashvamedha Ghat takes its name from a complicated ritual 'The Place of Ten Horse Sacrifices' that was performed by the King of Kashi, Divodasa, in the age of the gods. Divodasa had been appointed king by **Brahma**, God of Creation, at a time when the world was in chaos and he accepted the job only if all the god would leave Varanasi and let him do his job unhindered. Even **Siva** was forced to leave but he set the test for Divodasa confident that he would get the ceremony wrong and this would allow the God back into the city. Siva was wrong as the ritual was performed flawlessly. The ghat has thus become one of the holiest and bathing here is regarded as being almost as meritorious as making the sacrifice.

Upstream is the *Shivala Ghat* after the temple. The uninspiring temple houses an image that is sprinkled with Ganga water. The ghat is especially popular with women. Next is the **Munshi Ghat**, a place where some of the city's sizeable Muslim population (25% of the total) come to bathe. The river has no religious significance for them. Adjacent are the **Pandeya Ghat** and **Rana Ghat**, the latter built by the Maharana of Udaipur.

Professional washermen work at the **Dhobi Ghat**. Their method is to soak the clothes in the river mud, beat them around a bit, then rinse. There is religious merit in having your clothes washed in the sacred Ganga. Brahmins have their own washermen to avoid caste pollution. In the past the dhobi wallahs were generally illiterate and had a system of marking clients' clothes with special symbols.

The *Raja Ghat* is associated with the Raja of Pune and here the high-water levels are recorded. You can see from the flood level marked in Jul 1967 that at times the steps can be almost completely covered, difficult to imagine when the river is at its lowest ebb in Jan or Feb. Next is the *Kedara Ghat*, named after Kedarnath, a pilgrimage site in the U.P. Himalaya – **see page 210**. This ghat is especially popular with Bengalis and S Indians.

The *Harishchandra Ghat* is particularly holy and is dedicated to the king Harishchandra whose devotion to Brahma was given a series of rigourous of tests by the god. Harishchandra performed these, including becoming a servant at the Varanasi crematorium, so the impressed Brahma named this ghat after him. It is now the most sacred cremation ghat (Manikarnika is more popular). Behind the ghat is a *gopuram** of a Dravidian style temple. The Karnataka Ghat is one of many regional ghats. These are attended by priests who know the local languages, castes, customs and festivals.

The *Hanuman Ghat* is where *Vallabha*, the leader of a revival in the Krishna bhakti cult is believed to have been born at the end of the 15th century. This is popular with bodybuilders and wrestlers since Hanuman epitomises the qualities associated with these sports. **Chet Singh's Fort** stands behind the Sivala Ghat. The fort was the old palace of the Maharajas', was taken by the Muslims and retaken by Chet Singh. He later made an escape from the British who had imprisoned him in his own fort for tax evasion by climbing down to the river and swimming away. **Jain Ghat** is for members of that faith. **Anandamayi Ghat** is named after the Bengali Anandamayi who died in 1982. She was born into a poor family, received 'enlightenment' at the age of seventeen and spent her entire life teaching and setting up charitable missions. One of her ashrams is here. Her name Anandamayi Ma means 'Mother of Bliss'. Furthest upstream is the **Asi Ghat**, one of five that pilgrims should bathe from in a day. The order is: **Asi, Dasasvamedh, Barnasangam, Panchganga** and **Mainkarnika**.

Here the boat will turn to take you back to **Dasavamedh Ghat**. Upstream is the Ramnagar Fort, the Maharaja of Varanasi residence. From Dasavamedh Ghat you can go downstream past the following ghats. *Man Mandir Ghat* was built by Mahrajah Man Singh of Amber in 1600 and is one of the oldest in Varanasi. The palace here has been much restored in the last century with brick and plaster. The fine stone balcony on the NE corner gives an indication of how the original looked. Maharaja Jai Singh of Jaipur converted the palace into an observatory in 1710 – see also Jaipur (**page 355**). The instruments are inside but not used. Near the entrance is a small Siva Dalbhyeshvara Temple whose shrine is a lingam immersed in water. During droughts, water is added to the cistern to make it overflow for good luck. **Dom Raja's House** is next door. The *Doms* are the Untouchables of Varanasi who are integral to the cremation ceremony. As Untouchables they can handle the corpse, a ritually polluting act for Hindus. They also supply the flame from the temple for the funeral pyre. Their presence is essential and also lucrative since there are fees for the various services they provide. The Dom Raja is the hereditary title of the leader of these Untouchables. **Mir Ghat** leads to the Nepalese temple of **Vishalakshi**.

Jalasai and *Marnikarnika Ghat* **N.B. No photography is allowed here**. Above the ghat is a well into which Siva's dead wife Sati's earring is supposed to have fallen when Siva was carrying her after she committed suicide – **see page 204**. The Brahmins managed to find the jewel (marnikarnika) from the earring and returned it to Siva. He blessed the place. Offerings of bilva flowers, milk, sandalwood and sweetmeats are thrown into the tank. Between this and the ghat is Charandapuka, a stone slab with the footprints of Vishnu. A few privileged families are allowed cremations here. The Marnikarnika Ghat is immensely popular as a burning ghat. **Dattatreya Ghat** is named after a Brahmin who left his footprint here. Scindia's Ghat was originally built in 1830 but it was so huge that it collapsed and had to be done again. Ram Ghat was built by the Maharaja of Jaipur.

Five rivers are supposed to meet at the magnificent *Panchganga Ghat* – the Ganga, Sarasvati, Yamuna, Kirana and Dhutupapa. It is one of the five main pilgrimage ghats in Varanasi. The impressive flights of stone steps run up to the Smaller Mosque of Aurangzeb (late 17th century) which occupies the site of an earlier Vishnu temple. Early European visitors to India such as Tavernier, marvelled at the size and opulence of the temple and its images. It is, perhaps, not surprising that Aurangzeb knocked it down. At **Gaya Ghat** there is a stone statue of a sacred cow whilst at Trilochana Ghat there is a temple to Siva in his form as the 'Three-eyed' (Trilochana). There are two turrets sticking out of the water. **Raj Ghat** is the last on the boat journey. Excavations have revealed that there was a 9th century BC city situated on a grassy knoll near here. Raj Ghat was where the river was forded until bridges were built across the river.

Other places of interest *Benares Hindu University* is one of the largest campus universities in India to the S of the city and is almost opp Ramnagar Fort on the other bank. Founded at the turn of the century, it was originally intended for the study of Sanskrit, Indian art, music and culture and has a museum (see under Museums). The New Visvanath Temple is in the university semi circle and was financed by the Birla family. Pandit Madan Mohan Malaviya (1862-1942), long-serving chancellor of the university, was a great nationalist and wished to resurrect the idea of Hinduism without caste distinctions. Consequently, the marble temple, said to be modelled on the old Visvanath Temple destroyed by Aurangzeb, is open to all. **Ramnagar Fort** was the residence of the former

Maharaja of Varanasi where the Durbar Hall (hall of Public Audience) houses a museum (see under Museums). Beautiful situation, surrounded by narrow, crowded streets, but the Fort is run down.

Hotels Varanasi is poorly provided with top class hotels but has an enormous range of very cheap lodging houses. Beware, they can also be very nasty.
A *Taj Ganges*, Nadesar Palace Grounds. T 42485, Cable: Tajgan, Telex: 545-219 Taga-in. 104 rm. 22 km airport, 1 km rly, 2 km centre. All facilities, restaurant, drinks expensive and food can vary in quantity. A *Clarks Varanasi*, The Mall. T 42401-6, Cable: Clarkotel, Telex: 0545-204 Clak-in. 140 rm. 20 km airport, 4 km rly, 5 km centre. Large and bustling, good facilities and situation. Varied food in restaurant. B *Varanasi Ashok*, The Mall. T 46020-30, Cable: Tourism, Telex: 0545-205. 84 rm. 22 km airport, 2 km rly. C *Hotel Hindustan International*, C 12/3 Maldahia. T 57075, Telex: 0545-247. 52 rm. Restaurant, bar, 24 hr coffee shop, exchange, travel, TV. D *Pallavi International*, Hathwa Market, Chetganj. T 54894, 56939-42, Cable: Pallavi. 55 rm. 24 km airport, 2 km rly, centre location. D *Diamond*, Bhelupur. T 56561, Cable: Diamotel. 40 rm. 20 km airport, 5 km rly, 1 km centre. D *Hotel India*, 59 Patel Nagar, Cantt. T 43634. 33 rm. Restaurant, bar, 18 hr rm service, travel, TV, garden. Restaurant very popular so service can be slow in the evening but recommended as a hotel. Good value. D *Hotel de Paris*, 15 The Mall, T 43582-4, Cable: Hotel Paris, Telex: 545-323 Dpri-in 20 km airport, 4 km rly, 5 km centre. D *Gautam*, Ramkatora. T 44015-7, Cable: Suvega. 37 rm. 22 km airport, 3 km rly, centre location.
The following are inexpensive: E *Tourist Bungalow*, (UPSTDC) off Parade Kothi, Grand Trunk Rd, opp Rly Station. T 43413. 39 rm, some a/c, with and without bath, 'delux suites' plus dormitory. Restaurant, shady verandah. Simple, clean and efficient; E *Sandhya Guest House*, Close to Shivala Ghat. Rm with bath. New, clean, manager anxious to help: tours, airtickets. Rooftop restaurant with good views. Homemade brown bread, relaxed atmosphere, pleasant. E *Dak Bungalow*, Caravan Park, The Mall, T 42182; E *Central*, Dasaswamedh Rd, T 62776; E *Pushpanjali*, Lohurabir. T 54276; E *Ajaya*, Lohurabir. T 43707; E *Natraj*, Lohurabir. T 65817; E *International*, Lohurabir. T 57140; E *Pradeep*, Jagat Ganj. T 66362; E *K.V.M. Hotel*, Godaulia; E *Nur-Indira*, Parade Kothi. T 44686. 30 rm, some a/c with Indian style bathrooms. Simple but clean. F *Amar*, Parade Kothi. T 44686. A/c and no a/c rm. Its cheapness is its main attraction; F *Raj Kamal*, Parade Kothi. T 44607. 13 rm, some a/c with and without bath. Shabby; F *Park Villa*, Rathayatra Crossing. T 44607. 14 rm, 12D, 2S. Atmospheric, interesting and friendly; F *Divan*, Parade Kothi. No phone. Very basic. There are also *Railway Retiring Rooms* at Varanasi Cantt Rly Station. A/c and non a/c double rm and dormitory. The *YMCA* is also at the Cantonment. The *Circuit House* is usually reserved for government officers, T 43406.

Restaurants City restaurants are not allowed to serve alcohol. Hotels observe 'Dry Days" on the 1st and 7th of each month, and on certain Public holidays. **International**: *Darpan* Hotel Pallavi. *Satkar* Hotel Bombay. **Indian and Continental**: *Poonam*, Hotel Pradeep; *Nagina* Hotel Jaigangas; *Sagar*, Hotel Gaurav; *Amber*, Hotel India; *Kwality*, Lohurabir and the inexpensive *Blue Moon* in the Old City centre which, though simple, will often be open when others are shut. *Bombay International*, nr Shivala Ghat. Delicious food and pleasant surroundings but overpriced, slow service, lacking atmosphere. **Chinese**: *Canton's*, Hotel Surya, Varuna Bridge Rd, Cantt; *Winfa*, Lohurabir. **Continental**: *Konamey*, Bansphatak. **Indian vegetarian**: *Tulsi*, Chetganj.

Banks Open weekdays 1000-1400, Sat 1000-1200. At Bansphatak: *Andhra, State Bank, Canara*. At Godoulia: *Baroda, Union Bank of India*. At Chetgang: *New Bank of India*. There are also branches at *Hotel de Paris* (Mon 1300-1500, Wed- Sun 1300-1700. Closed Tues) and at *Hotel Clarks Varanasi* and *Varanasi Ashok*.

Shopping Varanasi is famous for silk weaving, fabrics and brassware, ivory and gold jewellery and hand block printed goods. Main shopping areas are Chowk, Godoulia, Viswanath Lane, Gyanvapi and Thatheri Bazaar. *UPICA*, Nadesar Cantt; *UP Handlooms*, Lohurabir, Nadesar and Neechi Bagh; *Tantuja*, Bengal Emporium, Dasaswamedh Rd; *Mahatex*, Godoulia.

Photography *Passi Studio*, Lohurabir, T 63580. *Bright Studio*, Godoulia, T 64345. @IS = **Local Transport** No yellow-top-taxis are available. Private taxis available from agencies, hotels. Tariff: Full day (90 km, 8 hr), A/c Rs 400, non-A/c Rs 275; Half day (45 km, 4 hr), A/c Rs 200, non-a/c Rs 140. Basic rate per km A/c Rs 4, non-A/c Rs 2.75. Airport/city transfer, A/c Rs 200, non-A/c Rs 140. **Tempo-rickshaws** and **auto-rickshaws** generally work on fixed routes point-to-point. Basic min Re 1 per stage. **Cycle-rickshaws** and **Horse-tongas** widely used, rates negotiable. **Ferry and Boats** are the best way to enjoy Varanasi. Available from Ghats, charges generally negotiable. Representative rates for sightseeing: big boat (20) Rs

100, small boat (10) Rs 50 per hr, river crossing approx. Re 1.25 per person – even less if you're lucky. **City buses** cover most of Varanasi. UPSRTC Bus Stand, opp Rly Station, Cantt. T 42011. Open 24 hr.

Sports **Swimming** pools at hotels Taj Ganges, Varanasi Ashok and Clarks Varanasi. Can be used with temporary membership.

Sports Stadia, Sampurna Nand Stadium, Vidyapeeth Rd and Multi-purpose Stadium, BHU.

Museums **Bharat Kala Bhavan**, Benaras Hindu University. Open Summer 0800-1200, Winter 0930-1630. Closed Sun and University holidays. Exhibits include various pieces representative of Varanasi through the ages plus sculptures from Mathura and Sarnath. **Ramnagar Fort** across the river. Open 0900-1200, 1400-1700. Small fee. The Durbar Hall is now a **royal museum** containing palanquins, elephant *howdahs*, costumes, arms and furniture.

Parks and Zoos Shahid Park, Sigra.

Useful Addresses Police: T 100 Fire: Chetganj, T 53333, Bhelupur, T 54444.

Hospitals and Medical Services Benares Hindu University Hospital, BHU, T 66833 Birla Hospital, Machhodari, T 56357. SSPG Hospital, T 62424.

Post and Telegraph Head Post and Telegraph Office, Bisheshwarganj, T 67150. Head Post Office, Cantt, T 42738. Central Telegraph Office, Cantt.

Places of Worship *Hindu*: Vishwanath Temple (BHU); Tulsi Manas Temple. *Muslim*: Alagir Mosque; Arhai Kangura Mosque. *Christian*: Catholic Church, Cantt; St Mary;s Protestant Church; Methodist Church; St Thomas Church. *Jain*: Jain Temples at Sarnath, Bhelupur and Maidagin. Sikh: Gurubag, Luxa; Gurudwara, Ashbhairo. *Buddhist*: Buddhist Temple, Sigar; Mulgandh Kuti Vihar, Sarnath.

Travel Agents and Tour Operators *Anisha Excursions* India (P) Ltd, Mint House, Cantt, T 44528, 44536. *Lohartara*, T 62244. *Cosmic Travels and Movers*, Hotel Diamond, T 56561, 56045. *Forvol Travels*, behind Hotel Varanasi Ashok, T 43135 *ITDC Transport Unit*, Hotel Varanasi Ashok, T 42565 *Mercury Travels*, Hotel Clarks Varanasi, T 42650. Telex: 0545-269. *Nepal Travels*, Parade Kothi (near UPSTDC Tourist Bungalow). *Sita World Travels,* Hotel Clarks Varanasi, T 42965. *Travel Bureau*, Hotel Clarks Varanasi, T 42401. *Travel Corporation of India,* Hotel Clarks Varanasi, T 43096.

Tourist Offices and Information *Govt. of India Tourist Office,* 15B The Mall, Cantt, T 43744. *Govt. of India Tourist Information Counter*, Babatpur Airport. *UP Govt. Tourist Office*, Parade Kothi, Cantt, T 43413. *UP Govt. Tourist Information Counter*, Varanasi Cantt Railway Station, T 43544. Open daily 0600-2000. *Bihar State Tourist Office*, Englishiya Market, Sher Shah Suri Marg, Cantt, T 43821. Open daily 0800-2000. **Conducted Tours** *UPSRTC* Tour I: River trip, temples, Benaras Hindu University. Daily, Summer 0530-1145, Winter 0600-1215. Tour II: Sarnath and Ramnagar Fort. Daily, Summer 1430-1825, Winter 1400-1755. Starts from UPSTDC Tourist Bungalow, picking up from Govt of India Tourist Office, The Mall. Tickets sold on bus. *Varuna Travels and Tours*, Pandey Haweli, also organise tours, mainly from Sep to Mar. T 52173.

Air Indian Airlines flies daily from/to Delhi via Agra and Khajuraho. 5 flights a week from/to Delhi via Allahabad and Patna. 3 times a week from Bombay en route to Lucknow. Two flights a week from Delhi en route to Bhubaneswar. Indian Airlines also flies daily between Varanasi and Kathmandu. **Vayudoot** links Varanasi to Delhi, Agra and Khajuraho. Because Indian Airlines flights to Varanasi mainly originate in Delhi and stop at intermediate places en route they are subject to severe delays, especially in Jan and early Feb when Delhi is often fogbound. Be prepared for a long wait if you are flying. *Indian Airlines*, Mint House, Varanasi Cantt, T 43116. Airport Office, T 43746. Open 1000-1300 and 1400-1630 *Vayudoot* Anisha Excursions India (P) Ltd, Mint House, Varanasi Cantt, T 44528, 44536. Telex: 0545-282. Open 1000-1800. Lohartara, T 62244.

Rail Allahabad: *Sarnath Exp* 4260, daily, 1155, 2 hr 55 min; *Bundelkhand Exp* 1108, daily, 1310, 4 hr 45 min. **Bombay (VT)**: *Mahanagri Exp* 1094, daily, 1135, 27 hr 15 min; *Varanasi-Bombay Ratnagiri Exp* 2166, Tue,Th,Fri, 1745, 29 hr 50 min. **Dehra Dun**: *Doon Exp* 3009, daily, 1945, 20 hr 30 min; *Dehra Dun-Varanasi Exp* 4265, daily, 0915, 24 hr 30 min. **New Delhi**: *A.C. Exp* 2381, Tue,Th,Sat, 2115, 13 hr 25 min; *Neelachal Exp* 8475, Mon,Wed,Sat, 0735, 13 hr 45 min.

Kanpur: *Neelachal Exp* 8475, Mon,Wed,Sat, 0735, 7 hr 20 min; *Ganga-Yamuna Exp*

4283, Mon,Wed,Th,Sat, 1245, 9 hr 35 min: *Ganga-Yamuna Exp* 4213, Tue,Th,Sun, 1245, 9 hr 35 min. **Lucknow**: *Varanasi-Lucknow Varuna Exp* 2427, daily, 0515, 4 hr 45 min; *Kashi-Vishwanath Exp* 4057, daily, 1400, 6 hr 25 min. **Calcutta** (Howrah): *Amritsar-Howrah Exp* 3050, daily, 1950, 19 hr 55 min; *Amritsar-Howrah Mail* 3006, daily, 1725, 14 hr 30 min; *Doon Exp* 3010, daily, 16 hr 25 min, 14 hr 55 min. **Gorakhpur (for Nepal)**: *Fast Passenger*, 82/1144, daily, 1340, 10 hr 35 min; *Triveni Exp* 5406/5205, daily, 2350, 7 hr 50 min; *Exp* 5450/5027, daily, 0700, 8 hr 55 min.

Road Varanasi is situated at the junction of **NH2**, **NH7**, and **NH29**. To: **Agra** (565 km); **Allahabad** (122 km); **Bhopal** (7791 km); **Bodhgaya** (240 km); **Kanpur** (320 km); **Khajuraho** (406 km); **Lucknow** (286 km); **Lumbini** (Nepal; 386 km); **Patna** (246 km); **Delhi** (765 km); **Calcutta** (677 km); **Bombay** (1590 km); **Madras** (1901 km); **Trivandrum** (2524 km); **Ahmedabad** (1329 km); **Hyderabad** (1197 km).

Bus UPSRTC Bus Stand, Station Rd, Varanasi Cantt, T 42011. Reservations for deluxe buses to Allahabad. Open 24 hr. UPSRTC and MPSRTC connect Varanasi to important neighbouring centres.

Excursions *Sarnath*, 10 km E of Varanasi, is one of Buddhism's major centres in India. Having achieved enlightenment at Bodh Gaya, the **Buddha** came to the deer park at Sarnath and delivered his first sermon, usually referred to as Dharmachakra (Turning the Wheel of Law). This was around 528 BC. Since then, the site has been revered.

Local Festival May. Buddha Purnima marks the birth of the Buddha. A huge fair is held when his relics (which are not on public display at any other time) are taken out in procession.

Both the Chinese travellers Fa-Hien and Hiuen Tsang visited Sarnath, the former at the beginning of the 5th century AD, the latter in 640 AD. Hiuen Tsang described the sangharama (monastery) as having 1500 monks, a 65 m high vihara, a figure of the Buddha represented by a wheel, a 22 m high stone stupa built by Asoka, a larger 90 m high stupa and three lakes. The remains here and the sculptures now housed at the Indian Museum, Calcutta and the National Museum, Delhi reveal that Sarnath was a centre of religious activity, learning and artistic endeavour continuously from the 4th century BC to its abandonment in the 9th century AD. Sarnath was probably destroyed when Muslim armies devastated the region in 1197.

The site is dominated by the *Dhamekh Stupa*, believed to be where the master gave his first discourse to the 5 ascetics became his first disciples. This event ranks along with his birth, enlightenment and death as one of the 4 most significant in his existence.

You enter the **Deer Park** by the E Gateway. On the right is a statue of **Anagarika Damapala**, the founder of the Mahabodhi Society which has assumed responsibility for the upkeep of Sarnath and Bodh Gaya – see Bihar (**page 665**). The modern temple on your right is the *Mula Gandhakuti Vihara* (1929-31) which contains frescoes by the Japanese artist Kosetsu Nosu depicting scenes from the Buddha's life. The **Bodhi tree** (pipal or Ficus religiosa) is a sapling of the tree in Sri Lanka which was grown from a cutting taken there in 240 BC by Asoka's nephew. It was planted here in 1931.

The **Dhamekh Stupa** (5th-6th century AD) is the most imposing monument at Sarnath. It consists of a 28 m diameter stone plinth which rises to a height of 13 m. There are 8 faces, each with an arched recess for an image. Above this base rises a 31 m high cylindrical tower. The upper part is brick and was probably unfinished. The central portion is elaborately decorated with Gupta designs, e.g. luxuriant foliation, geometric patterns, birds and flowers. Excavations have revealed that the stupa was enlarged on six occasions and the well known figures of boddhisattva standing and the Buddha teaching were found around the monument.

The Deer Park is holy to Jains because *Shreyamshanatha*, the 11th *Tirthankara** died here. The temple to your left as you move between the stupas commemorates him. The Monastery (5th century onwards) in the SW corner is one of 4 in the Deer Park. The other 3 are along the N edge. All are of brick with cells off a central courtyard. All are in ruins.

The *Dharmarajika Stupa* (3rd century BC and later) was built by the emperor **Asoka** to

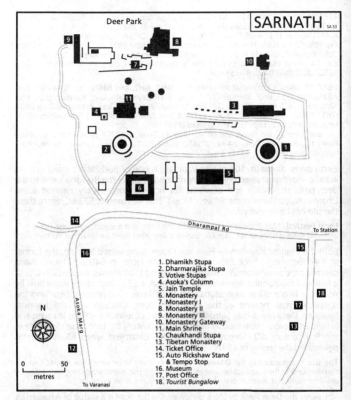

SARNATH SA 53

Deer Park

1. Dhamikh Stupa
2. Dharmarajika Stupa
3. Votive Stupas
4. Asoka's Column
5. Jain Temple
6. Monastery
7. Monastery I
8. Monastery II
9. Monastery III
10. Monastery Gateway
11. Main Shrine
12. Chaukhandi Stupa
13. Tibetan Monastery
14. Ticket Office
15. Auto Rickshaw Stand
    & Tempo Stop
16. Museum
17. Post Office
18. *Tourist Bungalow*

Dharampal Rd   To Station

Asoka Marg

0   50
metres

To Varanasi

contain relics of the Buddha. Like the Dhamekh Stupa this was enlarged on several occasions but was destroyed by Jagat Singh, the prime minister to the Maharaja of Benares in 1794. At its core was found a green marble casket containing human bones and pearls which Jagat Singh ordered to be thrown into the Ganga. Mr Duncan, British Resident at the Maharaja's court, published an account of the discovery thereby drawing Western scholars' attention to the site.

The Main Shrine (3rd century BC and 5th century AD) is a rectangular building 29 m by 27 m with doubly recessed corners and reaches 5.5 m in height. It is believed that this is where Buddha settled in the Deer Park. The building is attributed to Asoka and the later Guptas. The concrete path and interior brick walls were added later to reinforce the building. To the rear is the lower portion of a polished sandstone **Asokan Column** (3rd century BC). The original was about 15 m high and was topped by a capital which is now housed in the Archaeological Museum. This comprises four lions sitting back to back with the wheel of law between them. It is now the symbol of the Indian Union. The part remaining is only 5 m high. The column was one of many erected by Asoka to promulgate the faith and this contained a message to the monks and nuns not to create any schisms and to spread the word.

The Museum Open 1000-1700, closed Friday. Re 0.50. Contains a wide range of sculptures and pieces from the site, including the capital from the Asokan Column, a Sunga Period (1st century BC) stone railing, Kushana Period (2nd century AD) Boddhisattvas, Gupta Period (5th century AD) figures, including the magnificent seated Buddha, plus others from all stages until the 12th century.

At **Chaunkandi** about 1 km to the S is the site of a 5th century Stupa. On top of this is an octagonal brick tower built by Akbar in 1588 to commemorate the visit his father Humayun made to the site. The inscription above the doorway reads 'As Humayun, king of the Seven Climes, now residing in paradise, deigned to come and sit here one day, thereby increasing the splendour of the sun, so Akbar, his son and humble servant, resolved to build on this spot a lofty tower reaching to the blue sky'.

Hotels Sarnath can easily be visited in a day from Varanasi which has a good range of hotels. Sarnath has an **E** *Tourist Bungalow* with rooms and a dormitory.

Station Travel Reservations: UPSRTC Bus Stand, Charbagh; UPSRTC Bus Stand, Kaiserbagh, T 42503.

Excursions The **Dudhwa National Park**. The terrain and vegetation is that of the **terai***. With an area of 613 sq km and bordering the Sarda River, Dudhwa has tigers, leopards, sambar, swamp deer and nilgai. It is famous for its sloth bears (Melursus ursinus). Like Corbett, it has a rich bird life.

DELHI TO AGRA AND FATEHPUR SIKRI

On a day trip from Delhi it is quite feasible to visit the three major sites – **the Red Fort**, **Itimad-ud-daulah** and the **Taj Mahal** – and do some shopping, especially if you travel on the superfast Shatabdi Express (see Travel section). This will give you 12 hr in the city. If, however, you wish to visit Sikandra and/or Fatehpur Sikri (see **Excursions**) you need to stay at least one night in Agra. This makes it possible to see both the Taj Mahal and Fatehpur Sikri early in the day, which is strongly recommended. The suggested sequence for viewing the three major sites in one day is first the Red Fort, then Itimad-ud-daulah and finally the Taj Mahal.

Train is now the most comfortable way of travelling to Agra. Of the trains the Shatabdi Express is the quickest and most convenient. This takes only 1 hr 50 min to cover the 194 km and has airline type meals service aboard. By the time you have added in the airport waiting time and possible delays it is often faster than flying. The railway line follows the road for much of the distance. Buses are much slower and less comfortable. By bus the journey will take about 4 hr. Hired cars can be somewhat faster. However, many hired cars need frequent attention, and are no faster than buses. For the most part the journey passes through agricultural land watered by the Yamuna river. Here, rice and wheat are the principal crops, the former during the **kharif*** (rainy) and the latter during the **rabi*** (winter) season. The topography as seen from the road and train is flat and uninteresting, though there are some low hills at places like Radha Kund and Gobardhan on the W side towards Rajasthan.

The **NH2** leaves Delhi along the **Mathura road** and is entirely built up and very busy. 5 km after crossing the **Haryana border** there is a right turn to **Badhkal Village** (32 km S of Delhi) which has a motel **D** *Badhkal Lake*, T 22201. Deluxe motel and camper huts. A/c rm. Pool, boating. The Grand Trunk Rd continues to **Faridabad** (4 km), an industrial town in S Haryana. Just S the Haryana State Tourist Department has an attractive motel **D** *Magpie*, T 23473. A/c rm. The NH2 by-passes **Palwal** (23 km *Population* 60,000), one of many small sites at which *Painted Grey Ware* has been found dating from the end of the Harappan period to around the beginning of the Northern Black Polished Ware period, 800 BC (**see page 80**).

The Painted Grey Ware culture Ghose has given a clear view of what the cultures that produced the Painted Grey Ware must have been like. It was, he writes "essentially a village culture with an agricultural cum pastoral base. No sign of urbanisation – such as town planning, large-scale trade and commerce, coinage, writing etc – has as yet emerged. People lived in houses made of wattle and daub or mud and mud bricks. The settlements were of moderate size. Amongst the agricultural produce rice deserves to be specially mentioned. Likewise amongst the domesticated animals particular reference may be made to the horse, a favourite animal of the Aryans. The other domesticated animals include the cattle, buffalo, pig and sheep. The occurrence of cut and charred bones of animals indicate the inclusion of meat in the diet. The deer was also hunted for food and its antlers utilised for making thin pointed tools."

The road continues to **Hodal** (25 km), where there is another pleasant Haryana State Tourist Department motel. **D** *Dabchick*, T 91; *Dream Castle motel* and camper huts. A/c and no a/c rm. Elephant rides, boating, childrens' playground. Continue across the state border with Uttar Pradesh (6 km) to **Kosi Kalan** (8 km). There is a right turn to **Barsana**, 30 km NW of Mathura. This small town is revered as the home of Krishna's wife **Radha**, and lies at the foot of a low range of hills. The four prominent peaks are believed to be emblematic of the four-faced Brahma. Each has a shrine on top. The fine old buildings of the town were destroyed when Najaf Khan and his Mughal forces defeated the Jats in 1773.

You can continue S from Barsana to Govardhan or return to the Grand Trunk Rd at Kosi turn right to **Chhata** (11 km) where there is a road on the right leading to **Govardhan**, 26 km W of Mathura on the Deeg road. It lies in the narrow range of the **Girraj Hills**. The story goes that Indra caused a tremendous flood and Krishna raised these hills up above the flood for a week so that people could escape. By the Manasi Ganga river is the Harideva temple which was built by Raja Bhagwan Das in the reign of Akbar. On the opp bank are the chattris of Ranjit Singh and Balwant Singh, both rulers of Bharatpur – see Rajasthan (**see page 367**). On the way to *Radha Kund*, 5 km N, is a cenotaph to **Suraj Mal** of **Bharatpur** who attacked Delhi. Radha Kund consists of a small town around two lakes, Krishna Kund after the god and Radha Kund after his favourite milkmaid mistress. There are stone ghats on all sides and these were constructed in 1817. The legend is that Krishna ritually bathed here to purify himself from the pollution caused from killing the demon bull Arishta.

The **NH2** continues S from **Chhata** to **Chomar** (15 km) and for another 12 km to a road junction. A left turn goes to **Vrindavan** (4 km) where Krishna played with the *gopis* or cowgirls, stealing their clothes while they were bathing. Here you are entering perhaps the most sacred region of India for Vaishnavite Hindus, for it is here that many of the stories surrounding Krishna are set (**see page 56**). **Vrindavan** – "Forest of Basil Plants" – is the most famous of the holy sites around Mathura. At the entrance to the town is the **Red Temple** (1590) of Gobind Deo, the Divine Cowherd, i.e. Krishna himself. Fergusson writes quite ecstatically on the temple which he says is 'the only one, perhaps, from which a European architect might borrow a few hints'. Nearby there is a Dravidian style temple dedicated to **Sri Ranga,** one of Vishnu's names, with three *gopura**, each nearly 30 m high. The **Madan Mohan Temple** stands above a ghat on an arm of the river. There is a pavilion decorated with cobra carvings. Siva is believed to have struck Devi here and made it a place for curing snake bites.

If you return to the National Highway from Vrindavan turn left to **Mathura** (6 km; *Population* 210,00)

Mathura

Early history Mathura is one of the most sacred cities of Hinduism and is situated on the W bank of the Yamuna River. It is a great religious centre whose history dates back to 600 BC. **Ptolemy** mentions the town and it played an important role in the formation of the 1st-2nd century **Kushan Empire.** Kanishka and his successors used it as their capital. The Chinese traveller Hiuen Tsang visited it in

634 AD. At that time it was also important Buddhist centre with over 2,000 followers. By the time Mahmud of Ghazni came and sacked the city in 1017, Buddhism had virtually disappeared. It was Mahmud of Ghazni's practice to plunder and Mathura offered rich pickings: the city was burnt, temples destroyed and numerous jewel encrusted idols were carted off. **Sikander Lodi** did similar harm to the religious places in 1500 whilst the Mughal Emperor **Aurangzeb** used a local revolt in which his governor was killed as an opportunity to destroy all the main temples.

As the Mughal Empire declined, Jats and Marathas jostled for control. As it lay on the main Delhi-Agra artery it had great strategic value. At the beginning of the 19th century it came under British control. They laid out a cantonment in the S and left a cemetery and the Roman Catholic **Church of the Sacred Heart** (1870). Today Mathura is an important and rapidly growing industrial city. The opening of a big oil refinery on the outskirts of the city in 1975 caused great concern among environmentalists that atmospheric pollution would be carried by prevailing northwesterly winds and irreversibly damage the Taj Mahal only 50 km away.

The Vaishnavite city For Vaisnavaites Mathura is perhaps the supremely sacred city of India, being the reputed birth-place of Krishna. **Krishna** is the most human aspect of Vishnu and tends to be portrayed as multi-talented: the ideal lover, soldier, statesman. Localities commemorating episodes in this popular god's life are scattered throughout the area. Thus at **Gokul**, for example, Vishnu first appeared as Krishna and at **Govardhan** Krishna lifted a mountain to give shelter to people and livestock. During the monsoon theatrical groups perform the Banjatra (Pilgrimage of the Groves) and act out some of these episodes. Because of Muslim depredations, almost no monument of antiquity remains in Mathura. This, however, does not stop tens of thousands of pilgrims from visiting it each year since it is the religious association that is most important.

Places of interest The city is entered by the finely carved **Holi Gate** and in the centre is the **Jami Masjid** (1660-1) which was built by Abd-un-Nadi, the governor who was killed. This has four minarets, was once covered with brightly coloured enamel tiles. The courtyard is raised and above the façade are the ninety nine names of Allah.

Less than half a kilometre from here is the **Katra** which contains a mosque built by Aurangzeb. This stands over the ruins of one of Mathura's most famous temples, the Kesava Deo Mandir which, in turn had been built on the ruins of a Buddhist monastery dating back to the Kushan period. At the rear of this enclosure is a newer **Temple of Kesava**, built by Bir Singh of Orchha – see Orchha, Madhya Pradesh (page 294). Close by this is the **Potara Kund**, a tank in which Krishna's baby linen was washed. This has steps leading down to it, is capable of allowing cattle and horses access and is faced in the familiar local red sandstone.

The Yamuna The river is a focal point for Hindu pilgrims and a paved street runs the length of it. There are a number of bathing ghats though these are nothing like as extensive or many as in Varanasi. The **Vishram Ghat** is where Krishna rested after battle with Kamsa. The steps were reconstructed in 1814. The Sati Burj is a square tower of red sandstone with a plastered dome. It is said to have been built in the late 16th century to commemorate the *sati** of the wife of Raja Bhar Mal of Amber. Maharaja Jai Singh (see page 355) built an observatory in Mathura. Nothing has survived.

Cows, monkeys and turtles are fed at the **Vishant Ghat** when the *Arati* ceremony is performed. If you can, the best way to see the riverside activity is from a boat. The **Kans Qila** fort was built by **Raja Man Singh** of Amber and was rebuilt by Akbar but only the foundations remain.

Hotels The hotels in Mathura largely cater to pilgrims. The Western visitor can easily stay in Agra and make a day trip to Mathura and surrounding places. **C** *Madhuvan.* T 5058, 6414, Cable: Madhuvan. 28 rm, some a/c with bath. 3 km rly, 2 km centre. Pool, TV, 24 hr rm service, exchange,travel, health club, Amex, Diners. The other hotels are in the **E** and **F** category and are fairly basic: *Agra*, Bengali Ghat, T 3318; *Kwality*, near bus stand, T 3379; *Tourist Bungalow* (UP Tourism); *Braj Lodge*, Junction Rd. There are *Railway Retiring Rooms*.

Museums Government Museum, Dampier Nagar. An extensive and impressive collection of sculptures, terracottas, bronzes and coins is housed here. There is a 1st century headless Buddha, Kushana sculptures including one of Kanishka, again decapitated. Gandhara pieces from Pakistan were also discovered at Mathura indicating that links existed between the two regions. There are also numerous Gupta figures. Open 1030-1630 except April 16 – June 30 when 0730-1230. Closed Monday.

    Rail There are a number of trains from Delhi and Agra. The best is: New Delhi: *Taj Exp* 2179/2181, daily, 1940, 2 hr 20 min. **Agra Cantt.**: *Taj Exp* 2180/2182, daily, 0900, 50 min. Sawai Madhopur: *Paschim Exp* 2926, daily, 1920, 2 hr 50 min; *Frontier Mail* 2904, daily, 1040, 3 hr 35 min; *Bombay Exp* 9020, daily, 0125, 3 hr 40 min; *Bombay-Janata Exp* 9024, 1720, 3 hr 55 min.

Bus There are frequent buses to and from Delhi, Agra and neighbouring towns.

Excursions *Mahaban*, 9 km SE of Mathura on the E bank of the Yamuna, means 'a great forest'. There is no forest now, but in 1634 Shah Jahan is recorded as having held a hunt here and killed four tigers. The town was sacked by Mahmud of Ghazni and in 1234 was a rendezvous point for the armies of Shams-ud-din Altamish sent against Kalinjar. The **Palace of Nanda** Krishna was where Krishna was secretly raised. Each year in Aug Vaishnavite pilgrims come to visit the scenes of Krishna's infancy. His cradle stands in the hall, a hole in the wall is where the *gopis* hid his flute, one pillar is polished, apparently by his mother as she leaned against it when churning. **Gokul** is 2 km away and is associated with very early Hindu legends and is where Vishnu first appeared as Krishna. The place is approached by a long flight of steps (*ghat*) from the river. Members of the Valabhacharya Sect have this as their headquarters and have built some large temples. Their founder started the cult at Vrindaban.

Baldeo, 8 km SE of Mathura, is another place of pilgrimage , this time associated with Baladeva, Krishna's elder brother. There is a temple and Khirsagar tank (Sea of Milk). Other temples in Mathura include: **Gopi Nath**, now ruined; **Jugal Kishor** (reputedly 1027), near the Kesi Ghat; **Temple of Radha** which was partly demolished by Aurangzeb.

From Mathura rejoin the Grand Trunk Rd S. It passes through the small towns of **Naurangabad** (7 km), **Bad** (7 km) and **Farah** (11 km). 20 km further on is the *Baradari of Sikander Lodi*, one time King of Delhi, built in 1495, and the tomb of Mariam uz Zamani, a Hindu wife of Akbar's who is said to have been converted to Christianity. There is little supporting evidence.

The Grand Trunk Rd then passes the tomb of the Mughal Emperor **Akbar** at *Sikandra* (3 km). Open, sunrise to sunset. Rs 2. Ample parking in front of the Buland Darwaza (main entrance). Large gardens have deer, black buck and monkeys.

Akbar's tomb Following the Timurid tradition, Akbar (r1556-1605) had started to build his own tomb at Sikandra. He died during its construction and his son Jahangir completed it, though not before he had considerably modified the design and had much of the earlier work pulled down. The result is an impressive, large but architecturally confused tomb. A fine gateway, the Buland Darwaza, in the style of the massive Victory Gate at Fatehpur Sikri, leads to the great garden enclosure. The decoration on the gateway is strikingly bold, with its large mosaic patterns, shaped pieces of stone having been laid on a flat surface. This was a fore-runner of the pietra dura technique whereby recesses were cut into the bedding stone of marble or sandstone and pieces set into it. The white minarets surrounding the entrance were an innovation. They reappear, almost unchanged, at the Taj Mahal. The walled garden enclosure is laid out in the char bagh style, i.e. quadrants, with the mausoleum at the centre, and is considerably larger, though less well kept than that of the Taj Mahal.

    A broad paved causeway leads to the tomb which has four storeys and is 22.5 m high. The first three storeys of red sandstone are in the style of Fatehpur Sikri and on top of them sits a white marble courtyard containing a finely carved replica sepulchre (the real tomb is below ground level). This fourth storey is very beautiful and obviously points the way to the more extensive use of white marble at the Itimad-ud-daulah and the Taj Mahal. Unfortunately, visitors are not allowed up to this.

The lowest storey is 9 m high, 97.5 m long on each side and contains a massive cloister broken in the centre by a doorway. The one on the S side forms the entrance to the tomb chamber. The vaulted ceiling of the vestibule was ornately frescoed in gold and blue. A section has been restored. The Surah-i-mulk chapter from the Koran runs under the cornice. A gentle ramp leads down to the tomb chamber. Off it are sealed bays containing other tombs. In a niche opposite the entrance is an alabaster tablet inscribed with the 99 divine names of Allah.

The Grand Trunk Rd continues due S to Agra. 4 km S of Sikandra nearly opposite the high gateway of an ancient building called the Kach ki sarai, is a sculptured horse, believed to mark the spot where Akbar's favourite horse died. There are also two *kos minars* or milestones and several other tombs on the way. You enter **Agra** through the Delhi Gate, built in Shah Jahan's time (r1627-1658).

Agra

Population 950,000 *Altitude* 169 m *Best time for a visit* Oct to Mar. Indian Airlines connects Agra with Delhi (196 km, 30 min). The airport is 7 km from the city centre.

	Jan	Feb	Mar	Apr	May	Jun	Jul	Aug	Sep	Oct	Nov	Dec	Av/Tot
Max (°C)	22	26	32	38	42	41	35	33	33	33	29	24	32
Min (°C)	7	10	16	22	27	29	27	26	25	19	12	8	19
Rain (mm)	16	9	11	5	10	60	210	263	151	23	2	4	764

Early history Agra is one of the great Mughal cities of S Asia, and with minor interruptions alternated with Delhi as the capital of their empire. Little is known about it before the Muslim conquest. **Sikander Lodi** seized it from a rebellious governor and made it his capital in 1501. He died in Agra but is buried in Delhi (**see page 162**). Sikandra owes its name to him. **Babur**, the founder of the Mughal Empire in India, defeated Ibrahim's immensely larger army at Panipat on April 20 1526 (**see page 418**) and immediately sent his son and successor **Humayun** to Agra to secure the treasure there whilst he marched into Delhi. However, he only stayed long enough to have the *khutba** (Friday Sermon) read in his name before marching on to Agra. Here he was offered the **Koh-i-Noor** diamond by Humayun, but in his memoirs, Babur notes 'I just gave it him back'. Agra was Babur's capital and he is believed to have laid out a pleasure garden on the E bank opp the Taj Mahal. Humayun built a mosque here in 1530.

Akbar's reign Akbar lived in Agra in the early years of his reign. Ralph Fitch, the English Elizabethan traveller, described Agra as a "magnificent city, with broad streets and tall buildings". He also witnessed Akbar's new capital at Fatehpur Sikri, 40 km W of the city, commenting that the route to it from Agra was lined all the way with stalls and markets. Akbar moved his capital again N to Lahore before returning to Agra in 1599, where he spent the last six years of his life. Jahangir left Agra for Kashmir in 1618 and never returned. Under Shah Jahan, there was considerable building activity but he too moved away to his new city Shahjahanabad in Delhi for the period 1638-50. He spent his last years at Agra as his son Aurangzeb's prisoner. Aurangzeb, the last of the Great Mughals moved the seat of government permanently to Delhi. In the 18th century it suffered at the hands of the Jats, was taken, lost and retaken by the Marathas who, in turn were ousted by the British in 1803. It was the centre of much fighting in the Mutiny and was the administrative centre of the Northwest Provinces and Oudh until that too was transferred to Allahabad in 1877.

Agra today is one of Uttar Pradesh's larger cities, and its most visited. This is simply on account of the Taj Mahal and the presence nearby of Fatehpur Sikri. The

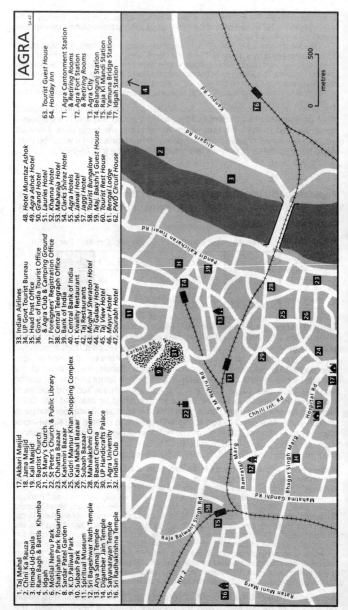

AGRA

1. Taj Mahal
2. Chini Ka Rauza
3. Itimad-Ud-Daula
4. Ram Bagh & Battis Khamba
5. Idgah
6. Motilal Nehru Park
7. Shahjahan Park Rosarium
8. Sardar Patel Garden
9. Gulab Patel Park
10. Subash Park
11. Spiritual Museum
12. Sri Bageshwar Nath Temple
13. Arya Samaj Temple
14. Digamber Jain Temple
15. Satyanarayan Temple
16. Sri Radhakrishna Temple
17. Akbari Masjid
18. Jama Masjid
19. Kali Masjid
20. Baptist Church
21. St Mary's Church
22. St Peter's Church & Public Library
23. Chhatta Bazaar
24. Cashmiri Bazaar
25. Kala Mahal Bazaar
25. Gulab & Subhash Khan Shopping Complex
27. Subash Park
28. Mahalakshmi Cinema
29. Basant Cinema
30. UP Handicrafts Palace
31. Agra University
32. Indian Club

33. Indian Airlines
34. UP Govt Tourist Bureau
35. Head Post Office
36. Govt. of India Tourist Office
    & Agra Club & Camping Ground
37. Foreigners' Registration Office
38. Central Telegraph Office
39. Central Bank of India
40. State Bank of India
41. Kwality Restaurant
42. Taj Restaurants
43. Mughal Sheraton Hotel
44. Taj Galaxy Hotel
45. Taj View Hotel
46. Mayur Hotel
47. Sourabh Hotel

48. Hotel Mumtaz Ashok
49. Agra Ashok Hotel
50. Grand Hotel
51. Lauries Hotel
52. Khanna Hotel
53. Maharaja Hotel
54. Clarks Shiraz Hotel
55. Atithi Hotels
56. Jaiwal Hotel
57. Jaggi Hotel
58. Tourist Bungalow
59. Maj. Bakshi's Guest House
60. Tourist Rest House
61. Bengal Lodge
62. PWD Circuit House
63. Tourist Guest House
64. Holiday Inn

T1. Agra Cantonment Station
    & Retiring Rooms
T2. Agra Fort Station
    & Retiring Rooms
T3. Agra City
T4. Belanganj Station
T5. Raja Ki Mandi Station
T6. Yamuna Bridge Station
T7. Idgah Station

0   500
metres

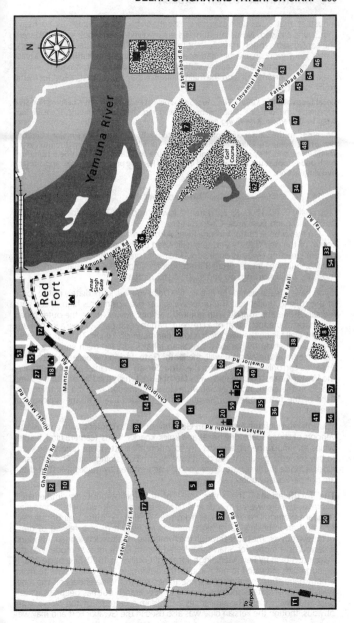

industries that have developed are essentially handicraft trades as no heavy industry is allowed. Numerous families are involved in activities associated with the considerable tourist traffic – in hotels, transport, the manufacture of carpets, pietra dura work in marble and soapstone, clothing and leather. It is a vast sprawling city with seven railway stations. Of these, Agra Cantonment (Cantt.) is the most important as it is on the main Delhi-Bombay line, and Agra Fort for traffic from Rajasthan.

Local Festivals *The Kailash Fair* (Aug/ Sep) is held at Kailash,(2 km). It is believed that **Siva** appeared in the form of a stone lingam, where a temple has now been built. There are four caves by the temple. *Kite-flying* every Sunday.

Warning: In the winter and spring the outer walls some of Agra's major buildings are often home to wild bees nests. While usually the bees keep themselves to themselves, and they should not give any cause for alarm, they can be a nuisance, both under foot at the Taj Mahal and in the Red Fort. Be prepared to take appropriate avoiding action.

The Red Fort

Open daily 0700-1800. Rs 2, Fri free. Allow 1 hr to 1 hr 30 min for a visit. Guide books and good postcards. Clean toilets.

On the W bank of the Yamuna River, **Akbar**'s magnificent fort dominates the centre of the city. The site was originally used by the son of **Sher Shah**, but the present structure owes its origins to Akbar who erected the walls and gates and the first buildings inside. **Shah Jahan** built the impressive imperial quarters and mosque, while **Aurangzeb** added the outer ramparts.

If you have already visited the Red Fort in Delhi you will immediately notice some of the striking similarities. The outer walls, just over 20 metres high, faced with red sandstone and topped with pointed merlons, tower above the outer moat. The shape of the fort is that of a crescent, flattened on the E to give a long nearly straight wall facing the river, with a total perimeter of 2.4 km. This is punctuated at regular intervals by bastions. Like Shah Jahan's fort the main entrance is also in the centre of the western wall, the **Delhi Gate**, facing the bazaar. However, in Agra you can only enter now from the **Amar Singh** gate in the S. A third entrance, the **Water Gate**, faces the river. The **Delhi Gate** which used to lead to the Jama Masjid in the city is now permanently closed. Although only the southern one third of the fort is open to the public this includes nearly all the buildings of interest.

You enter through the **Amar Singh Gate** having had to contend with enthusiastic vendors of cheap soapstone boxes and knick-knacks, 'films' (camera film), leather whips and macrame table cloths. Try to ignore their attentions unless you want to buy something – and if you do, it's well worth bargaining hard. The admission kiosk is inside the first gate. Here you will be pestered by guides. Most of these are not particularly good.

The fortifications The sheer scale of the fortifications are immediately impressive. There was a 9 m wide and 10 m deep moat (still evident but containing stagnant water) filled with water from the Yamuna, an outer wall on the river side and an imposing 22 m high inner, main wall. It gives a feeling of great defensive power. The route through the Amar Singh Gate is dog-legged. Although it served as a model for Shah Jahan's Red Fort in Delhi its own model was the Rajput fort built by Raja Man Singh Tomar of Gwalior in 1500. **See page 288.** If an aggressor managed to get through the outer gate they would have to make a right hand turn and thereby expose their flank to the defenders on the inner wall. The inner gate is solidly powerful in appearance but has been attractively decorated with tiles. The similarities with Islamic patterns of the tilework are obvious, though the Persian blue was also used in the Gwalior Fort and may well

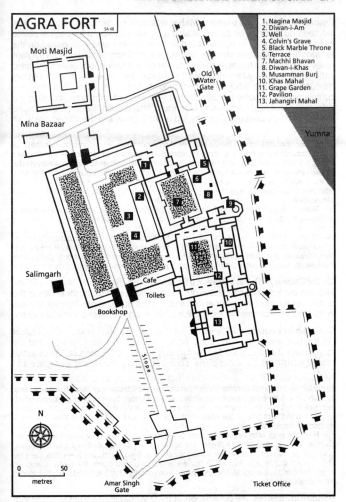

AGRA FORT SA 48

Moti Masjid

Mina Bazaar

Old Water Gate

Yumna

Salimgarh

Cafe

Toilets

Bookshop

Slope

N

0   50
metres

Amar Singh Gate

Ticket Office

1. Nagina Masjid
2. Diwan-i-Am
3. Well
4. Colvin's Grave
5. Black Marble Throne
6. Terrace
7. Machhi Bhavan
8. Diwan-i-Khas
9. Musamman Burj
10. Khas Mahal
11. Grape Garden
12. Pavilion
13. Jahangiri Mahal

have been imitated from that example. The incline up to this point and beyond was suitable for elephants and as you walk past the last gate and up the broad brick lined and paved ramp, it is easy to imagine arriving on elephant back.

At the top of this 100 m ramp is a map and description board on your left, a gate in front and a building and garden on your right. The toilets (in poor condition) are round to the right of the gate. There is a shop selling books, postcards and slides in the arcade within the gate and a refreshment kiosk on the right on the other side. The best route round the buildings is not to go thorough this gate but to start with the building on your right.

Despite its name, the **Jahangiri Mahal** was built by **Akbar** in about 1570 as women's quarters for his palace. Now it is all that survives of his original palace buildings. Almost 75 m square, it is built of stone and simply decorated on the exterior. In front is a large stone bowl which was probably used to contain fragrant rose water. Tillotson has pointed out that the blind arcade of pointed arches inlaid with white marble which decorate the façade are copied from 14th century monuments of the **Khilji** and **Tughluqs** in Delhi. He notes that they are complemented by some features derived from Hindu architecture, including the balconies (*jarokhas**) protruding from the central section, the sloping dripstone in place of eaves (*chajja**) along the top of the façade, and the domed *chattris** at its ends.

The presence of distinctively Hindu features should not be taken to indicate a synthesis of architectural styles at this early stage of Mughal architecture, as can be seen much more clearly from inside the Jahangiri Mahal. Here most of the features are straightforwardly Hindu; square headed arches and extraordinarily carved capitals and brackets illustrate the vivid work of local Hindu craftsmen employed by Akbar without any attempt either to curb their enthusiasm for florid decoration and mythical animals nor to produce a fusion of Hindu and Islamic ideas.

Tillotson argues that although there are a few Islamic touches the central courtyard is essentially Hindu, in significant contrast with most earlier Indo-Islamic buildings. In these, he points out, an Islamic scheme was modified by Hindu touches. He suggests therefore that the Jahangiri Mahal marks the start of a more fundamental kind of Hinduization, typical of several projects during Akbar's middle period of rule, including the palace complex in Fatehpur Sikri. However, it did not represent a real fusion of ideas, something that only came under Shah Jahan, simply a juxtaposition of sharply contrasting styles.

On the S side is **Jodh Bai's Drawing Room** (named after one of Jahangir's wives) while on the E the hall court leads onto a more open yard by the inner wall of the fort. In contrast to other palaces in the fort, this is quite simple. Through the slits in the wall you can see the Taj. There is a better place to take photos further on.

Shah Jahan's palace buildings Turn left through to Shah Jahan's **Khas Mahal** (1636). First there is an open tower from which you can view the walls and see to your left the decorated Mussaman Burj tower. The extensive use of white marble transforms the atmosphere, contributing to the new sense of grace and light.

To the left are the formal gardens of the 85 m square geometric *Anguri Bagh* (Grape Garden). In Shah Jahan's time the geometric patterns were enhanced by the choice of flowers which decorated the beds. The terrace on which the Khas Mahal stands has three. You can go down to this and in the middle of the white marble platform wall in front of the Khas Mahal is a decorative water slide.

From the pool with its bays for seating and its fountains, water would drain off along channels decorated to mimic a stream. The surface might be scalloped to produce a rippling waterfall, or inlaid to create a shimmering stream bed. Behind vertical water drops there are little cusped arch alcoves into which flowers would be placed during the day and lamps at night. The effect was magical. The open pavilion on your right has a splendid (and photogenic) view across to the Taj.

Bengali influences The curved roofs of the small pavilions are based on the roof shape of Bengali village huts designed to keep off heavy rain and constructed out of bamboo, curved to give its distinctive form. Such huts can still be seen in W Bengal and Bangladesh today, although the shape was first expressed in stone building by the Sultans of Bengal. Originally they were gilded. It is believed that these were ladies' bedrooms with deep holes in the walls that were so small that only a woman's hand could reach in to retrieve jewels stored there.

The Khas Mahal has some of the original interior decoration restored (1895) and gives an impression of how splendid the painted ceiling must have been. The Diwan-i-Khas at the Red Fort in Delhi was modelled on this. Underneath are rooms used to escape the summer heat. The Khas Mahal illustrates Shah Jahan's original architectural contribution.

These buildings retain some distinctively Islamic Persian features – the geometrical planning of the pavilions and the formal layout of the gardens, for example. They are matched by the normal range of Hindu features such as chattris. However, Tillotson point out that in Shah Jahan's buildings the "Hindu motifs are treated in a new manner, which is less directly imitative of the Hindu antecedents. The temple columns and corbel capitals have been stripped of their rich carving and turned into simpler, smoother forms. The supporting brackets of the *chajja** are similarly not replicas of those on an Indian temple but derived from them. And, as in the Delhi palace, the *chattris** have Islamic domes. Through these subtle changes " he goes on " the indigenous motifs have lost their specifically Hindu identity; they therefore contrast less strongly with the Islamic components, and are bound with them into a new style. The unity is assisted by the use of the cusped arch and the *bangaldar* roof – forms which had, in various versions, been widely used in India in the past, and so also had no exclusive association."

A true synthesis Seen in this light Tillotson claims that the Khas Mahal of Agra's Red Fort actually achieves a synthesis which eluded Akbar's designs. He writes that "Shah Jahan's palaces, no less than Akbar's, draw on India's two main traditions; but here the various parts are combined, not simply in a collage, but in a new and resolved style. It is that resolution which gives the buildings their appearance of purity. There is no longer an exuberant eclecticism suggesting delight of diversity, but instead a dignified unity suggesting confidence in a new order. The purity which some writers have supposed to be Persian is in fact Mughal, and in the pavilions of the Anguri Bagh it makes its debut: here Mughal architecture comes of age."

The **Mussaman Burj** On the left of the Khas Mahal is the Mussaman Burj (*Octagonal Tower*, though sometimes corrupted into Saman Burj, then translated as Jasmine Tower). It is a beautiful octagonal tower with an open pavilion. With its openness, elevation and the benefit of cooling evening breezes blowing in off the Yamuna river, this could well have been used as the emperor's bedroom. It has been suggested that this is where Shah Jahan lay on his deathbed, gazing at the Taj. Access to this tower is through a magnificently decorated and intimate apartment with a scalloped fountain in the centre. The inlay work here is exquisite, especially above the pillars. In front of the fountain is a sunken courtyard which could be flooded and in the **Shish Mahal** (Mirror Palace) opposite are further examples of decorative water engineering.

From the tower you can appreciate the defensive qualities of the site of the fort and the fortifications erected to take advantage of it. In the area between the outer rampart and the inner wall gladiatorial battles between man and tiger, or elephants were staged. The tower was the emperor's grandstand seat.

Next to the Mussaman Burj is the **Diwan-i-Khas** (Hall of Private Audience, 1637) which is approached on this route by a staircase which brings you out at the side. On the wall is a plaque to commemorate the fact that the British undertook some restoration work. The interior of the Diwan-i-Khas which is really a pavilion open on three sides is closed but the fine proportions of the building can still easily be appreciated. The interior was richly decorated with tapestries and carpets. The marble pillars are inlaid with semi-precious stones in delightful floral patterns in pietra dura, relieved by carving. It is smaller than the one at Delhi which was modelled on it.

The Macchi Bhavan On the terrace in front of the **Diwan-i-Khas** are two throne 'platforms'. The Emperor sat on the white marble platform facing the **Macchi Bhavan** (Fish building) waiting to meet visiting dignitaries. There was often a certain amount of one-upmanship in this exercise, the emperor wishing to be deified, the visitor not wanting to be too obsequious.

Gascoigne recounts an example of this at Shah Jahan's court when the emperor tried to trick a haughty Persian ambassador into bowing low as he approached the throne. He did this by erecting a fence with a small wicket gate so that his visitor would have to enter on hands and knees. The ambassador, with great agility of mind, did so but entered backwards, thus presenting his bottom first to the emperor. The black marble throne at the rear of the terrace is the one used by Salim (who later changed his name to Jahangir – 'Seizer of the World') when claiming to be emperor at Allahabad. It is now a popular prop for group photographs.

A reddish stain in one spot is alleged to be blood.

If you go to the corner opposite the Diwan-i-Khas you can go through two doorways and have a view over the small courtyards of the *zenana** (harem). Further round in the next corner is the **Nagina Masjid**. Shoes must be removed at the doorway. This was the private mosque of the ladies of the court and was built by Shah Jahan. Beneath this was a bazaar where merchants were invited to display their goods to the women.

The Diwan-i-Am The rooms around the Machhi Bhawan were imperial offices. Go down an internal staircase and you enter the **Diwan-i-Am** from the side. The clever positioning of the pillars gives the visitor arriving through the gate in the right hand hall of the courtyard an uninterrupted view of the throne. On the back wall of the pavilion are *jalis*, screens to enable the women of the court to watch the proceedings. The hall has three aisles of nine bays and is 64 m long and 23 m deep. The throne alcove is of richly decorated white marble. It used to house the extraordinary Peacock Throne, completed after seven years work in 1634. "It was built on the usual Mughal pattern, with a cushioned cradle shaded by a canopy. But in this case, the canopy was carved in enamel work and studded with individual gems, its interior was thickly encrusted with rubies, garnets and diamonds, and it was supported on twelve emerald covered columns" writes Tillotson. When Shah Jahan moved his capital to Delhi he took the throne with him to the Red Fort, only for it to be taken back to Persia as loot by Nadir Shah in 1739.

To the right of the Diwan-i-am as you look outwards you can see the domes of the **Moti Masjid** (Pearl Mosque, 1646-53), an extremely fine building closed to visitors because of structural problems. Opposite the Diwan-i-am are the barracks and **Mina Bazaar**, also closed to the public. In the paved area in front of the Diwan-i-am is the tomb of Mr John Russell Colvin, the Lieutenant Governor of the NW Provinces who died here during the 1857 Mutiny. Stylistically it is sadly out of place.

The tour ends back at the bookshop. The café is a pleasant place for a drink or ice-cream before leaving the Red Fort.

Itimad-ud-Daulah

This is the least visited of Agra's three great monuments and surprisingly ignored by many. Along with the Chaunsath Khamba in Delhi it set a startling precedent as the first Mughal building to be faced with white inlaid marble (inlaid with contrasting stones). It is set in the traditional garden. Unlike the Taj it is small, intimate and, because it is less frequented, has an air of serenity and peace that is quite in keeping with its purpose.

Entrance Rs 2 Open daily, sunrise to sunset. The tomb was built for **Ghiyas Beg**, a Persian who had obtained service in Akbar's court. On Jahangir's succession in 1605 he became *Wazir* (Chief Minister) and received the title of Itimad-ud-daulah ('Pillar of Government'). Jahangir fell in love with his daughter, Mehrunissa, who at the time was married to a Persian. When her husband died in 1607 (and it has been said, without substantiation, that Jahangir had a hand in his death) she entered Jahangir's court as a lady-in-waiting. Four years later Jahangir married her. Thereafter she was known first as **Nur Mahal** ('Light of the Palace'), later being promoted to **Nur Jahan** ('Light of the World') – see page 96.

Her family was almost an extension of the royal family. Her father was *Wazir**, her brother Asaf Khan was Jahangir's second most trusted adviser and later Shah Jahan's (r1627-58) wazir. Her niece Mumtaz married Shah Jahan (r1627-58). Asaf Khan's son, Shaishta Khan became Aurangzeb's (r1658-1707) wazir. In short, her family provided two successive first ladies and three successive chief ministers and as the Mughal historian Bamber Gascoigne noted, the two most perfect Mughal tombs, Itimad-ud-Daulah and the Taj Mahal, belong to the Persian adventurer and his granddaughter rather than to the great Mughal emperors themselves.

The plan Nur Jahan built the tomb for her father in the pleasure garden that he himself had laid out. It was constructed in the six years after her father died in 1622. Located 4 km upstream from the Taj Mahal and on the opposite bank of the river Yamuna, it is a beautifully conceived gem of white marble, mosaic and lattice. The enclosure is approached from the E through a red sandstone gateway embellished with marble mosaics. You can get a good view from the roof of the entrance. A sandstone pathway leads to the main tomb which stands on a low platform (4 m high and 45 m square) inlaid with marble decoration. The tomb itself is a low building (21 m square) with a dome-roofed octagonal minaret (12 m high) at each corner and a central rooftop pavilion in marble tracery. If it has a shortcoming it is that the minarets rather dwarf the central pavilion, making it appear squat, but such a weakness seems somehow irrelevant in the light of the superb decoration.

A young Scottish soldier serving in India in 1800, **Patrick Macleod**, gave a vivid description of a march to Agra and his first sight of the Itimad ud daulah in a letter home. He wrote: "This building appeared to me at the time I first beheld it as much more magnificent a structure than I had expected to have seen in Agra, but in this I was afterwards agreeably disappointed. This was a mausoleum in the centre of a large enclosed garden, of a square form, but what constituted its magnificence was its being all faced with high polished white marble inlaid as I then thought in the most masterly style with different coloured marbles forming that kind of ornament called mosaic work. In the interior of the buildings were the tombs of the vizier and his son in a very pretty kind of brown marble. Although there was nothing striking in the architecture of the building, still we could not but contemplate its magnificence as superior to any thing we had yet seen and unanimously agreed, that if we were to view nothing else, this was well worth the trouble of our jaunt." As he had just marched all the way from Kanpur that was no lightly given testimonial.

Pietra dura The main chamber contains the tomb of Itimad-ud-Daulah and his wife and is richly decorated with mosaics and semi-precious stones inlaid in the white marble. This technique, belonging more to the art of a jeweller than a stonemason, achieved popularity in Europe in the 16th century. Some have argued that the concept and skill must have travelled from its European home of Florence to India. However, there are differences between the two. Florentine pietra dura is figurative whereas the Indian version is essentially decorative and can be seen as a refinement its Indian predecessor, the patterned mosaic (see the S Gateway at Sikandra). **See page 171.**

The development of style Marble screens of geometric lattice work permit soft lighting of the inner chamber. The yellow marble caskets appear to have been carved out of wood. On the top of the woman's tomb is a replica of a slate, the implication being 'here is my heart, clear as a slate, write on it what you will'. On the engraved walls of the chamber is the recurring theme of a wine flask with snakes as handles. This was perhaps a reference by Nur Jahan, the tomb's creator, to her husband Jahangir's excessive drinking habits. The flanking chambers contain the tombs of other family members. Stylistically, the tomb marks a change from the sturdy and manly buildings of Akbar's reign to softer, more feminine lines. The roof retains a distinctive Hindu influence with its curved roof and broad eaves. In the rooftop pavilion there are replica tombs of the proper one in the main chamber below. This became a popular feature throughout N India (see the Taj Mahal).

Chini ka Rauza 1 km to the N of the Itimad ud daulah is the **Chini ka Rauza**. Literally translated as the 'China Tomb', this is the tomb of **Afzal Khan** who was in the service of both Jahangir and Shah Jahan. He died in Lahore in 1639 and was buried in Agra at this tomb which he had had constructed during his lifetime. The chamber has been severely damaged and the outside is decorated with enamelled plaster as were many Mughal buildings in Lahore. The Persian influence is quite strong.

Ram Bagh (3 km from Itimad-ud-daulah). Further upstream still is what is believed to be the first Mughal garden in India. Its name is a corruption of the original "Arambagh" – literally "garden of rest". It is reputed to have been laid out by Babur (r1526-30) as a pleasure garden and was the resting place of his body before its internment at Kabul. Now in ruins, little can be seen. There is the Battis Khamba, a tall octagonal red sandstone cupola supported on 36 (battis is the Hindi for this) pillars. Between the Chini ka Rauza and Rambagh is **Zuhara bagh**, another enclosed garden named after Zuhara, one of Babur's daughters. Little remains.

The Taj Mahal

Open daily, sunrise to 1930 hr. Rs 2 except on Fri when it is usually free (and consequently very busy). Best visited in early morning and late evening. Allow 1-2 hr. **Note** The Archaeological Survey of India explicitly asks visitors not to make donations to anyone in the Taj, including the custodians in the tomb itself, who often ask for money.

When the Taj Mahal was constructed, the Mughal Empire was already past its prime. The Taj, despite its unquestionable beauty was an extravagance which the empire could not pay for. Shah Jahan was imprisoned by his son Aurangzeb and confined to his marble palace at the Red Fort. Here he lived out his remaining eight years, a prisoner gazing across the Yamuna river at his beloved wife's memorial.

The state of the Taj declined with the fortunes of the Mughal Empire, the gardens becoming quite overgrown with weeds. In the 19th century the Taj was a favourite place for courting couples and open air balls were held by the British outside the tomb itself. Lord Bentinck, Governor General 1828-35 planned to have the Taj dismantled and sold off in pieces by auction in England. In this way, wealthy Victorians could have a bit of the Taj Mahal in their gardens. Cranes were even erected in the garden. The plan was only abandoned when a pilot auction of part of Agra's Red Fort failed to attract enough interest. Fortunately, Lord Curzon, one of Bentinck's successors (1899-1905), repaired much of the damage done over the centuries, reset the marble platform around the Taj, and cleaned up the gardens.

Viewing The best way of viewing the Taj is to do so at different times of the day and year. Unfortunately, it is now no longer possible to view it by moonlight. In winter (Dec-Feb), it is worth being there at sunrise. Then the mists that often lie over the river Yamuna lift as the sun rises and casts its golden rays over the pearl white tomb. It appears then as though the Taj Mahal, beautifully lit in the soft, warming light, is floating on air.

The approach You can approach the Taj from three directions. The E entrance is often used by groups arriving by coach, the S is from the township that sprang up during the construction of the Taj and the W entrance is that usually used by persons arriving by car or rickshaw from the Red Fort. The ticket offices are shown on the map. From these entrances you approach the gateway proper. On the W approach there are State Govt. emporia selling souvenirs and handicrafts. This used to be an arcade of shops during construction. On the E approach the flanking buildings were stables and accommodation for visitors to the Taj. Because of threats to bomb the Taj, bags are examined by security officials at the entrance. If you have a video camera you are required to hand this in for safe keeping.

The origin of the Taj To the poet Tagore it was 'a tear on the face of eternity', a building to echo the cry 'I have not forgotten, I have not forgotten, O beloved.' (*The Fight of Swans*). The Taj Mahal is an enduring monument to love, with a continually fulfilling beauty. **Shah Jahan** (1618-1707, r1627-58), fifth of the Great Mughals was devoted to his wife *Mumtaz Mahal* (Jewel of the Palace), though he still insisted that she travel with him in all states of health with the effect that she died at the age of 39 giving birth to her 14th child. On her deathbed it is said that she asked him to show the world how much they loved one another. It is also said that his hair went grey almost overnight, that he went into mourning for two years and observed a very simple life. At the same time he turned away from the business of running an empire and became more involved with his other great love, architecture, resolving to build his wife the most magnificent memorial on earth. It was to be placed along the river Yamuna in full view from his palace at the fort and it was to be known as the Taj-i-mahal (The Crown of the Palace).

The construction According to the French traveller **Tavernier** the Taj complex took 22 years to construct and employed a workforce of 20,000. The red sandstone used was available locally but the white marble was quarried at **Makrana**, near Jodhpur, 300 km away and transported by a fleet of 1,000 elephants, each capable of carrying a 2.25 tonne block. Precious stones for the inlay came from far and wide: carnelian (red) from Baghdad, jasper (red, yellow and brown) from the Punjab, jade (green) and crystal from China, Lapis lazuli (bright blue) from Afghanistan and Ceylon, turquoise from Tibet, chrysolite (gold) from Egypt, amethysts (violet) from Persia, agates (various colours) from the Yemen, malachite (dark green) from Russia, diamonds from Golconda in Central India and mother of pearl from the Indian ocean. A 3.2 km ramp was used to lift material up to the level of the dome and because of the river bank site and the sheer weight of the building, boreholes were filled with metal coins and fragments to provide suitable foundations.

Myths surround masterpieces and the Taj Mahal is no exception. On completion it is said that the emperor ordered the chief mason's right hand to be cut off to prevent him from repeating this masterpeice. A much more widely believed legend suggests that Shah Jahan intended to build a replica for himself in black marble on the other side of the river and that the two be connected by a bridge made in alternate blocks of black and white marble. Yet another suggests that the inlaid pietra dura work was carried out by Europeans. Historical evidence for these assertions is negligible. Although no one knows who drew up the plans, the overall work is so clearly the result of a flowering of architectural development that had been taking place through the Mughal period, fusing the traditions of Indian Hindu and Persian Muslim into a completely distinct form, that there is no escaping the conclusion that its designers must have had long experience on the developing Mughal tradition, working to meet the demands of their Indian Muslim patron.

The approach One aspect of the unique beauty of the Taj is the way in which subtlety is blended with grandeur and a massive overall design is matched with immaculately intricate execution. All these features contribute to the breathtaking first impression you gain as you pass through the arch of the entrance gateway. You will already have seen the dome of the tomb in the distance, looking almost like a miniature, but as you walk through the arcade of shops and into the open square before the main entrance the Taj itself is so well hidden that you almost wonder where it can be. The glorious surprise is kept until the last moment, and before you can experience it you are faced with the massive red sandstone gateway of the entrance, designed to guard the enormous wealth inside as well as to symbolise the divide between the secular world and paradise.

In the Koran, the garden is constantly cited as a symbol for paradise. Islam was born in the deserts of Arabia. Muslims venerate water, without which plants will not grow and the old Persian word pairidaeza means 'garden'. It is no coincidence then that green is the favourite colour of Muslims. To the Muslim entering the enclosed garden it is the nearest thing to heaven on earth. The inscription round the central arch is from the 89th chapter of the Koran and reads: 'O soul that art at rest, return to the Lord, at peace with Him and he at peace with you. So enter as one of his servants; and enter into His garden'.

The gateway The gateway, completed in 1648, stands 30 m high. The small domed pavilions (**chattris***) on top are Hindu in style and usually signify regality. The huge brass door is recent. The original doors were solid silver and decorated with 1100 nails whose heads were contemporary silver coins. Along with some other treasures, they were plundered by the Jats who ravaged the Mughal empire after its collapse. A final feature of the gateway is that if you look at the lettering, it appears to be the same size. The engravers skilfully enlarged and lengthened the letters as their distance from the ground increased. This created the illusion of consistency.

Although the gateway is remarkable in itself, one of its functions is to prevent you getting any glimpse of the tomb inside until you are right in the doorway itself. That first view suddenly unfolds from the framing archway. At first only the tomb is visible, stunning in its nearness, but as you move forward the minarets come into view. Beyond the entrance and into the sunlight, it is a good idea to move either right or left to avoid the inevitable crowds. From here, see how the people walking around the tomb are dwarfed by the 70 m high dome.

The Garden 'Gardens underneath which rivers flow' is a frequently used expression for the faithful, appearing more than 30 times in the Koran. Four main rivers of paradise are also specified: water, milk, wine and purified honey. This is the origin of the quartered garden (*char bagh**). The watercourses divided the garden into quadrants and all was enclosed behind a private wall. To the Muslim the beauty of creation and of the garden was held to be a reflection of God. The great Sufi poet *Rumi* used much garden imagery: 'The trees are engaged in ritual prayer and the birds in singing the litany'. Thus, the garden becomes as important as the tomb.

The Taj garden, well kept though it is nowadays, is nothing compared with its former glory. The whole of the Taj complex measures 580 x 300 m and the garden 300 x 300 m. The guiding principle is one of symmetry. The four quadrant lawns, separated by the watercourses (rivers of heaven) emanating from the central, raised pool, were divided into 16 flower beds, making a total of 64. Each bed was planted with 400 plants. The trees, all carefully planted to maintain the symmetry were either *cypress* (signifying death) or fruit trees (life). The channels were stocked with fish and the gardens with nightingales, peacocks and other colourful birds. Guards dressed in white robes patrolled the area, reputedly scaring off birds of prey with pea-shooters. Such was the air of tranquillity and joy. Nobles visited them for picnics and celebrations – that is why there are stables and guesthouses in the forecourt area. It is well worth wandering along the side avenues for not only is it much more peaceful but also good for framing photos of the tomb with foliage.

The mosque and its jawab On the E and W sides of the tomb are identical red sandstone buildings. On the W (left hand side) is a mosque. It is common in Islam to build one next to a tomb. It sanctifies the area and provides a place for worship. The replica on the other side is known as the **Jawab** (Answer). This cannot be used for prayer as it faces away from Mecca.

The tomb The four minarets (41.6 m high) at each corner of the plinth provide balance to the tomb. Minarets used in this fashion first appeared in India with Akbar's tomb at Sikandra. They are used again at Itimad-ud-daulah and are refined still further here. Each was constructed with a deliberate slant outwards – the SW by 20 cm, the others by 5 cm. This was so that in the unlikely event of an earthquake, they would fall away from the tomb, not onto it. On each pillar is written a letter (R,H,M,N) which together spell the word ar-Rahman (The All Merciful). This is one of the 99 names of Allah.

There is only one point of access to the plinth (6.7 m high and 95 m square) and tomb, a double staircase on the S side (facing the entrance). Here, visitors must either remove their shoes (socks can be kept on) or have cloth covers tied over them. There are attendants to look after shoes and they request some bakshish for doing so when you return. Payment is not required as the sign round the corner (moved deliberately, but by whom, one wonders?!) indicates. This also applies to the attendants inside the tomb. In hot weather the white marble gets very hot.

The tomb is square with bevelled corners. Each side is 56.6 m long with a large central arch flanked by two pointed arches. At each corner smaller domes rise while in the centre is the main dome topped by a brass finial. The dome is actually a double dome and this device, Central Asian in origin, was used to gain height. With the Taj, the Mughals brought to fruition an experiment first tried in Humayun's tomb in Delhi, 90 years earlier. The resemblance of the dome to a huge pearl is not coincidental. There is a saying of the Prophet that describes the throne of God as a dome of white pearl supported by four pillars. The exterior ornamentation is calligraphy (verses of the Koran, again calibrated), beautifully carved panels, e.g. by the entrance, and inlay work. The last, in the form of large floral sweeps and chevrons is immaculately proportioned.

Inside the tomb The interior of the mausoleum comprises a lofty central chamber, a crypt (*maqbara**) immediately below this and four octagonal corner rooms originally intended to house the graves of other family members. Shah Jahan's son and usurper, Aurangzeb (r1658-1707), failed to honour this wish. The central chamber contains replica tombs, the real ones being in the crypt. It was customary to have a public tomb and a private one. The public tomb was originally surrounded by a jewel encrusted silver screen. Aurangzeb removed this fearing it might be stolen and replaced it with an octagonal screen of marble and inlaid precious stones, the cost being Rs 50,000. It is a stupendous piece of workmanship. Examine the lattice (jali) screens. They are each carved from one block of marble. See the entrance to the tombs and the finials surmounting the screen. These curved surfaces have been inlaid, a most difficult task. Examine the flowers on the borders of the screens. By placing a flashlight on the surface you can see how luminescent the marble is and the intricacy of the inlay work. Some flowers have as many as 64 pieces making up the petals.

Hanging above the tombs is a cairene lamp whose flame is supposed to never go out. The original was stolen by the Jats. This one was given by **Lord Curzon**, Governor General of British India (1899-1905), who had it made in Egypt. The tomb of Mumtaz rests immediately beneath the dome. If you look from behind it back to the gateway, and assuming the view is uninterrupted, you can see how it lines up dead centre with the main entrance. Shah Jahan's tomb is larger and to the side, marked by a 'male' pen-box which was the sign of a cultured or noble person. Not originally intended to be placed there but squeezed in by Aurangzeb, this flaws the otherwise perfect symmetry of the whole complex. Both tombs are exquisitely inlaid with semi-precious stones. Identical, real ones are in the crypt below. Finally, the accoustics of the building are superb, the domed ceiling being designed to echo chants from the Koran and musicians' melodies. Take a walk round the outside the tomb before retrieving your shoes to appreciate it from all sides.

Museum The museum above the entrance has an interesting collection of photographs etc. on the Taj. It is worth a brief visit. See under Museums.

Hotels Most are 5-10 km from the airport and 2-5 km from Agra Cantt. Rly.
AL *Welcomgroup Mughal Sheraton*, Fatehabad Rd, Taj Ganj. T 64701-4, Cable: Welcotel, Telex: 0565-210. 282 rms, some with views of the Taj. 12 km airport, 1 km Taj Mahal. Excellent Nauratna restaurant serving Mughlai food (good Indian music), sports (badminton, mini-golf, tennis, archery), secretarial and telex services, elephant, camel and carriage rides. Beautiful hotel designed by Ramesh Khosla in the Mughal tradition (low brick and marble buildings, utilising open spaces, gardens and breezes) and one of India's finest. Well furnished and maintained. Winner of the 1980 Aga Khan Award for architecture. 25% of rms have Taj view. **A** *Taj View*, Fatehabad Rd, Taj Ganj. T 64171-5, Cable: Tajview, Telex: 0565-202 Tajv in. 100 rm. 12 km airport. Well run by the Taj Group, rooms pleasant, service good. Superior rooms (even nos) have a view of the Taj Mahal. **A** *Clarks Shiraz*, 54 Taj Rd. T 72421-6, Cable: Shiraz, Telex:0565-211. 147 rm. Good shops, croquet, golf, tennis, pleasant gardens, pool. Well established and comfortable, distant view of the Taj from 4th floor and excellent roof top restaurant. 'Tourist menu' can be boring. **A** *Agra Ashok*, 6B Mall Rd. T 76223-7. Cable: Ashokotel, Telex: 0565-313. 55 rm. 3 km Taj. Typical of Asoka Group (ITDC) hotels – quite

pleasant but slow service.

C *Mumtaz*, Fatehabad Rd. T 64771, Telex: 0565-222 Mmtz in. 50 rm, some with view of Taj. 1 km Taj. Central a/c. Pool, secretarial and telex services, bar, TV, shops, doctor. Guests are allowed to use the facilities at the Mughal Sheraton. **C** *Shahanshah Inn*, Fatehabad Rd. T 62609, Telex: 0565-299. 24 rm a/c and non a/c. Restaurant, pool, TV, travel desk. **C** *Amar*, Fatehabad Rd. T 65696, Telex:0565-341 Amar in, Cable: Hotel Amar. 68 rm, all doubles (a/c and non a/c). Restaurant, bar, TV, exchange. Good value.

D *Grand*, 137 Station Rd. T 74014, Cable Grandhotel. 46 rm all double (a/c and non a/c). A/c restaurant, camping, exchange, TV in lobby and some rooms. Tennis and badminton. A popular hotel. **D** *Mayur Tourist Complex*, Fatehabad Rd. T 67302, Cable: Mayur. 30 rm (most a/c) in bungalows. TV. Restaurant, bar, garden. Good value. **D** *Imperial*, M.G. Rd. T 72500. 8 rm non a/c. Restaurant, bar. **D** *Lauries*, M.G. Rd. T 72536, Cable: Lauries. 28 rm some aircooled. Bar, restaurant, pool, exchange, camping, car hire. Magic show available on request. Once a favourite, now much neglected. **D** *Col Bakshi's Guesthouse*, 5 Lakshman Nagar. T 61292. Rooms with bath. Newish, clean and well-run. A/c available at extra charge. **D** *Ranjit*, 263 Station Rd. T 64446, Cable: Ranjithotel. 30 rm non a/c. Restaurant, TV in lobby, car hire.

E *Agra*, 165 Cariappa Rd. T 72330,66987, Cable: Agra Hotel. 18 rm, mostly double, some have Taj view, 1 a/c rm. Good food. **E** *Jaiwal*, 3 Taj Rd, Sadar Bazaar. T 64141-2. 17 rm. Central a/c. **E** *Khanna*, 19 Ajmer Rd. T 66634. Not far from Tourist Rest House. Rms with bath. Pleasant but front rooms noisy. **E** *Major Bakshi's Guesthouse*, 33/83 Ajmer Rd. T 76828. rms with and without bath. **E** *Colonel Duggal's Guesthouse*, 155 Pertabpura (nr GPO and Tourist Office). **E** *Tourist Resthouse*. Restaurant. Air cooling inadequate in hot season. Fairly basic. **E** *Tourist Bungalow*, Raja Mandi area. T 72123. Long way from anywhere. Garden.

F *Ajay International*, 1 Daresi, nr Agra Fort rly. T 64427. Cheap and noisy. **F** *Jaggi*, The Mall. T 72370. Rms with bath available. Basic. **F** *Jai Hind*, Naulakha Rd (off Taj Rd, the main street of Sadar). T 73502 Basic and friendly. **F** *UPSTDC Taj Khema*, Eastern Gate, Taj Mahal. T 66150. 6 rm, 8 camping huts. Restaurant, travel service. Just behind the Taj Mahal. *Railway Retiring Rooms* at Agra Fort and Agra Cantt. Stations. Only for rail passengers. T 72121, 72515. Reservations in advance. Send money order/ draft to Railway Superintendent, Agra Cantt. Some A/c and an inexpensive dormitory.

Restaurants *Kwality*, Taj Rd, T 72525, popular, open 0900-2400; *Chung Wah*, Taj Rd, T 72370. Chinese. Open 1000-1500 and 1800-2300. *Prakash*, Taj Rd, T 74593. Indian, especially Mughlai. Open 1000-2300. *Taj*, outside the Taj Mahal, T 76644. Open 0800-2200.

All the larger hotels have restaurants most of which are pleasant and are multi-cuisine. *Nauratna* at the Mughal Sheraton is particularly good for N Indian food and has live music.

Banks *Allahabad*, Hotel Clarks Shiraz Taj Rd; *Andhra*, Taj Rd Sadar bazar; *Baroda*, M.G. Rd; *Canara*, M.G. Rd; *Central Bank of India*, M.G. Rd; *Indian Overseas Bank*, Hotel Taj View Fatehabad Rd; *Punjab*, Raja-ki-Mandi; *State Bank of India*, Chhipitola; *Vijaya*, Taj Rd, Sadar Bazar.

Shopping The handicrafts Agra specialises in are mostly related to the court, e.g. jewellery, inlaid and carved marble, carpets and clothes. If you are staying in Agra, it is best to make your own way to the various establishments mentioned if you want the best price. Tour guides, taxi drivers, rickshaw wallahs all receive commissions which is built into the price you pay. If

you go independently, you should get a better price. You will have to bargain hard anyway.
Warning If you do not find exactly what you want, you may be tempted to place an order for a carpet or an inlaid marble piece and have it posted on. Reports suggest that what you receive may not be exactly what you ordered.

Silk, silk/cotton mixed and woollen hand knotted **carpets** and woven woollen **dhurries** are all made in Agra. The quality is high and the prices tend to be better than in Delhi. *Harish Carpets*, Vibhav Nagar Rd, T 75598, has a very wide range and is conveniently located for major hotels. Also *Bansal Carpets*, Naulakha Market. Open 1000-1900 and *Mangalik* and Co. 5 Taj Rd, Sadar Bazar. Nearby are the *Modern Book Depot*, a chemist, *Kwality Restaurant* and *Sadar Bazar* itself. Closed on Mon.

Delicately inlaid **marble** made by generations of the same families as those who worked on the Taj is widely available. *U.P. Handicrafts Palace*, 49 Bansal Nagar, T 68214, has the widest selection imaginable from table tops to coasters, produces work of an exceptionally high quality and is good value. Will collect you from your hotel. Conveniently located near the *Taj View*. *Oswal*, 30 Munro Rd, Agra Cantt., T 75168 is also extremely good. Most other shops stock some marble and soapstones, often of indifferent quality. You may be able to see craftsmen working on the premises.

For **jewellery** try *Munshi Lal* next to U.P. Handicrafts Palace. There are also Government emporia in the arcade of shops near the Taj entrance. *Gangotri* (U.P.), T 63172. *Kairali* (Kerala), T 62893. *Rajasthali* (Rajasthan), T 73017. *Black Partridge* (Haryana), T 76992. *Kashmir*. Also *U.P. Handlooms* and *UPICA*, Sanjay Palace, Hari Parbat. The main shopping areas for everyday items as well as handicrafts are Sadar Bazaar, Kinari Bazaar, Gwalior Rd, Mahatma Gandhi Rd, and Pertap Pura.

Local Transport City Bus Service: covers most areas. Fare Re 0.50-1. Tempo-rickshaws: point-to-point service. Fare Re 1 per stage. Scooter rickshaws: Re 1.50 per km (usually negotiable). Cycle rickshaws and tongas: easily available. Fares negotiable. Rs 20-25 per day for cycle rickshaw for day from Agra Cantt. Rly Station.

Tourist taxis can be hired from: Travel Corporation (I) Pvt. Ltd., Hotel Clarks Shiraz, Taj Rd, T 64111. Ashok Tours and Travels, Agra Ashok, The Mall, T 681631. Taj Travels, Hotel Clarks Shiraz, T 75128. Tour Aids India, Gopichand Shivhare Rd, T 72338, 74957. Rainbow Travels, Hotel Mumtaz, Fatehabad Rd. T 74605. See also Travel Agents section. Tarriff: Non a/c car Rs 2 per km, full day Rs 240 (100 km), half day Rs 110 (45 km). A/c car rates negotiable.

Sports Golf is available at the Golf Course, Circuit House campus. Contact The Secretary, The Agra Club 191 The Mall T 74084. **Fishing** at Sur Sarovar (23 km). Permits from Executive Engineer, Lower Division, Agra Canal, The Mall Cantt. T 72215.

Museums Taj Mahal Museum. Opening hours same as monument. Small collection of Mughal memorabilia and photographs and miniatures on the Taj through the ages. Free.

Useful Numbers Police 200, Fire 201, Ambulance 202. *Foreigners' Registration Office* 16 Idgah Colony T 74167

Hospitals and Medical Services District Hospital, M.G. Rd, T 74236, Jaggi Nursing and Maternity Home, Vibhav Nagar, T 73315. Lady Lyall Hospital, Noori Gate Rd, T 72658. S.N. Hospital, Hospital Rd, T 72222. Asha Nursing and Maternity Home, Daulpur Hse, opp. State Bank of India, M.G. Rd, T 67153.

Post and Telegraph Head Post Office, The Mall, T 74000. Open 1000-1700 daily except Sun. Central Telegraph Office, The Mall, T 76914. Open 24 hr. Telecom Bureau and Post Office, Taj Mahal, T 68135, 74533. Open 1000-1700. Closed Sun.

Places of Worship *Hindu*: Mankameshwar Mandir, Rawatpura; Satyanarayan Mandir, Shahzadi Mandi; Radhasoami Temple, opp Dayal Bagh; Raoil Temple, M.G. Rd. *Jain*: Digamber Jain Temple, Hari Parbat. *Christian*: Central Methodist Church, M.G. Rd, T 74473; Roman Catholic Cathedral, Wazirpura, T 72407; St Mary's Church, Ajmer Rd, T 72500; Baptist Church, Pertap Pura; St John's Church, opp S.N. Hospital. *Sikh*: Guru ka Tal, near Sikandra; Gurudwara Kalgidhar, Sadar Bazar.

Travel Agents and Tour Operators *Ashok Tours and Travels*, Hotel Agra Ashok, T 76233. *Mercury Travels*, Fatehabad Rd, T 75282. *Sita World Travels*, Taj Rd, T 74922. *Taj Travels*, Beech-ka-Bazaar, Taj Rd, T 75128. See also agents under Local Transport.

Tourist Offices and Information Information Offices : Govt. of India Tourist Office, 191 The Mall, T 72377. Also at Kheria (Agra) Airport during flight times. UP Govt. Tourist Bureau, 64 Taj Rd, T 75034. UP Govt. Tourist Reception Counter, Agra Cantt. Rly Station, T 66438. UP Govt. Tourist Information Centre, UPSTDC Tourist Bungalow, Raja-ki-Mandi, T 77035. Rajasthan Govt. Tourist Office, Taj Mahal Shopping Arcade, T 64582. Haryana Govt. Tourist Office, Taj Mahal Shopping Arcade, T 65950.

Conducted Tours Uttar Pradesh State Tourism Development Corporation (UPSTDC), Taj Khema, Eastern Gate, Taj Mahal, T 66140, conducts the following tours : Sikandra-Fatehpur Sikri (half day) 0930-1400, Rs 35; Sikandra-Fatehpur Sikri-Taj Mahal-Agra Fort (full day), 0930-1800, Rs 50; Fatehpur Sikri (half day) 1030-1400, Rs 30; Fatehpur Sikri-Taj Mahal-Agra Fort (full day) 1030- 1800, Rs 40. UPSRTC, 96 Gwalior Rd, T 72206, and also at Plat form 1, Agra Cantt. Rly Station conducts a Fatehpur Sikri-Taj Mahal-Agra Fort (full day) 1030-1800. Deluxe Rs 45, Ordinary Rs 31. All the above tours commence and terminate at Agra Cantt. Rly Station.

Air Indian Airlines flies daily from Delhi to Agra and on to Khajuraho, Varanasi and Kathmandu, returning on the same route; also 4 times a week from Bombay and back via Jaipur. Long delays in flight departures and arrivals can be expected especially over the winter. Agra and Delhi airports are often closed due to fog. Train travel from Delhi is more reliable, see the (Shatabdi Express) and quicker. **Vayudoot** flies daily between Delhi and Agra. Information and reservations: Indian Airlines, Hotel Clarks Shiraz, Taj Rd, T 75949. Open 1000-1700. Indian Airlines, Airport, T 65950, Open at flight times Vayudoot, Alpha Travels, 18 The Mall (opp CTO Grounds), T 74453, Airport, T 73234 at flight times. Air India, Janta Travels, Hotel Clarks Shiraz, Taj Rd, T 76983. The airport is 7 km from the city centre.

Rail Unless stated otherwise all trains mentioned arrive and depart from Agra Cantt. **New Delhi:** *Shatabdi Exp* 2001, daily, 2021, 2 hr; *Taj Exp* 2179, daily, 1845, 3 hr 15 min. **Mathura:** *Taj Exp* 2179, daily, 1845, 1 hr 59 min. **Jaipur** (from Agra Fort): *Agra Fort Fast Passenger Exp* 9705, daily, 2015, 6 hr 30 min; *Agra-Barmer Exp* 9707, daily, 0815, 11 hr 15 min; *Agra-Jaipur Exp* 2921, daily, 1700, 5 hr. **Lucknow** (from Agra Fort): *Avadh Exp* 5064, daily, 2202, 8 hr 28 min. **Gwalior:** *Shatabdi Exp* 2002, daily, 0810, 1 hr 20 min; *Punjab Mail* 1038, daily, 1035, 2 hr 10 min; Malwa Exp 4068, daily, 2215, 1 hr 55 min. **Jhansi:** *Shatabdi Exp* 2002, daily, 0810, 2 hr 30 min; *Punjab Mail* 1038, daily, 1035, 4 hr 5 min; *Malwa Exp* 4068, daily, 2215, 3 hr 45 min.

Mathura *Taj Exp* 2179, daily, 1845, 55 min. **Bhopal:** *Shatabdi Exp* 2002, daily, 0810, 5 hr 50 min; *Punjab Mail* 1038, daily, 1035, 10 hr; *Malwa Exp* 4068, daily, 2215, 9 hr. **Bombay (VT):** *Punjab Mail* 1038, daily, 1035, 14 hr 15 min; 23 hr 50 min. **Kathgodam (for Nainital) from Agra Fort**: *Kumaon Exp* 5311, daily, 2200, 11 hr 50 min. **Kathgodam and Nainital (via Bareilly Junction):** *Kumaon Exp* 5311, daily, 2200. 11 hr 50 min. **Calcutta (Howrah)** : *Udyan Abha Toofan Exp* 3008, daily. 1235, 29 hr 40 min. Information and reservations: Agra Cantt. Rly Station, Enquiries T 72515, Reservations T 63787. open 0900-1640. Agra Fort Rly Station, T 76161, 72131. Raja-ki-Mandi Rly Station, T 73131. Agra City Rly Station, T 74260. Tundla Rly Station, T 72207.

Bus Most buses from Agra leave from the **Idgah Bus Station** and express buses leave daily for the following: **Delhi** (204 km via Mathura, 5 hr); **Jaipur** (240 km via Bharatpur and Mahua); **Kajuraho** (400 km via Jhansi, 12 hr); **Lucknow** (357 km via Shikohabad, Etawah and Kanpur), **Gwalior** (119 km via Dholpur and Morena); **Nainital** (376 km via Tundla, Etah, Bareilly and Haldwani, 10 hr). Bus information: UPSRTC Bus Stand, Idgah, Enquiries T 64198. UPSRTC Bus Stand, Ram Bagh Crossing (across river Yamuna), T 74141.

Excursions Akbar's tomb at Sikandra, 10 km N of Agra, is described above.

Fatehpur Sikri

37 km W of Agra. The journey itself is interesting. The first two Great Mughals, **Babur** (r1526-1530) and his son **Humayun** (r1530-1540 and 1555-56), both won (in Humayun's case it was won back) Hindustan at the end of their lives. What they left was essentially alien rule with occupation more like an armed camp. **Akbar**, the third and greatest of the Mughals changed that. By marrying a Hindu princess, forging alliances with the Rajput leaders and making the administration of India one of partnership with Hindu nobles and princes rather than armed foreign minority rule, Akbar consolidated his ancestors' gains, put his stamp on India and won the allegiance, loyalty and respect of its influential, and potentially troublesome, inhabitants. In short, Akbar became the accepted Emperor of the whole of N India.

This was the achievement of a man of great personal magnetism, the natural centre of any gathering, and, though formally illiterate, a man of great wisdom and learning as well as undoubted administrative and military skills. In the deserted city of Fatehpur Sikri you can gain a clear insight into this remarkable character.

The birth of Jahangir In spite of his ample supply of wives the 26 year old Akbar had no living heir; the children born to him had all died in infancy. It became his habit to visit holy men to enlist their prayers for a son and heir. A *Sheikh Salim Chishti* living at Sikri, a village 37 km SW of Agra, told the emperor that he would have three sons. Soon after, one of his wives, the daughter of the Raja of Amber, became pregnant, so Akbar sent her to live with the sage. A son Salim was born, later to be known as **Jahangir**. The prophecy was fulfilled when in 1570 another wife gave birth to Murad and in 1572, to Daniyal.

Akbar, so impressed by this sequence of events, resolved to build an entirely new capital at Sikri in honour of the saint. By a fortunate coincidence, the holy man had set up his hermitage on a low hill of hard red sandstone, an ideal location with good building material, easy to work and yet very durable. Over the next 14 years a new city would appear on this hill. For its name the word Fatehpur (town of victory) was added to that of the existing village Sikri.

Fatehpur Sikri is four hundred years old and, so far as the principal buildings are concerned, it is in a state of perfect preservation.

One feature is that they appear to be wooden houses made of stone, in that their techniques of construction and ornamentation are precisely those of craftsmen in wood in other countries. The palace buildings at Fatehpur Sikri consist of nothing but perfectly tailored chunks of stone resting on one another.

The Royal Palace

Entrance Rs 2. Open sunrise to sunset. Allow about 3 hr for a leisurely visit. Hawkers can be troublesome in the mosque and forecourt area. Toilets, fair.

It is most likely that you will approach Fatehpur Sikri through the **Agra Gate**. From Agra is the well-laid out and straight road that Akbar had laid out. It is said that there was a bazaar for its entire length. If approaching from Bharatpur you will pass the site of a lake 32 km in circumference. This provided one defensive barrier. On the other sides was a wall pierced by nine gates : Clockwise – Delhi, Lal (Red), Agra, Birbal, Chodanpol, Gwalior, Tehra (Crooked), Chor (Thief's), Ajmer.

From Agra Gate you enter the monument by the **Naubat Khana** (Music House) where drums were beaten to mark the Royal Approach. Past this you are in the garden of the **Diwan-i-am** (Hall of Public Audience). Akbar was an able administrator demonstrating a liberal-mindedness not common among invaders. The unpopular Poll Tax was abolished on non-Muslims, as was the Pilgrim Tax at Mathura and Akbar founded a public administration system that the British later based theirs on.

On the W wall is the platform for the Emperor's Throne. This backed onto the

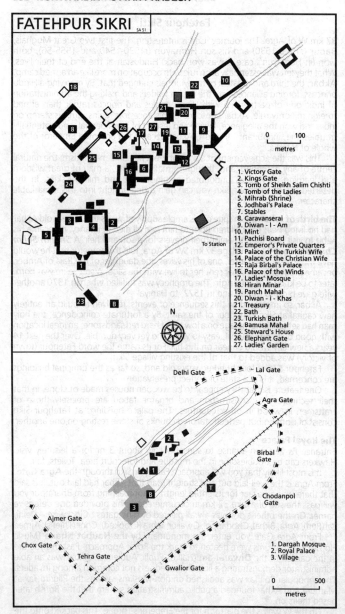

FATEHPUR SIKRI SA 51

0   100
metres

To Station

1. Victory Gate
2. Kings Gate
3. Tomb of Sheikh Salim Chishti
4. Tomb of the Ladies
5. Mihrab (Shrine)
6. Jodhbai's Palace
7. Stables
8. Caravanserai
9. Diwan - I - Am
10. Mint
11. Pachisi Board
12. Emperor's Private Quarters
13. Palace of the Turkish Wife
14. Palace of the Christian Wife
15. Raja Birbal's Palace
16. Palace of the Winds
17. Ladies' Mosque
18. Hiran Minar
19. Panch Mahal
20. Diwan - I - Khas
21. Treasury
22. Bath
23. Turkish Bath
24. Bamusa Mahal
25. Steward's House
26. Elephant Gate
27. Ladies' Garden

N

Delhi Gate
Lal Gate
Agra Gate
Birbal Gate
Chodanpol Gate
Dargah Mosque
Gwalior Gate
Ajmer Gate
Chox Gate
Tehra Gate

1. Dargah Mosque
2. Royal Palace
3. Village

0   500
metres

private palace. In the centre of the courtyard behind the throne is the ***Pachisi Board***. This game is nothing like chess even though it uses a similar board. It is said that Akbar had colourfully clothed slave girls as pieces!

The Diwan-i-Khas (Hall of Private Audience) In the centre of the side to your right, a two storey building stands on its own. It is a single room with a throne platform. Here Akbar would spend long hours in discussion with the Fathers from Goa, Jains, Buddhist Monks, Hindu Pandits (Teachers). They would sit along the walls of the balcony connected to the **Throne Pillar** by *jali** screened walkways, while courtiers could listen to the discussions from the ground floor. Always receptive to new ideas, Akbar developed eclectic beliefs. The decorative techniques and metaphysical labels are incorporated into Fatehpur Sikri. The pillar, for example is shaped like a lotus, a Hindu and Buddhist motif, a Hindu Royal Umbrella (***Chattri****), and the Tree of Life (Islam). The bottom of the pillar is carved in tiers; the first in Muslim designs, the second Hindu, the third Christian and the fourth Buddhist.

The Throne Pillar can be approached by steps from the outside. The design of the Hall deliberately followed the archaic universal pattern of establishing a hallowed spot from which spiritual influence could radiate. In his later years, Akbar developed a mystical cult around himself that saw him as being semi-divine. He appreciated that he could not draw Hindus and Muslims away from their religion but by raising himself to semi-divine status he realised that for his subjects it would be akin to a religious duty to obey and a sacrilege to oppose. In this way he won the allegiance of Hindus and Muslims alike.

The treasury In the NW corner of the courtyard is the **Treasury** which comprises three rooms each protected by a narrow corridor round it. This was for sentries to guard the money. The ceiling struts emerge from the jaws of the mythical sea dragons (makaras) who are the guardians of the treasures of the deep. The serpentine scrolls derive from Jain architecture from W India. Slightly in front of the Treasury is **The Astrologer's Seat**. Whilst not addicted to it like his father Humayun, astrology played an important role in the running of court affairs. Akbar kept Hindu (Jyotishis) and Muslim (Nunajjims) astrologers. It is also possible that it was used by the Court Treasurer.

The Palace of the Turkish Wife is directly opp beyond the Pachisi Board. Despite not being able to bear him any children the **Sultana Ruqayya Begum** was his favourite. Her palace, with a balcony on each side, is so richly carved that it is like entering a finely carved Chinese Box. The walls would originally have been set with semi-precious stones and mirrors to create a **Shish Mahal** (Mirror) Palace. The outside has pillars carved into vines, a very European motif. In the centre of this smaller S courtyard is the **Musicians Tank**. Akbar's favourite musician was the Hindu singer ***Tansen***, one of 'The Nine Jewels of the Court'. Much N Indian music bears his imprint.

In the E corner is the **Rosewater Fountain**. Next to this are the **Emperor's Private Quarters**. There are two main rooms on the ground floor. One certainly housed his library. Although unable to read or write himself, Akbar loved to have books read to him. It is said that wherever he went in the empire, his library of 50,000 manuscripts was taken with him. The recesses in the walls are for this. Behind this room is a larger room, his resting area. Records indicate that Akbar would have a Hindu Brahmin Pandit hoisted up to the balcony to instruct him on the finer points of Hindu thought. On the first floor is the *Khwabgah** (bedroom, or Palace of Dreams). Like the other rooms this was richly decorated in gold and ulramarine colours. Leaving the Private Quarters by the left you enter another courtyard which contained the **Zenana** (Harem) garden and the **Palace of the Christian Wife** (Maryam from Goa). The Persian inscriptions on the beams are verses by **Faizl**, Akbar's poet laureate and another the 'Nine Jewels of the Court'.

The Panch (Five) Mahal is the five storeyed building. This elegant pavilion was a pleasure palace. To counteract the Indian heat, all buildings had long overhanging eaves to increase shade. Shaded arcades were attached and open basements to allow cool air to flow into the building. There are 84 ground floor pillars, a particularly auspicious number as it is the seven planets multiplied by the 12 signs of the zodiac. The second floor pillars (56) all have a different design. There is the Muslim stalactite design (Muqarna) and the Hindu vase and foliage motif signifying harvest and material well-being. From the upper storeys there is a fine view of the rest of Fatehpur Sikri and the adjoining countryside.

Hawa Mahal Through the garden and to the S is the **Hawa Mahal** (Palace of Winds) and **Jodh Bai's Palace**. The first storey is open, the second enclosed by an elaborate jali screen which nevertheless still allowed free circulation of air. Akbar's Rajput princesses lived in this. *Jodh Bai*, the daughter of the Maharaja of Amber and mother of Jahangir, lived in the spacious palace in the centre of this area. Assured of privacy by a 9 m high gate, blending Hindu and Muslims styles. This was guarded by eunuchs. The word *harem* (also known as the zenana) derives from the Arabic Haram which means 'forbidden by law'.

The six-pointed stars enclosing a lotus, may be tantric motifs symbolizing the union of male and female. They are found elsewhere at Fatehpur Sikri (see Salim Chishti's tomb) and in other places too, e.g. Humayun's tomb in Delhi. They do not connote Jewish influence. The centre of the building is a quadrangle around which were the living quarters of other ladies of the harem. The N and S wings are roofed in azure tiles from Multan (Pakistan). As elsewhere in the city, the buildings give the impression of an encampment, of tents of stone, a clear reminder of the nomadic way of living of the Mughal's ancestral homeland in Central Asia.

Raja Birbal's house To the NW of Jodh Bai's Palace is **Raja Birbal's House**. Birbal, a Hindu Brahmin, was the brightest of Akbar's 'Nine Jewels'. Again the building is a combination of styles. The eaves and arches decorated with the lotus are typically Indian, the cusped arches Jain and the floral and geometric designs are Islamic. Some scholars believe that this building was not for Birbal, Akbar's Wazir (Chief Minister) but for his senior queens.

S of the Raja's house are the **Royal Stables**, though some have questioned why stables should be placed next door to the women's living quarters. The niches in the walls could have been used for fodder and the rings for tethering the emperor's camels and horses. Leaving the Royal Palace you now proceed across a car park to the Mosque, the second part of Fatehpur Sikri.

The Mosque
The King's Gate (Badshahi)
This is the entrance Akbar used. Shoes must be left at the gate. The porch is also packed with vendors. This can be irritating because they are aggressive salesmen.

Inside is the vast congregational courtyard (132 m x 111 m). To your right in the corner is the **Jamaat Khana Hall** and next to this the **Tomb of the Royal Ladies**. The mosque area (courtyard, mihrab [shrine], enclosing wall and the two gates on the S (Victory Gate) and E (Badshahi) was constructed in 1571-2 at a cost of Rs 700,000 and is modelled on the Bibi Khanam at Samarkand.

The **Tomb of Sheikh Salim Chishti,** in the brilliant white marble, dominates the N half of the courtyard. This is a masterpiece and one of the finest examples of marble work in India. Serpentine brackets support the eaves and the carved lattice screens surrounding the pavilion are stunning pieces of craftsmanship. The canopy over the tomb is inlaid with mother of pearl. On the cenotaph is the date of the saint's death (1571) and the date of the building's completion (1580). Around the arched entrance are inscribed the names of God, the Prophet and the 4 caliphs of Islam (rulers – derived from successors of Mohammad). The shrine is on the spot of the saint's hermitage. Originally the dome was red sandstone. It was marble veneered in 1806. The screens were added by Jahangir's foster brother in

1606. Both Hindu and Muslim women pray at the shrine, tying a cotton strip to the tomb and hoping for the same miracle of parenthood that befell Akbar.

The shrine In the centre of the W wall is the mihrab shrine which, of course, backs on to Mecca and orientates worshippers towards the Prophet's city. The central chamber is flanked by halls with Hindu style pillars, the first time for over 300 years that Muslim architects had incorporated a purely Hindu style into a mosque. The shafts are square, then octagonal, then 16-sided and culminate in a second octagonal section. The dome was painted in the Persian style. Also in this building are decorative panels of tiles and the Hindu *satkona** (six-pointed star).

Buland Darwasa The final feature dominating the S wall is the **Victory Gate**. Constructed in 1573 to celebrate Akbar's brilliant conquest of Gujarat, it sets the style for later gateways. The gate is approached from the outside by a 13 m flight of steps and the entrance rises 41 m high. Decoration is quite plain, thus emphasizing the military character of the gate. Standing in the central hall and facing the courtyard there is an inscription on the right. It is a famous verse from the Koran and reads:

> 'Said Jesus, on whom be peace: The world is but a
> bridge; pass over it but build no houses on it. He who
> hopes for an hour, hopes for Eternity, for the world is
> but an hour. Spend it in prayer, for the rest is
> unseen'.

Fatehpur Sikri was only fully occupied for 14 years. It has been generally stated that it was due to a failing in the water supply that the city was abandoned, but political motives may also have had a bearing on its desertion. In 1585 Akbar moved his court to Lahore and when he did move S again, it was to Agra and not Fatehpur Sikri. But it was at Fatehpur Sikri that Akbar spent the richest and most productive years of his long reign (49 yrs).

AGRA TO ALLAHABAD VIA GWALIOR, JHANSI, ORCHHA & KHAJURAHO

The route visits Gwalior, with its powerful, strategically important fort, the fortified palace at Orcha and Khajuraho whose temples contain many of the best examples of the craftman's art in the whole of India.

Leave Agra on the NH3 S. The road follows the railway line all the way to Jhansi. Often shaded with beautiful trees, it passes through **Jajua** (31 km), crossing into Rajasthan from Uttar Pradesh, and **Mania** (10 km) to **Dholpur** (15 km), the northeasternmost town in Rajasthan. A road on the right out of Dholpur leads to **Ramsagar** and the *Vanvihar Wild Life Reserve* (20 km). Continuing straight on down the NH3 there is an abrupt change of scenery as the road crosses the River *Chambal* (4 km), entrenched in a deep bed. In the dry season it is difficult to imagine that this river can be turned into a vast and turbulent flood. Successive bridges have been washed away or damaged.

To the S begins one of the most notorious regions of India for *dacoity* and *thuggee*, castes who make their living from armed robbery. The road climbs through the heavily dissected "badlands" on the southern flank of the Chambal, an arid looking sandy brown for much of the year but converted into a bright green during the monsoon. The river is the boundary between Rajasthan and Madhya Pradesh. The road climbs slightly and passes through **Morena** (21 km) and **Nurabad** (13 km) to **Gwalior** (20 km).

Gwalior

Population 725,000. *Altitude* 212 m. *Best Season* Oct to Mar.
Languages Hindi and English. Gwalior has daily air services to Delhi
(321 km, 1 hr 30 min). The airport is 12 km from the city centre.

	Jan	Feb	Mar	Apr	May	Jun	Jul	Aug	Sep	Oct	Nov	Dec	Av/Tot
Max (°C)	23	27	33	39	43	41	34	32	32	33	29	25	33
Min (°C)	7	10	16	22	28	30	27	25	34	18	11	7	20
Rain (mm)	18	7	8	3	9	83	274	259	192	35	2	8	898

Early history The distinctive and colourful hill fort of Gwalior on the N-S corridor from N to W India was the key to control of the Central Provinces. Gwalior's history is traced back to 8 A D when the chieftain **Suraj Sen** was stricken with a deadly disease, probably leprosy. He was cured by a hermit saint, **Gwalipa**, and in gratitude founded and named the city after him. An inscription in the fort records that during the 5th century reign of **Mihiragula the Hun** a temple of the sun was erected here. Later, Rajput clans took and held the fort. Muslim invaders like **Qutb-ud-din-Aibak** (12th century) ruled Gwalior before it passed into through a succession of **Tomar** (Rajput), **Mughal**, **Afghan** (Sher Shah), and **Maratha** hands. During the 1857 **Mutiny**, the Maharaja remained loyal to the British but his troops, 6,500 of them, mutinied on Sunday June 14th. Next year, there was fierce fighting round Gwalior, the rebels being led by Tantia Topi and the **Rani (Queen) of Jhansi**. When the fort was taken by the British, the Rani was found dressed in men's clothes among the slain. Although the Maharaja of Gwalior had remained loyal to the British they kept the fort for another thirty years.

Places of interest The fort area contains Jain sculptures, Jain and Hindu temples and the charming sandstone palace which is decorated with yellow ducks on blue tiles. In the town are the Maharaja's Palaces, the Moti Mahal and the 19th century Jai Vilas. The Maharaja (Scindia) of Gwalior was one of five Maharajas awarded the highest 21-gun salute by the British and was a man of enormous influence and wealth. The fact that these two huge palaces are within 1.5 km of each other is testimony to the latter.

The Fort
The fort is situated on a high sandstone precipice 91 m above the surrounding plain and 2.8 km long and 200-850 m wide. In places the cliff overhangs, in other it has been scarped to make it unscaleable. The main entrance to the N comprised a twisting, easily defended approach and of the original 7 gates (from bottom: Alamgiri, Hindola, Bhairon, Ganes, Lakshman, Hathiapur and Hawa) – only 5 remain. The walls are 9 m high and seen from the N present a formidable battlement. On the W is the **Urwahi gorge** and another well well-guarded entrance.

Apart from its natural defences, Gwalior had a further advantage with its unlimited supply of water. There are many tanks on the plateau and Gwalior earned itself the reputation of being one of the most impregnable fortresses of N and C India. The first Mughal Emperor **Babur** (r1526-30) described it as 'the pearl amongst fortresses of Hind'. If walking, the easiest entrance is by the **Alamgiri gate**. If travelling by car, it is the **Urwahi Gate**. From the latter, travel around the S half of the fort area and see the temples and city viewpoint. On the approach to the Urwahi Gate are 21 **Jain sculptures** dating from the 7th to 15th centuries and of various sizes up to 20 m tall. Babur was offended by them and ordered their faces and private parts to be destroyed. Modern restorers appear

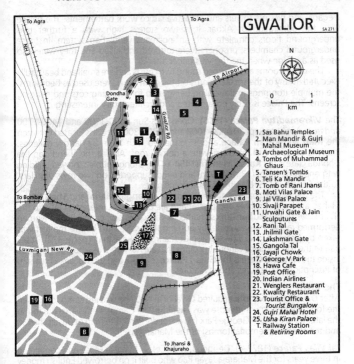

GWALIOR
SA 271

To Agra
To Agra
To Airport

N

0   1
km

1. Sas Bahu Temples
2. Man Mandir & Gujri Mahal Museum
3. Archaeological Museum
4. Tombs of Muhammad Ghaus
5. Tansen's Tombs
6. Teli Ka Mandir
7. Tomb of Rani Jhansi
8. Moti Vilas Palace
9. Jai Vilas Palace
10. Sivaji Parapet
11. Urwahi Gate & Jain Sculputures
12. Rani Tal
13. Jhilmil Gate
14. Lakshman Gate
15. Gangola Tal
16. Jayaji Chowk
17. George V Park
18. Hawa Cafe
19. Post Office
20. Indian Airlines
21. Wenglers Restaurant
22. Kwality Restaurant
23. Tourist Office & Tourist Bungalow
24. Gujri Mahal Hotel
25. Usha Kiran Palace
T. Railway Station & Retiring Rooms

Dondha Gate
Gwalior Rd
Gandhi Rd
Luxmiganj New Rd
To Bombay
To Jhansi & Khajuraho

to have been in partial agreement with him in that only the faces have been repaired.

Teli-ka Mandir and ***Sas Bahu Mandir*** The unique Teli-ka Mandir (30 m high) is a Pratihara (8th-11th centuries) Vishnu Temple and blends a number of regional styles. The shape of the roof is distinctively Dravidian (S Indian) while the decoration is typically Indo-Aryan (N Indian). The name appears to be a corruption of Telengana. A Garuda (Vishnu's transport) crowns the doorway. Also dedicated to Vishnu is the 11th century Sas Bahu (Mother and Daughter-in-law) temples. The larger of the two has an ornately carved base and four heavy pillars support the roof. Tillotson records how after the Mutiny the Maharaja "watched the British garrison paying scant respect to the ancient Hindu buildings within the Fort: the great medieval temple, the Teli ka Mandir, for example was put to service as a soda water factory and coffee shop. By such acts of desecration, the British showed Indian rulers how the ancient Hindu heritage was then regarded by those who laid claim to power and authority."

Suraj Kund is where Suraj Sen's leprosy was cured by the saint Gwalipa and is a large tank (107 m by 55 m) and reservoir.

The ***Man Mandir Palace*** is a pictorial delight since large areas of the red sandstone exterior is decorated with blue tiles, elephants, yellow ducks and peacocks. Built between 1486 and 1517 by Raja Man Singh (hence the name), the decorated walls are massive (The E face is 91 m long and 30 m high) yet elegant, and possess towers and attractive lattice work battlements. The palace won the admiration of Akbar. It is two storeys high with a further two underground floors complete with an ingenious ventilation system. In these underground chambers, prisoners were tortured and killed and they were also used as a refuge when the fort was under attack.

The upper rooms are arranged round two courts and are small and beautifully executed. Many of the smaller rooms off the main court were used as bedrooms, the multiple iron rings in the ceiling being used for swinging cots and hanging screens. The Palace is richly ornamented and architecturally interesting.

The *Vikramaditya Palace* (1516) Open Tues-Sun 0800-1100 and 1400-1700 and from April 1 to Sept 30 0700-1000 and 1500-1800. Free. It is located between the **Man** and **Karan Palace** and is connected with them by narrow galleries. Inside is an open hall (baradari) with a domed roof. Also at the N end opp the Dhonda Gate is the **Karan Mandir** (1454-1479), a long double-storeyed building with one large room (13 m by 9 m) and a roof supported on two rows of pillars. To the S is a hall (1516) with a Hindu dome roof.

The two Muslim palaces at the N end, the **Jahangiri Mahal** and **Shah Jahan** Mahal, are built of rubble and plaster and are of no great interest. A little to the NW of them is the **Jauhar Tank** so named because this is where the Rajput women performed *jauhar* (mass suicide) by burning themselves just before the fort was taken by Altamish in 1232 – see also Chittaurgarh, Rajasthan (**page 372**). The S part of the fort contains various buildings that are now used as a boarding school. Inside the **Hindola Gate** is the **Gujari Palace** (c.1500) and this houses a museum of inscriptions, sculptures and miniatures.

The Town
After **Daulat Rao Scindia** acquired Gwalior in 1809 he pitched camp to the S of the fort. The new city that arose was **Lashkar** (The Camp). In this area are found the later palaces, King George Park (now Gandhi Park), the market (Jayaji chowk) and the chattris (memorial tombs) of the Maharajas.

Jai Vilas Palace (1872-4) Designed by Lt-Col Sir Michael Filose and completed in three years for the Maharaja Jayaji Rao who built it on borrowed English money yet died leaving Rs 62 million in assets. The reason behind the rapid construction was that it was to be ready for the Prince of Wales' visit. It is a simply enormous place, built in an Italian palazzo style. In the Durbar Hall, which is approached by a crystal staircase, hang what are claimed to be the two largest chandeliers in the world. Elephants were used to test the strength of the ceiling before the chandeliers were hung. The rest of the palace is on a similarly grand scale. There is the largest carpet in Asia (made in the Gwalior jail), an electrically-lit rock garden, and a silver electric train set which transported cigars and port round the dinner table. With the Maharaja at the controls, it is said that he sent it past those guests he did not particularly like too fast for them to be able to take anything. Like some other Indian Princes, he also had his own private full-size train. Half the palace is still the residence of the the current Maharaja, the other a museum (See Museums). The other large palace is the **Moti Mahal** nearby and is used as offices.

The Tomb of Muhammad Ghaus Built in the form of a square with a hexagonal tower, the corners surmounted by small domes, the interior of the building is enclosed on all sides by carved stone lattice screens, elaborate and delicate in design. Muhammad Ghaus was a well-known Muslim saint in the 16th century and assisted Babur in his acquisition of the fort.

Nearby is the **Tomb of** *Tansen*, a famous musician who lived in Akbar's time and was one of the emperor's 'Nine Jewels of the Court' (see Fatehpur Sikri). A popular legend holds that beside this comparatively simple tomb there was a tree, the leaves of which musicians used to chew in the belief that their voices would be improved. No trace of the tree remains today and, in fact, there is an air of desolation about both these tombs as they stand in the middle of a piece of barren waste ground.

The Royal Chattris These are memorial tombs, each dedicated to a Maharaja of the ruling family. Situated near the Jayaji Chowk these ghostly buildings, empty except for a lighted image, are in various stages of disrepair and neglect.

Hotels B *Welcomgroup Usha Kiran Palace*, Jayendraganj, Lashkar T 23453, Cable; Usha Kiran, Telex: 566-225 Garg. 27 rm some A/c. 14 km airport, 4 km rly, 2 km downtown. Restaurant, TV, bar, garden, travel, post office, laundry, badminton, billiards, table tennis, buggy rides, archery, golf on request, credit cards. Situated next door to the Jai Vilas Palace, this was the Maharaja's guesthouse. Attractive location and gardens. The rooms are variable – either pokey or cavernous. Pleasant but over-priced. **D** *Fort View*, M.L.B. Rd, T 23409. A/c and non a/c rm. TV in a/c rm. **D** *Motel Tansen* (MPTDC), 6A Gandhi Rd, T 21568. 24 rm, some a/c, with phone 10 km airport, 0.5 km rly, 5 km downtown. Bar, multi-cuisine restaurant, garden, airport transfer, TV in suites, laundry. **D** *President*, Station Rd, T 24673. A/c and non a/c rm. **E** *Galav Guest House*, near Roop Singh Stadium, T 27531. 5 rm non a/c with bath. Restaurant, laundry. **E** *Vivek Continental*, Topi Bajar, T 27016, Cable: Hotvek. 30 rm. 14 km airport, 4 km rly, downtown location. A/c and non a/c rm with bath. Pool, restaurant (Indian), car hire, garden, credit cards. **F** *Metro*, Ganesh Bazar, near Gandhi Market, T 25530, Cable: Metro hotel. 29 rm. 16 km airport, 5 km rly, downtown location. Non a/c rm with bath. Indian cuisine

Restaurant Restaurants at both the Usha Kiran Palace Hotel and the Motel Tansen are open to non-residents from breakfast to dinner. *Kwality* Motilala Nehru Marg T 23243

Shopping *Kothari and Sons*, Sarafa Bazaar, T 23333. Brocade, *chanderi** (light and flimsy cotton and silk material), Banarasi and Kanjivaram silks. Closed Tues. *M.D. Fine Arts*, Subhash Market, T 22315. Paintings and objets d'art. Closed Tues. *M.P. Emporium*, T 22196. Handlooms. Closed Tues. *M.P.Khadi Sangh*, Sarafa Bazaar, T 22314. Handlooms. Closed Tues. *Ganpatlal Krishna Lal* Jewellers and Antiques, Sarafa Bazaar, T 24437.

Photography *Akar Studio*, Morar; *Goyal Studio*, Daulat Ganj, T 21588; *Sahani Studio*, near Roxy Cinema. T23138; *M.G.M. Studio*, Patankar Bazaar, T 22310.

Local Transport Taxis, Tempos, **Auto-rickshaws and Tongas** are available. Fares negotiable. MPSTDC Taxi **Private Taxi** Tarriff: Rs.2.50 per km.

Entertainment *Son et Lumière*, Man Singh Palace, Gwalior Fort. Information on times and admission available from MPSTDC.

Museums Gujari Mahal Archaeological Museum, inside Hindola Gate, Gwalior Fort, T 8641. Interesting collection – sculptures, archaeological pieces, terracottas (Besnagar, Ujjain) coins, and paintings , including copies of two frescoes from the Bagh caves). Good guide book available. Open 1000-1700, Closed Mon. Nominal admission fee. **Municipal Corporation Museum**, Moti Mahal Rd, T 22819. Collection of armoury and natural history. Open 1000-1630, closed Mon. Rs.1. Kala Vithika, M.P. Kala Parishad. Modern art collection. Open 0900-1700, closed Sun. Free. Jai Vilas Palace Museum, Open 1030-1700, Closed Mon. Maharaja's and Palace memorabilia and decorations. **Scindia Museum**, Scindia Palace, T 23453, Open 0900-1700, Rs 5.

Post and Telegraph General Post Office, Jiyaji Chowk, T 22642. Birla Nagar P.O., T 8244. Morar P.O., T 8350. Residency P.O. 8491.

Travel Agents and Tour Operators Tourist Taxis/ Private Cars available from M.P. Tourism, motel Tansen, T 21568. Welcomgroup Usha Kiran Palace, Jayendraganj, T 26636. *S.S. Travels*, Welcomgroup Usha Kiran Palace, Jayendraganj, T 26636. *Gooch Travels*, Shivaji Marg, T 24564. *Ambika Travels*, near Ramakrishna Ashram. **Tours** to Orchha and Shivpuri – transport only – Rs.850 (5 persons in an ambassador), same day return. Local sightseeing – M.P. Tourism – car Rs.200 S.S. Travels – car Rs.300. Airport transfer Rs.80 (car).

Tourist Offices and Information M.P. Tourism, Motel Tansen, 6A Gandhi Marg, T 21568.

Air Indian Airlines flies five times a week to Gwalior from Delhi, continuing to Bombay via Bhopal and Indore, and returning the same route. Indian Airlines, T 24433

Rail Gwalior is on the Central Railways main Delhi-Bombay and Madras-Delhi lines. **New Delhi:** *Punjab Mail* 1037, daily, 1415, 5 hr 55 min; *Amritsar Exp* 1057, daily, 2325, 7 hr 40

min; *Jhelum Exp* 4677, daily, 1537, 7 hr 30 min; *Karnataka Exp* 2628, daily, 2320, 4 hr. **Bombay (VT)**: *Punjab Mail* 1038, daily, 1255 (23 hr 30 min). **Bhopal**: *Shatabdi Exp* 2002, daily, 0933, 4 hr 30 min; *Jhelum Exp* 4678, daily, 1548, 6 hr 50 min; *Punjab Mail* 1038, daily, 1255, 7 hr 40 min; *Karnataka Exp* 2628, daily, 0336, 5 hr 15 min **Jhansi**: *Shatabdi Exp* 2002, daily, 0933, 1 hr 5 min; *Punjab Mail* 1038, daily, 1250, 23 hr 35 min; *Karnataka Exp* 2628, daily, 0336, 1 hr 16 min; *Jhelum Exp* 4678, daily, 1543, 6 hr 57 min. **Agra** *Shatabdi Exp* 2001, daily 1903, 1 hr 10 min; *Punjab Mail* 1037, daily, 1415, 1 hr 55 min; *Amritsar Exp* 1057, daily, 2325, 1 hr 50 min; *Malwa Exp* 4067, daily, 0347, 2 hr 5 min. Railway Station: Enquiries T 22544, Reservations T 25306

Road Gwalior is 114 km from Shivpuri and 119 km from Agra. It is accessible on NH3 (Agra-Bombay) and on the State Highway from Jhansi.

    Bus Regular bus services connect Gwalior with Agra via Morena and Dholpur, **Delhi** (321 km via Agra), **Jaipur** (338 km via Agra and Bharatpur), **Khajuraho** (278 km via Jhansi and Chhatarpur), **Shivpuri** (114 km), Lucknow and other towns in U.P., Rajasthan and M.P.: Rewa, Jabalpur, Panna, Indore, Ujjain, Etawah and Jhansi.

Excursions From Gwalior the NH3 to Bombay climbs gently S up onto the plateau, passing through *Shivpuri*, the summer capital of the Scindia Rulers and now a game reserve. From Gwalior take the NH3. After 9 km there is a left turn to **Tekanpur** (23 km), **Datia** (60 km) and **Jhansi** (94 km), while a road on the right leads to the **Tigra Dam** (14 km). Continue straight on, across the **River Punniar** (10 km) through the small town of **Ghatigaon** (11 km) to **Mohana** (26 km), where after a further 2 km the road crosses the **River Parvati** on a narrow road cum rail bridge. The three small towns of **Chorpura** (17 km), **Ghar Ghat** (8 km) and **Satanwara** (13 km) also lie on the main road, *Satanwara* being on the N edge of Shivpuri National Park. A turning on the left leads to **Narwar** fort (25 km).

Shivpuri National Park The dense forests of the Shivpuri National Park were the hunting grounds of the Mughal Emperors when great herds of elephants were captured for Emperor Akbar. The road to Shivpuri passes through the Shivpuri National Park which is similar to Ranthambhor in Rajasthan and consists of dry deciduous forest featuring *dhok* (Anogeissus peridula). There is also a large perennial lake. It used to be a well known *shikar* (hunting ground) for tigers which, though here, are seldom seen now. Its main mammals include nilgai, chinkara, chowsingha, sambar, cheetal and wild pig. Cheetal deer are the most common but the herds are not as large as in Kanha, not as well nourished. The lake attracts numerous waterbirds including migratory ducks and bar-headed geese which stay on until May. On its shores, you can see huge flocks of demoiselle cranes.

    The best months for a visit to Shivpuri National Park are Jan-Mar. After Mar it gets very hot and it is not worth going out except in the early mornings and at sundown. There is a regular bus service from Gwalior.

    In Shivpuri there are the tombs of the Scindia rulers. Set in formal Mughal style gardens with quiet nooks under flowering trees, intersecting pathways lit by ornamental Victorian lamps, is the complex of cenotaphs. Architecturally, they are a synthesis of Hindu and Islamic styles with their *shikhara*-type* spires and Mughal pavilions.

Hotels D *Tourist Village* (M.P. Tourism), 3 km off the Agra-Bombay highway, overlooking Sakhya Sagar Lake and adjacent to Bhadaiya Kund, T Shivpuri 2600. 20 cottages, some a/c, lounge, restaurant and bar. Attractive location, best accommodation available. **E** *Chinkara Motel* (M.P. Tourism), Agra-Bombay Rd, Shivpuri, T 297. 4 rm. Non a/c. Restaurant. Basic. **E** *Govt. Circuit House*. Basic. **E** *Harish Lodge*, Centre of Shivpuri. Simple, well-kept, restaurant.

Gwalior to Allahabad Take the road SE out of Gwalior, and at a road junction 9 km out of Gwalior bear left. The road to the right goes to Shivpuri. After 18 km pass through Makora to Tekanpur (5 km). There is then a succession of villages and small towns: **Dabra** (14 km) **Goraghat** (9 km) where there is a bridge across the **River Sindh**, **Uprain** (6 km) and **Sitapur** (4 km) to **Datia** (4 km). The road follows the railway line for the whole distance.

The Bundela chief, *Bir Singh Deo*, is responsible for the fortress palace at *Datia*, 24 km NW of Jhansi and 69 km SE of Gwalior. Bir Singh supported **Salim** (later **Jahangir**) against his father Akbar, and is held to be responsible for **Abul-Fazl's** death in 1602. Abu Fazl was Akbar's friend and biographer and was distrustful of Salim's ambitions. While returning from a campaign in the Deccan with a camel train of treasure he was ambushed by Bir Singh and killed. Bir Singh, fugitive from Akbar's wrath until the emperor's death three years later, is believed to have financed much of his building with his ill-gotten gain. His successors were loyal to the Mughals.

The *palace at Datia* blends Mughal and Rajput styles beautifully. It was one of the few Indian buildings admired by **Sir Edwin Lutyens**, architect of much of British New Delhi in the early 20th century See page 153. Unlike most Moghul palaces, it was conceived as a single unit. Its form and decoration are thus completely integrated. Built in 1620 on a rocky outcrop, the five storeyed palace known as the **Govind Mandir** appears much taller than its actual height of 39 m. It is square in plan with corner towers, and its balconies, bridges and oriel windows provide attractive panoramas of the surrounding countryside. In the central courtyard are the royal apartments which are connected with the buildings around the edges of the fort/palace by flying bridge corridors. The facades are richly ornamented with balconies, kiosks and recessed arches. With hardly a tourist in sight, Datia is well worth visiting. Occupied only intermittently by its owners, it is now a well preserved yet deserted monument.

Jhansi

30 km from Datia. Jhansi is best known for its fort and the involvement in the 1857 Mutiny of its woman ruler **Rani Lakshmi Bhai**. Today it is a useful stopping point if you are travelling from Delhi to Khajuraho. It remained a small village until it was taken in 1742 by Naru Shankar, a Maratha. He built the Shankar Fort. The East India Co acquired control in 1803. It then 'lapsed' – see Lucknow (**page 232**) in 1853 when there was no direct heir to succeed the Raja. The civil station dates from this time. The fort was seized in 1857 and most of the occupants slaughtered. The Rani, who had a $6,000 pension from the British still had a grievance with them because under this new system she was not allowed to adopt an heir. She joined the rebels and was killed on 18th June 1858 in a battle at Kotah-ki-Sarai 'dressed like a man.. holding her sword two-handed and holding the reins of her horse in her teeth.. and fighting with two female companions' (Hibbert). Five thousand people died in the siege and fighting around Jhansi. The British ceded the fort to the Maharaja of Scindia and exchanged it for Gwalior in 1866.

The nucleus of the Fort was built by **Bir Singh Deo** in 1613 (**see above**), and consists of a tier of ramparts which varies in height from 5.5 m to 9 m. They are built of solid masonry and have ten gates: Khanderao, Datia, Unao, Orchha, Baragaon, Lakshmi, Sagar, Sainyar, Bhander and Jhirna. The breach made by the British under Sir Hugh Rose is between the **Sainyar** and **Jhirna** gates. Inside is a whitewashed *mandir** (temple) attended by a *pujari** (worshipper). A road encircles the fort and there are good views from the walls. NE of the railway station is Retribution Hill, which marks the last stand of the Mutineers in 1858.

Hotels There are no top class hotels in Jhansi. If a degree of comfort is required, it is best to go to the *Shish Mahal* at Orchha, a 25 min taxi/45 min auto-rickshaw ride away – see Orchha Hotels, below. The *Railway Retiring Rooms* at the station and a handful of cheap establishments near it are the best that Jhansi has to offer. The **F** *Central* and **F** *Shipra* are 500 m to the left as you leave the station. The **F** *Ashok* near the Natraj Cinema is a little more expensive. The **E** *Jhansi Hotel* on Shastri Marg has a variety of rooms with and without bath.

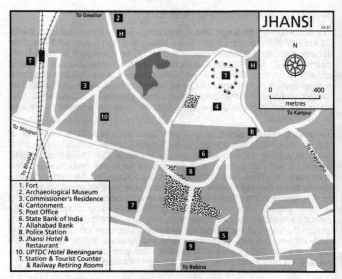

JHANSI SA 61

To Gwalior
To Shivpuri
To Bhopal
To Kanpur
To Khajuraho
To Babina

N

0   400
metres

1. Fort
2. Archaeological Museum
3. Commissioner's Residence
4. Cantonment
5. Post Office
6. State Bank of India
7. Allahabad Bank
8. Police Station
9. Jhansi Hotel & Restaurant
10. UPTDC Hotel Beerangana
T. Station & Tourist Counter & Railway Retiring Rooms

Rail New Delhi: *Karnataka Exp* 2627, daily, 0510; *Malwa Exp* 4067, daily, 0205, 7 hr 55 min; *Amritsar Exp* 1057, daily, 2130, 7 hr 35 min; *Jhelum Exp* 4677, daily, 1410, 7 hr 30 min; *Shatabdi Exp* 2002, daily, 1758, 4 hr; **Bombay (VT):** *Punjab Mail* 1038, daily, 1500, 21 hr 25 min. **Jabalpur (for Kanha):** *Mathakosal Exp* 1450, daily, 2235, 10 hr 15 min. *From Jabalpur: Mathakosal Exp* 1449, daily, 1435, 11 hr 35 min. **Lucknow:** *Kushi Nagar Exp* 1015, daily, 0900, 6 hr 25 min; *Gwalior-Chhapra Mail* 1143, daily, 1315, 6 hr 55 min; *Pushpak Exp* 2133, daily, 0335, 6 hr 25 min. **Agra** *Shatabdi Exp* 2001, daily 1758, 2 hr 15 min; *Punjab Mail* 1037, daily, 1240, 3 hr 25 min; *Amritsar Exp* 1057, daily, 2130, 3 hr 30 min; *Malwa Exp* 4067, daily, 0205, 3 hr 50 min. **Varanasi:** *Bundelkhand Exp* 1107, daily, 1700, 17 hr 15 min. **Indore:** *New Delhi-Indore Malwa Exp* 4068, daily, 0210, 10 hr 15 min.

Bus In addition to long distance bus connections to major N Indian cities there is a daily bus for **Khajuraho**. It leaves early and the journey takes 5 hr.

From Jhansi it is a three hour car drive to **Khajuraho**. The road runs along the edge of the hill region of Bundelkhand. Most is though agricultural land but the forested slopes of the hills are quite evident as you cross a number of rivers coming off the plateau, e.g. the Betwa and Dhasan. Half of the journey is in UP, half MP, but you keep alternating between the two. It is a very attractive route, through gentle scenery often like parkland, trees scattered between fields, and there is not much traffic on this back road. From Jhansi take the road East towards Barwar Sagar, Maurinapur and Chhatarpur. After 9 km there is a right turn to Orchha (10 km).

Orchha

The site The Bundela chief **Raja Rudra Pratap** (1501-31) chose an easily defended and beautiful site for his capital. Set on an island of rock on a bend in the **Betwa river**, which is usually nearly dry outside the monsoon season, it is elevated above the surrounding wooded countryside and approached by an arched bridge, Orchha was once capital of its own state. Unlike its near neighbour Datia, Orchha contains three palaces, each built by succeeding Maharajas in a similar style and combining to form a complex as imposing as that at Udaipur.

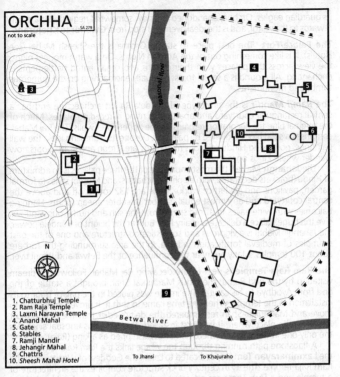

ORCHHA
SA 279
not to scale

Betwa River

1. Chatturbhuj Temple
2. Ram Raja Temple
3. Laxmi Narayan Temple
4. Anand Mahal
5. Gate
6. Stables
7. Ramji Mandir
8. Jehangir Mahal
9. Chattris
10. *Sheesh Mahal Hotel*

To Jhansi   To Khajuraho

The origins of the dynasty Garkhundar, once capital of the Bundela Rajas, fell to the **Tughluqs**, whose base was Delhi, just as that dynasty was weakening. Into the vacuum that they left, the Bundelas again expanded, moving their base in the early 16th century to Orchha. **Raja Rudra Pratap** threw a wall around the existing settlement and built the first palace, the **Ramji Mandir** (c.1525-30) and a bridge to it. Before his death, rescuing a cow from a tiger, he commenced the **Raj Mahal** (1554). This work was finally completed in 1591 by his successors, **Bharti Chand** and **Madhukar Shah**.

Links with the Mughals The continuing fortunes of the House of Orchha may be said to have stemmed from the rulers' diplomatic talents. Though **Madhukar Shah** was defeated in battle by Akbar, he nevertheless won the Mughal emperor's friendship. The later **Bir Singh Deo** (1605-26 – See Datia, above), while opposing Akbar, aligned himself with **Prince Salim** (Jahangir) and is believed to have killed **Abu Fazl**, one of Akbar's closest friends and supporters, at Jahangir's instigation. He was to be rewarded when Jahangir succeeded his father and thus ensured the ongoing prosperity of Orchha. The **Jahangir Mahal** was built to commemorate the emperor's visit to Orchha. However, Bir Singh's first son, **Jhujan**, ran foul of Shah Jahan and, ignoring orders, treacherously killed the neighbouring chief of **Chauragarh**. The imperial army routed Jhujan who in turn was killed in the jungle by Gonds. Orchha was then pillaged. In 1783 the Bundela capital was moved to **Tikamgarh**, leaving Orchha to the jade green dhak forests, the Betwa river and its guardian eagles. Orchha, abandoned and now somewhat neglected, pays rich rewards to the visitor, and is the ideal overnight stop from **Gwalior** to **Khajuraho**.

The Palace/Fort   The best place to stay in Orchha is the Sheesh Mahal (see Hotels). It is like something out of the Arabian Nights. On a warm moonlit night, the view across the palaces with their chattris and ornamented battlements is enchanting. All around is a sea of forest gradually encroaching on the numerous tombs and monuments.

The *Ramji Mandir* is the prototype of Bundela Rajput architecture and has a central rectangular courtyard and apartments rising in receding planes. Much of the original blue tile decoration remains on the upper outer walls. The Raj Mahal, comprises a solid block crowned by pavilions. Despite its crumbling look, the wall paintings, portraying Hindu religious mythology are strong and vivid. Goats now wander where kings once trod.

The **Jahangir Mahal,** the most impressive of the three palaces is an admixture of Hindu (brackets decorated with elephants, chattris) and Muslim styles (a formal garden, pavilions and jali lattice work). There are 132 rooms off and above the central courtyard and an almost equal number of subterranean rooms. Hanging balconies with wide eaves to afford shade from the sun and numerous windows give this huge palace a delicate and airy feel. Built at the height of Bundela power, the Jahangir Mahal is a vigorous and sophisticated structure and one of the best examples of medieval fortification in India. In the area surrounding the fort are about 100 temples. Many are near the confluence of the Betwa and Jamni river.

The Ram Raja Temple is next to the decaying Raj Mahal. Following a dream visitation by the god Rama, the pious Madhukar Shah brought a statue of the god from Ayodhya to his capital. The image was placed in the palace prior to its installation in the temple. When the time came to shift it, it proved impossible to move and Madhukar Shah remembered the deity's edict that the image must remain in the place where it was first installed. This temple is unusual since it is the only one in the country where Rama is worshipped as a king (Raja).

A flagstone path running through the village links the Ram Raja temple with the **Laxminarayan Temple**, dedicated to Laxmi the Goddess of Wealth, with the Ram Raja temple. The 17th century brick structure combines the architecture of a temple and a fort. There are attractive wall paintings of the developed phase of the Bundelkhand school of art. The temple is usually locked and information about its opening can be obtained from the staff at the Shish Mahal (see Hotels). There is a fine view looking back across the plain to the chattris and palace.

The Royal Chattris   There are 14 of these cenotaphs to former rulers grouped by the Kanchana Ghat of the river Betwa. Again, overgrown and neglected, fine views can be obtained from them.

Hotels D *Sheesh Mahal* (MP Tourism), T 24. 8 rm. 34 km from Jhansi railway station. A/c and non a/c with bath. Restaurant. The place to stay in Orchha. There's nowhere else and the views from the Sheesh Mahal, which is part of the palace complex, are magnificent. Ask for the deluxe room. Tariff very reasonable and staff charming.

From Orchha return N to the main Jhansi road. Turn right on joining it to **Maurinapur** (64 km). After 10 km the road crosses briefly into Madhya Pradesh to **Nowgong** (30 km) and **Chhatarpur**, the capital of a small princely state before Independence.

Khajuraho

Population 4,000 approx. *Altitude* 457 m. *Climate* Temp. Summer, Max. 47C, Min. 21C, Winter, Max. 32C, Min. 4C. Annual rainfall 1120 mm; monsoon Jul-Aug. *Best Season* Oct-Mar. In Apr-Jun it becomes

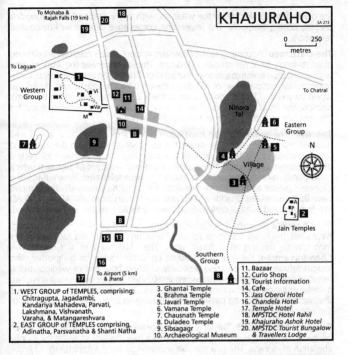

KHAJURAHO SA 273

To Mohaba &
Rajah Falls (19 km)

To Laguan

Western
Group

To Chatral

Ninora
Tal

Eastern
Group

N

Village

Jain Temples

Southern
Group

To Airport (5 km)
& Jhansi

1. WEST GROUP of TEMPLES, comprising;
   Chitragupta, Jagadambi,
   Kandariya Mahadeva, Parvati,
   Lakshmana, Vishvanath,
   Varaha, & Matangareshvara
2. EAST GROUP of TEMPLES comprising,
   Adinatha, Parsvanatha & Shanti Natha

3. Ghantai Temple
4. Brahma Temple
5. Javari Temple
6. Vamana Temple
7. Chausnath Temple
8. Duladeo Temple
9. Sibsagagr
10. Archaeological Museum

11. Bazaar
12. Curio Shops
13. Tourist Information
14. Cafe
15. Jass Oberoi Hotel
16. Chandela Hotel
17. Temple Hotel
18. MPSTDC Hotel Rahil
19. Khajuraho Ashok Hotel
20. MPSTDC Tourist Bungalow
    & Travellers Lodge

very hot, dry and dusty. Khajuraho has daily air services to Delhi (470 km, 1 hr 50 min) and is part of the popular Delhi - Agra - Khajuraho - Varanasi - Kathmandu flight route. Delays are common in winter due to fog at Delhi and Agra. The centre of Khajuraho is 5 km from the airport.

The temples at Khajuraho are among the finest examples of temple craftsmanship in the whole of India.

The presence of erotic sculptures in the temples at Khajuraho – even though they account for less than 10% of the total carvings – have sometimes been viewed as the work of a degenerate society obsessed with sex. Believed by some to be merely erotic in a pornographic sense, the sculptures are held by others to be an expression of the celebration of all human activity, displaying one aspect of nature of Hinduism itself, a genuine love of life.

Indian (Hindu) art contrasts strongly with that of Europe. The temple towers, though often tall, are solidly based on earth. Little imagination is needed to see the temple towers at Khajuraho as mountains, soaring like the Himalayas to the Abode of the Gods. The bases are broad, firm and solidly based in the land below. The Gods and demi-gods in temples all over India are young and handsome, their bodies rounded, often richly jewelled. They are often smiling and sorrow is rarely portrayed. With one or two exceptions (Siva dancing being one) the sacred icon is nearly always firmly planted on the ground. Also, temple sculpture makes full use of the female form as a decorative motif. Goddesses and female attendants are often shown naked from the waist up, with tiny waists and large, rounded breasts, posing languidly. The impression conveyed is one of well-being and relaxation.

The craftsmen According to A.L. Basham, ancient India's religious art differed quite strikingly from her religious literature. The literature was the work of men with vocations – brahmins, monks and ascetics. The art, on the other hand, came from secular craftsmen who, although they worked to instructions, loved the world they knew. This is usually seen in the fruits of their labours. In Basham's opinion, the usual inspiration of Indian art is not so much a ceaseless quest for the absolute as a delight in the world as they saw it.

The site The setting for the remarkable temples of Khajuraho is a rich well watered plain, miles from the nearest large urban centre, with the rocky and forested crags of the **Vindhya hills** as a backdrop. Khajuraho was formerly a place of great importance, the capital of the old kingdom of **Jajhauti** which corresponds with the region now known as **Bundelkhand**. Hiuen Tsang the Chinese traveller and chronicler mentions it in the 7th century AD. The temples were built under later Chandela kings over the century from 900 AD to 1050 AD in a truly inspired burst of creativity. Of the original 85 temples, 25 have survived.

The Chandela Rajputs The Chandela kings claimed descent from the moon. **Hemwati**, the lovely young daughter of a Brahmin priest, was seduced by the moon while bathing in a forest pool. The child born of this union was **Chandravarman**, the founder. Brought up in the forests by his mother who sought refuge from a censorious society, children born out of wedlock being frowned upon, Chandravarman, when established as ruler of the local area, had a dream visitation from his mother. It is said that she implored him to build temples that would reveal human passions and in doing so bring about a realisation of the emptiness of desire.

Tantrism See page 59. The Chandelas were followers of the Tantric cult which believes that gratification of earthly desires is a step towards attaining the infinite liberation of nirvana. This is a possible explanation for the importance of erotic sculpture. The belief in **Shakti** and worship, sexual expression and spiritual desire, were intermingled.

The Chandelas developed into a strong regional power in the early 10th century. Under their patronage **Jajhauti** was blessed with prosperity as the rulers decorated their kingdom with tanks, forts, palaces and temples, mainly concentrated in their strongholds of Mahoba, Kalinjar, Ajaigarh and also Dudhai, Chandpur, Madanpur and Deogarh (in Jhansi district). These men were great patrons of the arts and equally great builders.

With the fading of Chandela fortunes, the importance of Khajuraho waned, for the later kings concentrated their energies on the hill forts of Mahoba, Kalinjar and Ajaigarh for strategic reasons. However, temple construction continued until the 12th century but at a much reduced pace. Khajuraho can be regarded as the Chandelas' spiritual homeland and, perhaps, in this can be found the reason for the siting of the temples at this particular place. Far removed from the political centres of the kingdom, its out-of-the way location may have meant that it was unlikely to be threatened. This is in keeping with the idea of a celestial refuge.

Local Festivals Week long Dance Festival held each year in Mar. Critics suggest that this is contributing to the growing feeling in temple sites such as Khajuraho and Konarak that they are being converted into theme parks, with neatly laid out flower beds and organised "shows". This extravaganza of Indian classical dance tries to recreate the "lost symbiosis of dance and temple worship". However, many of the country's most accomplished dancers do per form in the spectacular setting of the Western Group of Temples. Buy tickets in advance. They are not expensive. Contact the Tourist Office for details.

Places of Interest The temples of Khajuraho can be conveniently divided into three groups: the western, eastern and southern. Of these the western group are the most impressive and the gardens the best kept. If you feel that temple fatigue is likely to set in quickly, then these are the ones to be seen, especially the **Lakshmana Temple**.

The Western Group
Open daily from 0800 -1800. Rs.1.50. Good Archaeological Survey of India Guide book available (Rs 5.00). The entrance to the Western group is opp a car park flanked by curio shops and a couple of restaurants. As usual, there is a throng of eager vendors to be dispensed with before one is through the gateway and into the peaceful surroundings of the beautiful gardens. The ticket office is slightly to the left of the entrance as you face it. One day does not do justice.

Ancient historical records indicate that the whole area now covered by the W group was originally a sacred lake with the temples rising like islands. At dawn on winter mornings they loom like mountains rising in the distance from the mist. The lake has gone – now there is something of a water shortage in Khajuraho – but notice how all the temples are built on plinths.

Temple Design The standard temple design which has persisted from 6th century AD to the present day was not fundamentally different from that of the ancient Greeks. The heart was a small dark shrine room (*garbha-griha*) containing the chief icon. This opened onto a hall for the worshippers (*mandapa*) originally a separate building but usually joined to the shrine room by a vestibule (*antarala*). This hall was approached through a porch (*ardha mandapa*). The shrine room was generally surmounted by a tower, while smaller towers rose from other parts of the building. The whole was set in a rectangular courtyard which might contain lesser shrines and, often, the whole was placed on a raised platform.
 The medieval period in India, like that of Europe, was an age of faith. Temples sprang up everywhere and better stonework techniques replaced previous wooden and brick works. Strict rules on design were laid down in textbooks (*silpasastra*). The techniques used in construction, though, were comparatively simple. Arches were constructed through corbelling (the building up of an arch by overlapping blocks of stone – see Qutb Minar, Delhi (**page 166**). Mortar was rarely used, perhaps because the archless and domeless architecture rendered it unnecessary.
 Temples were heavily and ornately decorated, but despite this the impression is one of great mass. Heavy cornices, strong, broad pillars and the wide base of the tower (sikhara) give to temple architecture the feeling of strength and solidity, only partly counteracted by the ornate friezes.

Varaha Temple (c.900 AD) is really more a shrine, dedicated to Vishnu in his third incarnation as Varaha the boar. Vishnu, The Preserver, at rest, is usually depicted as reclining on a bed of serpents, only wakened from his dreams when his help in saving the world from great danger is required.

The demon **Hiranyaksha** (The Golden-eyed) is said to have stolen the earth and dragged it down to his underwater home. The Gods begged Vishnu to do something about it. The Demon, however, hid himself deep in the underworld, and created a thousand replicas of himself to confuse any pursuer. But, Vishnu incarnated himself as a boar, able to dig deep with his tusks to winkle out his quarry and with his powerful sense of smell to sniff out the right rat. In this way, Hiranyaksha was destroyed and the world saved.
 The shrine is of highly polished sandstone and is huge, and covered with hundreds of tiny gods and goddesses. As a form of the all-pervading **Vishnu**, **Varaha** is Lord of the Three Worlds – water, earth and heaven. By his feet are creatures of the water, such as crocodiles, joined higher by humans and finally gods. On his jaws sit the nine planets, five on one side, four on the other and on his snout is **Sarasvati**, the patron goddess of artistic creativity. Between the boar's legs lies the cosmic serpent Shesha on whose head the world rests. The broken feet nearby belong to the missing (removed) figure of the earth goddess Prithvi, gratefully worshipping her saviour whilst above all is an exquisitely carved lotus ceiling.

Shakti Although each temple here is dedicated to a different deity, such as **Vishnu** or **Siva**, each of these expresses its own particular nature through the creative energy of **shakti**. Practising Hindus were divided into two main sects, **Vaishnavas** (Vaishnavites)and **Shaivas** (Shaivites), each claiming Vishnu or Siva as the supreme deity. The worshippers of Vishnu were more prevalent in N India. Tantric beliefs made an impression on Hindu worship and there developed the shakti cults with their basic belief that the male can be activated only by being united with the female. The gods, therefore, acquired wives who were worshipped in their own right; for example Lakshmi, the wife of Vishnu. This cult, according to Romila Thapar, appears to have been based on the persistent worship of the mother goddess (as in the Indus valley civilization of the 3rd millenium BC), which has remained an enduring feature of religion in India. Since this could not be suppressed it was given a priestly blessing and incorporated into the regular ritual in the guise of the shakti cult.

Move on to the **Lakshmana Temple** (c.950 AD) opposite. This is the earliest and best preserved of the large temples and the only one with all its subsidiary shrines intact. Leave your shoes at the entrance. You enter through a simple *makara-torana** of crocodiles cum serpents – mythical sea monsters. These are the guardians of the treasures of the deep and are very similar to those on Jain temples, for example at Mount Abu (Rajasthan). The ceiling of the porch (*ardha mandapa**) has an intricately worked opened lotus blossom. Entering the hall (*mandapa**) you see a raised platform. This was used for dancing and tantric sexual rituals in praise of the deity. These were disciplined sexual rites, the culmination of intensive training and performed under the supervision of a guru. Until this century, many temples kept *devadasis* (slaves of God), women whose duty it was to be the female partner in these rituals. But, as the Tantric practices declined, the *devadasi* increasingly tended to become a temple prostitute and a source of revenue for unscrupulous priests.

At each corner of the platform are pillars with carved brackets from which musicians and *apsaras** (heavenly nymphs) look down approvingly. The holes that you see indicate the manner of construction – bores into which iron rods were placed, thus holding together the stones and allowing carved blocks to be attached. There are 8 figures on each column, representing the 8 sects of Tantra while the entrance to the shrine room (*garbha-griha**) is framed by 108 figures, symbolic of the number of techniques Siva taught his wife Parvati for calming the mind. The image at the heart of the temple is a three headed and 4 armed **Vishnu**, the central head being human, the side ones of a boar and a lion.

The exterior On leaving the temple, shoes can be put back on for walking round the outside. The exterior of the temple is covered with hundreds of carvings and the designs have a sequence from bottom to top : lotus-leaf design (bottom) – floral motifs – sea creatures (guardians of the deep) – elephants (stability and royalty) – human and divine beings (top). Thus the whole of creation is represented. There are elephants at shoulder height, each one different, all beautifully carved. There are loving couples surrounded by nymphs which are shown either as attendants of the gods or as idealizations of woman representing a broad range of female activities – washing, brushing hair, beautifying themselves, playing music etc. Note how all the figures are in a state of relaxation, resting their weight on one leg, thus accentuating their curves. Their movements evince grace and charm. There is nothing formal or regimented about these figures and they are absorbed with one another. The delicacy with which the carver has produced the smallest of bodily characteristics – someone brushing their hair, standing on tiptoe, smiling – attests to their consummate skill.

The best examples are seen in the recesses below the main tower. With the loving couples the taut and elastic tension of flesh is well caught in the figure of a woman whose back is arched over the man's waist, her face twisted to meet his. And, again, there is a delicate crease of skin under her breasts as she twists round. The firm fullness of the lover's limbs is also very graceful. Around the base of the plinth are carvings depicting life on a military campaign and the excesses that deprivation and hardship produce, e.g. rape and sodomy.

Leaving the temple walk to the rear of the delightful gardens to the two temples at the rear. The **Kandariya Mahadeva Temple** (1030) is regarded as the most developed of the Khajuraho temples though it is the Lakshmana that has the greatest impact as it is seen first. The Khandariya Mahadeo is the largest and dedicated to Siva. There are over 800 statues of gods, goddesses, musicians and erotic groupings, carved into its internal and exterior surfaces. Some, like the Vajroli scene where a man is standing on his head and making love to a woman held over him by two attendants are sometimes interpreted as illustrating forms of tantric teachings on **shakti**.

The exterior walls of the temple rise in a series of seven bands of peaks to the summit of the central 31 m high tower. The smaller, subsidiary towers or *urushingras* are replicas of the main tower except on a smaller scale. The impression is one of great complexity but coherence. At the entrance there are mythical beasts and the ceilings are delicately carved. The elaborately carved doorway leads to an inner sanctum where there is a linga.

In between the **Kandariya Mahadeva Temple** and its partner the **Jagadambi Temple** is the ruined **Siva Temple** (11th century). Little remains except a porch, within which there is a person attending a lion-like beast. The **Jagadambi Temple** (mid 11th century) is similar in layout to the next temple, the **Chitragupta Temple**. The outer walls have no projecting balconies but are lavishly decorated with deities, very often Vishnu, and *mithunas* (loving couples). The ceiling panels inside are very fine. There is some debate over whether the image is of Parvati or Kali. Some regard this as Khajuraho's most erotic temple.

The **Chitragupta temple** This early 11th century temple is the only temple dedicated to **Surya**, the Sun God. (**see page 636**) It is also longer and lower than its companions and has received much restoration. In the *garbha griha** inner sanctum there is a carving of Surya driving his chariot, while on the S facade is a statue of Vishnu. The eleven heads signify **Vishnu** himself and his ten avatars (incarnations), see page 55. In the final corner of the garden are two buildings sharing the same raised base. The one nearest the road is the **Nandi Pavilion** which houses a large image of Nandi the bull, Shiva's vehicle. The temple behind is the Vishvanatha Temple (1002). In the chronology of temples at Khajuraho, this comes between the **Lakshmana** and the **Kandriya Mahadeva**. The basement is particularly deep but still well carved. This blends into the building itself and both have recessed and projecting bands giving the impression that the temple is made up of a number of layers. Each of the four sections of the temple, the *ardha mandapa* (porch), *mandapa* (hall), *antarala* (vestibule) and *garbha-griha* (sanctum) has a separate roof. These gradually increase in height to the tallest which is above the sanctum. On the top of each is a *kalasha* (a pot shaped finial) which signifies physical and spiritual well-being. There were originally five shrines within the temple. Now there are only two. The temple is dedicated to Siva. The word Vishvanatha means 'Lord of All'.

Outside this garden complex of temples and next to the Lakshmana temple is the **Matangesvara Temple** (900-925 AD), simpler in form and decoration than its neighbour and unlike all the others still in everyday use.

The **Chausath Yogini Temple** (late 9th century) is a ruined Jain temple standing apart from the rest of the W Group beyond the tank. It is constructed entirely of granite. Originally it had 64 shrines (chausath means 64) but only 35 remain. The temples in the Eastern and Southern Groups are remarkable and pleasing in their own right but not a match for the Western temple.

Eastern Group

The temples here fall into two groups: the collection of Jain temples in a walled enclosure and the others which are scattered around the village. In the enclosure there is the **Parshvanath Temple** (mid 10th century). This is the largest **Jain** temple of the Chandela period and one of its finest. The curvilinear tower dominates the structure and is beautifully carved. The walls contain panels set into recesses and these depict the deities, particularly Vishnu and amorous couples. Some of the best known non erotic sculptures in Khajuraho are found here. The interior is richly carved. There are elephants and lions at the entrance, sea goddesses and Jain figures. The temple was originally dedicated to Adinath but apparently changed to Parshvanath about a century ago.

Next to the Parshvanath temple on the left is the *Adinatha Temple* (late 11th century), smaller and simpler. The tower is covered with 'a mesh of arch-like motifs' according to Michell whilst below there are three bands of wall sculptures. The porch is a later addition. The whole has been much restored. The other temple in this group is the **Santinatha Temple** which is quite modern by Khajuraho standards having been built about 100 years ago. There is also a small Jain museum in the compound.

Around the village is the ruined **'Ghantai' Temple** (late 10th century). The richly ornamented doorway can be seen. Walk through Khajuraho village to the small **Javari Temple** (late 11th century) contains more female decoration. About 200 m N is the **Vamana Temple** (11th century). This is in the fully developed Chandela style and has a single tower without *urushringas* (subsidiary towers). The walls are adorned with the usual maidens and the interior houses a Vamana (Dwarf) image. Returning to the modern part of Khajuraho, you pass the **Brahma Temple** (early 10th century), one of the earliest, and actually a Vishnu temple wrongly attributed to Brahma.

Southern Group

There are only two temples in this 'group' and they stand on open land. The setting, attractive at sunset, lacks the overall ambience of the Western Group but the backdrop of the Vindhyas is impressive. The *Duladeo Temple* (early 12th century) is one of the last Chandela temples, when the temple building art was already in decline. The *Chaturbhuja Temple* (early 12th century) houses a large 2.7 m high Siva image.

Hotels **B** *Chandela*. T 54. 102 rm. Attractive hotel run by the Taj Group and popular with tour parties. **B** *Jass Oberoi*. T 66. 54 rm. Next door to Chandela. Very pleasant country atmosphere and equally attractive. Ground floor rm suitable for disabled. Friendly welcome and good food. Good pool and gardens. **C** *Khajuraho Ashok* T 24. 40 rm. Pool, bar, restaurant (Indian, Continental), coffee shop, room service, shops, exchange. Some rooms have temple views. Run by ITDC. Pleasant. MP Tourism has an impressive range of moderately priced accommodation. The **D** *Payal*, T 76, has 25 a/c and non a/c rooms with bath. **E** *Rahil*, T 62, 12 non a/c rooms and dormitory. Extensive gardens. **E** *Tourist Bungalow*, T 64, 6 single, double and four-bedded rooms. **E** *Tourist Village*, T 62. 13 well equipped 'ethnic' huts with bedroom and attached bathroom. All establishments have restaurants and the *Payal* a bar. All MP Tourism accommodation is good value and recommended. The Tourist Huts are especially attractive. **E** *Temple* T 49. 11 non a/c rm. Indian style bathrooms. **F** hotels include, *Jain Lodge*, T 52, *Bharat Lodge*, T 82 and *Sunset View*, T 77.

Restaurants *Raja's Cafe*, opp the W Group of Temples. Simple fare. Popular.

Bars None other than those at hotels. There is a bottle shop near Raja's Cafe. Open 1000-2100.

Shopping There are numerous gift shops: *Mrignayani Emporium, Jem House, Chandela Emporium, Chandela Art Palace, Indian Art Emporium, Jewel Art House, Khajuraho Handicrafts Emporium, Lavania and Sons*. All open daily. Most have cheap stone and bronze sculptures plus other handicrafts. Some of the gems are good. Panna diamond mines, the largest in the country are nearby.

Photography *Dosaj Photo Centre* and *Bajpai Photo Centre*, both in the market opp the W Group of Temples.

Local Transport Cycle rickshaws – fares negotiable. Bicycles may be hired near the main market. **Private taxis** are available at Rs 2.20 per km for local excursions. Approved **car hire** rates are Rs.80 per half day (4 hr) and Rs.160 per full day (8 hr). Contact *MPTDC* and *Khajuraho Tours*.

Museums Archaeological Museum, T 28. Collection of sculptures from the temples. Open daily 1000-1700, closed Fri.

Useful Addresses Police, T 32. Ambulance, T 41. *Foreigners' Regional Registration Office*, Superintendent of Police, Chhatarpur.

Hospitals and Medical Services Khajuraho Medical Centre.

Post and Telegraph Post and Telegraph Office, Bus Stand, T 22.

Places of Worship *Hindu*: Matangesvara Temple, adjacent to W Temple Group.

Tour Operators *Khajuraho Tours*, T 33.

Tourist Offices and Information (incl Conducted Tours) Government of India Tourist Office, Khajuraho. Opposite W Group of Temples, T 47. Tourist Information Centre, Bus Stand. Regional Tourist Office, Tourist Bungalow, T 51.
    Air Indian Airlines flies daily from Delhi to Khajuraho via Agra and on to Varanasi, returning the same route. **Vayudoot** flies daily from Bhopal to Khajuraho and on to Rewa, returning the same day. Also daily except Sun on Delhi-Agra Khajuraho-Varanasi route. The airport is 5 km from the village centre. Indian Airlines, Temple Hotel, T 35. Airport, T 36. Vayudoot Booking Office, Bus Stand.

Rail The nearest railheads are Jhansi (176 km, convenient for Agra, Delhi, Bhopal) and Satna (117 km, convenient for Calcutta)

Bus There are daily MPSRTC services to **Agra** (391 km, 12 hr), **Gwalior** (280 km, 9 hr), Jhansi (176 km, 6 hr), Bhopal, Indore, Jabalpur, Jhansi, Satna and Harpalpur. UPSRTC runs a service to Agra via Gwalior.

Excursions Mahoba and **Charkhari** in UP, approx 50 km N of **Khajuraho** and **Chhatarpur**. Mahoba overlooks the Madan Sagar lake.

Mahoba is believed to have existed under different names in all the successive cycles through which the world has passed. Its name in the present 'evil age' (Kala-Yuga), Mahoba is said to be derived from a great sacrifice (Mahot-Sava) performed by its reputed founder the Chandela Raja Chandra Varma in 800 AD. Architectural antiquities of the Chandela period abound throughout the neighbourhood. The Chandela kings, apparently, desired two earthly things after the safe possession of Bundelkhand : to build temples for their gods and to bring water to the land. The **Ram Kund** lake marks the place where the dynasty's founder died and on an island in *Madan Sagar*, the main lake, stands a Siva temple dating from the 12th century. The shores of the lakes and the islands are littered with ruined temples and large rock figures, Buddhist and Jain sculptures left abandoned since the Muslim invasions; a dancing Ganes of whitewashed granite in a mustard field here, a sun temple dedicated to Surya the Sun god there, a vast figure of Siva cut into the rock there.

Lakes and forts The Chandelas obviously had a liking for water. The area around the Khajuraho temples was flooded, and at Mahoba they constructed four lakes by damming valleys. **Madan Sagar**, 5 km in circumference, was made in the 12th century, **Vijay Sagar** in 11th century. The other two are **Kalyan Sagar** and **Kirat Sagar**. Defence seems to have been at the heart of the enterprise and the hill fort at **Charkhari** is surrounded on three sides by water. The landward approach to the fort is made through an imposing gate, its door studded with spikes to deter elephants from knocking it down. It leads to a courtyard and durbar hall decorated with portraits of the **Charkhari Rajas**. From there the ascent is long and gradual and this enabled elephants and heavy guns to be taken higher. There are cannons abandoned in nearly every bastion. Also within these walls are the temple gardens and well.

Parmadidev, the last Chandela king, was defeated by the Chauhan emperor **Prithviraj** in 1182, the latter making Delhi his strategic base. **Qutb-ud-Din** (See page 165) took the town in 1195. A number of Muslim remains survive. The tomb of **Jalhan Khan** is constructed from the remains of a Saivite temple, and a mosque whose Persian inscription indicates it was founded in 1322 during the reign of **Ghiyas-ud-din-Tughluq (see page 167)**. The fort fell into the hands of **Tantia Topi** during the Mutiny but the local **Raja Ratan Singh** remained loyal to the British and afterwards was awarded a hereditary 11 gun salute.

The view from Charkhari across the lakes and fields is spectacular. The ruins are of an Edwardian summer palace that was used as a hunting lodge for large shooting parties that terrorised the local wildfowl and, the villagers too.

From Khajuraho you can drive along the N boundary of Madhya Pradesh visiting various Chandela forts and finishing this journey at Allahabad. There are, in fact two routes. The northerly route goes via **Mahoba** (51 km), **Banda** (50 km), **Chitrakut** (69 km), **Allahabad** (120 km) and is less interesting scenically as the road runs N of the hills. The terrain is flat and tedious. The southerly route is more exciting.

From Khajuraho you drive across the cultivated plain. On the hillside to your right as you turn into the main road from the side road out of Khajuraho you can see the imposing hillside palace (ruined) of the Maharaja. Further along (20 km) you pass some attractive waterfalls and pools. On one side there was a small hermitage. Now, the area is a popular picnic spot. After crossing the **Ken River** you then begin to climb the Panna Hills. Once ascended, the forest thins out and there are some attractive. The **diamond mines** are off to the right as is the **Panna National Park**. Neither are worth bothering with, the first because it is difficult to obtain permission and the second because the wildlife is not very abundant.
At **Panna** (40 km) turn left and drive to **Ajaigarh**, about 80 km from Khajuraho and 26 km from Kalinjar. There is an alternative, shorter direct route from Khajuraho to Ajaigarh by a back road. Ask at the Tourist Information Office what conditions are like before using it.

Ajaigarh lies in rugged country (*Altitude* 500 m) on a granite outcrop and crowned by a 15 m perpendicular scarp. The excellent coffee table book *The Forts of India* by Virginia Fass and others note that although it lies deep in remote and difficult country and is only reached by a stiff 250 m climb, the fort repays the effort. Like most of the forts of N India, there are places of worship, rock carvings and sculptures to be seen as well, some before the climb is over. Ajaigarh was a self-contained forest hill fort, intended to withstand long sieges and be capable of housing the entire population of the region within its walls. This accounts for its size.
The Chandela kings' main defensive bases were **Mahoba** and **Kalinjar** (both now in U.P.), but these were complemented by other forts such as Ajaigarh as the kingdom expanded. In fact, there are a large number of forts in a comparatively small area : Kalinjar, Ajaigarh, Mahoba and Charkhari, Garkhundar, Orchha, Datia, Samthar, Talbehat, Deogarh and Chanderi, and many of these are Chandela forts. The Chandelas, like other kings and emperors, donated villages to maintain the families of soldiers who had died in war. This was an effective means of encouraging the continuing flow of soldiers which the system required. Heroic virtues were instilled into a child from birth so that any man who shirked combat was held in contempt. Women too were taught to admire men who fought well. A woman had to be ready to die should her husband be killed and the becoming of sati, whether forced or voluntary became fashionable (though not with the women concerned one suspects) throughout the region of NW India.
As the Chandela's fortunes declined, they lost **Mahoba** (1182) and **Kalinjar** (1203) and became confined to the area around **Ajaigarh**. Much later still, when the Bundela chief *Chattrasal* rose to prominence in the early 18th century, Ajaigarh fell. On his death in 1734 the area descended into factional conflicts until the Marathas under the Nawab of Banda took the fort after a six week siege in 1800. In 1808 it changed hands again, this time falling to Lakshman Daowa.

He showed no signs of acknowledging the British presence in Bundelkhand and in 1809 the battle lines were drawn again. Under Colonel Martindell, the British Indian army took the surrounding hills in fierce fighting, after which they used their artillery on the fort with devastating effect. Since then the forests of teak and ebony have been slowly and quietly invading the place.

Ajaigarh's battlements show little uniformity as the thickness of the walls never remains the same for more than a few metres. The Muslims are accredited with using carved pillars and door jambs from the Hindu and Jain temples to effect repairs and fortifications. Huge blocks of stone once formed steps for elephants on the steep track up to the fort and now only two of the former five gates are accessible. From **Ajaigarh** you can drive directly to **Kalinjar** (20 km). Again it is worth asking locally about road conditions. An alternative route is to go to **Naraini**, then approach **Kalinjar** from the N. This will add about 30 km to the journey. You can always miss out **Kalinjar** and continue on from Ajaigarh to **Atarra Basurg**.

Kalinjar, 53 km S of **Banda**, the fort stands on the last spur of the **Vindhya hills** overlooking the Gangetic plains, a plateau (*Altitude* 375 m) with a steep scarp on all sides. **Kalinjar** is one of the most ancient sites in Bundelkhand, referred to by the Greek Ptolemy as Kanagora. It combines the sanctity of remote hill tops with the defensive strength of a natural fortress.

Origins One legend proclaims Kalinjar as the Abode of **Siva**, the Lord of Destruction (*Kal*=death, *Jar*=decay). Its name, though, is linked with the Chandela kings, and it was one of their strongholds. In the second half of the 10th century the independent Chandelas joined a Hindu confederacy to repel an Afghan invasion led by *Amir Sabuktigrin*. His son, Mahmud of Ghazni, the 'Idol Breaker', made at least 17 of his almost annual plunder raids into India from 1000-1027. In 1019 he crossed the Yamuna river and approached Kalinjar. On this occasion neither side could claim victory but in 1022 he returned and took the title Lord of Kalinjar. Thereafter, it was a depressingly familiar story. Successive Muslim invasions weakened the forts defences and, then in 1182, the Chandela forces were crushed by the rival Hindu forces of Chauhan. In 1203 Kalinjar fell again to the Muslims and the last Chandela king, Parmadidev, was defeated. Yet Muslim power over the area remained unconsolidated until the rise of the Mughals.

The fort Like other forts of the ancient world, Kalinjar's design has a mystical significance, the idea being that it is a manifestation of a force greater than man's. The only approach is from the N but entry is through 7 gates, all of them with barbicans, and each corresponding to one of the 7 known planets and stations though which the soul must pass before being absorbed into Brahma. Only some of the names indicate Hindu significance. The succession is: **Alam Darwaza** or **Alamgir Gate** after the Mughal Emperor Aurangzeb; **Ganesh Gate**; **Chandi Darwaza** is a double gate; **Budh Budr Gate**, approached by a flight of steps; **Hanuman Gate**, surrounded by numerous sculptures and inscriptions; **Lal Darwaza**; **Bara Darwaza**. At the crest crumbling Hindu and Muslim monuments stand side by side on the 1.5 km long plateau. Beyond the last gate is a drop of about 3.6 m leading to **Sita Sej**, a stone couch set in a chamber hewn from the rock. The inscription over the door dates from 4th century AD. Beyond is a passage leading to Patalganga or underground Ganga, which runs through Kalinjar.

Koth Tirth at the centre of the fort is a large 90 m long tank with ghats (steps) leading down to it. Nearby are the ruins of **King Aman Singh's Palace**. Numerous stone relics are scattered about the site; a dancing Ganes, Nandi bulls, a model temple complete with figures like a miniature Khajuraho and a reclining Siva. Sati pillars are scattered about the fort, reminders of the tradition of self-immolation by Rajput women, and there are a number of lingams and yonis, symbols of male and female fertility.

Kalinjar was retaken from the Muslims by local chiefs and remained Hindu until 1545 when the Afghan Sher Shah, who dethroned the Mughal Humayun from Delhi besieged the fort. During the heavy fighting, Sher Shah was mortally wounded but he clung on for long enough to know that the Hindu king Kirat Singh had been executed. Humayun re-established Mughal rule in India at the end of his life and his son Akbar took Kalinjar in 1569. Kirat Singh married one of his daughters to a Gond Raja and for most of her married life she waged war against Akbar, earning for herself the reputation as heroine of Bundelkhand.

Towards the end of Aurangzeb's reign, the Bundela chief **Chattrasal** took Kalinjar and on his death in 1732 bequeathed it to the **Marathas**. This was surrendered to the British after Martindell breached the fort's defences in 1812. They later erected a monument to Andrew Wauchope, the first Commissioner of Bundelkhand. The ancient hill of Kalinjar, standing on the last range of the Vindhyas and overlooking the Ganges plain has long been a place of pilgrimage and worship for Hindu saddhus, rishis and pilgrims. It is rarely visited by other travellers. The town below is of little interest.

From Kalinjar it is about 150 km to Allahabad via *Chitrakut*, a Hindu pilgrimage site where Sita, Rama and Lakshman are said to have lived after their exile from Ayodhya. Before reaching Allahabad, visit Kausambi (see Allahabad **Excursions**).

MADHYA PRADESH

Madhya Pradesh, (the "Central Provinces") is, geographically, the heart of India. With an area larger than that of Germany, the state straddles the centre of the country from Rajasthan in the W to Orissa and Bihar in the E. Yet despite its central position it has all the characteristics of a marginal territory. It contains many of the tribal groups least touched by modernisation, most of India's remaining genuine forest and some of its least densely populated countryside. The western region has been part of the N-S corridor of population movement for over 4,000 years. Today's major towns in Madhya Pradesh (**Gwalior, Bhopal, Indore**) are all in this funnel. Indeed, the majority of the population and most of the industrial activity is here. In contrast the dense forests which cover much of the rest of the state, especially the wetter E, have been very difficult to penetrate. It has however been the home of some of India's earliest settlements. The magnificent paintings and other archaeological discoveries made in rock shelters and caves at Bhimbetka, for example, illustrate the continuity of settlement from before the Acheulian period to the recent historical past.

Social indicators Area 443,000 sq km **Population** 64 million **Literacy** M 40% F 15%
Birth rate *Rural* 40:1000 *Urban* 32:1000 **Death rate** *Rural* 16:1000 *Urban* 9:1000
Infant mortality *Rural* 145:1000 *Urban* 79:1000 **Registered graduate job seekers**
118,000 **Average annual income per head**: Rs 1130 **Inflation** *1981-87* 73% **Religion**
Hindu 93% *Muslim* 5% *Christian* 1% *Sikh* 0.3%.

INTRODUCTION

A zone of contact Madhya Pradesh has been a shatter belt between the northern and southern core regions of India's cultural development. Thus despite its central position in South Asia it has never been the home of a major Indian empire. Rather it has come under a succession of different rulers, most accepting the ultimate sovereignty of a power beyond the region itself. This political history is illustrated by the fact that when the British arrived they came to it relatively late, and left much of the region in the hands of its multitude of princes, many of them ruling tiny states.

A rich architecture The state has some magnificent archaeological and historical sites and some superb buildings. The stupa at **Sanchi**, whilst having no direct connection with the Buddha, is one of the faith's finest monuments in India. The Chandela temples at **Khajuraho** are testimony to a period of great artistic merit and the splendid fort and palaces at **Gwalior** a reminder of the magnificence of many Indian princely states. **Mandu** in Malwa (W Madhya Pradesh) occupied a strategic position on the important corridor from Delhi to the western seaboard. This delightful hilltop fort and citadel of palaces, mosques and tombs was fortified as early as the 6th century AD, and under the Muslim Sultans of Malwa it was named Shadiabad (City of Joy). **Ujjain** is one of the seven holy cities of India and a centre of Hindu pilgrimage. The **Kanha National Park** is a superb wildlife sanctuary covering the type of country that Kipling based the Jungle Books on.

Communications are well developed along the N-S corridor in the W but much less so elsewhere. This has hindered the industrial development of the state and the exploitation of its impressive mineral deposits. Madhya Pradesh thus has great potential for sustainable economic growth and is not hampered by an excessively large population like its two neighbours to the N, Bihar and Uttar Pradesh. Despite its central location, ease of access from Delhi, its wide range of sites and monuments and its freedom from violent political struggles that have afflicted other states, Madhya Pradesh is rarely visited by foreigners.

You can now reach **Bhopal** in the heart of Madhya Pradesh from Delhi in only 8 hours by travelling on the super fast Shatabdi Express which stops only in Agra, Jhansi and Gwalior. Whilst there are not many top class hotels in the region, there is good accommodation at reasonable prices. Madhya Pradesh Tourism, like its counterpart in Haryana, is a progressive organisation and has built up an impressive network of tourist complexes at most of the major destinations in the state. These are modest, reasonably comfortable and inexpensive.

The Land
Madhya Pradesh is the southernmost of the landlocked states in India and shares boundaries with seven states: Uttar Pradesh (N), Bihar (NE), Orissa (E), Andhra Pradesh (SE), Maharashtra (S and SW), Gujarat (W) and Rajasthan (NW). The state occupies the northern part of the Deccan plateau, has a number of hill ranges and is the source of some of the most important peninsular rivers, namely the **Narmada**, **Chambal**, **Mahanadi** and **Tapti**.

The **Vindhya** and **Kaimur ranges** Along the northern edge is an old erosion front joined in the W by the **Vindhya range** that runs diagonally across the state from around **Dhar** to **Khajuraho**. The **Kaimur range** runs through **Baghelkhand**, overlooking the Gangetic plain around Varanasi and Allahabad in UP. Both ranges are frequently broken by rivers, e.g. the Ken, and deep ravines. They are generally well wooded and rise to 600 m. Behind the Kaimur range is the **Baghelkhand plateau** with an average altitude of 300 m above sea-level. In the E the Hazaribagh range juts into the state and S of Raipur around Bastar is

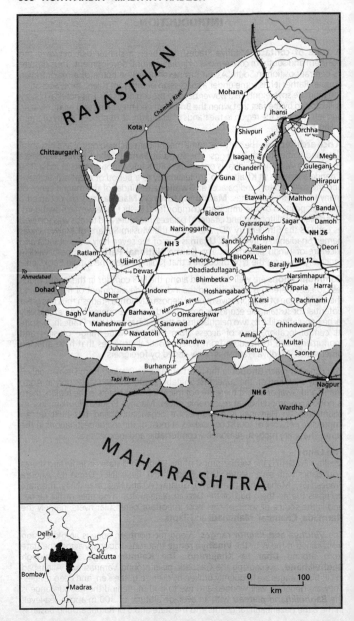

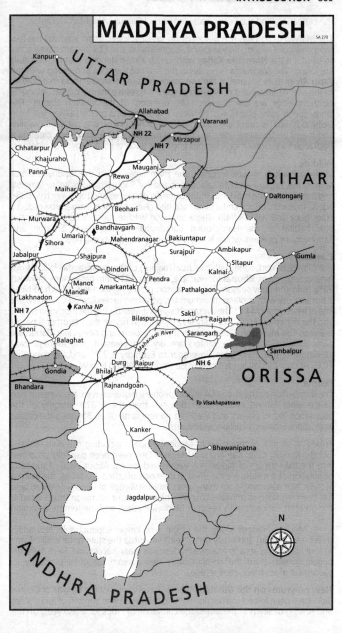

MADHYA PRADESH

SA 270

UTTAR PRADESH

Kanpur

Allahabad

NH 22

NH 7

Varanasi

Mirzapur

Mauganj

Chhatarpur

Khajuraho

Panna

Maihar

Rewa

BIHAR

Beohari

Daltonganj

Murwara

Bandhavgarh

Umaria

Mahendranagar

Bakiuntapur

Sihora

Surajpur

Ambikapur

Sitapur

Gumla

Jabalpur

Shajpura

Dindori

Pendra

Kalnai

Pathalgaon

Manot

Amarkantak

Mandla

Lakhnadon

Kanha NP

Bilaspur

Sakti

Raigarh

NH 7

Seoni

Makanadi River

Sarangarh

Sambalpur

Balaghat

Durg

Raipur

NH 6

Gondia

Bhilai

ORISSA

Bhandara

Rajnandgoan

To Visakhapatnam

Kanker

Bhawanipatna

Jagdalpur

N

ANDHRA PRADESH

the plateau behind the Eern Ghats. To the N of Raipur is the Maikala range.

The *Malwa* region has rich black cotton soil of volcanic origin whereas the low lying areas of Gwalior, Bundelkhand, Baghelkhand and Chattisgarh have lighter soil. But it is the **Narmada Valley** with its rich alluvial deposits that the best soils are found. The *Narmada* river rises in the heart of the state and, along with the *Tapti River* to its S is one of the two major rivers in peninsular India that flow W to the sea. At Jabalpur it runs through some impressive marble gorges. Along its northern edge are the Bhanrer Hills, outriders of the Vindhya Range. The landscape in some places, e.g. between Jhansi and Bina on the railway line from Delhi to Bhopal is stony and inhospitable. In other places, e.g. between Gwalior and Jhansi on the same line the Chambal river has dug deep gorges, creating a *badlands** area which local bandits known as **dacoits** have enjoyed as hideouts.

Wildlife
Madhya Pradesh is well forested, the main areas being the Vindhya-Kaimur ranges, the Satpura and Maikala ranges and the Baghelkhand plateau. Teak, sal and bamboo are the most important commercial species and there is rich wildlife: tigers, leopards, bison, chital (small spotted deer), sambhar (large brown deer), black buck and wild buffalo. There are good wildlife sanctuaries at Kanha, the only habitat of the Hardground Barasingha (swamp deer), Shivpuri and Bandhavgarh or Rewa which is known for its white (albinotic) tigers.

Climate
The climate is monsoonal with the usual majority of the yearly rainfall falling from June to September. **Bhopal** for example, receives 1210 mm per annum, of which 90% is in the rainy season. The dry season preceding the rains (March to May) is hot and dry with average maximum temperatures exceeding 33°C everywhere and often reaching 44°C. The average daily maximum during the monsoon is 30°C and the minimum 19°C. Humidity levels are much higher than at other times of the year. The monsoon causes luxuriant plant growth and places like Mandu are particularly attractive. The winters are dry and pleasant. The average daily maximum temperature from November to February is 27°C and the minimum 10°C. Annual rainfall tends to decrease from S to N and E to W.

People
The distribution of the state's 64 million people is highly uneven, the western part of the state having much higher densities than the E. The majority of the population live in villages and there are no very large cities. Bhopal is the capital with approximately 1 million inhabitants.

Tribes A variety of tribes live in Madhya Pradesh including the Bhils, Baigas, Gonds, Korkus, Kols, Kamars and Marias. Many have been painfully absorbed into the mainstream of Indian life, with mixed results. About 20% of the total population of the state are classified as members of scheduled tribes, the highest in India. Not surprisingly, for many years this vast wedge of densely forested land has been regarded as primitive country. There are about 20 million tribals in India, the greatest concentration being in Madhya Pradesh and the remote adjoining areas.

In Madhya Pradesh today, the jungle is no longer impenetrable. Nowadays travel may be long and dusty but at least you cross the state quite easily. Three to four hundred years ago Madhya Pradesh was really inaccessible. Here the tribal people, driven from the comparatively well-watered Gangetic plains by its succession of invaders, took refuge.

New pressures on the tribals In the not too distant past the *Baigas* of Central India have been forced to abandon shifting cultivation (the burning of forest strips and sowing of seeds in the ashes, the cultivation of crops for a few years on this land and its abandonment for regeneration; the rotation of fields rather than crops) and to move from this axe and hoe agriculture to the plough. Most of the 2 to 2.5 million Gonds in Madhya Pradesh retain their so-called 'primitive' ways. Traditionally, the tribals were semi-nomadic, some living solely off what they could hunt, others relying on shifting cultivation. Most have now been settled, many it would seem as unhappily as the Australian aborigines, for country liquor and drug dependency are said to be common among the men. Many cling to their older, deep set beliefs, such as burying their dead, rather than burning them according to Hindu tradition. Over the centuries, tribal territory has gradually been nibbled away, and everywhere their way of life is under threat.

The **Gonds**, the largest of the tribes, managed to maintain their independence until the last century. From 1200 AD there were as many as four Gond Kingdoms. One had an initiation ceremony centred on eating wild orchids. John Keay has suggested that Gond history is like J.R. Tolkien's *The Lord of The Rings*, and that the Hobbit heroes would have made friends with 'these gentle people and joined them on their travels'. Today one of the biggest threats to the tribals comes from that symbol of large scale modernisation, irrigation dams. With the proposed building of a succession of dams across the Narmada River in S Madhya Pradesh hundreds of thousands of hectares of tribal forest land will be inundated, and loud political protests are a feature of the state's current politics.

Some tribal traditions, especially mythology and folklore, have been preserved, though they have been exposed to outside cultural influences. The **Pandwani** and the **Lachmanjati** legends are the Gond equivalents of the Hindu **Mahabharata** and **Ramayana** epic poems. Songs and ceremonies mark life's milestones

Language Hindi is the most widely spoken language though Marathi is also popular. Urdu, Oriya, Gujarati and Punjabi are each spoken by sizeable numbers. The Bhils speak *Bhili* and the Gonds *Gondi*. Both these tribal languages are independent in origin of the Indo-European and Dravidian language groups.

Religion Hinduism is the majority religion and Islam is the largest of the minority faiths which include Sikhism, Christianity and Buddhism.

Economy
The economy of Madhya Pradesh is based on agriculture, the main agricultural regions being in the Chambal Valley, the Malwa Plateau, the Narmada Valley, the Rewa Plateau and the Chhattisgarh Plain. Nearly half of the land area is cultivable of which 15% is irrigated. Irrigation is carried out by means of canals, tanks and and wells. There are 22 major irrigation and power projects with plans to create an irrigation potential of 5.5 million ha. Along with the promotion of Higher Yielding Varieties the state government is attempting to overcome the problem of low agricultural productivity and the use of traditional methods of cultivation.

Agriculture The main food crops are *jowar* (sorghum), wheat and rice and coarse millets such as **kondo** and **kutki**. Pulses (beans, lentils and peas) and groundnuts (peanuts) are also grown. In the E where rainfall exceeds 1270 mm per annum rice is the favoured crop. In the drier eastern areas, wheat is preferred as the principal staple. Madhya Pradesh is the largest **soya bean** producer in India. Important among the commercial crops are oilseeds (linseed and sesame), cotton and sugarcane.The extensive forests are logged for **teak**, **sal**, bamboo and **salai** which yields a resin used for incense and medicines.

Minerals The state is also rich in **minerals.** The country's largest diamond mine is at **Panna** near **Khajuraho**. This has recoverable reserves of 1 million carats. Other minerals include high grade limestone, dolomite, iron ore, manganese ore, copper, coal, rock phosphate and bauxite. The state is also the country's only producer of tin ore. With improved communications, the potential of these resources will be realised. An extensive programme has been undertaken to explore gold deposits in Raipur and Raigarh districts.

Manufacturing industry Before planned development, most **manufacturing** enterprises were located in western Madhya Pradesh, particularly around Bhopal. State attempts at regional improvement have led to the establishment of large- and medium-scale industries at Indore, Ujjain, Gwalior and Jabalpur. The major industries in the state are the steel plant at **Bhilai**, the heavy electrical plant at Bhopal, an aluminium plant at Korba, paper mills at Hoshangabad and Nepanagar, an alkaloid battery factory at Neemuch and numerous cement works. There are 25 textile mills in the state, seven of them nationalised. Madhya Pradesh also has a strong traditional village **handicraft** industry. Handloom Chanderi and Maheshwar silks are especially sought after. The tribal population produce attractive handicrafts.

Hydro electricity The seven major river systems in the state (Narmada, Chambal, Tapti, Son, Betwa, Mahanadi and Indravati) offer good potential for hydro-electric power generation. The Chambal Valley project is jointly run with Rajasthan and other schemes include those at Rajghat, Bansagar, Mahanadi Reservoir, Hasdeo Bango and Bargi.

Communication Transport facilities in the state are uneven. Good road and rail communications exist in the western part of the state, particularly along the corridor running from Gwalior in the N to Bhopal in the centre and Khandwa in the S. The railways, originally laid to connect Bombay with Delhi and to a lesser extent Delhi with Madras and Calcutta, have since been extended to incorporate places like Jabalpur in the heart of Madhya Pradesh into the rail network. Bhopal is now highly accessible from Delhi. In many districts, however, the road network is very poor. This has obviously hindered development efforts.

History
Several remains of prehistoric cultures, including rock paintings and stone artefacts, have been found. One of the earliest states that existed in Madhya Pradesh was **Avanti** of which **Ujjain** was capital, part of the 4th-3rd century BC **Mauryan Empire**. From the 2nd century BC to the 16th century AD various dynasties ruled part or most of the state: the **Sunga** dynasty (185-73 BC) in Eastern Malwa; the **Andhras** (Satavahanas 1st Century BC to 3rd century AD); the **Ksaptrapas** and the **Nagas** (2nd-4th Centuries AD); the **Guptas** ruled the region to the N of the **Narmada** (4th-5th century AD); the **Hunas** (Huns) struggled to seize control of Malwa during this period while in the 7th century it became part of Harsha's N Indian empire.

In the 10th century a number of dynasties controlled different parts of the region: the **Kalachuris** in the Narmada Valley, the **Paramaras** in the W, the **Kachwahas** around Gwalior and the **Chandelas** at Khajuraho. Later the **Tomaras** took Gwalior. Gwalior was conquered by the Muslims in the 11th century. The **Delhi Sultanate** incorporated Hindu domains in 1231 and the **Khalji** dynasty took Malwa. Akbar annexed this into his empire in the mid 16th century. A large part came under **Maratha** rule with the decline of the **Mughal** empire in the 18th century. The **Scindia** and **Holkar** dynasties of Marathas established independent rule at Gwalior and Indore respectively.

In 1817-18 territories known as the 'Saugor-Nerbudda' were ceded to the **British**. Other districts were added in 1860 and the region became known as the Central Provinces. Berar was added in 1903. To the N and W the Central India Agency was formed in 1854 and comprised Malwa, Bundelkhand and Baghelkhand.

On independence, the **Central Provinces** and **Berar** became **Madhya Pradesh.** The Central India Agency was first divided into Madhya Bharat (Middle India) and Vindhya Pradesh (Vindhya Provinces) and then added to Madhya

Pradesh. Eight Marathi-speaking districts were detached and added to Bombay state.

Recent political developments Since it took its present form Madhya Pradesh has had a state legislature of 320 seats. With the exception of 1977 and 1989 the Congress Party has always held a comfortable majority of the seats, though the **BJP (Bharatiya Janata Party)** has always had a strong base of support, winning at least 50 seats in every election after 1967. In the post Emergency election of 1977 the Congress vote slumped from 48% to 36%, but its representation in the **Vidhan Sabha** fell from 220 seats to 84 seats. It suffered another reversal in the 1989 elections. The State elects 40 members to the Lok Sabha.

In 1980 and 1984 the Congress won 35 and 40 seats respectively, its then Chief Minister **Arjun Singh** playing a prominent part in Rajiv Gandhi's attempts to pacify the Punjab by being appointed Punjab's governor. In common with the other states of the Hindi belt the BJP contributed to sweeping the Congress from power in 1977 and again in 1989. In December 1989 they won 27 of the 40 seats, helped by a defection of Muslims from the Congress to their own independent Muslim candidates. **Bhopal** became known across the world in October 1984 for its terrible industrial accident at the Union Carbide pesticide plant. Thousands continue to suffer the effects.

BHOPAL

Population **671,018 (81 Census).** *Altitude* **523 m. Indian Airlines services connect Bhopal with Delhi (705 km, 1 hr 55 min) and Bombay (837 km, 2 hr). The airport is 7 km from the city centre.**

	Jan	Feb	Mar	Apr	May	Jun	Jul	Aug	Sep	Oct	Nov	Dec	Av/Tot
Max (°C)	26	29	34	38	41	37	30	29	30	31	29	26	32
Min (°C)	10	13	17	21	26	25	23	23	22	18	13	11	19
Rain (mm)	17	5	10	3	11	137	499	308	232	37	15	7	1281

Bhopal, the capital city of Madhya Pradesh (MP), is situated on the site of 11th century Bhojapal, founded by Raja Bhoj, an Afghan adventurer. He is accredited with the creation of the lakes (pal). The present city within the walls was laid out by *Dost Mohammad Khan* who had been one of Aurangzeb's governors and on his death in 1707 took advantage of the situation by carving out a kingdom for himself. He died in 1723 leaving an island state in Malwa. From 1857 until 1926, Bhopal was ruled by women, first *Sikander Begum* (r1857-1901) and then by *Shah Jahan Begum* (r1901-1926). The Taj-ul-Masjid, one of the largest mosques in India was begun but not completed by Shah Jahan Begum.

Situated round the two artificial lakes and on gently rolling hills, Bhopal is an attractive city. It achieved international notoriety in 1984 with the *Union Carbide* disaster. Poisonous gas escaped from the multi-national corporation's plant and killed over 1000 people and injured many thousands more. The case is as yet unresolved. Outside the infamous factory is a small memorial with the inscription "No Hiroshima. No Bhopal. We hope to live".

The city has a good range of hotels and is conveniently located for travel from Delhi (train and air) and to Sanchi. It is a very pleasant city to rest and relax.

Places of Interest The **Taj-ul Masjid** (19th century) is striking because of its 3

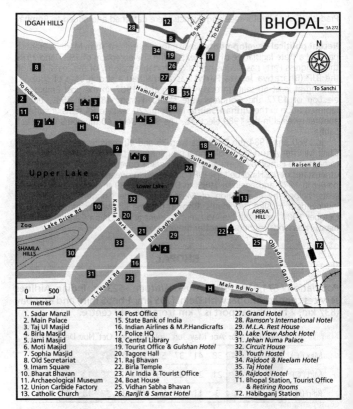

1. Sadar Manzil	14. Post Office	27. *Grand Hotel*
2. Main Palace	15. State Bank of India	28. *Ramson's International Hotel*
3. Taj Ul Masjid	16. Indian Airlines & M.P.Handicrafts	29. *M.L.A. Rest House*
4. Birla Masjid	17. Police HQ	30. *Lake View Ashok Hotel*
5. Jami Masjid	18. Central Library	31. *Jehan Numa Palace*
6. Moti Masjid	19. Tourist Office & *Gulshan Hotel*	32. *Circuit House*
7. Sophia Masjid	20. Tagore Hall	33. *Youth Hostel*
8. Old Secretariat	21. Raj Bhavan	34. *Rajdoot & Neelam Hotel*
9. Imam Square	22. Birla Temple	35. *Taj Hotel*
10. Bharat Bhavan	23. Air India & Tourist Office	36. *Rajdoot Hotel*
11. Archaeological Museum	24. Boat House	T1. Bhopal Station, Tourist Office
12. Union Carbide Factory	25. Vidhan Sabha Bhavan	& *Retiring Rooms*
13. Catholic Church	26. *Ranjit & Samrat Hotel*	T2. Habibganj Station

white domes and 2 massive minarets, this mosque is still being completed. The main hall is impressive. Gold spikes crown the minarets of the smaller and earlier **Jama Masjid** mosque. Built in 1837 by another woman ruler, Qudsia Begum, this is surrounded by a bazaar. The **Moti Masjid** (1860) was built by Qudsia Begum's daughter, Sikander Begum in similar style to the Jama Masjid in Delhi and has 2 red, gold topped minarets. At the entrance to the old city area is **Shaukta Mahal** designed by a Bourbon Frenchman, combining Post-Renaissance and Gothic styles. Nearby is the **Sadar Manzil**, the Hall of Public Audience of the former rulers of Bhopal. S of the Lower Lake is the modern **Laxmi Narayan Temple** (Vaishnavite). Open daily 8000-1200 and 1400-1800. Entry free.

Hotels The best hotels are in the quiet Shamla Hills (about 12 km from airport, 5 km from rly and 2 km from centre). In town there are a large number of hotels on Hamidia Rd and Berasia Rd. Along Station Rd there is less expensive accommodation.
   C *Jehan Numa Palace*, Shamla Hills, T 540100, Cable: Jehanuma, Telex: 0705 343 Jnph in. 60 rm, some in annexe. Central a/c. Restaurant, bar, 24 hr rm service, laundry, travel, exchange, credit cards, gift shop, TV. Very attractive, central courtyard and gardens, good position but no lake view. Pleasant rooms, friendly and efficient service. **C** *Lake View Ashok*, Shamla Hills, T 540452, Cable: Ashokotel, Telex: 0705-303. 47 rm. Central a/c. Restaurant, coffee shop, room service, bar, shopping, TV, laundry, exchange, wheelchair, credit cards,

doctor on call, shops. Newly opened (1990) by MPSTDC and ITDC Ashok Group. Good location with views of Upper Lake, comparable in most other respects with Jehan Numa. **C** *Panchanan* (MPSTDC), New Market Rd, T 63047. Central a/c. Restaurant.

C *Taj*, 52 Hamidia Rd, T 73161/2, Cable: Htltaj, Telex: 705-366 Htaj in. 48 rm. Some a/c rm. Restaurant, laundry, travel, doctor on call, credit cards,TV. Modern. **C** *Imperial Sabre*, Palace Grounds, T 72738. Converted palace guest house. Good location and recommended. **D** *Ramsons International*, Hamidia Rd, T 72298 Cable Sethibros, Telex: 705354. 26 d rm. Central a/c. Restaurant, Amex, TV. Good food. **D** *Mayur*, Berasia Rd, T 76418. A/c and non a/c rms. **D** *President International*, Berasia Rd. T 77291. Some a/c rm. Restaurant, bar. Comfortable, modern. **D** *Motel Shiraz*, Hamidia Rd, opp Board Office, Sivaji Nagar, T 64513. 22 rm, some a/c in cottages. Inexpensive and basic but comfortable. **D** *Palash*, nr '45 Bungalows', MPSTDC, T 68006. 9 a/c rm. Restaurant, bar. Used by VIPs and difficult to get in. **D** *Panchanen*, New Market, MPSTDC, T 551647. 5 s/v rm. Restaurant, bar. Like Palash for VIPS mainly. Bed tea and breakfast included.

D *Siddhartha*, Hamidia Rd, T 75680. 16 rm. A/c and non a/c. **D** *Surya Sheraton*, Hamidia Rd, T 76925. 36 rm, some a/c. **D** *Rajdoot*, 7 Hamidia Rd, T 72691. Some a/c rooms. Restaurant, exchange, travel, car hire. **E** *Ranjit*, 3 Hamidia Rd. T 75211, Cable: Ranjit Bhopal. 29 rm with bath. 6 km airport, near rly, 0.5 km centre. Restaurant, bar, car hire, TV. **E** *Hotel Jyoti*, 53 Hamidia Rd. Some rm with air coolers and TV. Restaurant (veg). On Station Rd: **E** *Sangam*, T 77161. Some a/c rm**. F** *Rainbow*, T 76395; *Meghdoot*, T 76961 with restaurant; *Samrat*, T 77023. **F** *Youth Hostel* (MP Tourism), TT Nagar, T 63671. Dormitory, far from town centre and very basic. **F** *Railway Retiring Rm.*

Restaurants The Hamidia Rd hotels are open to non-residents. You can sample Gujarati specialities at the *Jyoti*, Bhopali cuisine at *Madina Hotel*, Sultania Rd, *Afgani Hotel*, Pir Gate and at *Hakeem's* in Jummerati and New Market. The *Indian Coffee House* is in New Market, Hamidia Rd and Sivaji Nagar. *Bagicha* on Hamidia Rd with garden and bar, and *Dragon* next door for Chinese. *Tapti*, GTB Complex. *Kwality*, Hamidia Rd and Newmarket: cool and comfortable, reasonably priced. For fast food there is *Doodees*, No 10 Bus Stop, Arera Colony. Inexpensive meals at Rly Station and near Bus Stand.

Shopping The *Chowk* in Old Bhopal and the *New Market* in New Bhopal are the main shopping centres. *Mrignayani Emporium* in New Market and *Handicrafts Emporium* on Hamidia Rd stock souvenirs and local handicrafts. *The Women's Cooperative Zari Centre*, Peer Gate has bags richly embroidered with gold and silver thread, and chiffon saris. The *Madhya Pradesh State Emporium*, Sultania Rd, specializes in a local fabric called *chanderi*, a combination of cotton and silk so sheer that the Emperor Aurangzeb insisted that his daughter wear seven layers of it.

Photo Shops *Central Studio*, Hamidia Rd T 74015; *Jaimini Studio*, Ibrahimpura T72582; *Ajanta Photo Emp.*, Hamidia Rd T 74102; *Central Studio*, Marvadi Rd T 72582; also GTB Complex.

Local Transport Buses, tempos, taxis (unmetered), auto-rickshaws (metered) and tongas.

Entertainment Bharat Bhawan's *Rang Mahal* organises regular productions of a wide variety of plays in Hindi, English and regional languages.

Sports Boat Clubs on the Lower and Upper Lakes provide sail, paddle and motor boats. The Upper Lake Boat Club is also a training Centre for water sports.

Museums Below the Shamla hill to the S of the Lower Lake is **The State Museum** which houses sculptures from the 10-12th centuries. Open daily except Sun. Entry free. On the very pleasant **Shamla Hills** overlooking the Upper Lake (area 6 sq km) is **Bharat Bhawan**, centre for the creative and performing arts. Designed by the renowned Indian architect Charles Correa, the low-rise buildings merge with the contours of the landscape. Art gallery, crafts gallery, library and theatre. Entry Re 1.50. Open 1000-1700, closed Mon. **Birla Museum**. Rare sculptures. Open 0900-1700. Closed Mon.

Parks and Zoos *Van Vihar* (Bhopal National Park), adjacent to the Upper Lake has tiger, leopard, lion and bear, among others.

Useful Addresses/Numbers Police 63939, Fire 73333, Ambulance 72222. Passport Office (Ministry of External Affairs), Govt. of India, Gangotri, TT Nagar T 67278.

Hospitals and Medical Services *Hamidia Hospital*, Sultania Rd T 72222; *Sultania Ladies Hosp.*, Budhwara T 540849; *Jai Prakash Hosp.*, Tulsinagar T 62042, 62134; *Kasturba Hosp.*, BHEL T 551359; *Katju Hosp.*, TT Nagar T 62465, 64352.

Post and Telegraph *General P and T Office*, Sultania Rd T 72095; *Central P and T Office*, TT Nagar T 62465.

Places of Worship *Hindu*: Laxmi Narayan Mandir, Gopal Mandir, Kamali Mandir, Ram Mandir. *Jain*: Digamber Jain Mandir. *Muslim*: Jama Masjid, Moti Masjid, Taj-ul-Masjid. *Sikh*: Gurudwara, Hamidia Rd; Gurudwara, TT Nagar. *Christian*: St Francis Cathedral, Jehangirabad; St Joseph's Church, Berkheda.

Travels and Tour Operators MPSTDC has a fleet of vehicles, local and imported, a/c and non a/c, buses and mini coaches for hire for travel locally, within and out of the state. Full details on hire rates can be obtained from MPSTDC offices and hotels.

Tourist Offices and Information *M.P.State Tourism Development Corporation* (MPSTDC) Ltd, Gangotri, 4th Floor, TT Nagar, T 66383. Telex 0705-275 Tour In. **Conducted tours**: MPSTDC runs a tour round Bhopal on Sun, Tues and Thurs 0900-1600 for 24 (lunch not included). Contact MP Tourism, T 64338 for reservations and further information. Tours are also run to various places within the state. For full details contact Tours Section T 65154. Tourist Information (MPSTDC), Airport and Railway Station.

Air Indian Airlines flies daily from Bombay to Bhopal (2 hr) and back via Indore; daily from Bhopal to Raipur and back via Jabalpur; daily from Delhi via Bhopal (1 hr 55 min) to Nagpur and back and 5 times a week from Delhi to Bombay via Gwalior, Bhopal and Indore and back. **Indian Airlines**: City Office T 61633; Airport T 8524-25. **Vayudoot** links Bhopal with Delhi, Gwalior and Guna. **Air India**, GTB Complex, TT Nagar T 63468, 61108.

Rail Bhopal is on the main lines between Delhi and Bombay and the southern state capitals of Madras, Hyderabad (Secunderabad), Bangalore and Trivandrum. It is directly connected with Amritsar and Jammu Tawi in the N and also linked to major towns in MP. **New Delhi**: *Shatabdi Exp*, 2001, daily 1440, 7 hr 40 min; *Punjab Mail*, 1037, daily, 0723, 13 hr; *Jhelum Exp*, 4677, daily, 0930, 12 hr 10 min; *Malwa Exp*, 4067, daily, 2105, 13 hr. **Bombay (VT)**: *Punjab Mail*, 1038, daily, 2042, 15 hr 45 min. **Calcutta (H)**: *Shipra Exp*, 1172, Th and Fri, 0225, 27 hr.
  Lucknow: *Kushi Nagar Exp*, 1015, daily, 0323, 12 hr; *Pushpak Exp*, 2133, daily, 2215, 11 hr 45 min. **Jabalpur** *Amarkantak Exp*, 2854, Tues,Th,Fri,Sun, 1500, 5 hr 35 min; *Narmada Exp*, 8233, daily, 2235, 7 hr 30 min. Bhopal Railway Station, Enquiry and Reservation, T 55000/1/2/3. Booking Office on Plat form 1. Hamidia Rd is closest from Plat form 4 and 5 exit. **To Ujjain**: Narmada Exp, 8234, daily, 0600, 5 hr.

Bus Extensive services (private and state) to cities within the region: **Agra** (NH3 541 km), **Gwalior** (422 km), **Indore** (186 km), **Kanha** (540 km), **Khajuraho** (387 km), **Mandu** (290 km), **Ujjain** (189 km), **Jabalpur**, **Sanchi** (45 km), Nagpur (345 km), Jaipur (735 km). Bus Stand, T 540841.

Excursions It is possible to visit several of the sites that are described below as excursions from **Bhopal**. Sanchi and its neighbouring sites to the E and **Bhimbetka** to the S are particularly well worth visiting, and can comfortably be seen on a day trip. For details see below.

BHOPAL TO GWALIOR

The main route N to Gwalior leaves Bhopal to the northwest across the open plateau country immediately to the N of the main range of the Vindhyas. It is attractive countryside, crossing one of the driest regions of the state with only about 30 rainy days a year. Although there is little of interest on the way to Gwalior, it is the main road route to Agra and Delhi.

Follow the road out of Bhopal on the **Dewas** Road for 5 km, then fork right for **Shampur**. Almost immediately cross the railway. After 2 km there is a road junction the road on the left leading to **Bairagarh**. Continue along the main road. After a further 23 km a road on the right leads to **Durshi** (3 km) and **Ahmedpur** (18 km), then into **Shampur** (8 km). After 8 km the road crosses over a raised causeway the north-draining **River Parvati**, a tributary of the **River Chambal**. In 13 km it begins a 3 km climb through a ghat section of road before reaching **Narsinghgarh** (15 km). A road on the right leads to **Berasia** (37 km), **Vidisha** (81 km) and **Sanchi** (91 km) – see below. Follow the **NH12** northwest to **Biora** (34 km) on the main Delhi-Bombay National Highway.

From Biaora the **NH3** runs almost due N, following the railway line. It is the main Delhi Bombay road, and can be very busy with lorry traffic. From Biaora it goes through **Binaganj** (33 km) and **Khatkia** (18 km) before crossing the Parvati River again (2 km). Another long straight stretch of road passes through **Sarai** (23 km), a railway junction where the line from Kota comes in from the E, and **Guna** (25 km) to **Barauda** (18 km). From here it continues passing through the small towns of **Badarwas** (27 km) and **Lukwasa** (17 km) where a right turn leads to **Isagarh** (51 km), **Ashoknagar** (88 km), **Vidisha**, **Sanchi** and **Raisen**. Continue straight along the NH 3 through **Kolaras** (11 km) and **Parora** (8 km) to **Shivpuri** (17 km) – **see page 292**. The route from Shivpuri to Gwalior runs through the **Shivpuri National Park** to the N of the town, which begins at **Satanwara** (16 km). After passing the **Ghar** ghat section of road (13 km) to **Chorpura** (8 km) the road crosses the E flowing River Parvati (3 km), a tributary of the Sind, just before entering **Mohana** (2 km). After going through **Ghatigaon** (26 km) and crossing the **River Punniar** (11 km) the road reaches **Gwalior** (19 km).

BHOPAL TO JHANSI VIA RAISEN, SANCHI, UDAYAGIRI AND DEOGARH

A slower route from Bhopal to the N makes it possible to visit a number of Madhya Pradesh's more interesting sites.

Travel E out of Bhopal, crossing the River Betwa by high level causeway after 31 km to *Raisen* (14 km), a hilltop fort. Raisen was a site of some of the earliest inhabitants, as evidence of a Lower Palaeolithic tool factory and rock shelters have been found. The present settlement has temples, 3 palaces and a large tank. Built around 1200 AD it was later dependent on Mandu (MP), later still declaring its independence before conquest by the Mughal Bahadur Shah. It is a stiff climb.

From Raisen take the road to the left, N to *Sanchi* (10 km), a peaceful hill crowned by a group of stupas and abandoned monasteries that together are one of the most important Buddhist sites in India. Although the Buddha himself never came to Sanchi, the first evidence of any Buddhist activity dating from the time of the Emperor Asoka in the 3rd century BC, it has something of the quiet stillness now lost at many of the other famous places of religious pilgrimage. It is an atmosphere entirely in keeping with the spirit of the faith that underlay its building.

The imposing hilltop site has commanding views of the surrounding countryside. Sitting under the trees in the bright sunshine, it is easy to slip into quiet meditation and be moved by the experience of just being there, aided both by the nature of Buddhist belief and by the fact that comparatively few people visit Sanchi. For anyone prepared to make the journey, and from Delhi you can visit Sanchi via Bhopal quite comfortably in only two days, the rewards are great.

Places of Interest Sanchi was a centre of Hinayana (the "Lesser Vehicle") of Buddhism.

The Great Stupa Entrance at Main Gate (bottom of hill) – Re 0.50 (also allows entry to Museum). Allow at least 1 hr 30 min to see site. If in a hurry, visit Stupas 1,2 and 3, Temples 17 and 18, and Monasteries 45 and 51.

History The final form of the Great Stupa was the product of work from different periods. In Asoka's reign during the 3rd century BC, the stupa was constructed – of bricks and mud mortar. Just over a century later it was doubled in size, a balcony/walkway and a railing were added. 75 years later the gateways were built. Finally in 450 AD four images of the Buddha (belonging to the later period) were placed facing each of the four gateways. The entrances are staggered. This is because it was widely believed that evil spirits could only travel in a straight line. The wall was built for the same purpose. From the 14th century Sanchi lay half buried, virtually forgotten and deserted until 'rediscovered' by General Taylor in 1818, the year before the Ajanta caves were found. Amateur archaeologists and treasure hunters caused considerable damage. Some say a local landholder, others say General Taylor, used

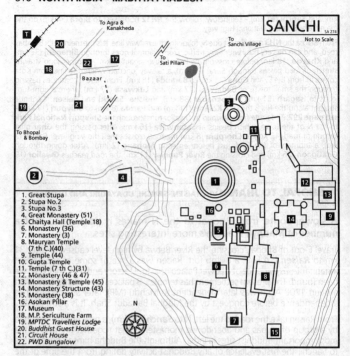

SANCHI SA 274
Not to Scale

1. Great Stupa
2. Stupa No.2
3. Stupa No.3
4. Great Monastery (51)
5. Chaitya Hall (Temple 18)
6. Monastery (36)
7. Monastery (3)
8. Mauryan Temple (7th C.)(40)
9. Temple (44)
10. Gupta Temple
11. Temple (7th C.)(31)
12. Monastery (46 & 47)
13. Monastery & Temple (45)
14. Monastery Structure (43)
15. Monastery (38)
16. Asokan Pillar
17. Museum
18. M.P. Sericulture Farm
19. *MPTDC Travellers Lodge*
20. *Buddhist Guest House*
21. *Circuit House*
22. *PWD Bungalow*

the Asoka Pillar to build a sugar cane press, breaking it up in the process. Sir John Marshall, Director General of Archaeology from 1912-1919, ordered the encroaching jungle to be cut back and extensive restoration to be effected, restoring it to its present condition.

The stupa began as an earthen burial mound which was revered by the local population. They were large hemispherical domes containing a small central chamber in which relics of the **Buddha** were put. The stupa was crowned by an umbrella of wood or stone and surrounded by a wooden fence enclosing a path for ceremonial clockwise circumambulation. That was the chief form of reverence paid to the relic. Later, these symbols were greatly decorated and beautified. The **gateways** leading into a stupa – the *torana* – are stone versions of the wood and bamboo gates that protected villages in ancient India.

The basic model consists of two pillars joined by three architraves (cross beams) built as if they actually passed through the upright posts. Originally, the brick and mortar domes were plastered and shone brilliant white in the tropical sunlight. The highlight is the carving, typically Indian in that every surface has been richly carved. The earliest decorative carving was done on wood and ivory but these craftsmen readily transferred the skills to stone. At Sanchi, the yellow sandstone lends itself to such intricate carving.

The carvings The principal subjects covered in the Sanchi carvings are scenes from the life of Buddha, events in the subsequent history of Buddhism and scenes from the Jataka stories. These were legends concerning the Buddha's previous lives before he was reincarnated as Siddhartha, Gautama the Buddha. The gateways have been so finely carved and with such inspiration that they are regarded as the finest of all Buddhist toranas.

The **E Gateway** depicts the young prince Siddhartha Gautama, leaving his father's palace and setting off on his journey towards enlightenment. It also contains the dream the his mother had before Gautama's birth. The **W Gateway** shows the 7 incarnations of the Buddha. The **N Gateway**, crowned by a wheel of law, illustrates the miracles associated with the Buddha as told in the Jatakas. The **S Gateway** reveals the birth of Gautama in a series of dramatically rich carvings. Just to the right of the S gate is the stump of the pillar erected by Asoka in the 3rd century BC. The capital, with its 4 lion heads, later adopted by the post Independence India as its national symbol, is in the local museum.

There are few Indian stupas larger than that at Sanchi – 37 m diameter and 16 m height. The ones at Sarnath (near Varanasi) where the Buddha preached his first sermon are also large and like the one at Sanchi were successively enlarged, but they do not compare with those in Sri Lanka where the stupa reached stupendous proportions. At **Anuradhapura**, the capital of the early kings was 100 metres in diameter – **see page 1427**. In India they became taller in proportion to their bases, in other countries the shape was modified further. In SE Asia, the stupas were often set on raised platforms and were constructed as stepped pyramids. These have been found in Burma but the largest example is at Borobodur in Java, Indonesia. Around the great stupas were lesser ones, often containing the ashes of monks famous for their piety and learning, plus a whole complex of buildings, e.g. monasteries, dining rooms, shrine-rooms, peaching halls and rest-houses for pilgrims. These can be seen at Sanchi.

Hotels The accommodation available in Sanchi is quite modest. For an overnight stay, the **D** MPSTDC *Traveller's Lodge* is the most comfortable. A/c and non a/c rm. Restaurant. Pleasant and within walking distance of rly station and monuments. Reservations: Manager. Also **F** *Railway Retiring Rm.* 2 d rm. Recommended. **F** *Buddhist Guest House*, nr rly station, T 39. 20 non a/c rm, also dormitory. For reservations write to Bhikku-in-charge, Mahabodhi Society, Sanchi, M.P. Pin 464661. Simple. Also the *Circuit House* and *Rest House*, both intended mainly for government workers and often unavailable.

Restaurants MPSTDC *Traveller's Lodge* and MPSTDC *Tourist Cafeteria*. If you are not staying in the Traveller's Lodge you need to give the Manager advance warning that you want to eat there. There are also food stalls by the crossroad. Little fruit available in Sanchi.

Local Transport The Stupa is within walking distance from the railway station.

Museum Archaeological Museum, nr entrance to monument. Exhibits include finds from the site (caskets, pottery, parts of gateway, images) dating from the Asokan period. Archaeological Survey guide books to site and museum available. Open 0900- 1700. Small fee, Fri free. Closed Mon.

Tourist Offices and Information Tourist Information available from Travellers Lodge. MPSTDC run tours to Sanchi – see Bhopal.

Travel Sanchi is best visited by car for a half day trip from Bhopal which has more comfortable hotels. Arrange through local travel or in advance from Delhi or elsewhere. Allow Rs 500 for the visit and approx 1 hr 15 min by car to Sanchi.

Rail Trains on the Jhansi-Itarsi section of the Central Railway stop in Sanchi if you are planning to stay there. The *Pathankot Exp* leaves Bhopal at 1530 and reaches Sanchi at 1630. **Note** The Shatabdi Exp does not stop at Sanchi. First Class passengers travelling over 161 km and 2nd class passengers (min group of 10) travelling over 400 km may request a stop at Sanchi on the Punjab Mail. Enquire and arrange this in advance.

Road 47 km E of Bhopal, the road follows the rly. You pass the Union Carbide factory in the outskirts. Once in the countryside the **Vindhya Hills** lie to your right.

Bus Regular service from Bhopal to Sanchi. The 47 km journey takes about 2 hr 30 min.

Excursions In the area around Sanchi there are a number of minor sites, some of which are Buddhist. None compare in quality and extent with Sanchi and only merit a visit by the enthusiast with plenty of time available.

From **Sanchi** drive NE following the railway line to **Vidisha** (8 km), situated between the Betwa and Bes rivers. In the 5th-6th centuries BC Vidisha was an important trade centre of the Sunga dynasty where Emperor Asoka was governor in the 3rd century BC. The citizens of Vidisha are recorded as acting as patrons of the monuments at Sanchi. Deserted after the 6th century AD it came into prominence again as Bhilsa during the medieval period (9th-12th centuries). It later passed on to the Malwa Sultans, the Mughals and the Scindias. The use of lime mortar in the construction of a shrine dedicated to Vishnu suggests this was one of the first structures in India to use "cement". It dates from 2nd century BC.

Vidisha has a small **museum** containing some of Besnagar's earliest antiquities. Near to the ruins of the **Bijamandal Mosque** and **Gumbaz-ka Makbara**, both dating from the Muslim period, are the remains of votive pillars. A monolithic, free-standing column, the inscription states that it was a Garuda pillar erected in honour of Vasudeva by Heliodorus, a resident of Taxila (now in Pakistan) who had been sent as an envoy to the court of Bhagabhadra. This is part of the evidence which shows that relations existed between the Greeks in their kingdoms on the Punjab and the kings of this area and that Heliodorus had become a follower of the Hindu god Vishnu. The **Heliodorus Pillar**, similar to Asokan pillars but much smaller in size has been dated to 140 BC.

Travel Bus from Sanchi (Bhopal-Vidisha and Raisen-Vidisha) approximately hourly. Fare Rs 3. As an add-on to the car hire, Rs 125 will include Vidisha and Udaygiri.

From Vidisha cross the railway line and go N to the **Udaygiri Caves** (13 km), a group of rock-cut sanctuaries carved into the sandstone hillside, an inscription in one indicating that they were produced during the reign of **Chandragupta II** (382-401 AD). The caves possess all the distinctive features that gave Gupta art its unique vitality, vigour and richness of expression: the beautifully moulded capitals, the design of the entrance, and the system of continuing the architrave as a string-course around the structure.

The caves have been numbered, probably in the sequence in which they were excavated. **Cave 1** has a frontage created out of a natural ledge of rock. The row of four pillars bear the 'vase and foliage' pattern about which the art historian Percy Brown wrote : 'the Gupta capital typifies a renewal of faith, the water nourishing the plant trailing from its brim, an allegory which has produced the vase and flower motif, one of the most graceful forms in Indian architecture'. The shrines become progressively more ornate. **Cave 5** depicts **Vishnu** in a massive carving in his Varaha (Boar) incarnation holding the earth goddess Prithvi aloft on one tusk. Another large sculpture is of the reclining Vishnu. Both reflect the grand vision and aspirations of the carvers. **Cave 9** is notable for its 2.5 m high pillars, its long portico and pillared hall.

Travel From **Vidisha** to **Udaygiri** you can take a tonga if you have no car. Allow Rs 15-20 travelling charge and the same again as a waiting charge. An auto-rickshaw will charge the same but will, of course, be quicker.

From **Udaygiri** continue to **Jarod** (40 km). A right turn goes to **Besnagar** (Basoda; 10 km) and *Udaypur* (10 km). The colossal **Neelkantheshwara** temple is the centre-piece of Udaypur and is an outstanding example of Parmara art and architecture of the 11th century AD. The beauty of the temple lies in its well proportioned and gracefully designed shikhar (spire) and the delicate carving adorning its sides. Some regard the spire as being unmatched in the whole array of N Indian temples. Built of red sandstone and standing on a lofty platform, the temple consists of a *garbha-griha* (shrine room), a *sabha mandap* (hall) and three *pravesha mandaps* (entrance porches). See section on Khajuraho for terms.

Travel To reach Udaypur, stay on the Pathankot Express from **Bhopal** (1530) until you reach **Ganjbasoda** (1830), then take a bus (Rs 5) or tonga (Rs 20) to Udaypur.

From **Udayapur** you can travel N to Shivpuri and Gwalior or to Jhansi and Orchha. From **Basoda** return to Jarod and travel N for 21 km to the crossroads with the main **Sagar** road. For **Shivpuri** go straight on through **Onder** (24 km), **Ashoknagar** (39 km) and **Isagarh** (37), then across **Kataura** (32 km) and across the **River Sindh** (13 km) to **Lukwasa** (6 km) and **Shivpuri**. For Jhansi turn right towards Sagar. Pass through **Bina-Etawa** (35 km), a railway junction, and **Kimlasa** (30 km). Continue straight, avoiding right turn to **Khurai** and **Sagar**, to **Malthon** (20 km).

In **Malthon** join NH 26 N through **Lalitpur** (45 km). **Painted Grey Ware** has been found at *Lalitpur*, indicating its early origins as a settlement. From **Lalitpur** you can travel W to *Chanderi* (37 km), an important town under the **Mandu** sultans. The road crosses the **Betwa River** by the Rajghat causeway (22 km), and climbs steeply in the approach to **Chanderi** itself. It is attractively placed in an embayment in the hills overlooking the Betwa, river, though the old town is 8 km N of the present town and is buried in jungle. It contains the ruins of some Jain temples dating from the 10th century. The old town has many ruins – palaces, market places, mosques and tombs, and the own is dominated by its hill fort. Jain statues have been carved in the Khandar Hill. *Dak Bungalow*. The **NH26** continues N from **Lalitpur** to **Jhansi** (92 km) through areas of jungle, now increasingly cleared for cultivation.

BHOPAL TO ALLAHABAD VIA GYARASPUR, SAGAR, AND CHHATARPUR

Passing through some of the most ancient sites of Madhya Pradesh, the route goes though farmland, then attractive open parkland and wooded hills.

Leave Bhopal to the E and follow the route through **Raisen** (45 km), **Sanchi** (10 km) and **Vidisha** (8 km). Continue to **Gyarspur** (35 km). Jains and Hindus were both active in this attractive site during the medieval period and there are several temple remains. The most striking is the Maladevi Temple on the hill above the village, with the ruins of a stupa to its W. Part of the temple was cut out of the rock, and at different periods it has served as both a Hindu and a Jain shrine. The ruins of an eight-pillared temple – **"Athakhambe "**(8 pillars) and a four pillared temple -**"Chaukhambe "**- (4 pillars) are the remains of two temples belonging to the 9th and 10th centuries AD, signifying that Gyarspur was a place of some importance. Other monuments are the 10th century Bajra Math and the Mala Devi temples.

Continue through **Rahatgarh** (36 km) to *Sagar* (32 km). **Sagar** is the centre of Sagar district and was founded by the **Bundela Raja Udaussa** (17th century). He commenced the fort (1660 onwards) which was completed by the Marathas in 1780. In 1829 it was used as a prison for Thugs. Today it is a university town and an important route centre. In **Sagar** take the road E towards **Damoh**. After 3 km a road to the right goes to **Narsinghpur**, and a further 4 km is another right turn to **Damoh**. Continue to **Banda** (24 km) and *Dalpatpur* (11 km; *altitude* 680 m). The road passes through stretches of open farmland alternating with forest northwards with a succession of small towns and villages – Burawan (5 km), Shahgarh (7 km) Hirapur (23 km) and a short ghat section to **Dargawan** (12 km). It is then 48 km to **Guleganj**, 16 km to **Meghawan** and a further 12 km to **Chhatarpur**. For the route onwards to Allahabad **see page 303**.

BHOPAL TO RANCHI VIA JABALPUR AND MANDLA

Leaving the National Park at Kanha in the country of Kipling's Jungle Book, the route from Mandla to Ranchi is through beautiful uncrowded areas with dense forests, parkland, hills and rivers.

There are two possible routes. The northern route goes through **Sanchi** (47 km) and **Sagar** (103 km) – see previous routes. From Sagar, follow the road E out of the town At the first road junction (3 km) bear left but bear right at the second road junction (4 km) to **Parsonaria** (15 km). Keep straight on through **Hiradnagar** (20 km) to **Garhkotta** (20 km) and continue to **Damoh** (23 km). This is a district headquarters and also a stone age site where stone axes with pointed handles have been discovered. There are several ruins, including temples. There is a *Circuit House* and a *Rest House*. Out of Damoh follow the road for **Jabalpur** to the SE. This goes through **Abhana** (14 km), **Nohta** (4 km) and **Jabera** (13 km). The next section of the route is both hilly and forested, passing through **Singagarh** (6 km) an old Gond fort, and a succession of small towns – **Singrampur** (4 km) **Gubra** (4 km), **Katangi** (13 km), **Pondi** (3 km) and **Belkharu Kalan** (17 km) **Jabalpur**, in the Narmada River valley.

The alternative route is to first drive S from Bhopal towards Hoshangabad. At **Obaidullaganj** (37 km) turn left and stay on NH12 which runs along the N side of the Narmada river valley via **Baraily** (111 km). The Marble Rocks – see below are 22 km before you reach **Jabalpur** (309 km approx)

Jabalpur

Population 650,000 *Altitude* 496 m. *Climate* See Kanha. 970 km from Delhi with daily air services via Bhopal. The airport is 15 km from the town centre.

Places of Interest In his 'Highlands of Central India', Capt. J. Forsyth wrote eloquently about the Marble Rocks at Jabalpur : 'The eye never wearies of the effect produced by the broken and reflected sunlight, glancing from a pinnacle of snow-white marble reared against the deep blue of the sky and again losing itself in the soft bluish greys of their recesses'. These rocks rise to 30 m on either side of the Narmada river and in moonlight produce a magical effect. Recently, floodlights have been added. Boats are available (Nov-May). The *Marble Rocks* are 24 km from Jabalpur and can be reached by bus or car. Cheap marble carvings are available at the site.

Other sights are the *Dhaundhar Falls*, **Hathi-ka-paon** (Elephant's Foot Rock) and **Monkey's Leap** ledge. Nearby is the **Chausath Yogini Mandir**, a 10th century temple with stone carvings. Legend has it that it is connected to the Gond queen Durgavati's palace by an underground passage – yet another of that mysterious group of legendary subways that are believed to tunnel under the sub-continent.

Jabalpur town was the capital and pleasure resort of the Gond kings during the 12th century. It was later the seat of the Kalchuri dynasty until it fell to the Marathas. The British took it in 1817 and left their mark with the cantonment residences and barracks. Jabalpur today is an important local centre. Its attractions are the **Madan Mahal Fort** (1116), built by the Gond ruler Madan Shah, the **Rani Durgavati Memorial** and **Museum** which houses a collection of sculptures and prehistoric relics and the *Tilwara Ghat* where **Mahatma Gandhi's** ashes were immersed in the Narmada. There are also Jain temples.

Jabalpur is the most convenient base for visits to **Kanha** (173 km) and **Bandhavgarh** (194 km) National Parks.

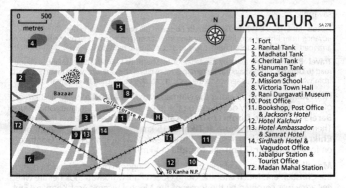

JABALPUR SA 278

1. Fort
2. Ranital Tank
3. Madhatal Tank
4. Cherital Tank
5. Hanuman Tank
6. Ganga Sagar
7. Mission School
8. Victoria Town Hall
9. Rani Durgavati Museum
10. Post Office
11. Bookshop, Post Office & *Jackson's Hotel*
12. *Hotel Kalchuri*
13. *Hotel Ambassador & Samrat Hotel*
14. *Sirdhath Hotel & Vagudoot Office*
T1. Jabalpur Station & Tourist Office
T2. Madan Mahal Station

Hotels D *Ashok Hotel*, Wright Town, T 22167, Cable: Ashokhot, Telex: 0756-256 Ahot. 45 rm. 16 km airport, 3 km rly, in centre of town. A/c and non a/c rm with bath with TV in some. Restaurant, bar, garden, laundry and dry cleaning, rm service, cars and taxis available. **D** *Jackson's Hotel*, Civil Lines, T 21320, Cable: Jackson's Hotel, Telex: 765-207. 44 rm, some a/c with bath. 14 km airport, 1 km rly, 1 km centre. Restaurant (Indian and Continental), post office, airline office, laundry, trips to Kanha, Khajuraho and Marble Rocks arranged. **D** *Ambassador*, Russell Crossing, T 21771/2, Cable: Ambassador, Telex: 0765-298 Amba in. 40 rm, some a/c with bath. 16 km airport, 1 km rly, near centre. Restaurant (Indian and Continental), car hire, railway reservation, Video, TV and refrigerator in some rm. **D** *Hotel Kalchuri* (MPSTDC), near Circuit House No.2, Tel. 27411. 30 rm, some a/c with bath. Restaurant, bar. Overlooking the gorge. **F** *Raja Gokuldas' Dharamshala*, nr rly station. Cheap but good. **F** *Rajhans Hotel* and *Sawhney Hotel* at Naudera Bridge, Jabalpur are both simple. There are other inexpensive hotels around the railway station.

Tourist Offices and Information T 2211.

Air Daily two connections with Bhopal and one with Raipur.
Rail Jabalpur is on the Bombay-Allahabad-Calcutta railway line. **Allahabad**: *Ganga-Kaveri Exp*, 6039, Mon,Sat, 2300, 6 hr 10 min; *Cochin/Tirupati-Varanasi Exp*, 7489/7491, Wed,Th,Sun, 1235, 4 hr 50 min. **Bhopal**: *Narmada Exp*, 8234, daily, 2215, 7 hr 15 min; *Amarkantak Exp*, 2853, Mon, Wed, Fri, Sat, 0250, 7 hr. **Delhi (Hazrat Nizamuddin)**: *Mahakoshal Exp*, 1449, 1030, 28 hr. **Lucknow**: *Chitrakoot Exp*, 5009, daily, 1840, 16 hr.
Bus Bus services connect Jabalpur with Allahabad, Khajuraho, Varanasi, Bhopal and other main centres.

Excursions

Bandhavgarh National Park (170 km *Altitude* 800 m). This compact park of 105 sq km is in the Vindhya hills. Though it involves quite a journey, it has a wide variety of game and has a longer 'season' than Kanha. Its main wild beasts are tiger, leopard, sloth bear, gaur, sambar, chital, muntjac, nilgai, chinkara and wild pigs. In 1990 a census revealed that the tiger population had grown from 9 in 1969 to 59, sambhar from 111 to over 4,500 and spotted deer from 78 to over 7,000. Bandhavgarh (pronounced Bandogarh) is not very far S of *Rewa*, which is famous as the place in which the white (albino) tiger originated. Now it is only found in zoos. The tigers at Bandhavgarh have normal coloured coats and, whilst elusive, are increasingly seen. There are many woodland birds. There are also interesting cave shrines scattered around the park as well as archaeological remains of a fort believed to be 2,000 years old.

The park has a dynamic leadership. Protection from disease, fire, grazing and poaching have all been factors in its recovery as a wildlife area. It is strictly monitored by gamewardens, who have virtually eliminated poaching, and fire has been strictly controlled. Set in extremely rugged terrain, and surrounding the fort itself the marshes which used to be perenniel now support a vast grassland savanna.

Hotels MPSTDC's E *White Tiger Forest Lodge* in the park has a/c and non a/c rm. Book in advance from Bhopal and Jabalpur. Restaurant. Car or jeep hire and elephant rides can be arranged in the park. Closed from 1 July to 31 Oct during monsoons.

Travel Bandhavgarh drive by car Jabalpur to **Shajpura** (144 km) then taking a country road to **Umaria**. From Shajpura the terrain is more hilly. The nearest railway station is Umaria from which there is a bus service to the park. It can also be reached from Satna.

From **Jabalpur** drive SE along the Narmada valley to **Mandla** (97 km). 3 km out of Jabalpur is a military dairy farm on the left and the road then goes on through **Barela** (12 km) and **Dhobi** (7 km) to **Kalpi** (19 km) where there is a *Rest House*. There is another *Rest House* at **Tikaria** (15 km), where you keep straight on to **Chikraidongri** (18 km). A road on the left leads to a hot spring (6 km). Go straight on for **Phoolsagar** (7 km) and **Mandla** (14 km).

Mandla was the capital of the ancient Gond Kingdom of Garha-Mandla early in the Christian era. Much later the Gond Queen Rani Durgavati took her life when her army was cornered by the forces of the Mughal Viceroy Asaf Khan in 1564. The fort was built in the late 17th century and is surrounded on three sides by the Narmada River. The Marathas took it and when Mandla was transferred to the British in 1818 the Maratha garrison refused to surrender. General Marshall stormed it in March 1818. The jungle has since taken over. There are a number of temples and ghats in the town. The national park is about 40 km from Mandla.

Kanha National Park

Area 1945 sq km. *Altitude* 450-950 m. *Climate* Temp. Summer Max. 43°C, Min. 11°C, Winter Max. 29°C, Min. 2°C. *Annual Rainfall* 1500 mm; monsoon July to October. The nearest airport and railhead is Jabalpur (173 km)

Places of Interest This is the country about which Kipling wrote so vividly in his *Jungle Books*. The same abundance of wildlife and variety of species still exists today and the park which forms the core of the Kanha **Tiger** Reserve (1945 sq km) created in 1974 is the only habitat of the rare hard ground *Barasingha* (Swamp Deer). It comprises sal and bamboo forests, rolling grasslands and meandering streams of the Banjar river. It lies in the Mandhla district in the Maikal hills which are the E part of the Satpura range. Originally the area was famed as a hunter's paradise and especially for its teeming herds of barasingha.

The valley has been well developed to accommodate visitors and display the rich fauna. Forest Department Guides accompany visitors around the Park on mapped out circuits which enable naturalists to see a good cross-section of Kanha's wildlife. The best areas are the meadows around Kanha where blackbuck, cheetal (spotted deer) and barasingha can be seen throughout the day. **Bamni Dadar** (Sunset Point) affords a view of the dense jungle and animals that can be sighted from here are typical of the mixed forest zone: sambhar, barking deer, gaur (bison) and chausingha (four-horned antelope).

Mammals: Kanha has 22 species and the most easily spotted are three-striped palm squirrel, common langur monkey, jackal, wild pig, cheetal, barasingha and blackbuck. Less commonly seen are tiger, Indian hare, dhole or Indian wild dog, barking deer and gaur. Rarely seen are Indian fox, sloth bear, striped hyena, jungle cat, panther (leopard), mouse deer, nilgai (blue bull) ratel (Indian porcupine), wolf (which actually live outside the park), Indian pangolin, the smooth Indian otter and civet.

Birds: Kanha has some 200 species. Good vantage points are in the hills where the mixed and bamboo forest harbours many species. The *sal* forests do not normally afford good viewing. Early morning and late afternoon are ideal times and binoculars are invaluable. Commonly seen species are: cattle egret, pond heron, black ibis, common peafowl, rachet-tailed drongo, hawk eagle, red-wattled lapwing, various species of flycatcher, woodpecker, pigeon, dove, parakeet, babbler, mynah, Indian roller, white breed kingfisher and grey hornbill.

Hotels D *Baghira Log Huts*, Kisli. Price includes breakfast. **D** *Kanha Safari Lodge*, Mukki. A/c and non a/c rm and dormitory. Price includes breakfast. **F** *Jungle Camp*, Kanha. Non a/c rm. *Tourist Lodge*, Khatia. Dormitory. For reservations more than 10 days in advance contact General Manager (Tours), MPSTDC, Gangotri, 4th Floor, T.T. Nagar, Bhopal, T 462003, Cable: MP Tour, Telex: 0705-275 Tour In. For reservations between 4 and 10 days in advance contact Regional Manager, MPSTDC, Railway Station Building, Jabalpur, T 22111. Less than 4 days in advance, see the Manager of the unit. Alternatively you can book a tent or chalet at *Kipling Camp* through Bob Wright, Tollygunge Club, Calcutta or *Sita Travels* in major cities. The camp is well located and recommended.

Restaurants *Baghira Log huts*, Kisli, *Kanha Safari Lodge*, Mukki and *Jungle Camp*, Khatia have restaurants attached to them. The canteen at Kisli serves meals and snacks to guests staying at the Tourist Hostel. If boiled water is required, ask for it specifically; water served at the lodges is generally filtered. Cold drinks are usually available but fresh fruit is not.

Banks There is no facility for cashing Travellers Cheques at Kanha, Kisli or Mukki. The nearest bank dealing in foreign exchange is the State Bank of India at Mandla.

Shopping Items of daily use are available at Baghira Log Huts. Markets at Mocha (Wed), Sarekha (Fri), Tatri (Tue) and Baihar (Sun).

Local Transport and Park Information Entry Fees. Minibus, van or station wagon (up to 15 persons): Rs 10 per vehicle for up to 5 members and extra for each additional person. Cars and jeeps, Rs 10. Motorcycles and bicycles are not allowed in the park.

  Jeep hire MPSTDC owned jeeps are available for hire from the log huts for touring the park at Rs 4 per km. for a maximum of 6 persons.

  Elephant hire Forest Dept. elephants can be hired from Kanha or Kisli at Rs 15 per hr. For bookings see the Range Officer (Kanha, Kisli or Mukki) or the Managers, Baghira Log huts, Kisli and Kanha Safari Lodge, Mukki. Guide charges: Rs 3 per head per hr.

  Tiger Sightseeing elephants are used for tiger tracking and should a tiger be located, they can take visitors to the site. Rate: Rs 15 per head (visitor) per hr.

  Photography Charges: 8 mm movie camera – Rs 10, 16 mm movie camera – Rs 50, 35 mm movie camera Rs 250. Films are available at the Kisli Baghira Log Huts. **Petrol pumps** are at Baihar and Kisli.

Hospitals and Medical Services Hospitals at Mukki, Mocha and Baihar.

Post and Telegraph Post Offices at Mocha and Mukki, Telegraph Offices and Telephones at Bamhni, Banjar and Baihar.

Tourist Offices and Information *MPSTDC Tourist Office*, Jabalpur Railway Station, T 22111. Can arrange car hire. For Bookings: MPSTDC, Gangotri, 4th Floor, T.T. Nagar, Bhopal, T 63552, Cable: MP Tour, Telex: 0705-275 Tour In. MPSTDC, 74 World Trade Centre, Cuffe Parade, Bombay, T 214860. MPSTDC, Kanishka Shopping Centre, Asoka Rd, New Delhi, T 3321187.

Air Nearest airport is at **Jabalpur** (173 km) and Nagpur (226 km). **Indian Airlines** flies to Jabalpur from Bhopal and Raipur and to Nagpur from Bombay, Calcutta and Bhubaneswar, Hyderabad Delhi and Bhopal. **Vayudoot** flies to Nagpur from Aurangabad. **Rail** The nearest railhead is **Jabalpur** (173 km) on the Bombay-Alllahabad-Calcutta, Delhi-Jabalpur and Madras-Varanasi main lines. **Road** Kanha is connected with Jabalpur, Nagpur and Bilaspur by motorable roads. **Daily bus service** connects Jabalpur with Kisle via Mandla and Chiraidongri which takes approx 7 hr, fare Rs 30. An overnight stop has to be made at Kisli as vehicles are not permitted within the park after dark.

From **Mandla** to **Ranchi** is 800 km, the road crossing some of the least densely populated parts of the peninsula. It is a journey for which you need to be prepared, but it contains some beautiful scenery, dense forests and open parkland, and passes the source of the River Narmada, one of peninsular India's most sacred rivers. There are only a few small towns along the way and virtually the only accommodation is in Rest Houses and official Bungalows, always fairly spartan.

The route goes E out of Mandla keeping to the N of the Narmada for 31 km where it is crossed by bridge at **Manot**. The confluence of the Narmada and Burhner Rivers is at **Deogaon** (14 km) and after crossing the River Gupta Ganga

(10 km) the road enters a forested ghat section of the road for 16 km. Through **Sakka** (37 km from Gupta Ganga) and **Dindori** (21 km). A long section follows with few villages; Garhasarai (17 km), the River Seoni (18 km) and Karanja (12 km), the last before the next section of ghat road climbs up to **Kabirchabutra** (*Altitude* 1,040 m) in the **Maikala Range**. Here a road to the right leads to **Amarkantak** (*Altitude* 1,050 m) where there is a dharamsala and temple at the source of the **Narmada River**. Continue E down the ghat from **Keonchi**, passing hills that reach 1,123 m on the left. Keonchi has an inspection bungalow.

Continue through **Pendra Road** (22 km) across the railway, bearing right at the road junction (2 km) and **Pendra** (8 km), bearing right again at the next road junction (5 km). After 9 km bear left at a road junction; the road to the right goes to **Pasan** (8 km). Continue to **Marwahi** (27 km) and bear right at the road junction 4 km out of the village. In 24 km turn right and turn right again at the next road junction in 3 km, now going due E. The road on the left goes to **Bijuri** and **Bharatpur**. Cross the railway after 3 km. In 10 km the road passes through **Mahendragarh**, 12 km to another level crossing before crossing the **River Hasdeo**, a S flowing tributary of the **Mahanadi River**, 6 km further on. This is bridged and there is a *Forest Rest House*.

The road passes through a forested ghat section for 4 km on the way to **Bakiunthpur** (25 km). Pass through **Surajpur** (37 km) and **Bisrampur** (13 km) to *Ambikpur* (26 km). Follow the road SE through a 5 km ghat section after 3 km. After 24 km the road crosses a causeway and then goes through **Sitaput** (22 km) and **Protabgarh** (7 km) on the **River Madh**. Cross the river and continue across the Mainpat Hills (highest point 1127 m) to **Pathalgaon** (23 km; also known as **Dharmjaygarh** and **Habkob**). In Pathalgaon turn sharp left, travelling NE to **Bandarchuan** (46 km) and across the **River Ib** (4 km). The road to Ranchi runs NE,close to the watershed between the northflowing rivers draining into the Ganga system and the S flowing rivers which runs into the Mahanadi. The *Ib River* flows S to the **Hirakud Dam** in Orissa – see page 644.

If you are going to **Sundargarh** for Rourkela or **Sambalpur** turn right to pass through **Kunkuri** and on to **Kunjara** (18 km) and **Tapakera** (18 km) which has a *Forest Rest House*. In 13 km the road passes an *Inspection Bungalow* on the banks of the **River Ib** at **Lawkera** before reaching the **Orissa/Madhya Pradesh** border, crossing a causeway in 6 km and passing through **Karamida** in 19 km to reach **Sundargarh** (8 km).

If you are going to Ranchi continue NE through **Jashpurnagar** and across the Madhya Pradesh Bihar border to **Gumla**. **Ranchi** is then 103 km NE on NH 23. See page 667.

BHOPAL TO NAGPUR VIA BHIMBETKA HILL AND HOSHANGABAD

The route from Bhopal to Nagpur follows the main Delhi-Madras railway line for much of the way. Just South of Bhopal it crosses the tableland of the Malwa plateau then cuts through the Vindhyans, crossing the Narmada River at Hoshangabad. It then crosses the Mahadeo Range of the Satpura Hills to Betul before turning SE to Nagpur.

Leave Bhopal travelling SE. Cross the railway (8 km) to **Misrodh** (7 km) and the bridge over the **River Betwa** (6 km) to *Obadiadullaganj* (15 km). In 7 km the road runs through the tribal village of **Bhiyanpur** by the railway line. 2 km further S is the **Bhimbetka Hill**, with its magnificent collection of rock caves and shelters.

Bhimbetka Hill has S Asia's richest collection of prehistoric paintings associated with many other archaeological discoveries. The site was discovered by V.S.

Wakanker of the Vikram University, Ujjain, in 1957 and systematic digging at the site has continued since 1971. Located in the middle of a dense deciduous forest there are over 30 species of trees with edible fruit, flowers seeds and tubers – a vital food for tribal people even today. There is also still a rich wildlife including several species of deer, wild boar, sloth bear, antelope, leopard, jackal, scaly anteater and a very wide range of bird species. Perennial springs provide the essential year round water supply. This is the setting for a total of more than 1000 shelters stretching for 10 km from the village of Kari Talai in the E to Jondra in the W. Over 500 of them contain prehistoric and later paintings and a smaller number have evidence of Stone Age habitation from the Lower Palaeolithic period to the late Mesolithic.

The earliest settlement Dating of the occupation is far from complete. In the bottom layers of the settlement sequence were a few pebble tools. There was a thin layer of bare material above this, followed by a thick layer of *Acheulian deposits* – see page 78. Over 2.5 metres of accumulated material were excavated in Cave III F-23 for example, bringing to light successive floors paved with stone, and large quantities of stone implements that were clearly being made in the cave. This period is dominated by flake tools – blades, scrapers, cleavers and handaxes. Many were damaged, suggesting that they were not only made on site but used there as well. Some of the core tools were found to weigh up to 40 kg and the high level of skill suggests that they come from the end of the Acheulian period.

This level is followed in many caves by *Middle Palaeolithic* materials (approximately 40,000 to 12,000 years before the present), and the evidence suggests that this culture developed on the same site out of the preceding Acheulian culture. The same raw materials are used, although the tools are generally smaller. The *Upper Palaeolithic* period (approximately 12,000 to 5,500 years before the present) was even shorter than the Middle, again growing out of it. Short thin blades made their appearance for the first time.

The rise in population It was in the period immediately following the Upper Palaeolithic that the largest number of caves were occupied. Ghose suggests that during this Mesolithic period there was a huge increase in population, and much more can be learned about the culture because there are many remains both of food stuffs and of skeletons, and some of the cave paintings can be correlated with this period. There may have been improvement in the climate, although there is evidence for climatic change even within the *Mesolithic* period, which at Bhimbetka has been Carbon-14 dated as running from 5500 – 1000 BC.

A brand new technology was introduced. Tiny stone tools – microliths -were made by blunting one or more sides into an enormous variety of specialised shapes for specific purposes – knives, arrow heads, spearheads and sickles. Hard, fine grained rocks like chert and chalcedony were the basic material.

An imported technology Ghose suggests that the technology was clearly introduced from outside the region and gradually supplanted the older technology. The raw materials for the new industry had to be brought in – the nearest source is near Barkhera, 7 km to the SE. From the skeletons that have been discovered it is clear that the dead were buried in caves still occupied by the living, usually though not always in a crouched position with the head to the E, with grave goods like antlers and stone tools buried alongside them. In the middle level of the deposits are copper tools and pottery, and at the very top early historical pottery.

Regular habitation seems to have come to an end at the end of the Mesolithic period, probably by the end of the 1st millenium BC. However, there are several circular structures on the hills around which have been interpreted as much later stupas. 20 km W of Bhimbetka an Asokan inscription has been found recently which supports this view.

Open air sites were also widely occupied in the area. At *Barkhera*, 7 km SE of Bhimbetka, is one of the richest Stone Age sites in S Asia. On the southern edge of the road there are thousands of Acheulian tools scattered in the thick teak forest, and fields on the N side of the road are equally rich in tools. Ghose concludes that it is clear that Barkhera was a large camp site of the final Acheulian hunter-gatherers.

Cave paintings By far the most striking remains today, however, are the *cave paintings*, covering walls and ceilings in over 500 shelters and in rocky hollows. Some are quite small, while some are as much as 10 metres long. Red and white are the dominant colours used, but green and occasionally yellow are also found.

The paintings belong to three periods. The prehistoric phase is dominated by wild life paintings – cattle, boar, tiger, deer, engaged in various activities, and varying from tiny miniatures to life size – and often very life-like – representations. Hunting is a common theme, the humans during this period being shown simply as "stick men". Some women are shown, occasionally pregnant.

This period was followed by what Ghose terms a "transitional period". Men are shown grazing or riding animals, but animals lose their proportions and naturalism. The later period is quite different, for animals and animal hunts are replaced by battle scenes with men riding on elephants and horses with spears, bows and arrows, and probably date from the early centuries AD.

Continue straight through **Bodhni** (21 km), passing an attractive and densely forested area, then cross the railway line (2 km) before reaching the bridge over the **Narmada River** (2 km) and *Hoshangabad* (4 km). Hoshangabad was named after the Mandu ruler Hoshang Ghori (1406-35), and was built to defend the Mandu kingdom against the Gond tribal incursions.

From **Hoshangabad** continue S to *Itarsi* (18 km), an important railway junction. From here the road passes through a forested and hilly region. The ghat section itself begins 5 km S of Itarsi, continuing for 7 km. Pass through **Kesla** (18 km from Itarsi) and **Suktawa** (7 km) and **Bhawra** (6 km). Between Bhawra and Shahpur is a left turn to **Pachmarhi** (90 km) a hill resort on the northern slopes of the Satpura range.

In 1857 Capt. Forsyth approached the plateau of the Satpura range at the head of a column of Bengal Lancers. At an altitude of 1,100 m, he viewed the surrounding tranquil forests of *wild bamboo*, *sal*, *jamun*, *aonla* and *gular* trees, interspersed with deep pools fed by the streams that ran across the red sandstone hills. Later, acting on Forsyth's advice, the British developed **Pachmarhi** as a sanatorium and Hot Weather Resort. Today, their legacy remains in Madhya Pradesh's only hill station.

Pachmarhi is an ideal place from which to escape the heat of Central India. There are numerous walks, requiring varying degrees of exertion, into the countryside. In the neighbouring **Mahadeo Hills** there is an astonishing wealth of **rock paintings**. Several have been found in Panchmarhi itself, others – at **Tamia**, **Son Bhadra** and **Jalai** – 32, 40 and 64 km away respectively. Gordon, who studied the paintings between 1935 and 1958, was reluctant to put a Stone Age date to any of the paintings, but more recent studies suggest that the earliest can be traced back to the Mesolithic period. Ghose suggests that "of the more interesting paintings at Panchmarhi are 'a Gilgamesh figure' subduing two wild animals at Monte Rosa and a scene of rare humour in which a monkey standing on its hind legs plays on a flute while a man lying on a cot too small for his size has raised arms, as if to keep time with the flute." This is in the so-called **Upper Dorothy shelter**.

Ghosh visited the Pachmari shelters in 1940 and discovered two additional important ones he called **Bania Beria** and **Dhuandhar**, near a waterfall. He writes that "in the Bania Beri cave, among other subjects is depicted a large cross around which is a group of men, most of them holding in their hands what may be raised umbrellas. The cross may be a primitive or conventionalised svastika. One of the cows appearing below the cross has her belly cut open to reveal a calf in a crouching position inside. In the same cave there is another painted cross composed of small triangles which look like having been made out of a stencil." The bulk of these have been placed in the 500-800 AD period but the earliest are an estimated 10,000 years old.

Hotels There are a number of establishments at Pachmarhi run by MP Tourism so you can be assured of a reasonable quality. **D** *Panchvati Cottages*, nr Tehsil, T 96. 5 two bedroom cottages and some non a/c one bedroom huts. Restaurant. **D** *Satpura Retreat*, Mahadeo Rd, T 97. 6 rm, non a/c. Restaurant. **D** *Amaltas*, nr Tehsil. 4 rm, non a/c. Restaurant, bar. **E** *Holiday Homes*, near Bus Stand, T 99. 40 rm non a/c. Restaurant.

Rail   The nearest railhead for Pachmarhi is Itarsi which can be reached from Allahabad, Bangalore, Bombay, Delhi, Gwalior, Indore and Lucknow.

Road   Leave Bhopal on the road to Hoshangabad and Itarsi which traverses the Vindhya Hills. At Hoshangabad (69 km) turn left and continue along the Narmada river valley to Piparia (72 km) where you turn right on the Chhindwara road. At Matkuli a secondary road climbs up to Pachmarhi which is situated in the Mahadeo range. **Bus**   There are daily bus services to Pachmarhi from Bhopal and Itarsi.

If you do not make the diversion to Pachmarhi continue S through **Shahpur** (12 km) through the **Baretha ghat** section (8 km) and **Nimpani** (6 km) to **Betul** (22 km). In Betul turn SE. The road runs through a long forested section after 11 km, where there is also a ghat section for 20 km. At the end of the ghat section cross the **River Tawa** by raised causeway to **Multai** (17 km). A left turn leads to **Chhindwara** (90 km), on a small coalfield. From **Multai** the road continues SE. After 15 km it passes through another forested ghat section for 8 km, 10 km later reaching **Pandhurna**. Continue to **Chicholi** (22 km) and the **Madhya Pradesh** border with **Maharashtra** (8 km). The market town of **Saoner** is a further 23 km, with ruins of a fort and temples. The road goes straight on to **Pipla** (18 km) and across the **River Kolar** (4 km) to **Nagpur** (14 km) – see page 977.

BHOPAL TO AHMADABAD VIA INDORE, MANDU, DOHAD AND GODHRA

From Bhopal it is a 3-4 hr drive to either the ancient city of Ujjain (199 km) or the palaces and tombs of Indore (198 km). The journey is across a broad, cultivated plain. In the distance to your left the flat topped Vindhya Hills rise.

At **Sehore** (37 km) there is the *Paradise Restaurant* which is quite attractive. Farmland gradually gives way to open scrub as you gain about 100 m in height. **Dewas** (152 km) is where **E.M. Forster** 'worked' in the court of the Raja of Dewas Senior in 1912 and 1921. Forster came to regard his stay in this now rather dusty town as the 'great opportunity' of his life and used this experience to good literary effect with the autobiographical *The Hill of Devi* and his most famous novel *A Passage to India*. It is worth going up the 'Hill of Devi' overlooking the town for the views. There is a temple at the top. You can drive all the way.

At **Dewas** turn right for **Ujjain** (see below) or left for **Indore**. You can easily drive from **Bhopal** to **Ujjain** to see the town and then continue to **Indore**, where there is better accommodation. There is a direct road from **Ujjain** to **Indore** (55 km) via **Sanwer**.

Indore

Population 1,100,000 *Altitude* 567 m. *Climate* Temp. Summer Max. 40°C, Min. 22°C, Winter Max. 29°C, Min. 10°C. Annual Rainfall 1050 mm, mostly July-Sep. *Best season* Oct to Mar, or June to Sep if proceeding to Mandu. The airport is 9 km from the city centre.

Indore is a textile town on the banks of the rivers *Sarasvati* and *Khan*, and is the second biggest city in Madhya Pradesh (after Bhopal). Its cotton textile industry is the fourth largest in India. It is also famous for its bangles, and is a notable centre of Hindustani classical music. The area that is now Indore was given to **Malhar Rao Holkar** in 1733 by the **Maratha Peshwas** (see page 973) in appreciation of his help in many of their battles. Malhar Rao left much of the statecraft in the capable hands of his widowed daughter-in-law who administered the area well and succeeded him to the throne. Indore was destroyed in 1801 but recovered and was the British headquarters of their Central India Agency. The ruling family of Indore, the **House of Holkar**, took the British side during the Mutiny in 1857. The Maharaja, **Tukuji Holkar Rao II**, then only 15 years old, gave assistance to the British and refused to surrender a number of Christians to whom he had given sanctuary in the Lal Bagh palace. The Old Palace with its many-storeyed gateway faces the chief square. On the N of it is the New Palace and garden. In the streets there are some good timber houses with deep recessed verandahs and carved pillars. Indore was also one of the first states to open temples, schools and public wells to **Harijans** (Untouchables) in support of Gandhi's campaign against untouchability.

Local Festivals *Sanghi Samaroh* (Nov), classical dance and music. *Mandir Festival* (Nov) for Kathak and Dhrupad.

Places of Interest

Kanch Mandir Shoes to be left at door. Entry after 1000. 30 mins is ample for a visit. On Jawahar Rd next to the aptly named Hotel Sheesh Mahal (Mirror Palace – not very appealing as a hotel) is the Jain temple. Just like all the other buildings in the street from the outside, inside there is not a plain surface in sight. Thousands of mirrors adorn the walls and ceilings supplemented by gaily patterned ceramic tiles, Chinese lantern-type glass lamps and cut glass chandeliers. All are exquisitely crafted and the pillars and some panels in particular give one a clear idea of how other Sheesh Mahals must have been, e.g. in the Delhi and Agra Red Forts and the Amber Palace.

There are 50 or so murals depicting scenes from Indian life – at the court, conversion to Jainism and life in the 19th century (from the costumes, uniforms and the number trains steaming out of stations. The use of glass beads and raised figures produces a pleasing 3-D effect. This mirrored palace is at variance with the austerity and simplicity of the Mahavira's supposed existence and teachings, a point clearly demonstrated by the image of the Mahavir in plain black onyx.

Chhatri Bagh The Chhatris are memorial tombs of the Holkar kings. Neglected and not easy to find, they are in an area called Chhatri Bagh. Many of local people seem unaware of the existence of the tombs. There are 7 in all on the banks of the Khan river. All the inner sanctums are locked so one cannot see the effigies. The largest and most impressive is that of **Malhar Rao Holkar I** and is lavishly decorated with frescoes. The other important tomb is that of Rani Ahilya Bai. Now overgrown and unkempt, this is a tranquil place but hardly worth a special detour. The chhatris at Gwalior are more accessible and their interiors open.

Lal Bagh (The Nehru Centre). Entry Re 1.50. Open daily 1000-1700. Once the residence of the Maharaja, built and decorated in a confusion of styles, now a museum and cultural centre named after Jawaharlal Nehru. The rooms have been restored and furnished and, overall, the place is pleasing and informative. Much of the furniture and ornamentation is in the late Regency, early Georgian style.

Queen Victoria, orb and sceptre in hand, looks on to the main entrance portico (you actually leave through this and enter through a side entrance after purchasing your entrance ticket) which is reminiscent of Warren Hasting's house at Alipur (see page 527). The entrance hall is in marble and gilt rococo. Two rooms on the ground floor are much more 'Indian' in flavour. One displays many high Mughal characteristics, the other more Akbarian in that it is a mixture of Hindu and Muslim styles. Both are attractive.

Sporting trophies There are a number of stuffed tigers in the *atrium** and on the landings, all looking menacing. The Maharaja was obviously a keen sport and in the small but fine collection of photographs can be variously seen rowing a boat across a lake and flying in an early aeroplane. Both these are in fact backdrop paintings with a hole for him to stand in to be photographed – like old seaside

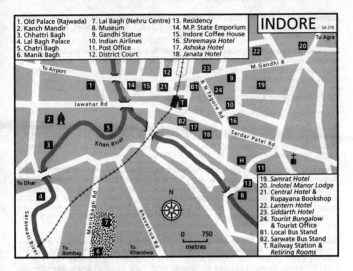

1. Old Palace (Rajwada)
2. Kanch Mandir
3. Chhattri Bagh
4. Lal Bagh Palace
5. Chatri Bagh
6. Manik Bagh
7. Lal Bagh (Nehru Centre)
8. Museum
9. Gandhi Statue
10. Indian Airlines
11. Post Office
12. District Court
13. Residency
14. M.P. State Emporium
15. Indore Coffee House
16. *Shreemaya Hotel*
17. *Ashoka Hotel*
18. *Janata Hotel*

INDORE SA 276

19. *Samrat Hotel*
20. *Indotel Manor Lodge*
21. *Central Hotel & Rupayana Bookshop*
22. *Lantern Hotel*
23. *Siddarth Hotel*
24. *Tourist Bungalow & Tourist Office*
B1. Local Bus Stand
B2. Sarwate Bus Stand
T. Railway Station & Retiring Rooms

snaps! Also in the collection are good prints of the Old Palace (mentioned in introduction to Indore).

On the first floor there is a good collection of coins dating mostly from the Muslim period as well as miniatures and a display of contemporary Indian artworks -paintings and sculptures. There are also Italian sculptures and in the same room as these some marvellous intricately inlaid boxes. On the ground floor at the entrance there is a display of prehistoric artifacts – better displayed than at the Central Museum. The Garden, though maintained, is dry and dusty suggesting that the gardeners are fighting a losing battle against nature.

The final words should be from the Guidebook, written by Kalyan Kumar Chakravarty and available at the exit for Rs 2.50. Lal Bagh: 'a certain hybridisation and artistic solecism were inevitable in the attempt to adapt the classical Graeco-Roman legacy through the self-righteous, interventionist British channels to the indigenous climatic and functional context. A blend of Italian villa, French château, traditional motifs and modern conveniences, the Lal Bagh palace is indeed a statement of riotous Victorian eclecticism not surprising, perhaps, for a ruler who supported the British'. How can one add to that !

Hotels C *Indotels Manor House* (formerly Suhag Hotel), Agra-Bombay Rd. T 33270, Telex: 0735-272. 75 rm. 11 km airport, 3 km rly. Central a/c. Restaurant, TV, rm service, pastry shop, laundry, exchange, pool. Comfortable Western style hotel. Courteous and helpful staff. Recommended. **D** *Shreemaya*, 12/1 R.N.T. Marg, T 34151, Cable: Shreemaya. 52 rm, half a/c with bath. 8 km airport, 1 km rly. Restaurant (S Indian), TV, exchange, laundry. Good Indian style hotel. **D** *Central*, Rampurawala Building, 70-71 M.G. Rd, T 32041. 43 rm, some a/c. 5 km airport. TV, laundry, car hire, Diners Club. Old fashioned, fairly well kept.

D *Tourist Bungalow* (MPSTDC), behind Ravindra Natya Griha, T 38888. 6 rm, 1 a/c with bath. No restaurant. Breakfast available. **D** *Kanchan*, Kanchan Bagh, T 33394. 28 rm. 6 km airport, 2 km rly. A/c and non a/c with bath. Rm service, TV. **D** *Lantern*, 28 Yashwant Niwas Rd, T 35327. 26 rm. 8 km airport, 1 km rly. A/c and non a/c. Restaurant, bar. **D** *Paras Regency*, 5 Murai Mahalla, Kibe Compound, T 65430. 30 rm. 20 km airport. A/c and non a/c with bath. Travel, Diners Club. **D** *Sundar*, Tukoganj, Tukoganj, T 33314. 30 rm. Restaurant. **D** *Surya*, Tukoganj, T 22640. 29 rm. Restaurant, bar.

There are a number of inexpensive hotels (**F**) close to the railway station and bus station. Consequently, they can be quite noisy. *Janta*, opp bus station, T 37695. Non a/c. *Standard*

Lodge, next to Janta Hotel, T 37370. *Ganesh Hind Lodge*, Chhoti Gwaltoli Rd. Shared bath. *Ashok*, on road parallel to and opp bus station, T 37391. Clean, pleasant. *Neelam*, 33/2 Chhoti Gwaltoli. T 37161. Non a/c rm with bath.

Restaurants There are a number of places around the bus stand and railway station, offering typically Indian traveller's fare. The more expensive hotels have their own restaurants, e.g. the *3 Seasons* at Indotels Manor House and the Shreemaya's *Apsara*, 1 RNT Tagore Marg, T 21081 is a/c and is recommended for vegetarian meals while *Mehfil*, 36 Sneh Nagar, Main Rd, T 63097, has a bar and good Indian food. *Indore Coffee House*, M.G. Rd; *Jaiswal*, near G.P.O.; *Hotel Hong Kong*, Palasia Chowk; *Volga*, Regal Talkies, M.G. Rd;

Clubs Rotary, T 21416, 62863. Lions, T 30488. Maharaja Yashwant, Race Course, T 23023.

Banks *Baroda*, S. Mata Bazaar, T 36219. *Maharashtra*, 484 M.G. Rd, T 35483. *Rajasthan*, New Palasia, T 5894. *Canara*, 207 M.G. Rd, T 35694. *Corporation Bank*, 24 M.G. Rd, T 37904. *Oriental Bank of Commerce*, 12/2 R.N.T. Marg, T 39022. *Saurashtra*, 22 Jawahar Marg, T 39018. *State Bank of India*, T 5136. *Indore*, T 30564.

Shopping *Sarafa Market* specialises in savoury snack foods and antique jewellery. *Kasera Bazaar* – metal pots and pans. *Cheap Jack*, Prince Yashwant Rd, antiques. *The Gallery*, 2-C Tukoganj, T 7741, antiques and curios. *Kilol Fabrics*, Chetak Arch, M.G. Rd, handlooms. *Gift House*, *Sweet House* and *Mrignayani Emporium*, all on M.G. Rd have handicrafts. *Rupmati*, M.G. Rd, handloom cloth and Chanderi and Maheshwari saris. *Recent and Decent*, M.G. Rd, leather garments. *Avanti*, MPLUN, M.G. Rd, handlooms. *Rupayan Bros.*, M.G. Rd, books.

Photography *Anant Photo Stores*, M.T.H. Compound; *Gopal Studio*, 30 Rajawada Chowk, T 32396; D. *Masands*, 78 Ushaganj, T 7126; *Lazor Colour Processing*, Lal Gali, M.G. Rd; *Eagle Studio*, 318 Jawahar Marg, T 31369; *Jeevan Photo Stores*, 105 M.G. Rd, T 33177; *Vippy Colour Labs*, Jail Rd; *Bhatia Arts*, Parsi Mohalla; *Bhalu Mondhe* (Art Photography), T 64946.

Local Transport Unmetered taxis, tempos, auto-rickshaws and cycle rickshaws are available. Fares negotiable.

Museums **Central Museum of Indore** (Archaeological Museum). Bombay-Agra Road Open 1000-1700 daily except Mon. Entry free and guides available with payment 'as you wish'. 30 mins is sufficient for a visit. Near the GPO, it has two main galleries plus statues in the grounds. The **first gallery** contains artefacts from Madhya Pradesh's prehistoric period, c 50,000 – 4,000 BC and some from western Malwa which are quite well displayed. There are stone tools, the use of quartz in sickles, ornaments and items of domestic use, as well as maps indicating the location of various archaeological sites. There has been quite extensive excavation in the Chambal valley and many rock shelters have been discovered in the central part of the province – **see Bhimbetka above**. In addition, there is an interesting model of the supposed first Hindu temple – at Barhut (another, slightly better one is also on display at the Lal Bagh Palace Museum). This is the earliest free-standing building of which there are traces and it comprises a small round hall made from brick and wood. Dated at around 3rd century BC, little but the foundations remain. This model gives a good indication of what it was probably like. The **second gallery** contains Hindu mythological carvings and more are found in the gardens of the Museum, said to have been a battlefield during the Mutiny.

If time is precious the Museum can be missed in favour of the riotously varied, but nevertheless fascinating Lal Bagh which has a selected range of early artefacts as well.

Useful Addresses Police, T 100, 35550. Fire, T 101. Ambulance, T 23201. MPSTDC Information Office, T 38888.

Hospitals and Medical Services Indore Cloth Market Hospital, Dhar Rd, T 62472. Pushpkunj Hospital, P.O. Kasturbagram, T 63353. Gokuldas Hospital, Gokul Building, Geeta Bhawan Rd. Noble Hospital, nr Nath Mandir, S Tukoganj. Robert's Nursing Home, Residency Area, T 23457. Sanjeevni Nursing Home, Phadnis Colony, T 38388. M.Y. Hospital, Agra Rd, T 23201. Greater Kailash Nursing Home, T 30888. Govt. Hospital, T 23465.

Chemists Anil Medical Stores, Maharani Rd, T 31766. Cash Chemists, Maharani Rd. Indian Medical Stores, Near T.B. Hospital, T 34943. R.B. Seth, Maharani Rd, T 33770. K.N. Khanna and Co., Ahilya Marg, T 32547.

Places of Worship *Hindu*: Annapurna Temple, M.G. Rd; Geeta Bhawan, Palasia; Gopal Mandir, Rajawada; Ramakrishna Ashram, Kila Maidan. *Sikh*: Imli Sahib Gurudwara, M.Y. Rd. *Jain*: Kanch Mandir, Itwariya Bazaar. *Christian*: White Church, Residency Area; Red Church, nr Nehru Stadium.

Travels and Tour Operators MPSTDC, Tourist Bungalow, T 38888. *Sharma Transport*, T 39199. *Sanghi Travels*, T 7361. *Vijayant Travels*, T 39771. *Sindh Travels*, T 39467.

Tourist Offices and Information *MPTDC Office,* Tourist Bungalow, behind Ravindra Natyagrih, T 38888. **Conducted Tours** for Mandu (see Mandu section), leave every Wed, Fri, Sat and Sun and Omkareshwar and Maheshwar (see Excursions) every Mon and Th. Both leave from the Madhya Pradesh Tourist Bungalow. Departure for both is 0730 and return 1900. Cost: Mandu Tour 70 (inclusive of lunch and tea) and Omkareshwar-Maheshwar 50 (exclusive of meals). Tours are also organised for Mandu by both Vijayant and Trimourti Travels every Sun.

Air Indian Airlines connects Indore with Jaipur, Gwalior, Ahmedabad, Pune and Bombay. Direct daily flights to Bombay (1 hr 5 min), Bhopal and Gwalior. **Indian Airlines**: city office, T 7069; airport, T 31244. **Vayudoot**: City office, T 36771; **Airport**, T 33161.

Rail Indore is not on the main broad gauge line between Delhi and Bombay but is on a spur that connects with Ujjain. There is also a metre gauge line that connects with Ajmer and Chittorgarh (N) and Khandwa, Nizamabad and Secunderabad (S). **New Delhi**: *Indore-New Delhi Malwa Exp*, 4067, daily, 1505, 18 hr 55 min. **Bombay Central**: *Indore-Bombay Exp*, 1962, daily, 2030, 14 hr 55 min. **Bilaspur**: *Narmada Exp*, 8233, daily, 1520, 26 hr 15 min. **Secunderabad**: *Meenakshi Exp*, 7569, daily, 0501, 13 hr 10 min. **Jaipur**: *Meenakshi Exp*, 7570, daily. 2226, 15 hr 19 min. **Ujjain**: *Narmada Exp*, 8234, daily, 1520, 1 hr 50 min.

Bus Buses run from Indore to **Ujjain** (55 km), **Bagh** and **Mandu** (100 km, Deluxe recommended) several times daily, and hourly to **Bhopal** (187 km). Buses to **Udaipur** (Rajasthan) take 12 hr. **Aurangabad** (for Ajanta and Ellora caves) one direct bus a day. Allow a full day for getting there.

The direct road from Indore to **Ujjain** (55 km) via Sanwer passes mainly through farming country.

Ujjain

Population 300,000 approx. *Altitude* 492 m. *Climate* same as Indore. Ujjain is 889 km from Delhi and 749 km from Bombay and is connected to both by rail and road. The nearest airport is at Indore (53 km). *Best season* Oct-Mar.

It is hard to believe that this comparatively quiet and relatively small provincial town is one of the greatest cities of ancient India and one of contemporary Hinduism's seven sacred cities (the other six are Varanasi, Mathura, Haridwar, Kanchipuram, Dwarka and Ayodhya). It is also one of the four towns in the triennial Kumbh Mela (the other three being Haridwar, Allahabad and Nasik) and thus plays host up to a million pilgrims who converge on the place every twelve years. At other times, there is a constant though smaller stream coming to bathe in the river Shipra and worship at the temples on its banks. For Hindus it is holy, for western visitors it offers no more than other towns and this is somewhat surprising when one considers its great antiquity.

Tracing its origins to the age of the great Hindu epics the Upanishads and the Puranas and known in the earliest times as **Avantika**, legend has it that Siva commemorated his victory over the demon ruler of **Tripuri** by changing the name of his capital to **Ujjaiyini** (One who Conquers with Pride).

Many dynasties ruled over this prosperous city – the Sakas, Guptas, Paramaras, the governors of the Slave Dynasty of Delhi, the Mughals and the Marathas. It is said to have been the seat of the viceroyalty of Asoka during the reign of his father at **Pataliputra** (Patna) in 275 BC. The emperor Asoka's sons were born here, and it was from here that they set out to preach Buddhism. The poet *Kalidasa*, one of the *Nava Ratna* (Nine Gems) of Hindu literature, wrote some of his works here and even the god Krishna is believed to have studied here.

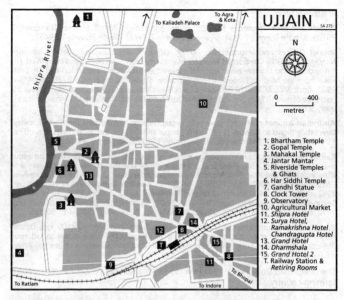

UJJAIN SA 275

N

0 ——— 400
metres

1. Bhartham Temple
2. Gopal Temple
3. Mahakal Temple
4. Jantar Mantar
5. Riverside Temples & Ghats
6. Har Siddhi Temple
7. Gandhi Statue
8. Clock Tower
9. Observatory
10. Agricultural Market
11. *Shipra Hotel*
12. *Surya Hotel, Ramakrishna Hotel Chandragupta Hotel*
13. *Grand Hotel*
14. *Dharmshala*
15. *Grand Hotel 2*
T. Railway Station & Retiring Rooms

To Kaliadeh Palace
To Agra & Kota
Shipra River
To Ratlam
To Indore
To Bhopal

Ujjain stands in N latitude 23° 11'10" the first meridian of longitude for Hindu astronomers, who believed that the **Tropic of Cancer** passed through the site. This explains the presence of the **observatory** (Vedha Shala) built much later by **Raja Jai Singh** of Jaipur in about 1725 when he was the Governor of Malwa under the Mughal Emperor Muhammad Shah. Even today the *Ephemeris* tables (predicted positions of the planets) are published here – see page 527.

In its heyday, Ujjain was on a trade route to Mesopotamia and Egypt and, consequently, trade flourished. Nowadays, it is little more than a provincial town. There are a reasonably large number of sites in Ujjain, the number reflecting its long history:

Local Festivals The triennial *Kumbh Mela* takes place here every 12 years (see page 248). The next one is in 1992. *Kartik Mela* (Nov). This fair, lasting a month, draws large crowds from surrounding villages.

Places of Interest

The *Mahalakeshwar Temple* with its soaring *shikhar** (tower) dominates the skyline and life of Ujjain. Here the god Siva reigns supreme and the temple lingam, one of the 12 *jyotirlingas* in India, is believed to be swayambhu (born of itself), deriving its *shakti** or power from within itself. The myths surrounding the jyoti linga (*linga of light*) go back to the 2nd century BC and were clearly developed in order to explain and justify linga worship. Wendy O'Flaherty has translated this story of antagonism and competition between the gods in which Siva (in the form of Rudra) terrorizes the other gods into worshipping him with a devotion to the linga. Her vivid translation of the Puranic myth is summarised in the introduction to S Asia, see page 58.

Close to the tank near Mahalakeshwar is enshrined a large sculpted image of Ganes in the **Bade Ganesji Ka Mandir**. Other noteworthy temples are **Chintaman Ganes, Harsiddhi Mandir** and **Gadkalika**. There are more, much smaller temples and shrines out of town along the river and the atmosphere at these is generally very restful and relaxed. About 8 km from the city centre and past the British built jail is the **Kaliadeh Palace**, built on the banks of the Shipra river. This once imposing building was built by Mahmud Khilji in 1458. Akbar stayed here in 1601. The riverside buildings are quite attractive but overall the palace, now used as a storeroom, is badly neglected. Except during the monsoon, the river level is quite low. The *Vedha Shala* (Observatory) is very small compared with Jai Singh's Jantar Mantars in Delhi and Jaipur and contains only five instruments.

Hotels Although MPSTDC run a very good chain of hotels and motels throughout the state Ujjain is not as well provided as many places, especially for the foreign visitor. If you are travelling by car, it is better to stay in Indore. None the less there are some cheap hotels that are good value. Recommended: **D** *Shipra Motel* (MPSTDC), University Rd, near the Madhav Club, T 4862. Restaurant, garden, travel information. **E** *Grand*, T 42. **E** *Savera*, T 403. **F** *Adarsh Gupta*. **F** *Chinar*, opp the railway station. **F** *Railway Retiring Rooms*.

Shopping The region is famous for its Maheshwari saris, a unique weave introduced to Maheshwar by Rani Ahilyabai. They are mostly woven in cotton with reversible borders.

Local Transport Unmetered taxis, auto-rickshaws, tempos, cycle rickshaws and tongas are widely available.

Air Nearest airport is Indore (53 km), connected by regular flights with Delhi, Gwalior, Bhopal and Bombay.

Rail Ujjain is on the Bhopal-Nagda sector of the Western Railway. **Ahmedabad:** *Bhopal-Rajkot Exp*, 1270, daily, 2350, 9 hr 10 min; *Sabarmati Exp*, 9186, daily, 2030, 10 hr 30 min: **Bhopal:** *Narmada Exp*, 8233, daily, 1735, 4 hr 40 min: *From Indore:* *Narmada Exp*, 8233, daily, 1520, 1 hr 50 min: **Indore:** *Narmada Exp*, 8234, daily, 1130, 2 hr 20 min: **Bombay Central:** *Indore-Bombay Exp*, 1962, daily, 2230, 12 hr 25 min: **New Delhi:** *Malwa Exp*, 4067, daily, 1655, 15 hr.

Road Regular bus services connect Ujjain with **Indore** (53 km), **Ratlam, Gwalior, Mandu** (149 km), **Dhar, Kota** and **Omkareshwar**.

Excursion to Mandu It is possible to visit Mandu (see below) in one day by either taking a hire car or one of the conducted tours mentioned above.

Leave Indore and drive W. The road first crosses a cultivated plain and then the headwaters of the Chambal river. *Dhar* (65 km), was originally the stronghold of the Paramara dynasty and the capital of Raja Bhoj from Ujjain. It has a number of ruined mosques dating from the 15th century and an imposing fort on the edge of the town. Leaving Dhar, the road gradually climbs onto a more open plateau which is still farmed though less intensively. The final half hour of the 2 hr 30 min drive is spectacular as the road reaches the N limits of the Western Ghats. Here and there the land falls steeply away and from the tops of ravines there are stupendous views of the the lowland country to the W and SW. The road entrance to **Mandu** is along an short razor back ridge dividing two deep valleys.

Mandu

Population 5,500 *Altitude* 634 m. *Climate* Temp, Summer Max. 36°C, Min. 28°C, Winter Max. 22°C, Min. 7°C. Annual rainfall same as Indore. *Best time for a visit* During the monsoon when the tanks are full and the rain turns the entire countryside a verdant green. Good Oct -Feb. Mandu is approximately 500 km from Bombay and 900 km from Delhi. There is no airport and the nearest railheads are at Ratlam (124 km) and Indore (99 km).

Perched along the **Vindhyan ranges** at 592 m, Mandu was fortified as early as the 6th century, but gained prominence in the 10th century as the fort capital of the Parmar rulers of Malwa. Later, towards the end of the 13th century it came

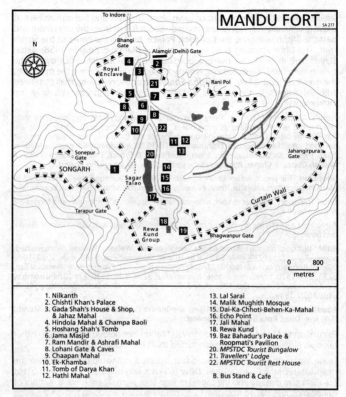

MANDU FORT SA 277

To Indore

Bhangi Gate

Alamgir (Delhi) Gate

Royal Enclave

Rani Pol

Sonepur Gate

SONGARH

Sagar Talao

Tarapur Gate

Rewa Kund Group

Bhagwanpur Gate

Jahangirpura Gate

Curtain Wall

0   800
metres

1. Nilkanth
2. Chishti Khan's Palace
3. Gada Shah's House & Shop, & Jahaz Mahal
4. Hindola Mahal & Champa Baoli
5. Hoshang Shah's Tomb
6. Jama Masjid
7. Ram Mandir & Ashrafi Mahal
8. Lohani Gate & Caves
9. Chaapan Mahal
10. Ek-Khamba
11. Tomb of Darya Khan
12. Hathi Mahal

13. Lal Sarai
14. Malik Mughith Mosque
15. Dai-Ka-Chhoti-Behen-Ka-Mahal
16. Echo Point
17. Jali Mahal
18. Rewa Kund
19. Baz Bahadur's Palace & Roopmati's Pavilion
20. *MPSTDC Tourist Bungalow*
21. *Travellers' Lodge*
22. *MPSTDC Tourist Rest House*

B. Bus Stand & Cafe

under the sway of the Sultans of Malwa, under whom it was named **Shadiabad** (The City of Joy). It has a fine architectural heritage and the buildings, spread over the naturally defensible plateau (area 21 sq km) exude a grace compatible with Mandu's other name. Its rulers built exquisite palaces (the **Jahaz** and **Hindola Mahals**), ornamental canals, baths and pavilions. Most of Mandu's buildings are superb but some are really outstanding like the large **Jama Masjid** and **Hoshang Shah's Tomb.** Under Mughal rule Humayun captured Mandu in a brilliant campaign in Malwa in 1534, and it became a pleasure resort, its lakes and palaces the scenes of magnificent festivities. However by the end of the Mughal period it had effectively been abandoned and in 1732, it passed into Maratha hands.

Architecturally, Mandu represents the best in a provincial Islamic style. Most of the existing buildings were constructed between 1401 and 1526, initially using stone salvaged from desecrated local Hindu temples. Perhaps as a consequence of numerous wars and the need for effective use of resources, the builders disdained the use of elaborate exterior ornamentation. A little imagination is therefore required to picture many as buildings for pleasure.

Places of Interest The 45 km parapet was built from rubble and boulders and is punctuated by 12 gateways. Most notable of these is **Delhi Gate** (1405-7), the main entrance to the city and testimony to the fort's history of violent sieges, for which the approach is through a series of well fortified subsidiary gates such as **Alamgir** and **Bhangi Darwaza.** The present road is along this route. There are six groups of buildings at Mandu, the first three being the most important.

The Royal Enclave

The **Mosque of Dilwar Khan** (1405) is the earliest Islamic building, comprising a central colonnaded courtyard. There are Hindu influences in the main entrances. The **Hathi Pol** (Elephant Gate) is the main entrance to the royal enclosure, the **Hindola Mahal** or **Swing Palace** (1425). The audience hall acquired its name from its inward sloping walls which give the impression of swaying. Behind and to the W of the Hindola Mahal is a jumble of ruins which was once the palace of the Malwa Sultans.

There is the **Champa Baoli,** an undergound well, so named because its water is said to have smelt like the *champak* flower, rooms for hot weather use, a **Hammam** (hot bath) and a **water pavilion**. The **Jahaz Mahal** or **Ship Palace** (late 15th century) reflects the spirit of romantic beauty characteristic of the palace life of the Muslim rulers of India. Popular imagination has given it a fitting tribute in its name. It is a long (122 m) and narrow (15 m) building built between two artificial lakes. Its shape and kiosks give it the impression of a stately ship. Built as a *harem*, it was 'crewed' entirely by women and consists of three great halls with a beautiful bath at the N end.

Other places of interest in this enclave are **Taveli Mahal** (stables and guardhouse), from which there is a wonderful panorama of the ruins of Mandu, two large wells called the **Ujali** (bright) and **Andheri** (dark) **Baolis** and **Gada Shah's Shop** and **House**.

The Central Group

Hoshang Shah's Tomb (c.1440) is India's first marble edifice and a refined example of Afghan architecture. Its features are a well proportioned dome, delicate marble latticework and porticoed courts and towers. Shah Jahan sent 4 of his architects, including Ustad Ahmed who is associated with the Taj Mahal (see Agra), to study its form for inspiration. The *Jama Masjid* (1454) was inspired by the great mosque at Damascus. Conceived on a grand scale on a high plinth (4.6 m) and a large domed porch ornamented with jali screens and bands of blue enamel tiles set as stars. The courtyard is flanked by colonnades. The western one is the Prayer Hall and is the most imposing of all with numerous rows of arches and pillars which support the ceilings of the 3 great domes and the 58 smaller ones. The central niche (*mihrab*) is beautifully designed and ornamented along its sides with a scroll of interwoven Arabic letters containing quotations from the Koran.

The **Ashrafi Mahal** palace of gold coins (c.1436-1440), now a ruin, was conceived as a *madrassa* (religious college). In the same complex, its builder Mahmud Shah Khilji (1436-69) built a seven-storeyed tower to celebrate his victory over Rana Khumba of Mewar (Udaipur). Only one storey has survived. Also in ruins is the tomb that was intended to be the largest building in Mandu.

Rewa Kund Group

This group is 3.2 km S of the village. **Rewa Kund** is a sacred tank whose waters were lifted to supply the **Palace of Baz Bahadur** (1508-9), the last Sultan of Malwa (1555) on the rising ground above. The palace was built before Baz Bahadur's time. The main portion of the palace consists of a spacious open court with halls and rooms on all sides and a beautiful cistern in its centre. On the terrace above are two beautiful *baradaris** (pavilions) from which there is an enchanting view of the surrounding countryside.

Beyond the palace and on higher ground at the S edge of the plateau is **Roopmati's Pavilion**, originally built as an army observation post but later modified and added to as a palace so that Baz Bahadur's mistress could have her *darshan* (view) of the sacred **Narmada river**, seen 305 m below winding like a white serpent across the plains. The shepherdess **Roopmati**, the story goes, agreed to go to Mandu with Baz Bahadur when she was promised that she should live in a palace within sight of her beloved river! The pavilions, square with hemispherical domes are the latest additions and these have added distinction to the building. To enjoy the romantic beauty of the setting, sunrise and sunset are particularly good times.

The *Sagar Talao Group* In the large group of monuments around the picturesque *Sagar Talao* lake is the **Malik Mughith mosque** built in 1432. In front of this is the **caravansarai** which was probably attached and built at the same time. It consists of an open courtyard with two halls with rooms at both ends. The rooms were probably for storage of goods while the halls provided living accommodation. The **Gumbad** building to the S is associated with some lady related to a certain wet-nurse of one of the Mandu princes. Although really a tomb, it is possible that it was once her house in which she was buried later. Such practices are not uncommon with Muslims. It is an octagonal building with arches and a shapely dome.

Between Sagar Talao and the village is the **Hathi Mahal** (Elephant Palace) which stands to the E of the road and takes its names from its stumpy pillars. It was probably a baradari (pleasure pavilion). Traces of old tile work can still be seen. The **Tomb of Darya Khan** (c.1526) is a red masonry mausoleum, once embellished with rich enamel patterns. More ruins lie nearby.

Others On the edge of the plateau is the **Lal Mahal** (Ruby Palace), once used as a royal summer retreat. **Chishti Khan's Palace** stands on a spur to its E. Now in ruins, this may have been used as a retreat during the monsoon. W of Sagar Talao is the *Nilkanth Palace* which was built on the site of a Saivite shrine. Situated on the scarp of one of the great ravines and commanding a magnificent view of the valleys below, it was used by the Mughals as a water palace. On one of the outer room walls is an inscription recording Akbar's expeditions into the Deccan.

There is an excellent guide to Mandu by D.R. Patil and published by the Archaeological Survey of India (Rs 4.50), available in Mandu.

Hotels D *Tourist Cottages* (MPSTDC), Roopmati Rd, T 35. 20 cottages, some a/c. Restaurant, bar, gardens. Very attractive location overlooking Sagar Talao lake. Recommended. **D** *Travellers' Lodge* (MPSTDC), T 21 is less expensive. 8 non a/c rm. Restaurant, bar. Nearer bus stand and very pleasant. **E** *SDA Guest House*, T 34. 7 rm. Simple. **F** *Taveli Mahal Guest House* (Archaeological Survey of India), nr Jahaz Mahal. Basic.

Restaurants Apart from the restaurants at the State Tourism establishments which need a few hours' advance notice, there are a number of small simple places (*dhabas*), nr the bus stand in the centre of the village.

Banks State Bank of India, T 36. No foreign exchange facilities.

Local Transport Mandu is essentially a small village. Everything worth visiting can be reached on foot although some of the distances are a few kilometres. No taxis or auto-rickshaws. Cycle rickshaws and bicycles are available for sightseeing.

Hospitals and Medical Service Government Hospital, Mandu is basic.

Post and Telegraph P and T Office, T 20.

Places of Worship *Hindu*, Neelkanth Mandir, Ram Mandir; *Jain*, Jain Mandir; *Muslim*, Jama Masjid.

Tourist Offices and Information (incl Conducted Tours and Excursions) MPSTDC Tourist Cottages and Travellers Lodge. Special Area Development Authority (SADA), T 34. Archaeological Survey of India, T 25.

Air Nearest airport is at Indore with Indian Airlines and Vayudoot connections to Bhopal,

Gwalior, Jaipur, Bombay and Delhi.

Rail The most convenient railheads are **Ratlam** (124 km) on the Bombay Delhi Broad gauge line, and **Indore** (99 km) on a branch route. Ratlam has connections from Bombay, Delhi, Allahabad, Vadodara, Jaipur, Ajmer, Bhopal, Kanpur, Lucknow, Varanasi, Amritsar and Gwalior.

Road Mandu lies just off NH3 from Agra to Bombay. It is most accessible from Indore. **Bus** Regular bus services connect Mandu with **Dhar** (35 km), **Indore** (99 km – 4-5 hr), **Ratlam** (124 km), **Ujjain** (152 km) and **Bhopal** (286 km). Conducted tours from Bhopal and Indore.

Return to the main road at *Gujri* (42 km) and turn right to travel S. In *Dhamnod* (11 km) there is a left turn for **Maheshwar** (13 km) and **Omkareshwar** (74 km) which can also be visited as a full day trip from Indore, either travelling independently by car or on a tour. To follow route direct to Ahmadabad, see below.

Maheshwar On the N bank of the Narmada, Maheshwar has been identified as *Mahishmati*, the ancient capital of King Kartivirarjun. Then it had a reputation as a spectacular city. The temple town on the banks of the Narmada is mentioned in the *Ramayana* and *Mahabharata* epics. The Holkar queen *Rani Ahilyabai of Indore* (d.1795) revived the city, and today Maheshwar's temples and fort complex stand reflected quietly in the river below.

The queen was widely revered, as was testified by Sir John Malcolm: "She sat every day for a considerable period in open durbar transacting business. Her first principle of government appears to have been moderate assessment and an almost sacred respect for native rights... she heard every complaint in person, and although she continually referred causes to courts of equity and arbitration and to her ministers for settlement, she was always accessible... Her charitable foundations extend all over India, from the Himalayas to Cape Comorin, and from Somnath to the Temple of Jagannath. She had the courage to watch her own daughter become *sati*, after vainly seeking to dissuade her."

The **Rajwada** is a life size statue of Rani Ahilyabai sitting on her throne in the **Rajgaddi** within the fort. This is the right place to begin a tour of the town as it was the queen who revived Maheshwar's fortunes. Relics and heirlooms of the Holkar family can be sen in other rooms which are open to the public. Within the complex is an exquisite small shrine which is installed on a palanquin and carried down from the fort to receive the towns people's homage during the ancient *Dassehra* ceremony.

Pilgrim ghats The **Peshwa**, **Fanese** and **Ahilya Ghats** on the river bank provide a fascinating kaleidoscope of rural India. Pilgrims and holy men sit in meditation, rows of graceful women carry gleaming brass pots to collect water and the ferries bring villagers to the town. Lining the banks too are stone memorials to the *sati's** of Maheshwar who perished on their husbands' funeral pyres. The temples to see are **Kalshwara**, **Rajarajeshwara**, **Vithaleshwara** and **Ahileshwar**.

The town is renowned throughout the region for its **Maheshwar** saris. Introduced 200 years ago by Rani Ahilyabai, these have a unique weave. Woven mostly in cotton, the Maheshwari sari has a plain body and sometimes stripes or checks in several variations. The borders have a wide range of leaf and floral designs. The *pallu* (end section of the sari) is particularly distinctive with five stripes, three coloured and two white alternating, running along its width. Maheshwari has a reversible border, known as *bugdi*.

Hotels Accommodation is basic. *Ahilya Trust Guest House, Govt. Rest House* and *dharamshalas.*

Travel Regular bus services from Barwaha, Khandwa, Dhar and Dhamnod. The nearest railhead is Barwaha (39 km) on the Western Railway.

Navdatoli, opposite Maheshwar on the S bank of the Narmada is an important archaeological. Since its first exploration in 1950, when painted pottery and microliths were found, a broad sequence of cultures have been discovered from the Lower Palaeolithic period up to the 18th century. The third period of occupation during the Chalcolithic has been dated at between 1500 BC and 1200 BC. House plans from this period have been excavated which show either circular or rectangular buildings, the circular houses having a circumference of about 3 metres. The walls and roof, made of split bamboo covered in mud, were supported by wooden poles.

Burnt grains of wheat and rice, legumes and oil seeds have all been found along with large numbers of bones of domesticated animals which show that the people ate beef, pork and venison. A wide range of ornaments has also been discovered from this third period. It ended with a great flood, and the site was abandoned temporarily. During the succeeding period a small stupa was built though probably left incomplete.

61 km E is *Omkareshwar*, a sacred island shaped like the holy Hindu symbol 'Om' in the middle of the Narmada, which has drawn pilgrims for centuries. The island is over 2 km long and 1 km wide and is divided N to S by a deep gully. The ground slopes gently along the northern edge but in the S and E there are cliffs over 150 metres high. The S bank of the Narmada is just as high at this point so the river is in effect forced through a narrow gorge. The village is built both on the S bank of the river and on the island, and the river between is reputedly very deep and full of crocodiles. A new bridge links the island with the southern bank.

In the **Sri Omkar Mandhata temple** is one of the twelve *jyotilinga* in India, natural rock features that are believed to be representations of *Siva* in the form of a linga. The oldest temple is at the E end of the island. Craftsmen have carved elaborate figures on the upper portion of the temple and its roof. Encircling the shrine are verandahs with columns carved in circles, polygons and squares. The **Siddhnath Temple** on the hill is a fine example of early medieval temple architecture, its main feature being a frieze of elephants over 1.5 metres high carved on a stone slab at its outer perimeter. There is a gigantic Nandi bull in front of the temple to Gauri Somnath at the W end of the island.

The temples were severely damaged after the Muslim invasions of **Mahmud of Ghazni**. Every dome was overturned and all the sculptured figures were mutilated. The long periods when they ceased to be used allowed them to get completely overgrown, and Murray's Guide records that when the Peshwa Baji Rao II wanted to repair the temple it couldn't be found, so he built a new one. Subsequently repairs were carried out to the part that was discovered.

Other places in or near Omkareshwar are the **24 Avatars***, a cluster of Hindu and Jain temples, the 10th century **Satmarika Temples** (6 km) and the **Kajal Rani Cave** (9 km), a picturesque scenic spot with a panoramic view of the gently undulating landscape.

Hotels Accommodation is limited and includes the *Holkar Guest House*, run by the Ahilyabai Charity Trust, Omkareshwar Temple and a number of *dharamshalas*.

Travel Omkareshwar is connected to Indore, Ujjain, Khandwa and Omkareshwar Road Railway Station (12 km) by regular bus services. The railhead is on the Ratlam-Khandwa section of the Western Railway.

To Ahmadabad Return to Guyri. Turn left off the NH3 to Dhar (44 km). From Dhar the road runs W through Sardarpur (41 km) to Dohad (79 km), just across the border of Gujarat. From Dohad continue W through Godhra (70 km) and Nadiad (82 km) to Ahmadabad (58 km) **see page 1040.**

RAJASTHAN

Rajasthan's many princely states, impressive forts and magnificent palaces, set in the often bleakly inhospitable surroundings of India's Thar desert, evoke uniquely colourful images of medieval India. Lack of rainfall has kept it poor whilst inaccessibility made it a region of refuge. Rajasthan means 'the land of the rajas (or kings)', but was also called **Rajputana** 'the country of the Rajputs'. Some families have ruled for centuries, often warring in an apparently endless round of clan feuds, vying with one another for supremacy, together appearing like the Knights of the Round Table. The colourful peasant population, the primitive methods of cultivation and camel trains, tales of heroism and chivalry, make Rajasthan a fascinating region to visit. It is particularly inviting as it is easily reached from both Delhi or Bombay.

Social indicators Area 342,000 sq km **Population** 46 million **Literacy** M 36% F 11% **Birth rate** *Rural* 42:1000 *Urban* 34:1000 **Death rate** *Rural* 14:1000 *Urban* 10:1000 **Infant mortality** *Rural* 105:1000 *Urban* 60:1000 **Registered graduate job seekers** 76,000 **Average annual income per head:** Rs 1238 **Inflation** *1981-87* 66% **Religion** *Hindu* 89% *Muslim* 7% *Christian* 0.1% *Sikh* 1.5% *Jain* 1.8%

INTRODUCTION

The Land
Rajasthan is bounded on the W and NW by Pakistan, Punjab and Haryana in the North, Uttar Pradesh in the E, Madhya Pradesh in the E and SE and Gujarat in the S and Southwest. It is almost exactly the same size as Germany.

Physically, Rajasthan comprises three areas. Running across the S of the state are the *Aravalli Hills*, one of the oldest mountain systems in the world. These form a series of jagged ridges made up of heavily folded synclines, stretching from their highest point, **Mt Abu** in the SW (1720 m) to **Kota** and **Bundi** in the E. Every visitor to Delhi sees their northernmost ridges break the surface of the plain in the Delhi Ridge on which New Delhi's government buildings now stand.

Mt. Abu itself is a granite massif but the range as a whole has a complex mixture of rocks. There are small hills of quartzite, nearly buried under the alluvium of the Ganga and alluvial embayments between the ridges, such as at Tonk. Rajasthan is also the source of the glittering white *Makrana marble* used in the Taj Mahal and the much later testament to Empire, the Victoria Jubilee Memorial in Calcutta. The route from Delhi to Jaipur gives an excellent view of the approach to the Aravallis. Within this region are numerous fort towns, e.g. Chittaurgarh, Kota, Bundi, Kumbhalgarh, the last commanding a very fine view over the plains to the north.

In the NW part of the state is the arid and forbidding **Thar Desert**, with its shifting sand dunes, high summer temperatures and poor access. Towns like **Jaisalmer** and **Bikaner** are important settlements on overland trade routes to

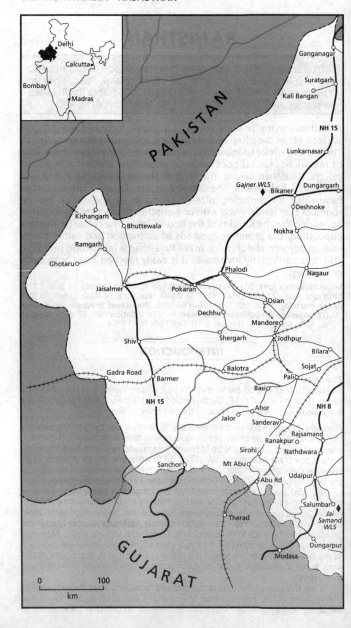

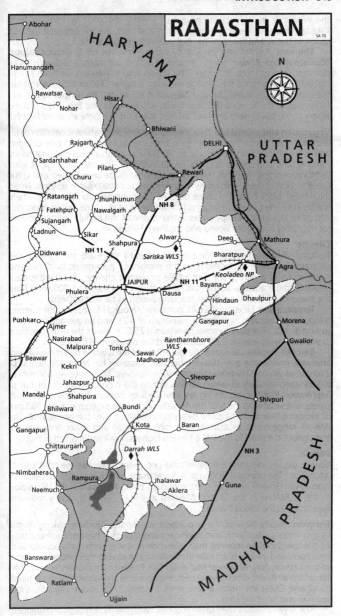

RASTHAN

SA 70

the W whose main functions have ben severely disrupted by Partition from Pakistan. **Jodhpur** lies on the edge of this arid tract, the link between the true desert to the W and the semi arid but cultivable regions to the E.

The east Rainfall and soil fertility increase towards the E. Around **Jaipur**, **Bharatpur** and **Alwar**, tracts of cultivated land are interspersed with rocky outcrops such as those at Amber. This region adjoins Haryana, Delhi and Uttar Pradesh. S of the range the average elevation is higher (330 to 1150 metres) but the topography is varied. Around **Mewar** it is hilly, but **Bharatpur** is flat and forms part of the Yamuna drainage basin. Around **Kota** and **Bundi** is a plateau where good, black, deep and well drained soils exist. All these areas are farmed.

Vegetation and animal life Over most of the state, the natural vegetation cover is scrub jungle. Trees are scarce except in areas such as Kumbhalgarh near Udaipur, and some of the SE and E parts, e.g. Sariska and Ranthambhor national parks. Tamarisk and arid zone plants are found in the W. The natural jungle is ideal territory for tigers, leopards, sloth bear, sambhar (large brown deer) and chital (smaller spotted deer). These now only rarely occur outside game reserves. Nilgai (blue bulls), black buck and ravine deer are fairly numerous on the plains. There is a great variety of birds. Bikaner is famous for its sand grouse, whilst Bharatpur and other low-lying swampy places in the southeast are popular winter grounds for migratory birds from Siberia and Northern Europe.

Climate
Although Rajasthan is the driest region of India there are still considerable contrasts in climate. Its locations on the margins of pure desert lands has also made much of it particularly susceptible to climatic change, and there is clear evidence of the advance and retreat of the desert over the last 5,000 years from the presence of fossil sand dunes reaching almost as far east as Delhi.

Temperature Except in the hills, particularly around Mount Abu, the summer temperatures are very high with a maximum of 46°C and an average from May to Aug of 38°C. The daily summer minimum is 25°C. In winter the daily maximum in most low lying areas is 22°C to 28°C and the minimum 8°C-14°C.

Rainfall Rainfall varies over the state. Parts of the western desert receive very little rain, on average only 100 mm per year. Jaisalmer has an annual rainfall of 210 mm of which 90% falls in the monsoon (Jul-Sep). Jaipur receives 650 mm of precipitation annually of which 80% is during the monsoon months of July to September. Jodhpur, occupying an intermediate position between these two places and situated to the N of the Aravallis and on the desert fringe has 380 mm of rainfall a year with the same heavy concentration over the wet season. The Aravalli range tends to experience a higher rainfall and lower temperatures throughout the year. To the SW there is higher rainfall and marked humidity.

People
Various groups, including a sizeable tribal population, comprise the state total of 34 million. The principal language is **Rajasthani,** which includes a number of Indo-Aryan dialects, the four most important being **Marwari** in the W, **Jaipuri** in the E, **Malwi** in the SE and **Mewati** in the NE. Hindi is rapidly replacing Rajasthani as the lingua franca.

Religion Nearly 90% of the population are Hindus, Muslims making up the largest minority. Jainism is also significant and though it has not been practised by the rulers it often received their toleration as it was particularly popular with merchants and traders. Islam extended into Rajasthan with the conquest of Ajmer in the 12th century. **Khwajah Mu'in-ud-Din Chishti**, a missionary or saint, had his refuge at Ajmer which has subsequently become a popular pilgrimage place. Sikhs and Christians form a very small minority. Until about 1400 BC tribes roamed and ruled the land.

The Aryan invaders were often in conflict with the tribal groups and gradually forced most of them back into the remote craggy and forested Aravallis. Successive invasions of the Sakas, Kusanas, Abhiras and Huns affected the region but the aboriginal tribes, whilst assimilating some of the ways and manners of the intruders nevertheless managed to preserve a clearly distinct culture.

Tribal peoples

Today, tribals constitute 12.21% of the state population which is higher than the national average of 7%. The dominant tribes are the Bhils and Minas plus the smaller and less well known Sahariyas, Damariyas, Garasias, Gaduliya Lohars and the Bhil-Minas. The tribes share common traits which seem to link their pasts together but it is the differences in their costumes and jewellery, their gods, fairs and festivals that set them apart from one another.

The **Bhils** comprise 39% of Rajasthan's tribal population and form an important group in the S part of the state around Dungapur, Udaipur and Chittaurgarh. Their stronghold is Banswara. The generic term derives from *bil** (bow) which describes their original talent and strength. The Hindu epic the Mahabharata mentions the Bhils and their archery skills. Today, the accepted head of all the Rajput Clans of Rajasthan – the Maharana of Udaipur – is crowned by anointing his forehead with blood drawn from the palm of a Bhil chieftain, affirming the alliance and loyalty of his tribe.

The Bhils maintained their numbers and strength by intermingling with rebellious outcast Rajputs. Rajput rulers came to value the guerilla tactics of the Bhils and Muslim and Maratha attacks could not have been repelled without their active support. However, they always remained a minority and offered no real threat to the city dwelling princes and their armies. Physically, they are short, stocky and dark with broad noses and thick lips. They marry within a narrow kinship group and the tribe has a patrilineal system of inheritance. Subsistence is not always easy for the Bhils who used to live off roots, leaves and fruits of the forest and the increasingly scarce game. Most now farm land and keep cattle, goats and sheep, while those who live near towns often work on daily wages to supplement their incomes.

Imperfectly absorbed into Hinduism, the Bhils have their own deities. **Nandevro**, a deity who presides over the corn, **Gwali**, the god of milk and **Hir Kulyo**, the god of agriculture, are three of the most important. The fact that these gods are worshipped indicates how much the Bhil way of living has changed form their original hunting and gathering existence. The Baneshwar fair in Jan/Feb is the best known seasonal gathering of the Bhils when thousands congregate near the confluence of the Mahi and Som rivers in Dungarpur district.

The **Minas** are Rajasthan's largest and most widely spread tribal group. It seems that the Minas may have been the original inhabitants of the Indus Valley civilization before they were ousted by the Aryans. The **Vedas** and the **Mahabharata** mention them, and it was the **Kachhawaha Rajputs** who finally dispersed them and forced them into the forests and hideouts of the Aravallis. The Minas have a tall, athletic build with sharp features, large eyes, thick lips and a light brown complexion.

Dress Their dress is casual and practical. The men wear a loincloth tied loosely round the waist, a waistcoat and a long piece of brightly coloured fabric on the head tied loosely like a turban. The women wear a long flared skirt with many gathers (*ghaghra**), a small blouse (*kurti-kanchali**) and a large square scarf.

Customs The Mina measure their wealth in cattle and other livestock. Most Mina are cultivators. The Mina worship Siva and have built a number of exquisite temples that are rich with stone carving. Other gods are worshipped including **Sheeta Mata**, the dreaded goddess of smallpox, although this as been eradicated. Like other tribal groups they have a tradition of looking after their own by donating grain, clothes, animals and jewellery to the needy. The forest dwellings, **Mewas,** comprise a cluster of huts called pal and each pal constitutes a family unit. The marriage ceremony performed round a fire is not very different from a Hindu one. Divorce, though, is not uncommon or particularly difficult. A man wishing to divorce his wife tears a piece of his clothes and gives this to the woman who moves away carrying two pitchers of water. Whoever helps her unload the pitchers becomes her new husband.

The *Gaduliya Lohars* receive their name from their beautiful bullock carts (*gadis**). These nomadic blacksmiths are said to have wandered from their homeland of Mewar because of a pledge made to their acknowledged lord, **Maharana Pratap**. He was ousted from **Chittaurgarh** by the Mughal emperor Akbar and the Gaduliya Lohars, a clan of warring Rajputs, vowed to re-enter the city only after the victory of Maharana Pratap. Unfortunately, he was killed on the battlefield. Despite the efforts of Prime Minister Jawaharlal Nehru to take a procession of Gaduliya Lohars back into Chittaurgarh in an effort to settle them in their homeland, most of them prefer to keep their vow to their Maharana.

The ***Garasias***, comprising only 2.7% of Rajasthan's tribals, have an interesting custom of marriage through elopement, which usually takes place at the annual Gaur fair held during the full moon of Mar. After the elopement which can be spontaneous or pre-arranged, a bride price of Rs 40-250 is paid to the bride's father. Should the arrangement not work out, the woman returns home to her father who receive Rs 15. Widows are forced to remarry, since their children – and not they – are given a share in the husband's property.

The ***Sahariyas*** are jungle dwellers and their name possibly derives from the Persian *sehr* (jungle). Simple, illiterate and open to exploitation, the Sahariyas are regarded as the most backward tribe in Rajasthan and eke out a living as shifting cultivators and hunting and fishing. More recently, they have also undertaken menial and manual work on daily wages. In most respects their rituals are those of Hindus but widow marriage, called *nata**, is permitted but only to a widdower or divorcee. Polygamy is permitted amongst men but not women.

The small tribal community of ***Damors*** seems to have migrated N from their original home in Gujarat to settle in Dungarpur and Udaipur districts. They are mainly cultivators and manual labourers.

The tribals are slowly being absorbed into the mainstream of Indian life and losing their distinctive originality. Travelling through Rajasthan, it is possible that you will see one or some of these communities and may do so without realising it. There is an Institute of Tribal Research near Shastri Circle, Udaipur, Rajasthan and the W Zone Cultural Centre in Udaipur (see Udaipur entry) will have further details for those that are interested.

Economy
Rajasthan is one of the least densely populated states in India. It is also one of the poorest, with low per capita incomes and low levels of literacy, especially among women. It is primarily an agricultural and pastoral economy, though it does have good mineral resources and an expanding industry. Tourism makes a large contribution to the regional economy.

Agriculture The total sown area of Rajasthan is approximately 20 million hectares of which about 20% is irrigated. With a low and erratic rainfall and most of the farmed area rainfed, increasing irrigation is highly desirable. A variety of crops are grown: wheat, hardy *bajra* (millet) in the more arid areas; *jowar* (sorghum), maize and pulses (peas, beans and lentils) in most areas. Improved varieties (HYVs) of rice have been introduced but these are only suitable in areas of assured water availability.

Cotton is an important cash crop in the N and S of the state. Rajasthan receives water from the Punjab rivers in the N, the Narmada in the S and from the Gurgaon and Agra canals from Haryana and Uttar Pradesh respectively. It shares the **Bhakra Dam** project with Punjab, and the **Chambal Valley** project with Madhya Pradesh. It has been estimated that with improved management techniques nearly a third of the sown area could be brought under irrigation. The largest canal within the state is the **Rajasthan canal**, though this is far from complete and is working much less efficiently than had originally been planned. Many of the areas too dry for cultivation are none the less used for grazing. Rajasthan has a very large livestock population and is the largest wool producing state. It also breeds camels.

Mineral resources Rajasthan accounts for the country's entire output of zinc concentrates, emeralds and garnets. It also produces 94% of India's gypsum, 76% of silver ore, 84% of asbestos, 68% of feldspar and 12% of mica. It has rich salt deposits at Sambhar and other places and copper mines at Khetri and Dariba. The white marble favoured by the Mughal emperor Shah Jahan, e.g. the Taj Mahal, is mined at Makrana near Jodhpur.

Industries The main industries are based on textiles, the manufacture of rugs and woollen goods, vegetable oil and dyes. Heavy industry includes the construction of railway rolling stock, copper and zinc smelting. The chemical industry also produces caustic soda, calcium carbides and sulphuric acid, fertiliser, pesticides and insecticides. There is a rapidly expanding light industry which includes precision instrument manufacture at Kota and television assembly. The principal industrial complexes are at Jaipur, Kota, Udaipur and Bhilwara. Traditional handicrafts such as pottery, jewellery, marble work, embossed brass, block printing, embroidery and decorative painting are now very good foreign exchange earners.

History

Archaeological excavations have revealed that humans lived along the **Banas river** 100,000 years ago. **Harappan** and **post-Harappan** (3rd-2nd millenium BC) cultures have been discovered. Pottery at Kalibangan has been dated to 2700 BC while rock inscriptions near Bairat reveal that the emperor Asoka controlled this part of the state. The Mauryas were succeeded by the Bactrian Greeks (2nd century BC), the Sakas (Scythians, 2nd-4th centuries AD), the Guptas (4th-6th centuries) and the Huns (6th century). Rajput dynasties rose from the 7th to the 11th centuries and until the end of the 12th century, control of N India was concentrated in the their hands.

The Rajputs claimed to be the original Kshatriyas – warriors – of the ancient **varna*** system, born out of the fire offering of the Gods on Mount Abu. They were probably descended from the Huns and Scythians who had entered India in the 6th century, and they modelled themselves on Rama, the hero of the Ramayan epic, seeing themselves as protectors of the Hindu **dharma*** against invaders. The Brahmins made considerable efforts to give them royal lineages and accorded them **kshatriya** (warrior) status. They were provided with genealogies which connected them with either the solar or lunar race e.g. Udaipur.

Previous dynasties had ruled irrespective of their caste status and were accepted by the high castes simply because they were the rulers. The Rajputs, however, went to great lengths to insist on their *kshatriya** status, thereby seeking some religious sanction for their rule, a means of demonstrating to their subjects that not only was it foolhardy but also sacreligious to oppose their authority. Associated with this was promotion of those qualities or attributes ascribed to the martial castes, e.g. chivalry, bravery and unquestioning loyalty.

A self sufficient economy In the medieval period between 800 AD and 1200 AD villages were based on a self-sufficient economy. Any surplus wealth was spent on richly ornamented palaces and magnificent temples. It is no wonder that both caught the eye of avaricious invaders and suggested to them the great productive worth of the region as a whole. The king granted the revenue from varying proportions of land to his office holders. They in turn leased land to peasant cultivators who handed over a fixed share of their produce to the landowner. Part of the land revenues was sent to the king.

The relationship of the feudal landowner to the king was close but always subordinate. He was bound to express his loyalty in various ways, from being called upon to give his daughter in marriage to the king to using the currency of his feudal lord. Attendance at court on certain occasions, such as the king's birthday, was obligatory. In return he was permitted the use of a title and various symbols of dignity. He was expected to supply troops when required and to send them of his own accord when the king declared war. These obligations tended to strengthen the martial aspect of the system which lent itself admirably to the rise of the Rajput clan system.

The Mughals and the Rajputs Rather than engage in costly campaigns to crush the Rajputs, the Mughal emperor **Akbar** (r1556-1605) sought appeasement and conciliation by inviting them to assist in the running of his empire. Many Rajput princes were given high office and privileges in return for loyalty and Akbar sealed this important strategic alliance by marrying a Rajput princess, **Jodh Bai**, the daughter of the Maharaja of Amber.

Recent political developments Before Independence in 1947, the state comprised 18 princely states, two chiefships and the small province of Ajmer-Marwar which the British administered. After Independence the princely states were gradually absorbed into the Provinces and then states of the Indian Union. The state assumed its present name and form on November 1 1956.

The Princes of India have lost their independence, titles and traditional revenues since Independence. Their former states have been absorbed into the national political and administrative system but still the regions maintain their individuality and the people show a loyalty and respect that given the duration of rule that the noble houses had is not surprising. The palaces, many of them converted to hotels, with varying degrees of success it must be added, maintain the memory of princely India.

Party political strength The influence of some of Rajasthan's royal families on politics since Independence has been very strong. Rajasthan now sends 25 members of the Lok Sabha. In 1984 the **Congress** captured nearly 53% of the vote and won every seat, an almost complete reversal of the election result in 1977, after Mrs. Gandhi's emergency, when it won only 1 of the 25 seats, despite winning 31% of the popular vote. Its place then was taken by the Janata Party, in which the **Jana Sangh**, the forerunner of the **BJP**, played a prominent part.

In the 1989 elections there was a resurgence of support for the BJP across Rajasthan when it won 13 and the Janata Dal 11 of the seats to the Lok Sabha, the CPI(M) winning the last. Reports suggested that the key to the BJP's success was its campaigning on the issue of building a temple on the supposed site of Ram's birthplace at Ayodhya – the Ram Janmabhoomi issue. Evidence of the recent revival of *sati** in the state has caused widespread controversy.

Festivals Rajasthan celebrates a number of festivals of its own quite apart from the standard Hindu festivals. *Gangaur* in Mar-Apr about two weeks after Holi is a festival of fertility and concerns Gauri, another name for Siva's wife Parvati. She is the Goddess of abundance. There is a singing procession as wooden images of Gauri are taken from the temple to the nearest lake or tank for a ritual bath. Siva then arrives to collect his bride on an elephant or horse.

Teej is celebrated at the onset of the monsoon rains and is thus associated with fertility. Associated with this is a celebration of the reunion of Siva and Parvati.

At Jaipur, there is a big procession with gaily caparisoned elephants. In the villages, there is much singing and dancing, and the women wear green striped veils. Women and children play on swings decorated with flowers.

At the festival of **Urs** in **Ajmer**, hundreds of Muslim pilgrims congregate at the mosques. The kite flying festival in **Jaipur** in mid Jan is spectacular. At **Pushkar** there is the famous *cattle and camel fair* in Nov-December. At **Jodhpur** in Jul-Aug there is *Nag Panchami* in honour of the serpent king Naga and women visit the snake charmers for worship.

The **Desert Festival** at Jaisalmer in Jan-Feb is essentially a commercial phenomenon with no established tradition. There are camel races, camel polo and desert music and dance.

Handicrafts *Bandhani* This is the ancient technique of tye-dying and is common throughout Rajasthan and Gujarat. The fabric is pinched together in selected places and tied round with twine or thread. It is then dyed. Afterwards the cords are removed to reveal a pattern in the original or preceding colour (the process can be repeated a number of times on a single piece of fabric so long as the dyeing sequence goes from light to dark colours). The commonly used colours are yellow for fertility and Spring, blue or indigo for Lord Krishna, Pale blue for water, saffron for renunciation as associated with pilgrims and sages.

Lacquered Brassware This is a combination of engraving and lacquering of bowls, dishes, vases, trays and goblets. Many are highly coloured and richly engraved.

Leatherwork Decorated and embroidered camel skin slippers, water bottles, handbags and purses.

Pottery The best known in Rajasthan is the Jaipur blue pottery which uses a course grey clay that is quite brittle even when fired. This is then decorated with floral and geometric patterns along Persian lines utilising rich ultramarines, turquoise and lapis colours on a plain offwhite/grey background. Worth purchasing but a problem to carry. In the villages, the common pot is made from a combination of earth, water and dung. The pots are coarse thrown on a simple stone wheel, partially dried then finished with a hammer before simple decoration, glazing and firing. Stalls selling these attractive terracotta pots are common in the small towns and villages and whilst quite rough they are incredibly cheap. The tendency nowadays, of course, is for village folk to use vessels made of more durable materials, e.g. aluminium, brass and plastic.

Block-printing This is very popular in Gujarat, Rajasthan and S India. Hand-held wood blocks are carefully cut to enable patterns in different colours to be printed and up to five blocks enable very elaborated designs to be finished. The most sophisticated of the designs are very fine indeed and good examples can be seen in the City Museum in Jaipur. Much of the block making is done with great manual dexterity. Children are apprenticed to block makers and printers; they master the craft by the age of 14 or 15. The colours used are traditionally based on vegetable dyes but nowadays, although those running emporia will insist on the authenticity of the process, many now use chemical dyes. Printing on the great lengths of cotton is done in a long shed and after the block printing is complete, the fabric will be boiled to make the dye fast. There are places between Jaipur and Amber that demonstrate the technique and tour guides and drivers will show no reluctance to take you there. Just S of Jaipur, **Sanganer** is regarded as the capital of block-printing. Delightfully unspoilt, a trip there is worthwhile (see Excursions from Jaipur).

*Khari** is embossed printing using gold and silver. Skirt borders, blouses, sari ends and the like can be done, floral patterns being the most common. Other crafts that are practised in Rajasthan are dhurri weaving, screen printing, cotton weaving and paper making.

Tours It is certainly worth trying to get away from the cities and forts and experience something of rural Rajasthan. There are half-day and full day tours offered in many places but you should be wary of these. Whilst some are good, others are shabby attempts at exploitation. Also, if the journey follows a well travelled route, as some are, what you experience is likely to be less authentic than if you were to organise your own itinerary, preferably from one of the less frequented towns of Rajasthan. In many villages you will see not only the methods of cultivation and subsistence practised but also typical housing, often simply but beautifully decorated and, of course, traditional rural handicrafts.

The best known tour is the so-called **Palace on Wheels.** About ten years ago, the Rajasthan Tourist Development Corporation (RTDC), Government of India Tourist Office and Indian Railways initiated what has become a highly popular means of touring Rajasthan. It is the Palace on Wheels train comprising the 'Desert Queen' railway engine and refurbished carriages belonging to former Maharaja's of the Princely States of India. There are weekly departures (Wednesday) from Oct to Mar (inclusive) The itinerary includes Jaipur and Amber Fort, followed by night travel to Chittaurgarh, Udaipur (Lake Palace Hotel), Jaisalmer, Jodhpur (Umaid Bhawan Palace) and Bharatpur.

It ends with visits to Fatehpur Sikri, Agra and Delhi. Each saloon has its own sleeping accommodation in two/four berth cabins, plus a lounge, kitchenette and mini-bar, bathroom and telephone link with the train superintendent. There is also two dining cars serving continental and Indian cuisine and a library/lounge/observation car with bar. For those interested in seeing a great deal in a short space of time and travelling in an unusual style in a fair degree of comfort, the Palace on Wheels is undoubtedly exotic and interesting. It is also expensive. On the negative side, it is a whistle stop tour giving only a brief introduction to the places in Rajasthan. On Day 7 for example, you will visit three places – Bharatpur Bird Sanctuary, Fatehpur Sikri and Agra. A day in each of these places would allow much better viewing, two in the case of Agra. All your time is accounted and you are only able to pursue independent daytime activities if you are prepared to forego the tours. Travelling by night means that you don't see much of the countryside between the cities. Also, at this time of year, travelling is very dusty. To keep the dust out, you will have to travel with the windows closed and the fans on.

Accommodation in Rajasthan The most popular tourist places of Jaipur, Jodhpur and Udaipur are well provided with hotels. Other places such as Bikaner have a very narrow range. Chittaurgarh does not have even one suitable Tourist Class Hotel. Expect variations in the quality and type of accommodation.

Palace hotels Since Independence, the changed circumstances of the Indian Princes resulted in many former palaces being converted into hotels. These have been furnished and run with varying degrees of efficiency and skill, so it pays to be discriminating. You can expect good service and facilities in addition to the undoubted thrill of being in a former palace. But you can get a very good room with excellent views or you can get a room with little or no view and which seems ill-suited to its new function. Not all the palaces have lent themselves easily to conversion into hotels. The Rambagh Palace and the Lake Palace Hotels in Jaipur and Udaipur respectively are good cases in point. This can be a big disappointment and the variability in rooms can be irritating.

Whether in a group or travelling independently, you can always try and change your room, but in the high season this is likely to be a time-consuming and ultimately unrewarding exercise. It is best therefore, to try and visit these hotels at the very beginning or end of the high season or during the off-season. With the right choice and a little bit of luck you can have a really memorable experience.

JAIPUR

Population 1,250,532 (1981). *Altitude* 431 m. *Best season* The winter season from Nov to Mar is best as it is cooler. Apr-Jun is very hot whilst Jul-Sep is the monsoon.

	Jan	Feb	Mar	Apr	May	Jun	Jul	Aug	Sep	Oct	Nov	Dec	Av/Tot
Max (°C)	22	25	31	37	41	39	34	32	33	33	29	24	32
Min (°C)	8	11	15	21	26	27	26	24	23	18	12	9	18
Rain (mm)	14	8	9	4	10	54	193	239	90	19	3	4	647

Jaipur was built by Sawai Jai Singh II, the Maharaja (Great Ruler) of the Kachhwaha clan of Rajputs who ruled from 1699-1744. The ancient capital was **Amber** (see below) but in 1727 the foundations were laid for a new capital, to be called **Jaipur** (City of Victory). Today it has become the most popular tourist destination in Rajasthan and comprises one corner of what is known as The Golden Triangle (Delhi-Jaipur-Agra).

Jai Singh, had inherited a kingdom under threat not only from the Great Mughal Aurangzeb but also the Maratha armies of Gujarat and Maharashtra. Victories over the latter and diplomacy with the former won back the favour of the ageing Aurangzeb so that the political stability Maharaja Jai Singh was instrumental in creating, allowed him to pursue his scientific and cultural interests. Jaipur is very much a product of his intellect and talent.

The charming story of the encounter between the Emperor **Aurangzeb** and the 10 year old Rajput prince tells of the reply made by the youngster when asked what punishment he deserved for his family's hostility and resistance to the Mughals. The boy answered 'Your Majesty, when the groom takes the bride's hand, he confers lifelong protection. Now that the Emperor has taken my hand, what have I to fear?' Impressed by his tact and intelligence, Aurangzeb bestowed the title of *Sewai* (one and a quarter) on him, signifying that he would be a leader.

Astronomy and science Foremost among his academic interests was a love of mathematics and science. A brilliant Brahmin scholar, *Vidyadhar Bhattacharya* from Bengal, worked in association with him to design the city. Jai Singh also studied ancient texts on astronomy, had the works of Ptolemy and Euclid translated into Sanskrit and sent emissaries to **Samarkand** where **Mirza Beg**, the grandson of Timur the Lame had built himself an observatory in 1425. When his throne was secure, i.e. from about 1720 onwards, he spent much of his time studying astronomy and this culminated in the construction of masonry observatories at Delhi, Varanasi, Ujjain and Mathura. The most impressive of these is the Jantar Mantar at Jaipur (see below).

A declining glory? Jaipur is a highly distinctive city and is easily visited by those with little time to spend in India. Built with ancient Hindu rules of town planning in mind, in a grid pattern with wide avenues and divided into nine areas, it was advanced for its time. Coming towards the end of the period of Rajput power many of its original buildings suggest a decline in architectural power and originality. Tillotson suggests that even in the earliest of them "the traditional architectural details lack vigour and depth; they are flattened so that they become relief sculpture on the building's surface, and sometimes they are simply drawn on in white outline. The 'pink', a traditional colour of welcome, was added in 1853 in honour of the visit by Prince Albert, and the tradition has survived to this

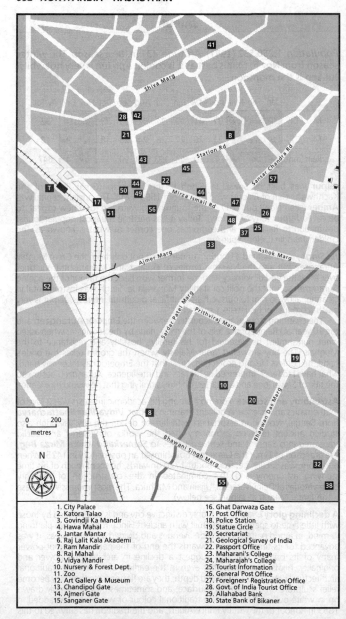

1. City Palace
2. Katora Talao
3. Govindji Ka Mandir
4. Hawa Mahal
5. Jantar Mantar
6. Raj Lalit Kala Akademi
7. Ram Mandir
8. Raj Mahal
9. Vidya Mandir
10. Nursery & Forest Dept.
11. Zoo
12. Art Gallery & Museum
13. Chandipol Gate
14. Ajmeri Gate
15. Sanganer Gate
16. Ghat Darwaza Gate
17. Post Office
18. Police Station
19. Statue Circle
20. Secretariat
21. Geological Survey of India
22. Passport Office
23. Maharani's College
24. Maharajah's College
25. Tourist Information
26. General Post Office
27. Foreigners' Registration Office
28. Govt. of India Tourist Office
29. Allahabad Bank
30. State Bank of Bikaner

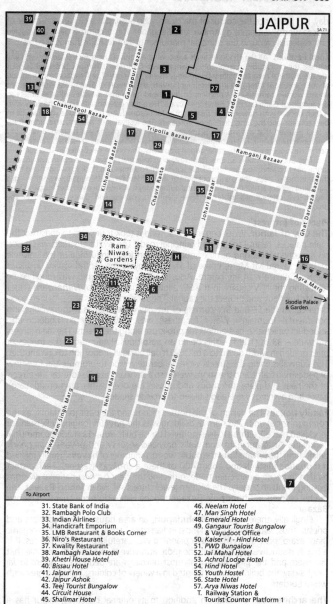

JAIPUR SA 71

Gangapuri Bazaar
Chandrapol Bazaar
Tripolia Bazaar
Siredeori Bazaar
Ramganj Bazaar
Kishanpol Bazaar
Chaura Rasta
Johari Bazaar
Ghat Darwaza Bazaar
Ram Niwas Gardens
Agra Marg
Sisodia Palace & Garden
Sawai Ram Singh Marg
J. Nehru Marg
Moti Dungri Rd
To Airport

31. State Bank of India
32. Rambagh Polo Club
33. Indian Airlines
34. Handicraft Emporium
35. LMB Restaurant & Books Corner
36. Niro's Restaurant
37. Kwality Restaurant
38. Rambagh Palace Hotel
39. Khetri House Hotel
40. Bissau Hotel
41. Jaipur Inn
42. Jaipur Ashok
43. Teej Tourist Bungalow
44. Circuit House
45. Shalimar Hotel
46. Neelam Hotel
47. Man Singh Hotel
48. Emerald Hotel
49. Gangaur Tourist Bungalow & Vayudoot Office
50. Kaiser - I - Hind Hotel
51. PWD Bungalow
52. Jai Mahal Hotel
53. Achrol Lodge Hotel
54. Hind Hotel
55. Youth Hostel
56. State Hotel
57. Arya Niwas Hotel
T. Railway Station & Tourist Counter Platform 1

day. It is paint, not the colour of the stone. Also around the city are a number of places worth visiting, e.g. Amber and Sanganer. It is a commercially aggressive city, especially around the principal monuments. Not all Rajasthan is like this.

Local Festivals All the Hindu festivals are celebrated plus: During *Holi* (Mar/Apr) you will witness the procession of elephants in fancy dress. *Gangaur* (Mar/Apr). Ishar and Gagaur are the mythical man and wife who embody marital harmony. The Gangaur festival is held about a fortnight after Holi in honour of **Parvati**, the consort of **Siva**. Colourfully dressed young women carrying brass pitchers on their head make their way through the streets to the temple of Gauri (another name for Parvati). Here they ceremonially bathe the deity who is then decked with flowers. The women pray for husbands 'such as the one you have been blessed with' and the long life of their husbands. The festival ends with much rejoicing for it is also believed that if a women is unhappy while she sings she will be landed with and ill-tempered husband. The festivities are concluded when Siva arrives to escort his bride Gauri home. He is accompanied by caparisoned elephants. This is also celebrated in Udaipur.

Teej (Jul/Aug). This is an important festival in Rajasthan to welcome the monsoon rains to the parched land. The womenfolk dress in bright costumes and flock to swings hung from the branches of trees. There is a procession of the goddess Parvati through towns and villages signifying her departure from the parental home to take up residence with her husband Siva. The special celebrations in Jaipur have elephants, camels and dancers joining in the processions.

Places of Interest
The City of Jaipur Work began in 1727 and it took four years to construct the main palaces, central square and principal roads. The layout of streets was based on a mathematical grid of nine squares, the ancient Hindu map of the universe with the sacred Mt Meru, home of Siva, occupying the central square. In Jaipur the royal palace is at the centre. Also, the 3 by 3 square grid was modified by relocating the NW square in the SE, allowing the hill fort of **Nahargarh** (Tiger Fort) to overlook and protect the capital. The surrounding hills also provided good defence. At the SE and SW corners of the city were squares with pavilions and ornamental fountains. Water for these was provided by an underground aqueduct which also had outlets for public use along the streets. The main streets are wide – 33 m (108 ft – this being an auspicious Hindu number) – the lesser ones graded in width down to 4 m (13.5 ft), all being in proportion to one another. The sidewalks lining the streets were deliberately wide to promote the free flow of pedestrian traffic and the shops were also a standard size. To counter the effects of the heat and glare, the shops and houses are deep rather than broad. Large eaves and awnings were also utilised to provide shade.

Family houses The design of the houses recognised the basic joint family as the common social unit. The normal building was the *haveli** (originally Persian for 'enclosed space'), a three to five-storeyed house built around a shaded communal courtyard. An outer gate and walls provided security and privacy thus clearly delineating the private from the public world. A number of **havelis** usually formed a *mohalla** (district) and about 400 of these a *chokra** (section). Each district tended to house a particular trade, reflecting the clear cut occupational divisions existing in Indian society. The Muslim jewel cutters still live in **Johori Bazaar**, the marble workers in **Chandpole Bazaar** and the Hindu cloth merchants in **Nehru Bazaar**.

Originally, there was also **Brahmapuri**, an area housing royal scholars and priests. Thus, Jaipur differs from most Indian cities, which were subject to organic (haphazard) growth, in that town planning was carefully practiced. The result is a highly distinctive city, made all the more attractive by the colourful people that live there and the pink wash that most buildings are periodically given. In Jai Singh's day, the buildings were painted in a variety of colours, including grey with white borders.

The architectural revival In addition to its original buildings, Jaipur has a number of examples of late 19th century public and private buildings which marked an attempt to revive Indian architectural skills. One of the key figures in this movement was *Sir Samuel Swinton Jacob*, a soldier with long family connections in India who transferred from the army to the Public Works Department in 1862. In 1867 he became Executive Engineer to the **Maharaja of Jaipur**, living there until 1902. The founding of a school of art in 1866 was one sign of the determination of a group of English officers employed by **Maharaja Sawai Madho Singh II** (r1880-1922) to encourage an interest in Indian tradition and its development.

A number of crafts were revived, a process fostered by the 1883 **Jaipur exhibition**. A museum was opened in 1881 in preparation for the exhibition and soon had more than 250,000 visitors a year. In February 1876 the Prince of Wales visited Jaipur, and work on the *Albert Hall* was begun to a design of Jacob. It was the first of a number in which Indian craftsmen and designers were actively employed, contributing not just to the building but also to the design. This ensured that the **Albert Hall** was not simply an Indo-Saracenic building of the type becoming popular elsewhere in India, though Jacob's contemporary De Fabek did build the Indo-Saracenic style *Mayo Hospital* in the city. However, the new opportunities for training provided under Jacob's auspices encouraged a new school of Indian architects and builders. One of the best examples of their work is the *Mubarak Mahal* (1900), designed by Lala Chiman Lal, director of the State Department responsible for palace buildings. These buildings repay a visit.

Jantar Mantar **(Observatory)**   Literally 'Instruments for measuring the harmony of the heavens, the Jantar Mantar was built between 1728 and 1734. Not content with brass, Jai Singh wanted things on a grand scale and chose stone with a marble facing on the important planes. Each of the instruments serves a particular function and each gives an accurate reading. The observatory is a fascinating and attractive site to walk round, but it gets extremely hot in the middle of the day.

In a clockwise fashion they are:

1   Small Samrat Yantra   This is a large sundial (the triangular structure) with flanking quadrants marked off in hours and minutes. The arc on your left will show the time from sunrise to midday, the one on the right midday to sundown. Read the time where the shadow is sharpest. The sundials are constructed on Lat. 27 degrees N (Jaipur's Lat.) and give solar time. To adjust the reading to Indian Standard Time (IST), between 1 min 15 secs to 32 mins must be added according to the time of year and solar position. There is a board indicating the right adjustment.

2   Dhruva Yantra   locates the position of the Pole Star at night and those of the twelve zodiac signs. The graduation and lettering is in Hindi and is based on a different system to that employed nowadays. The traditional unit of measurement is the human breath calculated to be of 6 seconds duration. Thus: 4 breaths = 1 pala (24 secs), 60 palas = 1 gati (24 mins), 60 gatis = 1 day (24).

3   Narivalya Yantra   sundial with two dials: S facing for when the sun is in the S hemisphere (Sept 21 – Mar 21) and the N facing for the rest of the year. At noon the sun falls on the North-S line. The time is read in the normal way.

4   Observer's Seat   (Jai Singh's).

5   Small Kranti Yantra, used for the direct measurement of of the longitude and latitude of the celestial bodies.

6   Raj Yantra (King of Instruments). Used once a year to calculate the Hindu calendar, all the details of which are based on the Jaipur Standard as they have been for 250 years. A telescope is attached over the central hole. The back of the Yantra is fitted with a bar for sighting purposes. The plain disk is used as a blackboard to record observations.

7   Unnathamsa Yantra   is used for finding the altitudes of the celestial bodies. Round the clock observations can be made and the sunken steps allow any part of the dial to be read.

8   Disha Yantra points to the North.

9   Dakshina Yantra, a wall aligned along the N-S meridian and used for observing the position and movement of heavenly bodies when passing over the meridian.

10   Large Samrat Yantra.   Operating on the same principle as the Small one (1) but ten times larger and thus accurate to 2 secs. instead of 20 secs. The sundial is 27.4 m high and the observer climbs the steps to make the reading. This instrument is used on guru purnima, a particularly holy full moon in Jul/Aug, to predict the length and heaviness of the monsoon for the local area.

11 Rashivalayas Yantra. Twelve sundials for the signs of the zodiac and operated in the same way as the Samrat Yantras. The instruments enable readings to be made at the instant each zodiacal sign crosses the meridian. Hindus embrace the universe and believe that their fated souls move to its rhythms. The matching of horoscopes is still an essential part in the marriage arrangements and the selection of partners. Astrologers occupy an important place in day to day life and are consulted for all occasions and decision-making.

12 Small Ram Yantra. A smaller version and a similar purpose.

13 Jai Prakash Yantra. This acts as a double check on all the other instruments. It measures the rotation of the sun and the two hemispheres together form a map of the heavens. The small iron plate strung between crosswires indicates the sun's longitude and latitude and which sign of the zodiac it is passing through.

14 Chakra Yantra. This gives the angle of an object from the equator.

15 Large Ram Yantra. As with the Small Ram Yantra (12), this is used to find the altitude and the azimuth (arc of the celestial great circle from Zenith to horizon).

16 Diganta Yantra. Another instrument for measuring the azimuth of any celestial body. **17 Large Kranti Yantra**. The same as the Small Kranti Yantra (5).

The City Palace (1728-1732) The city palace occupies the centre of Jaipur, covers one seventh of its area and is surrounded by a high wall. Entering through the main gate you find yourself in a large courtyard with a building in the centre. This was the Guest Pavilion and has a very attractive white marble frontage. On the first floor is the **Textile and Costume Museum**. When Jai Singh moved his court from Amber to the new palace, four out of the 36 imperial departments were devoted to costumes and textiles. In this collection there are fine examples of fabrics and costumes from all over India as well as musical instruments and toys from the royal nursery.

In the NW corner of the courtyard is the **Arms and Armour Museum** containing an impressive array of weaponry – pistols, blunderbusses, flintlocks, swords, rifles and daggers. This was originally the common room of the harem. Moving now to the gate to your right after leaving the museum you come to the gates to the inner courtyard. The gate itself is flanked by two elephants each carved from a single block of marble. Behind these are beautifully carved alcoves with delicate arches and jali screens. There is a fine pair of patterned brass doors.

Hall of Private Audience   Once through this fine gateway, directly opposite you and in the centre of the courtyard is the large **Hall of Private Audience** (c.1730). In it are two huge urns. **Sawai Madhu Singh**, the present Maharaja's grandfather was an extremely devout Hindu. There is a picture of him through the Krishna door (see Map). Any physical contact with a non-Hindu was deemed to be ritually defiling, so any contact with the British carried awkward and unwanted ritual problems. Whenever required to meet a Britisher, including the Viceroy, the Maharaja would wear white gloves, and after any meeting would ritually purify himself in a bath of Ganga water and have the clothes he wore burnt. When he went to England to celebrate Queen Victoria's Diamond Jubilee he had a P and O liner refitted to include a Krishna temple and carried sufficient Ganga water with him, in these two 309 kg silver urns, to last the trip.

Art Gallery and Museum   Entrance in the right hand corner of the inner courtyard. This was the Hall of Public Audience (c.1760). Today it houses a picture gallery with a fine collection of Persian and Indian miniatures, some of the carpets the Maharajas had made for them and an equally fine collection of manuscripts. Moving now across the courtyard to the opposite side, you enter through the **Ganesh Pol** to the **zenana** and the seven storey palace of the Maharaja. In this courtyard are some extremely attractive doors, rich and vivid in their peacock blue, aquamarine, amber and other colours. Each doorway has a small marble figure of a Hindu god watching over it.

The Chandra Mahal   In the NE corner of the courtyard is the Krishna door. This is so named because its surface is embossed with scenes of the God's life. The door is sealed in the traditional way with a rope sealed with wax over the lock. Near this and along the corridor is the portrait of Sawai Madhu Singh mentioned above. Along the NE side of the zenana courtyard is the **Chandra Mahal** (c.1724-34) with its **Chamber of the Privy Council** where the Maharaja would sit in consultation with his ministers.

The furniture is European – Bohemian glass chandeliers, furniture, the decoration Indian – scenes from the Kalidasa. Following the steps around you will see a *mandala** (circular diagram of the cosmos), made from rifles around the royal crest of Jaipur. The ceiling of this hall is in fine goldwork. Further on you reach the beautiful Mughal style fountains and the Jai Niwas gardens (1727), done in the char-bagh manner. The view extends across to the Maharaja's private Krishna temple and beyond the compound walls to the Nahargarh (Tiger Fort) on the hills beyond.

The *Hawa Mahal* Forming part of the eastern wall of the palace complex and seen to advantage only from the street outside the palace is the **Hawa Mahal** (Palace of the Winds, c.1799). This, the most famous building in Jaipur, is a pink sandstone facade rather than a building proper. It was built for the ladies of the harem by **Sawai Pratap Singh** and is a five storey frontage standing on a high podium with an entrance from the W. It contains 953 small casements in a huge curve, each with a balcony and crowning arch. The windows enabled cool air (hence the name) to circulate and the ladies to watch processions below without being seen. Tours to Amber often stop first at the Hawa Mahal.

The *Mubarak Mahal*, originally a guest house for the Maharaja and now part of the Palace Museum, is a small two-storied building on the southern side of the palace, immediately opposite the Jantar Mantar. It is designed on the same cosmological plan in miniature as the city itself – a square divided into nine by three square grid. Tillotson suggests that the "greater beauty of the design derives from the delicacy and depth of the facades...achieved by a number of devices: by the variation in the basic plan, with a verandah projecting in the centre of each side; by the cantilevered balconies, which project yet further; by the roof parapet, which rises above those balconies but is separated from them by a deep recession; by the pierced balustrade and the open arcade of the upper gallery. The open space above each arch in the gallery, an arrangement copied from traditional courtyard houses in the city," he goes on "make the building's roof appear to float weightlessly above it. The lightness and the depth are typically Rajput features."

Nahargarh (Tiger Fort, 1734) stands on a sheer rockface nearly 7 km from the city centre. It can be reached on a jeepable road from Amber. Auto rickshaws also make the journey. To reach the top you have to walk 1.5 km up a winding path. There is a small entry fee and restaurant. There are excellent views.

Hotels A *Rambagh Palace*, Bhawani Singh Rd (Taj group), T 75141-5, Cable: Rambagh, Telex: 0365-2254. 105 rm. 12 km airport, 4 km rly, 3 km centre. Maharaja Ram Singh's (1835-80) hunting lodge. Extensively modified by Madhi Singh II (1880-1922). Some excellent rm (royal suites), others can be cramped. Rms in main palace overlooking garden are best but not in the new wing. You may be able to choose if you can arrive early. The food is good and reasonably priced for the category. Superb gardens. Not so good when there is a large tour group staying. Good shops. Pool open to non-residents. **A** *Jaimahal Palace,* Jacob Rd, Civil Lines, (Taj group), T 73215-6, Cable: Jaimahal, Telex: 0365-2250. 102rm. 11 km airport, 1 km rly, 2 km centre. Tennis, horse riding, jogging track. Imaginative hotel development around small palace. Some high quality rooms, good restaurants and excellent service. Recommended. The gardens are especially lovely. Refurbishment on 1st floor (Spring 1991). Snack bar inadequate. No pool.

A *Mansingh*, Sansar Chandra Rd. T 78771, Cable: Welcomtel, Telex: 0365-2344 Wico In. 100 rm. 13 km airport, 3 km rly, 1 km centre. Open-air theatre, good puppet show. Modern. Excellent location for shopping, no garden or pool. **A** *Rajmahal Palace,* Jamnalal

Bajaj Marg, Civil Lines, T 61257, Cable: Residency, Telex: 0365-313. 11 rm. A/c. Once the British Residency. Limited facilities include restaurant, bar, 24 hr room service, exchange. **A Clarks Amer**, Jawaharal Nehru Marg, T 882616, Cable: Clarksamer, Telex: 0365-276. 118 rm. 5 km airport, 12 km rly, 8 km centre. All amenities, less 'exotic' since it didn't start out as a palace. Tall building in the middle of the desert, with friendly service, good shopping arcade, garden and pool, food occasionally inspired ('Tourist menu' boring), but rm a/c erratic and out of town. A favourite with tour groups.

B **Jaipur Ashok**, (ITDC), Collectorate Circle, Bani Park, T 75171, Cable: Ashoketel, Telex: 0365-2262. 63 rm. Modern, comfortable but unimaginative. **C Khasa Kothi**, M.I. Rd. T 75151-5, Cable: Khasa Kothi, Telex: 0365-431. 36 rm. 12 km airport, 1 km rly, 2 km centre. Restaurant (Indian and Continental), bar, tourist office, post office, exchange, Amex, Diners credit cards, pool, cultural shows on demand. Government run with rm in need of attention but attractive verandahs overlooking the beautiful lawns. **C Meru Palace**, Sawai Ram Singh Rd. T 61262-5, Cable: Hotelmeru, Telex: 0365-259. 48 rm. 8 km airport, 5 km rly, 1 km centre. Restaurant (Veg), coffee shop, bar, doctor on call, car hire shops, exchange, credit cards. New, not a palace but pleasant. **C Neelam**, Motilal Atal Rd. T 7773-4. 52 rm, some a/c with TV. Restaurant (Veg), 24 hr rm service, car hire, shops. Decor may not be to your liking!

Some interesting cheaper places to stay. **D Achrol Lodge**, Civil Lines, T 72254. 7 rm, non a/c. Breakfast and Indian evening meals, limited hr rm service, exchange. Camping facilities with toilet and power connections in large lawns in peaceful setting. **D Arya Niwas**, Sansar Chandra Rd, behind Amber Cinema. T 65524, Telex: 0365-2423. 30 rm, non a/c. 14 km airport, 2 km rly, close to bus stand. Restaurant (Veg), rm service, exchange, travel, credit cards. Part of hotel was an old palace but now modern. Clean, friendly and helpful management and very good vegetarian food. Recommended. **D Bissau Palace**, Chandpole Gate. T 74191, Cable: Hobi. 32 rm (most a/c). 15 km airport, 2 km rly, l km centre. Restaurant (Indian and Continental), rm service, pool, lawn tennis, shops, library and royal museum, credit cards. Once home of the Rawal (ruler) of Bissau. Bedrooms clean but a little rundown. Public rooms pleasant. Attractive views of Amber Fort.

D Narain Niwas, Kanota Bagh, Narain Singh Rd. T 65448, Cable: Narainniwas, telex: 1365-2482. 22 air-cooled rm. 11 km airport, 4 km rly, 2 km centre. Restaurant (Indian veg), pool, safe deposit, laundry, doctor on call, car hire, credit cards. The palace of Narain Singh, chieftain of Kanota. Many 19th century regal trappings – huge rooms, big fireplaces, Rajasthani portraits. **D Gangaur Tourist Bungalow**, (RTDC), M.I. Rd. T 60231-8. 63 rm, some a/c. Restaurant, 24 hr coffee shop, tours, car hire, travel. Convenient for bus and rly. **D Goyal**, Vanasthali Marg. T 61709, Cable: Hotelgoyal. Restaurant, TV and Video, 24 hr room service. **D Jaipur Emerald**, M.I. Rd, T 70476, Cable: Luxury. 14rm, a/c and non a/c. 13 km airport, 1 km rly. Restaurant, 24 hr rm service, exchange, travel. **D Kohinoor**, Vanasthali Marg. T 64687. Some a/c rm. Restaurant, TV and Video.

D L.M.B., Johari Bazar in Old City. T 48844, Cable: Alambe. 33 rm, a/c. 10 km airport, 6 km rly. Restaurant (Veg), TV, car hire, travel, exchange, Amex credit cards. Monkeys may be a nuisance! Excellent food. **D Lakshmi Vilas**, Sawai Ram Singh Rd. T 61368-9, Cable: Lakshmi. 21 rm, some a/c. Restaurant (Indian veg), 24 hr room service, car hire and travel, TV. **D Mangal**, Sansar Chandra Rd, T 75126. 65 rm, some a/c. 12 km aiport, 1 km rly. Restaurant (Veg), beauty parlour, bar, health club, doctor on call, travel, credit cards. Roof terrace with nightly barbecue. **D Megh Miwas**, C-9 Jai Singh Highway, Bani Park. T 74018, Telex: 0365-2110. 10 rm, some a/c. Meals on order, exchange, travel. **D Hotel Natraj**, Motilal Atal Rd, nr Polo Victory. T 61348, Cable: Hotnat. 18 rm, some a/c. Rm service, travel. **D Teej Tourist Bungalow**, Collectorate Rd. T 74206. 45 rm, some a/c. Restaurant, bar, tours and travel. Convenient for bus and rly.

E Broadway, Agra Rd. T 41765, Cable: Broadway. 22 rm, a/c and non a/c. 12 km airport, 6 km rly, 2 km centre. TV, restaurant (Indian, Continental), coffee shop, 24 hr rm service, safe deposit, laundry. **E Jaipur Inn**, Bani Park. T 66057. Non a/c without bath. Limited dining, camping facilities. **E Khetri House**, outside Chandpole Gate. T 69183. 13 rm, non a/c. 10 km airport, 1 km rly. Restaurant (Indian, Continental). **E Purohit**, 16 Vanathali Marg. T 61974. 27 non a/c rm, TV and refrigerator in some. Dining hall (Indian veg), restricted hr room service. **E Rajdeep**, Farsoia Market, Bapu Bazar. T 49141-2. 37 rm, non a/c. Restaurant (Indian, Continental).

E Swagatam Tourist Bungalow (RTDC), Station Rd. T 68938. 38 rm, a/c and non a/c. Restaurant, tours. **E Tourist Hostel** (RTDC), M.I. Rd. T 69013. Non a/c rm with bath. Restaurant, tours. Across from the GPO and down a little alley is a group of small, but basic and very cheap hotels **F** category hotels: **Ever Green Guest House** and **Ever Happy Guest House** are regarded as the best. Around the corner from the Teej Tourist Bungalow is the **Assam**. Near the rly station are the *Rajdhani* and *Chandralok*. Also *Rly Retiring Rooms*. The *Youth Hostel*, T 67576, is some way out of town. Discounts for YHA members.

Restaurants Mughlai food is best in the top hotels – *Shivir*, Mansingh's rooftop restaurant, T 788771 (lunchtime buffet) is highly recommended. Others are at the *Jai Mahal* and the Rambagh Palace's *Suvarna Maha*. You can get traditional Rajasthani food at *Chandralok* on M.I. Rd. Continental and Indian cuisine: *Aravali*, Hotel Ashok, T 75121 and *Kwality*, T 72275 and *Niros*, T 74493 both on M.I. Rd. Niros (which also serves Chinese dishes) is particularly recommended for good food in pleasant surroundings. *Golden Dragon* on M.I. Rd is a Chinese restaurant.

Veg. Indian: *Chanakya and LMB* are highly recommended. *Chanakya*, MI Rd, T 78461; *LMB*, Johari Bazar, T 48844 also has good ice creams and Indian sweets; *Natraj*, M.I. Rd, 75804; *Upwan*, Hotel Meru Palace, T 61212; *Rituraj*, Hotel Mangel, Sansar Chandra Rd, T 75126. For Fast food and confectionery: *Atithi*, M.I. Rd. *Deluxe*, Vegetarian food and confectioners. *Surya Mahal*, MI Rd and *Gauri* at Gangaur Tourist Bungalow nr All India Radio serve good coffee and snacks.

Banks *Bank of India*, T 75781, *Bank of Rajashtan*, T 76472 and *State Bank of India*, T 72912 all on MI Rd. Open 1000-1400, 1430-1630.

Shopping The traditional Bazaars are well worth a visit. *Bapu Bazaar* (closed Mon) specializes in printed cloth, *Johari* (Goldsmiths) *Bazaar* for jewellery and *Khajane Walon ka Rasta* for marble and stone ware. Try *Maniharon ka Rasta* for lac bangles which the city is famous for, *Tripolia Bazaar* at the three gates for inexpensive jewellery and *Nehru and Bapu Bazaars* for textiles. Jaipur is also famous for its jewellery, *Kundun* using uncut gemstones to set in gold and *meenakari* enamelling which often complements the setting on the reverse side of the pendant, locket or earring. You may be able to see the craftsmen at work, especially in *Gopalji ki Rasta* and *Haldiyon ka Rasta*. Similar work on silver and semi-precious stones, is more affordable.

You may also watch *Durrie* weavers at *Art Age*, Plot 2, Bhawani Singh Rd, T 75726. Jaipur also specializes in embroidered leather footwear and blue pottery'. *Handicrafts, Jewellery, Carpets and Durries*: *Rajasthali*, Rajasthan Govt. Handicrafts, M.I. Rd, Ajmeri Gate, T 67176. *Handloom House*, Rituraj Bldg., M.I. Rd, T 78214. *Amrapali Silver Shop*, Chameliwala Market, opp G.P.O., M.I. Rd, T 77140. *Art Age*, Plot 2, Bhawani Singh Rd, T 75726. *Arun's Emporium*, Silverware, M.I. Rd, T 74033. *Silver and Art Palace*, T 43980 and *Manglam Arts*, both on Amber Rd. *Jewellery* – In Johari Bazar, *Bhuramal Rajmal Surana*, Haldiyo ka Rasta, T 42628 and on MI Rd, Gem Palace and Lall Gems and Jewels. Also try *Gopalji ki Rasta* in Johari Bazaar. *Ambika Exports*, Naila House, M.D. Rd, T49821. *Art India*, B-180, Mangal Marg, T 61111 and *Neeta Enterprise*, B-50 Ganesh Marg, T 68240 both in Bapu Nagar. *Anokhi*, 2 Tilak Marg, opp. Udyog Bhawan, T 67619 is recommended.

Handloom Haveli, Lalpura House, Sansar Chandra Rd (various handloom emporia under one roof). *The Reject Shop*, Bhawani Singh Rd, for Shyam Ahuja collections. *Kripal Kumbha*, B-18, Shiv Marg, Bani Park, T 62227, for the world famous exclusive blue pottery. Good bookshops – *Arvind*, *Best Books*, *Usha* are Wof Chaura Rasta.

Photography *Tak Studio*, Chaura Rasta, T 73546. *Pictorials*, M.I. Rd, T 73834.

Local Transport City Buses in and around Jaipur, fares low. Tourist taxis available, but no yellow top taxis. Other transport includes three-wheelers, cycle rickshaws (which are not always well-maintained), tongas and mini buses. Coach and Car Hire *ITDC*, Hotel Khasa Kothi, T 65451. *RTDC*, Gangaur Tourist Bungalow, T60231-8. *Rajasthan Tours*, Hotel Rambagh Palace, T 76041. *Travel House*, Hotel Mansingh, T 78771.

Entertainment *Ravindra Rang Manch*, Ram Niwas Garden, T 47061, sometimes hosts cultural programmes and music shows.

Sports Most hotels will arrange golf, tennis, riding and squash. **Polo** enjoys a special place in the city's life: Spring (Mar) is the polo season when five polo tournaments are held – Sawai Madhosingh Gold Vase, Kots Cup, Sirnur Cup, Mysore Cup and Argentina Cup. Matches are organised at Polo Ground nr Rambagh Palace. Just before the *Holi* festival in the spring, you may even witness elephant polo!

Museums Hawa Mahal Museum, closed Friday. Entry Re 0.50, free on Mon. **City Palace Museum**, Entry Rs 6. **Central Museum** (Albert Hall), Ram Nivas Gardens. Closed on Fri. Entry Re 1, free on Mon. Mainly excellent miniature portraits and other art pieces. Also Rajasthani village life displayed through costumes, pottery, woodwork, brassware etc. Gallery of Modern Art nearby. **Dolls Museum**. Small entry fee.

Parks and Zoos *Zoological Garden*, situated in the Ram Niwas Gardens. Entry Re 1. Crocodile breeding farm attracts many.

Useful Numbers Police: T 100 Fire: T 101 Ambulance: T 102

Hospitals and Medical Services S.M.S. Hospital, S.M.S. Highway, T 72222. Santokba Durlabhji, T 68251. Jay Kay Lon Mother and Child Health Institute, Jawaharlal Nehru Marg, T 49827-28-30-33.

Post and Telegraph G.P.O., M.I. Rd, T 63707. Central Telegraph Office, M.I. Rd, T 67001. Rly Mail Service, Jaipur Rly Station, T 69561.

Places of Worship Govind Devji's Temple, temple of Radha-Krishna.

Travel Agents and Tour Operators *Sita World Travel*, Station Rd, T 68226. *Travel House*, Mansingh Hotel, T 78771. *Service*, M.I. Rd, T 61062. *Rajasthan Tours*, Rambagh Palace, T 76041. *Mayur Travels*, M.I. Rd, T 64058-59. *Rajasthan Travel Service*, Jalupura, T 65408. *Aravali Safari and Tours*, Civil Lines, T 72735.

Tourist Offices and Information Rajasthan Tourism Development Corporation, Tourist Office, Rly Station, T 69714. Ashok Travels and Tours (ITDC), Hotel Khasa Kothi, T 65451.

Tours Operated by Rajasthan Tourism Development Corporation. City Sightseeing, half day (0800-1300, 1130-1630, 1330-1830), Rs 20; Central Museum, City Palace, Amber Fort and Palace, Gaitore, Nawab ki Haveli, Jantar Mantar, Jal Mahal, Hawa Mahal. City Sightseeing, full day (0900-1800), Rs 40; places above plus Nahargarh Fort, Indology Museum, Dolls Museum, Galta, Sisodia Rani Garden. Jaigarh Tour (1430-1900), Rs 25; Gaitore, Jigarh, Nahargarh, Jal Mahal. Operated by Ashok Travels and Tours. City Sightseeing, half day (0800-1300, 1330-180), Rs20; Nawab ki Haveli, Amber Fort and Palace, Hawa Mahal, City Palace, Jantar Mantar, Jal Mahal, Gaitore, Central Museum.

Air Indian Airlines flies daily from Delhi to Jaipur and on via Jodhpur, Udaipur and Aurangabad to Bombay, returning similarly; 5 a week from Delhi to Jaipur and on via Jodhpur and Ahmadabad to Bombay, returning similarly; and 4 a week between Agra and Bombay via Jaipur. Vayudoot flies to/from Jaipur from/to Delhi, Jodhpur, Jaisalmer, Bikaner, Kota, Indore and Bhopal. Reservations: *Indian Airlines*, Mundhra Bhawan, M.I. Rd, T 74500; Airport, T 822222. *Vayudoot* handling agents, Mayur Travels, 10 Park St, off M.I. Rd, T 61269; Airport, T 822603; open 0930-1730.

Rail Old Delhi: *Pink City Exp*, 2902, daily, 1700, 5 hr 15 min; *Delhi Mail*, 9902, daily, 0030, 6 hr 55 min; *Chetak Exp*, 9616, daily, 0645, 7 hr 30 min; *Ashram Exp*, 2906, daily, 0435, 5 hr 35 min. **Agra Fort**: *Agra Fort Fast Passenger Exp*, 9706, daily, 0100, 6 hr 35 min; *Barmer-Agra Exp*, 9708, daily, 0730, 12 hr; *Jaipur-Agra Fort Exp*, 2922, daily, 0610, 4 hr 50 min. **Ahmadabad**: *Agra Fort Fast Passenger Exp*, 9705, daily, 0315, 25 hr; *Ashram Exp*, 2905, daily, 2345, 11 hr 30 min; *Ahmadabad Exp*, 9903, daily, 1750, 16 hr 10 min; *Ahmadabad Mail*, 9901, daily, 0500, 15 hr 15 min. **Bharatpur**: *Marudgar Exp*, 5314, daily, 1355, 4 hr; *Agra Fort Fast Passenger Exp*, 9706, daily, 0100, 4 hr 28 min; *Jaipur-Agra Fort Exp*, 2922, daily, 0610, 3 hr 16 min. **Bikaner**: *Bikaner Exp*, 4737, daily, 2105, 10 hr 5 min.

Indore: *Meenakshi Exp*, 7569, daily, 1350, 15 hr. **Chittaurgarh**: *Meenakshi Exp*, 7569, daily except Sun, 1350, 7 hr 35 min; *Garib Nawaz Exp*, 2915, daily, 1125, 6 hr 30 min; *Chetak Exp*, 9615, daily, 2055, 8 hr 10 min. **Mt. Abu** *Ahmadabad Exp*, 9903, daily, 1750, 11 hr; *Ahmadabad Mail*, 9901, daily, 0500, 10 hr 10 min. **Jodhpur**: *Mandore Exp*, 2461, daily, 2345, 6 hr; *Agra-Barmar Exp*, 9707, daily, 2230, 7 hr 50 min; *Marudhar Exp*, 5313, daily, 1415, 7 hr 10 min. **Udaipur**: *Garib Nawaz Exp*, 2915, daily except Sun, 1125, 10 hr 5 min; *Chetak Exp*, 9615, daily, 2055, 12 hr 20 min. **Ajmer**: *Garib Niwaz Exp*, 2901, daily, 1125, 2 hr 18 min; *Delhi-Ahmadabad Mail*, 9901, daily, 0500, 3 hr 15 min; *Delhi-Ahmadabad Exp*, 9903, daily, 1750, 3 hr 30 min; *Ashram Exp*, 2905, daily, 2345, 3 hr. **Indore**: *Meenakshi Exp*, 7569 (Jaipur-Secunderabad), daily, 1350, 15 hr.

Road Jaipur is on **NH8** (Delhi-Ahmadabad-Bombay) and **NH11** (Agra-Bikaner) and is connected to all parts of India by good roads. The distances from Jaipur are: **Delhi** (261 km); **Agra** (230 km); **Jodhpur** (332 km); **Udaipur** (374 km); **Ajmer** (131 km); **Bikaner** (321 km); **Jaisalmer** (654 km); **Calcutta** (1472 km); **Bombay** (1176 km); **Madras** (2187 km); **Bhopal** (735 km); **Trivandrum** (2674 km).

Bus Rajasthan Roadways, Haryana Roadways and ITDC run delux buses between Delhi and Jaipur. Rajasthan Roadways and ITDC between Agra and Jaipur. Rajasthan Roadways also connects Jaipur to other towns in Rajasthan. *Rajasthan Roadways*, Sindhi Camp, Jaipur, T 75834, 66579; Reservations open 24 hr.

Excursions from Jaipur

Amber, or *Amer*, lies 11 km N of Jaipur, the ancient capital of the **Kachhawaha Rajputs** from 1037 until Sawai Jai Singh II moved to newly created Jaipur. The building of the fort-palace was begun by Raja Man Singh, a noted Rajput general in Akbar's army, and was later added to by successive rulers. The architecture shows distinct Mughal influence. The route there is very attractive, leaving the town and travelling first across the surrounding plain. To your left are rocky outcrops, to your right is the *Jai Mahal* lake with the attractive but now abandoned **Water Palace** (1735) at its centre. During the monsoon the lake is filled with water hyacinth and looks very beautiful. Opposite the lake at *Gethur* are the marble and sandstone *chhattris* of the rulers of Jaipur. These are set in landscaped gardens. Leaving the plain the road begins to climb and passes through a number of of small but defensible rocky gaps before entering the area of flat ground below Amber Fort.

By the side of the road is a dramatic view of the hilltop palace, easily found because there will be a few vendors and entertainers hanging around. Across the **Maota Lake** tank, is a laid out garden connected to the *Jaigarh fort*, running up the steep escarpments to the long, narrow palace running along the top. Proceed along the road a little further and amidst a cluster of buildings is the first gate and ramp up to the palace. This is also easily recognised as usually there are hordes of people plus elephants. Because this is such a popular place to visit it is crowded with vendors. They can be extremely persistent, and unless you really want something it pays to try and ignore them.

The elephant ride From the bottom you can either walk or ride by elephant in the style of medieval royalty! If you have no head for heights this can be somewhat unnerving when the elephant comes close to the edge of the road, but it is perfectly safe and is now an infrequent opportunity outside the Wildlife Parks. You will have to buy a 'return ticket' even if you wish to walk down after seeing the hill top palace. In the high season there is a continuous train of these colourfully decorated elephants walking up and down with their human cargoes. You can also see snake chamers.

It has become very touristy and once on the elephant's back you will not be immune from people trying to sell you something, be it post cards, a mahout's stick or a photograph of you on the elephant (which will be presented to you when you get off). Only when you are inside the palace buildings will you be free from this high-pressure salesmanship. From the hill top you will get an excellent view of the gorge and hills around. **Warning** The monkeys here may try to steal your picnic lunch if given the chance.

The entrance After passing though a series of five defensive gates, you reach the first courtyard of the **Raj Mahal** or old Palace built by Man Singh I in 1600, entered through the **Suraj Pol** (Sun Gate). Here you can get a short ride around the courtyard on an elephant, but bargain very hard. There are some toilets near the dismounting platform. On the S side of the courtyard which has some flower beds in its centre, is a flight of steps leading up to the **Singh Pol** (Lion Gate) entrance to the upper courtyard of the palace.

On your right as you ascend these is the **Shri Sheela Devi Temple**, with its idol brought from Bengal by *Man Singh I* in 1604. In the left hand corner of the courtyard is the **Diwan-i-am** (Hall of Public Audience). This as built by **Mirza Raja Jai Singh I** in 1639 and is raised on a plinth. Originally, it was open on all sides but the E facade was closed when **Sawai Ram Singh II** added a room. The hall is Mughal-influenced, with grey marble pillars and a vaulted roof. The porticos are of red sandstone with carved elephants. On the S side of the courtyard is the **Ganes Pol** (c.1699-1725), covered in mosaics and painted in a variety of attractive colours, taking its name from the prominent figure of Ganes above the door.

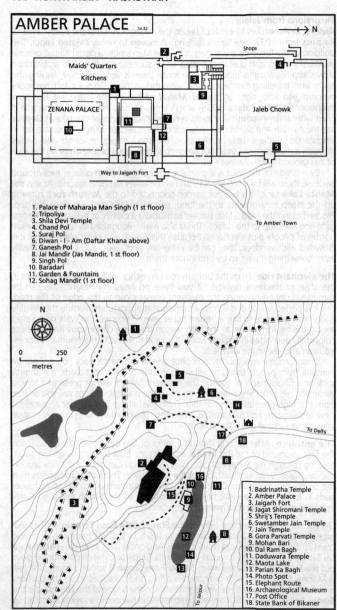

AMBER PALACE

1. Palace of Maharaja Man Singh (1st floor)
2. Tripoliya
3. Shila Devi Temple
4. Chand Pol
5. Suraj Pol
6. Diwan - I - Am (Daftar Khana above)
7. Ganesh Pol
8. Jai Mandir (Jas Mandir, 1st floor)
9. Singh Pol
10. Baradari
11. Garden & Fountains
12. Sohag Mandir (1st floor)

Maids' Quarters
Kitchens
Shops
ZENANA PALACE
Jaleb Chowk
Way to Jaigarh Fort
To Amber Town

0   250
metres

To Delhi
To Jaipur

1. Badrinatha Temple
2. Amber Palace
3. Jaigarh Fort
4. Jagat Shiromani Temple
5. Shriji's Temple
6. Swetamber Jain Temple
7. Jain Temple
8. Gora Parvati Temple
9. Mohan Bari
10. Dal Ram Bagh
11. Daduwara Temple
12. Maota Lake
13. Parian Ka Bagh
14. Photo Spot
15. Elephant Route
16. Archaeological Museum
17. Post Office
18. State Bank of Bikaner

This leads onto another courtyard around which are grouped the royal apartments. On your right hand side is the **Jai Mandir** or **Diwan-i-Khas** (Hall of Private Audience) within which is the **Sheesh Mahal** (Mirror Palace). Both are cool and the former with its white marble columns and painted ceiling has pleasant views across the lake to the hillside beyond. The Sheesh Mahal is faced with mirrors and by lighting a match or using a lighter, you get a brilliant starlit night effect all over the ceiling. Opposite these palaces is the **Sukh Niwas,** a pleasure palace with a marble cascade to beautify it and cool the air and doors inlaid with ivory and sandalwood.

Above the **Ganesh Pol** is the **Sohag Mandir**, an octagonal chamber with beautiful laticed windows and rectangular rooms to each side. To the NE is the **Jas Mahal** (1635-40) which is on the roof of the Jai Mahal. This has wonderful mosaics and was a cool summer pavilion. The marble jali screens facilitated the free movement of cooling breezes. From the rooftop there are stunning views over the palace, the town of Amber, the long curtain wall surrounding the town and further N to the plains beyond. This place is particularly good for photographs. Beyond this courtyard is the **Palace of Man Singh I**. A high wall separates it from the Jai Singh Palace. One passage leads to the **Sukh Niwas** and another to the **Jai Mandir.** In the centre of this complex is a **baradari** (pleasure pavilion) and the style of decoration is a combination of Mughal and Hindu influences.

The forbidding **Jaigarh Fort** nearby was never captured and so the massive **Jaivan** cannon there, believed to be one of the largest of its kind on wheels, was never used. It is very impressive when lit up at night. The smaller **Nahargarh Fort** though less impressive has the **Durg** cafe from which you can get excellent views of the city. **The Old Palace of Amber** (1216) lies at the base of Jaigarh fort. A stone path from the Chand Pol in the first courtyard leads to the ruins.

Sanganer 12 km SW of Jaipur. The road into this small town passes through two ruined Tripolias or triple gateways, beyond which is the ruined palace. The fortifications and four gates around the town are also in ruins. The greater attractions of **Sanganer** are being away from the hustle, bustle and hassle of Jaipur and being able to see paper-making and block-printing. *Paper-making* is practised in the *kagazi mohulla* (paper area) and uses waste cotton and silk rags which are churned into a pulp, sieved, strained and dried. The finished products are often speckled with gold and silver. *Block-printing* is done all around the town and you should be able to wander and watch the printers in many workshop and purchase samples, probably at a fraction of the price asked in commercially aggressive Jaipur. There are hourly buses from Jaipur to Sanganer.

Sisodia Rani Gardens, 8 km E of Jaipur on the Agra Rd. This palace, built for Jai Singh's second wife, has walls illustrated with the Krishna legend and hunting scenes and is surrounded by terraced gardens. **Vidhyadhar Bagh** is nestled in a narrow valley along the Agra Rd next to it and is a beautiful garden laid out in honour of Jai Singh's friend and city planner Vidyadhar Bhattacharya.

DELHI TO JAIPUR

If you are travelling by road from Delhi to Jaipur the normal and fastest route is Delhi-Gurgaon-Amber-Jaipur on NH 8. This is very busy with slow moving lorry traffic and a bus will normally take at least 5 hours. It is worth taking the alternative Delhi – Gurgaon – Alwar – Sariska – Amber – Jaipur route if you have the time to spare, as it is both more interesting and less busy. The first part of the journey skirts along the northen side of the Aravallis but at Tijara the road climbs into the hills.

Leave Delhi south from Connaught Place following signs to Gurgaon and the International Airport. After 12 km pass the Delhi Cantonment and follow signs left for Gurgaon. Pass the airport. Keep straight on at a succession of road junctions, with a right turn to the Airport (domestic terminal – 2 km), a left turn to **Mehrauli** (3 km) and two more right turns (3 km and 7 km) to **Najafgarh** and **Daulatabad** respectively. At the next junction (3 km) leave the main Jaipur Road and turn left for *Gurgaon*, formerly the Headquarters for S Eastern Punjab and now a District HQ in Haryana State. The road goes S across the plains to **Bhundsi** (12 km) and a further 11 km where there is a left turn to **Sohna**.

Sohna is known for its hot springs and there is an attractive **Haryana Tourism motel D** *Barbet*, T 56. Motel and camper huts. A/c rm. Pool, restaurant. The left turn in the town goes to **Palwal** (29 km) where it joins the main Delhi-Agra Road, while a road on the right goes to **Rewari** (46 km). Continue straight on to by-pass **Nuh** (20 km). At *Daruhera* (70 km S Wof Delhi) is the Haryana Topurism motel *Jungle Babbler*, T 25. **D** Motel. A/c and non a/c rm. Restaurant, camel rides.

The road goes straight on through **Bhadas** (20 km) and **Firozpur Jhirka** (19 km) to the Haryana Rajasthan border (12 km). After 13 km take the by-pass to the left of **Ramgarh** and continue a further 12 km to the next junction. Here a road to the left goes to **Nagar** (40 km), **Deeg** (65 km) – see below, **Mathura** (96 km) and **Bharatpur** (102 km). Continue straight on to Alwar (14 km).

Alwar was founded by **Rao Pratap Singhji** of Macheri in 1771 as capital of the state of Alwar. It is protected by a hilltop fort 308 m above the town from which there is a splendid view of the surrounding countryside. In the fort lie the remains of the palaces, 15 temples and 10 tanks built by the first rulers of Alwar. The fortifications extend 3 km along the hilltop. At **Siliserh**, 14 km to the W runs an aqueduct which supplies the city with water.

There are five gates to the walled city. The **Vinai Vilas City Palace** (1840) is now a fine museum with more than 7,000 manuscripts and miniature paintings in both Mughal and Rajasthani styles, armour, textiles and musical instruments. Open Sat-Th 1000-1630. The building itself is very fine and successfully blends Mughal proportions with Rajput decoration. The stables apparently could hold 3000 horses while in the treasury among the crown jewels there was a cup carved out of a single diamond. On the S side of the tank is the **Cenotaph of Maharaja Bakhtawar Singh** (1781-1815) which is of marble on a red sandstone base. The gardens around are alive with peacocks and other birds. To the R of the main entrance to the palace is the **House of the Elephant Carriage** which contains a two-storey processional carriage designed to carry 50 people and be hauled by four elephants.

Also worth seeing is the **Yeshwant Niwas** a palace built by Maharaja Jey Singh in the Italianate style. Apparently on its completion he disliked it and never lived in it. Instead he built the **Vijay Mandir** in 1927. The royal family still live in part of this 105-room palace beside Vijay Sagar. Part of it is open to the public. Nearby is Siliserh Lake, a local picnic spot with boats for hire. The lakeside palace is now a hotel.

Hotels There are no top class hotels in Alwar. **E** *Lake Castle Tourist Bungalow*, Siliserh, T 3764. Modest. Out of Alwar. **E** *The Alka* (T 2796), *Asoka* (T 2027) and *rly Retiring Rooms* are all basic.

Rail Old Delhi Delhi Mail, 9902, daily, 0340, 3 hr 50 min; *Delhi Exp*, 9904, daily, 1423, 4 hr; *Ashram Exp*, 2906, daily, 0647, 3 hr 15 min; *Ahemdabad-Jodhpur Exp*, 9965, daily, 1909, 3 hr 5 min.

Bus There are regular buses from Delhi and Jaipur.

Follow the **Sariska** road south out of the town. After 25 km the road climbs up a 5 km ghat section into the Aravallis then enters **Sariska** immediately after the ghat section ends, the gateway for the Sariska National Park.

Sariska National Park
The best time to visit is Feb-Jun and Oct-Nov. This 210 sq km sanctuary comprises dry deciduous forest set in a valley surrounded by the barren Aravalli hills. Open all year round. During the monsoon the vegetation is very lush and travel through the forest may be difficult. The place is alive with birds but many animals move to higher ground. Sariska's special feature is its **rhesus** and **langur** monkeys. All Indian monkeys are either macaques or langurs, and N of the Godavari river the commonest macaque is the rhesus. What is special about them at Sariska is that both are so tolerant of humans being close to them. That does not mean that they have been tamed. **Warning** It is not safe to play with them.

Talvriksh is where the main rhesus population live whilst at **Brat-Hari** the langur have become used to people being close to them. The *chowsingha*, or four-horned antelope, is found at Sariska but not at nearby Ranthambhor. Other deer include nilgai, chital and sambar. Jackals, hyenas, hares and porcupines are the other animals that may be seen here. Occasionally tigers are seen. The birdlife includes ground birds such as peafowl, jungle fowl, spur fowl and the grey partridge. Babblers, bulbuls and treepies are common round the lodges. There are two *machans* (tree platforms) and it may be possible to arrange to sit out in these, dawn and dusk being the best times for viewing game. You can also take an organised night ride into the jungle but reports of this are not promising.

Hotels C *Sariska Palace*. T Sariska 22 or Thanagazi 47, Cable: Palace. 40 km from Alwar rly. 31 rm, a/c and non a/c. Restaurant (Indian, Continental), 16 hr room service, exchange, Amex, Diners credit cards. A former Maharaja's hunting lodge. "Wonderful building, rather like a stately home, delightful staff, good food." **E** *Tiger Den Tourist Bungalow*, at the sanctuary. Booking and information from the Wildlife Warden, Sariska, T Alwar 2348.

Bus From Alwar there are buses to the sanctuary.

Follow the road out of Sariska to Thana Ghazi (11 km) and Bairat (15 km), then rejoin the NH 8 at **Shahpura** (25 km). The National Highway goes south with the arid ridges of the Aravallis getting increasingly close. It goes through **Chandwagi** (18 km) and **Achraul** (12 km) to **Amber** (20 km) and **Jaipur** (10 km). For information on Amber see **Excursions** from Jaipur.

JAIPUR TO AGRA

The second side of the tourist triangle runs from Jaipur to Agra via Bharatpur (which is best known for its bird sanctuary but also has a splendid city) and Fatehpur Sikri in Uttar Pradesh. Travelling time is around 4 hours by car, 5-6 hours by coach. There is also a 'Superfast' train from Jaipur to Agra which takes 5 hours 45 mins. The road journey is on NH11 which passes through cultivated areas for virtually the whole distance. The total distance is 230 km and the road is flat and straight.

From Jaipur the road runs E through a series of small towns and villages: **Kanota** (14 km) and **Daosa** (38 km), where a right turn leads to **Sawai Madhopur** (104 km) and **Ranthambor** (114 km). Continuing along the NH 11 there is a good roadside restaurant near **Sakrai** run by the Rajasthan Tourist Development Corporation (25 km) – very good toilets!. Continue straight to **Mahwah** (37 km), and through **Chonkarwalla** (15 km) to **Halena** (10 km) and to **Sewar** (30 km). A left turn leads to Deeg (33 km).

The fort and pleasure palace at **Deeg** are of major architectural importance.

BHARATPUR SA 72

To Kota
To Mathura
To Jaipur
To Jaipur via Sewar
To Deeg
To Agra
To Fatehpur Sikri

Circular Rd
Suijen Ganga
NH 11

N
Not to scale

1. Keoladeo Ghana National Park & Forest Lodge
2. Nehru Park
3. Museum
4. Gandhi Park
5. Goverdhan Gate
6. Anah Gate
7. Jaghina Gate
8. Ketari Gate
9. Asht-Dhatu Gate
10. Surajpol Gate
11. Lohiya Gate
12. Mathura Gate
13. Binarayan Gate
14. Atalbund Gate
15. Neemda Gate
16. Post Office & Telegraph Office
17. Post Office
18. Golbargh Palace Hotel
19. Tourist Office & Dak Bungalow
20. Eagles Nest Hotel
21. Saras Tourist Bungalow

Badan Singh (1722-56), a Sinsini Jat, began the development of the town into the capital of his newly founded Jat kingdom. The strong central citadel was built by his son **Suraj Mal** in 1730. In the late 18th century the town reverted to **the Raja of Bharatpur**. The British stormed the fort in December 1804, after which the fortifications were dismantled.

The **fort** is square, its 8 km long walls are of rubble and mud and it is encircled by 12 bastions and a moat. **The Palaces**, built as pleasure palaces, were begun by the Suraj Mal of Bharatpur. They are flanked by 2 reservoirs, the **Gopal Sagar** (W) and the **Rup Sagar** (E) and lie around a central garden. The main gate is the unfinished **Singh Pol** (Lion Gate). Other gates are the **Suraj Pol** (NE) and **Nanga Gate** (SW). The largest and main pavilion is the **Gopal Bhavan** (1763) which is oblong and contains a central hall and 2 side chambers. The **Sawon** and **Bhadon** pavilions (1760) flank this and the main arch was for a *hindola** (swing) and marble thrones. These were taken as booty when Suraj Mal attacked Delhi.

To the S of this is the **Suraj Bhavan** (c.1760), a single storey marble building, a tank, the **Kishan Bhavan** with its five central arches and fountains on the terrace, a temple and behind this the **Purana Mahal** (1722 onwards). This was built by Raja Badan Singh and has a curved roof with chattris. It is now used for government offices. There are around 500 fountains in the palace complex which are turned on for a festival in August.

The **Keshav Bhavan** on the W side of the Rup Sagar and is a *baradari* or garden pavilion. In the SE corner of the Rup Sagar is the **Sheesh Mahal** (Mirror Palace, 1725) whilst on the NW corner there is another temple. Finally, on the N side of the central garden or courtyard is the **Nand Bhavan** (c.1760), a large hall 45 m long, 24 m wide and 6 m high, raised on a terrace and enclosed by an arcade of seven arches leading up to overhanging eaves. There are frescoes inside but it all has a deserted feel. The palace is open 0800-1200 and 1300-1900. Entry free.

Hotels There is a *Dak Bungalow*, T 18 which is basic and cheap.

Take the road south to **Bharatpur** (7 km), a popular halting place on the 'Golden Triangle' famous for its **Kaladeo Ghana Bird Sanctuary** (which is simply referred to as *Bharatpur*). But there is also the old fort and town of Bharatpur which is rarely visited by foreign visitors but well worth the effort, particularly if you are staying overnight in the area.

The Fort and Palace Bharatpur is situated at the confluence of the Ruparel and Bangagga rivers. Its ruling family was Jat and along with other Jats they were quite a harassment to Aurangzeb. Under Badan Singh they controlled a large tract between Delhi and Agra, then led by Suraj Mal they seized Agra and marched on Delhi in 1763. The fort, built by **Suraj Mal** appears impregnable and Lord Lake suffered his most disastrous defeat when in 1803 he was repulsed. In 1825 the British took it after a month long siege. There are double ramparts, a 46 m wide moat and an inner moat around the palace. Much of the walls have been demolished but there are the remains of some of the gateways. Inside the fort there are three palaces: the Raja's palace, the Old Palace (1733) and the Kamra Palace. N of these are the Jewel House and Court of Justice. **Golbagh** (c.1905), the palace of the Maharaja, is 1.6 km outside the city and is what Davies has described as a 'beautiful piece of Victorian eclecticism executed in local sandstone'.

The Bird Sanctuary There are entrance fees to the park on a per person and vehicle basis but these are nominal – about Rs 10 per foreigner. You can either hire a bicycle in the town a few km away and cycle to and around the reserve or hire a cycle rickshaw (takes two passengers). The last is well worth the charge of around Rs 15 per hour because many of the rickshaw wallahs have binoculars which they are very willing to lend (not hire) and all are very knowledgeable about the birds and make identification easy. They also know where to look for the pythons. A small tip for the rickshaw wallah is in order.

Established in 1956, this 29 sq km piece of marshland is one of the finest bird sanctuaries in the world with over 360 species of birds. It used to be part of the private shooting reserve of the Maharaja of Bharatpur and during the season enormous numbers of birds were shot by him and his guests. Apparently, the Viceroy Lord Linlithgow holds the record bag with 4,273 in 1938. It is especially good in Nov to Feb when it is frequented by Northern hemisphere migratory birds, including the rare Siberian Crane. Sep to Oct is the breeding season. Early morning and dusk are the best times, not only for bird watching but for soaking up the delightful atmosphere. Among many other birds to be seen are egrets, ducks, Chinese coots, storks, kingfishers, spoonbills, Sarus cranes and Siberian cranes, Pallas' eagle. There are also chital deer, nilgai and wild boar whilst near the entrance there are usually one or two very large python.

It is worth buying the *Penguin Handbook of Indian Birds* by Martin Woodcock (available in hotel bookshops and booksellers in Delhi, Agra, Jaipur etc.) as an aid. The illustrations are very good. There is also a extremely good book entitled *Bharatpur: Bird Paradise* by Martin Ewans, Lustre Press, Delhi, price Rs 250-320 (depending on where you buy) if you want a keepsake of your visit.

Hotels D *The Bharatpur Forest Lodge* (ITDC), just inside the Sanctuary. T 2260/ 2232, Cable: Forestour. 8 km rly. Book in advance. 18 rm, some a/c. Restaurant, bar, rm service. Boats for bird watching. Basic but adequate. Animals such as wild boar wander into the compound providing entertainment in the evenings and mornings. The cheaper **E** *Seras Tourist Bungalow* (RTDC), is on Fatehpur Sikri Rd, T 3700. 20 rm, some a/c. Restaurant, bar, lawns, tours. Simple. In Bharatpur itself, **D** *Golbagh Palace Hotel*, T 3349. 18 rm, some a/c.

Restaurant, bar, 24 hr rm service, TV. Former palace which has been modernised without destroying its character. Good food and service. Recommended.

Rail Jaipur: *Marudhar Exp*, 5315, daily, 0936, 4 hr 4 min; *Agra Fort Fast Passenger Exp*, 9705, daily, 2155, 4 hr 50 min; *Agra-Jaipur Exp*, 2921, daily, 1805, 3 hr 50 min. **Sawai Madhopur**: *Paschim Exp*, 2926, daily, 1953, 2 hr 25 min; *Frontier Mail*, 2904, daily, 1115, 3 hr; *Bombay Exp*, 9020, daily, 0157, 3 hr 10 min; *Bombay-Janata Exp*, 9024, 1823, 3 hr 15 min.

12 km after leaving Bharatpur the road crosses the Rajasthan/UP border, an area of some historic significance as the borders between Rajput Mughal territory which **Fatehpur Sikri** (9 km) – **see page 282** – was designed, at least in part, to watch over. Continue straight on for **Agra** (35 km), **see page 267**.

JAIPUR TO UDAIPUR & AHMADABAD VIA RANTHAMBOR & CHITTAURGARH

There is a very pleasant journey from Jaipur through E Rajasthan to Gwalior or Jhansi. The route followed takes in **Sawai Madhopur, Ranthambhor** and **Shivpuri National Parks**. From Jhansi you can drive to **Orchha** and **Khajuraho** (see page 296). It is also possible to take the first part of this route as a long way round from Jaipur to Udaipur, allowing you to see several interesting sites in SE Rajasthan on the way.

Leaving Jaipur you take the road to Sanganer (13 km) **(see above)**. Here you take the road to **Chaksu** (28 km) and **Nawai** (27 km) where you cross the railway line from Jaipur to Sawai Madhopur. The road crosses the *River Banas* (21 km), which has given its name to the post-Harappan culture of the region, and proceeds through some very attractive scenery to *Tonk* (4 km). Before Independence Tonk was a tiny and unimportant Princely State ruled by Muslim Nawabs. The **Sunehri Kothi**, a late 19th century addition to the palace built by the Nawab, is a mixture of predominantly local architectural styles with European style additions such as imitation Ionic columns and false marbling of the columns. Some of the "doors" are also simply painted. There is also an old **Amirgarh Fort** built by Amir Khan.

From Tonk you have the choice of taking the SE route to **Sawai Madhopur**, **Shivpuri** and **Gwalior** or **Jhansi** or the SW route to **Bundi**, **Kota** and **Chittaurgarh**. For **Ranthambor** take the road SE out of Tonk.

Ranthambhor National Park
Ranthambhor (74 km) lies on the easternmost spur of the Aravallis. It has both the old fort and the Sawai Madhopur/ Ranthambhor wildlife sanctuary. Situated on a 215 m high rock 19 km N Eof Sawai Madhopur, the **Chauhan fort** was built in 944 and over the next six centuries changed hands on a number of occasions. Qutb-ud-din Aibak captured it in 1194 and later handed it back to the Rajputs. Ala-ud-din Khalji sacked it in 1301 and Akbar took it in 1569. It later passed to the house of Jaipur.

The only approach is along a narrow valley from the W and the path to the fort zig-zags up the steep outcrop in a series of steep ramps and through four impressive gateways. The fort wall runs round the summit and has a number of semi-circular bastions. This combined with the natural escarpment produce sheer drops of over 65 m in places. There are two tanks, a palace and pavilion and a few temples inside the walls. All are in various states of ruin but there are good views out over the surrounding countryside to warrant the effort of reaching the fort and it is a wonderfully peaceful place after noisy Jaipur.

Sawai Madhupur Set in 400 sq km of dry deciduous forest in and around the Aravalli and Vindhyan hills, this was the private tiger reserve of the Maharaja of Jaipur. It is studded with pavilions, watch-towers and is watched over by the fort at Ranthambor. Best time: Nov-Apr.

Hotels D *Castle Jhoomar Baori Forest Lodge*, T 620. A former hunting lodge for guests of the Maharaja of Jaipur. Few rooms, all large and airy, available. Book in advance. Good location on the top of a hill. 7 km rly. **E** *Hunting Lodge*. This was the Maharaja of Jaipur's personal lodge. 3 km rly. **E** *Jogi Mahal*. Small lodge on edge of a small lake covered with water-lilies overlooked by a fort on a hill. 15 km rly.

Travel Sawai Madhopur is on the main Delhi-Bombay railway line. It is midway between Bharatpur and Kota so if you have a car it is worth considering as a stopping place.
   Rail: New Delhi: *Paschim Exp*, 2925, daily, 0355, 6 hr 30 min; *Frontier Mail*, 2903, daily, 1255, 6 hr 5 min; *Dehra Dun Exp*, 9019, daily 2143, 8 hr; *Firozpur-Janata Exp*, 9023, daily, 0430, 8 hr. **Bombay Central**: *Paschim Exp*, 2926, daily, 2225, 16 hr 40 min; *Frontier Mail*, 2904, daily, 1423, 16 hr 20 min; *Bombay Exp*, 9020, daily, 0518, 23 hr 10 min; *Bombay-Janata Exp*, 9024, 2210, 22 hr 10 min. **Kota**: *Paschim Exp*, 2926, daily, 2225, 1 hr 20 min; *Frontier Mail*, 2904, daily, 1423, 1 hr 35 min; *Bombay Exp*, 9020, daily, 0518, 2 hr; *Bombay-Janata Exp*, 9024, 2210, 2 hr 10 min.
   Bharatpur: *Paschim Exp*, 2925, daily, 0355, 2 hr 50 min; *Frontier Mail*, 2903, daily, 1255, 2 hr 50 min; *Dehra Dun Exp*, 9019, daily 2143, 3 hr 40 min; *Firozpur-Janata Exp*, 9023, daily, 0430, 3 hr 40 min. **Mathura**: *Paschim Exp*, 2925, daily, 0355, 4 hr 5 min; *Frontier Mail*, 2903, daily, 1255, 3 hr 35 min; *Dehra Dun Exp*, 9019, daily 2143, 4 hr 30 min; *Firozpur-Janata Exp*, 9023, daily, 0430, 4 hr 40 min.

From Sawai Madhopur you can continue E to Shivpuri, Gwalior and Jhansi. To continue to Udaipur take the road S to **Lakheri** and **Kota**. The first part of the journey, following the railway line, runs along the Aravalli ridge (heights of about 500 m) to **Lakheri** (40 km) and on to Kota (55 km).

Situated on the E bank of the Chambal river below a deep gorge, *Kota* lies in a tract of country that straddled a major trade route from Delhi to Gujarat. It is now a rapidly expanding industrial area for processing chemicals, and there are hydro-electric power and a nuclear power plants nearby. In the past it was a small state surrounded by more powerful neighbours. Its fortunes and ambitions varied inversely with those of its neighbours. Under the guidance of the able **Zalim Singh** in the 19th century, Kota prospered but it then foundered on his death. The British reunited the territory in 1894 and imposed stability. Kota's existence as an independent state, then, depended more on the diplomatic skills of its rulers than military might.

Like most towns in Rajasthan, Kota has a **fort**. This was constructed from 1625 onwards. Like other forts, it is an example of organic growth and there is no overall plan to the development of the area within the walls. The **Bhim Mahal**, a large Durbar Hall, is early 18th century and is covered with Rajput miniatures documenting the towns periods of expansion and recording Kota's legends. **The Hathi Pol** (Elephant Gate 1625-48) had murals added to it at a later stage, one of which depicts a royal wedding procession. The exterior of the palace with its robust fortifications and delicate ornamental stonework summarises the town's changing fortunes.

Museums The fort has two museums. **The Akhade Ka Mahal** (1723-56) was added to the W of the inner court and was enlarged between 1888 and 1940. The **Hawa Mahal** (1864) is modelled on its more famous namesake in Jaipur.

The Umaid Bhawan (New Palace 1904) was built for the Maharao Umaid Singh II and designed by **Sir Samuel Swinton Jacob** in collaboration with the Indian designers. The finish reflects the the combination of European design for Indian taste. Its exterior is buff-coloured stone with a stucco finish and includes much typical Rajput detail. The interior, however, is Edwardian with a fine drawing-room, banquet hall and garden.

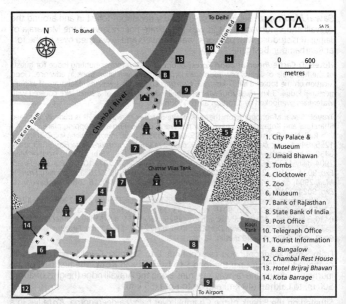

KOTA SA 75

0 — 600 metres

1. City Palace & Museum
2. Umaid Bhawan
3. Tombs
4. Clocktower
5. Zoo
6. Museum
7. Bank of Rajasthan
8. State Bank of India
9. Post Office
10. Telegraph Office
11. Tourist Information & Bungalow
12. *Chambal Rest House*
13. *Hotel Brijraj Bhavan*
14. *Kota Barrage*

The Chambal Gardens at Amar Niwas, S of the fort, are popular for picnics. The pond is well stocked with gharial crocodiles and somewhat surprisingly flamingoes share this with their reptilian neighbours. Upstream at **Bharatiya Kund** is a popular swimming spot whilst the Kota barrage controls the river level and is the headworks for an irrigation system downstream.

Hotels D *Brijraj Bhawan Palace*, Civil Lines. T 23071. 7 rm, air cooled. Restaurant, (Indian, Continental), room service, laundry, travel. A palace in small grounds by river, though homely and relaxing and with regal memorabilia. Used by small tour groups. Non-residents may be allowed to use the restaurant. Recommended. E *Navrang*, Civil Lines, Nayapura. T 23294, Cable: Navrang. 21 a/c rm. 8 km airport, 3 km rly. E *Chambal Tourist Bungalow* (RTDC), nr bus stand. T 26527. 49 rm, some a/c. Restaurant (limited menu), Tourist Office. Clean, simple but pleasant and good value. There is also the *Payal*, T 5401 at Nayapura and the *Rly Retiring Rooms*.

Rail New Delhi: *Rajdhani Exp*, 2951, daily except Mon, 0418, 4 hr 57 min; *Paschim Exp*, 2925, daily, 0220, 8 hr 5 min; *Dehra Dun Exp*, 9019, daily, 1940, 10 hr; *Frontier Mail*, 2903, daily, 1125, 7 hr 35 min. **Bombay (Central)**: *Paschim Exp*, 2926, daily, 2358, 15 hr; *Frontier Mail*, 2904, daily, 1610, 14 hr 50 min; *Bombay Exp*, 9020, daily, 0800, 20 hr 30 min; *Bombay-Janata Exp*, 9024, 0035, 19 hr 45 min. **Sawai Madhopur**: *Paschim Exp*, 2925, daily, 0220, 1 hr 30 min; *Frontier Mail*, 2903, daily, 1125, 1 hr 25 min; *Dehra Dun Exp*, 9019, daily 1940, 1 hr 55 min; *Firozpur-Janata Exp*, 9023, daily, 0244, 1 hr 30 min. *Awadh Exp*, 5064, daily, 1420, 1 hr 50 min.

Excursions *Jhalarapatan,* 85 south east of Kota has several fine Hindu temples dating from the 11th century, the **Surya Temple** being the best. This is Central Indian in style and has a curvilinear tower adorned with miniature tower-like motifs. There is a large *amalaka** at the crest. 2 km to the S is the ruined site of 7th century **Chandravati**. Here there are broken sculptures and derelict temples. Many of the sculptures have been removed to **Jhalawar** which is nearby.

Badoli , 40 km from Kota on the way to Pratap Sagar, has some of the finest examples of 10th century Pratihara temples in WIndia. They are now rather dilapidated but include the **Ghateshvara Temple**, the best preserved and finest example. It consists of an elaborately carved curvilinear towered sanctuary with a pot finial and a columned porch. Inside are sculptures of Siva dancing flanked by Brahma and Vishnu with river goddesses and dancing maidens beneath. Within the sanctuary is a square pedestal with five stone lingas, the central one being an upturned pot or *ghata** which gives the temple its name.

The **Mahishamardini Temple** is immediately SW and also has a finely carved curved tower. A smashed image of Durga is in the sanctuary. Trimurti Temple to the SE is derelict but houses a large triple-headed Siva image. The temple complex is about 100 m to the E of the bus stand.

From **Kota** you can drive SW along a picturesque route that skirts the Rana Pratap Sagar and Gandhi Sagar lakes. It is a 236 km drive but the views are very attractive and there a some beautiful picnic spots along the way. It is to 125 km **Rampura**, from there to **Neemuch** 55 km, and a further 56 km to Chittaurgarh. Alternatively, take the road NW out of Kota to **Bundi** (37 km), a very picturesque little town and former capital of a small state of the same name.

Bundi is sited in a beautiful narrow valley above which towers the **Taragarh Fort**. The drive into the town is particularly pleasing as the road runs along the hillside overlooking the valley and opposite the fort. It is well off the beaten tourist track and unspoilt. After the hustle and hassle of Jaipur it is a welcome haven. The (C Category) accommodation is quite limited: it's best to spend the night in Kota and make a day trip to Bundi.

The state was founded in 1342 and whilst neither wealthy nor powerful, it nevertheless ranked high in the Rajput hierarchy. The founding family belonged to the Hara Chauhan clan, one of the 4 Agnikula created by Vishnu at the fire-pit at Gaumukh (Cow's Mouth) on Mount Abu. The town lies on the side of a steep hill and the palace which is situated by a lake with little islands was begun around 1600. Former rulers lived in the **Taragarh (Star) Fort** which was built in 1342. In fact the palace complex is a jumble of smaller palaces. **The Chatar Mahal** (1660) is of green serpentine rock and is pure Rajput in style. A steep ramp provides access which is through the **Hazari (One Thousand) Gate** where the garrison lived. The palace entrance is through the **Hathi (Elephant) Pol** (1607-31).

The Chitra Mahal, an open courtyard with a gallery running around a garden of fountains, has a splendid collection of miniatures in the local style showing scenes from the Radhakrishna story. The 18th century murals are some of the finest examples of Rajput art. There is supposed to be a labyrinth of catacombs in which the state treasures are believed to have been stored. Each ruler was allowed one visit but when the last guide died in the 1940s the secret of its location was lost.

Sukh Niwas is a summer palace on the **Jait Sagar** lake. The square artificial *Nawal Sagar* lake has in its centre a half-submerged temple to Varuna, the god of water. The lake surface reflects the entire town and palace and is stunning. W of the Nawal Sagar is **Phool (Flower) Sagar**, a 'new' palace started in 1945 but not finished.

The Fort is square in plan with large corner bastions. There is a large gate in the E wall which like the others are crenellated with high ramparts. The main gate to the W is flanked by octagonal towers and the approach was difficult. The **Bhim Burj** tower dominates the fort and provided the platform for the **Garbh Ganjam**, a huge cannon. A pit to the side provided shelter for the artillerymen. The **Sabirna-Dha-ka-Kund** is a square stepped water tank and provided defenders with their water supply. It was built in 1654. Overall, the fort is rather sombre which contrasts sharply with the beauty of the town and the lakes below.

Hotels E *Circuit House* and the **F** *Dak Bungalow* nr the bus stand. These can be booked in advance but this will only give you preference over other visitors. Indian Govt officials have the right to lay claim to the rooms even after they have been occupied.

Travel Bundi is only accessible by road. It takes about 5 hours by **bus** from Ajmer (165 km) and one hour from Kota (37 km). Buses also to Chittaurgarh and Udaipur.

From Bundi you can drive directly to **Chittaurgarh** (143 km). At **Menal** (48 km) there is a complex of **Siva** temples. These were built during the Gupta period. At **Bijolia**, 16 km further on is another group. Originally there were over a hundred. Now only three stand. In one is a large statue of Ganes.

Chittaurgarh (***Chittor***) is one of the oldest cities in Rajasthan and was founded in 728 by **Bappu Rawal** who according to legend was reared by the Bhil tribe. Archaeological investigation at two sites near the **River Berach** has shown stone tools dating from the Lower Palaeolithic, the earliest period of human settlement. Buddhist relics from a period a few centuries BC. From the 7th century it was occupied by a succession of rulers. The imposing fort sited on a rocky outcrop of the Aravallis gave Chittaurgarh a great strategic importance which demanded attention from Muslim armies from the 12th century when it also became the centre of Mewar.

Excavations in the Mahasati area of the fort have shown 4 shrines with ashes and charred bones. The earliest of these dates from about the 11th century AD. There was a paved platform over which was a ***sati stone****, commemorating the self immolation of a widow, and 2 other loose sati stones were also discovered.

Rajput chivalry On three occasions during its long subsequent history its inhabitants conducted themselves according to the best traditions of the Rajput chivalric code. Three times her defenders preferred death to surrender, the women marching en masse into the flames of a funeral pyre in a form of ritual suicide known as ***jauhar**** before the men, who had donned the saffron robes associated with Hindu pilgrimage and marriage threw open the gates and charged towards a mightier enemy and annihilation. The first was in 1303 when **Ala-ud-din Khalji**, the King of Delhi, laid claim to the beautiful Padmini, wife of the Rana's uncle. When she refused, he laid siege to the fort. The women committed jauhar, Padmini entering last, and over 50,000 men were killed in battle. The fort was retaken in 1313.

In 1535 ***Bahadur Shah*** of Gujarat laid claim to Chittaurgarh. Every Rajput clan lost its leader in the battle in which over 32,000 lives were lost, and 13,000 women and children died in the sacred ***jauhar**** which preceded the the final charge. The third and final sack of Chittaurgarh occurred only 32 years later when Akbar stormed the fort. Again, the women and children committed themselves to the flames, and again all the clans lost their chiefs as 8,000 defenders burst out of the gates. When Akbar entered the city and saw that it had been transformed into a mass grave, he ordered the destruction of the buildings. In 1567 after this bloody episode in Chitaurgarh's history, it was abandoned and the capital of Mewar was moved to Udaipur. In 1615 Jahangir restored the city to the Rajputs.

The fort dominates the city and is itself 280 hectares in area. Until 1568 the town was situated within the walls. Today the lower Town sprawls to the W of the fort and straddles the **Berach** and **Gambheri** rivers.

Places of Interest The Fort This stands on a 152 m high rocky hill which rises abruptly above the surrounding plain. The great length of the walls (5 km), however, makes the elevation look lower than it really is. The ruins are deserted and the slopes are covered with thick scrubby jungle. The modern town of Chitor lies at the foot of the hill and is surrounded by a wall. Access is across a limestone bridge of ten arches (nine pointed and, curiously one semi-circular) over the Gambheri river. The winding 1.5 km ascent to the fort is defended by seven

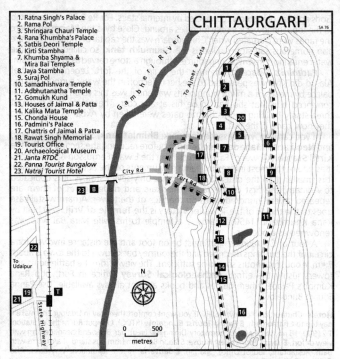

1. Ratna Singh's Palace
2. Rama Pol
3. Shringara Chauri Temple
4. Rana Khumba's Palace
5. Satbis Deori Temple
6. Kirti Stambha
7. Khumba Shyama & Mira Bai Temples
8. Jaya Stambha
9. Suraj Pol
10. Samadhishvara Temple
11. Adbhutanatha Temple
12. Gomukh Kund
13. Houses of Jaimal & Patta
14. Kalika Mata Temple
15. Chonda House
16. Padmini's Palace
17. Chattris of Jaimal & Patta
18. Rawat Singh Memorial
19. Tourist Office
20. Archaeological Museum
21. Janta RTDC
22. Panna Tourist Bungalow
23. Natraj Tourist Hotel

CHITTAURGARH

SA 76

impressive gates: the **Padal Pol** is where Bagh Singh, the Rajput leader, fell during the second siege; the **Bhairon or Tuta (broken) Pol** where Jaimal, one of the heroes of the third siege was killed by Akbar in 1567; the **Hanuman Pol** and Ganesh Pol; the **Jorla (Joined) Gate** whose upper arch is connected to the **Lakshman Pol**; finally the **Ram Pol** (1459) which is the main gate.

Inside the walls is a village and ruined palaces, towers and temples. When you enter the fort you turn right and come immediately to the ruins of the **Palace of Rana Khumba** (1433-68). It was originally built of dressed stone with a stucco covering and was approached by two gateways, the **Badi Pol** and the **Tripolia**. All is in ruins but once there were elephant and horse stables, a zenana and a Siva temple. The *jauhar* committed by Padmini and her followers is believed to have taken place beneath the courtyard. The N frontage of the palace contains a characteristically attractive combination of canopied balconies. Across from the palace is the archaeological office and the **Nau Lakha Bhandar** (900,000 Treasury). A little beyond the **Rana Khumba Palace** is the comparatively modern **Fateh Prakash Palace** built by Maharana Fateh Singh who died in 1930 which houses an interesting **museum** containing statues found on this site.

If you carry on in an anti-clockwise fashion, you come to **Jaya Stambh** (Tower of Victory). Along with the older Kirrti Stambh (Tower of Fame) this is one of the most interesting buildings within the fort and was built over a ten year period (1458-1468) by Rana Khumba to celebrate his victory over Mahmud Khilji of Malwa (Madhya Pradesh) in 1440. It stands on a base 14 m square and 3 m high and rises 37 m from a 9 m wide base. It is completely covered sculptures of Hindu

Gods and has nine storeys connected by internal stairs. For Re 0.50 you can climb to the top. The tower is visible for miles around. Close by is the **Mahasati** where the ranas were cremated when Chittaurgarh was the capital of Mewar. There are also numerous sati stones. Next is the **Gaumukh tank**, so called because the water entering it from its spring source is through a stone carved as a cow's mouth.

Padmini's Palace stands near the S tip of the fort. Legend has it that Ala-ud-din Khilji was permitted to see her reflection in the water surrounding the palace by means of a mirror hung on its wall and it was this vision of beauty that convinced him that she had to be his at any cost. The palace is a compact three-storey building and its bronze gates were taken by Akbar to Agra where they now hang in the fort.

If you carry on, you pass the deer park, **Bhimlat Tank, Suraj Pol** (Sun Gate) and **Neelkanth Mahadev Jain temple** before reaching the second tower, the **Kirtti Stambh** (Tower of Fame) which is on the E wall. Fergusson has described it as one of the most interesting Jaina monuments of the age (up to 1300 AD). It is smaller than the other (23 m) and has only seven storeys. It is dedicated to Adinath, the first of the Jain Tirthankars and nude figures of them are repeated several hundred times on the face of the tower. A narrow staircase goes to the top. N of the Tower of Victory is the **Temple of Vriji**, also built by Rana Khumba in 1450. Nearby is a temple to his wife Mira Bai who was renowned as a poetess.

A tour of Chittaurgarh fort must be on foot and the distance involved for a circuit of the buildings described and the journey back down to the town is about 7 km. About four hours should be sufficient. The views from the battlements and towers justify the effort. **Archaeological Survey** Office in Fort, opp Rana Kumbh's Palace, where guides and books are not always available. Use Panna Tourist Bungalow.

Hotels Chittaurgarh has few hotels. If you want comfort then stay in Udaipur and make a day trip to Chittaurgarh. **E** *Panna Tourist Bungalow* (RTDC), Udaipur Rd, nr the rly station. T 21900. 16 rm, some a/c plus dormitory. Dining hall (veg), bar. Basic and clean. Best rm with view of fort. **E** *Janta Tourist Rest House*, Station Rd. 2 km from bus stand. 4 a/c rooms with bath. Restaurant, Tourist Office. Spartan. **F** *Sanvaria*, nr the rly station. Very basic. Also *Railway Retiring Rooms*.

Local Transport It is over 6 km from the station to the fort which itself covers quite a large area. Unmetered **auto-rickshaws** and **cycle rickshaws** are available in the town. Fares negotiable. **Bicycles** can also be hired.

Information and Conducted Tours *Tourist Information Office* at the Janta Tourist Rest House, T 9. Open 0800-1200 and 1500-1800. RTDC (Rajasthan Tourist Development Corporation) runs two daily tours, 0800-1130 and 1500-1830. Summer (May,June), 0700-1030 and 1600-1930. Rs 12 per person.

Rail A 117 km branch line runs from **Chittaurgarh to Udaipur**. At **Mavli Junction** (72 km) another branch runs down the Aravallis scarp to **Marwar Junction** (150 km). The views along this line are very picturesque indeed. By taking this route you can visit **Udaipur, Ajmer** and **Jodhpur** in a circular journey.

Old Delhi: *Garib Nawaz Exp*, 2916, daily except Sat, 0920, 12 hr 55 min; *Chetak Exp*, 9616, daily, 2210, 16 hr 5 min. Jaipur: *Meenakshi Exp*, 7570, daily, 0540, 8 hr 5 min; *Garib Nawaz Exp*, 2916, daily, 0920, 6 hr 50 min; *Chetak Exp*, 9616, daily, 2210, 7 hr 50 min. Ajmer: *Meenakshi Exp*, 7570, daily, 0540, 4 hr 30 min; *Garib Nawaz Exp*, 2916, daily except Sat, 0920, 4 hr; *Chetak Exp*, 9616, daily, 2210, 4 hr 25 min. Indore: *Exp*, 9671, daily, 0125, 9 hr 15 min; *Fast Passenger*, 581, daily, 1427, 11 hr 10 min; *Meenakshi Exp*, 7569, daily, 2150, 7 hr 5 min.

Bus There are daily buses to Bundi, Kota, Ajmer and Udaipur. From Chittaurgarh you can travel N to Ajmer (187 km) or Wto Udaipur (N route via Fatehnagar 116 km, S route via Mangarwar 113 km). This is a ictureque drive. Along the way you might see fields of pink and white poppies, grown legally for opium. Just before you reach Udaipur you can stop at the remains of the the ancient city of **Ahar** – see page 378.

Udaipur

Population 300,000 (1981) *Altitude* 577 m. *Best Season* Oct-Mar. *Rainfall* mostly Jun-Sep. Indian airlines flies daily to Udaipur from Delhi (635 km) and Bombay (802 km).

	Jan	Feb	Mar	Apr	May	Jun	Jul	Aug	Sep	Oct	Nov	Dec	Av/Tot
Max (°C)	24	28	32	36	38	36	31	29	31	32	29	26	31
Min (°C)	8	10	15	20	25	25	24	23	22	19	11	8	18
Rain (mm)	9	4	3	3	5	87	197	207	120	16	6	3	660

Set in the Girwa valley amidst the Aravalli hills of S Rajasthan, **Udaipur** is a beautiful city, regarded by many Indians and foreign visitors as one of the most romantic in India. In contrast to some of its desert neighbours it presents an enchanting image of white marble palaces, placid blue lakes and green hills that keep the wilderness at bay. It is an oasis of colour in a stark and arid region.

The city of sunrise The legendary **Ranas of Mewar** who self-consciously traced their proud ancestry back to the Sun, first held sway over the region from their 7th century stronghold, the great Fort of Chittaurgarh. In 1586, Maharana Udai Singh founded a new capital on the shores of Lake Pichola and named it Udaipur, the 'abode of Udai' or 'the city of sunrise'. On the advice of a sage, Udai Singh built a temple above the lake and then his palace around it.

In contrast to the house of Jaipur, the rulers of Udaipur prided themselves on being independent from other more powerful regional neighbours, particularly the Mughals. In a piece of local princely one-upmanship, **Maharana Pratap**, heir apparent to the throne of **Udaipur**, invited **Raja Man Singh** of Jaipur to a lakeside picnic. Afterwards he had the ground Man Singh had trod on washed with sacred Ganga water and insisted that his generals take purificatory baths. **Man Singh** reaped appropriate revenge by preventing Pratap Singh from acceding to the throne. In fact, Udaipur for all its individuality remained one of the poorer princely states in Rajasthan, a consequence of being almost constantly at war. In 1818, **Mewar**, the kingdom of the Udaipur Maharanas, came under British political control but still managed to avoid almost all British cultural influence.

Fort palaces Udaipur is a traditionally planned walled city, its bastioned rampart walls pierced by five massive gates, each studded with iron spikes as protection against enemy war elephants. High on the hill overlooking the lake stands the palace of the Maharanas, an imposing edifice that is probably the largest palace in Rajasthan. From its rooftop gardens and balconies, you can look out over the Pichola Lake. Here 'adrift like a snowflake' is the Jag Niwas Palace, the summer palace of the Maharanas. Around the lake, the houses and temples of the old city stretch out in a pale honeycomb.

Local Festivals All the popular Hindu festivals are celebrated but *Gangaur* (Mar/Apr) is especially popular in Udaipur – see Jaipur (page 354).

Places of Interest The Old City was built in the 17th century on undulating ground, and surrounded by a large wall through which there were five main gates: **Hathi Pol** (*Elephant Gate*-North), **Kishan Gate** (South), **Delhi Gate** (N East), **Chand Pol** (*Moon Gate* West) and the **Suraj Pol** (*Sun Gate*-East). The W side of the town is bounded by the beautiful **Pichola Lake** and the E and N sides by moats. To the S is the fortified hill of **Eklingigarh**. The streets of the city are narrow and, generally, quite picturesque. The main street leads from the Hathi Pol to the City Palace (1567 onwards) which stands on a low ridge overlooking the Lake Pichola. This actually comprises a number of palaces, that despite

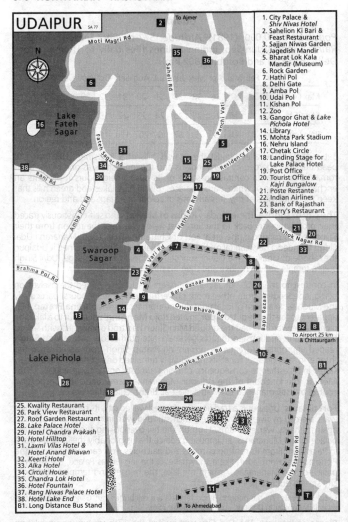

UDAIPUR SA 77

To Ajmer

Moti Magri Rd

Saheli Rd

Panchi Vati

Lake Fateh Sagar

Fateh Sagar Rd

Rani Rd

Residency Rd

Mohta Park Stadium

Amba Pol Rd

Brahma Pol Rd

Swaroop Sagar

H

Ashok Nagar Rd

Silawat Vari Rd

Bara Bazaar Mandi Rd

Bapu Bazaar

Oswal Bhavan Rd

To Airport 25 km & Chittaurgarh

Amalka Kanta Rd

Lake Pichola

Lake Palace Rd

B1

City Station Rd

NH 8

To Ahmedabad

1. City Palace & *Shiv Nivas Hotel*
2. Sahelion Ki Bari & *Feast Restaurant*
3. Sajjan Niwas Garden
4. Jagedish Mandir
5. Bharat Lok Kala Mandir (Museum)
6. Rock Garden
7. Hathi Pol
8. Delhi Gate
9. Amba Pol
10. Udai Pol
11. Kishan Pol
12. Zoo
13. Gangor Ghat & *Lake Pichola Hotel*
14. Library
15. Mohta Park Stadium
16. Nehru Island
17. Chetak Circle
18. Landing Stage for Lake Palace Hotel
19. Post Office
20. Tourist Office & *Kajri Bungalow*
21. Poste Restante
22. Indian Airlines
23. Bank of Rajasthan
24. Berry's Restaurant

25. Kwality Restaurant
26. Park View Restaurant
27. Roof Garden Restaurant
28. *Lake Palace Hotel*
29. *Hotel Chandra Prakash*
30. *Hotel Hilltop*
31. *Laxmi Vilas Hotel & Hotel Anand Bhavan*
32. *Keerti Hotel*
33. *Alka Hotel*
34. Circuit House
35. *Chandra Lok Hotel*
36. *Hotel Fountain*
37. *Rang Niwas Palace Hotel*
38. *Hotel Lake End*
B1. Long Distance Bus Stand

variations in design and ornamentation are integrated into an an impressive whole. It is built on a massive scale, with a blend of Rajput and Mughal influences.

The *Jagdish temple* Only 150 m to the N of the palace is the **Jagdish Temple** (1651), a fine example of Indo-Aryan architecture built by Maharana Jagat Singh. Now a little run down, in front of it is a brass Garuda and stone elephants flanking the steps to the entrance. Within the temple is a black stone image of Vishnu as Jagannath, the Lord of the Universe. The entrance is through the **Bari Pol** (Great Gate, 1600) which leads on to the **Tripolia Gate** (1725). Between them are eight

toranas, arches under which the rulers on their birthdays were weighed against gold and silver which was then distributed to the poor.

Beyond the Tripolia the **Ganes Deori Gate** leads S to the fine **Rai Angan** (Royal Courtyard, 1571) which is adjoined on the Eside by the Jewel Room. From here you can wander or be guided through a number of palace enclosures, some beautifully decorated, all comparatively small and picturesque. Here and there you will get pretty views out over the city or the lake. Of these palaces, the **Chhoti Chitra Shali** has brilliant peacock mosaics and the **Manak Mahal** (Ruby Palace) has been filled with figures of porcelain and glass. The **Moti Mahal** (Pearl Palace) is decorated with mirrors and the **Chini ki Chitra Mahal** (1711-34) has fine ornamentation of Dutch and Chinese made tiles counterpointed with mirror work. The **Bari Mahal** or **Amar Vilas** (1699-1711) has a pleasant garden in it.

On the W side of the Tripolia are the **Karan Vilas** (1620-28) and **Khush Mahal,** a pleasure palace for European guests with a 'grotesque mixture of European, Rajput and Mughal detailing' (Davies), whilst to the S lies the **Shambhu Niwas Palace**. Maharana Fateh Singh added the **Shiv Niwas Palace** to this. Now a small hotel, one room has crystal furniture.

Palace Museum   Half of the City Palace is still occupied by the royal family and is not accessible. There is a museum in the 'open' part of the City Palace, well worth visiting, and with some beautiful views across the lake. The museum includes the **Mor Chowk** with its beautiful late 19th century peacock mosaics. There is also armour worn by Pratap Singh against Akbar, narrative wall paintings, royal cradles, toys etc. There is also a government museum within the palace complex with a characteristically bizarre collection of exhibits which include a stuffed kangaroo and Siamese twin deer.

Lake Pichola   Fringed with hills, some of them wooded, gardens, havelis, ghats and temples, Lake Pichola is the scenic focus of Udaipur. Set in it are the **Jag Niwas** and the **Jag Mandir** Palaces. The S Island, The **Jag Mandir** is notable for the **Gul Mahal,** a domed pavilion built during the reign of Karan Singh (1621-28). **Prince Khurram,** later the Shah Jahan, lived on this island when he was in revolt against his father, the Emperor Jahangir. Refugee European ladies and children were also given sanctuary there by **Maharana Sarap Singh** during the Mutiny. It is now abandoned but there has been talk for some years now of converting it into a hotel.

The Lake Palace   N is the **Jag Niwas** island (1.5 ha) with the older **Dilaram** and **Bari Mahal** Palaces. They were built by *Maharana Jagat Singh II* in 1754 and covers the whole island. Once the royal summer residences, they seem to float like a dream ship on the blue waters of the lake. These now form the **Lake Palace Hotel**. The courtly atmosphere, elegance and opulence of princely times, the painted ceilings, antique furniture and stained glass windows combined with the truly magical setting make it the most romantic in India. If you are not staying in the hotel it is possible to go across on boat shuttle service for a visit but you will be required to have tea or a meal (see Hotels). The views from the Lake Palace hotel are superb.

The old city   The old city is a maze of narrow narrow winding lanes flanked by tall whitewashed houses with doorways, decorated with Mewar folk art, windows with stained glass or jali screens, majestic havelis with spacious inner courtyards and, of course, shops. Many of the houses within the city were given by the Maharana to retainers – barbers, priests, traders and artisans. Many landholders, titled *jagirdars**, in addition to an ancestral home in a far flung village had a townhouse conveniently located near the palace. One of the grandest of these is the **Bagor ki Haveli**, all glass work and a succession of cool shady courtyards. This is the **W Zone Cultural Centre** and is open to visitors during office hours.

Other Places within the City   The *Fateh Sagar* Lake, N of Lake Pichola, was constructed in 1678 during the reign of Maharana Jai Singh but has been modified since. There is a pleasant lakeside drive along the E bank but, overall, it lacks the charm of the Pichola. The **West Zone Cultural Centre** has created a village by the lake where village huts from Rajasthan, Gujarat, Maharashtra and Goa have been faithfully replicated. A small **museum** has a collection of colourful folk art. Free, no guide books. The 6 km trip from the Old City centre is well worth it.

Pratap Samak Open daily 0900-1800. Entry Re 1. Overlooking the Fateh Sagar is the **Moti Magri** (Pearl Hill) on which is a statue of Maharana Pratap astride his famous steed Chetak (there are numerous everyday items in the area bearing his name, including soap, and also a Chetak Express). Chetak possessed some fine equine qualities and these have been exaggerated by local guides, some of whom claim that he was able to jump an abyss of extraordinary width in the heat of the battle even after losing one leg! The path to the top winds through some attractive gardens.

The Bharatiya Lok Kala Museum Open daily 0900-1800. Entry Rs 2. It is charged with the preservation of folk arts, which abound in Rajasthan and has an interesting collection including dresses, dolls, masks, musical instruments, paintings and puppets. There are regular puppet shows.

Sahelion ki Bari Gardens open daily 0900-1800. Entry Re 0.50. This 'Garden of the Maids of Honour' is a small ornamental pleasure garden in the N of the city and contains an elegant lotus pool, gushing fountains, beautiful black marble kiosks on the corners of the pool and stunning bougainvilleas covering the walls of the enclosure. A very attractive place. In what was a pavilion opposite the entrance is a small 'children's' museum which has a curious collection of exhibits.

Ahar 3 km E of the city are the remains of the ancient city which contains some chattris (cenotaphs) and a small **museum**. The chhattris are in the Jain style and set on high plinths in the Mahasati or royal place of cremation. The museum contains pottery sherds and terracotta toys dating from the 1st Millenium BC plus exhibits from subsequent periods, e.g. 10th century sculptures. In the vicinity are the temples of Mira Bhai (10th century), Adinatha (11th century) and Mahavira (15th century). Nearby is the village of Ahar.

Hotels Most are 25 km from airport, 4 km from rly and 1-2 km from centre **AL** *Lake Palace Hotel*, Pichola Lake. T 23241-5, Cable: Lakepalace, Telex: 33-203 LPal In. 80 rm best with lake view. Superb situation. Very good Rajasthani folk dances, puppet shows, though swimming pool is disappointing. The most romantic hotel in India. Expensive but excellent. If you wish to visit the hotel without staying, buy a ferry cum lunch or dinner ticket (about Rs 180-225) which allows you several hours of luxury and an excellent meal. Mid afternoon, you may take the boat across for tea, for approx Rs 60.

 B *Shiv Niwas*, City Palace. T 28239-41. Cable: Palace, Telex: 033-126 Ipalin, Fax: 0294-23823. 31 rm. Pool, tennis, squash, billiards. Garden and boating. Former Royal guesthouse of the Maharana. Palatial. **B** *Laxmi Vilas Palace* (ITDC). T 24411-3, Cable: Tourism, Telex: 033-218. 54 rm. Former guesthouse for the Maharana's VIP guests, now rather down at heel. Good views.

 C *Shikarbadi*, Govardhan Vilas. T 83200-4, Cable: Imperial/ Shikarbadi, Telex: 033-227 Badi in. 25 rm. Restaurant (Indian, Marwari, Rajasthani and Tandoori, Continental), 24 hr room service, pool. Deer park and riding. Attractive turn of the century forest hunting lodge owned by the Maharaja. Good gardens. **C** *Anand Bhawan*, Fateh Sagar Rd. T 23256, Cable: Anandbhawan. 24 a/c rm. Restaurant, bar, exchange, car hire. Hilltop location with spectacular views. Another royal guesthouse. **C** *Lake Pichola*, Chandrapole. T 29197, Cable: Pichola. 20 rm. Restaurant, bar, rm 24 hr room service, exchange, shops, car hire, TV. Cultural shows on demand. New but in the traditional style. Good views. Boat rides.

 C *Chandralok*, Saheli Marg. T 29011-2, Cable: Chandralok. 4 a/c rm. Restaurant, doctor on call, car hire, TV. Folk dances and puppet shows on request. Well-kept rm. **C** *Hilltop*, 5 Ambavgarh. T 28708-9, Cable: Hilltop. 27 rm, central a/c. Restaurants, bar, exchange, shops, safe deposit, laundry, doctor on call, car hire, credit cards, TV and Video. Folk dances and puppet shows on request. **C** *Rajdarshan*, 18 Pannabai Marg, inside Hathipol. T 23271-3, Cable: Darshan. 34 rm, central a/c. Pool, bar, restaurant, 24 hr room service, exchange, shops, safe deposit, laundry, doctor on call, credit cards. Folk dances and puppet shows. Balconies and good views.

D *Fountain*, 2 Sukhadia Circle. T 26646, Cable: Fountain. 20 rm, some a/c. Restaurant, laundry, travel, Amex, Diners credit cards, secretarial service,TV and Video. Garden, folk dances and puppet shows. **D** *Kajri Tourist Bungalow* (RTDC), Shastri Circle. T 23509. 38 rm, some a/c and dormitory. Restaurant, bar, TV lounge, tours and sightseeing, gardens. Rm overlooking garden pleasanter. Restaurant rather dull and food mediocre though you can have breakfast and tea on the lawns. Helpful Tourist Office near entrance. **D** *Lakend*, Fateh Sagar. T 23841, Cable: Hilltop. 78 rm, a/c and non. Somewhat unusual restaurant, bar, credit cards, pool, TV. Modern with lakeside garden. Reasonably attractive rm with balconies overlooking the lake.

E *Ankur*, Gurdwara Marg, T 25355, 24355. 10 rm, non a/c. 24 hr room service. **E** *Alka*, Shastri Circle, opposite Tourist Bungalow. T 28611, 25130, Cable: Alka. 55 rm, non a/c, some with bath. 25 km airport, 2 km rly. Restaurant, laundry, Diners credit cards. **E** *Damanis*, nr Telegraph Office, Madhuban. T 25675-6, Cable: Hotel Damanis. 25 rm, some a/c. 22 km airport, 3 km rly. Restaurant (Indian, Continental), exchange, car hire, travel,credit cards, TV. Puppet shows. **E** *Keerti and Pratap Country Inn*, Airport Rd. T 23638-9, Cable: Hotelkeerti. 33 rm, mostly non a/c. Restaurant, horse and camel safaris and rides. **E** *Meera*, Meera Marg, nr Sukhadia Circle. T 27554, 24857. Some a/c rm. Restaurant, travel.

E *Rang Niwas Palace*, Lake Palace Rd, T 23891. 14 rm, some a/c, with and without bath. Restaurant, 24 hr room service. **E** *Lalghat Guest House*, behind the Jagdish temple on Lake Pichola. Rm with and without bath and cheaper dormitory beds. Restaurant food mediocre, but snacks and drinks fine. Good views from balconies and rooftop, and very relaxed atmosphere. Excellent value. Recommended. **E** *Raj Palace*, 103 Bhatiyani Chotta. Rm with bath. Garden, restaurant. Very highly recommended for clean rm, comfortable beds, excellent service and good food. Will organize city tour (5 hrs, RS100). **E** *Yatri Guest House*, 3/4 Punchkun Rd, helpful and knowledgeable owner, good value.

F *Badi Haveli*, nr the Jagdish temple. Non a/c rm with and without bath. Pleasant with good rooftop views. **F** *Chandra Prakash*, Lake Palace Rd, T 28109. Rm with and without bath. Garden. Good value. **F** *Ghunghru Guest House*, College Rd, behind the Keerti Hotel. Reasonable. Garden. **F** *Keerti*, Sarasvati Marg, nr Suraj Pol. T 3639. Non a/c rm with and without bath. Popular. Do not confuse it with the Keerti Tourist Hotel which is not as good. **F** *Mona Lisa*, City Palace Rd. Some rm with bath. **F** *Natural*, Rang Sagar Lake. Clean and cheap. **F** *Ratnadeep*, Lake Palace Rd. T 24730. Mostly non a/c rm. Nr the bus stand on city Station Rd is the **F** *Apsara*, T 23400 and **F** *Sonika*, T 25353. Nearby is the **F** *Raj*, T 28262. All are basic. Close by, the **F** *Shalimar*, T 26807 is good value. *Railway Retiring Rooms*.

Restaurants *Park View*, opp Town Hall, City Station Rd is widely regarded as the best in town. *The Coffee House*, Chetak Circle has good coffee and Indian snacks. Open 0730-2200. *Berrys*, Chetak Circle, T 25132. *Kajri*, T 25122. *Apsara*, T 23400. *Kwality*, T 25107. Open 1000-2300. *Delhi Darbar*, Hathipol.

Bars The larger hotels have bars and the one at the Lake Palace is especially pleasant.

Banks In Town Hall: *Dena*, T 25480; *Indian Overseas Bank*, T 24064; *Punjab and Sind*, T 27158; *Baroda*, T 23157; Also in Mandi Yard, T 26221; *Punjab National*, T 26118, Also in Bapu Bazaar, T 27136. In Delhi Gate: *Allahabad*, T 27014; *Central Bank of India*, T 23053; *Bank of India*, T 23935. In Chetak Circle: *New Bank of India*, T 24775; *Bikaner and Jaipur*, T 27087; *Hathipole, Kotwali*, T 25315. In Bapu Bazaar: *Oriental Bank of Commerce*, T 27436; *Vijay*, T 28162; *Syndicate*, T 27506. *Canara*, Sethji-ki-Bari, T 27635. *Rajasthan*, Shastri Marg, T 26059; Ashwini Marg, T 24835. *Bank of India*, Nyaya Marg, T 27359. *United Commercial Bank*, T 23795. *Union Bank of India*, New Fatehpura, T 27089. *State Bank of India*, Hospital Rd, T 26970, 26371. *Indian Bank*, opposite Surajpol, T 24725

Shopping The main shopping centres are Chetak Circle, Bapu Bazaar, Hathipole, Palace Rd, Clock Tower, Nehru Bazaar, Shastri Circle, Delhi Gate, Sindhi Bazaar, Bada Bazaar. The local handicrafts are wooden toys, colourful portable temples, *Bandhani* tie-and-dye fabrics, embroidery and Pichchwai paintings. Paintings are of three types: miniatures in the classical style of courtly Mewar; *phads** or folk art; and *pichchwais** or religious art. All three styles are widely available. *Rajasthali* (Rajasthan Govt. Emporium), Chetak Circle, nr Chetak Cinema. *Jagdish Emporium*, City Palace Rd. The best place to buy traditional Udaipur and Gujarati embroideries. The cushion covers are especially attractive and come in two price categories. The more expensive ones are claimed to be quite old – 20-30 years – and are in beautiful dusky colours. The cheaper ones are more garish. Friendly and persuasive staff.

Photography *Ajanta Studio and Colour Lab*, A Marg, T 26218.

Local Transport Private taxis are available from the airport and major hotels. They are unmetered and charges vary from Re 1.60 to Rs 2 per km. Negotiate rates. **Auto-rickshaws** are unmetered, fares negotiable. Min. fare Rs 3. **Bicycles** are available for hire at various places in the town. Try the shops nr the Tourist Information Office at the Tourist Bungalow. The hire charge should be approximately Rs 10 per day.

Entertainment The Department of Tourism (Govt. of Rajasthan) conducts regular cultural programmes in Udaipur from Sep to Mar. Details from Tourist Information Bureau, Kajri Tourist Bungalow, T 23605. Hotels also run cultural shows, notably folk dances and puppet shows.

Sports Golf, Field Club, Fatehpur.

Museums The Bharatiya Lok Kala Museum is charged with the preservation of folk arts, which abound in Rajasthan and has an interesting collection including dresses, dolls, masks, musical instruments, paintings and puppets. There are regular puppet shows. Open daily 0900-1800. Entry Rs 2. **WZone Cultural Centre** and **Village** on Fateh Sagar. Open during office hours. **City Palace Museum**. Entered through the Deoria Gate. Open 0930-1600. Entry Rs 3, Camera Fee, Rs 3 (still), Rs 10 (movie and video). Extensive, a little geared to the tourist but worth a visit.

Parks and Zoos Gulab Bagh a reasonably attractive park on Lake Palace Rd. Also contains a Zoo which is unremarkable and not worth a visit.

Useful Numbers Police: T 3000 Fire: T 27111 Ambulance: T 23333

Hospitals and Medical Services General Hospital, Chetak Circle, T 233319. Ayurveda Sewashram, Station Rd, T 23199. Kanchan Nursing Home, Bapu Bazaar, T 25520. Bakhatahar Lal Nursing Home, Bapu Bazaar. Udaipur Ayurveda Centre, Bhupalpura, T 25562. Seema Nursing Home, T 24491. Homoeopathic Hospital, Hathipole, T 23704.

Chemists Several on Hospital Rd.

Post and Telegraph General Post and Telegraph Office, Chetak Circle, T 23322.

Places of Worship Hindu – Jagdish Temple, Amba Mata Temple; Christian – Church of Scotland Mission, St Paul's Church, Church of N India; Sikh – Guru Singh Sabha.

Travel Agents Rajasthan Tours, Garden Hotel, T 23030 (Lake Palace branch, T 25533). Tourist Guide Service, Chetak Circle, T 23526. Peacock Travels, Lake Palace Rd, T 25757. Padmini Tours, Chandralok Hotel, Saheli Marg, T 23482. Mayur Travels, 59, Polo Ground, T 23482. Alka Travel Service, Hotel Damanis, T 22567, 25675. Lakend Tours and Travels, opp Shastri Circle, T 23611, 25130. RTDC, Kajri Tourist Bungalow, Shastri Circle, T 23509, 25122. Jai Mewar Transport Co., opp Commerce House, T 25289. On City Station Rd, Udiyapol, Taxi Stand, Chetak Circle, T 25112. Tourist Taxi Service, Lake Palace Rd, T 24169.

Tourist Offices and Information Tourist Information Bureau (Govt. of Rajasthan), Kajri Tourist Bungalow, T 23605. Open 1000-1700. Information Centre, Mohata Park, Chetak Circle, T 24924. Open 1000-1700. Counters at City Rly Station, T 25105. Open 0800-1200 and at Dabok Airport, T 23011. Open during flight times.
   Conducted Tours RTDC tours from Kajri Tourist Bungalow, Shastri Circle, T 23509, 25122.
   City Sightseeing: Half day (0800-1300), Pratap Smarak, Fateh Sagar, Sahelion-ki-Bari, Lok Kala Mandal, Sukhadia Circle, City Palace, Jagdish Temple, Gulab Bagh. Rs 20. Excursion: Half day (1400-1900), Haldighati, Nathdwara, Eklingji. Rs 45.

Air Indian Airlines flies daily from Delhi to Bombay via Jaipur, Jodhpur, Udaipur and Aurangabad, and back on the same route. Reservations: Indian Airlines, Delhi Gate, T 23952. Open 1000-1315 and 1400-1700. Airport, T 23011. Dabok Airport is 23 km from centre Udaipur. The security staff are very particular about hand luggage and check it thoroughly. Do not take any batteries or knives in you hand luggage. There are only taxis operating the Airport/City transfer. Fare approx Rs 75.

Rail Ahmadabad: Udaipur-Ahmadabad Exp, 9643, daily, 1845, 9 hr 55 min. Old Delhi: Pink City Exp/Garib Nawaz Exp, 2902/2916, daily except Sun, 0530, 16 hr 45 min; Chetak Exp, 9616, daily, 1815, 20 hr. Jaipur: Garib Nawaz Exp, 2916, daily except Sun, 0530, 10 hr 40 min; Chetak Exp, 9616, daily, 1815, 11 hr 45 min. Jodhpur: Udaipur-Jodhpur Passenger, 252, daily, 2015, 11 hr 45 min. Ajmer Garib Nawaz Exp, 2916, daily except Sun, 0530, 7 hr 50 min; Chetak Exp, 9616, daily, 1815, 8 hr 20 min.

Road Udaipur is on NH8. Jaipur (405 km); Jodhpur (275 km); Ajmer (274 km); Ahmadabad (252 km); Mount Abu (270 km); Indore (635 km); Hyderabad (1471 km); Bhopal (765 km); Delhi (635 km); Bombay (802 km); Calcutta (1755 km); Madras (2099 km); **Varanasi** (1078 km).

Bus State Transport Bus Stand, City Station Rd (NH 8), Udiyapol. Enquiries, T 27191, Reservations open 0700-2100. The Rajasthan, Gujarat, Uttar Pradesh and Madhya Pradesh SRTC operate buses to Udaipur from various centres in the region, such as Ahmadabad, Vadodara, Surat, Brindavan, Bharatpur, Agra, Mathura, Jaipur, Jodhpur, Delhi, Bikaner, Ujjain, Ratlam and Bhopal. Private bus companies also operate to/from destinations in the region. Luxury coaches run at night.

Excursions

Monsoon Palace 15 km. Fantastic views from deserted, run down palace on hilltop which is now a radio transmitting centre. The 3-4 hr round trip costs about Rs 70 per head in auto rickshaw and more in a taxi.

Kumbhalgarh

To reach Kumbhalgarh it is best to hire a car for an afternoon. The drive goes due N out of Udaipur. It will take about 2 hours and is through the Rajasthani countryside. You may encounter camel trains on the roads and groups of colourfully dressed Rajasthani women and children returning to their villages. The small fields are well kept and wherever possible are irrigated from the streams and tanks that are dotted across the landscape. At the natural reservoirs among the rocks you will see the Persian Wheel type of irrigation as water is lifted from the lake level often up to 20m below. It is worth stopping and watching. In the fields there will be wheat and mustard over winter and everywhere you will see groups of people working. As you return to Udaipur at sundown, they will be returning to their villages. Around, the sand and honey coloured rocks will turn golden as the sun sinks. All this combines to make the journey there and back every bit as magical and fascinating as the fort itself.

The fort of **Kumbhalgarh** (*Altitude* 1,087 m) 84 km N of Udaipur, was the second most important fort of the **Mewar Kingdom** after Chittaurgarh. Built mostly by the **Maharana Khumba** in the 15th century, it is situated on the northernmost ridge of the Aravallis and commands a great strategic and scenic view of the lower land to the N and stands 213 m above the pass leading towards Udaipur. It is one of those many places in India that is off the beaten tourist track yet accessible enough from a major tourist centre to make a visit practicable.

Places of interest en route At *Nagda*, 21 km out of Udaipur, are three temples: the ruined Jain temple of **Adbudji** and the **Sasbahu** temples. These two 'Mother' and 'Daughter in law' temples are Vaishnavite and are raised on a terrace to face E towards the tank. The larger temple is surrounded by ten subsidiary shrines, the smaller by only four. The complex, though comparatively small, has some very intricate carving. You can hire bicycles in *Eklingi* (1 km) to reach these temples and there is a regular, approx. hourly bus service to Eklingi from Udaipur. Small cheap and basic *Guest House* in the village. Eklingi and Nagda are set in a deep ravine, in which is the Eklingi lake, with a white marble temple sacred to the family deity of the Maharana's family. The two storeyed **Ekalinga Temple** to Siva in the village dates from 734 AD, although its present form is due to **Maharana Raimal** (r.1473-1509). The walled complex houses a four-faced Siva image of black marble. Open daily 0500-0700, 1000-1300 and 1700-1900. Evenings draw crowds of worshippers (few tourists). No photography. In the vicinity is the large but simple **Lalkulisha Temple** (972), and other ruined semi-submerged temples. Lots of waterbirds – and very quiet. *Nathdwara*, 48 km is a centre of the Krishna worshipping Community of Gujarati merchants who are followers of Vallabhacharya (15th century). Non-Hindus usually not allowed inside but the outside has interesting paintings. Bazaar sells temple hangings (*pichwais*) which are painted on cloth.

The approach The final dramatic approach to the **Kumbhalgarh fort** (63 km) is across deep ravines and through thick scrubby jungle. Seven gates guard the approaches while seven ramparts, reinforced by bastions and towers, make the palace impregnable. The first gate is the **Arait Pol**,some distance from the main fort. Signals would be flashed by mirror in times of emergency and danger. **Hulla Pol** (Gate of Disturbance) is named after the point reached by invading Mughal armies in 1567. **Hanuman Pol** contains a shrine and temple, The **Bhairava Pol** has a plaque ordering the exile of a treacherous Prime Minister in the 19th century.

The fifth gate, the **Paghra (Stirrup) Pol** is where the cavalry assembled and the Star tower nearby has walls 8 m thick. The **Top-Khana** or Cannon Gate is alleged to have a secret escape tunnel. The last gate the **Nimbu (Lemon) Pol** has the Chaimundi temple beside it. The walls of the fort stretch over 30 km enclosing a large plateau within which there is the palace and garrison, 365 temples and shrines and a village. This enabled the occupants to be self-sufficient in foodstuffs and well supplied with water. The dominant location of Kumbhalgarh enabled its defenders to see aggressors approaching from a great distance.

The palace Tiers of inner ramparts rise to the summit and the appropriately named **Badal Mahal** (Cloud Palace) perched on it. There is a chaukidar who holds the keys to the palace which by Rajput standards is small and he will show you round. A small tip of Rs 10 is appropriate when you sign the visitors book at the end. The views from the palace down below the sinuous walls to the jungle-covered hillsides (now a wildlife reserve containing tiger and leopard, the chaukidar will tell you) and across the deserts of Marwar beyond towards Jodhpur are stunning. The palace rooms are decorated in pastel colours in a 19th century style and a number have very attractive more boldly coloured friezes, but are unfurnished. After the maze-like palace at Udaipur, this is marvellously compact.

The winter months are best for visiting the fort and Mar-Jun is the best time for the reserve, which you can go through to **Ranakpur**. The little known and visited Kumbhalgarh is one of the finest examples of defensive fortification in Rajasthan and a trip there is likely to be a highlight of any trip to India. In addition to the palace you can wander round the many temples and along the walls to savour the great panoramic views.

Accommodation You can stay in the *PWD Rest House* at Kumbhalgarh or in the *Aodhi Lodge* tourist complex run by one of Mewar's old noble families. The **Aodhi** Lodge has a restaurant serving authentic Mewari food and has delightful cottages built of stone. Aodhi ('The Watchtower') can organise horse safaris to the fort and surrounding areas. A very pleasant place for an out of town stay.

Ranakpur, 25 km SW of Kumbhalgarh as the crow flies was built in 1367 by Rana Khumbha's prime minister, Ranakpur has one of best known Jain temples in the country. Vaguely reminiscent of the other Jain temples in Rajasthan, e.g. the Dilwara temples at Mt. Abu, the complexity and elaborate ornamentation demonstrate the western Indian style in full flower. The secluded wooded setting complements the building wonderfully. There are three temples worth visiting: **The *Adinatha* Temple** (1439), **The Parshvantha** and the **Surya Narayana Temples** (mid-15th century). Of these the Adinatha is the most noteworthy. The sanctuary is symmetrically planned around the central shrine and is within a 100 m x 100 m square enclosure raised on a terrace. The gateways consist of triple-storey porches approached by steep flights of steps. Above the enclosure walls are rows of spires topping the subsidiary shrines that line the compound.

The main sanctuary has a clustered central tower with smaller towers at each corner. The central chamber with its quadruple image of **Adinatha** is approached through four doorways. It contains an extraordinarily complex array of pillars and balconies, intricately decorated with depictions of Jain saints, narrative scenes, and plaques depicting sacred sites. Ranakpur is 39 km from Palna Junction on the

Ajmer-Mt Abu railway line and road. From Udaipur there are about six buses a day, each taking a very long time. From Ranakpur you can proceed by bus to Jodhpur or Mt Abu.

Jaisamand Lake, 52 km SE of Udaipur, was constructed in the late 17th century. Before the recent building of huge dams in S Asia like the Tarbela or Hirakud, it was the second largest artificial lake in Asia (15 km by 10 km) and is surrounded by the summer palaces of the **Ranis of Udaipur** and by low hills stretching as far as the eye can see. The highest two hills are topped by palaces – the **Hawa Mahal** and **Ruti Rani**. Both stand empty but are worth a visit for the architecture and the view. **E** *The RTDC Bungalow* – 4 rm with enormous bathrooms as as well as dormitory facilities. Ideal for an overnight stay. Very reasonable.

From Udaipur a road goes SW through the Aravallis to **Som** (69 km), then turns NW to **Mt Abu**. The total distance is 165 km. The road to Ahmadabad goes south.

JAIPUR TO JODHPUR, ABU RD & AHMADABAD VIA AJMER & PUSHKAR

It is a very pleasant drive from Jaipur to Jodhpur with a number of interesting places en route. Leaving Jaipur on NH8 it is 108 km to Kishangarh. The first part of the journey is across relatively low lying land. Beyond Kishangarh you enter the Aravalli Hills. The direct rly line from Jaipur to Jodhpur bypasses Ajmer and Pushkar and on leaving Jaipur passes by the Sambhar salt lake. Further on is Makrana, where the white marble used on the Taj Mahal, other Mughal masterpieces such as the Red Forts in Delhi and Agra, and today in marble souvenirs, is quarried. From Makrana to Jodhpur the countryside is quite featureless.

Leave Jaipur to the SW on **NH8** to Ajmer. After 5 km there is a left turn to **Ramgarh Lake** (28 km). **NH8** goes straight on through **Dhami** (24 km) and **Dudu** (39 km) to Kishangarh (39 km).

Kishangarh was a tiny princely state surrounded by the larger and infinitely more powerful states of Amber, Marwar and Mewar. Founded in 1597 by Kishan Singh, son of the Maharaja of Jodhpur, the state served the Mughals and later accepted British protection. Kishangarh is chiefly known for its school of miniature painting and the temple within the fort houses a very fine collection depicting the religious epics. The main gate, the **Hathi Pol** (Elephant Gate) has a very high pointed arch which is appropriately flanked by elephants painted on the walls. Situated on the shores of **Lake Gandalan**, the fort and palace, although in a state of disrepair, are undeniably picturesque and hint at a real, if modest, former glory: battlements, courtyards with gardens, shady balconies, windows with brightly coloured panes of glass, brass doors flanked by paintings.

From Kishangarh you continue on **NH8** to Ajmer (27 km). If you are travelling by car (your own or hired) it is worth breaking the journey at Ajmer, seeing the town, making the short drive to nearby **Pushkar**, then proceeding on to Jodhpur the following day. An afternoon drive will bring you to Jodhpur before dark.

Ajmer Population 440,000 Altitude 480 m.

Places of Interest It is said that seven pilgrimages to Ajmer equal one to Mecca. Every year, especially at the annual Islamic festivals of **Id** and **Mohurram** thousands of pilgrims converge on this ancient town on the banks of the Ana

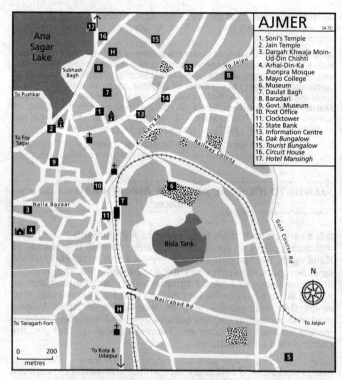

AJMER SA 73

1. Soni's Temple
2. Jain Temple
3. Dargah Khwaja Moin-Ud-Din Chishti
4. Arhai-Din-Ka Jhonpra Mosque
5. Mayo College
6. Museum
7. Daulat Bagh
8. Baradari
9. Govt. Museum
10. Post Office
11. Clocktower
12. State Bank
13. Information Centre
14. *Dak Bungalow*
15. *Tourist Bungalow*
16. *Circuit House*
17. *Hotel Mansingh*

Ana Sagar Lake

Subhash Bagh

To Pushkar

To Foy Sagar

Nalla Bazaar

To Taragarh Fort

Kutchery Rd

Railway Colony

To Jaipu

To Jaipu

Bisla Tank

Golf Course Rd

Nasirabad Rd

To Jaipur

To Kota & Udaipur

N

0   200
metres

Sagar Lake in Rajasthan. Ajmer has become sanctified and renowned throughout the Muslim world as the burial place of Muin-ud-din Chishti who claimed descent from the son-in-law of Mohammed. Born in Afghanistan in the middle of the 12th century at a time when Islam was on the threshold of expanding into India, he visited Ajmer (1192) and died here in 1235, his tomb becoming famous almost overnight. Mosques, pavilions and other tombs were subsequently erected here, the area around the saint's tomb becoming known as the **Dargah Khwaja Sahib**.

Early history The city is situated in a basin at the foot of **Taragarh Hill** (870 m) and is surrounded by a stone wall with five gateways. According to tradition it was founded in 145 AD by **Raja Ajaipal**, one of the Chauhan kings. After numerous dynastic changes it was sacked by Mahmud of Ghazni in 1024 and again by Muhammad Ghuri in 1193. Later it was held by the **Rana Khumbha of Mewar** and then by the rulers of Malwa (1470-1531). Fully aware of its strategic importance, **Akbar** annexed the city in 1556 and made it his royal residence. **Jahangir** and **Shah Jahan** both lived here for long periods.

With the disintegration of the Mughal Empire, it passed to the **House of Jodhpur** and later to the **Marathas**. In 1818 it was annexed by the British and was one of the few places in the region governed by them rather than the Indian princes. The lake was created in the 12th century by damming the Luni river. The town developed around it. On the bank is the fine **Daulat Bagh** garden with its marble pavilions built in 1637 by Shah Jahan. A hill rises behind the garden. Good views from the top.

Taragarh (Star Fort) stands on the hilltop overlooking the town. It is rectangular with walls 4.5 m thick. The view is good but the walk up tiring. Along the way is a graveyard of Muslim 'martyrs' who died storming the fort. The **Dargah of Khwaja Muin-ud-din Chishti** (1143-1235) is the tomb of the Sufi saint who became known as 'The Sun of the Realm of India'. It was commenced by Iltutmish of Delhi and completed by Humayun. So great was the pilgrim traffic from **Agra** and **Fatehpur Sikri** that Akbar, who made several pilgrimages himself on foot, erected *kos** minars (two-mile milestones) along the route.

The entrance is a high gateway painted blue and white. Here visitors must remove their shoes. In the courtyard are two large cauldrons. Rich Muslims on their first visit will pay for a feast of rice, ghee, sugar, almonds, raisins and spices to be cooked in one of these. Local families 'loot the pot', literally climbing in to collect the food which will then be distributed. On the right is the **Akbar Masjid** (c.1570) with drums and candlesticks presented by the Great Mughal. To the left is an assembly hall for the poor.

In the inner courtyard is the **Shah Jahan Masjid** (c.1750), characteristically in white marble, 33 m long and with 11 front arches. On 3 sides there is a carved balustrade. In the centre of the 2nd court is the **Dargah** (tomb). Also in white marble, this is square with a domed roof and 2 entrances. The ceiling is gold-embossed velvet, and silver rails and gates enclose the tomb which pilgrims sprinkle with rose petals. The doors to the shrine, like those at Fatehpur Sikri are covered with votive horseshoes, nailed there by horse-dealers to commemorate successful deals.

Nearby is a small enclosure with marble latticework. This is the **Mazar** or tomb of Bibi Hafiz Jamal, daughter of the saint, and close by is that of Chimni Begum, daughter of Shah Jahan. She never married, refusing to leave her father during the seven years he was held captive by his own son and usurper, Aurangzeb. She spent her last days in Ajmer, as did another daughter who probably died of tuberculosis. At the S end of the Dargah is the **Jhalra**, a deep tank.

Akbar's Palace lies in the heart of the city near the E wall and the railway station. It is large rectangular building with a fine entrance gate. Today it houses the **Ajmer museum**. Owing to its troubled past, Ajmer has comparatively few archaeological treasures. One building illustrates that the city has been a Hindu as well as Muslim stronghold. The **Arhai-din-ka Jhonpra Mosque** (The Hut of two and a half days) lies just outside the **Dargah**. Originally a Jain college built in 1153, it was partially destroyed by Muhammad of Ghori in 1192 and in 1200 turned into a mosque by building a massive screen of seven arches in front of the many pillared hall. This was done by **Qutb-ud-din-Aibak**, allegedly in 2½ days. The mosque is now ruined and only part of the 67 m screen and the Jain hall behind remain. Some restoration work was undertaken in 1875-78 and 1900-03. The mosque proper measures 79 m by 17 m and has ten domes supported by 124 columns.

Mayo College (1873), one of several throughout the country founded to provide young Indian princes with a liberal education, is one of two genuinely Indo-Saracenic buildings designed by **De Fabeck** in Ajmer, the other being the **Mayo Hospital** (1870). The College was known as the 'Eton' of Rajputana and was run along the lines of an English Public School. It is now open to all.

Local Fairs and Festivals The festival commemorating **Khhwaja Muin-ud-din Chishti's** death is celebrated with six days of almost continuous music, and devotees from all over India and the Middle East make the pilgrimage. *Qawwalis** and other Urdu music developed in the courts of rulers can be heard. Roses cover the tomb. On the final day, women wash the tomb clean with their hair, then squeeze the rose water into bottles as medicine for the sick.

Hotels C *Mansingh Palace*. Vaishali Nagar. T 30855/6. 60 rm. 3 km rly, 1 km downtown. Central a/c. TV and Video in all suites. Restaurant, room service, exchange, shops, safe deposit, beauty parlour, doctor on call, credit cards, secretarial service. Golf, polo, swimming and tennis as well as folk dances and puppet show on request. **E** *Khadim Tourist Bungalow*, Savitri Girls' College Rd, nr the rly station and bus stand. T 20490. 49 rm, some a/c, plus dormitory. Restaurant (limited menu), bar. Pleasant setting. The *Circuit House* overlooks the Ana Sagar lake. There is a group of **F** category hotels offering rm with bath, by the rly station: *Nagpal Tourist Hotel*, T 21603; *Anand*, T 20090; *Malwa*, T 23343.

Restaurants *Honey Dew* for good veg food throughout the day. Also *Kwality* for Indian and continental, *Italia*, *Vikram* and *Khadim Tourist Bungalow* open to non-residents.

Banks *Bank of Baroda* and *Punjab National Bank* on Prithviraj Rd, *State Bank of India* at the Collectorate, Bank of Bikaner, Jaipur Station Rd.

Shopping Fine local silver jewellery, tie and dye textiles and camel hide articles are best buys. The shopping areas are Madar Gate, Station Rd, Purani Mandi, Naya Bazaar and Kaisarganj.

Museum housed in the octagonal building which was Akbar's fort-palace. It contains a very good collection of old Rajput and Mughal armour, coins and some fine sculpture.

The **Tourist Office** is in the Khadim Tourist Bungalow, T 20430 which is nr the bus stand on Jaipur Rd

Rail Old Delhi: *Aravalli Exp*, 9932, daily, 1905, 10 hr 25 min; *Delhi Mail*, 9902, daily, 2040, 10 hr 50 min; *Delhi Exp*, 9904, daily, 0710, 11 hr 50 min; *Ashram Exp*, 2906, daily, 0135, 8 hr 25 min. **Agra (Fort)**: *Agra Fort Fast Passenger Exp*, 9706, daily, 2000, 10 hr 35 min. **Ahmadabad**: *Agra Fort Fast Passenger Exp*, 9705, daily, 0740, 20 hr 30 min; *Ahmadabad Exp*, 9903, daily, 2150, 12 hr 10 min; *Ahmadabad Mail*, 9901, daily, 0835, 11 hr 40 min; *Aravalli Exp*, 9931, daily, 0315, 13 hr; *Ashram Exp*, 2905, daily, 0250, 8 hr 25 min. **Beawar**: *Ahmadabad Exp*, 9903, daily, 2150, 57 min; *Ahmadabad Mail*, 9901, daily, 0835, 1 hr; *Aravalli Exp*, 9931, daily, 0315, 53 min.

Jaipur: *Pink City Exp*, 2916, daily except Sat, 1350, 2 hr 20 min; *Delhi-Ahmadabad Mail*, 9902, daily, 2000, 3 hr 35 min; *Delhi-Ahmadabad Exp*, 9904, daily, 0710, 3 hr 45 min; *Ashram Exp*, 2906, daily, 0137, 2 hr 48 min. **Udaipur**: *Garib Nawaz Exp*, 2915, daily, 1358, 7 hr 32 min; *Chetak Exp*, 9615, daily, 0030, 8 hr 45 min. **Chittaurgarh** *Meenakshi Exp*, 7569, daily, 1720, 4 hr 5 min; *Garib Nawaz Exp*, 2915, daily except Sun, 1358, 3 hr 56 min; *Chetak Exp*, 9615, daily, 0030, 4 hr 30 min.

Bus There are buses every half hour from Jaipur. The journey takes about 3 hr. There are daily buses to **Jodhpur** (198 km), **Chittaurgarh** (190 km), **Udaipur** (302 km) via Chittaurgarh, **Kota** (200 km) via Bundi and Bikaner. Also buses for Agra and Delhi.

Excursions Ajmer is a good base from which to visit **Pushkar** (11 km W of the city). Buses leave from outside the railway station.

For most of the year, *Pushkar* is a gentle and peaceful lakeside village on the edge of the desert. It has become a very popular place for foreigners travelling round India to relax in. From Ajmer, the usual access point, the road skirts the W shore of the Ana Sagar and at 5 km passes the village of Nausar and through a striking 2 km long pass through the Nag Pahar (Snake Hills) that divide Pushkar from Ajmer. Pushkar lies in a narrow valley overshadowed by these impressive rocky hills and the lake is one of India's most sacred.

Fa Hien, the Chinese traveller who visited Pushkar in the 4th century AD, commented on the number of pilgrims. Even though the Mughal Emperor Aurangzeb destroyed many of the ancient temples, they are still numerous. There are also ghats leading down to the water to enable pilgrims to bathe. The temple to Brahma, at the farther end of the lake, is regarded as a particularly holy shrine since it marks the spot where the incarnation of the god took place. It is said to be the only such place in India. The lake apparently sprang from a lotus blossom dropped by him. If you climb the hills around the village at sunset you will be rewarded with spectacular views of the desert stretching out before you.

Local Fairs and Festivals Every year at the full moon of *Kartik Poornima* in Oct/Nov, there is a cattle and camel *mela* (fair) and the village is roused from its dreamy existence by the influx of up to 100,000 visitors and pilgrims and hordes of cattle and camels with their part nomadic drivers and food stock to last the

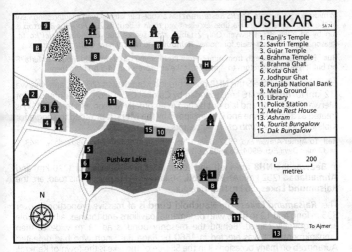

PUSHKAR SA 74

1. Ranji's Temple
2. Savitri Temple
3. Gujar Temple
4. Brahma Temple
5. Brahma Ghat
6. Kota Ghat
7. Jodhpur Ghat
8. Punjab National Bank
9. Mela Ground
10. Library
11. Police Station
12. Mela Rest House
13. Ashram
14. Tourist Bungalow
15. Dak Bungalow

Pushkar Lake

0   200
metres

N

To Ajmer

period. The RTDC caters for this by erecting a tent city.

The huge **cattle market** is Pushkar's biggest draw. Farmers, breeders and camel traders buy and sell. Sales in leather whips, bits, shoes, embroidered animal covers soar, whilst for the women it is a chance to bargain over bangles, clothes, pots, necklaces of glass beads from Nagaur, ivory work from **Merta** and printed cloth from Jodhpur and Ajmer. Thousands of people travel long distances to participate, and entertainment is richly provided. There are horse and camel races on all days and betting is heavy. The **Ladhu Umt** is a race in which teams of up to 10 men will cling to the camel and one another in a hilarious spectacle of chaos and frivolity. There are also sideshows of jugglers, acrobats, magicians and folk dancing. On the devotional side, there is the opportunity to bathe in the lake, the night of the full moon being the most auspicious time. Pilgrims launch boats of marigold and rose petals in the moonlight. The official programme cannot always be trusted as some events fail to materialise! A very colourful spectacle, but dusty and crowded too.

Hotels Like most of the smaller, less patronised centres in Rajasthan, Pushkar suffers from a poor range of accommodation and prices vary, being lower outside the Festival season.
E *Sarovar Tourist Bungalow* (RTDC). T 40, Cable: Sarovar. 0.5 km from bus stand. Non a/c rooms with bath plus dormitory. 36 rm non a/c rm around courtyard in former lakeside palace with splendid views from rm overlooking lake. Otherwise, unremarkable. Restaurant. **E** *Peacock Holiday Resort*. On edge of town, convenient for buses to Ajmer. Non a/c, with a choice of beds in tents, dormitory to rm with bath in **D** category complex. Beautiful shady courtyard, pool but little sign of peacocks! Friendly staff, adequate food and bearable amenities. **E** *Pushkar*, lakeside location. Non a/c rooms plus dormitory. Non veg food is not permitted in hotel. Pleasant lawn leading down to the water's edge.

There are a number of **F** category hotels around the town offering the basics: *Krishna*, T 43; *Natraj Guest House*, in the bazaar; *Gopal Rest House*. During the annual fair RTDC erects a remarkable tent city capable of housing about 100,000 people. There are deluxe tents costing approx. Rs 500 (with meals), ordinary and dormitory tents at Rs 30-40 per bed. Hotel charges all over town rise dramatically over this period. It is essential to book in advance through Central Reservation Office, Chandralok Building, 36 Jan Path, New Delhi 110001, T 32180 or through a travel.

Restaurants Apparently a lot of travellers get sick in Pushkar, especially during the fair. It is wise to be very careful and eat only freshly cooked food. There are a number of inexpensive to mid-price restaurants. The *RS Restaurant* has an open air kitchen with an interesting view of the food preparation. *Siva* does excellent veg *thalis* (about Rs 20). *Poppins Rooftop* is run by an effervescent lawyer. Only 2 tables, slow service but very good *Malai kofta*. Reasonable choice and value for money. *Rainbow* and *Navraj* have rooftop restaurants.

Bus Buses run frequently from Ajmer. From Pushkar you can travel to Jodhpur via Merta (8 hr) but it is quicker to return to Ajmer and take an express bus (4-5 hr) from there.

Leaving Ajmer to the S the **NH8** goes through Mangliawas (26 km), and Kharwa (12 km) to *Beawar* (16 km), founded by Colonel C.G. Dixon, Superintendent of Merwara (1836-48) and laid out by him in an orderly fashion. His tomb (1857) is treated as a local shrine and is worshipped by the **Mers**. It provided the origin for Kipling's story *The Tomb of His Ancestors*.

Rail To Ajmer *Aravalli Exp*, 9932, daily, 1705, 1 hr 30 min; *Delhi Mail*, 9902, daily, 1843, 1 hr 37 min; *Delhi Exp*, 9904, daily, 0520, 1 hr 15 min.

In **Beawar** the **NH8** forks left and continues south to **Udaipur** (220 km) and **Ahmadabad** (252 km). At **Kankroli**, 56 km N of Udaipur on this road, are the **Rajsamund Lakes**, 56 km N of Udaipur.

The *Rajsamand Lakes* The **Nauchoki Bund** is of massive proportions – over 335 m long and 13 m high, with ornamental pavilions and toranas, all of marble and exquisitely carved. Behind the masonry bund is an 11 m wide earthen embankment that was erected in 1660 by Rana Raj Singh who had defeated Aurangzeb on many occasions. On the SE side of the lake is the town of Kankroli with a beautiful temple.

For **Jodhpur** fork right, following road to Barr. After 14 km pass through Sendra and a further 12 km enter Barr. At this point there is another junction. The left fork leads through Pali (83 km), Sanderao (53), Sirohi (56 km) and Sarupganj (44 km) to Abu Road (28 km). The road to Jodhpur goes off to the right. It passes through the small town of Bilara (55 km) to **Jodhpur** (64 km).

Jodhpur

Population 725,000. *Altitude* 216 m. *Area* 23 sq km. *Rainfall* mostly in Jun-Sep. *Best Season* Nov-Mar. *Languages spoken* Rajasthani, Hindi and English.

	Jan	Feb	Mar	Apr	May	Jun	Jul	Aug	Sep	Oct	Nov	Dec	Av/Tot
Max (°C)	25	28	33	38	42	40	36	33	35	36	31	27	34
Min (°C)	9	12	17	22	27	29	27	25	24	20	14	11	20
Rain (mm)	7	5	2	2	6	31	122	145	47	7	3	1	378

The city was once the capital of the ominously named princely state of Marwar ('Land of Death') and lies on the edge of the Thar Desert. It is the second largest city in Rajasthan after Jaipur. It was founded in 1459 by Rao Jodha although the area had been won by his Rathore Rajput clan in 1211 who had moved there after their defeat at Kanauj by Muslim invaders. **Rao Jodha** moved to the more easily defended Jodhpur site after the older capital of **Mandor** 8 km to the N had been shown to be too vulnerable. On the sandstone bluff that dominates the immediate locality, a huge city developed with the Meherangarh Fort brooding 122 m over it.

Development of the state The descendants of Rao Jodha include the princes of Bikaner, Kishangarh, Idar, Ratlam, Jhabua, Sailana and Sitamau, so the ruling

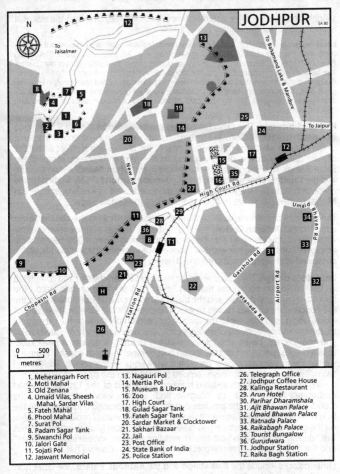

JODHPUR SA 80

1. Meherangarh Fort	13. Nagauri Pol
2. Moti Mahal	14. Mertia Pol
3. Old Zenana	15. Museum & Library
4. Umaid Vilas, Sheesh Mahal, Sardar Vilas	16. Zoo
5. Fateh Mahal	17. High Court
6. Phool Mahal	18. Gulad Sagar Tank
7. Surat Pol	19. Fateh Sagar Tank
8. Padam Sagar Tank	20. Sardar Market & Clocktower
9. Siwanchi Pol	21. Sakhari Bazaar
10. Jalori Gate	22. Jail
11. Sojati Pol	23. Post Office
12. Jaswant Memorial	24. State Bank of India
	25. Police Station

26. Telegraph Office
27. Jodhpur Coffee House
28. Kalinga Restaurant
29. Arun Hotel
30. Parihar Dharamshala
31. Ajit Bhawan Palace
32. Umaid Bhawan Palace
33. Ratnada Palace
34. Raikabagh Palace
35. Tourist Bungalow
36. Gurudwara
T1. Jodhpur Station
T2. Raika Bagh Station

family could claim great regional influence. **Rao Udai Singh** of Jodhpur (d.1581) received the title of Raja from the Mughal Akbar, and his son, **Sawai Raja Sur Singh** (d.1595), conquered Gujarat and part of the Deccan for Akbar. This is a good example of the government in partnership that Akbar succeeded in achieving with the Muslims' traditional enemies the Rajputs of Rajasthan. **Maharaja Jaswant Singh** (d.1678) died commanding Shah Jahan's armies against the forces of Aurangzeb and Murad in 1658 but his son, Maharaja Ajit Singh (d.1731), alert to the decline in Mughal fortunes, drove them out of Ajmer and his successor, Maharaja Abhai Singh (d.1750) took Ahmadabad. The State came into treaty relations with the British in 1818.

Jodhpur lies on the once strategic Delhi-Gujarat trading route and the Marwaris managed and benefitted from the passing traffic of opium, copper, silk, sandalwood, dates, coffee and much more besides. They provided the essential economic base for the military power of the state.

Local Festivals In addition to the common Hindu festivals celebrated throughout N India, there are a number especially popular in Rajasthan, e.g. Teej (See Jaipur **page 354**). *Naag Panchami* (Jul/Aug). Reverence for the cobra (naag) is shown by people all over the country. The festival day is dedicated to Sesha, the thousand-headed god or Anant ('infinite') Vishnu, the great god of preservation who is often depicted reclining on a bed of serpents in between great acts or incarnations (avatars). In Jodhpur huge effigies of the mythical serpent are displayed in a colourful fair. In other parts of India, idols of hooded serpents are fed with milk and sweets.

Places of Interest The City The old city is surrounded by a huge 9.5 km long wall which has 101 bastions and seven gates, above which are inscribed the name of the place to which the road leads. Some of the houses and temples within the city are of richly carved stone, in particular the red sandstone buildings of the Sadar Bazaar. Also important are the temple in the **Dhan Mandi** (Grain Market) and the **Talaiti Mahal** which was built by **Jaswant Singh I** (1638-81) and is now a women's hospital. The **Kunjebehari** temple dedicated to **Krishna** and the **Raj Mahal** garden palace are both on the banks of the **Gulab Sagar**.

The new city beyond the walls is of interest too. Overlooking the **Umaid Sagar** is the **Umaid Bhawan Palace**. Building started in 1929 as a famine relief exercise when the monsoon failed for the third year running. Over 3,000 people were employed constructing this vast 347 room palace of sandstone and marble, which possessed all the latest mod cons and 8 dining rooms.

Indo-deco design The Palace was designed by *H.V. Lanchester* and completed in 1944. Tillotson comments that it is "the finest example of Indo-Deco...The forms are crisp and precise, and the bland monochrome of the stone makes the eye concentrate on their carved shapes. The details of the exterior are mostly of Indian origin, and they evoke the spirit of art deco simply through their sculptural treatment and consequent chill elegance." It is now a luxury hotel (see Hotels), and the interior, based strongly on western models, produces a remarkable sensation of separation from the Indian environment in which it is set. There is a subterranean swimming pool decorated with signs of the zodiac. The Gemini twins, Tillotson observes, "have stepped straight from the pages of Vogue".

Whereas much British inspired building at the end of the 19th century had deliberately gone back to Mughal and Islamic idioms, cultivating the Indo-Saracenic style on the grounds that this was recapturing and developing the best of Indian traditional architecture, Lanchester deliberately avoided such a style on the grounds that Rajasthan had never been fully under Muslim influence. Thus the "dripstones or *chajjis** are ribbed, recalling those of ancient Indian temples" and the dining hall is "a reinterpretation of a Buddhist Chaitya hall".

Other palaces include the **Raikabagh** and the **Ratnada Palace**, the latter now used by the military. Near the former are the Jubilee Buildings, public offices designed by Sir Samuel Swinton Jacob in the Indo-Saracenic style.

The **Mahamandir** (2 km NE of the city) is a huge temple set in a housing colony. Visit *Balsamand Lake* ; it is surrounded by gardens laid out in 1936.

The Fort

The *Meherangarh* (Majestic Fort) sprawls out on top of a steep escarpment with a 37 m sheer drop at the S end. It was built by Rao Jodha in 1459. It stands 121 m above the plains, with walls which in places 36 m high and 3 to 21 m wide. The summit is divided into three areas: the palace (NW), a wide terrace to the E of the Palace and the strongly fortified area to the S edge of the the cliff. The approach is by a winding path up the W side and, (which is possible by rickshaw) Extensive views from the top.

En route there is the cremation ground of the former rulers and their cenotaphs (chattris). Distinctive among these is the white marble memorial (1899) to Jaswant Singh II. Open Summer 0800-1800, Winter 0900-1700. Entry fee Rs 10 (includes local musicians), Camera fee Rs 25. Guides available.

The gateways Typically, there were seven gateways. The first gate, the **Fateh Gate** is pockmarked with cannon shot and heavily fortified with a spikes and a barbican that forces a 45 degree turn. The smaller **Gopal Gate** is second, followed by the **Bhairon Gate** which has extensive guardrooms. The fourth, **Toati Gate,** has been demolished but the fifth, **Dodhkangra Gate** stands over a turn in the path and has loopholed battlements for easy defence. In the NE of the Palace is the sixth gate, the **Amarti Gate** which is essentially a long passageway protected on both sides by guardrooms. The last, **Loha (Iron) Gate,** controls the final turn into the fort and has the handprints of 15 royal *satis**, the wives of Maharajas, particularly of **Ajit Singh** who expelled the Mughals. **See page 47**. It is said that 6 queens and 58 concubines became satis on his funeral pyre. Though illegal since 1829, there have been satis in Jodhpur in the last decade. All *satis** carry the Bhagavad Gita with them into the flames and legend has it that the holy book will never perish.

A further gate, the **Suraj (Sun) Gate** leads into the durbar hall. The climb to the top through all these gates is quite arduous. Within the fort are two small tanks: the **Rani Talao** (Queen's Lake) and the **Gulab Sagar** (Rose-Water Lake). Despite these there was a scarcity of water and the women had to fetch it daily from Mandor. Now it is brought up to the top in pipes from a 140 m deep well. In the city below, the fear of water scarcity has been removed with the creation over time of the Rani Sagar, Akherajii ka Talao, Kailana Tank, the Umaid Sagar Lake and its supplement the Takht Sagar.

The Old Palaces are a series of inter-connecting courtyards within building complexes of intricately carved and filigreed stonework. Though the first was commenced in 1499, the surviving apartments date from 1640 onwards. From the **Loha Gate** you enter the Meherangarh Museum.

Meherangarh Museum This is a series of palaces, a typically haphazard extension of buildings, of courtyards within courtyards, beautifully designed and decorated windows and walls, and inside a magnificent collection of the Maharajas' memorabilia. It is superbly maintained and presented.

The **Jewel House** has a wonderful collection of jewellery, including diamond eyebrows held by hooks over the ears. There are also palanquins, howdahs and ornate royal cradles, all marvellously preserved and maintained. The **Phool Mahal** (Flower Palace) upstairs was built by Akhai Singh (1730-50) as a hall of private audience, displays the increasingly decorated and opulent style of the 18th century. This Durbar-e-Khash is especially noteworthy for the portraits of former rulers, the lavishly gilded ceiling and the Jodhpur coat of arms displayed above the royal couch. Following the **Umaid Vilas,** which houses Rajput miniatures, you then walk through the **Sheesh Mahal** (Mirror Palace 1702-24) to the **Ajit Vilas** where you will find a fascinating collection of musical instruments and costumes. **Sardar Vilas, Khabka Mahal, Chandan Mahal, Long Balcony,** the **Moti Mahal** (Pearl Palace), were probably built at the very end of the 16th century. The zenana has an exquisite stone screen and a carved marble throne.

The Armoury with its variety of Indian weapons has no equal. **Kamangars** (bowmakers), **dhabdars** (armourers) and **sikligars** (swordsmiths) all lived in the fort and were famed for both their skill and artistry: swords and daggers could be leaf shaped, curved, pointed and the handles decorated with calligraphy and other designs. There are shields of rhino hide, crocodile skin, wood and steel and body armour for man and beast, including the pakhar for an elephant's trunk. **Abai Singh's** tent from his highly successful Deccan campaign is also displayed.

Along the ramparts antique cannonry can be seen. In the **Tent Room** you will see Shah Jahan's, and later, Aurangzeb's red silk and velvet tent, lavishly embroidered with gold thread, which they used in the Imperial Mughal campaign.

From the windows of the palaces you can see the town below. The houses painted blue belong to Brahmins. On a clear day the towers of **Kumbhalgarh fort** – see Udaipur excursions (**see page 381**) – can be seen 144 km away. Like all the most spectacular Rajput Palaces and forts, Jodhpur provides a very picturesque and memorable contrast between the exigencies of defence and the flamboyance of prosperity.

Hotels A *Welcomgroup Umaid Bhawan Palace*. T 22316, Cable: Palace, Telex: 0552-202 Ubp in. 78 rm, mostly a/c. 3 km airport, 5 km rly, 3 km centre. Pool, tennis, squash, badminton, golf, billiards, croquet. Private museum, a folly erected for the best possible motives (poor relief) on a site recommended by Hindu astrologers. Hydrologists might have suggested somewhere else, as there is a problem with the water supply. The royal family still occupy part of the palace.
 B *Ratanada Ashok*, Residency Rd. T 25910-4, Cable: Polo, Telex: 552-233 Polo in. 50 rm central a/c. Near airport, 3 km rly, 3 km centre. Pool, tennis.
 D *Ajit Bhawan*, nr Circuit House. T 20409. 50 rm, mostly air-cooled, including individual cottage units, furnished in the local style. 5 km airport, 2 km rly, 3 km centre. Restaurant (Indian) with meals included in price, tennis, squash, golf, riding. 'Village safari' to see the real Rajasthan. Charming family house built for Maharaja Ajit Singh's younger brother, now owned and partly run by two of his descendants who treat clients as personal guests. Lots of period furniture. Recommended. **D** *Karni Bhawan*, Defence Laboratory Rd, Ratanada. T 20157, Cable: Karnima. 15 non a/c rm. Restaurant. **D** *Ghoomar Tourist Bungalow* (RTDC), High Court Rd. T 21900. 60 rm some a/c. Bar, restaurant, shops, Indian Airlines Office, Tourist information Bureau, travel. **D** *Adarsh Niwas*, opposite rly station. T 26936, 23658, Cable: Kalinga. 26 non a/c rm. Multi-cuisine restaurant, laundry, car hire. **D** *Priya*, 181 Nai Sarak, Sojati Gate. T 26363. A/c and non a/c rm. Limited hr room service. TV lounge. **D** *Marudhar*, 12 Nai Sarak. T 22736. 17 rm, some a/c. Limited hr room service. **E** *Maharaja Kenya*, Nai Sarak, Sojati Gate. T 28242. A/c and non a/c rm without bath. Dormitory. Room service (breakfast and snacks). **E** *Galaxy*, outside Sojati Gate, opposite Tempo stand. T 25098, 20796, Cable: Galaxy. 60 rm, some a/c, with and without bath. Restaurant (Indian vegetarian), TV in some rm. **E** *Arun*, outside Sojati gate. T 20238, Cable: Arunotel. 47 non a/c rm with and without bath. Dormitory. Limited hr rm service, TV lounge, car hire and travel.

Guest Houses These are essentially budget hotels. Many have shared bathrooms. **E** *Marudhar Guest House*, opposite K.N. Hall, Raikabagh. T 23208. 14 rm, some a/c. Restaurant (Indian), laundry,TV in some rm. **E** *Shanti Bhawan Lodge*, opp rly station. T 21689. 86 rm, some a/c, with and without bath. Restaurant (Indian vegetarian), travel, beauty parlour,TV in some rm. **E** *Golchha*, Station Rd. T 28447. Non a/c rm with bath. Rm service. **E** *Shree Laxmee*, 132-3 Nai Sarak, T 22047. 18 non a/c rm without bath. Rm service, TV lounge. **E** *Mayur*, Nai Sarak. T 27511. 9 non a/c rm without bath. Rm service (breakfast), car hire, travel. **E** *Raj*, Station Rd, T 28447. 27 non a/c rm without bath. Limited hr rm service, TV lounge, car hire and travel. **F** *Chander Lok*, 1 Nai Sarak, Sojati Gate. T 20624. Non a/c rm without bath. Rm service. *Dak Bungalow* opp the Rly Station. **F** *Rly Retiring Rooms*, Jodhpur Rly Station. Non a/c double and dormitory.

Restaurants Millets are basic to local cooking. Thick chapattis – *Sogra* – are very popular, particularly served with ghee, which makes them extremely filling. Mutton cooked with millet – *Sohita* and mutton kebabs cooked over charcoal – *sulla* are also favourites. Rabbit *Khud khar ghosh* is one of the popular non-vegetarian dishes. *Krer kumidai saliria* uses three kinds of beans cooked with cumin and chillies. *Mawaki-kachori* is a particularly rich dessert consisting of pastry stuffed with nuts and coconut and smothered in syrup. As with all Indian sweets, you need a very sweet tooth to enjoy it fully!
 The best restaurants are in *Ajit Bhawan Hotel*, where you get an excellent meal outside with entertainment (evenings) in very pleasant surroundings. The *Umaid Bhavan* has a palatial formal dining rm, with occasional barbecues in the courtyard. The restaurant at the *Ratanada International* is less expensive. Non-residents should reserve in advance.
 Outside hotels, *Kalinga*, nr the rly station is popular and offers W Rajasthani dishes as well as Mughlai food, the *Coffee House* serves S Indian snacks, *Kashmiri* nr the Anand Cinema serves hot and spicy Indian food, *Manglam*, Residency Rd and *Uttam*, High Court Rd. For fast food try *Frigo* in Sardarpura. *Pankaj* is a veg restaurant in Jalori Gate. The *Agra Sweet Home* nr Sojati Gate has splendid *makhania lassi*, creamy and saffron flavoured

and a local favourite. *Rawat Mishtan Bhandar* nr Anand Cinema and the Clock Tower has a tempting selection of Indian sweets and drinks.

Bars There are bars at the Welcomgroup Umaid Bhawan Palace, Ratanada Ashok hotels and Ghoomar Tourist Bungalow.

Clubs *Sardar Club*, nr Polo Ground, Ratanada, T 20010. *Umaid Club*, Gaushala, Old Park, T 24610. Branches of Lions and Rotary.

Banks In Jodhpur there are the following: *State Bank of India, State Bank of Bikaner and Jaipur, Bank of Baroda, Canara Bank, Dena Bank, Indian Bank, Allahabad Bank.*

Shopping Jodhpur is famous for its Jodhpuri coats and breeches (riding trousers), *safas** (turbans), *badle** (water bottles), tie-and-dye fabrics, embroidered camel leather footwear, lacquer work, cast toys and decorations. The main shopping areas of the city are *Sojati Gate* for gift shops and emporia, *Station Rd* for jewellery, *Tripolia Bazaar* for handicrafts, *Khanda Falsa* for tie and dye, *Lakhara Bazaar* for lac bangles, *Sardarpura* and *Clock Tower*. Shoemakers can be found around *Mochi* (Shoe) *Bazaar*. *Bandhanas** are mostly made by Muslim families in Bambamola. There are also 'factories' around *Siwanchai* and *Jalori Gates*. *Bhagatram Ishwarlal, Lucky Silk Shop* and *Prakash Silk Stores* are good. There are numerous antique shops in Jodhpur but the opportunities for good hard bargaining are quite limited.

Dhurries* are woven at Salavas village, 18 km out of town. Shops include: *Rajasthan Khadi Sangathan*, BK Ka Bagh, T 23978 and in the Industrial Area, T 21375. The *Khadi Sangh* is on Station Rd, T 20479. *Abani Handicrafts*, nr Tourist Bungalow and at Umaid Bhawan Palace is good but expensive. *Arvind Handicrafts, Haswani Handicrafts* and *Lalji Handicrafts*, Umaid Bhawan Palace Rd, T 22472 (very good for local crafts). *Maharani Boutique, Oasis, Rajasthan Art Emporium.* Good. *Rajasthan Arts and Crafts, The Paradise* and *Sunderam Art Emporium* in the Fort. *Universal Book Depot*, Jalori Gate has a reasonable selection.

Photography : *The Regal Studio, Tak Studio* and *Famous Studio* are all in Sojati Gate.

Local Transport Tourist taxis are available from taxi stands at Rly Station, Ghoomar Tourist Bungalow, Sojati Gate, etc. Fixed tariffs for popular destinations displayed at taxi stands. Other rates negotiable. **Auto-rickshaws**, first km Rs 2.60, subsequently Re 1.50 per km. **Tempo-rickshaws** and **mini-buses** on fixed route, min Re 0.60. Tongas, rates negotiable.

Museums Mehrangarh Fort Palace Museum see above in Places of Interest.

Govt. Museum, Umaid Park. Open 1000-1700 hr. Entry Re 1. The Museum could almost be called a time capsule from the British Raj in that since Independence hardly anything has been added. There are some moth eaten stuffed animals, some almost featherless birds, one of which has fallen off its perch, plus some model aeroplanes, a brass battleship, images of Jain *Tirthankars*, textiles, local crafts, miniature portraits and some excavations from sites in the state. The gardens contain a small zoo which has a few rare exotic species.

Umaid Bhawan Palace Museum, Umaid Bhawan Palace Hotel. This fine museum includes the Durbar Hall with the flaking murals that were painted by by a Polish artist who did not seal the walls afterwards. A good collection of miniatures, armour and old clocks. Open daily 0900-1700.

The Old Fort Museum is fascinating. Palanquins, royal *howdahs* (seats for elephant backs) lavishly upholstered and one of silver, a golden throne, pearl encrusted shoes, paintings and mirrors among the exhibits. Open Summer 0800- 1800, Winter 0900- 1700. Usually tours with English speaking guides included in price.

Parks and Zoos *Umaid Park*, High Court Rd. *Mandore Gardens* – see Excursions.

Useful Numbers Police: T 20200 Fire: T 101 Ambulance: T 102

Hospitals and Medical Services *M.G. Hospital*, Jalori Gate, T 24479. *Umaid Hospital*, Sivanchi Gate Rd, T 22567. *Government Dispensary*, Paota, Residency, T 22666. Hospital Hours: 0800-1200 and 1700-1900. On Sundays, 0800-1200.

Posts and Telegraphs *G.P.O.*, nr Rly Hospital, nr U.I.T. *Telegraph Office*, nr Telephone Exchange, Sardarpura.

Places of Worship *Hindu:* Laxmi Nath Temple, Old City, Ratan Bihari Temple opp Head PO, Park Temple opp Bus Stand. *Jain:* Bhanda Sagar Temple. *Sikh:* Gurdwara, Cantonment Area. *Muslim* – Mosque, Cantonment Area. *Christian:* Church nr Circuit House.

Travel Agents and Tour Operators *Rajasthan Tours*, Tourist Bungalow, T 27464, Cable: Raj Tour, Telex: 0552-288. *Tourist Guide Service*, 15 Old Public Park, Cable: Excursion

Jodhpur, Telex: 0552-284. *Peacock Travels (P) Ltd*, 2 Raikabagh, T 27176. *Aravalli Safari and Tours*, 2 Raikabagh, T 27176. *Mayur Travels*, Handling agents for Vayudoot, Kalyan Singh Bldg, Sojati Gate, T 20909.

Tourist Offices and Information *Tourist Office, Govt. of Rajasthan*, Ghoomar Tourist Bungalow, High Court Rd, T 25183. Open 0800-1200 and 1500-1800. **Conducted Tours** Operated by RTDC from Ghoomar Tourist Bungalow. City Sightseeing, half day (0830-1300 and 1400-1800). Fort and palaces, Jaswant Thada, Mandore Gardens, Govt Museum. Rs 20.

Air Indian Airlines flies daily from Delhi to Bombay via Jaipur, Jodhpur, Udaipur and Aurangabad, and back on the same route. There are also flights five times a week from Delhi to Bombay via Jaipur, Jodhpur and Ahmadabad, and back on the same route. **Vayudoot** flies to Jodhpur from Delhi, Jaipur, Bikaner and Jaisalmer. Indian Airlines, City Office, Ghoomar Tourist Bungalow, High Court Rd, T 28600, Airport T 20617. Open 0930-1315 and 1400-1700. Vayudoot handling agents, Mayur Travels, Kalyan Singh Bldg, Sojati Gate, T 20909. Open 0930-1730.

Rail Jodhpur is on the Western Railways' metre gauge line. **Old Delhi**: *Mandore Exp*, 242, daily, 2145, 12 hr 15 min; *Jodhpur Mail*, 4894, 1545, 14 hr 5 min; **Jaipur**: *Mandore Exp*, 2462, daily, 2145, 6 hr 40 min; *Marudhar Exp*, 5314, daily, 0630, 6 hr 55 min. **Jaisalmer**: *4 JPJ Exp*, 2305, daily, 2235, 8 hr 55 min; *2 JPJ*, 4791, daily, 0820, 9 hr 50 min. **Agra**: *Barmar-Agra Exp*, 9708, daily, 2200, 21 hr 30 min. *From Agra: Agra-Barmer Exp*, 9707, daily, 0815, 22 hr 5 min. **Mt. Abu** *Surya Nagri Exp*, 2907, daily, 2245, 4 hr 35 min; *Ranakpur-Marwar Exp*, 4727, daily, 0725, 6 hr 40 min. **Udaipur** *Jodhpur-Udaipur Passenger*, 251, daily, 2035, 10 hr 20 min.

Road Jodhpur is linked to by State Highways to **NH8** (Delhi-Jaipur-Ahmadabad-Bombay), **NH11** (Agra-Jaipur-Bikaner) and **NH15** (Pathankot-Amritsar-Jaisalmer-Samakhiali). From: **Jaipur** (340 km); **Ajmer** (208 km); **Mt Abu** (292 km); **Bikaner** (256 km); **Udaipur** (275 km); **Kota** (360 km); **Jaisalmer** (305 km); **Bharatpur** (520 km); **Agra** (575 km); **Delhi** (594 km); **Bombay** (1,077 km); **Ahmadabad** (526 km).

Bus Jodhpur Bus Stand, nr Raikabagh Rly Station, T 22986. Open 1000-1700. The State Road Transport Corporations of Rajasthan and neighbouring states connect Jodhpur to regional centres such as Ahmadabad, Jaipur, Abu Road, Ajmer, Bikaner, Jaisalmer, Udaipur by regular and frequent bus services. **Private Bus Operators:** Sun City Tours and Travels, Hotel Shanti Bhawan, opp. Rly Station, T 26572. Sethi Yatra Co., opp. Rly Station, T 24397 PP. Several private bus companies run deluxe video coaches between Jodhpur and Delhi, Ahmadabad, Jaipur, Bikaner, Bhilwara and Jaisalmer. Earplugs are recommended!

Excursions *Village Safaris* These are becoming quite popular and is recommended for those who are not travelling around Rajasthan by car. **Warning** there are some unscrupulous operators who charge dearly, e.g Rs 500 for an afternoon and then wander around a couple of villages not really showing much that is interesting. It is much better to go through a reputable agency or to ask the managements at good hotels such as the Ajit Bhawan Hotel.

Jodhpur to Bikaner There are a number of interesting to visit if you are travelling by car to Bikaner. Alternatively, they can be treated as day trips from each place.

Mandor 8 km N of Jodhpur, is the old capital of Marwar, set on a plateau over the *Mandor* Gardens. The gardens, set around the former cremation ground of the Rathor rulers and their dark red sandstone chhattris are very attractive. **The Shrine of the 33 Crore** (330 Million) **Gods** is a large pillared hall containing huge painted figures of heroes and gods and is the pantheon of the Rathors. The largest chattri is that of Ajit Singh (c.1724) who also had a pleasure palace built. There are also the remains of an 8th century Hindu temple at the top of a nearby hill. There are regular buses to Mandor from Jodhpur.

About 30 km out of Jodhpur you come to a road junction. Take the left hand road to the villages of **Khari** and **Umaidnagar**. *Osian*, 58 km from Jodhpur is an ancient town in the Thar desert and contains the largest group of 8th-9th century Hindu and Jain temples in Rajasthan. The typical Osian temple is set on a terrace whose walls are decorated with mouldings and miniatures. The sanctuary walls have central projections with carved panels and above these rise curved towers topped by an amalaka and pot finial. The doorways are usually decorated with river goddesses, serpents and scrollwork. The temples are grouped in several sites North, W and S of the town. The S group includes three **Harihara Hindu** temples. The W group contains a mixture of Hindu (Surya, Vishnu and Pippala Devi) temples, an 8th century tank and an 11th century Jain (Mahavira) temple. The S group includes the **Surya Temple** (early 8th century) and the **Sachiya Mata Temple** (11th-12th century). There are half a dozen buses a day from Jodhpur and the journey takes about two hours.

Khimsar, 100 km N of Jodhpur, 130 km N if you take the detour to Osian. Khimsar is a remote 15th century Rajput fort in the desert. The moated **B** *Royal Castle* (T 28, Telex: 0552-202 Ubp in) is now a hotel run by the Welcomgroup. 14 rm, some a/c, all with bath. Restaurant (Mughlai, Rajasthani, Continental), outdoor barbecue. Desert tours can be arranged on camel back or by jeep. Book through Umaid Bhawan Palace, Jodhpur. The castle was built as a fortified home by Karam Singh, the fifth son of Rao Jodha.

The dull stretch of desert is enlivened at *Nagaur,* 137km N of Jodhpur by the fort, palace and mosque. Akbar built the Mosque and there is a shrine of the disciple of Muin-ud-din Chishti of Ajmer (**see page 385**). A raucous and highly authentic cattle fair takes place just outside the town in Jan/Feb during which there are camel races, cock fights, folk dancing and puppet shows. Unfortunately, Nagaur has no suitable accommodation, so it is best to stay at Khimsar.

About 70 km N of Nagaur and 31 km S of Bikaner on the main Jodhpur-Bikaner road is **Deshnoke** with its bizarre rat inhabited Karni Devi temple – see Bikaner Excursions.

Jodhpur to Mount Abu Take the road to **Pali** (69 km) then **Sirohi** (113 km) where you can take a country road and reach Mount Abu directly via the villages of Mero and Anadra. This will save about 50 km. The other route is to go from Sirohi to **Pindwara** (23 km), then Abu Road (40 km) and finally up to Mount Abu (27 km). The shorter route is approximately 200 km, the longer via Abu Road 270 km. Allow the best part of a day.

There are no historical sites worth visiting en route and for the most part the way is across the plains. Once into the Abu Hills, it becomes more scenic and the views more interesting.

JAIPUR TO BIKANER, JAISALMER AND BARMER VIA SIKAR

It is 275 km by road from Jodhpur to Jaisalmer and scenically it is quite tedious. There are day and night trains. The day train can be a hot, dusty and dirty experience, especially if a steam engine is pulling it. It can also get quite cold travelling across the desert at night in the winter months, so a sleeping bag or blanket is recommended. This section of the northern railway is one of the most neglected in India's whole rail network. Although bedding is available as on all overnight trains it is rarely clean, even if ordered well in advance. The trains have a wholly uncared for feel, and maintenance is made more difficult by the very dusty journey. None the less, the night train journey is recommended, and arrival at Jaisalmer at dawn can be a tremendously exciting experience. Much of the journey by road and rail is across unrelenting scrubby desert, relieved only by the occasional village, camel trains, flocks of sheep and goats or a rare glimpse of gazelle. Allow a full day for the car journey. The train journey takes 10 hours.

At **Pokaran**, 165 km from Jodhpur you may wish to visit the old fort. This magnificent yellow sandstone fort overlooks a confusion of streets in the town below. Pokaran is also the site of India's first nuclear test explosion which took place on Mar 18, 1974. They switch the locomotive from the front to the back of the train here for the final leg of the journey to Jaisalmer so don't be alarmed. Bikaner is a full day's drive (342 km) from Jaipur on NH11. The journey can be broken by visiting the Shekhavati region and staying at **Mandawa** which is approximately 170 km from Jaipur.

 Shekhavati is a region of NE Rajasthan, the Indian 'homeland' of many Marwari families. Its name means 'Garden of Shekha'and is named after a 15th century ruler. The **Marwaris** form one of the most important merchant and business groups in India. Originally from Marwar, further W, they developed their business acumen on the trade routes between Delhi and the coast and between India and Central Asia. Anxious to serve their rulers and be protected by them, they were often the Maharaja's financiers and extravagant patrons of the arts. Many built grand *havelis** in the 360 villages of Shekhavati.

 The *havelis** are mansions, elaborately and attractively decorated but introverted to protect the inhabitants. Usually there is a strong main entrance leading onto one or a series of courtyards. The walls were often covered with murals, local legends and religious scenes being favourites.

From **Jaipur** take the **NH11** NW to **Chaumu** (35 km) and **Ringus** (28 km), through **Palsana** (22 km) to **Sikar** (26 km). You can visit the old quarter and see the Wedgwood blue Biyani Havelis. 27 km further on at **Lachmangarh** is an old fort, worth going up to for the views of the surrounding region. Continue straight to **Fatehpur** (21 km) which has more very attractive havelis, in particular the Derva and Singhani havelis. If you wish to make an overnight stop, consider **Mandawa**, a town has a busy market.

 At **Fatehpur**, turn right down a country road for about 20 km before reaching **Mandawa**. The large fort here (c 1755), is now a hotel with excellent views. **C** *Castle Mandawa*, District Jhunjhunu. T Mandawa 24, Jaipur 75358, Cable: Castle Mandawa. 49 rm, non a/c with bath. 14 km Mukandgarh rly, 25 km Jhunjhunu Junction rly. Restaurant (Indian, Rajasthani), laundry, house doctor, credit cards, camel, horse, jeep rides and camel safari. Puppet show, folk dances. Popular with Delhi diplomats for weekend trips. The Maharaja also runs a hill-top Indian village style **hotel complex** at nearby **Dundlod Fort**. Less expensive than the Mandawa hotel but good. Alternatively, there is the **Roop Nivas Haveli** in Nawalgarh which lacks age and character of the other two. Around **Mandawa** there is **Jhunjhunu** (25 km east) with the Modi and Tibdiwala havelis, the **Chhe Haveli** complex and the Rani Sati temple. This is the scene of an annual Marwari fair. *Mukundgarh* (approx 10 km south) has a good handicrafts market. *Bissau* (approx 15 km north) has painted chattris and a fort.

If you carry straight on from Fatehpur it is 35 km to **Ratangarh** (35 km), a market town with some basic facilities, including a Rest House. The road continues along the **NH11** through **Rajaldesar** (13 km) to **Sri Dungargah** (43 km) and **Seruna** (29 km) to **Bikaner** (42 km).

Bikaner

Population **350,000** *Altitude* **237 m.** *Area* **18 sq. km.** *Climate* Temp. Summer Max. 41°C Min. 28°C, Winter Max. 23°C Min. 10°C. Annual rainfall 440 mm, mostly Jun-Sep. Bikaner has daily Vayudoot air services from Delhi (435 km).

Bikaner is the fourth largest town in Rajasthan and was founded in 1488 by Bhika, the sixth son of Rao Jodha, the founder of Jodhpur. Bhika had left his father's

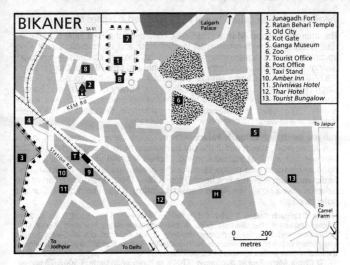

BIKANER SA 81

1. Junagadh Fort
2. Ratan Behari Temple
3. Old City
4. Kot Gate
5. Ganga Museum
6. Zoo
7. Tourist Office
8. Post Office
9. Taxi Stand
10. Amber Inn
11. *Shivniwas Hotel*
12. *Thar Hotel*
13. *Tourist Bungalow*

capital in 1459 and after 30 years had carved out a kingdom for himself and his followers. Rising out of the arid desert of W Rajasthan, it was an important staging post on the caravan route west. The impressive fort is the town's principal feature but like Jaisalmer to the S, many of the houses within the separate old city area have very fine stone carving. The Bikaner area is chiefly agricultural and a fine wool is obtained from its sheep. The Bikaner Gang Canal (1925-7) enabled an area of 285,000 hectares of previously arid scrubland to be irrigated for crop production. Camel rearing is also practiced and there is a government breeding station near the city. Bikaner's Marwari traders are noted throughout N India for their business acumen.

Local Festivals *Desert Festival* for 2 days in Nov. Folk music and dance. Fire Dance is the special attraction in the evenings. *Gangaur, Dasserah* and *Diwali* are especially spectacular in Junagarh Fort, in the Old City near Kote Gate and some smaller palaces.

Places of Interest **Junagarh Fort** Open daily 1000-1600. Closed Fri. Entry Rs 5 and Rs 10 for a camera. Raja Rai Singh (1571-1611), one of Akbar's generals, built the 986 m. long fort of pink sandstone between 1588 and 1593. The wall has 37 pavilions which look very impressive silhouetted against the morning and evening sky. Its huge columns, arches, screens and minarets and the wealth of carving and painting draw visitors to the fort.

The gate The main entrance is the **Suraj Pol** (Sun Gate)(1593) which is guarded by Jaimal and Patta, warriors mounted on painted stone elephants. Within the walls and to the S is a picturesque collection of palaces, pavilions, courtyards and towers, all well preserved and built by a succession of rulers.

The **Karan Mahal** (1631-9) lies in the second courtyard and was built by **Karan Singh** to commemorate an important victory over Aurangzeb. Over this is the **Gaj Mandir** (1745-1787) which was built as royal apartments. The **Chatra Niwas**(1872-87), a later addition, is a small pavilion on the roof decorated with English plates embedded in the plaster walls.

The **Chandra Mahal** (Moon Palace) and the **Phul Palace** (Flower Palace) are lavishly ornamented with mirrors and elaborate carved marble panels. The latter contains Bhika's bed, reputedly made small to allow him to get up in a hurry, thereby avoiding his father's fate of being murdered in his bed by a courtesan.

The impressive **Anup Mahal** (1669-98), containing the Raja Tilak Coronation Hall, is decorated with ornamental lacquer work and opaque glass inlay. One adjoining room is aquamarine and gilt whilst another contains a *hindola** (swing). Other palaces include the **Chetar Mahal** and **Chini Burj** of Dungar Singh (1872-87) and the **Ganga Niwas**, a beautiful audience hall added by Ganga Singh (1887-1943). The fort also contains a fine **library** of Sanskrit and Persian books and an armoury which includes the Maharajas' palanquins. The well nearby is over 130 m deep. **Har Mandir** is the royal temple, dedicated to Siva where their birth and wedding ceremonies were celebrated.

The red sandstone **Lalgarh Palace** with its superb carvings, particularly in the fine lattice work, stands out in the city surrounded by rocks and sand dunes. The banquet hall is full of stuffed hunting trophies and old photographs and the bougainvillea and wild peacocks make the gardens particularly attractive. The **Sadul museum** is on the first floor. Open 1000 – 1700, closed Wed. Part of the palace is now a hotel. The **Anup Sanskrit Library** is open on request. Contact hotel manager.

Hotels **C** *Lalgarh Palace*. T 3263, Cable: Palace. 34 a/c rm. 13 km airport, 3 km rly, 2 km centre. Restaurant, bar, billiards, pool. A red sandstone palace, excellent Rajput style architecture and beautiful landscaped gardens. It was financed out of Ganga Singh's enlightened policy of modernization. He founded the Bikaner Camel Corps and developed the local railway system to exploit local coal deposits. **D** *Dhola Maru Tourist Bungalow* (RTDC), nr Puran Singh Circle. T 5002. 26 non a/c rm with bath. Dormitory. Restaurant (Indian, Continental), bar, restricted hours rm service, TV lounge, handicrafts shop. Pleasant but some way out of town. **D** *Gajner Palace*, Gajner. T 3239. 15 rm. 18 hole golf course, clay and skeet shooting ranges, bird watching and photography on the lake. **D** *Joshi*, Station Rd. T 6162. 40 rm. A/c. Dining Hall (Indian, Continental, Veg). 24 hr room service, TV, terrace garden, car hire. **D** *Karni Bhawan Palace*. T 3308. 10 a/c rm. Clay pigeon, trap and skeet shooting ranges, 9 hole golf course. **D** *Thar*, Ambedkar Circle. 23 non a/c rm with bath. Restaurant (Indian, Veg), 24 hr coffee shop, laundry, car hire.
  E *Delux*, Station Rd. T 3292. Non a/c rm with bath. Restaurant (Indian, Veg), 24 hr room service, car rental, travel. **E** *Green*, Station Rd. T 3396. 16 rm, non a/c. Restaurant (Indian), 24 hr room service.
  F *Haryana*, Ganga Shahr Rd. T 5282. 50 rm, non a/c without bath. Dormitory. Restaurant (Indian), 24 hr room service, TV in hall. **F** *Shri Shanti Niwas*, Ganga Shahr Rd. T 5025. 50 rm, non a/c without bath and Dormitory. Restricted hr room service. **F** *Sankhla Rest House*, nr Rly Crossing, Station Rd. T 3949. Non a/c rm without bath. 24 hr room service. *Railway Retiring Rooms*. Bookings: Enquiry Counter, T 4887.

Restaurants Vegetarian restaurants on Station Rd: *Amber Restaurant* is usually crowded with foreigners as it does some western dishes. Fast service, good value for money. Also *Chhotu Motoo*, T 4466 and *Anand*. Try the local speciality – *Bikaneri Bhujia* a spicy snack made out of gram and pulses.

Clubs *Sardul Club* and *Ganga Golden Jubilee Club* which have theatres and swimming at the former. There is also a public pool.

Banks The following are all located on M.G Rd (KEM Rd). *Union Bank of India; Bank of India; Dena; Central Bank of India; Oriental Bank of Commerce; Allahabad*.

Shopping Bikaner is famous for and specialises in *Usta** work (camel leather wares painted in colours) which includes footwear, purses and cushions. You can also get local carpets and woodwork. The main shopping centres are on K.E.M. Rd which starts from nr the Fort, and the nearby roads and lanes, Kote Gate in the Old City and Mahatma Gandhi Rd, Modern Market. *Cottage Industries Institute*, nr Junagarh Fort. *Government emporium*, Rajasthali counter at the Information Centre in Giani Area, T 4595. Private emporia at Kote Gate and Modern Market. Shop hours: 0900-1930.

Photography: *Studio India*, M.G. Rd; *K Studio*, M.G. Rd.

Local Transport Only **tourist taxis** available at Rly Station, opp Dak Bungalow or at Bus Stand, S End, Junagarh Rd, or through hotels and agencies. Rates negotiable. Auto-rickshaws are available all over the city. Rates negotiable. Bicycles can also be hired at various places around town

Museums Ganga Golden Jubilee Museum, Public Park. Open 1000-1700. Closed Fri. A small but fine collection of pottery, paintings and weapons. There is some pre-Harappan exhibits and a group of terracottas from the Gupta (4-5th century) and Kushan periods. Separate section of local crafts and a gallery of artefacts. *Junagarh Fort*. Open daily 1000-1630. Closed Fri. Entry Rs 4, Camera fee Rs 10. *Sadul Museum*, Lalgarh Palace, Civil Lines. Open 1000-1700. Closed Wed. Entry Rs 2.

Parks and Zoos *Ganga Nivas Public Park* nr Modern Market. Open 0800-1800. *Ratan Bihari Temple Park* nr Shopping Centre. *Bhawan Palace Park* nr Bus Stand. *Nathji Park* nr Museum.

Useful Numbers Police: T 3840. Ambulance: T 4175.

Hospitals and Medical Services *P.B.M. Hospital*, Hospital Rd. T 4175.

Post and Telegraph *GPO*, behind Junagarh Fort. *Telegraph and Telephone Office*, behind Collectorate, Public Park. Post Office inside Kote Gate.

Places of Worship *Hindu*: Laxmi Narainji Temple, inside walled city. Nagnechiji Temple, 3 km W of city. *Jain*: temples inside walled city. *Sikh*: Gurudwara, Jodhpur Rd. *Muslim*: Mosque inside city wall. *Christian*: Church nr Public Park.

Travel Agents and Tour Operators *Rajasthan Tours*, Daudsar House, T 4834. *Mayur Travels*, 148 Sadul Ganj. *Desert Tours*, behind Head Post Office. *Victorian Travels*, Ganga Shahr Rd, T 5626.

Tourist Offices and Information *Tourist Office*, Govt. of Rajasthan, Suraj Pol, Junagarh Fort main entrance, T 5445. Open 1000-1700. *Information Centre*, Old Ghinani Area, T 4595. *Tourist Information Bureau* and RTDC Office at Dhola-Maru Tourist Bungalow, Poonam Singh Circle, T 5445. Open 0800-1800, Oct – Mar.

Air Vayudoot flies daily to Bikaner from Delhi, Jaipur, Jodhpur and Jaisalmer, and returns to Delhi, Jaipur and Jodhpur. Vayudoot handling agents, Mayur Travels, 148 Sadul Ganj, T 431. Open 1000-1700.

Rail Jaipur: *Bikaner Exp*, 4738, daily, 2000, 9 hr 55 min. Old Delhi: *Bikaner-Delhi Exp*, 4790, daily, 0845, 11 hr; *Bikaner-Delhi Mail*, 4792, daily, 1930, 11 hr 30 min.

Bus Rajasthan Roadways run daily delux bus services connecting Bikaner to Jaipur, Jodhpur, Ajmer, Sriganganagar, Jaisalmer (8-9 hr), Udaipur, Kota, etc. Ordinary bus service to all district headquarters, daily. Two daily buses connect Delhi to Bikaner via Hissar. The RTDC runs a delux coach service between Jaipur and Bikaner. Central Bus Stand, K.E.M. Rd, T 6688. Reservations open 0600-2200. RTDC, Dhola-Maru Tourist Bungalow, T 5002.

Road: National Highways **NH8** and **NH11** pass through Bikaner. From: **Delhi** (435 km); **Jaipur** (330 km); **Jodhpur** (250 km); **Jaisalmer** (320 km); **Ajmer** (280 km); **Sriganganagar** (250 km); **Bombay** (1250 km).

Excursions *Bhand Sagar* (5 km), a group of colourful temples of which the 16th century Jain temple is the most important. Guides from city only, none at site. A little difficult to find on your own and numerous steps but wonderful views. Entry Rs 5. *Devi Kund* (8 km). This is the site of the Bhika rulers' *chattris**. The white marble chattris of Surat Singh with its ceiling decorations of Rajpur paintings, is the most impressive.

Camel Breeding Farm (10 km). Claims to be the only one in Asia. Rides available. Camels returning from grazing at sunset are an especially good sight.

Gajner Wildlife Sanctuary (33 km on the Jaisalmer Rd). A number of animals can be seen including nilgai, chinkara and blackbuck whilst in winter the Imperial Sand Grouse migrates here. On the banks of the lake stands the old royal summer palace which is now a hotel. You can visit with prior permission – Contact Manager at the Lalgarh Palace, T 3263.

Karni Mata Mandir (33 km at *Deshnoke* on the Jodhpur Rd). Entry Rs 10 plus camera fee. No guides. Mice and rats, revered and fed in the belief that they are reincarnations of mystics, swarm over the temple and your bare feet. Huge silver gates and marble carvings were donated by Maharaja Ganga Singh who had the temple dedicated to a 15th century female saint who is revered as an incarnation of Durga. The temple is in a late Mughal style. Travel there can be either by the hourly bus from Bikaner (Rs 5 fare), by cycle rickshaw (Rs 100) taxi (approximately Rs 120 for the round trip).

From Bikaner there is a road due south to **Jodhpur** through **Nokha** (51 km) and **Nagaur** (48 km). The total distance is 236 km, and there are regular buses. The NH 15 goes south west to Jaisalmer, a total distance of 331 km.

From Bikaner take the road for Gajner (30 km) where there is a National Wildlife Park. Through **Mar** (22 km) and **Deatri** (12 km) to **Nokhra** (24 km) and **Bap** (42 km). In Bap the main road bends left in a curve to the south which takes it to **Phalodi** (31 km) **Ramdeora** (50 km) and **Pokaran** (10 km) the site of India's underground nuclear explosion in 1974. Follow the Jaisalmer road out of Pokaran to **Khetolai** (24 km), **Lathi** (22 km) and **Chandan** (19 km) to **Jaisalmer** (47 km).

Jaisalmer

Population 26,000 *Altitude* 793 m. Rainfall mostly Jul-Sep. *Best season* Nov-Mar.

	Jan	Feb	Mar	Apr	May	Jun	Jul	Aug	Sep	Oct	Nov	Dec	Av/Tot
Max (°C)	24	28	33	38	42	41	38	36	36	36	31	26	34
Min (°C)	8	11	17	21	25	27	27	25	25	20	13	9	19
Rain (mm)	2	1	3	1	5	7	89	86	14	1	5	2	216

The Medieval city of **Jaisalmer**, the farthest W of Rajasthan's cities, has long been a favourite with travellers who revel in its medieval feel, its crenellated golden sandstone walls and its narrow streets lined with exquisitely carved buildings. It is 275 km from Jodhpur and the final approach to it across the hot barren desert is magical as the city shimmers as if a mirage. The town was founded by Prince Jaisal in 1156 and it grew to be a major staging post on the trade route across the forbidding Thar desert from India to the Middle E and Europe. Architecturally the buildings are a magnificent blend of Rajput and Islamic styles, all, including new structures, built out of the local honey-coloured sandstone. Against this captivating backdrop are handsome Rajasthanis, the men in bright loosely tied turbans and white kurta pajamas, the women in vivid skirts and blouses.

Jaisalmer is the westernmost town of any significance in India. It built up its prosperity by acting as a centre for trade across the desert from far to the west in Afghanistan and Iran through to the Ganga valley. The growth of maritime trade between India and the west caused a decline in trade across the desert. This came to a complete end with Partition in 1947, but the 1965 and 1971 Indo-Pakistan wars resulted in Jaisalmer being linked by paved road and railway to the central cities of Rajasthan. This facilitated troop movements and rendered the town more accessible to foreign visitors. Today, the army and tourism are mainstays of the local economy. However, despite its popularity, it is to many still a relaxing haven and well worth the effort involved in reaching it.

The town is mostly on the N side of the citadel and was enclosed by a wall in 1750. There are four major gateways to the city: **Malka Pol** (N), **Amar Sagar Pol, Baron-ki-Pol** and **Gadhisar Pol** (SE). Two other S gateways have been sealed.

Local Festivals *Holi* (Feb/Mar) is especially colourful, as are the other Hindu festivals popular in Rajasthan and N India. The *Desert Festival* (Jan/Feb) is a recent Tourism Dept promotion.

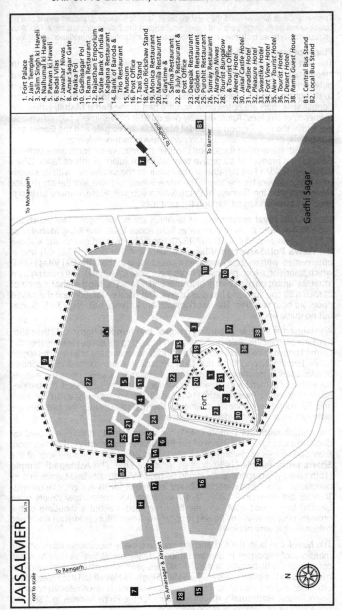

JAISALMER
not to scale

1. Fort Palace
2. Jain Temples
3. Salim Singh ki Haveli
4. Nalhumal ki Haveli
5. Patwan ki Haveli
6. Badal Vilas
7. Jawahar Niwas
8. Amar Sagar Gate
9. Malka Pol
10. Gadhisagar Pol
11. Rama Restaurant
12. Rajasthan Emporium
13. State Bank of India & Kalpana Restaurant
14. Bank of Baroda & Trio Restaurant
15. Museum
16. Post Office
17. Taxi Stand
18. Auto Rickshaw Stand
19. Monica Restaurant
20. Manila Restaurant
21. Gaytime &
    Safina Restaurant
22. 8 July Restaurant & Post Office
23. Deepak Restaurant
24. Golden Restaurant
25. Purohit Restaurant
26. Sunray Restaurant
27. Narayan Niwas
28. Tourist Bungalow
    & Tourist Office
29. Neeraj Hotel
30. Jaisal Castle Hotel
31. Paradise Hotel
32. Pleasure Hotel
33. Swastika Hotel
34. Fort View Hotel
35. New Tourist Hotel
36. Tourist Hotel
37. Desert Hotel
38. Rama Guest House

B1. Central Bus Stand
B2. Local Bus Stand

To Mohangarh
To Jodhpur
To Barmer
To Ramgarh
To Amarsagar & Airport

Gadhi Sagar

Fort

N

There is a *son et lumière* amid the sand dunes at Sam, folk dancing, puppet shows and of course camel races, camel polo and camel acrobatics at the 3-day event, usually in Feb. Also an opportunity to see craftsmen at work. Rail bookings and hotel accommodation are difficult

Places of Interest The Fort

The Fort on Tricuta Hill stands 76 m above the town and is enclosed by a 9 m crenellated wall reinforced with 99 bastions, the vast majority constructed between 1633 and 1647. The **Suraj Pol** (Sun Gate:1594) faces the rising sun and to its right is the delicately carved five storeyed **Tazia Tower**. Its gently curved Bengali style roofs are noteworthy and it is part of the **Badal Mahal**, where the former ruler still lives. Approximately one quarter of Jaisalmer's population also live within the fort. Beyond the **Badal Mahal**, a spiked gate and the **Ganes** and **Rang Pols,** plus a second outer rampart, provide further defences.

As with many other Rajput forts, within the massive defences are a series of palaces, the product of successive generations of rulers' flights of fancy. Often called the Golden Fort because of the colour of the sandstone, with its superb position, it dominates the town. The stone is easy to carve and the dry climate has meant that the fineness of detail (which you will notice in many buildings here) has been preserved through the centuries.

The splendid **royal apartments** at Jaisalmer are no exception. The oldest, the **Juna Mahal**, with its *jali* screens dates from about 1500. The **Rang Mahal** built during the reign of Mulraj II (1762-1820) has highly detailed murals and is above the **Hawa Pol**. **Sarvotam Vilas** was built by Akhai Singh (1722-62) and is ornamented with blue tiles and glass mosaics. Next to this is the **Gaj Vilas** (1884) which stands on a high plinth and faces the square (*chauhata*). The building is an attractive amalgam of pavilions, balconies and pillars. The **Moti Mahal** is another of Mulraj II's creations and has two storeys. The floral decoration and the carved doors are both very fine. The first floor was an audience hall. Entry Rs 5. Guides but no guide books.

Also within the fort is an interesting group of **Jain temples** from the 12th to 15th Centuries. Whilst the Rajput of Rajasthan tended to be devout Hindus they did permit Jainism to be practiced. It is no coincidence that many towns in this region house temples belonging to that faith because in sharp contrast to Buddhism, Jainism appealed to merchants. Because of Jaisalmer's situation on a trade route, the wishes of its merchants were acknowledged and accommodated. The temples found here are the **Parsvanatha** (1417) which has fine gateway, an ornate porch and 52 subsidiary shrines surrounding the main structure. The brackets are elaborately carved as maidens and dancers.

The **Sambhavanatha Temple** (1431) has vaults beneath it that were used for document storage. The exterior of the **Rishbhanatha Temple** (1479) has more than 600 images as decoration whilst clusters of towers form the roof of the **Shantinatha Temple** (1480) built at the same time. The **Ashtapadi Temple** (16th century) incorporates the Hindu deities of Vishnu, Kali and Laksmi into its decoration. The *Gyan Bhandar* **Library** is famous for its ancient manuscripts. Temples are open until 1200. Take a walk through the narrow streets often blocked by the odd goat, and see how even today about a thousand of the ordinary people live in tiny houses yet often with beautiful carvings on doors and balconies. It is easy get lost!

The *havelis* In both the fort and the town are many exceptional *havelis**, the mansions of important nobles and traders. Many are as fine as their Venetian counterpart with beautifully carved facades, *jali** screens and oriel windows overhanging the streets below. The **Salim Singh-ki-Haveli** (c.1815) is especially attractive and because of its distinctive upper portion is often referred to as the Ship's Palace. **Nathumal's Haveli** was built for the Prime Minister in 1885 and has an entrance flanked by stone elephants.

Two craftsmen, Hathi and Lulu were responsible for its construction, each undertaking one half of the house which is even more unusual for the fact that it is carved from rock. The front door is stunning. Two of the five **Patwon-ki-Haveli** (1805) are open to the public from 1030-1700 and have beautiful murals and carved pillars. Where the *havelis* are occupied, you may be allowed in on a polite request. Otherwise, your guide (not necessarily an official one) will help you gain access into one or more of these, often at no cost.

The *Gadi Sagar* tank, SE of the city walls, has many small shrines around it and is also popular with migratory birds during winter. The delightful archway is said to have been built by a distinguished courtesan. Also outside the city walls is the **Jawahar Niwas** (1900) and opulent guest-house, the pleasure palace of Amar Singh (1661-1703) on the banks of the *Ana Sagar,* 5 km W of the town, whilst to the N at Bada Bagh are the **Royal Chattris.**

Hotels Jaisalmer does not have many hotels, particularly at the top end. Jaisalmer is included in many package tour itineraries and this means that it can often be difficult for the independent traveller to get a booking during the season unless it is done very early. When choosing, consider your means of access. A car is useless inside the city walls. That may mean carrying your luggage to the hotel. Also, many of the hotels in the city do not have the wonderful views often claimed.
C *Himmatgarh Palace*, 1 Ramgarh Rd, T 2213. 35 rm, non a/c. Restaurant, room service, shopping, travel counter, camel safaris and jeep tours, exchange, occasional cultural shows. **C** *Jawahar Niwas Palace*, T 2208, Cable: Jawahar. 15 rm, non a/c. Restaurant, open-air coffee shop, billiards room, car hire and sightseeing on camel cart, cultural show. A beautiful old haveli with spacious rooms, high ceilings and big bathrooms and plenty of atmosphere. In large open grounds (you might catch sight of curious 'desert rats' in a corner!) but needs refurbishing. **C** *Narayan Niwas Palace*, Malka Rd, T 2408, Cable: Jaisal. 38 rm, non a/c. 5 km airport, 3 km rly, city location. Restaurant, bar, 24 hr rm service, car hire and travel, tours and safaris, exchange, occasional cultural shows, credit cards, car parking. An old caravansarai with a large hall where camels slept! Modern extension built into the structure. Very popular with more affluent visitors and tour groups.
D *Narayan Vilas*, Malka Rd, nr Khadi Bhandar, T 2283. 8 rm, non a/c. Restaurant, 24 hr rm service, car hire and travel, tours and safaris, exchange, credit cards accepted. **D** *Moomal Tourist Bungalow* (RTDC), Amar Sagar, T 2392. 51 rm, including round huts, some a/c. Restaurant, bar, room service, travel, tours, Tourist Information Office. Concrete, modern and architecturally uninspiring, outside the city walls, close to Jawahar Niwas. Comfortable, but restaurant very mediocre. **D** *Neeraj*, Station Rd, T 2442. 15 rm, non a/c. Dining room (Indian and Continental), 24 hr room service, travel, tours and safaris, cultural shows sometimes. **D** *Rama*, Salam Singh Haveli Marg, Dibba Para, T 2570 PP. 12 rm, non a/c. Restaurant (Indian and Vegetarian), 24 hr rm service, travel and car hire, safaris, check-out 0900. **D** *Jaisal Castle*, Fort, T 2362, Cable: Jaisal. 11 rm, non a/c. Restaurant (Indian and Continental), 24 hr rm service, travel and car hire, tours and safaris, exchange, credit cards accepted. Right on the ramparts of the wall. Not easy to reach if you are carrying a lot of luggage. Most rm overlook desert. **D** *Haveli*, Station Rd, Dibba Para, T 2552, Cable: Haveli. 16 rm, non a/c. Restaurants (Indian and Continental), travel, cultural shows on demand.
E *Hotel Suraj*, Old Haveli, next highest after fort. 5 rm with bath. Restaurant, travel, camel safaris and jeep tours. Highly recommended for excellent service from helpful owner, and value for money. **E** *Paradise*, Fort, opp Fort Palaces, T 2569. 19 rm, non a/c. 24 hr rm service (breakfast and snacks), some rms with balconies, car hire, safaris, check-out 0900. The **E** *Golden Rest House*, T 226, has clean basic rms with bath, a friendly atmosphere and low rates. The *Swastika Guest House*, opp State Bank of India, Chainpura, nr Amar Sagar Gate, T 2483 is well kept with 8 non a/c rms with bath and a dormitory. R m service, travel.
Also nr Amar Sagar Gate is the **F** *Deepak Rest House,* behind Jain temples in fort. Large rm, good atmosphere, local food. Recommended. **F** *Pleasure*, Gandhi Chowk, T 2323 which is basic but friendly. 5 non a/c rm. Car rental and travel. Very basic and very cheap accommodation can be found at **F** *Fort View,* Central Market, T 2214. Restaurant, car hire and travel. **F** *Rama Guest House,* **F** *Sun Ray* and **F** *Sunil Bhatia Rest House.* Many of these are clustered round the rly station. The best place nr the station is **E** *Neeraj,* T 142 with plain but adequate rooms.

Restaurants All in the fort area offering a varied menu. *The Trio*, Sri Narayan Vilas Hotel, Amar Singh Pol, Gandhi Chowk. Partly open-air, tented restaurant with a small terrace from which you can watch the bread being cooked, occasional cultural shows, good atmosphere and food. Popular and so usually crowded in the evening. Highly recommended. Also *Kalpana* and *Gay Time*, *Monika*, opp Main Gate and Manila at Main Gate. The *Sky Restaurant* is slightly more expensive, but large helpings. Serves mainly Indian, some Italian dishes and 'English' breakfasts. Rajasthani dancers and musicians, colourful and noisy!

Banks *Baroda*, Gandhi Chowk, Amar Sagar Pol. *Rajasthan*, nr Patwon ki Haweli. *Bikaner and Jaipur*, Sadar Bazaar, Air Force Rd. *State Bank of India*, nr Nachana House, Gandhi Chowk. Banks are usually 1000 -1400, Mon-Fri, 1000- 1200, Sat. Closed Sun.

Shopping Jaisalmer is famous for its handicrafts – stone carved statues, leather ware, embroidery work on fabrics, brass enamel engraving specially on camel Palan (camel seats), Heerawal Pattu shawls, tie-and-dye word on woollen shawls and cotton fabrics, block printing on fabrics, Barmer-style furniture, etc. Main shopping areas are Gandhi Chowk: *Rajasthali*, Rajasthan Emporium, T 2461. Open 1000-1330 and 1500-1930, closed Tues. *Rajasthan Handloom*. Open 1030-1330 and 1400-1900, closed Sun. *Gandhi Darshan Emporium*. Also look in Sadar Bazaar, Sonaron Ka Bas and the narrow lanes of the Old City including the *Khadi Parishad* in the Old Fort. Moomal Tourist Bungalow has a branch of *Rajasthali*.

Photography *Ajanta Studio*, Bhatia Market, T 2177.

Local Transport **Scooter rickshaws** are easily available, rates negotiable. **Jeeps/Jongas** are easily available everywhere, rates negotiable within city. **Tourist taxis** very few available, rates negotiable. **Bicycles** can be hired in the central market. Rates negotiable.

Entertainment Most restaurants in the Fort have visiting dancers and musicians each evening in the tourist season.

Sports Poonam Stadium and Open-Air theatre, Station Rd.

Museums Govt. Museum, nr Moomal Tourist Bungalow. Open 0900-1600. Closed Fri. **Jaisalmer Folklore Museum** (private collection), Garhsisar. Entry Rs 2.

Useful Numbers Police: T 23322 Fire (Civil Defence): T 2352.

Post and Telegraphs Head P.O. and Telegraph Office, nr Badal Vilas, Kotwali, T 2407.

Places of Worship *Hindu*: Ashapandi ka Mandir, Surya Mandir, Ganesh Mandir. *Jain*: Rikabdevji Temple, Sambhavnathji Temple.

Hospitals and Medical Services Sri Jawahar Hospital (SJ Hospital), Gandhi Marg, T 2343.

Travel Agents and Tour Operators *Rajasthan Tours*, Gandhi Chowk, Amar Sagar Pol, T 2561. *Tourist Guide Service*, nr Patwon ki Haweli, T 2450. *Jaisal Tours*, Hotel Narayan Niwas, Malka Rd, T 2408, 2397.

Tourist Offices and Information *Tourist Office*, Govt. of Rajasthan, Moomal Tourist Bungalow, Amar Sagar Rd, T 2406. Open 0800-1200 and 1500-1800. *Tourist Information Office*, Rly Station. Open during train times. **Conducted Tours** Operated by RTDC, Moomal Tourist Bungalow, T 2392. City Sightseeing, half day (0930-1230). Fort, havelis, Garhisisar Lake. Rs 15. Sam Sand-dunes, half day (1530-1930). Rs 30.

Air Vayudoot connects Jaisalmer with Delhi, Jaipur and Jodhpur and with a flight to Bikaner (no return service from Bikaner). Vayudoot handling agents, Mayur Travels, Moomal Tourist Bungalow, Amar Sagar Rd, T 2392, 2406. Open 0930-1300 and 1330-1730.

Rail There is only one line to Jaisalmer, from Jodhpur. The services offered are therefore very limited. The trains are sometimes not well maintained or clean and the bedding on hire for the overnight journey is often dirty. Jeeps and rickshaws to town (often shared). Jodhpur: *3 J.P.J.*, daily, 2115, 9 hr 45 min; *J.P.J. Passenger*, 1, daily, 0900, 9 hr 35 min.

Road Jaisalmer is connected by way of **NH15** (Pathankot-Samakhiali) to other parts of the country. The distances are: **Jodhpur** (285 km); **Bikaner** (330 km); **Ajmer** (500 km); **Delhi** (897 km); **Jaipur** (638 km); **Udaipur** (663 km); **Bombay** (1465 km); **Calcutta** (2110 km); **Madras** (2762 km); **Trivandrum** (2963 km); **Agra** (868 km).

Bus RTDC runs a coach service between Jaisalmer and Jodhpur. Rajasthan Roadways buses connect Jaisalmer with other important centres in the region like Jaipur, Jodhpur, Barmer, Bikaner and Ajmer. RTDC, Moomal Tourist Bungalow, T 2392 for bookings and reservations. *Private operators: Marudhara Travels*, opp Notified Area Committee Office, Station Rd, T 2351. *National Tours*, Hanuman Choraha, T 2348. Private bus companies run delux coach services between Jaisalmer and Jodhpur, Bikaner.

Excursions
Camel Safaris   As you might expect, this charming desert outpost is the starting point for camel safaris into the surrounding wilderness. These can be one day, one week or longer, for example there is an 11-day trek to Bikaner.

The camel safari business in Jaisalmer is flourishing and an important element in the local economy. It is no problem arranging a trip, though it pays to choose carefully. All the camels are privately owned. The hotels and agents act as middlemen: it often depends on their integrity whether you get good arrangements. The larger hotels have reputations to maintain and you may feel that it is worth paying more for that, but reports indicate that many small hoteliers do organise good outings. Seek some local assistance, especially if you are planning a longer trip. *Mahendra Tours* at the *New Tourist Hotel*, nr Fort Gate, T 282 and the *Narayan Niwas Hotel*, T 2408 organise safaris. The *Fort View Hotel* has had many satisfied customers. It is not necessary to stay at these places, though obviously it helps.

There are day long trips which usually include the **Sam sand dunes**. The usual tours take 4 days and 3 nights and are on a circuit around Jaisalmer via Mool Sagar, the Sam sand dunes and Lodruva. En route you will pass through a few Muslim, Rajput and tribal villages, occupied and abandoned. You will see fields of hardy millet and come across flocks of sheep and goats with their tinkling bells.

Meals and camping equipment are usually provided but check beforehand. On safari there will probably be 1 camel per person plus 1 each for luggage. The camel may be led, you may 'steer' or the driver will sit behind you on the fodder bags. Radios are usually taken, for contact with the police is important in this sensitive border area.

The following items are useful: **cushion** – the curious swaying gait of the camel and the fact that it may cover 20-30 km per day can render your backside tender; **fruit (citrus)** – to quench the thirst; **water bottle; suntan lotion** and **sunburn cream; sunhat, large scarf** or **bandhana** to use as an Arab-style headcloth; **sunglasses**; some **cash** – the camel wallah will expect a tip.

Bada Bagh, a few km N of Jaisalmer. Fruit and vegetables are grown here in the oasis around a large old dam. There are also royal chattris. This is a popular place to visit at sundown to view Jaisalmer. ***Amar Sagar***, 5 km NW of Jaisalmer is a formal garden gone to seed. The lake dries up during the hot season but there is a Jain temple currently under restoration. ***Lodruva***, 15 km NW of Jaisalmer, contains a number of Jain temples that are the only remains of a once flourishing town. The road beyond Lodruva is unsealed.

Mool Sagar, 9 km W of Jaisalmer on the road to Sam is another small garden around a tank. ***Sam*** (also *Sain*), 40 km W of Jaisalmer. Popular with camel treks as there are proper sand dunes. There is a Thar Desert national park near the village. If short of time, you can also visit it by jeep and take a short camel ride, visiting desert villages on the way. ***Khuri***, 40 km SW of Jaisalmer, is a small picturesque desert village of decorated mud thatched buildings.

About 14 km S of town on the road (**NH15**) towards **Barmer** you can see 180 million year old fossils of trees at the **Wood Fossil Park**.

Jaisalmer to Mount Abu   It is a long (400 km), hot, dry and dusty road journey to Jaisalmer and one of little interest unless miles of desert holds an appeal. The road goes via Barmer (158 km).

Barmer, is on the now disused railway line from Jodhpur to Hyderabad in Pakistan (it was supposed to have been reopened in 1986; it remains closed). It is a centre for wood carving (surprisingly in a desert region), carpets, embroidery and block printing. Suitable accommodation along this route is non-existent and it is a very long way to travel in a day. Please be careful and try and take some emergency supplies, e.g. water, food, blankets/sleeping bags just in case.

UDAIPUR TO MOUNT ABU

Most of the road journey is through hill country, first the Aravallis up to Abu Road, then the Abu Hills. The distance is 192 km and plenty of time should be allowed to negotiate the winding road which leaves Udaipur and travels south west to Som (69 km). Here you turn right and go 75 km to the junction with the Pindwara-Abu Road highway. Turn left and continue as per the above route description. You will pass through a number of villages but no towns of any note.

Mount Abu Population 20,000 approx, though swells considerably during season. Altitude 1,720 m. Climate because of its altitude it benefits not only from lower temperatures but also cooling breezes. In summer when it is 32-34°C on the plains below it is 27-28°C in Mount Abu. In winter (Nov-Feb) the maximum is 22°C and minimum 10°C.

Mt Abu is Rajasthan's only hill resort and is situated in the SW part of the state. Like other hill stations or 'Hot Weather Resorts' it is very popular locally, many people coming from Rajasthan and Gujarat who find the atmosphere cool and the pace relaxed and easy-going. It stretches along a plateau roughly 22 km long and 6 km wide and is approached from Abu Road in the SE. Abu is well wooded and has a good variety of birdlife and flowering trees in its jungles. During the monsoon there are numerous orchids. The surface of Abu is hilly and the views over the plains are very good. The Crags and Sunset Point are 2 good spots.

In ancient times, Mount Abu was the home of the sage **Vasishtha**. His companion was **Nandini**, a wish-fulfilling cow, and the place was known as **Nandivardhan** (Place that Increases Joy). One day she fell into a great lake. Vasishtha requested the gods in the Himalaya to save her and they sent Arbuda, a cobra who carried a rock on his head, dropped it into the lake, displacing the water and saving Nandini. Thereafter the place became known as Arbudachala 'The Hill of Arbuda'. Vasishtha also created the 4 powerful 'five-born' Rajput tribes, including the houses of Jaipur and Udaipur, out of a ritual fire ceremony on the mount.

A summer resort Abu was leased by the British Government from the Maharao of Sirohi and was used as the HQ for the Resident of Rajputana until 1947. Its beneficial climate was recognised and it was used as a sanatorium for troops. Many of the rulers from surrounding princely states had summer houses here. The main part of the town is around the **Nakki Talao** (Lake) which takes its name from a legend that states that it was formed by a god who scooped out a depression using only his nails (nakk). There is a pleasant and easy walk around it. You will see rock formations bearing names such as Toad Rock, Nun Rock, Nandi Rock and Camel Rock. You can hire rowing boats to row yourself or be rowed. A 14th century Raghunath Temple stands by the lake.

The natural beauty of the area is enhanced by the group of Jain temples at Dilwara. They contain some superb marble-carving, and are set in beautiful surroundings of mango trees and wooded hills .

Local Festivals Diwali is especially popular.

Places of Interest The **Dilwara Temples** , 5 km from the town centre, are Mount Abu's finest architectural attraction and equally popular with tourists and pilgrims alike. Open 1200-1800. Rs 5 camera charge (though you are not supposed to take photographs inside). Leave all leather items at entrance. It takes about an hour to walk to the temples from town.

The complex is surrounded by a high wall. There is a rest-house for pilgrims on the approach road. Through the entrance on your left is the **Chaumukha** or

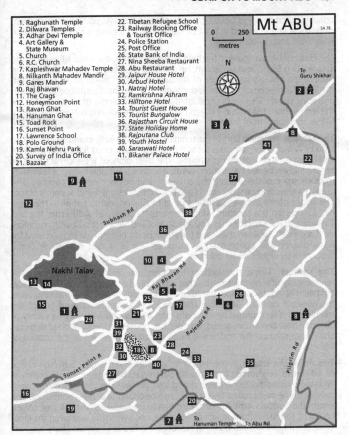

Mt ABU SA 78

1. Raghunath Temple
2. Dilwara Temples
3. Adhar Devi Temple
4. Art Gallery & State Museum
5. Church
6. R.C. Church
7. Kapleshwar Mahadev Temple
8. Nilkanth Mahadev Mandir
9. Ganes Mandir
10. Raj Bhavan
11. The Crags
12. Honeymoon Point
13. Ravan Ghat
14. Hanuman Ghat
15. Toad Rock
16. Sunset Point
17. Lawrence School
18. Polo Ground
19. Kamla Nehru Park
20. Survey of India Office
21. Bazaar
22. Tibetan Refugee School
23. Railway Booking Office & Tourist Office
24. Police Station
25. Post Office
26. State Bank of India
27. Nina Sheeba Restaurant
28. Abu Restaurant
29. Jaipur House Hotel
30. Arbud Hotel
31. Natraj Hotel
32. Ramkrishna Ashram
33. Hilltone Hotel
34. Tourist Guest House
35. Tourist Bungalow
36. Rajasthan Circuit House
37. State Holiday Home
38. Rajputana Club
39. Youth Hostel
40. Saraswati Hotel
41. Bikaner Palace Hotel

Nakhi Talav

Subhash Rd

Raj Bhavan Rd

Rajendra Rd

Sunset Point R

Pilgrim Rd

To Guru Shikhar

To Hanuman Temple   To Abu Rd

Stone Cutters Temple, said to have been built free of charge by the masons in their free time. It is in a mixture of 13th and 15th century styles and is generally regarded as inferior to the two main temples. The ground floor has a colonnaded hall in which there is a shrine of the 23rd Tirthankara.

Along the entrance avenue on the right is a statue of **Ganes**, very popular with the merchants of Gujarat and Rajasthan. Directly ahead is the **Vimala Shah Temple**. The entrance is shaded by a champak tree with its yellow musky flowers. **Kama**, the God of physical love, applied the oil of the champak flowers to his arrows. The pilgrim, by offering these symbols of sensual desire, demonstrates a willingness to surrender to the gods.

The Vimala Shah Temple The entrance contains an image of Mahavira, the last of the 24 Tirthankaras of the present age. He is naked and the energy centres on his body are picked out and the most important of these is the *heart chakra* or *srivasta*. On the left of the shrine is a white marble tablet showing Mahavira surrounded by the other Tirthankaras. The sanctuary door has a silver chest for donations across it and beside it is a camphor holder. As part of Jain worship, camphor is lit and waved in front of the image. The ceiling is carved in a typical Rajasthani and Gujarati design.

The **Hall** contains a figure of the patron, **Vimala Shah**, the Chief Minister of the Solanki King Bhim Deva of Gujarat. He commissioned the temple in 1031. At the back of the hall is a small figure of **Ambika**, a form of the goddess Durga, and the Shah family deity. The room is decorated with elephants, symbols of strength and royal power. Elephants undoubtedly hauled the blocks of white marble for the temple from **Makrana**, 110 km W of Jaipur. The building material for the Taj Mahal also came from there.

The temple The main part of the temple is one of the early examples of the Jain style in W India. The temple is set within a rectangular court lined with a row of small shrines and a double colonnade. The chief glory of the architecture is its ornate and exuberant decoration. Hardly a surface is left unadorned. *Makaras**, mythical sea monsters, guard the entrance, and below them are conches. The cusped arches and ornate capitals are beautifully designed and superbly made. The layout of the temple is similar to that of Gujarati Hindu temples. The main hall focuses on the sanctum which contains the image of **Adinatha**, the first Tirthankara. The **sanctum** has a pyramidal roof and has a vestibule with entrances on three sides. Between these and the entrance is a platform which was used for ritual dances and congregational purposes. Above it is a 6 m wide dome supported by eight slender columns.

The shrines Lining the walls of the main hall are fifty two shrines, each representing one of the temples that stood on the mountain of the mythical continent Nandishvaradvipa 'the Abode of the Lords of Joy'. The *Chakrasuri* was the personal deity of Adinatha. The goddess is attractively carved out of the marble and is surrounded by musicians. She is six-armed and carries a variety of objects – bow and arrow, discus, thunderbolt, noose and elephant goad or mace. She is mounted on the mythical Garuda so can be identified as the consort of Vishnu.

The *Adinatha image* In the SW corner is a shrine and large 2.5 m high image of **Adinatha**. Legend has it that the land at Dilwara belonged to Hindu Brahmins who were unwilling to part with it and told Vimala Shah that he could have it only when he had proved that it had once belonged to a Jain community. In a dream the goddess **Ambika** instructed him to dig under a champak tree. When he did he found the huge image of Adinatha, upon which he was given the land. Opposite the image are figures representing the family of Vimala Shah.

Along the N side of the main hall are a number of interesting *friezes* showing **Krishna and the Serpent**, **Krishna and the Gopis**, a well-known and immensely popular myth of the young god and his favourite cowgirl. The **Goddesses of the Four Directions** align the temple in space. **Shitala** is the goddess of smallpox and commands widespread worship. **Saraswati** is the patron of the arts and wife of Brahma, the creator. **Padmavati** is a tantric deity and carries the *trishula** and the snake which are both symbols of Siva. **Narasingha** is the man-lion and Vishnu's fourth incarnation who destroyed the demon **Hiranyaksha**. Narasingha was popular with the warriors who converted to Jainism. In contrast to the tedious repetition of the Jain shrines, these Hindu panels are bursting with energy. The final highlight of the temple is the **Mandapa**. This domed lotus ceiling rises in eleven concentric circles, all exquisitely carved.

Opposite the Vimala Temple is the **Adinatha Temple**, a 14th century structure that encloses a huge brass **Tirthankara** image reputed to weigh 4.3 tonnes and made of *panchadhatu* (five metals) – gold, silver, copper, brass and zinc. The temple was commenced in the late 13th century by Brahma Shah, the Maharana of Udaipur's chief minister. Building activity was curtailed by war with Gujarat and never recommenced.

The large **Neminatha Temple** (1230) on your right as you leave the Adinatha Temple, was erected by two wealthy merchants, Vastupala and Tejapala and dedicated to the 22nd Tirthankar. They also built a similar Neminatha temple at Girnar. This imitates the Adinatha temple but is complete. The decoration and jali screens are profuse yet extremely pleasing. The ceiling mandapas and colonnades are especially good. Portrait sculptures of the donors and their wives have been placed in the entrance porch.

Adhar Devi, 3 km from town, is a Durga Temple approached by 200 steep steps. There are very good views.

Achalgarh (11 km) The view from here is very good. At the **Achaleshwar Temple** there is the toe of Siva, a brass Nandi and a deep hole claimed to reach into the netherworld. Outside by the car park is a tank. On the bank is an image of **Adi Pal,** the **Paramara** king and near him are three large stone buffaloes pierced with arrows. Legend has it that the tank was once filled with *ghee* (clarified butter) and these buffalo, who were really demons in disguise, came every night to drink from it until they were shot by Adi Pal. A path leads up to a group of temples. The whole site is quite picturesque.

Guru Shikhar (1,720 m), 15 km, is the highest peak in the area and there is a road almost to the top. The views all round are good.

Gaumukh (Cow's Mouth), 8 km south east, on the Mt Abu- Abu Road road. Here a small stream flows from the mouth of a marble cow. There is also a Nandi bull, Siva's vehicle and the tank here is believed to be the site of Vasishtha's fire from which the four great Rajput clans were created – see Introduction. An image of the sage is flanked by ones of Rama and Krishna.

Hotels mostly 27 km from Abu Rd rly, central. **C** *Hilltone*, T 127, Cable: Hilltone, Telex: 3752700 Attention Hilltone. 46 rm, mostly non a/c. Restaurant, health club, doctor on call, car parking, pool, garden. **C** *Palace Hotel* (Bikaner House), Dilwara Rd. T 21 and 23, Cable: Palace. 28 non a/c rm. Restaurant, exchange, billiards, table tennis and tennis, gardens. Imposing granite and sandstone mansion, many antique furnishings in a large garden with lake. **C** *Savera*, Sunset Rd. T 254, Cable: Savera. 24 non a/c rm. Swimming, restaurant.

D *Connaught House*, Rajendra Marg, T 20941. Owned by the Maharaja of Jodhpur and former summer residence of the chief minister of Marwar-Jodhpur. 12 rm. Simple but adequately furnished. **D** *Abu International*, opp Polo Ground. T 177, Cable: savera. 43 rm. Simple but clean. Restaurant (Punjabi, Gujarati). **D** *Mount*, Dilwara Rd. T 55, Cable: Mounthotel. 7 non a/c rm. Restaurant (Indian, Continental, Parsi, Gujarati), doctor on call, car parking, sightseeing tours, Amex, Diners and Mastercard Credit Cards, garden. Once a British officer's bungalow. Clean and cosy. **D** *Samrat International*, nr Bus Stand. T 73 and 53, Cable: Samrat. 30 non a/c rm. Restaurant, exchange, video hall, travel, Amex, Diners credit cards. Modern. Shares reception area with **D** *Navjihan*, T 53, the cheaper of the two hotels. **D** *Madhuban*, nr the Bus Stand, T 121. 10 non a/c rm. Nearby **D** *Sheratone*, T 273. 40 non a/c rm with baths (Western or Indian style). Cheerful and unprofessional.

E *Saraswati*, opp. the taxi stand, T 7. Clean and plain. Nearby is **E** *Maharaja* which is clean but over-priced by comparison. On the road into town is **E** *Shikhar Tourist Bungalow* (RTDC). 79 rm non a/c rm with Indian style bathrooms, some cottages. Restaurant, bar, boating. Good views from hill. Opposite is the **D** *Aravalli*, nr the Veterinary Hospital, T 216. 18 non a/c rm that are pleasantly furnished and well maintained. Pretty terraced garden. There is also a **F** *Youth Hostel* which is central. Dormitories are quite cramped.

Restaurants *Handi*, Hilltone Hotel. Specialises in Indian dishes cooked in small clay pots (*handis*), though others available. Open for breakfast 0700-1000, lunch 1200-1500 and dinner 1900-2300, Bar open 1000-2300. *Angan Dining Hall*, Navjivan Hotel and the *Mount Hotel* are plain but serve a good Gujarati veg *thali*. Open 1300-1430 and 1900-2100. *Maharashtra International* serves *thalis* . *Dilwara*, nr Samrat Hotel.

Shopping *Rajasthan Emporium*, Raj Bhavan Rd. Trinkets, carved agate boxes, marble figures. *Chacha Museum*. Not a museum but a source of unusual items. Open 0930-2200 daily. *Roopali*, nr Nakki Lake. Sells silver. Open 0900-2100 daily.

Local Transport Taxis with posted fares to anywhere round about. **Large Baby Prams** that you sit in and a wheeled around in are unique to Mount Abu. Buses leave for Dilwara and/or Achalgarh. Check first.

Museums Art Museum and Gallery, Raj Bhavan Rd. Small collection which includes some textiles and stone sculptures from the 9th and 10th centuries. Open 1000-1700, Closed Fri. Entry free.

Tourist Offices and Information *Rajasthan Tourist Development Corporation* (RTDC) Bureau, opposite the bus stand, T 51. Open 0800-1100 and 1600-2000 in season and 1000-1700 out of season. Supplies guides. RTDC runs daily tours to Dilwara, Achalgrah, Guru Shikhar, Nakki Lake, Sunset Point and Adhar Devi. Times 0800-1300 and 1400-1900. Depart from bus stand. Price Rs 14. *Gujarat Travels*, T 218, organise tours by jeep.

Travel Abu Road is the railhead for Mount Abu. Many buses go straight to Mount Abu, others terminate at Abu Road. Check when buying your ticket.

Air The nearest airport is at Udaipur, 165 km to the E.

Rail Jodhpur: *Marwar-Ranakpur Exp*, 4728, daily, 1220, 6 hr 50 min; *Surya Nagri Exp*, 2908, daily, 0048, 5 hr 12 min. Jaipur: *Delhi Mail*, 9902, daily, 1308, 10 hr 52 min; *Delhi Exp*, 9904, daily, 2250, 11 hr 30 min; *Ashram Exp*, 2906, daily, 2030, 7 hr 55 min. **Agra Fort**: *Agra Fort Fast Passenger Exp*, 9706, daily, 0650, 24 hr 45 min. From Agra Fort: *Agra Fort Fast Passenger Exp*, 9705, daily, 2020, 23 hr 40 min. **Old Delhi**: *Aravalli Exp*, 9932, daily, 1105, 18 hr 25 min; *Delhi Mail*, 9902, daily, 1308, 18 hr 22 min; *Delhi Exp*, 9904, daily, 2250, 20 hr 10 min; *Ashram Exp*, 2906, daily, 2030, 13 hr 30 min. **Ahmadabad**: *Ahmadabad Exp*, 9903, daily, 5.05, 4 hr 55 min; *Ahmadabad Mail*, 9901, daily, 1525, 4 hr 50 min; *Aravalli Exp*, 9931, daily, 1016, 6 hr; *Surya Nagri Exp*, 2907, daily, 0335, 3 hr 25 min.

Bus There is an extensive service from Mount Abu to various destinations. It is often quicker to take a bus all the way rather than go by bus to Abu Road, then take the train. To Ahmadabad (250 km) and Udaipur (165 km) takes about 7 hr. The local bus takes about an hour to make the 27 km climb from Abu Road

HARYANA AND PUNJAB

Before the arrival of irrigation Haryana and Punjab were not especially fertile areas. Their distinction was as a battlefield. Here on the flat plains NW of Delhi, the history of N India was largely determined. At Panipat three decisive battles were fought whilst at nearby Kurukshetra the great battle between the Kauravas and Pandavas in the Hindu epic the *Mahabharata* took place. The Jat community still has a strong martial tradition to which the sixth Sikh Guru, Hargobind, turned when looking for ways of protecting the Sikhs from Mughal attacks. Looking at Haryana and Punjab today, which over the summer months appear monotonous, tired and dusty, it is hard to believe why wave upon wave of invaders rushed down from the heights of the Khyber Pass to stake their claim in N India. The climate is one of extremes. In winter cold 'snaps' can take hundreds of lives whilst in the summer the heat is often stifling.

Warning In the last decade it has been difficult to travel around Punjab unhindered. Given the continuing violence in the state, permission is difficult to obtain. Tourists have great difficulty in obtaining permits which are issued by the Home Ministry. Applications are through Indian High Commissions worldwide.

Social indicators Haryana Area 44,000 sq km **Population** 16 million **Literacy** M 48% F 22% **Newspaper circulation** 329,000 **Birth rate** *Rural* 38:1000 *Urban* 30:1000 **Death rate** *Rural* 10:1000 *Urban* 7:1000 **Infant mortality** *Rural* 100:1000 *Urban* 62:1000 **Registered graduate job seekers** 473,000 **Average annual income per head** Rs 2330 **Inflation** *1981-87* 66% **Religion** *Hindu* 89% *Sikh* 6% *Muslim* 4% *Christian* 0.1% **Punjab Area** 50,000 sq km **Population** 21 million **Literacy** M 47% F 34% **Birth rate** *Rural* 31:1000 *Urban* 29:1000 **Death rate** *Rural* 10:1000 *Urban* 7:1000 **Infant mortality** *Rural* 82:1000 *Urban* 53:1000 **Registered graduate job seekers** 67,000 **Average annual income per head:** Rs 2770 **Religion** *Hindu* 37% Sikh 61% *Muslim* 1% *Christian* 1%

Towns and cities 23% and 30% of Haryana's and Punjab's population respectively is urban, Chandigarh, the joint capital, being the largest town.

INTRODUCTION

Agricultural conditions have improved greatly with the development of canal and tube well irrigation, and the promotion of modern crop technologies. Now, Haryana and Punjab are one of India's most important agricultural regions. The countryside around Delhi is also close to the soul of India, with countless villages and, seemingly, innumerable people. It is here that you see the Indian tradition being played out in many aspects of daily life; festivals, building styles and house decoration, the regional handicrafts and the cuisine. It is well worth visiting villages to get a sense of this life.

The region has few truly great monuments, and its historical past is to be seen in the pages of books rather than on the ground. Despite this natural disadvantage, the Haryana state tourist department has worked hard to appreciate travellers' requirements and has done a great deal to provide for them. It has developed an extensive chain of tourist complexes, named after different species of birds, modestly priced, all well run and easily accessible, especially to road users.

Not surprisingly, the towns and cities of the region are mostly route centres associated with the *Grand Trunk Road*, the great highway from Peshawar to Calcutta. **Rudyard Kipling** described this as 'the backbone of all Hind' and 'such a river of life as nowhere else exists in the world' on which he saw 'all castes and kinds of men...all the world going and coming'. Much of *Kim* was set along it.

N.B. The well-watered and fertile land of the Punjab is the homeland of the **Sikhs**, one of India's most distinctive regional and religious groups. There has been extensive political unrest through much of the 1980s and the problems have still not been resolved. This has often made travel in Punjab difficult. **Permits are sometimes required and you need to take advice before visiting.**

The Land
Haryana is 44,222 sq km in area and roughly triangular in shape. Rajasthan and Punjab border it to the W and NW, Himachal Pradesh and Uttar Pradesh to the N and E, with Delhi encapsulated on its eastern side. Apart from a small portion of the state in the N which lies in the Siwalik Hills, Haryana is on the Gangetic plain and is unrelentingly flat, lying at a height of between 220-270 m. The river Yamuna forms the eastern boundary of Haryana and its waters feed the extensive irrigation network. A number of small rivers, including the Ghaggar, flow S across it from the foothills of the Himalayas.

Punjab occupies a strategic position on India's border with Pakistan. Its

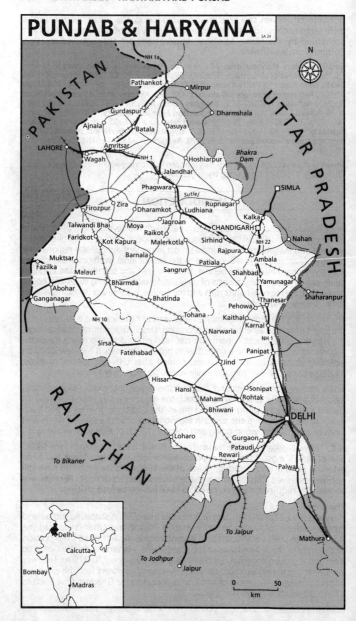

PUNJAB & HARYANA

SA 24

neighbours are: Pakistan (W), Rajasthan (S) and Haryana (S), Himachal Pradesh and Jammu & Kashmir (N). The area of the state is 50,362 sq km. Nearly all of the Punjab is a gently sloping plain, highest in the NE at 275 m and falling to 167 m in the SW. There are three regions. The **Siwalik Hills** in the NE vary in altitude from 275 m to 915 metres and occupy only a very small part of the state. Between the hills and the plain is a narrow **transitional zone** of gently undulating foothills, broken up in places by seasonal streams. Most of the state is on the low-lying, well watered and highly fertile alluvial soils which make up **the plains**. There are one or two distinguishable upland areas between the main watercourses. The two major rivers are the **Sutlej** and the **Beas** which rise in the Himalaya. In the SW, near the border with Rajasthan, there are sand dunes.

Vegetation
Nearly all the natural vegetation cover has gone. The Siwaliks once supported tropical deciduous forests of *shisham** (a valued building timber), pipal, jujube, *kikar** (gum arabic) but are now covered in bush and scrub. Wild animal life is correspondingly rare and includes the occasional nilgai (blue bull), wild boar, rabbits, jackals, foxes and various species of deer. The birdlife is richer and includes heron, cranes and geese. Like Haryana, Punjab receives migratory birds from the Northern hemisphere over the winter. Cobras, vipers and kraits are all poisonous snakes and relatively common in summer (May and Jun).

Climate
Haryana and Punjab have an inland continental climate. The winters are quite cold, with daily minimum temperatures ranging from 5°C to 9°C between Nov and Feb. Occasionally it reaches freezing point. The daily maximum temperatures over the same period are 19°C to 27°C. Humidity at this time is usually low, but depressions moving in from the W sometimes bring rain and a chill dampness to the air. The summers are hot. In May and Jun the average daily temperature is 40°C although it can reach 45°C on extreme days. Amritsar, situated very near the border with Pakistan receives 650 mm rainfall per annum, of which 70% is during the monsoon months of Jul, Aug and Sep. Annual rainfall totals are higher in the Siwaliks.

People
Haryana was created when the state of Punjab was divided in 1966. 90% of the population of 13 million are Hindu, the majority living in rural areas. By South Asian standards there are no large cities, although many of the smaller market towns have grown rapidly as Delhi's industrialisation has spilled over into the surrounding states. The main language is Hindi. Urdu and Punjabi are spoken by many of the minority Muslims and Sikhs. All the Hindu festivals are important in this region. **See page 154.**

The inhabitants of the Haryana and Punjab are mainly descended from the Aryan tribes that invaded NW India from around 1500 BC. Successive invaders became assimilated with the early Aryans. The Jats, Rajputs and Punjabis are a product of this movement of peoples. Two-thirds of the 21 million people in Punjab speak **Punjabi,** an Indo-Aryan language which is a close relative of Hindi. The remainder speak Hindi. Punjab is the homeland of the Sikhs and the only state where they form the majority.

Punjabi culture is strongly influenced by Hinduism and Islam yet it displays a distinctive character of its own. Its literature has strong connections with Sufism. **See page 1090.** Guru Nanak used the Punjabi language as a medium for poetic expression. Typically Hindu celebrations and festivals such as Dasara and Diwali are enthusiastically observed as are the birth and death anniversaries of the gurus and saints. Sikh music, much of it like the Mughal *ghazal** and *qawwali** is immensely popular.

In dress, the Punjabi *salwar kamiz**, a long *kurta* (shirt) and baggy trousers drawn in at the ankle are traditional and popular forms of dress with men and women alike, women usually having an accompanying *dupatta** (long scarf or shawl). Males are distinctive, of course, for their turbans and beards. **See page 72**.

Many people think that the Sikhs are endowed with an almost mystical affinity with machines. The Sikhs were among the first in India to use and understand all manner of machines from tractors to tubewells, threshing machines to grinders. Sikhs are now found driving buses, taxis, hire cars and tanks (they were the drivers in the Indian army and have maintained this role ever since).

Economy

Agriculture is **Haryana's** main economic activity and the state government has invested heavily in developing farming. The canal irrigation network has been increased and the rapid increase in the use of deep wells, powered by electric or diesel pumpsets, has encouraged the rapid adoption of modern crop technologies. Now 91% of the total area is cultivated, with wheat, gram, barley and mustard grown over the winter (the *rabi** season) and rice, millet, maize, sugarcane and cotton over the summer (the *kharif** season). The state is also known for the quality of its bullocks and dairy cattle. Cotton and sugar processing have developed into important agro-industries.

There are no sizable mineral resources for exploitation. Haryana has no heavy industry but around Faridabad in the S a major light industrial zone has been established and it is the largest producer of automobile spare parts in India. Other products include paper, cement and bicycles. As a result of these developments in both agriculture and industry Haryana is one of India's fastest growing states.

About 85% of the total area of **Punjab** is under cultivation and 70% of the population are engaged in agriculture. The state produces a surplus of foodgrains, especially wheat and rice. The other main foodgrains are maize, gram, barley and pulses (peas, beans and lentils).

Irrigation Over 90% of Punjab's agricultural land is now irrigated. Canals serve about half the area. There are over half a million electric and diesel pumpsets in use. Important irrigation works implemented since 1947 include the Bhakra Nangal multi-purpose river valley project, the largest of its kind in Asia and the Madhopur-Beas and the Sutlej-Beas Links for the redistribution of water.

The soil is rich and well watered and the Punjabi's skill in harnessing resources and adopting new crop technologies (the much talked-of "Green Revolution",) have turned the region into the breadbasket of India. Indian wheat production has risen from 7 million tonnes in 1947 to nearly 50 million tonnes in 1991. Landholdings average 15-20 hectares, large enough to sustain capital-intensive farming, but small enough to spur farmers to maximise returns. Major cash crops are oilseeds, sugar-cane, cotton and potatoes. The consolidation of holdings and the formation of cooperative societies and community development programmes has made the agrarian class the most affluent in India. Higher per capita incomes, increased spending power and reinvestment has promoted the development of agriculture-related and non-farm industries.

Minerals Punjab has practically no mineral resources. Industrial development is associated with agriculture and the production of consumer goods. Bicycles and bicycle parts, sewing machines, hand tools, machine tools, auto parts, electronic equipment, surgical goods, leather goods, hosiery, knitwear and textiles are all manufactured in the state. Ludhiana accounts for 90% of the country's woollen hosiery industry, Jalandhar is an important centre for the production of sports goods and Batala is noted for its manufacture of agricultural implements.

Punjab also has large remittances sent from abroad and elsewhere in India which have helped to pay for the necessary investment.

The state is well served with roads and railways. The remotest parts of the state are incorporated into the road network, thus facilitating the collection and distribution of agriculture produce as well as promoting social mobility. Amritsar is well connected with Delhi and other N Indian centres. There is also a rail link with Pakistan which is 24 km to the W of Amritsar. See page 1260.

History

Early settlement The *Ghaggar Valley*, running from the Siwaliks down to the Rajasthan desert, was the home of fortified urban settlements before the rise of the Harappan civilisation and go back to before 3000 BC. After approximately 1700 BC, it came under the influence of successive waves of Aryan invaders. The territory became the region in which many of the fundamental beliefs and ideas of the **Vedas** took shape. Incorporated into the Mauryan Empire during the 3rd century BC, it became a vital region for the Muslim kings of the Delhi Sultanate 1500 years later and was part of the Mughal's core region of power. It has long been famous as a battleground. Culturally it is a region of legends. In **Kurukshetra** the epic struggle between the **Pandavas** and **Kauravas** took place and **Karnal** is the site of a number of episodes in the *Mahabharata*, including that where Krishna is believed to have given Arjuna lessons in moral welfare. See page 46.

The Sikhs The community of Sikhs or 'disciples' (from the Sanskrit *shishya**) began with the preaching of the Hindu ascetic Nanak who lived in the Punjab from 1469 to 1539. Nanak taught that God is one and accessible to all and before his death chose one of his disciples to be his successor. He was followed by 9 Gurus – see page 71. Aurangzeb tried to put down Sikhism by force, encouraging the Sikhs to become militant. The Punjab experienced several periods of extreme violence. In 1799 **Ranjit Singh** set up a Sikh confederacy which governed until the late 1830s. Two wars with the British ended in 1849, after which the Sikh community played an important role in British India, see page 46.

Jallianwallah Bagh Relations with the British soured in 1919. During the Nationalist movement *hartals** (strikes) became a customary form of demonstration. The Punjab which had supplied 60% of Indian troops committed to the First World War was one of hardest hit economically in 1918. The feeling the British were not doing enough prompted demonstrations throughout the country and some of the most energetic were in the Punjab. Here, the Lieutenant Governor of the province decided on a 'fist force' to repulse the essentially non-violent but vigorous demonstrations. Some looting occurred in Amritsar and the British called in reinforcements. These arrived under the command of *General Dyer*. His heavy-handed and callous approach prompted further indignation.

Dyer's first act was to ban all meetings but in spite of this people were reported to be gathering on Sunday April 13 1919 as thousands of pilgrims poured into Amritsar to celebrate Baisakhi, a holy day in the Sikh calendar. That afternoon thousands were crammed into Jallianwala Bagh, a piece of waste ground popular with travellers, surrounded on all sides by high walls with only a narrow alley for access. Dyer personally led some troops to the place, gave the crowd no warning and simply ordered his men to open fire. When 1650 rounds had been spent he ordered them to about turn and marched off leaving 379 dead and 1200 wounded behind.

This act and others of a similarly brutal and nature such as the flogging of six youths suspected of beating an English woman Miss Sherwood who escaped only because a Hindu family treated her injuries and smuggled her into British hands, compounded matters. Related to the Miss Sherwood incident (modified in Paul Scott's *Jewel in the Crown* epic novel) was Dyer's order that every Indian who lived in the street where she was attacked must go down it on all fours.

The British response The Jallianwala Bagh massacre was hushed up and London only got to know of it six months later at which time the Hunter Committee was set up to investigate the incident. It did not accept Dyer's excuse that he acted as he did to prevent another insurrection throughout India on the scale of the Mutiny of 1857. He was asked to resign, and returned to England where he died in 1927. However, he was not universally condemned. A debate in the House of Lords produced a majority of 126 to 86 in his favour and the Morning Post newspaper launched a fund for 'The Man who Saved India'. Over UK £26,000 was raised to comfort the dying General.

This was not the end of the affair. O'Dwyer, the Governor of the Province was shot dead at a meeting in Caxton Hall, London by a survivor of Jallianwala Bagh who was hanged for the offence.

India was outraged by Dyer's massacre. Gandhi, who had called the nation-wide *hartal* (strike) in March, did as many Indians did and threw back decorations given by the British, in his case for serving as a stretcher bearer in S Africa. This was the beginning of the non-cooperation movement, which was to be a vital feature of the struggle for Independence.

Partition The next bloody chapter in the Punjab's history occurred during Partition in 1947. The Muslim League's demand for a separate state for Muslims encouraged some Sikhs to press for an independent state for Sikhs as well. In the event it was clear that the overwhelming majority of Sikhs would opt to be with India. In the atmosphere of increasing intransigence and communal violence, the Radcliffe Commission was set up to draw a boundary separating those districts with a Muslim majority from the remainder. The result was that the Punjab was divided in two, leaving as many as 5 million Sikhs and Hindus in Muslim W Pakistan and as many Muslims in predominantly Hindu India. Many of these groups, terrified by the prospect of losing all that they had worked for, turned on each other in frenzied rage. All across the state villages and bazaars were reduced to rubble as men women and children were butchered.

Amritsar witnessed some of the worst carnage, situated as it is 24 km from the border. It is the principal railway station on the line between Delhi and Lahore. All that summer the roads and trains were filled with refugees. Decimated by cholera, the situation was further aggravated when the long overdue monsoon broke causing extensive flooding. In six terrible weeks from Aug to mid-Sep it is estimated that half a million people died, maybe more. During Partition, there was a movement of 11 million people across the new borders of India and Pakistan.

After Independence Sikh political opinion in Punjab continued to stress the need for a measure of autonomy within India's federal constitution. The creation of linguistic states in 1956 encouraged the Sikh *Akali Dal* to press for the further division of Punjab on the basis of the distinctiveness of Punjabi from Hindi. Punjabi agitation in 1966 resulted in the further sub division of the Punjab into the present states of Punjab (predominantly Sikh), Haryana (predominantly Hindu) and Himachal Pradesh (a purely mountain state, 96% Hindu).

Sikh fundamentalism and party politics Despite economic success, political discontent simmered. Some orthodox Sikhs bitterly opposed the liberalism which they saw as a threat to Sikh identity. They attacked the extent to which "modern" habits of dress and behaviour, such as smoking, were being adopted. However, the main causes of Sikh unrest were party political. The Akali Dal party had a majority in the State Assembly between 1969-72 and again between 1977 and 1980. However, in 1980 it was routed by the Congress when Mrs. Gandhi returned to power on a national landslide. The disheartened Akali Dal was torn by factionalism as well as by opposition to the Congress Party.

The Akali demands The Akalis presented a list of demands to the central government. First, Amritsar, home of the Golden Temple, the Sikh Holy of Holies should be recognised as the holy capital of Punjab. Second, Article 25 of the Constitution should be amended to recognize Sikhism as an independent religion and not an offshoot of Hinduism. Third, there should be a daily 90 minute broadcast of readings from the **Granth Sahib**, the Sikh holy book, over national radio. Fourth, Chandigarh should become the exclusive administrative capital of Punjab. Fifth, certain Sikh lands given by Central Government to Haryana should be returned and sixth, the restoration of water rights from the **Ravi** and **Beas** rivers which had been diverted to Haryana and Rajasthan.

Operation Blue Star Fundamentalist inspired violence increased across the state and their demands became steadily more extreme, making hopes of conciliation fade the longer the agitation persisted. Eventually in July 1984 **Mrs Gandhi** launched 'Operation Blue Star' in which she told the army to capture the Golden Temple. In the brief but fierce fighting that followed Bhindranwale was killed, 259 Sikh militants and 59 soldiers died, 90 Sikhs and 110 troops were wounded and 450 militants were arrested. Although the action gained the support of many Hindus, Sikhs were appalled and outraged at the desecration. Two months later, on October 31 1984, Mrs Gandhi was shot in the grounds of the Prime Minister's residence in Delhi by two Sikh bodyguards. That was immediately followed by what many saw as officially sponsored attacks on Sikhs in many cities, especially Delhi.

Recent political developments
Punjab's trauma has not been ended. In 1989 the continuing violence claimed 1800 lives, including 699 'terrorists', 18 police, 100 women and children and 38 politicians. Even with the defeat of Rajiv Gandhi's Congress (I) Party in the 1989 national elections and a subsequent change of leadership following V.P. Singh's resignation, the Punjab problem, like that in Northern Ireland, remains intractable.

Administration
Like the other states in the Union Punjab's governor is the constitutional head of government and is appointed by the president of India. He is advised by the chief minister and his cabinet who are elected from the democratically elected legislature. Punjab has 13 seats in the Lok Sabha (Lower House) and 7 seats in the Rajya Sabha (Upper House) in the national parliament in New Delhi. In recent years Punjab has had several periods of direct rule from New Delhi.

In 1947, the Indian government built **Chandigarh** as the modern administrative capital for the Punjab. When Haryana was created in 1966 Chandigarh became the capital for both states. Arbitration was promised to decide its ultimate allocation, but the political upheavals in Punjab have made it impossible to reach acceptable agreement. For administration Haryana has a governor who is appointed by the president of India on a five year term. He is aided by a council of ministers drawn from the legislative assembly. The state has 10 seats in the Lok Sabha (Lower House) and 5 seats in the Rajya Sabha (Upper House) in the national parliament in New Delhi. There are 12 districts, each administered by a collector. The *panchayat raj* (village rule) includes all 7,000 villages in Haryana. The capital, shared with Punjab, is Chandigarh which is a Union Territory like Delhi.

The state has undergone several major changes in government. The Congress Party held 7 of the 9 Lok Sabha seats in 1967 and 1871, taking about 50% of the vote. However, it was particularly severely affected by Sanjay Gandhi's campaign of enforced sterilisation during the emergency of 1975-77, and the Congress Party won only 18% of the vote in 1977. Rajiv Gandhi came back to win all 10 seats with 55% of the vote in 1984, but the Jats are a powerful political force in the state and the Congress suffered another big defeat at the hands of the peasant dominated Janata Dal in 1989.

DELHI TO AMRITSAR VIA CHANDIGARH

The intensively cultivated fields now show all the benefits which can come with irrigation. Around Delhi many of the fields are now planted with vegetables for the Delhi market. Further out from December to March the fields are green with wheat, often irrigated by tube wells and canal irrigation. The small brick huts built to house the electric or diesel pumps in the fields are a common sight. The Grand Trunk Road itself has long stretches lined with magnificent trees, all numbered, for the products of the trees are extremely valuable and villagers have to buy rights to the leaves and wood.

Leave Delhi on **NH1** (The Grand Trunk Road) which runs parallel to the Yamuna River which forms the boundary between Haryana and Uttar Pradesh. 8 km out of Delhi bear left to keep on NH 1. Rai (25 km), Bahalgarh (3 km) and Samalka (32 km) are passed before reaching Panipat (18 km).

Panipat *(Population* 138,000) is the first historic site of importance after leaving Delhi, and is a battlefield town near the old bank of the river Yamuna. Like many other towns on the Ganga plains the town lies on the higher ground made up of the debris of earlier settlements. It overlooks the old river course. Three great battles were fought here though virtually no evidence remains to suggest their importance for India and for the establishment of the Mughal Empire.

The first battle On 21 April 1526 **Babur** fought **Ibrahim Lodi** the Sultan of Delhi. Babur had entered India with about 12,000 men (**see page 91**). By the time he reached Panipat his forces had swelled to perhaps 25,000 men. Ibrahim's army was said to number 100,000 men and 1,000 elephants. Babur dug himself in using a formation which Babur claimed to have adapted from Turkish practice. As many as 700 carts were gathered together and strung together with ropes of rawhide, thus creating a barricade similar to those used in N America three centuries later. From behind this, the matchlockmen would fire on the advancing enemy.

It took several days before Ibrahim could be provoked into attacking but when he did his army came to a grinding halt before the fusillade of musket fire. In the meantime, Babur's cavalry attacked on both flanks in a pincer movement, raining arrows on the Indian army caught on three sides and too cumbersome to about turn and retreat. When the battle ceased, about 20,000 of the sultan's army were dead, including their leader.

The second battle of Panipat took place on 5 Nov 1556. **Akbar**, who had just succeeded his father Humayun, and his general-cum-guardian **Bairam Khan**, defeated **Hemu**, the general of the Afghan **Sher Shah**. The battle was going badly for Akbar until Hemu was hit in the eye by an arrow, and although it did not kill him outright, it made him unconscious. The sight of the tiny Hemu slumped in the howdah of his famous elephant Hawai (the wind) caused his troops to flee. Hemu was brought unconscious before Akbar and Bairam Khan and beheaded, the head then being sent to Kabul and the body to be hung on a gibbet at Delhi. There was a mass slaughter of those unfortunate enough to have been caught, and in the gruesome tradition of *Genghis Khan* and **Timur** a victory pillar was built and their heads plastered in.

The third battle took place two centuries later on 13 January 1761. The remnants of the once great Mughal Empire was threatened from the W by the resurgent **Rajputs** and from the NW by the **Afghans,** who sacked Delhi in 1756-57. The distracted Mughal minister called in the Marathas and, according to Percival Spear ' the triangular power struggle between the Mughals, Marathas and Afghans became a duel between the Marathas and the Afghans'. The battle at Panipat was fought between these two forces. The Maratha army was said to number 15,000 infantry, 55,000 cavalry, 200 guns. These were supported by 200,000 Pindaris and camp followers. The Afghans comprised 38,000 infantry, 42,000 cavalry and 70 guns, besides numerous irregulars.

Despite their numbers the Marathas lost and their soldiers fled. However, the Afghan leader *Ahmad Shah Durrani* was unable to take advantage of his victory as his followers mutinied for the two-years arrears of pay he owed them. Thus, the former Mughal empire was denied to both the Afghans and Marathas, leaving N India in a political vacuum which

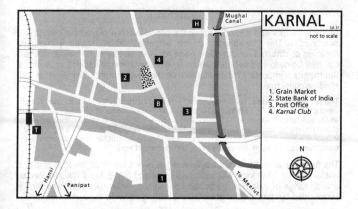

KARNAL SA 31
not to scale

1. Grain Market
2. State Bank of India
3. Post Office
4. Karnal Club

N

adventurers tried to fill during the next 40 years.

The main old building in Panipat is a shrine to the Muslim saint **Abu Ali Kalandhar**. One of the stories about him is reminiscent of the Old Testament story of Moses in Egypt, for he was said to have banished all flies from Panipat. However, people complained so he ordered 1000 times as many to come back. Panipat is not the only small town in India where this story might seem to have the ring of truth.

Hotels D *Skylark Motel* (Haryana Tourism), T 3579. Motel and dormitory. A/c rm. Restaurant.

The route from **Panipat** continues N to **Karnal** (34 km *Population* 132,000) which is an ancient town. Legend suggests that it was founded by one of the leaders of the **Kauravas** in the great battle recorded in the *Mahabharata* (see below). It was seized by the Raja of Jind around 1763 and taken from him by George Thomas in 1797. A British cantonment was established in 1811 but was abandoned in 1841 due to the unhealthiness of the site, caused by the W Jumna canal interfering with natural drainage and promoting malarial fever. The canal was re-aligned in 1875. At nearby **Uchana** (3 km N) there is the **D** *Oasis Motel* (Haryana Tourism), T 4249. Tourist huts.

From Karnal it is possible to divert from **NH1** to **Kaithal** (63 km). This was quite an important town during Akbar's reign (r1556-1605), and is located by the picturesque man-made **Bidkiar Lake**. Bathing steps lead down into the tank. In 1767 it passed to the Sikh leader Bhai Desu Singh whose descendants, the Bhais of Kaithal, achieved some prominence on the Indian side of the Sutlej before the British acquired the territory in 1843. The old ruined fort of the Bhais overlooks the lake. For accommodation use the **D** *Koel Motel* (Haryana Tourism), T 2170.

From **Kaithal** you can re-join the **NH1** either by taking the road NE through the totally uninspiring small town and pilgrimage centre of **Pehowa** (30 km) to **Ambala** (50 km), or by going due N to **Patiala** (90 km) and then to **Rajpura** (26 km).

The road N from Karnal passes through the village of **Pipli** (34 km), the turn off point to **Kurukshetra**. where there is the **D** *Parakeet Motel* (Haryana Tourism), T 250. A/c rm. Restaurant, camping facilities.

Kurukshetra

Modern Kurukshetra has no trace of the period when it played the central role described in The *Mahabharata* as the battlefield where Arjuna learned the meaning of **dharma**, or duty. See page 46. A small town, the modern temple can best be described as kitsch, an artificial reproduction of earlier temple styles. But the site is important for its influence on the development of Hindu ideas, not Hindu architecture.

The nature of dharma The Mahabharata is revered by Hindus today for its code of right conduct or *dharma*. The Mahabharata talks of ten embodiments of dharma: good name, truth, self-control, cleanness of mind and body, simplicity, endurance, resoluteness of character, giving and sharing, austerities and continence. In Dharmic thinking these are inseparable from five patterns of behaviour: non-violence, an attitude of equality, peace and tranquillity, lack of aggression and cruelty, and absence of envy.

The **Brahmasar** or **Kurukshetra Tank** is just over 1 km W of the township and is a lake about 1 km long. Many pilgrims come and bathe, but it is also visited by a wide range of wildfowl, particularly during the winter (Dec-Feb). The tank is surrounded by temples and *ghats* (steps) leading down to the water's edge.

Like many other sacred sites it becomes the special focus of pilgrimage at the time of exceptional astronomical events. In Kurukshetra it is eclipses of the sun are marked by special pilgrimages, when over one million people come to the tank from across northern India. It is believed that the waters of all India's sacred tanks meet together in the Kurukshetra tank at the moment of eclipse, giving extra merit to anyone who can bathe in it at that moment. The arrangements which are made to maintain basic health standards in the water and around the tank are remarkable.

The flat plain around Kurukshetra is described in Sanskrit literature as '**Brahmavarta**' (Land of the Sages) and is regarded as particularly sacred. There are also the remains of a **Muslim Fort**, including the **Tomb of Shaikh Chilli Jalal** (d 1582) and **Lal Masjid**, a small red sandstone mosque. The carving on the domes is similar to that at Fatehpur Sikri.

Excursion *Thanesar*, near Kurukshetra, is an ancient town and birthplace of the ruler *Harsa Vardhana* (590-647 AD). Thanesar (originally known as *Sthanvisvara*) became the launching pad for Harsha's campaigns. Harsa's father, a local chief had fought off the Huns besides feuding with his neighbours.

Harsa was 16 years old when came to the throne. His father had already begun to establish his power in the key strategic region between the Rivers Yamuna and Sutlej. In his forty one year rule Harsa earned a reputation for fairness and an open-handedness. Unlike many other Indian kings Harsha's reign was remarkably fully recorded, especially by the remarkable Chinese traveller Hiuen Tsang. From his capital in **Thanesar** Harsa extended his territory from Bengal to Gujarat, and he received tribute from as far afield as Assam, but many of the regional kings retaining their thrones.

Sati Harsa shared his throne with the widowed sister whom he had rescued from self-immolation on her husband's funeral pyre. This rite, known in the W as **suttee** (a word which simply means a good or virtuous woman, and not the act of self-immolation) is recorded in the Vedas, but probably did not become accepted practice until the early centuries BC. Even then it was mainly restricted to those of the ksatriya, or warrior, caste. By Harsa's time sati had become widespread and tantric cults had also begun to grow rapidly, suggesting Buddhism was already on the decline. Harsa himself however appeared to model himself on **Asoka** and leaned towards Buddhism, adding a new monastic building to the Buddhist monastery at Nalanda. This earned him the opposition of brahmins and in 647 AD he fell victim to a murder plot organised by a Brahmin minister and carried out by the army. Thanesar became a Hindu pilgrimage centre and was one of the towns sacked by **Mahmud of Ghazni** in 1011 AD.

Driving N the road passes through **Ambala Sadar** (formerly Ambala Cantonment and still known as such) *Population* 80,000) to **Ambala** (50 km (*Altitude* 274 m *Population* 105,000) which lies on the Haryana/Punjab border on the road from

Delhi to Chandigarh.

Ambala During British times it became a large cantonment area covering 78 sq km, laid out from 1843 onwards in grid fashion. The famous Gupta iron pillar which is now at the Qutb Minar in Delhi was originally placed on the hill just outside Ambala town before being moved by the Muslim rulers to its present position. **Paget Park** on the N side of the city is a pleasant open space with the shell of St. Johns cathedral, designed in 14th century Gothic style. It was bombed in the 1965 Indo-Pakistan war. The city is the headquarters of the district and an important wheat market.

From Ambala the Grand Trunk Road (NH1) carries on to **Rajpura** and the Punjab border. A right fork after 5 km leads to **Chandigarh** (36 km) on **NH22**.

Chandigarh

Population 379,660 (1981). *Altitude* 320 m. Chandigarh is connected by Indian Airlines services with Delhi (230 km), Jammu, Srinagar and Leh. The airport is 11 km from the city centre.

	Jan	Feb	Mar	Apr	May	Jun	Jul	Aug	Sep	Oct	Nov	Dec	Av/Tot
Max (°C)	20	23	29	34	38	39	34	33	33	31	27	22	29
Min (°C)	7	9	14	19	24	26	24	23	22	17	10	7	17
Rain (mm)	56	25	26	10	13	62	277	263	226	82	5	18	1063

At the time of Partition in 1947 the old state of Punjab was divided between Pakistan and India and its former capital Lahore was allocated to Pakistan. The Indian government decided to build a new modern capital for the new Indian state of the Punjab, just as later the Pakistan government decided to build a new national capital at Islamabad, Lahore remaining the provincial capital for Pakistani Punjab. The result is Chandigarh which now serves as the administrative centre for both Punjab and Haryana which were the products of a further sub-division of the Indian Punjab in 1966.

The plans The initial plans were drawn in New York by Albert Mayer and Matthew Novicki. When the latter died in an air crash in 1950 the work was entrusted to the internationally renowned architect **Le Corbusier**. He supervised the layout and was responsible for the grand buildings whilst Maxwell Fry and Jane Drew designed the residential and commercial areas. They laid out city adopting the latest principles of town planning.

As an exercise in civic design it shares with Jaipur, Fatehpur Sikri and New Delhi the merit of having avoided the unwanted products of haphazard organic growth that typify most Indian cities. Yet many regard it as a failure and characterless. The style of buildings is post-war modernism. In marked contrast to the attractively landscaped and planted open areas in New Delhi there are too many spaces that have been allowed to go to waste. The impression gained by many is that ugly buildings have been carefully laid out in a grid fashion on an unimproved site. It is not a delightful garden city and has not taken advantage of its location on the edge of Siwalik hills.

For all that, Chandigarh is a pleasant enough place to stop en route to Shimla and obviously an attraction for anyone interested in town planning.

Local Festivals All the Hindu festivals are celebrated especially *Baisakhi*, the Hindu New Year' Day (April/May). Bhangra dancers per form with great enthusiasm, standing on each other's shoulders, and displaying all the joie de vivre for which the peoples of the old Punjab are renowned.

Places of interest The city's major works areas are: the capital complex

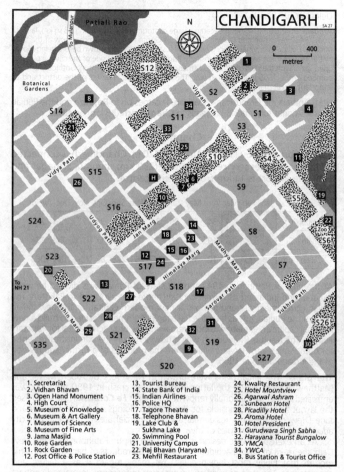

CHANGIGARH SA 27

1. Secretariat
2. Vidhan Bhavan
3. Open Hand Monument
4. High Court
5. Museum of Knowledge
6. Museum & Art Gallery
7. Museum of Science
8. Museum of Fine Arts
9. Jama Masjid
10. Rose Garden
11. Rock Garden
12. Post Office & Police Station
13. Tourist Bureau
14. State Bank of India
15. Indian Airlines
16. Police HQ
17. Tagore Theatre
18. Telephone Bhavan
19. Lake Club &
    Sukhna Lake
20. Swimming Pool
21. University Campus
22. Raj Bhavan (Haryana)
23. Mehfil Restaurant
24. Kwality Restaurant
25. *Hotel Mountview*
26. *Agarwal Ashram*
27. *Sunbeam Hotel*
28. *Picadilly Hotel*
29. *Aroma Hotel*
30. *Hotel President*
31. *Gurudwara Singh Sabha*
32. *Harayana Tourist Bungalow*
33. *YMCA*
34. *YWCA*
B. Bus Station & Tourist Office

consisting of the **Secretariat, Legislative Assembly** and **High Court** to the N with the Siwalik Hills as a backdrop; **Sector 17**, the central business district with administrative and state government offices, shopping areas and banks; a **Cultural Zone** for education which includes a museum, campus university with institutions for engineering, architecture, Asian studies and medicine.

The city was planned to accommodate half a million. Informal housing has already helped to take the total past that figure. For housing there are 14 carefully graded categories for ministers down to the lowest-paid public sector employees. Each sector was built with self-sufficiency in mind, i.e. to cater to the community's immediate needs. In this sense they are like traditional Indian villages. Villagers seeking work in Chandigarh live outside the town.

The Government buildings The Government complex is at the city's N end.

The elongated **Secretariat** cost Rs 14 million to build. Tours are given every half hour. Ask at the Main Reception. From the rooftop there is a good panorama of the city and the hills and plain beyond. The multi-pillared **High Court** stands nearby with a reflective pool in front. Primary colour panels break up the vast expanses of grey concrete but it all looks rather dated. Its cost was Rs 6.5 million.

The **Legislative Assembly** has a removable dome (why, you may ask?) and a mural by Le Corbusier that symbolizes evolution. There are tours on the half hour from 1030-1230 and 1420-1630. Ask at the public reception desk. The assembly cost Rs 12 million.

In the same sector is the **Open Hand** monument which symbolizes the unity of humankind, a tragically unfulfilled hope in modern Punjab. **Jawaharlal Nehru,** Independent India's first Prime Minister said of Chandigarh 'Let this be a new town symbolic of the freedom of India, unfettered by the traditions of the past..an expression of the nation's faith in the future'. In many respects it is with its use of readily available concrete, the material of the post war years, and there are numerous buildings around the country that are in keeping with the Chandigarh style. Its detractors say that Chandigarh is a concrete prairie, the product of 'the ivory tower school of architecture', certainly unfettered by the past, in that it seems to have learnt nothing from over two millenia of building tradition.

Hotels **C** *Chandigarh Mountview*, Sector 10, T 21257, Cable: Mountview, Telex: 0395-337. 33 rm. 15 km airport, 10 km rly. Central a/c. Restaurant, 24 hr rm service, exchange, doctor on call, TV. **C** *Piccadilly*, Sector 22-B, T 32223-7, Cable: Piccotel, Telex: 0395-256 Piccin. 48 rm. 8 km airport, 6 km rly. Restaurant, bar, 24 hr rm service, travel, car hire. **C** *President*, Sector 26, T 40840-4, Cable: Comforts, Telex: 0395-490 Hyg in. 20 rm. 9 km airport, 4 km rly. Central a/c. Restaurant, 24 hr coffee shop, bar, health club, bookshop, beauty parlour. **C** *Sunbeam*, Sector 22, T 32057, Cable: Sunbeam, Telex: 0395-444. 57 rm. 10 km airport, 8 km rly. Central a/c. Restaurant, 24 hr rm service, car hire, secretarial service, beauty parlour, health club.

   D *Pankaj*, Sector 22, T 41906, Cable: Hotpankaj, Telex: 0395-367 Hot Pankaj. 14 rm. 8 km airport, 6 km rly. A/c and non a/c rm. Restaurant, bar, car hire, secretarial services, exchange, golf can be arranged, TV & Video. Amex, Diners cards. Comfortable. **D** *Rikhy's International*, Sector 35-B, T 26764, Cable: Rikhy's. 16 rm. 6 km airport, 8 km rly, 2 km downtown. A/c and non a/c rm. Restaurant, bar, car hire, Amex and Diners cards. **D** *Kapil*, 303-304 Sector 35-B, T 33366. 13 rm. 8 km airport, 8 km rly. Central a/c. Restaurant (Chinese and Indian), bar, TV. Owned by Kapil Dev, the cricketer. **D** *Dhillon's*, Sector 35, T 32118. 12 rm. 8 km airport, 8 km rly. A/c rm. Restaurant, bar, discotheque, 18 hr rm service, car hire, Diners cards, TV & Video. **D** *Samrat*, Sector 22-D, T 32846. A/c and non a/c rm. 24 hr rm service, TV in some rooms. **D** *Amar*, Sector 22, T 26608. A/c and non a/c rm. Restaurant (Indian), TV & Video in lobby, 18 hr rm service.

   E *Aroma*, Sector 22, T 23854. 32 rm. Restaurant, bar, car hire, TV in some rooms. Clean and well-kept. **E** *Jullundur*, Sector 22, T 32721. 15 rm. Non a/c. Restaurant (Indian). **E** *Chandigarh*, Sector 22, T 41708. 16 rm, some a/c. Restaurant, TV in lobby. **E** *Diyadeep*, Sector 22-B, T 43191, 14 rm, some a/c. Restaurant (Indian Veg), car hire. **E** *Alankar*, Sector 22, T 21303. 14 rm, some a/c. 16 hr rm service.

Guesthouses Most have shared bathrooms and generally are more basic – and cheaper – than registered hotels. However, these **E** and **F category** guest houses are often very good value. *Tourist Rest House*, 2nd Floor, Bus Stand, Sector 17, T 22548. *Panchayat Bhawan*, Sector 18, T 23698. 4 rm. *Union Territory Guest House*, Sector 6, T 27231. 27 rm. Central a/c. *Puffin Guest House* (Haryana Tourism), Sector 3, T 27653. 12 rm. *Yatri Niwas*, Sector 24, T 24540. 48 rm. Hostel-like with shared bathrooms. *YMCA*, Sector 11. T 26532. Members only. *YWCA*, Sector 11, T 43224. Members only. *Shivalik Lodge*, Sector 18.

Restaurants There is a large number of restaurants in Sector 17: *Mehfil*, T 29439; *Mandarin*; *Kwality*; *Lyon's*, T 20537; *Shangrila*, T 23026; *Sindhi Sweets*, T 21057; *Ghazal*, T 29396; *The Hot Million*, T 32200; *Indian Coffee House*, T 25804; *Mahak* (multi-cuisine). *Ginza*, Sector 14 (University Campus); *Hong Kong*, Sector 11; *Mamamia*, Sector 35-B; *The Chef* (CITCO), Inter State bus Terminal (Fast food and multi-cuisine).

Banks All the banks are in Sector 17: *Allahabad*, T 20913; *Bank of India*, T 26853; *Canara*, T 22016; *Central Bank of India*, T 28292; *Haryana State Co-op*, T 29059; *Punjab National*, T 26758; *State Bank of India*, T 28541-3; Syndicate Bank, T 29089.

Shopping The main shopping centres are in Sectors 17 and 22. Shop hours 1000-1945. **Sector 17**: Black Partridge (Haryana), Chandigarh (CITCO), Co-operative, Co-Optex (Tamil Nadu), Gram Shilpa Khadi Ashram, Handloom Emporium, Kashmir Government Arts, Rajasthan Government Handicrafts, The Weaver (Haryana Govt.), U.P. Handloom, Punsup Clothes (Punjab Govt.), Charma Shilpa (footwear), Super Bazar. **Sector 22**: Haryana State Handlooms, Punjab State Handloom and Textiles Development Corporation, SEAVCO (Punjab State Handloom Weavers Apex Co-op Society, UPICA Handloom, Leathera (Punjab Govt.), Bharat Leather Emporium. Madras Handloom House is in **Sector 28**.

Photography *A-One Studio*, Sector 22, T 23558; *Batra Colour Lab*, S 27, T 26395.

Local Transport Private taxis (un-metered), **auto rickshaws**, officially metered with a min. fare of Rs 3.50, but always negotiable. The Chandigarh Transport Undertaking (CTU) runs a reasonably good **bus** service. Min. fare Rs 0.50. **Cycle rickshaws** are widely available. Fares negotiable.

Entertainment *Tagore Theatre*, Sector 18, T 26533. *Open Air Theatre*, Sector 10. *Auditorium*, University Campus, Post Graduate Institute, Sector 14, T 32351.

Sports *Athletic club*, Sector 7. *Hockey Stadium*, Sector 18. *Football Stadium*, Sectors 17 & 45. *Cricket Ground*, Sector 16. *Roller Skating Rink*, Sector 10. *Swimming Pool*, Sector 23, 14 (University). *Lake Pool Complex*, Sector 23. Temporary membership available. *Boat Club*, Sector 1. Rowing and paddle boats available for hire.

Museums International Dolls Museum Bal Bhawan, **Sector 23**. Government Museum & Art Gallery **Sector 10**, T 25568. Open 1000-1630, Closed Mon. The Art Gallery contains a modest collection of stone sculptures dating back to the Gandhara period and miniatures and modern art. The museum has prehistoric fossils and artefacts.
Museum of Evolution of Life **Sector 10**. The exhibits cover 5,000 years of N Indian history from the Indus Valley Civilization to the present day. Open 1000-1630, Closed Mon. Admission Rs 0.20. Fine Arts Museum Punjab University, **Sector 14**. National Gallery of Portraits Central Library Building, **Sector 17**.

Parks & Zoos Raj Bhawan Mini Zoo, **Sector 7**. Rose Gardens, **Sector 16**. Containing over 1,000 varieties of roses it claims to be the largest in Asia.
Rock Garden or *Garden of Nek Chand*, **Sector 1**. Described as 'a concrete maze with a lot of rocks and very little garden', this contains a large number of interesting statues and sculptures made out of discarded items of everyday use, e.g. bottle tops, fluorescent lights, mud guards etc. The creation of Nek Chand, now in his fifties, who began these interesting sculptures thirty years ago. Highly imaginative, amusing and enjoyable. The low archways are so that visitors have to bow to the gods who have blessed the park. Open 0900-1300 and 1500-1900 April 1 – September 30. Admission Re 0.50. **Sukhna Lake**, Sector 1.

Useful Addresses Foreigners' Regional Registration Office, Town Hall Bldg, Sector 17. Police 25600. Ambulance 26165, Fire 101.

Hospitals and Medical Services General Hospital, Sector 16, T 44697,42756. Post Graduate Medical Institute of Medical Sciences, Sector 12, T 22513,26513. Chandigarh Medical & Research Centre, Sector 17, T 32152.

Chemists *Sahib Singh & Sons*, Sector 17, T 26574. *Venus Medical Stores*, Sector 17, T28675. *Paul Medical Stores*, Sector 22, T 25467.

Post and Telegraph GPO Sector 17, T 217070. Central PO, Sector 17, T 23033/25400.

Places of Worship Sikh: Gurudwara in Sectors 8, 19 & 21: *Hindu*: Sector 23: Jain: Sector 27. *Muslim*: Sector 20. *Christian*: Church of N India Sector 18; Catholic Sector 19.

Travel Agents & Tour Operators The agents listed below with the airline initials after their name, e.g. *Onkar* (JAL) are GSAs (General Sales Agents) for the airline indicated. *Bajaj*, Sector 17, T 28500. *Delta* Sector 8, T 31985. *STIC*, S 17-A, T 28585 *Onkar* (JAL), S 17-B, T 32630 *Madhur*, S 22-A, T 28991 *Amber* (PIA), S 17-A, T 31752 *Bird* (Lufthansa), S 17-C, T 29337 *Janta* (Air India), S 17-C, T 31510 *Delhi Express* (Thai, PIA), S 17-A, T 27054 *Trans Air* (Kuwait), S 17, T 28333.

Private Taxis and Tour Operators *Bangla Tourist Service*, Sector 21, T 29952 *Guru Nanak Tourist Service*, S 21, T 26668 *Tourist Syndicate*, S 27, T 28159 *Aroma Taxi Stand*, S 22, T 26433 *Capital Taxi Stand*, S 17, T 20495 *Tara Brothers*, S 17, T 27164 *Cosy Tours*, S 10, T 28638 *Kulwant Taxi Service*, S 35, T 21517 *Labh Taxi Service*, Bus Stand, S 17, T 45521 *Haryana Tourism Taxi Fleet*, S 17, T 21955,32899 *Chandigarh Tourism*

Taxi Service, (CITCO), S 22, T 31256.

Tourist Offices & Information (incl Conducted Tours & Excursions) Tourist Information Office, Chandigarh Administration, 1st Floor, Main Bus Terminal, Sector 17, T 22548 Uttar Pradesh Tourism Development Corporation, Sector 22, T 41649 Himachal Pradesh Tourism Development Corporation, Sector 22, T 26494 Directorate of Tourism, Punjab, Sector 22, T 20869. Directorate of Tourism, Haryana, Sector 17, T 21955-6,31022.

Conducted Tours Tours are organised by the Tourism wing of the Chandigarh Industrial and Tourism Development Corporation whose booking office is at the Chandigarh Emporium Building, Sector 17, T 25839. Local tours are conducted as well are tours further afield to Pinjore Gardens, Bhakra dam, Shimla, Kulu and Manali and the Golden Temple at Amritsar. For all tours there is a minimum requirement of 20 persons. You may have to wait around until adequate numbers are reached.

Air Indian Airlines connects Chandigarh with with Delhi, Jammu, Srinagar and Leh. Reservations, City Office, Sector 17, T 40539, 1000-1630. Airport, T 43304. **Vayudoot** connects Chandigarh with Delhi and Kulu. Handling and Booking Agents: Shivalik Travellers, Mini Hall, Hotel Piccadilly, Sector 22-B, T 44996, Telex: Vayu-in-495 or Picc-In 395-296; Airport, T 43304 Extn. 462.

Rail New Delhi: *Himalayan Queen*, 4096, daily, 1722, 4 hr 33 min; *Shatabi exp*, 2006, daily, 0625, 3 hr 20 min; **Old Delhi**: *Kalka-Howrah Mail* 2312, daily, 0050, 5 hr 40 min **Shimla**: *Himalayan Queen* 4095 (Change at Kalka to Express 257), daily, 1030, 6 hr 50 min; *Howrah-Kalka Mail* 2311 (Change at Kalka to Mail 253), daily, 0505, 7 hr 20 min. The railway station at Chandigarh is 8 km from the centre of town. Enquiries, T 22105. Reservations, T 22260 1000-1700; City Booking Office, 1st Floor Inter-State Bus Terminal, Sector 17, T 32696, 0900-1600.

Bus There are many buses per day from ISBT in Delhi to Chandigarh and the journey takes about 5 hr. There are buses from Chandigarh to **Shimla** (5 hr), **Amritsar** (6 hr), **Pathankot** (7 hr), **Dharamsala** (10 hr), **Kulu** (12 hr) and **Manali** (14 hr).

Excursions *Pinjore*, 20 km from Chandigarh on Kalka road. The Mughal gardens were laid out by Aurangzeb's foster brother Fidai Khan, who also designed the Badshahi Mosque in Lahore. Within the gardens are a number of palaces in a Mughal-Rajasthani style, i.e. **Shish Mahal, Rang Mahal** and **Jai Mahal**. Cool and delightful. A popular picnic spot.

Hotels D *Yadavindra Gardens Budgerigar Motel*, T Kalka 455. Deluxe Motel. A/c rm. Restaurant, open-air cafe, dosa shop, mini-zoo, childrens' playground.

The **Bhakra-Nangal Dam,** on the **River Sutlej**, is approximately 70 km NW of Chandigarh in Punjab. It is claimed to be the highest dam in the world at 225 m. The multi-purpose river-valley project (electrical energy and irrigation) is certainly the largest irrigation system of its kind in Asia, and was built as part of the **Indus Waters Treaty** between India and Pakistan, signed in September 1960. Two other massive dams, the Mangla dam on the Jhelum and the Tarbela Dam on the Indus, both in Pakistan, were built under the terms of the same treaty, financed by the World Bank – see page 1118.

The Treaty allocated the water of the Rivers **Sutlej**, **Beas** and **Ravi** to India. The building of the Bhakra Nangal Dam, which had already been agreed in 1959, was supervised by the well-known American dam builder Harvey Slocum. It provides electricity for Punjab, Haryana and as far away as Delhi. It is also the source for the **Rajasthan Canal project**, which is designed to take water over 1500 km S to the Thar desert, a scheme which is still far from complete. The sharing of the water between Punjab, Haryana and Rajasthan remains a problem which successive governments have failed to solve and which has been made more complicated by the crisis in the Punjab.

For Shimla, Kulu and Manali see Himachal Pradesh section, **page 435**. From Chandigarh you can continue to Amritsar through Ludhiana, due W, or you can return to the NH 1 at **Rajpura** (36 km). 26 km to the S of Rajpura is Patiala.

Patiala (*Population* 240,000) was once the capital of an independent state whose ruling Jind and Nabha houses were both Sikh. It suffered at the hands of the European Adventurer George Thomas and was later consolidated into the Sikh Empire of Ranjit Singh who included it in treaty arrangements made with the British in 1809. Thereafter, the Maharaja remained loyal to the British.

The most impressive building in this well-kept town of approximately 250,000 people is the fort which was the creation of *Maharaja Ala Singh* in the late 18th century. It is a huge concentric fort with two walls surrounded by a moat, and is 8 km to the NE of the town on the Chandigarh road. Known as the **Bahadurgarh**, it is a good example of a *nara durg**, a large fort built on a plain and capable of housing a garrison large enough to repulse strong attacks, such as the unsuccessful but nevertheless fierce Maratha attempt in 1794. Looking majestic from the air and now surrounded by intensively cultivated fields, Patiala has no palaces or pleasure gardens.

In the town there is the **Old Motibagh Palace** (late 19th Century), perhaps one of the largest homes in Asia. The huge and rambling central building is surrounded by lawns and trees. A combination of European, Rajput and Mughal styles, part of it is now the National Institute for Sports. There are 15 dining halls and numerous outbuildings.

Air Daily **Vayudoot** service with Delhi.

Train Patiala is on the metre gauge branch line to Bhatinda and Firozpur. **Bus** Daily services to Delhi, other towns in Punjab and neighbouring states.

Return to **NH1** at Rajpura and turn left. *Rajpura* has a Rest House and a railway station on the main Delhi-Amritsar line. **NH1** crosses the railway line and a road on the right leads to **Chandigarh** (38 km) and **Kalka** (56 km). **NH1** passes through **Turkhanmajra** (24 km) where there is a right turn to *Sirhind* (5 km), once capital of the **Pathan Sur Dynasty,** whose army was defeated by Humayun in 1555. A year later Akbar completed the downfall of the dynasty with his victory at Panipat.

There is little left of the fort which commanded the Sar-i-Hind – the "Frontier of India". The town's period of greatest splendour was between 1556 and 1707, i.e. after the Mughals had wrested control. The **Haveli** of **Salbat Beg** is a large and well preserved Mughal house whilst the Sarai of the Mughal emperors is in the SW of the town and is now a public hall. There is also a mosque in the N, a number of Mughal tombs and a Gurudwara.

The road continues through the small market towns of **Mandi Govindgarh** (10 km), **Khanna** (8 km) and **Doraha** (21 km) before reaching

Ludhiana (20 km *Population* 800,000), a rapidly growing town is on the S bank of the **Sutlej river** and is a major textile and light engineering centre. Hero bicycles are manufactured here. The rich agricultural area around it supports a large grain market. Founded in 1480 by Lodi princes from Delhi (hence its name), it subsequently passed through a number of hands and around it at Aliwal, Ferozeshah, Mudki and Sobraon are important battlegrounds from the First Sikh War (1845).

In the NW is the fort which includes the Shrine of **Piri-i-Dastgir** who was also known as Abdul Kadir Galani. There is an annual pilgrimage of Muslims and Hindus to the Muslim Saint's tomb. There are other tombs belonging to members of Shah Shuja's family while they were in exile from Afghanistan.

The town is also the home of the Christian Medical College Hospital, which along with the CMC hospital in Vellore, with which it is in partnership, is one of SAsia's major teaching and research hospitals.

Hotels C *Amaltas*, Via Netaji Nagar, T 23794. 22 rm. 18 km airport, 8 km rly, 7 km downtown. A/c and non a/c rooms with bath. **C** City Heart, T 50240-3, Cable: City heart. 31 rm. 10 km airport, near rly. A/c rm with bath. Restaurant (Indian, Chinese, Continental), Diners cards. **D** *Grewalz*, 148 Ferozepur Rd, T 27978, Telex: 0386-425. 28 rm. 12 km airport,

2 km rly, 1 km downtown. Central a/c. Restaurant (Indian, Chinese, Continental), travel agency. **D** *Gulmor*, Ferozepur Rd, T 51742-7, Cable: Gulmor. 28 rm. 10 km airport, 2 km rly, 2 km downtown. Central a/c. Restaurant (Indian, Chinese, Continental), refrigerator in rooms, laundry, baby sitting, exchange, Amex and Diners cards. **D** *Shiraz*, Ferozepur Rd, T 25252, Cable: Hoshiraz. 21 rm. 10 km airport, near rly and downtown. Central a/c. Restaurant (English, Indian, Chinese), TV in some rooms.

Restaurants *Gazebo*, 15 Bhadaur House, T 21831. A/c. *Kabab Corner*, 186 Rani Jhasi Rd, Civil Lines, T23786. *Kashmir restaurant and bar*, G.T. Rd, Doraha District, T 70.

Air Daily Vayudoot service with Delhi.

Road Daily bus services connect Ludhiana with Delhi and other towns in Punjab and neighbouring states.

Take the **NH1** N out of Ludhiana. After 13 km cross the old bed of the Sutlej, now largely dry. Pass through **Phillaur** (1 km) on the right bank of the Sutlej, **Goraya** (11 km) and **Phagwara**, following the main railway line all the way. The road then runs NW through **Chiheru** (7 km) to **Jalandhar Cantonment** (10 km) and **Jalandhar** (6 km).

Jalandhar (formerly Jullundur) is a very ancient city of which very little survives. It was sacked by Mahmud of Ghazni and under the Mughals it was an important centre administering the area between the Beas and Sutlej rivers. The **Sarai** (1857) is a comparatively late addition.

The cantonment area was established in 1846 to house army units after the treaties signed in Lahore in March and December 1846 which brought an end to the first Sikh War. It covers an area of 20 sq km. The 'modern' city consists of a number of wards, each originally enclosed by a wall.

Hotels D *Kamal Palace*, EH-192, Civil Lines, T 76315-6, Cable: Kamalplace. 20 rm. 3 km rly, 1 km downtown. Central a/c. Restaurant (Indian Chinese, Continental), laundry, TV & Video. **D** *Sky Lark*, Circuit House Rd, T 75891-3, Cable: Skylark. 72 rm. 3 km rly, near bus stand. A/c and non a/c rooms with bath. TV, Bar, Restaurant (Indian, Continental, Chinese), Diners cards. **D** *Plaza*, Civil Lines, T 75886-7, Cable: Plaza. 22 rm. 1 km rly. A/c and non a/c rooms with bath. Bar, restaurants (Indian, Continental, Chinese), TV in rooms, laundry, drive-in snacks bar!, generator. **E** *Ramji Dass*, Model town Rd, T 3252. 10 rm. 1 km rly, 1 km downtown. A/c rooms with bath. Restaurant (Indian, Chinese, Continental).

Restaurants *Moti Mahal*, Grand Trunk (GT) Rd, T 74677. Multi-cuisine.

Jalandhar is a major road and rail junction. The main road N to **Pathankot** (112 km) takes off from here From Pathankot you can travel to **Dalhousie, Chamba, Dharamsala** and **Kangra**, all of which are in Himachal Pradesh or to Jammu and Srinagar in Kashmir. See relevant sections.

A short diversion to the S off the **NH1** allows you to visit the capital of the former Sikh princely state of *Kapurthala* (19 km from Jalandhar). This was the home town of the **Ahluwalia** family who conquered it in 1747. Its army fought against the British at Aliwal in the first Sikh War but took the British side during the **Second Sikh War** (1848) and the Mutiny (1857).

Later governed as a model city-state, the ruler *Jagajit Singh* who ascended the throne in 1890 and was educated in France, attempted to turn the city into 'a scrap of Paris'. The **Jalaukhana**, designed by Monsieur Marcel and based in part on Fontainebleau, started in red sandstone but finished in pink stucco when funds ran out, was the Maharaja's palace. It is now a boys school. Gallic in design and decoration, it fulfilled its creator's wish. However, his regional preferences changed when he married a Spanish dancer. The **Villa Buona Vista** (1894) designed by the local engineer J. Elmore is more Iberian in flavour.

Rail Kapurthala is on the line to Ferozepur and can be reached by changing at Jalandhar.
Bus There are daily services from Jalandhar and Amritsar.

The **NH1** continues WNW from **Jalandhar** through **Kartapur** (14 km), which has a Rest house and gurudwara, to the **River Beas**. On the N side of the bridge is a right turn to **Batala** (35 km). The road goes on through **Jandiala** (28 km) to **Amritsar** (19 km). Bypass if you do not wish to go into the town.

Amritsar

Population 790,000 *Altitude* 234 m. *Best Season* Avoid May and June. Amritsar is connected by Indian Airlines services with Delhi (447 km, 50 min) and Jammu and Srinagar. The airport is 11 km from the city centre.

	Jan	Feb	Mar	Apr	May	Jun	Jul	Aug	Sep	Oct	Nov	Dec	Av/Tot
Max (°C)	21	22	28	35	40	41	38	36	36	35	28	23	32
Min (°C)	4	7	12	17	22	26	27	26	23	15	8	4	16
Rain (mm)	43	36	30	26	15	48	142	153	83	10	5	12	598

Amritsar (meaning 'Pool of Nectar') is named after the sacred pool in the Golden Temple, the holiest of Sikh sites. The largest town and effective capital (Chandigarh is the actual administrative capital) of the Punjab, Amritsar is only 24 km from the Pakistani border. It is a traditional junction of trade routes and the different people found here – Yarkandis, Turkomens, Kashmiris, Tibetans and Iranians indicate its connections with the Old Silk Road and the trade routes of Central Asia. Overland travellers have to go through Amritsar for the only land crossing open between India and Pakistan. It therefore, has an unmistakable frontier town atmosphere.

Early history The original site for the city was granted by the Mughal Emperor Akbar (r 1556-1605) who also visited the temple and the then Sikh guru, Amar Das (Guru 1552-1574). In 1761 the Afghan Ahmad Shah Durrani sacked the town and destroyed the temple. The temple was rebuilt in 1764 and during the reign of Ranjit Singh was roofed over with gilded copper plates, thereby giving rise to the name 'The Golden Temple'.

Permits Foreigners sometimes need a permit to visit Punjab. No permit is required for Chandigarh and if you are merely travelling through, e.g. by train to Pathankot for Jammu and Kashmir or from Chandigarh to Dharamsala, you do not need a permit. However, if travellers intend to stay in Punjab and/or are travelling through Amritsar to the border and intending an overnight stay or longer, a permit is required. These are obtained from the Home Ministry in New Delhi. The address is Lok Nayak Bhawan, near Khan Market. Opening hours Monday – Friday 1400-1600.

Local Festivals *Baisakhi* is the Hindu solar New Year's Day and is observed over all N India. It is a religious festival when people bathe in rivers and worship at temples. The river Ganga is believed to have descended to earth on this day. To the Sikh community, Baisakhi is of special significance because on this day in 1689 Guru Gobind Singh organised the Sikhs into the Khalsa or 'pure one' – see page 72. In Punjab, farmers start harvesting with great jubilation. The vigorous *Bhangra* dance is a common sight in the villages. The birth anniversaries of the ten gurus are observed as holy days and those of Guru Nanak, the first (Oct/Nov), and Guru Gobind Singh, the last (Dec/Jan), are celebrated as festivals. The celebrations are *Akhand Path*, the recitation of the Guru's verses and processions carrying the Granth Sahib.

Places of Interest

The **Golden Temple** The spiritual nerve centre of the Sikh faith, every Sikh tries to make a visit here and bathe in the holy water. It is the Sikh Varanasi. The site has been sacred to the Sikhs since the time of the fourth guru, **Ram Das** (Guru 1574-1581). In 1577 he heard that a cripple had been miraculously cured while bathing in the pool here. This was enlarged and named **Amrit Sovar** ("Pool of the Nectar of Immortality"). The Mughal Emperor Akbar granted the land but

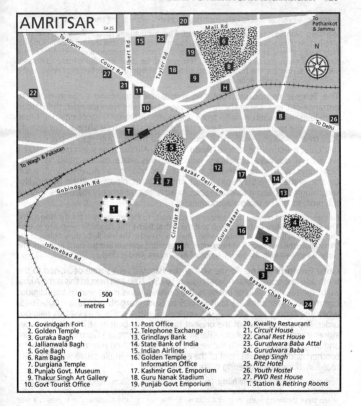

AMRITSAR SA 25

1. Govindgarh Fort
2. Golden Temple
3. Guraka Bagh
4. Jallianwala Bagh
5. Gole Bagh
6. Ram Bagh
7. Durgiana Temple
8. Punjab Govt. Museum
9. Thakur Singh Art Gallery
10. Govt Tourist Office
11. Post Office
12. Telephone Exchange
13. Grindlays Bank
14. State Bank of India
15. Indian Airlines
16. Golden Temple
    Information Office
17. Kashmir Govt. Emporium
18. Guru Nanak Stadium
19. Punjab Govt Emporium
20. Kwality Restaurant
21. *Circuit House*
22. *Canal Rest House*
23. Gurudwara Baba Attal
24. Gurudwara Baba
    Deep Singh
25. *Ritz Hotel*
26. *Youth Hostel*
27. *PWD Rest House*
T. Station & *Retiring Rooms*

Ram Das insisted on paying its value to the local Jats who owned it, thereby eliminating the possibility of future disputes on ownership. Ram Das then invited local merchants to live and trade in the immediate vicinity and the subsequent township became **Amritsar**. **Arjun Das** (Guru 1581-1601), Ram Das' son and successor enlarged the tank further and built the original temple at its centre from 1589-1601.

The Golden Temple suffered twice at the hands of the Afghan **Ahmad Shah Durrani,** who invaded northern India in 1747. The temple was occupied in 1757 and desecrated. The Sikhs united and drove him out, but four years later he returned and defeated the Sikh armies at **Ghallughara**. This time the town was sacked and the temple blown up. After his departure, the Sikhs re-conquered the Punjab and restored the temple and tank. Under their greatest secular leader, **Maharaja Ranjit Singh**, the roof was gilt. In 1830 he donated 100 kgs (220 lbs) of gold which was applied to the copper sheets on the roof and much of the exterior of the building.

Behaviour in the temple Tobacco, narcotics and intoxicants are not allowed to be carried or consumed. Shoes, sticks and umbrellas are to be left outside at the cloakroom where they are looked after free of charge. Visitors without socks should wash their feet outside the entrance. All visitors should keep their heads covered while in the temple precincts.

Worship Singing is central to Sikh worship. After building the temple, Arjun Das compiled a collection of hymns of the great medieval saints and this became the *Adi Granth* (Original Holy book). It was installed in the temple as the focus of devotion and teaching. Gobind Singh, the tenth and last guru (1675-1708) revised the book and also refused to name a successor saying that the book itself would be the Sikh guru. It thus became known as the *Granth Sahib* (The Holy Book as Guru).

The Temple compound Entering the temple compound through the main entrance or Clock Tower the first thing you see is the *Hari mandir*, the Golden Temple itself, beautifully reflected in the water of the tank surrounding it. Move to your right round the tank. Along this pathway is the **Tree Shrine**. This gnarled *jubi tree* is 450 years old and is reputed to be the favourite resting place of the first chief priest of the temple, *Baba Gujhaji*. Although he was chief priest, he would still do **seva** (voluntary work) and his share of the building work. Nowadays, women tie strings to the branches hoping to be blessed with a son by the primeval fertility spirits that choose such places as their home. Not surprisingly, it is also a favourite spot to arrange and sanctify marriages, despite the protests of the temple authorities.

Further round and on your right before the causeway to the temple itself are the **Flagstaffs, The Shrine of Guru Gobind Singh** and the **Akhal Takht**. The flagstaffs symbolize religion and politics, in the Sikh case intertwined. They are joined in the middle by the emblem of the Sikh nation, the two swords of Hargobind, representing spiritual and temporal authority. The circle is inscribed with the Sikh rallying call *Ek Omkara* (God is One).

Guru Gobind's shrine To the side of the flagstaffs is a shrine dedicated to the tenth and last guru, Gobind Singh (Guru 1675-1708) and next to this is the Akhal Takht temple. Standing opposite to the causeway this is the seat of the religious committee. It was originally built in 1609 by **Guru Hargobind** (Guru 1606-1645) when the brotherhood was being organised into a political as well as religious order. The ground floor of the present building was built in 1874 and the upper stories were added by Maharaja Ranjit Singh. In the temple is Guru Gobind's sword and an golden ark in which the vessels used for initiating new members into the brotherhood are kept. In front of the entrance to the temple causeway is a square that functions as a gathering place for visitors.

Sometimes you may see *Nihang* (meaning "crocodile") Sikhs, followers of the militant Gobind Singh, dressed in blue and armed with swords, lances, curved daggers and razor sharp steel throwing irons in their turbans. To the right of the causeway entrance is a tree shrine and booth where the **Guru Granth Sahib** is read. The tree was a favourite spot of Arjun Dev (Guru 1581-1606). The marble causeway is 62 m long and lined on each side with nine gilded lamps.

The Hari Mandir (The Golden Temple) is the centre of the Sikh universe, a refuge from the world and a place of peace and calm. With its four doors, always open, like the Muslim Ka'ba at Mecca and the Hindu temple, it signifies the division of the cosmos into four. When it was built, **Arjun Dev** likened it to a ship crossing the ocean of ignorance.

The *Guru Granth Sahib* The temple has three floors. The ground floor with its fine silver doors contains the Holy Book which has been placed on a platform under a jewel encrusted canopy. Professional singers and musicians take turns performing verses from the book and the singing is continuous from 0400-2300 in the summer and 0500-2200 in winter. Each evening the holy book is taken with due pomp and circumstance to the Akhal Takhat and brought back the next morning. The palanquin set with emeralds, rubies, diamonds silver poles and golden canopy used for this can be seen in the treasury on the first floor of the entrance to the temple. The **Guru Granth Sahib** contains approximately 3,500 hymns.

Throughout the day, pilgrims place their offerings of flowers or money around the book. There is no ritual in the worship and no pressure from temple officials to donate money. The marble walls are decorated with mirrorwork, gold leaf and designs of birds animals and flowers in semiprecious stones in the Mughal style. The rest of the temple is covered with gilt copper inscribed with quotations from the *Granth*.

The unbroken reading On the first floor is a balcony on which three respected Sikhs are always performing the *Akhand Path** (Unbroken Reading). In order to preserve unity and maintain continuity, there must always be someone practising devotions. The top floor is where the gurus used to sit and here again someone is performing the *Akhand Path*.

Leaving the temple, crossing back along the causeway, continue walking round the tank. The next shrine is that of *Baba Deep Singh*. When Ahmad Shah Durrani attacked Amritsar in 1758, Baba Deep Singh was copying out the Granth Sahib. On hearing of the attack he went out to fight with his followers, vowing to defend the temple with his life. Six kilometres from town he was mortally wounded, some saying that his head was hacked from his body. Grimly determined and holding his head on with one hand he fought on and back to the temple. He finally died on this spot which ever since has been regarded as sacred.

The holy places In the SE corner is an area screened off from public view for ladies to bathe. Further round on the eastern side are the **Sixty Eight Holy Places** which comprises a number of shrines and booths. This takes its name from the 68 Hindu pilgrimage spots. When the tank was built Arjun Singh told his followers that rather than visit all the orthodox Hindu places, they should just bathe here. The merit that they would acquire would be equivalent to visiting all 68 places. There is a shrine built round a *jubi* tree and is believed to be where the cripple received his miraculous cure. Now similarly afflicted people bathe, hoping for a similar cure. There is a covered ladies' changing area nearby.

Next is a **Shrine** containing a copy of the Granth Sahib. Here and at other booths round the tank the Holy Book is read for devotees. Sikhs can arrange with the temple authorities to have the book read in their name in exchange for a donation. The reader (*granthi*) is a temple employee and a standard reading lasts for three hours. A complete reading of the Granth Sahib takes 48 hours.

Dining Hall, Kitchen, Assembly Hall and **Guesthouse** Sikhs have a custom of having a community kitchen where all temple visitors, Sikh, Hindu, Muslims and others, men and women alike can eat together. The third Guru, **Amar Das** (1552-1574), noticed that his disciples ate separately, as dictated by Hindu caste rules. He abolished this, saying that all should eat the same food together, thus establishing an egalitarian principle that has been continued. The Mughal Emperor Akbar visited Amar Das to obtain his blessing, which was given only on condition that Akbar ate with the common people. Akbar did so. The kitchen is run by volunteers and voluntary service (seva) is an important part of the Sikh faith. The food is paid for out of temple funds. The same practice is found at other Sikh temples and shrines.

The Amritsar kitchen feeds 10,000 people a day, holds 3,000 at a sitting, is free of charge and vegetarian (even though many Sikhs eat meat). Lunch is 1100-1500 hours and dinner 1900 onwards. Next to the kitchen and dining room is the residence of Baba Karak Singh who is hailed by Sikhs as a saint. His followers are distinguished by their orange turbans. Temple employees and members of the militant Akali sect wear blue or black turbans. Also in the vicinity is the large assembly hall whilst behind are the guesthouses (*dharamsalas**) which are for pilgrims who can stay for three days and nights free.

The administrative offices of the temple trust are also in this area. The trust is staffed by 140 unpaid members and in addition to running the temple administers schools, colleges, hospitals and other temples throughout India.

The Town

The old city is S of the main railway station and is encircled by a ring road which traces the line of the city walls constructed during the reign of Ranjit Singh. The Golden Temple is inside the old city.

The modern part of Amritsar is NE of the railway station and contains the **Ram Bagh** gardens, **The Mall** and **Lawrence Street** shopping areas. The Ram Bagh Gardens contains a museum housing weapons dating from the Mughal times plus some portraits of rulers of Punjab. The building is a small palace built by Maharaja Ranjit Singh. Closed on Wednesdays. *Jallianwala Bagh* where General Dyer instigated the massacre is five minutes walk from the Golden Temple – **see page 415**. The walls are pockmarked with bullets and the well which some tried to hide in can be seen. The film 'Gandhi' dramatically recreates this shameful episode in British Indian history. A number of mosques and Hindu temples, e.g. the **Durgiana Temple** dedicated to the goddess Durga (16th century), and also the **Laxmi** and **Narayan Temples** are also found in the city whilst to the southwest is *Govindgarh fort*, built by Ranjit Singh in 1805-1809.

Hotels C *Mohan International*, Albert Rd, T 66484-7, Cable: Luxury-in. 39 rm. 13 km airport, 1 km rly, 2 km downtown. Central a/c. Restaurant, TV, shops, car hire, Amex cards, pool.

D *Amritsar International*, City Centre, T 31991-2. 56 rm. 12 km airport, 2 km rly, 1 km downtown. Central a/c. Restaurant, bar, shops, Diners and Amex cards. **D** *Airlines*, Cooper Rd, T 64848, Cable: Pankaj. 25 rm. 11 km airport, 1 km rly. A/c and non a/c rm with bath. Restaurants. Clinic for Ayurvedic treatment for grey hair and baldness!, credit cards. **D** *Astoria*, 1 Queens Rd, T 66046, Cable: Astoria. 27 rm. 10 km airport, 0.5 km rly. A/c and non a/c rm with bath. Restaurant, laundry, travel agent, car hire, Diners and Amex cards, TV & Video. **D** *Blue Moon*, The Mall, T 20416. 20 rm. 12 km airport, 2 km rly, 1 km downtown. A/c and non a/c rm with bath. Restaurant, laundry, car hire, Diners card. **D** *Grand*, Queens Rd, opposite Railway Station, T 64111-2, Cable: Grand Hotel. 44 rm with bath. 10 km airport. Restaurant, bar, TV & Video, laundry, car hire, Diners card. **D** *Mrs Bhandari's Guest House*, Rec. for good food and interesting decor – Heath Robinson baths and sepia prints of English Lake district for nostaglia.

E *Skylark* and *Chinar*, Station Links Rd. Both moderately priced. **E** *Palace*, Station Links Rd. State Tourist Office. **E** *Tourist Guest House*, opp railway station. Popular with budget travellers.

F *Temple View*, lives up to its name. **F** *Youth Hostel*, T 48165. 3 km from centre on Amritsar- Delhi road. Double rm, dormitory and camping. Concessions for YHA members. **Regarded as one of the best Youth Hostels in India. F** *Vikas Guest House* and *Amritsar Majestic*, around the Golden Temple.

Restaurants Indian, Chinese and Continental and a/c: *Crystal*, Crystal Chowk, T 26666; *Kwality*, The Mall, T 22849. Also Mughlai; *Madira*, *Manbhawan* and *Pankaj Coffee Shop*, Mohan International, Albert Rd, T 66122, Also bar; *Napoli*, Queens Rd, T 66094. Also Tandoori.

Shopping Locally manufactured woollen blankets and sweaters are supposed to be cheaper here than in other parts of India. *Katra Jaimal Singh* is a good shopping area and is near the telephone exchange in the old city.

Local Transport Taxis and auto-rickshaws are widely available. Fares negotiable.

Parks & Zoos Rambagh.

Places of Worship *Sikh*: Golden Temple. *Hindu*: Durgiana, Laxmi and Narayan Temples.

Tourist Offices & Information Punjab State Tourism Office, opp the rly station.

Air Indian Airlines have daily flights with Delhi, Jammu and Srinagar

Rail New Delhi: *Amritsar-New Delhi Exp* 2460, daily, 0630, 7 hr 10 min; *Amritsar-Dadar Exp* 1058, daily, 0825, 11 hr 35 min; *Flying Mail* 4648, daily, 1200, 8 hr 20 min; *Shane Punjab Exp* 2498, daily, 1410, 8 hr. Pathankot: *Ravi Exp* 4633, daily, 0910, 2 hr 10 min. **From Pathankot:** *Ravi Exp* 4634, daily, 1535, 2 hr 10 min.

   Lahore: *I.P. (India-Pakistan) Exp* 4607, daily, 0930, 4 hr 5 min. This train is seriously affected by the state of political relations between India and Pakistan. When running it is a slow, relatively gentle way of entering Pakistan, with sometimes protracted customs and immigration formalities. However, it has often been severely disrupted. Check in Delhi for information before leaving.

Bus There are daily services with **Delhi** (447 km, 10 hr), **Pathankot** (112 km, 3 hr), Chandigarh (230 km, 5 hr), **Jammu** (215 km, 5 hr) and **Dharamsala** (250 km, 7 hr).

AMRITSAR TO JAMMU VIA PATHANKOT

The road leaves Amritsar to the NE. It crosses one of the first areas in northern India to benefit from the enormous irrigation systems that were built in the Punjab from the late 1830s onwards. Pathankot is the gateway to Kashmir and a gateway to Himachal Pradesh, e.g. to Dharamsala and Dalhousie.

The road goes through the small town of **Verka** (9 km) and after a further 10 km cross the *Bari Doab Canal*, see page 1117. This part of the canal, which carries water from the **Beas River** SW into Pakistan, was built by Maharaja Ranjit Singh to fill the tank of the Golden Temple in Amritsar. "Bari" is a shortened form of the Rivers Beas and Ravi, the doab being the land between the "two waters".

1 km after crossing the canal the road passes through Kathua Nangal, then goes on to **Batala** (20 km) and the district headquarters of *Gurdaspur* (32 km). 25 km to the W of **Gurdaspur** is the small town of **Kalanaur**, noted as the place at which Akbar was proclaimed Emperor. The 13 metre long, 3 metre high **Jhulna Mahal monument** is reputed to sway wildly if sat on. The main road continues NW through **Dinanagar** (13 km) and then crosses the **Upper Bari Doab Canal**. This was one of the first canals to be completed in the new irrigation system of the Punjab. In the early 19th century much of the land to the E of the Amritsar-Pathankot road had been very heavily populated and was suffering declining fertility. After the Anglo-Sikh wars at the end of the 1840s the British decided to try and provide new opportunities for the Sikhs by bringing new land into cultivation further W through extending the canal irrigation system. In doing so they built the system that ultimately transformed the whole of W Punjab from semi-desert into fertile agricultural land. The canal flows across the Pakistan border and through Lahore.

The road continues to *Pathankot* (16 km), a crossroads town and trading centre on the main route from N India to Srinagar. 13 km to the N is the *Shapur Kandi Fort* (16th Century) on the banks of the Ravi river, once the stronghold of the **Rajas of Pathan** who fought against and were driven into the hills by the Mughals. The site is picturesque.

Hotels E *Gulmohar Tourist Bungalow*, T 292. A/c and non a/c rooms. Dormitory also. **F** *Green Hotel* and *Imperial Hotel*.

Travel The bus and railway stations are 100 m apart so transfers are convenient. There are buses to all the important destinations nearby. Shared taxis can be taken if the prospect of hill bus journeys fails to thrill. These can be found near the railway station.
   Rail The rail times to and from Amritsar are given in the Amritsar section. A really spectacular mountain railway, built in 1928, runs to **Jogindarnagar**, 56 km NW of **Mandi** in Himachal Pradesh.

From **Pathankot** it is 108 km on **NH1** to **Jammu**, the winter capital of Jammu and Kashmir. The route is along the border between hill and plain, with the Pakistan border always nearby. This is a sensitive, highly strategic area. Approximately 25 km out of Pathankot you cross the **Ravi River**. The small town of **Kathua** is just across the river.

DELHI TO FIROZPUR

An alternative route from Delhi to the W and Pakistan is **NH10**. It allows access to several remote archaeological sites and India's most important early settlement region.

The road goes out of Delhi along the Rohtak Road to *Rohtak* (77 km Population 167,000 1981). The archaeological sites at Khokhra Kot and Ramala Ala have revealed pottery from pre-Harappan and early historical times after 1500 BC. Coin moulds from the 1st century which have thrown valuable light on the processes of minting coins. In the 18th century Rohtak was a border town between the Sikh and Maratha empires and had a series of local chieftains.

Craft industry Rohtak is well known for its turbans, interwoven with gold and silver thread.

Hotels D *Myna* (Haryana Tourism), T 4594. Camper huts. **Restaurant D** *Tilyar* (Haryana Tourism), T 4606. Tourist Rest House. A/c and non a/c rm. Restaurant, boating.

The road W goes on through the small medieval town of *Meham* (30 km). It contains an attractive well approached down a series of steps. It was built in 1656 by **Saidu Kalal**, Shah Jahan's mace-bearer. In the war between the Rajputs and Aurangzeb, the town was plundered and fell into decline. It still has high walls and attractive brick houses. Despite its small size it became widely known across N India in 1990 as the site of a major election fraud during elections to the Haryana State Assembly, thugs being used to beat up anyone who showed signs of opposing the then Chief Minister of the State.

Hansi (37 km), dating from the 8th century AD, was once the capital of the region. *Colonel James Skinner*, the son of a Scotsman and a Rajput woman, and founder of the most famous Indian Cavalry regiment, Skinner's Horse, died in the town in 1841. **See page 702.** Skinner was a commander of such stature that his troops, the 'yellow boys' on account of their canary coats, called him Sikander Sahib, likening him to Alexander the Great – **see page 176**. Good Haryana State Tourism accommodation can be found at **Jind** (43 km NE of Hansi) **D** *Bulbul*, T 293. Camper huts. Restaurant.

Continue W to *Hissar* (24 km), founded in 1354 by **Firuz Shah Tughlaq**. Firuz Shah constructed a canal specifically to bring water to his hunting ground. This was renovated in the 19th century and incorporated into the W Jumna canal. The city was reputedly one of his favourite homes, and he fortified it. The **Gujari Mahal** in the old fort was built from the remains of a Jain temple. The citadel contains the **Mosque of Firuz Shah** (late 14th century) and the **Jahaz** ("ship") which takes its name from its shape (reminiscent of that at Mandu – **see page 337**. This lies to the E of the city.

Festivals Like Hirsa Hissar is also widely known for its cattle fairs, held twice a year and exporting cattle all over India.

Hotels E *Flamingo* (Haryana Tourism), T 2606. Guest House and Camper Huts. A/c rm. Restaurant.

Continuing, you pass through the village of **Badopal** (45 km) and the small market town of *Fatehabad* (15 km). An archaeological site at *Sirsa* (a further 30 km) has shown that there was a settlement on the present site of the town from around 1500 BC and has revealed pottery known as Rang Mahal Ware. Thus it was clearly occupied long before the traditional date of its founding – the 6th Century AD – when it was known as Sarasvati. There is a large cattle fair here in August/September.

Kalibangan and Harappan sites Just N of *Sirsa* the road crosses the usually dry bed of the *Ghaggar River*. There is little to tell from the river today that its valley has been one of northern India's most important early settlement regions. Some have identified the Ghaggar with the *River Sarasvati*, known from early literature. The valley stretches from the Shimla hills down past the important Harappan sites of **Hanumangarh** and **Kalibangan** in Rajasthan, to the S of Bahawalpur in Pakistan. It has been explored by archaeologists, notably A. Ghosh, since 1962.

Late Harappan sites were identified in the upper part of the valley, the easternmost region of the Indus Valley civilisation. Sadly in the present state of Indian – Pakistani relations it is not possible to cross the border by land to visit the sites of Harappa 200 km to the NW or Moenjo Daro 450 km to the south. The most impressive of the sites today is that of **Kalibangan**, on the S bank of the Ghaggar River just across the state border in Rajasthan. The site was extensively explored in 1959, and as in **Kot Diji** in Pakistan it is clear that there were several pre-Harappan phases. The site was a heavily fortified citadel mound, rising about 10 metres above the level of the plain. **See page 1178.**

Allchin and Allchin record that the bricks of the early phase were already standardised, though not to the same size as later Harappan bricks. The ramparts were made of mud brick and a range of pottery and ornaments have been found. The early pottery is especially interesting, predominantly red or pink with black painting. It has been possible to date the levels discovered at Kalibangan using radiocarbon dating. The finds in the pre-Harappan phase have been dated at between 2920 to 2550 BC, while a group of six dates of between 2550 to 2440 BC for the beginning of the mature Harappan phase are, Allchin and Allchin suggest, "provocatively close to that obtained at Kot Diji" in Pakistan.

Indus valley "fossil fields" One of the most extraordinary discoveries at Kalibangan has been the unearthing of a field which had clearly been ploughed in two directions. This had been covered by builders' debris. Allchin and Allchin comment that the pattern of having one narrowly spaced set of furrows at right angles to a broader set of furrows, probably made with a wooden plough, is identical to the technique still used in the region for planting two crops at once in the same field. Ghosh suggests that the wide range of investigations in the valley that have now been carried out make it possible to distinguish a series of settlement periods, from the pre-Harappan around 3000 BC right through to the early medieval period.

Kalibangan is right off the beaten track. You can reach it by taking the road from Sirsa or Mandi Dabwala to **Hanumangarh**, then W SW to **Suratgarh** (60 km). Take the road to **Anupgarh**, passing through the very small settlements of **Sardargarh** (15 km) **Bughian** (10 km) and **Raghunathpura** (20 km) before reaching **Kalibangan** (10 km), about 30 km short of Anupgarh. Anupgarh is the terminus of the railway line, and is about 15 km from the Pakistan border.

If you do not wish to make the diversion to Kalibangan you cross into Punjab at the border town of *Mandi Dabwali* (57 km). Just after Mandi Dabwali the road crosses the Rajasthan Canal, which carries water from the Bhakra Nangal Dam as far Sas the Jaisalmer region another 700 km to the south. From **Malout** (34 km, and where you can turn W to **Abohar** (29 km) and **Ganganagar** (44 km) just over the border into Rajasthan) The NH 10 goes N through **Muktsar** (29 km) to **Firozpur** (85 km). For the first half of this last section the road keeps close to the Rajasthan Canal on its right.

HIMACHAL PRADESH

Himachal Pradesh (Himalayan Provinces) is one of India's most beautiful states and is becoming increasingly accessible. The Kulu valley can be reached easily from Delhi. It is particularly well known throughout N India for its pleasant climate and deliciously cool mountain streams, and as the region which supplies India with all its temperate fruit. Throughout the state there is good trekking. The state was created out of the Punjab in 1966 and awarded statehood in 1971. Shimla is the state capital and its most important town. Along with Darjiling in the E it is the most famous British Hill Station and worth a visit to see the lengths to which the British went in trying to recreate a part of England on foreign soil.

Himachal Pradesh has been far less affected by tourism than have Kashmir and Nepal. This is quickly changing as the region attracts more foreigners and Indian visitors alike. The scourge of the daily video coach has reached Shimla and the Kulu Valley, and there are plans to develop skiing and other adventure sports and a widening range of accommodation.

Social indicators **Area** 56,000 sq km **Population** 5 million **Literacy** M 53% F 31% **Birth rate** *Rural* 40:1000 *Urban* 30:1000 **Death rate** *Rural* 10:1000 *Urban* 7:1000 **Infant mortality** *Rural* 100:1000 *Urban* 62:1000 **Registered graduate job seekers** 16,000 **Average annual income per head:** Rs 1520 **Religion** *Hindu* 96% *Muslim* 2% *Christian* 0.1% *Sikh* 1% *Buddhist* 1%

INTRODUCTION

The Land

Himachal Pradesh is 55,673 sq km in area, or one third as large again as Switzerland. It lies between Kashmir (NW) and Uttar Pradesh (SE) in the western Himalaya. To the NE is Tibet/China whilst to the SW are Haryana and Punjab. The state is wholly mountainous, stretching from the outer ranges of the Shiwaliks in the south to peaks of more than 6,700 metres above sea level. The **Dhaula Dhar** range runs from the northwest to the Kulu Valley. The **Pir Panjal** is farther N and parallel to it. To the N of these are the regions of **Lahul** and **Spiti** which are beyond the influence of the monsoon. Consequently they share similar climatic characteristics with **Ladakh**. High, remote, arid and starkly beautiful, Lahul and Spiti are sparsely populated. They contrast strongly with the well-wooded lushness of Himachal Pradesh lying south of the Himalayan Axis.

Rivers The major rivers in Himachal Pradesh are the Chenab, Ravi and Beas in the W and the Sutlej and Yamuna in E. Some such as the Uhl river, a tributary of the Beas, has been dammed to generate hydro-electricity, and the largest lake in the region has been formed by the the **Bhakra Dam** across the Sutlej.

Climate

At lower altitudes the summers can be very hot and humid whereas the tops of the higher mountains are permanently under snow. In Shimla, the Kangra Valley, Chamba and the Kulu Valley, the monsoon arrives in mid-Jun and lasts until mid-Sep. Shimla, at an altitude of 2,000 m, has an average daily minimum temperature in Jan of 2°C and a maximum of 9°C. Snow is common. In June the average daily maximum is 24°C and the minimum 16°C. Shimla receives 1480 mm of rain a year, of which 77% is between Jun and Sep. As in many hill stations there are often sharp contrasts between sun and shade temperatures, particularly noticeable in spring and autumn when the average temperatures are lower, but the sun can be very warm.

People

The population comprises a mixture of hill tribes which includes the Gaddis, Gujars, Kinners, Lahaulis and Pangwalas. All have been assimilated into the dominant Hindu culture. The majority of the population are Hindu but its social corollary, the caste system, is simpler and less rigid. In Lahul and Spiti there are some Buddhists, giving a further indication of this region's cultural heritage. In the other Himachal towns too, there are Buddhists, many refugees from Tibet, plus Sikhs, Muslims and Christians.

Their folk lore has the common theme of heroism and legends of love and are sung solo, as duets or by groups. *Natti,* the attractive folk dance of the high hills is performed with great fervour.

The dominant local language is **Pahari**, a Hindi dialect derived from **Sanskrit** and **Prakrit** but largely unintelligible to plains dweller. **Hindi** is the medium for instruction in schools and is widely spoken.

After Arunachal Pradesh the state is the least urbanised in India, with only 10% of the total population of 4.28 million (1981 Census) living in towns. There are over 40 towns but by Indian standards they are small. Only Shimla has more than 50,000 inhabitants.

Economy
The economy is based on agriculture. Terrace cultivation is practised wherever possible and at higher altitudes farming is supplemented by animal husbandry. Only 15% of the sown area is irrigated. Wheat, rice, maize, barley and potatoes are the main staples. The potato was introduced in the 19th century by the British, who planted it wherever they went. Apples are an important cash crop, as are other fruits (plums, peaches, pomegranates and ginger) and mushrooms.

Pashmina wool Sheep and goat rearing is common and the fine and soft *pashmina* wool is highly sought after. Migratory groups such as the Gaddis and Gujars have traditional grazing routes that criss-cross the state.

Forests According to official statistics, forests occupy one third of the area. In reality the coverage is less with some regions facing considerable problems of erosion caused in large part by excessive deforestation. The forests are an important source of state revenue and the main products are construction timber, fuel wood, gum and resin.

Minerals There is some mining but this is on a relatively small scale. Slate, gypsum, limestone, baryte, dolomite and pyrite are quarried. Himachal Pradesh has very little industry although the government is making a concerted effort to rectify this. The major industries are the Nahan iron foundry, resin and turpentine factories and breweries. Commercial production of fertilisers has recently begun and an electronics complex has been established near Shimla. Village industries include wood carving, spinning wool, leather tanning, pottery and bamboo crafts.

Handicrafts Wool products are the most common local manufactures. It is a common sight in the hills to see men spinning wool by hand as they watch over their flocks or as they are walking along. The wool is later used for blankets and clothing. In the villages, men often knit. Good quality shawls made from the fine hair from pashmina goats, particularly in Kulu, are highly sought after. Fleecy soft blankets called *gudmas**, heavier *namdas** (rugs) and rich pile carpets in Tibetan designs are also produced.

Chappals* (leather sandals) are made in Chamba and Chamba *rumals** are beautiful 'handkerchiefs' with scenes embroidered on them imitating the famous miniature paintings of the region. Now, Buddhist *Tankhas**, silver ware and chunky tribal silver jewellery is popular with tourists which are sold in bazaars throughout the state.

Migration to the plains Himachal Pradesh produces less than half of its food requirements, but at the same time there is little alternative employment outside agriculture. Consequently, there is heavy male migration out of the district. Within the family, secondary education is often given high priority for males. This can be seen as equipping them to migrate and improving their chances of securing employment outside the village and district. The army has always been popular but there are limits its capacity for offering employment. Government service also

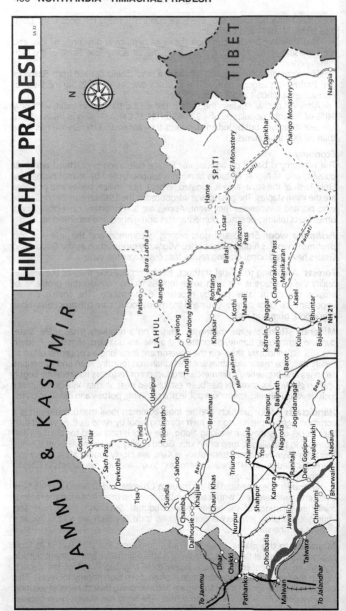

HIMACHAL PRADESH

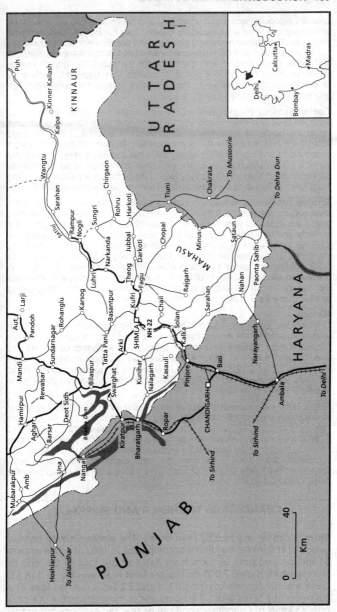

provides a popular, secure, but uninspiring alternative. Migrants are now found in towns across N India but especially in Delhi. They live frugally, save and remit money to village-based household members who use the cash to buy foodstuffs.

Migrants make periodic trips home for weddings, annual leave etc. and have sufficiently strong contact with the village for the population growth rate to remain unaffected by their long periods of absence. On retirement from the army or public service, most return to the hills. Many villages are really remittance economies supported by subsistence agriculture.

Communication The principal lines of communication are roads and footpaths. After the 1962 Sino-Indian Border War the Indian government pushed good roads up to the border to serve their strategic needs. A by-product was improved accessibility and mobility for the local population. This has facilitated the import of foodstuffs and made it easier to migrate. It has also linked Himachal with the wider N Indian economic system. There is a small commercial airport at Bhuntar, 10 km south of Kulu and the only railway is the picturesque narrow gauge line from Kalka in Punjab to the state capital of Shimla. The distance is 96 km.

Tourism has become increasingly important with Shimla, Kulu and Manali the most popular destinations. Trekking, rock climbing and mountaineering are being promoted, especially since the virtual closure of Kashmir in 1990. Much of the traffic bound for Kashmir and Ladakh has been diverted to Himachal and many Kashmiri travel agents have relocated in the Kulu Valley. The area is also being developed as a winter sports centre. There is skiing in Manali and Narkanda (courses from Jan), winter carnival in Manali in the second week, heli-skiing in the second and third week of Feb and ice skating and ice hockey in Shimla from Dec to Feb. Tourists are also being attracted to adventure sports – hang gliding at Bilking near Bir and exciting river rafting.

History
Originally the region was inhabited by a tribal group called the Dasas who were later assimilated by the Aryans. Parts were occupied by the Muslims when they invaded N India. **Kangra**, for example, submitted to **Mahmud of Ghazni** and later became a Mughal Province. The **Gurkhas** of Nepal invaded Himachal Pradesh in the early 19th century and incorporated it into their kingdom as did the Sikhs some years later. The British finally took over the princely states in the middle of the 19th century.

Shimla came into existence in 1819 after the Gurkha War. The climate appealed to the British and it rapidly developed into a hot weather resort. In the mid 19th century, it became the Summer Headquarters of the government who shifted 1760 kilometres from Calcutta for four months each year. After the British, Shimla served as the temporary capital of E Punjab until the new city of Chandigarh was completed. Since 1966 it has been the state capital of Himachal Pradesh. Following the Chinese takeover of Tibet in the 1950s, Dharamsala has been the home of the Dalai Lama since 1959.

CHANDIGARH TO SHIMLA AND SHIPKI-LA

Shimla can be reached by road or rail. The **Kalka-Shimla** narrow gauge (2 ft 6 in) railway line was completed in 1903 at a cost of over $1 million and runs 96.5 km from Kalka at the foot of the hills to Shimla which is over 2,000 m. The gradient is an average of 1 in 33, there are 107 tunnels covering 8 km and 3.2 km is over bridges. The train journey takes around 6 hours and is most enjoyable. Kalka is only 35 km N of Chandigarh and can be reached easily by bus or taxi from there. For train times, see **Shimla Travel.** By car the route is virtually the same.

Take the **NH1** out of **Ambala** towards **Ludhiana**. After 5 km turn right. Pass through **Baldevnagar** (2 km), **Dhulkot** (4 km) and **Lalru** (10 km) to **Basi** (11 km). After 4 km the road crosses the **River Ghaggar** and passes through **Panchkola** (11 km), where there is a left turn to **Chandigarh** (3 km), before reaching **Pinjore** (8 km).

It is worth stopping briefly at **Pinjore** to see the Mughal summerhouse and garden built by **Fidai Khan**. At **Kalka** (6 km) the climb up the ghat section of road begins. Across the border from Haryana, at **Parwanoo**, there is the **C** *Timber Trail Resort*, T 497. 25 rm, 10 tents. Reached by road, with a restaurant, cafe, bar and good rooms. *Timber Trail Heights*, reached by rope way, also with restaurant. Excellent setting with gardens. Good place to stop. Open 24 hr.

The road passes through **Dharampur** (24 km 1,500 m) and **Barogh** (8 km 1,760 m) to **Solan** (9 km 1,750 m), the half way point of the journey, and on both the road and railway line. It is noted for its brewery and mineral water springs. **E** *Tourist Bungalow* (HiPTDC)) here for travellers wishing to break their journey. The road continues down to **Kandaghat** (16 km 1,350 m) then climbs up to **Tara Devi** (22 km 1,820 m) and **Shimla** (11 km).

Shimla

Population 50,000 approx. *Altitude* 2,213 m *Area* 18 sq km. *Best season* Oct and Nov are exceptionally pleasant, with hot days and cool nights. Dec-Feb is cold and there are snowfalls. Mar-Apr is pleasant but the weather can be quite changeable, storms are not infrequent and the air can still feel very chill. May-June is good but this is the height of the Indian tourist season and accommodation is hard to find. Jul-Sep is the monsoon.

Shimla is one of the more important hill stations in the W Himalaya, but it is a matter of taste whether you consider its undoubted charm more regal than others.

	Jan	Feb	Mar	Apr	May	Jun	Jul	Aug	Sep	Oct	Nov	Dec	Av/Tot
Max (°C)	9	10	14	19	23	24	21	20	20	18	15	11	17
Min (°C)	2	3	7	11	15	16	16	15	14	10	7	4	10
Rain (mm)	65	48	58	38	54	147	415	385	195	45	7	24	1481

The early history For the British, the only sure way of beating the hot weather on the plains in May and June was to avoid it. The British therefore established a number of hill stations in the Lesser Himalaya and elsewhere (**Ooty** in the Nilgiris, **Mount Abu** in Rajasthan, **Murree** in Pakistan, **Darjiling** in W Bengal) which developed into hot weather resorts. These developed some of the features of English county towns or seaside resorts. Bandstands, mock Elizabethan houses with exotic names like Harrow on the Hill and Runnymede, pavilions and picnic spots, a main street invariably called the Mall, churches and clubs, with clouds replacing the waves on the beach.

The seasonal move of government So beneficial were the effects of the cooler mountain air that Shimla, 'discovered' by the British in 1819, became the summer seat of government from the mid 19th century until Independence. The capital was shifted there from Calcutta and later from Delhi (1912 onwards) and all business was transacted from this cool mountain retreat. As Kipling wrote in 'A Tale of Two Cities':

> But the rulers in that City by the Sea
> Turned to flee–
> Fled with each returning Spring and tide from its ills
> To the Hills.

Huge baggage trains were required to transport the mountains of files and the whole operation cost thousands of rupees. At the end of the season back they would all go. Other hill stations, such as Nainital in U.P. became summer seats of state governments.

Rest and relaxation The emphasis was on rest and relaxation and a holiday atmosphere developed. They were places where females heavily outnumbered males, for the simple reason that many British men had to run the empire and therefore were not able to get away for as long as their womenfolk. Army officers spent their leave there. Social life in hill stations became something of a whirlpool: parties, balls, formal promenades along the Mall, and brief flirtations.

Colonels of Indian army regiments would not allow their subalterns to go to certain hill stations. Many were said to come down from the hills fighting rearguard actions against the husbands coming up. They became known as 'poodle fakers'. At the height of the Victorian period of propriety in England, Shimla was considered a very sinful place.

Since Independence the hill stations have continued to function as hot weather resorts, and as the temperatures on the plains soar, so do the population and room rents in these hilltop retreats. They are best avoided then. Paul Scott's Booker Prize winning novel *Staying On* was set in post Independence Shimla. J.G. Farell's last unfinished novel *The Hill Station,* which was set in colonial Shimla of 1871, is also worth reading.

Local Festivals June *Summer Festival* is celebrated when numerous cultural programmes are staged by performers from Himachal Pradesh and neighbouring states. Exhibitions of art and handicrafts are held and you will get the opportunity to sample different local dishes.

Places of Interest The Town Shimla is strung out on a long crescent-shaped ridge which connects a number of hilltops: Jakko (2,453 m), Prospect Hill (2,176 m), Observatory Hill (2,148 m), Elysium Hill (2,255 m) and Summer Hill (2,103 m). Good views of the snow-capped peaks to the N can be obtained from Jakko and others. The Mall runs along the ridge, often giving beautiful views. All the walks are lined with magnificent pines, giving a beautifully fresh scent to the air.

Jakhu Temple Dedicated to Hanuman the monkey god and well frequented by monkeys, the temple is at an altitude of 2,455 m and near the highest point of the Shimla Ridge at the E end of the town beyond Christ Church. It takes 45 minutes to walk there from the Mall and the views are magnificent.

Christchurch (1844 onwards) dominates the E end of town. This was designed by Col. J. T. Boileau, consecrated in 1857 and later extended with the addition of a clock (1860) and porch (1873). The original chancel window was designed by **Lockwood Kipling**, Rudyard Kipling's father. No trace remains. Next door is the **Library** (c.1910) designed by James Ransome in the Elizabethan style. Where the Mall joins the Ridge is Kipling's '*Scandal Point*'.

Down the road towards the railway station is the **Gaiety Theatre** (1887), the **Town Hall** (c.1910) which Davies describes as being done in an Arts and Crafts style and the timber **General Post Office** (1886) in a style best described as Wild West Swiss. Nearby are the YWCA, St Andrew's Church (1885) and the Telegraph Office. Beyond is the Grand Hotel. Further down you pass the sinister looking **Gorton Castle**, designed by Sir Samuel Swinton Jacob and much modified during its construction. This once housed the Civil Secretariat. A road to the left leads to the railway station, while one to the right goes to Annandale and the racecourse and cricket ground.

Past the station on the way to **Viceregal Lodge** you pass the **Cecil Hotel** (1877). From here it is 800 m to the **Viceregal Lodge** (1888) on Observatory Hill. Now

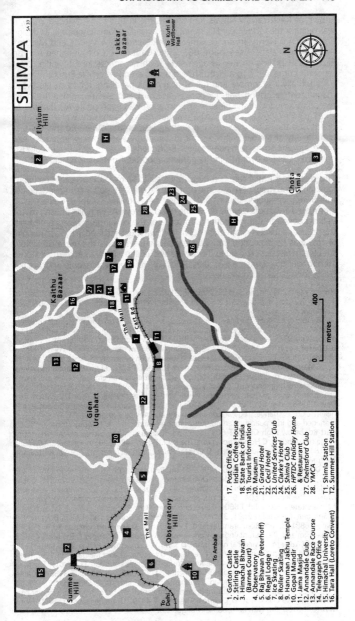

SHIMLA SA.33

1. Gorton Castle
2. Stirling Castle
3. Himachal Bhavan
   (Barnes Court)
4. Observatory
5. Raj Bhavan (Peterhoff)
6. Regal Lodge
7. Ice Skating
8. Roller Skating
9. Hanuman Jakhu Temple
10. Hope Mandir
11. Jama Masjid
12. Annandale Club
13. Annandale Race Course
14. Telegraph Office
15. Himachal University
16. Tara Hall (Loreto Convent)
17. Post Office &
    Indian Coffee House
18. State Bank of India
19. Tourist Information
20. Museum
21. Grand Hotel
22. Cecil Hotel
23. United Services Club
24. Clarke's Hotel
25. Shimla Club
26. HPTDC Holiday Home
27. Chelmsford Club
28. YMCA

T1. Shimla Station
T2. Summer Hill Station

known as **Rashtrapati Niwas** and used as the Institute of Advanced Study, it was built for the Viceroy Lord Dufferin, who played a prominent part in its design and building. **Henry Irwin**, designer of the Madras Law Courts and Mysore's Ambar Vilas Palace – **see page 863** – and Capt. H.H. Cole designed it in an Elizabethan or English Renaissance style, with no concessions to India. Later residents compared it to a 'Scottish Hydro' and even Pentonville Prison.

Internally it is sombre and full of heavy teak panelling. It had six storeys, a magnificent reception hall, indoor tennis court and electric lights. The main reception rooms can still be seen. The location was appropriate for the lord of 'The Little Tin Gods' as the hill is a natural watershed. On one side, water ultimately drains into the Sutlej river and the Arabian Sea, on the other into the Yamuna and the Bay of Bengal. Many historic and important decisions were made here. There are still some reminders of its British origins such as the meticulously polished brass fire hydrants in the garden, imported from Manchester.

The decaying Raj There is a ramshackle air to Shimla. The wooden buildings look more and more rickety, some of the stone ones are slowly crumbling. Below the British creations strung out along the ridgeline, shabby houses with corrugated iron roofs tumble down the hillside below. As with all "British" towns in India although the inspiration and some of the design may have come from the colonial outsiders much of the town itself was built and lived in by local people. Shimla was no exception. Immediately below the ridge is the maze of narrow streets and bazaars clinging to the hillside as if it might slip away in the next storm. Throughout the tourist season these lines are crowded with people up from the plains for a break from the heat.

Hotels May and June can be difficult for those looking for modest accommodation, especially if you arrive after mid-day, so it is best to book beforehand. Most down to C category have a car park.

B *Oberoi Clarkes*, The Mall. T 6091-5, Cable: Obhotel. 48 rm. This mock Tudor building in a pleasant garden setting is where the enterprising Mohan Singh Oberoi started his chain of hotels in 1935. Very pleasant, well run with good views, good food and in a central location. **B** *Oberoi Cecil*, The Mall. T 2073, Cable: Obcecil. 33 rm, mostly suites, garden. Colonial grandeur on the edge of town, with superb views. Open in season.

C *Woodville Palace*, Himachal Bhavan Rd, The Mall. T 2712. 11 rm. Restaurant, gardens, indoor sports. Good views. Spacious house in large grounds with croquet, tennis and lawns. Restaurant recommended. **C** *Chapslee*, Lakkar Bazaar, T 3242. 7 suites. Old mansion with character in large grounds with good views. Very good restaurant. **C** *Asia The Dawn*, Tara Devi. T 5858, Telex: 0391-205. 37 rm. 4 km from Mall. Restaurant and terrace barbecue, bar, health club, exchange, regular complimentary bus service into Shimla, TV. Modern, well managed and in a peaceful setting. Restaurant recommended. **C** *Holiday Home* (HPTDC), Cart Rd, below High Court. T 6031-6. 65 rm. Restaurants, bar, exchange, car hire, tours. Large clean rooms. **C** *Honeymoon Inn*, The Mall. T 4967, 4880. 20 rm. Restaurant (Indian), TV, 18 hr rm service, indoor sports. **D** *Crystal Palace*, Cart Rd (near lift). T 5088. Restaurant, TV, travel, car hire.

D *Surya*, Circular Rd. T 4762, 4962. 41 rm. Restaurant, TV, 16 hr rm service, travel and tours, car parking, Diners . Modern. **D** *Auckland*, Circular Rd, Lakkar Bazaar. T 6315, Cable: Auckland. Restaurant, car hire. **D** *White*, Lakkar Bazaar. T 5276. 26 rm. Room service. **D** *Mayur*, The Ridge. T 6047-9. 32 rm. Restaurant, TV, lift. Modern and clean. **D** *Pineview*, Mythe Estate, Circular Rd. T 6606, Cable: Snowline. 28 rm. Restaurant (Indian), TV, exchange. **D** *Shingar*, The Mall. T 2881. 32 rm. Restaurant (Indian, Continental), TV, lift. **D** *Hans*, The Mall. T 6881. 32 rm. Restaurant (Indian), TV, car rental. **D** *Himland*, Circular Rd. T 3595-6, Cable: Himland. Restaurant (Indian, Continental), TV in suites. **D** *Sangeet*, The Mall. T 5823. 10 rm. TV, 18 hr rm service, car hire, travel. **D** *Samrat*, Cambermere Bridge, The Mall. T 4172. Restaurant (Indian, Chinese), TV, car hire, travel. **D** *Harsha*, Chaura Maidan. T 3016-7, Telex: 0391-221. 20 rm. 1.5 km from Mall. Restaurant, TV. Simple but clean. **D** *Victory*, The Mall. T 2600. 34 rm. Restaurant (Indian, Continental). **D** *Gulmarg*, The Mall. T 3168-9, Cable: Gulmarg. 48 rm. Restaurant (Indian, Continental), credit cards, TV. **D** *Diplomat*, The Ridge. T 3033. 23 rm with bath. Restaurant (Indian, Continental), 18 hr rm service, travel, car hire. Rooms vary, so check first. **D** *Cosmos*, The Mall. T 4429. 18 rm. Restaurant, TV. **D** *Hotel White*, T 6136. Rm with bath, some with good views.

E *Prashant*, The Mall. T 6715. 12 rm. TV, 15 hr rm service. E *Ridge View*, The Ridge. T 4859. 20 rm. 18 hr rm service. E *Chanakya*, The Mall. T 3388. 12 rm. 24 hr rm service. E *Flora*, The Ridge. T 2027. 22 rm. TV, 16 hr rm service, car hire, travel. E *Bridge View*, Cambermere Bridge, The Mall. T 4137. 50 rm. Restaurant (Indian, Continental), lift, car hire, TV. E *Kwality*, The Mall. T 6440. 16 hr rm service, travel, car hire. E *Sharda*, Lakkar Bazaar. T 2188. Restaurant, 24 hr rm service, credit cards. E *Marina*, The Mall. T 3557, in dining hall (meals on order), billiards, terrace. Older hotel. E *Dalziel*, The Mall. T 2691. 29 rm. Restaurant (Indian), TV. E *Capital*, The Mall. T 3581-3. 45 rm. Restaurant, 16 hr rm service. E *Rock Sea*, The Mall. T 2748. 24 hr rm service. F *Tashkent*, The Mall. T 2482. 25 rm. Restaurant, 24 hr rm service. Very basic.

F *Ganga*, Melrose Lodge Estate, The Mall. T 4503. 24 hr rm service. F *YMCA*, above Christ Church. Quiet location. Temporary membership, electricity, extra. Dining hall.

Accommodation near Shimla

B *Kufri Holiday Resort*, Kufri, 16 km from Shimla. T 8-341 to 8-344. 8 cottages. TV, bar, Restaurant, sports and skiing. Beyond Kufri, Chail on a direct bus route, 45 km SE from Shimla at an altitude of 2250 m has an old Patiala palace which has been converted to a comfortable hotel. B *Chail Palace Hotel*, T Chail 37. 19 suites and 10 cottages with 1 to 4 bedrooms. Restaurant. Former palace but modest and has character. D *Wildflower Hall* (HPTDC), Chharabra. T 8-212, 13 km from Shimla. 34 rm and 11 rustic cottages with sitting rooms and kitchens. Restaurant, outdoor cafe, bar, rm service, childrens playground, car parking. The gardens are particularly attractive, with lovely walks. Also HPTDC D *Log huts* and *cottages*. Chail is popular with birdwatchers and claims to have the country's highest cricket ground!

Restaurants Nearly all the restaurants in Shimla offer Indian, Continental and Chinese food. Hotels recommended for their restaurants are *Asia the Dawn* and *Honey Dew*, both excellent for lunch and dinner. *Woodville Palace* and *Chapslee* are more intimate, and equally good. *Holiday Home* has the *Golden Dragon*.

Outside hotels, *Ashiana* above *Goofa* on The Ridge, T 4264, circular with good views, recommended for Indian and Chinese dishes while *Goofa*, better for snacks, especially pizzas. On the Mall, *Fascination*, T 2202, above *Baljee's*, T 2202, popular with local people. Others nearby are *Alfa*, T 5142; *Himani*, T 6070; *Embassy*, T 2271; *Ajay*, opp Telegraph Office, recommended; *Indian Coffee House*, T 2080, good for south Indian food and snacks.

Bars Some of the higher category hotels have bars

Banks *Baroda*, T 5968. *Bank of India*, T 3600. *United Commercial*, T 3035. *State Bank of India*, T 2480, 5503. *State Bank of Patiala*, T 2153. *Punjab National Bank*, T 5310. *Punjab and Sind Bank*, T 3603. *Indian Bank*, T 5433. *Indian Overseas Bank*, T 5358. *Jammu and Kashmir Bank*, T 3085. *Central Bank of India*, T 3703. *Grindlays*, T 2925. *H.P. State Co-Op Bank*, T 3815. *New Bank of India*, T 2051. *Central Bank of India*, T 3703. *Syndicate*, The Mall.

Shopping Major shopping areas are The Mall, Lower Bazar, and Lakkar Bazar. *Himachal Emporium*, The Mall, for locally made woollen items. Books, maps and prints at *Maria Bookshop*, 78 The Mall.

Local Transport Taxi Union Service, near Himachal Tourism Lift on the Cart Rd, T 5123. **Private taxis**, mini buses and Himachal Road Transport Corporation buses are available for local sightseeing in and around Shimla. **Buses** from Cart Rd. The Lift, nr Hotel Samrat, takes passengers to the Mall.

Sports *Skating rinks*: Ice Skating Rink, Below Rivoli, T 2344. *Roller Skating Rink*, Regal Bldg, T 3300. *Skiing*, from the first week in Jan till mid-Mar. Ski courses at Narkanda are organised by HPTDC. *Fishing* for trout at Rohru, Seema and Baspa, for mahseer at Tattapani. Licence fee Rs 10. per person. Off season: 15 Jun-15 Aug and 1 Nov-15 Feb. Licensing authority: Assistant Director, Fisheries, Khalini, T 4732, 6985. *Golfing* at Naldera, 9-hole. For casual members green fee Rs 15, golf set Rs 10, caddie Rs 10, balls Rs 16- 25. *Trekking* on the Shimla-Kinnaur belt, one to ten day options.

Museums The State Museum is nr Chaura Maidan. Open 1000-1330, 1400 -1700, closed Mon. It is a pleasant walk down the road to the northwest from the Cecil Hotel. The collection of stone statues from different places in Himachal Pradesh is interesting as are the miniatures from the Kangra School of painting. Also costumes, jewellery and textiles.

Useful Numbers Police: T 100, 2444 Fire: T 101 Ambulance: T 3464, 2888

Hospitals and Medical Services Kamala Nehru Hospital, T 2841. Indira Gandhi Medical College, T 2646.

Post and Telegraph Head Office, The Mall (nr Scandal Point). Post Office, The Mall (nr State Bank of India). Post Office, Cambermere Bridge. Central Telegraph Office, The Mall.

Places of Worship *Hindu*: Kali Bari Temple; Krishna Mandir; Hanuman Temples at Jakko and Sankat Mochan; Iara Devi; Shiva Temple near Baljee's; Dheengu Mata Mandir at Sanjauli. *Muslim*: Jama Masjid; Kashmiri Masjid. *Christian*: Cathedral Church; Catholic Church; Baptist Church; Christ Church. *Buddhist*: Monastery at Sanjauli.

Travel Agents and Tour Operators *Himalayan Travels*, The Mall, T 2411. *Devi Travels*, The Mall, T 3492. *Destinations Inc*, 35 Upper Flat, The Mall. *Asia and International Travel and Tourist Agencies*, 90 The Mall. *Ambassador Travels*, 58 The Mall, T 4662. Telex: 0391-212. *South East Asia Travels*, Room 7, Masonic Guest House, The Ridge.

Tourist Office and Information HPTDC Tourist Information Office, The Mall, T 3311. Open 1000-1800. Tourist Information Office, Dept of Tourism, Govt of H.P., Panchayat Bhawan, Cart Rd, T 4589. Open 1000-1700. Tourist Information Office, The Mall, Shimla, T 3311. HPTDC has a fleet of a/c and non a/c cars and luxury and delux coaches.

Conducted Tours are well run. Full day (1000-1700), daily. Shimla Wildflower Hall, Kufri, Indira Holiday Home, Fagu, Mashobra, Craignano, Fruit Research Station, Naldehra. Rs 315 per car for 5 people, Rs 40 per seat by luxury coach. Full day (1000-1700) Wed, Fri and Sun. Shimla, Fagu, Theog, Matiana, Narkanda. Rs 450 by car for 5 persons, Rs 50 per seat by luxury coach. Full day (1000-1700) Mon, Th and Sat. Shimla, Chail, Kufri, Indira Holiday Home, Kiarai Bungalow. Rs 420 by car for 5 people, Rs 50 per seat by luxury coach.

Air Services Shimla has a new airport at Jabbar Hatti. *Vayudoot* operates Dornier fights on the Shimla-Delhi and Shimla-Kulu sectors Vayudoot (handling and booking agents), HPTDC, Tourist Office, The Mall, T 32336, 3311, 77646. Airport enquiries T Sairi Exchange 39.

Rail Travel by rail to Shimla involves a change of gauge at Kalka. The narrow gauge 'toy' train takes 4 hr 10 min on rail car (sometimes nearly 6 hrs), but is enjoyable. Travel by bus is quicker but also requires a stronger stomach. **Chandigarh**: *Kalka-Howrah Mail* 2312 (change at Kalka to 254), daily, 1745, 6 hr 35 min; *Himalayan Queen*, 4096 (change at Kalka to 258), daily, 1722, 4 hr 33 min. **New Delhi**: *Himalayan Queen*, 4096 (change at Kalka to 258), daily, 1055, 6 hr 21 min. **Old Delhi**: *Kalka-Howrah Mail* 2312 (change at Kalka to 254 Mail), daily, 1745, 12 hr 45 min.

Road **Kalka** (90 km); **Chandigarh** (117 km); **Ambala** (166 km); **Delhi** (370 km); **Dehra Dun** (240 km); **Amritsar** (453 km); **Jammu** (495 km).

Bus Services to **Delhi** (10-12 hr), **Chandigarh** (4 hr), **Manali** (11 hr), **Dharamshala** (12 hr), **Dehra Dun** (9 hr) and from other places within the state. HPTDC runs delux buses between Shimla and Delhi in the summer months. Transport Enquiry, T 2887, 3566. You may not be able to avoid the video coach. Remarkably, if the video is not working, you get a discount.

Excursions There are a number of pleasant walks in and around Shimla. **The Glen** (1,830 m) is a popular picnic spot and a 4 km walk from the centre of town. Go via the Cecil Hotel. **Summer Hill** (1,983 m) is a pleasant 'suburb' 5 km from town. 3 km further on are the 67 m **Chadwick Falls**. **Prospect Hill**, 5 km from Shimla, is a 15-20 minute walk from Boileauganj. There is a temple and good views. **Tara Devi** (1,851 m) is 7 km but can be reached by car or train.

The road to the Tibetan border (a total of 520 km from Shimla) continues northeast from the bus stand to **Dhali** (8 km) where there is a road on the left to **Mashobra** (6 km, 2,150 m). This is an attractive picnic spot with good forest walks. 3 km further on is **Craignano** (2,280 m) which has a hilltop *Rest House*. Go straight on to **Kufri** (2,500 m), Himachal's best-known ski resort.

The best time is Jan and Feb. There is an annual winter sports festival held during the first week of Feb. C *Kufri Holiday Resort*, T 8341. 21 rm in 8 cottages. Modern with facilities of a Western holiday resort – Restaurant (Indian, Continental), barbecue, 24 hr coffee shop, health club, 24 hr rm service, Meditation Centre. Good for walks. At weekends, the outdoor barbecue has the option of allowing you to cook while they provide! *Rest House* can be booked through Tourist Officer, The Ridge, Shimla.

At *Danes Folly*, 5 km away at an altitude of 2550 m is a government run orchard. The road continues through **Fagu** (6 km, 2,500 m) to **Naldhera** (2,050 m), which has a 9 hole golf course which claims to be the oldest in India. The temple to

Mahung is beautiful. In June there is the colourful **Sipi fair** which attracts crowds from the surrounding villages who bring handicrafts to sell. *Tourist Bungalow* and cafeteria.

The road then drops a little to **Theog** (10 km, 2,230 m), where there is a right turn to **Chella** (11 km) and **Chakrata** (154 km). The road goes straight on through **Mathiana** (17 km), **Narkanda** (17 km, 2,660 m) and then drops to **Nirth** (32 km, 1,150 m). It remains at approximately this height for the next 20 km to **Rampur-Busayar**, then climbs again to **Gaora** (13 km, 1,960 m).

Winding its way through a series of tiny hamlets at around 2000 m altitude – **Sarhan** (18 km), **Choura** (14 km – *Forest Rest House*), **Paunda** (16 km) and **Wangtu** (13 km) the road then descends to **Tapri** (8 km 1,470), then climbs steeply to the highest part of the route through **Urni** (6 km) to **Rogi** (15 km, 2,810 m) and **Kalpa** (5 km 2,775 m).

Warning Travellers are not allowed beyond this point without an Inner Line Permit from the District magistrate at Shimla. Contact police in Shimla.

If you are lucky enough to do so, the road continues through **Pangi** (11 km) and *Morang* (11 km – *Forest Rest House*), to *Shipki* (47 km) and the delightfully named **Pooh** (25 km), finally going through **Namgia** (16 km) and **Tasi Gang** (6 km) to *Shipki La* (10 km 3,185 m). Sadly there is then no choice but to turn round and come back the same way.

SHIMLA TO MANALI, LAHUL AND SPITI VIA MANDI AND KULU

From Shimla the route runs through the Shiwalik hills to *Bilaspur*, then N to Mandi. The road continues N into Kashmir, though foreigners need frontline permits to travel in this region.

Leave Shimla on the **NH22** W, the main road to **Kalka** and **Ambala**. After 3 km take the right turn, leaving the Kalka road which goes straight on. The road winds its way down for much of the way from Shimla, through **Jutogh** (4 km) where you take a right fork to **Ghanna Hatti** (7 km 1,530 m) and **Kheri Ghat** (8 km 1,280 m). Continue through small villages and hamlets: **Shala Ghat** (4 km), **Dano Ghat** and **Darla Ghat** (3 km and 9 km respectively) and then 11 km to a road junction where you take the right turn. After 2 km the road passes through **Bharari Ghat** and then to *Namhol* (6 km) where there is a *Rest House* and a checkpost.

After a further 16 km there is a junction. The road to **Bilaspur** (18 km) is the right fork. The road to the left leads to **Swarghat** (33 km), where there is a *Forest Rest House*, and **Naina Devi** (56 km 910 m) where there is also a forest rest house and a tourist inn. This road connects with the **NH21** at **Kiratpur**, where you can go on SW to **Rupar** or NW to **Nangal**.

From **Bilaspur** go N to **Dehar** (25 km) where the road cross the **River Sutlej**, which now feeds into the *Govind Sagar* lake, and follow the road to **Sundernagar** ("Beautiful city"; 18 km). 18 km beyond Sundernagar a road on the left leads to **Tanda** (29 km), the road on the right to **Tatapani**, where there is a hot spring. The road straight on continues to Mandi (8 km)

Mandi (760 m) is at the southern end of the Kangra Valley and is a gateway into the Kulu Valley, which is reached by climbing the narrow and spectacular gorge of Beas river.

It is very much a crossroads town. The **Triloknath Temple** (1520), built in the Nagara style, is centre of a group of shrines overlooking the river. It has a protective tiled roof. Outside the old town in a walled enclosure are more than 100 memorial slabs commemorating members of the royal household. These date from the 13th-20th century. Also near Mandi in the **Uhl river** valley is a hydroelectric dam with a power station downstream at Jogindernagar.

Rewabar Lake, 24 km southeast of Mandi is a popular multi-faith pilgrimage centre for Hindus, Buddhists and Sikhs. The mountain cave refuge is used by visiting Buddhists and there is also a monastery. Feb/Mar. *Sivaratri Fair* is very special. Dance, music and drama during celebrations. Temple deities congregate

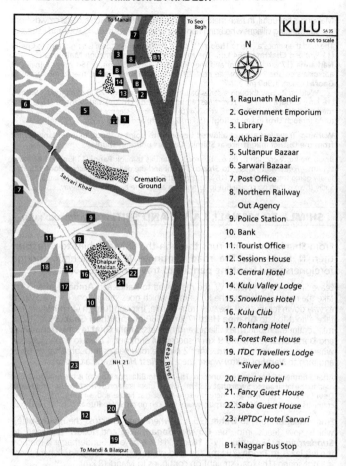

KULU SA 35

not to scale

N

1. Ragunath Mandir
2. Government Emporium
3. Library
4. Akhari Bazaar
5. Sultanpur Bazaar
6. Sarwari Bazaar
7. Post Office
8. Northern Railway Out Agency
9. Police Station
10. Bank
11. Tourist Office
12. Sessions House
13. Central Hotel
14. Kulu Valley Lodge
15. Snowlines Hotel
16. Kulu Club
17. Rohtang Hotel
18. Forest Rest House
19. ITDC Travellers Lodge "Silver Moo"
20. Empire Hotel
21. Fancy Guest House
22. Saba Guest House
23. HPTDC Hotel Sarvari

B1. Naggar Bus Stop

and there are processions with chariots and palanquins.

Hotels Mandi has a HPTDC **E** *Tourist Bungalow*, T 575. 7 rm, some with balcony and a dormitory. Simple, clean and peaceful. The **E** *Raj Mahal*, a former Maharaja's Palace (though not in the same class as most Rajasthani palaces), single and double rooms with bath. In need of attention. There are also a number of cheap and basic **F** hotels in town of which the *Adarsh* is quite good. Clean rooms with baths.

The HPTDC *Café Shiraz* is probably the most suitable Restaurant. If you take the road S of Mandi, 8 km out of town towards Sundarnagar, you can treat yourself to excellent milk shakes at the *Roadside Milk Bar*.

The *valley of the gods* There is a route W from Mandi which goes to **Kangra** (130 km) and **Dharamshala** (14 km). These are described below. From **Mandi** the road N enters the **Kulu Valley**. The Kulu region is set in the **Beas** river valley, rising from **Mandi** and culminating in the **Rohtang Pass** (3,915 m). It is enclosed to the N by the **Pir Panjal** range, to the W by the **Bara Bangahal** and to the E by the **Parvati range**. The approach to it is through a narrow funnel or gorge but in the upper part it extends outwards to almost 80 km width. The name Kulu is derived from **Kulantapith** which means 'the end of the habitable world'. To many it is the Valley of the Gods. It is steeped in Hindu religious tradition and it almost seems that every stream, rock and blade of grass is imbued with some religious significance.

For a long time the **Kulu kingdom** was restricted to the upper Beas Valley and the original capital was at **Jagatsukh**, a few kilometres to the S of Manali. In the 15th century it was extended S to Mandi. In the 17th century the capital was shifted to Kulu and the kingdom's boundaries extended into Lahul and Spiti and as far east as the Sutlej. Kulu was strategically located on trade routes from N India to Ladakh and beyond, so was bound to attract outside interest. The Sikhs, for example contested Kulu's control of this section of the trade route. In 1847, Kulu came under British control and was governed from Dharamshala.

The **Kulu valley** is famous for its apple orchards, beautiful women, wooden temples and folk music and dance. It is one of the most accessible of the Central Himalayan valleys which is one reason for its popularity. It is now a very popular alternative to Kashmir and, in fact, since the eruption of political troubles and the virtual closure of Jammu and Kashmir (which also includes Ladakh), many tourist and trekking companies have relocated to the Kulu Valley. Whilst it is not the secluded backwater that it was, it is nevertheless a pleasant and restful haven after the rigours of travel.

From Mandi take the NH 21 NE to **Pandoh** (19 km) where there is now a dam on the **River Beas**. Continue to **Aut** (22 km, 910 m; pronounced 'out') where there is trout fishing. The season is Mar and Apr. The Tourist Office issues licences. The road then climbs through **Baijuara** (14 km 1,100 m) and Bhuntar (5 km), where a jeepable road goes off to the right to **Jari** (20 km) and **Shoja** (40 km) to the **Jalori Pass** (4,330 m). NH 21 continues straight to Kulu (10 km 1,200 m).

Kulu is the district headquarters but not the main tourist centre. It sprawls along the W bank of the Beas and the grassy *maidans* on the S side are the sites for annual festivals such as **Dasara** which is usually vivid and colourful. If you are planning to travel to **Manali**, you can give this a miss unless it is Dasara.

Local Festivals End of Apr. Colourful 3 day *Cattle Fair* attracts villagers from the surrounding area who attend to trade. Numerous cultural events accompany.

Dasara is a festival sacred to the goddess **Durga**. Elsewhere in India it is an occasion that tends to be overshadowed by **Diwali** which follows a few weeks later. In this part of the Himalaya it is a great social event and a get-together of the Gods. Every village has one and they all come to Kulu. The festival starts on the 10th day of the rising moon – **Vijay Dashmi** – and continues for a week.

N.B.   In recent years what was once a great social and religious event has become commercialised, with the stalls and traders outnumbering the gods and the ceremonies being performed on a sound stage.

Dasara celebrates Rama's victory over the demon Ravana. Elsewhere Ravana's effigy is burnt. In Kulu it isn't. From their various high perches the gods come to Kulu, drawn in their *rath* (chariot) by their villagers, to pay homage to Raghunathji who is ceremoniously brought from his temple in Kulu. The goddess Hadimba, patron deity of the Kulu Rajas has to come before any other lesser deities is allowed near. Her chariot is the fastest and her departure marks the end of the festivities. All converge on the maidan on the first evening of the festival in a long procession with shrill trumpeters loudly proclaiming the advance. Thereafter there are dances, music and a market. During the high point of the fair a buffalo is sacrificed in front of a jostling crowd. Jamlu, the village God of Malana, high up in the hills, follows an old tradition. He watches the festivities from across the river, but refuses to take part! On the last day Raghunathji's *rath* is taken to the river bank where a small bonfire is lit to symbolise the burning of Ravana. Raghunathji is then carried back to his temple in a wooden palanquin.

Places of Interest Sultanpur Palace contained some very fine examples of the

Kulu style of miniature painting where the characteristic features are the simple rural nature of the scenes and the lack of sophistication of the human subject, a reflection that the artists were comparatively simple people. Most have been removed to Delhi.

The Temples   These bulky curvilinear structures seem well suited to the environment. They are like the huge boulders that are often found in river beds and on hillsides. A peculiar feature of these Nagara temples is the umbrella-shaped covering made of wood or zinc sheets placed over and around the *amalaka* stone which forms the top of the spire.

The **Raghunathji Temple**, in Raghunathpura, 1 km from **Dhalpur**. This is the temple of the principal god of the Dasara festival (see above). Inside there is little of interest except the shrine. It is a stiff climb to the village of **Bhekhli**, 3 km from Kulu, to see the **Jagannathi Temple**. The views are very good. **Vaishno Devi Temple**, 4 km N on the **Kulu-Manali** road is really a small cave with an image of the goddess Vaishno.

Bijli Mahadev is connected by jeepable road, 8 km from **Kulu** at 2435 m. The temple is sited on a high bluff and has a 20 m iron rod on top which is reputedly struck by *bijli* (lightning), shattering the stone *lingam* inside. The priests put the lingam together each time with *ghee* (clarified butter) and a grain mixture, until the next strike breaks it apart again!

The *Bajaura Temple* is located on the banks of the Beas river, about 200 m off the Kulu-Mandi road. Its ancient name was **Hat** or Hatta and it is a massive structure magnificently decorated with images of Durga, Mahishamardini, Vishnu and Ganesh in the three sided niches. Floriated scrollwork adorn the outer walls. Inside is a large *yoni-lingam*. PWD Rest House at Bajaura.

Hotels   The choice is quite limited and the accommodation basic. The **C** *Silver Moon Travellers Lodge* (HPTDC) is probably the best. It is perched on a hill at the entrance to the town and is quite small. 6 doubles with baths and rm heaters.
   The newish **D** *Rohtang*, Dhalpur, T 2303 has 12 rm with bath. Restaurant (Indian and Chinese). Simple, clean and good value. **E** *Empire*, T 97, is close to the Travellers Lodge. 6 doubles, 3 triples. **D** *Sarvari* (HPTDC), T 2471, is a little way S from the maidan. 8 rm and dormitory. Dining hall, TV, gardens, good views. **E** *Bijeshwar View*. New. **F** *Sa-ba*, T 118 and *Fancy Guest House* have only low prices to recommend them. Also **F** *Daulat*, nr the maidan. Around the bus stand are the **F** *Kulu Valley Hotel* and **F** *Central*.

Restaurants   The *Travellers Lodge* and *Rohtang* have restaurants. The Tourist Department's *Monal Cafe* is near the Tourist Office which offers simple meals.

Shopping   Best buys are shawls, caps, *gadmas*. Ankhara Bazaar has a *Govt Handicrafts Emporium*, *HP Khadi Emporium* and *Khadi Gramudyog*. *Charm Shilp* is good for sandals. *Bhutti Weavers Cooperative Colony* is 6 km away but they have a retail outlet in town.

Tourist Offices and Information   HPTDC Tourist Office, T 2349, is by the maidan. Open 1000-1700. Local maps available. All the HPTDC properties are nearby.

Air Services   Vayudoot fly Delhi-Kulu a few times per week (55 min). The airport is at Bhuntar, 10 km S of Kulu.

Road   There are direct **buses** to Kulu from **Shimla** (235 km), **Dharamshala**, **Chandigarh** (bypassing Shimla, 270 km, 12 hr) and **Delhi** (512 km, 15-18 hr). Most services continue on to **Manali**. For Delhi there is a range of services up to super deluxe. **Taxis** also run between Kulu, Chandigarh and Shimla.

Excursions *Parvati Valley / Manikaran,* 45 km can be walked or there is a 'luxury' coach service – details from Tourist Office. This valley runs NE from Bhuntar which is about 8 km S of Kulu. Manikaran is a hot sulphur spring, purportedly the hottest in the world. Attractive orchards and river valley scenery en route. The locals cook their food by the springs and there are male and female baths and a Sikh temple. Unfortunately, this is a popular place for dropouts. Accommodation is limited. A local bus service runs from Kulu to Bhuntar and another from Bhuntar to Manikaran.

The climb continues from Kulu to Manali. There are two roads running between them. The direct, smoother road runs along the W bank of the Beas. The old road, runs along the other side and is rougher, more circuitous and more interesting. Buses travel both routes, every two hours direct and twice a day by the old road. Don't take the latter if it is wet. En route there are the following places:

8 km N of Kulu, **Raison** is a grassy meadow favoured by trekking groups. HPTDC has 14 double rm in *Tourist Huts* by the Beas river, in a peaceful setting, bookable through the Information Office in Kulu.

Mid-way between Kulu and Manali, **Katrain and Naggar** are on opposite sides of the river. This is the widest part of the Kulu Valley and is overlooked by **Baragarh Peak** (3,325 m). **Katrain** has good accommodation at the **D** *Hotel Apple Blossom*. 9 rm in 4 stone cottages with impressive views. Spartan inside but with bathrooms. Book through the Tourist Office, Kulu, T 2349. The expensive **A** *Span Resort*, T 38, is very comfortable, but with **C** category facilities. It is very westernized with little local colour. Accommodation is in 8 attractive stone cottages with 24 rm, overlooking the river. Restaurant, bar, lounge, video room, table tennis, fishing, horse riding, travel, badminton, mini golf, Amex. Resort dining room and Riverside Restaurant have good views. Trout hatchery nearby ensures good river fishing. Reservations through travel agents or Span Motels, GF-7, Surya Kiran, 19 Kasturba Gandhi Marg, New Delhi, T 3311434.

Across the bridge at Patli Kuhl, the road climbs through dark *deodar* forests to **Naggar** which is situated high above Katrain, with its castle. It is traditionally believed to have been built by Raja Sidh Singh in the early 16th century and was used as a royal residence and state headquarters until the 17th century when Raja Jagat Singh transferred the capital to Sultanpur (see Kulu). It continued to be used as a summer palace by subsequent rulers until the British took over the region in 1846, when it was sold to the Major Hay, the first Assistant Commissioner, for next to nothing. He Europeanised part of it – fitted staircases, fireplaces etc. This quaint rough stone fort is built round a courtyard with verandahs all round the outside. The views over the valley are stunning. It is now the **D** *Hotel Castle Naggar.* Book in advance (as it it popular) through the Tourist Office, Kulu, T 2349. 7 rm. Very spartan. The *Poonam Fruit Garden Hotel* with 6 rm is a comparatively new enterprise. Also a *Forest Rest House.*

There are a number of temples around the castle. The 11th century **Gauri Shankar Shiva Temple**, near the market is on the approach to the castle. Opposite the front of the castle is the **Chatar Bhuj Temple** to Vishnu. Higher up are two more, the **Tripura Sundri Temple** with a multi-level roof in the Himachal style, and above that the **Murlidhar Krishna Temple**.

    Also above the castle is the **Nicholas Roerich museum/gallery**. Roerich was born in St Petersburg, studied law to please his father, then switched to painting and archaeology. In Russia he achieved great renown as an artist and set and costume designer for *Prince Igor* and other ballets. Shortly after the Russian Revolution, he left Russia and spent time in Finland, England, America before embarking on two Trans-Himalayan Expeditions and settling in Kulu. Here he spent the remainder of his life. He died in Dec 1947. The views from this fine little museum are excellent. Check at the Kulu Tourist Information Office, T 2349, for opening times.

If you are travelling on the old road, 12 km N of Naggar and only 6 km S of Manali, is **Jagatsukh**, the capital of Kulu before Naggar. There are some very fine stone temples here.

Manali

Population 20,000 approx. 1,926 m *Climate.* Temp. Summer Max 25°C, Min 12°C. Winter Max 15°C, Min 3°C. Average annual rainfall 1780 mm. *Best season* Spring (Mar-Apr) and post monsoon (Sep-Nov) are the best periods.

At the northern end of the valley, **Manali** is the principal town and tourist destination of the Kulu Valley but it is not a hill station and there are few Raj-style buildings. If anything, this adds to its charm. in the summer it is packed with Pahari-speaking Kulus, Lahoulis, Nepali labourers, Tibetan refugees and foreign and Indian tourists. Apples are to Kulu what apricots are to Hunza, and Manali is the centre of a flourishing orchard industry. It is also the trailhead for a number of interesting and popular treks. The town of Manali is comparatively new, and not particularly attractive. The old town, 2 km away, is well worth a visit.

Local Festivals Feb – Week-long winter sports carnival. May – Annual colourful *Doongri Forest festival* at Hadimba Devi Temple which is celebrated by hill women.

Places of Interest Hadimba Devi Temple (1553) is about 2 km from the Tourist Office. The walk to this temple in a forest clearing, is pleasant. The temple built by Maharaja Bahadur Singh in 1553 looks a little like a pagoda with its triple roof with a carved wooden doorway which has inscriptions. The goddess Hadimba plays an important part in the annual festival at Kulu. Another major festival here in May. The **Tibetan Monastery** is not old but is attractive and the centre of a small carpet making industry. Rugs and other handicrafts are for sale. The colourful **Market** is worth visiting, where you can buy Tibetan souvenirs.

Hotels Few hotels have a/c rm, since it is not needed. If you are travelling in winter, heating is desirable. There are large discounts in the winter while the peak period is May to Aug, with hotels charging most in May and June when it can be very difficult to find accommodation. The modest hotels may only provide hot water in buckets. Many have a simple, rustic charm.
A/B Log Huts (HPTDC). T 39. 12 huts with 2 bedrooms, sitting rm, bath and fully furnished with kitchen and refrigerator. Don't be fooled by the name. These are fully equipped cottages in a beautiful setting. Cafeteria nearby and rm service. Peaceful.
C *Piccadilly*, The Mall. T 113-4, Cable: Piccotel, Telex: 03904-205. 44 rm. Centrally heated. Restaurant bar, coffee shop, car hire and travel, TV. **C** *Ambassador Resorts*. T 173, Cable: Holiday. 40 rm **C** *Honeymoon Inn*, Aleo. T 233. 37 rm. Restaurant, discotheque, special arrangements for honeymooners, games room, tours, TV. **C** *Preet*, HN21, T 129, Telex: 03904-206. 34 rm. Restaurant, 24 hr coffee shop, indoor games, TV. **C** *Panchratan Resorts*, near Log Huts, T 163. 30 rm. Centrally heated. Restaurant, bar, coffee shop, travel and car hire.
C *Honeymoon Cottages* (HPTDC), T 34. 12 fully furnished cottages. **C** *John Banon's Guesthouse*, near Circuit House, The Mall. T 35, Cable: John Banon. 12 rm. Full board, rm service, garden. The Banon family has been in the valley for the last century and many of them are now running guesthouses. Popular with trekkers. Peaceful, simple and rustic but very pleasant.
D *Hotel Holiday Home*, near Circuit House, The Mall. T 101, Cable: Neemal. 16 rm. Restaurant, car hire, TV. Good bath rooms and good views. **D** *Pinewood*, The Mall, T 118. 9 rm. Full board available, gardens. Run by the Banon family. Attractive rooms, good views, quiet. Closed in winter. **D** *New Hope*, The Mall, T 78. 14 rm with phone and some with good mountain views. Restaurant, tours and trekking, winter sports. Has seen better days. Simple, rustic, quiet, away from centre. **D** *Chetna*, near Log Huts. T 245. 13 rm. Restaurant, TV. **D** *Highland*, near Log Huts. T 99. 15 rm. Restaurant with TV. A stone building with cheerful rooms. **D** *Ashok Travellers Lodge* (ITDC), Naggar Rd, T 31. 10 rm and suites with bath. Restaurant (Indian, Continental), 18 hr rm service, TV lounge. Away from centre but quiet, with superb views. **D** *Rohtang Manaslu* (HPTDC), near Circuit House, The Mall, T 32. 27 rm, incl some 4-bedded. Restaurant, 18 hr rm service. Away from centre but with views. **D** *Highway Inn*, The Mall, T 220. 15 rm. Restaurant, TV lounge. **D** *Moonlight*, The Mall, T 205, Cable: Moonlight. 8 rm. Restaurant, TV, 24 hr rm service, car hire and travel. **D** *Pineview*, The Mall, T 144. 8 rm. Restaurant, 24 hr rm service. **D** *Central View Tourist Hotel*. 16 rm, TV in some. 18 hr rm service, car hire and tours. **D** *Anupam*, The Mall, T 181. 14 rm. Restaurant 24 hr rm service, TV. **D** *Woodlines*, The Mall, T 52. Restaurant, car hire. **D** *Samrat*, The Mall, T 56. 36 rm. Restaurant, 24 hr rm service, car hire. **D** *Lhasa*, Model Town, T 134. Restaurant (Indian), 24 hr rm service. **D** *Naveen*, The Mall, T 211, Cable: Naveen. 22 rm. Restaurant, TV, car hire. **D** *Marble*, The Mall. T 86. 18 rm. Restaurant, 18 hr rm service. **D** *Paradise*, The Mall, T 65. 15 rm. Restaurant, TV, 18 hr rm service. **D** *Aroma*, Model Town, nr Tibetan monastery, T 12. 12 rm with bath. Restaurant TV. **D** *Solang*, School Road, T 190. 12 rm. 24 hr rm service, TV.
E *Tourist Lodge* (HPTDC). 32 rm. 4-bedded rooms available. Spartan but acceptable. Bring your own towel. Situated on bank of Beas. **E** *Beas*, (HPTDC), nr Tourist Office. Room service. Magnificent river view is the main recommendation **E** *Snowlines*, The Mall, T 205. Room service. **E** *New Neel Kamal*, T 62. 31 rm. Restaurant 24 hr rm service. **E** *Ashiana*, The Mall, T 232. Restaurant 24 hr rm service, TV. **E** *Hill Top*, School Rd, T 140. 9 rm. 18 hr rm service. Hilltop location. Modest accommodation **E** *Pujara Shiraz*, School Rd. 9 rm. 18 hr rm service. **E** *Silmog*, The Mall, T 73. 15 rm. **E** *Ajanta*, Model Town, T 5. 10 rm. 24 hr rm service. **E** *Sunshine Guest House*, The Mall, T 20. 10 rm. Restaurant (Indian, Continental), rm service. Away from centre, so quiet. Family atmosphere, rustic but with comfortable public rm. Good value. **E** *Taj Palace*, Model Town, T 243. 8 rm. 24 hr rm service. **E** *Shivalik*, The Mall, T 22. 16 rm. 24 hr rm service, TV lounge. **E** *Hill Queen*, 48 Model Town, T 162. 24 hr

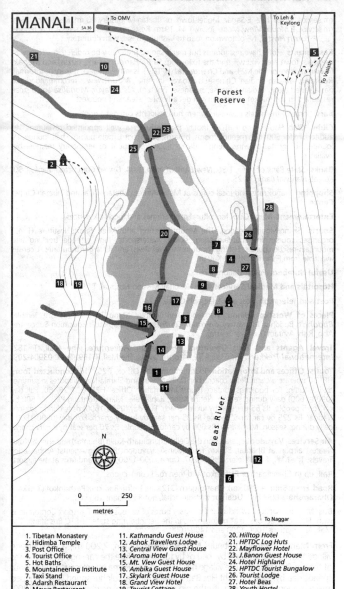

MANALI   SA 36

To OMV

To Leh & Keylong

To Vasisth

Forest Reserve

Beas River

To Naggar

N

0   250
metres

1. Tibetan Monastery
2. Hidimba Temple
3. Post Office
4. Tourist Office
5. Hot Baths
6. Mountaineering Institute
7. Taxi Stand
8. Adarsh Restaurant
9. Mayur Restaurant
10. Rohtang Cafe

11. *Kathmandu Guest House*
12. *Ashok Travellers Lodge*
13. *Central View Guest House*
14. *Aroma Hotel*
15. *Mt. View Guest House*
16. *Ambika Guest House*
17. *Skylark Guest House*
18. *Grand View Hotel*
19. *Tourist Cottage*

20. *Hilltop Hotel*
21. *HPTDC Log Huts*
22. *Mayflower Hotel*
23. *J.Banon Guest House*
24. *Hotel Highland*
25. *HPTDC Tourist Bungalow*
26. *Tourist Lodge*
27. *Hotel Beas*
28. *Youth Hostel*

rm service, TV, car hire. **E** *Sagar*, Model Town, nr Tibetan Monastery. 10 rm. Restaurant 18 hr rm service. **E** *Mount View*, Model Town, T 44. 19 rm. Restaurant 24 hr rm service, roof terrace.
   F *Youth Hostel*, NE of town on road to Vashisht. Basic, with dormitory.

Restaurants Hotel have restaurants but meals should preferably be ordered in advance. In the main town area you will find the following: *Sa Ba Parlour* (snack, pizzas) and *Mehak*, (Indian veg) are on the Mall, and *Chandratal* (HPTDC), is in the town centre and is informal. *Rohtang, Adarsh* (Indian, Chinese) is also very informal; *Mountview* is recommended and has a varied menu (Indian, Chinese, Japanese, Tibetan). Also *Mayur, Monalisa* and a small restaurant in the market where you can get a bowl of steaming noodles!

Bars Some of the hotels have bars where non residents can get a drink.

Clubs *Club House*, and HPTDC facility that includes a well appointed restaurant, an auditorium for 500, two meeting rooms, billiards, cards room, multi-purpose hall, lounge, TV lounge, library, table tennis, tennis, dance floor. Permanent or temporary membership available.

Banks *State Bank of India*, T 36. *New Bank of India*, T 64. *United Commercial Bank*, T 30. *Punjab National Bank*, T 125.

Shopping Handicrafts and local curios at Main Market, Tibetan Bazar and Tibetan Carpet Centre.

Entertainment *Manu Club*, for cultural programmes and local folk dances.

Sports Skiing/Mountaineering. The Mountaineering and Allied Sports Institute (T 42) organises courses in mountaineering, skiing, watersports, high altitude trekking and mountain-rescue courses. Fishing: Trout in the river Beas, and its larger tributaries. Licenses available from Fisheries Officer, Katrain.

Useful Numbers Police Station: T 26.

Hospitals and Medical Services Civil Hospital; Mission Hospital, T 79.

Post and Telegraph Post and Telegraph Office, T 24.

Places of Worship *Hindu*: Hadimba Devi Temple; Manu Temple; Vashisht Temple. *Buddhist*: Buddhist Monastery. *Spiritual Centres*: Rajyoga Spiritual Education Subcentre, Also; Rishi Ashram (Tapasya Centre).

Travel Agents and Tour Operators *Himalayan Adventure*, The Mall, T 182. *International Trekkers*, The Mall, T 72. *Arohi Travels*, The Mall, T 139. Telex: 03904-209.

Tourist Offices and Information Tourist Information Office, T 25, 116. **Conducted Tours** HPTDC operate a/c and delux coaches on Delhi-Manali and Shimla-Manali routes in summer and autumn. For bookings contact Tourist Information Office, HPTDC, T 25, 60. Full day (0900-1600) daily during season. Nehru Kund, Rahla Falls, Marhi, Rohtang Pass. Rs 500 by car for 5 people, Rs 65 per seat by luxury coach. Full day (0900-1600) daily during season. Naggar. Rs 225 by car for 5 people, Rs 35 per seat by luxury coach. Full day (0900-1800) daily during season. Manikaran. Rs 600 by car for 5 people, Rs 70 per seat by luxury coach.

Air Services Vayudoot operates on the Delhi-Chandigarh-Kullu (Bhuntar) and Shimla-Kulu. Nearest airport at Bhuntar, 50 km from Manali. Vayudoot Booking Agents: Ambassador Travels, The Mall, T 110. Telex: 03904-207. Open 1000-1700. Buses and taxis at the airport.

Rail up to Chandigarh or Pathankot and then road connections.

Road From: **Shimla** (280 km); **Chandigarh** (312 km); **Delhi** (838 km); **Pathankot** (326 km); **Dharamshala** (253 km), **Udaipur** (**NB** Himachal, not Rajasthan; 166 km).

Bus Manali is serviced by delux and ordinary buses of various State Transport Corporations with direct connections to all major towns in the neighbouring states. HRTC Bus Stand, The Mall. Reservations,1000-1200 and 1400-1600.

From Manali the road continues N to *Vashisht* (3 km; 2,200 m), a small hillside village that can be reached by road or by footpath. Note the carvings on the houses of the wealthy farmers. The village has Vashisht and Rama temples with the sulphur springs nearby – the Vashisht Hot Baths where natural sulphur spring water is piped into a modern bath-house with the old stone lined pool nearby. Open 0700-1300, 1400-1600, 1800-2200. Small charge for a 20-30 minute bath. Café serves hot and cold drinks, 0700- 2200. Recommended after trekking or rigourous road travel.

The road then climbs steeply through **Rahala** (15 km, 2,600 m) to the **Rohtang Pass** (14 km, 4,075 m). This is the only route for foreigners into the region of Lahul and Spiti. Follow the road a further 18 km to a road junction, the road on the right leading to **Futuruni**, **Losar** and **Kaza**. Bear left to **Khoksar** (3 km, 3,170 m). The road remains at this height all the way to **Patsea** (92 km).

Lahul and Spiti

These two regions lie N of the Himalayan Axis in a rain shadow area. The climate and terrain is very similar to Ladakh's. Upper Lahul comprises the Bhaga and Chandra valleys, Lower Lahul the region below the confluence. Spiti and Kinnaur lie to the E. The whole region is approached by road from three directions: **i.** From Shimla on the road which runs up to the Tibetan border through Kinnaur. **ii.** From Manali over the Rohtang Pass (Altitude 3,915 m) into Upper Lahul. **iii.** From Zanskar and Ladakh. Travellers can only enter by road over the Rohtang Pass. There is a trekking route from Manali to Zanskar.

A high altitude culture The atmosphere in Lahul and Spiti is much drier than in the Kulu valley. The air is crisp, biting when windy. The temperatures are more extreme both in summer and winter and most of the landscape is barren and bleak. The annual rainfall is very low so cultivation is restricted to the ribbons of land that fringe rivers with irrigation potential. The crops grown are chosen for their hardiness and ability to withstand the arid conditions. They include potatoes, wheat, barley and millet. The local inhabitants farm suitable land, raise goats and traditionally have combined this with some Tibetan trading. The people are of Mongol origin, which is evident from their facial features. In Lahul, most are Hindus or Buddhists, while Spiti is almost completely Buddhist, the religion being a Tibetan form of **Buddhism**.

Early history Historically there are similarities between this region and Ladakh since in the 10th century Lahul, Spiti and Zanskar were part of the Ladakh kingdom. The Hindu Rajas in Kulu paid tribute to Ladakh. In the 17th century Ladakh was defeated by a combined Mongol – Tibetan force. Later Lahul was separated into Upper Lahul which fell under the control of Kulu, and Lower Lahul which came under the Chamba Rajas. The whole region came under the Sikhs as their empire expanded whilst under the British Lahul and Kulu were part of the administrative area centred on Kangra. Spiti was part of the Maharaja of Kashmir's state of Kashmir and Ladakh but was later exchanged for territories formerly belonging to Kangra. Under the British, communications were improved and little else. Strategic considerations were far more important than economic development.

It is possible to travel from **Manali** over the 3915 m Rohtang Pass to **Keylong**, the principal town of the region. The road is only open from the end of June to the end of October. Traders and trekkers negotiate the pass out of season. In season, HPTDC run a daily tour by bus from Manali to the pass and back. It costs approximately Rs 60 and is popular with Indian tourists who want to see and feel snow. Details from the Tourist Office, Manali.

Warning It is not possible to go beyond Keylong by vehicle if you are a foreigner, though you are free to trek.

SHIMLA TO KANGRA, DHARAMSHALA AND CHAMBA

It is possible to reach the Kangra Valley from **Shimla** and **Mandi** to the E, **Hoshiarpur** to the S or **Pathankot** to the W. The fastest route by road from New Delhi is via Ambala, Ludhiana and Hoshiarpur.

From **Shimla** take the road to **Bilashpur** (66 km) and **Mandi** (58 km) – see page 447. Out of Mandi continue northwest through **Drang** (19 km) and **Urla** (12 km) to **Jogindernagar** (25 km 1,220 m). The road continues at the same height through **Chowntra** (17 km) and **Baijnath** (5 km), where there is a PWD Rest House, to **Palampur** (16 km).

Palampur (1,260 m), 35 km E of Dharamshala. A pleasant little town surrounded by old tea plantations established by the British. The temples at **Baijnath**, 16 km E of Palampur are old by hill standards, and date from at least 1204. Originally known as **Kirangama**, it's name was changed after the temple was built to **Siva** in his form as Vaidyanath, the Lord of Physicians. It is the best example of the Nagara style of temple architecture. The walls have the characteristic niches, and the *shikhara** (tower) has an *amalaka** and pot finial at the summit.

The **Vaidyanatha Temple** stands by the roadside on the **Palampur-Mandi** road within a vast rectangular enclosure.

The temple faces W and has an *mandala** (antechamber) supported by four pillars. Note the graceful balcony window on the N wall. The niches enshrine the images of **Chamunda**, **Surya** and **Karttikeya** and a life-size stone statue of Nandi stands at the entrance. There are miniature shrines and memorial stones within the complex.

Accommodation At Palampur, there is the HPTDC **E** *Hotel T-Bud* which is about 1 km from the bus stand. 12 rm and a dormitory. Restaurant, rm service, garden, terrace. Clean and quiet. **E** *Palace Motel*, Taragarh, Kangra, nearby. T Baijnath 34. 12 rm. Good restaurant, rm service. Former palace with period furniture.

From Palampur the road continues winding westwards, closely following and crossing the railway line. It passes through **Nagrota** (22 km) and **Mataur** (12 km) where there is a left turn to **Kangra** (6 km, 450 m). The Kangra Valley is situated between the Dhaula Dhar and the Siwalik foothills, starts near Mandi, runs northwest to Shahpur near Pathankot. It is named after the town of **Kangra**, but now the largest and main centre is **Dharamshala.**

Formerly **Kangra**, 18 km S of Dharamashala, was much more extensive and at one time was the second most important kingdom in the W Himalayas after Kashmir. The capital, Kangra was also known as Bhawan or Nagarkot, and overlooks the Banganga River. The fort stands on a steep rock dominating the valley. The temple of **Bajeshwari Devi** achieved a reputation for wealth and attracted some of the invaders of N India. **Mahmud of Ghazni** sacked it in 1008 and **Firoz Tughluq** plundered it in 1360. During Mahmud's invasion, many of the court artists fled to neighbouring **Chamba** and **Kulu**. The Rajas submitted to Mughal rule.

In 1620 **Shah Jahan** captured the fort for his father the **Emperor Jahangir**. Kangra became a Mughal province. On its decline they reasserted their independence and under Sanser Chand Kangra sought to extend its boundaries into the Chamba and Kulu Valleys. This was forestalled when the vigorous and powerful Gurkhas appeared on the scene from Nepal and conquered what is now the hill region of UP and Himachal Pradesh.

Under **Sanser Chand** the region prospered and the **Kangra** school of miniature painting developed. This is in the style of Mughal miniature painting, but the subject matter is different. Usually the Rajas and the gods and their followers are depicted in a local setting. With the rise of the Sikh Empire, the valley was occupied until the Treaty of Amritsar. Under the British, **Dharamshala** was made the administrative capital of the region, which led to the decline of the town Kangra. Both the fort and the temple were destroyed in the great earthquake of 1905.

Excursions *Masrur*, 15 km S of Kangra, has fifteen 9-10th century temples excavated out of solid rock. They are badly eroded and partly ruined but show similarities with the larger temples at Ellora in Maharashtra. Several panels from these temples are at the State Museum, Shimla.

Jawalamukhi, 34 km S of Kangra, is one of the most popular Hindu pilgrimage sites in Himachal Pradesh. A temple is set against a cliff and from a fissure comes an inflammable gas. This has given rise to the eternal flame. Note Emperor Akbar's gift of the golden dome. In Mar/Apr there are colourful celebrations during the *Shakti Festival*. The HPTDC **D** *Hotel Jwalaji* has a/c and non a/c rooms and a dormitory. Also a *PWD Rest House*. The road N climbs the 18 km to **Dharamshala.**

Dharamshala

Population approx. 16,000. 1,250 -1,980 m. *Climate* Summer Max 38°C, Min 22°C, Winter Max 15°C, Min 0°C. Annual rainfall 2900 -3800 mm, mostly Jun-Sep.

Places of Interest Founded in 1855, it has one of the most spectacular settings for a Hill Station. It is built along a spur of the **Dhauladhar** range and varies in height from 1200 m at the bazaar to 1800 m at *Macleodganj*. It is surrounded by trees and is set against a backdrop of peaks rising to over 4,750 m on three sides. The great granite mountains almost overhang the town. Views are superb, not only of the mountains but also over the Kangra Valley and Siwaliks.

There are two sections to the town, the upper McLeodganj and the lower Dharamshala, one 450 m higher than the other. As a result temperatures vary sharply. The distance between them is almost 10 km by road from centre to centre but there is a shorter, steeper path that takes about 40 minutes to cover.

Tibetan influence In Dharamshala there is a strong Tibetan influence although some visitors are disappointed that it did not strike them as a particularly Buddhist town. The **Dalai Lama** settled here after his flight across the Himalaya following the Chinese invasion of Tibet in October 1959. There is a monastery at Mcleodganj a short distance along from the Dalai Lama's residence and a Library on the way to Mcleodganj from Dharamshala.

Mcleodganj has attracted the hippy community and represents Kathmandu on a small scale with its cheap hotels and little Tibetan-run Restaurants with all the old favourites like banana pancakes. In fact, most visitors tend to stay in Mcleodganj where the Tibetan community has tended to takeover the hospitality business and provide cheap but clean and friendly little establishments.

Dharamshala was one of the eighty hill stations established by the British between 1815 and 1847 though it was not on a par with Shimla, Nainital and Mussoorie in terms of popularity and size.

The Church of **St John-in-the-Wilderness** (1860) is a short distance below Mcleodganj on the way to Forsythganj. Along with other buildings in the area it was destroyed by the earthquake of 1905 but has been rebuilt. The 8th Lord of Elgin, one of the few Viceroys to die in office, is buried here. Apparently, it was his wish as it reminded him of his beloved native Scotland. There are some very attractive stained glass windows.

Hotels There are two accommodation areas, Dharamshala and Mcleodganj. There are no a/c rms as it is unnecessary. In May and June, accommodation may be difficult to find.

In Dharamshala: **D** *Dhauladhar* (HPTDC), Kotwali Bazar. T 2256. 21 double rm with bath and phone and inexpensive Dormitory. Restaurant, bar, pleasant garden. Terrace for meals. The cheap **E** and **F** hotels are all Tibetan run. The *Rising Moon* is relaxed and basic with a dormitory, rooms with and without bathrooms. The *Tibet United Association Hotel* is similar. Near the fountain is the *Deyki Palber* and the *Shimla* is opposite the Tourist Office and downhill beyond the Bus Stand is the *Sun and Snow*.

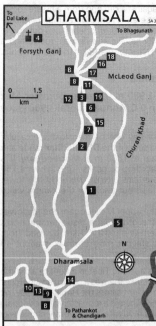

DHARMSALA SA 34

To Dal Lake
To Bhagsunath
Forsyth Ganj
McLeod Ganj
0   1.5
km
Churan Khad
N
Dharamsala
To Pathankot
& Chandigarh

1. Dalai Lama's Residence
2. Tibetan Monastery
3. Chorten
4. Church of St John
   in the Wilderness
5. Tibetan Library
6. Handicrafts Shop
7. Post Office
8. Bank
9. Tourist Office
10. Rising Moon Restaurant
11. Tashi's Restaurant
12. Om Restaurant
13. Dhauladhar Hotel
14. Dekyi Palber Hotel
15. Hotel Bhagsu
16. Namgyal
    Guest House
17. Hotel Tibet
18. Green Hotel
19. Toepa Hotel &
    Restaurants

In Mcleodganj: D *Bhagsu* (HPTDC). T 2290. Doubles with bath and dormitory. Restaurant, rm service, large lawns, good views. Cheap hotels along Bhagsu Rd are extremely popular and often full. The **E** *Tibet* has the most luxurious rooms, some with bath and TV, and a restaurant. The *Koko Nor* and *Green Guest House* are more basic but less expensive. The *Tibetan Himalayan Restaurant* has a few rooms and the *Namgyal* is similar. Away from Bhagsu Rd the *Om* is very popular and the *Toepa* on the main street is comparably priced.

Restaurants   Because of Western demand and the willingness of the Tibetan community to try and accommodate it, the cuisine of Dharamshala caters to those whose palates have become rather jaded with Indian food. You can be adventurous and try Tibetan soups, noodle dishes, fried *momos* and *shabakleb.* In Dharamshala there is the *Cafe Dhauladhar*, Kotwali Bazar~has a good selection of western, Indian and Tibetan dishes. You can eat out on the terrace with good views. The *Rising Moon* is pleasant but no place for a quick bite.

Mcleodganj has more to offer. The *Om* is popular, relaxed and inexpensive, the *Tibet* is busy, the *Tibetan Himalaya Restaurant* has good food and the *Green* is also popular. *Teopas's* is very informal and serves very good Tibetan dishes and also has good cakes. Near the bus stand is *Sangey Pasang*, *Tashi's* and *Shambala*. All do good breakfasts.

Banks   *Bank of India*, T 2577. *New Bank of India*, T 2201. *Punjab National Bank*, T 2340. *State Bank of India*, T 2778. *Kangra Central Bank*, T 2357. *State Bank of Patiala*, T 2355.

Shopping   Kotwali Bazar and Mcleodganj are major shopping areas in Dharamshala. There are a lot of Tibetan handicrafts for sale including wool carpets. At the Sunday market in Dharamshala you can buy good handicrafts, handwoven cloth and garments.

Entertainment   *Tibetan Institute of Performing Arts,* Dharamshala, stages occasional music and dance performances. Details at Tourist Office.

Local Transport   Buses and taxis are available for various places in and around Dharamshala. It is about 10 km from Dharamshala to McLeodganj by road, a 45 min bus ride costing approx Rs 2 per person. You can **walk** by taking the right hand road which is steep and passes by the Tibetan Library which takes about 40 min.

Sports   Fishing. At Nadaun and Dehra Gopipur, for mahaseer. Best season mid-Feb to end-Apr and Oct to end-Nov. Licensing authority: Assistant Warden of Fisheries, Dehra-Gopipur. **Trekking** equipment can be hired from a branch of the Mountaineering Institute (Manali) at Dharamshala. Best season Apr-Jun and Sep-Nov.

Useful Number Police: T 2303.

Hospitals and Medical Services District Hospital, T 2333. Tibetan Welfare Hospital, T 2453. Of interest to followers of alternative medicine. Dr Dolma's Clinic (for Tibetan treatment).

Post and Telegraph GPO, below the bus stand on the main road from Chandigarh.

Tourist Offices and Information HPTDC Tourist Information Office, Kotwali Bazar, T 2363. HP Department of Tourism Information Office, T 2107.

Air Service Nearest airport at **Amritsar** (200 km).

Rail Nearest railway station is at **Pathankot**.

Bus All buses start at Dharamsala and most leave early. About 4 buses a day to **Simla** (317 km, 10 hr) and **Delhi** (521 km, 15 hr). Direct and regular State and private bus services link Dharamshala with **Chandigarh** (248 km, 9 hr), **Jalandhar** (197 km, 8 hr), **Pathankot** (90 km, 4 hr), **Kulu** (214 km, 10 hr) and **Manali** (253 km, 13 hr).

Road Dharamshala is linked by State Highways to Pathankot and Jalandhar, on NH1, and NH1A. To: **Madras** (2,678 km); **Bombay** (1,929 km); **Calcutta** (1,763 km).

Warning It is dangerous to drive at night in the hills – anywhere. The roads are not lit and the risks of running off the edge are great. Few local drivers drive at night.

Excursions in the Kangra Valley From Mcleodganj there are a number of interesting walks. There is a 2 km stroll to *Bhagsu* where there is a spring and a temple. you can continue on towards the snowline. *Lake Dal*, 3 km down from Mcleodganj is rather uninteresting. *Dharamkot*, also about 3 km from Mcleodganj has very fine views.

It is an 8 km trek from Mcleodganj to **Triund** (2,827 m) which is at the foot of **Dhauladhar**. A further 5 km brings you to the snowline where there is a *Forest Rest House*.

To travel W from Dharmashala or Kangra rejoin the Mandi-Pathankot road at Gaggal. From Gaggal the road drops steadily through Shahpur (12 km) and Kotla (18 km) to **Nurpur** (22 km 420 m). Emperor **Jahangir** named this after his wife in 1622, two years after Kangra had been taken from him by his son **Shah Jahan**. The fort is now in ruins. Some fine carving remains visible along with a Krishna temple, also in ruins. Nurpur has a *PWD Rest House*.

From Nurpur continue to **Chakki** (13 km). The main road continues to Pathankot (11 km) and the main road up into Kashmir. The road to the right leads up to Dalhousie and Chamba. Chamba State occupied the upper part of the Ravi river valley and some of the Chenab Valley. Founded in the 9th century, it occupied an important position on the trade route from Lahul to Kashmir and was known as 'The Middle Kingdom'. Its relative isolation led to the nurturing of the arts – painting, temple sculpture, *rumal* embroidery imitating typical miniature paintings and handicrafts. In the first half of the 19th century (1810-46) it was under Sikh rule.

From **Chakki** (370 m) the road climbs to **Dhar** (14 km, 680 m) where a road to the left leads to **Udhampur** and Kashmir. At Dunera (17 km) there is a barrier gate to keep traffic to a one way system for the next 28 km to **Banikhet** (1,680 m). The road continues 8 km to **Dalhousie**.

Dalhousie

Population approx 8,000 2,030 m *Climate*. Temp. Summer Max

24°C, Min 16°C. Winter Max 10°C, Min 1°C. Annual rainfall 1500 mm.

Purchased by the British in 1853 from the Raja of Chamba, Dalhousie, named after the Governor-General (1848-56), sprawls out over five hills just E of the *Ravi river*. Lt-Col Napier (later Lord Napier of Magdala) selected the site. By 1867 it was a municipality and a sanatorium. It reached its zenith in the 1920s and 1930s as a cheaper, but arguably more attractive, alternative to Shimla. Its popularity has declined since Independence and now it is a quiet hill station. The town, however, is surrounded by forest and the distances between places make it a pleasant and relaxing place. **Rabindranath Tagore**, wrote his first poem here as a boy and **Subhash Chandra Bose** came secretly to plan his strategies during the second World War, **see page 515**. Its main importance is due to the number of educational institutions and the presence of the army.

The town centres on **Gandhi Chowk** (formerly Post Office Sq). It has an significant population of industrious Tibetans who make and sell various handicrafts, woollens jackets, cardigans and rugs. There are no buildings of great interest but a number of pleasant walks over the 5 hills. Just over 2 km from the square is **Martyr's Memorial** which commemorates **Ajit Singh**, a supporter of Subhash Chandra Bose and the Indian National Army during World War II. **Jhandra Ghat** is the old palace of Chamba rulers and is set among tall pine trees.

Hotels There are plenty of hotels in Dalhousie but many look rather down at heel, sometimes because the cost of maintaining the Raj-built structures is prohibitive, sometimes due to laziness and neglect. Nearly all, however, have good mountain views and offer discounts out of season.

D *Geetanjali*, (HPTDC), T 55. The Tourist Bungalow. **E** *Youth Hostel* (HPTDC). T 59. Good discounts for YHAI Members. Reservations: Area Manager, Tourist Information Office, T 36. **D** *Aroma-n-Clairs*, The Mall, T 99. 20 rm, large but spartan. Restaurant, bank, shop, library, TV. Generally regarded the best available with good views and character. **E** *Grand View*, above Mount View. T 23. 20 rm. Restaurant. Rather run down. **E** *Mountview*, nr Bus Stand, T 27. 24 large rm. Restaurant. Better managed than most and has good views. **E** *King's*. T 111. **F** *Fairview*, Mall Rd. T 106. **F** *Mehar's*, The Mall. T 79. **F** *New Metro*, Subhash Chowk. **F** *Lill Resort*. Dormitories and good views. Near the bus stand are *Glory* and *Lall's*, both of which are very cheap and basic.

Restaurants *Moti Mahal*, Subhash Chowk. *Metro*, Subhash Chowk *Lovely*, Subhash Chowk. *Lovely Dhaba*, GPO. *Sharma Dhaba*, GPO.

Clubs *Dalhousie Club (Army)*. Temporary membership is open to all. Rooms available and a self-contained cottage.

Banks and Exchanges *State Bank of India*, T 24; *Punjab National Bank*, T 90

Shopping *Tibetan Handicrafts Centre*, Gandhi Chowk; *Himachal Handicrafts Emporium*.

Local Transport Jeeps, ponies and *dandis* are available for visiting Khajjiar and other places in and around Dalhousie. Rates may be obtained from the local Tourist Office.

Sports Golf at Khajjiar.

Useful Addresses Police, T 26; Civil Hospital, T 26; GPO, Gandhi Chowk.

Places of Worship *Hindu*: Lakshmi Narayan Temple, Sadar Bazar; Radha Krishna Temple, Baloon Bazar. *Sikh*: Gurudwara Singh Sabha, Sadar and Baloon Bazar. *Muslim*: Mosque, Cantonment. *Christian*: St Francis Church, Subhash Chowk; St Patrick Church, Baloon Bazar; Convent Church, Subhash Chowk.

Tourist Offices and Information Himachal Tourism, Tourist Information Office, by the Bus Stand. T 36. Conducted Tours Full day (0900-1500) during the tourist season to Khajjiar by HPTDC. Rs 225 by car for 5 people, Rs 35 per seat by luxury coach.

Travel Air Nearest airport at Amritsar (200 km). **Rail** Nearest railway station at Pathankot.

Bus State and private buses connect Dalhousie with many towns and cities in the region. From Dalhousie to **Chamba** (56 km, 2 hr), **Pathankot** (80 km, 4 hr), **Dharamshala** (8-9 hr) on a very poor road.

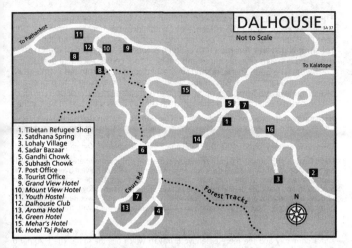

DALHOUSIE SA 37

Not to Scale

To Pathankot

To Kalatope

To Pathankot

1. Tibetan Refugee Shop
2. Satdhana Spring
3. Lohaly Village
4. Sadar Bazaar
5. Gandhi Chowk
6. Subhash Chowk
7. Post Office
8. Tourist Office
9. Grand View Hotel
10. Mount View Hotel
11. Youth Hostel
12. Dalhousie Club
13. Aroma Hotel
14. Green Hotel
15. Mehar's Hotel
16. Hotel Taj Palace

Court Rd

Forest Tracks

N

Road Dalhousie is linked by State Highway to Pathankot in Punjab on NH 1A. From: **Pathankot** (78 km); **Delhi** (559 km); **Chandigarh** (336 km); **Shimla** (414 km); **Bombay** (1967 km); **Calcutta** (1801 km); **Madras** (2716 km); **Ahmedabad** (1445 km).

Excursions *Khajjiar*, 22 km, is a long and wide *marg* or 'way' ringed by cedars with a lake in the centre. There is a golf course and a temple. The **E** *Deodar* Tourist Bungalow (HPTDC) has 11 clean rm and a dormitory. Simple restaurant, horse riding. Good setting with fields, pond and pine forest. There is also a **F** *Youth Hostel* and a *PWD Rest House*. Regular buses and more expensive tourist buses run by HPTDC. It is also a day's walk and this can be made into a short trek to Dharamshala over two days.

From Dalhousie it is a very pleasant drive to the medieval town of **Chamba** (26 km; 760 m) The higher road, at about 1800 m, passes through some beautiful forests and the small town of Khajjiar (see above). The other, winter road, takes a lower route. The distances are similar.

Chamba is situated on the S bank of the Ravi, its stone houses clinging to the hillside. The river ultimately makes its way past Lahore and the ancient site of Harappa to join the Chenab. Some see the town as having an almost Italian feel, surrounded by lush forests. In the centre is the **Chaugan**, the grassy *maidan* with a promenade.

Places of interest The **Rang Mahal** was built by Raja Umed Singh in the mid 18th century. He had been a prisoner of the Mughals for 16 years and was obviously influenced by their architectural style. Additions were made by Jit Singh (1794-1804) and Charat Singh (1808-44), neither of which enhanced the original style of the palace. It became the residence of the women of the Maharajas' until 1947. The wall paintings are splendid and represent one of the most extensive hill collections. The theme is usually religious, the Krishna stories being particularly popular. The **Bhuri Singh Museum** has a fine collection of Chamba, Kangra and Basholi schools of miniature paintings. The older ones are found in the **Devi-ri-Kothi** temple but the best were in the Rang Mahal (mentioned above). Some murals were removed to the museum after a fire, as well as wood carvings and manuscripts.

The temples There are a number of old temples in Chamba, their great curvilinear stone towers indicating the influence of Central Indian architecture from the 10th century Pratihara period. The overhanging wooden roofs are later additions. The **Lakshmi Narayana Temple** (14th century) is opposite the palace of the Chamba rulers and contains several shrines and a tank in four courts, each higher than the one before. The Gauri Shankara shrine in the third court dates from the 11th century. There are also large Shiva, Parvati and Nandi images of brass inlaid with copper and silver. The **Hariraya Temple**, S of the *chaugan* or *maidan* (meadow or open ground) is 14th century and contains a fine 9th -10th century brass sculpture of Vaikuntha.

Nomadic pastoralists Chamba is the centre of the *Gaddis*, traditionally shepherds who move their flocks with the seasons, from lower pastures during winter to higher ones after snowmelt and during the monsoon. In the winter they can be found round Kangra, Mandi and Bilaspur. The Gaddis are only found in the Dhauladhar range which separates Kangra from Chamba.

Local festivals Chaugan, the grassy meadow in the centre of town is where fairs and festivals are held. Apr – *Suhi Mela* lasts 3 days. Jul- Aug – *Minjar* to celebrate harvest over 7 days when people offer thanks to the rain gods. Decorated horses and banners are taken out in procession and mark the beginning of the festival. Sri Raghuvira is followed by other images of gods in palanquins and the festival ends with a procession to the River Ravi for immersion of *minjars* (tassels of corn). Also numerous cultural events take place with the Gaddis, Batlis and Gujjars taking part.

Hotels HPTDC has 2 establishments, the **F** *Champak* Tourist Bungalow which has doubles and a dormitory and the more expensive **E** *Iravati* which has the same. The **F** *Akhand Chandi*, College Rd, T 171 has a restaurant. There is also the **F** *Janta*.

Restaurants Apart from the ubiquitous tea shops, *Akhand Chandi* has a restaurant and there is the *Ravi View Cafe*.

Travel Bus Daily service with Dalhousie (2-3 hr). Jeeps for hire but relatively expensive.

From Chamba you can proceed up the Ravi Valley or go over the Sach Pass to Kashmir.

TREKKING FROM SHIMLA

From Shimla there are opportunities for short and long treks. Shimla is on the Hindustan-Tibet Highway. *Wildflower Hall*, 13 km beyond Shimla at 2,593 m, was the residence of Lord Kitchener, Commander-in-Chief of the Indian Army. The original building has gone but HPTDC has changed the present one into a hotel. It is set in lovely gardens, surrounded by pine forest and there are some pleasant walks from it. Further on at Naldhera, 23 km from Shimla, was **Curzon's** summer retreat. There is a HPTDC *hotel* here.

Still further on at Narkanda, 64 km from Shimla, is another. The walks from here are very good, especially up Hattu Peak. From Narkanda the highway runs down to the Sutlej valley and enters Kinnaur and Spiti. Foreigners are not allowed into these restricted areas.

From just beyond **Narkhanda** you can trek northwest over the *Jalori Pass* into the lower part of the **Kulu Valley**, joining the Kulu-Manali road at **Aut**. There is a jeepable road over much of this route. An alternative is to proceed about 35 km from **Narkhanda** to **Rampur** and then trek into the Kulu Valley via the *Bashleo Pass* (3,600 m). There are *Forest Rest Houses* en route so a tent is not essential. The pass is crossed on the third day of this five day trek.

TREKKING FROM CHAMBA

There are several short and longer treks that can be undertaken from **Chamba and Brahmaur** in the Upper Ravi Valley. To the N there are three main passes over the Pir Panjal into **Lahul**: the Kalicho, Kugti and Chobia Passes. At least 5 days should be allowed for crossing them as their heights are around 5,000 m and acclimatisation is highly desirable. All the first stages of the walks are along the Budhil River which flows through Brahmaur and is a tributary of the Ravi river. After the first two days, the services of a guide or porters are recommended for picking the right trail. Views from the passes are very good both of the Himalaya to the N and the Chenab Valley to the S. The descent from the passes is very steep. On reaching the road you can take a bus from Udaipur or Triloknath to the Kulu Valley over the Rohtang Pass.

Another trek from Brahmaur is to **Manimahesh Lake** in the Manimahesh Dhar which is essentially a spur running off the Pir Panjal. The lake is revered by locals as a resting place of Siva. The trek takes three days.

The Chamba region receives the monsoon rains but the amount is less than in the Kangra Valley to the S. A trek, particularly over the Pir Panjal into Lahul can be undertaken with the possibility of good conditions during the monsoon months of Jun-Sep. The ideal season, though, is just after the monsoon.

TREKKING IN LAHUL AND SPITI

Note Anyone trekking in this region has to take food from outside simply because Lahul does not have a surplus and there is very little available locally. This dictates the sort of trekking possible. The 'freedom' walking popular in Nepal is not really feasible. As provisions have to be taken along, porters and/or horses are required. These are not always easily available and prices fluctuate considerably. A good arrangement is to go on an organised trek with a group and thereby unload this logistical responsibility onto someone else. With this in mind the Trek into or from Zanskar is strongly recommended for the vigorously fit. You can, of course, do it independently but it requires greater planning and takes more time.

Lahul, **Zanskar** and **Ladakh** are ideal trekking destinations during the monsoon which does not affect the region, and the best season is mid-June to mid-October.

You can take a trek from Keylong up the Bhaga valley to Darcha, over the Shingo La and on to Padum, the capital of the Zanskar region. Padum is linked with Leh. The **Shingo La** is over 5,000 m so some acclimatisation is desirable. The route is well marked.

An alternative route to Zanskar is up the Chandra valley and over Baralacha La. This is a more gradual ascent and includes much fine scenery. The route taken from Manali is over the Hampta Pass to Chatru village in the Chandra Valley. To save time you can take the bus over the Rohtang Pass to the village of Chandra. The next stage of both variations is to Chandratal and then over the Baralacha Pass into Zanskar. From here you can continue on to Padum or return to Darcha in Lahul. This second option makes for a very good circular trek.

A third possibility is to trek down the Chenab Valley and either cross the Pir Panjal by one of a number of passes into the Ravi Valley to **Chamba** or carry on to **Kishtwar**.

All these treks are immensely enjoyable. There are stone huts and the occasional PWD or Forest Rest House. Always carry a tent in this area.

TREKKING IN THE KULU VALLEY

There is a variety of treks in the Kulu Valley in terms of duration and degree of difficulty. There are pleasant walks up the subsidiary valleys from Aut and Katrain with the opportunity to camp in spectacular and high locations without having to spend very long getting there. An easy option is to take the bus up to the Rohtang Pass, which is very spectacular and then walk down. There is a path, and it only takes a few hours. There are also longer treks which offer a wider variety of scenery.

Season The post-monsoon period, i.e. Sep-Nov is the most reliable season. Longer treks with crossings of high passes can be undertaken before the winter snows arrive. During the monsoon (Jun-Sep) it is wet but the rain is not continuous. It may rain all day or for only an hour or two. Visibility is affected and glimpses of mountains through the clouds are more likely than broad clear panoramic views. The compensation is that there are many flowering plants at their best. There is trekking in the spring, i.e. Apr-May but the weather is more unsettled and the higher passes may still have quite a lot of winter snow on them. There can be very good spells of fine weather during this period and it can get quite hot in May.

Acclimatisation Reasonable fitness beforehand can only enhance the experience of trekking, especially as you will be starting from only a few hundred metres above sea level. It is quite a climb up to the passes. Acclimatisation, in the form of gradual progress and preferably a rest day at around 3,500 m is strongly recommended for those intending to negotiate higher passes such as the Tentu La which is just under 5,000 m.

Equipment You will need to take your own as there are few good agencies in the Kulu Valley and what equipment there is, is often of an inferior quality. Also, there are no pony-wallah unions as in Kashmir and no fixed rates for guides, porters and horses. Ask at the hotels, Tourist Office and the Mountaineering Institute for information and assistance, **see page 454.**

Treks to the North From **Manali** you can go N into **Lahul and Spiti** by crossing the **Rohtang Pass** or the **Hampta Pass** (4,200 m). Once over the great divide of the **Pir Panjal** the treks are as briefly described later – see Trekking in Lahul (see above). W of Manali are the routes into the **Chamba and Kangra Valleys**.

The most popular route, and trek in Kulu, is from Manali up the **Solang Valley** to Beas Kund beneath **Hanuman Tibba**. From here you can return making it a pleasant four day trip. Alternatively you can proceed over the Solang Pass (also known as the **Tentu La**) and on to **Bara Bangahal.** Here you have the choice of continuing – see Trekking in Chamba above – or returning to the Kulu Valley. If you choose the second you do not have to return the same way but can backtrack to **Kaori Got** and then go over the **Manali Pass**, or you can walk from Bara Bangahal and go over the Sagar Pass. This will return you to Katrain which is halfway between Kulu and Manali.

Treks to the East The trekking E from Manali is good too with the trek to **Malana Valley** offering a good opportunity to see a relatively isolated and comparatively unspoilt hill community. From Manali you go to **Nangar** and stay at **Rumsu** (2,377 m) which is somewhat higher. The **Chanderkani Pass** (3,500 m) takes you into the Malana Valley. On the third day you can reach **Malana** (2,650 m) which is 7 km further on.

Until recently you needed a permit to enter the village, now you can stay but you will need the verbal permission of the villagers who may also provide food. You camp outside the village boundary. On the fourth day you can trek from **Malana** to **Jari** (1,500 m) where you can catch a bus to Kulu. The whole of the Malana Valley is dominated by **Deo Tibba** peak in the N.

The origin of Malana is difficult to trace. Legend has it that it was founded by a band of renegade soldiers who deserted Alexander's army in the 4th century BC. The language called Kanashi has no script and is said to include some Tibetan. However, it is more probable that their antecedents were from the plains of India.

The important deity in the valley is **Jamlu** who is believed to be a pre-Aryan god. There is a myth which says that Jamlu was carrying a casket containing all the important deities of Hinduism and while he was crossing the mountains into the Kulu Valley a strong gust of wind blew open the box and spread the deities all over the valley. Since then Malana has been known as 'The Valley of the Gods'.

TREKKING IN THE KANGRA VALLEY

There are very pleasant day walks throughout the Kangra Valley. Longer, more arduous treks are N over the Dhauladhar to Chamba or the Kulu Valley in the E.

Baijnath, **Palampur** and **Dharamshala** are popular starting points. From here you go over the **Dhauladhar** at passes such as the Indrahar and Minkiani (both from Dharamshala) and the Waru (from Palampur) then enter a feeder of the Upper Ravi Valley. Midway up the valley which lies between the Manimahesh Dhar and Dhaula Dhar ranges is Bara Bangahol.

From here you can go downstream to **Chamba** or upstream which offers the choice of at least 3 passes for crossing into the Kulu Valley. The northernmost of these is the Solang Pass which passes Beas Kund beneath Hanuman Tibba. In the middle is the Manali Pass whilst the southernmost is Sagar Pass. A good trip which includes the upper part of this valley is the round trip trek from Manali – see Trekking in the Kulu Valley above.

JAMMU AND KASHMIR

Kashmir, the treasured jewel of South Asia's northernmost region, has seen its astonishingly beautiful valleys and mountains repeatedly scarred by violence and political dispute. Its lakes, fertile valleys and remote, snow-covered peaks have drawn rulers, pilgrims and ordinary travellers from the Mughals onwards. Fought over in 1948, 1965 and 1971 by India and Pakistan, its territory is still disputed. Politically it is divided by a Line of Control between India and Pakistan. The easternmost part of that boundary across the Siachen Glacier, at over 6,000 metres, was left undemarcated. It was the scene of sporadic fighting throughout the late 1980s.

Note In late 1989 violence erupted in the Vale of Kashmir which at the time the Indian press put down to discontent with corrupt election practices of the state government. Through 1990 the Indian government also blamed the violence on Pakistani-sponsored terrorism. Throughout 1990 visitors to India were being advised not to travel to Kashmir, a recommendation which has remained in force through 1991. All foreigners entering Jammu and Kashmir and required to register their arrival.

Social indicators Area 222,000 sq km **Population** 9 million **Literacy** M 36% F 16% **Birth rate** Rural 33:1000 Urban 25:1000 **Death rate** Rural 9:1000 Urban 7:1000 **Infant mortality** Rural 74:1000 Urban 43:1000 **Registered graduate job seekers** 9,000 **Average annual income per head** : Rs 1500 **Inflation** 1981-87 82% **Religion** Hindu 32% Muslim 64% Christian 0.2% Sikh 2% Buddhist 1.2%

INTRODUCTION

The State comprises three distinct regions: Jammu, the predominantly Hindu foothills in the S, Srinagar and the Vale of Kashmir, predominantly Muslim in the centre; and Leh and Ladakh, forming the eastern highlands across the great Himalayan axis, predominantly Buddhist. Together they comprise the largest of India's Himalayan states and contain over 6 million inhabitants.

Kashmir has been one of the most visited states of India and consequently has many facilities to offer the visitor. The **Vale of Kashmir** has always been the main focus, with a superb summer climate and glorious scenery, and increasing opportunities for skiing in winter. However, there are many other attractions. **Gulmarg** and **Pahalgam** draw large numbers of visitors and offer outdoor activities such as trout fishing and trekking. Adventure sports such as white water rafting are being added to trekking in **Ladakh**. In both regions tourism is an important source of income. Most travellers to Ladakh are also attracted by its **Buddhist** and **Tibetan** culture. Tragically, the state has also experienced repeated political upheaval, and since late 1989 it has been virtually impossible for travellers to visit. In mid 1991 it seemed that there may be some chance of an improvement in the situation but it was far from clear. It will be essential for foreigners to take advice in Delhi from Indian Tourist Information and from their consulates before leaving.

The Land
The state is 222,236 sq km in area – slightly smaller than New Zealand – and is joined to the rest of India by a 30 km long boundary with **Punjab** and a 300 km boundary with **Himachal Pradesh**. Its other neighbours are foreign countries: Pakistan to the E, Tibet/China to the N and NE.

The three regions Geographically the region falls into three parts. The southern region stretches from the plains to the Pir Panjal. **Jammu** is the borderland with the Punjab, and the transitional zone between the plains and the mountains. It comprises the edge of the Punjab between the Chenab and Ravi rivers and the Siwalik hills, a band of low hills running NW to SE. In contrast to the fertile plains, these have thin, thirsty soils that are liable to erosion. Irrigation is limited and the water-table is deep. To the N the **Siwaliks** give onto the **Pir Panjal** which attain heights of 5,000 metres. These form the southern wall to the Vale of Kashmir. **The Pir Panjal** is really a double range. The northern part stretches from **Kishtwar** to **Kulu** (Himachal Pradesh) and separates the **Chenab** and **Ravi** rivers. The southern part, or **Dhauladhar**, separates the Ravi and Beas rivers and continues to Dalhousie (Himachal Pradesh). The Pir Panjal is breached only once by the combined waters of the Marwa-Warvan and Chenab.

The Vale of Kashmir, the second region, lies between the **Pir Panjal** and the **High Himalaya,** at an average altitude of 1,580 metres. It is a great syncline

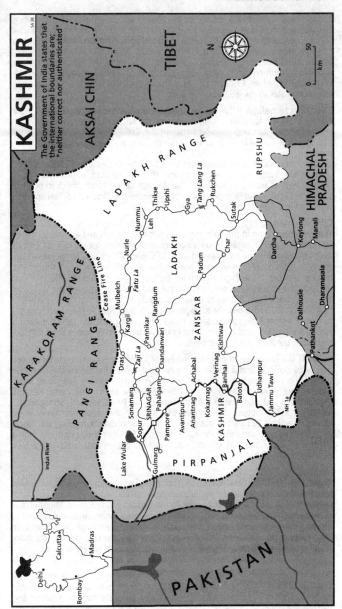

containing a number of lakes fed by the Jhelum and other rivers. Rising behind the Vale are the Great Himalaya which culminate in the W with Nanga Parbat ("Naked Mountain" – 8,125 metres). **The Nagin and Dal lakes** dominate Srinagar. Nearby is **Anchar Lake**. Thirty kilometres NW is **Wular Lake**, the largest in Kashmir, 17 km long and up to 5 km wide. It is fed by the river Jhelum. There are a large number of smaller lakes. Of these Sheshnag is sacred for Hindu pilgrims. The Jhelum, Chenab, Ravi and Beas rivers, all of which later provide vital irrigation water to Punjab, cross the state.

The Trans Himalaya Between the Ganga plains and the Tibetan Plateau are the Trans-Himalaya , forming a rugged zone of transition. Across it runs the Indus river, rising in Tibet and running between the Zanskar range to the S and the Ladakh range to the N. Both of these ranges have an average altitude of 5,000 metres.

Leh, the capital, is at an altitude of 3,521 metres. As the mountains were uplifted the Indus maintained its course through erosion, carving very deep gorges, e.g. at Hunza in Pakistan. The Zanskar range forms the backbone of southern Ladakh and is broken only once where the **Doda** and **Tsarap** rivers converge and flow N to the Indus river.

Climate
Temperature Even in the Vale, the air in summer is fresh and at night can even be quite brisk. In Srinagar the daily average maximum temperature is 31°C in Jul and 4°C in Jan and the minimum in Jul is 18°C and -2°C in Jan. Temperatures can reach as high as 37°C in summer and as low as -11°C in winter. A short climb quickly reduces these high maximum temperatures. In Ladakh the sun cuts through the thin atmosphere, and diurnal and seasonal temperature variations are even wider. Even the rocks break up rapidly in the alternating extremes of heat and cold, and a bare-headed person with their feet in the shade can get sunstroke and frostbite at the same time! There are great contrasts between N and S facing slopes and even in summer many streams only flow a few hours per day when the ice melts in their beds.

Rainfall The climates of the various regions of Jammu and Kashmir are influenced mainly by position and altitude. Although Kashmir is affected by the monsoon system the rain bearing clouds drifting in from the Arabian Sea never reach Ladakh, where they are blocked out by the Himalaya. Even in the Vale of Kashmir the rainfall is reduced due to the influence of the Pir Panjal. Still, Srinagar, at a height of 1,730 metres, receives over 650 mm per annum on average whereas Leh at a height 3,521 metres has only 85 mm, evenly distributed over the whole year. Even though the monsoon rains do reach Srinagar they bring less than a third of its total, over half coming with westerly depressions crossing the Vale between Jan and Apr.

Vegetation
Vegetation is very thin and apart from thorny bushes able to cope with low water supplies, it is confined to the watercourses. In contrast to Kashmir where about one third of the land area is still under forest, Ladakh has few trees. The shortage of timber and fuel are a pressing problem for the local inhabitants. In Kashmir the forests provide the Government with a significant income though there is concern that they are being over-exploited. Among them are the chenar tree (the giant Asian Plane Tree, *Platanus orientalis*), willows and a wide variety of pines.

People
The 9 million people are divided unequally between Jammu, Kashmir and Ladakh. The Vale of Kashmir is the most densely populated with over half the total number whilst Ladakh is the most sparsely populated. Culturally Jammu, Kashmir and Ladakh are poles apart. Jammu was traditionally the seat of Dogra power and

serves a largely Hindu population. Its affinities are more with the Punjab than with the Vale of Kashmir.

Kashmir with its dominant Muslim population marks the northernmost advance of Islam in the Himalaya while Ladakh is aptly named 'Little Tibet'. Ethnically the Ladakhis are of Tibetan stock. The early 'history of Ladakh is that of Tibet itself as it was a province of Tibet. It was governed in secular matters by an independent prince and in spiritual affairs it was guided by the Dalai Lama.

The **Kashmiri language** is influenced by Sanskrit and belongs to the Dardic branch of the Indo-Aryan languages. Linguistically and physically Kashmiris are similar to the tribes around Gilgit in Pakistan. The Ladakhi's features reveal a mixture of Tibetan-Mongolian and Indo-Aryan elements. In Ladakh, the majority (52%) of the population are Lamaistic Buddhists. Among the followers of Islam (47% of the total), are immigrant Kashmiris and Dards who speak their own languages. Ladakhi belongs to the Tibetan-Burmese language group and differs significantly from the Lhasa dialect.

Economy

Agriculture Only 20% of Jammu and Kashmir is cultivated but this is farmed intensively. Wherever possible irrigation is practised. This is most striking in the starkly beautiful, almost lunar landscape of Ladakh where stream water is carefully tapped by constructing headworks and running channels (*yura** along the natural contours to fields up to 8 kilometres away.

Rainfed crops About 80% of the people depend on agriculture. As the road winds up the steep hillsides to the Banihal Pass, for example, you see tiny plots of rice, wheat and maize, the major crops of the region as a whole. Barley, *bajra* (millet) and *jowar* (sorghum) are grown in some parts, and pulses (peas, beans and lentils) are also cultivated in market gardens and well-watered areas. A wide variety of temperate vegetables are grown. The floating market gardens of Lake Dal are especially fertile. In the Vale of Kashmir there are large orchards of apples, peaches, pears, apricots, walnuts and almonds. The Vale is also the only S Asian producer of **saffron**, prized as a delicate spice and worth its weight in gold.

Ladakhi farming Cultivation in Ladakh is restricted to the areas immediately around streams and rivers. Altitude and topography determine the choice of crop. Barley is the most common and is roasted, ground and combined with water to form the staple. This can also be eaten dry. Peas are the most common vegetable and apples and apricots the most popular fruits. Because of the harshness of the climate and lack of rain, there is only one cropping season. This lasts from Mar to Nov. Agriculture is therefore supplemented by pastoralism. Sheep, goats and yaks are taken to alpine pastures at altitudes of 4,000 metres and more over the summer months. This occurs to a lesser extent in Kashmir. From both is obtained the wool of the Pashmina goats. This has achieved international fame as 'cashmere' wool.

Minerals There are no commercially important mines. Some tin is mined, as is lapis lazuli (sodium aluminium silicate-sulphate), which has traditionally been valued as decoration for Ladakhi headdresses. Turquoise is also found.

Handicrafts Small-scale handicraft enterprises dominate the pattern of manufacturing in Kashmir. Products include carpets, papier mâché objects, woollen shawls and brassware. Many of these developed when Srinagar was an important entrepot on the ancient trans-Himalayan trade route. They later grew in response to the demands of the court and tourism. Today Kashmiri handicrafts are available all over the world.

Communication Kashmir and Ladakh have air connections with peninsular India; airports are at Jammu, Srinagar and Leh. Bad weather over winter often closes Srinagar and Leh. The railhead for Kashmir is Jammu which is well connected with other N Indian cities.

The Indian government having invested heavily in communications for strategic reasons. The Jawahar tunnel which links Jammu with the Vale of Kashmir is one of the longest in Asia. Beyond the Vale road construction has been just as costly. The road from Srinagar to Leh via Kargil is a magnificent piece of engineering and the means by which most people travel between the two places. The journey takes two days and the overnight halting place is Kargil. It is a route used heavily by the Indian military who have approximately 200,000 men stationed in Kashmir and Ladakh.

History of Ladakh

Rock carvings indicate that the region has been used for thousands of years by nomadic tribesmen. These have included the Mons of N India, the Dards of Dardistan in Pakistan, the Mongols and Champa shepherds from Tibet. The Mons introduced Buddhism and established settlements in the valleys while the Dards from Gilgit introduced irrigation. Kashmir and Ladakh lay on a feeder of the great Silk Road that ran from China to the Mediterranean in Roman times.

Early political development By the end of the 10th century, Ladakh was controlled by the **Thi** dynasty who founded a capital at Shey and built many forts throughout their domain. **Tibetan Lamaistic Buddhism** took hold in the 10th century and over 100 gompas were built. Ladakh's golden age began in 1533 when **Soyang Namgyal** united the whole region up to the outskirts of Lhasa and made his capital at Leh. The **Namgyal** dynasty still exists today. **The Rani (Queen) of Stok** was elected to the Indian Parliament.

Medieval expansion During the reigns of **Senge Namgyal** (c1570-1620) and **Deldan Namgyal** (c1620-60) the country was expanded. During this time Ladakh was threatened from the S and W by the Baltis who had enlisted the assistance of the Mughals. They were beaten back. The expansionist era came to an end when the fifth Dalai Lama of Tibet, **Nawang Lobsang Gyatso** (1617-82) convinced the Mongolians whom he had converted to Buddhism to enter a military campaign against western Tibet and Ladakh. The Ladakhis were unable to repel the invading Mongol forces. **Delegs Namgyal** turned to Kashmir for help. The Mughal Governor of Kashmir sent troops to help the King of Leh regain his throne but in return he had to pay regular tribute to the King of Delhi and build a mosque. From then on the country became an extension of the Islamic empire of the Great Mughals. In 1834 Ladakh was invaded by the **Dogra** forces of **Zorawar Singh** and placed under various governors appointed by the Maharaja of Jammu. The dethroned royal family received the Stok Palace where they still live today.

Recent political developments Following India's independence and partition in 1947 Ladakh, like Kashmir, was divided. Indian and Chinese troops have been stationed on the eastern border since the Chinese invasion of Tibet in 1950. From the early 1950s Chinese troops were stationed in the Aksai Chin, which India also claimed, and without Indian knowledge built a road linking Tibet with their southwesternmost province of Xinjiang. This was one of the two fronts in China's war with India in 1962, which confirmed China's de facto hold on the territory. India still disputes the legality of China's hold.

History of Kashmir

Early history For many years Kashmir was ruled by **Scythian Hindu princes** who were succeeded by **Tartars**. **Shams-ud-din** gained possession in 1341 and was responsible for the spread of Islam. In 1588 the Mughal emperor **Akbar** conquered Kashmir and built the fort on **Hari Parbat Hill** in Srinagar. His son and successor **Jahangir** (1605-27) was captivated by the beauty of the Vale of Kashmir and did much to make it a man-made paradise by planting chenar trees and constructing pleasure gardens.

In 1739 **Nadir Shah** the Persian annexed Kashmir. The Hindu **Misr Chand**, who served as a General in the army of the Sikh **Ranjit Singh**, took it in 1819 and was granted effective control over the territory in exchange for his loyal service. At the close of the first Sikh War in 1846 it was assigned to the *Maharaja Gulab Singh of Jammu* who founded a dynasty of *Dogra Rajputs*. Thus, Hindus ruled a mainly Muslim population. **Gulab Singh**'s territory included his home base of Jammu, the Vale of Kashmir and its mainly Muslim population, Ladakh and its small Buddhist population and the Muslim frontier districts of Baltistan and Gilgit.

19th century development During the 19th century Kashmir became popular with the British. Hunters enjoyed the rich wildlife and many visitors stayed in houseboats which came into existence to provide hotel accommodation when non-Kashmiris were forbidden from owning land. These are still extremely popular with visitors.

Independence Before Independence Kashmir had already developed a distinct political base, with the secular Congress Party, led in Kashmir by **Sheikh Abdullah**, establishing itself as the leading democratic political force in the state. Although the **Muslim League** favoured joining Pakistan the Congress had a clear preference for joining India, or even of remaining independent of both new states, a wish seemingly shared by the Maharaja. The question was still not resolved when India and Pakistan gained their independence in August 1947. In the autumn, tribes in the northern territories of **Gilgit** and **Baltistan** revolted and joined Pakistan. In SW Kashmir Muslims rebelled, declared '**Azad Kashmir**' (Free Kashmir) and forged links with Pakistan, who then proceeded to invade Kashmir. When the Pakistanis were very near to Srinagar, the Maharaja threw in his hand with India who quickly despatched troops there. Hostilities between India and Pakistan continued until 30 Dec 1948 when a ceasefire was agreed upon. That ceasefire line has become the *de facto* frontier separating the Indian State of Jammu and Kashmir from the Pakistani Azad Kashmir.

Kashmir's special status The state enjoys a special status within the union. As defined in Article 370 of the constitution, since 1956 Jammu and Kashmir has had its own constitution that affirms its own integrity. The central government has direct control over defence, external affairs and communications within the state and indirect influence over citizenship, Supreme Court jurisdiction and emergency powers. The governor of the state is appointed by the president of India while executive power rests with the Chief Minister and his council of ministers. Srinagar is the summer capital and Jammu the winter. The state sends six representatives to the Lok Sabha and two members who are nominated by the governor to the Rajya Sabha.

The plebiscite After the 1948 war a plebiscite was agreed to by India on condition that the armies of both parties withdrew from all the territories of the former state, and that peace and normalcy were restored first. Those conditions were never met and the plebiscite was never held. When **Sheikh Abdullah** resurrected the idea of one in 1953, he was imprisoned. The Kashmir Assembly declared the state to be a part of India in 1957. In 1965 **President Ayub Khan** of Pakistan launched a military attack on India in the hope of capturing Kashmir by force, but the war rapidly ground to a stalemate.

The *Simla Agreement* This contributed to his own subsequent political defeat in Pakistan, and the crushing defeat of Pakistan in the 1971 war over Bangladesh led **Zulfikar Ali Bhutto**, the new Pakistan Prime Minister, to believe that Pakistan could no longer look to take Kashmir from India by force. In 1972 he signed the **Shimla Agreement** with **Mrs. Gandhi**, under which both countries recognised the line of control between them and agreed that the dispute would be resolved through bilateral negotiations. Following the Shimla Agreement Mrs. Gandhi released Sheikh Abdullah from prison, came to an agreement with him and allowed elections.

Handicrafts

Despite the problems in Kashmir many Kashmiri products are still available outside the State. Kashmir is renowned for its distinctive and finely executed handicrafts. High quality craftsmanship in S Asia initially owed much to the patronage of the court and Kashmir was no exception. From the 15th century onwards, carpet making, shawl weaving and decorative techniques were actively encouraged. This developed into the tradition that persists today and forms an invaluable part of the local economy. At the end of the 19th century, for example, the estimated population of the Vale was 800,000 of which 30,000 were weavers.

Carpets Hand knotted *carpets* are available in wool (often imported from New Zealand), wool and cotton mix or silk. The patterns tend to the traditional, the Persian and Bukhara styles being especially common, though figurative designs such as The Tree of Life are becoming increasingly popular.

Young boys do the hard work under the guidance or in tandem with a master and it is common to hear them calling out the colour changes in a chant. The use of child labour in carpet-making across N India is increasingly widely criticised. Government attempts to insist on limiting hours of work and the provision of schooling often seem to be ignored.

A large carpet will take months to complete and the price will depend on the density of knots and the material used, silk being by far the most expensive. The salesmen usually claim that only vegetable dyes are used and whilst this is true in some instances, more readily available and cheaper chemical dyes are commonplace. After knotting, the pile is trimmed with scissors, loose threads burnt off and the carpet washed and dried.

Prices vary tremendously and you must bargain hard. Agra is another carpet making centre – weaving same designs and the quality is just as good despite what you are told. In both places, the usual practice is to ply customers with tea or cold drinks to soften them up. Carpets can be shipped back though if you are about to leave India and intend making a purchase, check your country's customs regulations to see what the duty is and whether there is an advantage in carrying the article home with you. Carpets of up to 2m by 3m fold well and are suitably wrapped in compact packages. They can be taken on the plane as hand luggage. Payment by credit card is usually acceptable but there is a surcharge. Be wary of people approaching you in the street or shikhara wallahs inviting you to visit a factory. They will receive a commission on the sale and this will be built into the price you are quoted.

Papier mâché work is extremely popular and comes in many forms – boxes, trays, egg cups, serviette rings etc. Paper is soaked, dried in a mould, then painted. The traditional style is on a black background. Natural colouring is used, e.g. lapis lazuli for blue, a gold leaf and salt mix for gold, charcoal for black. The patterns can be highly intricate and the finish exquisite. When the painting has been completed, the item is lacquered.

Pashmina and **shahtush** Kashmir shawls are world renowned for their softness and warmth. The best are **pashmina*** (Cashmere) and **shahtush***, the latter being the warmest, the rarest and, consequently, the most expensive. Prized by Moghuls and Maharajas they found their way to Europe and through Napoleon's Egyptian campaign became an item of fashion in France. Josephine is said to have had nearly 400. The craft was possibly introduced from Persia in the 15th century. Originally a fine shawl would take months to complete especially if up to 100 colours were used. The soft fleece of the pashmina goat or the fine under hairs of an antelope were used, the former for cashmere shawls, the latter for *shahtush*. The very best were soft and warm and yet so fine that they could be drawn through a ring. The designs changed over the years from floral patterns in the 17th century to Paisley in the 19th century. The Mughals, especially Akbar, used them as gifts. However, with the introduction of the Jacquard loom, cheap imitations were mass produced at a fraction of the price. The Kashmir shawls thus became luxury items, their manufacture remaining an important source of employment in the Vale. However, they were no longer the major export.

Other crafts include **crewel work*** (chain stitching) on fabric, *fur coats* and 'Kashmiri *silver*' *jewellery*. The Kashmiri *silk* industry and *woodcarving*, particularly on walnut wood, provides employment for many.

Cuisine
The rich cuisine of Kashmir is at its best in the ceremonial *wazwan** which is a formal meal prepared in the home to mark a special occasion. The *waza* is the chief cook who supervises the serving of about a dozen (but up to 2 or 3 dozen, depending on the importance of the occasion) specially prepared dishes which are offered to guests who are usually seated on the floor in groups of four, the meal being eaten with the fingers.

The menu is planned days in advance and the preparations take hours, using the very best of fresh produce and spices and herbs. The meal begins with the passing around of the *Tash-t-Nari* for guests to wash their hands, followed by numerous delicacies – *methi*, *Rogan Josh*, kebabs, vegetables – finishing with the very special *gushtaba* which no guest refuses. The dessert is usually *phirni* and finally a drink of *kahwah,* the green tea, flavoured with saffron, cardamom and almonds.

PATHANKOT TO SRINAGAR VIA JAMMU AND UDHAMPUR

From Pathankot there are two main routes to Udhampur, the starting point for the road across the Banihal Pass into Kashmir. The shortest goes up the **NH1** for 74 km before branching right to **Samba**. From this junction a slightly more circuitous route via Jammu is possible. The alternative goes E from **Pathankot** to **Chakki** (11 km), then N to **Dhar** (12 km), where a road runs the 130 km on to Udhampur.

The fastest route described here follows the NH 1 out of Pathankot through **Sujanpur** (10 km), **Kathua** (8 km) and **Khanal** (32 km). The road keeps close to the railway line to Jammu. After 24 km there is a right turn to Samba (10 km) and Udhampur (52 km). For Jammu (34 km) keep straight on.

Jammu

Population 223,361 (1981) *Altitude* 305 m

	Jan	Feb	Mar	Apr	May	Jun	Jul	Aug	Sep	Oct	Nov	Dec	Av/Tot
Max (°C)	18	21	26	33	39	40	35	33	33	31	26	21	30
Min (°C)	8	11	15	21	26	28	26	25	24	19	13	9	19
Rain (mm)	71	54	57	25	17	61	321	319	151	29	8	29	1142

Jammu is the homeland of the **Dogras**, the Rajput clans of the hill region N of the Ravi River. They are descended from the **Katoch** branch of the lunar race of **Rajputs**. These people have a well deserved reputation as a martial caste. Under

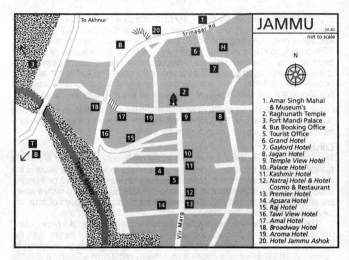

JAMMU SA 40
not to scale

To Akhnur
Srinagar Rd

N

1. Amar Singh Mahal & Museum's
2. Raghunath Temple
3. Fort Mandi Palace
4. Bus Booking Office
5. Tourist Office
6. Grand Hotel
7. Gaylord Hotel
8. Jagan Hotel
9. Temple View Hotel
10. Palace Hotel
11. Kashmir Hotel
12. Natraj Hotel & Hotel Cosmo & Restaurant
13. Premier Hotel
14. Apsara Hotel
15. Raj Hotel
16. Tawi View Hotel
17. Amal Hotel
18. Broadway Hotel
19. Aroma Hotel
20. Hotel Jammu Ashok

the Mughal Akbar's policy of conciliation and religious toleration, the dogras became loyal feudatories of the Mughal Emperors. They have been described as 'having courtly manners, great courage and strong powers of physical endurance' and 'it is their characteristic to be faithful and loyal to any paramount power which offers them opportunities of honourable employment' (Jackson).

The city of Jammu is the second largest in the state and is the winter capital of the government. Until the late 18th century the fortunes of Jammu were closely associated with events in the Punjab.

During the rule of the Sikh Ranjit Singh the Dogras of Jammu were allowed a a large degree of independence. Their ruler was the resourceful Gulab Singh. At the close of the Sikh War in 1846 and by virtue of a treaty with the British he became the ruler of the combined states of Jammu and Kashmir.

Gulab Singh's wish was to establish Jammu as a religious centre that compared favourably with Varanasi. He commissioned the Raghunath Temple which was completed by his son Ranbir Singh who in turn commissioned the Rambireshwar Temple, the largest Siva Temple in N India. Nearby is the the important cave temple of Vaishno Devi – see Excursions It is often called the City of Temples. At Partition, Hari Singh, the Maharaja of Kashmir, decided to side with India. This resulted in the creation of the state of Jammu and Kashmir.

Local Festivals *Lohri* (Jan) is an important festival throughout N India and is celebrated with *havan yagyas* in temples and houses. *Baisakhi* (Apr) is the harvest festival. A large celebration is held at Nagbani temple.

Places of Interest Most travellers usually just pass through Jammu on their way to Kashmir, the lakes and a more equable summer climate. However, it does have some places of interest. Jammu comprises two distinct parts. The hilltop **Old Town** overlooks the **Tawi River** and the **New Town**.

The *Raghunath Temple* (1857) in the city centre, is the focus of the town's religious attentions. It is one of the largest temple complexes in N India. The temple consists of seven shrines each with a simple tower, the one over the central shrine being curvilinear. Its fluted surface, arches and niches indicate a Mughal influence. The interior is gold plated and the principal sanctuary is dedicated to Rama, Vishnu's eighth incarnation, the hero of the popular *Ramayana* and the **Dogras'** patron deity.

Morning and evening *aartis** are ritually attended and there is also a stone lingam here and in the other shrines for this is a centre for Shakti worship. A portrait of Ranbir Singh, the temple patron and a sculpture of Hanuman are at the entrance. The other shrines have images of Vishnu in various incarnations, Siva and Surya. The Sanskrit Library here contains numerous rare manuscripts.

The Rambireshwar Temple (1883) opposite the **Dogra Art Gallery**, is also centrally located and is dedicated to **Siva**. It is a local landmark on account of its 75 m tower and has extraordinary crystal linga.

Overlooking the river are the ruined ramparts of the **Bahu Fort**. Situated on a rock face, it is the oldest remaining building in the region. The existing structure was later improved and rebuilt as the **Mondi Palace** (c.1880) by the Dogra rulers. It is situated in the NE of the city and is entered through a large quadrangle. A reception room stands to the right. The Old Palace is now the **High Court**.

The **Kali Temple** inside the fort attracts large crowds at a big festival held twice a year in Mar/Apr and Sep/Oct. The newer **Amar Singh Mahal** (early 20th century) is just off the Srinagar road and has been described by Davies as an art deco creation. In fact, it is more like a French chateau with its sloping roofs and turrets. This is hardly surprising since it was designed by a Frenchman. The museum has a portrait gallery.

Hotels Jammu is well provided for with hotels. Many are in the **E** and **F** category and reflect Jammu's significance as a transit, break of journey, town. It makes the overland journey to Kashmir more comfortable and enjoyable if you stay a night in Jammu. There are, however, buses which connect with arriving trains. These tend to stop at Banihal which has very little to offer. In season there is a big demand for accommodation so it is important to either book in advance or obtain a room as soon as possible after arriving.

C *Asia Jammu-Tawi*, Nehru Market. T 43930, Cable: Asiaotel, Telex: 0377-224 Asia In. 51 rm a/c. 4 km airport, 2 km rly, 1 km centre. Restaurant, shops, exchange, parking. **C** *Jammu Ashok*, opp Amar Mahal, P.B. 60. T 43127, Cable: Tourism, Telex: 0377-277 Asok In. 48 rm a/c. 9 km airport, 8 km rly. Restaurant, shops, pool, doctor on call, credit cards.

D *Cosmopolitan Hotel*, Vir Marg. T 47561, Cable: Cosmohotel. 28 rm, some a/c. Restaurant, bar, coffee shop, rm service, Diners card. Good restaurant. **D** *Mansar*, Denis Gate. T 46161. 22 rm, some a/c. 5.5 km airport, 4 km rly, close to centre. Restaurant, bar. **D** *Premier*, Sherwani Rd. T 43234. 21 rm, some a/c. 5 km airport, 5 km rly, central. Restaurants, bar, Diners card. Recommended. **D** *Tourist Reception Centre*, Vir Marg. T 5421. 128 rm with bath, a few air cooled, and dormitory. Restaurant. Good value with best rm in Blocks NA and A. Dormitory not so good. **D** *Jahangir*, Shaheedi Chowk. 23 rm. **D** *Samrat*, nr General Bus Stand, T 47402. 20 rm. **D** *Vardaan*, J.P. Chowk, T 43212, Cable: Vardaan. 23 rm.

E *Airlines Lodge*, 299 Canal Rd, T 42910. 20 rm. **E** *City Centre Lodge*, Jewel Chowk, T 43295. 38 rm. **E** *Indra Lodge*, Vinayak Bazar, near Jewel Cinema, T 46069. **E** *Jagan Lodge*, Raghunath Bazar, T 43243. 16 rm. **E** *Naaz Hotel*, Jogi Gate, Shaheedi Chowk. **E** *Natraj*, Vir Marg, T 7450. Non a/c rms. **E** *New Naz Hotel*, Shaheedi Chowk. 11 rm. **E** *Picnic Lodge*, Idgah Rd, T 43931. 20 rm. **E** *Standard Hotel*, Shaheedi Chowk, T 5455. **E** *Tourist Reception Centre*, Jammu Tawi Railway Station, T 43803. 4 rm. Dormitory not recommended. **F** *Railway Retiring Rooms*, Jammu Tawi Railway Station. Rooms and dormitory. A/c available. Reservations: Office of the Senior Superintendent, Counter No 2, Jammu Railway Station. **F** *Retiring Rooms*, General Bus Stand, T 47078. Booking: Retiring Rooms Booking Counter, General Bus Stand. Some bad reports.

Restaurants Asia Jammu Tawi Hotels *Bar-e-Kabab,* which is outdoor, with entertainment, is open Apr-Sep, 1900-2300. Cosmopolitan Hotel's *Cosmo* is good for Chinese and Kashmiri food. *Tourist Reception Centre Canteen,* Veer Marg is recommended for simple Indian and Continental dishes.

Others: *Dragon*, Veer Marg for Chinese; *Rachna*, Shalimar Rd for Vegetarian; *Capri Coffee House*, Old Hospital Rd, T 5805 and *India Coffee House*, Exhibition Grounds. *Silver Inn*, Veer Marg for Indian. Fast Food: *Kailash*, Raghunath Bazar, T 5969; *Kwality*, Veer Marg, T 5116; *Hungry Hops* and *Hot Pot*, both in Gole Market, Gandhi Nagar.

Clubs *Jammu Club*, nr Stadium, NH 1A. T 48009.

Banks *State Bank of India*, Raghunath Bazar, T 5894 *Canara*, Gulab Bhavan, T 43107 *Dena*, Raghunath Bazar, T 5811 *Baroda*, Purani Mandi, T 43854 *Bank of India*, Veer Marg, T 42040

UCO, Asoka Market *J and K*, Town Hall, T 46032 *Punjab National Bank*, Shalimar Rd, T 5835 *United Bank of India*, Veer Marg, T 42442.

Shopping Jammu has a number of fascinating markets: Raghunath Bazar, Hari Bazar, Upper Gumat, Below Gumat *J & K Government Arts Emporium*, T 5315 and *Khadi Gramudyog* are both on Veer Marg.

Local Transport City bus services run frequently on fixed routes. Low fares. Popular **Matador Mini-buses** and **tempos** operate on point-to-point fixed routes. Fare Re 0.50- 1. **Taxis and auto-rickshaws** are easily available but unmetered. The railway station is on the other side of the Tawi River. Allow approx Rs 10 by auto rickshaw. Information on appropriate tariffs at TRCs.

Entertainment *Cultural Academy*, Jewel Chowk. Information on cultural programmes from TRC, Veer Marg.

Sports Swimming Temporary membership for non-residents for the pool at Jammu Tawi Hotel. Maulana Azad Stadium Complex has a large pool, T 42038. Also other **indoor sports** – Badminton, Basketball, Volleyball, Table tennis and roller skating. **Tennis** Temporary membership at Jammu Club. **Fishing** The Tawi River is famous for a variety of fish, e.g. mahseer, mali and seeng. Permits obtainable from the Deputy Director, Fisheries Dept, Old Secretariat, Jammu Tawi, T 46211. Fishing equipment is not available for hire.

Museums Amar Mahal Palace Museum, Ramnagar, T 5676. Open winter 1000-1200 and 1500-1700, summer 1700-1900. Sunday 1000-1200. Closed Mon. Standing in a superb site above the Tawi river. Contains paintings of *Mahabharata* scenes. **Dogra Art Gallery**, Gandhi Bhawan, opp Old Secretariat. Free. Open winter 1100-1700, summer 0800-1330. Closed Mon. Contains a fine collection of Pahari miniatures, terracottas, manuscripts and sculptures from various sites including 6th century terracotta heads.

Parks and Zoos *Bage Bahu*, Bahu Fort.

Useful Addresses Police Control Room: T 100 Fire Service: T 101 Ambulance: T 5080, 442779 *Foreigners' Regional Registration Office*, Superintendent of Police (CID), Canal Rd, T 42676.

Hospitals and Medical Services SMGS Hospital, Jammu City, T 5080. Government Hospital for Children, T 5622.

Post and Telegraph GPO, Pacca Danga Raja Ram, T 5677, 43726. PO, Raghunath Bazar, T 47044 and Jewel Chowk.

Places of Worship *Hindu*: Siva Temple, Raghunath Group of Temples; Bahu Fort Temple; Kali Temple; Ranbireshwar Temple. *Muslim*: Ibrahim Masjid; Jamia Masjid. *Sikh*: Singh Sabha Gurudwara; Sundar Singh Gurudwara. *Christian*: Catholic Church, NH1A; St Paul's Church, Near Police Headquarters.

Travel Agents On Veer Marg: *Alpine India Travels*, *Gouri Travels* and *India Travels*. *Kumar Travels*, Hotel Gulmour and *Pushp Travels*, Hotel Rightway, Chand Nagar, both below Gumat. *Globe Travels*, Canal Rd. *Summerland Travels*, Idgah Rd. *Travel Care*, Hotel Ambassador, Raghunath Bazaar, T 47455.

Tour Operators *Asoka Travels*, Hotel Diamond, below Gumat. *B.T. Gupta Travels*, Hari Market. *International Travels*, Shastri Nagar. *P.K. Vaid Travels*, Hari Market. *Heaven Kashmir Travels*, Chand Nagar, below Gumat. *Shalimar Travels*, Near General Bus Stand. *Picnic Travels*, Idgah Rd, behind TRC. *Shakti Travels* and *Wing Tours and Travels*, Veer Marg.

Tourist Offices and Information Tourist Reception Centre, Veer Marg, T 5421. TRC, Jammu Tawi Railway Station, T 43803.

Air Indian Airlines flies daily between Delhi and Jammu. Five times from Delhi via Chandigarh and on to Srinagar. Two times a week via Amritsar and on to Srinagar. The nearest international airport is at Delhi, Air India Offices at Amritsar, T 33692, and Srinagar, T 77141. Indian Airlines, Tourist Reception Centre, Veer Marg, T 42735.

Rail Bombay Central: *Jammu Tawi Exp*, 2972, Tue,Wed,Fri, Sat, Dep. 1035, 31 hr 35 min. **Old Delhi:** *Jammu Tawi Mail*, 4034, daily, Dep. 1500, 14 hr 15 min. **New Delhi:** *Jhelum Exp*, 4678, daily, Dep. 1935, 14 hr 40 min; *Jammu Tawi-Bombay Exp*, Tue,Wed,Fri,Sat, Dep. 1035, 10 hr 30 min; *Shalimar Exp*, 4646, daily, Dep. 1845, 16 hr 20 min. **Calcutta (Sealdah):** *Jammu Tawi Exp*, 3152, daily, Dep. 1815, 46 hr 15 min.

Road Jammu is on National Highway 1A (Jalandhar-Srinagar-Uri), is linked beyond Jalandhar to Delhi by NH1. Jammu is connected to destinations in Jammu and Kashmir, by all-weather roads, and to Ladakh via Srinagar from May to October. From: **Srinagar** (293 km); **Kargil** (497 km); **Leh** (727 km); **Amritsar** (214 km); **Chandigarh** (363 km); **Agra** (786 km); **Jaipur** (847 km); **Patnitop** (112 km); **Kishtwar High Altitude National Park** (248 km); **Delhi** (586 km); **Bombay** (1994 km); **Calcutta** (1828 km); **Madras** (2743 km); **Varanasi** (1351 km).

Bus There are direct buses to Srinagar, Katra (for Vaishno Devi), Pathankot and Kishtwar, all run by J & K SRTC, Tourist Reception Centre, Veer Marg, Jammu, T 46851, 7095. Open 1000-1700. General Bus Stand, Jammu, T 47078, 47475. J & K State Road Transport Corporation (J&KSRTC) runs delux and ordinary buses from Delhi to Jammu daily. The Punjab, Haryana, and Himachal Pradesh SRTCs run buses to Jammu from Delhi and important towns in N India.

All **inter-state buses** operate from the General Bus Stand in Jammu. Super deluxe, deluxe, video and A-class coaches to Srinagar leave from the Railway Station, usually between 0600 and 0700. B-class buses to Srinagar leave from the General Bus Stand. These also touch the railway station en route but to be sure of a seat go to the point of departure.

Excursions **Vaishno Devi**, 48 km N of Jammu, can be visited from Jammu or en route to Srinagar. Vaishno Devi, a cave situated at 1,700 m, is 30 m long and is dedicated to the three mother goddesses of Hinduism.

According to legend Vaishno Devi used the cave as a refuge when she was fleeing form the demon Bhairon who apparently wanted to marry her. She would have nothing to do with this and so killed him. A pilgrimage to the cave should be accompanied by a visit to the temple of Bhairon who was absolved of his sins before he died. Pilgrims greet each other with the cry 'Jai Mataki' (Victory to the Mother Goddess).

You can drive, or go by bus as far as Katra, an attractive town at the foot of the Trikuta Hills. From here it is a 12 km climb to the cave temple. Another road from Lower Sanjichat to the Dabba brings you 2 km closer with 300 m less to climb. Ponies, **dandies*** and porters are available from Katra at fixed rates. The pilgrimage season lasts from Mar to Jul.

Akhnoor, 32 km NW of Jammu, is where the Chenab river meets the plains and was on the route to Kashmir in Mughal times.

Surinsar and Mansar Lakes, 80 km and 42 km E of Jammu. Picturesque forest fringed lakes. *Tourist Bungalow* and *Huts*.

Jammu is the railhead for Kashmir and from here visitors can either fly or travel by road to Srinagar. Before the Jawahar tunnel (named after Nehru) was completed, the journey took two days with an overnight stop at Batote. Now it can be covered in one long day. You begin on the plains (Jammu is only 305 m) and go through the low lying foothills, some with pine forests to the boulder strewn slopes near Udhampur.

From **Jammu** the road climbs through **Jhajjar** (32 km) to **Udhampur** (29 km Altitude 680 m), where it is joined by a road on the right from **Dhar** (125 km). It continues climbing through Dharmthal (20 km) to **Kud** (18 km, 1,738 m), a small hill station and also a popular lunch stop. The **Swamai Hi Bauli** is a well known spring 1.5 km from the road.

From **Kud** there is a side road to **Sanasar**, an attractive valley at just over 2,000 m and a centre for Gujar shepherds each summer. The main road continues through **Patnitop** (8 km, 2,024 m), another popular hill station with a *Tourist Rest House* and a *Youth Hostel*. **Batote** (1,560 m) is 12 km further on and has a *Tourist Bungalow* and several hotels. The road to Kishtwar (109 km) branches off to the right here.

From **Batote** the road falls rapidly, running along the deeply cut **River Chenab** which is bridged at **Ramban** (30 km *Altitude* 675 m). From this point it climbs steeply through **Digdole** (14 km) to **Banihal** (25 km, 1,720 m) which has a *Tourist Bungalow*. This is the last place of consequence before the Jawahar tunnel and the overnight stop for buses leaving Jammu after the morning trains have arrived.

The *Jawahar Tunnel* (*Altitude* 2,200 m) is 200 km from Jammu and 93 km from Srinagar. There are two passages through the hill and the 2.5 km tunnel was used in David Lean's 'Passage to India'. When you emerge from the darkness you are in the verdant Vale of Kashmir. The road drops gently to **Qazi Gund** (16 km) and **Khanabal** (19 km Altitude 1,600 m). Just out of Khanabal is a right turn to **Anantnag** (2 km) **Pahalgam** (44 km) and **Amarnath** (92 km). The NH1 A to Srinagar goes straight on through **Awantipur** (21 km) and **Pampur** (16 km), a town surrounded by fields of saffron. **Srinagar** is a further 13 km.

The Vale of Kashmir

Who has not heard of the Vale of Cashmere
With its roses the brightest that earth ever gave
Its temples, and grottoes, and fountains as clear
As the love-lighted eyes that hang over their wave

Thomas Moore wrote *Lalla Rookh, An Oriental Romance* in 1826 in a sentimental style typical of the Persian poets. His poem captured the English public's imagination of this, the most famous valley in the Himalayas, adored by Mughal Emperors and, it would seem, by nearly every other visitor since. Interestingly, Moore had never been to Kashmir but obviously did a bit of homework and let his imagination run riot. *Lalla Rookh* sold 85,000 copies and ran to 55 editions before the copyright expired in 1880.

The Mughals The origins of Kashmir's popularity date back to the Mughals. Akbar's first visit was in 1586 after its conquest. The journey took six weeks, largely because and army of stone cutters and navvies prepared the way for him. On this visit, floating gardens and river palaces were prepared for him. **Akbar** paid three visits to the Valley and liked to refer to it as his private garden.

The Mughals found the heat and dust of the Indian plains in summer oppressive and depressing. Babur longed for the streams and cool mountain air of N of the Hindu Kush and improvised by laying out gardens, thus starting a family tradition. Babur would have liked Kashmir. When Akbar was there he would go water-fowling, watch the fields of saffron being harvested and relax. His son Jahangir also found the natural paradise of Kashmir captivating and did much to make it a man made one as well. He is responsible for many of Srinagar's finest creations.

The British found most places away from the plains attractive and Kashmir was no exception. The small trickle of visitors became a steady stream after *Lalla Rookh*. Until 1990 when political disturbances effectively closed the state, this stream had developed into a raging flood. Kashmir was one of S Asia's most popular tourist destinations, on a par with Rajasthan and even more popular with Indian tourists.

The origins of the valley There is a popular legend that says that all the Vale of Kashmir was a lake and that a wise man succeeded in draining it by throwing gold coins into the water near Baramula. Some energetic youths then dredged an opening – where the Jhelum river is now – in order to get the coins. Scientists would agree that less than 1 million years ago the valley was submerged. It drained, however, because of local earthquakes. Today, of the lakes that remain, the *Wular* and Dal are the most important. When it floods in spring and summer, the Wular reaches 260 sq km in size making it one of the largest lakes in India. In winter, it decreases considerably in size. *Lake Dal* is much smaller at 38 sq km. Srinagar is situated around it.

Srinagar

Population 570,195 (1981)   *Altitude* 1,730 m   *Best Season* Throughout the year, Feb to Apr are wet. Indian Airlines connects **Srinagar** with Delhi (876 km, 1 hr 15 min), Amritsar, Jammu, Leh,

Chandigarh, Bombay and Ahmedabad. The airport is 14 km from the city centre.

	Jan	Feb	Mar	Apr	May	Jun	Jul	Aug	Sep	Oct	Nov	Dec	Av/Tot
Max (°C)	4	8	13	19	25	29	31	30	28	23	15	9	20
Min (°C)	-2	-1	3	7	11	14	18	18	13	6	0	-2	7
Rain (mm)	73	72	104	78	63	36	61	63	32	29	17	36	664

Srinagar is beautifully located around a number of lakes, of which Lake Dal is the most well known. The city is divided in two by the river Jhelum which is crossed by a number of bridges (**kadal***), nine of them wooden and built on a cantilever principle. There are also a number of canals but here the obvious comparison with Venice ends. The city was built by Raja Pravarasen in the 6th century. Its name was once mistakenly thought to be derived from Suryanagar (The City of Surya or the Sun god). Its true derivation is *Shri Nagar* – 'beautiful city'. It had a strategic as well as economic importance as it stands on the ancient trade route to Central Asia. Akbar reinforced the massive fort on Hari Parbat which dominates the surrounding countryside.

The lakes The Jhelum river and Dal and Nagin lakes dominate Srinagar's daily life. Here, there are lush wild gardens of lotus and waterlily amidst bustling lanes. There are countless floating market gardens. By the lakeside spread the gardens of the Mughals in their patterned beauty and the distinctive *shikharas** (boats) criss-cross the lake ferrying passengers, carrying reclining tourists and performing the function of a floating vegetable garden and market. The **Mihrbahri** people have lived around the lake for centuries and are market gardeners, carefully tending the floating beds of vegetables and flowers that they have made and cleverly shielded with weeds to make them unobtrusive.

When political conditions permit Srinagar is an ideal place for a holiday. It is not as quiet and restful as one might think as the Kashmiris have a well deserved notoriety for being keen businessmen, prepared to sell almost anything. The Vale of Kashmir is suitable as a base for winter sports and for trekking in the surrounding valleys. It is also en route to Ladakh.

Local Festivals The following festivals, enjoyed in other parts of N India have a special local significance.
Baisakhi (mid April). This is also known as the 'Blossom Festival' and marks the end of winter and beginning of spring. Large crowds gather in the gardens. *Id-ul-Milad* (Oct/Nov). The Prophet Muhammad's birthday. Celebrated with prayers and festivities. *Shab-e-Miraj* (Mar/Apr). The day the Prophet Mohammed departed for heaven. Relics of the Prophet are displayed. *Navratri* (Mar/Apr). The Festival of the Nine Nights marks the beginning of the New Year. *Amarnath Yatra* (Jul/Aug). One of the most important pilgrimages in the state when thousands of Hindu devotees make a 5 day trek to Amarnath in the Lidder Valley to offer prayers to Siva in a cave (3,880 m) in which there is an ice lingam. This is where Siva explained the secret of salvation to his wife Parvati. See Excursions.

Places of Interest *Hari Parbat Fort* (1592 onwards). Legend suggests that this hill was once a lake as large as a sea and was inhabited by the abominable demon Jalobhava, who spread ruination among the local people. They called on Sati Mata for her help and, taking the form of a bird, dropped a pebble on his head. The pebble increased in size as it fell and crushed him. Hari Parbat is revered as that pebble and it became the residence for all 33 crore (330 million) gods of the Hindu pantheon.

The entrance The ramparts are just under 5 km in circumference and are made from local grey sandstone. An original structure was built between 1592 and 1598 by Akbar's Pathan Governor **Azim Khan**. You enter through the domed **Kathi Darwaza** which is decorated by

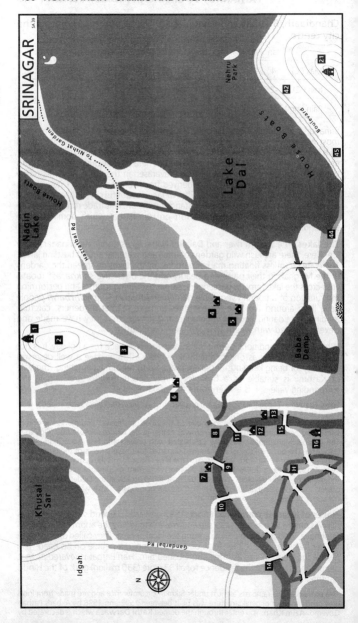

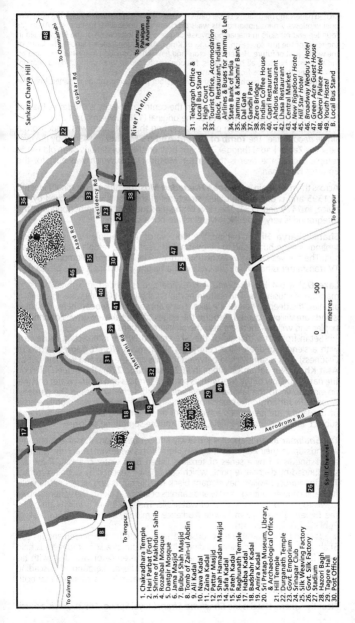

1. Chakradhara Temple
2. Hari Parbat (Fort)
3. Shrine of Makhdum Sahib
4. Rozabhal Mosque
5. Dastgir Mosque
6. Jama Masjid
7. Bulbul Shah Masjid
8. Tomb of Zain-ul Abdin
9. Ali Kadal
10. Nava Kadal
11. Zaina Kadal
12. Pattar Masjid
13. Shah Hamadan Masjid
14. Safa Kadal
15. Fateh Kadal
16. Raghunath Temple
17. Abi Kadal
18. Badshah Kadal
19. Amira Kadal
20. Sri Pratap Museum, Library, & Archaeological Office
21. Hill Temple
22. Durganath Temple
23. Govt. Emporium
24. Srinagar Club
25. Silk Weaving Factory
26. Govt. Silk Factory
27. Stadium
28. Hazori Bagh
29. Tagore Hall
30. Post Office
31. Telegraph Office & Local Bus Stand
32. High Court
33. Tourist Office, Accomodation Block, Restaurant, Indian Airlines & Buses for Jammu & Leh
34. State Bank of India
35. Jammu & Kashmir Bank
36. Dal Gate
37. Gandhi Park
38. Zero Bridge
39. Indian Coffee House
40. Capri Restaurant
41. Ahdous Restaurant
42. Lhasa Restaurant
43. Central Market
44. New Brigadoon Hotel
45. Hotel Star
46. Broadway Nedou's Hotel
47. Green Acre Guest House
48. Oberoi Palace Hotel
49. Youth Hostel
B. Local Bus Stand

arched panels and medallions. Lesser gates include the **Sangin Darwaza** which has attractive oriel windows. An inscription on its walls proclaims the unequalled greatness of Akbar, its founder, and his skills in managing diverse peoples: 'The foundation of the fort was aid in the reign of the just sovereign, the King of Kings, Akbar, unparalleled among the kings of the world, past or future. He sent one crore and ten lakhs from his treasury and two hundred Indian master builders, all his servants. No one was forced to work without remuneration. All obtained their wages from his treasury'.

Note The fort is normally closed to visitors but permission can be obtained from the Director of Tourism.

The Jama Masjid Beneath the hill in the centre of the city is the **Jama Masjid** (1674). This was built on the site of the original (1385) which burnt down twice. It is notable for the wooden pillars supporting the roof. Each was made from a single *deodar* tree. The **Tomb of Zain-ul-Abdin's Mother** (c.1430) is by the river near the **Zaina kadal** (bridge). This was built on the foundations of an old Hindu temple. Across the river is the **Pattar Masjid** (1623) which was built for the Empress Nur Jahan.

Across the river again is the *Shah Hamadan Mosque*, this was originally erected in 1395 and is one of the oldest structures in the city. It was destroyed by fire twice, in 1479 and 1731. The view of the mosque with the timber bridge in the foreground is very good. Non-Muslims are not allowed in.

Shankacharya Hill is behind the Boulevard. The temple was built during Jahangir's reign but is said to be over a 2nd Century BC temple built by Asoka's son. The hill was known as Takht-i-Sulaiman – The Throne of Solomon. The local TV transmitter is here also. The walk up (a height of 400 m) is quite pleasant.

Lake Dal is 6.4 km long and 4 km wide and is divided into three parts by man-made causeways. The eastern portion is the Lokut (Small) Lake. In the W is an inlet, the deepest part of the lake. There are some houseboats here. The small islands are willow covered. Around the edges of the Lake are groves of *chenar*, poplar and willow. There are also the pleasure gardens.

Set in front of a triangle of the lake created by the intersecting causeways with a slender bridge at the centre lies the famous *Nishat Bagh* (Garden of Gladness). This is sandwiched between the hills and the lake and was laid out by **Asaf Khan, Nur Jahan's** brother, in 1632 (**see page 274**). This garden relies on the natural beauty of the site with its series of terraces and central water channel flowing down to the lakeside. There are splendid *chenar* trees in the gardens. Apparently **Jahangir**, the creator of the nearby Shalimar Bagh was slightly jealous of the landscape gardener's achievement and expressed pained surprise that a subject, albeit his brother-in-law, could produce something so lovely.

The *Shalimar Bagh* is about 4 km away and set back from the lake. A channel extends up to their edge. Built by Jahangir for his wife Nur Jahan, the gardens are distinguished by a series of terraces linked by a water channel. These are surrounded by decorative pools which can only be reached by stepping stones. The uppermost pavilion has elegant black marble pillars and niches in the walls for dahlia flowers during the day and candles or lamps at night. The water tumbles down to the bottom in a series of waterfalls. The two lower pavilions are called the Diwan-i-Khas (Hall of Private Audience – middle) and Diwan-i-Am (Hall of Public Audience – lowest).

Jahangir is responsible for choosing the ideal site for the garden and his son Shah Jahan for the exquisite buildings. In normal times a *son et lumière* is held here from May to October . In Jahangir's day the emperor would sit with his beloved wife while musicians played to the gentle background of cascading fountains, the air rich with the bouquet of rose water. It was intended that both the gardens were approached by water.

Near the Oberoi Hotel is the *Chashma Shahi* (Royal Spring, 1632). This is a much smaller garden and was built around the course of a renowned water source. The garden was laid out in 1632 and is attributed to **Shah Jahan**. It has been much altered over the centuries. Originally, the water bubbled into a marble lotus basin in a central pavilion. This was removed with the effect that the garden has lost its piece de resistance and focal point. There is a small entry fee.

Just above the Chashma Shahi is the **Pari Mahal** (the Fairies Palace). This was a school of astrology and was built by **Dara Shikoh**, Aurangzeb's brother, for his tutor Akhund Mullah Shah. Several levels of the garden have recently been restored. Originally, there was a central building with flanking pavilions. This is one of the loveliest sites around Srinagar and the view down to the Lake and across to the hills beyond is captivating.

Hazratbal (Majestic Place) is on the west shore of the lake and commands an excellent view of the countryside. The mosque is modern and has a special sanctity as a hair of the prophet **Mohammed** is preserved here. This is displayed to the public on special occasions. Just beyond is the **Nazim Bagh** (Garden of the Morning Breeze), one of the earliest Mughal Gardens and attributed to Akbar. Little remains of the original buildings but some of the trees are believed to be those planted by the Emperor. It is now part of an Engineering College.

Anchar Lake lies 11 km N of Srinagar and is a popular excursion.

Hotels Note Seasonal discounts are often available and always worth asking for. **A** *Centaur Lake View Hotel*, Cheshma Shahi. T 75631-33, Cable: Centaur, Telex: 375-205 CLVH IN. 284 rm. 7 km airport, 5 km centre. 2 restaurants, coffee shop, 24-hr rm service, travel, pool, health club, billiards, golf, jogging, tennis. **A** *Oberoi Palace*, Gupkar Rd. T 71241-2, 75651-2, Cable: Obhotel, Telex: 375-201 LXSR. 101 rm. 15 km airport, 6 km centre. Shops, badminton. The former palace of the Maharaja with excellent garden but uninspiring buildings. First floor rm with lake view best.

B *Broadway*, Maulana Azad Rd. T 75621-3, Cable: Broadway, Telex: 375-212. 106 rm. Central heating. 12 km airport, 3 km centre. 3 restaurants. Modern, well run. **B** *Shahenshah Palace*, Boulevard. T 71345-6, Cable: Shahenshah, Telex:375-335. Overlooking Lake Dal. 74 rm. Central heating. 2 restaurants, bar, coffee shop, pool.

C *Asia Brown Palace*, Boulevard. T 73903, Cable: Asiaotels. 33 rm. 14 km airport, 3-4 km centre. Restaurant. **C** *Nehrus*, Boulevard. T 73621, Cable: Nehruguest. 35 rm. 16 km airport, 4 km centre, travel. **C** *Pamposh*, Sherwani Rd. T 75601-2, Cable: Pamotel. 48 rm. 9 km airport, 0.5 km bus stand and tourist reception centre. Restaurants (one open air), coffee shop, car hire, exchange. **C** *Shah Abbas*, Boulevard. T 79334, Cable: Restwell, Telex: 375-273 Yali ln. 84 rm. 14 km airport, centrally located. Restaurant, 24-hr coffee shop, exchange, travel, doctor on call, shops, TV. **C** *Tramboo Continental*, Boulevard. T 73914, Cable: Host. 54 rm. 8 km airport, 1 km centre. Restaurant, doctor on call, 24 hr rm service, TV. Clean, comfortable, good value.

D *Jahangir*, Jahangir Chowk. T 71830-1, Cable: Jehanotel. 66 rm. 8 km airport, 1.5 km tourist reception centre. Restaurant, safe deposit facilities, bank, car hire. **D** *Lake Isle Resort*, Nagin. T 78446. 9 rm. Closed in winter. **D** *Parimahal*, Dal Lake Boulevard, T 75351. 35 rm Restaurant, 24 hr rm service. Good. **D** *Gulmarg*, Dal Lake Boulevard, T 71331. 1.5 km centre. 49 rm. Restaurant, bar. Good older hotel. **D** *Sabena*, Sherwani Rd. T 78046, Cable: Sabena, Telex: 375-214 Fair ln. 32 rm. Travel, 24-hr rm service. **D** *Shangrila*, Sonwar Bagh. T 72422, Cable: Shangrila. 59 rm. Restaurant, exchange, rm service, exchange, car hire, shops, doctor on call. Diners, Visa. **D** *Zabarvan*, Boulevard. T 71441-2, Cable: Feelhome. 26 rm. Central heating. Closed in winter. Car hire. **D** *Dukes*, T 79427. **D** *Lake Side*, T 75892. **D** *Malik*, T 73672. **D** *Ornate Nehrus*, T 73641. **D** *Zamrud*, T 75263. **E** *Lalla Rukh Hotel*, Lal Chowk, T 72378. **E** *Tibetan Guest House* Gagrabal Road off Buchwara Road. Good value for the price, but no food and like most of the hotels in this area you may get woken by the muezzin.

J&KTDC provides a varied selection of accommodation which you can reserve through the *Tourist Reception Centre*, T 76107. **D** *Cheshma Shahi Huts*, Cheshma Shahi, T 73688. 53 huts, 1-3 bedrooms with bath, kitchen and sitting rm. Need transport to reach them. Very popular so book early. **D** *Tourist Reception Centre*, Maulana Azad Rd and Sherwani Rd, T 72644. Hotel Blocks with Deluxe suites and **E** Double rm. **E** *Tourist Bungalow*, Nagin Lake, T 76517. 4 rm. **E** *Budshah Hotel*, Lal Chowk, T 76063. **F** *Tourist Hostel* for dormitory accommodation. No bedding.

Guest Houses and Lodges E *Angles Inn*, Indra Nagar, T 77043. E *Aziz*, Boulevard, T 77675. Closed in winter. E *Boulevard*, Boulevard, T 77153. 80 rm. E *International*, Sonwar Bagh, T 78604. 60 rm. 2 restaurants, car hire. E *Madhuban*, Old Gagribal Rd, T 72478. Closed in winter. E *New Shalimar*, Dal Lake, T 74427. 30 rm. E *Surya*, Sherwani Rd, T 78778. 18 rm. E *Zero Inn*, Zero Bridge, T 77904.

Houseboats are peculiar to Srinagar and came into existence as a way to circumvent a royal edict which prohibited the ownership of land by non-Kashmiris. The answer was to build on water. Today, there are over 1,000 houseboats moored along the shores of the Dal and Nagin Lakes and along the **Jhelum**. Each range in length from 25-45 m and 3-6 m width. Some are delightfully cosy with one bedroom, others are sumptuously deluxe with 2-3 bedrooms and well appointed living areas. The larger ones are therefore capable of accommodating separate groups of guests prepared to share. Built of fragrant cedar planks, the interiors are intricately (some think fussily) carved and display the artistry of the Kashmiri craftsmen. The furnishings tend to take no regard of matching and rugs, bedspreads, walls, curtains, lamps etc all tend to be classically and busily ornate. Houseboats usually come with their own staff, e.g. a cook and often a boatman for your shikara, who usually live in the adjoining 'kitchen boat'. All meals are included.

Categories The State government has categorised the houseboats into 5 price categories : Deluxe, A,B,C and D according to the comfort provided. There is variation in quality and value for money in each. Recommended for Nagin Lake *Roshu Doktoo*, Suleiman Shipping Corp, Dal Lake, T 74547 and small boats from Abdul Rashid Major, Nagin Bagh, Nagin Lake. Also good boats from *Butts Claremont*, Nasim Bagh, Hazratbal, T 72325. For close to centre *Sieh Group*, Box 76, T 74044.

The following are listed according to the South Asia Handbook price category: **C** *Welcomgroup Gurkha Houseboats*, PO Box 57, Srinagar-190 001. T 75229, 73848, Cable: Guides, Srinagar, Telex: 0375-286 GRKA IN. 17 rm in all. 16 km airport, 7 km centre. Each houseboat has a sitting and dinning room, sun deck. Meal service (Mughlai, Continental), shikara rides, sight seeing, folk entertainment on request.

Others you might try: **C** *Alps Houseboats*, PO Box 390, Dal Lake. T 78669. 6 houseboats. *California Group of Houseboats*, PO Box 19, Dal Lake. T 73549, 78079, 78045, Cable: Vale, Telex: 375-223 Vale In. 16 houseboats. **C** *Lion of Kashmir Houseboats*, PO Box 61, Nagin Lake. T 74253, 73075, Telex: 375-270 Aill In. 12 houseboats. **C** *Meena Bazaar Group of Houseboats*, PO Box 433, Srinagar-190 001. T 74044, 77662, 7051, Cable: Fabulous, Telex: 375-358. 25 rm. 16 km airport, 5 km centre. Car rental, travel agents, laundry. Amex, Diners.

Note If you book ahead with a reputable group such as Welcomgroup, which has a chain of hotels throughout India and an instant reservations network, you will get what they advertise. If you arrive in Srinagar and arrange houseboat hire yourself, there are some points worth bearing in mind. Houseboat touts can be very pushy.

Bargain for what you want since, with the increase in the number of hotels, there are more houseboats than clients. Try to establish precisely what you will be getting for your money. Is the shikhara included and for what? Will hot water be provided? What extras are there? What do you get for meals? **Above all, insist of looking over the vessel before deciding.**

Life on a houseboat is not always peaceful. As tourists you are prospective buyers so there will be a constant stream of shikharas paddling by selling all sorts of handicrafts, flowers, chocoloates and sweets, razor blades etc. The houseboat owners receive a commission on the merchandise sold to their clients so you may have to **assert your right to privacy**. If you are sharing a houseboat with other guests (not of your choosing but because it is a large houseboat) their company may be pleasant or tedious. You can always move unless, of course, you have booked and paid in advance. You are therefore, advised not to pay in advance. If you would like to choose your boat without being harrassed on arrival in Srinagar, it is best to spend one night in a hotel. **Leave your luggage there to look around a selection before making up your mind.**

Warning It can be a nightmare trying to get a suitable houseboat if you have not made advance bookings. You need time, preferably some knowledge and experience, and the willingness to bargain hard. Location is also important. The E bank of Nagin Lake is the most peaceful and also gets the sun, but is far from the centre. The W bank of Lake Dal, particularly beyond Nehru Park is pleasant and good for sunsets – the SW corner known as boulevard is crowded. The Jhelum is not so popular so you can find a bargain there.

Agents in the country of origin can book houseboats in advance. The major travel agencies in the metropolitan centres in India are also reliable.

Restaurants The restaurants at the Oberioi Palace and Broadway Hotels are the best for comfort and food but expensive. The Dining Room has a more comprehensive menu than the lunch selection offered on the lawns at the Oberoi, but both are excellent. The Centaur Lake View has *Dawatkhana*, an Indian Restaurant and a 24 hr coffee shop but you may have a problem getting transport back late in the evening. *Lhasa*, Boulevard, T 71438 and the small, popular *Alka Salka*, Sherwani Rd, are good for Chinese with the latter serving Indian dishes as well.

The following specialize in Kashmiri food: *Mughal Darbar*, Sherwani Rd, T 72934 next to Suffering Moses has a drab exterior but is recommended for good food at a reasonable price. Also *Ahdoo's*, Sherwani Rd, T 75688. *Mahalaxmi*, Lal Chowk, T 76286; *Juniper*, Lal Chowk, T 72253; *Neelam*, Neelam Chowk, T 75929; *Royal*, Sherwani Rd; *Ruby*, Lambert Lane, T 74724.

For N Indian food: *Broad View*, New Secretariat Rd, T 78866. *Hollywood*, Sherwani Rd, T 75606 and *Indian Coffee House* which also does snacks; *Kailash*, Amirs Kadal, T 73631; *Kwality*, Hari Singh High St, T 7508. Continental cuisine at *Solace*, Sherwani Rd, T 72913. Gujarati food at *Surti*, Lal Chowk, T 72811. *Grand*, Sherwani Rd, T 73242 is a vegetarian restaurant.

Glocken Bakery serves hot and cold drinks and is recommended. Close by, near Dal Gate *Sultan's Bakery* is recommended for western delicacies. *Dimple* is good for milk shakes.

Banks Normal working hours 1000-1400. *State Bank of India*, Shervani Rd, T 76996, 77233. *Grindlays*, Shervani Rd, T 74092, 766935. *Canara*, The Bund, T 78598. *Baroda*, Shervani Rd, T 78332. *Bank of India*, Boulevard, T 75673. *Bombay Mercantile Co-operative*, Maulana Azad Rd, T 75629. *Bank of Maharashtra*, Maulana Azad Rd, T 71426. *Jammu and Kashmir Bank*, Divisional Branch, Shervani Rd, T 72430. Evening Bank: *State Bank of India*, Shervani Rd. Hours 1600-1800 Winter, 1600-1900 Summer.

Shopping Major shopping centres are located at the Bund, Boulevard, Dalgate, Lal Chowk, Polo View, Maulana Azad Rd and Sherwani Rd. On Sherwani Rd: *Government Arts Emporium*, T 73011-12, *Khadi Bhandar*, T 73321 and *Rajasthan Emporium*. *Arts Emporium*, Government Central Market, Boulevard, T 77466. Exhibition Grounds *Art Emporium*, T 77466. Carpets: *Indo-Kashmiri Carpet Factory*, Shah Mollah and *Roshu Doktoo*, Dal Gate. *Shyam Brothers*, Hotel Rd for furs. *Darson's*, opposite Lhasa restaurant, Boulevard Lane II. Walnut woodcarving, shawls and Papier mâché: *Langoo and Co.*, T 78860. *Suffering Moses* is well known for quality goods and is aware of their reputation. Shop shikharas 'patrol Dal lake like sharks'. **Bargain very hard for anything you like.**

Photography *Preco Studios*, T 72483. *Mahattas*, T 72572. *Royal*, T 73901.

Local Transport Auto-rickshaws are readily available. Fares negotiable. **Matador Mini-Bus** service covers most areas in the city. Minimum fare Re 0.50. **City Bus service** covers all places in the citty. **Main bus** stand at Lal chowk, T 77308.

Some routes of interest to tourists are: Lal Chowk to Shalimar and return (Double decker service); No 5 Lal Chowk to Harwan via Dalgate, Boulevard, Nehru Park, Oberoi Palace Hotel, Centaur Lake View Hotel, Shailamr Gardens, Nishat Gardens and Cheshma Shahi and return; No 12 Lal Chowk to Hazratbal via Nagin Lake and return; Lal Chowk to Satpura via Manasbal.

Bicycles can be hired quite resaonably from several shops along Boulevard close to Dalgate.

Shikharas are water taxis operating on the lakes and Jhelum river. There are various shikhara stands and an official fare to most destinations. In practice the fare can be variable so be wary. You can hire shikharas by the hour, part of or all day.

Entertainment Son et Lumière, run May-October by ITDC, at Shalimar Bagh. Time 2000-2100. *Sher-i-Kashmiri International Conference Centre,* Chema Shahi, T 72449, is one of the country's most modern complexes of its kind.

Sports *Sher-e-Kashmir Sports Complex*, Hazuriburg. Facilities for tennis, basketball, badminton, table tennis, gymnastics, boxing, archery. Restaurant and snack bar. *Amar Singh Club*, Ram Munshi Barg, T 76848. Temporary membership available; squash, tennis. **Golf**: *Kashmir Govt. Golf Club*, Maulana Azad Rd, T 76527. 18-hole golf course, temporary membership accepted. **Swimming and boating**: Water Sports Institute, Nagin Lake, T 76517. Hotels Broadway and Centaur Lake View have pools. **Billiards**: *Srinagar Club*, Zero Bridge, T 72132. *Amar Singh Club*, T 76848. Temporary membership accepted.

Museums *Partap Singh Museum*, Lal Mandi. Entrance free. Open 1000-1700. Closed Wed and holidays. A fine collection of miniature paintings, weapons, tapestries and sculpture. A small donation is appreciated to maintain the collection.

Parks and Zoos Apart from the gardens mentioned in the Places of Interest section, there is the *Nehru Memorial Park*., Shirazi Bagh, *Nehru Park*, Dal Lake, *Gandhi Park*, nr New Secretariat and the *Polo Grounds*, netween Maulana Azad Rd and Sherwani Rd.

Useful Addresses Foreigners' Regional Registration Office, CID Special Branch, Sherwani Rd, nr the Bund, T 77298. Open 1000-1600. Also at New Airport, T 31521. Police: T 100. Fire: T100, 72222. Ambulance: T 74591, 74594. Tourist Police: T 77303.

Hospitals and Medical Services Jawaharlal Nehru Memorial Hospital, T 77332. Kashmir Nursing Home, T 77518. Lalded Hospital, T 77526-7 (for women). Sher-e-Kashmir Institute of Medical Services, T 77467. S.M.H.S. Hospital, T 79226-7.

Post and Telegraph GPO, T 76494. Central Telegraph Office, Maulana Azad Rd, T 76549. open 24 hrs. Post Offices at: New Airport, 31521-9; Govt. Central Market, T 76481; Hazratbal, T 74637; Lal Chowk, T 76409; Nehru Park, T 76550; Tourist Reception Centre, T 76458.

Places of Worship *Hindu*: Durga Temple; Raghunath Temple; Shankaracharya Temple. *Muslim*: Hazratbal; Imambara, Hassanabad; Imambara, on Zadibal; Jama Masjid; Shahi Masjid; Makhdoon Sahib; Khangahi Mir; Syed Abdul Qadir Jalani; Dastgir Sahib. *Sikh*: Gurudwara Singh Sahib, Chanti Padshahi. *Christian*: Protestant Church, Munshi Bagh; Roman Catholic Church, Maulana Azad Rd.

Travel Agents and Tour Operators *Ladakh Safari Travels*, Bund, T 72000. *Mercury Travels*, Oberoi Palace, T 78786, *Sita World Travels*, M.A. Rd, T 78891 and at Hotel Broadway, T 77186, *Tiger Tops/Mountain Travel*, Bund, T 73015.and *Travel Corporation of India*, Maulana Azad Rd, T 73525, 76714 have been recommended. Numerous others include: *Adventure Tours*, Dalgate. *M.M. Butt and Sons*, Dalgate, T 72175. *Kashmir Himalayan Expedition*, Hotel Broadway, T 73913. *Trade Winds*, Boulevard. *Travel Centre*, Polo View, T 75373.

Air Lines Offices *Indian Airlines* City Office, Tourist Reception Centre, T 73270, 73538. *Alitalia*, Sherwani Rd, T 72392. *Indo Arab Air Services*, Zero Bridge, T 75399. Open 0930-1730.

Tourist Offices and Information J & K Tourism Development Corporation, Tourist Reception Centre, T 76107. Open 1000- 1700. Govt Dept of Tourism, Veer Marg. Open 0800- 2000. Govt Tourist Reception Centre, T 77303, 77305, 73648. Kashmir Motor Drivers Association, T 72798, 76504. Hotel Association Booking Counter, Tourist Reception Centre, T 76631. Also at New Airport.

Conducted Tours. J&KSRTC City Forest and Shopping Tour – Shankaracharya Hill, Cheshmashahi Garden and Zeathyar, Central Market, Weaving Factory and Museum. Others to Mughal gardens and Shankaracharya Temple; Daksum via Achhabal and Kokernag; Gulmarg; Pahalgam; Sonamarg; Wular Lake; Yusmarg, Verinag, Shikargah. T 72698.

Air Indian Airlines flies twice daily between Delhi and Srinagar, five times a week via Amritsar; Chandigarh and Jammu, twice a week via Amritsar and Jammu and five times a week between Srinagar and Leh. *Indian Airlines* City Office, Tourist Reception Centre, T 73270, 73538. Airport, T 31521, 31529. The airport is 14 km from the City Centre.

Rail The nearest railhead is at **Jammu**. Govt Tourist Reception Counter, 0700-1900. City Office, TRC, T 72698 for freservation of 2nd Cl Sleeper and a/c only. Summer 0830-1900, Winter 1000- 1800. Also City Booking Office at *Radhakrishnan*, Budhah Chowk, T 72929, 72798.

Road Srinagar is situated on **NH1A**, which connects to all parts of the **country by all-weather roads.** From: **Jammu** (293 km); **Gulmarg** (56 km); **Pahalgam** (96 km); **Sonamarg** (87 km); **Manasbal** (30 km); **Kargil** (204 km); **Leh** (434 km); **Delhi** (876 km); **Bombay** (2299 km); **Calcutta** (2133 km); **Madras** (3048 km); **Trivandrum** (3671 km); **Chandigarh** (630 km); **Jaipur** (1152 km); **Agra** (1091 km).

Bus *J&KSRTC* and the STRCs of Punjab, Haryana, Delhi and Himachal Pradesh regularly run to Jammu from major northern cities like Delhi, Chandigarh and Amritsar. Some continue to Srinagar, while there are many connections from Jammu. J&KSRTC, TRC, Srinagar, T 72698. Summer 0600- 1800, Winter 0700- 1700.

Excursions *Achabal* (Peaceful Place, 1,677 m), 58 km on the old route from

Jammu to Srinagar. This garden is set into the mountains and is supposedly the work of Nur Jahan. It is smaller than the Shalimar and Nishat Baghs but incorporate features of both. The rushing waters make it seem lively yet at the same time, like being beside a river, it is restful too. The original Mughal buildings have been replaced by Kashmiri style structures, the smaller ones lacking any distinction. The massive chenars produce a highly pleasing dappled effect of light and shade. There is a massive waterfalls gushing into a large tanks containing a pavilion. The source was renowned for its sweet water and was a place of pilgrimage before the garden was laid out. The view from this pavilion is delightful. There are *Tourist Huts* and a *Tourist Bungalow*.

Kokernag is 6 km E of Achabal and has a stream whose water is said to contain curative properties for indigestion. Across the wall that encloses the spring are five temples.

Verinag (1,876 m), 80 km S of Srinagar, was a stopping place en route to Srinagar from Jammu and is at the foot of the Banihal Pass. This is the most dramatic example of a spring tamed for the use of a Mughal garden. The **Bihat River** has its source here welling up in a clear pool that Jahangir calculated was 14 m deep. Originally circular, it was transformed into an octagonal basin in 1620 and surrounded by a brick wall. The waters are a turquoise blue. A 300 m channel led off the water to the stream. A set of octagonal pavilions were set around the tank and on its completion, Jahangir is said to have given a party there, plying his guests with alcohol and peaches brought by runners from Kabul. The pool was stocked with carp, some of which had gold rings attached by the emperor and empress. According to Gascoigne, when Francois Bernier visited Verinag forty years later he found that the largest still had gold rings through their noses. There is a *Tourist Bungalow* here.

SRINAGAR TO PAHALGAM

Pahalgam is 96 km from Srinagar and the journey to it along roads lined with poplar is very attractive. *Pampore*, 16 km from Srinagar is the centre of Kashmir's *saffron* industry.

There are few places in the world where this plant is grown, so production is small. Consequently the price of this delicate flavouring and colouring in cooking is high, as costly by weight as gold. Spain is another producer. Hiuen Tsang, the famous Buddhist pilgrim and Chinese traveller, visited Kashmir in 631 AD and commented then on the how rich the country was agirculturally, noting the abundant fruits and flowers as well as the medicinal herbs and saffron. He also admired the Kashmiris' good looks and their love of learning, but also felt that they were too frivolous and given to cunning.

Sangram (35 km) is a centre for the manufacture of cricket bats and driving past you can see them lined up in their thousands. **Avantipur**, 29 km from Srinagar, and famous for its ruined temples. Avantipur was the capital of Avantivarman (855-83), the first ruler of the Utpala dynasty of Kashmir. Several sculptures from the Avantisvamin and Avantishvara temples (both 9th century) are housed in the Shri Pratap Museum in Srinagar.

At the foot of the Lidder Valley is **Anantnag** (54 km), a spring town surrounded by a flower garden. A myth associates Anantnag with Indra. **Achabal** and **Verinag** (see Excursions above) can be visited as detours.

Martand is situated 8 km from **Anantnag** in the lower Lidder Valley, and is famous for its 8th century **Surya Temple**. Like the town, it is on a plateau which affords a splendid view of the Vale of Kashmir. It is dedeicated to the Sun God Surya and despite its rather dilapidated condition is an impressive example of the early Kashmir style of temple. **Lalitaditya** (724-60), the best known of the **Karkota dynasty**, is accredited with it. **Paraspora**, NW of Srinagar, is also associated with him, and was his capital.

The temple is set in the eastern half of an 80 m by 60 m colonnaded courtyard which is mostly in ruins. Originally there were 84 columns, a sacred Hindu number. The sanctuary is approached by a broad flight of steps and comprises a main sanctum and two minor shrines. Damaged images of Ganga (N) and Vishnu (S) can still be seen. The roof has gone but this may have been gabled in two tiers, similar to those found protecting temples in the Western Himalaya – see Chamba, Himachal Pradesh (**see page 461**).

Pahalgam

(2,130 m) One of Kashmir's major resorts. The best season for a visit to Pahalgam is mid-April to mid-Nov.

The **Lidder River** runs through the town which is surrounded by snow-capped mountains with pine and fir forests on their lower slops. In fact it is little more than a main street but is a pleasant place to stay away from noisier and busier Srinagar and ideal for short walks. It is also the base for launching a trekking trip – **see page 493**. The area around Pahalgam is also famous for its shepherds who more than anyone are responsible for maintaining the tracks and bridges over much of the trekking country as they herd their flocks from pasture to pasture.

There is trout fishing (fly only) in the river and permits have to be obtained in Srinagar and each year in July and Aug the town is thronged with thousands of pilgrims en route to the holy cave at Amarnath. Around the town there are luxuriant meadows and groves of poplar, willow and mulberry, the last of which is important for Kashmiri sericulture.

The walk to **Baisaren**, 2 km, a small glen about 150 m above the valley and set in a pine and fir forest is pleasing and offers good views. A further 11 km brings you to **Tulian Lake** (3,353 m) which is ice-covered for most of the year. However, for most people this would be an overnight camping trip and there are plenty of other attractive trekking destinations. The small village of **Aru**, 11 km up the Lidder River is the first stage for the **Kolahoi Glacier** trek. The main track takes cars so you can drive there but it does make a very interesting day walk. The **Mamaleswara** temple is only 1 km downstream after crossing the Sheshnag and Lidder Rivers. The small Siva temple (12th century) has a square stone tank.

Hotels C *Pahalgam*, Main St, nr Bazaar, T 26. 46 rm, some suites. Health club, heated indoor pool and sauna. Rm with river view best. Good views. C *Woodstock*, closer to river than the *Pahalgam*, T 27. Health club, occasional disco. Well run with a good restaurant. Good views of the river. C *Heaven*, far side of Aru River, T 17. 15 rm. Restaurant. Modern and offers free transport to town. C *Mansion*. 20 rm. Restaurant. Modern.

D *Natraj*. T 25. Rm and self-contained cottages. D *Plaza*. T 39. Double rm with bath. Pleasant views. Garden. D *Shepherd's*. T 74. D *Pine View*. T 70. D *Mountain View*, T 21. D *Tourist Bungalow and Cottages*. The 'Bungalow' (really a large house) has 7 pleasant rm with bath. Also 10 huts with bedroom, sitting rm, bath and kitchen. In the high season there are furnished tents set up in the grounds. Very popular, so reserve early through J&KTDC, Tourist Reception Centre, Srinagar, T 76107.

E *Windrush* One recent visitor wrote 'absolutely superb situation, inexpensive good food, lovely garden, but facilities very basic – no showers". Other E hotels include *Bente's* and *Aksa Lodge*. Out of town on a hill top is *Hill Park*. Further still is the *White House* on Laripora Rd. There are no really cheap F category establishments in Pahalgam but reasonable.

Restaurants *Pinegrove* at the Woodstock Hotel is recommended. Chinese: *Pahalgam* and *Natraj*. Continental: *Mountview, Pine View* and *Volga*. Indian: *Poornima* restaurant. Kashmiri food is served in most restaurants.

Bars Prohibition is not in force, Bar facilities are available at the *Woodstock, Pahalgam, Natraj* and Government Pahalgam Club.

Clubs The Government Pahalgam Club, T 22, 51. Operated by the Govt. Tourist Office. Table tennis, badminton, a card room and bar. Open all year round. Temporary Membership Rs 3

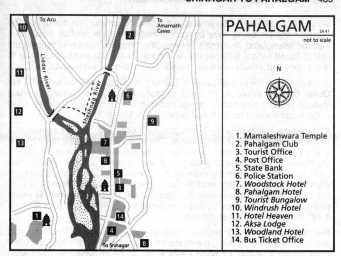

To Aru
To Amarnath Caves

PAHALGAM SA 41

not to scale

N

1. Mamaleshwara Temple
2. Pahalgam Club
3. Tourist Office
4. Post Office
5. State Bank
6. Police Station
7. *Woodstock Hotel*
8. *Pahalgam Hotel*
9. *Tourist Bungalow*
10. *Windrush Hotel*
11. *Hotel Heaven*
12. *Aksa Lodge*
13. *Woodland Hotel*
14. Bus Ticket Office

Lidder River
Sheshnag River

To Srinagar B

per day. Three rooms available to non-members.

There is a branch of **State Bank of India**, a **Post Office** (open 1000-1700) and a **Government Hospital**.

Shopping Pahalgam was originally a shepherds' village. Wool products such as *gadbas** and *namdas* (blankets) can be bought in local shops.

Photography: *RK, Delhi, Soni, Pitam and Longman Studios.*

Horse riding Ponies can be hired through the Tourist Office, T 24.

Sports Golf The Govt Pahalgam Club has a golf course open to non-members. **Fishing** The Lidder River has some excellent fishing beats. Season: Apr-Sep. Permits at approx Rs 75 per day per rod and for a maximum of three days at a time. Contact Directorate of Fisheries, Tourist Reception Centre, Srinagar, T 72862. Fishing tackle can be hired in Srinagar. Live baits and spinning are prohibited.

Places of Worship *Christian*: Catholic Church. *Hindu*: Siva Temple. *Muslim*: Jama Masjid. *Sikh*: Gurdwara.

Travel Agents and Tour Operators J&KSTDC runs tours to Wular Lake (depart 0900, Rs 38 per person), Yusmarg in the Pir Panjal range (depart 0900, Rs 38 per person) and Sonamarg (depart 0830. Rs 43 per person). All leave from the Tourist Reception Centre. The fares are for the round trip. You can get one-way tickets to all depending on the number they have booked.

Travel Bus You can take a sightseeing coach to Gulmarg and pay a one-way fare if you intend spending a few nights there. There are also local buses from Srinagar tio Pahalgam. **Taxi:** One way costs Rs 300-350. Return is not much more expensive.

Excursions

Gulmarg (2,730 m) is 52 km W of Srinagar on the N side of the Pir Panjal. It stands in a broad upland meadow – the name means 'flower path'. From surrounding vantage points you can see the entire Vale of Kashmir and admire the surrounding mountains. It is a good base for treks into the Pir Panjal but is best known as India's major winter sports resort. Compared with the fields of Europe and N America, the facilities are neither advanced nor sophisticated ('utilitarian' is how one promotional brochure describes them), especially some of the equipment for hire, but it is comparatively cheap. The slopes immediately around Gulmarg are for beginners, but Heli-skiing is beng introduced and the opportunities for skiing were being improved before the political situation in Kashmir deteriorated. As a resort, however, the increasing number of tourists, the cost of hotels (which is higher than in Pahalgam) and the constant pressure to hire a pony had already made Gulmarg less attractive than in the past.

There are a number of walks around Gulmarg, the best known being the 11 km **Outer Circular Walk**. As its name suggests, this runs right round Gulmarg through pleasant pine forests. Nanga Parbat (8,126 m), the eighth highest peak in the world is visible to the N and Haramukh (5,148 m) to the S.

Khilanmarg is a small valley, 5 km uphill from **Gulmarg**, that is carpeted with flowers in spring and a ski run in winter. The walk up there can be quite muddy if you catch the snow melt as the path has also been over used by ponies. Otherwise, it is an exhilarating steep walk with beautiful scenery, which is best undertaken fairly early in the morning. Further on and 13 km from Gulmarg is *Alpather* (3,843 m) which lies at the foot of the main Apharwat Peak (4,511 m). The lake is frozen until mid-June. A ridge separates this from the main Gulmarg valley so a walk there entails going over the Apharwat Ridge (3,810 m). There is a well graded pony track all the way.

Ferozepore Nallah, 5 km from Gulmarg, and reached from the Tangmarg road and the Outer Circular Walk, is a mountain stream that is said to be particularly good for trout. **Ziarat of Baba Reshi** is the shrine of tomb (*ziarat*) of Baba Payam-ud-Din, a noted Muslim saint. Before renouncing the world he was a courtier to the Kashmiri King Zain-il-Abidin in the 15th century. He is revered by both Hindus and Muslims. The path leads through thick forest.

Hotels (Gulmarg) Some hotels close for the winter months. The best is **B** *Hotel Hilltop*, T 245, Cable: Hilltop. 35 rm. Shops, health club, TV. **C** *Highlands Park*, T 230, 291, Cable: Highlands, Telex: 0375-320 HHPF IN. 39 rm in bungalows. 1 km centre. Health club, table tennis, billiards, badminton in summer. Meals (which are mediocre) included in price. Lovely building in a fine garden with terraces for sitting out to enjoy the views. **C** *Nedous*, T 223. 20 rm, 3 huts. Putting green. Good views, pleasant, with character. **C** *Asia Green Heights*, T 204, Cable: Asiaotel. 16 rm, garden. **C** *Ornate Woodlands*, T 268, Cable: Ornateclub, Telex: 73146 (Bombay). 14 rm in 3 rustic huts. 3 km centre. Restaurant (incl Gujurat Thali), bar, TV room, car hire, doctor on call. Diners. Hilly location. **C** *Affarwat*, T 202. 18 rm. Simple but well managed. **C** *Pine Palace*, Nr ski Lift, T 266. 21 rm. Gardens. Simple but good.
   D *New Zum-Zum*, T 215. 20 wood-panelled rm with bath and balcony. Restaurant, 24 hr rm service. Recommended. There is reasonably priced accommodation provided in government **D** *Tourist Huts,* T 39187. 14 huts, 1 to 4 bedrooms with bath, sitting rm and kitchen. Charming wooden insulated huts with heating. Popular, so book early through J&KTDC or travel agent. Also a new **D** *Tourist Bungalow*, T 241. Clean, open all year round. 24 d rm with Indian style bathrooms. No restaurant. Good value. **D** *Yamberzal*. 4 rm. Restaurant.

Restaurants Indian, Continental, Chinese and Kashmiri cuisine is available in the restaurants. One at *Highlands Park* is expensive but not exceptional. Also *khailan* at Affarwat Hotel is pleasant. Others at *Nedou's, Woodlands* and *Yumberzal*. Near the Bus Stand, *Ahdoos* does good meals.

Bars Some of the hotels have bars. Try the lounge bar at the *Highlands Park*. There is also a bar at the Government club, T 99.

Clubs The Government Club, T 99. Sports and bar. Temporary membership available.

Banks State Bank of India. J & K Bank.

Local Transport Ponies can be hired through the Tourist Offices at Tangmarg and Gulmarg. Reasonable rates on a daily and hourly basis. Porters can also be arranged through the Tourist Office.

Trekking Equipment can be hired from the Tourist Reception Centre, Srinagar on fairly nominal charges, T 77305. Horse riding: Ponies can be hired through the Tourist Office, T 99.

Golf 18-hole course maintained by the J&K Dept. of Tourism. Claims to be one of the highest greens in the world at 2652 m. Temporary membership is available from the local Tourist Reception Centre which also has equipment and caddies for hire. The course has recently been relaid by the Australian golfer Peter Thompson and now offers a greater challenge. *Golf Club*, T 224. 2 rm for guests. Tennis: Government Club. Visitors with temporary membership may use it.

Skiing Some of the best slopes in the country are at Gulmarg. However, India is not a skiing nation so do not expect too much. There is a 500 m chair lift (allowing a 900 m run), and a 200 m T-bar. Passes are very cheap. In summer the chair lift is used for sightseeing. Basic ski equipment and toboggans can be hired from the Ski Shop, Tourist Office, T 299. *Indian Institute of Ski and Mountaineering*, T 246.

Services There is a *Police Station*, a *Government Hospital* and a *Post Office*.

Places of Worship There is a Hindu temple, a mosque and Sikh gurdwara.

Tourist Offices and Information J&K Govt. Tourist Office, Club Building, Gulmarg, T 299. Open 0930-1800. J&K Govt. Tourist Office, Tangmarg, T 236. Information is also available from the J&K Tourist Reception Centres at: Srinagar, T 77303; Jammu, T 5421; Delhi, T 3325373.

Air J&K Dept of Tourism runs a helicopter service to Gulmarg. Frequency depends on weather conditions. Fare Rs 500 per person for return flight.

 Bus J&KSRT offers regular deluxe sightseeing (Rs 46 return) and ordinary bus services (Rs 13 one way, 3 hr) from Srinagar. In winter it is only up to Tangmarg (13 km from Gulmarg). The remaining distance is by jeep – Rs 150 one way for full load. **Taxi** Full taxi from Srinagar Rs 300 approx. Fix price before departure. As always in Kashmir, bargain hard.

TREKKING IN KASHMIR

Trekking in Kashmir and Ladakh differs quite markedly from trekking in Nepal in three important respects. Before the recent disturbances, no special permission was required, i.e. you did not need permits for Kashmir or Ladakh. It is currently impossible to trek from the Vale of Kashmir, though it is still possible to get into Ladakh.

There are more wide open spaces in Kashmir and Ladakh and a sparser population in much of the trekking area. This obviously results in less crowding and means that you will be walking through countryside that is used for grazing as opposed to farming. The feeling of being in a wilderness area is very obvious in Kashmir and Ladakh whereas in Nepal, a large part of many treks is through heavily populated, intensively farmed countryside.

Porters are far less common in Kashmir than in Nepal. Ponies are usually used to transport loads. At night these are hobbled and as most have little bells, these can tinkle all night. You may find this irritating at first but after a few nights you will get used to it. The Government is making great efforts to develop alternatives to Kashmir in Himachal Pradesh, **see page 462**.

There are two 'Trekking Maps' of Jammu and Kashmir available from the Survey of India. Both are 1:250,000 so are not very good for route finding in a precise manner but they do give a general indication of the lie of the land. Obtainable from the Government Map Shop on Janpath, Delhi. Price Rs 5 each – see Delhi Shopping (**page 185**).

Trekking From Kishtwar To Kashmir

Kishtwar, approx 226 km NE of Jammu. Kishtwar is an isolated district of Jammu and Kashmir and, despite its physical proximity to Srinagar it is administered from Jammu.

Both Hinduism and Islam are strong in Kishtwar. Rajputs controlled the area before the establishment of Islam which gained a firm hold under the Mughals. Both religions survive today. The great Zorawar Singh was appointed governor in the 1820s and used it as a base for mounting his Dogra military campaigns in Ladakh and Western Tibet.

Today, this is a splendidly spectacular region of mountains in the Pir Panjal, with cascading waterfalls. Good quality saffron is grown on the plateau above the Chenab River and in spring and summer presents a very colourful sight. It is well off the beaten track and has few facilities. The hotels are all around the bus stands and are cheap and 'ethnic'. It takes over 10 hours by bus from Jammu and 15 hours from Srinagar. There is a jeep road from the Vale of Kashmir via the Sythen Pass and eventually this will be used for bus services which will reduce the journey time by half.

Trekking in Kishtwar The region offers some very fine trekking which can be undertaken out of Jammu. Supplies of basic foodstuffs and fuel can be obtained in Kishtwar. Horses and porters can also be recruited, the cost varying with the destination. The rates for Zanskar bound routes are almost twice those for Kashmir. There are no foreign exchange facilities so you will have to change enough money in Jammu. You can start trekking from Kishtwar or take buses and trucks some distance further.

Routes There are two routes into Kashmir, either by way of the **Chatru Valley** and **Sythen Pass** or the **Marwa/Warvan Valleys** and the **Margan Pass**. From Kishtwar you can bus or walk to **Palmer** village. Suitable camping is a few kilometres further on the road to **Ikhala**. From **Ikhala** the mule track passes through forested gorge country before reaching **Sundar** and **Sirshi** villages which are located in the valley at the confluence of the **Kiar** and **Kibar Rivers**. This is the northernmost limit of rice cultivation and also Hinduism. From here you can make a satisfying side trip to the base camp of *Brammah* or **Sickle Moon**. Both require 3-4 days for the round trip. If you are going to Brammah you will need porters as horses cannot negotiate the route.

Two relatively short stages go from **Sirshi** to **Yourdu** via **Hanzal** where a hydro-electric scheme for the lower part of the river are under way. From Yourdu it is a comparatively long walk along the Warvan Valley to Inshin. There are some very attractive camp sites en route for those who do not want to cover the full distance in one day. The ascent to the **Margan Pass** from **Inshin** is quite steep. The views back down the **Warvan Valley** to **Brammah** and **Sickle Moon** are excellent. This is a long pass and a major route of the goat-rearing *Bakrawallahs* (*bakra* is Hindi for goat), so expect well fertilised camp sites for most of the trek!

There is a jeep track over the pass but you do not need to follow it. From **Lehinvan** you can take the bus to **Anantnag** and **Srinagar**. Along the trekking route are *Forest Rest Houses*. Without the side trips to **Brammah** and **Sickle Moon**, this trek can be completed comfortably in a week. Each day's walking is about 6 hours.

Kishtwar To Chamba

A day should be allowed to reach *Padyarna* (6 hr walk) because the bus service is often disrupted. It is a warm day's walk but there are tea stalls along the route. Horses can be obtained in **Padyarna** or the next village of **Galhar** though they usually come in multiples, i.e. it is difficult to get only one at a time. From **Galhar** it is uphill to **Shasho** with good views on the *Chenab Valley*. Much of the area is heavily forested and there are a number of gorges. At **Shasho** there is a big waterfall and a pleasant camp site. It is a long day's trek so you may choose to break it up by stopping at **Nunhoto**. **Atholi** is the next destination and is a Hindu and Muslim town. On the opposite bank is **Gularbagh** whose population includes Buddhist traders from Zanskar. You can stock up with more provisions at **Atholi**.

From **Atholi** there are two trails, one leading to the **Umasi La** and **Zanskar**, the other continuing up the Chenab Valley to **Chamba** passing through **Shoal** and **Istahari** in two stages before reaching the border with Himachal Pradesh. It is then three stages to the **Sach Pass** (4,400 m). There are excellent views of the Pir Panjal on the Kishtwar side and of the distant Dhaula Dhar and the Ravi Valley on the Himachal side. The trek ends at the roadhead at **Tarila**.

This trek can be completed in 10 days though an extra couple of days would make it much more relaxed. The daily walking time is just under 6 hours. It is not as arduous as the treks in Zanskar and Ladakh.

Kishtwar To Zanskar

You follow the same route as above to Atholi. You can hire horses at Gularbagh from the Ladakhi traders who will make cheerful trekking companions. It is three stages up the **Pardar Valley** (the Umasi La is known as the Pardar La by the people of Atholi and Kishtwar) to the base of the pass. **Suncham** is the last village and 4 km beyond on the plateau above the terminal moraine is the **Hogshu Base Camp**. From here it is a long steady grind and another camp to the pass (5,340 m).

With such a high crossing, acclimatisation is essential. The last part will be through snow. The views of the Zanskar range are magnificent. The descent, however, is steep and difficult and an ice-axe or stick is essential. If you have hired horses you will have the services of a guide. From the camp at **Nabil** it is an easy day's walk to **Asing** in the Zanskar Valley. From there you can continue to **Karsha** or **Padum** and catch a bus or truck out over the **Pensi La.**

This trek is certainly spectacular but it is also demanding, simply because you have to cross a high pass. The average daily walking time is 6 hours and the trek can be completed in 10 stages. An extra one or two days are recommended to allow flexibility and make it easier.

The Sindh And Lidder Valleys

This is the most popular trekking area in Kashmir and offers a variety of routes from the very easy to the longer yet still not very difficult. It is also the easiest place in Jammu and Kashmir for making suitable trekking arrangements. The season lasts from mid-June to late October. Jul and Aug are good months but there can be some heavy rainfall even though Kashmir does not receive a 'full' monsoon. Sep and Oct are ideal as the weather is settled, the atmosphere clear and the temperatures not too high.

Making arrangements There is a pony wallah union in Kashmir and the rates are more or less fixed. Pahalgam is the best place for this and there is a board displaying the rates. You will have to budget for the pony wallah's return journey. Provisions can be obtained in Pahalgam. Basics such as rice, dal and potatoes are generally available at **Aru** though this cannot be relied upon.

Equipment is not so readily available but enquiries at trekking hotels may elicit a response. It is, of course, much better to bring your own, well tried and proven equipment. Some rope will be required in case river crossing have to be made and when doing these caution must be exercised at all times.

N.B. Due to the immense popularity of camp sites such as those at **Aru**, **Lidderwat** and **Gangobal**, there is now a problem with litter. Please do not add to it. Unfortunately, there is no official policy on removing, burying or burning garbage and no permit system which would create funds for clean-up operations. The emphasis is on each individual and group being responsible. Some are more diligent than others. There are a number of medium length treks worth considering.

The Lidder to Sindh Valley trek via the Yemhar Pass

The Lidder to Sindh Valley trek via the Yemhar Pass leaves from Pahalgam and follows the road almost to Aru. There are excellent views looking back down the valley. The meadow camp site has a number of trekking lodges and some interesting day trips can be undertaken from here.

From **Aru** the trail climbs through pine forest to a Gujar grazing meadow and follows the **Lidder River**. There is a *Government Rest House* at **Lidderwat** and a number of other lodges which tend to mar the scenic beauty of the meadow.

The next stage is quite short (3 hr) to **Satlanjan**, the largest Gujar village in the Lidder Valley. From this camp site you can make a long round trip up to the **Kolahoi glacier**. An early start is essential if you are to get good views. **Sekiwas** is the next camping ground on the trek and can be reached from Lidderwat in only 3 hours.

If you are there from mid-June onwards there is a profusion of wild flowers which include marsh marigolds, gentians, buttercups and up in the crags, occasionally Himalayan Blue Poppy. There is another optional side trip to the 2 km by 1 km **Tarsar Lake**, one of the most beautiful in Kashmir. From the ridge beyond the lake you get good views into the **Dachigam Sanctuary**. The round trip from Sekiwas will take about 8 hours including reasonable stops.

From Sekiwas the valley splits into three. The left hand path goes over the **Sonamous Pass** (3,960 m), the centre one over an unnamed pass (4,200 m) and the right hand one over the **Yemhar Pass** (4,350 m). The ascent to the Yemhar should take about 3 hr and from the top there are excellent views. The camping ground is by a small glacial lake. The following day's walk is an easy stretch down to **Kulan** where you can get transport back to **Srinagar** or **Sonamarg**.

There are a number of variations to this trek which take in different passes. E.g. from Sekiwas you can go over the Sonamous Pass – passable when the snow on the Yemhar Pass is too soft. Local shepherds and trekkers will be able to advise. Also there is a route from Aru to Sonamarg via the Harbaghwan Pass (4,200 m).

The Lidder to Sindh Valley trek via Mahguna Pass and Amarnath

This is another popular route. On this one you have to contend with a sizeable Hindu pilgrim traffic. It is the most important trek in Kashmir since each year at August full moon, about 25,000 pilgrims make their way to the cave at Amarnath which is where Siva related his theory of immortality to his wife Parvati. There is an ice lingam there which changes size according to the season.

For pilgrims, the trek takes about 5 days. Transport can be hired in the form of ponies and *dandies** which are wooden palanquins carried by bearers. The pony rates are about half as much again as at other times during the season. The first stage is the **Chandanwadi**, the second to the glacial lake at **Sheshnag**, the third to **Panchtarni** via the **Mahgunas Pass** (4,580 m), the fourth to the cave (3,600 m) and back to **Sheshnag** and the final day back to **Pahalgam**. It is certainly an experience to be part of this *yatra** (pilgrimage) but you have to like noise, crowds, be prepared for cramped conditions and poor sanitation. It helps immensely if you are Hindu.

The whole trek can, of course, be done at other times and this is recommended if you want to feel more a part of the countryside. It is an attractive and spectacular trek. Go before the annual *yatra* and the camp sites and track will be less polluted with litter.

The Sonamarg to Haramukh Trek

This can be treated as an extension of the Lidder-Sindh Valley Trek. It can be completed in a week and includes wonderful scenery, opportunities for fishing and the chance to get lost. If you are travelling without local guides, you should check your route with shepherds as the trail bifurcates frequently.

You will get views of the *Zoji La* and of *Baltoro* and *K2* from the *Nichinni Bar* (4,000 m), *Nanga Parbat* from *Vishenagar Pass* (4,300 m), glacial lakes, Gujar shepherd encampments, Gangobal Lake, Haramukh peak (5,755 m) and the Vale of Kashmir. Each day's walking will take 5 hours and there are plenty of ups and downs. It is recommended for those with a reasonable level of fitness.

Kashmir To Ladakh

There are a number of routes, the most popular being along the *Warvan Valley*. The *Boktol Pass* (4,420 m) is the most popular pass, another is the *Chilung Pass* (5,200 m). Treks to Ladakh should not be started until mid-June and the season ends in mid October when the passes are blocked with snow.

Before going over the passes, time should be allowed for acclimatisation. Basic food supplies can usually be obtained from the larger villages in the Warvan Valley. Ponies are available and also porters if farm labour demands are not too high. From **Sheshnag** (Amarnath trek) you can reach Ladakh via the *Gulgali Pass* (4,500 m). Allow six days and take a local guide if you are doing this early in the season.

LADAKH

Approx 98,000 sq km. *Population* 135,000. 2,500-4,500 m with passes at 6,000 and peaks up to 7,500 m all around.

INTRODUCTION

The mountains of Ladakh are not particularly spectacular. Because Leh is already at an altitude of 3,500 m the summits are only 3,000 m higher and do not look any bigger than the Alps. Because it is desert there is little snow on them and they look like big brown hills – a bit bigger than the Scottish Highlands, for example, but not a lot. When you get into them they are dry and dusty, with clusters of willows and desert roses along the streams. Yet successive visitors still find that Ladakh is a completely magical place. It is remote, with delightful, gentle, ungrasping people.

By natural inclination and with the exception of those places on trade routes, Ladakhi society has been very introverted. The economy has been surprisingly self-sufficient in what is a hostile environment. Ladakh also developed a very distinct culture. Polyandry was common, many men (and in the past, women) became monks. The harsh climate contributed to very high death rates, which resulted in a stable population based on subsistence agriculture.

That is rapidly changing. Imported goods are increasingly widely available and more and more people are taking part in the monetary economy. Traditional Ladakh is being quickly brought more is step with the 20th century. Ladakh and Leh, the capital, have been open to tourists only since 1974. Some argue that already there have been too many.

Travel by road gives you an advantage over flying into Leh as it enables you to acclimatise to a high altitude plateau and if you are able to hire a jeep or car it will give you the flexibility of stopping to see the several sights on the way.

Land

Four mountain ranges pass though the region – Gt Himalayan, Zanskar, Ladakh and Karakoram. It also has the world's largest glaciers outside the poles. The towns and villages occur along the river valleys – the Indus and its tributaries, Zanskar, Shingo and Shyok. There is the large beautiful lake **Pangong Tso**, 150 km long and 4 km wide at a height of 4,000 m.

Vegetation

Out of necessity, the people, particularly the Baltis, are expert irrigation engineers, cutting granite to channel melt water to the fields. The barley grown is turned into **tsampa*** after roasting and grinding, **gur gur*** is the salted butter tea. Apple and apricots grow well, with the latter being dried for the winter, the kernel yielding oil for burning in prayer lamps. At lower altitudes, grape, mulberry and walnut is grown. The willow and poplar grow in profusion and provide fuel and timber, as well as fodder and material for basket making. The fragrant **juniper** is reserved for religious ceremonies.

Wildlife

The area with its unique terrain and climate supports some rare species of animals and birds. You will have the chance to see red foxes, wolves, ibex, mouse hare and marmots and the bird watcher be able to spot the black necked cranes, Bactrian magpies, Turkoman rock pigeon, desert wheatears, buntings, larks, kite, kestrel and many kinds of finches, ducks and geese among the hundred or so species that inhabit the region. Some of the mammals are only found in Ladakh, among them the *brong drong* (wild yak), *kyang* (wild horse) and *nyan* (the large-horned sheep). The snow leopard is the rarest wild animal and you are unlikely to see some of the others, like the musk deer, the Tibetan gazelle or the Tibetan antelope which is prized for its fleece which produces **Shahtoosh***, the very best wool.

Climate

The temperature goes down to -30°C in Leh and Kargil and -50°C in Dras, remaining sub-zero for 3 months, from Dec to Feb. Yet on clear sunny days, it can be scorching hot and you can get sun burnt. Rainfall is minimal, 50 mm annually, the melting snow sustaining life. In the desert like landscape, you may come across sand dunes and there are even occasional dust storms.

Communication

Though the area is virtually cut off for 6 months, it nevertheless has always retained cultural links with its neighbouring regions in Himachal Pradesh, Kashmir, Tibet and Central Asia and traded in valuable **Pashm***, carpets, apricots, tea, and small amounts of salt, boraz, sulphur, pearls and metals. Animal transportation is provided by yaks, ponies, Bactrian camels and *hunia* sheep with broad backs.

Economy

Livestock is precious, especially the **yak** and goat. The yak provides meat, milk for butter, hair and hide for tents, boots, ropes, horns for agricultural tools and dung for fuel. Goats, especially in the eastern region, produce fine *pashm* for export. The Zanskar pony is fast and strong and therefore used for transport – and for the special game of Ladakhi polo!

People

There are four main groups. The **Mons** who are of Aryan stock are usually professional entertainers, often musicians. The **Dards** are found along the Indus valley, many converted to Islam, though some remained Buddhist. **Tibetans** form the bulk of the population in Central and Eastern Ladakh, though they have assumed the Ladakhi identity over generations. The **Baltis** who are thought to have originated in Central Asia, mostly live in the Kargil region.

Ladakhis are hardy, cheerful and live close to nature. They dress in **gonchas*** which is a loose woollen robe tied at the waist with a wide coloured band. Buddhists usually wear dark red while Muslims and nomadic tribes often use undyed material. A variety of head dress is worn, from the simple woollen cap with a rolled brim worn by the Baltis to the ornate black **peraks*** studded with turquoise and lapis lazuli, worn by some Ladakhi women.

Religion

The majority follow **Mahayana Buddhism** (*Vajrayana*), with a mixture of animistic pre-Buddhist **Bon** origins and influence of **Tantrism** from Hinduism. W Ladakh also has a large number of **Shia** Muslims, their mosques influenced by Persian architecture. The Buddhist *gompas* or monasteries are places of worship, of meditation and religious instruction and the structures, often sited in spectacular mountain ridges add to the attraction of the landscape while remaining a central part of the Ladakhi life. Travellers to Ladakh will find visits to *gompas* a rewarding experience, especially as some are within easy reach of Leh.

Winter festivals The festivals usually take place in the bleak winter months when villagers gather together, stalls spring up around the *gompas* and colourful dance dramas and masked dances are performed in the courtyard. Musical instruments, weapons and religious objects are brought out during these dance performances. The high priest (the **Kushak**) is accompanied by monks in recitation while others play cymbals, trumpets and drums. The serious theme of the victory of Good over Evil is lightened by comic interludes. Although most of the annual festivals are celebrated in Jan and Feb, you may be lucky to be at one of the few that celebrates their's in a warmer month, for example Lamayuru – end Apr/ early May; Hemis – end Jun/ early Jul; Phyang – Jul. Thikse – mid Jul/ early Aug.

The gompas When you approach the *gompas* you will notice walls of stones inscribed with prayers and figures called *manis*, as well as *chortens* which are shrines containing relics of some religious significance. Each monastery has a courtyard and on the outer walls, you will notice lines of 'prayer wheels' which are wood and metal cylinders with prayers written on pieces of paper inside. Every turn of each cylinder is equated to prayers being said and so adds to the religious merit of the pilgrim or every travelling Buddhist. You will notice smaller hand-held individual ones used for the same purpose and can be bought as souvenirs. Inside the **gompas*** the walls are decorated with paintings and **tankhas*** and many house precious manuscripts, statues of the Buddha, as well as musical instruments and masks used for ceremonies. Outside (and inside), buntings and prayer flags, which are colourful pieces of cloth, decorate the building.

Visitors to a *gompa* will be often expected to pay an entry fee (since they would be entering it as though it were a museum), which goes towards the maintenance and restoration work. As they are places of worship and are considered holy, visitors are expected to dress in a fitting manner, remove their shoes, and not eat, drink or smoke. The paintings and other objects should not be touched or flash used for photography.

Recent History

Since 1962 when trouble with the Chinese flared up, a large contingent of the Indian army has maintained a presence in Ladakh. This will have been most striking on the journey by road to Leh with all the convoys and the large army camp and airfield on the edge of town. Whilst their presence has not produced devastating effects, the strategic requirements of better links with the rest of India have resulted in Ladakh being 'opened up' and have had some corrosive effects.

SRINAGAR TO LEH

The journey from Srinagar to Leh must be one of the most fascinating road journeys in the world. There are dramatic scenic and cultural

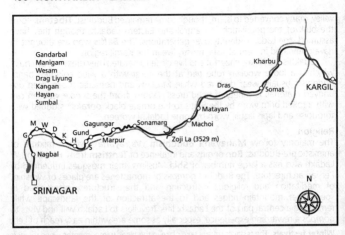

changes as you go from Muslim, verdant Kashmir to Buddhist, ascetic Ladakh. The engineering skill employed in constructing the road is stunning as it negotiates high passes and brittle mountainsides. This will be a trip to remember and your adrenalin is going to get good exercise. However, see warning below. The route is not open to foreign visitors in 1991.

Places en route are: **Gandarbal** (19 km from Srinagar), **Kangan** (19 km), **Sumbal** (16 km). *Sonamarg* (30 km - "Path of Gold" 2,740 m), is the last major town in Kashmir before the **Zoji La** and **Ladakh**. Its name may derive from the fact that it was on this important feeder to the Great Silk Road or, more likely, because of its carpet of spring flowers.

Legend has it that it is the spring which has the power to turn anything into gold. Whatever, this valley by the Sindh river has been regarded by many as a close rival to Gulmarg in beauty, grandeur and picturesque scenery with its forests of silver fir and blue pine. Accommodation is available here during the summer. **D** *Sonamarg Glacier Hotel*. Newly opened. Also, a range of Government **E** *Tourist Huts* with double rm, kitchen and sitting rm, an **F** *Rest House* nr the Tourist Office, and *Tourist Bungalow* outside the town.

The small village of *Baltal* (43 km), is the last Kashmiri settlement and is at the foot of the pass. It is 13 km from here to the pass itself. *Zoji La* (3,529 m) marks the boundary between Kashmir and Ladakh. The road here is unsurfaced, narrow and with steep unprotected drops which can be a little worrying. This is the first of the passes on the Srinagar-Leh Highway to be blocked by snow each year even though it is not the highest. There are higher ones but these are nearer Leh and in a rainshadow area. The approach is a long haul across a slate mountainside which looks as though it might shear off at any moment.

From **Zoji la** the road descends to *Minamarg* meadow, rich in rare Alpine flora and then on to **Dras** (50 km from Baltal),which is the first village after the Zoji La pass. This is where the convoys over the pass start and end and is also the base for the road clearing gangs. The winter temperatures go down to -50°C, and heavy snow and strong winds cut off the town. The inhabitants here are Dard Muslims. There is a bank and a *Tourist Bungalow*. You travel along the Dras river and pass **Kharbu**. As you approach **Kargil** , (30 km, 2,740 m) you will notice the careful channelling of water in the inhospitable granite irrigating terraces to make the area support apple and apricot orchards, fields of buckwheat and barley and

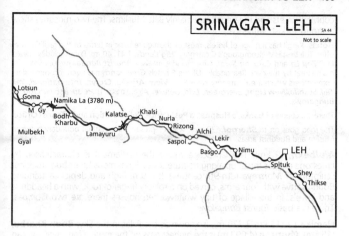

groves of willow and poplar. The town sits on the bank of the river Suru.

Kargil was an important trading post on two routes, from Srinagar to Leh and to Gilgit and the lower Indus Valley. Nowadays, it is the overnight stopping place of the Srinagar-Leh highway. All J&KSRT buses on the Srinagar to Leh route stop here for the night. You arrive hot, dusty and tired in the early evening and depart early the next day. To cater for the more demanding and affluent tourist there is one good hotel. Otherwise, the establishments are dingy. The broad Kargil basin and its wide terraces is separated from the Mulbekh valley by the 12 km long **Wakha Gorge**. Kargil is also the starting point of trekking expeditions lasting 7 to 12 days and mountaineers attempting to climb the Nun and Kun, both over 7,000 m high, start from here. The town has a medieval atmosphere with narrow

1. Tourist Reception Centre	8. Telephone Exchange	15. *Ruby Hotel*
2. Post Office	9. *New Light Hotel*	16. *Naktul Hotel*
3. Police Station	10. *Argali Hotel*	17. *Greenland Hotel*
4. Bank	11. *Deluxe Hotel*	18. *Suzu Hotel*
5. Taxi Stand	12. *Tourist Bungalow*	19. *Evergreen Hotel*
6. Bus Booking Station	13. *Nun-Kun Hotel*	20. *Crown Hotel*
7. Govt. Handicrafts Emporium	14. *Lyle Hotel*	21. *International Hotel*

cobbled streets and the people are mainly Balti Muslims. The two mosques show a strong Turkish influence.

Hotels Kargil has a range of hotels, most of them quite basic in terms of the facilities they offer. The best is Welcomgroup's **C** category *Highlands*, T 41. 40 rm. Price includes meals. **D** *D'Zoji La* and *Caravan Sarai*. Price includes meals. **E** *Tourist Bungalow*, 0.5 km from main street by the river. Reasonable. Of the **E** hotels *Greenlands* has been recommended. Some others which are **F** category are – *Suru View, Argalia, Crown, International, Yak Tail, Sushila, New Light, Evergreen, Lylo, Deluxe.* All are basic. There are also two *Tourist Bungalows.*

There is a couple of **banks**, a **Hospital**, a **Post Office**, **Police Station** and a **Tourist Office**.

The road goes on to **_Shergol_**, (30 km), which represents the cultural boundary between Muslim and Buddhist areas.

Mulbekh, (9 km). The landscape round the settlement is characterised by limestone masses thrust up along fracture zones. It is famous for its huge rock-cut sculpture of *Maitreya* (8th-9th century). It is 9 m high and depicts a standing Boddhisattva with four arms, carved on a solitary finger of rock, with a headdress and jewels. In the village of tidy whitewashed houses there are two *Gompas.* There is a basic *Tourist Bungalow.*

Namika La (13 km 3,720 m), is known as the Pillar in the Sky; **Bodh Kharbu**, (15 km); **Photu La** (4,093 m) is the highest pass on the route. From here you can catch sight of the monastery at Lamayuru. **Khalsi** (36 km) is where the road meets the milky green **Indus river** which leaves the wide valley of Ladakh and disappears into a deep granite gorge. The village has abundant apricots.

At *Lamayuru,* (10 km) the monastery is perched on a crag overlooking the Indus River. The complex, thought to be the oldest in the region, was founded in the 11th century and belongs to the Tibetan Kagyupa sect. It was partly destroyed in the 19th century. Some of the murals, however, which mix Indian and Tibetan styles have been preserved and along with the recently redecorated *dukhang* (hall) is worth a visit if you have the opportunity. There are caves carved out of the mountain wall and some of the rooms are richly furnished with carpets, Tibetan tables and butter lamps.

Rizong (53 km), has a monastery and nunnery, each apparently able to accommodate members of their respective sexes. After passing the caves at **Saspol** you arrive at **Alchi** (7 km), which has a large temple complex and is regarded as one of the most important Buddhist centres in Ladakh and a jewel of monastic skill. There are five shrines in the **Choskor** complex (11th century) which has some splendid wall paintings. The flood plain at Alchi is very fertile and provides good and relatively extensive agricultural land.

The next monastery is at **Lekir** (12 km) and you then reach the fortress of **_Basgo_** (10 km) which contains the ruins of a Buddhist citadel impressively sited on a spur overlooking the Indus Valley. It served as a royal residence for several periods between the 15th and 17th Centuries. Tibetan and Mongol armies besieged it. There are two Buddhist temples, numerous *chortens** and *mani** walls beyond the village. The Maitreya Temple (16th century) was contructed by the Namgyal rulers. There is a large sculpture of Maitreya at the rear of the hall. The Serzang (Gold and Copper) Temple (17th century) is the other and contains murals depicting the Buddha though these have suffered much from water damage.

From here the road rises to another bare plateau to give you the first glimpse of **Leh**, still 30 km away. You then pass *Phyang* with its 16th century *gompa* housing hundreds of statues on wooden shelves, and finally to *Spituk* (29 km). The Buddhist monastery here was founded in the 11th century but the buildings here are later. It is constructed in a series of tiers with courtyards and steps. The long **Dukhang hall** (16th-17th century) is the largest building and has two rows of seats running the length of the walls to a throne at the far end. Sculptures and miniature chortens are displayed on the altar. The **'Mahakal Temple'** (16th-17th century) contains a shrine of **Vajrabhairava** which is often mistaken for the Hindu goddess Kali. Her terrifying face is only unveiled once a year in Jan. This chamber also contains a collection of ancient masks.

The final approach to Leh can be disappointing after such a spectacular ride. Amidst stark mountains, the Indus valley widens and before entering the city 'proper' you go through a vast expanse of army huts. Then you see Leh, the buildings all piled up on one another and topped by the ancient, but unused, palace.

LEH

Population 8,718 (1981) *Altitude* 3,521 m *Best season* May to Nov. *Clothing* Plenty of layers. When the sun is up it gets quite hot but in the shade it can still be very cold. Weather permitting and when the political situation in Kashmir is normal, Indian Airlines connects **Leh** with **Delhi** (1,310 km, 2 hr) via **Srinagar** (434 km). Flights are now available from **Manali**. The airport is 8 km from the city centre.

	Jan	Feb	Mar	Apr	May	Jun	Jul	Aug	Sep	Oct	Nov	Dec	Av/Tot
Max (°C)	-3	1	6	12	17	21	25	24	21	14	8	2	12
Min (°C)	-14	-12	-6	-1	3	7	10	10	5	-1	-7	-11	-1
Rain (mm)	12	9	12	7	7	4	16	20	12	7	3	8	117

Warning Arriving in Leh (Altitude 3,521 m) by plane after spending a few days in Srinagar (1,768 m) or Manali, or after flying straight from Delhi (Altitude 216 m) or Jammu (305 m) will mean that you have experienced a substantial increase in altitude. You need to acclimatise by not exerting yourself too much. Rest is very important. If you have travelled by road from Srinagar you will have acclimatised better. Still, a mild headache is common and can be treated with aspirin or paracetomol. After a couple of days you will feel more energetic as your body adjusts to the changed atmospheric conditions. If you have a heart condition, consult your doctor on the feasibility of your going to Leh before you book.

If you want to acclimatise slowly the best way to travel to Leh is to go by road and return by air, weather permitting. The ordinary buses are inexpensive although the delux buses charge considerably more. Alternatively, you can hire a taxi which works out more expensive than flying but gives you the freedom to stop when you want to, especially to visit *gompas* on the way. You may sometimes be able to hire a taxi for a fraction of the quoted rate for the return journey, should you choose to fly out from Srinagar (see Travel below).

Health warning Many people suffer from stomach upsets. There is no clean water or sewage sytem for a town which may have a population of 25,000 in the summer. Furthermore, most meat is brought in unrefrigerated lorries, a two day journey from Srinagar. It is best avoided. Because of these problems it is necessary to be even more careful about food and hygiene than elsewhere in South Asia.

Note on Security As a matter of course, you should carry your passport with you. This is especially so in Ladakh which is a sensitive border region. there are checkpoints on some routes and from Srinagar to Leh via Kargil you pass very close to the *de facto* border with Pakistan.

Leh is situated in a fertile side valley of the Indus about 10 km from the river. It

LEH SA 45
Not to scale

To Sankar Gumpa→

N

To Nubra Valley

Polo Ground

To Thikse, Shey, Hemis

To Airport
Kargil
Srinagar

13. National Archery Stadium
14. Petrol Station
15. Handicraft Training Centre
16. Tourist Taxi Stand
17. Taxi Stand
18. Potala Restaurant
19. Burman Restaurant
20. *Tak Guest House*
21. *Old Ladakh Guest House*
22. *Hilltop Hotel*
23. *Kidar Hotel*
24. *Tsemo La Hotel & Library*
    & Ecological Centre
25. *Himalaya Hotel*
26. *Shangri La Hotel*
27. *Hotel Kang La*
28. *Circuit House*
29. *Hotels Lha Ri Mo & K Sar*

1. Leh & Tsemo Gompas
2. Buddha Picture
3. Chorten
4. Palace
5. Book Store
6. Mani Wall
7. Post Office & Card Shop
8. Bank
9. Police Station
10. Tourist Information
    & *DAK Bungalow*
11. Indian Airlines
12. Vegetable Market

developed as an important trading post and market and attracted a wide variety of merchants – from Yarkand, Kashgar, Kashmir, Tibet and northern India. Tea, salt, household articles, wool and semi-precious stones were all transacted in the market. Buddhism travelled along the Silk Road and the Kashmir and Ladakh feeder, and so have soldiers, spies, explorers and latter day pilgrims. Today, Leh is important as a military base and a tourist centre and it is these two groups who contribute most to the urban economy.

Local Festivals Ladakh's monasteries hold colourful festivals in the summer months – **see page 497** under Ladakh religion. Notable are the *Ladakh Festival* in Aug and the Hemis Festival in Jun. The *Hemis festival* is held to commemorate the birth of Guru Padmasambhava who is believed to have fought local demons to protect the local people. Young and old of both sexes, Lamas and commoners take part in which there are masked dances. Stalls are also set up selling handicrafts and other wares. *Losar* is celebrated in the eleventh month of the Buddhist year and dates back to the 15th century. It was held before a battle to enlist protection for the people of Ladakh.

Places of Interest The town is quite small and consists of a main street running up to the palace with small side streets running off it.

Leh Palace in the NW has been described as a miniature version of Lhasa's **Potala Palace**, with which this 17th century building is contemporary. It has nine storeys, sloping buttresses and projecting wooden balconies. The impression is that it is massively solid yet graceful as it rises up like a mountain. From the town below it is dazzling in the morning sun and ghostly at night. Built by King Singe Namgyal and still owned by the royal family, it is now unoccupied – they live in the palace at Stok. Visible damage was caused during the invasion from Zorawar Singh's invasion from Kashmir last century. If you visit the palace, be careful of the many holes in the floor.

Inside, it is like the Potala with numerous rooms. steps and narrow passages lined with old *tankhas*, paintings, arms and constitutes a museum. The central prayer room, usually locked but opened on request, is unused but has numerous religious texts lining the walls. From the roof of the palace are magnificent views of the Zanskar Range. Officially Open 0600-0900 and 1700-1900 but don't be surprised if it doesn't open at these times.

High above the Palace is the older and even more ruined **Palace/Fort** and the remains of the **Temple of the Guardian of the Deities.** The temple houses a large golden Budhha, many scrolls, murals and old manuscripts. Of the monasteries, the **Soma Gompa** (1957) in the centre of town is a new building erected to commemorate the 2,500th anniversary of the birth of Buddha.

The *Tsemo (Red) Gompa* (15th century onwards) is a strenuous walk N of the city and has a colossal three-storey high image of Bodhisattva flanked by figures of Avalokiteshvara (right) and Manjushri (left). It was founded by the Namgyal rulers and a portrait of Tashi Namgyal hangs on the left at the entrance. The **Sankar Gompa** (17th-18th Centuries) is quite modest and is the residence of the chief lama of Spituk. There are a number of sculptures here. The **Leh Mosque** (1594) was built by Singe Namgyal to pay tribute to his Muslim mother. It is in the main bazaar and is architecturally striking.

From the Radio station there are two long *mani** walls. **Rongo Tajng** is in the centre of the open plain and was built as a memorial to Queen Skalzang Dolma by her son Dalden Namgyal. It is about 500 metres long and was constructed in 1635. The stones have been meticulously carved. The other *mani* wall which is down the hill is believed to have been built by Tsetan Namgyal in 1785 as a memorial to his father the king. This is about 350 metres long.

Hotels Electricity is supplied for only about 4 hours per day in Leh – 1900-2300. A flashlight is recommended, partly for hotel use but mainly if you are visiting the gompas. The most expensive in the area is **C** *Ladakh Sarai,* Stok, T 181. 11 km. 15 rather fancy circular tents set among willows in a very peaceful location. Convenient for short treks, visiting monasteries and river rafting. Reservations: Tiger Tops Mountain Travels Enterprise at Srinagar or through their Delhi office at 1/1 Rani Jhansi Rd, T 523057.

    C The following are good in their class. *Tsemo La,* Karzoo, T 84. Once a private villa. Rooms, clean and tidy with bath. Restaurant and very pleasant garden. Popular with tour groups. *Kangri,* Nehru Park, T 51. 22 rm, with bath. Restaurant (Indian, Chinese, Ladakhi). *Kang-Lha-Chien,* T 144. 24 rm, most with baths. Restaurant. *K-Sar,* T 67, 184. Large rooms with pleasant views. Restaurant. *Lharimo,* T 101. 30 rms, all double with baths. Attractive lobby and restaurant. Good views from verandahs. Central. Recommended. Others: *Shambala,* Skara, T 67. Once run by Oberoi group, now in need of attention. Large rms. Restaurant. *Indus,* T 166 and *Lingzi,* T 20.

    C Class *Bijoo,* T 131. Two-storey white building enclosed by high wall. Rm with bath. *Dragon Leh,* T 139. 16 rm with bath. Almost always filled with trekking parties. *Himalayan,* T 104. 16 rm, 12 with western style bathrooms. Set in a shady willow grove. Camping in courtyard. *Ibex,* T 212. Restaurant, coffee shop, shop and travel. Pleasant terrace. *Omasila.* Double rm, garden. *Ra-Rab.* Clean simple rooms with baths. Also *Gai-dan Continental, Ladakh Sarai,* Stok, T 181, *Lung-Se-Jung,* T 193, *Mandala.*

    D Class *Choskor, Singe Palace, Tibet,* T 149, *Yak-Tail,* T 118. **E Class** *Hills View,* T 58, *Chospa, Delux, Dreamland* T 89, *Firdous, Khababs Khaltsi, Khayal, Phonsog-Ling, Snow View, Tsemo View.*

Tourist Bungalows and **Rest Houses** are very simple where you should use your own sleeping bags. You can also get very basic accommodation for under Rs 60 for double rm. Fleas and bed bugs can be a problem. *Lung Snon Guest House,* Sheynam Chulli Chan.

Delightful family guest house. Clean and friendly, but simple and basic. Earth toilet, cold water only. Run by teacher. *Palace View Kidar Hotel*, nr Polo Ground, T 161. *New Antelope Guest House*, Main Street. *Manzor Guest House* and *Two Star Guest House* are nr Tsemo La. *Old Ladakh Guest House, Moonland Guest House.*

Restaurants Local restaurants serve a variety of cuisines: Chinese, Tibetan, Mughlai, S Indian, Ladakhi. One of the best is the *Dreamland Restaurant* (not connected to the Hotel Dreamland next door). Central, good atmosphere, good food and reasonable. *Mentokling Restaurant* Pleasant, low cost, tables in garden. European and local food. *Tibetan Friend* Clean, simple and very friendly service – much used by local people. The *Shambala* is also recommended but is more expensive.

Banks *State Bank of India*, T 52. *J & K Bank*.

Shopping Leh Bazaar is full of shops selling curios and knick-knacks. There are tight restrictions on the export of anything over 100 years old. Baggage is checked at the airport partly for this reason, but mainly for security purposes. But don't worry. Even though most items are antique looking in fact they are fresh from the backstreet workshops. If you walk down the narrow lanes, you will probably find an artisan at work, from whom you can buy direct. Chang (the local home brew) and tea vessels, cups, butter churns, knitted carpets with Tibetan designs, Tibetan jewellery, prayer flags etc. are all available. Prices are quite high so bargain vigorously. Try to have lots of small change. There does not appear to be much in general circulation in Ladakh. In general, it is better to buy Ladakhi jewellery and souvenirs from Ladakhis instead of the Kashmiri traders who have moved in. *Artou Bookshop*, Zangsti, T 146. *Ladakh Medicate*, behind Post Office, T 136. *Dragon* Curio. *Tibetan Arts* and *Ladakhi Village Curios* have a good selection of *tankhas*, inlaid bowls, baubles, bangles and beads. *Imtaz* on Main Street is Kashmiri run and reasonable. Take a plastic bag for apples and apricots as the recycled paper ones have a habit of breaking. Peanuts are cheap in season.

Photography *Eureka Studio, Dijoo Studio, Lalit Studio, New Light Studio, Yountan Studio.*

Local Transport Tourist taxis, jeeps, tongas available with Ladakh Taxi Operators Union, Leh. Fixed fares point-to-point. Ponies and mules, check with Tourist Office, T 97. A day's taxi hire to visit nearby *gompas* costs about Rs 500.

Sports Information on mountaineering from Indian Mountaineering Federation, Benito Juarez Marg, New Delhi, T 671211. **Adventure Institutes in India**, contact the Tourist Office, T 97.

Polo The polo club – the highest in the world? – is well worth a visit.

Useful Numbers Police: T 18 Ambulance: T 14

Hospitals and Medical Services Sonam Narbu Memorial Hospital, T 14. Soway Clinic, T 117. Kunfan Octsnang Clinic.

Post and Telegraph Head Post Office and Telegraph Office, Leh. Post Offices at Choglamsar, Thiksey, Shey, Sakti, Chemray, Hemis, Karu, Matho.

Places of Worship *Buddhist*: All monasteries. *Muslim*: Mosque, Leh Bazar. *Christian*: Moravian Mission Church, Karzu.

Travel Agents and Tour Operators *Artou Travels*, T 146. *Dragon Tours*, Zangsti, T 8. *Rigyal Travels*, Hotel Omasila. *Fargo; Kang-chan Trek and Tours; Ladakh Safari Tours; Mamsothong Hing Adventure; Yuva Treks.*

Tourist Office and Information Tourist Information Centre, T 97. Foreigners' Regional Registration Office, Superintendent of Police, T 18.

Air Indian Airlines, City Office nr Dak Bungalow, T 76. Airport, through Army Exchange. Indian Airlines flies 5 times a week between Srinagar and Leh. Twice a week between Delhi and Leh and between Chandigarh and Leh. In winter months, this is the only link between Ladakh and the outside world. The flight over the Himalayas is very spectacular. Airport bus service and Jeep taxis available.

Warning Weather conditions can deteriorate even in the summer, which might lead to flight cancellations (especially outside Jul and Aug) so you should always be prepared to face a delay or take the alternative, that is road transport, out of Ladakh. Furthermore, Indian Airlines fly quite full planes into Leh but can take fewer passengers out because of the high altitude for take-off. That adds to the difficulty of getting a flight out. If you fail to get on the flight you had booked you do not get an immediate refund from the airline but have to reclaim it from the travel agent. It is also essential therefore to have enough money to travel out by road. Allow 4 days to get to Delhi by taxi.

Make sure that you are not connecting with an onward flight or train, immediately after your visit to Ladakh. Be prepared to take a taxi if your return is imperative. It is best to book air tickets at least 2 weeks in advance. Occasionally, Srinagar houseboat owners will offer to get 'VIP tickets' at short notice, for which there will be a surcharge of about Rs 60 a ticket. Despite the difficulties, even if you do not have a firm outward booking you may sometimes get on a flight at short notice if weather conditions prove to be better than expected. It is worth asking.

Rail The nearest railhead is Jammu.

Road Leh is connected to **Srinagar**, via **Kargil**, by a State Highway (closed Oct-May). Information on road conditions from the Traffic Police Headquarters, Maulana Azad Rd, Srinagar. From: **Kargil** (230 km); **Srinagar** (434 km); **Jammu** (739 km).

NB Since the security clamp down in Kashmir, the road route to Leh goes from Manali.

Warning Many travellers find the mountain roads extremely frightening, and objectively they are comparatively dangerous. Perhaps 1 vehicle in 10,000 falls off the road into a river or deep valley. Much of it is cut out of extremely unstable hillsides, usually with nothing between the road's edge and the often nearly vertical drop below. The road is often covered by landslides. It is also a long and uncomfortable journey. The compensations are some spectacular scenery.

Taxis are recommended for the journey from Srinagar, although it is expensive, as it gives you the chance to stop en route. The one-way hire charge for the 2 day trip is about Rs 3,500 (Rs 6,000 return). However, it is often possible to find one returning empty to Srinagar which you may be able to hire for as little as quarter of the regular charge. **Bus** J & K SRTC runs regular deluxe and ordinary bus services between Srinagar and Leh, from May to Oct. The overnight stop is Kargil. J & K SRTC, Tourist Reception Centre, Srinagar, T 72698. The fare on a delux bus is about Rs 300. Local buses run to **Kargil** (daily in summer), **Choglamsar** (frequently), **Hemis** (daily), **Spituk** (twice daily), **Shey** (3 times a day), **Stok** (twice daily), **Phyang** (daily), **Lamayuru** (daily, take the Kargil bus), **Matho** (daily). The vehicles are ramshackle but the fares are low.

Excursions

If you hire a car or jeep you can visit all the places below in one day. If you are short of time, try to visit Thikse and Hemis, at least.

Shey, 15 km S of Leh on the eastern (same as Leh) bank of the Indus. Open 0700-0900 and 1700-1800. Rs 5. Until the 16th century, Shey was the royal residence and was located at an important vantage point in the Indus Valley. It has a large victory *stupa* which is topped with gold. The royal family moved to Stok in order to escape advancing Dogra forces. Much of the palace and fort have fallen into disrepair but there are extensive grounds to the E with a large number of *chortens*. Shey along with Thikse is regarded as an auspicious place for cremation. The palace gompa has a 12 m high Maitreya Buddha which was commissioned by Senge Namgyal and is attended by Drukpa monks from Hemis. It is made of copper and brass but splendidly gilded and studded with precious gem stones.

Stok, 10 km S of Leh on the W bank of the Indus and close to the Choglamsar bridge. Rs 20. This is the royal palace dating from the 1840s when the King of Ladakh was deposed by the invading Dogra forces. The last king died in 1974 but his widow is still alive and his son continues the royal line and will ascend the throne in a few years at a suitably auspicious time. The Palace **Museum** at Stok is a showpiece for the royal *tankhas**, royal crown, dresses, coins, precious stones and turquoise head dresses. A rambling building with a small museum, well worth a visit, T 131. Open 0700-1800. Rs 25. A 3 hr walk up the valley behind Stok takes you to some extraordinary mountain scenery.

Thikse, 25 km S of Leh on a crag overlooking the desert on the E bank of the Indus, Thikse is one of the most imposing monasteries in Ladakh and was part of the original **Delgupat** order in the 15th century. The monastery has 12 storeys,

10 temples, a nunnery and 60 Lamas in residence. It contains numerous *stupas*, statues, *tankhas*, wall paintings, swords and a large pillar engraved with the teachings of the Buddha. The interior is dominated by a giant figure of the Buddha. There is an entry fee of Rs 10 the proceeds in large part going towards the restoration and maintenance of the monastery. Beside the car park is a small **Zan-La** temple. Thikse Monastery is a good place to watch religious ceremonies which are usually around 0630 or 1200. They are preceded by the playing of the long horns similar to *alpenstock*. Across the valley is the **Drukpa** monastery of Stakna which was built at the same time as Hemis.

Hemis, 45 km S of Leh on the west bank of the Indus. The monastery here is the biggest in Ladakh and is perched on top of a pleasant green hill surrounded by spectacular mountain scenery. Colourful flags flutter in the breeze from the four pillars in the courtyard and against the white walls of the buildings and the clear blue sky make a very pretty sight. The complex is entered through a gate on the eastern side and leads into a large 40 m long 20 m wide courtyard. This is where the sacred dances are performed during the annual festival – see Leh Festivals. Stones inserted into the wall are painted with saintly figures.

On the N side are two assembly halls approached by a flight of steep steps. The paintings and murals depict guardian deities and the Wheel of Life and are in a good state of preservation. At the upper level are a number of shrines, one of the most important being the bust of the first Lama. The Gompa has an important library of Tibetan style books and an impressive collection of *tankhas**, the largest of which is displayed every 11 years (last display 1991).

The **Hemis High Altitude National Park** covers 600 sq km and contains some rare species of flora and fauna, some, like the snow leopard, ibex, *bhral* and *shapu,* are endangered. There are camping sites where you can reserve accommodation through the Divisional Forest Officer, Wildlife Warden, Leh.

You can visit Hemis from Leh comfortably in one day if you are travelling by car or jeep. If you are reliant on public transport, an overnight stay is necessary. There is a rather grubby but cheap *Tourist Hotel* but many householders have overnight accommodation.

Phayang Gompa 20 km from Leh A traditional monastery, setting for a spectacular religious festival with masked dancing.

TREKKING IN LADAKH

Geographically, Ladakh can be divided into three regions : Little Baltistan (the Suru Dras, Wakka and Bodkarbu Valleys), the Indus Valley and Zanskar. See 'Trekking in Kashmir' for maps.

Little Baltistan is the region just beyond the **Zoji La** which marks the climatic and cultural watershed between Ladakh and Kashmir. It is part of the larger region of Baltistan which was divided on Independence and has an interesting past.

The Dards were among the earliest settlers and they absorbed Buddhism before 500 AD. When Tibetan forces invaded Ladakh a new culture was introduced. Later, in the 15th century, most Dardic communities were converted to Islam. Some Buddhist pockets remained. Trade links were strong with Gilgit and affinities were more with that area than with Kashmir and Ladakh. It was incorporated into the Dogra Zorawar Singh's Kashmir Empire in the mid 19th century.

The **Suru Valley** offers some very good trekking and **Kargil** is the jumping off point for treks in this region. There is a road along the valley now but this can be avoided for large sections of the trek. The metalled part extends to **Parachik** which is beyond **Pannikher**. An unmetalled road runs over the **Pensi La** – see Trekking in Zanskar below. The road to **Padum** is generally open by the beginning of July.

Sanko is a good starting point for a trek. From here you have the choice of continuing along the valley past the **Nun Kun Massif** to the S and on towards the **Pensi La**, or going over the **Wakka La** and **Sapi La** to **Mulbec**. You can also reach **Dras** via the **Umba La**.

Sanko to Dras This route goes through some very picturesque villages, especially in spring when all the wild flowers are out. **Umba** is the highest village. From the pass above it (3,350 m) there are very good panoramas of the Himalaya and Nun Kun. There is an intermediary ridge between the **Umba La** and **Dras**. Allow 3 days to do this trek comfortably.

Sanko to *Mulbec* This trek should take about 4 days and could be combined with a **Dras-Sanko** trek. From **Sanko** the route follows the **Thargam Valley**. The climb to the **Wakka La** (4,930 m) is steep. For the sake of acclimatisation, two camps are recommended before crossing the pass. Two more stages are necessary for crossing the **Sapi La** and descending to **Mulbec** on the **Kargil-Leh** Highway.

Rangdum To Heniskot

Rangdum is further down the Suru Valley towards the Pensi La and the trek runs NE over the Zanskar range to Heniskot on the Kargil-Leh Highway. The Kanji La (5,270 m) needs to be approached gradually because of its height and you should acclimatise well. If the ascent is undertaken too quickly there will be little enjoyment. Four or five days should be allowed for the trek.

The first stage follows the valley E of *Rangdum*. A guide is recommended as the trail divides and that used by yak herders skirts the southern edge of the Zanskar range and goes over the **Pingdom La**, **Kesi La** and **Netuke La** to **Lingshet**. Camp at the confluence of the two rivers in the **Rangdum valley**. From this plateau camp there is a gradual 4 hour ascent to the pass. In late spring there are snow bridges. By late Sep the going is over scree which can be very tiring.

From the *Kanji La* there are fine views of the Karakoram and Ladakh ranges. Care is needed on the north descent as it is heavily corniced. The camp is near the valley floor. The third stage follows the watercourse downstream and eventually *Kanji village* is reached. Here the path splits again.

It takes another four days to cross the *Yogma La*, travel down the *Shilakong Valley* and then on to *Lamayuru*. From *Kanji* to *Heniskot* is a spectacular descent through impressive gorges. Unfortunately, there are over a dozen river crossings. As always, extreme care is needed.

The Indus Valley Leh is the major town in this valley and the destination of many visitors. For trekking in this region, Jul and Aug are pleasant months. Go earlier and you will be wading through snow much of the time. Sep and Oct are also good months though colder at night.

Spituk To Hemis

Another popular trek. Whilst both places are in the Indus Valley and only 30 km apart a very satisfying 9-10 day can be undertaken by traversing the Stok range to the Markha Valley, walking up the valley and then back over the Zanskar range again to Hemis.

There is an interesting monastery at *Spituk*, a short drive from Leh. This was built by Delgupta monks in the 15th century who created the precedent in Ladakh of building on mountain tops rather than valley floors. From **Spituk** you proceed SW of the Indus along a trail passing through barren countryside. After about 7 km you reach the *Jinchan Valley* and from here is is a further five hours to **Rumbak village**. Camp below the settlement. You can also reach this place from **Stok** and that will require two days and a steep ascent of the **Namlung La** (4,570 m).

From Rumbak it is a five hour walk to **Utse** village. The camp is two hours further on and at the base of the ***Gandha La*** . To go up and over the pass takes about 3 hours, then it is the same time again to negotiate the wooded ravine to Skiu. Here the path meets the Markha Valley.

You can make a half day round trip from **Skiu** to see the impressive gorges on the Zanskar River. The stage to **Markha** where there is an impressive fort, takes a full day.

The next destination is **Hankar** village and from here the path climbs quite steeply to a plateau. There are good views of **Nimaling Peak** (6,000 m) and a number of mani walls en route. From ***Nimaling*** it is a two hour climb to **Gongmaru La** (5,030 m) and views of the Stok range and the Indus Valley. The descent is less arduous and involves stream crossings. There is a camp site at **Shogdu** and another at **Sumda** village, 3 km further on. The final stage is down the valley to the **Leh-Manali** road. The daily walking time on this trek is 5-6 hours so you must be fit and enjoy walking.

Lamayuru To Alchi

This is a shorter trek of 5-6 days. The average daily walking time is 6½ hours so do not imagine that because the shortness of the trek equates with less effort. Three passes, the ***Printiki La*** (3,500 m), ***Konke La*** (4,570 m) and ***Stapski La*** (5,200 m) are crossed rewarding the exertion of reaching them with excellent views.

The first stage involves walking from the usual camp site just below the monastery down the valley for 2 km then over the **Printiki La** (3,500 m). You then descend the ***Shilakong Valley*** and climb to **Phangi** village, passing huge boulders brought down by a landslide and impressive irrigation is such a forbidding landscape.

From Phangi you walk up the Ripchar Valley to **Halsi**, crossing the river a number of times. There are a number of small settlements until you reach the summer grazing ground a few kilometres below the pass. The **Konke La** (4,570 m) is a steep two hour climb. From here you will see the Zanskar river and gorge and the Stok range. At **Sumdahchenmo** village there is a large wooden statue of the Buddha.

The fourth stage should be with a guide since the trail splits, one leading to **Chillung** on the Zanskar River, the other to **Sumdahchoon**, the latter being quite treacherous as it involves many river crossings. About three hours below Sumdahchenmo there is a path which climbs the ridge above the river to **Sumdahchoon**. It is quite easy to miss this, hence the guide. There is a monastery at Sumdahchoon with an impressive statue of the Buddha and some attractive wall paintings. Just beyond the village are some camping areas. The last stage of the trek is long, about 8 hours walking, and takes you over the ***Stapski La*** to **Alchi**. Needless to say, the views from the top are splendid. From Alchi you can get a bus to Leh.

ZANSKAR

The land

Zanskar is a sub region of Ladakh and is a remote area contained by the Zanskar range to the N and the Himalaya to the S. There are two subsidiary valleys, the Stod (Doda Chu) and the Linak (Tsarap Chu) which converge below Padum the capital. The Zanskar flows along the valley from Padum to Zangla, then cuts through the Zanskar range in a series of impressive gorges to join the Indus. The main valley is approximately 300 km long and is ringed by mountains. Access to it is therefore over one of the high passes. The most important are the Pensi La connecting Zanskar with the Suru Valley in the W, the Umasi La with the Chenab Valley in the S and the Shingo La with Lahul in the E. This, of course, makes for very spectacular trekking country. The long Zanskar Valley was 'opened' up for tourism even later than Ladakh and quickly became popular with trekkers. There is now river rafting on the Zanskar river. There is a jeep road from Kargil to Padum over the Pensi La. This is closed for over half the year.

People

The Zanskaris are of the same stock as the Ladakhis and because of the sheer isolation of their homeland were able to preserve their Buddhist culture against the onslaughts of Islam. There are some old Muslim families in Padum, the capital, but these date from the Dogra invasion.

An almost total lack of precipitation has meant that cultivation must rely on irrigation. As in Ladakh, the rivers have been harnessed but with difficulty. The deep gorges presented a problem. Headworks were constructed and irrigation channels (yura) were contoured along to the fields, some up to 5 km away. Barley is the most suitable crop as it is very hardy, copes well with poor soils and can be roasted to form the staple **ngamphe** (*tsampa*) which can be eaten without cooking. This is useful in winter when fuel is scarce. Animal husbandry complements agriculture which only produces one crop per year. Sheep and goats are taken to high meadows in the summer after the snow melt and grazed while the shepherds live in small stone huts.

The foundation of **Sani** in the 11th century is recognised as the first monastery in Zanskar. **Phugyal** and **Karsha** date from the same period. The sects developed alongside those in Ladakh. The **Delgupta** order was established in the 15th century and monasteries at **Karsha**, **Linshet** and **Mune** belong to this. The **Drukpa** sect set up monasteries at **Bardan** and **Zangla** and 'occupied' that at Sani. These have links with **Stakna** near Leh and the **Delgupta** ones are associated with the Likir monastery. Zanskar became an administrative part of Ladakh under **Singe Namgyal** whose three sons became the rulers of Ladakh, Guge and Zanskar/Spiti. This arrangement collapsed after Ladakh's war with Tibet and the Zanskar royal house divided, one part administering Padum, the other Zangla. Under the Dogras, the rulers were reduced to puppets as the marauding army wreaked on the villages, monasteries and population.

Traditional Ladakhi and Zanskari life, even today, bears a striking similarity with Mahatma Gandhi's Utopian society, the ideal he believed existed in Ancient India: a small republic of villages, each self-sufficient, everyone playing a valuable part, with no crime and discrimination with regard to caste or religion and where disparities in wealth would not exist.

Padum has a population of about 1,000 of whom a sizeable minority are Sunni Muslim (see above). On arrival you must report to the Tourist Officer and accommodation is limited, to say the least, being mostly dormitory style. You can, of course camp. Access is either by the jeep road already mentioned which is generally open for four months from mid June until mid October. The alternative method is to trek in.

TREKKING IN ZANSKAR

As part of the Indian Government's aim of incorporating peripheral areas into the country, a road has been constructed over the **Pensi La** from **Kargil** to **Padum**. This tenuous link with the rest of the country can only be used in the summer months. Ladakh can be covered with snow for as much as 7 months each year, so for half the year at least it is cut off. This isolation has helped it to preserve its cultural identity, although this is now being insidiously eroded. Traditional values include a strong belief in Buddhism, frugal use of resources and population control. For centuries, the Zanskaris have been able to live in harmony with their hostile and yet nevertheless fragile environment.

Trekking in Zanskar is not easy. The paths are often rough, the ascents and descents steep, the passes high and the climate one of extremes. Provisions, fuel and camping equipment should be taken along from Srinagar, Kishtwar and Manali. You may be able to get basic necessities such as dried milk, biscuits and sugar from Padum but do not expect this at the beginning of the season. See 'Trekking in Kashmir' for Maps.

In **Padum** you must register at the Tourist Office. The Tourism Officer and Government Development Officer will be able to advise and maybe even assist in hiring horses. Porters can be hired at **Sani** village for the traverse of the **Umasi La** into Kishtwar. Horses cannot use this pass. In Padum you may also be able to hire porters. The advantage of porters over horses is that you can traverse rougher terrain.

There are four treks in Ladakh worth considering:

Pensi La to Padum (3 stages).

If you trek this route before the road is open (June to Oct) then obviously it will be free of vehicles.

Karsha to Lamayuru (9 stages).

This is a demanding trek which includes seven passes, five of which are over 4,500 m. The highest is the Singi La (5,100 m). A high level of fitness is therefore necessary before commencing the trek. Each day's walking should take an average of 5 hr 30 min. When you add time for rests and lunch this adds up to a full day. An extra day allows for flexibility.

The Buddhist monastery of the **Tibetan Gelugpa** (Red Hat) sect is the largest in the Zanskar Valley and is occupied by nearly 100 monks. It dates from the 13th century. The first two stages more or less follow the Zanskar River. Then it is a steady climb up to the **Purfi La** . The camp site is halfway down the other side. The next pass is the **Haluma La** (4,800 m) which provides a very good view of the last pass, the **Singi La**, and the distant **Stok Range**. Then it is a steep descent to **Lingshet** which has a monastery which is similar but smaller (30 monks) to that at **Karsha**. On the fifth stage you can camp below the **Singi La**.

This is the highest on the route to **Lamayuru** and gives a good view of where you have come from and where you are going. On the seventh stage you should cross the **Shirshi La** then descend though an area that supports abundant wildlife. In the **Photang Valley** that you reach next, some river crossings may be necessary. The final stage follows the **Shiulakong Valley** upstream to the **Prinkiti La**. The descent takes about an hour and the village often has cold beers!

Padum to Leh

This is another demanding trek which also takes about 10 days. Some is through the spectacular gorges between **Markha** and **Zangla**. A local guide is recommended as this is truly a wilderness area. In Jul and Aug river crossings are necessary.

It is 7 hours walking from **Padum** to **Zangla** and this includes crossing the **Zanskar River** by a string and twig bridge that spans over 40 m. Ponies are not allowed on it and if it is windy sensible humans don't. At **Zangla** you can see the King's palace. The third stage takes you over the **Charcha La** (5,200 m). On the next stage river crossings are again necessary. This is time consuming and if you are travelling in mid-summer, an extra day may be called for.
You then follow the **Khurna River** to a narrow gorge that marks the ancient border between **Zanskar** and Ladakh and end up below the **Rubarung La**. When you cross this you get good views of the **Stok** range. You then descend into the **Markha Valley** and from here you can reach Leh in four stages, either by going down the **Markha Valley** and going over the **Gandha La** and **Namlung La** to **Leh** or by crossing the **Gongmaru La** to **Hemis** and **Leh**.

Padum to Darcha

This is a week long trek and starts with a walk along the **Tsarap Chu** to **Bardan** and **Reru**.

After two stages you reach **Purni** where you can stay two nights and make a side trip to the impressive 11th century **Phugtal monastery** . The location of this is spectacular as it has been carved out of the mountainside around a limestone cave. Usually there are about 50 monks in attendance. From **Purnia** you continue on to **Kargya**, the last village before the **Shingo La**. It is still another day's walk to the camp below this high pass (5,200 m).
The mountain scenery is stunning with 6,000 m plus peaks all around. Once over the pass you can stop at **Rumjack** where there is a camp site used by shepherds or you can go further to the confluence of the **Shingo River** and the **Barai River**. By Jul and Aug this is quite a torrent and great care is required when crossing it. From here the trail passes through grazing land and it is about 15 km from the river to Darcha, the end of the trek. Keen trekkers can, of course combine this with a trek from **Darcha** to **Manali**. The average daily walking time of the **Padum – Darcha** trek is 6 hours so this is also a very full trip to be undertaken only by people with a high level of fitness.

EAST INDIA

GEOGRAPHY

E India covers 10 states. The population of W Bengal, Bihar and Orissa is over 180 million in 1991, representing over 85% of the region's total population of 210 million. The remaining seven states are the much smaller states of the N E, Assam, and the tribal hill states of Arunachal Pradesh, Manipur, Meghalaya, Mizoram, Nagaland and Tripura, all of which have received full statehood comparatively recently. The total area of the eastern region is 673,000 sq km, almost exactly the size of Texas, or of France, England and Wales combined. Calcutta is at the hub of the region; as the crow flies it is 1100 km from Assam's N border with China, 960 km from the SE tip of Orissa, and 700 km from the NW tip of Bihar. By land routes the distances are much greater.

The land
Within its area E India encapsulates some of the most striking contrasts in the sub-continent. Its northernmost section comprises the Himalayan ranges. Unlike the Himalayan ranges further W the mountains are not fronted by the comparatively low Siwaliks. Darjiling in northern W Bengal is thus overlooked by the main front of the Himalayas themselves, with Kangchendzonga dominating the immediate skyline and, weather permitting, Everest visible from Tiger Hill.

Immediately to the S of the mountain ranges are the plains of the Ganga (in the W) and the Brahmaputra (in Assam). N Bihar and W Bengal occupy the alluvial plains of the Ganga, which has created a monotonously flat landscape on alluvial beds over 3,000 m thick. Like the Himalayas the plains are of very recent origin, and the silt brought down by the frequent floods that devastate large areas of Bihar and W Bengal has also contributed to the fertility of the soil. After

Bangladesh, it is one of the most densely populated regions in the world.

To the S again is a land of further major contrasts. The plateau lands of Chota Nagpur in S Bihar and of Orissa are part of the ancient rocks of peninsular India. While the coastal districts of Orissa have broad flat delta landscapes, the interior has hills rising to over 1500 m. The forest cover of Orissa has been cleared much more recently than elsewhere in the region, and it is still widely populatedby tribal peoples.

The same can be said for the NE hill states. Assam and the states that used to comprise the NE Frontier Agency are quite different, physically as well as culturally from the plains areas of W Bengal and Bihar. In medieval India Assam was regarded as "foreign" to the rest of India, and it is still distinct today. The **Brahmaputra**, which flows through the Assam valley on its route from its deeply cut valley to the N down to Bangladesh in the S, is one of the most remarkable rivers in the world. Nearly 3,000 km long from its source in the high Himalayas to the junction with the **Meghna**, it flows from W to E for the major part of its course before taking a hairpin turn to run S W through Assam. The change in direction is almost certainly the result of earth movements. Before it reaches Assam proper it passes through gorges over 5,000 m deep. Even in the dry season it is broader, 1600 km from the sea, than is the Rhine near its mouth. In the snow melt and wet season the river flow increases dramatically. At **Guwahati**, where the river is nearly 1.5 km wide, it rises between 4 and 5 m during the wet season. It often floods, forcing settlements back from its banks.

The distinctiveness of the N E is provided not just by the Brahmaputra Valley or by the scenery to its S of low, forest covered hills, but by the prevalence of Mongoloid tribes, barely assimilated into mainstream Indian culture and life. Many still have strong ethnic connections with Burma and other regions of S E Asia. Many have also converted to Christianity, and in Nagaland and Mizoram, for example, Christians make up the majority of the population.

CLIMATE

The eastern region contains some of the wettest places in the world. The whole area is affected by the monsoon, getting most of its rain between Jun and Oct, but amounts of rain vary considerably. Orissa and W Bengal receive between 120 cm and 150 cm, decreasing generally from E to W, so that W Bihar receives less than 100 cm. The whole of Bengal is subject to storms between Mar and May, and cyclones can devastate any part of the coastal region from Orissa round to the state of Tripura and the Burmese coast in May and between Oct and Dec. Altitude makes a tremendous difference to rainfall. **Meghalaya** ('abode of clouds') is appropriately named, for in Cherrapunji it has the wettest weather station anywhere in the world. Between Jun and Oct, it receives over 10 m of rain on average - and in a wet year, more than double that figure. See page 596.

Calcutta's climate is moderate by comparison, but shows the strong seasonal contrasts typical of the region as a whole. Between Nov and Feb the weather can be very pleasant, cool at night and warm in the daytime. Further S into Orissa the same pattern holds, but both minimum and maximum temperatures are higher the nearer you get to the Tropic of Cancer. Altitude has its cooling effects, though, and around Ranchi in Bihar as well as further S into the Eastern Ghats of Orissa winter temperatures are also very pleasant. From Mar onwards the temperatures throughout the region rise sharply, and in all the lowlying and coastal areas high humidity makes it extremely uncomfortable. Temperatures can rise to between 40°C and 47°C, with humidity levels at around 80%. This is not a time for sightseeing on the plains, though Darjiling and the hills are magnificent through to the end of May. The arrival of the rains brings a slight lowering of the temperatures but a marked increase in humidity.

THE ECONOMY

Industry and resources The eastern region is of great strategic significance for India today, having a vital external border with China, along which war broke out in 1962, as well as with Burma, Bhutan, Nepal, and Bangladesh, whose territory it almost completely surrounds. It also has some of India's most vital resources. Oil has been exploited in Assam for over 50 years, and it has contributed a major share of India's home produced oil which now accounts for over 30% of total requirements. In the peninsular region of Orissa, Bihar and W Bengal there are huge reserves of iron ore, coal and minerals. The existence of these raw materials in abundance contributed to the decision of **Jamshedji Tata**, founder of the Tata Iron and Steel Company, to locate India's first steel mill at Jamshedpur in 1908. Particularly since Independence in 1947, the region has seen a huge expansion in heavy engineering industry, coal mining, power generation and a range of related activities, making it one of the most important industrial regions of S Asia.

Calcutta played a vital role in much of this expansion, offering demand for industrial products to feed its own engineering and related activities, and its port and other transport links, notably rail connections, to the rest of India and the outside world. In the 1960s and 1970s Calcutta handled nearly half of all India's trade, and its network of broadgauge railway links with the rest of India make it the pivotal point for the region as a whole. For over 100 years it has also been a centre for migrants coming in search of work, and there are communities from all over India living in the city.

Agriculture Underlying the comparatively recent expansion of the region's industrial base has been the continuing importance of agriculture. As a whole it is one of India's poorest regions, and although there have been significant developments in some parts of the region, agriculture has shown little improvement in others, notably many parts of Bihar,

Tea, grown in both W Bengal and Assam, is far and away the region's most important cash crop. Indigenous tea plants were discovered in the northeast corner of Assam in 1823. The East India Company began to exploit it when it lost the monopoly of the Chinese trade in 1833. As the geographers Spate and Learmonth have said, "the early days of the industry were marked by frantic speculation, non-existent estates in the midst of unmapped jungle being sold over and over again, and the acute shortage of local labour being met by beguiling Biharis and Madrassis with glowing promises, convoying them under guard, and keeping them in what were virtually concentration camps. In eighteen months over 18,000 out of 50,000 coolies died or vanished into the jungle. "Darjiling tea is now world famous, and production has risen steadily over the last three decades in response to growing demand from within India as well as from abroad. Assam alone accounts for virtually all of Indian production..

However, for most of the region rice is the staple crop, cultivated both for subsistence and for sale. W Bengal, Bihar and Orissa account for 30% of India's total rice production. Wheat is much less important, and accounts for only 8% of India's total wheat area. Throughout the region wheat is grown as a winter crop while rice is predominantly a monsoon crop. Thus the same land sometimes produces both crops at different times of year. Jute, the dominant cash crop in Bangladesh, has also become important on the much less well suited soils of W Bengal and Orissa, in order to provide raw materials for the jute industry whose supplies were cut off soon after the creation of Pakistan in 1947.

There is obvious pressure on the resources of the land. The average farm size in W Bengal and Bihar is under 2 ha and over 20% of the village working population has no land at all. The great majority of people thus remain poor, although there have been important agricultural developments, particularly where irrigation is available.

HISTORY

The eastern region has some of India's most important historical sites. By the 6th century BC the northern plains of modern Bihar were the developing heartland of Indian political power. Here both the **Buddha** and **Mahavir**, founder of Jainism, were born into royal families. Within a night's train journey from Calcutta it is possible to reach many of the most sacred sites associated with the Buddha's life.

Two centuries later the plains and their margins were the hearth from which the Mauryan Empire expanded to conquer the major part of the sub-continent. Under Asoka, the third Mauryan Emperor who reigned from 272-232 BC, the influence of Buddhism spread far beyond its original home. Modern Orissa was the only territory conquered by Asoka himself, the bloody defeat of which converted him to non-violent Buddhist beliefs.

Despite the importance of the eastern region as the home of Buddhism and Jainism, it was also the hearth of a succession of Hindu kings and emperors. The **Guptas** of the 4th to 6th centuries AD controlled great areas of N India from their cities of the plains of modern Bihar, creating an artistic tradition by which Hindu art has come to be judged. Much later, from the 9th to the 13th century AD, Orissa became the centre of a regional power responsible for some of India's most outstanding architectural and religious monuments, the temple complexes of Bhubaneshwar, Puri and Konarak.

The arrival of the Muslims That period marked the high water mark of Hindu kingdoms in E India. Very soon after the Delhi Sultanate was established in 1206, Muslim power spread right across the Ganga plains into Bengal. A succession of Muslim powers were established in Bengal itself whose influence stretched from Bihar in the W to Assam in the E. Often these were dependent on the main power in India's political heartland, focused on Delhi and Agra.

Under the Mughals from the 16th century onwards that power was consolidated. It also contributed to the shift in the religious balance of population in the region as a whole. Anxious to increase both their revenues and their political security the Mughal emperors offered incentives to clear and settle new lands. The Ganga plains between Delhi and Varanasi were already densely populated and cultivated. Further E great tracts of jungle remained uncleared, the Bengal delta, now the most densely populated region in the world, was covered in untamed forest. Muslim nobles set about clearing and settling forested tracts. Associated with the new settlements Muslim **pirs*** set up shrines and carried the word of Islam, that all are equal in the eyes of God, to poor and outcaste Hindus. Thus they created a second core of Muslim population, separated from that in NW India by the Hindu belt of the central Ganga plains.

Periodically there was also a destructive element in the extension of Muslim power across the E. Particularly under Aurangzeb many Hindu temples were desecrated or destroyed, some having mosques built on their sites. The eviction of the Brahmin priests from the major temples in Bhubaneshwar and Puri caused a reaction which is still powerful today, and is reflected in the refusal to allow non-Hindus into the shrines of the Lingaraj and the Jagannath temples.

The British The arrival of the British rapidly transformed the economy and the social character of the entire region. From the first settlement of Calcutta in 1690 to the permanent control of Bengal established after the Battle of Plassey in 1757, the traders of the East India Company developed networks of influence to protect their trading rights and powers. These increasingly involved political deals with princes who themselves were trying to protect their local power as the Mughal Empire began to collapse. During the next hundred years the East India Company converted Calcutta and a widening region around it into the chief centre of its economic and political power in India. Agriculture was channelled into producing goods, notably indigo, opium and later jute, for sale to Europe, and so produced tax revenue for the support of the Company, its servants and its army.

It was elements of the Bengal army that mutinied first in 1857, though they were stationed in Meerut, far to the NW, and Bengal itself remained unaffected. Calcutta had already been the pre-eminent city of the British East India Company's territories for 150 years. From 1857 it became the first capital of "British" India, which it remained until 1911, when the capital was moved to Delhi.

The role of Calcutta By then the economy of E India had been permanently re-shaped. Calcutta developed into India's largest manufacturing city, and much of the eastern region was tributary to it. If all roads in the Roman Empire led to Rome, all railways in the eastern part of the British Indian Empire centred on Calcutta. New lines stretched across Bengal to the hills of Assam to allow tea to be sold on the Calcutta market, ready for export. Coal from W Bengal and Bihar supplied the city and passed through it to other Indian destinations. Every fibre of jute grown in E Bengal was either exported through Calcutta or was processed there before export. It was a regional capital par excellence.

Calcutta had also become the centre of the newly emerging educated Bengali elite. Many obtained government jobs and moved to other parts of the region as administrators and clerks. The government administration in Assam, Bihar and Orissa was dominated by the new educated class of Bengalis. That was just one element of new population movements encouraged by the economic changes which were the hallmark of the later British period. The massive migration of labour into the tea estates from Bihar and Orissa was another. They led to changes which remain politically important today. Periodically troubles erupted, sometimes as a result of industrial disputes, sometimes because the intellectual Bengali population, who were kept at a distance by the ruling British, began to feel strongly a sense of discrimination against them.

The partition of 1905 Troubles were brought to a head by **Lord Curzon's** 1905 plan to divide the area which included Bengal, Bihar and Orissa. Bengal was divided into E and W, the former being predominantly Muslim. The action in 1905 resulted in a strong reaction in Calcutta where the call to boycott British goods and buy *Swadeshi** had begun a revolt which was sustained until Independence in 1947. Bengalis played an increasingly prominent role in leading the movement for independence.

The most prominent was *Subhas Chandra Bose*, who forty-five years after he disappeared aboard a Japanese plane is still revered throughout W Bengal. Originally a leading figure and one-time President of the Indian National Congress, Bose argued that India should side with the Axis powers and Japan during the Second World War in order to speed up the eviction of the British. After bitter disagreements with Gandhi and Nehru, Bose fled to Japan, returning to Burma to head the Indian National Army alongside the Japanese.

Recent developments The eastern region has undergone a series of traumatic events since India and Pakistan achieved independence in 1947. On the economic front the partition of India and Pakistan created great problems for the economy of Calcutta, cutting of access to supplies of raw jute. The war with China in 1962 opened up the whole of the Brahmaputra Valley to a Chinese invasion, and although the Chinese army withdrew the Indian army's defeat sent shock waves through the entire region. Then in late 1970 E Pakistan entered a crisis in its relations with the western wing of the country which resulted in a military crackdown on March 25, 1971. In the nine months that followed 10 million Hindu refugees fled into India, only returning after the brief war of December 1971 which created the independent state of Bangladesh.

Until the middle 1970s the NE hill states were ruled as a special Frontier Agency of the Government of India. Throughout the period many of the tribal peoples were fighting guerrilla wars against the Indian army, trying to establish their own right to autonomy. Assam has its own individuality. It is one of the very few areas in the whole of S Asia that until very recently had cultivable land to spare. As a result there had been continuous movements of agriculturalists from Bengal into the **Brahmaputra Valley**. Bengalis colonised much of the lower land, cultivating rice as in the deltas of Bengal from which they came. Land below 1500 m above sea level was severely malarial until the 1950s, which contributed to the sparseness of the population. In the late 1970s the native born Assamese mounted huge political protests against the immigrant non-Assamese. The problems have only partially been resolved. Elsewhere in the N E the major tribal groups have now been given their own states. Long periods of violent protest against the central Indian government in Nagaland and Mizoram were brought to an end in the late 1980s.

CALCUTTA

Population 10.86 m (1991). *Altitude* 5.3 m. *Area* 104 square km (city core), 1,380 square km (Metropolitan district) Calcutta's position on the low-lying, marshy delta often leads to high humidity levels – over 80% between Mar and Nov. *Best Season* Nov to Feb. Distance of city centre to Dum Dum airport – 15 km.

	Jan	Feb	Mar	Apr	May	Jun	Jul	Aug	Sep	Oct	Nov	Dec	Av/Tot
Max (°C)	26	29	34	36	36	34	32	32	32	31	29	27	31
Min (°C)	12	15	20	24	26	26	26	26	26	24	18	13	21
Rain (mm)	13	22	30	50	135	263	320	318	253	134	29	4	1571

INTRODUCTION

Calcutta, India's largest city, is capital of W Bengal. It was founded by the remarkable English merchant trader Job Charnock in 1690. In the 17th century there was a group of 3 villages along the river Hugli, Kalikata, Govindapur and Sutanuti, where communities of weavers lived.

The site was particularly holy to Hindus. According to one myth, **King Daksa** was enraged when his daughter **Kali** married **Siva**. He organised a *Yajna** (grand sacrifice) to which he invited everyone in the kingdom – except his son-in-law. Kali was distraught to hear that her husband had been so insulted by her father and threw herself on the sacrificial flames. Siva in turn arrived on the scene to find his wife's body already burnt. Tearing it from the flames, he started his dance of cosmic destruction. All the other gods, witnessing the devastation that Siva was causing in his anguish, pleaded with Vishnu to step in and end the chaos. Vishnu intercepted him with his flailing *chakra** (a discus-like weapon) and, in order to dislodge Kali's body from Siva's shoulder, chopped it into fifty nine pieces, which were flung far. The place where each one fell became a place of pilgrimage – a *pithasthana**. The toe of Kali's right foot fell at Kali Ghat. Thus, Kalikshetra or Kalikata gave the city its name.

Job Charnock was in charge of the East India Company factory (or warehouse) in **Hugli**, then the centre of British trade from Eastern India. He found it increasingly impossible to remain there owing to the attacks from the local Muslim ruler and was forced to flee – first down river to Sutanuti and then 1500 km S to Madras. However, in 1690 he selected the 3 villages where Armenian and Portuguese traders had already settled, leased them from Emperor Aurangzeb and returned to what was to become the capital of British India. Charnock became the first Governor of Calcutta, where he lived with his Indian wife, whom he had rescued from committing *sati** on her first husband's funeral pyre.

Calcutta has inspired passionate views. By 1780 the high quality of the British housing in Calcutta led to the nickname "village of palaces", but the Indian settlement was already desperately squalid. The traveller **William Macintosh** wrote in 1782 that "from the western extremity of California to the eastern coast of Japan there is not a spot where judgment, taste, decency, and convenience are so grossly insulted as in that scattered and confused chaos of houses, huts, sheds, streets, lanes, alleys, windings, gullies, sinks, and tanks, which, jumbled into an undistinguished mass of filth and corruption, equally offensive to human sense and health, compose the capital of the English Company's government in India".

Just over 100 years later the 20 year old **Kipling** borrowed James Thomson's description of Calcutta as the 'City of dreadful night':

> Thus the midday halt of Charnock – more's the pity!
> Grew a City
> As the fungus sprouts chaotic from its bed
> So it Spread
> Chance-directed, chance-erected, laid and built
> On the silt
> Palace, byre, hovel – poverty and pride -
> Side by side

Kipling's other verse in the 'Song of the Cities' speaks of the Calcutta

> the Sea-captain loved, the River built,
> Wealth sought and Kings adventured life to hold.
> Hail, England! I am Asia – Power on silt,
> Death in my hands, but Gold!

Calcutta still has areas of appalling poverty and squalor, but it is also an extraordinarily vibrant and lively city. Many people would not choose to live anywhere else in spite of its physical handicaps.

The first Fort was on the site of the present BBD Bagh. Named after King William III, it was completed in 1707 but was weak and badly designed "for the entire length was only 710 ft and the breadth at the northern end 340 ft, widening to 485 ft in the S". In 1742 the chief threat to Calcutta's safety was posed by the **Marathas**, and thus a deep defensive moat was dug, known as the Maratha ditch (**see page 973**). This is now followed by the Lower Circular Rd (Acharya Jagdish Chandra Bose Rd). That threat never materialised. However, the city fell easily when the 20 year-old **Siraj-ud-Daula**, the new Nawab of Bengal, stormed Calcutta in 1756. The tragedy of the '**Black Hole**' took place when the 146 British residents who could not flee (most having escaped by way of the river gate) were imprisoned for a night in a small guard room measuring about "18 feet by 14 feet 10 inches" (less than 6 m x 5 m) with only one window. Only 23 are believed to have survived. Some believe there had been 64 prisoners held in the room.

For a brief period Siraj ud Daula called the city Alinagar but it was re-taken early in the following year by **Clive**. In 1772 it became the capital of British administration in India with Warren Hastings as the first Governor of Bengal (**see page 99**). The new Fort William was built on its present site to the S between 1757 and 1770. In 1770 itself there was a catastrophic famine in Bengal and an estimated 76,000 people died in Calcutta alone. A heavy chain was run across the river, roughly opposite the present site of the Botanical gardens, to prevent pirates attacking the city.

Some of modern Calcutta's most impressive colonial buildings date from the years that followed. The Writer's Building, designed by Thomas Lyon, was built in 1780 as the trading headquarters of the East India Company, though its present terracotta facing dates from 1880. Government House was built between 1799-1802, St Andrew's Kirk in 1818. It was a period of intense activity, in which Calcutta established itself as the first city of British India. The Asiatic Society had been founded in 1784, and in 1813 the Bishopric of Calcutta was created. The first 2 Bishops, Middleton and Heber, made a profound impact. It was also a time

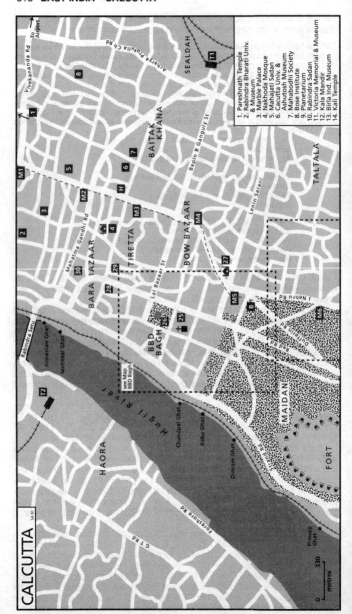

CALCUTTA

1. Pareshnath Temple
2. Rabindra Bharati Univ. & Museum
3. Marble Palace
4. Nakhoda Mosque
5. Mahajati Sadan
6. Cacutta Univ. & Ashutosh Museum
7. Mahabodhi Society
8. Bose Institute
9. Planetarium
10. Rabindra Sadan
11. Victoria Memorial & Museum
12. Kala Mandir
13. Birla Ind. Museum
14. Kali Temple

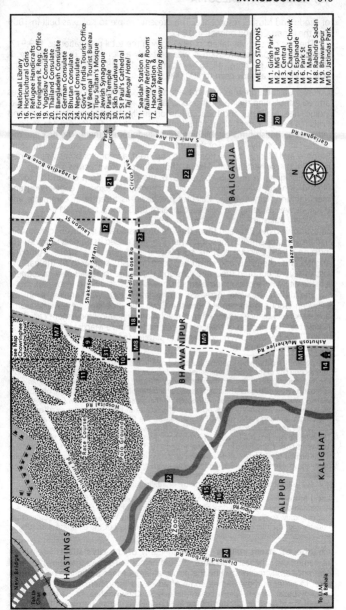

15. National Library
16. Horticultural Gdns
17. Refugee Handicrafts
18. Foreigners R. Reg. Office
19. Yugoslav Consulate
20. Thailand Consulate
21. Bangladesh Consulate
22. Sri Lanka Consulate
23. Bhutan Consulate
24. Nepal Consulate
25. Govt. of India Tourist Office
26. W Bengal Tourist Bureau
27. Tipu Sultan's Mosque
28. Jewish Synagogue
29. Parsi Temple
30. Sikh Gurudwara
31. St Paul's Cathedral
32. Taj Bengal Hotel

T1. Sealdah Station &
    Railway Retiring Rooms
T2. Haora Station &
    Railway Retiring Rooms

METRO STATIONS

M 1. Girish Park
M 2. MG Rd
M 3. Central
M 4. Chandni Chowk
M 5. Esplanade
M 6. Park St
M 7. Maidan
M 8. Rabindra Sadan
M 9. Bhawanipur
M10. Jatindas Park

of Hindu and Muslim resurgence. The present temple to Kali was built in 1809 and the Hindu College opened in 1817.

The first census was taken in 1821, giving the total population as 179,917. Despite the apparent precision it was probably a significant underestimate. It showed 118,203 Hindus, 48,162 Muslims and 13,138 Christians. By 1850 the population had already risen to 400,000.

Colonial Calcutta grew as new traders, soldiers, administrators and their wives arrived establishing their exclusive social and sports clubs. Trade in cloth, silk, lac, indigo, rice, areca nut and tobacco had originally attracted the Portuguese and British to Bengal. Later Calcutta's hinterland producing jute, iron ore, tea and coal led to large British firms establishing their headquarters there. The first jute mill opened in 1854. By the end of the 19th century Calcutta was connected to Delhi, Bombay and Madras by rail. Roads had improved, a bridge of boats was opened in 1874 to connect it with Haora, the industrial town across the river, and townships grew in the suburbs. In 1876, the Calcutta Corp began to provide filtered drinking water and a drainage scheme. The biggest engineering and manufacturing city in India, Calcutta prospered as a centre of commerce and trade, as well as being the political capital of British India up to 1911.

When Pakistan was created in 1947 Calcutta's economy suffered a catastrophic blow. Between them the jute processing and engineering industries had provided one million jobs, but when Pakistan closed its borders to trade with India in 1949 Calcutta lost its supplies of raw jute at a stroke. Although engineering, chemicals and consumer goods industries grew to fill the gap the loss of several hundred thousand jobs and the failure to attract new investment left the city with economic problems from which it has still not recovered.

The difficulties were increased in the late 1960s with endless problems between labour, management and the Govt. The problems were worsened by outbreaks of violence organised by a revolutionary political movement called the **Naxalites**. The election of the Communist Party of India Marxist (**CPM**) to power in 1977 has been followed by a period of stability for the city, and there are some signs of renewed growth.

The port of Calcutta which had played a vital role in British trade for 2 centuries making it 'the second city of the British Empire' has also declined in importance. 150 km upstream from the sea, the Hugli up to Calcutta was always difficult to navigate, and only suitable for comparatively small boats. The river was also silting steadily, with decreasing amounts of fresh water coming down even in the wet season. In the dry season the flow was so low that sea water was travelling many miles upstream of Calcutta at high tide, seriously affecting the city's main drinking water supply. For that reason the Govt of India built a barrage on the Ganga at *Farakka*, over 150 km to the N, so that water could be diverted down the Hugli. The scheme was first put forward by British engineers in the 1850s but wasn't taken up until 100 years later. Completed in 1971, water began to flow down the Hugli in 1975. Although it has helped to alleviate Calcutta's water problems it has caused major disagreements with Bangladesh ever since, as Bangladesh also needs the dry season flow of the Ganga for irrigation. Despite its colossal problems, however, Calcutta retains its commercial importance. It is also undoubtedly India's leading centre of intellectual, cultural, and artistic activity.

Local Industries   The trade in jute, tea and the industries that flourished in the city's hinterland owing to the rich deposits of coal and iron continue to play an important role in the economy some of which are detailed in the section W Bengal below. Some heavy engineering, car manufacture and ship building continues, but the emphasis is shifting to electronics and lighter consumer industries.

Change of street names   Although many of the city's streets have been re-named over the last 3 decades, the old names still survive in popular use and are more easily recognized by the public at large. Maps and guide books often refer to either of these names, some of which are listed here.

Bowbazar Street – Bepin Behary Ganguly St; **Chowringhee** – J.L. Nehru Rd; **Free School St** – Mirza Ghalib St; **Harrington St** – Ho-Chi-Minh Sarani; **Harrison Rd** – Mahatma Gandhi Rd; **Howrah** – Haora; **Kyd Street** – Dr. M. Ishaque Rd; **Landsdowne Rd** – Sarat

Bose Rd; **Lindsay St** – Nelly Sengupta Sarani; **Lower Chitpur Rd** – Rabindra Sarani; **Lower Circular Rd** – Acharya J.C. Bose Rd; **Theatre Rd** – Shakespeare Sarani; **Wellesley St** – Rafi Ahmed Kidwai Rd.

Telephone numbers Exchange numbers are being altered by area and you may need to check those listed with 44, 46 and 47.

Local Festivals *Durga Puja* (Sep – Oct) The most important Hindu festival of Bengal. Celebrations of music, dance and drama last for 10 days. Govt offices remain closed. Educational institutions and law courts close for 3 weeks (Puja holidays). Images of the ten-armed Goddess Durga (**see page 59**) with her 4 children are worshipped throughout the city in hundreds of beautifully illuminated and decorated *pandals** – marquees made of bamboo and coloured cloth. The priests perform prayers at appointed times while devotees flock throughout the day and loudspeakers relay Indian film and traditional music into the small hours. On the last day of festivities, processions, often emotionally charged, carry the clay figures to be immersed in the river at many points along the banks. *Ganga Sagar Mela* (Jan) is at Sagar, 105 km S of Calcutta where the river Hugli joins the sea. Vast numbers of Hindu pilgrims bathe in the holy water. *The Mahesh Yatra* (Jun-Jul) car festival at Serampore is particularly famous, 25 km from Calcutta. *Id* is celebrated by thousands of the city's Muslims in congregational prayer on the Maidan. During *Muharram* (meaning 'the sacred') they process beating their chests, chanting the names of Hassan and Hussain, the 2 murdered grandsons of Muhammad. They carry replicas of the Mecca tombs. *Christmas* is also celebrated in a big way. The numerous churches hold special services, including Midnight Mass, and the New Market takes on a new look in Dec as 'Barra Din' (Big Day) approaches with temporary stalls selling trees, pre-packed traditional stockings, baubles, streamers, and glitter. All other major religious festivals are observed as elsewhere in India.

Places of interest Sightseeing takes time, and outside Nov to early Mar can be very hot. Calcutta traffic is often extremely slow moving, and while the metro has greatly improved travel S of the Esplanade, the line N to Dum Dum will not open completely until the mid 1990s. Traffic N of BBD Bagh is often held up both by road works on Chittaranjan Ave, where the metro is being extended by cut-and-fill down the middle of the road, and by periodic hold ups on Haora Bridge.

NORTH CALCUTTA

Dakshineswar Kali Temple On the opposite side of the river from Belur Math alongside the Vivekananda Bridge, the temple was built in 1847 by Rani Rashmoni. The Kali temple has 12 spires and 12 other smaller temples in the large courtyard are dedicated to Siva and Radha Krishna. **Ramakrishna** achieved his spiritual vision of the unity of all religions while a priest here. Non-Hindus are not permitted inside. Accessible by buses from BBD Bagh. Allow about 20 min.

S of the Dakshineshwar Kali Temple is Chitpur and *Kumartuli*. Off Chitpur Rd in N Calcutta are the '*kumars**' or potters who work throughout the year preparing clay images around cores of bamboo and straw. The life size idols are of gods and goddesses, particularly of Durga on her vehicle the lion slaying the demon Asura, for the pujas or festivals. The images are usually unbaked since they are immersed in the holy river at the culmination of the festival. Often very brightly painted and gaudily dressed, as the time of the pujas approach thousands of images are stacked awaiting the final finishing touch by the master painter, before they are ready to be sold. There are also *shola* artists (**see page 546**) who make images for the pujas and floral decorations for weddings. The material is the pith of Bengal's sponge wood tree.

Immediately to the N of the new Belgachia metro station, on the N side of Belgachia Rd, is the *Paresnath Jain Temple*. This Digambar Jain temple is highly ornate, built in the central Indian style by a jeweller in 1867, and dedicated to the 10th *Tirthankara**, Sitalanatha. The interior is impressively decorated in European baroque and Italianate styles, with mirrors and Venetian glass mosaics, while the gardens have formal geometric flower beds and a gold fish tank. Open 0600-1200, 1500-1900. Free. Allow 15 min.

Running parallel with, but one street to the E of Chittaranjan Ave is **College Street**, "the heart of intellectual Calcutta". On a short stretch of this street stands the University with its various associated institutions, including the old **Sanskrit College** and the highly thought of **Presidency College**. Its Centenary Building was opened in 1817 as the Hindu College to provide "a liberal education" through the efforts of European and Indian benefactors. The Bloomsbury of Calcutta, this was the centre for Bengali writers, artists, religious and social reformers and thinkers of the 19th century. It was also the spawning ground of the nationalist **Swadeshi*** movement at the beginning of this century. The College Sq water tank is to the S of the Hindu School and Sanskrit College, and to the N, in a 3 storeyed building, are the principle book companies, an auditorium and the famous smoke filled **Calcutta Coffee House**.

Opened in 1944, the 'Coffee House' have been the haunt of the city's intelligentsia ever since. You can still get an excellent cup of coffee and soak in the atmosphere among 300 or so other people, watch some greying old-timers and regulars in their reserved chairs who may spend their whole day arguing, joking and discussing the events of the day. All along are the second-hand book stalls displaying their 'treasure' on wooden shelving which takes up every space along the iron railings.

Haora Bridge ("Rabindra Setu"). Opened in 1943, this single span cantilever bridge replaced the old pontoon bridge which joined the city with its main railway station and the industrial town of Howrah. It remains a prominent landmark. To avoid affecting river currents and silting, the 2 80 m high piers rise from the road level; the span between them is 450 m, increasing by a metre on a hot day. Considered one of the busiest bridges in the world, there are 8 lanes of traffic and 2 foot paths which are nearly always packed with vehicles and pedestrians.

Marble Palace 46 Muktaram Babu St. (Travelling N up Chittaranjan Ave, the 3rd turning on the left after crossing Mahatma Gandhi Rd) Open 1000-1600. Closed Mon and Th. Photography allowed for documentary purposes. Visitors free on obtaining passes from the W Bengal Tourist Bureau, 3/2 BBD Bag, 24 hr in advance. It is possible to get in without a permit, though a tip will be expected. Shoes must be removed before entering the reception hall.

It was built in the 'Chor Bagan' or 'Thieves' Garden area of N Calcutta in 1835, an ornate building with Italianate courtyard, classical columns a large tank with fountain and Egyptian sphinxes. It houses the one-man collection of Raja Rajendra Mullick Bahadur. There is some interesting statuary in the garden with 6 sleeping marble lions gracing the lawns. The entrance is through a courtyard where one is greeted by mynahs and macaws from the aviary. There are also stuffed birds inside. Befitting its name there are said to be ninety different kinds of marble from near and far, used in every part of the 'palace' especially to great effect on the patterned floors and cool white walls. The long galleries are crammed with statues, pottery, mirrors, chandeliers and English, Dutch and Italian paintings, disorganised and gathering dust. The Reynolds, Titian and Rubens are not generally on display. Part of the mansion is still lived in by the Raja's descendants, the present owners, who continue to keep up the tradition of feeding the poor at their gates at noon. The rambling museum on 2 floors has curiosity appeal but would benefit from better organization and upkeep. Allow about 40 min.

To its N is the Tagore family seat at **Jorasanko**, the home of the wealthy merchant **Dwarkanath Tagore** whose grandson was the gifted Rabindranath (see page 552). This is also the Rabindra Bharati University and Museum (see Museums below). Further N on Baghbazar St is the **Girish Mancha**, the new Govt theatre complex. Returning S and across Mahatma Gandhi Rd it is possible to visit the **Nakhoda Mosque** on Rabindra Sarani. It is the largest mosque in the city, able to accommodate 10,000 worshippers. Built between 1926 and 1942 of red sandstone, it is a four-storeyed structure reminiscent of Akbar's tomb in Sikandra, near Agra, and has huge blue and white painted domes flanked by 2 46 m minarets. Near the Mosque and just to the S of Haora Bridge is the **Armenian Church of Holy Nazareth** (1724), a reminder of the important role that the small

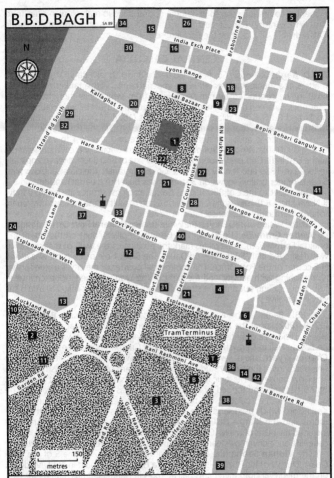

B.B.D.BAGH SA 89

1. BBD Bagh
2. Eden Garden
3. Ochterlony Monument
4. State Library
5. Parsi Temple
6. Tipu Sultan's Mosque
7. High Court
8. Writers' Building
9. St Andrew's Church
10. Netaji Stadium
11. Ranji Stadium
12. Raj Bhavan
13. Vidhan Sabha
14. US Information Service (Library)
15. Grindlay's Bank
16. Chartered Bank
17. Citibank
18. Bank of Tokyo
19. Hongkong & Shanghai Bank
20. GPO & Philatelic Bureau
21. Post Office
22. Telephone Bhavan
23. Police HQ
24. Calcutta Swimming Club
25. Alitalia
26. UP Tourist Office
27. W Bengal Tourist Office
28. Govt of India Tourist Office
29. East Railway Booking Office (1st Class)
30. East Railway Booking Office (2nd Class & Tourist)
31. SE Railway Booking Office
32. Shipping Corporation of India
33. Everett Travel Service
34. Mackinnon Travel Service
35. Amber Restaurant
36. Cottage Industries Emporium
37. Govt of India Publications
38. Kashmir Emporium & *Ritz Continental Hotel*
39. *Oberoi Grand Hotel* & Frank Ross (Chemist)
40. *Great Eastern Hotel*
41. *Hotel Minerva*
42. Y.W.C.A.

Armenian community played in commerce and trade in major Indian cities from the 17th century. Almost next door, on its E side, is the **Roman Catholic Cathedral** (1797), built by the Portuguese.

CENTRAL CALCUTTA

B.B.D. Bagh (Dalhousie Sq) Renamed Benoy Badal Dinesh Bagh after 3 Bengali martyrs, the square was created in the imperial capital with a tank (small artificial lake) in the centre fed by natural springs, from which it is thought that Job Charnock obtained drinking water. N of the square and just beyond Haora Bridge on Strand Rd N is the dilapidated Silver Mint (1824-31); opposite is the Mint Master's House, built at the same time. They are both in the Greek style.

Many historic buildings surround the square and it is best to visit the area before 0900. The **Writers' Building** (1780), where originally the clerks ('*writers*') of the East India Company worked, is on the N side of BBD Bagh. It was completely re-faced in 1880 and is now the state Govt secretariat. The classical block with 57 sets of identical windows on 3 storeys was built like a barrack inside.

One street to the E of BBD Bagh is Calcutta's oldest street, Mission Row (now R.N. Mukharji Rd). Here is the Old Mission Church, built by the Swedish missionary Johann Kiernander and consecrated in 1770.

On the W side of BBD Bagh is the white-domed **General Post Office** designed by **Walter Granville** (1868), with its Corinthian pillars, built on the site of the original Fort William. Brass plates mark the position of the walls of the fort which was destroyed in 1756 by Siraj ud Daula. The Black Hole of Calcutta was at the N-E corner of the Post Office. The commercial quarter of the city is a little further N, throbbing with activity, and the sight of the Lyon's Range stock exchange in full swing, spilling out onto the street, confirms that commercially, Calcutta is still very much alive.

S of BBD Bagh, at the N end of the Maidan, is the imposing **Raj Bhavan (1799-1802)**, now the residence of the Governor of W Bengal, formerly Govt House, residence of British Governors-General and Viceroys. It was modelled on Kedleston Hall in Derbyshire, (later to be Lord Curzon's home), and designed by **Charles Wyatt**, one of several Bengal Engineers who acted as architects of many fine buildings in the city by studying books and plans of famous British buildings. The Govt house with its Ionic facades and its processional staircase, set in grounds of 2.5 hectares and topped by a massive dome, was built so that India could be governed from a "palace". It is built of brick with cream-washed plaster, unlike Kedleston, which used sandstone. The interior is lavishly decorated with stately rooms and the Marble Hall containing several curiosities (which until recently included the busts of twelve Caesars, now removed), **Tipu Sultan's** throne, a 'bird cage' lift once driven by steam, and some artistic treasures. Entry is restricted.

The **Vidhan Sabha** (the State Legislative Assembly) is to the S of the High Court. Due W of Raj Bhavan is the **Calcutta High Court**, built in l872. Modelled on the medieval cloth merchants hall at Ypres in Flanders, it has a 55 metre high tower. It has been described as "the most important Gothic building in the city". Next door to it, at the junction of Council House St and Hastings St is **St. John's Church** (1787) (open 0900-1200, 1700-1800). Like the later **St Andrew's Kirk** (1818), which is at the N-E corner of BBD Bagh, and St. Andrew's Kirk in Madras, it was modelled on St. Martin-in-the-Fields, London, **see page 702**. The soft sub-soil meant that the height of St John's spire had to be restricted, and architecturally the church was thought to be 'full of blunders'. Verandahs were added to the N and S in 1811 to reduce the glare of the sun. The church contains a desk and chair belonging to Warren Hastings. Memorials inside include that to Major Kirkpatrick, Resident of Hyderabad from 1789-1805 and the tomb of Bishop Middleton, first Bishop of Calcutta.

The Last Supper by **Zoffany**, which shows Calcutta residents dressed as the

Apostles, was moved from its original place behind the altar because of rising damp to its present position in the S aisle. Charnock who died in 1692 is buried in the old cemetery. His mausoleum, the oldest piece of masonry in the city, is an octagonal structure, topped by a smaller octagon. The stone used is Pallavaram granite from Madras, which takes its name 'charnockite' from Calcutta's founder. The monument to the Black Hole of Calcutta was removed in 1940 from Dalhousie Sq (BBD Bagh) to its present location in St. John's churchyard.

PARK STREET AREA

South Park Street Cemetery Opened in 1767 to accommodate the large number of the British who died serving their country. The heavily inscribed, decaying headstones, elaborate classical temples, obelisks, pyramids and urns have been somewhat restored and the cemetery, which is the resting ground for many of the old capital city's Europeans, is a quiet space on the S side of one of Calcutta's busiest streets. Death, often untimely, came from tropical diseases or other hazards such as battles on land and at sea, melancholia and childbirth. More uncommonly there was death through a surfeit of alcohol, or smoking the 'hookah' or as in the case of Rose Aylmer, of eating too many pineapples! Tombs include those of **Col. Kyd** the founder of the Botanical Gardens, the great linguist and oriental scholar **Sir William Jones**, and the father of William Makepeace Thackeray, author of Vanity Fair. A good booklet is available. Open at all times. Allow about 30 min. Best early in the morning.

The Maidan It is difficult to believe that 200 years ago the maidan was still covered in dense jungle. Tigers, crocodiles and many other wild animals were common. Today it is Calcutta's lifeline, a unique 'green', covering over 400 ha in the heart of the city, extending from Esplanade in the N, the Race Course in the S, Chowringhee (J.L. Nehru Rd) in the E and the river to the W. In it stands Fort William, the Ochterlony Monument and numerous club houses providing tennis, football, rugby, cricket and even crown green bowls. It claims the distinction of being the largest urban park in the world – larger, than New York's Central Park!

The **Ochterlony Monument**, now known as Shahid Minar (Martyrs' Memorial), was erected in 1828 as a memorial to Sir David Ochterlony, who led East India Company troops against the Nepalese in the war of 1814-16.

The 46 m tall Greek Doric column rises from an Egyptian base and is topped by a Turkish cupola. It used to be possible to get a permit to climb the monument from the Police Headquarters in Lal Bazar (in the NE corner of BBD Bagh). Recent visitors have not been fortunate, but if you can face 223 steps, there is a magnificent view at the top, so it may be worth trying. Often called the 'lungs' of the city, the maidan is used by thousands each day to pursue a hundred different interests – from early morning yogis, riders, men exercising dogs, model plane enthusiasts, late evening lovers, weekend cricketers and the performers earning their living – snake charmers, jugglers and acrobats, to Calcutta's vast political gatherings. The Second Hugli Bridge was started at Hastings, the S end of the Maidan, in 1970. Approach works are complete but it is likely to be at least 1992 before the bridge itself is finished.

Chowringhee (Jawaharlal Nehru Rd) The city's main thoroughfare with shops, hotels, offices and residential buildings. Some of the old Palladian buildings with pillared verandahs (designed by Italian architects as residences of prominent Englishmen) can still be seen from the Maidan. Modern high rise blocks have transformed the skyline of the old pilgrim route to Kalighat. The **Indian Museum** is on Chowringhee between Mirza Ghalib St and Sudder St (see under Museums). 600 m S of the Museum is the **Birla Planetarium** (In Maidan immediately opposite Shakespeare Sarani, next to St Paul's Cathedral). T 441554. S Asia's largest planetarium seats 500 and has 3 shows between 1230-1830 daily (except Mon). Commentaries are in Bengali, Hindi and English. There are exhibits pertaining to astronomy, astrophysics and celestial mechanics. Entry fee Rs 5.

Directly opposite the Planetarium is **St. Paul's Cathedral.** Also close to the Victoria Memorial, it is the original metropolitan church of British India. Completed in 1847, it has a gothic tower modelled on the Bell Harry tower of England's Canterbury Cathedral, designed to replace the earlier steeples which were destroyed by earthquakes in the 1897 and 1934. The cathedral has a fine altar piece, 3 Gothic stained glass windows, 2 Florentine frescoes and the great W window by **Burne Jones**. Sadly, the original stained-glass E window which was intended for St. George's, Windsor was destroyed by cyclone in 1964 and was replaced by the present one 4 years later. The candle light service on Christmas eve, when the cathedral is full, is very moving. Open 0900-1200, 1500-1800. Five services on Sundays. Allow about 20 min.

The **Victoria Memorial** stands on the southern side of the Maidan. T 445154. Mar-Oct.1000-1530. Nov-Feb 1000-1630. Museum 1000-1530 (opening occasionally delayed due to late arrival of clerk holding the vital keys!). Closed Mon. Entry Rs 2. Cameras and electronic equipment are not permitted. Free guided tours start at 1030. Postcards, catalogues and brief guidebooks available.

Sometimes called the Taj Mahal of the Raj it was designed in Italian Renaissance-Mughal style and built of white Makrana marble from Rajasthan, in commemoration of Queen Victoria and as a symbol of her Indian Empire. Completed in 1921, it stands in well kept grounds of 64 acres with ornamental pools. A seated bronze statue of Queen Victoria dominates the approach, while another, of marble, is in the centre of the main hall, below the dome. Flowers are sometimes to be seen left at the feet of the latter!

The statues over the entrance porches, including those of Motherhood, Prudence and Learning, and around the central dome, of Art, Architecture, Justice, Charity etc., came from Italy. The entrance is through large ornate iron gates and it has an impressive 'weather vane' in the form of a 5 m. tall bronze winged figure of Victory, weighing 3 tons. There are over 3,500 exhibits in 25 galleries, some rather musty, including a wealth of Raj memorabilia. From galleries exhibiting portraits, paintings, sculpture, arms and armoury downstairs and ones devoted to prints of old Calcutta, to documents tracing the history of the East India Company and also a wealth of watercolours and engravings of Indian scenes.

You will come across Queen Victoria's rosewood piano and desk, books, portraits and paintings by Reynolds, Zoffany, **Daniells** and Emily Eden which hark back to the days of Empire. There are also fine miniatures, a rare collection of Persian manuscripts, portraits of national leaders and many reminders of military conflicts. There is a first class reference library. In all gives an excellent impression of the Raj days. Allow at least 1 hr. **Superb illumination** in the evening – worth another visit after dark. In Jan 1991, "musical fountains" were added – 3 fountains lit by coloured lights which are quite spectacular.

Fort William After the defeat in 1756 the British built a new massive fort to replace the original one at Kalikata and named it after King William III. It was completed around 1781 on the site of the old village of Govindapur. Designed to be impregnable, it was shaped in a roughly octagonal plan about 500 m in diameter. This was to make it large enough to house all the Europeans in the city in case of an attack, which never materialized. It stood on the edge of the river Hugli from which water was channelled to fill the wide moat. One of the 5 entrances to the fort was in fact a water jetty. The church of St. Peter, the barracks and stables, the arsenal, prison and strong rooms still stand. The jungle around it was cleared to give a field of fire. This became the Maidan. Today the Fort is the Eastern Region's Military Headquarters. Permission needed to enter.

SOUTH CALCUTTA

Kali Temple (Open 0500-2000) Dedicated to **Kali**, the patron goddess of Calcutta, who is usually portrayed with blood dripping from her tongue and garlanded with skulls. It was re-built in 1809 over the site of an older temple which marked the spot where one of the goddesses toes is said to have fallen when **Siva** carried her charred corpse in a frenzied dance of mourning and she was cut into pieces by Vishnu's *chakra**. Kalighat remains an important Hindu pilgrimage centre. Only Hindus are permitted inside. In the past human sacrifices are said to have been made but now only goats are offered daily on 2 wooden blocks to the S of the temple. Legend has it that '*thugs*' would offer their prayers to Kali here before a robbery. Next door is 'Nirmal Hriday' the home for the dying started by Mother Teresa (see below) who, with her sisters from the Missionaries of Charity now run many more institutions for the poor and abandoned elsewhere in the city. Allow about 30 min.

Mother Teresa's Homes Mother Teresa was born of Albanian parents in Yugoslavia and as a Loreto Sister went to teach in a Calcutta school in 1931. Nineteen years later she obtained permission from the Pope to start her Order of the Missionaries of Charity to serve the destitute and dying among the poorest. You may see the nuns always in pairs in their white cotton saris with blue borders busy working in different parts of the city in the many homes, clinics and orphanages. 'Nirmal Hriday' (pure heart), near the Kali Temple, the first 'home' was opened in 1952 for the dying among the poorest which is open to anyone who needs a place to find peace. Today there are nearly 300 different homes and refuges.

National Library Just S of the Maidan in Alipur, the former winter residence of the Lieutenant Governors of Bengal on Belvedere Rd was originally the property which was given by Mir Jafar to **Warren Hastings** on which the latter erected an "ordinary Anglo-Indian building". Later additions made it more impressive. Built in the Renaissance Italian style, with a double row of classical columns, it is surrounded by 12 ha of wooded grounds. Approached through a triple arched gateway, through a drive between mahoganies and mango trees, to the sweeping staircase to the S which is the entrance to the Durbar Hall where the card catalogue is housed. The ground floor has 15 km of closed stacks while the reading room in the old Banquet Hall where you have access to 10,000 reference books and Gazetteers. There is a new annexe with an auditorium and canteen as well as a readers' hostel. The air-conditioned Rare Books Section contains some very rare documents while the **Asutosh Mookerjee** collection, the world's largest personal collection is also here (open 1000-1800 weekdays). The library has the largest collection in the country, approaching 2 million books and manuscripts, some very rare and includes all published material in India. Open between 0900-2000 on weekdays and between 1000-1800 at weekends and holidays. In addition there is a collection of 11,000 bound volumes of newspapers in a separate reading room at Esplanade E.

Rabindra Sarobar The lake in S Calcutta is a peaceful haven surrounded by shaded walks and palm trees and has small islands. The city's rowing clubs hold their regattas here and there is a stadium for concerts. To the S is the 'lily pool' and the southeast, the Japanese Buddhist temple.

HAORA AND THE WEST BANK

North 16 km N of the city across the Ganga from Calcutta is ***Belur Math***, the international headquarters of the Ramakrishna Mission, founded in 1899 by Swami Vivekananda who was a disciple of the great 19th century Hindu saint **Ramakrishna (see page 792)**. He preached the unity of all religions. Symbolising its belief the *Math* (or *shrine*) synthesises Hindu, Christian and Islamic architectural styles. Open daily from 0630 to 1100 and 1600-1930 and in winter 1530-1900. Admission free. Allow about 20 min.

South ***Botanical Gardens*** On the W bank of the Hugli, 20 km from BBD Bagh. Founded in 1787 by the East India Company, the gardens cover more than 100 ha. The major attraction is a flourishing 200 year old ***banyan tree*** with a circumference of over 380 m, said to be the largest in the world (Guinness Book

CHOWRINGHEE

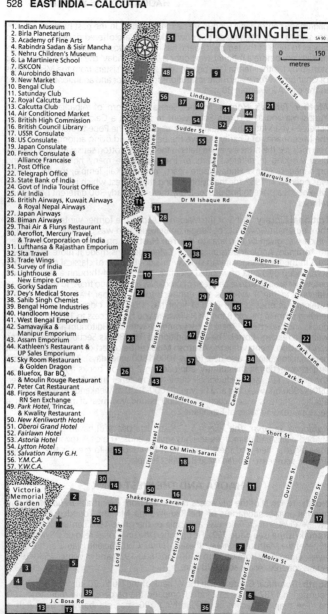

1. Indian Museum
2. Birla Planetarium
3. Academy of Fine Arts
4. Rabindra Sadan & Sisir Mancha
5. Nehru Children's Museum
6. La Martiniere School
7. ISKCON
8. Aurobindo Bhavan
9. New Market
10. Bengal Club
11. Satunday Club
12. Royal Calcutta Turf Club
13. Calcutta Club
14. Air Conditioned Market
15. British High Commission
16. British Council Library
17. USSR Consulate
18. US Consulate
19. Japan Consulate
20. French Consulate &
    Alliance Francaise
21. Post Office
22. Telegraph Office
23. State Bank of India
24. Govt of India Tourist Office
25. Air India
26. British Airways, Kuwait Airways
    & Royal Nepal Airways
27. Japan Airways
28. Biman Airways
29. Thai Air & Flurys Restaurant
30. Aeroflot, Mercury Travel,
    & Travel Corporation of India
31. Lufthansa & Rajasthan Emporium
32. Sita Travel
33. Trade Wings
34. Survey of India
35. Lighthouse &
    New Empire Cinemas
36. Gorky Sadam
37. Dey's Medical Stores
38. Sahib Singh Chemist
39. Bengal Home Industries
40. Handloom House
41. West Bengal Emporium
42. Samavayika &
    Manipur Emporium
43. Assam Emporium
44. Kathleen's Restaurant &
    UP Sales Emporium
45. Sky Room Restaurant
    & Golden Dragon
46. Bluefox, Bar BQ,
    & Moulin Rouge Restaurant
47. Peter Cat Restaurant
48. Firpos Restaurant &
    RN Sen Exchange
49. *Park Hotel*, Trincas,
    & Kwality Restaurant
50. *New Kenliworth Hotel*
51. *Oberoi Grand Hotel*
52. *Fairlawn Hotel*
53. *Astoria Hotel*
54. *Lytton Hotel*
55. *Salvation Army G.H.*
56. *Y.M.C.A.*
57. *Y.W.C.A.*

SA 90

0   150
metres

of Records) – not an uncontested claim! The original trunk was struck by lightning in 1919 and had to be removed, but more than 1500 offshoots form an impressive sight. The tea grown in Darjiling and Assam was developed here. The avenues of Royal Cuban palms and mahogany trees are impressive and there are interesting and exotic specimens in the herbarium, fern, cacti, orchid houses and the 16 m domed palm house. Parts are ill-tended, though the pleasant and cool gardens can make a welcome change from the city for the long term visitor.

Avoid on Sun and public holidays when it is very overcrowded. May be reached by ferry from Chandpal, Metiabruz or Takta Ghat or by road across Haora Bridge and through Haora which may take an hr. **This road journey can be very slow, hot and bumpy.** Entry free. Open from sunrise to sunset usually 0700-1700. Permits for cars are obtainable from Govt. of India Tourist Office, 4 Shakespeare Sarani. T 441402. The *Central National Herbarium* is situated here (see Museums). Of real interest only to botanists. Allow at least 1 hr.

Zoological Gardens 4 km from BBD Bagh. See under Parks and Zoos.

SERVICES

Hotels Note 10% Luxury tax, 10% Service Charge and 20% Expenditure tax are charged at most hotels. If you occupy an a/c room and do not make use of the facility in a hotel which is not centrally air-conditioned, when you have requested a room without a/c, the hotel may still pass on an extra tax payable to the Tax authority. Infants sharing a room with parents (without an extra cot) are usually accommodated free. For facilities in AL, A and B categories, see page 134.

AL *Oberoi Grand*, 15 J.L. Nehru Rd. T 292323/290181, Cable: Obhotel, Telex: 7248.. 300 rm. 16 km airport, 5 km rly. centrally sited opposite the Maidan, a grand white Victorian edifice exquisitely restored, outdoor swimming pool, suites have giant four-posters, new tea lounge, international disco and some of the best restaurants in town. 'The Rotisserie' for pricey French delicacies although the 'set lunch' is more affordable; the low-seating expensive 'Mughul Room' for N Indian food where you can even sit cross-legged Indian style and listen to live Indian music and the new 'Ming Court' for Szechuan. Some may feel a little lost amongst the grandeur. **AL** *Taj Bengal*, 34B Belvedere Rd, Alipore. T 283939, Telex: 021 5718, Fax: 033281766. 250 rm. 20 km airport, 10 km rly. Newly opened, close to Calcutta Race Course and Zoo, personal valet service and a resident astrologer available! 'The Chinoiserie' for Szechuan, Cantonese and Peking and the 'Sonargaon' for N Indian. Plush, imaginative, intimate with good food, but expensive. The Indian Restaurant has authentic village decor, where food is served on metal plates and cutlery is optional! Excellent coffee-shop serving substantial snacks. Poolside barbecue in winter. Suites have unique works of modern art. You can order an unusual Bengali breakfast of "luchi and cholar daal" (wheat fried 'bread' and a savoury lentil dish). **A** *Airport Ashok*, Calcutta Airport. T 575111, Cable: Airportel, Telex: 021 2271. 150 rm. 18 km Haora rly. Modern luxury hotel, soundproofed against aircraft noise, restaurant with 'frontier cuisine', health club, tennis court. 'Durbar' has reasonably priced good food but is not easily accessible except from the airport.

There are a few other good hotels which have recently undergone extensive improvement. They are modern, centrally located, efficient and with some good restaurants, but in general lack atmosphere and character. **A** *Hindusthan International*, 235/1 A.J.C. Bose Rd. T 442394 (20 lines), Cable: Modern, Telex: 021 7164. 212 rm. 15 km airport, 12 km rly. Architecturally plain. 'Golden Peacock' for a wide choice and the new 'Kalash' for regional Indian cuisine in very ethnic surroundings: good food and a buffet at lunchtime. 'The Palm Court' is their 24 hr coffee shop which also serves meals in comfortable surroundings. Service can be slow but good value. **A** *Park Hotel*, 17 Park St. T 297336/7941, Cable: Parkotel, Telex: 021 5912. 155 rm. 15 km airport, 5 km rly. Lacks style and ambience. 'Celebrity' for Indian, Continental and Chinese and 'Maples' for Veg food and Fresh fruit bar. **B** *Great Eastern Hotel*, 1-3 Old Court House St. T 282331, Cable: Greastern, Telex: 021 7571. 200 rm. 17 km Airport, 2 km Rly. Station. Central a/c. The old Raj style hotel has lost its former splendour but is undergoing reconstruction. 'Shah-en-Shah' serves tandoori dishes. Live Indian music. **B** *New Kenilworth International*, 1 & 2 Little Russell St. T 448394/99, Cable: Newken, Telex: 021 3395. 15 km airport, 6 km rly. Central a/c. Recommended. In an excellent location, well appointed and good value. Very popular so must book. Only few credit cards accepted so check in advance. 'Marble Room' for good Indian food in pleasant surrounding and 'Maikhana' open air Indian Barbecue on the lawn. Extra courteous service and good value for money. 'Crystals' open 24 hrs for fast food and 'R.B.'s Cafeteria' for bakery and fast food.

C *Hotel Rutt Deen*, 21B Louden St. T 431691, Cable: Rutt-Deen, Telex: 021 8163. 50 rm. 15 km airport, 5 km rly. Central a/c.

In the city centre, about 15 km from the airport and 5 km from the railway, there are several medium range hotels providing comfortable accommodation in a/c rooms. **C** *Fairlawn Hotel*, 13/A Sudder St. T 244460/183, Cable: Fairotel. 20 rm some a/c. Old fashioned and unmodernised. Meals (included in the price) are semi-formal and served at set times. Trades on its reputation as a relic of the Raj. **C** *Lytton Hotel*, 14 Sudder St. T 291872, Cable: Lyttotel, Telex: 01 3562. 59 rm. Recommended. **C** *The Astor*, 15 Shakespeare Sarani. T 449957, Cable: Kingcole, Telex: 021 2020. 32 rm. 'Serai' restaurant and open air 'Kebab-e-que' in the garden has a trio of musicians and despite the toe-curling name serves tender and delicious fish, chicken and meat kebabs cooked in a 'tandoor' or charcoal grill: good value. **C** *Hotel Shalimar*, 3 S.N. Banerjee Rd. T 285030. 22 rm. **C** *Hotel Minerva*, 11 Ganesh Ch. Av. T 263365. 38 rm some a/c. A/c restaurant, travel, business services. Price includes English breakfast. Popular with business clients and families.

There are several moderately priced places to stay. Some include breakfast, others all meals. A few have a/c rooms but unlike the larger hotels which have their own generators, these may suffer from hours of power cuts, especially in the hot season. Most of these are in the down town area, about 15 km from the airport and 5 km from the railway station. **D** *Astoria Hotel*, 6/2,3 Sudder St. T 241359/2615/9361. 30 rm some a/c. **D** *YMCA*, 25 J.L. Nehru Rd. T 292192, Cable: Manhood. Large gloomy building but rooms have attached baths and breakfast and dinner are included. Table tennis, snooker and billiard tables in the lounge! **D** *Udaychal Tourist Hostel*, (WBTDC) DG Block Sector II, Salt Lake. T 378246. A/c or less expensive non-a/c double rm as well as dormitory with cheap accommodation. One meal compulsory. **E** *YMCA*, 42 S.N. Banerjee Rd. T 292192. **E** *YWCA*, 1 Middleton Row. T 297033. 75 rm. For women only. Special wing for married couples. **E** *Salvation Army Guest House*, 2 Sudder St. T 242895. Modest but clean, water supply erratic. Popular with backpackers.

Youth Hostels and very simple hotels Several cheap hotels in the Sudder St area are popular with low budget back packers, some with dormitories. **E** *Railway Retiring Rooms* at both stations (Sealdah has a/c double) for railway passengers only. *Airport Rest Rooms* are also available where prices vary. **D** *Rest House III* and **E** *Rest Houses I and II*. Meals at airport restaurant. The **F** *Youth Hostel* is at 10J Ananda Dutta Lane in Haora across the river.

There are some *Dharamsalas* run by religious foundations in the city which provide very simple accommodation (often free) for one or more nights for travellers. Alcoholic drinks not permitted. Some are restricted to Hindus only. One open to all (smoking not allowed) is Bara Sikh Sangat, 172 Mahatma Gandhi Rd. T 385227. Others at 51B Sir Hari Ram Goenka St, 37 Kalakar St, 41 Kali Krishna Tagore St., 242 Kalighat Rd, 15 Hazra Rd, 42 Sarat Bose Rd and 34 Ezra St.

Club Accommodation It is also possible to stay in one of Calcutta 's clubs, each with a character of its own. **Note** Technically membership of an affiliated club is necessary or an introduction by a member which is possible at short notice. *The Bengal Club*, 1/1 Russell St. T 299233. Contact Col. N. Sarkar. Ideally situated opp the Maidan, comfortable with excellent dining room (try their steak), Chinese restaurant, pastry shop. Established 1827; a former home of Lord Macaulay. *The Calcutta Club*, 241 Acharya J.C. Bose Rd. T 443318, contact Commander M. Fernandes. Started for the Indian 'upper classes' in period when the Bengal Club refused them entry (until 1970). Pool, tennis, pleasant public rooms and a very popular bakery. Only male members may stay overnight. Busy at lunchtime. *Saturday Club*, 7 Wood St. T 445411. Contact Brig. C.S. Mehta. Good bar and dining room. Rm well appointed but no phones. *The Tollygunge Club*, 120 Deshapran Sasmal Rd. T 463141. Contact Mr. Bob Wright. 18 hole golf course, riding, tennis and swimming. Away from city centre; atmosphere and location compensate for average accommodation and dining room. The building was the residence of the family of Tipu Sultan after he was killed at Seringapatam. It was on the site of an old indigo plantation.

Omar Village Resort at Vasa on Diamond Harbour Rd is fast becoming a popular escape for city dwellers, but out-of-the-way.

Restaurants Thurs are 'meatless' days, but chicken and fish are available. Calcutta restaurants are allowed to serve alcoholic drinks to all patrons in licensed restaurants. As a result some of Calcutta's good restaurants have changed in character. Some are no longer very pleasant places to eat since the emphasis is on drink rather than on food. However, there are still a number which provide excellent food and service, though at a price. **Note** Be prepared for a large surcharge for live music (and sometimes even for recorded music) at a restaurant. This and other taxes can mean that the bill is often double the price on the menu.

Many restaurants, outside hotels, do not accept credit cards.

There are several **multi-cuisine** a/c restaurants in the Park St area and a few further afield. *Skyroom*, 57 Park St (closed Tue). T 294362/299029. Slightly cramped surroundings are compensated by excellent food and charming extras. Try the smoked 'Hilsa' fish. Highly recommended. *Blue Fox*, 55 Park St. T 297948. Bar. Pleasantly quiet. *Kwality*, 17 Park St (closed Th). T 297849 and 2 Gariahat Rd (closed Wed) T 482982. Famous for ice creams but also for Indian and continental (baked fish, chicken kiev, vegetable gratin). Usually crowded. Good value. *Kathleen's*, 12 Mirza Ghalib St (closed Th) with the 'Princess' suitable for families. T 242548. Excellent pastry shop. *Tandoor*, 43 Park St (closed Wed). T 298006. *Bar-B-Q*, 43 Park St (closed Th). T 299345. Bar. *Trinca's- The Other Room*, 17B Park St (closed Th). T 298947. Bar. *Oasis*, 33 Park St, 2 Madge Lane, (closed Th). T 299003. Small, good value, quick lunches. *Peter Cat*, 18 Park St (closed Th). T 298841. Good Indian food, crowded, reasonably priced. Bar.

Indian *Suruchi*, 89 Elliot Rd. (close Sat 1700 and Sun 1500). T 291783. Only authentic Bengali restaurant. Excellent inexpensive food on **thalis*** in simple and unpretentious surroundings. Restricted menu but very tasty food, especially the fish. Also snacks all day. Entirely run by women at the institution. Highly recommended. *Amber*, 11 Waterloo St in the business district (closed Th). T 283477. Said to be the largest Indian restaurant in the country. Excellent Tandoori dishes; reservations essential. Bar. Fast efficient service, generous helpings. Highly recommended. *Shiraz Golden Restaurant*, 56 Park St. T 447702. Recommended for Muslim cuisine. *Badshah*, in the heart of the shopping centre, well known for *Kebab rolls*. Bar. *Rung Mahal*, 15 J.L. Nehru Rd (closed Mon). T 292323. *J's Shop*, 123B Rashbehari Av. Bengali cuisine. *Lahore*, 140 SN Bannerjee Rd. *Amina*, 1 Corporation Place.

    Vegetarian *Vineet*, 1 Shakespeare Sarani. T 440788 (located in basement of shopping complex) with live Indian Pop Music in the evenings. Some continental dishes also available. Good for ice creams. Slightly expensive. *Jyoti Vihar*, 3A Ho Chi Minh Sarani. T 449791. Near British High Commission and American Consulate. Quick service and good S Indian cuisine. Very good value. *Gupta Brothers*, 18B Park St. T 299687. 'Thalis' and Indian sweets. *Invader Centre*, 12 Loudon St. T 448552. *Friends' Home*, 1 Chowringhee Centre. T 283737.

Chinese Calcutta is not as good a centre for Chinese food as in the past. Connoisseurs now travel to S Tangra Rd (off the Eastern Metropolitan Bypass) where many Chinese have moved to from old China Town. Food excellent but surroundings not so pleasant. *Blue Diamond, Ka Fa Lok* and *Sin Fa* for excellent soups, jumbo prawns and honey chicken. Best to go early, by noon for lunch and 2000 for dinner. More central but not as good: *How Hua*, 10 Mirza Ghalib St. (closed Tue). T 297819. *Golden Dragon*, 40 Park Mansions, Park St (closed Wed). *Eau Chew*, P32 Mission Row Extension. *Chin Wah*, Temple St. *Mandarin*, 217 Landsdowne Rd. T 462276. *Mayfair China Bowl*, 122 Meghnad Saha Sarani (closed Th), T 465042 is a small and intimate restaurant in S Calcutta which offers Chinese and other Far Eastern cuisine. *Jimmy's kitchen*, AJC Bose Rd and Shakespeare Sarani crossing. Rec.

Others Swiss confectionery *Kathleen's*, 12 Mirza Ghalib St. T 242548. *Kookie Jar*, Express Towers, Rawdon St. Flury's, 18 Park St (closed Mon) T 297664. Traditional English breakfasts, morning coffee, afternoon teas and pastry counter but has lost its old charm. *Nahoum's*, New Market. T 243033. **Fast Food** *Super Dooper*, 18C Park St. T 296119. *Health Food Centre*, 21 Park St. *Big Max*, 1 Russell St. *Garden Cafe*, Alipore Rd for pizzas and 'dosas', burgers and Chinese fast food. Highly recommended. *Super Snack Bar*, 14 Old Court House St. *Corner Cafe*, Lower Circular Rd for pizzas and burgers. **Ice Creams** *Upvan, Sub-Zero* and *Tulika* all on Little Russell St and *Yankee* in Ballygunge Circular Rd with its 42 varieties. *Gay Rendezvous*, 71 Strand Rd, Man-o-War Jetty. T 285680. On the riverside with terrace, popular with families.

    Less expensive food is available in several places in the Sudder St area, among them are; *Nizam's* (22/25 Hogg Market) with *UP* and *Bihar* nearby, *Taj Continental, Blue Sky, Khalsa Restaurant* and *Mughul Durbar*. Others are *Shiraz Golden Restaurant*, 56 Park St, *Royal Indian Hotel*, 99 Lower Circular Rd and *Sabir's* in Chandni Chowk. The excellent Moghlai food of *Kathi-kebab*, the tender meat on bamboo skewers in a *paratha* (rich unleavened 'bread'), is hard to beat. You, in company with the elite, will find them at *Nizam's* and stalls in Zakaria St, Park Circus and around the cinemas off Esplanade.

Bengali sweets worth sampling (they are often very sweet!) are *Sandesh, Roshogolla, barfi, roshomalai, pantua* and the sweet yoghurt *mishti doi*. *Mithai*, 48B Syed Amir Ali Av. T 443590, *Bhim Chandra Nag*, 8 Vivekananda Rd. T 344333, *K.C. Das*, 11 Esplanade E, T 285920 and 1/433 Gariahat Rd, T 410182. *Sen Mahasay*, 171H Rashbehari Av, T 462360. *Girish Chandra Dey*, 167N Rashbehari Av, 460162. *Jadav Chandra Das*, 127A Rashbehari

Av, T 466373. *Ganguram*, 46C J.L. Nehru Rd. T 442077. *Mukherjee Sweets*, 29/1 Ballygunge Place. Tasty **savoury snacks** are sold fresh every afternoon from about 1600-1730. Try *singaras*, *kachuris* and *nimkis*. *Radhu's*, Lake Market serves superb savoury snacks – the Bengali *fish fry* and *chicken* or *'prawn cutlet '*(which are fillets, crumbed and fried) as well as rich *Moghlai paratha* and *aloor dum* (potato curry).

Bars These are situated in all the larger hotels and up-market restaurants. In addition there are independent bars which are open usually till midnight. Atmosphere is not very sociable. *Asoka*, 3B J.L. Nehru Rd. T 282248. *Olympia*, 21 Park St. T 249525. *Shenaz*, 2A Middleton Row. T 295750. *Saki* 177 Lenin Sarani. T 273061. *New Central*, 99 Chittaranjan Ave.

Clubs The 4 prominent clubs listed under places to stay above are affiliated to a number of clubs in India and some foreign clubs covering the 5 continents, among them Royal Overseas League, Travellers', St. James', The National Liberal and United Oxford and Cambridge University Clubs, London, Sind Club, Karachi, Hong Kong Club, Wellington Club, New Zealand, Dubai Country Club, Doha Club, The American Club, Singapore and Columbia Club, Indianapolis. In addition several sports clubs attract a large and active membership.

Banks Banking hours – Mon-Fri 1000-1400,Sat 1000-1200. *State Bank of India*, 1 Strand Rd. T 289331. 43 J.L. Nehru Rd. T 434337. 1 Middleton St. T 293649. 11 & 13 Shakespeare Sarani. T 449076. *United Bank of India*, 16 Old Court House St. T 287471. United Commercial Bank 10 Brabourne Rd. T 260120. *Central Bank of India*, 13 Netaji Subhas Rd. T 208921. *Andhra*, 58 J.L. Nehru Rd. T 445660. *Allahabad*, 2 Netaji Subhas Rd. T 208375. *Bank of India*, 15A Hemanta Basu Sarani. T 202301.

Foreign Banks *American Express*, 21 Old Court House St. T 286281. *Bank of America*, 8 India Exchange Place. T 272824. *Bank of Tokyo*, 2 Brabourne Rd. T 261125. *Citibank*, 43 J.L. Nehru Rd. T 299220. *Grindlays*, 19 Netaji Subhas Rd. T 205264. *Standard Chartered*, 4 Netaji Subhas Rd. T 206907. *Algemeene Bank Nederlands*, 18A Brabourne Rd. T 262160. *Banque Nationale de Paris*, 4A B.B.D. Bagh E. T 202318. *Hong Kong & Shanghai*, 8 Netaji Subhas Rd. T 201833. 24 hr teller service.

Exchanges *R.N. Dutta*, Stephen House, 4 & 5 B.B.D. Bagh E. T 236975. 5 & 7 Kidderpore Dock. T 453725. Calcutta Airport. T 575425. *Maneek Lal Sen*, New Market. *R.R. Sen & Bros.*, 18A,B & C J.L. Nehru Rd. T 296077.

Shopping Most shops open 1000-1730 or later (some break for lunch) on weekdays and between 1000-1300 on Saturdays. Central and State **Government Emporia** are mainly situated in the down town area and are fixed price shops. *Central Cottage Industries*, 7 J.L. Nehru Rd. *Handloom House*, 2 Lindsay St. *Khadi Gramodyog*, 28 Chittaranjan Av. *Assam*, 8 Russell St. *Bihar*, 145 Rashbehari Ave. *Cauvery*, 7 J.L. Nehru Rd. *Kashmir Art*, 12 J.L. Nehru Rd. *Manipur*, 15L Lindsay St. *Manjusha*, 7/1D Lindsay St. *Meghalaya*, 9 Russell St. *Phulkari*, 26B Camac St. *Rajasthali*, 30E J.L. Nehru Rd. *Tripura*, 58 J.L. Nehru Rd. *Refugee Handicrafts*, 2A & 3A Gariahat Rd. *Uttar Pradesh*, 12B Lindsay St. *Dakshinapan*, nr Dhakuria Bridge. Open Mon-Fri 1030-1930, Sat 1030-1300. Very convenient. Excellent selection of quality handloom and handicrafts at fixed prices.

   There are a lot of **Boutiques and handicrafts** shops in Park St and streets leading off it. *Bengal Home Industries*, 57 J.L. Nehru Rd, *Good Companions*, 13C Russell St, *Ritu's Boutique*, 46A Rafi Ahmed Kidwai Rd, *Ananda*, 13 Russell St, *Guy's N' Dolls*, 14 Sudder St, *Jete*, Park Centre, Park St and *Women's Friendly Society*, 29 Park Lane are all centrally located and will provide unusual gifts. Womens' self-help centres which have shops and also give you the opportunity to see techniques such as handloom weaving, batik printing, embroidery, handblock printing being practised are specially recommended. Visit *All Bengal Womens' Union*, 89 Elliot Rd, *Karma Kutir*, 32 Ballygunge Place ('kantha' making), and *Nari Seva Sangha* in Jodhpur Park. *Sasha*, 27 Mirza Ghalib St (off the Rd). Open Tue-Sat, 1000-1900, Sun, Mon 1000-1300. Excellent handicrafts by women's voluntary organisation. Cane, bamboo, *Dokra**, *kantha**, leather amd crafts from E and NE India.

Photography Camera films, accessories and quality printing services are easily available. Only some listed here. *IPC Ltd* (Kodak Affiliate), 115 Park St. T 295711. Bombay Photo Stores, 33-34 Park Mansions, Park St. T 299711. *Frank Ross* (Photo Division), 7 Park St. T 240308. *Narain's*, 20H Park St. T 298320. *Colour Photo Studio*, 113/2 Rashbehari Av. T 460589.

Bookshops *Cambridge Book & Stationery Co.*, 20D Park St. *Oxford Book Shop*, Park St. *Bookmark*, 56D, Free School St. A wealth of second-hand pavement bookstalls along *College Street* caters for students but may equally reveal an interesting first edition for a keen collector (see under Places of interest). For a fortnight every January the Calcutta Book Fair takes over a part of the Maidan near the Victoria Memorial where last year there were

300 book stalls selling paperback fiction to antiquarian books.

Laundry Plenty of dry-cleaners, some Chinese, can be found all across the city.

Markets The *New Market*, Lindsay St, the old Hogg Market over a century old, was partially burnt down in 1985. Now largely rebuilt, it has over 2,500 shops covering an area of thirteen acres. Be prepared to be pestered by porters insisting on offering their services. If you want to wander round on your own you have to make up your mind to be firm. It used to be said that you could buy anything from a needle to an elephant (on order) in one of its stalls. Today it is still worth a visit, preferably early in the morning, to watch it come alive, selling from the dull mundane everyday needs of the city dweller to the most exotic luxuries. The produce and wares have their separate sections to make shopping easier, but it will pay to simply wander around to breathe in the atmosphere.

Calcutta has a number of *bazaars* each with a character of its own. In *Bentinck Street* you will see Muslim tailors, Chinese shoemakers interspersed with Indian sweet meat shops and tea stalls. *Gariahat* market has an enormous range of fish; also very diverse clientele; city businessmen, professors, cooks, servants. Best in early morning. In *Shyambazar* the coconut market starts business at 5 in the morning and you will miss it if you arrive 2 hr later. The fragrant flower market is in *Bapu Ghat* on the river bank. There are dozens of others equally interesting. The old *China Bazar* no longer exists although a trip to the Tiretta Bazar area still retains its ethnic flavour; exceptional Chinese breakfasts are available off street stalls. In the city centre you can shop in air-conditioned comfort in the *Market* on Shakespeare Sarani, *Park Centre* on Park St or *Vardaan Market* on Camac St.

Local Transport Buses run by W Bengal State Transport provide a regular service throughout the city and suburbs from 0500-2030; always overcrowded, very cheap; minimum fare Re.0.50. The alternative private maroon minibus service covers major routes; faster, only slightly more expensive with fares starting at Re.1. They will often stop on request. Very limited headroom! **Trams** Many people's favourite transport: this is the only Indian city to run them. Extensive network, running from 0400 terminating at 2300. Often crowded except on Sun.; very cheap – fares starting at Re.0.50. **Taxis** Yellow top taxis are available throughout the city. Meters often out of date which you can tell because they start at Rs4. The driver has a card showing conversion rate – add 60% to meter figure. The rate is Rs 5 for first 2 km. and Re.1 for subsequent 200 m. There is also a waiting charge. It is sometimes possible to stop a taxi with a passenger, even at traffic lights, and agree to share the cost if it happens to be travelling in the direction required. Three wheeler taxis are less comfortable but cheaper, charging a minimum fare of Rs 1.60 with a surcharge of 60%.

Metro The only city in India to have one and rightly very proud of it. The Metro opened in 1984, is clean, efficient and punctual: stations are air-conditioned. There is piped music and TV screens on platforms to entertain you while you wait! Only covers 10 km of the main N-S trunk route from Tollygunge to Esplanade with a further extension due for completion in 1991. It operates from 0800-2100, takes 17 min for this section of route and costs Rs 1.50. Excavation work now in progress along Chittaranjan Ave. **Rickshaws** Calcutta is the only city to have hand-pulled rickshaws (of which there are supposed to be 40,000) many of which are hired for the day by the 'pullers'. Any attempt by the Govt to ban them is met with strong protests as jobs are vital. Can be as expensive as taxis, especially when wet. When the streets are flooded they become indispensible. A few auto-rickshaws have been introduced and in the suburbs they are cycle-powered.

Ferry services are available from 0815-2000 from Chandpal Ghat and operate at 15 min. intervals except on Sun; can be used to cross the river to Haora station or the Botanical Gardens. Often both more comfortable and quicker than Haora Bridge. **Luxury launches** can be hired for short cruises. Tourist Bureau, Rs 2,200 for first 4 hr. Omar Resort, 135 Canning St. T 251379. Rs 300 per hr. Max 50 people. Candida Customer Services, Mercantile Building, 9/12 Baghbazar St. T 202382. Rs 1,500 per weekday, Rs 2,000 for holidays. Max. 15 people. **Private taxi operators** Rent-a-Car Service, 1/5 Dover Lane. T 467186. A & E Pvt. Ltd., 16B Gurusaday Rd. T 446161. Ashai International, 12/12 Hungerford St. T 441987. **Car Rent Services**, 1/5 Dover Lane. T 467186. A & E Pvt., 16B Gurusaday Rd. T 446161. Ashai International, 12/12 Hungerford St. T 441987. Car Rent Services, 233/4A Acharya J.C. Bose Rd. T441285. Durgapur Automobiles, 113 Park St. T 294044. Wheels on Road, 150 Lenin Sarani. T 273081. Hertz are expected to introduce hire of self-drive cars soon. W Bengal Tourist Bureau, 3/2 BBD Bagh, may be contacted for car, coach and launch rental on T 288272. Ambassador cars (seating 4), Rs 2.40 per km, Rs 20.60 per hr, Min. Rs 55.

Entertainment 'Calcutta: this Fortnight' is distributed free by the W Bengal Tourist Office. The monthly 'Calcutta Skyline' also carries information of all major events in the city. The 'Sunday Telegraph' and English language dailies carry a comprehensive list of what is showing in the air-conditioned cinemas and theatres.

Cinemas which are a/c and comfortable, showing English language films 3 or 4 times a day are situated in the down town area off J.L. Nehru Rd near Esplanade and near Hogg Market. **Elite**, S.N. Banerjee Rd. T 241383. **Globe**, Lindsay St. T 296665. **Lighthouse**, Humayun Place. T 241402. **Metro**, J.L. Nehru Rd. T 233541. **Minerva**, Chowringhee Place. T 241052. It would be worth enquiring if a film by one of the top Bengali film-makers (Satyajit Ray, Mrinal Sen, Aparna Sen, Ritwick Ghatak) is showing, although since there would be no sub-titles you would ideally need to be accompanied by a Bengali.

Auditoria Regular performances of dance, music and theatre at *Rabindra Sadan*, Acharya J.C. Bose Rd, T 449937. *Kala Mandir*, 48 Shakespeare Sarani, T 449086, *Ramakrishna Mission Institute of Culture*, Golpark and *Gorky Sadan*, Gorky Terrace, nr Minto Park, T 442791. Some of these also put on art exhibitions as at *Academy of Fine Arts*, Cathedral Rd next to Rabindra Sadan, T 444205 and the Ramakrishna Mission which also has a library, International Guest House and a language teaching centre. *Nandan*, Acharya JC Bose Rd is the Govt film complex with an auditorium and exhibition area. Other venues for Bengali theatre of a high standard are *Children's Little Theatre*, Aban Mahal, T 461200, *Biswaroopa*, 2A Raja Raj Kissen St, T 553210 and *Star Theatre*, 79/34 Bidhan Sarani, T 551139 (productions by Bahuroopi and People's Little Theatre are highly recommended).

English-language stage productions are less frequent as they are dependent on amateur drama groups, touring groups organized by the *British Council* and local educational institutions. Cultural programmes are also staged by *United States Information Service*, 7 J.L. Nehru Rd, T 287413. The *Sangeet Research Academy* set up in 1970 is a national centre for training in Indian Classical music. On Wednesday evenings there is a free concert. *Rabindra Bharati University*, 6/4 Dwarakanath Tagore Lane holds performances, particularly during the winter, of the performing arts including Rabindra Sangeet (songs) and Dance and 'Jatras', the folk theatre of Bengal which is enjoying a revival. 'Jatra' is community theatre in the round, highly colourful and exaggerated both in style of delivery and make-up, drawing for its subject either the old romantic favourites from mythology or more up-to-date social, political and religious themes.

Sports There are numerous sports clubs. Calcutta has some noted golf courses. The *Royal Calcutta Golf Club* was founded in 1829, and is the oldest golf club in the world outside Great Britain. It moved to its present course in 1910. It took the radical step of admitting women in 1886. The Club also has a Bowling Green section at 18 Golf Club Rd. T 421352. *The Tollygunge Club* also has an 18 hole golf course, on land that was once an indigo plantation. Although the course as a whole is not difficult, some of the holes cross large water bodies; the 14th is even known as "hydrophobia"! Calcutta also claims the only women only golf club in India, founded in 1891 by a Mrs. Peddler, who "could no longer take the humiliation of not being allowed to play golf at will at the Royal and Tollygunge Clubs." They were allowed to lay out a 9 hole course in the maidan as long as they did not build any permanent structures. To overcome that problem they constructed a club house on wheels. *Calcutta Polo Club*, 51 J.L. Nehru Rd. T 442031. *Calcutta Racquet Club*, Maidan near St. Paul's Cathedral. T 441152. *Royal Calcutta Turf Club*, 1 Russell St. T 291103. *Calcutta South Club*, 1 Woodburn Park for tennis. T 444478. *Calcutta Swimming Club*, 1 Strand Rd. T 232894. *Calcutta Rowing Club*, 15 Rabindra Sarobar. T 463343. *Bengal Rowing Club*, Rabindra Sarobar. T 411751. *Lake Club* (Rowing), Rabindra Sarobar. T 462538. *Mohan Bagan Athletic Club*, C.F.C. Ground. T 281634. *E Bengal Club* (Football), Maidan. T 284642. *Calcutta Cricket and Football Club*, 19/1 Gurusaday Rd. T 478721. *Eden Gardens* (see Parks and zoos below) is mainly a cricket stadium which can accommodate 100,000 spectators. *Netaji Indoor Stadium*, an indoor stadium and *Khudiram Anushilan Kendra* also for indoor sports are in the Eden Gardens area.

Calcutta is the venue of cricket test matches, international tennis tournaments, important football fixtures and other sports championships throughout the year.

Museums Indian Museum, 27 J.L. Nehru Rd. T 299853. Mar-Nov 1000-1700, Dec-Feb 1000-1630. Closed Mon. Entry Re.1. Fri Free. Possibly Asia's largest, founded in 1814 and known locally as Jadu Ghar (magic house). Excellent collection, much – though not all – well displayed. The colonnaded Italianate building completed in 1875 stands opposite the Maidan and surrounds an open grassed area. 36 galleries, about 10,000 items, divided into 6 sections; art, archaeology, anthropology, geology, zoology and economic botany. The last has the interesting section on 'plants in the service of man' with details of herbs, plants and woods. It has a very large geological gallery (Siwalik fossils from lower Himalaya) and an excellent natural history section. Outstanding archaeological exhibits include fine examples of Indian ware from the Harappa and Moenjodaro periods as well as Buddhist art (Barhut gallery to the S of the entrance), a reconstruction of a part of the 180 BC Buddhist stupa and ancient sculptural pieces from Sanchi, Gandhara, Amaravati and Sarnath. The chronological coin collection is exceptional but requires special permission to view; sections displaying miniature paintings and the Art and Textile gallery with ivory, bone, glass and silverware also particularly notable. The new Egyptian gallery boasts a popular exhibit – a partially exposed mummy. There is a good guide book. Some galleries are poorly lit and gathering dust. Best to be selective and allow at least 2 hours. Photography allowed on payment of fee.

Academy of Fine Arts, Cathedral Rd. T 444205. 1500-1800. Closed Mon. Entry Re.1. Founded in 1933, the collection includes Indian miniature paintings, textiles, works of contemporary Indian artists including Jaimini Roy and Desmond Doig and also Tagore's paintings and manuscripts. Guide service and films once a month and photography with permission. Two galleries also hold exhibitions of works of local artists.

Asiatic Society, 1 Park St. T 231158. Open 1000-2000 weekdays, 1000-1700 weekends. Entry free. The oldest institution of Oriental studies in the world was described by the founder and great Orientalist Sir William Jones in 1784 as the platform for "Man and Nature, whatever is performed by one or produced by the other within the geographical limits of Asia". Originally restricted to Europeans; opened its doors to Indians in the 19th century. The library was started when a valuable collection from Fort William was transferred together with Tipu Sultan's libraries from Mysore. Today includes a treasure house of books, documents and ancient manuscripts in most Asian languages, some dating back to the 7th century. The museum, opened in 1814, includes a rare collection of coins although much of the original archaeological, geological and zoological exhibits have been transferred to the Indian Museum nearby. Gallery of paintings includes works by Reynolds, Canaletti, Rubens and Guido. One hopes that the many items which could not be viewed while the building underwent repairs will now be displayed.

Asutosh Museum, Centenary Building, Calcutta University, College St. T 347472. 1030-1630 weekdays. Sat 1030-1500. Closed Sun and Univ. holidays. Entry free. Small museum with objects of eastern Indian art and antiquity including textiles and terracotta figures, with particular emphasis on Bengali folk art. Good booklet. **Bangiya Sahitya Parishad**, 243/1 Acharya P.C. Rd. T 353743. 1300-1900. Closed on Th and public holidays. Entry free. Imposition of English as the medium of instruction by Macaulay in 1834 later led many Bengalis to return to the riches in their own literature and language. In 1894 a group of 30 intellectuals founded the *Parishad*. Collection of books, rare manuscripts, antiques, icons, metal and stone inscriptions. Memorabilia of Rammohun Roy, Vidyasagar and Sister Nivedita. **Birla Academy of Art & Culture**, 108/109 Southern Ave. T 467843. 1600-2000. Closed Mon. Entry Re.0.50. Mainly medieval and contemporary paintings and sculpture.

Central National Herbarium, Botanical Gardens, Haora. T 67323. 10.15-1600. Closed Sundays, 2nd Saturdays and Central Govt holidays. Entry free. The largest collection of dried plants in S and S E Asia of some 1.5 million specimens and including the collections of eminent botanists of the last 200 years. Centre for taxonomic research in India. **Marble Palace** (see under Places of interest). **Nehru Children's Museum**, 94/1 J.L. Nehru Rd. T 443516. 1200-2000. Closed Mon. Entry Adults Rs 2 and children under 12, Re.1. Tales from the Ramayana and Mahabharata are depicted in miniature clay figures from Krishnagar. Well displayed in glass cabinets, convenient for children to view. Allow about 30 min. **Netaji Research Bureau**, Elgin Rd, is in his home which is now a museum and containls photographs and memorabilia of Netaji and the freedom struggle. **See page 515**. **Rabindra Bharati Museum**, 6/4 Dwarakanath Tagore Lane. T 345241. 1000-1700. Sat 1000-1400. Sun and holidays 1100-1400. Entry free. Located in the ancestral home of **Rabindranath Tagore**, writer, artist and philosopher who won the Nobel prize for literature in 1913. A major section is devoted to his life and works, and the Renaissance movement in Bengal in the 19th century. **Victoria Memorial** (see under Places of interest above).

Parks and Zoos *Botanical Gardens* (see under Places of interest) *Eden Gardens*, N-W corner of the Maidan. Established in 1836 a part forms the Ranji Stadium, enclosing the Calcutta cricket grounds where international Test Matches are played. Only open during matches. It contains pleasant walks, an artificial lake, tropical palms and a small Burmese pagoda (about average size for this type of *Pyatthat*). *The Zoo* 0600-1700. Entry Re.1. Opened in 1876, the 16 ha. grounds house a wide variety of animal and bird life. The white tigers from Rewa and the '**tigon**', a cross between a tiger and a lion are the rarest animals. A reptile house, children's zoo and aquarium are across the road. Migratory birds crowd the zoo lakes each winter. There are 4 restaurants; picnics are permitted. Vehicles are only allowed in for the disabled.

The Horticultural Gardens, alongside the National Library near the Zoo. The Horticultural Society was started in 1820 by the Baptist missionary **William Carey**. 0600-1000, 1400-1700. Closed Mon. Entry Re.0.50. Pleasant and quiet with Flower Show at the beginning of Feb.

Useful addresses *Foreigners Regional Registration Office*, 237 Acharya J.C. Bose Rd. T 443301. *Home Political Department*, 1st Floor, Block 2, Writers' Building, B.B.D. Bagh.

Foreign missions and Trade representations *Austria*, 96/1 Sarat Bose Rd. T 472795. *Bangladesh*, 9 Circus Av. T 444458. *Belgium*, 5/1A Hungerford St. T 443886. *Bhutan*, 48 Tivoli Court, Pramothesh Barua Sarani. T 441302. *France*, 26 Park Mansions, Park St. T 240958. *Germany*, 1 Hastings Park Rd. T 459141. *Greece*, 41 J.L. Nehru Rd. T 238194. *Indonesia*, 128 Rashbehari Ave. T 460297. *Italy*, 3 Raja Santosh Rd. T 451411. *Japan*, 12 Pretoria St. T 442241. *Nepal*, 19 National Library Ave. T 452024. *Netherlands*, 18A Brabourne Rd. T 262160. *Norway*, 11 R.N. Mukherjee Rd. T 237005. *Spain*, 1 Taratolla Rd. T 455771. *Sweden*, 5/2 Russell St. T 213621. *Thailand*, 18B Mandeville Gardens. T 460836. *Turkey*, 2 Nazar Ali Lane. T 445605. *United Kingdom*, 1 Ho-Chi-Minh Sarani. T 445171. *USA*, 5/1 Ho-Chi-Minh Sarani. T 443611. *USSR*, 31 Shakespeare Sarani. T 444982.

Others *Alliance Française*, Park Mansions, Park St. *British Council* Library, 5 Shakespeare Sarani. T 445379. *Max Mueller Bhavan*, Ballygunge Circular Rd. *US Information Services*, 7 J.L. Nehru Rd. T 287413. Library 287411. *Indo-American Society*, 17 Camac St. *Indo-Soviet, Gorky Sadan*, Gorky Terrace nr Minto Park. T 442791.

Hospitals & Medical Services **Government** *Calcutta Hospital & Medical Research Institute*, 7/2 Diamond Harbour Rd. T 453921. *Calcutta National Medical College & Hospital*, 24 Gorachand Rd. T 441012. *Medical College Hospital*, 88 College St. T 359252. *N.R.S. Medical College & Hospital*, 138 Acharya J.C. Bose Rd. T 243213. *R.G. Kar Medical College & Hospital*, 1 Belgachia Rd. T 554311. *SSKM Hospital*, 244 Lower Circular Rd. T 449753. **Private** Belle Vue Clinic, 9 Dr. U.N. Brahmachari St. T 442321. *Woodlands Nursing Home*, 8/6 Alipore Rd. T 453951. *Park Nursing Home*, 4 Victoria Terrace. T 443586. *Metropolitan Laboratory and Nursing Home*, 18 Shakespeare Sarani. T 432487.

Ambulance Dhanwantary Clinic, 1 National Library Ave. T 456265. Emergency Doctors' Service, A 165 Lake Gardens. T 466770.

Chemists *Dey's Medical Stores*, 20A Nelly Sengupta Sarani. T 299810. *Frank Ross & Co. Ltd.*, 15/8 J.L. Nehru Rd. T 234565. 57 Park St. T 240308. 55 Gariahat Rd. T 475595. 41/A Block A New Alipore. T 454829. *Sahib Singh*, Park St, nr Trinca's. *Blue Print*, 1 Old Court House St. T 233281. *King & Co.* (Homeopath), 29 Shyama Prasad Mukherjee Rd. T 271366. *Singh & Roy*, 4/1 Sambhunath Pandit St. T 433770. 24 hr Wed-Sun. *Sterling & Co.* (Homeopath), 91-C Elliot Rd. *Welmed*, 4/1 Sambhunath Pandit St. T 446939. 24 hr Mon, Tue.

Opticians *Himalaya Opticals*, 25 Camac St. *Presidency Optical Co.*, 306 Bepin Behari Ganguly St (Lal Bazar).

Chambers of Commerce Bengal Chamber of Commerce, 6 Netaji Subhas Rd. T 228393. Bengal National Chamber of Commerce and Industry, 23 RN Mukherjee Rd. T 282951. Bharat Chamber of Commerce, 8 Old Court House St. T 280023. Indian Chamber of Commerce, 5 Exchange Place. T 223242. Calcutta Chamber of Commerce, 18H Park St. T 290758. Merchants Chamber of Commerce, 3-1 Armenian St. T 265246.

Post & Telegraphs There are numerous post offices throughout the city which are usually open from 1000-1700. General Post Office, B.B.D. Bagh (W). T 221451. Post Restante here. Telex facilities at the Philatelic Bureau. Central Telegraph Office, 8 Red Cross Place. T 234223. Open 24 hr for International calls, Telex and cable. Speed Post for foreign mail is available here. Park St Post Office, 65 Park St. T 294770. Telex facilities (0900-2000, Sun and holidays 1000-1700). International calls from a public phone from Park St Telegraph Office, Park Lane off Rafi Ahmed Kidwai Rd and from Telephone Bhavan, BBD Bagh (S). For international telex, telegrams and phone go to Overseas Communications Services, 18 Rabindra Sadan. T 266264. Speed Post for mail within Indian cities is available from the major post offices.

Places of Worship *Hindu* Kali Temple, Kalighat Rd. T 411413. Dakshineswar Kali Temple. T 582222. Ramakrishna Mission Belur Math, Howrah. T 663619. *Muslim* Nakhoda Mosque, Junction of Rabindra Sarani and Zakaria St and many others. *Christian* St. Paul's Cathedral, Cathedral Rd. T 445756. Five services on Sunday. St. Andrew's Church, 15 B.B.D. Bagh. T 221994. Baptist Mission Chapel, Acharya J.C. Bose Rd. T 244654. Assembly of God Church, Elliot Rd. St. John's Church, 2/1 Council House St. The Cathedral, Portuguese Church St. St. Thomas' Church, 7 Middleton Row. St. Xavier College Church, Park St. *Buddhist* Mahabodhi Society, 4A Bankim Chandra Chatterjee St. T 341091. Japan Saddharma Vihasa, 60/2/1 Lake Rd, Rabindra Sarobar. T 469725. *Jain* Badridas Mookim's Temple, Badridas Temple St. Parsvanath Temple, 26 Belgachia Rd. T 554681. *Sikh* Gurdwara Bara Sikh Sangat, 172 Mahatma Gandhi Rd. T 335227. Gurudwara Jagat Sudhar, 31 Rashbehari Av. T 411727. Gurdwara Sant Kutiya, 10A Harish Mukherjee Rd. T 474977. *Jewish* Shalome Jewish

Synagogue, Synagogue St. *Parsi* Rustomji Cawasji Agiary. T 239857.

Travel Agents *American Express*, 21 Old Court House St. T 288896, 280266. *Balmer Lawrie & Co.*, 21 Netaji Subhas Rd. T 226871. *Chetak Travels* (railway tickets), 12/1A Lindsay St (1st Floor). T 213450. *Everett Travel Service*, 4 Govt Place (N). T 236295. *Gladstone Lyall & Co.*, Camac Court, Camac St. T 451794. *Globe Travels*, 11 Ho-Chi-Minh Sarani. T 446038. *Indian Air Travels*, 28 Chittaranjan Ave. T 272040. *James Warren*, 31 J.L. Nehru Rd. T 240131. *Kundu Special*, 1 Chittaranjan Ave. T 275734. *Mackinnon Travel Service*, 16 Strand Rd T 236381. *Mercury Travels*, 46C J.L. Nehru Rd. T 443555. *Sita World Travels*, 3B Camac St. T 293003. *Speedways International*, 3 Chowringhee Sq. T 236337. *Trade Wings*, 32 J.L. Nehru Rd. T 299531. *Travel Corporation of India*, 46C J.L. Nehru Rd. T 445469.

Tour Operators *Charson Tours*, 6 J.L. Nehru Rd. T 239384. *Indo-Culture Tours*, 18 A-C J.L. Nehru Rd. T 234732. *Panurge & Co.*, 20B J.L. Nehru Rd. T 247873.

Tourist Offices, Information and City Tours *India Tourism Development Corporation*, 4 Shakespeare Sarani. T 441402, 440922. The office conducts 2 tours with a break for lunch of one hour. The morning tour covers the commercial area, Jain Temple, Dakshineswar Temple, Belur Math and Botanical Gardens. In the afternoon it covers Indian Museum, Nehru Children's Museum, Victoria Memorial, The Zoo and Rabindra Sarobar. These may be booked at Ashok Travel & Tours, 3-G Everest Buildings, 46 O J.L. Nehru Rd. T 440901. ITDC Airport Counter. T 572611 Extn. 444. *W Bengal Tourism Development Corporation*, 1 Sarat Bose Rd. T 448187.

W Bengal Tourist Bureau, 3/2 B.B.D. Bagh E. T 288271. Airport Counter. T 572611 Extn. 440. Howrah Rly. Station Counter. T 663518. The bureau organises daily coach tours in and around Calcutta starting at their city office. 0730-1140 and 1240-1700. A/c half day ticket Rs 35 and full day Rs 45. Non-a/c half day ticket Rs 25 and full day Rs 30. Morning tour departs at 0730 and covers Eden Gardens, High Court, Writers' Building, Botanical Gardens, Belur Math, Dakshineswar, Jain Temple and Esplanade. Afternoon tour departs at 1240 and covers Esplanade, Indian Museum, Nehru Children's Museum, Victoria Memorial, The Zoo, Rabindra Sarobar and Birla Academy. Passengers are required to pay entry fees where applicable. The morning tour goes further and is better value; most of the sights visited in the afternoon are within easy reach of the centre. At weekends and on public holidays only full day tours may be available and it is always best to check nearer the time if these will be operating. Private tour operators listed above also conduct similar city tours.

Tours Long distance tourist coach services are available to several destinations. Digha. Santiniketan – Bakreswar. Malda – Murshidabad – Gaur – Pandua. Antpur -Vishnupur – Mukutmanipur – Kakrajhore – Jhargram. Shaktapithas. Jairambati – Kamarpukur – Tarakeswar. Mayapur(ISKON) – Krishnagar – Bethuadari Deer Park. Sundarbans – Tiger and Crocodile projects. Tourist Guides approved by the Department of Tourism are available from the Regional Tourist Office, the charges varying according to the size of the group, starting from Rs 40 for half day to Rs 80 for the full day.

Indian states tourist offices The different State Governments have their own Information Centres in the city. *Andaman & Nicobar Islands*, 3A Auckland Place (2nd Floor). T 442604. *Arunachal Pradesh*, 4B Chowringhee Place. T 236500. *Assam*, 8 Russell St. T 291711. *Bihar*, 26B Camac St (1st Floor). T 446821. *Haryana*, 49 Muktaram Babu St. T 347190. *Himachal Pradesh*, 25 Camac St (2nd Floor). T 446847. *Jammu & Kashmir*, 12 J.L. Nehru Rd. T 225790. *Madhya Pradesh*, 8 Camac St (8th Floor). T 448543. *Manipur*, 26 Rowland Rd. T 478358. *Meghalaya*, 9 Russell St. T 290797. *Mizoram*, 24 Old Ballygunge Rd. T 757034. *Nagaland*, 13 Shakespeare Sarani. T 445269. *Orissa*, 55 Lenin Sarani. T 243653. *Punjab*, 5 Lower Rawdon St. T 751790. *Rajasthan*, 2 Ganesh Chandra Av. T 279051. *Sikkim*, 5/2 Russell St (4th Floor). T 295476. *Tripura*, 1 Pretoria St. T 443856. *Uttar Pradesh*, 12A Netaji Subhas Rd. T 227855.

National airlines *Air India*, 50 J.L. Nehru Rd. T 442356. Airport. T 572611, Extn. 346. *Indian Airlines*, 39 Chittaranjan Av. T 26-3390/0730. Airport Counter. T 57-2567/2633. Indian Airlines Booking Counters at Hotel Hindusthan International, 235/1 Acharya J.C. Bose Rd and Great Eastern Hotel, 1,2 &3 Old Court House St. T 280324. *Vayudoot*, 28B Nilambar Buildings, Shakespeare Sarani. T 447062, 432316. Airport Counter. T 572611 Extn. 472.

Foreign airlines *Aeroflot*, 58 J.L. Nehru Rd. T 449831. *Air Canada*, 35A J.L. Nehru Rd. T 248371. *Air France*, 41 J.L. Nehru Rd. T 296161. *Air Lanka*, c/o STIC Travels, New Kenilworth Hotel, 1 Little Russell St. T 448394. *Alitalia*, 2/3 Chitrakoot Building, 230A Acharya J.C. Bose Rd. T 447394. *Bangladesh Biman*, 1 Park St. T 442356. *British Airways*, 41 J.L. Nehru Rd. T 248181. *Cathay Pacific*, 1 Middleton Row. T 293211. *Druk Air* (Bhutan Airlines), 1A

Ballygunge Circular Rd. T 441301. *Japan Airlines*, 35A J.L. Nehru Rd. T 248371/3. *KLM*, 1 Middleton Row. T 441221/4. *Kuwait Airways*, 230A Acharya J.C. Bose Rd. T 444697. *Lufthansa*, 30A/B J.L. Nehru Rd. T 248611/13. *Pan Am*, 42 J.L. Nehru Rd. T 443251. *Qantas*, Hotel Hindusthan International, 235/1 Acharya J.C. Bose Rd. T 440718. *Royal Nepal Airlines*, 41 J.L. Nehru Rd. T 243949. *SAS*, 18G Park St. T 249696/8. *Swissair*, 46C J.L. Nehru Rd. T 444643/4. *Thai Airways*, 18G Park St. T 299846. *Gulf Air, Singapore Airlines, Philippine Airlines* are represented by GSA Jet Air Pvt. Ltd., 230A Acharya J.C. Bose Rd. T 447783.

Air Services   Indian Airlines connects Calcutta many Indian destinations and with Bangkok, Chittagong, Dhaka and Katmandu. Indian Airlines **Agartala**, daily (+ 2 others), 0700, 45 min; **Ahmedabad**, daily, 1700, 1 hr 10 min, change at Dehli (20 min wait) then daily, 1930, 1 hr 15 min (total time 2 hr 45 min); **Bagdogra**, daily, 1100, 55 min; **Bangalore**, Tue-Sun, 1500, 2 hr 20 min; **Bombay**, Daily (+ 1 other), 0855, 2 hr 30 min; **Car Nicobar**, Monday, 0545, 3 hr 15 min; **Delhi**, daily (+ 1 other), 0630, 2 hr 10 min; **Dibrugarh**, Mon-Sat, 1130, 1 hr 30 min; **Dimapur**, Mon, Wed, Fri & Sat, 1120, 2 hr 5 min; **Guwahati**, daily (+ 2 others), 1250, 1 hr; **Hyderabad**, Mon, Tue & Sun (+ 1 other), 1745, 2 hr; **Imphal**, daily (+ 1 other), 0600, 2 hr.
Jaipur daily except Tue, 0830, 4 hr 40 change at Dehli (5 hr 30 wait) then Mon, Wed, Th & Sat (+ 1 other), 1840, 35 min (Total time 10 hr 45 min); **Jorhat**, Wed, Fri & Sun, 1030, 2 hr 30 min; **Lucknow**, Daily except Tue, Th, 0830, 3 hr 20 min; **Madras**, daily, 1700, 2 hr 5 min; **Nagpur**, Wed, Fri & Sat, 1710, 2 hr 40 min; **Patna**, daily except Tue, 0830, 1 hr 55 min; **Port Blair**, Tue & Th (+ 1 other), 0545, 1 hr 55 min; **Ranchi**, daily except Tue, 0830, 45 min; **Silchar**, daily, 0600, 1 hr, **Tezpur**, Wed, Fri & Sun, 1030, 1 hr 35 min; **Varanasi**, daily, 0630, 2 hr 10 min change at Delhi (2 hr 20 min wait) then daily, 1100, 30 min (Total time 5 hr); **Visakhapatnam**, Mon, Tue, Th & Sun, 0730, 1 hr 20 min; **Bangkok** (Thailand), Sat, 1330, 1 hr 20 min; **Chittagong** (B'desh), Sat, 1330, 1 hr 20 min; **Dhaka** (B'desh), Mon & Sun (+ one other), 1340, 1 hr 10 min; **Kathmandu**, Tue, Th, Sat & Sun, 1600, 1 hr 30 min; **Dhanbad & Gaya** – no flights. Indian Airlines Enquiries, T 263390. Reservations, T 260731.
Vayudoot   Vayudoot flights are subject major modifications at the time of going to press. Confirm details. **Jamshedpur**, Mon-Sat, 0615, 50 min; **Malda**, Tue, Thur & Sat, 0600, 1 hr; **Patna**, Mon, Wed, Fri, 0550, 2 hr 20 min; **Ranchi**, Mon, Wed & Fri, 0600, 1 hr 5 min; **Shillong**, Mon-Sat, 1350, 1 hr 500 min. Vayudoot Enquiries, T 569582. Reservations, T 433091. Indian Airlines, 39 Chittaranjan Av. T 260730. Airport. T 572633. *Vayudoot* sometimes connects Calcutta with Agartala, Aizawl, Aling, Balurghat, Coochbehar,arizo, Dhanbad, Dibrugarh, Guwahati, Imphal, Jamshedpur, Jorhat, Kailashar, Kamalpur, Lilabari, Malda, Passighat, Ranchi, Rourkela, Shillong, Tezu and Ziro. Confirm with Vayudoot, 28B Nilambar Buildings, Shakespeare Sarani. T 447062. Airport, Esso Sub-station Building. T 572611, Extn. 472. *Air India*, City office, T 442356. Airport, T 572031.
International carriers connect Calcutta with Amman, Bangkok, Belgrade, Beijing, Chittagong, Dhaka, Dubai, Frankfurt, Hongkong, Kathmandu, London, Moscow, New York, Osaka, Paris, Paro, Rome, Singapore, Tokyo. International Flight Enquiry, T 569364.

Rail Calcutta is served by 2 Railway stations, **Howrah** and **Sealdah**, and is connected to major cities all over the country. From Haora a/c Expresses (via Gaya) go to **New Delhi** on Tue and Wed and to **Amritsar** on Sat, and via Patna to New Delhi on Th and to Amritsar of Sun. The Rajdhani Exp (a/c) to New Delhi runs on Mon, Tue, Th, Fri, Sun. There are fast trains to Bombay and Madras daily from both Rly stations, as well as to numerous other destinations through the week including Darjiling, Ranchi, Guwahati, Puri, Hyderabad, Bangalore, Cochin, Trivandrum, Ahmedabad and Jammu. **Delhi (D)**: *Kalka Mail*, 2311 (AC/II), daily, 1900, 24 hr 55 min; *A.C. Exp*, 2303 (AC/CC), Mon, Wed, Fri, Sun, daily, 0915, 25 hr 20 min; **Bombay (VT)**: *Gitanjali Exp*, 2860 (AC/II), 1310, 32 hr 35 min; *Bombay Mail*, 8002 (AC/CC), daily, 2000, 35 hr 40 min; **Madras (MC)**: *Coromandal Exp*, 2841 (AC/II), daily, 1445, 26 hr 50 min; *Madras Mail*, 6003 (AC/II), daily, 2045, 32 hr; **Varanasi**: *A.C. Exp*, 2381 (AC/CC&AC/II), Tue, Th, Sat, 0915, 10 hr 45 min; *Amritsar Mail*, 3005 (AC/II), daily, 1920, 14 hr 45 min; **Patna**: *A.C. Exp*, 2303 (AC/CC&AC/II), daily, 0915, 8 hr 55 min; *Delhi Exp*, 3011, daily, 2045, 10 hr 25 min; **Gaya**: *A.C. Exp*, 2381 (AC/CC&AC/II), Mon, Wed, Fri, Sun, 0915, 7 hr 29 min; *Jammu Tani Exp*, 3151 (AC/II), daily, 1120, 9 hr 16 min; **Darjiling**: *Kamrup Exp*, 5659 (AC/II), daily, 1735, 21 hr 55 min; *Darjiling Mail*, 3143 (AC/CC&AC/II), daily, 1900, 22 hr 30 min; **Allahabad**: *Kalka Mail*, 2311 (AC/II), daily, 1900, 14 hr; *Bombay Mail*, 3003 (AC/II), daily, 2000, 14 hr 40 min; **Agra**: *Toofan-Udyanabha Exp*, 3007, daily, 0945, 29 hr 20 min; **Bhuban**: *Coromandal Exp*, 2841 (AC/II), daily, 1445, 7 hr 8 min; **Puri**: *Howrah-Puri Exp*, 8007, daily, 2215, 10 hr 45 min; *Sri Jagannath Exp*, 8409 (AC/II), daily, 1920, 10 hr; **Trivandrum**: *Guwahati-Trivandrum*, 2602 (AC/II), Mon, 2235, 47 hr 55 min; **Ranchi**: *Hatia Exp*, 8015, daily, 2115, 9 hr 40 min; **Guwahati**: *Trivandrum-Guwahati*, 2601 (AC/II), Sat, 1410, 22 hr 20 min; *Cochin-Guwahati Exp*, 2649 (AC/II), Th, 1410, 22 hr 20 min; *Bangalore-Guwahati Exp*, 2674

(AC/II), Mon, 1410, 22 hr 20 min.

Round-the-clock railway information for incoming trains. T 203445-203454. Other information. T 203535-203544. For reservations. T 280370 (0900-2100 weekdays and 0900-1400 Sun).

Computerised Booking Office, 61 J.L. Nehru Rd. Railway Booking and Information Centre, 6 Fairlie Place, B.B.D. Bagh. T 204025. Haora Station T 263535. Sealdah Station T 359213. Tourists are often still automatically told to go to the tourist counter at Fairlie Place, which is the upstairs booking hall. However, unless you are travelling on an Indrail Pass or buying a pass, it is worth checking whether seats are available for the trains you want downstairs first as it can now be much quicker than using the special tourist counter. It is also easier to get a refund if you want to change your ticket, since if you buy the ticket at the tourist counter you may only be allowed a refund by going back to that counter. However, there are still quotas for tourists, so if the trains you want are listed as full it is worth trying the tourist counter.

Be prepared for **at least** half an hour's wait, and check when you enter which queue to join for the region you want to travel in. There are separate queues for N and SE Railways respectively, and you need to check on entering to avoid additional frustration. SE Railway Booking and Information Centre, Esplanade Mansions. T 289530.

Ship The Shipping Corporation of India, 13 Strand Rd. T 232354. It operates steamer service from Calcutta to Port Blair in the Andamans.

Road Calcutta is connected by an extensive network of National Highways with the major cities and towns of tourist interest nearby. Calcutta State Transport Corporation Booking Office is at Esplanade Bus Terminus. T 231916. The buses operate on routes similar to the tours detailed above under Tourist Offices and Information.

EXCURSIONS AND PLACES OF INTEREST NEARBY

There are several places of interest within reach of a day's outing from Calcutta. However, road travel is very slow in and around Calcutta, and it is best to leave central Calcutta before 0800 to avoid the worst traffic. To visit places on the W bank of the Hugli from Belur northwards it is possible cross the Haora Bridge and join the Grand Trunk Road. Haora itself is extremely congested. The Barrackpur Trunk Road on the E bank of the river is not much better. It is possible to visit Barrackpur and then to cross the Hugli over the Vivekananda road and rail bridge which runs from the Dakshineshwar Temple. Suburban trains from Haora are fast and frequent. Buses leave Esplanade, but the journey is a lot slower.

Barrackpur 25 km. As the name suggests, Barrackpur was a cantonment town of the East India Company. Originally planned as the site for building the extravagant country house of the governor, only a large 'bungalow' was built on the E bank which is now the hospital. You may visit the grounds to see the bronze Raj statues which have been removed from their pedestals in prime positions in Central Calcutta and have been brought to Barrackpur. Permission from the Secretariat at Raj Bhavan in Calcutta. Gandhi Ghat is by the river side where there is a museum. There is a pleasant garden in memory of Jawaharlal Nehru. W Bengal **E** *Tourist Bureau Cottages* have 8 double rooms.

British East India Company apart, the Danish, Dutch, French and Portuguese each had their outpost along the river Hugli. The Hugli District has a rich history with many independent kingdoms with great achievements in art and architecture. In time they fell to the Pathan, Mughal and Bargi invaders. When the Mughals lost their hold on several of the ancient seats of past rulers of Bengal, they became centres of foreign trade. The Portuguese and British settled at Hugli, the Dutch chose Chinsura, the French, Chandernagore, the Danes, Serampore, the Greeks had an outpost at Rishra and the Germans and Austrians at Bhadreswar!

Serampore **(Shrirampur)** and **Mahesh** are 5 km on across the river from Barrackpore is this old Danish settlement, known originally as Fredricnagore. Serampore was the centre of missionary activity from the beginning of the 19th century until sold to the East India Company in 1845. **Government House**, the **Roman Catholic Church** and **St. Olaf's Church** and the **Danish cemetery** retain a feeling of the past. Serampore is particularly well known for the work of the Baptist missionaries Carey, Marshman and Ward who came to the Danish port since they were not welcomed by the English administrators in Calcutta. They set up the Baptist Mission Press, which by 1805 was capable of printing in 7 Indian languages and was responsible for the first vernacular newspaper.

The **Serampore College**, founded in 1818, stands on the river bank with its imposing 7 columned classical portico. Several interesting portraits hang in the great hall. It was the first Christian Theological college in India though today perhaps only 60 of the 2,000 students there read theology. The library has rare Sanskrit, Pali and Tibetan manuscripts, over 40 translations of the Bible into Asian languages, and also the treasured 17th century Persian manuscript of the lives of the apostles. Open Mon-Fri 1000-1600 and Sat 1000-1300. You can get permission to visit from the Principal.

The **College of Textile Technology** at 12 Carey Rd, T 618248. Open weekdays 1000-1630 and on Sat 1000-1300.

At nearby **Mahesh**, 3 km away, there is a large Jagannath temple. The annual Rathjatra, 'Car' Festival, which takes place in June/July is second only to the one in Puri and draws very large crowds.

Travelling N a further 4 km along the river is **Chandernagore**. The former French colony, which dates back to 1673, was one of the tiny pockets of "non-British India" that did not gain Independence in 1947. It was handed over to India after a referendum in 1950. The French traded from here from 1673 except for 2 periods when the British took control. Attractively laid out with a promenade along the river Hugli, the churches, convents and cemeteries of the French in Chandernagore still remain. The **Bhubanesvari and Nandadulal temples** too are worth visiting, especially when *Jagaddhatri Puja* is celebrated. The Institute Chandernagar at the **Residency** has an interesting collection of documents and relics of the French in India as well as paintings, terracottas and antiques. Open weekdays 1600-1830 and Sun 1100-1700. Closed Th. The orange painted Italian missionary Church of the Sacred Heart built in 1726 also stands witness of Chandernagore's European past although the old French street names and shops have given way to Bengali.

A further 2 km N is **Chinsura**. It was originally held by the Dutch who settled there in 1653 and built the **Fort Gustavus**. It was later exchanged with Sumatra in Indonesia and became British in 1825. The octagonal **Dutch church** to the N dating from 1678, with its cemetery a short distance to the W and 3 East India Company barracks are remains of its colonial past. There is the Armenian church of **St. John the Baptist** which was built at the end of the 17th century and the **Shandesvar Siva** temple, important to Hindus. At the temple, the Dutch are still remembered on occasions when the *lingam* is decked in western clothes and a sword presented by the former rulers.

Hugli is right next door, 1 km N of Chinsura. The village was important as a trading port in the 16th century and a factory was set up by the Portuguese in 1537. However, Emperor Shah Jahan, who disliked the Portuguese for refusing to help him against his father, took the town after a siege in 1632 and made Hugli a royal port. The British were granted permission to trade from Bengal in the 17th century under a royal 'firman' and built a factory at Hugli in 1651. Fighting between the Mughals and the British broke out and much of the town was burnt, including Charnock's East India Company factory. After the Mahrattas sacked it Clive regained it for the British in 1757.

The **Imambara of Hazi Mohammed Mohasin,** built in 1836, belonging to the Shi'a sect, is the principal sight. The large facade has a central gateway with 2 35 m minarets on either side. The mosque proper stands on the N side of the quadrangular courtyard which has halls and rooms all around it. Texts from the Koran decorate the walls of the Imambara, while the interior has rich marble inlay, a silver pulpit and elaborate lanterns and chandeliers. The library has a rare collection of old manuscripts. The **Old Imambara** built in 1776 is on the opposite side of the road. The **Amulya Pratnasala Museum** in Rajbalhat village has a collection of Sculpture, coins, terracottas and manuscripts. Open 1400-2100 daily. Closed 2nd and 4th Tue and Wed.

Continuing a further 3 km you reach *Bandel*. The Portuguese settlers built **Bandel Church** dedicated to Our Lady of the Rosary around 1660 on the foundations of an older church and monastery built by Augustinian friars. The keystone dating back to 1599 can be seen on the riverside gate of the monastery and it is believed to be one of the earliest Christian churches in W Bengal. Destroyed in 1640 by Emperor Shah Jahan it was reinstated 20 years later. It always had a close association with the seafaring Portuguese, who believed that the statue of the Virgin, 'Our Lady of Happy Voyages' on top of the church's belltower, could work miracles. One story relates how the statue, which was being carried across the river to save it from the Emperor's soldiers, was lost and then in 1842 appeared on the river bank. There are fine cloisters to the S and a priory with an impressive hall dedicated in 1820 to St. Augustine. The **Hanseswari Temple** is 4 km away, built of stone and terracotta in the 18th century.

Tribeni is 5 km N of Bandel. An ancient seat of culture, it is now a straggling village. Originally known as 'Saptagram', 7 villages, it acquired great sanctity being sited at the confluence of the 3 rivers Ganga, Saraswati and Kunti, and several temples were built in the area. A mound near the river houses several monuments including tombs and a ruined mosque. There appear to have been some structures of Vaishnavite and Buddhist origin of the Pala-Sena period of the 11th and 12th centuries. The remains of the **Mazar of Zafarkhan Ghazi** illustrates the way black basalt sculpture and columns of the earlier temples and palaces were incorporated into the later masonry. It is the earliest mausoleum in eastern India, dating back to 1313. The mosque bears the Arabic inscription 1298, possibly the date of the original structure, although it certainly underwent alteration. There is a group of small temples surrounding the **Benimadhava Temple** near the 'ghat' on the river bank.

Pandua **(Hugli District)** Going a further 20 km up the Grand Trunk Rd, is Pandua, the seat of a former Hindu ruler. Once a fortified town with a wall and moat, it has several architectural remains of the Pala and Sena periods. Aamong them are a tower, 2 mosques, a tomb and 2 tanks. The most important of these is the 39 m 5 storeyed **Tower** which has a circular base of 18 m diameter narrowing to 5 m at the top. The outer surface is fluted and the inner walls have enamelled decoration. A circular staircase rises to the top with doorways leading to a narrow balcony on each storey which circles the tower. It has a court house at its base and is believed to have been ascended by a 'muezzin' who would call the faithful to prayer. Shah Sufi-ud-din is said to have erected the tower to commemorate his victory over the local Hindu ruler in 1340.

The last stop on this northern excursion is *Antpur*, 62 km from Calcutta. The 18th century temples for which Antpur is known were mainly built by Krishnaram Mitra, a local zamindar. The **Radha-Govinda temple**, dedicated to the family deity, is the most ornately decorated. The terracotta panels that appear on the front wall as well as walls of the prayer hall or *jagamohan* which forms a part of the large temple structure, depict scenes from the epics as well as contemporary life. Inside, the vaulted ceiling of the *jagamohan* has coloured murals. The whole is on a raised platform with additional sections of the 'Dolmancha' and 'Rasmancha'. Apart from several other temples, the structure of 'Chandimandap' is unique for its artistry in wood. There is also a temple to commemorate the birth place of Swami Premananda of the Ramakrishna Mission in whose home Swami Vivekananda and 8 other disciples took their vows of 'sannyasa',

Longer tours With Calcutta as the regional centre tours by road can be a way of seeing more of the area. Places of interest en route are listed, details about which appear in the relevant sections of the handbook under W Bengal, Bihar and Orissa. Accommodation is available at most places for over night stops.

Calcutta to Darjiling (W Bengal): 674 km. NH34, NH34. Barakpur (20 km) – Ranaghat via Chakdaha (80 km), Mayapur ISKCON complex, Krishnagar (35 km) for clay dolls (Dak Bungalow and Circuit House). Continue up NH 34 to Bethuadari Deer Park (20 km – Forest Rest House) to Plassey battle field (30 km), Murshidabad (50 km) for silk, ivory carvings, bell-metal utensils, Harzarduari Palace, and Behrampur (Tourist Lodge), – Jangipur (50 km) and Dhulian (30 km) – Farakka Barrage (20 km) – Malda (45 km, Tourist Lodge) for Gaur and Pandua's ancient sites, then up the NH 34 via Gajol (26 km) – Rajganj (50 km) Dalkhola (66 km) Kishanganj and Islampur to Siliguri (134 km, Tourist Lodge, Hotels).

Calcutta to Bodh Gaya (Bihar): 467 km. NH2. Durgapur steel town, (Tourist Lodge, Hotel), Asansol (Hotel), Burnpur iron and steel plant, Barakar (Inspection Bungalow), Barhi. Gaya, Rajgir for sulphur springs, Nalanda for ancient university.

Calcutta to Puri (Orissa): 489 km. NH6, NH5. Kharagpur, (Inspection Bungalow, Hotel), Balasore (Inspection Bungalow), Markona (Inspection Bungalow), Cuttack (Rest House, Hotel), Bhubaneswar (Tourist Lodge, Hotel).

WEST BENGAL

> **Introduction, 544; Calcutta to Santiniketan via Bishnupur, 549; Calcutta to Malda and Gaur, 554; Calcutta to Darjiling and the North, 559; Calcutta to the mouth of the Hugli, 568.**

West Bengal covers 88,000 sq km, more than double the area of Switzerland, but its population of 65 million in 1991 (more than three times that of California) makes it India's fifth largest state. Urban population 19 m 1991 (29%) 11.0 m 1971 (25%). Created in virtually its present form in 1947, W Bengal stretches 600 km from the Bay of Bengal in the S to the borders of Sikkim in the N. Bengali and several minor and tribal languages, such as *Santali*, are spoken. All the major languages of India are spoken in Calcutta.

Social indicators *Literacy* M 41% F 30% *Newspaper circulation:* 1,802,000 *Birth rate* Rural 36:1000 Urban 21:1000 *Death rate* Rural 11:1000 Urban 6:1000 *Infant mortality* Rural 93:1000, Urban 52:1000 *In-migrants* 5,700,000 *Out-migrants* 980,000 *Registered graduate job seekers* 4,118,000 *Average annual income per head* : Rs 1553 *Inflation 1981-87* 74%

Religion *Hindu* 76% *Muslim* 22% *Christian* 1% *Sikh* 0.3%

Towns and cities 29% of W Bengal's population is classified as urban, but that reflects the overwhelming dominance of Calcutta, W Bengal's capital, which is more than ten times the size of the next largest city in the state. Its population in 1991 was 9.4 million. It lies surrounded by poorly drained marsh, still often flooded. Newly industrialising cities include Asansol (250,000) Durgapur (410,000) and Barddhaman (227,000), while in the N, Darjiling (70,000) is E India's most important hill station and centre of India's major tea growing region.

WEST BENGAL

SA 93

Delhi
Bombay
Madras
Calcutta

0   50
km

N

Darjiling
Kalimpong
Bagdogra
Siliguri
Jalpaiguri
Jaldapara
WLP

Katihar
Raiganj
NH 34

B A N G L A D E S H

Pandua
Malda
Gaur

B I H A R

Dhuliad

Rampurhat
Murshidabad
Baharampur

Siuri
Santiniketan
Asansol
Bolpur
Ondal
Durgapur
NH 2
Krishnagar
Bankura
Barddhaman
Naihati
Bishnupur
Tarakeswar
NH 34
Arambagh
Srirampur
Haora
Dum Dum
CALCUTTA
NH 6
Kharagpur
Diamond Harbour
Haldia
Kanthi
Digha

O R I S S A

S U N D E R B A N S

Mouths of
the Ganga

INTRODUCTION

The land

Most of the state lies on the flat W delta of the Ganga. At this E end of the Ganga valley the great alluvial-filled trough which fronts the Himalayas becomes much shallower. The basalt **Rajmahal Hills**, in the centre of the state, are a projection NE of the Peninsula rocks. However, like Bangladesh, which forms the E half of the delta, W Bengal is made up largely of "new mud, old mud and marsh". That mud – some of the most fertile silt in the world – was originally densely forested. Over the last 1,000 years it has been cleared, and now the only jungle that remains is in the mangrove swamps of the **Sundarbans** in the far S and on the slopes of the Himalayas in the N. Elsewhere the flat alluvial plains have been converted into an intensively cultivated rice growing landscape.

Even here there is great variety. Driving N from Calcutta the national highway crosses the apparently dead flat plains of what is called the 'moribund delta'. Here the rivers that used to carry the bulk of the Ganga's water have progressively silted up, leaving old channels, often dry in the winter, sometimes with old meanders and shallow cut-off lakes left as wild swamp. Coconut-fringed village ponds break up the scenery and villages often stand surrounded by orchards with mangoes, papayas and palmyra palms.

Rivers The Ganga delta is still highly active, and rivers continue to change their course frequently. Over the last 300 years the main course of the Ganga has shifted progressively further E, leaving the Bhagirathi-Hooghly as a minor channel. The front margins of the Himalayas are one of the great belts of earth movement, and these shifts in the river courses may have been caused both by earth movements and by silting of the western rivers. Certainly in the 16th century the **Bhagirathi** was the main course followed by the Ganga to the sea. In 1770 the Damodar River, which used to flow from Bihar to join the Bhagirathi N of Calcutta shifted its course 130 km southwards – just one of several major changes of course made by the delta rivers.

The road N and a new railway now cross the **Farakka Barrage**, opened in 1972 to divert the Ganga waters in the dry season back down their old course in order to supply more water for Calcutta and to flush silt from the river bed. It also reopens the rail route to northern W Bengal and Assam which had run across the Hardinge Bridge through what is now Bangladesh.

The ease with which rivers have changed their courses suggests how flat the land is. Despite the flatness of the terrain minor variations in height make enormous differences to the quality of the land for farming. Houses cluster along old river banks and any slightly higher ground that gives protection against floods, microcosms of Calcutta's own built up area which hugs the banks of the Hughly, slightly raised above the surrounding marsh. But the chief variety in the landscape of the plains of Bengal comes from the contrasting greens of the different varieties of rice and the clusters of tree-shaded hamlets, often producing startlingly attractive countryside.

Much greater variety of scenery is provided by the mountains on the northern fringes of the state and the plateau and hills of the SW. The gently rising, often lateritic, slopes, which lead from the delta to the peninsular rocks of Bihar and Orissa, are still the home of some of India's most primitive tribal peoples such as the Santals, although their forest habitat has been severely eroded.

Climate

Hot and humid summers are followed by much cooler and clearer winters over most of W Bengal. The most distinctive feature of W Bengal's climate are the heavy storms occurring in late Mar and Apr. Known as Nor'Westers, these electric storms are marked by massive cloud formations, often reaching over 15 km above the ground, strong winds, and heavy rain. Occasionally tropical cyclones also strike coastal areas at this time of year, though they are far more common after the main season of the rains, between Oct and Dec.

People

The majority of the people are Bengalis. There are also significant tribal groups, notably Santals, Oraons and Mundas in the plains and the borders of Chota Nagpur and Lepchas and Bhutias in the Himalayas. Over 85% of the population speak Bengali. Hindi, Urdu, and tribal languages account for most of the remainder, though all India's major languages are represented in Calcutta.

Economy

Agriculture Rice is the dominant food crop, but there are dozens of varieties suited to the small contrasts in height, soil type and season of growth which are extremely important for successful cultivation. Jute has become an important cash crop since Independence. The jute plant (*Corchorus*) grows to a height of between 3 and 4 m. Even today the best jute grows on freshly deposited river silt, found far more widely in Bangladesh than in W Bengal. Tea is the second major cash crop. See under Darjiling **page 560**.

Industry and Resources Bengal became famous for its **jute**, which is twisted to produce a variety of household items. Jute production was mechanised in 1855 with powerlooms being introduced 4 years later and a large number of prosperous mills were established along the banks of the Hugli. After 1947, and the partition of E Bengal (now Bangladesh) from the W, problems arose since the jute mills in the Indian side were separated from the jute growing areas and Pakistan made it impossible to export raw jute to India. However, this was overcome by increased production of jute as a cash crop in eastern India, while Bangladesh has set up its own jute mills.

Across the margins of W Bengal, Bihar and Orissa lie India's richest *mineral resources* in deposits of coal and iron ore. Coal was first exploited at Raniganj in 1774-75, but has been mined continuously since 1815. The development of the railways boosted demand, and in the 1970s they accounted for 20% of the total coal output. Since Independence there has been an enormous increase in output from mines across the region. In 1991 the total coal output had reached nearly 200 million tonnes. Early development focused on the **Damodar Valley**. In the 1950s the Damodar River was dammed in a scheme to bring wide-ranging, integrated development, modelled on the Tennesseee Valley Authority in the United States. Flood control in downstream areas of W Bengal, irrigation and power development have made it a major economic region. A new steel mill was commissioned at Durgapur in 1957, and Asansol, Burdwan and Burnpur have all become important industrial towns. Calcutta was the first industrial centre in India, and from the middle of the 19th century became the leading jute processing centre in the world. Alongside that industry it developed a range of engineering industries, diversifying into production of cars and lorries and more recently into electronics. However, the devastating effect of the loss of raw jute supplies from E Pakistan coupled with a very hostile climate for investment in the 1960s and 1970s contributed to very slow overall growth, especially compared to other Indian cities.

Despite the growth of industrial capacity and in particular of power generation, demand has constantly outstripped supply. Much of W Bengal, including Calcutta, suffers major power cuts (referred to as "loadshedding"), especially during the summer. This adds to the unpleasantness of the big cities in the hot season.

Craft industries

Silk is known to have been woven in India for more than 3500 years and there are references to Bengal and Assam silk in manuscripts of the 2nd century. The tradition continues with the weaving of the natural coloured wild silk called 'tassar'. Bengal silk, commonly found as block-printed saris, has had a revival in the exquisite brocade weaving of '*baluchari*' which was produced in past centuries under royal patronage, and is carried out today in Bankura. The saris are woven in traditional style with untwisted silk and have beautiful borders and '*pallu*' (the end section), which often depict horses, peacocks, flowers and human figures. Fine cotton is woven into saris, fabrics and articles for everyday use.

'Kantha' embroidery, again very typically Bengali, uses a quilting technique of running stitches to make patterns of birds, flowers and animals or scenes from mythology. Several layers of old cotton '*dhoti**', the long piece of fine white cloth worn by men, were traditionally stitched together to form the basis for a quilt or 'shawl' which would then be embroidered from the centre outwards with thicker coloured threads retrieved from the borders of old '*saris**' worn by the women. The outlines of the patterns would be filled in by lines of close stitches, often in another colour, while the ground would have similar stitches in white, the whole reinforcing the old cloth and at the same time producing attractive useful articles. Villages would often develop their distinctive designs, although each item produced would be unique, often the work of several pairs of hands as women might have sat around to work on a single piece. Today, 'kanthas' offered for sale are of new cloth and usually made up into small pictures, cushion covers, bedcovers and *kurtas**.

The **'Bankura horse'** has become a symbol of pottery in W Bengal which still flourishes in the districts of Bankura (**see page 550**), Midnapore and Birbhum. 'Shola' pith, the core of the sponge wood that grows in marshy areas of Bengal, is fashioned into delicate flowers, toys and deities by 'Malakars' and are in great demand during festivals. The '*Sola Topee*' or the pith helmet, so inseparable from the colonial era of India, was derived from this '*shola**', not the 'solar' of the sun! The art of carving flourishes using soft soap-stone for carving out copies of temple images and for making small boxes and plates. Shell craft is another speciality since it is considered auspicious for women to wear conch shell bangles. The ivory carvers produce superb decorative items, a skill developed in the Mughal period and then during British rule for the European market. Ivory export is now banned, however, and plastic has largely replaced ivory as the material used in inlay work. Metal workers produce **brass** and **bell-metal** ware while the tribal Dokra casters still follow the ancient '**cire perdu**' or lost-wax method. High quality jewellery is made, as it has been for centuries, and very fine items of gold and silver are available. In contrast, the Kalighat '*pat' paintings* are in a primitive style using bold colours and mythological themes. The origin of the 'pats' go back to time when travelling 'patuas', painter-storytellers, went from village to village entertaining folk with their tales, using illustrated scrolls.

History

In pre-historic times Bengal was peopled with Dravidian tribes. They were hunter-gatherers and lived in small communities. In the 1st millenium BC, the Aryans from Central Asia, who had by then absorbed the agricultural techniques of the Indus Valley civilization and learnt the art of weaving and pottery, spread towards the E under pressure from tribal warfare and arrived in the region of Bengal bringing with them the Sanskrit language. From about the 5th century BC trade in cotton, silk and coral from the port of Ganga Nagar in one of the estuaries, flourished and made the region prosperous although little is known of those who ruled. In the 3rd century BC Bengal was part of the Mauryan Empire, but it remained densely forested and comparatively sparsely populated.

The classical age The **Guptas** conquered Bengal in the 4th century AD and trade with the Mediterranean expanded for the next 200 years, particularly with Rome. However, with the fall of the Roman Empire in the 5th century, the increasing importance of Arab and Persian traders led to a change in Bengal's fortunes. It was only with the founding of the *Pala* dynasty in 750 AD that the region was united once again and for the next 450 years many cities emerged along the great river Ganga. Bengal became a centre of Buddhism, and art and learning flourished.

Muslim rule The Pala dynasty was followed by the *Senas* who were great patrons of the arts and ruled for half a century untilosed by the invading Turks. They began a century of Muslim rule under the Khiljis of the Delhi Sultanate. Pathan kings who came originally from Afghanistan followed. The most notable was **Sher Shah**, who took advantage of the death of the first Mughal Emperor, Babur, to extend his territory from Bihar into Bengal, and then westwards to displace Humayun in 1540. However, Bengal was ultimately taken back under Mughal rule by Akbar, anxious to obtain the rich resources of rice, silk and salt-petre, between 1574 and 1576.

During the lengthy period of Muslim rule, the birth of *Chaitanya* in 1486, believed by many to be an incarnation of Lord Krishna, brought a new dimension in Hinduism and a revival of interest in Vedic literature.

European trade Although **Vasco da Gama** had reached Goa in 1498 the Portuguese did not begin to trade with Bengal until the middle of the 16th century. The increasing power of the Muslims, both in terms of trade (in spices, cotton and silk cloth, and indigo) as well as religion spurred the Portuguese towards the subcontinent. Before long they faced competition for trading opportunities from the Dutch and the British and in 1632 the subsequent attack on their port near Calcutta by Emperor Shah Jahan reduced their merchant power.

In 1634 one of **Shah Jahan's** daughters was badly burned in a fire. For weeks her life was in danger, but she was finally saved under the guidance of an English surgeon, Gabriel Boughton, who was visiting the court. In gratitude for this Shah Jahan granted the British permission to trade from Bengal and establish 'factories', or trading posts, there. English surgeons repeatedly played a part in securing more than the health of the Company's servants. Eighty years later another surgeon, William Hamilton, cured the Emperor Farukhsiyar of venereal disease, and was granted effective control of trading rights for the Company in Bengal. A plaque commemorates him in the tomb of Job Charnock in Calcutta. In 1690 the purchase of the 3 villages which grew into Calcutta gave the British greater power. They built a fort and consolidated their position.

The Presidency In 1700, Bengal became an independent Presidency and the city of Calcutta prospered. The *firmans** granted were for trading from the ports but the British took the opportunity of gaining a monopoly over internal trade as well. The internal waterways gave them access to rich resources and to the other commodities was added the export of saltpetre to fuel the wars in Europe.

The Mughals ruled from Delhi through the Nawabs they appointed in the distant parts of their Empire. In the case of Bengal they made individual gains in the name of the Emperor and following the death of Aurangzeb the authority of the throne slowly crumbled. In 1756, the 20-old **Siraj-ud-Daula**, the then Nawab of Bengal began to take note of Calcutta's growing wealth and finding the British strengthening the fortifications (apparently against the French, which he chose not to believe), he attacked Fort William, finding little difficulty in capturing the city. This victory was short lived and within a year Clive took the city back and also defeated the Nawab at **Plassey** – a turning point for the British in India.

Through the 19th century W Bengal became the economic and political centre of British India. Agricultural raw materials – indigo and opium in the first half of the century, jute in the second – became staples of trade. Manufacturing and processing developed in the late 19th century, along with engineering industries which grew up with Calcutta's port activities and focus as a railway centre.

Religious and social reform Calcutta also developed as the major centre of cultural and political activity in modern India. Bengali literature, drama, art and music flourished. Religious reform movements such as the Brahmo Samaj, under the original leadership of **Raja Ram Mohan Roy** in the 1830s, grew out of the juxtaposition of traditional Hinduism with Christian missionary activity, of which Calcutta was a major centre in the early 19th century. At the end of the century and into the 20th, one of India's greatest poets, Nobel Prize winner **Rabindranath Tagore** (1861-1941), dominated India's cultural world, breathing moral and spiritual life into the political movement for independence from colonial rule.

The two partitions Until 1905 Bengal had included much of modern Bihar and Orissa, as well as the whole of Bengal. Lord Curzon's partition of Bengal in 1905 created 2 new states; E Bengal and Assam, and W Bengal, Bihar and Orissa. It roused fierce political opposition among Bengalis, who played prominent roles in the national movement for independence. It also encouraged the split between Muslims and Hindus which finally resulted in Bengali Muslim support for the creation of Pakistan and Partition in 1947. The division into the 2 new states was accompanied by the migration of over 5 million people and appalling massacres as Hindus and Muslims fled. W Bengal was directly affected by the struggle to create Bangladesh in 1971, when about 10 million refugees fled into the state from E Pakistan after 25 Mar 1971. Most of them returned after Bangladesh gained its independence in Dec 1971.

Modern political development W Bengal has 42 seats in the Lok Sabha and a State Assembly of 294 seats. Since the mid 1960s political life has been dominated by the confrontation between the Communist Party of India Marxist (the CPM) and the Congress Party. The CPM has held power in the State Assembly continuously since June 1977 when the present chief minister, **Jyoti Basu**, took power. In 1987 it held 187 out of 294 seats. The Congress is the second largest party, winning 40 seats in the 1987 State Assembly elections. It has performed consistently better in the Lok Sabha parliamentary elections. Its poorest performance since Independence was in 1971 and 1977 when it obtained around 29% of the vote but as few as 3 seats. In 1984, a high water mark, it polled over 48% of the popular vote but still only won 16 out of the 42 seats. In contrast the CPM won 18 seats on the strength of 36% of the vote.

Cuisine

The Bengali is said to be obsessed about what he eats and it is not unusual for the man of the house to take a keen interest in the business of buying the most important elements of the days meal, namely fresh fish from the bazaar. Typically, it is river fish, the most popular being **Hilsa** and **Bekti** or the more widely available shell fish, especially king prawns. Bekti is grilled or fried (tastier than the 'fried fish' of the W as it has often been marinated in mild spices first) and the prized smoked Hilsa, although delicious, requires patience as it has thousands of fine bones which are best removed with the help of your teeth and fingers. Fish comes in many forms as *macher jhol* in a thin gravy, *macher jhal* spicy and hot, or prepared with coconut milk and spices to produce *malai curry* 'chop' with a covering of mashed potato and crumbs or *chingri macher* 'cutlet', flattened king prawn 'fillets', crumbed and fried. 'Chop' and 'cutlet' (as with the *macher* 'fry') are hang overs from the days of the Raj but bear little resemblance to the original!

Another feature of Bengali cooking is the use of mustard oil and mustard which grows in abundance and the subtle mixture of spices. An example is **Panch Phoron**, a mixture of 5 spices (cumin, mustard, fennel, onion seed and fenugreek) is used in some vegetable preparations. You will only find the true flavour of Bengali cooking in someone's home (or a special restaurant like *Suruchi* in Calcutta's Elliot Rd, since others fight shy of the subtle taste and tend to offer the universally available N Indian cuisine).

An item which assumes great importance in a Bengali household is *mishti**, the sweetmeats you can buy from a shop. Many are milk based and the famous sandesh, *roshogolla, roshomalai, pantua* and Lady Kenny are prepared with a kind of cottage cheese. (Indians in the West attempt to replace the authentic ingredients with milk powder, semolina, flour and butter!). There are dozens on offer with different textures, shapes, colours and taste, but nearly all of them, though delicious, are very sweet for the Western palate. One which needs a special mention is pale pinkish brown *mishti doi*, an excellent sweet yoghurt eaten as a dessert, typically sold in hand-thrown clay pots.

Unfortunately, it is not safe to buy sweets on the road side as they are often covered with flies. However, the good sweet shops have glass display cases or you may catch a sweet meat maker at his work in front of his shop and buy your favourite as it emerges from the boiling syrup! If travelling outside Calcutta, try the specialities – *mihidana* and *sitabhog* in Barddhaman, *sarpuria* in Krishnanagar and Lady Kenny in Ranaghat.

REGIONAL TOURS

The major places of interest in West Bengal, other than those in and around Calcutta, are in four areas; the W, north-central, far N and S. Each of the groups of places described below could make a self-contained tour of 2 or 3 days by train, car or bus, centred on Calcutta, though flying from Calcutta to Bagdogra shortens the time necessary to see Darjiling. In a more extended tour it would be possible to link the groups together without returning to Calcutta.

CALCUTTA TO SANTINIKETAN VIA BISHNUPUR

The route crosses the flood plains W of Calcutta to Bishnapur, with its Bengal terracota temples. The modern steel town of Durgapur has massive plants for steel ingots and high-tech alloys. By contrast, the route ends in Santiniketan with the Vishva Bharati University ('Abode of Peace') and many local festivities.

Immediately to the W of Calcutta are the flat floodplains of the Damodar River, once ravaged by periodic floods but now protected by the massive Damodar Valley Project scheme. The main road to the northwest, the NH 2 leaves Calcutta travelling due N before turning W N W for the administrative and industrial town of Barddhaman (formerly Burdwan), Durgapur and Asansol, now the heavy industrial belt of W Bengal. The NH 2 can be a busy road with a lot of heavy traffic. There is also a quieter road W which leaves the NH 2 N of *Shrirampur* (Serampore) and passes through **Tarkeshwar** (30 km), **Chanpadanga** (10 km) and **Arambagh** (52 km). If you follow this route you reach *Jairambati* (11 km) and *Kamarpukur* (5 km) en route. Both these small towns are noted as the birth places of Sri **Ramakrishna** and his wife Sri Saradamani. The Ramakrishna Mission has an Ashram in spacious gardens at Kamarpukur and the place where Ramakrishna was born is marked by a marble statue. A few kilometres from Kamarpukur are the ruins of the **Garh Mandaran fort**. Simple accommodation is available at the *Ramakrishna Mission Guest House* which can be reserved through the Secretary. The road continues W to Bishnupur (45 km).

Bishnupur *(Altitude* 70 m 152 km from Calcutta) was the seat of the kings of the Malla dynasty, the warrior rulers who administered this part of Bengal for over 200 years from the late 16th century until the British sold it by auction to the Maharajah of Burdwan. The Mallas were great patrons of the arts, architecture, sculpture and music. Bishnupur is also the birth place of the **Dhrupad** style of classical Indian vocal music and is famous for the 17th and 18th century Bengal terracotta temples.

Local industry Local handicrafts include silk, tassar, conch-shell and bell-metal ware and the famous terracotta 'Bankura horse', *Dokra** and also slate statues and artefacts. Bengali sweetmeats and flavoured tobacco are Bishnupuri specialities.

Local festival The most famous local festival, *Jhapan* takes place in August in honour of the serpent goddess 'Manasa', the daughter of Siva. A regional harvest festival it is linked with the fertility cult and is a unique occasion; snake-charmers display tricks and amazing feats with live, venomous snakes on decorated bullock carts. Cobras, pythons, vipers, rat snakes, kraits and flying snakes are brought in baskets made of cane or grass. The origin of the festival is believed to date back to the 17th century when King Bir Hambir Malla was greeted with great rejoicing on his victorious return after a battle.

Places of interest The exceptionally ornamental temple architecture which is distinctive of the Malla's reign survives today. The temples have walls built on a square plan but topped with a gently curved roof like Bengali thatched huts, which are built of bamboo and mud. The style was taken across India by the Mughals and later by the Rajputs, and was used to great effect in forts such as that in Lahore and Agra. The temples are usually built of brick but sometimes of laterite. The terracotta tiles depict episodes from the epics Ramayana and Mahabharata, but occasionally there are scenes from daily life. The interior consists of a single hall (*thakur bari*) and has a platform (*vedi*) for the image on one side. The upper storey has a gallery topped by one, 5 or even 9 towers.

There are more than two dozen temples mostly dedicated to **Krishna** and **Radha** in Bishnupur. Most are concentrated within the fort, (built later by Muslim rulers) while a few stand outside. Distances are given from the Tourist Lodge. The **Rasmancha** (3 km) is unique as a Vishnu shrine. A squat, stepped pyramid, the *thakurbari* (sanctuary) is surrounded by passageways. It was built by Bir Hambir in 1587 to provide a place for all the local Vaishnavite deities to be brought together in a procession from the other temples during the annual Ras festival. The well preserved cannons, in particular the 4 m long **Dalmadal** to the S of the Rasmancha, date back to the time of the Mallas. The **Jora Mandir** (5 km), a pair of hut-shaped structures with a single 'sikhara', built of brick in 1655 by Raghunath Singh, is highly ornamented and of architectural interest. The panels illustrate battle scenes from the epics, hunters with wild animals, maritime scenes and life at court.

The **Madan Mohan Temple** (5 km), although not as elaborate is one of the largest, standing in a compound, on a 16 m square base with a white facade. It was built of brick with terracotta panels in 1694 by King Durjan. **Shyam Rai Temple** (7 km) also built by Raghunath Singh is perhaps the earliest example of the 'pancharatna' style, with five towers built together in brick with a fine 'sikhara'. Each facade is triple arched and the terracotta panels depict stories from the Ramayana and Lord Krishna's life. The **Lalji** and **Madan Gopal** are 17th century examples of temples built of laterite, the former with a single tower and the latter in the 'pancha ratna' style.

The **Mrinmoyee Mandir** (3 km) is an ancient place of worship dating from AD 997. The temple deity, Durga, is a clay idol and in the courtyard there is a curious sight of nine trees growing together. The **Malla Kings' Fort** (3.5 km) was built by Bir Singh but little remains. The gate of laterite, '*pathar durwaza*', has holes drilled in different directions through which the king's soldiers would fire shots. A stone chariot is believed to date back to the 13th century. The moat which used to be served by 7 lakes is partially dry although the water reservoirs ('*bundhs*') can still be seen.

Hotels E *The Tourist Lodge* has non a/c single and double rooms and also an **F** *dormitory*. One meal is compulsory. Reservations: Tourist Lodge, Bishnupur or Calcutta Tourist Bureau, 3/2 B.B.D. Bagh, Calcutta 700001, T 238271.

Restaurant *Guest N Rest*, near Rabindranath Tagore's statue serves Bengali food only.

Banks The *State Bank of India*, T 51, will convert foreign exchange. *United Bank of India*, T 27, and *Bank of India* (T 188) also have branches in the town.

Shopping The local cottage industries flourish in the different 'paras' or quarters of the town each devoted to a specialized craft – pottery in Kamarpara, conch shell or 'sankha' cutting in Sankharipara and weaving, particularly Baluchari silk saris in Tantipara. You may purchase silks from *Silk Khadi Seva Mandal*, Boltala, T 45 or Bankura horses and clay dolls and folk toys from *Terracotta Crafts*, ½ km from the Tourist Lodge. *Shri Hari Sankha Bhandar* and *Ma Durga Sankha Bhandar*, both in Sankharipara, specialize in conch shell craft. Camera films are available in *Chitriniketan* in Matukgunge.

Local Transport The Tourist Lodge will arrange hire of cars or jeeps. Cars can be hired from Kiron Homeo Hall, Matukgunge for Rs 2 per km. Otherwise most temples can be visited by cycle rickshaws.

Museum *Jogesh Chandra Pura Kirti Bhavan* is within walking distance from the Tourist Lodge. Open daily 1000-1200, 1400-1800 or by request to the Manager, Tourist Lodge.

Hospitals and medical services The Bishnupur Sub-Division Hospital (near the Court); Vishnu Pharmacy in Maruee Bazar; Kiron Homeo Hall in Matukgunge.

Travel Rail Trains from Haora (Calcutta): Fast Chari Car to Bankura, daily, 1600, 4 hr. Asansol, Gomoh and Purulia Passenger. **Road** The WB State Transport Corporation buses leave Esplanade Terminus in Calcutta daily at 0745 and 0845. Fare Rs 14.60. Durgapur State Transport Super Express buses leave Durgapur daily at 1115 (journey time 1 hr). Fare Rs 24.

To visit **Durgapur** (72 km) from Bishnupur take the road N to Sonamukhi and Kaksa, which is on the NH 2.

Durgapur

Altitude 69 m. *Population* 410,000. *Climate* Temp. Summer Max. 46°C Min. 38°C, Winter Max. 32°C Min. 29°C. Annual rainfall 1500 mm mostly from Jun to Sep.

If you take the NH 2 all the way Durgapur is 176 km from Calcutta. The route along NH2 goes N from Haora (keep to the western highway and avoid the riverside road N through the suburbs of Haora) to Magra and then northwest through Memari to **Barddhaman** (Burdwan, an administrative and commercial centre). Much of the land on either side of the road is irrigated from the Damodar Valley scheme. The road runs close to the Damodar Canal all the way from Memari to Durgapur. In stark contrast to the other places of cultural interest suggested to the tourist, this steel town was built in the mid-1950s within easy reach of the rich belt of coal and iron ore. The steel plant, the thermal power projects, and the Fertilizer and Allied Machinery Corporation are the places of interest. **Maithan**, 66 km away has a massive dam and a hydro-electric project.

Places of interest Durgapur is a planned city, with land use zoned for different kinds of use. It is also quite widely spaced out. Distances are given from the railway station. The steel plant (10 km) was commissioned in 1957 and now produces over 1.6 million tonnes of ingot steel. The coke oven by-products unit processes crude tar, ammonium sulphate and crude benzol from the residual gases. A 176 km gas pipe supplies Calcutta with domestic gas from Durgapur. The AVB Heavy Engineering Plant (6 km) an Indo-British enterprise is the largest in the private sector. A joint Japanese-Canadian venture provided technical cooperation to set up the Alloy Steel Project (10 km) which produces tool steel, stainless steel and heat resistant steel. The 692 m Durgapur Barrage (3 km), constructed by the Damodar Valley Corporation, is vital for the 2,500 km canal network in the region. Permits to visit are issued by the Public Relations Office. T 483, personal application only. Visiting: 1030-1230, 1430-1630 on weekdays, 0930-1215 on Sat.

Hotels The Government has an **E** *Tourist Lodge* (T 5476) with 24 rooms (some air-conditioned) and a restaurant and a very inexpensive **F** *Youth Hostel* near the railway station. Reserve through the Calcutta office of the WBTDC, 3/2, B.B.D. Bagh (E), T 235917. The Steel Plant also has accommodation at **E** *Durgapur House*, reserve by contacting the Public Relations Officer, T 3611, Ext 315 or Manager, T 2517. Some private hotels including the **E** *Durgapur Lodge* near the railway station, T 5921.

Restaurants The *Tourist Lodge*, T 5476 has a bar, *Kwality* near the Steel Plant, T 2777 and *Qaiser* in Nachan Rd, T 2466 have restaurants.

Banks There are several in the town including the *State Bank of India*, T 2589, *Bank of India*, T 2472 and *Central Bank of India*, T 5156.

Shopping The main shopping centres are Benachitti Market, the City Centre and the Sector Market of the township. Handicrafts are available from *Gramin* and *Rehabilitation Industries Corporation* both in Benachitti.

Tourist office and Information The Public Relations Officer at the Durgapur Steel Plant, T 3611, Ext 315 provides information for tourists.

Travel Durgapur is on the main railway line to Calcutta. There are also frequent buses, both to Calcutta and to neighbouring towns, including Santiniketan.

To reach Santiniketan return to the NH 2. Turn right, and after 16 km (just before the road crosses the railway line) turn left for *Bolpur*, the railway station for Santiniketan. Bolpur is connected to Calcutta by rail from both Haora and Sealdah (147 km). Fast trains from Haora: Kanchenjunga Exp, Santiniketan Exp, Danapur Fast Passenger and Viswa Bharati Exp. To Calcutta (H): Shantiniketan Exp, 3016, daily, 1300, 2 hr 40 min.

Santiniketan, 2 km away, can be reached by taxi or cycle rickshaw. The road journey on NH2 takes longer (213 km), and can be very slow, but may be a useful way of visiting other places of interest en route.

Santiniketan

Population 34,600 *Altitude* 32 m. *Climate* Temp. Summer Max. 39°C Min. 34 °C, Winter Max.16°C Min. 12°C. Annual rainfall 1250 mm, mainly June-Sep but particularly heavy in July/Aug.

Santiniketan was founded by **Maharishi Debendranath Tagore**, father of **Rabindranath Tagore**, the Nobel Laureate, who first started an *ashram* here, later named the 'Abode of Peace'. In 1901 his son started an experimental place of learning with a 'classroom' under the trees, and a group of five pupils. It went on to become the **Vishva Bharati University** in 1921 which attracts students from all over the world and aspires to be a spiritual meeting ground in a serene, culturally rich and artistic environment. There are faculties in all major disciplines, although the humanities and performing arts dominate, particularly philosophy, Sanskrit, art, Indian music and drama. It also includes agriculture and cottage industries, thus providing employment within the campus. **Satyajit Ray**, **Indira Gandhi** and the Maharani of Jaipur are among the famous who studied here. An interesting feature of Santiniketan is the number of sculptures, frescoes, paintings and murals that are to be found around the campus, particularly paintings by Rabindranath, Nandalal Bose and Ramkinkar.

Local Festivals *Poush Mela*, (23-25 Dec) is Santiniketan's most important fair. It coincides with the village's Foundation Day and brings thousands of visitors. You have the opportunity not only to see a large number of *Santals*, the tribal group in this region, who may be seen performing dances, but also to hear the *bauls*, Bengal's wandering minstrels. They are worshippers of Lord Krishna who believe that there is divinity in every being and travel from village to village singing their songs, often accompanied by the strumming on a single string, '*ektara*', and a tiny drum. Tribal silver and 'Dokra' metal crafts make attractive buys.

The *Convocation* (Samabartan Utsav) of the University is usually held in Dec when the Prime Minister of India presides, but it is not open to the general public for security reasons. *Magh Mela* at Sriniketan marks the anniversary of the *Brahmo Samaj* and the founding of

SANTINIKETAN SA 94
not to scale

Deer Park
Uttarayan Complex
Malancha
Old Mela Ground

1a. Punascha
1b. Shamali
1c. Konarak
1d. Udichi
1e. Udyana
1f. Vichitra
2. Chatimtola
3. Sadhana Prayer Hall
4. Silpa Mandir
5. Natya Ghar
6. Kala Bhavana
7. Sangeet Bhavana
8. Patha Bhavana
9. Shikshar Vidya Bhavana
10. China Bhavana
11. Hindi Bhavana
12. Darshan Bhavana
13. Santasalay
14. Science Dept.
15. Granthagar (Library)
16. Central Library
17. Central Office
18. State Bank
19. Coop Bank
20. Post Office
21. Railway Booking Office
22. PRO Tourist Office
23. Ratan Kuti
24. Guest House
25. Tourist Lodge

Bakul Bithi
Kitchen
Amra Kunja
Chaity
Gour Prangana
Benukunja
Canteen
Hati Bagan
Mela Ground
Gurupalli
To Bolpur

N

Sriniketan. It is an agricultural and rural crafts fair held at the end of Jan. *Vasanta Utsav* in Mar coincides with Holi, *Varsha Mangal* in Jul/Aug during the rainy months and *Saradotsava* in the autumn marks the end of term before the Pujas. Programmes of dance, music and singing are held throughout the year, particularly good during the various festivals.

Places of interest The University, where classes are still held in the open-air, is unique. Among the many *Bhavans* there are those concentrating on art (Kala Bhavan), music and dance (Sangit Bhavan), Chinese studies, the humanities and the sciences. Vinaya Bhavan is the Teachers' Training College. **Sightseeing is permitted only after university hours.** In the summer from 1430-1730, winter from 1400-1700 and during vacations from 0730-1100. Photography is not permitted. The **Uttarayan Complex** where the poet lived consists of several buildings in a distinct architectural style. There is a **Prayer Hall**, founded in 1863 where Brahmo prayers are held on Wed (**See page 61**). It has a polished marble floor usually decorated with *alpana* designs and is surrounded by glass doors with patterns picked out in stained glass.

Chatimtala, where Maharishi Debendranath sat and meditated, is the site at Convocation time of special prayers. In keeping with its simplicity, graduates are presented with a twig with five leaves from the *Saptaparni* trees which grow freely in the area. **Sriniketan**, 3 km away, has the Department of Rural Reconstruction where the country's socio-economic problems are studied and is also a College of Agriculture. Activities include weaving, leather craft, pottery, *Kantha* embroidery and *Batik*. Open 0800-1000, 1030-1230. Photography with prior permission from the PRO, Viswa Bharati.

Hotels D *Santiniketan Tourist Lodge*, Bolpur, a/c and non a/c rooms as well as **E** and **F** inexpensive dorms (4 and 13 bedded). T 398/399. **F** *University Guest House* in Purba Palli,

Santiniketan (T 751, Ext. 87), simple rms, book through the PRO, Vishva Bharati. Also the inexpensive *Poushali Hotel* in Purba Palli, a *Youth Hostel* and 2 simple hotels in Bolpur.

Restaurants The *Tourist Lodge, Happy Lodge* and *Poushali* have restaurants but may require prior notice. *Kalor Dokan* is an 'institution' which has become a meeting place for intellectuals and is open all hours. Indian sweet shops have sprung up in its neighbourhood.

Banks State Bank of India in Bolpur and Santiniketan (T 465) have foreign exchange facilities but do not cash foreign Travellers Cheques. Also branches of Allahabad Bank, United Bank of India (T 225) and United Commercial Bank.

Shopping The local embossed leather handbags, purses and belts are particularly popular. Handicrafts are available at *Gramin* and *Sarvodaya Ashram* in Bolpur and the Vishva Bharati *Silpa Sadans* in Santiniketan and Sriniketan. Books are available at *Manisha Granthalaya* on Sriniketan Road, Bolpur and *Subarnarekha* in Santiniketan sells rare books. Camera films are sold by *Studio Vichitra, Chitrangan, Photolita* and *Ruprekha*, all in Bolpur.

Local Transport Autorickshaws and cycle rickshaws, occasionally taxis.

Museums Rabindra Bhavan (Bichitra), a museum and research centre containing paintings, manuscripts and many objects of interest, including personal belongings which give a picture of Tagore's life and times. Open daily 1030-1300, 1400-1630. Tue, mornings only. Closed Wed. No photography. **Kala Bhavan Gallery**. A rich collection of 20th century Indian art, particularly sculptures, murals and paintings by famous Bengali artists. 1500-1700. Closed Wed. **Nandan Museum**, Vishva Bharati. T 451. 0730-1200, 1400-1600. Closed Wed and University holidays. Entry free. Collection of terracotta, paintings and original tracings of Ajanta murals.

Parks and zoos *Ballavpur Deer Park*. 3 km. The area of rapidly eroding 'khowai' has been reclaimed and now forms a large wooded area with herds of black buck and spotted deer and a natural bird sanctuary. The *Uttarayan Garden* is delightful, particularly when the roses are blooming.

Hospitals and medical services Pearson Memorial Hospital, Santiniketan. Bolpur Hospital. T 605. Subdivisional Hospital, Bolpur. T 685. Janata Pharmacy, Chowrasta, Santiniketan.

Post & Telegraphs Main P.O., Santiniketan Rd, Bolpur. Santiniketan P.O., Chowrasta.

Places of Worship *Hindu* Lakshmi Narayan Temple, Bolpur. Dangali Kali Temple, Bolpur. *Brahmo* Prayer Hall, Santiniketan. *Muslim* Mosque, Bolpur. *Christian* Methodist Church, Santiniketan.

Travel agents *Uttarayan Travels*, Ram Krishna Mandir Rd, Bolpur. T 430.

Tourist offices and Information The Tourist Lodge Manager. T 398/9. PRO, Vishva Bharati Office. T 651.

Tours Enquire at the Tourist Lodge.

Bakresvar, 58 km NW of Santiniketan, lies between Siuri and Chinpai. It is known for its sulphurous hot springs, said to have medicinal properties. There are seven important '*kunds*' (springs) where the temperature varies from 36˚C to 67˚C, the hottest being **'Agnikunda'** ("fire spring"). Rare halogen gases have been found here too. Therapeutic qualities of the spring water led the West Bengal Mineral Development Corp. to market it under the brand name '**Tirtha Salil**'.

There are temples to Siva, Sakti and Vishnu making it a Hindu pilgrimage centre for the 3 principle sects. The 2 important temples are Bakresvar Siva Temple and the Mahishamardini Temple.

Hotels There is a W Bengal **E** *Tourist Lodge*, a **F** *Youth Hostel* providing simple accommodation as well as an *Inspection Bungalow* which may be booked through Executive Engineer, PWD (Roads), Birbhum, Suri.

CALCUTTA TO MALDA AND GAUR

NH 34 is the main route N from Calcutta, passing many sites of interest. The first 250 km lies across the flat Ganga delta to the new Farakka Barrage, then crosses the rather drier plains of N Bengal en route to Sikkim, Darjiling and E to Assam. Distances given are from Calcutta.

Plassey (Palashi) 172 km. It became famous after the battle between **Robert Clive** and **Siraj-ud-Daula** with his French supporters in 1757, where the British enjoyed their first significant victory, although it was not great in terms of time and lives lost. The monuments on the battlefield include a mound by the river bank which marks the position of the British forces but the meandering Bhagirati river has eroded away much of the site. An *Inspection Bungalow* can be reserved.

The NH 34 continues N to **Baharampur**, formerly an important junction of roads crossing into what is now Bangladesh with routes to the N and W. Leave the NH 34 to travel N for 6 km to Murshidabad.

Murshidabad (*Population* 25,000 221 km from Calcutta) is connected to the regional capital both by rail and road. Hiuen-Tsang, on his travels in the 7th century described *Subarna Rekha*, the first capital of ancient Bengal, which was nearby. Named after Nawab Murshid Kuli Khan, a Diwan of Bengal, Bihar and Orissa under Emperor Aurangzeb, it became the capital of Bengal in 1705 and remained so up to the time of the battle of Plassey, which led to the rise of British supremacy in Bengal. During the following 3 decades the judicial and revenue functions were moved to Calcutta.

Places of interest The **Nizamat Kila** on the river bank near the centre of town, encloses the Nawabs' old **Hazarduari** (thousand doors) **Palace** built in the Italian style by one of Mir Jafar's descendants and designed by one of the Bengal Engineers in 1837. It has an imposing domed banqueting hall with mirrored doors, an impressive chandelier and an ivory throne. It is now a splendid museum with a portrait gallery, a circular durbar hall and a library and contains a rare collection of old arms, curios, china and paintings. Closed Fri.

The **Imambara** (1847) within the walls is one of the largest in the region. Also Italianate in style, it is believed to have replaced the original built by Siraj-ud-Daula. The domed, square pavilion with a verandah nearby may be what remains of the original Imambara that reputedly contains earth from the Karbala in Mecca, justifying the inscription found on the new Imambara. There are numerous 18th century monuments in the city. **Jafaragunj Deorhi** known as the traitor's gate was where Mir Jafar, and later his son Miran lived and where the latter is believed to have murdered Siraj-ud-daula. The **Kat-gola** which was the garden-house of a rich Jain merchant houses a collection of curios and has an old Jain temple. The **Palace of Jagat Sett**, one of the richest financiers of the 18th century is 2 km from the Jafargunj Cemetery which is to the N of the palace and where lie buried many of the Nawabs. The **Katra Mosque** (1724) outside the city proper, modelled on the Great Mosque at Mecca was built by Murshid Kuli Khan where he lies buried under the staircase. You can still see some of the decorative panels on the outside of the ruins as well as 2 octagonal minarets. It was once an important centre of learning.

3 km S of the city is **Moti Jheel** (pearl lake) which is an ox-bow lake, and the ruins of **Begum Ghatesi's palace**. Only a mosque and a room remain. Another important sight is **Khosbagh** or the Garden of Delight across the river. There are 3 walled enclosures and you enter the outer enclosure, a flower garden, from the E. The 2nd enclosure is the cemetery where **Siraj-ud-Daula** of 'Black Hole' fame, and Alivardi Khan are buried. The 3rd enclosure has a tank and what was once a 'travellers' rest house'.

Hotels WBTDC has an **E** *Tourist Lodge* at Berhampore, 12 km away. 26 rms, some a/c, restaurant. Reservations from Calcutta, T 285917. **F** *Youth Hostels* at Lalbagh and Murhsidabad, reserve through Youth Services, 32/1 BBD Bagh S, Calcutta. T 280626.

Shopping Woven and handblock printed Bengal silk saris, bell metal ware and ivory carving are the main local industries. Murshidabad also produces excellent mangoes, of which there are more than 55 varieties, in season.

Travel Rail Murshidabad can be reached by the Lalgola Passenger train from Calcutta (Sealdah). **Road** Buses leave the Esplanade Terminus, Calcutta for Baharampur, 12 km away, from where you can get a taxi, bus or cycle rickshaw. To hire a tourist car or taxi, contact Tourist Bureau or ITDC.

From Murshidabad return to Baharampur to rejoin the NH 34 northwards. It passes through Jangipur (50 km) and Dhulian (30 km) before crossing Ganga by the Farakka Barrage (15 km). Immediately to the W are the *Rajmahal Hills*, ranging in height between 460 and 575 m. They are the northeasternmost extension of the Peninsula proper, made up of black basalts much used in the building of Malda. Although the surface features remain flat throughout this route, the alluvium which makes up the surface of the Ganga Plain is at its thinnest at this point. There is a series of historically important sites on the road northwards. The first of these on the road to **Ingraj ("English") Bazar** is Gaur (20 km), followed by Malda and Pandua, both to the N of Ingraj Bazar.

Gaur, on the ancient site of Lakhnauti Gaur, now almost lost, was the capital of the Senas where an exceptional complex of basalt buildings once stood. Its situation on the Ganga bank within easy reach of the Rajmahal hills, with their fine black basalt, made it possible for the gifted stone masons to construct both religious and secular buildings of great beauty and architectural skill. It was the capital of King Sasanka in the 7th century, followed by the Buddhist Pala and Hindu Sena kings. Gaur became famous as a centre of education art and culture during the reign of the latter in the 12th century. Its fortunes fluctuated from the beginning of the 13th century when it was invaded by Bhaktiar Khalji. The Fakhr-ud-din, founders of an Afghan dynasty, captured it in the 14th century and transferred their capital to Pandua for a time, plundering the temples to construct their own mosques and tombs, and destroying most of these buildings. Gaur regained its importance as a capital in 1500 for a short time until it was sacked by **Sher Shah Suri** in 1537 (**See page 92**). The city's population was wiped out by plague in 1575 after which it became a part of the Mughal empire.

Places of interest Now mainly Muslim monuments of the Sultanate period displaying various architectural styles can be seen strewn around the deserted city. The Fort was to the S on the bank of the Bhagirati where you can still see the remains of the embankments. The **Dakhil Darwaza**, the main gateway to the fort with its 5-storeyed towers in the 4 corners, was constructed in the early part of the 15th century out of small red bricks which were embossed with decorations. The façade is broken up by turrets and circular bastions, producing a striking contrast of light and shade, with decorative motifs of suns, rosettes, lamps and fretted borders. During the 15th century. a number of mosques and mausolea were built in the new architectural style. The usual courtyard of the mosque gave way to a covered hall, possibly as a practical measure against monsoon rains. The length of the façade was broken up by several pointed arches, while the interior was divided into arched aisles supported by pillars giving the impression of a church nave. The intersections of the aisles were marked by a dome and the important W wall of the mosque had several recessed *mihrabs**.

Inside the Fort, in the SE corner is the **Baisgazi Wall** which enclosed the Old Palace and got its name from its height of '22 yards' (20 m). This high brick wall is 5 m broad at its base decreasing to about 3 m at the top. The Royal Palace with its *darbar*, private quarters and *harem* were supposed to have stood within the enclosure. **Kadam Rasul** is to the E of the Palace within the perimeter of the fort. The domed square building with the Bengali thatch style roof was erected in 1513 to house the relic of The Prophet, a footprint in stone. The Royal Eastern Gate or **Lukochuri Darwaza** (hide-and-seek gate) is a large 2 storeyed structure about 20 m long and 13 m wide although the entrance itself is only 3 m across. Believed

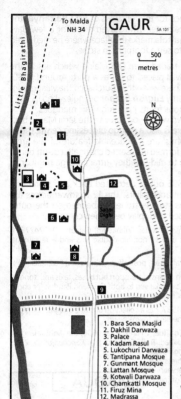

To Malda
NH 34

GAUR SA 101

0   500
metres

Little Bhagirathi

N

1. Bara Sona Masjid
2. Dakhil Darwaza
3. Palace
4. Kadam Rasul
5. Lukochuri Darwaza
6. Tantipana Mosque
7. Gunmant Mosque
8. Lattan Mosque
9. Kotwali Darwaza
10. Chamkatti Mosque
11. Firuz Mina
12. Madrassa

to have been built by Shah Shuja around 1655 it is in a later Mughal style. The **Kotawali Darwaza** (late 15th century), in the S wall is now in ruins but once had a magnificent archway. It is close to the border with Bangladesh.

1 km or so E from the SE corner of the fort, on the main road, is the **Tantipara Mosque**, built around 1475 in what was probably the 'tanti' or weavers' quarter of the town. It is in superbly decorated red brick with five entrance arches and octagonal turrets in the corners. Another km S is the **Lattan** or the Painted Mosque built by Yusuf Shah in 1475 although the legend would have you believe that a dancing girl of the Royal Court was responsible for it. It is notable for its elegant structure and the decorative bands of blue, green yellow and white glazed tiles which were used to adorn it.

About a km outside the fort's E wall is the **Firuz Minar** which was probably built as a victory tower by Sultan Firuz Shah in 1486 but was also used to call the faithful to prayer. It is about 26 m high in 5-storeys and 19 m in circumference. The lower 3 storeys are 12 sided while the upper 2 are circular. The striking feature of the tower is the introduction of blue and white glazed tiles which are used in addition to the terracotta and brick. The crude quality of the tiles contrasts with the excellence achieved by the Hindu craftsmen in producing terracotta decorations by that time. A spiral staircase inside leads to the top chamber with its 4 windows.

Bara Sona Masjid, also known as Baroduari, is outside the fort, to the NE, and is the largest of the monuments. The great golden mosque was built in 1526 and is an enormous rectangular structure built of brick with stone facing with a large open square in front. There were arched gateways on 3 sides and you enter through one 8 m high and 2 m wide. There appear to have been 44 domes over the 4 arched colonnades and you can see the quality of the carving in marble in what remains of the minarets.

The **Chika Mosque,** (bat mosque) not far from the Kadam Rasul is a single domed structure which must have freely used Hindu idols in its construction. Although this early 15th century building is in ruins, you can still see evidence of this in the stone work of the doors and lintels. Nearby is the **Chamkati Mosque,** probably built in 1475. The remains still show the vaulted ceiling of the verandah and there are medallions visible between the arches in the main chamber.

Ramkeli not far from the Bara Sona Masjid has the Madan Mohan Jiu Mandir and is of particular religious significance for the followers of **Sri Chaitanya**, the great 14th century Bengali religious reformer, who stayed there for a few days and made some famous converts. **Tamaltola** marks the place where he meditated under a tree and pilgrims come here to see a footprint in stone.

Malda Once the Dutch and French traded from Old Malda which lies at the confluence of 2 rivers and was thus well placed to act as a port. Around 1680, the English established a market town here when they purchased the village from a local landlord and then moved to nearby **English Bazaar** or Englezabad in 1771 where they built a fort. Now only famous for its juicy large Fajli mangoes.

Old Malda is 4 km from Malda Town where you can visit the Jami Masjid built in 1596 and the Nimasarai Tower. There is also a mango processing centre there. The low-lying marshy tracts called **'bhils'** are a noticeable feature of the area. Typical of the moribund delta, they are formed in deserted channels, cut-off bends and ox-bows of the Ganga. From Nov to mid-Feb they attract a large number of wild fowl including the Siberian goose.

The **Jami Masjid** was built in 1596 out of decorated brick and stone and displays some good carving on the entrance pillars. The 17 m tower across the river dating from the same period has strange stones embedded on the outer surface which may have once been used to display beheaded criminals.

Hotels D Hotel Purbanchal. Reservations: 18 Netaji Subhas Rd, Calcutta. T 224278. **E** Malda Tourist Lodge, T 2213, has 2 a/c and 11 non-a/c double rms and a restaurant. Reservations: WBTDC. T 285917.

Malda has all essential amenities with several banks, post offices, shops and hospitals.

Local Transport Rickshaws are the common means of transport but buses, taxis and 'tongas' are available for visiting Gaur and Pandua. Taxis take you to both Gaur and Pandua for about Rs 200. Seats on local buses only cost a few rupees.

Museums Malda Museum established in 1937, has a collection of stone images, coins and inscriptions from Gaur and Pandua, the 2 medieval towns nearby.

Air Vayudoot flies to Malda from Calcutta on Tue, Th and Sat at 0600, the flight taking an hour. You can get a taxi or bus to Murshidabad. **Rail** Calcutta (H): Kanchenjunga, 2558 (AC/II), daily, 1410, 6 hr 40 min. **Road** N Bengal State Transport Corporation operate regular express bus services which take approximately 8 hr. Reservations: Esplanade Terminus, Calcutta or the Malda office on Krishna Jiban Sanyal Rd. T 2465.

18 km from Malda, **Pandua** alternated with Gaur as a capital of Bengal between 1338 and 1500, when it was abandoned. Some ruins show clearly how the Muslims made free use of material from Hindu temples near Malda. The old brick-paved road, nearly 4 m wide and about 10 km long, passes through the town and most of the monuments stand close to it.

Places of interest The **Adina Masjid** (1369) Perhaps the most outstanding mosque of eastern India, the mosque is sadly in a poor state of repair, but still gives an idea of Muslim architecture in medieval Bengal, with evidence of Sena architecture of the 12th century. The enormous structure, 154 m from N to S and 86 m from E to W, which is compared to the great 8th century mosque at Damascus, was built between 1364 and 1374 by Sultan Sikander Shah. The space is enclosed by

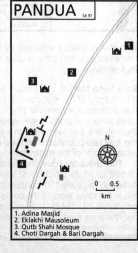

PANDUA SA 97

N

0   0.5
km

1. Adina Masjid
2. Eklakhi Mausoleum
3. Qutb Shahi Mosque
4. Choti Dargah & Bari Dargah

pillared aisles, 5 bays deep on the western sanctuary side and 3 on the others, using 260 pillars in all. In the interior is a screen of 88 arches enclosing an open quadrangle with the mosque to the W. It seems to have incorporated the 'sikhara', a tall ornate tiered structure, and trefoil arches and is remarkable in the absence of a large entrance gateway.

Although the upper part of the building and the arches and domes were built of brick, most of the substructure was of basalt masonry plundered from existing Hindu temples and palaces; in many instances the carved surfaces were inserted into walls. The pillars may have been taken from earlier Hindu structures too. A small doorway in the W back wall of the mosque clearly shows evidence of having been removed from an earlier Vishnu temple which exhibited not only the stone masons' skill but the exceptional advance made by the metal workers of the time.

The **Eklakhi Mausoleum** built of brick around 1412 with a large single dome, has a Hindu idol carved on its front lintel. The octagonal chamber housing 3 tombs, has outer walls decorated with finely carved terracotta bricks and the ceiling inside ribbed and plastered with decorations. The **Qutb Shahi Mosque** also called the 'Sona' or golden mosque was built in 1582 in brick and stone and had ten domes. Further along are the **Chhoti and Bari Dargah**, the 17th century shrines to Saint Nur Qutbul Alam and Harazarat Shah Jalal Tabrizi. They are in ruins but within their campus are relics of various quarters, baths, prayer stations, kitchens and the Bibi Mahal.

Percy Brown's volumes on Indian Architecture have detailed descriptions of Bengal's temples and Muslim tombs and mosques.

Hotels The WBTDC has a *Tourist Bungalow* in Pandua.

CALCUTTA TO DARJILING AND THE NORTH

The northern hill stations of Darjiling and Kalimpong have spectacular scenery and views of the Himalayas. Darjiling is the centre for trekking and monasteries can be visited, one by the second highest railway in the world. Rhino, elephants, leopards and tigers can be seen in the Jaldapara wildlife sanctuary in Bhutan.

The road route to Darjiling from Ingraj Bazar continues up the NH 34, a distance of 334 km. Alternatively it is possible to travel by air or train (see below).

Darjiling

Population 56,857 (1981). Nepali, Lepcha, Tibetan, Bhutia, Bengali. *Altitude* 2,134 m *Best Season* April to mid-June and Oct-Nov. June to September when the monsoons arrive may bring heavy downpours, sometimes causing landslides.

	Jan	Feb	Mar	Apr	May	Jun	Jul	Aug	Sep	Oct	Nov	Dec	Av/Tot
Max (°C)	9	11	15	18	19	19	20	20	20	19	15	12	16
Min (°C)	3	4	8	11	13	15	15	15	15	11	7	4	10
Rain (mm)	22	27	52	109	187	522	713	573	419	116	14	5	2759

Calcutta is 651 km. The flight via the nearest airport at **Bagdogra** (90 km) takes 55 min but the transfer by road adds a further 2 hr 30 min to 3 hr 30 min.

Entry requirements Foreign tourists travelling by air through Bagdogra airport may stay in the area for up to 15 days without a permit but must report to the FRRO at the airport on arrival and departure to get their passports endorsed. Those visiting Darjiling by rail or road for a period of 7 days (and visitors to Kalimpong) must obtain a permit from Foreigners' Registration Offices at Calcutta, Delhi, Bombay or Madras. Special permits are also available from the Under Secretary, Govt of West Bengal, Home (Political), Writers Building, Calcutta (T 221681) or from the Deputy Commissioner of Police (Security Control). 237 Acharya P.C. Bose Road, Calcutta (T 443301). Alternatively, contact Indian Missions abroad before departing or Ministry of Home Affairs, Govt of India, N Block, New Delhi. For requirements for entering Sikkim see under separate section under Sikkim.

Darjiling (formerly "**Darjeeling**") – "*place of the thunderbolt*" or possibly "*Dorja the mystical*", and the surrounding area once belonged to the Rajas of Sikkim although parts were annexed from time to time by the Bhutanese and Nepalis. The East India Company's intervention and the subsequent return of the territory's sovereignty to the Rajas of Sikkim, however, led to the British obtaining permission to gain the site of the hill-station called *Darjiling* in 1833, in return for an annual payment. At that time it was practically uninhabited and thickly forested – "a worthless, uninhabited mountain". It soon grew into a popular health resort after a road and several houses were built and tea growing was introduced. It is a favourite tourist resort for Bengalis, although in the late 1980s the political disturbances associated with demands for the creation of a separate state for the Gorkhas greatly decreased its popularity. Many people commented on its "run-down" condition and shabby appearance, but from 1989 the situation has improved again.

Built on a crescent shaped ridge, it faces the Himalayas with surrounding hills thickly covered with coniferous forests or terraced tea gardens. The upper reaches of the popular hill station were originally occupied by the Europeans who built houses with commanding views. Down the hillside on terraces sprawled the humbler huts, tenements and bazaars of the Indian town. The Bengal Government escaped from the Calcutta heat to take up its official summer residence here, the Shrubbery or Government House being at the N end on Birch Hill with St. Andrew's Church built at the highest point.

The railway station is in the lower part of town on Cart Rd, with the taxi and bus stands. The Chowrasta is a focal point with the busy Mall and Nehru Rd leading off it. The lower and upper roads have a series of connecting roads and steps joining them.

Local Festival *Buddha Jayanti* in April-May, celebrates the birth of the Buddha and is observed with much ceremony in the monasteries.

Local Industry *Tea* An ancient Chinese legend suggests that 'tay', tea, originated in India, although tea was known to have been grown in China around 2700 BC. It is a species of Camellia, *Camellia thea*. After 1833, when its monopoly on importing tea from China was abolished, the East India Company made attempts to grow tea in Assam using wild 'chai' plants found growing there and later introduced it in the Darjiling area and in the Nilgiri hills in the S. Some believe that plants were smuggled in from China. Certainly, Chinese experts had to be asked to advise on improving the method of processing the leaves in the early days while horticulturists at the Botanical Gardens in Calcutta worked on improving the varieties. There are now varieties available which will grow at much lower altitudes, for example at Bagdogra or in Sylhet in Bangladesh. Today India is the largest producer of tea in the world. Assam grows over half and Darjiling about a quarter of the nation's output. Once drunk only by the tribal people it has now become India's national drink although the amount consumed per head is a fraction of that drunk by an Englishman!

The old 'orthodox' method of tea processing, which can still be seen by visiting the **Happy Valley Tea Estate** near Darjiling, among others, produces the aromatic lighter coloured liquor of the Golden Flowery Orange Pekoe in its most superior grade. The fresh leaves are dried by fans on 'withering troughs' to reduce the moisture content and then rolled and pressed to express the juices which coat the leaves. These are then left to ferment in a controlled humid environment in order to produce the desired aroma. Finally the leaves are dried by passing them through a heated drying chamber and then graded – the unbroken being the best quality, down to the 'fannings' and 'dust'.

The more common 'crushing, tearing, curling' (CTC) method produces tea which gives a much darker liquor. It uses a machine which was invented in Assam in 1930. The process

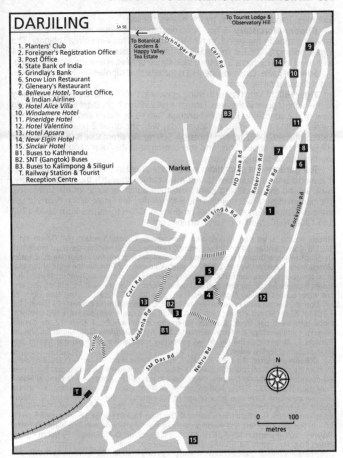

DARJILING
SA 98

1. Planters' Club
2. Foreigner's Registration Office
3. Post Office
4. State Bank of India
5. Grindlay's Bank
6. Snow Lion Restaurant
7. Gleneary's Restaurant
8. *Bellevue Hotel*, Tourist Office,
   & Indian Airlines
9. *Hotel Alice Villa*
10. *Windamere Hotel*
11. *Pineridge Hotel*
12. *Hotel Valentino*
13. *Hotel Apsara*
14. *New Elgin Hotel*
15. *Sinclair Hotel*
B1. Buses to Kathmandu
B2. SNT (Gangtok) Buses
B3. Buses to Kalimpong & Siliguri
T. Railway Station & Tourist
   Reception Centre

To Tourist Lodge &
Observatory Hill

To Botanical
Gardens &
Happy Valley
Tea Estate

Lochnagar Rd
Cart Rd
HD Lama Rd
Robertson Rd
Nehru Rd
Rockville Rd
NB Singh Rd
Market
Cart Rd
Ladenla Rd
SM Das Rd
Nehru Rd

N

0   100
metres

allows the withered leaves to be given a short light roll before engraved metal rollers distort the leaves in a fraction of a second.

Most of Darjiling's tea is sold through auction houses, the largest centre being in Calcutta. Tea tasting and blending are skills which have developed over a long period of time and are highly prized. The industry provides vital employment in the hill areas and is an assured foreign exchange earner. India as a whole produces over a quarter of the world's tea and is easily the largest single producer. There has been concern over the deteriorating state of the plantations and a great deal is being done to use improved varieties when replanting. As a result productivity has risen steadily during the last decade.

Places of interest Believed to be the site of the Makhala cave, **Observatory Hill**, sacred to Siva, offers an excellent viewing point for the twin peaks of Kangchendzonga. A Red Hat Buddhist monastery which stood here was destroyed in the 19th century but gave its name to the hill station.

Aloobari Monastery on Tenzing Norgay Rd is open to visitors. Tibetan and

Sikkimese handicrafts, made by the monks, for sale.

Ghoom Monastery 8 km. According to some Indian sources, the highest railway station in the world. In fact the Andean railway in Bolivia is higher. The Yiga-Choliang Gompa, a Yellow Hat Buddhist Monastery, the most famous in the area, built in 1875, has a 5 metre gilded statue of *Maitreya* or the future Buddha.

Senchal Lake Close to Tiger Hill is the lake that supplies Darjiling with water. It is a pleasant picnic spot.

Tiger Hill 11 km. It is worth rising as early as 0400 to make the hour's journey to the highest point in the area. From the hill 2590 m high, there is a breathtaking view of the sunrise on Kangchendzonga flanked by Kabru and Pandim. Mount Everest (8,842 m) is visible on a clear day with the other 2 peaks of the Three Sisters, Makalu (8,482 m) and Lhotse (8,500 m). An alternative is to walk to Tiger Hill which takes about 2 hrs, and stay overnight at the Tourist Lodge. The return journey can be through Ghoom.

Tea gardens Tea plantations were started here in the 1840s and still thrive. It is worth setting aside time to visit a tea garden to watch the pickers at work, walk around the processing plants and then purchase some locally grown tea. The garden closest to Darjiling is the Happy Valley Tea Estate which claims to use the old 'orthodox' method of tea production. Open to visitors from 0800-1200 and 1300-1630. Mon and Sun mornings only.

Hotels Mostly 90 km from airport, 1 km from railway **C Hotel Sinclair**, 18/1 Gandhi Rd. T 3431/2, Cable: Sinclair. 54 rm. 90 km airport, 1 km rly. Central heating. The most modern of Darjiling's Hotels with good service. Restaurant, bar, shops, travel and indoor games. **C Hotel Windamere**, Observatory Hill. T 2397, Cable: Windamere. 27 rm. On the edge of the Mall in an enviable position, comfortable but old-fashioned. Good reputation for continental and Indian food. Exchange, garden, golf and games room. No central heating, but log fires and hot water bottles! **C New Elgin Hotel**, H.D. Lama Rd. T 3314,3316, Cable: New Elgin. 22 rm. Non a/c. Restaurant bar, exchange and travel. **C Oberoi Mount Everest**, 29 Gandhi Rd. T 26716. 28 rm. 90 km airport, 1 km rly. A/c. Built like a castle, with old fashioned comforts. Good restaurant, bar, travel. **C Hotel Valentino**, 6 Rockville Rd. T 2228. 17 rm. Central heating. Chinese restaurant recommended, bar, travel. **C Darjiling Club**, Nehru Rd. The old Planters' Club, a relic of the Raj, allows temporary membership Rs 15 per day. Dining, bar, billiards, tennis, library, video.

D Bellevue Hotel, The Mall. T 2129, Cable: Bellevue Hotel. 43 rm. Non a/c. Best views in town including Kangchendzonga on a clear day. Conveniently situated and has a new economy block. Restaurant, shops, travel, Govt tourist offices, pony rides. **D Central Hotel**, Robertson Rd. T 2033, Cable: Nadam. 50 rm. Non-a/c. Good restaurant, bar. Comfortable rm. Out of season there may be shortage of hot water, but discounts available. **D Tiffany Hotel**, 4 Franklyn Prestage Rd (below Gymkhana Club). T 2840. 7 rm. Not a/c. Restaurant, tours and car hire. First floor rooms better. **D Darjiling Tourist Lodge**, Bhanu Sarani. T 2611. 15 rm. Not a/c. Breakfast and evening meals compulsory. Good views and warm. **D Hotel Polynia**, 12/1 Robertson Rd. T 2705. 34 rm. Indian cuisine. **D Pineridge**, 19 Nehru Rd and **Hotel Cosy Inn**, Nehru Rd. T 2073. 28 rm. Restaurant, travel.

There are several cheaper hotels where prices vary from Rs 100 for single to Rs 200-300 for double rms. Some also offer 3 or 4 bedded rms and most have restaurants and dining halls. **Hotel Tara**, 125 Gandhi Rd. T 3060. 27 rm. Indian and Chinese. **Hotel Apsara**, 61 Laden La Rd. T 2983. Veg. **Hotels Broadway, La Bella, Surja Bhawan**, 3 Coochbehar Rd, T 2319. 29 rm. **Hotel Purnima**, 2A Coochbehar Rd, T 3110. 20 rm. **Hotel Springburn**, 70 Gandhi Rd, T 2054. 12 rm. Indian cuisine. Cheaper still are the WBTDC's **Maple Tourist Lodge** on Kutchery Rd, T 2092, **Lewis Jubilee Sanatorium**, Dr S.K. Paul Rd, T 2127 and the very inexpensive **Youth Hostel** on Dr. Zakir Hussain Rd, T 2290 which can accommodate 46. No restaurant. Reservations direct to the lodge or hostel or through WBTDC, 3/1 BBD Bagh (E), Calcutta, T 28591 or Tourist Bureau, 1 Nehru Rd, Darjiling, T 2050. The Mohanlal Shivlal **Dharamsala** is on Cart Rd.

Restaurants Hotels with restaurants will usually serve non-residents. Apart from these there are only a few good places to eat. **Glenary's** on Nehru Rd, T 2055, one of the best tea-rooms with excellent confectionery. Also has a licensed multi-cuisine restaurant. **Keventer's** on Nehru Rd, T 2026, a well-patronized snack bar, popular with youngsters from public schools. Also serves full English breakfasts. The terrace above is particularly pleasant. The open-air **S Indian Restaurant** on Chowrasta serves very good vegetarian meals. **Shangri La** on Nehru

Road has Indian and Chinese food while *Silver Fir*, H.D. Lama Rd is multi-cuisine. *Snow Lion Restaurant*. Good Chinese and Tibetan food. Near the railway station is a multi-cuisine restaurant *Simla*. *Chopstix*, Judge Bazaar serves only Indian and Chinese food and *Lunar* on Gandhi Rd does snacks. *Gol Ghar*, Main Bazaar area does excellent Indian meat dishes with chapatis, naan and rotis.

Bars There are bars in the following hotels – Sinclairs, New Elgin, Mount Everest, Windamere, Central and Valentino.

Clubs The old *Gymkhana Club* provides indoor sports facilities including roller skating, snooker, badminton and squash as well as tennis courts. Temporary membership on a weekly or daily basis available.

Banks *Baroda*, H.D. Lama Rd. *Indian Bank*, Hotel Polynia, Robertson Rd. *Grindlays* and *State Bank of India*, Laden La Rd. *United Bank of India*, Chowk Bazaar. *Union Bank of India* and *United Commercial*, Robertson Rd. *Vijaya*, Gandhi Rd.

Shopping There are plenty of curio and handicrafts shops which provide you with an overwhelming choice. The main shopping areas are Chowrasta, Nehru Rd, Laden La Rd and Chowk Bazaar. The local handicrafts sold widely include Buddhist *tankhas* which are hand painted scrolls surrounded by Chinese brocade, good wood carving, carpets, handwoven cloth, jewellery, copper, brass and white metal religious curios such as prayer wheels, bowls and statues. The Chowrasta shops are closed on Sun and Chowk Bazar on Th. *The Tibetan Refugee Self-Help Centre* is on Gandhi Road with its temple, school and hospital. After the Chinese invasion, thousands of Tibetan refugees settled in Darjiling (many having accompanied the Dalai Lama) and the rehabilitation centre was established in 1959 to enable them to continue to practise their skills and provide an outlet for their goods. It is possible to watch the craftspeople at work and then buy carpet, textiles, curios or jewellery in the shop. Well worth a visit. At *Hayden Hall* in Laden La Rd, colourful woollen goods are sold by local women. The West Bengal Government's *Manjusha Emporium* on Nehru Rd is recommended for silk and cotton handloom as well as handicrafts. The *Markets* are very colourful and worth a visit. *Darjiling Photo Stores*, 13 Nehru Rd T 2361, and *Das Studios* along the same rd, T 2204 and on Gandhi Rd T 3415, are reputable shops selling films and interesting black-and-white prints. *Singh Studios* is also on Nehru Road.

Bookshops *The Cambridge Bookshop* is on Laden La Rd and the *Oxford Bookshop* on Chowrasta has old books on India and Tibet.

Local Transport **Tourist Taxis, Landrovers** and **Jeeps** are readily available for both short or long journeys. Prices vary according to the season and rates are negotiable. **Private taxis** charge approximately Rs 2 per person Nehru Rd to Top Station. Clubside Motors, Robertson Rd, T 2123. Siddique Motors, Robertson Rd, T 2370. Darjiling Transport Corporation, Laden La Rd, T 2074. Kalimpong Motor Transport Syndicate, Motor Stand, T 2269. **Bus** operators. N Bengal State Transport Corporation, T 3133. Gorkha Parvatiya Anachalik Bus Karamchari Union, Chowk Bazar Bus Stand, T 3487. Darjiling Siliguri Motor Syndicate, Motor Stand. Singamari Syndicate, Main Taxi Stand, T 2820. The **Ropeway Cable Car**, the first of its kind to be built in India to carry passengers, connects Top Station with Tukvar Station in Singla Valley on the Little Ranjit River. When operating fully, it runs a virtual hourly service in both directions in the morning up to mid-afternoon.

Entertainment The local papers carry programmes at Cinemas and Theatres which sometimes include performances in English. *Capitol*, Laden La Rd. T 2171. *Rink*, Dr. S.M. Das Rd. T 2651. In addition there are mini-cinemas which show video films (often in English). Gorkha Duka Nivarak Sammelan Hall on N.C. Goenka Rd. T 2089. *NNHP Hall*, J.N. Mitra Rd. T 2303. Gorkha Rangmanch, Bhanu Sarani.

Sports The facilities available at the *Gymkhana Club* are detailed above. Pony rides are popular on the Mall starting at Chowrasta. The Tibetan 'guides' charge approximately Rs 15 per hour. Pony races are held during the spring and autumn at the *Lebong Race Course*, one of the smallest and highest in the world.

Trekking, for which Darjiling has become rightly famous, offers many options and details are available from the W Bengal Tourist Bureau on 1 Nehru Rd. See **Treks below**.

Museums & Galleries *Natural History Museum* near Chowrasta. Open daily 1000-1600. Afternoons only on Wed and closed Th. Entry Re.1. Recommended. Large collection of fauna of the region. *Himalayan Mountaineering Institute* and *Everest Museum*. T 2438. Entrance is through the Zoo on Jawahar Road W. The institute, previously headed by the late Tenzing Norgay who jointly conquered Everest in 1953, trains mountaineers and holds demonstrations during the season. The museum has old mountaineering equipment including that used on that historic climb, a model of the Himalayas and a display of Himalayan flora and fauna. Among the curiosities is a telescope that belonged to Adolf Hitler! Open 0900-1300, 1400-1600. Closed Tue in winter. Entry Re.1 main museum and Re 0.50 Everest Museum. Telescope Re.1. Movie Re 1. *Ava Art Gallery*, Ghoom. T 2469. Open 0800-1200, 1230-1800. *Hayden Hall*, Laden La Rd is where you can buy woollen goods from local women.

Parks & Zoos The *Lloyds Botanical Gardens* nr the market was laid out on land given by the Bank in 1878 and has an interesting collection of Himalayan and Alpine flora including banks of azaleas and rhododendrons, magnolias, a very large collection of orchids and a hot house. The herbarium has rare botanical specimens. 0600-1700. Closed Sun. and bank holidays. Entry free. Victoria Falls which is only impressive in the monsoons provides added interest to a ½-hr nature trail. The *Zoological Park* next to the Mountaineering Institute has among its high-altitude wildlife Himalayan black bear, Siberian tiger, red pandas, yaks and llama although they are kept in depressingly small enclosures. 0800-1630. Entry Re.1. The *Shrubbery* behind Raj Bhawan on Jawahar Parbat (Birch Hill) affords spectacular views of Kangchendzonga.

Useful addresses Foreigners' Registration Office is on Laden La Rd where permits for Darjiling may be extended without formalities and for Kalimpong only a form is needed.

Hospitals and medical services There are 3 hospitals in town. The Sadar Hospital, T 2218. Shahid Durgamaull Hospital. T 2131. Darjiling and Dooars Medical Association Hospital. T 2302/2306.

Post Offices General Post Office, Laden La Rd. T 2076. Telegraph Office, Gandhi Rd. T 2185.

Places of worship *Hindu* Dhirdham Temple near railway station modelled loosely on Kathmandu's famous Pashupatinath and Bara Thakur Bari, Chowk Bazar. *Buddhist* Nepali Tamrg Buddhist Monastery. Bhutia Busti Monastery, C.R. Das Rd. Sherpa Buddhist Monastery, Tenzing Norgay Rd. *Christian* Church of N India, Mall Rd. Union Church, Gandhi Rd. *Others* Brar Masjid is on Dr. Zakir Hussain Rd, the Sikh Gurudwara on Jala Pahar and the Baha'i Centre on Hermitage Rd.

Travel agents and Tour operators Travel Corporation (India), Gandhi Rd. T 2694. Himalayan Travels, Hotel Sinclairs, Gandhi Rd. Juniper Tour and Travels, 14 H.L. Ghosh Rd. Summit Tours, Indrani Lodge, Chowrasta. Singamari Syndicate, Main Taxi Stand. T 2820.

Tourist offices and information *W Bengal Tourist Office*, Hotel Belle Vue Complex, 1st Floor, Chowrasta. T 2050. In season 0930-1730. Off season 1000-1630.

Tours The following conducted tours are organized by the Tourist office.
Tour 1: Tiger Hill, Senchal Lake, Ghoom Monastery, Batasia Loop. 0400-0730. Min. 8 persons. Rs 20 per person. *Tour II*: Local sightseeing. Ava Gallery, Manjusha Bengal Emporium, Dhirdham Temple, Himalayan Mountaineering Institute, Zoological Park, Ropeway, Lebong Race Course, Tibetan Refugee Self-help Centre. 0930-1230 and 1330-1630. Min. 8 persons. Rs 20 per person. *Tour III*: Mirik. 0830-1730. Min. 12 persons. Rs 45 per person. *Tour IV*: Gangtok and Kalimpong. Min. 12 persons. 2 days. 0800-1730 following day. Rs 135 per person for transport only. *Tour V*: Kalimpong. Min. 12 persons. 0800-1730. Rs 60 per person.

Air Nearest airport, *Bagdogra*, is 90 km away and Indian Airlines daily flights connect it to **Calcutta** (55 min), **Delhi** (1 hr 50 min). The transfer by car or coach adds another 2 hr 30 min to 3 hr 30 min. Taxis charge approx Rs 50 per person when carrying 7 passengers and the coach operated by W Bengal Tourism costs Rs 30 per head. Indian Airlines, Belle Vue Properties, Chowrasta. T 2355. Weekdays 1000-1700, Sundays 1000-1300.

Rail *Siliguri*, which is 80 km away, and *New Jalpaiguri* nearby, are the nearest railway stations to Darjiling, and each is connected by a good network to other parts of the country. The 566 km rail journey from Calcutta to New Jalpaiguri takes about 13 hrs.

When functioning, the toy train, with its 0.6 m (2 foot) gauge track and hauled by sparkling engines, some originally built in Glasgow, is a rewarding experience. It travels at 6 kph, and the journey can take as much as 7 hrs. The railway has been in existence since 1878, and climbs up to **Ghoom** at 2438 m and then descends 305 m to Darjiling. The views en route, the mountain villages and the Batasia Loop can of course also be enjoyed by travelling up the State Highway, a journey of 3 hr 30 min to 4 hrs. It is possible to do a short rail journey from Darjiling to Ghoom and back.

New Jalpaiguri: *Darjiling Mail*, 3144 (AC/CC&AC/II), daily, 1000, 7 hr 45 min; **Calcutta (H):** *Kamrup Exp*, 5660 (AC/II), daily, 0825, 22 hr 5 min. **New Jalpaiguri Calcutta (H):** *Kanchenjunga Exp*, 2558 (AC/II), daily, 0945, 11 hr 5 min; **Darjiling:** *3D (N.G.)*, 0715, 8 hr

DARJILING TREKS SA 99
(not to scale)

Legend:
- Main Roads
- Jeepable Road
- Treks
- Distance in km 16

15 min. Darjiling Railway Station: Reservations and Enquiries, T 2555. Enquiries open 1000-1200, 1300-1600.

Road NH31 connects Siliguri with other parts of India. You may wish to drive from Calcutta, a distance of 570 km and visit other places of interest on the way. The overnight N Bengal State Transport Corporation's 'Rocket' bus service is faster than the train and you can reserve seats in Calcutta, T 231854 or in Siliguri, T 20531. They can be very full and noisy – not a relaxing way to travel! The journey from Siliguri to Darjiling is possible either by taxi or by W Bengal State Transport bus. The taxi stand is opp Air View Hotel on Hill Cart Rd, Siliguri. At Darjiling the main taxi stand is at Chowk Bazar.

Excursions may be privately arranged to Bijanbari (38 km), Kalimpong (51 km), Kurseong (32 km), Majitar (32 km, Sandakphu (58 km), Senchal Lake (10 km, Singlatakdah (26 km) and Mirik (45 km).

Treks

The eastern Himalayas attract the seasoned trekker as much as those without any previous experience as it is possible to walk up to altitudes of 3,660 m in stages, along safe roads through wooded hills, provided you are fit. The best trekking season is in Apr-May or Oct-Nov. In the spring there may be the occasional shower but the disadvantage is more than compensated for by the beauty of the magnolias and rhododendrons in full bloom. In the autumn the air is dry and the visibility excellent and although early December is not too late, it may turn rather cold.

A one day trek can be undertaken to Tiger Hill about 5 km away but if you have more time, the trekking agents in Darjiling can organize 4 to 7 day programmes. *Summit Tours*, Indrani Lodge on Chowrasta Rd and *Tenzing Kanchenjunga Tours* are trekking agents. The *Tourist Bureau* in Darjiling, will provide detailed information, plan the trek and book your accommodation and also obtain necessary equipment (sleeping bag, wind-jacket etc.) and arrange a Sherpa guide. **NB** Trekking gear can be hired from the *Youth Hostel* where there is a very useful book of helpful suggestions by past trekkers.

Most trekkers take in Phalut at the junction of Nepal, Sikkim and W Bengal and Sandakphu from which one can get a fantastic view of four of the world's highest peaks – **Everest** (8,842 m), *Kangchendzonga* (8,585 m), **Makalu** and **Lhotse**. Everest is 140 km from Sandakphu as the crow flies and you can see about 3,700 m of its slopes from there. The route takes you through fragrant forests of conifers with rhododendron, primulas and a great variety of orchids. A bird-watchers' dream with 600 species including orioles, minivets, flycatchers, finches, sunbirds, piculets, emerald cuckoos, falconets and Hoodson's imperial pigeons.

The longer 160 km trek takes you to Manaybhanjang and Tonglu as well, although parts of the journey to and from Darjiling can be undertaken by bus. For those wanting the added challenge an optional extension to Raman, Rimbik and Jhepi is possible. You can hire a Landrover or Jeep and be driven early in the morning to Manaybhanjang, 26 km away to start a 2 day trek to Sandhakphu (3,636 m), 33 km away returning to your starting point in a day or 2 if you are short of time. Alternatively, you can carry on for another 21 km to Phalut (3,600 m) and return the same way. Those with 3 more days to spare can return by the Raman-Rimbik-Jhepi-Bijanbari route. From Bijanbari it is possible to return to Darjiling 36 km away, in a Jeep or climb a further 2 km to Pulbazar and then return to Darjiling 16 km away. Those wishing to only go to Rimbik may return to Manaybhanjang via Palmajua and Batasi, which takes a day.

There are very simple *Bungalows* and *Youth hostels* for overnight accommodation but it is advisable to book bungalows in advance before starting from Darjiling. Dak Bungalows at Phalut, Sandakphu, Tonglu and Jorepokhri may be booked through the deputy Commissioner, Improvement Fund Department. The one at *Jhepi* should by reserved through the District Land Revenue Officer. The Forest Bungalows at Palmajua and Batasi may be booked through the Divisional Manager, W Bengal Forest Development Corp while for the Inspection Bungalow at Bijanbari, applications must be made to the Divisional Engineer, State Electricity Board at Siliguri. It is not necessary to apply in advance for overnight stays in Raman, Rimbik, Sandakphu and Manaybhanjang youth hostels.

Kalimpong

Population 28,591 (1981). *Altitude* 1,250 m. *Best season* Mar-Jun, Sep-Feb. A permit, obtainable from the Foreigners' Registration Office in Darjiling, usually allows a 2 day stay and is checked at Teesta bridge.

A remote hill station, Kalimpong has been a meeting point of the once 'three Closed Lands' on the trade route to Tibet, a meeting of the northern neighbours, Bhutan and Nepal. The gentle climate with warm summers with temperatures around 30°C and cool winters (down to 7°C), the beautiful mountain scenery and the abundance of flowers have made Kalimpong an attractive resort. The lifestyle of the local people reflect the social and religious influences of its neighbouring nations, Nepal, Tibet, Sikkim and Bhutan.

From Darjiling 51 km away, it is possible to make the trip by taxi or Landrover in about 2 hr 30 min, taking in beautiful scenery. Buses are less frequent, slower and not much cheaper. The taxi stand is on Robertson Rd/Laden La Rd and

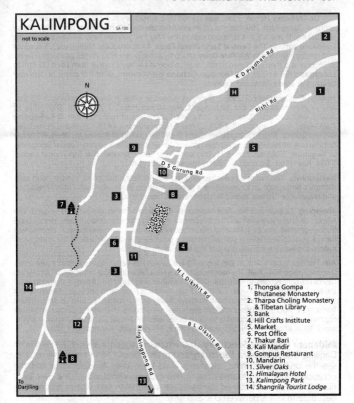

KALIMPONG SA 100

not to scale

N

D S Gurung Rd

K D Pradhan Rd

Rishi Rd

H L Dikshit Rd

B L Dikshit Rd

Ringkingpong Rd

To Darjiling

1. Thongsa Gompa
   Bhutanese Monastery
2. Tharpa Choling Monastery
   & Tibetan Library
3. Bank
4. Hill Crafts Institute
5. Market
6. Post Office
7. Thakur Bari
8. Kali Mandir
9. Gompus Restaurant
10. Mandarin
11. *Silver Oaks*
12. *Himalayan Hotel*
13. *Kalimpong Park*
14. *Shangrila Tourist Lodge*

Landrovers and buses depart from the Bazar Motor stand. The road, which is variable but improves with distance, descends to 200 m at Pashoke where it crosses the river on a single lane bridge. The road winds through the Pashoke and Lopchu tea estates and a halt at View Point will give you a superb view of the Rangeet and Teesta rivers ringed by mountains.

Places of interest A centre for the commercial nursery trade, Kalimpong excels in producing orchids, amaryllis, roses, cacti, dahlias and gladioli among others for export. The Standard, Sri L.B. Pradhan and Sri Ganesh Moni Pradhan are considered to be the best nurseries in the field. The Tourist office in Darjiling will arrange a visit to one.

Monasteries The oldest in the area is the ***Thongsa Gompa*** Bhutanese monastery founded in 1692 which has been restored and is now brightly painted. Further up and to the N is the Yellow Hat Tibetan monastery at Tirpai, the ***Tharpa Choling***, which houses a library of Tibetan manuscripts and Tankhas. It belongs to the Yellow Hat sect, to which the present Dalai Lama belongs and was built in 1837. The ***Pedong*** Bhutanese monastery was established in the same year near the old fort of Damsang where ceremonial dances are held every February. At Darpin Dara, the highest point in Kalimpong with superb views over the plains, the Teesta and Reang rivers, stands the ***Zang-Dog Palri Fo-Brang.*** It is the only one of its kind outside Tibet, retaining its special lamaistic order with a school of Tibetan Medicine and a religious debating society.

Dr.Graham's Home, 3 km, was started by a missionary in 1900 when he admitted six orphans. Today it has 700 students on an extensive site on Delo hill with its own dairy, poultry and bakery. If you are in Kalimpong during the May Fair you will have a chance to see the Lucie King cottage. The **Central Sericultural Farm**, 4 km, produces high-grade silk cocoons and nearby is the **Swiss Welfare Dairy** set up by a missionary who started producing cheese in Pedong and then expanded to this large co-operative. You can trek from **Lava** (32 km) or **Lolaygaon** (56 km) or visit **Mungpo Cichona plantation** (26 km) or picnic on the river beaches at Teesta Bazar and Kalijhora.

Hotels C *Silver Oaks* (T 296) is the most expensive hotel in town. Central with 25 rms. Multi-cuisine restaurant, bar, exchange. C *Himalayan Hotel*, T 248. 9 rm. Old-fashioned though with character. One visitor complained about lack of running water. D *Kalimpong Park Hotel*, Ringkingpong Rd, T 304, 20 rms. E *Hotel Gompu*, T 418. Larger and inexpensive, with restaurant. *Tourist Bungalows* run by the W Bengal Tourist Bureau are clean and simple but you may be required to have breakfast and dinner there. The E *Luxury Tourist Bungalow* at Singamari, T 384 has 7 rm. 6 rm Tashding Tourist Lodge Annexe. *Hill Top Tourist Lodge*, T 654, has 10 rm. *Shangri La*, T 304, cheaper in dormitory.

Restaurants The hotels all have restaurants. The *Maharaja* has good S Indian food only. *Gompu's* Restaurant on Chowrasta is a popular meeting place, attempts English breakfasts and reasonable Chinese food. *Mandarin* serves Chinese food.

Shopping Tibetan and Nepalese handicrafts and woven fabrics are particularly good. *The Market* or *haat* every Wed and Sat becomes a meeting place for colourful villagers who sell fruit, vegetables, spices, traditional medicines, woollen cloth, yarn and musk. A place to visit for the atmosphere (even if you do not make purchases) and think back of the times when Kalimpong was the starting point of the trade route to Lhasa.

Air The nearest airport is at Bagdogra, 80 km, which has daily flight to Calcutta (see under Darjiling, page 564). **Rail** The nearest railhead is New Jalpaiguri/Siliguri station, 67 km, which has direct connections to Calcutta, Delhi, Guwahati and Lucknow. **Road** Kalimpong is off the National Highway 31-A to Gangtok. From there it is possible to get buses, Landrovers or taxis to Siliguri and Bagdogra, both journeys taking approximately 3 hours. N Bengal State Transport Corporation buses and private buses run services to Darjiling, Siliguri and other regional centres. It is also possible to catch buses from the Motor Stand to Gangtok in Sikkim which takes about 4 hrs. NBSTC Booking Office, Motor Stand, Kalimpong. T 525.

Jaldapara Wild Life Sanctuary 160 km from Bagdogra airport, 224 km from Darjiling. The *Jaldapara Sanctuary* covers an area of 116 sq km where you can see the one-horned rhino, elephants, wild boar, deer, leopard, gaur and the occasional tiger. It is situated close to Phuntsoling in Bhutan with the river Torsa flowing through and trained elephants are available to take visitors around. The best time to visit is between Dec and May.

Hotels Very simple and inexpensive accommodation is available at the *Hollong Forest Lodge*, Madarihat or at the Madarihat Lodge, Dist. Jalpaiguri, T 30 which has 8 rms and a restaurant. The *Forest Lodge*, built of timber on stilts has 7 double rms and is very popular since it is close to the sanctuary and also en route to Phuntsholing in Bhutan. Book well in advance through the Calcutta Tourist Office at 3/2 B.B.D. Bagh, or the Darjiling or Siliguri office. *Nilpara Forest Bungalow* at Hasimara, 2 rms, very basic accommodation. Facilities for cooking are available and the caretaker will oblige with preparing a simple meal if requested: remember to bring all provisions.

Travel The nearest air field is at Hasimara 5 km away, which is also connected by the Northern Frontier Railway. Indian Airlines daily flight to Bagdogra, then scenic drive through tea gardens to Jaldapara. Express buses run from Calcutta to Madarihat. Forest Department transport to Hollong inside the sanctuary.

CALCUTTA TO THE MOUTH OF THE HUGLI

Short trips are possible to the S of Calcutta to the mouth of the Hugli and to the Sundarbans in the Ganga/Brahmaputra delta.

Diamond Harbour, Sagardwip and Bakkhali Follow the road due S from

Calcutta to **Diamond Harbour** (51 km) which lies on the bend of the river where it turns S towards the sea. Once the ships of the East India Company anchored here: the ruins of a fort is said to date back to the days of the Portuguese pirates. Today it is a favourite picnic spot for day-trippers. Motor launches take passengers to Sagar island or country boat trips go rounds of the estuary.

Hotels WBTDC **E** *Sagarika Tourist Lodge*, a/c and non a/c double rms and suites, and cheap dormitory. The *Irrigation Department Bungalow* can be reserved through the Irrigation Department, 11A Mirza Ghalib St, Calcutta.

Continue S to Kulpi (18 km) and Kakdwip (26 km) en route to **Bakkhali**. This small village has a pleasant unspoilt palm fringed beach close to the Sunderbans. From Calcutta, you can get as far as Namkhana by bus (3 hr), take a ferry across the **Hatania-Doania** river and then another bus for 90 min. Alternatively, there is train to Diamond Harbour, stopping en route at the pleasant Tourist Centre overlooking the widening Ganga and proceed for Bakkhali the following day.

Hotels WBTDC has a **F** *Tourist Lodge* (T Kakdwip 76) with very basic accommodation for 48 in double rms and dorms. The beach house is among casuarina groves and has a restaurant. Boat trips are available to Jambu Dwip.

Sagardwip, the island at the mouth of the Ganga is where the Ganga Sagar Mela is held in mid-January. It attracts over half a million pilgrims each year who come to bathe and then visit the **Kapil Muni Temple**.

The island has been devastated many times by cyclones and floods often killing large numbers of inhabitants. There is a lighthouse to aid navigation in the SW tip. WBTDC organizes 2 day boat trips with accommodation on board.

Sundarbans and Sajnekhali The best season to visit the Sundarbans is from Aug to Mar, though heavy rains and occasional severe storms can make a visit impossible in the first half of the season.

The unique **Sundarbans** (meaning "beautiful forests") with their mangrove swamps covering over 2,500 sq km in the Ganga/Brahmaputra delta, spread across to Bangladesh, **see page 1388**. They are said to be the largest estuarine forests in the world. The **biosphere reserve** still preserves the natural habitat of over 200 or so Bengal tigers which can swim and still attack fishermen. Spotted deer, wild boar, monkeys, snakes, sea turtles and large crocodiles are the other wildlife to be seen, particularly on Lothian Island and Chamta block. **Sajnekhali** has a **famous bird sanctuary** and can be approached from Canning or Basanti by motor launch.

Hotels The *Sunder Chital Tourist Lodge*, simple accommodation can be booked through the Tourist Board which also organizes 2-day trips twice a month or 1-day cruises more frequently. You must be accompanied by armed forest rangers in order to view the wildlife from watch towers.

Digha *Climate* Temp. Summer Max. 32°C Min. 15°C, Winter Max. 23°C Min. 10°C. *Best season* October to March. Digha is 185 km from Calcutta on the W bank of the Hugli estuary where it has already become indistinguishable from the Bay of Bengal. Warren Hastings, nearly 2 centuries ago, visited Digha and called it the 'Brighton of the East'. It is rather difficult to see why, as there is not a pebble for at least 2000 km! The casuarina-lined hard wide beach is very popular with Bengalis but can not compare with Puri further S.

Places of interest nearby Junpur Beach 8 km from Contai and 40 km from Digha has a fishing research station and duck breeding centre. **Chandaneshwar** 8 km from Digha has a Siva Temple which can be reached by going to the Orissa border by bus and then completing the last 3 km by rickshaw.

Hotels **D** *Hotel Sea Hawk* has Western style a/c and non-a/c double rooms. Cottages and cheap dormitory accommodation is also available. T 35/46/47. Calcutta T 572048. **E** *Hotel Dolphin*, B.B. Ganguly St has non-a/c dle rms. WBTDC **E** *Luxury Tourist Lodge* has both non-a/c single and double rooms. T 55/56.

Travel Rail The nearest railway halts are at Kharagpur (116 km) and Contai Road (151 km) Stations on the S Eastern Railway. **Road** Express buses and Tourist Bureau luxury buses do the journey from Calcutta in about 6 hrs, the route having been shortened by the Norghat Bridge. The services Calcutta-Digha-Calcutta start at around 0700 from Esplanade, the fare for the return journey (any day) is Rs 40, single Rs 20.

SIKKIM

> Introduction, 570; Gangtok, 574; Trekking in Sikkim, 578

Sikkim is famous for Kangchendzonga (8,586 m) the third highest mountain in the world, a rich flora and fauna and a diverse ethnic and cultural population. The original inhabitants, the Lepchas, call the region *Nye-mae-el* ('Paradise'). To the later Bhutias it is *Beymul Denjong* ('The Hidden Valley of Rice'). The word Sikkim is commonly attributed to the Tsong word *Sukkum* meaning New or Happy House.

Basic indicators Population 400,000; Urban 18%; Literacy 34% (M 42%, F 21%); Birth rate per '000 *Urban* 27, *Rural* 36; Death rate per '000 *Urban* 4.8 *Rural* 12.2 Religion *Hindu* 67% *Muslim* 1% *Christian* 2% *Buddhist* 29%.

INTRODUCTION

Geography
The Land Sikkim is in the E Himalaya, sandwiched between Nepal to its W and Bhutan to the E. In the N is Tibet/China. To the S is the Indian state of West Bengal. It is the second smallest state in India (*Area* 7,298 sq km), only 112 km length and 64 km width. Flat land is a rarity.

It encompasses the upper valley of the Tista river, a tributary of the Brahmaputra. The watershed ridges form the borders with Tibet/China and Nepal. The Rangit and Rangpo rivers form the border with West Bengal. The Singalila range separates Sikkim from Nepal to the W and the Dongkya range forms the border in the N and NE. In the E the Chumbi valley lies between Sikkim and Bhutan, a tongue of Tibetan land that has given Sikkim its strategic and political sensitivity.

Sikkim once covered a much larger area but now begins at the foot of the mountains. It is dominated by **Kangchendzonga** (formerly *Kanchenjunga*), which means the 'Five Treasures of the Great Snows'. According to Sikkimese belief it is the repository of minerals, grains, salt, weapons and holy scriptures. On its W side is the massive 31 km long **Zemu** glacier. Various explorers and mountaineers have claimed to have seen yeti or their prints in the vicinity of the mountain and its glacier, and in common with other regions of the Himalaya and Karakoram the 'abominable snowman' has its place in folklore.

Rivers and lakes The *Tista river* valley traverses the whole country from N to S, and allows the monsoon rains to penetrate the northernmost parts. As a result of high monsoonal rainfall, tributaries of the Tista have cut numerous deep valleys out of the soft slate in the S. In the N is an area of rock, glacial debris and snow, with only occasional thin grass cover. This forms the transitional zone between the Himalaya and the Tibetan plateau.

Vegetation has been influenced by altitude, aspect and rainfall. In the lowest

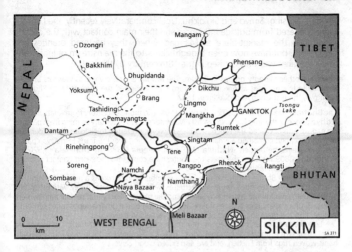

parts there is wet *sal* (Shorea Robusta) forest with 660 species of **orchids** and 20 species of bamboo. This gives way to tropical evergreen mountain and rain forests (tree ferns, epiphytes, bamboo, oak, beech, chestnut, tree fern, giant magnolia, rhododendron and conifers (firs, pines) up to the treeline at 3,600-4,200 m.

The **alpine forests** 3,900-5,000 m are characterised by such beautiful flowering plants as primulas, gentians, blue poppies, and wild strawberry, raspberry and rhubarb. Sikkim is a botanist's delight.

Wildlife The animal and bird life is correspondingly rich, with 81 species of mammals, 600 species of birds and 631 species of butterflies – wild asses and yaks in the N, bears, lesser (red) pandas, silver foxes and leopards in the tropical forests. The birdlife is also rich, with pheasants, teal, partridges, cuckoos, babblers and thrushes among many others.

Climate
Temperatures In the lower valleys Sikkim's climate is sub-tropical. Above 1,000 m the climate is temperate, while the tops of the higher mountains are permanently under snow.

Rainfall Sikkim is one of the wettest regions of the Himalayas. It has the same seasonal rainfall pattern, dominated by the monsoon, as the rest of the E Himalaya. Total rainfall is more than 3,000 mm.

People and Languages
Three tribes – the Naong, Chang and Mon are believed to have inhabited Sikkim in prehistoric times. The **Lepchas**, who have no myths or legends of migration, may have come from Tibet well before the 8th century and brought Lamaistic Buddhism, which is still practised. They completely assimilated the earlier tribes and are now regarded as the indigenous peoples. They are a deeply religious, shy, and peaceful people, but at the same time cheerful. Most have accepted Mahayana Buddhism, while retaining the pre-Buddhist Bon practices.

The government has reserved the ***Dzongu*** area in N and Central Sikkim for Lepchas only, now numerically smaller than the later Nepali immigrant population, making up less than 10%. It is a heavily forested region bounded by the the rivers Tista and Tolung, and surrounded by the mountain ranges of Kangchendzonga,

Pandim, Narsing, Simvo and Siniolchu. Until comparatively recently, the Lepchas were sheltered from outside influence, and their main contact with the outside world was the market-place at Mangan, where they bartered oranges and cardamom, but have now been brought closer to the mainstream of Indian life. Their alphabet was only devised in the 18th century by the king.

There are other minority groups in Sikkim. The **Magar** are renowned as warriors and are mentioned in chronicles as one of the groups that celebrated the coronation of Phuntsog Namgyal, the first Chogyal of Sikkim in 1642.

The **Bhutias** (meaning 'of Bhot/Tibet') entered Sikkim in the 13th century from Kham in Tibet, led by a prince of the later Namgyal dynasty. Many adapted to sedentary farming from pastoral nomadism and displaced the Lepchas. Some, however, preferred to cling to their older style of exisitence, and combined animal husbandry with trading over the Trans-Himalayan passes that punctuate the border: **Nathula** (4,392 m), **Jelepla** (4388 m), **Donkiala** (5,520 m), **Kongrala** (4,809 m). Over the years the Bhutia have come into increased contact with the Lepcha and intermarried with them.

Nearly every Bhutia family has one family member who becomes a monk. Traditionally, the priesthood was regarded as the intellectual as well as spiritual elite. Today, with the spread of the Indian educational system into Sikkim and the social mobility that secular employment offers, Bhutia society is in a state of flux. The monasteries remain the repositories of Bhutia culture, and the main social events are the festivals held in them.

Like the Lepchas and the Nepalis, the Bhutias are fond of their *chhang**, a fermented millet, that is the unofficial national drink. They are famous for their weaving, especially hand-woven rugs from Lachen, and are also skilled wood carvers.

The largest migration into Sikkim took place in the 19th century and was from Nepal. The **Newars**, skilled in metal and wood work, were granted the right by the *chogyal* to mine copper and mint the Sikkimese coinage. They were followed by other Nepali groups: the Sherpas, Gurung, Tamang and Rai. All had developed high altitude farming skills in Nepal and settled new lands. As population pressure increased, terraced farming and wherever possible irrigation, were practised with the introduction of rice cultivation. Their houses were built directly on the ground, unlike the Lepcha custom of building on stilts.

The Newars were followed by the Chettris, Bahun and Bishu Karma clans of Nepal, who introduced Hinduism, which became more popular as their numbers swelled. Yet it was Hinduism of the Himalayan type, which included a pantheon of Buddhist bodhisattvas as well as Hindu deities. In Sikkim, as in Nepal, Buddhist and Hindu beliefs have traditionally interacted and amalgamated. See Nepal, **page 1273**

Economy

Agriculture is the main economic activity, and is practised on terraced fields that have been laboriously created from the steep hillsides. Wherever possible irrigation has been introduced. Maize, wheat and barley are grown as winter crops and rice in the summer. Potatoes, oranges and and tea are grown in the foothills. Sikkim is the largest producer of **cardamom** in India. Cardamom is exported, and fruit farming has led to the development of a small canned fruit industry, also for export.

Animal husbandry is important in upper Sikkim, with sheep and yak being shepherded to the high pastures over 3,500 metres over the summer. Forests cover one third of the state and have enormous economic potential.

Resources and industry Sikkim is rich in minerals and has deposits of copper, lead, zinc, coal, iron ore, garnet, graphite, pyrites and marble, all of which are mined. There are also high grade reserves of gold and silver.

Manufacturing Traditional handicrafts and carpet weaving are important. A distillery was set up in 1956. The Government of India has declared Sikkim an industrially backward area and has set up a flour mill and tannery, watch assembly, tea processing, cable and soap factories.

Tourism The comparatively small number of tourists reflects the lack of accessibility. The trekking industry is still in its infancy.

History

The Lepchas claim to be the original inhabitants of Sikkim and call themselves

Rongpas. From the 13th century Tibetans immigrated into the area, including the Namgyal clan in the 15th century, who gradually won political control over Sikkim. In 1642 Phuntsog Namgyal (1604-70) became the **Chogyal** (king). He presided over a social system based on Tibetan Lamaistic Buddhism, and divided the land into 12 *Dzongs* (fortified districts).

In the 18th century Sikkim was much reduced in size, losing land to Nepal, Bhutan and the British. Armies from Bhutan and the newly consolidated Gurkha empire of Nepal invaded and took considerable areas of Sikkim. When the Gurkhas launched a campaign into Tibet and were defeated by the Chinese in 1791-2, Sikkim won back its N territories. The thin Chumbi valley that separates Sikkim from Bhutan remained with Tibet.

When the British defeated Nepal in 1817, the southern part of the country was given back to Sikkim. However, in the next conflict with Nepal, **Darjiling**, was handed over to the British in return for their assistance. Later in 1848 the Terai region at the foot of the mountains was annexed by the British.

Nepalis migrated into Sikkim from the beginning of the 19th century, eventually becoming more numerous than the local inhabitants. This led to internal conflict which subsequently also involved the British and the Tibetans. When the British refused to stop the influx of Nepalis the *Gyalpos* (Kings, *gyalmos* – Queens) enlisted Tibetan help . The British won the ensuing battles and declared Sikkim a protectorate in 1890. The state was controlled by a British Political Officer who effectively stripped the Gyalpos of executive power. It was many years before the Sikkimese regained control.

The Indian Government took over effective control of political life in Sikkim in 1950. The Gyalpos lost their power as a result of the new democratic constitution, and the pro-India Nepali population gained the upper hand. Sikkim was formally annexed by India in 1973 and became the 22nd state in the Union through an amendment to the constitution in 1975.

Local Festivals

Hindu and Buddhist rituals form the basis for Sikkim's festivals and the same annual *pujas* as in India and Nepal are performed. The animist tradition also prescribes that evil spirits be propitiated. Each ethnic group has an impressive repertoire of folk songs and dances with one for almost every occasion. Since the 22 major festivals are dictated by the agricultural cycle and the Hindu-Buddhist calendar, it is best to check dates with the Tourist office.

Feb *Losar* Tibetan New Year – preceded by Lama dances in Rumtek.

Jun *Saga Dawn* A Buddha festival – huge religious processions round Gangtok. *Rumtek chaams* Dance festival in commemoration of the eight manifestations of Guru Padmasambhava, the teacher who is thought to have established Buddhism in Tibet.

Aug/Sep *Pang Lhabsol* commemorates the consecration of Kangchendzonga as Sikkim's guardian deity, and has its origins in the Lepcha belief of the mountain as their place of birth. However, the actual origin of the festival is said to be the blood brotherhood covenant between the Bhutias and Lepchas at Kabi between the Lepcha *bongthing* and the ancestors oof the Namgyal royal family. The masked warrior dance is especially spectacular. Kangchendzonga is represented by a red mask and her commander a black one. The warriors who accompany wear traditional armour of helmets, swords and shields. The dramatic entry of *Mahakala* (Protector of the Dharma) is one of the highlights of the festival.

Sep/Oct *Dasain* and *Deepavali* is the biggest and most important festival celebrated by the Hindu Nepali population. It coincides with *Dussehra* in N India and *Durga Puja* in Bengal. [C] See festivals in India and Nepal. It begins on the first day of the bright half of the lunar month of *Aswin*. Barley seeds are planted in prayer rooms, invocations are made to Durga and on the 8th day buffaloes and goats are ritually sacrificed. *Diwali* (the Festival of Lights) is celebrated after Dasain.

Nov-Dec *Losoog* (*Namsoong* to the Lepchas) is the Sikkimese New Year and may also be called *Sonam Losar*, for this is the farmers' celebration of their harvest and beginning of their new cropping calendar. Both Lossong and Losar are exuberant family celebrations.

Dec *Kagyat Dances* enact various themes from the Buddhist mythology and culiminate with the burning of effigies made of flour, wood and paper. This symbolises the exorcism of evil and the ushering in of prosperity for the coming year. The dancers of this extremely popular

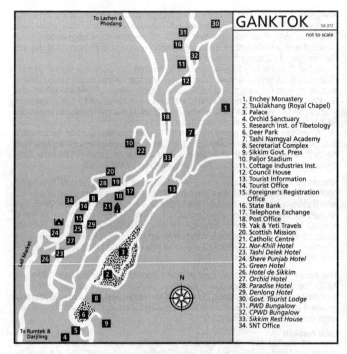

GANGTOK SA 372

not to scale

To Lachen & Phodang

1. Enchey Monastery
2. Tsuklakhang (Royal Chapel)
3. Palace
4. Orchid Sanctuary
5. Research Inst. of Tibetology
6. Deer Park
7. Tashi Namgyal Academy
8. Secretariat Complex
9. Sikkim Govt. Press
10. Paljor Stadium
11. Cottage Industries Inst.
12. Council House
13. Tourist Information
14. Tourist Office
15. Foreigner's Registration Office
16. State Bank
17. Telephone Exchange
18. Post Office
19. Yak & Yeti Travels
20. Scottish Mission
21. Catholic Centre
22. *Nor-Khill Hotel*
23. *Tashi Delek Hotel*
24. *Shere Punjab Hotel*
25. *Green Hotel*
26. *Hotel de Sikkim*
27. *Orchid Hotel*
28. *Paradise Hotel*
29. *Denlong Hotel*
30. *Govt. Tourist Lodge*
31. *PWD Bungalow*
32. *CPWD Bungalow*
33. *Sikkim Rest House*
34. SNT Office

To Rumtek & Darjiling

chaam are always monks who are accompanied by liturgical music and chanting.

Information for Visitors Inner Line Permits for foreigners from Inspector Gen of Police, Gangtok for 7 days extendable by 3 days. Groups of up to 20 may apply to trek for a max of 15 days. Apply at Indian missions 6 weeks in advance or from Ministry of Home Affairs in New Delhi (can take months). No charge but you need 3 photos with the form.

GANGTOK

The capital of Sikkim lies on a ridge overlooking the Ranipool River. Its name means 'High Hill'. The setting is spectacular with fine views of the Kangchendzonga range, but the town itself has long since lost its quaint charm. It is now rather dusty and uninspiring, and sprawls over the hillside. New and invariably ugly buildings dominate the urban landscape.

Population 75,000 *Altitude* 1,547 m. *Area* 2.54 sq km. *Best season* Mid-Feb to Mid-June and Oct to Dec. *Clothing* Summer – light woollens and cotton, Winter – heavy woollens.

Gangtok has only a road connection with the rest of India. The nearest airport is at Bagdogra (124 km), and the nearest railhead at Siliguri (114 km).

	Jan	Feb	Mar	Apr	May	Jun	Jul	Aug	Sep	Oct	Nov	Dec	Av/Tot
Max (°C)	14	15	19	22	22	23	23	23	23	22	19	15	20
Min (°C)	4	5	9	12	14	16	17	17	16	12	9	6	11
Rain (mm)	44	56	142	222	493	644	663	588	476	152	35	15	3530

All the main facilities including hotels, cafes, bazaar, bus stand and post office are along the main road from Darjiling which ultimately merges with the old Hindustan-Tibet road.

Local Festivals Most of the festivals above are celebrated with great fervour in Gangtok.

Places of Interest

At the N end of the town is the **Government Institute of Cottage Industries** where a wide range of local handicrafts are produced, many with a distinctive Tibetan and Chinese look and feel to them, e.g. woollen carpets, blankets, shawls, dolls, decorative papers and carved and painted wooden tables. Open 0900-1230 and 1330-1530 daily. Closed Sun and every 2nd Sat of the month.

Enchey Monastery is 3 km to the SE of the main bazaar, and next to the Tourist Lodge. Believed to be 200 years old, though the present building dates from 1909. Religious dance performances in Jan.

The *Palace of the Chogyal* is only open once a year in the last week of Dec for the *Pang Lhabsol* festival. Below this is the **Tsuklakhang** or Royal Chapel, standing on a high ridge. This is the major place of worship and has a large and impressive collection of scriptures. Coronations and royal marriages took place here. The interior is lavishly decorated with woodcarving and murals and houses a number of Buddha images. Not always open to visitors and photography prohibited. Moving S along the road you pass the **Secretariat** complex on your left. Beyond this is the **Deer Park,** loosely modelled on the famous one at Sarnath (with a statue of the Buddha, see page 261).

The unique **Research Institute of Tibetology** on a hilltop was established in 1958 to promote research on Tibet and Mahayana Buddhism. Open 1000-1600 daily except Sun. Free. The library maintains a large and important Buddhist collection. Many fine *thangkas**, icons and art treasures on display.

The *Orchid Sanctuary*, 14 km, S of the Institute and lower down, contains over 500 indigenous species in what is more like a botanical garden with large orchidariums. At any one time over half are in bloom, but the best times are Apr-May and Dec-Jan although vistors in late were disappointed. In Sikkim, orchids are found mostly in tropical regions up to 2,100 m, though there are some at 3,000 m. With over 600 species, it is an orchid lovers paradise.

The **Do-drul Chorten** on one of the southern approaches to the town has a comparatively large gold topped stupa with 108 prayer wheels, and is a local landmark. Nearby is a monastery for young lamas.

Hotels Because of Gangtok's altitude, air-conditioning is unnecessary. **C** *Nor Khill*, Paljor Stadium Rd, T 3186/7, Cable: Nor Khill. 35 rm with baths. Restaurant, bar, 24 hr rm service, exchange, shops, car hire, travel, Amex, Diners. **C** *Tashi Delek*, MG Marg. T 2991, Cable:Tashidelek. 50 rm, with bath. Central. Restaurant, bar, exchange, shops, car hire, travel (incl airlines counter), roof garden, Amex, Diners. Free audio visual programme. Rooftop garden. **C** *Mayur*, Paljor Stadium Rd, T 2825, Cable: Sikkim Tourism. 27 rm with bath. Restaurant, bar, tours, car hire, Diners. Bookings for all Tourism Dept units. **D** *Tibet*, Paljor Stadium Rd. T 2523, Cable: Hotel Tibet. 28 rm, some with bath. Restaurant (incl Japanese), bar, exchange, car hire, Diners. **D** *Siniolchu Lodge*, near Enchey Monastery. T 2074. Cable: Sikkim Tourism. Some rm with bath. Restaurant, bar, car hire, tours.
  E *Green*, MG Rd, T 2554. 45 rm, some with bath. Restaurant. **E** *Orchid*, National

Highway, T 2381. 21 rm. Restaurant, bar. **E** *Swagat*, Lall Bazar Rd. T 2991, Cable: Motila. 16 rm with bath. Indian restaurant. **E** *Karma*, MG Marg, nr Gandhi Statue. 17 rm. Restaurant, bar. **F** *Deeki*, Lall Market, T 2301. 18 rm, some with bath. Restaurant, bar. **F** *Laden*, Lall Market, T 3058. 13 rm. Chinese restaurant, bar, limited room service. **F** *Sher-e-Punjab*, National Highway, T 2823. 10 rm. Restaurant, bar. **F** *Woodlands*, MG Rd. 16 rm. **F** *Kanchen View*, PO Tadong, National Highway, T 2086. 24 rm. **F** *Doma*, MG Rd. 14 rm.

There is also the *Sikkim Rest House*. The *CPWD Bungalow* and the *Tourist Lodge* are at the N end of town.

Restaurants in hotels offer Indian, Chinese, Continental and sometimes Sikkimese and Tibetan specialties. *Blue Sheep*, next to the Tourist Information Centre. *House of Bamboo* (Tibetan specialities) and *Cooks Inn* on MG Rd. *Dreamland*, Stadium Rd. *Hungry Jack*, National Highway (near Bansi Lal petrol pump). *Windshore*, Deorali. Chinese at *Khoo Chi*, MG Rd, vegetarian at *Snip 'n Bite*, Taxi Stand on National Highway and *Marwari Bhojanalay*, MG Rd.

Local Sikkimese rum and other spirits are made in Rangpo.

Banks State Bank of Sikkim, National Highway, T 2465. **State Bank of India**, MG Rd, T 2824, **Central Bank of India**, T 2235 and **United Commercial Bank**, T 2464 on Stadium Rd.

Shopping Sikkim is famous for traditional crafts. Carpet weaving, Thangka wall hangings, shirts, boots, fur caps and other clothing, and wood carving all offer good buys. *Cottage Industries Sales Outlet* Mon-Sat 0930-1230; 1300-1530. Also at **Old Bazar**, **Naya Bazar** and **Lall market** ('*Haat*' on Sun). Markets close on Tues. Several camera shops on MG Rd.

Local Transport Taxis: Unmetered. Rates negotiable for sightseeing and local running. The Department of Tourism, MG Rd, T 2064. **Car hire**. Tarriff per day exclusive of fuel: Car (max. 5 persons) – Rs 500 for travel outside Sikkim, Rs 400 within Sikkim, night halt Rs 200; **Mini-coach** for 16 persons, Land Rovers and Jeeps also available.

Sports *Mountaineering* Himalayan Mountaineering Institute based in Yuksom offers climbing courses in stunning surroundings. *Trekking* information from Tourist offices in Gangtok and Pemayangtse for W Sikkim. *River rafting* on Rivers Teesta and Rangeel arranged by Dept Tourism and private travel agents.

Useful Services Police T 2022. Fire T 2001. Ambulance T 2924. S.T.N.M. Hospital, National Highway, T 2944.

Post and Telegraphs G.P.O., Stadium Rd, T 2385 and PO in Gangtok Bazaar.

Places of Worship *Buddhist*: Enchey Monastery; Guru Lhakhang Chorten; Rumtek Monastery. *Christian*: The Church of North India, Church Rd; St Thomas Catholic Church, National Highway. *Hindu*: Thakurbari Temple. *Muslim*: Anjuman Mosque, National Highway.

Travel Agents Yak & Yeti Travels, Snow Lion Travels and Sikkim Himalayan Adventures all organise treks.

Tourist Offices and Information Tourism Information Centre, MG Rd, Gangtok Bazaar, T 2064. Open in season 0900-1700, off season 1000-1600. Also offices in: Hill Cart Rd, Siliguri, West Bengal, T 24602; Bagdogra Airport; 4C Poonam, 5/2 Russell Street, Calcutta, T 295476; Room No. 10, Hotel Janpath, Janpath, New Delhi 110001.

Tours starting from the Tourist Information Centre. Gangtok **1. Morning tour** – Govt. Institute of Cottage Industries, Deer Park, Chorten, Research Institute of Tibetology, Orchid Sanctuary and Enchey Monastery. In season daily 0930-1230. Rs 25. **2 Afternoon Tour** – Orchidarium and Rumtek Monastery. In season daily 1400/1430-1700. Rs 35. **3. Phodong Tour**. Rs 50. Tours by car are more expensive.

Mountain Flight to view Kangchendzonga. 35 min. Daily in season weather permitting. Minimum 12 persons. Fare Rs 350.

Package tours to W Sikkim, (min 16 persons), Fri at 1030 returning Sun 1600 (3 days 2 night). Rs 500.

Tourist Information Centre, Pemayangtse, organises **treks in W Sikkim** and helps with information and equipment.

Air Nearest airport is Bagdogra (124 km), daily Indian Airlines connections with Calcutta (direct) and Delhi (Delhi-Patna-Bagdogra-Gauhati-Imphal). Indian Airlines, Tibet Rd, Gangtok, T 3099. Open 1000-1600. Taxi to Gangtok, about Rs 125 (Rs 600 for full taxi, max 5 persons) or Snow-Lion mini-bus. **Helicopter** between Gangtok and Siliguri daily, about Rs 400, one way. Book at Tourist Information Office, MG Rd, T 2097, 2064.

Rail Nearest railway stations are at **Siliguri** (114 km) and **New Jalpaiguri** (126 km) which are well connected with other centres in N and E India. Reservations: Sikkim Nationalised Transport (SNT), T 2016; 0930-1100, 1330-1430 for transport to stations.

Road Gangtok is on the NH 31A. Darjiling (139 km) and Kalimpong (72 km). **Bus** SNT services to Darjiling, Kalimpong and Bagdogra (5-6 hr) in N Bengal and Rumtek, Namchi, Namok, Chungthang and Mangan in Sikkim. Private buses also run between Gangtok, Kalimpong and Siliguri. Opp W Point Bus Stand, NH 31 A, T 2858. SNT Bus Stand, National Highway, T 2016. Private buses from West Point Taxi Stand, National Highway. Also N Bengal STC, Burdwan Rd Bus Stand, Siliguri.

Excursions

Rumtek Monastery, 24 km. Situated in one of the lower valleys, SW of Gangtok, it is the headquarters of the Kagyupa (Red Hat) sect of Tibetan Lamaistic Buddhism. The 16th Gwalpa Karmapa took refuge in Sikkim after the Chinese invaded Tibet. He and his followers brought with them whatever statues, thangkas and scriptures they could and at the invitation of the Chogyal, the Karmapa settled in Rumtek and the lamasery was built. The original monastery built by the 4th Chogyal and destroyed by an earthquake, was rebuilt in the 1960s in the traditional style as a faithful copy of the Kagyu headquarters in Chhofuk, Tibet and now houses the Dharma Chakra Centre.

The important **chaam*** (religious masked dance) of Rumtek is performed on the 10th day of the 5th month of the Tibetan calendar, and presents 8 manifestations of the Guru Rimpoche. This is highly colourful and spectacular and draws many pilgrims and visitors. From Gangtok, Rumtek can be visited in a day by car. The public bus leaves Gangtok late afternoon and reaches Rumtek at nightfall; return early morning.

In W Sikkim is **Pemayangtse** (2,085 m), Sikkim's 2nd oldest monastery, near the start of the the Dzongri trek. A full day's trip by car from Gangtok, Pemayangste (The Perfect Sublime Lotus) was built during the reign of the 3rd Chogyal Chador Namgyal in 1705. The walls and ceilings have innumerable paintings and there is an exceptional collection of religious artworks, including an exquisite wooden sculpture depicting the resting place of Guru Rimpoche.

There are approximately 100 monks in residence and according to tradition they have been recruited from the leading families in Sikkim as this is the 'headquarters' of the **Nyingama sect**. Annual chaam dances, at the end of Feb, 12th month of the Tibetan calendar.

Beautiful views of Kanchendzongha from the comfortable Tourist Lodge **D** Mount Padim, Pelling, T 73. All meals provided. Reservations: Tourist Office in Gangtok.

Yuksom nearby, where the coronation of the country's first ruler took place in 1641, has a stupa and is in a picturesque pine forest with a lake.

Gezing, 6 km S of the monastery. About 8 hr by car or bus from Gangtok. Gezing has basic Guesthouses and 2 km along the track to Pemayangtse is a PWD Rest House. Reservations: CPWD, Gangtok nr Cottage Industries Institute.

From Gezing it is about a 2 hr climb up to the monastery. Forest Dept Resthouse. Bring your own bedding. Local meals available in the village. Reservations: Tourist Office in Gangtok.

Tashiding in W Sikkim was built by the half sister of Chador Namgyal in 1716 on a spot consecrated by Guru Rimpoche, between the Ratong and Rangit rivers on a ridge overlooking both. Considered to be the most sacred chorten in Sikkim, the sight of which is thought to be bring blessing. Pilgrims come each spring for the Bumchu festival to drink water from the sacred pot which has never run dry for over 300 years.

TREKKING IN SIKKIM

Trekking is in its infancy and many of the routes are through areas that seldom see foreigners. As a consequence, facilities for independent trekkers are poorly developed. Best time mid-Feb to late-May and Oct to early Dec. You do not need previous experience since most treks are between 2,000 to 3,800 m. in altitude. The paths are usually clear and the huts for overnight stops are clean, having been recently built, although the toilets are basic. An added attraction are that *dzos** (cross between a cow and a yak) will carry your gear instead of porters. The trekking routes also pass through villages which will give an insight into the tribal people's life-style.

Maps The U 502 sheets for Sikkim are NG 45-3 and NG 45-4. P.P. Karan published a map at the scale of 1:150,000 in 1969. Price US$3.00, available from the Program Director of Geography, George Mason University, Fairfax, VA 22030, USA. Sikkim Himalaya (Swiss Alpine Club) – Huber 1:50,000. Very detailed. £16.

It is possible to trek from Gangtok (6-18 days), Pemayangtse (8-15 days) or Naya Bazar (7-8 days) with several options of routing. From Darjiling, a shorter trek goes to Singla and Pemayangtse. **See Darjiling Treks, page 565**, for details of others.

Warning Anyone contemplating a trek should aim to be self-sufficient. For this reason, and the likelihood of getting lost and being unable to communicate sufficiently well to re-orientate oneself, the organised group trek is recommended. Foreigners must make up a group of 4 at least before applying for a permit. A Govt of India Liaison Officer will usually accompany the group. A number of international companies operate trips to Sikkim. Local agents in Darjiling and Gangtok will organise a trek. Govt of India Tourist Offices overseas can often supply a list of tour operators in the country with an accompanying note of special interest tours organized by each.

Gangtok – Pemayangtse

The route is from Gangtok to Pemayangtse via Rumtek, then on to Yaksum, Bakhim and Dzongri. Although it is not a long trek there are excellent views throughout as you travel up the Rathong Chu river to the amphitheatre of peaks at the head of the valley. This includes Kotang (6,150 m), Ratong (6,683 m), Kabru Dome (6,604 m), and Forked Peak (6,116 m).

    Yuksom is the base for the trek (2 hr drive from Gangtok) and from here it is 12 km to Bakhim (2,740 m). You will climb through pine forests with rhododendron, azalea, orchid and should see monkeys and a large variety of butterflies and birds. Not far from here is Tsoka, the last village on the trekking route where many Tibetan refugees have settled. For the most part the route beyond Tsoka is through forests of rhododedron and silver fir. The highpoint of this 6-7 day trek is *Dzongri* (4,030 m) reached after a more challenging climb, where nomadic yak herders stay in huts. There is also a *Tourist Lodge*. It is considered specially important for its *chortens* containing Buddhist relics and so attracts occasional pilgrims. From this exposed and windswept spot you can get a good panoramic view of the surrounding mountains and see a spectacular sunset. A longer 10 day trek will allow you to descend to Thangshing through the Onglathang valley where you cross the Pregchu river by a bridge. The added attractions are bird watching and the large glacial lake, *Samiti* by which you will camp in Thanshing. The gentle climb to the next campsite at *Zemathang* is particularly beautiful. From there you return to Yuksam.

Note See Nepal Trekking for detailed advice, **see page 1302**. **Leeches** can be a special problem in the wet season, below 2,000 m. They can be a nuisance as a bite can become septic. To remove do not pull away but use a spray (eg Waspeeze), some salt, a lighted cigarette or match or, as a last resort, a sharp knife to encourage it to drop off. It is a good idea to spray socks and boot laces well with an insect repellant before setting off each morning.

NORTH-EASTERN HILL STATES

The NE is a frontier region in every sense. It has over 800 km of border with Burma and at least that distance again with China and Bhutan. But although the northern border runs through the easternmost extension of the Himalayas and the border to the SE with Burma also runs through mountain ranges the NE hill states are a region of transition. Even Assam, now confined largely to the Brahmaputra Valley, is highly distinct.

Visiting the north east

The NE has always been a politically sensitive region. After Independence in 1947 large parts were governed directly from New Delhi as a special region, the NE Frontier Agency, although **Assam** has been a state since 1947. In 1962, the year of India's crushing military defeat in its war with China, the Naga Hills district was separated to form Nagaland. Political pressures for autonomy in the tribal areas remained high and ten years later Meghalaya became a separate state and Arunachal Pradesh and Mizoram became Union Territories. In the 1980s these too were given statehood. Throughout the 1980s Assam was the centre of agitations against the central government in New Delhi. These focused on the issue of immigration from Bangladesh and the eligibility of over 2 million immigrants to vote in elections. In 1985 Rajiv Gandhi signed an accord through which elections were held on the basis of old electoral registers, and since then agitations have been much more subdued.

Documents

Foreigners intending to visit the two states in the region accessible to tourists, Assam and Meghalaya, must obtain Restricted Area Permits from the Secretary, Ministry of Home Affairs, Govt. of India, N Block, New Delhi 110001, well in advance. Applications must state details of name, passport number with issuing authority and expiry date, place of birth, profession, duration of stay and the purpose of the visit. However, Foreigners Registration Offices in Calcutta, Delhi, Bombay and Madras are authorised to grant permits to organized groups for visits only to Shillong in Meghalaya, and Guwahati and the game reserve at Kaziranga in Assam. Visits must be organized by recognized travel agencies, be accompanied by a State Government Liaison Officer along a prescribed route and last no more than 7 days. Permit holders must travel to Guwahati and back by air.

    Indians wishing to visit the other states, Arunachal Pradesh, Manipur, Mizoram, Nagaland and Tripura have to obtain Inner Line Permits from the Ministry of Home Affairs. **Please check rules before departing.**

INTRODUCTION

The land

Geographically even this outlying section of the S Asian landmass has elements of all three major physical features of the sub-continent. The northern mountains are a continuation of the Himalayas, not quite as high as the ranges immediately to their W but still with many peaks over 6,500 m on both the Indian and Chinese sides of the border. To the immediate S of the northern mountain ranges, the Brahmaputra Valley is part of the same trough that, filled with silt, makes up the Ganga basin. To its S lies the Shillong Plateau, now Meghalaya State, which is an

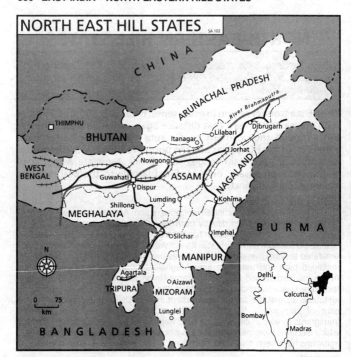

outlier of the ancient peninsular rocks of southern India. These became detached in the northwards push of the Indian plate **see page 30**, leaving a shallow gap of about 240 km between it and the main peninsular block in Bihar. Through that gap pour the waters of the Brahmaputra and the Ganga. Like the Peninsula, the Shillong Plateau is made up of ancient quartzites, shales, schists, and granites, reaching heights of around 1,800 m.

These hills marked the sharp end of the advancing Indian plate as it forced itself NE under the Asian landmass. In doing so it grossly distorted the easternmost hills of the Arakan so that they now run N-S in parallel ridges. Heights rarely exceed 2,100 m, although the highest point on the Indo-Burmese border, **Saramati** (formerly Mount Victoria) is 3,810 m.

Climate

The whole region is in one of the wettest monsoon belts in the world. The driest area, a tiny pocket in central Assam, affected by the rainshadow of the Shillong Plateau, has over 1600 mm rain a year. The rest of the Assam Valley has between 1600 mm and 3200 mm a year, while the wettest parts of the Shillong Plateau has received well over double that.

Given that rainfall, and the warm temperatures at lower altitudes, many of the hills are covered with dense forest, now much degraded. This has stemmed partly from the shifting cultivation practised by tribal peoples who have been forced into ever more intensive use of land by their own increased population, and by the spread of settled agriculture from the plains into the valleys of the hills. On top of these pressures has come commercial forestry. Bamboo forest is common – in places it has been described by Oscar Spate as "like a hayfield over 10 metres high". Elsewhere mixed deciduous and evergreen forest is common. Assam still has more forest than any other state in India.

People

People of the NE are as diverse in origin as in any other part of S Asia. They show strong Mongoloid elements, and the tribal people who comprise the overwhelming majority of the population of the region have been welded together from Aryan and mongoloid races who originally came from China, Tibet, Thailand and Burma and possess very distinct cultures with a variety of musical, dance and folk traditions and religious practices with Hindu, Buddhist and animist backgrounds.

A wide range of tribal people – Garo, Khasi, Jaintia in Meghalaya, Nagas and Mizos to the S, to give just a few examples, have until recently tried to keep themselves to themselves, and have resisted integration into the wider political unit of India. The local *Ahom* population of the Assam Valley itself has long been intermixed with immigrant Bengalis, Hindus from Calcutta and Muslims from Sylhet and the northern regions of what is now Bangladesh. The towns have minorities from further afield in India, notably Marwari businessmen from Rajasthan, who control trade throughout the region.

Economy

Agriculture The economy of the NE is sharply divided between the settled agricultural economy of the rice growing valleys, notably the Brahmaputra, and the tribal economy of the hills, with its dependence on the forests and forest products, and a tradition of shifting cultivation. Increasing population pressure is forcing changes in agriculture, less and less land being available in the hill tracts and in the Brahmaputra Valley for extending land under cultivation.

Industry and resources Oil and natural gas are by far the most important natural resources, and have been exploited for over fifty years, but most of the product is exported from the region. There is little heavy industry, though some engineering work related to the oil industry is carried out.

Craft industries Handloom weaving is the major cottage industry and unlike other regions here the women are the principal weavers. A young girl's dowry usually includes a loom. Tribal designs and weaves make the items of clothing and table linen unique. The patterns may reflect the courage and valour of the Naga warrior, the tragic tales in local folklore or the coils of a legendary snake. The wild silks are especially noteworthy of the region, in particular the golden 'muga' of Assam as well as the 'endi' and 'tassar'. It is believed that the finer mulberry silk industry was also already established in Manipur long before the British are thought to have introduced it into India.

In Manipur, cushions and mats are made of a locally grown spongy reed called 'kounaphak'. Cane and bamboo, of which there is a plentiful supply, has led to the hill-states producing a wide range of basketry, both useful and ornamental, including the traditional 'sitalpatti' or cool floor covering. Fine wood carving too has an old tradition, especially in Assam.

Tribal dances performed by the 60 or so groups that live in the region are performed in locally woven costumes, exotic head dresses of feathers and animal relics, ornaments of cowrie shells and beads and gleaming spears.

ASSAM

Assam's area of 78,438 sq km, a little smaller than Portugal, makes it the largest of the hill-states in the NE, and its population in 1991 of 24 million, dwarfs that of the surrounding ring of tribal states.

Social indicators *Literacy* was estimated at 37% in 1981 but there has been no accurate assessment for two decades. *Newspaper circulation*: 5:1000, the lowest but one in India. *Birth rate-rural* 35:100 *urban* 24:1000 *Infant mortality-rural* 103:1000 *births, urban* at 72:1000 – among the highest in India. Yet population growth has been faster than almost anywhere else in the country. If its average growth had been the same as that in the rest of India throughout this century its present population would be less than half its current size. *Registered graduate job seekers* (1985) 510,000. *Average annual income per head* : Rs 1200 in 1981, ranking sixteenth among Indian states. *Inflation 1981-87* 66%.

Religion 72% Hindu, 26% Muslim, 2% others.

Towns and cities Less than 12% of Assam's population lives in towns. Guwahati is the largest city with an estimated population of 500,000.

Transport Inland transport locally has focused strongly on the river, for the Brahmaputra is navigable up to the point at which it enters the State. A metalled road, the Assam High Road, now runs the length of the State. Guwahati is connected by air to Calcutta with a flight time is 1 hour. The old rail links with Calcutta and with Chittagong ran through East Bengal and the links were cut when Pakistan was created in 1947. A new but very roundabout link has been created through W Bengal.

The Land
Occupying the long narrow floor of the **Brahmaputra Valley**, Assam lies just to the N of 26°N. It stretches nearly 800 kms from E to W but on average is only 80 kms wide. The Himalayas to the N and the **Shillong Plateau** to the S can be clearly seen. The valley floor, even in the rainshadow of the Shillong Plateau, still receives heavy rainfall during the monsoon season of June to October. This is often more than 1800 mm, while elsewhere rainfall exceeds 2500 mm.

Physically Assam is dominated by the mighty **Brahmaputra**, one of the great rivers of the world. Having flowed eastwards to the N of the Himalayas it turns sharply S and then passes through the Assam valley from E to W for over 700 km before entering Bangladesh. Rarely more than 80 km wide, the river valley not only has a fertile alluvial plain growing rice, but is also famous for its tea and for the two game reserves at Kaziranga and Manas. The valley floor is covered in recent alluvium, often rather coarse. *Earthquakes* are common, the 1950 earthquake which had its epicentre on the border between Assam and Tibet being estimated as the fifth largest earthquake in the world.

Although most of Assam is low-lying it has some beautiful scenery and some outstanding game reserves. On the banks of the Brahmaputra, the Kaziranga park occupies an area of approximately 430 square km and combines grassland with thorny rattan cane, elephant grass and evergreen forest as well as areas of swampy ground and extensive ponds and lakes. It was declared a game sanctuary in 1926, to save the Indian one-horned rhino which had become threatened with extinction at the turn of the century. The present rhino population has grown to over 1,100 although poachers still kill the animal for its horn. The park also harbours wild buffalo, bison, sambar, swamp deer, hog deer, wild pig, hoolock gibbon, elephants and tiger. There are otters in the river as well as the long-snouted fish-eating crocodile, the *gharial*.

People
Ethnically their origin varies widely, being based on the same mixture of Mongoloid tribes with those of directly India stock, but the predominant language is Assamese. Although the Ahom settlers who came into the valley from Burma were Buddhist most converted to Hinduism. There has been a steady flow of Muslim settlers from Bengal since the late 19th century, a flow which was not stopped by the Partition of India and Pakistan or the creation of Bangladesh. The overwhelming majority of the people continue to live in rural areas, towns accounting for less than 10% of the total population. Literacy was estimated at 37% in 1981 but there has been no accurate assessment for 2 decades.

Economy Agriculture
In addition to rice cultivation, on which peasant farming is based, and a limited amount of maize, Assam is famous for its tea gardens. Rice farming has been less touched by agricultural modernisation than almost

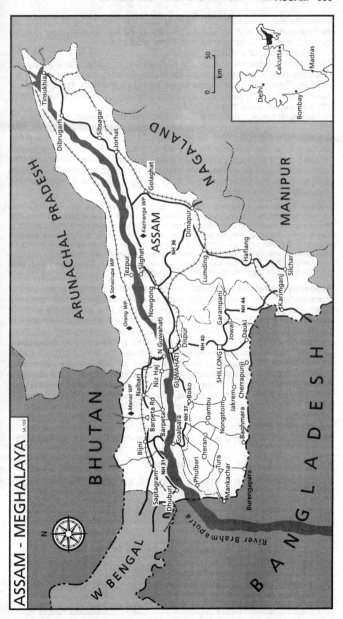

anywhere else in India. In 1991 farmers used less than 10 kg of fertilizer per hectare compared with an all-India average of 60 kg. There are over 800 tea gardens, responsible for over half India's tea production.

Resources and industry Extensive oil reserves were found in the 19th century and *Digboi* became the site of Asia's first oil refinery. Low quality coal resources have also been exploited for several decades, mainly for use on the railways. Potentially there is great scope for Hydro electricity, but the costs of development in a major earthquake area are enormous. Assam remains one of the least industrialised states in the country.

Manufacturing Traditional industries have been based on handicrafts, notably weaving, which continue to be important. Assam's oil industry received a boost from the building of the Guwahati Oil Refinery. The first in the public sector in India, the Noonmati Refinery was erected with Rumanian collaboration in 1961 and it produces petrol, light diesel, aviation fuel and furnace oil. The forests continue to provide essential resources, not just of timber but of products such as resins and tanning material from tree bark. Bamboo is very important, especially for paper making.

History The Ahoms, a Thai Buddhist tribe arrived in the area in the first part of the 13th century, deposed the ruler and established a kingdom with its capital in Sibsagar. They called their kingdom Assam and later adopted Hinduism. The Mughals made several attempts to invade in the following centuries without success, but the Burmese finally invaded Assam at the end of the 18th century. As a result of these invasions much of the valley became virtually depopulated, and the Burmese held it almost continuously until it was ceded to the East India Company in 1826. The British administered it in name until 1947, though many areas were effectively beyond the reach of normal British government.

Modern political development At Partition, Sylhet district was allocated to Pakistan. Since then Assam has also lost most of its tribal areas which have been given independent statehood. The Assam Valley is in a strategically sensitive corridor for India, lying close to the Chinese frontier. Its sensitivity has been increased by the tension between local Assamese and immigrant groups. Since the late 1970s attention has focused on Muslim immigrants from Bangladesh, and severe political disturbances occurred through the early 1980s. The then Prime Minister Rajiv Gandhi achieved an Accord in 1985 with the *Asom Gana Parishad*, the new opposition party which emerged as a result of the struggles. The AGP is still in power. However, for most of the period since Independence the Congress Party dominated politics. The State sends 14 members to the Lok Sabha. In five of the seven elections held until 1980 the Congress won over 50% of the vote and at least 9 of the seats. After the Accord in 1985 the Asom Gana Parishad won 33% of the vote and 7 seats in the Lok Sabha elections. In the 126 member State Assembly it won 65 of the 126 seats to the Congress Party's 25.

Guwahati

Until recently Guwahati (formerly *Gauhati*) was the capital. (The new capital is *Dispur*, just S of the city) *Population* 500,000 approx. Assamese, Bengalis, people from other NE hill states. *Altitude* 55 m. Monsoon months May to Sept. *Best season* October to March to avoid heavy rains. *Clothing* Summer – cottons, Winter – light woollens.

	Jan	Feb	Mar	Apr	May	Jun	Jul	Aug	Sep	Oct	Nov	Dec	Av/Tot
Max (°C)	23	27	30	32	31	32	32	32	30	27	25	27	29
Min (°C)	10	12	16	20	23	25	26	26	25	22	17	12	20
Rain (mm)	17	9	73	136	276	351	373	294	190	86	8	7	1820

Local Festival *Magh Bihu* in January and *Bohag Bihu* and *Rongali Bihu* in mid-April, the week-long New Year festivities are celebrated with singing and dancing. Mar – *Sivratri* is celebrated on Peacock Island at the Umananda Temple with all night vigil and hymns and prayers. Sep – *Manasa Festival* at the Kamakshya Temple in honour of the Snake goddess. You can watch devotees in unusual costumes dancing and going into trances from galleries built for the purpose on the hillside above the temple.

Travel Guwahati is connected by air to Calcutta by both Indian Airlines and Vayudoot and the flight time is 1 hour. Transfer coaches or taxis are available from the airport to the city centre which is 25 km away.

Guwahati, on the site of the ancient capital of many kingdoms, was once known as *Pragjyotishpur*, ("the city of astrology"). It stands in a commanding position on the river Brahamaputra and features in the Indian epics. For centuries it was ruled by local chieftains. It has been, since very early times, a vital link with the N E for both communication and trade, and was also a seat of learning and a centre of Hindu pilgrimage. As early as the 7th century, Hiuen Tsang, the Chinese traveller described its beautiful mountains, forests and wildlife.

Places of interest 12 km from Guwahati is the beautiful site of the **Basistha Ashram**. The ashram believed to occupy the site where the sage **Vasistha** lived is a natural beauty spot with three mountain streams flowing nearby. **Guwahati Oil Refinery** The first in the public sector in India, the Noonmati Refinery was erected with Rumanian collaboration in 1961 and produces petrol, light diesel, aviation fuel and furnace oil. **Janardhan Temple** In the heart of the city atop the hillock Suklesvar the temple was rebuilt in the 17th century having been consecrated in the 10th. It has an image of the Lord Buddha which is an unique blend of Hinduism and Buddhism.

Kamakshya Temple 8 km NW of Guwahati by bus or taxi. Believed to be an ancient Khasi sacrificial site it has the temple on the sacred Nilachal Hill which is dedicated to the goddess Kamakshya and has been a well known centre for Tantric Hinduism and worshippers of Sakti (a part of her body is said to have fallen here when Siva was carrying her to Mount Kailasa). Re-built in 1665 after the original 10th century temple was destroyed by a Brahmin who had become a Muslim convert in the 16th century, it typifies Assamese temple architecture with its distinctive sikhara or spire in the shape of a beehive, the nymph motifs and the long turtle back hall. The hill top also affords a panoramic view of the Brahmaputra and the surrounding region. **Navagrah Temple** The temple of nine planets, W of Chitrachal Hill was the ancient seat of astronomy and astrology for which Pragjyotishpur was named.

Umananda Temple Dedicated to Siva, it stands on Peacock Island in the Brahmaputra as it flows through the city and can be reached by ferry. An Ahom king built the temple in 1594 believing Siva's consort, Uma, to have stayed.

Services

Hotels Mostly around 20 km. from airport and close to railway. **C** *Brahmaputra Ashok*, M.G. Rd. T 32632/3, Cable: Brahmashok, Telex: 0235-2422. 50 rm. Central a/c. *Ushaban* restaurant and bar, exchange, shops, travel. **C** *Chitral Regency*, H.P. Brahmachari Rd, Paltan Bazar. T 26877, Cable: Regency, Telex: 0235-2401. 44 rm. *Mahal* restaurant, bar, exchange, TV. **C** *Prag Continental*, Motilal Nehru Rd, Pan Bazar. T 33785/7, Cable: Atithi, Telex: 0235-2403. 62 rm. All public areas and some rooms are a/c. Restaurants *Davat* and *Bagicha* on terrace, *Continental Café*, beauty parlour, travel, TV. **C** *Coronet Dynasty*, S.S. Rd. T 24353. 68 rm. 2 restaurants and bar (*Snack House* for meals and buffet and *Tandoor* for Indian). **C** *Urvashi*, near the airport. T 28893. 25 rm. Central a/c. Restaurant for residents, exchange, TV, complimentary airport transfer.

D *Kuber International*, Hem Barua Rd. T 32601, Cable: Hotelkumber, Telex: 0235-2251. 75 rm. all a/c. Well appointed, revolving restaurant '*Orbit*', *Parag*, and terrace barbecue *Panorama*, bar, terrace top barbecue, shops, TV. **D** *Nandan*, Paltan Bazar, G.S. Rd. T 32621/9, Cable: Nandan, Telex: 0235-2267. 55 rm. A/c. 2 restaurants, *Upavan* snack bar, bar, shops, travel, TV. Tourist luxury buses to other hill states. Recommended. **D** *Belle Vue*, M.G. Rd. T

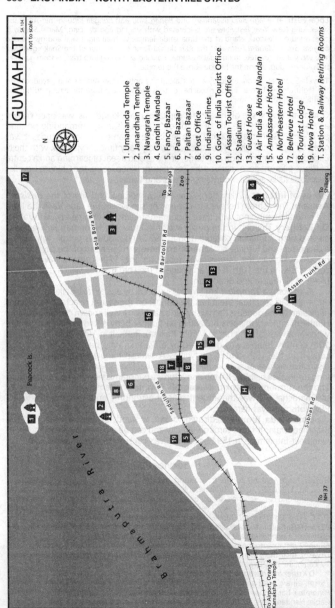

GUWAHATI

not to scale

SA 104

N

1. Umananda Temple
2. Janardhan Temple
3. Navagrah Temple
4. Gandhi Mandap
5. Fancy Bazaar
6. Pan Bazaar
7. Paltan Bazaar
8. Post Office
9. Indian Airlines
10. Govt. of India Tourist Office
11. Assam Tourist Office
12. Stadium
13. Guest House
14. Air India & Hotel Nandan
15. Ambassador Hotel
16. Northeastern Hotel
17. Bellevue Hotel
18. Tourist Lodge
19. Nova Hotel
T. Station & Railway Retiring Rooms

Brahmaputra River

Peacock Is.

Bola Bora Rd

G N Bardoloi Rd

To Kaziranga

Zoo

Saolihan Rd

Assam Trunk Rd

Subhas Rd

To Shillong

To NH 37

To Airport, Orang & Kamakhya Temple

28291/2, Cable: Belleview, Guwahati, Telex: 0235-2322. 45 rm. A/c. Simple. Located on river front. *Renee* restaurant and permit room, exchange. **D** *Siddharth*, Hem Barua Rd, Fancy Bazar, opp. Taxi Stand. T 33746/49, Cable: Siddarth. 36 rm. A/c. Restaurant, exchange, travel, TV. **D** *Samrat*, Assam Trunk Rd, Santipur. T 31479. 18 rm. A/c. Restaurant and bar, travel. **D** *North Eastern*, G.N.B. Rd. T 28281/2. 18 rm. A/c. Licensed dining room serving Indian and Chinese food, billiards. **D** *Ambassador*, Paltan Bazar. T 28341/2. A/c. and non-a/c rm. Indian dining hall. **E** *Maruti*, Radha Bazar, Fancy Bazar. T 34811/13. 66 rm some a/c. Vegetarian meals only. **E** *Mayur*, Paltan Bazar. T 26288. 158 double rm some a/c. Indian vegetarian restaurant, travel.

The hotels above, except *Brahmaputra Ashok* and *Urvashi* which are centrally air-conditioned, also provide less expensive non a/c accommodation. Most medium priced and budget hotels tend to provide Indian meals only.

F *Railway Retiring Rooms*, book at the Enquiry Counter. T 34831/2. Double rms and 4-bedded dormitories. **F** *Tourist Lodge* (Govt. of Assam), opp. Railway Station. T 24475. 5 rm. Conveniently situated, fairly clean with good toilet facilities. Service indifferent and no catering. Good value for short stay. Contact Tourist Information Officer, Guwahati. **F** *Hotel Joydurga*, K.C. Sen Rd, Paltan Bazar. T 24138. 30 rm. Rooms small, Indian food only. *Circuit House* and *Dak Bungalow* and a *YMCA Hostel* on Chatribari Christian Hospital Compound with double rms. Simple and inexpensive hotels in Paltan Bazar with single rooms: *Rajdoot Palace*. T 24298. 57 rm. *Sukhmani*, K.C. Sen Rd. T33235. 53 rm. *Embassy*. T 32927.

Restaurants The restaurants in the larger hotels are the only ones that offer continental cuisine and also Indian or Chinese meals. There are a few other restaurants serving Indian and Chinese food. *Paradise* on Moniram Dewan Rd, *Silpukhuri* does Assamese *thalis* as well as Chinese and Indian. T 26904. *Piccadilly* and *Sunflower* (a/c) restaurants are in Pan Bazar and offer Chinese and Indian menus.

Bars Again these are situated in the top hotels.

Banks Central Bank of India, T 25980. United Bank of India, T 23270 are in Panbazar. Punjab National Bank, T 32443, United Commercial Bank, T 23171 and State Bank of India, T 25436, Foreign Exchange, T 23484 are in Fancy Bazar. Grindlays Bank is in Lakhotia, T 31704. The banks provide foreign exchange facilities.

Shopping Assamese Muga, Pat and Endi silks, hats, bamboo and cane baskets, flutes, drums, pipes and ivory carvings are typical of the area (though as elsewhere in S Asia ivory exports are now banned). *Pragjyotika Assam Emporium* at Ambari, sells silks, bamboo, wood, brass and ceramics. T 23439. *Purbashree*, G.N. Bardoloi Rd has traditional craft items from all the NE hill-states. *Assam Co-operative Silk House* on Hem Barua Rd, Pan Bazar has pure silk items including saris with typical geometric patterns in cotton ranging from Rs 500 to over Rs 2000. *The Manipur Emporium* is in Paltan Bazar and *Tantuja* for Bengal handloom is in Ulubari. There are many other shops in Panbazar and Fancy Bazar where it may be necessary to bargain. *Camera films* are available at the following stores: S. Ghoshal, H.B. Rd. T 28095. Apsara Studio, Pan Bazar. Hara Kamani Studio, Pan Bazar.

Local transport Airport to city transfer by *taxi* costs Rs 25 per head or Rs 125 for the taxi and city sightseeing. Rs 55 per hr. A day's hire which allows for trips outside the city limits costs Rs 300 plus fuel for 10 hrs. *Auto-rickshaws* are available for the transfer from the airport as well as city sightseeing and costs about half the rate for taxis, Rs 60 for the airport transfer and Rs 25 per hr city sightseeing. There is a city *bus service* but for flexibility the State Government's Department of Tourism has *cars*, jeeps and mini-buses for hire. There is a complicated system of charging but overall amounts to approximately Rs 3-4 per km with a minimum of Rs 50 for first hour, Rs 30 for subsequent hours but a minimum charge of Rs 240 for out-station journeys by car. Extras for waiting, night halts and hill running. The Inland Waterways Transport Corporation runs a *ferry* to Raja Duar and Madhya Khanda from M.G. Rd Ferry Station. Re 0.50 one way.

Entertainment The local daily carries programme information on cinemas and theatres. *Apsara Cinema* at M Basti is a/c and *Anuradha* at Bamuni Maidan is air-cooled. There are 2 auditoria in Ambari-Rabindra Bhawan and the District Library Auditorium.

Sports Assam Swimming Club, Ambari. B.P. Chaliha Swimming Pool. Nehru Stadium for outdoor sports and there is also a Flying Club on Station Rd.

Museums Assam Forest Museum, S Kamrup Division has collections of timber, cane and ivory work, tusks and horns, and models of buildings and bridges. Open 1000-1600 on weekdays and 1000-1330 on Sat. Guide service. **Assam Government Cottage Industries Museum** is open 1000-1600 weekdays and 1000-1300 Sat. **Assam State Museum** has collections of archaeology, sculpture, paintings, metal, ivory and woodwork, costumes and ethnology. Open 1000-1630, Tue-Sat and 0800-1200 on Sun. Closed Mon and on second Sat. Entry Re 0.50. A small museum, well lit and thoughtfully displayed with notes in Assamese and English where you can get a good idea of Ahom and neighbouring cultures. Guide book available. Guide service and films occasionally. Photography with permission. The **Veterinary College museum**, open 1000-1600. Closed Sun. **Commercial Museum**, Guwahati University has collections of art and craft, commercial products, minerals and rocks, coins etc. Open 1230-1830, Mon-Sat., closed Sun and University holidays. Entry free. No photography.

Parks and Zoos   The *Assam State Zoo and Botanical Gardens* has swamp tapirs, rhinos, tigers, lions, panthers among other species as well as rich birdlife, particularly interesting because there are animals and birds of NE India which are not often seen elsewhere. It is largely an open-enclosure zoo with landscaped gardens. There are restaurants and souvenir shops. Opening times vary according to the season but usually Sep – Mar 0700-1600, Apr to Oct 0800-1730. Entry Re 1. Access by bus, taxi and auto rickshaw.

Hospitals and Medical services   Medical College and Hospital, Bhangagarh. T 87477. M.M. Choudhury Hospital, Pan Bazar. T 32446. Satribari Christian Hospital. T 24469. Red Cross Society, Chandmari. T 25144.

Post and Telegraphs   *GPO*, Pan Bazar. T 23534. *Central Telegraph Office*, Pan Bazar. T 24604. Several other post offices in different parts of the city including Fancy and Paltan Bazar.

Places of worship   *Hindu* temples are listed under places of interest above. Others are Silpukhri, Kalibari, Noormati and Ganesh Mandir near High Court Building. *Christian* – St. Joseph's Catholic Church, Anandaram Baruah Road and the Baptist Church are in Pan Bazar. *Others* There is a Jain Temple and a Sikh gurdwara at Fancy Bazar. Muslims have several mosques in different parts of the city.

Travel Agents and Tour Operators   *Rhino Travels*, Motilal Nehru Rd, Pan Bazar. T 27838. *Sheba Travels*, G.N.B. Rd, Ambari. T 23280. *BSS Travels*, Fancy Bazar. T 23544. These act as agents for Indian Airlines and Vayudoot and as handling agents for other operators organizing tours to the game reserves and Shillong. *Pelican Travels* in the Hotel Brahmaputra Ashok are agents for British Airways. *Blue Hill Travels*, Paltan Bazar. T 31427. Hotel Brahmaputra Ashok. T 32632. In season, hr long cruises on the river Brahmaputra cost Rs 25 per person (min 5). *Assam Valley Tour and Travels*, G.S. Rd, Paltan Bazar. **Green Valley Travels**, G.S. Rd. T 25289.

Tourist Offices and Information   Government of India Tourist Office, B.K. Kakati Rd, Ulubari. T 31381. Airport counter. T 82204. Government of Assam, Director of Tourism, Station Rd. T 27102. Information Office. T 24475. 1000-1700. Also counters at the airport and the Main Hall at the Rly Station.

Government of Meghalaya, Tourist Information Office, ASTC Bus Stand, Paltan Bazar. 1000-1700. Assam Information Centre, 8 Russell St, Calcutta, T 248341 and at A6 State Emporia Building, Baba Kharak Singh Marg, New Delhi, T 343961.

Tours   State Department of Tourism runs tours from the Tourist Lodge on Station Rd. *City sightseeing*: Basistha Ashram, Zoo, Museum, Kamakshya Temple, Govt. Sales Emporium. Wed and Sun. 0800-1600. Rs 25 (adult), Rs 20 (child). *Shillong*: Day trip. Wed and Sun. Rs 60 (adult), Rs 45 (child). *Kaziranga*: Overnight trip departing at 1100 and returning at 1500 on the following day. Sanctuary visit on elephant. Mon,Th, Sat, Sun. October to May. Rs 197 (adult), Rs 147 (child). *Manas*: Tiger Reserve visit. Fri. Rs 155 (adult), Rs 100 (child).

Air   This is the only means of travel permitted for foreign tourists entering the region. **Indian Airlines** Calcutta, daily (+ 3 others), 1450, 1 hr; **Delhi**, Tue, Thur and Sun (+ 1 other), 1000, 2 hr 25 min; **Dibrugarh**, Mon, Wed, Fri and Sat, 1000, 45 min; **Dimapur**, Mon, Wed, Fri and Sat, 1250, 35 min; **Bagdogra**, Mon, Wed, Fri and Sat, 1445, 45 min; **Imphal**, Tue, Wed and Fri, 0700, 45 min; **Patna** – no flights; **Agartala**, Wed, Fri, Sat and Sun, 0825, 40 min.

Vayudoot (NB These services are under review at the time of going to press and may not be available.) **Jorhat**, Mon, Wed and Fri (+ 1 other), 0900, 1 hr 20 min; **Calcutta**, Mon-Sat, 1700, 1 hr 50 min; **Shillong**, daily, 1635, 10 min; From **Silchar**, Tue, Thur and Sat (+ 1 other), 0630, 50 min. In addition **Pawan Hans** operates a helicopter service to Shillong and Tura. The airport is 25 km from the centre of town and the IAC transfer coach and Assam T222ourism Coach connect with Calcutta flights, the charges are Rs 25 and Rs 15 per head respectively. Rhino Travels and Brahmaputra Ashok also provide coach transfers. Taxis are also available and can be shared. Indian Airlines, Paltan Bazar, G.S. Rd, (T 31640), Reservations (T 33616) and airport (T 82235). Open 0900-1600. Vayudoot, Parmeshwari Building,

Chhatribari. T 33194. 0900-1700. Pawan Hans Handling Agents, Rhino Travels, Motilal Nehru Rd, Pan Bazar. T 26016. 0900-1800.

Rail The town is linked with all parts of the country by broad gauge and metre gauge railway. **Dibrugarh Town**: *Tinsukia Mail*, 5907, daily, 1315, 17 hr 45 min; **Calcutta (H)**: *Kanchenjunga Exp*, 2558 (AC/II), daily, 2230, 22 hr 20 min; *Kamrup Exp*, 5660 (AC/II), daily, 0745, 22 hr 45 min; To **Delhi (D)**: *Tinsukia Mail*, 2455 (AC/II), daily, 1315, 40 hr 40 min. Enquiries: T 26644. Reservations: T 32288. 0945-1700.

Road 1,151 km from Calcutta by road, Guwahati is well connected by road to all major centres of the NE region being at the junction of National Highways 31, 37 and 40.

Buses State Transport Corporations of the neighbouring hill states all provide good links with the capital of Assam with Deluxe and Express buses. Assam State Transport Corporation Bus Stand, Paltan Bazar. T 24709. Reservations 0630-1230,1330-1700. Private coaches and taxi services are also available and some companies operating from Paltan Bazar provide extra facilities such as waiting rooms, left-luggage counters and snack bars. Blue Hill Travels. T 31427. Hotel Brahmaputra Ashok. T 32632. Green Valley Travels. T 25289. Network Tours and Travels, Paltan Bazar. Daily services to the following towns: **Silchar** 1730. **Shillong** from 0630 to 1730 (3 hr 30 min). **Kohima** 2000, 2015, 2030 (13 hr). **Itanagar** 1830 (11 hr). **Aizawl** 1830 (11 hr). **Imphal** 2000, 2015, 2030. **Siliguri** 1830, 1845, 1900. **Tezpur** 0700.

    Distances between Guwahati and some places of interest in the region: Shillong 103 km, Kaziranga National Park 233 km, Manas Wildlife Sanctuary 176 km, Itanagar 401 km, Imphal 579 km.

Excursions 24 km across the river is **Hajo**, a centre for different religions. The Hayagriba Madhab, the best known in the group of Hindu temples is believed by a section of Buddhists to be where the Buddha attained Nirvana. It is also a Muslim pilgrimage centre since the mosque known as Pao Mecca built by Pir Ghiasuddin Aulia, is supposed to have one fourth (pao) of the sanctity of Mecca.

    24 km away on the N bank of the Brahmaputra is **Sualkashi**, the famous silk-producing village. Every household is involved with weaving of *Muga*, *Endi* or *tassar* silk. There are also brass-workers here. **Ferry services** operate between Guwahati and N Guwahati.

Guwahati to Kaziranga

The road from Guwahati runs through forest covered hills, small villages, low-lying fields with stands of coconut palms before entering tea estates. Even in the tea growing areas there are a low-lying shallow-water expanses before the road begins to rise quite sharply as it approaches the **Kaziranga National Park**.

    Altitude 65 m. *Climate* Temp. Summer Max. 35°C Min. 18°C Winter Max. 24°C Min. 7°C. Annual rainfall 2300 mm, heavy in summer. *Best Season* Nov-mid April. Closed mid April-mid Oct during monsoons. *Clothing* Cottons but carry a jacket for sudden cool weather. Woollens in the winter. Guwahati is 215 km from Kohora, the entry point of the Kaziranga Wildlife Sanctuary on the NH37 and 1,300 km from Calcutta.

    On the banks of the Brahmaputra, the park occupies an area of approximately 430 square km and combines grassland with thorny rattan cane, elephant grass and evergreen forest, as well as areas of swampy ground and extensive ponds and lakes. The Karbi Anglong Hills rise around the park, while the river flows as its northern boundary. There are a number of rivulets which flow down to the flood plain, bringing down rich silt and spreading out into shallow lakes called **bheels***. The habitat varies from swamps and marshes to grassland, savannah woodland, rising to drier deciduous forests and finally to tropical evergreen forests. It is therefore able to support a large variety of wildlife.

    Kaziranga was declared a game sanctuary in 1908, to save the Indian one-horned rhino which had become threatened with extinction at the turn of the century. The present **rhino** population is over 1,100 although poachers still kill the animal for its horn, and you can easily see them in the marshes and grasslands. The park also harbours wild buffalo, bison, sambar, swamp deer, hog deer, wild pig, hoolock gibbon, elephants and tiger. The weaver birds make interesting bottle-shaped straw nests which you can spot hanging from the branches. There is a rich variety of shallow-water fowl including egrets, pond herons, river terns, black-necked stork, fishing eagles, and adjutant storks which breed in the park and a pelicanry. The grey pelican can be seen nesting in tall trees near the village. There are otters in the river and long-snouted fish-eating crocodile, the *gharial*.

Jeeps, minibuses and elephants may be hired for seeing the game reserve. Whereas the elephants cover less ground than motor vehicles, they can get a lot closer to the wildlife than the vehicles. The Deputy Director, Department of Tourism, Kaziranga has jeeps for hire by the hr, the rates take into account a given distance. The rate for 1 hr at Rs 50 covers 15 km and for 5 hrs at Rs 125, 60 km. Elephants carry 4 and a seat may be booked through the Forest Range Officer for Rs 18 per adult or Rs 12 per child. **NB** Those taking a car or a jeep around the sanctuary **must be accompanied by a Forest Department guide**, provided free, who can give directions as well as spot wild life. Cars and jeeps are charged an entry fee plus a charge per person for forest viewing which is Rs 5 for adults, Re 1 for students. Fees for cameras start at Rs 5 for a simple still camera without telephoto lens rising to Rs 500 for a 35 mm Ciné camera.

The park roads are open 0800-1100 and 1400-1630. Elephant rides between 0500-0600, 0630-0730 and 1530-1630. There are three road routes for visiting the park. The *Kaziranga Range* – Kohora, Daflang, Foliomari; the *Western Range* – Baguri, Monabeel, Bimoli, Kanchanjuri; and the *Eastern Range* – Agortoli, Sohola, Rangamatia. The *observation towers* are situated at Sohola, Mihimukh, Kathpara, Foliamari and Harmoti.

Tours from Guwahati Assam Tourism offers a two-day tour from Guwahati during the season, starting on Th, Sat and Sun which includes food, accommodation, transport and sanctuary visit on elephant back. Adults Rs 197, Children Rs 147.

Hotels D *Kaziranga Forest Lodge*. T 29, Cable:Tourism. A/c and non a/c single and double rms. Restaurant with reasonable meals and bar. Best rms with private balconies overlooking the Karbi hills (more comfortable, suitable for elderly or those travelling with children). Reservations: Manager, ITDC. **E** *Kaziranga Tourist Lodge* has 2 bungalows. No.1 (western style) has 5 rms. Rates vary according to whether they are on the upper (better) or lower floor, a/c or non a/c. No. 2 (Indian style) has 7 rm. Surcharge for a/c, clean, good upkeep and catering. *Dormitory* at Kohora, rates between Rs 15 without and Rs 25 with linen. Two 12 bedded rms and two with 3 beds only. Reasonably clean but no cupboards or lockers. Shared toilet facilities. Meals, both Indian and Western at Tourist Lodge. Suitable for the young prepared to rough it. Reservations with the Deputy Director of Tourism, Kaziranga Sanctuary, Sibsagar District. T 23, Cable: Tourism.

Post Office There are post offices nr the Tourist Lodge and at the Park. The Wildlife Society has a **library** of books and magazines and can organize wildlife films for large groups of foreign tourists.

Air Jorhat, 88 km away is the nearest airport. Daily Indian Airlines flights to Jorhat from Calcutta via Guwahati, Calcutta having the nearest international airport. See **page 589. NB Groups of foreign tourists may only use Guwahati airport. See page 579.**

Rail Nearest railway station is at Furkating, 75 km away with a metre gauge line to Guwahati. Buses connect Furkating with Kaziranga via Golaghat. The Chaparmukh – Silghat Town branch line of the Northern Frontier Railway stops at Jakhalbandha 45 km away.

Road Kaziranga is on the National Highway 37 which crosses the Brahmaputra from Goalpara Ghat in Western Assam. Assam Road Transport operates buses from Guwahati and Jorhat which stop at Kohora where the accommodation is located. Private companies operating long-distance coaches make request stops at Kohora. The *Forest Lodge* at Kaziranga has 10 seats reserved on the Express coach between Golaghat and Guwahati.

Manas Wildlife Sanctuary *Altitude* 70 m. *Area* 2,800 square km. *Climate* Temp. Summer Max. 35°C Min. 18°C, Winter Max. 24°C Min. 7°C. Annual rainfall 410 cm, July-Sep. *Season* Nov to Apr. *Clothing* Summer Cottons, Winter Woollens. Closed during the monsoons from July to Sep.

Scenically the **Manas Wildlife Sanctuary** is one of India's most beautiful. It lies in the foothills of the Himalayas, S-E of the river Manas, which with its associated rivers *Hakua* and *Beki* separate India from the neighbouring kingdom of Bhutan. Over half the area is covered with tall grass and scattered patches of woodland with *simul*, *khoir*, *udal*, *sida*, *bohera* and *kanchan* trees. This changes to dense semi-evergreen forest in the upper reaches and even to conifer on hills abutting Bhutan.

The forests are home to most of the larger animals found in Kaziranga, most common being wild buffalo, swamp deer, hog deer, sambar and elephant. In addition it also has pigmy hog, the hispid hare, the rare capped golden langur and the tiger. The **Manas Tiger Reserve**, a core area of 360 sq km was demarcated in 1927/8 when the preservation programme 'Project Tiger' was launched. The sanctuary is also rich in birdlife attracting many migratory flocks including redstarts, forktails, cormorants and ruddy shelduck. Otters are frequently seen in the Manas river it is possible to take a boat ride. Between Dec and Mar the river fish made it an angler's paradise but this has been banned since 1988. Boats for 2 to 8 people can be hired for 4 to 8 hr from the Forest Beat Officer, Mothanguri. To see the animals from close range it is advisable to take an elephant ride which starts from Mothanguri, inside the sanctuary. The ride takes 3 hr and for 3 people the cost is Rs 30. The timings are 0900-1200, 1400-1700. The visiting arrangements by car, taxi or minibus, and charges for entry and camera fees are similar to Kaziranga (see above).

Guwahati, 176 km away is the nearest airport. **NB** Foreign tourists must at present travel in groups through approved tour agents and via Guwahati. **See page 579.** The nearest railway station is at Barpeta Road, 40 km from Mothanguri, with connections to Guwahati and Calcutta. There is a good fair weather road from Manas to Barpeta which in turn has a very good road to Guwahati. Barpeta Road is the nearest place with medical facilities, a Tourist Information Office, Banks and a Post Office.

Hotels *Manas Forest Lodge* which is built on a hill overlooking the river and the Forest Department's *Forest Lodge* and *Bhutan Tourist Lodge*, Mothanguri provide very simple and inexpensive accommodation which is clean and well maintained and must be booked well in advance. Cook available but visitors must carry their own provisions. Camp site available for visitors with tents. The prefabricated *Rest House* provides linen but has no electricity. Open Oct-May. Reservations: Divisional Forest Officer, Wildlife Division, PO Barpeta Rd, Assam, T 19 or Field Director, Manas Tiger Reserve, PO Barpeta Rd, Assam.

MEGHALAYA

Meghalaya means "abode of the clouds". The name is appropriate, for the S-facing slopes overlooking Bangladesh are also the wettest place on earth. Just S of the Brahmaputra River, Meghalaya is a compact and isolated state. It is bordered on the N by Assam and on the S by Bangladesh. It covers 22,500 square kilometres of rolling plateau, and lies in a severe earthquake belt. The entire town of Shillong was destroyed in an earthquake in 1896. It is one of the smallest States in India having a population of only 1 million.

Social indicators *Literacy* Male 35%, Female 30% *Newspaper circulation* 3,000 *Birth rate*-rural 33:1000,urban 17:1000 *Death rate* Rural 9% *Death rate* urban 4% *Registered graduate job seekers* (1985) 13,000 *Average annual income per head:* Rs 1400

Religion Hindu 18%, Muslim 3%, Christian 53%, Tribal and animist religions 26%.

Towns and cities 20% of the population live in towns. Shillong, the capital, is the only large town, with a population of 220,000.

Transport The nearest railway is over 100 km away at Guwahati. The state has less than 1000 km of surfaced roads and there is only one major road, from Guwahati to Shillong.

Shillong is connected to Calcutta by air.

The land Meghalaya has been referred to as the 'Scotland of the East' in view of similarity of the climate, terrain and scenery with pine clad hills, beautiful lakes and waterfalls. Much of the plateau is made up of the same ancient granites as are found in peninsular India. Its south facing slope, overlooking Bangladesh, is very steep. The hills rise to heights just under 2,000 m which makes it pleasantly cool despite the fact that it is so close to the tropics. Much is still densely forested.

Climate The altitude of the plateau at 1,500 m moderates the temperatures, but also causes tremendously heavy rainfall as the monsoon winds come N from the Bay of Bengal laden with moisture. **Cherrapunji** has received more than 20,000 mm in one year.

People The people come mainly from three tribes, the **Garos** (who are also found in Bangladesh), the **Khasis** and the **Jaintias**. Each has their own tribal language, Garo, Khasi and Jaintia. Shillong is the only important town, and 80% of the people live in villages.

Economy Agriculture The tribal people practise shifting cultivation. They grow oranges and potatoes as cash crops. Rice, maize and vegetables are grown as food crops.

Mining There are rich mineral deposits, including mica, gypsum and coal, but they are not yet being used.

Manufacturing There is no large scale modern industry. Handicrafts and weaving are as important in Meghalaya as in the other Hill States. Brightly coloured textiles are a speciality.

History Meghalaya is the home of the Khasi, Jaintia and Garo tribes of ancient origin and each with their distinctive cultural heritage and tradition. They had their own small kingdoms until the 19th century when the British annexed them one by one. The Garos were originally from Tibet. They were animists, and once practised human sacrifice. Since the mid-19th century have stopped displaying human skulls in their houses. The Khasis are believed to be Austro-Asiatic. Jaintias are Mongolian and similar to the Shans of Burma. The believed in the universal presence of god and hence they built no temples. The dead are commemorated by erecting **monoliths** and groups of these can be seen in Khasi villages in central Meghalaya on your way from Shillong to Cherrapunji.

Similar monoliths erected by ancient peoples in other parts of the world, as in Brittany, Corsica, Cornwall and Wales are called cromlechs, dolmens or menhirs, the 'men' from the word for 'stone'. Curiously, the Khasi word for stone is also 'men'! In the 19th century many were converted to Christianity by missionaries, although they continued many of their old traditions. They have several distinctive customs. All 3 tribes are matrilineal passing down wealth and property through the female line.

Recent history The hill-state was created on 21 Jan 1972 out of Assam. The Congress Party came to dominate elections to the Lok Sabha after claiming only 36% of the vote in 1977, winning 74% in 1980 and 62% in 1984. However, it has never won more than 25 of the 60 State Assembly seats, local opposition parties, most recently the Hill Peoples Union, claiming the largest minority of seats.

Local festivals A major folk-dance festival, 'Shad Suk Mynsiem', is held each year in Shillong in Apr. In Ashanagiri near Tura, the harvest is celebrated in Nov with the 'Wangala', the hundred drums festival by the Garos. Jowai celebrates the harvest with 'Laho' dances and the 'Behdeinkhlam' in Jun-Jul when Smit hosts the Khasi 'Shed Nongkrem' dance festival.

Shillong

Population 230,000. Khasi, Garo, Jaintia, other hill-tribes and Bengalis *Altitude* 1,496 m. *Climate* Temp Summer Max. 23°C Min. 15°C, Winter Max.16°C Min. 4°C. Annual rainfall 2030 mm, mostly Jun-Sep. *Best Season* October to May. *Clothing* Summer cottons with light woollens, Winter Woollens. Umroi airport is 16 km from the city centre of Shillong.

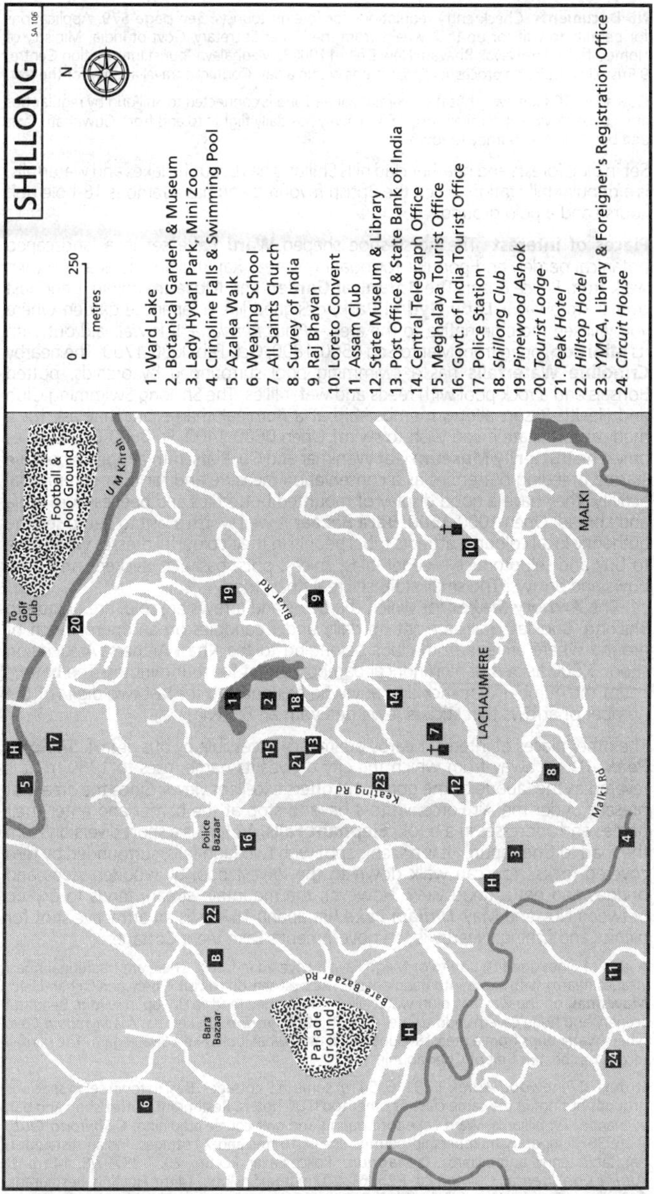

SHILLONG

N

0   250
metres

1. Ward Lake
2. Botanical Garden & Museum
3. Lady Hydari Park, Mini Zoo
4. Crinoline Falls & Swimming Pool
5. Azalea Walk
6. Weaving School
7. All Saints Church
8. Survey of India
9. Raj Bhavan
10. Loreto Convent
11. Assam Club
12. State Museum & Library
13. Post Office & State Bank of India
14. Central Telegraph Office
15. Meghalaya Tourist Office
16. Govt. of India Tourist Office
17. Police Station
18. *Shillong Club*
19. *Pinewood Ashok*
20. *Tourist Lodge*
21. *Peak Hotel*
22. *Hilltop Hotel*
23. YMCA, Library & Foreigner's Registration Office
24. *Circuit House*

Football & Polo Ground

U M Khrah

Golf Club

To

Bivar Rd

MALKI

LACHAUMIERE

Malki Rd

Keating Rd

Police Bazaar

Bara Bazaar Rd

Bara Bazaar

Parade Ground

SA 106

NB Documents Check entry regulations for foreign tourists. **See page 579.** Applications for permits to visit for up to 2 weeks from the Under Secretary, Govt of India, Ministry of Home Affairs, Lok Nayak Bhavan, New Delhi 110003. Meghalaya Tourist Information Centre, 9 Russell St, Calcutta processes applications within a day. Contact a travel agency for the rest.

Guwahati, 103 km away has the nearest railhead and is connected to Shillong by regular bus and coach services. Umroi airport, 16 km away has daily flights to and from Guwahati. Taxis and buses do the journey to town.

Set in pine forests and heather clad hills Shillong has beautiful lakes and waterfalls. is a popular hill-station which the British favoured and has a famous 18-hole golf course and a polo ground.

Places of interest The horse-shoe shaped **Ward Lake** set in a landscaped botanical garden and popular for boating is near Raj Bhavan and is a two min. walk from Police Bazar. The **Botanical Garden** and **Museum** adjoin it and just over a km away is **Lady Hydari Park**, designed like a Japanese garden where you will see the pine native to the area – *Pinus khasiana*. It is well laid out with its **Mini Zoo**, open from Mar to Sep 0500-1800, Oct- Feb 0630-1700. The nearby **Crinoline Waterfalls** has a swimming pool surrounded by orchids, potted Bonsais and a rock pool with reeds and water lilies. The Shillong Swimming Club and Health Resort allows membership at a nominal charge but may ask for a medical certificate if you wish to swim! Open 0600-1400, Fri 0600-0800 Ladies only. **The Butterfly Museum** is at Wankhar and Co, Riatsamthiahopen who have started breeding butterflies as a conservation measure and for their commercial activity. They have a good display of mounted butterflies and beetles from India and abroad. Open 1000-1600. **Bara Bazaar** is well worth a visit to get to see the authentic local colour. It attracts tribal people in their colourful dresses who come to buy and sell produce – vegetables, spices, pots, baskets, chickens and even bows and arrows. The small stalls sell real Khasi food.

The ***Archery Stakes*** for which the bows and arrows are sold, are unique to Shillong. Bookies' stalls are set up daily under canopies on an open stretch of ground where archers from clubs belonging to the Khasi Archers' Association shoot 1,500 arrows at a cylindrical bamboo target for four minutes. The betters count the number that stick and any who has guessed the last two digits of the number of arrows that stick is rewarded with an 8:1 win!

The other places of interest nearby are mostly accessible by bus or taxi. ***Shillong Peak***, 10 km away from which the city derives its name, rises to 1960 m. It is revered as the 'abode of the gods' and offers excellent views. Since the area is at present under the Air Force, visitors have to stop at the barrier and enter their names and addresses in a book. **Elephant Falls,** 12 km, is a short diversion from the road to Cherrapunji. It is a scenic spot with two high falls, surrounded by fern covered rocks. You can walk down to the lowest pool by wooden steps and bridges and get a good view. However, the mountain stream tends to dry up between Nov and May. ***Umiam Lake*** (Barapani) 16 km, is an attractive spot for picnics and fishing. Nearby is the government's Lake View Cottage.

A land of pines and firs, a third of Meghalaya is covered in forest. There are traditional Khasi villages nearby with views into Bangladesh. The best season to visit is between Oct and Feb. **Mawsmai,** on the way has high waterfalls, though they tend to dry up in winter. Beautiful scenery and huge caverns add to the interest. **Mawsynram**, 55 km, has *Mawjymbuin Cave* where water drips from a breast shaped stone onto what looks like a Siva lingam. The rainfall record has beaten that of Cherrapunji.

Hotels C *Pinewood Ashok* T 23116. 54 rm some in 9 cottages. Best in town set in spacious grounds but not in the same class as other top ITDC hotels. Restaurant, coffee shop and bar, exchange, TV, billiards. Ward Lake for boating and golf-course adjoining. **C** *Shillong Club*. T 26938. Temporary membership permits use of 10 rms and 2 cottages. Indian restaurant, bar, table tennis and billiards. **D** *Magnum*, Police Bazar, PO Box 20. T 27797/8. 14 rm. **D** *Alpine Continental*, Quinton Rd, T 25361. 20 km from Shillong. 14 rm. Heating. Restaurant. **E** *Shillong Tourist Hotel*, Polo Rd, T 24933. 60 rm and also very inexpensive dormitory.

Restaurant serving Indian and Chinese food. Also two Assam Tourism's **Tourist Bungalows** on cliff top. Reservations at the office in Police Bazar.

There are several simple hotels charging from around Rs 80-100 for single and Rs 150 for double, some with an Indian restaurant. **Broadway**, G.S. Rd. T 26996. **Godwin**, G.S. Rd. T 26516. **Monsoon**, G.S. Rd, T 23316. **Liza**, Malki Point, Lower Lachumiere, T 27328. No restaurant.

Restaurants *Pinewood Ashok* and the *Tourist Hotel* have good restaurants. Continental cuisine is available at *Ambrosia* on Red Hill Rd, which also serves fast foods and has a pastry shop. There are some Chinese restaurants in Bara Bazar – **Sterling**, **York** and **Abba** in Lower Lachumiere. *Regal* in Police Bazar serves S Indian specialities. There are **bars** in the *Pinewood Ashok* and at the *Shillong Club*.

Banks Several provide exchange facilities. *Bank of Baroda*, Police Bazar. T 26995. *Bank Of India*, Lachumiere. T 26605. *Canara*, Mirullah Building. T 26061. *Central Bank of India*, 29 Cantonment. T 24872. *Indian*, G.S. Rd. T 26990. *Indian Overseas*, Morello Building. T 24616. *Punjab National*, G.S. Rd. T 24848. *State Bank of India*, Gari Khana. T 25491. *Evening Branch at Police Bazar*. T 25391. *Syndicate*, GS Rd. T 23551. *Vijaya*, GS Rd. T 26904.

Shopping You can get handwoven shawls, canework and beautiful butterflies mounted in glass, handicrafts, orange flower honey. The Khasi women's dress, the 'jainsem' is also suitable as a western dress. The emporia are good places to make purchases. **Meghalaya Handicrafts Emporium**, **Purbashree** India Emporium, **Khadi Gramodyog** and the **Manipur Emporium** are on Jail Rd, Police Bazar. **Assam Government Sales Emporium** is on G.S. Rd while *Arunachal Museum* is on Cantonment Rd. **Assam Co-operative Silk House** is in Bara Bazar. The main shopping areas are in Police Bazar, Bara Bazar and Laitumukhra. The **Bara Bazar** market where tribal people gather wearing their traditional costumes, is particularly interesting. They sell attractive Nepali silver and Khasi gold and amber jewellery.

Photography Camera films are available from the following: *Photo Studio*, T 24436 and *Assam Studio*, T 23289 are on GS Rd while *Karuz Photographers* is in Police Bazar, T 24977.

Local Transport Meghalaya Tourism Development Corporation has taxis for hire which can be booked either through Hotel Pinewood Ashok or the Tourist Hotel. Local sightseeing costs Rs 40 per hour and Rs 430 for any destination (up to 8 hours, 100 km). The trip to Guwahati airport costs Rs 450. Yellow-top taxis charge Rs 5 for the first km and Re 1 for subsequent half km with a waiting charge of Re 1 for every 10 min.

Entertainment The local cinemas usually have four shows, at 1130, 1330, 1730 and 2030. The daily newspaper carries a detailed programme. *Dreamland*, *Bijou* and *Kelvin* are in Police Bazar, *Anjali* is on Cantonment Rd and *Payal* on Thana Rd.

Sports The **Golf Club** has an 18-hole course where competitions are held and a Polo ground, restaurant and bar. The course has the reputation of being the wettest but one of the most beautiful in the world. The club was founded in 1898, the present 5,873 yard 18 hole course dating from 1924. In an undulating valley covered with pine and rhododendron the fairways are covered in a tough variety of local grass. Despite the wetness the greens have the reputation of being extremely fast. The **Shillong Club** has billiards, table tennis, bar and restaurant and charges a daily temporary membership fee of Rs 10. There is a **Swimming Club** and Health Resort near Crinoline Waterfalls. The water sports complex is being developed at Bara Pani, Umiam Lake (16 km) with water skiing, boating and fishing; Lake View Tourist Bungalow for accommodation and Orchid Restaurant for meals. NSCA Indoor Stadium, Upper Lachumiere provides outdoor sports facilities.

Museums Central Museum, Lachumiere has ethnographic and archaeological objects. Open 1000-1600, Mon-Sat. except 2nd Sat and all government holidays. Entry free. Guide service, occasional film shows. No photography. **Tribal Research Institute**, Mawlai has indigenous specimens and articles of the tribal people. Open 1000-1600, Mon-Sat. Entry free. **Zonal Anthropological Museum**, Lachumiere. T 3459. Open 1000-1630, Mon-Sat. except 2nd Sat.

Useful address Foreigners' Registration Office is in Lachumiere near the State Museum.

Hospitals and Medical services Civil Hospital, G.S. Rd. T 24100. Nazareth Hospital, Laitumukhrah. T 24052. Ganesh Das Hospital, Polo Rd. T 23350.

Post and Telegraphs GPO, Postal enquiries, T 22162, Telegraph enquiries, T 22146.

Places of worship *Christian* – churches of all principal denominations in various parts of the town. *Buddhist* – The Buddhist Monastery is in Upper Lumparing and the Buddha Vihar in the Polo Ground. *Hindu* – Kali Mandir is also in the Polo Ground and Krishna Mandir in Police Bazar. *Others* – The mosques are at Fire Brigade, Police Bazar and Garikhana and the Sikh Gurdwara is near Raj Bhavan. Seng Khasi is in Mawkhar.

Travel agents and Tour operators Sheba Travels, Police Bazar. T 23015. Agents for Indian Airlines and Vayudoot and also run coach services to the airport. ACSCO Travels at Shillong Club. T 23354. Airlines agents. Blue Hill Travels and several other coach companies operate coaches to all major centres of the NE.

Tourist Offices and Information Government of India Tourist Office, G.S. Rd, Police Bazar. T 25632. 1000-1700. Government of Meghalaya Tourist Office, Jail Rd, Police Bazar. T 26220. 0700-1900. Director of Tourism, MTC Building. T 26054. Meghalaya Tourism Development Corporation, Polo Ground. T 24933.
   Government of India Tourist Office, B.K. Kakati Rd, Ulubari, Guwahati 781107. T 31381. Tourist Information Centre, Government of Meghalaya, Ulubari, Guwahati. T 27276. Also at 9 Russell St, Calcutta, T 290797 and at 9 Aurangzeb Road, New Delhi, T 3014417.

Tours City sight seeing tours from 0900-1600 cost Rs 40 per head. The trip to Cherrapunji is from 0830-1630 and costs Rs 45.

Air Shillong has a daily **Vayudoot** flight to Calcutta (1 hr 40 min) which in turn in connected to Delhi and all major centres in the NE by Indian Airlines. Daily Vayudoot flights between Guwahati and Shillong (20 min). Vayudoot To Calcutta, Mon-Sat, 1350, 1 hr 50 min. Sheba Travels, Police Bazar. T 23015. 0930-1630. (Handling agents for Vayudoot and Indian Airlines). **Pawan Hans** runs a helicopter service to and from Guwahati to Shillong. Meghalaya Tourism Corporation, Jail Road, Police Bazar. T 26054. (Handling agents).

   Rail Guwahati, the nearest railhead is well connected to the rest of the country. Rly Booking Out Agency, MTC Bus Station, T 23200. Current booking: 0600-1100, 1300-1600. For advance reservations 1130-1300.

   Road Buses, both Deluxe and ordinary, run services from Guwahati from 0600-1700. Meghalaya Road Transport, T 23200. Bus stands on Jail Rd, Police Bazar, and Anjali Cinema, Bara Bazar. Fare Rs 25 (Deluxe) and Rs 16. Meghalaya Tourism Development Corporation operates daily coaches from Guwahati Airport to Shillong. from Shillong for Guwahati Airport at 0900, Fare Rs 45. for Guwahati Railway Station daily at 0800, Fare Rs 25.

Excursions *Cherrapunji* 56 km, the old administrative headquarters of the Khasis can be reached by bus or taxi. It once held the record as the wettest place on earth according to the Guinness Book of Records and has an annual average rainfall of nearly 11,000 mm, although nearby Mawsynram is now said to have broken the record. Despite the Shillong plateau's exceptionally heavy rainfall it still has a four month dry season from Nov to Feb.

	Jan	Feb	Mar	Apr	May	Jun	Jul	Aug	Sep	Oct	Nov	Dec	Av/Tot
Max (°C)	16	17	21	22	22	22	22	23	23	22	19	17	21
Min (°C)	8	9	13	15	16	18	18	18	18	16	12	9	14
Rain (mm)	18	53	185	666	1280	2695	2446	1781	1100	493	69	13	10799

ARUNACHAL PRADESH

Arunachal Pradesh has a population of under 800,000, scattered very sparsely across over more than 84,000 square kilometres, approximately twice the size of the Netherlands. This gives the state a very low population density in comparison with other parts of India, under 10 per square kilometre. It is India's largest NE state and also its remotest as it has no railways and only air services to three of its towns. The State, located in the extreme NE of India, is not at present open to foreign visitors due to its strategic location bordering Bhutan, China and Burma.

Documents Inner line permits are required by all visitors which can be obtained from the Liaison Commission, New Delhi, Calcutta, Guwahati, Lilabari, Mohonbari and Tezpur, The Secretary, Ministry of Home Affairs in New Delhi or the Deputy Secretary, Itanagar.

Social indicators *Literacy*: M 23% F 11% *Birth rate*: Rural 37:1000 Urban 20:1000 *Death rate* Rural 19:1000 Urban 2:1000 *Urban* 8%.

Religion *Hindu* 29%, *Muslim* 1%, *Christian* 4%, *Buddhist* 14% (one of the highest figures in India), *Tribal and Animist* 52%.

Towns and cities Arunachal Pradesh is one of the least urban states in India, with only 8% of its population living in towns.The capital and largest town is **Itanagar**. Others with air links to towns in the neighbouring states are Tezu, Ziro and Pasighat.

Transport Arunachal Pradesh has very limited connections by commercial transport with the rest of India. **Air** Access to the state from Calcutta is through Dibrugarh in neighbouring Assam, Lilabari and Guwahati. **Road** Itanagar, the capital, and other small towns are connected by motorable roads and there is a road from Tezpur to Bomdila and Tawang. The old road to Mandalay ran from Ledo crossing the Burmese border through the Pangso Pass.

Land Located on the NE frontier of India Arunachal Pradesh stretches from the foothills of the E Himalayas to their peaks. The Brahmaputra, known in the state as the Dihang River, enters the E of the state from China and flows through a deeply cut valley from N to S.

Arunachal Pradesh's main attraction is its natural beauty, with a wide range of flora and fauna. The variety of terrain stretching from the snow capped mountains of the Himalayas to the steamy plains of the Brahmaputra valley, has led to an extraordinary range of forests from the Alpine to the sub-tropical – from rhododendrons to cacti and bamboo. It is an orchid lovers paradise with over 550 species identified. The wildlife includes elephants, clouded leopard, snow leopard, tiger, sloth, Himalayan black bear, red panda and musk deer. The **Miao wildlife sanctuary** is in the Tirap district on the Indo-Burmese border.

People The people of the India's NE are as diverse in origin as in any other part of S Asia. The tribal people who comprise the overwhelming majority of the population have been welded together from Aryan and Mongoloid races who originally came from China, Tibet, Thailand and Burma. There are 20 major **tribal groups** and they have very distinct cultures with a variety of musical, dance and folk traditions and religious practices with Hindu, Buddhist and animist backgrounds who are worshippers of the Sun and the Moon. Tribal dances are highly developed and range from martial warrior dances to religious dance-drama of the Buddhist tribes.

The Arunachali people are said to be the state's greatest attraction. An account describes their diversity "There are gentle and cultured **Monpas** of W Kameng who received Buddhism from Padma Sambhava; The **Thongi** whose chiefs trace their treaty relationships with the powers in the valley to a 1,000 years back; the **Hrusso** who for 30 generations have patronised Vaishnava scholars; the proud *Bangni-Nishi* and the *Tagin* typifying the ancient Indian ideal of the honourable warrior; the *Adis* and *Mishmis* who are eager to build academic careers; the **Apatanis** with their marvels of wet-rice cultivation; the **Khampti** in their magnificent ceremonial robes and peaceful, progressive *Nocte, Wancho* and *Tangsa*".

The people are highly "civilized", enjoying good health, a very strong community sense which goes beyond the bounds of narrow tribalism, no land disputes and a strong sense of justice. India's first Prime Minister, Jawaharlal Nehru struck a warning note when he spoke of India's tribal people – "not to treat them as anthropological specimens for study.....nor allow them to be engulfed by masses of India's humanity.....not to interfere with their way of life but want to help them live it". In the capital Itanagar you may see Nishi warriors wearing their hornbill caps, carrying bearskin bags and their knives in monkey-skin scabbards.

Economy Agriculture Main food crop is rice, grown on valley bottoms and on some terraced slopes. **Industry and resources** No large scale manufacturing industry, though some coal and lignite are mined. Forest products, and especially bamboo, are vital resources. Weaving is the universal craft as in other parts of the NE, with beautiful, highly coloured fabrics being made largely by women.

History Most Arunachalis have an oral tradition of recording their historic and cultural past by memorizing verses handed down through generations. Some Buddhist tribes have however maintained written records. These are largely concerned with the State's Buddhist history, still vibrantly alive and shown in buildings such as the **Tawang Monastery** (see below).

Itanagar

Population Altitude 750 m. *Rainfall* 2660 mm. *Best season* Oct – Mar. *Clothing* Summer Cottons, Winter Woollens. The nearest airport is Lilabari in Assam, 67 km away, a 2 hr journey by road.

The capital, **Itanagar** has been identified as **Mayapur**, the capital of the 11th century Jitri dynasty and there is a fort dating back to the 14th or 15th centuries which is believed to have been built by King Ramachandra. Naharlagun at 200 m and the new capital, Itanagar at 750 m are 10 km apart but together provide the capital's administrative offices. Itanagar's new light earthquake proof wooden buildings are mixed with the traditional huts built on the slopes of the hill. On one peak is the Residence of the Lt Governor while on the other there is a new Buddhist temple: in between are shops, bazaar, old huts and new administrative buildings.

Places of interest In Naharlagun – The **Polo Park** is on top of a ridge with interesting botanical specimens including the cane thicket, which looks like palm as well as a small zoo. In Itanagar – The new yellow-roofed **Buddhist Temple** stands in well kept gardens on top of the hill. The shrine is behind a *stupa* and on one side has a tree planted by the Dalai Lama. The **Ganga Sekhi Lake** is 6 km away and provides a drive through jungle with bamboo, tree ferns and orchids growing on tall trees. When the road reaches the foot of the hill you walk across a bamboo bridge, up steps cut on the red clay of the hill to reach a ridge which looks down on the forest lake which you can row across on a boat.

Hotels The only accommodation is for government officers primarily so you need to reserve rooms at least a month in advance. **F** *Inspection Bungalow*, Naharlagun. 24 rm. Reservations: Superintendent Engineer, Naharlagun. **F** *Field Hostel*, Itanagar, T ITN 275. 24 rm. Reservations: Chief Engineer, CPWD, Itanagar.

Local transport Taxis can be hired for the day for about Rs 400 plus fuel. Others do the journey between Itanagar and Naharlagun which you can usually share. **Cycle rickshaws** are only available in Naharlagun. **Buses** run a frequent service between Itanagar and Naharlagun between 0600 and 2000.

Shopping The cotton textiles are colourful and are beautifully patterned. You can also get wooden masks and figures, and cane belts and caps. The **Handicrafts Centre** has a sales section where you can buy shawls, *thankas*, handloom articles, wood carvings, cane and bamboo work and carpets. Next to the show room you can watch tribal craftsmen trimming, cutting and weaving cane.

There are **banks, hospitals** and **post offices** at both Itanagar and Naharlagun.

Tourist office and Information *Government of India Tourist Office*, Sector 'C', Naharlagun, T 328. *Government of Arunachal Pradesh*, Public Relations and Tourism,, Naharlagun, T 371. Also Arunachal Pradesh Information Centre, 4B Chowringhee Place, Calcutta, T 236500 and at Arunachal Bhawan, Kautilya Marg, New Delhi, T 3013915.

Travel agents and Tour operators *Arunachal Travels*, Itanagar T ITN 411 are agents for Indian Airlines. *Blue Hills Travels*, Naharlagun runs a night coach service to Guwahati. 1730, Arr Guwahati 0500. Rs 75.

Air Nearest airport is Lilabari in Assam, 57 km from Naharlagun, 67 km from Itanagar. Access to the state from Calcutta is through Dibrugarh (1 hr 30 min) by **Indian Airlines** daily flights via Tezpur which are extended to Tezu 3 a week. 4 flights a week from Guwahati (Mon, Th, Fri, Sun) and 3 from Tezu (Tue, Wed, Sat). **Vayudoot** has daily flights from Calcutta to Lilabari (2 hr 50 min – 3 hr 45 min) and 3 a week via Guwahati to Ziro (3 hr 25 min) on Tue, Th and Sat and 4 times weekly via Dibrugarh to Tezu (5 hr 15 min) on Mon, Wed, Fri and Sun.

Rail The nearest convenient railhead is N Lakhimpur in Assam, 50 km from Naharlagun and 60 km from Itanagar served by Nos 2 9 and 10 Arunachal Fast Passenger and other local trains. The nearest railheads for the bigger towns are as follows: Itanagar: Harmutty, Along: Silapathar, Tezu: Tinsukhia, Miao-Namdhapa: Margharita and Khansa: Naharkatia. Taxis are available for the connections.

Road Reasonable road connections with other towns in the region. Some distances: Agartala 980 km, Aizawl 901 km, Kohima 350 km, Guwahati 381 km, Imphal 495 km, Shillong 481 km. These towns are connected by motorable roads and there is a road from Tezpur to Bomdila and Tawang. The old road to Mandalay ran from Ledo crossing the Burmese border through the Pangso Pass.

Buses State Transport buses run services from Naharlagun Bus Station, T 221. Guwahati, daily, except Tue, 0630 (8 hr). Shillong, Wed, 0630. Lilabari Airport, daily except Mon, 0630 (2 hr). Ziro, daily 0700 (6 hr) and non-stop service on Tue, Th, Sat, 0800. N Lakhimpur, daily 0745, 1100, 1430, 1800. Bomdila, Mon and Th, 0630 (12 hr). *Blue Hills Travels* has an overnight coach to Guwahati 1730 (11 hr 30 min).

Excursions To reach Tawang, from Tezpur which is the nearest airport, you first travel to Bomdila 160 km away. The road passes through low wooded slopes for about 60 km. On the bank of the Bharali River in the upper plains, is Tipi at an altitude of 190 m, a glass house with more than 7,500 orchids. From there the road rises sharply to reach Bomdila at 2,530 m from where you get marvellous views of the snow capped mountains. It has a craft centre, apple orchards and Buddhist *gompas* and you can spend the night at the **F Tourist** Lodge which has 4 rm, before continuing the following morning to Tawang. Reservations: Deputy Commissioner, Bomdila. The next stretch of the journey of 180 km, passes through the pretty Dirang Valley and pine woods, then climbs to the Sela Pass at 4,215 m which presents a far starker view. You see a high-altitude lake and the trout hatchery at Nuranang just below the pass before reaching Tawang.

The **Tawang Monastery**, in a breathtakingly beautiful setting at over 3,000 m, is one of the largest in India. Constructed in the 17th century with 65 residential buildings around the main temple structure, it still houses over 500 *lamas** belonging to the Gelugpa or Reformed Sect of Mahayana Buddhist monks. It is where the sixth Dalai Lama was born and houses a very large Buddha and many priceless manuscripts, books and *tankhas**. **F** *Inspection Bungalow*. Reservations: Deputy Commissioner, Tawang.

In the foothills of W Siang, old granite images of Hindu deities were found in **Malinithan** while in Dibang Valley the ruins of **Bismaknagar Palace** are thought to date from the 12th century. The state is best known for its famous **Parasuram Kund**, a lake near Tezu where at Makar Sankranti in mid-Jan thousands of pilgrims come to the mela (fair) and take a dip in the holy water to wash away their sins. Spartan accommodation is available in Government *Tourist Lodge* at Tezu. It is advisable to book well in advance through the Deputy Commissioner, Tezu.

Museums There are *District Museums* in Along, Bomdila, Khonsa, Pasighat, Tezu and Ziro which hold collections of art and craft objects. They are open from 1000-1700 and admission is free. Photography is prohibited.

NAGALAND

Another of India's very small states with an area of 16,579 sq km – half the size of Belgium. Nagaland has a population of 800,000. *Altitude* Between 900-1,200 m.

Social indicators *Literacy* M 43% F 34% *Birth rate* Rural 24:1000 Urban 19:1000 *Death* *rate* Rural 8:1000 Urban 2:1000 *Registered graduate job seekers* 14,000 *Average annual income per head* : Rs 1400

Religion *Hindu* 14% *Muslim* 2% *Christian* 80% *Animist* 4%

Towns and cities The *Capital* is **Kohima**. Dimapur is the town in the plains which acts as the entry point for Nagaland and neighbouring Manipur.

The Land The narrow strip of mountain territory has Assam to the W, Burma to the E, Arunachal Pradesh and Assam to the N and Manipur to the S. From Dimapur which is in the plains and the gateway to the state, the road leaves the tea gardens and rises up wooded mountains. There are green valleys with meandering streams, high mountains with deep gorges and a rich variety of flora and fauna.

People It is almost entirely inhabited by 16 groups of the Tibeto-Burmese tribes among them are the Angamis, Aos, Konyaks, Kukis, Lothas, Semas and Wanchus. The *Nagas*, who were once head hunters, have been known for their fierceness and the regular raids they made on Assam and Burma. The warring tribes believed that since the enemy's animated soul 'yaha' in Wanchu dialect, was to be found at the nape of the neck, it could only be set free once beheaded. However, since the spiritual soul '*mio*', resided in the head and brought good fortune by way of prosperity and fertility, it was thought important to add to a community's own store of dead ancestors by acquiring extra '*mio*' by taking enemy heads. Nagas therefore attempted to carry home the heads of dead comrades while 'welcoming' any alien spirits of enemies killed in battle by ceremonial rituals. Evidence of their culture and practices can be gauged from wooden images, masks, jewellery and headgear which are displayed in several museums across the country, particularly in New Delhi.

The villages even today are situated on hill tops and ridges and are protected by stone walls. Often the first building one comes across in a village is the '*morung*', a building with a single huge cross beam often as much as 20 m long and 10 m high which served as the most important meeting house in the community. It was also used as a boys' dormitory, for storing weapons and displaying the prizes of war in the form of enemy heads, often as many as 150 in any *morung*. Since the longhouses were constructed out of timber, bamboo and thatch, the record in the form of skulls would often be destroyed in a fire, when it would be substituted by carving small replicas to retain the good fortune which otherwise would be lost. The huge sacred drum which stood by each *morung* was hollowed out of a tree trunk and carved appropriately to resemble a buffalo head.

Religion Originally animists, missionaries were so successful in converting the Nagas that today 90% are Christians. The Bible was translated into many of the Naga dialects, nearly every village boasts a church and yet the people have retained many of their old customs. There are also remains of the Hindu kingdom of the Cacharis at Dimapur near the present capital Kohima, which was destroyed by the Assamese Ahoms in the 16th century.

Economy Agriculture Primarily agricultural, the Nagas have now become dependent on the timber industry. The practice of 'Jhuming' still continues where shifting cultivation allowed for 'slash and burn'. Land cultivated for 2 years used to be left to regenerate for 10 to 15 years by lying fallow. Now the period between cultivation has diminished to a couple of years and the larger trees which remained untouched are now felled for valuable timber, changing the look of the land. Rice and maize are the dominant crops.

Manufacturing Timber is the most important product from the state, but traditional handicrafts are still made. The ancient craft of weaving on portable looms is still practised by the women. The strips of colourful cloth are stitched together to produce shawls in different patterns which distinguish each tribe, the shawl being a universal garment worn by Nagas all over the state.

Local crafts The ancient craft of weaving on portable looms is still practised by the women. The strips of colourful cloth are stitched together to produce shawls in different patterns which distinguish each tribe, the shawl being a universal garment worn by Nagas all over the state. The Ao warrior wears the Tsungkotepsu, a red and black striped shawl with a white band in the middle embroidered with symbols.

History The British reached peace with the Nagas at the end of the 19th century and found them useful allies in the war against the Japanese, who reached Kohima before finally retreating from the region. After Indian independence, Nagaland became a separate state on 31 December 1963. A separatist movement continued to demand fully independent status but this was abandoned when in 1975 they accepted the Indian Constitution.

Kohima

Population 53,000 *Altitude* 1500 m. *Best season* Nov to Apr. *Clothing* Summer Cottons, Winter Light woollens.

	Jan	Feb	Mar	Apr	May	Jun	Jul	Aug	Sep	Oct	Nov	Dec	Av/Tot
Max (°C)	15	17	21	23	25	24	24	25	24	22	19	10	21
Min (°C)	8	10	13	17	18	19	19	19	19	17	13	10	15
Rain (mm)	18	18	55	63	177	319	382	353	270	143	39	4	1841

Kohima is 74 km from the nearest airport at Dimapur, a 3 hr drive (4 hr by bus). Kohima attracted world attention during the Second World War because it was here that the Japanese advance was halted by the British and Indian forces.

Local festivals Feb Sekrenyi is celebrated by Angamis for 10 days when all work in the field cease. On one particular day the young people sit and songs traditional songs throughout the day. Mar-Apr *Aoling* Konyaks observe the six day festival after the sowing is completed in March. It marks the end of the winter and beginning of the new year with the appearance of the spring flowers. May *Moatsu* is a similar 6 day festival marking the beginning of the growing season after the hard work of clearing the fields, burning the jungles and sowing of seeds. The year continues with different tribes celebrating their special festivals – *Tutuni* and *Naknyulum* in July, the harvest festival of *Metemneo* in August, *Amongmong* in Sep, *Tsokum* in Oct and *Tokhu Emong* in Nov. The priests perform ceremonies and there is lot of dancing, singing and drinking of rice beer.

Places of interest The **Second World War Cemetery** is in a beautiful setting, with well maintained lawns where rose bushes bloom in the season. Two tall crosses stand out at the lowest and highest points. The stone markers each have a polished bronze plaque commemorating the men who fell here. The flowering cherry tree which was used by Japanese soldiers as a snipers' post was destroyed and what you see is what grew from the old stump, marking the limit of the enemy advance. The upper cross carries the following inscription: "Here, around the tennis court of the Deputy Commissioner lie men who fought in the battle of Kohima in which they and their comrades finally halted the invasion of India by the forces of Japan in April 1944." At the base of the lower cross there are four lines:

> When you go home
> Tell them of us and say
> For your tomorrow
> We gave our today.

The Market outside the Supermarket brings tribal women in their colourful dress who come to buy and sell their produce from farms, rivers and forests. **Kohima Village (Bara Basti)** is the old village which was the origin of Kohima. It has a traditional Naga ceremonial gateway carved with motifs of guns, warriors and symbols of prosperity at the entrance to the village that rise steeply up the hill. The traditional Naga house with its crossed 'horns' on the gables, carved heads to signify the status of the family, a huge basket to hold the grain in front of the house and a trough where rice beer is made for the whole village community.

Hotels **E** *Government Tourist Lodge*, T 2417. 10 rm. Also a few Indian style **F** category hotels. *Hotel Meyase*, Mission Compound Rd. *Razhu Hotel* nr Supermarket. *Travel Lodge*, Assam Rifles Rd. *Regal Hotel* nr Ao Church. *Evergreen Hotel* nr Nagaland Emporium.

Restaurants There are a few restaurants serving Indian and Chinese food – *Le Baron*, *Relax* opp Emporium and *Midland* which also does Continental food.

Shopping Warm and colourful Naga shawls are excellent. you can also get shoulder bags, decorative spears, table mats, wood carvings and bamboo baskets. The *Sales Emporium* of Nagaland Handloom and Handicrafts Development Corporation is opp the State Transport Bus Station. There are also shops in the Supermarket.

There are **banks, a post office** and a **hospital**.

Museums The **Nagaland State Museum** is in Kohima, Directorate of Art and Culture, Kohima. T 770. Open 1000-1500. Closed Sun and holidays. Collection of anthropological exhibits of the different Naga tribes. Gateposts, status pillars, jewellery, a ceremonial drum which looks like a dugout war canoe in a separate shed. There is a strong belief that the Nagas' ancestors came from the seafaring nation of Sumatra and retain their link with their island past in their legends, village drums and ceremonial jewellery which uses shells. In the basement you can see birds and animals of the NE Hill states.

The **Zoo** built into a wooded hill side has most of its animals kept in cages. To the left of the entrance are the semi-wild Naga *mithun* bison. There are also golden langurs and the rare tragopan pheasant in a cage at the top of the hill. Open Summer 0900-1100, 1300-1700. Winter 0900-1100, 1300-1600. Closed Mon. Small entry fee.

Travel agent and tour operator *Green Hills Travel*, Taxi Stand, Kohima, T 2279 run coaches and do internal flight bookings.

Tourist office and Information *Tourist Information Centre*, Kohima, T 607. Also at Dimapur Tourist Bungalow, T 2147. Nagaland Information Centre, 13 Shakespeare Sarani, Calcutta, T 445269 and at 29 Aurangzeb Road, New Delhi, T 3014289.

Air Daily flights from Guwahati to Dimapur which has the nearest airport, 74 km and 3 hr drive.

Rail Dimapur has the nearest railhead on the NE Frontier Rly. From Dibrugarh **Guwahati**: *Tinsokia Mail*, 5908, daily, 1745, 18 hr; **Calcutta (H)**: *Kamrup Exp*, 5906 (AC/II), daily, 1000, 18 hr 30 min, change at Guwahati (3 hr 15 min wait), then *Kamrup Exp*, 5660 (AC/II), daily, 0745, 22 hr 45 min (total time 44 hr 30 min). From Dimapur **Guwahati**: *Assam Mail*, 5904, daily, 0025, 6 hr 20 min; **Dibrugarh Town**: *Tinsukia Mail*, 5907, daily, 2030, 10 hr 30 min. Guwahati–*Dimapur Exp* No 207. Dibrugarh–*Guwahati Assam Mail* No 3. Calcutta (Howrah)-*Dibrugarh Kamrup Exp* No 5.

Road Nagaland State Transport runs services from Dimapur to Kohima from 0530-1530 (2 hr 30 min). Bus Station, T 2094. Blue Hills Travels runs luxury coaches from Guwahati which connect with Kohima and all other state capitals of the NE Hill states.

MANIPUR

Further S from Nagaland is the former princely state of Manipur. It covers 22,327 sq km (just half the size of the Netherlands) has a population of just over 1 million. Manipur lies about 700 kilometres NE of Calcutta. It has an international border on its E with Burma and State borders with Nagaland, Assam and Mizoram.

Social indicators *Literacy* M 41% F 29% *Newspaper circulation:* 24,000 *Birth rate* Rural 30:1000 Urban 24:1000 *Death rate* Rural 7:1000 Urban 6:1000 *Registered graduate job seekers* 190,000 *Average annual income per head* : Rs 1050

Religion *Hindu* 60% *Muslim* 7% *Christian* 30%.

Towns and cities The capital is **Imphal**, with a population of 270,000. Flights connect it to Calcutta via Silchar and also to Guwahati. Imphal can be reached by road from Kohima, 130 km away, on the famous road to Mandalay. The 'land of jewels', Manipur shares an international boundary with Burma and is bounded by Nagaland to the N, Assam to the W and Mizoram to the S. The majority of the population is Hindu, worshippers of Vishnu. They belong to the *Meithe* tribe and are related to the *Shans* of Burma, who live in the valleys. The 20 or so hill-tribes who constitute about a third of the population are mainly Christian.

Manipuri Dance Isolated for years, the ancient musical forms of the valley dwellers are closely connected to the worship of Vishnu which finds expression in the Manipuri school of Indian dancing. The 'Rasa' dances usually adopting a Krishna- Gopi theme are performed at every ceremony and are characterised by graceful light and restrained movements and delicate hand gestures. The ornate costumes worn by the women are glittering and colourful. The 'Sankirtanas', a second group of Manipuri dance often precede the 'Rasa'. They are usually performed by men and are vigorous, rhythmic and athletic, requiring them to play on the Manipuri drums called 'pung' and cymbals while they dance. The tribal ritual dances, some of which are performed by priests and priestesses before deities, are very different and may end in a trance. Others can last several days observing a strict form and accompanied by the drone of a bowed instrument called the 'pana'.

Like the Nagas, the Manipuris too have a reputation for being great warriors, still practising their skills of wrestling, sword fighting and martial arts. The game of *polo* is said to have originated here. Most of the wars were fought across the border in Burma. British sovereignty over Manipur was recognized in 1891. After Indian independence it became a Union Territory and subsequently achieved statehood in 1972.

The Land Much of Manipur lies above 2000 m. However, the heart of the populated area is a low lying basin. In its centre is the reedy Lake Loktak, and the flat bottomed basin and river valleys that drain into it are extremely beautiful.

Rivers and lakes There are several large lakes in the central area where the rivers drain southwards. They are used for fishing and duck shooting as well as for special boat races.

Economy Agriculture Subsistence agriculture provides the basis of living for the majority of the rural population who make up over 70% of the total.

Manufacturing Weaving and other handicrafts are as important in Manipur as elsewhere in the NE. No mineral deposits to speak of have yet been exploited, but as elsewhere in the hill regions forest products are important, and there is a significant local stoneware industry.

History Tradition has it that Imphal, capital of Manipur, was founded at the beginning of the 1st century AD. Imphal derives its name from 'yumpham' meaning homestead and is believed to be one of the oldest state capitals of the country.

Manipur has always been quite independent of its neighbouring tribal areas. Although the main historical landmarks are few and far between, we do know that the Bishnupur temple, nearly 30 km from Imphal, was built in AD 1467 during the reign of King Kiyamba. Manipur was often invaded from Burma but it also enjoyed long periods of quite stable government. In 1826 it was brought into India by the Treaty of Yandabo at the end of the Indo-Burmese War. During World War II Imphal was occupied by the Japanese.

Imphal

Population 210,000. *Altitude* 785 m. Imphal has direct flights to Calcutta which takes 1 hr 15 min.

	Jan	Feb	Mar	Apr	May	Jun	Jul	Aug	Sep	Oct	Nov	Dec	Av/Tot
Max (°C)	21	23	27	29	29	29	28	29	29	29	28	25	22
Min (°C)	4	7	10	15	19	21	22	22	21	17	11	5	15
Rain (mm)	17	31	51	91	231	278	253	189	136	117	28	3	1425

Local festivals Feb-Mar *Yaosang* on full-moon night, boys and girls dance the Thabal Chongba and sing in a circle in the moonlight. May-June is celebrated in honour of forest gods. Sep: *Heikru Hitongba* is mainly non-religious, when there are boat races along a 16 m wide moat in narrow boats with large number of rowers.

Places of interest The Old Palace In the heart of town, has ruins of the old fortress and a palace. As it is occupied by paramilitary forces, you have to convince the guard that you are visiting the ruins. The **Shri Govindaji Temple** adjoins the palace and is a Vaishnavite centre. It has two golden domes, a large raised hall. The presiding deity Vishnu has on one side shrines to Balaram and Krishna and to Jagannath on the other side. Well patronized performances of ceremonial dancing are held there regularly. Overlooking the University, 8 km, the historic palace on the Indo-Burma road of **Langthaband**, with its ceremonial houses and temples, stands on the hills among formally planted pine and jackfruit trees.

Khwairamband Bazar, in the town centre is the largest women's bazaar to be seen perhaps anywhere in the country. It is an excellent place for handicrafts and handlooms.

Hotels F *Tourist Lodge*, inexpensive, reserve through the Director of Tourism, T 459, very basic accommodation. There are a few **F** Indian style hotels – *Ranjit* in Thangal Bazar, T 382, *Grand* in Paona Bazar, T 777 and *Diplomat* on B.T. Road, T 588. There is also a Marwari *Dharamsala* T 1175.

Museums The Manipur State Museum is nr Polo Ground, T 709. Open 1000-1630 on weekdays. Closed Sun and holidays. Entry free. Collection of art, archaeology, natural history, geology and textiles.

Parks and zoos The *Zoological Gardens* are 6 km away at Lamphelpat to the W. The rare brow-antlered deer seen in the wild at Keibul Lamjao Sanctuary can be seen here in captivity. The *Khonghampat Orchid Yard* is 7 km on the NH 39 away is best visited in April-May. Set up by the State Forest Dept, it has well over a hundred varieties of orchids including some rare species. Best season Apr-May.

Banks Allahabad, T 902 and United Bank of India Branch, T 1206 on Paona Bazar; Baroda, T 1396, Central Bank of India, T 1094 and United Commercial, T 1145 on Thengal Bazar; State Bank of India, T 14 and United Bank of India, T 130 on MG Avenue.

Shopping The handloom textiles have a distinct Manipuri design. Paona Bazar is the main area where fixed-price shops make purchases easier. *Sales Emporium* of the Manipur Handloom and Handicrafts Development Corporation, *Handloom House* selling goods produced by the Handloom Weavers' Cooperative Society and the *Tribal Emporium* are all in the same area. The Khwairamband Bazar is the other major centre for shopping.

Local Transport Tourist taxis are available through the Tourist Information Centre but otherwise taxis are un-metred. Auto-rickshaws and rickshaws are also available but rates should be negotiated for journeys.

Tourist offices and Information Tourist Information Centre, Govt of Manipur, Imphal. T 802. Govt of India Tourist Office, Old Lambulane, Jail Rd, Imphal. T 21131. Manipur Information Centre, 26 Rowland Road, Calcutta, T 478358 and at C7, Baba Kharak Singh Marg, New Delhi, T 344026.

Air Indian Airlines flies daily to Delhi (4 hr) via Guwahati (45 min), Calcutta (1 hr 15 min) and Silchar (30 min). Indian Airlines, MG Ave. T 28. There are also **Vayudoot** flights to Calcutta (2 hr 10 min) and Dimapur (35 min) on Tue, Th and Sat. T 22119.

Rail Dimapur on the Northern Frontier Railway is the nearest railhead for Manipur. Regular buses connect Dimapur with Imphal, the journey normally taking 8 to 9 hours.

Road Imphal is well connected by a good network of roads with major centres in the NE. Some of the road distances are Agartala 465 km, Aizawl 374 km, Guwahati 579 km, Itanagar 413 km, Kohima 123 km, Shillong 643 km and Silchar 198 km.

Excursions

The first three places can be visited in a circuit from Imphal. *Bishenpur*, 27 km away, named after a temple to Bishnu (Vishnu), is a picturesque town at the foot of a hill. The temple was built in AD 1467 during the reign of King Kiyamba and the very thin bricks used in its construction are said to have been influenced by the Chinese. There is a significant stoneware industry here. *Moirang*, 45 km from Imphal, stands on the western fringe of the Loktak lake, noted for its early Manipuri folk-culture. The ancient love story of Khambha and Thoibi is said to have given birth to traditional folk dance form in this city. There is a temple to the forest god, Thankgjing, where garments of the 12th century Moirang kings are preserved.

During World War II Moirang was the headquarters of the Indian National Army for a short time and the Congress flag is believed to have been raised here as a symbol of national independence for the first time on 12 April, 1944. (Note: the Congress flag and the National flag can easily be confused, having the same colours. The Congress flag has at its centre the *charkha* (spinning wheel), while the national flag uses the Asokan *chakra wheel*. The national flag was designed in 1947). There is an INA memorial and a war museum.

Keibul Lam Jao National Park The park covering 25 sq km, 53 km from Imphal, is the only floating sanctuary of its kind in India. It has a small population of brow-antlered deer, one of the most endangered species of deer in the world, as well as wild boar, panther and water birds. There is an observatory tower on Babet Ching, a small hillock within the park and also a *Forest Lodge*. **Kaina**, 29 km, is a Hindu pilgrimage centre because of its association with Shri Govindaji who was said to have appeared in a dream to his disciple Jai Singh, Maharaja of Manipur. He requested that a temple be built to him enshrining an image carved out of a jackfruit tree. The dream is enacted in ceremonial dances at the *Rasa Mandapa*.

MIZORAM

The southern-most of the hill states, Mizoram juts down between Burma and Bangladesh. Previously it had been Lushai Hills, a district of Assam. Covering 21,000 sq km, Mizoram is twice the size of its neighbour Tripura, but still has a population of only just over 500,000 and a density of under 25 per sq km. It has State borders with Manipur, Assam and Tripura to its N, and its western border with the Chittagong Hill Tracts of Bangladesh. Houses often have front doors at level with streets cut on steep slopes, while the backs stand precariously on stilts. The Mizo people love flowers, and every home proudly displays orchids and pots of geranium, begonia and balsam.

Social indicators *Literacy* M 60% F 55% *Registered graduate job seekers* 19,000.

Religion *Hindu* 7% *Muslim* 1% *Christian* 84%.

Towns and cities 25% of population lives in towns. Aizawl, the capital, is the biggest city.

The half a dozen or so parallel N-S ranges of hills rising to over 2,000 m near the Burmese border are covered in dense forests of bamboo and wild banana. At the bottom of the deep gorges run the rivers in narrow ribbons. The villages perch on top of the ridges with Aizawl, the capital, considered to be on the steepest slopes in the country.

Economy Agriculture Rice and maize are supplemented by shifting cultivation. They provide the chief means of support for about three quarters of the population. There are no mineral resources exploited as yet. **Manufacturing** Handicrafts and handwoven textiles predominate, and there are no large scale industries. The Government has sponsored some light industrial development in Aizawl.

History Mizo is derived from 'mi'(man) and 'zo' (mountain or cold), a collective name given by their neighbours to a number of tribes which settled in the area. The different groups of tribal people are thought to have originally come from NW China who were gradually pushed southward towards Tibet and Burma in the 7th century and finally reached their present homeland less than 300 years ago. The raiding of British tea-plantations which carried on until around the end of the last century led to the introduction of Inner Line permits which gave free access to missionaries to visit the area. They not only carried out their religious duties but also introduced literacy which is exceptionally high in this state, the language having adopted the Roman script. The great majority of the self reliant and music loving Mizos are Christian converts and have built up a strong tradition of Western choral singing. The remainder, mainly nomadic Chakmas along the western border, practise a religion which combines Hinduism, Buddhism and animism.

Aizawl

Population 95,000 *Altitude* 1,132 m. *Climate* Temp. Summer Max. 29°C Min. 20°C. Winter Max. 21°C Min. 11°C. Annual rainfall 3000 mm

The flight to **Aizawl** from Calcutta takes 1 hr 35 min. The bus journey from the airport 27 km away takes about an hour.

The town, built on the central ridge, stands out like a citadel and dominates the scenery. The Assam Rifles Centre is an important landmark with the administrative buildings and Raj Bhavan nearby. On the E side is the Zoo with birds and animals from Mizoram, Burma and the Chittagong area in Bangladesh.

Local festivals *Chapchar Kut* is a traditional spring festival held at the beginning of March celebrated with dancing and feasting. *Cheraw*, a Mizo dance for this joyous occasion and also to speed the souls of the dead on their way, is performed by nimble-footed girls who dance in and out of bamboo poles which are clapped together by teams of young men. Similar dances are found in Burma, Thailand and the Philippines.

Places of interest Bora Bazar, the main shopping centre is on the other side of the ridge, with the steep Zion St lined with stalls selling garments and vendors trying to impress customers with Mizo recordings on music cassettes! The main bazaar is where the people are best seen in their traditional costumes selling produce from farms and homesteads including river crab in little wicker baskets. The **Weaving Centre** is above the Bata shoe shop where one can watch women at their looms weaving traditional shawls which are available for sale. **Luangmual Handicrafts Centre**, 7 km away takes ½ hour to reach by car. The 'khumbou' ceremonial bamboo hat is made here using waterproof with 'H'manthial' leaves. The **Museum** is in Bora Bazar (see below).

Hotels and restaurants E *Embassy Hotel*, Chandmari with 11 basic rm and an 'Indian Extension'. The **E** Tourist Bungalow or Tourist Lodge at Chaltlang has 14 rm. Reserve both through the Deputy Director of Information, PR and Tourism, State Secretariat, Treasury Square, Aizawl 796001. T 449, 306. The *Labyrinth Restaurant* in Chandmari serves Chinese and Indian food.

Banks Mizoram Co-operative Bank is at Tuikal, T 644. State Bank of India at Khatla, T 2533. In Bora Bazar are Vijaya Bank T 2562 and United Commercial Bank T 710.

Shopping The *District Industries Centre* in Upper Bazar, T 2368, has shawls, bags and fine bamboo articles for sale. In Bora Bazar, the *Bata* stockist sells Mizo shawls which are woven on the premises in the *Weaving Centre*, while in Zion St you can buy locally produced music cassettes. The *Photo House* is in Bungkawn, T 2363.

Local transport There are un-metred taxis charging about Rs 75 for 2 hr sightseeing within the town and city buses.

Cinema Zodin Cinema Hall, Tuikual.

Museums Mizoram State Museum on Canteen Kual is in the town centre. Open Mon 1200-1600 and Tue-Fri 0930-1600. Entry free. Though small it has an interesting collection of historical relics, ancient costumes and traditional implements.

Hospital Civil Hospital. T 2518.

Post and Telegraphs GPO, Khatla. Post Master T 2233.

Places of worship Catholic Church, T 2260; Presbyterian Church; Salvation Army at Rust Memorial Hall and United Pentecostal Church, Sikulpuikawn. Hindu Temple. Muslim mosque in Bora Bazar.

Travel Agents Thanginkhuma, Khatla. Indian Airlines and Vayudoot agents. T 2297, 448.

Tourist Offices and Information Director of Information, PR and Tourism, Aizawl. T 449. Deputy Director. T 306. There are Mizoram Houses at Rangir Kharia, Silchar, Assam, T 87091, Zoo Rd, Guwahati 781005, T 87091, Chanakyapuri, behind Sri Lanka Embassy, New Delhi, T 301595 and at 24 Ballygunge Rd, Calcutta, 700019, T 477034.

Air Aizawl has daily **Vayudoot** flights to and from Calcutta (1 hr 35 min) and Silchar (30 min) every day except Sun. T 2297. **Bus** The Mizoram State Transport has bus services (ordinary and deluxe) to **Silchar** (8-9 hr).

TRIPURA

The former princely state is surrounded on three sides by Bangladesh. It is partly mountainous, carved by several river valleys and being in the monsoon belt with over 4000 mm of annual rainfall is covered in rich green vegetation.

Social indicators Literacy M 42% F 52% Newspaper circulation: 39,000 Birth rate Rural 25:1000 Urban 17:100 Death rate Rural 8:1000 Urban 5:1000 In-migrants 555,000 Out-migrants 29,000 Registered graduate job seekers 95,000 Average annual income per head : Rs 1200.

Religion Hindu 89% Muslim 7% Christian 1%.

Towns and cities 11% of the population lives in towns, Agartala the capital having a population of 170,000.

Tripura is the smallest of the hill states in NE India. Covering just under 10,500 square kms, it is almost surrounded on the N, W and S by Bangladesh.

Land The N of the state falls into four valleys, separated by hills that rise to just under 1000 metres. The more open land of the S is still forested. Indian hardwoods include sal (*Shorea robusta*), which is economically important.

    Rivers and lakes There are many small streams. N draining rivers include the Deo, the Khowai and the Dhalai while the Gumti is the biggest river flowing S.

People Tripura remains a predominantly tribal society, even though the great majority of the population are now described as Hindu. One typical old tribal custom of welcoming a visitor to a village is still carried out, for example. A bamboo arch is built and the guest is garlanded and greeted with wafting of incense. An egg is held in front of the person which is believed to absorb any evil spirits which is then rubbed in paddy, dipped in water and then thrown away.

Economy Agriculture Rice is the main crop. It is well suited to the marshy conditions of the northern basin. Jute, cotton, tea and fruit are important cash crops. Sugar cane, mustard and potatoes are also grown.

    Manufacturing There is very little industry, though in the last ten years the Indian Government has encouraged small industries. Weaving, carpentry, pottery and basket making are common.

History Legend has it that Tripura existed in the times of the epic Mahabharata but recent history confirms that around the end of the 14th century it came under the rule of the **Manikya dynasty** of Indo-Mongolian origin. Permanently feuding with her neighbours, particularly the Nawabs of Bengal, the British found a means of gaining influence in the area by coming to the help of the Maharaja and establishing a protectorate separating the princely state from tribal lands outside the control of the Hindu rajas. The Manikyas ruled continuously right up to India's independence when Tripura joined it as a Union Territory later to become a state in 1972. **Rabindranath Tagore's** play 'Visarjan' and novel 'Rajarsi' based on the legends of the Manikyas is said to reflect the friendship that existed between the poet and the Maharaja Virehandra Manikya who was a great patron of the arts, **see page 552**. Tagore's university at Santiniketan found patrons among the royal family.

    Tripura began a period of modernisation in the 1930s and Maharaja Bir Bikram made his kingdom more accessible by opening an airport in Agartala. He also designed the college named after him which stands on a hillock by a lake on the E part of the city. The town is noticeable for the well kept gardens, intricately woven cane fences and official buildings of red brick favoured by the royal family. However, evidence of British fondness for white can be seen in a few important structures, notably the one designed to be the palace for the Maharaja in 1901.

Agartala

Population 175,000 (1991) *Altitude* 1,280 m. *Climate* Temp. Summer Max. 35°C Min. 24°C Winter Max. 27°C Min. 13°C. Annual rainfall 2240 mm, June to August. *Best Season* September to March. Clothing cottons in summer, woollens in winter.

Agartala has 3 flights daily to and from Calcutta (1 hr) and also Silchar. Vayudoot flights connect it to Kailashar and Kamalpur.

Places of interest Ujjayant Palace Built in the Mughal style by Maharaja Radha Kishore Manikya in 1901 is now the State Legislative Assembly. It is reputedly the largest building in the state covering 1 sq km, which once stood amidst formal Mughal gardens with pools and fountains. The magnificent tiled floors, the ceiling of the Chinese room and the beautifully carved front doors are particularly notable. The late 19th century **Jagannath temple** is across one of the artificial lakes in front of the palace. It rises from an octagonal base to a striking orange four-storeyed 'sikhara' or tower.

Sipahijala 33 km. A botanical garden with a small zoo and a boating lake. The **F** *Forest Bungalow* may be reserved through the Chief Conservator of Forests, Agartala. Hourly buses run from the city between 0700-1600.

Neer Mahal 60 km. A water-palace built for one of the Maharajas in Rudrasagar Lake is like a fairytale castle with tower and pavilions, moats and bridges.

Tripura Sundari Temple 67 km. Known as Matabari, the temple in the ancient capital, Udaipur was built on top of a hillock Dhanisagar in the middle of the 16th century. Claimed to be one of the 51 holy 'pithas' mentioned in the *Tantras*. The temple of the Mother Goddess, is served by red-robed priests and is the location of a large fair during Diwali in Oct/Nov. Temple of Chaturdasa Devata 8 km. As the name suggests the temple near old Agartala is dedicated to 14 gods and goddesses who are represented by their heads only. It is built in the Bankura style of Bengali temple architecture but has a Buddhist stupa type structure on top. In July worshippers come from all over Tripura for *Kharchi Puja* which has evolved from a tribal festival.

Hotels Only fairly basic accommodation is available in Agartala in small **D**, **E** and **F** category hotels with limited availability of a/c rooms. **D** *Agartala Club*. T 1375. **D** Broadway Guest House, Col. Chowmohini Palace Compound. T 3122. 12 d rm. No dining rm, though you can have Indian and Chinese food served in you rm. **D** *Meenakshi*, Khushbagan. T 5721. Indian food. *Royal Guest House*, Kunjaban. T 526. *Minakshi*, Hawkers Corner, H.G. Basak Rd. T 1433. **E** *Sonal Rest House*, GB Hospital Rd, T 5322. 12 rm. Indian and Chinese food. There is also a *Circuit House*, Tel 41 (apply to Resident District Magistrate, Tripura, West) and a *Dak Bungalow* (Resident Chief Manager, PWD, Agartala).

Restaurants There are a few Indian Restaurants in town. *OK Restaurant*, HG Basak Rd; *Ambar*, Sakuntala Rd; *Insrapuri*, Akhaura Rd.

Banks The following are on HG Basak Rd: State Bank of India, T 5809. United Bank of India, T 5874. Union Bank of India, T 4298. Allahabad Bank, T 3403. Indian Bank, T 4742. 3 on Central Rd: United Commercial Bank, T 5250. Central Bank of India, T 4837. Punjab and Sind Bank, T 4715. Bank of Baroda is on Kaman Chowmuhani. T 4744.

Shopping Tripura is noted for its exceptional bamboo, cane and palm leaf handicrafts, among the finest in India and handloom fabrics. *Purbasha*, Tripura Handloom and Handicrafts Development Corporation, MMB Sarani, T 3496. *Tripura Handicrafts*, Akhaura Rd. Films available at Sen and Sen, Kaman Chowmuhani, T 3950.

Local Transport Unmetred taxis are available from the airport (about Rs 75) as well for sightseeing and excursions, which can cost about Rs 200 for a full day plus a charge per km. The Directorate of Information has Tourist Cars and coaches. Auto-rickshaws and Cycle-rickshaws are available for the airport run and for city sightseeing only. The journey to and from the airport can cost upto Rs 30 or Rs 7 per person. Sightseeing is charged by the hr – about Rs 25 and Rs 8 respectively. The city also has a bus service.

Entertainment The *Rupasi Cinema*, Netaji Rd Ext shows films at 1500, 1800 and 2100.

Museums Tripura Government Museum, PO West. T 4344. Weekdays 1000-1700. Entry free. Collection includes rare stone images, old coins, Bengal *kantha* embroidery, archaeological finds from Tripura and adjoining areas. A small museum but sculptures, including 8th-10th century Buddhist sculptures from Pilak, are very well displayed.

Hospitals and medical services VM Hospital, AK Rd, T 3331. GB Hospital, Kunjaban, T 3385. **Post and Telegraphs** General Post Office. T 5489. Chowmuhani Post Office. T 5666.

Places of worship *Hindu* – Laxminarayan Bari; Jagganath Bari. *Buddhist* – Buddha Vihar. *Muslim* – Shibnagar Mosque. *Christian* – St Paul's Church, Arundhuti Nagar; Holy Cross Church, Luchubagan.

Travel agents Ramkanai Travels, Motor Stand Rd. T 3633. **Tourist Offices and Information** Directorate of Information, Cultural Affairs and Tourism, Government of Tripura, Gandhighat. T 3839.

Tours Agartala – Sipahijala – Neermahal, 0800-1930, Sun. Agartala – Kamalasagar Matabari (Tripura Sundari), – Sipahijala, 0800-1930, Tue. Agartala – Bhuvenswari Matabari – Sipahijala, 0800-1930, Fri.

There are Tripura Bhavans at Lachit Nagar, Guwahati 7810007, T 28767, 1 Pretoria St, Calcutta 700016, T 442801 and at Kautilya Marg, Chanakyapuri, New Delhi 110021, T 3015157.

Air This is the only convenient means of travel to Agartala. **Indian Airlines** To **Calcutta**, daily, 0815, 45 min; To **Guwahati**, Wed, Fri, Sat and Sun, 0715, 40 min. Indian Airlines, Palace Compound, T 5588 and Airport, T 3128. In addition there are daily Vayudoot flights from **Agartala to Calcutta** (1 hr 10 min) and also to **Kailashar** (1 hr) via Kamalpur (25 min) on Tue, Th and Sat. T 3937.

Rail The nearest railway station is at **Dharmanagar**, 200 km away which in turn is connected to Lumding Station. Guwahati is connected to Lumding by the Cachar Exp, Kamrup Exp, Tinsukia Mail and Barak Valley Exp.

Road The distances are Calcutta 1808 km, Guwahati, 599 km, Shillong 499 km, Imphal 539 km, Kohima 683 km, Silchar 317 km, Itanagar 980 km and Siliguri 1074 km. Tripura Road Transport Corporation runs four buses from Dharmanagar to Agartala daily, an 8 hour journey. A private tourist coach operates Silchar to Agartala once daily.

ORISSA

Despite the fame of the Sun Temple at Konarak and of the Jagannath Temple in Puri, *Orissa* remains one of the least visited parts of India. Fewer than 3% of tourists visiting India at the end of the 1980s went to the state, and some of its outstanding sites remain little known. Yet Orissa has had a long and distinctive history, and contains some of India's most outstandingly beautiful scenery. Although it is little visited, it is quite easily accessible.

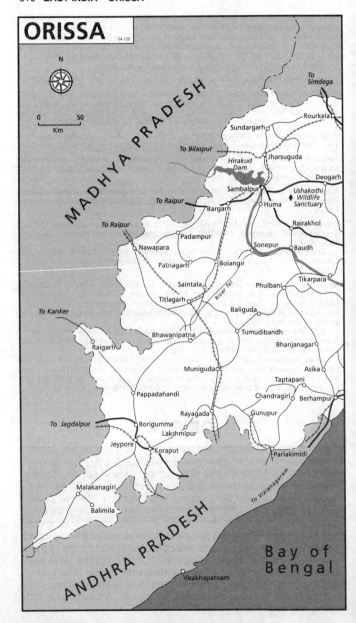

Social indicators *Literacy* M 34% F 21% *Newspaper circulation:* 231,000 *Birth rate* Rural 34:1000 Urban 29:1000 *Death rate* Rural 13:1000 Urban 9:1000 *Infant mortality* Rural 139:1000, Urban 64:1000 *In-migrants* 807,000 *Out-migrants* 528,000 *Registered graduate job seekers* 574,000 *Average annual income per head* : Rs 1100 *Inflation 1981-87* 73%.

Religion *Hindu* 95% *Muslim* 2% *Christian* 2%.

Towns and cities Orissa has only 13% of its population living in towns, making it one of the least urbanised states in India. Bhubaneshwar is the modern capital, with a population of 289,000, but the former capital Cuttack still has a larger population, of 400,000.

INTRODUCTION

The land

The train or road journey from Calcutta to Bhubaneshwar enters Orissa from the NE. The road from Midnapore turns sharply S after entering the State passing to the E of the ancient volcanic Simlipal Massif, which rises to a height of more than

1000 m. From Balasore southwestwards the road crosses the flat alluvial plains of the **Brahmani** and **Mahanadi** rivers, one of the rich rice growing deltas of the E coast. Just to the N of Cuttack, the old capital of Orissa, the road crosses some of the striking red lateritic soils that run in a band some 40 or 50 km wide from Balasore to Bhubaneshwar and beyond. They provided one of the building materials for Bhubaneshwar itself.

If you just visit the cities of Bhubaneshwar and Puri and the Sun Temple at Konarak it is easy to get the impression that Orissa is nothing but a flat alluvial plain. On any of the roads between that famous triangle of sites the view stretches for mile after mile over flat paddy fields. Occasional low mounds of granite, such as the hill at Dhauli on which a new Buddhist stupa now stands, overshadowing the ancient edicts of Asoka carved on a bare outcrop, break the otherwise straight horizon. If you have the chance it is worth going to the top, for in morning and evening light you get breathtaking views.

The delta stretches nearly 170 km from its northernmost point southwards to the Chilika Lake, and it is often over 80 km wide. It is formed of the alluvium which, until the Hirakud dam was completed in 1957, the Mahanadi River used to deposit with devastating frequency through its annual flooding. In the S is the **Chilika Lake**, only a few metres deep but covering between 900 and 1,200 sq km according to the season, with water which alternates between fresh and brackish.

But the image of an overwhelmingly flat, intensively cultivated State with settled and long established villages, is misleading. The delta accounts for no more than 10% of Orissa's surface area. The whole of the area inland of Bhubaneshwar, to the W of a line running from Balasore in the N to Chatrapore in the S, is made up of the ancient rocks of peninsular India. Among them are some of India's richest mineral resources. Coal is mined in thick seams 100 km NW of Bhubaneshwar. Around Bhubaneshwar itself and at several other sites in the interior are important bauxite deposits, which began to be exploited in the 1980s for aluminium smelting. In the far N of the state, especially between Keonjhar and Rourkela, are enormous reserves of very high grade iron. They frequently occur as outcropping hills of almost solid iron ore. These are now exploited in the iron and steel mill, built with help initially from Germany, at Rourkela itself. In addition to these basic mineral resources there are also important reserves of manganese, graphite and mica.

Such a list of resources might suggest an unattractive industrial landscape. In fact nothing could be further from the reality of interior Orissa. Until recently much of the State was inaccessible. Densely forested hills, rising in the SW to over 1500 m, were made inhospitable to settlers from the plains both by the difficulty of clearing the forest and by the devastating prevalence of malaria. Although the total annual rainfall along the coast decreases southeastwards from nearly 1600 mm at Balasore to just over 1100 mm at Chatrapur, the inland hills in the far SW receive much more than their nearby coastal strip. Furthermore, most of Orissa has one of the shortest dry seasons in India, only Jan and Feb being virtually rainless.

The combination of climate and relief resulted in dense natural deciduous forest, with *sal** common, peopled only by tribal groups, living in isolation, with a stone age culture, and barely touched by the societies and events on the coast. Shifting cultivation, in which clearings were made in the forest, cultivated for a few years and then left to recover their natural vegetation, was widely practised.

Today the hills have been extensively opened up. If you drive inland there are stunningly beautiful routes via **Keonjhar** to **Sambalpur**, crossing the Brahmani river, and then S through Bolangir to **Bhawanipatna** and **Koraput**. The forests have given way to an open parkland scenery, interspersed with open fields.

These are still rarely travelled roads, but the scenic rewards for the slowness of parts of the journey are great. The lakes to the S of Koraput, in hills which at

3,000 million years old are among the earth's oldest, are particularly striking. Though much of the forest has now been severely thinned and cultivation has spread up many of the valleys there remain remote and sparsely populated areas, and an atmosphere of quiet stillness unimaginable when you are on the plains.

Climate
N Orissa lies full in the track of the main monsoon current bringing over 1500 mm of rain, but the southern part of the state receives less than 1250 mm. Most of Orissa has a typical Indian monsoon distribution, the main rains starting in Jun and tailing off in Nov. Lying just S of the Tropic of Cancer, Orissa is very warm throughout the year, though the hills are sufficiently high (1500 m) to moderate the temperatures significantly.

People
The tribal population, about a quarter of the total, live mainly in the Koraput, Phulbani, Sundargarh and Mayurbhanj districts. There are some 60 *Adivasi* ('ancient inhabitants') or tribal groups living in forest and remote hill regions of the state, some of whom still remain virtually untouched by modern civilization and have kept their tribal traditions alive. Each has a distinct language, pattern of social customs, and artistic and musical tradition including dance forms.

The **konds** who are mostly to be found in the western districts are famous because they carried out human sacrifice in the past. Today this has been replaced by animal sacrifice at the time of sowing seeds to ensure a good crop. They, in common with several other groups, still use bows and arrows to defend themselves from wild animals.

In the southern districts, especially in Koraput you may still come across the **bondas** or naked people of Tibeto-Burmese origin who speak an Austro-Asiatic language and come to trade at local markets. They live on high hills, growing rice by the shifting cultivation method, irrigating and terracing paddy fields and have domesticated cows and goats. The women wear striking silver necklets which cover the neck completely.

The **koya** who live in villages in clearings in the middle of dense forest are distinguished by their headgear made of bison horn.

The **santals** come from the northern districts of Mayurbhanj and Balasore particularly from around the Simlipal National Park area. Their language is one of the oldest in India. In the northwestern industrial belt have abandoned their aboriginal lifestyle to go and work in the steel mills.

Music and dance, especially at marriages and religious ceremonies, are a common and distinct feature of the tribal life style. Tribal and folk dances are performed throughout the year in the villages but more particularly during festival time in Oct-Nov and Mar-Apr.

Economy
Agriculture Shifting cultivation, in which clearings were made in the forest, cultivated for a few years and then left to recover their natural vegetation, used to be widely practised. Even in the 1960s it was estimated that over 3 million hectares of forest was cut every year by shifting cultivators. Today the hills have been extensively opened up to settled farming. In the S colonisation schemes have been introduced for Indian emigrants returning from Burma and Sri Lanka. Rice and some millets dominate the farming in the interior. Rice is grown on 90% of the fertile plains of the Mahanadi delta. There are also small areas of jute, ragi, oilseeds and gram.

Resources and industry Among the ancient rocks of inland Orissa are some of India's richest mineral resources. Coal is mined in thick seams at **Talcher**, 100 km to the NW of Bhubaneshwar. Around Bhubaneshwar itself and at several other sites in the interior are important bauxite deposits. They began to be exploited in the 1980s for aluminium smelting. In the far N of the state, especially between Keonjhar and Rourkela, are enormous reserves of very high grade iron. They frequently occur as outcropping hills of almost solid iron ore. In addition to these basic mineral resources there are also important reserves of manganese, graphite and mica. Mining began only after Independence in 1947. A new port was built at Paradwip to handle the export of minerals from Orissa.

In the last 20 years Orissa has seen major developments of industry. Aluminium works, using local bauxite and hydro-electricity, and the steel works at Rourkela, are now on stream. There has been increasing investment from within India, but some of the development has taken place with the help of foreign aid. Despite recent growth, Orissa still provides only 3% of India's factory employment.

Craft industries Stone carving has been a highly developed skill in Orissa for over 2,000 years, as can be seen from the rock cut cave sculpture in the Udayagiri and Khandagiri caves, which date from the 1st century BC. The artistry that produced these early sculptures and the superb carvings on Orissan temples in Bhubaneswar, Puri and Konarak is still alive in modern craftsmen. Sculpting in stone, which reached such magnificence in the temples nearly a thousand years ago, can be seen today in the delicate images carved out of soft soapstone, hard konchila or multicoloured serpentine from Khiching or turned into bowls and plates. In Puri the sculptors' quarter is in Pathuria Sahi or Stone carvers' Street. Orissa also has a tradition of hornwork in Parlakhemundi and Cuttack, buffalo horn being carved into the usual small flat figures of animals and birds.

Silver filigree, *Tarkashi* is perhaps one of the most unique and exquisite works of the Cuttack jewellers who turn fine silver wire into beautiful, fragile objects with floral patterns. Small boxes, trays and most of all jewellery are the popular items. The silver used is close to sterling silver which is drawn through finer and finer holes.

Everyday domestic utensils are widely available in brass and bell-metal. The same craftsmen also produce small figurines, vases and plates. The **tribal metal casting** in the *dokra** style by the lost wax process is carried out in the Mayurbhanj district. A clay shell is created around a wax core and molten metal is poured into the shape, displacing the wax.

Wood carving and inlay work on wood is still practised, the most common example of the former being the brightly coloured replicas of the deities in the Jagannath temple, and other figures of animals and birds sold as toys. Ivory inlay, now replaced by plastic inlays, was traditionally carried out for making gifts for the Puri temples by rich patrons and also for making illustrated wooden covers for narrow palm leaf manuscripts. The tradition of using papier-mâché masks of deities and animal characters, to tell stories from the epics also comes from Orissa.

The *chitrakars** (picture makers), particularly from the village of Raghurajpur near Puri, paint the *pattachitras** on specially prepared cloth, coated with earth to stiffen it and finally finished with lacquer after painting, producing not only pictures but attractive playing cards in the form of discs. Old sets of 'ganjapa' consisted of 96 cards. The bold curved and angular lines and vibrant colours which traditionally came from earth, stone, leaves and flowers, depict the tales from the Vedas and Puranas, but mainly of Radha and Krishna and of course Lord Jagannath. The best 'chitrakars' hold the coveted post of painting the Puri temple deities and their 'cars' each year. They also produce fine murals for the temples and manuscripts on paper and palm-leaf, commissioned by the rich. However, what is commonly available in the bazaars are cruder examples for pilgrims to take home as mementos.

Palm leaf etching is another skill that is still practised. An iron stylus is held stationary while moving the leaf to produce illustrated manuscripts. It was a technology that helped to give the Oriya script its rounded form. Manuscripts from the 16th century have been found, most of which are secular. The leaves had to be prepared by drying, boiling, drying again and flattening before coating with shell. After inscribing, the grooves would be rubbed with soot or powdered charcoal while colour was added with a brush. The leaves would be stacked and strung together and placed between decorative covers made of wood. The artists who work on 'pattachitras' in Raghurajpur have also revived this art form.

Pipli, a small town about 32 km SW of Bhubaneswar on the Puri road is famous for its colourful **appliqué** work, one of the centres for production of a special kind of brightly coloured embroidered cloth probably originally designed for use in the Jagannath temple. The shops on the road side sell items for the house and garden – sun umbrellas, canopies, cushion covers, wall-hangings and heart-shaped cloth shields called *tarasa*, which use primary colours to make patterns of animals, birds and flowers on a backcloth. Unfortunately the attempt to churn out goods for a growing market has resulted in the loss of attention to detail of the original fine Pipli work which picked out motifs of appliqué by cleverly stuffing sections of the pattern. The best pieces now tend to be sent away to the government emporia in Bhubaneswar and New Delhi.

Textile weaving has been a traditional handicraft throughout Orissa for generations and thousands are still employed in this cottage industry in different parts of the state. In common with other parts of India which have developed a textile of its own, it is one of the few regions producing **ikat***, the technique of 'resist-dyeing' the warp or weft thread, or both, before weaving, so that the fabric that emerges from the loom has a delicate enmeshed pattern. The favourite designs include rows of flowers, birds and animals (particularly elephants) as well as geometric shapes, using either tussar or cotton yarn. Berhampore, Sambalpur, Mayurbhanj and Naupatana are all prominent centres producing silk and cotton saris. Some also produce tapestry, bedspreads and embroidered fabric.

Crafts villages There are several villages where craftsmen are grouped together. In **Raghurajpur** (12 km from Puri) you can watch villagers painting the 'Pattachitras' in bright folk-art style or etching palm leaves. **Pipli,** on the Bhubaneswar-Puri Road, specialises in appliqué work, **Belakati** (10 km from Bhubaneswar) in bell-metal, and there is a community of Tibetan carpet weavers at **Chandragiri** near the Taptapani Hot Springs in tribal country. Adjacent to the Buddhist site of **Lalitagiri** is a stone-carvers' village, while master-weavers work at their looms in the Buddhist villages of **Nuapatna** and **Maniabhanda** (70 km from Bhubaneswar) or down the narrow streets next to the temple at **Berhampur**. **Cuttack** remains famous for silver filigree work.

History

It was the coastal plains that were the focus of early settlement and the first development of politically organised kingdoms in the region. Orissa, a part of the ancient kingdom of Kalinga which also comprised of a part of what is now Andhra Pradesh, grew prosperous through trading, using its port of Kalingnagar, as early as the 4th century BC. Their colonial influence extended beyond the seas to lands as distant as Java, Sumatra, Borneo and Bali where they left the mark of Indian civilization. The rulers of the Maurya dynasty with their capital near modern Patna in Bihar held sway over most of N India and up to this eastern region of India.

The Mauryan king **Asoka** who crushed the *Kalingan kingdom* around 260 BC underwent a total reformation after experiencing the horrors of war and the bloodshed that accompanied the conquering of this region. He became a fervent Buddhist and preached the philosophy of peace and although Buddhism flowered in his time, his tolerance permitted the continuance of Jainism and Hinduism. After Asoka, Orissa regained independence once again in the 1st century BC under the native **King Kharavela**, a fervent Jain, who was perhaps the greatest of the Kalinga kings; his achievements in extending his empire and descriptions of his capital remain recorded for posterity in the Udayagiri caves near Bhubaneswar, which show an exceptional development in cave sculpture.

After Kharavela there appear to have emerged separate areas to the N and centre of the region which went under the names of Utkal ('land where the arts excelled') and Toshali. Maritime trade flourished and Buddhism once again became a popular religion. The Buddhist caves being excavated in Lalitagiri, Ratnagiri and Udayagiri near Cuttack may date from the early 2nd century and do not, as believed until recently, only go back to around the 5th century.

The greatest period of temple building in Bhubaneswar coincided with the Kesaris (7th-12th century) to be followed by **Ganga dynasty** (12th-15th century) who were responsible for the Jagannath Temple in Puri (c1100) and the Sun Temple at Konarak (c1250), the 3 sites making the 'golden triangle' in Orissa. The most significant years were between 750-1250 AD which saw the flowering of the distinctive Northern or Indo-Aryan style of Orissan temple architecture. The affluence of the Gangas who became rich and powerful on trade gave them the means to support an ambitious programme of developing temple architecture.

Orissa with her military might resisted the annexation of her territory by Muslims from the N. For a time the Afghans held Orissa in the 16th century until finally the powerful Mughals arrived as conquerors in 1592 and during their reign destroyed many of the temples that once stood in Bhubaneswar. It was their violent disruption of temple life in Puri and Bhubaneshwar that led the Brahmin community to ban all non-Hindus from the precincts of the Lingaraj and Jagannath temples when they were allowed to return. The Mughals were followed by the Marathas in 1751. In 1765 after Clive's win at Plassey, parts of Orissa, Bihar and Bengal were acquired by the East India Company with further gains in Cuttack and Puri at the beginning of the following century, thus by 1803 British Rule extended over the whole region.

Temple architecture

The temples of Bhubaneshwar, along with those of Puri and Konarak, represent a remarkably full record of the development of Orissan architecture from the 7th century AD to the 13th century AD. Although some of the temples have suffered structural damage from a variety of causes, many are virtually intact and some are still in everyday use. These are living shrines, centres of active pilgrimage, worship and faith. Although, non-Hindus are excluded from 2 of the most famous, the Lingaraja Temple in Bhubaneshwar and the Jagannath Temple in Puri, it is possible to gain some impression of both from views over the external walls. But even with these restrictions those temples that are open provide plentiful opportunity to follow in detail the development of Orissan artistic and architectural traditions. Furthermore, they are all easily accessible. The temples in Bhubaneshwar are within 2 km of each other and are very easy to reach from any of the main hotels on foot, by rickshaw or by car.

The most obvious features of Orissan temples are the tall, curvilinear tower or spire, and a much lower, more open structure or porch in front of the entrance to the tower. The taller tower, which rises over the sanctuary, is known as the *deul** (pronounced day-ool) or *rekha deul*, while the porch is usually referred to as the *jagamohana.** The interior of the sanctuary is quite dark and is designed to allow only a glimpse of the presiding deity and to enable priests to conduct ritual worship. It is usually considerably smaller than the more open porch, where worshippers may meditate or simply wait. In later temples 2 further halls were often added, the dancing hall (*nata mandira**) and the hall of offering (*bhoga mandira**), sometimes referred to as *nata mandapam* and *bhoga mandapam*.

The main sanctuary tower and the porch are both normally square in plan. However, the square plan is broken vertically by the inward curving upwards form of the main tower. Furthermore each exterior face of the sanctuary tower is divided by vertical, flat-faced, projections (*rathas**). In the early temples in Bhubaneshwar there was just one such projection, dividing each face into 3 parts – giving rise to the term *tri-rathas*. As temples became more ornate with increasing technical and artistic sophistication the number of projections increased, creating 5 or 7 sections- *panch-rathas* or *sapta-rathas* – or more.

Both the sanctuary and the porch are divided vertically as well as horizontally. Some Orissan

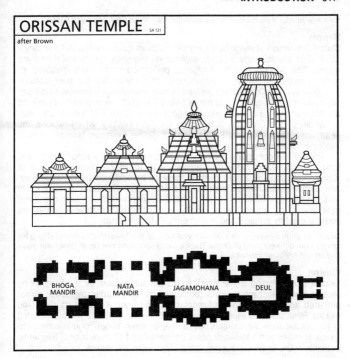

ORISSAN TEMPLE SA 121
after Brown

BHOGA MANDIR · NATA MANDIR · JAGAMOHANA · DEUL

architects likened the structure of the temple to that of the human body, and the names given to the vertical sections correspond to the main parts of the body. Fuller architectural details are given in the Archaeological Survey's publications, but the chief features may be summarised as follows:

1. A platform. Early temples had no platform, and even some important temples are also without one. In contrast, in highly developed temples such as the Surya temple at Konarak, the platform is a prominent feature, often being built up to a height of more than 3 m.

2. The lower storey, seen as corresponding to the lower limbs. In early temples this was divided into 3 parts, the base, above which was a perpendicular section corresponding to the shin. This was topped by a set of mouldings. In some mature temples the scale of this section was greatly elongated and was itself then divided into 5 layers.

3. The upper storey takes the shape of a curvilinear spire in the case of the sanctuary, or a pyramidal roof in the case of the porch, and is seen as corresponding to the human trunk.

4. A head with crowning features. The head itself is divided into a series of regular elements: The "head" or *mastaka** of the sanctuary developed over time, as did the other elements of the temple. The first standard feature is the "neck" (*beki**) a recessed cylindrical portion which is surmounted by the skull. This is represented by a symbolic fruit, the *amla**. On the *amla* rests a "water pot", which is an auspicious symbol, and then on top of all comes the sacred weapon of the deity.

The real distinction between the sanctuary and the porch lies in the development of the upper sections. Over the porch or *jagamohana* the upper storey tapers rapidly in a pyramidal shape made up of a series of flat layers decreasing in size from the bottom upwards. The upper storey of the main sanctuary tower has a convex curve upwards, very gentle at first but increasing sharply at the top.

There is a third type of temple sanctuary in which the *deul* has a barrel-vaulted and elongated roof, though it is comparatively rare in Bhubaneshwar. This type is called *kakharu*, the name of a local pumpkin. The best example is the Vaital Deul (**see page 623**).

Dances

Odissi The region of magnificent temple sculpture gave rise to a classical dance form which shadows the postures, expressions and lyrical qualities of the carved figures. The dance was a ritual offering performed in the '*nata mandiras*' of temples by the temple dancers (*maharis* in Orissa) resplendent in their costume and jewellery. The Odissi which evolved as a religious dance follows strict rules of position for the body, feet and hands falling into postures and attitudes akin to the figures sculpted in rock centuries ago. A favourite subject for interpretation is Jayadev's 'Gita Govinda' dating from the 12th century, which explores the depths of Krishna's love for Radha, and the dancer expresses both the sensual and devotional with great lyricism.

The *folk dances* usually performed during festivals take various forms – day long 'Danda Nata' are ritual dances, the traditional fishermen's dance 'Chaitighoda' requires a horse dummy, there is a battle dance called 'Paika Nritya' and 'Chhau' is the masked dance-drama reminiscent of Orissa's martial past. In addition there are tribal dances which are often performed with distinctive head gear made of animal horns shells and colourful costumes, sometimes accompanied by simple string instruments, flutes and drums.

Tribal Fair Bhubaneswar holds a fair each year from 26 Jan-2 Feb which is attended by tribal groups from different parts of Orissa. There are excellent performances of dance and music and art and crafts exhibitions.

Cuisine

Orissa's principal crop is rice which forms the staple food, with wheat taking second place. Most meals are accompanied by fairly lightly spiced side dishes prepared from a large variety of vegetables and pulses as well as chutneys and pickles. Fresh sea-food especially prawns and the flat 'pomfret' fish are included in the coastal areas. Restaurants will sometimes offer Orissan food in addition to typical N Indian and S Indian dishes. Continental and Chinese food is frequently available in the larger restaurants in the major cities and towns.

Orissa is particularly noted for its sweetmeats prepared from milk. Try from rasagolla, rasamalai, chenapoda, khiramohan, rajbhoga, rabidi, jilabi and kalakhanda. Khiri is prepared with milk and rice (similar to rice pudding) or semolina or vermicelli for festive occasions. There are also the pithas which are often filled with sweetened coconut.

Although tea is the common drink, coffee is freely available in hotels and restaurants. Fruit juices (mango, sugar cane, bel) and the very refreshing green coconut 'milk' is worth trying. The last is sold on the roadside – safe and ready-to-drink, the top sliced off and a straw put in when you ask for it.

Hotel accommodation

Bhubaneswar and Puri each have an excellent A grade hotel. Few others in B and C categories are very good. Most places however only have good value but lower grade hotels often Indian style in the smaller towns. OTDC however have a number of Pantha Nivas hotels which vary from excellent in Chandipur on the sea to spartan in out of the way places. It is sometimes possible to stay in Inspection Bungalows or Circuit Houses (which give priority to government officers) provided they are not booked. These are also very convenient for a rest stop – the caretaker will often allow you to use the facilities if they are vacant.

BHUBANESHWAR

Population 310,000. *Altitude* 45 m. *Best season* October to March.
Languages Oriya, Hindi and English

	Jan	Feb	Mar	Apr	May	Jun	Jul	Aug	Sep	Oct	Nov	Dec	Av/Tot
Max (°C)	29	32	35	38	38	35	31	31	31	31	29	28	32
Min (°C)	16	19	22	26	27	26	25	25	25	23	18	16	22
Rain (mm)	12	25	17	12	61	223	301	336	305	266	51	3	1612

Bhubaneshwar (a name meaning "The Lord of the Universe") is the modern capital of Orissa, chosen in 1948 in place of Cuttack some 29 km to the NE. One of the reasons for the decision lay in the antiquity of Bhubaneshwar's role as capital of the Kalinga Empire. It is the architectural legacy of that period which remains Bhubaneshwar's greatest attraction. However, there are several sites in the vicinity which testify the importance of the region far earlier than the 7th to 11th centuries when the Kalinga kings ruled Orissa and regions beyond. Both Jain and Buddhist shrines give clear evidence of important settlements around Bhubaneshwar in the first 2 centuries BC, and one of the most complete edicts of the Mauryan Emperor Asoka, dating from between 272-236 BC, remains carved in rock just 5 miles to the SW of the modern city. The remains of a ruined city, Sisupalgarh (under 3 km from the centre of modern Bhubaneshwar), have been excavated to show that it was occupied from the beginning of the 3rd century BC to the middle of the 4th century AD.

Local Festival *Asokashtami* The Lingaraja Car Festival when the image of Lord Siva (Lingaraja) is drawn on a chariot from his own temple to visit the Ramesvara temple for 4 days takes place in Mar/Apr on the 8th day of the waxing moon in the month of 'Chaitra'.

Places of interest Once the city with 7000 temples which were built over centuries around the Bindusagar tank, Bhubaneswar still attracts pilgrims and tourists to the 500 that still survive.

The Parasuramesvera Temple This is an excellent place to start a tour of the temples. It is easily found just 200 m down a lane to the right off the main road to Puri, about 1 km S of the museum. In order to reach it you pass the Muktesvara Temple, to which you should return.

The Parasuramesvara Temple has been dated to the 7th century. It is a small but highly decorated temple, and although it is not the oldest, is the best preserved of the early Bhubaneswar temples. Its early date is indicated partly by the nature of the porch, which is rectangular rather than square, and which has a stepped roof rather than a pyramidal structure typical of later development. Even so, the porch was probably built after the sanctuary itself, as is suggested by the rather crude junction between the 2.

The early date of the temple is also illustrated by the building technique used, in which masonry was kept in place by weight and balance and without any form of cement. Another feature which marks this out as an early temple is the carving of the lintel over the doorway into the sanctuary. Traditionally this entrance is topped by carvings of the 9 planets, but in the Parasuramesvara temple there are only 8.

The temple marks an important stage in the development of Hindu power at the expense of Buddhism in 7th century Orissa. One illustration of this transfer is the frequent representation of the figure of *Lakulisa*, the seventh century priest responsible for Hindu proselytism, sculpted in Buddha-like form, often surrounded by disciples. A second illustration of the borrowing from Buddhist traditions is the use made of distinctive window shaped motifs developed earlier in Buddhist chaitya halls, such as those at Ajanta. In Bhubaneshwar's temples these are described as *chaitya** windows. On the front of the sanctuary tower the central section has 2 obvious examples. The lower shows **Siva** tackling **Ravana**, with Ravana, the demon king of Lanka desperately trying to root out Mount Kailasa,

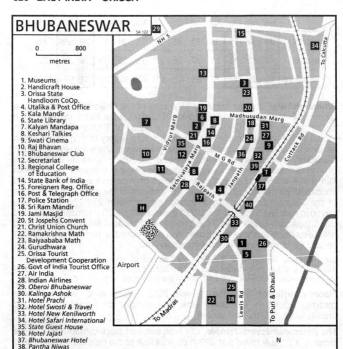

BHUBANESWAR

SA 122

0   800
metres

1. Museums
2. Handicraft House
3. Orissa State
   Handloom CoOp.
4. Utalika & Post Office
5. Kala Mandir
6. State Library
7. Kalyan Mandapa
8. Keshari Talkies
9. Swati Cinema
10. Raj Bhavan
11. Bhubaneswar Club
12. Secretariat
13. Regional College
    of Education
14. State Bank of India
15. Foreigners Reg. Office
16. Post & Telegraph Office
17. Police Station
18. Sri Ram Mandir
19. Jami Masjid
20. St Josephs Convent
21. Christ Union Church
22. Ramakrishna Math
23. Baiyaababa Math
24. Gurudhwara
25. Orissa Tourist
    Development Cooperation
26. Govt of India Tourist Office
27. Air India
28. Indian Airlines
29. Oberoi Bhubaneswar
30. Kalinga Ashok
31. Hotel Prachi
32. Hotel Swosti & Travel
33. Hotel New Kenilworth
34. Hotel Safari International
35. State Guest House
36. Hotel Jajati
37. Bhubaneswar Hotel
38. Pantha Niwas
39. Hotel Anarkali
40. Hotel Pushpak
41. PWD Inspection Bungalow
T. Train Station & Retiring
   Rooms & Tourist Information

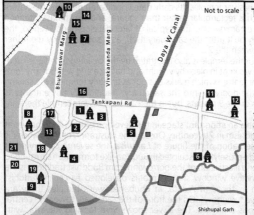

Not to scale

N

Temple Area

1. Parasuramesvara
2. Svarnajalesvara
3. Muktesvara,
   Siddhesvara
   & Kedaresvara
4. Ananta-Vasudeva
5. Rajarani
6. Brahmesvara
7. Satrughnesvara
8. Vaital Deul
   & Sisiresvara
9. Lingaraja
10. Ramesvara
11. Bhaskaresvara
12. Meghesvara
13. Bindu Sarovara
14. Lakshmanesvara
15. Bharatesvara
16. Navakesvara
17. Uttaresvara
18. Markandeyesvara,
    Mohini & Sarideul
19. Makaresvara,
    Mitresvara,
    & Chitrakarini
20. Yamesvara
21. Bakesvara

Shishupal Garh

Siva's home. **Ganesa** and **Karttikeya** are ready to fight while Siva is comforting his wife, Parvati. This is a universally known Hindu story, familiar to any Hindu today just as it was when the temple was built. The upper *chaitya* window shows Siva as Nataraja, the Lord of the Dance.

The sanctuary is just under 13 m high and does not have a platform. Both horizontally and vertically it is divided into 3 sections. Several features of the carving give an excellent idea of motifs and styles which were to reach their full flowering in later temples. The base, for example, has a top moulding (just a few cm above the ground) which is decorated with scrollwork, tiny round motifs encircling figures in cameo-like form, and birds, human beings and floral motifs.

At about eye level, the moulding also has features that were developed in later temples. The recessed decorative frieze (which itself was discarded in later designs) is embossed with human figures, including early examples of the amorous couples which were to become such a prominent feature of the Konarak temple. In between the human figures are panels with **vyalas*** – rampant lions, head swung right round, usually astride a crouching elephant.

In addition to the main entrance to the porch there is a door on the S side and 4 latticed windows. But it is the carvings on each side of the W doorway that are outstanding. They are vigorous and graceful sculptures of musicians and dancers, executed with exceptional skill.

Walking round the sanctuary you can see a further common feature of temples in the Orissan style, the placing of sculptures of the main accessory deities in niches on each side of the sanctuary tower related to the deity to whom the sanctuary itself is dedicated. The Parasuramesvara temple was dedicated to Siva. Only 2 of the 3 original deities survive. On the S side of the sanctuary, at eye level in the middle of the sanctuary tower, is a statue of the 4-armed elephant-headed god Ganesa. His trunk is curled towards a bowl of laddhus, a sweet of which tradition has it Ganesa was particularly fond. In his upper left hand he holds a hatchet. In the S niche is the 2 armed brother of Ganesa, Karttikeya, known in S India as Subrahmanya. His hair is arranged in 3 locks. He carries a citrus fruit in his right hand and a spear in his left, the symbol of his role as warrior of the gods. Beneath him is his vehicle, the peacock.

In the words of the Archaeological Survey, the carvings are "chaste and elegant". The lintel above the niche showing Karttikeya illustrates the marriage of Siva and **Parvati**. They are standing to the left of Agni, the fire god, with the kneeling figure of Brahma to the right of Agni, probably pouring ghee with a ladle. To the right of Brahma is Surya.

In the NW corner of the temple compound is a "lingam of one thousand *lingas**" – the phallic symbol of Siva with 1,000 lingas engraved on its surface.

The Svarnajalesvara Temple If you have plenty of time it is possible to walk some 50 metres to the S to see the Svarnajalesvara temple. Architecturally and sculpturally this is almost a duplicate of the Parasuramesvara temple, but sadly it is badly dilapidated. There are fragments on the N and W sides of friezes showing stories from the Ramayana.

Muktesvara and Siddhesvara Temples Retrace your steps and walk back towards the main Puri road. On your left you come to another compound with 2 temples. On your right is the Muktesvara temple and ahead to your left is the Siddhesvara temple.

Muktesvara temple, described by George Michell as "the most exquisitely ornamented temple in the Bhubaneswar series", takes us forward in time to the end of the first phase of temple building, the late 10th century. Although it still has features of the earlier buildings, such as the 3 fold horizontal division of the *bada*, and the absence of lions supporting the crowning *amla* on top of the sanctuary, the plan of the sanctuary is now divided into the 5-sectioned form. Also the plinth on which the temple stands consists of 5 mouldings, like later temples.

New designs are in evidence, with graceful female figures and **pilasters*** carved with snake figures – *nagas* and *naginis*. Most strikingly, the porch is taking on a new and more dramatic layered form, although the pyramidal roof is not yet topped with the full range of elements. To set the seal on the transition, **Ketu** has been introduced as the ninth planet and Ganesa is joined by his mount, the mouse, unlike his depiction in the Parasuramesvara Temple.

The first impression of the Muktesvara temple is given by the unique gateway arch or

*Torana,** which has been dated at about AD 900. Although the upper portion of the arch is restored, the original skill can still be seen in the graceful female figures. But the compactness of the temple is also very striking. The rectangular tank at its E end, in use today by priests and devotees, and the well on the southern side of the compound into which women still toss coins in the hope of curing infertility, symbolise the continued holiness of the site. On the door frame of the well is carved the figure of a local saint, Lakulisa, whose image is found on several of Bhubaneswar's early temples, for he played a major part in replacing Buddhist with Hindu worship in the region.

But it is the carvings which make the sharpest impression. The *chaitya* windows carved in the vertical *rathas* of the sanctuary are crowned by a decorative motif showing the grinning face of a lion. A string of beaded tassels often comes out of the lion's mouth, and the whole is flanked by 2 dwarves in an ensemble that is known as a *bho** motif. It finds its finest expression in the Muktesvara Temple.

The decoration of the porch walls imitates some of the scenes from the main vertical section of the sanctuary. On the N and S walls is a diamond-shaped latticed window. Notice the monkey scenes on the outer frame. There is also an unusual degree of carving on the interior of the porch.

Immediately to the NW of the Muktesvara Temple is the later **Siddhesvara Temple**. It shows the mature Orissan temple form almost complete. Unlike the earlier temples, the vertical lower section is now divided into 5 parts. Furthermore, on top of the sanctuary the *amla* is supported by 4 squatting figures. However, the overall effect is comparatively plain, as sculptures which were marked out on the rock were never executed, a feature evident also in the porch of the Rajarani temple.

If you have plenty of time it is possible to walk S to the Gauri temple, which probably dates from a similar period to the Muktesvara temple. However, not only is it built in the **khakara*** form, like the Vaital Deul (see below) but it has been substantially repaired. The porch was rebuilt in the early years of this century, but there are a few original sculptures of real merit. Note the girl shown leaning against a post, on which is perched a bird, on the S face of the eastern projection of the sanctuary. On the W projection there is an equally beautiful sculpture of a girl removing her anklets.

The Rajarani Temple You need to go back up the main road towards Bhubaneswar a very short distance and then follow the road to the right. The entrance to the Rajarani Temple is about 300 m on the right. The Brahmesvara Temple is a further 1 km down the same road. The Rajarani temple is set back 200 m from the road in an open space. Both are representatives of later styles, the Rajarani being early 11th century and the Brahmesvara precisely datable to AD 1060. However, the Rajarani Temple no longer has an image of the presiding deity in the sanctuary and it is therefore out of use, while the Brahmesvara continues to be an active temple for worship.

Even as you approach the Rajarani temple down the path the form of the sanctuary is striking, for the main sanctuary tower, nearly 18 m high, is surrounded by 4 miniature copies. These give the sanctuary an almost circular appearance, which perhaps detracts from the impression of the heavenwards projection of the main sanctuary. The example was not followed in other temples. They have the further effect of concealing the diagonal placing of the sanctuary against the porch in a form which is not uncommon elsewhere in India but which is unique in Orissan temples. The diagonally placed square plan of the sanctuary is further concealed by the intricacy of the carving which adds to the sanctuary's almost circular appearance.

On approaching closer it is also obvious that the porch, or *jagmohana**, is comparatively plain, even though it has the mature style of pyramidal roof. This simplicity reflects the fact that much of the sculpture was unfinished. However, it is possible to see the way in which Orissan sculptors started their work by cutting the stone into sections ("blocking out") which were then roughly shaped ("boasted"), to be finished later by the master sculptor. The finished work is visible in the sculpture of the main sanctuary which is extremely fine.

Perhaps the best preserved features of the temple, not nearly as clearly visible on the other temples, are the statues of the "guardians of the 8 cardinal directions", the *Dikpalakas*. These are the deities whose responsibility it is to protect the central shrine from every quarter. They are placed in pairs about 3 m above ground level, carved in the lower section of the main sanctuary tower.

If you approach the main sanctuary tower by passing to the left (S) of the porch you come across them in the following order:

1. Facing E is **Indra**, the Guardian of the East. He holds a thunderbolt and an elephant goad, and has his vehicle, the elephant, beneath.

2. At right angles to Indra, facing S, is the pot-bellied and bearded figure of **Agni**, god of fire and Guardian of the Southeast. He rides a ram.

3. Moving a few yards along the wall, on the far side of the projection, is the S facing figure of **Yama**, holding a staff and a noose. In the staff is a skull, a symbol associated with Tantrism, as is his vehicle the buffalo.

4. Again at right angles to the figure of Yama is the W facing figure of **Nirritti**, Guardian of the Southwest. Nirriti, the god of misery, holds a severed head and a sword over a figure lying beneath.

5. Again facing W, but on the N side of the sanctuary's central projection, is the image of the Guardian of the West, **Varuna**. He holds the noose associated with fate or destiny in his left hand, while his right hand is in the gesture of giving.

6. At right angles to **Varuna**, facing N, is Vayu (meaning "wind"), Guardian of the Northwest. He holds a banner, clearly fluttering.

7. The last pair of guardians are on the further side of the central projection, on the N and E facing sides respectively. First you come to **Kubera**, Guardian of the North, pot-bellied to signify prosperity, and placed above 7 jars of precious stones.

8. **Isana**, Guardian of the Northeast, is shown as was customary with an erect phallus and accompanied by an emaciated figure.

The Brahmesvara Temple

Like the Muktesvara Temple, the Brahmesvara is in use today. As you enter from the N you pass through the 2 enclosure walls, the inner one of which forms a compact surround for the temple complex which is raised on a platform. Immediately facing you on the N wall of the porch see a well-oiled image of Lakshmi, covered in cloth, and often with incense sticks burning in front of it. The sanctuary itself houses a Siva linga, and it is from an inscription, now missing, that the precise date of the temple's building is known. In addition to the main central sanctuary you see 4 minor shrines, one in each corner of the compound.

The sanctuary tower is over 18 m high. The vertical wall of the sanctuary follows the pattern of mature temples in having a 5-fold division. Looking at the base and at the top of the wall (the *pabhaga** and the *varanda**) you see the rich carvings with which they are decorated. The wall itself is divided into upper and lower sections by a single broad moulding. The lower section is decorated alternately by miniature representations of the *khakara* style temples, such as the *Vaital Deul* which you may visit next. Alternating with these sculptures are those showing rampant lions. Although the central niches of the miniature temple carvings which decorate the corners of the lower section have the guardians of the cardinal directions, they are less prominent than in the Rajarani temple.

In the corresponding spaces of the upper section are miniature representations of the normal temple sanctuary towers, and graceful women. These are not deities but are secular images. The scenes in the niches of the miniature temples of the upper section are mainly erotic couples and female figures. A Nataraja playing on a vina above a bull, shown on the W face, is one of the rare depictions at this level of a deity.

The Satrughnesvara group

(the Mohini, Uttaresvara, Gauri-Sankara-Ganesa and Paschimesvara temples). Despite their ruined state, with only the cores remaining visible, the first 3 temples deserve mention as almost certainly the oldest in Bhubaneshwar. They probably date from the late AD 6th century. The southernmost temple in the group has been rebuilt by the State Archaeological Department of Orissa.

Vaital Deul

To reach the Vaital Deul you retrace your steps and return towards the main temple complex surrounding the tank. 2 features mark out this small, late 8th century, temple for special attention. The first and most obvious is its form. Seen from the road the semi-cylindrical shape in section of the *deul* (which is just over 11 m high) is immediately obvious, marking it out as belonging to the *khakhara* type of temple. As such, it derives as Percy Brown says, from a quite different tradition than the Parasamesvara temple. The shape of the tower is similar to that of the gopurams of Dravida temples in S India. Like them, it takes this shape originally from the Buddhist chaitya halls referred to above. Yet the porch, with its miniature "sanctuary towers" at each corner suggests that the Vaital Deul was a forerunner of the 5-shrined type of temple common later in N India.

The second is its tantric associations, marked by its presiding deity, **Chamunda** (a form of **Durga**) and by other features visible on closer viewing. The first external view of Durga can be obtained from the carving on the northern face of the *bada* where she is shown as the 8 armed **Mahishasuramardini** (slayer of the buffalo demon). She holds a snake, a bow, a shield, a sword, a trident, a thunderbolt and an arrow, and she is piercing the neck of the buffalo demon.

There are excellent carvings elsewhere on the exterior. On the eastern face of the deul there are 2 *chaitya* windows. The lower of these has a beautifully carved figure of the sun god Surya, with Usha and Pratyusha shooting arrows on either side of him while *Aruna* (goddess of the dawn) drives a chariot in front. It has a certain incongruity in view of the image within the sanctum itself. The upper *chaitya*-window has a 10 armed Nataraja, or dancing Siva.

Further evidence of the tantric basis of the temple comes from the stone post to which sacrifices were tethered, just in front of the jagamohana, but more importantly from the image of the deity Chamunda in the central niche of the deul. This is extremely difficult to see without artificial light, though very early morning sun penetrates the gloom of the interior. In Mitra's words "The sanctum is pervaded by a weird atmosphere, the image..of the 8-armed Chamunda is depicted in her most terrifying aspect conceivable. Seated on a corpse with an owl on the right and a jackal on the left, she has an emaciated body with only skin and bones, a shrunken belly, an open mouth and sunken eyes and decorated with a garland of skulls." There are numerous other figures, the most chilling being that of "a male figure on the N wall in the attitude of rising from the ground after filling his skull-cup with the blood of a person whose severed head lies on the right; on the pedestal is an offering of 2 more heads on a tray resting on a tripod, flanked by a jackal feasting on a corpse on the right and a woman holding a head on the left".

The Lingaraja Temple Along with the Jagannatha Temple at Puri the Lingaraja Temple represents the peak of achievement of the Orissan middle period. Built in 1,000 AD, 100 years before the Jagannath Temple, Brown suggests that the Lingaraja Temple is one of India's most remarkable architectural achievements. Although non-Hindus are not allowed inside it is possible to get an impression of the main features of the temple from a specially constructed viewing platform outside the N perimeter wall. If you wish to take photographs, note that early morning and late afternoon are by far the best times.

Even from a distance the sanctuary tower (known in this case as the *Sri Mandir*) dominates the landscape, rising to a height of 54 m. From the viewing platform it is possible to see that it is just one of the 4 main buildings in the temple compound, though there are many other subsidiary shrines. Immediately to the left of the tower is the pillared hall of the jagamohan, then the *Nata Mandir* (dance temple) and finally the *Bhoga Mandir* (hall of offering). Although they all lie on the same E-W axis the latter 2 buildings were added a century after the sanctuary and the porch.

The tower itself is a monumental piece of work. In plan it is just under 17 m square, although the projecting faces take its form out of the true square. Approximately 1/3 of its height is vertical. From 15 m above ground level the sanctuary tower begins to curve inwards, gently at first and then rapidly at the top to produce a graceful parabolic curve at 37.5 m above ground level. The *amla* head is supported by 4 mythical gryphons, surmounted by the pot-shaped pinnacle, in turn carrying the trident of Siva. According to Brown the inner sanctuary is highly unusual. Just under 6 m sq, the small chamber housing the deity has no ceiling, but rises like a chimney up the centre of the tower, only capped by the top of the sanctuary tower itself. Externally the middle section is textured by horizontal mouldings, the background to individual motifs which stand in sharp relief. These comprise a vertical line of miniature towers. On each of the 4 sides there is massive protruding sculpture of a lion crushing an elephant – a common symbol in Orissan architecture.

This section relies on the excellent account given by Debala Mitra in the Archaeological Survey of India's booklet on Bhubaneshwar. This gives far fuller explanations than space permits here, and copies are available from the Archaeological Survey of India and from the Orissa State Museum in Bhubaneshwar.

Udayagiri and Khandagiri caves

Only 6 km from modern Bhubaneshwar, the caves on the 2 low hills of Kumargiri and Kumarigiri known as **Udayagiri** and **Khandagiri** bear witness to the Jain and Buddhist occupation of the region at least by the 2nd century BC. A narrow valley winds between the hills, the route of an early Buddhist pilgrim track leading to a stupa which probably stood on the present site of Bhubaneshwar.

The coarse-grained sandstone which forms Khandagiri ("broken hill") and Udayagiri ("hill of the sunrise") stands out nearly 40 m above the surrounding lateritic and infertile plain. The hills are very easy to visit by car, public transport, rickshaw or bicycle from Bhubaneshwar. The crumbling nature of the sandstone into which they were carved has exposed them to severe damage over time. In recent years the Archaeological Survey of India has done extensive work repairing vital supporting features of the caves and protecting the most important carvings. While some of these works have a rather crude effect their necessity is obvious. The need is even greater as the site has become the focus both of contemporary religious activity and an increasing flow of pilgrims and tourists. The Archaeology Department has now numbered the caves, and this numbering is used below.

The **Jain caves** are among the earliest in India. Furthermore, the inscriptions found on some of the rock surfaces, especially that above *Hathi Gumpha*, the elephant cave (No.14), provide historical evidence of a dynasty known as the Chedis who ruled the region of Kalinga from their capital. This is probably identifiable with the site of present-day Sisupalgarh, 9 km SE of Khandagiri.

Kharavela, the only king of the dynasty about whom there is any detailed information, according to his own record took the power of the Kalingas across a large part of N, central and S India. But in addition to his military achievements he also devoted great efforts to civil works at home. Among these were the improvements of canals, rebuilding his capital city of Kalinganagara, and, in his 13th year of rule, excavating some of the caves for Jaina ascetics at Udayagiri-Khandagiri which we see now. Probably all the caves now visible were constructed in the 150 years preceding the birth of Christ. They were designed for the ascetic life of Jain monks, with no concessions to any form of comfort other than an attempt to provide dry shelter. Too low to stand, the cells are nothing more than sleeping compartments, cramped even for that purpose.

Although the Jains did not enjoy royal patronage after the fall of Kharavela's dynasty, Jain occupation was continuous throughout successive Buddhist and Hindu periods in Bhubaneshwar and the region. The Parsvanatha temple on top of Khandagiri was built at some time in the early 19th century, while the Hindu temple was built in the 1970s.

Visiting the caves

Access to the caves is now controlled and entry is only permitted between 0800-1800.

It is simplest to follow the route indicated in the plan below, as the numbering of the caves is then easiest to follow. First follow the path up towards **Udayagiri,** the right hand of the hills as you face them. Take the right hand path to **cave number 1, the Rani Gumpha**. This is the largest and most impressive of the caves, a double-storeyed monastery cut on 3 sides of a quadrangle. Some of the pillars have now been restored. Note particularly the sculptured friezes on the walls of the caves. On the lower storey the right hand wing is flanked by 2 sentries. The pilasters at the entrance to the cell and the arches are very richly carved, illustrating both religious and royal scenes. The whole series of sculptures in the main, central wing of the caves celebrates the king's victory march. 2 small guard rooms with richly decorated outer faces are placed where the right and the left wings meet the main wing.

7 of the pillars of the upper storey are modern replacements. As in the lower storey the doorway arches to the cells are ornately carved. Auspicious Jain symbols like the snake and the lotus are common, and the friezes vigorously depict stories which seem to have

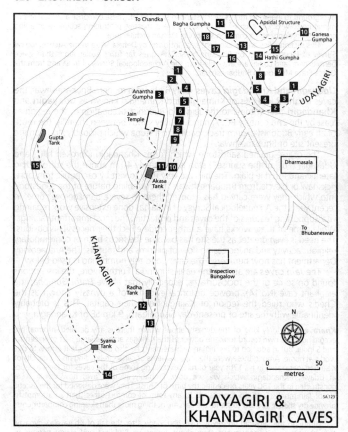

UDAYAGIRI & KHANDAGIRI CAVES

SA 123

little religious content.

Retrace your steps. **Cave 3**, above and to the left of **Cave 2**, has 3 elephants carved on either side. **Cave 4** has 2 cells one above the other, the upper cell reached by a flight of steps in front of **cave 5**. The pillars are mainly modern, though the inner brackets are original with good carvings – including a lion with prey and an elephant entwined by a serpent. As in several caves the floor of **cave 6** has been lowered significantly (perhaps by as much as a metre) by comparatively recent quarrying. **Cave 8** is unusually high-ceilinged. Behind it and up to the right is Cave 9. The lower storey has 2 wings, guarded by armed doorkeepers carved against the pilasters. The caves include a badly damaged relief showing the worship of a Jain religious symbol by figures including a king. On the roofline of the lower storey is a royal inscription. The upper storey carries an important 3 line inscription declaring that the cave was dedicated by the chief queen of King Kharavela.

Return to the steps and turn right at the top. About 50 m on is **Cave 10**, *Ganesa Gumpha*, deriving its name from the figure of Ganesa carved on the back of its right cell. The friezes vividly depict scenes such as a woman's abduction, an elopement, and a duel between a man and a woman ending in the man's carrying off the defeated woman.

From Cave 10 go to the top of the hill by a path up to the right, where an apsidal structure was unearthed in 1958. Its plan is very similar to that of Buddhist *chaitya** halls, and the structure was almost certainly a place of worship for the Jain monks living in the caves.

Continuing down the path takes you past the small **Caves 11, 12 and 13**. Cave 12 is carved bizarrely into the shape of a tiger's open mouth and has an inscription showing it to have been the cave of the town judge. However, it is **Cave 14**, the last important Cave on Udayagiri, the **Hathi Gumpha** or elephant cave, which has the most important inscription, that of King Kharavela. Protected now by a masonry shelter built in 1902, it is in the Magadhi script.

You can either come down the steps in front of Cave 17 to the main road or down the flight of steps in front of caves 2 to 7 and out of the main entrance. If you take the first route you can go about 20 m up the road and then up the footpath to cave 1 of **Khandagiri**. The steps opposite the main entrance take you up between caves 5 and 6.

Cave 1 and Cave 2 are known as Tatowa-Gumpha from the parrots carved on the arches of their doorways. 2 sentries wearing dhotis guard the entrance to cave 1, and between the arches a short inscription names the cave as that of Kusuma. The modern steps lead up from cave 1 to **cave 2** on the left, which is both larger and more elaborately carved than cave 1. It has 3 doorways which have arches and pilasters. The pilasters have octagonal bases, and there are lively carvings of animals including 4 elephants and a pair of very lifelike bulls. You can see under the arches ribs which are shaped like the rafters that were typical of the wooden models that preceded these caves. Most of the 2 pillars which support the ceiling of the verandah are modern restoration. On the back of the cell are letters written in the Brahmi script in red pigment, dating from the 1st century BC to the 1st century AD. Debala Mitra suggests that they are evidence that "perhaps one of the recluses was trying to improve his handwriting".

At the top of the flight of steps is **cave 3**, Ananta Gumpha, taking its name from the 2 serpents on the door arches. The reliefs on this cave make it one of the most interesting on the Khandagiri hill. Although there are similarities with those in Cave 2 and with some on Udayagiri some of the motifs are unique. Note especially the sculpted façade of the cell. The 4 doorways are flanked by pilasters. On the back wall of the cell note among the various symbols the svastika, regarded as auspicious by the Jains. The partially finished sculpture of a Tirthankara on the right hand side was a medieval addition. The ornamentation of the pilasters is particularly distinctive. The faces of the arches have numerous carvings. The central arches have a frieze of boys chasing lions, bulls and other animals. The first arch has rosettes in loops of garlands while the fourth has a line of 12 geese carrying a lotus in their beaks "as if to offer it to the sacred tree depicted below the arch" as Mitra says.

The tympanums also have unique motifs, including royal elephants, a turbaned royal person, identified as Surya the sun God, attended by a woman with a fly whisk. The next tympanum shows Lakshmi in the lotus lake, lotus stalks round her arms and elephants holding pots from which she is bathing. A fourth tympanum shows a sacred tree with a woman worshipping, a man and 2 dwarfs. An inscription on the outside of the architrave between the left pilaster and the first pillar of the verandah says that the cave belonged to Dohada.

You can follow the footpath on up the hill to the Jain temple at the top, or you can retrace your steps to Cave 2 and then follow the path round to the right past caves 4 and 5. **Cave 4** is a single small cell with 2 entrances, while **cave 5** at the top of the modern flight of steps from the road is called khandagiri from the cracks (khanda) in it. Both its cells are damaged. The path continues past caves 6,7,8 and 9, in a row facing an artificial terrace. **Cave 7**, Navamuni Gumpha, gets its name from the 9 Tirthankaras (munis) carved on the back and right walls. It has been substantially modified since it was first formed as a residential cell. The last of the 5 inscriptions in the cell mentions Subhachandra, a renowned teacher of the 11th century. On the back wall of what was originally the right hand cell are sculptures of 7 Tirthankaras in high relief. There are 2 reliefs on the right wall of the cave, one of Parsvanatha (last but one of the 24 Tirthankaras) and the other of the sage Rishabanatha. Parsvanath sits under the 7-hooded canopy on either side of which is a flying figure holding a garland. Rishabanatha has a halo and beneath his seat is a bull.

Cave 8 has 2 12-armed figures on the side walls of the veranda. Again, originally it was a dormitory but was converted into sanctuary by carving images. At the same time as this was done the floor was scooped out. The pillars are modern, replacing old ones. The 24 are sculpted, with Parsvanatha being shown twice. Adjoining cave 8 is **cave 9**, the Trisula Gumpha. The figures carved are much later than those in cave 7, probably from the 15th century at the earliest. The masonry altar at the back of the chamber has 3 chlorite images of Rishabhanatha. Mitra suggests that "the facial expression of the figures is highly pleasing; so also is the youthful modelling of the body. Particularly noteworthy is their coiffure where the artist has lavished all his skill."

Caves 10 and 11 are a further 40 m S, both almost destroyed by large scale quarrying though some carvings are still visible. Other minor monuments are found 200 m further on and on the other side of the hill.

You can reach the **Jain temple** on top of the hill either by taking the steep path up past cave 10 or by going back to cave 5 and climbing the steps. According to Debala Mitra the temple was built in the first quarter of the 19th century by Manju Chowdhury and his nephew Bhavani Dadu of Cuttack. The central white marble image in the shrine, dedicated to Rishabanath, was placed there quite recently, probably in the 1930s. There was a much earlier temple on the site. It is well worth climbing to the temple to get the view both of Udayagiri and of the plains surrounding Bhubaneshwar. The modern peace pagoda at Dhauli is clearly visible about 10 km away, built on the hillock next to one of Asoka's rock edicts. (See below)

A pleasant short extension of the trip to Udayagiri and Khandagiri can be made by going on to **Atri**, 42 km W of Bhubaneswar. Follow NH 5 S to **Khorda**, then turn right. Atri is famous for the hot sulphur springs whose temperature remains at 55°C. The water is supposed to cure skin disorders. There is a shrine to Hatakesvara. The drive through avenues of **neem***, peepul and plantains is picturesque. OTDC plans to improve bathing facilities.

Hotels A *Oberoi Bhubaneswar*, Nayapalli. T 56116, Cable: Obhotel, Telex 0675-348. 70 rm. 9 km airport, 4 km rly, 5 km downtown. Central a/c. New luxury hotel in temple architecture style, tastefully decorated using Orissan handicrafts and set in well kept gardens. Tennis, jogging track. **C** *Kalinga Ashok*, Gautam Nagar, ITDC. T 53318, Cable: Tourism, Telex: 0675-282. 64 rm. Central a/c. Restaurant, bar, coffee shop, exchange, shop, TV. Opp the Museum and about a km from the main group of temples. New, well designed, accommodation and service similar to other ITDC hotels. Good value though slow service in restaurant. **C** *Hotel Prachi*, 6 Janpath. T 52689, Cable: Destiny, Telex: 0675-278. 48 rm. Restaurant, terrace barbecue, pool, exchange, travel, tennis, health club, shops. Well placed, old favourite with tour groups. **C** *Hotel Swosti*, 103 Janpath. T 54179, Cable: Swosti, Telex: 0675-321. 51 rm. Central a/c. Restaurant, bar, coffee shop, exchange, travel, beauty parlour, TV. **C** *Hotel New Kenilworth*, 86A-1 Gautam Nagar. T 53330, Cable: Newken, Telex: 0675-343.. 72 rm. Central a/c. Restaurant, coffee shop, exchange, travel, pool, beauty parlour, TV. Was Hotel Konark but was taken over in 1989 and stylishly refurbished. Close to Museum and Tourist office.

D *Hotel Safari International*, 721 Rasulgarh. T 53443, Cable: Safari, Telex: 345 STAY IN. 60 rm and restaurant air-cooled, bar, open-air cafeteria. **D** *Hotel Meghdoot*, 5B Shaheed Nagar. T 55802. 27 rm. 5 km airport, 2 km rly. A/c. Restaurant, bar, TV. **D** *State Guest House*. T 51919. Meals included in price. Some a/c rooms. **D** *Hotel Jajati*, Station Sq, Unit III. T 50288. 21 rm, some a/c. Restaurant. **D** *Bhubaneswar Hotel*, Cuttack Rd. T 51977. 30 rm, some a/c. **E** *Pantha Niwas*, Jayadev Marg (Lewis Rd) OTDC. T 54515. 76 rm some a/c. Restaurant, bar, Tourist information and conducted tours. Modest but clean, very reasonable rates conveniently situated. Good restaurant, friendly service.

Other simple **E** hotel accommodation in Bhubaneswar is available in the following. *Hotel Anarkali*, Kharabela Nagar, Unit III. 22 rm. non a/c. Restaurant. *Hotel Pushpak*, Kalpana Sq. T 50545. 22 rm a few a/c. **F** *Hotel Nandan*, Station Sq. T 50997. 18 rm.

Restaurants Best restaurants are situated in the top hotels – The *Oberoi* Bhubaneswar and Kalinga Ashok's '*Ganjapati*' serve excellent food in comfortable surroundings. Hotel *Swosti* and *Panthaniwas* have multi-cuisine restaurant while Hotel Prachi has the Chinese '*Golden Dragon*'. Hotel *Swapanpuri* in Sahid Nagar serves Indian meals and snacks and *New Gunguram Sweets* in Brit Market, Station Sq has delicious Indian sweets and snacks.

Bars The only comfortable bars are again to be found in the hotels. The Oberoi Bhubaneswar and Kalinga Ashok and also Hotel Swosti and Panthaniwas.

Shopping The introduction to the Orissa section describes the rich heritage of art and craft in the region and the capital is a good place to shop if you are unlikely to travel to the special villages where the skills are practised, sometimes exclusively.

The Market Building has a number of shops which are fixed priced and recommended. *Utkalika*, (E Tower), T 50187 sells Orissa handloom and handicrafts. Closed Th. *Orissa State Handloom Co-operative Society*, (West Market), T 50741 (Closed Th) and *Kala Mandir*, T 52456 (Closed Sun) are good for handloom fabrics. You can gifts and stationery from *Lalchand and Sons* (Closed Th).

Bookshop *Modern Books*, New Market has a good selection of books on the region's history and art.

Camera Films are sold by *Studio Neel Kamal*, Western Tower Market, *Sujata Photo Studio*, Sahid Nagar, *Art Studio*, Bapuji Nagar and *Studio Sonali*, Lewis Rd.

Local Transport Yellow-top taxis are not available but **auto-rickshaws** and **cycle-rickshaws** are widely available though it is best to negotiate the fare in advance. City **buses** are inexpensive and cover major routes charging Re.0.50 up to 3 km and Re.1 for longer journeys. OTDC (Transport Division), T 55515, hires out **Tourist Taxis** the rates depending on whether a/c or non a/c and the type of car. The tariff for a/c varies from Rs 45 to Rs 50 for 1 hr/10 km and rises to Rs 310 to Rs 500 for 8 hr/80 km within the city. Outside Bhubaneswar charges range from about Rs 3 to 4.50 per km. The tariff for non a/c cars is Rs 30 for 1 hr/10 km and Rs 250 for 8 hr/80 km within the city and Rs 2.40 per km outside. **Coaches** and mini-buses both with and without a/c are also available for hire. It is also possible to hire **motor launches** and yachts at the seaside resorts and for Chilika Lake at the Panthanivas, Barkul.

Entertainment There are several cinema halls where films are usually shown 4 times a day, at 1200, 1500, 1800, 2100. The local paper carries details of programmes. *Keshari Talkies* on Sachivalaya Marg (T 50546), *Sriya Talkies* and *Swati* both at Unit-3 and *Ravi Talkies* in the Old Town. Programmes of Odissi and folk dances and folk drama are staged regularly and worth seeking out.

Sports *Bhubaneswar Club*, Unit-6, Rajpath. T 52277. Table tennis, billiards, badminton and bridge. Contact Secretary for temporary membership.

Museums Orissa State Museum. T 52897. Open daily from 1000-1700. Closed on Mon and government holidays. The collection includes some archaeological exhibits of stone inscriptions and tools, copperplates, coins, sculptures from temples, portraits and models, musical instruments and particularly, rare palm leaf manuscripts. The Harijan and Tribal Research Institute's **Tribal Museum of Man**. T 51635. Open 1000-1700 except Sun. Collection of tribal dress, weapons and jewellery and tribal dwellings. **Handicrafts Museum**, Secretariat Rd. T 50484. Open 1000-1700 except Sun. Large collection of traditional art and crafts including stone sculptures, *pattachitras**, brass and horn ware, toys, masks, playing cards, silver filigree and dowry boxes.

Parks and zoo See Nandankanan under excursions (below).

Useful addresses Foreigners Registration Office, Superintendent of Police, District Intelligence Bureau, Sahid Nagar. T 51816.

Post and Telegraph The General PO and Central Telegraph Office are on Sachivalaya Marg.

Places of worship *Hindu* Apart from the Lingaraja Temple there is the Sri Ram Mandir in Janpath Unit 3. *Muslim* – The Masjid is in Sachivalaya Marg, Unit 4. *Christian* – There is a Catholic Church (T 50187) and the Christ Union Church Unit 4. *Others* – The Ramakrishna Math is in Vivekananda Marg, The Gauranga Ashram near Baiyaabada Math, Sahid Nagar and the Arya Samaj opposite Sahid Nagar Market Building near Maharsi College. There is also the Sri Aurobindo Ashram.

Hospital and Medical services Capital Hospital, Unit 6. T 50688.

Travel agents and tour operators Larger hotels have helpful travel counters. *Swosti Travels*, Hotel Swosti, Janpath. T 56617. They offer city sightseeing and other specialist tours such as architectural tours, wildlife tours and beach resorts. *Sita Travels*, Hotel Kenilworth. T 53330. *Mercury Travels*, Hotel Oberoi. T 54216. *Arya Travels*, Hotel Prachi. T 53668.

Tourist offices and information The Orissa Tourism Development Corp (OTDC) office is on Jayadev Marg near Panthanivas. T 50099. Open 1000-1700. Airport Tourist counter. T 54006. Railway station tourist counter. T 54715. A large **Tourist Map of Orissa**, available at the Bhubaneswar Tourist Office (Pantha Niwas) or from the Delhi office at Baba Kharak Singh Marg, is very helpful as it lists typical Orissan crafts and textiles and indicates where they are produced. Govt of India Tourist Office, B 21, Kalpana Area. T 54203.

Tours Conducted sightseeing tours by luxury coach are available from Panthanivas. *Nandankanan – Khandagiri and Udayagiri – Temples and Museum – Handicraft Emporium – Dhauli*. 0900-1730. Daily except Mon. Rs 50, no guide. *Puri – Konarak*. 0900-1800. Daily. Rs 60. Also a number of package tours provided there are at least 30 people. The rates quoted often includes accommodation at the Panthanivas and have to be booked at least a month ahead. *Bhubaneswar – Puri – Konarak*. 1 night 2 days. Rs 160. *Bhubaneswar – Chilika – Gopalpur*. 1 night 2 days. Rs 200. *Bhubaneswar – Puri – Konarak*. 2 nights 3 days. Rs 230. *Bhubaneswar – Puri – Konarak – Chilika*. 2 nights 3 days. Rs 275; 4 nights 5 days. Rs 407; 5 nights 6 days. Rs 487. **Children are charged half price.**

Air Indian Airlines connects the following places with Boeing flights: **Calcutta**, daily (55 min), **Delhi**, daily (3 hr), via Raipur (50 min), **Varanasi, Hyderabad**, Wed, Fri, Sat (2 hr 45 min) via Nagpur (1 hr 15 min) and also **Bombay** (2 hr 55 min). Indian Airlines, Airport, T 51084; City, T 52380; Reservations, T 50533. **Vayudoot** links Bhubaneswar with **Hyderabad**, Tue, Th, Sat (4 hr 15 min) via Jeypore (1 hr 20 min) and **Vishakapatnam** (2 hr 10 min). Vayudoot, City, T 57985. Tourist Information Counter, Airport, T 54006.

Rail Indian Railways has "superfast" connections linking Bhubaneswar with major regional centres. **Calcutta (H)**: *Dhauli Exp*, 2822 (AC/CC), daily, 1345, 7 hr 35 min; *Haora Mail*, 6004 (AC/II), daily, 2215, 8 hr 30 min; **Madras**: *Coromandal Exp*, 2841 (AC/II), daily, 2200, 19 hr 35 min; *Guwahati-Trivandrum Exp*, 2602 (AC/II), Tue, 0626, 21 hr 44 min; **Bangalore**: *Howrah-Bangalore Exp*, 2611 (AC/II), Wed, 0626, 21 hr 44 min; *Guwahati-Bangalore Exp*, 2674 (AC/II), Mon, Th, 0626, 21 hr 44 min; **Cochin**: *Haora/Patna-Cochin Exp*, 2652 (AC/II), Fri and Sat, 0626, 21 hr 44 min; *Guwahati-Cochin Exp*, 2650 (AC/II), Sun, 0626, 21 hr 44 min; **Cuttack**: *Puri-Howrah Exp*, 8008, daily, 2100, 10 min.

Puri: *Kalingutkal Exp*, 8478 (AC/II), daily, 0538, 2 hr 22 min; **Delhi (ND)**: *Puri-New Delhi*, 2815 (AC/II), Mon, Wed, Th, Sat, 1052, 30 hr 8 min; *Neelachal Exp*, 8475 (AC/II), Tue, Fri, Sun, 1052, 34 hr 23 min. At Bhubaneswar Railway Station, Station Supt., T 51637; Enquiry, T 52233; Tourist Information Counter T 54715.

Road Bhubaneswar is situated on NH 5 which links Calcutta and Madras and has good connections by road to other important regional centres. Some distances to other tourist centres are: Calcutta 480 km, New Delhi 1,745 km, Madras 1,225 km, Bombay 1,691 km, Bangalore 1,430 km, Ahmedabad 1,829 km. Within Orissa: Cuttack 32 km, Puri 62 km, Konarak 65 km, Chilika Lake 130 km.

REGIONAL TOURS

Bhubaneshwar is a base from which it is possible to make day trips and longer excursions. Bhubaneshwar, Puri and Konarak are being pushed very hard as "Orissa's golden triangle" to rival Delhi Agra and Jaipur in the northwest. However, Orissa has a great deal to offer if you have more time. Northern and western Orissa remain largely unvisited, yet they are quite accessible by car or bus and offer a tremendous contrast to the densely populated – and intensively visited – towns of the coastal plain. For convenience, suggested tours take Bhubaneshwar as the starting point. After describing the Bhubaneshwar, Puri, Konarak triangle they are grouped into northern, western and southern Orissa. A number of places of interest can be visited in day trips from Bhubaneshwar. In a more extended visit it is possible to link the longer tours together.

BHUBANESHWAR TO PURI AND KONARAK

The journey to Puri is most rewarding for the Jagannath Temple, one of the 4 holiest Pilgrimage centres for Hindus, and the superb surfing beaches. Konarak, one of the world's wonders according to Mark Twain, is amongst the most vivid architectural treasures of Hindu India.

The route S from Bhubaneshwar to Puri passes through ***Dhauli***, (8 km S of Bhubaneshwar). It was here that the horrors of the Kalinga war brought about a transformation in Emperor Asoka and led to his acknowledging the value of Buddhist teachings. The rock edicts at the bottom of the hill, which date from approximately 260 BC, give detailed instructions to his administrators to rule his subjects with gentleness and fairness. " ..... You are in charge of many thousand living beings. You should gain the affection of men. All men are my children, and as I desire for my children that they obtain welfare and happiness both in this world and next, the same do I desire for all men........" Above the inscription you can see the front of an elephant carved out of an enormous rock. It may have been placed there to mark the position of the edicts. All around there is a magnificent view, even better from the hill now topped by the Peace Pagoda, of the flat rice growing landscape. This is particularly attractive in the early morning or late evening.

Now the rock edicts are almost ignored by the bus loads of tourists who are taken on up the hill to the Buddhist Peace Pagoda and the Hindu temple beyond. Known as the Santi Stupa the Pagoda was built in the early 1970s by the Japan Buddha Sanga and Kalinga Nippon Buddha Sangha. The old temple of Lord Dhavaleswar which was reconstructed in 1972 is also on the hill top here.

A further 15 km S on the Puri road is the small village of **Pipli**. This is famous for its appliqué work, and houses and shops are covered in samples of the brightly coloured work. Well worth a visit if time permits – **see page 615**.

Puri

Population 380,000 (1991) *Altitude* Sea level *Best season* Nov to Mar. It gets very hot from Mar to the end of May, then very wet until Nov.

	Jan	Feb	Mar	Apr	May	Jun	Jul	Aug	Sep	Oct	Nov	Dec	Av/Tot
Max (°C)	27	28	30	31	32	31	31	31	31	31	29	27	30
Min (°C)	18	21	25	27	27	27	27	27	27	25	21	18	24
Rain (mm)	9	20	14	12	63	187	296	256	258	242	75	8	1440

Bhubaneswar 60 km away has the nearest airport where you can get buses or taxis to Puri. The bus service is half hourly throughout the day and takes approximately 1 hr 30 min. Alternatively, there are rail connections from Bhubaneswar but the journey between the 2 takes approximately 2 hrs.

The **Sabaras**, an 'adivasi' tribal group who predated the Dravidian and Aryans were believed to have inhabited the area around Puri which was thickly wooded. The ancient site of **Dantapura**, 'town of the Tooth', is believed to be in the region of Puri although no proof exists. Its name was derived from the left canine tooth of The **Buddha** which was for a time enshrined there before being taken to Sri Lanka. According to Murray, in Japan and Sri Lanka, the Tooth Festival of Buddha was celebrated with 3 cars and the similarity with the *Rath Yatra* at Puri further strengthens the theory that the deities in Puri evolved from Buddhist symbols.

Puri is one of the 4 most important pilgrimage centres for Hindus. The temple of Jagannath, the Lord of the Universe, attracts thousands on feast days and particularly at the time of the 'Rath-Yatra', the Car Festival.

Local festivals *Rath-Yatra** takes place each year in June/July when massive *raths* or 'chariots' carrying wooden images of **Jagannath**, his brother **Balabhadra** and his sister **Subhadra** process through the streets to spend 7 days at Gundicha Ghar, or Garden House, a temple 1.5 km away. It is believed to commemorate **Krishna's** journey from Gokul to Mathura. Each is brightly decorated and take on the shape of a temple sanctuary. Lord Jagannath's 'car', 13 m tall on a base which is more than 10 m sq and with 16 wheels each 2 m in diameter, is the largest and most impressive. Loud gongs announce the boarding of the deities onto the chariots with the arrival, accompanied by bedecked elephants, of the Raja of Puri who even today plays an important religious role in representing the old rulers. On this occasion he fulfils his role as the 'sweeper of the gods', symbolizing that all castes are equal before God. The Raja sweeps the floor of the *raths* with a ceremonial broom and sprinkles holy water and the procession then starts, led by the one carrying Balabhadra

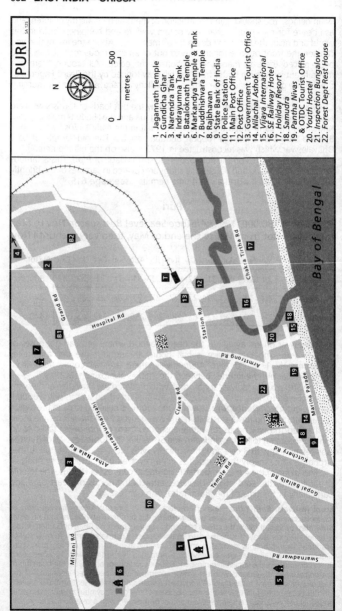

PURI

SA 125

0   500
metres

N

Bay of Bengal

1. Jagannath Temple
2. Gundicha Ghar
3. Narendra Tank
4. Indrayumna Tank
5. Bataloknath Temple
6. Markandya Temple & Tank
7. Buddhishvara Temple
8. Rajbhavan
9. State Bank of India
10. Police Station
11. Main Post Office
12. Post Office
13. Government Tourist Office
14. Nilachal Ashok
15. Vijaya International
16. SE Railway Hotel
17. Holiday Resort
18. Samudra
19. Pantha Nivas
20. Youth Hostel
   & OTDC Tourist Office
21. Inspection Bungalow
22. Forest Dept Rest House

Grand Rd
Hospital Rd
Station Rd
Chakra Tirtha Rd
Armstrong Rd
Clarke Rd
Heragauri Sahi
Athar Nala Rd
Marina Parade
Kutchery Rd
Temple Rd
Gopal Balabh Rd
Mitrani Rd
Swarnadwar Rd

followed by Subhadra's and lastly Lord Jagannath's. The fabrics used to decorate the different *raths* are green, black and yellow respectively. About 4,000 are needed to draw each chariot, which is accompanied by devotional dances and music.

After a week the journey is retraced with a similar procession. During the week away, the deities are treated to *padoapitha*, special rice cakes and are dressed in new garments each day before returning home to their own temple. The festival attracts more that 200,000 devotees to Puri each year. In the past some were said to have thrown themselves under a massive wheel to die a blessed death. The journey is slow and to cover the short distance through the crowds may take as much as 24 hrs. After the festival, the *raths* are broken up and bits are sold to pilgrims as relics. Incidentally, the massive 'car' has given the English language the word *juggernaut**!

Chandan-Yatra This coincides with the Hindu new year in mid-April when the images of Jagannath accompanied by his brother and sister are taken in decorated boats with swan-heads on a daily ride in the Narendra tank for 21 days. The festival derives its name from the use of sandal paste, *chandan*, to annoint the deities and the celebrations include music, dancing and singing of devotional songs.

Snana Yatra follows the Chandan Yatra and marks the ritual bathing of the 3 deities from the temple, on a special barge. For 4 days the gods are said to convalesce out of sight and is a period when worshippers must be satisfied with praying before paintings or 'pattachitras'. This festival which precedes the Rath-Yatra is missed every so many years (the number being decided by astrological calculations) when new images of the deities are carved from specially selected trees and the old ones are secretly buried by the temple priests.

Places of interest *Jagannath Temple* The temple to the 'Lord of the Universe' is the major attraction of Puri. To remain here for 3 days and 3 nights is considered particularly rewarding and the fact that in the eyes of Jagannath there are no caste distinctions, has made Puri a very popular destination with the devout. The wooden figures of the 3 deities, Jagannath, Balabhadra and Subhadra stand in the sanctuary garlanded and decorated by the priests. The extraordinary form that Jagannath takes, according to legend, is the unfinished work of the craftsman god Viswakarma, who in anger left this portrayal of Lord Vishnu incomplete. Small wooden replicas of the 3 images are available around the temple.

The temple which has been referred to by some as the 'white pagoda' (the Konarak temple being known as the 'black pagoda') is only open to Hindus. Records suggest that a victory pillar was erected by the conqueror of Kalinga, Chorda Ganga in 1030 which was consecrated nearly a century later and possibly the temple was only completed at the end of the 12th century. The original temple built in the Kalinga style, consisted of the '*deul*' or sanctuary and the '*jagamohan*' or audience hall in front of it. It was only in the 14th or 15th century that the '*nata mandir*' (dance hall) and the '*bhoga mandir*' (hall of offerings) were added in alignment, in the style of other Orissan temples, making it 95 m in length and 25 m in width. The 'nata mandir' is unusual in that it has 16 pillars in 4 rows to support the large ceiling. Unfortunately there are signs of decline in the quality of craftsmanship by the time of the later additions. It is also a pity that in order to deal with the deterioration of the original stone work large quantities of plaster were used to carry out the restoration in the last century which has inevitably masked the finer details in places. Fortunately, the Archaeological Survey of India has undertaken to restore the temple to its original splendour.

The site of the temple is a virtual 200 m sq enclosed within an outer wall 6 m high. Within is another concentric wall which may have acted as fortification, inside which stands the tallest temple in Orissa, reaching a height of 65 m where it is crowned by the wheel of Vishnu and a flag. On the higher ground in the enclosure are 30 small shrines, including those to Vimala, Vishnu and Lakshmi, much in the Buddhist stupa tradition. Pilgrims are expected to visit these smaller temples and even those with limited time must visit 3 before proceeding to the main temple. According to Percy Brown, its elevated position gives it added eminence and have led some to conjecture that it is indeed the site of Dantapura, which for a time was sanctified by the holy Buddhist relic.

The outer wall has a gateway with pyramidal roofs on each side with 2 lions guarding the main 'Lion' entrance. On this E side there is an intricately carved 10 m high free-standing stone pillar with a small figure of *Aruna*, the charioteer of the Sun. This once stood in front of the *Nata Mandir* at Konarak but was moved to its present site about 200 years ago by the Raja of Khurda, **see page 636**. To the left of the main entrance is the temple kitchen which daily prepares 56 varieties of food making up the *Bhogas* for the deities which are offered 5 times a day and then distributed from the *Ananda Bazar*. Literally meaning 'pleasure market', this is a food where 'Mahaprasad' or the meals, are served to thousands. At festival times as many as 250,000 visitors can be served in a day.

Although non-Hindus are not permitted inside, there are vantage points from which tourists may view the temple, one being the roof of the Raghunandan Library opp the main entrance to the E or from the Jaya Balia Lodge nearby. A small donation is expected in return. The temple is supposed to be a self-sufficient community, served by some 6,000 priests and more than 10,000 others who depend on it for their livelihood.

The 4 sacred **tanks*** in Puri provide thousands of pilgrims with the opportunity to take a holy dip. The Narendra Tank is particularly famous since the deities are taken there during the *Snana Yatra*.

Gundicha Ghar where the Ratha Yatra takes the deities from the Jagannath Temple to spend a week at their 'aunt's house'. It is open to Hindus only and is an example of the Orissan style demonstrating the unique and ingenious use of wrought iron to form a framework to support the laterite lintels of the massive structures of the other temples. Since no mortar was used the great blocks of laterite used in construction were finely balanced by means of counterpoise. To make it practically possible, stone lintels were used which had to be reinforced with metal bars, some of which, as in the case of the Jagamohan in Konarak, measured 10 m in length and nearly 20 cm in thickness.

The Beach The other major attraction is the long stretch of golden beach, shallow enough to walk out a long distance, with **superb surf**. Sunrise is particularly striking. The currents can be treacherous at times but you can swim safely on your own if you take care. The customary 'nulia', fisherman turned life-saver in a distinctive conical straw hat, may offer his services for either half or full day at a small price for those not used to bathing in the sea. The best hotels have a stretch of sand which is clean.

Sadly, the beach tends to get progressively unpleasant underfoot as you move away from the tourist hotel area and although it may be interesting to walk to the nearby fishing villages along the coast to watch the fisherfolk set out in their colourful boats early in the morning, you have to be prepared to pick your way carefully.

Sakshigopal 22 km from Puri has a temple with a charming image of Gopal or Child Krishna who in legend was called here as witness in a dispute between 2 Brahmins and then remained here because of its attraction and therefore is a pilgrim centre.

If you are interested in an ancient engineering marvel, go and see the 85 m **Atharnala Bridge** over the Madupur stream. It was built in the 13th century and is still in use.

Hotels C *Toshali Sands* – Orissa's Ethnic Village Resort, Konarak Marine Drive, PO Baliguali. T 2888,2999, Cable: Yellow Sand, Telex: 0675-395. 24 d rms in cottages and 18 in villas. A/c public areas. Good restaurant, bar, pool, shops, exchange, travel, sports, health club. Recently opened and highly recommended, good service. Tastefully designed in superb location, access to a deserted beach through pleasant casuarina groves. Courtesy transport is available to beach and Puri centre. **C** *Nilachal Ashok*, adjoining Raj Bhawan Complex, VIP Rd. T 2973, Cable: Nilashok, Telex: 0675-335. 42 rm. 65 km airport, 1 km rly. Restaurant, bar, coffee-shop, pool, shops, exchange, travel.

D *Vijaya International*, Chakratirtha Rd. T 2701/2, Cable: Manisa. 44 double rooms some a/c. Pleasant seafacing restaurant, travel. **D** *South Eastern Railway Hotel*, Chakratirtha Rd. T 2063, Cable: Surf. 36 double rooms, few with a/c. Price includes all meals. Restaurant, bar. 200 m from beach, well-maintained gardens. First floor rms have greater privacy, most with wide verandahs overlooking sea. Siestas are encouraged with silence expected from co-operating residents between 1400 and 1600 hr! Old-world atmosphere with courteous service, although it has lost its old grandeur and superb 5-course meals with the passage of time. No credit cards. Raw sewage in sea opp reported 1991.

D *Holiday Resort*, Sandy Village, Chakratirtha Rd. T 2919,2440, Cable: Sandy, Telex: 0675-370. 97 double rooms in cottages some a/c. Complex of small cottages in beautiful gardens has a/c restaurant, bar, exchange, air ticketing and helipad. **D** *Prachi*, Swargadwar, Gourbarsahi. T 2638, Cable: Prachi,Telex: 0675-278. 36 rooms. Central a/c. Ground floor rooms have verandahs right on the beach. Casual restaurant, shops. Fairly simple but comfortable. **D** *Samudra* on Chakratirtha Rd (T 2705) has 30 rms, a couple a/c with balconies and an a/c restaurant.

There are several beachside hotels with restaurants, mostly with no a/c, which offer reasonable accommodation at about Rs 100-120 for double rooms. OTDC has 2 other hotels, the larger is **E** *Panthanivas* (T 2562), 48 rms and the smaller *Mahodadhinivas* (T 2507), 9 rms. Both have restaurant and a travel counter. The Panthanivas has large rms in the old wing but the rms in the new wing are better and closer to the sea though a little more expensive. In addition it has a bar and coffee shop. Reservations: Manager of the hotel with a day's room rent in advance.

The very inexpensive **F** *Youth Hostel* has segregated pleasant dormitories, some of which are conveniently for 2 or 3, but guests are expected to be in by 2200. Dining room. The **F** *Railway Retiring Rooms* are equally inexpensive.

There are some *Dharamsalas* in the town and a *camping* site on Marine Drive between Puri and Konarak.

Restaurants and Bars It is usual to dine where one is staying but the larger hotels will happily accommodate extra diners. The abundance of fresh fish is worth taking advantage of although an unaccustomed stomach might well object to daily intake of seafood. The 3 govt run hotels and Holiday Resort have bars.

Shopping Handicrafts are available at *Utkalika* and *Crafts Complex* at Mochi Sahi Sq and at *Sun Crafts* in Tinikonia Bagicha while *Sudarshan* on Station Rd specialises in stoneware. Handlooms are sold at the *Weavers' Co-operative Society* on Grand Rd and at *Odissi* in Dolamandap Sahi.

You can get very good buys in the vast *bazaar* around the Jagannath Temple, along Bada Danda and Swargadwara, but prices there are not fixed and you are expected to spend time bargaining. *Hawkers* on the beach sell shells and bead jewellery (often passing on glass beads for coral!). If you have more time, a visit to the villages and neighbourhoods where the craftsmen and weavers can be seen at work will be rewarding. In Puri itself, Pathuria Sahi is the area where the stone carvers live and nearby, Raghurajpur produces 'pattachitras' and etchings on palm leaf (**see page 614**). Photo Life on Grand Rd (T 2697) and Metro Studio, Mochi Sahi (T 2853) sell **camera film**.

Local Transport Tourist taxis may be hired from the larger hotels, from *Dullu Tours* (T 2171) and from the Taxi Stand (T 2161). The daily rates vary between Rs 300 and Rs 500 depending on the car, whether it is air-conditioned and the distance travelled. **Cycle-rickshaws** are freely available around Puri but bargain and fix fare in advance.

Entertainment Classical *Odissi* dances and folk dances and drama which are always performed for festivals are also staged from time to time and are worth seeking out.

Hospitals and medical services District HQ Hospital, T 2062. I.D. Hospital, Red Cross Rd, T 2094. Gopabandhu Ayurvedic Hospital, Armstrong Rd, T 2072.

Places of worship *Hindu* Jagannath Temple, Shyamakali Temple, Lokanath Temple, Siddha Mahavira. *Others* There is the Muslim Nazar Khana Masjid and 2 Christian churches.

Travel agents and Tour operators N.N. *Mukherjee*, Chakratirtha Rd, T 2267. *Mohapatra Tour Travel*, Swargadwar, T 2661. *Konarak Travels*, Sea Beach, T 2465.

Tourist Office and Information OTDC, Pantha Bhawan, T 2507. *Govt of Orissa Tourist Office*, Station Rd, T 2131, Cable: Orissatour. Tourist Counter, Rly Station, T 2519. *OTDC* and private tour operators conduct daily sightseeing tours (except Mon) to Konarak, Pipli, Dhauli, Bhubaneswar temples, Nandan Kanan, Udayagiri and Khandagiri, Sakshigopal. The fares are approximately Rs 55. The Chilka Lake tour is offered on Mon, Wed and Fri for Rs 70.

Air Bhubaneswar 60 km away is the nearest airport and has Indian Airlines daily services to Calcutta. For details see section on Bhubaneswar **page 630**. Indian Airlines, Airport T 51084, Bhubaneswar City T 52380, Reservations T 50533.

Rail The main Calcutta-Madras broad gauge line branches to Puri linking it to all parts of country by Express trains. New Delhi and Calcutta have direct trains while Hyderabad, Madras and Bombay have fast trains connections at Bhubaneswar. **Calcutta (H):** *Puri-Haora Exp*, 8008, daily, 1800, 11 hr 30 min; *Sri Jagannath Exp*, 8410 (AC/II), daily, 2045, 11 hr; **Bhubaneshwar,** *Puri-New Delhi Exp*, 2815 (AC/II), Mon, Wed, Th, Sat, 0915, 1 hr 30 min; *Neelachal Exp*, 8475 (AC/II), Tue, Fri, Sun; 0915, 1 hr 30 min; **Bombay:** *New Delhi Exp*, 2815, AC/II, Mon, Wed, Th, Sat; 0915, 7 hr 20 and *Neelachal Exp*, 8475 (AC/II), Tue, Fri and Sun; 0915, 7 hr 20 min change at Kharagpur (5 hr 20 min wait), then *Bombay Mail*, 8002, daily, 2155, 33 hr 45 min; (total time = 46 hr 25 min); **Madras:** *Coromandal Exp*, 2841, daily, 2200,

19 hr 35 min; **Delhi (ND)**: *Puri-New Delhi*, 2815 (AC/II), Mon, Wed, Th and Sat; 0915, 31 hr 45 min. For further details see Bhubaneswar section **page 630**. Puri Railway Station T 2065 which is about 2 km N of the town.

Road The junction with the Madras-Calcutta NH 5 is again at Bhubaneswar. The distance from Puri to Calcutta is 541 km, and from Madras 1,285 km. Bus services run regularly between Puri and Bhubaneswar and also to Cuttack, Visakhapatnam and Calcutta.

Konarak The drive from Puri to Konarak is along a recently-built road running close to the coast. The thin, lateritic soils of the coastal belt, overlain by sand in places, are being brought into use by extending cashew, casuarina and eucalyptus plantations in between the cultivated fields. The drive of 35 kilometres takes nearly an hour, but despite the flat landscape there are very attractive views. It is also possible to get to Konarak from Bhubaneswar, 65 km away, and there are conducted tours by 'luxury' coach organized by OTDC from both towns (details in Bhubaneswar section, **see pages 629** and **635**).

Konarak is one of the most vivid architectural treasures of Hindu India. It no longer stands as a landmark on the sea shore since the land has risen and the sea is now some 3 km away. Despite the fact the the main sanctuary, the 'black pagoda' as it was called by European sailors, to distinguish it from the whitewashed 'pagoda' of the Jagannath temple in Puri, now lies in ruins, the remaining porch or *jagamohana* and the other structures in the complex are still magnificent, representing the culmination of Orissan art. It is best to see it after visiting the temples in Bhubaneswar, for then it is possible to appreciate in full the development both of style and of technical skill which the **Surya** temple of Konarak represents.

One of the legends surrounding the building of the temple relates the story of Samba who was cursed by his father Lord Krishna and suffered from leprosy for 12 years before being cured by the Sun god and so built a temple to *Surya*. It was in fact built by King **Langula Narasimha Deva** in the 13th century, when Orissan temple building had reached its peak, although there may have been an older temple to the Sun god here dating back to the 9th century. It is said to have taken 1,200 masons sixteen years to complete. It is built of *khondalite**.

The sculptures draw for their subject from every aspect of life – dancers, musicians, figures from mythology, scenes of love and war, of court life, hunting, elephant fights – the list goes on. Since the temple was conceived to reflect a rounded picture of life and since *mithuna** or union in love is a part of that, a significant section of the sculpture is erotic art. Konarak is unusual in that the carvings are found both on the outer and inner surfaces.

It was only in 1906 that the first tentative steps were taken to reclaim the ruins of the temple from the encroaching sand. By that stage not only had the sanctuary or *deul* collapsed but a number of the statues had been removed, notably in the 1830s by the Hindu Raja of Khurda, who wanted them to decorate temples he was building in his own fort about 100 km away and at Puri. Kittoe, an English visitor, wrote in 1838 that "The Kurda Raja has demolished all 3 entrances and is removing stones to Puri; the masons pick out the figures and throw them down to take their chance of being broken to pieces (which most of them are); such they leave on the spot, those that escape uninjured are taken away. The elegant doorway called the Navagriha has been completely destroyed."

In recent years there has been substantial renovation, some of it protective, some replacing fallen stone work and sculptures, so that the appearance of the whole temple complex is now very different from that of even a few years ago.

Guides Like many famous sites in India Konarak is now the focus of rapidly growing tourist interest. It is increasingly difficult to wander peacefully and at your own pace round the temple. Guides recognised by the Archaeological Survey are available and will take visitors round in a tour lasting under an hour. Unofficial guides will also press their services, but can be extremely unreliable. One such guide was heard telling his listeners that the magnificent chlorite sculptures of Surya, the deity to whom the temple was dedicated, were of the Buddha!

The temple compound The Surya temple is now set back some 180 m from the road and is reached by a wide laterite path. This is lined with stalls, and there

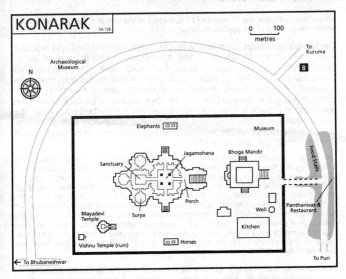

are plenty of places to buy soft drinks and snacks on the way in and out of the temple. The image of the deity has long since been removed and the sanctuary is no longer therefore regarded as a holy place. Shoes may thus be worn throughout. The exception to this is in the small modern building in the northeast corner of the compound which houses the old doorway arch showing the 9 planets, removed from the temple. In recent years these have become objects of veneration, and Brahmin priests are now in charge of this building as a place of worship. The path to the temple is increasingly lined with beggars, as is common in major centres of Hindu pilgrimage.

The temple is set in the middle of a spacious compound which lies about 2 metres below the level of the surrounding land. It is easy to see how the lower parts of the ruins were covered with wind blown sand. An excellent way to appreciate the overall scale of the buildings and their layout is to start the tour by walking round the outer perimeter wall. The light is naturally best from the S, and by going along the wall to the left at the entrance to the compound, the layout and design of the remaining buildings becomes clear. Excellent views for photographs; a telephoto lens is strongly recommended.

Walking along the S wall of the compound you get an excellent view of the temple's basic structure. At the E entrance to the complex of buildings is the *bhoga mandir**, an isolated hall with massive pillars, raised on a richly decorated platform. To its W is an open space, leading to the porch, or *jagamohana**. This still rises magnificently to its original height of 39 m, and is now the dominant building in the temple complex. To its E is the massive lower section of the the original sanctuary, or *deul**. Estimates based on its known architectural style and existing base suggest that originally it was over 60 m tall. Walking round the compound it is possible to get some sense of what the original sanctuary must have been like, though its roof has long since collapsed.

From the S wall of the compound you can see that the temple was built in the form of a war chariot. 12 pairs of great wheels were sculpted on either side of the 4 m high platform on which the temple stands. In front of the E entrance a team of 7 horses were shown straining to pull the chariot towards the dawn. In Hindu mythology the Sun god is believed to traverse the sky in a chariot drawn by 7 horses each representing a day of the week; the 12 pairs of wheels may symbolize the 12 months (24 fortnights) of the year and the 8 spokes in each wheel, the divisions of the day into 8 *prahars*.

The temple buildings You enter the temple compound from the E end, reaching first the hall of offering (*bhoga mandir*). Its walls are covered by carvings, but as Debala Mitra writes, you "rather feel tired with the monotonous over-ornamentation, lack of balanced composition and mediocre quality in the sculpture." Most of the sculptures are of dancers and musicians. From the platform you get an excellent view of the steps leading up to the E door of the porch and of the whole E front of the main temple. It is the best place to see the eastern doorway of the porch and the large and remarkably vivid sculptures, carved in the round, on the terraces of its pyramidal roof. They are unique in Orissan architecture. **See page 616**.

The roof of the porch is divided into 3 tiers, separated by terraces. Above the bottom and middle tiers is a series of some life-sized and some larger than life-sized musicians, vividly captured in a variety of rhythmic poses, and playing instruments ranging from drums and cymbals to *vinas*. The figures on the bottom tier at either end of the central segments (*rahas*) are dramatically carved sculptures of *Siva* in the form of Bhairava. In Mitra's words "he has an awe-inspiring facial expression, open mouth with teeth displayed, a garland of chopped heads and flaming hair. Dancing in ecstasy on a boat, he carries in his left hand a mace, a club made of a human bone headed with a human skull, and a kettle drum and in the right skull cap, a trident and a wheel. " The top of the porch is crowned with the flattened spheres typical of Orissan temples. The top one is supported by 8 figures seated on their haunches. The lower is held up by 8 lions.

The porch and sanctuary At Konarak the porch and the sanctuary are designed as an integrated whole. Although there is a wealth of detail the broad structures are clear. One of the remarkable features of the temple is that the skill and quality of the craftsmanship is displayed down to tiny details of stone carving. It is impossible to see everything of note in a short visit. Mitra estimates that on the narrow plinth alone, at the base of the platform, are carvings of over 1700 elephants – each different!

The plinth, a few cm high, runs right round the base of the temple, and is decorated with a variety of friezes – elephants, notably wild elephants being trapped, military marches, hunting, journeys, and a variety of other animals, including, on the S side, crocodiles and a giraffe.

The platform is divided into the same 5 horizontal layers that characterise the division of the temple itself. It is carved in such magnificent detail that if you have time it is well worth walking round it before viewing the porch and what remains of the sanctuary. Above the plinth is a series of 5 horizontal mouldings, connected at intervals of every m or so by vertical bands. These are richly decorated with creepers and scrolls, and end with tiny motifs of *chaitya* windows. Along the lower mouldings are spaced miniature temple-like facades – **khakhara-mundis*** – which contain niches. Set into these are a variety of figures, often young women – caressing a bird, washing hair, playing the *vina* and so on. The slabs between are sculpted with a further variety of figures. Some are erotic, some are *nagas* or **nagis***, each with a human head but with the tail of a snake. Others are sexually provocative women, or miscellaneous figures illustrating a wide variety of scenes.

The middle of the platform has 3 horizontal mouldings at about eye level. Above these are the 2 remaining sections, the *upper jangha* and the *verandah*. The former is as richly sculpted as the lower section, sometimes with religious scenes such as the gods *Mahishasuramardini* (or the Goddess of destruction, Durga) and *Jagannatha*, enshrined in a temple. Other sculptures show royal or simple family scenes. Along the top of the platform is the verandah, consisting of 2 mouldings separated by a narrow recess. These are severely damaged, but even these mouldings are decorated with friezes.

While going round the platform it is well worth examining the wheels. Intricately carved, each 16-spoked wheel is shown with its axle, a decorated hub, and an axle pin. Floral motifs, creepers and the widely shown chaitya windows cover the stonework. Medallions with gods like Surya and Vishnu, erotic figures, noblemen, animals – all add immense life to the structure.

The upper sections The collapse of much of the sanctuary has left the porch, or *jagmohana*, as the dominant building of the complex. However, the scale of the sanctuary is still evident, and the climb up the outer walls and then down into the sanctuary itself, which is possible for the reasonably agile, allows you to see at close quarters both the remarkable chlorite statures of Surya on the outer S wall of the sanctuary and the interior of the sanctuary. This is particularly interesting as it gives an almost unique opportunity to see the inside of a temple sanctuary in full light.

It is best to climb up the main E steps of the porch and to walk round it to the left, or S side. The E door of the porch is the best preserved. Each door jamb is divided into 8 facets, all carved with a variety of reliefs which repay a close examination. Climbing up to the more than life sized statue of Surya it is possible to see clearly how even the larger sculptures show an attention to minute detail. Made of grey-green chlorite which stands in sharp contrast with the surrounding yellowish orange *khondalite* stone, Surya stands on a chariot drawn by his 7 horses, lashed by Aruna, the charioteer, shown down to the waist. Shown around the central figure of Surya are 2 4-armed gods, a pot-bellied Brahma on the right and possibly Vishnu on the left. Below them are 4 women, possibly the wives of Surya.

The sanctum sanctorum It is possible to go down into the holy of holies by a recent flight of steps from the western end of the temple. The route is clearly indicated. The original approach was through the porch.

The main feature is the chlorite platform at the western end of the 10 m square room which used to support the presiding deity. Even when the debris from the fallen tower was cleared the pedestal was empty, for the image had already been moved to the Jagannath Temple at Puri. It is possible that it is now in the Virinchi temple within the complex at Puri, but can only be seen by Hindus. The platform which remains is none the less outstanding. Some of the central carvings almost certainly show the king, the donor of the temple, in the company of priests. Note the hollows on top of the platforms E edge, caused by the placing of pots over a long period.

The temple grounds: the colossi Originally each of the 3 staircases to the porch was guarded by a pair of colossi. The E stairway had 2 rampant lions on top of a crouching elephant, the N 2 fully harnessed and decorated elephants, and the S 2 war horses. Those on the N and S sides have been remounted a short distance from their original sites. The lions have been put in front of the E steps up to the *Bhoga mandir*, nr the entrance.

Hotels As Konarak is easy to visit from both Puri and Bhubaneswar, in the past most visitors have only spent the day at Konarak. 3 of the major hotel chains (Taj, Oberoi and Welcom) have now obtained land to build hotels on the beach about 3 km from Konarak itself but there have been objections. The first is planned to open by the end of 1993. **F** *Panthanivas*, T Konarak 31 and the **F** *Ashok Travellers' Lodge*, T Konarak 23 are govt guest houses. The accommodation is very simple in non-a/c double rooms or family rooms. Restaurant and a fast food counter. There is a 4 rm **F** *PWD Inspection Bungalow*, T Konarak 34 and there is a camping ground.

Museum The *Archaeological Museum*, T 22. Open daily, 0900-1700. Close to the Travellers' Lodge. Entry free. Although the museum is small, the collection includes many important pieces of loose sculpture from the Sun Temple complex. Exhibitions with lectures and film shows are held occasionally. The Archeological Society publications on Konarak and other monuments are available for sale.

The **Tourist Office** is located at the Panthanivas nearby.

BHUBANESHWAR TO CUTTACK AND THE NORTH EAST

The road from Bhubaneshwar passes Nandankanan, a large well laid-out zoological park, to Cuttack, the medieval regional capital. Amid the idyllic hillsides of Ratnagiri and Lalitgiri, ancient Buddhist sites are being excavated.

Driving N along NH 5 20 km out of Bhubaneshwar is **Nandankanan**. The 'Pleasure Garden of the Gods' is on the road to Cuttack and is a zoological park and botanical garden set in 400 hectares in the dense Chandaka forest. There are

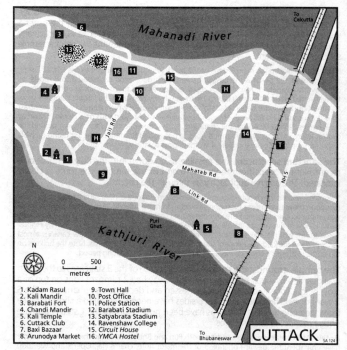

Map legend:
1. Kadam Rasul
2. Kali Mandir
3. Barabati Fort
4. Chandi Mandir
5. Kali Temple
6. Cuttack Club
7. Baxi Bazaar
8. Arunodya Market
9. Town Hall
10. Post Office
11. Police Station
12. Barabati Stadium
13. Satyabrata Stadium
14. Ravenshaw College
15. *Circuit House*
16. *YMCA Hostel*

N 0 500 metres

To Calcutta
Mahanadi River
Jail Rd
Mahatab Rd
Link Rd
Puri Ghat
Kathjuri River
NH 5
To Bhubaneswar

CUTTACK SA 124

tigers, including the rare white ones, a lion safari, rhinos, panthers, leopards and a variety of wild fowl and reptiles in their natural surroundings. In 1967, Nandankanan made news when a wild tiger jumped into the enclosure to find her mate, suggesting the attraction of the zoo even to a wild animal! It has also succeeded in breeding black panthers and *gharials* in captivity. The botanical gardens with its cactus house and rosarium are across the lake which separates it from the zoo. There is a *Guest House* and a lakeside cafeteria where you can get refreshments. Open daily except Mon.

Cuttack 30 km N of Bhubaneswar along the NH 5 is the medieval capital Cuttack, one of the oldest towns in Orissa. It was founded by Nripati Kesari who ruled from 920-935 AD and remained the administrative centre until the end of the British Raj. It occupies an important strategic position in relation to the network of canals in the region. Situated at the head of the Mahanadi delta and surrounded by the great river and its tributary the Kathajuri, the town is almost an island.

Places of interest To the S of the town, the ancient stone embankment was built in the 11th century by the Kesari ruler to protect the town from flooding by the Kathajuri river in spate. It still stands as a reminder of the engineering skills which went into its construction 900 years ago.

The 13th century **Barabati Fort** built of blue granite is in ruins. Its wide moat, a gateway and a mosque inside can still be seen although the 9-storeyed palace is no longer there. Built probably by one of Ganga rulers in the 14th century, it was in Marhatta hands when it was taken by the British in 1803. Close to the fort is the vast Barabati Stadium where major sporting and cultural events are held.

The **Kadam Rasul** in the centre of the city has 3 18th century mosques with beautiful domes and a music gallery within a walled enclosure with towers at each corner. The Muslim shrines contain relics of the Prophet Mohammed as well as the Prophet's foot print carved on a circular stone. Interestingly, it is visited by both Muslim and Hindu pilgrims.

Hotels D *Hotel Trimurti International*, Link Rd. T 22918. 38 rm. Central a/c. Restaurant, bar, travel counter. D *Akbari Continental*, Dolmundai, Haripur Rd. T 25242, Cable: AKBARCON, Telex: 0676-272. 34 rm. Central a/c. Restaurant, bar, exchange, shop, travel counter, TV. D *Hotel Asoka*, Ice Factory Rd, College Sq. T 25708, Cable: HOTASH. 50 rm. A/c. and non-a/c. Restaurant, bar, exchange, travel counter. D *Oriental*, Baxi Bazar. T 24249, Cable: COMFORT. 20 d rm. a/c and non-a/c. Restaurant, bar, exchange, travel. D *Panthanivas*, Baxi Bazar Chouk. T 23867. 32 rm (8 a/c). A/c restaurant, bar, TV, central.

Shopping The *Utkalika Govt Emporium* on Jail Rd, T 21961, has a very good selection of textiles and handicrafts including horn and brass objects and jewellery. The famous silver filigree shops line the streets in Nahasarak and Balu Bazaar.

Travel agent Majestic Travels, Mahatab Rd, Opp Basanti Hotel. Tirupati Travels, Chauliaganj. People Travels, Makaraba Sahi.

Tourist office is in Arunodya Market Building, Link Rd. T 23525. Tourist Counter at the Railway Station. T 25107.

Travel Air The nearest airport is at Bhubaneswar 29 km away. **See page 630**.

Rail Cuttack is on the SE Railways and has direct connections to Bhubaneswar, Calcutta, Delhi, Hyderabad, Madras and Puri. **Calcutta (H)**: *Dhauli Exp*, 2822 (AC/CC), daily, 1425, 6 hr 55 min; **Bhubaneswar**: *Haora-Tirupati Exp*, 8079, daily, 0855, 1 hr 10 min; *E Coast Exp*, 8045, daily, 1900, 40 min; **Puri**: *Haora-Puri Exp*, 8007, daily, 0550, 3 hr 10 min. See also **page 630**.

Road NH5 passes through city. Regular buses to Bhubaneswar and other major towns nearby.

The NH 5 passes through Cuttack NE. At Patharajpur turn right for **Ratnagiri**, **Lalitgiri** and the **Udaigiri Hills**. The hills are about 65 km from Cuttack. To the NE is an ancient Buddhist complex which can only be reached by rough road. You can take a car to the bottom of the Lalitgiri and Udaigiri hills and climb to the sites.

Ratnagiri, which has produced the best finds, is more difficult to reach since you must cross a narrow river by ferry and spend another 15 min on a rickshaw. Bhubaneswar is 90 km. It is possible to do a day excursion from there, but allow at least 2 hrs each way. Extensive remains have been excavated, which show an excellence in the quality of sculpture combining different coloured stones; from blue-green chlorite with the purple-red garnets in brownish silver khondalite. The finds include 3 monasteries, 8 temples and several stupas believed to date from the 7th century. The largest monastery is 55 m sq with a surrounding verandah with 60 pillars built around a courtyard. It appears to have about 2 dozen cells for monks. Look for the intricate carving on the doorway of the back porch wall. The 7th century University of *Pushpagiri* flourished here and the famous Chinese traveller Hiuen Tsang visited it in AD 639 and described it as one of Orissa's 2 Buddhist centres of learning. However, by the 13th century the excavations at the 3 sites have revealed numerous Buddhist structures, both stupas and monasteries, as well as sculptures and Buddha images. The Lokesvar image at **Udaigiri** is 3 m high and has an 8th century inscription on it.

Lalitgiri is at present being excavated by the Archaeological Department and although you are welcome to walk around, photography is not allowed. Large architectural remains including a 20 m high apsidal temple has been found while a stone platform suggests a date closer to the 2nd century. The stone casket containing silver and gold artefacts found in a stupa is believed to hold Buddha's relics; a small museum displays some of the finds. There is the stone-carvers' village at the base of Lalitgiri which traces its connections back to ancient times and produces excellent pieces of sculpture. Worth a visit.

The whole area with its hills rich with excavated Buddhist remains is in an idyllic situation, surrounded by green fields. OTDC Tourist Complex planned.

Paradwip, 94 km from Cuttack on the NH 5 or 86 km along the State Highway that follows the S bank of the Mahanadi. It is a pleasant beach resort and active port at the mouth of the Mahanadi river, with a marine drive. Thousands of giant **sea turtles** migrate very long distances every year (said to be from as far as S America) to lay their eggs and then return. There are regular buses from Cuttack and Bhubaneswar.

BHUBANESHWAR TO SIMLIPAL AND NORTHERN ORISSA

In visits of between 3 and 7 days it is possible to visit several places of historic and religious interest in northern and northwestern Orissa as well as to see outstandingly beautiful scenery and the **Simlipal National Park**. There is some accommodation which offers excellent value en route (particularly at Chandipur), though in places the accommodation is very basic. It is possible to travel either by bus or by car. Cars can be hired (with driver) in Bhubaneshwar.

Travelling NE from Bhubaneshwar along the NH 5 the road passes through Baleshwar (**Balasore**). This medieval maritime trading port first established by the British in 1642 with subsequent competition from the French who called it 'Farasidinga' and the Dutch 'Dinamardinga'. Ruins of Dutch tombs can still be seen. It is on the SE Railway between Calcutta and Madras and is 5 km off the NH5. Regular buses from Bhubaneshwar and Calcutta. Tourist Office, T 48.

Chandipur is a further 16 km from Baleshwar on the coast. It has one of Orissa's finest beaches with the tide receding 5 km daily. The sand dunes and casuarina groves make it particularly attractive. **D** Pantha Nivas, T 2151. On the beach, is very well run with helpful staff and good food (freshly caught sea fish a speciality). It makes an excellent stopping place and is a good point from which to go on to Simlipal and Khiching.

The NH 5 turns N in Baleshwar and enters **Mayurbhanj District** approximately 20 km N of Baleshwar. Do not take the right turn to Kharagpur 10 km N of Baleshwar, but follow road to Baripada. The district is thickly forested with hills, waterfalls and streams and is the home of much of India's wildlife which can now be seen at Simlipal. Apart from its natural beauty, there are prehistoric sites at Kuchai and Kuliana and students of history and archaeology would find Khiching, Baripada and Haripur, where the Bhanja rulers have left their mark, of particular interest. The area produces excellent 'tussar' silk, carvings of images and utensils on multi-coloured translucent serpentine stone from Khiching and tribal metal casting of toys and cult images. The tribal people have enriched the culture of the district particularly with their traditional dances.

Accommodation throughout the district is very basic.

Haripur is 16 km SE of Baripada. There is a regular bus service. Previously called Hariharpur, it was founded by Maharaja Harihar in 1400 as the capital of the Bhanja dynasty. A later king built the magnificent **Rasikaraya Temple** which, though now in ruins, still stands as a unique example of a brick built Orissan temple. The area is still fascinating as it has several other historic buildings in the vicinity of the temple. The ruins of Ranihamsapur, the inner apartment of the queen, can be seen to the N of the courtyard. To the E are the remains of the Durbar Hall with its beautiful sculptured stone columns and arches. The brick-built **Radhamohan Temple** and 14th century **Jagannath Temple** are architecturally interesting although the deities were moved and are now worshipped in a neighbouring village **Pratapur**.

The district headquarters, **Baripada** has all basic facilities including a hospital, P.O., branch of the State Bank of India and shops selling local handicrafts and handloom (Central Tussar Depot). **Tourist Office** is here. T 2710. Baripada has a *Circuit House*, which can be reserved through the District Magistrate and a *PWD Inspection Bungalow* for which contact Executive Engineer (R and B).

Museum *Baripada Museum* Open Summer 0700-1200, Winter 1000-1700. Closed Mon and govt holidays. Entry free. Collection of stone sculpture, coins, seals, terracottas, inscriptions.

Festival The Rath Yatra or 'car' festival held in Jun/Jul is unique because the chariot carrying *Subhadra* is drawn by women. The 'Chhau' dance festival is held at the palace during Mar/Apr.

Travel Bus services connect all major towns in the region but you can also hire private taxis or travel by deluxe coaches to visit the sights.

8 km N from Baripada on the road to Simlipal, **Kuchai**, has been excavated to reveal a prehistoric site yielding pottery and neolithic and microlithic implements. **Kuliana**, 17 km further N, is rich in palaeolithic finds.

Simlipal National Park

There is a regular bus service from Baripada 50 km away. The park can be reached from Baripada by road at Lulung, 30 km W of Baripada. However, it is also possible to enter directly from the NH 6, either at Bangiposi or at the Joshipur entrance, where there is a crocodile sanctuary. The nearest railway stations to the Park are on the SE Railways at Tatanagar and Balasore.

Simlipal is Orissa's principal wildlife sanctuary. It extends over an area of 2,750 square km at the heart of which is one of the country's earliest tiger reserves covering about 300 sq km. The area has majestic *sal* forests, expanses of grassland, waterfalls, gorges and valleys through which run streams which attract the animals. The fauna includes tiger, elephant, leopard, wolf, chital, sambar, deer, gaur, flying squirrel and a variety of wild fowl including mynas, parakeet and peacocks. The Barehapani waterfall with a drop of 400 m and the Joranda Falls (150 m) are both very impressive as are the Bachhuriachara grassland, where you might see a herd of elephants and the 1,158 m peak of Meghasani. Prior permission is required before visiting Simlipal. Contact the Assistant Conservator of Forests, Joshipur, Dt. Mayurbhanj. The Field Director, Simlipal Tiger Reserve, Baripada is able to issue Restricted Permits for visiting **Barehapani** and **Joranda** waterfalls and the **Chahala** woodland and **Nawana** valley which are situated in the core area. Jeeps with spotlights can be arranged through the Assistant Conservator of Forests, Joshipur.

Hotels There are very spartan *Forest Rest Houses* at Chahala, Nawana, Joranda, Barehapani with a view of the waterfall, Jenabil and Upper Barkamra. Reservations through the Field Director, Simlipal Tiger Reserve, PO Baripada well in advance. There are others at Gudgudia, Lulung, Jamuari, Dhudruchampa (which is a log house), Kanchhida and Talabandha. Reservations through Simlipal Forest Development Corporation, PO Karanjia. *Panthasala* Tourist Bungalow at Bangriposi can be reserved through the Tourist Officer, Baripada. Take your own food; the caretaker/cook will help to prepare the meal. Alternatively you can visit the park as an excursion from the beach resort Chandipur near Balasore, see page 642 above. The *OTDC Tourist Complex* nearing completion is at the entrance to the park and completely run on solar power in order to retain its natural ecology. The stone lodges and catering facilities will make a stay more comfortable since you need to spend 2 or 3 days to make a visit to the park worthwhile.

Khiching is approximately 20 km W of Joshipur along the NH 6. The capital of the Bhanja rulers in the 10th-11th century, Khiching is just N of the NH 6 nearly half way between Kharagpur in W Bengal and Sambalpur. Baripada,150 km away, has a regular bus service to the town. By rail, although the nearest station is at Rajrangpur 96 km away, it is better to get down at Balasore, 210 km, which has a fast service on the SE Railway. Otherwise, combine it with an excursion to Simlipal from Chandipur near Balasore as mentioned above.

The local deity **Kichangesvari**, once the family goddess of the Mayurbhanj royal family, has a unique temple built entirely of chlorite slabs. The reconstructed 20th c temple which has fine carvings is believed to have used the traditional temple building skills which date back to 8th c. Nearby there are a number of other temples built in the Kalinga style, some of which are still in use.

Hotels There is a *PWD Inspection Bungalow* which can be reserved through the Executive Engineer (R and B). PO Baripada. For the *Revenue Rest Shed*, PO Sukruli contact the District Magistrate, PO Baripada.

Museum The Khiching Museum, PO Sukruli. Open Summer 0700-1200, Winter 1000-1700. Closed Mon and government holidays. Entry free. Though small, it has a rare collection of art, sculpture and pottery.

Shopping The *Khiching Stone Workers Society* sells the locally produced carvings out of translucent coloured serpentine stone.

BHUBANESHWAR TO SAMBALPUR AND WESTERN ORISSA

The route passes through Sambalpur, famous for its textiles, dance and music. The gigantic Hirakud Dam can be visited as well as the densely forested Ushakothi Wildlife Sanctuary. The road to the steel town of Rourkela runs by the Brahmini river through glorious scenery.

It is possible to travel directly to Sambalpur, Hirakud and the northwest from Bhubaneshwar by crossing the Mahanadi at Cuttack and taking the State Highway through Denkanal and Angul to Sambalpur. If you have already visited Khiching it is also easy to continue W along the NH 6.

Sambalpur District This part of Orissa to the NW of the state was settled in ancient times. An undeciphered pictograph found at Vikramkhol, N of the Hirakud reservoir is evidence of such settlement. The region also features in Ptolemy's text of the 2nd century and was once the centre for trading in diamonds. In the 8th century King Indrabhuti became a Buddhist and a preacher of the Vajrayana sect. Its present name probably comes from the presiding deity Samalesvari to whom a temple was built by the Chouhans in the mid-16th century.

Sambalpur is famous for its textiles, particularly Sambalpuri saris from Bargarh, its tie and dye work, folk dance and music. It also produces some of the finest rice in the country. 20 km away at Hirakud is one of the longest mainstream dams in the world and the vast reservoir can be seen if you climb the Gandhi Minar or the Jawahar Minar in Sambalpur town.

Hotels E *Panthanivas*, T 21482. 12 a/c and 12 non-a/c double rms, restaurant and bar. Organised tours offered. Inexpensive **F** hotels: *Nataraj Hotel*, T 456, *Chandramani Lodge*, T 1040 and *Ashok Hotel*, T 760. The *Inspection Bungalow* where the cook will prepare a meal if you take provisions. Reservations: Executive Engineer (R and B), Sambalpur.

Tourist offices There is an *OTDC Tourist Office*, T 268. Counter at the Rly station T 1661.

Hirakud Dam The Mahanadi created enormous problems every year through devastating floods of the delta region. In order to combat these the Dam was built some 20 km northwest of Sambalpur. The key section is an over 1,100 m long masonry dam, with a further earthen dam of over 3,500 m. It is a colossal structure, over 60 m high and so drains an area of 133,000 sq km, twice the size of Sri Lanka! Since it was completed in 1957 there have been no serious floods in the Mahanadi delta. The dam has a 270 MW hydro electric power station and also allows the irrigation of nearly 750,000 ha of high quality land. Some of this is on the right bank of the Mahanadi S of Sambalpur and the remainder in the delta itself. Contact the Deputy Supt of Police, Security Force, Hirakud before visiting. There is a good Guest House, *Ashok Nivas*, at one end of the dam. You get an excellent view from the revolving tower, Gandhi Minar at the other end.

Ushakothi Wildlife Sanctuary 48 km E of Sambalpur on the NH 6, is a densely forested national park covering 130 sq km. Wild elephant, panther, leopard, tiger, bison, wild boar and many kinds of deer inhabit the sanctuary. Best to visit the sanctuary at night between 2000 and 0200 from Nov to June, accompanied by a guide with search lights and see the wildlife from the watch-towers sited near watering points to which the animals come. Open hooded jeeps recommended. Permits to visit from the Forest Range Officer, PO Badrama. Very basic accommodation (no electricity) at the *Forest Rest House*, Badrama, 3 km away. Reservation: Divisional Forest Officer, Bamra, Sambalpur.

About 32 km S of Sambalpur is *Huma*, where there is a famous leaning temple on the bank of the Mahanadi, dedicated to Lord Siva. The Kudo fish which thrive in the river is believed to belong to the deity so is never caught by fishermen. Country boat rides available at a small fee.

To the N of Sambalpur is *Sundargarh District*. In the tribal heartland it is an area of undulating hills with the richest deposits of mineral wealth in the state. Cave paintings are evidence of the existence of early man in this region. Once relatively untouched by modern civilisation and with a rich tribal culture, notable for many dances, the district was chosen for the siting of the first public sector steel plant at Rourkela. The route from Sambalpur to Rourkela runs E 115 km to Barakot, then N up the E bank of the Brahmani River. It passes through some glorious scenery. The Brahmani itself flows along a wide rocky and sandy bed, a torrent in the monsoon, with forested hills on either side.

The modern township of *Rourkela* is reached by a direct rail connection from Bhubaneswar, 470 km away. It can also be reached by regular bus services from both the state capital and Sambalpur 192 km away. A large industrial town girdled by a range of hills and encircled by rivers, Rourkela was selected for its prime position, as a steel plant in 1955 and has a Fertilizer Complex attached to it. The power for the steel plant comes from Hirakud. Both plants can be visited with permission from the PRO. The Gandhi Park and Zoo are the other attractions.

Hotels There is a wider choice of accommodation here. The western style *Rourkela House* T 5076 is best. The *Ispat Guest House*, Sector 2 and the *Atithi Bhavan*, Sector 4 are alternatives. Reservations through the PRO, Rourkela Steel Plant. **D** *OTDC Panthanivas*, Sector 5. T 5065, modern, with 12 a/c, some with TV and 8 non-a/c double rms. A/c restaurant and bar, car hire. There are several small hotels and *dharamsalas* as well as *PWD Inspection Bungalows* in Sector 4 and Panposh. For the last 2, contact Executive Engineer, R and B Div, Uditnagar, Rourkela.

Services Within the township buses, taxis, auto-rickshaws and cycle-rickshaws are available. Rourkela is well provided with banks, post offices, shops and medical facilities. *Orissan Handicrafts*, Sector 5 is worth visiting for stone statues, shell ornaments, horn craft, silver filigree, clay and wooden toys and silks. *OTDC Tourist Office* is at UGIE Square, Uditnagar, T 3923. Counter at the rly station, T 4150.

BHUBANESHWAR TO CHILIKA LAKE AND SOUTH ORISSA

Chilika Lake is India's largest, and has an abundance of bird and marine wildlife. Several excursions to the hills and coast can be made from Berhampur, a trading centre for silk fabric.

NH 5 passes southeast across the narrowing coastal plain of the Mahanadi before reaching *Chilika Lake* about a 100 km SE of Bhubaneswar en route to Berhampur.

Chilika, in the heart of coastal Orissa, is the largest inland lake in the country. It covers an area of 1,100 sq km stretching across the Puri and Ganjam districts and forms an enormous lagoon as it is joined to the Bay of Bengal with a narrow mouth, a sandy ridge separating it from the sea. The lake has a number of lush green islands and is the winter home of migratory birds, particularly on Nalabana island, some flying great distances from Persia and Siberia. During the winter months when it is best to visit Orissa, you can watch cranes, ospreys, golden plovers, sandpipers, flamingoes pelicans and gulls. Sadly the sound from the army guns practising may deter the birds.

Its aquatic fauna has made it a rich source for fisherman who come in search of mackerel, prawn and crab. The presiding deity of the lake has a shrine at the Kalijai temple on one of the tiny rock islands. The government plans to improve the facilities on the lake and introduce a centre for water sports at one end.

It is easiest to reach by road from Barkul, 6 km N of Balugaon or Rambha, at the S end of the lake. Both are on the Madras-Calcutta NH 5. The Calcutta-Madras rail route touches the Lake at Balugaon, Chilika, Khallikote and Rambha.

Hotels Accommodation is available at the OTDC **E** *Panthanivas* at Rambha, T 46, a 2-storeyed building with restaurant, 18 a/c and non-a/c double rms. **E** *Panthanivas* bungalow at Barkul, T Balugaon 6, very small, with restaurant and bar, 2 a/c and 9 non-a/c d rms. There are 2 hotels in Balugaon, *Asoka*, T 8 and *Chilka* T 68.

Boating OTDC motor launches for cruising on the lake through the marshes and backwaters, are available from Barkul and Launches belonging to the Revenue Dept at Balugaon. Country boats can be hired from private operators from Barkul, Rambha and Balugaon.

ML 'Sagarika' (34 seater) can be chartered for Rs 300 per hr or Rs 10 per seat. The smaller ML 'Paryataka' (8 seater) can be chartered for Rs 40 per hr or you pay Rs 10 per seat when there are at least 4 passengers. A 2 hr cruise goes to the Kalijai Temple and a 4 hr one to Nalabana Island. Reservations through Manager, Panthanivas, Barkul, T Balugaon 60.

There is an *OTDC Tourist Office* at Rambha, T 44, as well as a post office and a government dispensary.

Travelling S of Chilika Lake is ***Ganjam District***. Much of the district is covered in dense forest. Settled in prehistoric times, it also came under the influence of Emperor Asoka's rule. The handicrafts of the region include brass and bell-metal ware, horn work, wood carvings, silks and carpets.

Berhampur, on the NH 5, a trading centre for silk fabric, is the major commercial town of Ganjam District. An important station on the SE Railway where there is an OTDC Tourist counter (T 3870, Open 0500-2100), it is on the Madras-Calcutta highway and has a good bus network to other towns in the region.

Places of interest The **Thakurani, Jagannath, Nilakanthesvar Siva temples** are worth visiting. It is also a good place to shop for silks.

Hotels Accommodation is in simple hotels and guest houses. *Hotel Moti*, Gandhinagar Rd. T 2003. *Berhampur Rest House*, Convent School Rd. T 2244. *Udipi Hotel*, Fire Station Rd. T 2196. Government *Municipal Guest House*, Town Hall Rd. T 3318; *Circuit House* on Station Rd, and an *Inspection Bungalow* (Revenue) on Engineering School Rd. Reservations for the last 2 through the Sub-Divisional Officer. T 2103. The *PWD Inspection Bungalow*, Courtpetta can be booked through SE Southern Circle. T 2082.

Museum The **Berhampur Branch Museum**. Open Summer 0700-1400, Winter 1000-1700. Closed Mon and government holidays. Entry free. Collection of sculpture, armoury, anthropological and natural history specimens. No photography.

Tourist office The *OTDC Tourist Office* is on Old Christian St. T 3226. Tourist Counter at the Rly Station. T 3870.

Banks The State Bank of India has a branch among others and there are several shops, post offices and a hospital.

Local transport Private cars and taxis are available for hire for excursions from Berhampur to places like Gopalpur-on-Sea, Jaugada and Taptapani.

Rail Bhubaneshwar: *Haora Mail*, 6004 (AC/II), daily, 1855, 3 hr 10 min; **Vijayawada**: *Coromandal Exp*, 2841 (AC/II), daily, 0011, 10 hr 14 min; *Haora Mail*, 6003 (AC/II), daily, 0705, 12 hr 35 min; **Madras (MC)**: *Coromandal Exp*, 2841 (AC/II), daily, 0011, 17 hr 35 min; **To Calcutta (H)**: *Coromandal Exp*, 2842 (AC/II), daily, 0119, 10 hr 11 min.

Gopalpur-on-Sea offers a seaside alternative to staying in Berhampur. 16 km E of the town, Gopalpur was an ancient sea port from which early settlers from Kalinga sailed as far as Java, Bali and Sumatra. It became a popular seaside resort offering a beautiful sandy beach which has a regular bus service from Berhampur. Though it has the rather faded feeling and appearance of many seaside resorts, almost as if it were permanently out of season, it has its attractions. Sand dunes, groves of coconut palm and casuarinas separate the small town from the beach on the Bay of Bengal. The backwaters, creeks and lagoons give some variety.

Hotels B *Oberoi Palm Beach*. T 21, Cable: OBHOTEL, Telex: 673-261. 20 double rms, 4 a/c. Good restaurants, bar, private beach, tennis court, surfing. Run like a British country house. The **F** *Youth Hostel* has accommodation for 16 (members only). Some inexpensive hotels are **E** *Sea View Lodge*, 6 rm, **E** *Sea Breeze*, T 56, **E** *Holiday Home*, 11 rm, T 49, **E** *Motel Mermaid*, on the beach with restaurant, T 50 and *Kalinga*, T 33.

It is possible to visit a number of places of interest in the neighbourhood of Berhampur. **Taptapani**, 50 km along the state highway to the NW is at an altitude of 500 m, and has a regular bus service from Berhampur and Koraput. There is also a direct bus from Bhubaneswar 240 km away. Water from the the hot sulphur springs which were discovered in a forest setting are channelled to a pond for bathing. There is a shrine to goddess Kandhi inside the original 'kund'.

Hotels Piped sulphur spring water also supplies hot water to the govt **E** *Panthanivas* bath rms. 8 rm. Accommodation may be reserved in the 2-storeyed Travellers' Lodge which has a restaurant and a/c or non a/c double rooms. T Digaphandi 21. **F** *Youth Hostel*. Reservations through the Secretary.

At **Chandragiri** 32 km S of Taptapani in the tribal hills, the Tibetan carpet weavers have settled in a refugee colony after fleeing from Tibet in the 1950s. The temple and Buddhist prayer flags lend a distinctive atmosphere. The carpets and handicrafts can be seen being woven; prices are very reasonable.

35 km N of Berhampur, is **Jaugada** in the Malati Hills, famous for the Asoka edicts found inscribed in granite, which is more difficult to get to. It can be reached by a jeepable road from Purusottampur, which has a regular bus service from Berhampur. Emperor Asoka's doctrine of conquest through love instead of the sword and his declaration "All men are my children" appear here. The old fort which is believed to date back to the 6th century contains images of the 5 Pandavas in stone which are worshipped in the temple of Guptesvar. There are several other interesting sites nearby especially those in **Buguda**, a few km away, where there is the **Viranchinarayan Temple** with its beautifully carved wooden *Jagamohan**, and its murals depicting stories from the epic Ramayana. Also, close by in **Buddhakhol** are Buddhist sculptures and shrines to Siva.

BIHAR

Bihar took its present form at Independence, and apart from losing Purnea and Manbhum districts to W Bengal was unaffected by the process of states reorganisation. Its area of 174,000 sq km and population in 1991 of 84 million makes it half the size of the re-united Germany but with 10 million more people.

Social indicators *Literacy* M 42% F 26% (1991) *Newspaper circulation*: 498,000 *Birth rate* Rural 38:1000 Urban 32:1000 *Death rate* Rural 14:1000 Urban 7:1000 *Infant mortality* Rural 116:1000, Urban 60:1000 *In-migrants* 1,348,000 *Out-migrants* 2,537,000 *Registered*

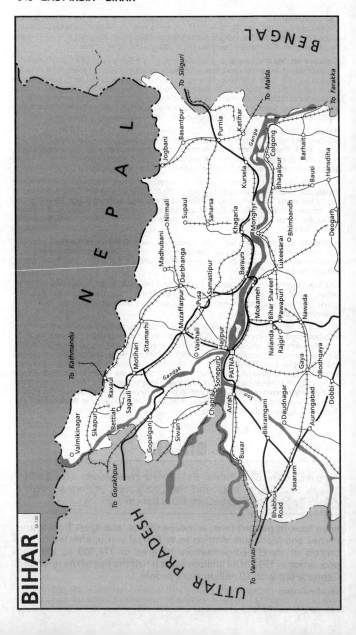

BIHAR SA 130

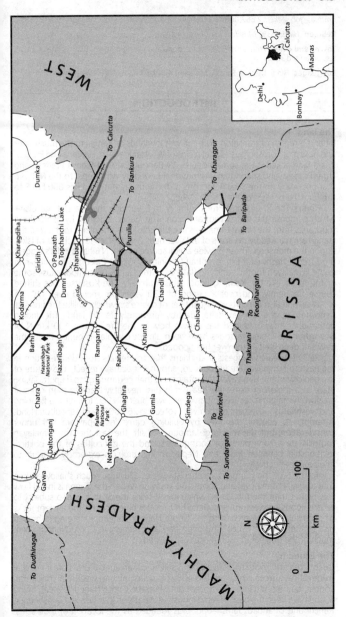

graduate job seekers 2,662,000 *Av annual income per head* : Rs 927 *Inflation 1981-87* 68%.

Religion *Hindu* 83% *Muslim* 14% *Christian* 1%.

Towns and cities With under 13% of the population living in towns Bihar is one of India's less urbanised states.

Languages Hindi, Maithili, Santali, Mundari, Kurukh

INTRODUCTION

The land

Bihar is a region of transition from the wet lowlands of Bengal to the much drier and now more prosperous alluvial plains of W Uttar Pradesh, Haryana and Punjab. It is a landlocked state, surrounded by W Bengal, Orissa, Madhya Pradesh and Uttar Pradesh and sharing an international boundary with Nepal to the N. From that boundary on the Siwalik foothills of the Himalayas it stretches 600 km S to the forested borders of the Chota Nagpur plateau.

Rivers The River Ganga runs from W to E through the heart of the plains which comprise the state's central region. The Ganga is joined by its northern tributaries from the Nepal Himalayas like the Son-Kosi. The plains to the N of the Ganga are marked by the scars of old river beds which often form chains of lakes during the monsoon. These provide a vital source of fish. N Bihar is India's biggest producer of freshwater fish, over half of which is sold to Calcutta. Torrential rain in the Himalayan foothills and the flatness of the Ganga valley cause some of the rivers, like the *Kosi*, to flood catastrophically. The Kosi itself has shifted course frequently, and over a period of 130 years has moved over 110 km westwards. It also deposits vast quantities of coarse silt which, unlike the fine silts deposited in the Bengal delta, destroy previously fertile land. The Indian geographer Enayat Ahmed has shown how in the area about 100 km N of *Monghyr* old indigo factories have been almost completely buried under the new silt, deposited as the river has flooded.

Recent research suggests that claims that this results from deforestation in the eastern Himalayas are unfounded, and that it actually reflects the nature of the geology of the Himalayan mountains and their continuing rapid uplift. Taking place in a region of extremely heavy rain this inevitably leads to high rates of erosion. A major protective embankment was built in 1960 to limit the flooding and westwards movement of the river, protecting 265,000 ha of agricultural land. Attempts to control the Kosi by building dams in Nepal are still under consideration, but the very large amounts of silt, the fact that the Himalayan foothills are a zone of major earthquakes, and the difficulties of the political relationship between India and Nepal, makes projects extremely difficult to implement effectively.

To the S of the Ganga is another stretch of alluvium, much shallower than that to the N of the river and about 150 km wide. When the Ganga is in full flow it is higher than the tributaries which join it from the S, so it is also subject to severe floods between Jul and Oct. The alluvium barely covers the ancient rocks of peninsular India which form the Chota Nagpur plateau, emerging in broken hills to the S. There is beautiful open parkland scenery in Chota Nagpur itself, much of the original forest having been cleared.

The Economy

Resources and industry While Bihar is still mainly an agricultural state it has vital **mineral resources**. The state has 40% of India's mineral wealth in coal, mica, copper, bauxite and iron. These deposits lie on the Chota Nagpur plateau in the S, and have been the basis of rapid industrial expansion in towns like Jamshedpur, Ranchi and Dhanbad. Jamshedpur was founded as the location of India's first integrated iron and steel mill, opened by Jamshedji Tata in 1908.

Since Independence major industrial projects have been undertaken by the Govt of India, often using foreign aid. Bokaro steel mill in the Damodar Valley project area was one of such developments. Bharat Heavy Electricals at Ranchi is another, built with Soviet aid in the 1960s. India is the world's leading mica producer, Bihar accounting for 50% of that production, but the decline in world demand for mica has hit the industry hard. Production dropped from 15,000 tonnes in 1971 to under 3,500 tonnes in 1991. The industry is focused on Hazaribagh, about 70 km N of Ranchi, where women and children work at splitting the mica sheets, reportedly to thicknesses of 1/25 mm. In the same period bauxite production has more than doubled. It is mined in laterites at Lohardaga, 50 km W of Ranchi and moved by metre gauge train to Luri, S of the Damodar River, for processing.

Craft industry Bihar is the home of the **Madhubani** painting. Its origins are in paintings by women from Mithila who pass down the skill from mother to daughter. On ceremonial or religious occasions centuries ago, they created a striking folk art on the walls and floors of their mud huts often drawing from mythology for their subject and using bright colours with strong lines. The very elaborate Kobhar Ghar design for weddings used figures of a god and goddess with symbols of long life and fertility such as the fish and the tortoise. Originally vegetable dyes prepared from leaves, flowers and sap were used and black was obtained from the soot underneath their cooking pots. The rules laid down meant they could not spend money on material or use any edible plants. Now the paintings in red, blue, green, black and yellow use coloured powder bought in the bazaar mixed with goats milk and are done on handmade paper or fabric. The white is often powdered rice and the black, burnt straw. They are unique items and make good gifts, eg. greeting cards and wall hangings showing Krishna with gopis (milkmaids), country scenes and animals. From the same Madhubani district a special **Sikki grass** is dyed in bright colours and woven with the natural grass to make attractive boxes, baskets and figures.

Floral 'Alpana' patterns which are usually painted on the floor with chalk or rice powder have been transferred to paper, cloth or wood to sell as decorative items. Around Bodh Gaya, **miniature paintings** on leaves or paper depicting the lives of the Buddha or Mahavira are sold to pilgrims and tourists.

Bihar is also well known for wooden toys, small white metal figures and leather goods. Wood inlay is another ancient craft which has been practised in the Patna region. The craftsman uses different woods, ivory, metal and horn to create inlaid designs for table tops, trays and wall plaques.

History

The name **Bihar** is derived from 'vihara' ('monastery'), and is indicative of its wealth of religious monuments. All the major religions of India have left a mark, but Bihar is particularly famous as the home of the Buddha and of Mahavira, founder of Jainism. The world's first university of Buddhist learning was founded at Nalanda, (now an easy bus ride 50 km to the SE of Patna).

Bihar was settled from the W as Aryan tribes moved down the Ganga valley, clearing the forest and developing cultivation. Agriculture provided the base for the Magadhan kings who ruled what is now S Bihar from the 6th to the 4th centuries BC. Some of these kings were clearly outstanding administrators. **Bimbisara**, for example, travelled widely through his kingdom, maintained good relations with neighbouring states and contacts as far afield as Taxila in the NW and Tamil Nadu in the S. He was deposed and murdered in about 490 BC, 7 years before the Buddha died.

The early Magadhan kings had their capital at **Rajagriha**, 100 km SE of modern Patna. It was surrounded by stone walls with a perimeter of about 40 km, which can still be seen. An early example of a garden city, only the centre was built up. Later they moved their capital to

Pataliputra, the site of modern **Patna**. From that base the last of the Magadhan kings, the unpopular tyrant Nalanda, was overthrown by **Chandragupta Maurya**, some time between 324 and 313 BC. Modern Bihar thus became the centre of the first empire to unite most of India under one ruler. Even then Pataliputra had taken much the shape of modern Patna, being a long narrow city, strung about 12 kms along the bank of the Ganga.

It was over 600 years after the death of the **Emperor Asoka** in 232 BC before Bihar moved back into centre stage in India's history. The Guptas, who played a central role in the flowering of Hindu culture of the classical period, regained power for Magadha in the 4th and 5th centuries AD. They were followed by the Palas of Bengal who ruled until defeated by the Muslims in 1197. The Delhi sultans and a succession of Muslim rulers independent of Delhi controlled the region until the Mughals brought it into their territory. A variety of Muslim place names such as Aliganj, Hajipur are evidence of the 5 centuries of Muslim political dominance that is still marked in the fact that 14% of the population today is Muslim.

The Mughals under **Babur** overran the Lodis, the last in the line of Delhi Sultans, in 1529. When **Akbar** re-took it from the Afghan **Sher Shah** the Mughals retained it until the British won the Battle of Buxar in 1764. Subsequently Bihar was separated from Bengal and became a province under British rule until India's independence in 1947.

Modern political development From its pre-eminent position in the culture and politics of early and classical India, Bihar has declined today to one of India's poorest and most badly administered states. Throughout the 1980s there have been outbreaks of caste-based violence in the countryside. Many of the tribal peoples have felt themselves increasingly under pressure by agricultural settlers from the plains, and have found little scope for taking up work in new industries, where jobs have tended to go to the more educated and qualified Hindi speaking Biharis. For over 100 years emigration from the state has exceeded immigration, as the poor have moved to cities like Calcutta and Bombay or to work on tea estates. Hundreds of thousands of Biharis also migrate seasonally to regions like Punjab and Haryana to work in harvesting periods, as well as to Nepal.

The state has been dominated for long periods by the Congress Party. In all Lok Sabha elections except 1977 (when Congress won no seats) it has obtained a majority of the 54 seats. In the landslide of Rajiv Gandhi's election in 1984 it won 48 of the 54 seats with 51.8% of the vote. The chief alternative has come from the Janata Party, which won all the seats in 1977 in the rout of Mrs. Gandhi at the end of India's emergency, though even then the Congress held on to 23% of the vote. None of the other parties have made a significant impact either in the Lok Sabha elections or the State assembly elections, where there are 324 seats.

Local Festivals
Bodh Gaya and **Rajagriha** attract Buddhists from all over the world who come to celebrate *Buddha Jayanti*, the birth of the Buddha in Apr/May while *Mahavira Jayanti* in Apr brings Jains to the sacred Parasnath Hill where 22 tirthankaras are believed to have attained salvation. A unique *marriage market* takes place for a fortnight each June when the nation's Mithila Brahmins gather in Saurath in the Madubani district and parents come with horoscopes, arrange the future of their marriagable children in a large mango grove. The annual *Pataliputra Festival* starts with Dasara in Oct and concludes with the Sonepur fair. Dasara is celebrated for 10 days as elsewhere in India, firstly with the worship of goddess Durga for 9 days before the immersion of the image on the 10th and simultaneously enormous paper effigies of the demon Ravana filled with fire-crackers are set alight.

Diwali, the festival of lights, follows 20 days later with lamps lit to remember the return of Rama after his exile and is accompanied with grand fireworks.

Six days later *Chhath* or Surya Puja is celebrated to worship the Sun God. To mark the harvest, fresh paddy, sweets and fruit are the offerings made by devotees who process through the streets. Thousands of women offer homage at sunrise and sunset by the river Ganga standing waist deep in water. *Sonepur Fair* Across the river from Patna is the scene of Asia's largest cattle fair which coincides with a Hindu festival at Kartik Purnima, the first full moon after Diwali, in Nov. See Sonepur below.

Cuisine
Bihar does not have a particularly distinctive style of cooking. The typical meal consists of boiled rice, unleavened bread, lentils and vegetables cooked with hot

spices. *Sattoo* which is combination of grains is often made into a dough and eaten either as a savoury or a sweet when mixed with sugar or jaggery. You may notice Biharis in other parts of India taking this as a mid-day meal under a shady tree (taxi-drivers in Calcutta for example). The mixture can also be taken as a drink when mixed with milk or water and flavoured with cardamoms and cloves. You can get snacks of *Puri-aloo,* deep fried Indian bread with potatoes cooked with onions and garlic and *kachoris* made with wheat and lentil flour and served with *kala chana* (black gram).

PATNA

Population 1,200,000 (1991). *Altitude* 53 m. Clothing Cottons in summer, light woollens in hill stations in winter.

	Jan	Feb	Mar	Apr	May	Jun	Jul	Aug	Sep	Oct	Nov	Dec	Av/Tot
Max (°C)	24	26	33	38	39	37	33	32	32	32	29	25	32
Min (°C)	11	13	19	23	26	27	27	27	26	23	16	12	21
Rain (mm)	21	20	7	8	28	139	266	307	243	63	6	2	1110

At the confluence of the rivers **Son**, Punpun and **Ganga**, **Patna** is an ancient city with a history that can be traced back 2,500 years. **Ajatasatru**, the second Magadha king who ruled from Rajagriha, built a small fort at Pataligrama. Later **Chandragupta Maurya** (who according to Greek classical sources had advised Alexander the Great in his campaigns in NW India) founded the Mauryan Empire with Pataliputra as its capital, **see page 81**. Buddhist histories suggest that it was here that Asoka usurped the throne of his father, Bindusara, murdering all his rivals and starting a reign of terror, before a conversion 8 years later. It marked the beginning of perhaps the greatest reforming kingship the world has known. The Greek ambassador *Megasthenes*, who visited Chandragupta's court at Pataliputra was deeply impressed by the efficiency of the Emperor's administration and the splendour of the city. Ruins can be seen at Kumrahar, Bhiknapahari and Bulandhi Bagh with its 75 m wooden passage. Excavations date the site back to the pre-Mauryan times of 600 BC.

In the 16th century the Pathan **Sher Shah Suri** revolted against the Mughal Emperor Humayun who then ruled the region and established the foundations of a new Patna, building a majestic mosque in 1540 which dominates the skyline.

Modern Patna stretches along the S bank of the Ganga for about 15 km. It is a pleasant city divided in 2 by the Maidan, a large open park with the airport to the W as well as Patna Junction station. Patna has the buildings which reflect its important administrative and educational functions. The collectorate, Judge's court, Medical College and Hospital, Patna College, the University, the Law College and the College of Engineering are all close to the river banks in the western part of the city. Also on this side lies the Governor's state house, Raj Bhavan, the Maharaja's palace, the High Court and the Museum as well as the finer residential quarters. To the E is Old Patna with its bazaars, the old mosques, Har Mandir and Padri-ki-Haveli or St. Mary's, the oldest Roman Catholic church in Patna, which was built in 1775.

Some streets have been renamed although they continue to be referred to by their old names, eg. Fraser Rd now Nazharul Huque Path and Exhibition Rd now Braj Kishore Path, although Beer Chand Patel Path has replaced Gardiner Rd.

Patna is directly linked to Delhi (1 hr 25 min) and Calcutta (55 min) by Indian

Airlines' daily flights. Also connected to Calcutta via Jamshedpur by Vayudoot 6 times a week. The flight takes 2 hr 15 min. The airport is 7 km from the city centre.

Places of interest *Golghar* The Gola or round house is the extraordinary 29 m high bee-hive shaped structure which stands between the Maidan and the river Ganga. It was built of stone slabs in 1786 by Capt. John Garstin of the Bengal Engineers, as a grain store for the British army in case of a famine similar to the one of 1770. It has a base 125 m wide where the wall is 3.6 m thick, with 2 brick staircases which spiral up the outside. The grain was to be carried up one side, poured in through the hole at the top and then the workforce was to descend the other staircase to collect more. The last line of the inscription 'First filled and publicly closed by___' was never completed. Although now empty, it is well worth climbing the steps for an excellent view of the city and the Ganga. Between Jul and Sep the river can be over 10 km wide at this point with a current of 8 to 10 knots in places. Inside, the Gola provides a marvellous echoing chamber.

Gulzaribagh About 8 km E of the Golghar near Kumrahar is the former East India Company's principal opium *godown* (warehouse), now a Government printing press. Strategically placed by the river, the 3 long buildings with porticoes on each side, were easily accessible to boats which would carry the opium down to Calcutta from these N Indian headquarters. The old opium godowns, ballroom and hall are open to visitors.

Har Mandir is in the Chowk area of old Patna. The gurdwara built by

1. Golghar
2. Gulzaribagh & Old Opium Godown
3. Kumrahar Excavations
4. Bulandibagh Excavations
5. Qila House or Jalan Museum
6. Saif Khan's Mosque
7. Sher Shah's Mosque
8. Raj Bhavan
9. Secretariat
10. Reserve Bank
11. State Bank
12. Khadi Emporium
13. Cottage Industries Institute
14. Moinul Haque Stadium
15. New Patna Club
16. Khuda Baksh Oriental Library
17. Rajendra Museum & Sadaquat Ashram
18. Gandhi Maidan
19. Sanjay Biological Park
20. General Post Office
21. Har Mandir
22. Ram Krishna Mission
23. Catholic Cathedral
24. Government of India Tourist Office
25. Patna Museum
26. British Library
27. Patna University
28. Indian Airlines & Maurya Patna
29. Samrat International
30. Satkar International & Mayfair Restaurant
31. Hotel Republic
32. Hotel Rajasthan & Ashok Restaurant
33. Hotel Pataliputra Ashok
T1. Patna Junction Station
T2. Gulzaribagh Station
T3. Patna City Station

Maharaja Ranjit Singh is the second of the 4 great *takhts* or thrones in the Sikh world and consecrates the birth place of the 10th Guru Gobind Singh. The shrine of white marble with kiosks on the terrace above has a museum on the ground floor exhibiting photos, holy scriptures and personal possessions of the Guru.

Kumrahar Excavations at the site of the ancient capital on the bypass between Patna Sahib and Patna junction stations, have revealed ruins enclosed within a high brick wall. These date back to 600 BC, the first of 4 distinct periods up to AD 600. The buildings were devastated by a fire and lay hidden in the silt. The more recent fifth phase dates from the beginning of the 17th century.

The most important finds are rare wooden ramparts and a large Mauryan assembly hall with highly polished sandstone pillars which date back to 400-300 BC. In the 5th century AD, when the Chinese pilgrim Fa-hien visited the area, he commented on the brilliant enamel-like finish achieved by the Mauryan stone-cutters and wrote of it "shining bright as glass". The evidence of their skill can be gauged even today from the ruins at Kumrahar and elsewhere. The excavations suggest that the immense pillared hall was 3-storeyed and covered an area of 77 m sq. There were probably 15 rows of 5 pillars, each 4.6 m apart. From the single complete column found they are estimated to have been about 6 m high. The fact that much of the building was wooden explains why so little has survived after the fire. The excavations also point to the possibility of one of the ceilings having been supported by immense *caryatid** figures which, taken together with the use of numerous columns, show a marked similarity with the palaces at Persepolis in S Iran.

Qila House or Jalan Museum. Across the road from Har Mandir, the private house was built over the ruins of Sher Shah's fort and is a museum containing Chinese paintings, a valuable collection of jade and silver filigree work of the Mughal period. Prior permission must be obtained from the owner. **Saif Khan's Mosque** or Pather-ki-Masjid. It is situated on the bank of the Ganga and was built in 1621 by Parwez Shah, the son of the Mughal Emperor Jahangir.

Hotels B *Maurya Patna*, Fraser Rd. T 22067/9, Cable: Maurya, Telex: 022 352. 80 rm. The best hotel in town has 2 restaurants (*Vaishali* and *Angara*), pool, poolside barbecue **C** *Pataliputra Ashok*, Beer Chand Patel Path. T 26270/9, Cable: Ashokotel, Telex: 022 311. 56 rm. 6 km airport, 2½ km rly. Day rms for half-day use available. Restaurant (*Pali*), bar, exchange, travel, Bihar Tourism office **C** *Chanakya*, Beer Chand Patel Path. T 23141/2, 31845/8, Cable: Swagat. 40 rm. Restaurant (*Samrat*), bar, exchange, travel, shops **C** *Samrat International*, Fraser Rd. T 31841/3, Cable: Samrat, Telex: 022 405. 68 rm some with TV. 2 restaurants (Haveli and roof-top barbecue Upwan), bar, 24 hr coffee shop, exchange.

D *Satkar International*, Fraser Rd. T 31886/8, Cable: Satkar. 50 rm. central a/c. Restaurant (*Amrita*), exchange, shops **D** *Republic*, Lawleys Building, Exhibition Rd. T 55021/4, Cable: Lyswal, Telex: 022 261. 35 rm some a/c. Dining hall, exchange, roof garden **D** *Marwari Awas Griha*, Fraser Rd. T 31866, Cable: Awasgriha, Telex: 022 241. 42 rm some a/c. Indian vegetarian restaurant, travel, TV. **D** *Avantee*, opp. Dak Bungalow, Fraser Rd. T 31851/5, Cable: Avantee. 40 rm some a/c. Restaurant, travel, shops **D** *President*, off Fraser Rd. T 31891. 36 rm some a/c. Restaurant (*Woodlands*), travel. **D** *Rajasthan*, Fraser Rd. T 25102. 20 double rm some a/c. Restaurant, travel, TV. **D** *Chaitanya*, Exhibition Rd. T 55123, Cable: Chaitanya, Telex: 022 213. 48 rm some a/c. Restaurant (*Samiana*), bar, attach. bath. **D** *Anand Lok*, opp. Patna Jn. Rly Station. T 223960. 43 rm some a/c. **D** *Tourist Bhawan* (BSTDC), Birchand Patel Path. T 25320. 44 rm some a/c. Cheap dormitory beds. A/c restaurant (*Amrapali*), exchange, travel.

There are several inexpensive hotels especially on Fraser Rd and Ashok Rajpath, providing non a/c accommodation for approximately Rs 80(s), Rs 120(d). Some have a restaurant and occasionally a bar. **E** *Railway Retiring Rooms* at Patna Junction d rm (some a/c) and non a/c d, triple and cheap dormitory beds. Reservations: Enquiry Supervisor. *Dharamsalas* Pataliputra and Birla Mandir are at Subji Bagh. Ram Piari Kunwar is at Kadam Kuan and Arya Athithi Grih at Naya Tola.

Restaurants and Bars The top hotels all have good multi-cuisine restaurants and bars which are listed above. There are some Indian Restaurants on Fraser Road – *Ashok* is dimly lit but serves good food; also Amber, *Palji*, *Krishna Chowk* and *Chef. Mayfair* serves inexpensive snacks and ice creams. *Sheesh Mahal* is on S Gandhi Maidan and *Vasant Vihar* on Maurya Lok Complex, Buddha Marg.

Banks and Exchange Allahabad Bank and Central Bank of India (Maurya Lok Complex) and United Bank of India (Hotel Pataliputra Ashok) on Bailey Rd; Bank of Baroda, Vijaya Bank and Bank of India on Fraser Rd; Bank of Maharashtra, Exhibition Rd.

Shopping Patna and its surrounding villages are known for **wooden toys and inlay work**, silver jewellery in beaten rustic style, tussar silk, beaten white metal figures, bamboo and leather goods (including shoes). Madhubani paintings, lacquerware and papier mâché goods are other good buys. The government emporia are *Amrapali*, Dak Bungalow Rd and *Bihar State Handloom and Handicrafts* on E Gandhi Maidan. There is also a *Bihar Khadi Gramodyog Kendra* and shops at Patna Market, New Market, Maurya Lok Complex and Boring Canal Rd. **Camera films** and accessories from Foto Daffodils, opp. Maurya Lok Complex, on Bailey Rd.

Bookshops There are some bookshops on Fraser Rd.

Local Transport Taxis No yellow-top taxis. Private un-metered taxis are available from the airport, railway station, some hotels and important tourist sites Rates should be agreed before the journey. **Auto rickshaws** are easily available charging a Re.1 per stage on a fixed route basis. **Cycle-rickshaws and horse-drawn 'tongas'** are available everywhere but fares must be negotiated in advance. There is a city **bus** service. The Bihar State Road Transport Corporation runs an hour-long **cruise** on the river from Mahendra ghat on its floating restaurant 'Sagarika'.

Car hire Ashok Travels and Tours (Hotel Pataliputra Asoka) hire out cars and coaches. The airport transfer costs Rs 55 (a/c), Rs 45 (non-a/c) and the Railway Station transfer Rs 45 (a/c), Rs 35 (non-a/c). Car hire charges vary from Rs 150 to Rs 250 for 4 hours, Rs 300 to Rs 450 for 8 hours and Rs 400 to Rs 600 for 12 hours for a/c and non a/c respectively. The charges relate to 10 km travel per hour. A/c coaches may be hired for half a day for Rs 500 or for a full day for Rs 1000.

Entertainment Local English language papers carry details of programmes at cinemas and auditoria. Cinemas in Gandhi Maidan are Mona and Elphinstone and on Exhibition Rd are Apsara and Chanakya. There are 3 auditoria in Gandhi Maidan – Kalidas Rangalay, Sri Krishna Memorial Hall and Prem Chand Rangalay. Bharatiya Nritya Kala Kendra at Fraser Rd.

Sports There is a swimming pool in Hotel Maurya with a poolside barbecue. The golf club is on Bailey Rd and the Moinul Haque Stadium in Rajendra Nagar. The clubs in Patna permit temporary membership for facilities of indoor games and swimming where available. Bankipur Club is on Judges Court Rd, New Patna Club on Beer Chand Patel Path.

Museums Khuda Baksh Oriental Public Library One of the largest one-man collections of books and rare Persian and Arabic manuscripts was founded in 1900. It also contains Mughal and Rajput paintings and the only books rescued from the Moorish University of Cordoba in Spain and an inch-wide Koran. It is now one of India's national libraries.

  Patna Museum, Buddha Marg. T 23332. 1030-1630. Closed Mon. Entry free except Fri. Collection of coins, paintings, terracotta, bronze and stone sculptures including the famous Mauryan Didarganji Yakshi (c 200 BC), Jain sculptures (2nd, 3rd centuries) and finds from Bodh Gaya, Nalanda and Kukrihar. It has Chinese and Tibetan sections and a 15 m long fossil tree. **Rajendra Smriti Museum**, Sadaquat Ashram. T 25800. Summer 0700-1100 and 1400-1900, winter 0800-1200 and 1400-1800. Closed Mon. Entry free. A small museum containing the former Indian President Rajendra Prasad's personal belongings. The ashram itself is the seat of Bihar Vidyapith, the national university established in 1921

Parks and zoos The Gandhi Maidan is the often crowded with people. The Vir Kunwar Singh Park is on Station Rd. The Sanjay Gandhi Biological Park which is a zoo cum botanical garden is open every day, except Mon, from sunrise to sunset. Entry Re 0.50.

Useful addresses British Library Bank Rd, nr Gandhi Maidan, T 24198. Open 1100-1800 Tue-Sat.

Hospitals and medical services Patna Medical College Hospital, Ashok Rajpath E. T 52301. Nalanda Medical College Hospital and Upadhyaya Nursing Home, T 52203 are on Kankar Bagh Rd. Getwell Nursing Home is on Jamal Rd. T 34183.

Post & Telegraphs General Post Office, Station Rd. T 24000. Central Telegraph Office, Buddha Marg. T 31000. Telex Enquiries: T 26858.

Places of worship *Hindu* Hanuman Mandir, nr Patna Jn Rly Station, Kali Mandir at Darbhanga House, Patna University and Patna Devi Temple. *Muslim* Jumma Masjid near Rly Station and Sher Shah Mosque and Pathar-ki-Masjid in Patna City. *Christian* Roman Catholic Church; at Bankipore and St. Xavier's Church at Danapur Cantonment. Protestant; Church of N India Christ Church, on the Maidan *Sikh* Har Mandir Sahib Gurdwara.

Travel agents and tour Operators In Hotel Pataliputra Ashok, *Ashok Travels and Tours*, T 26271 and *Indo-Saudi Services*, T 26270. In Hotel Maurya, *Arya Travels*, T 21247, *Holiday Nepal* (Room 410), T 22061 and *Travel Corporation of India*, T 31016. Nearby is *Swan Travel* on Biscauman Building, T 23700. *Jet Age Travel Services* is in Tourist Bhawan, Beer Chand Patel Path, (Room 154) T 34225 and the *Tourist Bureau* is in Hotel Menka in Kadam Kuan. Patna Tours and Travels is on Fraser Rd, T 26846.

Tourist offices and Information Government of India Tourist Office, Room 151, Tourist Bhawan, Beer Chand Patel Path. T 26721. Open 1000-1700. Bihar State Tourism Information is on Fraser Rd. T 25295. Open 0800-2200. Airport counter, T 23199. Hotel Pataliputra Ashok counter, T 26270. Tourist Information Centre also at Patna Junction Railway Station.

  During the tourist season from October to March conducted tours are operated by the Bihar State Tourist Development Corporation (BSTDC), Ashok Travels and Tours and Patna Tours and Travels. The tour includes city sightseeing, Rajgir, Nalanda and Pawapuri, starting from 0800 returning at 2200. Fare Rs 40. Tours to Vaishali, Bodh Gaya, Buxar and Sasaram are only operated by the BSTDC when there are sufficient number of passengers.

Air Indian Airlines Delhi, daily except Tue (+ 1 other), 1055, 2 hr 14 min, **Lucknow**, daily except Tue, 1055, 55 min; **Ranchi**, daily except Tue, 1310, 45 min; **Calcutta**, daily except Tue, 1310, 2 hr; **Guwahati, Bombay, Ahmedabad, Allahabad, Kanpur** – no flights; **Kathmandu**, daily except Tue, 1310, 45 min change at Calcutta (2 hr 5 min wait) then Tue, Th, Sat & Sun, 1600, 1 hr 30 min (Total time 4 hr 20 min). Calcutta, Jamshedpur, Gaya & Dhanbad no Vayudoot flights. Indian Airlines, S Gandhi Maidan. T 22554. Airport Office. T 23199. Open 1000-1300 and 1400-1600. Vayudoot Handling Agents, Arya Travels, Hotel

Maurya. T 21247. 0930-1300 and 1400-1730. Coach from Patna Airport to the Indian Airlines City Office (7 km) stops at various hotels. T 63354. Rs 8 per person.

Rail Patna is well connected to major cities all over India, particularly in the N and NE. Express trains, a few a/c, run between Patna and Delhi, Calcutta, Varanasi, Bhagalpur, Amritsar, Jammu Tawi, Guwahati, Bombay and Madras among others. **Calcutta (H):** *A.C. Exp*, 2304, Mon, Tue, Th & Sat, 0815, 9 hr 45 min; *Amritsar-Haora Mail*, 3006 (AC/II), daily, 2208, 9 hr 57 min; **Delhi (ND):** *NE Exp*, 2521 (AC/II), daily, 0500, 15 hr 15 min; *A.C. Exp*, 2303, Mon, Wed, Fri & Sun; 1820, 16 hr 15 min; **Varanasi:** *Amritsar Mail*, 3005, daily, 0520, 4 hr 45 min; **Gaya:** *Palamu Exp*, 3348, daily, 1910, 3 hr 15 min; **Guwahati:** *NE Exp*, 2522 (AC/II), daily, 2120, 20 hr 55 min; **Bombay (VT):** *Chapra-Bombay Exp*, 5114 (AC/II), Mon, Th & Sat, 2345, 36 hr 55 min; **Madras (MC):** *Patna-Madras Exp*, 6044, Sat, 1535, 43 hr 15 min. Patna Jn Rly Station: Enquiries, T 22012/4. Reservations: Class I, T 22016 and Class II, T 23300. Patna City Railway Station. Enquiries: T 41383.

Road A good network of roads make Patna (on NH 30) easily accessible. Distances by road to major cities: Delhi 1,011 km, Calcutta 595 km, Bombay 1,824 km and Madras 2,099 km. Other important tourist sites are Bodh Gaya 125 km, Nalanda 90 km, Rajgir 107 km, Sasaram 152 km, Betla National Park 316 km, Ranchi 326 km and Varanasi 246 km. Bihar, W Bengal and UPSTC run Luxury and Exp bus services between Patna and their regional centres, including Calcutta, Siliguri, Bhagalpur, Ranchi, Hazaribagh, Mungher and Gumra. Bihar STRC, Bus Stand, Gandhi Maidan. Enquiries, T 51682. Reservations open from 1030-1800. Private bus companies also have services to neighbouring towns and tourist sites.

Excursions From Patna

The Mahatma Gandhi Bridge, one of the world's longest river bridges, crosses the Ganga to the E of Patna and has made tourist sites to the N of the city more easily accessible. **N.B.** Even recent maps often do not show this road connection, opened in the 1980s. Several interesting excursions are possible from Patna. Bihar is cut in 2 by the Ganga, but the new bridge across the river at Patna has made both the road route to Nepal and short excursions to the N of the river much more practicable by bus or car.

Sonepur and Vaisali If you are in Patna in late Oct or early Nov it is worth visiting *Sonepur*. 22 km across the Ganga, near its confluence with the Gandak, Sonepur witnesses Asia's biggest cattle market which begins on Kartik Purnima, the first full moon after Diwali (Oct/Nov). The month long fair which accompanies the trading in livestock and grain draws thousands to the magic shows, folk dances and contests of skill and stalls selling handicrafts and handlooms. Legend has it that Sonepur was the site of a battle between Gaj (elephant), the lord of the forest and Garh (crocodile), the lord of the waterways. Elephants (as well as camels, horses and birds) are still bought and sold at this fair but their numbers are dwindling. The Harihar Kshetra Mela commemorates the coming together of devotees of Siva and Vishnu who perform their Puja at Hariharnath Temple after bathing in the river on the day of the full moon. Sonepur is a station on the NE Railway.

Vaishali is 55 km to the N of Patna, about 1 hour by car or bus. It is a small town of about 10,000 people. You can easily see its main sights of interest in 3 hours. Even including Sonepur it makes a comfortable day excursion, and can be managed in less. If you are driving, cross the Ganga on the Mahatma Gandhi Setu (bridge) and take the road to Lalganj (not the state highway to Muzaffarpur). Vaishali's name is derived from King Visala, mentioned in the epic Ramayana, and it has a history dating back to the 6th century BC when it was a flourishing city of the Lichchavis. Reputedly it was one of the first cities in the world to adopt a republican form of government. It was visited by the great Chinese travellers Fa-hien and by Hiuen-Tsang, who took back a piece of sculpture from one of the stupas. The Buddha, who visited the city many times, preached his last sermon there announcing his approaching Nirvana. An Asoka pillar commemorates this. A century later, in 383 BC, it was the venue of the 2nd Buddhist Council, when

2 stupas were erected. Jains of the Svetambara sect believe that Lord Mahavir was born in Vaishali in 599BC.

Also at Vaishali are the **Asoka Pillar** at **Kolhua**, also known as Bhimsen-ki-Lathi (stick). It is a single piece of very highly polished red sandstone with a bell-shaped inverted lotus capital 18.3 m high which has a life size lion carved on top.

Asoka pillars or '*stambhas*' were un-ornamented shafts with a circular section which tapered like the trunk of a palm tree. It suggested that columns of this sort were forerunners of temples, developed from the ancient form of worshipping in the forest. The idea of sacred sites developed as early as Vedic times when rocks, trees and water, having a powerful significance, would be made more prominent by cutting and defining them. The Mauryan capitals bear some resemblance to those found in Persepolis, while the practice of obtaining high polish by rubbing, shows the influence of the Greeks. Many of the pillars were erected in places sanctified by the Buddha, or they marked the ancient royal route northwards from Pataliputra to the border region of Nepal. This is one of 2 Asoka pillars which remain *in situ*. Of the thirty or so monoliths that the Emperor was believed to have erected, remains of about 10 have been found and those with capitals have been moved to the Indian Museum. The Wheel of the Law which tops many of the pillars is the mark of the social and political order laid down by the Emperor, who drew a distinction between that and the Buddhist Law.

Ramkund, the small tank is also known as Monkey Tank, is believed in legend to have been dug by monkeys who offered the Buddha a bowl of honey. The 2 Buddhist **Stupas** are said to hold urns containing the Buddha's ashes, the second only having been excavated as recently as 1958. The ancient **Coronation Tank** or Kharauna Pokhar, containing holy water used for anointing the ruler of Vaisali at the coronation can also be visited. The half-kilometre long **Lotus Tank** nearby was said to be a picnic spot in the 6th century BC.

Miranji-ki-Dargah The ruins of a brick stupa has Muslim tombs on top. It contains the relics of Sheik Muhammed Qazin, celebrated local saint of the 15th c.

Raja Vishala ka Garh The ruin occupies an area enclosed by a wall about a kilometre in length and 2 m high. The moat surrounding the ancient Parliament House which could hold an assembly of 7,707 representatives is 43 m wide. There are some interesting temples in the area including the Chaumukhi Mahadeva, the 4-faced Lord Siva which dates from the 4th century AD at Kamman Chapra. Another is at Basarh, by Bavan Pokhar an ancient tank, which was built in the Pala period and enshrines beautiful images of Hindu deities.

Museum Vaishali Archeological Museum. Open 1000-1700. Closed Fri. Entry free. The collection includes terracottas, pottery, seals, coins, sculpture and antiquities.

Hotels *Tourist Bungalow*, 10 beds and Dormitory. *PWD Inspection Bungalow*.

Tourist Information Centre T 3.

Travel Buses and taxis do the short trip from Patna.

REGIONAL TOURS

Although it is possible to visit some of the major sites in Bihar like Bodh Gaya in day trips from Patna, if time permits it is better to spread out the visits into 2 or 3 days. The area to the S of Patna has many major Buddhist sites, and there are also Muslim and Hindu sites of interest. These can be visited easily by road from Patna, though it is also possible to fly to Gaya, and to visit Bodh Gaya from there.

PATNA TO NALANDA AND BODH GAYA

This circular route to the SW of Patna visits the ruins of Nalanda, the world's oldest University, Rajgit, royal capital of the Magadha Empire, the Barabara Caves and Gaya. At Bodh Gaya, one of the holiest Buddhist Pilgrim sites, Prince Gautama became the Buddha. The return to Patna is by the immense tombs of Sher Shaha at Sasarem.

Travelling from Patna leave on the NH 31 (travelling E). Keep on the NH 31 along the S bank of the Ganga to Bakhtiyapur, then follow it S to Bihar Sharif. **Biharsharif**, 13 km from Nalanda, is a Muslim pilgrim centre particularly during the annual Urs fair. The *dargah* (tomb) of Mukhdoom Shah, a 13th century Muslim saint and Malik Ibrahim Baya are sited here. It remained an Islamic cultural centre up to the 16th century. In Bihar Sharif you turn right for **Nalanda** and **Rajgir**, but it is possible to continue straight on down the NH 31 about 15 km to visit **Pawapuri**. It bears another name, *Apapuri* (sinless town), and Pawapuri is particularly sacred to the Jains since Lord Mahavir, the founder of Jainism, gained enlightenment there. The lotus pond where Lord Mahavir bathed and on whose bank he was cremated has a white marble temple, the *Jalamandir*, in its centre. **Samosharan** is another Jain temple built here. If you take the detour and do not want to retrace your steps to Bihar Sharif, continue through Pawapuri to Giriuk, then turn right for Rajgir.

Nalanda has the ruins of the world's oldest university, founded in the 5th century AD on an ancient site of pilgrimage and teaching which had been visited by both the Buddha and Lord Mahavir. The complex is open 0900-1700. Entry Re 0.50. Photography restricted.

Since Fa-hien, the Chinese pilgrim who visited the area in the early 5th century makes no mention of the structures, it is assumed that the Gupta Emperors were responsible for the first monasteries. In the 7th century the Chinese scholar Hiuen-Tsang spent 12 years both as a student and a teacher at Nalanda which once had over 3,000 teachers and philosophers. The monks were supported by 200 villages, and a library of 9 million manuscripts attracted men from countries as far flung as Java, Sumatra, Korea and Japan apart from China. Great honour was attached to a Nalanda student and admission was restricted with 7 or 8 out of

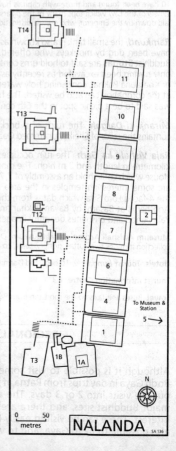

0   50
metres
NALANDA   SA 136

10 applicants failing to gain a place. I-Tsing, another Chinese scholar, arrived here in AD 673 and also kept detailed records, describing the severe life-style of the monks. The divisions of the day were measured by a water-clock, and the syllabus involved the study of Buddhist and Brahmanical scriptures, logic, metaphysics, medicine and Sanskrit grammar. Asoka built a *vihara* (monastery), King Harshavardhana donated a 26 m high copper image of the Buddha, and Kumaragupta endowed a college of fine arts. The University flourished until the 12th century when the Afghan Bhaktiar Khilji sacked it in 1199, burning and pillaging and driving the surviving residents into hiding. It was the end of living Buddhism in India until the modern revival.

The greatness of Nalanda was hidden under a vast mound for centuries where excavations have revealed a sequence of building and rebuilding on the same site. Its archaeological importance was only established in the 1860s with most of the excavation taking place over about 20 years from 1916. The monasteries went through varying periods of occupation, and in one case 9 different levels of building have been discovered. The Buddhist monastic movement resulted in large communities withdrawing into retreats of the kind seen at Nalanda. Even in the 7th century, according to Hiuen-Tsang, Buddhism was declining except in Bihar and Bengal where it enjoyed royal patronage and the support of the laity. The sanctuaries were often vast in size, as is the one here, which is nearly 500 m in length and 250 m in width.

The remains of 11 monasteries and several *chaityas* (temples) built by kings of different periods mainly in red brick, have been found as well as a large stairway, a library, lecture halls, dormitories, cells, ovens and wells. The buildings are in several storeys and tiers on massive terraces of solid brick with stucco decorations of the Buddha as well as Hindu divinities and secular figures of warriors, dancers, musicians, animals and birds. Several of the monasteries are aligned S to N, with a guarded entrance on the W wall with the monks' cells around a central quadrangular courtyard with a wide verandah which was replaced by a high wall in some cases. Opposite the entrance, a shrine is found in the centre of the E wall which must have contained an impressive image. Drains are found which carried sewage to the E and there are staircases giving access to the different storeys. The row of temples to the W of the monasteries left an open space where there were possibly smaller shrines.

A stupa built by Asoka, possibly in remembrance of the Buddha's first disciple Ananda, who was born in Nalanda, is an extremely impressive structure. New excavations to the northeast in Sarai Mound show evidence of a brick temple with frescoes of elephants and horses of the Pala period. The immediate surroundings and villages of Bargaon and Begampur to the N and Jagadishpur to the SW contain several impressive Buddhist and Hindu images.

The Archeological Survey's booklet by A. Ghosh gives excellent detailed description of the site and the Museum.

The **Nava Nalanda Mahavihar**, 2 km from the principal site, is a post-graduate institute for research into Buddhism and Pali literature set up by the Government of Bihar and has many rare manuscripts in its collection. It is now the site of the Indira Gandhi Open University. There is a colourful Thai temple built recently in the typical style.

Kundalpur 1.6 km N of Nalanda, is believed by the Digambara sect of Jains to be the birth place of Lord Mahavir.

Museum The **Archaeological Museum** is open daily from 0900-1700. Entry Re 0.50. It has a good collection of antiquities, Buddhist and Hindu stone sculptures, terracottas and bronzes particularly of the Gupta and Pala periods and also includes coins, inscriptions, plaques, seals, pottery and samples of burnt rice found in the ruins at Nalanda as well as Rajgir.

Hotels *Nalanda Rest House*. Very spartan rm for Rs 25. Reservations through the Divisional Officer, PWD and similar accommodation may be booked at the Inspection Bungalow, through the Supt, Archaeological Survey of India, Eastern Survey, Patna. Meals to order. There is also a very inexpensive *Youth Hostel* and rms at the *Pali Institute*.

Travel 90 km S of Patna, which has the nearest airport, Nalanda has regular bus services from the capital and from Rajagriha, 15 km away, which also has the nearest railway station.

Local transport Cycle-rickshaws and 'tongas' are available and at the Tourist Information Centre. T 20.

Continue S out of Nalanda to *Rajgir* or *Rajagriha*. 'Rajagriha' (or Royal Palace), 15 km S of Nalanda, was the capital of the Magadha empire before Pataliputra, from around 800 BC. Encircled by hills it sits in a valley with lush forests around it. It is held sacred by both Buddhists and Jains for its association with the Buddha and Lord Mahavir, who taught here for many years.

The Buddha is believed to have converted the Magadhan King **Bimbisara** on **Gridhrakuta,** the 'Hill of Vultures'. It was one of his favourite places, and he delivered many important sermons there. The old stone road leading up the hill is attributed to Bimbisara. It was used by Hiuen-Tsang in the 7th century and still provides the best access. There are rock-cut steps leading to the 2 natural caves; several plaques and Buddhist shrines were found in the area which are now in Nalanda Museum. The first Buddhist Council was held in the **Saptaparni Cave** on Vaibhara Hill, 6 months after the Buddha's death, and his teachings were written down for the first time. On the way to the Saptaparni Cave is the **Pippala stone house** or *Machan* (watch tower), an extraordinary structure built of blocks of stone. It is about 24 m sq and 7 m high. On all sides there are small cells which may have been shelters for guards later used by monks.

The 40 km cyclopean dry stone wall that encircled the ancient city is in ruins as is the Ajatasatru Fort dating back to the 5th century BC. The outer wall is significant as it was built with large blocks of stone, 1 m to 1.5 m long, carefully fitted together without mortar, with smaller boulders and pieces in its core. In places it reached a height of nearly 4 m, finished at the top with smaller stones while the width was about 5.5 m. At intervals, on the outer side were bastions to strengthen the wall while on the inner side there were ramps giving access to the top with watch-towers added later. Of the 32 large gates (and 64 small ones) mentioned in ancient texts, only one to the N can be seen. Of the inner city wall which was about 5 km long and roughly pentagonal, only a section to the S survives with 3 gaps through which the old roads ran. A part of the deep moat which was cut into the rock can also be seen. In the valley is a circular brick structure, about 6 m high, decorated with stucco figures all around it, which had an old Jain shrine called **Maniyar Math.**

Nearby is *Venuvana*, the bamboo grove where the Buddha spent some time where excavations have revealed a room and some stupas, and the Karanda Tank where he bathed. It is now a deer park with a small zoo. To the S of Venuvana there are Jain and Hindu temples among the hot springs. Ruins of Buddha's favourite retreat within the valley, the *Jivakamarvana Monastery* (4th-3rd century BC) with elliptical walls have been found which show remains of 4 halls and several rooms.

An aerial cable chair-lift leads to the **Visva Santi Stupa**, which was built by the Japanese on top of Ratnagiri hill. Dedicated to world peace, the large white monastery has 4 golden statues of the Buddha representing his birth, enlightenment, preaching and death. Japanese Buddhists have built a large temple, the *Nipponzan Myohoji*.

Lord Mahavir spent 14 rainy seasons in Rajagriha and the twentieth Tirthankara was born here so today Rajgir is also a major Jain pilgrimage centre, with temples on most of the hill-tops. It has also become a popular health resort, the hot springs being a special attraction.

Hotels The 2 govt *Tourist Bungalows* have double bedrooms with bathrooms. Contact Bihar State Tourism Information Centre, Fraser Rd, T 25295. The PWD has an inexpensive *Rest House* and a *Youth Hostel*. The *District Board Rest House* and *Inspection Bungalow*, a km to the SW of the rly station may be booked through the Board Engineer, Biharsharif. Also *Centaur Hokke Hotel*, primarily for Japanese pilgrims, open Nov to Mar and several *Jain Dharamsalas* near the station.

Tourist Information Centre 2 Kund Market. T 36.

Travel S from Rajgir to Hisua, then turn right along the State Highway to *Gaya*, 92 km S of Patna. Gaya is the city which **Vishnu** is said to have blessed with power to absolve all temporal sins in the same way as Varanasi is sanctified. It draws

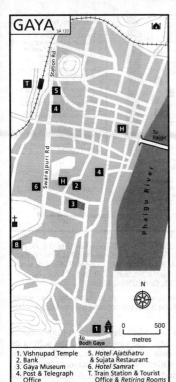

GAYA

1. Vishnupad Temple
2. Bank
3. Gaya Museum
4. Post & Telegraph Office
5. Hotel Ajatshatru & Sujata Restaurant
6. Hotel Samrat
T. Train Station & Tourist Office & Retiring Rooms

believers to the many sacred shrines where prayers are offered for the dead before pilgrims take a dip in the holy river Phalgu having brought with them 'pindas' or funeral rice cakes and sweets. Cremations take place on funeral pyres in the burning ghats along the river.

Places of interest In the centre of the town is the *Vishnupad Temple* supposed to have been built over the Lord's footprint which is imprinted on a rock inside set in a silver basin.

The 30 m high temple has 8 rows of beautifully carved pillars which support the 'mandapa' or pavilion which were refurbished in 1787 by Rani Ahalyabai of Indore. Hindus only are permitted into the sanctum. Within the temple grounds stands the immortal banyan tree 'Akshayabat' where the final puja for the dead takes place. It is believed to be the one under which the Buddha meditated for 6 years. A kilometre to the SW is Brahmayoni Hill with its 1000 stone steps which lead to a vantage point for viewing both Gaya and Bodh Gaya.

The **Surya temple** at *Deo* 20 km away, dedicated to the Sun God, attracts large crowds in Nov when *Chhatt* Puja is celebrated.

Museum Gaya Museum is Open 1000-1700. Closed Mon. Entry free. Collection of sculptures, bronzes, terracottas, paintings, arms and manuscripts.

Hotels and restaurants Very basic accommodation is available in a few hotels most of which offer non a/c double rooms for around Rs 70. *Ajatshatru*, opp. Rly Station. T 22514. *Sri Kailash Guest House*, N Azad Park. *Hotel Samrat*, Swarajpuri Rd. T 20770. *Railway Retiring Rooms* at Gaya Junction are available for Rs 125 (d) a/c and Rs 70 (d) non-a/c. There are several large *Dharamsalas* for pilgrims.

Sujata in Hotel Ajatsatru is a multi-cuisine restaurant while Punjab Restaurant on Station Rd only serves Indian food.

Local Transport Tourist taxis from Sri Kailash Hotel, Hotel Shyam and Sakun Tourist View, Ramna Rd. T 22416. Negotiate rate before journey unless visiting major sites for which a fixed price is quoted. **Auto-rickshaws, cycle-rickshaws** and horse-drawn 'tongas' are easily available. The buses, mini-buses and auto-rickshaws which run services to Bodh Gaya from the Zila School Bus Stand are always very crowded.

Tourist office and Information Bihar Govt Tourist Office, Gaya Jn Rly Station Main Hall. T 20155. Open 0600-2100.

Travel agent Sakun Tourist View, Shyam Bazar, Ramna Rd, T 22416, offers conducted tours.

Air Services Vayudoot flights connect Gaya with Calcutta and Dhanbad in addition to Patna 3 times a week. Handling Agents, Hotel Shyam, Ramna Rd. T 22416. Airport 8 km from town centre. Transfer to city by taxi (approx Rs 50) or rickshaw.

Rail Superfast and express trains connect the city to other regions of the country as it is on

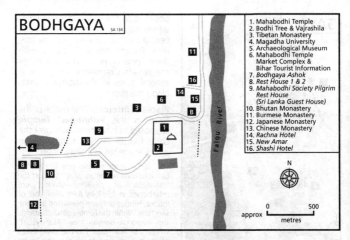

BODHGAYA SA 134

1. Mahabodhi Temple
2. Bodhi Tree & Vajrashila
3. Tibetan Monastery
4. Magadha University
5. Archaeological Museum
6. Mahabodhi Temple
   Market Complex &
   Bihar Tourist Information
7. *Bodhgaya Ashok*
8. *Rest House 1 & 2*
9. *Mahabodhi Society Pilgrim
   Rest House
   (Sri Lanka Guest House)*
10. Bhutan Monastery
11. Burmese Monastery
12. Japanese Monastery
13. Chinese Monastery
14. *Rachna Hotel*
15. *New Amar*
16. *Shashi Hotel*

Falgu River

N

approx   0   500
           metres

the Grand Chord line of the Delhi-Calcutta section of Eastern Railway. **Calcutta (H):** *AC Exp*, 2382 AC/CC&AC/II), Wed, Fri & Sun; 0930, 8 hr 30 min; *Kalka-Haora Mail*, 2312 (AC/II), daily, 2340, 8 hr 50 min; **Varanasi:** *AC Exp*, 2381 (AC/CC&AC/II), Tue, Th & Sat, 1659, 4 hr 1 min; **Delhi (ND):** *Puri-New Delhi Exp*, 2815 (AC/II), Tue, Th, Fri, Sun, 0129, 15 hr 31 min. Gaya Jn. Rly Station. Enquiries and Reservations: T 20031. Open 0900-1600.

Road Bihar State Transport Corporation buses operate services to Patna and other tourist centres at Rajgir, Ranchi and Hazaribagh from the Bus Stand opposite Gandhi Maidan while private coaches run between Calcutta and Gaya.

Excursion from Gaya It is possible to take a half day excursion from Gaya to visit the ***Barabar Caves***. 35 km N of Gaya, the caves inspired the setting of E.M.Forster's *A Passage to India*. They date from the 3rd century BC, the same period as the Asokan pillars, and are the earliest examples of rock-cut sanctuaries. With the tolerance required by Buddhism, Emperor Asoka permitted non-Buddhists to practise their religion, which led to creation of the rock-cut temples in a form of reverse architecture.

The whale-backed quartzite gneiss hill stands in wild and rugged country. Inscriptions reveal that, on instructions from Emperor Asoka, 4 chambers were excavated, cut and chiselled to a high polish by the stone masons. They were to provide retreats for ascetics who belonged to a sect related to Jainism. As Percy Brown points out, the extraordinary caves, particularly the *Lomas Rishi* and the *Sudama*, are exact copies of ordinary beehive shaped huts built with bamboo, wood and thatch, the stone mason having imitated the carpenter in every detail. The barrel-vaulted chamber inside the *Sudama* is 10 m long, 6 m wide and 3.5 m high which through a doorway leads to a circular cell of 6 m diameter. The most impressive craftsmanship is seen on the facade of the *Lomas Rishi* which replicates the horse-shoe shaped gable end of a wooden structure with 2 lunettes which have very fine carvings of lattice-work and rows of elephants paying homage to Buddhist stupas. Excavation is incomplete as there was a possibility of the cave collapsing. There is also a Siva temple on the Siddheshwar peak.

Nagarjuna Hill 1 km NE from Barabar there are 3 further rock-cut sanctuaries. The 'Gopi' or Milk-maid's cave has the largest chamber measuring 13.5 m in length, 6 m in width and 3 m in height. Inscriptions date these to about 50 years after the excavations at Barabar and clearly indicate that they were cut when Asoka's grandson Dasaratha acceded to the Mauryan throne.

Continue S from Gaya to reach ***Bodh Gaya***. *Population* 27,000 (1991) *Altitude* 113 m. *Climate* Temp. Summer Max. 47°C Min. 28°C, Winter Max. 28°C Min. 4°C. Annual rainfall 186 cm.

Bodh Gaya, a quiet village near the river Niranjana (Phalgu), is one of the holiest Buddhist pilgrimage centres since it was here under the Bo tree that Gautama, the prince, attained enlightenment to become the Buddha.

Places of interest The original **Bodhi tree** was said to have been destroyed originally by Emperor Asoka before he himself was converted, and others which replaced it met with a similar fate or withered away, although the present tree is believed to have grown from a sapling from the original stock, **see page 1427**. The story of Prince Mahinda, the Emperor's son describes him carrying a sapling from the sacred Bo or pipal tree to Sri Lanka when Buddhism spread there, which in turn produced a sapling which was brought back to Bodh Gaya. The red sandstone slab, the **Vajrasila**, under the tree marks the place where Gautama sat in meditation. Today pilgrims tie pieces of coloured cloth on its branches when they come to pray.

Mahabodhi Temple Asoka erected a shrine near the Bodhi tree which was replaced by this temple in the 2nd century which in turn went through several alterations. The temple on a high and broad plinth, with a soaring 54 m high pyramidal spire with a square cross-section and 4 smaller spires, houses a gilded image of the Buddha in the *asana* (pose) signifying enlightenment. The smaller spires appear to have been added to the original when Burmese Buddhists attempted extensive rebuilding in the 14th century.

An ornately carved stone railing in *bas relief,* once believed to have been erected by Asoka, surrounds the temple on 3 sides and several carved Buddhist stupas depict tales from the Buddha's early life. Unlike earlier circular railings this had to conform to the quadrangle of the temple structure and its height of 2 m and lighter proportions together with the quality of its carving suggests that it was constructed in the Sunga period in the early part of 1st century BC. The entrance is through a *torana* or ornamental archway on the eastern side. The lotus pond where the Buddha may have bathed is to the S of the temple. To the N is the 'Chankramana', a raised platform dating from the 1st century with lotus flowers carved on it, which marks the consecrated promenade where the Buddha walked back and forth while meditating on whether he should reveal his Message to the world. This appears to have been later converted into a covered passage with pillars of which only one survives.

The numerous attempts to reconstruct and restore the temple have obscured the original although fragments are now housed in various museums. 'Animeshlochana' another sacred spot where the Buddha stood to gaze in gratitude at the Bodhi tree for a week. The temple also attracts Hindu pilgrims since the Buddha is considered to be one of the 'avatars' or incarnations of Vishnu. Pilgrims from many lands have built their own temples here so there are Tibetan, Thai, Japanese Chinese, Bhutanese and Burmese shrines to visit.

The Tibetan Monastery built in 1938 is the most interesting as it has a *Dharma Chakra* or wheel of law, which must be turned 3 times when praying for forgiveness of sins. A large 2 m metal ceremonial drum in red and gold is also on display. **Magadha University**, an international centre for studies in history, culture and philosophy is less than a km from the Mahabodhi Temple.

Hotels C *Bodh Gaya Ashok* near Archeological Museum. T 22708/9 (Gaya) 25 (Bodh Gaya), Cable: Tourism. 30 rm. a/c. Restaurant, bar, exchange, shops, TV. BSTDC **D** *Rest House* II, near Thai Temple. 7 rm. Dining hall provides meals on order. *Rest House* I has 9 dorms with 40 beds charging a small fee. *Mahabodhi Society Pilgrim Rest House* (Sri Lanka Guest House). T 42. 6 rm and 3 dormitories. Voluntary donations. Vegetarian canteen. **E** *Bhutan Monastery* (Druk Do Nagcholing Monastery) maintains 18 rms in guest houses.

The **Burmese and Japanese monasteries** also provide accommodation primarily for pilgrims from their respective countries but rooms may be made available to others if vacant. All the religious organisations expect guests to conform to certain rules of conduct and good behaviour. Reservations: Contact Monk-in-Charge. On the Main Rd near the Temple there are a few very simple hotels: *Rachna, New Amar* and *Shashi.*

Shopping Miniature paintings are specially prepared to be sold as mementos. **Mahabodhi Temple Market Complex** and the **New Tibetan Market** have a number of shops selling the soft-stone articles handcrafted in Patthalkatti nearby. One can pick up small images of the Buddha and Hindu divinities as well as utilitarian tableware. There is a **bank, post-office**

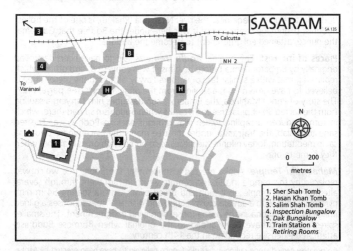

SASARAM SA 135

To Calcutta
NH 2
To Varanasi

N

0   200
metres

1. Sher Shah Tomb
2. Hasan Khan Tomb
3. Salim Shah Tomb
4. Inspection Bungalow
5. Dak Bungalow
T. Train Station & Retiring Rooms

and **police station** on the Main Road. A few auto-rickshaws and plenty of cycle-rickshaws and 'tongas' are available. Rates must be negotiated.

Museum The Archaeological Museum. Open 1000-1700 but closed Fri. Entry free. The collection of antiquities includes sculptures and fragments of railings and posts from the original temple as well as gold, bronze and stone images of the Buddha and Hindu deities.

Tourist Office and Information   Govt of Bihar Tourist Information Centre, 34-35 Mahabodhi Temple Market Complex. T 26. Open 1000-1700.

Travel **Air** Patna, 125 km, is the nearest airport with regular flights to all major cities by Indian Airlines and Vayudoot. Calcutta, 482 km, has an international airport. Buses and auto-rickshaws which take about ½ hour to Bodh Gaya are usually very crowded. **Rail** Gaya, 16 km away has the nearest station. **Road** Dobhi, 22 km away is on the Delhi-Calcutta NH2. Delhi is 1,052 km and Calcutta, 482 km away. Patna is 125 km to the N. Bihar SRTC. has bus services to Gaya, Patna, Nalanda and Rajgir. The main bus stand is opp the Mahabodhi Temple.

A round tour from Patna can continue by visiting the Muslim sites of **Sasaram** and **Maner**. Continue S from Bodh Gaya about 20 km to **Sherghati** on NH 2. Turn right and travel W approximately 100 km. You reach Sasaram 19 km after crossing the **River Son**. The empire of the Mughals was interrupted for about 15 years by the Sur dynasty who, for that brief period of rule, left a surprising mark of the architectural style begun by the Lodis in India. The tombs at Sasaram and in Delhi would in their turn affect the style of the later Mughuls.

The driving force behind the erection of the tombs at **Sasaram** was **Sher Shah Suri** who around 1535 obtained the services of the master-builder Aliwal Khan to construct a tomb for his father Hasan Khan. This in itself was not remarkable but laid the foundations for the second tomb for Sher Shah himself – see page 92. The first imitated the octagonal structure and walled enclosure of the earlier Lodi tombs but lacked a plinth and had rather a plain appearance without any ornamentation in its middle storey. What followed however was extraordinary not only in its size, which was 75 m wide at its base and 45 m high, but also in its conception and execution. The mausoleum was set in an artificial lake 430 m sq so it appeared to float while it cast its reflection on the water. It is approached by a causeway through first entering a guard room on the N bank. This may have been an afterthought as it would appear that the original plan may have been for visitors to approach by barge from the ghat on the E side of the tank.

Percy Brown describes the construction in 5 stages, starting with the lower 2 on a square plan rising out of the water and forming a terrace with pillared pavilions in each corner with steps down to the water. The third is octagonal with 3 arches on each side with doorways to enter the mausoleum except to the W where the *mihrab** is positioned, the whole being surrounded by a verandah. The storey immediately above follows the same horizontal plan with its simple plainness broken by ornamental kiosks at each of the 8 angles. The final stage is the dome itself which cleverly loses the angles and arises circular leading up to the lotus at the top. The tomb chamber which is 20 m wide thus rises to a height of 27.5 m without a break. A curious fact is that the base itself was not correctly positioned for the faces of the structure to coincide with the points of the compass but with a clever correction of 8 degrees, the planned orientation of the upper storeys was achieved!

The use of fine grey sandstone for construction, quarried at **Chunar** nearby gives the tomb a fitting sense of gravity. However, a closer examination reveals that geometrical patterns in red, yellow, blue and white adorned the exterior in places and the dome itself was painted white with a golden lotus at its crown. It was sited close to the main highway so would have been an impressive monument to be seen by all who passed.

The third tomb for Sher Shah's son Salim was to have been even larger and is again set within a lake, was never completed because of his untimely death. There is a memorial to the architect Aliwal Khan and a further tomb to Bhakiyar Khan in Chainpur nearby.

Hotels There are 2 *Rest Houses*, a Government *Youth Hostel* and small hotels.

Tourist Information Centre. T 203.

From Sasaram take the road NE to **Bikramganj** (40 km), where you join the NH 30, and **Piro** (20 km). Continue to **Arrah**, which was the scene of a fierce siege during the 1857 mutiny. The Little House at Arrah, in the grounds of the Judge's House, was held by 50 Sikh and 12 English soldiers against over 2000 attacking mutineers for a week at the end of Jul 1857. It can still be visited, as can the church in the town, which contains several plaques. Arrah is on a branch of one of the great irrigation works in Bihar, the Son Canals.

Leave Arrah travelling E on the NH 30, and approximately 10 km after crossing the River Son the National Highway turns sharply N to **Maner**. One of the earliest Islamic centres in Bihar, it was named after the 13th century Sufi saint, Hazrat Makhdum Yahiya Maneri. His tomb known as the Badi Dargah is a very sacred shrine. The Chhoti Dargah, a mausoleum commemorating the Muslim saint's disciple Shah Daulat is famous for its architectural interest. The annual Urs fair is held here. From Maner it is 30 km to Patna.

SOUTH BIHAR AND THE CHOTA NAGPUR PLATEAU

Ranchi, the area's main town, is in beautiful countryside with many waterfalls and lakes. The Belta National Park and Hazaribagh Wildlife Sanctuary suport tiger, leopard, elephant and many other species. There are several hydro electric dams, some suitable for boating and swimming.

Ranchi

Altitude 658 m. *Population* 670,000 (1991). With an airport nearby, and a railway station Ranchi has good air and rail connections with Patna the capital.

Once the summer capital of Bihar, the town still attracts holiday makers for its location on higher ground in the heart of the Chotanagpur tribal country and its proximity to beautiful waterfalls and lakes. Like many middle ranking Indian towns it has been growing very fast in the last 20 years, though it has few of the public buildings which might be expected to accompany its size and present importance. Part of its growth has stemmed from the Govt of India's decision to build the

Bharat Heavy Engineering plant in Ranchi (with Soviet financial and technical support), and along with associated industry this has contributed to its dynamism. It has also become a major educational centre for S Bihar and is well known for its mental asylum at Kanke, the largest in India.

Note Some telephone numbers may have been changed.

Hotels C *Ranchi Ashok*, Doranda, PO Hinoo. T 300037, Cable: Ashokotel. 30 rm. Central a/c. Restaurant, bar, exchange, shops, TV. **C** *Hindustan*, Makhija Towers, Main Rd. T 27988, Cable: Makgroup, Telex 625-283. 36 rm. A/c. Restaurant, shopping, exchange, travel, TV. **C** *Kwality Inns*, Station Rd. T 26821, Cable: Kwality Inns. 36 rm some a/c. A/c restaurant, bar, exchange, TV. **C** *SE Railway Hotel*. 22 rm. Tennis. **C** *Yuvraj Palace*, Doranda. T 300805. 25 rm. 2 km airport, 1 km rly. Central a/c. Restaurant, bar, exchange, travel, TV. **D** *Arya*, H.B. Rd, Lalpur. T 20355, Cable: Arya, Telex 625-253. 32 rm, some a/c. Good a/c restaurant with live music, travel,TV. **D** *Yuvraj*, Doranda. T 300403, Cable: Yuvraj, Telex: 625-229. 45 rm some a/c. A/c restaurant. **D** *Hotel Raj*, 57A Main Rd. T 22613. 18 rm. Veg restaurant, TV.

Museums **Ranchi Museum**, Tribal Research Institute Building, Morabadi Rd. T 21160. 1030-1700. Closed Sun. Entry free. Collection of stone sculpture, terracottas and arms as well as ethnological objects at the Institute itself. **Ranchi University**, Dept of Anthropology. T 23695. 1100-1700. Closed Sun and University holidays. Entry free. Ethnographic collections of central Indian states and Andaman and Nicobar Islands.

Tourist Information Centre Court Compound, Circular Rd. T 20426.

Air Indian Airlines has daily connections from Ranchi to **Patna** (40 min), **Calcutta** (30 min) going on to Rourkela and Delhi (2 hr 45 min). In addition to links with Patna, Ranchi has direct air connections to **Calcutta** by Vayudoot on Mon, Wed, Fri (2 hr). It is also linked by air to **Delhi** and **Lucknow**. Indian Airlines, Main Rd, Vayudoot, T 24900.

Rail To Calcutta (H): *Hathia-Ranchi Haora Exp*, 8016, daily, 1659, 4 hr 1 min.

Road The distance by road is 598 km from Calcutta on the NH 33. Other regional centres have access to Ranchi by rail and road.

Excursions Ranchi is surrounded by some beautiful rural landscapes. Formerly densely forested, tribal territory, much land has been cleared for cultivation. There are several very attractive short excursions that can be made from the town. The Subhanarekha River, which rises SE of the town, is interrupted by several impressive waterfalls, within easy range of Ranchi. *Hundru Falls* (45 km E of Ranchi), one of the highest in Asia, is formed by the 100 m drop of Subarnarekha river and is particularly impressive just after the monsoons. You can picnic and bathe in the pools at the bottom. The others falls in the area include *Jonha Falls* (40 km E of Ranchi on the Purulia road) and *Dassamghagh Falls* (34 km).

Jagannathpur, 10 km SW of Ranchi, has a temple dedicated to Lord Jagannath, very much in the style of the great temple in Puri.

Wildlife Sanctuaries Reached From Ranchi

There are game reserves set in often stunningly beautiful and remote scenery on the Chota Nagpur plateau which can be easily reached from Ranchi. *Palamau*, also known as the *Betla National Park*, is about 120 km due W of Ranchi. Take the road W NW out of Ranchi for Kuru (57 km). In Kuru fork right to Tori, then left towards Daltonganj. Palamau is a further 70 km. The National Park covers an area of 930 sq km of dry deciduous forest. It is the second major wildlife sanctuary in Bihar which participates in the Project Tiger scheme. The world's first tiger census was taken here in 1932. Access by air is through Ranchi (115 km) or by rail from *Chipadohar* (80 km).

The wildlife includes tiger, leopard, gaur, sambar, muntjac and nilghai as well as the Indian wolf. Elephants can be seen after the monsoons and until the waterholes begin to dry up in Mar. There is a rich variety of birdlife and to add to the attraction a number of waterfalls and hot springs. 2 masonry watch-towers and the Swiss Family Robinson Tree Top at Kamaldan with ground level 'hides'

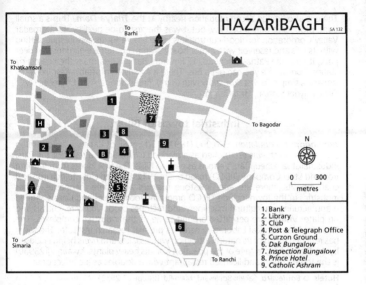

HAZARIBAGH SA 132

To Barhi
To Khatkamsari
To Bagodar
To Simaria
To Ranchi

N

0   300
metres

1. Bank
2. Library
3. Club
4. Post & Telegraph Office
5. Curzon Ground
6. *Dak Bungalow*
7. *Inspection Bungalow*
8. *Prince Hotel*
9. *Catholic Ashram*

are good vantage points. There is also evidence of the Ghero kings who once ruled from here in the form of monuments and a fort in the forest. Although open throughout the year, it is best between Feb and Apr. Jeeps for viewing the animals can be hired from the Forest Dept.

Rest Houses and cottages provide basic accommodation but the new a/c *Forest Lodge* at Betla is more comfortable. Reservations: Field Director, Project Tiger, Palamau, Daltonganj. For *Rest Houses* at Mundu, Barwadih and Lat, contact Div Forest Officer, S Forest Div, Daltonganj.

Hazaribagh *Altitude* 615 m. Travel N from Ranchi on the NH 33 through Ramgarh to Hazaribagh. Named 'thousand tigers' and set amidst hilly and still forested country, it has attracted visitors who also use it as a base to see the wild life sanctuary, water falls and dams in the vicinity. Tilaiya Dam is 55 km and Konar, 51 km away.

The **Hazaribagh Wildlife Sanctuary** is approached either from railway stations at Hazaribagh Road (66 km) or by air from Ranchi (115 km). By road it is 26 km from Hazaribagh and NH 33 takes you up to the main gate at Pokharia.
Set at an altitude of 550 m on hilly terrain, it is a part of the Chotanagpur plateau, heavily forested with grass meadows and deep waterways and covering an area of 186 sq km. Best season Feb – Apr. With the name 'thousand gardens', the park supports a large number of sambar in addition to nilghai, deer, chital, leopard, tiger, wild boar and wild cat. Roads permit easy access to large sections of the forest. There are 10 watch towers for viewing but accommodation in *Forest Rest Houses* at Rajdewra and Harhad within the sanctuary area is very spartan. Reservations: Div Forest Officer, Hazaribagh.

Hotels *Tourist Lodge*, T 236. Reservations: Tourist Information Centre, Govt of Bihar, Hazaribagh or Bihar STDC, Beerchand Patel Path, Patna. *Inspection Bungalow* through the Collector, PWD, Hazaribagh. There are a few inexpensive Indian style hotels with restaurants in the town centre nr the bazaar. *Magadh, Ashok* and *Standard*.

There is also limited accommodation nearby at the **Tilaiya Dam**. This is a small dam, producing only 4,000 kw, but it was the first to be built by the Damodar Valley Corporation for flood control. It is visited more for its picturesque setting with its hills and reservoir with motor boats, swimming, terrace gardens and deer park. It is on the Patna-Ranchi Rd, 17 km from Barhi. Kodarma is the nearest rly station from where you can get a bus. There is a fairly comfortable *Rest House* (6 rm) and a simple *Tourist Bungalow* with (8 rm). Reservations: Asst. Engineer, DVC, Tilaiya Hydel Station, Hazaribagh.

Industrial towns of Bihar

Jamshedpur, *Population* 670,000 (1991). 130 km SE of Ranchi is a flourishing steel town which was established as a planned township as a result of the Parsi industrialist Jamshedji Tata's efforts as early as l908. The first ingots from the Tata Iron and Steel Company (TISCO) rolled out in 1912. Located close to rich iron and coal deposits, there are also limestone quarries and some magnesite. Other industries in the town include TELCO producing locomotives and boilers, Agrico manufacturing agricultural machinery and factories producing wire, chassis and tin plate. Visitors are permitted around some of the industrial complexes. The National Metallurgical Laboratory here is a premier research institute. The town has retained much of its natural attraction with its lakes and rivers being enclosed by the Dolma hills, in spite of the pollution from its heavy plants. *Kwality* (T 23930) is the town's only good licensed restaurant which doubles as a confectioner.

Hotels D *Boulevard*, Sakehi Boulevard, Main Rd, Bistupur. T 25321. 43 rm some a/c. 3 km from airport, 4.5 km from rly. A/c restaurant (Indian and Chinese), bar. *Nataraj*, Main Rd. *TISCO Guest House*, 7 B Rd mainly for company guests. Restaurant. There is also a *Circuit House*, *Dak Bungalow*, *Forest Rest House* and a *Lake House* on Dimna Lake.

Air Vayudoot flights from Calcutta daily except Sun (50 min) and on Tue, Th, Sat to Patna (1 hr 15 min). **Rail** Tatanagar station is on the SE Rly on the Calcutta (Haora) – Bombay line. **Road** Very well connected.

Other centres have emerged along the Damodar Valley which cuts through the Chotanagpur plateau through rocky, thickly wooded areas which are the home of the many aboriginal tribal people of Bihar. The Santals, Bedia, Khond, Munda and Oraon were the original inhabitants and though a few still live an isolated villages, most have been influenced by developments in the region to abandon their old lifestyle and many have joined the workforce in the industrial townships. The river valley (DVC) has a number of hydro-electric power stations and with them large dams as at Maithon, Panchet and Tilaiya (see under Hazaribagh above). These have become centres offering recreational water-sports. The main centres of activity are Dhanbad for coal, Chittaranjan for locomotives and Bokaro for steel.

Dhanbad *Population* 885,000 (1991) has the highest concentration of mineral wealth in India with collieries, technical and research institutions in the town. A major industrial town, with little to recommend it for the sightseer. The DVC Maithon and Panchet dams are within easy reach (about 50 km) and Topchanchi Lake is 37 km away.

Excursions Maithon Dam was designed for flood control but has the unique underground power station, the first in S. Asia. Permits to visit are obtained from Assistant PRO for guided tours. Accommodation in *Inspection Bungalow*, 10 rm (6 a/c) or *Rest House* with 12 rm. Reservations: Executive Engineer, Maithon Division, DVC.

Panchet Dam 6 km with a hydro electric power station. The DVC Inspection Bungalow (4 rm) can be booked through PRO, DVC, Anderson House, Calcutta 700027.

The nearest convenient rly station for both is at Barakar (8 and 12 km away). There are buses or taxis from there, and from Dhanbad and Asansol (35 km).

ANDAMAN AND NICOBAR ISLANDS

Area 8,293 sq km *Population* 260,000 *Climate* Tropical. Temp. 20°C to 32°C. Sea breeze has a cooling effect. *Annual rainfall* 254 cm. Monsoons – mid-May to mid-Sep and Nov to mid-Dec. *Best Season* mid-Dec to mid-May. *Languages* Hindi, Bengali, Tamil, Malayalam, English. *Population* 200,000.

Social indicators *Literacy* M 52% F 42% *Birth rate* Rural 34:1000 Urban 26:1000 *Death rate* Rural 9:1000 Urban 4:1000 *Registered graduate job seekers* 11,000.

Religion Hindu 29% Muslim 1% Christian 4%.

Towns & cities 26% of the population live in towns. Port Blair is the capital and only large town.

Entry regulations Foreigners arriving by air with tourist visas for India are allowed a maximum stay of 15 days on arrival at Port Blair, the principal harbour and capital, but they not are permitted to visit tribal areas or restricted islands including Nicobar. Permits are obtainable from Indian Missions abroad or the Ministry of Home Affairs (ANL Div.), Government of India, North Block, 2nd Floor, New Delhi, 110 001, which may take up to 6 weeks by post. However, a personal visit may cut it down to 48 hours. Alternatively, Foreigners' Regional Registration Offices in Delhi, Calcutta and Bombay and the Chief Immigration Officer, 9 Village Road, off Nungambakkam High Rd, Madras can grant permits but there may be delay due to queues.

If you arrive without a permit you will have to get your passport endorsed on arrival by the Duty Officer who you may have to ask to see since there is no official counter. Permits are given to visit Jolly Buoy, Cinque, Red Skin, Neil and Havelock Islands. Organised groups may visit Grab and Boat Islands as well. Since the government is likely to encourage tourism, it is worth checking whether the rules have been relaxed with regard to visiting the restricted islands.

Indians may visit the Andamans without a permit but must obtain a permit for the Nicobars on arrival at Car Nicobar or from the Deputy Commissioner (Nicobar) at Port Blair.

INTRODUCTION

The Andaman and Nicobar group is made up of a string of about 300 islands formed by a submarine mountain range which divides the Bay of Bengal from the Andaman Sea. The islands lie between latitudes 6° to 14° N (about level with southernmost tip of Sri Lanka and Madras and longitudes 92°-94° E, a span of 725 km. The Andamans to the N is separated from the Nicobars by a (90 m) 150 km strait. The Andamans group has 204 islands with its 3 main islands of North, Middle and South, which are separated by mangrove-fringed islets and are together called **Great Andaman** as they virtually join each other. Only 26 of these are inhabited. The **Nicobar Islands** comprise 12 inhabited and 7 uninhabited islands including the three groups, **Car Nicobar** in the N, **Camorta** and **Nancowry** in the middle and the largest, **Great Nicobar** in the S. The land rises to 730 m (Saddle Peak), formed mainly of limestones, sandstones and clays.

The islands have brilliant tropical flora and are thickly forested with evergreen, deciduous rainforest and tropical trees, with mangrove swamps on the waters' edge. Hilly in parts, they have superb palm-fringed white sand beaches and coral reefs. The sparkling clear water is excellent for snorkelling and you can see the rich marine life among the reefs. The Andamans are also a bird-watchers' paradise with 242 species

ANDAMAN &
NICOBAR ISLANDS

SA 426

recorded and the wild life includes 46 species of mammals and 78 of reptiles.

People The tribal population has been dwindling. Most of the inhabitants are Indians, Burmese and Malays – some, descendants of the criminals who were transported here. Since the 1950s, refugees from East Pakistan (now Bangladesh), Burma and Indian emigrants from Guyana have settled on the main islands to be followed more recently by Tamils from Sri Lanka. The total population is around 223,000, the largest concentration is around the capital, Port Blair, with the majority of the tribal people who comprise about 15% of the population living in the Nicobars.

Tribals The origin of the name Andaman may be linked to the monkey god *Hanuman* who is believed to have arrived there on his way to Lanka (Sri Lanka) is search of Sita who had been abducted by *Ravana* in the epic Ramayana. The islands have been inhabited by Aboriginal tribes (some Negrito) for thousands of years but remained unexplored because anyone attempting to land would be attacked. The isolation up to the mid 19th century meant the tribal people lived a Stone Age existence. Today there are only a few *Andamanese* who once inhabited the Great Andamans, some *Onges* in Little Andaman who traditionally painted their naked bodies, the fierce *Jarawas* on S Andaman, the *Sentinelese* on N Sentinel and the mongoloid *Nicobaris* who are the most numerous group and *Shompens* who may have been of pre-Dravidian stock in Car Nicobar and Great Nicobar respectively.

The islanders practised hunting and gathering, using bows and arrows to kill wild pigs, fishing with nets and catching turtles with harpoons from dug-out canoes. In past centuries the iron for the arrowheads and harpoons came from the metal collected from wrecks. The 'Shompens' used digging sticks for agriculture and Burmese iron choppers they may have raided. Some tribes made pottery but the 'Andamanese' particularly were exceptional since they had not discovered fire-making. Not a lot is known about some tribes. The Anthropological Survey of India and the Andaman Administration have been jointly trying to establish friendly contact with the Jarawas and Sentinelese since the '60s. 5

'Jarawas' first appeared in Port Blair in the late 1960's but have not made much contact with the civilised world since, while the 'Sentinelese' consistently repelled groups of explorers with poisoned arrows. More recently, groups of tribals have picked up coconuts that were floated towards them or left on the each as a gesture of friendship by anthropologists in a boat. In Feb 1991, a few Sentinelese boarded a lifeboat to accept gifts of coconuts. This may signal the beginning of contact with these 'mysterious' islanders. The attempt to rehabilitate some friendly tribals and encourage them to fish for sea slugs and collect edible birds nests for the Chinese market did not succeed.

The Government of India has a strict policy of keeping the Primitive Tribal Reserve Areas out of bounds though Indian tourists may be able to get permission to visit some of the islands. However, you may get a chance to see some who have been integrated into the immigrant population who now dress up in their tribal costume and perform dances for tourists.

The **Andamanese Language** which bears no resemblance to any other language uses prefixes and suffixes to indicate the function of a word and is extraordinary in using simply two concepts of number, 'one' and 'greater than one'.

Economy Local seafood (lobsters, prawns and sea fish) is good. Tropical fruit like pineapples, variety of bananas and the extra sweet papaya is plentiful and the green coconut water very refreshing. Rice is also cultivated.

Resources and industry Tourism is rapidly becoming the Andamans most important industry. Forests represent an important resource. The government has divided 40% of the forests into Primitive Tribal Reserve areas which are only open to Indian visitors with permits and the remaining 60% as Protected Areas from which timber is obtained for export in the form of plywoods, hardwoods and matchwoods. To improve the economy, rubber and mahogany have been planted in addition to teak and rosewood which are commercially in demand.

Local Crafts Mother-of-pearl jewellery, shell and exotic woods crafted for the tourist trade, palm mats and beautiful natural shells which are collected for sale.

History Lying in the trade route between Burma and India the islands' existence was known to early sailors. They appeared on Ptolemy's 2nd century map and were also recorded by the Chinese traveller I-Tsing in the 7th century. By the end of the 17th century the Mahrathas established a base there to attack the trading British, Dutch and Portuguese ships. Dutch pirates and French Jesuits had made contact with the islands before the Danish East India Company made attempts to evangelize the islands in the mid-18th century. The reputation of ferocity attributed to the Nicobarese may have been partly due to Malay pirates who attacked and killed sailors of any trading vessel that came ashore. The first British attempt to occupy them was made in 1788 when the Governor General of India sent Lt. Blair (whose name was given to the first port) and although the first convicts were sent there in 1794, it was abandoned within a couple of years.

After the Indian mutiny in 1857 the British gained control of most of the islands and used them as a penal colony for its prisoners who until then had been sent to Sumatra, right up to Indian Independence with a short break from 1942-45, when the Japanese occupied the islands. However, the political prisoners were sent in large numbers only after the completion of the **Cellular Jail** in 1910 and each revolt in the colony resulted in certain groups of people being sent there, hence the presence of Bengalis, Keralans and Burmese among others. Subhas Chandra Bose, the Indian Nationalist first raised the Indian tricolour here in 1943. The British used it primarily as a penal colony to send the Indian freedom-fighters and criminals for life imprisonment. The name 'Kalapani' or 'black water' by which the islands were known referred to the blood shed by the nationalists.

PORT BLAIR

The capital is 1,255 km from Calcutta and 1,191 km from Madras. *Population* 67,000 (1991).

The small town has changed in the last three decades from one which saw a ship from the mainland once a month if the weather permitted, to a place connected by flights from Madras, Delhi, Bhubaneswar and Calcutta several times a week. It now has a hospital, a co-operative stores, schools, a college of higher education and a few museums, in addition to resort hotels and water sports facilities. The central area of Aberdeen Bazaar is where you will find most of the hotels, the bus station and shops. The airport is a few km S of Port Blair.

There are only a handful of sights in Port Blair but as a tourist you will find enough to do particularly if you enjoy a beach holiday with its related water sports, especially the fascinating marine life on the reefs, or bird watching and fishing.

Places of interest Cellular Jail N of Aberdeen Jetty, it was built between 1886-1906 by the British to house dangerous criminals. Subsequently it was used to place Indian freedom fighters until Independence in 1947. Open 0900-1200, 1400-1700. Mon-Sat. Once it could hold 698 solitary prisoners in small narrow cells. There is a site museum, photographs and lists of 'convicts' held, a 'death house' and the gallows, where you can get an impression of the conditions within the prison and the implements used in torture. Three of the original seven wings which extended from the central guard tower survive. A wing is still in use as the local jail until a new one being built is completed. Allow about 1½ hrs.

Chatham Saw Mill One of the oldest in Asia. Tours take you through the different stages and processes of turning logs into 'seasoned' graded planks. Photography is not allowed. You can also visit the museum (listed below). Allow about 1 hr for both.

Mini Zoo has specimens of unusual island fauna including a sea crocodile farm. Open 0700-1200, 1300-1700, daily except Mon.

Sippighat Farm (14 km) Government demonstration farm where you can see cash crops such as spices and other plants being propagated. Open 0600-1100, 1200-1600, daily except Mon.

Chiriya Tapu or Bird Island (30 km) on the southern tip of South Andaman is very picturesque and is also rich in butterflies in addition to birdlife and has a beach covered in interesting shapes of driftwood. You may visit it if you get a permit to visit Cinque Island, which takes about 2 hr by boat.

Wandoor Beach (28 km) on the W coast is particularly good for snorkelling and diving where you can get a boat to uninhabited Jolly Buoy (1 hr). The National Marine Park includes Jolly Buoy and several other islands. Small fee to enter beach.

Madhuban (14 km) is on the seaside on the E side where young elephants are trained for forestry and **Burma Nalla** (17 km) where they are used for lumbering.

Hotels C *Andaman Beach Resort*, (Travel Corporation of India), Corbyn's Cove. T 2599, Cable: Travelaids. 52 rm, beautiful gardens, restaurant, bar, very good travel counter, car hire, TV, most watersports including scuba diving, wind surfing, snorkelling and sailing, tennis. Reduced fares off season (May -Sep). **C** *Bay Island* (Welcomgroup), Marine Hill. T 2881/8, Cable: Welcotel. 48 rm most with balconies, some a/c and some suites. On a steep hill with superb views hence not too close to a beach, rms imaginatively designed to imitate local huts, facilities in main building. Good open-air restaurant and bar, travel, video, sea-water pool (at bottom of hill) and watersports (snorkelling and fishing). Indoor and outdoor games. The most expensive hotel on the islands. **D** *Asiana*, South Point, T 2937, new resort hotel in elevated location on road to Corbyn's Cove but not too close to a beach and **D** *Hotel Shompen*, 2 Middle Point, T 2360. Both have a/c single and double rm, harbour facing ones with balconies, restaurants and some facilities, free transport from airport. In most hotels there is

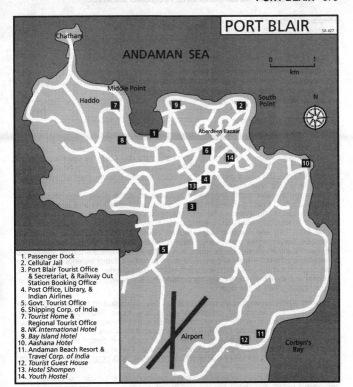

PORT BLAIR

SA 427

ANDAMAN SEA

Chatham

Middle Point

Haddo 7

9 2 South Point

1

8 Aberdeen Bazaar

6

14

10

13

4

3

5

N

0   1
km

1. Passenger Dock
2. Cellular Jail
3. Port Blair Tourist Office
   & Secretariat, & Railway Out
   Station Booking Office
4. Post Office, Library, &
   Indian Airlines
5. Govt. Tourist Office
6. Shipping Corp. of India
7. Tourist Home &
   Regional Tourist Office
8. NK International Hotel
9. Bay Island Hotel
10. Aashana Hotel
11. Andaman Beach Resort &
    Travel Corp. of India
12. Tourist Guest House
13. Hotel Shompen
14. Youth Hostel

Airport

12 11 Corbyn's Bay

only a small difference between a/c and non-a/c rm, so go for the former.

The simpler government tourism authority accommodation is good value. **E** *Guest House* in a good location at Corbyn's Cove, past the Andaman Beach Resort. **E** *Nicobarese Cottages* and **E** *Megapode Nest* which have superb views, both at Haddo with some a/c accommodation are recommended. Also two **F** *Tourist Homes* at Haddo about 20 min walk from the centre and which has the Regional Tourist Office, and at Marine Hill. Reservations: Deputy Director of Tourism, Port Blair.

There are other very inexpensive **E** and **F** hotels and guest houses which only provide very simple accommodation and where you can get a good reduction out of season. The new **E** *Dhanalaxmi* in Aberdeen Bazar, T 21306, and the slightly less expensive **E** *Hotel NK International*, T 21066, has some a/c double rm with attached baths. *Tourist Cottage*, Babu Lane, Aberdeen Bazaar, *Ram Nivas Lodge, Hotel Sampat, Phoenix* and *Central Lodge*. Also a very inexpensive *Youth Hostel* and two *Guest Houses*. You can book the latter through the Executive Engineer, Port Blair Division, but be prepared to really rough it.

At **Chiriya Tapu** in the S of the island and at Wandoor Beach, there are very cheap *Forest Rest Houses*, though most people would choose to visit them on a day excursion.

Middle Andaman has *Rest Houses* at Betapur, and Kangal and North Andaman at Aerial Bay, Diglipur, Kundantala, Mayabunder, Parangara and Tugapur.

Restaurants Most of the hotels down to **E** grade have restaurants. The best are at the more expensive hotels which offer continental, Indian, Chinese and Burmese food. The restaurant in the *Dhanalaxmi* (Aberdeen Bazar) is popular with the young and is recommended for its food. *Annapurna Cafe* on the same road is recommended. Meals (most ingredients have to be brought from the mainland), and drinks, are expensive.

Shopping *Cottage Industries Emporium*. Open 0900-1300,1330-1700. Closed Mon and Fri. Small selection of souvenirs in wood and shell. *Aberdeen Bazaar* is a good place with small shops selling local crafts where you can bargain down the asking price.

Local transport **Taxis** are the most convenient means and you can hire one through the hotel or by contacting the Taxi Stand which is open until 2000. **Bicycles** can be hired at around Re 1 per hr but you need to be very fit to manage the hilly island. The hire shop is between Aberdeen Bazar and the Bus Stop. **Bus** tours are cheap and do the capitals sights and Corbyn's Cove. **Ferry** Three services daily around South Andaman operated by the Marine Department. Local boat hire from Oceanic Company, M.G. Rd, Middle Point or Marine Department. **Helicopters** are also available for island hopping if you have a permit. Services from Port Blair to Rangat, Mayabunder, Hut Bay, Car Nicobar, Kamotra and Campbell Bay.

Entertainment Occasional tribal dance performances for tourists.

Sports **Swimming** is excellent. The best spot is the crescent shaped Corbyn's Cove or one of the uninhabited islands which tourists may visit for the day. *Corbyn's Cove* is to the S of South Andaman, 10 km from Port Blair and 4 km from the Airport where the Andaman Beach Resort is situated and where you can get a snack. The water is warm, clear with gentle surf and the white sand beaches are clean and palm fringed.

A variety of water sports are offered by the resort hotels where some equipment is available. It is best to bring your own mask and snorkel. **Snorkelling and skin diving** are particularly good in the Wandoor National Marine Park where you will see a rich variety of tropical fish, including angelfish, green parrot, yellow butterfly, black surgeon and blue damsel fish. There are also silver jacks, squirrel, clown fish and sweetlips as well as sea cucumbers, sea anemones, starfish and a variety of shells – cowries, turbots, conches and the rarer giant clam which can be as much as a metre wide. There are turtles, sharks and barracudas on the outer reefs and beautiful corals of many different varieties including the brain, finger and antler coral, the colours derived from the algae that thrive in the living coral. **NB Coral and shell collecting is strictly forbidden.** Fishing can be rewarding and you can get your catch grilled on the beach.

Museums **Anthropological Museum** Small but very informative on tribal life with model villages, artefacts, records of exploratory expeditions. Open 0900-1200, 1300-1600, weekdays. Publications on sale. Comprehensive Research Library with books and periodicals on the islands on the second floor which is open until 1700. Allow 1 hr. A visit is strongly recommended. **Marine Museum** with collection of corals and display of 350 species of marine life including tropical fish, sea crocodiles, barracudas, pearl oysters and dolphins which you may be lucky enough to see live, on a boat trip. Open 0830-1600, weekdays. Allow 30 min.

Forest Museum near the Saw Mill has unusual local woods including red paduk, satin and marble woods and shows the use of different woods in the timber industry and the methods of lumbering and finishing. Open 0830-1600, daily. Allow 30 min.

Post and telegraphs Near the centre by the Indian Airlines office. 0700-2200 weekdays, 0800-1800 weekend.

Useful addresses PRO, Andaman and Nicobar Administration. T 20694. Also Resident Commissioner, Curzon Rd Hostel, F105 Kasturba Gandhi Marg, New Delhi, T 387015 and 3A Auckland Place, Calcutta, T 442604.

Travel agents & tour operators Island Travel, Aberdeen Bazaar. Good for excursions and hire of water sports equipment. Travel Corporation of India, Andaman Beach Resort. T 3381.

Tourist offices and information Government of India Tourist Office, VIP Rd, T 21006 which is on the way to the airport. Deputy Director, Information, Publicity and Tourism, Secretariat. T 20933, 20694. The Port Blair Tourist Office at the Secretariat and the Regional Tourist Office at the Tourist Home, Haddo, T 20380. The Regional Office screens occasional films about the islands (1730 on Mon, Wed, Fri).

Tours Half day sightseeing tour of Port Blair and on Sun to Corbyn's Cove. Daily Harbour cruises from Marine Jetty at 1500 (2 hr) including Viper Island. Marine Department trips to Jolly Buoy from Wandoor Beach usually in the morning returning around 1500. The Andaman Beach Resort can arrange trips to Wandoor National Park for a min 4. Travel agents also arrange tours.

Air **Indian Airlines** flies from **Calcutta** to Port Blair on Tue, Th, Sat departing 0545 (2 hr) returning back at 1015 and extended to Car Nicobar on Mon (3 hr 15 min) returning at 1235.

Also from **Madras** on Tue, Wed, Fri, Sun departing 0635 (2 hr 20 min) returning at 1125. Indian Airlines, G55 Middle Point, Port Blair. The journey to the hotel is by taxi either sent by the hotel or you can hire one from the stand but fix the fare before starting which should be around Rs 30.

Ship Sailings from Calcutta and Madras which run to a schedule of sorts (usually fortnightly) and occasional ships from Visakhapatnam. Journey time 2-3 days so you would need to allow about 10 days for the round trip. Travel in a deluxe a/c Cabin costs up to about Rs 850 plus Rs 45 for meals per day and Port Toll Tax, with slightly cheaper cabins in A, B and C Class. The least expensive is an 'Ordinary Bunk' for about Rs 100. Contact Shipping Corporation of India at 3 Strand Rd, Calcutta 700001, T 239466, Port Trust, Old Warehouse Building near Customs House, Rajaji Salai, Madras 600001, T 514401, or Aberdeen Bazar, Port Blair 744101. Agents in Madras: KPV Sheik Md. Rowther and Co., 41 Linghi Chetty St, T 510346; in Vishakapatnam: Bhanojiraw and Guruda, Pattabirmaya and Co., Post Box 17.

WANDOOR NATIONAL MARINE PARK & THE OFF ISLANDS

Excursions The coral beds and underwater life is exceptional off the the two uninhabited islands of **Cinque** which can be reached by boat from Port Blair (3 hr 30 min) or **Chirya Tapu** in the S (2 hr) with a special permit and **Jolly Buoy** which is now a part of the Marine Park.

Wandoor National Marine Park about 30 km SW of Port Blair is well worth visiting. It is a group of about a dozen islands with deep blue waters separating them. It includes Grub, Redskin, Jolly Buoy, Pluto, Boat Island, with Tarmugli on the W, Kalapahar or Rutland to the E and the Twins to the S. Very rich not only in marine life but also in the variety of tropical flowers and birds. The dense forests come down to the beach where the mangrove thrives on the water's edge.

You will need a permit unless just visiting Jolly Buoy which is at the centre of the park and is encircled by a coral reef. The boat lands visitors on the beach in the N and it is possible to see some sea life in the tidal pools but the best is underwater on the reefs. Only supervised diving is advised because of the the strong currents. **Redskin** has a colony of spotted deer introduced by the British, with caves to the rocky N and mangrove swamps to the S and E but with sandy beaches on the W coast where you will probably land. **Tarmugli** is good for snorkelling and diving, with a stretch of coral reef on the SW while the tiny island of **Grub** has good sandy beaches.

Ross Island, once the island with the British Residence, is now only inhabited by peacocks and spotted deer. It has ruins of the Government House, churches, clubs, dungeons, bungalows and bakeries. **NB Remember to pack lunch and drinks for the day. Viper Island** is at the mouth of Port Blair harbour where convicts were interned before the Cellular Jail was built, with its gallows. Indian nationals can apply to visit Dugong Creek where 'Onges' have been rehabilitated in wooden huts.

SOUTH INDIA

Maps: **Madras City**, 694-5; George Town, 697; Anna Salai, 705; Madras Government Museum, 712; Kanchipuram, 718; **Tamil Nadu State**, 722-3; Mamallapuram, 728; Pondicherry, 734-5; Kumbakonam, 743; Thanjavur, 746; Trichy, 750; Tiruvannamalai, 755; Salem, 757; Coimbatore, 761; Ooty, 766; Vellore, 773; Madurai, 779; Tirunelveli, 790; Kanniyakumari, 792; Kodaikkanal, 797; **Kerala State**, 802; Trivandrum, 808; Padmanabhapuram, 813; Kovalam, 815; Quilon, 818; Cochin-Ernakulam, 822-3; Thekkadi, 835; **Karnataka State**, 840-1; Bangalore, 846-7; Bangalore Centre, 849; Guntakal, 857; Srirangapatnam, 860; Mysore, 862; Hassan, 869; Mangalore, 872; Hubli-Dharwood, 876; Gadag-Betgeri, 878; Hospet, 879; Hampi, 881; Badami, 884; Bijapur, 887; Gulbarga, 889; **Andhra Pradesh**, 892-3; Hyderabad, 898-9; Hyderabad Centre, 903; Golconda, 908; Qutb Shahi Tombs, 910; Tirupati, 921; Visakhapatnam, 926; Lakshadweep, Minicoy and Amindivi Islands, 930.

GEOGRAPHY

South India is made up of the 4 states of Andhra Pradesh, Karnataka, Kerala and Tamil Nadu. They all lie in the southern part of the Indian Peninsula. Geologically this is simply an extension of the region immediately to its N. The Western Ghats are rather higher in Kerala and Tamil Nadu than they are inland of Bombay, and the volcanic Deccan lavas which give the black soils of Maharashtra barely reach the 4 southern states. But despite these differences, it would be wrong to imagine that there is a clear and sharp division between the 4 southern states and the region to their N. Most of the states are made up of the same ancient granites found further N. Many are over 3000 million years old, and are part of the old Gondwana land mass that has moved across the Indian Ocean as part of the Indian Plate over the last 100 million years.

The **Western Ghats**, which form a spine along the W coast, are at their highest in S India, where in the Nilgiri Hills of Tamil Nadu they reach heights of over 2,500 m. The Indian plateau falls away to the E, and as a result all the major rivers of S India rise within 100 km of the W coast but reach the sea in the Bay of Bengal. Here the most important of them – the **Krishna** , the **Godavari**, the **Kaveri** – have created broad alluvial deltas which contrast sharply with the higher land of the interior, often covered with dry, thin red soils. Where the possibility of irrigation has been exploited, sometimes for over 2,000 years, the alluvial soils have supported rich rice cultivation. In the far S the Kaveri and **Tamraparni** deltas were the centres of major southern kingdoms while the river valleys of the centre, such as the Krishna, had been the focus of highly developed Buddhist kingdoms in the Nagarjunakonda region.

The **peninsular plateau** falls gradually eastwards from the high crest of the Western Ghats. From N to S, the central plateau is often marked by extraordinary outcrops of granite boulders. The 14th century capital of the Vijayanagar Empire at Hampi is surrounded by the natural fortification of such inhospitable terrain, and the outcrops are also particularly striking between Bangalore and Mysore in S Karnataka or around Hyderabad in Andhra Pradesh. They create a bizarre landscape. Their dramatic effect is heightened when they are interspersed with small patches of bright green paddy growing in irrigated low lying plots between.

The slope from the Ghats to the E coast is also interrupted by massive outlying blocks of hills, from N Andhra Pradesh, where they are an extension of the Orissa Hills, to S Tamil Nadu. These hills are sometimes called the **Eastern Ghats**, but that suggests too great a continuity in what is essentially a disconnected series of hills. The highest rise to over 1500 m, and have often enjoyed sufficient isolation and distinctive climate to produce quite distinct micro regions. The Javadi Hills, about 150 km west of Madras are just one example.

CLIMATE

On a small scale S India experiences almost as wide a range of climates as the wider S Asian region. In common with the rest of the region the climate is dominated by the monsoon system. However, the height of the Western Ghats and the southern position of the 4 states have a major influence on local climates.

Temperature All of S India is S of the Tropic of Cancer. Thus even in places like Udhagamandalam (Ooty) and Kodaikkanal, at altitudes of more than 2,000 m, daytime temperatures in the coldest months remain above 15°C. At sea level the lowest temperatures seldom fall below 21°C and mean temperatures in Jan are around 26°C and 28°C. Thus while the whole of the S is much warmer than the N in winter, in summer the pattern is reversed. Cooling breezes from the sea and much greater cloud cover help to keep summer temperatures lower than in the N, and mean maximum temperatures at sea level are in the low 30s. On the coast itself these temperatures are accompanied by very high humidity, making the climate from Mar through to Oct uncomfortable except where altitude brings greater freshness. Even Bangalore, at a height of just under 1000 m, is noticeably cooler and fresher for most of the year than coastal cities like Madras.

Rainfall The S experiences great contrasts in rainfall. In most of the region the dry season lasts from Jan through to May. The onset of the south west monsoon, which reaches the southernmost point of Kerala in mid-May, gradually moving N towards Bombay into June, transforms the weather pattern. The warm, wet winds, having crossed over 3000 km of the Indian Ocean, are suddenly forced to rise and cool by the mountains near the coast. As a result, on the W coast itself and on the Ghats very heavy rain falls, often for several days at a time. Total rainfall is often more than 4000 mm a year. In Jun 1990 Bombay and some other places on the west coast had as much as 400 mm in 15 hours of torrential rain. Such rain can produce spectacular results – the 250 m high Jog Falls at Shimoga, in W Karnataka, are a magnificent sight in full spate.

The picture immediately to the E of the Ghats is very different. Protected by the rainshadow effect of the mountains themselves, the plains to the E have strong winds through the early monsoon period, but as they come down the eastern slopes of the hills they warm up and become drier. The contrasts with the west are often striking. In the extreme S of Tamil Nadu, for example, the districts around Madurai receive less than 750 mm annually, and the extreme SE experiences almost semi-desert conditions. The journey by land from Trivandrum to Madurai round India's southern tip illustrates the dramatic effects on vegetation and agriculture of this sudden decrease in rainfall.

Retreating Monsoon Tamil Nadu, and particularly the area around Madras, has a quite exceptional rainfall pattern, as it receives the bulk of its rain in what is sometimes called the retreating monsoon. From Oct through to Dec depressions move across the E coast around Madras from the Bay of Bengal. They bring heavy rains, often accompanied by storms, to the coastal belt, decreasing inland and southwards from Madras. It is a season when cyclonic storms, originating much further to the E and SE over Malaysia, may also strike any part of the S Indian coast as they move first W and then N up the Bay of Bengal. Such cyclones can cause enormous disruption, damage and loss of life, particularly when they strike densely populated parts of the country. Landing at Madras during this season can be an extraordinary experience, for all the small irrigation tanks of the district around Madras are full, and the main rice crop is under water.

Best Time Nov through to Mar is far and away the best time to visit the S. Even then you need to be prepared for the heat, which in the daytime can be oppressive. The sun is never very far from being overhead, and is very intense.

THE ECONOMY

Agriculture Even though S India has some of India's most industrialised regions agriculture remains vitally important, and over 70% of the total population still lives in villages. Rice is the most important single crop in all the coastal regions and the deltas of the four southern states, supplemented in some irrigated areas by sugar as a cash crop. Inland is a much more varied picture, with millets such as *ragi* (finger millet) and *sorghum* (known in Hindi as *jowar* and in Tamil as *cholam*) important cereals. They are supplemented by cash crops such as groundnuts and cotton on the plains, and tea, coffee, cardamom, ginger and pepper in the hills.

Resources and industry S India has nothing like the rich mineral resources of the NE of the Indian Peninsula. None the less, there are important deposits of iron ore in Tamil Nadu, Andhra Pradesh and Karnataka, now being exploited for the manufacture of steel, magnesite, coal and lignite, and gold and gemstones from the Kolar Gold Fields northwards. Modern industrialisation can be traced back to the late 19th century in Madras, and the textile industry expanded rapidly in Coimbatore and Madurai before the Second World War. Since Independence Bangalore and Hyderabad have developed a widening range of high technology industries, especially in the field of communications, computing and aeronautics.

Local industries and handicrafts The southern states are particularly famous for both silk and cotton handloom products. Kanchipuram silk, Bangalore silk and *ikats** from Andhra Pradesh are renowned and of extremely high quality. Apart from traditional saris these fabrics can be bought by the metre. Lacemaking by women, which was introduced by the British, is a flourishing cottage industry in the Godavari delta area.

Palms grow in profusion in the south which has led to the production of household goods with the fibres. Cane, reed and coir are transformed into furniture, mats and baskets. Wood inlay and carving is carried out with rosewood and sandalwood, the latter also being used to produce soap, incense and perfume. Handcarved wooden blocks are also produced for printing fabrics to produce Machlipatnam (Masulipatam) '**kalamkari**'. In Kalahasti, they practise the traditional method of using a *kalam* or bamboo pen to introduce the dyes on the material.

Bidri work which comes from Hyderabad in Andhra Pradesh has silver inlay on a black metal alloy and you can buy small bowls, boxes, vases or items of jewellery. Bangalore has a well developed leather industry producing shoes, bags and cases as well as being a centre for exporting garments. Channapatna, also in Karnataka, has long been famous for its wood-turning industry. You can purchase delightful and colourful traditional toys there: miniature carts, swings, roundabouts and furniture.

SOUTH INDIAN TEMPLE ARCHITECTURE

Temple architecture is always the expression of belief, sometimes clearly structured, sometimes only loosely articulated. The heart of South Indian religious and temple development for two thousand years has been Tamil Nadu, although other regions such as central Karnataka have made important contributions to the development of temple styles. Temple building was a comparatively late development in Hindu worship, **see page 616**. For long before the first temple was built shrines were dotted across the land. Such shrines were the focus of **pilgrimage**, and every shrine developed its own mythology to justify its existence as a centre to which pilgrims should come. Even the most majestic of S Indian temples have basic features in common with these original shrines, and many of them have simply grown by a process of accretion around a shrine which may have been in that spot for centuries.

Mythology The myths that grew around the shrines were expressed first by word of mouth, then often written down. Most temples today still have versions of the stories which were held to justify their existence in the eyes of pilgrims. There are several basic features in common. David Shulman has written that the story will include "the (usually miraculous) discovery of the site and the adventures of those important exemplars (such as gods, demons, serpents, and men) who were freed from sorrow of one kind or another by worshipping there." The shrine which is the object of the story nearly always claims to be supreme, better than all others. Many stories illustrate these claims of superiority: for example, we are often told that the **Ganges** itself is forced to worship in a south Indian shrine in order to become free of the sins deposited by evildoers who bathe in the river at Benares.

Worship See page 53. David Shulman gives an excellent idea of the way in which a pilgrim approaches the temple which is ultimately the focus of his worship. He writes: "There is often to begin with, the long, uncomfortable journey to the shrine, which may be defined as a form of asceticism, *tapas**. The journey is, however, only the prelude to a deeper sense of self-sacrifice. Once the pilgrim arrives at the shrine, he sees before him the towering gopuras or gates set in the walls that enclose the sacred area. He leaves his shoes outside the gate; he will also usually undergo an initial purification by bathing, which prepares him for contact with the powerful forces inside. Once the pilgrim goes through the gopuram the real journey begins. This is a journey of the self, and backwards in time. The tall gopurams of the S Indian temple create a sense of dynamism, of movement away from the gate and towards the centre, which is locked inside the stone heart of the main shrine. There lies the sacred force contained within the walls, rendered accessible only through the strong ties that bound it, and through the ritual ordering of the universe within."

So the physical form of the temple has direct spiritual significance. Shulman goes on to illustrate how the pilgrim approaches the central shrine. "The worshipper first circles around the temple compound, offering obeisance at minor shrines, always keeping the main sanctuary on his right; he circumscribes the centre in an individual act of demarcation, just as the stone walls forever mark its limits. At length he will penetrate into the recesses of the main shrine and come to rest before the *garbhagrha**, where the image of the deity is located. Here he has arrived at the farthest reach of his wandering; hidden away in stone and darkness, as in a cave in the bowels of the earth, lies the symbol of the god, which is imbued with the divine power whose deeds are related in myths. Knowledge, or truth, is, in the eyes of the Hindus, by nature esoteric; it is buried, lost, to be recovered from the depths of the sea or from the darkness of the earth. The temple expresses in its very structure this search for hidden wisdom: the *gopuras** point us inward, to the cave. But the *garbhagrha* is, literally, a "house of the womb"; at this spot the pilgrim is conceived afresh, to be reborn without taint, with all the powers latent in the newborn child. He is not, indeed, alone in this experience; the very deity whom he worships also suffers in this site a new birth preceded by violent conception. Life enters the womb in darkness, out of the disintegration into chaos and death of an earlier existence."

He goes on to ask what pilgrims hope to achieve by their pilgrimage. Usually there is a very practical aim – the worshipper comes into contact with a power that helps him in his ordinary life. By offering his own sacrifice to the god, he hopes that the god will reward him by meeting his wishes – for good health, for a suitable husband or wife, for the birth of a child, for prosperity. As Shulman says "It is important to realise that no one in Tamil Nadu goes on pilgrimage in order to attain release from this world (*moksha**). What has happened in the Tamil tradition is that the world renouncing goal of the ascetic has been re-defined as equivalent to *bhakti** (worship and praise). Pilgrimage came to be a substitute for *sannyasa**." The Hindu *bhakti* movements which developed personal worship and praise of a personal Lord, often directed the worshipper back to the world in which they live rather than to seek release from it.

Early Architecture Through all its great diversity Hindu temple architecture repeatedly expresses these beliefs, shared though not necessarily expressed, by the millions who make visiting temples such a vital and living part of life for Hindus today. In architecture as in religious philosophy, the S has derived much from its northern Hindu relations. The Buddhist *chaitya** hall with its apsidal plan had been the common form of most religious shrines up to the time of the Chalukyans in Karnataka, who in the 6th century, started experimenting with what the Guptas in the north had already achieved by elaborating the simple square plan of earlier shrines. Developments at Aihole, Badami and Pattadakal led to the divergence of the two styles of Hindu temples and this became obvious in the shape of the spire. In the N, the *sikhara* was a smooth pyramidal structure, rising to a rounded top with a pointed end, while in the S the *vimana** was more like a stepped pyramid, usually square in plan and had at its top a rounded cupola. You can see examples of both types of tower at Aihole and Badami.

The southern *Dravida* or **Dravidian style** underwent several changes during the reign of the different dynasties that held sway for about a thousand years from the time of the Pallavas who laid the foundation. In Mamallapuram, rock-cut cave temples, *mandapams** or small excavated columned halls and the 'rathas' or monoliths in the shape of temple chariots, were carved out by the early *Pallavas* in the 7th century. These were followed by structural temples and bas relief sculptures on giant rocks, which added another dimension. The Shore Temple (**see page 730**) built there in the 8th century and the Kailasanatha at Kanchipuram (**page 719**) were structural expressions of the Pallava style with the distinctive 'lion pillar' which became a hall mark of the period, as well as the rectangular enclosure. The Ekambaranatha Temple in Kanchipuram shows the evolution of the Dravidian style – the shrine with its pyramidal tower, the separate *mandapa* all within the courtyard with its high enclosure wall made up of cells. Six centuries later the two separate structures were joined by the covered hall or *antarala**. In the Kailasanatha, whereas the substructure was solid granite the upper portion was in sandstone which allowed more freedom to the sculptor. A large subsidiary shrine there which took the place of an entrance gateway also hinted at the later *gopuram*.

Various dynasties fought for the Tamil lands until the **Cholas** gained supremacy in the 9th century and established their kingdom in the Kaveri river valley later extending their realm to become rulers overs a vast area from the Ganga in the north to Sri Lanka in the south. They did away with the rampant lion pilasters, introduced high relief, half-size sculptures of deities and also the gryphon motifs. Their greatest achievements are seen in the early 11th century temples at Gangaikondacholapuram and at Thanjavur with huge pyramidal towers on high vertical bases with exquisitely carved figures in niches on the walls. The Cholas are also remembered for the fine bronzes which adorned their temples.

Development of Gopurams The *Pandiyas* succeeded the Cholas a century later and although no outstanding changes were made they introduced the practice of building tall and prominent watch towers, the *gopurams* and concentric, often battlemented fortress walls which enclosed the courtyards with shrines. Percy Brown observes that the reason for this change may have been due to the inability of the Pandiyas structurally to alter or remove any insignificant holy shrine which they found to be of no artistic merit but in order to draw attention to them and give them prominence they constructed the high walls and massive, richly ornamented gateways. The *gopuram* took its name from the 'cow gate' of the Vedic village, which later became the city gate and finally the monumental temple entrance. This type of tower is distinguished from the **vimana** by its oblong plan at the top which is an elongated vaulted roof with gable ends. Its has pronounced sloping sides, usually 65°, so that the section at the top is about half the size of the base. Although the first two storeys are usually built solidly of stone masonry, the rest is of lighter material, usually brick and plaster. You can see examples of Pandiya gopurams at Jambukesvara near Tiruchirappalli and in Chidambaram and Tirumalai, **see page 739**. The temple at Airavatesvara Temple at Darasuram in Thanjavur District built in the 12th century, towards the end of Chola rule under King Rajaraja II, is a more complete example of the period, **see page 744**. Not only does it have the central temple with its tower but the enclosure also includes a number of smaller shrines. You will be interested to see the reappearance of the lion pilasters and the gryphons of the earlier periods which will be replaced by the horses and dragons of later temples. In the Ramesvaram region on the coast in S Tamil Nadu, open courtyards, trefoil arches and chariot forms became distinguishing features.

The Muslim incursions from the north from the 13th century and their power over a part of the south resulted in a period when large scale temple building was not undertaken for 200 years. However by the 15th century the *Vijayanagar* kings established their empire across southern India and built their fortressed city at Hampi in a barren rocky landscape. Their temples adopted this backdrop and were carved out in harmony with the rock with exceptional skill. Their flat roofed halls had numerous highly sculpted pillars and are marked by their distinctive style. The changes that took place during the period reflect the changes in the ceremonial observances in temple worship. The marked move towards having a number of buildings within the enclosure each having a separate purpose is noticeable. Around the central temple, a subsidiary shrine was built (usually to the NW) to house the consort of the main deity and to celebrate their marriage anniversary, a many-pillared open hall with a central altar, or *kalyana mandapa,* made its appearance close to the east entrance. The temples at Kanchipuram, Tadpatri, Srirangam, Lepakshi and Vellore are also in the Vijayanagara style. The development of the temple complex with several shrines to different deities in the courtyard, the tradition of building *gopurams* in each of the concentric enclosure walls and the remarkable use of the horse motif (and sometimes lions or dragons), mark the Vijayanagara period. The *kalyana **mandapams*** of the temples at Vellore and Kanchipuram are particularly significant in the use of hippogryphs in its pillars and in the Srirangam temple it reaches its full expression in the *Seshagiri mandapam* or 'Horse Court'.

17th century After the fall of Vijayanagar at the hands of the Muslim sultans of the Deccan, the Hindu rulers were pushed further S. The **Nayakas** emerged in the 17th century with their capital at Madurai and continued the practice of building temple complexes with tall *gopurams*. These increased in height to become dominating structures covered profusely with plaster decorations. The fort cities of Madurai and Srirangam show a profusion of defensive walls, lengthy colonnades of the 'thousand pillar' halls and these towering *gopurams*. The tall *gopurams* of Vijayanagara and *Nayaka* periods may have served a strategic purpose, but they moved away from the earlier *Chola* practice of giving the central shrine the tallest tower. The *kalyana mandapa* or marriage hall with a 'hundred' or 'thousand' pillars, and the temple tank with steps on all four sides, were introduced in some southern temples. Another feature which is typical of the south is the *Nandi* bull, Siva's 'vehicle' which occupies a prominent position at the entrance to the main Saivite shrine. In some temples you will see the sacrificial altar with a pole which may have small bells attached.

In Karnataka, at Belur, Halebid and Somnathpur, the *Hoysalas* from the 12th century developed their own style. The temples had a high star-shaped platform, providing an ambulatory, or walking path around a pillared hall with columns which were hand-lathe turned and intricately carved. The temples had parallel bands of exquisitely carved friezes and figures of deities which went around the exterior walls. The quality of the craftsmen in stone reached a peak during this period.

Kerala developed its own style of temple architecture resulting from the need to keep off the heavy rain. The temple roof imitated the functional tiled house roof and sometimes these were covered in metal sheets, occasionally golden as in the case of Guruvayur. The pagoda type tiered roof with gable windows are distinctive of the style as is the circular plan of some Kerala temples.

Details of architectural styles are given in the introduction to the states and within the text.

SOUTH INDIAN MUSIC AND DANCE

Indian music shared a common heritage although within the basic framework of *raga-tala-prabandha* which was well established by the 7th century, changes constantly occurred in different schools of music within the country. From the 13th century the division between the *Hindustani* or the northern system (which included the western and eastern regions as well) and the *Carnatic* or the southern system, became pronounced. The southern school has a more scale-based structure of **raga** where as the the northern school has greater flexibility and thus continued to develop through the centuries. The *tala* too is much more precise. In its content it is also nearly always devotional or didactic where the northern system also includes non-religious, every-day themes which are sometimes sensuous. The language that lends itself naturally to the southern system is Telugu and the only bowed instrument that is used to accompany vocal music is the violin, imported from the west but played rather differently.

The fundamental form in **Carnatic music** is the **varnam***. This is like an étude which conforms to phrases and melodic movements of a particular *raga*. They all have lyrics. The complex structure reaches its height in the **kritis*** which are usually devotional, particularly in the 18th century with singers like Shyama Shastri and Tyagaraja. Unlike some north Indian musical forms in which the melody became more important than the lyric, *kriti* restored the balance between words and music.

Dance *Bharata Natyam* is thought to be the oldest from of classical dance in India having started with the temple dancers in the S. It originated in Tamil Nadu and is essentially a highly stylised solo feminine dance which combines movement, music and mime with *nritta* (pure dance) and *nritya* (expression), the theme being usually spiritual love. The opening *alarippu* shows the dancer unfolding her body in strict rhythm and order accompanied by the *mridangam* (drum) and the singing of the *nattuvanar* (conductor) and the dancer's own ankle bells, while the middle section *varnam* allows her to display her greatest skill and is very demanding, physically and emotionally. The two related dance forms, the *Bhagavata Mela*, performed by men in some important temples and the *Kuravanji*, a dance-opera for women for certain temple festivals also come from Tamil Nadu. Institutions excelling in the teaching of this form are Kalakshetra, Madras, Darpana, Ahmedabad, Rajarajeswar Kala Mandir, Bombay, MS University, Baroda and Triveni Kala Sangam, New Delhi.

Dance-Drama Rhythmic singing naturally leads to dancing. The *tillana** is like abstract dance while the *padams** tell a story by attitudes, gestures and facial expression. *Kuchipudi* takes its name from a village in Andhra Pradesh where it started as a religious dance-drama performed by men (although women now take part) where acting and speaking are also a part of the performance. The most important in this form is *Kathakali* which comes from Kerala and in its traditional form relates stories from the epics Ramayana and Mahabharata and with the performance lasting the whole night. It may appear rather strange and exaggerated with the highly elaborate make-up in green, red and white, with stylised beards made of rice paste and head dress giving the impression of a mask and accompanied by shrill music. The eyes convey the subtlest of expressions. The dancers are all male taking the part of gods and demons with make up and costumes (including large skirts) conforming to strict convention. Being based partly on traditional martial arts, the dancers sometimes carry weapons and the dancing is expressive and vigorous requiring long and rigorous training, **see page 806.**

The simpler **Ottan Thullal** combines classical with folk. Kerala has several institutions specializing in Kathakali – Kala Mandalam, PSW Natya Sangam, Unnayi Warrior Kala Nilayam. New Delhi has the International Centre, Calcutta Rabindra Bharati and Viswa Bharati in Santiniketan near Calcutta. **Mohiniyattam**, a secular dance has combined elements of both Kathakali and Bharat Natyam and the dance of an enchantress. Karnataka has its own folk theatre style of dance-drama in *Yakshagana* and is considered by some to out-do Kathakali in make up and costume! Its theme draws from strength, valour and anger in contrast to other forms which concentrate on the gentler emotions, the *nava rasas* (the nine sentiments). Details in Introduction to the different states.

Percussion The unusual southern percussionists' contest takes place during the *Tala Vadya Kacheri* when instrumentalists compete with each other while keeping within the framework of a rhythm and finally come together in a delightful finale.

SOUTH INDIAN CUISINE

This region of India excels in vegetarian food. The strict S Indian Brahmin is vegetarian and the meal avoids garlic and onion and in some cases even tomatoes. The cuisine reflects what grows in abundance in the South – particularly coconut, chillies, tamarind and bananas. Although most Tamilians tend to be vegetarians there are many in S India who are not. However, the choice of vegetarian food is particularly wide in this part of the country. Favourites for breakfast or 'tiffin' (snack) include **dosai*** (thin crisp pancakes, plain or 'masala' when stuffed with potatoes), **idli*** (soft steamed fermented rice cakes) and *vadai* (savoury lentil doughnuts) which are all served with a coconut chutney and **sambhar*** (a spicy lentil and vegetable broth). *Dosais* and *idlis* have become universally popular and you may now find it on the menu of restaurants all over India.

Try a typical meal at a Lunch Home or Udipi restaurant. *Thalis* here are served on literally a stainless steel plate or more commonly on green plantain leaf, a natural disposable product! You will be offered *rasam* (a clear peppery lentil soup), an unlimited quantity of boiled rice, two or three vegetable preparations often cooked with yoghurt and coconut, *sambar**, plain yoghurt and chutney. The dessert usually is *payasam** (similar to rice or vermicelli pudding, prepared with thickened milk). Coffee is a treat in the S. It is freshly roasted and ground, carefully filtered and then served mixed with hot milk, frothy and aromatic as it is poured from tumbler to a bowl, locally spoken of as being sold by the yard!

The four states in the region tend to have a certain uniformity, although Hyderabadi cuisine remains distinct because of its history of Muslim rule. Specialities include an aubergine dish *baghara baigan** and *haleem** which is a mutton and wheat preparation. Other non-vegetarian specialities which you can try in some restaurants or in 'military hotels' include Mughlai dishes of *biriyani* (rice cooked with meat), *paya**, a soup, egg *paratha*, the rich unleavened bread and spicy pepper chicken *Chettinad* style.

HISTORY

The origins of settlement With its social, economic and political core in the delta of the Kaveri River around Thanjavur, S India has had its own distinctive history within the wider S Asian region. Today the major point of entry to the S for most visitors is Madras. Founded in 1639 it is one of S India's newer cities. Colonial both in origin and function, its development contributed to the transformation of the political and economic development of S India after the 17th century. However, long before that the region that now comprises the 4 southern states – Tamil Nadu, Andhra Pradesh, Karnataka and Kerala – had developed a cultural identity rooted in its Dravidian languages. Although the latest of these, Malayalam, did not emerge fully until the 14th century AD, about the same time as modern English was developing, the oldest, Tamil, had a literary tradition going back 1,500 years before that.

Pre-History S India as a whole has long been the home of distinctive cultural traditions within India. Evidence from various sites in S India shows that there were stone age settlers at the end of the Acheulean period a million years ago. By the 2nd century BC, S India was the home of Iron Age megalithic cultures, and **megalithic burial sites** are common in several parts of the region. Recent analysis of skeletons discovered near Hyderabad on 16 Dec 1931, has shed new light on the life style, illnesses and causes of death of the early megalith builders. The skeletons of 4 males and 6 females from Raigir, nr Hyderabad, were found by chance in the wardrobe of an elderly Londoner on 17 Oct 1983. A number of fascinating conclusions can be drawn from the analysis of skeletal remains. It has been shown from studying the pattern of wear and disease on the teeth, for example, that the megalithic peoples of the area after 1100 BC were settled food producers. Equally it is possible to be certain that osteoarthritic conditions, which were widespread in humans across S Asia, was also present in Raigir, but the Raigir remains are unique in so far as one of the dead clearly suffered from spina bifida.

Since at least the 4th millenium BC, the S had been inhabited by the Dravidians who now make up the great majority of its people. The 4 major Dravidian languages of the S – Tamil, Telugu, Malayalam and Kanarese – developed from the earlier and unknown languages of these people, who were superseded from northern S Asia by the invading Aryans from 2000 BC to 1500 BC.

Early political development By the 4th century BC it is possible to be far clearer about the emerging political and cultural development of the South. From that time Tamil Nadu was under the rule of 3 dynasties. The *Cholas* occupied the coastal area east of Thanjavur and inland to the head of the Kaveri Delta at Tiruchi. Periodically they were a strong military power, one of their princes, Elara, for example conquering the island of Sri Lanka in the 2nd century BC. The centre – Madurai, Tirunelveli and a part of S Kerala were under the *Pandiyas* while the *Cheras* controlled much of what is now Kerala on the west coast of the peninsula. The three kingdoms are mentioned in Ashokan edicts of c. 257 B.C., although not a great deal is known other than that the Pandiyas had good relations with the Mauryan Emperor.

From a very early period S Indians used the sea to trade. Chinese records from the 2nd century BC identify Kanchipuram as an important trading centre. Western classical sources mention ports such as Kaveripatnam, Pondicherry, Malakkanam and Masulipatnam. Indian merchants organised themselves in guilds, trading with the Kra Isthmus and other SE Asian ports.

Literature From around the 2nd century AD a poets' academy known as the *Sangam* was established in Madurai. From the beginning of the Christian era a fundamental development began to take place in Tamil religious thought and writing, transforming Krishna from a remote and heroic figure of the epics to the focus of a new and passionate devotional worship – *bhakti*. The American scholar J.T.F. Jordens has written that this new worship was "emotional, ardent, ecstatic, often using erotic imagery" and it began to appear in Tamil Nadu in the 7th century. From the 7th to the 10th century there was a surge of writing new hymns of praise, sometimes referred to as "the Tamil *Veda*". The view of **Krishna** underwent a transformation, and attention focused on the "marvels of his birth and infancy and his heroic and amorous exploits as a youth among the cowherds and cowherdesses of Gokula". In the 9th century Vaishnavite Brahmans produced the *Bhagavata Purana*, which, through frequent translation into all India's major languages, became the vehicle for the new worship of Krishna, **see page 265**. Its tenth book has been called "one of the truly great books of Hinduism". There are over forty translations into Bengali alone.

Religious orders The new message was not restricted to Tamil Nadu. Followers of both Siva and Vishnu (*Saivites* and *Vaishnavites*) formed religious orders. Monks travelled all over India, preaching and converting, giving the lie to the widely held view that Hinduism is not a proselytising religion. The Vaishnava mystic and saint **Ramanuja** (died 1137) was the first and perhaps the greatest of these. Fleeing from the Shaivite Cholas in Tamil Nadu he founded the *Srivaishnava* sect. It developed a strong following in Karnataka as well as in Tamil Nadu itself. The whole of the south was involved in the new movement. *Madhva*, a Kanarese brahmin, founded the Madhva sect in the 13th century. The Telugu brahmins **Nimbarka** (13th century) and **Vallabhacharya** (1479-1531) carried the message to Varanasi.

The facts of S Indian religious development are often surrounded in myth. It is said for example that Tamil literature was put through an extraordinary test, **see page 780**. Books would be thrown into the sacred tank of the Minakshi Temple at Madurai and those that floated would be deemed worthy, while those that were useless would sink! (This might suggest that this would produce a very small body of worthy literature, until it is remembered that books were written on leaves of the Palmyra palm!), **see page 44**. The writings of the Sangam literature suggest that life in Tamil society had a different system of hierarchy from that in the north, with the sages at the top, followed by peasants, hunters, artisans, soldiers, fishermen and scavengers – quite different from the caste system that existed in the rest of the subcontinent.

Political Development In the early centuries of the Christian era S India thus experienced its own powerful religious development. Politically too it saw the rise of regional powers who contested with each other and on the wider Indian and SE Asian stage. The *Pandiyas* became a great maritime trading power who had connections with the Roman Empire up to the time of Nero and well beyond. Later they returned to power in the Tamil area after the decline of the Cholas and ruled from 1175 to 1300. In the 13th century, international trade flourished under their control and was only superseded by the rise of Vijayanagar.

The Telugu speaking area, was under the rule of the **Andhras** from about 230 BC. They too were a powerful dynasty who reigned for four and a half centuries and traded with many nations from Rome in the W to the countries of SE Asia in the E. Buddhism flourished under their patronage, as did art and craft. The Amaravati stupa in their second capital is attributed to them, but the work of their craftsmen travelled round the world, illustrated by an ivory carving found in the ruins of Pompeii.

To the S of the Andhras, the **Pallavas** of Kanchi, during whose reign the sage poets flourished, came to power in the 4th century AD. They held power over much of the S for 4 centuries. They are thought to have come from the north and may have had connections with Parthians. **Mamallapuram** (*Mahabalipuram*) became an important port and naval base in the 7th century and it was during this period that the famous *rathas* were carved. The Pallavas were mainly Saivites and this was followed in the next century by the building of the Mamallapuram shoretemple, during the reign of Narasimhavarman II who also built the great Kailasanatha temple at Kanchipuram which for 150 years was not only the administrative centre but also a literary and artistic capital where Sanskrit and the Vedas were studied.

The **Chalukyas** 543-755 The Chalukyas with their fortified capital at Badami, ruled the Deccan for two centuries from around the middle of the 6th century and at their peak controlled the vast region between the Narmada and the Kaveri rivers including present-day Maharashtra, Karnataka and western Andhra Pradesh. Although they were great warriors, the Chalukyas were also great temple builders and you can see some of their finest examples at Badami, Aihole and Pattadakal.

The **Cholas** returned to power with the decline of the Pallavas in 850 and were a dominant political force until 1173. Within a century, during the reign of **Rajaraja I**, they defeated the Pandiyas and the Cheras (whose home base was in Kerala) and their great empire at one time expanded to cover the whole Tamil area, Sri Lanka, the region of the Andhras, southern Karnataka and the islands of Laccadives and the Maldives. Further expansion followed during the 11th century during the reign of **Rajendra Chola** (1013-44) which covered Kerala and the Pandiya lands and to the north east across Orissa and up to the Ganga in Bengal. His naval expeditions to the Malayan Peninsula resulted in Chola domination over the trade routes in that entire area of the Indian Ocean and control of the sea routes to Java, Sumatra and China. The control over such a vast area continued for nearly a century until the Pandiyas became powerful again and in Karnataka the Hoysalas emerged as a strong power at the beginning of the 11th century.

The **Hoysalas** (1022-1342) extended their empire from the Krishna to the Kaveri rivers and during the 12th century, after the conversion of king Vishnuvardhana from Jainism to Vaishnavism by the saint Ramanuja, great temples were built. These include the finest in the kingdom at Belur and Halebid. They failed to organise effectively to resist the spread of Muslim power from the north in the mid 14th century and the empire collapsed.

The Left Hand and Right Hand Division In the 11th century a major social division developed which spread across S India through succeeding centuries and remained powerful into the nineteenth century under the labels "right hand" and "left hand" castes, given the Tamil names **Valangai** and **Idangai** respectively. An account of 1072 records a fight between 2 groups which says that "in the second year of the King Kulottunga I there was a clash between the right-hand and left-hand communities in which the village was burnt down, the sacred places destroyed, and the images of deities and the treasure of the temple looted."

Probably originating in Tamil Nadu, the division spread across Karnataka and Andhra Pradesh. Both the origins and the functions of the division are imperfectly understood. At some periods and places, as for instance 17th century Madras, the division was a major feature of the social organisation of communities, where in comon with much earlier periods the left hand groups were identified with particular types of artisan activity, in contrast with the right-handed groups more commonly engaged in agricultural work.

Burton Stein quotes an inscription dated AD 1218 found at the **Uttamacholan Temple** 25 km N of the Kaveri River near Trichy which vividly ilustrates the incorporation of a group into the idangai division: "In order to kill the demons that disturbed the sacrifices of Kasyapa (the priest of Visvakarma, the patron god of artisans) we were made to appear from the sacrificial fire pit and while we were thus protecting the said sacrifice, Chakravartin Arindama honoured the officiating priests by carrying them in a car and led them to a Brahmana colony. On this occasion we were made to take our seats on the back of the car and to carry the slippers and umbrellas of these sages. Eventually with these Brahman sages we were made to settle down in the same villages...We received the clan name idangai because the sages (while they got down from their cars) were supported by us on their left side. The ancestors of this our sect having lost their credentials and insignia in the jungles and bushes, we were ignorant of our origins. Having now once learnt it, we the members of the 98 subsects enter into a compact, in the fortieth year of the king Kulottunga III that we shall hereafter behave like sons of the same parents and what good and evil may befall any one of us, will be shared by all. If anything derogatory happens to the idangai class, we shall jointly assert our rights until we establish them. It is understood that only those who, during their congregational meetings to settle communal disputes, display the insignia horn, bugle, and parasol shall belong to our class. Those who have to recognise us now and hereafter, in public, must do so from our distinguishing symbols – the feather of the crane and the loose hanging hair. The horn and the conch shell shall also be sounded in front of us and the bugle blown according to the fashion obtaining among the idangai people. Those who act in contravention of these rules shall be treated as enemies of our class. Those who behave differently from the rules thus prescribed for the conduct of the idangai classes shall be excommunicated and shall not be recognised as members of the community. They will be considered slaves of the classes opposed to us."

That colourful description does little to help identify the real reasons underlying the designation left and right for the two groups, which embraced many different castes across the region. The impurity associated with left-handedness may suggest ritual connections, though why those called "left-handed" should have accepted such a damaging description is not clear. Stein suggests that perhaps the usefulness of the label came to outweigh the underlying stigma of its associations, but that to disadvantaged groups of both poorer agriculturalists and artisan-traders alliances across wide regions gave a measure of security and political leverage.

The **Muslims** 1296-1347 The Delhi Sultanate's advance was led by **Malik Kafur** who conquered first the N Deccan establishing strongholds in Devagiri and Warangal. Later they took control of the Tamil lands. However, in 1347 the Muslim officers in what is now N Karnataka and Andhra Pradesh rebelled against Delhi. Their leader Hasan Kangu set up the independent Bahmani Kingdom after adopting the name Ala ud-Din Hasan Bahman Shah. Myths about his origins continue to circulate. The court genealogists were persuaded to trace his ancestry back to the Iranian king Bahman Isfander, while another myth asserted that he was the servant of Gangu Brahmin of Delhi. In fact he was the nephew of one of the Delhi sultanate's greatest generals, Hizabru'd Din Zafar Khan.

Ala ud Din founded the **Bahmani dynasty** (1347) setting up their first capital in Gulbarga where a great mosque was built. He extended his control over much of northern and central Karnataka and Andhra Pradesh, a process of expansion consolidated by his successor Muhammad I (1358-1375). A succession of five sultans ruled after Ala ud Din's death in 1375 up to 1397. The early Muslim rulers encouraged immigration from Iran and Arabia, but as the historian S.A.A. Rizvi has argued, the high positions occupied by many such immigrants often caused intense jealousy and conflict, being resented both by local people and by immigrants from N India. Such tensions encouraged divisions within the ruling family, and the sultanate was constantly fighting against the rising power of the Vijayanagar Empire and against internal factions. In 1422 Ahmad I (1422-36), having won one such battle over the **Raja of Warangal**, N of Hyderabad, moved the capital to **Bidar**. However the gains he made were frittered away by his son and successor Ala ud Din, and the dynasty continued to be beset with internal and external conflicts.

Rizvi quotes the Russian traveller Athanasius Nikhitin, who visited the Deccan between 1469 and 1474 (travelling under the Muslim name Khwaja Yusuf Khurasani), illustrating the nature of life at the Bahmani court. "The Sultan of Bedar is a little man, twenty years old, in the power of the nobles. Khorassanians rule the country and serve in war. There is a Khorassanian Boyar, Melik-Tuchar, who keeps an army of 200,000 men; Melik Khan keeps 100,000; Kharat Khan, 20,000, and many are the khans that keep 10,000 armed men. The Sultan goes out with 300,000 men of his own troops. The land is overstocked with people; but those in the country are very miserable, whilst the nobles are extremely opulent and delight in luxury. They are wont to be carried on their silver beds, preceded by some twenty chargers caparisoned in gold, and followed by 300 men on horseback and 500 on foot, and by horn-men, ten torchbearers and ten musicians."

The kingdom split up at the end of the 15th century resulting in the formation of five independent states of **Berar, Ahmednagar, Bijapur, Golconda** and **Bidar**.

Vijayanagar Empire (1336-1565) At the same time as the Muslim sultanates were pressing south the *Vijayanagar Empire* was re-asserting Hindu political power from its capital, Hampi in Karnataka across the southern peninsula of India. The last Hindu Empire was named after its capital on the **Tungabhadra river**. It rose out of the break away from Delhi by the Madurai Sultanate in Tamil Nadu, the separation of power into smaller Muslim sultanates and the resistance to Islam by the Hindu kingdoms which soon came to include the Hoysalas. Under the founder of the Empire, **Harihara I**, the region S of the Kaveri river came under the rule of a single king which was to extend over the whole of the S.

For the next two centuries the Vijayanagar kings flourished and for a time their influence spread as far as Orissa. They were patrons of a vigorous expansion of temple building across S India. Although they were frequently at war with the Muslim kingdoms to their N they capitalised on the rivalries between the Muslim sultans and periodically they sided with one or other of the five kingdoms as self interest suggested prudent.

Between 1559-61 Bijapur and Vijayanagar were on one side against the sultanate of Ahmadnagar, but the Vijayanagar king **Ramaraja** so disgusted his allies by playing off one kingdom against another that the Muslim states formed a coalition to take on the Vijayanagar forces. For the first and only time they came together as an effective force on 24 December 1564. They marched to fight the Vijayanagar army on 23 February 1565 at **Talikota**. Ramaraja himself was captured and executed, the Vijayanagar army comprehensively defeated and the capital city pillaged. Even after their forces were routed by a confederacy of the Muslim states of the Deccan in 1565 their kings continued to rule from further S into the next century.

The Deccan sultanates held on to their independent states until the arrival of the Mughals under Aurangzeb while the Tamil areas broke up into independent principalities to be fought over by foreign empires attempting to establish first their trading bases and then colonies. The advent of the Muslims in N India had less impact in this part of the subcontinent but its history changed after 1639 with the arrival of the British as a trading company.

The Europeans The fall of the Roman Empire in the 5th century AD ended the direct trade between Europe and India which had flourished for six centuries. The Arabs, Byzantians and Venetian and Genoese traders acted as middle men before goods reached Europe. The hunger for spices and exotic goods increased so **Vasco da Gama** sailed from Lisbon for the East.

The **Portuguese** were the first to establish trade with the Vijayanagars as early as 1498 arriving at the port of Calicut in search of 'Christians and spices' thus ending the long held Arab monopoly of sea trade with India. It was to be bloody takeover in the fighting that followed the attacks on Calicut over the next few years. In 1510, the seizure of Goa by **Alberquerque** established the Portuguese empire. He built many forts at strategic places along the coast and dominated sea trade in the Indian Ocean for the next half century until the fall of Vijayanagar in 1565. During this period **St Francis Xavier** was sent by the Society of Jesus 'to convert the Indians'. He arrived in Goa in 1542, spending a few years before going further east to Malacca. He returned briefly to Goa in 1547 and again in 1551 before going further E again. His name lives on in the several Jesuit educational institutions to be found all over India.

Up to the end of the 16th century the sailors had depended on the monsoon winds to traverse the Indian Ocean. In 1595 the **Dutch** published navigation maps which made sailing eastwards quicker. The Dutch East India Company was set up in 1602 in Amsterdam and they subsequently established themselves in **Surat**, the Mughal port north of Bombay and later seized Pondicherry from the French in 1693 only to return it in 6 years. They, however, unlike the other European trading companies had not sought to establish an empire in India.

The Danes arrived in **Tranquebar** on the E coast of the peninsula, between Karikal and Pondicherry in 1620 but their activities remained very limited unlike the English. In 1600 the English merchants' companies in London obtained permission to hold monopoly of trade with the Indies from Queen Elizabeth I. The East India Company's first counting house was set up in Surat in 1619, followed by settlement near Madras with the building of Fort St. George in 1639. A century later the French in India under Dupleix seized Madras and held it for a few years until the the treaty of Aix-la-Chapelle forced its return to the English in 1749. In 1751 Clive's victory over the French in Arcot was a turning point and following the French example he placed his own Indian agent on the throne there. Trouble for the English emerged with the coming to power of Haidar Ali on the throne of Mysore in 1761.

Haidar Ali was exceptional not only as a military strategist on both land and sea but also as a patron of the arts. He defeated the English and their ally the Nizam of Hyderabad in the first Mysore war. He and his son *Tipu Sultan* fought and won many battles against the English with the help of the French at a vast expense, during the Second Mysore War which started in 1780. The victories extended the rule of the Sultan of Mysore over most of S India including Malabar (Kerala). However, Haidar Ali was defeated in 1781 and died the following year when his son acceded to the throne. But the Treaty of Versailles in 1783 brought the French and English together and Tipu was forced to make peace. The English took Malabar in 1792 and finally marched on Tipu's capital in Srirangapatna (Seringapatam) near Mysore where the Sultan was killed in his fort in 1799. In 1801, Lord Wellesley succeeded in bringing together most of the S under the Madras Presidency with the exception of Hyderabad and Mysore, see page 860.

The 17th and 18th centuries The French established their East India Company in 1664, their ships arriving at the port of Surat to set up the first counting house there where the English and the Dutch had already established themselves. This was followed by the acquisition of land at Pondicherry in 1673 and Masulipatnam, N of Madras 14 years later. In 1742, Dupleix who had been administering Chandernagore near Calcutta in E India was named Governor of the French India Company and took up residence at **Pondicherry**. He seized Madras within a few years but was forced to fight against the Nawab of Arcot who demanded its return. Having won his victory he made grand plans for the empire by installing his chosen men on the thrones of the Nawabs of Arcot in the S and Nizams of Hyderabad in the N of the region.

However, in 1751 **Clive** attacked Arcot and won it for the English which was the beginning of the end of the French in India. The Treaty of Paris brought their Empire to a close in 1763 although they retained five counting houses. Louis XIV and Louis XV had not shown any interest in the Orient so the English gained an increasing advantage in trade which made them the foremost colonial power in India. English power spread from Madras northwards up the coast of modern Andhra to Visakhapatnam and the borders of Orissa, southwards to include the whole of modern Tamil Nadu and westwards to the coast at Mangalore.

Recent political development At Independence the old province of Madras which included Andhra Pradesh and part of Kerala in addition to present day Tamil Nadu, became the State of Madras. In 1969, the name was changed to Tamil Nadu. Sixteen years earlier Andhra Pradesh itself had become the first state to be re-organised on the basis of a common language when the coastal districts of Andhra were joined with the interior districts of Telangana to become one State. Kerala was formed out of the former Princely States of Travancore and Cochin joined with some of the western coastal districts of Madras Presidency. Similarly Karnataka was formed by a re-grouping of districts which had previously been in different states, uniting all those districts where Kannada was the majority language.

MADRAS

Population 5.36 million (1991). *Altitude* Sea level. *Climate* Temp. Summer Max. 37°C Min. 28°C, Winter Max. 32°C Min. 20°C. Annual rainfall 127 cm. The international airport is 15 km from the city centre with taxis and coaches available for the transfer.

	Jan	Feb	Mar	Apr	May	Jun	Jul	Aug	Sep	Oct	Nov	Dec	Av/Tot
Max (°C)	29	31	33	35	38	37	35	35	34	32	29	28	33
Min (°C)	20	21	23	23	28	28	26	26	25	24	23	21	24
Rain (mm)	24	7	15	15	52	53	83	124	118	267	309	139	1216

The villages of Triplicane, Mylapore, Tiruvottiyur, Pallavaram etc. have a long historical past, some even going to centuries before Christ, but the city of Madras is just over 350 years old, being founded by the East India Company trader, Francis Day, in 1639.

INTRODUCTION

Before the arrival of the British, there was a Portuguese settlement in the San Thome area as well as Armenian traders. In 1639, *Francis Day*, a trader with the East India Company, negotiated the grant of a tiny plot of sandy land to the N of the Cooum River as the base for a warehouse or "factory" which consisted of a mere strip "3 miles long and a mile at its widest". By 1640 a few thatched houses had been built, close to the beach and was protected by walls on 4 sides and since it was St George's Day on 23 April, it was christened Fort St George. There was no natural harbour, and there was nothing in the site of Madras itself to attract a settlement. Its choice was dictated partly by local politics – Francis Day's friendship with Dharmala Ayyappa Nayak provided a useful lever with the *Raja of Chandragiri*, the last in the line of Vijayanagar chiefs who still controlled that section of coast – but more importantly by the local price of cotton goods, which was better than anywhere else along India's eastern seaboard.

By 1654 the settlement had grown and been fortified. **Fort St. George** had a church and English residences and it came to be known as 'White Town' or Madraspatnam. To its N was what the British referred to as 'Black Town', which the local people called Chennapatnam after Nayak's father. The two towns merged and Madraspatnam grew with the acquisition of neighbouring villages of *Tiru-alli-keni* or Lily Tank (Triplicane) in 1676. In 1693, Governor Yale (founder of Yale University in the USA) acquired Egmore, Purasawalkam and Tondiarpet from Emperor Aurangzeb, who had by that time extended Moghul power to the far S, at the expense of the last Vijayanagar rulers. Initially they were acquired on an annual lease until they were all brought in to the city in 1720. Successive wars with the French, and developing British ambitions in Bengal and N India, led to fluctuations in the fortunes of the city. In 1746 it was captured by the French and largely destroyed, to be returned to British control as a result of the **Treaty of Aix la Chapelle** in 1748. By the middle of the 18th century many other villages such as Nungambakkam, Ennore, Perambur, San Thome and Mylapore (the "city of the peacock") were purchased or added with the help of friendly Nawabs. By this time Calcutta had already become the chief focus of British ambitions in India, and in 1793 Calcutta became the chief centre of British administration in India. However, Madras continued to grow, and it became the centre of the E India Company's expanding power through the late 18th and early 19th centuries.

The city is still growing with Greater Madras comprising of Ennore, Avadi, Tambaram and extensions to satellite towns such as Maraimalainagar, between Madras and Chingleput. Since 1971 there has been a succession of attempts to tackle the massive problems of housing and services. In the 1970s the state government embarked on an ambitious rehousing programme for so-called "slum dwellers". It was estimated then that there were nearly 1 million people living in the thatched roofed colonies that lined the open spaces along canal and river banks, roads and railway lines. Travelling round Madras today you see the 4 and 5 storey tenements that were built to replace the informal housing. The programme proved far too costly to meet the ambition of replacing all slum housing by 1977.

In the years since attention has shifted to improving services in many of the colonies. Provision even of basic services remains extremely limited. The water supply, served by the Red Hills lake to the N of the city, has been grossly inadequate for many years. In the late 1960s the then government embarked on a plan to pipe water into the city from over 150 km to the W. The unfinished concrete pipe line still lies by the roadside on the inland road S to Mamallapuram.

An agreement was signed in Feb 1990 between Tamil Nadu and Andhra Pradesh to divert waters from the Krishna River to Madras at a cost of Rs.900 crore in a project to be completed by 1993. It is possible to see something of the work of city redevelopment by visiting the headquarters of the Madras Metropolitan Development Authority, next door to Egmore Railway station.

Change of road names As in the case of the other capital cities with a colonial past, some old street names in Madras have been changed to commemorate national and local personalities. The 4 main roads leading out of Fort St George take you towards ancient villages that existed long before the fort was built. The southern road, the **S Beach Rd** has been renamed **Kamaraj Salai** while the one to the SW, the old **Mount Rd** which leads to St Thomas' Mount is now called **Anna Salai**. The latter becomes NH45 which heads towards Kanniyakumari on the peninsula's southern tip. The western road led to the old villages of Wandiwash and Poonamallee whose local governors were responsible for the British settlement in the 17th century. **Poonamallee High Rd** is now **Periyar EVR Salai** while the road N, **North Beach Rd**, which has existed since the harbour was built by the British, is now called **Rajaji Salai**. Occasionally, both names are in common use.

Some of the other changes are: **Edward Elliot's Rd** now **Dr. Radhakrishnan Rd**; **Elliot's Beach Rd** now **Sardar Vallabhai Patel Rd**; **Lloyds Rd** now **Avvai Shanmugham Salai**;

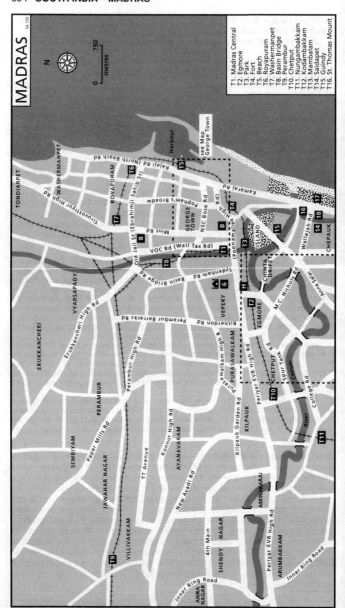

MADRAS

N

0   750
metres

T1. Madras Central
T2. Egmore
T3. Park
T4. Fort
T5. Beach
T6. Royapuram
T7. Washermanpet
T8. Basin Bridge
T9. Perambur
T10. Chetput
T11. Nungambakkam
T12. Kodambakkam
T13. Mambalam
T14. Saidapet
T15. Guindy
T16. St. Thomas Mount

Harbour

see Map
George Town

TONDIARPET

WASHERMANPET

Tiruvottiyur High Rd

Rajaji Rd (North Beach Rd)

Kamaraj Rd

ROYAPURAM

Old Jail St (Ebrahimji Sahib St)

Popham's Broadway

Mint Rd

NSC Bose Rd

GEORGE TOWN

VOC Rd (Wall Tax Rd)

(Poonamallee)

ISLAND

CHINTA DRIPET

ERUKKANCHERI

VYASARPADY

Erukkancheri High Rd

Basin Bridge Rd

Sydenham Rd

Perambur Barracks Rd

VEPERY

PURASAWALKAM

Ritherdon Rd

Purasawalkam High Rd

EGMORE

M.C. Nichols Rd

Anna Salai

PERAMBUR

Perambur High Rd

Konnur High Rd

Kilpauk Garden Rd

KILPAUK

Periyar EVR High Rd

CHETPUT

Chetput Rd

Spur Tank

Cooum

SEMBIYAM

Paper Mills Rd

TT Avenue

AYANAVARAM

New Avadi Rd

River

College Rd

JAWAHAR NAGAR

VILLIVAKKAM

4th Main

SHENOY NAGAR

AMBIKARAI

Periyar EVR High Rd

ARUMBAKKAM

Inner Ring Road

ANNA NAGAR

Inner Ring Road

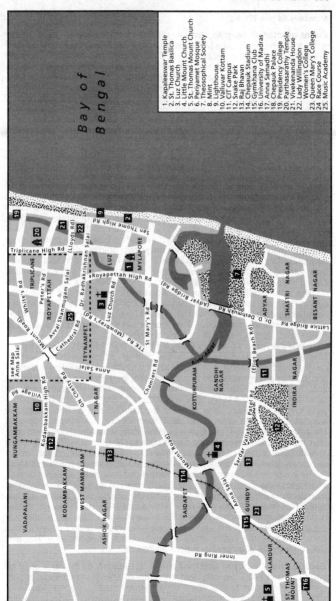

1. Kapaleeswar Temple
2. St. Thomas Basilica
3. Luz Church
4. Little Mount Church
5. St. Thomas Mount Church
6. Periyamet Mosque
7. Theosophical Society
8. Mint
9. Lighthouse
10. Valluvar Kottam
11. IIT Campus
12. Snake Park
13. Raj Bhavan
14. Chepauk Stadium
15. Gymkhana Club
16. University of Madras
17. Anna Samadhi
18. Chepauk Palace
19. Presidency College
20. Parthasarathy Temple
21. Vivekenanda House
22. Queen Willingdon Women's College
23. Queen Mary's College
24. Race Course
25. Music Academy

Mowbray Rd now TTK Rd.

Places of interest (with approximate distances from the Tourist Office). Of the 3 major British colonial cities Madras is the most accessible. While it does not have the major buildings of either Bombay or Calcutta some features of its history can be much more easily seen and the overlay of modern development has not completely obliterated the traces of its earlier history.

The city falls into 3 main areas, the north, central and southern sections. The N was the original centre of British trade and subsequently of British political power. Mylapore in the S was the first Portuguese settlement. Between the two, and inland stretching down Mount Rd (now *Anna Salai*) through Guindy to St. Thomas' Mount the city gradually expanded through the 19th century as its political base became secure.

NORTH

Fort St. George and **St Mary's Church** (3 km) The beginning of the city of Madras was marked by the building of the Factory House with its fortifications on the beach. Completed by the British in 1654 but rebuilt several times, it now houses the Tamil Nadu Secretariat and Legislative Assembly. The present structure, which is a fine example of British military architecture of the 17th century was mostly built in 1666. The country's tallest flagstaff is here and is thought to be over 300 years old. The 24 shiny black Pallavaram granite or Charnockite (**see page 32**) pillars are those reclaimed by the British in 1762 of the original 32 which once formed the colonnade of the present Secretariat building (the French had carried them off to Pondicherry after their victory in 1746).

The State Legislative Hall has fine wood work and black and white stone paving. You can also see the old barracks and officers' quarters including the house occupied by Lord **Clive** which he rented from an Armenian merchant and where you can see one room; Clive's Corner has small exhibits. The Duke of Wellington's residence has collapsed and is now closed.

Inside the Fort is *St. Mary's Church* (3 km) Built 1678-80 by **Streynsham Master** in solid masonry to a simple plan of 3 aisles with semi-circular cannon-proof roofs and 1.3 m thick walls. It was the safest building in the Fort and in times of siege was used as a military dormitory and store house. The first English church in India, it was entirely re-built in 1759 after being severely damaged in a siege. A fluted spire was added and the tower and belfry which were originally detached were linked to the main church. Well-known people associated with the church include Robert Clive, who married Margaret Maskelyne here in 1753, and Governor *Elihu Yale*, who was also married here, later founded Yale University and gave a plate to the Church in 1687. The most remarkable monument is the one erected by the E India Company to the famous missionary Schwartz, at one time the intermediary between the British and Haidar Ali. He is represented dying on his bed surrounded by a group of friends with an angel appearing above (Murray). The church now has an active congregation in membership with the Church of S India and the original black granite font has been in continuous use. Job Charnock, who founded Calcutta, is thought to have had his 3 daughters baptized here in 1689. The painting of the Last Supper over the altar is attributed to the school of Raphael and was originally believed to have been looted by the British from a French church in Pondicherry. The teak balustrade in the W gallery has curious oriental carvings.

George Town, re-named after the future King George V on the occasion of his visit to India in 1905, has long been the centre of Madras's commercial activity. Lying to the E and N E of the Central Railway station, George Town was substantially developed – from the densely packed labyrinth of lanes and gullies which characterised it in the late 18th century.

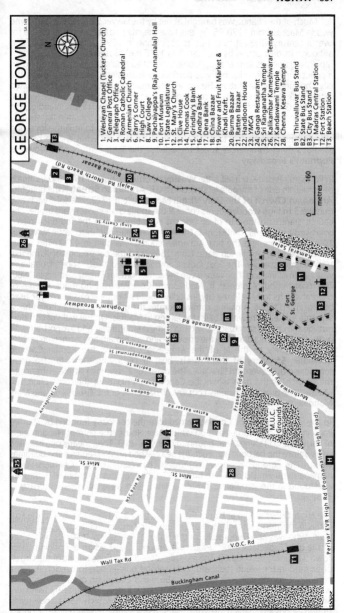

GEORGE TOWN

N

1. Wesleyan Chapel (Tucker's Church)
2. General Post Office
3. Telegraph Office
4. Roman Catholic Cathedral
5. Armenian Church
6. Parry's Corner
7. High Court
8. Law College
9. Pachaiyappa's (Raja Annamalai) Hall
10. Fort Museum
11. State Legislature
12. St. Mary's Church
13. Clive House
14. Thomas Cook
15. Grindlay's Bank
16. Andhra Bank
17. Dena Bank
18. China Bazaar
19. Flower and Fruit Market &
    Khadi Kraft.
20. Burma Bazaar
21. Ratten Bazaar
22. Handloom House
23. GMCA
24. Ganga Restaurant
25. Sri Ranganatha Temple
26. Kalikambar Kameshwarar Temple
27. Kandaswami Temple
28. Chenna Kesava Temple

B1. Thiruvalluvar Bus Stand
B2. State Bus Stand
B3. City Bus Stand
T1. Madras Central Station
T2. Fort Station
T3. Beach Station

0   160
    metres

Much of the change was brought about by the lawyer Stephen Popham, who was in Madras from 1778-95. By this time the city had been a major centre for over a century. One estimate put its population in 1690 at over 300,000, and although its destruction by the French in 1746 had caused a mass evacuation it rapidly regained its former size. Popham had already laid the basis for setting up a police force in the city, but was particularly enthusiastic about improving the city's housing and sanitation. He argued that main drains should be constructed in the Black Town to carry away the stagnant waters. The scheme could be realised when the Governor finally insisted on the removal of a low hill just inland of Fort St. George, then known as Hog Hill, which was thought to threaten the security of the Fort. The work was carried out, and the earth used to infill the low-lying marshy land immediately to its N. Here Popham laid out what was to become Madras's main commercial street throughout the 19th century, still known as **Popham's Broadway**.

In Popham's Broadway itself is the **Wesleyan Church**, built in 1820 (now Church of S India). In one of the parallel streets to the E, **Armenian Street**, is the beautiful **Armenian Church of the Holy Virgin Mary**, built in 1772. The solid walls and massive 3 m high wooden doors conceal the spotless open courtyard inside. The church stands on the site of an ancient cemetery and in the red-brick paved courtyard are several tombstones. The Armenians had begun to settle in Madras 100 years before and the first Armenian church was built in 1712. The oldest tombstone of an Armenian dates from 1663, and the community of Armenian traders grew steadily. The East India Company valued their "sober, frugal and wise" style of life and they were given the same rights as English settlers in 1688. The most famous Armenian in Madras was Coja Petrus, who made a series of charitable gifts to benefit the city, including the first bridge across the Adyar, used by Mount Rd today. A plaque commemorates the gift. The present church has a separate white belfry with 6 bells, the largest in Madras. On the walls of corridors outside the church sanctuary now hang some beautiful pen and ink portraits and pictures of Armenia drawn by the present – and last remaining – Armenian sexton.

Immediately to the N of the Armenian Church is the Roman Catholic Cathedral, **St. Mary of the Angels**, built in 1675 with the help of a grant sanctioned by Governor Elihu Yale. The date 1642, inscribed at the entrance to the Church, is the date when the Capuchin monks built their first church in Madras. The present sanctuary contains oil paintings of the Crucifixion and Mary Magdalene.

To the E again is **Parry's Corner**, named after the company founded by Thomas Parry in 1790. The corner plot on which Dare House (the current Headquarters of Parry and Co.) stands, was bought by Parry in 1803. Then, nearly one hundred years before the harbour was built, the sea washed right up against the buildings walls. The group is now controlled by Nattukkottai Chettiars from Ramanathapuram District – see page 739. Other famous commercial names are also found in the same area, including Binny, who were established as early as 1682.

The **High Court** (5 km) at Parry's Corner was built in 1892 is to the N of the Fort and is in the Indo-Saracenic style of the late 19th century architects such as Henry Irwin, who was also responsible for the National Art Gallery. It stands on the site of the old "Esplanade Park", which was made in 1757 when the original Black Town was finally demolished. The red judicial building, said to be one of the largest of its kind in the world (believed to be second only in size to London's), has a number of domes, minarets and spires above and a labyrinth of vaulted corridors within. You are allowed to visit the courtrooms in the lawcourts by using the entrance on the left. A fine example is Court No. 13 which has stained glass, fretted woodwork, carved furniture, silvered panels and a painted ceiling. Contact

Registrar for visit and guide. Open 1045-1345, 1430-1630. Mon-Sat.

The huge red central tower nearly 50 m tall built like a domed minaret to serve as a **lighthouse** can be seen 30 km out at sea. It took over from the Esplanade lighthouse in 1894 as the city's third lighthouse and was in use until 1977 when the new one was built on the Marina. You can climb to the top of the lighthouse for a good view. The *Esplanade Lighthouse* SE of the High Court is in the form of a large Doric pillar which took over from the Fort lighthouse in 1841. It is used as the standard bench mark for Madras.

W of the High Court is the **Law College** with its twin minarets which stands on the site of the old cemetery of Fort St George. Behind it is the **Yale Obelisk** which marks the grave of Elihu Yale's 4 year old son and his wife's first husband Edward Hynmers.

To the W of the Law Courts are the Law College (opened in 1892 on the site of the European settlers' first burial ground) and the *Pachaiyappa's Hall*, built in 1850 and modelled on the Athenian Temple of Theseus. Pachaiyappa Mudaliar was a Hindu who was one of the first Indians to leave a will. Born in 1748 in a destitute family, he had made a fortune by the age of 21. He wished a major share of his wealth to go to charity, and his will was contested for 47 years after his death in 1794. In the event the court decided that Rs 450,000 should be held in trust to provide education for poor Hindus. The trust now administers charities across India, sponsoring six colleges, a polytechnic and 16 schools in Tamil Nadu.

The 19th century growth of Madras can be traced N from Parry's corner. *First Line Beach* (N Beach Rd) was built on reclaimed land in 1814, and at that time it was what its name implied – the road fronting the beach. The General Post Office, designed by Robert Fellowes Chisholm and "an inventive piece of tropical Gothic", as Philip Davies has described it, was finished in 1884. By then the first harbour pier had been in use for over twenty years, and the harbour which was to transform the economy of the city was begun in 1876. The whole structure was washed away in a catastrophic cyclone in 1881, but the work was renewed, to be completed in 1896. From the end of the 18th century the city behind the beach had flourished.

There are several reminders of this wealth. Major commercial expansion took place between First Line Beach and *Mint Road*. The Mint from which the road takes its name was first opened in 1640, from the end of the 17th century minting gold coins under licence for the Mughals, though it did not move to Mint St until 1841-2.

Today the Mint is part of the Government Printing Press. S. Muthiah writes that in 1699 Thomas Salmon had written of the "Black Town" that the streets are wide, and trees planted in some of them; and having the sea on one side and a river on the other, there are few towns so pleasantly situated or better supplied; but except for some few brick houses the rest are miserable cottages, built with clay and thatched and not so much as a window to be seen on the outside... but I must say, notwithstanding all their appearance of poverty, I never was in a place where wealth abounded more, or where ready money was more plentiful about 20 years ago... Beyond the Black Town are gardens for half a mile together planted with mangoes, coconuts, guavas, oranges, where everybody has the liberty of walking and may purchase the most delicious fruit for a trifle ". Standing on the banks of the Buckingham Canal today it is difficult to imagine that it could ever have been an attractive scene.

Immediately to the N runs *Wall Tax Road*. It takes its name from an unsuccessful plan to raise money by taxation to pay for the defensive wall constructed between 1764-69 to ward off the attacks of Haider Ali. At *Basin Bridge* it reaches one of the early experiments to provide Madras with a secure drinking water supply, Charles Trevelyan's "basin" dug out to act as a reservoir.

"Interior" George Town is much the same now as the early 19th century town, except, as Muthiah says, "it just keeps getting more and more congested". He goes on to say "in the northern half there still remain the country-tilled houses with pillared verandahs, short and heavy doors inches thick and 'caste marks' at the entrance. The southern half, mainly in

Peddanaickanpet, is Madras's wholesale market, street after street, narrow and crowded, specialising on street level in particular goods, with palatially equipped homes often occupying the upper reaches of these same dingy buildings." Paper in Anderson St, fireworks in Badrian st, fruit in Bunder St, vegetables in Malayaperumal St, turmeric and *kumkum* powder, silk thread for charms, false hair, glass and mica in Devaraj Mudali St. The list of specialist wholesalers is seemingly endless. The pavements of the main streets are now lined with trinket sellers

CENTRAL

Triplicane and ***Chepauk*** contain some of the finest examples of late 19th century Indo-Saracenic architecture in India, focused on the University of Madras just to the S of the Cooum. From that point S Beach Rd (now *Kamarajar Salai*, after the well known Tamil Congress politician), laid out in 1846, runs 3.5 km due S to Mylapore. Until the end of the 19th century the beach had been ignored by settlers moving S from Fort St. George. Then the Governor of Madras Mountstuart Elphinstone Grant-Duff (1881-86) decided to develop the Marina, especially as a promenade. Ever since the early years of the 20th century it has been a lung for the city and a favourite places for thousands of city dwellers to walk on Sun evenings.

Over a century before that the **Chepauk Palace** had been built for Wallajah Muhammad Ali, Nawab of the Carnatic. It marked the move of the Nawab to Madras and became the focus for a growing Muslim population in the city which remains focused on Triplicane and Wallajah Rd. See below.

Marina Beach and **Aquarium** (3 km) The fine sandy beach which stretches to about 5 km from the harbour to St.Thome, is also impressively wide. Its width is artificial, for until the harbour was built to the N at the end of the 19th century the sea washed up close to the present road. The northward drifting current has progressively widened the beach since the harbour walls were constructed out into the sea in 1876, intercepting the current.

On the beach itself are the *Anna Park* and *MGR Samadhi*, named after the founder of the DMK party and the Chief Minister of its first administration in 1967, and M.G. Ramachandran, the film star and charismatic Chief Minister during the 1980s. The latter has become a focus of pilgrimage from all over Tamil Nadu. If you wish it is quite possible to get a ride on one of the fishermen's catamarans at dawn for a few rupees.

There is an aquarium, described by one Madras resident as something "Madras should be ashamed of". The swimming pools are not recommended. Open 1400-2000 weekdays, 0800-2000 holidays. Small fee.

Warning Swimming unattended along Marina beach is dangerous.

The University Building and **Presidency College**. The University of Madras was incorporated in 1857 and is one of India's oldest modern universities. In 1864 Robert Chisholm won a competition to design the University and Presidency College buildings. The two-storeyed Presidency College, "combining Italianate with Saracenic" styles, making full use of red brick, was completed in 1870. The Senate House, the Foundation stone of which was laid by Lord Napier KT, was begun in 1874 and completed 5 years later. The Senate Hall was built to seat 1600 people. In the words of S. Muthiah "the ceiling is elaborately carved and the stained glass windows were, in their day, the finest in Madras."

Chepauk Palace (4.5 km) on the Beach Rd was the residence of the Nawab of Carnatic and now houses the Public Works Department. Designed by Philip Stowey in 1768, it is one of the earlier of the city's buildings in the Mughal style. It was originally built in two sections, the two storeyed Khalsa Mahal with four small domes and the Humayun Mahal which had the grand *durbar* hall, but after the Government took over the palace in 1855, a tower was built between the two. The original building is now hidden from the road by the modern Public Works Department building, *Ezhilagam*.

Immediately behind these is the **Chepauk cricket ground** where cricket test matches are played. Lining the S Beach Rd to the S is a succession of University buildings, including a University Guest House and Postgraduate Hostel, the Lady Willingdon Teacher Training College and further S on the corner of Edward Elliot's Rd and S Beach Rd Queen Mary College. This women's college was founded in 1914.

Almost next door to the Lady Willingdon Teacher Training College is the unimpressive-looking **Vivekenanda House**, but despite its looks as S. Muthiah points out, it has an interesting history, for it was Madras's first "ice house", built for storing ice imported from abroad.

The first ice arrived in Calcutta from New England in 1833, and followed on the discovery by Frederic Tudor of Boston that ice would remain frozen if covered in sawdust. Tudor organised the cutting and storing of ice blocks during the New England winter and their transport around the world. The "ice house" in Madras was built in the early 1840s. The business survived for thirty years, until refrigeration was invented. The building then changed hands several times before becoming the home for a few months of Swami Vivekenanda in 1892. On the other side of the beach is the sculpture "the triumph of labour" the work of K.C.S. Pannicker. He was the successor to the architect Robert Fellowes Chisholm as Principal of the School of Industrial Art. When he retired in 1966 he founded the Cholamandal artists colony, which can be visited on the road S to Mamallapuram.

The Island and *Anna Salai* (*Mount Road*) Immediately to the S of Fort St. George is the Island, created between 1696 and 1705. First the grounds for a Governor's residence, it later became a military camp, and it has retained its military ownership ever since. In the SW corner is the Gymkhana Club, and a range of sporting facilities including a golf course. Beyond the Willingdon Bridge is the bronze statue of the former governor Sir Thomas Munro, cast in 1839. Shown on horseback, it has the curious feature that he is shown riding without stirrups.

Near the Round Tana is the Banqueting Hall of the old Government House, now known as **Rajaji Hall**. Set back from Anna Salai where it crosses the River Cooum, it was built at the instruction of Robert Clive's son Edward to mark the British victory over Tipu Sultan. It is in a very attractive setting and was used as a banqueting hall. Designed by Danish astronomer, Goldingham, who had been working with the E India Company since 1786, it was completed in 1802, though subsequently it was altered in the mid 19th century. It is in the Greek temple style with impressive columns and stairway. The surrounding compound is often used for trade fairs and exhibitions.

Parthasarathi Temple (3 km) on Triplicane High Rd and the tank which gives its name to the locality is the oldest temple structure in Madras. Built in the 8th century by Pallava kings, it was renovated in the 16th by Vijayanagara rulers. Dedicated to Krishna as the royal charioteer, it shows five of Vishnu's ten incarnations and is the only one dedicated to Parthasarathi whose legend is told in Tamil and Telugu inscriptions on the outer wall. Open 0600-1200, 1600-2200.

Wallajah Mosque (3.5 km) On Triplicane Rd, the 'Big Mosque' was built in 1795 by the Nawab of the Carnatic and is large enough to house thousands. The two slender minarets with golden domes on either side and a wide set of steps across the front.

Chintadripet, Egmore and the western inner suburbs Almost enclosed by a loop on the S side of the Cooum River, just to the S of the Central Railway station, **Chintadripet** is one of Madras's earliest suburbs. Today it is a densely packed collection of single and double storey houses, enclosing courtyards. Founded in 1734, it was set up as a weavers' settlement when the E India Company was finding it difficult to get enough good cloth to meet the demand in England. The Tamil words *chinna tari pettai* mean "village of small looms", and by 1737 230 weaving families were settled in the suburb. The area remains a centre of small scale industry. A Jain shrine was built in 1985.

Egmore A bridge across the Cooum at Egmore – the Egmore Bridge – was opened in 1700. In the last quarter of the 18th century the area to the S of the Poonamallee High Rd between the bends of the Cooum became a popular new residential area. Pantheon Rd, laid out in the late 1780s, became the centre of Madras's social and cultural life for 200 years. Now focussing on the metre gauge railway station that connects Madras with stations to the S, **Egmore** was first developed in 1715 with the construction of a "garden house" for Richard Horden. In the hundred years after 1720 all the major roads of contemporary Egmore – *Casa Major Rd*, *Marshall's Rd*, *Hall's Rd* and *Montieth Rd* – were laid out, taking their names from senior army officers.

The most important still keeps the name *Pantheon Rd*, although the "pantheon" – or public assembly rooms – to which the name refers, standing on the site of the present museum and Connemara Library, was almost completely replaced in the late 1880s. The museum site contains some striking late 19th century buildings. The **Connemara Library** was opened in 1896 and is one of India's National Libraries, though the origins of the library in Madras go back to 1662, "when a bale of calico from Madras was exchanged for books in London".

At the southwest corner of the site stands Irwin's Indo-Saracenic Victoria Memorial Hall, now the **Art Gallery**, which Tillotson describes as one of "the proudest expressions of the Indo-Saracenic movement".

Also on the site are the **Museum** itself, housing one of the world's finest collections of S Indian bronzes (**see page 711**). Egmore has a number of other reminders of the Indo Saracenic period of the 19th and early 20th centuries, the station itself, built in the 1930s, being one of the last.

Across the railway line to the N E of the station is the splendid *St. Andrew's Church*, still standing in a spacious compound. You can get an excellent view from the footbridge over the railway line just E of the station. Consecrated in 1821, the church still has a highly active congregation. The building was another of the Indian churches modelled on St Martin-in-the-Fields in London, working designs of which had been published at the end of the 18th century and which were available to the British engineers who were given the job of building churches for the British community in India in the early 19th century. However, apart from the façade the church is essentially circular, 25 m in diameter, and has a magnificent shallow-domed ceiling. The spire is 51 m high, and there used to be a set of bells, the biggest ever cast in Madras.

Thousand Lights* and *Nungambakkam In the 18th and 19th centuries the region which now lies on either side of Anna Salai from the Island to the southern end of TTK Rd (Mowbray's Rd) was known as the Great Choultry Plain. It became the focus for high class residential European settlement. The first large house in the area was built in 1758, just N of the Thousand Lights Mosque. When the threat to the security of Madras posed by Haidar Ali and his son Tipu Sultan was removed at the end of the 18th century British administrators and merchants began to move in ever larger numbers, and many built splendid houses. **Arthur Wellesley**, the future Duke of Wellington, was one, building his house on the E side of what is now the Nungambakkam High Rd, just N of the *Anna* flyover.

Immediately to the S of Anna Salai is the Church of S India **Cathedral**, built originally as the Anglican cathedral in 1816. Now concealed from Anna Salai by offices and other modern buildings in the compound, the church is well worth visiting. The Cathedral spire is over 40 m high.

Nungambakkam today is a prestigious residential area. College Rd, with Madras Christian College, a very highly regarded school, and the Director of Public Instruction's offices are next door to Doveton House (one of Madras's few remaining "garden houses" and the *Meteorological Centre*.

Equipped now with high technology forecasting equipment, particularly important in this cyclone prone region, the grounds of the meteorological centres have two commemorative pillars marking the first ever base line for *surveying in India*. Here too are India's earliest bench marks. The inscription, in Tamil, Telugu, Urdu and Latin as well as English, reads "the Geoditic position (Lat 13°4'3" 0.5N Long 80°14'54".20E) of Col William Lambton is primary original of the Survey of India. Fixed by him in 1802, was at a point 6 feet to the S and 1 foot to the W of the centre of this pillar. 2. The centre of the meridian circle of the Madras Observatory was at a point 12 feet to the E of the centre of this pillar." From that minutely precise beginning spread the extraordinary undertaking of surveying S Asia from the southern tip of Kanniyakumari to the heights of Mount Everest, named after the surveyor *George Everest* who completed the first survey.

The Thousand Lights Mosque with its cream washed façade is a landmark on the corner of Anna Salai and Peters Rd. The old mosque was built by the Wallajah family in the early 17th century but had to be replaced by the new 5 domed mosque, as it was unsafe. The name recalls the 1,000 oil lamps that used to be lit in the old mosque.

Valluvar Kottam (4 km) is near the junction of Nungambakkam Tank Rd and Kodambakkam High Rd and was built in 1976 as a memorial to a Tamil poet and philosopher Thiruvalluvar. He wrote the great Tamil classic Thirukkural in 1,330 verses which is inscribed on 133 granite slabs mounted on 67 pillars. It has a vast auditorium with a capacity of 4,000 and is one of Madras's important cultural centres. A special feature is the 2,700 tonne 35 m granite replica of the temple chariot of Tiruvarur which carries a statue of the poet. Its pale pink dome which is reflected in the two large pools in the terrace garden can be seen from a long distance. Open 0900-1900.

SOUTH

The **Basilica of San Thome** (6 km) at the S end of Marina Beach, surrounded now by the massive tenement re-housing scheme of a fishermen's colony. The church is claimed as one of very few churches to be built over an apostle's tomb. St. Thomas Didymus (Doubting Thomas) is believed to have come to India in AD 52. According to one legend, having landed on the W coast, he travelled across the peninsula, arriving in *Mylapore* ("town of peacocks") where he lived and preached. To escape persecution he took shelter in Little Mount (see below). An alternative story recalls how he was invited to visit the King Gondophernes in Taxila, where he converted the king and his court before moving to S India.

A few hundred m to the E is the *Kapaleeswarar Temple* (4 km) off Kutchery Rd. It is a 16th century Siva temple with a 40 m *gopuram*, built after the original was destroyed by the Portuguese in 1566 on an older site which may date back to the 7th. It is very sacred to Tamil Shaivites so non-Hindus are only allowed in outer courtyard where there are several bronze statues. There is also a shrine to a saint with a sculpture of the miracle of bringing back a dead girl to life. Open 0600-1200, 1600-2200.

From the temple in the heart of Mylapore you can go W to Mowbray's Rd to the *Luz Church*, probably the oldest church in Madras. It was built by the Portuguese in 1516, according to the inscription, in honour of Our Lady of Light. The actual date is probably between 1547 and 1582. The Tamil name for the church, *Kattu Kovil*, means "jungle temple", and a story suggests that Portuguese sailors were rescued from a storm by following a light. They traced it on shore, where it disappeared, and on the spot they built the church. The neighbourhood has become a busy shopping centre. From the church you can continue W, then S to the **Madras Club**. This is housed in a late 18th century house owned then by George Mowbray, and is surrounded by very attractive gardens. Admission is no longer restricted to European men, but you still need to be invited by a member.

Cross the **Adyar River** by the Elphinstone Bridge, built to provide work during the catastrophic famine in S India in 1876-78. The river itself has a sailing club, but capsizing is not recommended. A survey of pollution in the Adyar River has suggested that it is 98% effluent, and all three waterways of Madras – the Adyar, the Cooum and the Buckingham Canal remain appallingly heavily polluted.

On the S banks of the river is the **Theosophical Society** (8 km), which has its world headquarters in 120 ha gardens. These contain several shrines of different faiths and a Serene Garden of Remembrance for the founders, Madam Blavatsky and Colonel Olcott who founded the society in New York in 1875 and moved its headquarters to Madras in 1882. The 400 year old magnificent banyan tree is of particular interest in the garden which also has specimens of exotic shrubs and trees and which is the home of several species of birds and wildlife. There are several buildings on the estate including the Olcott Memorial School, the press, a child welfare centre, a museum, the Adyar Library and Research Centre and a Hall of Meditation. Scouts and Guides may use the camping ground but the accommodation at the Leadbeater Chambers and Indian style *Bhojansala* is restricted to visiting members.

Due W of the Theosophical Society is the old **Government House,** built in 1817 in the style of a Raj bungalow. It is now Raj Bhawan, the Governor's house. It has superb grounds, now a national park.

Little Mount, on the S bank of the Adyar where St. Thomas is believed to have spent some time. You will see two churches, the older, with its small vaulted chapel having been built by the Portuguese in 1551. The modern circular church was built in 1971. To the SW of the city is **Great Mount** where the apostle is believed to have been martyred and bled to death in AD 52. Some believe he was accidentally killed by a hunter's arrow. On top of the 90 m high 'mount' is the **Church of Our Lady of Expectation**, where the altar marks the spot where Thomas fell and the cross one of which he had himself carved. The Madonna and Child over the altar is said to be one painted by St. Luke. It is believed that the original church was built by Armenians in AD 530 but was replaced by the Portuguese in 1523. The latter forms the core of the present church which was subsequently extended.

The **Armenian Christians** who came from Persia are believed to have found St. Thomas's grave and built a tomb and a church over it. The village was called San Thome. One school of thought says that the original burial site and the church have disappeared under the sea. Marco Polo in his travels recorded the chapel and a monastery on a hill to the N where the apostle was put to death. In 1523, when the Portuguese started to rebuild the church they discovered the tomb containing the relics consisting of a few bones, a lance head and an earthen pot containing bloodstained earth. The church was replaced by the neo-Gothic structure which has two spires and was granted the status of a basilica in 1956. The relics are kept in the sacristy and can be seen on request. There are 13th century wall plaques, a modern stained glass window, a 450 year old Madonna brought from Portugal and a 16th century stone sundial.

The **Snake Park** at Guindy is in the grounds of the Guindy national park, the Raj Bhavan Estate. Quite a wide collection of snakes and other reptiles but not worth visiting if you have been to a good one in Africa. The cages are poorly lit and some wrongly labelled. There is an hourly display from 1000 near the entrance, to inaudible taped recording in English, Tamil and Hindi. Brave visitors may be allowed to handle one! Government has banned 'milking'. Open 0830-1730. Small fee. Trains from Egmore or Beach rly station or buses from town centre. Also has deer park (see under Parks and Gardens below).

NB Snake skins are sold by hawkers but Indian Government does not allow it and most countries have banned import of articles.

Local industries In the 45 years since Independence industrial activity in Madras has expanded and diversified rapidly. From its strength in cotton textiles and a long established leather industry Madras and its suburbs have become the centres of heavy and light

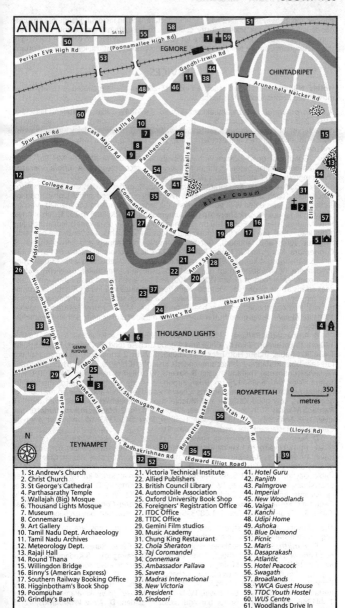

ANNA SALAI SA 151

1. St Andrew's Church
2. Christ Church
3. St George's Cathedral
4. Parthasarathy Temple
5. Wallajah (Big) Mosque
6. Thousand Lights Mosque
7. Museum
8. Connemara Library
9. Art Gallery
10. Tamil Nadu Dept. Archaeology
11. Tamil Nadu Archives
12. Meteorology Dept.
13. Rajaji Hall
14. Round Thana
15. Willingdon Bridge
16. Binny's (American Express)
17. Southern Railway Booking Office
18. Higginbotham's Book Shop
19. Poompuhar
20. Grindlay's Bank

21. Victoria Technical Institute
22. Allied Publishers
23. British Council Library
24. Automobile Association
25. Oxford University Book Shop
26. Foreigners' Registration Office
27. ITDC Office
28. TTDC Office
29. Gemini Film studios
30. Music Academy
31. Chung King Restaurant
32. Chola Sheraton
33. Taj Coromandel
34. Connemara
35. Ambassador Pallava
36. Savera
37. Madras International
38. New Victoria
39. President
40. Sindoori

41. Hotel Guru
42. Ranjith
43. Palmgrove
44. Imperial
45. New Woodlands
46. Vaigai
47. Kanchi
48. Udipi Home
49. Ashoka
50. Blue Diamond
51. Picnic
52. Maris
53. Dasaprakash
54. Atlantic
55. Hotel Peacock
56. Swagath
57. Broadlands
58. YWCA Guest House
59. TTDC Youth Hostel
60. WUS Centre
61. Woodlands Drive In

engineering, railway equipment and car manufacture, and an increasing range of consumer goods industries. Small scale industry continues to be extremely important. In the 19th Century Madras became a major centre for cotton textile manufacture with the opening of the Buckingham Carnatic Mills in 1885. They are now closed, but textiles remain important.

SERVICES

Hotels NB All A class hotels collect an extra 15-20% of the rate quoted as Luxury Tax. In most hotels *Permit Room* refers to the bar.

A *Taj Coromandel*, 17 Nungambakkam High Rd. T 474849, Cable: Hotelorient, Telex: 041 7194. 240 rm. 12 km airport, 8 km rly. Possibly the best modern luxury hotel. Slightly characterless but excellent restaurants, *Golden Dragon* (Chinese-speciality jumbo prawns), *Mysore* (business lunches and excellent Indian food, evening Bharat Natyam dance recitals) and the 24 hour coffee shop *Pavilion* which also serves snacks and has a dance floor with live music. Good pool, good location with new high quality shops nearby. The MH Taxi, Travel and Transport Service, based in the hotel's arcade, is recommended. **A** *Chola Sheraton* (Welcomgroup), 10 Cathedral Rd. T 473347, Cable: Hotel Chola, Telex: 041 7200. 135 rm. 13 km airport, 6 km rly. Restaurants: *Sagari* (Chinese), buffet lunches and has a roof-top dance floor (open until 0100); *Yali* serving (Indian and continental); *Mercara* (24 hr coffee shop). **A** *Park Sheraton* (Welcomgroup), 132 T.T.K. Rd. T 452525, Cable: Adyar Hotel Madras, Telex: 041 6868. 140 rm. 13 km airport, *Dakshin* restaurant (S Indian including 'Chettinad' style), live lunch time music and discos on Sat nights, *Khyber* by the pool side, barbecue (grills and tandoori), *Gatsby* live music for dancing and serves snacks. **A** *Connemara*, Binny's Rd (Off Mount Rd). T 860123, Cable: Connemara, Telex: 041 8197. 138 rm. 15 km airport, 4 km rly. 1989-90 major renovation and rebuilding without destroying atmosphere. Retains splendid art deco features. Extremely comfortable, excellent location, good continental food at *Kolam* (1100-2400) and has a very good pastry shop which also does salads at the *Cookie Jar*. Outdoor *Rain Tree* specializes in S Indian 'Chettinad' cuisine (evenings only) with S Indian music and dance in a garden setting. One of the best pools in the city. First class bookshop. Very heavily booked Dec-Mar. **A** *Hotel Residency*, opened 1991. *Restaurant* serves good buffet lunches, live music at dinner time, *Salt and Pepper* (24 hr coffee shop).

B *Ambassador Pallava*, 53 Montieth Rd. T 868584, Cable: Palambas, Telex: 041 7453. 120 rm. 15 km airport, 2 km rly. *Chop Sticks*, good Chinese food. **B** *Trident*, 1/24 G.S.T. Rd. T 434747, Cable: Trident Hot, Telex: 041 26055. 172 rm. 2 km airport, 15 km rly. Half day rates available. Restaurants (all recommended): *Shanghai* (Chinese), *Tanjore* (Hyderabadi) and *Maratha* (continental, Thai and snacks). **B** *Savera*, 69 Dr. Radhakrishnan Rd. T 474700, Cable: Savera, Telex: 041 6896. 125 rm. 9 km airport, 2 km rly. Central a/c. Recommended for location, pool and excellent restaurants: *Chakra* has a dance floor and *Minar* on the roof top, good views, very good Kashmiri and Mughlai food accompanied by music from the N. **B** *Ramada Madras*, St Thomas Mount (near airport). 174 rm. **C** *Madras International* (Indian style), 693 Anna Salai. T 861811, Cable: Hotliner, Telex: 041 7373. 14 km airport, 4 km rly. Central a/c. Restaurant, bar, exchange, travel, TV.

D *New Victoria*, 3 Kennet La, Egmore. T 8253638, Cable: Hotel Vicky, Telex: 041 7897. 50 a/c rm. 15 km airport, 1 km rly. Restaurant (dimly lit but meals good value), bar, exchange, travel, TV. Best in its class with excellent location, 200 m from Egmore Station. Quiet in spite of busy area, clean with good service. **D** *President*, 16 Dr. Radhakrishnan Rd. T 832211, Cable: Gaytime, Telex: 041 6699. 144 rm some a/c. 12 km airport, 4 km rly. Restaurant, bar, pool, shops, exchange, travel, TV. Seaview. Poor value for money. **D** *Sindoori*, 24 Greames La, Greames Rd. T 477197, Cable: Sindotel, Telex: 041 8859. 79 rm. 20 km airport, 7 km rly. Central a/c. Restaurant, shops, car hire, TV. **D** *Shrilekha Inter-Continental*, 564 Anna Salai. T 453132, Cable: Lekha,Telex: 041 6873. Some a/c rm. Restaurant, bar, exchange, TV.

The following are Indian style hotels which have basic furnishings, are uncarpeted with vegetarian restaurants only unless otherwise mentioned.

D *Ranjith*, 9 Nungambakkam High Rd. T 470521, Cable: Ranjitotel. Restaurant (also good non-veg continental), shops, travel, exchange. **D** *Palmgrove*, 5 Kodambakkam High Rd. T 471881, Cable: Hotel Palm, Telex: 041 7115. 89 rm some a/c (some cottages). 11 km airport, 5 km rly. Restaurant (veg), bar, exchange, travel,TV. **D** *Imperial*, 14 Whannels Rd, Egmore. T 566176, Cable: Majestic. 68 rm some a/c, best at rear. 15 km airport, 1 km rly. Restaurant (also non-veg), bar, travel, TV. **D** *Transit House*, 26 Venkataraman St, T Nagar. T 441346. Some a/c rm. Snack bar and pleasant garden. **D** *New Woodlands*, 72/75 Radhakrishnan Rd. T 473111, Telex: 041 6914. Some a/c rm. Good restaurant

(Indian/continental veg) excellent for S Indian food, exchange, small but pleasant pool. Good value. **D** *Peacock*, 1089 Poonamallee High Rd. T 39081, Cable: Gopikas, Telex: 041 8169. 73 rm some a/c, quieter at rear. 20 km airport, 1 km rly. Restaurant, exchange, travel, TV.

Some hotels in the same category are significantly cheaper and when on the main rd have a problem with noise except at rear of the building.

    D *Vaigai*, 3 Gandhi Irwin Rd, Egmore. T 567373, Cable: Hotelvygai. 50 rm some a/c. 14 km airport, 1 km rly. Restaurant, exchange, travel. **D** *Shrilekha*, 49 Anna Salai. T 840081, Cable:Your Choice. 77 rm some a/c. 16 km airport, 3 km rly. Restaurant (vegetarian), bar, exchange, travel. **D** *Kanchi*, 28 Commander-in-Chief Rd. T 471100, Cable: Hotel Kanchi. 75 rm some a/c. 12 km airport, 2 km rly. Roof top restaurant (Indian vegetarian), bar, exchange, travel, TV. Good value and modern. **D** *Peninsula*, 26 G.N. Rd, T Nagar. T 8252700. 144 rm some a/c. 12 km airport, 4 km rly. Restaurant (Indian vegetarian), bar, exchange, travel, TV. **D** *Udipi Home*, 1 Halls Rd, Egmore. T 567191, Cable: Udipi Home. Some a/c rm. Restaurant (vegetarian). **D** *Madras Hotel Ashoka*, 33 Pantheon Rd, Egmore. T 568977, Cable: Hotelashok, Telex: 041 7510. 113 rm some a/c. 18 km airport, 1 km rly. Restaurant (Indian/ continental vegetarian), bar, travel, exchange. **D** *Blue Diamond*, 934 Poonammallee High Rd. T 665981/5, Cable: Jewelbox, Telex: 041 6406. 33 rm some a/c, quieter at rear. 20 km airport, 2 km rly. Restaurant (Indian, continental, Chinese), exchange, travel, no credit cards. **D** *Picnic*, 1132 Poonammallee High Rd (near Madras Central). T 589715, Cable: Picnic. Restaurant (vegetarian), bar, exchange, travel.

    D *Maris*, 9 Cathedral Rd. T 470541, Cable: Hotelmaris, Telex: 041 3680. 70 rm some a/c. 13 km airport, 5 km rly. Restaurant, bar, travel, exchange, TV. **D** *Dasaprakash*, 100 Poonammallee High Rd. T 661111, Cable: Dasprakash, Telex: 041 7837. 100 rm some a/c. 19 km airport, 2 km rly. Restaurant (Indian/ continental vegetarian), bar, exchange, no credit cards, travel. Good grounds and public area but in need of refurbishing. **D** *Atlantic*, 2 Montieth Rd, Egmore. T 860461, Cable: Rose Garden. 60 rm some a/c. 16 km airport, 3 km rly. Restaurant (mixed cuisine, but not recommended), shops, exchange, travel,TV. A recent visitor advises against trying the attached New Tandoor Restaurant here – Rs 21 for fish and chips comprising 8 cold chips. Complaints brought the promise to improve "next time". **D** *Harrisons Hotel*, 154/5 Village Rd. T 475271, Cable: Queenhotel. Some a/c rm. Restaurant (S Indian / Chinese), bar. **D** *Swagath*, 243 Royapettah High Rd. T 868466, Cable: Subaswagat. 110 rm some a/c. 15 km airport, 5 km rly. Restaurant, exchange, travel.

Youth hostels and very simple hotels. The most popular perhaps is **E** *Broadlands*, 16 Vallabha Agraharam St. T 845573. Within walking distance of the Tourist Office. Set around lovely shady courtyards, it is clean with good service and is reasonably quiet (avoid ground floor). Few rm with baths. Very friendly and helpful management. **E** *Tourist Hostel*, Andhra Mahila Sabha, 3B Adyar Bridge Rd. T 416001. Some a/c rm. Vegetarian restaurant. Good guest houses in this category at **F** *YWCA Guest House*, 1086 Poonamallee High Rd. T 39920. Restaurant, for men and women. Small membership fee and includes breakfast but is popular so book early. Very good value if you can get in. Also *camping ground*. Reservations: Secretary. *Laharry Transit Hostel*, is for women under 30 only. *YMCA*, 14 Westcott Rd, Royapettah, T 811158 and at 17 Ritherdon Rd, Vepery. T 32831 where there are d rm with bath. Nearby *Salvation Army's Red Shield Guest House* has clean d rm with bath and dormitory (for men) at 15 Ritherdon Rd, Vepery. T 38148. Contact Warden. Other dormitory beds are at *Youth Hostel*, Indira Nagar.T 412882. Reservations: Warden. TTDC *Youth Hostel*, EVR Rd, Park (near Central Rly Station). T 30332. Reasonably quiet. Also at **F** *World University Service Centre*, Spur Tank Rd. T 663991. Single, double and dormitory (some s rm with attached bath. International Students' cards needed. Reservations: Director. This is very good value, with a reasonable canteen and well located for Egmore and S central Madras. *Railway Retiring Rooms*. **E** Central Station, T 32218. Rm (some s and d a/c). Also **F** dormitory. **F** Egmore Station, T 848533.

    The Automobile Association of S India has guest house for members. **F** *'Choultries'* or rest houses and *'Dharamsalas'* are in the **F** category but may be restricted to certain religious groups or low earners.

Restaurants The greatest choice is in S Indian vegetarian food. Those serving non-vegetarian dishes are often the more expensive and in the top hotels. Most are open from 1200-1500 and 1900-2400.

    Spencer's *Fiesta*, T 810051 Extn 893 (0800-2400) serves Continental and Chinese food and has a dance floor with recorded music plus a fast food counter. Recommended. Some places are open almost throughout the day. The less expensive *Mayur* at Hotel Ganpat is one (0600-2200) and at Madras International *Shangrila* opens at 1000. *Blue Diamond* at 934 Poonamallee High Rd is good for breakfasts from 0700 and is open till 2400. *Buhari's* at 83

Anna Salai has a terrace and a/c dining room (0700-0130) with unusual decor, good food even if rather dark. Try their crab curry, also good egg rotis and other Muslim dishes. Opp it for S Indian 'Udipi' veg food is Woodland's *Mathura*, Tarapore Towers, 2nd Floor, Anna Salai, T 831777, (1000-2300) which lacks style but makes up with good variety of food. *Dasprakash*, 100 Poonamallee High Rd, T 661111 (0900-2400) and *Woodlands Drive-In Restaurant*, 30 Cathedral Rd, T 471981 (0600-2100) are recommended for veg food, the former also has a very good salad bar. The a/c restaurants *Eskimo* in Building, 827 Anna Salai, T 82784 (0900-2200) has a varied menu while *Pals* at 42 Anna Salai, T 849814 (1330-2400) has N Indian and continental dishes. Hotel Atlantic's *New Tandoor* is best avoided for quality of food and service.

Chinese Particularly good at *Golden Dragon* (Taj Coromandel), *Shangahai* (Trident), also *Chopsticks* (Ambassador Pallava) and *Sagari* (Chola Sheraton). *Chunking*, 67 Anna Salai (opp Anna Rd Post Office), T 86134 (1030-2200) where lack of atmosphere (after dark the lighting is very dim) is compensated by good food. Also *China Town*, 74 Cathedral Rd, T 476221 (a/c) and *Dynasty* at Harrison's Hotel, recommended. The last 3 are less expensive and very popular. **Thai** *Cascade*, Kakani Towers, 15 Khaderi Nawaz Khan Rd, T 471412. Open for lunch and dinner and also offers Chinese, Japanese and Malay cuisine.

Fast food places are *Cakes 'n' Bakes*, 22 Nungambakkam High Rd, T 447075 (0930-2200), *Chit Chat*, 557 Anna Salai, T 451880 (1000-1400), *Maratha* (Trident) and *Snappy*, 74 Cathedral Rd, T 475770 (1100-2400), *Cake Walk* and *Hot Breads*. *Avin* is a milk bar on Anna Salai. You can get good Indian sweets and savoury snacks from *Nala's* on Cathedral Rd and *Naga's* in Village Rd.

Bars Although technically prohibition is in force in Tamil Nadu in practice it is possible to obtain alcoholic drinks without any difficulty. If you are going to buy alcohol elsewhere it is best to get an All India Liquor Permit from either an Indian mission or a Govt of India Tourist office abroad or in one of the regional capitals. A recent development has been the spread of "wine bars" and "wine shops" in many parts of the city. This should not be interpreted in the western sense! Such shops sell locally made spirits and beers. Foreign wines are not available at all, and although some wines are now made in India they are reputed to rasp the palate. The only exception is the sparkling white "Omar Khayyam", produced from French stock in Maharashtra, which has won international prizes and is now selling well in Europe.

Clubs There are local chapters and branches of Rotary, Round Table (T 474094), Lions, Jaycees (T 38069) and Freemasons in different parts of the city. They usually meet in hotels, eg Madras Central Lions, Hotel Connemara, 2nd and 4th Mon at 1930.
    Madras Gymkhana Club, Anna Salai. T 447863. Tennis, swimming, cricket, billiards, library, bar. Golf at Guindy Race Course. Temporary membership. *Cosmopolitan Club*, Anna Salai. T 849946. Tennis, billiards, golf, library, bar. Temporary membership for golf only. *Madras Boat Club*, Adyar. T 453190. Bar. Temporary membership. *Madras Club*, Chamiers Rd. T 450121. Tennis, swimming, billiards, mini golf, bar. Temporary membership when introduced by member. *Madras Cricket Club*, Chepauk. T 842886. Tennis, cricket, billiards, bar. Temporary membership for games only. *Madras United Club*, 3 Fraser Bridge Rd. T 562946. Temporary membership when introduced by member. *Madras Riders Club*, Race View, Race Course, Velachery Rd. T 431171. Riding (including lessons) throughout the year except June. *S India Philatelists Association.*, T 39645, 2nd Sun. *Yoga Brotherhood*, Express Estate, Anna Salai. *Public Relations Society of India*, T 473661, meets at Hotel Connemara.

Banks Most banks listed are open from 1000-1400 on weekdays and from 1000-1200 on Sat and deal in foreign exchange. They close on Sun, national holidays and June 30 and Dec 31. Several branches are near hotels. Most big hotels will cash Travellers' cheques and a few have 24 hr banks.
    Foreign Banks Bank of America, 748 Anna Salai, T 863586. **Citibank**, 768 Anna Salai, T 860856. **Grindlays**, 19 Rajaji Salai, T 589131 and 164 Anna Salai, T 844784. **Hong Kong and Shanghai**, 30 Rajaji Salai, T 512626. **Standard Chartered**, 58 NSC Bose Rd, T 581301. *Indian Banks* Andhra, 265 TTK Salai, T 451868. **Bank of India**, 46 Cathedral Rd, T 478091. **Central Bank of India**, 803 Mount Rd, T 566817. **Indian Overseas**, 762 Anna Salai, T 82041, 58 Pantheon Rd, T 867234, 32 Radhakrishnan Rd, Mylapore, T 843984, 109 Nungambakkam High Rd, T 473989 (0900-1300, Sat 0900-1100) and 15 Hunters Rd, T 31889 (0830-1230, Sat 0830-1030). **State Bank of India**, 103 Mount Rd, T 840393. **United Bank of India**, 217 RK Mutt Rd, T 71834. **Union Bank of India**, 39 Chalmiers Rd, T 452203 (0900-1300 and Sat 0900-1100) and at 35 Mount Rd, T 861846. **United Commercial**, 835 Anna Salai, T 844784.
    NB Some banks have extended hours Grindlays, 3A Padmanabha Nagar, Adyar, T

411092 (0830-1230, Sun 0830-1030, closed Mon) is nr the Tourist Hostel. **Indian Overseas**, 473 Poonammallee High Rd, T 666141 (0830-1530, Sat 0830-1230). **Indian**, Puraswalkam High Rd (nr Hotel Picnic), T 661413 (0830-1230, 1600-1800, Sat 0830-1030, 1600-1800).

Exchange facilities are available at the International Airport, T 431254 (0630-2400) and Meenambakkam Airport. You should get your Currency forms endorsed by the money changer. **Thomas Cook**, 112 Nungambakkam High Rd, T 473092. **Credit Cards American Express**, c/o Binny Ltd, 16 Armenian St, T 29361. **Diners Club**, Greenmore, 16 Haddows Rd, T 472748. **Mastercard**, International call in case of loss, 1-314 275 66990.

Shopping Shopping in Madras has been changing rapidly in the last 5 years. The best known landmark of old Madras's shopping, Moore Market, was destroyed in a fire in 1985 in suspicious circumstances and has made way for the new Railway Central Reservation Office and associated car parking. New shopping space is planned in the immediate vicinity but has not yet been opened. A similar fate has overtaken one of Madras's most famous shops, Spencer's, just round the corner from the Connemara Hotel. What is left after a fire has still been described as "one of the finest Victorian Gothic buildings in Madras", but it is unclear how long it will survive.

A range of new shopping centres has been developed both in the 2 central parts of the city (Parry's corner and Anna Salai) and in a number of suburbs. The commercial centre of gravity has been shifted rapidly southwestwards from the old commercial heart of the city, which in the British period grew up to the N of the Fort St George in the area known as George Town. In the 1970s the development of new 5 star hotels some 5 to 7 km S W along Anna Salai encouraged the transformation of that area. Although there are no large department stores there are many new specialised shops both on Anna Salai itself and in complexes around.

Most shops are open Mon to Sat 0900-2000 with a lunch break from 1300-1500 although some remain open through out the day. Weekly holidays may differ for shops in the same locality. You should ask for a receipt and check what you buy carefully because it may be difficult to return or exchange goods. There are often discount sales during the festival seasons of Pongal, Diwali and Christmas.

Silks, cottons and clothes Madras was founded because of the excellence and cheap prices of the local cotton. In this respect nothing has changed since Francis Day established the first small trading post for the East India Company in 1639. Furthermore some of India's best silk and silks come from Kanchipuram, 65 km away, and can readily be bought in the city. In 1990 ready made garments from Madras were poised to become a major element in India's exports. Today both Govt run and private retailers have excellent stocks of traditional Indian clothes, including some of the best silk and silk saris available in India, and some western fashioned clothes. The Govt's Co-optex all over Madras have a wide variety of handloom silks and cottons while their Khadi (handspun and handwoven cotton) stores specialise in the rather coarse but lightweight cotton.

It is now possible to buy good clothes at shopping centres in various parts of the city. However, three shops are still regarded as particularly good for silks in terms of quality and value. *Radha Silk Emporium*, 1 Sannathi St, Mylapore, is near the Sri Kapaleshwarar Temple, *Kumaran* and *Nalli Chinnasami Chetty* (opp Panagal Park), both in Theagaraya Nagar (universally known as T.Nagar). *Amrapali* in Fountain Plaza and Adyar and *Shilpi*, and *Urvashi* on Mowbrays Rd are good for cottons. *Handloom House* is in 7 Rattan Bazaar while *India Silk House* and a number of Government Emporia are along Anna Salai. They are at numbers 121 Andhra Pradesh, 700 Haryana, LIC Building, Karnataka, 42 Kashmir, 138 Kerala, 189 N Eastern Region, 818 Tamil Nadu, 834 W Bengal).

Jewellery Traditional S Indian jewellery in gold or with diamond and stone setting is best. Also available is the 'Madras Diamond' which is zircon jewellery and the larger than life artificial stone products used by dancers and stage performers. Some recommended shops for gold are *Thangamaligai*, T Nagar, *Bapalal & Co.*, 24/1 Cathedral Rd and *Fashion 'n Gems*, 9 Nungambakkam High Rd while *Vummidi Bangaru Kanna*, Anna Flyover and *Taj Gems* in Hotel Taj Coromandel and *Gem Palace* in Hotel Adyar Park are good for stone set jewellery.

Crafts For many years it has been possible to obtain excellent S Indian handicrafts (wood carving, inlaid work, ivory, sandalwood) at very reasonable (fixed) prices from the *Victoria Technical Institute*. This Govt-backed shop is Anna Salai close to the Spencer's complex and the Connemara Hotel. Another Govt managed craft store is *Poompuhar* also on the same street, which specialises in first class bronzes. Other recommended shops are the excellent *Cane & Bamboo*, 26 Commander-in-Chief Rd, *Firdusi*, Fountain Plaza (miniatures paintings), *Jamal's Corner Shop*, 44 Devraja Mudali St (antiques,bric-a-brac), *Cottage Industries Exposition* opposite Taj Coromandel Hotel and *Contemporary Arts and Crafts* off

Cathedral Rd. The *Kalakshetra* at Thiruvanmiyur excels in kalamkari and traditional weaving and their range includes good household linen.

Department Stores such as *Mini Cauvery*, 21 Madloy Rd, *Supermarket*, 112 Davidson St and TNHB Building, Annanagar (closed Fri), *Harringtons*, 99 Harrington Rd, Chetput and *Five Stars*, 60 Pantheon Rd, Egmore have made shopping easier for the city dweller. However, although they open by 0900 some close from 1330-1600 to stay open until 2000.

Bookshops Books are often extremely good value in India. Western books in English are widely available, often at much lower prices than in Europe or the United States. *Higginbothams*, 814 Anna Salai and F 39 Anna Nagar E, near Chintamani Market was the city's main bookshop for many years and inn 1989 underwent major reorganisation. There is now a range of good bookshops. The most recently opened is *Landmark* in Apex Plaza, 3 Nungambakkam High Rd. This is in one of the shopping complexes which are now scattered through the city. Many publishing houses also have bookselling departments. The *Oxford Book House* in the grounds of the Cathedral (Anna Salai) and *Allied Publishers* (off Anna Salai) have extensive collections. The big hotels have branches of *Danai Bookshops* which are open through out the day sometimes 0830-2300. Most others are open from 0900-1900.

Camera and Film *GK Vale*, 107 Anna Salai, T 849613. (0900-1230, 1430-1830).

Local transport The city has inexpensive and convenient bus service. Walking, however, within the crowded areas is unavoidable especially in Broadway, George Town and Anna Salai for shopping. Yellow top *Taxis* are available at stands near the top-class hotels. There are some 'stands' elsewhere, but taxis are not as widely used as in some major Indian cities. If you want a taxi from a hotel ask the bell-boy to call it as that is the only way you stand a chance of using the meter (check it is cleared and insist on seeing a chart before paying any supplementary charge). Some absolutely refuse to go a short distance or to go a long distance after 2000! Others may demand a 20% surcharge between 2200-0500. Drivers often refuse to use meters, and their first asking price will often be up to 4 or 5 times the metered fare.

Buses Pallavan Transport Corporation (PTC), Anna Salai, T 566063, runs an excellent network of buses from 0500-2300 and a skeleton service through the night (timetables from major bookshops) and you can get a month's bus pass at a bus depot. Avoid the rush hr (0800-1000, 1700-1900) when buses are very crowded, and make sure you know route numbers as most bus signs are in Tamil. 'M' Service on mini-buses are good for the route between Central and Egmore stations and journeys to the suburban rly stations. The 'V' service operates fast buses with fewer stops and have a yellow board with the route number and LSS (Limited Stop Service). PTC has a half-hourly luxury mini-bus service between Egmore Station, Indian Airlines Marshalls Rd office and Meenambakkam Airport picking up passengers from certain hotels (inform time keeper at Egmore in advance, T 561284. The fare is about Rs.20.

Suburban Rly Fast and inexpensive but crowded at peak times. Stops between Beach Rly Station and Tambaram (5 min in rush hr) are Fort, Park, Egmore, Chetpet, Nungambakkam, Kodambakkam, Mambalam, Saidapet, Guindy, St.Thomas Mount. Also serves suburbs of Perambur and Villivakkam. Convenient stop at Tirusoolam for Meenambakkam Airport, Domestic Terminal. The *Metro* is being built but will take some time to complete.

Auto Rickshaws Three-wheeler scooter taxis take 2 adults and a child, extra passengers negotiable. Usual extra night charge of 25% between 2200-0500. Negotiations can be difficult at any time but particularly out of normal hours. *Cycle Rickshaws* Often no cheaper than autorickshaws. Fix the fare first.

Car hire Chauffeur driven a/c or ordinary cars are good value and convenient for sightseeing, especially for short journeys out of the city, when shared between 3 and 5 people, otherwise costly. Ashok Travels, ITDC, Transport Unit, 29 Victoria Crescent Rd, Commander-in-Chief Rd,T 478884. Bajaji Tourist, 270 Anna Salai, T 453628. Balakrishna Tourist Taxi, 882 Poonamallee High Rd, Egmore. T 663340. Ganesh Travels, 36 Police Commissioner's Office Rd, T 561941. Travel Wings, 98 Alagappa Rd, T 666344. TS Narayanan, 1/35 Luz Church Rd, Mylapore. T 72883. TTDC, 143 Anna Salai, T 849803, Time Central, T 583351. Wheels, 499 Pantheon Rd, T 568327.

Entertainment *Cinemas* which show foreign (usually English language) films are mostly in the centre of town on Anna Salai. They are a/c and quite comfortable and you may appreciate a break on a hot day! English language newspapers carry details of all entertainments in the city. Best to book in advance. *Abhirami*, T 663377. *Alankar*, T 849666. *Blue Diamond*, T 478766. *Casino*, T 567430. *Devi Paradise*, T 840747. *Pilot*, T 868934. *Safire*, T 478766. *Santham*, T 867813.

Music and Dance – The *Madras Music Academy* auditoria is the scene of numerous performances of Indian music, dance and theatre, not only during the prestigious 3 week Music Festival in from mid-Dec but right through the year. The *sabhas* are membership societies that offer cultural programmes four times a month to its members, but occasionally tickets are available at the door. There are several other auditoria – *Raja Annamalai Hall, Mylapore Fine Arts Club, Narada, Brahma and Krishna Gana Sabhas* and the little *Sittraragam*.

Sports Facilities in clubs (addresses in Clubs section above) are for members only. You can either go as a guest or take out temporary membership on being recommended by a permanent member. Your country's Foreign Representation may be able to help. Some hotels allow facilities such as pools and courts to be used on payment of a fee.

Swimming The larger hotels have pools which you may be able to use by paying a fee. Taj Coromandel, Chola Sheraton, Park Sheraton, Trident, Connemara, Adyar Park, Ambassador Pallava, Savera, New Woodlands, President. Madras Club, Gymkhana Club and the Indian Institute of Technology at Guindy have pools. Others open to the public are at Marina Beach and the YMCA pool at Saidapet. Sea bathing is safe at Elliot's Beach, though this has now become completely surrounded by the suburban development of Besant Nagar and is not nearly as attractive as it was up to the late 1970s.

Tennis Clubs allowing members' guest and temporary members to use courts are Madras Club, Gymkhana Club, Cricket Club, Cosmopolitan Club, Presidency Club and Lady Willingdon Club. YMCA at Saidapet also has courts.

Boating Marina Boat Club near Anna statue on Beach Rd has rowing boats, pedal boats and motor boats for hire. Muttukadu Boat House, Injambakkam has facilities for windsurfing and also has boats for hire. Yachting is possible at Ennore. Contact Captain, Royal Madras Yacht Club. The Taj Group's Fisherman's Cove Hotel in Covelong has windsurfing, yachting and sailing.

Fishing Madras offers ample opportunity for good fishing especially in Chetpet Lake, YWCA International Guest House grounds, backwaters of Ennore and Covelong but it is not possible to hire equipment.

Museums The Government Museum and Art Gallery, Pantheon Rd. Open 0900-1700. Closed Fri. Entry Free. (The Pantheon had been a "place of public entertainment and balls" in the late 18th century. The museum is a circular red-brick rotunda surrounded by an Italianate pillared arcade. Started in 1851 as Museum of Practical Geology and Natural History it comprises three separate buildings: Archaeology, Art, Bronzes. You will need to spend some time in the museum to do it full justice but look for the excellent collection of bronzes and the interesting exhibits of Stone and Iron Age hunting and cooking implements which have been excavated locally. There is also an excellent numismatic collection and sections on botany (500 year old teak and engineering designs inspired by plants), zoology (18.5 m whale skeleton) and arms and armoury. The section on anthropology has the Meriah Sacrifice Post which carries the story of being used for tying human victims whose flesh would be sliced off by 'Khond' farmers who buried it in their fields as offering to the gods. There is a separate children's gallery with a model railway.

Archaeology This features early stone sculptures from the Deccan and the beginnings of Buddhist artistic traditions. Fragments from Jaggayyapeta (in Andhra Pradesh, between Vijayawada and Hyderabad), including the depiction of a royal figure (10). There is a long frieze of Vessantara Jataka from Goli. Both are dated from the 2nd and 3rd centuries and are carved in limestone. Amaravati is represented by a large number of damaged limestone panels, posts and railings from dismantled stupa. Several figures date from 2nd century BC. Include a representation of a multi-storey tree shrine with flying celestials(IB.11). Remainder mainly 2nd and 3rd centuries. Episodes in life of Buddha – Master subduing elephant (IIIA.15) and the bowl of the Buddha uplifted by devotees (IIIA.6). Jataka stories also illustrated. Elaborate lotus medallions and garlands, and picture of the stupa itself. Also some rare free-standing Buddha figures, wearing finely fluted robes.

There are numerous Hindu images from later periods of southern India. 10th century sculptures from Kodambalur – Siva and the Goddess "fine examples of the early Chola style. Contemporary sculptures part of panel from Hemavati (104.38) also Siva and Parvati together in elliptical frame from Penukonda. Hoysala style represented by an ornate doorway. Sage leaning on staff (Tadpatri) and figure of Durga standing on buffalo are Vijayanagar period.

Bronzes The largest collection in country including some of finest Chola examples exhibited in Art Gallery, excellently displayed so as to show the iconography of the principal deities, Siva and Vishnu. 11th century Nataraja from Tiruvengadu; seated images of Siva and Parvati from Kilaiyur. Large standing figures of Rama, Lakshmana and Sita from Vadakkuppanaiyur. Other metal images in Bronze gallery. Hindu figures from 9th century Pallava period, small, 11th-12th century Chola period represented by numerous seated and dancing images of Siva. Also later Chola bronzes. Buddhist bronzes from Nagapattinam –

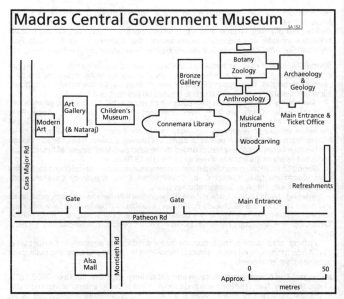

Madras Central Government Museum

SA 152

Botany
Zoology

Bronze
Gallery

Archaeology
&
Geology

Anthropology

Art
Gallery

Children's
Museum

Modern
Art

(& Nataraj)

Connemara Library

Musical
Instruments

Main Entrance &
Ticket Office

Woodcarving

Casa Major Rd

Refreshments

Gate

Gate

Main Entrance

Patheon Rd

Montieth Rd

Alsa
Mall

0   50

Approx.

metres

assigned to Chola and later periods.

The National Art Gallery has a good collection of old paintings and sculptures. Tanjore paintings on glass, Rajput and Mughal miniatures, 17th century Deccan paintings. Also 11th and 12th century handicrafts, metalware and ivory carvings. Fine 13th and 14th century bronzes are housed in a separate building at rear. **The Gallery of Modern Art** (opened in 1984) has a permanent collection of contemporary art with temporary exhibitions on the first floor.

Fort Museum, S Beach Rd (within Fort St. George). The 18th century building houses exhibits from 300 years of British Indian history. Includes prints, documents, paintings, sculpture, arms (medieval weapons with instructions on their use) and uniforms. Indo-French gallery has some Louis XIV furniture and clocks. Clive Corner which includes letters and photographs particularly good. Open 0900-1700. Closed Fri. Entry free.

Development Centre for Musical Instruments, 86 Mundakanni Koil St, Mylapore. A collection of ancient and modern instruments which you may touch and play. Some curiously ornamental (sitars and veenas carved into fish and peacock shape) and some modern experiments (violin made out of a walking stick). Of special interest are those reconstructed with the help of ancient literary texts and temple sculptures. **Tamil Isai Sangam**, Raja Annamalai Hall (2nd floor), Esplanade. T 561425. Open 1630-2000. Closed Sun. Interesting and rare collection of folk and classical musical instruments, ancient and modern from all over India and a few from abroad.

Parks and zoos *Agri-Horticultural Society Gardens* are next to the Cathedral and cover about 10 ha. A small haven lawns, trees, flower beds and a collection of *bonsai**. Open 0800-1200, 1330-1730. Closed Th. *Guindy National Park*, adjacent to the governor's house. 231 ha game reserve containing the endangered Indian antelope or black buck. Also spotted deer, white buck, bonnet monkey, civet cat, jackals and common mongoose and many species of birds.

Useful addresses Consular offices Most open 0830-1330. Mon-Fri. **Austria**, 114 Nungambakkam High Rd, T 472131. **Belgium**, 1/E Spur Tank Rd, Chetput, T 665495. **Brazil**, 1B 1st Main Rd, Gandhi Nagar, T 412397. **Czechoslovakia**, 31A Haddows Rd, T 479754. **Denmark**, 8 Cathedral Rd, T 85116. **Finland**, 762 Anna Salai, T 867611 (1000-1700). **France**, 111 Floor, 26 Cathedral Rd, T 476854 (0930-1700). **Germany**, 22 Commander-in-Chief Rd, T 471747. **Greece**, 9 Harley's Rd, Kilpauk, T 869194. **Hungary**, 3A

Sivaganga Rd (off Sterling Rd), T 478803. **Italy**, 5th Floor, 86 Chamiers Rd, T 452329 (1000-1700). **Japan**, 60 Spur Tank Rd, Chetput, T 865594. **Malaysia**, 287 TTK Rd, T 453580. **Norway**, 44-45 Rajaji Salai, T 517950. **Philippines**, 86 Radhakrishnan Rd, T 470160. **Romania**, 27 Khadar Nawaz Khan Rd, T 478387. **Singapore**, 2nd Floor, Apex Plaza, 3 Nungambakkam High Rd, T 473795. **Spain**, 8 Nimmo Rd, San Thome, T 72008. **Sri Lanka**, 9D Nawab Habibulla Av, off Anderson Rd, T 472270 (0900-1700). **Sweden**, 6 Cathedral Rd, T 472040 Extn 60. **Turkey**, 202 Linghi Chetty St, T 25756. **UK**, 24 Anderson Rd, Nungambakkam, T 473136 (0830-1600). **USA**, 220 Anna Salai, T 473040 (0830-1715). **USSR**, 14 San Thome High Rd, T 71112.

Cultural centres International Institute of Tamil Studies, Central Polytechnic Campus, T 412992. **Bharatiya Vidya Bhavan**, 38/39 R E Mada St, T 74674. Some of the foreign cultural centres have libraries and arrange film shows. **Alliance Française**, 3/4 A College Rd, Nungambakkam, T 472650. **American Centre**, 220 Anna Salai, T 477825. Library Open 0930-1800, closed Sun. **British Library**, (British Council Division), 737 Anna Salai, T 89402. Open 1000-1900, closed Mon. **Max Mueller Bhawan**, Express Estate, T 861314. Open 0900-1900, closed Sun. **Indo-Nippon Cultural Exchange Society**, 10 Chittaranjan Rd, T 451439. **House of Soviet Culture**, 27 Kasturi Rangan Rd, T 454050.

Post and Telegraph The GPO and major post offices which also accept Speed Post Mail are in Anna Rd, T Nagar, Meenambakkam, Nungambakkam High Rd, Flower Bazar and Adyar. Fax The P & T service is between New Delhi, Calcutta, Bombay and Madras. Documents (not photos) can be sent from Central Telegraph Office, Rajaji Salai (near Parry's Corner). You can send also Fax to private Fax machines (G-II or G-III). **Warning** Beware of con-men claiming to be Sri Lankan refugees needing help to pay for a telegram 'home to Sri Lanka'. Many people have lost money.

Places of worship *Hindu* – There are several temples in the city apart from the famous Kapaleeswarar in Mylapore and Parthasathi in Triplicane detailed under Places of interest above. The former allows non-Hindus except in the sanctum sanctorum. One of the newest is the Ashtalakshmi temple, built in Besantnagar in 1976. Highly regarded for its architecture, it has been described as one of only three shore temples still open for worship on the E coast. Most temples are open from 0600-1200, 1600-2200. Sri Channadesawa and Chenna, near Flower Bazar, Mini St, Sri Kandaswamy Koil and Sri Vadapalani Andavar temples, Mahalakshmi temple in Besant Nagar and Sri Satya Sai Baba temple in RK Mutt Rd. *Muslim* – In addition to The Big Mosque and Thousand Lights Mosque listed under Places of interest, there is also the Perimet Mosque in Sydenhams Rd.

Christian Church of S India: St. Mary's, Fort St. George, T 583097; St. George's Cathedral, Cathedral Road, T 561266; St. Andrew's, Poonamallee High Road, Egmore, T 33508. **Roman Catholic**: St. Thomas' Cathedral Basilica, 24 San Thome High Rd, T74925. St. Mary's Cathedral, 2 Armenian St, T 23097. St. Theresa's Nungambakkam. *Armenian* Armenian Church, 60 Armenian St, T 26223.

Jain – Temples in Mint St, GN Chetty Rd, T Nagar and in Puzhal near Red Hills. *Parsi* – W Mazda St, Royapuram. *Sikh* – Gurdwara in GN Chetty Rd, Thyagaraya Nagar.

Hospital and medical services The following are open to all including foreigners with Casualty open 24 hr. **Government** *Kilpauk Medical College and Hospital*, Poonammallee High Rd, T 666631. *Stanley Hospital*, 8 Old Jail Rd, 513311. *Hospital for Women and Children*, Pantheon Rd, Egmore, 821982. *General Hospital*, Park Town, T 39181. **Private** *Apollo Hospital*, 21/22 Greames Lane, off Greames Rd, T 476566. *Devaki Hospital*, 148 Luz Church Rd, Mylapore, T 77707. *Kalyani Hospital*, Edward Elliot's Rd (Dr. Radhakrishnan Rd); *Lady Willingdon Nursing Home*, 21 Pycrofts Garden Rd, T 4768983. *St. Isabel's Hospital*, Oliver Rd, T 71082. *Voluntary Health Services Medical Centre*, TTTI Post Office, T 412018. **Specialist** *Ophthalmic Hospital*, Marshalls Rd, Egmore, T 89081/2. *Government Dental College Hospital*, T 564341. *Dental Clinic*, 109 Dr. Radhakrishnan Rd, T 845678. *Cancer Institute*, Canal Bank Rd, Adyar, T 412714. *ENT Nursing Home*, 827 Poonamallee High Rd, Egmore, T 666224. **Ambulance** *Government* T 102, *Devali Hospital*, Mylapore, T 73935. *National Hospital*, T 511405. *St. John's Ambulance*, 1 E Spur Tank Rd, T 664630. 1000-1700.

Chambers of Commerce Southern India Chamber of Commerce and Industries, Esplanade, T 562228. Andhra Chamber of Commerce, T 583798. Hindustan Chamber of Commerce, T 586394. National Chamber of Commerce, T 583214. Indo-German Chamber of Commerce, 5 Kasturi Ranga Rd, T 454498. **Others** Madras Stock Exchange, 513081. All India Manufacturers' Organization, 69 NH Rd, T 471966. Clothing Manufacturers' Association of India, 2 Errabalu St, T 581042. Cotton Textiles Export Promotions Council, 26 Stringer St, T 583681. Gem and Jewellery Export Promotion Council, High Towers, NH Rd, T 476188.

Federation of the Association of Small Industries of India, 10 GST Rd, T 433413.

Travel agents and Tour operators Ashok Travels, 34 Pantheon Rd, T 566587. **Asian Travels**, 39 Anna Salai, T 476451. **Bharat Travels**, 159 Linghi Chetty St, T 580276. **Cox & Kings (India)**, A15 Kodambakkam High Rd, T 470162. **Gay Travels**, 61 Nungambakkam High Rd, T 471550. **Govan Travels**, Kannakai Building, 612 Anna Salai, T 477416. **Mercury Travels**, Mohan Mansion, 191 Anna Salai, T 869498. **Orient Express**, 150 Anna Salai, T 869616. **Ram Mohan**, 224 NSC Bose Rd, T 581256. **Ravel Tours and Travels**, 34 Rajaji Salai, T 511350. **Richfield Agencies**, Trade Centre, 100 Wallajah Rd, T 840135. **Sheriff Travel**, 22 Second Line Beach, T 511421. **Sita World Travel**, Fagun Mansion, 26 Commander-in-Chief Rd, T 478861. **Thomas Cook**, Eldorado Building, 112 Nungambakkam High Rd, T 473092 and **Freight Office**, 20 Rajaji Salai, T 584976. **Trade Wings**, 752 Anna Salai, T 864961. **Travel Corporation of India**, 734 Anna Salai, T 868813.

Tourist offices and information Govt of India Tourist Office, (GITO), 154 Anna Salai, T 88685/6. Weekdays 0900-1800, Sat 0900-1300. Domestic Airport Counter, T 431686. Open 24 hr and International Airport Counter open at flight times. India Tourism Development Corporation (ITDC), 29 Victoria Crescent, Commander-in-Chief Rd, T 478884. Weekdays 0600-2000, Sat and Sun 0600-1400. Government of Tamil Nadu Tourist Office (TTDC), 143 Anna Salai, T 840752. Weekdays 1000-1730. Tamil Nadu Tourism Development Corporation (Tours and Travels), 143 Anna Salai, T 849803 and at Central Rly Station, T 563351 (Sales Counter on Sun only).

State Government Tourist Bureaux and Information Centres are open from 1030-1700 on weekdays, closed on Sun and 2nd Sat. Haryana, 700 Anna Salai, T 860475. Himachal Pradesh (T 472966), Kerala (T 479862), Rajasthan (T 472093) and UP (T 479726) are at 28 Commander-in-Chief Rd. Jammu and Kashmir, 1st Floor, 837 Anna Salai. W Bengal, 787 Anna Salai, T 87612.

Tours These are on deluxe coaches and accompanied by a guide. Tamil Nadu Tourist Development Corporation **(TTDC)** *City sightseeing*: Half-day. Daily 0830-1330, 1400-1800. Fort St. George, Government Museum, Valluvar Kottam, Snake Park, Kapaleeswarar Temple, Elliot's Beach and a drive along Marina Beach. (Government Museum closed on Fri.) Fare Rs.40. Full-day. Daily 0810-1900. Drive along Marina Beach, Kapaleeswarar Temple, Snake Park, Vallavur Kottam, Museum, Fort St. George, St. Mary's Church, Birla Planetarium, Muttukadu Boat House and VGP Golden Beach. Fare Rs. 60 (includes vegetarian meal). Reservations: Sales Counters at 143, Anna Salai, T 849803 and at Express Bus Stand near High Court compound, T 560982 (0600-2100), the two places you may start the tour. Tourist Information Centre, Central Rly Station, T 563351 (24 hr). There are also separate day tours to *Mamallapuram* (strongly recommended) and *Tirupati*. *A weekend Tour*. Dep. Fri 2100, Arr. Sun 1930. Covers Thanjavur, Velankanni, Nagore, Tirunallar, Poompuhar, Vaitheeswaran Koil, Chidambaram (night at hotel), Pitchavaram, Pondicherry. Fare Twin sharing Rs.180, Single Rs.210. Longer tours cover sites in Tamil Nadu and Karnataka and also Goa.

ITDC *City Sightseeing* Daily 1330-1830. Fort St. George, St. Mary's Church, Fort Museum, Government Museum, National Art Gallery, Vallavur Kottam, Gandhiji, Rajaji & Kamaraj Memorials, Children's Park, Snake Park, Kapaleeswarar Temple, Marina Beach. On Fri The Government Museum and Art Gallery are closed so the visit includes the Botanical Garden and Parthasarathi Temple. Fare Rs.30. Reservations: ITDC, 29 Victoria Crescent, Commander-in-Chief Rd, T 478884. Booking counters at 154 Anna Salai, T 478884, Express Bus Stand, Esplanade, T 561830, Central Rly Station, T 566438. Garage, 5 -6 Chamiers Rd, T 454056. Also offers *Kanchipuram, Tirukalikundram, Mamallapuram* Tour (0730-1900). Fare A/c coach Rs.90, Non-a/c Rs.60. *Tirupati, Tiruchanur* Tour (0630-2030). Fare A/c coach Rs. 200, Child Rs.175. Non-a/c Rs.150, Child Rs.125 (includes *Darshan* Fee at Tirumala, breakfast and lunch). The *5-day S India Panorama* Tour covers Bangalore, Mysore, Mudumalai, Ooty, Coimbatore, Salem and Tiruvannamalai. Dep. Sun 0630, Arr. Th 2030. Fare: Twin sharing Rs.895, Single Rs.995, Child Rs.695 which does not include meals. The *8-day S India Safari Tour* covers Trichy, Kodaikkanal, Kanyakumari, Trivandrum, Madurai, Ramesvaram, Tanjore, Kumbakonam, Chidambaram and Pondicherry. Dep. Fri 0630, Arr. Fri 2030. Fare: Twin sharing Rs.1195, Single Rs.1295, Child Rs.945.

Airlines Most are open 0930-1730 Mon-Fri, 0930-1300 Sat. **Air India**, 19 Marshalls Rd, T 474477. Airport T 474488. **Air France**, 769 Anna Salai, T 88377. **Air Lanka**, Hotel Connemara Annex, Binny's Rd, T 89701. **British Airways**, Fagun Mansion, 26 Commander-in-Chief Rd, T 474272. **Indian Airlines**, 19 Marshalls Rd, T 478333. **Iraqi Airways**, 1-30 Pantheon Rd, T 811740. **Lufthansa**, 171 Anna Salai, T 81483. **Malaysian Airlines**, 189 Anna Salai, T 88970. **N W Airlines**, 1 Whites Rd, T 87703. **Qantas**, Eldorado Building, Nungambakkam High Rd, T 478649. **Sabena**, Regency House, 250 Anna Salai, T

451598. **Singapore Airlines**, 167 Anna Salai, T 82871. **Swissair**, 40 Anna Salai, T 82583.
Several Airlines operate through a General Sales Agency (GSA). **Air Canada, Air Kenya, Garuda Airways, Japan Airlines** are all c/o Global Travels, 733 Anna Salai, T 87957. **Alitalia** and **Zambia Airways**, c/o Ajanta Travels & Tours, Kivraj Mansion, 738 Anna Salai, T 810936. **Bangladesh Biman, Philippines Airways**, c/o Jet Air Transportation, 55 Monteith Rd, T 861810. **Cathay Pacific** and **KLM**, c/o Spencer & Co., Hotel Connemara, Binny's Rd, T 811051. **Ethiopian Airlines, Iberian Airways, LOT Polish Airways** and **Royal Nepal Airlines**, c/o STIC Travels, Hotel Chola Sheraton, 10 Cathedral Rd, T 473347. **Egypt Air** and **Yemen Air**, c/o BAP Travels, 135 Anna Salai, T 849913. **Kuwait Airways**, c/o National Travel Service, Embassy Towers, 50 Monteith Rd, T 811810. **Maldive Airways**, c/o Crossworld Tours, 7 Rosy Tower, Nungambakkam High Rd, T 471497. **Pakistan International Airways**, c/o Swaman, 63 Pantheon Rd, T 810619. **Pan Am**, c/o Indam Travels, 163 Anna Salai, T 811209. **Saudi Arabian Airlines**, c/o Arajaath Travels, 3 Monteith Rd, T 811370. **Thai International**, c/o Swan Travels, Aarti Building, 189 Anna Salai, T 812775. **TWA**, c/o Air Transportation, Hardevi Chambers, 68 Pantheon Rd, T 812775.

Air Services Madras has an international airport with two terminals, Meenambakkam International (15 km) and Domestic (17 km). **Indian Airlines** Delhi, daily (+ 1 other), 0600, 3 hr 45 min; **Bombay**, daily (+ 1 other), 1100, 1 hr 40 min; **Bangalore**, daily, 1930, 40 min; **Calcutta**, Tue, Th & Sat (+ 1 other), 1010, 3 hr; **Visakhapatnam**, Mon (+ 1 other), 0645, 1 hr 10 min; **Ahmedabad**, Wed, Fri & Sun, 1520, 3 hr 10 min; **Coimbatore**, Mon, Thur & Sat (+ 1 other), 0610, 1 hr 45 min; **Madurai**, daily except Mon, 0630, 1 hr 40 min; **Tiruchirappalli**, daily except Mon, 0630, 45 min; **Trivandrum**, Wed, Fri & Sun (+ 1 other), 1115, 1 hr 5 min; **Cochin**, Wed, Fri & Sun (+ 1 other), 1115, 2 hr 5 min; **Port Blair**, Tue, Wed, Fri & Sun, 0635, 2 hr; **Hyderabad**, daily (+ 1 other), 0600, 1 hr.
Vayudoot Tirupati, Mon-Sat, 0700, 35 min; **Coimbatore**, Mon-Sat, 1600, 1 hr 25 min; **Cochin**, Mon-Sat, 0630, 2 hr 25 min; **Agatti**, Mon-Sat, 0630, 4 hr 10 min.
Indian Airlines Reservations, 19 Marshalls Rd, T 478833 (0630-1900). Enquiries T 477977. Flight information: Airport, T 433954, General, T 433131. Mini Booking Offices: Mena Building, 57 Dr. Radhakrishnan Rd, T 479799. Umpherson St (nr Broadway), T 583321. 57 Venkatanarayana Rd, T Nagar, T 447555. Reservations and Cancellations 24 hr. Ticketing 0900-1700. *Vayudoot* connects Madras with Agati, Calicut, Cochin, Coimbatore, Hubli, Madurai, Pondicherry, Rajahmundry, Tanjore, Tirupati, Trichy and Vijayawada. Booking office, 1st Floor, Wellington Estate, Commander-in-Chief Rd, T 869901 (0900-1800). Airport, T 435521.
International *Air India* has one flight a week to New York and once to Kuwait and Jeddah, twice a week to London and Kuala Lumpur and 5 times a week to Singapore.

Airport Connections Special Taxis are available from national and international airports to anywhere in the city (flat rate of Rs.95 within 20 km). *Pallavan Transport Corporation* runs "deluxe" coaches (far from deluxe by non-Indian standards) to Egmore Rly Station from the airport via the big hotels. If you're in any hurry this can be a very slow way of getting into town, as the bus tends to go very slowly on a very roundabout route. Not too bad late in the evening. Fare Rs.20. Airport, T 432534. Egmore, T 561284 (see Local Transport above).

Rail Madras has 2 rly stations, Madras Central for broad gauge trains to all parts of India and Egmore for metre gauge trains to other towns in the southern region. *Madras Central* General Enquiry, T 563535. Train Arrival, T 567575. Current Reservations: Upper Class, T 563545. Second Class, T 564455. Reservations open 0700-1300, 1330-1900. Sun 0700-1300. Indrail Passes are available here at the Central Reservations Office, Southern Rly to foreigners and Indian resident abroad. *Egmore* General Enquiry and Current Reservations, T 566565. Upper Class, T 564010. Second Class, T 566555/7.
There are several *Southern Rly Booking Offices* in addition to the ones at the stations. Annanagar, T 615132. Anna Salai, T 849642. Esplanade, T 563672. George Town, T 23553. Guindy, T 431319. Ambattur, T 653387. Mylapore, T 72750. T Nagar, T 441491. Triplicane, T 842529. Meenambakkam Airport has a Rail Booking Counter.
You may reserve 60 days in advance, except for Inter-city Day Expresses to Bangalore, Coimbatore, Madurai, Mysore, Tirupati and Trichy which can only be reserved 30 days in advance.
Delhi (ND): *Tamil Nadu Exp*, 2621 (AC/CC & AC/II), daily, 2100, 33 hr 45 min; *Grand Trunk Exp*, 2615 (AC/II), daily, 2115; 36 hrs 50 mins; **Calcutta (H):** *Coromandal Exp*, 2842 (AC/II), daily, 0810, 27 hr 20 min; *Haora Mail*, 6004 (AC/II), daily, 2230, 33 hr 15 min; **Bombay (VT):** *Madras-Bombay Mail*, 7010 (AC/II), daily, 2220, 30 hr 30 min; **Bombay (Dadar):** *Madras-Dadar Exp*, 6512 (AC/II), daily, 0915, 26 hr 45 min; **Hyderabad:** *Madras-Hyderabad*, 7053 (AC/II), daily, 1530, 16 hr; **Bangalore:** *Madras-Bangalore*, 6023 (AC/II), daily, 1330, 7

hr 15 min; **Cochin**: *Madras-Cochin Exp*, 6041 (AC/II), daily, 1935, 14 hr; **Trivandrum**: *Trivandrum Mail*, 6319 (AC/II), daily, 1855, 16 hr 50 min; **Trichy**: *Pallavan Exp*, 2605 (AC/II), daily, 1225, 7 hr 45 min; **Ramesvaram**: *Rameswaram Exp*, 6101, Daily, 2020, 16 hr 40.

Road Four National Highways originate in Madras. NH 5 to Calcutta via Vijayawada, Visakhapatnam and Bhubaneswar, NH 4 to Bombay via Bangalore, NH 45 to Dindigul, Ramesvaram and Trivandrum and NH 46 to Krishnagiri, Salem and Trichur. The National Highways are motorable, the state Highways are reasonably well-maintained but condition of other roads vary. You can hire cars (at present with driver) through ITDC or take the Tourist offices' conducted coach tour. Distances to some major towns in the region: Bangalore 334 km, Cochin 669 km, Coimbatore 486 km, Hyderabad 620 km, Kanchipuram 75 km, Madurai 461 km, Mamallapuram 64 km, Mysore 465 km, Periyar 554 km, Pondicherry 162 km, Ramesvaram 613 km, Salem 326 km, Tirupati 143 km, Trichy 319 km, Trivandrum 710 km, Visakhapatnam 800 km.

Long Distance Buses The *Thiruvalluvar Transport Corporation (TTC)* offers good connections within the whole region and the service is efficient and inexpensive. Best to take a/c coaches or super delux a/c. Buses originate from Parry's (Esplanade), T 561835 picking up from T Nagar, Egmore, T 561284, Broadway, T 561144 and Basin Bridge, T 519527. Bookings 0700-2100. Other offices at Bangalore, T 76974, Coimbatore, T 25949, Madurai, T 41730, Pondicherry, T 6513, Salem, T 62960, Thanjavur, T 175, Trichy, T 23680 and Tirupati, T 2162.

   Other state and private companies cover the region but you may wish to avoid their video coaches which make listening, if not viewing, compulsory as there are no headphones! Interstate Bus Depot, Broadway Bus Stand handles enquiries and reservations. Computer reservations are now made on long distance routes.

Ship Regular passenger ships to the Andaman and Nicobar Islands charge from about Rs.600 for a/c Delux Cabins down to Rs 400 for C Class. Agents: The Shipping Corporation of India, Rajaji Salai, T 514401. A passenger line is reputed to be opening to Singapore. Check with a local travel agent for details.

EXCURSIONS

Anna Zoological Park, Vandalur. 32 km. 520 ha. Attempts to provide a natural environment and breed some endangered species. Hippos, zebras, chimpanzees, elephants, Nilgiri langurs, Rhesus macaque, jackals and spotted deer among 28 species of mammals and includes a nocturnal animal house. Also 61 species of birds include macaw parrot, blossom headed parakeet and Manila duck and 8 species of reptiles. There is a ropeway and monorail, and a lion and bison safari park. Small battery operated 'cars' and bicycles for hire. Open 0800-1700, daily except Tues. Camera fee Rs.3.

Cholamandal Artists' village, T 412892. 20 km out of Madras on the road S and close to the sea. Started in 1969, the community of artists who live and work here, exhibit and sell their paintings, graphics, sculptures, pottery and batik. Occasional dance performances in small open-air theatre. Stop for a short visit. Open daily 0600-2000.

Muttukadu 30 km is being developed as a rowing, boating and wind surfing resort.

Covelong fishing village and beach is 38 km away, the road having branched off at Kelambakkam (16 km). You may wish to stop for a drink and snacks at *Fisherman's Cove Hotel.*

Continuing S, 42 km from Madras is the **Crocodile Bank** where Indian and African species are bred in addition to native species of turtle. It was set up in 1976 by Romulus Whittaker who was also founder of Guindy Snake Park and has saved the endangered *gharial* and marsh crocodile. One of the largest crocodiles in the world, over 7 m long is here. Entry – Re.1. Cameras Rs 5. Allow 30 min stop.

NB A shop has crocodile skin articles for sale but you may not export it out of the country and import it into your own.

The Madras to Trichy coastal route takes you to Mamallapuram and beyond. **See page 727.**

60 km from Madras and 16 km from Mamallapuram on the Chingleput road, *Tirukkalukundram* **(Pakshitirtham)** has a small finely carved Siva temple dedicated to Bhaktavatsleesvara on the hill top with its *gopuram* or gateway standing out like a beacon. About 400 steps take you to the top of the 160 m hill and at mid-day you will see two Neophran vultures (*Pharaoh's chickens*) fly down to be fed by the priests. The tank is considered holy and said to produce a conch every 12 years. The temple here and the larger Siva temple in the village below have made this a Hindu pilgrim centre. A range of small shops in the village, cold drinks available. Good views from hill top.

On the Trichy Rd, *Vedanthangal Bird Sanctuary* is 85 km from Madras and 60 km from Mamallapuram. Best season Nov-Feb for migratory birds which include blue-winged teals, pintails, shovellers, numbering about 100,000. Best time dawn and 1500-1800. Viewing from observation tower near the small lake. The sanctuary is said to have been in existence as a protected area for about 250 years. A marshy 30 ha site attracting numerous water fowl, has a small lake and a grove of Kadappamaram (Barrintonia acutangula) trees part of which remains submerged in the rainy season and provide the main nesting site for the birds. Visitors and residents include crested cormorants, night herons, grey pelicans, sand pipers, grey wagtails, pelicans, open-billed storks, white ibis, egrets, little grebe and purple moorhens. You can walk along a shaded raised path along the W bank of the lake to see the nesting colonies of birds from late Oct until Feb.

It is possible to attempt a long day-trip from Madras but if you wish to stay the night, the very simple **F** *Forest Rest House* which has electricity, bath and running water, has suites of rooms. The cook will prepare an Indian meal to order. Reservations in advance: Wildlife Warden, 49, Fourth Main Rd, Adyar, Madras. T 413947. Advance payment for rm and food to Forester in Charge of the Rest House, Vedanthangal.

Travel You can get there by rail to Chingleput and then take one of the regular buses to the sanctuary. Alternatively, travel by road from Madras either by car or take a bus from the Broadway Bus Stand, Madras which only runs at weekends or one from Mamallapuram. It is also included in some of the coach tours.

Kanchipuram, *Population* 175,000. *Altitude* 20 m, 'The golden city of a thousand temples' is 71 km from Madras. Its history can be traced back to the early Cholas in the 2nd century, although Buddhism is believed to have reached here in the 3rd century BC. However, none of the 3rd century BC Ashokan stupas which were supposed to have existed, now remain. Successive dynasties of Pallavas, Cholas and Vijayanagar made it their capital and built over a hundred temples. Temple building started as early as the 4th century with the best examples dating from the 6th and 7th centuries. It is one of India's seven most sacred cities for Hindus (others being Ayodhya, Dwarka, Hardwar, Mathura, Ujjain and Varanasi) but apart from being a pilgrimage centre, it was also a centre of learning, culture and philosophy. Sankaracharya and the Buddhist monk Bodhidharma lived and worked here.

From the 16th century the silk weavers have produced high quality silk in beautiful colours and patterns on their handlooms. Nowadays, about 20,000 work with silk and another 10,000 with cotton. To visit the weavers at work in their spotless huts, contact Weavers' Service Centre, 20 Railway Station Rd, T 2530. The main town is W of the rly.

Local Festivals Throughout the year at the temples. The important ones are mentioned under each temple.

Places of interest Temples It would only be practicable to attempt to see only a few of the 70 or so temples in a day's visit and some of the most important are listed here. *Ekambaresvara Temple* is in the NW of the town between W and N Made St about a km from the Bus Stand. It is the largest of the temples covering an area of 9 ha and has five enclosures and a 'Thousand-pillared Hall' (actually

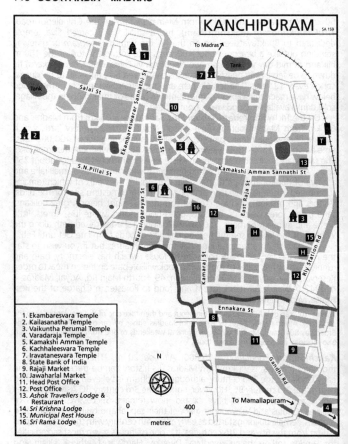

KANCHIPURAM SA 159

To Madras ↗

Tank

Salai St

Ekambareswarar Sannathi St

Raja St

Tank

S.N.Pillai St

Kamakshi Amman Sannathi St

Narasingarayar St

Kamaraj St

East Raja St

Rly Station Rd

Ennakara St

Gandhi Rd

To Mamallapuram →

1. Ekambaresvara Temple
2. Kailasanatha Temple
3. Vaikuntha Perumal Temple
4. Varadaraja Temple
5. Kamakshi Amman Temple
6. Kachhaleesvara Temple
7. Iravatanesvara Temple
8. State Bank of India
9. Rajaji Market
10. Jawaharlal Market
11. Head Post Office
12. Post Office
13. *Ashok Travellers Lodge &
    Restaurant*
14. *Sri Krishna Lodge*
15. *Municipal Rest House*
16. *Sri Rama Lodge*

N

0   400
└──────┘
metres

540). Dedicated to Siva in his ascetic form it was first built by the Pallavas, developed by the Cholas with further additions by the Vijayanagara **King Krishna Deva Raya**. At the beginning of the 16th century he built the high stone wall which surrounds the temple and the 59 m tall *rajagopuram* or main tower (one of the tallest in S India) on which is sculpted several figures of him and his consort. Some find the temple rather eerie, with decaying statues, lots of bats and a feeling of being trapped in time.

The main sanctuary has a *lingam* made of earth (**Siva** as one of the elements) and the story of its origin is told on a carved panel. The teasing **Parvati** is believed to have unthinkingly covered her husband Siva's eyes for a moment with her hands which resulted in the earth being enveloped in darkness for years. The incident enraged Siva and he ordered Parvati to do severe penance during which time she worshipped her husband in the form of an earth *lingam* which she created. When Siva sent a flood to test her, she clung to the lingam with her hands until the waters subsided and some devotees claim they can see her finger prints on the temple *lingam*. The old mango tree in one of the enclosures is claimed to be 1,000 years old (3,500 according to some!) and still bears fruit.

The temple's historical connections include Clive's Arcot campaign when it served as a fortress. Non-Hindus are not allowed to enter the sanctum sanctorum. There is a very small charge for entry and also for cameras (Rs 2 for still and Rs 5 for movie). *Panguni Uthiram Festival* in Mar-Apr.

At the W end of the city (1.6 km), the **Kailasanatha**, said to be the most beautiful of the town's temples, was built out of sandstone in the early 7th century by the Pallava King Narasimha Varman II with the front completed by his son Mahendra III. The outer wall has a dividing wall with a shrine and doorways, separating a large courtyard from a smaller. The unusual enclosure wall has 58 small raised shrines with a *nandi* in each pavilion. The 7 shrines in the temple complex are similar to the *rathas* in Mamallapuram and have images of different forms of Siva while the intricately carved panels on the walls depict legends about Siva from mythology with accompanying text in ancient Grantha script. Closed 1230-1600. *Mahashivaratri festival* in Feb.

Vaikuntha Perumal Temple (1 km) SW of the station, nr the crossing of E Raja St and Kamakshi Ammman Sannathi St. Dedicated to Vishnu this was built in the 8th century by the Pallava king Nandivarman just after the Kailasanatha and illustrates the progress of Dravidian temple architecture. As Brown points out, the 2 temples (together with the Shore Temple at Mamallapuram) are examples of dressed stones being used for structural temples. Here too the sanctuary is separated from the *mandapa* by an open space. The cloisters are built out of lines of lion pillars. Panels of bas relief accompanied by lines in old Tamil, trace the history of the wars between the Pallavas and Chalukyas. There is an unusual *vimana* (tower) with shrines in 3 tiers with figures of Vishnu in each. Murray has a very detailed description of this temple.

Varadaraja (Devarajasvami) (3.2 km) in the SE of the town. Built by the Vijayanagara kings possibly in the 16th century superb sculpture in its hundred-pillared marriage hall (actually 96 pillars). Note the massive flexible chain carved out of supposedly one piece of granite although now it is no longer in one piece. The mutilation of the figures and the chains is attributed to Muslim invaders and particularly to Haider Ali. The main shrine is on an elephant shaped rock. There are also small shrines in the courtyard with painted roofs. The two tanks in the temple enclosures have granite steps sloping down. Entry fee Re.0.50, Camera fees Rs.2 for still, Rs.5 for movie. Details in Murrays Handbook. Festivals – *Float Festival* in Feb and Nov, *Brahmotsavam* in May, *Garuda Sevai* in June.

Kamakshi Amman on Odai St in the centre of town built probably first before the 7th century and later by the Cholas in the 14th century. It is dedicated to Parvati and is one of the three holiest places of *sakti* worship, the others being Madurai and Varanasi. There is a shrine to Sri Sankara who founded a monastery and a golden *gopuram*. The 'Amai' *mandapa* is beautifully sculpted. The annual 'car' festival when other deities are drawn to this temple in their wooden temple chariots, draws large crowds in Feb-Mar.

Jaina Kanchi is just outside the town. The two temples worth visiting are **Vardhamana Temple** with beautiful paintings and the smaller **Chandraprabha**.

You can also watch the **weavers** at work in their homes. See above in introduction.

Hotels E *Ashok Travellers' Lodge*, (TTDC), 78 Kamakshi Amman Sannathi St. T 2561. Near the rly station, it is a western style hotel with non-a/c rm. Restaurant, garden. Reservations: Manager or through TTDC, 143 Anna Salai, Madras. T 849803. E *Sri Rama Lodge*, 19-20 Nellukkara St. T 2395. Has some a/c rm is fairly basic but close to the Bus Station. Opp is the **F** *Sri Krishna*, T 2831 with non-a/c rm. The **F** *Municipal Rest House* is basic (no food) and only available when not required by govt officers. Advance booking with payment to Commissioner, Kanchipuram Municipality. T 2301.

Restaurants *Ashok Travellers' Lodge* has a reasonable restaurant but the service can be slow. Others are small *Thali Bhawans* in the centre of town nr the Bus Stand, inexpensive veg *thali* meals.

Shopping Silk and cotton fabrics with designs of birds, animals and temples or in plain beautiful colours sometimes 'shot', are sold by the metre in addition of course to saris. Weavers do not sell directly but it is best to buy from Govt shops or Co-operative Society stores. *Srinivas & Co*, 135 Thirukatchi Nambi St, *Thiruvalluvar Co-Operative Society*, 207 Gandhi Rd, *Co-Optex*, *B.M. Silks*.

Tourist information at the Ashok Travellers' Lodge, 78 Kamakshi Amman Sannathi St, T 2461. Head **Post Office**, 27 Gandhi Rd, T 2534. Others on Station Rd and near Bus Stand. **Banks** State Bank of India on Gandhi Rd, T 2521.

Air Services Nearest airport is Madras (Indian Airlines Enquiries, T 477977. Reservations T 477098. Vayudoot Enquiries, T 435521. Reservations, T 861422.)

Rail Trains to Madras Beach Station and to Arakkonam on the Madras-Bangalore line.

Road Direct Thiruvalluvar (TTC) buses to Madras 71 km (No.828), Bangalore 263 km (No.828), Kanyakumari (No.193), Pondicherry 109 km (No.804) and Trichy (No.122). To get to Mamallapuram (65 km), either take a direct bus or quicker still take a bus to Chingleput (35 km) which are frequent and catch one from there. Other buses go to Tirupati, Tiruttani and Vellore.

TAMIL NADU

Tamil Nadu is in the SE corner of India. Lying between latitudes 8°N and 14°N, to its E and S is the Bay of Bengal and the Indian Ocean. Across the Palk Straits in the SE is Sri Lanka. To its N and W are the Indian states of Andhra Pradesh, Karnataka and Kerala. The state covers an area of 130,000 sq km, making it approximately the same size as England.

One of the four Dravidian States of India, it has over 2000 years of continuous cultural history. Tamil is one of the oldest literary languages in India, some of its poetry dating back before the birth of Christ. Tamil Nadu also has some of the most remarkable temple architecture in India, and a living tradition of music and dance.

Social indicators *Literacy* M 47% F 35% *Newspaper circulation:* 1,130,000 *Birth rate* Rural 29:1000 Urban 26:1000 *Death rate* Rural 13:1000 Urban 8:1000 *Infant mortality* Rural 97:1000, Urban 51:1000 *Registered graduate job seekers* 1,755,000 *Average annual income per head* : Rs 1200 *Inflation 1981-87* 71%.

Religion *Hindu* 89% *Muslim* 5% *Christian* 6%.

Towns and cities 32% of the population of Tamil Nadu live in towns and cities. Although

Madras, the state capital and by far the largest city, developed as a result of British power, Tamil Nadu has a very long urban tradition. Madurai, Coimbatore, Tiruchirappalli and Salem are all major regional centres.

Administration There are now 18 administrative districts. Tamil Nadu sends 39 Members to the Indian Parliament, the Lok Sabha. It elects 234 Members to its own Legislative Assembly and a further 63 to its Legislative Council.

INTRODUCTION

The Land

Tamil Nadu falls into 3 main regions. The western flank is dominated by the Western Ghats. These hills fall into 2 main blocks, the **Nilgiris** in the N and the Palani, Cardomom and Anamalai hills in the S. The Nilgiris cover an area of about 2,500 sq km. Ootacamund, one of India's most famous hill resorts, is in their centre. The hill blocks are of rocks over 3,000 million years old, and they rise to heights of over 2,500 m. The highest mountain in S India, Anaimudi (2,694 m), is in Kerala, and the second highest, Dodabetta, in in Tamil Nadu. To the E of the hills are the plains. In the N of the State isolated blocks like the Shevaroy and Javadi hills reach heights of over 1,500 m. On the coast itself is the flat alluvial plain. Where major rivers have deposited alluvium over many hundreds of years, especially the Kaveri, deltas have formed. These were the centres of the major Tamil kingdoms and often called the rice bowls of Tamil Nadu.

Climate Because most of Tamil Nadu lies to the E of the Ghats the climate is very different from that on the W coast, even though it is less than 100 km away. Protected by the rainshadow effect of the mountains themselves, the plains to the E have strong winds through the early monsoon period, but as they come down the eastern slopes of the hills they warm up and become drier. The contrasts with the W are often striking. In the extreme S of Tamil Nadu, for example, the districts around Madurai receive less than 750 mm annually, and the extreme SE experiences almost semi-desert conditions. The journey by land from Trivandrum to Madurai round India's southern tip illustrates the dramatic effects on vegetation and agriculture of this sudden decrease in rainfall.

Tamil Nadu, and particularly the area around Madras, has a quite exceptional rainfall pattern, as it receives the bulk of its rain in what is sometimes called the retreating monsoon. **See page 680**.

Rivers and lakes Tamil Nadu's most important river is the **Kaveri** (formerly Cauvery). Rising in Karnataka within 100 km of the W coast, the major part of its water is used to irrigate the Thanjavur delta between Tiruchirappalli and the sea. It is used so effectively that it is possible to walk across it ankle deep at its mouth. Other rivers include the Palar in the N and the **Tamramparni** in the S. Like all rivers in peninsular India they are often dry, reflecting the seasonal nature of the rainfall pattern. Tamil Nadu's biggest lake is that created behind the Dam. This was built in 1926 to improve the efficiency of use of the River Kaveri.

People

The population of Tamil Nadu is now 53 million. The great majority of Tamilians are Dravidians, with Mediterranean ethnic origins. They have been settled in Tamil Nadu for several thousand years. Tamil, the main language of the State, is spoken by over 85% of the population. In the N of the state, especially around Madras, many people speak Telugu, another Dravidian language. They make up a further 10% of the population. Hindus make up nearly 90% of the population. Over 5% are Christian, a group especially strong in the S where Roman Catholic and Protestant missions have been active for over 500 years. However, the origins of Christianity in the S traditionally go back to 52 AD, when **St Thomas the Apostle**

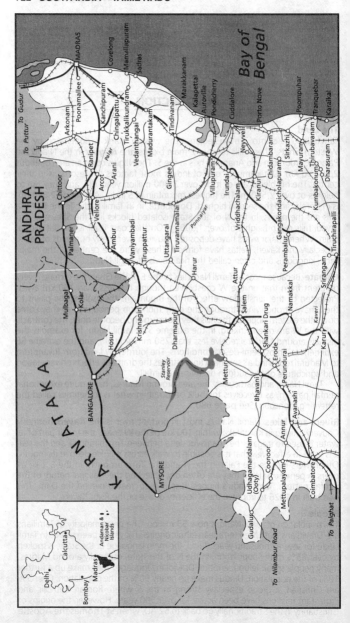

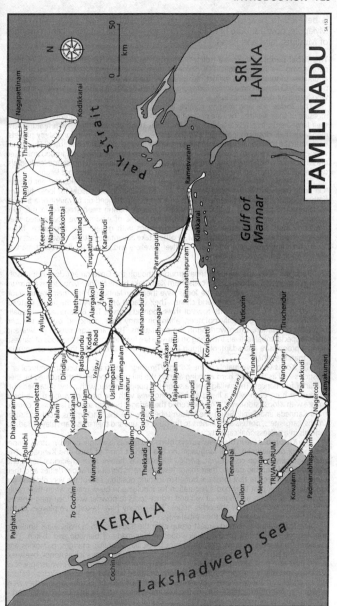

is believed to have come to India. He is believed to have been martyred in Mylapore, now a suburb of Madras. There are also small but significant minorities of Muslims, Jains and Parsis.

The Tribal people There are isolated groups of as many as 18 different types of tribal people, who live in the Nilgiri Hills. Some of them are of aboriginal stock although local antiquities suggest that an extinct race preceded them. Most travellers to the hill stations, particularly Ooty, will come across *Toda* culture, but besides them there are a few other groups who lead their own distinct lives.

The **Todas'** life and religion revolve around their long-horned buffalo which are a measure of their wealth. They are pastoralists, with the men occupied in grazing and milking their large herds. In physical appearance the Todas stand out with their sharp features, the men with their close cropped hair, and the women who wear theirs in long shiny ringlets. Both wrap the traditional **puthukuli*** toga style shawl which is brightly patterned. Their small villages are called **munds*** with half a dozen or so igloo-like, windowless bamboo and dried grass huts into which they crawl through tiny entrances. The animist temples and 'cathedrals' or *boa*, which only men are allowed to enter, are of similar construction but larger.

Their chief goddess 'Tiekirzi', the creator of the indispensable buffalo, and her brother 'On', rule the world of the dead and the living. Marriage customs allow for loose ties and 'fatherhood' is a social requirement, with partners being changed on payment of a price in buffaloes. The practice is declining, female infanticide having been stopped in the 19th century. There are only about a 1,000 Todas left, some of whom have abandoned their traditional huts and adopted conventional dwellings with government assistance. Many young people now leave their *munds* while others take advantage of their close contact with 'civilization' and produce articles such as silver jewellery and shawls for the tourist market. (Gift Shop at Charing Cross, Ooty).

The **Badagas** form the principal tribal group (although the Government does not classify them as a tribe) and appear to have come from Karnataka to the N. Their language is a mixture of Kannada and Tamil, (whereas the Todas have their own language) and their oral tradition is rich in folktales, poetry, songs and chants. Their villages are mainly in the upper plateau, perched usually on hillocks, with rows of three-roomed houses. The Badagas are principally agriculturists growing mainly potatoes, although many have branched out to tea and vegetable cultivation, often working in the plantations. They are worshippers of Siva and observe special tribal festivals including an unusual fire feast in honour of the gods of harvest. Being a progressive and adaptable group they are being absorbed into the local community faster than the others.

The **Kotas** who live mainly in the Kotagiri/Tiruchigadi area are particularly musical and artistic as well as the most hard working among the hill tribes and are distinguished by their colourful folk dances. Their villages are also on the upper plateau, with a few detached huts or rows of huts, each with a living and sleeping area with the place of worship in a large square with a loose stone wall. They preceded the Badagas but also speak a language derived from Kannada and Tamil. Being the artisan tribe, they are the blacksmiths, gold and silver smiths, carpenters, potters and tanners to the other groups and their musicians play at Badaga funerals in a professional capacity.

The **Kurumbas** live in the lower valleys, glens and forests in villages called 'mothas' under the control of headmen. Their language too is a corrupt form of Tamil and Kannada. This hunter-gatherer group collect fruit, particularly bananas, honey, resin, medicinal herbs and also hunt and trap big game. Their major festivals are in honour of tribal deities and their burial customs require that most are buried in a sitting position, except the very old who are cremated. In the past they had a reputation for indulging in black magic when they could conjure up elephants and tigers at will and reduce rocks to powder with their magic herbs, and so were murdered by the other tribes. Today many have become employees in the plantations and have given up their tribal ways.

The **Irulas** are the second largest group after the Badagas and in many ways similar to the Kurumbas. They live on the lower slopes in huts made of bamboo and thatch. They cultivate small areas to grow *ragi*, and various fruit like plantains, oranges, pumpkins and jackfruit and also hunt and ensnare wild animals. They take produce such as honey, beeswax, gum, dyes and fruit, down to towns in the plains to trade. The Irulas are worshippers of Vishnu, especially in the form of Rangaswamy, and their temples are simple circles of stone which enclose an upright stone with a trident. In common with other tribal people they wear a large number of ornaments but like the Kurumbas also have a reputation for witchcraft – there are stories of women leaving their babies and children in the care of tigresses when they go out to work!

The Economy

Agriculture Nearly three quarters of the population of Tamil Nadu still depend on agriculture, although it only contributes one third of the State's economic wealth. There are great contrasts between irrigated agriculture and dry farming. Irrigation has been practised in the region for over 2,000 years. *Tanks* – large, shallow reservoirs – were built as early as the 8th century AD in the areas around Madras. Further S the River Kaveri has been used for irrigation for over 1,000 years. There are over 20,000 km of irrigation channels (known in Tamil as "anicuts") in Tamil Nadu. In both regions rice is the most important crop. Tamil Nadu accounts for over 10% of India's rice production. Sugar cane is also a vital cash crop, as are groundnuts and other oilseeds. Cotton and bananas are also grown for market. In the hills of the Western Ghats tea makes a major contribution to exports and domestic consumption. The hills are also famous for cardamom, pepper, ginger and other spices. Potatoes are widely grown in the Nilgiris for sale in India's big cities.

Resources and industry Tamil Nadu does not have rich mineral resources. There are extensive deposits of lignite, exploited at Neyveli, iron ore is now being used in the steel mill at Salem, and magnesite has been mined for many years in Salem district. The E facing slopes of the Western Ghats have also offered considerable potential for the development of hydro electricity.

Tamil Nadu is one of India's most industrialised states. In the 1980s it was second, after Maharashtra, in terms of the value-added in manufacturing industry. It also has 10% of India's industrial labour force. The first industrial venture in the state was the setting up of a small steel mill at Porto Novo in 1820. That was a failure, and the only successful venture in the next fifty years was the setting up of sugar mills, converting *gur* into white sugar in S Arcot District. However, the biggest development was to come in cotton milling.

The disruption to Europe's cotton supplies caused by the American Civil War led to a great expansion of the area under cotton in Tamil Nadu. However, when the war ended and American supplies were resumed there was a glut of raw cotton on the market, and both British and Indian investment looked to setting up mills in India. Mills were built in Madurai, Tuticorin, Madras and Coimbatore in the 1870s and early 1880s. During the same period the sugar industry expanded and the leather industry grew rapidly from its traditional small scale base. All three industries remain pillars of the modern Tamil Nadu economy. In the 1930s hydro-electric power was developed in the hills of the S W, and Coimbatore rapidly became a major industrial centre for the textile industry. By Independence Tamil Nadu had over 80 cotton textile mills, five sugar factories and over 300 leather manufacturing units.

Rapid industrialisation followed. Tamil Nadu has become the centre of engineering works making a range of products – cars, buses, lorries and railway rolling stock, alongside motorbikes and precision tools. More traditional industries remain important; of these, leather is one of India's major export earners. There are also oil refining and fertiliser industries. The most striking change has been the rise of chemical industries to second position by the end of the 1980s, with fertilisers accounting for nearly 50% of their value. Over half the fixed industrial capital in Tamil Nadu is concentrated in the three districts of Coimbatore, Madras and Salem, but most districts have some factory-based industry.

Power At Independence in 1947 $\frac{2}{3}$ of Tamil Nadu's total installed electric capacity came from hydro schemes, the remainder being coal fired power stations. Production capacity has gone up from 156 MW then to over 4000 MW in 1991. Of this hydro still contributes a major share, over 1400 MW. However, demand has risen so fast that there remain major shortages. A nuclear power station was commissioned in the late 1980s at Kalpakkam, 70 km S of Madras, but it it still not producing to its 500 MW capacity.

Transport Tamil Nadu has some of the best road and rail connections in India. Madras is the focus for the transport system, linking the State with other major centres in India and abroad. The broad gauge rail system links Madras with Bangalore, Cochin, Bombay, Delhi, Calcutta and the N. The metre gauge system serves the S. Tamil Nadu also has 111 km of roads per 100 sq km, the second highest density in the country. It is served by the national highway network as well as a good network of all-weather state highways.

History
Although there is much evidence of Stone and Iron Age settlements, Tamil Nadu's cultural identity has been shaped by the Dravidians, who had inhabitated the S since the 4th millenium BC. Tamil, its oldest language, developed from the earlier and unknow languages of people displaced from northern Asia by invading Aryans from 2000 BC to 1500 BC.

Tamil Nadu was under the rule of three dynasties from the 4th century. The *Cholas* occupied the coastal area E of Thanjavur and inland to the head of the Kaveri Delta at Tiruchi. Periodically they were a strong military power. One of their princes, Elara, for example conquered the island of Sri Lanka in the 2nd century BC. The centre – Madurai, Tirunelveli and a part of S Kerala, were under the *Pandiyas* . The *Cheras* controlled much of what is now Kerala on the W coast of the peninsula, but they also penetrated S Tamil Nadu.

From around the 2nd century AD a poets' academy known as the *Sangam* was established in Madurai. The writings describe life in Tamil society as belonging to a different system of hierarchy from that in the N. In Tamil Nadu the sages were at the top, followed by peasants, hunters, artisans, soldiers, fishermen and scavengers. This was quite different from the caste system that existed in the rest of the subcontinent.

In turn the Pallavas (AD 550-869), Cholas again(AD 850-1173), Pandiyas (AD 1175-1300) and finally the Vijayanagar Empire all had considerable influence over the area.

However, it was the arrival of the British that brought the most major changes. Madras, was founded in 1639. It is thus one of S India's most recent cities. It is also certainly one of the least representative. Colonial both in origin and function, its development contributed to the transformation of the political and economic development of S India after the 17th century. Today it is India's 4th largest city. In the late 19th century Tamil political leaders played a prominent part in creating the movement for Independence.

Recent political developments Tamil Nadu took its present form as a result of the States Reorganisation Act of 1956. Already by that time the earlier British Presidency of Madras had been greatly reduced in size. It had lost its northern districts to Andhra Pradesh and its western districts to Mysore, now Karnataka. Under the 1956 Act it lost 2 districts from Malabar but gained 4 from Travancore when the new state of Kerala was formed, and thus assumed its present shape. Until 1967 the Assembly was dominated by the Indian National Congress. However, after an attempt by the central government to impose Hindi as a national language the Congress Party was routed by a regional party, the Dravida Munnetra Kazhagam (the DMK). Since then either the DMK or a splinter party, the All India Anna DMK, has been in power in the State.

Routes Tamil Nadu has one of the best road networks in S Asia (though the quality of the surface often leaves a lot to be desired). The routes outlined below are suggestions as to convenient ways of seeing some of the state's most interesting places, but it is easy to find alternatives as bus transport goes within range of virtually every village.

MADRAS TO TRICHY (Coastal Route)

The suburbs of S Madras give way to casuarina groves along the increasingly developed road to Mamallapuram. Crossing the attractive salt flats to Tirukkalukundram, the quiet district road then passes through fascinating villages and the coconut fringed coast to Pondicherry.

The road out of Madras via **Tiruvanmiyur** and the coast road goes past the Cholamandalam Artists colony, in the suburbs of southern Madras, the VGP Golden Beach Resort, and Fisherman's Cove.

Tiruvanmiyur is noted for its temple dedicated to the Goddess Tripurasundari, who is believed to have been worshipped here by one of Tamil Nadu's most revered poets, **Valmiki**. The temple is packed with worshippers on Fridays, and the temple has 108 Sivalinga images.

A great deal of development has taken place alongside the road in the last 10 years. The city now stretches down to the VGP Golden Beach resort complex and all the way to Mamallapuram the land on either side is divided up into plots ready for building or commercial use. The VGP beach resort is a tacky commercial "fair". Through Tiruvanmiyur are numerous small temples and shrines. New houses and blocks of flats line the narrow road. Coconut and casuarina trees are common on both sides. Note the use of windmills for water pumping. Development along coast side of the road is taking place fast, represented by buildings like that of the National Institute of Port Management 26 km from Madras. Travelling in the early Feb morning the air is still fresh, and there is often a heavy dew.

Travelling S you see casuarina plantations on right. For many years these have provided firewood for Madras, which used to be shipped up the Buckingham Canal. Shortage of fuel has meant a sharp increase in wood prices, and the poor sandy soils produce an extremely valuable harvest. (Firewood still accounts for nearly 30% of India's total energy requirement.) Note the round concrete buildings built for protection in case of natural calamities. They are a reminder that this coast is subject to catastrophic **cyclones**, and have been built to provide safe refuge for villagers. Many are now used to house Tamil refugees from Sri Lanka. There are some very good looking new houses on both sides of the road before a view of Fisherman's Cove across the water to the left. All the land has either been developed or marked into plots for development. Traditional means of raising water – **picottahs*** – used to be working on the salt pans between here and Mamallapuram, but they have now been replaced by power pumps. The red soil so typical of many parts of Tamil Nadu makes its first appearance here. Beyond Covelong, 16 km out from Mamallapuram are extensive casuarina groves, which are interspersed with palmyra palms.

More very exclusive houses down by the sea. 4 km from Mamallapuram is another circular building for protection. There are attractive views to right across extensive paddy fields. Across the plains as you approach Mamallapuram is the outline to the W of Tirukkalukundram hill – the first glimpse of the 3000 million year old Charnockite rocks that outcrop across Tamil Nadu. The town of Mamallapuram is still a rather scruffy little place, though there are comfortable places to stay.

Mamallapuram (64 km from Madras. *Population* 9,500) was previously called **Mahabalipuram** after the legend of **Vishnu** conquering the giant Mahabali, it has been renamed as the town of 'Mamalla' (great wrestler) the name given to **Narasimhavarman I Pallavamalla** (r AD 630-668) the Pallava ruler who made the port famous in the 7th century and was largely responsible for the temples. There are 14 cave temples and 9 monolithic *rathas* (shrines in the shape of rathas

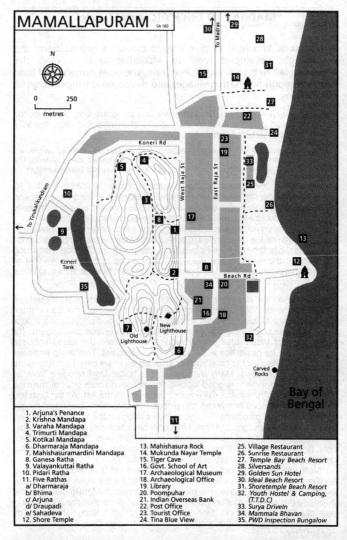

MAMALLAPURAM

SA 160

N

0   250
metres

To Madras

To Tirukalikundram

To Madras

Koneri Rd

West Raja St

East Raja St

Koneri Tank

Beach Rd

New Lighthouse

Old Lighthouse

Carved Rocks

Bay of Bengal

1. Arjuna's Penance
2. Krishna Mandapa
3. Varaha Mandapa
4. Trimurti Mandapa
5. Kotikal Mandapa
6. Dharmaraja Mandapa
7. Mahishasuramardini Mandapa
8. Ganesa Ratha
9. Valayankuttai Ratha
10. Pidari Ratha
11. Five Rathas
   a/ Dharmaraja
   b/ Bhima
   c/ Arjuna
   d/ Draupadi
   e/ Sahadeva
12. Shore Temple

13. Mahishasura Rock
14. Mukunda Nayar Temple
15. Tiger Cave
16. Govt. School of Art
17. Archaeological Museum
18. Archaeological Office
19. Library
20. Poompuhar
21. Indian Overseas Bank
22. Post Office
23. Tourist Office
24. Tina Blue View

25. Village Restaurant
26. Sunrise Restaurant
27. *Temple Bay Beach Resort*
28. *Silversands*
29. *Golden Sun Hotel*
30. *Ideal Beach Resort*
31. *Shoretemple Beach Resort*
32. *Youth Hostel & Camping,*
    (T.T.D.C)
33. *Surya Driveln*
34. *Mammala Bhavan*
35. *PWD Inspection Bungalow*

or temple chariots), 3 stone temples and 4 relief sculptured rock panels. The nature of the area with its 2 vast natural granite-gneiss mounds lent itself to rock cut architecture although there were also structural temples in this spot.

Another characteristic feature of the temples here was the system of water channels and tanks, drawn from the **Palar river**, which made it particularly suitable as a site of religious worship apart from providing water supply for household use. The *naga* or serpent cult associated with water worship can be seen given prominence at Arjuna's Penance.

Local Festival 10 day festival in Jan. Masi Magam in Mar attracts large crowds of pilgrims. Brahmotsava for 10 days in Apr-May. The *Palanquin Festival* is held in Oct-Nov at the Salasayana Perumal Temple.

Places of interest (Distances from the Bus Stand). **Arjuna's Penance (Descent of the Ganga)**, bas relief sculpted on the face of two enormous adjacent rocks, is 29 m long and 7 m high. It shows realistic life size figures of animals, gods and saints watching the descent of the river from the Himalayas. A contrived water fall fed from a collecting chamber above, issuing from the natural crack between the two rocks is believed to have originally represented Ganga. Some see the figure of an ascetic as representing Arjuna's penance when praying for powers from Siva. The animals are particularly curious and show a humorous scene of a cat imitating the solemn posture of a saint in meditation while rats dance around him. The two large elephants are remarkable and there are also scenes from the fables in the *Panchatantra* and a small shrine to Vishnu.

Mandapas There are 10 cave temples or *mandapas** (of which 2 are unfinished) in an area about a km away which are cut out of rock on the main hill to make shallow halls (porticos). They are very distinctive architecturally and show a progression in the Dravidian temple style. The pillared halls are a means of providing space for the sculptures depicting tales from mythology. However, they too, with the rest of the architectural devices, are superbly executed. The temples are fairly small – mostly 8 m wide, and 8 m deep and about 6 m high with pillars which are 3 m tall and 50 cm in diameter.

The **Krishna** Mandapa (mid-7th century) has a bas relief scene of Krishna lifting Mount Govardhana to protect a crowd of his kinsmen from the anger of the Rain God, Indra. The **Varaha** Mandapa shows two incarnations of Vishnu – Varaha (boar) and Vamana (dwarf), among other scenes of kings and queens and has the distinctive architectural feature where the base forms a narrow receptacle for water for pilgrims to use before entering the temple. The **Trimurthi** caves have three shrines to Brahma, Vishnu and Siva, the last with a lingam. The **Kotikal** Mandapa may be the earliest of them dating from the beginning of the 7th century, roughly carved out with a small shrine with no image inside.

S of the new lighthouse, beyond the unfinished Arjuna's Penance, is the early 7th century **Dharamaja** cave which is simpler and contains 3 empty shrines. To its W is the **Mahishasuramardini** mandapa (mid-7th century) which has particularly fine bas relief and finely carved columns which show the introduction of the lion to the base of the pillars. It is named after the scene of the goddess Durga slaying the buffalo demon Mahishasura which is beside one of the 3 shrines. Another shows Vishnu lying under the hood of Adishesha the 7-hooded serpent. These panels are particularly good examples of Pallava art.

The **Rathas** (1.5 km) are monolithic temples to the S, which were sculpted out of the rock in the mid-7th century and are influenced by Buddhist architecture in resembling the *vihara* (monastery) and *chaitya* hall (temple). They point to the evolution of different kinds of Dravidian temples with *gopurams*, *vimanas* and *mandapas*. The purpose of imitating in granite, temple structures that were built of wood is not known.

The **Ganesa** ratha is a rectangular shrine with pillars which have lions at their base. It is double-storeyed and has a vaulted roof. To the W are the **Valayankuttai** and twin **Pidari** rathas which are small monolithic temples. There is a set of 5 *rathas* **Pancha Pandava**, in the monastery style, named after the 5 Pandava brothers, the heroes in the epic Mahabharata and their wife Draupadi. The largest is the domed *Dharmaraja*, then the barrel vaulted *Bhima* which is followed by another dome shaped ratha *Arjuna*. The *Draupadi* ratha is the smallest and simplest and in the form of a thatched hut with a lion in front as though carrying that, which may suggest that it is a replica of a portable shrine.
To its W is the apsidal *Nakula Sahadeva* ratha with a free-standing elephant nearby. The

Dharmaraja and Arjuna are particularly well sculpted. The Bhima, Sahadeva and Ganesa rathas follow the form of the Buddhist *chaitya* hall, and are oblong in plan and built to 2 or more storeys, a precursor to the *gopuram*, the entrance gateway.

The *Shore Temple* (1 km) has been transformed by the building of an enormous protective sea wall barrier of granite boulders about 50 m out to sea. The space has been filled in and is being grassed. There are signs declaring it to be a national monument and part of the world heritage. The whole promontory has been fenced off, and access is only through a gate. The whole has a strange effect. It largely loses its romantic appeal, for the sea is now felt to be far distant rather than crashing right up against the temple, and there is the slightly ominous sense that as the flower beds and gardens are developed it will become something of a theme park. On the other hand it is possible to see it – all round – far more comfortably. There are very large numbers of Indian tourists coming through from early morning. The road to the five *rathas* is lined with stalls and carving factories. For details see below.

A compact temple with 2 spires, built at the end of the 7th century by king Rajasimha, it is based on the Dharmaraja Ratha and is unusual in that it has shrines to both Siva and Vishnu. Its position on the sea shore and the purpose of making the altar face E to catch the rising sun as well as provide a lamp light (a stone pillar to hold the beacon for sailors is evident) at night meant there was no space for a forecourt or entrance gateway. Two additional shrines were built to the W, asymmetrically. The second smaller spire adds to the unusual structure of this temple.

This early temple shows the introduction of the lion figure at the base of *pilasters** – an architectural style which was to become significant. Some of the temple has been reclaimed from the sea and it seems that the central shrine could be surrounded by water by the flooding of the outer enclosure. The outer parapet wall has lines of *nandi* or sacred bulls and lion pilasters.

5 km N of Mamallapuram, on the coast, is the excavated temple at **Saluvankuppam** which has the **Tiger Cave** mandapam with carvings of tigers' heads. The cave is not signposted from the beach; it is 10 min N of *Ideal Beach Hotel*. Secluded and very peaceful – a lovely place for a picnic. On the way you will see the **Mukunda Nayar Temple**.

NB One recent visitor writes: "If you're white, female and wearing shorts, you have to be prepared to star in lots of photos".

Hotels B *Fisherman's Cove*, Covelong. T 04114 268 (Madras 474849). 80 rm some a/c cottages, and rm with sea view. 38 km from Madras and 20 km from Mamallapuram. Pool for residents only but bar open to visitors. Excellent value, on a beautiful site with very good facilities. **C** *Temple Bay Ashok* (ITDC). T 251, Cable: Tourism. 23 rm some a/c. Restaurant (Indian and continental), occasional barbecue, bar, exchange, travel, pool, TV. Some cottages with kitchenette and fridge. 'Resort hotel'. **C** *Silversands*, Covelong Rd. T 283, (Madras 477444), Cable: Veecumsees, Telex: 041 8082. 65 rm (best are a/c, on beach and with sea view). Restaurant, bar, exchange, travel, fridge, 'swing', balcony and TV with deluxe rm, cultural shows. No pool. Occasional free shuttle service into Madras. Less expensive **E** *Silver Inn* with accommodation in huts away from the beach. **D** *VGP Golden Beach Resort*, E Coast Rd, Injabakkam. T 412893. 15 km from Madras, 39 km from Mamallapuram). Restaurant, bar, exchange. Popular with Indian day tourists. **D** *Golden Sun Hotel*, 59 Kovalam Rd. T 245. 35 rm. Restaurant (Indian, Chinese), bar, exchange, TV, cultural shows. Fairly simple but in pleasant surroundings. **NB** Visitors are charged for access to sea although half is coupon for food and drink at stalls. Sewer runs into sea. **D** *Ideal Beach Resort*, Kovalam Rd is 3½ km from Mamallapuram. T 240. 15 rm. Restaurant (generous portions), travel, good pool and gardens. Reduced rate May-Aug. Clean, comfortable, friendly and relaxed. **D** *Shore Temple Beach Resort* (TTDC). T 235. 48 cottages (new split-level ones best), some a/c with telephones and TV. Multi-cuisine restaurant (slow service, not recommended), bar, travel, pool. Good value. **D** *Buharis Blue Lagoon Hotel*, E Coast Rd, Neelankarai. T 414525. 14 km airport. A/c rm and cottages. Restaurant, pool, sports. **E E** *Mammala House*, 105 E Raja St. 20 rm some a/c. Restaurant (Indian veg). **E** *Surya* **F** *Mammala Bhavan* (opp Bus Stand). T 250. 20 rm. Restaurant (S Indian veg).

There are also some cheap guest houses nr the Bus Stand and on E Raja St and the **F** *Nemmeli Alavander Naicker Dharamsala* near the Bus Stand. T 229. The **F** *PWD Inspection Bungalow* is very basic (electricity but no running water) and can only be reserved through the Collector, Chingleput District, Kanchipuram, a week in advance, if not booked for govt officials.

Youth Hostel and Camping *Shore Temple Youth Hostel and Camping Site* (TTDC), Temple Rd nr the Shore Temple. T 287. 18 cottages and 45 dorm beds. Restaurant, bar, exchange, rm service. Clean, good value, (no mosquito nets), well placed though not on beach. Recommended. *Drive-in Camp Site*, 1 Thirukula St. T 290. 8 cottages and 2 rm. Restaurant, travel. Camping available.

Restaurants The best are in the top hotels. The outdoor café at *Silver Sands* is popular and recommended. Two specializing in sea food are *Sunrise Restaurant* (multi-cuisine), on Shore Temple Rd which is simple and under thatch, serves good fish dishes and the *Village Restaurant* nr the Bus Stand (recommended). Other multi-cuisine restaurants are *Tina Blue View*, Othavadai St (view from balcony upstairs, which also catches the breeze) with good food, *Gazebo* E Raja St and *Honeyfalls*, Shore Temple Rd. *Ashok* and the *Youth Camp* have snack bars on Shore Temple Rd.

Bank There is a branch of Indian Overseas Bank, T 222, a Sub Post Office, T 230 and a small library nr the Tourist Office.

Shopping *Poompuhar Govt Sales Emporium*, (nr the Shore Temple) on Beach Rd and shops nr the Five Rathas complex sell small statues in soapstone and metal, shell jewellery and trinkets and palm leaf baskets. The *Govt School of Sculpture* is nr the Bus Stand and continues to practise the skills which flourished centuries ago. Open 0900-1300, 1400-1830. Closed Tue.

Local Transport Un-metered private taxis, cycle and motorcycle rickshaws.

Museums The small **Archeological Museum** on W Raja St, nr the Ganesa Ratha has granite sculptures and fragments which have been found nearby.

Tourist office and information Government of Tamil Nadu Tourist Office, E Raja St. T 232. Open 1000-1730. TTDC guides can be hired from Madras. The *Archaeological Survey of India Office* nr the Bus Stand to the S, has a guide lecturer who can guide visitors on request. His services are free.

Travel Several regular daily buses from Madras which also go to Tirukkalukundram and Pondicherry. Nos. 19C, 68, 119A. The nearest station is Chingleput, 29 km away. (STD 004113). The bus tour organized by TTDC includes Kanchipuram and Mamallapuram in one day. Dep 0500, return 1900. Tiring, but good value if you do not mind being rushed. It also includes a stop at the appallingly garish VGP Beach Resort.

Bicycle Hire If you're staying in Mamallapuram you can hire bikes to get to Tirukkalukundram – from Dec to Feb this is a comfortable and very attractive ride.

The road to Tirukkalukundram (16 km) first crosses salt flats and the Buckingham Canal, which stretches over 350 km into Andhra Pradesh. Patches of land under rice cultivation are irrigated by wells visible from the roadside. This is a really attractive landscape, illustrating important contrasts between wet and dry land in much of S India. Small wells – the water table here is very high – and tanks allow irrigation of low lying areas; slightly higher land or land beyond the range of such irrigation is uncultivated. This pattern continues southwards.

Another feature common throughout India is the widespread numbering of trees, indicating their great value – for fuel, fodder, building and other purposes. On the dry land a thorn scrub, *Prosopis juliflora*, is now very common. Introduced as a fencing plant to keep cattle off the fields by an enthusiastic District Collector at the turn of the century, this has run riot on dry, thin soils. For a long time it was regarded as a menace, but in some areas is now being used to make charcoal.

On the road between Mamallapuram and Tirukkalukundram is an experimental tree-planting scheme for tribal women. There is a growing number of such schemes sponsored both by the government and by Non-Governmental Organisations. Much of this re-afforestation has been with eucalyptus, introduced to India from Australia a century ago. There are examples on both sides of the road between 5 and 6 km S of Tirukkalukundram on the road to Madurantakam. Such plantations have attracted fierce criticism from some experts, who believe that they take a lot of water from the soil around and that they do not supply the products needed by poor people which are supplied by local varieties of trees.

Hilltops, springs, trees, are all imbued by Hindus with special significance as places where the divine has been revealed. **Tirukkalukundram** (*Population* 26,000) illustrates the dramatic potential of hilltop sites for temples. For details see page 717.

Leaving Tirukkalukundram on the Madurantakam road, a brief detour to **Sadras** (14 km) is possible. The ruined Dutch fort is close to the sea and a cemetery going back to 1679. In line with many other small European territories in India, its fate depended largely on events outside India. Sadras was taken by the British in 1781, but given back to the Dutch in 1818. It was finally ceded to the British in exchange for British-held territories in Sumatra.

Otherwise go straight to Madurantakam (14 km *Population* 29,000), crossing the broad, sandy bed of the **Palar** river approximately half way. The Palar rises in Andhra Pradesh and flows through **Vellore** and past **Kanchipuram**. Though it rarely has surface water its bed is tapped along its length for ground water, now seriously polluted, particularly by Tamil Nadu's economically very important leather tanning industry.

Join briefly the NH 45 at **Madurantakam**, which has a very large irrigation tank. This is seen from the new by-pass, though not from the town itself which lies stretched along the foot of the tank *bund* or embankment. Typical of the irrigation tanks built from the 8th century AD onwards in the districts around Madras, these very shallow storage reservoirs dry out completely for up to eight months of the year, but provide an insurance for the main crop and extend the growing season for the area irrigated (known in Tamil as the *ayacut*).

The road is a narrow but quiet district road with a moderate surface. Unlike the main Madras Trichy road, NH 45, there is little heavy traffic, though some local buses come this way. Follow it down to the village of **Chunampettai** (30 km), then take road to **Malakkanam** (12 km *Population* 16,000), mentioned in Roman records as an important port in the 1st century AD. The village has an ancient, quite well worked, Siva temple, with many inscriptions. The road then goes on to **Kalapettai** (16 km).

All the way down the coast the villages depend largely on agriculture, but there are communities of fishermen who live along the beach itself, selling their catch at small markets inland. From Malakkanam the road follows the coast again, passing through some fascinating villages and beautiful scenery. The coast is coconut fringed, and although the road is often a km or so from the sea's edge the glimpses of azure water are captivating.

Approaching Pondicherry (16 km), sometimes shortened to Pondy, you pass the new University of Pondicherry buildings (a central Govt of India university) and then 8 km from Pondicherry the turning to Auroville (see below under Excursions). Inland from the road is a clear view of the sharply defined ridge of red soil, evidence that the coastline has been raised significantly from the sea since the ending of the last Ice Age. These bright red soils, typical of much of S Arcot District, provide a striking contrast with the golden sands of the shoreline. 5 km out of Pondicherry the road passes under a canopy of coconut trees, sheltering scattered thatched village huts. In Jan and Feb, when the rice is being harvested, you drive across the straw spread out across the road to winnow the chaff.

Enter Pondicherry down Anna Salai which is the W Boulevard.

Pondicherry

Population 162,697. *Altitude* Sea level. *Climate* Temp. Summer Max. 41°C Min. 31°C, Winter Max. 31°C Min 25°C. Annual rainfall 135 cm. *Clothing* Cottons. Regular rly connections from Madras, 160 km away, via Villupuram.

	Jan	Feb	Mar	Apr	May	Jun	Jul	Aug	Sep	Oct	Nov	Dec
Max (°C)	28	29	30	32	34	36	35	34	33	31	29	28	32
Min (°C)	21	21	23	26	26	25	25	25	24	23	22	24
Rain (mm)	13	6	52	21	45	28	62	74	135	327	380	210	1351

Pondicherry is believed to be the site of ancient Vedapuri where **Agastya muni** (sage) had his hermitage in 1500 BC. In the 1st century AD Romans traded from nearby Arikamedu and in the 9th century, well after the decline of the University of Nalanda in Bihar, a Sanskrit University flourished here. Nearer our time, the small coastal village fishermen's village called Pulicherri which existed in 1673 was set up as a trading post by the French and renamed it Pondicherry.

The town, planned in a grid, acquired a distinct French atmosphere amidst the surrounding Tamil country. French was spoken with a noticeable accent and street names were in French. Except for short periods when the colony passed into Dutch and British hands, it was retained by the French until 1954. It was then voluntarily handed over to the Indian Govt and became the Union Territory of Pondicherry together with Karaikal, the other French enclave in the state and Mahe in Kerala and Yanam in Andhra Pradesh.

Today, many visitors are attracted by the Ashram founded by Sri Aurobindo and the Mother. *Sri Aurobindo* was a Bengali revolutionary and philosopher who struggled for freedom from British colonial power, **see page 62**. In 1910 he left Calcutta as it proved too difficult for him to continue with his political activities, and was welcomed by this far corner of French territory. He had a vision of an age of the super mind and developed a system of 'integral yoga' which combined the ancient yogic philosophy with what he then knew of modern science. He started the Ashram where he could put into practice his ideals of a peaceful community living. In this aim he found a lifelong French companion in the Mother, who helped, supported and guided him from 1920 until his death in 1950 and then continued as the spiritual successor and charismatic figure of Pondicherry until her death in 1973. *Auroville*, or the City of Dawn 8 km away, was set up 1968 as a tribute to Sri Aurobindo, and is still evolving (see under Excursions).

The grid pattern of the planned town has the waterfront to the E, along which runs Goubert Salai sometimes called Beach Rd, with a good beach over a km long which is easily accessible. There you will see the statue of Mahatma Gandhi among the eight carved pillars of the War Memorial which commemorates those who died in the first World War. On the other three sides, the main town is contained in a semicircular boulevard with a NS canal along Gingee St. On the W side you will find most of the accommodation and to the E which retains much of its former attraction, most of the public buildings, Government Place, Ashram offices and the International Guest House. The NH45A enters the town past the bus station through Lal Bahadur St while the Rly Station is to the S off S Boulevard.

Note The beach looks attractive in places, but take care. Avoid walking too close to the New Pier, which is used as a public toilet.

Local festivals Feb/Mar. *Masi Magam* On the full moon day of the Tamil month of Masi, pilgrims take a holy dip in the sea when deities from about 40 temples from the surrounding area are taken in colourful procession to the seaside for a ceremonial immersion. 'Fire walking' sometimes accompanies festivals here, 3 or 4 times a year.

Places of interest *Sri Aurobindo Ashram* has its main centre in Rue de la Marine where you can see the marble *Samadhi* where Sri Aurobindo's and the Mother's remains are kept, as well as their houses. The International Centre is across the road which has occasional films, lectures and other performances (free) and also several Ashram shops and workshops scattered around the town. **Auroville** See below under Excursions. Otherwise Museum, Parks, Churches, Libraries listed below.

Local crafts and industries Dolls of papier mâché, terracotta and plaster are produced at Kosapalayam where you can buy them. The local grass is woven into *Korai* mats. Craftsmen at the Ashram produce marbled silk, hand dyed cloths, hand made paper, rugs, perfumes and incense sticks. Well worth visiting the hand-made paper 'factory' – enquiries at the Ashram.

Hotels Western style hotels are fairly comfortable and have a/c rm. **C** *Pondicherry Ashok*,

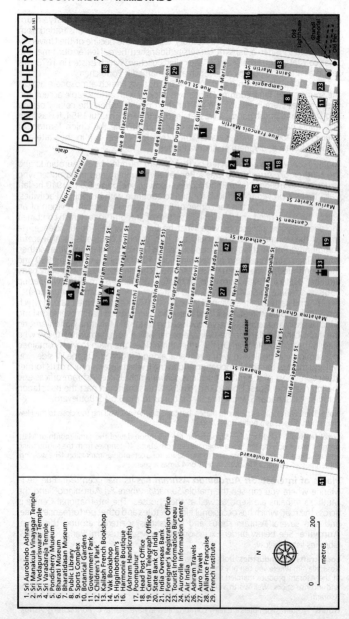

PONDICHERRY

1. Sri Aurobindo Ashram
2. Manakula Vinayagar Temple
3. Sri Vedapurisvarar Temple
4. Sri Varadaraja Temple
5. Pondicherry Museum
6. Bharati Museum
7. Bharatidasan Museum
8. Public Library
9. Sports Complex
10. Botanical Gardens
11. Children's Park
12. Vailash French Bookshop
13. Vak Bookshop
14. Higginbotham's
15. Harmonie Boutique
16. Harmonie Boutique
    (Ashram Handicrafts)
17. Poompuhar
18. Head Post Office
19. Central Telegraph Office
20. State Bank of India
21. India Overseas Bank
22. Foreigner's Registration Office
23. Tourist Information Bureau
24. Auroville Information Centre
25. Ashram Travels
26. Auro Travels
27. Alliance Française
28. French Institute

0   200
metres

N

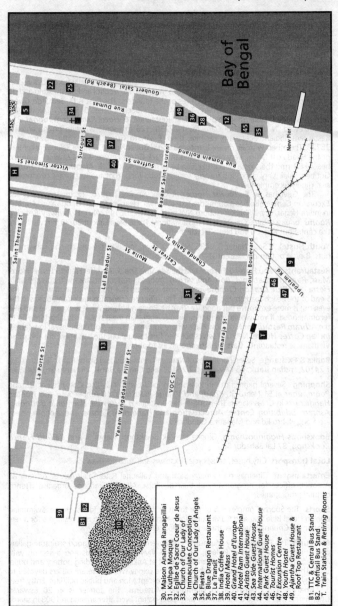

Bay of Bengal

30. Maison Ananda Rangapillai
31. Kutijai Mosque
32. Eglise Sacré Coeur de Jesus
33. Church of Our Lady of Immaculate Conception
34. Church of Our Lady of Angels
35. Fiesta
36. Blue Dragon Restaurant
37. Le Transit
38. India Coffee House
39. Hotel Mass
40. Grand Hotel d'Europe
41. Hotel Ram International
42. Aristo Guest House
43. Sea Side Guest House
44. International Guest House
45. Park Guest House
46. Tourist Homes
47. Excursion Centre
48. Youth Hostel
49. Ajantha Guest House & Roof Top Restaurant

B1. TTC & Central Bus Stand
B2. Mofussil Bus Stand
T. Train Station & Retiring Rooms

Chinnakalapet, Kalapet Exchange 460, Cable: Pondyashok, Telex: 0469-239. 20 rm. 12 km rly. Central a/c. Restaurant, bar, coffee shop, exchange, travel, TV. **D** *Hotel Mass*, Maraimalai Adigal Salai, T 27221, Cable: Mass. Just off the NH 45A and nr the New Mofussil Bus Stand, short distance from the centre. 35 rm. New, 2 restaurants, bar, exchange, travel, shops, TV. **D** *Grand Hotel d'Europe*, 12 Rue Suffern off Lal Bahadur St. Very central but quiet. T 404. 6 rm. Restaurant recommended – excellent French family cooking. Opened in 1891 by Frenchman, clean, sparse but with very attractive character.

The Aurobindo Ashram has several guest houses which are primarily for official visitors to the Ashram but also open to others (not to 'hippies'). No alcohol and no smoking and do not be put off by the presence of pictures of the founders. The best is **D** *Sea Side Guest House*, 10 Goubert Salai (Beach Rd), T 6494, Cable: Society, Telex: 0459-221 SAS In. Very central. 8 large double rm in an old building. Restaurant. **E** *Hotel Ram International*, 212 W Boulevard, N of Botanical Gardens, T 27230. 120 rm, some a/c with phone and TV. Restaurant (Indian vegetarian), car hire, shop. **E** *Aristo Guest House*, 50A Mission St, T 26728. The others with a/c rm are **E** *International Guest House*, Gingee Salai, very central, nr the Head Post Office, very popular, and the *Park Guest House*, T 4412, which is on the beach. 80 rm. The Fiesta Snack Bar nearby is recommended. **E** *Ajantha Guest House*, Goubert Salai. Very clean and freindly service, good food, roof top restaurant overlooking sea. Highly recommended.

The Govt has an **E** *Tourist Homes* at Uppalam Rd, T 6376. 12 rm some a/c. The *Excursion Centre* also has a dormitory. S of the town, clean and quiet. Good value. Another in Indira Nagar, opp JIPMER in suburb NW of the town, T 6145. Also **F** *Railway Retiring Rooms* for passengers. Quieter than most stations! These are all about 20-30 min walk from the centre but easier if you hire a bicycle.

Youth Hostel F Solai Nagar, T 3495, N of the town, close to the sea among fishermen's huts. Bicycle or transport essential.

Restaurants *Grand Hotel d'Europe* and the *Sea Side Snack Bar* offer French cuisine. *Hotel Mass, Ram International, Bon Ami, Aristo* (roof top restaurant) are multi-cuisine, while *Fiesta* and *Blue Dragon Chinese Restaurant*, both on Rue Dumas nr the New Pier at the S end of the beach road are recommended. The *Alliance Française* restaurant, opens in the evening, is more expensive but good. *La Transit*, Romain Roland St is less expensive and also recommended. If you would like to try a simple vegetarian meal in an unusual setting, go to the *Ashram Restaurant* N of Govt Place where you will be seated on cushions, at low tables. *Indian Coffee House*, Nehru St serves non-veg fare throughout the day. There are also some Vietnamese restaurants. **Bars** In larger hotels listed above.

Banks & Exchange Several branches of National banks including **State Bank**, 5 Suffren St, T 24102, **Indian Bank**, 65 Mission St, T 26403 and **Canara Bank**, 16 Nehru St, T 24354.

Shopping Several handicraft emporia selling local crafts including *Co-optex* at 28 and *Poompuhar* at 51 Nehru St, *Khadi and Village Industries*, 10 Amber Salai and *Tibetan Handicrafts* in Colas Nagar. The Ashram has Boutique *d'Auroville, Harmonie Boutique, Ashram Exhibition Centre, Aurocreation* and *Handloom Centre*. The shopping areas are along Nehru Rd and Mahatma Gandhi Rd.

Bookshops *Higginbotham's*, Gingee St, *Vak Bookshop*, Nehru St and *Kailash French Bookshop*, 87 Lal Bahadur St.

Local transport City buses, taxis, cycle rickshaws and auto rickshaws.

Entertainment Cinemas on Kamaraj Salai and Vallabhai Patel Salai. Ask at Ashram an Auroville offices for programmes at their auditoria. Alliance Française organises French cultural programmes.

Sports The Sports Complex is S of the town nr the Government Tourist Home. Swimming pool in Hotel Blue Star and Calva Bungalow, Kamaraj Salai open to non-residents for a fee. Boating on Chunnambar river through the Boat Club, 10 km away.

Museums The **Pondicherry Museum** S of Government Park has a good sculpture gallery containing items from the Pallava, Chola and Vijayanagara periods and a section with archaeological finds from the Roman settlement at Arikamedu including pottery and burial urns. The French gallery charts the history of the colony while there are others devoted to geology, art and handicrafts. Open 1000-1700, except Mon and public holidays. Entry free.

Bharati and **Bharatidasan Memorial Museums**. The former is in 20 Eswaran Dharmaraja Koil St where the famous Tamil poet-patriot lived after arriving in 1908 in search of refuge. The latter is in 95, Perumal Koil St, the home of Kanakasubburatnam who adopted the name meaning disciple of Bharati which has become the second place of literary pilgrimage. **Ananda Rangapillai** on Rangapillai St has material on French India from 1736-1760.

Parks and zoos The *Botanical Gardens* which was opened in 1826 has a variety of rare and exotic plants and also an aquarium with ornamental fish and exhibits showing local methods of coastal fishing. The *Government Park* which is laid out with lawns and flower beds and fountains(one at the centre is of Napoleon III period), is in front of the Raj Niwas, the residence of the Lieutenant Governor. *Children's Park*, N of New Pier.

Useful addresses Foreigners' Regional Registration Office, Goubert Salai (Beach Rd). *French Consulate*, 2 Marine St, T 24058. The *French Institute*, Rue St Louis, close to the N end of Goubert Salai, was set up in 1955 for the study of Indian culture, and **Alliance Française** at the S end of Goubert Salai for cultural programmes.

Post and telegraph The *Head Post Office* is on the NW corner of Government Place. *Central Telegraph Office* is on Nidarajapayer St.

Places of worship *Hindu* – Sri Manakula Vinayagar Temple, Manakula Vinayagar Koil St and on MG Rd; Sri Vedapuriswarar Temple and Sri Varadaraja Perumal Temple. *Muslim* – Kulthapa Mosque, Mulla St. *Christian* – Eglise de Sacré Coeur de Jesus, S Boulevard; Church of Our Lady of Immaculate Conception, Cathedral Rd; Church of Our Lady of the Angels, Rue Dumas.

Hospitals and medical services *General Hospital*, Rue Victor Simone, T 27070. *Jawaharlal Institute of Post Graduate Medical Education and Research* (JIPMER), Gorimedu to the NW of town, T 263880.

Travel agents and tour operators *Auro Travels*, Nehru St, T 25128. *Amsham Travels*, Chetty St, T 23717. *Air India* office is on Beach Rd.

Tourist offices and information *Tourist Information Bureau*, Old Secretariate in Compagnie St, E of Government Place, has limited information. The *Auroville Information Centre* is on Nehru St, W of the canal. *Pondicherry Tourism Development Corporation*, (PTDC), Goubert Salai (Beach Rd), T 23590. *Ashram Reception Service*, Main Building, Rue de la Marine, T 24836.

Rail Connects only with Villupuram which is on the main line and in turn has connections to Madras. Rly Station, Enquiries: T 26684. Open 0900-1200, 1500-1800. Reservations for Villupuram and Madras connections.

Road Good network through NH 45A which extends to Pondicherry. Villupuram 39 km, Cuddalore 22 km, Madras 150 km.

Buses Thiruvalluvar (TTC) buses run from the bus stand on NH 45A about 500 W of the traffic circle. Hourly buses for Madras, 7 daily to Chidambaram, and daily to Bangalore (7 hr 30 min), Madurai (8 hr) and Ooty (12 hr). Bus Stand Enquiries: T 26513. Computerised Reservations: Open 0700-2100. The Moffusil Bus Stand serves all other bus companies, State and Private, and is a further 500 m to the W which run services to the major cities in the region. Bus Stand Thanthai Periyar Transport Corporation Enquiries: T 26919. Open 0430-1230, 1330-2130.

Excursions It is possible to extend this trip by visiting **Auroville** taking either of the 2 roads N from Pondicherry to Madras. Taxi or bicycle hire is possible from Pondicherry. In Pondicherry La Boutique d'Auroville, 12 Nehru St, T 27264, can give you directions. There are conducted tours to Auroville 3 times a week.

The Mother, as Sri Aurobindo Ghose's chief disciple was universally known, died at the age of 93 in 1973. She had seen the building of Auroville as a centre for world brotherhood, hoping that it would become a major focus for meditation and spiritual regeneration. Futuristically designed, the layout of the city and its major buildings, notably the Matri Mandir, were to reflect the principles of Sri Aurobindo's philosophy. The Charter says "To live in Auroville one must be a willing servitor of the Divine Consciousness" and describes it as belonging "to humanity as a whole......the place of an unending education, of constant progress ....a bridge between the past and the future......a site of material and spiritual researches."

Development after its inauguration in 1968 has been very slow. The city was planned in the form of a spiral nebula, symbolising the universality of its faith. The central meditation building remains to be completed and the crystal of meditation which is to be placed in its centre is ready for installation after the internal work is finished. The city itself remains largely unfinished.

The population in 1990 was still less than 700, drawn mainly from a range of European nations. Designed by a French architect, Auroville has over 50 settlements spread across about 50 sq km. With Matrimandir at the centre, you will come across names like Sincerity, Shanti (peace), Grace, Verite, Horizon, Transition, Recueillement, Gratitude, Fertile etc. Activities include village work, education, 'Green work' (17 different kinds of windmills, afforestation), food growing, dairies, alternative technology and handicrafts. The settlements are widely spaced out and can only be visited comfortably by cycle or by car. Tourist facilities are very limited with 2 restaurants, tea shops, a bank, a post office and two shops.

It was the vision of Sri Aurobindo and the Mother to achieve the ideal international commune, and you may get a glimpse of what the supporters believe in from what is written about Mother's Agenda now published in 13 volumes. "Mother's prodigious exploration into the body's cellular consciousness.......as narration of twenty three years' experimentation strikes deep into the most recent discoveries of modern physics. Step by step we uncover what may well be Man's passage to the next species upon earth: how to change the law of death and the old genetic programme of cells."

The community at Auroville welcomes visitors who have a genuine interest in the philosophical basis of the community, though it does not encourage general sight-seeing. There are three **E** Guest Houses *Fraternity, Swagatham* and *Utility Repose* where food is included in rm charges. Since accommodation is limited it is best to make enquiries in advance if you propose to spend the night. Contact Boutique d'Auroville, Aspiration, PO Koilapalayam via Kattakuppam, S Arcot District, Tamil Nadu.

PONDICHERRY TO TRICHY

Early morning is an excellent time to travel in most places in India, but especially in the S. The air is fresh and cool, the light limpid. Southwards from Pondy on the road to Cuddalore there are alternating groves of casuarina trees, many recently planted, with coconut and palmyra palms. In Jan-Feb at harvest time there is also a delightful scent of fresh straw in the air. Paddy, groundnut and sugar cane are all found in the fields along the road to Cuddalore, and S Arcot district is one of the main sugar producing districts of S India.

Development is taking place fast along the roadside. The road passes a small steel rolling mill (E Coast Steel) on the left. The second wide river to be crossed is the **Ponnaiyar**, which rises nearly 500 km to the N W just N of Bangalore. Its flow is now controlled by the Sathanur Dam just W of Tiruvannamalai, but it remains very variable, coming down in short floods which rapidly dry up. It is held to be a scared river, especially so during the first five days of the Tamil month of *Tai*, when bathing in it is thought to be particularly meritorious. There are beautiful views crossing the river early in the morning and again in late afternoon.

Signs of the changing economic face of Tamil Nadu are evident in **Cuddalore** itself (21 km; *Population* 167,000) with the presence of shops selling motor bikes, electric pumpsets, even videos. But there are also obvious features of continuity with the past, though not many of its origins as an E India Company trading settlement in 1684, nor of **Fort St. David** which was built soon after. This was destroyed by the French General Lally in 1758. All that remains is the ditch, and some ruins of walls. The oldest part of the town is the commercial centre, at the junction of the 2 rivers the Gadilam and the Uppanar, from which the town took its name. The second oldest section is 4 km to the northwest, followed by the district of *Manjikuppam*, where today's district offices are located. This is the official city centre.

In the middle is an open *maidan*, referred to in old records as "the lawn" or "the green", recalling images of village England. Round it are several shaded avenues and the old Collector's house, completed in 1733. Fort St David is the most recent sector. Soon after their arrival the traders of the English E India Company began to set up new suburbs (*pettahs*) for weavers, some of whom were brought in from as far afield as Kalahasti nearly 100 km N of Madras. *Brookespettah*, *Lathomspet* and *Cumingspet* are 3 examples of such late 18th century settlements. At one time the "new" town of Tiruppapuliyur was a major Jain centre. The present large temple enshrines the deity Patalesvara, and there are several Chola inscriptions. The temple has been richly endowed by the *Nattukkottai Chettiyars* (**see page 776**) and among its valuables are a silver car and a gold palanquin.

Between 43 km and 29 km from Chidambaram, the land becomes a totally flat plain, but the irrigated rice fields make it a beautiful sight. Tamarind trees line much of the road – all carefully numbered, along with all the other trees on the roadside. The rich fertile irrigated soils alternate with much poorer land. The difference lies in the availability of irrigation. Land slightly above the irrigation channels or beyond their reach remains sparsely cultivated or waste. Soon after dawn the roads begin to fill with pedestrians, cyclists, lorries and buses. Villages and towns come alive – and are much slower to get through.

You can take a short detour back to the coast again to visit **Porto Novo** (21 km), a port established by the Portuguese in 1575, the first Europeans to land on the Coromandel coast. They were followed by the Dutch, who occupied it in 1643 with a two year gap, until 1781. War having broken out in Europe between the British and Dutch the British captured it (along with all the other Dutch factories along the Indian coast) and made it a trading post. On 1 July 1781 the British military Commander Sir Eyre Coote won a battle for the port over **Haidar Ali** of Mysore that in the view of some historians ensured the possibility of British expansion in S India. It changed hands twice more before finally being ceded to the British in 1824. Today the town has a large Muslim population, mainly involved in sea based trade. 10 km N of Chidambaram the road crosses the **Vellar River** ("white river").

Chidambaram (15 km) *Population* 72,000, the capital of the *Cholas* from AD 907 to 1310, Chidambaram lies on the N edge of the Coleroon River, which in itself marks the northern limit of the Thanjavur delta. In Tamil Nadu Chidambaram is regarded as a holy town of great importance, and has been the home of noted Tamil poets and saints.

Local festivals Jun/Jul: Ani Tirumanjanam Festival. Dec/Jan: Markazhi Tiruvathirai Festival.

Places of interest The best known temple is the **Nataraja Temple,** which is dedicated to the dancing Lord Siva, a favourite deity of the Chola kings. One legend surrounding its construction suggests that it was built by "the golden coloured Emperor", **Hiranya Varna Chakravarti**, who suffered from leprosy. He came to Chidambaram on a pilgrimage from Kashmir in about 500 A.D. After bathing in the temple tank he was reputed to have recovered from the disease, and as a thank-offering rebuilt and enlarged the temples.

One of the most basic ideas of Hinduism "is the identification of a sacred site with the centre or navel of the universe, the spot though which passes the axis connecting the heavens, the earth and the subterranean world of *Patala*" writes David Shulman. **Siva** is quoted as saying: "The day I danced in the forest of Tillai while **Vishnu** looked on, I saw the spot that could not support me... But there is a site which can sustain the dance ... the world is analogous to the body. The left channel (of the 'subtle body') goes straight to Lanka, and the right channel pierces the Himalaya. The central channel goes directly through the great *Tillai*, the site of the original linga." This myth refers back to the story of the founding of Chidambaram, for Tillai is the ancient name of Chidambaram, "where Siva performed his dance of joy; so powerful is this dance, which represents the entire cosmic process of creation and dissolution, that it can be performed only at the very centre of the cosmos.... Chidambaram , which sees itself as the heart of the universe, locates an invisible Akasalinga in its innermost sanctum, the Chitsabha ("room of consciousness"). The centre thus proclaims its identity as the centre which, like the hidden source of life within man, is directly linked to the infinite."

The imagery dates back to the myth of the origin of the Chidambaram temple itself. The S Arcot District Gazetteer recounts it as follows: "In the forest of Tillai was an ancient shrine to Siva and another to the Goddess **Kali** which was built where the Nritta Sabha now stands. Siva came down to his shrine to manifest himself to two very fervent devotees there, and Kali objected to his trespassing on her domains. They eventually agreed to settle the question by seeing which could dance the better, it being agreed that the defeated party should leave the site entirely to the winner. Vishnu acted as the umpire, and for a long time the honours were evenly divided. At length Vishnu suggested to Siva that he should do his well known steps in which he danced with one leg high above his head. Kali was unable to imitate or beat this style of dancing, Siva was proclaimed the winner and Kali departed outside the town, where her temple is still to be seen."

Enter the temple by the E gate. Shoes can be left with the door keeper just outside. No fee is usually demanded. A slow walk round takes about 1 hour, though you could spend much longer. Written notice boards outside the inner sanctum say that non-Hindus are not allowed, especially at times of Puja, but that rule seemed to be readily waived. Groups or individuals may be taken straight in. Open 0400-1200. 1630-2100. The evening puja at 1800 is interesting to watch. The guide *Anandan* is extremely helpful if you can find him. Also ask to meet the priest *Raja*.

This is a highly active temple, with Brahmins at every shrine – though they all belong to a local Brahmin community, unrelated to the 3000 Brahmins Hiranya Varna Chakravarti is reputed to have brought with him from Kashmir. Some of them make repeated and insistent requests for donations. Although this can be irritating it needs to be understood against the background of the very unusual form of temple management. The S Arcot District Gazetteer explains the system. "The Chidambaram temple has never had landed or other endowments, and it belongs to a group of Brahmans called *Dikshitars** ("those who make oblations"). They are peculiar to Chidambaram and are regarded locally with very high respect. You may notice that they have the single Brahmin style tuft of hair at the front rather than the back of their heads, and they marry only among themselves. Temple ritual is more like family worship than normal temple ritual.

Theoretically all the married males have a say in the running of the temple. They support the temple by going round the district asking for alms and offerings for themselves. Each has his own particular clients, and in return for the alms he receives he undertakes to make offerings at the shrine of his benefactors. From time to time he will send them holy ash or an invitation to a special festival. 20 dikshitars are always on duty at the temple, each of the males doing the work which is divided into 20 day rotas. The 20 divide themselves into 5 parties of 4, each of which is on duty for 4 days at one of the 5 shrines at which daily puja is made, sleeps there at night and becomes the owner of the routine offerings of food made at it. Large presents of food made to the temple as a whole are divided among all the *Dikshitars*. The right to the other oblations is sold by auction every 20 days to one of the Dikshitars at a meeting of the community. These periodical meetings take place in the Deva Sabha."

At each shrine the visitor will be daubed with vibhuti (sacred ash) and paste. It is not easy to see some of the sculptures. All Hindu temples are very dark inside and it takes time for eyes to adjust. If you are accompanied by a tour guide and are going round in a group you are less likely to be pressed by others to accept their services, but you may need patience and persuasive powers if you want to take your own time and to look round on your own.

The effort will be repaid. Although some of the buildings date from the late Chola period the group as a whole was built over several centuries. There are definite records of its existence before the 10th century and inscriptions from the 11th century. At the N, S, E and W are 4 enormous *gopurams*, the N and S ones being about 45 m high. The E gopuram, through which you enter the temple, is the oldest, being erected in 1250 AD. Large sculptures in the upper niches are of Saiva deities. The N gopuram has an inscription which shows that it was built by the great Vijayanagar king **Krishna Deva Raya** (1509-30). The temple compound of over 12 ha is surrounded by 2 high walls, outside which run the streets used for the temple car processions, nearly 20 m wide.

On entering the E gate you see immediately in front and to the right the large *Sivaganga* tank, with still further to the right the Raja Sabha, a 1000 columned hall or *mandapam*, built between 1595 and 1685. In the N-W of the compound are temples dedicated to **Subrahmanya** (second half of the 13th century AD), and to its S, the 12th century shrine to *Sivakumasundari* or *Parvati*, the wife of Siva. According to Michell this is the oldest building in the complex, though other authorities suggest that it is a 14th century building. The ceiling paintings are 17th Century.

At the S end of this outer compound is what is said to be the largest shrine to *Ganes* in India. The next inner compound has been filled with colonnades and passageways, some used to store images used in processions. In the innermost shrine are 2 images of Siva, the Nataraja and the lingam. A later Vishnu shrine was added to Govindaraja by the Vijayanagar kings.

The inner enclosure is the most sacred and contains four important *sabhas* (halls), the *Deva Sabha*, where the temple managers hold their meetings; the *chit sabha* or *chit ambalam* (from which the temple and the town get their names), meaning the hall of wisdom; the *kanakha sabha*, or golden hall; and the *nritta sabha*, or hall of dancing. Siva is worshipped in the *Chit ambalam*, a plain wooden building standing on a stone base, in his form as Lord of the Dance, Nataraja. The area of the shrine immediately over the deity's head is gold plated. Immediately behind the idol is the focus of the temple's power, the "Akasa Lingam". It represents the invisible element, "space", and hence is itself invisible. Known as the "Chidambaram secret", it is believed to be situated immediately behind the idol. A curtain and a long string of golden *bilva* leaves are hung in front of it.

Hotels **E** *Hotel Tamil Nadu*, Railway Feeder Rd. T 2323. Some a/c rm. Restaurant. Best in town. There is also a *Youth Hostel*. Other simpler and cheaper hotels are in the centre of town, further from the station. **F** *Star Lodge*, 101 S Car St, T 2743, near the Bus Station, basic but clean. *Raja Rajan*, 163 W Car St, T 2690 has rm with bath for a slightly higher price. Also **F** *Railway Retiring Rooms*.

Restaurants You can get non-vegetarian meals at Hotel Tamil Nadu, Hotel Mahalakshmi or Udipi Hotel.

The **Shopping** area is around the temple in Car St. The Head **Post Office** is in N Car St. **Banks** State Bank of India in Pava Mudali St, T 2284, Central Bank, 62/63 Bazaar St, T 2278 and Indian Bank, 64 S Car St, T 2244. Government of Tamil Nadu **Tourist Office** in Railway Feeder Rd, T 2739.

Travel The nearest airport is at Trichy 167 km away. The metre gauge railway links Chidambaram with Madras, Kumbakonam, Thanjavur and Trichy among others. There are also daily buses to the above cities and to Nagapattinam and Pondicherry.

Travelling S from Chidambaram to Kumbakonam you enter the Thanjavur delta some 10 minutes S of Chidambaram. After 9 km you cross the Coleroon River, the northern edge of the delta proper. A large modern rice mill on the left illustrates the present day importance of this area to the economy of the state. Sugar cane and paddy remain dominant, but the landscape is quite heavily wooded. Village ponds are scattered occasionally, with beautiful lotuses. There are occasional wayside shrines where drivers will often stop to make an offering to their chosen deity.

From Chidambaram take right turn out of town to Komarakshi, Mannargudi and **Gangakondaicholapuram** (30 km). This, the capital of the Chola **King Rajendra** (1012-1044) has now all but disappeared, though recent archaeological work suggests that interesting remains lie buried, especially at the site of the palace less than 2 km from the temple.

In 1942 Percy Brown wrote "this fine structure now stands in solitary state, except for the mud huts of a village straggling around it, as centuries ago the tide of life receded from these parts, leaving it like a great stranded shell. Nature with artistic hand has endeavoured to veil its abraded surfaces, not always to its structural good, with festoons of foliage, so that it appears as a lovely grey-green pile slumbering amidst the tangled verdure of a wide neglected garden."

The whole site has now been restored, although it is still in an isolated backwater of Trichy District. It is well worth visiting. The temple which Rajendra built to celebrate his victory march up the Ganga Valley remains a magnificent testimonial to the skill of his Chola architects and builders. The name itself means "The city of the Chola who conquered the Ganga", reference to his supposedly filling the temple tank with water brought from the Ganga. (It was an achievement that recent governments of Tamil Nadu have planned to emulate with proposals for a World Bank funded project to build a canal from the Ganga to the Kaveri.) The temple was built to rival the *Brihadisvara* temple built by Rajendra's father *Rajaraja* in Thanjavur. The 2 temples have important similarities, though the temple here has not been as extensively repaired or altered by subsequent builders as happened at Thanjavur. The enclosure is even larger than that at Thanjavur and was surrounded by a wall that may have had defence at least partly in mind. Note the bastion at the SE corner.

You enter the rectangular compound by the ruined E gopuram and see the huge Nandi placed facing the mandapam and sanctuary. Unlike the Nandi in Thanjavur this is not carved out of one block of stone. As in Thanjavur the mandapam and sanctuary are raised on a high platform, oriented from W to E and climbed by steps at the right and left sides. The whole building is over 100 m long and over 40 m wide. 2 massive doorkeepers (*dvara-palas**) stand guard at the entrance to the long closed mandapam, its roof supported by comparatively ordinary slender pillars. (This hall is the first of the many subsequent mandapams which expanded to "halls of 1000 pillars".) The plinth of the mandapam is original. The narrow colonnaded hall linking the entrance mandapam and the shrine (the *mukha-mandapa**) are similarly guarded, as is the shrine itself.

On the E side of this hall are various carvings of Siva such as bestowing grace on Vishnu, who worships him with his lotus-eye, and Kalyanasundara-murti (going out for his marriage attended by goblins) and many others. On the northeast is a large panel, described as a masterpiece of Chola art, showing Siva blessing Chandikesvara (the steward of Siva's household). The temple, though not as highly decorated as the Brihadisvara Temple in Thanjavur, has many similar figures. There are many single figure subjects. The dancing Nataraja is shown in a panelled recess of the SW corner, Siva within a flaming lingam on the W, Ganes on the S.

At the centre of the shrine is a huge lingam on a round stand. As in Thanjavur there is a magnificent pyramidal *vimana** (tower) above the sanctuary, nearly 55 m high. Its vertical base has 2 sections, succeeded upwards by 8 tiers. Unlike the austere straight line of the Thanjavur temple, however, here gentle curves are introduced, giving it "all the sensuous passion of an eastern lyric". The space on the temple base below the frieze is covered in inscriptions. Also in the enclosure are subsidiary shrines. Immediately to the N of the mandapam is a shrine dedicated to Chandikesvara, with an excellent carving showing the steward of Siva's household. To N and S are 2 shrines dedicated to Kailasanatha, erected by two of Rajendra's queens. There are excellent sculptures on the walls. In the SW corner is a small shrine to Ganes.

From Gangaikondaicholapuram take the road due S across the **Coleroon**.

If you go straight from Chidambaram to Kumbakonam you follow the road through Shirgali (9 km after crossing the Coleroon) where there is a good Inspection Bungalow. A road on the left goes to Thirumulaivasal (13 km away on the coast). The main road goes through Vaitheswaran Koil (7 km) and Mayavaram (13 km). A road on the left leads to Tiruvarur (42 km) and Nagapattinam (72 km). Straight on to Kuttalam (10 km) and a further 10 km where you turn left at the road junction. It is 14 km to **Kumbakonum**, of ancient origin. It got its name from the legend where Siva was said to have broken a *kumbh* (water pot) after it was brought here by a great flood. The water from the pot is reputed to have filled the Mahamakam Tank. Today Kumbakonam is a very busy town.

Places of interest There are 18 temples in the town centre and a monastery of the Kanchipuram Sankaracharya here. The temples are closed between 1200-1630. The oldest of the temples is the **Nagesvara Swami Temple**, a Saivite temple begun in 886 AD. It had several later additions and has recently been repainted. The small Nataraja shrine on the right before you reach the main sanctum is designed to look like a chariot being pulled by horses and elephants. There are some superb statues on the outside walls of the inner shrine; *Dakshinamurti* (exterior S wall) *Ardinarisvara* (W facing) and *Brahma* (N) are in the central panels. They have been described as among the best works of sculpture of the Chola period, and are worth a visit in themselves. Above the sanctuary is a pyramidal tower.

Sarangapani is the largest of Kumbakonam's 18 shrines. Dedicated to

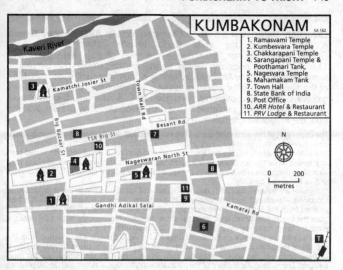

KUMBAKONAM SA 162

1. Ramasvami Temple
2. Kumbesvara Temple
3. Chakkarapani Temple
4. Sarangapani Temple & Poothamari Tank
5. Nagesvara Temple
6. Mahamakam Tank
7. Town Hall
8. State Bank of India
9. Post Office
10. *ARR Hotel* & Restaurant
11. *PRV Lodge* & Restaurant

Vishnu, the temple is dominated by its eleven storey main *gopuram,* 44 metres tall. The mandapam, built during the Nayaka period, is inside the first court, which then leads through a second, smaller gopuram to a further mandapam. There is a small vaulted shrine to Lakshmi, Vishnu's consort, on the N. The main central shrine is the oldest, dating from the end of the Chola period. In common with a number of other shrines such as those in Chidambaram or distant Konarak, it resembles a chariot, with horses and elephants carved in relief. The shrine is covered by a vaulted roof and the walls are richly carved.

The **Kumbesvara** temple dates mainly from the 17th century and is the largest Siva temple in the town. It has a a long colonnaded *mandapam* and a magnificent collection of silver *vahanas* (vehicles) for carrying the deities during festivals. The **Ramasvami** temple is another Nayaka period building, with beautiful carvings in its pillared mandapam. The rearing horses are typical of the Vijayanagar sculptures. and the frescoes on the walls depict events from the Ramayana. The Navaratri Festival is observed with great colour.

Note The temples in this region contain some exceptional pieces of jewellery which can be seen on payment of a small fee.

The *Mahamakam Tank* which is towards the rly station is visited by huge numbers of pilgrims every 12 years when 'Jupiter passes over the sign of Leo' (Feb 1992 being the next) when they come to take a holy dip when the Ganga is supposed to flow into it!

Local industries include textiles, gold and silver jewellery, and the high quality betel vines provide the essential raw material for the chewing *pan*.

Hotels F *ARR*, 21 Big St, T 21234. Simple but clean. Some a/c rm with bath. Restaurant with reasonably good veg food. **F** *PRV Lodge*, 32 Head Post Office Rd, T 21820. New but absolutely bottom end of market. Reportedly clean, best rooms have attached shower or bath. Restaurant (veg). **F** *Railway retiring rooms*.

Banks The State Bank of India on Big St is nr the ARR Hotel **Post Office** GPO is close to the Mahamakham Tank on Head Post Office St.

Travel Rail Station 2 km from town centre. Trains to Madras, Chidambaram, Thanjavur and Trichy. **Road** TTC buses to Madras (No.305, 4 daily, 7½ hr). Several daily to Thanjavur.

Excursion *Darasuram* is 5 km S of Kumbakonam. Its *Airavatesvara Temple* is the third of the great Chola temples, after Thanjavur and Gangakondaicholapuram, built during the reign of **Raja Raja II** between 1146-72. It was originally named Rajarajesvaram. Unlike the temples in Kumbakonam itself the Airavatesvara temple is open from sunrise to sunset. Most of the temple is constructed out of granite. You enter the temple through two gateways. A full description has been given by C. Sivaramamurti in his booklet on the Chola Temples, published by the Archaeological Survey of India, available from the Brihadisvara Temple in Thanjavur.

The upper part of the outermost gopura has now been lost. Inside this first gateway is a small inner gateway which gives onto a rectangular court at the centre of which is the main temple. The outer wall, which follows the line of the second gopura, is decorated with seated bulls at intervals while the gopura itself is supported by beautifully carved *apsaras*. Beyond is an altar place decorated with lotus petal carvings, and on one side the carving of a dwarf devotee of Siva blowing a conch.

Inside are friezes full of lively dancing figures and musicians. The entrance is flanked by crocodiles – *makara** – often portrayed as guardians. Inside is a mandapa which is best entered from the S, though there were steps on the E and W. Though the steps have now gone the balustrades which lined them still show their decoration on the outer side. Note the elephant being ridden by dwarfs whose trunk is lost down the jaws of a crocodile.

You can see evidence of the development of style in the late Chola period from the capitals of the pillars in the mandapa, which show the first signs of being carved into flower corbels, typical of the later Vijayanagar style when they were developed into full lotus patterns. The rectangular sections of the pillars show mythological stories such as the penance of Parvati and Siva's marriage. On either side of the extension of the mandapa through which you enter are superbly carved galloping horses.

The front base of the extension has more decorated panels illustrating stories such as that of **Siva** burning **Kama** who had dared to attack him with his bow, and Siva fighting the Tripuras from a chariot. Above in 5 niches are the gods Agni, Indra, Brahma, Vishnu and Vayu, all shown paying homage to Siva.

The main mandapa is completely enclosed and is joined to the central shrine. Its outer face has niches and pilasters, in which are figures carved in black basalt. The pillars of the main mandapa are decorated with naturalistic creepers enclosing dancing figures, musicians and deities. The ceilings are also richly decorated, and the capitals of the pillars show the same development of flower emblems as in the outer mandapa. Moving through from the outer mandapa towards the main shrine are niches which have some outstanding sculptures. Some of the openings in the main mandapa have been bricked up in recent years. The sculpted guardians on the N are particularly well carved.

At the entrance to the main shrine is a nandi, smaller than that at the entrance to the main mandapa itself. The sculpted door-keepers have massive clubs. Some of the niches inside contain superb early Chola sculptures, including a unique sculpture of **Ardhanarisvara** with three faces and eight arms; a four-armed **Nagaraja**, easily recognised from the snake-hoods above his head, and a very unusual sculpture of Siva destroying Narasimha (seen by climbing a small flight of steps). There are also many other sculptures, including those of Durga with eight arms and seated on the severed head of the buffalo and of Siva carrying an axe, deer, bow and arrow. The sides of the main shrine are covered in sculpture, with a long frieze on the lower half of the base. The sculptures are all of polished black basalt.

The outer walls are also covered in decorative sculpture. Siva as Dakshinamurti on the S wall, Brahma on the N wall and Siva appearing out of the linga on the W wall are all accompanied by appropriate figures. The inner wall of the encircling walkway, or *prakara*, is divided into cells, each of which used to house a deity. Some have disappeared.

The corners of the courtyard have been enlarged to make four mandapas, again with beautiful decoration. There is a small museum in the northeast corner, but the mandapa in the northwest corner probably has the best collection of sculptures. This appears to have been the mandapa reserved for dance, the *nata mandapa**, which according to Sivaramamurthy probably housed a bronze Nataraja. Immediately to the W is a group of large sculptures representing Siva as a beggar, and a number of attendants. Beyond are Siva saints with their names and a short description inscribed.

Tirubvanam (28 km) on the road to Tiruvidaimarudur has another famous Chola temple dedicated to Kampahareswara which has a remarkably high base. The spacious Mahalingasvami temple has a sacred tank. The *gopuram* is modelled on the one on the Thanjavur temple.

Thanjavur (*Tanjore*)

38 km. *Population* **(244,000)** *Altitude* **59 m.** *Climate* **Temp Summer Max. 37°C Min. 33°C, Winter Max. 24°C Min. 23C. Annual rainfall 940 mm** *Best season* **Oct – Mar.** *Clothing* **Cottons.**

Capital of the great Chola Empire and later of the ***Thanjavur*** Nayaka and Maratha rulers. The Chola kings built numerous temples, including the majority of Thanjavur's 93 temples. The treasures gained from defeating the Chalukyas were used to enrich the temple. Stein wrote that "The Brihadisvara Temple was built and maintained through the demands by Raja Raja I upon villages in throughout the Kaveri Delta core of Chola power as well as from the 'booty in the conquests of Chera, Pandiya...and Chalukya kings. Such warfare tended to enhance the prestige of a few warriors, and this was an important secondary objective of the activity, but it also brought fame and fortune to the corporate groups who made up the armies led by such warriors – soldiers of the left and right divisions of castes, certain artisan groups, guilds – thus it strengthened the vigorous corporate structure of S Indian political relations at least until the fourteenth century." The Chola kings were great patrons of the arts and while they lavished their wealth to build temples, they encouraged the belief in the divine right of kings. The practice of donating a part of one's wealth to the temple for spiritual gain was encouraged and there is some evidence of it even today.

Local festivals Jan. *Thyagaraja Music Festival* to commemorate one of the three most important personalities of Carnatic music at Thiruvaiyaru, 13 km away. Buses from Thanjavur. Oct *Raja Raja Chola's* birth anniversary celebrations.

Places of interest The ***Brihadisvara Temple***, known as the big temple, is the achievement of the Chola king **Rajaraja I** who ruled from AD 985-1012. It is one of the World Heritage monuments and very well worth seeing. The Brihadisvara Temple with its tank, fortified by a wall and moat, stands to the SW of the old town, near the Grand Anicut Canal.

The main temple is Chola and considered to be one of the most magnificent in the country, with a 14 storey, 62 m high *vimana* (the tallest in India) topped by a dome carved from a block of granite, the whole so cleverly designed that it never casts a shadow at noon, throughout the year. The 80 ton block is believed to have taken a 6.5 km ramp to raise it to the top.

After crossing the moat you enter through 2 *gopurams*, the second guarded by two guardians (*dvara palakas*). This design is representative of the early Chola period, when the gopuras on the outer enclosure walls were dwarfed by the scale of the *vimana* over the main shrine. Shulman has suggested that "in cases such as this the pilgrim's passage toward the central shrine is a form of ascent – as of course, it is in the many shrines built upon hills or mountains. Yet even here the **garbhagrha*** remains remote, in the chamber of stone, and the worshipper seems to enter and re-emerge from a womb."

An enormous *Nandi* which too is carved out of a single block of granite 6 m long, guards the entrance to the sanctuary. It is the second largest in the country. According to one of the many myths that revolve around the image of a wounded *Nandin*, the Thanjavur Nandi was growing larger and larger, threatening the temple, until a nail was driven in its back. The same idea of dangerous growth was applied to the Siva linga itself. The architecture, sculpture and painting are all of exceptional quality. Built mainly with large granite blocks there are superb inscriptions and sculptures of Siva, Vishnu and Durga on 3 sides of the massive plinth. To the S there are images of other deities. To the N, W and S of the sanctuary there are three huge sculptures of Siva in three forms, the dancer with 10 arms, the seated figure with a sword and trident and Siva bearing a spear. The carvings of dancers showing the 81 different Bharat Natyam poses are the first to record classical dance form in this manner.

The main shrine has a large *lingam*. In the inner courtyard you will see Chola frescoes on

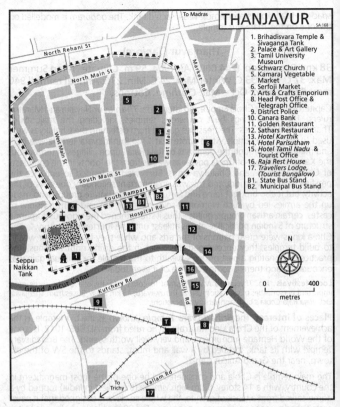

THANJAVUR
SA 168

1. Brihadisvara Temple & Sivaganga Tank
2. Palace & Art Gallery
3. Tamil University Museum
4. Schwarz Church
5. Kamaraj Vegetable Market
6. Serfoji Market
7. Arts & Crafts Emporium
8. Head Post Office & Telegraph Office
9. District Police
10. Canara Bank
11. Golden Restaurant
12. Sathars Restaurant
13. Hotel Karthik
14. Hotel Parisutham
15. Hotel Tamil Nadu & Tourist Office
16. Raja Rest House
17. Travellers Lodge, (Tourist Bungalow)
B1. State Bus Stand
B2. Municipal Bus Stand

walls prepared with lime plaster, smoothed and polished and then painted while the surface was wet. These were hidden under later Nayak paintings. Chambers 7 and 9 are well preserved and have fresco paintings of kings, queens and musicians. Open 0600-1200, 1600-2030. One of the unique records inscribed on the walls of the temple lists gifts from the royal family, details of how the temple was to be maintained including the payments granted to certain shepherds who would be responsible for providing clarified butter for the temple lamps.

The permanent exhibition in the temple complex which has reproductions of the paintings and a record of the Archaeological Survey of India's conservation programme, is worth a visit. Open 0900-1200, 1600-2000. Since music and dance (this being the cradle of Bharat Natyam) were a vital part of temple life and dancing in the temple would accompany the chanting of the holy scriptures which the community attended, Raja Raja also built two housing colonies nearby to accommodate 400 deva (temple dancers). Subsidiary shrines were added to the main temple at different periods. The Vijayanagara kings built the Amman shrine, the Nayaks the Subrahmanya shrine with intricate carvings and the Mahrathas the Ganesa shrine.

The Palace Though part in ruins, this is one of the principal buildings which once stood within the fort, built by the Nayakas in the mid-16th century, and later completed by the Mahrathas. You enter from E Main St, proceed towards the police station and the entrance is to your left. The evidence of the splendour of the original palace can be seen in its ornate Durbar Hall (left of Library) which has some bronzes on display, long corridors and towers which are worth climbing for a good view. The Art Gallery, Saraswati Mahal Library and the Tamil University Museum are here, together with some government offices.

The **Schwarz Church** is just N of the Sivaganga Tank next to a landscaped garden. It is dedicated to the Danish missionary **F.C.Schwarz** (whose life is also commemorated in St. Mary's Church, Madras) who died in 1798. There is a particularly striking painting at the W end of the church by Flaxman of Schwarz on his deathbed, showing him surrounded by the family of Raja Serfoji to whom he was tutor.

Local crafts and industries Stone carving, particularly in granite is an ancient craft that is being revived by the government through centres which produce superbly sculpted images and columns for Hindu temples. Blocks of stone are cut, chiselled, rubbed and polished, which takes months to produce the finished work of art. Also wood carving, bronze and brass casting, decorative copper plates with silver and brass patterns in relief (repoussé) or inlaid, papier mâché dolls. Revived painting on wood and on glass.

Hotels D *Parisutham*, 55 Grand Anicut Canal Rd. T 21466, Cable: Staydine, Telex: 0468 220 PTS IN. 36 rm some a/c. 15 min drive airport, close to rly. Restaurant, bar, coffee shop, exchange, travel, shop, garden, TV. **E** *Travellers' Lodge* (ITDC), Vallam Rd, garden setting, restaurant. **E** *Hotel Tamil Nadu* (TNDC), Gandhiji Rd, heavily booked, very good value. Comfortable rm, some a/c, with bath, in pleasant setting around a cool inner courtyard. Restaurant rather simple, bar, Tourist Office. The govt's *Raja Rest House* behind Hotel Tamil Nadu, quiet, a little run-down. Both about 10 min walk from station and Bus Stands.

Restaurants Hotel Parisutham serves Chinese and non-veg Indian food in *Les Repas* and Indian veg in *Geetha*, both good. The a/c *Golden Restaurant* on Hospital Rd is recommended for veg food. *Sathars* nr the Bus Stand serves good Tandoori food until midnight. For traditional meal off a banana leaf try *Hotel Karthik*, 73 S Rampart St.

Local transport There are un-metred and tourist taxis. Auto rickshaws and cycle rickshaws are available as well as a city bus service. **Shopping** *Poompuhar* the Arts and Crafts Emporium is on Gandhiji Rd, nr the Hotel Tamil Nadu. Several other shops sell crafts items in the Gandhiji Rd Bazaar.

Museums Raja Raja Museum and Art Gallery is housed in the Thanjavur Palace. Large collection of Chola sculptures in bronze (lost wax process) and granite, lithic pieces. Look for Bhairava, Umasahita Siva, Kali, Somaskanda and the Rama Lakshmana group. Open daily 0900-1200, 1500-1800, closed Fri. Also in the Palace buildings is the **Saraswati Mahal Library** containing over 40,000 rare books, several first editions and manuscripts, about 8,000 of which are on palm leaf. Considered to be one of the country's major reference library, it contains books and manuscripts in many foreign languages including French, German, Italian, Greek and Latin covering Literature, Art, Philosophy, Music, Astrology, Sciences and particularly Medicine. Open 1000-1300, 1400-1700 except Wed. **Tamil University Library** has a numismatic section and a collection of old musical instruments.

Useful addresses The District Police Office is S of the Big Temple between the canal and the rly. **Banks** The Canara Bank is on S Main St, with branches of **Indian Bank** and **Indian Overseas Bank**. The **State Bank of India** is on Hospital Rd. **Post and telegraph** The Head Post Office and Telegraph Office are S of the old city off the Rly Station Rd. **Hospital** The *Raja Mirasdas Government Hospital* is on Hospital Rd, S of the old town.

Tourist office and information The Tourist office, Gandhiji Rd (Hotel Tamil Nadu Complex) is open daily 0800-1100, 1600-2000 except Mon.

Travel Air *Vayudoot* connects Thanjavur with Madras and Madurai. **Rail** Tiruchirappalli: *Cholan Exp*, 6153, daily, 1800, 1 hr 15 min; *Madras Tirunelveli Janata Exp*, 6179, daily, 2210, 1 hr 20 min; **Madras (ME)**: *Cholan Exp*, 6154, daily, 0845, 8 hr 45 min; *Ramesvaram Exp*, 6102, daily, 2042, 9 hr 23 min. **Road** *Thiruvalluvar* (TTC) service runs 12 buses daily to Madras (8 hr) and others daily to Pondicherry, Madurai and Tirupathi. The TTC Bus Stand is N of Hospital Rd, S of the old town. While opp the Municipal Bus Stand runs a frequent service to Kumbakonam (1 hr) and Trichy (1 hr 15 min).

Excursions The Thyagaraja Temple at *Tiruvarur*, 55 km on the road to Nagapattinam, is one of the largest in S India. The town was one of the ancient

Chola capitals. The palace here had a 'calling bell' hung which any citizen could ring in an emergency and gain the attention of the King for justice for a crime committed. The legend of the prince running over a calf with his chariot relates how the Chola king sought to deliver justice on the bell being rung, by ordering that a chariot run over his own son. Happily, Siva intervened and revived both the calf and the prince. The stone chariot of Tiruvarur is famous.

The Tyagaraja temple was built over a period of more than three centuries from the 13th century. Founded by the Cholas, it was added to periodically, the most important additions being those made by the Nayaka kings in the 17th century. There are magnificent gopurams in the outer enclosures, the northern and western gateways being late additions of the Vijayanagar and Nayaka periods. Just inside the second enclosure wall on the S side is the 10th century shrine of Achalesvara.

The W facing temple follows the early Chola pattern, with a simple base, pilasters on the walls and a pyramidal tower. The roof is hemispherical. The name *Achalesvara* means "immovable Lord" because Siva promised never to abandon it. The story goes that the king Samatkara "performed *tapas* and, when Siva appeared to him, begged him to be present forever in the holy site. The god said that he would remain, immovable, in that place. The king set up a linga, and a voice from heaven announced: "I will dwell eternally in this linga; even its shadow will never move." So it happened: the shadow of the Achalesvara linga is ever stationary. Only he who is to die within six months is unable to perceive this marvel." As David Shulman points out, "the miracle is made secure by terror – he who doubts it will die!" In the innermost court are the shrines of *Vanmikanatha* and *Tyagaraja*, both E facing. Most of the external plaster decoration on the former is a late addition to what is mainly a 10th century shrine. The latter dates from the 13th century.

Tiruvarur celebrates a *car festival* to continue the tradition when in the past the 23 m high old temple chariot needed 10,000 devotees, led by the King, to pull it on festival days. Today the chariot is smaller and no longer needs thousands of devotees to pull. This is also the birth place of the saint Tyagaraja (1767-1847), one of the three music composers of note who lived in Tamil Nadu in the 18th century.

A popular excursion among many Tamil tourists is to **Poompuhar**, at the mouth of the **Kaveri**. At this point the flooding waters of the Kaveri are reduced to a trickle as they enter the sea. It was once an important port of the Cholas but most of the city of Kaveripoompattinam (as it was then called) was lost under the sea. There is a good beach. The Government of Tamil Nadu has built a tourist complex with a number of genuinely bizarre buildings in modern S Indian style or art imitating kitsch. There is a seven storeyed Art Gallery which tells the story of the Tamil classic, Silappadikaram, in stone carvings. Next door the Government of Tamil Nadu has a F *Tourist Bungalow*, T 39. You can get a bus from Chidambaram or Thanjavur. The name Poompuhar has been adopted for the Tamil Nadu government emporia throughout the country.

Point Calimere (Kodikkarai). 80 km from Thanjavur to the SE and 11 km from Vedaranyam, *Point Calimere Bird Sanctuary* on the coast, is open throughout the year. Best season – Nov to Feb for flamingoes. The sanctuary is famous for its migratory water birds, especially flamingoes and covers 17 sq km, half of which consists of tidal swamps. Known as the Great Swamp, it attracts one of the largest colonies of flamingoes in Asia, numbering between 5,000 and 10,000 during the season.

In the spring when the berries are available on the trees and shrubs, the green pigeons, rosy pastors, koels, mynahs and barbets can be seen. In the winter the availability of vegetable food and insects attracts paradise fly catchers, Indian pittas, shrikes, swallows, drongos, minivets, blue jays, wood-peckers, robins among others. Spotted deer, black buck and wild boar are also supported.

Accommodation in F *Poonarai Rest House* (10 suites) and F *Calimere Rest House* (4 suites) which you can reserve through the District Forest Officer, Thanjavur Division.

MADRAS TO TRICHY (Main Road NH 45 all the way)

The NH 45 runs direct from Madras to Trichy, and is the route followed by the express buses. The total distance 320 km. In a modern, well-sprung car this can be done comfortably in under four hours driving, but the road can be much slower than you might expect. The surface is often poor and in the 1980s heavy traffic has increased enormously. Allow up to five hours travel time.

Leave Madras past Meenambakkam airport for **Chengalpattu** (58 km) _Population_ 59,000. The chief focus of interest is the fort, built by the Vijayanagar king Thimmu Raya after his defeat at the Battle of Talikota in 1565. After 1687 it was absorbed into the Mughal Empire. 63 years later it was taken by the French, who held it for a year until it was captured by Clive in 1752. Its control in British hands was not finally established until the defeat of Haidar Ali in 1781.

Although the fort is now almost totally destroyed (the railway runs through the middle of it) the _Raja Mahal_ ("King's Palace") remains. It is an extraordinary design, having been modelled on the temple car in Kanchipuram. The five storey structure was said to be particularly tall so that Thimmu Raya's queens could worship at midday within sight of the great gopuram of the Kanchi temple. Some of the architecture was "Islamised" during the Muslim control. The bus stand has the usual array of fruit stalls and tea and coffee shops.

Immediately S of Chingleput cross the Palar River, a stretch of sand over 1 km wide, usually with no running water visible on the surface. The region around Madras has its main wet season between October and December, and this area close to the coast depends heavily on tank irrigation. Just outside Chingleput is one of S India's largest tanks, a beautiful sight and an invaluable source of irrigation water, built in the 8th century AD.

Driving S to **Madurantakam** (21 km _Population_ 27,000) a new road by-passes the town along the _bund_ of another great tank. Madurantakam is a typical medium sized town strung out along the roadside. Tea/coffee stalls around the bus stand. Through **Tindivanam** (40 km _Population_ 70,000) to **Villupuram** (37 km _Population_ 102,000), just to the S of which the road crosses the Ponnaiyar River. To the right, between the Ponnaiyar and Velar Rivers is the distant block of the Kalrayan Hills.

Neyveli, (_Population_ 113,000) where lignite has been mined open cast since 1961 as part of an integrated power and fertilizer production scheme, is off to the left after passing through **Ulundurpetttai**. Continuing on the NH 45 the road crosses the Velar river before reaching **Perambalur** (69 km _Population_ 24,000). Visible on the right are the Pachamalai and Kollamalai Hills. Rising from the plains to the S is the dramatic rock, over 70 m high, on which Trichy fort stands.

Tiruchirappalli

Population 480,000. Altitude 88 metres. Known as **Trichy** or **Tiruchi** for short, **Tiruchirappalli**, (3 km) in the heart of Tamil Nadu, is in the Kaveri delta, formed where the Kaveri's distributary the Coleroon (Kollidam) branches away to the N. The airport is 8 km away.

56 km W of Thanjavur the land near the delta around Trichy is very fertile and productive. The town was mentioned by Ptolemy, the 2nd century BC Alexandrian geographer. A Chola fortification from the 2nd century, it came to prominence under the Nayakas from Madurai who built the fort and the town, but saw the ravages of war through the centuries because of its important strategic position. Different powers fought to gain control including the Muslims who ended Chola

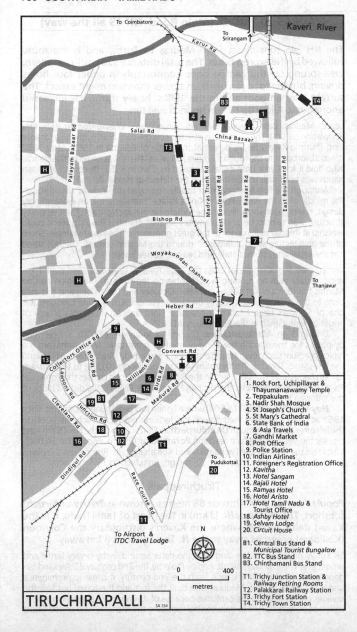

1. Rock Fort, Uchipillayar & Thayumanaswamy Temple
2. Teppakulam
3. Nadir Shah Mosque
4. St Joseph's Church
5. St Mary's Cathedral
6. State Bank of India & Asia Travels
7. Gandhi Market
8. Post Office
9. Police Station
10. Indian Airlines
11. Foreigner's Registration Office
12. Kavitha
13. Hotel Sangam
14. Rajali Hotel
15. Ramyas Hotel
16. Hotel Aristo
17. Hotel Tamil Nadu & Tourist Office
18. Ashby Hotel
19. Selvam Lodge
20. Circuit House

B1. Central Bus Stand & Municipal Tourist Bungalow
B2. TTC Bus Stand
B3. Chinthamani Bus Stand

T1. Trichy Junction Station & Railway Retiring Rooms
T2. Palakkarai Railway Station
T3. Trichy Fort Station
T4. Trichy Town Station

TIRUCHIRAPALLI

SA 154

rule in the 14th century. It also saw the Mahratta Wars and the wars between the British and the French for over a hundred years. One of the sources for its name is traced to a legendary three-headed demon Trisiras who terrorised both men and the gods until Siva overpowered him in the place called Tiruchi.

The railways came to Trichy in 1862 and it became an important junction in the S. It was the headquarters of the privately owned S Indian Railway until nationalization. There are 4 stations – The Town, The Golden Rock, Palakkarai and The Junction, the last being the most important. Most of the hotels, restaurants and offices needed by the tourist are in the the Junction or Cantonment area to the S, near the Junction Rly Station. The sights are near the Town Station 1.5 km to the N. The Golden Rock area is an industrial suburb.

Local festivals Mar – The *Festival of Floats* on the Teppakulam when the temple deities are taken out onto the sacred lake on rafts. Several at Srirangam (see Excursions below).

Places of interest The **Rock Fort** was built on an 84 m high rock in the centre of town in about 1660. The **Vinayaka Temple** or Ucchi Pillayar Koil with a shrine to *Ganesa* is at the its highest point from which you get marvellous views although you need to climb 437 rock cut steps to reach it. Open 0600-2000. On your way up you come to the main 11th century defence line and the remains of a thousand pillar hall which was destroyed in 1772, at the top of the first flight of steps. Further up is a hundred pillar hall where civic receptions are held. At the end of last flight is the **Tayumanasvami Temple** dedicated to Siva which has a golden *vimana* and a lingam which is carved out of the rock on which the temple stands. There are also other 7th century Pallava cave temples which have beautifully carved pillars and panels. It is worth while discovering the old city on foot, particularly **Big Bazaar Street** and **China Bazaar**.

Teppakulam at the foot of the rock is a large artificial *tank* surrounded by colourful stalls and a flower market. Among the dozen or so mosques in the town, the **Nadir Shah Mosque** near the Teppakulam and city railway station stands out with its white dome and metal steeple. Chanda Sahib who is said to have built it with material taken from a Hindu temple is buried there. **St Joseph's College Church** (Church of our Lady of Lourdes) is one of many Catholic churches in Trichy and was designed as a smaller version of the Basilica at Lourdes in S France. Its unusual sandalwood altar is interesting. The 18th century **Christ Church** in the Fort, N of the Teppakulam is the first English church built through raising money from the British officers, by Schwarz the Danish missionary.

Local crafts and industries With the industrial district of Coimbatore to the W and the agricultural one of Thanjavur to the E, Trichy gains advantage from both. Handloom *textiles* are manufactured in Woraiyur and Karur. *Cigar* making became prosperous between the two Word Wars and supplied the British while the indigenous *bidis** the poor man's cigarette continues to be made here, following a tradition started in the 18th century.

More importantly Trichy is the country's largest centre manufacturing *artificial diamonds* having taken over from centres in Switzerland and Rangoon in Burma which provided most of the artificial gems until the second World War. The processes of cleaving, shaping, faceting and polishing of the synthetic gems are carried out in and around the city (Jaffersha St is commonly known as 'Diamond Bazaar') providing employment for thousands of local people including a large number of women. They are not only used in everyday jewellery but also to produce the brilliant ornaments worn by dancers and are also in demand abroad. In addition the town produces glass bangles, carpets, mats, palm leaf boxes and high quality string instruments, particularly *veenas* and *violins*.

Heavy engineering includes the Boiler Plant (Bharat Heavy Electricals Ltd) at Tiruvembur 11 km away, steel mills and the old established *Railway Workshop* at Golden Rock. Sembattu, nearby, is an important centre for *leather tanning*.

Hotels The most expensive is **C** *Sangam* on Collector's Office Rd. T 41514, Cable: Sangu, Telex: 0455-221. 58 comfortable a/c rm. close to rly, about 4 km from the town centre. A/c restaurants and bar, exchange, car hire, shops, spacious lawns, TV. **D** *Rajali*, 2/14 Macdonalds Rd. T 41301, Cable: Hotrajali, Telex: 0445-279. 78 rm, most a/c. Close to rly, central. Restaurants, bar, travel, health club, shops, pool, TV. Excellent food. Recommended. **D**

Femina, 14C Williams Rd. T 41551, Cable: Femina, Telex: 0455-333 Fmna In. 72 rm, 42 a/c. Close to rly, central. A/c restaurants and bar, 24 hr coffee shop, travel, beauty parlour, TV. **D** *Ramyas*, Williams Rd, T 31470. A new hotel in the centre of town, close to the Tourist Office and the Bus Stand. Some a/c rm.

E *Aristo*, 2 Dindigul Rd, T 26565. 31 rm (including interesting 'theme' cottages), some a/c with bath. Close to rly, 4 km centre. Restaurant, exchange, travel, shops, attractive lawns. Highly recommended for the price. **E** *Abirami*, 10 Macdonalds Rd, opp Central Bus Stand. T 40001, Cable: Vasantham, Telex: 0445-329 Muna In. 55 rm, some a/c with bath. 5 km rly, 4 km centre. A/c restaurant (vegetarian), exchange, travel, car hire, shops. **E** *Tamil Nadu*, TTDC, Cantonment. T 25383, Cable: Tamil Tour. 12 rm, some a/c with bath. Close to the Bus Stand and rly station. Restaurant recommended, bar and Tourist Office. Basic but clean and very good value. **E** *Ashok Travellers Lodge*, Race Course Rd. T 23498, Cable: Tourism. 4 rm. **E** *Ashby*, Junction Rd, T 23652, Cable: Ashby. 11 rm, 8 a/c. with bath. Close to rly, 3 km centre. Restaurant, bar, car hire. Old fashioned, with Raj character and can be a little noisy. **E** *Aanand*, 1 Racquet Court Lane, Cantonment. T 240545. 71 rm, some a/c with TV and bath. Close to rly, 4 km centre. Restaurant (S Indian veg), lawn. **E** *Lakshmi*, 3A Alexandria Rd, Cantonment. T 25298, Cable: Hotelax. 48 rm, 7 a/c. Close to rly. Restaurant, 24 hr coffee shop, Air Lanka office, car hire. **E** *Sevana*, 5 Royal Rd, Cantonment. T 41201, Cable: Hotelsevana. 44 rm, some a/c with phone, TV and bath. A/c restaurant (Indian) and bar. **E** *Midland Lodge*, 20 Macdonalds Rd, Cantonment. T 23911. **F** *Mayaram Lodge*, 87 Vanapattrai St. T 24089. Nr the Rock Fort. **F** *Municipal Tourist Bungalow*, Central Bus Stand, T 27680. **F** *Railway Retiring Rooms*, some a/c.

Restaurants *Rajali Hotel* (multi-cuisine), highly recommended especially the Chinese. Reservations advised. *Sangam's* restaurant for Indian and continental food, recommended . Hotel Abbirami's part a/c *Vasanta Bhavan* serves vegetarian continental and Indian food from 0600-2200. *Hotel Skylord*, Municipal Office Rd, T 24662 has an a/c multi-cuisine restaurant open 1000-2200. Outside hotels, there are very good inexpensive Indian veg restaurants on China Bazaar, particularly the *Vasantha Bhavan* opp the Tourist Office recommended for its *thalis* and *Sree Ranga Bhavan* which has local character. Near the Tourist Office the *Kanchana* serves non-veg. The *Selvam Lodge* on Junction Rd serves good S Indian food in its roof top restaurant. At the corner of Junction Rd and Williams Rd is the a/c *Kavitha* which is also recommended for its veg *thalis*.

Banks & Exchange The State Bank of India is on Dindigul Rd just N of the Rajali Hotel, T 25172.

Shopping Artificial diamonds, cigars, wood and clay toys, bangles and textiles make attractive buys. You will also find pith temple models in Big Bazaar St. In the Srirangam Temple precinct, there are shops selling brass figures and handicrafts. Government Emporia – *Poompuhar*, nr Main Guard Gate and *Khadi Kraft* opp Rly Station.

Local transport *Taxis* Unmetred taxis and Tourist Taxis. You can hire the latter from Kavria Travels, Hotel Sangam, Collector's Office Rd, T 25202. Good city *Bus* Service. The journey from the airport takes about 30 min (Nos 7, 63, 122, 128). The State Bus Stand is in the corner of Williams Rd and Royal Rd across from the Tourist Office. From there the No 1 Bus will take you to all the sights. Cycle rickshaws and auto rickshaws are also available.

The **Museum** is on Bharatiyar Rd, 19/2 Promenade Rd, Cantonment. The collection is displayed in sculpture, art, archaeology, handicrafts, numismatic, geology and science galleries. Open 0900-1230, 1400-1700. Closed Fri. Entry free.

Parks and zoos *Lourdhswamy Pillai Park.*

Places of worship *Hindu* – In Trichy the Tayumanasvami and Uchipillayar Temples and in Srirangam the Ranganathasvami Temple and Jambukesvara Temples at Tiruvanaikkaval. *Muslim* – Nadir Shah Mosque nr Teppakulam. *Christian* – Christ Church, St Paul's Church, St John's Church, All Saints Church. St. Joseph's College Church.

Travel agents and tour operators *Asian Travels*, LIC Building, Cantonment, T 27660.

Tourist offices and information Information office at the *Hotel Tamil Nadu Complex*, Cantonment, T 25336. Open 1030-1730, Closed Sun. Also counters at the Airport and the Trichy Railway Junction Station. Open 0700-2100.

Air *Indian Airlines* and *Air Lanka* connects the international airport with Colombo 4 times and twice weekly, respectively. In addition Indian Airlines has direct flights to and from Madras daily as well as to Madurai and Trivandrum. Indian Airlines **Madurai** Daily, except Mon, 0740, 30 min; **Madras** Daily, except Mon, 0740, 1 hr 50 min. Indian Airlines, Rly Cooperative

Mansion, Dindigul Rd opp Aristo Hotel, T 23116. Air Lanka, Hotel Lakshmi, 3a Alexandria Rd, Cantonment. T 27952.

Rail An important railway junction connecting the city with major towns in the region. **Madras** *Vaigai Exp* takes 5 hr and is the fastest. *Rock Fort Exp* (night train) takes 8 hr and *Quilon Exp* 9 hr. **Madurai**: *Vaigai Exp*, 2635 (AC/CC), daily, 1743, 2 hr 27 min; *Nellai Exp*, 6119 (AC/II), daily, 0135, 3 hr 10 min; **Madras (ME)**: *Pallavan Exp*, 2606 (AC/II), daily, 0615, 5 hr 20 min; *Vaigai Exp*, 2636 (AC/CC), daily, 0911, 5 hr 14 min; **Quilon**: *Quilon Mail*, 6105 (AC/II), daily, 0325, 11 hr 15 min; *6161 Exp*, daily, 1610, 12 hr 20 min.

Road Good road connections to all major towns in the S. Some distances – Chidambaram 156 km, Coimbatore 205 km, Kumbakonam 92 km, Madras 330 km, Madurai 161 km, Palani 152 km, Kanniyakumari 396 km. **Buses** The Thiruvalluvar buses – 30 daily to Madras (8 hr), 2 daily to Kanniyakumari (9 hr) and Tirupati (9 hr 30 min). Others go to Coimbatore, Kodai, Madurai, Nagercoil, Ramesvaram and Nagapattinam.

Excursions 3 km to the N, on an island in the Kaveri is the temple town of **Srirangam** (*Population* 85,000) surrounded by seven concentric walled courtyards, with magnificent gateways and several shrines which you reach by an arched bridge. The **Ranganathasvami Temple** is one of the largest temples in India dedicated to **Vishnu**.

The original small temple built by Raja Dharma Varman was enlarged by successive Chola, Pandiya and Vijayanagara kings. The fact that it faces S, unlike most other Hindu temples, is explained by the legend that **Rama** presented the image of Ranganatha initially for a temple in Sri Lanka but this was impossible since the deity became fixed inside but still honours the original destination.

The temple is famous for its superb sculpture and its 21 impressive *gopurams*. and its rich collection of temple jewellery. Its 'thousand' pillared hall (904 columns) stands beyond the 4th wall and in the 5th enclosure there is the unusual shrine to Tulukka Nachiyar the God's Muslim consort. Some of the pillars have beautiful carvings out of a single block of stone. It lacks any grand plan since it was expanded by different rulers through the centuries (mostly between the 14th and the 17th), each of whom left the central shrine untouched but competed with their predecessors by building further walls with taller *gopurams*. The restoration of the deteriorating granite walls and the unfinished 7th *gopuram* was undertaken with the help of UNESCO and completed in the 1980s. Non-Hindus are not allowed into the sanctuary but can enter the fourth courtyard where the famous sculptures of *gopis* (*Radha's* milk maids) in the Venugopala shrine can be seen. You will need to leave you shoes here and can hire a guide. A camera fee is also charged.

There is also a **Museum** with an interesting collection of copper plates, ivory sculptures, bronze casting, weapons and coins. From the top of the wall you can get an excellent view. The **festival** of *Vaikunta Ekadasi* in Dec/Jan draws thousands of pilgrims who witness the transfer of the image of the deity from the inner sanctum under the golden *vimana* to the *mandapa*. In the same period the car festival is also celebrated.

9 km from Trichy, E of Srirangam, is **Tiruvanaikkaval** (so named because a legendary elephant worshipped the lingam) which has the architecturally finer **Jambukesvara** temple with its five walls and 7 *gopurams*. It is one of the oldest and largest Siva temples in Tamil Nadu where the unusual lingam under a *jambu* tree, always remains under water. There are special festivals in Jan and in the Spring. In Aug, *Pancha Piraharam* is celebrated in *Panguni* the images of Siva and his consort Akhilandesvari exchange their dress.

A major Siva temple in the heart of Vaishnava territory, the temple here, according to the noted architectural historian Percy Brown, gives a clearer "idea of the Dravidian style at its best" than any other temple in S India. Open 0600-1300, 1600-2130. Non-Hindus are not allowed into the sanctuary. Nominal entry fee, Cameras Rs 10.

There are numerous Chola temples in the area. **Kothamangalam** At **Thiruthavathurai** with its Chola temple was renamed Lalgudi by the Muslims, because of its colour ('Lal' red, 'gudi' temple).

Not far from Trichy is the **Grand Anicut Barrage** which was originally built in the 2nd century by the Chola king Karikalan. It was reinforced by successive kings in the centuries that followed and stills functions as a 320 m long barrage across the river Kaveri.

Also nearby at **Chittanavasal** are Jain cave temples with famous frescoes where Jain monks took shelter when they fled from persecution in the N. The *Brahmi* inscriptions are dated from the 2nd century BC.

About 20 km N on the Turaiyur road, is the small village of **Tiruvellarai** which has a Pallava temple on top of rocky hill with its ancient well, its rock cut walls and steps in the form of a swastika. There are several other Pallava monuments including a rock cut Siva temple to the E.

MADRAS TO COIMBATORE AND OOTY

The shortest route to Coimbatore and Ooty from Madras follows the NH45 S through Chingleput to Tindivanam (119 km). (For a description of this section of the route see page 749).

Turn right in Tindivanam for **Gingee** (27 km) and the 15th century Vijayanagar fort. If you are going by bus to Gingee take a rickshaw from the bus stand to the hills. It should not cost more than Rs 20 for the round trip. Although it had Chola foundations, the "most famous fort in the Carnatic", was almost entirely re-built in 1442. It is set on 3 *Charnockite* hills, all strongly fortified and connected by walls 5 km round. In places the hills on which the fort stands are sheer cliffs over 150 m high. The highest is *Rajagiri* ("king's hill") which has a S facing overhanging cliff face, on top of which is the citadel. The fort was protected on the N by a deep narrow ravine, crossed by a wooden bridge. The citadel is approached from the E through a series of defensive lines, 2 of which have impressive triple arches. In all there are 7 gateways, some with large courtyards between them.

There are several interesting remains in the fort itself; 2 temples and a square court used by the women of the Governor's household known as the *Kalyana Mahal*. On top of the citadel is a huge gun, a smooth granite slab known as the Raja's bathing stone. An extraordinary stone about 7 m high and balanced precariously on a rock, surrounded by a low brick wall, is referred to as the prisoner's well. The fort was intensely contested by successive powers. The Vijayanagar king lost it to the **Sultan of Bijapur** in 1638, 18 years before the catastrophic defeat of the Vijayanagar Empire at the Battle of Talikota in Karnataka, **see page 885**. In 1677 it was taken by the Marathas under **Sivaji**, **see page 937**, but they only held it for thirteen years before it was captured for the Mughals by Zulfikar Khan. It was taken by the French in 1750 who held it until it was taken by an East India Company force in 1762.

Continue on the road due W from Gingee to **Tiruvannamalai** (37 km *Population* 119,000), one of the holy towns of Tamil Nadu and widely thought of in the region as the home of **Siva** and his consort **Parvati**. As such it is a major pilgrimage centre, and its location at the foot of the rocky *Arunachala Hill* gives it a striking setting.

The hill is centre of a powerful myth as to its origins. The Tamil scholar Arunachalam writes: "*Brahma* and *Vishnu* quarrelled over who was superior. *Siva* appeared to them in a *linga* of fire. *Vishnu* tried to find its base by digging in the form of a boar, while Brahma became a goose and flew towards the top. Neither could find any limit to the *linga*. They recognised it as a form of *Siva*, who made the fiery *linga* into the mountain Tiruvannamalai."

There are over 100 temples in the town below the hill, but by far the most important, and possibly the largest in S India, is the **Arunachala Temple** itself. It is approximately 1 km SE of the railway station. Built mainly in the 16th and 17th centuries under the patronage of the Vijayanagar kings, its massive

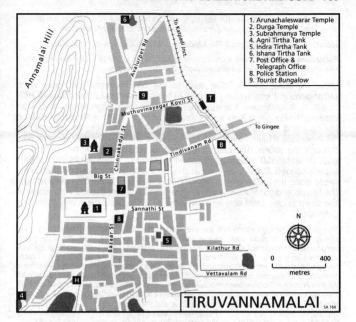

1. Arunachaleswarar Temple
2. Durga Temple
3. Subrahmanya Temple
4. Agni Tirtha Tank
5. Indra Tirtha Tank
6. Ishana Tirtha Tank
7. Post Office & Telegraph Office
8. Police Station
9. *Tourist Bungalow*

Annamalai Hill

Avalurpet Rd

To Katpadi Jnc.

9

Muthuvinayagar Kovil St

To Gingee

3

2

Chinnakadai St

Tindivanam Rd

Big St

7

Sannathi St

1

Bazaar St

8

5

Kilathur Rd

Vettavalam Rd

N

0   400

metres

H

4

TIRUVANNAMALAI SA 164

gopurams, the tallest of which is 66 m high, dominate the centre of the town. It is dedicated to Siva as God incarnate as Fire.

The temple has 3 sets of walls forming a series of nested rectangles, built at quite different periods and illustrating the way in which many Dravidian temples grew by accretion rather than by overall design. The E end of each is extended to make a court, and the main entrance is at the E end of the temple. The lower parts of the gopurams date from the late Vijayanagar period but have been added to subsequently. As is common with Dravidian temples, the lower parts of these towers are built of granite while the upper parts (10 storeys) and the decoration are of lighter materials – brick and plaster.

There are some remarkable carvings on the gopurams. On the outer wall of the E gopuram, Siva is shown in the centre of the N wall while in the S corner he is shown dancing with an elephant's skin. The design of the temple illustrates the effect produced in later Dravidian temples of progressive abasement produced by moving from the grandest and greatest of gateways through ever smaller doorways until the very modest inner shrine is reached. Inside the E doorway of the first courtyard is the 1000 pillared *mandapam* built late in the Vijayanagar period. To the S of the court is a small shrine dedicated to *Subrahmanya* (known in northern India as *Kartikkeya*). To the S again is a large tank. The pillars in the mandapam are carved with typically vigorous horses and riders and *yalis* (lion-like images).

The middle court has 4 much earlier gopurams (mid 14th century). Again the entrance is at the E end. This court also contains a large columned mandapam and a tank. The innermost court may date from as early as the 11th century and the main sanctuary is certainly of Chola origin. There are images of deities carved in stone on the exterior walls of the sanctuary. In the S is Dakshinamurti, the W shows Siva appearing out of a lingam and the N has Brahma. The outer porch has small shrines to Ganesa and Subrahmanya. In front of the main shrine are a brass column lamp and the *Nandi* bull.

Places of interest The much-visited ashram of the **Guru Ramana Maharishi**, who died in 1950 is on the edge of town.

Local festivals *Karthikai Deepam* Full moon day in Nov-Dec. A huge beacon is lit on top of the hill behind the temple. The flames, which can be seen for miles around, are thought of as Shiva's lingam of fire, joining the immeasurable depths to the limitless skies.

Hotels F The *Park Hotel* and F The *Modern cafe*, simple and clean, good value.

Excursions Sathanur Dam, a small power project 35 km to the W on the Ponnaiyar River, has attractive gardens and is a popular picnic and day outing site.

Leave the town on the Salem road to the SW. The main road goes W to **Uttangarai** (62 km), passing to the S of the massive blocks of the **Javadi Hills** to the N. In Uttangarai the road joins the main Tirupattur- Salem road. After crossing the Ponnaiyar River it rises steadily, with the 1,100 m **Shevaroy Hills** on the right and the **Kalrayan Hills** on the left. All these blocks are separated by great geological faults which have controlled the alignment of the rivers that flow through the valleys. The hills were raised as flat-topped *horsts**, pushed up possibly some 300 million years ago in a period of mountain building. Some experts suggest that it took place at the same time as the Western Ghats were raised along the fault line from the Arabian Sea. Driving along the road past both the Javadis and the Shevaroys you can see areas of forest that still cover some of the steep slopes. Until very recently some of these were the scene of shifting cultivation.

The gently rolling tops of the hills are intensively cultivated, though their height alters the climate enough to allow crops such as coffee to be grown in the Shevaroys. Ragi, gram, **sorghum** (known as *cholam* in Tamil) are the most common crops, and forest products have also been an important source of income. Particularly striking is the development of cattle breeding in the districts of Dharmapuri and Salem. Dharmapuri-Krishnagiri cattle are famous throughout S India and are the main source of heavy draught cattle from Kerala to southern Andhra Pradesh. 'The breeding herds live on the forests for the greater part of the year, where they are kept in pens at night time. They are brought back to the village at harvest, when the harvested fields provide grazing for some time, and the cattle supply the necessary manure for the succeeding ragi crop.... The breeders cannot be considered *ryots* (farmers). They certainly grow crops for their own requirements but by profession they are breeders of cattle, dependent on the sale of their calves for their livelihood... A good number of breeding bulls live in a semi-wild state.' Littlewood's description of the situation in the mid 1930s still applies.

On the low land of the valley floors small scale irrigation has always been important. You may notice wells being operated by bullocks moving up and down a ramp, pulling a large bucket from a well. This *kavalai** system is widespread in northern Tamil Nadu, and is particularly distinctive as it can be operated by only one man, unlike the similar systems in N India which need two people. The most important crop is groundnut. **Uttangarai** has a small rest house at the cross roads with the Tiruppattur road. The road S to **Harur** (27 km; *Population* 21,000; *Rest House* available) passes through a small area of Reserved Forest. Enter Harur and take the Salem Rd out of the town to the SW. A left turn in Harur itself crosses the Vaniyar River and leads up onto the Reserved Forests of the westernmost block of the *Kalrayan Hills*.

Salem *Population* 480,000 *Altitude* 280 m The approaching road passes the impressive Shevaroy Hills on the right. The town (58 km) itself is at the junction of roads from Bangalore to the N and Trichy to the S, and is surrounded by the Shevaroy and Nagaramalai Hills to the N, the Jerumumalai Hills to the S, the Godumalai Hills to the E and the Kanjamalai Hills to the W. The town of Salem is divided into 2 parts by the River Tirumanimuttar, the old town being on the left or E bank, with Shevapet being on the opposite side. One tradition holds that the town takes its name from *Sela* or *Shalya*, a corruption of Chera, named because a Chera king from the S was believed to have rested at Salem. The town is also one of many places held to be the birthplace of the Tamil poetess Avvaiyar.

Historically Salem was a defensive site. The fort, of which only the E wall remains, is the oldest part of the town. Situated on the right bank, a bridge crosses the river from its NE corner. The main administrative buildings such as the

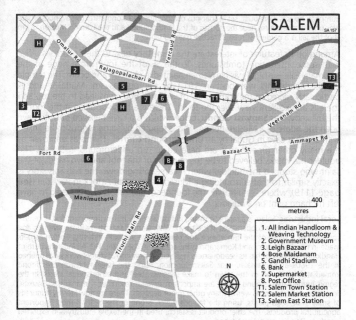

1. All Indian Handloom &
   Weaving Technology
2. Government Museum
3. Leigh Bazaar
4. Bose Maidanam
5. Gandhi Stadium
6. Bank
7. Supermarket
8. Post Office
T1. Salem Town Station
T2. Salem Market Station
T3. Salem East Station

Collector's Office and the Town Hall are just N of the fort, near to Christ Church, which was consecrated in 1875. A seated Jain figure is opposite the old Collector's bungalow known at the *Talaivetti Muniappan*, or "Muniappan with the broken head". Devotees bring offerings of the blood of goats and chickens. Near the Jain statue is a shrine to Tipanja Amman which contains a stone slab with a round top on which are carved 2 human figures, reputedly erected to commemorate two women who burned themselves on the spot when they learned of their husbands' death in battle.

Also near the centre of the town are the compound of the old **London Missionary Society**, now part of the Church of S India, and to its W the market of **Shevapet**. This takes its name from the Tamil word Sevvai, the name for the planet Mars. The market is held on Tue (Mars' day) every week and is still attended by thousands of people from all around the town.

There are several important temples in the town itself. The **Siva** temple is dedicated to *Sukavaneswara*, the "Lord of the Parrot Forest", though one inscription describes him as the "parrot coloured Lord". The main entrance to the temple has a pillared portico. N of the portico is a *kalyanamandapam* named after the British Collector who gave it, W.D. Davis. To the N of the hall is a deep round well called "the **frogless spring**", because it is said that all the frogs were frightened away by Adisesha who once visited the well. In addition to the temples there are several mosques, the oldest of which is in the fort. A Friday Mosque was built by **Tipu Sultan** on the bank of the river. The mosque in Shevapet was built in 1882, causing riots among objectors.

The Salem District Gazetteer records that to the S of Shevapet is a hamlet called **Gugai** which "takes its name from a cave, the entrance to which is marked by the Muniappa temple. The cave is said to have been the abode of a Hindu hermit who for some inscrutable reason was petrified into the idol of Muniappan. The idol is seated cross-legged in the attitude of meditation and at its feet is seated a bearded devotee in a similar posture." To the N of the town the Yercaud road leads from Christ Church through the area where most of the old

European houses were built, set in spacious compounds and along attractive avenues. There was once a race course near the houses of the District Judge and the London Mission. 2 km N of the jail is a garden with an attractive bathing tank.

Among other features of interest are the **cemetery** next to the Collector's office with some interesting tombstones. To the SE of the town on a ridge of the Jerumalai Hills is a highly visible *Naman* painted in chunam and ochre. The temple on the nearby hill was built in 1919 by Karuppanasvami Mudaliar and is particularly sacred to the community of weavers. 600 steps lead to the top and there is an excellent view over the town. There is a huge boulder at the foot of the hill known as **Sanyasi Gundu**, below which is a cave believed once to have been the home of a Muslim hermit. This is reputed by some Hindus to be linked with another cave in Gugai by an **underground tunnel**. That is as unproven as the many other tunnels that are believed to run underground in S Asia. The boulder has marks believed to be the imprints of the foot and two hands of the saint who stopped the boulder when it came rolling down the hill. This story is exactly similar to that surrounding a Muslim shrine near Attock in Pakistan (**see page 1119**), where Guru Nanak, the founder of Sikhism, is also believed to have left his hand print on a boulder..

Local industries Salem is a rapidly growing industrial town. It is an important textile centre, with over 130 *textile* cooperatives in the town. Walk along Bazar Street in the evening and you will get a sense of the importance and range of the weaving industry. *Cotton carpets* made in nearby Bhavani and Komarapalayam are sold in the Bazar. The All India Institute of Handloom Technology has its headquarters in the city. A new *iron and steel* works was opened in the 1980s at Kanjamalai, near Salem Junction, using the haematite iron ores found immediately to the W of the town to make stainless steel and other special steels. In the region immediately around Salem are important *mineral resources* – magnesite, bauxite, limestone and iron ore as well as many other minor deposits. There are now literally hundreds of small scale sago plants, using the tapioca which is one of the districts most important agricultural products. The chief product is starch, used in the textile industry and exported largely to Bombay and Ahmadabad.

Hotels D *National*, Omalur Rd. T 54100, Cable: National, Telex: 0450-228 Otel In. 105 rm, 40 a/c. 3.5 km rly, 1 km downtown. Restaurant, a/c bar, travel, roof garden. **E** *Hotel Apsara*, 19 Car St. T 63075, Cable: Himalyas. 37 rm, 3 a/c. Close to rly. Restaurant (Indian, Continental), coffee shop, exchange. **E** *Woodlands*, Five Rds. T 7272, Cable: Woodlands. 40 rm, some a/c. 2 km downtown. A/c restaurant (Indian). **E** *Maduthi Hotel*, Salem, T 64214. Some a/c double rm. **E** *Hotel Gokulam*, Mayyanur Rd, T 7071. Some a/c rm.

Museums Government Museum Omalur Rd, open 0900-1230, 1300-1700. Closed Fri, 2nd Sat and national holidays. The collection has archaeological, zoological and botanical exhibits. There is a library, guide service, lectures and films. Photography is allowed except of the collection of bronzes. **Planetarium** The South's first planetarium, housed in the Govt College of Engineering. Fixed shows, apply at the college.

Places of worship *Hindu* Sukavanesvarar Temple for the Lord of the Parrot Forests; Saundara Raja Perumal Temple; Kottain Mariamman Temple; Ramakrishna Mutt. *Christian* CSI. *Muslim* The Jama Masjid (built by Tipu Sultan). The *Theosophical Society* also has a meeting hall.

Air An airport is under construction for Vayudoot services, due for completion in 1992.

Rail Madras (MC): *W Coast Exp*, 6028, daily, 0800, 5 hr 55 min; *Kovai Exp*, 2676, daily, 1640, 5 hr 15 min; **Coimbatore**: *W Coast Exp*, 6027, daily, 1740, 3 hr 10 min. **Road** Salem is well connected by bus with all major towns in Tamil Nadu, Kerala and S Karnataka.

Excursions The *Mettur Dam* Built between 1925-1934, the dam is still one of the world's largest. Its reservoir holds 3 times as much water as the Aswan Dam on the River Nile, over 2,600 million cubic metres. The dam is 1.6 km long and 54 m high, and the lake it impounds is over 155 sq km. The water provides irrigation to Salem and Coimbatore and the Mettur Hydroelectric Project is situated here. It can be visited by leaving Salem at the Salem Jn Rly station, and via Taramangalam to Pottaneri. There are also regular buses from Salem. There are 2 **F** *Circuit Houses*. Reservations: Sub-Divisional Officer, PWD, Stanley Dam,

Sub Division, PO Mettur Dam.

Salem is an excellent base from which to visit the **Shevaroy Hills** and the small hill town of **Yercaud** (33 km). *Altitude* 1515 m. *Climate* Temp. Summer Average 29°C, Winter Average 13°C. Annual rainfall 168 cm. Clothing Summer Cottons, Winter Woollens. Season Throughout the year.

Described by Murray's Guide in 1904 as "essentially a place for a quiet holiday – smaller and less expensive than Ootacamund or Kodaikkanal" the description holds today, though a day trip is also very pleasant. The drive up the steep and sharply winding ghat road is beautiful, but the whole journey from Salem takes under an hour. There are several points of interest all within 3 km of Yercaud itself. There is a small artificial **lake** with a park nearby. Just outside the town is **Lady's Seat**, which overlooks the Ghat road and gives wonderful views across the Salem plains.

In May there is a special festival focused on the **Shevaroyan Temple**, on top of the third highest peak in the hill range. Many tribal people take part, but access is only possible on foot. Ask for details in the Tamil Nadu Tourist Office in Madras. Near the Norton Bungalow, the oldest bungalow in Yercaud on the Shevaroyan Temple Rd, is another well known local spot, **Bear's Cave**. Formed by two huge boulders, it is now occupied by huge colonies of bats. The whole area is full of botanical interest, the altitude of over 1,500 m allowing a quite different range of species to grow from those common on the intensively cultivated plains below. There is an **Orchidarium-cum-Nursery** and a **Horticultural Research Station**, many varieties of flowers flourish in the relative coolness, along with pear, jack and orange trees.

Hotels Most offer off season discounts. **F** *Hotel Tamil Nadu* (TTDC), Salem–Yercaud Ghat Rd, behind Panchayat Union Office, T 273. Cable: Tamil Tour. 12 rm, some a/c . *Youth Hostel*, dormitory beds and an a/c dormitory, simple, good value. Reservations: Manager, Hotel or Commercial Manager, TTDC, 143 Anna Salai, Madras. T 849803. **E** *Hotel Shevaroys*, Main Rd, Yercaud, T 288. **E** *Hotel Select*, nr Bus Stand, T 296. Only double rm.

Namakkal *Population* 53,000. You can see the ruins of an extraordinary hill top fort 50 kilometres S of Salem which dominates the busy market town below and is believed to have been built by Tipu Sultan. It is equally famous in Tamil Nadu for its Vishnu temple. Opposite the temple is a huge statue of Hanuman worshipping. The bare rock to the N of the main tank (*Kamalalayam Tank*) covers 2 ha. The district played a leading part in the Indian independence movement in the S, and Mahatma Gandhi addressed a huge meeting from this spot in 1933, still remembered by some. Within the shrine of the **Narasimhasvami Temple** there are 4 particularly remarkable Pallava bas reliefs.

From Salem Join the NH 47 S W to **Shankari Drug** (35 km), passing the 750 metre high rock fort on your right. Haider Ali was reputed to have kept hoards of gold in the rock fort at the top of the hill, 500 m above the plain. From the top you have magnificent views over the Shevaroy Hills and to the Kaveri River. The fort has various gruesome associations. It is said that "undesirable persons" were rolled down the almost vertical 500 m cliff on the Swestern side of the hill. The hill has several springs with medicinal properties, the most famous being the *Maan Sunai* or Deer Spring which is never touched by the sun's rays. The main road crosses the Kaveri at **Bhavani** (21 km, *Population* 37,000) which straddles the rocky banks of the river just above its confluence with the Bhavani. The town is a centre of pilgrimage, especially from Palghat.

The Nayaka **Sangamesvara Temple** at the confluence of the 2 rivers has bathing ghats going down into the mixing waters of both rivers. 6 km to the W of Bhavani is an open cast mica mine, yielding good quality green mica.

From here on the route enters a region of great historical importance as an area of contact between the plains of Tamil Nadu to the E, the plateaus of Mysore to the N and the coastal plains of Kerala, reached through the Palghat gap to the S. Notice the frequency with which the word *"palayam"* ("encampment") occurs in place names, indicating the extent to which this was also a region of conflict between the three major regional powers of the *Cholas*, the *Pandiyas* and the *Cheras*. From Bhavani the main road goes SW to **Perundurai** (23 km). Asbestos is mined nearby.

Erode (15 km S of Bhavani on the banks of the Kaveri; *Population* 187,000), is noted as the home of the great Tamil nationalist, social reformer and political leader Periyar E.V. Ramaswamy Naicker. The town is also famous for its handloom products. The road from Bhavani westwards crosses some of the districts most fertile areas, the 'granary of Kongu country'. Paddy, sugar cane, groundnut, cotton, turmeric, tobacco, bananas, and various millets are all grown in what is regarded as one of the most progressive agricultural areas of Tamil Nadu.

Avinashi (36 km, *Population* 21,000) has a widely visited Siva temple, dedicated to *Avinasisvara*, noted partly for its colossal *Nandi*. The outer porch of the temple has 2 stone alligators, each shown vomiting a child. They recall a local story which told how a local saint, Sundaramurti Nayanar, interceded on behalf of a child who had been swallowed by an alligator, and the infant was disgorged unhurt. There is a shrine to the saint inside the temple and on the bund of the Tamaraikulam tank (pond of lotuses). The temple gopurams were renovated in 1756, but inscriptions indicate that the temple goes back to at least the early 13th century. The biggest temple tower lost its top 5 storeys in 1860. To some local chiefs it was known as the *Kasi* (Varanasi) of the S.

If you are going direct to Ooty from Avinashi you can take the right turn a few km out of Avinashi on the Coimbatore road and go direct to Mettupalayam, via Annur. Frequent local buses. Otherwise go straight to Coimbatore (40 km).

Coimbatore

Population 1.1 million. *Altitude* 425 m.

	Jan	Feb	Mar	Apr	May	Jun	Jul	Aug	Sep	Oct	Nov	Dec	Av/Tot
Max (°C)	30	33	35	35	34	31	30	31	32	31	29	29	32
Min (°C)	19	19	21	23	23	22	22	22	22	22	21	19	21
Rain (mm)	7	4	5	70	76	35	37	18	42	127	127	25	573

The city owes its rapid growth in the last fifty years to the development of Hydro Electricity from the **Pykara Falls** in the 1930s. This led to a boom in cotton textile milling, Coimbatore often being called the Manchester of S India. The industry had started in 1888 with 2 mills, but until electric power became available it could not compete with the much larger scale production in Bombay and Gujarat. Related industries have also developed, including a range of engineering industries. Pump sets for irrigation and motor parts and assembly have been added in recent years. The centre of a rich agricultural area, Coimbatore has a noted agricultural university. The nucleus was an Agricultural Demonstration Farm started on the outskirts of Madras in 1868. This was shifted to Coimbatore in 1907 and became an internationally known centre of agricultural research. It was converted into an agricultural university in 1971. It is a centre for seed breeding experiments and has been responsible for a wide range of cross bred varieties of major crops grown in S India. Travelling across Tamil Nadu you will often see advertisements for seeds in fields and painted on walls. Some have the prefix "CO" and a number, indicating its origin in the Coimbatore Agricultural University.

Places of interest The Tamil Nadu Agricultural University **Botanical Garden.**

Dear Editor

WILL YOU HELP US?

We do all we can to get our facts right in the **SOUTH ASIAN HANDBOOK**. Each section is thoroughly revised each year, but the territory covered is vast and our eyes cannot be everywhere.

Your information may be more up to date than ours and if you have enjoyed a tour, trek, hotel, restaurant or any other activity or establishment and would like others to share it, please write with the details.

When writing, it will be very helpful if you can give the year on the cover of your Handbook and the page number referred to.

If your letter reaches us early enough in the year, it will be used in the next annual edition, but write whenever you want to, for all your information will be used.

Thank you very much indeed for your help.

Write to: The Editor, The South Asian Handbook,
Trade & Travel Publications
6 Riverside Court, Lower Bristol Road,
Bath BA2 3DZ England.

THE BEST IN
TRAVEL GUIDES

THE TRAVELLER'S HANDBOOK

1992
SOUTH ASIAN HANDBOOK
INDIA
PAKISTAN, NEPAL, BANGLADESH,
SRI LANKA, BHUTAN, THE MALDIVES

A traveller's guide
to the
Indian Sub-Continent
from the Himalayas to the Indian Ocean

1992
CARIBBEAN ISLANDS HANDBOOK

1992
MEXICO & CENTRAL AMERICAN HANDBOOK

SECOND EDITION
Mexico, Guatemala, Belize, Honduras,
El Salvador, Nicaragua, Costa Rica, Panama
From the Rio Grande to the Darién Gap

1992
SOUTH AMERICAN HANDBOOK

SIXTY EIGHTH EDITION

Winner of the first ever Thomas Cook Best Travel Guide Award
The definitive guide for South America
From the Darién Gap to Tierra del Fuego

**TRADE & TRAVEL
PUBLICATIONS**

KEY TO MAP SECTION

© Bartholomew 1990

adrachalam
gūdem
Tuni
Anakapalle
ahmundry
Kākināda
Yanam
Bhimavaram
Machilipatnam
et

③

15
Preparis I.

Preparis South Channel

Gt Coco I.
(Burma)

Coco Channel

North
Andaman

Karen

A N D A M A N

Middle
Andaman

I S L A N D S
(India)

Ritchie's
Archipelago

South
Andaman

Port Blair

N. Sentinel

Rutland

Duncan Passage

Palalankwe

Little
Andaman

Ignoitijala

10N

Ten Degree Channel

Car Nicobar

Batti Malv

Chaura
Tillanchong

Teressa
Camorta

Katchall
Nancowry

N I C O B A R

Sombrero Channel

Little Nicobar

I S L A N D S
(India)

Great Nicobar

Bananga

Mullaittvu

niya
Trincomalee

SRI LANKA

Polonnaruwa
Batticaloa

tale
ctoria Dam
ndy
Badulla
uwara-Eliya
pura

Hambantota
adra Hd

95E

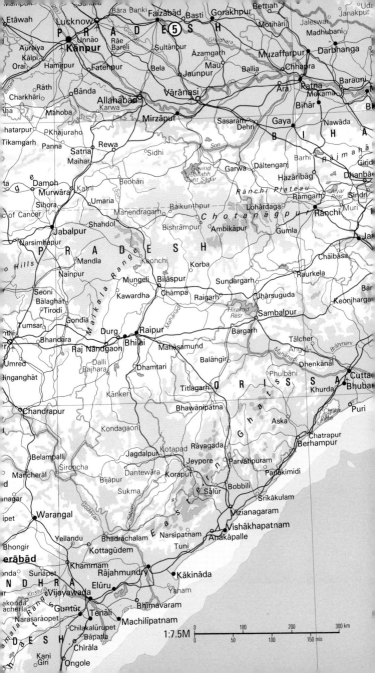

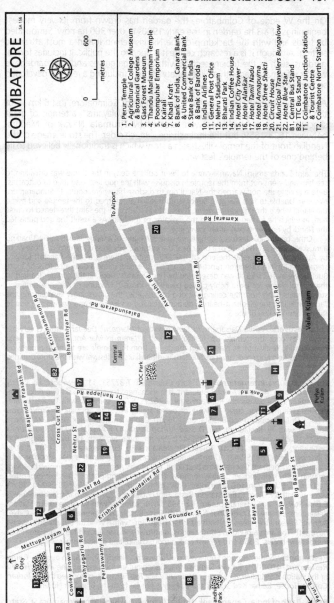

COIMBATORE

SA 156

N

0   600
metres

1. Perur Temple
2. Agricultural College Museum
3. Botanical Gardens
4. Gass Forest Museum
5. Thandu Mariammam Temple
6. Poompuhar Emporium
7. Kairali
8. Khadi Kraft
8. Bank of India, Canara Bank, & United Commercial Bank
9. State Bank of India & Bank of Baroda
10. Indian Airlines
11. General Post Office
12. Nehru Stadium
13. Bharati Park
14. Indian Coffee House
15. Hotel City Tower
16. Hotel Alankar
17. Hotel Tamil Nadu
18. Hotel Annapurna
19. Hotel Shree Shakti
20. Circuit House
21. Municipal Travellers Bungalow
22. Hotel Blue Star
B1. Central Bus Stand
B2. TTC Bus Stand
T1. Tourist Centre & Coimbatore Junction Station
T2. Coimbatore North Station

To Airport

Kamaraj Rd

V K Krishnamenon Rd

Bharathiyar Rd

Balasundaram Rd

Avanashi Rd

Race Course Rd

Central Jail

VOC Park

Dr Rajendra Prasath Rd

Cross Cut Rd

Nehru St

Dr Nanjappa Rd

Bank Rd

Tiruchi Rd

Valan Kulam

Perija Kulam

Mettupalayam Rd

To Ooty

Cowley Brown Rd

Bashyagarlu Rd

Perlaswamy Rd

Patel Rd

Krishnasvami Mudalier Rd

Rangai Gounder St

Sukrawarpettai Mill St

Edayar St

Raja St

Big Bazaar St

Gandhi Park

Perur Rd

On the W edge of Coimbatore, the garden has grown from its very modest beginnings of a 3 ha garden in the early 1900s to over 300 ha now. Surrounded by fields and with the backdrop of the Nilgiris behind it is in a most attractive setting. Although it is a research centre it is open to the public. It includes formal gardens, such as the topiary section with casuarina groves and rose gardens as well as informal areas with a wide variety of trees, including a recently developed section of flowering trees.

Perur *Population* 9,000 Now almost a suburb of Coimbatore, just 6 km W of the city centre, Perur has one of seven "Kongu Sivalayams", a temple of great sanctity. The outer buildings were erected by **Tirumala Nayak** of Madurai between 1623-1659, but the inner shrine is much older. The stone image of the Nandi in front of the temple illustrates a story which is traditionally believed to lie behind one of the temple's festivals.

The saint Sundaramurti Nayanar came to Perur but the deity in the shrine was unwilling to see him and went out from the temple in disguise with the goddess, disguised as outcastes. Before leaving the god warned the Nandi not to disclose his whereabouts to Sundaramurti Nayanar. Unable to find the god, Sundaramurti Nayanar returned to the temple and asked the Nandi where the deities had gone. The bull kept silent until the saint threatened to curse him, at which he turned his head in the direction of the field. As a result the god punished the Nandi by removing part of his lower jaw.

Other remarkable features of the temple are the figure of a sepoy (Indian soldier) loading a musket carved on the base of a pillar near the entrance. His dress is identical to those worn by Aurangzeb's soldiers at the end of the 17th century. There is a stone flagstaff (*dhvaja stambha*) 11 m high at the entrance to the temple, the main shrine is dedicated to *Sabhapati*. Built between 1623-59, it was desecrated by Tipu Sultan's troops. In the corridor leading to the central shrine are eight richly carved pillars like those in Madurai or Kanchipuram, and stone chains hang from the ceiling. Among other scenes the pillars show Siva dancing the *Tandava*; killing the elephant-headed demon, treading on his head and waving the skin in the air; and the lion of the S.

Local festivals *Arudra Darsanam* in Tamil month of *Margazhi*, Dec-Jan. Attracts very big crowds, as does the temple car festival *Panguni Uttaram* in Mar-Apr. In Jun-Jul a seed transplanting festival takes place when the deities from the temple are taken in procession to a nearby field and seeds are transplanted. Tradition links the festival with the story outlined above.

Hotels D *Surya International*, 105 Race Course Rd. T 37751. 11 km airport, 1.5 km rly and downtown. 44 rm, 37 a/c. Restaurant, bar, exchange, travel, shops, skating rink, lawn. **D** *Alankar* 10 Dr Sivaswamy Rd, Ramnagar. T 26293. 57 rm, some a/c with TV. Restaurant, bar, ice-cream parlour, travel. Beware of overcharging in dining 'special'. **D** *Tamil Nadu* (TTDC) Dr Nanjappa Rd opp Bus Station. T 36310, Cable: Tamiltour, Telex: 0885-224. 49 rm, some a/c with TV. Restaurant, bar. **D** *Sree Annapoorna*, 47 E Arokiasamy Rd, RS Puram, T 47621, Cable: Poornam, Telex: 0855-447. 56 rm some a/c with TV. Indian vegetarian restaurant, bar, travel. **D** *City Tower*, Dr Nanjappa Rd, Gandhipuram. T 37681, Cable: Citytower, Telex: 0855-543. 97 rm some a/c. 2 restaurants, travel, shops. Popular with businessmen, perhaps Coimbatore's best hotel. **D** *Railway Retiring Rooms*, in new building, rm with bath, including a/c double rm, noisy. The dormitory off platform 1 is less expensive. Restaurant. **E** *Janaranjani*, Janaranjani Cross off N H Rd. T 34101, Telex: 0855-234. 36 rm some a/c with TV. Close to Bus Station. Restaurant (Indian veg, Chinese), bar, snack bar, travel. **E** *Blue Star*, Nehru St, Gandhipuram. T 26395. 50 rm, some a/c with TV. Close to Bus Station. Restaurant, car hire. **E** *Shree Shakti*, on Shastri Rd nr Bus Station, Ramnagar. T 34225, Cable: Rajnivit. Reasonable, clean rm with attached bath. Rm "with TV" extra but doesn't always have set! The area around the bus stations, particularly Shastri Rd and Nehru Rd are full of inexpensive hotels. **F** *SBS Lodge*, just opp. airport, cheap, and good in emergency.

Restaurants Some outside hotels are *Udhaya*, Nehru St, Gandhipuram. *China Restaurant*, 410 Trichy Rd. *Sri Sampoorna*, Gandhipuram for S Indian. The *Royal Hindu* nr the station is an Indian vegetarian restaurant while *Top Form* offers non-veg meals. *Indian Coffee House*, Ramar Koil St. *Pushpa Bakery* is not far from the Blue Star Hotel.

Banks Bank of India, Canara Bank, United Commercial Bank all on Oppankara St. State Bank of India, T 36251 and Bank of Baroda are on Bank Rd.

Shopping Famous for handloom and handicrafts. *Poompuhar Emporium*, Big Bazar St, *Kairali* off Mettupalayam Rd and *Khadi Kraft* on Dr Nanjappa Rd. Several other shops along the street and in Shukravar Pettai and Gandhipuram.

Local Transport *Tourist Taxis* and un-metred yellow top taxis at the Bus Station, Rly Station and Taxi stands. About Rs 40 per hr. Out-station hill journeys more expensive. *City Buses* run a good service, with No 12 connecting the Bus Stations with the Coimbatore Junction Rly Station and No 20 with the airport (Rs 20). Central (Cheran) Bus Stand, T 26309. *Auto rickshaws* – negotiate fare before journey. Min Rs 5 per km.

Museums College Museum Tamil Nadu Agricultural University, Coimbatore 641003, T 35461 Open 0900-1200, 1400-1700. Closed Sun and Government holidays. Special collections of minerals, rocks, insects pests, fungal diseases, snakes, silver and gold medals. Guide service. **Gass Forest Museum** Southern Forest Rangers' College and Research Centre, Coimbatore 641002, T 22642 Open 1900-1300, 1400-1630 Closed Sun, second Sat and public holidays. Exhibits of forestry and forest products. Library.

Parks and zoos The *VOC Park* and *Zoo* nr the Stadium has a toy train circuit. *Bharati Park*, Bharati Park Main Rd. 1 Sai Baba Colony. *Botanical Garden*, nr Agriculture University.

Post Office and telegraph The Head Post Office and Telegraph Office, T 36151 is nr the fly over on Rly Feeder Rd. Fax service available.

Hospital The *Government Medical College and Hospital* is on Trichy Rd.

The **Tourist Information Centre** is at Coimbatore Junction Rly Station, open weekdays 1000-1930, Sat and Sun 1000-1700.

Air Indian Airlines Madras Mon, Th & Sat (+ 1 other), 0825, 1 hr 45 min. Mon, Tue, Th & Sat, 1535, 1 hr 45 min; **Bangalore** Mon, Th & Sat (+ 1 other), 0825, 35 min; Mon, Tue, Th & Sat, 1535, 35 min; **Bombay** Daily, 1225, 1 hr 35 min. **Vayudoot Madras** Mon-Sat, 1740, 1 hr 25 min. Indian Airlines and Air India Office, Trichy Rd. Enquiries T 22743, Reservations T 22208. Open 1000-1300, 1345-1730. Airport T 73396. Vayudoot flies from Madras to Coimbatore. Vayudoot Booking Agents, Kasturi Travels, 218 Avanashi Rd nr fly-over Bridge. T 22413. Peelamedu Airport (30 km from centre). Cheran Transport runs an airport coach to several hotels and parts of the city. **Air Asiatic** to Bombay, Sue, Th, Fri & Sat.

Rail Junction Rly Station **Madras**: *Kovai Exp*, 2676 (AC/CC), daily, 1415, 8 hr 40 min; *Trivandrum-Guwahati Exp*, 2601, Thurs, 2215, 7 hr 40 min; **Bangalore**: *Nagercoil-Bangalore Exp*, 6525 (AC/II), 2055, 9 hr 30 min; **Cochin** (HT): *Trichy-Cochin Exp*, 6365, daily, 0045, 5 hr 30 min; *Haora/Patna-Cochin*, 2652/2610 (AC/II), Tue, Sat, Sun, 1315, 5 hr 15 min; *Guwahati-Cochin*, 2650 (AC/II), Fri, 1315, 5 hr 15 min; **Delhi** (ND): *Mangala Link Exp*, 2625/2625A (AC/II), daily, 1925, 43 hr 5 min. **Madurai** (5 hr 30 min) and **Ramesvaram** (12 hr) *Ramesvaram Exp*, daily. *Kanniyakumari Exp*, daily, 13 hr 30 min. Other trains: W Coast Exp (Madras – Coimbatore – Calicut – Bangalore), daily. to Calicut (4 hr 30 min) and Bangalore (9 hr). **Ooty**: train at 0630 connects with narrow gauge train from Mettupalayam. Coimbatore Junction Rly Station. Enquiries, T 36224. Reservations, T 24157. Open 0700-1300, 1400-2030.

Road Coimbatore is on the NH 47 and there are good roads to other towns in the region. Some Distances: Bangalore 312 km, Cochin 184 km, Kaniyakumari 469 km, Kodaikkanal 172 km, Madras 492 km, Madurai 227 km, Ooty 90 km, Trivandrum 400 km.

Buses TTC and the SRTCs of the neighbouring states as well as private companies run regular services to many cities. Frequent buses to Ooty (5 hr) between 0400 and 2400. TTC also runs frequent buses to Madurai and Trichy (5 hr 30 min) and 5 daily to Madras (12 hr). The 2 Bus Stands for out-station services are in the Gandhipuram area on Dr Nanjappa Rd. TTC Bus Stand, Cross Cut Rd, Enquiries, T 44969. Computerised reservations 0700-2100. Corporation Bus Stand, T 26309. Reservations 0900-1200, 1600-1800.

From Coimbatore there is an excellent road N to Mettupalayam (53 km) *Population* 80,000. **Mettupalayam** is a centre of the *areca* nut trade, and between the town and the bottom of the ghat road up to Coonoor and Ooty the road passes through magnificent groves of tall slender areca nut palms. These are an immensely valuable tree, and the nut is used across India wrapped in betel vine leaves as two of the essential ingredients in India's universal after-meal digestive agent, *pan**. The town is the starting point of the ghat railway line up to Ooty (**see page 792**). On the banks of the Bhavani river, it has also become the centre for a range of new industrial units, notably the production of synthetic gems. The ghat road up to Coonoor (32 km) is one of the most famous in India, the views over the plains below, glimpsed through the thick woodland, being very striking.

Coonoor

Population 56,000 *Altitude* 1800 m. *Climate* Temp Summer Max. 24°C Min 14°C, Winter Max. 19°C Min. 9°C. Annual rainfall 130 cm. *Best season* Apr-June, Sep-Oct. *Clothing* Summer Light woollens, Winter Woollens.

The second largest of the 3 Nilgiri hill stations but has little to offer except as a place to relax. It is quieter and has a milder climate than Ooty. The increase in population is partly due to the arrival of Tamils from Sri Lanka. The town is physically divided into upper and lower Coonoor.

Places of interest At its heart is **Sim's Park** which was founded in the mid-19th century as an amusement park for Coonoor and the cantonment at Wellington nearby. The 12 ha park in Upper Coonoor is on the slopes of a ravine and has been developed into a botanical garden partly in the Japanese style. The fruit and vegetable show is held in May, after the Flower Show in Ooty. Coonoor also has the *Pomological Station* where the State Agricultural Department researches both common and uncommon fruits including persimmon, apricot and pomegranates. Surplus fruit is sold to the public, T 6008. There are 2 other research stations in the Nilgiris, at Burliar and Kallar. The **Pasteur Institute** opp the main entrance to Sim's Park was established in 1907, researches into rabies and manufactures polio vaccine. You can take a tour with a guide on Sat between 1030 and 1115. Otherwise you may visit with permission of the Director.

Next door is the **Silkworm Rearing Station** of the Central Silk Board. You should contact the United Planters' Association of Southern India (UPASI), Glenview if you wish to visit **tea and coffee plantations**. There are several view points nearby some of which can be reached by road. **Lamb's Rock** 6 km away is on a high precipice from which you can see the plains of Coimbatore and the coffee and tea estates on the slopes. **Dolphin's Nose** 12 km, is another, 10 km away, from which you can see Catherine Falls, and **Droog** 13 km which has ruins of a 16th century fort used by Tipu Sultan as an outpost, requires a 3 km walk. **Law's Falls** 5 km, is near the junction of Coonoor and Katteri rivers on the road to Mettupalayam. There are several very attractive local shady walks in Coonoor, including **Tiger's Hill**, **Walker's Hill** and **Brookland's Road**.

Hotels D *Ritz*, T 6242, Cable: Ritz. 20 rm, some with TV. Restaurant, bar, car hire, garden. Recommended. **D** *Hampton Manor*. T 6244, Cable: Hampton. 31 rm. Restaurant, exchange, car hire. **D** *Blue Hills*, Mount Rd. T 6130. 40 rm. Restaurant, car hire, TV. Fairly basic, less expensive in its category with a reasonable food. There are also Indian style hotels. **E** *Vivek Tourist Home*, Figure of 8 Rd, nr UPASI. T 6658, Cable: Vee-tech. 60 rm with bath. Restaurant, credit cards. **E** *Sri Lakshmi Tourist Home*, Kamrajpuram, Rockby. T 7022. 35 rm. Indian restaurant, car hire and TV lounge. **E** *YWCA Guest House*, Wyoming. 12 rm. Dining hall, garden. **F** *Venkateswara Lodge*, Cash Bazar nr Bus Stand. T 6740. 40 rm.

Shopping *Spencer's*, Figure of 8 Rd, *Variety Hall*, Jubilee Bridge and *Shanthi Mahal* nr the Bus Stand. *Issu Book Centre*, Bedford.

Hospitals Govt Lawley Hospital, Mount Rd, T 2223. The Emmanuel Eye Hospital has an excellent reputation.

Travel Rail A Mountain Rly connects Coonoor with Coimbatore via Mettupalayam. See below under Ooty. **Road** Frequent buses connect Coonoor with Ooty (every 10 min) some via Sim's Park and many via Wellington. Also regular services to Kotagiri and Coimbatore through Mettupalayam.

Wellington (3 km) *Population* 28,000 The barracks which gave the raison d'etre for Wellington's existence were built in 1852. It is now the headquarters of the Indian Defence Services Staff College with an excellent library. It is also the headquarters of the Madras Regiment, which is over 250 years old, the oldest in the Indian Army. Follow the road up to Ooty (17 km).

Ooty (*Udhagamandalam*)

Population 105,000 *Altitude* 2,286 m *Climate* Temperature Summer Max. 25°C Min. 10°C, Winter Max. 21°C Min. 5°C. Rainfall 121 cm. Season April – June. *Languages* Tamil, English, Kannada, Malayalam, Hindi. *Clothing* Light woollens in the day, occasionally, Warm woollens in the evenings and during the monsoons.

Near the junction of the three states of Tamil Nadu, Karnataka and Kerala, Ooty was mentioned in the Madras Gazette of 1821 as "Wotokymund". It had been inhabited by *Toda* tribal people who lived in villages or 'munds' consisting of a handful of huts. **See page 724**. The origin of the name is disputed. Some think it comes from the Tamil word 'votai', a dwarf bamboo, 'kai' meaning vegetable or unripe fruit, and the Toda word 'mund'. Others believe it is 'one-stone-village' in the Toda language. The English shortened it to 'Ooty'. The 'Queen of the Blue Mountains', along with Kotagiri and Coonoor nearby, is famous for its rolling hills covered in pine and eucalyptus forests and its coffee and tea plantations. Because of its climate it was developed by the British as a hill station to provide a summer retreat after a Collector from Coimbatore, John Sullivan, 'discovered' it. A Government House was built there, and the British life style followed with cottages, clubs: tennis, golf, riding and teas on the lawn. The Indian Maharajahs followed, built their grand houses and came here to shoot.

Local festivals Jan Ooty celebrates Pongal. May – The Annual Flower and Dog Shows in the Botanical Gardens. Summer Festival of cultural programmes with stars from all over India.

Places of interest The **Botanical Gardens** are 2 km E of Rly station, over 20 hectares planted with more than a thousand varieties of plants, shrubs and trees including orchids, ferns, alpines and medicinal plants among beautiful lawns and glass houses. There is a small lake with a 20 million-year old fossil tree trunk by it. It started life as a kitchen garden of a few residents, was developed by the Marquis of Tweeddale in 1847 who got a Kew gardener to transform it into an ornamental garden and 10 years later was taken over by the government in Madras. To the E of the garden in a Toda *mund* with a group of huts and to the N is the Woodhouse made of logs from which you can get good views. The Raj Bhavan is next door. The Annual Flower Show (mainly exotics) with its accompanying exhibition is held in the third week of May. Unless you are attending the flower show, Ooty is best avoided at this time. It cannot cope with the thousands of extra visitors.

Ooty Lake was constructed between 1823 and 1825 through the initiative of the Collector Mr. John Sullivan as an irrigation tank. Although artificial, the winding lake looks beautifully natural. It has been shrinking for decades and is now about 2.5 km long and between 100 and 140 m wide. Part of the land which was under water in the last century has been reclaimed to provide recreational facilities, including the race course. The Boat House is maintained by the Dept of Tourism. Open 0800-1800. The lake is polluted and is likely to be drained.

Raj Bhavan Built by the Duke of Buckingham and Chandos in 1877, when Governor of Madras, in the style of his family home at Stowe. The Government House, now the Raj Bhavan, is superbly positioned on the Dodabetta Ridge to the SE of Ooty and is approached through the Botanical Gardens. The grounds are very well maintained and open to visitors, though the building is now only

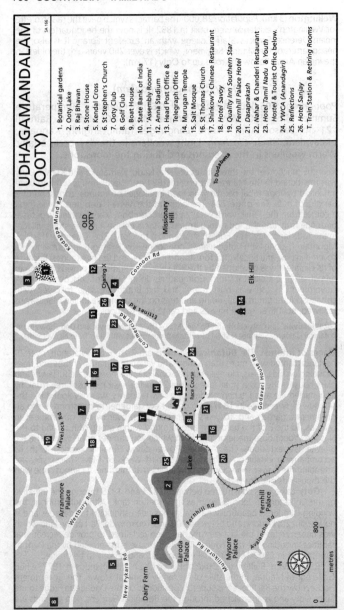

UDHAGAMANDALAM (OOTY)

SA 166

1. Botanical gardens
2. Ooty Lake
3. Raj Bhavan
4. Stone House
5. Kendal Cross
6. St Stephen's Church
7. Ooty Club
8. Golf Club
9. Boat House
10. State Bank of India
11. 'Assembly Rooms'
12. Anna Stadium
13. Head Post Office & Telegraph Office
14. Murugan Temple
15. Sait Mosque
16. St Thomas Church
17. Shinkow's Chinese Restaurant
18. Hotel Savoy
19. Quality Inn Southern Star
20. Fernhill Palace Hotel
21. Dasaprakash
22. Nahar & Chanderi Restaurant
23. Hotel Tamil Nadu & Youth Hostel & Tourist Office below.
24. YWCA (Anandagiri)
25. Reflections
26. Hotel Sanjay
T. Train Station & Retiring Rooms

occasionally used for official entertaining. Among the Victorian portraits of the Raj days hangs a modern full length painting of Gandhiji. **Stone House** The first bungalow built here by the town's founder, John Sullivan, is the residence of the principal of the Govt Art College which has its campus opposite. The house which gives its name to the hill above the market place where it stands, was called *Kal Bangla* (stone bungalow) by the tribals.

Kandal Cross 3 km W of the rly station is a Roman Catholic shrine considered the 'Jerusalem of the E'. During the clearing of the area as a graveyard in 1927 an enormous 4 m high boulder was found and since then a cross was erected. Today, a relic of the True Cross brought to India by an Apostolic delegate is shown to pilgrims every day. The annual feast is in May. **St Stephen's Church** Ooty's first church built in the 1820s in a gothic style occupies the site of a Toda temple. Much of the wood is said to be from Tipu Sultan's Lal Bagh Palace in Srirangapatnam, after his final defeat, which had to be hauled up by elephants from the plains up Sigur Ghat. The clock tower and gallery were added in 1851 and the nine tubular bells in 1894. The inside of the church and the graveyard (with its poignant colonial plaques and head stones) at the rear are worth a look even though the church does not look very impressive.

Palaces With the development of Ooty as a hill resort the Maharajahs and Nawabs soon built their summer palaces and mansions here, the most impressive among them were those of the rulers of Baroda, Hyderabad, Jodhpur and Mysore but many have been turned into hotels. *Fernhill*, built by the Maharajah of Mysore is now a hotel (see below) while *Arranmore Palace* was sold by the Maharani of Jodhpur and is now a Govt Guest House, Tamizhagam. Open to visitors.

Local crafts and industries Numerous large as well as small **tea** estates clothe the hill sides to produce the famous Nilgiri tea with about 65 factories and 94 others catering for the 20,000 'small growers'. The **Cordite** factory manufacturing explosives was set up in 1904 and was served by its own hydro-electric power station at Katery Falls. The factory is in the Aravankadu Valley off the Ooty-Coonoor road. The **Hindusthan Photo Films** Unit, 8 km away in the Wenlock Downs, on the Gudalur Bus route, is a Govt of India enterprise undertaken in 1960. It produces roll film, bromide paper and high quality X-Ray film and special films for CAT scanners and space photography and is hoping to start producing magnetic tape. The **Needle Industries** factory is in Yellanhalli village about 8 km away at a height of over 2,200 m. Started in 1949 with production of the simple hand sewing needle it has become leader in the field producing the highest quality needs for medicine and is now exporting know how to the Far E. In addition there are units producing gelatine, mushroom and the more common vegetables and fruit. More unusual is the local cottage industry of extraction of **Eucalyptus Oil** as well as oils from citrioda, lemon grass, camphor and vetiver manufactured by the Govt Cinchona Department.

Hotels Most offer off season discounts from 1 July- 31 Mar. Virtually all have car parking. **B** *Savoy* (Taj Group), Club Rd. T 4142, Cable: Savoy, Telex: 0853 240 Saho In. 40 rm, some in cottages with fireplaces and verandahs. 1.5 km rly, close to centre. Restaurant, bar, exchange, travel, good gardens (tea on the lawn), tennis, billiards, children's playground, TV. Pony rides, trekking, fishing arranged. The old section supposedly has timbers from Tipu Sultan's palace in Srirangapatnam! Old fashioned atmosphere, Taj standards. **C** *Quality Inn Southern Star*, Havelock Rd. T 3601/9, Cable: Quality Inn, Telex: 0853 249 Qsso In. 67 rm. 2 km rly, 2 km centre. Restaurant, bar, tea garden, exchange, travel, shops, health club, table tennis, billiards, pony rides, TV. **D** *Fernhill Palace*, T 3910 (10 lines), Cable: Palaschain, Telex: 0853 246 Fern In. 56 rm with log fires and heaters (not always enough). 1.5 km rly and Bus Stand, 2 km Downtown. Restaurant (very poor service, food fair) in the old ball room, bar, exchange, travel, shops, lawns, tennis, squash, children's playground. Built in 1842 as the Mysore Maharajahs' summer retreat in wooded surroundings needs modernisation, but with character. Excellent views from cottages Nos. 301-304. Popular with stars from Bombay's silver screen! **D** *Dasaprakash*, S of Racecourse. T 2434, Cable: Dasaprakash. 100 rm. Close to rly, Bus Stand. Off season 15 June-10 Apr. Discounts also for student groups. 2 restaurants (vegetarian), 24 hr coffee shop, ice cream parlour, exchange, travel, children's playground. Comfortable, quiet location. **D** *Lake View*, W Lake Rd. T 3904, Cable: Lakeview. 117 rm all double cottages most without a 'view'. Restaurant, bar, exchange, travel, phones, TV. Riding arranged. **D** *Nahar*, 52 A Charing Cross. T 2173. 88 rm with heaters. 1 km rly, central. Off season 15 June-15 Mar. Restaurant (Indian vegetarian), travel, shops. **D** *Snowdon Inn*, Snowdon Rd. T 2138. 12 rm. Restaurant, exchange, travel. Golf and pony rides arranged. There are several middle range hotels in the Charing Cross area, near the Post Office. they include: **D Durga** and **D** *Prithi Palace*.

   E *Tamil Nadu*, above the Tourist Office near the centre. T 2543. Restaurant, bar, indoor games. **F** *Youth Hostel* near Tourist Office. Dormitory beds. Restaurant. Four **E** *Railway Retiring Rooms*. **E** *YWCA* Ettines Rd. Popular with the young, though not central. Restaurant. **E** *Reflections*, N Lake Rd, T 3834. 6 rm, clean, homely guest house with good views, friendly owners, pleasant dining room. Not rec. for females travelling alone. **E** *Sanjay*, Charing Cross. T 3160. Rm with spacious balcony. Clean rooms. Somewhat noisy at night. Excellent room service. recommended. **E** *Ritz*, Orange Grove Rd. T 6242. 20 rm. Good restaurant, bar.

Restaurants *Savoy*, highly recommended for its relaxed atmosphere and good, not too spicy food. Buffets are more affordable. The *Southern Star* has over attentive service! Inexpensive non-veg food at *Hotel Kaveri* and at *Blue Hills* in Charing Cross. The *Ritz* hotel, good, inexpensive food, excellent lemon sodas. Good Indian veg food at *Chandan* in Nahar Hotel on Charing Cross and several inexpensive places on Commercial Rd. *Shinkow's Chinese Restaurant*, 42 Commissioner's Rd (near Collector's Office), T 2811, good authentic dishes, reasonably price. Popular, especially late evening. *Chung Wah*, Commercial Rd, less good.

Bars In larger hotels. *Southern Star* recommended, though expensive. **Clubs** There are branches of Rotary, Lions and Jaycees, T 2703.

Banks & Exchange State Bank of India on Bank Rd. Several national banks deal in foreign exchange. You can also change money at the TTDC Hotel Tamil Nadu on Charing Cross Rd.

Shopping Most shops open from 0900-2000 but close for a long lunch break from 1200-1500 although the smaller shops keep longer hours. *Poompuhar* and *Kairali Emporia*. Charing Cross has the *Toda Showroom* which sells silver and tribal shawls. *Kashmir Emporium*, Garden Gate and *Kashmir House*, Charing Cross sell mainly Kashmiri handicrafts but also stock Toda jewellery. *Higginbotham's Bookshop*, Charing Cross. Municipal Market and Cooperative Super Market and Upper and Lower Bazar Roads are other shopping areas. Nilgiri Dairy Farms outlets sell quality milk products. *Variety Hall* in the Silver Market for cloth/silk. Takes some credit cards.

Local transport Taxis and the cheaper cycle rickshaws can take you to your hotel. To explore, other than on foot, you can also hire bicycles. Autorickshaws are unmetered.

Entertainment There are a number of cinemas including the recently renovated 100 year old 'Assembly Rooms', Garden Rd, T 2250. Shows western films. Check local paper for programme of English language films. Most of the annual events take place in May – Summer Festival, Dog Show, Flower Show, Vegetable Show in the Botanical Gardens, Boat Race and Pageant on the lake.

Sports Gymkhana Club, T 2254 allows temporary membership for a fee. Beautifully situated in the middle of the 18-hole Golf course which is superbly maintained. **Ootacamund Cricket Club**, T 2846. Anna Stadium has good facilities for badminton and table tennis. **Lawley Institute**, T 2249, for tennis, badminton, billiards, bridge. Boating and rowing on Ooty Lake. **Fishing** is good at Avalanche, 25 km away, where there is a trout hatchery. Forestry Guest House for overnight accommodation. Licenses for hired tackle from Assistant Director of Fisheries, Fishdale. T 2232.

Hiking or simply **walking**, is excellent in the Nilgiris. Climbing Dodabetta, the highest peak in the range and Mukurthi, is hardly a challenge and there are several equally straightforward alternatives. Try Kalahatti Falls, Wenlock Downs or one of the dams, which are shorter and have regular buses from the town. The longer walks through the *sholas* are best undertaken with a guide.

Parks and zoos *Botanical Gardens*, see under Places of interest above.

Post and telegraph Head PO, Collectorate, T 3796 and Telegraph Office, Town W Circle. International direct dialling and Fax facility. PO at Charing Cross.

Places of worship *Hindu* – Mariamman Temple near the market, Subrahmanya Temple in Lower Bazaar Rd, Ayyappan Temple in Jail Hill, Srinivasa Perumal Temple in Old Agraharam. *Muslim* – Sait Mosque in Lower Bazaar Rd. *Christian* – St Stephen's Church nr Collector's Office, St Thomas Church nr Ooty Lake, St Mary's Church on Convent Hill.

Hospitals and medical services Govt Headquarters Hospital, Hospital Rd. T 2212.

Travel agents and tour operators *Blue Mountain Travel*, Nahar Shopping Centre, Charing Cross. Luxury Coach bookings to neighbouring states. *George Hawkes Travels and Tours*, 52 C Nahar Complex, Charing Cross. T 2756, 3560 (out of office hours) for tourist taxis. *MB Travel*, Commercial Rd, next to Higginbothams.

Tourist offices and information Tourist Office, Super Market Building, Charing Cross, T 3964. **Tours** *Ooty and Mudumalai* Ooty Lake, Dodabetta Peak, Botanical Gardens, Mudumalai Wildlife Sanctuary. Daily 0830-2000. About Rs.70. *Kotagiri and Coonoor* Kotagiri, Kodanad View Point, Lamb's Rock, Dolphin's Nose, Sim's Park. Daily 0830-1830. About Rs.75. Reservations TNTDC, Hotel Tamil Nadu, T 2543.

Air Services The nearest airport is at Coimbatore, 105 km away. Taxi fare approx Rs 600. Reservations through MB and Co. Super Market Complex, MB Rd, T 2604.

Rail *Blue Mountain Express* travels overnight from Madras to Coimbatore and Mettupalayam and from there you can reach Ooty by road or by the 'toy train' from the latter. The delightful narrow gauge Mountain Railway in its blue and cream livery goes from Mettupalayam to Ooty via Coonoor. The railway scenes of the 'Marabar Express' in the film of *A Passage to India* were shot here. The whole 5 hr journey through tea plantations and lush forests is highly recommended for the scenery, but if short of time just try the Coonoor – Ooty section. Trains are scheduled to leave Mettupalayam at 0730 and 0800 and arrive at Ooty soon after midday.

Road Good road connections to other towns in the region. Roads to Mettupalayam and Gudalur are well maintained but being Ghat roads have numerous hairpin bends which can have fairly heavy traffic at times. The Gudalur road passes through Mudumalai and Bandipur sanctuaries and you may catch sight of an elephant herd and other wildlife especially at night. From Bangalore, the road is via Mysore.

Buses Frequent buses to Coonoor (every 10 min) and Coimbatore (every 20 min from 0600-2100), 3 hr 30 min, about Rs.10. Several a day to Bangalore (5 between 0630 and 2000), Mysore (5 between 0800 and 1530) and Calicut (8 between 0530 and 1515) and daily buses to Cannanore (0900, 2030), Madras (1600), Kannyakumari (1630), Pondicherry (1700) and Palani (0810) with connection to Kodaikkanal. Cheran Transport Corp, T 2352.

Excursions *Wenlock Downs* 8 km from the station on the Gudalur road, the area of about 8,000 ha of grassland with *sholas** or 'gallery forests' is described in the Madras Gazetteer of 1908. "In the *sholas* grow rhododendron, ilex, ferns of many varieties, bracken, tree-orchids with delicate blossoms, the hill gooseberry, blackberries, the sweet scented Nilgiri lily, the alpine wild strawberry..... Hedges are often made of heliotrope, fuchsia, and geraniums". It has changed since those days with the planting of eucalyptus and wattle forests to provide firewood and siting of factories in a part of the downs, but it is very pleasant for walks especially if you can get well into the interior (it is possible to take a car in). The 'Ooty Hunt' with horses, hounds and the jackal and the Hunt Ball, is still resurrected but not in quite the style of the past. The downs are also where the golf links are situated.

Mount Dodabetta About km 10 E of the rly station, off the Kotagiri road, the 'big mountain' reaches 2,638 m, the second highest in the Western Ghats. It therefore shelters Coonoor from the SW monsoons from Jun-Sep when Ooty gets its heavy rains and vice versa during the NE Monsoon in Oct and Nov. The peak is easily accessible by road and on a clear day you can see as far as the Coimbatore plain and the Mysore plateau although unfortunately the top is often shrouded in mist. There is a viewing platform at the summit which is covered by red-flowered Rhodendron arboreum, truly wild and not a 'garden escape'.

Mukurti Peak 36 km. Turn left off the Gudalur road after 25 km which brings you to the Hydro-Electricity Board's *Inspection Bungalow* and another km to the right, Mukurti Lake, which is surrounded by high hills and is 6 km long. The name is derived from 'muku' (nose) and 'ardha' (half) suggesting a severed nose for the shape of the peak. The Electricity Department and Nilgiris Game Association *Bungalows* are on the S side of the lake, half way along, and you can go fishing and boating is permitted. You need to book the Bungalows early as they are popular as an excellent place to escape for walking and view the occasional wildlife. Mukurti Peak which is not an easy climb is to the W. The Todas believe that the peak is sacred as it is from there that the souls of the dead and the sacrificed buffaloes leap to the next world.

Avalanche 24 km. The "avalanche" in 1823 gave the valley its name. A beautiful part of the *shola* with plenty of rhododendron, magnolia and orchids and a trout stream running through. Excellent for walking and superb scenery. Forestry Department *Guest House*, clean with good food. Avalanche Top is 4 km from bungalow.

Pykara 19 km. You can get there by car, bus or bicycle. The river has a dam and power plant. Breathtaking scenery. The Falls, about 6 km from the bridge on the main road, are best in July, though it is very wet then, but are also worth visiting from Aug to Dec.

Kotagiri 29 km (*Population* 29,000) is the oldest of the three Nilgiri hill resorts and sits on the N eastern crest of the plateau overlooking the plains. At 1983 m is milder than Ooty, but more bracing than Coonoor as a hill resort and is also protected by the Doddabetta range from the worst of the SW Monsoon rains. The name comes from Kotar-Keri, the street of the *Kotas* who were one of the original hill tribes and have a village to the W of the town (**see page 724**). There is a Handicrafts Centre of the Women's Welfare Department. You can visit some scenic spots – St Catherine Falls, 8 km and Elk Falls, 7 km, or one of the peaks Kodanad Viewpoint 16 km which you reach through the tea estates or Rangaswamy Pillar which is an isolated rock and the conical Rangaswamy Peak. **Hotel** F *Queen's Hill Christian Guest House*. Very clean, bath, hot water, beautiful surroundings. Proprietress Mrs Rose very friendly. Superb breakfasts, Highly recommended. There are regular bus services from Mettupalayam Rly Station, Ooty and Coonoor.

Mudumalai Wildlife Sanctuary 67 km from Ooty on the road to Mysore (94 km) adjoining Kerala and Karnataka states, the sanctuary is a part of a larger national park that includes Wynad and Bandipur. It covers 321 sq km at an altitude of 885 -1,000 m. Open through the year but best time to visit is Dec to Jun when the undergrowth has died down and it is easier to see the animals particularly when they are on the move at dawn. The sanctuary has large herds of elephant, bison, sambar, barking deer, wild dog, Nilgiri Langur, bonnet monkey, wild boar, four-horned antelope and the rarer tiger and leopard. There are also smaller mammals including the scaly anteater, the pangolin, and mouse deer, civet, giant Malabar flying squirrels and a rich variety of bird life (jungle fowl, peacock, Malabar hornbill, woodpeckers, Malabar whistling thrush, paradise flycatchers, warblers, babblers and a number of birds of prey and nocturnals). Reptiles include python, saw scaled viper, Hamadryad (King cobra), seen by one visitor in Jan 1990, crocodile and large monitor lizards. The vegetation is mixed deciduous and conifer and also bamboo.

It is on the bus route from Madras to Ooty and there are regular services from Ooty and Mysore. You can hire a jeep or van, or take elephant rides between 0600 and 0800 or 1630 and 1800. The Elephant Camp at Theppakadu 5 km, where wild elephants are tamed and some are bred in captivity and trained for working in the forest for the timber industry, is particularly interesting. You can see baby elephants do acrobatics (and puja at the temple!) and also watch others come to be fed in the afternoon, learn about each individual elephant's diet and specially prepared blocks of food. In the wild, elephants spend most of the 24 hr foraging but in captivity they have to adapt to a totally alien life style.

Hotels E *Bamboo Banks Farm Guest House*, Masinagudi. T Masinagudi 22 via Ooty. The Forest Dept has several Forest Houses. Theppakkadu *Log House*, Abayaranyam *Sylvan Lodge* and *Annexe*, Masinagudi *Log House* and *Red House*, Kargudi *Rest House* and *Annexe*. There is also a **F** TNTDC *Youth Hostel* at Theppakadu. **F** *Dormitories* (*Munnivet*, *Morgan* and *Peacock*). Reservations: Wildlife Warden, Kargudi, The Nilgiris or the District Forest Officer, Nilgiris (N Div), Ooty. The Mudumalai Wildlife Office is in the N Mahalingam & Co Building on the Ooty- Coonoor Rd, T 3114, where there is a Reception Range Officer.

MADRAS TO BANGALORE (Northern Route)

The northern route to Bangalore follows NH 4 all the way. Allow at least five hours driving time. For the first 150 kilometres the road crosses the flat Coromandel coastal plain through Chingleput district into N Arcot. It leaves the much more densely populated southern route at Ranipet, enters Andhra Pradesh and then climbs gently up the plateau towards Kolar.

The stretch of road out of Madras along E.V.Ramaswami Naicker Rd (formerly Poonamallee High Rd) is now extremely busy. It runs along the often stagnant waters of the Cooum River before passing through the village of **Poonamallee** (16 km *Population* 29,000) and into open country. Chingleput and N Arcot districts are typical "tank" country, each having over 3,000 of the shallow reservoirs dotted over the landscape, irrigating over 260,000 ha. Some date back to the Pallava period of the 6th to 8th centuries AD, and many were added by the Chola kings. The smaller tanks are simply fed by rainwater, but some have springs or streams flowing into them for part or all of the year.

The NH 4 forms the W boundary of one of the biggest of these tanks, the **Chembarambakkam Tank**, between 30 and 32 km from Madras. One of India's most ancient tanks (though no accurate date is available), it is fed by the Palar River. The water is dammed by an embankment of nearly 9 km running from some high ground in the N to bare rocky soils in the S. It often has water throughout the year, though its surface area fluctuates enormously. When it is full it is nearly 10 km long and has an area of over 2,500 ha, but its shallowness and the great surface area result in over half the stored water being lost through evaporation. In 10 km the road passes through the small town of **Sriporumbadur**, where Rajiv Gandhi was assassinated in May 1991.

The NH 4 by-passes **Kanchipuram** (55 km; described as an excursion from Madras see page 717). At the approach to Ranipet is a typical roadside village deity, complete with offering box (*undi*) – and a prohibition on taking photographs. At **Ranipet** (42 km *Population* 52,000) the NH4 turns N to Chittoor. Ranipet was founded by the Nawab of Arcot in 1771 and takes its name from the Rani of Gingee who performed *sati** on her husband's funeral pyre. It was an important East India Company cantonment, later becoming a centre of Christian mission work, notably a hospital. Today it is a rapidly growing town with a large industrial estate built in the 1980s. Enfield Motorbikes are among the modern industrial products of the town, which has received significant Tamil Nadu govt aid under its programme for developing "backward areas".

5 km away on the S bank of the Palar River is the historically important town of **Arcot** (*Population* 50,000) formerly the capital of the 18th century Nawabs of Arcot. Virtually nothing of the old town remains except the Delhi gate, on the banks of the Palar. The moat which used to surround the citadel is dry and filled with trees. Beyond the Jami Masjid to the W are the ruins of the palace of the Nawabs. Yet in these now insignificant surroundings **Robert Clive** made his reputation, capturing and then holding the fort during a siege which lasted nearly 2 months until 15 Nov 1751 – some 6 years before the Battle of Plassey.

The southern route continues to Vellore, but in Ranipet the NH4 turns N to **Chittoor** (43 km *Population* 112,000 *Altitude* 315 m). A monument at **Narsingh Rayanpet**, near Chittoor, marks the place where *Haidar Ali* died on 7 December 1782. The cemetery in the town contains a number of striking tombs. The road now passes through some of the least densely populated parts of S Andhra Pradesh. To the right are the southernmost limits of the *Vellikonda Ranges*, terminating very strikingly in *Nagari Nose*, an escarpment visible on a clear day even from Madras 90 km away. Light brown soils are cultivated with millets, but travelling W the road passes through some extraordinary landscapes of huge outcropping granite boulders.

In the 19th century **Palmaner** (39 km *Population* 32,000 *Altitude* 700 m) was regarded almost as a hill station, as it has a lower temperature than the areas of N Arcot District to the S. Before the Nilgiris were opened up officials from Madras and others visited the town to provide a break from the intense heat of the lower plains. The road goes on to **Mulbagal** (42 km *Population* 35,000) and to **Kolar** (31 km *Population* 85,000). **See page 844**. The NH 4 by-passes Kolar and Kolar Gold Fields, passing through Hoskote (40 km) to Bangalore (26 km).

MADRAS TO BANGALORE (Southern Route)

The southern route follows the NH 46 via Ambur to Bangalore. Although only about 30 km longer than the northern route via Chittoor and Kolar it is very much slower, passing through the densely populated – and intensively cultivated – **Palar valley**. It is a route of considerable historical interest. The Vijayanagar Empire left one of its finest temples, albeit a miniature, in Vellore. Later the whole valley became the scene of Anglo-French-Indian contest at the end of the 18th century. The valley is the centre of S India's vitally important leather industry, especially the towns of Ambur and Vaniyambadi.

For the section to **Ranipet and Arcot** see the previous route above. The road approaches **Vellore** (27 km; Population 234,000 Altitude 220 m) along the S bank of the dry sandy bed of the *Palar River*. It passes through a region which has experienced rapid agricultural development, especially since the early 1970s. The widespread use of well irrigation has been increased by the use of electric pumpsets. The guarantee of reliable water supply has encouraged farmers to invest in new varieties of seeds, especially of paddy. There has been a long tradition of experimentation in the region, and several improved varieties of rice were introduced in the 1930s. Today every farm plants cross-bred high yielding varieties, usually with considerable inputs of fertiliser. This is one of the centres from which the Govt hoped to spread "green revolution" technology to Indian farming. There are growing signs of its effectiveness in the development of a widening range of small scale industries and shops selling consumer goods that would have been completely unavailable 20 years ago – from soap to torch batteries.

Vellore is a thriving market town on the S bank of the Palar river, growing extremely fast. The fort is a major attraction in its own right, but Vellore is now world famous for its Christian Medical College and Hospital, the best place for treatment in S India.

Places of interest Vijayanagar architecture is beautifully illustrated in the temple at **Vellore Fort**. The fort itself is a perfect example of military architecture and a *jala durga* or water fort. The main rampart of the small fort, which is believed to have been built by the Vijayanagara kings, dating from the 14th century, is built out of imposing blue granite, has round towers and huge gateways along its double wall which has Hindu motifs. The moat which is still filled with water by a subterranean drain, followed ancient principles of defence with a colony of crocodiles, and it was possible for the defenders to flood the causeways at times of attack. A wooden draw-bridge crosses the moat at the southeast. It was the scene of many battles and sieges.

In the 17th century it fell to the Muslim **Adi Shahis** of Bijapur and then to the Marathas. The 18th century saw the Karnatic Wars and Vellore came under

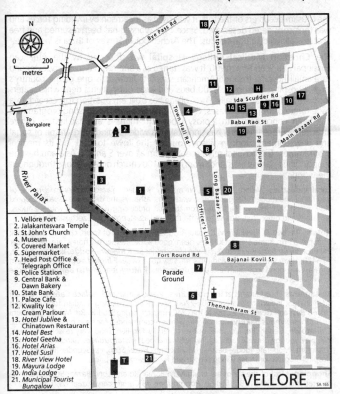

1. Vellore Fort
2. Jalakantesvara Temple
3. St John's Church
4. Museum
5. Covered Market
6. Supermarket
7. Head Post Office & Telegraph Office
8. Police Station
9. Central Bank & Dawn Bakery
10. State Bank
11. Palace Cafe
12. Kwality Ice Cream Parlour
13. Hotel Jubliee & Chinatown Restaurant
14. Hotel Best
15. Hotel Geetha
16. Hotel Arias
17. Hotel Susil
18. River View Hotel
19. Mayura Lodge
20. India Lodge
21. Municipal Tourist Bungalow

VELLORE

the control of the British in 1768 who defended it against **Haidar Ali** in 1782. After the victory in Seringapatnam in 1799, **Tipu Sultan's** family was imprisoned here and a *sepoy* mutiny of 1806 in which many British and Indian mutineers were killed, left many scars. In the fort is a parade ground, the CSI church, the Temple and two-storeyed *mahals* which are used as Govt offices. The moat was refilled and is used for fishing and swimming. The wide promenade between the lower outer wall and inner wall is at one point, a tennis court.

Jalakantesvara Temple (enter from the S). Considerable restoration work has been undertaken on the temple in recent years, especially to the 7-storeyed granite gopuram, over 30 m high. Inside on the left, the *kalyana mandapam* (wedding hall) is considered by some to be the most beautiful structure of its kind, with dramatic and vivid sculptures of dragons and 'hippogryphs' on its pillars. The central pillars show the much older motif of the seated lion, a Pallava symbol going back more than 6 centuries but elaborated to match its Vijayanagar surroundings. Note the impressive stepped entrances and the free hanging chains. Surrounding the temple is a high wall, embossed with small but immaculately carved animal figures. The temple consists of a shrine to Nataraja in the N and a lingam shrine in the W. The *nandi* bull is in the courtyard. Typical giant guardians stand at the door of the main shrine. Although the temple was not touched by the Muslim occupiers of the fort, it was used as a garrison by invading forces and was thus considered desecrated. Since 1981 worship has been resumed and free access is allowed to non-Hindus. The Archeological Survey of India is in charge.

The **Christian Medical College Hospital** was founded by the American missionary Ira Scudder in 1900. It was started as a one-room dispensary, extended to a small hospital through American support. Today it is one of the country's largest hospitals with over 1,200 beds and large out-patients dept which caters for over 2,000 patients daily. The College has built a reputation for research in a wide range of tropical diseases. One of its earliest and most lasting programmes has been concerned with leprosy work and there is a rehabilitation centre attached. In recent years it has undertaken a wide ranging programme of social and development work in villages outside the town to back up its medical programmes. The hospital serves people from all over S and SE Asia and has the support and financial assistance from nearly 100 church organizations throughout the world.

Local industries Vellore specialises in making 'Karigari' glazed pottery in a range of traditional and modern designs. Vases, water jugs, ashtrays and dishes are usually coloured blue, green and yellow. The local automatic fruit processing unit dealing with mangoes, tomatoes and other fruit, was set up with technical assistance from Czechoslovakia.

Hotels The best **D** *River View*, Katpadi Rd, T 25768. 1 km N of town, close to the Nakkal Channel. 31 rm, some a/c, restaurants, clean, good value. Inexpensive hotels, are mainly near the hospital on Babu Rao St and a few in Ida Scudder St. **F** *Mayura Lodge*, 85 Babu Rao St, T 25488, clean single, double and triple rm, very good value. **F** *India Lodge*, inexpensive rm and *Raj Cafe*, good vegetarian restaurant downstairs. **F** *Municipal Tourist Bungalow* is close to the Vellore Rly Station.

Restaurants 3 restaurants at the *Hotel River View*, Katpadi Rd. *Palace Cafe*, 21 Katpadi Rd, T 20125, Indian, open from 0600-2200. Several others serving S Indian food including *Hotels Best* and *Geetha* are close to the CMC Hospital, on Ida Scudder Rd. *Nanking*, Gandhi Rd, Chinese. *Venus Bakery* opp the Hospital is recommended for fresh bread and biscuits. *Chinatown*, Gandhi Rd, a/c, small but very friendly. Excellent food, very reasonable prices. Will play your own music tapes, highly recommended. *Hotel Jubilee*, Gandhi Rd. Rooftop restaurant. Moderate food – best early in evening. *Hotel Susil*, Ida Scudder Rd, opp CMC Hospital. Rooftop or inside. Good service and food, reasonable price.

Shopping Most of the shops are along Main Bazaar Rd and Long Bazaar St with a large covered market S of the Bus Station. *Poompuhar*, 48 Commissary Bazaar Rd, T 21173.

Rail Katpadi Jn to the N of town is on the broad gauge line between Madras and Bangalore. The bus into Vellore takes between 10 to 30 min. **Madras** (MC): *Bangalore-Madras Exp*, 6024 (AC/II), Daily, 1202, 2 hr 28 min; *Brindavan Exp*, 2640 (AC/CC), daily, 1743, 2 hr 7 min; **Bangalore** (C): *Brindavan Exp*, 2639 (AC/CC), daily, 0915, 4 hr 35 min; *Madras-Bangalore Exp*, 6023 (AC/II), daily, 1558, 4 hr 47 min; it is also on the metre gauge line to **Villupuram** to the S, with daily passenger trains to **Tirupathi**, **Tiruvannamalai** and **Pondicherry**. The Cantonment Station is about a km S of the GPO.

Buses The Bus Station is off Long Bazaar St, E of the Fort. TTC runs buses to Trichy and Tiruvannamalai and Vellore is en route for buses from Bangalore, Madras, Ooty, Thanjavur and Tirupathi. The regional state bus company PATC run frequent services to Kanchipuram from 0500 (2 hr 30 min) and also several a day to Madras and Bangalore.

The NH 45 goes W through ***Ambur*** (50 km *Population* 88,000), an important centre of the leather tanning industry. There is also a large sugar milling co-operative, and sugar cane is widely grown along the length of the valley. Ambur is the headquarters of the Syrian and Orthodox Apostolic Church of the Indies. There is a large Muslim population throughout the Palar valley and a significant Christian minority. Churches, mosques and madrassas are common sights in the villages along the road. The NH 45 passes SW through the intensively cultivated valley bottom of the Palar River, the same route followed by the broad gauge railway line to Bangalore. To the S and E are the rising mass of the Javadi Hills and their outliers, reaching up towards Vellore. Shortly after passing

Vaniyambadi (16 km *Population* 80,000), another major centre of the leather industry, there is a left turn to the district market town of *Tiruppattur* (*Population* 67,000) and S to Salem. The NH 45 turns W to *Krishnagiri* (51 km *Population* 63,000).

Excursion The route S from here to the district capital of Dharmapuri is also the most convenient way of getting to the remote Hoganekal Falls on the Kaveri. If you are looking for peace and quiet and an undisturbed day or two, the falls provide an ideal spot. The point at which the Kaveri takes its last plunge down the plateau edge to the plains, 250 m above sea level. There is a beautiful forested drive down from Pennargaram to the falls, where the water drops 20 m through a long zig zag canyon. *Hogenakkal* is a Kannada word meaning "smoke that thunders", an apt description. **F** *Hotel Tamil Nadu* offers clean and very reasonable accommodation.

From Krishnagiri the road goes NW to *Hosur* (50 km *Population* 40,000). Until the early 1970s Hosur was a sleepy town in a backward district. Since then a huge industrial estate has been opened by the Tamil Nadu Government, bringing large scale industrial investment from other parts of India and abroad. The town has grown rapidly, benefiting partly from the nearness of **Bangalore** (40 km) (see page 844). Many people in management still commute out from Bangalore in the day and return to the city at night.

TRICHY TO MADURAI (Eastern Route)

There are several possible options for travelling S from Trichy to Madurai. Local buses run over all the routes, and the eastern and central routes have the advantage of being much less busy than the national highway which runs through Dindigul and to the W of the beautiful Sirumalai Hills. The eastern route goes through the former small princely state of Pudukkottai and the district known as *Chettinadu*, (the land of the Chettiyars). The trading community of Chettiyars, numbering perhaps 90,000 people, has the reputation as one of India's wealthiest clans, and although the sources of some of that wealth -trade from Burma and Malaysia – have long since dried up, remarkable houses remain in the district.

Leave Trichy past the aerodrome on the *Kiranur* road (30 km *Population* 8,000), cutting straight across the unirrigated land beyond the reach of the Kaveri canals. Some of the barren land on both sides of the road has been taken up by industries. Close by Kiranur is the Kunnandarkoil cave temple, built in the 8th century AD, with the later addition of a Vijayanagar mandapam. Some of the bronzes in the temple are also excellent. Straight on to *Narthamalai* (8 km), which has an important Chola temple. Some of the most significant stone figures from the temple are in the govt museum in Pudukkottai. In the hills near Narthamalai are some Jain caves.

Pudukkottai (12 km *Population* 115,000) was the capital of the former Princely State ruled by the Tondaiman Rajas, founded by Raghunatha Raya Tondaiman in 1686. At one entrance to the town is a ceremonial arch raised by the Raja in honour of Queen Victoria's jubilee celebrations, still kept in good order. Its broad streets suggest a planned history. The **temple** is at the centre, with the old palace and a tank. The **new palace** where the Maharajah lived has become the office of the District Collector.

Local festivals The area has bullock races (*manju virattu*) in Jan-Feb.

Places of interest There are several pre historic burial sites as well as Neolithic and Iron Age in the area. The natural rock shelters and caves suggest there were very early human occupation here. ***Sittannavasal*** where Jain monks found refuge nearby, is rich in Pallava finds, especially the very fine frescoes in the shrine. The triangle ***Pudukottai-Kiranur-Kodumbalur*** has a number of early Chola and late Pallava monuments.

Local industries There is a major TVS bus factory, making luxury buses for export.

Museum The museum has a wide range of exhibits, including sections on geology, zoology and the economy as well as sculptures and the arts. The archaeology section of the museum has some excellent sculptures from nearby temples, including stone sculptures from Narthamalai. There is a notable carving of Siva as *Dakshinamurti*. There are also some fine bronzes from Pudukottai itself.

Rail Madras (ME): *Sethu Exp*, 6114, daily, 2101, 9 hr 19 min; Ramesvaram: *Ramesvaram Exp*, 6101, daily, 0751, 5 hr 31 min. **Road** Pudukkottai is well connected by bus with Trichy, Thanjavur, Madurai, Ramnad and Ramesvaram.

The road S to ***Karaikkudi*** (39 km *Population* 88,000) goes through the heart of Chettinad country. Many of the villages that were once the homes of fabulously wealthy merchant families are now semi-deserted. ***Kanadukathan*** (*Population* 6,500) for example, 5 km N of Karaikkudi, has a number of magnificent mansions, some of them empty except for bats, monkeys – and as India Today put it "marauding antique dealers". It has been estimated that the Burma teak and satinwood pillars in just one of the village's **Chettiar** houses weighed 300 tonnes. The plaster on the walls is made from a mixture of lime, eggwhite, powdered shells and myrobalan fruit (the astringent fruit of the tree *Phyllantles emblica*), mixed into a paste which, when dried, gave a gleaming finish. One of the specialities of the houses was the quality of their woodcarving, notably on the doors. Although many of the Chettiars themselves have now left, they are still a powerful force in many of the cities of the S. Traditionally in the jewellery and trading business, they now own a variety of large companies. The existence of 11 banks in the town illustrates the wealth that has flowed into it. Some of that money continues to be channelled back to this remote region, but there is an air of decay and dilapidation about many of the finest houses.

Local industry Karaikkudi is quite an important industrial centre. Processing betelnuts and chewing tobacco. There are noted diamond cutters and goldsmiths, over 2,000 handlooms and several dyeing factories, and a wide range of food processing industries. Today Karaikkudi is the home of a modern Electro Chemical Research Institute, which is open to visitors.

Rail The *Ramesvaram Exp* connects Madras with Pudukottai. **Road** Bus routes link the town with every part of the State.

The road goes S to ***Tiruppatur*** (21 km *Population* 67,000) and ***Melur*** (31 km Population 34,500) across open agricultural land. Bright red soils are common – generally the result of deep weathering of the iron rich gneiss underneath. During the rains it tends to become very marshy but bakes hard as rock during the long hot and dry periods. There are patches of laterites, almost impossible to cultivate and giving rise to expanses of bare flat land. Isolated tanks, such as the particularly beautiful tank W of Melur, add light, colour and coolness to an otherwise often dry landscape. On the land beyond the reach of reliable irrigation thorny scrub, *Prosopis juliflora* is common. From place to place you may see the work of charcoal burners, clearing the scrub and converting it into highly priced charcoal for sale as a cooking fuel in the urban market of Madurai (29 km).

TRICHY TO MADURAI (Central Route)

A second alternative route to Madurai which avoids the National Highway but is considerably shorter than the route via Pudukottai can be taken by following District roads.

Leaving Trichy on the main Dindigul road, take a left fork to *Viralimalai* (26 km) after under 2 km. This small town is noted for its peacock sanctuary, and there is a shrine to *Subrahmanya* (whose divine vehicle is a peacock) on the top of the hill outside the town. It is also known for a dance drama form, the *Viralimalai Kuravanji*, which originated here.

Just 5 kilometres to the S is **Kodumbalur**, whose *Moovar Koil* temple illustrates the evolution of Dravidian temple architecture. Although the village is now something of a backwater, it is on the route that used to connect the Pandiyan and Chola kingdoms. It has over 100 temples, and was once the capital of the *Irukkuvels*, a local dynasty.

The road passes through attractive open country and the road is comparatively quiet, although it is used by local buses and longer distance buses connecting Trichy and Madurai. It passes through *Tovarankurichchi* (32 km) and **Natham** (18 km), where drinks and fruit are available at the bus stand. The road continues over the rolling country and unirrigated farm land to **Madurai** (37 km). The local bus ride over the whole route is easy and often quite uncrowded, and gives an interesting view of an area off the beaten track. The road from Natham crosses the Periyar Main channel about 6 km after passing through the village of Chattrapatti. It enters Madurai at the junction by the Pandiyan Hotel, Tamil Nadu Tourist Complex, and the Ashok Hotel, all just N E of the city.

TRICHY – MADURAI (Western Route)

There are two options, the first of which follows the **NH 45** all the way. From Trichy the road goes SW to **Manapparai** (37 km *Population* 36,000) The town is particularly famous for its cattle fairs and markets, held on Wednesdays. The cattle are often highly decorated, with bells and painted horns. Continue through Ayilur (30 km) to Dindigul (26 km).

Dindigul Population 209,000 *Altitude* 300 metres. Now a large market town, it commands a strategic gap between the **Sirumalai Hills** to its E and the *Palani Hills* to the W, both formed out of Charnockite rising from the plateau of granite. The market handles the produce of the Sirumalai Hills, mainly fruit. Sirumalai and the Palanis used to be famous for a particular variety of hill banana with a pinkish skin and a very distinctive flavour. Growing at a very limited range of altitude, their production has been decimated by disease.

Places of interest The fort The massive granite rock towers over 90 m above the plain, an ideal site for a fort. Under the first Nayaka kings the near vertical sides were fortified, controlling the western province of the Nayaka kingdom. The importance of the site encouraged the Mysore army to attack and capture it in 1745 and **Haidar Ali** was appointed Governor in 1755. He used it as the base from which to capture Madurai itself, and is reputed to have disposed of the prisoners he took by throwing them over the side of the cliff. It changed hands with the British twice in the late 1780s before being ceded to the British under the Treaty of Seringapatam. There are magnificent views of the town the valley and the hills on either side from the top of the rock fort.

Our Lady of Dolours church, is one of several Christian churches, both Catholic and Protestant, in the town. It is over 250 years old, and was rebuilt in 1970.

Local industries Tobacco, tanning and cotton industries are all important. Dindigul is particularly known for its cheroots. Iron safes and locks are also made in the town.

Hotels and restaurants Several tea shops and small restaurants nr the bus stand.

Travel Rail Madras (ME): *Vaigai Exp*, 2636 (AC/CC), daily, 0745, 6 hr 40 min; **Trichy:** *Vaigai*

Exp, 2636 (AC/CC), daily, 0745, 1 hr 24 min; **Madurai**: *Vaigai Exp*, 2635 (AC/CC), daily, 1900, 1 hr 10 min. **Road** Good and frequent bus service to Trichy, Madras, Salem and Coimbatore as well as longer distance connections.

From Dindigul the NH 45 goes S through **Ambatturai** and **Orutattu** with the 500 metre *Rishimalai* ("Rishi Hill") hill on the right. Just past Orutattu is the Kodai Road railway station, where buses leave for **Kodaikkanal**. It then runs through beautiful and lush countryside, irrigated by the *Peranai Main* channel which the road crosses near the village of Andipatti.

This channel, built in 1897, takes off from the Vaigai and was made possible by the Periyar River scheme at Thekkadi. Such a scheme of reversing the flow of the Periyar by digging a tunnel under the top of the Cardamom Hills was first mooted at the beginning of the 19th century. It diverted water that would otherwise have flowed to the W coast eastwards down the channel of the Vaigai. When completed it irrigated over 50,000 ha mainly in Madurai District. The water has the unusual quality of being almost entirely silt free. In the 1960s a new dam was built near Periyakulam which has helped to regulate the flow still further and to increase the area under irrigation.

A magnificent view of the *Vaigai Dam* is obtained from the ghat road up to Kodaikkanal. See page 796. The *Vaigai River* itself, on which much of the agriculture to the E partly depends, has always been notoriously unreliable. The Ramnad District Gazetteer for 1910 reported the flow of the Vaigai with repeated comments like "No water in the Vaigai" (1823-24, 1834-35, 1885-86) or alternatively "Vaigai full – filled all the tanks in the district" (1841-42) and even "Extraordinary freshes – several tanks breached" (1843-44). That kind of variability has always been a handicap, and the benefits of increased control can be seen from the fields around Madurai which receive the channelled water. The alluvium of the Vaigai reaches up the valleys from the sea almost as far as Madurai and northeastwards in a broad band across the low tableland inshore from the sea. To the right of the road after Andipatti is the long spine of *Nagamalai* (snake hill), a ridge of pink granite running SE towards Madurai (63 km).

Madurai

Population 844,000. *Altitude* 100 m. *Climate* Temp. Summer Max. 37°C Min 26°C, Winter Max. 30°C Min. 21°C. Annual rainfall 905 mm.

	Jan	Feb	Mar	Apr	May	Jun	Jul	Aug	Sep	Oct	Nov	Dec	Av/Tot
Max (°C)	30	32	35	36	37	37	36	35	35	33	31	30	34
Min (°C)	21	22	23	25	26	26	26	25	25	24	23	22	24
Rain (mm)	26	16	21	81	59	31	48	117	123	179	161	43	905

Madurai is situated on the banks of the river Vaigai. Sometimes referred to as the Athens of the E, Madurai's history goes back to the 6th century BC when it traded with Greece and Rome. The name is attributed to a legend according to which drops of nectar fell from Siva's locks on the spot, so it was named 'Madhuram' Madurai, or the nectar city. Ancient Madurai was a centre of Tamil culture, famous for its writers, poets and temple builders and was the literary and cultural centre during the last of the 3 *Sangam* periods (Tamil Academies) nearly 2,000 years ago (see page 726). The **Pandiyas** made it their capital and held it for several centuries against their neighbours, the **Pallavas** and **Cholas** to the the E, and the **Cheras** to the W, becoming a major power from the 6th to the beginning of the 10th century. They remained in their capital Madurai until the 14th century although they were subservient to the Cholas who gained control over the area from the beginning of the 10th century and ruled for nearly 300 years, after which the Pandiyans returned to power. With the arrival of the Muslims from the N, Malik Kafur completely destroyed the city in 1310, following which there was a short period when it became a Sultanate. This was followed in 1364 by the rule of the

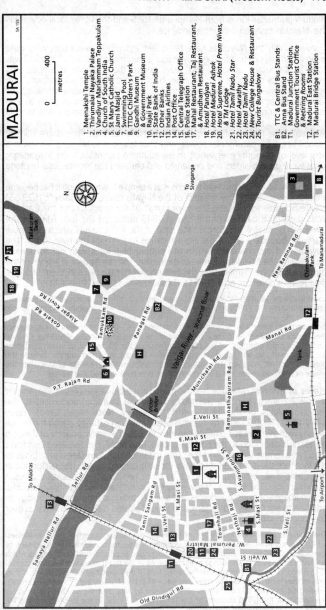

MADURAI

SA 155

```
0          400
|----------|
   metres
```

1. Meenakshi Temple
2. Thirumalai Nayaka Palace
3. Vandiyur Mariamman Teppakulam
4. Church of South India
5. St Marys Catholic Church
6. Jami Masjid
7. Swimming Pool
8. TDPC Children's Park
9. Gandhi Museum
   & Government Museum
10. Rajaji Park
11. State Bank of India
12. Other Banks
13. Indian Airlines
14. Post Office
15. Central Telegraph Office
16. Police Station
17. Mahal Restaurant, Taj Restaurant,
    & Ruckmani Restaurant
18. Hotel Pandyan
19. Hotel Madurai Ashok
20. Hotel Supreme, Hotel Prem Nivas,
    & TM Lodge
21. Hotel Tamil Nadu Star
22. Hotel Aarathy
23. Hotel Tamil Nadu
24. New College House & Restaurant
25. Tourist Bungalow

B1. TTC & Central Bus Stands
B2. Anna Bus Stand
T1. Madurai Junction Station,
    Government Tourist Office
    & Retiring Rooms
T2. Madurai East Station
T3. Madurai Bridge Station

Hindu Vijayanagar Kings from Hampi until 1565 and then their local governors the Nayakas asserted their independence.

Conventionally the **Nayakas** have been seen essentially as warriors who were given an official position by the Vijayanagar government. The term "nayaka" was used in Karnataka at least 300 years before the Vijayanagar empire was established. Its origins lie much further back than that, for it is a Sanskrit term applied to someone of prominence and leadership. Although some scholars have suggested that in the mid-16th century there may have been as many as 200 nayakas, throughout the Vijayanagar period only 27 have been mentioned in inscriptions. As Burton Stein comments, "the history of the Vijayanagara state is essentially the history of the great Telugu Nayakas, their formidable military capabilities, their patrimonial power, and their relations to religious leaders in a new level of authority everywhere in the southern peninsula." The Vijayanagar kings were great builders and preserved and enriched the architectural heritage of the town.

Today Madurai's main claim to fame is as a temple town, though it has become a major industrial city. The greatest of the Nayaka rulers, **Tirumalai** (r 1623-55) was responsible for building the **gopurams*** of the temple. After the Carnatic Wars the British gained control and in 1840 destroyed the fort, filling in the surrounding moat which formed the base of the 4 Veli streets which even now mark the boundary of the old city which lies to the S of the river Vaigai. The Nayakas laid out the old town in the pattern of a lotus with narrow streets surrounding the Minakshi Temple at the centre. The streets on the 4 sides of the central temple are named after the festivals which take place in them and give their relative direction, eg S Masi St, E Avanimoola St and E Chitrai St.

Local festivals Jan/Feb. At Vandiyur Mariammam Teppakulam. The annual *Float Festival* is celebrated to mark the birth anniversary of Thirumalai Nayak, who originated it. Many temple deities in silks and jewels, including Minakshi and Sundaresvarar, are taken out on a full moon night, on floats colourfully decorated with hundreds of oil lamps and flowers. The floats carry them to the central shrine to the accompaniment of music and chanting. **Apr/May** *Chithrai Festival* The most important at the Minakshi Temple is the 10 day festival which celebrates the marriage of Siva and Minakshi in the Kalyana Mandapam, when pilgrims come to the banks of the river. **Aug/Sep** The *Avanimoolam* is the Coronation Festival of Siva when the image of Lord Sundareswarar is taken out to the river bank dressed as a worker.

Places of interest Madurai has the most outstanding examples of Vijayanagar temple architecture in the **Minakshi Temple**, a standing monument to the temple builders of the 16th and 17th century. **Note** Inner Temple open 0430-1230, 1600-2130. The massive gopurams are profusely decorated (some will say with as many as 33 million carvings, including an encyclopaedia of dancing poses). It is dedicated to the consort of Siva, **Minakshi**, the 'fish-eyed goddess', who has a temple to the S and the other to her consort **Sundaresvarar** (Siva) to the W. Since she is the presiding deity the daily ceremonies are first performed in her shrine and, unlike the practice at other temples, Sundareswarar plays a secondary role. The temple's 9 towering gopurams stand out with their colourful stucco images of gods, goddesses and animals, telling stories from mythology. In addition to the Golden Lotus tank and various pillared halls it has 5 vimanas over the sanctum sanctorums.

The main entrance to the temple proper is through a small door (porch of the 8 goddesses) which projects from the wall, S of the E *gopuram*. Inside, to your left is the sacred tank of the Golden Lotus, with a lamp in the centre, surrounded by pillared cloisters and steps which go down to the waters. The Sangam legend speaks of the test that ancient manuscripts had to undergo – they were thrown into the sacred tank, if they sank they were worthless, if they floated they were considered worthy! (**see page 687**) The N gallery has 17th century murals, relating 64 miracles said to have been performed by Siva, and the southern has marble inscriptions of the 1,330 couplets of the Tamil Book of Ethics. To the W of the tank is the *Kulikka* or *Yali Mandapam*, the pavilion leading to the Minakshi shrine. Here the pillars are carved in the form of the mythical beast *yali* which recurs in temples throughout the region. You will also see parrots, Minakshi's green bird which brings luck, in cages hanging from the ceiling. The Minakshi shrine stands in its own enclosure with smaller shrines around it. To the N of the tank is another enclosure with smaller *gopurams* on 4 sides within which is the Sundareswarar shrine. The sculpture of the divine marriage of Minakshi and Sundareswarar being blessed by Vishnu and Brahma and Siva in his 24 forms are in the *Kambathadi Mandapam* (19th century), around the flagstaff in front of the Sundareswarar Shrine.

In the NE corner is the 'thousand pillared hall' which dates from the mid-16th century. It is the most remarkable feature here with each column carved exquisitely. Note Siva riding a peacock, Parvati as a huntress playing the *vina*, a gypsy leading a monkey. It now also houses a good museum for displaying exhibits related to temple art and architecture with fine brass and stone images, friezes and photos though the labelling could be improved. Open 0800-2000. Entry Re 1, Camera Rs 5. Near the N *gopuram* you will see 5 clusters of musical pillars each set carved out of a single stone. By striking each pillar with a wooden stick or a hand you can produce a different note and feel the column vibrate. In the Nayaka period musicians could play on these as an instrument. The *Nandi* pavilion is to the E and is often occupied by flower sellers. The long *Pudhu Mandapam* or New Mandapam, with its beautiful sculptures of *yalis* and Nayaka rulers and their ministers, is outside the enclosure wall, between the E tower and the base of the unfinished *Raya Gopuram* which was planned to be the tallest in the country.

The temple is a hive of activity, with thousands of worshippers in a day, a colourful temple elephant, flower sellers, and performances by musicians, who are often excellent, from 1800-1930, 2100-2200. At 2115 there is a special ceremony when an image of Sundareswarar is carried from the shrine near the E *gopuram* to Minakshi to sleep by her side, which is returned the next morning. Camera fee Rs 10 at the temple office near the S Tower. Good views from the top of the S Gate which you can climb but now often closed.

About a km to the SE of the Minakshi temple is the **Tirumalai Nayaka Palace**, built in the 1636 in the Indo-Mughal style. Only the central section remains, because Tirumala's grandson dismantled the rest when he moved to Tiruchirappalli. Its 15 domes, some of which are huge, and arches are adorned with stucco work while some of its 240 columns rise to 12 m. Its *Swarga Vilasam* (Celestial Pavilion), which is an arcaded octagonal structural is curiously constructed with brick and mortar without any supporting rafters. The Tamil Nadu Archaeological Dept has done extensive renovation work using special artisans with skills in the use of traditional lime plaster and powdered sea shell and quartz. The original complex had a shrine, an armoury, a theatre, royal quarters, a royal bandstand, a harem, a pond and a garden but only about a quarter survives since Tirumalai's grandson planned to use the sections he removed in order to build another palace in Tiruchirappalli. Open 0900-1300, 1400-1700. 10 min walk from the Temple. Bus 17, 17a, 11, 11 A. Museum and Sound and Light Show (see below under Museums and Entertainment). **Vandiyur Mariammam Teppakulam** to the SE of town, which has a small shrine in its centre where the annual float festival takes place in Jan/Feb. Bus No 4 and 4 A takes 10 min from the Bus Stand and Rly Station.

Local industries Several spinning mills produce a variety of yarn for the handloom and industrial sectors. The range covers fine cottons, embroidery threads to sophisticated blends for medical sutures, tyre cord and supplying fibres for Air Force parachutes. Other engineering industries include sugar and chemicals.

Hotels The better hotels are N of the river, about 1.5 km from the town centre. Auto rickshaws should charge about Rs 10 but often ask a lot more. Alternatively, several City Buses will take you there. *Pandiyan*, (formerly Taj Group) Race Course. T 42471, Cable: Templecity, Telex: 0445-214. 57 rm. 14 km airport, 4 km rly, 3 km downtown. Restaurant (multi-cuisine), bar, exchange, travel, car hire, shops, TV. The best in town, with comfortable rm and pleasant garden. C *Madurai Ashok*, Alagarkoil Rd. T 42531. Cable: Tourism, Telex: 0445-297. 43 double rm. 14 km airport 4 km rly. Central a/c. Restaurant, bar, exchange, shops, pool, TV. D *Supreme*, 110 W Perumal Maistry St. T 36331, Cable: Supreme, Telex: 0445-232. 69 rm,some a/c. 10 km airport, 0.5 km to rly and downtown. Restaurants, exchange, travel, shops, TV. Recommended. D *Tamil Nadu Star*, Alagarkoil Rd. T 42461, Telex: 0445-238. 51 rm, some a/c. 14 km airport, 4 km rly. Restaurant, bar, exchange, travel, shop. Not conveniently placed, though quiet. E *Prem Nivas*, 102 W Perumal Maistry St, T 37531, clean rm with bath, some a/c. **E** *Aarathy*, 9 Perumalkoil W Mada St, T 31571. Close to Bus Station, clean, comfortable rm, some a/c, all with bath. Some rm with balcony, friendly staff. Restaurant. Recommended. **E** *Arima*, 4 TB Rd, T 23261. 37 rm, some a/c doubles. **E** *TM Lodge*, 50 W Perumal Maistry St. T 31481, Telex: 0445-280. 57 rm, some a/c, some with TV. **E** *Tamil Nadu*, W Veli St. T 37470. 44 rm, some a/c. Close to centre and the Bus Stands. Restaurant, bar, exchange, travel. Rather dingy rms, can be noisy (last resort).

Several other Indian style inexpensive hotels on W Perumal Maistry St and Town Hall Rd, in the heart of town, W of the temple, with plenty of places to eat in the locality. **E** *Railway Retiring Rooms*, Madurai Jn Station, 1st floor above Platform 1. 13 double rm, some a/c. Can be very noisy. **E** *New College House*, 2 Town Hall Rd, T 24311. 193 rm, some a/c. Restaurant (Indian veg) recommended, travel. Basic, reasonably clean with better rm on upper floors. Behind the Rly Station there is a Municipal **F** *Tourist Bungalow*, 33 rm.

Restaurants Hotels particularly good on S Indian dishes, including *Pandiya, Madurai Ashok, Tamil Nadu Star* and *New College House*. There are a number of restaurants mostly serving Indian food to the W of the temple, mainly along Town Hall Rd and W Veli St. On Town Hall Rd, the a/c *Mahal* and *Amudham Restaurant* both are multi-cuisine and recommended and the Indian *Taj Restaurant* and the *Indo-Ceylon Restaurant* (good non-veg food). Prohibition in the state requires you to get a temporary liquor permit from the Tourist Office. There are **bars** in some of the hotels listed above.

Banks Branches of national banks with several on E Avanimoola St, including **Bank of India**, T 30930 and **United Commercial Bank**, T 22010. Also **Central Bank of India**, 15 Minakshi Koil St, T 31457, Foreign Exchange T 33576. **State Bank of India**, 6 W Veli St, T 22850.

Shopping Best buys are textiles, carvings in wood and stone, brass images, jewellery and appliqué work for temple chariots. Most of the shops are on S Avanimoola St (for jewellery), Town Hall Rd and Masi St, in and around the Temple, where you will find the *All India Handicrafts Emporium* at 39-41 Town Hall Rd , T 30742. *Poompuhar Sales Emporium*, T 25517, *Khadi Gramodyog Bhandar* and *Surabhi* (Kerala Handicrafts) on W Veli St. Also Cooptex shops on W Tower St and S Chitrai St and *Pandiyan Co-operative Supermarket*, Palace Rd, T 31582. *Hajee Moosa*, 18-19 E Chitrai St, T 32118, nr the E Gate is a large textile department store which stocks ready made garments. Tailoring in 8 hrs. Others facilities at the store include exchange, export enquiries, hotel and travel reservations and laundry! They also have a Cutpiece Centre at 15 Chitrai St and the House of Readymades, *Shabnam* at No 17. Another similar store selling textiles, clothing and gifts is *Femina*, 10 -11 W Chitrai St, T 32485. They invite you to take aerial view photos of the Minakshi Temple from their rooftop. Near the new *mandapam* there are tailors' shops where you can choose some material and have a made-to-measure item of clothing sewn up in a few hours.

Local transport Taxis are un-metred and charge according to type of journey, more for ghat roads, some by distance or by time. From airport to Central Bus Stand, approx Rs 50, to Alagar Koil Rd hotels, Rs 75. For city sight seeing Rs 35 -40 per hr,y Rs 275 -300 per day. **Cycle rickshaws and auto rickshaws** are available but you must fix the charge before hiring. **Buses** City service is run by Pandiyan Roadways Corporation which has a good network within the city and the suburbs.

Entertainment *Sound and Light Show* at the Thirumalai Nayaka Palace, T 26945. Organised by the Department of Tourism, Govt of Tamil Nadu. It tells the story of *Silappathikaram* and the life of the Nayaka King Thirumalai. Timings: English 1845-1945. Tamil 2000-2100. Entry Rs 2, Rs 3. During the day there are performances of dance drama and concerts in the courtyard. Auditoria – *Raja Muthaia Mandaram*, opp District Court. *Lakshmi Sundaram Hall*, Tallakulam, T 25858. Several cinemas in Satamanglam and Chairman Muthuramalingam. Check newspaper for programme.

Sports *Swimming* Public Pool nr Gandhi Museum, Rs 10 per hr. TTDC Children's Park, *Vandiyur Kanmoy* with restaurant, toy train and boating. Boat hire – 2 seater, Rs 10, 4 seater, Rs 20 both for 30 min.

Museums Gandhi Museum, Old Palace of Rani Mangammal built 300 years ago, contains an art gallery, relics, a Khadi and Village Industries Section and another on S Indian handicrafts. Open 0900-1300, 1300-1830, closed Wed. **Government Museum** in the same complex was opened in 1981. Open 1030-1300, 1400-1730, closed Fri. Bus No 1, 2 and 3. The **Museum** at the Thirumalai Nayak Palace concentrates on the history of Madurai with galleries on the famous Nayaka King and the art and architecture of Tamil Nadu. Bus No 4.

Parks and zoos *Rajaji Park* opp Temkum Ground.

Post and telegraph The town GPO is at the N end of W Veli St. In Tallakulam there is another Head Post Office, T 42263 and the *Central Telegraph Office*, on Gokhale Rd, T 42275.

Places of worship *Hindu* – Minakshi Temple, Mariamman Temple, Manmai Tharuvarkoil, Koodal Alagar Temple. *Muslim* – Pallivasal Mashmir Theru, S Gate, Sai Pallivasal, S Masi St, Sangam Pallivasal, Vaigai Bridge. *Christian* – Rosary Church, St Mary's Church, Mahal, W Gate Church, YMCA Church, Lutheran Church.

Hospitals and medical services *Christian Mission Hospital*, E Veli St, T 22458. *Govt Rajaji Hospital*, Panagal Rd, T 43231. *Grace Kennet Foundation Hospital*, 34 Kennet Rd, T 22279.

Travel agents *Trade Wings*, 279 N Masi St, T 30271. *Travel Lok*, Kamaraj Rd, Vilakunthun, T 34343. *Natarajan Pillai Travels*, Sukikulam, T 42061. *S India Travel Agency*, W Veli St, T 22345.

Airlines offices *Air India*, opp Rly Station, W Veli St, T 24947. *Indian Airlines*, 7A W Veli St, T 22795.

Tourist offices and information *Govt of Tamil Nadu Tourist Office,* W Veli St, T 22957. Open 1000-1750, Closed Sun, 2nd Sat, Government holidays. Useful maps. Also at Madurai Jn Rly Station, Main Hall, T 24535. Open daily 0630-2030. Information Counter at the Airport is open during flight times. Guides are available through the Tourist Office. **Tour** Apr-Jun TTDC. *Kodaikkanal.* 0700-2100.

Air Indian Airlines Madras Daily, except Mon, 0840, 50 min. Indian Airlines, TVS Building, W Veli St, T 22795. Airport, T 37433. Open 1000-1300, 1400-1700. **Vayudoot** Agents, Travel Lok, Kamaraj Rd, Vilakunthun, T 42061. Open 0930-1830. Madurai airport to city centre by Pandiyan Roadways Corp transfer coach (calls at top hotels) costs Rs 12

Rail Madurai is on the Madras – Tiruchirappalli – Dindigul – Quilon line. **Madras** (ME): *Vaigai Exp*, 2636 (AC/CC), daily, 0645, 7 hr 40 min; *Pearl City*: 6104 (AC/II), daily, 2045, 11 hr; **Ramesvaram**: *Tirupati-Ramesvaram Exp,* 6799, daily, 1030, 4 hr 40 min; *Ramesvaram Fast Pass,* 6115, daily, 0520, 6 hr; **Quilon**: *Quilon Mail,* 6105 (AC/II), daily, 0650, 7 hr 50 min; *6161 Exp,* daily, 2035, 7 hr 55 min; **Tirupati**: *Ramesvaram Exp,* 6800, daily, 1040, 18 hr 20 min. *Tirupati Madurai Exp.* Madurai Jn Rly Station, W Veli St, Enquiries, T 37597. Reservations: I Class T 23535, II Class T 33535. Open 0700-1300, 1330-2000.

Road The NH 45 and 7 cross at Madurai providing it with good links to the rest of the region.

Buses State and Private Bus Companies such as TTC, MPTC, PRC run services to other cities in the S including Bangalore 427 km, Coimbatore 227 km, Kanniyakumari 242 km, Madras 447 km, Ramesvaram 167 km, Trichy 128 km, Trivandrum 259 km. There are 4 main Bus Stations. The 3 Bus Stands for TTC, Mofussil and Central are in the centre on W Veli St. Buses to Kodai leave from here. The Anna Bus Stand is 3 km away. TTC Enquiries, T 25354. Reservations: 0700-2100. Computerised reservation, Anna Bus Stand, T 43380. Mofussil Bus Stand Enquiries, T 36818. Periyar Bus Stand, T 35293. Pandiyan Roadways Corp, Anna Bus Stand, T 43622. Rani Mungammal Transport, T 33740.

Excursions There are some excellent walks and scrambles around Madurai. One of the most accessible is up *Yanai Malai* (*elephant hill*), the granite outcrop to the E of Madurai that looks like a seated elephant. Take the road out of Madurai across the Vaigai and turn right immediately. The road leaves Madurai and runs along the southern edge of the hill. Approximately 1 km after reaching the western end of the hill a road turns sharp left straight to a village at the bottom of the hill. Paths lead up a scramble to the top, which gives superb views across the cultivated plain below. It is a beautiful early morning outing between Dec and Mar, but gets very hot later in the day.

Koodal Alagar Temple 20 km to the W of Madurai (Bus No 44) is an ancient Vaishnavite Temple with beautiful sculptures. **Vishnu** is shown in his special poses, sitting, standing and reclining, one above the other.

MADURAI TO RAMESVARAM

The NH 49 runs in a virtually straight line SE across the flat plains of the **Vaigai River**. Seen from the air the landscape is one of the most remarkable in India, for it is what has been called "tank country supreme'. There are over 5,000 tanks in the District, and tank irrigation has been so widely developed that it seems not a drop of water is wasted, other than by evaporation and seepage into the soil.

Although it is primarily an agricultural area the coastal districts of *Ramnad* have their own highly distinct economic and social features. Both Hindu and Muslim communities have long established trading links across the Bay of Bengal – to Malaysia and SE Asia and traditionally to Sri Lanka, though these have been severely interrupted by the civil war in Sri Lanka. Small towns and villages along the coast such as Kilakkarai, S of Ramnad, have long been associated with smuggling as well as with a wide range of legal activities.

Between Madurai and **Manamadurai** (45 km *Population* 22,000) the road crosses and re-crosses one of the 96 canals which take off from the Vaigai river. Although the Vaigai is often dry by the time it reaches Madurai for months at a time the canals serve the vital function of leading flood water both directly to the fields and into the tanks for storage. When full the Vaigai itself presents a beautiful and imposing sight. The effect of a major river may be spoiled somewhat by the sight of villagers wading less than knee deep across it!

Manamadurai takes its name from the story of the Ramayana, which tells how Hanuman the monkey god stopped here with his monkey allies on his way to the island of Lanka to rescue Sita. In the **Perumal** temple **Hanuman** is enshrined, with the highly unusual feature of a crown on his head, reflecting the local belief that Hanuman was crowned here before leaving for Lanka. According to one account the name of the town is derived from this visit, which in Tamil is described as *Vanara Veera Madurai*, which has been corrupted to become Manamadurai. There are other possible derivations.

The town has three large temples. The biggest is the Somanathasvami temple, which has a gopuram of 15 m and was built by 2 brothers between 1783-1801. Inside the *Nandimandapam* and the *Kalyanamandapam* were added in 1900. The crowned Hanuman is enshrined nr the entrance of the Vaishnavite Veera Alagar Koil temple on the E bank of the river. The bridge which crosses the river at this point was opened in 1927, which both symbolised and encouraged the development of the town.

It is particularly noted for its ceramics, the red clay soil being well suited to pottery, tiles and bricks. Along the road you may well see bricks being fired in the local way, which is to build a large hollow pile of bricks, as large as a big house, covered with thatch and with wood and charcoal underneath. This is then set fire and burns for many hours until the bricks are baked. Modern industries include cement pipe manufacture and brass ware. There are several small restaurants, the best vegetarian. There is also a post and telegraph office near the centre.

The road continues SE to **Paramagudi** (30 km Population 80,000), probably taking its name ("embankment town") from its position on the Vaigai. There are small restaurants and tea shops and a traveller's bungalow, post and telegraph office. The road and rail run side by side SE through a scatter of villages and farming landscape on either side. Tanks remain vital to the success of agriculture. Although there are few signs of change in this remote part of SE Ramnad, and it is widely regarded as one of S India's most backward districts, the area has opened up dramatically in the last 30 years. The frequent bus service has brought all the villagers within easy reach of Madurai, and the town of Ramnad has become an important market. Whereas even in the 1960s most farmers had no choice but to sell their crops to travelling merchants – usually getting a very low price – many are now able to take their crop direct to market.

As a result there have been big changes in the cropping pattern. E of Paramagudi is one of the driest regions of SE India – though if you are travelling in October or November you might not believe it, as 500 mm of rain has been known to fall in 24 hours. However, beyond the reach of tank irrigation crops have to resist drought. Traditionally that meant growing varieties of rice that would survive long periods without water and still give some return. Now however it is common to find oilseeds and millets being grown for market as quick growing crops for sale in the market. Another important crop in this area is chillies, again bringing a very good cash return from sale in the cities. An additional problem for the farmers is that although many could now afford pumpsets the groundwater is very salty in many areas, and therefore unusable for drinking or irrigation.

The nearest market is **Ramanathapuram** (37 km) *Population* 57,000, *Altitude* 10 m, only 16 km from the sea, and now an important market town for the region, with a bustling market and associated shops, restaurants and cinema. It is the terminus for several bus routes. Since the eruption of the civil war in Sri Lanka the district has become the centre for Tamil refugees from Sri Lanka. Between 1985 and 1987 there were over 160,000 refugees in camps through the district. Those numbers decreased sharply after the Indo-Sri Lankan Accord of July 1987, but rose again in mid 1990.

Places of interest Between 1674 and 1710 Raghunatha Setupati, a local chieftain, built a *fort* of brick and stone (a commodity in short supply in these alluvial plains) nearly 2 km W of the present town, but it now lies in ruins. In the centre was an extensive palace with high stone walls, still visible, along with some of the artillery. The Protestant *Christ Church* (now CSI) was built by Colonel Martinez, a French Catholic army officer, but handed over and dedicated as a Protestant Church in 1804 under the governorship of Lord William Bentinck.

Local industry Coarse cloth is made in the town and there is a recently built spinning mill. Palm leaf products are made as a cottage industry, and Ramnad is centre for the chilli trade.

Hotels F *Traveller's Bungalow* 3 rms, comfortable.

Post office and telegraph office Near the town centre.

Excursion *Kilakkarai* (16 km *Population* 33,000) is a strikingly distinct small coastal settlement, reached by the road that goes due S from Ramnad town. The entire coastline here has been emerging steadily from the sea, perhaps by as much as 15 m. Fossils of various species of oysters, which now live at depths of 10 m, are found inland at heights of up to 5 m. The uplift is responsible for converting the living coral into solid rock, and made the link between **Ramesvaram** and **Pamban Island**. (This was followed by the railway line until a catastrophic cyclone and storm surge destroyed it in 1963.) The name *Kilakkarai* simply means "E coast". The majority of the population is Muslim and there are 12 mosques in the town as well as a 16th century temple dedicated to Siva, and a number of other temples. From 1759 the **Setupati** chiefs gave the Dutch East India Company permission to trade, and in the following decade the Dutch built a fortified settlement. Some of the buildings are still visible

The town is particularly famous for its Muslim *pearl divers*. Many of the Muslims are jewel traders, one of the major specialities being the cutting and polishing of *chank* shells. There is one major factory employing about 100 people in finishing chank products. All the coastal area to the S has many palmyra palms, a source of toddy and palm sugar (*gur*). Coconut and mango groves are also an important source of income.

Continuing to **Ramesvaram** the road crosses the railway, crossing the dead flat and marshy land of the narrow peninsular before reaching **Mandapam** (30 km *Population* 18,000). Since the mid 1960s this has been the main port of entry for Tamil tea estate workers from the central highlands of Sri Lanka who have been repatriated to India under the agreement signed between the Indian and Sri Lankan govts in 1965. The was a Sri Lankan govt quarantine camp here. However, as a result of the Sri Lankan crisis in 1983 access to Mandapam, one of the main crossing points from Sri Lanka and camps for "returnees" is now strictly controlled.

The village is predominantly a Muslim fishing village, the long Ramesvaram island providing sheltered fishing even during the strong NE monsoon. The main catch is silverbelly, a non-edible variety of fish converted into fish meal. An Indo-Norwegian project has established a plant that sells fish meal across the country. Prawns have also become an important source of foreign exchange. The

Marine Biological Research Centre is also here. To the S lie a chain of small coral islands, one of the few coral areas of India. **Kurusadai Islands** W of the Pamban bridge, between the mainland and Ramesvaram and you can get there via Mandapam. They are surrounded by coral reefs and the shallow waters harbour a wealth of marine life of interest to scientists – starfish, crabs, sponges, sea cucumbers, algae and sea cow. Approach the Fisheries Dept for permission.

Hotels TTDC F *Youth Hostel*, T 92, with a dormitory at Mandapam. Reservations: Manager, Youth Hostel, Mandapam or TTDC, 143 Anna Salai, Madras, T 849803.

Museum The Central Marine Fisheries Research Institute has a museum and aquarium at Mandapam, which includes a pair of live sea cows (*dugongs*).

Ramesvaram

20 km *Population* **36,500** *Altitude* **Sea level. The nearest airport is at Madurai, 154 km.** *Best Season* **Jan – Mar.**

	Jan	Feb	Mar	Apr	May	Jun	Jul	Aug	Sep	Oct	Nov	Dec	Av/Tot
Max (°C)	28	29	32	33	33	32	32	32	32	31	29	28	31
Min (°C)	24	24	25	27	27	27	26	26	26	26	24	24	26
Rain (mm)	66	23	18	46	25	3	13	15	28	216	297	193	943

Ramayana tells how the monkey king Hanuman built the bridges linking Ramnad to *Pamban* and *Danushkodi* (the spot where *Rama* is believed to have bathed; the name means "Rama's bow", taken probably from the gently curving shape of the shoreline) in order to help in the rescue of *Sita* from the demon king *Ravana*. When he returned he was told by the *rishis* that he must purify himself after committing the sin of Brahmanicide, for *Ravana* was the son of a Brahman. To do this he was advised to set up a lingam and worship it. Rama, the story goes, fixed an auspicious time and sent Hanuman to Mount Kailasa to fetch a *lingam*. Hanuman failed to return on time, so again on the advice of the *rishis* he set up a lingam made by Sita. Soon Hanuman returned with a lingam, but was dejected to discover a lingam already in place. His journey had been in vain. He threatened to kill himself because of the dishonour shown him by Rama. Rama instructed him in the virtue of detachment; then he told the monkey that he could remove the linga fashioned by Sita and install in its place the one he had brought. Hanuman took hold of the sand linga with his hands and tried to move it; it would not budge. Then he wrapped his tail around it, touched the earth with his hands and jumped high in the heavens. The earth with its mountains and islands shook, and the monkey fell senseless near the lingas, his mouth, eyes, nostrils, ears and anus streaming with blood. Sita wept over the fallen monkey; Rama picked up his body and stroked it as he wept, covering Hanuman with his tears. Hanuman awoke from his faint, and seeing Rama in this state, sang his praises and those of Sita. Rama said: "This act of violence was committed by you in ignorance. None of the Gods could move this linga; you fell because you offended against Siva. This place where you fell will be known by your name; the Ganga, Yamuna and Sarasvati will unite there, and whoever bathes there will be free of evil. At Rama's command Hanuman set up the linga he had brought. The other linga still bears the marks of the monkey's tail." – David Shulman.

The red image of **Hanuman** to the N of the main E gate illustrates this story, and according to popular belief the marks visible on the lingam today resulted from Hanuman's struggle. In order to pacify him Rama asked Hanuman to fix his lingam a little to the N of that made by Sita and ordered that all pujas should be offered first to the Hanuman lingam. Some say that as the Ramayana has been dated to the 3rd century BC the lingams must be over 2,200 years old. Certainly the original shrine long predates the present great Ramesvaram temple, though there is no evidence as to the real age of the lingams. It is one of India's most sacred shrines, being visited by pilgrims from all over India and one of the 14 sacred temples of the Pandiyas. The temple benefitted from enormous donations from the Rajas of Ramanathapuram, the 17th century **Setupatis**. (Their name means "guardian of the causeway", and they derived their wealth from being granted the right to levy taxes on crossing to the island.) The island on which the temple stands is covered in low acacia shrubs, coconut palm and umbrella pines, and the temple stands on slightly higher ground, surrounded by a freshwater lake.

Places of interest The *Ramalingesvara temple* (also known as Ramanathasvami temple) was founded by the Cholas but most of the temple was built in the Nayaka period of the 16th-17th centuries. It is a massive structure, enclosed by a huge rectangular wall with gopurams in the middle of 3 sides. Entrances through the E wall are approached through columned mandapams and the E gopuram is on the wall of the inner enclosure rather than the outer wall. This gopuram, over 45 m high, was begun in 1640 but left incomplete until recently. The W gopuram is comparatively recent. In contrast the N and S gopurams are considerably older, built by **Keerana Rayar** of the Deccan about 1420 AD.

The most remarkable feature of the temple is its pillared mandapams. In total these have been estimated to stretch for 1,200 m. The longest single corridor is over 200 m long. The pillars, nearly 4 m tall, are raised on moulded bases and the shafts are decorated with scrollwork and lotus motifs. They give an impression of almost unending perspective, those on the N and S being particularly striking. There are two gateways on the E side which give access to the Parvati and Ramalinga shrines at the centre. The masonry shrine is probably the oldest building on the site, going back to 1173.

On entering the E gate you see the statue of Hanuman, then the Nandi flanked by statues of the Nayaka kings of Madurai *Visvanatha* and *Krishnama*. Non Hindus are not allowed beyond the first enclosure. The Sphatikalinga Puja is performed daily at 0500. Worshippers take a holy bath in the sea in a very calm bay 25 km away, where the waters are believed to wash away their sins. Fishermen will occasionally offer to take visitors for a boat ride, staying fairly close to land.

Gandhamadana Parvatam Just over 2 km N of Ramesvaram is an unimpressive looking single storeyed building on a low sand hill about 30 m high, reached by a black top road from the temple. Its name is derived from the Sanskrit words *gandha* (fragrance) and *mad* (intoxicate), "highly fragrant hill place". Dedicated to Rama's feet, this is the spot from which Hanuman is believed to have surveyed the area before taking his leap across the narrow Palk strait to Sri Lanka. You can get an excellent view from the top of the mandapam.

Kotandaramasvami Temple 8 km. The 1964 cyclone completely washed away the southernmost tip of the Dhanuskodi island but the temple was untouched. The legend marks it as the spot where Ravana's brother Vibhishana surrendered to Rama hence the images of Rama, Sita, Lakshmana, Hanuman and Vibhishana.

Hotels E *Tamil Nadu*, (TTDC), Kamatchi Sannathi St nr Rly. T 277, Cable: Tamiltour. 18 double rm, some a/c. Clean, balconies overlook the sea. Restaurant. Sea bathing is possible nearby (when calm). **F** *Youth Hostel* with dormitory accommodation. Both, especially the hotel, are heavily booked so you should book well in advance. Reservations: Manager, Hotel Tamil Nadu, Ramesvaram or Commercial Manager, TTDC, 143 Anna Salai, Madras, T 849803. **E** *Maharaja's*, 7 Middle St, W of the Temple. T 271, Cable: Maharaja's. 30 double rm, some a/c with bath. Travel. Recommended but beware of temple music broadcast on loudspeakers. **E** *Santhya Lodge*, 1 W Car St, T 329. 22 double rm, some a/c with bath. Travel. *Devasthanam Lodges and Cottages*, T 241. 115 cottages some of which are **E** category, modern with a/c rm. Reservations: Executive Officer, Devasthanam, Ramesvaram, T 223. **F** *Railway Retiring Rooms*, T 226. 9 rm and a dormitory. Several other small Indian style hotels without restaurants, some of which offer triple or family rm on W Car St, N Car St, S Car St and Bazaar St. In addition there are *dharmasalas* most of which cater for religious groups.

Restaurants *Hotel Tamil Nadu*, multi-cuisine restaurant open to non-residents but you may need to order in advance. The *Devasthanam Trust* has a canteen opp the E gate of the temple. For Indian veg food, some specializing in food from Gujarat, Rajasthan and Andhra try *Ashok Bhawan* and *Vasantha Vihar* on W Car St and *Vasantha Bhawan* at the Central Bus Stand. Others are *Arya Bhawan* and *Lakshmi Mess*.

Local transport Taxis A few cars and jeeps are available from the Rly Station and hotels. **Tongas, Cycle rickshaws** and **Auto rickshaws** are easily available. You can hire a bicycle by the hour from W Car St. **Bus** Services of the Marudhu Pandiyan Transport Corporation (MPTC) cover the town and its surrounding area. The Bus Station is 2 km W of the town. You can get a bus from the Rly Station to the Ramalingesvara Temple, to Pamban via the temple or to Dhanushkodi via the temple. Also services from outside the Temple's main E Gate to Dhanushkodi roadhead every 1 hr 30 min and to Gandhamadhana Parvatham every 2 hr.

Shopping Local crafts include conch shells, beads and articles made of banana fibre and palm leaf can be bought from shops near the E Gate of the Temple. *Khadi Kraft*, E Car St, close to the temple; *Cottage Industries* and *Sea Shell Industries*, Middle St. Tamil Nadu Handicrafts Development Corp shop, *Poompuhar* operates during festival time.

Hospital There is a *Govt Hospital* nr the Railway Station, T 233.

Bank The State Bank is N Car St, T 282 and **Indian Bank** is W Car St, T 234.

Post office The *Post and Telegraph Office* is on Mela St, T 225. Open 0930-1730.

Tourist Office and information *Government of Tamil Nadu Tourist Office*, E Car St, T 371. Open daily 1000-1700. Also at the Railway Station, T 373. Open daily 0700-0800, 1030-1400, 1500-1620,1900-2030.

Air The nearest airport is at Madurai, 154 km away.

Rail Ramesvaram is on the metre gauge section of the Southern Rly. **Madurai**: *Ramesvaram Exp*, 6800, daily, 0600, 4 hr 25 min; *Coimbatore Fast Pass*, 6116, daily, 1610, 5 hr 40 min; **Madras**: *Sethu Exp*, 6114, daily, 1545, 14 hr 35 min; **Trichy**: *Ramesvaram Exp*, 6102, daily, 1230, 6 hr 35 min; **Coimbatore**: *Coimbatore Fast Pass*, 6116, daily, 1610, 12 hr 10 min; **Tirupati**: *Ramesvaram-Tirupati*, 6800, daily, 0600, 23 hr. Ramesvaram Rly Station, Enquiries and Reservations T 226. Open 0800-1300, 1330-1730.

Road Mandapam 19 km away, is connected by road to various towns in the S. The Indira Gandhi road bridge across the Pamban Strait which was opened in 1988 has made Ramesvaram accessible by road from other parts of the S via the NH 49.

Buses The State owned TTC, MPTC and private bus companies run regular bus services via Mandapam to several towns in the region. There are frequent buses to Madurai (4 hr), 2 to Pondicherry and one to Thanjavur. Other services include Kanniyakumari 300 km, Madras 592 km, Ramanathapuram 37 km, Tiruchendur 205 km and 6 daily to Tiruchirappalli 258 km (3 hr 30 min). The Central Bus Stand is 2 km from the main temple gate. TTC Reservations, N Car St. Open 0700-2100. MPTC, Central Bus Stand, Kartupilyar Kovil, T 251 does not offer a reservation service.

MADURAI TO TRIVANDRUM (Eastern Route)

The route S along the NH 7 crosses the central part of southern Tamil Nadu, the heart of the Pandiyan kingdoms from the 8th century. It passes through the major educational centre of Tirunelveli, with four centuries of Christian missionary activity and a large Christian population.

Almost on the outskirts of Madurai are the Pandiyan rock cut shrines of the 8th century AD, and the much later Nayaka Hindu temple at *Tiruparankunram* (5 km *Population* 30,000), with a wide range of Hindu gods carved on the walls. The Subrahmanya cave temple, dated to 773, has a shrine dedicated to Durga, with the figures of Ganes and Subrahmanya on either side. Other carvings show Siva dancing on the dwarf on the right hand side and Parvati and the Nandi with musicians on the left.

In *Tirumangalam* (12 km) *Population* 36,000, *Altitude* 120 m , a busy market town, the NH 7 forks left to *Virudhunagar* (30 km *Population* 88,000). Meaning "city of banners". The town has a considerable history of civic pride and self-awareness. The municipality changed its name to Virudhunagar from *Virudhupatti* ("hamlet of banners") in 1915, and was upgraded to a full municipality in 1957. These moves reflected the upwardly mobile social status of the towns dominant local caste, the *Nadars*. Originally low caste toddy tappers, the Nadars have established a wide reputation as a dynamic and enterprising group. The best known political leader to emerge from the caste was **Kamaraj Nadar**, the powerful Congress leader chiefly responsible for Mrs. Gandhi's selection as Prime Minister.

Local industries Virudhunagar has become an extremely important commercial and industrial town. Many cotton ginning factories, textile mills, a steel rolling mill, paper and match factories have been joined by a range of new industries.

Hotels F There is a well furnished traveller's bungalow as well as several hotels in the town.

The road continues S through **Sattur** (23 km *Population* 33,000), a district headquarters, situated on the banks of the **Vaipar River**. Although this is often dry, occasional floods devastate the town. 21 kilometres S is **Kovilpatti** (*Population* 84,000) in the heart of the southern black cotton soil district. To the E is the driest region in the whole of S India, with as little as 550 mm rain a year in the port city of Tuticorin. The black soils (known as *regur*) around Kovilpatti are developed not from lavas but from the underlying gneiss, and are well suited to the the common rotation of cotton, *bajra* and *sorghum*, the two millets providing both foodgrain and fodder for animals. Cotton is widely irrigated, but the difference between fields where irrigation is available and those that depend entirely on rainfall is often dramatic. Electrification has encouraged the use of electric pumps to increase the efficiency of well irrigation.

If you take the road to **Tuticorin** (*Population* 250,000) and the coast from Kovilpatti you cross the startlingly red soils leading to the *teri* of the coast. Much is just waste, but the *palmyra palm* is everywhere. One estimate suggests that there may be 10 million palmyra palms in Tirunelveli district alone. They are a vital resource for village economies. The broad fan-shaped leaves were used for writing early Tamil literature, but today they still serve for thatching, fencing, sunshades, basket making and mats. The fibres of the stem are used for making string or rope and for brushes. The extremely sweet sap is sometimes drunk fresh, but more commonly it is allowed to ferment into the highly potent *toddy* or converted into sugar, or *jaggery*.

The red *teri** soils themselves are wind blown sands, although the dunes on the coast have often been fixed. They form small rolling plateaus covering about 50 sq km, often occurring as thin deposits over the underlying sandstones which occur at heights of about 60 m, suggesting that since the last ice age the land may have risen by this amount. They are a rich source of stone age tools.

Six kilometres S of Kovilpatti, just after passing through the village of **Nalattinputtur** a road turns right off the NH 7 to **Kalugumalai** (20 km *Population* 13,500). This small town has some magnificent Jain figures and an unfinished monolithic temple, with turtle back roofs, dating from about 950 AD. They are well worth the detour.

Tirunelveli (*Population* 173,000 *Altitude* 50 metres) is now joined with the twin settlement of **Palayamkottai**, (*population* 117,000) located on the banks of the only perennial river of the S, the **Tamramparni**. The irrigation from the river has created "a splash of green in the naturally dull brown of the vegetation map" of the area. Rising only 60 km to the E at an altitude of over 1700 m, the river benefits from both the SW and the SE monsoons. It tumbles down to the plains and follows a narrow strip of land which itself gets more rain – an annual average of about 850 mm – than the belts on either side. Thus a narrow strip of rich paddy growing land has been created.

Tirunelveli is a market town but also one of the oldest Christian centres in Tamil Nadu. St Francis Xavier settled here to begin his ministry in India in the early 16th century, but it has also been a centre of Protestant missionary activity for a long period. In 1896 it became the head of an Anglican diocese, now Church of S India. There is a **temple** divided into 2 equal parts, the northern being dedicated to Siva and the southern to Parvati. Each has enclosures over 150 m by 120 m. Going into the Parvati temple is a porch, to the right a tank and to the left a 1,000

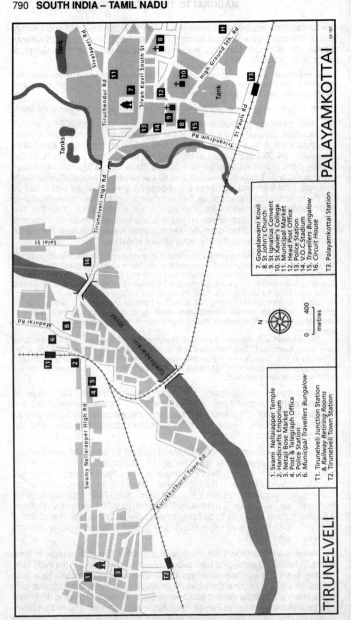

PALAYAMKOTTAI

TIRUNELVELI

SA 167

1. Swami Nellaiapper Temple
2. Handicrafts Emporium
3. Netaji Bose Market
4. Post & Telegraph Office
5. Police Station
6. Municipal Travellers Bungalow

7. Gopalasvami Kovil
8. St John's Church
9. St Ignatius Convent
10. St Xavier's College
11. Municipal Market
12. Head Post Office
13. Police Station
14. V.O.C.Stadium
15. Travellers Bungalow
16. Circuit House

T1. Tirunelveli Junction Station
      & Railway Retiring Rooms
T2. Tirunelveli Town Station
T3. Palayamkottai Station

N

0   400
metres

pillared mandapam. **Palayamkottai** has a **Church Missionary Society church** with a spire 35 m high, a landmark for miles around.

Excursion *Tiruchendur*, (*Population* 28,000) 32 km to the southeast of Tirunelveli, has a famous temple dedicated to Subrahmanya and a cave with rock cut sculptures. To the S is **Kulasekharapatnam** (*Population* 8,500) a predominantly Roman Catholic village where St Francis Xavier is said to have landed and lived in a cave near the headland.

Rail Madras (ME): *Nellai Exp*, 6120 (AC/CC), daily, 1735, 14 hr 55 min. **Road** Good bus connections to Kanniyakumari and Trivandrum, and to Madurai, Trichy and Madras.

Continuing down the NH 7 from Tirunelveli the western Ghats loom ever larger to the right of the road. Village houses are often white painted, and the patches of bright green rice against the blue backdrop of the hills creates a beautiful succession of views. The road passes through **Nanguneri** (31 km *Population* 25,000) and **Panakkudi** (27 km) before reaching Kanniyakumari (23 km) or **Cape Comorin** as the British named it at the southernmost tip of India.

Kanniyakumari *Population* 17,000. *Altitude* Sea level. *Climate* Temp. Summer Max. 39°C Min 22°C, Winter Max. 33°C Min 20°C. Annual rainfall 1020 mm. *Best season* Throughout the year. *Clothing* Cottons. The nearest airport is at Trivandrum 86 km away.

One of India's holiest sites, Kanniyakumari has become a highly commercialised pilgrimage centre, associated as its name implies with the Goddess **Kumari**, the virgin. The memorial to **Swami Vivekenanda**, on a rocky promontory just over 400 m off shore, now dominates the view. There is a ban on photography of the best views "for security reasons". The Bay of Bengal, the Indian Ocean and the Arabian Sea meet here. The sunrise, sunset and moonrise are particularly spectacular. At full moon you can see the sun set and the moon rise, at the same time! The full moon in Apr is especially unusual when you should be able to see the sun and the moon on the same horizon. The beach sands here are of different colours, having been deposited from different directions. Prominent on the beach are the black monazite and red garnet sands, the former exploited further N in Kerala for its radioactive properties.

Local festivals Apr, 2nd week. *Chitra Purnima* is a special full moon celebration at the temple. Also special locally is the festival of *Navarathri* in the first week of Oct.

Places of interest The **Kanniyakumari Temple** overlooks the shoreline. The legend tells of the Devi Kanya, one of the incarnations of Parvati, who sought to marry Siva by doing penance and when she was unsuccessful she vowed to remain an unmarried virgin. The deity who is the 'protector of India's shores' has an exceptionally brilliant diamond on her nose ring which is supposed to shine out to sea. The E gate is opened only on special occasions. Open 0430-1130, 1730-2030. Non-Hindus are not allowed into the sanctuary and men must wear a *dhoti* to enter. You must leave your shoes outside.

The **Gandhi Mandapam** commemorates the Father of the Nation. Mahatma Gandhi's ashes were placed in public view before immersion in the sea and the memorial was built in a way that the sun shines on the spot where the ashes were placed, on his birthday, 2nd Oct at mid day. Visitors from the W may find the concrete rather unaesthetic.

Vivekananda Memorial which stands on one of two rocks separated by about 70 m, is about 500 m from the mainland which you can reach by a half-hourly ferry. The Bengali religious leader and philosopher Swami Vivekananda who came here as a simple monk and devotee of the Devi, swam out to the rocks out at sea and sat in long and deep meditation on one of the rocks in 1892. He left transformed and divinely inspired to speak on Hinduism at the Parliament of Religions in Chicago. There his eloquence held every one spell bound while he

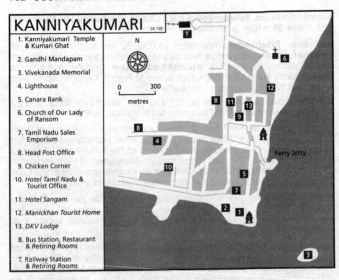

KANNIYAKUMARI SA 159

1. Kanniyakumari Temple & Kumari Ghat
2. Gandhi Mandapam
3. Vivekananda Memorial
4. Lighthouse
5. Canara Bank
6. Church of Our Lady of Ransom
7. Tamil Nadu Sales Emporium
8. Head Post Office
9. Chicken Corner
10. Hotel Tamil Nadu & Tourist Office
11. Hotel Sangam
12. Manickhan Tourist Home
13. DKV Lodge

B. Bus Station, Restaurant & Retiring Rooms
T. Railway Station & Retiring Rooms

N

0   300
metres

Ferry Jetty

preached for universal tolerance and human brotherhood. His belief that all religions are equally true and that each is merely a different approach to the Lord "He is one, but the sages describe Him differently." He looked on religion as the most powerful instrument of social regeneration and individual development, believing in practical Vedanta, **see page 527**. On his return, he founded the Ramakrishna Mission in Madras, which now has spread across world. The rock was renamed Vivekananda Rock and a memorial was built in 1970. The design of the *mandapam* incorporates different styles of temple architecture from all over India and now also houses a statue of Vivekananda. People also come to see Sri Pada Parai, the 'foot print' of the Devi where she did her penance on the rock (divine foot prints are believed to be raised when enshrined on rock). You are not allowed to smoke or eat and must take off you shoes before entering. Open daily except Tues, 0700-1700. Entry Re 1, Ferry Rs 3. You can get excellent views from the **Lighthouse.** Open 1500-1900. Small entry fee. No photography.

Hotels The hotels are in heavy demand: book well in advance. **D** *Cape* (TTDC), T 222. 45 rm, some a/c. Reservations: Direct to the Manager, Cape Hotel or through Commercial Manager, TTDC, 143 Anna Salai, Madras, T 849803. **E** *Tamil Nadu*, T 257. 45 rm, some a/c and dormitory in cheaper *Youth Hostel*. **E** *Sangam*, Main Rd opp the Post Office, T 351, has double rm with bath. N of the Vinayaka Kovil Temple on the shore to the E are **E** *Manickhan Tourist Home* (fairly new) and **F** *DKV Lodge* both have comfortable double rm and are recommended.

Restaurants TTDC restaurant (non-veg), which looks like a barrack, serves excellent Indian meals also several places serving S Indian veg food. Non-veg menu at the *Manickhan Tourist Home* and the *Chicken Corner*. There is a restaurant at the Bus Station.

Banks Branches of *Canara Bank, State Bank of India* and *State Bank of Travancore*.

Shopping *Tamil Nadu Co-optex Sales Emporium* nr the Gandhi Mandapam. *Khadi Krafts*, S Car St. *Indco Products*, Beach Rd. *Poompuhar Handicrafts Emporium*, Sannathi St.

Local transport *Taxis* and *Cycle rickshaws* are available. The *ferry service* to the Vivekananda Rock is half-hourly and runs from 0700-1100, 1400-1700. Fare Rs 3.

Post and Telegraph   Head Post Office is on the the Main Rd, T 21. Branches at Vivekandandapuram, T 8, open 1100-1600 and in Sannathi St, open 1000-1400.

Tourist Office at Hotel Tamil Nadu Complex, on Beach Rd nr the Gandhi Mandapam.

Rail   The Station to the N off the Trivandrum Rd, is large and well organized. **Madras**: *Him Sagar Exp*, 6017, Th, 2330, 23 hr 40 min. If you take this train to its ultimate destination of Jammu the journey lasts 3 days 14 hrs, the longest in India. **Bombay** (VT): *Kanniyakuman*, 1081 (AC/II), daily, 1535, 47 hr 15 min; **Delhi** (ND): *Him Sagar Exp*, 6017, Th, 2330, 71 hr 50 min; **Trivandrum**: *Him Sagar Exp*, 6017, Thurs, 2330, 2 hr 15 min; *Kanniyakuman*, 1082 (AC/II), daily, 0515, 2 hr 20 min.

Road   The Bus Station is to the W of town, about 15 min walk from the centre. It has a restaurant, waiting room and *Retiring Rooms* upstairs. Local buses have frequent services to Nagercoil, Kovalam and Trivandrum. The State TTC buses go to other major towns in the S including Madras (16 hr), Madurai (6 hr), Ramesvaram (8 hr 30 min) and Trivandrum (2hr 30 min).

From Kanniyakumari the road (NH 47) runs northwest through **Suchindram** (12 km). The temple was originally founded during the Pandiyan period but was expanded under Tirumala Nayak in the 17th century. It was also used later as a sanctuary for the rulers of Travancore to the W and so contains treasures from many kingdoms. One of few temples dedicated to the Hindu Trinity, Brahma, Vishnu and Siva. The temple is in a rectangular enclosure which you enter through the massive ornate seven-storeyed gopuram. N of the temple is a large tank with a small shelter in the middle while round the walls is the typically broad street used for car festivals. Leading to the entrance is a long colonnade with musical pillars and with sculptures of *Siva*, *Parvati*, *Ganes* and *Subrahmanya* on the front. The main sanctuary, at the centre of which is a lingam, dates from the 9th century, but many of the other structures and sculptures date from the 13th century and later. There are special temple ceremonies at sunset on Fridays.

The road passes on through Suchindram to **Nagercoil** (19 km *Population* 215,000). Already the landscape begins to feel more like Kerala than Tamil Nadu. Nagercoil is set with a stunning backcloth of the Western Ghats, reflected from place to place in the broad tanks dotted with lotuses. It is an important railway junction and bus terminal. The old town of **Kottar** which is now a suburb was a centre of art, culture and pilgrimage. The temple to Nagaraja, after which the town is named, is unique in that although the presiding deity is the Serpent God *Naga*, there are also shrines to Siva and Vishnu as well as images of Jain *Teerthankaras*, Mahavira and Parswanatha on the pillars. Christian missionaries played an important part in the town's development and have left their mark in schools, colleges, hospitals and of course churches of different denominations. There is also a prominent Muslim community in Kottar which is reflected in the closure of shops on Fri, remaining open on Sun. The NH 47 continues past **Padmanabhapuram** (15 km) see page 813 to **Trivandrum** (53 km), page 807.

MADURAI TO TRIVANDRUM (Western Route)

A much shorter route from Madurai to Trivandrum runs to the W of the NH 7 through the Western Ghats at the Shenkottai gap. In addition to beautiful scenery as the road climbs through the ghats there are some interesting towns en route that are completely off the normal beaten track. This is roughly the route followed by the metre gauge line from Madurai to Quilon.

The road journey is much more interesting than the rail trip. If you are going through to Quilon from Madurai without stopping two recent travellers, Katherine and Sian Floyd, write that the rail trip is definitely not as spectacular as it is made out to be, and it is better to take the night train. On the Tamil Nadu side of the state border it is a much less busy road than the national highway, but overall the route is no quicker than the comparatively straight and flat main route, followed by all the express buses. Once onto the Kerala side of the border the road becomes far more heavily used and much slower, running through the rubber plantations of S Kerala to Trivandrum.

From Madurai follow the NH 7 to **Tirumangalam** (17 km *Population* 40,000), then take the right fork to **Kallupatti** (18 km) and **Srivilliputtur** (35 km *Population* 78,000).

One of 108 sacred Vaishnavite sites, the gopuram of the **Vishnu Vadabadrasaikoil** in Srivilliputtur towering nearly 60 m is a landmark for the whole district. Built of wood, brick and plaster it comprises 13 storeys high excluding the superstructure which forms its roof. The superstructure itself is, in the words of Percy Brown, an "excessively tall composition resembling a hall with a chaitya roof, elaborately ornamented with a great *suraj mukh* ("sun face") above its gable end and a row of huge pinnacles along its ridge." It has a slightly concave curvature, emphasising its upward curving grace while lessening the feeling of power and strength. During this century there have been increasing signs of stress. In 1904 major cracks were noticed, and by the early 1970s 25 cracks had opened up from the foundations to varying heights. The NW corner of the tower seems to have settled more than 15 cm. The whole tower is supported by a timber frame of teak, the whole built on foundations that go no deeper than 2.3 m. There is an enormous temple car associated with the temple, built over 100 years ago, which takes 3,000 people to pull it. Srivilliputtur is revered throughout Tamil Nadu as the birthplace of the Tamil poetess and devotee **Andal**. In the town is an **old palace** of Tirumala Nayak, partly converted into the *Taluk* office. There is an important handloom industry, and brass and other utensils are made.

Excursions The **Srivilliputtur Reserved Forest** has a wild life sanctuary which is the only known habitat in the world of the grizzled squirrel. There is no guarantee that you will see one! 19 km SE of Srivilliputtur is the important industrial town of **Sivakasi** (*Population* 81,000) On the main Trivandrum-Madras railway line and well connected by road, Sivakasi is famous for modern industries such as litho printing, but it has also gained a degree of notoriety for the extensive use of child labour in its match and firework factories, ignoring all health hazards, **see page 472**. There are over 70 fireworks factories in the town, and most of the *firecrackers* used in India are produced in Sivakasi. At the turn of the 20th century it was an area of rivalry between the low caste **Nadar** community and the higher castes, reflected in the continuing struggles today over caste discrimination in India.

The history is illuminating. In 1874 Nadars tried to enter the Minakshi temple in Madurai, but were refused permission. In 1876 they tried to enter the Tirumangalam temple, but again were refused. In 1899 they petitioned to gain entry to the *Visvanathasvami* temple in Sivakasi but were turned down once more. They then tried to gain entry to temples wherever they were numerous enough. High caste Hindus began to object strongly, and on 26 April 1899 Sivakasi Nadars burnt 55 houses belong to a higher caste group, the *Maravars*. As a reprisal, on 6 June 1899 the Maravar community organised a huge demonstration which led to widespread rioting. Nadar houses were looted and set on fire and police and the army had to be called from as far afield as Trichy. 1,958 people were arrested, 552 were convicted and 7 were executed.

Rajapalayam (*Population* 130,000) 11 km to the S W of Srivilliputtur, the town owes its origins to the dispersal of the Vijayanagar families after 1565 **See page 843**. The Western Ghats rise to heights of over 1,200 m immediately behind the town. Wild elephants continue to come down through the forests, causing devastation to farm land. The town has become a centre of small scale industry, including engineering and food processing industries. The road over the Ghats is narrow and winding, though nowhere particularly steep. It passes through **Puliangudi** (39 km *Population* 54,000) and **Ilattur** to **Tenkasi** (37 km Population 65,000). A small railway town, Tenkasi is nearest town to the **Kuttalam Falls** (Courtallam Falls). These are an extremely popular health resort, especially between

Jun and Sep. The River Chittar cascades over 92 m. With average temperatures of 22°-23°C, the waters are widely believed to have great curative powers.

From Tenkasi the road heads NW through **Shenkottai** (10 km *Population* 32,000) to the pass across the Ghats. The town has major saw mills using timber from the surrounding hills. There are magnificent views from this road as it approaches the narrow pass, much better than from the metre gauge railway line below, which heads for the tunnel through which it passes into Kerala. Stretched out is a panoramic view of intensively cultivated and lush green paddy fields, interspersed with irrigation tanks, leading down onto the open plains below. From **Tenmalai** (21 km) you can either take the direct but slow road through **Nedumangad** (51 km) to **Trivandrum** (18 km).or the longer alternative route from Tenmalai via **Punalur** (21 km) to **Kottarakara** (21 km), **Ayur** (20 km), and **Kilimanur** (20 km) to **Trivandrum** (40 km).

MADURAI TO COCHIN (Via Thekkadi And Kottayam)

The most direct route from Madurai to Cochin crosses the Western Ghats at the Periyar-Thekkadi game reserve, then going down through **Permed** and **Kottayam**. From Thekkadi it is equally possible to go S to Trivandrum. Allow three hours by road up to Thekkadi. In all the small towns there are tea shops and cold drink stalls.

From Madurai take the NH 7 W to **Usilampatti** (39 km *Population* 32,000), skirting the northern end of the Andipatti Hills as they stretch northeastwards from the Western Ghats. At **Teni** (35 km *Population* 70,000), an important market town at the head of the artificial lake created by the *Vaigai Dam*, turn left and travel up the Kambam Valley. The road passes through a succession of market towns. Irrigation supports paddy and sugar cane as well as some cotton on the rich valley floor soils, which are both well watered and well drained. Away from the river and its irrigation the soils are thinner and poorer, and on the dry land sorghum, bajra, groundnut and cotton are grown. The *Suruli River* is supplemented by the waters of the *Periyar*, which were diverted eastwards through the crest of the Ghats by the Periyar scheme, completed in 1897. **Chinnamanur** (22 km *Population* 40,000), **Uttampalayam** (6 km) and **Kambam** (11 km *Population* 64,000) lie on the valley floor, but from **Gudalur** (10 km *Population* 48,000) the road rises steeply up the Ghat.

The Ghat section of the road continues for 70 km across to **Mundakayam** in Kerala. As is true with many of the Ghat roads it gives wonderful views on the 14 kilometres stretch up to **Kumili** and **Thekkadi**. The road to Thekkadi (*Altitude* 1000 m) is a left turn 1 km after passing through Kumili. (**See page 835.**) The road through Kerala passes down through tea (on the higher slopes) and rubber plantations (at middle levels). Cardamom is grown in lightly shaded areas, often on small holdings, as is ginger, coffee and pepper. On flat land, even at high altitude, rice is grown. After 14 km the road passes through **Vandiperiyar** (*Altitude* 900 m) and a further 19 km **Peermed** (*Altitude* 1130 m). There is a further 22 km of ghat road. After passing through **Mundakayam** (22 km from Peermed) it goes through **Kanjirapalli** (16 km), where it is joined by a road on the left from **Changanacherry**. Lower down approaching **Kottayam** (39 km) there are gardens of areca nut, coconut, banana, pepper and cashew. For the remainder of the route to **Cochin** (38 km) **See page 821.**

MADURAI TO COCHIN (Via Kodaikkanal, Palani &Trichur)

The bus journey from Madurai to Kodaikkanal takes 3 hours. The route follows the NH 45 northwest to Kodai Road, then branches off to Batlagundu. It moves from the fertile and shaded irrigated lowlands around Madurai, to the upper dry land on the land to the N of the Vaigai River.

Kodai Road (40 km) is nothing but a railway halt, change here if travelling from Madras to Kodai. *Batlagundu* (20 km *Population* 24,000) is an attractive small town, with an active market, a busy shopping area and a range of tea and cold drink shops. Surrounded by irrigated land, with sugar cane and rice occupying the best land, millets the upper land, just outside Batlagundu is a boys' orphanage (*Boys' Town*) which supports itself by producing a range of products from food stuffs and spices to handcrafts. You'll see their products widely available.

The ghat road to begins about 20 km out of Batlagundu. It is one of the most rapid ascents anywhere across the Ghats. Be prepared with some warm clothing for the increasing coolness, particularly if you are travelling between December and March, and if you are going up in the late afternoon. The views are stunning, and there are several excellent places to stop, though the buses usually only stop occasionally, and not at places to admire the view. In the lower reaches of the climb you look down over the *Kambam valley*, the *Vaigai Lake* and across to the *Varushanad Hills* beyond. The road twists and winds up through rapidly changing vegetation, but generally wooded slopes.

Kodaikkanal

40 km. *Population* 26,500. *Altitude* 2,343 m. *Climate* Temp. Summer Max. 21°C Min. 11°C, Winter Max. 17°C Min. 5°C. (Frosts are not uncommon at night) *Best Season* Apr-June, Aug-Sep. Heavy rains from Oct to Dec. *Clothing* Summer Light woollens, Winter Warm woollens. The nearest airport is at Madurai 124 km away and the nearest Railway Station is a Kodai Road 80 km away.

	Jan	Feb	Mar	Apr	May	Jun	Jul	Aug	Sep	Oct	Nov	Dec	Av/Tot
Max (°C)	18	19	20	20	21	18	15	17	18	19	19	18	19
Min (°C)	5	6	8	10	11	11	11	10	10	10	9	7	9
Rain (mm)	43	21	73	231	169	96	129	122	157	263	237	123	1664

The *Palani Hills* were first surveyed by British administrators in 1821, but the surveyor's report was not published until 1837 – 10 years after Ooty had become the official " sanitorium" for the British in S India. A proposal to build a sanitorium was made in 1861-2, when Colonel Hamilton reported that "the climate of the Upper Palanis is considered to be exceedingly salubrious: and no sickness of any kind is known to be endemic or epidemic upon them. They are too lofty to be visited by the ordinary malarious fever of India; too sparsely populated to be scourged by typhus and typhoids. And having a much drier air and more equable temperature than the Nilgiris, they are said to be far better suited to children and invalids. " Despite the warmth of that recommendation the sanitarium was never built because the site was so difficult to get to from the plains below. Yet it was the freedom from malaria that was the greatest incentive to opening a hill station

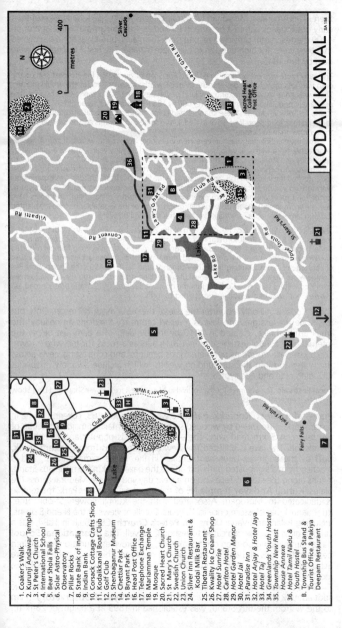

KODAIKKANAL SA 158

1. Coaker's Walk
2. Kurunji Andawar Temple
3. St Peter's Church
4. International School
5. Bear Shola Falls
6. Solar Astro-Physical Observatory
7. Pillar Rocks
8. State Bank of India
9. Indian Bank
10. Corsack Cottage Crafts Shop
11. Kodaikkanal Boat Club
12. Golf Club
13. Shenbaganur Museum
14. Chettiar Park
15. Bryant Park
16. Head Post Office
17. Telephone Exchange
18. Mariamman Temple
19. Mosque
20. Sacred Heart Church
21. St Mary's Church
22. Swedish Church
23. Union Church
24. Silver Inn Restaurant & Kodai Milk Bar
25. Tibetan Restaurant
26. Kwality Ice Cream Shop
27. Hotel Sunrise
28. Carlton Hotel
29. Hotel Garden Manor
30. Hotel Jai
31. Paradise Inn
32. Hotel Anjay & Hotel/Jaya
33. Hotel Taj
34. Greenlands Youth Hostel
35. Township New Rest House Annexe
36. Hotel Tamil Nadu & Youth Hostel
B. Township Bus Stand & Tourist Office & Pakiya Deepam Restaurant

there. The American Mission in Madurai, established in 1834, had lost 6 of their early missionaries within a decade. It looked as if the **Sirumalai Hills**, at around 1300 metres, might provide a respite from the plains, but it was soon discovered that they were not high enough to eliminate malaria. The first 2 bungalows were built by Jun 1845.

The early route was extraordinarily difficult. For 5 km of zig-zag on the steepest section the path was less than 1 m wide, and the average width was only 2 m for the whole journey. There was no question of getting any kind of vehicle up the hills. Despite the obstacles, the permanent population had reached over 600 by 1883. 7 years later it stood at 1,743 according to the first official census. These changes had come about partly because Europeans began to spend their long periods of leave in Kodai, and some civil servants and missionaries retired there rather than to Europe.

The most influential was Sir Vere Henry Levinge, and in the words of the American geographer Nora Mitchell, who herself lived in Kodai for many years, "it was acclaimed by Europeans and Americans alike that most of the improvements in Kodaikkanal were due to his interest and generosity. He constructed the bund which dammed the stream to form Kodai lake, stocked the lake with fish, and brought up the first boat from Tuticorin. His experiments with foreign varieties of trees, fruits, and flowers have had enduring results as eucalyptus, wattle, and pines are now grown extensively by the forestry department, and pears have become an important export from the hill station. many of the vegetables he tried are planted today in large quantities in Kodaikkanal and the surrounding villages."

The major transformation came at the turn of the 20th century with the arrival of the car and the bus. The **Raja of Pudukkottai** had a French car in 1904, but could not use it to get to Kodai because of the lack of a road (**see page 775**). Although a new road had been started in 1876, along the line of the present road from Vatlagundu, it was left incomplete because of shortage of funds resulting from the Afghan War in 1876. In 1905 the Trichinopoly Bus Company set up a bus service to Periyakulam, making it possible to do the whole journey from Kodai Road station to Kodai within the hours of daylight. In 1914 the present road, up "Law's Ghat" was begun again, and opened to traffic in 1916.

Today Kodai is still only a quarter the size of the other major hill resort, Ooty, but it is none the less growing fast as a resort centre for S Indians on holiday. The small artificial lake, created in 1910 by the building of a dam just below the International School (established in 1901), acts as a focus for the whole town. The 5 km walk around its perimeter gives beautiful and contrasting views across the water and into the surrounding woods, which include a variety of species including pine and eucalyptus.

Local Festivals The Summer Tourist Festival in May. Boat Race, Flower Show and Dog Show and other entertainments.

Places of interest *Kodaikkanal Lake* was formed in 1863, covering 24 ha in a star shape surrounded by wooded slopes, and it remains a major attraction of the resort. A 5 km road skirts the edge. Boating is popular and fishing with permission. The lake is polluted.The view over the plains from **Coaker's walk,** built by the engineer Lieutenant Coaker in the 1870s is magnificent, and is reached from a signposted path just above the bazaar, a km from the Bus Stand. It runs along the steep S face and on a clear day you can see Madurai across the plains. **Kurinji Andavar Temple** NE of the town, past Chettiar Park, the temple is dedicated to Murugan. Associated with the kurinji flower (Strobilanthes kunthianus) that blossom once in 12 years. Excellent views of the N and S plains, including Palani and Vagai Dams. **St. Peter's Church** (CSI) built in 1884, has a stained glass window dedicated to Bishop Caldwell. **The International School** has a commanding position on the lakeside, and provides education for children between the ages of 5 and 18 from India and abroad. There is also the Highclere School for Girls and the Bhavan's Gandhi Vidyasram School, founded in 1983, located on the way to Pillar Rocks.

Bear Shola Falls, named because it once attracted bears, is a favourite picnic spot about 2 km from the Bus Stand. **Solar Astro-Physical Observatory** 6 km to the W from the Bus Stand, was established in 1899 at a height of 2347 m.

Open to the public on weekdays between 1000-1230, 1900-2100 during season. Otherwise Fri between 1000-1200. **Pillar Rocks**, 7 km from the lake, is another striking viewpoint. There are three granite formations over 120 m high. **Dolmens** and other megalithic remains. There are over 100 dolmens that have been discovered in the Palanis, all datable to around the 2nd century AD.

NB Whenever you are in Kodai the mist can come down, especially in the afternoon, so you cannot guarantee the wonderful views.

Hotels Most offer off-season discounts from 1st July to 14th Oct and 15th Jan to 31st Mar. The majority have double rm with bath in the **B** to **D** categories, only a few have single rm. The more expensive hotels are some distance from the centre.

B *Carlton*, Boat Club Rd. T 252, Cable: Carlton, Telex: 0445-285 Carl In. 93 rm. Restaurant, bar, barbecue, exchange, travel, shops, health club, putting green, TV. Tennis, golf and boating on the lake arranged. Excellent position overlooking the lake. **C** *Sornam Apartments*, Fern Hill Rd. T 431, Cable: Sornapuri. 6 apartments. Restaurant (Indian), coffee shop. **D** *Garden Manor*, Lake Rd. T 525, Cable: Garden. Restaurant. Good lakeside location. **D** *Jai* Lloyds Rd, T 344. **E** *Tamil Nadu*, TTDC, Fern Hill Rd, T 481. Inconveniently located at least 15 min on foot from Bus Station and the most interesting walks. Restaurant and bar, with cheap **F** *Youth Hostel*. Reservations: Manager Hotels, or Youth Hostel, TNTDC, 143 Anna Salai, Madras, T 849803. **E** *Anjay*, Anna Salai, T 489. **E** *Jaya*, Anna Salai nr Bazaar. **E** *Taj*, Coakers Walk nr the centre has pleasant double rm in an old building. **F** *Youth Hostel*, Greenlands, end of Coakers Walk. Very basic but superb views. Dormitory and two double rm with bath. **F** *Township New Rest House Annexe*, Poet Thyagaraja Rd. **F** *Township Bus Stand Rest House*, Anna Salai. **F** *Tay Lodge*, end of Coaker's Walk. Very primitive and rustic, but friendly staff.

Restaurants Best at the *Carlton Hotel*. Multi-cuisine at *Garden Manor* and *Tamil Nadu* and Indian vegetarian at Sornam. *Pakiya Deepam* opp the Bus Stand and *Apna Punjab* in 7 Rd are Indian restaurants. On Hospital Rd are *Silver Inn Restaurant*, the *Kodai Milk Bar*, *Tibetan Restaurant* and *Kwality Ice Creams* opp Kodai International School. There are a few bakeries – *Jacob* in the Main Bazar, PO Rd, *Vasu* on Lake Rd nr the Telephone Exchange, and the tiny *Manna Bakery* on Bear Shola Rd which also serves pizzas and western veg food.

Banks State Bank of India, T 468 and Indian Bank, T 442. and others on the main Bazaar Rd, Anna Salai.

Shopping *Kashmir Handicrafts Centre*, 2 N Shopping Complex, Anna Salai for shawls, jewellery, brass, leather, marble, bone and walnut wood articles and 'Numdah' rugs. *Khadi Emporium, Handloom Cooperative Stores, Travancore Craft Works*, Post Office Rd. *Government Sales Emporium* nr Township Bus Stand is only open during the season. The *Cottage Crafts Shop*, Anna Salai (Council for Social Concerns in Kodai) is run by volunteers. *Philco's Cold Storage*, opp Kodai International School for Confectionery, cakes, frozen foods, delicatessen. **Books** – *CLS Bookshop*, Anna Salai, T 229.

Local transport *Taxi* Unmetred taxis available. Tourist Taxis only from Madurai. *Bicycles* can be hired at the top of the Bazaar.

Sports Boating – **Kodaikkanal Boat Club**, T 315 which allows daily membership with club facilities. **Golf Club**, T 323. **Riding** You can hire ponies by the hour near the Boat House and may have to bargain down the price. Going rate approximately Rs 20 per hour during season.

Museums Shenbaganur Museum is maintained by the Sacred Heart College, a theological seminary founded in 1895. In addition to local flora and fauna it has archaeological remains. The Orchid House has an excellent collection with more than 300 species. Open 1000-1130, 1530-1700, closed Sun. Attractive walk down hill from the town passing waterfalls.

Parks and zoos *Chettiar Park* is in the NE of the town on the way to the Kurinji Andavar Temple. *Bryant Park* on the lakeside is where the annual horticultural show is held in May.

Post and telegraph You can make STD calls from the Telephone Exchange, the Boat Club and the kiosk at the back of the Tourist Information Office at Township Rest House in the Main Bazaar. *Head Post Office* on Post Office Rd, T 241. Others in Main Bazar, Observatory, Lake View, Anantha Giri, Pambapuram and Shenbaganur.

Places of worship *Hindu* – Kurinji Andavar Temple, Mariamman Temple, Vinayakar Temple, Murugan Temple. *Muslim* – Mosque, Bliss Villa, Mosque in Munjikal. *Christian* – Sacred Heart Church, Munjikal, Mount Zion Church, St Peter's, Swedish Church, Francis Xavier Church, St Mary's Church.

Hospitals and medical services Government Hospital, T 292. Van Allan Hospital, T 273. Hindu Mission Clinic, Observatory Rd. Dental Clinic, Lake Rd. Chemists – Anand Medical, 5 Shopping Complex.

Tourist Office and information Government of Tamil Nadu, Department of Tourism, Township Bus Stand, Rest House Complex. Open 1000-1700, Mon-Fri.

Rail Reservations for Kodai Road Station trains from the agents at Jayaraj Hall, Coakers Walk Rd.

Bus Direct buses to Cuddalore, Dindigul (90 km), Kodai Road (80 km), Madras (497 km), Madurai (120 km), Palani (65 km), Trichy (197 km), Coimbatore (171 km) during the season, among others. Frequent service to Madurai (3 to 4 hr journey) and several to the other destinations. Also one daily to Kumili for the Periyar Wildlife Sanctuary, 4½ hrs. Bangalore has an overnight service by the Karnataka SRTC. RMTC Bus Stand.

Excursions *Berijam Lake* A road runs W past the golf course and **Pillar rocks** to Berijam Lake, some 15 km away. The road itself has beautiful views, especially over Berijam Lake, before running down to the lakeside. Apart from timber lorries the road is little used. Some maps show the road as going through to **Munnar**, one of the most attractive routes in the whole of S India. Unfortunately in recent years it has been made impassable to ordinary cars by the heavy traffic of the timber lorries, and a four wheel drive vehicle is essential to complete the journey across the highest road in peninsular India into Kerala.

The ghat road to Palani was opened in the 1970s. It is not heavily used, and gives superb views of the lower Palani Hills. It passes through the mixture of coffee, orange and banana smallholdings typical of this range of hills. Since the mid 1980s some of these have seen major improvements and considerable investment. Interplanting of crops such as pepper are further increasing the yields from what can be highly productive land, even on steep slopes. The dangers of incautious cultivation however are of greatly increased erosion. This road was built in part with money given by the Palani Temple Fund (*devasthanam*).

Palani (35 km *Population* 85,000) The hill top shrine to **Murugan** is a very important site of pilgrimage. At full moon in Jan-Feb pilgrims walk from up to 80 km around to the shrine. Many carry shoulder-poles with elaborate bamboo or wooden structures on each end, living out the myth which surrounds the origin of the shrine.

David Shulman tells how the sage **Agastya** "was given two hills, *Shivagiri* and *Shaktigiri*, as sites of worship, with permission to take them S. One day he met the demon, Itumpan... Seeing he was of a good nature, Agastya sent him to bring the hills. When Itumpan arrived at the hills, a shoulder-pole appeared, and the eight serpents which support the world took the form of ropes so he could tie the hills to the support. In this way he lifted the mountains and carried them southwards until he reached Palani. Suddenly he felt faint; he put the hills down and rested, but when he tried to lift them again he could not move them. Puzzled and sorrowful, he climbed one of the trees, and there he noticed a child under a tree. "Go away" he said to the child, and added that he was a murderous demon. "This is my home," said the child; "pick it up if you can!" "You may be small in size but you tell big lies," cried Itumpan as he leaped at the boy. But the child was **Murugan**, playing his games; he killed Itumpan at a stroke. When Itumpan's wife Itumpi heard of her husband's death, she prayed to Murugan, who revived him. Agastya came to worship Murugan at that spot, and he ordered the demon to serve Murugan there for his salvation."

Accommodation in **F** Sri Venkateswara Lodge, Adivaram, T 220. **F** Devasthanam Rest House, Dandapani Nilayam, T 325.

The route to the W coast continues through **Udumalpet** (32 km *Population* 70,000) – **Pollachi** (29 km *Population* 107,000) – **Alathur** (50 km) then to **Trichur** (40 km); S down NH 47 to Angamaly (43 km) – Alwaye (11 km) – Cochin (21 km). A highly picturesque alternative is available from Udumalpet via Munnar (87 km) – Perumbavur (97 km) – Alwaye (15 km) – Cochin (21 km).

COIMBATORE TO BANGALORE (Via Palghat)

The major route to Bangalore is along NH 47 and NH 7. The shortest route is across the Nilgiris via Ooty and Mysore. However, there is another very attractive alternative via the Palghat gap, Coorg and Mysore. This is as follows:

Coimbatore to **Palghat** (48 km) This important route town commands the most important gap through the southern part of the Western Ghats which has been used by traders since before Roman times. The railway line from Karnataka and Tamil Nadu to Kerala passes through Palghat.

Rail Coimbatore: *Kerala-Mangala Link Exp*, 2625/2625A (AC/II), daily, 1800, 1 hr 15 min; **Madras**: *Madras Exp*, 6042 (AC/II), daily, 2015, 9 hr 50 min; **Ernakulam Jn**: *Kerala-Mangala Exp*, 2626 (AC/II), daily, 0845, 2 hr 55 min; **Cochin**: *Guwahati/Haora Exp*, 2650/2652 (AC/II), Mon, Sat, Sun, 1440, 3 hr 50 min.

From Palghat the road goes through Mannarkhad (40 km) – Mannerji (42 km) – Kozhikode (Calicut; 33 km) – Tellicherry (67 km) – Cannanore (21 km) – Virajpet (63 km) – Mercara (43 km) – Periyapatna (40 km) – Hunsur (24 km) – Mysore (59 km) – Srirangapatnam (14 km) – Mandya (23 km) – Channapatna (45 km) – Bangalore (48 km). These places are described separately under the routes from Cochin to Cannanore and Bangalore.

KERALA

The name Kerala is recorded in Asoka's edicts before the start of the Christian era, over a thousand years before the Malayalam language of contemporary Kerala took shape, and was applied to the area known in Tamil as *Seranadu*. For many this is India's most idyllic state. "Overall our favourite state in India – very lush, beautiful scenery, coastline and backwaters" wrote two recent travellers. Although it is India's most densely populated region it has a distinctive charm which belies the statistics which suggest that it is also one of India's poorest states. High levels of education and health care have given Kerala an enviable reputation elsewhere in India, and its unique balance of Hindu, Muslim and Christian sets it apart even from next door neighbours Tamil Nadu and Karnataka.

Population 30 million. *Area* 39,000 sq km. *Chief cities* Cochin 900,000, Trivandrum 650,000. *Literacy* 90% (female 85%) (1991).

Social indicators *Literacy* M 70% F 66% *Newspaper circulation:* 1,496,000 *Birth rate* Rural 25:1000 Urban 25:1000 *Death rate* Rural 7:1000 Urban 7:1000. *Infant mortality* Rural 32:1000, Urban 24:1000 *Registered graduate job seekers* 2,457,000 *Average annual income per head* : Rs 1379 *Inflation 1981-87* 67% *Newspaper circulation* 60:1000 (nearly 3 x national av.)

Religion *Hindu* 58% *Muslim* 21% *Christian* 21%

Towns and cities 21% of the population lives in towns. The twin towns of

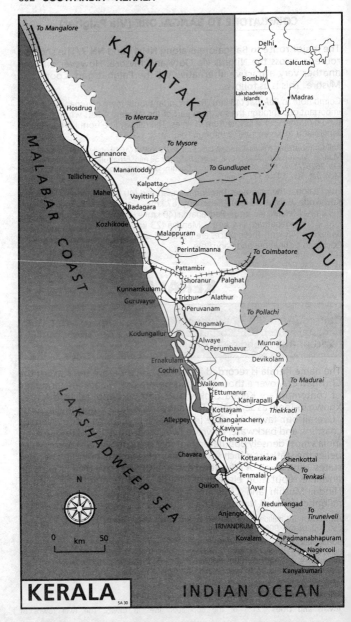

Cochin-Ernakulam are the largest in the state, with the state capital Trivandrum third.

INTRODUCTION

The land
Kerala is formed on the W slopes and coastal plains of the Western Ghats. The steep face of the Ghats was formed by the sliding of the ocean floor along the fault line of the Ghats as the Indian Peninsula moved NE across the Arabian Sea from its old position attached to Southern Africa. However, in recent geological time the coastline has been raised, causing the narrow coastal fringe that makes up Kerala and the shoreline to its N to emerge from the sea. This is proved partly by the discovery of coral formations under the alluvium of Kerala several km inland. The land is continuing to extend seawards, for example around Cochin. Physically the state can be divided into 3 parallel regions. On the coast itself is a narrow band of alluvium, visible for example around Trivandrum airport. Immediately inland are low, rolling hills of laterite, then inland again the ancient gneisses of the Peninsula which form the backbone of the Western Ghats.

Climate
Kerala has an almost equatorial climate. Maximum temperatures are always moderated by the sea and rarely rise above 32°C. Minimum temperatures at sea level are never below 20°C. The annual range at Cochin is 6°C. The hill slopes have very heavy rainfall, especially in the N. The crest of the Western Ghats receives over 3,000 mm a year, mainly from May to Nov.

Trivandrum in the S has about half that total rainfall. Although Kerala is strongly affected by the monsoon it does not have the extended dry season characteristic of the rest of India. 40% of its rain falls between Jun and Aug, 33% from Sep to Nov and a further 28% from Dec to May.

People
Malayalam, the State language, is the most recent of the Dravidian languages, developing its present form from the thirteenth century. However, the region has been distinct from its neighbours for far longer than that might suggest. Its coastline stretches over 550 km from Karnataka to within 100 km of the S tip of India, but nowhere is it more than 120 km wide. Both its wet climate and its inaccessibility by land from the rest of peninsular India have helped to make Kerala one of India's most distinctive regions. That distinctiveness is still highly visible today. If you enter Kerala from neighbouring Tamil Nadu you are immediately struck by the rich greenness of the vegetation and the sheer number of people. Every cm of available land is used – for agriculture, for plantations, for forestry or for settlements. There does not seem to be a single road that is not crowded with people. But the distinctiveness goes far beyond either the nature of the landscape or the density of population. Although Hinduism is still dominant, as much as a quarter of the population is Christian, the majority tracing their Christian roots back at least 1,500 years. There is a also a significant Muslim population.

Many of the social indicators suggest a relatively high quality of life. Kerala has more than twice the literacy rate than any other state in India and an infant mortality less than one quarter that of the national average. Women enjoy a high social status, perhaps partly a reflection of the matrilineal system which was common in pre-modern times. Yet in the hills are some of India's most primitive tribes, and on the coastal plains there remain too few economic opportunities for the growing population. Very large numbers of Malayalis have emigrated to find work, in recent years to the Gulf. It is one of the 2 Indian states, along with W Bengal, where Communists have played a major part in government for several periods since Independence, perhaps reflecting the high rate of literacy and sophistication in both states.

Economy

Despite its progressive social character, by some economic indicators Kerala is only a middle ranking Indian State – 7th in the mid 1970s and 9th in the mid 1980s. Since the middle 1970s the flow of migrants from Kerala to the Gulf increased rapidly, and remittances have played an increasing role in the lives of many villagers. Kerala accounted for over half the total Indian emigration to the Gulf up to the end of the 1980s. However, remittances have not been invested in productive industry apart from building, the evidence of which can be seen in many parts of the State. Ironically, the greater the flow of remittances, the slower has been Kerala's economic growth, particularly in the productive sectors of the economy. There are some exceptions, the most notable being banking and insurance and transport and communications. The returned Kerala migrants' liking for cars and motorbikes is well known! Most migrants came from the coastal districts of Trivandrum, Trichur, Malappuram, Kozhikode and Cannanore. In these areas land prices rocketed tenfold in the years 1975-86. The Gulf War in 1991 caused a severe drop in remittances and the return of thousands of migrants.

Although unemployment has remained extremely high, in some semi-skilled areas there have been labour shortages that have pushed up wage rates and encouraged migrants to come in from neighbouring states, especially Tamil Nadu. Most of the new money from remittances has gone on consumption. Strikingly it is the poorer families who have benefited most, even though there has been a significant drain of skilled workers as well. Most of the increases in demand for consumer goods in Kerala have been met by imports from other states of India – rice, pulses, sugar, medicine, clothing, cosmetics and construction materials. That trade has produced a huge State financial deficit. Ironically Kerala's trade overseas – tea, cardamom, ginger, rubber, produces big surpluses.

Industry and resources The traditional coir industry which has supported the Malabar coastal economy still thrives. The **coconut palm** which grows in abundance is made use of in a dozen different ways. Annually, each palm produces around 80 nuts which are harvested and the fibrous outer covering is removed. The coir is obtained by soaking the fibres in water for some months, dried and beaten with a stick, then the coir is woven into mats or twisted into rope. Each part of the tree is put to use, the trunk for building houses or boats, the leaves for thatching or baskets, the 'milk' for drink, fresh or fermented. The fleshy white kernel is eaten or used for oil or soap making and the hard outer shell dried to be turned into bowls or pots or simply burnt as fuel.

Handicrafts The availability of *wood* in the lush forests of Kerala has made the state excel in wood work. You can see excellent carving in temples and palaces and also buy articles made out of rose wood and inlaid with other woods or bone or plastics (to replace the traditional ivory), or wooden boxes with brass binding where plain or patterned strips of brass are used for decoration. A popular item for the tourists is carved models of the snake boats. The home of Kathakali dance, Kerala also produces *masks* and *theatrical ornaments*, particularly the *Krishnattam* masks which resemble the mask-like make up of the Kathakali dancers. *Conch shells* which are also available in great numbers are carved out in relief.

History

Early History Kerala, "the land of the Cheras" is referred to in Asoka's rock inscriptions between 273-236 BC, but although other outsiders made fleeting references to the region, and the Romans carried on extensive trade through it, very little is known about the Cheras before the 8th century AD. Unlike many other parts of India there are virtually no archaeological remains before the **megalithic monuments** of the 2nd century BC and after. Although such remains are common elsewhere in S India Kerala developed its own distinctive types, most strikingly the so-called hood-stones (*kudaikal*) and hat-stones (*topi-kal*) and rock cut tombs. All three have umbrella-like forms, which was a symbol of authority and power. Many can still be seen.

Periodically the region had been under Tamil control, whether of the **Pandiyans** or the **Cholas**, but in about AD 800 the *Cheras* re-established themselves. This second dynasty ruled over various parts of what is now modern Kerala until 1102, developing considerable economic prosperity and a wide network of trading relationships, in which both the long established Christian community and the Jewish community participated fully. However, the neighbouring Cholas launched several successful attacks against Chera power from AD 985 onwards, preventing the emergence of a united Kerala kingdom. When Chola power itself disintegrated at the end of the 11th century minor principalities emerged, dominated by a new group, the Nambudiri Brahmans. Up until the arrival of the Portuguese in 1498 three chieftains had control over the major ports and hence the region's vital trade in spices – pepper, ginger, cardamom and cinnamon. Venadu formed the southern, Calicut the central and Kolattiri the northern region respectively. Of these **Calicut** gradually became dominant under its ruler, the **Zamorin** (literally "*Lord of the Sea*"). He had well established contacts with the Arab world, and by some accounts was the wealthiest ruler in contemporary India.

The *Zamorin* was unable to use these advantages to unite Kerala, and during the sixteenth century the Portuguese were able to exploit the rivalry of the Raja of Kolattiri with the Zamorin of Calicut, being granted permission to trade from Cochin in 1499. Over the following century there was fierce competition and sometimes open warfare between the Portuguese, bent on eliminating Arab trading competition, and the Zamorin of Calicut, whose prosperity depended on that Arab trade. The competition was encouraged by the rulers of Cochin, in the hope that by keeping the hands of both tied in conflict their own independence would be strengthened. After a century of hostility and intermittent conflict a new force arrived on the W coast in the shape of the Dutch. The Zamorin of Calicut seized the opportunity of gaining external support, and on 11 November 1614 concluded a Treaty giving the Dutch full trading rights. In 1615 the British E India Company was also given the right to trade by the Zamorin. By 1633 the Dutch had captured all the Portuguese forts of Quilon, Cranganore, Purakkad, Cochin and Cannanore. The ruler of Cochin rapidly made friends with the Dutch, in exchange having the new Mattancheri Palace built for him, and inevitably facing renewed conflict with Calicut as a result.

***Travancore* and the British** In the decade after 1740 a new force emerged in Travancore (now S Kerala). King Martanda Varma succeeded in uniting a number of petty states around Trivandrum and led them to a crushing victory over the Dutch in the Battle of Kolachel in 1741. By 1758 the Zamorin of Calicut was forced to withdraw from Cochin, but the Travancore rulers' reign was brief. In 1766 **Haidar Ali** had led his cavalry troops down onto the western coastal plain, and he and his son **Tipu Sultan** pushed further and further S with a violence that is still bitterly remembered. In 1789, as Tipu was preparing to launch a final assault on the S of Travancore, the British attacked him from the E. He withdrew his army from Kerala and the Zamorin and other Kerala leaders looked to the British to take control of the forts previously held by Tipu's officers. Tipu Sultan's first defeat at the hands of **Lord Cornwallis** led to the Treaty of Seringapatam in 1792, under which Tipu surrendered all his captured territory in Malabar, the N part of Kerala, to direct British rule. Travancore and Cochin became Princely states under ultimate British authority.

Modern History The reorganisation of the Indian States in 1956 brought together the Malayalam language area of Kerala into one political unit for the first time. It comprises all except some of the Kanniyakumari districts of

Travancore, Cochin, Malabar and a part of S Kanara District from Karnataka.

Religion

Kerala has had an unusually peaceful history of relations among its different religious communities. There is no conflict between the varying Hindu sects, and most temples have shrines to each of the major Hindu divinities. Christianity, which is thought to have been brought by **St Thomas the Apostle** to the coast of Kerala at Cranganore in AD 52, has its own very long tradition. The Portuguese tried to convert the Syrian Christians to Roman Catholicism, but although they established a thriving Catholic Church the Syrian tradition survived in various forms. The equally large Muslim community traces its origins back to the spread of Islam across the Indian Ocean with Arab traders from the 7th century, and is particularly strong in the N of the state. In the last 15 years the Muslim community responded quickly to the new opportunities in the Gulf. It suffered correspondingly from the dramatic repatriation of Indian workers in 1990-91.

Local festivals

Kerala has several distinctive festivals. In Jan-Feb *Ulsavam* is celebrated with an eight-day celebration at the Ernakulam Siva Temple. An elephant procession and folk dance and musical performances are staged. In **Guruvayur** this festival is celebrated at the end of Feb. In Apr-May *Vishukani* celebrates the start of the rainy season and the sowing of the main paddy crop. The fire crackers exploded to ward off evil spirits can be quite terrifyingly loud if you're close to them. On the eve of the festival families place a large bell metal container between 2 lamps and filled with rice and *Nava Dhanyas* or 9 kinds of grain each in a banana leaf cup, a picture of a favourite goddess, cash, jewellery and fruit. Next day, at dawn the family first look at the gifts of nature, in the hope that it will bring prosperity through the year.

In **Trichur** the festival of *Pooram* occurs in April-May. 30 elaborately bedecked elephants carrying priests and deities are taken out in procession through streets specially decorated with lamps and palm leaves with the accompaniment of music and terminating with a grand display of fireworks. The biggest and most important festival is held in Aug-Sep. *Onam* is a harvest festival, celebrated throughout Kerala in the month of *Chingom* (Aug/Sep) and lasts for four days. According to legend it is on the first day that the good Asura king Mahabali who once ruled Kerala, comes from exile to visit his beloved people. Homes are prepared for his visit, decorated with flowers. It is accompanied by elephant processions, Kathakali dances, fire works, water carnivals and *vallam kalli*, the famous snake boat races, sometimes with over 100 oarsmen per boat. The last is held at several places, including **Alleppey**, **Kottayam**, **Cochin**, **Aranmula** and **Payipad**.

Dance

Kathakali See page 685. The special dance form of Kerala has its origins in the *Theyyam*, a ritual tribal dance of N Kerala and *kalarippayattu*, the highly skilled martial arts practised by the high-caste Nayars, which go back 1,500 years. In its present form of sacred dance-drama, Kathakali has evolved over the last 400 years. The performance is usually out of doors, the stage is bare but for a lamp (now helped by electric lighting), with the drummers on one side and the singers with cymbal and gong, who act as narrators, on the other. The art of mime reaches its peak in these highly stylised performances which last through the night. For the performers the preparations begin several hours in advance, since putting on the elaborate make-up and costumes is very time consuming. The final application of a flower seed in the lower eye-lid results in the red eyes you will see on stage.

This classical dance form requires lengthy and hard training to make the body supple, the eyes expressive and the dancer master the 24 *mudras** to express the nine emotions of serenity, wonder, kindness, love, valour, fear, contempt, loathing and anger and a mime vocabulary of several hundred, in addition to music and drumming. They must learn all the major character parts of the core repertoire of about three dozen plays and be able to change roles frequently. The gods and mortals play out their roles and chaos brought about by human ambition but ends in peace and harmony restored by the gods.

Every 12 years N Malabar village communities organize a *Theyyam* festival in which the dancer wears a 9 m tall head dress made of decorated cloth stretched over a bamboo framework. The ancient rituals at a *kavu* shrine preceding the performance, gives the dancer a divine significance even though they all come from the group of *Untouchables**, and the festival of dancing and singing ends with the scattering of rice and blessings and a final feast. *Kavus* were once dedicated to ancient animistic deities.

Kalaripayattu is still practised in kalaris or gymnasia which teaches the special Keralan form of martial arts of unarmed combat.

Mohiniyattam performed by women, is known as the dance of the charmer or temptress and is particularly sensuous. It evolved through the influence of Tamil dancers who brought Bharata Natyam to the Kerala royal courts and the local Kathakali school. It is performed solo as in Bharata Natyam with a similar core repertoire and musical accompaniments but with the addition of *idakkai*, a percussion instrument. **Tullal**, again peculiar to Kerala, is another classical solo dance form which is more popular as it comes closer to contemporary life, and is marked for its simplicity, wit and humour. In addition there are a number of dance forms which are special to each locality and in general all are performed in very colourful, often gaudy, costumes and ornaments and accompanied by singing and drumming.

TRIVANDRUM

Population 550,000. *Altitude* 64 m. *Climate* Temp. Summer Max. 36°C Min. 21°C, Winter Max. 35°C Min. 18°C. Annual rainfall 170 cm. Monsoons from June to Sep. *Clothing* Cottons. *Airport* is 6 km away, 15 min from town centre

	Jan	Feb	Mar	Apr	May	Jun	Jul	Aug	Sep	Oct	Nov	Dec	Av/Tot
Max (°C)	31	32	33	32	31	29	29	29	30	30	30	31	31
Min (°C)	22	23	24	25	25	24	23	22	23	23	23	23	23
Rain (mm)	20	20	43	122	249	331	215	164	123	271	207	73	1838

Trivandrum (*Tiruvananatpuram*) is 87 km from Kanniyakumari, the southern tip of India. It became the capital of the Raja of Travancore in 1750 when the then Raja moved from Padmanabhapuram. The name is derived from *Tiru Ananta Puram*, the abode of the sacred serpent **Ananta** upon whose coils Vishnu lies in the main temple. It is a peaceful, attractive city built on low hills by the sea, very relaxed for a state capital. Away from the centre, you can walk through narrow winding streets with whitewashed houses with red tiled roofs in cool, green gardens. The typical gabled pagoda-like roof style is unique to Kerala and coastal Karnataka. Despite its size it still has the feel of an overgrown village or market town. Although it is simply a stopover en route to other places like the Maldives or Kovalam beach for many people it is an attractive place to get an impression of Kerala town life. Public amenities such as museums, parks, gardens and some shops are usually closed on Mon.

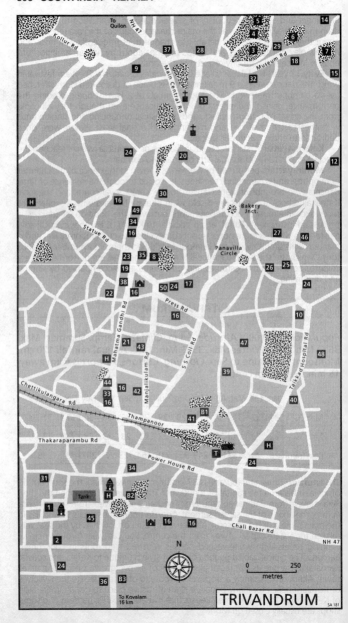

TRIVANDRUM

Local festivals Mar. *Chandanakumad* at Bemmapalli for local Muslims process to the mosque, holding incense sticks and pots. Marked by sword play, singing, dancing, elephant procession and fireworks. Mar/Apr. *Ulsavam* Celebrated at Padmanabhasvami Temple for 10 days with music and dance and procession of elephants. *Arat* Image of Vishnu is taken to the sea for immersion. Also in Oct/Nov. Sep/Oct. *Navaratri* at the special mandapam in Padmanabhasvami Temple. Several concerts which draw famous musicians.

Places of interest **The *Sri Padmanabhasvami Temple*** Only open to Hindus. Unlike Tamil Nadu where non-Hindus may enter a temple complex but not the inner sanctuary, the Kerala Brahmins are stricter and have rules of clothing even for Hindus who must enter wearing only a white *dhoti*. According to legend the temple was built in stages to house the statue which was found in the forest. The original temple where the presiding deity is Vishnu seen reclining on the sacred serpent *Anantha* gives the city its name. It was rebuilt in 1733 by Raja Marthanda Varma who dedicated the whole kingdom, including his rights and possessions, to the deity. Unlike some other famous temples in Kerala, it is in the Dravidian style with beautiful murals, sculptures and 368 carved granite pillars which support the main pavilion or *Kulashekhara Mandapa*. You can see the seven storeyed *gopuram* with its sacred pool from outside. The **Kanakakunnu Palace**, 800 m NE of the Museum: spectacular wooden building in traditional Kerala style which now belongs to the government. **Museum** and **Botanical Gardens, Art Gallery** and the **Zoo** are described below. **Shankhumukham Beach** close to the airport has a stretch of clean sand and is good for relaxing but not suitable for sea bathing.

Local crafts and industries Ivory carving used to be carried out until restrictions imposed by the govt. Wood carving (sandal and rosewood).

Hotels (See also under Kovalam) The central area and the railway station have many very cheap hotels, some excellent value. Even the better hotels are very reasonably priced compared with larger cities elsewhere in India. Attached bath often indicates showers, although a few have bath tubs.

D *Luciya Continental*, E Fort. T 73443, Cable: LUCIYA, Telex: 0884 330 LUCY IN. 104 rm some a/c, in fun decor in 'fantasy suites' with Keralan or old English, and more unusual Chinese and Arab decor. The suites are large with dining area and tubs in bathrooms, with the Kerala Suite particularly recommended. 3 km airport, 1 km rly and bus. Restaurant, coffee shop, exchange, travel, shop, TV. Another good value hotel, rather more expensive than the Mascot or Pankaj. **D** *Mascot* (KTDC), Mascot Junction nr Museum. T 68990, Telex: 0884 229 KTDC IN. 42 rm some a/c. 7 km airport, 4 km rly. Dark and sombre appearance inside, though most of hotel modern construction. Restaurant, bar, exchange, pool. Restaurant, competent without being exciting, but very good value for money. Coffee shop is not always open and the open air Barbecue restaurant is open in the evenings. Close to the Museum, Tourist Office and next to the Indian Airlines office. **D** *Pankaj*, MG Rd, opp Govt Secretariat. T 76257,

---

Trivandrum - Key to map

1. Sri Padmanabhasvami Temple, 2. Bhajanapura Palace, 3. Napier Museum, Open Air Theatre, & natural History Museum, 4. Sri Chitra Art Gallery, 5. Zoo, 6. Kanakunna Palace, 7. Vellayambalum Palace, 8. Secretariat, 9. Museum of Science & Technology, 10. Children's Museum, 11. Forest Museum, 12. Tagore Theatre, 13. Public Library, 14. Cosmopolitan Club, 15. Swimming Pool, 16. Bank, 17. SMSM Handicrafts Emporium, 18. Handicrafts Design Centre, 19. Kairali Handicrafts Emporium, 20. Victoria Jubliee Market, 21. Antiquants, 22. main Post Office, 23. Telegraph Office, 24. Post Office, 25. Foreigner's Registration Office, 26. Maldives Airways, 27. Air Lanka, 28. Indian Airlines, 29. Air India, 30. Kerala Travels, 31. Verma Travels, 32. Govt. of Kerala Tourist Office, 33. Kalandriya Restaurant, 34. Indian Coffee House, 35. Arul Jyoti Restaurant, 36. Hotel Luciya Contiinental, 37. Mascot Hotel, 38. Hotel Pankaj, 39. Hotel Horizon, 40. Hotel Shanthi Woodlands & Annapurna Restaurant, 41. Hotel Chaithram & Tourist Office, 42. Hotel Highlands, 43. Bhaskara Bhavan Tourist Paradise, 44. Omkar Lodge & Safari Restaurant, 45. Rajdhani Tourist Home, 46. Hotel Magnet & Jaihind Travels, 47. Residency Guest House, 48. PWD Rest House, 49. YMCA, 50. YMCA & British Council Library, B1. KSRTC & TTC Bus Station, B2. Fort Bus Station, B3. Bus Station for Kovalam, T. Central Station & Railway Retiring Rooms

Cable: PANKAJ, Telex: 0884 323 PNKJ IN. 50 rm some a/c. 5 km airport, 1 km rly. Multicuisine, two restaurants including rooftop, bar, exchange, TV. very central, first class value for money. **D** *Horizon*, Aristo Rd. T 66888. 47 rm, some a/c with showers. 5 km airport, central. Restaurants, bar, bookshop, TV. Built in 1985, comfortable though simple – suites with sitting rm and bath. The Mira restaurant is multi-cuisine, while the roof top Galaxie is open on weekend evenings but only in the dry season. **D** *Shanthi Woodlands*, Thycaud. T 67415, Telex: 0884 358. Part of the Woodlands chain. Small hotel, 16 rm some a/c. 5 km airport, central. Veg restaurant. **D** *Jazeera*, Medical College. T 76582. **D** *Chaithram*, (KTDC hotel), Station Rd next to station. 88 rm some a/c. 2 restaurants, bar. Very clean. **D** *Highlands*, Manjalikulam Rd, Thampanoor. T 78440. 85 rm, some a/c. Very central, good value.

F *Bhaskara Bhavan Tourist Paradise*, nr Ayurveda College. T 79662. 40 rm. Sombre but clean. Good value. **F** *Omkar Lodge*, MG Rd, opp SMV School. T 78503. 15 rm. Basic. **F** *Rajdhani Tourist Home*, E Fort. T 73353. 50 rm. **F** *Government Rest House*, Thycaud. T 63711. As usual extremely cheap if you can get in.

Youth Hostels F *YMCA Guest House*, Palatam is behind Secretariat, T 68059. **F** *Youth Hostel*, Veli. T 71364. Boating on the lake at the leisure complex. Perhaps the cheapest in Trivandrum! Even cheaper than the dormitory in the **F** *Railway Retiring Rooms*, T 63869.

Restaurants *Hotel Luciya Continental* serves good S Indian food. *Hotel Pankaj*. Excellent food, with sweet stall cum restaurant at its entrance as well as hotel restaurant. *Hotel Horizon's* 2 restaurants, a/c *Mira* and *Galaxie* on roof top. *Safari Restaurant* is multi-cuisine, a/c, with Peeusha bar. *Kalandriya* on MG Rd is a N Indian restaurant nr the Overbridge Jn. *Azad Hotel*, MG Rd, Statue Jn specializes in Muslim dishes and *Annapurna* at Shanthi Woodlands, Thycaud and *Arul Jyoti*, MG Rd, opp Secretariat, Statue Junction, in good S Indian veg. *Indian Coffee House* has 2 branches on MG Rd, one nr YWCA, N of the Secretariat and the other nr E Fort. Several of the hotels and the larger restaurants have **Bars.**

Banks and Exchange Banks in Kerala are open from 1000-1400 from Mon to Fri, and from 1000-1200 on Sat. If you need to change money outside these hours the Airport now has a bank normally open 24 hours. *Baroda*, MG Rd, T 65923. *Canara*, Spencer Junction, T 68051. *Central Bank of India*, MG Rd, T 68547. *Federal*, Palayam, T 62645. *Indian Overseas Bank*, Ayurveda College Junction, T 68489. *Punjab National*, Statue Junction, T 61697. *Reserve Bank of India*, Kowkidar, T 60676. *State Bank of India*, nr Secretariat, T 66683. *State Bank of Travancore*, Marikar Building, T 68344.

Shopping Shops are open usually from 0900 to 2000, though some take a long lunch break. Although ivory goods have now been banned carving of wood and marquetry using other materials such as plastic continue to flourish, and are the hallmark of traditional Kerala handcrafts. These and items such as *Kathakali* masks and traditional fabrics can be bought at a number of shops, including the Government run *SBMS Handcrafts* emporium behind the Secretariat T 63358. *Natesan Antique Arts* and *Gift Corner* on MG Rd have a wide collection of high quality goods including old dowry boxes, carved wooden panels from old temple 'cars' or chariots, miniature paintings, old ivory carvings and bronzes. *Kairali* is another Government handicrafts emporium, opp the Secretariat in MG Road T 60127. Kairali also produces items of banana fibre, coconut, screw pine, mainly utilitarian. Also excellent sandalwood carvings and bell-metal lamps, utensils. A new *Spencers* supermarket is opening on MG Rd. Shopping areas include the Chalai Bazar, the Connemara market and the Main Rd from Palayam to the E Fort.

Bookshops *Higginbothams*, T 79122, *Pai & Co*, T 75116, *India Book House*, T 75443 and *National Book Stall*, T 78881 all on MG Rd.

Photography Several on MG Rd. *Paramount, Sundaram Studio, Baven's Studio* also *Sivaram* in Press Rd and *Minerva* in Rly Station Rd.

Local transport Buses are extremely crowded but a feasible and very cheap way of getting about. There are many auto rickshaws, but it is often necessary to bargain, especially outside normal daytime hours. Frequent buses to Kovalam leave from the Fort Bus Depot between 0630 and 2100 and it takes 30 min.

Car Hire Luxury cars and Tourist Taxis can be hired through several firms – ITDC Transport Section, Chettikulamkara, T 61783. Verma Travels, E Fort, T 71400, Blaze Car Rentals, E Fort, Airport Rd, T 71622. Jai Hind Travels, Hotel Magnet, Thycaud, T 64445. Kerala Travels, LMS Building, T 63212.

Entertainment Children's films screened at Open Air Theatre in the Museum Complex, daily except Mon from 1800-1930. Several cinemas especially nr Station and Overbridge Junction on MG Rd some showing English language films.

Sports *Trivandrum Golf Club*, Kowkidar, T 60834; *Trivandrum Tennis Club*, Kowkidar, T 62737; *Indoor Recreation Centre*, Shankumugham, T 5349; *Kerala Flying Club*, Airport, T 3814; *Trivandrum Boat Club*, Veli, T 2349. Swimming at *Waterworks* pool nr the Museum. 0430-1000, 1015-1200, 1400-1530, 1815-2000. Closed Mon. Also at *Mascot Hotel*.

Museums The Napier Museum. N of the city, in the same grounds as the park, zoo and art galleries, 400 m E of Indian Airlines Office and the Mascot Hotel. Closed Mon. Open all other days from 0900 until 1700 except Wed, when it is open from 1300 to 1645. The building itself is something of a landmark, built in Kerala style. The main feature is the collection of S Indian bronzes, mainly from the 8th to the 18th centuries. Some are superb. Rules for sculpting deities such as Siva, Vishnu, Parvati and Lakshmi were laid down in the *Silpa Sastras*. Sculpture in Kerala was strongly influenced by Tamil styles, but there are distinctive features evident in some of the sculptures on display. Most of the 400 bronzes in the Museum are from the Chola, Vijayanagar and Nayak periods. There are a few Jain and Buddhist sculptures. Among other exhibits are some excellent wood carvings, for which Kerala is particularly famous in India. Ceilings, gables and doors of both homes and temples were usually built of wood and richly decorated. Ivory carvings and Kathakali costumes are also displayed. A printed guide is available at the Museum.

   Natural History Museum Immediately to the E of the Napier Museum. In addition to its natural history collection this museum houses a small ethnographical collection. It includes a beautifully made replica of a typical Kerala Nayar wooden house (*nalukettu*) with an account of the principles of its construction. These houses were particularly common in the N of Travancore among the wealthy Nayar families, a highly regarded Hindu warrior caste whose members inter-married with Brahmins. The Nayars were noted for their matrilineal pattern of descent.

   Sri Chitra Art Gallery An excellent collection of Indian art with examples from early to modern schools. Paintings by Raja Ravi Verma, who exhibited widely in the W. Includes paintings from Java, Bali, China and Japan. The Indian section has Mughal and Rajput miniature paintings and Tanjore paintings embellished with semi-precious stones. Open 1000-1700. Closed Mon and Wed mornings. Entry Rs.2. Well worth a visit, as is the new gallery devoted to modern art next door.

Museum of Science and Technology Located nr the Mascot Hotel. Highlights science, technology and electronics. Open 1000-1700, closed Mon. Small entry fee. **Children's Museum**, Thycaud, T 64939. Dolls, masks, paintings. Open 1000-1700. **Oriental Research Institute and Manuscripts Library**, University, Kariavattom. Literary treasures including vast collection of palm leaf manuscripts.

Parks and zoos *Botanical Gardens* and *Zoo*. Open daily except Mon, 0900-1645. Entry Rs.2, Video/cine cameras Rs 5. Entrance at SW corner of the park, 400 m E of Indian airlines office. The zoo is one of the most attractive in India. Set in wooded gently hilly parkland it is spaciously set out and offers delightful shaded walks. The park also houses the botanical gardens, and many of the trees are clearly labelled. The zoo has a wide collection of animals, including several species of monkey, lions, tigers, leopards, giraffes, deer, zebra. Sadly some of the animals do not look well cared for. There are other parks and gardens in the city – around the Secretariat, Gandhi Park, Waterworks Gardens and at Veli Tourist Village. **NB** The Aquarium nr the beach has closed.

Clubs *Trivandrum Club*, Vazhuthacud, T 62980. *Automobile Association of S India*, VJT Hall Rd, T 76081; *Press Club*, behind Secretariat, T 61642; *National Club*, behind Secretariat, T 63128.

Post and telegraph The *GPO*, Palayam, is in a narrow street just to the W of MG Road opp the Central Bank of India, T 3071. Poste Restante is here, open 0800-1800. The Telegraph Office, Statue Rd, is 200 m to its N, T 61494. Open 24 hours.

Places of worship *Hindu* (Note: Non Hindus are not allowed) Bhagavati Temple, Attukal; Ganapati Temple, Pazhavangudi; Padmanabhasvami Temple, E Fort; Srikantesvaram Temple, Fort *Muslim* Beemapalli Mosque nr Airport; Jama Masjid Palayam; Thampanoor Mosque. *Christian Roman Catholic* Lourdes Church Near PMG junction; *Protestant Mateer Memorial Church* Church of S India Near Museum; Salvation Army Central Hall, Kowkidar; St. Peter's Jacobite Syrian Church; St Thomas Mar Thoma Church.

Hospitals and medical services *General Hospital*, Vanchiyoor, T 70870. *Cosmopolitan Hospital*, Maurinja Palayam, T 78182. *Ramakrishna Mission Hospital*, Sasthamangalam.

Useful addresses Visa extension *City Police Commissioner*, Residency Rd, nr Women's College, Thyacaud, T 60555; *Superintendent of Police* (Rural), Kowkidar, T 61296. The former is a better bet. Allow up to a week, though it can take less. Open 1000-1700 Mon-Sat. **Cultural Centres** British Library, nr Secretariat, T 68716. *Alliance Française*, Vellayambalam, T 67776. *House of Soviet Culture*, Vanros Junction, T 64550. *Indian Council of Cultural Relations*, Vellayambam, T 62489. **Air Carriers** Air Lanka, Vazhuthacaud, T 44495. *Gulf Air*, Jet Air, Panavila Jn, T 67514. *Kuwait Airways*, National Travel Service, Panavila Jn, T 63436. *Saudi Airways*, Arafath Travels, Pattom, T 78101.

Travel agents *Aries Travels*, Ayswarya Building Press Road, Trivandrum 695001; *Jaihind Travels*, Hotel Magnet, Thycaud, T 64454; *Kerala Travels*, MG Road, T 63212

Tourist offices and information *Govt of India Tourist Information Counter* and *Tourist Information Counter Govt of Kerala*, Trivandrum Airport, T 71085. There are also Tourist Information counters at the Rly station and bus station T 67224. Kerala Tourism Development Corporation (KTDC), Tourist Reception Centre, Thampanoor. T 75031 and 64261. *Govt of Kerala, Tourist Information Centre*, Park View, T 61132. You will find the Kerala Tourist offices particularly well supplied with leaflets and information sheets and very helpful.

Air Indian Airlines International air connections from Trivandrum Colombo (Sri Lanka) and Male (The Maldives). Indian Airlines **Madras** Mon, Fri & Sun (+ one other), 1730, 1 hr 5 min; Wed, Fri & Sun (+ 1 other), 1730, 1 hr 5 min; **Delhi** Daily, 1455, 4 hr 45 min; **Bombay** Daily, 1455, 1 hr 55 min. **Bangalore** Wed, Fri & Sun (+ 1 other), 1730, 55 min, change at Madras (65 min) then Daily, 1930, 40 min (Total time 2 hr 40 min); **Cochin**, Wed, Fri & Sun, 1250, 30 min; **Colombo**, Mon, 1950, 50 min; **Male**, Mon, Thur & Sat, 1420, 30 min. Indian Airlines, Mascot Junction, T 66370, Airport T 72228, Enquiries T 73537, Duty Officer T 71470. **Vayudoot** Bangalore Mon, Wed, Fri 1100 2r 5 min This flight may continue to Hyderabad. Handling agents: Airtravel Enterprises, LMS Junction. T 60690, Airport T 71351.

Air India flies to London, New York, Frankfurt and Paris and several destination as in the Gulf. Air India, Velayambalam, T 64837, Airport T 71426, Duty Officer T 70281. List of other carriers under Travel Agents above.

Trivandrum airport is located on the beach 6 km away, but very poorly signposted, seemingly on the assumption that everybody knows how to get there. The airport has new terminal buildings, but their management leaves a great deal to be desired. Arrangements for booking into flights are rudimetary, queues may often become crushes, labelling and signposting are negligible and spoken directions are inaudible in the echoing building. Even with confirmed international bookings it pays to arrive in good time. Individually the staff are usually very helpful, but the system lets them down. If in doubt, ask frequently. Transfer by local bus No. 14 is very cheap. Alternatively you can get a taxi or auto rickshaw – about Rs 20.

Rail Broad gauge line connects Trivandrum with the rest of the country. Often the rail journey is slower than by bus but it is more comfortable. Some important fast trains: **Madras**: *Trivandrum-Guwahati Exp*, 2601 (AC/II), Th, 1250, 18 hr 15 min; *Madras Mail*, 6320 (AC/II), daily, 1330, 17 hr 45 min; **Calcutta** (H): *Trivandrum-Guwahati Exp*, 2601 (AC/II), Th, 1250, 48 hr 55 min; **Delhi** (ND): *Kerala-Mangala Link Exp*, 2625 (AC/II), daily, 0940, 52 hr 50 min; **Bombay** (VT): *Kanniyakuman Exp*, 1082 (AC/II), daily, 0755, 45 hr 10 min. **Quilon**: *Kerala-Mangala*, 2625/2625A (AC/II), daily, 0940, 1 hr 20 min **Mangalore**: *Malabar Exp*, 16 hr. **Bangalore**: *Island Exp*, 18 hr. Trivandrum Central Enquiry T 62966, after 1800 T 63066. Reservations open 0700-1300,1330-1930, Sun 0900-1700.

Road Good network of roads since several National Highways connect Trivandrum with other cities in the S. NH 7 (Kanyakumari to Varanasi), NH 17 (Trichur to Bombay), NH 45 (Dindigul to Madras) and NH 47 (Kanyakumari to Salem). Some distances: Kanyakumari 85 km, Cochin 219 km, Coimbatore 410 km, Madurai 307 km, Tekkadi for Periyar 271 km.

Buses Kerala State Road Transport Corporation (KSRTC) operates a comprehensive service from Trivandrum, throughout the state and Tamil Nadu. Central Bus Station, Thampanoor, T 63886. No.11 from MG Road, S of the Bus Station for Kovalam Beach about every 30 min, from 0630 to 2100. Kanyakumari via Nagercoil or direct (10 daily), frequent dep., 2hr 30 min. Buses to Cochin via Quilon start at 0730, 2 hr; Tekkadi, 3 daily, 8 hr. Thiruvalluvar Transport Corporation (TTC) and the other Tamil Nadu Govt Co, Nesamony connects the city with many other centres – Coimbatore, Cuddalore, Erode, Kanyakumari, Madurai and Madras. The Termini are opp Trivandrum Central Rly Station, at the Central Bus Station. TTC T 67756.

Excursions Trivandrum has several places of interest (see above). There is an excellent day trip from Kovalam to the old palace of the Rajas of Travancore at

Plan of PADMANABHAPURAM PALACE <small>SA 183</small>

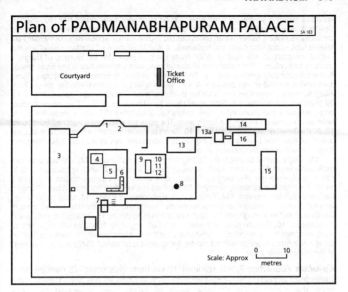

Courtyard

Ticket Office

Scale: Approx 0   10
metres

Padmanabhapuram. Leave Trivandrum on NH 47 S to Nagercoil and Kaniyakumari. After 20 km pass through the busy market town of Neyyattinkera. A road on the right leads to Puvar (10 km) and a road on the left goes to Nedumangad. After a further 16 km pass through Marthandam, the road passing through gently rolling countryside the 17 km to Padmanabhapuram. The palace is beautifully kept and contains some fascinating architecture and paintings. Padmanabhapuram was capital of the kings of Travancore from 1550 until 1750 (then moved to Trivandrum). (*Padma*, lotus; *nabha*, navel; *puram*, town; the name refers to the image of the lotus coming from the navel of **Vishnu**. Although the Rajas of Travancore were Vaishnavite kings, they did not neglect Siva, as can be seen from various sculptures and paintings in the Palace.)

The King never officially married, and the heir to the throne was his eldest sister's oldest son. This form of "matrilineal descent" was characteristic of the earlier Chera empire of Kerala (who ruled for 200 years from the early 12th century). The palace shows the superb craftsmanship, especially in woodworking, that has been characteristic of Kerala's art and architecture. (Modern examples of traditional styles of carving are obtainable from several shops in Trivandrum – see below) There are also some superb frescoes and excellent stone-sculpted figures.

Open 0900-1700 (last tickets 1630) Closed Mon. Tickets Rs 2, still cameras Rs 5, **video Rs 500** (Some complaints have been raised at the scale of this charge, and it may be lowered, but be prepared). **N.B.** It is difficult to photograph in the palace without flash or fast film. It is compulsory to take the tour with a guide. These are provided as you enter the main building and are very competent.

1. *The main entrance*. A granite bed (notably cool) is in one corner and ceremonial bows line one wall. The carving on the royal chair is Chinese, illustrating the commercial contact between China and the Kerala kings. 90 different flowers are carved in the teak ceiling. **2.** 1st floor, the *durbar hall* where the king met with his ministers. The floor is made of egg-white, cement and lime, coconut water, charcoal, river sand, giving a smooth, hard, black finish. It is very well ventilated with wooden slatted surrounds, and has some coloured mica in windows giving a simple coloured effect. **3.** An enormous two-floored hall (30' x 270'), designed as a *dining hall* where 2,000 Brahmins were fed free once daily. Its long low cross-beams make it rather like an enormous old English barn in appearance. Downstairs are granite tubs – cool – for curds and buttermilk. **4.** The *Thaikottam* – "Mother palace" – is the original structure. It was built in 1550. There is a *puja* room for the worship of Durga, a jackfruit tree column. The woodwork is stained teak, with whitewashed stone work below. **5.** A small *courtyard* (open to the sky). This is typical of Keralan domestic architecture. There is an **underground secret passage**, 4' x 8', which is said to run from another palace 2 km away. **6.** Houses large urns for pickle for Brahmins' meals: lime, mango, gooseberry, and a list of others. **7.** Steps down to bath, room above for oil massage. **8.** The 38 kg stone standing on a pedestal in the courtyard at chest height had to be lifted 101 times consecutively over head as qualification to join the king's army. The potential recruit was watched from room 10. **9.** The *Treasury* on the ground floor. **10.** *King's bedroom* contains a four poster medicinal bed of 64 ayurvedic healing woods e.g. sandalwood, presented by the East India Company. It has the serpent of Hippocrates at its head.

11. King's special bedroom for fasting times, balcony all round. **12.** Vishnu's bedroom (teak beds) vegetable oil tints and frescoes of deities all round, 2 hanging brass lanterns lit continuously since the 18th century. Coconut oil is added twice daily, a cotton wick once a week. The room has a balcony all round. **13** The King's sister's *dressing room*; it has 2 hanging beds and Belgian mirrors. **13a.** King's sister's bedroom and toilets **14.** Used to be ladies' quarters, then an armoury. It includes a gruesome "hanging cage" (rather like a suit of armour, but slats of metal) through which eagles tore criminals to death. **15.** A room for scribes and accountants. **16.** Granite pillar and roof dance hall, eggwhite floor, women kept behind wooden screen. It is connected to what was once the *Sarasvati* temple. The outer cyclopean stone wall is fitted together without mortar. It encloses a total area of 75 ha, and the buildings of the palace cover 2 ha.

Kovalam *Population* 2,500, sea level. 10 km from Trivandrum (25 minutes from Trivandrum airport). The world-famous beach at Kovalam has been transformed since the early 1980s. Once a series of sandy bays separated by rocky promontories, deserted except for the scattered fishing villages under the coconut palms, it is becoming one of the Govt's major tourist centres. Despite the development it is still "a super beach, a very good place to relax for a few days, uncrowded and unspoilt – not be missed for the world".

There are plenty of local buses from the main bus stand in Trivandrum to Kovalam. The cost is under Rs 2. There are also taxis and auto rickshaws, but they either wait to fill up with passengers or charge what they think you can afford. The target price is around Rs 20 per head. To get to Kovalam from Trivandrum follow signs either to Kovalam or to Vizhinjam. The road to Kovalam has been enormously developed in the last 5 years. The laterite has been cut back and back to create building plots. The signs are not always clear. *Hotel Samudra* is the first sign, to the N of Kovalam. **NB** *Vizhinjam* is to the S of Kovalam, not the N as shown on the maps.

There are 4 main stretches of beach, each about a 400 m long, with a rocky promontory, on which stands Charles Correa's award-winning *Ashok Kovalam Hotel*, dividing them into N and S sections. The hotel has its own small section of beach immediately to the N of the promontory, giving the most sheltered bathing and the clearest water. The *Ashok Hotel* cottages are just behind this stretch of the beach. The southern beaches are much more populated, but although there are now life guard patrols along these beaches you need to be careful. There can be a current, and the sea can get rough, particularly between Apr and Oct. The best season is between Dec and Mar, and even at the end of Mar it can get very hot in the middle of the day. A wide range of new building has taken place in the last 5 years, and the government is planning to widen the beach by 100 m, demolishing the line of small restaurants and shops that have sprung up. Thatched parasols have been provided along the beach.

Hotels There is now a wide range of accommodation. In season (October – March) prices more than double those of the off-season period, but it is still possible to obtain very cheap rooms in cottages behind the beach.

A *Kovalam Hotel*. ITDC Previously poorly-rated service now much improved. However, the pricing still reflects the stunning location rather than the range or quality of services. The

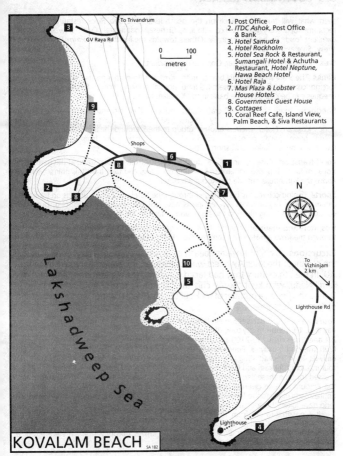

To Trivandrum

GV Raya Rd

0   100
metres

1. Post Office
2. ITDC Ashok, Post Office
   & Bank
3. Hotel Samudra
4. Hotel Rockholm
5. Hotel Sea Rock & Restaurant,
   Sumangali Hotel & Achutha
   Restaurant, Hotel Neptune,
   Hawa Beach Hotel
6. Hotel Raja
7. Mas Plaza & Lobster
   House Hotels
8. Government Guest House
9. Cottages
10. Coral Reef Cafe, Island View,
    Palm Beach, & Siva Restaurants

Shops

N

To
Vizhinjam
2 km

Lighthouse Rd

Lakshadweep Sea

Lighthouse

KOVALAM BEACH

overall value for money depends on the assessment of the value to put on its glorious position and comparative isolation from the crowds down below. (How can a 5-star hotel not even have a weighing machine in its health centre, let alone any other equipment?) 72 rms, a further 72 are being added on the head of the promontory. Now that the top ITDC hotels have been merged with the international hotel group standards may improve further. **D** *Raja* Off beach location, reasonably priced Indian style hotel. **C** *Rockholm* Excellent position on S end of beach just above lighthouse. Good restaurant, beautiful views, especially early morning. **D** *Sea Rock*. Right on the beach. New clean hotel, sea facing rooms twice the price of back rooms.

There is now a large number of cottages and rooms to let, broadly of a similar standard. Many have scouts out at the bus stand to greet arrivals, but you are likely to pay up to 25% more if you use their services. If you are staying for any length of time you can get big reductions in price – it pays to bargain. You will find several small hotels by walking from the *Sea Rock* towards the lighthouse. Inexpensive clean though simple. **E** *Sumangali* with Achhuta Restaurant, **E** *Neptune* and **E** *Hawa Beach*

Restaurants Many of the beach restaurants are likely to be cleared away. It has yet to be seen what will take their place on the beach itself. The *Sea Rock* restaurant is highly recommended. Very wide choice – Indian, Chinese, continental. Quite slow service, but excellent food. Try banana pancake. Others towards the lighthouse – *Palm Beach*, *Island View*, *Siva* and *Coral Reef*.

Bars　*Kovalam Hotel* has a bar. Open to non-residents.

Banks　The State Bank of India branch in the Kovalam Hotel changes travellers cheques and foreign currency for non-residents during normal banking hours. **Exchange** Travellers cheques can be cashed at the bank in the Kovalam Hotel.

Shopping　There are about 40 craft shops, including Kashmiri and Tibetan shops selling a wide range of goods. The majority are clustered around the bus stand at the gate of the *Ashok Kovalam Hotel*. There is another group to the S around the lighthouse. It is possible to get good quality paintings, metalwork, carpets, woodwork from all over India, at reasonable prices. Tailoring at short notice.

Local transport　Buses go into Trivandrum frequently from the bus stand at the gate of the *Kovalam Hotel*. It is also possible to hire auto rickshaws and taxis from this point, also from above the lighthouse outside the Rockholm Hotel.

Sports　Fishing can readily be arranged through the hotels, as can excursions on traditional catamarans or motor boats. Water sports have not yet been fully developed, but active consideration is being given to the expansion of facilities by the Kerala Tourist Board.

Hospitals and medical services　In an emergency it is possible to obtain assistance either through the Kovalam Hotel or from the Govt Hospital in Trivandrum.

Excursions　Just S of Kovalam beach is the small village of *Vizhinjam*. This was the capital of the later *Ay* rulers who dominated S Travancore in the 8th century AD. In the 7th century they had faced constant pressure from the Pandiyans of S Tamil Nadu, who kept the Ay chieftains under a firm control for long periods. During this period a number of rock cut temples were constructed using a number of Tamilian features.

Tours　The KTDC organises 5 main tours from Trivandrum ranging from day trips to a three day tour. **1** Trivandrum city tour, 0800-1800, including Kovalam Beach (125 km) Rs 40 daily; **2** Cape Comorin 0730-2100 including Kovalam, Padmanabhapuram and Kanniyakumari (200 km) Rs 60 daily; **3** Ponmudi 0830-1900 daily Golden Valley and Ponmudi (125 km) daily Rs 40 **4** Tekkadi Wild Life Sat 0630 return Sun 2100 (520 km) **5** Kodaikanal 3 day tour including Tekkadi and Cape Comorin Sat 0630 Return Mon 2100 (800 km) Rs 250. If pressed for time these can be worth considering, but they can be very exhausting tours and the amount of time given to individual stops at sites of interest is often very limited. This applies particularly to the Tekkadi tour, most of which is spent in the bus. A number of people who have taken this tour say "don't". The journey is 9 hr each way.

　　It is possible to get from Trivandrum to Cochin in a day, including one section of the backwaters. Leave Kovalam (or Trivandrum) at 0730. Allow 2½ hrs to Quinlon. The boat jetty is very near the bus station. Boat leaves at 1030, arrives Alleppey 1830. There are regular buses from there to Cochin every 10 min.

TRIVANDRUM TO COCHIN (The Coastal Route)

There are two main routes through Kerala from Trivandrum. They run nearly parallel and very close to each other so it is possible to make detours to places of particular interest from one route to the other if you wish. Kerala is India's most densely populated state, and even the main roads are often crowded with people. Road transport is slow (though bus travel often feels dangerously fast!). The NH 47 tends to by-pass more of the small towns and villages. The inland route is slower, but both pass through some beautiful scenery.

Most of this route follows **NH 47**, leaving Trivandrum from the Indian Airlines Offices and the *Mascot Hotel* along the Quilon Rd. Initially through the winding and very busy town street. The road crosses low rolling hills covered in coconut, jack, eucalyptus, cashew, mangoes, papaya, and under the wood cover cassava. The land itself is very intensively prepared. 18 kms from Trivandrum the road crosses a toll bridge. In **Attingal** (25 km, capital of the Travancore Tamburetti princes until 1758) take a left turn off the NH 47 to **Kadakaur** and **Anjengo** (5 km). Initially held by the Portuguese this massive laterite fort has an English cemetery, the earliest tomb of which is dated 1704. An English warehouse and trading post had been set up 20 years earlier, but was abandoned in 1810. For a coast line fringed almost its entire length with coconut palms it is slightly ironical that *Anjengo* should mean "five coconut trees". Return to the NH 47.

30 km out of Trivandrum there is an excellent view of the lateritic rocks. Along the road is one of Kerala's tree planting schemes with the usual slogans; "forests preceedes civilisation, deserts succeed them". There are views of a succession of low ranges, no more than 15 m to 30 m, but with a regular succession of rice growing, flat river valleys with wooded slopes. The French geographer Pierre Gourou pointed out that "the better-off rice farmers live in the valley bottoms, while only thirty metres or so up the slope live a very wretched (and mainly Christian) peasantry." Occasional rubber plantations stretch as far down towards the coast as NH47, but most lie further inland. After 50 km you reach Quilon.

Quilon (Kollam)

Population 175,000. *Altitude* sea level. *Climate* Temperature Summer Max. 35°C Min. 25°C, Winter Max. 34°C Min. 24°C. Annual rainfall 2800 mm. *Best Season* Oct – Mar. *Clothing* Cottons. Trivandrum 71 km, which has an airport.

Quilon is a shaded, gentle town on the side of the Ashtamudi Lake, though it has a growing industrial activity and at times it can be very busy. It is one of Kerala's most ancient settlements, going back to the 9th century AD. The Malayalam calendar is calculated from the founding the town. It was also associated with the early history of Christianity. There is a wide range of new goods and services offered by shops along roadside – electronics, video, and medicals. Its traditional industries include cashew nut processing and fisheries. If you're familiar with autorickshaws in other parts of India the hard-topped autorickshaws with roof racks come as a surprise. The District Headquarters, Quilon has been an important centre of Travancore administration under successive different rulers.

It was known to Marco Polo (as *Koilum*) and its port traded with Phoenicians, Persians, Greeks, Romans and Arabs to the W and the Chinese to the E. Superb chinaware has been found in the area. If you arrive from Trivandrum this is the start of the marvellous backwater of Kerala.

Local Festivals Apr. Colourful 10 day *Vishnu festival* in Asram Temple with procession and fireworks. Aug – Sep. Avadayattukotta Temple celebrates a 5 day *Ashtami Rohani* festival. *Muharram* too is observed with processions at the town mosque.

Places of interest 3 km from the centre of Quilon, **Tangasseri** (*Changana Cheri*) was once a British outpost, covering under 40 ha. Before that the Portuguese Fort Thomas, built in 1503, taken later by the Dutch, dominated the shore, but most has now collapsed and been washed away. There is a ruined belfry in the middle of the Protestant graveyard. Light House. Open daily 1530-1730. Small entry fee.

Backwaters Ashtamudi Lake with coconut palms on its banks and picturesque promontories extends N from the town. You might see some 'Chinese' fishing nets and in wider sections large sailed dugouts carrying the local coir, copra and cashew. Boats for hire for cruising from the *Quilon Boat Club*, T 2519 or from the *Tourism Promotion Council*, Guest House Compound, T 76456. From the latter pedal or rowing boats cost about Rs 5 per hour and speed boats for 4, 8 or 10

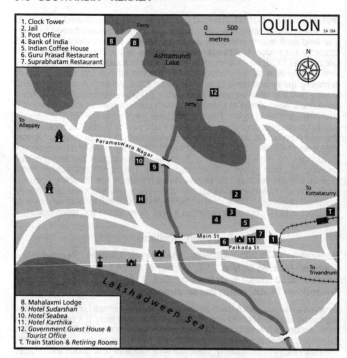

1. Clock Tower
2. Jail
3. Post Office
4. Bank of India
5. Indian Coffee House
6. Guru Prasad Restaurant
7. Suprabhatam Restaurant

QUILON SA 184

0   500
metres

Ashtamundi Lake

Ferry

Jetty

To Alleppey

Parameswara Nagar

To Kottatacurry

Main St

Paikada St

To Trivandrum

Lakshadweep Sea

8. Mahalaxmi Lodge
9. Hotel Sudarshan
10. Hotel Seabea
11. Hotel Karthika
12. Government Guest House & Tourist Office
T. Train Station & Retiring Rooms

persons cost from Rs 40 to Rs 60 per hour. The boat jetty is opposite the Bus Station.

Short trips to **Kapapuzha** (twice a day) and **Guhanandapuram** several trips a day. Daily trip to Alleppey in each direction which takes over 8 hr with 2 stops, but can be very interesting if you have the time.

Thirumullavaram Beach and model park at **Kochupilamoodu Beach**.

Local industries Coir, ceramics, cashew nuts, aluminium and fisheries.

Hotels E *Sudarshan*, Parameswar Nagar. T 3755, Cable: Comfort, Telex: 0886 292. 63 rm some a/c with attached baths. 2 restaurants (one a/c), bar. E *Shah International*, T 75360, Cable: Shahinn, Telex: 0886 267. 72 rm some a/c. E *Karthika*, Paikada Rd. T 74240, Cable: Karthika, Telex: 0886 284. 40 rm with attached bath some a/c. Restaurant. Very central. E *Neela*, Quilon Cantonment, T 3616. Some a/c rm. E *Seabea*, T 2192. 35 rm some a/c. Restaurant. Central.

E *Government Guest House*, T 76456. Children's pool. 8 rm and restaurant. A beautiful place to stay, it is a 200-year-old former palace with a garden on the edge of the lagoon. It was the British Residency and has a small waterfront park, an example of excellent value for money. 2 km from town centre, which can be a disadvantage. Reservation: Executive Engineer, PWD. Also *YMCA*, T 76933 and *YWCA*, T 77010. Reservations: General Secretary.

Restaurants The *Indian Coffee House*, Main St good for coffee and snacks. The restaurant at the *Iswarya Lodge* to the E of town has a good veg restaurant. *Guru Prasad*, Main St also is recommended. Others are *Village Restaurant* (Town centre), *Suprabhatam* (opp Clock Tower), *Noorjahan, Koya's*.

Banks Open Mon – Fri 1000 – 1400, Sat 1000 – 1200. Number of branches of national banks.

Shopping The main areas are on the Main Rd. Chinnakkada, Municipal Shopping Complex and Supreme Supermarket.

Local transport Buses and auto rickshaws are plentiful. Bikes for hire.

Post and telegraphs Head Post Office open Mon-Sat to 2000, Sun to 1800.

Tourist information Tourism Promotion Council, at the Government Guest House. T 76456.

Rail Trains to Madras via Madurai and Bombay via Cochin. Quilon Junction rly station N of town, is about 3 km from Boat Jetty and Bus Station. **Trivandrum**: *Kerala-Mangala Exp*, 2626 (AC/II), daily, 1530, 1 hr 20 min; **Madras (MC)**: *Madras Mail*, 6320 (AC/II), daily, 1457, 16 hr 18 min; **Madurai**: *Quilon Mail*, 6106 (AC/II), daily, 1220, 7 hr 45 min.

Road Buses run frequent services to Trivandrum, Cochin and Alleppey (85 km) and other towns on the coast. Daily bus to Kumily village for Periyar National Park, change at Kottayam. Also buses to Kanyakumari.

Excursions Boat cruises along the backwaters provide one of the most delightful tours in India. It is possible to go all the way to Alleppey. This takes about 8 hrs and costs under Rs 10 per person. It leaves Quilon at 1030. Even in the coolest times of year (Dec to Feb) this journey can get very hot in the day time, and along the coconut fringed backwaters there is often little breeze. However, it does give an almost uniquely quiet view of Kerala village life, impossible to get simply from the road. Agriculture in Kerala has always taken advantage of the comparatively long rainy season. While the coconut provides both a vital economic resource – nuts, with the copra of mature nuts a vital source of coconut oil, coir and the wood of the trees themselves – and shelter, the land underneath is often intensively cultivated.

From the boat you see some of the different fruit crops – papaya, mangoes, jack fruit – and cassava (*tapioca*), now a staple of village peoples' diet. As tapioca was only introduced to Kerala in 1920 its popularity is particularly striking, and reflects the fact that it gives remarkably high yields from lateritic soils that have been picturesquely described by Oscar Spate as about as fertile as railway ballast. Some people find the full journey from Quilon to Alleppey too long. Shorter trips are possible, either round trips returning to Quilon or by picking up the trip closer to Alleppey. **Changanacherry** and **Kottayam** are two alternatives.

Tips There are 2 options. **1** The "luxury" KTDC boat costs Rs 60, even if you join half way. Crowded with westerners, 2 stops for food. **2** The local ferry costs Rs 7, many travellers strongly recommend it. Resist the pressure to take the Tourist boat.

Rejoin the NH 47. **Chavara** 16 km N of Quilon is the very large plant of *Kerala Minerals and Metals*, Titanium Oxide Pigment Plant, a Kerala Govt enterprise. This makes use of the radioactive ilmenite and monazite sands which were found along the beach in the early part of this century. The concentrations are very high and known reserves exceed 1.5 million tonnes. Even the waste of early extractions were richer than fresh deposits exploited in Australia, and they contain 8% to 10% thorium oxide. Titanium from the ilmenite sands is essential for some highly specialised electrical and chemical industries – electrodes, tracer bullets, and as a catalyst. Although they have been exploited since the early part of this century production today is very important. The monazite sands of the Kerala coast are particularly important for India's nuclear power programme. The view from the air shows an enormous slick of pollutants drifting S from the factory down the coast. There is also an Indo-Norwegian Fishing project.

If you have come from Tamil Nadu by road you will appreciate the much better surface, but it is still generally very slow. If you're driving, it is extremely difficult to predict what people are going to do, and the road seems a mass of random movements. Bus drivers weave their way through regardless. There are literally thousands of people who have other things on their minds than avoiding the traffic. Between Quilon and Alleppey the road passes through more coconut groves, (orange as well as green) but also a great variety of trees; jack fruit, mango, eucalyptus along road sides. There is an atmosphere of prosperity quite different from the neighbouring states. Just 20 km N of Quilon is one of several new mosques. This is just one reflection of the money beng sent to Kerala by migrants working in the Gulf. Income from these sources began to dry up at the end of the 1980s, and the area has suffered considerable retrenchment. You reach Alleppey in (90 km).

Alleppey (Alappuzha)

Population 200,000. *Altitude* Sea level. *Climate* Temp. Summer Max. 35°C Mln. 22°C, Winter Max. 32°C Min. 22°C. Annual rainfall 250 mm. *Best Season* Dec – Mar. The nearest airport and railway station are at Cochin 64 km away where you can get a bus or taxi. Alleppey is centre for backwater cruises and also the state's coir industry. A large network of canals pass through the town and there is a long sandy beach.

Local Festivals Jan. *Cheruppu* is celebrated in the Mullakkal Devi Temple with procession of elephants, music and fireworks. Aug. Alleppey is the site of one of Kerala's most famous boat races.

The Nehru Cup, inaugurated in 1952, is the largest *Snake Boat Race* in the state. It takes place on the 2nd Sat in Aug, and is an extraordinary event. As many as 40 snake boats (long narrow boats) as well as others, with highly decorated and carved prows, are rowed by several dozen oarsmen before huge crowds. Naval helicopters do mock rescue operations and stunt flying. Entry by ticket. The *Champakulam Boat Race* takes place 16 km ferry ride away on 'Moolam' day in Jun/Jul.

Places of interest The **backwaters** are the major tourist attraction. Apart from the cruise to Quilon detailed above, there are several others you can choose from. To **Champakulam**, 16 km. 1 hr 30 min. 9 Dep. from 0430 – 2300. To **Kottayam**, 29 km. 2 hr 30 min. 14 Dep. from 0500 – 2230. Some visitors feel that this trip is so different from the Quilon-Alleppey trip that it is worth doing both if you have the time. To **Ernakulam**, 74 km. 7 hr. Dep. 0030. The journeys in the daytime are obviously much more interesting for watching unspoilt village life of Kerala. Fares are only few rupees. If you wish to hire a motor boat for a short time, the best hourly rate of Rs 50 is offered by the *State Water Transport Dept*, Contact Traffic Supt, T 2110. *Vembanad Tourist Service*, Akkarakalam Buildings, Jetty Rd, T 3395 and *Kuttanadan Travels*, Boat Jetty, T 3453 charge 2 to 3 times the rate but may offer larger boats.

Local industries The headquarters of Kerala's coir industry, cashew nuts.

Hotels D *Alleppey Prince*, A.S.Road (2 km N of centre), T 3762, Cable: Prinzo, Telex: 883 202 Jons In. Hotel uses local woods and coir in its furnishings. Central a/c. 30 rm with bath and phone. Restaurant, pool (not well-maintained). Luxury boat for backwaters trips. E *Komala*, nr Municipal Maidan, Opp jetty N of canal, T 3631, Cable: Komalbar. Some a/c rooms. Has one of the best restaurants in Alleppey, the *Arun Restaurant* E *Kuttanad Tourist Home* Next to bus station. New, clean and recommended. F *PWD Rest House*, Beach Rd, T 3445. Excellent value, cheap and reasonable food (order in advance. Reservations: District Collector, Alleppey. If calling in person apply at the Collectorate, District Headquarters. E *Narasimhapuram Lodge*, Cullen Rd, Mullakkal, T 3698. A/c doubles. F *Karthika Tourist Home*, N of canal, opp Jetty, T 2554. Clean, some large rooms with baths, good value. Also *YWCA*, T 3313.

Restaurants *Arun* in Komala Hotel opp Jetty and Prince Hotel's *Vemanad* serve very good food. There is an *Indian Coffee House* there too. *Gokul*, Mullakal Rd (main St). Good veg S Indian food.

Banks Open Mon to Fri 1000 – 1400, Sat 1000 – 1200. Banks near the Post Office and the Telegraph Office.

Post and telegraph Head Post office, off Mullakal Road in town centre. Telegraph office, on corner of NH 47 and Beach Rd, just over canal.

Shopping Coir mats a local speciality. Mullakal Rd and Market Rd are the shopping centres.

Local transport Tourist and other taxis, and auto-rickshaws. Boat hire is listed under 'Backwaters' in Places of interest above.

Tourist Information Officer, Collectorate. T 2549.

Road On NH 47, with good road connections with important cities in the S. Bus services to Quilon, Trivandrum, Kanyakumari, Cochin, Calicut, Trichur. **Note** that here as elsewhere in Kerala "Non-stop" buses are faster than "Express" buses.

Excursions The starting point of backwater boat trips to Quilon, Kottayam and Cochin, and the main centre for cruises on the backwaters. See above under Places of Interest.

After 14 km you pass through **Ambalapuzha**. The temple dedicated to Lord Krishna celebrates 10 day festival in Mar – April when a number of dances from Kerala are performed. **Haripad** (33 km) has a Subrahmanya Temple and Snake Boat Race at **Payipad** (3 km by bus) for three days. 'Jalotsav' during Onam in Aug/Sept. Boat processions on first 2 days followed by competitive races on 3rd day. Entry by ticket. **Mannarsala** (36 km) has a Nagaraja Temple in forest. Festivals in Aug and Nov/Dec. All 3 places are on NH 47, S of Alleppy (on the road from Quilon) and have regular services from the town centre.

From Alleppey the NH 47 goes N to Cochin (56 km)and Willingdon Island. (223 km to Trivandrum, total of about 3.5 hrs driving, allow 4 hrs by express bus.)

Cochin-Ernakulam

Population 850,000. *Altitude* Sea level. *Climate* Temp. Summer Max. 35°C Min. 23°C, Winter Max. 32°C Min. 20°C. Annual rainfall 25 cm. *Best season* Dec–Mar. *Clothing* Cottons. Airport on Willingdon Island, 5 km from Ernakulam, its sister city on the mainland, with daily air services to Trivandrum. Taxis from airport to Ernakulam centre about Rs 30.

	Jan	Feb	Mar	Apr	May	Jun	Jul	Aug	Sep	Oct	Nov	Dec	Av/Tot
Max (°C)	31	31	31	31	31	29	28	28	28	29	30	30	30
Min (°C)	23	24	26	26	24	24	24	24	24	24	24	23	24
Rain (mm)	9	34	50	139	364	756	572	386	235	333	184	37	3099

Cochin is one of the most interesting towns in S India. Historically it has been a trading port since at least Roman times. On the main trade route between Europe and China it shows evidence of long contact with both E and W. The town is in three main parts. Fort Cochin occupies the southern promontory on the seaward or westernmost side of the Bay. It is the first point of contact coming N up the coast road from Alleppey. **Willingdon Island** is an artificial island created in the 1920s by dredging the Bay to increase the depth of the entrance to the harbour to over 11 m. It is the HQ of the Southern Command of the Indian Navy, and has the airport, the railway terminus and at its northern tip the Malabar Hotel.

Across the causeway from Willingdon Island is **Ernakulam**, the first point of contact if coming by road either from the N or by the inland route from the S. Immediately opposite the jetty at Ernakulam is **Bolghatty Island**, strictly speaking a long narrow peninsula, and beyond it a **Vypeen Island** Island (also a peninsula).

The separate settlements have been of more than purely geographical interest. Until India's Independence in 1947 the long outer sand spit, with its narrow breach leadng to the wide bay inland, was under British political control from 1795. However, the inner harbour was in Cochin State, while most of the

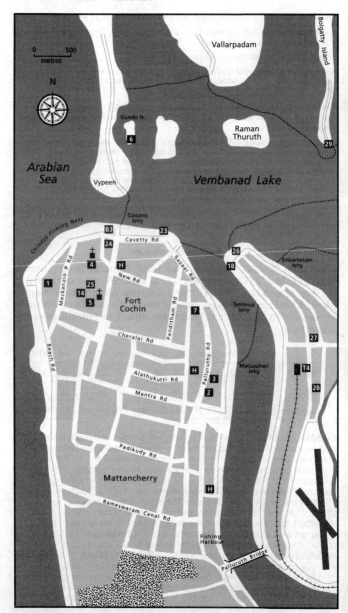

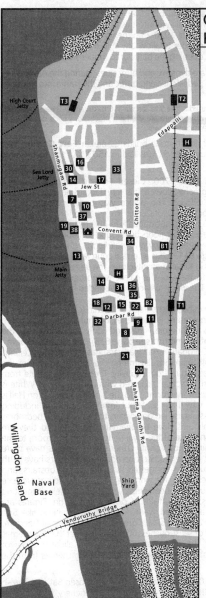

COCHIN & ERNAKULAM

SA 185

1. Dutch Cemetery
2. Mattancheri Palace & Museum.
3. Jewish Synagoge
4. St Francis Church
5. Santa Cruz Cathedral
6. Coir Factory
7. State Bank
8. Kerala Handicrafts Emporium
9. Kairali & Central Telegraph Office
10. Pai & Co. Bookshop
11. See India Foundation
12. Museum
13. Children's Traffic Park
14. Head Post Office
15. Siva Temple
16. St Mary's Syrian Church
17. Jami Masjid
18. Tourist Office
19. KTDC
20. Air India
21. Chinese Restaurant
22. Indian Coffee House
23. *Hotel Seagull*
24. *PWD Bungalow*
25. *Elite Hotel & Bakery*
26. *Malabar Hotel*
27. *Hotel Casino*
28. *Hotel Maharaj*
29. *Bolgatty Palace Hotel*
30. *Hotel Sea Lord*
31. *Woodlands*
32. *Bharat Tourtist Home & Indian Airlines*
33. *Blue Diamond*
34. *Hotel Luciya*
35. *YMCA*
36. *YWCA & Pandhal Rest*
37. *Ernakulam Rest House*
38. *Guest House*

B1. KSRTC
B2. Buses to Fort Cochin
B3. Fort Cochin Bus Stand

T1. Ernakulam City (S) & Rly Retiring Rm
T2. Ernakulam Town (N).
T3. Goods Station.
T4. Cochin Harbour.

hinterland was in the separate state of Travancore. The division of political authority delayed development until well into this century. Development of the harbour facilities did not begin until 1920-23, when the approach channel was dredged to a depth of 11 m in order to allow any ship that could pass through the Suez Canal to dock safely, opening the harbour to modern western shipping.

Today Ernakulam and Cochin are dynamic and busy cities. During the day the city centre streets are packed with pedestrians and traffic and the traffic into the cities is often reduced to a crawl.

Local festivals *Ulsavam* is celebrated at the Siva Temple in Ernakulam for 8 days in Jan/Feb and at Tripunithura Temple in Nov/Dec. There are elephant processions each day and folk dance and music performances. Aug/Sept. Onam.

Places of interest Most of the historic buildings are in **Fort Cochin** The foundation stone of the Portuguese fort was laid in 1503, but the fort itself is now completely ruined.

Mattancheri Palace Open 0900-1700. Closed Fri and national holidays. Entrance free, no flash photography allowed. It is very dark inside; you need fast film to get any worthwhile photos. The palace was built originally by the Portuguese in 1557 as a gift for the Raja of Cochin in exchange for trading rights. Just over 100 years later, in 1663, it was substantially re-built by the new occupants of Cochin, the Dutch. The palace is on 2 floors built round a quadrangle. The plan follows the traditional Kerala pattern known as *nalukettus* ("four buildings"). See Trivandrum Museum (**page 811**. It has a central courtyard, in common with most well constructed houses in Keralan architecture. The temple in the centre is dedicated to *Bhagavati*, and to the S of the palace is another temple complex dedicated to *Siva* and *Vishnu*. The whole palace is surrounded by high walls, with gates in the E and W.

Although the Palace has exhibits of the Rajas of Cochin (clothes, palanquins, weapons, furniture) the main feature is the series of murals painted on the wooden walls. These are remarkable, matched only by those in the Padmanabhapuram Palace S of Trivandrum (**see page 813**). The "royal bedroom" immediately to the W of the Coronation Hall (*palliyara*) has low wooden ceilings and walls covered in about 45 paintings illustrating the *Ramayana*, from the beginning to the point of Sita's return from captivity. These paintings date from the late 16th century. Every cm of space is covered with darkish colour. White is very rarely used and blue is used very sparingly. To the S of the Coronation Hall is *kovinithilam* (staircase room), which has six 18th century large murals including the coronation of Rama. (The staircase led downstairs to the women's bedrooms on the ground floor). The pictures have no thematic content, and they are somewhat lighter in tone than those of the royal bedchamber. The room to the N of the *kovinitilam* has a painting of Vishnu. Other rooms upstairs have more exhibits of the royal house. 2 of the women's bedrooms downstairs have 19th century murals. These are much less congested than the murals upstairs, and details are shown much more clearly. In the words of H. Sarkar, "shadings produce tonal effects and realistic colours have been employed, thus minutely delineating even minor features like nails, fingers, folds of clothes and so on. Figures are comparatively slimmer with attenuated waist... All the panels here, like Siva dallying with Mohini, Krishna and Gopis, and others breathe an air of freedom, charged with an undercurrent of sensuousness in spite of the fact that the themes are mythological." One of the rooms shows the poet Kalidasa's story of *Kumarasambava*, while the other has 5 large murals relating themes from the *Puranas*.

Jewish Synagogue Open 1000-1200 and 1500-1700. Closed Sat and Jewish holidays. Entrance Re 0.50. The Jews quarter is in S Mattanchery, next door to the Mattancheri Palace. The story of the Cochin Jews is fascinating, if far from clear in all its details. For several centuries there were 2 Jewish communities. The older was that of the "black" Jews. According to one source they claimed to have settled in 587 BC. The earliest sure evidence of their presence and importance is a copper inscription dated AD 388 (or possibly as much as a century later) by the Prince of Malabar. The White Jews came much later, and eventually in larger numbers, possibly totalling as many as 4,000 at their peak. The synagogue of the White Jews is next to the Mattancheri Palace. Stepping inside is an extraordinary experience of light and airiness, given partly by the flooring of eighteenth century light blue Chinese ceramic tiles, hand made and each one different. In addition to the trade links with China implied by this purchase from Canton, the Jewish community may also have had strong links with Babylonian Jews. It is possible to see the Great Scrolls of the Old Testament and the copper plates on which privileges were granted to the Jewish community by the Cochin rulers. Since Indian Independence and the contemporary founding of the State of Israel the Jewish community has now shrunk to fewer than fifty. However, the nameplates on a few of the houses still witness to their continuing presence. The second Jewish synagogue (in Ernakulam) is deserted.

St. Francis Church Originally named Santo Antonio, St. Francis Church is the first church to have been built in the new, European influenced tradition. It is in Fort Cochin and was probably first built in 1510. It is said to have been built of wood, but within a few years had been replaced by the present stone building. (There is no authority for the widely quoted date of 1546.) Vasco da Gama died on the site in 1524 and was originally buried in the cemetery. 14 years later his body was removed to Portugal. The church has an impressive façade; inside, the chancel is separated from the nave by a plain arch. The use of the arch is in sharp contrast to traditional Indian use of flat overlapping slabs, or **corbelling***, to produce gateways. The church was taken over by the Dutch and converted into a Protestant chapel after they captured Cochin in 1663. The British converted it into an Anglican church after they took power in 1795, and in 1949 the congregation joined the Church of S India. **Santa Cruz Cathedral**, Fort Cochin, close to St Francis Church, contains some attractive paintings.

Chinese fishing nets Not unique to Cochin, but uniquely accessible to the short stay visitor, the fishing cantilevered fishing nets line the entrance to the harbour mouth. They can best be seen either on the N end of the fort promontory, a few metres from the fort Cochin bus stand, or from a boat tour of the harbour.

Gundu Island On the inshore side of Vypeen island, with only 2 ha Gundu is the smallest island in the bay. It has a co-operative coir factory where you can try your hand at making mats. Visit through KSTDC tour.

Bolghatty Island The "palace" now converted into a hotel was originally built in 1744 by the Dutch. It became the home of the British Resident at the court of the Raja of Cochin after 1799. Set in about 3 ha of gardens, the Kerala State Tourist Corporation has now added new "honeymoon suites" at the water's edge and has a golf course in the grounds. Despite the attempt it has not completely ruined the atmosphere of colonial decay which haunted the old building in its pre-modernised form.

Willingdon Island The artificial island created when Cochin port was dredged to deepen it has become the hub of one of India's busiest ports. The custom's house, Government of India tourist office and *Malabar Hotel* lie to the N of the airport and the main railway terminus. You can take a pleasant and inexpensive ferry ride around the lake.

Local industries Cochin is still famous for its coir products. Now the centre of a ship repairing industry there is a growing range of associated engineering industries, making Cochin-Ernakulam the centre of Kerala's industrial economy.

Services

Hotels Most hotels are in Ernakulam, with very limited accommodation in Fort Cochin. It is also worth considering staying outside Cochin at the Govt Guest House in Alwaye, one of the most attractive in Kerala (see under Alwaye below).

A *Malabar*. Taj Group. Willingdon Island. T 6811, Cable: Comfort, Telex: 0885 6661 Mlbr In. 100 rm. 3 km rly, 12 km centre. Excellent hotel and service, superb setting with lawns on the waterfront, range of facilities being developed. Beautifully furnished rm – those on the upper floors have sitting areas. Two suites decorated in Kerala and Chinese styles! Snacks on the lawn, multi-cuisine Rice Boats restaurant and Jade Pavilion Chinese. Strange that pineapple not available on the menu for breakfast in Kerala! Regular ferry service from Ernakulam to its own jetty. **C** *Presidency Ashok*, 47 Paramara Rd, Ernakulam Town. R 363100, Cable: Ashok, Telex: 0885 6201 Tour In. 47 rm, deluxe with fridge. 3 km rly, central. Central a/c. Restaurant, bar, coffee shop, exchange, travel, TV. **C** *Abad Plaza*, MG Rd, Ernakulam. T 361636. Cable: Abadplaza, Telex, 0885 6587. 41 rm, some deluxe with fridge. 2 km rly, central. Central a/c. Restaurant (seafood specialities), bar, exchange, travel, shops, TV. **C** *Casino*, Willingdon Island. T 6821, Cable: Casino, Telex: 0885 6314 Safe In. 71 rm, better in the older building. close to rly, 5 km centre. Central a/c. Restaurant (multi-cuisine and an outdoor seafood restaurant), exchange, travel, shops, outdoor pool in large garden. Not on the water front.

D *Sealord*, Shanmugam Rd, Ernakulam. T 352682, Cable: Sealord, Telex: 0885 6643 Tour In. 40 rm. 7 km airport, 2 km rly. Central a/c. Restaurant, TV. **D** *Bolghatty Palace* (KTDC), Bolghatty Island, Mulavukad. T 355003, Cable: Relax. Former British Residency (18th century palace) has 12 rm some a/c. Restaurant, bar, lawns on the waterfront, small golf course. Menu off-season rather limited. Ferries every 20 min from High Court Jetty and frequent sightseeing boat tours. The old fashioned 'Suites' are enormous with sitting rm and large marble floored bathrooms. In addition, simple waterside tree house, 'honeymoon' cottages with round beds and own staircases! **D** *Grand*, MG Rd, Ernakulam, T 353211, Cable: Grand. 24 rm, some a/c. 1 km rly, Central. A/c restaurants, bar, exchange, travel, garden. Comfortable with good food. **D** *International*, MG Rd, Ernakulam. T 353911, Cable: Turistome. 26 rm 1 km rly, close to centre. Central a/c. Restaurant (Kerala specialities), bar, coffee shop, exchange, travel, TV. **D** *Woodlands*, MG Rd, Ernakulam. T 351372, Cable: Woodlands, Telex: 0885 6316. 65 rm, 21 a/c with bath. close to rly. Very central. A/c veg restaurant. Good value. **D** *Bharat Tourist Home*, Durbar Hall Rd, Ernakulam. T 353501, Cable: Bharathome, Telex: 0885 6461 Bth In. 92 rm some a/c. Close to Ernakulam Jn. rly. A/c restaurants (N and S Indian veg), coffee shop, exchange. Good value.

E *Sea Gull*, Calvetty Rd, Fort Cochin, NE between the 2 ferry stops. T 28128. 8 rm, ask for a/c. Converted old warehouses and houses on the waterside, between the 2 ferry stops. **E** *Biju's Tourist Home*, Market Rd, nr Canon Shed Rd corner, Ernakulam. T 369881. 28 rm. No restaurant. Good position, clean and comfortable. Friendly. **E** *Sangeetha*, Chitoor Rd, Ernakulam. T 368736, Cable: Excellent. 48 rm some a/c. Close to rly, central. A/c veg restaurant. **E** *Blue Diamond*, Market Rd, Ernakulam. T 353221, Cable: Bludiamond. 42 rm some a/c. Restaurant, a/c bar, roof garden. **E** *Piazza Lodge*, nr S rly station, Ernakulam. T 367408. a/c rm. Clean and recommended. **E** *Luciya*, Stadium Rd, close to Bus Station, Ernakulam. T 354433, Cable: Luciya. 106 rm with bath, some a/c. 2 km rly, central. A/c restaurant and bar.

Other inexpensive non-a/c accommodation – **E** *Bosoto Lodge*, Press Club Rd, nr jetty. Drably decorated, friendly staff. Beware mosquitoes and bed bugs. **F** *Railway Retiring Rooms*. 5 single rm. Contact Station Master. **F** *Govt Rest House*, opp Guest House, Ernakulam. T 361265. Reservations: District Collector, Collectorate Trikkakara. **F** *PWD Inspection Bungalow*, nr Fort Cochin beach. T 25797. Large rm but run down. Reservations: Executive Engineer, PWD (Buildings & Roads), Ernakulam. **F** *YMCA*, Chittor Rd, Ernakulam. T 355620. Reservations: General Secretary.

Restaurants Ernakulam has a number of good restaurants, some in hotels. The *Sealord's* Roof top restaurant on Shanmugam Rd (good fish dishes and Chinese), The *Regency* also includes Chinese, in Abad Plaza Hotel, the Grand Hotel offers Japanese dishes on its menu and *Presidency Ashok's* Restaurant serves Continental, Indian and Chinese. Other restaurants serving non-veg food is the *Chinese Garden* off MG Rd and *Pandhal* on MG Rd which is also good for snacks. *Whizz* in the Abad Plaza Complex, MG Rd and *Jancy's Café* on Shanmugam Rd serves S Indian snacks. *Bimbi's*, nr the corner of Durbar Hall Rd and MG Rd, also offers fast-food, the *Khyber* upstairs serves meals. The *Indian Coffee House* has 2 branches, one near the rly station opp Bimbi's and the other at the corner of Park Av and Canon Shed Rd and lives up to its reputation. *Fort Cochin* has the Govt *Sabala* Restaurant and the *Elite Hotel* near St. Francis Church. **Willingdon** The *Malabar* offers excellent food in its expensive restaurant, *Rice Boats*. *Ceylon Bake House*, Ernakulam. Great fish and chips, excellent service – lovely place.

Bars Recommended in the major hotels only, although prohibition is not in force.

Banks & Exchange Several banks on MG Rd (Allahabad, Baroda, Central Bank, Reserve Bank), Shanmugam Rd (Bank of India, State Bank, Syndicate Bank) and on Broadway, Ernakulam (Canara and State Bank of Travancore). Branches of Chartered, Grindlays and State Bank of India on Willingdon Island and Punjab National Bank in Mattancheri and State Bank of Mysore on Palace Rd, Cochin Rd.

Shopping Coir products (eg mats), Carvings on rosewood, buffalo horn, ivory and models of snake boats. Several Govt Emporia on MG Rd, Ernakulam, including *Kerala State Handicraft Emporium*, (T 353063), *Kairali* (T 354507), *Khadi Bhavan* (T 355279), *Handloom House and National Textiles* (which also has a shop in Banerji Rd (T 354470). Other shopping areas are in Broadway, Super Bazaar, Anand Bazaar, Prince St and New Rd. *Bhavi Books* has a good selection in Convent Rd and you can pick up gifts from *Curio Palace* on MG Rd.

Local transport Yellow top and Tourist *taxis*, both luxury and ordinary, can be hired by the hour or on a charge based per km. Extra charges for waiting. Kumar Taxis, Palace Rd, Mattancheri, T 245558, Ensign Taxis, MG Rd, T 353080, Collin Travels, Lissie Jn, T 368064 among others. KTDC, Tourist Reception Centre, Shanmugham Rd, Ernakulam, T 353234 and Princey Travels, nr N Overbridge, Ernakulam, T 352751 also offer coach hire. *Buses* are fairly frequent and cheap in Ernakulam. Journeys between Ernakulam, Willingdon and Fort Cochin useful after ferries stop running. *Auto-rickshaws* usually ask for a minimum charge.

Ferries are the best way of getting about between the islands – faster, cheaper and much more comfortable than buses or autos. Ferry stops are clearly named. *Fort Cochin* 'Customs' (main stop) with a separate one for Vypeen Island, *Willingdon Island* 'Embarkation' to the N and 'Terminus' on W side towards Mattancheri.

From **Ernakulam** To Fort Cochin Customs, Willingdon Terminus and Mattancheri – Half-hourly from 0630 to 2130. To Bolgatty Island – Every 20 min from High Court Jetty from 0600-2200. To Vypeen Island via Willingdon Embarkation, ½-hr or more, from 0530-2230.

From **Fort Cochin** Customs to Malabar Hotel, ½-hr approx and to Vypeen Island, very frequent with about 2 car ferries an hour.

Entertainment You can visit a couple of centres where there are daily performances of Kathakali and you can arrive early to watch the extraordinary make-up being applied. See India Foundation, XXX/111 Kalathi Parambil Lane off Chittor Rd, behind Laxman Theatre, T 369471. Make up 1830, Performance with English commentary, 1900-2030. Rs 25. Cochin Cultural Centre, (XXXV/1521 Sangamom, Manniath Rd, Ernakulam, T 353732). Performances at Darbar Hall Grounds by the Museum, Theatre T 367866. Demonstration with explanations1830-2000. Rs 25. Art Kerala, Ravipuram, Ernakulam. 1900-2030. Check with Tourist Office for date of monthly performance at Kathakali Clun, Layam Rd, Ernakulam.

Museums Parishath Thamburan Museum, Darbar Hall Rd Ernakulam T 369047. In Old Durbar Hall with typical Kerala architecture. 19th century oil paintings, old coins, sculptures, some collections from Cochin Royal family. Open 0930 – 1200 and 1500-1730, closed Mon and national holidays. **Hill Palace Museum**, Tripunithura T 857113 Royal exhibits, paintings, carvings, arms Open 0900-1700, closed Mon. Small entry fee, extra for car. **Kerala Fine Arts Society**, Fine Arts Ave, T 352730. **Museum of Kerala History and its Makers**, Edappally, Cochin. Open 1000-1600, closed Mon and national holidays. Starting with Neolithic man through St. Thomas, Vasco da Gama and historical personalities of Kerala are represented with sound and light. Entry Rs 2, Child Re.1. **Archaeological Museum**, Mattancheri Palace. Ornaments, weapons, clothes and paintings. Open daily 1000-1700. Closed Fri. Entry free.

Parks and zoos Children's Traffic Park and Subhas Chandra Bose Park in Ernakulam and Nehru Memorial Children's Park in Fort Cochin.

Useful addresses For visa extension, City Police Commissioner, Marine Drive, T 31700.

Post and telegraph Central Telegraph Office, Jos Junction Building, 2nd Floor, MG Rd, Ernakulam, T 355601. Open 24 hr. Cochin, Matancherry T 25554; Ernakulam Head Post Office, Hospital Road, T 355467, Cochin Head Post Office, Fort Cochin (for Poste Restante), T 24247. N End Post Office, Willingdon Island, T 6270.

Places of worship *Hindu* Siva Temple and Tirumalai Dewaswom, Ernakulam; Tirumalai Dewaswom Temple, Cochin; Palliyarakavu Temple, Cochin; Paramara Devi Temple Ernakulam;

Aiyappa Temple, Willingdon Island. (**NB** Non-Hindus are not allowed inside the Hindu temples) *Christian* St Francis Church (Church of S India) Fort Cochin; Santa Cruz Cathedral (Roman Catholic), Fort Cochin; Stella Maris Church (Roman Catholic), Willingdon Island; Emmanuel Church, Broadway, Ernakulam; St. Mary's Orthodox Syrian Church, near Boat Jetty, Ernakulam. *Muslim* New Mosque, Bazar Road, Mattancheri; Pullapadi Mosque Ernakulam *Jain* Jain Temple, Palace Road *Jewish* Jewish synagogue, Jew Town Fort Cochin.

Hospitals and medical services Several hospitals include General Hospital, Hospital Rd, T 361251, Lissie Hospital, Lissie Junction, T 352006, Lourdes Hospital, Pachalam, T 351507.

Travel agents Govan Travels, Hospital Rd, T 354970. Harrison Malayalam, Willingdon Island, T 6007, and several on MG Rd, Ernakulam – Jail Hind Travels, T 361011, Kerala Travels, T 367738, Travel Corporation of India, Telstar Building, T 351646.

Tourist offices and information Govt of India Tourist Office, next to Malabar Hotel, nr Jetty on Willingdon Island, T 6045, where you can pick up maps and small booklets. Govt of Kerala Tourist Information Office, Old Collectorate, Park Avenue, Ernakulam. KTDC, Shanmugam Rd, Ernakulam. T 353234 where you can get a small booklet 'Kerala Travel Facts' with useful listings and 3 rather small scale maps. 0800-1800. *Guides* are available through the Govt of India Tourist Office, the rates vary according to the number in the group. For up to 4 persons, half day (4 hr) Rs 40 and full day (8 hr) Rs 80. For journeys outside the city additional charges are made of about Rs 40.

Tours KTDC offers daily *Boat Cruise and Sightseeing* tours visiting Dutch Palace, Jewish Synagogue, Francis Church, Chinese Fishing Nets, Gundu Island, Bolghatty Island. Dep. from Boat Jetty opp Sealord Hotel, Shanmugam Rd, Ernakulam. 0930-1300, 1330-1700. Rs. 15. Highly recommended. Overnight *Tekkadi Wildlife Tour* by coach visiting Kadamattam Church, Moolamattom Power House, Idukki Dam, Periyar. Dep. from Tourist Reception Centre, every Sat 0730 returning 2000 Sun. Rs.100 plus food and accommodation. 3 day Velankanni Tour by coach visiting Thanjavur, Madurai and Tekkadi. Dep. from Tourist Reception Centre, First Fri every month 0800 returning following Sun 2100. Rs.175 plus food and accommodation. Reservations through KTDC.

Air Indian Airlines Bombay Daily (+ 1 other), 0755, 1 hr 45 min; **Delhi** Daily, 1725, 3 hr 55 min; **Trivandrum** Wed, Fri & Sun, 1630, 30 min; **Goa** Daily, 1725, 1 hr 5 min; **Madras** Wed, Fri & Sun (+ 1 other), 1630, 2 hr 5 min; **Bangalore** Mon, Tue, Th & Sat, 1700, 50 min. **Vayudoot** Madras Mon-Sat, 1245, 2 hr 25 min; **Agatti**, Mon-Sat, 0910, 1 hr 30 min. Indian Airlines, Durbar Hall Rd, nr Bharat Hotel. T 352065. Airport. T 6486. **Air Asiatic** To Kozhikode and Bombay.

Rail Cochin is on the broad gauge line joining the Trivandrum to Mangalore, Bangalore and Madras lines. Trains from the important cities in the N stop alternately at Cochin and Ernakulam Junction, the latter continuing to Trivandrum. Enquiries: Cochin Harbour Terminus, T 6050. Ernakulam Jn, S, T 353100, Public Information, T 369119, Town (N Station), T 353920.
   Ernakulam to Trivandrum: *Vanchinad Exp*, 6303, daily, 0600, 4 hr 20 min; *Venad Exp*, 6301 (AC/CC), daily, 1710, 4 hr 50 min; **Cochin to Madras (MC)**: *Madras Exp*, 6042 (AC/II), 1620 (from Ernakulam 1655), 13 hr 55 min; **Ernakulam to Delhi (ND)**: *Kerala Mangala Exp*, 2625/2625A (AC/II), daily, 1440, 47 hr 50 min; **Cochin to Bombay (VT)**: *Netravati Exp*, 2136 (AC/II), Mon, Wed, Fri, 1725 (from Ernakulam 1750), 36 hr 20 min; **Ernakulam to Bombay (VT)**: *Kanniya Kumari Exp*, 1082 (AC/II), daily, 1330, 39 hr 35 min; **Ernakulam to Mangalore**: *Trivandrum-Mangalore Exp*, 6349 (AC/CC), daily, 1100, 10 hr.

Road Cochin is junction of 2 National Highways, 17 and 47, the former to Panvel (Bombay) and the latter to Kanniyakumari. Other major highways lead to Bangalore and Madras and other cities beyond. Distances to some are Madras 675 km, Bombay 1,400 km, Alleppey 64 km, Trivandrum 223 km, Kanniyakumari 309 km, Ooty 312 km, Kodaikkanal 330 km, Tekkadi (Periyar National Park) 190 km, Trichur 80 km and Madurai 324 km.

Buses of the Kerala SRTC run Express and Fast services from Ernakulam Bus Terminus to other major cities within Kerala and into the neighbouring states with reciprocal services from other State Transport Corp. Enquiries: Bus Terminus, T 352033. Indira Travels, DH Rd, T 360693 and SB Travels, c/o Ensign Agencies, MG Rd, opp Joss Annexe, T 353080, run overnight video coaches (12 hr) to Bangalore.

Ship Cruises to Lakshadweep organised by SPORT, Harbour Rd, Willingdon Island, T 69755.

Excursions *Kalady* 45 km from Cochin, Kalady, on the bank of the Periyar River, is a major Hindu pilgrimage centre as it is the birthplace of one of India's most influential philosophers, Sankaracharya. Living in the 8th century, **Sankaracharya** founded the school of *advaita* philosophy (**see page 50**) which spread widely across southern India. There are now 2 shrines in his memory, one as Dakshinamurti and the other to the Goddess Sarada, open 0530-1230, 1530-2000. The Adi Sankara Kirti Stambha Mandapam is 9 storeyed octagonal tower, 46 m high, and details Sri Sankara's life and works and the Shan Mathas or 6 ways to worship. Open 0700-1900. Small entry fee.

Kalady can easily be visited in an afternoon from Cochin. However, accommodation is available in Sri Sankaracharya *New Guest House* which is basic and cheap. T 345. Alternatively, for the *PWD Rest House* apply to Assistant Engineer, PWD, Angalamlai.

COCHIN TO CANNANORE

Initially going inland, this route goes through Kerala's most sacred pilgrimage centre at Guruvayur and the many megalithic monuments around the western end of the Palghat gap. It rejoins the coast at the major commercial, but historically important, town of Kozhikode. The road then follows the attractive coastline to Cannanore.

Leave Ernakulam on NH 17 **Alwaye**, 21 km N of Ernakulam, is an important industrial town; the radioactive monazite sands of the beach here are processed for India's nuclear power programme. Other industries include chemicals, glass, aluminium, rayon, tyres, fertilisers. Despite its industrial activity the **Periyar River** on which it stands is still very attractive, and good for river swimming. There is a Siva lingam on the sand bank.

Accommodation in **E** *Periyar Ltd*, New By Pass Rd, T 5465. 10 rm, some a/c. Government **E** *Guest House*, which also has Tourist Information. T 3637. This is one of the best Government Guest Houses in Kerala. An old palace on the banks of the river, it has a beautiful circular verandah, large rm and efficient staff. Apply to Manager. Cheaper **F** *Rest House* which you can reserve through the District Collector, Ernakulam or direct.

From Alwaye return to coast road and **Kodungallur** (30 km, formerly Cranganore). The Syrian orthodox church here has some striking features, illustrating a blending of early Christian architecture in Kerala with surrounding Hindu traditions. Thus the images of Peter and Paul are placed where the *dvarapalas* (door-keepers) of Hindu temples would be found, and a portico is placed in front of the church for pilgrims. These and other features suggest that, in the words of H. Sarkar of the Archaeological Survey of India, "the **church architecture** in Kerala evolved out of an indigenous building tradition, and basically the same trend continued until recently despite the impact of later ecclesiastical architecture of Europe." At one time Cranganore was the W coast's major port, and the capital of the Chera king Cheraman Perumal. **Muziris**, on the shore, is the point at which St. Thomas is believed to have landed. It is worth visiting the Tiruvanchikulam Temple, the Bhagavati Temple and the Portuguese fort. But **Cranganore** is also associated by tradition with the arrival of the first Muslims to reach India by sea. Malik-ibn-Dinar is reputed to have built India's first mosque here. There is no evidence that the present mosque can be dated as early as the 7th century AD, but it does have some interesting features. The outer walls have a moulded base similar to that of Brahmanical temples, for example.

Accommodation in **F** PWD *Resthouse*. Apply to the District Collector at Trichur or the Manager of the Rest House itself.

Continue N through **Chakkavad** to one of Kerala's most sacred pilgrimage centres, to **Guruvayur** (50 km). The temple to Krishna which probably dates from at least the 16th century makes this a very sacred place and an important pilgrimage centre. The image of **Krishna** has 4 arms with the conch, the discus, the mace and the lotus.

One devotee has written that "Adoringing himself with the divine tulais garland and pearl necklace, the Lord here appears in all his radiance. His eyes stream forth the milk of compassion and kindness. To millions, *Gurvayurappan* is a living deity who answers all their prayers. He is *Sri Krishna*, the divine cowherd who played his flute in Gokulam and Vrindhavan and enchanted the whole world with his music. It is not only the gopis or milkmaids who yearn for oneness with him, but all men and women who wish to be liberated from *samsara*."

In the outer enclosure there is a tall gold plated flagpost and a pillar of lamps. The sanctum sanctorum is in the 2-storeyed *srikoil*, with the image of the 4 armed Krishna garlanded with pearls and marigolds. Punnathur Kotta, 4 km away, houses the 40 temple elephants. An unusual feature of the temple at Guruvayur is the timing of the rituals. The sanctum opens at 0300 and closes at 2100. Except between 1300 and 1600, when it is closed, a continuous series of pujas and processions is performed. The darshan at 0300 is believed to be particularly auspicious. It is called the *nirnalaya* darshan, when the image is decked out with the previous day's flowers. Non-Hindus are not allowed inside the Sri Krishna Svami Temple, where the devotional poet Melpattur Narayan Bhattathiri composed a famous Sanskrit devotional poem, *Narayaniyam*.

Festivals Feb/Mar *Ulsavam*. 10 days of festivities start with an elephant race and continue with colourful elephant processions and performances of Krishattam dances. Details of the timing can be obtained from Kerala Tourist offices. In Nov-Dec Guruvayur is famous for its recitals of classical music at the temple.

Hotels Accommodation in a/c rm in the **E** category available in *Elite Tourist Home*, T 6215 in E Nada and in W Nada; *Surya*, T 6505, Maharaja Hotel, T 6369 and Namaskar Tourist Home, T 6355. Similar accommodation also available at KTDC *Tourist Bungalow*, E Nada, T 6266. Reservations: Manager. *Rest Houses* of the Guruvayur Devaswom, T 6535 including a VIP Guest House *Sreevalsam*. Reservations, Administrator.

Restaurants in the hotels listed above and also an Indian Coffee House and Ramakrishna Lunch Home.

The road goes inland to **Kunnamkulam** (10 km). This area is noted for its wide range of **megalithic monuments**. On the western side of the Palghat gap; it has been one of the few easy routes through the western Ghats in both directions for 3,000 years.

Megalithic cultures spread from the Tamil Nad plains down into Kerala, but developed their own local forms. The small villages of Eyyal, Chovvanur, Kakkad, Porkalam, Kattakampala and Kadamsseri, between Guruvayur and Kunnamkulam, have *hoodstones*, *hatstones*, *dolmens*, *burial urns* and *menhirs*. **Chovannur** in particular has many *Topikals* (hat stones), one of the particularly distinctive iron age megalithic remains of Kerala. Nearby **Porkalam** has a wide range of monuments side by side within an area of less than 1 ha. Hoodstones (kudaikal) are made of dressed granite and are like a handleless umbrella made of palm leaf used locally. It is shaped into a dome and covers a burial pit. The hat-stones, made of dressed laterite, have a circular top stone resting on four pieces of stone placed upright in an almost circular form, looking like a giant mushroom. They did not have any burial chamber.

Continue N The road keeps away from the coast, to Kozhikode (77 km).

Kozhikode (Calicut)

Population 450,000. *Altitude* Sea level. *Climate* Temp. Summer Max. 35°C Min. 23°C, Winter Max. 32°C Min. 22°C. Annual rainfall 2500 mm. *Best season* Oct – May. *Clothing* Cottons. Kozhikode has direct flights to Bombay; the airport is 30 km away.

Kozhikode (meaning literally "cock crowing") played a vital role in Kerala's history as the capital of the Zamorin Rajas. According to the early 19th century historian Buchanan-Hamilton "when Cheruman Perumal had divided Malabar, and had no principality remaining to bestow on the ancestors of the Tamuri, he gave that chief his sword, with all the territory in which a cock crowing at a small temple here could be heard. This formed the original dominions of the Tamuri, and was called Colicudu, or the cock crowing". That romantic derivation of the name is not unchallenged, but the story is suggestive of the tiny states that existed in medieval Kerala. In 1498 Vasco da Gama landed at the port, starting a turbulent, often violent, 150 years of contact with European powers.

When the Portuguese arrived Calicut was under the control of the **Vijayanagar Empire (see page 879)**, based in Hampi over 500 km to the NE. After a decade of violent raids the local **Zamorin** made peace with the Portuguese and gave them trading rights and the right to build a fort. It remained a centre of Portuguese economic and political power and influence for over a century. In 1766 the city was threatened not by Europeans from the sea but by the Muslim Raja from Mysore, **Haidar Ali**. The Zamorin offered peace, but when the offer was rejected barricaded himself and his family in the palace and burnt it to the ground. Although Haidar Ali soon left, his son Tipu Sultan returned twenty three years later and devastated the entire region. British rule was imposed in 1792 by the Treaty of Seringapatam.

Its name during the British period, **Calicut**, was given to the *calico* cloth, a block printed cotton exported round the world. Today Kozhikode is a major commercial centre for N-central Kerala.

Local festivals Feb. *Ulsavam* at Srikantesvara Temple for 7 days during Sivaratri week. Elephant processions, exhibitions, fair and fireworks.

Places of interest *Kakkai* (6 km from town centre) is the main centre of the timber industry. Elephants are still widely used for hauling timber. The timber yard is said to be the second largest in the world.

Local crafts and industries The major centre for Kerala's timber industry. Boat building is also important. The textile mill started by the Basel Mission in the 19th century is now state owned.

Hotels D *Seaqueen*, Beach Rd. T 60201, Cable: Seaqueen, Telex: 0804 216. 25 rm, 15 a/c. 1.5 km rly. Restaurant, a/c bar, credit cards. **D** *Hyson*, Bank Rd. T 65221. 51 double rm, some a/c. **E** *NCK Tourist Home*, Mavoor Rd. T 65331, Cable: Enceekay. 54 rm, some a/c with bath. Close to centre. Good veg restaurant. **E** *Alakapuri Guest House*, Maulana Md Ali Rd. T 73361, Telex: 0854 223. 39 rm some a/c with bath and telephone. 1 km rly, central. Restaurant, bar, garden, credit cards. **E** *Kalpaka Tourist Home*, Town Hall Rd. T 76171, Cable: Kalpalodge, Telex: 854 295 Kala In. 100 rm, some a/c with bath. Close to rly. Restaurant. **E** *Foura*, Mazoor Rd. T 63601. 33 rm, some double a/c. Central. Restaurant. The **E** *Government Guest House* is on W Hill with a/c rm. T 73002. Apply to Manager. The *Rest House* is cheaper and can be reserved through the District Collector.

Restaurants There are restaurants in the hotels listed and other eating places on Beech Rd, and Mavoor (Indira Gandhi) Rd. *India Coffee Houses* on Kallai Rd and Mavoor Rd, *Woodlands* on the latter, Snack bars, including *French Bakery* and Restaurant on Beech Rd, *Park* open air restaurant, Bank Rd.

Banks & Exchange State Bank on Bank Rd, T 73626. Several others in town.

Shopping Local handicrafts are rosewood, ivory, buffalo horn carvings, coir products and model snake boats. Supermarket nr Mavoor Rd and Big Bazaar in SM St.

Local transport Tourist taxis, Yellow top taxis, auto-ricksaws and SKS Luxury Buses from Jail Rd.

Sports Yoga. Kerala Yogasanam Centre is on New Rd.

Museums Pazhassiraja Museum 5 km on E Hill. The Archaeological Department Museum, located at E Hill. Exhibits include copies of original murals, plus bronzes, old coins and models of the different types of megalithic monuments widespread in the area. **The Art Gallery and Krishna Menon Museum** (named after the Kerala politician who became a leading left wing figure in India's post-Independence Congress Government) Located next door to the Pazhassiraja Museum, it has an excellent collection of paintings by Indian artists and also wood and ivory carvings. A section of the museum is dedicated to the personal belongings of V.K. Krishna Menon. Open 0930-1230, 1430-1730. Daily except Mon. Entry free.

Tourist office and information is at the District Information Office, Civil Station. T 73096.

Air Indian Airlines Bombay Daily, 1420, 1 hr 35 min. Indian Airlines, Cherroty Rd. Air India, Beach Rd. Airport is 25 km from centre.

Rail Trains to Mangalore 3 hr, Ernakulam about 5 hr, Trivandrum about 10 hr. Also to Madras and Bangalore and Coimbatore.

Road Well connected to other important towns in Kerala and neighbouring states, including Mangalore 246 km, Cochin 225 km, Trivandrum, Bangalore, and Madurai.

Excursions There is a very picturesque journey over Western Ghats to Ooty and Mysore 214 km (5.5 hrs). This goes up through **Vayittiri** (65 km) and **Manantoddy** (Manantavadi – 25 km, altitude 750 m) 3 km before Manantoddy is the Vallurvaku or "fish pagoda", dedicated to Durga. The tank has sacred carp. **Hotel** F *Deluxe Tourist Home*, Described by one recent visitor as "clean, comfortable but not deluxe! " It has a fairly good restaurant. Rm have attached and clean, en-suite Indian toilets.

A branch road 10 km from Vayittiri leads to **Sultan's Battery** (now spelt Sultan's batary: 22 km, population 27,000), an 18th century fort built by Tipu Sultan in the heart of the Wynad coffee and cardamom growing region. Not much of the fort itself remains. 6 km E of the fort is a natural deep crack in the rock on which four inscriptions have been carved and some crude drawings. **Hotels F** *Modern Tourist Home* Quite modern and reasonable.

Leave Kozhikode on NH 17. After 23 km the road goes through Kovilandi, a road on the right leading to Tamarasseri (28 km). Keep on the road straight on which goes through Kollam (3 km) to **Badagara** (19 km). **Mahe** is a further 13 km, just one more village in the apparently endless palm fringed beach of Kerala. It was named after M. Mahe de Labourdonnais, when he captured it for the French in 1725. A tiny settlement of 7 sq km, Mahe is beautifully positioned on a slight hill overlooking the river. From the neighbouring hill where the Basel Mission house was built there are very attractive views of the Wynad hills inland. It is still part of the State of Pondicherry.

Continue N along the coast road, often with attractive views of the sea, to **Tellicherry** (6 km) a British E India Company settlement dating from 1683. It was set up to export pepper and cardamom, and in 1708 the Company obtained permission to build a fort. It survived a siege laid by Haidar Ali and today is still standing on a rocky promontory about 15 metres above sea level. The N W of the Fort citadel is occupied by an old building. The town is on a beautiful site, with good swimming and a fascinating bazar. Few visitors come to the town but it is well worth seeing. The NH 17 continues N to Cannanore (22 km).

Cannanore is the centre of the Moplah community, a group of Arab descent. Cannanore was also the capital of the N Kolathiri Rajas for several hundred years, their palace is at **Chirakkal**, 6 km away. As with so many coastal sites in Kerala the town stands on low hills and cliffs at the sea face, no more than 10 to 15 m above sea level. At the end of the northwestern promontory is the Fort St Angelo, built by the Portuguese in 1505, later taken over by the British as their most important military base in the S. It is a massive building, constructed out of laterite blocks and is surrounded by the sea on three sides and a dry ditch on its landward side. The British cantonment area was on the northwest side of the bay while the highly picturesque Moplah town are round the bay to the S of the fort.

Rail Mangalore: *Mangalore Mail*, 6001 (AC/II), Daily, 1020, 2 hr 55 min; *Trivandrum-Mangalore Exp*, 6349 (AC/CC), daily, 1805, 2 hr 55 min; **Palghat:** *Kerala-Mangalore Exp*, 2625/2625A(AC/CC), daily, 1140, 6 hr; *Madras Mail*, 6002 (AC/CC), daily, 1515, 5 hr 10 min; **Coimbatore:** *Kerala-Mangala Exp*, 2625/2625A (AC/II), daily, 1140, 7 hr 35 min; *Netravati Exp*, 2136 (AC/II), Mon, Wed, Fri, 1600, 6 hr 32 min; **Madras (MC):** *Madras Mail*, 6002 (AC/II), daily, 1515, 15 hr 20 min.

Excursion *Madayi*, 22 km away, has a famous 12th century mosque built by Malik Ibn Dinar with white marble which is claimed to be from Arabia. The coast road now continues N through **Hosdrug** (60 km) to **Mangalore** (71 km).

TRIVANDRUM TO TRICHUR (THE INLAND ROUTE N)

The two routes N are never widely separated, and it is possible to divert from one to the other at several places according to time and interest. The road N out of Trivandrum winds through apparently endless settlements, villages without beginning or end. Through all the hours of daylight people are visible on every section of road. Some parts of this route run through rubber plantations, and the lush vegetation makes it a very attractive route, and includes the Periyar Wildlife Sanctuary at Thekkadi.

45 kilometres N of Trivandrum is **Chengannur** which has a small Narasimha temple dating from the 18th century. The **Mahadeva Temple** uses the base of an older shrine as its *kuttambalam*, (a building where dance, music and other rituals are performed). It illustrates the elliptical shape that was found again in the early Siva temple at Vaikom 60 km to the N. In the heart of the town is a famous *Bhagvati* temple, described by the arch over its main entrance on the W side of the Trivandrum-Alwaye road as the *Mahadeva* temple. The shrine is dedicated to Parvati (facing W) and Parameswara (facing E).

K.R.Vaidyanathan recounts a widely believed legend about the image of **Parvati** enshrined in the temple as follows: "There is a legend describing how **Siva** and Parvati came to reside in Chengannur. It was the wedding of Parvati and Parameswara at Mount Kailas. All the thirty three crores of *devas* and *asuras* had assembled for the occasion. It looked as though the earth would tilt towards the N because of the undue weight that side. Siva grew anxious. He summoned the sage Agastya and requested him to proceed to the S to maintain the balance. Sage Agastya felt sorely disappointed that he would miss the celestial wedding. Parameshwara understood his feelings, He assured him that he would see everything through divine sight. Further, he promised that after the marriage ceremony he with his consort would come to the S and grant him *darshan* – **see page 50**. Accordingly sage **Agastya** journeyed towards the S and selected that part of the Sahyadri Hills called Sonadri for his meditation. True to his word, Siva went there with Parvati and blessed Agastya. While there, the goddess had her period. The divine couple therefore stayed here for twenty eight days after the purificatory bath." Vaidyanathan goes on to tell the development of the story. "Wonder of wonders " he writes " even today the deity which is cast in *panchaloha* gets her periods, a phenomenon which is not heard of in any other temple." He reports that the head priest of the temple describes what happens as follows. The head priest or his assistant "on opening the shrine in the early morning removes the previous day's decoration and hands it over to the attendant along with the white petticoat without looking at it. The attendant examines the dress closely and if there are signs of bleeding sends it to the home of the temple *tantri*. There the lady of the house scrutinises the cloth again and confirms the period." He goes on: "The petticoat, after the occurrence, is available for sale to the public. Though the rate fixed by the temple management is only Rs 10/-, due to its being a rarity it is grabbed by devotees paying hundreds of rupees, booking it well in advance. Among the dignitaries who bought this, we are told, are the late Sir C.P. Ramaswami Aiyer and ex-President V.V. Giri." The Tamil scholar John Marr has described this as "a fascinating example of myth appropriation, as this story is a variation of the Tamil myth of Agastya and Podiyilmalai, which recounts how the sage came S (for the same reason of maintaining balance) and taught the first Tamil grammar!"

In case you are sceptical, Vaidyanathan recounts the story of the British adviser to the Raja of Travancore between 1810-14, Colonel Munro. "When carrying out his duty of checking the temple accounts to regulate their expenses Colonel Munro found expenses relating to replacement of garments soiled by the period. He is reported to have laughed at the naivete of the people. "How can a metal deity get its periods?" he mused. It is not only absurd but obscene" he said, and cut out the budget provision with a stroke of his pen. At the same time the goddess had her period. But the Colonel learnt his lesson. His wife started to have heavy bleeding and their children took ill." Fortunately he is reported to have repented of his doubts and ensured the full recovery of all his family.

Kaviyur (5 km) is noted for the best preserved rock cut cave in Kerala, dating from the 8th century. The small shrine, dedicated to Siva, is decorated with strikingly well carved reliefs. The cave has a shrine and *linga*, with a pillared hall immediately in front of it, all aligned E-W. The walls of the pillared entrance hall have reliefs showing either a chieftain or donor of the temple, a bearded ascetic, a four-armed *Ganesa* and at the entrance the 2 doorkeepers. The chieftain is an impressive, strong-looking figure, standing with arms folded. The temple is a link between the Pandiyan kingdom of S Tamil Nadu and that of S Kerala, having much in common with temples in Ramanathapuram and Tirunelveli Districts.

From Kaviyur the road passes through Changanacherry (13 km) and then *Kottayam* (18 km), the main Christian centre in Kerala. Kottayam is surrounded by some of the most fertile and beautiful scenery in Kerala, with the hills to its E and backwaters to the W. The foothills of the Ghats are intensively cultivated with cash crops, notably rubber, tea, coffee, cardamom and pepper, while the valley bottoms are given over to paddy. Despite very low yields when compared with Malayan rubber production the area planted to rubber has grown dramatically.

The Christians in Kerala largely owed their allegiance to the Orthodox Syrian tradition until the arrival of the Portuguese in the 16th century. Indeed, bishops continued to be sent out from Syria to lead the church. After the Inquisition was introduced in 1560 the Portuguese tried to encourage the conversion of Syrian Christians in India to Roman Catholicism. One of the cruder means was by intercepting ships carrying Syrian bishops and preventing them from joining their churches in Kerala. At the same time efforts were made to train Indian priests, and in 1599 the Thomas Christians were allowed to use the Syriac liturgy. A formal split occurred in the Syrian church in 1665 (the year of London's great plague) when the Roman Syrians split from the Syrian Christians under their Bishop Mar Gregory. He was a Jacobite, which resulted in the name Jacobite Christians being applied to his branch of the Syrian Church. Subsequent divisions occurred in the 18th and 19th centuries, but several of the Protestant Syrian churches came back together when the Church of S India was formed in 1947.

Places of interest Two of the Syrian churches a little away from the town centre give an indication of Christian church architecture. The **Cheria Palli** (Small Church) which has beautiful paintings over the alter and **Vallia Palli** (Big Church) on a hillock 5 km out of town are both 700 years old. In the Vallia Palli Church two "Nestorian" crosses are carved on plaques inserted behind two side altars. They may be the oldest Christian artefacts in India. One has a Pahlavi inscription on it, the other a Syriac. On Sun Mass at Cheria Palli at 0730 and Vallia Palli at 0900 and on Wed at Cheria Palli at 0730.

Local crafts and industries The town is the centre of Kerala's rubber industry.

Hotels E *Kumarakom Tourist Complex*, KTDC, Vembanad Lake. 4 double rm with bath. Restaurant with limited menu. Set in large woodland on the shores of the lake, the 50 year old mansion has simple rm overlooking the lotus pond. The woodland attracts a variety of birds. 1 km Path through the woods leads you to the lake where you can hire a boat for about Rs 60 an hr. **E** *Pallathaya Tourist Complex*, on the water's edge. 10 rm 'motel'. Simple. **E** *Aida* MG Road T 61391 Some A/c rooms **E** *Ambassador* KK Road T 3294 Some a/c rooms. Pleasant Indian style hotel and comfortable restaurant. Very good value. **F** *Kaycees Lodge* YMCA Road T 3440. Good quality for the price, and clean. **F** *PWD Rest House* Reservations from the District Collector, Kottayam or Executive Engineer, PWD Kottayam. **F** *Railway retiring rooms* Railway station

Restaurants *Pallathaya Tourist Complex Restaurant* is recommended with its out door setting by the lake. The KTDC *Kumarakom Tourist Complex* on the lake for simple food. *The Indian Coffee House*, TB Road opp the bus station. *Hotel Black Stone* Good veg.

Rail Quilon: *Mangalore-Trivandrum Exp*, 6350 (AC/CC), daily, 1518, 2 hr 4 min; *Vanchinad Exp*, 6303, daily, 0705, 1 hr 53 min; Trivandrum: *Vanchinad Exp*, 6303, daily, 0705, 3 hr 15 min; *Guwahati-Trivandrum Exp*, 2602 (AC/II), Wed, 1908, 3 hr 22 min.

Road Fast and frequent bus connections with Trivandrum, Cochin, Thekkadi and 3 buses a day to Madurai. This takes 7 hrs and goes over the Thekkadi pass, with superb views down

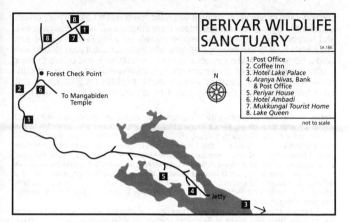

PERIYAR WILDLIFE SANCTUARY

SA 186

1. Post Office
2. Coffee Inn
3. Hotel Lake Palace
4. Aranya Nivas, Bank & Post Office
5. Periyar House
6. Hotel Ambadi
7. Mukkungal Tourist Home
8. Lake Queen

N

not to scale

Forest Check Point

To Mangabiden Temple

Jetty

the E side of the Ghats onto the Tamil Nad plains. The bus station in Kottayam has been described as "especially chaotic, even for India, and there is a mad scramble to get on the Periyar bus". The route from Thekkadi to Kottayam is described on page 795.

Excursions Kottayam is a good place to take a trip on the **backwaters**. It takes under three hours to Alleppey, the first boat leaving at 0630. Shorter trips are also possible, and the route is very attractive.

Kumarakom A KTDC development on an old rubber plantation.

Periyar wildlife sanctuary, Thekkadi

Area 777 sq km. *Climate* Temp Summer Max. 29°C Min. 18°C, Winter Max. 21°C Min. 16°C. Annual rainfall 2600 mm. *Season* Dec – May, *Best* Mar – May. *Clothing* Summer – cottons, winter – light woollens. The nearest airport is at Madurai 140 km away.

Set on attractive lake side, the 780 sq km sanctuary was created by the old Travancore State govt in 1934 and can easily be reached from Kottayam. The drive goes up through Kanjirapalli, Mundakayam and Peermed (where there is a Traveller's Bungalow). The road rises from the plains, through tropical forests, rubber and spice plantations, pepper on the low land gives rise to tea and cardamom plantations. Be prepared for a rapid change in temperature. Above 1500 m the air freshens and you may need warm clothing. In 1895 the lake was created by building a dam. A 180 metre long tunnel led the water which had flowed W into the Arabian Sea E into the **Suruli** and **Vaigai** Rivers, irrigating extensive areas of Ramanathapuram and Madurai districts. To see the dam, no entry fee but permission from Executive Engineer, PWD Periyar Project, Tallakulam, PO Madurai.

The sanctuary, near the border with Tamil Nadu, is in a beautiful setting and was designated a part of **Project Tiger** in 1973. It is best to avoid weekends and holidays since the park gets crowded with visitors and the ideal times are dawn and dusk, so an overnight stop is recommended. You can view the wildlife best by taking a motor launch trip on the lake – but "**not** the one for about 60 people, which is too noisy scaring animals away. Book a boat for 8-12 people from the Aranya Nivas Hotel (where the buses terminate) There is usually no trouble finding other tourists wanting to share it with you."

The elephants, bison, sambar, wild oxen, wild boar and spotted deer are common and in periods of drought when the forest water holes dry up, on rare occasions a tiger or leopard is sighted. There are plenty of water fowl and owls and hornbills in the forests and smaller animals including Black Nilgiri langurs. The forests have special viewing platforms which you can use if you prefer to walk with a Game Ranger who can act as guide. This costs Rs 5, and is "worth doing – but it can get quite hot so take something to drink (we didn't and regretted it)" writes a recent visitor. Elephant rides are readily available (Rs 30 per elephant). Book from Information Centre by lake. 1 hr ride allows you to see much more wildlife than boat trip.

Hotels At Thekkadi, where the KTDC has accommodation nearest the lake, it is best to book well in advance through any Kerala Tourist office. Well into the park and accessible by free ferry from the Aranya Nivas jetty (last trip 1600) is the **D** *Lake Palace*, T Kumily 24. Beautiful island setting with superb views of this former hunting lodge gives it character. 6 comfortable rm in the bungalow and good restaurant with fixed menus (price includes meals). Bar, bank, shop, post. Recommended. Non-residents must reserve in advance for meals at the restaurant – the Indian dishes are better. **D** *Aranya Nivas*, T Kumily 23, Cable: Aranyanivas. 26 rm of different categories, cheaper ordinary to a/c VIP. Accommodation is in an old stone building – simple but comfortable. Restaurant, (multi-cuisine, fairly simple), bar, exchange, small shop and post. Close to lake.

   E *Periyar House*, KTDC 5 min walk from lake, T Kumily 26. 40 rm. Simple, clean and comfortable. Dorm also available. Reasonable restaurant. Alternative accommodation is in the charming government *Forest Rest House*, 3 rm, which is well placed for walks and listening to the animals at night. Recommended, but book well ahead. Otherwise try the privately owned **E** *Ambadi*, T Kumily 11, nr the Forest Checkpost at the entrance 2 km away which has a reasonable restaurant. The village of Kumily, 3 km away has cheaper **F** category hotels including the *Mukkungal Tourist Home*, T Kumily 70 which has a vegetarian restaurant, but where rm at the rear are noisy, the *Rani Lodge*, T Kumily 33 and *Lake Queen*, T Kumily 83.

Restaurants The hotels in Thekkadi have their own restaurants and those just outside too welcome non-residents. *The Coffee Inn*, about half km inside the park from the check post, half way between Kumily village and the lake, serves good food from 0700-2200.

Local transport **Buses** between Kumily and Thekkadi. Jeeps are more costly although you can share one. **Bicycles** are available for hire in Kumily village. On the lake, **motor launches** for 2 hr trips are inexpensive but you may need to wait for the boat to fill on a quiet day although they are scheduled to start every 2 hr from 0700 – 1500. Aranya Nivas also has boats for private hire (for 60, 40 or 30 persons) which is not too expensive if there are several to share the small one. Contact Manager, Aranya Nivas, Thekkadi, or Wildlife Preservation Officer, Thekkadi. There is a small charge made per head in addition to the boat hire charge or ticket and you will also have to pay for cameras.

There is a **post office**, a **bank** and **hospitals** at Kumily.

Air Nearest airports with road connections are Madurai (140 km) and Cochin (208 km).

Road Regular buses run between Kumily and other important towns nearby. Kottayam 116 km, has 6 daily (4 hr), 4 daily to Madurai (4 hr), 3 daily to Trivandrum, 285 km (8 hr) and Cochin/ Ernakulam (6 hr), and one daily to Kodaikanal (4½ hr) and Kovalam (9 hr). Buses from Kumily go down to Aranya Nivas in Thekkadi on the lakeside.

Many Hindu pilgrims make the journey to the forest shrine dedicated to Sri Aiyappan at **Sabarimala** on a route through Kottayam. Aiyappan is a particularly favoured deity in Kerala, though it seems that there are growing numbers of devotees. The pilgrims are readily visible in many parts of S India as they wear **black dhotis** as a symbol of the penance they must undergo for 41 days before they make the pilgrimage.

The pilgrimage itself is deliberately hard, writes Vaidyanathan, because "the pilgrimage to the shrine symbolises the struggle of the individual soul in its onward journey to the abode of bliss and beatitude. The path of the spiritual aspirant is always long, arduous and hazardous. And so is the pilgrimage to Sabarimala, what with the observance of severe austerities and trekking up forested mountains, risking attacks from wild animals." The route from **Kottayam** goes through **Erumeli** (35 km) **Chalakkayam** (10 km) **Pamba** (5 km). There is then a 4 hr walk through the jungle to the shrine. Pilgrims carry their own food, and there are only temporary sheds provided at the temple itself.

The road from Kottayam goes through Ettumanur (11 km) and **Vaikom** (23 km), which has a famous Hindu temple, but non Hindus are not allowed inside. Then across the flat marshy and backwater terrain of the Cochin backwaters to Cochin (45 km) – **see page 819**. Leave Cochin on NH 47 and drive through **Alwaye** (21 km), and Angamaly (11 km). Alwaye has one of the best Government guest houses in Kerala – **See page 829**. Between Cochin and Trichur is a beautiful backwater, and the journey can be made by boat. By road **Peruvanam** is 33 km, then a further 10 km to **Trichur**.

Trichur

Population 250,000. *Altitude* Sea level. *Climate* Temp Summer Max 35°C Min 23°C Winter Max. 32°C Min 20°C. Annual rainfall 2540 mm. *Clothing* cottons. The nearest airport is at Cochin 78 km away.

Trichur is on the western end of the Palghat gap through the low pass between the Nilgiri and the Palani Hills. Thus it has been on the most important routeway into Peninsular India since pre-Roman times. Once the capital of Cochin State it was captured by the Zamorin of Calicut and in the 18th century by Tipu Sultan.

Local festivals The *Pooram* Festival in Apr-May in the Tekkinkadu maidan outside the temple is marked by huge, colourful and very noisy processions with temple elephants and nightlong fireworks and is one of the most spectacular in Kerala. The district also celebrates Kamdassamkadavu Boat Races at Onam (Aug/Sep).

Places of interest   Trichur is built round a hill on which stands the **Vadakkunnatha Temple,** is a multi-shrined complex with three principal shrines dedicated to Vadakkunnatha (Ten-Kailasanatha) where the Mahalingam is covered by centuries of offerings of *ghee** (clarified butter), Sankaranarayana and Rama. The shrine to Sankaranarayana has superb murals depicting stories from the Mahabharata which appear to have been renovated in 1731. Other subsidiary shrines were added, including the apsidal Ayyapan shrine and the shrine dedicated to Krishna. It is a classic example of the Kerala style of architecture with its special pagoda-like *gopura* roof which is richly decorated with fine wood carving. Open 0400 -1030, 1700 – 2030. Non-Hindus are not permitted inside. The large and impressive **Lourdes Church** with an interesting underground shrine. **Town Hall** which is an impressive building housing an art gallery with murals from other parts of the state. **Local crafts and industries** Cotton spinning, weaving and textile industries, silk saris and brass lamps.

Hotels D *Casino*, TB Road, T 24699, Cable: Casinotels, Telex: 0887 237. 25 rm, 14 a/c. Close to rly. Restaurant, Pastry shop, exchange, tourist taxis, shop, TV. D *Luciya Palace*, Marar. T 24731. D *Elite International*, 22 Chembottil La, T 21033, Cable: Hotelite, Telex: 0887 202 Elitein. 90 rm with phones, some a/c. close to rly and centre. A/c restaurants, bar, tourist taxis. E *Skylord*, Municipal Office Rd. T 24662, Cable: Manuelsons, Telex: 0887 221 PTMS In. 10 rm with bath, some a/c. 1 km rly, central. Restaurant. E Government *Guest Home (Ramanilayam)*, Palace Rd, T 20300. Some a/c rm. Restaurant. Also a *YMCA* on the same rd, T 21190 and *YWCA* in Chemukkavu, T 21818. F *Railway Retiring Rooms* and a *PWD Rest House*. Reservation: District Collector.

Restaurants The hotels above have reasonable restaurants. *Hotel Bharat* serves good S Indian food.

Local transport Yellow top and Tourist Taxis, autorickshaws and buses.

Shopping Kerala State Handicraft Emporium *Surabhi*, and shopping areas in Rounds S, W, N and MO Rd, High Rd and MG Rd.

Museums State Museum, Chembukkavu, T 20566. 1000 -1700. Closed Mon. Free. **Art Museum**, Zoo compound has a collection of wood carvings, metal sculptures, an excellent collection of traditional lamps and old jewellery. Open daily 1000 – 1700, closed Mon.

Parks and Zoos *Trichur Zoo,* nr the Art Museum is reputed to have one of the best snake collections in India. Open 1500 – 1715. Small entry and camera fee. Filming only with prior permisiion of the Director of Museums and Zoos, Govt. of Kerala, Trivandrum. There is an *Aquarium* nr Nehru Park which is open daily 1500-2000. **Tourist information** in the Government Guest House, Palace Rd. T 20300.

Rail Connections to coastal cities in Kerala and through Coimbatore and Salem to Madras. Even Express trains stop at Trichur. **Cochin**: *Madras-Cochin Exp,* 6041 (AC/II), daily, 0705, 2 hr 30 min; **Madras (MC)**: *Madras Exp,* 6042 (AC/II), daily, 1840, 11 hr 35 min; **or**: *Cochin-Gorakhpur Exp,* 5011 (AC/II), Mon & Fri, 1155, 11 hr 25 min.

Road Kerala State Road Transport Corporation and private buses connect to major towns in the state with direct services to Palani, Madurai, Bangalore, Mysore, Erode and Madras.

Excursions *Cheruthuruthy* 29 km N of Trichur nr Shoranur Junction. Famous for the Kerala Kalamandalam which led to a revival of Kathakali dancing. Centre for teaching music, drama and Mohiniyattam and Ottam Thullal in addition to Kathakali. You can watch training sessions from 0430 – 0630!, 0830 – 1200 and 1530 – 1730. Closed Sat, Sun, 31 Mar, 15 June and public holidays. The centre is closed in Apr and May. Entry free. *Peechy Dam,* 23 km, has accommodation, boating facilities and you may on occasions see wild elephants in the sanctuary there. Buses from Trichur.

KARNATAKA

The modern state of Karnataka is made up of the Kannada langauge areas of south western and central southern India. The southern part of the state was the former princely state of Mysore. In 1953 and 1956, the old Mysore State's boundary was redrawn to include areas with Kanarese speakers bringing in districts which had previously been administered by Maharashtra and Andhra Pradesh. The new boundaries also gave Karnataka access to the sea by the addition of the coastal areas of N and S Kanara Districts, areas formerly administered by Madras Presidency. On the W coast of India, bounded by the Arabian Sea, Karnataka is the seventh largest Indian state (191,757 sq km).

Social indicators *Literacy* M 39% F 28% *Newspaper circulation:* 748,000 *Birth rate* R 30:1000 U 26:1000 *Death rate* R 11:1000 U 6:1000 *Infant mortality* R 71:1000, U 47:1000 *Registered graduate job seekers* 788,000 *Average annual income per head* : Rs 1314 *Inflation 1981-87* 62%.

Religion *Hindu* 86% *Muslim* 11% *Christian* 2%.

Towns and cities 30% of the population lives in towns and cities. Bangalore, the capital, has a population of 4.1 million.

Administration There are 19 districts which are grouped into 4 divisions of Bangalore, Mysore, Belgaum and Gulbarga. The state legislature, which has its assembly hall, the remarkable Vidhana Soudha, in Bangalore, has a legislative assembly of 208 directly elected members and a legislative council of 63 indirectly elected members. Chief Minister assisted by a council of ministers.

Education Over 35% of the population is literate, yet there are more than 34,000 schools. There are universities in Mysore, Karnatak (at Dharwad), and Bangalore as well as a University of Agricultural Sciences there.

INTRODUCTION

The land

Karnataka has a lush green coastline which is 320 km long. Inland are the Western Ghats, called the Malnad or hill country, which have beautiful forests with waterfalls and wildlife parks, and to the E stretches across the Mysore Plateau. Three great rivers originate in the Ghats and flow over the plateau – the *Kaveri*, the *Tungabhadra*, and the *Krishna*. Some, like the short westward flowing *Sharavati*, have very impressive waterfalls, Jog Falls being one of the highest in the world. Parts of northern Karnataka are almost barren, rocky and covered with scrub.

People

The population are mainly speakers of the Dravidian langauge **Kannada** (Kanarese). However, there has been a lot a intermixture with speakers of Indo-Aryan languages, evident in the N of the state. The other southern languages are spoken in the border regions while Hindi is often used for business and trade. While the **Lingayats** are the dominant caste group in N Karnataka a peasant caste, the *Vokkaligas*, is dominant in the S. Their rivalry still runs through Karnataka politics. Karnataka has its share of tribal people. The nomadic *Lambanis* live mostly in the N and W, just one among several tribal peoples in the remoter hill regions.

Literature Kannada has the second oldest Dravidian literary tradition. The earliest classic known to us is *Kavirajamarga* which dates from the 9th century. A treatise on the writing of poetry, it refers to several earlier works which suggests that the langauge had been in existence for some centuries. Kannada inscriptions dating from 5th and 6th centuries support this view. Early writings in both Telugu and Kannada owe a lot to Jain influence. Kannada made a distinctive contribution in its very early development of prose writing.

From the 10th to the 12th centuries a mixed poetry and prose form was developed by the writers *Pampa*, *Ponna* and *Ranna* – the "three gems of Kannada literature". Towards the end of the 12th century the Saivite saint **Basava** started a new Hindu renaissance. His sect, the *Lingayats*, used simple rhythmic prose, the *vachanas*, to spread its teaching. The American scholar Jordens gives the following example: "*Oh pay your worship to God now – before the cheek turns wan, and the neck is wrinkled, and the body shrinks – before the teeth fall out and the back is bowed, and you are wholly dependent on others – before you need to lean on a staff, and to raise yourself by your hands on your thighs – before your beauty is destroyed by age and Death itself arrives. Oh now worship Kudala-sangama-deva.*" The Lingayats started as a reforming and egalitarian group, becoming highly influential especially across N Karnataka. They remain a dominant group across the N part of the state.

The Hindu-Sanskrit tradition was greatly strengthened by the rise of Vijayanagar Empire. One of their greatest kings, *Krishna Deva Raya* (who ruled from 1509-29), was also a poet in Telugu and Sanskrit, though through his influence poetry reflected the life of the court rather than of the people outside. From the 16th century onwards Vaishnavism produced a rich crop of devotional songs. However after the fall of the Vijayanagar Empire, the quality of literature declined. Muslim power encouraged Hindu art forms almost to go underground, and expressions of Hindu devotion and faith became associated with song and dance for popular entertainment – the *Yakshagana* in Kannada, and the remarkable *Kathakali* in Kerala, see page 806.

The Economy

Karnataka has the benefit of abundant hydroelectric power. In the early years of Independence this allowed it to produce enough to sell to neighbouring states. However, in recent years the growth of industrial demand has been so rapid that at the end of the 1980s it had a higher deficit than any other Indian state, over

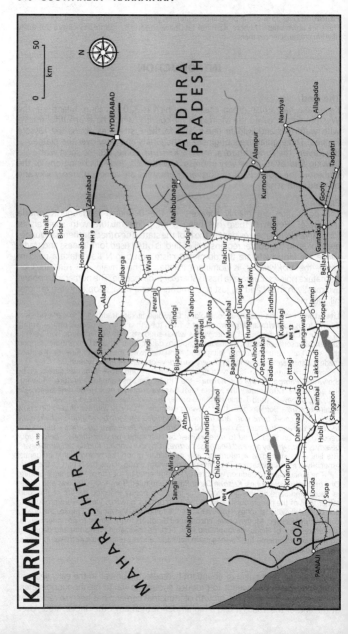

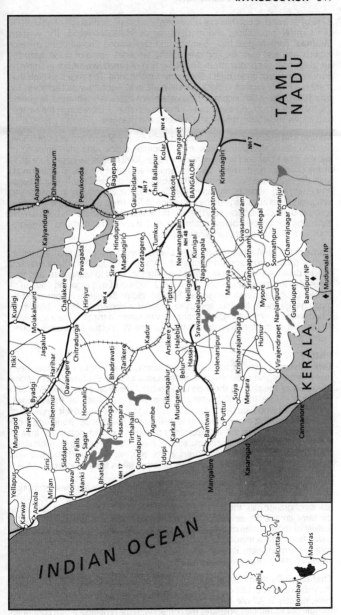

27% of demand. It also has extensive forests, is India's chief source of gold, 90% of its coffee production, and most of the world's sandalwood. The western *'**Malnad' forests*** yield teak, bamboo and sandalwood (the oil being a major export), and also gum, lac and dyes for the tanneries. Some of these resources are also under enormous stress. The harvesting of **sandalwood**, for example, is now illegal except under direct Government monitoring. The price is so high that there is a highly profitable black market trade in it. Agriculture still accounts for over 50% of the state's income. The coastal plains intensively cultivated, rice being the main food crop and sugar cane a major cash crop. Cultivation in the eastern part allows sugarcane, rubber also bananas and oranges.

Mining and industry The Precambrian rocks (over 3,500 million years old) have rich deposits of manganese, iron, mica, chromite, copper, and small amounts of bauxite. The Kolar gold fields, with mines over 3000 metres deep, produce 85% of the country's gold. There has been an iron and steel industry at **Bhadravati** since the 1920s and heavy engineering works in Bangalore. Cotton milling, sugar processing and cement and paper manufacture. The silk industry in Mysore and Bangalore takes advantage of the cultivation of *Tuti* trees, on which the silk worm feeds, and which produces very fine silk. In the last decade there has been a rapid expansion of high technology communication industries in and around Bangalore, from jet aircraft to computers and watches.

Transport The Western Ghats have always been a major cultural as well as physical divide, and transport through them is still difficult. The only railway line directly down to the Karnataka coast from the plateau is to Mangalore, and that is closed in the monsoon season. There are 2,700 km of m gauge and 150 km of narrow gauge line, with Bangalore the main focus. Bangalore is connected by broad gauge line to Madras, and there is talk of widening the line to Mysore to broad gauge as well. Mangalore connects with Kerala in the SW. There are nearly 40,000 km of road, mainly on the plateau. The W is often impassable during heavy rains.

History
Early History Some of the earliest settlements in peninsular India have been found in the region between the **Tungabhadra** and the **Krishna** Rivers. At one site just N of the Krishna these go back to the Acheulean period over 500,000 years ago. More than 300 artefacts have been discovered at *Rangampet*. Communities who lived by hunting and gathering their food also left evidence of their settlements at a later period at several sites. By the Middle Stone Age there was already a regional division appearing between the black cotton soil area of the N and the granite-quartzite plateaus of the S. The division appears between the Krishna and Tungabhadra Rivers in the modern districts of **Raichur** and **Bellary**. In the N hunters used pebbles of jasper taken from river beds; to the S quartz tools were developed.

The first agricultural communities of the peninsula have also been identified from what is now N Karnataka. Located in the region of black cotton soils with islands of granite hills, the Neolithic communities of N Karnataka lived at roughly the same time as the early Indus valley civilisations. Radio carbon datings put the earliest of these settlements at about 3,000 BC. Although agriculture appears to have played only a minor role evidence from later sites in Karnataka shows that millets and gram were already widely grown by the first millenium BC. They have remained staple crops ever since.

Chalukyan Dynasty Karnataka's role as a border territory was illustrated in the magnificent architecture of the Chalukyan dynasty from the 450 A.D. to 650 A.D. Here, notably in **Aihole**, were the first stirrings of **Brahman temple design**. A mixture of Jain temples illustrates the contact with the N of India which continued to influence the development of the Dravidian temples which grew alongside them. Visiting this small area of N Karnataka it is possible to see examples in the one village of Pattadakal alone four temples built on N Indian "**Nagari**" principles and six built on S Indian "**Dravida**" lines. Nothing could more clearly illustrate the region's position as a major area of contact. Architecturally that contact was developed through the later Hoysala styles.

Vijayanagar Empire Less than a thousand years after the Chalukyan dynasty had left their indelible mark the region became the heart of the Vijayanagar Empire from 1336 to 1565. But Muslim influence had already been felt with the attacks of **Muhammad bin Tughlaq** in the 13th century – **see page 147** – and even during the Vijayanagar period the Muslim sultanates to the N were extending their influence. The Bidar period (1422-1526) of **Bahmani rule** was marked by wars with Gujarat and Malwa, continued campaigns against Vijayanagara, and expeditions against Orissa. **Mahmud Gawan**, the Wazir of the Bahmani sultanate, seized Karnatak between 1466 and 1481, and also took Goa, formerly guarded by Vijayanagar kings. Goa itself was seized by **Albuquerque** for the Portuguese in 1510. But the struggle between administrators brought in to the Bahmani sultanate from outside who usurped the power of the Deccani king weakened the kingdom, which by 1530 had split into five independent sultanates: *Adil Shahis* of Bijapur, the *Qutb Shahi* of Bidar, the *Imad Shahi* of Ahmadnagar, the *Barid Shahi* of Bidar, and the *Imad Shahi* of Berar. From time to time they still came together to defend common interests, and in 1565 they co-operated to oust the Vijayanagar Raja, but Bijapur and Golconda gathered the lion's share of the spoils.

Falling apart among themselves they were rapidly succeeded by the later Mughals and then the British. Thus what had for most of history been a marchland between different cultures and powers retained its significance as a region of contact and conflict right up to Independence. The creation of linguistic states in 1956 made explicit the linguistic and cultural significance of Karnataka's N border as the limit of Dravidian cultures in the western part of peninsular India.

The Dynasties Karnataka was named after the region occupied by the Kanarese speaking people. There is various evidence of Aryans' conflict and contact with the southern Dravidians in early history. Tradition in Karnataka states that **Chandragupta Maurya**, India's first emperor became a Jain, renounced all worldly possessions and retired to **Sravanabelagola** between Mysore and the Western Ghats. Dynasties, rising both from within the region and outside it, exercised varying degrees of control. The *Western Gangas* from the 3rd to 11th centuries and the Banas (under Pallavas) from 4th to 9th centuries controlled large parts of modern Karnataka. The *Chalukyas* of central Karnatak took some of the lands between the Tungabhadra and Krishna rivers in the 6th century and built great temples in Badami. They and the *Rashtrakutas* tried to unite the plateau and the coastal areas while there were Tamil incursions in the S and E. The break up of the Tamil Chola empire allowed new powers in the neighbouring regions to take control. In Karnataka the *Hoysalas* (11th – 14th centuries) took advantage of the new opportunity, and built the magnificent temples at Belur, Halebid and Somnathpur, symbolising both their power and their religious authority.

They were followed by the Sangama and Tuluva kings of the *Vijayanagara* empire, which reached its peak in the mid-16th century, had its capital where Hampi now stands. The fortresses of Bijapur, Gulbarga and Bidar are a result of *Muslim* invasions from the N from the 13th century. In the 16th century the *Deccan Sultans* ruled in the N with the rajas of Mysore in the S. In the following century the *Wodeyars* of Mysore expanded their rule while the Mughals fought off the Marathas, taking Srirangapatnam and then Bangalore. They lost control to *Haidar Ali*, the opportunist commander-in-chief in 1761 who with French help extended control and made Srirangapatnam the capital. The Mysore Wars followed and with Haidar Ali's, and then his son Tipu Sultan's death in 1799, came the *British* who re-established rule of the *Wodeyars*. The Hindu royal family from Mysore (with the exception of a 50 year period from 1831 when a British Commissioner was appointed) continued to administer the state even up to the reorganization of the state in the '50s when the Maharaja was appointed State Governor.

Temple architecture

You can see the evolution of temple architecture in the S by visiting some of the ancient capital cities in the state. At *Badami* and *Aihole* and later at *Pattadakal*, both the N *sikhara* and the southern *vimana* are evident in the early 6th century temples built by the Chalukya Dynasty.

Four centuries later came the Hoysalas and the temples built during the 11th to 14th centuries at *Belur*, *Halebid* and *Somnathpur* the two styles are combined to produce the distinctive creations of this dynasty. The star-shaped plan of the base and the shrine with the bell-shaped tower above with the exterior and interior surfaces exquisitely crafted became a hall mark of their temples.

They were followed by the Vijayanagara kings who advanced temple architecture to blend in the rocky, boulder ridden landscape at *Hampi* where you can see the flat-roofed pavilions and intricately carved pillars which characterised their style.

To see the monuments of the Muslim rulers in the state travel to *Bijapur* where you will see the austere style of the Turkish rulers, the refinement in some of the pavilions and the world's second largest dome at the Gol Gumbaz.

Theatre

Bayalata or open-air folk theatre of Karnataka has adapted itself from religious ritual and is performed in honour of the local deity. Unlike the literary theatre, the plays evolve and are improvised by the actors. The stage is often improvised too, and the performances usually start at night and last often into the early hours. The famous **Yakshagana** or **Parijata** usually has a single narrator while the other forms of Bayalata have four or five assisted by a jester. The plots of the **Dasarata** which enacts several stories and **Sannata**, which elaborates one theme, are taken loosely from mythology but sometimes highlights real-life incidents and are performed by a company of actors and actresses. There is at least one star singer and dancer in each company and a troupe of dancers who not only perform in these dance-dramas but are also asked to perform at religious festivals and family celebrations.

The **Doddata** is less refined than the *Yakshagana* but both have much in common, beginning with a prayer to the god Ganesa, using verse and prose and drawing from the stories of the epics Ramayana and Mahabharata. The costumes are very elaborate with fantastic stage effects, loud noises and war cries and vigorous dances. It all amounts to a memorable experience but requires stamina as you will have to sit up all night!

BANGALORE

Population 4.11 (1991) *Altitude* 921 m. *Climate* Temp Summer Max. 33°C Min. 29°C, Winter Max. 27°C Min. 15°C. Rainfall 820 mm mainly June to Sep. *Best season* Oct to Mar. Capital of Karnataka. *Clothing* Cottons in summer, light woollens on winter evenings. *Languages* Kannada, Tamil, Hindi and English. The *airport* is 7 km from the city centre.

	Jan	Feb	Mar	Apr	May	Jun	Jul	Aug	Sep	Oct	Nov	Dec	Av/Tot
Max (°C)	28	31	33	34	33	30	28	29	28	28	27	27	30
Min (°C)	15	16	19	21	21	20	19	19	19	19	17	15	18
Rain (mm)	4	14	6	37	119	65	93	95	129	195	46	16	819

Kempe Gowda, a Magadi chieftain (1513-1569) founded Bangalore in 1537, building a mud fort and marking the limits of the city by his four watch towers and called it Bengaluru. His statue stands in front of the City Corporation Buildings. It was extended by **Haidar Ali** and **Tipu Sultan** and became not only a fortress city although little evidence now remains, but also one with the beautiful garden of Lalbagh. When the British gained control after 1799 they installed the *Wodeyar* of Mysore as the ruler and the Rajas saw that it developed into a major city of the nation.

In 1831 the British took over the administration for a period of 50 years and made this a spacious garrison town, planting impressive avenues and creating parks, building comfortable bungalows surrounded by beautiful lawns with tennis courts as well as churches and museums. When the *Wodeyars* returned they handed over the cantonment area which is called (Civil Area) and only after Independence were the city and cantonment areas amalgamated.

Today it is India's fifth largest and one of its fastest growing, a busy commercial and industrial centre. It is also rightly called 'The Garden City' with its numerous parks and avenues of jacaranda, gulmohur and cassia, and because of its enviable situation and climate has attracted people to retire there.

The origin of the name is lost in legend but some believe that one of the Vijayanagar kings, lost and hungry in the forest was given some boiled beans by a humble old woman. Touched by this gesture he called it 'Bendakalooru' (town of boiled beans) which was distorted to Bengalooru and hence Bangalore!

The old part of the city is to the S of the City Rly Station with most of the sights further S, while the Cubbon Park area with Mahatma Gandhi Rd to its E is where you will find the Tourist office, Government buildings and the bigger hotels and restaurants, book shops and government emporia. MG Road is very pleasant to wander round, with excellent shops, eating and drinking places.

Local Festivals Apr – Karaga. Sakti (Mother Goddess) worshipped as **Draupadi**, the daughter of Fire. To test one's strength of character, a number of pots are balanced, one on top of the other. Nov-Dec – At the Bull Temple, the Kadalekaye Parishe (Groundnut Fair) includes a competition of eating groundnuts.

Places of interest 4 km to the S of the city, the **Lalbagh Gardens** is one of the country's best botanical gardens. See below under Parks and zoos. One of Kempe Gowda's 1537 four Towers is here. Open 0800-2000. The **Bull Temple** further SW at *Basavanagudi*, built in the Kempe Gowda period in mid 16th century is one of the city's oldest. The monolithic *Nandi*, Siva's bull, is believed to have grown in size since and now measure nearly 5 m in height and over 6 m in length. It is made of grey granite polished with a mixture of groundnut oil and charcoal which makes it appear black. In Nov/Dec a groundnut festival marks the harvesting and the farmers' first collection is offered to the Nandi. The priests are friendly and don't press for donations. "Showing interest in the restoration work was rewarded with being allowed to take a closer look by being allowed up the scaffolding" writes a recent visitor. Buses 34 and 37 will take you there. Nearby is one of Kempe Gowda's four towers.

The Kempe Gowda **Fort** 4 km, S of the City Market on Krishnarajendra Rd, was built of mud in 1537 with a Ganapathi Temple, and was rebuilt in stone two centuries later by Tipu Sultan. It is not open to the public at present.

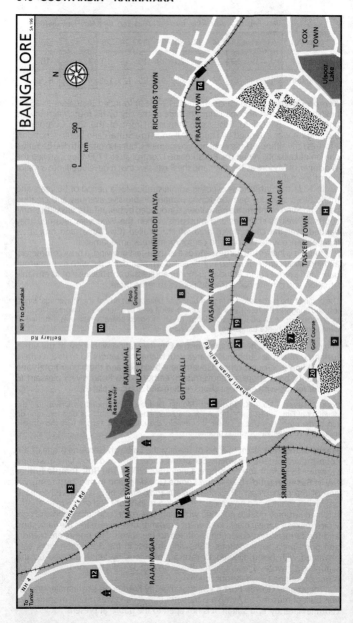

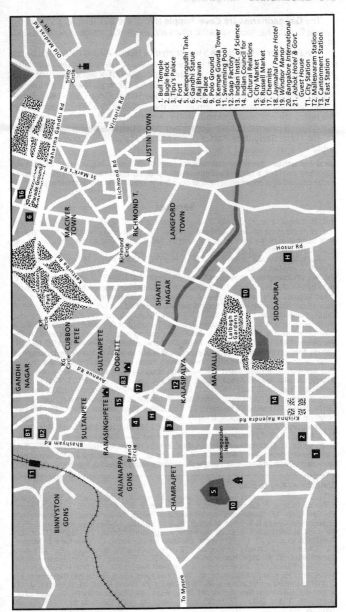

1. Bull Temple
2. Bugle Rock
3. Tipu's Palace
4. Fort
5. Kempengudhi Tank
6. Gandhi Satrue
7. Raj Bhavan
8. Palace
9. Polo Ground
10. Kempe Gowda Tower
11. Swimming Pool
12. Soap Factory
13. Indian Instit. of Science
14. Indian Council for
    Cultural Relations
15. City Market
16. Russell Market
17. Chemists
18. Jaymahal Palace Hotel
19. Windsor Manor
20. Bangalore International
    Guest House
21. Ashok Hotel & Govt.

T1. City Station
T2. Mallesvaram Station
T3. Cantonment Station
T4. East Station

The **Gangadharesvara Cave Temple** NW of the Bull Temple, also built by Kempe Gowda, has four monolithic pillars and an unusual image of *Agni* the God of Fire.

The **summer Palace** to the S was started by Haidar Ali and completed by his son Tipu Sultan in 1789. Based on the Daria Daulat Palace in Srirangapatnam, the two storeyed ornate palace has a substantial amount of wood with walls and ceilings painted in brilliant colours with beautiful carvings. There is a museum tracing the life and times of Haider Ali and Tipu Sultan. Open 0800-1800. There is the Venkataramanasvami Temple in the Dravida style which, when the Wodeyars dynasty was restored at the end of the 18th century, the new Maharajah is believed to have worshipped in first before entering the palace.

The grand **Bangalore Palace** of the Mysore Maharajahs is only open to the public for a week around 1 Nov.

Local industries Bangalore has become one of S India's major industrial centres. Telecommunications, a range of industries related to defence, including aircraft manufacture, electronics and light engineering have all been boom industries in the last twenty years.

Services

Hotels Bangalore appears to lack a range of medium priced hotels. The ones at the Luxury end are nearly as expensive as Delhi and Bombay. ITDC Hotels make no charge for service. A large number of hotels are clustered around the MG Rd area close to the centre where the restaurants, cinemas and shops are also nearby.

AL *Holiday Inn*, 28 Sankey Rd. T 79451, Telex 0845 354 March In. 162 rm. 11 km airport, 3 km rly. Super Deluxe suites Rs 3,500. Executive Suites up to Rs 2,000 per person. Close to golf. **AL** *Welcomgroup Windsor Manor*, 25 Sankey Rd. T 79431, Cable: Welcotel, Telex: 0845 8209 WIND IN. 140 rm. 10 km airport, 8 km rly. Deluxe suites up to Rs 5,000. In plush Indian/Regency style with marble and chintz. Good restaurants (including NW Frontier cuisine), poolside barbecue and 'English' bar. **AL** *West End* (Taj Group), Race Course Rd. T 29281, Cable: Westend, Telex: 0845 337 WEND IN. 135 rm. 9 km airport, 1½ km rly. Spacious site (8 ha), near golf course with superb lawns and good pool. Rm with verandahs around a lawn better than in the new block. Riding and golfing arranged. Recommended. **A** *Taj Residency*, 14 MG Rd (Trinity Circle). T 568888, Cable: Resident, Telex: 0845 8367 TBLR IN. 180 rm. Modern exterior, but tastefully conceived public areas with marble and fountain at entrance. Southern Comfort Coffee Shop serves S Indian specialities among others , Jockey Club Bar with a Club style menu. Balconies with bougainvilleas to complement room colour scheme. **A** *Bangalore Ashok* (ITDC), Kumara Krupa High Grounds. T 79411, Telex: Ashokotel, Telex: 0845 2433. 187 rm. 13 km airport, 3 km rly. Suites upto Rs 4,000. Spacious grounds with tennis courts (golf nearby). Very central but as with some other Ashoks, service can be slow. **C** *Gateway*, 66 Residency Rd. T 573265, Cable: Getaway, Telex: 845 2567 LUX IN. 96 rm some a/c. 9 km airport, 6 km rly. Restaurant, bar, coffee shop, pool, health club.

D *Maurya*, 22/4 Race Course Rd, Gandhinagar. T 72774, Cable: Hotmaruthi, Telex: 0845 2119. 88 rm, 20 a/c. 12 km airport, close to rly and downtown. Restaurant (Indian), exchange, travel, shops, TV. **D** *Bangalore International*, 2A-2B Crescent Rd, High Grounds. T 258001, Cable: Sweethome, Telex: 0845 2340. 57 rm some a/c. 12 km airport, 2 km rly. Restaurant, secretarial services, travel, TV. **D** *Harsha*, 11 Venkataswamy Naidu Rd, Sivajinagar. T 565566,

Bangalore - Key to map

1. Tipu's Palace, 2. Cubbon Park, 3. Maz Mueller Bhavan, 4. Vidhana Saudha, 5. Raj Bhavan, 6. Parade Ground, 7. Kantirava Stadium, 8. Parsi Temple, 9. Public Library, 10. British Library, 11. Golf Club, 12. Bangalore Club, 13. National Theatre, 14. University, 15. Government Museum, Art Gallery, & Technical Museum, 16. Janata Bazaar, 17. City Market, 18. Post Office, 19. Central Telegraph Office, 20. Foreigner's Registration Office, 21. Tourist Office, 22. Karnataka Tourism, 23. K.S.T.D.Centre, 24. State Bank of India, 25. State Bank of Mysore, 26. Chemist, 27.Cauvery Emporium, 28. Higginbotham's Bookstore, 29. Kalpataru Supermarket, 30. Air India, Handloom House, & KSTDC Booking Office, 31. Indian Airlines, 32. Khadi Bhavan, 33. Thomas Cook & Rice Bowl Restaurant, 34. Blue Heaven Chinese Restaurant, 35. Koshy's Restaurant, 36. Mac's Fast Food, Oasis, & The Pub Restaurant, 37. Chit Chat Restaurant & Lakeview, 38. Taj Residency, 39. Grand Hotel, 40. Taj West End, 41. Tourist Hotel, 42. Hotel New Victoria, 43. Shilton Hotel, 44. Woodlands Hotel, 45. Sudarashan Lodge, 46. Sudha Lodge, 47. Hotel Nilgiri's Nest, 48. Hotel Gautam, 49. Y.M.C.A., 50. Y.W.C.A.

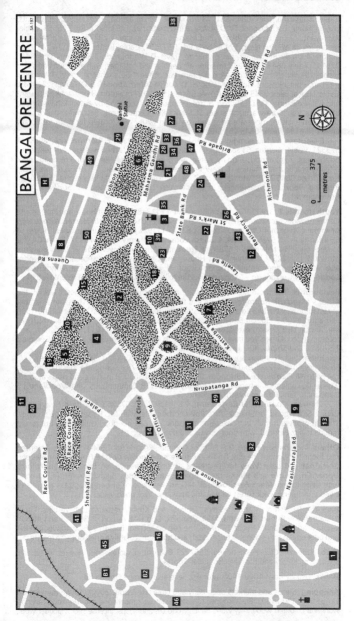

BANGALORE CENTRE

SA 197

Gandhi Statue

Cubbon Rd

Mahatma Gandhi Rd

Brigade Rd

Victoria Rd

Richmond Rd

State Bank Rd

St Mark's Rd

Residency Rd

Lavelle Rd

Queens Rd

Vidhan Vidhi

Kasturba Rd

Nrupatanga Rd

Palace Rd

Race Course Rd

Race Course

Sheshadri Rd

KR Circle

Post Office Rd

Avenue Rd

Narasimharaja Rd

N

0   375
metres

H   49   8   50   15   2   4   20   5   19   11   40

38   29   27   28   33   36   34   37   21   48   42   47   24   3   35   10   39   23   18   22   26   43   12   44   7   6   46   49   30   9   13   31   14   25   32   41   45   16   B1   B2   17   1   H   6

Cable: Hotharsha, Telex: 0845 561. 78 rm, 40 a/c. 10 km airport, 1 km rly. A/c restaurants, bar, exchange, car hire, pool, TV. **D** *Ashraya International*, 149 Infantry Rd. T 75569, Cable: Ashrayant. 72 rm. **D** *Kanishka*, 2 2nd Main St, Gandhinagar. T 29275, Cable: Hotkanish. No a/c rm. **D** *Nilgiris Nest*, 171 Brigade Rd. T 577501, Cable: Butter. 24 rm ,14 a/c. 7 km airport, 4 km rly. Restaurant, bar, exchange, travel. **D** *Woodlands*, 5 Sampangi Tank Rd. T 225111, Telex: 0845 2399. 247 rm some a/c doubles and cottages, with attached baths and fridge. 10 km airport, 4 km rly. A/c restaurant, bar, coffee shop, exchange, travel, TV in delux rm. Large but pleasant Indian style hotel. **D** *Luciya International*, 6 OTC Rd. T 224148, Cable: Luciya, Telex: 0845 8360 LUCY IN. 66 rm, 15 a/c. 12 km airport, 3 km rly. A/c restaurant and bar, exchange, TV. **D** *Shilton Hotel* (pronounced "sheeton" by autorickshaw drivers, otherwise you'll draw a blank stare) St Mark's Rd Cantonment. Recommended as very comfortable, clean, moderate price and very good value. Well located for main restaurant area. T 568184 Telex: 0845-251 SHIL-IN.

E *Gautam*, 17 Museum Rd. T 577461, Cable: Staygautam. **E** *Ajanta*, 22A MG Rd. T 573321. Cable: Ajanta. 61 spacious rm and cottages with attached western style toilets but no showers. 7 km airport, 7 km rly. Restaurant (S Indian), travel. Very helpful reception desk offering practical information. **E** *New Victoria*, 47-48 Regency Rd. T 570336, Cable: Vicky Hotel, Telex: 0845 2298 Attn N3. 21 rm, 1 a/c. 7 km airport, 3 km rly. Very central. **E** *Railway Retiring Rooms* for passengers in transit. Also 15 dormitory beds. **F** *Sudha Lodge*, Cottonpet Rd.

Youth Hostels F *City YMCA*, Nrupathunga Rd. T 211848. The Guest House and Programme Centre provides accommodation for the Karnataka Branch of the *Youth Hostels Association of India* (Office at 4 Obalapa Garden, B 82. T 611292). Also *Bourdillon Guest House* at 65 Infantry Rd, T 572681. *YWCA Guest House*, 86 Infantry Rd, T 570997. **F** *YMCA* (for families only) 57 Millers Rd T 57885 **F** *Students Christian Movement*, 2E Unity Building, Mission Rd, T 223761. Other Guest Houses and Dharamsalas (for short stays only) offer alternative fairly inexpensive accommodation. If you have a choice, avoid *New Citizens Lodge*, Lady Curzons Rd – 'dingy, dirty' is the mildest description of some recent visitors.

Restaurants The top hotel restaurants are good, particularly at the Windsor Manor, the Ashok's *Mandarin Room* for Chinese and the barbecue at the W End. There are a number of restaurants in the MG Rd area, most listed here are a/c and are open between 1200-1530 and again 1900-2330. On Brigade Road, *Prince's* at No.9, first floor, T 565678, which has the Knock Out Disco next door and *Kwality's* at 44, T 571633, multi-cuisine and recommended. Others you might try are *Blue Fox*, 80 MG Rd, Shrungar Shopping Complex, T 570608 and *Shipla*, 40/2 Lavelle Rd, T 578273.

Indian For N Indian specialities try *Tandoor*, 28 MG Rd, T 563330, Khyber, 17/1 Residency Rd, T 212205 and *Koshy's*, St Mark's Rd, T 213793. For good S Indian dishes you can go to *RR Plantain Leaf Brigades*, 55/1 Church St, T 563060 (part a/c and closes at 2230) where you can eat off a banana leaf, *Woody's*, 177/178 Commercial St and *Woodlands*, 5 Sampanghi Tank Rd. *Amarvathi*, Residency Rd.

Chinese *Continental Restaurant*, 4 Brigade Rd, T 570263 and *Blue Heavens* on Church St are good for Chinese. *Rice Bowl* nr the corner with MG Rd serves large portions. The atmosphere is lively with western music and you can get good chilled beer but recent reports it is overpriced, with poor service and dirty toilets.

Others *Indiana Fast Foods*, 9 St Patrick's Complex, Brigade Rd, T 566176, serves American fast foods throughout the day. On MG Rd there is the *Indian Coffee House* for snacks and *Chit Chat* and *Lake View* for ice-creams. Opposite Kwality's, on Brigade Road, *Nilgiris Upper Crust Café* sells snacks, breads, pastries and cheeses. Slightly expensive but good with clean toilets. *Mac's Fast Food*, off MG Rd, wide choice of burgers, pizzas and lots of sweets, including Black Forest gateau and apple pie. Very good value.

Bars The larger hotels and Kwality's, Tandoor and Khyber restaurants have bars. Other Restaurants with bars are *Fiesta*, MSIL Complex, Opp HAL Airport, T 563025 and *Napoli*, Gupta Market, Gandhi Nagar, T 70748. *The Pub* off MG Rd. English style, with wooden bar and beer on tap for reasonable prices. Staff and pub immaculately turned out – "a real treat".

Clubs *Bangalore Club*, Residency Rd, T 567223. Badminton, table tennis, lawn tennis, squash, swimming, library and bar. See also under **Sports.**

Banks Usually open 1000-1400, Mon-Fri. Several on Kempe Gowda Rd.

Shopping Shops and markets open early and close late (about 2000) though they remain closed from 1300-1600. Brass, copper, soapstone statues, sandalwood and rosewood carvings, ivory and coloured wood inlay work. Sandalwood oils and soaps, incense sticks, lacquer work, ceramics, carpets. Also fabrics (silk, cotton, georgette), watches and silver jewellery.

MG Rd (especially the Public Utility Building) with *Cottage Industries Emporium, Manjusha, Cauvery,* and *Shrungar.* Shopping Complex and Brigade Rd with *Nilgiris* Department Stores, are the main shopping streets. Residency Rd and Avenue Rd also have several shops. *Khadi Gramudyog Bhavan* is Silver Jubilee Park Rd, nr City Market, *Karnataka Silk Industries Corporation* in Gupta Market on Kempe Gowda Rd, Mysore Silk Showroom, Leo Complex, MG Rd, T 561718, *UP Handlooms,* 8 Mahaveer Shopping Complex, Kempe Gowda Rd, T 258457 and *Janardhana Silk House,* Unity Building, JC Rd. *Vijayalakshmi Silk Kendra,* Kempe Gowda Rd, T 27155. Will also make shirts.

Silver and Goldsmiths have shops in Commercial St where you will find the family shop of *C Krishnaiah Chetty and Sons* at No. 35. There is also *KR Market* on Residency Rd and *Jayanagar* Shopping Complex. If you want to see a colourful local market with plenty of atmosphere, selling fruit, vegetables and flowers go to the *City Market* or *Russell Market.*

Bookshops *Higginbothams* and *International Book House* on MG Rd.

Local transport *City Buses* run a frequent and inexpensive service throughout the city. *Taxis* are easily available and also *auto rickshaws* which are not much cheaper.

Entertainment A/c cinema *Santosh* on Kempe Gowda Rd shows English films.

Sports *United Services Club.* Swimming, tennis, squash, badminton and billiards. Members'/guests welcome, but hotels can sometimes help. *Bangalore Tennis Club,* Cubbon Park, T 564538.

Golf *The Bangalore Golf Club* celebrated its centenary in 1976. In the early days, competitions drew enthusiasts from far and wide and golfers would travel by bullock cart and on horseback sometimes as much as 300 km. The original 18 hole course was '6550 yards' (Par 71). The new International Championship Golf Course is a KSTDC and the Golf Association and covers a site of 50 ha around the airport. *Bangalore Golf Club,* High Ground, T 27121. Open 0600-1800. Closed Mon. Bangalore is also famous for horse racing and stud farms. *Bangalore Turf Club,* Race Course Rd, T 72391. The racing season is May-July and Nov-Mar.

Swimming There are pools in *Hotel Ashok,* Kumara Krupa High Grounds, *Hotel Harsha,* Shivaji Nagar and *Windsor Manor Sheraton,* Sankey Rd. Pools at Corporation Office premises, NR Square, Kensington Park Rd, nr Ulsoor Lake, Sankey Tank, Sadhiv Nagar, Jayanagar 3rd Block.

Museums Government Museum, Kasturba Gandhi Rd, Cubbon Park. Opened in 1886, one of the oldest in the country has 18 galleries including Neolithic finds from the Chandravalli excavations, and from the Indus Valley, especially Moenjodaro antiquities. Also antique jewellery, textiles, coins, art (especially miniature paintings) and geology. Open daily 1000-1700 except Wed. Small entry fee. The Venkatappa Art Gallery next door displays the works of the Karnataka painter. Visveswaraya Industrial and Technological Museum, Kasturba Gandhi Rd, next to Museum. Open daily 1000-1700 except Mon. The Trade Centre is next door and includes permanent exhibition of what the state produces.

Parks and zoos Lalbagh Gardens The superb 100 ha Botanical Gardens were laid out by Haidar Ali in 1760 while his son Tipu Sultan added a wealth of plants and trees from many countries. It has a very good collection of tropical and subtropical and medicinal plants with over a 1,800 species and a Floral Clock. The Glass House, based on London's Crystal Palace is a venue for exhibitions. Flower Shows in Republic Day (26 Jan) and Independence Day (15 Aug) weeks. One of Kempe Gowda's 1537 four Towers is here. Open 0800-2000.

Cubbon Park, a 120 ha wooded site was laid out in the Cantonment in 1864 with flower beds and lawns. Fountains, a bandstand and statues were added and so were a number of official buildings which included *Attara Kacheri,* the High Court (finished in red stucco with an Ionian facade), the State Library and the museums. The Vidhan Soudha is on the N boundary, a post Independence granite building in the neo-Dravida style which houses the State Legislature and Secretariat. The Cabinet Room has a huge sandalwood door. The gardens are open to the public but you need prior permission to enter the Legislature and Secretariat.

Bal Bhavan, is a children's park with a theatre, toy train, pony rides, boat rides and other attractions. Toy train rides from 0930-1800 on Sun, 0930-2000 Public holidays. Closed on Mon, second Tues of month. T 564189.

The **Aquarium** on Kasturba Rd with a good collection of fish is open daily from 1000-1730. Entry free for children under 12, others pay a small fee. T 577440.

Useful addresses For Visa Extensions, Commissioner of Police, Infantry Rd (N of Cubbon Park). T 75272.

Cultural Centres *Alliance Française,* Millers Tank Bund Rd, Off Thimmaiah Rd, opp

Cantonment Rly Station, T 28762. *American Cultural Centre, British Library*, St Mark's Rd, corner of MG Rd and Kasturba Rd, T 573485. Open 1030-1830, Tues-Sat. *Max Mueller Bhavan*, Almas Centre, 87 MG Rd, T 572135. *Bharattiya Vidya Bhavan*, Race Course Rd, T 27421. *Indian Council for Cultural Relations*, 1, 12th Main Rd, Vasanth Nagar, T 71485. *Indian Institute of World Culture*, 6 BP Wadia Rd, T 602581. *Karnataka Sangeeta Nataka Academy*, Canara Financial Corporation Complex, Nrupathunga Rd, T 72509.

Post and Telegraph *General Post Office*, Raj Bhawan Rd, T 24772. STD available. Brigade Rd Post and Telegraph Office, T 573005 and Museum Rd Post and Telegraph Office, T 573011. Branch Post Offices at several locations in the city.

Places of worship *Hindu – Sri Venkataramana Swamy Temple* nr Bangalore Medical College; Bull Temple, Basavangudi; *Gavi Ganagdharesware* Cave Temple, *Visvesarapuram* and *Malleswaram*; *Subramanyaswamy Temple*, Kumara Park W, *Dharamraja Temple*. *Muslim – Akbar Masjid*, Avenue Rd, Mosque, OPH Rd; *Jami Masjid* off Cavalry Rd. . *Sikh –* Gurudwara, Kensington Rd, Ulsoor Lake. *Christian – St Mary's Basilica* (RC), Sivajinagar; *Infant Jesus Church*, Viveknagar; *St Andrew's Church* (CSI) Cubbon Rd, *St John's Church.*; *All Saints*, Trinity (Methodist). *Buddhist – Buddhavihar* at Coxtown; *Mahabodhi Society*, Gandhinagar. *Jain – Digambara* and *Swetambara* Temples at Chickpet. *Parsi – Fire Temple*, Queens Rd.

Hospitals and medical services There are several Hospitals and Nursing Homes in the city. *Baptist Mission Hospital*, T 330321; *Bowring and Lady Curzon Hospital*, Hospital Rd, T 570782 is N of Cubbon Park, *St John's Hospital*, T 565183. *Victoria Hospital* opp City Market, T 606575, *Sanjay Gandhi Memorial Hospital*, Jayanagar, T 643402. *Chemists* at City Market, corner of Krishnaraja Rd and Narasimharaja Rd and Pancha Shila Medical Store on Brigade Rd. *Siddique Medical Shop*, opp Jamia Masjid, nr City Market, is open 24 hr.

Others are at 5 Queens Rd, 2 St Mark's Rd, 131 Residency Rd, 249 Cavalry Rd and 18 Hospital Rd.

Chamber of Commerce and Industry Post Office St.

Travel agents *Bharat Travels*, St Mark's Rd, T 572251. *Mercury Travels*, Infantry Rd, T 577730. *Sita World Travels*, St Mark's Rd, T 578091. *Thomas Cook*, 55 MG Rd. *Trade Wings*, Lavelle Rd, T 574595. *Travel Corporation of India*, Richmond Circle.

Airlines offices *Air India*, Unity Building, JC Rd. T 224143. *Indian Airlines*, City Office, Karnataka Housing Board Buildings, T T 567525. *Vayudoot*, 11 Crescent Rd, T 24436. *Air France*, St Mark's Rd, T 214060. *British Airways*, TT Travels, Sophia Complex, St Marks Rd, T 214034. *Cathay Pacific, KLM*, W End Hotel, T 29745. *Japan Airlines*, 9/1, 2 Residency Rd, T 215416. *Lufthansa*, Ulsoor Rd, T 570740. *Alitalia*, Ajanta Travels, St Patrick's Complex, Residency Rd, T 215416.

Tourist offices and information *Government of India Tourist Office*, KFC Building, 48 Church St. T 579517. 1000-1800 Mon-Fri, 0900-1300, Sat. Helpful. *Directorate of Tourism*, F Block, 1st Floor, Cauvery Bhavan. T 215489. *Karnataka State Tourism Development Corporation*, 10/4 Kasturba Rd (near MG Rd Corner). T 212091/3. Also at Badami House, Narasimharaja Sq. (opp Corporation Office). T 221299. Where tours originate. Tourist Information Counter, 64 St Mark's Rd. 0900-1900. City Rly Station Counter, T 70068. 0600-2100. Airport Counter, HAL Airport. T 571467. 0700-2030.

Tours KSTDC offers a number of tours starting from Badami House, Narasimharaja Sq. *Bangalore City Sightseeing* Tipu's Palace, Bull Temple, Lalbagh, Ulsoor Lake, Soap Factory, Vidhana Soudha, Museums also stops at Govt Emporia. Twice daily, 0730-1330 and 1400-1930. Rs. 37. There is a large choice of trips out of the city. One day trips to *Nandi Hill* daily during summer, *Sravanabelagola, Belur and Halebid* daily, *Mysore* and *Tirupati* every Fri and at weekends to *Muthyalamlavedu and Bannerghatta* and *Sivangange and Devarayanadurga*. 2 day tours to *Jog Falls* every 2nd Sat, *Subramanya and Dharamsthala* every Sat. 3 day tours to *Mantralaya, Tungabhadra Dam and Hampi*, every Fri and to *Ooty and Mysore* on Mon and Fri, Oct to Jan. Longer 4-day tours to *Goa* every Th and 5-day tours *Bijapur, Badami, Aihole, Pattadakal, Hampi and Tungabhadra Dam* every Fri from Oct to Jan costing Rs 400 including accommodation, and a 10-day S. India tour every Fri which costs Rs 1,000.

Air Indian Airlines Delhi Daily, 1405, 2 hr 30 min; **Bombay** Daily (+ 2 others), 0910, 1 hr 30 min; **Calcutta** Tues-Sun, 1800, 2 hr 25 min; **Madras** Daily (+ 5 others), 0710, 40 min; **Hyderabad** Tues, Wed, Fri & Sat (+ one other), 1445, 1 hr; **Goa** Mon, Thur, & Sun, 1445, 55 min; **Mangalore** Tues, Wed, Fri & Sun, 100, 40 min; **Coimbatore** Mon, Thur & Sat (+ one other), 0720, 35 min; **Cochin** Wed, Fri & Sun (+ one other), 1510, 50 min; **Ahmedabad** Wed, Fri & Sun, 1630, 2 hr. **Vayudoot** Belgaum, Tues, Thur & Sat, 0900, 30 min; **Trivandrum**

Mon, Wed & Fri, 0900, 1 hr 50 min. **Cochin and Agatti** Mon to Sat, 0745, 1 hr 10 min to Cochin, 2 hr 55 min to Agatti; **Hyderabad** Tue, Th, Sat 0820 1 hr 50 min; **Madras** Mon to Sat 1410 1 hr; Indian Airlines, Cauvery Bhavan, Kempe Gowda Rd, T 76851, Airport T 566233. KSRTC operate coach service from airport to major hotels, MG Rd and bus station.

Rail Several Express trains connect Bangalore on the broad gauge line with important cities in the rest of India. On the metre gauge line there are connections with other cities in the S. **Madras**: *Brindavan Exp*, 2640 (AC/CC), daily, 1355, 5 hr 55 min; **Madras**: *Bangalore-Madras*, 6024 (AC/II), daily, 0725, 7 hr 5 min; **Delhi**: *Karnakata Exp*, 2627 (AC/II), daily, 1815, 41 hr 40 min; **Bombay** (VT): *Udyan Exp*, 6530 (AC/II), daily, 2030, 23 hr 55 min; **Calcutta** (H): Bangalore-Guwahati, 2674 (AC/II), Sat, 2330, 14 hr 15 min; **Calcutta** (H): *Bangalore-Haora*, 2612 (AC/II), Fri, 2330, 38 hr 15 min; **Hyderabad**: *Bangalore-Hyderabad Exp*, 7086 (AC/II), daily, 1715, 16 hr; **Goa** (Vasco-da-Gama), *6201 Mail*, daily, 1710, 20 hr. City Rly Station. Enquiry (Arrivals and Departures), T 74173. Reservations, T 76351/3 for 1st Class and T 74172/4 for 2nd Class. Cantonment, General Enquiry, T 27000.

Road Situated at the intersection of three National Highways, Bangalore is at the centre of a good road network: NH 4 (Bombay – Pune – Madras), NH 7 (Varanasi – Nagpur – Kanniyakumari), NH 48 (to Mangalore).

Buses The Central Bus Station, opp the City Rly Station is extremely busy but well organised. State buses of Karnataka (KSRTC), Andhra (APSRTC) and Tamil Nadu (TTC) run efficient, frequent and inexpensive services to all major cities in S and Central India. Very frequent service to Mysore (3 hr 30 min), to Madras (9 hr), to Madurai and to Hassan, 6 daily to Hyderabad, 4 daily to Mangalore (8 hr) and Bombay (24 hr). Several others have two to four buses daily, eg Bijapur, Calicut, Goa, Jog Falls, Kodaikkanal and Ooty. KSRTC, Transport House, Kengal Hanumanthaiah Rd, T 73377. Bangalore Bus Station Enquiry, T 73377. Private bus operators offer Deluxe or Ordinary coaches which are usually more comfortable though slightly more expensive, but it is well worth avoiding the Video Coaches (often overnight) which can be noisy and irritating.

Excursions *Bannerghatta National Park* 21 km on Anekal Rd, covering over a 100 sq km, has a lion and tiger safari, a crocodile and snake farm and offers elephant rides. Picturesque scenery and a temple here. KSTDC's *Mayura Vanashree Restaurant*, T 42. Buses from Bangalore – No 366 from City Market, 365 from City Bus Stand, 368 from Sivajinagar. Open daily except Tues. Small entry fee. *Kolar Gold Fields* 98 km has the world's deepest gold mines, some 2,400 m below the surface, which are the oldest and largest in the country. Open to visitors with prior permission on Mon, Wed and Sat only. Children under 10 are not allowed. There is a *PWD Guest House* and you can get there by buses from the KSRTC Bus Stand in the city which will take you there via NH 4.

BANGALORE TO HYDERABAD

For much of the way, with minor diversions, this route follows NH 7. Leave Bangalore on **NH 7**. The route goes N across the boulder covered plateau of the ancient peninsula granites and gneisses. On either side reddish or light brown soils are cultivated with millets like ragi or sorghum, with rice on the patches of land irrigated by tanks or wells. There are broad views across the gently rolling plateau, interspersed with isolated granite blocks.

Pass through Yelahanka and Devanahalli to *Chikballapur* (56 km). It is then possible to divert 10 km to *Nandidrug* (a hill of ancient granite, named after Siva's bull) in the Nandi Hills.

The hills are regarded as a minor hill resort today, rising over 1000 metres above sea level. It was a once a summer retreat for **Tipu Sultan**, who thought it would be impossible to capture. Guarded on three sides by almost sheer cliffs, on one side over 300 m high, Tipu massively fortified the western approach. There are superb views from the top. The temple at foot of the hill is an important example of the Nolamba style which then had extensions built during the Vijayanagar period. The ***Bhoganandisvara Temple*** (9th & 16th centuries) is entered from the E side. The gopuram at the entrance was built during the Vijayanagar period. Passing through a second gate leads to colonnaded enclosure. There are twin Siva shrines. The early style is suggested by the plainness of the walls, but the stone windows have carvings of Nataraj and Durga. The *Bhoganandishvara* shrine has pyramidal towers and an octagonal roof.

Hotels *Hotel Mayura Pine Top*, KSTDC, T 1. Reservations Manager or through KSTDC, 10/4 Kasturba Rd, Bangalore, T 212901. *Rest Houses*, Dept of Horticulture, Govt of Karnataka, T 21. Reservations: Special Officer, Dept of Horticulture, Nandi Hills, or Director of Horticulture, Lalbagh, Bangalore, T 602231.

From Nandidrug return to the NH 7 at Chikballapur and continue N. After approximately 55 kilometres turn left for ***Chilamattur*** (5 km) to visit Lepakshi (10 km), which has a noted Vijayanagar temple. Approaching the temple at Lepakshi from Chilamattur you see a massive sculpture of Siva's bull (*Nandi*), carved out of granite boulder. It is 5 metres high and 8 metres long.

Lepakshi (10 km) is a very small village, but has a temple of outstanding interest for its murals. According to an inscription the *Virabhadra Temple* was built in 1538 under the Vijayanagar emperor Achutyadeva Raya. There are well preserved Vijayanagara sculptures, but the mural paintings are particularly striking. They depict popular legends from the **Puranas (see page 47)** and epics. George Michell has written that they show "Elegant linework and vibrant colours (mostly browns and ochres) and details of costumes and facial types are of outstanding interest". Built on rocky outcrop of gneiss, the main temple is entered from the N through 2 gopurams, with unfinished brick towers. There are pyramidal brick towers over the main sanctuary and Vishnu shrine. Inside are large sculptures of Nataraja and Bhikshatanamurti on columns of the central bays. Narrative reliefs on the S walls illustrate Siva legends, including Arjuna's penance. In the principal sanctuary is a life size image of Virabhadra, decked with skulls and carrying weapons, appropriate to this form of Siva as a deity bent on revenge.

Drive W from Lepakshi along the narrow minor road to ***Hindupur*** (10 km). From Hindupur continue N to ***Penukonda***. A steep path goes to the top, while at the base of the eastern side of the hill are some huge walls and gateways of the old fortifications. The Jain *Parsvanatha Temple* has "an 11th century sculpture of the naked Parshvanatha in front of an undulating serpent" in late Chalukyan style. There are also two granite Hindu temples from the early Vijayanagar period dedicated to Rama and Siva. There are also remnants of the Muslim period. These include the mosque of Sher Ali, built about 1600, and the Gagan Mahal (*Ancient Palace*). Davies suggests that this was built in the "courtly style of the period, with Islamic style arches, vaults and plaster decoration combined with temple-like elements".

Penukonda became the headquarters of the districts ceded to the E India Company by the Nizam of Hyderabad in 1800 under the first principal collectorship of Thomas Munro. A tablet on the walls of the Collector's guest house commemorates him. There is a well carved stambha 10 m high in compound of the sub-collector's office.

The road continues N to Anantapur, cutting through the granite hills towards ***Nagasamudram*** (26 km). Off to the right is the railway junction and silk producing town of ***Dharmavaram*** (13 km). The main road crosses the railway before Nagasamudram and continues N. In the hills to the W of the road before reaching Anantapur are extensive deposits of corundum and mica, and small deposits of gold. Join the road from Kadiri 3 km S of ***Anantapur*** (39 km). Anantapur is on the eastern edge of a quite distinct geographical region, the Anantapur-Chittoor basins and the hill ranges of Cuddapah. The most direct route to Hyderabad continues N through **Gooty** (55 km; see below) across the unbroken stretch of granites that the road follows all the way from Bangalore. The Seshachamal Hills are clearly visible to your right driving N from Anantapur. Beyond Gooty they are followed by the N ranges of the group, the Erramala Hills.

If you take a short diversion to ***Tadpatri*** (54 km) to the N E you cross a distinctive landscape. The Tadpatri road passes through Singanamalla and then crosses the N tip of the **Seshachalam Hills**. Formed of massive quartzites, but with layers of slates and volcanic lavas, they present a steep scarp face to the W. Crossing the scarp towards Tadpatri you enter a region of limestones and shales intruded into the sedimentary rocks, they are the westernmost range of a dramatic, crescent shaped range of hills. To their E, out of sight though clearly visible from the air on the flight from Hyderabad to Madras, are the **Nallamalais** and the **Vellikondas** in the N and the **Pallikondas** in the S, stretching down to the famous temple town of Tirumalai. The western scarp of the Seshachalam Hills which you cross on the way to Tadpatri have rich mineral deposits: copper, barytes, talc and graphite.

Although the region is dry for much of the year the major rivers – the **Pennar**, the **Cheyyuru** and the **Krishna** – have cut deep gorges through the hills on their path to the E coast. Of these only the Krishna rises in the Western Ghats, guaranteeing it much more reliable water supply for at least six months a year. The others are often completely dry. The hills themselves are thinly wooded, much of it destroyed by overgrazing a landscape which has marginal rainfall of around 1,000 mm a year.

Tadpatri has two interesting temples. Founded in 1485 under the Vijayanagar Empire, its two main temples were built at the same time. The **Ramalingesvara temple**, on the S bank of the **Pennar River**, is the more impressive of the two according to Fergusson, who wrote that "The wonders of the place are the two gopurams belonging to the Rameshwara temple, which is now deserted on the banks of the river. One of these was apparently quite finished." This temple houses a Siva lingam in a stand filled with spring water. There are two sanctuaries in the southern temple of the complex with images of Parvati and Rama, Lakshmana and Sita. According to Michell "the architectural elements include double basements, pilastered walls, niches framed by multi-lobed arches or surmounted by tower like pediments, and pilasters standing in pots. All of these are encrusted with friezes of jewels and petals, scrollwork and miniature animals and birds..... the resulting sculptural density is unparalleled." About 1 km to its S is the equally highly decorated Venkataramana Temple. The **Venkataramana Temple** is about 1 km N E of the bus station, and the Ramalingesvara Temple a further kilometre N. The Venkataramana Temple dates from the mid 16th century. The main shrine is dedicated to Vishnu. Sculptures relate stories of Krishna, Rama and Sita. The gopuram is partly ruined but still impressive.

From **Tadpatri** it is possible to continue via **Gooty** and to rejoin the NH 7 to reach **Kurnool**.

Train Kurnool Town to Madras (MC) via Tirupati: *Venkatadri Exp*, 7597, daily, 2122, 12 hr 8 min plus 55 min waiting; **then** *Tirupati-Madras Exp*, 6054, daily, 1025, 3 hr 20 min (total time 16 hr 23 min; **Guntakal**: *Venkatadri Exp*, 7597, daily, 2122, 2 hr 43 min; **Secunderabad**: *Tungabhadra Exp*, 7058 (AC/II), daily, 1415, 6 hr 5 min.

Alternatively go N to Banganapalle and Kurnool via **Ahobilam** and **Gandikot**. Both routes have places of interest. The road to **Gooty** (50 km) runs N E, at first along the Pennar, then through the gap between the Seshachalam Hills to the S and the Erramalai Hills to the N. Gooty has a dramatic Vijayanagar fort. Built on an isolated granite outcrop 300 m high, in the 18th century the fort fell into the hands of the Maratha chief Murari Rao Ghorpade. Murray's Guide records that "in 1776 it was captured by Haidar Ali after a siege of 9 months. Water having failed Ghorpade surrendered the fort and soon died." Sir Thomas Munro, Governor of Madras died nearby in 1827.

Train Guntakal: *Madras-Bombay Mail*, 7010 (AC/II), daily, 07.55, 40 min; *Madras-Dadar Exp*, 6512 (AC/II), daily, 1803, 27 min; **Madras (MC)**: *Dadar-Madras Exp*, 6511 (AC/II), daily, 0803, 8 hr 32 min.

From Gooty you can go W through the major railway junction town of **Guntakal** and **Bellary** to visit Hampi and Hospet, (**see page 879**). It is around Bellary that the first agricultural communities of the peninsula have also been identified. The climate is typical of the central peninsula.

	Jan	Feb	Mar	Apr	May	Jun	Jul	Aug	Sep	Oct	Nov	Dec	Av/Tot
Max (°C)	31	34	37	39	39	34	32	32	32	32	31	29	34
Min (°C)	17	19	23	26	26	24	24	23	23	22	19	17	22
Rain (mm)	3	5	5	20	48	43	41	61	125	107	51	3	512

The black cotton soils are pierced by islands of granite hills, and the **Neolithic communities** here lived at roughly the same time as the early Indus valley civilisations. Radio carbon datings put the earliest of these settlements at about 3000 BC. Hill tops were favoured for settlement, and caves or rock shelters were used for living space. A distinctive feature has been the discovery of *ash mounds* at 4 places in this area, close to the confluence of the *Krishna* and *Tungabhadra*, and to the S of **Bellary.** The mounds are where cattle were herded together. Some of the pens are near permanent settlements but others are isolated. They looked very like the traps used for catching wild elephants much nearer to the modern period. Although agriculture appears to have played only a minor role evidence from later sites in Karnataka shows that millets and gram were already widely grown by the first millenium BC. They have remained staple crops ever since.

Rail Gadag: *Guntur-Hubli Exp*, 7825, daily, 0845, 3 hr 30 min; **Guntakal**: *Hubli-Guntur Exp*, daily, 1720, 1 hr 10 min.

Guntakal is a medium sized town but an important railway junction.

Train Madras (MC): *Dadar-Madras Exp*, 6511 (AC/II), daily, 0738, 8 hr 57 min; or *Chennai Exp*, 6063 (AC/II), daily except Tue and Sun, 1140, 8 hr 20 min; **Bangalore**: *Karnataka Exp*, 2628 (AC/II), daily, 0939, 5 hr 36 min; or *Ahmadabad-Bangalore Exp*, 6501 (AC/II), daily, 1108, 6 hr 52 min; **Secunderabad**: *Venkatadra Exp*, 7598, daily, 0030, 8 hr 55 min; **Hyderabad**: *Rayalaseema Exp*, 7430 (AC/II), daily, 2303, 8 hr 57 min; **Bombay (VT)**, *Udyan Exp*, 6530 (AC/II), daily, 0315, 17 hr 10 min; or *Netravati Exp*, 2136 (AC/II), Mon, Wed, Fri, 1236, 17 hr 9 min; **From Guntakal to Goa (Vasco-da-Gama)**: *7829*, 0300, 16 hr 15 min; **Hubli**: *Guntur-Hubli Amravati Exp*, 7825, daily, 0745, 6 hr 30 min; **Cochin** (HT): *Ahmadabad Cochin Exp*, 2637, Th, 1108, 20 hr 52 min.

If you do not wish to make this diversion, in Gooty rejoin the NH 7 and travel N to **Kurnool** (96 km). For the first half of the journey the road runs close to the scarp of the Erramalai Hills. The alternative route from Tadpatri allows you to visit the Vijayanagar temples of **Ahobilam** and the fort at **Gandikot**. The former is an important Hindu pilgrimage centre while the latter has another famous fort, the so-called "fort of the gorge".

To reach Ahobilam you have to turn S E In Banganapalle to Koilkuntla (about 15 km) across the nandyal plains. The road crosses the Cuddapah River (often dry) before reaching Allagudda. Then follow a minor road N E to *Ahobilam*. The shrines are dedicated to Narasimha, where local legend has it the man-lion incarnation of Vishnu actually took form to defeat the demon Hiranyakasipu. There are two main sets of temple complexes, one in the town, and Upper Abohilam 8 km away. Abohilam is in the heart of the limestone region. As a result there are many natural caves, some of which are used for temples. The main shrine in the town of Lower Abohilam was begun in the 14th century but developed and completed by the Vijayanagar kings in typically Vijayanagar style. Michell writes that "the inner gopuram, which is the better preserved of the two, has its outer walls adorned with elongated pilasters. The successive storeys of the steeply rising pyramidal tower and also the vaulted capping form with arched ends have been renovated recently." In Upper Abohilam the Narasimha temple has been made in a natural cave. It is entered from the E or W sides.

From **Ahobilam** return to **Allaguda**. In the town turn sharp right and travel due N to **Nandyal** (43 km). After 40 km you reach the turning on the left for **Gandikot**. Built in 1589 at a height of more than 500 metres above sea level, Gandikot fort proved far from as impregnable as its position might suggest. It fell in succession to the Golconda kings, to the Nawab of Cuddappah, to Haidar Ali and finally to the British. The remains hang precariously, just to the W of the flat Nandyal Valley through which the Kurnool River flows S to join the Pennar. It is part of a route that has always been strategically significant.

From Gandikot return N. Turn left at the main Nandyal-Kurnool road. After 40 km you reach **Kurnool** (50 km. *Pop* 180,000). Between 1950-56 Kurnool was capital of the state of Andhra Desa before Hyderabad was chosen as the capital of the new state of Andhra Pradesh in 1956. Located at the junction of the Hindri and Tungabhadra rivers, Kurnool was an administrative centre for the Nawabs of

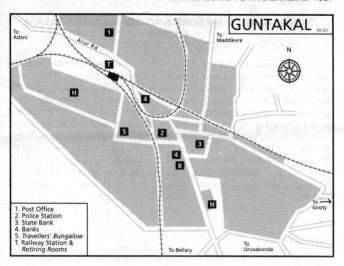

1. Post Office
2. Police Station
3. State Bank
4. Banks
5. *Travellers' Bungalow*
T. Railway Station &
   Retiring Rooms

Kurnool. Muslim influence is still evident in the ruined palace of the Nawabs on the steep bank of the Tungabhadra.

Hotels *Hotel Raviprakash* at Kurnool is ½ km from the station on Railway Station Rd. T 21116. It has 46 rm some of which are a/c with attached baths. The Restaurants serve only Indian food. Conveniently located with lawns.

Excursion From Kurnool you can visit the early Chalukyan site of **Alampur** with its nine 7th and 8th century temples. Take the minor road N out of Kurnool with the railway line to Hyderabad on your left. After 6 km take a right turn for Alampur (4 km). The temples overlook the Tungabhadra river near its confluence with the Krishna. Together, the Krishna-Tungabhadra cut through the N range of the Nallamalai Hills just to the E. A huge dam built just to the S E of Kolhapur at the entrance to the hills has created a lake which has threatened the site, now protected by very large embankments. The site was defended with fortifications. The nine temples of Alampur are dedicated to Siva. However, they are known as the nine Brahma temples – the *Nava Brahma* – for the nine 'mind-born' sons of Brahma. The temples are in very good condition, beautifully carved. The layout conforms to a standard pattern: the sanctuary faces E and is surrounded by a passage and a mandapam. Over the sanctuary is a tower with curved sides, similar to central Indian temples. An *amalaka** motif (like a flattened gourd) caps the tower. Alampur also has a small but very good museum in the middle of the site.

A longer excursion can be made to **Srisailam**, a popular site of Hindu (Saivite) pilgrimage. This is 170 km E of Kurnool on the route through Doranala. The wooded hills of the Nallamalai Hills are home to the Chenchu tribes. The Srisailam township has been built for workers on another massive dam construction project. The pilgrimage site lies on the banks of the Krishna to the N. Its origins are obscure, and the Mallikarjuna Temple (14th century) has often been attacked and damaged. It is surrounded by a 5 m wall 300 m long (dated to 1456). The outer face is richly decorated with carved figures. These include a portrait of **Krishna Deva Raya**, the Vijayanagar Emperor who visited the site in 1514. From Srisailam it is possible to go straight on to Hyderabad (200 km) without returning to Kurnool. The route crosses the wide open *Telangana Plateau*.

The route from Kurnool to Hyderabad passes through **Badepalli** (51 km), then follows the railway line N across the Telangana Plateau to **Farooqnagar** (34 km), before entering **Hyderabad** (51 km).

BANGALORE TO MYSORE AND UDHAGAMANDALAM (OOTY)

There are two routes to Mysore. The southern route through Harehalli, Kanakapura and Malvalli is longer and slower. The newer and more northerly road to Mysore is relatively good and quick by Indian standards. Allow 2 hours driving time. It crosses the open parkland of the *Mysore maidan*. The ancient rocks of one of the oldest series of granites in India, the Dharwad system give reddish or brown soils, often outcropped by extraordinary hills and boulders. These plateaus of the S are the highest in Karnataka, rising to over 1200 m. To the S of Mysore the road enters the forests of the N slopes of the Nilgiris. After passing through two game reserves it climbs steeply through the forests, now heavily cut and replanted with non-local species.

The open plateau land of the Mysore *Maidan* was fiercely contested by various powers. The Vijayanagar Kings controlled it through much of its own ascendancy in the 15th and early 16th centuries. After the collapse of the Empire it came under the control of the Hindu **Wodeyar Princes**, who in turn were displaced by **Haidar Ali** in the mid 18th century. It was returned to them by the British in 1799. The route passes through several towns which show the marks of their successive rulers, from Vijayanagar temples to Muslim Forts and British settlements.

Leave **Bangalore** on the Mysore road to **Ramanagaram** (48 km). It was formerly known as Closepet after the first British Resident in Mysore to hold the post after the fall of Tipu Sultan in 1799, Sir Barry Close. Locally it is still often called *Kalispet*, a corruption of its original name. The settlement was established in 1800 to open up previously dense jungle and to help secure the road to Srirangapatnam. It takes its more recent name from the nearby hill, Ramgiri. The name *Closepet* was given to the local granite, which runs in a band 20 km wide due N through Tumkur into Andhra Pradesh.

The main road continues to **Channapatna** (10 km), a small town famous for its painted wooden dolls, made as toys. It is well worth a stop. Dry farming predominates on both sides of the road, on flat land between the bizarre granite boulders. Ragi (*finger millet*), other millets and gram are common crops on the poorer land, though there are also patches of irrigated ragi. Channapatna is a busy small market town, known particularly for its lacquer ware. Small dolls with nodding heads are a speciality. The craftsmen are now producing a wider range of lacquered wood ware, including educational toys. From the late 1980s the World Bank was giving assistance to producers, along with external design guidance. Steel strings are also made for musical instruments. Tipu Sultan's religious teacher is buried in one of the two large Muslim tombs just N of the town. The ruined fort in the town was built by Jagadura Rai in 1580. Across India and through much of its history emperors and kings granted land to minor chiefs in gratitude for various services performed on their behalf. **Jagadura Rai** was given land around Channapatna by the Vijayanagar King in gratitude for his military support in defending Penukonda in 1577 – see page 854.

In 19 km the road passes through **Maddur**, on the banks of the River *Shimsha*. For a short time Maddur was the Headquarters of a Vijayanagar Viceroy. There are two Vaishnava Temples dedicated to Narasimhasvami and Varadaraja. The brick bridge was built in 1850. A diversion is possible from here to the **Sivasamudrum Falls** on the Kaveri. Its total length is just over 100 km. It can be taken as an excursion from Mysore.

After leaving Maddur on the Mysore road there is a clearly signed fork to the left for Sivasamudram. The road passes through **Malvalli** (23 km) where it crosses the southern road from Bangalore to Mysore. This was the battlefield on which Tipu Sultan's army was defeated in March 1799, leading to his retreat to Srirangapatnam. After just over 10 km there is a left turn to the falls at **Sivasamudram**. This is the edge of the plateau region, and the Kaveri plunges over a total drop of 100 m into a series of wild and inaccessible gorges. At the top of the falls the river divides around the island of *Sivasamudram* into two channels, the *Barachukki* on the E and the *Gaganchukki* on the W. The hydro electricity project was completed in 1902, the first HEP scheme of any size in India. During the wet season the falls are an impressive sight, water cascading over a wide area of otherwise bare rock in a series of leaps. The discharge at peak flow can be as high as 12,000 cubic m per second although the average monsoon flow is less than one tenth of this figure. In front of the Gaganchukki fall are the water pipes which feed the generators 125 m below. *Guest Houses* can be reserved through Executive Engineer, KEB and Asst Executive Engineer, PWD at Bluff, Malavalli Taluk, Mandya District. Food to be ordered in advance. Tea stalls available.

From the falls take the road W, before crossing the bridge over the Kaveri, towards **Sosale** (25 km) and **Thirumakudla Narasipur** (5 km). At Sosale turn right to reach **Somnathpur** (12 km). This tiny village has one of the best preserved of the 80 or so *Hoysala* temples found in the Mysore region. Built in 1268, late in the Hoysala period, the small temple to **Kesava** shows the distinctive features of the late Hoysala style, having its roof intact where other famous temples have lost theirs. It has 3 sanctuaries with the *trikutachala* or triple shrine and stands in the middle of its rectangular courtyard about 70 m long and 55 m wide, with cloisters containing 64 cells around it. You enter through the eastern gateway and get a view of the perfect whole. The temple stands on a raised platform in the form of a 16 pointed star, with an ambulatory in the Hoysala style. There is a pillared hall in the centre with the 3 shrines to the W which give it the form of a cross in plan. Walk around the temple to see the bands of sculptured figures which are particularly fine and are again typical of the style. Brown describes them as "animated continuous designs" which go right around the temple. The lowest of the 6 show a line of elephants for strength and stability, then horsemen for speed to be followed by a floral scroll. The next band of beautifully carved figures (which is at eye level) is the most fascinating and interesting of all and tells stories from the epics which is followed by the *yali** frieze, the monsters and foliage may depict the river Ganga and finally on the uppermost is a line of *hamsa*, the legendary geese. A guide book on the Hoysalas by Mishra is available from the custodian. Toilet but no refreshments.

Hotel KSTDC *Hotel Mayura Keshava*, T 85, Bannur.

Leave Somnathpur N to **Bannur** (5 km) and **Srirangapatnam** (20 km). At **Maddur** the road enters a totally different landscape, transformed by canal irrigation. Maddur is on the eastern edge of the great tract of land irrigated from the **Krishnarajasagar Dam**, W of Mysore – see page 865. From Maddur to Mandya sugar cane becomes a dominant crop, but rice is also common. **Mandya** (16 km) itself is an important market town, especially for sugar.

The completion of the Krishnarajasagar Dam in 1927 transformed the local economy. The main benefits were greatly increased cash returns on farming and a boost to local processing industries. The villages around Mandya shared in the changes. We know from the records of one village outside Mandya, **Chikkamaralli**, that one hundred years ago the land that now looks so fertile was largely unirrigated, with a few wells to give protection against drought. By the time the new canal irrigation was established nearly 80% was irrigated by a canal that guaranteed water from 1 Jun to 30 Nov. In the dry season from 1 Dec to 31 May the village receives water in rotation, ten days with water and four days without. Farmers can thus rely on the timing and the amount of water they receive. The low yielding but hardy crops like millets were rapidly replaced by rice and sugar cane. Sugar cane takes twelve months to mature, so guaranteed water supply is essential. However, poor drainage of the canal irrigated land often led to increases in malaria. Until 1950 this stopped population growth and much of the village's land was left fallow because there was not enough labour to work it. Malaria was not tackled effectively until DDT was introduced after World War II. Even then, while poor land was improved, some previously good land suffered from poor drainage and had to be abandoned.

Since the early 1950s there have been major changes – use of chemical fertilisers and high yielding varieties of rice, the use of electric pumpsets for irrigation to supplement canal

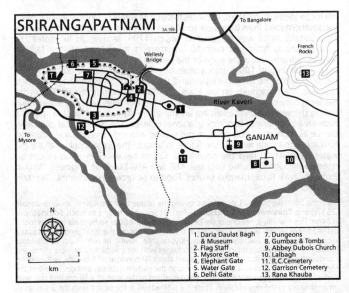

1. Daria Daulat Bagh & Museum	7. Dungeons
2. Flag Staff	8. Gumbaz & Tombs
3. Mysore Gate	9. Abbey Dubois Church
4. Elephant Gate	10. Lalbagh
5. Water Gate	11. R.C.Cemetery
6. Delhi Gate	12. Garrison Cemetery
	13. Rana Khauba

water. Villagers have been willing to experiment. The Japanese method of transplanting rice seedlings in straight lines was tried in the 1970s as against the local method of intensive but random transplanting. Although line transplanting was shown to increase yields, the benefit was more than offset by the increased costs of labour, so the experiment was abandoned.

Mandya became the centre of the Mysore Sugar Company, which has made refined sugar and spirit since 1930. The road passes straight through the main street of Mandya (tea and coffee shops, cold drinks, S Indian meals all available in town centre) to:

Srirangapatnam (23 km; otherwise *Seringapatam*). The name comes from the temple of *Vishnu Sri Rangam*, which has been here far longer than the fort or the town. It has played a crucial part in the history of the region at several points since its origins in the 10th century. Since the arrival then of the great Vaishnavite philosopher and reformer **Ramanuja** in 1133 (**see page 55**), who had fled from the Saivite Chola kings in Tamil Nadu, the site has been a focal point in S India's political development. The fort was first built under the Vijayanagar kings in 1454. 150 years later the last Vijayanagar king handed over authority to the Hindu Wodeyars of Mysore, who made it their capital. In the second half of the 18th century it became the capital of **Haidar Ali**, who defended the fort against the Marathas in 1759, laying the foundations of his expanding power across S India. He was succeeded by his son **Tipu Sultan**, who also used the town as his headquarters.

As a result of the battle in which Tipu Sultan was finally killed on 4 May 1799, Colonel Wellesley, the future **Duke of Wellington**, established his military reputation, **see page 100**. The fighting itself was exceptionally fierce, and Tipu Sultan died at the N gate of the Fort, "shot dead by a British soldier who fancied the jewel in his turban" according to the Duke of Wellington's biographer Elizabeth Longford. She also records that in his pocket book was found a prayer: "I am full of sin; thou art a sea of mercy. Where thy mercy is, what became of my sin?" For Wellesley it was the beginning of a five year governorship of Seringapatam. Within fifteen years he was to fight Napoleon at the Battle of Waterloo.

The advantages of the site for a military fortress at **Srirangapatnam** are quite different from those of the many hill top forts which are scattered across the Mysore plateau. The fort and town lie on a low but rocky island 5 km and 1 km wide in the middle of the **Kaveri River**. Bridges carry the main road across the island. The fort has triple fortifications which enclose the town and what remains of the fort. The British destroyed most of the fort and you can see the battle scars on the ramparts. The Jama Masjid mosque, built by Tipu Sultan, has delicate minarets, and there are two Hindu temples, Narasimha Temple (17th century) and Gangadhareswara Temple (16th century). Outside the fort, 1 km to the E, is the **Daria Daulat Bagh** (Splendour of the Sea), Tipu Sultan's summer palace built in 1784, in its beautiful garden. There are colourful frescoes of battle scenes between the French, British and Mysore armies, ornamental arches and gilded paintings on the teak walls and ceiling which are full of interesting detail. The small museum upstairs has 19th century European paintings and Tipu's belongings is open daily. The buildings are excellently maintained by the Archaeological Survey of India.

The family mausoleum is 3 km away and was built by Tipu in remembrance of his father. The ornate white domed **Gumbaz** which has beautiful ivory-on-wood inlay and Tipu's tiger stripe-emblem. Some of his swords and shields are kept here. To visit the sights there are tongas and rickshaws. Also bicycle hire from shops on the main road.

Hotels KSTDC **F** *Hotel Mayura River View*, T 114 is a little out of town. Accommodation in cottages. Restaurant.

Trains between Bangalore and Mysore stop here. Many buses daily from Central Bus Station, Mysore.

Continue S to **Mysore** (14 km)

Mysore

The former capital of the Princely State, Mysore is Karnataka's third largest city. *Population* 600,000. *Altitude* 776 m. *Climate* Temp Summer Max. 28°C, Winter Max 22°C. Rainfall 74 cm. *Best season* Oct (Dussera Festival) to March, but much more pleasant than on the lower plains throughout the year.

General introduction The city of royal palaces (there were five plus a dozen mansions) and sandalwood and a centre for the manufacture of incense sticks. An attractive city with a pleasant climate, it is clean with beautiful parks and shady avenues. Scent of jasmine, for which the city is famous, in the air in the spring.

Local festivals End Sept-early Oct – For 10 days *Dasara* is celebrated with medieval pageantry. Although the Dasara festival can be traced back to the Puranas and is widely observed across India, in the S it achieved its special prominence under the Vijayanagar kings. As the Mahanavami festival it has been celebrated every year since it was sponsored by Raja Wodeyar in late September 1610 at Seringapatam. It symbolises the victory of goddess Chamundeswari (Durga) over the demon Mahishasura. The 16th century Portuguese visitor Paes described the Vijayanagara celebrations in vivid terms. As Burton Stein has written, "throughout the nine days, festivities are centred on the 'citadel' area of Vijayanagara, before the palace and on two large permanent structures... Here the king observed the many processions, displays, and games, and here he accepted the homage and the gifts of throngs of notables as he sat upon his bejewelled throne."

Today the festival is still enormously colourful. On the last day, with the sound of guns and bands, colourfully bedecked elephant with a golden *howdah* carrying the statue of Bharatmata starts from the palace to process with palace chariots, and units of the army through the city to Banni Mantap about 5 km away where the Banni tree is worshipped. The temple float festival takes place at a tank at the foot of **Chamundi Hill** and a car festival on top. In the evening there is a torchlight parade by the mounted guards who provide an exciting display of horsemanship and the night ends with a great display of fireworks. A good time for cultural programmes particularly at the Palace Durbar Hall and Exhibition Grounds which with other public buildings, are ablaze with illuminations during this period. *Feast of St. Philomena* 11th August each year, the statue of the saint is taken out in procession through

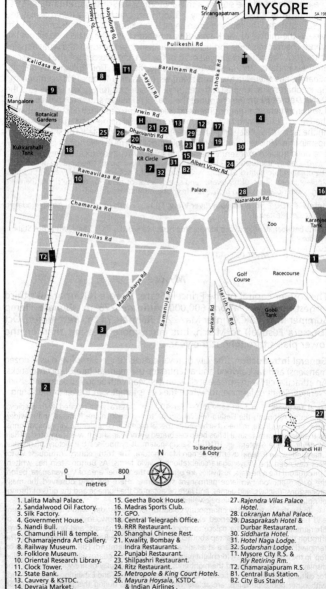

MYSORE SA 198

0   800
metres

N

1. Lalita Mahal Palace.
2. Sandalwood Oil Factory.
3. Silk Factory.
4. Government House.
5. Nandi Bull.
6. Chamundi Hill & temple.
7. Chamarajendra Art Gallery.
8. Railway Museum.
9. Folklore Museum.
10. Oriental Research Library.
11. Clock Tower.
12. State Bank.
13. Cauvery & KSTDC.
14. Devraja Market.

15. Geetha Book House.
16. Madras Sports Club.
17. GPO.
18. Central Telegraph Office.
19. RRR Restaurant.
20. Shanghai Chinese Rest.
21. Kwality, Bombay & Indra Restaurants.
22. Punjabi Restaurant.
23. Shilpashri Restaurant.
24. Ritz Restaurant.
25. *Metropole & King Court Hotels.*
26. *Mayura Hoysala,* KSTDC & Indian Airlines .

27. *Rajendra Vilas Palace Hotel.*
28. *Lokranjan Mahal Palace.*
29. *Dasaprakash Hotel & Durbar Restaurant.*
30. *Siddharta Hotel.*
31. *Hotel Naga Lodge.*
32. *Sudarshan Lodge.*
T1. Mysore City R.S. & Rly Retiring Rm.
T2. Chamarajapuram R.S.
B1. Central Bus Station.
B2. City Bus Stand.

the city streets ending with a service at the cathedral.

At **Nanjangud** 23 km. Mar – Apr. Temple car festival with a 15 day fair. **Melkote** Temple 52 km. Mar – Apr. Vairamudi festival which lasts 6 days when deities are adorned with 3 diamond crowns.

Places of interest The City Palace, **Amber Vilas** was designed by **Henry Irwin** and built in 1897 as the new palace after a fire which burnt down the old wooden one. It is built in the **Indo-Saracenic** style in grand proportions, with domes, arches and colonnades of carved pillars and shiny marble floors. It is one of the largest palaces in the country, beautifully maintained and contains some artistic treasures. The architectural historian Philip Davies comments that "It is a glorious Indo-Saracenic pile in grey granite dominated by a 5 storey minaret with a gilded dome. On Sunday nights and during festivals the entire exterior is lit by over 50,000 light bulbs, like some sort of Oriental Harrods." Look at the stained glass (from Glasgow), the wall paintings, the red and gold walls, carved silver, teak and rosewood doors, ornamental wooden ceiling and the stone-studded solid golden throne (now displayed during Dasara). The *Kalyana Mandap* or marriage hall where women sat behind a screen has paintings of the times when the family were the rulers. On the 2nd floor is the great Durbar Hall, 47 m long by nearly 14 m wide, described by Davies as "one of the most exuberant rooms in India, a blaze of colour and sinuous forms, like a setting from *A Thousand and One Nights.*"

The last in the line of Wodeyar rulers decided in late 1990 to put his families' fabulous collection of jewels on permanent display. Enter by the gate to the S. T 23083. Open 1030-1730. Rs 2 for each section plus a charge for leaving shoes and camera with attendant. Allow about 1 hr, 2 if you wish to see everything. Security guards-cum-guides tend to rush you and expect a tip – take your time. No photography indoors. Downstairs is fairly accessible to the disabled. It can be very crowded at weekends although illuminations on Sunday night worth seeing.

Chamundi Hill The hill immediately to the SE of the town has a temple to Durga (Chamundeswari) celebrating her victory over the buffalo god. She became the guardian deity of the Wodeyars. Below the temple on the road to the top is the giant Nandi, carved in 1659. Unless you have transport and it is a very clear day, the journey is hardly worthwhile.

With prior permission you can visit two government factories. In the **Sandalwood Oil Factory** you can see the extraction of oil and see how incense is made. The factory produces more than half the country's output. Sales counter. Open 0900-1100, 1400-1600. T 22856. **Silk Factory**, Manathandy Rd. T 21803, where you can watch weavers using their skill to produce Mysore silk saris. Open 0900-1100, 1230-1630 on weekdays.

Local crafts and industries Sandalwood, rosewood carving. Sandalwood oil, incense, soaps, ivory inlay on wood. *Agarbatti* (incense sticks). Women and children produce *agarbatti* at home, producing thousands each day with thin bamboo sticks covered with putty and powdered incense. Silk weaving.

Hotels Note In the higher class hotels Sales Tax (usually 5%) is charged for food and Luxury Tax (5-15%) on rooms plus a Service Charge which is often 10%.

A *Lalitha Mahal Palace* (ITDC), T Narasipur Rd. T 26316, Cable: Tourism, Telex: 0846 217. 54 rm. 8 km rly. Built in 1931 to a design by E.W. Fritchley in superb gardens to offer hospitality to the Maharaja's non-veg foreign guests! The central dome is modelled on St. Paul's Cathedral in London. Grand and old-fashioned. The main palace rooms have verandahs, some have original baths with extraordinary system of spraying! If you are looking for nostalgia stay in the old building and not in the new annexe behind. Sports facilities include billiards, badminton, tennis and table tennis but pool not well kept. Restaurant service is slow and the hotel is out-of-town. **C** *Quality Inn Southern Star*, Vinobha Rd. T 22717, Telex: 0846 256. 108 rm. 0.5 km rly. Speciality restaurant, bar, 24 hr coffee shop, exchange, travel, shops, pool side barbecue, health club, TV. New smart hotel in convenient location. Recommended for excellent restaurant, pool and friendly staff, though evening entertainment of dance and music considered mediocre. C *Metropole*, 5 Jhansi Lakshmibai Rd. T 10681, Cable: Metropole, Telex: 0846 214 Ritz In. 22 rm with dressing rm and bath, 4 a/c. 1 km rly. Very good restaurant, travel, curio shop, TV. Attractive and in spacious grounds but you may be slightly disturbed by the traffic noise. Helpful staff.

D *Highway*, New Bannimantap Extension. T 21117, Cable: Highway. 40 rm some a/c. 2 km rly. Restaurant, bar, coffee shop, exchange, travel, shop. D *Rajendra Vilas Palace*, Chamundi Hills. T 22050. Cable: Palaschain, Telex: 0846 231 Hrvi In. 29 rm, 17 a/c. 10 km rly. Restaurant, bar, exchange, travel, tennis. Built in 1939 to allow the Majarajah to escape from the city proper and you can book the royal suite. Run by the family with the help of old retainers, now somewhat dilapidated. The out-of-town hilltop situation sounds attractive but you have to allow 30 min to get into the city centre. D *Dasaprakash Paradise*, 105 Vivekananda Rd, Yadavgiri. T 26666, Cable: Paradise, Telex: 0846 266 Dasa In. 90 rm, 36 a/c. 2 km rly. Restaurant, bar, travel, TV. D *Kings Kourt*, Jhansi Lakshmi Bai Rd. T 25250, Cable: Kingskourt, Telex: 0846 263 King In. 20 rm, 12 a/c, with bath. Close to rly. A/c restaurant, exchange, travel, Beauty Parlour. Very central, new hotel. D *Lokranjan Mahal Palace*, Lokranjan Mahal Rd. T 21868, Cable: Palaschin Mgr. 31 rm part a/c. 3 km rly. Restaurant, bar, exchange, travel, pool, TV.

The **Gandhi Square** area has some Indian style hotels which are clean and good value. Others in Dhanvanthi Rd. E *Dasaprakash* Gandhi Square. T 24444, Cable: Dasprakash, Telex: 0846 257. 145 rm most with attached bath and a few a/c. 1 km rly. Restaurant (Indian Vegetarian), travel. E *Mayura Hoysala* KSTDC 2 JLB Rd (opp Hotel Metropole). T 25349. 21 rm. Close to rly in the heart of the city. Restaurant, bar. E *Siddharta*, 73/1 Guest House Rd, Nazarbad. T 26869, Cable: Comforstay, Telex: 0846 312 Hotl In. 76 rm some a/c. 2 km rly, close to centre. Restaurant (Indian veg), Exchange. New, clean, good value. E *Calinga*, 23 KR Circle (opp City Bus Stand). T 31310, Cable: Calinga. 80 rm single to 6 bedded (3 tier cot!) with attached baths (occasional hot water) and Indian toilets. Restaurant (Indian veg), travel, phone, TV. Fairly basic, clean, central and popular. E *Railway Retiring Rooms* are reasonable. Dormitory beds very inexpensive. E *Park Lane* 2720 Curzon Park, Sri Harsha Rd, Mysore 570001. Beautiful and very well-kept hotel; lovely, if cramped rooms. Staff slow and unhelpful, prices of food and drink high, but very attractive courtyard restaurant and good food. F *Youth Hostel* is rather inconvenient, 5 km NW of city centre.

Restaurants *RRR*, Gandhi Sq, Gun Hill Imperial, Bangalore Nilgiri Hill Rd and *Punjabi Bombay Juice Centre*, 397 Dhanvantri Rd are recommended. There are two on Sayaji Rao Rd – *Bombay Indra Bhavan* and Indra Cafe's *Paras Restaurant*. *Gaylord* and *Quality* Restaurants, Dhanvanthri Rd are recommended. *Kings Court* Restaurant which has a bar. Near the Central Bus Station is the *Ritz* which has good inexpensive restaurant and serves excellent lime sodas! For vegetarian food try *Hotel Dasaprakash*. You can get good Chinese food at Hotel Metropole and also at Rajendra Vilas, Quality Inn Southern Star, King's Kourt, Lokranjan Mahal Palace and *Shanghai Chinese* Restaurant on Vinobha Rd.

Bars Best in the hotels. You can try *Lalitha Mahal Palace, Lokranjan Mahal Palace* and *Gun Hill Imperial*.

Banks & Exchange State Bank of Mysore, corner of Sayaji Rao Rd and Sardar Patel Rd. Mysore Bank is almost opposite the GPO in the city centre.

Shopping Superb carved figures, sandalwood and rosewood items, silks, incense-sticks, handicrafts. The main shopping area is Sayaji Rao Rd which runs N from the centre, just N of the Maharaja's Palace. *Cauvery Arts & Crafts Emporium* for sandalwood, ivory and rosewood items. *Devaraja Market* with its lanes of stalls selling spices, perfumes among all else. *Sri Lakshmi Fine Arts & Crafts* (opp. the zoo) also has an outlet at their factory in 2226 Sawday Rd, Mandi Mohalla. *Ancient Curios* is at 12 Dhanvanthari Rd and *Ganesh* is at No. 532 on the same rd. For silks go to *Karnataka Silk Industry's* shop on Visweswara Bhavan, RKR Circle or better still the factory shop on Mananthody Rd where you can watch machine weaving. 0730-1130. 1230-1630, Mon-Sat. Bookshops *Geetha Book House* on KR Circle and Ashok Book Centre, Dhanvanthari Rd.

Local transport Frequent city buses to the Government Silk Weaving Centre and the Sandalwood Oil Factory (No 1A goes to both). No 150 leaves about every 30 min for the Krishnarajasagar Dam and Brindavan Gardens. No. 101 goes to Chamundi Hill. Autorickshaws are also easily available.

Sports *The Madras Sports Club* is on Lalitha Mahal Palace Rd just before you get to the hotel.

Museums **Chamarajendra Art Gallery** at the Jaganmohan Palace. The palace itself was built in 1861. Indian Miniature paintings and others, including Ravi Varma and Nicholas

Roerich. Also exhibition of ceramics, stone, ivory, sandalwood, antique furniture and old musical instruments. No descriptions or guide book; many items randomly displayed, but pleasant atmosphere. T 23693. Open daily, 0800-1100, 1400-1700. Entry Rs.2. No photography. The Technical Institute produces high class rosewood and sandalwood articles. T 23883. The **Railway Museum** is small but will interest an enthusiast. Includes a royal carriage over a hundred years old. Open 1000-1300, 1500-1700. **Folklore Museum**, University of Mysore, Manasa Gangotri. Open 1030-1730, closed 2nd Sat and Sun. Entry free. Collection includes weapons, jewellery, folk toys, utensils. Photography with permission of Director. **Art & Archaeology Museum**, PG Department of Ancient History, University of Mysore, Manasa Gangotri. Open 1030-1730, closed Sun. Entry free. Collection includes antiquities, sculpture, inscriptions, coins. Photography with permission. **Medical College Museum**. Open 1830-1300, 1400-1700. Sun 0800-1300. Entry free. Collection includes botanical paintings, charts, models, weapons.

Parks and zoos *The Zoological Gardens* established in 1892, in the town centre on a 5 sq km site with well kept lawns and gardens. Contains the usual variety of fauna and has also bred wild animals in captivity especially tigers. Well managed in spacious enclosures. You are encouraged to feed some animals, eg rhinos and elephants in return for a tip! Open 0900-1400, 1500-1800 on weekdays. 0900-1800 on Sun. Entry Re 2. Camera charge extra. Accessible to the disabled.

Useful addresses *Indian Airlines,* Hotel Hoysala Complex, JLB Rd, T 21846.

Post and telegraph GPO on corner of Ashok Rd and Irwin Rd. Poste Restante mail here. Central Telegraph Office, open 24 hr, is to the E of Maharajah's Palace.

Places of worship *Hindu – Chamundeswari Temple* in the Chamundi Hills; *Kali Temple,* Kali Temple Rd N of the Palace. *Christian – Karuhapura Church* (CSI), *St Bartholomew's Church* and *St Joseph's Cathedral* off Church Rd. *St Philomena's Church,* Hyder Ali Rd which is worth visiting.

Hospitals and medical services The Medical College, corner of Irwin Rd and Saiyaji Rao Rd and KR Hospital, S of Irwin Rd. The Mary Holdsworth Hospital (in a striking building dating from 1906) was established as a Methodist Mission Hospital.

Travel agents and tour operators KSTDC Transport Wing, Hotel Mayura Hoysala, Jhansi Lakshmi Bai Rd. T 23652. Shri Raghavendra Travels, Narayanshastri Rd.

Tourist offices and information Deputy Director of Tourism, Regional Tourist Office, Old Exhibition Building (corner of Irwin Rd). T 22096. 1000-1730. Rly Station, T 30719. KSTDC Tours *City sightseeing including Somnathpur* Daily 0730-2030. Rs. 85. *Ooty Tour* Daily Apr-July. One day tours to Belur, Halebid and Sravanabelagola. Fri and Sun. Other tours to Hampi and Aihole, Badami, Pattadakal and Bijapur.

Air Mysore currently has no scheduled flights as Vayudoot cancelled its services in 1990. They may be re-started. Vayudoot City Office, T 20031. Indian Airlines Office, Hotel Mayura Hoysala, T 25349.

Rail At present on the metre gauge network but after the section to Bangalore is upgraded to broad gauge, Mysore will have good connections with rest of the country. Several Express trains run between Bangalore and Mysore **Bangalore**: Tipu Exp, 6205, daily, 0955, 3 hr 35 min. Rly Station Enquiries, T 20100.

Road Mysore has a number of state highways radiating to major cities and towns in Karnataka, Tamil Nadu and Kerala and connects to NH 48.

Buses The State Transport Corporation buses of Karnataka, Tamil Nadu and Kerala run regular services to Mysore with a network covering several major cities including Bangalore, Coimbatore, Cochin, Madras, Mangalore, Mercara and Trivandrum. Every ten min from Bangalore. Towns within the state are served by the State buses.

Excursions The Brindavan Gardens and *Krishnarajasagar dam* 19 km from Mysore, an extremely popular outing for people from the city, **see page 859**. The 2 km dam is one of the biggest in India and forms a 130 sq km lake. It is a rock filled dam built by Maharaja Krishnaraja Wodeyar to provide continuous water supply for the Sivasamudram Power Station. The terrace gardens have numerous fountains including 'musical' ones which are turned on for 10 min at 1930. Special lighting 1900-2100 on Sun and holidays, an hour on weekdays. Entry Rs 2 but costly to take camera or car. You can take a boat ride across the river Kaveri, from one end of the lake to the other. Refreshments from a former royal guest house verandah.

Hotels D *Krishnarajasagar* T Belagola 22. Some a/c rm and usual facilities. Restaurant. Reservations at Hotel Metropole in Mysore. **D** *Ritz*, Telex: 0846 214 Ritz In. A/c and non-a/c rm. Restaurant. **F** KSTDC *Hotel Mayura Cauvery*, T Belagola 52. Inexpensive, good value, double rm with bath. Restaurant. Bus No 150 every 30 min from Mysore City Bus Stand.

Somnathpur, Sivasamudram and Srirangapatnam

From Mysore continue S to the small town Nanjangud (23 km). This is famous throughout Karnataka for the three day temple-car festival held in March. The temple itself is over 110 m long and is supported by 147 columns. Cross the railway and take a right turn to continue S to Gundlupet (35 km).

From **Gundlupet** take the left fork, the road S to **Bandipur** and **Mudumalai** Wildlife Sanctuaries. Bandipur is on the Karnataka side of the border while Mudumalai is in Tamil Nadu, but they are extensions of the same forest reserve which also stretches W to include the Kerala reserve of Wynad. These were the Maharaja of Mysore's game reserves. It is possible to spend a day or more in the forest rest houses and to take organised trips into the reserves on elephant back or jeep.

Bandipur National Park Altitude 780 -1455 m. Area 874 sq km. Best season May-June, Sep-Nov. Open 0600-0900, 1600-1800. **Bandipur** was the first park in S India to be chosen for the Project Tiger scheme. You will probably not see any but will more easily spot bison, *chital* or spotted deer, elephant and sambar in the mixed deciduous forest. Also good variety of bird life. Jeeps and vans available through Forestry Department and viewing is from *machans* or raised platforms near watering places. Otherwise elephant rides for up to 4 at a time. Boats for hire on the river.

Accommodation in inexpensive but excellent value **F** *Forest Lodges*, *Guest Houses* which have attached baths, and 3 *Wooden Cottages* each with 12 beds. A couple of VIP lodges – Rajendra I and II, available. Food to order. Bookings for bungalows and jeeps to Assistant Conservator of Forests, Bandipur National Park. T 21 or Forest Officer, Forest Dept, Woodyard, Ashokpuram, Mysore which is to the S of Mysore city (Bus No. 61 from city centre). Also possible through Field Director, Project Tiger, Government House Complex, Mysore. T 20901.

The road climbs through Bandipur to one of the highest parts of the Mysore Plateau before dropping sharply into the deeply cut straight gash of the Moyar Valley, the floor of which is only between 300 and 500 metres above sea level. The River is the boundary between Karnataka and Tamil Nadu, but it also marks the N edge of the Nilgiri Hills. From here on the road climbs, first to **Gudalur** (49 km) at the base of the hills. Turn left up to **Naduvattam** (10 km), the road climbing through mixed woodland, which has been managed through this century by the Forest Department. Many imported species have been experimented with, including fragrant and medicinal trees such as eucalyptus and chinchona, the bark of which was used for extracting quinine. The drive often gives beautiful views, and as with all the hill climbs in India the rapid change in altitude quickly brings a freshening coolness. Udhagamandalam (25 km) is set in rolling downland on the plateau top of the Nilgiris – see page 765.

Nagarhole National Park 96 km SW of Mysore and 225 km from Bangalore. Area 572 sq km. Best Season Oct – May. Open 0600-0900, 1600-1830. **Nagarhole** was once the Maharajas' reserved forest and includes swampland, salt licks and streams. The Kabini river which is a tributary of the Kaveri flows through the deciduous forest the upper canopy reaching 30 m. The timber here is valuable and includes teak and rosewood and also stands of giant bamboo. Wildlife includes elephants, *gaur* (Indian bison), *dhole* (Indian wild dogs), wild cats, 4-horned antelopes, flying squirrels, sloth bears, monkeys, sambar and panthers. Many varieties of birds including the rare Malabar *trogan*, great black woodpecker, Indian pitta, pied hornbill, whistling thrush and green imperial pigeon. Also waterfowl and reptiles. Jeeps, vans and guides through the Forest

Dept. Viewing from raised platforms near water holes. Trekking possible with permission. Entry Rs.2. Extra for camera. You can also visit the govt's Haballa camp for training elephants. Number of tribesmen, particularly Kurubas, live here.

Hotels From Sept – June **B** *Kabini River Lodges*. 14 double rm. 80 km airport and rly. Good restaurant, exchange. A government of Karnataka Tourism Venture. Converted from the Maharajas' Hunting Lodge and the Viceregal Bungalow. Package includes sailing, boat rides in coracles (buffalo hide boats), jeep tours. Price charged for foreigners is double that for Indians. Reservations: Jungle Lodges and Resorts, 348/9 Brooklands, 13th Main, Rajmahal Vilas Extn, Bangalore, T 362820, Cable: Brooklands. **F** *Forest Lodges*.

BANGALORE TO MANGALORE (SOUTHERN DIRECT ROUTE)

This route crosses the open plains of the Mysore plateau. Agriculture is carried out on flat and low lying land, intensively cultivated where irrigation is possible from tanks or occasionally wells. It is the land of the *Vokkaliga* caste, the dominant agricultural community of southern Karnataka, traditionally at loggerheads with the reformist Lingayats of the N districts of the state.

Leave Bangalore on NH 4, the main route to Bombay. In **Nelamangala** (26 km) turn left on to NH48. After 20 km the road passes through the southern end of the **Devarayadurga hills** (highest point 1387 m) formed out of the underlying Closepet granites to **Kunigal** (45) and **Nelligere** (35 km). From Nelligere you can take a short diversion to see the 10th century Jain shrines at **Kambadahalli** (15 km) and **Sravana Belagola** (20 km). Ignore the right turn taken by NH 48 in Nelligere and continue S to **Nagamangala**.

Kambadahalli The shrines at Kambadahalli have many features in common with the Chola temples built at the same period in Tamil Nadu. They have clearly defined mouldings on the base, the walls are divided by pilasters, and the shrines have stepped towers rising above them. The *Panchakutu Basti* has three shrines, housing *Adinatha* (the father of the Jain saint Gommateshwara) in the S shrine, *Neminatha* in the E and *Santinatha* in the W. There are many excellent sculptures, including a seated Jain figure. Note also the high relief carvings on the ceiling of the Santinatha shrine.

A visit to Kambadahalli can serve as an hors d'oeuvre to seeing one of the marvels of Jain sculpture, the colossal monolithic statue of Shri Gommatesvara at **Sravanabelagola** (20 km). It is one of the most visited pilgrimage sites in India and a centre for Digambara Jains. To reach the village continue along the road from Nagamangala towards Channarayapatna. Sravana Belagola lies between two bare granite hills. The statue of **Gommatesvara** stands on *Vindhyagiri* (sometimes known as *Indrabetta* or *Indragiri*) to the S, while there is a group of other shrines on *Chandragiri* to the N. Vindhyagiri rises nearly 150 metres above the plain while Chandragiri is just under half that height.

The statue was erected at some time between AD 980 and 983. Standing just over 17 metres high, it represents the saintly prince **Bahubali**, son of the first *Tirthankara*, after he had gained enlightenment. Having fought a fierce war with his brother *Bharata* over the rights to succession, Prince Bahubali accepted defeat when he had won the battle because he recognised its futility. Passing on his kingdom to his defeated brother, Bahubali adopted a life of meditation. The statue is nude (possibly as he is a Digambara or 'sky clad') and captures the tranquillity typical of much Buddhist and Jain art. The depth of the saint's meditation and withdrawal from the world is suggested by the spiralling creepers shown growing up his legs and arms, and by the ant hills and snakes at his feet. He is shown standing on a lotus. While the features are finely carved, the overall proportions are odd, with greatly enlarged shoulders and lengthened arms but shortened legs.

To reach the statue climb up the 189 steps carved in the steep granite slope. These start near the village tank. There is often a constant succession of pilgrims making their way to the top and the path up gives excellent views. There are several small shrines on the way to the statue itself on top. In order these are the *Odeagal Basti*, the *Brahmadeva mandapa*, the *Akhanda Bagilu* and the *Siddhara Basti*. All of these were built in the 12th century except the Brahmadeva Mandapa which is two centuries older. Several are intricately carved. A good example of a freestanding pillar or *manastambha* stands in front of the *Parsvanathasvami Basti*. These pillars, which could sometimes reach 15 m in height, were placed at the temple entrance and in this example shows the steps at its base with a square cross-section in the lower part of the column which transforms to a circular section and is then topped by a capital.

There is a collection of 15 shrines on **Chandragiri** and the Mauryan Emperor **Chandragupta**, who is believed by some to have become a Jain and left his Empire to fast and meditate, is buried here. In the town itself is the *Bhandari basti*, built in 1159 and added to later. It is about 200 metres to the left from the bottom of the path leading up to the Gommatesvara statue. Inside are twenty-four images of Tirthankaras in a spacious sanctuary. There are 500 rock-cut steps to the top of the hill and it takes about half and hour to climb up. It is safe to leave luggage at the Tourist Office which has a branch office at the entrance which is closed from 1300-1415.

Sravanabelagola is often crowded with visitors. Every twelfth year however it is the focus for Jain pilgrims from across India to celebrate the **Mastakabhisheka** – the sacred head-anointing ceremony. In February 1982, celebrated as the one thousandth anniversary of the sculpture's completion, hundreds of thousands of pilgrims converged at the hill. Scaffolding is specially erected to pour *ghi*, milk, coconut water, turmeric paste, honey and vermilion powder over the statue. Some even sprinkle gold dust. The next celebration will be in 1994. It's an interesting village to wander round.

Hotels All facilities are very basic. **F** *Tourist Canteen cum Rest House*, T 54. 50 rm. Reserve direct or through Department of Tourism, Government of Karnataka, 9 St Mark's Rd, Bangalore. T 579139. **F** *Travellers Bungalow*. Reservations: Chief Executive Officer, Talum Board, Chennarayapatna, Hassan District. Several tea and coffee shops, cold drink stalls. Canteen at the bus station. Vegetarian restaurants and **F** *Shriyans Prasad Guest House*, a pilgrim's guest house, at foot of hill.

Leave Sravanabelagola from the middle of town on the Hassan road. In 10 km you reach the ancient settlement of **Channarayapatna** and rejoin NH 48 to Hassan (36 km). .

Hassan is a good base from which to see **Belur** and **Halebid** if you have time to stop. A railway junction with connections to Bangalore (via Arsikere), Mangalore and Mysore, Hassan is also the focus of several long distance and local bus routes.

Hotels **C** *Hassan Ashok* (ITDC) BM Road, opposite end of Race Course Rd. T 8731. 46 rm some a/c. 1 km rly. Restaurant, bar. The best in Hassan. **D** *Amblee Palika* , Race Course Rd. T 7145. 34 rm New Indian style hotel, in the style of many being built in the S. Clean and comfortable. **F** *Inspection Bungalow and Travellers Bungalow*, BM Rd. T 8437. 7 rm. Reservation: Executive Engineer, PWD, Hassan Division, BM Rd, Hassan. T 8437. No facilities, but typical cheap accommodation for government servants on tour of duty. Available for travellers when not in official use. **F** *Railway Retiring Room* 1 rm only (2 km out of town centre). **F** *Vaishnavi Lodging* T 7413 Clean, spacious, new. 100 m N of bus station. **F** *Satyaprakash Lodge*, Bus Stand Rd. T 8521. Excellent value, less than 100 m S of bus station. **F** *Lakshmi Prasanna*, T 8391. Large rooms, cheap, clean. 300 m S of bus station, nearly opp *Abiruchi Restaurant*.

Restaurants Several reasonable places to eat, mainly S Indian and vegetarian food, all grouped close by 200 metres S of bus station. *Hotel Hassan Ashok*, the most expensive but good. *Abiruchi Restaurant*, N Indian and Chinese *Hotel New Star*, non vegetarian Indian food, cheap but good. *Shantala Restaurant*, very near bus station. Good S Indian meals.

Banks & Exchange State Bank of India, Aurobindo Complex. T 8210. State Bank of Mysore, PN 27, 3291 Narasimharaja Circle. T 8407. Canara Bank, PB 45 Narasimharaja Circle. T 8238.

Local transport The Bus Stand, T 8418. Private Tourist Taxis can be hire from Cauvery Tourist Centre, Old Race Course Rd, T 8026. Tongas are also available.

Museum District Museum, Maharaja Park. Open 0900-1700. Closed Mon and government holidays. Entry free. Collection includes sculpture, paintings, weapons, coins and inscriptions.

Post Office, T 20, 100 m from town centre bus stand in and there is a General **Hospital**, T 3.

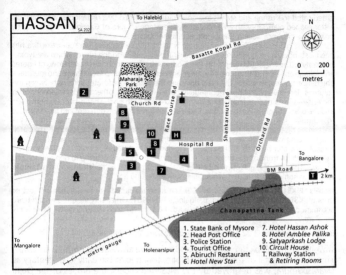

```
HASSAN  SA 202

To Halebid                                    N

                    Basatte Kopal Rd

                                              0      200
        Maharaja                                metres
          Park

        Church Rd

    2                    +

       B
       9                                  To
    6     10                             Bangalore
          8    H
    5     1    Hospital Rd
    3     7                    BM Road    T  2 km

                              Chanapattna Tank

                                    metre gauge

To                To
Mangalore         Holenarsipur
```

1. State Bank of Mysore   7. *Hotel Hassan Ashok*
2. Head Post Office   8. *Hotel Amblee Palika*
3. Police Station   9. *Satyaprkash Lodge*
4. Tourist Office   10. *Circuit House*
5. *Abiruchi Restaurant*   T. Railway Station
6. *Hotel New Star*   & Retiring Rooms

Tourist office is on BM Rd, T 8862 and there is a **Tour Operator**, Cauvery Tourist Centre, Old Race Course Rd, T 8026. The Government Tourist Office has daily conducted tours from Bangalore and thrice weekly from Mysore.

Travel Hassan Rly Station, T 8222 has trains to Bangalore, Mangalore and Mysore. Regular buses to Sravanabelagola, Belur and Halebid and Bangalore, Mangalore, Mysore and others.

Excursions If you stay in Hassan it is possible to visit Belur, Halebid, Sravanabelagola and other small sites on an excursion. There are frequent buses as well as organised tours. These sites are described in the route description.

Leave Hassan on NH 48, turn right for **Doddagaddavahalli** (10 km) on the Belur road. The comparatively plain Lakshmidevi Temple, built in 1113 in the early Hoysala style, is contemporary with the Belur temple. However, there is virtually no sculpture on the outside. The temple has 4 shrines leading off a common square mandapa. The N shrine has an image of *Kali*, followed clockwise by *Mahalakshmi*, *Bhairava* (a form of *Siva*) and *Bhutanatha*. Continue NW to **Belur** (20 km).

The **Hoysalas** who ruled a large kingdom between the rivers Krishna and the Kaveri, made **Belur** and Halebid their capital. Although great warriors, at times of peace and plenty, culture and art flourished. The temples here rank with those at Khajuraho, famous for their architecture and their sculpture, typifying the the style of the Hoysalas who built them. The artisans were encouraged to rival each other and even sign their names on their work of art. Steatite gave the sculptors the opportunity to work with intricate detail since the rock is initially comparatively soft when quarried but hardens with exposure to air. The temples they built as prayers to god to help them to be victorious in battle, are relatively small structures but are superbly conceived. See also Somnathpur **page 859**.

On the banks of the Yagachi river, **Belur** was the capital of the dynasty before it was moved to Halebid. The group of temples here stand in a courtyard with the **Chennakesava Temple** near the centre. One of the earliest of its type, this was started in 1116 (during the period when the great cathedrals of Europe – Lincoln, Wells, Chartres and Rheims were built) and took a century to complete. It celebrated the Hoysala victory over the Cholas at Talakad and is dedicated to Krishna and stands in a courtyard surrounded by a rectangular wall, built on a star shaped platform with an ambulatory. The winged figure of *Garuda*, Vishnu's carrier, guards the entrance, facing the temple with joined palms.

At first glance the view of the temple is unimpressive because the superstructure has been lost, however exquisite sculptures cover the exterior with the friezes which are typical of the style. The line of 650 elephants (each different) surround the base, with rows of figures and foliage above. The 38 figures of women are perfect in detail. Look at the young musicians and dancers on either side of the main door and the unusual perforated screens between the columns. Ten have typical bold geometrical patterns while the other ten depict scenes from the *Puranas* in its tracery. Inside the carving is excellent both on the hand-lathe-turned pillars and the bracket-figures on the ceiling. Each round filigreed pillar is different and bears witness to individual sculptors producing a masterpiece in competition with each other. The unique Narasimha pillar at the centre of the hall is particularly fine and could be rotated! The detail is astounding when you see the jewellery on the figures is hollow and moveable and the droplets of water hanging at the ends of the dancer's wet hair on a bracket above you. On the platform in front of the shrine is the figure of Santalesvara dancing in homage to Lord Krishna. The annual Car Festival is held in Mar-Apr. To the W is the **Viranarayana Temple** which has some fine sculpture and smaller shrines around it.

Hotels F KSTDC *Mayura Velapuri*, T 9. 2 rm simple but clean. Reservations: Direct or through KSTDC. 10/4 Kasturba Rd, Bangalore. T 578901. Other very inexpensive and basic accommodation in **F** *Vishnuprasad*, Main Rd. T 63. 12 rm and **F** *New Gayatri*, Main Rd. T 55. 7 rm.

Banks Canara Bank, T 22 and State Bank of Mysore, 1017 Temple Rd, T 41.

Travelling through picturesque hilly landscape you arrive at **Halebid** 12 km away. The ancient capital of the Hoysala Empire, founded in the early 11th century as *Dvarasaumdra*, was destroyed by the Muslim invaders, the armies of the Delhi Sultanate in 1311 and 1327 after which it was deserted and later renamed Halebid (Old Capital). Fortunately the great temple survived.

The **Hoysalesvara Temple** set with lawns around, has two shrines, one dedicated to Siva and the other to Santelesvara with a *Nandi* bull facing each. The largest of the Hoysala temples, it was started in 1121 but remained unfinished even after 86 years. In structure it is similar to the one at Belur and sadly because its superstructure was never completed; one can only imagine it in its full glory. There are extraordinary half life-size statues of Hindu deities, with minute details of each, all around the temple. These, and the six bands of sculpture below, show the excellence of the artisans' craft. The lines of elephants at the base, followed by lions and then horsemen, a floral scroll and then most impressive of all, at eye level, stories from the epics and the Bhagavata Purana. This frieze relates incidents from the Ramayana and Mahabharata among them Krishna lifting Mount Govardhana, Rama defeating the demon god Ravana. The friezes above show *yalis* and *hamsa* or geese.

There is a small museum on the lawn near the S entrance with a large Ganes statue and where the Archaeological Survey of India maintains a gallery of 12th-13th century sculptures and gold coins of the time, while to the W is a small lake.

Archaeological Museum Open 1000-1700. Closed Fri. Entry free. Collection includes sculpture, wood carvings, idols, coins and inscriptions. Curator, T 27. Guides available.

Hotels F *Tourist Cottages*, T 24, in the Inspection Bungalow compound in nice garden overlooking temple. 4 rm with fan and mosquito nets and bathroom. Simple, modern, limited kitchen facilities. Restaurant. *Travellers Bungalow*. Reservations: Assistant Engineer, PWD, Halebid. Also some tea stalls nearby.

There is a branch of Canara **Bank**, T 15, a **Post Office**, T 21, a Primary **Health Centre** and a **Photography shop**.

Travel Regular Karnataka State Road Transport bus connections with Hassan and from there to Bangalore, Mangalore and Mysore.

Return via Belur to the hill station of **Chikmagalur** (35 km). From here the road runs S W along the E facing slopes of the Western Ghats. To the right of the road they rise to heights of over 1800 m. This is one of India's major coffee growing areas. At **Mudigere** (35 km) the road turns sharply W to cut through the hills.

The difference between the wet and densely forested hills and the open, cultivated and comparatively dry rolling countryside is particularly sharp. This strip of the Western Ghats is one of the wettest regions of India and the road enters dense tropical forest. Wildlife abounds. Lungur monkeys hang in the trees and squat by the roadside. Occasionally King Cobras up to 3 m in length slide across the road. The narrow strip of true tropical evergreen forest – no more than 20 km wide – is rich in varied species. Giant bamboos, often 40 m high, arch gracefully, and even in the dry season the forest feels comparatively cool and damp.

The road drops quite steeply down to *Beltangadi* (45 km) where it enters the small embayment around **Mangalore** formed by the *Netravati River*. This is one of the longest westward flowing rivers S of the Narmada and Tapti, rising just N of Mercara. The road from Beltangadi crosses a low laterite plateau at between 50 and 120 m above sea level, giving the bright red soils typical of the heavy rainfall belt of the W coast. It has laid some alluvium over the ancient granites, but these break the surface from place to place. But although rice becomes the dominant crop again, forestry is vital to the district as a whole. Teak, mainly as a plantation crop, and other timbers, plus bamboos, canes, honey and wax are important products. Cashew nuts, introduced by the Portuguese in the 16th century, grow wild as well as cultivated. The nuts are exported and processed for a variety of industrial uses – in paints and varnishes and for caulking boats. On the laterites, which are not fertile enough for rice, ragi and pulses are common. The road from **Bantval** (30 km) to **Mangalore** (23 km) runs between the railway line from Hassan to Mangalore and the right bank of the Netravati River.

Mangalore Population Approx 400,000. Capital of S Kanara District. Situated on the Arabian sea it is a minor port with very limited harbour facilities but handling 75% of India's coffee exports. Today the modern port is 10 km N of the town.

In the 14th and 15th centuries **Mangalore** saw trade with Persian and Arab merchants and since it was then an important port it was fought over by the different powers. For a time it was in the hands of the Nayaka princes and the Portuguese, then in the 18th century alternated between the **Haidar Ali** (who made it his centre for shipbuilding) and his son Tipu Sultan on the one hand, and the British on the other, thus suffering the ravages of war several times.

Mangalore's other claim to fame is that it produces Ganesh *Bidis* (the cheap alternative to cigarettes), a tobacco leaf tied with a thread around a few pieces of tobacco.

Places of interest St Aloysius College Chapel with 19th century frescoes. **Mangaladevi Temple** 10th century. **Kadri Caves and Temple,** Lakes which have water with medicinal properties, and the Old Lighthouse. There is fascinating boat building and river traffic on the Netravati River. You can take a trip out to the sand bar at the river mouth.

Hotels C *Manjarun*, Bunder Rd, T 31791, Cable: Welcotel, Mangalore, Telex: 0832 316 Welh in. It is a new Welcomgroup hotel overlooking the sea and harbour. 100 a/c rm, some with sea view. 8 km airport. Restaurant, bar, coffee shop, pool. The older **D** *Moti Mahal*, Fahnir Rd, T 22211, Cable: Moti Mahal, Telex: 0832 314 Moti In. It has 90 rm, 53 a/c. 21 km airport, 1 km rly, close to centre. A/c restaurant and bar, coffee shop, shops, pool. **D** *Srinivas*, GHS Rd. T 22381, Cable Myhome, Telex 0842 328 Siri. 50 rm, 23 a/c. 16 km airport, 1 km rly. Restaurant, bar, exchange, travel, shops, indoor games.

E *Navaratna*, KS Rao Rd. T 27941, Cable: Navaratna. 66 rm, 13 a/c with TV. 20 km airport, 1 km rly, very central. A/c restaurant, bar, exchange, travel. **F** KSTDC *Tourist Home*, Kadri Hills (3 km). 18 rm and dormitory. **E** *Summer Sands Beach Resort* at Chotamangalore, Ullal (10 km), T 6253, Cable: Summersand. 128 rm, 29 a/c in cottages and bungalows. 30 km airport, 12 km rly. Restaurant, bar, travel, good pool, mini golf, tennis. Sailing and deep sea fishing arranged. Imaginatively designed in the local style with a superb beach. There are also some Indian style hotels and a *Circuit House*. **E** *Railway Retiring Rooms* with cheaper dormitory beds.

Restaurants *Embers* on Old Port Rd, T 575001 with open-air dinners by the pool and The *Galley* restaurant at the Manjarun, T 25465. They are both expensive but good, and reservations are recommended. The lantern lit restaurant at the **Summer Sands Resort**, T

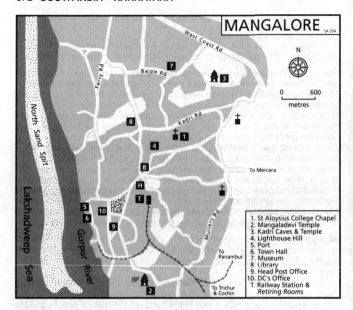

MANGALORE SA 204

1. St Aloysius College Chapel
2. Mangaladevi Temple
3. Kadri Caves & Temple
4. Lighthouse Hill
5. Port
6. Town Hall
7. Museum
8. Library
9. Head Post Office
10. DC's Office
T. Railway Station & Retiring Rooms

6253, though outside Mangalore, does very good food including seafood and local dishes, at a more reasonable price. *Taj Mahal* and *Navratna* both nr the Bus Stand, serve veg meals.

Bars In the big hotels.

Sports Sailing, boating and tennis at the *Summer Sands Beach Resort* at Chotamangalore.

Museums Shremmanti Bai Memorial Museum. Open 0900-1700, closed Mon. Entry free. Collection includes archaeology, ethnology, porcelain and wood carvings. **Mahatma Gandhi Museum**, Canara High School. Open 0930-1230, 1400-1730. Closed Sun and holidays. Entry free. Collection includes zoology, anthropology, sculpture, art, coins and manuscripts.

Air Bajpe airport is 25 km out of town. **Indian Airlines** Bangalore, Tues, Wed, Fri & Sat, 1110, 40 min; **Bombay**, daily (+ 1 other), 0745, 1 hr 15 min. Indian Airlines office is in the Moti Mahal Hotel, T 4669.

Rail Mangalore is at the N end of the broad gauge line which goes down the coast to Kozhikode and then inland to Coimbatore, connecting with all major destinations. **Cannanore**: *Madras Mail*, 6002 (AC/II), daily, 1240, 2 hr 30 min; **Madras**: *Madras Mail*, 6002 (AC/II), daily, 1240, 17 hr 55 min.

Road Bus connections to the E and N are much shorter and quicker than train.

BANGALORE TO MANGALORE (THE NORTHERN ROUTE)

After the open plains of the Mysore plateau, the route passes the Baba Bhudan hills and the impressive Jog Falls. A small diversion leads to some beautiful, unspoilt beaches, whilst the coastal road goes through several historic ports. If you wish to visit the sites described in the southern route to Mangalore then follow the road to Chikmagalur, then divert as follows:

Take the road N to **Tarikere** (55 km) and on to **Bhadravati** (19 km) an industrial town with a population of over 150,000 people in Shimoga District. Bhadravati is on the edge of the **Baba Bhudan Hills**. Apart from their physical attractiveness the Baba Bhudan Hills are important today as one of S India's most important sources of iron ore as well as being the centre of one of India's main coffee growing regions. The Mysore Iron and Steel Co set up a plant here in 1923, one of the first successful steel plants in India. It made extensive use of charcoal in the smelting process. As a side process it had a wood-distillation plant that was one of the biggest in Asia, producing 136,000 litres of distillate every day, the source of calcium acetate, methyl alcohol and formaldehyde. The plant has expanded into production of ferro-manganese, iron castings and pipes, steel ingots and tar products.

It is worth asking at the District Commissioner's Office in **Shimoga** (16 km) whether there is accommodation available at the Inspection Bungalow at **Jog Falls**. This is often heavily booked and best reserved in advance if you want to stay overnight at the falls. The road from Shimoga runs in the lee of the Western Ghats but close enough to the ridge to benefit from higher rainfall than the plateau to the E. Open woodland and rice cultivation on gently terraced slopes are common. They give way to some magnificent forest, often with bamboo. In **Sagar** (77 km) turn left to visit the 16th century temples at **Ikkeri** (3 km) for a brief period the capital of an independent Nayaka kingdom. The largest and most interesting is the *Aghoresvara* Temple. The influence of Vijayanagar style is evident in the vigorously sculpted animals rearing up, but there is also evidence of Muslim influence in the parapets of some of the smaller buildings. Return through Sagar to visit the **Jog Falls** (30 km).

At the start of the cool season just after the rains have finished the **Jog Falls** are a magnificently spectacular sight. The 50 km long *Hirebhasgar Reservoir* now regulates the flow of the **Sharavati River** in order to generate hydro-electricity, but there is still an enormous difference between wet and dry season flow. Often during the monsoon the falls are shrouded in mist. Dampness envelopes everything, water drips or pours from the trees, leeches seem to attach themselves to you at every step if you walk down the paths to the base of the falls, and rooms in the guest houses have a permanently musty smell. In the dry season the water is often reduced to a trickle. Late November to early January are strongly recommended as the best times to visit.

There are 4 falls. The highest is the Raja, with a straight fall of 250 m and a pool below it 40 m deep. Next to it is the Roarer, while a short distance to the S is the Rocket, which spurts great shafts of water out into the air. In contrast the Rani (what used to be called the White Lady or Dame Blanche) cascades over the rocks. The Inspection Bungalow has excellent views and the walk to the bottom of the falls is highly recommended for the fit.

Hotels The F *Inspection Bungalows*, near the Falls and in the colony, are often heavily booked and therefore difficult for people other than officials to get in. See above about reservations in Shimoga. The alternatives are unexciting. F *Woodlands*, T 22. Simple. Poorly maintained, poor food and service. The Tourist Department F *Jog Falls Guest House* reserve through Resident Manager. F *Guest House* near the Falls reservations through the Resident Superintending Engineer (Elec), Mahatma Gandhi Hydro-electric Works, Jog Falls.

Travel Buses run to Karwar daily, leaving Jog in the morning. Many buses to Sagar, and the S. Jog is also near the end of the railway line at Talguppa. Two trains a day, one to Bangalore and one coach of the train for Mysore. Choose the right one. From Jog Falls you can retrace your steps to Shimoga and turn right to **Tirthahalli**. Then through the Ghats to Agumbe, Udupi and Mangalore.

Alternatively go N through **Siddapur** to **Sirsi** (52 km), then through the Ghats to **Mirjan** (61 km). The shortest route to Mangalore is down the greatly improved coast road, **NH 17**, via **Kumta** (12 km). The whole of the National Highway has been upgraded, not least by building bridges across the many inlets which previously were only crossed by ferries.

Diversion If you have time the short journey N to **Ankola** (30 km) and **Karwar** (37 Km) has its attractions. Both have beautiful beaches to rival those of Goa less than 100 km to the N, but still deserted. The road runs along the coconut fringed W coast, studded with inlets and bays. **Ankola** has the remains of a fort. **Karwar** has a deep water port, now to be developed for naval use, and superb beaches. It is the administrative headquarters of N Kanara District on the banks of the Kalinadi River. From 1638 to 1752 there was an English settlement, surviving on the pepper trade. Then the Portuguese held it for nearly fifty years from 1752 before the old town was destroyed in 1801.

Main route Turn S at Mirjan, across new bridge over a tidal estuary to **Kumta**. The NH 17 passes through **Honavar** (18 km) across another new bridge over the Sharavati estuary, with Jog Falls just 20 km inland, accessible only to 4 wheel drive vehicles, and even then with difficulty from **Manki** (20 km). The W coast has a long wet season and high total rainfall, as shown by the figures for Honavar. The contrast with the peninsula, as shown by Bellary (**see page 855**), is striking:

	Jan	Feb	Mar	Apr	May	Jun	Jul	Aug	Sep	Oct	Nov	Dec	Av/Tot
Max (°C)	29	29	31	32	32	31	29	28	28	29	30	29	30
Min (°C)	21	22	24	26	27	25	24	24	24	24	23	21	24
Rain (mm)	2	2	2	18	66	752	793	404	241	97	33	5	2415

There is one of the many bullock cart tracks that used to be the chief means of access from the coast over the often apparently impenetrable Western Ghats. **Bhatkal** (30 km) is now only a small town, but in the 16th century was the main port of the **Vijayanagar Empire**. It also has two interesting small temples, one Jain and one Hindu. From the N the Jain *Chandranatha Basti* is approached first. Built in the 17th century it has two buildings linked by a porch. The use of stone tiling is a particularly striking reflection of local climatic conditions, and is a feature of the Hindu *Ketapai Narayana Temple* to its S. This is a 17th century Vijayanagar temple with typical animal carvings.

Continue S through **Bainduru** (15 km) and **Gangoli** (25 km) to **Coondapur** (10 km; formerly Kandapur). This was another small port, serving the rajas of Bednur about 50 km inland. The 16th century Portuguese fort survives. A further 27 km to the S is **Udupi**, one of Karnataka's most important pilgrimage sites. It commemorates the birthplace of the 12th century saint Madhva. The *Rashtrakavi Govind Pai Museum* is at the MGM College with a collection of sculpture, bronze, inscriptions and coins. Today it is almost as well known as the home of a family of Kanarese Brahmins who have established a chain of coffee house/hotels across S India. Just 5 km W is **Malpe**, one of the best port sites in southern Karnataka. Across the bay is the island of **Darya Bahadurgarh** and five km to the SW is **St. Mary's Isle**, composed of dramatic hexagonal basalt. Inaugurating a new era for S Asia, Vasco da Gama made his first landfall in India on this island and set up a cross.

From Udupi either go straight down coast to Mangalore (58 km) or take a diversion inland to see the Jain temples at **Karkal** (40 km) and **Mudabidri** (12 km) en route to **Mangalore** (20 km). **Karkal** has a statue modelled on the Gommateshwara statue at Sravanabelagola as well as many Jain shrines. **Mudabidri** has twenty Jain **bastis*** and excellent sculptures. The buildings are in the S Kanara style, with sloping roofs to allow easy drainage of the torrential rains that fall during at least five months of the year. Metal and stone sculptures from the 11th century onwards are found in the bastis, but the Jain Matha near the centre of the town also houses a collection of 12th and 13th century manuscripts and palm leaf paintings.

BANGALORE TO GOA

NH 4 runs direct from Bangalore to Hubli-Dharwad (and beyond up to Pune and Bombay). It crosses the rolling plateau of central Karnataka, and as it reaches Hubli-Dharwad follows one of the main routes for trade and military movement over centuries. To the E of the crest line of the Western Ghats it runs across high, open country. Even before the spread of cultivation the forest was comparatively light and easy to penetrate. Bullock cart tracks came up from the small W coast ports through the dense jungles of the ghats and then joined the much easier route of the plateau edge.

Leave **Bangalore** through the N of the city on the Tumkur road through **Nelamangala** (26 km) and **Dobbspet** (30 km). From here to **Tumkur** (46 km) the road passes through the *Devarayadurga Hills*, which just to the S of *Dobbspet* reach 1347 m above sea level. From **Tumkur** goes N through *Sira* (51 km) and *Hiriyur* (45 km) Uncultivated land is common on those areas without irrigation water. Wood cover is often thin and periodically bare outcrops of granite break the surface.

Chitradurga (40 km) is at the foot of a group of granite hills, rising to the S to 1175 m. The forts were built in the 17th century by Nayak *Poligars* (semi-independent landlords). They were crushed by Haidar Ali in 1779 who captured the fort and scattered the population. Haidar Ali replaced the Nayaka's mud fort with stone and Tipu built a palace in it. These can still be seen, along with as many as fourteen temples and pits dug for storing food. In the town are tea and coffee shops, soft drinks and simple S Indian 'meals' hotels.

The NH 4 continues to *Davanagere* (61 km), an important market town for cotton, groundnut and millets, all of which are important crops in the district. **Harihar**, reached in 10 km, takes its name from the combined image, half Siva, half Vishnu, enshrined in the Sri Harihareswara temple built in 1223. It is now a small industrial town with a Dak Bungalow. *Ranibennur* (30 km), a small market town, has a rocky hill to the S known as Scorpion Hill, and the NH 4 then passes through **Haveri** (20 km) and **Bankapur** (23 km) en route for the twin city of **Hubli** (53 km) and **Dharwad** (21 km).

Hubli-Dharwad Population 700,000. Hubli has some importance as a centre for the textile industry and also has a big a medical school while Dharwad has the State University, but in themselves the two towns are not of particular interest.

Hotels Only basic accommodation in Indian style hotels. **E** *Ayodhaya*, PB Rd, opp Central Bus Stand. T 66251. 104 rm, some a/c. 2 km rly. **D** *Hubli Woodlands*, Keshwapur. T 62246, Cable: Woodlands. 50 rm, 6 a/c with attached baths. 0.5 km rly. A/c restaurant (Indian), bar. **D** *Ashok*, Lamington Rd. T 62271, Cable: Ashok Hotel, Telex: 0865-305 VPRA IN. 87 rm, 1 a/c. 0.5 km rly and Bus Stand. Restaurant (vegetarian), exchange. **D** *Shree*, Poona Bangalore National Highway, Hosur-Hubli. T 2015. Some a/c rm. **F** *Railway Retiring Rooms*, s and d and dormitory.

Museums Kannada Research Institute Museum, Karnataka University. Open 1100-1800, closed Tues afternoon and University holidays. Entry free. Collection includes sculpture, paintings and manuscripts.

Rail Hubli and Dharwad are on main rail routes. **Dharwad to Bangalore**: *Kittur Exp*, 1007 (AC/CC), daily, 11 hr 25 min; **Hubli to Goa** (Vasco-da-Gama): *6201 Mail*, daily, 0555 (Dharwad 0631), 7 hr 15 min; **Dharwad to Goa** (Vasco de Gamma: *6201 Mail*, daily, 0631, 6 hr 39 min; **Hubli to Bombay (VT)**: *Mahalaxmi/Sahyadri Exp*, 6203/7304, daily, 1505 (Dharwad 1538), 21 hr; **Hubli to Secunderabad (H)**: *Vijaynagar/Venkatadri Exp*, 7830/7598 (AC/II), daily, 1625, 5 hr 55 min; **Hubli to Hospet**: *Hubli-Guntur-Amravati Exp*, 7826, daily, 1215, 3 hr 30 min; **Gadag** 1 hr 25 min; **Guntakal** 6 hr 15 min.

Excursions Alnavar (29 km) – Nangad (28 km) – Degamve (5 km). *Dandeli Wildlife sanctuary* (80 km).

From Hubli the road keeps close to the railway line to **Alnavar** (29 km) and **Londa** (32 km), which is a railway junction with the line N through *Belgaum*, an important town on the border with Maharashtra.

Rail Belgaum to Pune via Miraj: *Mahalaxmi Exp*, 6203, daily, 1900, 2 hr 50 min, change

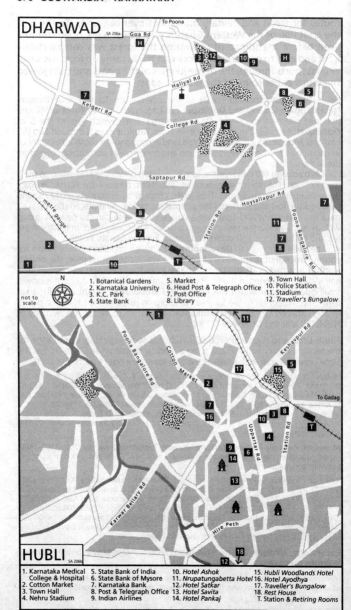

DHARWAD SA 206a

To Poona

Goa Rd

Haliyal Rd

Kelgeri Rd

College Rd

Saptapur Rd

Hoysallapur Rd

metre gauge

Station Rd

Poona Bangalore Rd

N
not to
scale

1. Botanical Gardens
2. Karnataka University
3. K.C. Park
4. State Bank
5. Market
6. Head Post & Telegraph Office
7. Post Office
8. Library
9. Town Hall
10. Police Station
11. Stadium
12. *Traveller's Bungalow*

Poona Bangalore Rd

Cotton Market

Keshavpur Rd

To Gagad

Uppatkar Rd

Station Rd

Karwar Bellary Rd

Hire Peth

HUBLI SA 206b

1. Karnataka Medical
   College & Hospital
2. Cotton Market
3. Town Hall
4. Nehru Stadium
5. State Bank of India
6. State Bank of Mysore
7. Karnataka Bank
8. Post & Telegraph Office
9. Indian Airlines
10. Hotel Ashok
11. Nrupatungabetta Hotel
12. Hotel Satkar
13. Hotel Savita
14. Hotel Pankaj
15. Hubli Woodlands Hotel
16. Hotel Ayodhya
17. *Traveller's Bungalow*
18. *Rest House*
T. Station & Retiring Rooms

at Miraj (1 hr 50 wait): Sahyadhri, 7304, daily, 2340, 7 hr 15 min; (total time 11 hr 55 min); **Goa** (Vasco-da-Gama): *Mandovi Exp*, 7898, daily, 1015, 7 hr; **Bombay (VT) via Miraj**: *Mahalaxmi Exp*, 6203, daily, 1900, 2 hr 50, change at Miraj (1 hr 50 min wait): Sahyadhri, 7304, daily, 2340, 12 hr 25 min (total time 17 hr 5 min); **Bangalore**: *Kittur Exp*, 7808, daily, 1655, 16 hr 25 min.

The road then passes through magnificent forested scenery down the steep face of the Ghats to **Molem** (35 km) and **Ponda** (37 km). Again the dramatic contrast between the wet W coast and the much drier to the E of the Ghats crest is strikingly visible. While the scenery is often stunning be prepared for the moist, hot air of the coast as you descend to sea level. **Panaji** (34 m).

HUBLI TO BANGALORE

It is possible to convert the route from Bangalore to Goa into a return trip to Bangalore, visiting some fascinating historical sites en route. N Karnataka has several features that distinguish it from the southern and central regions of the state. On a line running E N E from *Belgaum* to *Shorapur* the ancient granites which dominate the plateaus of Karnataka are overlain by the volcanic lavas of the Deccan. Black "cotton" soils stretch as far as the eye can see, giving a quite different ecological environment for farming and settlement. Historically the region also has a distinctive place.

Follow the route to Hubli. From Hubli take the road to **Gadag-Betgeri** (sometimes referred to just as " **Gadag**") via Annigeri (30 km). Hubli is in a region of black soils and has developed a range of cotton industries to match the agriculture of the surrounding area. *Gadag-Betgeri* (23 km) is an important and typical **cotton** collection market. The Indian geographer C.D. Deshpande has described it vividly: " Gadag dominates the southern cotton tract and cotton dominates the town and its annual rhythm of activity. Its cotton market is the focus of urban life. By the beginning of the picking season the town bursts into activity; commercial agents flock in; there is a flow in cart caravans bringing cotton into the market; the market bustles with activity and the rest of the town follows the pace; ginning mills and cotton presses lying idle for a long time are now set to work; cotton finds its way out in a compact and well-graded form to the metropolitan city of Bombay or for export, or to cities like Solapur for industrial consumption. By the middle of June this activity is at its zenith. The town accomplishes its major ambition and settles down to a quiet life during the next eight months."

The cotton market is well worth a visit. There is a Vaishnavite temple in the NW corner with a 15 m high gopuram at its entrance. The fort at Gadag has a Saivite temple of *Trimbakeshwar*, "Lord of the Three Peaks", elaborately carved, and an enormous carved bull. An inscription dates the temple at AD 868. Behind the main part of the temple is a shrine to Saraswati. The porch is perhaps the best feature of the temple. The black hornblende pillars have been smoothed to a remarkable finish with superbly detailed carving, sharp and clear. Gadag, a railway junction, has tea stalls, cold drinks and simple restaurants and a Dak Bungalow.

Rail Guntakal: *Hubli-Guntur-Amravati Exp*, 7826, daily, 1350, 4 hr 40 min; **Hubli**: *Link Exp*, 7837, daily, 2045, 1 hr 35 min; **Solapur**: *Golgumbaz Exp*, 6542, daily, 2300, 7 hr 25 min; **Bijapur**: *Bijapur Exp*, 7789, daily, 1555, 4 hr 50 min.

It is possible to take a diversion to the S E to visit the 12th century *Dodda Basappa* temple at **Dambal** (10 km). This is a late Chalukyan temple with a plan similar to the Hoysala temples further S. There is a highly polished *Nandi* at the E end. The sanctuary has a multi storeyed tower above it, and there is some decoration on the otherwise polished stone work. Return to **Gadag** and turn right out of the town before crossing the railway to visit the 17 Hindu and Jain temples at **Lakkandi** (15 km) which date from the 11th and 12th centuries. The stone used for the temples in Dambal, Gadag and Lakkandi is the schist brought from the

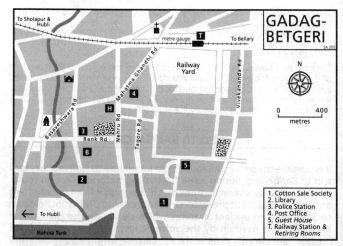

GADAG-BETGERI

SA 205

To Sholapur & Hubli

metre gauge

To Bellary

Railway Yard

To Hubli

Bishma Tank

N

0   400
metres

1. Cotton Sale Society
2. Library
3. Police Station
4. Post Office
5. Guest House
T. Railway Station & Retiring Rooms

Silasankar Hill in Dharwad. The sculpture was carried out at the quarry and the near finished work then transported to the temple to be erected. In this the method used differed from that in Orissa, for example, where raw stone was moved to the temple site before sculpting. Basements are moulded, walls have pilasters and there is remarkable detail on the ceilings. The late 11th century *Jain basti* is the largest of the temples, with a five storeyed pyramidal tower and square roof. Especially fine carving is found on the incomplete *Kasivisvesvara Temple*, dating from the 12th century. Both temples are near the tank in the southwest of the town, which is no more than 1 km across, and there is a small museum between them.

To the N of **Lakkandi** are two more sites with temples of the same period, **Kuknur** (15 km) and **Ittagi** (10 km). The Mahadeva temple in Ittagi, built in 1112 has similarly finely finished columns with beautifully finished miniature carvings. Two temples at Kuknur represent the transition from a Rashtrakuta style to a Chalukyan style taking place in the 11th century AD. The earliest is the *Navalinga* complex, dated the late 9th century. It has nine shrines, originally dedicated to female deities. The two gateways are Vijayanagar. The Kallesvara Temple (10th century) has a square sanctuary topped by a three storey tower. Ganesa and Durga are enshrined .

Return to the main Hospet road to **Koppal** (55 km), noted for two impressive forts. On the margins of Maratha, Hyderabad and Mysore power, this territory was once under the control of the Nizams of Hyderabad and Koppal was given to Salar Jung, one of the Nizam's nobles, as a *jagir* (a land gift). The upper fort is over 120 metres above the plains while the lower one was rebuilt by French engineers when it had been captured by Tipu Sultan from the Marathas. The road continues to Hospet (40 km).

Hospet (population 140,000) is used as a base by many visitors to Hampi since it offers a variety of accommodation and is the nearest station for Hampi.

Local festivals There is a significant Muslim population in Hospet and Muharram is celebrated with vigour. Firewalkers walk across burning embers and there are noisy celebrations. The custom may go back to long before the arrival of Islam. Villagers in the region still celebrate events such as the beginning or end of migrations to seasonal feeding grounds with huge bonfires. Cattle are driven through such fires to protect them from disease. The archaeologists Allchin and Allchin have suggested that ash mounds around Hospet dating from the neolithic period could have resulted from similar celebrations over 5000 years ago.

Hotels E *Mayura Vijayanagara* (KSTDC) T 8270. 2 a/c rm, basic with fans, mosquito nets and bath. Restaurant. E *Priyadarshini*, 45A Station Rd , T 8838. Some a/c rm. F *Sudarshan*, Station Rd, T 8128. F *Melligi Tourist Home*, Bellary Road, T 8101. 64 rm. Good value. F *Railway Retiring Rooms*, T 360. F *Vishwa*, Station Rd, opposite bus station. One of the new style S Indian hotels, clean and excellent value. **Note**: Station Road has been re-named Mahatma Gandhi Rd.

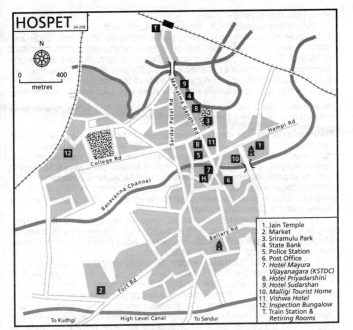

HOSPET SA 208

N

0   400
metres

Mahatma Gandhi Rd

Sardar Patel Rd

Hampi Rd

College Rd

Basavanna Channel

Bellary Rd

Fort Rd

To Kudhgi   High Level Canal   To Sandur

1. Jain Temple
2. Market
3. Sriramulu Park
4. State Bank
5. Police Station
6. Post Office
7. Hotel Mayura
   Vijayanagara (KSTDC)
8. Hotel Priyadarshini
9. Hotel Sudarshan
10. Malligi Tourist Home
11. Vishwa Hotel
12. Inspection Bungalow
T. Train Station &
   Retiring Rooms

At **Hampi: F** *Hampi Power Station Guest House*. See below. **Tungabhadra** is by far the better place to stay. Accommodation is listed below under Excursions.

Restaurants Hotel Mayura Vijayanagar's restaurant serves both veg and non-veg. *Amrut Garden* at Malligi Tourist Home does veg meals. *Shanti Restaurant* in Vishwa Hotel. *Shanbag Cafe*, in the town centre has good Indian food.

Local transport Frequent local buses to Hampi (to Hampi Bazar and Kamalapuram, the two entry points to the site). Also to Tungabhadra Dam. **Cycle hire** recommended in Hospet to visit Hampi (13 km) but check carefully the state of the bike. Not available in Hampi itself. Taxis available and you can share one with other tourists.

Post and telegraph *Post office* opposite vegetable market. *Telegraph office* in Hotel Sudarshan.

Tourist offices and information Karnataka State Tourist Office, Station Road. Free map and leaflets and occasionally guides for the sites.

Rail Secunderabad via Guntakal: *Tungabhadra Exp*, 7508, daily, 2015, 2 hr 45 min, change at Guntakal (1 hr 30 min wait): *Venkatadri Exp*, 7598, daily, 0030, 8 hr 55 min (total time 13 hr 10 min); Guntakal: *Hubli-Guntur-Amravati Exp*, 7826, daily, 1550, 2 hr 40 min.

Buses Express buses from Bangalore, 12 departures daily from 0700. Overnight KSTDC luxury coach. The State Transport KSRTC buses run regular services to Hampi, 13 km.

Excursions *Hampi*, also named 'the town of victory', *Vijayanagara*, is 13 km N of Hospet town *(Altitude* 467 m. *Best season* Oct-Mar). It was once the seat of the Vijayanagara Empire and a great centre of Hindu rule for two centuries from its foundation in 1336 although it is thought that there may have been a settlement in the area as early as a 1000 years before then. You can get a bus from Hospet to Hampi Bazaar via Kamalapuram (where you can get off to enter the site if you wish). Several buses from about 0630 (30 min journey) and last return from Hampi around 2000.

The city was incredibly rich, 'greater than Rome', with a market full of jewels and palaces plated with gold, having held a monopoly of trade in spices and cotton. It was very well fortified and defended by a large army. With the defeat in 1565 at Talikota at the hands of the Deccan Sultans, the city was largely destroyed and is sometimes referred to as the Pompeii of India. Today the stark and barren area of 26 sq km on the right bank of the river Tungabhadra has the ruins of the great Empire strewn across it and will take a full day to cover on foot.

Local Festival Jan – Feb. Virupaksha Temple Car festival. Also annual Purandaradasa Aradhana Music festival at Vithala Temple.

Places of interest The site for the capital was chosen for strategic reasons but the craftsmen adopted an ingenious style to blend in their architectural masterpieces with the barren and rocky landscape. Most of the sites are early 16th century, built during the 20 year reign of Krishna Deva Raya (1509-1529) with the **citadel** standing of the bank of the river. Excavations undertaken by the Archaeological Survey of India and the state Government in 1976 are still in progress. You can enter the area at Hampi Bazar, near the Bus Stop or from the southern end at Kamalapuram village.

Of the famous Market Place which was known across the world, you can now only see the wide pathway running eastwards from the towering **Virupaksha (Pampapati) Temple** with its 9 storey *gopuram*, along the river where the bazaar hummed with activity. The temple is still in use.

Further E is the **Vitthala Temple** dedicated to Vishnu, standing in its rectangular courtyard with its superb chariot carved out of a single piece of granite, its wheels raised off the ground so that they could be revolved! It was probably built in the mid-15th century and is one of the oldest and most intricately carved with its three *gopurams* and *mandapa* which has 56 superbly sculpted slender pillars which can be struck to produce different musical notes and the elephants on the balustrades and horses at the entrance. It is a World Heritage Monument.

Away from the temples, in the palace complex you will see the two storeyed **Lotus Mahal** in the *Zenana* or ladies' quarter screened off by its high walls and the **Queen's Bath** in the open air which is surrounded by a narrow moat and had scented water fill the bath from lotus shaped fountains. It measures about 15 m by 2 m and has interesting stucco work around it. The watch tower is in ruins but you can still see the **domed stables** for eleven elephants and the guardhouse and the specially built decorated platform of the **Mahanavami Dibba**, from which the royal family watched the pageants and tournaments during the 9 nights of *dasara* festivities. It originally had a covering of bricks, timber and metal but what remains still shows superb carvings of hunting and battle scenes as well as dancers and musicians. There is the small **Hazara Rama Temple**, the 'chapel royal'. which has statues of Vishnu in many forms. The exterior has carvings of men and animals (elephants, camels and horses) while the interior is devoted to stories from the epics, *Ramayana* and *Mahabharata*.

It is not difficult to imagine the magnificence of the Vijayanagar court or of some of its special occasions. Burton Stein has suggested that "in nothing else is the ritual focus of the Vijayanagar kings so clear as in the *Mahanavami festival*, an annual royal ceremony of the 15th and 16th century "occurring from mid Sep-mid Oct". The festival lives on across S India today, now often known as *Nava ratri*. The festival provided a ritual through which the power of the Vijayanagar kings was given validity. Paes, the Portuguese traveller, suggested that the activities in Hampi focussed on the Palace, what Paes called the "House of Victory" but which today is called locally the *mahanavami dibba* and the King's Audience Hall. Today they are just vast granite platforms, which almost certainly carried wooden building. Through the festivities Stein records that the king sometimes shared his throne , or sat at its foot while it was occupied by a richly decorated processional image of the god, while at other times he was alone.

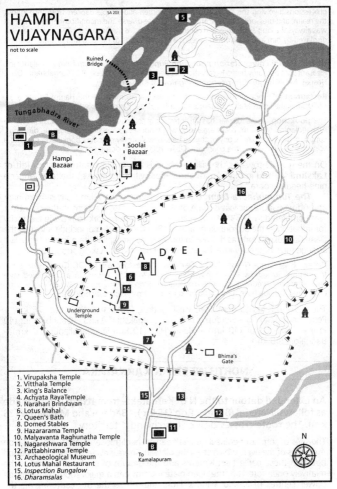

HAMPI - VIJAYNAGARA

SA 203

not to scale

Tungabhadra River

Ruined Bridge

Soolai Bazaar

Hampi Bazaar

C I T A D E L

Underground Temple

Bhima's Gate

To Kamalapuram

N

1. Virupaksha Temple
2. Vitthala Temple
3. King's Balance
4. Achyata RayaTemple
5. Narahari Brindavan
6. Lotus Mahal
7. Queen's Bath
8. Domed Stables
9. Hazararama Temple
10. Malyavanta Raghunatha Temple
11. Nagareshwara Temple
12. Pattabhirama Temple
13. Archaeological Museum
14. Lotus Mahal Restaurant
15. *Inspection Bungalow*
16. *Dharamsalas*

"In front of the two structures which were the centre of the festival activities", Stein writes, "were constructed a number of pavilions which contributed to the aura of wealth and sumptuousness of the festival as a whole. They were elaborately decorated, in among other ways, with 'devices', symbols of the grandee occupants. ...There were nine major pavilions for the most illustrious notables, and each military commander also had to erect one in the broad space before the palace. Access to the guarded, central arena of festival activity' he goes on "was gained by passage through several gates enclosing wells of the temple precincts....What was viewed was a combination of great durbar with its offerings of homage and wealth to the king and return of gifts from the king – exchanges of honours; the sacrificial re-consecration of the King's arms – his soldiers, horses, elephants – in which hundreds of thousands of animals were slaughtered; *darshana** and *puja** of the King's tutelary – the goddess – as well as his closest kinsmen; and a variety of athletic contests, dancing and singing processions involving the King's caparisoned women and temple dancers from throughout the realm, and fireworks displays. The focus of these diverse and magnificent entertainments was always the king as glorious and conquering warrior, as the possessor of vast riches lavishly displayed by him and his women (queens and their maids of honour) and distributed to his followers."

Hotels *Hampi Power Station Inspection Bungalow*, T 8272, 3 km from Kamalapuram. Pleasant spot but fairly basic. Reservation: Superintending Engineer, HES, Tungabhadra Dam, Hospet. Meals to order. *Inspection Bungalow* at Kamalapuram.

Restaurants Several simple places offering vegetarian meals in the Hampi Bazaar area. KSTDC has the Lotus Mahal Restaurant near the Hazar Rama Temple among the ruins.

The **bookshop** in the bazaar has an interesting collection and also sells postcards. The Archaeological **Museum** is at Kamalapur, which houses a collection of sculpture, paintings, copper plates and coins. Copy of the Archaeological Survey of India's booklet on sale and a scale model of Hampi in the courtyard. Open 1000-1700, closed Fri.

On the road N towards the village, there is a 6 m high statue on your left of **Lakshmi-Vishnu** in the form of a man-lion with bulging eyes sheltered under a nine-headed cobra.

The Tungabhadra Dam 6 km further where the 2 km Dam is 49 m high and offers panoramic views. One of the largest masonry dams in the country it was completed in 1953 after 8 years of construction work to provide electricity for irrigation in the surrounding districts. Bus tours to Hampi include a visit to the Dam. Can take as long as the visit to the Vijayanagar capital. State Tourist Office will arrange trips, but many local buses go every day, the trip taking about 15 min.

Hotels E *Vaikunta Guest House, Dam View Guest House*, KSTDC *Guest House* and *Inspection Bungalow* (Tungabhadra Dam), T 8241. This is built in a crenellated style reminiscent of Balmoral. It occupies a beautiful hill top site, but out of town above the dam. Only suitable if you have transport and sometimes rm occupied by officials.

The route returns to Bangalore via Rayadrug (55 km) – Anantpur (76 km) – Penukonda (74 km) – Hindupur (70 km) – Lepakshi (10 km) – Gauribidanur (40 km) – Chikballapur (40 km) – Nandi Hills (10 km) Doddaballapur (20 km) – Bangalore (40 km).

NORTH WESTERN KARNATAKA

An extended detour to the N of Karnataka from **Ittagi** can be made as follows- Naregal (8 km) – Ron (15 km) – Badami and Manakuta (25 km). The route crosses classic "marchlands" territory.

The sites of some of peninsular India's earliest neolithic settlements are found on the banks of the rivers which cross the plateau. There is evidence that in the period between those earliest settlements and the growth of medieval kingdoms the relatively open forests of the open plateaus provided a major route between the power centres of N and S India. From the 4th to the 8th centuries AD the **Chalukyas** ruled over this part of the Deccan. They made the three cities of **Aihole**, **Badami** and **Pattadakal** their capitals. Apart from some of the monolithic cave temples at Ellora such as the Kailasa Temple (cave 16), they became among the Nernmost centres of Dravida temple architecture. The villages are very attractive and unspoilt, and retain their traditional character. The sites themselves are well preserved and maintained in attractive gardens and are close enough to each other to be visited over 2 to 3 days by making either Aihole or Badami the base. Alternatively you can stay in Bagalkot. Buses connect the villages. During the medieval period the region was a historic battleground between the Hindu Vijayanagar Empire immediately to its S and the Muslim sultanates to the N. As you leave Ittagi for Badami you cross a landscape that was contested repeatedly from the 14th century through to the ascendancy of Aurangzeb's Mughal thrust in the late 17th century.

The **Bahmani Dynasty** was the most powerful in the Deccan, ruling from **Gulbarga** from 1347 until 1422, then making **Bidar** the capital. The founder, Ala'u'd-Din Bahman Shah, divided the kingdom into four quarters (*taraf*) and assigned each one to a trusted officer (*tarafdar*). The **Raichur doab** (the land between the Krishna and the Tungabhadra rivers) was contested between the *Vijayanagara* and the *Bahmani* rulers. In the eventful reign of *Firuz Shah Bahmani* (1397-1422) three major battles were fought between the two powers without disturbing the status quo. Firuz developed **Chaul** and **Abhol** as ports for trading ships from the Red Sea and Persian Gulf carrying luxury goods not only from the Persian, Arabian, and African coasts, but also (through Egypt) from Europe. Persians, Turks, and Arabs were given a ready welcome by the Bahmanids, ultimately producing conflicts between the sons of the soil and the foreigners (*pardesis*).

The Bidar period (1422-1526) was marked by wars with Gujarat and Malwa, continued campaigns against Vijayanagara, and expeditions against Orissa. Mahmud Gawan, Wazir of Bahmani sultanate, seized Karnatak between 1466 and 1481, and seized Goa, formerly guarded by Vijayanagar kings. But the struggle between *pardesis* and Deccani kings weakened the kingdom, split into five independent sultanates by 1530: the Adil Shahi of Bijapur, the Qutb Shahi of Bidar, the Imad Shahi of Ahmadnagar, the Barid Shahi of Bidar, and the Imad Shahi of Berar. In 1565 they co-operated to oust the Vijayanagar Raja, but Bijapur and Golconda gathered the lion's share of the spoil.

From Ittagi the route goes through Narega and Ron to Badami.

Badami *Population* 15,023 (1981). *Altitude* 177 m. *Climate* Summer Max. 38°C Min. 23°C, Winter Max. 29°C Min.15°C. *Annual rainfall* 50 cm.

Badami, also called *Vatapi* after a demon, was the Chalukyan capital from 543 – 757. It is a land of sandstone hills and cliffs with a natural gorge which leads to the ancient city with several Hindu and Jain temples and a Buddhist cave. The Chalukyas for a short period lost control of Badami to the Pallavas in the mid-7th century and were finally defeated by the *Rashtrakutas*. This was followed by the Western Chalukyas, the Yadavas, the Vijayanagaras, the Bijapur emperors and the Marathas.

Places to visit It is famous for its **cave temples** four of which were cut out of the hill side. You climb some 40 steps to get to the Cave 1 which has the Nataraja with 18 arms who is seen is some 81 dancing poses. The next two are dedicated to Vishnu (note the frescoes in the upper cave) and No 4 which is older, is the only Jain cave, with the statue of the seated Mahavira. The Buddhist temple is in the natural cave. The ancient artificial *Bhutanatha Lake*, where the mossy green water is considered to cure illnesses, has two temples to Siva, one as Bhutanatha (God of souls). In this form he appears angry in the dark inner sanctuary. The **fort temples** and a number of inscriptions give an insight into the history of this place as it passed through invading powers. Steep steps, almost a metre high, take you to 'gun point' at the top of the fort, which has remains of large granaries, a treasury and a watchtower. The village with its busy bazaar has white-washed houses clustered together along narrow winding lanes up the hill side.

Hotels The KSTDC **E** *Mayura Chalukya*, T 46, 28 rm with attached baths and a restaurant Indian and simple continental food. It is clean, well placed, in a wooded surrounding about half a km from the village, and in front of it is the *Inspection Bungalow* with only 2 suites. Reservation recommended. There is also a PWD *Guest House* and a Malaprabha Irrigation Department Bungalow. The village has a few places serving snacks near the Tonga stand, the best place for a vegetarian meal is *Laxmi Vilas*.

Museum The Archaeological Survey has a **medieval sculpture gallery** on the N of the tank which houses a collection of fine specimens from Badami, Aihole and Pattadakal. There is also a model of the natural bridge at Sidilinapadi, 5 km away. Open 1000-1700, closed Fri. Free.

Air Belgaum, 192 km, is the nearest airport with Indian Airlines services to Bombay. **Rail** The station 5 km away has passenger trains on the Hubli-Solapur metre gauge route, Hubli

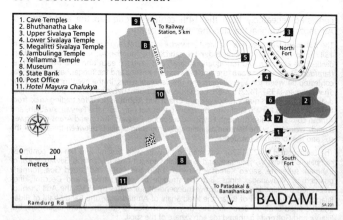

being 128 km away and Bijapur 163 km which takes about 3½ hr. Also connections to Bangalore and Bagalkot. Tongas to town centre are available at the station.

On the road to Pattadakal there is a village named after the goddess **Banasankari**. At the temple with its unusual three-levels and its slender tower, you can see her rather terrifying black image riding a fierce golden lion. She was said to have been transformed into the lake alongside the temple. *Local Festival* Jan – Feb. 20 day fair at the Temple.

Pattadakal (15 km) on the banks of the Malaprabha river, was the second capital of the Chalukyan kings between the 7th and 8th centuries and the city where the kings were crowned. Ptolemy referred to it as 'Petrigal' in the 1st century AD. Two of their queens imported sculptors from *Kanchipuram* in modern Tamil Nadu to carve some of the masterpieces. Most of the temples cluster at the foot of a hill, built out of the pink-tinged gold sandstone which display a succession of styles of southern *Dravida* temple architecture (even miniature scaled-down models) as well as the N *Nagara* style, vividly illustrating the region's position at the cross roads of N and S Indian traditions.

Local Festivals Mar – April Temple car festivals at Virupaksha and Mallikarjuna temples.

Places of interest The earliest temple here dates from the 3rd-4th century when the **Sangamesvara Temple** was built with its experimental brick pillared hall or *mandapa* and the last in the 9th century when the Rashtrakutas arrived and built a Jain temple with its two stone elephants a short distance from the centre. The carvings on the temples, particularly on the **Papanatha** near the village which has interesting sculpture on the ceiling and pillars synthesises N and southern architectural styles, **Virupaksha** which is the largest, with its three-storeyed *vimana* and the **Mallikarjuna** dedicated to Krishna typify the Dravida style are very delicate and depict episodes from the *Ramayana* and *Mahabharata* and the *Puranas* as well as giving an insight into the life of the Chalukyas. You will see a 2.6 m high *Nandi* bull carved out of a dark green chlorite with a red floral covering sitting in front of the Virupaksha (or Lokesvari) Temple, which is still in use. There is no accommodation available here. You can stay either in Badami, Aihole (see above) or Bagalkot.

Aihole is 46 km from Badami and 19 km from Pattadakal. It was the first Chalukyan capital. On approaching the old city you will see the solid-looking, flat-roofed temples which have been excavated by a French archaeologist with the help of the local villagers. There are about a hundred temples here – half within the fort walls, and in one place you can see a range of developing styles from Hoysala, Dravida, Jain, Buddhist, Nagara and Rekhanagara. One of oldest structures here is the 5th century **Lad Khan Temple** which was originally an assembly hall and *Kalyana Mandapa* (marriage hall) and was named after Lad Khan, a Muslim prince who chose to live there. A stone ladder through the roof leads to a shrine with Surya and Vishnu carved on its walls. It bears a striking resemblance to the megalithic caves which were still being hewn in this part of the Deccan at the beginning of the period. You can also get a good view of the village from here.

A particularly unusual example is the **Durgigudi temple,** so named because it is close to the *durga* or fort (not because of any connection with the goddess Durga) with its early *gopuram* structure and its semi-circular apse. A small temple nearby has the first model of the intricately carved Hoysala pillar which reached its perfection in Belur, Halebid and Somnathpur. There is also the **Meguti Temple** built out of 630 small stone blocks. There are several groups of temples with examples of Vishnu on a cobra (in the Chalukyan style), Brahma on a swan or a lotus, the Nandi bull. A winding road leads to a rock cut temple in the 6th century **Ravana Phadi Cave** with carvings of Siva both outside and inside. One of his figures is in the *Ardhanarisvara* form, half Siva, half Parvati. A hill has the rather plain two-storeyed Buddhist Temple with the serene smiling Buddha with the Bodhi Tree emerging from his head, on the ceiling of the upper floor. You climb further uphill to the Jain temple, a plain structure lacking the decorations on the plinth, columns and no gopuram as found on some of the Hindu temples. It has a statue of Mahavira in the shrine within. You can again climb up through the roof for a good view of Aihole. The **Ramalinga Temple Car Festival** is held every Feb/Mar.

Hotels KSTDC **E** *Tourist Lodge*, T Amingad 41, close to the temples. 6 rm with bath but simple food on giving prior notice. You may request a meal here even if you are not staying.

Museum Archaeological Museum. Open 1000-1700, closed Fri. Entry free. Collection includes early Western Chalukyan sculpture of 7th-8th century. Photography with permission.

From Aihole N the road crosses the River Krishna just S of **Tangadgi**, near the historic site of the battle of **Talikota** (35 km), where the Vijayanagar Empire was swept aside by the combined force of the Deccan Sultanates in 1565. 50 km to the E of Talikota is **Hunsigi**, where some of earliest remains of human settlement were found in 1974 in Gulbarga District. They include Acheulean period tools, limestone and quartzite. The road continues N through Mudebihal and Basavana Bagewadi to Bijapur.

Bijapur The Chalukyas who ruled over Bijapur were overthrown at the end of the 12th century. In the early years of the 14th century the Delhi Sultans took it for a time until the Bahmanis, with their capital in Gulbarga, held sway with a governor in Bijapur who declared independence in 1489 and founded the Adil Shahi dynasty, of Turkish origin, which held power until 1686. Bijapur has the air of a N Muslim city with its mausolea, masjids and palaces.

Local Festivals Jan *Siddhesvara Temple festival*. Sept *Asar Mahal Urs festival* in memory of saints.

Places of interest The **Jama Masjid** is one of the finest in the Deccan with a large shallow, onion-shaped dome and arcaded court. It was built by Ali Adil Shah I (r 1557-79) during Bijapur's rise to power and displays a classic restraint. During his reign the citadel was built with its moat as well as palaces, pleasure gardens and a conduit system. The Emperor Aurangzeb added a grand entrance to the masjid and also had a square painted for each of the 2,250 worshippers that it can accommodate, within. The **Citadel** with its own wall has few of its grand buildings intact. One is the Durbar Hall, **Gagan Mahal** open to the N so that the citizens gathered outside were not excluded. It had royal residential quarters on either side. Another worth visiting is the **Jala Manzil** or the water pavilion which provided a cool sanctuary.

The palatial 17th century **Ibrahim Rauza**, outside the city wall to the W, which is so beautifully proportioned that it is said to have inspired the **Taj Mahal.**

It has slender minarets and carved decorative panels with lotus, wheel and cross patterns as well as bold Arabic calligraphy, bearing witness to the tolerance of the Adil Shahi dynasty towards other religions. Built during the dynasty's most prosperous period when the arts and culture flourished, it also contains the tomb of Ibrahim Adil Shah II (r 1580-1626) who had it built for his wife but predeceased her.

To the E of the city, near the Rly Station is the vast **Gol Gumbaz**, Mohammed Adil Shah's tomb has the world's second largest dome (unsupported by pillars) and the wide **whispering gallery** carries a message across 38 m which is repeated 10 times! You climb up numerous narrow steps in one of the 50 m high, 7 storeyed corner towers, to come to the 3 m wide gallery which can seat 1,000. It is believed that the plaster was made out of eggs, cowdung, grass and jaggery! Excellent view of the city with its walls, from the base of the dome. Adil Shah is buried here with his wife, daughter and favourite court dancer. Open 0600-1800, small entry fee except Fri when it is free. Quietest early in the morning.

The **Nagar Khana**, the gate house, which almost seems a part of the tomb from a distance, is a Museum now. The **Asar Mahal** just E of the citadel was built c1646 with a tank watered by the old conduit system. It was used as a court house and has teak pillars and interesting frescoes in the upper floor. The **Mehtar Mahal** with its delicate minarets and carved stone trellises and brackets supporting the balconies which forms a decorative gateway, was supposed to have been built for the palace sweepers.

The **Bara Kaman** only has an impressive base and magnificent lines of arches to stand as witness of the last Adil Shah's great project which was never completed. The fort wall which is about 10 km long has at a point on the W side, the enormous 55 tonne, 4.3 m long, 1.5 m in diameter cannon **Malik-i-Maidan** (Ruler of the Plains). The gunner to avoid being deafened is believed to have dived into the tank on the platform! It was cast in the mid-16th century and was brought back as a prize of war needing 400 bullocks, 10 elephants to pull and hundreds of soldiers. Note the muzzle which is a lion's head with open jaws and within is an elephant being crushed to death. Inside the city wall, close to the famous cannon is **Upli Burj**, the 24 m high watch tower on high ground with its long guns and water tanks. You can climb up the winding staircase outside to get a good view of Bijapur.

Hotels If you wish to spend a night in this pleasant 'city' to see the monuments in comfort, there are a few places to stay in Bijapur, most located fairly close to the bus station. KSTDC **E** *Mayura Adil Shahi*, Anandamahal Rd, at the entrance to the citadel, T 934. 15 rm with attached bath, clean though fairly basic. Within a pleasant courtyard with a restaurant. The **Tourist Office** here is open 1030-1330, 1415-1730, Mon-Sat. The annexe is the old Tourist Lodge on the other side of the road in a well kept garden, with 4 rm which are slightly more expensive. The State Road Transport Corporation's *Guest House* near Sainik School, *Inspection Bungalow* on Station Rd. Reservations: Executive Engineer, PWD, Bijapur Division. **F** *Railway Retiring Rooms* (dormitory beds also available) and **F** *Samrat* and *Lalita Mahal* near the Bus Station (rm at rear quieter). Places to eat are at the *Mayura Adil Shahi*, *Hotel Tourist* on Gandhi Rd and next door, the *Swapna Restaurant* upstairs for meals and *Prabhu* for snacks downstairs.

The State **Bank** is in the citadel, other banks in the city outside. A local **Bus** runs from the station 2 km E of the town centre to the W end of town and back. **Shopping** Handlooms, toys and Lambadi gypsy jewellery.

The Archaeological **Museum** in the gatehouse of the Gol Gumbaz has an excellent collection of Chinese porcelain, parchments, paintings, armoury, miniatures, stone sculpture and old Bijapur carpets. Open 1000-1700, closed Fri. Entry free.

Rail Bijapur has a train to Badami which takes about 3½ hr. **Hyderabad via Solapur**: Regional timetable: 1506, 3 hr 24 min, change at Solapur (4 hr 15 min wait): *Bombay-Hyderabad Exp*, 7031 (AC/II), daily, 2245, 7 hr 45 min (total time 15 hr 24 min); **Gadag**: *Bijapur Exp*, 7790, daily, 0615, 4 hr 50 min.

Road Buses are frequent between Bijapur and Bidar, Hubli, Belgaum and Solapur. There are

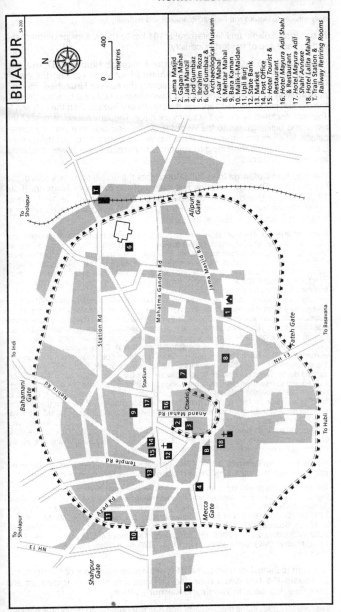

BIJAPUR

N

0   400
metres

1. Jama Masjid
2. Gagan Mahal
3. Jala Manzil
4. Jod Gumbaz
5. Ibrahim Roza
6. Gol Gumbaz & Archaeological Museum
7. Asar Mahal
8. Mehtar Mahal
9. Bara Kaman
10. Malik-i-Maidan
11. Upli Burj
12. State Bank
13. Market
14. Post Office
15. Hotel Tourist & Restaurant
16. Hotel Mayura Adil Shahi & Restaurant
17. Hotel Mayura Adil Shahi Annexe
18. Hotel Lalita Mahal
T. Train Station & Railway Retiring Rooms

To Sholapur

To Indi

To Sholapur

Bahamani Gate

Nehru Rd

Station Rd

Mahatma Gandhi Rd

Jama Masjid Rd

Alipur Gate

To Basavana

Fateh Gate

NH 13

Stadium

Temple Rd

Anand Mahal Rd

Citadel

Azad Rd

Shahpur Gate

Mecca Gate

To Hubli

daily services to Hospet and Badami, Bangalore and Hyderabad.

Excursions Solapur (in Maharashtra) is 101 km to the N, a major centre of the cotton trade and of the textile industry.

From Bijapur the road to Gulbarga passes E through **Hippargi** (37 km), and **Jevargi** (69 km) before crossing the *Bhima River*. After crossing the river it follows it N on its eastern side before reaching the ruins of **Firuzabad** 25 km S of **Gulbarga**. On a bend in the Bhima River where is takes a U turn from N to S, the massive stone fort walls enclose the old city of *Firuzabad* on the E, N and S. The area enclosed by the fortifications are huge. The *Jami Masjid*, largest of the remaining buildings, lies to the W of the centre, and behind it was the former palace. Much of the history of the city has yet to be recovered, but stylistically it is clear that it owes something to influences from central Asia as well as to more local Hindu traditions.

The road N to *Gulbarga* (pop 200,000) crosses the undulating black soils of the Deccan lavas. The town was the first capital of the *Bahmani kingdom* (from 1347-1525). It is also widely known among S Indian Muslims as the home of *Saiyid Muhammad Gesu Daraz Chisti* (1320-1422), who was instrumental in spreading pious Islamic faith in the Deccan.

Places of interest The most striking remains in the town are the **fort**, with its citadel and Mosque, the **Jami Masjid**, and the **great tombs** in its eastern quarter, massive, fortress like buildings with their distinctive domes over 30 m high. The fort is just 1 km W of the centre of the present town. Most of the outer structures and many of the buildings are in ruins, although the outer door of the W gate is still intact. The *Bala Hissar* (citadel) remains almost intact. It is a massive structure. A flight of ruined steps leads up to the entrance in the N wall, and the citadel has turrets at the sides and corners.

The Jami Masjid is unique among Indian mosques in having its whole area of 3500 sq m covered by a dome over the *mihrab*, 4 corner domes and 75 minor domes. The tombs of the Bahmani sultans are in 2 groups. One lies 600 m to the W of the fort, the other on the eastern side of the town. The tombs of the eastern quarter have no remaining exterior decoration, though the interiors show some evidence of decorative finishing. The tomb of the Chishti saint Gesu Daraz, (also known as the **Dargah of Hazrat Gesu Nawaz**) who came to Gulbarga in 1413 during the reign of **Firoz Shah Tughlaq** is open to visitors – see page 88. It is surrounded by a complex of buildings. The tomb is 2 storeyed with a highly decorated painted dome. There is a mother of pearl canopy over the grave which was a late addition. It is reputed to have been built during the reign of Mahmud Adil Shah. Firoz Shah Tughlaq's brother was a devoted follower of the saint and gave him huge areas of land, as well as building a college for him. It is said that some of his descendants still live near the tomb.

The most striking of all the tombs near this eastern group is that of *Taj ud Din Firuz* (1422) known as Haft Gumbaz. Unlike the other tombs it is highly ornamented, with geometrical patterns developed in the masonry. The tombs to the N W of the fort are those of the earliest Bahmani rulers, and to their N the Dargah of Shaikh Suraj ud Din Junyadi, the teacher of the early sultans. It has a monumental gateway.

Hotels F *Maurya Bahmani* (KSTDC) This is probably the best of several small hotels in the town. *Railway Retiring Rooms* offer a choice of standards for passengers in transit.

Travel Gulbarga is 190 km from Hyderabad in neighbouring Andhra Pradesh. There are regular train and bus connections to Hyderabad and Solapur. **Rail** Hyderabad: *Bombay-Hyderabad Exp*, 7031 (AC/II), daily, 0050, 5 hr 40 min; Secunderabad: *Minar Exp*, 2101 (AC/II), daily, 0745, 4 hr 30 min; Solapur: *Kanniyakumari*, 1082 (AC/II), daily, 1633, 1 hr 32 min; **Bombay (VT):** *Udyan Exp*, 6530 (AC/II), daily, 0905, 11 hr 20 min; **or:** *Minar Exp*, 2102 (AC/II), daily, 2010, 10 hr 5 min; **Bangalore**, *Karnataka Exp*, 2628 (AC/II), daily, 0415, 11 hr; **Madras (MC):** Dadar-Madras Exp, 6063 (AC/II), Mon, Wed, Thurs, Fri, Sat, 0617, 13 hr 43 min.

To return to Bangalore from Gulbarga take the main road E out of the city centre to **Sedam** (54 km) which is on the main rail link between Hyderabad and Bangalore. Continue to **Yadgir** and **Raichur** (120 km).

For two centuries in the mediaeval period *Raichur* dominated the central plateaus

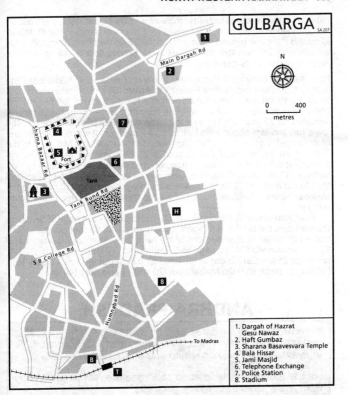

GULBARGA
SA 207

Main Dargah Rd

N

0   400
metres

Shama Bazaar Rd

Fort

Tank

Tank Bund Rd

S B College Rd

Hummabad Rd

To Madras

1. Dargah of Hazrat
   Gesu Nawaz
2. Haft Gumbaz
3. Sharana Basavesvara Temple
4. Bala Hissar
5. Jami Masjid
6. Telephone Exchange
7. Police Station
8. Stadium

of the **Krishna-Tungabhadra doab**. It is still at a crossroads of the regional cultures of Karnataka, Andhra Pradesh and Maharashtra. As Kanarese is the dominant langauge it was allocated to Karnataka after the reorganisation of the states in 1956. Now it is an important market town in the middle of a cotton growing area. Cotton takes up more than 20% of the sown area, followed by groundnuts.

Places of interest The site of the fort's citadel at Raichur gives magnificent views over the vast open spaces of the Deccan plateaus nearly 100 m below. Built in the mid 14th century Raichur became the first capital of the Bijapur kingdom when it broke away from the Bahmani Sultans in 1489. Much of the fort itself is now in ruins, but there are some interesting remains. The N gate is flanked by towers, a carved elephant standing about 40 m away. On the inner walls are some carvings, and a tunnel reputedly built to enable soldiers access to barricade the gate in emergency. Near the W gate is the old palace.

The climb to the citadel begins from near the N gate. In the citadel is a shrine with a row of cells with the Jani Masjid in the E. Its eastern gateway has 3 domes. The top of the citadel is barely 20 m sq. There are some other interesting buildings in the fort below the hill, including the *Daftar ki Masjid* (Office Mosque), built around 1510 out of masonry removed from Hindu temples. It is one of the earliest mosques in the Deccan to be built in this way, with the bizarre result of producing flat ceilinged mosques with pillars carved for Chalukyan temples. The **Ek Minar ki masjid** ("the one minaret mosque") is in the S E corner of the courtyard. It has a distinctively *Bahmani* style dome. The *Railway Retiring Rooms* offer a choice of accommodation in its rooms and dormitory.

From **Raichur** continue S through Madhavaram (where the road crosses the Tungabhadra River into Andhra Pradesh), to **Adoni** (80 km). Another marchland town, Adoni today is a major cotton market. After the Battle of Talikota in 1565 Malik Rahman Khan, the Abyssinian, was appointed Governor by the Sultan. He remained for 39 years. His tomb on the Talibanda Hill is a pilgrimage centre. The lower fort and Jami Masjid were built by his adopted son. It was captured by one of Aurangzeb's generals in 1690 after fierce fighting, and in 1740 it fell to the Nizam of Hyderabad, **Asaf Jha**. Its position at the borders of warring regional powers exposed it to a turbulent history, which culminated in its capture by Tipu Sultan in 1786 and its demolition, ultimately to be returned to the Nizam and then to the British in 1800. The citadel is built on 5 hills, rising 250 m above the plateau. There is an excellent tank half way up the rocks that is reputed never to run dry.

From Adoni drive SE through Aspari (20 km) to Gooty – **see page 855** – where the road joins the NH 7 S to Bangalore. The route passes through several sites of interest discussed in other sections of the handbook; **Anantpur** (50 km, **page 854**) – Penukonda (74 km, **page 854**) – Hindupur (70 km) – Lepakshi (10 km, **see page 854**) – Gauribidanur (40 km) – **Chikballapur** (40 km) – **Nandi Hills** (10 km **see page 853**) Doddaballapur (20 km) – **Bangalore** (40 km).

ANDHRA PRADESH

For the route from **Hyderabad to Bangalore**, see page 853 and from **Hyderabad to Bombay**, page 998.

Andhra Pradesh is India's fifth largest state. Set in the heart of peninsular India, it lies entirely within the Tropics. It has a longer stretch of coastline than any other Indian state. Andhra Pradesh was created in its present form in 1956. It was the first state in India to be defined on the basis of language. This set a pattern for the reorganisation of Indian States which followed its own creation in 1953 and the assumption of its present boundaries in 1956.

Social indicators *Literacy* M 30% F 20% *Newspaper circulation:* 695,000 *Birth rate* R 32:1000 U 28:1000 *Death rate* R 11:1000 U 7:1000 *Infant mortality* R 86:1000, U 50:1000 *Registered graduate job seekers* 2,203,000 *Average annual income per head :* Rs 1300 *Inflation 1981-87* 58%

Religion *Hindu* 88% *Muslim* 9% *Christian* 3%

Towns and cities 23% of the population is urban. Hyderabad, the state capital, and its twin city of Secunderabad were the fifth largest city in India when the Nizam of Hyderabad had his capital there at the end of the 19th century and into the twentieth century. Coastal Andhra is much more densely populated than the interior, however, and has a number of important towns, notably Visakhapatnam and Vijayawada.

Administration Andhra Pradesh elects 42 members to the Lok Sabha, the lower house of

Parliament in New Delhi. It has a Legislative Assembly of 294 seats and a Legislative Council as a second chamber elected by university graduates, representatives of local bodies and Members of the Legislative Assembly. It has 23 administrative districts.

INTRODUCTION

People Most of Andhra Pradesh's 65 million people are Dravidians. Ethnically of Mediterranean stock, the "Dravidian" peoples of S India had already been in India many years before the first Indo-Aryans came after 2000 BC. Andhra Pradesh is now the northernmost region of Dravidian culture and language. Telugu, the State language, is one of the four main Dravidian languages of India.

Over 85% of the population speak Telugu. However, there are important minorities. Tamil is widely spoken in the extreme S, and on the border of Karnataka there are pockets of Kanarese speakers. In the urban areas, particularly in **Hyderabad**, the State capital, there are large numbers of Urdu speakers. In all they make up 7% of Andhra Pradesh's population. They represent the result of Muslim influence, which spread rapidly after the Muslim Turks took power in Delhi at the beginning of the 13th century. Hyderabad, the capital of modern Andhra Pradesh, was the seat of government of the Muslim Nizams of Hyderabad. Under their rule in what is now central Andhra Pradesh many Muslims came to work in the court, both from N India and from abroad. In many respects the Nizam's capital was a highly cosmopolitan centre, drawing extensively on Islamic contacts both in N India and in W Asia – notably Persia. Its links with the Islamic world and the long tradition of political power that the Nizams had enjoyed encouraged them to hope that they might gain complete Independence from India in 1947. That option was foreclosed by the Indian Government's decision to remove the Nizam by force in 1948 after a half-hearted insurrection.

Although Hyderabad is still India's seventh largest city and there are other growing industrial towns in the state, nearly 80% of the population of Andhra Pradesh live in villages. There remains quite a large tribal population in remote areas of the state. The **Chenchus**, for example, live in the Vellikonda Hills of the S E. Forest cover is thin, and the Chenchus live by a mixture of pastoralism and collecting produce like honey, bamboos and wood for fuel.

Land and rivers

Andhra Pradesh occupies an area of 275,000 sq km. It stretches over 1,200 km along the eastern seaboard of India and more than 700 km inland from the coast at Masulipatnam to the W of Hyderabad, its capital. Along the coast it runs from Berhampur in Orissa more than 1,200 km, almost reaching Madras. Lying entirely S of the Tropic of Cancer, it is one of India's truly tropical states.

It can be divided into three main regions. Along the coast is a long, narrow and flat strip of land. The alluvial soils can be very fertile when they are irrigated, as in the deltas of the Godavari and Krishna Rivers. However, the deltas are subject to some of the worst cyclones in S Asia. A catastrophic cyclone in 1977 resulted in many thousands of deaths. Protective measures have now been taken by the government to provide sheltered housing, but similar severe storms in 1989 still caused heavy damage and some loss of life. Immediately inland is a series of hill ranges. These run nearly parallel with the coast, though they have large gaps leading up to the plateau behind. The plateau itself has some of India's oldest rocks, now known to be more than 3500 million years old. They give generally very thin red soils.

For much of the year many areas of Andhra look hot, dry and desolate. While the great delta of the Krishna and Godavari Rivers retains its lush greenness by virtue of their irrigation water, great tracts of the granitic plateaus of the interior are

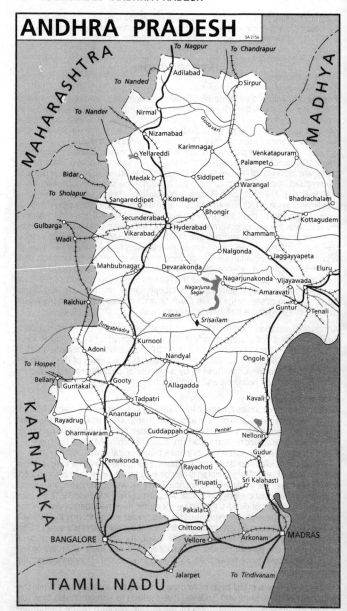

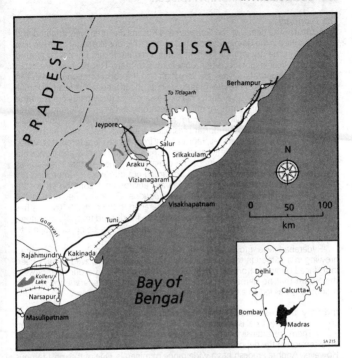

baked dry by unremitting sunshine. Yet the **Godavari** and the **Krishna** are two great rivers, crossing the state and dominating its drainage pattern. Both rise close to India's W coast. The Godavari rises less than 200 km N of Bombay and flows nearly 1,500 kilometres S E across the Deccan Plateau. It drains over 300,000 sq km, and is the largest of the peninsular rivers. 15% of its catchment area is now irrigated. The Krishna rises near **Mahabaleshwar** at an altitude of 1,360 m. It then flows 1,400 km to the Bay of Bengal. In all it drains an area of 260,000 sq km, only the lowest quarter of which is in Andhra Pradesh.

After the Ganga these two rivers have the largest watersheds in India, and between them they irrigate nearly 6 million ha of farm land. The much smaller rivers of the **Pennar** and **Cheyyar** are important locally, but like many peninsular rivers are more often broad bands of sand than they are stretches of running water. The largest lakes in the State are the man-made lakes behind the dams built since Independence. The largest of these is the Nagarjunasagar Dam on the Krishna. On the delta between the Krishna and the Godavari is the *Kolleru Lake*. During the wet season this covers nearly 260 sq km and is now a bird sanctuary.

Climate

Lying entirely S of the Tropic of Cancer Andhra Pradesh is hot throughout the year. The interior of the state is in the rain shadow of the Western Ghats and receives less rainfall than much of the coast. All regions have most of their rain between Jun and Oct, although the S gets the benefit of the retreating monsoon which brings Madras most of its rain between Oct and Dec.

The Economy

Agriculture The deltas of the Godavari and Krishna are intensively irrigated and cultivated. Rice is the dominant crop, but some cash crops like sugar cane are also important. In the dry interior farming is much more difficult. Rainfall of around 1000 mm a year might not seem ungenerous to many European or American farmers, but evaporation rates are very high and the concentration of rainfall in three or four months of the year greatly limits its effectiveness. The relatively small amount of rain and its unreliability make it essential to grow hardy crops. In the *Telengana* region of central Andhra Pradesh only between 20% and 40% of the area is cultivated. Millets, sorghum and gram are grown on the unirrigated land. Oil seeds are the most important cash crop, especially groundnuts and castor. On the areas brought under well, tank or canal irrigation rice predominates. Valley floors are often intensively cultivated while the surrounding hills and slopes are completely barren. The difficulty of the climate in interior Andhra Pradesh has encouraged considerable research to be carried out into ways of improving dry farming. Its comparatively harsh "dry land" environment contributed to the United Nations' decision to set up the *International Centre for Research in the Semi Arid Tropics* (ICRISAT) just outside Hyderabad in the early 1970s. This has now become the world's leading research centre for dryland tropical agriculture. Crop breeding and experimental farming techniques are being developed to improve yields with very considerable success.

Hyderabad also grows a special variety of grape which was discovered growing in a garden in the early part of the 20th century, believed to have been introduced originally from the Middle E, by *Haj* pilgrims. Its flavour so impressed the Nizam that he named it the King of *Grapes* or *Anab-e-Shahi* and its high productivity has led to a flourishing viticulture industry.

Industry and Resources The state's most important *mineral resources* today are coal and iron ore. Coal is mined in the **Singareni** field along the lower Godavari valley. There are extensive deposits of high quality iron ore in the far N. These are an extension of the deposits found in Orissa, but as yet are not developed as fully. However, Andhra Pradesh has a wide range of minerals. One of the most famous diamonds in the world, the Koh-i-Noor, was found at Golconda, just W of Hyderabad. Diamond mines are being opened up again after a long period of closure. Iron ore, copper, asbestos and barytes are also found, but are too scattered to be of great economic value.

Andhra Pradesh has seen a rapid growth of employment in factory employment. It now has nearly 10% of India's total industrial employment. It ranks fifth in India. Much of that growth has taken place in high tech industries which have grown up around the state capital Hyderabad. However, shipbuilding, heavy engineering and iron and steel are important in the coastal belt, especially at Visakhapatnam. On top of that it has nearly 60,000 people employed in small scale units.

Craft industries Andhra's *Bidriware*, uses dark matt gunmetal (an alloy of zinc and copper) with silver damascening in beautiful flowing floral and arabesque patterns and illustrates the Persian influence on Indian motifs. The articles vary from large vases and boxes, jewellery and plates to tiny buttons and cuff links. The name is derived from Bidar in Karnataka and dates back to the Bahmani rulers. **Toys** Miniature wooden figures, animals, fruit, vegetables and birds are common subjects of the *Kondapalli* toy maker which are known for their use of light wood with bright colours. *Nirmal* toys look more natural and are finished with a herbal extract which gives it a golden sheen, *Tirupati* toys are in a red wood while Ethikoppaka toys are finished in coloured lacquer. Andhra also produces fine figurines of deities in sandalwood. **Jewellery** Hyderabadi jewellers work in gold and precious stones which are often uncut, giving them a distinctive look. The craftsmen can often be seen working in the lanes around the Char Minar. On the W side are the shops selling the typical local bangles set with glass. Pearl ornaments of Hyderabad and silver filigree ware from Karimnagar are another speciality.

Textiles The state is famous for **Himru** shawls and fabrics produced in cotton/silk mixes with rich woven patterns on a special handloom. The use of silver or gold threads produce even richer 'brocade' cloth. A young boy is sometimes seen sitting with the weavers 'calling out' the intricate pattern. The art of weaving special **Ikat** fabrics (see page 615) has been revived through the efforts of the All India Handicrafts Board in the villages of Pochampalli, Chirala, Puttapaka and Koyyalagudem among others. The practice of dyeing the warp and weft threads before weaving in such a way as to produce a pattern, additionally used oil in the process when it was woven into pieces of cloth *Teli rumal* (literally oil kerchief) to be used as garments. and other towns produce their own special weaves. **Kalamkari paintings** (*kalam* refers to the pen used) produced in Kalahasti have a distinctive style, using indigo and vegetable dyes extracted from turmeric, pomegranate skin etc, on cloth. Originally designed to tell stories from mythology, they make good wall hangings. In addition hand block printed textiles are also produced. **Carpets** are produced in Warangal and Eluru and are known as 'Deccan rugs' with designs that reflect a Persian influence.

Transport Despite its central geographical position in the S Indian Peninsula, and the fact that it had been capital of the Princely State, Hyderabad had been largely by-passed by the transport developments of the late 19th century. The main railway lines linked the capital cities of British-held Indian territory – Madras, Bombay and Calcutta. Hyderabad remained comparatively poorly connected. It is now on main railway lines to Bombay and Madras, and is linked via Warangal with Delhi. There are over 2,500 km of national highway and over 50,000 km of state and minor roads, but most of these are unsurfaced. The road density is exactly the Indian average. Hyderabad and other major towns are connected by air to the national network. On the coast Visakhapatnam has been greatly expanded as one of the country's major ports. It is the Eastern Headquarters for the Indian Navy. It has facilities for shipbuilding is now a major outlet for exports.

History

The prehistoric settlements of Andhra have been outlined in the introduction to S India, see page 686. The first historical evidence of a people called the "Andhras" came from **Emperor Asoka Maurya**. After his victory in the Kalinga war he sent envoys to the S. They took with them Buddhism, which was to bear remarkable fruit. The first known Andhra power, the **Satavahanas**, encouraged various religious groups including Buddhists. Their capital at Amaravati shows evidence of the great skill and artistry of early Andhra artists and builders. In the fifty years before AD 200 there was also a fine university at Nagarjunakonda.

Literature Although the name Andhra was by then well known the Telugu language did not emerge until the 11th century AD. There developed a vigorous literary tradition, not always simply in the hands of the brahmin priesthood. Two figures, **Potana** (1400-75) a poor man who lived in the countryside, translated the Bhagavata – immediately popular, combined simple language with deep devotion. **Vemana** (15th century) was a low caste Saivite, very much an individualist and a revolutionary. The American scholar J.T.F. Jordens has pointed out that "His sataka (century) of gnomic verse is known to all Telugus and to most S Indians. His verses bristle with sarcastic attacks on the brahmans, on polytheism, idolatry, and pilgrimages.

> The solitariness of a dog! the meditation of a crane!
> The chanting of an ass! The bathing of a frog!
> Ah, why will ye not try to know your own hearts?
>
> What are you the better for smearing your body with ashes?
> Your thoughts should be set on God alone;
> For the rest, an ass can wallow in dirt as well as you.

The books that are called the Vedas are like courtesans,
Deluding men, and wholly unfathomable;
But the hidden knowledge of God is like an honourable wife.

He that fasts shall become (in his next birth) a village pig;
He that embraces poverty shall become a beggar;
And he that bows to a stone shall become like a lifeless image."

Vijayanagar Well before Vemana wrote those lines Muslim power had begun to be felt across India. In 1323 Warangal, just to the N E of the present city of Hyderabad, was captured by the armies of **Muhammad bin Tughlaq**. Muslim expansion further S was prevented for two centuries by the rise of the Vijayanagar Empire. Vijayanagar – the "city of victory" – was an empire based on military achievement (**see page 879**). *Krishna Deva Raya* (r 1509-1529) presided over an expansion of Hindu territorial power and literary development across S India from its capital at Hampi, 80 km W of the present border between Andhra Pradesh and Karnataka. A poet himself, Krishna Devaraya encouraged others such as the great Kannada poet *Allasani Peddana*. However, his empire was crushed at the Battle of Talikota in 1565 by a short-lived federation of Muslim States and the cultural life it supported had to seek fresh soil.

The Muslim states From then on Muslim rulers played a major role in the politics of central Andhra, the region now known as **Telengana**. The Bahmani kingdoms in the region around modern Hyderabad controlled central Telengana in the 16th century. They were even able to keep the Mughals at bay until Aurangzeb finally forced them into submission at the end of the 17th century. **Hyderabad**, now India's sixth largest city, was the most important centre of Muslim power in central and S India from the 17th to the 19th centuries. It was founded by the 5th in line of an earlier Muslim dynasty, **Mohammad Quli Qutb Shah**, in 1591. His tomb and those of his successors standing outside Hyderabad next to Golconda Fort, are an impressive testimony to the power in the region. Through their successors Hyderabad became the capital of a Princely State the size of France, ruled by a succession of Muslim Nizams from 1724 till after India's Independence in 1947.

The arrival of the Europeans That rule was not without strings. Through the 18th century British and French traders were spreading their influence up the coast. Increasingly they came into conflict and looked for alliances with regional powers. At the end of the 18th century the British reached an agreement with the **Nizam of Hyderabad** whereby he accepted British support in exchange for recognition of British rights to trade and political control of the coastal districts. Thus Hyderabad became one of the 550 Princely States of India which retained a measure of Independence until 1947 while accepting British suzerainty.

Independence At Independence in 1947 the present State of Andhra was divided between the British Presidency of Madras and the Nizam of Hyderabad's Princely State. There was doubt as to whether the Princely State would accede to India after Partition. The Nizam of Hyderabad would have liked to join fellow Muslims in the newly created Muslim State of Pakistan. However, political disturbances in 1949 gave the Indian government the excuse to take direct control, and the state was incorporated into the Indian Union.

Modern political development In 1953 Andhra Pradesh was created on the basis of the Telugu-speaking districts of Madras Presidency. However, this was not enough for those who were demanding statehood for a united Telugu-speaking region. One political leader, *Potti Sreeramulu*, starved himself to death in protest at the government's refusal to grant the demand. Finally, in 1956, Andhra Pradesh took its present form. It was the first State to be re-organised when the Indian Government decided to re-shape the political map inherited from the British period. In 1956 all Telugu-speaking areas were grouped together in the new State of Andhra Pradesh. This brought together the eastern parts of the old Nizam's territories and the coastal districts which had formerly been in Madras Presidency. Hyderabad became the capital of the new state. It became the centre both for the rapidly expanding Osmania University (to the N of the city in Secunderabad) but also of a huge increase in the number of government jobs.

Despite the growth in the economy many areas of the state remain extremely poor. Some regions have continued to see political unrest. The **Naxalite** movement, which started in Bengal, has a hold in NE Andhra Pradesh, particularly among the poor. Andhra Pradesh was regarded as a stronghold of the Congress Party until 1983 when a regional party, the Telugu Desam, won a crushing victory in the State Assembly elections. The Leader of the Telugu Desam, N.T. Rama Rao was following in the footsteps of the then Chief Minister of Tamil Nadu, M.G. Ramachandran, in using fame as film star as a stepping stone to political power. N.T. Rama Rao had made his name playing popular gods, and in the late 1980s his hold seemed unbreakable. However, the Congress continued to do well in Lok Sabha elections, and in the 1989 elections the Telugu Desam suffered its own resounding defeat. On June 20th 1991, Andhra Pradesh provided India's first ever South Indian Prime Minister, when P.V. Narasunha Rao was selected by the Congress Party take over the leadership and asked to form a Government.

Cuisine
The kitchens in the four southern states have much in common but Andhra stands out as distinct because of its northern influence and larger number of non-vegetarians. The rule of the Muslim Nawabs for centuries is reflected in the rich, spicy local dishes, especially in the area around the capital. **Haleem** is a dish produced with pounded wheat with spiced mutton, **Baghara Baigan** with aubergines. Rice and meat *Biryani, Nahari* and *Kababs* have a lot in common with the northern Mughlai cuisine. The growing of hot chillies has led to its liberal use in the food prepared so that the good quality locally grown grapes (especially *Anab e Shahi*), provide a welcome neutralising effect.

HYDERABAD

Population 4.27m (1991) *Altitude* 537 m. *Climate* Temp. Summer Max. 39°C Min. 26°C, Winter Max. 28°C Min 13°C. Annual rainfall 760 mm. Monsoons June-Sep. Hyderabad's small international airport (at Begampet in the "twin city" of Secunderabad) is only twenty minutes from most hotels and half an hour from the centre of the old city.

	Jan	Feb	Mar	Apr	May	Jun	Jul	Aug	Sep	Oct	Nov	Dec	Av/To'
Max (°C)	29	31	35	37	39	34	30	29	30	30	29	28	32
Min (°C)	15	17	20	24	26	24	22	22	22	20	16	13	20
Rain (mm)	2	11	13	24	30	107	165	147	163	71	25	5	763

Approaching Hyderabad from the air it is often possible to obtain magnificent views of the extraordinary landscape in which Hyderabad is at the heart. Set at a height of over 500 m, enough to ameliorate the semi arid tropical climate except at the height of the hot season, the city is almost in the middle of the S Indian Peninsula. Over 400 km E of the crest line of the Western Ghats, Hyderabad lies in the rain shadow of the hills. It is built on the ancient granites and gneisses of the Peninsula, which outcrop in bizarre shapes on hills in many parts of the city and its surrounds, and which provide building stone for some of the city's most

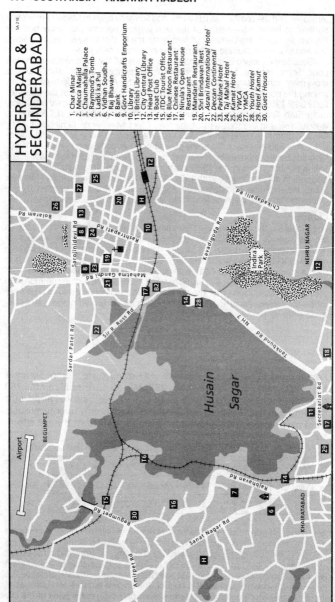

HYDERABAD & SECUNDERABAD

1. Char Minar
2. Mecca Masjid
3. Chaumahalla Palace
4. Raymond's Tomb
5. Ladki ka Pul
6. Vidhan Soudha
7. Raj Bhavan
8. Bank
9. Govt Handicrafts Emporium
10. Library
11. British Library
12. City Central Library
13. Head Post Office
14. Boat Club
15. ITDC Tourist Office
16. Blue Moon Restaurant
17. Chinese Restaurant
18. Nirula's Open House Restaurant
19. Mandarin Restaurant
20. Shri Brindavan Rest
21. Asrani International Hotel
22. Deccan Continental
23. Parklane Hotel
24. Taj Mahal Hotel
25. Kamat Hotel
26. YMCA
27. YWCA
28. Youth Hostel
29. Hotel Kamut
30. Guest House

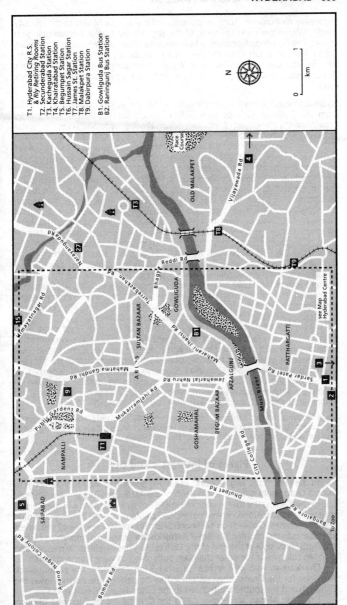

T1. Hyderabad City R.S. & Rly Retiring Rooms
T2. Secunderabad Station
T3. Kacheguda Station
T4. Khairatabad Station
T5. Begumpet Station
T6. Hussain Sagar Station
T7. James St. Station
T8. Malakpet Station
T9. Dabirpura Station

B1. Gowliguda Bus Station
B2. Raningunj Bus Station

impressive monuments, such as the pillars of the Mecca Masjid in the old city centre. Within the rocks lay some of the region's most valued resources, gem stones. The Golconda kingdoms which preceded those of Hyderabad and whose capital lies just 8 km from the present city, produced magnificent diamonds, including the **Koh-i-Noor**. This legendary jewel was given to the Mughal Emperor **Aurangzeb**, subsequently to be cut and dispersed, a part into the English royal crown.

Hyderabad was the most important centre of Muslim power in central and S India from the 15th to 19th centuries. Even though the population was always predominantly composed of Telugu-speaking Hindus, Hyderabad was the capital of a Princely State the size of France, ruled by a succession of Muslim Nizams from 1724. That was the year that the *Nizam-ul-Mulk* ("Regulator of the Land") *Asaf Jha*, seized power from the Mughal Governor of the Deccan district of Khandesh, founding the dynasty that included some of the "richest men in the world" and who ruled up to India's Independence in 1947. He inherited Hyderabad as his capital, which had been founded by the fifth Sultan of Golconda of an earlier Muslim dynasty, Muhammad Quli Qutb Shah, in 1589, under the original name of *Bhagnagar*. The founders were apparently famous for their beautiful "monuments, mosques and mistresses" and also for their diamond markets. Hyderabad stood on the S bank of the river Musi, in a prime military position.

Unlike other Mughal cities, it was planned in a grid pattern with enormous arches and the Char Minar was built in 1591 by the Sultan as the city's prime monument. The streets were lined with stone buildings which had shops below and living quarters above (many are still standing). If you come out through the western arch of the Char Minar you enter Lad Bazaar where shops sell the typical Hyderabadi glass embedded bangles while to the N you will find the jewellers including those with pearls, and cloth merchants. To the S the craftsmen in their tiny shops still prepare thin silver 'leaf' by pounding the metal.

During the Asaf Jahi rule the city expanded N of the river. Then in the early 19th century, during the reign of **Sikander Jah** (1803-30), the cantonment of Secunderabad was developed by the British, further up river. Close to the Salar Jung Museum, you can see examples of Asaf Jahi architecture. N of the river are the Asafia State Library and Osmania General Hospital and on the S bank the City College and the High Court. Other typical examples are in the Public Gardens behind the Archaeological Museum, where you will find the Ajanta Pavilion, the elaborate Jubilee Hall, the State Assembly Hall and the Health Museum.

Local festivals *Makara Sankranti* Mid-January (usually 13th-15th). Houses bring out all their collection of dolls. *Ugadi* March-April New year in Andhra Pradesh – Chaitra Sudda Padyami *Muharram and Ramzan* are celebrated distinctively in Hyderabad.

Places of interest – Old city

Facing the river, is the **High Court**, a splendid building in the Mughal style is in the old Qutb Shahi gardens Amin Bagh nr the Afzal Ganj Bridge (New Bridge), one of the 4 across the river. It was built in 1916 of pink granite. It is in the Mughal style with red sandstone carved panels and columns, a large archway and blue and gold domes. Going S, on Mahboob Shahi Rd you will see one of the oldest imambaras in the country. The Royal **Ashurkhana** or house of mourning built in the Qutb Shahi style at the end of the 16th century has excellent tile mosaics and wooden columns in the outer chamber, both of which were later additions.

Charkaman with its 4 arches is further S from the river. The eastern Black Arch was for the Drums, the western led to the palaces, the northern was the Fish Arch and the southern which led to the Char Minar, the fruit sellers'.

The **Char Minar**, sometimes called the Oriental Arc de Triomphe (though certainly not on account of its physical appearance), was built between 1591 and

1612 by Sultan **Mohammad Quli Qutb Shah** as a showpiece at the centre of his beautiful city and has become the city's symbol – and the brand name for one of India's best selling cigarettes. With its 56 m tall slender minarets with spiral staircases and huge arches on each side (the whole plastered with lime mortar) it stood at the entrance to the palace complex. Now it guards the entry to the main bazaar. There is a beautiful mosque on the second floor and a large water tank in the middle. Some believe it was built to commemorate the eradication of the plague from the city. Special market day is Thursday. Daily illuminations in the evening from 1900-2100. Small entry fee.

Mecca Masjid immediately to the SW. The grand mosque, the most impressive in S India, was started in 1614 by the sixth Sultan Abdulla Qutb Shah and completed by Aurangzeb when he annexed Golconda in 1692. Built of enormous black granite slabs quarried nearby it has tall pillars, stucco decorations and red bricks on its entrance arches believed to have been made from clay from Mecca mixed with red colouring. The vast mosque, one of the largest in India, can accommodate 10,000 at prayers. The tombs of the Asaf Jahi rulers, the Nizams of Hyderabad, are in a roofed enclosure to the left of the courtyard. To the NE also on the E of Sardar Patel Rd, the **Jami Masjid** in a narrow lane was the second mosque built in the old city at the end of the 16th century.

To the W of the Char Minar the **Lad Bazaar** area has interesting buildings with wood and stone carvings and the pink elephant gates. You arrive at the **Chowk** which has a mosque and a Victorian Clock Tower. SE of the Lad Bazaar is the huge complex of the palaces which were built by the different Nizams, including the grand **Chaumahalla Palace** around a quadrangle.

About 2 km S along Sardar Patel Rd and Kishan Prasad Rd, on Kohi Tur Hill, stands the **Falaknuma Palace** which was originally a rich nobleman's house mainly built in a mixture of classical and Mughal styles in 1873 but bought by the Nizam at the end of the last century. It has a superb interior (particularly the state reception room) with a lot of marble, chandeliers and paintings. The palace houses all manner of treasures, both oriental and European including a collection of jade, crystal and precious stones and a superb library. Prior permission is required to visit.

NE of Char Minar is the **Purani Haveli** or the Old Palace which is a vast mansion, worth visiting. (Prior permission required to visit).

The **Tomb of Michel Raymond** is off the Vijayawada Rd, about 3 km from the Oliphant Bridge. The Frenchman joined the Second Nizam's army in 1786 as a common soldier and rose to command 15,000 troops. His popularity with the people earned him the combined Muslim-Hindu name 'Moosa Ram' and even today they remember him by holding a commemorative *Urs* fair at his grey granite tomb which is 7 m high and bears the initials 'JR'.

Mir Alam Tank to the SW of the old city, about 2.5 km from the Char Minar is approached by Bangalore Rd. An artificial lake covering over 20 sq km, it was built by French engineers under instructions of the grandfather of Salar Jung III and is a popular picnic spot. It is now a part of the **Nehru Zoological Park** which is to its N (see below under Parks and Zoos).

New city

The **Osmania General Hospital** is an impressive building across the river, opp the High Court. In 1925, the 200 m long building was one of the largest hospitals in the world. To its E, also on the river, is the imposing **State Central Library** with its priceless collection of Arabic, Persian and Urdu books and manuscripts.

The **Public Gardens** in Nampally, N of Hyderabad Station is the largest in Asia and contains many important buildings including the Archaeological Museum and Art Galleries and the State Legislative Assembly. The **Naubat Pahad** (Kala Pahad or Neeladri) are 2 hillocks to the N of the Public Gardens. The Qutb Shahis are believed to have had their proclamations read from the hill tops accompanied by the beating of drums. In 1940 pavilions were built and then a hanging garden was laid out on top of one. The marble **Venkatesvara Temple** with an intricately carved ceiling which overlooks a vast lake, was built on the other by the Birlas. Completed in 1976, the images of the deities are S Indian, although the building itself drew craftsmen from the N as well, among them some who claimed to have ancestors who built the Taj Mahal. Open 0800-1200, 1600-2000.

Hussain Sagar is further N. The lake was built in the 16th century and named to mark the gratitude of the Qutb Shahi Sultan, Ibrahim Quli Qutb Shah to Hussain Shah Wali who helped him recover from his illness. Hyderabad has grown around the lake and the *bund* is a favourite promenade for the city dwellers. At the far end of the lake is the Nizamia Observatory.

Osmania University is just outside the city limits to the E of Secunderabad. Inaugurated in 1917 in temporary buildings, its sprawling campus with its black granite Arts College combining Moorish and Hindu Kakatiya architectural styles. It was built by the Nizam in 1939 and occupies a large site which is beautifully landscaped. There is a botanical garden and the **State Archives**.

Race Course was once an 'occasional track' in the 19th century. Today the Malakpet Race Course, S of the river, is one of the major centres of racing in the country and one of the most modern.

Secunderabad The Mahakali Temple where the *Bonalu* festival is held in June/July.

Local industries *Bidriware* (silver inlay on dull black 'gunmetal') articles such as cuff links, buttons, bangles, boxes and vases are named after Bidar in Karnataka (see State Introduction, **page 894**). Stone setting and silver jewellery can be seen being produced in the lanes around Char Minar. *Nirmal* industries use old Ajanta, Mughal and other motifs to produce unusual household furniture. Embroidered cloth decorated with beads, shells, mirrors and metal discs are stitched into bags and belts.

Services

Hotels AL *Oberoi Krishna*, Banjara Hills, T 222121, Cable: OBHOTEL, Telex: 0425 6931 Obh In, Fax: 091-0842-223079. 274 rm. 5 km airport, 7 km rly, 5 km downtown. Very luxuriously appointed. Three restaurants (Indian, Chinese, Continental), all looking out on an artificial waterfall. Large swimming pool and beautiful gardens. Immaculately kept. Opened 1988. **A** *Gateway Banjara*, Road 1, Banjara Hills. T 222222, Cable: Gateway, Telex: 0425 6947 BANJ IN. 124 rm. 7 km airport, 8 km rly, 5 km centre. Taken over by Taj group in 1989 from Welcom. Comparatively modest and some renovation undertaken in 1990. Service and food excellent. **A** *Bhaskar Palace Ashok*, Banjara Hills. T 226141, Telex: 0425 6182 Bpa. 222 rm. Opened in 1988.

C *Ritz*, Hillfort Palace. T 233571, Cable: Ritz, Telex: 0425 6215. 40 rm. 6 km airport, 1 km rly, central. Central a/c. Restaurant, bar, exchange, travel, pool, tennis, pleasant lawns. Old palace which has seen better days. Rm on ground floor in the main wing best and retains character. **C** *Baseraa*, 9-1, 167/168 Sarojini Devi Rd. T 823200, Cable: Baseraa, Telex: 0425 6152. 75 rm. 5 km airport, 1 km rly, central. Central a/c. Restaurant, bar, exchange, travel, beauty parlour, TV. **D** *Asrani International*, 1-7-179 MG Rd, Secunderabad. T 842267, Cable: Asranis, Telex: 0425-6115 ASRN IN. 65 a/c rm with phone. 2 km airport, 5 km rly,

---

Hyderabad - Key to map

1. Naubat Pahar, 2. Archaeological Museum, 3. Yelleshwaram Museum, 4. Yusufkhan's Tomb, 5. Gandhi Bhavan, 6. King Kothi Palace, 7. State Library, 8. Osmania General Hospital, 9. Salar Jung Museum, 10. Purana Haveli Palace, 11. Jami Masjid, 12. Bank, 13. Ashad Books & Grindlay's Bank, 14. Lepakshi, 15. APTDC Tourist Office, 16. Govt. Handicrafts Emporium, 17. Mercury Travels & Trade Wings, 18. Sita Travels, 19. Indian Airlines, 20. Air India, 21. Post Office, 22. Liberty Restaurant, 23. Priya & Swagat Restaurant, & Palace Hotel, 24. Ritz Hotel, 25. Nagarjuna Hotel, 26. Emerald Hotel, 27. Royal & Yatrik Hotels, & New Punjab Restaurant, 28. Brindavan Hotel & State Bank of India, 29. Hotel Annapurna, 30. Hotel Siddhartha, 31. Grand Hotel, 32. Jaya International, 33. Everest Lodge, 34. Taj Mahal Hotel, 35. Y.W.C.A., T. Hyderabad Station & Retiring Rooms.

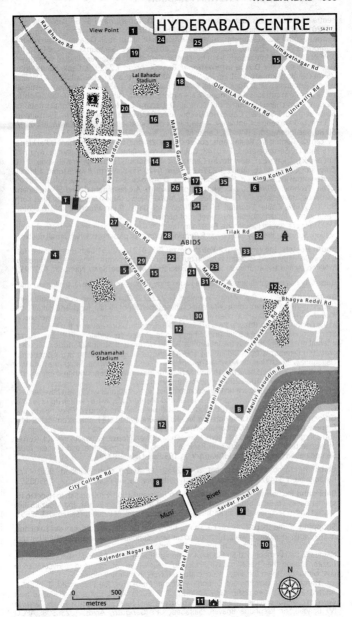

HYDERABAD CENTRE

central. A/c restaurants, bar, exchange, travel, TV. **D** *Nagarjuna*, 3-6-356 Basheerbagh. T 237201, Cable: Magnifique, Telex: 0425-6260 HONA IN. 60 rm. 7 km airport, 2 km rly, 1 km centre. Central a/c. Restaurants, travel, beauty parlour, shop, pool. On a busy main road. **D** *Sampurna International*, Mukramjahi Rd. T 40165, Cable: Sampurna, Telex: 0425 2132 JOY IN. 120 rm. 8 km airport, 1 km rly, central. Central a/c. Restaurant (Indian vegetarian), bar, travel, shop, TV. **D** *Jaya International*, Bank St, Abids. T 232929, Cable Neeba Hotel. 75 rm, 18 a/c. 9 km airport, 1 km rly, Central. A/c public rm and restaurant, (S and N Indian vegetarian), travel, TV. **D** *Rock Castle*, Road 6, Banjara Hills. T 33541, Cable: Rock Castle. 22 rm, some a/c in cottages with phone. 7 km airport, 6 km rly. Restaurant, bar, large delightful gardens. Has character, but is not central. **D** *Deccan Continental*, Sir Ronald Ross Rd, Secunderabad. T 840981, Cable: Hot Decon, Telex: 0425 6665 Home In. 70 rm. 1 km airport, 1.5 km rly, 1 km centre. Central a/c. Restaurant, pool. Good value. **D** *Hotel Karan*, 1-2-261/1 SD Rd, Secunderabad. T 840191, Cable: Malwala, Telex: 0425 6319. 44 rm. 2 km airport and rly, central. Central a/c. Restaurants, coffee shop, exchange, travel, roof garden. **D** *Parklane*, 115 Park Le, Secunderabad. T 70148, Cable: Hiarches, Telex: 0425 6679 Park In. 47 rm 2 km airport, 1 km rly, nr downtown. Central a/c. Restaurants, exchange, travel, shop, TV. **D** *Emerald*, Chirag Ali Le, Abids. T 237835, Telex: 0425 6578. 69 rm. 8 km airport, 1 km rly, nr downtown. Central a/c. Restaurant, shop. **D** *Ashoka*, 6-1-70 Lakdi ka pul. T 230105, Cable: Prohotel. 90 rm, 50 a/c. 5 km airport, 2 km rly. A/c restaurant (N and SI vegetarian), exchange, travel, shop, TV. Good value. **E** *Taj Mahal*, Nehru (Abids) Rd, corner of King Kothi Rd. T 237988, Cable: Courtesy. 69 rm, 20 a/c with baths. 9 km airport, 2 km rly, central. Restaurant (S Indian vegetarian), travel, roof garden, TV.

There are several inexpensive **F** category hotels in the Abids Circle area, nr Hyderabad Rly Station. Secunderabad Rly Station has **F** *Retiring Rooms* for passengers which are all double.

Youth Hostels The very cheap **F** *Youth Hostel*, T 220121, with 51 beds is behind the Boat Club in Secunderabad. Pleasant position but too far from the centre. There are *Dharamsalas* in Nampally and also at Grain Bazaar in Secunderabad. *Municipal Sarai*, Nampally, T 220930.

Bars City has no prohibition. There is a wide range of bars, most in the larger hotels.

Restaurants Best in top hotels. Gateway's (T 222222) *Dakhni* serves good Andhra and Deccan dishes, *Shahnaz* continental and Chinese (open for breakfast, lunch and dinner), the *Kebab-e-Bahar* is a lakeside open air barbecue open in the evenings and you can get snacks at the *Lobby Lounge*. Bhaskar Palace (T 226141) has multi-cuisine *Revathi*, Ritz's (T 233571), *Star* is good for Continental and Chinese and *Prince* for Indian and Italian. Asrani International (T 842267) has the Indian Restaurant *Ganga* and Mughlai *Tandoor*. Baseraa's (840200) *Dawaat* is for S Indian veg and *Mehfil* for Mughlai, Chinese and Continental. Nagarjuna (237201) has the Mughlai *Gulmohar* and the Chinese *Ming*. Sampurna (T 40165) has the multi cuisine *Shahenshah* and *Satkar* for Indian veg (open lunch and dinner) and *Samptrupthi* open 1100-2200 for inexpensive veg food.

Outside hotels there are several recommended a/c restaurants which also have bars – *E and W*, Saifabad (T) opp Telephone Bhavan and *Manju Cafe*, 4-1-873 Tilak Rd (233180). On Abid Rd, *Palace Heights* (8th floor of a tall building) and *Golden Deer* nearby and *Golden Dragon* nr Park Lane Hotel off MG Rd, Secunderabad are highly recommended for Chinese cuisine. *Mughal Durbar* and *Nilgara* are two recommended on Basheerbagh Rd. You can get Western style fast foods from Nirula's *Open House*, Himayatnagar Rd, (corner of Basheerbagh) while *Liberty's* on Bank St (Abids) serves Continental and Chinese food. Secunderabad has a branch of *Kwality's* at 103 Park Lane, T 847735.

Clubs *AP Flying Club*, Begumpet, T 842759. *AP Riding Club*, Saifabad. *Boat Club*, Kavadiguda, T 844978. *Golf Club*, Bolarum. *Hyderabad Racing Club*, Malakpet, T 550055.

Banks and Exchange Open 1000-1400, Mon to Fri and 1000-1200 on Sat. In Hyderabad, several banks on Bank St (including State Bank of India), Sultan Bazaar and Moazam Jahi Market and in Secunderabad on Rashtrapati Rd. Reserve Bank of India is in Saifabad, T 32551.

Shopping Some shops close on Fri. Pearls, Bidriware, Crochet work, Kalamkari paintings, filigree work, inlaid wood work, himroo and silk saris, Kondapalli toys and Hyderabadi bangles nr Charminar (see introduction above). The shopping areas in Hyderabad are Abid Rd, Nampally, Basheerbagh and Sultan Bazaar and Rashtrapati Rd in Secunderabad. Fascinating *bazaar* around the Char Minar with colourful stalls where you can imagine Hyderabad in past centuries. Down the alleys, silver craftsmen work in their tiny rooms.

Handicrafts Government Emporia – *Nirmal Industries*, Raj Bhavan Rd, T 232157. Andhra Pradesh's *Lepakshi*, Gun Foundry, T 235028. Kerala's *Kairali*, Saifabad and *Coircraft*, Mayur complex, Gun Factory. *Cooptex* (Tamil Nadu Handlooms), Abids. *Tantua* (W Bengal), nr Telephone Bhavan, Saifabad. UP's *Gangotri*, Abids, T 236308. APCO

Handloom Houses on Mukharam Jahi Rd, Abids, MG Rd, Amerpeth Kothi among others. *Khadi Bhandar*, Sultan Bazar. *Khadi Crafts*, Municipal Complex, Rashtrapati Rd, Secunderabad. Privately owned *Jewelbox*, SD Rd, T 845395, *Baba Handicrafts*, MG Rd, Secunderabad, T 843572, *Canaud House*, Shastri Stadium, T 238031, *Sheelas*, Lal Bahadur Shastri Stadium, T 236944 and *Bidri Crafts*, Abids.

Antiques from *Govind Mukandas*, Bank St, T 556389, *Humayana* at Hotel Gateway, T 222222, *Rizvi*, Darus Shafa, T 525200. **Jewellery** from *Mangatrai Ramkumar* at Hotel Gateway and Pathergatti, T 521405, *Sri Jangadamba Pearls*, MG Rd, Secunderabad, T 842883, *Tibrumal*, Basheebagh and *Totaram Sagarlal*, Abids.

Bookshops A A Hussain, MG Rd good for guide books.

Local transport Metred yellow top or *Auto rickshaws* and *cycle rickshaws.*

Car Hire You can hire Tourist taxis and luxury cars from APTDC, Gagan Vihar, 1st Floor, MG Rd, T 556493, *Ashok Travels*, Lal Bahadur Stadium, T 230766, *Travel Express*, Saifabad, T 234035.

Buses City buses are very crowded. The Gowliguda Bus Station is on the Maulavi Alauddin Rd on the N Bank of the river, E of Afzalgunj Bridge. Bus No. 1 takes you from Afzalgunj to Secunderabad Station (No.7 does the return journey) No. 80 goes to Golconda Fort. No 8 goes from Secunderabad Station to Char Minar. From Char Minar No. 87 goes to Nampally. Nos.119 and 142 go from Nampally to Golconda Fort.

Entertainment The city proudly claims to have the largest number of cinemas in the country, most screening four times daily. Check papers for English language films. *Ravindra Bharati* stages dance, theatre and music programmes, *Lalit Kala Thoranam*, Public Gardens, free film shows daily and *Max Mueller Bhavan*, Eden Bagh, theatre and film shows.

Sports *Swimming* BV Gurumoorthy Swimming Pool, Sardar Patel Rd, and Hanuman Vyayamshala, Sultan Bazar, T 41660. Some hotels have pools – Ritz, Parklane, Nagarjuna and Deccan. *Yoga* – Yoga Academy, Vijayanagar, T 60187. Vemana Yoga Research Institute, Secunderabad.

The Salar Jung Museum, Afzal Ganj, T 523211. Open 1000-1700, closed Fri and public holidays. Entry Rs.2, Children and students half price. Tape recorded guides are available for Rs 5 from the ticket office.

Sir Salar Jung was the Wazir (Prime Minister) to the Nizam between 1899-1949, and his collection forms the basis of the modern museum, one of the three national museums in India. Originally housed on the edge of the city in one of the palaces, it was re-housed in a purpose-built if singularly dull and unattractive building just inside the northern boundary of the city in the early 1970s. In the early period after the move the displays left a great deal to be desired, but major improvements have been made. Work is continuing, and some of the rooms are closed from time to time.

There is as yet no printed guide or plan to the museum, although there are now informative descriptions of the exhibits in English, Urdu, Hindi and Telugu in each of the rooms. However, the museum can be confusing.

The museum is built to a semi-circular plan. Cameras and bags are not allowed. They may be left at the special counter on the right. Tickets Rs.2 may be bought at counters on the left. It is also possible to buy some specialist publications from the counter immediately inside the door, but no general plan or guide is available. There are free guided tours six times a day at half past the hour, starting at 1030. However, it is often difficult to hear what is being said and to see the objects when going round in a group, so an individual visit is recommended.

Enter the museum from the left hand corner of the reception area. Along the verandah,19th century copies of European statuary overlooking small open space. **Rooms 1 and 2** on left, currently closed. At end of verandah turn right, and room 3 is immediately on the left.

Room 3 Indian textiles and bronzes This room houses late Pallava bronzes, 9th C AD, Vishnu, Vijayanagar. Some of the Vaishnavite images in this gallery belong to the period of the Cholas (AD 846-1216). There are also Jain images. The earliest is a standing figure of Parthavananda and a 9 headed cobra holding a canopy over Jaina's head from Maharashtra, end of 8th century. *Kalamkaris* and *Picchwais* – temple hangings which were used to cover the walls behind the deities. Fabric patterned through the medium of dye, then glued. Most of the *Picchwais* show Krishna in one form or another. They come from Sri Kalahasti in the extreme S of Andhra where they were exported from the S E coast of India. They illustrated stories from Mahabharata and Ramayana. *Pallakollu* and *Masulipatam* were particularly famous for printing and painting of floral designs. The blues stand out markedly from the otherwise dullish ochre colours. *Jain statues* include some of Mahavira from Karnataka and Gujarat. There is also a dancing Nataraja, S India 14th C and a very fine small Tamil Nadu Nataraja 14th century. The Dancing Nataraja symbolises Siva performing the *Anandatandava* – the five attributes of the Lord: creation, preservation, destruction, salvation and omnipotence. The movement of Nataraja himself symbolises the rhythmic movement of the cosmos. There is an unusual dancing Ganes from Mysore 15th C.

R3a Indian sculpture (not numbered on the door) opposite Room 3. Early development of the plastic arts in India. Stone carving from rock pillars (Asokan edicts) – development from Sungan art (1st C BC), abounding with the organic forms of nature, through Gupta period. *Mathura*, see page 264, was the first major centre for carving stone. Sandstone was used in the Kushan period, drawing inspiration from Buddhist art in *Bodh Gaya*. See page 664. Broken stone slab carved with lotus medallion, dated to 1st C BC. Amaravati and Nagarjunakonda had a soft grey limestone, popularly known as *Palna* marble. In the S the Pallava dynasty kings were devotees of Vishnu, though Siva worship also flourished. An early Gupta *Mukhalinga* (3rd C AD) is given pride of place in the room with an effective mounting. **Room 4   Minor arts of S India** Wood carving – one of most ancient crafts of the S – sandalwood and rose wood. Temple carving. **Room 6   Printed fabrics and glass** Temple cloths – freehand designs in Rajasthan, with glue then appliqué. Wood block printing also used in Rajasthan, and some scrolls used as visual aids by itinerant "preachers" and storytellers. Some clothing, including 18th C Dacca muslin. There is some attractive Mughal glass characterised by gilt paint, flowers, coniferous trees and other motifs common.

Go through **Room 6.** Out at other end the small open space is counted as **Room 7.** Turn right. The small open space on the right with large pots counts as **Room 8.** Retrace steps. On the right as you retrace your steps are **Rooms 9,10,11 Children's sections. Room 12** is a very shallow porch with stags, deer etc in glass cabinets. The children's sections contain some very crude models, but they also contain some toys that are real collectors' pieces. Possibly the only model flying boat brought out by W. Bristow's in 1939 left in the world is in the collection. From a collectors' point of view many of these exhibits have been devalued by putting museum numbers on them, and some suffer from the usual metal-fatigue that attacks pre-War zinc alloy "Mazah"!

14 The ivory room Ivory chairs, inlaid tables. Delhi, Mysore, Travancore and Visakhapatnam are current centres. The cuckoo clock is a great attraction. **16 Armaments** 17th century chain mail, Blunderbusses, matchlock guns etc. Persian swords 17th C. Amazing variety and enormous quantity of old arms, including firearms. **15 Metal ware** There are some excellent examples of Bidri ware, local to the region. **17a Modern Indian painting** 19th & 20th century with some examples of leading Indian artists such as Ravi Varma, Amanindra Tagore, Sunil Prakash. **18 Indian miniatures** Representatives of major schools, Mughal Deccani, Rajasthani, Mewar, Amber etc.

Upstairs   Room 20   European art There is not a great deal here to excite interest. A Landseer perhaps the best in a mediocre collection. **21 European porcelain** Examples from Dresden, Sèvres and Wedgwood, as well as some Italian and Austrian porcelain. A porcelain mirror, belonging to Marie Antoinette is displayed. **Room 25 Jade** Some outstandingly beautiful examples of Indian and Chinese jade. **26 European bronzes** All 19th C copies of classical sculpture **28 Clock room** Some bizarre examples, many French, some English grandmother clocks.

29 Manuscripts This includes some magnificent early Islamic scripts. A 9th century AD Qu'ran, a script on Unani medicine. No 6 is the oldest in collection. One copy of the Qu'ran, written in 1288, has the signatures of Jehangir, Shah Jahan and Aurangzeb on it. There is also a large copy of Qu'ran written in Arcot. **31 Far Eastern Porcelain** Sung Dynasty. Marco Polo compared pottery to Porcella, the white shell. Celadon – brought to Europe at same time as French play featuring. 12th century onwards. Switch to cobalt derived blue "Mohammadan blue" from Persia and Baluchistan. Replaced celadon. **32 Kashmiri room** **33 Far Eastern statuary** Various Buddhist sculptures recounting the birth of Buddha at Lumbini.

Other Museums   Government Archaeological Museum Public Gardens. Small museum, located by Lal Bahadur Stadium. 10 minutes by car from Banjara Hills hotels, 2 minutes from Ritz. Open 1030 -1700. Entry Adults Re.0.50. children Re. 0.25   Closed Mon and public holidays. Publications section, but no publications on archaeology. The museum was opened in 1930 in the specially constructed two storeyed, semi-circular building. Sections on pre-historic implements, sculptures, paintings, inscriptions, illuminated manuscripts, coins, arms, bidri ware, china, textiles and the crowd drawing 4,000 year old Egyptian mummy. Behind the museum, in the Ajanta Pavilion are life size copies of Ajanta frescoes while the Nizam's collection of rare artefacts are housed in the Jubilee Hall. The Public gardens open daily except Mon.

Birla Archaeological Museum   Malakpet, T 558347. Collection of finds from excavations of historic sites, housed in Asman Ghad Palace, 9 km away. Open daily.

Birla Planetarium   Believed to be "the most modern planetarium in the country". Naubat Pahad. Six shows daily, 8 on Sat, Sun and holidays. Entry Rs.5.

Khazana Museum   On the way to Golconda – stone sculptures (see Excursions).

Parks and zoos   *Nehru Zoological Park* occupies 13 ha of a low hilly area with remarkable boulders. The animals are kept in natural surroundings. The Natural History Museum, Ancient Life Museum, Pre-historic Animals Park, a Lion Safari Park and a children's train are here. Open 0900-1800, closed Mon. Small entry fee. Cars Rs.10. *Nampally Public Gardens* N of the Station, close to the Lal Bahadur Stadium, is the largest in Asia. Lotus ponds and Children's Playground. There are municipal parks in Tank Bund Rd, Club Rd, Secunderabad, Indira Park below Tank Bund Rd and Public Gardens in Saifabad.

Useful addresses   Foreigners' Regional Registration Office, Commissioner of Police, Purani Haveli, Hyderabad T 230191.

Cultural centres   Alliance Française, T 220296. Max Mueller Bhavan, Ramkote, T 43938. Bharatiya Vidya Bhavan, King Kothi Rd, T 237825.

Airlines   *Air India*, 1st Floor, Samrat Complex, Secretariat Rd, T 232858. *Air France*, Nasir Arcade, Secretariat Rd, T 236947. *British Airways*, Chapel Rd, T 234927. *Cathay Pacific*, Spencers Travel Division, 89 SD Rd, Secunderabad. T 840234. *Egypt Air*, Safina International, Public Garden Rd, T 230778. *Kuwait Airways*, National Travel Service, United House. *KLM*, Gemini Travels, Chapel Rd, T 236042. *Lufthansa*, 86 Shantinagar, T 220352. *PanAm*, Indam Travels, T 235142. *Saudia*, Arafath Travels, Basheerbagh, T 238175. *Singapore Airlines* and *Swissair*, Regency Buildings, Begumpet. *Thai International*, Swan Travels, Chapel Rd, T 236042.

Hospitals and medical services   There are three general hospitals as well as several government specialist hospitals which are open to foreigners. Most are open for out-patients from 0900-1400, Casualty 24 hr. General Hospitals in Nampally, T 234344, LKing Kothi Rd, T 36085 and Golconda, T 231776. Dental, Afzalganj, T 45830, Chest Diseases, Irramnuma, T 261431, ENT, 5-1-714 King Kothi Rd, T 557845, Homoeopathic, Malakpeta, T 41320, Maternity, Amenbagh City, T 523641, Orthopaedics, Somajiguda, T 232564, Eye Hospital, Asifnagar, T 220752. Osmania General Hospital is in Afzalganj, T 45286.

Post and Telegraphs   In **Hyderabad,** General Post Office and Central Telegraph Office, Abids. In **Secunderabad**, Head Post Office in RP Rd and Central Telegraph Office on MG Rd.

Places of worship   *Hindu* Ram Mandir, Hanuman Mandir, Mahakali Temple, Sri Venkatesvara Temple, Birla Mandir and Hare Krishna Temple. *Muslim* – Mecca Masjid, Jama Masjid, Qutb Shahi Masjid. *Christian* St Paul's, St George's, All Saints Church, Our Lady of Health. *Jain* – Jain temple in Sultan Bazar.

Travel agents   *Blaze Tours*, Basheerbagh, T 233055. *India Travels*, Chapel Rd, T 230052. *Mercury Travels*, Public Gardens Rd, T 234441. *Sheriff Travels*, Basheerhagh, T 237914. *Thomas Cook*, Saifabad, T 222689. *TCI*, Regency House, Somajiguda. *Trade Wings*, Public Gardens Rd, T 230545. *Travel Express*, Saifabad, T 234035.

Tourist offices and information   *Government of India Tourist Office*, Sandozi Building, Himayat Nagar, T 66877. *Tourist Information Bureau*, Government of Andhra Pradesh, Lidcap House, Himayatnagar, T 223384, 223385. *Andhra Pradesh Travel and Tourism Development Corporation* (APTTDC) Gagan Vihar First Floor, Mukaram Jahi Rd, T 556493, 556303. Opp Anand Theatre, SP Rd, Secunderabad, T 843942. Approved guides from Tourist Information Bureau, Lidcap House, Himayatnagar, T 223384/5. Also information centres at Hyderabad Rly Station, T 221352, Secunderabad Rly Station, T 70144 and at the Begumpet Airport, T 77192.

Tours   APTTDC *City sightseeing* half day or full day. Rather unsatisfactory as it allows about an hr at the Fort and includes sights which could be omitted. *Hyderabad-Pochampalli* Sat, 0800-1300. Twice daily *Yadagirigutta* for Laxmi Narayan Temple. 1 day tours to *Nagarjunasagar* Dam and Museum, Ethipothala Falls. 2 day *Mantralayam* for Sri Raghavendra temple, Alampur and *Srisailam* for Mallikarjuna Svami Temple, Pathal Ganga falls, Sikharam Power House. The other tours cover a range of options and last from 3 to 15 days.

Air Indian Airlines Delhi Daily (+ 1 other), 0745, 2 hr, **Madras** Daily (+ 1 other), 0805, 2 hr; **Bombay** Daily, (+ 1 other), 0600, 1 hr 10 min; **Bhubaneshwar** Wed, Fri & Sat, 1630, 2 hr 45 min; **Nagpur** Wed, Fri & Sat, 1630, 1 hr; **Bangalore** Daily, 1315, 1 hr; **Visakhapatnam** Mon, Tues, Thurs, Fri & Sun, 1005, 1 hr; **Vayudoot** Tirupati Mon, Wed

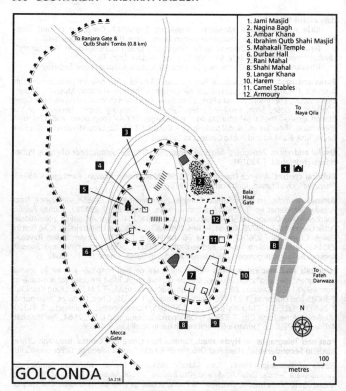

1. Jami Masjid
2. Nagina Bagh
3. Ambar Khana
4. Ibrahim Qutb Shahi Masjid
5. Mahakali Temple
6. Durbar Hall
7. Rani Mahal
8. Shahi Mahal
9. Langar Khana
10. Harem
11. Camel Stables
12. Armoury

To Banjara Gate &
Qutb Shahi Tombs (0.8 km)

To Naya Qila

Bala Hisar Gate

To Fateh Darwaza

N

Mecca Gate

0   100
metres

GOLCONDA SA 218

& Fri (+ 1 other), 0630, 1 hr 30 min; Vijayawada Mon, Wed & Fri (+2 others), **Rajahmundry** Mon, Wed & Fri, 1030, 1 hr 45 min. Indian Airlines, City Office, Saifabad, T 236902. Airport, T 842051. **Vayudoot** supplements with 3 flights a week to Mysore via Bellary and Bangalore, Bhubaneswar via Rajahmundry, and Jeypore (Orissa), Goa and Solapur. Vayudoot, 2nd Floor, Samrat Complex, Saifabad, T 234717, Airport, T 842855. The airport is at Begumpet, Secunderabad.

Rail The broad gauge lines Delhi-Madras, Calcutta-Madras and Bombay-Madras all serve the city. **From Hyderabad** Bangalore: *Hyderabad Exp*, 7085 (AC/II), daily, 1750, 17 hr 5 min; **Bombay (VT)**: *Hyderabad-Bombay Exp*, 7032, daily, 1935, 17 hr 20 min; **Madras (MC)**: *Charminar Exp*, 6060 (AC/II), daily, 1830, 14 hr 50 min; **Tirupati**: *Rayalaseema*, 7429 (AC.II), daily, 1700, 16 hr 15 min; **Vijayawada**: *Godavari Exp*, 7008 (AC/II), daily, 1715, 6 hr 25 min.
   From Secunderabad Aurangabad, *Ajanta Exp*, 7551 (AC/II), daily, 1830, 12 hr 20 min. **Bombay (VT)**: *Minar Exp*, 2102 (AC/II), daily, 1535, 14 hr 30 min; **Delhi (ND)**: *A.P. Exp*, 2723, daily, 0635, 26 hr 5 min; **Tirupati**: *Venkatadri*, 7597, daily, 1530, 18 hr; **Vijayawada**: Godavari Exp, 7008 (AC/II), daily, 1745, 5 hr 55 min.

Road Hyderabad and Secunderabad are on the NH 7 (Varanasi – Nagpur – Bangalore – Kanniyakumari) and NH 9 (Bombay – Pune – Solapur – Vijayawada). Some distances – Aurangabad 599 km, Bombay 739 km, Bangalore 566 km, Madras 704 km, Nagpur 468 km, Tirupati 651 km, Vijayawada 271 km, Visakhapatnam 637 km.

Long Distance Buses APSTRC, Musheerbad, T 64571. The main bus station is at Gowliguda and the service covers the state. Private coaches run services to Aurangabad, Bangalore, Bombay, Madras and Tirupati. Reservations: Royal Lodge, Entrance to Hyderabad Rly Station.

Excursions *Golconda* (11 km from Hyderabad) was the capital of the Qutb Shahi kings who ruled over the area from 1507 to 1687 of the Qutb Shahi kings. Originally built of mud in the 12th century by the Hindu **Kakatiyas** who ruled from Warangal nearby, the fort was reinforced by masonry by the Bahamanis who occupied it from 1363. The massive fort was built on a granite hill occupying a good defensive site and surrounded by three walls. One encircled the town, another the hill on which the citadel stood and the last joined huge boulders on the high ridge with parts of masonry wall. The citadel's double wall had 87 bastions with cannons and 8 huge gates which have outer and inner doors and guardrooms between. The total circumference of the outer curtain wall is 5 km. Each of the gateways carries relief ornamentation of birds and animals, and some of the guns of the Qutb Shahi's are still on the walls. The *Fateh Darwaza* or Victory Gate made of teak, with a Hindu deity engraved, is studded with iron spikes as a defence against war elephants.

The fort had an ingenious system of laminated clay pipes and huge *'Persian Wheels*'* to carry water to cool the palace chambers and up to the height of 61 m where there were hanging gardens. It also had superb acoustics which enabled a drum beat or bugle call or even a clap under the canopy of the *Fateh Darwaza*, to be heard by someone at the palace at the very top. There are plenty of people trying it out! The famous diamond vault once held the **Koh-i-noor** and the **Hope diamonds**. The fort fell to Emperor Aurangzeb, when the Delhi Mughals set their sights to expanding southwards. It took two attempts, an 8 month siege and the help of a Qutb Shahi General who turned a traitor before the fort could be captured. By the early 19th century the fort was in ruins. The English traveller Walter Hamilton who visited it in 1820 described it as being almost completely deserted, "the dungeons being used by the Nizam of Hyderabad as a prison for his worst enemies, among whom were several of his sons and two of his wives."

Though in ruins (parts having been destroyed during the Mughal attacks), you can still see mosques, temples, the three-storeyed armoury, the harem, the Hall of Public Audience and the Rani Mahal with its royal baths. The central hill, the Bala Hissar, is over 110 m high, making a vigorous climb to the top. There are fortifications at various levels on the way up. There is a good map mounted at the entrance to the fort. As you enter the gate you see the remains of the armoury and the women's palaces on the left. The suggested route is clearly marked. About half way up is a large and rather unhealthy looking water tank or well, near the King's storehouse. A Persian inscription on black basalt states that the Ambar khana was built during the reign of Abdullah Qutb Shah (1626-72), and to the N is what was once the most densely populated part of the city. Near the top of the fort the path passes the Hindu Mahakali temple on the way to the Durbar Hall on the summit. Another of S Asia's supposed **underground tunnels** is believed by some to run from a corner of the summit about 8 km to Gosha Mahal. It is well worth climbing the stairs onto the roof of the Durbar Hall. The path down is clearly signed to take you on a circular route through the ruins back to the main gate.

The Archaeological Department has taken up the management of the site. It is steadily being "sanitised", with stone paths, properly made steps and a large flow of visitors. Equipment for sound and light shows is being installed. The old mint on the road to Golconda is the **Khazana Museum** of the Archaeological Department which exhibits stone sculptures.

One road leaves Golconda Fort to the N through the Banjara Gate. 800 metres NNW of the fort on a low plateau are the **Qutb Shahi Tombs**, each of black granite or greenstone with plaster decoration, built on a square or octagonal base. Each has a large onion dome and arches with fine sculptures, inscriptions and remains of glazed decoration. The larger tombs have their own mosque attached which usually comprises an eastward opening hall with a *mihrab* to the W. The sides have inscriptions in beautiful Naksh script, and remnants of the glazed tiles which used to cover them can still be seen in places. The tombs of the rulers were built during their lifetime, under their supervision. They fell into disrepair and the gardens ran wild until the end of the 19th century when **Sir Salar Jang** (who founded the museum which takes his name in Hyderabad) restored the tombs and replanted the gardens. It is now managed and kept in an excellent state of repair by the Archaeological Survey of India, who have labelled the buildings. It is a popular place to visit, and from 1000 can get busy with busloads of schoolchildren and tourists from Hyderabad and beyond.

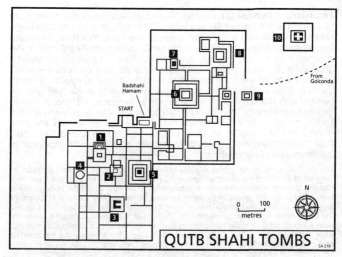

Badshahi Hamam

START

From Golconda

Abul Hasan

0   100
metres

N

QUTB SHAHI TOMBS
SA 219

The road from Golconda fort goes N, passing the tomb of Abdullah Qutb Shah as it approaches the entrance to the tombs, which is at the eastern gate of the compound. On the left hand side of the road just outside the compound is the tomb of Abul Hasan Tana Qutb Shahi (r 1672-1687). He was the last of the kings to be buried here as the final king in the line of the Qutb Shahi dynasty, *Abul Hasan*, died in the fort at Daulatabad in 1704, see page 987. You enter the formal gardens in the middle of the eastern wall. To the right are the tomb of Princess Hayat Baksh Begum (d. 1617), the daughter of Ibrahim Qutb Shah, and a smaller mosque, while about 100 metres directly ahead is the granite tomb of Muhammad Qutb Shah (r 1612-1626). Tucked away due N of this tomb is that of Pemamati, one of the mistresses of Abdullah Qutb Shah, dating from 1663. The path turns S and W around the tomb of Abdullah Qutb Shah. About 100 m to the S is a tank which is still open. The ramp up and down which the bullocks walked to draw the water is typical of those found in villages across southern India where *kavalai** irrigation is practised.

The path turns right again from near the corner of the tank and runs W to the oldest structure in the compound, the Badshahi Hammam, the 'bath' where the body of the king was washed before burial. You can still see the channels for the water and the special platforms for washing the body. The Badshahi kings were Shi'a Muslims, and the twelve small baths in the Hammam stand symbolically for the twelve imams revered by the Shi'a community.

To the S of the Hammam is the second main area of the compound, with a series of major tombs. The most striking lies due S, the 54 m high mausoleum of *Mohammed Quli Qutb Shah* (r 1581-1612), the poet king who was the founder of Baghnagar (Hyderabad). It is appropriate that the man responsible for creating a number of beautiful buildings in Hyderabad should be commemorated by such a remarkable tomb. The underground excavations here have been turned into a Summer House. You can walk right through the tomb and on to the tomb of the fourth king of the dynasty, Ibrahim Qutb Shah (r 1550-1580) another 100 m to the S.

At the W edge of the compound is the octagonal tomb of Kulsum Begum (d 1608), granddaughter of Mohammad Quli Qutb Shah. To its E is the tomb of Jamshid Quli Qutb Shah (r 1543-1550), who was responsible for the murder of his 90 year old father and founder of the dynasty, Sultan Quli Qutb Shah (r 1512-1543). This has the appearance of a two storey building though it is in fact a single storey structure with no inscription. A number of other small tombs are found in the compound.

Allow half a day for a leisurely exploration. Guidebook available. The bus (Nos 119 or 142) takes an hour from Nampally, Hyderabad. Nizam-ul-Mulk repossessed it in 1724 and restored it to its former glory for a time. Open daily 0900-1630 except Fri. Entry Re.0.50, camera fee Rs 2.

The ancient city of **Nagarjunakonda**, one of India's richest Buddhist sites now lies almost entirely under the lake created by the Nagarjunasagar Dam, completed in 1960.It is possible to take an excursion from Hyderabad. For details and site description see route from Hyderabad to Vijayawada (**see page 913**).

Osman Sagar 22 km. It was the name given in honour of the last Nizam, to the 46 sq km reservoir which was constructed at great cost to avoid a repetition of the devastation caused by the flooding of the Musi river in 1908. Hyderabad's water supply comes from this lake which is also known as Gandipet. There are very pleasant landscaped gardens and a swimming pool. Guest Houses Sagar Mahal and Visranti Dormitory can be reserved through Andhra Pradesh Tourism. **Himayat Sagar**, a large 85 sq km lake named after the Nizam's eldest son, is close to Osman Sagar can only be reached by a separate road 22 km from Hyderabad. There is a Dak Bungalow with a cook available. Reservations: Supt Engineer, PWD, Water Works, Gosha Mahal, Hyderabad. T 48011.

Vanasthalipuram Deer Park 13 km on the Hyderabad- Vijayawada road. 125 ha park also known as Mahavir Harin Vanashtali is also a wildlife sanctuary with spotted deer, black buck, chinkara, wild boar, porcupines and python and over a hundred species of birds.

Warangal

140 km to the N, Warangal was the capital of the Hindu Kakatiya Empire in the 12th and 13th centuries who were also great temple builders. The name is derived from the Oranallu (one stone) Hill. This is the massive boulder with ancient religious significance which stands on the W side where the modern town is situated. When he visited Warangal, Marco Polo was highly impressed by the riches. Warangal is famous for its temples, lakes and wildlife and for its 2 circular fortifications, the outer, an earthen rampart and the inner of stone. 4 roads enter the city from the N E S and W through decorative gateways in the inner wall which have become symbols of Kakatiya architecture. The roads meet at the ruins of the Siva temple in the centre where you can still see the typical carvings and motifs of the period on the 4 gateways. There are several other Siva shrines nearby.

The 'thousand pillar' Siva (Rudresvar) temple in the Chalukya style on the slopes of the **Hanamakonda Hill** to the N of Warangal, has beautiful carvings with subsidiary shrines to the N and S. In contrast to the sprawling, high Dravida temples, this is a low, compact temple, built on several stepped platforms. There are subsidiary shrines to Vishnu and the Sun God Surya. You can see rock cut elephants, a large superbly carved nandi in the courtyard and an ancient well where villagers have drawn water for 800 years. The underground passage which is believed to have connected the temple with the Fort 11 km away, cannot be seen! The Bhadrakali Temple stands on the hill top overlooking a shallow lake. In the 1970s Hanamakonda was the Parliamentary Constituency held by the newly elected Indian Prime Minister P.V. Navasimha Rao.

Hotels There is a **D** Ashoka on the Main Rd, T 85491 with 40 a/c rm and a restaurant, bar. The food is recommended. The **Government Tourist Rest House** is on Kazipet Rd, T 6201 which has been recently renovated. 4 a/c rm.

Rail Nagpur Tamil Nadu Exp, 2621 (AC/CC&AC/II), daily, 0653, 7 hr 7 min; **Delhi (ND)**: Tamil Nadu Exp, 2621 (AC/CC&AC/II), daily, 0653, 23 hr 52 min; **Vijaywada**: Kerala-Mangala Exp, 2626 (AC/II), daily, 1154, 3 hr 21 min; G.T. Exp, 2616 (AC/CC&AC/II), daily, 2032, 3 hr 18 min; **Madras (MC)**: Cochin-Bilaspur Exp, 7058 (AC/II), Th, 1323, 11 hr 37 min; **Secunderabad**: Konark Exp, 2119 (AC/II), daily, 1204, 3 hr 6 min; **or** Golconda Exp, 7201 (AC/CC), daily, 1005, 3 hr 20 min.

Excursions Ramappa, Pakkal, Lakhnavaram and Ghanpur lakes are a result of the Kakatiya rulers' management of water resources in the 12th and 13th centuries. They created the artificial lakes by bridging gaps between river valleys by building walls of earth. There are game sanctuaries at *Pakhal*, *Ethumagaram* and *Lakhnavaram* nearby. This is the richest area for wildlife in the state with tiger, panther, hyena, wild dogs, wild boars, gaur, foxes, spotted deer, jackals, muntjacks, sloth bears and pythons. The is also a large variety of water birds and fish, otters and alligators in the vast lakes.

Close to the Ramappa Dam is *Palampet* 64 km from Warangal. The *Ramappa Temple*, to Siva as Rudreswara, was built in 1234 and is one of the finest medieval Deccan temples. The sculpture decoration and paintings are excellent (even richer than that at the thousand-pillar temple) with famous Mandakini figures of female dancers which appear on brackets at the four entrances. The base of the temple has the typical bands of sculpture, the lowest of elephants, the second a lotus scroll, the third which is the most interesting depicting figures opening a window on the life of the times and finally another floral scroll. More fine sculpture inside, some displaying a subtle sense of humour in common with some of the figures outside, and paintings of scenes from the epics on the ceiling. *Vanavihar Tourist Rest House* nearby, also overlooking the lake, serves snacks. There are 4 simple and clean rm. Cook available but bring own provisions.

ROUTES FROM HYDERABAD

All the routes from Hyderabad are off the major tourist tracks. This does not mean that they are inaccessible or difficult, though accommodation is often limited and basic. However, there are attractive and very lightly travelled roads, and even if you are simply travelling on to another city there are interesting sites all round the city. The routes N to Nagpur and S E to Vijayawada are outlined first. These are followed by the route from Vijayawada through Vishakapatnam to the northeast and from Vijayawada to Madras. The route from Hyderabad to Bangalore and Hyderabad to Bombay are described in the sections on Karnataka and Maharashtra respectively

---

HYDERABAD TO NAGPUR

The route from Hyderabad to Nagpur runs almost due N, first across the northernmost section of the granite Telangana plateau, with its thin red soils, rock strewn landscape and scattered vegetation, then across the great expanse of black Deccan lavas that are typical of Maharashtra. The road crosses the boundary between Andhra Pradesh and Maharashtra at the Penganga River, one of the tributaries of the Godavari.

The road from Hyderabad (the NH 7) goes through a series of small towns. 90 km N of Hyderabad is the "town of mounds", *Kondapur*. Now referred in the official tourist brochures as the "Taxila of the S" there are the remains of a great Buddhist complex. Nearly 2000 coins have been discovered – gold, silver, copper and lead – as well as fine glass beads, coming from as far afield as Rome.

The first important town is *Medak* (96 km) some 10 km W of NH7. To reach it take a left turn 80 km N of Hyderabad. It has an extraordinary Gothic style cathedral, complete with stained glass windows and a spire over 60 m high, begun in 1914 and completed ten years later. The artificial lake, Nizam Sagar, which covers 130 sq km and irrigates rice, sugarcane and turmeric lies a further 30 km N W of Medak and can be seen from *Yellareddi*.

If you want to continue N from Medak you can go straight back to the NH 7 at Ramayampet. If you go to Yellareddi you can return to the NH 7 northwards at **Kamareddi**. From time to time the road passes through forest of teak and sal, now often broken up by cultivated land, giving a parkland appearance. Kamareddi has important iron ore deposits, in common with several areas immediately to its N. NH 7 goes on to the market town of **Nizamabad** (26 km).

Rail Secunderabad: 7592 Exp, daily, 1340, 3 hr 45 min; **Aurangabad**: Ajanta Exp, 7551 (AC/II), daily, 2225, 8 hr 25 min.

From Nizamabad the road continues N to **Armur** (29 km) and then across the Godavari River to **Nirmal** (33 km). Nirmal is particularly well known for its local craft of painting on light wood, for which it became famous in the sixteenth century during the reign of the Qutb Shahis. Today the painters and craftsmen of Nirmal are making furniture as well as painting portraits and pageants for which they are more commonly known.

11 km from Nirmal are the **Kuntala Falls**. These 46 metre waterfalls on the River Kadam, a tributary of the Godavari, plunge into the wooded valley below, an impressive sight immediately after the heavy rains of the monsoon. To the E are the important coal reserves of **Singareni**.

Once across the Godavari the focus of economic life is northwards towards Nagpur. **Adilabad** (81 km) is the last major town before crossing the Penganga into Maharashtra. The road goes through **Umri** (50 km), **Karanji** (7 km) and Hinganhat (61 km) before reaching the turning left to **Wardha** (36 km), the centre of the Gandhi ashram movement. It is possible to go direct from Hinganghat to Nagpur (74 km) if you do not want to visit Mahatma Gandhi's ashram at Sevagram or Vinobe Bhave's ashram nearby.

HYDERABAD TO VIJAYAWADA

The road route from Hyderabad to Vijayawada is off the beaten tourist track, although parts are heavily used by goods traffic. The route along the NH 9 from Hyderabad to Madras descends gently eastwards down the Telangana plateau slope to the flat rice-growing delta of the Krishna, with Vijayawada at a vital crossing point.

It passes through a series of small towns, none of which is of major significance. Suryapet (115 km); Kodad (60 km), through Jaggayyapeta to Vijayawada (96 km) The whole journey along the main road is approximately 4 to 5 hours driving. This route is still relatively quiet. There are regular and frequent buses between all the towns along the route, as well as express buses linking the major cities.

An interesting though longer route can be taken via Nagarjunakonda. Leave Hyderabad on NH 9 towards Vijayawada (the Vijayawada Road). After 6 km take the right fork to Ibrahimpatam, Kulkulapalli and **Mailepalli** (101 km from Hyderabad). In Mailepalli take the left turn towards Miryalguda. After 35 km turn right to **Vijayapuri** S (30 km).

Nagarjunakonda, one of India's richest Buddhist sites, now lies almost entirely under the lake created by the Nagarjunasagar Dam, completed in 1960. Rising from the middle of the artificial lake is the Nagarjuna Hill (konda is the Telugu word for hill) which had been nearly 200 m above the floor of the secluded valley in which the remains of a highly cultured Buddhist civilisation had remained almost undisturbed for 1600 years until their discovery by A.R.Saraswati in March 1926. A full account of Nagarjunakonda is available from the Archaeological Survey of India Guide published in 1987. Some of the popular tourist literature suggests that Nagarjunakonda is another Abu Simbel, rescued from the rising tide of an artificial reservoir. While the scale of archaeological work that was carried out was remarkable, don't imagine that the visual effect of the reconstruction is remotely on a scale to match that of the Egyptian reconstruction above the Aswan Dam. Nagarjunakonda is a most attractive site, set in one of India's biggest artificial lakes, but the reconstructed buildings are on a comparatively small scale, set in a peaceful setting on top of the hill top fort, now an island. Below is a brief summary of the main discoveries on the site.

The valley lies in the northern ranges of the **Nallamalais** ("black hills") which surround it on three sides. On the fourth side was the great **River Krishna**, superimposed on the hills as it flows W to E towards the Bay of Bengal. Early archaeological work showed the remnants of Buddhist monasteries, many limestone sculptures and other remains. In the early 1950s the government decided to go ahead with building the Nagarjunasagar Dam in order to provide irrigation water for the arid plains to the E and to improve control of the Krishna's waters in the economically vital delta region. The archaeological site had by that time barely been touched, and the Archaeological Survey of India carried out a six year programme of fully excavating the sites in the valley before they were to be covered by the rising waters of the lake. The excavations discovered more than 100 distinct sites ranging from the prehistoric early stone age period to the late medieval.

Today some of the most important remains have been moved and reconstructed above the water line. Nine monuments have been rebuilt in their original form and there are fourteen large replicas of the excavated ruins shown on what is now the island hill-top.

Pre-history The valley site has probably been occupied for almost 200,000 years. Crude stone tools were found – points, scrapers and handaxes, made out of quartzite pebbles – on the banks of the Krishna. Developments in the tools founds suggest that the site was occupied during the middle and late **Stone Ages**. In the 3rd millenium BC rural settlements began to take shape. One of the sites excavated showed a neolithic cemetery, suggesting the development of permanent settlement rather than simply a nomadic existence. Many pits were found, though no satisfactory explanation has yet been given for them. From around 400 BC a new culture appeared, that of the **Megalith builders**. The remains were all stone circles under which were pits for the dead, often in groups. Just a few had any ornamentation. One site showed the bodies of women, one of which had gold spiral earrings and a necklace. In all nineteen skeletons were discovered.

Ikshvakus period A lapse of perhaps four hundred years in the site's importance followed. Then from the 3rd century AD under the brief rule of a group called the Ikshvakus Nagarjunakonda became the centre of extraordinary political and artistic activity. Knowledge of their activities comes from inscriptions which have been found at a number of sites. They suggest that the first king, Chamtamula followed the Hindu god of war, **Karttikeya**, known in the S as Subrahmanyam. However, his sister, Chamsatri, strongly supported Buddhism, creating the first Buddhist establishment found at Nagarjunakonda. The support of both Buddhism and Brahmanism side by side throughout the reign of the Ikshvaku rulers encouraged the building of monuments and development of art which reflected both traditions at the same time. It would seem that the supremacy of the Ikshvakus in the region was unchallenged over a long period. Datable records show that the building of monuments in the valley started in the sixth year of the reign of Virapurushadatta and ended abruptly in the 11th year of Rudrapurushadatta's reign.

In the mid 4th century AD it seems certain that the **Pallavas** pushed northwards from their centre in northern Tamil Nadu and eclipsed the Ikshvaku kingdom, reducing Nagarjunakonda to a deserted village. However, the site was occupied again. During the **Chalukya** period between the 7th and 12th centuries AD there was a Saiva centre built at Yellaswaram, on the other bank of the Krishna.

In the 15th and 16th centuries the hill became a fortress in the contest for supremacy between the Vijayanagar, Bahmani and Gajapati kings. After the fall of the Vijayanagar Empire both the hill and the valley below lost all importance.

The site The capital of the Ikshvakus was a planned city on the right bank of the Krishna known as **Vijayapuri** ("city of victory"). The citadel had rampart walls on three sides with the river serving as protection on the fourth. The buildings inside the citadel included houses, barracks, baths and wells. Although the palace couldn't be precisely identified there was a complex bathing area and tank. There is strong evidence that the buildings were destroyed by a great fire. Most people lived outside the citadel in houses made of rubble bound by mud. One of the houses discovered was clearly a goldsmith's workshop, and an inscription nearby showed that there were guilds of craftsmen – sweet makers, masons, artisans. There was a shell cutting industry near the Brahman shrines, and many fragments of shell bangles were discovered. The most striking secular building was the amphitheatre which could seat about 1000 people. It isn't clear whether it was just used for music and drama, or whether the wrestling scenes depicted in some of Nagarjunakonda's art were enacted in the theatre as well. People obviously enjoyed themselves – dice, game boards and dancing were all common.

Some of the most interesting discoveries on the site are those of the temples, for they show the earliest developments of Brahmanical temple architecture in S India. Just one of the nine temples was dedicated to Vishnu, while five were definitely dedicated to Siva or Karttikeya. The Vishnu temple, which can be dated precisely to AD 278 from an inscription, housed an eight-armed wooden statue. Two beautifully carved pillars were recovered from its site.

2 km upstream was a shrine clearly associated with a *burning ghat*. One sculpture recovered shows a woman as if lying in state while a second seems to show *sati* taking place – a woman throwing herself onto her husband's funeral pyre. The main bathing ghat on the banks of the Krishna was remarkable, and has been moved to its new site above the lake. The river bank was dotted with **Brahmanical shrines**. The largest temple complex was nearly 150 m sq, with an apsidal sanctuary, and was clearly a centre of pilgrimage for long after the decline of the Ikshvaku kingdom. One of the features of the Brahmanical temples of this period is that as yet they had not developed a standard form. Some had a single shrine, others more than one, each with a pillared hall in front of it. Oblong, apsidal and square shrines are all found, and while brick was used for the building of shrines, stone was prominent in the construction of the *mandapas*, which were flat roofed.

In addition to the Brahmanical temples there are over 30 Buddhist buildings throughout the valley, spanning a period of about 100 years. The earliest dated structure in the whole of Nagarjunakonda, the *Maha chaitya*, was in the centre of the site, and was built between the 6th and 18th years of King Virapurushadatta's reign. It was a stupa with a wheel shaped plan with a diameter of over 27 m. It had a **tooth relic** among other relics, and the inscription refers to the bodily remains of **the Buddha**. In their earliest phases none of the stupas had image shrines, and there were several small stupas unconnected with other buildings. However, some later monasteries did have shrines. There were nine monastic buildings around the citadel itself and a further 10 in the NE part of the valley. These were undoubtedly later, and show two new trends; the development of circular image shrines, and a memorial pillar opposite a *stupa-chaitya* which was put up in honour of the Queen's mother.

It is clear from the remains that were found in the valley that both the early **Hinayana Buddhism** and the later **Mahayana** schools were represented, see page 66. The Hinayana schools never introduced images into worship and therefore resisted also the development of temple forms which allowed and encouraged image worship. The early Buddhist monasteries had simply a stupa and a vihara for the monks to live in. Apsidal shrines were introduced later, possibly from the northwest. The **Gandharan sites** in modern Pakistan had innovations that clearly came before they were introduced at Nagarjunakonda – quadrangular monasteries, square or oblong image shrines, a pillared hall for the congregation, miniature stupas and a square platform for the stupa all appear to have come from the N W. The most striking development within Nagarjunakonda itself was that of the wheel-shaped plan of stupas. In doing so the architects transformed a Buddhist symbol into an architectural plan. Dr. John Marr suggests that this too may be a Gandharan development, as the Dharmarajika stupa at Taxila is so constructed, (see page 1111). The other development in Nagarjunakonda in stupa architecture was that of building *ayaka* platforms* at N, S, E and W, the cardinal directions. Each platform was designed to have five pillars symbolizing the five stages of the Buddha's life – Birth, Great Renunciation, Enlightenment, First Sermon and Extinction.

Another major feature of the Nagarjunakonda excavations was the discovery of some of India's finest early sculptures and memorial pillars. Over twenty pillars were raised in the memory not just of rulers and nobles but also of artisans and religious leaders. The sculptures represent the final phase of artistic development begun further E in the Krishna delta at Amaravati and Jaggayyapeta in the 2nd century BC. The first phase included carvings on drum slabs and a few memorial pillars. The Buddha was always represented by symbols – wheel, feet, column of fire, throne with a swastika and others. Later figures have much greater boldness, rhythm and clarity, and capture pathos, joy and sorrow. The major themes were all taken out of a dozen *Jataka** stories of Buddhist literature, but there were probably several different groups of sculptors at work.

Particularly striking is the fact that there was a significant amount of secular art. These, which include the carvings on memorial pillars, may relate simply to the deeds of an individual, and battle scenes are particularly popular. One shows an elephant with its rider, and the most vivid description of a battle is on three minutely carved pillars from Site 37.

The hill fort dates from the first part of the 14th century and has remnants of a quite different culture, that of the medieval kings of the Vijayanagar period. The ruins of the fort run the entire length of the hill. The main entrance was from the northeast, near where the ferry now lands on the island. In places the walls are still over 6 m high, with regular bastions and 6 gateways, and in all it covered nearly 4 sq km. There are two temples in the eastern part, where the museum now stands. After the foundation by the Reddi kings of Andhra, it was taken over by the Gajapatis of Orissa before falling to the Vijayanagar kings. The present layout of the fort probably dates from as recently as 1565, the year in which the Vijayanagar Empire was crushed at the Battle of Talikota. The earliest of the three temples remaining in the fort was probably built in the mid 14th century. Standing near the rebuilt Maha stupa, it was originally a Jain shrine, and was then converted to a Vaishnavite temple. The image of a Jain *Tirthankara** in black stone remains just outside the temple. There is another Jain Tirthankara near the bathing ghat, shown seated.

Museum Open from 0900. Closed on Fridays. Because the entire ancient site was covered by the waters of the Nagarjunasagar lake the remains visible today have largely had to be built on a new site. Most are around the museum on the northeast, now an island in the lake itself planted with low trees. The island is 11 km from Vijayapuri, and there are two ferries a day from the jetty there. The first ferry leaves at 0930, the second at 1330. Other ferries serve tours organised either from Hyderabad or locally by the APTTDC. Unlike many Indian museums there is a plan at the entrance.

There are several important and beautiful exhibits. They include beads, coins, relic caskets and a variety of ornaments, but the most important are the sculptures. A 3 metres high standing Buddha, put together from several fragments, is one of the few figures carved in the round. The are several panels and friezes depicting Buddhist scenes. The museum also contains prehistoric and protohistoric remains.

The ***Nagarjunasagar Dam*** Project is the largest on the Krishna River and one of the largest in India. Together with the other dams on the Krishna it will irrigate over 5 million hectares of land when the whole scheme is completed of which the Nagarjunasagar scheme alone contributes nearly 1 million hectares in the first phase. The dam itself is constructed out of stone masonry. The Government opted for this method of construction for two reasons. Although it would have taken several years less to build a concrete dam it would have involved the use of much more foreign exchange. It would also have created far less employment for labourers than the stone masonry method. Now completed, the scheme generates 400 MW of electricity, and nearly 800 km of canals lead irrigation water onto the fields below the dam. Two tunnels are said to be among the longest irrigation tunnels in the world. The Jawahar Canal (right bank) has an overall length of 12 km, while the Lal Bahadur Canal (left bank), is 3 km long with an internal diameter of 9 m. They are named after India's first two Prime Ministers.

Hotels There are no western style hotels but a variety of inexpensive, basic accommodation. **E** *Soundarya Tourist Annexe*, Hill Colony has 8 double rm which are a/c or air cooled and **F** *Vijaya Vihar Complex*, (APTTDC) has 8 a/c double rm. Reservations: Assistant Manager, T 69. **F** *The Project House* (APTTDC), T 3633. The ground floor has 25 rm, the upstairs has 18 rm which are cheaper. **F** *River View Rest House* On the right bank. There are also furnished cottages on Hill Colony which are a little more expensive and much cheaper cottages on the Right Bank.

Youth Hostel The *Youth Hostel* has 12 rm. Contact the Executive Engineer B & R Hill Colony T 2672, Residence 2635.

Restaurants *Vijaya Vihar Guest House* and a few others.

Banks and **Post Offices** at Hill Colony and Pylon (4 km). The **Tourist Office** is at the Andhra Pradesh Guest House, Hill Colony, T 3633 (Office), T 3634 (Residence). There is one guide available through this office. Others from the Hyderabad Tourist Office.

The largest of the State's Wildlife Sanctuaries is near Nagarjunasagar at **Srisailam Wildlife Sanctuary** (201 km from Hyderabad) which covers 5 neighbouring districts at an altitude of 200 m to 900 m. There are tiger, panther, wild dogs, civet, hyena, jackals, wolves, pangolins, giant squirrels, crocodiles, lizards, python, vipers, kraits and a rich variety of birds.

Srisailam also attracts visitors to its fort and temple with one of 12 **Jyotirlinga*** in the country which are special as they are believed to have been formed through divine power, **see page 334**. The ancient Bharamaramba – Mallikarjunasvami or **Mahakali Temple** on a hill rising from the Nallamalai forest contains the rare *lingam* which draws large crowds of pilgrims daily and especially at *Sivaratri*. The original temple is said to date from the 2nd century AD. The walls and gates have carvings depicting stories from the epics. Non-Hindus are allowed into the inner sanctuary to witness the daily puja ceremony conducted by the priests. It is a worthwhile experience and in order to avoid the long queue in the middle of the day, it is best to arrive early. The first prayers are at 0545!

En route to Guntur from Nagarjunakonda it is possible to take a short diversion to the other major Buddhist site of S India, **Amaravati**. This was the capital of the medieval Reddi kings of Andhra, but 1500 years before they wielded power a great Mahayana Buddhist centre (**see page 66**) had grown up on the site. Initially the shrine was dedicated to the Hinayana sect but under Nagarjuna was changed into a Mahayana sanctuary where the Buddha was revered as **Amareswara**.

The **Great Stupa** (Maha Chaitya), supposed to have been 32 m in height and 32 m diameter, was larger than that at Sanchi, **see page 317**, in modern Madhya Pradesh. Its origins go back to the 3rd-2nd centuries BC, though it was enlarged between the 1st and 4th centuries AD when the 5 m wide ambulatory path and 4.5 m high railings were added. The whole dome was faced with intricately carved marble slabs. At festival time, pilgrims circled the Stupa, carrying lamps which gave rise to its other name 'Deepadinne' (dome of light).

Today very little remains. Excavations began in 1797 and most of the magnificent sculpted friezes, medallions and railings have been removed, the majority to the museums at Madras (see Amaravati Gallery which has finds from excavations from 1797-1905) and Calcutta. Half of the finds went to the British Museum, London.

There is an **Archaeological Museum** on the site itself. This contains panels, mainly broken, railings and sculptures of the Bodhi Tree, *chakras* and caskets containing relics. Episodes from the life of the Buddha are common, and there are some free standing images of the Buddha. Some of the sculptures are exquisitely carved. Also galleries containing pottery, coins, bangles and terracotta. Apart from items excavated since 1905, there are some exhibits from other sites in the Krishna and Visakhaptnam Districts. Open daily 0900-1700 except Fri. Entry free. There is a *PWD Guest House*.

Vijayawada

Population 700,000, *Altitude* 20 m. *Climate* Temp. Summer Max. 41°C Min. 29°C, Winter Max. 30°C, Min. 20°C.

Standing at the head of the **Krishna delta** just over 70 km from the sea, the city is surrounded by bare, rounded granite hills. During the hot dry season these radiate heat, contributing to the considerable discomfort implied in Vijayawada's position of being one of India's hottest places. Temperatures of over 45°C are not uncommon in April and May. The Krishna cuts through a gap less than 1,200 m wide in the ridge of gneissic rocks, exposed as bare hills. This gap gave the opportunity to create the Krishna Delta canal scheme, one of the earliest major irrigation developments of the British period in S India, completed in 1855 and which now irrigates nearly a million ha. In the words of one Indian authority, K.L. Rao, "this banished famine from the delta and converted it into one of the richest granaries of the country". The dam (*anicut*) now known as the **Prakasam**

Barrage, over 1000 m long, carries the road and railways southwards.

The name of this ancient city, over 2,000 years old, is derived from the goddess Kanakdurga, the presiding deity of the city, also called Vijaya. There is a temple to her on a hill along the river. There are several sites with caves and temples with inscriptions from the 1st century AD. The **Mogalarajapuram Temple** has an *Ardhanarisvara** statue which is thought to be the earliest in S India. There are two 1,000 year old **Jain temples** and the **Hazratbal Mosque** which has a relic of the Prophet Mohammed.

The **Qutb Shahi** rulers made Vijayawada an important inland port. Today it has retained its importance as a trading and commercial town, and has capitalised on its position as the link between the interior and the main N-S route between Madras and Calcutta.

The **Victoria Jubilee Museum** contains a colossal granite statue of the Buddha, just one of the reminders that the site of the modern town was an important Buddhist religious centre even before the 7th century AD, when it was visited by Hiuen Tsang.

Hotels **D** *Kandhari International*, MG Rd. T 471311, Cable: Hotkan, Telex: 475-271. 73 rm all a/c. 22 km airport, 3 km rly, 1 km downtown. A/c restaurants, bar, coffee shop, travel, shops, TV. **D** *Mamata*, 45-15-478 Eluru Hotel opp Bus Stand. T 61251, Cable: Comfortstay. 59 rm, most a/c with bath. 20 km airport, 1 km rly, central. A/c restaurants (one roof top), bar, TV. The owners have alternative accommodation at the cheaper *Sri Durga Bhavan* which has 42 rm and a vegetarian restaurant. **D** *Manorama*, 27-38-61 Bander Rd, T 77221, Cable: Bliss. 69 rm, 19 a/c. 22 km airport, 2 km rly, central. A/c restaurants, exchange, car hire, shops, TV. **D** *Tilotthama*, nr Bus Stand, Governorpet. T 73201, Cable: Starhotel. 53 rm, some a/c with phone. Restaurant (vegetarian). Central. **E** *Chaya*, 27-8-1 Governorpet. T 61336, Cable: Hotel Chaya. 39 rm, 12 a/c with phone. 22 km, 1 km rly, nr downtown. Restaurants (S Indian vegetarian), travel. **E** *Sree Lakshmi Vilas*, Besant Rd, Governorpet. T 62525. 50 rm some with bath and phone. 18 km airport, 1 km rly, central. A/c restaurant.

There are several inexpensive hotels near the Bus Stand on Bandar Rd and a few near the Railway Station. The station has *Retiring Rooms* and a reasonable restaurant which opens at 0600. The Government *Guest Houses* are on Surya Rao Pet, T 61241 and on Bandar Rd – *Canal Guest House*, R & B Guest house and Zila Parishad Guest.

Restaurants Both *Hotel Kandhari* and *Mamata* have good multicuisine restaurants. In addition there is *Greenlands* at 40-17-191/1 Bhavani Gardens, Labbipet, T 73081 where you can dine out of doors in the Garden Restaurant with 7 huts set in lawns. Open 1100-1400, 1830-2300.

Banks There are several branches of banks. The *State Bank of India* is in Babu Rajendra Prasad Rd, T 63502.

Local Transport Tourist taxis, auto rickshaws, cycle rickshaws and tongas are available. Very few metred yellow-top taxis. Good network of city buses but overcrowded. Ferry service to Bhavani Islands from 0930 to 1730. Tourist Taxis can be hired from APTTDC, Krishnaveni Motel, Seethanagaram, T 75382.

Shopping Local Kondapalli toys and Machilipatnam Kalamkari paintings are especially popular. *Apco*, Besant Rd, *Aptex*, Andhra Pradesh Handlooms, Eluru Rd, *Handicrafts Shop*, Krishnavani Motel, *Lepakshi*, Gandhi Nagar.

Sports Water sports and boating. K L Rao Vihara Kendram, Bhavani Island on Prakasham Barrage Lake offers a variety of water sports including rowing, canoeing, water scooters, pedal boats to visitors. Open 0930-1830. Charges vary from Rs 5 to Rs 15. Contact Assistant Manager, Water Sports Unit, Krishnaveni Motel, T 75382.

Museums Victoria Jubilee Museum, Bandar Rd, T 64299. Collection includes sculpture and paintings. Open daily 1030-1700 except Fri. Entry free. Camera fee Rs 3.

Useful addresses *Foreigners' Regional Registration Office*, Superintendent of Police, Bandar Rd, T 77772.

Post and Telegraphs Head Post Office, Kaleswara Rao Rd, T 75645.

Tourist Office and Information is at Krishnaveni Motel, Sitanagaram, T 75382. Open

0600-2000. APTTDC counter at RTC Bus Stand, Machilipatnam Rd, T 61220.

Air Vayudoot Hyderabad Tue, Th, Sat, 1515 and 1745; Mon, Wed, Fri 1510; 1 hr. **Rajahmaundry** (1 hr) and **Vizag** (1 hr 25 min) Mon, Wed, Fri 1145; **Vizag** Tu, Th, Sat 1515 1 hr. **Tirupati** Tue, Th & Sat, 1205, 1 hr 10 min. Indian Airlines have an office opposite Old RTO Office, Bandar Rd, T 472218. Open 1000-1315, 1400-1700. Vayudoot, Smita World Travels, T 475020. Open 0930-1300, 1400-1800. Transfer by car between airport and city Rs 30.

Rail Vijayawada is an important junction and is connected to most major cities by express and superfast trains. **Bhubaneshwar**: *Coromandel Exp*, 2842 (AC/II), daily, 1520, 12 hr 40 min; *Konark Exp*, 2120 (AC/II), daily, 1900, 14 hr 10 min; **Calcutta (H)**: *Coromandel Exp*, 2842 (AC/II), daily, 1520, 20 hr 10 min; **Madras (MC)**: *Tamil Nadu Exp*, 2622 (AC/CC&AC/II), daily, 0110, 6 hr 40 min; or *Coromandel Exp*, 2841 (AC/II), daily, 1045, 6 hr 50 min; **Delhi (ND)**: *Tamil Nadu Exp*, 2621 (AC/CC&AC/II), daily, 0350, 26 hr 55 min; *Kerala Mangala Exp*, 2625 (AC/II), daily, 1035, 27 hr 55 min; **Secunderabad**: *Konarak Exp*, 2119 (AC/II), daily, 0845, 6 hr 25 min; **Hyderabad**: *E Coast Exp*, 8045, daily, 1200, 6 hr 55 min. Vijayawada Rly Station Enquiries, T 67771. Reservations, A/c and I Class, T 74302, II Class T 73555. Open 0800-1300, 1300-2000. Tokens issued 30 min earlier.

Road Linked to other regions by NH 5 and 9. Some distances – Bangalore 638 km, Bombay 1,012 km, Calcutta 1,193 km, Delhi 1,724 km, Hyderabad 270 km, Madras 444 km, Nagpur 679 km, Tirupati 380 km, Visakhapatnam 366 km. **Buses** Andhra Pradesh, Karnataka, Madhya Pradesh SRTC Buses offer Vijayawada a good service to and from cities in the three states. RTC Bus Stand, Machilipatnam Rd in the city centre, T 76988. Enquiries T 73333. Reservations open 0730-2100. **Ferry** Services between Krishnaveni Motel and Amaravati. Daily 0800. Fare Adult Rs 50, Child Rs 25. Reservations, AP Tourism, Krishnaveni Motel, Seethanagaram, T 75382 or Counter at RTC Bus Station.

Excursions 20 km out of Vijayawada, just N of the NH 9 to Hyderabad, is the famous toy-making centre in the village of **Kondapalli**. The toys are usually made of light wood and laquered in brilliant colours. Craftsmen can be seen working on carvings of human, animal and religious figures.

A rock temple close to the village of **Sitanagaram** and a five storeyed Brahman cave temple at **Undavali** were discovered in 1797. The upper storeys are set back, while the lowest storey has three rows of pillars partly cut out of the rock. They probably date from the same period as the Mamallapuram shore temples. One compartment has a shrine cell with an altar, another has a relief of Vishnu and his wives. There are friezes of geese, elephants and lions. The third storey has a hall over 15 metres by 10 metres, with a figure of **Vishnu** seated on the snake Ananta. Another shows **Narayana** on the snake Sesha. The top storey has barrel vaulted roofs. To reach the temple, cross the barrage going S out of Vijayawada, then turn right up the course of the river for nearly 3 km beyond and W of Sitanagaram.

VIJAYAWADA TO MADRAS

In Vijayawada the NH 9 joins the main Calcutta-Madras NH 5. It becomes much busier, and is slow moving, particularly around Vijayawada and Guntur and between Nellore and Madras in the S. It is about seven hours travelling by road to Madras. You can divert to Tirupati before completing the short journey to Madras.

From the approaches to Vijayawada southwards the landscape changes dramatically. The journey becomes extremely uncomfortable during the hot weather from early Mar, and in Oct-Nov the whole eastern coastline is subject to severe cyclones. **If you are travelling at that time of year check the weather forecasts**. The deltas and the flat coastal plains are fringed with palmyra palms and occasional coconut palms, rice and tobacco. Inland the often poor soils have sparse vegetation, and barely 40% of the surface area is cultivated. The coast itself is either fringed by mangroves or lined with wind blown dunes and casuarina trees. About 120 kilometres to the W of the road run the Vellikonda ranges, only visible in very clear weather, and in the southern sections of the route where they come closer to the coast.

From Vijayawada the road crosses the barrage (giving a magnificent view over the Krishna at sunset) to **Guntur** (32 km), a major commercial town (Population 400,000). It lies right at the junction of the ancient charnockite rocks of the Peninsula on its W and the alluvium of the coastal plain to the E. It is also a junction for the rail line crossing central Andhra Pradesh to Guntakal. In the 18th century it was important as the capital of the region known as the Northern Circars, and was under Muslim rule from 1766 subservient to the Nizam of Hyderabad. From 1759 onwards there remained French officers in his army.

Hotel: F *Railway Retiring Rooms*, single and double.

Train Secunderabad: *Golconda Exp*, 7201 (AC/CC), daily, 0525, 8 hr 10 min; **Calcutta via Vijayawada**: *Golconda Exp*, 7201 (AC/CC), daily, 0525, 55 min, change at Vijayawada (15 min wait), then *Howrah Mail*, 6004 (AC/II), daily, 0635, 15 hr 30 min (total time 16 hr 40 min); **Madras via Vijayawada** *Golconda Exp*, 7201 (AC/CC), daily, 0525, 55 min, change at Vijayawada (4 hr 5 min wait), then *Coromandel Exp*, 2841, daily, 1025, 7 hr 10 min (Total time 14 hr 10 min).

The road S through Ongole (113 km) and Kavali (60 km) to Nellore (53 km) runs across the stony lateritic coastal plain, often covered with thin scrub and occasional palmyra palms.

Nellore (population 175,000) is another administrative and commercial town. Along the roadside are some good S Indian restaurants – excellent coffee, dosai, idli and puris available in the mornings, meals at lunch time and in the evenings, near the bus stand.

Rail Madras (MC): *Bokaro-Madras Exp*, 8689, daily, 0456, 4 hr 9 min; or *Navjivan Exp*, 2641 (AC/II), Tue, Wed, Sat, Sun, 1405, 3 hr 10 min; **Vijayawada**: *Navjivan Exp*, 2642 (AC/II), Mon, Wed, Th, Sun, 1310, 4 hr; **Secunderabad**: *Charminar Exp*, 6059 (AC/II), daily, 2127, 10 hr 28 min.

The NH 5 continues S through **Gudur** (27 km) to **Naidupet** (27 km) where it is possible to take a diversion to **Sri Kalahasti** (27 km) and **Tirupati** (27 km). Even though the border between Telugu speaking and Tamil areas is only 35 km from Madras the influence of the city begins to be noticeable well before that. The main road to Madras goes through Gudumallam, Puttur and Arani.

The world-famous Sri Venkatesvara temple of Tirumalai is built in the Dravida style, as are those of **Sri Kalahasti** (or **Kalahasti**). Sri Kalahasti is very attractively sited on the banks of the Svarnamukhi River at the foot of the extreme southern end **Vellikonda Ranges**, known locally as the Kailasa Hills. The Kalahastishvara Temple dominates the town with its gopuram facing the river. The town and temple developed largely as a result of the patronage of the Vijayanagar kings, and the **Kalahastisvara Temple** was built in the 16th and 17th centuries.

The magnificent detached gopuram was built by the Vijayanagar emperor Krishnadeva Raya. Although it does not compare with the neighbouring centre of Tirumalai, it is still a considerable pilgrimage town. The bathing ghats of the Swarnamukhi (golden) river and the temple have a steady flow of pilgrims, but in addition to its function as a pilgrim centre the town is known throughout S India for its production of *Kalamkaris*, the brightly coloured hand painted textiles used as temple decoration. There are fine examples in the Salar Jung Museum in Hyderabad, **see page 905**.

The temple is set within four high walls with a single entrance in the S wall. The temple is particularly revered for the white stone Siva lingam in the western shrine, believed to be worshipped by *kala* (King Cobra) and *Hasti* (Elephant). The Nayaka style is typified by the columns carved into the shape of rearing animals and the riders. The temple to the Wind God *Vayudeva* is the only one of its kind in India. A further 27 km from Sri Kalahasti is Tirupati.

Tirupati *Population* 151,000. *Altitude* 152 m. **Tirumalai** *Population* 28,000.

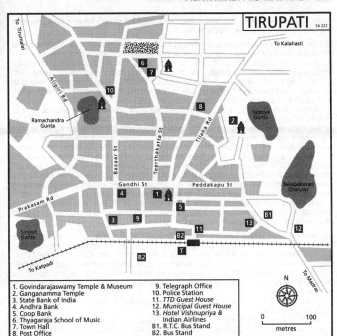

TIRUPATI SA 222

To Tirumalai

To Kalahasti

Alipiri Rd

Ramachandra
Gunta

Bazaar St

Teerthakatta St

Tilaka Rd

Tatayya
Gunta

Gandhi St

Peddakapu St

Tallapakaram
Cheruvu

Prakasam Rd

Singeri
Gunta

To Katpadi

To Madras

N

0   100
metres

1. Govindarajaswamy Temple & Museum	9. Telegraph Office
2. Ganganamma Temple	10. Police Station
3. State Bank of India	11. TTD Guest House
4. Andhra Bank	12. Municipal Guest House
5. Coop Bank	13. Hotel Vishnupriya &
6. Thyagaraja School of Music	Indian Airlines
7. Town Hall	B1. R.T.C. Bus Stand
8. Post Office	B2. Bus Stand

Altitude 860 m. *Climate* Temp. Summer Max. 40°C, Min. 22°C, Winter Max. 32°C Min. 15°C. Annual rainfall 71 cm, mainly Oct-Dec.

The Tirumalai Hills provide a picture-book setting for the famous temple here. The main town of **Tirupati** lies at the bottom of the hill where there are several temples, some centres of pilgrimage in their own right. The seven hills are compared to the seven headed Serpent God Adidesha who protects the sleeping Vishnu under his hood.

Local festivals Numerous festivals throughout the year. Most important is the *Brahmotsavam* in Sept, especially grand every third year when it is called *Navarathri Brahmotsavam*. On the third day the Temple Car Festival *Rathotsavam* is particularly popular.

Places of interest The main destination of pilgrims, the *Sri Venkatesvara Temple*, is in *Tirumalai* 22 km away at the top of the ghat road. In the N the temple complex is called Balaji and in the S, Srinivasa Perumalai. Pilgrims usually walk up the wooded slope to the top of the hill 700 m up above the plains through mango groves and sandal wood forest chanting "Om namo Venkatesaya" or "Govinda, Govinda". There is, however, a road that runs all the way and there is a bus stand at the top of the hill.

Of all India's temples, this draws the largest number of pilgrims and some sort of order is maintained by providing 'Q sheds' under which pilgrims assemble. Two types of queues for *Darshan** or special viewing are allowed. 'Sarvadarsan' is open to all while 'Special darshan' is offered to those paying Rs 25 who are allowed to join a separate shorter queue. The actual *darshan* itself lasts a precious second and a half even though the 'day' at the temple lasts 21 hr. Every day is festival day with shops remaining open 24 hr. Sri Venkatesvara's image is widely seen across S India, in private homes, cars and taxis and in public places, and is instantly recognisable from its black face and covered eyes, shielded so that the deity's piercing gaze may not blind any who look directly at him.

Architecturally the temple is unremarkable, but in other respects is extraordinary. The temple is probably the wealthiest in India, and the **devasthanam*** (or temple trust) now sponsor a huge range of activities, from the Sri Venkatesvara University at Tirupati to hospitals, orphanages and schools. The temple's wealth comes largely from its pilgrims, on average over 10,000 a day but at major festivals many times that number. All pilgrims will make gifts to the temple, and the **hundi*** (offering) box in front of the shrine is stuffed full with notes, gold ornaments and other gifts.

Another important source of income is the **haircutting service**. Many pilgrims come to Tirupati to seek a special favour – to seek a suitable wife or husband, to have a child, to recover from illness – and it is regarded as auspicious to grow the hair long and then to offer the hair as a sacrifice. You may see many pilgrims fully shaven at the temple when appearing before the deity. Lines of barbers wait for arriving pilgrims in order to shave their heads. Notice how when coaches unload their pilgrims one barber will line up customers and shave one strip of hair off as many heads as possible in order to maximise the number of customers committed to him before he returns and finishes off the job! The custom has had an unexpected commercial spin off. The hair is collected, washed and softened before being exported to the American and Japanese markets for wig making.

Another custom at the temple is the anointing of the deity's body with camphor, saffron and musk. The holy **prasadam*** or consecrated sweet is distributed to around 50,000 pilgrims on an ordinary day, and many more for a festival.

The deity is Sri Venkatesvara, a form of Vishnu. Theoretically the inner shrines of the Tirumalai temple are open only to Hindus. However, foreigners may be invited to sign a form stating that they are Hindus, and if they are willing to do that they are allowed in. The Tourist Information publicity leaflet states that "All are welcome. The temple welcomes all devotees regardless of formal religions. The only criterion for admission is faith in God and respect for the temple's conventions and rituals". The Venkatesvara Temple dates from the 10th century, with later additions. The atmosphere is unlike any other temple in India. Turnstiles control the flow of pilgrims into the main temple complex, which is through an intricately carved gopuram on the E wall.

Much of the gopuram is rebuilt. There are three enclosures. The first, where there are portrait sculptures of the **Vijayanagar** patrons, including Krishnadeva Raya and his queen and a gold covered pillar and the *vahanas or* sacred 'vehicles'. Several rituals are performed daily. The outer colonnades are Vijayanagar; the gateway leading to the inner enclosure may be of **Chola** origin. The second enclosure has more shrines, a sacred well and the kitchen. The inner enclosure is opened only once every year. The main temple and shrine is on the W side of the inner enclosure.

The sanctuary, which dates from the 9th-10th centuries, has a domed *vimana* entirely covered with gold plate which is known as 'Ananda Nilayam' and there are gold covered gates that guard the sanctum sanctorum. The image in the shrine is a standing Vishnu, richly ornamented with gold and jewels. The 2 m high image stands on a lotus, two of his four arms carry a conch shell and a *chakra* or discus and he wears a diamond crown which is said to be the most precious single ornament in the world. It is flanked by *Sridevi* and *Bhudevi*, Vishnu's consorts. There is a small **museum** with a collection of stone, metal and wooden images (see below).

Just a kilometre away there are strange rock formations in a naturally formed arch which is thought to have been the source of the idol in the temple. You can see shapes resembling a hood of a serpent, a conch and a discus. There is a sacred waterfall **Akasa Ganga** 3 km S of the temple. The Papa Vinasanam Dam is 5 km N. **Chandragiri** (11 km) was the last capital during the last days of the Vijayanagaras. The fort was built on a 180 m high rock where you can still see the well preserved fortifications and some palaces and temples. Visit the Rani Mahal and Raja Mahal with its pretty lily pond.

In Tirupati itself the **Govindarajasvami Temple**, dating from the 16th and 17th centuries, is the most widely visited. Built by the Nayakas, the successors to the Vijayanagar Empire in the extreme S after its defeat in N Karnataka in 1565, the temple has an impressive outer gopuram, though the temple as a whole can't be seen from the nearby streets. Of the three gopurams the innermost is also the earliest, dating from the 14th-15th centuries. The main sanctuaries are dedicated to Vishnu and Krishna. The other temple is **Kapilesvarasvami** in a very attractive setting has a sacred waterfall.

Local crafts Copper and brass idols are produced at **Perumallapalli** Village 8 km away. Wooden toy making are also a local industry.

Hotels The thousands of pilgrims are usually housed in well maintained Temple Trust's *choultries* which can accommodate about 20,000. They vary from Luxury suites, well-furnished cottages, dormitories to unfurnished accommodation some of which is free. Contact PRO, TT Devasthanams, T 2753 or Reception Officer 1, T 2571. The TTD *New Guest House, Travellers' Bungalow, Modi Bhavan, Shriniketan, India, Balakuteeram, Padmavati, Gokulam Guest Houses* are graded as Deluxe. The private hotels here are Indian style, usually with vegetarian restaurants. You will find a number around the Central Bus Station, on Govindraja Car St and in the TP Area.

D *Mayura*, 209 TP Area, T 20901, Cable: Kamath. 65 rm, some a/c with phone. Restaurant (S Indian vegetarian), exchange, travel, TV. **D** *Sri Oorvasi International*, Renigunta Rd. T 20202, Cable: Oorvasi. 78 rm, some a/c with TV. 12 km airport, 1 km rly. Restaurant (vegetarian), travel, indoor games. **D** *Vishnu Priya*, opp APSRTC Central Bus Stand. T 20300, Cable: Srivish, Telex: 0403-246 Hsvp In. 134 rm, some a/c double. Restaurants, travel (Indian Airlines office), exchange, shops, TV. **D** *Bhimas Deluxe*, Govindraja Car St. T 20121, Cable: Kayarvee. 60 rm, 30 a/c double. 15 km airport, close to rly station and downtown. A/c restaurant (N and S Indian), car hire, TV. **D** *Bhimas*, 42 Govindraja Car St. T 20766, Cable: Bhimas. 40 rm, some a/c. 14 km airport, close to rly, Central. Restaurant (S Indian vegetarian), roof garden, sweet stall.

Restaurants at the better hotels are reasonable. Outside hotels the vegetarian restaurants *Laxmi Narayan Bhawan* and *Hotel Dwarka*, opp RTC Bus Stand and the *Konark Bar and Restaurant* on Rly Station Rd and *New Triveni Bar and Restaurant*, 139 TP Area have been recommended. The Tirupathi- Tirumalai Devasthanams Trust (TTD) provides free vegetarian meals at its guest houses. In Tirumalai particularly, the Trust prohibits non-vegetarian food, alcohol and smoking. Near the TTD Canteen and the APSRTC Bus Stand there is an *Indian Coffee House* and a *Tea Board Restaurant*. There is also a Woodlands Restaurant in the TB Area.

Banks Most of the banks are on Gandhi Rd. *State Bank of India* opp AP State Road Transport Corporation, T 20268.

Shopping The brass and copper idols and utensils for which the area is famous and also wooden toys can be bought at the Handicrafts Emporia *Poompuhar* (Tamil Nadu) on Gandhi Rd and *Lepakshi* (Andhra Pradesh) in the TP Area.

Local transport Tourist Taxis from the Bus Stand and Rly Station. Taxi sharing is common between Tirupati and Tirumalai and can cost about Rs 25 per person. Auto rickshaws point to point fares fixed and displayed. Cycle rickshaws, fares negotiable.

APSRTC Bus Service between Tirupati and Tirumalai every three minutes from 0330 to 2200. the Padmavati Bus Stand, opp Rly Station for passengers with through tickets to Tirumalai and the Sri Venkateswara Bus Stand in TP Area. Enquiries: Padmawati Bus Stand, 3rd Choultry, T 20132 and Sri Venkateswara Bus Stand, TP Area, T 20203. Long queues for buses but buying a return ticket from Tirupati saves time at the ticket queue (past the Rly foot bridge). The journey is up the slow winding hill road and takes about 45 min.

Museums At Tirupati, the TTD **Sri Venkateswara Museum** of Temple art at the Sri Govindraja Swamy Temple compound. Open 0800-2000. Entry Re 1, Child Re 0.50. at the entrance to the temple in Tirumalai has among other exhibits an interesting collection of Indian musical instruments. Open daily 0800-2000. Entry Re 1. Sri Venkateswara University Oriental Research Institute. Collection includes images of stone, wood and metal, pottery, coins, inscriptions. Open 1000-1630. Entry free.

At Tirumalai a small museum, **Hall of Antiquities**, opp Sri Venkateswara Temple. Open 0800-2000. Entry Re 1, Child Re 0.50.

Useful addresses *Foreigners' Regional Registration Office*, Inspector Intelligence, 499 Reddy Colony, T 20503.

Tourist Offices and Information *AP Tourism Regional Tourist Information Bureau*, 139 TP Area, T 23208. *AP Government State Information Centre*, Govindraja Car St, T 4818. *TTD Information Centres,* 1 New Chowltry, T 22777 and also at Rly Station and Airport.

Tours *AP Travel and Tourism Development Corporation* (APTTDC), Rm 15, Srinivasa Chowltry, T 20602. Local sightseeing Tour starts at the APSRTC Central Bus Stand at 1000.

Fare Rs 30. Tirupati, Kalahasti, Tiruchanur, Chandragiri and Srinivasamangapuram.

Air Vayudoot Madras Mon-Sat, 1425, 35 min; **Vijayawada** Tues, Thur & Sat, 1345, 1 hr 10 min; **Hyderabad** Mon, Wed & Fri (+ 1 other), Tues, Thur & Sat, 1345, 1 hr 30 min. **Indian Airlines**, Hotel Vishnupriya opp Central Bus Stand, T 22349. Open 1000-1730. Vayudoot Agents, Travel Express, 10 SV Guest House, Tirupati, T 22030, Telex: 0403-223. Airport, T 5493. Open 0900-1730. Also at 302D SNC opp Central Reception Office, T 7212. Tirupati Airport is 15 km from the city centre. RTC coach between airport and Tirupati (Rs 7) and Tirumalai (Rs 13).

Rail Good rail links with rest of the region. Broad gauge trains: **Madras (MC)**: *Tirupati-Madras Mail*, 6054, daily, 1025, 3 hr 20 min; **Hyderabad**: *Rayalaseema Exp*, 7430 (AC/II), daily, 1530, 16 hr 30 min; **Bombay (VT) via Madras (MC)**: *Saptagiri Exp*, 6058, daily, 1810, 3 hr 25 min, change at Madras (45 min wait), then *Madras-Bombay Mail*, 7010 (AC/II), daily, 2220, 30 hr 30 min, (total time = 34 hr 40 min); **Guntakal**: *Rayalaseema Exp*, 7430 (AC/II), daily, 1530, 7 hr 23 min.

Road Tirupati is on the NH 4 (Madras – Bangalore – Bombay) and NH5 (Madras – Bhubaneswar – Calcutta) which provide good links with other parts of the region and the country. Some distances to major towns: Bangalore 247 km, Hyderabad 617 km, Madras 172 km, Trivandrum 675 km and Bombay 1,245 km and Calcutta 1,690 km further afield. The State Road Transport Corporations of Andhra Pradesh, Tamil Nadu and Karnataka connect Tirupati with other cities in the neighbouring states. APSRTC, Central Bus Stand Enquiries T 22333.

VIJAYAWADA TO VISAKHAPATNAM AND BHUBANESHWAR

From Vijayawada the NH 5 crosses the lush and fertile delta of the Krishna and Godavari. Rice is the dominant crop, though sugar cane is also important as a cash crop. Travelling NE the road crosses the broad plain to Rajahmundry and then the narrowing coastal plain with the beautiful hills of the Eastern Ghats rising sharply inland.

The whole pattern of life contrasts sharply with that of the S. Higher rainfall and a longer wet season, alongside the greater fertility of the alluvial soils, contribute to an air of prosperity. Village house styles are quite different. Even thatched roofed cottages, often with white painted walls, look comparatively prosperous. Going N E towards Orissa distinctive house types are matched by equally distinctive bullock carts, and the canals of the delta have their own economic and social role, visible in their importance as avenues of boat traffic.

  The distinctiveness of this area applies too to its history. It was brought under Muslim rule by the Golconda kings of the **Bahmani Sultanate** in 1575 and ceded to the French in 1753. In 1765 the Mughal Emperor granted the whole area to the **East India Company**, its first major territorial acquisition in India. The region is also the most urbanised part of Andhra Pradesh, with a string of a dozen towns with more than 100,000 people. Most are commercial and administrative centres with neither the functions nor the appearance of industrial cities, but they serve as important regional centres for trade, especially in agricultural commodities, and they are the homes of some of the wealthiest and most powerful families in Andhra.

Although the building of dams on both the Krishna and the Godavari has eliminated the problem of catastrophic flooding which often devastated the otherwise fertile fields until the mid-19th century, it has proved much more difficult to provide protection against *cyclones*. In 1864 a cyclone claimed over 34,000 lives. The totally flat delta, lying virtually at sea level, suffered another major natural catastrophe in 1883 when the volcano of Mount Krakatoa blew up 5000 km away it was completely engulfed by a tidal wave. In 1977 a cyclone just E of Vijayawada resulted in over 25,000 deaths, and there have been disasters on a smaller scale since. **From a practical point of view it is essential to read the weather forecasts if you are travelling along the coast between October and December.** You may notice the increasing number of small concrete buildings on raised platforms along the roadside designed to give temporary shelter to villagers during cyclones.

For much of the way to *Eluru* (63 km; population 160,000) the road runs sandwiched between the Kommanur canal on the right and the railway on the left. The canal is part of the coastal canal system that stretches all the way down to the southern end of the Buckingham Canal 100 km S of Madras. Eluru is a trading and administrative centre with little by way of industry apart from carpet making. The nearby Kolleru Lake has been a site visited by migrating water birds for many years and is now a sanctuary.

Rajahmundry (67 km population 340,000) was the capital of the Eastern Chalukyas. It was captured by the Muslims from the Vengi kings in 1471. Returned to the Orissan kingdom in 1512 it was retaken by the Deccan Muslims in 1571 and was the scene of repeated bitter hostilities until being granted to the French in 1753. It is remembered for the poet Nannayya who wrote the first Telugu classic 'Andhra Mahabharathamu'. Every twelve years the Pushkaram celebration is held by the river bank. The **Markandaya** and **Kotilingeswara Temples** on the river bank draw pilgrims.

There are several other Eastern Chalukya temples in the area but Rajahmundry is more noted for its carpets and sandalwood products and also because it is convenient to visit the coastal districts from here.

It is one of two points along this route where you can divert towards the hills of the Eastern Ghats. 80 km northwest of the town the Godavari cuts through a gorge and there is a succession of stunningly beautiful lakes, as Murray's guide suggested many years ago, reminiscent of Scottish lochs rather than India. You can take boat trips on the lakes.

Museum Sri Rallabandi Subbarao Government Museum, Godavari Bund Rd. Open 1030-1700. Closed Fri and AP Government holidays. Entry free. Collection of coins, sculpture, pottery, palm leaf manuscripts and inscriptions. Photography with permission. **Sri RSR Government Museum**, Ullithota St. Collection of Archaeological material and sculpture. Open 1030-1700. Closed Fri and Bank holidays. Camera fee Rs 3.

Rail Vijayawada: *Coromandel Exp*, 2841 (AC/II), daily, 0747, 2 hr 38 min; *Guwahati-Trivandrum Exp*, 2602 (AC/II), Tue, 1825, 2 hr 25 min; **Calcutta (H)**: *Coromandel Exp*, 2842 (AC/II), daily, 1750, 17 hr 40 min; **Visakhapatnam**: *Coromandel Exp*, 2842 (AC/II), daily, 1750, 3 hr 20 min; or *Haora Mail*, 6004 (AC/II), daily, 0935, 3 hr 55 min; or *E Coast Exp*, 8046, daily, 1645, 3 hr 45 min.

Excursions 15 km E of Rajahmundry is the small 10th century Chalukyan temple of **Samalkot**. It is unusual, being arranged on two levels. A two storey tower with a dome roof rises above the roof. There is no sculpture on the walls but some of the columns have figures.

The NH 5 passes through *Jaggampetta* (48 km), Thamayapeta (32 km), to *Talapalem* (99 km), the road being increasingly hedged in by the hills. The scenery is often outstandingly attractive, with the flat-floored valleys, planted with rice, surrounded by steep hills. The road finally passes through low hills into the very rapidly growing industrial port of Visakhapatnam (49 km).

Visakhapatnam

Population 800,000. *Altitude* sea level. *Climate* Temp. Summer Max. 34°C Min. 21°C, Winter Max. 28°C Min. 19°C. Annual rainfall 125 cm.

	Jan	Feb	Mar	Apr	May	Jun	Jul	Aug	Sep	Oct	Nov	Dec	Av/Tot
Max (°C)	28	29	31	33	34	34	32	32	32	31	29	28	31
Min (°C)	17	19	23	26	28	27	26	26	26	25	21	18	24
Rain (mm)	7	15	9	13	53	88	122	132	167	259	91	17	973

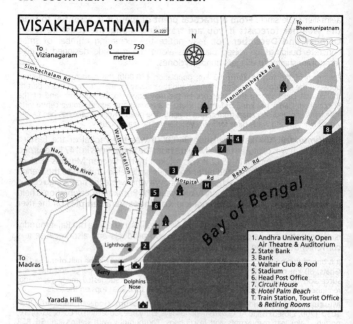

VISAKHAPATNAM SA 220

To Bheemunipatnam
N
To Vizianagaram
Simhachalam Rd
0   750
metres
Waltair Station Rd
Hanumanthayaka Rd
Narayagedda River
Hospital Rd
Beach Rd
Bay of Bengal
T
Lighthouse
To Madras
Ferry
Dolphins Nose
Yarada Hills

1. Andhra University, Open Air Theatre & Auditorium
2. State Bank
3. Bank
4. Waltair Club & Pool
5. Stadium
6. Head Post Office
7. *Circuit House*
8. *Hotel Palm Beach*
T. Train Station, Tourist Office & *Retiring Rooms*

Set in a bay with rocky promontories, "*Vizag*" has become one of India's most rapidly growing cities. It is already India's 4th largest port, and in addition to its role as Eastern Headquarters of the Indian Navy it has developed ship building, oil refining, fertiliser, petrochemical, sugar refinery and jute industries as well as one of India's newest and largest steel mills. On the Dolphin's Nose, a cliff rising 174 m from the sea, is a lighthouse whose beam can be seen 64 km out to sea. The airport is 12 km from the centre.

Its twin town of **Waltair** to the N used to be thought of as a health resort with fine beaches, though increasing atmospheric pollution may be taking its toll of that reputation. The good beaches are Ramakrishna Beach, along the 8 km Lawson's Bay and below 300 m Mt Kailasa 6 km away.

Places of interest The **Andhra University** founded in 1926 is in the Uplands area of Waltair. The red stone buildings are built like a fortress and are well laid out on a large campus. The country's major **Ship Building Yard** at Gandhigram makes all types of ocean going vessels – passenger liners, cargo vessels as well naval ships. The **Zoo** is large and attempts to avoid cages, keeping its animals in enclosures which are close to their natural habitat.

Each of the three hills here is sacred to a different religion. The Hindu Venkateswara temple on the the Venkateswa Konda was built in 1866 by the European Captain Blackmoor. The Muslims have a mausoleum of the saint Baba Ishaq Madina on the Darga Konda, while the highest Rose Hill has a Roman Catholic Church. A Buddhist relic was discovered at **Dhanipura** nearby.

Hotels C *Park*, Beach Rd. T 63081, Cable: Parkotel, Telex: 0495-230. 64 rm. 4 km rly. Central a/c. Restaurant, bar, exchange, travel, bookshop, pool, TV. Recommended beach side hotel. **C** *Dolphin*, Dabagardens. T 64811, Cable: Dolphin, Telex: 0495-316. 147 rm. 2 km rly, central location. Central a/c. Restaurants (one roof-top), bar, exchange, travel, shops, pool, TV.

Recommended. **C** *Sea Pearl*, Beach Rd. T 64371, Cable: Coho, Telex: 0495-395 Sea In. 42 rm, all sea facing. 4 km rly, 2 km centre. Central a/c. Restaurant, bar, travel, TV.

D *Apsara*, 12-1-17 Waltair Main Rd. T 64861, Cable: Apsara, Telex: 0495-404. 130 rm. 14 km airport, 2 km rly, central. Central a/c. Restaurants, bar, 24 coffee shop, exchange, travel, shops, health club, childrens' play area, TV. **D** *Palm Beach*, Beach Rd. T 63006, Cable: Palmbeach, Telex: 0495-436. 34 rm, 27 a/c. 4 km rly, 3 km central. Restaurant, beer garden, pool. **D** *Daspalla*, Suryabagh. T 63141, Cable: Daspalla, Telex: 0495-503. 72 rm. 3 km rly, downtown. Central a/c. 2 good restaurants (one serving good range of western dishes, the other, Indian, for thali meals), bar, exchange, travel, TV. Excellent rm service, helpful staff, recommended. **D** *Ocean View Inn*, Kirlampudi, T 54828, Cable: Oceanview, Telex: 0495-388. 30 rm, some a/c rm with TV. 30 rm, some a/c. 3 km rly, 4 km centre. A/c restaurant, car hire, TV. Clean and comfortable. In good location at the northern end of the beach. **E** *Lakshmi*, next to St Joseph's Hospital, Maryland, 10 rm a/c, some with bath and TV. Newly opened, clean and welcoming. Good Indian restaurant. **E** *Saga Lodge*, off Hospital Rd towards beach. Rm with balcony, some with bath and seaview. No restaurant but very good rm service. Recommended.

E *Virat*, Indira Gandhi Stadium Rd, Old Bus Stand. T 64821, Cable: Hotvik, Telex: 0495-367. 42 rm, some a/c, bath and TV in all rm. 2 km rly, central. A/c restaurant and bar, exchange and travel. The Bus Station has good **E** *Retiring Rooms*. The Rly Station has a *Rest House*.

Restaurants Most have bars and serve veg and non-veg food. Outside hotels, there are some on Station Rd, *Diwanjee*, *Imperial* and *Golden Phoenix*, others in Surya Bagh – *Sky Room*, *Black Dog* (nr Jagdamba Theatre) and several in Dabagardens – *Omst Khayyam*, *The Pink Elephant* and *Shangrila*. *Delight* is on Beach Rd and *Blue Diamond* opp RTC.

Banks Most national banks have branches. *State Bank of India* is at Old Post Office, T 62697. Several on Surya Bagh.

Shopping The main areas are Jagadamba Jn and Waltair Uplands, Main Rd. The AP Government Emporium *Lepakshi* is on Hospital Down Rd and *UP Handlooms* in the Saraswati Centre.

Local transport You can hire Tourist taxis at the airport, rly station or from hotels. *Auto rickshaws* are very common but cycle rickshaws are also available in the centre. Rates negotiable for all.

Ferry runs from 0800-1700 between the Harbour and Yarada Hills. You can take one to visit the Dolphin Lighthouse.

Sports Swimming pools in some hotels are open to non-residents. *Hotel Park* charges Rs 40 per day and *Palm Beach* Rs 20 for 2 hr. Waltair Club also has a pool. Roller skating at VUDA Park nr Park Hotel where you can hire skates.

Entertainment *Andhra University* has an open-air theatre and two other auditoria at Waltair, T 63324. *Gurjada Kala Mandir* nr Collector's Office and *Samba Murti Kala Mandir* in Port Grounds stage live performances. Check newspapers for films at local cinemas.

Useful addresses *Foreigners' Regional Registration Office*, SP Police, T 62709.

Post and telegraph *Head Post Office*, Vellum Peta, T 63554. Also at Waltair Rly Station, T 63436.

Places of worship *Hindu* – Sri Venkateswara Temple, Harbour, Pandurangasvami Temple, Beach Rd, Sai Baba Temple, Sitamamdhara. *Muslim* – Mosque, Darga Konda. *Christian* – St Anthony's Church, Waltair Main Rd, St Joseph's Church, I Town, Union Chapel, Waltair Uplands. *Sikh* – Gurdwara at Sitampetta.

Hospitals and medical services Seven Hills Hospital, Rockdale Layout, T 63081. King George Hospital, Hospital Rd, Maharani Peta, T 64891. St Joseph's Hospital, Maryland, T 62974.

Tourist office and information *Andhra Pradesh Regional Tourist Information Bureau*, Hotel Apsara Arcade, Waltair Main Rd, T 63016. Open 1000-1700, closed Sun and 2nd Sat. *AP Tourism Information Counter*, Visakhapatnam Railway Station which is near the city centre. Transport Unit, 8 RTC Complex, Dwarka Nagar, T 61985.

Air Indian Airlines Hyderabad Mon, Tues, Thur, Fri & Sun, 1135, 1 hr; *Calcutta* Mon (+ 1 other), 0825, 1 hr 20 min; *Madras* Mon, Tues, Thur & Sat, 0920, 1 hr 5 min; Indian Airlines, LIC Building, T 62673. Open 1000-1300, 1345-1700. **Vayudoot** *Rajahmundry, Vijayawada and Hyderabad* (40 min; 1 hr 40 min and 2 hr 40 min) Mon, Wed, Fri 1330;

Vijayawada and Hyderabad (1 hr and 2 hr 15 min) Tu, Thur, Sat. Vayudoot Agents, Frontline Travel, Shop No 1, Udyog Bhavan, VUDA Complex, T 54333. Open 0930-1730. Branch at Gajuwaka, T 57093. Airport is 12 km from city centre. You can get a taxi or a auto rickshaw into town. Approx fare Rs 80 for a taxi.

Rail Well connected by broad gauge line Express and Superfast trains to other parts of the country as it is on the main route between Calcutta and Madras. **Calcutta (H):** *Coromandel Exp* (Calcutta – Madras) 13 hr, *Madras Mail* 17 hr. *Irupati Exp Haora – Bangalore Exp, Guwahati – Trivandrum Exp* **Hyderabad** *Godavari Exp* 12 hr, *E Coast Exp* (Calcutta – Hyderabad) *Konark Exp* (Bhubaneswar – Secunderabad). Connections to Bombay at Hyderabad and Nagpur. Railway Enquiries, T 69421: Reservations T 63555. Open 0900-1300, 1400-1700. City Railway Extension Counter at Turner's Chowltry for reservations.

Road Good road network through NH 5. Distances – Bangalore 1,004 km, Bombay 1,376 km, Calcutta 879 km, Delhi 1,861 km, Hyderabad 638 km, Madras 799 km, Puri 442 km.

Bus The new bus station is well organised. APSRTC run services to main towns in the state including Rajahmundry, Srikakulam, Araku Valley, Kakinda, Rajahmundry, Vijayawada and Hyderabad and also to Puri and Bhubaneswar. APSRTC Enquiries, T 65038. Reservations open 0600-2000.

Ship Occasional service to Port Blair in the Andaman Islands. Announcements in the press but sometimes giving short notice.

Excursions *Simhachalam* (16 km) is the hilly site of several Chola temples among them the temple to Vishnu (originally a Siva shrine) has an image of the deity in the form combining a lion and a boar giving rise to the name. Devotees celebrate the cleansing of the sandalwood paste that is applied to the deity in a ceremony of *Chandan Visarjan* in Apr/May. The temple also has a finely carved horse-drawn stone chariot.

Bhimunipatnam (24 km) at the mouth of the river Gostani, is a popular beach resort, which unlike some other coastal spots is safe from sharks and not steeply shelved. The old Dutch East India Company settlement Vallanda Bhoomi, known as Hollanders' Green, has ruins of a fort, armoury and cemetery among banana plantations and palm groves. A simple *Guest House* provides accommodation.

The densely wooded Chintapalli forest, at an altitude of 1680 m is the highest point in Andhra and is rich in bird life. A large number of migratory waterbirds can be seen between October and November on the vast lake at Kondakarla Ava, 48 km away. At *Sankaram* (45 km) are the *Kotilingams* or ten million lingams, which are natural rock pinnacles which between 300 BC and AD 700 were turned into Buddhist stupas, caves and monasteries.

Vizianagaram to the N has a huge Vijayanagara fort. *Srikakulam* (68 km) which was the capital of the Kalingas in the 2nd century has an old temple where the Vijayanagara king Krishna Deva Raya was inspired in a dream when visiting it in 1509, to write down his memoirs. This resulted in the Telugu classic 'Amakutamalyada'.

To reach *Anantagiri* (85 km) you travel on scenic Ghat roads which rise and fall through coffee plantations, mango groves, water falls and mountain streams. The Ghat rail line is one of the highest broad gauge routes in the world. The area of limestone hills is rich in mica, and you can see impressive stalactite and stalagmites at the Burrah Caves (90 km) reached by a bridle path. The *Araku Valley* (115 km) which is inhabited by some seventeen tribal groups in about 70 villages is an area of grassland which rises from 1,000 to 1,300 m. The tribes still keep their traditions alive with ancestor worship, folk dances (*Dhimsa*, their most colourful) and hunting festivals (*Itika Pongal* in April). It is a beautiful drive, off the beaten track and far quieter than many Indian roads, with gentle scenery.

The road N to the Orissa border goes through **Chittivalasa** (30 km), **Narsannapet** (24 km) and **Tekkali** (29 km).

LAKSHADWEEP, MINICOY & AMINDIVI ISLANDS

Population 50,000 *Altitude* Sea level *Climate* Temp Summer Max.
35°C Min. 25°C, Winter Max. 32°C Min 20°C. Annual rainfall 160 cm.
Agatti is the airport which has flights from Cochin.
The archipelago comprises 22 coral islands and 5 islets off the Kerala
coast, spread across about 32 sq km and but only half of these are
fairly densely populated, although there are fishing stations on some
of the uninhabited ones. The islands are long, stretching N to S, with
lagoons to the W and beaches on the E. Androth, the island closest
to the mainland, is 235 km from Calicut.

INTRODUCTION

Entry regulations

You can only visit the islands on a package tour as individuals may not book
independently. The Society for Promotion of Recreational Tourism and Sports
(SPORTS) organises trips. Their offices are at Kavaratti, Lakshadweep and Harbour
Rd, Willingdon Island Cochin. T 6311. Entry permits from The Liaison Officer,
Lakshadweep Office, F 306 Curzon Rd Hostel, Kasturba Gandhi Marg, New Delhi
110001. T 386807. *Bangaram Islands* has been opened to foreign tourists and
is being developed. You can get information from the Travel Agents listed below.

History

The islands are mentioned in the writing of a 1st century Greek sailor in his Periplus
of the Erythrean Sea as a source of tortoise shell which was obtained by the Tamils.
It was by chance that he was taken off course by the monsoon winds and
discovered a route from the Arab ports to the peninsular coast.

The ruling dynasties of the S, the **Cheras**, **Pandyas** and **Cholas**, each tried to
exert their power over the islands, the last succeeding in the 11th century.
However, from the beginning of the 13th century the powerful Muslim family of
Cannanore, the *Arakkals*, for a time controlled the islands by appointing
administrators. The Portuguese 'discovered' the islands in 1498 and built a fort
there, and for some time guarded their rights over the island's coir production by
keeping an army. There was, however, an uprising led by the islanders in 1545.
After the Treaty of Srirangapatnam in 1792, the southern group was allowed to
be administered by the local chiefs. It was only in 1854, that the British **East India
Company** replaced them by *amins* who were chosen from the native families on
the Laccadive Islands (the name being an anglicized form). This was altered in
1908 when a Resident Aministrator in Calicut was given authority over the islands
until Indian independence in 1947. The islands became a Union Territory in 1956
and were renamed Lakshadweep in 1973. The original name meant 'one *lakh*
islands' (a *lakh* being a hundred thousand), and referred to the chain including
the Maldives to the S. Minicoy retains its Maldivian character even today.

People

Up to the 10th century, Hindus from three castes from the Cannanore area of
Kerala settled there and the groups are distinguishable even today – Koya (land
owners), Malmi (sailors) and Melachery (farmers). With the exception of Minicoy,
most of the people speak a sort of Malayalam (the language of Kerala). Even

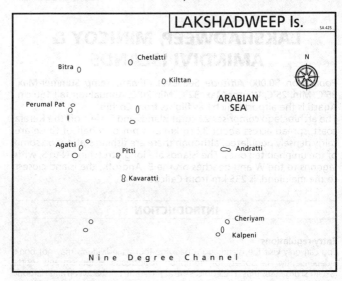

LAKSHADWEEP Is.

SA 425

Bitra

Chetlatti

Kilttan

Perumal Pat

ARABIAN
SEA

Agatti

Pitti

Andratti

Kavaratti

Cheriyam
Kalpeni

Nine Degree Channel

N

today the southernmost and largest island Minicoy (Maliku) is populated by
Maldivian speakers whose ancesters were Buddhists up to the 12th century. The
Moplahs of mixed Indian and Arab descent are nearly all Muslims having been
converted around the 9th century (although the local legend claims that in the
middle of the 7th century, Ubeidulla when returning from a pilgrimage to Mecca
arrived there by accident. He was shipwrecked on Amini Island and performed
miracles which led the population to convert to his faith).

Agriculture and Economy
The local industries depend on the natural resources. Sea fishing (especially tuna),
with coconut production provide the main income for the islanders. Palm trees
and jack fruit trees abound. The coconut palm is a vital part of the island's economy
since every bit of the palm plays an important role – the trunk providing wood
for building, the fruit, a drink either fresh or fermented, coir is used for mats and
ropes, the kernel for eating or making oil, the hard shell for bowls and the leaves
provide thatching. Bananas, grains, pulses and vegetables are also grown. There
is also some fruit canning and a small amount of dairy and poultry farming.
Tourism is the latest idustry to take advantage of the islands' unspoilt beauty,
lagoons, coral reefs and the possiblity of offering watersports.

THE ISLANDS

Tourism is being developed, although foreign tourists may only visit
uninhabited Bangaram Island and Indians, Kadmat, Kavaratti,
Kalpeni and Minicoy. Permits usually only granted to groups.
Application from Administrator, Union Territory of Lakshadweep,
Indira Gandhi Rd, Willingdon Island, Cochin, Kerala.

Kavaratti is in the centre of the archipelago and the Administrative Headquarters and there is a bank on the island. The Ajjara and Jamath mosques, the Aquarium, the lake nearby and the tombs are the sights. The wood carving in the Ajjara is an example of the superb craftsmen and masons who inhabit Kavaratti. Basic *Dak Bungalow* with 2 rm and a *Rest House* with 4 rm may be reserved through the Administrator, Union Territory of Lakshadweep, Calicut 1.

Bangaram is being developed for tourism. It has superb beaches, beautiful lagoons with a great variety of tropical fish and the green and hawkbill turtle. At the right time of the year you may be able to watch them laying eggs. The turtles arrive on the beach at night, each laying 100 to 200 eggs in the holes they make in the sand. *Centaur Bangaram Beach Resort*. 16 d rm in bungalows. Restaurant, bar. Reservation: Travel Corporation of India, MG Rd, Ernakulam, Cochin (opp Kavitha Theatre). T 31646 or at TCI's Bombay office at Chander Mukhi, Nariman Point. T 231881. Also Casino Hotel, Willingdon Island, Cochin, T 6821.

Some of the other islands in the group are, *Androth*, one of the largest which was first to be converted to Islam, *Agatti*, which neighbours Bangaram and also has a beatiful lagoon, *Piiti* which is tiny and only has birds, *Cheriam* and *Kalpeni* which have suffered most from storm damage.

Minicoy, the southernmost and largest is interesting because of its unique Maldivian character having become a part of the archipelago more recently. The people speak Maldivian, follow many of their customs and are matrilineal. There is a superb lagoon and a lighthouse you can visit.

The **Amindivi** group consists of, with a few others, the northern islands of *Chetlat, Bitra* the smallest (heavily populated by birds,which for a long time was a rich source of birds eggs), *Kiltan* where ships from Aden called en route to Colombo, *Kadmat* and the densely populated *Amini*, rich in coconut palms, which was occupied by the Portuguese.

Package Tours Tourism is still in its infancy and the facilities are limited on the islands you will be allowed to visit. The package tours which are still the only way to book a holiday are relatively expensive. They operate during Feb and Mar and only go to Kadmat, Minicoy and Kalpeni for Indian tourists and to Bangaram island for foreigners.

    Kadmat Accommodation in "family huts" or on board ship. Travel from Cochin. *Swaying Palms*. 6 days (including 2 days sailing). Rs. 3,000. *Silver Sands*. 5 days (including 1 day sailing and return by air or speedboat). Rs.3,000- Rs.3,500. *Coral Reef*. 5 days visiting Minicoy, Kavaratti, Kalpeni and Kadmat. *Coconut Grove*. Travel from Beypore. 4 days (including 2 day journey). Rs.1,300.

Travel Agents In **New Delhi**: *Ashok Tours and Travels* (ITDC), Kanishka Plaza, 19 Ashok Rd. T 3324422 Extn 2321, Telex: 031-61858 ATT IN. *SITA World Travel*, F 12 Connaught Place. T 3311133, Cable: Sitatur, Telex: 3165141 SITA IN, Fax: (011) 3324652.
    In **Bombay**: *Travel Corporation of India*, Chander Mukhi, Nariman Point. T 2021881, Cable: Turing, Telex: 11-2366 TOUR IN, Fax: (91) 22-2029424. *Raj Travels*, 27 B Panchratna, Ground Floor, Opera House, Mama Parmanand Marg. T 9117000, Telex: 011-76310 VIVA IN. *Lakshadweep Travelinks*, Passport Studio, Jermahal 1st Floor, Dhobitalso. T 254231. In **Madras**: *Sita World Travel*, Fagun Mansion, 26 C-in-C Rd. T 478861, Telex: 041-7891 SITA IN. *Mercury Travels*, 191 Mount Rd. T 869993, Telex: 041-7899. In **Calcutta**: *Ashok Tours and Travels* (ITDC), 3 G Everest Building, 46 JL Nehru Rd. T 440901, Telex: 021-2307 ITDC IN. *Mercury Travels*, Everest Building, 46 JL Nehru Rd, 443555, Cable: Merctravel. In **Calicut:** *Lakshadweep Tours and Travels*, YMCA, Cross Rd. T 66204. In **Cochin**: *SPORTS*, Lakshadweep Office, Indira Gandhi Rd. T 69755, Res. T 366612, Telex: Care 0885 6511 DEEP IN. *Lagoon Travels*, Shop 44, Kadavanthara Shopping Complex. T 351910.

Useful addresses Secretary to the Administration, Lakshadweep, Harbour Rd, Cochin 3.

Travel Air Vayudoot flights 3 times a week from Cochin to Agatti, which is the island nearest to Bangaram where you can get a boat. **Ship** MV Tippu Sultan/Bharat Seema sails from Cochin for Kavaratti. The First and Executive class passengers have a/c cabins while 2nd class passengers are accommodated in a/c halls.

WEST INDIA

GEOGRAPHY

Gujarat, Maharashtra and Goa, cover an area on India's NW seaboard the size of Spain, 507,000 sq km. Together they make up one sixth of India. Goa, formerly the Portuguese territory of Goa, Daman and Diu, with 3,814 sq km, is the smallest state in India. Maharashtra, with 308,000 sq km is the third largest, while Gujarat – 196,000 sq km – is about average. Each is distinctive in terms of scenery, language, history and culture. **Bombay** is the dominant city of the region and the commercial capital of the country. It is a major industrial centre, India's second most important gateway city, film capital and most westernised of all South Asia's cities. The population is around 9 million.

With under 200 people per sq km West India as a whole is less densely populated than the Indian average. However, there are some very densely populated regions, e.g. Bombay, the Konkan strip, and around Ahmadabad, as well as sparsely populated areas such as Kutch, the Western Ghats and large parts of interior Maharashtra. Maharashtra had 62 million inhabitants in 1981 making it third largest state in India, Gujarat had 34 million and Goa, Daman and Diu just over 1 million. Together, this was 97 million, or 14% of India's total. Because of Bombay, Maharashtra is India's most urbanised state.

The north
Kutch, in the north of the region, occupies the transition between the Indian peninsula and the Indus delta in Pakistan. The ***Rann of Kutch***, is an apparently limitless stretch of tidal mudflats, occasional patches of white salts lightening the otherwise dark surface. In it is India's most remote and inhospitable wildlife sanctuary. Here wild asses share the same terrain with Indian army units patrolling the highly sensitive border with Pakistan. To the N the desert of mud and the desert of sand merge imperceptibly. In the monsoon, as the floodwaters rise, the upland area between the Great Rann and the Little Rann becomes an island. It is literally a world apart.

The Kasthiawad peninsula Immediately to the S is **Saurashtra**. Gujarat proper lies to the East. The peninsula area has a central core of low lying hills and a long coastline. Further East are more fertile areas that have benefitted from the alluvium deposited by the rivers Narmada, Sabarmati and Mahi. The Government has plans to build at least 30 dams along the 1,000 km long **Narmada River** and 41 of its tributaries, submerging 2.5 million ha and displacing perhaps as many as 1 million people. By comparison the Tennessee Valley Authority flooded 1.6 million ha and displaced 70,000 residents. The World Bank has committed US$450 million to the project, which is intended to provide drinking water, irrigation for rainfed lands and electricity for industrial development, but it is proving a highly controversial scheme and has roused fierce local opposition in those areas which which will suffer the costs without gaining any of the benefits.

Economically the most important geological feature in West India is the series of oil bearing Tertiary sediments in the Gulf of Cambay, north of Bombay. These run from inland S to some distance from the shoreline in an area known as the Bombay High.

The Konkan

To the S again is the Konkan, a coastal lowland that stretches from around Surat as far as Goa. Although this 530 km long and 50 – 80 km wide ribbon is low, it is broken up by hills. Short rivers running off the mountains behind are straight and take direct routes to the sea. Rising dramatically behind them is the wall of the western Ghats which cause the incoming clouds to drop much of their rain before reaching the interior. Given the high year-round temperatures, the vegetation of the Konkan is sub-tropical. Coconut palms fringe much of the coast all the way down to Kerala, and play an important part in the economy.

Bombay, built on the site of seven former islands but now linked together by draining and filling the marshes, is the geographical focus of the region. Near the northern boundary of Goa the Deccan lava gives way to the ancient Archean rocks of the Peninsula, and the change is marked by a series of breaches in the mountain wall. S from **Ratnagiri** laterite is more common and is very noticeable in Goa where you can go the 100 km length of the state alternating between red crusted uplands and lush green deltaic lowlands.

The Western Ghats and the Deccan plateau form a stunning mountain wall,
rising dramatically to over 1,300 m in places. On the seaward side they present steep sided ravines and deep canyons. On the landward side the flat-topped spurs are intersected by valleys so gentle that sometimes the slopes are imperceptible. The Maratha leader **Sivaji**, named 'the Mountain Rat' by the Mughal Emperor Aurangzeb, built hilltop forts to dominate the interior and coastal strip. In places there are still patches of dense forests of teak, a material prized by the makers of wooden ships.

Interior Maharashtra dips gently eastwards from the scarp of the Western Ghats. The great rivers that flow into the Bay of Bengal – the **Krishna** and **Godavari** – have their sources in the Western Ghats and have broad gently undulating valleys. Rainfed agriculture gives a precarious existence. Travelling across the plateau there are often tremendous views across what sometimes seems a treeless plain. Maharashtra thus encompasses coastal Konkan, the mountainous Ghats and gently undulating Deccan plateau, liberally scattered with hilltop forts and cave temples.

CLIMATE

The climate reflects the region's position just S of the Tropic of Cancer. The overall climatic pattern is dominated by the monsoon, and rainfall distribution is strongly influenced by position relative to the Western Ghats, coastal regions, especially in the S, receiving very heavy rain from Jun to Oct.

Temperatures Temperatures vary much less through the year than they do further N in India. The greatest contrast is between the N and S of the region. Minimum winter temperatures in N Gujarat may be as low as 10°C, though daytime temperatures are twice that, while Goa, in the extreme S of the region has minimum winter temperatures of 20°C and daytime temperatures throughout the year of at least 28°C. Although the monsoon season is also very humid the W coast as a rule does not suffer the stifling humid heat of the E coast from Calcutta to Madras.

Rainfall The coast is extremely wet, and correspondingly more humid, than inland. Heaviest rainfall is between Bombay and Goa, total amounts diminishing N into Gujarat and towards the deserts of Rajasthan and Sind in Pakistan. E of the Western Ghats rainfall diminishes rapidly, though the monsoon season is still humid, overcast and often windy. The tops of the hills themselves are often shrouded in mist and cloud from Jun to Oct.

ECONOMY

Subsistence agriculture dominated the interior until the railways penetrated the Deccan Plateau in the second part of the 19th century. This stimulated a major development of cotton production for direct export and, from the end of the 19th century, for milling in India. Long before that much of the coastal economy of the region was geared towards overseas trade. Surat, Goa, Daman, Diu, Cambay and Broach were all important ports, some like **Surat** as much for their role in the annual Muslim pilgrim traffic to Mecca as for trade. In the post-Independence period many areas have seen rapid industrial development.

Agriculture In common with nearly all Indian states, agriculture employs the largest number of people. Irrigation is comparatively restricted, and today the Indian government is caught up in fierce arguments over proposals to build the world's largest irrigation system through constructing a series of dams on the **Narmada River** (see above).

Gujarat is a fertile land of wheat, cotton and bananas, irrigated by a complex of rivers. Southwards, in coastal Maharashtra and Goa, rice becomes the dominant crop, bananas and coconuts becoming important cash crops. Interior Maharashtra is much drier. Only one eighth of the state is irrigated, mostly in the Konkan, and the crops grown reflect this – sorghum (*jowar*), pearl millet (*bajra*), wheat and pulses. Coconuts, copra and fish are all coastal products, along with groundnuts, cashew nuts and bananas.

Cash crops W India is particularly noted as the major centre of Indian cotton production. Cotton is ideally suited to the rich black soils and climate of interior Maharashtra and eastern Gujarat, and the Indian cotton textile industry centred on Ahmadabad and Bombay developed on the strength of it. Tobacco is grown in Gujarat whilst the forest of N Maharashtra yield teak, a hardwood prized in shipbuilding by the British, who constructed their first warships outside England in the fledgling dockyards of Bombay.

Energy, Oil and natural gas Exploration in W India for oil and natural gas started in 1955 with the setting up of the Oil and Natural Gas Commission. Extensive finds have been made both onshore in Gujarat, around the head of the Gulf of Cambay, and offshore to the S. Exploitation was very slow getting started and development has remained below early expectations, but both gas and petroleum are now being extracted on a significant scale. Oil production meets approximately half of India's current demand. Some coal is mined in Eastern

Maharashtra, and W India has been in the forefront of nuclear power development. The atomic power station at Tarapur was India's first nuclear power plant.

Manufacturing Manufacturing is centred on Bombay, Thane, Kolhapur and Sholapur in Maharashtra and Ahmadabad, 'the Manchester of India', in Gujarat. Due in large part to the size and output of Bombay's light, medium and heavy engineering, manufacturing, food processing and textile industries, Maharashtra alone accounts for a quarter of the nation's industrial output by value. Ahmadabad is the region's second most important industrial city.

HISTORY

The **Indus Valley Civilization** influenced the NW corner of the region. Almost no historic monuments belonging to this period are preserved. Lothal, 80 km south of Ahmadabad in Gujarat, dates from the 3rd millenium BC and displays many characteristic features of the Harappan culture, **see page 1186**. Junagadh, on the Saurashtra peninsula, also dates from pre-Harappan times. Kaira, 32 km SW of Ahmadabad dates from 1400 BC.

Buddhism and Jainism Although they originated over 1000 km to the NE, Buddhism and Jainism flourished in the western region. From an early period Jains became influential in trade and commerce in Gujarat and Maharashtra, being restricted to those activities as the least likely to harm any form of life. Girnar Hill nearby has been an important Jain site since the 3rd Century BC and Asokan Edicts from the Mauryan period (400-200BC) indicate its importance in 250 BC. The temples are later, dating from the 12th Century AD.

Buddhism also exerted a strong influence from the 3rd century BC. Under the **Satavahanas** (200 BC-200 AD) the first Buddhist temples were constructed at Ajanta and Bhaja in Maharashtra. The later **Kshatrapas** (100-300 AD) were patrons of the cave dwelling monastic communities at Karli which is en route from Bombay to Pune. Junnar, east of Bombay also possesses caves that are contemporaneous with the early ones at Ajanta.

More Buddhist cave development occurred at the Maharashtran sites of Ajanta, Aurangabad and Ramtek under the Vakatakas (300-500 AD) but now the Mahayana sect of Buddhism had achieved popularity. Thus, what makes the caves at Ajanta impressive is that they span the development of Buddhism from the early Hinayana to the later Mahayana period up to the virtual disappearance of the faith from peninsula India.

Hindu sites There are important Hindu sites in the region dating from the early centuries of the Christian period. One of the earliest examples of Hindu temple design is at **Gop**, 50 km NE of Porbandar in Gujarat. Under the Kalachuris (500-600 AD) the caves on the island of Elephanta, a short boat ride from Bombay, were excavated. The Ellora group of cave temples and monasteries include 17 Hindu ones dating from 600-900 AD. The most magnificent is the rock temple of Kailasa (mid 8th Century onwards). Impressive wall panels illustrate stories from the Ramayana and Mahabharata.

From 900-1200 AD the Solankis emerged as the most powerful rulers in Gujarat and South Rajasthan. Patan, Prabhas Patan, Modhera and Girnar, all in Gujarat, developed under their patronage. Patan, 130 km N of Gujarat was the 8th Century capital of the Hindu Kings of Gujarat and once had over 100 Jain temples. A distinctive Western Indian architectural style emerged which is well displayed in the temples and step wells at Modhera and Patan. Later *baolis* had cool pavilions incorporated into the wells and an especially fine 16th Century example can be seen at Adalaj, 19 km N of Ahmadabad. Dwarka, on the tip of the Kathiawar Peninsula in Gujarat, was closely associated with the **Krishna** legend, and is regarded as one of the four holy abodes of the gods – **see page 54**. The present town and 12th Century temples are built on the sites of four former cities.

The Muslims Early Muslim raids under Mahmud of Ghazni in the 11th Century caused much damage to important religious monuments. By the 14th Century most of the region had come under Muslim control. Khalji Sultans of Delhi established themselves in the coastal towns along the western seaboard, demolishing earlier Hindu temples and utilising the materials for their own mosques and buildings (see Qutb Minar, Delhi **page 165**). **Ahmadabad** was founded in 1411 and became a Muslim stronghold. It flourished in second half of 15th Century and now contains the largest concentration of Muslim buildings in W India.

In 1328 Muhammad Tughluq Shah II of Delhi became moved his entire capital from Delhi to Daulatabad, near Aurangabad. The ordinary citizens of Delhi did not enjoy being subjected to the trauma of relocation, but it showed his sense of the strategic benefits stemming from control of the western peninsula.

Later governors asserted independence from Delhi. The Bahmani Sultans of Deccan were dominant until late 15th Century when they split into five kingdoms – Ahmadnagar, Berar, Bidar, Bijapur and Golconda. The Bhamanis of Maharashtra (1390-1485) had strong links with the Hindu kingdom of Vijyanagar in present day Karnataka. The Ahmad Shahis were dominant in Gujarat over the period 1451-1526. Early buildings are the mosques at the important ports of Surat and Broach and also at Patan.

Trade with the west Historically India's W coast has naturally had far more contact with the maritime trading regions to the W than it has with the E. The geographer Spate noted the importance of its numerous havens, its narrow immediate hinterland and the few well defined routes into the interior. However, its W facing shoreline made it readily accessible to trading Arabs and later to the Europeans. Thus, while India's E coast exported Indian ideas and political power to South East Asia with little by way of return, the W coast was a region of contact with foreigners. This is a direct result of the monsoon wind system which brought Arab dhows and early European traders across the Arabian Sea and the Indian Ocean. Similarly the SW monsoon carried sailing boats across the Bay of Bengal which then had to make their way back with much more difficulty.

The Portuguese Trade with the Middle East, the spread of Islam from the the deserts of Arabia, and later European interest in the Indies all had an impact on W India. In the 16th Century the Portuguese established themselves at **Daman, Diu** and **Goa**. Their conquests brought a distinctive Mediterranean flavour to the W coast that extended to architecture and culture. After dominating the trade routes to Europe, the Portuguese lost their maritime supremacy to the Dutch in the East Indies and to the British in the Indian Ocean. Thereafter, Goa became a 'somnolent colonial backwater', past its prime. It remained a foreign enclave on Indian soil until Jawarharlal Nehru ordered to Indian Army to march in in 1961, ending 4½ centuries of Portuguese influence.

The Mughals At the same time as the Portuguese were establishing their small settlements on the coast the Mughals were expanding their territories in the interior. Gujarat was taken in 1534-5 by Humayun who subsequently let it slip from his grasp. It was retaken by Akbar in 1572 and remained firmly in Mughal hands for the next 180 years bringing cotton, indigo, and trading links with Arabia, Persian Gulf and Egypt to their expanding Empire. Later attacks on the Deccan kingdoms were neither as swiftly executed as the conquest of Gujarat nor as effective. By Akbar's death in (1605) the region up to the **Godavari river** had been absorbed (**see page 91**).

The Deccan states   The Deccan at this time consisted of mostly Muslim independent states. The Muslim States were successors of the Bahmani Kingdom which in turn was a splinter of the Delhi Sultanate. The power that ruled Delhi could claim tenuous justification in seeking to annex these rebel territories. The most orthodox of the emperors, Aurangzeb, was also the most implacable of annexers. It took him nearly to the end of the 18th century to extinguish the last Deccan Muslim Kingdom, by which time a new Hindu power, the Marathas, had risen on the W flank. Akbar had captured the fort at Ahmadnagar in 1599. Aurangzeb brought the rest of the kingdom under Mughal rule, followed by Bijapur and Golconda, which fell in 1686 and 1687 – see page 91. Thereafter, Aurangzeb campaigned against the Marathas until his death in 1707.

The Marathas   Under Shivaji, a man of low-caste later elevated to power through his daring exploits and ambition, a new Hindu empire was created that centred on Maharashtra. In 1656 Shivaji took the fort of **Pratapgarh**, and proceeded to capture others in the Western Ghats. Maratha power was based on mobility, which they used to remarkable effect from their secure bases. Shivaji built as many as one hundred fortresses, but he also waged naval warfare against the Arab admirals in the Mughal imperial service.

Some of his main forts were Malangarh, Lohagen near Lonavla, Sinhagarh near Pune, Purandhar on the Pune-Mahabaleshwar road, Pandavgad which is said to have been visited by the Pandava brothers, Pratapgarh and above all his capital Raigarh, near Mahabaleshwar. Wasota near Satara, Panhala near Kolhapur, Junnar and Shivner near Thane as well as Vijayadrug and Janjira on the coast south of Bombay were also important. In addition he captured forts like Deogiri, a fort developed by the Khaljis and Tughluqs.

As Frances Watson has noted 'on land the zestful opportunism of hard-riding commando tactics and deceptive skills was given, under his excellent discipline, and with the fervour of a cause (Hindu), the promise of something more substantial'. When Shivaji died in 1680 he had brought into being a Hindu Raj which under an able successor might have achieved the permanence and authority of an indigenous empire.

After his death, the Marathas became more predatory, and though they extended their presence over great distances, it was 'more often as a scourge than as an inspiration'. Individual leaders of ability were to appear in the succession of states of their first empire – Nagpur, Baroda, Indore, Gwalior, together forming what has been coined the "Maratha Confederacy", but it was their failure to secure the central power of Delhi that led to their downfall.

The British   The British were latecomers to the Deccan. Like the Portuguese, their early activities were confined to the coast. Their first factory was at Surat. As the East India Company extended its trading influence from its original centres in Eastern India there was a need to link the three Presidencies of Bombay, Bengal and Madras. With territorial acquisition and the elimination of Maratha power, communications across the Deccan improved.

From the 1850s railway lines were pushed inland and the hinterland of Bombay was dramatically expanded. Mahabaleshwar was established as a hill station and the old Maratha capital of Pune became a fashionable summer retreat. The British garrison was across the river at Kirkee.

Gujarat was never fully absorbed into British India but fragmented into 200 petty princely states which included Porbandar, Morvi, Wankaner, Rajkot, Jamnagar, Bhavnagar and dominant Baroda (Vadodara). Outside Bombay British buildings are comparatively few in Gujarat and Maharashtra. There are palaces at all the places mentioned above as well as Surat.

Independence and after Mohandas Karamchand Gandhi – the Mahatma, the major philosophical influence on India's independence movement, was born in Gujarat. The beliefs he espoused were in part influenced by the tenets of pacifism inherent in Buddhism and Jainism. Both had an enduring influence on the region's development. The Salt March which he led from his ashram at Ahmadabad to the coast in protest against not only the law enacted by the British against domestic production of salt but against foreign rule in India drew world-wide attention to the non-violent movement in the struggle for independence.

After independence the old Princely States were absorbed into the new federal structure of Independent India. The creation of linguistic states in 1956 led to the separation of Gujarat and Maharashtra. Goa, Daman and Diu were forcibly absorbed into the Indian Union after Portugal had declined to recognize the end of an era initiated by Vasco da Gama and Alfonso Albuquerque.

BOMBAY

Population 12.57 million (1991) *Altitude* Sea level. *Best Season* The temperatures are fairly constant throughout the year. June to the early part of October are extremely wet, hot and humid. Best avoided if possible. *Clothing* Cottons throughout the year. *Languages spoken* Marathi, Gujarati, Hindi and English.

	Jan	Feb	Mar	Apr	May	Jun	Jul	Aug	Sep	Oct	Nov	Dec	Av/Tot
Max (°C)	31	32	33	33	33	32	30	29	30	32	33	32	32
Min (°C)	16	17	20	24	26	26	25	24	24	23	20	18	22
Rain (mm)	0	1	0	0	20	647	945	660	309	117	7	1	2707

Nearly all Bombay's foreign visitors now arrive by plane, but during the British period it was more usual to arrive by ship. For many travellers from Europe, the Gateway of India, built to commemorate the Prince of Wales' visit in 1911, was the point of disembarkation. Appropriately, the Taj Mahal hotel, one of India's finest, is located immediately behind it. Bombay has a wide range of accommodation, but prices tend to be high. There are not many really cheap hotels or guest houses suitable for travellers on very tight budgets. Transport around the city can be expensive if you are not prepared to travel on buses and suburban trains.

Bombay is well connected with other parts of the country by air, road and rail. The two major railway stations are Bombay Central and Victoria Terminus, the latter a fine example of British late Victorian architectural style in India. Opened during Queen Victoria's Golden Jubilee year, it combines Venetian, Gothic and Indo-Islamic styles as well as columns of granite brought all the way from Aberdeen. These stations are orderly and well-managed, and are good starting off points for travels inland.

INTRODUCTION

Travelling into Bombay 'proper' from Santa Cruz airport, it is hard to believe that 300 years ago, the area occupied by this great metropolis was seven islands inhabited by Koli fishermen and their families. To these original inhabitants we owe the word 'coolie', for many were later absorbed into the burgeoning urban economy as manual, unskilled labourers and porters.

Land reclamation   With subsequent land reclamation the islands were connected, so that now Bombay occupies a thin isthmus. The British acquired these marshy and malarial islands for a pittance. **Mumbadevi** or **Mumbai** (from which Bombay gets its name), was part of Catherine of Braganza's marriage dowry when she married Charles II in 1661. Four years later, the British took possession of the remaining islands and neighbouring mainland area and in 1688 the East India Company leased the whole area for £10 sterling in gold per year.

In the early years of British involvement in S Asia, Bombay was rivalled by **Surat** in Gujarat where the first English headquarters in India had been established in 1612. Until the early 19th century, Bombay's fortunes rested on the shipbuilding yards established by progressive Parsis. Durable Malabar teak was used, and the yards received the first orders for ships placed outside England.

Bombay before the Suez Canal   Bombay remained isolated from Madras and the E coast by the sharp face of the Western Ghats, the difficult terrain inland and the constantly hostile Maratha tribes. Bombay's wealth, therefore, depended on trade and this focus of economic activity, and the cosmopolitan city this created, resulted in a social system much freer from prejudice than elsewhere. Parsis, Sephardic Jews and the British shared common interests and responded to the same incentives. The legacy of this mutual cooperation can be seen in the numerous buildings made possible through benefactions.

To begin with the small British community lived within the confines of the old Fort area. After a devastating fire on 17th February 1803, a new town with wider streets was built. Then, with the abolition of the Company's trade monopoly, the doors to rapid expansion were flung open and Bombay flourished. Trade with England boomed. Annual exports of raw cotton trebled over the period 1809-1816, and with the defeat of the Marathas at Kirkee in November 1817, the economic hinterland of Bombay was able to expand along revitalised old trade routes onto the Deccan plateau and beyond.

After the opening of the Suez Canal in 1870 Bombay's greater proximity to European markets gave it an advantage over Calcutta. The port became the commercial centre of the Arabian Sea. The population in 1864 was 816,000, and grew rapidly.

The first railway line   The opening of India's first railway line from Bombay to Thana in 1854 was a prelude to penetrating the Western Ghats and gaining access to the Deccan Plateau. Bombay became the hub of regional and international trade, an ideal environment for the cosmopolitan community to develop great wealth and influence. Victoria Terminus, and indeed many other stations around India, were the product of a magnificent era of railway building at the end of the 19th century when the British Raj was striding confidently towards the 20th century.

Lord Dalhousie encouraged the East India Company to establish two private companies, the East Indian Railways and the **Great Indian Peninsula Railway** (GIPR). But with the disappearance of the East India Company after the Mutiny, the government of India took over the responsibility for running the railways.

On 16 April 1853 the GIPR's first train made its run from Bombay along 32 km of line to Thana. Subsequent advances were rapid but often incredible natural obstacles presented great challenges to the railway builders. The 263 km line from Bombay to Surat encountered 18 rivers and some of the foundations for the bridges had to be driven 45 m into the ground to cope with the monsoon floodwaters.

The challenge of the Ghats   The Western Ghats which rise to 800 m behind Bombay posed different problems. As many as 40,000 navvies worked to create 22 bridges, 25 tunnels on a gradient of 1 in 37 over much of the distance. Nearly one third died from disease or accidents.

The railways transformed the movement of goods and people across India. This enabled more Indians to make long pilgrimages to holy places. In areas they made possible extensive famine relief, which after the catastrophic Maharashtra famine in the 1870s became a widely used argument for speeding up the railway building programme. More than this, they encouraged cash crop production and transport and the development of heavy industry. As the journalist Sir Edwin Arnold noted very early on: 'Railways may do for India what dynasties have never done – what the genius of Akbar..could not effect by government, nor...Tippoo Sahib by violence. They make India a nation'.

Commerce and industry Bombay rapidly became the centre of an entrepreneurial as well as a commercial class, drawing from the Parsi as well as the **Bania** Hindu business community. Bombay is now the commercial capital of India, home of India's stock exchange and headquarters for many national and international companies. This is most apparent in the town centre, with its soaring skyscrapers and more traditional buildings in the British colonial style. The red double decker buses add to the sensation that you could almost be in London.

Bombay is also a major industrial centre. A cotton mill was established here in 1854 and by 1885 there were nearly 50 employing over 30,000 workers. The expansion of the railway system into the cotton producing areas of Maharashtra was a strong stimulus not only to milling but to engineering industries. Originally these were concentrated round the ports and railway facilities but have become more diversified with the growth of light and medium engineering installations. This, in turn, has made Bombay more resistant to national recession than Calcutta, for example, with its strong reliance on the jute industry. Other important activities are printing, furniture manufacture, ceramics, food, pharmaceuticals, tobacco and jewellery.

The pressures of growth With population pressure in the surrounding agricultural hinterland, Bombay is still growing fast. Many migrants cannot find suitable accommodation, and as with Calcutta's bustees, Bombay's desperately squalid chawls of cramped, makeshift and miserable hovels occupy nearly every spare piece of land. Perhaps one third of the population lives in these, and in addition there are many thousands of pavement dwellers. Wasteland does not remain vacant for long. In many places the chawls are alongside high-rise dwellings. Even those who live in what look like temporary huts often pay high "protection money" to local strong men to make sure that they are not removed by force. Due to heavy demand for building space, property values are exceedingly high, well beyond the reach of many of the city's workers. Flying in to Bombay you will see more permanent houses of mud, brick and daub with slate or corrugated iron roof cling to the hillsides and confirm the view that Bombay is far more crowded than Delhi, which has opportunities for almost limitless spatial expansion. The alleys between the houses can scarcely be seen.

Poverty and planning Concerns over the quality of life are hardly new to Bombay's planners, who have been trying to find new ways to decentralize the metropolitan region and create more living space, served with proper amenities. The Maharashtra government has promoted industrial dispersal in successive plans since the 1960s and this has had a strong impact. Another plan has sought to alleviate congestion in S Bombay by developing a massive market complex (Bandra-Kurla) in the northern part of Bombay Island. Also New Bombay across the Thana Creek and Bombay Harbour are being developed to ease the pressure on the isthmus. Greater Bombay now has a population of approximately 11 million.

Despite the extreme poverty of millions of people living in Bombay, for many it remains a city of hope. Like Delhi, it is full of contrasts. It has none of the old monuments which are scattered across Delhi. "Bombayites" are far more westernized and it has mass rapid transit system, all be it often desperately overcrowded. There is a very good suburban train network, a good bus service and only in the suburbs will you see the autorickshaws, which buzz like flies all around Delhi. Bombay often claims to be the most modern and cosmopolitan of India's cities.

Film capital Bombay is also the film capital of India and with its production of 300 films per year, is the world's second largest film maker after Hong Kong. Yet today, with the spread and huge popularity of videos and declining cinema attendances nationwide, this Indian Hollywood is under threat. The stars still live in sumptuous dwellings, many of which are on Malabar Hill, Bombay's Beverly Hills, and judging by the number of movie magazines on the newsstands their popularity seems undiminished.

Local Festivals In addition to the national Hindu and Muslim festivals there are: *Janmashtami* (Jul-Aug) celebrates the birth of Lord Krishna. Boys and young men form human pyramids and break pots of curd hung up high between buildings. *Coconut Day* (August). The angry monsoon seas are propitiated by devotees throwing coconuts into the ocean. *Ganes Chaturthi* (Aug-Sep). Massive figures of Ganes are worshipped and immersed in the sea on several days days following the festival. *Mount Mary's Feast* (Sep) celebrated at St Mary's Church, Bandra. A fair is also held.

Dasara (Sep-Oct). During this nationwide festival, in Bombay there are group dances by Gujarati women in all the auditoria. There are also Ramlila celebrations at Chowpatty Beach. *Diwali* (The Festival of Lights) is particularly popular in mercantile Bombay when the business community celebrate their New Year and open new account books. *Jamshed Navroz* (Mar). This is New Years Day for the Parsi followers of the Fasli calendar. The celebrations which include offering prayers at temples, exchanging greetings, alms-giving and feasting at home, date back to Jamshed, the legendary king of Persia. *Christmas* (25 Dec). Christians across Bombay celebrate the birth of Christ. A pontifical High Mass is held at midnight in the open air at the Cooperage Grounds

APOLLO BUNDER AND THE GATEWAY OF INDIA

The *Gateway of India* (1927) was designed by George Wittet to commemorate the visit of George V and Queen Mary in 1911. Architecturally it is built in the Indo-Saracenic style, and modelled on 16th century Gujarati work. The building material is honey-coloured basalt. The great gateway comprises an archway with halls on each side capable of seating 600 at important receptions. The arch replaces an earlier, lighter building. The present structure, though heavy in appearance, when viewed from the sea looks quite distinctive set against the imposing Taj Mahal Hotel. It was the point from which the last British regiment serving in India signalled the end of Empire when it left on 28 February 1948.

The area around the Gateway is popular among Bombayites for evening strolls and is a pleasant place to visit at sundown. A short distance behind the Gateway is an impressive statue of **Sivaji** which was erected in 1960. See page 972.

The *Taj Mahal Hotel* can rightly claim to be one of India's modern institutions. It comprises two distinct buildings, the older, original and red-domed hotel, and a modern skyscraper adjunct (called the Taj Mahal Inter-Continental). Both are owned and run by the prestigious Taj Group of Hotels. Jamshetji Nusserwanji Tata, a Bombay Parsi, is the man behind the enterprise and the hotel, designed by W. Chambers, is now one of the world's leading hotels. Close by are the Prince of Wales Museum and the Jahangir Art Gallery (See Museums & Art Galleries).

Colaba S of the Gateway of India is the crowded southern section of **Shahid Bhagat Singh Rd** which leads 3 km down to Colaba and the southern tip of the peninsula. ('Shahid' means martyr. The road is named after Bhagat Singh.) **The Afghan Memorial Church of St John the Baptist** (1847-58) is at the northern edge of Colaba itself, immediately behind Sassoon Dock. Early English in style,

CENTRAL BOMBAY

1. St. John's Church
2. Castle
3. Bombay University & Library
4. Gateway of India
5. Sculpture
6. Prince of Wales Museum
7. Jahangir Art Gallery
8. Horniman Circle
9. St. Thomas' Cathedral
10. Town Hall
11. Mint
12. Gurudwara
13. Hutatma Chowk (Flora Fountain)
14. Municipal Offices
15. Police Court
16. St. Xaviers College
17. School of Art
18. Dhule Market
19. Mangal Das (cloth market)
20. Jama Masjid
21. Jhaveri Bazaar
22. Mumbadevi Temple
23. British Council
24. St. Xavier's & Elphinstone schools
25. Aquarium
26. Banaji Fire Temple
27. Wadiaji Fire Temple
28. Anjuman Fire Temple
29. David Sassoon Library
30. High Court
31. Rajabhai Tower
32. Government dockyard
33. American Express
34. Old Customs House
35. Regional Passport Office
36. Taj Mahal & Intercontinental
37. Royal Bombay Yacht Club
38. Govt. Gujarat Tourist Office
39. Cottage Industries
40. Council Hall – Legislature
40. Tamil Nadu Handicrafts

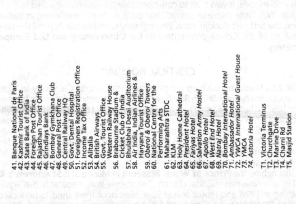

with a 58 m spire, it was built to commemorate the soldiers who died in the First Afghan War. Fishermen still unload their catch early in the morning at **Sassoon Dock,** the first wet dock in India. Photography is prohibited. Beyond the church at the tip of the Colaba promontory lie the **Observatory** and **Old European cemetery.**

CENTRAL BOMBAY

In the area stretching back up the peninsula from Colaba Causeway to Victoria Terminus is the heart of British Bombay. Most of the buildings date from the period after 1862, when Sir Bartle Frere became Governor (1862-7), and under whose enthusiastic guidance Bombay became a great civic centre. It is an extravaganza of Victorian Gothic architecture, modified by the Indo-Saracenic influences which were then being developed. From the **Gateway of India**, proceed along **Sivaji Marg** to **Mahatma Gandhi Rd** and you will see many of these buildings. Most of these are still in use as offices.

Just behind the **Prince of Wales Museum** in Marine St is *St Andrew's Kirk* (1819), a simple neo-classical church. The steeple was irreparably damaged by lightning in 1826 and rebuilt a year later. Next door there used to be a circular building (1840) for storing imported American ice (there is a similar one in Madras, see page 701). Local ice plants appeared in the 1880s. At the S end of Mahatma Gandhi (MG) Rd is the Renaissance style *Institute of Science* (1911) designed by George Wittet. The Institute, which includes a scientific library, a public hall and examination halls, was built with gifts from the Parsi and Jewish communities.

The Oval Maidan Immediately to the N, on the E side of **K.B. Patel Marg** (Mayo Rd) and the Oval Maidan, is a series of striking buildings, bringing together a range of European styles from the early English Gothic to the Romanesque. From S to N they are the old **Secretariat**, the **University**, **Library** and **clocktower**, the **High Court** and the **Public Works Office**.

The Venetian Gothic style old **Secretariat** (1874) is 143 m long, with a façade of arcaded verandahs and porticos. It is faced in buff-coloured Porbander stone from Gujarat. Decorated with red and blue basalt, the carvings are in white Hemnagar stone. The **University Convocation Hall** (1874) to its N was designed by Sir George Gilbert Scott in a 15th century French Decorated style. Scott also designed the adjacent **University Library** and **Rajabai Clocktower** (1870s) next door. The 79 m high Rajabhai Tower is based on Giotto's campanile in Florence. The sculpted figures in niches on the exterior walls of the tower were designed to represent the castes of India. Originally the clock could chime 12 tunes such as Rule Britannia.

The *High Court* (1871-9), in Early English Gothic style, has a 57 m high central tower flanked by lower octagonal towers topped by the figures of Justice and Mercy. The Venetian Gothic **Public Works Office** (1869-72) is to its N. Opposite, and with its main façade to Vir Nariman Rd, is the former General Post Office (1869-72). Now called the **Telegraph office**, it stands next to the original Telegraph Office and to add to the extraordinary mixture of European architectural styles the ·it is Romanesque. Both buildings are finished in honey-coloured sandstone from Kurla.

HORNIMAN CIRCLE

Turn right at the *Flora* **(or Frere)** *Fountain* (1869), now known as Huatatma Chowk, along **Vir Nariman Rd** to the Custom House, Town Hall and Mint on the imposing Horniman (Elphinstone) Circle. By Bombay standards the **Custom House** is an old building and is believed to incorporate a Portuguese barrack block of 1665. Over the entrance is the crest of the **East India Company**. Parts of the old Portuguese fort's walls can be seen; more exist in the Naval Dockyards which are inaccessible to the tourist. Many Malabar teak 'East Indiamen' ships were built here.

The Mint (1824-9) was built on the Fort rubbish dump, has Ionic columns and a water tank in front of it. The **Town Hall** (1820-3) has been widely admired as one of the best neo-classical buildings in India. The Doric columns that give the Town Hall its grandeur were shipped from England, and it was originally intended to use twice the number. The original idea of paired columns was abandoned as being too monumental and half were used at Christ Church, Byculla. The Corinthian interior houses the **Assembly Rooms** and the learned and once influential **Bombay Asiatic Society**.

Horniman Circle itself was laid out in 1860. On the W edge are the Venetian Gothic **Elphinstone Buildings** (1870), built of brown sandstone. Immediately to the W of these is the **Cathedral Church of St Thomas,** begun in 1672, opened in 1718, and subject to a number of later additions. Inside are a number of monuments combining to form a heroic "who's who of India".

Behind Horniman circle on the water's edge lies the **Old Castle**. Entry is not permitted. Proceeding N to Victoria Terminus you pass the **Port Trust Office** on your right, while a little farther on, to your right by the station is the **General Post Office** (1909), based on the architecture of **Bijapur** (Karnataka) in the Indo-Saracenic style.

THE VICTORIA TERMINUS AREA

Immediately to the N of the General Post Office is the **Victoria Terminus** (1878-1887), the most remarkable example of Victorian Gothic architecture in India, opened during Queen Victoria's Golden Jubilee year. Today it is known by everybody as 'VT'.

The frontage is symmetrical with a large central dome flanked by two wings. The dome is capped by a 4 m high statue of Progress by Thomas Earp, who also carved the Imperial lion and Indian tiger on the gate piers, nearly all executed by the Bombay School of Art. The booking hall with its arcades, stained glass and glazed tiles was inspired by London's St Pancras station.

It was built at a time when fierce debate was taking place among British architects working in India as to the most appropriate style to develop for the buildings increasingly in demand. One view held that the British should restrict themselves to models derived from the best in western tradition, as the British were to be seen as a "civilising force" in India. Others argued that architects should draw on Indian models, trying to bring out the best of Indian tradition and encourage its development. By and large, the former were dominant, but as Tillotson argues, the introduction of Gothic allowed a blending of western traditions with Indian (often Islamic Indian) motifs, which became known as the **Indo-Saracenic style**.

At the junction of Dadabhoy Naoroji Marg and Mahapalika Marg are the grand Municipal Buildings (1893), built by **Stevens**. The tower is 78 m high and the statue crowning the gable is designed to represent "Urbs Prima in Indis" (*The first city in India*). If you want to see more British buildings walk up **Mahapalika Marg** (Cruickshank Rd). On your right you will see the **Police Courts** (1888), **Cama Albless Hospital** which has interesting Gothic windows with conical iron hoods to provide shade, **St Xavier's College** founded in 1867 and **Elphinstone High School** (1872) standing among the trees.

Turning right into **Lokmanya Tilak Marg** (Camac Rd), on your right is **St Xavier's School, Gokuldas Tejpal Hospital** (1877) money for which was given by Parsi benefactors. On the SE and SW faces are medallions by Rudyard Kipling's father

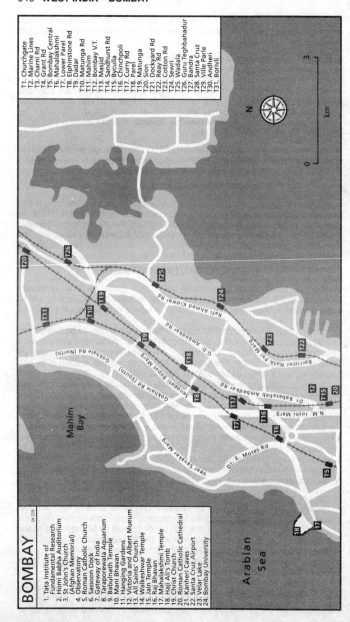

BOMBAY

SA 229

1. Tata Institute of Fundamental Research
2. Homi Babha Auditorium
3. St John's Church
4. Observatory (Aghyari Memorial)
5. Roman Catholic Church
6. Sassoon Dock
7. Gateway of India
8. Taraporewala Aquarium
9. Babulnath Temple
10. Mani Bhavan
11. Hanging Gardens
12. Victoria and Albert Mueum
13. All Saints' Church
14. Walkeshwar Temple
15. Jain Temple
16. Raj Bhavan
17. Mahalakshmi Temple
18. Haji Ali's Tomb
19. Christ Church
20. Roman Catholic Cathedral
21. Kanheri Caves
22. Santa Cruz Airport
23. Velar Lake
24. Bombay University

T1. Churchgate
T2. Marine Lines
T3. Charni Rd
T4. Grant Rd
T5. Bombay Central
T6. Mahalakshmi
T7. Lower Parel
T8. Elphinstone Rd
T9. Dadar
T10. Matunga Rd
T11. Mahim
T12. Bombay V.T.
T13. Masjid
T14. Sandhurst Rd
T15. Byculla
T16. Chinchpoli
T17. Curry Rd
T18. Parel
T19. Matunga
T20. Sion
T21. Dockyard Rd
T22. Reay Rd
T23. Cotton Rd
T24. Sewri
T25. Wadala
T26. Guru Teghbahadur
T27. Bandra
T28. Santa Cruz
T29. Ville Parle
T30. Andheri
T31. Borivli

N

km
0   3

Mahim Bay

Arabian Sea

Gokhale Rd (North)
Gokhale Rd (South)
Senapati Bapat Marg
Veer Savakar Marg
Dr. E. Moses Rd
N.M. Joshi Marg
Dr Babasaheb Ambedkar Rd
Barrister Nath Pai Marg
G.D Ambedkar Rd
Rafi Ahmed Kidwai Rd

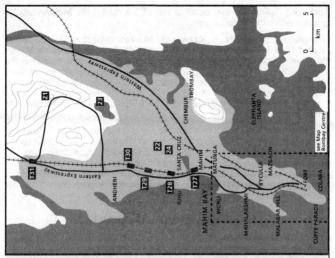

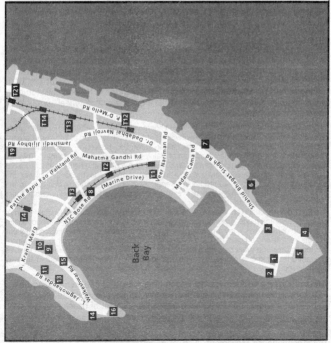

Lockwood Kipling. On the opposite side of the road is the **Maidan**, always popular with cricketers of all ages.

Immediately to the N is **Crawford Market** (Mahatma Jyotiba Phule Market,1865-71), at the junction of Lokmanya Tilak Marg and Dadabhoy Naoroji Rd. It was designed by Emerson in the 12th century French Gothic style. Over the entrance is more of Lockwood Kiplings' work. The paving stones are from Caithness! The market is divided into sections for fruit, vegetables, fish, mutton and poultry. From Crawford Market you can return to the Gateway of India or take a taxi to either the **Victoria and Albert Museum** at Byculla or **Malabar Hill.**

Between Crawford Market and Bombay Central Railway Station is **Falkland Road,** the centre of Bombay's red-light district. Prostitutes stand behind barred windows, giving the area its other name 'The Cages'. The much-praised film *Salaam Bombay* gave a striking insight into the life of a child prostitute in Falkland Street. Many of the girls and women are sold or abducted as forced labour from various parts of India and Nepal. Recent medical reports suggest that AIDS is now very widespread.

MARINE DRIVE AND MALABAR HILL

You can do an interesting half day trip from Churchgate Station, along Marine Drive to the Taraporewala Aquarium, Mani Bhawan (Gandhi Museum), the Babulnath temple, past the Parsi Towers of Silence to Kamla Nehru Park, the Hanging Gardens and the Jain Temple. If you wish you can go further towards Malabar Point to get a glimpse of Raj Bhawan and the Walkeshwar temple, before returning north via the Mahalaxmi Temple and Haji Ali's tomb on the W shore.

Churchgate Station (1894-6) designed by F.W. Stevens for the Bombay, Baroda and Central India Railway, is at the W end of Vir Nariman Road. Stevens was one of the great protagonists of what became known as the Indo-Saracenic style, a term which had earlier been applied inappropriately to Mughal architecture. With its domes and facades Churchgate station is Byzantine in flavour. The statue on the W gable shows a figure holding a locomotive and wheel, symbols of technological progress.

The "Dabbawallahs" If you go inside Churchgate station at mid-morning or after lunch, you will see the *dabbawallahs*. They are members of the Bombay Union of Tiffin Box Carriers. Each morning, the 2,500 dabbawallahs call on suburban housewives who pack freshly cooked lunch into small circular aluminium or stainless steel containers – "dabbas". They are divided into about four compartments, stacked one on the other and held together by a clip with a handle (they are widely available in general stores and bazaars). Typically the *dabbawallah* will collect 30-40 tiffin boxes, range them out on a long pole and cycle to the nearest station. Here he will hand them over to a fellow *dabbawallah* who will transport them into the city for delivery to the consumer.

Each day this goes on with over 100,000 lunches of maybe *sabze* (vegetable curry), *chappattis, dal* and pickle, making their way across town to the breadwinner and back again. The service which costs a few rupees a week, is a good example of the fine division of labour in India, reliable and efficient for the *dabbawallahs* pride themselves on never losing a lunch. It is Indian Meals on Wheels. Viewed in terms of traditional Hindu ritual pollution, it enables the family to rest knowing that carefully prepared 'pukka' (proper) food has not in any way been defiled.

Marine Drive and Chowpatty Beach The long stretch of white sand beach looks attractive from a distance, but on closer examination is polluted. Swimming here is not recommended. Like Juhu Beach there is a lot of beach activity.

Chowpatty has witnessed some significant events in India's comtemporary history as it was the scene for a number of important 'Quit India' rallies during the Independence Movement. Also, at important festivals like *Ganes Chaturthi* and *Dasara* (see Festivals), it is thronged with jubilant Hindu devotees. Netaji Subhash Rd, better known as Marine Drive, runs round the unimaginatively named **Back Bay** along Chowpatty from just below the Hanging Gardens on Malabar Hill to Nariman Point. At night, lined with lights, it is a very attractive sight from Malabar Hill, a view which gave rise to the description of it as 'Queen Victoria's Necklace'.

Towards the N end of Back Bay is the **Taraporewala Aquarium** Open 1100-2000, Closed Mon. Re 1. Regarded as one of the best aquariums in India for fresh and salt water fish. The latter has water piped from Back Bay. Shells and shell crafts on sale. Snacks are also widely available.

Gandhi Museum Further N just SW of Nana Chowk off Ramabai Rd is the Gandhi museum at **Mani Bhawan.** The nearest station is Grant Road. See Museums below.

The Towers of Silence are in secluded gardens 500 m to the W of the Gandhi Museum. This very private place is not accessible to tourists but it can be glimpsed from the road. Sir Jamshetji Jeejeebhoy gave a large area of land around the towers, thus affording them privacy and allowing the creation of a tranquil garden. Parsis believe that the elements of water, fire and earth must not be polluted by the dead, so they lay their 'vestments of flesh and bone' out on the top of the towers to be picked clean by vultures. See page 76. Some guides claim that the reason the Hanging gardens were created was to protect Bombay's water supply from being polluted by half-eaten corpses dropped by vultures. There is no truth in this.

The *Hanging Gardens* Immediately S of the Towers of Silence are **The Hanging Gardens** (Pherozeshah Mehta Gardens), in the centre of a low hill, so named since they are located on top of a series of tanks that supply water to Bombay. These are formal gardens with some interesting animal topiary with good views over the city.

Nearby is the Church of N India **All Saints' Church** (1882). Across the road from the Hanging gardens is the **Kamla Nehru Park,** a children's park that was laid out in 1952 and named after the wife of India's first Prime Minister with very good views over Back Bay. The *Naaz* café next door and the top terrace is a particularly good vantage point.

Jain Temple (1904). Built of marble and dedicated to the first Jain *Tirthankar*. Much of the decoration depicts the lives of the Tirthankars but overall the temple is not of great interest.

Raj Bhawan (Government House) is the Governor's official residence. Sir Evan Nepean (1812-1819) was the first to live there and succeeding Governors made various extensions and alterations. Entry is not permitted.

The Walkeshwar Temple (Lord of Sand) One of the oldest buildings in Bombay (few of which are old) is the Walkeshwar Temple (built about 1000 AD). In legend this was one of the resting points for Rama on his journey to Lanka to free his wife Sita from the demon king of Lanka, Ravana. The myths are retold in various ways in different parts of India. See page 786.

Here, the story goes that **Rama**, on his way from **Ayodhya** (Uttar Pradesh) to Lanka, stopped to rest. One day his brother **Lakshman** failed to return from Varanasi at the usual time with a lingam which he always fetched daily for Rama's worship. Rama then made a lingam from the beach sand to worship **Siva**. There is a small but attractive tank among the shrines and Brahmins' houses, believed to have been created when Rama shot an arrow into the ground.

From here you can return to Nariman Point and the Gateway of India, or you can continue along Laxmibai Jagmohandas Rd to Haji Ali's Tomb, the Rajabai Tower and maybe the Victoria Gardens. On **Bhulabhai Desai Rd** (Warden Rd) on Cumballa Hill there are the **Mahalaxmi temples**, the oldest in Bombay and dedicated to three goddesses whose images were found in the sea.

Haji Ali's Tomb and mosque are devoted to a Muslim saint who drowned here. They are reached by a long causeway usable only at low tide. Note the moneychangers willing to exchange One Rupee coins into individual paise coins, enabling pilgrims to make many individual gifts to beggars rather than one large one, thereby reputedly increasing the merit of the gift.

From Haji Ali's Tomb go along **Keshavrao Khade Rd** to **SG Maharaj Chowk** (Jacob's Circle). Go down Maulana Azad Rd then turn left into Clare Rd. On your right is **Christ Church, Byculla** (1835), which incorporated half the pillars originally intended for the Town Hall (See Central Bombay). Clare Rd leads onto **Babasaheb Ambedkar Rd** which runs along the side of the Victoria Gardens. There is a juice bar at the end.

The Victoria Gardens and Museum The Museum is a two storey Palladian building, and as such is unusual in a city dominated by Victorian Gothic (see Central Bombay). The museum, which houses an interesting display on the history of Bombay, was completed in 1872. In front of the museum is a clocktower (1865) The four faces show morning, noon, evening and night. Next door are the Victoria Gardens.

SERVICES

Hotels Broadly speaking, there are two concentrations of hotels in Bombay: the central area and Juhu. The central area includes Marine Drive, Nariman Point, Apollo Bunder and Colaba. Prices tend to be high but there are a large number of cheap hotels immediately behind the Taj. Prices though are higher than elsewhere in India.

Juhu is convenient for the airport and here there are a number of B and C category hotels, none of which has much character. Juhu Beach used to be quite an attractive and relaxed seaside area. It has now been absorbed into the metropolis and the Juhu's principal advantage is that it is close to the airports and therefore very convenient for early morning departures to Aurangabad for example. The sea is polluted and the beach is not pleasant enough for sunbathing but there is a lot happening on Sunday evenings when it has a fairground atmosphere. For services in **AL**, **A** and **B** hotels, see page 134.

Warning: Accommodation in Bombay is extremely heavily booked. Whenever possible make reservations in advance. If you have not, arrive as early in the day as possible.

Airport and Juhu Beach Hotels

All less than 10 km from the airport and approximately 20-25 km from the centre. Most are close to a suburban railway station

AL *Leela Kempinski*, Sahar. T 6363636, Cable: The Leela, Telex: 79236, 79241 Kemp in, Fax: 6360606. 280 rm. Excellent restaurants include Chinese-Hunan. Good sports facilities. **AL** *Welcomgroup Sea Rock Sheraton*. T 6425454, Cable: Searock, Telex: 71230, 71140 Rock in, 74599 Selc in. 398 rm. 6 restaurants (inc NW Frontier, Seafood and a Far-eastern revolving rooftop restaurant), live entertainment and dancing, squash, tennis and courtesy coach. Not well located for the city, but on water's edge and excellent for a relaxing stay or for an overnight stop from the airport. Best views from upper floors.

A *Centaur Juhu Beach*, Juhu Tara Rd, Juhu Beach, T 6143040, Cable: Centjuhu, Telex: 78181. 370 rm. **A** *Centaur*, Bombay Airport. T 6126660, Cable: Centaur, Telex: 71171 Chtl in, 288 rm. Floodlit tennis, jogging track, putting green. Very close to domestic airport. **A** *Holiday Inn*, Balraj Sahani Marg, Juhu Beach. T 6204444, Cable: Holiday Inn, Telex: 71432 Holi-in, Fax: 6204452. 210 rm. 2 pools, windsurfing, squash, tennis, courtesy coach to town. **A** *Ramada Inn Palm Grove*, Juhu Beach. T 6149361, Cable: Palmfronds, Telex: 71419 Palm in, Fax: 6142105. 113 rm. Full facilities plus windsurfing. **A** *Sun-n-Sand*, 39 Juhu Beach, Juhu. T 6201811, Cable: Sunandsand, Telex: 71282. 118 rm. Comfortable though cramped poolside. **A** *The Resort*, 11 Madh Marve Rd, Malad (W). T 682331, Cable: Aksabeach, Telex: 78127 Rahe in. 58 rm. 42 km centre. Wide range of sports. On the beach.

B *Sea Princess*, 969 Juhu Beach, Juhu. T 6122661, Cable: Seajuhu, Telex: 78160 Sph in. 72 rm. **B** *Airport Plaza*, 70C Nehru Rd, Ville Parle (E). T 6123390-3, Cable: Hotelplaza, Telex: 71365 Plza-in. 79 rm. Close to airport. Disco. Convenient for domestic airport. Comfortable, efficient, modern. **B** *Horizon*, 37 Juhu Beach. T 6148100, Cable: Beachrest, Telex: 71218 Horz in. 161 rm. Facilities incl disco. Good but no sea view. **B** *Sands*, 39/2 Juhu Beach. T 6204511, Cable: Chekinsand (SZ), Telex: 78046 Chek in. 40 rm. Courtesy coach to airport.

C *Airport Kohinoor*, JB Nagara, Andheri-Kurla Rd, Andheri (E). T 6348548-9, Telex: 79279 Haka in. 48 rm. Central a/c. Restaurant, courtesy coach. **C** *Ajanta*, 8 Juhu Rd, Juhu. T 6124890-1, Cable: Beach side, Telex: 78302 Rbex in. 32 a/c rm. Restaurant, 24 hr coach service to airport, TV, credit cards. **C** *Citizen*, 960 Juhu Beach, Juhu. T 6123790, Cable: Cit Hotel, Telex: 75590. 45 rm. 24 hr coffee shop. **C** *Jal*, Nehru Rd, Ville Parle (E). T 6123820, Cable: Hoteljal, Telex: 79006 Jal in. 40 a/c rm. Close to domestic airport. Restaurant, (Veg Indian & Chinese), coffee shop, rm service. **C** *Kumaria Presidency*, Andheri-Kurla Rd, facing International Airport, Marol Naka, Andheri (E). T 6042025-6, Cable: Kumpresi. 32 a/c rm. 8 km Bandra shopping centre. Restaurant, coffee shop, 24 hr exchange, travel. **C** *Parle International*, Agarwal Market, Ville Parle (E). T 6144335, Cable: Staywithus, Telex: 78208 Rama in. 39 a/c rm. Restaurant, bar, exchange, courtesy coach. **C** *Royal Inn*, opp Khar telephone exchange, Linking Rd, Khar (W). T 6495151. 23 a/c rm. Close to centre. Restaurant, exchange, travel, car hire, courtesy coach, TV. **C** *Transit*, Off Nehru Rd, Ville Parle (E). T 6129325. 46 a/c rm. Restaurant, bar, exchange, shops.

D *Atlantic*, 18B Juhu Tara Rd, Juhu. T 6122440-1, Cable: hotlantic. 27 a/c rm. Restaurants, bar, exchange, travel, courtesy coach, TV, credit cards. **D** *Caesars Palace*, 313 Linking Rd, Khar. T 542311-3, Cable: Homely. 20 a/c rm. Restaurants, bar, exchange. **D** *Jay Shree*, 197 Dayaldas Rd, Ville Parle (E). T 6127799. 30 a/c rm. Travel, car hire, courtesy coach, credit cards. **D** *King's*, 5 Juhu Tara Rd. T 6149775, Cable: Kings Juhu. 47 a/c rm. Restaurant, bar, courtesy coach to airport, TV, credit cards. Comfortable. **D** *Mayura*, 352 Linking Rd, Khar. T 6494416, Cable: Linkmayur. 28 rm. A/c rm. Restaurants, bar, 24 hr rm service, exchange, travel, TV, credit cards. **D** *Metro Palace*, Junction of Hill Rd and Waterfield Rd, Bandra (W). T 6427311, Cable: Hotel Metro, Telex: 78227 Metro in. 34 a/c rm. TV, bar, 24 hr rm service, laundry, travel, credit cards. **D** *Seaside*, 39/2 Juhu Rd, Juhu. T 6200923-7, Cable: Finestay. 36 a/c rm. Rm service, Diners, Visa. No sea view! **D** *Tunga International*, Plot B-11, MIDC, off Mahakali Caves Rd, Andheri (E). T 6366010, Cable: Hotel Hegde. 16 a/c rm. Restaurant, bar, rm service, car hire, Diners.

The less expensive hotels often have no restaurant but some will provide meals in rm. **E** *Galaxy*, 113 Prabhat Colony, Santa Cruz (W). T 6125223, Cable: Hot Galaxy. 24 rm, some a/c. Rm service, Amex. **E** *South End*, 11 Juhu Tara Rd, Juhu. T 6125213, Cable: Southendju. 38 rm, some a/c. Light refreshments. **E** *Manali*, Manchhubhai Rd, Malad (E). T 692004. 44 rm, some a/c. **E** *Rang Mahal*, Station Rd, Santa Cruz. T 6490303. 22 rm. Rm service (Indian).

Note: The Domestic terminal has retiring rooms for stays of under 24 hr. Bookings through Airport Manager.

Town hotels

All 25-30 km from airport, close to Victoria Terminus railway, with central locations.
AL *The Oberoi*, Nariman Point. T 2025757, Cable: Obhotel, Telex: 2337, 4153/4, 2334/5. 337 large rm. The newer Oberoi combining modern technology with period furniture. 4 restaurants (inc French), pool, health club, shops. **AL** *The Oberoi Towers*, Nariman Point. T 2024343, Cable: Obhotel, Telex: 4153/4, 2337, 2340, 2334/5. 594 rm. Excellent views. 9 restaurants/ bars plus discotheque, a garden pool on the 9th floor, vast shopping complex combined with excellent service. **AL** *Taj Mahal* and *Taj Mahal Intercontinental*, Apollo Bunder (Gateway of India). T 2023366, Cable: Inhotels, Telex: 3837, 6176, 2442, 6175, Fax: 2822711. 599 rm. Every facility with restaurants (inc French), excellent shopping parade and pastry shop. The former, the one to choose for style and character (wicker chairs still in the verandah). The latter is a plush, modern, world class 5 star hotel. Visit if you are not staying. **AL** *President*, 90 Cuffe Parade (Taj Group). T 4950808, Cable: Piemhotel, Telex: 4135, 5769, 3125 Pres In, Fax: 495-1201. 299 rm. Every facility with restaurants (inc Italian and Thai), excellent Indian 'Gulzar'. Good service, informal but lacks great character. Business hotel but others will find it equally comfortable and welcoming.

A *Ambassador*, Churchgate Extension, Vir Nariman Rd. T 2041131, Cable: Embassy, Telex: 2918 Amba in. 127 rm. All facilities, including revolving restaurant and pastry shop. Attractive rm.

B *Fariyas*, 25 Arthur Rd, off Bunder Rd, Colaba. T 2042911, Cable: Fariyas, Telex: 3272 Aban. 80 rm. Good restaurants, roof garden. **B** *Midtown Pritam*, Pritam Estates, Dadar. T 4300019, Telex: 76857 Prtm in. 63 rm. Terrace garden. **B** *Natraj*, 135 Netaji Subhash Rd. T 2044161, Cable: Hotelraja, Telex: 2302. 83 rm. Some rm have good views over the Bay, but otherwise lacks character. **B** *Ritz*, 5 Jamshedji Tata Rd. T 220141, 220116, Cable: Ritz, Telex: 2520. 72 rm, some a/c. Tourist Office and Churchgate Rly station.

C *Apollo*, 22 Lansdowne Rd, Apollo Bunder, Colaba, behind Taj Mahal Hotel (Gateway of

India). T 2020223, Cable: Apollotel, Telex: c/o 5929 Bl km in. 32 rm, some a/c, best with sea view. Restaurant, bar, car hire, TV. Very comfortable. **C** *Ascot*, 38 Garden Rd. T 240020, Cable: Ascohotel, Telex: 71361. 26 a/c rm, some with bath. Restaurant (Indian), Amex, Mastercard. **C** *Godwin*, 41 Garden Rd, Colaba. T 241226, Cable: Hoshee, Telex: 5929 Bl km in. 48 a/c rm. Restaurant, bar, rooftop garden, Amex. **C** *Grand*, 17 Sprott Rd, Ballard Estate. T 268211, Cable: Grandhotel. 72 a/c rm. Restaurant, exchange, bookshop. Old fashioned, built around a central courtyard but relaxing. **C** *Hilltop*, 43 Pochkanwala Rd, Worli. T 4930860, Telex: 71361. 70 a/c rm. Restaurant. **C** *Shalimar*, August Kranti Marg. T 8221311, Cable: Nicehotel, Telex: 75087. 74 a/c rm. Restaurant, bar, exchange, bookshop. **C** *West End*, 45 New Marine Lines. T 299121, Cable: Besthotel, Telex: 2892 Best in. 80 a/c rm. Restaurant (Indian, Continental), bar, 24 hr rm service, exchange, shops, laundry, house doctor, credit cards.

D *Astoria*, 4 JT Rd, Churchgate. T 221514-7, Cable: Casablanca. 70 a/c rm. Restaurant, bar, car hire. **D** *Diplomat*, 24-26 BK Bonam Behram Marg, Colaba. T 2021661, Cable: Bedi-hotels. 52 a/c rm. 25 km airport, 2 km VT rly, close to centre. Restaurants, bar, exchange, credit cards. Behind Taj, quiet and homely. **D** *Garden*, 42 Garden Rd, Colaba. T 241476, 241700, Cable: Gardenotel. 32 a/c rm. Restaurant, TV. **D** *Heritage*, Sant Savta Marg, Byculla. T 8514981-5, Cable: Lascalla. 84 a/c rm. Restaurant, bar, Amex, Diners. **D** *Kemps Corner*, 131 August Kranti Marg. T 8224646. 35 a/c rm. Breakfast only, travel, TV, credit cards. **D** *Samraj*, Chakala Rd, Andheri (E). T 6349311-5, Telex: 79107 Pscj in. 32 a/c rm. Restaurant, exchange, car hire, credit cards. **D** *Nagina*, 53 Dr Ambedkar Rd, Byculla. T 8517799. 52 a/c rm. TV, exchange, credit cards. **D** *Parkway*, Sivaji Park, Renade Rd, Dadar. T 45361-3, Cable: Parkwaves, Telex: 76857. 15 a/c rm. **D** *Rajdoot*, 19 Jackeria Bunder Rd, Cotton Green. T 8514442-4, Cable: Superotel. 56 rm, some a/c. Restaurant. **D** *Rosewood*, 99C Tulsiwadi, opp A/c market. T 4940320-7, Cable: Rosegotel, Telex: 76396 Rose in. 50 rm, some with TV. Central a/c. Restaurant, exchange, doctor on call, car hire, credit cards. **D** *Sea Green*, 145 Marine Drive. T 222294, 222235, Cable: Seahotel. 34 rm, some a/c, with sea view best. TV lounge, credit cards. **D** *Sea Palace*, 26 PJ Ramchandani Marg (Strand Rd). T 241828, Cable: silverend, Telex: Lxry 3252. 48 rm, some a/c. Restaurant, credit cards. **D** *Chateau Windsor Guest House*, 86 Vir Nariman Rd, next to Ambassador Hotel, T 2043376. 36 rm good clean rm. Friendly, good value. **D** *Lord Hotel*, 301 Mangalore St, Fort, Near P D'Mello Rd, T 262600. 36 good rm. Beer parlour. **E** *Norman's Guest House*, 2 Firdaus, 127 Marine Drive. T 294234. 6 rm, some a/c. Car hire. **D** *Anukool*, 292-8 Maulana Skaukatali Rd (in Shri Ram Smitri Building, corner of Grant Rd. T 392401, Cable: Staymore. 23 rm, some a/c. Coffee shop, credit cards. Good value.

E *Aroma*, 190 Dr Ambedkar Rd, Dadar. T 4111761, Cable: Hotel Aroma. 37 rm, some a/c. Terrace garden. **E** *Balwas*, 323 Maulana Shoukat Ali Rd, Grant Rd. T 363313, Cable: Balwas, Telex: 75879 Seal in. 27 rm, some a/c. **E** *Bentley's*, 17 Oliver Rd, nr the Harbour, Colaba. T 241474, Cable: Kakagroup. 37 rm, some a/c. Breakfast incl in rate, exchange, car hire, Mastercard. Good value. **E** *Lawrence Hotel* Rope Walk La. Behind Prince of Wales Museum. T 243618 Tiny, usually full, good value. **E** *Manora*, 243-245 PD Mello Rd. T 267509, Cable: Welcostay. 54 rm, some a/c with TV. Car hire. **E** *Nalanda*, CP Rd, Kandivali (E). T 6886538. 32 rm, some a/c. TV in lobby, Diners. **E** *Pals*, Reay Rd, Cotton Green, Kalachowki. T 8511951, Cable: Resthaven. 59 rm. A/c restaurant. **E** *Parklane*, 95 Dadasaheb Phalke Rd, near Dadar Central Railway Station, Dadar. T 448241, Cable: Parkotel. 23 rm, some a/c. Rm service. **E** *Rupam*, 239 P D'Mello Rd, Victoria Terminus. T 266226, Cable: Superotel. 37 rm, some a/c with phone. Clean, friendly, comfortable beds. **E** *Sea Green South*, 145A Marine Drive. T 221613, Cable: Hotelsouth. 36 rm, some a/c. TV lounge, credit cards. **E** *Railway Hotel*, Raja Rammohan Rd. T 351028. 31 rm. Non a/c rm. Beer parlour. Very basic. **E** *Sahara*, 35 Tribhuvan Rd (above Sher-e-Punjab restaurant). T 361491. 31 rm, some a/c. 19 km airport, 2 km rly, 1 km centre. Laundry, car hire. **E** *Whalley's Guest House*, Jaji Mansion, 41 Mereweather Rd. T 221802. 25 rm, some a/c with balcony and bath. 20 km airport, 2 km rly. Inc breakfast, accepts Traveller's Cheques. **E** *Seashore*, T 2874237, has good rm, facing sea.

The *YMCA International House and Programme Centre*, 18 YMCA Rd, nr Bombay Central, Bombay 400008. T 891191. Non a/c s and d without baths. Meals included. Rs 40 Temporary Membership Charge. Very good value. It is usually booked up three months in advance so book early. The *YWCA International Guest House*, 18 Madame Cama Rd, Fort, Bombay 400039. T 2020445. Pleasant non a/c rooms with bath and continental breakfast. For men and women. Temporary Membership needed – Rs 10 per month. Deposit required for advance reservations. Also *YWCA* at 34 Mostibai St, Byculla, T 372744.

Budget hotels The majority are clustered around the Taj Mahal Hotel, an interesting contrast. *Rex & Stiffles*, 8 Ormiston St, T 231518. Stiffles on 1st and 2nd floors, Rex on 3rd and 4th. Simple. Some a/c rm, many cramped but secure. Be there early. The *Salvation Army Red Shield Hostel*, 30 Mereweather Rd, T 241824. Mostly dormitories and some rooms, incl large doubles. Lockers for hire. Check out 0900. Meals included. Book in advance or be there early, i.e. to check in as others check out. Another Guest House at *Social Service Centre*, 122 Maulana Azad Rd, Byculla, T 241824. *Carlton*, 12 Mereweather Rd, T230642 and *Prosser*, corner of Henry Rd and PJ Ramchandani Marg, T 241715 and *Oliver Guest House*, Walton Rd have non a/c rooms without baths. On Arthur Bunder Rd there are several all basically the same: *Mukund, Gulf and Al-Hijaz hotels, Janata, Imperial, India and Gateway Guest Houses.*

Accommodation In Clubs C *Royal Bombay Yacht Club*, Apollo Bunder. 30 rm, s and d. A bearer in attendance for small extra charge. Temporary membership needed, about Rs 270 for 10 days. A club with character. **C** *Cricket Club of India*, D Vacha Rd, T 220262. 40 rm, s and d. Central, spacious grounds, good restaurant and excellent service. In demand so book in advance. Temporary membership, approx Rs 170 for 15 days. Popular so book well in advance.

Both clubs have comfortable accommodation at reasonable rates for visitors. Not plush but relaxing, in spacious surroundings. More details under clubs. Apply to Secretary of each for membership and to reserve rm.

Restaurants

Recommended restaurants are marked with an *.
Buffet Lunches: Becoming increasingly popular with visitors and local people. Plenty to eat and good value. Usually 1230-1500 unless indicated and about Rs 60-150 excluding beverages.

Ballroom*, Taj Mahal, T 202366, reservations advised; *Outrigger** (Polynesian) and *Mughal Room* *(Indian), Oberoi Towers, T 2024343. Not on Sun; *Gourmet*, West End Hotel, T 299121; *Rangoli*, Performing Arts Complex, T 234678. Daily; *Real McKoy* (Mon-Sat) and *Trattoria* (Sun), President Hotel, T 4950808; Grand Hotel, T 268211. Mon-Sat. *The Top*, Ambassador Hotel, T 291131; *Chopsticks* (Chinese), 90 Vir Nariman Rd, T 2049284; *Talk of the Town* (Indian and continental), 143 Netaji Subhash Rd, T 2230883; *Dasaprakash*, Lakshmi Building, Sir P.M. Rd, T2861753. Mon-Sat.

Out of Town: *Palace of the West Empress* (Chinese), Searock Hotel, T 6425454 Ext. 270, *Holiday Inn**, T 571425. Poolside, *Sunset Room*, Sun-n-Sand Hotel, T 571481, *Centaur Hotel*, T 612660 are on Sun only; *Iskcon**, T 626860, Gujarati vegetarian. Good value. Daily.

Continental and Indian *The Abanara*, Fariyas Hotel, 25, Off Arthur Bunder Rd, Colaba, T 2042911; *Berrys*, Churchgate, T 253954; *Cafe Royal*, Oberoi Towers, T 2024343. Bonaparte colour scheme – green and purple. Entirely French (ingredients flown from Paris). Very expensive. 1230-1500, 2000-2400; *Delhi Durbar**, Holland House, Shahid Bhagat Singh Rd, Colaba, T 2020235. Also in Falkland Road, the 'Red Light' district. Good and cheap; *Gallops*, Western India Turf Club, Mahalaxmi, T 397884; *Gaylord*, Vir Nariman Rd, Churchgate, T 221231. Tables inside and out, with barbecue for Tandoori or western. Pleasantly refurbished, good bar. Daily 1230-1500, 2000-2400; *Kobe Sizzlers*, Hughes Rd, T 8115174; *The Library*, Hotel President, T 4950808; *Lido Bar*, Ritz Hotel, J Tata Rd, T 220141. Oldest Italian restaurant in town. 1200-1500, 1830-2400; *Mela*, Dr Annie Besant Rd, Worli, T 4945656; *Menage à Trois**, The Taj Mahal Inter-Continental Hotel, T 2023366. Mainly nouvelle cuisine. 1230-1500, reservations rec; *Moti Mahal*, Bandra, T 6401161; *Rangoli, Rendezvous* and *The Sea Lounge*, Taj Mahal Hotel, T 2023366.

Rendezvous* French cuisine under the guidance of Les Trois Frères, London. Excellent views, fine service and elegant atmosphere. Expensive with dance band at night. 1230-1500, 1930-2400; *La Rotisserie**, Oberoi Hotel, T 2024343. Subtle decor of cream and rust, light wood furniture and decorative flower arrangements. Emphasis on Continental food. Very expensive. 1230-1500, 2000-2400; *Samovar*, Jehangir Art Gallery, Kala Ghoda; *The Wayside Inn*, 38 K Dubhash Marg, T 244324; *The Society*, Ambassador Hotel, T 2041131; *Supper Club*, Oberoi Towers, T 2024343. Good views, nightly cabaret and dancing. Expensive; *Talk of the Town*, 143 Netaji Subhash Rd, T 221074. Elaborate wall hangings from Nepal and S India. Accent on continental food but Indian dishes available. Band nightly for dancing except Mon. Pleasant outdoor cafe for coffee and snacks. Open 1100-2400; *Tanjore**, Taj Mahal Hotel, T 2023306. Beautiful surroundings, excellent food and wide variety of regional dishes. Indian classical music and dance. Expensive but good; *Trattoria**, President Hotel, T 4950808. Terracotta tiles, whitewashed walls decorated with colourful plates give it a pleasant airy feel. Italian food and ice-creams, quite reasonable.

Out of Town: *Indian Harvest*, Leela Kempinski Hotel, T 6363636; *Lobster Pot**,

Searock Hotel, T 6425454. Striking decor in black and white. Good sea food dishes, plus salmon and pomfret. Evening entertainment. Expensive. Open 1230-1500 and 200-2400; *Neptune*, Holiday Inn, T 6204444.

Mughlai and Tandoori *Balwa's*, Maker Bhawan, 3 Thackersey Marg, New Marine Lines, T 251108. Inexpensive, well-prepared food. Daily 0930-2300; *Berry's*, Vir Nariman Rd, near Churchgate Station, T 2046041. Tandoori specialities. Good *kulfi**. Reasonable prices; *Copper Chimney**, Annie Besant Rd, Worli T 22513. Window into kitchen so you can see how it is done. Very good food, from extensive menu. Reasonable prices. 1200-1600, 1900-0100; *Copper Chimney**, K Dubhash Marg, T 4924488, behind Prince of Wales Building. Different management to the above. Subdued lighting and quietly tasteful. Good N Indian dishes. Kitchen visible. 1230-1500, 1930-0030; *Delhi Durbar**, 197 Falkland Rd, nr Regal. Good biryanis. 0830-0300!

Golden Gate, Madame Cama Rd, T 2027989; *Gulzar**, President Hotel, T 4950808. Excellent Hyderabadi and Mughlai dishes and biryanis. Pleasant ethnic decor, dinner time entertainment; *Gulshan**, Palton Rd, Crawford Market. Downstairs for men. Popular for breakfasts. 0700-0200! *Khyber**, Kala Ghoda, Fort. Good Punjabi food, pleasant atmosphere; *Kabab Corner**, Natraj Hotel, T 2044261. Rustic looking interior with thatched roof alcoves. Kebabs a speciality. Breakfast 0700-1000, 1200-1530, 1530-1900 (snacks), 2000-0030; *Kwality* has branches at 252C, Dr Annie Besant Rd, T 4936369, India House, Kemps Corner, T 364991 and Worli. Indian and Continental. Medium priced. Daily 1030-2400.

Kandahar and *The Moghul Room*, The Oberoi Hotel, T 2025757. *The Moghul Room** has classic Mughlai dishes and entertainment (folk dances). Very good fish *makhani**, mutton *begum bahar* and handkerchief-thin *roomali roti*. 2000-2400. Also lunchtime buffets.

Kandahar* has a more hushed atmosphere and specialises in NW Frontier foods – kebabs, tandoori dishes and breads. Attentive service. Expensive but excellent. *Manjit da Dhaba**, corner of West and Main Avenue, opp Grindlays Bank, Linking Rd, Santa Cruz, T 539362. Simple atmosphere – eating around a mango tree on rush seats round simple wooden tables. Emphasis on authentic N Indian food. Many dishes are served in *handis* (casserole dishes). Quite expensive. 2000-2400. Reservations essential, popular with young people; *Pritam Da Dhaba*, Dadar, T 457817; *Santoor*, Maker Arcade, Cuffe Parade, nr President Hotel, T 215449. Small. Mughlai and Kashmiri specialities. Chicken *malai* chop (with cream), *chana* Peshawari (puri with chickpeas), Kashmiri soda made with salt and pepper recommended. 1130-1500, 1930-2330; *Sapna*, Vir Nariman Rd, T 2043687. Very traditional Mughlai delicacies, bar. Some tables outside. Attentive service, good value. 1200-2330; *Sheetal*, 648 Khar Pali Rd. Excellent sea-food too; *Sher-e Punjab**, 389 B Dr DB Marg, (Lamington Rd), T 361491. Wide choice of tandoori, Mughlai and Continental dishes. Pleasant, with recorded music. Also at 261/4 S Bhagat Singh Rd, T 265284, 260431. Good food in simple surroundings. Try *makai ki roti*, *saag* and *tandoori* chicken; *Yogi*, Sion, T 483972; *Vaishali*, Chembur, T 5516597. **Out of town:** *The Bageecha*, Holiday Inn, T 6204444; *Daavat**, 21-25 Natasha Shopping Centre, 52 Hill Rd, Bandra, T 6402625, nr Welcomgroup Searock Hotel. Look for small sign on dark door. Marble floor and pleasant garden. Authentic traditional N India food. Quite expensive. 1230-1530, 1930-2330; *Earthen Oven*, Searock Hotel, T 6425454; *Gazebo*, Bandra, T 6421075; *Oceanwide*, Centaur Hotel, Juhu, T 6143040.

Goanese These are all simple but inexpensive, serving authentic Goan food. New *Martin's**, 21 Glamour House, Strand Rd, Colaba. Excellent sea food and pork Sorpotel. Very busy; *City Kitchen*, 301 Shahid Bhagat Singh Rd, Fort Market. T 260002. Closed Sun and holidays.

Out of town: *St Mary Hotel**, 120 St Mary Rd, Mazgaon, T 868475. Small inexpensive upstairs restaurant with 6 tables. Chutney fish fry and beef tongue, specialities. *Goa Portuguesa* is one of the newer ethnic restaurants which attracts people who matter in the city and visiting VIPs. It brings authentic dishes to a comfortable restaurant where you can try *sungto* (prawn) served between *papads*, *kalwa* (oyster), *teesryo* (shell) and clams and to end the meal *bibinca*. Lobsters cooked with tomatoes, onions and spices. Others are *O Balcao* and *Saayba**, Bhatiya Building, opp Bandra Masjid, SV Rd. Mainly seafood. Closed Mon.

Gujarati and Western Indian: *The Village*, Poonam Intercontinental, near the Mahalaxmi race-course. Set up like a Gujarati village Sea views, good food; *Rajdhani**, nr Crawford Market; *Samrat**, behind Eros cinema, J Tata Rd; *Chetna**, 34K Dubash Marg, opp Jehangir Art Gallery. Veg dishes; *Thacker's**, corner M Karve Rd and 1st Marine St, T 8229290, 8111784. Good *thalis*. Home cooked specialities at *Thaili**, Tara Baug Estate, Chasrni Rd, T 355934. *Purohits**, Vir Naviman.

Parsi Bombay has the heaviest concentration of Parsis in the country, so try their cuisine here

– *Dhansak*, a special lentil curry with lamb or chicken, *Patrani machli* is fish (often pomfret) stuffed with coconut chutney and coriander, steamed in banana leaves, Bombay Duck, a salted dried white fish. *Piccolo Café**, 11A Sir Homi Mody St, T 274537. Open 0900-1800, closed Sat pm and Sun. Profits to charity. Homely, clean, good *dhansak*. *Landmark*, 35 S Patkar Marg, T 8226077. Both Piccolo and this, run by Ratan Tata Institute but the latter is a fully fledged restaurant. Open 1030-2330, Closed Mon. Parsi and Continental. Try kid *gosht* cooked with cashew nuts in coconut milk or the vegetarian stew *lagasara*. Takeaway shop next door. *Dorabjee's Ram Panjab**, Ambedkar Rd; *Hotel Heritage*, Sant Savta Marg, Byculla, T 8514891. Extensive range, including *dhansak*, *sale boti* (meat, spicy gravy, poppyseeds and cashew nuts), prawns patia (prawns, garlic, tomato and onion). 0700-2400. Another is *Bombay A1**, 7 Proctor Rd (Grant Rd Junc), T 381146. Closed National Holidays. Cheerful, varied cuisine, incl Parsi speciality – *Patrani machli. Rasna* and *Purohit**, nr Churchgate; Two family run restaurants are also recommended – *Britannia and Goa**, Wakefield House, Sprott Rd, Ballard Estate (0900-1800) and *Paradise**, Sindh Chambers, Colaba Causeway (closed Mon). On Mahatma Gandhi Rd (N end), you can have a good traditional breakfast, often as early 0600 at *Bastani*, *Kyani* or the *Sassanian Restaurant* .

South Indian *New Indian Coffee Shop*, Kittridge Rd, Sassoon Dock. Good Kerala breakfast; *Woodlands**, Mittal Chambers, Nariman Point, nr Oberoi Towers, T2023499. Closed Sun. Excellent *Idli* and *dosai* and good *thalis*. Busy at lunchtime. 1100-2300. *Kamat**, Electric House, Colaba, T 2874734. Very inexpensive *thalis* and vegetarian snacks. 0830-2230. *Bristol Grill*, Lakshmi Building, 22A Sir PM Rd, T 258462. S Indian vegetarian.

Chinese Some close for 3 days over Chinese New Year. *China Garden**, 123 August Kranti Marg, T 8280842. Bar. Interesting, imaginative menu, incl Thai and Japanese. Reasonably expensive, service can be slow. 1230-1500 1930-2400; *Chinatown*, 99 August Kranti Marg, Kemps Corner, T 8227147. Upstairs more comfortable. Szechwan, Cantonese and Mandarin dishes. 27 soups to choose from; *Chinese Palace*, Tardeo A/c Market, T 4940777; *Chinese Room*, Kemp's Corner, T 8225068; *Chopsticks**, 354 Vithal Bhai Patel Rd (Linking Rd), W Bombay, T 5377789. Mainly Cantonese. Some tables in garden. 1200-1500, 1700-1900. Generous helpings; *Chopsticks**, 90 A Vir Nariman Rd, Churchgate, T 2049284. Good food. Moderately priced, offering unusual dishes, e.g. taro nest, date pancakes and toffee bananas. 1230-1500, 1700-2400. Other branches at Jewel Mahal A/c Shopping Complex and Seven Bungalows, Versova, T 625750.

 Flora, Worli Seaface, A Gaffar Khan Rd, nr Hilltop Hotel, T 4937690. Over 200 dishes available. 1130-2330; *Golden Dragon**, Taj Mahal Hotel, T 2023366; Szechwan dishes. Expensive. 1230-1500, 1930-2400; *Golden Gate*, Madame Cama Rd, T 2026306; *HongKong*, Apollo Bunder, T 2022919; *Kamling**, 82 Vir Nariman Rd, T 2042618; Cantonese. Simple and good, often busy. Wide selection of ice creams. 1200-2330; *Mandarin**, Dhanraj Mahal, Sivaji Maharaj Marg, Apollo Bunder, T 2023186; *Nanking**, Apollo Bunder, nr Gateway of India, T 2020594. Good choice of Cantonese dishes. Very good food, reasonable prices. Fish ball soup, Whole Pomfret Nanking (for two), Pickled fish with rice and Beef with watercress. 1230-1500, 1930-2400; *Tuktuks*, 9 Dharaun Palace, Hughes Rd, T 8113958. *Out of town*: *Great Wall of China*, Leela Kempinski Hotel, T 6363636; *Sampan*, Holiday Inn Hotel, T 6204444.

24-Hr Coffee Shops *Cafe au lait**, President Hotel, T 4950808; *La Brasserie**, The Oberoi Hotel, T 2025757; *Oceanic*, Searock Hotel, T 6425454; *Samarkhand**, Oberoi Towers Hotel, T 2024343; *Shamiana**, The Taj Mahal Hotel, T 2023366; *Sea Lounge*, Taj Inter-Continental Hotel, T 2023366; *Trattoria**, President Hotel, T 4950808; Decked out like a rustic tavern. Reasonable pasta dishes; *Waterfall Cafe*, Leela Kempinski Hotel, T 6363636; *Shoreline*, Centaur Hotel, Juhu, T 6143040; *Coffee Shop*, T 571435 and *Sidewalk*, Holiday Inn Hotel, T 6204444.

Vegetarian *Landmark*, S Patkar Marg, T 8226077; *Kamats Restaurant**, Navrose Mansion Tardeo Rd, T 388586; *Dasa Prakash*, at Bristol Grill, Sir PM Rd, T 254862 (S Indian Buffet); *Kubera*, Churchgate; *Purohits Hotel**, Vir Nariman Rd, T 2046241. Excellent for *thalis*. 1030-2300; *Rasna**, Churchgate Reclamation, J Tata Rd, T 220995. Closed Sun; *Sahyadri*, M Karve Rd; *Samarambh*, next to BEST House, Bhagat Singh Rd, T 2874734. Good *thalis*, *chola battura*, a *puri* topped with spiced chickpeas 0800-2200; *Samrat**, Prem Court, J Tata Rd, Churchgate, T 220022. Large Gujarati *thalis*; *Sanman*, Churchgate, T 258777; *Satkar*, Indian Express Building, Churchgate, 293259. Delicious individual vegetarian dishes. Prices higher in a/c section. 0830-2200.

 Shilpa, 112/A Panchratna, 1st Floor Opera Building, T 388427. 1100-2245, Sun 1100-1445, 1800-2245; *Status*, Nariman Point, T 2872821; *Tavern*, Nariman Point; *The Sun*, B Desai Rd, T 8229663; *Woodlands*, Nariman Point; Madras style *thalis*. 0600-2300,

Sun 1200-1500, 1800-2300; *Thacker's**, Birla Krida Kendra, Chowpatty, T 8112859, 8111614. **Out of town:** *Shakahari*, Centaur Hotel, Juhu, T T 6143040; *Woodland's Garden Cafe**, Juhu Scheme, Vaikuntial Mehta Rd, T 6145886. *Vega*, Searock Hotel, T 6425454.

Snacks, Light Meals and Beverages

Pizzas and Burgers *Gazebo Open House*, 537 Vithal Bhai Patel Rd (Linking Rd), T 546118. Burgers, pizzas, confectionery and ice-creams, recorded Western music. Also takeaway and branch at Vir Nariman Rd, opp Churchgate station; *New Yorker*, 25 Chowpatty Sea Face, T 356018. Pizzas, sandwiches and Mexican fast food, ice-cream; *Pizza King*, Nylor House, 245 Dr Annie Besant Rd, Worli, T 4939757 and 6 Tirupati Shopping Centre, Warden Rd, T 4926058; *Waikiki*, 16 Murzban Rd, T 2044112. Clean and cheerful. burgers and ice-creams. 1000-2400. Others at *Kobe Sizzlers*, Hughes Rd nr Sukh Sagar and *Sundance Cafe*, Eros Building, Churchgate which also has Mexican and Continental food. *Akbarally's Snack Bar*, Vir Nariman Rd, T 2043921.

Western Ice-Cream *Snowmans*, B Desai Rd. Rich western style ice-creams. There are also ice-cream parlours by the Natraj Hotel on Netaji Subhash Rd and *K. Rustom's & Co*, Brabourne Stadium, Churchgate, opp Ambassador Hotel.

Indian Snacks Snacks are also available on Chowpatty Beach and are cheap. Better to eat from a banana leaf than from a crockery plate that has been washed in a bucket of dubious looking water. Stalls open 1500-2400. *Indian Fast Food*, Vithal Bhai Patel (Linking) Rd, opp the National College. *Fountain Dry Fruit Stall* at Flora Fountain. Badami (rich almond collection), pedah (milk and sugar sweet) and nuts. *Rasna Restaurant*, nr KC College, Churchgate, T 220995. Indian, Chinese and vegetarian snacks. Garden cafe, packed lunches. *Chimney Restaurant and Bar*, Filka Building, Daftary Rd nr E Bombay Rly Station also does snacks and packed lunches. Behind Taj Mahal Hotel, *Sheekh Kabab Stall** on Tulloch Rd does excellent Muslim snacks. Opens 1900.

Sweetmeats and kulfis *Brijwasi*, all over Bombay. High quality Indian sweets and savouries; *Dave Farshan and Sweet Mart*, Malabar Hill near Babulnath Temple. Excellent *jalebis* (batter whirls, dipped in syrup). 0630-2100; *Mathura Dairy*, nr Ambassador Hotel for a variety of sweets; *Princess Kulfi House*, Samaldas Marg (Princess St). Sweets and ice-creams; *Parsi Dairy Farm*, Shamaldas Gandhi Rd, T 313634 for excellent ice-creams. *Badshah's** opp Crawford Market and *Kailash Parbat**, *Third Pasta Le*, Colaba for *kulfi* sundaes.

Fruit and Fruit Juice *Sukh Sagar*, opp Chowpatty on S.V.P. Rd. Fresh fruit juices and ice-creams plus other snacks. 0900-0100; *Dipty's* opp Rex Hotel, good for drink, ice-creams and light snacks. *Edward VIII*, 113A Bhagat Singh Rd and *Canteena Juice Centre* nr Delhi Durbar are good for juices and *falooda** (ice-cream, milk and fruit syrup). *Badshah's** opp Crawford Market and *Kailash Parbat** in Colaba offer exotic pressed fruit. *Haji Ali's* juice Bar.

Beverages *Coffee Centre*, Homi Mody St. Three doors down from the Piccolo. Good fresh-brewed Indian coffee and snacks; *Cream Centre*, 25B, Chowpatty Sea Face, T 8112025; *Tea Centre*, Resham Bhawan, Vir Nariman Rd. 1100-1900, Closed Sun; *Ritz Coffee Bar*, Churchgate. Tea: *Gaylords Sea Lounge*, *Jahangir's Gallery*, *Chuchgate Station café*.

Bars All the major hotels and the top restaurants have bars but others may only serve beer. *The Ambassador* has excellent all-round views, as do the *Taj* and *Oberoi* hotels, but at a price. If you are happy to just drink beer, try the *Naaz Café* on Malabar Hill, *Golkuli* in Colaba or the small Irani restaurants in Churchgate or Fort which are allowed to serve beer.

Clubs *Bombay Gymkhana Club*, Main Mahatma Gandhi Rd, T 2040311. *National Sports Club of India*, Lajpatrai Marg, Worli, T 4938827. *Radio Club*, 15 Arthur Bunder Rd, T 245025. *Cricket Club of India*, Brabourne Stadium, Dinshaw Wacha Rd, T 235313. 40 rm (see under Hotels). Temporary membership about Rs 170 for 15 days open to anyone. For membership and rm booking, contact The Secretary. Affiliated clubs are the Royal Overseas League, London and the Caledonian Club, Edinburgh. Cricket, badminton, tennis, pool, squash, table tennis and cards. Central with large and pleasant grounds. *Royal Bombay Yacht Club*, Apollo Bunder. 30 rm (see under Hotels). Temporary membership about Rs 270 for 10 days. Contact the Secretary for details and room bookings. Library, billiards, table tennis. Pleasant garden. *Willingdon Club*, Haji Ali Rd, T 4945754.

Changing money

Banks Most are open from 1000-1400, Mon – Fri and 1000-1200, Sat. Closed on National holidays, 30 June and 31 Dec.

Foreign Banks *American Express* DN Rd, T 2048196. *Bank of America*, Express Towers, Nariman Po,, T 2023431. *Bank of Tokyo*, Jeevan Prakesh, PM Rd, T 2860564. *Banque Nationale de Paris*, 62 Homji St, T 253487. *Barclays*, Maker Tower F, Cuffe Parade, T 212797. *British Bank of Middle East*, 16 Vir Nariman Rd, T 296077. *Chartered Bank*, 25 MG Rd, T 2047198. *Citibank*, 239 DN Rd, T 258853. *Grindlays*, MG Rd, T 270162. *Hongkong and Shanghai*, 52 MG Rd, T 275319.

Indian Banks *State Bank of India*, Bombay Samachar Marg (at Centaur Airport Hotel until 2200), T 2863896 and at Churchgate, behind Govt Of India Tourist Office among others. *Reserve Bank of India*, Foreign Exchange Dept, New Central Office Building, Bhagat Singh Rd, T 295602. *ABN Bank*, 19 Vir Nariman Rd, T 252331. *Andhra Bank*, 18 Homi Modi St, Fort, T 2046160.*Bank of India*, Express Towers, Nariman Pt, T 2023020. *Union Bank of India*, 239 Backbay Reclamation, Nariman Pt, T 2024033.

Credit Cards *American Express* Majithia Chambers, 276 Dr DN Rd, T 2048291. *Diners Club*, Raheka Chambers, 213 Nariman Pt, T 244949. *VISA*, ANZ Grindlays Bank, 90 MG Rd, T 270007. *Mastercard*, Bank of America, Express Towers.

Shopping

Most shops are open for business on weekdays 1000-1900, the bazaars sometimes staying open as late as 2100. Best buys in Bombay are textiles, particularly tie and dye from Gujarat, hand-block printed cottons, Aurangabad and 'Patola' silks, and gold bordered saris from Surat and Khambat. Wood carving and brass ware and handicrafts of all kinds make good gifts. Jewellery and leather goods also attract the Western shopper. The hotel arcade shops often stock a good selection of high quality goods but prices are usually higher than you would pay elsewhere in the city. The *Oberoi* has 200 shops in a two storeyed 'arcade' while those at the *Taj Mahal* are along corridors in the main building.

Popular bazaars are *Crawford Market*, Mata Ramabai Ambedkar Rd, (fun for the bargain hunter) and *Zaveri Bazaar*, both with lines of shops, selling under the sun. For clothing try Dr Dadabhai Naoroji Rd, *Colaba Causeway shops* starting near the Taj Mahal Hotel.

For a different experience try *Chor (Thieves') Bazaar*, on Maulana Shaukat Ali Rd in central Bombay, full of finds – from Raj left-overs to precious jewellery. Some claim that the infamous name is unjustified since the original was "Shor" (noisy) bazaar! Fridays allow 'junk' carts to sell less expensive "antiques" and fakes. *Phillips Antiques*, Indian Merchants Mansions, Madame Cama Rd opp Regal Cinema is an Aladdin's Cave of bric-a-brac and curios.

You can buy silver by weight at the *silver bazaar* at Mumbadevi. Other shopping streets are Shahid Bhagat Singh Rd, Mangaldas Market, M Karve Rd and Linking Rd, Bandra.

Leather Try Dhaboo St bazaar for bargains or pay higher prices at the arcade shops in top hotels. Ask taxi driver for 'Bendi Bazaar'. Good quality and wide selection and at a fraction of the price paid for the real thing. Also *Rasalbhai Adamji*, on Colabra causeway, behind Taj.

Musical instruments If you are keen on Indian musical instruments, the approved shops on the Tourist Office list are RS *Mayeka* at No 386, *Haribhau Vishwanath* at No 419 and *Ram Singh and Sons* at Bharati Sadan, all on Sardar V Patel Rd,

Government Emporia All good for handicrafts and textiles at fixed prices. Most representative of the region is *Gurjari*, 27 Khaitan Bhavan, JN Tata Rd, T 296292. Particularly good for textiles, furnishings, wood carving and brassware. *Central Cottage Industries Emporium*, Apollo Bunder, T 2022491, represents a nationwide selection. Good selection of Kashmiri (particularly embroidery), S Indian handicrafts and Rajasthani textiles; *Handloom House*, D Naoroji Rd; *Bihar Emporium*, Dhun Nur, Sir PM Rd; Kairali, Nirmal, Nariman Point, T 2026817; *Kashmir Government Arts Emporium*, Co-op Insurance Building, Sir PM Rd, T 2863822; *Phulkari*, World Trade Centre, Cuffe Parade, T 215084; *Purbashree*, Khira Bhavan, Sandhurst Bridge; *UP Emporium*, Sir PM Rd for silks, cottons and brocades; *Black Partridge* (Haryana), Air India Building, Nariman Point, T 2023536; *Gangotri*, UP Export Corporation, World Trade Centre, Cuffe Parade, T 215497; *Mrignayanee*, MP Government Emporium, World Trade Centre, Cuffe Parade, T 212114; also at same address *Shikha*, T 211725 and *Trimurti* (Maharashtra), T 216283. *Khadi and Village Industries*, D Naoroji Rd. *Cottage Industries Emporium* stocks crafts from all the states.

Books The *Nalanda* in the Taj Mahal Hotel is one of the best for Art Books. The one at the Oberoi is also very good. *New Secondhand* Bookstore, Kalbadevi and *Strand* Books, off Pherozshah Mehta Rd nr HMV have an excellent selection. Will also arrange shipping (reliable), and offer 20% discount on airfreight. For Antiquarian books and prints try *Jimmy Ollia*,

Cumballa Chambers (1st Floor), Cumballa Hill Rd, T 350649. Along Churchgate St and near the University are the lines of second-hand book stalls. Religious books at *Chetna* Restaurant, 34K Dubash Rd, Rampart Row. *Bhavatiya Vidya Bhavan*, Chowpatty.

Photography *Central Camera*, 195 DN Rd, T264426; *Continental Photo Stores*, 243 DN Rd, T 262059; *India Photographic Co.*, DN Rd, T 269440; *Photokina*, Subh Sagar, T 8111290; *Photo Commercial*, Gunbow St, T 258991; *Photo Emporium*, 19 Bora Bazar St, T 261099; *Photo Guide*, Jeswani Niwas, Manohar Das St, T 265344; *Photomaster*, 23 Hama St, T 272014.

Local Transport

To and from the airport Coach service connects both the domestic (Santa Cruz), Rs 20, and international (Sahar), Rs 25, terminals with the city. Drop off and pick up points in town are the Air India, Indian Airlines offices and the Taj Mahal Hotel.

Prepaid taxis into town best, from counter at the international terminal. Retain your receipt as the driver requires this at the end of the journey. Be prepared for small additional charges for luggage. The cost to Nariman Point will be in the region of Rs 120. As yet there are no prepaid taxis from the domestic terminal though they may be introduced shortly. Check, otherwise use above figure as a guide.

Taxis (Yellow Top): Easily available. Metered charge about Rs 4 for first 1.6 km, additional fare as per revised tarriff card carried by driver. **Private Taxis and Car Hire**: A/c (luxury cars) Rs 750 for 8 hr or 80 km, each additional hr Rs 35 and Rs 8.50 per km; Non a/c (luxury cars): Rs 600 for 8 hr or 80 km, each additional hr Rs 20 and Rs 6.50 per km; A/c Ambassador cars Rs 500 for 8 hr or 80 km and Rs15 each additional hr and Rs 5.50 per km; Non a/c Ambassador cars Rs 275 for 8 hr or 80 km and Rs 12 each additional hr and Rs 3.50 per km.

Private **car hire** firms: Makson Auto Hirers, Sagar Kunj, L Jagmohandas Marg, T 8121701; Bhuta Travels, Nagardas Park, Old Nagardas Rd, Andheri East, T 6325334; Blaze Car hires, Eucharistic Congress Building, No 2, 3rd Floor, Colaba, T 2020073.

Auto-rickshaws Not available in central area. Metered charge about Rs 2.50 for first 1.6 km, additional fare as per revised tarriff card held by the driver. **Victorias** (Horse drawn carriages): Available at Bombay Central, Chowpatty and Gateway of India. Rates negotiable.

Buses Bombay Electrical Supply Co (BEST) buses are available in most parts of Greater Bombay. Special buses operating within the Central Business District (Central area) are marked 'CBD'.

Trains Suburban electric trains are fast and economical. Trains start from Churchgate for the W suburbs and Victoria Terminus for the eastern suburbs. They are often desperately crowded. Official capacity is 1500 per train, but official surveys show that they often carry more than 5000. Trains leaving central Bombay often have seats at the terminus but fill up at the next three or four stops. If you are using the suburban line out of Bombay it is best to get on at the terminus if possible.

Warning Avoid the rush hr, and keep a tight hold on valuables. The difference between 1st and 2nd class is not immediately obvious, as both are often equally full of standing passengers. Inspectors fine people for travelling in the wrong class. Note the class on the side of the compartment.

Entertainment

Bombay, a fortnightly glossy magazine has listings of plays, films and other cultural activities as well as sports fixtures. *This Fortnight for You!*, published by the Government of India Tourist Office and free from their office. Many hotels carries similar information.

Discotheques Hotel discotheques are open to non-residents who have to pay for admission. Residents often have to pay a nominal entrance fee. Typically drinks are quite expensive. *Cellar*,Oberoi Towers Hotel, T 2024343; *Studio 29*, Bombay International, T 2026060. Foreign visitors can usually get temporary membership without difficulty. *Nineteen Hundreds*, Taj Mahal Inter-Continental Hotel, T 2023366. Open 2130-0400.

Out of town *Cavern*, Welcomgroup Sea Rock, T 642524, Rs 35 (weekdays) and Rs 60 (weekends) for non-residents. Open 2130-0200; *Scorpio's*, Holiday Inn Hotel, T 571425; *Take Off*, Airport Plaza, T 6123390; *Xanadu*, Horizon Hotel, Juhu Beach, T 6148100. Rs 50 (weekdays) and Rs 100 charge for non-residents. Opens 2230.

Theatres Western India has a strong creative tradition much like that in W Bengal. Plays are performed in English, Hindi, Marathi and Gujarati. Local cultural events such as singing and dancing can be seen at the following theatres. Performances usually begin at 1815-1900. Check *Bombay* or *This Fortnight* first: *Homi Bhabha Auditorium*, Navy Nagar, Colaba; *ISCKON*

Auditorium, Juhu; *Prithvij*, Juhu; *Little Theatre*, Nariman Point; *National Centre for the Performing Arts*, Nariman Point; Patkar Hall, New Marine Lines; *Shanmukhananda Hall*, King Circle; *Tata Theatre*, Nariman Point; *Tejpal Auditorium*, Gowalia Tank.

The following are some **cinemas** in town: *Apsara*, Lamington Rd; *Dreamland*, New Charni Rd; *Ganga*, Tardeo; *Grover*, Lajpatrai Marg; *New Excelsior*, Bastion Rd; *Regal*, Museum; *Sophia Bhabha*, Bhulabhai Desai Rd; *Sterling*, Waudby Rd.

Horse racing The Mahalaxmi Race Course, opp Haji Ali. Season Nov-Mar. Sundays and Public holidays, 1400-1700. The course is delightful and the many of India's top races are held here, including the Derby in Feb/Mar. The original Bombay race course was established at Byculla in 1800. The Mahalaxmi course was opened in 1878 named after Laxmi, the Goddess of wealth! Bombay used to be famous for horse trading, especially Arab horses but was banned in 1948 thus encouraging the development of a local breeding industry. India today has around 80 studs.

Sports Bridge: Islam Gymkhana, Netaji Subhash Rd, T 313292. **Gymnasia**: Talwakars Gymnasium Club; Charni Rd, T 352618; Talwakars Gymnasium, Gohil House, Jamshetji Rd, T 457548. **Table Tennis**: Khar Gymkhana, 15th Rd, Khar, T 530884, 536955. **Wrestling**: National Sports Club, Lajpatrai Marg, T 4921412. **Yoga**: The Yoga Institute, Praghat Colony, Santa Cruz East, T 6122185; Kaivalyadham Iswardas Health Centre, Subash Rd, near Taraporewalla Aquarium, T 310494; Yoga Training Centre, 51 Jai hind Club, Juhu Scheme, T 536254; Yoga Vidhya Niketan, Sane Guruji Marg, Dadar, T 4226258.

Tennis: Maharashtra State Lawn Tennis Association, Cooper, Colaba, T T 2023872. **Squash**: Cricket Club of India, Brabourne Stadium, Dinshaw Wacha Rd, T 235313. Also Billiards, Snooker and Badminton.

Soccer (Football): Western India Football Association, Cooperage, Colaba, T 2024020. **Rugby**: Bombay Gymkhana, Mahatma Gandhi Rd, T 204101. **Hockey**: Bombay hockey Association, Charni Rd, T 291271.

Cricket: Bombay Cricket Association, Wankhede Stadium, Churchgate, T 251562.

Cycling, National Sports Club, Lajpatrai Marg, T4938818. **Golf**: Bombay Presidency Golf Club' Chembur, T 5513670.

Museums

Mani Bhawan Open 0930-0600. Free. This private house, at 19 Laburnum Rd, where Mahatma Gandhi used to stay on visits to Bombay, is now a memorial museum and research library with 20,000 volumes. Not easy to find – many taxi drivers don't seem to know it – but well worth a visit. Display on top floor very good, especially diorama depicting important scenes from Gandhi's life – slides of it are available for Rs100 at the entrance – you will have to mount them yourself. Cards, pamphlets etc at the door. Best seen on your own so if you are in a tour group it is worth coming back later. Allow an hour.

Victoria and Albert Museum N end of Mahatma Gandhi Rd. Closed Wed. Open Mon, Tue, Fri, Sat 1030-1700, Th 1000-1645, Sun 0830-1645. Small fee. This was inspired by the Victoria and Albert Museum in S Kensington, London. Financed by public subscription, it was built in 1871 in a Palladian style. Sir George Birdwood, a noted physician and authority on Indian crafts, was the driving force behind it and became its first curator. The collection covers the history of Bombay and contains prints, maps and models.

In front of the Museum is a Clocktower (1865). Also outside is a stone statue of an elephant found by the Portuguese in the harbour. Elephanta Island was named after it. The gardens are very attractive and were laid out by Birdwood on drained swamp land. A list at the entrance indicates which trees and shrubs are in blossom. A stroll in Victoria Gardens is very much a part of Bombay life. The statue of Queen Victoria used to stand in what is now Mahatma Gandhi Rd.

Prince of Wales Museum S end of Mahatma Gandhi Rd. Closed Mon. Open 1015-1730 (Oct-Feb), 1015-1800 (Jul-Sep), 1015-1830 (Mar-Jun). Rs 2, Tue free. Designed by George Wittet to commemorate the visit of the Prince of Wales (later King George V) to India in 1905. A bronze statue of the king stands outside and an equestrian statue of Edward VII on the other, all set in a landscaped garden. The most striking external feature is the dome of glazed blue tiles, very Persian and Central Asian in flavour. The whole is Indo-Saracenic, and thus in keeping with the Gateway of India which was built at the same time.

There are three sections inside – Archaeology, Art and Natural History. The archaeological section has three main groups: Brahminical; Buddhist and Jain, Prehistoric and Foreign. The Indus Valley section is well displayed. The art section includes an excellent collection of Indian miniatures and well displayed *tankhas*. There are also works by Gainsborough, Poussin and Titian as well as Indian silver, jade and tapestries and a collection of arms. The Natural History section is based on the collection of the Bombay Natural History Society founded in 1833 and includes dioramas. Good guide books, pamphlets, cards and reproductions on sale.

Jehangir Art Gallery Closed Mon. Open 1030-1800. Within the complex of the Prince of Wales Museum . Bombay's principal art gallery, often staging exhibitions of modern art. The 'Samovar' café is good with a terrace overlooking the museum gardens. Public phones and toilets. **Gallery Chermould** on 1st Floor

Nehru Planetarium, Dr Annie Besant Rd, nr Haji Ali, Worli. Closed Sun. Rs 5. Shows in English at 1500 and 1800, closed Mon. In the same grounds, **Nehru Science Museum**, Lala Lajpat Rai Rd, T 493266. Science Park and permanent gallery. Closed Mon. **National Maritime Museum**, Middle Ground off Gateway of India. Sat, Sun and holidays. Ask at boat operators at Gateway.

Art Galleries Commercially run art galleries that have works for sale: *Taj Art Gallery,* Taj Mahal Hotel; *Centaur Art Gallery,* Hotel Centaur; *Pundole Art Gallery*, Hutatma Chowk; *JJ Art Gallery,* Dadabhoy Naoroji Rd; *Aakar Art Gallery,* Bhulabhai Desai Rd; *Cymroza Art Gallery,* Bhulabhai Desai Rd.

Parks and Zoos Parks are by no means as plentiful or spacious as in Delhi since Bombay developed on an isthmus. The opportunities for relaxing under a tree away from the crowds are therefore limited.

Marine Drive, Chowpatty Beach and the *Hanging Gardens* are open expanses but afford little shade in the heat of the day. The *maidans** in the centre of town are quiet in the early morning but crowded with cricketers and office workers just relaxing at other times. There are large gardens at the *Willingdon* and *Gymkhana Clubs* but temporary membership is required (See under Clubs). *The Victoria Gardens* are very pleasant. There is a small *zoo* there. Open sunrise to sunset, usually 0800-1800. Closed Wed. Small fee. Elephant, camel and pony rides are available for children. *Kamla Nehru Park*, Bal Gangadhar Kher Rd, Malabar Hill.

Useful Addresses/ Numbers Santa Cruz Airport, T 6144433. Sahar Airport, Enquiries, T 6329090, 6329293 Foreign Exchange Department, Reserve Bank, T 2861602.

Fire, T 101. Police Emergency, T 100. Ambulance, T 102, Telephone Enquiry, T 197. STD Service, T 182. Telephone Assistance, T 199 Foreigners' Regional Registration Office, Annex 2, Office of the Commissioner of Police, Dadabhoy Naoroji Rd, near Mahatma Phule Market, T 268111.

Consulates and Embassies Australia, Maker Tower E, 16th Floor, Cuffe Parade, T 217366. **Austria**, Taj Building, DN Rd, T 2042044. **Belgium**, Morena, 11 Dahanukar Mar, T 4929261. **Egypt**, 12/B Maker Tower, 1st Floor, Cuffe Parade, T 212425. **France**, Mercantile Bank Building, M Gandhi Rd, T 271528. **Germany**, 10th Floor, Hoechst House, Nariman Point, T 232422. **Indonesia**, Lincoln Annexe, S Barodawala Marg, T 368678. **Italy**, Vaswani Mansion, D Wachha Rd, T 222192.

Japan, 1 ML Dahanukar Marg, T 4923847. **Netherlands**, The International, 16 M Karve Rd, T 296840. **Philippines**, Industry House, J Tata Rd, T 2026340. **Spain**, 6 K Dubash Marg, T 244644. **Sweden**, Indian Mercantile Chambers, R Kamani Marg, T 262583. **Switzerland**, Manek Mahal, Vir Nariman Rd, Churchgate, T 293550. **UK**, 2nd Floor, Mercantile Bank Building, M Gandhi Rd, T 274874. **USA**, Lincoln House, Bhulabhai Desai Rd, T 823611. **Yugoslavia**, Vaswani Mansion, D Wachha Rd, T 222050.

Address and phone number of a country not listed here which has a representation in Bombay, can be obtained from the Bombay telephone directory.

Hospitals and Medical Services The larger hotels usually have a house doctor, the others invariably have a doctor on call. Enlist the assistance of hotel staff for prompt action. The telephone directory lists hospitals and General Practitioners.

Chemists There are many around the city. Kemp & Co, Taj Mahal Hotel, Apollo Bunder. Wordell, Vir Nariman Rd.

Post and Telegraph Usually open 1000-1700. Sahar Airport 24 hr. Post offices all over the city and most 5 star hotels. GPO, Nagar Chowk. Mon-Sat, 0800-2000 (Poste Restante Facilities 0800-1800) and Sun 1000-1730 . Central Telegraph Office, Hutatma Chowk. Churchgate PO, 'A' Rd. Colaba PO, Colaba Bus Station and also at Mandlik Rd, behind Taj Mahal Hotel. Foreign PO, Ballard Pier. Counter at Santa Cruz.

Places of Worship Hindu: *Babulnath Temple*, Ban Ganga; *Walkeshwar* Malabar Hill; *Laxmi Naryan Temple*, Madhav Devi; *Mahalaxmi; Mumba Devi*, Round Temple; *Venkatesh Mandir*, *Kartikeya Temple*, Cheda Nagar, Chembur. **Muslim**: Mosque at Bandra; Minara Masjid,

Mohammed Ali Rd; Jama Masjid, Mahatma Phule Rd; Zakaria Masjid, Zakaria St. **Parsi**: Anjuman, Banaji, Wadiaji Fire Temples. **Sikh**: Guru Govind Singh Sabha, Kalbadevi; Dadar Gurudwara.

Christian: Roman Catholic: Pro Cathedral, N Parekh Marg, Colaba; Mount Mary's, Bandra; Gloria, Byculla; St Andrew's Church, Bandra; St Michael's, Mahim; Salvaco Portuguese Church. Protestant: *St Thomas' Cathedral*; *All Saints Church* Malabar Hill; *St John's (Afghan Memorial)* Colaba. **Jewish**: *Knesseth Ellyahoo*, Fort; Magen David, Byculla; *Magen Hasidim*, Abdul Hamid Ansari Marg, near Jacob Circle; *Tifereth Israel*, Clerk Rd, near Jacob Circle. *Buddhist*: Temple at Worli.

Chambers of Commerce *Bombay Chamber of Commerce and Industry*, Mackinnon Mackenzie Building, 4 Shoorji Vallabhdas Marg, Ballard Estate, T 264681. *Maharashtra Chamber of Commerce*, Oricon House, 6th Floor, 12K Dubash Marg, Fort, T 244548. *Directorate of Industries*, Govt of Maharashtra, New Administrative Building, Madam Cama Rd, T 2028616.

Travel and Tour Operators

The well established agents have offices in the city: **American Express International Travel**, Majithia Chamber, DN Rd, T 2048291; **Cox and Kings**, PO Box 398, Grindlays Bank Building, D N Rd, T 2043065; **Everett Travel Service**,1 Regent Chambers, Nariman Point, T 245133. **Freight Carriers**, P Mehta Rd, T 253212; **Mercury Travels Ltd**, 70VB Gandhi Rd, T 273275; **Sita World Travel**, 8 Atlanta, 1st Floor, Nariman Point, T 240666. **Thomas Cook**, Cooks Building, DN Rd, PO Box 46, T 2048556; **Trade Wings**, 30 K Dubash Marg, T 2044233. **Space Travels**, 4th floor, Sir PM Rd, T 2864773 offer discounted flights and special offers for students. Mon-Fri, 1000-1700, Sat 1030-1500.

Ambassador Travels, 14 Embassy Centre, Nariman Point, T 231046. **Asiatic Travel Service**, 12 Murzban Rd, T 2048151. **Balmer Lawrie & Co**, 5 JN Heredia Marg, Ballard Estate, PO Box 245, T 268106. **Bap Travels**, Mittal Towers 'A', Nariman Point, T 244058. **Bathjia Travel**, New Sil Bazar, 491 Kalbadevi Rd, T 311207-8. **Blue Skies**, 28 K Dubash Marg, T 242771. **Diners World Travel**, Raheja Chambers, 213 Nariman Point, T 224949. **Eastman Travel and Tours**, 21 Dalmal Chambers, New Marine Lines, T 317343. **Game Garden Tours and Travels**, C-4 Pink Rose, MM Chhotani Marg, Mahim, T 458072. **Govan Travels**, Poonam Apartments, Dr Annie Besant Rd, T 4934588. **Happy Travels**, Century Bhavan, Dr Annie Besant Rd, T 4304290. **Hermes Travel and Cargo**, Dhiraj Chambers, 9 Hazariwal Somani Marg, T 2040666. **Hind Musafair Agency**, Sir PM Rd, T 2861544. **Indtravels Division of Airfreight Ltd**, Neville House, Ballard Estate, T 265761, 264524. **Mackinnon Mackenzie & Co.**, 4 Shoorji, Vallabhdas Marg, T 260031.

Orient Express, 359 DN Rd, T 2871047. **Park Travels**, Tulsiani Chambers, T 2870209. **Patvolk Travel Services**, Volkart Building, Graham Rd, T 263714. **Sanghi International**, 39 A Patkar Rd, T 8225061. **SOTC Travel and Tours**, Vaswani Chambers, D Wlacha Rd, T 243775. **Raj Travels and Tours**, 27 Panchratna, Ground Floor, Mama Parmanand Marg, Opera House, T 8117000. **Trans Travel**, 4 Jain Chambers, 557 SV Rd, Bandra, T 6425411. **Travel Corporation Ltd**, Chandermukhi, 1st Floor, Nariman Point, T 2021881, 2027120. **Travelera**, Nariman Bhavan, Nariman Point, T 2023187 **Tressa Travels**, 9 Homi Mody St, T 271336. **Trimurti Travels and Tours**, Shale Building, 28 Bank St, T 2861413, 2860813. **Universal Express Travels and Tours**, 14 K Dubhash Rd, T2047982. **Vensimal Bassarmal & Bros**, 521 Kishore Building, Kalbadevi Rd, T 314233.

Tourist Offices & Information

Government of India Tourist Office, 123 M Karve Rd, T 293144. Open Mon-Sat 0830-1730 (closed every second Sat of the month from 1230, also on public holidays). Counters open 24 hr at Sahar and Santa Cruz airports, and at the Taj Mahal Hotel Mon-Sat 0830-1530 (closed every second Sat and public holidays from 1230). Helpful staff who can also issue Liquor Permits (essential for Gujarat). **MTDC**: CDO Hutments, Madame Cama Rd, T 2026713; Express Towers, 9th Floor, Nariman Point, T 2024482. **Government of Gujarat Tourist Office**, Dhanraj Mahal, C Sivaji Rd, T 243886. **Government of Goa, Daman and Diu Tourist Counter**, Bombay Central Station, T 396288. **Government of Rajasthan Tourist Office**, 230 DN Rd, T 267162. **Madhya Pradesh Tourist Development Corporation**, 74 World Trade Centre, Cuffe Parade, Colaba. T 214860, 219191 Ext. 299, Telex: 217603.

Tours There are a number of tour operators providing conducted tours of Bombay. The **City Tour** usually includes visits to The Gateway of India, Aquarium (except on Mondays), the Prince of Wales Museum (closed Mondays), Jain temple, Hanging Gardens, Kamla Nehru Park and Mani Bhawan (Gandhi Museum). Some tours do not operate during the monsoon. The **Suburban Tour** includes Sahar International Airport, Juhu Beach, Observation Point, Tulsi

Lake National Park, Kanheri Caves and Lion Safari Park (closed Mondays). A guide and Entry charges are included in the fare. Recent visitors have described the tour as 'awful'.

India Tourism Development Corporation, Nirmal Building, Nariman Point, T 2026679. Booking also at Government of India Tourist Office, 123 Maharshi Karve Rd, T 293144. City Tour – Daily except Mon, 0900-1300 and 1345-1745. Rs 35. **MTDC**, Madame Cama Rd, T 2026713. City tour – Daily except Mon, 0900-1400 and 1400-1900. Rs 40. Suburban Tour 1000-1900. Rs 65. **Travel Corporation of India (TCI)**, Chander Mukhi, Nariman Point, T 2021881 City tour – Daily 1430-1630. Rs 35. **Bombay Electrical Supply Transport (BEST)** Undertaking, Transport house, S Bhagat Singh Rd, Colaba Causeway, T 240601. Suburban Tour – Sun only, 0830-1730.

Tours to Elephanta (see Excursions) by **Elephanta Jal-Vahatuk Sahakari Sanstha Maryadit** and **Orient Charters** from the Gateway of India, departures every hr from 0900 until 1400.

If you wish to sightsee independently with a guide, the Tourist Office can arrange this. Rs 48 for 1- 4 persons for 4 hr and Rs 72 for 4-7 hr, with each additional hr thereafter at Rs 10 per hr. Lunch allowance – Rs 20 for full day and foreign language supplement (not English) of Rs 25. Extra Rs 15 to take a private guide to Elephanta and Rs 30 for the Kanheri caves.

Ajanta and Ellora MTDC runs a tour to the famous caves at Ajanta and Ellora. Daily departures for 4 day tour. Dep 0830, return 0800 four days later. About Rs 900 for transport, entry fee and guide charges, meals and accommodation at good hotels (Rs 765 for lower category hotel. One-way fare, also possible. Reservations and further information: T 2023343. For details of caves **see page 987**. If you want to see the caves at your leisure, it is much better to make your own arrangements.

Airlines

Domestic Indian Airlines, Air India Building, Nariman Point, T 2023031, Airport T 6144433. **Vayudoot**, Airbus Wing Terminal, T 6146583.

International Air India, Air India Building, 1st Floor, Nariman Point (Counters also at Taj Mahal Hotel, Centaur Hotel and Santa Cruz), T 2024142, Airport T 6329090. **Aeroflot**, 241-2, Nirmal Building, Nariman Point, T 221743, Airport T 6320178 **Air Canada**, Oberoi Towers Hotel, Nariman Point, T 2021111, Airport T 6435653. **Air France**, Taj Mahal Hotel, Apollo Bunder, T 2025021, Airport T 6328070. **Air Lanka**, Mittal Towers, Ground Floor, C Wing, Nariman Point, T 223288, Airport T 6322829, 6327050. **Air Mauritius**, Air India Building, Nariman Point, T 2028487, Airport T 6366767.

Alitalia, Industrial Assurance Building, Vir Nariman Rd, Churchgate, T 222112, Airport T 6329082 **Alyemba**, F-99, Shopping Arcade, 2nd Floor Oberoi Towers Hotel, Nariman Point, T 2024229, Airport T 6320700 Ext. 522. **Bangladesh Biman**, Jet Air Transportation Ltd, Airlines Hotel, 199 J Tata Rd, Churchgate, T 224580, Airport T 6366700 Ext. 524. **British Airways**, 202-B, Vulcan Insurance Building, Vir Nariman Rd, T 220888, Airport T 6329061/3/4. **Canadian Pacific**, Taj Mahal Hotel, Apollo Bunder Rd, T 2029112/3, Airport T 6321965/6. **Continental, Eastern, Iberia and MAS** (Malaysian Airline System), STIC Travel & Tours, 6 Maker Arcade, Cuffe Parade, T 211431.

JAL (Japan Airlines), Ground Floor, No 3 Raheja Centre, Nariman Point, T 233136 **KLM (Royal Dutch Airlines)**, 198 JN Tata Rd, Khaitan Bhavan, T 221372. **Lufthansa**, Express Towers, Nariman Point, T 2020887, Airport T 6321485. **PIA (Pakistan International Airlines)**, Oberoi Towers Hotel, Nariman Point, T 2021480, Airport T 6300328. **Pan Am**, Taj Mahal Hotel, Apollo Bunder, T 2024024, airport T 6324955. **Philippines Airlines**, 199 J Tata Rd, Churchgate, T 224580. **QANTAS**, Oberoi Towers Hotel, Nariman Point, T 2029297, Airport T 6127219. **Sabena** (Belgium), Nirmal Building, Nariman Point, T 2022724, Airport T 6348847. **Saudia** (Saudi Arabia), Express Towers, Nariman Point, T 2020457, Airport T 6323126. **SAS (Scandinavian Airline System)**, 15 World Trade Centre, Cuffe Parade, T 215207. **Singapore Airlines**, Air India Building, Nariman Point, T 2023365, Airport T 6327861. **Swissair**, Maker Chambers, 220 Nariman Point, T 222402, Airport, 6326084. **Thai Airways**, 15 World Trade Centre, Cuffe Parade, T 215207. **TWA (Trans World Airlines)**, Airlines Hotel Building, 199 J Tata Rd, T 224580.

Shipping Offices Mughal Lines, Shipping House, N Cama Rd, T 234861. Anchor Line (Agents: Lloyd Trestino), Neville House, JN Heredia Marg, Ballard Estate, T 262294. British India Steam Navigation Co., 4 Vallabhas Marg, T 268021. Forbes Forbes Campbell & Co., Forbes Building, Charanjit Rai Marg, T 2048081. P&O Lines, c/o Mackinnon Mackenzie & Co, 4 Ballard Estate, T 268081. Patel Volkart India, Volkart Building, JN Heredia Marg, T 266751 Scindia Steam Navigation Co, Scindia House, Ballard Estate, T 268161. Shipping Corporation of India, Shipping House, Madame Cama Rd, T 2026666. United Liner Agencies of India, Mahindra Spicer Building, JN Heredia Marg, T 266451.

Travel

Times for trains and planes are published each Saturday in the Indian Express newspaper.

Air Indian Airlines connects Bombay by regular flights with Agra, Ahmedabad (55 min), Aurangabad (40 min), Bangalore (1 hr 30 min), Belgaum (1 hr 25 min), Bhavnagar, Bhuj, Bhopal (2 hr, 1 stop), Bhubaneswar (2 hr 55 min, 1 stop), Calcutta (2 hr 20 min), Cochin (1 hr 45 min), Coimbatore (1 hr 35 min), Delhi (1 hr 50 min), Goa (55 min), Hyderabad (1 hr 10 min), Indore (1 hr 5 min), Jaipur (1 hr 30 min), Jamnagar, Jodhpur (2 hr 10 min, 1 stop), Keshod (1 hr 20 min), Lucknow (3 hr 5 min, 1 stop), Madras (1 hr 40 min), Patna (3 hr 25 min, 1 stop), Pune (30 min), Srinagar (4 hr 35 min, 2 stops), Trivandrum (2 hr), Udaipur (2 hr 15 min, 1 stop), Varanasi (1 hr 55 min).

Indian Airlines also has international connections with Colombo and Karachi. The airport is 26 km from centre Bombay and an hour should be allowed for travel by taxi. At peak traffic hours it can take much longer. Indian Airlines, Air India Building, Nariman Point, T 2021441, 2021626, 2023031.

Rail Bombay is the headquarters of the Central and Western Railways. Reservations: Central Railways, Victoria Terminus Station, Bori Bunder, T 264321, 0900-1230, 1300-1630; Western Railways, Western Railways Reservation Office, Churchgate, T 291952 and Bombay Central Station, T 375986, both open 0800-1345 and 1445-2000. All for First Class bookings and Indrail Passes. Foreign tourists may seek assistance of the Railway Tourist Guide at Victoria Terminus or Churchgate.

Note: The following list is by no means exhaustive. The trains included are generally the fastest available, have daily departures and do not involve changing trains en route, hence they are recommended. For all trains, book as early as possible. All leave from Victoria Terminus unless stated.

Ahmadabad *(from Bombay Central)*: *Bombay-Gandhidham Kutch Exp* 9031, daily, 1715, 7hr 53 min; *Gujarat Exp* 9011, daily, 0600, 9 hr 15 min; *Bombay-Ahmedabad Janata Exp* 9007, daily, 1935, 9 hr; Gujarat Mail 9001, daily, 2130, 9 hr. **Allahabad**: *Haora Mail* 3004, daily, 2110, 23 hr 35 min; *Mahanagiri Exp* 1093, daily, 2355, 23 hr 55 min; *Bombay-Bhagalpur Exp* 3418, Tue,Th,Fri,Sun, 1935, 27 hr 40 min. **Agra**: *Punjab Mail* 1037, daily, 1615, 23 hr 50 min. **Bangalore**: *Udyan Exp* 6529, daily, 0755, 24 hr 15 min. **Cochin**: *Netravati Exp* 2135, Tue,Th,Sun, 2015, 35 hr 25 min. **New Delhi**: *Punjab Mail* 1037, daily, 1615, 27 hr 55 min. *From Bombay Central*: *Rajdhani Exp* 2951, daily except Mon, 1700, 16 hr 15 min; *Paschim Exp* 2925, daily, 1130, 22 hr 55 min; *Frontier Mail* 2903, daily, 2115, 21 hr 45 min. **Bhopal**: *Punjab Mail* 1037, daily, 1615, 15 hr. **Gorakhpur** *(for Nepal)*: *Kushi Nagar Exp* 1015, daily, 1120, 33 hr 40 min. **Gwalior**: *Punjab Mail* 1037, daily, 1615, 21 hr 50 min. **Calcutta (Haora)**: *Gitanjali Exp* 2859, daily, 0605, 32 hr 10 min; *Haora Exp* 8029, daily, 2130, 41 hr 45 min; *Calcutta Mail* 8001, daily, 1910, 35 hr 50 min; *Haora Mail* 3004, daily, 2110, 40 hr 5 min **Lucknow**: *Kushi Nagar Exp* 1015, daily, 1120, 28 hr 5 min **Allahabad** *Haora Mail* 3004, daily, 2110, 23 hr 35 min; *Mahanagri Exp* 1093, daily, 2355, 23 hr 55 min; *Bombay-Varanasi Ratnagiri Exp* 2165, Mon, Wed, Th, 0500, 24 hr 10 min. **Madras Central**: *Bombay-Madras Mail* 7009, daily, 2315, 30 hr 30 min. **Pune**: *Bombay-Madras Mail* 7009, daily, 2315, 4 hr 17 min; *Udyan Exp* 6529, daily, 0755, 4 hr 7 min; *Deccan Queen Exp* 2123, daily, 1710, 3 hr 25 min; *Bombay-Hyderabad Exp* 7031, daily, 1235, 4 hr 20 min; *Sinhagad Exp* 1009, daily, 1435, 4 hr 30 min. **Ujjain** *(from Central)*: *Bombay-Indore Exp* 5064, daily, 2000, 12 hr 15 min: **Secunderabad/Hyderabad**: *Minar Exp* 2101, daily, 2155, 14 hr 20 min **Trivandrum** *Kanniya Kumar Exp* 1081, daily, 1535, 44 hr 45 min. **Varanasi**: *Mahanagiri Exp* 1093, daily, 2355, 28 hr 5 min; *Bombay-Varanasi-Ratnagiri Exp* 2165, Mon, Wed, Th, 0500, 27 hr 30 min.

Road Bombay is connected by good motorable roads to all major regional tourist and business centres: **Pune** (163 km), **Bhilwandi** (184 km), **Mahabaleshwar** (239 km), **Aurangabad** (392 km), **Vadodara** (432 km), **Ahmedabad** (597 km), **Panaji** (Goa – 597 km), **Hyderabad** (711 km), **Bangalore** (998 km), **Madras** (1367 km), **Delhi** (1460 km), **Calcutta** (2081 km).

The following National Highways connect Bombay: **NH8** with Vadodara – Ahmedabad – Udaipur – Jaipur – Delhi; **NH3** with Dhule – Indore – Agra; **NH6** with Dhule – Nagpur – Calcutta; **NH17** with Goa – Mangalore – Trichur; **NH9** Pune – Hyderabad -Vijayawada; **NH4** Thane – Pune – Bangalore.

Bus The Maharashtra State Road Transport Corporation operates bus services to all the major centres and district headquarters in the state as well as to Ahmedabad, Bangalore, Goa, Mangalore, Indore, Vadodara and Hyderabad in other states. Information on services can be obtained from the MRTC, Central Bus Stand, Bombay Central or Parel Depot.

Ship Mughal Lines operates a regular service between Bombay and Goa, normally suspended during the monsoon season. At present it has been suspended indefinitely. Check with Mughal Lines, Shipping House, N Cama Rd, T 234861.

SHORT EXCURSIONS FROM BOMBAY

There are several short excursions possible from Bombay. Both the Hindu caves of Elephanta and the earlier, Buddhist caves of Kanheri, are within easy reach. It is also possible to cross the bay to Chaul or to go north to the old Portuguese fort of Bassein, and further afield to Bombay's hill station of Matheran.

Chaul, a group of Moorish and Portuguese forts to the S at the mouth of Bombay harbour. On the N side of the creek, it was taken in 1522 by the Portuguese. Although it is similar to Bassein and has a very attractive fort it never equalled it in importance. The Marathas took it in 1739 and in 1818 it passed into British hands.

Little remains of the settlement apart from ruined churches and broken walls. If you look across the creek you will see the hilltop Muslim fort of Korlai. From the New Ferry Wharf it is a 90 minute trip to Revas. From there you can take a 30 km bus ride to Chaul and then continue by road to Mahabaleswar or join the Bombay-Pune road.

Matheran This is the nearest hill station to Bombay (171 km) (See Maharashtra page 987).

Ajanta and Ellora See above under Tours for transport details; for description of caves, see page 988.

Elephanta Caves 10 km by boat from the Gateway of India. Attractive but not as splendid as the caves at Ajanta and Ellora. Tour launches with guides leave the Gateway of India, hourly from 0900 until 1400 and the trip lasts 4 hours (Journey time to island, one hr). Rs 30 per adult, Rs 20 for children. Reservations, T 2026384. It is an extremely popular day trip for Bombayites so avoid the weekend rush and go on a weekday.

Ordinary launches without guides leave from the same place and cost Rs 16 per adult and Rs 10 for children aged 2-7 years. During the monsoon the seas can be very rough and the service is suspended. It is quite a stiff climb of about 125 sloping steps from the old landing place on the S of the island. Today boats normally land in the NW, about 400 m from the caves, which are at a height of about 75 m. Palanquins available. The island is formed of two parallel ridges separated by a valley. The highest point is 173 m.

More than 1,200 cave sites have been discovered across India. The vast majority of these were purpose built as temples and monasteries. They were still excavated and decorated long after building techniques were developed that allowed substantial and durable structures to be erected on the ground. being excavated over the period from 3rd century BC to the 10th century AD. Jain, Buddhist and Hindu caves often stand side by side in the same rock formation. Although Ajanta and Ellora in Maharashtra are the most highly developed, the Elephanta caves are also well worth visiting.

Elephanta Island

The temple cave on Elephanta island, dedicated to Siva, was probably excavated during the 8th century by the Rashtrakuta dynasty which ruled the Deccan from 757 to 973 AD. The Portuguese who were active along the coast in the 16th century desecrated it. They are believed to have removed an important stone panel which probably gave more precise information on its excavation and ornamentation. They also removed a damaged stone elephant, now housed at the Prince of Wales Museum. Muslim rulers and the British were not blameless for damage either, although the most recent threat comes from the blasting carried out for the new port on the mainland, opposite Elephanta. The Archaeological Survey of India is doing its best to preserve the site.

The symbolic significance of the setting is that the sea is the ocean of life, a world of change (*Samsara**) in which is set an island of spiritual and physical refuge. The journey to it was also important. In the rough seas of the monsoon it could be both difficult and dangerous. It was therefore a voyage of determination as well as discovery. As it is not in everyday use as a temple, shoes only have to be removed at the inner sanctum.

The Entrance Originally there were three entrances (see Plan), and 28 pillars, 8 of which have been destroyed or collapsed. The two side entrances on the E and W have subsidiary shrines which may have been excavated and used for different ceremonies. The main entrance is from the N. At dawn the rising sun casts its rays on the approach to the main shrine (*garbha-griha*) which is housed in a square structure at the W end of the main hall. On you left as you enter is a carving of **Siva** as Nataraj (**see page 57**).

On your right hand side is a much damaged carving of **Siva as Lakulisa**. Seated on a lotus, the symbol of the unconscious mind and enlightenment, the figure has a Buddha-like feel found also in the Orissan temples where Lakulisa played a prominent role in efforts to bring Buddhists back into Hinduism – **see page 619**. From the steps at the entrance you can see the *yoni-lingam**, the focus of a Siva temple which is the symbol of the creative power of the deity.

The Main Hall The pillars in the main hall, which form a cruciform pattern, have a square base from which rises a thick column that is topped by a cushion-like capital. They vary in height between 5 and 6 m, but they have no structural importance. At the corner of each pillar is a dwarf signifying the earth spirit (*gana**). There are also figures of Ganes, the elephant-headed son of Siva. To the right is the main **Linga Shrine** in the *garbha-griha*, 6 m square and 1 m above the floor of the temple. It has four entrances, each corresponding to a cardinal point. Symbolically they represent the threshold from the secular to the spiritual world and guard the idol from external influences.

Each doorway is flanked by guardians (*dwarapala**). The best preserved is on the W entrance to the shrine, and shows a tall elegant figure with a sacred thread over his left shoulder and a sword at his side. The foot is touched by pilgrims as an act of reverence when they enter the sanctum. In the centre of the shrine is a 1 m high smooth lingam. To worship the *yoni-lingam* the devotee must walk around it clockwise. To go the wrong way round is to invite bad luck. The yoni is the female symbol of creation and the lingam is the male phallus. Together they are in harmony or equilibrium as the creative forces of energy and spirit. The interior of the sanctum is bare, drawing attention more firmly to the *yoni-lingam*.

The wall panels To the N of the *garbha-griha* is a panel of **Bhairava killing the demon Andhakasura.** This extraordinarily vivid carving shows Siva at his most fearsome, with a necklace of skulls and a skull and cobra on his head. In this form he is known as **Bhairava**, and he is shown crushing the power of **Andhaka**, the chief of darkness. It was held that if he was wounded each drop of his blood would create a new demon. So Siva impaled him and collected his blood with a cup which he then offered to his consort Shakti to drink. In winter the best time to see this panel is in the early afternoon as the light plays on it.

Opposite, on the S side of the *garbha-griha* is the badly damaged panel of the **Marriage of Siva and Parvati**. Siva stands with Parvati on his right, a sign that it is their wedding for normally a Hindu wife stands on her husband's left hand side. She looks demurely at the floor, perhaps out of shyness or merely respect, but her body is inclined or drawn to him. Behind Parvati stands her father Himalaya and to his left is Chandramas, the god of the moon who is carrying a pot of *soma**, the food of the gods, as a gift. On Siva's left is Vishnu and below is Brahma. They are witness and priest respectively.

On the wall at the extreme W end of the temple are carvings showing **Siva as the Yogi** (on the right) and **Siva as Nataraja** (on the left). The latter shows a beautifully executed figure of **Ganes** above and Parvati on his left. All the other gods watch him. Above his right shoulder is the four headed god of creation and intellect, **Brahma**. Below Brahma is the elephant-headed god Ganes, Siva's son. Opposite by the left shoulder of Siva is Vishnu, the god of preservation. Behind him is Indra who is riding an elephant, and beneath him is Parvati. Dance has played an important part in Hindu worship since the earliest times and Siva is the principal exponent of it.

The *Descent of the Ganga* On the S wall, opposite the entrance, are three panels. On the W is that of The Descent of Ganga. Originally India's holiest river flowed only in heaven but was brought to earth by her father King Bhagiratha who is kneeling at Siva's right foot. Some of Bhagiratha's ancestors had disturbed a sage while he was meditating and in anger he destroyed them.

Since that time, the family had tried to have the curse revoked by getting Ganga to flow down from heaven over their bodies. However, Ganga was reluctant to leave heaven until

Siva commanded her and the waters were let loose, flooding the plains and destroying land. When she came to Siva at the holy Kailasa mountain, he broke her fall from heaven with his head. Ever since, Ganga is seen flowing from his hair. In this sculpture Ganga is shown in the centre and her two tributaries, Yamuna and Saraswati on either side. These three rivers are believed to meet at Allahabad (see page 247).

The triple headed Siva (Trimurti) To the left of the Descent of the Ganga is the centre piece of the whole temple, the remarkable sculpture of Siva as **Lord of the Universe** (*Maheshwara*). Nearly 6 m high, it shows Siva uniting all the functions of creation, preservation and destruction. Some have seen the head on the left (your right) as representing Vishnu, while others suggest that it shows a more feminine aspect of Siva and may be that of **Uma**.

To the right (your left) is **Rudra** or **Bhairava** . He has snakes in his hair, a skull to represent ageing from which only Siva is free, and has a look of anger and vengefulness. The central face is **Siva Swarupa**, Siva as his true self, balancing out creation and destruction. In this mode he is passive, serene and unperturbed. He radiates peace and wisdom like the Buddha. He wears a tall crown and his right hand is held up in a calming gesture. In his left hand is a lotus bud.

The left hand panel is the 5 m tall carving of **Siva as Arddhanarishvara** (Androgyne). This depicts Siva as the embodiment of male and female. Arddhanirishvara represents wholeness and the harmony of opposites. To the pilgrim, the ideal is to combine the best of both halves. In the rock sculpture the female half is relaxed and gentle, the male has Siva with his vehicle, Nandi. There is a particularly good statue of Siva as Arddhanarishwara in the museum at Madras (see page 711).

The final two panels are at the E entrance, opposite the *garbha-griha*. On the N is **Siva and Parvati on Mount Kailash**, while on the S is **Ravana Shaking Mount Kailash.** Siva and his consort Parvati is a popular subject. Kailash is believed to be the centre of the universe, in Tibet. It has always been a place of pilgrimage but has not been as popular as many of the other sites, largely due to the physical hardships in getting there. Siva is the faceless figure with Parvati on his left. They are surrounded by the divine Nandi, celestial beings, an attendant carrying a child, an ascetic with his begging bowl. Siva and Parvati are shown playing at dice. Parvati has lost and is sulking.

Ravana (see the other panel),the demon king of Lanka, arrives on the scene. Although he is a demon he also worships Siva. However, he was not content to go up to Mount Kailash to worship and wanted to bring Kailash back to his own kingdom (Sri Lanka) so that he could worship Siva at home. The panel shows him trying to uproot the mountain. Siva is shown sitting on the mountain supported by two attendants who are there to prevent him falling off. He is quite calm and unperturbed by Ravana's show of brute strength. Ravana fails to move the mountain, begs Siva's forgiveness and receives it.

The Subsidiary Shrines The larger shrine on the E side has a lingam shrine. There are also damaged images of **Karttikeya**, **Ganes** and the **Matrikas**.

Kanheri caves and Bassein

Kanheri Caves, 42 km N of central Bombay, the caves are on a low hill midway between Borivli and Thana. Even on recent maps the countryside around Kanheri is shown as dense jungle, and until quite recently the surroundings must have looked quite like those at Ajanta today. The hills used to form the central part of Salsette Island, but the surrounding land has long since been drained and extensively built on, connecting it with the rest of Bombay. Further up the ravine from the caves there are some fine views out to sea. Although not as impressive as the caves at Ajanta and Ellora, if time is limited, a visit to Kanheri is a compensation. They can be visited on the regular suburban tours or by train to Borivli station from Bombay Central. From here you can take a taxi for the 10 km journey to the caves. On Sundays and public holidays there is a bus service from the station.

The major caves There are 109 Buddhist caves, dating from the end of the 2nd to the 9th century AD with flights of steps joining them. The most significant is the **Chaitya cave** (No 3) which is probably 6th century. It is entered through a forecourt and verandah and comprises a 28 m long, 13 m wide colonnaded hall of 34 pillars At one end these encircle the 5 m high dagoba. Some of the pillars have carvings of elephants and trees.

50 m up the ravine is Darbar of the **Maharajah Cave** (No 10). This was a dharamsala,

a chapter house or resthouse. It is 22 m long and 10 m wide and has two stone benches running down the sides and some cells off the left and back walls. Above Cave No 10 is No 35 which was a *vihara* (monastery). This is 12 m by 14 m and has reliefs of a Buddha seated on a lotus and of a disciple spreading his cloak for him to walk on. Cave No 14 further up on the left has some traces of painting and No 21 has columns similar to some of those at Elephanta, a Buddhist litany and a figure of Padmapani.

60 km N of central Bombay, *Bassein* is situated at the mouth of the Ulhas river on the mainland. It was a Portuguese city (**Vasai**) from 1534 to 1739 when it became so prosperous that it was called the Court of the North. As a walled city it contained a cathedral, five convents, thirteen churches and the splendid houses and palaces of the aristocracy, or **Hidalgos**, who with members of the religious orders, alone were allowed to live within the walls. Stone and timber were available locally in large quantities so buildings were grand. The Marathas took Vasai in February 1739 after a long and desperate siege. Almost the whole Portuguese garrison of 800 was killed in the battle, the Marathas are thought to have lost 5000 men. In 1780 the British evicted the Marathas, only to return it to them three years later under the Treaty of Salbai. It is well worth walking round the sea face of the fort walls. The fort itself is entered from the N.

Due to silting, the fort on the Bassein Creek is now some distance from the sea. The Old Town, which you approach from the N contains the ruins of the Cathedral of St Joseph dating from 1536, the Church of St Anthony, the Jesuits' church and the convents, all belonging to Franciscans, Dominicans, Jesuits or Augustinians. You can reach Bassein by car or by train from Bombay Central to Bassein (or Vasai) Road station. From the station you can hire a car for 11 km journey to the town.

MAHARASHTRA

Maharashtra, India's third largest State, dominates the heart of the Peninsula. With over 500 km of coastline, from the former Portuguese territories of Daman in the N to Goa in the S, it stretches over 900 km E to border with the tribal territories on the edge of the Chota Nagpur plateau. Many foreign visitors see just two or three of the State's most striking sights – the densely packed, former colonial city of Bombay, for example, or the astonishing carved temples and paintings of Ellora and Ajanta, but there is much more to Maharashtra. Along the sea coast there are some attractive towns such as Ratnagiri. In the Western Ghats, Maratha forts are perched precariously on the hilltops, once the home of the charismatic and daring Sivaji, the 'Mountain Rat' as Aurangzeb called him.

From these fastnesses, in the late 17th century the Marathas, masters in the art of guerilla warfare, carved out a Hindu dominated territory that stretched the width of India. In Sivaji's time, the country was governed by a confederacy of Marathas. Later the region was divided into **Swarajya** (Homeland) and **Mughlai**, territory con-

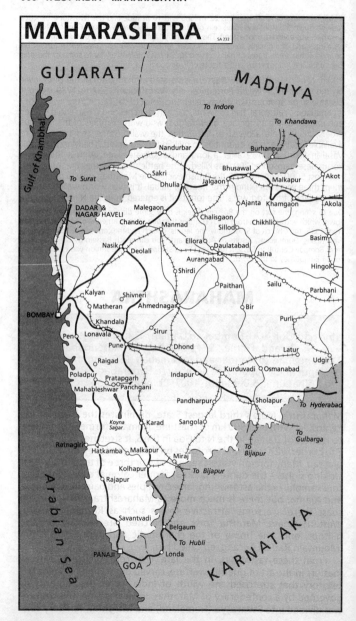

MAHARASHTRA

SA 232

GUJARAT

MADHYA

To Indore

To Khandawa

Nandurbar

Burhanpur

Sakri

Bhusawal

Malkapur

Akot

To Surat

Dhulia

Jalgaon

Ajanta

Khamgaon

Akola

DADAR &
NAGAR HAVELI

Malegaon

Chalisgaon

Sillod

Chikhli

Basim

Chandor

Manmad

Nasik

Ellora

Daulatabad

Jaina

Hingol

Deolali

Aurangabad

Shirdi

Paithan

Sailu

Parbhani

Gulf of Khambhat

Kalyan

Shivneri

Ahmednagar

Bir

Purli

BOMBAY

Matheran

Khandala

Sirur

Dhond

Latur

Pen

Lonavala

Pune

Kurduvadi

Osmanabad

Udgir

Raigad

Indapur

Poladpur

Pratapgarh

Mahableshwar

Panchgani

Pandharpur

Sholapur

To Hyderabad

Koyna
Sagar

Karad

Sangola

To
Gulbarga

Ratnagiri

Hatkamba

Malkapur

Miraj

To
Bijapur

Kolhapur

To Bijapur

Arabian Sea

Rajapur

Savantvadi

Belgaum

KARNATAKA

PANAJI

To Hubli

GOA

Londa

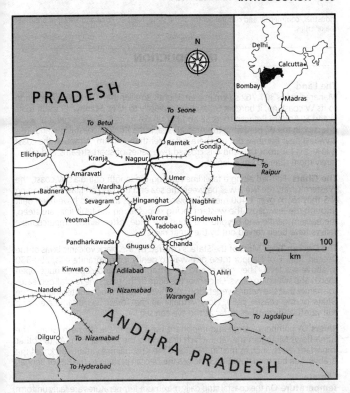

trolled by foreigners that was the legitimate object of raids. Swaraj ('home rule') re-emerged as one of the watchwords of the Independence struggle in the 20th century.

Maharashtra dominates the northern part of the India's western seaboard. Its principal centre is Bombay, now the commercial capital of India with approximately 9 million people. Bombay apart, Maharashtra is predominantly agricultural, but has a well developed industrial sector. It is a distinct cultural region, Marathi, the state language, being spoken by 90% of the population.

Social indicators *Area* 308,000 sq km *Population* 79 million Urban 35% Literacy M 59% F 35% *Birth rate* Rural 31:1000 Urban 26:1000 *Death rate* Rural 10:1000 Urban 7:1000 Infant mortality Rural 77:1000 Urban 55:1000 Registered graduate job seekers 146,000 *Average annual income* per head : Rs 2260 Inflation 1981-87 67% *Religion* Hindu 81% Muslim 9% Christian 1% Sikh 0.2% Buddhist 6%

Language Marathi is the regional language. In addition, English (particularly in Bombay), Gujarati, Hindi, Telugu, Kannada, Urdu, Bengali and Malayalam are spoken. There are also a large number of dialects: Konkani on the W coast, Gondi in the northern regions.

Towns and cities Maharashtra is one of the more urbanised states of India with two-fifths of its population of 62.7 million (1981 Census) living in towns and cities. Bombay is the major industrial, commercial and cultural centre of the state. Nagpur, Pune and Sholapur are other major cities.

INTRODUCTION

The Land
Maharashtra is 307,762 sq km in area, slightly smaller than Germany. In addition to its W coastline, it borders Gujarat immediately to its N, Madhya Pradesh to its N and E, Andhra Pradesh to its SE and Karnataka to its S. There is great physical diversity. In the W, bordering the Arabian Sea, is the Konkan coastal lowland. This is widest near Bombay, but nowhere is it wider than 100 km. Although the coast is low it is far from flat, and it is crossed by a series of short streams and rivers, rarely more than 80 km in length.

The Ghats Formed along a fault line running the length of India's W coast, the Western Ghats rise like a wall between the sea and the Deccan plateau. Running N-S they reach over 1,400 metres in places. Railways and roads have been built through the few gaps. The western facing slopes along the fault line, are steep, the eastern gentle and beyond the ridge line wide, often almost imperceptible valleys have been carved out by the great rivers.

The Deccan Trap Most of the State is covered by the black volcanic lavas of the Deccan Trap. E of Nagpur these give way to gently rolling granite hills, 250-350 m above sea level. They give rise to an extraordinary landscape of huge open spaces and sweeping views. Once over the ridge of the ghats the rainfall decreases so sharply that the natural vegetation cover was always much lighter than on the Ghats or the coastal plain. Now virtually all the forest has disappeared and cultivated land stretches as far as the eye can see.

Rivers A number of large and important rivers rise in the Western Ghats. The Girna flows NE to join the Tapti which drains into the Arabian Sea. All the other important rivers, such as the Godavari and the Krishna, rise within 100 km of the Arabian Sea but then flow E or SE across the Deccan plateau to the Bay of Bengal.

Climate
Temperature On the coastal strip daily maximum temperatures are fairly uniform throughout the year at an average of 31.5°C. The daily minimum temperature is 16°C in Jan and 26°C in Jun. In Aurangabad the average daily maximum temperature in May is 40°C and 29°C in Jan whilst the minimum is 14°C in Jan and 25°C in May.

Rainfall The SW monsoon breaks on the coast in the first week of June and finishes in September. Four-fifths of the annual rainfall is received over this period. While the coastal Konkan strip is wet while the interior upland area behind them is much drier. Bombay receives over 2,700 mm per year, 95% of which is from June to September. Nagpur on the other hand receives 1,128 mm per year, 87% of which is during the monsoon. Aurangabad occupies an intermediate position between Bombay and Nagpur and receives only 792 mm of rain per year, 82% during the monsoon.

Vegetation The natural vegetation is determined largely by the amount of rain an area receives. On the coast mango, coconut, bamboo, teak and myrabolan (for dyeing) are found. On the plateau, in areas that receive heavy rain, magnolia, chestnut and bamboo are common. Areas with less than 650 mm of rain per year have thorny, savanna-like vegetation, though none of the original natural vegetation remains.

Wildlife Tiger, leopard, bison, panther, sambhar, chital, barking deer, hyena and monkeys are found in the forests of the state which now cover less than 15% of the total area. In Sivaji's time they were, of course, more extensive and provided excellent ground cover for his troops. Snakes are common, though you will be lucky if you see one. Birds are numerous, particularly duck and peacock. The sanctuaries harbour drongo, paradise flycatchers and winter migrants.

People

Ethnically, Maharashtra contains a variety of peoples. The **Bhil**, Warli, Gond, Korku and Gowari tribal groups living in the Satpura and Sahyadri ranges in the north are Australoid aboriginals and the true inhabitants of the region.

The Kunbi Marathas are found all over the state and are believed to be the descendants of immigrants from the north at the beginning of the Christian era. Parsis arrived in the region in the 11th century from Persia.

Just over 80% of the people are Hindus with Islam and Buddhism the most numerous minority religions. The Buddhists are recent converts from among formerly outcaste Hindus, although ancient links with the religion can be traced through the many caves that became centres of Buddhist art, sculpture and worship. The paintings and sculptures at the Buddhist and Hindu caves at Ajanta and Ellora cover the period from the 2nd century BC to the virtual disappearance of Buddhism from India around 650 AD. The murals are stunning in their delicacy, the caves, especially the Kailadasa temple at Ellora, show extraordinary power in their execution.

Festivals There are many festivals throughout the year, the majority of them Hindu. The *Ranga panchami* is highly colourful. *Dasara* is significant because it was the day on which the Marathas usually began their military campaigns. *Holi*, marking the beginning of spring is very popular. *Janmashtami* in Jul and Aug celebrates the birth of Lord Krishna. Men and boys form human pyramids to break pots of curds that have been hung from high places.

On *Ganes Chaturthi* in Bombay in Aug and Sep massive figures of the ever popular elephant god Ganesh, the bringer of good fortune are immersed in the sea. The Muslim festival of *Mohurram* which commemorates the martyrs of Islam, is often observed by Hindus as well.

Economy

Agriculture is the mainstay of the economy with about 70% of the population dependent on farming for a living. Nearly two thirds of the total area of Maharashtra is cultivated but of this only one eighth is irrigated. The main crops are rice, jowar, bajra, wheat and pulses (peas, beans, lentils). Rice is not as well suited to the dry conditions and lower rainfall as these hardy crops. The state is also a major producer of oilseeds including groundnuts (peanuts) and sunflowers. Important cash crops are cotton, sugarcane, tobacco, turmeric and a variety of vegetables. The state also produces fruits and has a substantial area devoted to oranges, bananas, mangoes, grapes and limes. In recent years an attractive Methode Champenoise sparkling wine called *Omar Khayyam* has been produced with French assistance and expertise. Sugar refining is important among the food processing industries.

A major problem in Maharashtra is water scarcity but the state government has taken several successful steps to bring about a more diversified agricultural system. Farmers are given assistance to improve the productivity of their farms. Higher Yielding Varieties of rice and wheat have been promoted. Irrigation dams in rain shadow areas have encouraged good sugarcane crops. Forest products include timber, bamboo, sandalwood and tendu leaves which are used for making cheap cigarettes.

Mineral resources Manganese, iron ore, limestone, copper, bauxite, silica salt and common salt are extracted. Bhandara, Nagpur and Chandrapur districts in the east have rich coal deposits. This is bituminous coal and is used by the railways and power stations. There is off-shore oil at the *Bombay High* and the nearby Basin North fields. Bombay High was first developed in 1976. Although the state has only 9% of India's population, it accounts for about 11% of the industrial units, 17% of the industrial labour force, 16% of industrial investment and 23% of the value of the nation's industrial output.

Industry The Bombay-Pune complex is the state's major industrial area. Nagpur, Aurangabad, Sholapur, Thane and Kolhapur are also important. Maharashtra's industrial production includes chemicals, pharmaceuticals, plastic ware, machine tools, electrical and non-electrical machinery, petroleum and chemicals. The oldest and largest industry in the state is textiles. Maharashtra also leads the country in the manufacture of sophisticated electronics equipment. Maharashtra produces both thermal and hydro-electricity. The atomic power station at Tarapur, 112 km N of Bombay, was India's first nuclear power plant. The transport network centres on Bombay which is well connected by air, rail and road with other parts of the country. From the late 1970s the state government has been encouraging industry to decentralise away from Bombay. Centres such as Nasik have grown very rapidly.

History
Early settlement The dry W margins of the plateau have sites from the earliest pre-historic settlements in India. **Nevasa** and **Chirki**, on the banks of the **River Pravara** in the Godavari valley, have Paleolithic remains and a complete succession of cultural artefacts up to the modern period.

The name **Maharashtra** was first noticed in a 7th century AD inscription. Its origins are unclear. One view is that it is derived from the word **rathi** (chariot) whose drivers formed an army (maharathis). They are thought to have migrated south and settled in the upland area where they mingled with aboriginal tribes.

A marchland The relatively open lands in the lee of the Ghats were one of the major routes from N to S India. Constantly disputed, the region lacked the resources to become the centre of a major political power. In the early period from the 8th to the 14th century there were a number of Hindu kingdoms: Satavahana, Kalacuri, Rastrakuta, Chalukya and Yadavas. The first Muslim dynasty was founded in 1307 and was followed by a string of others. The Muslims used Persian as the language of the court, which left its mark on the development of the Marathi language.

Sivaji and Maratha power Sivaji was born into a low caste family. He rose rapidly to weld different Hindu groups into a powerful force. Initially attacking its neighbouring Muslim states, it rapidly expanded its power to confront the Mughal Empire which dominated the N. The Marathas developed the skills of lightning raids and highly mobile military manoeuvres, enabling them to threaten the greater power of the Mughals themselves. The last Great Mughal, Aurangzeb spent nearly the whole of the second half of his reign (1658-1707) fighting the Marathas in the Deccan Plateau. Aurangabad is named after him.

A regional hero Born in 1627, **Sivaji** was born in the then Muslim Sultanate of **Ahmadnagar**. In 1646, at the age of 19, Sivaji gathered an army, took Pratapgad fort near Pune and rapidly established a powerful base. He made his reputation by a combination of brilliant campaigns, physical courage and occasional acts of astonishing cruelty towards his opponents.

Sivaji made his capital at Raigarh, and championing the Hindu cause gained the reputation of being an Indian Robin Hood. In 1664 he sacked the Mughal port of Surat thereby drawing the Mughals into the fray. In 1666, the Rajput Jai Singh, sent by Aurangzeb to curb Sivaji's power, succeeded in defeating him and bringing him back to the Mughal court. At this stage Sivaji obviously thought that he could not take on the Mughals and win, so he agreed to relinquish 23 of the 35 forts he had taken and to accompany Jai Singh to Agra to pay his respects to Aurangzeb.

His reception at the great Mughal's court was muddled. Aurangzeb intended to make him a gift of an elephant but was caught up in his own 50th birthday party celebrations and ignored Sivaji. The Maratha stormed out in protest but was kept under house arrest. By deceiving his guards into thinking that every day he sent a large basket of sweetmeats to Brahmins in the city, he smuggled himself out and returned to Maharashtra, dressed much of the time like a Hindu ascetic to avoid recapture. He returned to his own people and was crowned King with due pomp and splendour.

The Maratha confederacy Within four years Sivaji had begun to re-take the forts ceded under the treaty with Aurangzeb, and by his death in 1680 he had re-established a powerful base around Pune. Sivaji died of dysentery at the age of 53. For the next twenty seven years Aurangzeb battled to maintain and extend Mughal authority across the whole of his S territory. However, on his death in 1707, Sivaji's former kingdom became a confederacy under the charge of a hereditary minister called the Peshwa and four main Maratha chiefs – Holkar, Scindia, Gaekwad and Bhonsla. By 1750 their power reached across India to Orissa, which they occupied, and Bengal, which they attacked.

Maratha power was only decisively curbed when they were defeated at Panipat by the Afghan Ahmad Shah Abdali. In 1772, on the death of the young Peshwa, *Madhao Rao I*, the 5 Maratha powers became increasingly independent of one another as the five Deccani sultanates had done 2 centuries earlier. Weakened and divided, they were unable to resist the advance of British power.

The British period Under the British, western India came under the Bombay Presidency. In 1688 The East India Company leased all of the islands of Bombay from the British Government for £10 in gold per year. To begin with, Bombay's fortunes rested on shipbuilding. Locally available Malabar teak proved to be very durable and an ideal timber. Later Bombay took over from Surat in Gujarat as the Company's main centre on the western coast of India. Thereafter its growth was dramatic. On Independence in 1947, Bombay Presidency became Bombay state.

Independence Bombay Presidency had never coincided with the area in which Marathi was the dominant language. In 1948 the former princely state of Vadodara (Baroda) and some others were merged into Bombay. The present state did not take shape until 1960, when Gujarati areas in the N and Kannada speaking areas in the S were allocated to Gujarat and Karnataka respectively.

Government
Maharashtra, a state in the federal union, has a governor as its head. The Chief Minister and Council of Ministers are elected from the state legislature and are responsible for policy formulation and implementation. The Chief Minister is invariably the leader of the largest party in the state parliament. The legislature has two houses; the Vidhan Parishad (legislative council) and Vidhan Sabha (legislative assembly). Except for an annual meeting at Nagpur, the old Maratha capital, these meet in Bombay. The state is represented by 48 members in the Lok Sabha (Lower House) and 19 members in Rajya Sabha (Upper House) of the national parliament in New Delhi.

BOMBAY TO DAMAN

This short journey leaves Bombay by the crowded W Expressway, then travels inland from the Konkan coast over low hills and across the short streams that run into the Arabian Sea from the W Ghats. The NH8 by-passes formerly rich Portuguese settlements such as Bassein and Thana which can make interesting short diversions. It is the main road to Vadodara and Ahmedabad (see Gujarat, below), and is very busy.

Leave Bombay on the road to **Mahim** (15 km). Bear left, keeping on the Western Expressway, which ends at **Dahisar** (27 km). 3 km before Dahisar a right turn leads to the **Kanheri National Park** and the **Kanheri caves** (see above – excursions from Bombay, **page 966**). From Dahisar the road goes N. A right turn after 6 km leads to the old Portuguese settlement of **Thana**. Thana's most recent claim to fame is as the terminus of the first railway in India, built from Bombay in 1856. As early as 1298, however, Marco Polo had written of Thana's fame as "a great kingdom...there is much traffic here and many ships and merchants frequent the place." It was an important Portuguese centre until the Marathas captured it in 1739. The English church in the town dates from 1825.

After a further 18 km along the **NH8** a road on the left leads to **Bassein**, another town in Portuguese hands from 1534 to 1739. The walls are still standing, and it is an interesting place to stop, see page 967.

The **NH8** goes on from the Bassein junction with the NH8 to **Shirsad** (6 km). In Shirsad a right turn leads to the **Vrajeshwari Temple** (14 km) and hot springs, **Ambadi** (23 km) and **Bhiwandi** (42 km; *Population* 145,000). Keep on the **NH8**, by-passing **Manor** (32 km) and continue to **Kasa** (Charoti; 23 km). A right turn leads over the ghats to **Nasik**. The **NH8** goes on through **Mahalaxmi** (4 km) and **Talasari** (20 km) to the Gujarat-Maharashtra border (13 km). In 14 km it crosses the **Damanganga River**, and a further 2 km there is a left turn off the **NH8** to **Daman** (12 km). The route N is described below under routes from **Ahmadabad** to **Bombay**.

BOMBAY TO NAGPUR Via Nasik and Dhule

Today the route through the Western Ghats from Bombay to Nasik (the NH3) is one of the busiest in India. After following the Ulhas River, for over 50 km from Shahapur to Igatpuri it climbs through the forested slopes of the Western Ghats. Since the 19th century streams on the wet slopes of the ghats have been dammed to provide hydro electricity for Bombay. The lakes offer some attractive picnic spots off the main route. The climb through the ghats is particularly beautiful before the end of the rains in September. Wild flowers are everywhere, and rivers and waterfalls are full. Although it is repaired periodically, sections of the road are often damaged by the volume of traffic and the heavy rains, and may be in poor condition.

The **NH3** leaves Bombay via **Thana** (43 km) and **Bhiwandi** (15 km) following the **Ulhas River.** A left turn in Bhiwandi goes to the temple and hot springs of **Vrajeshwari** (19 km). The ghat section of road starts in Bhiwandi, though the real climb does not begin until the NH3 reaches **Shahapur** (33 km). After 5 km a road on the left leads to the **Tansa Lake** (13 km) where there is a forest rest house. The road continues climbing to **Khardi** (17 km), where a left turn leads to the **Vaiturna Dam** (16 km). After 7 km the main road crosses the railway line, then passes through **Kasara** (6 km; altitude 300 m).

The steepest part of the climb begins here, gaining 320 m in 15 km. The railway through the ghats, which in this section alone passes through ten tunnels, and over five viaducts and eleven bridges, was completed in 1865. It starts the Thul ghat section after 7 km, passing through **Vihigaon** (2 km) before reaching the end of the ghat section at **Igatpuri** (10 km; altitude 580 m) – the "town of difficulties". **Kalsubai** (1540 m), the highest mountain in Maharashtra, is visible to the S. 1 km beyond the village of **Igatpuri** you drive past the S end of the beautiful **Beale Lake,** at the head of one the streams that joins the Godavari downstream from Nasik.

From Igatpuri the NH3 goes through **Ghoti** (8 km) where a road on the right leads to the 80 m high Wilson Dam at *Bhandardara* (32 km). NH3 goes on to **Nasik** (32 km).

Nasik Rd (*Population* 340,000 *Altitude* 610 m) is the railhead for the holy city of **Nasik,** one of Hinduism's most holy sites. It shares the triennial **Kumbh Mela** with **Ujjain**, **Haridwar** and **Allahabad**, see page 247. Associated with rivers from the Ramayana legend, every twelve years thousands of pilgrims converge on the River Godavari, sometimes referred to as the Ganga of the Deccan, to bathe. The Godavari is believed to have a common underground source with the Ganga itself.

Early settlement The town itself is undoubtedly ancient, and Ghose suggests that it has an unbroken history of over 2500 years. At **Panda Lenu**, within a few km of the town centre, palaeolithic settlements have been discovered. Excavations at Gangawadi, 15 km NW of Nasik, have shown five periods of settlement. The first has pottery from the Chalcolithic period, the second dates from the 5th to 3rd centuries BC up to the 1st century AD, with a great deal of Northern Black Polished Ware pottery typical of settlements further N – see page 263. Roman pottery has been found in the third period levels. Period four covers Muslim to Maratha periods and includes coins from Akbar's empire and polychrome glass bangles.

None of the temples are very old. The **Narayana Temple** (1756) is built on the W bank and has a ghat. Inside there are three black Vishnu images. The **Ramesvara Temple** (18th century) is built on the E bank. Nearby is **Rama Kund** where the god is said to have bathed. It is a popular place to throw ashes into the river.

On the E side of town is **Sita Gupha**, a cave near a large group of banyan trees (Ficus Indica) is where the Goddess hid from Ravana the demon. Nearby is the **Kala Rama Temple** (Black Rama, 1782) which stands in an enclosure with 96 pillars and has a 25 m high *shikhara**.

Today Nasik has a thriving modern industrial estate. Benefitting from Government incentives in the 1970s to re-locate outside Bombay, private industry rapidly took up all the spaces allotted on the industrial estate.

Hotels (Airport 5 km, railway 9 km) **D** *Green View*, 1363 Mt Trimbak Rd, T 72231-3. 24 rm. 2 km centre, Doctor on call, Diners. **D** *Holiday Cottages*, Bombay Agra Rd, Vilhouli, T 2376, Cable: Cottage. 40 rm. 13 km airport, 20 km rly, 10 km centre. Indoor games, pool, Diners. **D** *Panchavati*, 430 Vakil Wadi (Chandak Wadi), T 75771-3. 41 rm. 5 Courtesy coach service to airport and railway, Diners. **D** *Panchavati Yatri*, nr Panchvati Hotel, 430 Vakilwadi (Chandawadi), T 7124-6, Cable: Yatri. 54 rm. Bar, courtesy bus service, refreshment rm. **D** *Samrat*, nr Central Bus and Taxi Stand, opp Indian Airlines Office, Old Agra Rd, T 77211. 14 rm. Restaurant, permit rm, doctor on call, ticket booking office, tourist cars. **D** *Wasan's Inn*, Old Agra Rd, T 77881-6, Cable: Kundanco, Telex: 752 280 Wasn In. 24 rm. Diners. **E** *Siddhartha*, Nasik Pune Rd, nr Airport, T 73288. 32 rm. 1 km airport, 6 km rly, 3 km centre, Diners.

Rail Bombay (VT): *Punjab Mail* 1038, daily, 0754, 4 hr 30 min; *Kushinagar Exp* 1016, daily, 1104, 5 hr 15 min; *Bombay Mail* 3003, daily, 0630, 4 hr 55 min. **Bhopal**: *Kushinagar Exp* 1015, daily, 1547, 11 hr 35 min; *Punjab Mail* 1037, daily, 2017, 11 hr; *Amritsar Exp* 1057, daily, 0245, 12 hr 50 min.

Bus Good connections with other centres in the state.

Excursions *Pandu Lena*, 8 km SW of Nasik and just off **NH3** to Bombay is a group of 24 rock cut Buddhist monuments dating from the 1st century BC to the 3rd Century AD. **Cave 3** is one of the largest monasteries. It has a colonnaded balcony and 19 cells leading off the Main Hall. The group are cut into the NE facing escarpment and overlook the road.

Deolali, 7 km SE on **NH50** to Pune, was the transfer camp for British soldiers waiting for transport home during the First and Second World Wars. To go 'Doolally Tap' was to go crazy with boredom waiting there in the transit camp. There was a mental hospital to accommodate these casualties.

Trimbak, 29 km W of Nasik, is centred around the **Gangasagar Tank**, and 690 steps lead up the hill behind Trimbak to the source of the Godavari itself. The town is partly surrounded by a fantastic semi-circle of hills, topped by a near vertical scarp of about 40 m. The impressive **Fort** is situated 550 m above the village at 1,295 m.

There are two gateways, and the **Temple of Trimbakeshwar**, an 18th century Siva sanctuary, is a pilgrimage site. Only Hindus are allowed to enter, but non-Hindus are allowed to climb steps to look inside. *Prayag Tirth*, on the road to Trimbak, has a beautiful stone-lined tank with two temples. Further on near *Anjaneri* two 300 m high conical hills are on either side of the road, sweeping round in a broad arc behind the town of Trimbak.

The **NH3** continues NE from **Nasik** across the broad open agricultural land of the Deccan plateau. It passes through **Adgaon** (10 km), **Ojhar** (9 km) and **Pimpalgaon Basant** (12 km) and several small settlements to **Chandvad** (Chandore; 30 km), crossing the low-rising **Satmala Hills** which reach a height of 1376 m near **Chandvad**. 6 km N of **Chandvad** is a 2 km ghat section of road (**Davis Ghat**), NH3 then going through **Saundane** (18 km) and across the **River Girna** (16 km) to **Malegaon** (2 km), with nothing but the most basic facilities.

Dhule (48 km) has grown extremely fast since 1971, from a population of 137,000 to its current size of 280,000. Accommodation **E** *Hotel Dina* Sakri Rd. Reasonable modern hotel in town with little competition. In Dhule the **NH3** continues N through **Songi** (20 km) to cross the **River Tapti** at **Sukhwad** (26 km). The Maharashtra-Madhya Pradesh border is reached after 45 km. The route to **Indore** (167 km) goes NE, see page 329.

At the crossroads in Dhule you leave NH3 and turn right onto NH6 which runs along the valley of the Tapti River to Nagpur. Although this is the main Bombay to Calcutta road it is much less heavily used than the Bombay-Delhi NH3. Passing through largely open, extensively cultivated countryside, there is a scatter of towns, some growing rapidly but still largely lacking much in the way of facilities for travellers.

24 km out of **Dhule** cross the **River Bori** by high level causeway, then through the small towns of **Mhasva** (8 km) and **Ernandol** (20 km). Another high level causeway crosses the **River Girna** (28 km), continuing to **Jalgaon** (6 km).

Jalgaon (*Altitude* 820 m *Population* 185,000) is the rail junction for the Ajanta Caves (56km). The town was once at the centre of a savannah forest region, the habitat of tigers, leopards and other game animals. Now it has become an important cotton growing area, and the town has several cotton processing plants.

Hotels D *Moroko*, 364 Nevi Path and **E** *Natraj*, Nehru Chowk have some a/c rm. There are less expensive *Guest Houses*, *Traveller's Bungalow* and *Railway Retiring Rooms*.

Air The nearest airport is as Aurangabad, 154 km S of Jalgaon.

Rail Bombay (VT): *Punjab Mail* 1038, daily, 0433, 7 hr 50 min; *Kushinagar Exp* 1015, daily, 1120, 8 hr 40 min; *Bombay Mail* 3003, daily, 0305, 8 hr 20 min. Bhopal: *Punjab Mail* 1037, daily, 2325, 7 hr 40 min. *Amritsar Exp* 1057, daily, 0615, 9 hr 20 min.

   Bus Good connections with other centres.

The 437 km from Jalgaon to **Nagpur** runs from W to E. The road crosses from the S side of the Tapti valley into the catchment area of the S flowing tributaries of the Godavari. It lies in the core of the rainshadow area of the Western Ghats, with less than 750 mm of rain a year, increasing slowly to the E. On the lower land the soils are some of the best in the Peninsula – rich black soils derived from the lava, overlying basalt rocks, though on the higher land the much poorer red soils surface. Given the relative dryness of the region and the lack of irrigation, an extraordinarily high percentage is cultivated, in some districts as much as 80% of the total area, though the poorer soils are often left fallow. Another extraordinary feature is the lack of rice cultivation – less than 2% of the entire region. Sorghum (jowar) and cotton dominate, cotton being a short stapled variety. In the W pearl millet (bajra) becomes more important than sorghum. The whole route is on **NH6**.

Bhusawal (27 km) is an important railway junction. The road then enters what used to be the princely state of **Berar**, see page 689 which stretched as far as Nagpur. In 1858 the ruler was dispossessed for lending support to the 1857 Mutiny. His lands, long claimed by **Hyderabad** state, were awarded to the Nizam as a mark of gratitude. Around here are some of the finest cotton fields in India.

Continuing, you pass through **Varangaon** (13 km) and Edalabad (18 km), across the River Nalanga (22 km) to **Malkapur** (8 km). In Malkapur there is a right turn to **Buldhana** (Altitude 630 m), which had a reputation as one of the coolest and pleasantest spots in the Berar district. The road continues through **Nandura** (30 km), **Khamgaon** (19 km), and **Balapur** (23 km), to **Akola** (27 km; *Population* 295,000 *Altitude* 290 m). A lower Palaeolithic site has been discovered revealing a range of tools. The town is a major cotton and grain handling centre.

From **Akola** the NH6 continues through **Murtazapur** (41km) and **Badnera** (44 km) before reaching **Amraoti** (10 km), which has a very large cotton market. After a further 15 km it passes through **Nandgaon Peth** (15 km) and **Tiwsa** (26 km) to **Barwadi** (10 km), the bridging point of the **River Wardha**. In Telegaon (6 km) there is a right turn to **Wardha** (71 km). The **NH6** continues through **Karanja** (24 km) and **Kondahalli** (26 km) to **Gondkheri** (28 km) and **Nagpur** (20 km).

Nagpur

Altitude 312 m. *Population* 1,607,000. *Best season* Sep-Mar.

	Jan	Feb	Mar	Apr	May	Jun	Jul	Aug	Sep	Oct	Nov	Dec	Av/Tot
Max (°C)	29	33	36	40	43	38	31	30	31	32	30	29	34
Min (°C)	13	15	19	24	28	27	24	24	23	20	14	12	20
Rain (mm)	15	2	25	20	10	174	351	277	181	62	9	2	1128

Nagpur was the former capital of the Central Provinces (now mostly Madhya Pradesh) and is one of the older towns of Central India. The Chanda dynasty of aboriginal **Gonds** ruled the area in the 10th-11th Centuries – see page 311). Muhammad Bahmani (1463-82) wrested it from the Kherla rulers. The gonds rose again in the 16th century and in 1740 Nagpur was taken by Raghuji Bhonsla. Finally, in 1861 the British annexed it on the Principle of Lapse see page 232, Lucknow), along with the Saugor and Narbada Provinces.

The site The city stands on the *Nag river* and centres on the Sitabaldi Fort which is surrounded by cliffs and a moat. At the highest point there is a memorial to those who fell in the Battle of Sitabaldi between the Marathas and the British.

British buildings are to be found mainly in the Western half of the the city: the red brick **Council Hall** (1912-13); the Anglican **Cathedral of All Saints** (1851)**; the High Court** (1937-42) is comparatively recent and was designed by one of the architects who contributed designs to parts of New Delhi, Henry Medd. On the other high hill in the town is the **Raj Bhawan** (Government House). In the Eastern half of the town, near the Nag River, were the **Bhonsla's Palace** and the Gond Rajah's Palace. The former was damaged by fire in 1864 and now little remains of both.

The *Bhonsla Chattris* are in the Sukrawari area S of the old city. Around the town there are also a number of tanks, the **Maharaj Bagh**, a park/zoo which also has statues of the Indian Mutiny heroine Rani Laxmi Bai of Jhansi and one the Indian Nationalist patriot Sankar. Nagpur was famous for its oranges which enjoy a wide distribution. The Nagpur region's extensive coal reserves are mined and the city is an important industrial centre of the state.

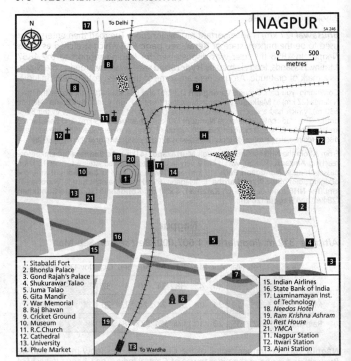

Map legend:

1. Sitabaldi Fort
2. Bhonsla Palace
3. Gond Rajah's Palace
4. Shukurawar Talao
5. Juma Talao
6. Gita Mandir
7. War Memorial
8. Raj Bhavan
9. Cricket Ground
10. Museum
11. R.C.Church
12. Cathedral
13. University
14. Phule Market

15. Indian Airlines
16. State Bank of India
17. Laxminamayan Inst. of Technology
18. Needos Hotel
19. Ram Krishna Ashram
20. Rest House
21. YMCA
T1. Nagpur Station
T2. Itwari Station
T3. Ajani Station

Hotels (Aiport 7-10 km, railway 2 km, most 2-3 km from centre) **C** *Rawell Continental*, 7 Dhantoli, Wardha Rd, T 23845, Cable: Rawcon, Telex: 0715 358 (INAG). 19 rm. central. Restaurant, travel. **D** *Pal Palace*, 25 Central Ave, T 44724-26. 32 rm, some a/c. **D** *Skylark*, 119 Central Avenue Rd, T 44654-58, Cable: Pleasure. 48 rm, some a/c. Restaurant, car hire, exchange, 10% travel discount, credit cards. **D** *Radhika*, Wardha Rd, Panchsheel Sq, T 22011-16, 22117, 24388, Cable: Khemka, Telex: 0715 459 RDKA In. 60 rm, some a/c, central. Restaurant, bar, car hire, exchange, Diners. **D** *Blue Diamond*, 113 Doser Chowk , Central Ave, T 47460-69, Cable: Diamond. 71 rm. Restaurant, bar. **D** *Bluemoon*, opp Mayo Hospital, Central Avenue Rd, T 46061-65, 48765-69. 30 rm, some a/c. Restaurant, bar, car hire, exchange, Diners. **D** *Jagsons*, 30 Back Central Ave, T 48611-19, Cable: Hoteljagso, Telex: 0715 369 Jags In. 25 rm. 13 km airport, 4 km centre. Restaurant, travel, exchange, credit cards. **D** *Midland*, opp Mayo Hospital, Central Avenue Rd, T 46131-35, Cable: Hotmid, Telex: c/- 715 438 Blue In. 36 rm, some a/c. Restaurant, bar, car hire, exchange, Diners. **E** *Shyam*, Pandit Malaviya Rd, Sitabuldi, T 24073, Cable: Comfort. 36 rm, central. Restaurant, rm service. **E** *Upvan*, 64 Mount Rd, Sadar, T 34704-5, Cable: Papyrus. 9 rm. central. Restaurant, car hire.

Restaurants Outside hotels in the Sadar area are Ashoka and *Moti Mahal* for Indian Chinese and Continental; *Nanking* is Chinese. In Sitabuldi: *Golden Gate, Anand Bhandar* for Indian; *Khyber* and *Sher Punjab* for tandoori); Others in Dharampeth, Ramdaspeth (inc *Indian Coffee House*) and Central Ave.

Banks State Bank of India, Punjab National Bank and Bank of India in Kingsway; Reserve Bank of India and Allahabad Bank in Civil Lines and several others in Dharampeth, Sitalbudi and Central Ave.

Shopping Main areas are Sitalbudi, Dharpeth, Sadar, Itwari, Mahatma Phule Market.

Gangotri UP Handicrafts in Sadar and *Khadi Gramudyog* in Mahal.

Local Transport Unmetred taxis from Stand opp Rly Station, T 33460 or Blaze Car Rentals, Sitalbudi, T 22792. Extensive coverage by city buses. **Coaches** from Tourist Office for sightseeing. Auto-rickshaws, Cycle-rickshaws and tongas available. Negotiate fares.

Post and Telegraph GPO and Central Telegraph Office nr Govt Printing Press, Itwari.

Tourist Office and Information Maharashtra Tourism Development Corporation, Deshmukh House, 96 Buty Rd, Sitalbudi, T 33325.

Air Indian Airlines connects Nagpur with Bombay, Delhi and Bhubaneshwar. Indian Airlines, T 33962, Air India, T 26300. 242A Manohar Nivas, Rabindra Tagore Rd, Civil Lines. Airport, T 24870.

Rail Bombay (VT): *Bombay Mail* 8002, daily, 1600, 15 hr 40 min; *Bombay Exp* 8030, daily, 1230, 17 hr; *Gitanjali Exp* 2860, daily, 0750, 13 hr 55 min. Enquiry, T 25743, Reservations, T 25633 (Class I), T 31019 (Class II).

Road Good bus services to places within the state and to neighbouring states' centres. Road Nagpur is connected with **Bhopal** (345 km), **Jabalpur** (240 km) on **NH7**. Maharashtra SRTC, Mor Bhawan Sitalbudi, T 46221. MPSRTC, nr Rly Station, T 33695.

Excursions *Ramtek*, 40 km NE of Nagpur just off the main road N to Jabalpur, has a fort with several Hindu temples with several dating back to the 5th century AD. The 'Hill of Rama', the fort walls were built in 1740 by Raghoji I, the first Bhonsla of Nagpur. The citadel is older and the principal temples are those of Rama and Sita. It was the capital of the Vakatakas who ruled the area between Ramtek and Ajanta and Aurangabad in the 4th-6th Centuries.

Wardha Mahatma Gandhi established his *Sevagram Ashram* (Gandhian Village of Service) in 1933, 6 km from Wardha, (62 km SW of Nagpur) where he spent 15 years. It is now a national institution where you can visit the various residences (*Nivases* and *Kutirs*), see the Mahatma's personal belongings, watch hand-spinning and attend prayers at the open-air multi-faith Prayer Ground (0430 and 1800). The **Mahatma Gandhi Research Institute of Medical Sciences** and **Kasturba Hospital**, with 325 beds, draws patients from neighbouring areas.

Accommodation The Ashram has a *Guest House* and *Yatri Niwas* where you can get meals. **Tourist Information**, voluntary guides. Reservations: Secretary, Ashram Pratishthan. **Post Office** nearby. Khadi cloth is sold through shops.

Note Alcohol, smoking and non-vegetarian food are prohibited.

Road You can get to Sevagram by bus from Wardha and Nagpur.

The *Magan Sanghralaya* (Centre of Science for Villages) is an alternative technology museum 6 km from **Wardha** (362 km), on the Nagpur Rd. 10 km away at **Pauna**, *Vinoba Bhave*, one of Gandhi's keenest disciples, set up his **Ashram.** He championed the **Bhoodan Movement.**

Hotels E *Holiday Resort* nr the Bus Stand. Rm with bath, dormitory. Restaurant. Also cheaper rm in *Lodges* and *Ashrams* and *Govt Circuit House* and *PWD Rest House* in Civil Line. *Annapurna Restaurant* is nr the Station and *Ambika* and *Rambharose* in Saraf Lines.

Rail Wardha is on the Central Railway. **Road** You can also get buses from other major cities in Maharashtra.

Taroba National Park

Approx 100 km S of Nagpur and 45 km N of the nearest town. This compact 117 sq km park, at an altitude of 200 m, is in the teak belt. Best season Nov-Jun. Once in the possession of the Gond Kings, it comprises deciduous forest with a circular perennial lake at the centre with a road around, while other roads radiate to the park perimeter. The dry-forest type of teak occurs abundantly but does not dominate the forest. Gardenia, satinwood (Chloroxylon swietenia) mango and jamun all occur. Bamboo is also common.

The wildlife consists of several troops of langur monkeys, civets, gaur, jackal, wild pigs, chital, various deer, bison and sambar and a few tigers but it is more likely that you will see a leopard if you take a late evening drive. As in Madhya Pradesh and Andhra Pradesh, there are no wild elephants in Maharashtra. There is a **crocodile farm** to conserve the Paul Strus species.

Of the bird life, cattle egrets are frequently seen along with purple moorhens and jacanas at the lake edge, particularly in the evening. Owls are forest dwellers. You can go around the park in a Mini bus.

Note No official guides but if you hire a search light, you will be accompanied by a forest guard who will act as guide.

Hotels E *Mayur,* Mayur Complex, Mul Rd, T 3712. 27 rm. 5 km airport, 1 km rly. Restaurant, bar, parking. **F** *Forest Rest Houses,* built around the lake. For reservations and further information contact The Divisional Forest Officer, W Chanda Division, Chandrapur. Canteen where you should give a day's notice.

From **Nagpur** the NH6 continues E across the **Nag Nadi River** (14 km), through **Maunda** (19 km) to **Bhandara** (27 km). Across the **Wainganga River** (2 km) it continues through open parkland scenery, interspersed with cultivated fields and areas of thicker forest, to **Sakholi** (37 km), **Khomara** (17 km) and the **Maharashtra-Madhya Pradesh** border (32 km). Running through one of the major tribal areas of Madhya Pradesh, the road goes through **Tappa** (16 km), crosses the **River Sheonath** 24 km after passing through **Raj-Nandgaon** (23 km), immediately followed by the **River Puthra** (2 km) and the town of *Durg* (2 km; Population 155,000). It is a further 13 km to the modern steel town of *Bhilai*, which has one of the few large hotels in the whole of the region, run essentially for visitors to the Hindustan Steel works at Bhilai. Accommodation **D** *Bhilai Hotel*, 124 rm, all a/c. **Raipur** is a further 24 km.

Raipur Population 490,000 *Altitude* 300 m The town has more than doubled its population since 1971 and is the regional centre for much of SE Madhya Pradesh. A fort, built by Raja Bhubaneshwar Singh in 1460, has long since disappeared. The city Museum records the major events in the town's history. A tank near the fort covered 3 sq km; the 18th century Maharajbandh Tank was built during the Maratha period, and the Dudhari Temple in 1775. The Kankali Tank which is in the middle of the town was built in the late 17th century. A railway line branches off to the S, crossing some of the few remaining dense jungles in India and the Eastern Ghats down to the coast of Andhra Pradesh. The main railway line to Calcutta turns N to Bilaspur before going E again.

BOMBAY TO AURANGABAD

There are several possible routes by road from Bombay to Aurangabad, the seat of power of the last great Mughal, Aurangzeb. Although the town is interesting, it is best known as the access point for the caves at Ellora, with the splendid Kailasa Temple, and Ajanta.

The easiest road route to Aurangabad is to take the NH3 to Igatpuri (see above), but a few km beyond Igatpuri, turn right for **Sangammer** (216 km). The road climbs up the Western Ghats to nearly 1,600 m and then from *Arthur Hill Lake* gradually descends to Sangammer following the **Pravara River**. From **Sangammer** it is 86 km across the upper valley of the **Godavari River** to the Ahmednagar-Aurangabad crossroads (302 km) via **Shrirampur**. Here you turn left, cross the Godavari at *Kalgaon*, and to your right is a large reservoir filled by the great river, and continue NE to Aurangabad (357 km). The journey can be completed in a very long day.

An attractive alternative is to leave the **NH3** at **Bhiwandi** (56 km) turn right for **Kalyan** (72 km), once an important town and port in Thana district. The ruined fort of **Malangarh** lies 16 km to the S. Kalyan rose to prominence at the end of the 2nd century and soon became one of W India's chief markets. The Muslims renamed it Kalyan Islamabad in the 14th century. The Portuguese and British occupied the town for periods between the 16th and 18th centuries though the Marathas were only defeated finally at the end of the 18th century. There are several ruined monuments nearby which suggest its earlier magnificence.

From Kalyan drive to **Junnar** (approx 182 km), turning right just before the village of **Otur** which is around 170 km from Bombay. A few km to the SE of **Ulhasnagar** is the very fine 11th century **Yadava temple** at **Ambarnath.** It is partly ruined but has very good sculptures of Siva dancing, Brahma, Bhairava and graceful female figures.

Junnar is another rock cut cave temple site, as well as being the birthplace of **Sivaji**. The hill fort dominating the town contains a monument commemorating Sivaji and a temple. On the E side of the hill there are more than 50 Buddhist caves. Most are *viharas** (monasteries) and date from the 2nd century BC to the 3rd Century AD. They are therefore contemporaneous with the early caves at Ajanta.

They comprise the **Tulja Lena Group**, 2 km W of the town, which includes an unusual circular *chaitya** (chapel, Cave 3) which a dome ceiling. The **Bhuta Lena Group** are on the side of **Manmodi Hill**, 1.5 km S of the town. The unfinished chaitya hall (Cave 40) has a well preserved façade containing reliefs of **Laxmi**. The **Ganes Lena Group** are 4 km S of Junnar on the **Lenyadri Hill**. Cave 7 is a vihara with 19 cells leading off the main congregational hall and a colonnaded verandah. The octagonal columns are repeated in the chaitya hall next door (Cave 6).

The fort of **Shivner** rises over 300 m above the plain and is approached from the S by a track that passes over the moat, through four gates then dog-legs up the final stretch to the plateau. Sivaji's birthplace is to the N, and not far from it is a ruined mosque. There are four tanks running down the centre. In the 3rd century the site was a Buddhist vihara and on the E face there are about 50 rock cells. **Maloji Bhonsla**, Sivaji's grandfather, was granted the fort in 1599. Sivaji was born in 1627 but did not remain long as it was taken and garrisoned by the Mughals from the early 1630s. Several attempts to win it back failed.

Drive down from Junnar by the SE road to join **NH50** which runs from Pune to **Nasik**. At the intersection at **Narayangaon**, turn left for **Sangammer** where you can continue on by the first route. Alternatively, at **Ghargaon**, midway between Narayangaon and Sangammer you can turn right and take a country road to Ahmadnagar (70 km). A longer way but on better roads is from Dolasne beyond Ghargaon, 72 km SE to **Supe**, crossing the **Mula River** and passing through the villages of **Kadakvadi**, **Takli Dhokeshwar** and **Parner**, the intersection with the shorter country road. **Supe** is in the **Harischandra Range** running SE from nr Nasik and the southernmost of the two ridges running either side of **Ahmadnagar**, 27 km from Supe.

Ahmadnagar (Population 170,000), an historic Muslim town, was founded in 1490 by Ahmad Nizam Shah Bahri, the son a Brahman from Vijayanagar who converted to Islam. The dynasty he founded ruled the region until 1636, their territory stretching from Aurangabad to Bassein, just N of Bombay. Akbar captured the fort in 1599 after a long siege. The widow of Ali Adil Shah was killed leading the defence of the fort and is buried on a hill 10 km E of the city in the **Tomb of Salabat Khan**.

Aurangzeb died here on March 3 1707. **Alamgir's Dargah** is a small enclosure near the cantonment and marks his temporary resting place before his body was moved to Aurangabad (Ahmednagar was where Aurangzeb had begun his long Deccan campaign 24 years earlier). The tomb faces a mosque, while to the E is a white marble **Darbar Hall**, well worth visiting for the view from the roof.

The Fort, almost 1 km to the E of the city, built in 1559, is circular in shape and has an 18 m high wall reinforced with 22 bastions. Among the numerous mosques inside are: the small but attractive **Qasim Mosque** (1500-8); the **Husaini Mosque,** with a Persian style dome; the **Farhad Khani Mosque** (1560) with minarets, the **Damadi Mosque** (1567) with its splendid carved stonework and the large domed **Jamal Khan's Mosque** are others.

The **Malik-i-Maidan** (Lord of the Plain) iron cannon now standing on the Lion Bastion at Bijapur – **see page 885**, was cast at Ahmadnagar by Rumi Khan, Nizam Shah's Turkish artillery officer. He also constructed the **Mecca Mosque** (c1515). **The Farah Baksh Palace**, built between 1508 and 1583 is now in ruins. The well preserved **Tomb of Nizam Shah** is situated in a large garden on the left bank of the Sina River. **Pariabagh** (Fairy Garden) the old palace of Burhan Nizam Shah (1508-53) is 3 km S of the city.

Hotels **E** Asoka Tourist, Kings Rd, T 3607-8. 32 rm, some a/c. 2 km rly, 1 km centre. Out of town: **D** Bhagyalaxmi, Post: Shirdi, Tal: Kopargaon, T 261-3. 58 rm. Close to Kopargaon rly, central. Diners. **D** Natraj, Nagar Aurangabad Rd, T 6576-80. 24 rm. Taxi services, Diners. **E** Suvidha, Nim Gaon Jali, Via Loni, T Ashwi 75. 6 rm. Bar.

Air Service Nearest airport is at Aurangabad (110 km).

Rail Pune: Maharashtra Exp 7384, daily, 0140, 4 hr 20 min. Bhopal: Jhelum Exp 4677, daily, 2046, 12 hr 35 min. The fort is 4 km NE of the station

Road Regular buses to Bombay, Pune and other places in the state.

From **Ahmadnagar** to **Aurangabad** (110 km) the most direct route is NE. The road goes through **Bhorwadi** (24 km), **Godhegaon** (10 km) and **Vadal Bhairoba** (9 km). It crosses the **River Godavari** at **Pravara Sangam** (24 km) and then passes through **Kaigaon** (2 km) and **Dahigaon** (16 km before reaching Aurangabad (24 km). You can also go by a longer route which takes in **Paithan** (85 km) which is 63 km S of **Aurangabad**.

Paithan is one of the oldest cities of the Deccan and is situated on the N bank of the **Godavari River** as it leaves the Nath Sagar reservoir to the W. It is mentioned in Asoka's Edicts and was visited by Greek traders in the 3rd Century BC. From the 2nd century BC to 2nd century AD it was the capital of the Satvahana dynasty and was known as Pratisthan. Earlier remains have been dated to the third millenium BC. This little town is famous for its Shrine of **Sant Eknath**.

Every year on *Nath Shastri* (usually in March) the 10-day Paithan Yatra fair is held drawing pilgrims in their thousands. Paithan is also famous for a special kind of silk sari with brocaded gold borders and *pallu** (end-piece). Motifs of geese, parrots, peacocks and stylised leaves flowers and creepers in dark greens, red and blue are brocaded against the golden background of the fabric.

The **Jaikwadi Project** at *Nath Sagar* is a large earthen dam and reservoir. Over 35,000 ha have been submerged. Around **Paithan** and Jaikwadi a large garden is being developed (the **Gyaneshwar Udyan** garden) along the lies of the Brindavan Gardens in Mysore. At the S and N ends of the dam are two viewing stations for watching indigenous and migratory birds (Best season Oct-Mar)

Aurangabad

Population 600,000   Best time for a visit Nov to Feb.

	Jan	Feb	Mar	Apr	May	Jun	Jul	Aug	Sep	Oct	Nov	Dec	Av/Tot
Max (°C)	29	32	36	38	40	35	29	29	30	31	30	29	32
Min (°C)	14	16	20	24	25	23	22	21	21	20	16	14	20
Rain (mm)	3	3	4	7	17	141	189	146	179	62	32	9	792

Aurangabad is the best known town on the inland plateau of Maharashtra, largely because it is the base for visiting the wonderful caves at Ellora and Ajanta. However, the town itself is of interest too. Aurangabad was first known as **Khadke** and was founded in 1610 by Malik Ambar, an Abyssinian slave who became the wazir (Prime Minister) of the King of Ahmadnagar. It was later changed to Aurangabad in honour of the last Great Mughal, Aurangzeb, who built a new citadel. His wife is buried in the *Bibi-ka Maqbara* and he is buried in a simple grave at Rauza – see Excursions. It acted as the centre of operations for his Deccan campaign which occupied him for the second half of his 49 year reign.

The British **cantonment** area is in the SW quadrant of the city and lies on the left bank of the Kham River. To the N is the Begumpura district in which there is the attractive Pan Chakki water mill and the Bibi-ka-Maqbara, the mausoleum of Aurangzeb's wife. Both are worth visiting.

Aurangabad has since experienced the usual growth of most Indian cities and has a university, medical and engineering colleges and an airport to complement its industrial and commercial activities.

Local Festivals Feb/Mar. *Mahashivratri* Large fair at the Grineshwara Temple, nr Ellora and the *Ellora Yatra*.

Places of Interest Aurangzeb built the 4.5 m high, crenellated city walls in 1682 to provide defence against the Marathas. There were four main gates: Delhi (N), Jalna (E), Pathan (S) and Mecca (W). In addition there were nine subsidiary gates.

The *Killa Arrak* (1692) was Aurangzeb's citadel and lay between the Delhi and Mecca Gates. Little remains though when it was Aurangzeb's Delhi of the South over fifty Maharajahs and Princes attended the court. With Aurangzeb gone, the city paled into relative insignificance. At the centre in a grove of trees lies the **Jama Masjid**, a low building with minarets and a broad band carved with Koranic inscriptions running the length of the façade. Malik Ambar built half the mosque, Aurangzeb the other.

Other monuments in the old city are **Kali Masjid** (1600) a six pillared stone mosque built by Malik Ambar who also constructed the ruined **Naukonda Palace** (1616) which contained a zenana, Halls of Public and Private Audience, mosque and baths. In the market square is the **Shah Ganj Mosque** (c.1720) which has shops on three sides. The **Chauk Masjid** (1665) was built by Shayista Khan, Aurangzeb's uncle and has five domes. The Lal **Masjid** (1655) is in red-painted basalt.

Beyond the Mecca Gate lies the **Bibi-ka Maqbara** (1678), the mausoleum of Aurangzeb's wife Rabia Daurani. Open Sunrise to 2000. Re 0.75, Free on Fri. Floodlit at night. Shoes must be taken off before entering the mausoleum.

Mughal style in decline The classic lines of a garden tomb give it an impressive setting. Yet close inspection disappoints. Modelled on the Taj Mahal, which was completed 25 years earlier, it is about half its size, standing in a 137,000 sq m walled area, **see page 147**. Far less money was spent – 1⁄300th, by some estimates – and the comparative poverty of the finish is immediately obvious. It uses marble in the mausoleum itself but plaster elsewhere. The proportions are less graceful, the design appearing cramped for space, nor do the most of the carvings approach the quality of the Taj Mahal. Although the minarets are more than

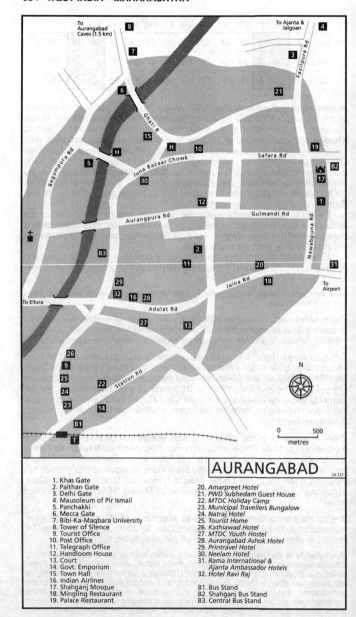

AURANGABAD

1. Khas Gate
2. Paithan Gate
3. Delhi Gate
4. Mausoleum of Pir Ismail
5. Panchakki
6. Mecca Gate
7. Bibi-Ka-Maqbara University
8. Tower of Silence
9. Tourist Office
10. Post Office
11. Telegraph Office
12. Handloom House
13. Court
14. Govt. Emporium
15. Town Hall
16. Indian Airlines
17. Shahganj Mosque
18. Mingling Restaurant
19. Palace Restaurant

20. *Amarpreet Hotel*
21. *PWD Subhedam Guest House*
22. *MTDC Holiday Camp*
23. *Municipal Travellers Bungalow*
24. *Natraj Hotel*
25. *Tourist Home*
26. *Kathiawad Hotel*
27. *MTDC Youth Hostel*
28. *Aurangabad Ashok Hotel*
29. *Printravel Hotel*
30. *Neelam Hotel*
31. *Rama International & Ajanta Ambassador Hotels*
32. *Hotel Ravi Raj*

B1. Bus Stand
B2. Shahganj Bus Stand
B3. Central Bus Stand

SA 237

adequate in themselves, they are too heavy in relation to the main mausoleum. The decoration has become over fussy and the lines weak.

Yet despite all its failings it is widely held to be one of the finest buildings of its period. The brass door carries an inscription which says Ata Ullah was the chief architect and Haibat Rai the maker of the door. An octagonal white marble *jali** screen surrounds the grave. On the tomb itself, in place of a marble slab, there is bare earth, a sign of humility. The second tomb in the corner is said to be Rabi'a Daurani's nurse. To the W is a mosque.

On the same side of the **Kham River** is the *Pan Chakki* (1696, Water Mill), which has a white marble shrine to Baba Shah Muzaffar, the devout Aurangzeb's spiritual adviser. The pre-Mughal 17th century mill for turning large grinding stones was powered by water channelled from a spring some distance away and released through a dam. Open sunrise to 2000. Re 0.75. Pleasant garden with fish pond and a refreshment stand under an ancient Banyan tree.

Aurangabad Caves 3 km N of Aurangabad. An auto-rickshaw will cover the distance in about 20 min.

Warning Waiting charges can be high, negotiate before and bargain. Alternatively, if it is cool enough and you feel fit, you can walk back to the edge of town and get an auto-rickshaw back to your hotel.

The caves are very interesting, but visit them first as they are not a substitute to Ajanta and Ellora. They were excavated out of a S facing hillside overlooking the town which came much later and fall into two groups about 1 km apart. They date from the Vakataka (4th and 5th Centuries AD) and the succeeding Kalachuri dynasties (6th to 8th centuries) though the older Hinayana Cave 4 is believed to date back to at least 1st century, if not earlier. In all there are ten caves, five in each group.

The **Western Group** are all *viharas** except for the earlier Cave 4 which is a *chaitya**. **Cave 1** is incomplete but has finely carved pillars with figures on brackets and ornamentation around doorways and walls. Good views of the country around. **Cave 2** has a shrine and columned hallways, with a large Buddha as Teacher, in a seated position with intricately carved panels. The larger **Cave 3** has a plain exterior but has superb carvings on twelve pillars of the hallway which leads to the sanctuary cut deep into the rock. Panels illustrating *jataka* stories and a fine large Buddha figure on his throne with attendant devotees who represent contemporary dress and style. **Cave 4**, the *chaitya* has a rib vaulting of the ceiling with a stupa containing relics while the Buddha figure is seated on a throne outside. **Cave 5** is damaged and has not much of its original carvings intact.

The **Eastern Group** has more sculptures of women and Bodhisattvas and **Cave 6** has a large Buddha supporting Ganes, indicating that this is of the later period when Hinduism was gaining the ascendancy over Buddhism. Note the mural on the ceiling of the balcony. **Cave 7** is regarded as the most interesting of both groups. Columned shrines at each end of the verandah house images of Hariti (right) and six goddesses, including Padmini (left). Here the shrine is central with an ambulatory passage around it. In the rear of the hall is a large Buddha in a preaching position, and walls have carvings depicting deliverance and a profusion of female figures including dancers and musicians. Not a lot to see in **Cave 9** which was not finished but has some carvings which suggest pre-Nirvana figures and Buddhism was waning. The incomplete **Cave 10** illustrates the first stages of cave excavation.

Hotels Some offer discounts between Apr and Sep. Most will provide packed-lunch for trip to the caves. **B** *Welcomgroup Rama International*, R 3 Chikalthana. T 82340-44, Cable: Welcotel, Telex: 0745 212 Rama In. 100 rm, suites. 4 km centre. Restaurant (rather poor), car hire, shops, travel, sports, gardens. Quiet, large gardens, off-season discount, some rms could be cleaner. **B** *Ajanta Ambassador*, Chikalthana. T 82211-15, Cable: Embassy, Telex: 745 211 Amba In. 125 rm. 4 km centre. Restaurant, bar, car hire, shops, travel, tennis. Excellent food. Quiet "country" hotel, good service, pool in pleasant gardens. **C** *Aurangabad Ashok*, Dr Rajendra Prasad Marg, T 4520-29. Cable: Tourism (DN), Telex: 745 229. 66 a/c rm. Restaurant, bar, travel, car hire, shops, sports, Amex, Diners. Comfortable and recommended. **C** *Amarpreet*, PJL Nehru Marg. T 23422, 24615, Cable: Aphotel, Telex: 754 307 Buxs In. 30 rm. 7 km airport, 1.5 km rly, 1.5 km Bus Stand, 0.5 km centre. Restaurants, garden bar, travel, car hire, play ground.

D *Raviraj,* Dr Rajendra Prasad Marg, T 27501-04, Cable: Rajotel. 40 rm, some a/c. 7 km airport, 1 km rly, 1 km centre. Restaurant, bar, Diners. **D** *Nandavan,* Station Rd,T 3311-3. 29 rm, few a/c. Restaurants, bar, car hire. **E** *MTDC Holiday Resort,* Station Rd. Some a/c rm with bath and mosquito nets, Tourist office. Good value rm. **Note:** checkout at 0800. **E** *Tourist Home,* Station Rd. Best in station area. **E** *New Punjab,* nr station. **E** *Natraj,* Station Rd, below Tourist Home. Simple rm with bath. **E** *Neelam,* Juna Bazaar Chawk, T 4561-2. 28 rm with bath, some a/c. Restaurant. **E** *Printravel,* Dr Ambedkar Rd, T 2707. Non a/c. Old fashioned rm with baths and mosquito nets.

F *Youth Hostel,* Station Rd, (mid way between Rly Station and town). Clean, well run, good segregated dormitories, roof terrace. Breakfast/evening meals. Recommended. **F** *Asoka* and *Ambika,* nr the station and are basic but cheap. Also *Railway Retiring Rm.*

Restaurants Aurangabad Ashok's *Albela* is very good with wide choice. On Airport Rd offering Chinese, Continental, and Indian: *Diwan-e-Am,* Ambassador Hotel; *Madhuban,* Rama International; *Kailash Restaurant,* Amarpreet Hotel, *Minglin,* opp Amarpreet, reasonably priced Chinese rec. *Palace,* Shahgunj. Indian (Mughlai); *Panchavati,* Padampura; *Neelam,* Jubilee Park; *Foodwala Bhoj Restaurant,* Printravel Hotel, Dr. Ambedkar Rd; Best value *thalis* at the Youth Hostel. Indian restaurants on Station Rd: *Tandoor,* Chanakya; *Radhika* and *Rathi,* Nandavan Hotel. also snack bar and *Guru;* Inexpensive *Pinky's; New Punjab* and *Kailash,* MTDC Holiday Resort, nr Rly Station.

Bars *The Rama International, Ambassador, Ashok* and *Amarpreet Hotels* have bars.

Banks and Exchanges Central Bank and State Bank of India in Kranti Chowk, State Bank of Hyderabad in Shahganj and Rly Station.

Shopping Usually open 1000-2000, closed Sun. The city is known for its handwoven Himru shawls (brocades occasionally with Ajanta motifs), and special textile weaves – *Mashru, Pathani silk* and *Kimkhab* as well as artificial silk. You can also get good decorative lacquer work, Bidriware and agate articles.

Main shopping areas are City Chowk, Gulmandi, Nawabpura, Station Rd, Shahgunj, Sarafa, Mondha. In Shahgunj: *Cottage Industries* and *Himroo Factory Emporium,* nr Bus Stand. Station Rd: *Silk Loom Fabrics* and *Tourist Emporium,* opp Holiday Camp. At Nawabpura: Shawl factory and Silk showroom. *Khadi Gramudyog* in Sarafa and *Sajawat* at Eknath Mandir.

Photography *Mohammed Bhoy,* Chowk, T 5402. *Paul Studio,* Cantonment, T 3592. *Rex Photo Studio,* Juna Bazar, T 3434.

Local Transport Local taxis are available. Rates Rs 100 for 4 hr, 40 km. Rs 200 for 8 hr, 80 km. Additional Rs 2.40 per km. **Tongas** (no fixed rate) and auto-rickshaws (Rs 2 per km).

Sports Aurangabad has a race course which is located in the cantonment area.

Museums History Museum, Marathwada University to the NW of town.

Useful Services Police: T 100 Fire: T 101 Ambulance: T 102

Hospitals and Medical Services Medical College Hospital, T 4411. Bhagwat Nursing Home, T 6109. Hazari Nursing Home Sanjeevani Hospital

Post and Telegraph GPO, Juna Bazaar Chowk. Cantonment Post Office, T 5460. City Colony Post Office, T 4685. S Block Colony Post Office, T 3888. Osmanpura, T 4490. Sessions Court, T 4688. Chikalthana (Mukundwadi), T 8382. Telegraph Office, T 5400.

Places of Worship *Hindu:* Nath Mandir, Aurangapura. *Muslim:* Shahnoormiya Dargah, Usmanpura. *Sikh:* Gurudwara, Usmanpura. *Christian:* Christ Church, Cantonment.

Travel Agents and Tour Operators Aurangabad Transport Syndicate, Rama International Hotel, T 4872. Tourist Guide Service, Shastri Nagar, Jawahar Colony, T 4262. Print Travel, Adalat Rd, T 4707. Amarmaya Travels, T 6300.

Tourist Offices and Information Govt. of India Tourist Office, Krishna Vilas, Station Rd, T 4817. Open 0830-1800 weekdays, 0830-1230 Sat. Airport Counter open at flight times. Maharashtra TDCL, Holiday Camp, T 4713. Open 1000-1700.

Tours MTDC, ITDC and ST all operate good sightseeing to Ajanta, Ellora and City sightseeing. Ellora and City Sightseeing: Daily (0800-1630) from Central Bus Stand. Daily (0930-1830) from MTDC Holiday Resort. Ajanta Excursions: Daily (0730-1730) from Central Bus Stand. Daily (0800-1800) from MTDC Holiday Resort. The ITDC tour tickets are also available from Hotel Aurangabad Ashok.

Air Indian Airlines connects Aurangabad with Bombay and New Delhi via Udaipur, Jodhpur and Jaipur daily. Vayudoot flies three times a week to Bombay-Nanded and three times a week to Bombay-Pune, and three times a week to Nagpur. Indian Airlines City Office, Adalat Rd, T 4864, 4008. Airport Office, Jalna Rd, Chikalthana, T 82223.

Rail Secunderabad (Hyderabad): *Ajanta Exp* 7552, daily,2153, 12 hr 40 min; There is no direct line to Bombay. If travelling by train you must go to Manmad, approx 120 km NE. A branch line connects Manmad with Aurangabad.

Road Aurangabad is the focus of a number of State Highways between Bombay, Hyderabad, Nagpur and Dhule. State Transport Bus Service operates a/c coaches to Bombay and Gatge Patil. State Transport bus services also connect Aurangabad with Pune, Hyderabad, Nasik and Nagpur.

Excursions There are two recognised excursions from Aurangabad, the first to the caves at Ellora via Daulatabad and the second to the caves at Ajanta. If time is limited, a choice may have to be made. Ellora is nearer and there is Daulatabad and Rauza on the way. For spectacle visit Ellora, especially the Kailasa Temple, but for scenic setting, Ajanta is more impressive. Allow a day for each tour. Conducted tours leave early.

Note for visiting the caves. Take packed lunch and drinks, wear a sun hat and comfortable shoes, take a strong torch. Flash photography (but no tripods) is allowed but permission needed for professional cine cameras. Guides (in a number of foreign languages) and at Ajanta ' flash lights passes' for groups wishing to see darker caves illuminated, are available (best to join a group if on your own). Painted caves open at 1000, others at 0900 – light is better in the afternoon. For the elderly and infirm, dhoolies (chairs carried by men) are available.

To Ellora

The very pleasant drive to Ellora, 30 km NW of Aurangabad, passes through some exciting countryside with two interesting sites en route. You leave Aurangabad and travel W along the Malegaon road. Initially the road is tree lined with cultivated fields either side. Then, as height is gradually gained, the vegetation becomes drier and often thorny scrub.

Daulatabad, 13 km from Aurangabad, is a local landmark. On the granite rock towering 250 m above the surrounding countryside is the fort of **Deogiri**. This dates from the Yadava period of the 11th-14th centuries although the first fort had probably been constructed in the 9th century, and before that had been a Buddhist monastery. It is an extraordinary engineering feat, making use of the natural features and enhancing them with a succession of fearsome obstacles.

The Chand Minar stands at the bottom of the fort, towering as a celebration of victory like the Qutb Minar in Delhi. Like the Mughals who followed him two centuries later, **Muhammad Tughluq – see page 168** – was determined to extend his power S into the Deccan Plateau. He seized Daulatabad and decided top make it his capital and populate it with the residents of his existing capital in Delhi. Thousands died as a result of the shortlived experiment.

The fortifications The hillside around the fort was made steeper to make scaling extremely difficult. The three concentric walls had strong gates and the surrounding moat could be flooded. The attacker would then face an L-shaped keep, a long tortuous tunnel which could be sealed by an iron cover at the top after firing with hot coals, and a chamber which could be filled with noxious fumes. Despite the sophistication of the design the fort was still captured a number of times.

The buildings From Ala-ud-din Khalji's capture of **Deogiri** in 1296 until Independence in 1947, by which time it was under the control of the Nizam of Hyderabad, the fort remained in Muslim hands. The outermost of the four main ring walls and the bastion gates were probably built by the Muslims.

The **Jami Masjid** (1318) at the W end has 106 pillars taken from a Hindu temple. Opposite is the well-preserved pink and white, four storey Persian style **Chand Minar** (1435) and was once thought to be covered in Persian tiles. The 31 m high victory tower built by Ala-ud-din Bahmani to celebrate his capture of the fort has at its base 24 chambers and a small mosque. To the right of the third gate is the **Chini Mahal** where Abdul Hasan Tana Shah, the last King of Golconda was imprisoned in 1687 for 13 years.

The 6.6m long **Kila Shikan** (Fort Breaker) iron cannon is on the bastion nearby. At the end of the tunnel inside the citadel, is a flight of steps leading up to the **Hindu Pavilion**, said to be the palace of the Yadavi Queen and later Shah Jahan. The **citadel** is reached by climbing one hundred further steps and passing through two more gateways. At the top is another cannon with a ram's head on the butt. The Persian inscription around the muzzle reads 'Creator of Storms'.

Beyond **Daulatabad** the road climbs onto a plateau and at various bends on the ascent there are good views looking back towards Daulatabad and Aurangabad. At **Rauza** (833 m), 24 km from Aurangabad, and only 6 km from Ellora, is the simple tomb of **Aurangzeb**. The other name for Rauza is **Khuldabad** (Heavenly Abode), a pilgrimage centre of the Deccan Muslims. There are over twenty tombs in the town including those of Aurangzeb and his son Azam Shah, and his family. There is also a carefully preserved robe, said to be the Prophet Mohammed's. This is displayed once a year to the faithful.

Rauza was once an important town with a large population. Aurangzeb built the wall around it with seven gates and a paved avenue leading up to it. it became a favourite Muslim burial ground, and tombs are scattered widely. The most significant is that of Aurangzeb himself(1707), who died at the age of 89. He had died as he had hoped on a Fri, 20 Feb 1707. He wanted a simple grave, a sign of humility, to be paid for by money obtained from the sale of his carefully copied korans. As an orthodox Muslim, he wanted a grave open to the sky. The grave on a stone platform has no canopy and the marble screen around it was erected later by Curzon and the Nizam of Hyderabad.

Slightly to the right is the **Dargah of Saiyad Zain-ud-din** (1370), a Muslim saint. The doors are inlaid with silver plates and there are decorated steps. A little to the rear is a locked room where you may still be told that the Prophet Mohammed's robe is kept. Across the road and beyond a courtyard, among other tombs, is the **Dargah of Saiyad Burhan-ud-din** (1344), a saint whose shrine is said to contain hairs from the Prophet's beard.

Hotels E *Kailash Hotel* nr the caves has non a/c rm and a good restaurant. **F** *Khuldabad Guest House* (3 km from Ellora caves) and *Local Fund Traveller's Bungalow* can be reserved through the Executive Engineer, Padampura and Zila Parishad, respectively, if free. Cook available.

Ellora

The caves at **Ellora** are among the finest in India and are a popular destination for travellers en route from Bombay to Udaipur and W Rajasthan. Over 1200 man-made caves have been discovered in India. Those at Ellora and Ajanta are miles from anywhere and you would be justified in wondering why they were excavated and decorated in the first place. They represent not one faith but three, **Hinduism, Jainism** and **Buddhism**. The fact that they are alongside one another indicates that at the time of their creation and occupation there must have been considerable mutual tolerance.

It has been suggested that the caves at Ellora lie near an important ancient trade route between Ujjain in Madhya Pradesh and the W coast. They are the work of priests and pilgrims who would have used the route for travel between pilgrimage sites thus benefitting from the patronage of passers by.

Unlike the caves at Ajanta, Ellora's caves were never 'lost', but they were abandoned and forgotten. There are 34 caves at Ellora, cut out of the volcanic lavas of the Deccan Trap. 12 are Buddhist (created from approximately 600-800 AD), 17 Hindu (600-900 AD) and 5 Jain (800-1100 AD). The land slopes so that most have courtyards in front. They face west and are best seen in the afternoon. This is convenient if you are hiring your own car, as the plane from Bombay arrives in the early morning leaving enough time to look round Aurangabad and visit the caves in one long day.

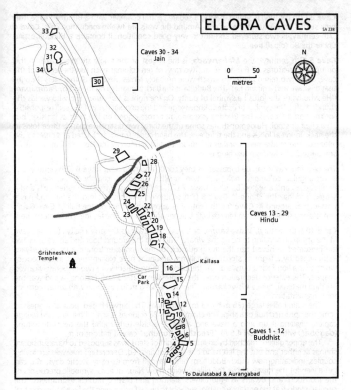

ELLORA CAVES SA 238

Caves 30 - 34 Jain

N

0   50
metres

29

28
27
26
25
24   22
23   21
20
19
18
17

Grishneshvara
Temple

Kailasa

16

Car
Park

15

14
13   12
11   10
9
8
7   6
5
4
3
2
1

Caves 13 - 29
Hindu

Caves 1 - 12
Buddhist

To Daulatabad & Aurangabad

The caves are not all equally interesting, but in order to see them in chronological order it is advisable if possible to stop at the E end of the caves so that you can see the Buddhist Viharas first. In this way the magnificent Hindu Kailasa temple is seen towards the end. However, tour buses often stop at the car park, directly in front of the temple itself.

Note MTDC has opened a restaurant. Unexciting food, slow service. Toilets and garden. Souvenirs and postcards are available. Very attractive countryside. Not suitable for disabled.

The Buddhist Caves (Nos. 1-12)
These belong to the **Vajrayana** sect of the Mahayana (Greater Vehicle) School. The caves include *viharas** (monasteries) and *chaityas** (chapels) where the monks worshipped. It has been suggested that the stone cut structures were ideally suited to the climate which experienced monsoons and rapidly became the preferred medium over more flimsy and less durable wood.

Cave 1 (7th century) is a simple vihara with no pillars and no carving. There are four cells in the S and E walls around a 13 m square assembly hall. The adjoining **Cave 2** (7th century) was a hall for worship and is reached by flight of steps. At the door of the cave are *dwarapala** (guardians) flanked by windows. The interior is slightly larger (14.5 m sq) and comprises a hall supported by twelve pillars with a gallery running down each side. All the columns are richly decorated and display the characteristic fertility motif of a pot and foliage. In the centre of the back wall is a 3 m high seated Buddha while along each of the side wall are five Buddhas accompanied by Boddhisattvas and *apsaras** (celestial nymphs).

Cave 3 (7th century) is similar, having a square central chamber with a Buddha image, this time seated on a lotus at the far end. Around the walls are twelve meditation cells. **Cave 4** (7th century) is two storeyed and not in very good condition. It contains a Buddha sitting under the Bo (pipal) tree.

Cave 5 (7th century), the **Maharwada**, is the largest of the single storeyed caves in this group and measures 17.6 m by 36 m. Two rows of ten columns each run the length of the cave, as do two raised platforms which were probably tables. Because of these it is thought that this cave was a dining hall. The Buddha at the back is guarded on the left by **Padmapani** ('He who holds the lotus') a symbol of purity. On the right is **Vajrapani** (He who wields the thunderbolt'), the symbol of esoteric knowledge and the popular deity of the sect responsible for creating the caves. The Buddha is seated, not cross-legged on the floor as is usual, but on a chair or stool. He demonstrates some of the thirty two distinctive marks: three folds in the neck, long ear lobes and the third eye. The hand codes (**mudras***) acted as signals to the initiated. The mudra here signifies the Buddha's first sermon at the Deer Park at Sarnath – see page 261 – and is a teaching pose.

The next four caves can be bypassed as they contain nothing new. **Cave 6** (7th century) has a rectangular columned hall with two smaller subsidiary chambers, decorations of Bodhisattvas and a seated Buddha. **Cave 7** (7th century) has twelve unfinished cells and a seated Buddha. The shrine in **Cave 8** (7th century) is brought out into the hall and has a passageway around it. **Cave 9** (7th century) is approached through the hall of Cave 6 and consists of a small hall, open terrace with balcony and a shrine. The façade is richly decorated.

Cave 10 (7th century), **Viswakarma,** or Carpenter's Cave, is the only chaitya (chapel) cave in the group, in addition to being the **vihara**. This is on the ground floor and above are what are presumed to have been the living quarters of the monks. In front is a large courtyard approached by a flight of steps. The galleries around it have elegant pillars at the foot of which was a lion facing outwards. At the back of these galleries are two elaborately carved chapels. The exterior decoration gives the impression that instead of stone, wood was the building material, hence **Viswakarma**. The façade has a trefoil window with **apsara** groups for ornamentation.

The main hall is large (26 m by 13 m, 10 m high). The curved fluted 'beams' suggest to some the upturned hull of a ship. The chamber has 28 columns, each with a vase and foliage capital, dividing it up into a nave and aisles. The aisle runs round the decorated stupa (**dagoba***) with a colossal 4.5 m "**Preaching Buddha**" carved in front of it.

The upper gallery, reached by an internal flight of steps, was supposed to have subsidiary shrines at either end but the left hand one was not finished. Decorating the walls are loving couples, indicating how much Buddhism had changed from its early ascetic days. You can get a view of the friezes above the pillars which show Naga queens, symbolic precursors of the monsoon, and dwarfs as entertainers, dancing and playing musical instruments. The circular window at the entrance enables sunlight to be cast on it giving the face a truly spiritual and ethereal quality.

Caves 11 and 12 (both 8th century) are three-storeyed and illustrate the use of the upper levels of these caves as a residence for monks and pilgrim hostels. **Cave 11** (Do Thal – two storeyed) was found to have a third storey in 1876 when the basement was discovered. The lowest level is a verandah with a shrine and two cells at the back of it. The middle level has eight front pillars and five rear cells of which only the central three are completed and decorated. The upper level has a porch opening into a long colonnaded hall with a Buddha shrine at the rear. Images of Durga and Ganesh suggest that the cave was later used by Hindus. **Cave 12** (Tin Thal – three storeyed) has cells for sleeping (note stone benches) on the lower floors but it is the figures of the Buddha which are of particular interest. The rows of seven Buddhas are symbolic of the belief that he appears on earth every 5,000 years and has already visited it 7 times.

The **Hindu Caves (Nos. 13-29)**

These lie in the centre of the group and are the most numerous. With the exception of a few most can be missed.

Cave 13 is a plain room only while **Cave 14** (Ravana ki khai, 7th century), is single storeyed and the last of the collection from the early period. River goddesses and guardians stand at the doorway while inside is a broken image of Durga and figurative panels on the walls depicted by carvings of the principle deities, Vishnu, Siva, Lakshmi and Parvati. **Cave 15** (Das Avatara, mid 8th century) is reached by a flight of steps and has a large courtyard and is two storeyed.

Cave 16, *Kailasanatha Temple* (mid 8th century onwards) There is a car park in front of the temple. The Kailasanatha Temple is the most magnificent of all the rock cut structures at Ellora. It differs from all the others in that it is not a cave but a temple cut out of the rock and open to the elements. One aspect of its uniqueness is that it is the only building that was begun from the top.

Carved out of 85,000 cu m of rock, the design and execution of the full temple plan is an extraordinary triumph of imagination and craftsmanship. Excavating three deep trenches into the rock, carving started from the top of the cliff and worked down to the base. Enormous blocks were left intact from which the porch, the free standing pillars and other shrines were subsequently carved. The main shrine was carved on what became the upper storey, as the lower floor was cut out below. It is impossible not to be awe-struck by the spectacle. It is attributed to the Rashtrakuta King *Dantidurga* (725-55) and must have taken years to complete.

Mount Kailasa (6,700 m), the home of Siva, is a real mountain on the Tibetan plateau beyond the Himalaya. Its distinctive pyramidal shape, its isolation from other mountains, and the appearance of a swastika symbol etched by snow and ice on its rock face, imbued the mountain with great religious significance to Hindus and Buddhists alike. Kailasa was seen as the centre of the universe, and Siva is lord of Kailasa, Kailasanatha. To imitate the real snow covered peaks, the sikharas here were once covered with white plaster.

The entrance The temple is 50 m long and 33 m wide and the tower rises 29 m above the level of the court. As with other sacred places the entrance gate is the threshold between the profane and sacred worlds. The goddesses **Ganga** and **Yamuna** form the door jambs. Just inside there are two seated sages: **Vyasa**, the legendary author of the Mahabharata and **Valmiki** to whom the Ramayana has been ascribed. In the porch there are four columns carrying the N Indian vase and foliage motif, a symbol of fertility and well-being. On each side of the doorway there are images of **Kubera**, the god of wealth, with other symbols of well-being such as the conch shell and the lotus. Two more figures complete the welcoming party. They are **Ganes** (left), the elephant headed son of Siva, the bringer of good fortune, and **Durga** (right), the vengeful form of Siva's wife Parvati.

In the antechamber opposite is **Lakshmi**, the goddess of wealth. In the courtyard, to your right and left are free standing elephants. On the left round the corner is a panel depicting **Kama**, the god of desire, carrying his bow and five arrows, one for each of the senses. On the far wall to your left of the entrance behind the pillars is the shrine of the Three River Goddesses – **Ganga** (centre), **Yamuna** (left) and **Sarasvati** (right). Symbolically they stand for purity, devotion and wisdom respectively. This is a good place to photograph the central shrine. The two carved monolithic pillars are interpreted by some as stylized flagstaffs indicating royal patronage – a practice that Asoka popularised in the third century BC.

There are two distinct levels taking the worshipper from the courtyard by two staircases flanking the central hall to the lower level with its processional path and then rising even higher to the upper level of the *mandapa*.

The Central Assembly Hall Around the central shrine is a colonnaded hall gouged from the rock, which in places overhangs menacingly. Inside this cloister are a series of panels portraying Siva and Vishnu myths. The whole can be viewed as a sort of instructional picture gallery, a purpose it served for worshippers from ancient times, who could not read.

The S facing wall has Ramayana stories – **Ravana** offering his heads, **Siva** and **Parvati** with **Nandi** the bull and the lingam (creative power); **Siva and Parvati** playing the vina; **Siva and Parvati** playing dice in a spirit of harmony; the marriage of **Siva** and **Parvati**; the origin of the *lingam*, the symbol of **Siva** and creative (male) energy; **Siva** dancing and **Siva** tricking **Parvati**. Note the panel on the S of the *mandapa* of **Ravana** shaking **Mount Kailasa** attempting to carry it off, disturbing Parvati and her attendants, one of whom is seen frightened and fleeing, and Siva restoring order with the movement of his toe.

Along the N facing wall are stories from the Mahabharata above and Krishna legends below. The panels include, **Krishna** (Vishnu's eighth incarnation) stealing buttermilk; and **Vishnu** as **Narasimha** (fourth incarnation) as half-man, half lion; **Vishnu** reclining on **Ananda** the serpent in between incarnations; **Vishnu** the Preserver. Finally there is **Annapurna**, Goddess of Plenty.

The inner porch contains two panels, Siva as Lord of Knowledge and Siva as Bhairava Killing the Elephant Demon.

The Main Shrine. Steps lead to the upper floor which contains a *mandapa** (central hall,

17 m by 16 m) of a 16 stout pillars arranged in groups of four with aisles corresponding to the cardinal points leading to an open central area. At the far end is the garbha *griha* * (shrine) with **Ganga** and **Yamuna** as door guardians. Inside is the yoni lingam, symbol of Siva's creative power. Running around the back is a passageway with five small shrines rm of it, each with a replica of the main temple. Note the Nataraja painting on the *mandapa* ceiling. There are remnants of paintings on the porch ceilings (particularly to the W) where you will see *apsaras*, dwarfs and animals.

The exterior of the temple rises in a pyramid, heavier and more squat looking than later towers in the north. The shape suggests enormous strength in a seemingly impossible site. As you leave the temple, walk round to your left where you will find a path that leads up and around temple. This is worth doing to gain a birds-eye view of the magnificent temple complex.

Cave 21 (**Ramesvara**, late 6th century) has a court with a stone Nandi bull in the middle and side shrines. A linga sanctuary leads off the verandah. This cave is celebrated for its fine sculptures of amorous couples and the gods. **Cave 29** (Dhumar Lena, late 6th century) is very similar to Elephanta – see Bombay Excursions **page 964** – in concept. Access is from three sides, there is a spacious hall with a separate small sanctuary with a *lingam* at the end. Wall panels depict Siva legends especially as Destroyer.

The **Jain Caves (Nos 30-34)** are something of an anti-climax after the Hindu ones, but they have an aura of peace and simplicity.

Cave 30 (Chhota Kailasa, early 9th century) was intended as a smaller scale replica of the Kailasanatha temple but was not completed. The columned shrine has 22 *tirthankaras* with *Mahavira* in the sanctuary.

Cave 32 (Indra Sabha, early 9th century) is the finest of the Jain series and is dedicated to **Mahavira**. A simple gateway leads into an open court in the middle of which stands the shrine. The walls have carvings of elephants, lions and *tirthankaras*. The lower of the two is incomplete but the upper has carvings of Ambika and also Mahavira flanked by guardians of earlier *tirthankaras* *. The ceiling is richly carved with a massive lotus at the centre and you can see signs of painted figures among clouds.

Ajanta

The drive to Ajanta (100 km) takes about 2 hr 30 min. You leave Aurangabad on the Jalgaon road and first drive across the relatively fertile plain surrounding the city. Then the road climbs the hills behind Aurangabad and interspersed with areas growing sugar cane maize and cotton are patches of scrub. There is extensive small scale irrigation in this area. *Shilod* (63 km) is a popular halting place and has a number of restaurants. About 10 km from Ajanta, you descend from this plateau region and looking to your right you can see the dramatic view of the Waghora valley, where the caves are located.

There is a small settlement with a *Tourist Lodge*, restaurant, curio market and aggressive salesmen at the foot of the approach to the caves, which are carved in a horseshoe shaped cliff face. Rocks and cheap handicrafts are for sale. Bargain hard if you want to buy. It is a short uphill walk along a well-made, stepped concrete path to the entrance, and, mercifully, more peace and quiet. Not suitable for disabled, but there are *dhoolis* available for hire if you wish to be carried. The admission kiosk is at the mouth of the valley at the top of the steps. Open 0900-1730, Re 0.50, free on Fri. A light pass (Rs 5.00) is necessary if you want the guides to turn on the lights.

You can approach the caves from the river bed in the bottom of the valley, where the bus stops. However, you have to buy your ticket from the kiosk, a little way up the hill, first, and if there is water in the stream at the bottom you have to walk through it. However, it is much shadier than the path cut out of the cliff.

The history

The caves date from about 200 BC to 650 AD and are therefore older than those at Ellora. They are cut from the volcanic lavas of the Deccan Trap in a steep crescent shaped hillside in a forested ravine of the Sahyadri hills. After the disappearance of Buddhism from India in the late 7th century, the jungle took over and they lay unnoticed for centuries. Wild animals took over the caves and the local tribal Bhils (see page 345) were hostile to strangers. Hiuen-Tsang, recorded in the 7th century (although he didn't visit it) a description of the 'monastery in a deep defile...large temple with a huge stone image of the Buddha with a tier of seven canopies.'

In 1819, a party of British army officers from the Madras while tiger hunting, noticed the top of the façade of Cave 10. They investigated and discovered some of the caves, describing seeing 'figures with curled wigs'. Others made exploratory trips to the fascinating caves. In 1843, James Fergusson, who reported at length on them, and horrified by the ravage of the elements, requested that the East India Company do something to preserve and protect the deteriorating caves.

In 1844 Captain **Robert Gill**, an artist, was sent to copy the paintings on the cave walls. He spent 27 years living in a small encampment outside, sending each new batch of paintings to Bombay and London. After nearly 20 years his work was almost complete. His collection was displayed in the Crystal Palace in S London. In Dec 1866 all but a few of the paintings were destroyed in a fire. Gill soldiered on for another 5 years before giving up, and died from illness soon afterwards. He is buried in the small European cemetery at **Bhusawal**, 60 km to the N.

Since 1951 the caves have been carefully restored and protected by the Archaeological Survey of India. They have also discovered new ones. Today they are on the World Heritage list of monuments.

The technique To prepare the rock for painting it was chiselled to leave a rough surface. 2 layers of mud-plaster containing fibrous material (grain-husk, vegetable fibres and rock grit), was applied, the first coarse, the second fine. Metal mirrors must have been used by the artists, to reflect sunlight into the dark caves.

It is thought that the tempera technique was used. On a dry surface, a red cinnabar outline defined the picture, filled in, possibly initially with grey and then numerous colour pigments usually mixed with glue and the completed painting burnished to give a lustrous finish. The pigments were mainly taken from the land around, the principle ones being red and yellow ochre, white from lime and kaoline, green from glauconite, black from lamp-black and blue from imported lapis lazuli.

The Caves Where the caves at Ellora are excavated from a series of low hills, here the terrain was a sheer cliff requiring different engineering skills. At the height of its importance the caves are thought to have housed about 200 monks (some of them artists), and numerous artists, craftsmen and labourers. The masterpieces retell the life-story of the Buddha and reveal the life and culture of the people of the times, royal court settings, family life, street scenes and superb studies of animals and birds. The Jatakas relate the Buddhas previous births – showing the progress of the soul. The painted narratives are broken by carved forms and architectural features.

Originally the entrance to the caves was along the riverbed and most had a flight of stairs leading up to them. The first to be excavated was Cave 10, followed by the first Hinayana (Lesser Vehicle in which the Buddha is not depicted in human form) caves either side. These are the earliest caves. Later Mahayana (Greater Vehicle) caves were discovered, thereby completing the spectrum of Buddhist development in India.

There is a round trip walk, up the side of the valley where all the caves are located then down to the river to cross to the other side. An attractive low level walk through forest brings you back to the roadhead. You will probably not want to visit all the caves. **Caves 1, 2, 10, 11, 16, 17, 19** and **26** are good examples and a representative sample.

Warning Flash photography is forbidden because of the damage that is caused by direct light to the paintings. Please obey this ban. It is possible to buy excellent postcards very cheaply. The lampholders in these caves expect a small tip. In the Mahayana caves with paintings there is a restriction on the number of visitors allowed in at any one time. Some caves have electricity supplied to them and lights for illuminating the paintings. These are only turned on for brief moments.

The Mahayana group
Cave 1 (Late 5th century), is one of the finest viharas (monasteries) remarkable for the

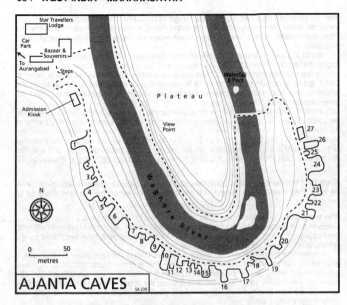

AJANTA CAVES SA 239

number and quality of its murals. A verandah with cells and porches either side has six columns and three entrances leading into a pillared hall. Above the verandah are friezes depicting the sick man, old man, corpse and saint encountered by the Buddha, who is shown above the left porch The hall measures 19.5 m sq and has twenty ornamented pillars, a feature of the late period caves. Five small monks' cells lead off three sides, and in the centre of the back wall is a large shrine of Buddha supported by Indra, the rain god. At the entrance are the river goddesses Yamuna and Ganga and two snake-hooded guardians at the base.

The murals The murals are among the finest at Ajanta. In the four corners are panels representing groups of foreigners. The **Mahajanaka jataka** (where the Buddha took the form of an able and just ruler) covers much of the left hand wall including Renunciation, and the scenes where he is enticed by beautiful dancing girls.

On both sides of the entrance to the antechamber of the shrine room are two of the best known murals at Ajanta. On the left is the **Bodhisattva Padmapani** (here holding a blue lotus) in a pose of spiritual of detachment, whilst on the right is the **Boddhisattva Avalokitesvara**. Together compassion and knowledge complement one another and are the basis of Mahayana Buddhism. Their size dwarf the attendants to enhance the godlike stature of the boddhisattva.

The Buddha inside the shrine is seated in the teaching position, flanked by the two carved boddhisattvas. Under the throne appears the **Wheel of Life**, with deer representing **Sarnath** where he preached his first sermon. **See page 261.**

One of the sculptural tricks that a guide will display is that when the statue is lit from the left side (as you face it), the facial expression is solemn suggesting contemplation. Yet from the other side, there is a smile of joy while from below it suggests tranquillity and peace. Note the paintings on the ceiling, particularly the elephant scattering the lotus as it rushes out of the pond and the charging bull. Also look for the 'black princess' and the row of the dancer with musicians. On the way out look for the pillar that has four deer sculpted skilfully, sharing the same head.

Cave 2 (6th century) has the same layout as Cave 1 though on a smaller scale. It is a vihara hall 14.6 m sq with 12 pillars, five cells on each side of the left and right hand walls and two chapels on each side of the antechamber and shrine room. At the front is a verandah with a side chapel at each end. The doorway is richly carved. On the left hand wall is the mural depicting The Birth of The Buddha. Next to this is The 'Thousand' Buddhas', which illustrates the miracle when the Buddha multiplied himself to confuse a heretic.

The cave is remarkable for its painted ceiling. The mandala (circular diagram of the cosmos) is supported by demon-like figures. The Greek key designs on the border are possibly influenced by Gandharan art, 1st-3rd centuries AD. The ceiling decorations portray a number of figures of Persian appearance apparent from the style of beard and whiskers and their clothing.

The *Yaksha* (nature spirits) Shrine in the left chapel is associated with fertility and wealth The main shrine is that of Buddha in the teaching position, again flanked by the two boddhisattvas, both holding the royal fly whisk. The Hariti Shrine on the right is to the ogress who liked eating children! The panel on your left as you leave the hall is a jataka telling the story of the Boddhisattva's life as the Pandit Vidhura.

Cave 3 (late 5th century) has no verandah and **Cave 4** (late 5th century) is the largest vihara at Ajanta, planned on an ambitious scale and not completed. The hall is 27 m sq and supported on 28 pillars. Along the walls are cells whilst at the rear is a large shrine. **Cave 5** (late 5th century) is also unfinished while **Cave 6** (late 5th century) is on two levels with only 7 of the 16 octagonal pillars standing. A shrine contains a seated Buddha. **Cave 7** (late 5th century) has no hall. The verandah has two porches each supported by heavy octagonal Elephanta-type columns. These lead to four cells. These and the antechamber are profusely carved. The shrine is that of Buddha, his hand raised in blessing.

A Hinayana group comes next (**Caves 6-10** and **12,13 and 15**) dating from the 2nd century BC.

Cave 8 (1st century BC) is a small vihara (10 m by 5 m and 3 m high) and of no great interest. **Cave 9** (c. 100 BC) is a *chaitya* is 14 m long 7 m wide and 7 m high with fourteen columns running the length of each side and eleven continuing round the stupa. The vaulted roof was once wooden ribbed and leads back from a huge 3.4 m arched *chaitya sun* window which throws light on the stupa at the rear. Two phases of wall painting have been identified. The earlier ones dating from the construction of the cave can be seen at the far left side and consist of a procession to a stupa as well as a thin band above the left colonnade. Above this are later Buddha figures from the Mahayana period when the figures of the Buddha on either side of the entrance were painted.

Cave 10 (c.150 BC) is much larger and measures 30 m by 12.4 m and is 11 m high. Like the previous cave the roof was once fitted with wooden ribs. The long hall with an apse housing the stupa was one of the first excavated and first rediscovered by army officers. An inscription above the façade, now destroyed, dated the excavation to the 2nd century BC through a generous donation by the king. The dagoba or stupa resembles that of Cave 9 and is a double storey drum. There are also paintings dating from the Hinayana and Mahayana periods. The early ones depict figures in costumes resembling those seen at Sanchi - **see page 317**. Traces of later paintings survive on the pillars and aisle ceilings and later Buddha figures are often superimposed on earlier works.

The main subjects of the Hinayana paintings are *jataka* stories. On the rear wall is the King (in a ceremonial headdress) and Queen approaching the Sacred Bodhi Tree, one of the earliest Ajanta paintings.

Cave 11 (originally 2nd century BC, with 6th century alterations) has a verandah and roof painted with birds and flowers, a hall supported by four heavy pillars and a stone bench running along the right side. There are five cells and a shrine of a seated Buddha. **Caves 12,13** (2nd century BC) are small viharas . **Cave 14** (5th century AD) was planned on a grand scale but not completed and can be missed along with **Cave 15** (5th century) which is a long hall with a Buddha carved out of the rock.

The remaining caves all belong to the **Later Mahayana period** and date from the 5th century.

Cave 16 has a 20 m long and 3.5 m deep verandah that carries six plain octagonal pillars. There is a good view of the ravine from here. The 20 m long columned hall inside has six cells on each side and a beamed ceiling. The Teaching Buddha is seated on a lion throne. On the left the 'Dying Princess' portrays Nanda's new bride being told that he has been ordained a monk and renounced the world. Her misery is shared by all and everything around her. On the right wall are the remains of a picture of Prince Siddhartha, later the Buddha, using a bow.

Cave 17 (late 5th century) is very similar to No. 16 in layout and preserves the greatest number of murals. On the left of the verandah is a painted Wheel of Life. Over the entrance door is a row of seven Past Buddhas and the eighth, the **Maitreya** or Future Buddha, above a row of amorous Yaksha couples. Sculpted deities are carved on either side.

Murals show scenes from a number of jatakas: the worship of Buddha where even the god Indra descends through clouds with other celestial figures; Buddha's preaching; Hansa jataka, with paintings of geese; Vessantara jataka where the greedy Brahmin is portrayed, grinning; the miraculous 'Subjugation of the rogue elephant', sent to kill the Buddha; the ogress who turns into a beautiful maiden by day! There are also panels showing royal processions, warriors, an assembled congregation from which you can get an accurate and detailed picture of the times. **Cave 18** (late 5th century) has little of merit and can be missed.

Cave 19 (late 5th century) is a chaitya hall and was painted throughout. The façade is considered to be one of the most elegant in terms of execution and elaborate ornamentation and has the arched chaitya window set into it. The interior (14 m long, 7.3 m high and wide) is in the layout seen before, two rows of richly decorated columns leading up to and around the back of the standing Buddha which here is in front of the slender stupa. This tall shrine has a triple stone umbrella above it. Note the seated Nagaraja with attendants.

Cave 20 is comparatively small (8.5 m by 7.6 m) and has imitation beams carved into the ceiling.

Later caves The final few caves belong to the 7th century and are a separate and distinct group at the farthest end of the horseshoe nr the waterfall. Only one, Cave 26 need be visited. **Cave 21** (early 7th century) has a fallen verandah with flanking chapels. The jewel or necklace patterns on the frieze is a characteristic of the period. Cave 24 was intended to be the largest vihara but was not completed.

Cave 26 is a large *chaitya* hall*. A partly damaged columned façade stretches across the front with the customary side chambers at each end. The 3 m high window is flanked by sculptured Buddha reliefs. Inside, 26 pillars run in an elongated semi circle around the cylindrical stupa which is decorated with Buddhas. The walls are decorated with sculpture, including the temptations by Mara's daughters but the most striking being a 9 m reclining image of the Parinirvana Buddha, about to enter Nirvana, his death mourned by his followers.

Note The walk back along the rather clumsily built, and in places ugly, promenade connecting the shrines is pleasant enough but the return via the river, waterfall and forest walkway is delightful. The hilltop opposite the caves offers a fine view of the horseshoe shaped gorge.

Preservation of the murals
Preservation of the murals poses enormous challenges. Repeated attempts to reproduce and to restore have faced major problems. After all but five of Robert Gill's paintings were destroyed by fire, the Bombay School of Arts sent out a team to copy the paintings under the guidance of the principal John Griffiths in the 1870s. He advocated that photographic plates be made of the facsimiles as soon as they reached London. However, the expense was considered too great. The paintings were stored in the Victoria and Albert Museum in London. This also had a fire in 1885, when eighty seven were destroyed.

In 1918 a team from Kyoto University Oriental Arts Faculty arrived at Ajanta to copy the sculptures. This they did by pressing wet rice paper against the surface to make casts which were then shipped back to Japan. In the early 1920s they were all destroyed by an earthquake.

In 1920 the paintings were cleaned by the former Hyderabad Government under whose jurisdiction the caves lay. Two Italian restorers were commissioned, whose first priority was to fix the peeling paintings to the walls of the caves. They first injected casein between the paintings and the plastered wall, then applied shellac as a fixative. The Griffiths team from Bombay had also applied a coat of varnish to bring out the colours of the paintings.

However, these varnishes darkened over the years, rendering the murals less, not more visible. They also cracked, aiding the peeling process and the accumulation of moisture between the wall and the outer membrane. The Archaeological Survey of India is now responsible for all restoration at the site.

Note Although there are toilets at the caves they are poorly maintained.

Hotels E MTDC *Holiday Resort,* Fardapur, 5 km from Ajanta caves. Non a/c rm with bath. Restaurant. Inexpensive, simple but recommended. Also Guest House and Traveller's Bungalow, with cook but these are less comfortable. Reservations: Executive Engineer, PWD, Padampura, Aurangabad, if free. Forest Rest House with cook. Reservations: Div Forest Officer, Osmanpura, Aurangabad.

Road Regular bus service and taxis from Aurangabad. Buses to Fardapur. The caves can also be visited from Jalgaon, which has the nearest railway station.

AURANGABAD TO NANDER AND NIZAMABAD

Following the main railway route to Hyderabad, the road goes down the gentle slope of the great basin of the Godavari, running about 50 km N of the Godavari itself then turning sharply S and crossing the river at Nander. Vast open spaces, ancient erosion surfaces covered in some of India's richest black lava soils, a remarkably high proportion of which are under cultivation, dominate the landscape.

Warning During the monsoon the causeways over the rivers may be flooded. Enquire in advance.

From **Aurangabad** pass the airport (11 km), and after crossing the railway line (10 km) and the **River Balamarai** (by causeway; 11 km) go through **Badnapur** (12 km) to **Selgaon** (6 km). After a further 213 km the road crosses the **River Kunlika** by another causeway and enters *Jalna*. Noted as the town to which **Abul Fazl**, who wrote the *Ain i Akbari*, was exiled and ultimately murdered by Bir Singh Deo of Orchha – see page 294 – at the instigation of **Jahangir**. The Jalna region is dotted with forts. There is a *Dak Bungalow* and a *Rest House* in the town.

Continue E through **Watoor** (46 km) to **Mantha** (12 km) and **Deogaon** (9 km). The road reaches *Jintur* in 25 km, but you can turn right 1 km before the town to go to Nander. 50 km beyond the town of Jintur is the remarkable meteor crater of **Lonar**, which can be reached by bus from Jintur. Leave the town on the Nander road. After 30 km a road left turn leads to the **Sideshwar Dam** (4 km). Continue straight on across the **River Purna** (1 km) to a road junction in 4 km where you turn right for Nander. The road continues through **Chondi** (18 km) and across wide open cultivated land, interspersed with occasional small settlements, mainly off the road itself. After 35 km turn right at a road junction for Nander, passing through **Dhabar** (3 km after the junction). Cross the *River Ashna* (6 km) to **Nander** (8 km).

Nander (*Population* 250,000) is a particularly important town for the Sikhs, remembered as the place where Guru Gobind Singh, the tenth guru, was assassinated in 1708 – see page 72. There is a gurudwara 1.5 km from the station. Today it is an important regional centre, administrative and commercial town. It is on the **River Godavari**, which is bridged.

Take the road S across the river and after 4 km fork left onto the **Nizamabad** road. Through **Naigaon** (36 km) and **Warshi** (5 km). Turn left for Nizamabad. The road then goes through **Biloli** (21 km) to the Maharashtra-Andhra Pradesh border (10 km). It continues through **Bodhan** (11 km) to **Nizamabad** (24 km). See page 913.

AURANGABAD TO SOLAPUR AND BIJAPUR

This journey of 325 km crosses from the great river basin of the Godavari River to the Bhima River, a tributary of the Krishna. It is the shortest route from Aurangabad to the important Muslim capitals of N Karnataka, Bijapur and Gulbarga.

The slopes are often imperceptible, occasional flat-topped tablelands separated from the valley floors by short steep sided escarpments. It is a classic example of an ancient erosion surface. The altitude falls gently moving SE, from 525 m at Aurangabad to 475 m around Sholapur. This is still the heart of the black lava soil region which stretches down to northern Karnataka. The roads are generally quiet, sometimes passing through short forested sections. The only towns are small market centres with very limited facilities.

Leave **Aurangabad** on the road past the airport (11 km) to **Adul** (37 km) and **Pachod** (19 km). Continue through **Wari-Godri** (20 km) and **Shahgad** (8 km) to cross the **Godavari River** (2 km). After passing through **Gevrai** (11 km) the road crosses the E flowing **River Sindhpana** (17 km), a tributary of the Godavari, and goes on to **Bir** (14 km). Shortly after it runs through a forested and ghat area for 11 km, then crosses the **River Ganes** (15 km) to **Chausala** (6 km) and **Yermala** (47 km). Continue to **Yedshi** (16 km). 5km S the road crosses the Barsi Light Railway, the narrow gauge railway line that links *Miraj*, 220 km to the SW, with the tiny town of **Latur** 70 km E.

After 21 km there is a 3 km ghat section of road before reaching *Osmanabad* (4 km). There are groups of Jain and Vaishnavaite caves around the town, dating from the 5th and 6th centuries AD. Between Osmanabad and *Tuljapur* (20 km) the road crosses the watershed between the **Godavari** and the **Krishna** river basins. In the town of Tuljapur the **Tulja Bhawani** temple, dedicated to Durga, is a focus for pilgrims from all over India. 11 km S of the town the road passes through a ghat section of road for 1 km, then runs SW to **Solapur** (42 km). See page 1007.

In Solapur cross the **NH9** (Bombay to Hyderabad) and continue S on the **NH13**. IN 16 km the road crosses the River Sina and 14 km further on the important tributary of the Krishna, the River Bhima. Continue through **Jhalki** (19 km) and **Horti** (16 km) to **Bijapur** (34 km). See page 885.

BOMBAY TO PUNE, SOLAPUR AND HYDERABAD

The main **NH4** crosses the narrow lowland out of Bombay to Thana then SE to the foot of the Ghats. It climbs steeply through the forested slopes of the ghats onto the plateau, a diversion from the main road going to the very attractive hill resort of Matheran. Pune, just in the lee of the ghats, has become a sprawling city with more than 2.5 million people. The **NH4** then runs across the vast open spaces of the cultivated plateau region, with spectacularly broad views of the black soil regions of the plateau en route to the cotton textile centre of Solapur.

Leave Bombay through Thana (28 km), then turn SE on the **NH4**, passing a short ghat section after 11 km. To the E of Mumbra crowning the steeply scarped plateau is the Maratha fort of **Malangarh**. Continue to **Panvel**, 23 km from the Thana creek bridge. 3 km out of Panvel there is a right turn for the route S to Mahabaleshwar and Panaji, and the climb up the ghats begins. After a further 16 km a road on the left leads to **Neral** (51 km) and **Matheran** (21 km).

Matheran (*Altitude* 750 m) Bombay's nearest hill station. The views and the cooler air and pleasant walks, are its main attractions. It is situated in the *Sahyadari range*, meaning 'Mother Forest' or 'Wooded Head'.

The most scenic route for this diversion is by light railway through the ghats from Neral. The journey is spectacular. From Bombay take the Pune trains as far as **Neral** then transfer to the narrow gauge Toy Train. Each sector of the journey is about 2 hours. On this route you appreciate the problems facing the early railway engineers – see page 939. There are also trains from Karjat Junction.

The town sprawls out along a N-S ridge and from rocky promontories such as **The Hart, Panorama Point, Chauk, Duke's Nose** and **Garbat** there are splendid views down the almost sheer hillsides to the valleys below. From the northernmost vantage points such as The Hart you can see the lights of Bombay on a clear night. The layout of the town conforms with standard British Hill Station planning with all the usual central civic buildings and widely dispersed bungalows.

Hotels The hotels here are all central and nr the Rly Station. **B** *Lord's Central*, T 28. To book in Bombay, T 318008. 23 rm. Restaurant, bar, children's park. Not plush but clean. **B** *Regal*, opp Post Office, Kasturba Rd, T 42,87. To book in Bombay, T 325342. 75 rm, some a/c. Indoor games, play ground. **C** *Rugby*, Vithalrao Kotwal Rd, T 91, 92, Cable: Rugby. 55 rm, some a/c. Indoor and outdoor games, library, tourist taxi service, Visa.

D *Alexander*, T 51,90. 23 rm. Restaurant car hire, health club, indoor and outdoor games, Diners. **D** *Brightlands Resorts*, Maulana Azad Rd, T 44. To book in Bombay, T 6423856. 28 rm. Sports. **D** *Royal Hotel*, T 47. To book in Bombay, T 352784, 368840. 50 rm. Restaurant, bar, coffee shop, travel, health club, library, bank, indoor and outdoor games, children park, information counter, credit cards. **D** *Tourist Towers*, B.P. No 187, MG Rd, T 71, Cable: Kakagroup. 24 rm. Restaurant, table tennis, riding. **D** *Bombay View*, Cutting Rd, T 79. To book in Bombay T 6145993, 451008. 22 rm. Close to rly. Restaurant, travel. **D** *Silvan*, Acharya Atre Marg, nr Charlotte Lake. T 74. 16 rm. Games, horse riding. **D** *Divadkar*, opp Rly Station. Rm with bath and verandah. **D** *Silvan*, nr Charlotte lake, T 74.

E *Gujarat Bhavan*, Maulana Azad Rd, T 78. 22 rm. Local folk dances, indoor and outdoor games. **E** *Giririhar*, Sivaji Rd. Peaceful, spacious gardens, some rm with balconies. **E** *Laxmi*, M Gandhi Rd, next to PO. Rm with bath. **F** *Holiday Camp*, 1 km before Matheran (Train stops at camp). Dormitory.

Restaurants *Kwality Fruit Juice House*, MG Rd, S of Rly Station among many. Excellent honey and *chikki**. Partial prohibition permits restaurants to sell beer without a permit.

Local Transport Ponies and rickshaws are available for hire at negotiable rates.

Tourist Information Centre and **Post Office** (opp Rly Station) and are on MG Rd.

From Matheran you can proceed to **Lonavla** via **Khandala**. The ravined countryside between is stunning. On the railway line gradients of 1 in 37 were used to overcome the problems posed by "the big step "(Ghat) the hills presented. At the **Bhor Ghat** near **Karjat** there was a reversing station. During the monsoon waterfalls are commonplace.

The **NH4** continues from the **Matheran – Neral** junction to **Shilpata** (16 km) and **Khopoli** (3 km), climbing through a ghat section for a further 5 km. It passes through a single track tunnel to **Khandala** (3 km).

Khandala (*Altitude* 615 m) is a quiet village overlooking a great ravine from which the Konkan region S of Bombay can be seen, 2.5 hr drive from Bombay.

Hotels On Bombay-Poona Rd: **C** *Fun-n-Food*, 61 Hilltop Colony, T 2854. 35 rm. 1 km rly. Restaurant bar, pool, doctor on call, sightseeing, tourist bus and cars, Diners. **C** *Mount View*, Plot No 415, T 2335, Cable: Mount In. 16 rm. 1 km Khandala. Restaurants (Indian, Veg Gujarati), bar, doctor on call, car hire, children's park, Diners. **C** *Duke's Retreat*, T 2336. 62 rm. 4 km Lonavla rly. Restaurant, pool, health club, children's park, indoor and outdoor sports, Diners.

Other hotels include the reasonably cheap **D** *Khandala*, T 239 and **D** *Hotel on the Rocks*.

Lonavla is a further 5 km. *Population* 45,000 *Altitude* 625 m. *Climate* Summer Max 36°C, Min 19°C, Winter Max 31°C, Min 12.3°C.

Like Mahabaleshwar and Matheran, **Lonavla** is regarded as a hill station for Bombay and so has a reasonable range of hotels. It is good as a base for the **Karla and Bhaja Caves** and also the **Rajmachi, Lohagen** and **Visapur Forts** nearby. It is situated on the tableland of Khandala which has a number of depressions, now used as lakes. Lonavla itself has little intrinsic interest.

Local Festivals Feb/Mar *Sivaratri* is celebrated at the Mahadev Temple with great ceremony and a fair.

Hotels **B** *Fariyas Holiday Resort*, Finchley Hill, Tungarli, T 2701-5. 90 rm. Restaurants, bar, coffee shop, health club, pool, amusement park. **C** *Adarsh*, Sivaji Rd, close to Bus Stop. T 2353. 50 rm. Close to rly. Chidrens' park, sightseeing, Diners. **C** *Biji's Ingleside Inn*, New Tungardi Rd, off Bombay-Pune Rd, T 2638, Cable: Bijis Lonavla. 37 rm. Restaurant, bar, pool, chidrens' park. **C** *Lions Den*, Tungarli Lake Rd, T 2954, 16 rm. 2.5 km Lonavla rly. Restaurant, games, Diners. **C** *Span Hill Resort*, Tungarli Valley, Anand Giri Society, T 2153. To book in Bombay, T 6145166. Restaurant, mini zoo. **D** *Ceeking*, nr Valvan Dam Bridge, T Bombay 398164. 30 rm, 5 cottages. Restaurant, car parking.

E *Peshwa Hotels and Holiday Resort*, nr Karla Caves, T 55. 15 rm. Restaurant, children's park. **E** *Vishwabharat*, 80 Tungarli (nr H.P.Pump), Bombay-Pune Rd, T 2686. 18 rm. **E** *Girikunj*, T 2529, rm with bath **E** *Purohit*, behind PO. T 2695, some rm with bath **F** *Pitale Lodge*, Bombay-Pune Rd, T 2657. 7 rm with bath. Charming old stone and wood colonial-style bungalow with verandah. Restaurant, bar. **F** *Sahani Holiday Home*, nr Lonavla Station, T 2784. 57 rm. Children's park. **F** *Woodlands*, Ryewood Rd, T 2417. 10 rm, 3 cottages. **F** *Chandralok*, T2294. Veg restaurant. **F** *Janata*, opp Girikunj. T 2689. Cheap but drab. **F** *Highway*, Main road. T 2321.

Restaurants On Bombay-Pune Rd: *Diamond Garden Restaurant*, opp Flyover Bridge,T 2969 (Inc *tandoori*)*; Lonavla*, T 2914; *Café*; *Sind Punjab Restaurant*; *Tandoor House*, Plaza, T 2806 (Veg, snacks). Also the *Central*, opp Rly Station, *Gulistan*, T 2321 and *Swad* (snacks only).

Clubs Municipal Sports Club, Municipal Office, T 285. Rotary Club, Lonavla.

Banks and Exchanges Bank of Baroda, T 46. Bank of Maharashtra, Lokmanya Tilak Rd, T 85. Canara Bank, G Ward, T 211. Pune District Cooperative Bank, T 874. State Bank of India, Lokmanya Tilak Rd, T 384. Syndicate Bank, T 462.

Shopping *The National Chikki Mart*, Marker Manzil, T 2421. *Super Chikki*, Bombay-Pune Rd, T 2438. *Santosh Chikki*, Bombay-Pune Rd, T 2978. *Favourite Medical Stores*, Tilak Rd, T 2728. *Maharashtra Medical & General Stores*, nr State Bank. *Mahavir Medical & General Store*, Jaychand Chowk.

Local Transport Rickshaws available – no fixed price. To the Caves by auto-rickshaw: Lonavla-Karla Rs 25, approx return Rs 60. To Rajmachi Fort: there is a local bus service but it is infrequent and erratic.

Sports Swimming pools at Biji's Ingleside Inn and Gajanan Mahimtura.

Useful Services Municipal Office & Fire Brigade, T 2286. Rly Station & Enquiry, T 2215. S.T. Stand, T 2742. Police Station, T 2233.

Hospitals and Medical Services Shri Babasheb Dahanukar Municipal Hospital, T 2673. Parmar Hospital, T 2631. Oswal Hospital, T 2871. Ashirward Hospital, T 2846. Sarawati Hospital, T 2475.

Post and Telegraph Post Office, T 2231.

Places of Worship Hindu: Hanuman Temple, Mahadev Temple, Siddheshwari Devi Temple

Tourist Information Bureau, nr Lonavla Rly Station, T 2428.

Air Pune (66km) and Bombay are the nearest airports.

Rail Bombay (VT): *Madras-Bombay Mail* 7010, daily, 0140, 3 hr 10 min; *Udyan Exp* 6530, daily, 1720, 3 hr 5 min; *Hyderabad-Bombay Exp* 7032, daily, 0955, 3 hr; *Deccan Exp* 1008, daily, 1628, 3 hr 15 min. **Pune**: *Indrayani Exp* 2113, daily, 0815, 1 hr 10 min; *Deccan Queen Exp* 2123, daily, 1925, 1 hr 10 min; *Sinhagad Exp* 1009, daily, 1745, 1 hr 20 min; *Sahyadahri Exp* 7311, daily, 2340, 1 hr 20 min.

Road Served by NH4 to **Bombay** (101 km) and **Pune** (62 km).

Bus Daily Maharashtra SRTC buses to Lonavla from Pune and Bombay.

The **NH4** continues E from Lonavla through the village of Karla (8 km). A left turn leads to the remarkable **Karla** caves (4 km) and the **Bhaja** caves (7 km).

Karli (or Karla) has the largest and best preserved Buddhist *chaitya*** (chapel) cave in India, dating from the 2nd-1st century BC. Unlike Ajanta and Ellora it is off the beaten tourist track for foreigners, though it is much visited at weekends.

The approach is across an excavated court. At the massive entrance stands a stone column topped with four lions (*sinha stambha*). There is also a Hindu temple just outside the entrance which may have been built over the remains of a second pillar. The façade contains a large horse-shoe shaped window above the three doorways (one for the priest and the other two for pilgrims). In front of the side doors were shallow water-filled troughs through which the pilgrims walked to cleanse their feet. The remarkable sun window diffused the light into the hall, falling gently onto the stupa at the end. Buddha images partly decorate the exterior but these are considered a later addition (c 5th century). There are also panels between the doorways depicting six pairs of donors.

The main chamber (38 m by 14 m), entered through a large outer porch, is supported by 37 pillars. It is 8 m from floor to ceiling which is barrel vaulted and ribbed with teak beams. There are 15 octagonal columns along either side, each capital having kneeling elephants carrying an embracing couple carved on it. The stupa is similar to that in Cave No 10 at Ellora but here is topped by a wooden umbrella which is carved with delicate patterns. The other caves to the right of the entrance are of little interest.

For on site accommodation there is the **F** *Holiday Camp*, off Bombay-Pune Road, T 30. Huts for 5, and dorms. Restaurant. Reserve through Maharashtra TDC at Bombay or Poona.

Bhaja, has 18 caves dating from the 2nd century BC. **Cave No 12** is the best and possibly the first apsidal *chaitya* (a long hall with a semi-circular end) in India.

The apse contains a **dagoba*** and the vaulted roof of the chapel is supported by twenty seven columns. The exterior was once covered in a bas-relief but unfortunately much of this has been defaced. The last cave to the S has very fine sculptures, including the 'Dancing Couple'. On either side of the main cave are others which were probably nuns' cells and working quarters. To the S there is a collection of fourteen stupas, five of which are inside the cave.

The ruined **Lohagen Fort** is about 4 km from the caves and was twice taken and lost by Sivaji. **Visapur Fort** which stands 600m from the foot of the hill is nearby.

There are more Buddhist rock-cut caves at **Bedsa** which is 6 km S of Kamshet Station. The chaitya with 4 columns with animal carvings is like the one at Karli but may have been built later. The rib vaulted roof is supported by 26 pillars.

The NH4 continues E from Karla to **Kamshet** (9 km), a turning to the right leading to the **Bedsa** caves (6.5 km). It passes through **Kirkee** (38 km) to **Pune** (7 km).

Pune

Population 2,500,000 *Altitude* 560 m. **Indian Airlines connects Pune with Bombay (184 km, 30 min), Delhi (1,424 km, 1 hr 55 min), Hyderabad (722 km) and Bangalore (840 km). The airport is 8 km from the city centre.**

	Jan	Feb	Mar	Apr	May	Jun	Jul	Aug	Sep	Oct	Nov	Dec	Av/Tot
Max (°C)	31	33	36	38	37	32	28	28	29	32	31	30	323
Min (°C)	12	13	17	21	23	23	22	21	21	19	15	12	18
Rain (mm)	2	0	3	18	35	103	187	106	127	92	37	5	715

Pune (also spelt Poona) was where Sivaji was brought up, and it later became the Maratha capital. After their demise the British developed it as a summer capital for Bombay and as a military cantonment. Since 1971 it has more than doubled in size, developing as a major industrial base. The climatic contrast between Pune and the ghats just 70 km away is astonishing. The monsoon winds of June to September drop most of their rain on the ghats themselves, and rainfall totals fall from over 3500 mm a year to Pune's 715 mm. Description of the city's site range from "absolutely flat" to "surrounded by hills", as Spate and Learmonth point out, the contrast depending on the direction from which you approach the city.

Pune became the Maratha capital in 1750 and after a period under the **Nizam of Hyderabad's** rule came under British control in 1817. For all its connections with the Marathas there are few physical reminders of their power. The city is known for its wide streets and there is much more of a British colonial feel to the the town, renowned for its military cantonment, educational and scientific institutions and as a place for relaxation. More recently Pune became known as the centre of the Bhagwan Rajneesh's movement which attracted many disenchanted young westerners. Rajneesh left India (to avoid paying taxes, it is claimed) founding a commune in Oregon. He returned to India and died in 1990.

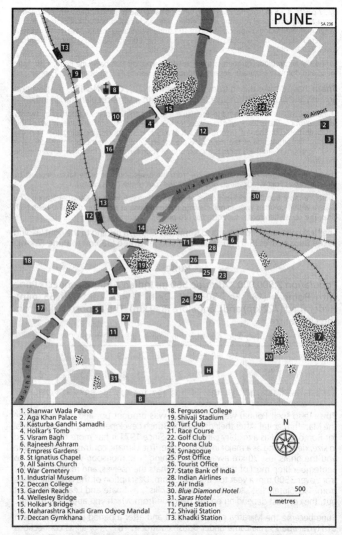

PUNE SA 236

To Airport

Mula River

Mutha River

N

0   500
metres

1. Shanwar Wada Palace
2. Aga Khan Palace
3. Kasturba Gandhi Samadhi
4. Holkar's Tomb
5. Visram Bagh
6. Rajneesh Ashram
7. Empress Gardens
8. St Ignatius Chapel
9. All Saints Church
10. War Cemetery
11. Industrial Museum
12. Deccan College
13. Garden Reach
14. Wellesley Bridge
15. Holkar's Bridge
16. Maharashtra Khadi Gram Odyog Mandal
17. Deccan Gymkhana
18. Fergusson College
19. Shivaji Stadium
20. Turf Club
21. Race Course
22. Golf Club
23. Poona Club
24. Synagogue
25. Post Office
26. Tourist Office
27. State Bank of India
28. Indian Airlines
29. Air India
30. *Blue Diamond Hotel*
31. *Saras Hotel*
T1. Pune Station
T2. Shivaji Station
T3. Khadki Station

Places of Interest The city stands on the right bank of the *Mutha River* before its confluence with the Mula and was divided up into 19 peths (wards). Some were named after the days of their weekly market, others such as Sadashiv Peth after well known people like the Maratha General. In the S in the Hill of Parbati after the temple on its summit. In the E and SE are hills leading up to the plateau around Satara.

The majority of the British buildings are to the S of both rivers. Near the Rly Station is the English gothic style **Sassoon Hospital** (1867) Nearby is the Collectorate and the old Treasury. To the SW is the **Synagogue** (1867) and Sir David Sassoon's Tomb. **St Paul's Church** (1867) was consecrated by Bishop Harding and **St. Mary's Church** (1825) to the S by Bishop Heber, who toured the country extensively in the 1830s. St Patrick's Cathedral is on the other side of the Racecourse. To the N are the **Empress Gardens** which have a fine collection of tropical trees and a small zoo.

Moving back to the W by the river are **Visram Bagh**, a very attractive Maratha Palace now used as a college, high school and court, and the **Shanwar Wada Palace** (Saturday Palace,1736). The palace was built by Baji Rao, the last Peshwa's grandfather, and unfortunately burnt down in 1827. Only the massive outer walls remain. The main entrance is the Delhi Gate. The gates were iron spiked, the usual method of deterring elephants from knocking them down. Elephants were used for crushing people to death in the nearby street (see below for Tomb of Vithoji Holkar).

The gardens were irrigated and contained the **Hazari Karanje** (Fountain of a Thousand Jets). In fact there were only 197 jets.

Cross the river by **Lloyd Bridge**, the main bridge for Bombay traffic, and you are on **Sivaji Rd**. Along this are the **Panchaleshwar Temple** and **Sivaji Memorial Hall** and **Military College** (1922). A large 9 m high statue of Maharashtra's favourite son stands in front and was sculpted by V.P. Karkomar. Sivaji Rd leads down to Lloyd Bridge.

To the N is **Wellesley Bridge** (1875) near the tongue of land called **Sangam** (see Allahabad, **page 247**) at the confluence of the rivers. Near the bridge is the Engineering College and 300 m beyond this is **Garden Reach** (1862-4), the family house of the influential Sassoon family, designed by Sir Henry St Clair Wilkins, who was also responsible for the Secretariat and Public works Office in Bombay. The main road then passes the **Institute of Tropical Meteorology** and the white domed **Observatory,** which was opened when the Meteorological Department was transferred to Pune from Simla in 1928.

Raj Bhawan (1866, Government House) designed by James Trubshawe is in the Ganesh Khind neighbourhood. Further on still are the **Botanical Gardens** on Aundha Rd. If you now continue in an easterly direction you will come to Kirkee Rly Station . From here on the way to Holkar's bridge is **All Saints Church** (1841) which contains the regimental colours of the 23rd Bombay Light Infantry. Almost one km to the SE is the Roman Catholic **Chapel of St Ignatius.** Cross the river by the Holkar's Bridge to the **Tomb of Vithoji Holkar** who was trampled by an elephant in 1802, and the adjacent Mahadeo Temple built in his memory.

Sir Henry St Clair Wilkins designed the Deccan College (1864). Beyond the Fitzgerald Bridge on the Talegaon Rd is the **Palace of the Aga Khan** (1860) who was attracted to Pune by the horse racing. **Mahatma Gandhi** was placed under house arrest here and his wife **Kasturba** died here. Her memorial tomb (samadhi) is on the estate. Backtrack to Nagar Rd and cross the Fitzgerald Bridge to the riverside **Bund Gardens**, a popular place for an evening stroll.

Hotels Airport about 10 km, railway approx 3 km, all within 2 km of centre.
B *Blue Diamond*, 11 Koregaon Rd, T 663 775, Cable: Bluediamond, Telex: 0145 369, Fax: 212 66 101. 114 rm. Restaurants, bar, pool, health club, travel, shops, car hire, sports, cultural shows for groups, Amex, Diners, Mastercard. Modern, good food. **B** *Executive Ashok*, 5 University Rd, Sivajinagar. T 57391, 50463, Cable: Executive, Telex: 0145 565 Heap In. 71 rm. 0.5 km Sivajinagar rly, 4 km centre. Restaurant, bar, shops, health club, travel, credit cards. **B** *Sagar Plaza*, 1 Bund Garden Rd, T 661 880, Cable: Staywithus, Telex: 145 645 Sagr In. 80 rm. 3 km airport. Restaurant, health club, shops, Amex, Diners.
   C *Amer-al-Asian*, 15 Connaught Rd, T (0212) 661 840, Cable: Hotelamir, Telex: 145 292 Amer In. 100 rm. Restaurants, bar, 24 hr coffee shop, rm service, exchange, TV, health

club, car hire, shops. **C** *Ashirwad*, 16 Connaught Rd, T 666 142, Cable: Hotel Ashirwad. 44 rm. Restaurant, 24 hr rm service, bank, travel. **C** *Amir*, 15 Connaught Rd, T 661 840, Cable: Hotelamir, Telex: 145 292 Amirin. 100 rm, most a/c with TV. Restaurants (inc outdoor), bar, 24 hr rm service, coffee shop and exchange, health club, travel, car hire, shops, chemist shop, credit cards. **C** *Regency*, 192 Dhole Patil Rd, T 669411, 669415, Cable: Regency, Telex: 0145 609 Hotr In. 25 rm. Restaurant, bar, 24 hr rm service, exchange, Amex, Diners, Mastercard, Visa. **C** *Span Executive*, Revenue Colony, Sivajinagar, T 59192-95. Restaurants, bar, coffee shop, 24 hr rm service. **C** *Regency*, 389/1 Ghorpodi Peth, Shankar Seth Rd, T 27847, Cable: Loveseven. 14 rm. Restaurant, car hire.

D *Ajit*, 775/2 Deccan Gymkhana, T 339076-79. 20 rm. Restaurant, travel, car hire. **D** *Ashiyana*, 1198 FC Rd, Sivajinagar, T 52426. 37 rm. Restaurant, car parking. **D** *Deccan Park*, FC Rd, opp Vaishali, Sivajinagar, T 59065, Cable: Deccanpark. 21 rm. Restaurant, bar, 24 hr rm service, garden coffee shop, exchange, travel, car hire, doctor on call, Diners. **D** *Dreamland*, 2/14 Connaught Rd, opp Rly Station, T 662121. 35 rm. Restaurant, car hire, doctor on call. **D** *Jawahar*, 1302 Shukrawar Peth, T 441019. 31 rm. **D** *Kapila*, 174 Dhole Patil Rd, T 661272. 25 rm. **D** *Marina*, 77 MG Rd, T 669141-4. 12 rm, Restaurant, bar, travel, car hire, doctor, Diners. **D** *Meru*, Ladkatwadi Rd, off Dhole Patil Rd, T 667878, Telex: 0145454 Wood In Care Meru. 40 rm. Exchange, car hire, parking, travel, doctor on call, airport transfer. **D** *Nandanvan*, Apte Rd & Shirole Rd Junction, Deccan Gymkhana. T 55251-52, Telex: 0145 454 Wood In care Nandanvan, Fax: (0212) 660 688. 27 rm. Restaurant, doctor on call, car hire, parking. **D** *Pathik*, 1263/4B, off Jungali Maharaj Rd, T 59085. 18 rm. Doctor on call. **D** *Ranajeet*, 870/7 Bhandarkar Institute Rd, T 59012. 25 rm. Restaurant, 18 hr rm service, Diners.

D *Raviraj*, 790 Bhandarkar Institute Rd, T 339581-4. 15 rm. Restaurant, coffee shop, Diners, Visa. **D** *Sahara*, Senapati Bapat Marg, T 59906. **D** *Shreyas*, 1242 B Apte Rd, Deccan Gymkhana, T 59023 for reservations, Cable: Shreyas, Telex: 0145 212 Srys In. 48 rm. Restaurants, tourist taxi, Diners. **D** *Silver Inn*, 1973 Gafferbeg St, nr Contonment Market, Poona Camp, T 25041, Cable: Silver Inn. 35 rm. 8 km Lohegaon airport, Restaurant, 24 hr rm service. **D** *Srimaan*, Bund Garden Rd, T 662 367. 28 rm. Restaurant, coffee shop. **D** *Sunderban*, 19 Koregaon Park, next to Rajaneesh Ashram, T 661 919, Telex: 0145 454 Wood In Care Sunderban. 23 rm. Restaurant, exchange, travel. **D** *Suyash*, 1547 B, Sadashiv Peth, opp Tilak Rd, T 439377, Cable: Suyash. 39 rm, some a/cRestaurant, city-airport coach. **D** *Swaroop*, 38, 3 Erandavane, Prabhat Rd, Lane No 10, T 335 661-64. 28 rm. **D** *Tej Regency*, 5 MG Rd, T 669 251-3, Cable: Hotel Tej, Telex: 368 Tej In. 21 rm. Travel, shops, Diners, Visa. **D** *Vandana*, opp Sambhaji Park, off Jangli Maharaj Rd, Deccan Gymkhana, T 59090, Telex: 0145 454 Wood In Care Vandana, Fax:(0212) 660 688. 23 rm. Restaurant (Veg), travel, exchange, airport transfer. **D** *Woodland*, Sadhu Vaswani Circle, nr Poona Rly Station, T 661111, Telex: 0145 454 Wood In, Fax: 60688. 50 rm. Restaurant (Veg), 24 hr rm service, travel, doctor on call, exchange, car hire, parking, airport transfer, Amex, Visa.

E *Alankar*, 14 Motilal Talera Rd, T 660484-89, Cable: Hot Alankar. 50 rm. Car hire. **E** *Ashwamedth*, behind Sivajinagar Telephone Exchange, T 59192. **E** *Central Lodge*, 13 Wilson Garden, Motilal Talera Marg, T 661628, Telex: 0145454 Wood In Care Central, Fax: (0212) 660 688. 45 rm. Restaurant (Veg). **E** *Gauri*, nr Chinchwad Rly Station, Pune Bombay Rd, T 85588, Telex: 0145454 Wood In Care *Gauri*, Fax: 660688. 22 rm. Restaurant (Veg), car hire, doctor on call. **E** *Gulmohr*, 15A/1 Connaught Rd, T 661773-5, Cable: Gulmohr. 32 rm. Restaurant, bar. **E** *Jawahar*, 426/B Somawar Peth, opp State Bank of India, T 21150. 26 rm. **E** *Parichay*, 1199/2A FC Rd, T 59901, Cable: Parichay. 20 rm. Restaurant, tourist taxi service. **E** *Pearl*, opp Balgandharva Rangmandir, J.M. Rd, T 53247-49, Cable: Hotel Pearl. 15 rm. Buffet dinner, taxi service, Diners **E** *Rupam*, Apte Rd, Deccan Gymkhana, T 54455, Telex: 0145 454 Wood In Care Rupam, Fax: (0212) 660688. 26 rm. **E** *Saras* (MTDC), Nehru Stadium, Swargate, T 30499. Close to bus station. Pleasant **E** *Yatrik*, 438 Raviwar Peth, Moti Chowk, T 446 566. **E** *Amar*, 47/1 Karve Rd, T 447445. Restaurant, coffee shop. **E** *Chetak*, 1100/2 Model Colony, T 51681. 18 rm. **E** *Farmer's Inn*, Uruli-Kanchan 412202, Pune-Sholapur Rd, Distt, T 256 241, Cable: Farmer's Inn. 6 rm. 36 km airport. Restaurant (Veg). **E** *Ketan*, 917/19 A Sivajinagar, FC Rd, T 59081-82, 59003-04. 15 rm. Restaurant (Indian). **E** *Mayur*, S No 201A/2A Bombay Pune Rd, Chinchwad, T 82071. 24 rm. 28 km airport. **E** *Poonam*, Jangli Maharaj Rd, Deccan Gymkhana, T 54584. 6 rm. **E** *Rajdoot*, 694 Pune Satara Rd, T 434011, Cable: Rajdoot. 39 rm. Diners. **E** *Safari*, Safari Hotel Bldg, Sivajinagar, T 50522-25. 22 rm. 16 km airport. **E** *Shalimar*, 12A Connaught Rd, T 69191, Telex: 0145333 or 0145505 MCCI Talera. 45 rm. Car hire, parking, safe deposit. **F** *National*, opp Wilson Garden. Helpful staff, good value.

Restaurants There are many restaurants in hotels with extensive menus as well as outside: *Coffee House*, N Molodina Rd, a large a/c restaurant (0800-2300); *Poona Coffee House*, 1256/2 Deccan Gymkhana. Large, live music, 0900-2400; *Mazdana*, 22 Amludhur Rd. In pleasant garden, has character; *Apsara*, Udyog Bhavan, Tilak Rd (a/c, bar); *George*, 2436 Gen Thimaya Rd. Part a/c, snacks and ice-creams; *Status*, 6 Parmar Chambers, Sadhu Vaswani Chowk; *Dicy-Spicy*, Senapati Bapat Rd (Punjabi); Indian: Khyber, Alankar Theatre (inc Continental, beer bar and ice-creams) *Panchali, Ruchira* (live music) and *Poonam* on Jangli Maharaj Rd, Deccan Gymkhana; *Supriya*, Ambedkar Rd; *Chalukya*, Garware Bridge, Deccan Gymkhana; *Valshali* and *Amrapali*, FC Rd.

Maharashtra specialities *Shreyas*, Apte Rd with open-air terrace; *Anand Dining Hall*, Prabhat Rd, Lane 10, Deccan Gymkhana; *Shabri*, Hotel Parichay, FC Rd; **Good thalis**: *Mathura*, Metro Building; *Suvarna Rekha Lodge*, 96B Prabhat Rd. Chinese: *Chinese Room Oriental,* Karve Rd (bar, ice-creams); *Cafe Nanking*, opp Poona Club, Bund Garden Rd; *Chinese Room*, 2434 E St, a/c. Recommended (*Latif's Cafetaria* in the same building); *Eddies Kitchen*, Synagogue St. *Dorabjee*, Dastur Meher Rd (Parsee); Good Luck and Lucky, nr Deccan Gymkhana are good cafés.

Spices Health Foods, MG Rd for brown bread, peanut butter and tofu. *Darshon*, 759 Prabhat Rd for fruit juices, milkshakes and western meals.

Banks *State Bank of India* Laxmi Rd

Shopping The three main shopping centres in Pune are at MG Rd in the Camp area, Deccan Gymkhana, and Laxmi Rd. Pune is known for its **handlooms**, especially Poona saris (cotton-silk weave). **Textiles** On MG Rd: *Poona Saree Centre* and *Indo-Foreign Stores*. *Kundan Saree Centre*, Bhawani Peth, Ramoshi Gate. **Boutiques and Garment Stores** On MG Rd: *Sirocco, Figleaf, Fairdeal, Weekenders*. Also *Sunny's Sports Boutique*, 766/3 Deccan Gymkhana, Pune. **Department Stores** On MG Rd: *Shan Hira, Chandan Stores*. *Dorabjee & Co*, Moledina Rd.

Photography *Pahiyar Studios*, Tilak Rd. *Colour Photo Studio*, MG Rd, Camp.

Local Transport Taxis, rates negotiable. **Auto-rickshaws** are readily available. Extra charges for journeys outside the Municipal Corporation and Cantonment limits, and between 2400-0500.

Buses **City Buses** operated by Pune Municipal Transport on all important routes in the city and suburbs. Pune has three bus stations. **Rly Bus Stand** for the S: Goa, Belgaum, Panaji, Kolhapur, Mahabaleshwar, Ratnagiri, Panchgani. **Satara and Solapur**. **Sivaji Nagar Bus Stand** for the N/NE: Ahmednagar, Amravati, Aurangabad, Belgaum, Dehu, Jalgaon, Lonavla, Murud, Nander and Nasik. **Swargate Bus Stand** for Baneshwar, Bhargar, Daund, Khodakwasla, Morgaon, Purandhar, Saswad, Sivapur and Sinhagad.

Bicycles are available for rental from many places.

Sports Racing is Pune's most popular sport. The Royal Western India Turf Club on Race Course Rd. Tickets available at the race course.

Museums Raja Kellar Museum, 1378 Shukrawar Peth, T 444 466. Open daily 0830-1230 and 1500-1830. Re 1. Good catalogue. This private museum collection is the work of Dinkar Kelkar and focuses on traditional Indian arts. There are 36 sections and the exhibits include carved temple doors, musical instruments, pottery, miniature paintings, nutcrackers, brass padlocks and lamps. The collection is so vast it can only be displayed on a rotational basis but Sri Kelkar is often on hand and personally guides visitors around his wonderful display.

Mahatma Phule Vastu Sangrahalaya, 1203 Sivaji Nagar, T 56570. Open daily 0800-1730. Re 1 adults, Re 0.50 children. **Kasturba Samadhi**, Aga Khan Palace, Nagar Rd. Open daily till 1700. Rs 2. A memorial to Mahatma Gandhi, his wife Kasturba and the Independence Movement.

Parks and Zoos There is a small zoo at the Empress Gardens.

Useful services Police: T 100 Fire: T 101 Ambulance: T 101

Hospitals and Medical Services Pune Cantonment Hospital, Shankareth Rd, Golibar Maidan, T 20530. Pune Chest Hospital, Aundh Camp, T 57937. Jehangir Nursing Home, 32 Sassoon Rd, T 662 3391. KEM Hospital, Rasta Peth, T 27221. Ruby Hall Nursing House, 40 Sassoon Rd, T 663 391. Sassoon Hospital, Jayaprakash Narayan Rd, T 664 764. Wadia Hospital, 283 Shukrawar Peth, T 442 363.

Post and Telegraph GPO, Vaswani Rd, T 660 757. Head Post Office (city), Laxmi Rd, T 445 058. Sivajinagar Head Post Office, T 59936.

Places of Worship *Hindu*: Ram Tekri Mandir, Solapur Rd; Parvati Mandir, nr Swargate; Chaturshringi Mandir, Senapati Bapat Marg; Ganapati Mandir, Sarabaug. *Parse*: Agiari Temple, MG Rd. *Muslim*: there are several mosques on Central St, Pune Camp. *Christian*: St Mary's Church, Gen Bhagat Marg; St Paul's Church, nr GPO; St Patrick's Cathedral, Prince of Wales Rd. *Jewish*: Ohel David Synagogue, Synagogue St, Camp.

Travel Agents and Tour Operators *Trade Wings*, 321 MG Rd, T 667 783. City booking, T 58431. *Travel Corner*, Deccan Gymkhana, T 54369. *Travel Corporation (India)*, Hotel Blue Diamond, T 662 494. *Travel Gem*, 12 Vasvani Rd, T 663 245. *Indtravels*, Atur House, Moledina Rd. *Starline Travels*, Darshan, 1 B.J. Rd, T 662 741.

Tourist Offices and Information Maharashtra TDC, T. Barrack, Central Bldg, T 666 697. Tourist Information Counter, Pune Rly Station.

Tours MTDC operate a number of tours from the Tourist Information Counter, Rly Station, opp 1st Class booking office. Pune Darshan. Daily (0800-1100 and 1500-1800). Rs 16. Suburban Pune Tour. Th and Sun (0800-1200 and 1400-1800). Places of interest within the city as well as on the outskirts. Rs 35.

Air Indian Airlines flies daily non-stop to Pune from Delhi and returns via Nagpur. Twice daily (Tues) and six other times a week non-stop from Bombay to Pune. Four times a week non-stop between Bangalore and Pune. Indian Airlines, enquiries T 664840.

Rail Bombay (VT): *Madras-Bombay Mail* 7010, daily, 0033, 4 hr 15 min; *Udyan Exp* 6530, daily, 1618, 4 hr 5 min; *Hyderabad-Bombay Exp* 7032, daily, 0853, 4 hr; *Pune-Bombay Indrayani Exp* 2114, daily, 1845, 4 hr 30 min. **Hyderabad**: *Bombay-Hyderabad Exp* 7031, daily, 1715, 13 hr 15 min.

Road Pune is on NH4, NH9 and NH3. From: **Bombay** (184 km); **Nasik** (184 km); **Mahabaleshwar** (120 km); **Belgaum** (336 km); **Delhi** (1424 km); **Calcutta** (1948 km); **Madras** (1356 km); **Bangalore** (840 km).

Bus Maharashtra SRTC, Rly Station Bus Stand, T 665360. Sivajinagar Bus Stand, T 51970. Swargate, T 441591. Maharashtra TDC (Central Bldg, T 666 697). Sohrab Tours and Travels, 94A MG Rd, T 664 670, 664 671. Southern Travels, Hotel Jagannath, Somwar, T 27209. MSRTC connects Pune by regular bus services with all major towns within the state. Asiad Buses ply daily to Bombay from Pune Rly Station every 15 mins from 0530 to 2330. Rs 40. Bookings should be made to ensure a seat. MTDC connects Pune with Panaji daily 1800, Rs 160. Kolhapur daily 0130, Rs 58. Aurangabad daily 0130, Rs 95. Southern Travels operates luxury coaches to Ahmedabad, Panaji, and Indore.

Excursions *Sinhagarh* (1,317 m), 24 km SW of Pune. The 'Lion Fort', situated in the relatively high Bhuleshwar range of the Western Ghats. On the way you pass the *Kharakwasla reservoir* on the **Mutha river**. The dam was constructed in 1879 and was the first of the large dams of the Deccan.

The **fort** is roughly triangular in shape on a hill 700 m above the land below. The ascent is steep. To the N and S are cliffs topped with 12 m high basalt walls. There were two entrances, the **Pune Gate** (NE) and **Kalyan Gate** (SW), both protected by three successive gates. On the W side of the hill the wall was continued across a gorge, creating a dam. It was called **Kondana** until its name change in 1647. Muhammad Tughluq (**see page 168**), besieged and captured the fort in 1328. In 1486 Malik Ahmad, founder of Ahmadnagar took it, along with Shivner, and in the 17th century it changed hands on a number of occasions. The Marathas captured it in a brilliant assault in 1670 when they scaled the cliffs at night and took the garrison by surprise. Near the dammed gorge is a monument (1937) to the leader of the campaign, Tanaji Malusara. The plateau is undulating and there are few buildings on it, most having been reduced to ruins, but the setting is wonderful.

From Pune the **NH4** goes E and SE across the plateau. The vast open fields and scattered settlements give the impression that this is a sparsely populated region. Only the very high proportion of land under cultivation makes clear the extent to which land throughout this rainfed agricultural belt is heavily used.

From **Pune** the **NH4** goes through **Loni-Kalbhor** (18 km), **Uruli** (12 km) and **Yavat** (14 km) to **Ravangaon** (41 km; the "village of Ravana"). After passing through a further series of small towns it crosses the **River Bhima** (62 km), a tributary of the Krishna, and continues through **Tembhurni** (11 km) and **Vengaon** (4 km). A right turn in **Vengaon** leads to the pilgrimage centre of **Pandharpur** (31 km).

Pandharpur, on the S bank of the Bhima River, has a shrine to Vithoba, an incarnation of Vishnu dating from 1228. There are a dozen bathing ghats on the river bank, and during the main pilgrimage season of July (the Ekadashi Fair) tens of thousands of pilgrims converge on the town.

From Vengaon **NH4** continues through **Shetphal** (23 km), **Yavli** (20 km) and **Mohol** (6 km) to the **River Sina** (8 km). Solapur is a further 24 km.

Solapur (Population 635,000; Altitude 450 m) is a cotton textile town. In the heart of the cotton growing area it has been a focus of the cotton trade for over a century, it is unusual among Indian towns in being almost entirely an industrial city. The town has benefitted from being on the main railway line between Madras and Bombay.

Hotels There are plenty of small, cheap boarding houses and lodges, all very basic. The best places to stay are probably: **F** *Rajdhani*, nr Rly Station. **F** *Railway Retiring Rooms* D rm and Dorm.

Travel Bombay (Dadar) *Chennai Exp* 6064, daily except Th and Sat, 2240, 8 hr 25 min. **Bombay (VT)** *Madras-Bombay Mail* 7010, daily, 1830, 10 hr 20 min **Madras** *Dadar-Madras Chennai Exp* 6063, Daily except Sat and Sun, 0435, 15 hr 25 min; *Dadar-Madras Exp* 6511, daily, 2345, 16hr 55min **Hyderabad** *Minar Exp* 2101, daily, 0605, 6 hr 10min **Bangalore** *Udyan Exp* 6529, daily, 1653, 15 hr 20 min.

Road Solapur is very well placed on the road network, with excellent connections to Bombay, Hyderabad, Aurangabad to the N and Bijapur to the S.

Bus Long distance Express bus services connect Solapur with Bombay, Aurangabad, Hyderabad and Bangalore.

BOMBAY TO KOLHAPUR AND BELGAUM VIA PUNE

This route climbs the Ghats up to Pune (see above) then runs virtually due S at an altitude of about 700 m along the E edge of the Ghats. The scenery is often spectacular, and the road still runs through some dense forests.

Leave Pune S on **NH9** through Swar Gate (6 km), then after 7 km across a ghat section of road for 5 km, ending in a tunnel at Katraj Ghat. After 17 km the road passes through **Nasrapur** to **Kapurwahal** (12 km). Turn left onto a country road that leads to **Purandhar** (13 km).

Purandhar Fort (1,220 m) commands a high point on the Western Ghats. Legends say that the citadel was built by Purandara or Indra, king of the gods. It is a double fort, the lower one, **Vajragad** to the E and **Purandhar** itself, which together command a narrow passage through the hills. Like other hill forts, Purandhar was defended by curtain walls, in this case 42 km in extent, relieved by three gateways and six bastions. The earliest fortifications date from 1350. On the summit of the hill farthest from Delhi Gate is the **Mahadev temple.**

From Purandhar return to **NH9** at **Kapurwahal**. The road loses height to cross the river at **Shirwal** (12 km), then climbs again to **Khandala** (12 km). In **Surul** (14 km) a left turn leads to **Mahabaleshwar** (43 km; see below). Take the right hand road for **Wai** (11 km), situated on the left bank of the **Krishna River**. The riverside is very attractive, lined with shady temples, and behind the town the hills rise sharply. Note particularly the finely carved mandapam in front of the Mahadev temple. On top of one is the fort of **Pandavgad**, which according to local tradition was visited by the Pandava Brothers of the Mahabharata. The town's sanctity is enhanced by its proximity to the source of the Krishna.

From Surul continue on the **NH9** through **Panchwad** (12 km) and **Udtara** (6 km) to **Satara**.

Satara (*Altitude* 670 m) The town lies in a hollow near the confluence of the **Krishna** and **Venna rivers,** considered a place of great sanctity. Consequently there are a number of temples on the banks at *Mahuli*. There is a cantonment containing Sir Bartle Frere's **Residency** (1820). **A "New Palace"** (1838-44) was built by the engineer responsible for the bridges over the two rivers.

The ruling house of Satara was descended from **Sahu**, Sivaji's grandson, who was brought up at the Mughal court. Their **mansion**, 200 m from the New Palace, contains a number of **Sivaji's** weapons. These are said to include the notorious "tigers' claws" (*waghnakh*) with which Sivaji is reputed to have disembowelled the Bijapur General, *Afzal Khan*. Other weapons include Jai Bhawani, his favourite sword, which was made in Genoa, and his rhinoceros hide shield. In addition to this storehouse of Sivaji's possessions there is an **Historical Museum** (1930) which contains a fine collection of archival material on the Marathas.

Wasota Fort is on the S side of the town and can be reached by footpath. It was allegedly built by the Raja of Panhala in the 12th century and behind its 14 m high walls and buttresses contains the remains of the Rajah's Palace, a small temple and a bungalow. It passed to the Mughals under Aurangzeb, for a time, after he besieged the fort in 1699 but returned to the Marathas in 1705 with the help of a Brahmin agent who tricked the Mughals.

The road continues S through **Atit** (21 km) and **Umbraj** (14 km) to **Karad** (18 km). A road on the right in Karad leads to the Koyna Dam (58 km) Through **Kasegaon** (16 km) the road goes to **Peth** (9 km) where there is a left turn to **Miraj** (54 km), an important railway junction. The **NH9** goes S through **Wather** (25 km) and **Shirol** (14 km) to **Kolhapur** (6 km).

Kolhapur (*Population* 450,000, *Altitude* 563 m) Kolhapur was once one of the most important Maratha states, ruled by Sivaji's younger son. Its history goes back to the 10th century and the Yadavas. It is now one of the major industrial centres of Maharashtra. It is the centre of rich bauxite deposits. The damming of the Koyna, a tributary of the Krishna, is providing electricity for production of aluminium.

Places of interest The *Panchganga River* is considered sacred and ghats and temples, including the **Amba Bhai Temple** (10th century onwards) stands on its banks. In the Western part of the is **Brahmapuri Hill** where Brahmins are cremated.

The **New Palace** (1881) belongs to the period when all the succession disputes had been resolved and Kolhapur was being governed as a model state. Built out of grey stone around a central courtyard dominated by a clocktower it contains elements from Jain temples and Deeg Palace.

Major *Charles Mant* of the Royal Engineers designed this and the **cenotaph** on the banks of the Arno River for Maharajah Rajaram and **Rajwada** (Old Palace) which was badly damaged by fire in 1810. There is a Durbar Hall and armoury which contains one of Aurangzeb's swords. Mant also designed the **Town Hall** (1873), **General Library** (1875), **Albert Edward Hospital** (1878) and **High School** (1879). The **Irwin Museum** has a bell taken from the Portuguese at Bassein in 1739. Near Brahmapuri Hill is the **Rani's Garden** where the royal family have memorial *chattris*.

Hotels D *Pearl*, New Sahupuri. T 20451, Cable: Pearl. 28 rm, some a/c. 8 km airport, 1 km rly, 2 km centre. TV, bar, restaurant, exchange, car hire, Diners. D *Shalini Palace Ashok*, Rankala, A Ward. T 20401, Cable: Shalotel, Telex: 195-258. 41rm. 5 km rly, 3 km centre. Restaurant, car hire, TV, Diners. D *Woodlands*, 204-E Tarabai Park. T 20941. 25rm, mostly non a/c. Nr rly and centre. Restaurant, bar, TV, Diners . **E** *Tourist*, 204 E Shahupuri. T 20421. 29 rm, some a/c. Nr rly. Bar, restaurant, car hire, lawn. **E** *Lishan*, Ward E. T 21804. 22 rm, a/c doubles only, rest non a/c. Restaurant (veg), 24 hr rm service.

In the **E/F** category are the: *Maharaja*, 514E, opp Central Bus Station, T 20829. 26 non a/c rm. Opal, Poona-Bangalore Rd, T 23622. 9 non a/c rm each with colour TV. Restaurant (Indian); *Samrat*, Station Rd, nr State Terminal Stand. T 27101, Cable: Samrat. 20 rm, all non a/c doubles. Restaurant; *Tapasya*, 517E Kawala Naka. T 27213. 11 non a/c rm. Restaurant.

Air There is a Vayudoot flight to/from Pune.

Rail Trains to Kolhapur arrive via Miraj (see Goa Travel). **Bombay (VT)**: Konya Express 7308, daily, 0800, 13 hr 15 min; Mahalaxmi Express 7304, daily, 2150, 14 hr 15 min.

Excursions *Panhala* (922 m), 19km NW of Kolhapur, is where the Rajah Bhoj II whose territory extended to the Mahadeo Hills N of Satara, had his fort. The Marathas and Mughals occupied it in turn until The British took it in 1844.

Like Raigarh it is triangular with a 7 km wall with 3 gates around it, in places rising to 9 m. The **Tin Darwaza** (Three Doors) Gate has two outer doors leading to a central courtyard and 'killing chamber' while the inner gate leads to the Guard Room. The **Wagh Gate** adopts similar principles of defence but is partly ruined. By the ruins is a **temple to Maruti**, the Wind god. Inside the fort are vast granaries, the largest the **Ganga Kothi** covers 950 sq m and has 11 m high walls and enabled Sivaji to withstand a 5 month siege. To the N is the two storey **Palace**.

The **NH9** continues S through **Kagal** (17 km) to the Maharashtra-Karnatak border at **Saundalga** (10 km). A left turn leads to **Miraj** (54 km). Continue straight on through **Nipani** (9 km) and **Sankeshwar** (20 km), **Gotur** (3 km) and **Sutgatti** (20 km) to **Belgaum** (24 km). See page 875.

BOMBAY TO PANAJI

The 593 km coast road from Bombay to Panaji, the NH17, runs S through the Konkan region, generally between 15 and 30 km inland of the coast itself. It connects a string of small towns which developed at the heads of estuaries. These acted as the transhipment points for cargos brought by ship, then hauled by pack animals over the Ghats. Although it is lowland it is far from flat. Many of the densely wooded slopes have been cleared, leaving the laterites bare and unproductive, alternating with patches of intensive rice cultivation and coconut groves. The coastal estuaries support mangrove swamps. It is one of the poorest and most densely populated parts of Maharashtra, and one of the main sources of migrant workers to Bombay. The **NH17** is not a fast road, and from late May to October is often flooded.

Follow the route to **Panvel** (see above). 3 km out of Panvel turn right onto the West Coast Road, **NH17**. After 9 km it runs through a forested and hilly stretch for a further 8 km, then passes **Karnala Fort** (1 km). There is a further ghat section before reaching Vadkhal Naka (25 km). Keep on the **NH17** through **Nagotana** (20 km) and **Indapur** (30 km) to **Mahad** (38 km). In Mahad there is a left turn off the **NH17** to Sivaji's former capital of **Raigarh**, high up in the Ghats (27 km).

Raigarh (869 m) The fort town was **Sivaji's** headquarters during the latter part of his reign. The views from the triangular hilltop fort are magnificent, especially the stunningly beautiful panorama across the lakes to the N and the hills around Lonavla. The Western Ghats are particularly attractive. Access to the fort is not easy and consequently it is little visited. The ascent begins at *Wadi.*

The history The flat hilltop is approx 2,500 m long and 1,500 m at the widest central point. A bastioned wall encloses it while two outer curtain walls contour round the hillsides 60 m and 120 m below. Each of the three corners of this irregular triangle are heavily fortified and command fine panoramas. In Sivaji's day it was regarded as one of the strongest in India. Raigarh dates from around the 12th century when it was known as Rairi and was the seat of a Maratha chief. Later it came under the suzerainty of Vijayanagar and in 1479 passed to the Nizam of Ahmadnagar. The Nizam Shahi dynasty held it until 1636 when it was ceded to the Adil Shah's of Bijapur. Sivaji took it in 1648 and died here in 1680. Aurangzeb acquired it in 1690 but it soon reverted back to the Marathas who surrendered it to the British in 1818.

The fort The main gate the **Maha Darwaza** is flanked by two large bastions, both 21 m high, one concave, the other convex. Inside the fort there are a number of buildings. The **Palace** and **Queen's Chamber** are both extensive, placed between the **Gangasagar** and **Kushwatra** tanks. In the courtyard is a low platform where the throne of Chattrapati stood.

In 1670 Sivaji was enthroned here, and assumed the tile *Chattrapati* – Lord of the Umbrella, a regal symbol. In the centre of the town was a market which had more than 40 shops in two parallel rows. The fort housed around 2,000 people. To the NE is **Sivaji's Samadhi** (cremation monument), as well as a chattri for his dog. The adjacent **Temple of Jagadishwara** has a Nandi Bull outside and and inscription to Hanuman inside.

There are 1400 steps up to it. A *doolie* (basket chair carried by four bearers) can be hired, and if you go up at sunset when the heat has died down, there is a small *Rest House* where you can stay overnight.

From **Raigarh** you have to return to the main road **NH17**. Continue S to Podalpur (20 km) where a left turn leads up to the fort of Pratapgarh (18 km) and the hill station of Mahabaleshwar (24 km).

Pratapgarh The setting for this Maratha **fort** is spectacular. From the summit of the hill (1,080 m) on which it is sited there is a splendid view down the hillside which falls away steeply from the crest and is forested. A road leads to the foot of the hill. Then 500 steps run up to the top. One of the most frequently recounted tales of Sivaji's cunning occurred near here when the Bijapur General Afzal Khan was invited to come unarmed to a meeting after threatening Sivaji's territory. Neither honoured the conditions and Sivaji killed his opponent with a *Waghnakh* (Tiger's Claw), a knuckleduster with sharpened spikes. Afzal Khan's head was cut off and buried beneath the Afzal Burj in the fort.

The fort comprises a double wall with corner bastions. The gates are studded with iron spikes. Inside are two *dipmal* (lantern towers), so called because of their exteriors are covered with regularly placed projections like giant coat hooks. Presumably lanterns were placed on these or hung from them, the towers then acting as beacons.

Due E of Pratapgarh is *Mahabaleshwar* (1,220 m), sited on a wooded plateau. It is the main hill station for Bombay, 250 km away. Best season Oct-May. It was declared an official British sanatorium in 1828.

The altitude and proximity to the sea make the climate very pleasant during the dry season, especially after muggy Bombay. From **Bombay Point** and the hills around the town you can see the sea on a clear day. There are pleasant walks and waterfalls within walking distance. **Arthur's Seat** (12km) looks out over a 600 m precipice to the Konkan.

There are several British hill station buildings: **Christchurch** (1842, enlarged 1867); the cemetery; **Frere Hall** (1864) with its mullioned windows and the **Club**, founded in 1882; **Government House** (1829) on Mount Malcolm, now privately owned; The **Lodwick Monument** (1874) in honour of the town's founder and the **Beckwith Monument.**

The old town contains three temples including the **Krishnabai** or Panchganga, said to have five streams, including the Krishna flowing from it. After Bombay, Mahabaleshwar is pleasantly cool and relaxed and an ideal place to have an overnight stop on the way back to the great metropolis from Pune. The Krishna rises from a spring at an altitude of 1,360 m near Mahabaleshwar, starting its 1400 km journey across the Deccan to the sea.

Hotels B *Brightland Holiday Village*, Nakhinda Village Kates Point Rd, T 353. 30 rm. 4 km centre. Other hotels close to town centre: **B** *Dreamland*, T 228. 64 rm. Car hire. **C** *Anarkali*, T 336. 37 rm. Car hire, horse riding. **D** *Fountain*, opp Koyna Valley, T PBX 227, 300, 425-27, Cable: Fountain Hotel. 106 rm, some a/c. Banquet, rm service, rent-a-car. **D** *Lake View*, Satara Rd, T 412. 36 rm. Car hire. **D** *Mayfair*, Mazda Bungalow, L.C. D'Souza Rd, nr S.T. Bus Stand, T 366. 13 rm. Buffet, car hire. **D** *Regal*, T 444, Cable: Regal. **D** *Belmont Park Hill Resort*, Wilson Point, T 414, Cable: Belmont. 14 rm. **D** *Executive Inn*, L.C. D'Souza Rd, T 432, Cable: Executinn. 8 rm. **D** *Fredrick*, T 240, Cable: Fredrick. 32 rm. Restaurant, car hire. Bungalow hotel. **F** *Holiday Camp*, T 218. State Govt operated. Rm and dorms.
    In Club: *Mahabaleshwar Club* has rm. Quiet, with character. You can get temporary membership to stay.

Banks Mahabaleshwar Urban Coop Bank and Satara Urban Coop Bank (exchange) on Dr Sabbana Rd.

There are **Tourist information centres** at the Bus Stand (T 271) and the Holiday Camp (T 7318). Reservations can be made at Maharashtra TDC (T 234522-482) Express Towers, Nariman Point, Bombay.

Rail Pune is the nearest railhead.

Bus Buses available from Pune. About Rs 15. Also State deluxe buses and taxis.

Return to the **NH17** at **Podalpur**. The road S runs through a succession of ghat sections to **Chiplun** (70 km) and **Aravalli** (31 km) where the **River Gad** is crossed. In **Hatkamba** (52 km) there is a right turn to *Ratnagiri* (13 km; "jewel hill"). Population 52,000. The birthplace of two leaders of the Independence movement, *Gangadhar Tilak* and *G.K. Gokhale*, Ratnagiri was also the internment home for the last king of Burma, King Thibaw, who was held here between 1886 and his death in 1916. It is the only town of any importance in S Konkan, though it is one of the slowest growing.

From **Hatkamba** the road S goes through **Lanja** (29 km), a series of ghat sections and then **Rajapur** (31 km), to **Talera** (33 km). A right turn in Talera offers one of the comparatively rare chances to get to the coast itself, at *Vijayadrug* (**Viziadurg**; 52 km). The formidable structure guarding the river is on an ancient site. The Sultans of Bijapur enlarged it and Sivaji further strengthened it by adding the three outer walls. It has 27 bastions, an inner moat, good water supply and carried 278 guns in 1682. The Maratha pirate Kanhoji Angria made it his base in 1698, plundered European shipping and withstood assaults by the Portuguese and the British.

You have to return on the same road to the NH17, then S to **Kankauli** (24 km). The **NH17** crosses the *River Petdhaval* (22 km) by causeway (**Warning** Often submerged during the monsoon). It continues through the small settlements of **Kudal** (11 km), **Akheri** (15 km), **Banda** (19 km) and **Morgaon** (11 km) to the **Maharashtra-Goa** border after *Dodamarg* (14 km). Panaji is a further 32 km.

Warning The Mandovi Bridge has still not been repaired; the ferry crossing can be chaotic – see page 1015.

GOA

Brilliant lush green fields of irrigated paddy surround villages and hamlets, white painted churches standing out against occasional empty patches of startling red soil or an isolated tin shack. In the background are the jungle-clad hills. It might be the setting for a Graham Greene novel. In fact, Goa is a tiny part of India touched by Mediterranean culture and climate. Piazzas with whitewashed churches and elegant mansions splashed with the colour of bougainvillea lend the atmosphere of southern Italian villages. Despite its great antiquity there are comparatively few sights. Perhaps this contributes to its air of lethargy and encourages its visitors to enjoy themselves through inactivity.

With some of India's finest beaches, Goa has long been popular as a place for relaxation. It gained the reputation for being free and

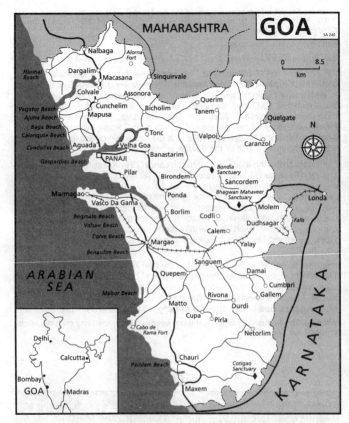

easy. It is still a restful haven, but now it attracts more affluent tourists, and has the facilities to meet their demands. Cheap accommodation is still widely available.

Indian Airlines connects Goa with Bombay (582 km, 55 min), Bangalore (570 km, 1 hr), Cochin and Trivandrum and Delhi (1,904 km, 2 hr 25 min). Dabolim airport is 30 km from Panaji.

Social indicators Area 3,800 sq km *Population* 1.3 million Urban 35% Literacy M 66% F 48% Birth rate Rural 22:1000 Urban 20:1000 Death rate Rural 8:1000 Urban 6:1000 Registered graduate job seekers 3,000 Average annual income per head : Rs 3,000 Religion *Hindu* 66% *Muslim* 5% *Christian* 29% *Sikh* 0.1%

INTRODUCTION

The Land

Goa has a 97 km coastline and is quite hilly with a portion of the Western Ghats rising to nearly 1300 m on the E margins. Clad mostly in lush forest these sweep down to the gently undulating coastal strip. The two largest rivers are the **Mandovi** and **Juari**. An inland creek joins them together at high tide so that they encircle the island of Goa (Ilhas). Spate noted how Alfonso de Albuquerque grasped the advantages of the island site which was large enough to give a secure food-producing base but with a defensible moat, at the same time well placed with respect to the important NW sector of the Arabian Sea. This island is roughly triangular in shape with a rocky headland and has the added advantage of having two harbours. It was given the name **Ilhas** (island in Portuguese).

The soils are rich and have a high mineral content, and the red laterite is quite apparent if you drive down through Goa, appearing like bald patches in the upland areas between the lower lying fertile deltas. In recent years huge reserves of manganese have been discovered and mined, along with iron ore. While the income derived from this has helped to boost Goa's foreign exchange, it scars the landscape and has had a bad effect on neighbouring agriculture.

Climate
In common with all the W coast of India Goa experiences the full force of the SW monsoon. Temperatures are virtually the same throughout the year, but humidity and rainfall vary sharply. In April and May minimum temperatures are notably higher than in the rest of the year, though average maximum temperatures rarely rise much above 33°C. April to October is the season to avoid if possible. The monsoon period itself is very wet and often experiences strong winds. The rainfall and temperature pattern for **Panaji** is shown below:

	Jan	Feb	Mar	Apr	May	Jun	Jul	Aug	Sep	Oct	Nov	Dec	Av/Tot
Max (°C)	31	32	32	33	33	31	29	29	29	31	33	33	31
Min (°C)	19	20	23	25	27	25	24	24	24	23	22	21	23
Rain (mm)	2	0	4	17	18	580	892	341	277	122	20	37	2310

The People
The Goan population is a mixture of Hindu, Christian and Muslim. The Christians generally spoke Portuguese but now speak Konkani and English. The Hindus speak Konkani, Marathi and Hindi. Declining economic conditions in the past caused large numbers of Goans to emigrate. Many are found in Bombay, Mozambique, Natal and elsewhere. Most are of part Portuguese descent and bear Portuguese names like de Silva and Fernandes. This is a direct result of Portugal's policy of encouraging inter-marriage which was seen as a way of maintaining settler populations in climates that exacted a high toll on Europeans. This intermingling has spread to the church – the complexions of the saints and madonnas are those of South Asia.

The cities There are three principal cities in Goa: **Old Goa** (Velha Goa), **Panaji** (Panjim) or New Goa and **Margao**. Old Goa has a melancholy beauty, a city of Baroque churches half-hidden by jungle, dead except for the great pilgrimage to the tomb of St Francis Xavier in the magnificent cathedral of Bom Jesus.

Panaji was originally a suburb of Old Goa and is built on the left bank of the Mandovi Estuary. It contains the archbishop's palace, a modern port, government buildings, a few hotels, bars and shops set around a number of plazas.

Margao is the best port between Bombay and Kozhikode (Calicut). A railway connects it with Castle Rock on the Western Ghats. Vasco da Gama is Goa's principal commercial port and the terminus of the Central Goa branch line.

History

Early Goa Goa has a long and chequered history. Some identify it the *Mahabharata* as **Gomant**, where **Vishnu**, reincarnated as Parasurama, shot an arrow from the Western Ghats into the Arabian Sea and with the help of the god of the sea reclaimed the beautiful land of Gomant. **Siva** is also supposed to have stayed in Goa on a visit to bless seven great sages who had performed penance for seven million years. In the *Puranas* the small enclave of low lying land enclosed by the Ghats is referred to as Govapuri, Gove and Gomant. The ancient Hindu city of Goa was built at the southernmost point of the island. The jungle has taken over and virtually nothing survives.

Contact with the Muslim world Arabian geographers knew it as Sindabur. It was ruled by the Kadamba dynasty from the 2nd century AD to 1312 and by Muslim invaders from 1312 to 1367. It was then annexed by the Hindu kingdom of **Vijayanagar** and later conquered by the **Bahmani dynasty** of Bidar in N Karnataka who founded Old Goa in 1440. It had already become an important centre for the trade in horses with the Vijayanagar Empire. When the Portuguese arrived, Yusuf Adil Shah, the Muslim King of **Bijapur**, was the ruler. At this time Goa was an important starting point for Mecca bound pilgrims, as well as continuing to be a centre for the import of Arab horses and as a major market on the W coast of India.

The Portuguese arrival The Portuguese in their quest for control of the lucrative spice trade from the East Indies, were intent on setting up a string of coastal stations from the home country to the Far East. Goa was the first Portuguese possession in Asia and was taken by **Alfonso de Alburquerque** in March 1510, the city surrendering without a struggle. Three months later Yusif Adil Shah blockaded it with 60,000 men. In November Albuquerque returned with reinforcements, recaptured the city after a bloody struggle, massacred all the Muslims and appointed a Hindu as Governor.

The Portuguese rarely interfered with local customs except for forbidding the burning of widows (*sati**). At first they employed Hindus as officials and troops. Mutual hostility towards Muslims encouraged cordiality and trade links between Goa and the Hindu kingdom of Vijayanagar. Religion only became an issue in later years when missionary activity in India increased. Franciscans, Dominicans and Jesuits arrived, carrying with them both religious zeal and intolerance. The Inquisition was introduced in 1540.

Goa as capital Goa became the capital of the Portuguese empire in the East and was granted the same civic privileges as Lisbon. It reached its greatest splendour between 1575 and 1600, to decline when the Dutch with their superior seafaring skills began to control trade in the Indian Ocean. The fall of the Vijayanagar empire in 1565 caused the lucrative trade between Goa and the Hindu state to dry up. The Dutch blockaded Goa in 1603 and 1639. They weakened but did not succeed in taking it. To add to its woes, it was ravaged by an epidemic in 1635. Manpower was severely depleted and the Portuguese were forced to bring criminals from their Lisbon prisons to maintain their numbers.

Distracted by the Mughals in 1683, the Marathas called off their attack on Goa which remained safe in its isolation, though it was threatened again briefly in 1739. The seat of government was shifted first to Margao and then in 1759 to Panaji mainly because of outbreaks of cholera. Over this period (1695 to 1775) the population of Old Goa dwindled from 20,000 to 1,600 and by the mid 19th century only a few priests and nuns remained.

Independence The Portuguese came under increasing pressure in 1948 and 1949 to cede their territories of Goa, Daman and Diu to India. In 1955 *satyagrahis** (non violent demonstrators) attempted to enter Goa, who were deported but later when larger numbers tried, the Portuguese used force to repel them. The problem festered on until the Indian Army supported by a naval blockade marched in in 1961 and brought to an end four and a half centuries of Portuguese rule. This act certainly tarnished then Prime Minister Jawaharlal Nehru's international reputation but it did mean that all land in India was Indian.

Economy
Goa exports coconuts, fruit, spices, manganese and iron ores, bauxite fish and salt. Its manufacturers produce fertilizers, sugar, textiles, chemicals, iron pellets and pharmaceuticals. Rice is the staple product with fruit, salt, coconuts, pulses and betel (areca nut) also produced.

Tourism Tourism plays an important role in the economy and is a growth industry. By the end of the decade the number of hotel beds is expected to rise tenfold from the present 10,000. The concept of homestays for visitors is being examined and householders are being encouraged to add an extra room to their home to accommodate paying guests.

In the S of Goa beyond the Majorda Resort, five hotel complexes are being developed on Colva beach. These are situated between the sea and the river so that during the monsoon, when the sea is too rough and dangerous for swimming, water sports can proceed on the river. Charter flights are bringing groups of Germans and Britons mainly for 2-3 week package tours.

Although tourism brings money into the Goan economy, there is considerable opposition to the expansion of facilities for tourists. Some Goanese criticise the Government's expansion plans as bringing little benefit to the local economy, while threatening to reduce access to both agricultural land and to the sea for local people, and to threaten traditional social and cultural values. The spread of hippy colonies in the late 1960s and 1970s was deeply resented by some, and more recently the rapid development of power, including current plans to generate nuclear power on the coast south of Panaji, have raised some protests.

Communications Communications internally and with the rest of India remain underdeveloped. The bridge across the **Mandovi** at Panaji collapsed in 1986 and the new one is still not finished. At peak periods this results in long delays as vehicles wait to use the chaotic ferries. The **Bombay-Goa** steamer service has been suspended indefinitely but there is talk of introducing an 8 hour hovercraft service from Bombay.

Goan Food
Goan food tends to be similar to that in the rest of India – rice, meat and vegetable curries and *dal* although many local specialities have Latin names. Spicy pork *vindaloo*, marinated in vinegar, is very popular. Goa's Christians had no qualms about using pork (not eaten by Muslims and most Hindus) in their culinary dishes. *Chourisso* is Goan sausage and *sarpotel* a hot, pickled pig's liver dish. The food in this region is hot on account of the small birds-eye chillies that are grown locally. *Xacutti* is a hot chicken or meat dish prepared with coconuts.

Seafood is plentiful; *Apa de camarao* is a spicy prawn-pie and *Recheiado* prepared with king prawns. You will find lobsters, baked oysters, boiled clams and stuffed crabs as specialities. *Bangra* is Goa mackerel and fish *Balchao* is cooked in a spicy chilli sauce. Goan bread is good and there are pleasant European style biscuits. The special dessert is *Bebinca*, a layered coconut and jaggery delicacy.

Cashew nuts are grown in abundance and form the basis of the local brew *feni* which can also be made from coconut. Beer is cheaper here than in most other part of India. Goan wines tend to be of the fortified variety and are sweet.

Local Festivals
With its large non-Hindu population, Christian festivals such as Christmas and Easter are popular.

Feast of the Three Kings (Jan 6) – celebrated in Cuelim, Chandler and Reis Magos, nr

Fort Aguada, where there is also a fair.

Carnival, 4 days in Feb or Mar, i.e. preceding Lent. In Panaji there are colourful street parades with spectacularly costumes, floats and dancing along the lines of mardi gras and Rio's carnival. On the Monday after the *5th Sunday in Lent* there is a procession in which all 26 statues of the saints from St Andrew's in Old Goa. This dates from the 17th century and is the only one of its kind outside Rome. It is accompanied by a large fair where old fashioned hand held fans, a local handicraft, are sold. Also actors and musicians perform in villages. *Feast of Our Lady of Miracles*, the nearest Sunday 16 days after Easter. A huge fair and market at Mapusa. Also celebrated by Hindus in honour of the Goddess Lairaya.

Feast of St Anthony, 13 Jun. Songs in honour of the saint requesting the gift of rain. *Feast of St John the Baptist*, 24 Jun, at Calangute. A thanksgiving for the arrival of the monsoon. Young men tour the area singing for gifts. They also jump into wells! *Festival of St Peter*, 29 Jun, Fort Aguada. A floating stage is erected on fishing boats tied together and a pageant is held as they float downstream .

Feast of St Lawrence, 10 Aug, celebrates the opening of the sandbars in the Mandovi River. *Harvest Festival of Novidade*, 21 and 24 Aug. The first sheaves of rice are offered to the priests on the 21st and to the Governor and Archbishop and placed in the Cathedral on the 24th. The festival includes a re-enactment of one of the battles between Alburquerque and the Adil Shah on the lawns of the Lieutenant Governor's Palace.

The major local Hindu festivals include: The *Birth of Lord Krishna*, late Aug. Mass bathing in the Mandovi River off Diwadi Island. *Diwali*, end of Oct. Celebrated with a big procession and fireworks.

PANAJI

Panaji (also called *Panjim*) is the capital of the Union Territory of Goa, Daman and Diu. Daman and Diu are now in Gujarat. Panaji is a small town by Indian standards, and a miniscule state capital, with only 50,000 inhabitants. It is laid out on a grid pattern.

Places of Interest

The **campal** is a riverside boulevard with picturesque views across the Mandovi. At the E end is the **Idalcao Palace** of the Adil Shahs and was once their castle. The Portuguese rebuilt it in 1615 and until 1759 was the Viceregal Palace. In 1843 it became the Secretariat.

Largo da Igreja , the main square, is behind the Secretariat. This is dominated by the **Church of Immaculate Conception** (1541) which is in the Portuguese Baroque style and modelled on the church at Reis Magos. The **Jama Masjid** (mid 18th century) lies near the square and has no dome. The Hindu **Mahalaxmi Temple** is further up Dr Dada Vaidya Rd on which all these places of worship are situated. Other places of interest in Goa are described in the **Excursions** section.

Services

Hotels The hotels listed here are those in Panaji, Margao and Vasco da Gama. The beach hotels are listed along with the beaches under places of interest below.

Many top hotels offer off-season discounts from mid-Feb or Mar to mid-Dec, the more modest offer reductions between Jul and Sep. The principal beach resorts, mostly located away from the town, have been grouped together, others listed by towns. There are other innumerable small 'hotels', often only a couple of rooms in a private house or a shack by the beach.

Note As in many coastal sites, you can often bargain big discounts if you are staying for any length of time.

Panaji

C *Fidalgo*, 18th June Rd, Panaji. T 6291-99, 6267, 3330-32, Cable: Maberest Panaji, Telex: 0194-213 Rest in. 123 rm. 2 km centre. Restaurant (Indian, Continental, Goan), bar, 24 hr coffee shop, pastry shop, 24 hr rm service, pool, health club, TV, doctor on call, car hire, shops, Air India office, Amex, Diners, Visa. Sometimes noisy and service slow. C *Golden Goa*,

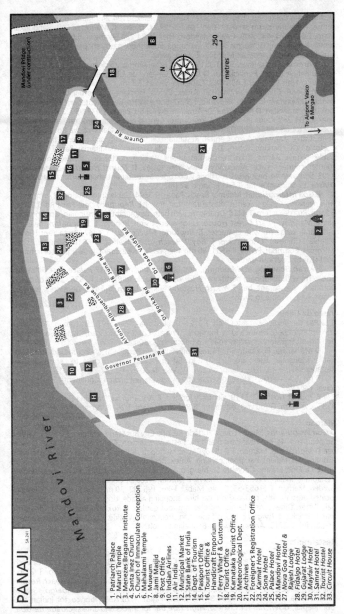

PANAJI
SA 241

Mandovi River

Mandovi Bridges
(under construction)

To Airport, Vasco
& Margao

Ourem Rd

Dr Dada Vaidya Rd

Dr Boskar Rd

Antonio Albuquerque Rd

18 Junie Rd

Governor Pestana Rd

0   250
metres
N

1. Patriarch Palace
2. Maruti Temple
3. Menezes Braganza Institute
4. Santa Inez Church
5. Church of Immaculate Conception
6. Mahalaxmi Temple
7. Museum
8. Jami Masjid
9. Post Office
10. Indian Airlines
11. Air India
12. Municipal Market
13. State Bank of India
14. Dept. of Tourism
15. Passport Office
16. Tourist Office &
    Handicraft Emporium
17. Ferry Wharf & Customs
18. Tourist Office
19. Karnataka Tourist Office
20. Meteorological Dept.
21. Archives
22. Foreigner's Registration Office
23. Karmat Hotel
24. Sona Hotel
25. Palace Hotel
26. Mandovi Hotel
27. Nova Goa Hotel &
    Rajesh Lodge
28. Fidalgo Hotel
29. Gujarat Lodge
30. Mayfair Hotel
31. Samrat Hotel
32. Tourist Hostel
33. Circuit House

Dr Atmaram Borker Rd. T 6231, Cable: Kambros, Telex: 0194-249 Kams in. 36 rm. 1 km centre. Restaurants, rm service, pool, sauna, Amex, Diners. **C** *Mandovi*, D.B. Bandodkar Marg. T 6270-74, 4405-09, Cable: Mandovi, Telex: 0194 229 Shome in. 63 rm. 4 km. Close to centre. Restaurant, TV, doctor on call, exchange, book shop, pastry shop, courier service, car hire, Diners, Visa. Overlooks Mandovi River, relaxing.

D *Aroma*, Cunha Rivara Rd. T 3519, Cable: Hotel Aroma. 26 clean rm. Centrally located. Restaurant a/c (Goan, Punjabi), bar. **D** *Delmar*, Caetano de Albuquerque Rd. T 5616. Clean. **D** *Keni's*, 18th June Rd. T 4581-83, Cable: Kenihotel. 38 rm. Centrally located. Restaurant (Indian, Goan, Chinese, Continental), Amex, Diners. Pleasant rm and bar overlooking the garden. **D** *Mayfair*, Dr Dada Vaidya Rd. T 5952. Some a/c rm. Restaurant, bar. Old Portuguese look, recommended. **D** *Nova Goa*, Dr Atmaram Borker Rd, Panaji. T 6231-39, Cable: Kamros, Telex: 0194-249 Kams in. 49 rm. 1 km centre. Central a/c. Restaurant, rm service, sauna, pool, doctor on call, Amex, Diners. Good value. **D** *Samrat*, Dr Dada Vaidya Rd. T 3318-19, 4546, Cable: Samrat. 44 rm. Central. Restaurant (Indian, Goan), sight seeing, boat cruiser, doctor on call, parking, Diners. **D** *Solmar*, Avenida Gaspar Dias-Miramar, Panaji. T 6555-6, Cable: Solmar. 24 rm. 3 km centre. Restaurant, Parking, doctor on call, exchange, travel counter, courier service, Amex, Visa. Very close to sea. **D** *Tourist Hostel*, nr Secretariat. T 2303. Some a/c rm, best views, top floor. Good open air restaurant, shops. Often fully booked. **D** *Vista*, Dr Shirgaokar Rd. T 5411. Some a/c rm.

E *Goa International*, Miramar Beach, Panaji. T 5804, Cable: International. 27 rm, some with riverview. Close to centre. Restaurant, bar, travel. **E** *Republica*, Jose Falca Rd. T 2638. **E** *Sona*, Rua de Ourem, T 4426. Double rm with bath. Restaurant (Goan, Indian, Continental), bar. **E** *Mandovi Pearl Guest House*. Large spacious rm. Popular. **E** *Panjim Inn*, near the Cathedral. Large rm with character. **E** *Neptune*, Malacca Rd. T 4447. Restaurant (Goan, Mughlai, Chinese). Good value. **E** *Royal Beach*, opp Miramar, T 6316. Some rm with balconies. **E** *Campal*, Panaji. T 4531. 46 rm. 1 km centre. Restaurant, local sight seeing tours, boat cruises. Spacious gardens.

F *Kiran Boarding and Lodging*, opp Bombay steamer jetty. **F** *Palace*, Jose Falca Rd. Cheap rm with hardboard partitions. **F** *Tourist Home*, Pato Bridge. T 2535, 3183 or 4215. Dormitory. Restaurant, bar. **F** *Youth Hostel*, Miramar Beach. T 5433. Dormitory. Next to beach, on bus route to town.

Vasco da Gama

C *La Paz Gardens*, Swatantra Path. T 2121, Cable: Lapaz, Telex: 191-291 Lpaz in. 74 rm. 4.5 km airport, close to centre and rly. Restaurant (Indian, Continental, Goan, Chinese), exchange, free airport transfers, courtesy coach to beach, Amex, Diners.

D *Maharaja*, Rua Leopoldo Flores, opp Hindustan Petroleum, Vasco da Gama. T 2559, Cable: Maharaja, Telex: c/o 191 221 In. 50 rm. 4 km airport, close to centre and rly. Restaurants, bar, car hire, doctor on call, TV, Visa. **D** *Zuari*, T 2127-29, Telex: 191-291 Lpaz in. 18 rm. 5 km airport, close to centre and rly. Restaurant (Indian, Continental, Goan), bar, travel, car hire.

E *Tourist Hostel*. T 3119. Centrally located. **E** *Annapurna*, Dattatria Deshpande Rd. T 3185. Clean rm. Good veg restaurant. **E** *Rebelo*, Vadem. T 2620. A/c and non a/c rm.

Margao

D *Goa Woodlands*, Miguel Loyola Furtado Rd, opp City Bus Stand, Margao. T 21121, Cable: Goawudland. 46 rm. near centre and rly. Restaurant (Indian, Continental, Chinese, Goan), bar. **D** *Metropole*, Margao. T 21516, Cable: Metropole. 50 rm. 2 km rly, central. Restaurant (Continental, Indian), bar, pool, parking, Amex. Roof garden.

E *La Flor*, Erasmo Carvalho St, Margao. T 21381-82, Cable: Laflor. 34 rm. near centre. Restaurant (Indian, Continental), Diners. **E** *Mabai*, Praca Dr George Barreto, opp Municipal Garden, Margao. T 21653-55, Cable: Mabai, Telex: 196 232. 30 rm, a/c and non a/c. centrally located. Restaurants, coffee shop, car hire, shopping arcade, doctor on call, entertainment hall, Amex, Diners, Visa. Large and pleasant roof garden. **E** *Rukrish*, Station Rd. Clean rm with balconies. **E** *Twiga Lodge*, off the main street on the W side. Pleasant. **E** *Milan Kamat*, Station Rd. T 2715. *Annapurna*, nr Benuelim turnoff.

Restaurants

In Hotels: *The Taj Group*, Sinquerim, Bardez, T 7501-03: *Sea Shell* for French, Indian, Chinese and Goan cuisine; *Anchor Bar and Coffee Shop and Beach House* - rustic beach shack ambience, Goan and Indian cuisine. *Oberoi Bogmalo Beach*, Bogmalo, T 2191: *Palmera* for Indian, Continental, Chinese. Barbecues and live music. *Majorda Beach Resort*, Majorda, Salcete, T 20751, 20203; *Laguna* with bar and barbecue. *Fidalgo*, Swami Vivekananda Rd, Panaji, T 6291-9. *Mandovi*, Panaji, T 6270-9: *Riorico* for Indian and Continental, *Goenchin* for Chinese, *High Tide Bar* for snacks and drinks. *Cidade de Goa*,

Vainguinim Beach, Dona Paula, T 3301. *Chit Chat* at the Tourist Hostel, Panaji, does good *tandooris*, is pleasant and popular

Outside Hotels: Panaji Indian, Continental and Goan: *Shalimar, Sher-e-Punjab*, 18th June Rd, T 3775. Indian Veg: *Kamat Hotel*, top of Municipal Gardens, T 3443 is recommended. Also *Taj Mahal*, M.G. Rd, *Gujarat Lodge*, 18th June Rd, T 3931 and *Shanbag Cafe*, Municipal Garden Square, T 3477. *Goenchin*, Dr Dada Vaidya Rd, nr Mahalxmi Temple in Ponda, T 5718 is recommended for Chinese. Expensive Chinese also at Riverdeck, nr Jetty. For a comprehensive menu: *Shalimar*, M.G. Rd, T 5446 and Captain's*Cabin*, Mandovi Park. *Eurasia*, Dr Dada Vaidya Rd has Italian.

Margao Indian, Continental and Goan: *Longuinhos* and *La Marina*. *Kamat Milan*, Station Rd for S Indian Veg. *Shalimar Cellar*, T 22888. *Gaylin*, Varde Valaulikar Rd for Chinese.

Vasco da Gama, seafood at *Zuari Hotel* and *La Paz*. At Colva, try *Dolphin* and *Matol Baiai do Sol*. There are also numerous small cafes along the various beaches.

Bars Beer is cheap and plentiful in Goa and in addition to hotels and restaurants there are a number of bars and liquor shops around. The bars in Panaji bear some resemblance to Mediterranean cafes. Some are very pleasant.

Clubs Lions and Rotary, c/o Hotel Dandovi, Panaji, T 6270.

Banks Most of the larger hotels and beach resorts have foreign exchange facilities for guests. In fact, you are supposed to pay your bill in foreign currency unless you have an Encashment Certificate from a previous transaction. In Panaji and the other towns there are banks.

Shopping Handicrafts (some of which still bear a Portuguese hall mark), jewellery, particularly malachite set in gold filigree and clothes, are good buys. The bazaars are worth browsing through for pottery and copper goods. Some resort hotels have clothes, jewellery, rugs and carvings (e.g. shell 'roses') while Goa Govt handicrafts shops are at Tourist Hostels and the Interstate Terminus, which also has the Madhya Pradesh Emporium. There are *Handicrafts Emporium* in all major towns.

Kashmir and Kerala handicrafts shops at Hotel Fidalgo, Swami Vivekananda Rd, Panaji. Mapusa has a colourful Friday market from 0800-1800. Worth a visit.

Photography Panaji: *Central Studio*, Tourist Hostel, T 3396 PP; *Lisbon Studio*, Church Sq.

Local Transport Private (yellow top) taxis, unmetered. Fares negotiable. Taxis do not run to neighbouring states. **Tourist Taxis**, non a/c Rs 2 per km, a/c Rs 3.50 per km, min 100 km. The Goa Tourism Development Corporation have all-India permits so can run to neighbouring states. Contact Tourist Hostel, T 3396. Share taxis are available near the ferry wharves, main hotels and market places. Pay by the seat. Maximum 5 persons. Approx. Rs 4 from Panaji to Mapusa and Rs 2 from Colva to Margao. **City bus service**, available from Panaji Bus Stand (Main Terminal) to the city, fare Re 0.35. **Auto-rickshaws** and **Motorcycle taxis** are easily available. Fares negotiable.

Ferries There are a number of ferries in Goa running from 0700-2300. *Agassaim-Cortalim*. Every 10-15 min. Passengers free, cars Rs 3. *Colvale-Macasana*. Re 0.40 .

Old Goa-Divar Island. Re 0.40. *Panaji-Betim* ferry has replaced the collapsed the Mandovi bridge which ironically replaced it. Long delays for vehicles can be expected at peak periods. Cars Rs 8, vans Rs 10, bicycles Re 1. *Dona Paula-Mormugao*. Fair weather service only, September-May, takes 45 mins approximately. Re 1.50 per person First Class, Re 0.90 Second Class. Buses meet the ferry at each side.

Coach and Car Hire Available from Goa Tourism Development Corporation (GTDC), Panaji T 3396, 3903. *A/c Deluxe Car* Rs 8, *A/c Contessa* Rs 4.50 per km and *A/c Ambassador* Rs 4 per km, min 8hr/100 km, Waiting charges Rs 15 per hour, night halt Rs 50 for all. *Ambassador (5)* Rs 2.50 per km, min 8hr/100 km, waiting charges Rs 10 per hour, night halt Rs 50. *Mini-bus* (15 and 23 seater) Rs 4 per km, min 8hr/100 km. Night halt charge Rs 75 inside Goa, Rs 100 outside the state. 31-, 35- and 41-seater, luxury and semi-luxury coaches also available.

Bicycles can be rented at the popular beaches and in Panaji for around Rs 1 per hour. Motorcycles can also be hired at approximately Rs 100-150 per day.

Entertainment A large variety of local drama presentations are performed in Goa, many during the festivals. The Kala Academy arranges a programme of drama contests for Marathi and Konkani plays. *Haystack*, Arpora Bardez, live music and cultural programmes on Friday.

Sports The most popular local sports are football and cricket. Water sports are what attract the tourists and the better beach resorts have a range of activities on offer. Goa Bridge

Association, c/o Club Tennis de Gaspar Dias, Miramar, Panaji. Yachting Association, PO Box 33, Panaji, Goa, T 3261. Aqua Sport, 2nd Floor, Ghanekar Building, Jose Falcao Rd, T 4706.

Walking There are some beautiful walks through the forested areas of Goa. Contact the Hiking Association of Goa, Daman and Diu, 6 Anand Niwas, Swami Vivekenanda Rd, Panaji, or c/o Capt. A. Rebello (President), Captain of Ports Office, Government of Goa, Daman and Diu, Panaji. T 5070.

Museums Archaeological Museum and Portrait Gallery, The Convent of St Francis of Assisi, Old Goa., T 5941. Open 1000-1200, 1300-1700, closed Fri. Entry free. Collection of sculptures covers the period from before the arrival of the Portuguese. Many date from the 12th-13th centuries when Goa came under the rule of the Kadamba dynasty. Also a fine collection of portraits of Portuguese Governors on the 1st floor which provides an interesting study in the evolution of court dress.

Gallery Experanca, opp Merces Church, Vadi Merces. **Archives Museum of Goa,** Ashirwad Building, 1st Floor, Santa Inez, Panaji, T 6006. Open 0930-1300, 1400-1730 weekdays. Galleries at See Cathedral, Convent of St Francis of Assisi and Basilica Bom Jesus. Open 0900-1230, 1500-1830, opens Sun at 1000.

Parks and Zoos Goa Children's Park; Municipal Garden; Manezes Braganza Park, Paraji. Mini zoo at Bondla Forest Sanctuary, 55 km E of Panaji – see Excursions.

Useful Addresses Foreigners' Regional Registration Office, Police Headquarters, Panaji, T 5360. **Police:** Panaji T 100; Mapusa T 2231; Margao T 22175; Vasco da Gama T 2304. **Fire:** Panaji, T 101, Mapusa T 2231, Margao T 22175, Vasco da Gama T 2300. **Hospital:** Panaji T 4566, Mapusa T 2372, Margao T 22164, Vasco da Gama T 2454. **Ambulance:** Panaji T 31026. Blood Bank, Panaji T 3037, Margao T 22164.

Hospitals and Medical Services Goa Medical College Hospital, Panaji. CMM Poly Clinic, Altituho Panaji, T 5918. Dmt. Laxmibai Talaulikar Memorial Hospital, Panaji, T 5626. Dr JJ Costa Hospital, Fatorda, Margao, T 2586. Mandovi Clinic, Alto Porvorim, Bardez. Mapusa Clinic, Mapusa, T 2350. Salgaocar Medical Research Centre, Vasco da Gama, T 2524.

Posts and Telegraph GPO, Panaji, T 3706. Telegraph Office, Dr Atmaram Borkar Rd, Panaji, T 3742, also STD, ISD and trunk services. Post Offices at Vasco da Gama, T 2764, Margao, Mapusa, Calangute, Colva and all towns. PCO Overseas and STD Delhi, T 5029.

Places of Worship *Roman Catholic*: Basilica of Bom Jesus, Old Goa; Se Cathedral, Old Goa; Colva Church, Colva; St Andrew's Church, Vasco da Gama; Madre de Deus Church, Saligao. *Protestant*: Goa Medical College Chapel, Panaji; Ponda Chapel, Ponda; Hospicio de Clero Chapel, Margao. *Hindu*: Mahalaxmi Temple, Panaji; Shri Gomateshwar, Old Goa; Shri Mahalakshmi, Bandora, Ponda; Shri Manguesh; *Priol; Sri Shantadurga Temple, Kavle*. *Muslim*: Jama Masjid, Panaji; Madina Masjid, Vasco da Gama; Safa Masjid, Ponda. *Sikh*: Gurudwara Singh Sabha, Mangor Hill, Vasco da Gama; Gurudwara, Betim, Bardez.

Chambers of Commerce Chamber of Commerce and Industry, Rua De Ormuz, Panaji, T 4223. Economic Development Corporation, Atmaram Borker Rd, Panaji, T 4541. Goa, Daman and Diu Industrial Development Corporation, Saraswati Mandir Building, 18th June Rd, Panaji, T 6201. Small Handicrafts Development Corporation, next to Don Bosco School, Gov Pestana Rd, Panaji, T 5702.

Travel and Tour Operators There are many travel and tour operators in Panaji. Outside the town are: *Merces Travels*, 6 Vasco Tower, Vasco da Gama, T 2077. *Rau Ruje Desprahu*, Panaji, T 5763, Margao, T 22477, also Vasco da Gama T 2403 and Mapuso T 2240.

International Air Carriers agents *Jet Air*, Jesuit House, Municipal Garden Square, Panaji, T 3891, Cable: Jetair: Biman Bangladesh, Air France, Gulf air. Philippine Airlines, TWA. *Chowgule Brothers*, opp Captain of Ports Office, Panaji, T 5266, 4596, Telex: 0194-237 Chbr In: British Airways, Kenya Airways. *Thakkers Travel Service*, Thakker House, Swatantrya Path, Vasco da Gama, T 2298-9, 2861, 2453, Cable: Thakerserv, Telex: 0191-204, 268: KLM. *National Travel Service* 2 Jesuit House, Municipal Garden Square, Panaji, T 3324, Cable: Air Kuwait, Telex: 0194-278. Kuwait Airways. *ABC International*, B-24 Trionora Apartments, Panaji, T 6190: PIA. *Pantours*, 8 Junta House, 18th June Rd, Panaji, T 4788: PanAm.

Tourist Offices and Information Government of India Tourist Office, Municipal Building, Church Square, Panaji, T 3412. State Government Tourist Office, Department of Tourism, Tourist Home, Patto, Panaji, T 4757. Also at Tourist Hostel, Margao, T 22513, Vasco da Gama, T 2673, Western Railway Station, Bombay Central T 396288 and Counter at GTDC, Stall no 5, Kadamba Bus Station, Panaji, T 6515. Tourist Information Centres of Govt of Maharashtra

Tourist Hostel, Panaji, T 3572, Govt of Karnataka, Velho Building, Panaji, T 4110, Govt of Andhra Pradesh, Rua de Ourem, Panaji.

Tours Goa Tourism Development Corporation conducts the following Tours which leave from the Tourist Hostel, Panaji T 3396, 3903: *North Goa Tour* (0900-1800): Altinho Hill, Arvalem Waterfalls, Sanquelim Temples, Mayem Lake, Mapusa, Vagator, Anjuna and Calangute beaches, Fort Aguada. Rs 35. *South Goa Tour* (0930-1800): Old Goa Churches, Priol and Kavle Temples, Margao, Colva Beach, Marmagao harbour, Vasco da Gama, Pilar Seminary, Dona Paula, Miramar Beach. Rs 35; *Pilgrim Special* (0930-1230): Panaji, Old Goa Churches, Temples. Rs 20; *Beach Special* (0930-1900): Calangute, Anjuna, Vagator beaches. Price Rs 20 per person. *Goa Darshan Tour* (0930-1800): Colva Beach, Marmagao Harbour, Vasco da Gama, Pilar Seminary, Dona Paula, Miramar Beach, Panaji, Old Goa Churches, Temples, Margao. Rs 35; *Holiday Special* (0930-1700): Bondla, Tambdi Surla. Rs 35; *Dudhsagar Packages* (0700, 0800 and 0715). Rs 20, Rs 15 and Rs 35 respectively. Weekdays from Vasco da Gama and Margao. Sat and Sun from Panaji.

River Cruises by luxury launch on Mandovi river with live cultural programmes: *Sunset Cruise* (1800), Rs 35. *Sundown Cruise* (1915), Rs 35. *Full moon Cruise* (2000-2200), Rs 50.

Air Indian Airlines flies daily from Delhi to Dabolim Airport (Goa) and on to Cochin and Trivandrum, and return on the same route. Three times a week from/to Bombay (25 min by Airbus). Four times a week non-stop from/to Bangalore. *Vayudoot* flies four times a week between Hyderabad and Pune via Dabolim. *Air India* flies on Tues between Dabolim and Kuwait via Bombay. *Indian Airlines City Office*, Dempo House Bldg, D.B. Bandodkar Marg, Panaji, T 3826, 3831, 4067. Reservations 1000-1300 and 1400-1600. Dabolim Airport, Vasco-da-Gama, T 2788, 3251. *Vayudoot*, c/o United Air Travels, opp Old Bus Stand, Panaji, T 4911, 6336. Cable: United. Telex: 0194-218 Rupa In. *Air India*, Dabolim Airport, T 4081, 5172. There is an airport/city transfer service run by Indian Airlines/ Air India, Rs 15 per person. Rs 150-200 for a taxi. Fares negotiable.

Goa is becoming increasingly popular as a package tour destination. There are direct charter flights from England and Germany so it is worth enquiring at your local travel agent.

Rail The line through Goa enters and stops at **Caranzol** in the Bhagwan Mahaveer Sanctuary then proceeds in a crescent through the central part of the state. There are stations at the following places: **DudhSagar** (for Waterfalls), **Sonauli, Colem (Kolamb), Sanvordem, Chandorgoa, Margao** (for Colva, Benaulim and S beaches), **Majorda** (for beach), **Cansaulim, Dabolim** (for airport and Oberoi Bogmalo), **Vasco da Gama** Railway Station is linked by metre gauge line to Miraj which is linked with Bombay and Bangalore by broad gauge lines. Suitable trains are given for both stations.

To Miraj: Shimoga Town-Bangalore Express 6587, daily, 2100, 12 hr 10 min; Mandovi Express 7897, daily, 1130, 10 hr 20 min. To Belgaum: Shimoga Town-Bangalore Express 6587, daily, 2100, 6 hr 40 min; Mandovi Express 7897, daily, 1130, 6 hr 30 min. To Bangalore: 6202 Mail 6202, daily, 1010, 20 hr 10 min. Vasco da Gama Railway Station, T 2398. Margao, T 22252, Panaji agency, T 5620 (Reservations 0930-1300 and 1430-1730).

Road National Highways **NH4A, NH17** and **NH17A** connect Goa with neighbouring states. From Panaji: **Delhi** (1,904 km), **Bombay** (582 km), **Calcutta** (2,114 km), **Madras** (904 km), **Bangalore** (570 km), **Hyderabad** (712 km), **Mysore** (645 km), **Pune** (505 km). **Bus**: Karnataka State Road Transport Corporation, Maharashtra SRTC, Maharashtra Tourism Development Corporation and private operators link Panaji by regular services to Bombay, **Bangalore, Pune, Mangalore, Mysore, Miraj, Margao, Malim, Betim** and other destinations in the region. *KSRTC*, Bus Terminus, Panaji, T 5126. *MSTRC*, Bus Complex, Panaji, T 4363; Bombay Central,Bombay. *MTDC*, Tourist Hostel, Panaji, T 3572; opp LIC Bldg, Madame Cama Rd, Nariman Point, Bombay. *Kadamba Transport Corp.*, Bus Terminus, Panaji, T 3334. *West Coast Travels*, Old Bus Stand, Panaji, T 5723.

Sea At present the steamer service (cabin and deck classes) to/from Bombay is suspended Journey time 20 hr. An 8 hour hovercraft service with Bombay may be introduced. Enquiries: *The Shipping Corporation of India*, New Ferry Wharf, Mallet Bunder, Bombay; Moghul Line Ltd, V.S. Dempo and Co, Customs Wharf, Panaji, T 3842.

Goa Velha (Old Goa)

When Richard Burton, the explorer, arrived in Goa on sick leave from his Indian army unit in 1850 he described Old Goa as being a place of 'utter desolation' and the people 'as sepulchral looking as the spectacle around them'. The vegetation was dense and he had difficulty reaching the ruins. He compared the churches

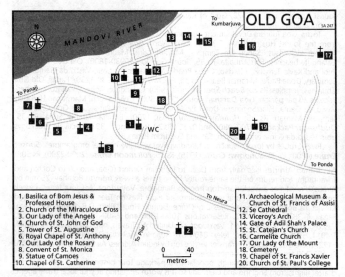

OLD GOA SA 247

To Kumbarjuva

To Panaji

To Ponda

To Neura

To Pilar

1. Basilica of Bom Jesus &
   Professed House
2. Church of the Miraculous Cross
3. Our Lady of the Angels
4. Church of St. John of God
5. Tower of St. Augustine
6. Royal Chapel of St. Anthony
7. Our Lady of the Rosary
8. Convent of St. Monica
9. Statue of Camoes
10. Chapel of St. Catherine

11. Archaeological Museum &
    Church of St. Francis of Assisi
12. Se Cathedral
13. Viceroy's Arch
14. Gate of Adil Shah's Palace
15. St. Catejan's Church
16. Carmelite Church
17. Our Lady of the Mount
18. Cemetery
19. Chapel of St. Francis Xavier
20. Church of St. Paul's College

0   40
metres

unfavourably with those in Italian villages, but was impressed by their size. His published account was *Goa and the Blue Mountains: Six Months of Sick Leave*. Burton may well have started the trend of going to Goa for rest and relaxation.

Old Goa is 8 km from Panaji and may be regarded as the spiritual heart of the territory. It lies on the S bank of the Mandovi on the crest of a low lying hill. It owes its origin as Portuguese capital to Alfonso de Alburquerque, and some of its early ecclesiastical development to **St Francis Xavier** who was here in the mid 16th century. However, before the Portuguese arrived it was the second capital of the Bijapur kingdom. All the mosques and fortifications of that period have disappeared, only a fragment of the Sultan's palace walls remaining.

The city Old Goa was protected by a fortified wall. In the W lay the barracks, mint, foundry and arsenal, hospital and prison. On the banks of the river were the shipyards of Ribeira des Gales and adjacent to these was the administrative and commercial centre. To the E was the market and fortress of Adil Shah whilst the true centre of the town was filled with magnificent churches. It is to these that most visitors come.

All of the churches of Old Goa used the local red laterite as the basic building material. Basalt and fine white limestone were imported from **Bassein**, N of Bombay, for decorative detail, (**see page 967**). The laterite exteriors were coated with a lime plaster to protect them from the weather and this lime-wash had to be renewed after each monsoon. When maintenance was allowed to lapse, the buildings literally crumbled away.

The Archaeological Survey of India is responsible for the upkeep of the churches and has published a small inexpensive booklet on the monuments: *Old Goa* by S Rajagopalan, available from the Archaeological Museum at Old Goa. There is also an attractive and much more extensive, richly illustrated book, *Goa: A Traveller's Historical and Architectural Guide* by Anthony Hutt, available from many hotel bookshops (Rs 150 at Bombay's Taj Mahal Hotel, up to Rs 225 elsewhere).

Holy Hill As you approach the the large central monuments you go over the '**Holy Hill**' with a number of churches. The **Chapel of Our Lady of the Rosary** (1526) belongs to the earliest period of church building and is described as **Manueline**. At the time of the conquest of Goa, Portugal was enjoying a period of prosperity under King Manuel I (r.1495-1521), hence the term. The architectural style that evolved borrowed from Iberian decoration, but also included many local naturalistic motifs as well as Islamic elements, seen on the marble cenotaph owing to the Hindu and Muslim craftsmen employed. The church here has a two storey entrance, a single tower and low flanking turrets. From this site Albuquerque directed the battle against the Adil Shahi forces in 1510.

Behind is the **Royal Chapel of *St Anthony*** (1543), the national saint of Portugal and **Tower and Church of St Augustine**. St Anthony's was restored by the Portuguese Government in 1961. St Augustine's is now in ruins, except for the belfry. The church, which once boasted eight chapels, and convent were first erected in 1512, but abandoned in 1835 due to religious persecution. The church vault collapsed in 1842 burying the image, followed by the façade and main tower in 1931.

Further on is the ***Convent of St Monica*** (1607-27), the biggest in E Asia. The huge square building is three storeys high and was built around a sunken central courtyard which contained a formal garden. The church is in the southern part of the building. At one time it enjoyed the status of Royal Monastery, now it is the Mater Dei Institute for Nuns founded in 1964 for theological studies. The only other building on the Holy Hill is the ***Church and Convent of St John of God*** built in 1685 and abandoned in 1835. Descending from the Holy Hill you enter a broad tree lined plaza with large buildings on either side. On conducted tours this is where you leave your transport and walk.

The ***Basilica of Bom (the Good) Jesus*** (1594). Open 0900-1830. No photography. The world renowned church contains the body of ***St Francis Xavier***, a former pupil of soldier-turned-saint, Ignatius Loyola, the founder of the Order of Jesuits. St Francis Xavier's remains form the principal spiritual treasure of the territory, (**see page 74**). The Jesuits began work on their own church in 1594. By 1605 it was finished and consecrated. In 1613 the body of St Francis was brought there from the College of St Paul. It was moved into the church in 1624 and its present chapel in 1655 where it has remained ever since. St Francis was canonised by Pope Gregory XV in 1622 and in 1964 Pope Pius XII raised the church to a minor basilica. The order of Jesuits was suppressed in 1759 and its property confiscated by the state. The church, however, was allowed to continue services.

The church is not white like all the others in Goa. It was originally lime plastered but this was recently removed to reveal the laterite base. The granite decorative elements which have always been unadorned. The façade is the richest in Goa and also the least Goan in character. There are no flanking towers. It appears that the church was modelled on the earlier but now destroyed church of St Paul which in turn was based on the Gesu, the mother church in Rome. There is only one tower in the building and that is placed at the E end, giving it a more Italian look. On the pediment of the façade is a tablet with I.H.S (Jesus in Greek or *Iaeus Hominum Salvator*). Apart from the elaborate gilded altars, and the twisted Bernini columns, the interior of the church is very simple.

The *Tomb of St Francis Xavier* (1696) was the gift of one of the last of the **Medicis**, Cosimo III, the Grand Duke of Tuscany, and was carved by the Florentine sculptor Giovanni Batista Foggini. It took ten years to complete. It comprises three tiers of marble and jasper, the upper tier having panels depicting scenes from the saint's life. The casket containing his remains is silver and has three locks, the keys being held by the Governor, Archbishop and Convent Administrator. Every 10 years on the anniversary of the saint's death the holy relics are displayed to the public. The next showing is in 1994.

The body of St Francis has suffered much over the years and has been gradually reduced by the removal of various parts. One female devotee is reputed to have bitten off a toe and carried it away in her mouth to Lisbon where it is still supposed to be kept by her family. In

1890 another toe fell off and is displayed in the Sacristy. Part of the arm was sent to Rome in 1615 where it is idolised in the Gesu. Part of the right hand was sent to Japan in 1619.

Next to the church and connected with it is the house for Jesuit fathers, a handsome two storey building with a typically Mediterranean open courtyard garden. It is also built of plaster-coated laterite, and was built in 1589 despite much local opposition to the Jesuits. There was a fire in 1633 and it was only partially rebuilt. It now houses a few Jesuit fathers who run a small college. There is a modern **art gallery** next to the church.

The Cathedral

Across the square is the Cathedral dedicated to **St Catherine.** This is the largest church in Old Goa, dedicated to the saint on whose day Goa was recaptured. Apparently it is the largest Christian church in Asia with a barrel vaulted ceiling.

It was built by the Dominicans in a Tuscan style on the exterior and Corinthian inside, commenced in 1562 and completed in 1623. The main façade faces east and had the characteristic twin towers one of which collapsed in 1776. The remaining one contains the Golden Bell (rung 0530, the 'Mid-day' Angelus at 1230, 1830) which was cast at nearby Cuncolim in 1652. Good views from the top.

The vast interior is divided into a nave and two side aisles. To your right is the granite baptismal font St Francis is believed to have used to baptise followers. On each side of the church are four chapels: on the right to St Anthony, St Bernard, The Cross of Miracles and the Holy Spirit; on the left to Nossa Senhora de Necessidades, the Blessed Sacrament and Nossa Senora de Boa Vida. The main altar is superbly gilded and painted. There are further altars in the transept.

The Inquisition in Goa

As you leave the cathedral by the front door, to your right, i.e. SW, is a pile of ruins that once used to be the *Palace of the Inquisition*. In the splendid hall that once existed over 16,000 cases were heard between 1561 and 1774. The Inquisition was finally suppressed in 1814. Beneath the hall were dungeons.

Further round to your right at the intersection is a **Statue of Mahatma Gandhi**. In the heyday of Old Goa this was where five roads converged and was thus the centre. Moving back towards the main thoroughfare you can see the **Church and Convent of St Francis of Assisi**, the **Chapel of St Catherine** and the **Archaeological Museum**. All these are in the same complex as the Cathedral.

The Church and *Convent of St Francis of Assisi* is a broad vault of a church with two octagonal towers, beautifully lit by the sun. The floor is paved with tombstones and the walls around the High Altar are decorated with paintings on wood depicting scenes from St Francis' life. The convent was begun by Franciscan friars in 1517, and later restored 1762-5. The style is Portuguese Gothic. The convent now houses the **Archaeological Museum** (open 1000-1700, closed Fri) which has an impressive range of stone sculptures from different ages in Goa's history and some portraits of former Viceroys. **St Catherine's' Chapel** was built on the orders of Albuquerque as an act of gratitude at having beaten the forces of Bijapur in 1510. The original church was of mud and straw. Two years later a stone chapel was erected.

To the NE of the cathedral on the road towards the Mandovi River is **The Arch of the Viceroys (Ribeira dos Viceroys)** which was built at the end of the 16th century to commemorate the centenary of Vasco da Gama's discovery of the sea route to India. His grandson, Francisco da Gama was Viceroy (1597-1600). On the arrival of each new viceroy this would be decorated. The ornamentation includes a statue of Vasco da Gama. The arch was rebuilt in 1954.

To the east of this lies the splendid domed Baroque **Convent and Church of St Catejan** (1665) built by Italian friars of the Theatine order who were sent to India by Pope Urban III. Shaped like a Greek cross, the church was modelled on St Peter's in Rome.

Beyond this is **Gate of the Fortress of the Adil Shahs**. This comprises a lintel supported on moulded pillars mounted on a plinth and was probably built by Sabaji, the Hindu ruler of Goa before the Muslim conquest of 1471. The now ruined palace was occupied by Adil Shahi sultans of Bijapur who occupied Goa before the arrival of the Portuguese in 1510. It then became the Palace of the Viceroys from 1554 to 1695.

Excursions

Albuquerque's original conquest was of the island of Tiswaldi (now called Ilhas) where Goa Velha is situated, plus the neighbouring areas – current talukas of Bardez (N of the Mandovi), Ponda, Mormugao and Salcete. The coastal provinces formed the heart of the Portuguese territory and are known as the *Old Conquests*.

The *New Conquests* cover the remaining peripheral areas which came into Portuguese possession considerably later, either by conquest or treaty. Initially they provided a refuge for not only the peoples driven from the Old Conquest but also their faith. By the time they were absorbed the full intolerant force of the Inquisition had passed. Consequently, the New Conquests did not suffer as much cultural and spiritual devastation.

All the important Christian churches are in the Old Conquests whereas the New Conquests have a large number of Hindu temples and, to a lesser extent, Muslim mosques. A tour of Goa will give the visitor more insight into not only the variety of scenery but also the depth and diversity of Goan culture.

BEACHES

For many visitors beaches are the major attraction of the state. Most offer some watersports – water skiing, sailing, para sailing, snorkelling, diving, water scooter and trips in glass bottom launches. There are no private beaches in Goa. Public access is guaranteed. On the popular stretches of sand such as Calangute there is a seemingly endless stream of local entrepreneurs selling food and simple handicrafts, or offering a massage or to tell your fortune. The more exclusive beach resorts try to protect their clients by discouraging these purveyors of goods and services.

In many respects the whole coastline of Goa is one long coconut-fringed beach, indented by occasional inlets and estuaries. The road runs slightly inland, with spurs leading down to the main popular sections of beach. From N to S the beaches are are:

The north

The northernmost beach is *Arambol*, well beyond the main tourist track and the crowds. There is simple and spartan accommodation in the small village, three hours by bus from *Mapusa*. The nearest provincial town is **Pernem** (13 km). **Mandrem** is about 1.5 km S and is deserted, while **Morgim** is at the mouth of the Chapora river. *Vagator* is a popular beach dominated by *Chapora Fort* at the N end.

Hotels C *Vagator Beach Resort*, Vagator, Bardez. T 41 Siolim. 46 a/c rm. 8 km from Mapusa centre. Restaurant (Indian, Continental, Chinese); pool. Red tiled cottages in a garden setting. **F** *Noble Nest* Restaurant and Boarding, opp the church nr Post Office, Vagator.

S of Vagator Beach is **Anjuna**, now one of Goa's best known beaches and which has taken over from Calangute as the centre for hippies. Some are still here, living in cheap rooms near the beach. In Anjuna itself is the splendid **Albuquerque mansion** built in the 1920s by an expatriate Goan who had worked as a doctor in Zanzibar and, like most Goans, wished to return home.

Restaurant *Haystack*, Arpora Bardez, nr Anjuna. Live music and cultural programmes on Fri from 2030; *O Coqueiro*, Porvorim, on Mapusa Rd, T 7271. Bar, tables in or out, excellent Goanese food, but avoid pork when the temp is high.

To the S, **Baga** is really the top end of **Calangute beach**. A former hippie hideaway, it has become more sedate and offers some cheap accommodation, beachside restaurants and shops. **Calangute** beach is similar in ambience and services. Neither is very picturesque nor deserves the title 'Queen' of Goa's beaches as there are comparatively few palm trees and little atmosphere. Calangute village has a post office, bank, tourist office, travels, restaurants and shops selling clothes and handicrafts and is quite a bustling place. Mapusa is 10 km away. Calangute runs into **Candolim** beach and then becomes **Sanquerim**.

Hotels C *Concha Beach Resort*, Umtawaddo, Calangute Beach, Bardez. T 56, 74, 78, 83, Cable: Concha Calangute. 14 rm. 1.5 km centre. Restaurant (Goan, Continental, N. Indian, Chinese), travel, car and motorcycle hire, library, wind surfing, Visa.

D *Baia Do Sol*, Baga Beach, Calangute. T 84/85, Cable: Resorts, Margao, Telex: 0194 303 Sol in. 23 rm, a/c cottages. 2 km centre. Restaurant (Goan, Portuguese, Indian, Continental), car hire, sight seeing, water sports, Diners, Visa. Excellent seafood and entertainment. Simple but good in attractive garden setting. **D** *Varma's Beach Resort*, Calangute Beach, behind Bus Stand. T 22,77. Clean a/c rm with verandahs facing pleasant garden. **D** *Estrelo do Mar*, Calangute-Baga Rd. Quiet. pleasant garden. **D** *Vila Bomfim*, Calangute-Baga Rd. Large and airy a/c and non a/c rm.

E *Riverside*, Baga Beach, Calangute. T 62. 12 rm. 40 km airport, 2 km centre. Restaurant (Goan, Continental). Cottages in garden setting, beautiful location. **E** *Sea View Cottages*. On the beach. Pleasant rm. **E** *Tourist Hostel*, Calangute Beach, T 24. Rm, cottages and dormitory. Restaurant, bar. Can be noisy. **E** *Meena's Lodge*, Calangute Beach. Noisy. **E** *Calangute Beach Guest House*, S of Beach Rd. Spacious rm. Restaurant. **E** *Coco Banana*. Back from beach. **E** *Oseas Tourist Home*, Calangute-Baga Rd. T 65. Quiet and shady. Restaurant, bar. **E** *Sunshine Beach Resort*, Calangute-Baga Rd. Attractive rm around a shady courtyard. **E** *Chalston*, Cobro Vaddo, Calangute, Bardez. T 80. 12 rm. 7 km centre. Restaurant (Chinese, Continental, Goan), water sports, bike and car hires. **E** *Calangute Beach Resort*, Umta-Vaddo, Calangute Bardez. T 63, Cable: Beach Resort. 28 rm, 9 with attached bath. 14 km centre. Restaurant (Indian, Continental), bar, conducted tours of Goa, Parking, doctor on call, exchange.

Mapusa E *Bardez*. T 2607. **E** *Tourist Hostel*, at the roundabout. **E** *Satyabara*, nr Post Office. Some rm with a/c and TV. **D** *Noah's Ark*, Bamboo Motels and Hotels, Verem, Reis Magos. T 7321-24, Cable: Bambomotel. 30 rm facing pool. 1.5 km from Betin, Bardez centre. Restaurant (Goan, Indian, Continental), pool.

The south

In contrast to the northern end, the beaches to the south are the most fashionable. The Taj Hotel group has set up its fabulous Holiday Village, **Fort Aguada** and **Hermitage Hotel Complex** and has made every effort to provide beautiful accommodation with a full range of services. Aguada Fort dominates the headland. Panaji, 13 km by road and a ferry ride away.

Hotels AL *Aguada Hermitage*, **A** *Fort Aguada Beach Resort,* T (0832) 7501-07 and **A** *Taj Holiday Village*, T 7515-17 (Holiday Village), Cable: Fortaguada, Telex: 0294 291 Taj In. These are the three Taj hotels at Sinquerim, Bardez. 45 km airport, 17 km centre. The Hermitage has 20 exclusive and luxurious self contained and fully serviced cottages, each in its own spacious, well kept tropical garden. The hideaway of the rich, famous and reclusive. The Fort Aguada Beach Resort has 125 cm in a standard hotel setting whilst the Holiday Village has 56 villas which are less pricy than the Hermitage. Bus to airport and Panaji, 17 km. Imaginative use of space to provide several types of accommodation in different settings sensitively dispersed in beautiful gardens on bougainvillea and palms. The hotel lobby is open to the elements on the seaward side, thus giving a magnificent view. Helpful staff, efficient service. Highly recommended. Very tasteful development around the historic Fort Aguada – see Excursions.

Miramar Panaji's beach on the Mandovi estuary is pleasant, with good views over the sea but very 'urban' in character. Although you can wade out a long way, there can be an undertow.

Dona Paula on the Zuari estuary has a small palm fringed beach, casuarina groves and very peaceful. **Vainguinim** beach is close by and is part occupied by Welcomgroup's stylish **Cidade de Goa** complex.

Hotels A *Cidade De Goa*, Vainguinim Beach, Dona Paula. T 3301-3308, Cable: Cidade, Telex: 194-257 Dona in. 101 rm. 26 km airport, 28 km rly, 7 km centre. 3 restaurants (Indian, Continental, Goan), 2 bars, pool, health club, TV, car hire, exchange, water sports, indoor games, shops, sightseeing. Another delightful and imaginative modern development designed by the noted Indian architect Charles Correa – see Kovalam Beach Resort, Trivandrum (**page 814**). Rm at various levels opening out onto balconies and small communal areas. Very pleasant and secluded beach.

Restaurant *O Pescador*, Dona Paula, T 4255. Recommended; seafood.

Bogmalo is the nearest beach to the airport – small, palm fringed and attractive. It backs onto the bald upland area of Mormugao peninsula which presents a stark contrast. At the S end of the beach is the beautifully appointed **Oberoi Bogmalo hotel. Vasco da Gama** is approximately 8 km away.

Hotels A *Oberoi Bogmalo Beach*, Bogmalo. T 2192, Cable: Obhotel, Telex: 0191 297. 121 rm, with balcony and sea view. 4 km airport, 9 km rly, 9 km centre. Restaurant. Older development, showing its age in rather dated furnishings. Nevertheless, a very attractive hotel on small pretty beach. Convenient for airport, close to Colva beach.

Velsao beach nestles at the top of the broad sweep of beaches running from Cabo de Rama in the S to Mormugao peninsula. There is little development here. **Majorda** beach is broad flat and somewhat windswept. The Majorda Resort is located by it though hardly at the water's edge. Margao is the nearest town (12 km) via Colva.

Hotels B *Majorda Beach Resort*, Majorda, Salcette. T 20751, Cable: Mbr goa, Telex: 196-234 Mbr. 108 rm. 18 km airport, 8 km rly. Restaurants. Designed on a grand scale with a barn like public area and Holiday camp like accommodation in the gardens behind. More modest and less select, it is popular with Soviet tour parties. Beach 2 min walk.

Colva is one of the most popular beaches in Goa and shows it. The village is a mass of cheap restaurants with names such as Johnny Cool and Vincy's Hotel, very much the product of rapid development. The beach itself is magnificent with beautiful white sand, coconut palms gently swaying in the breeze and blue waters (which can sometimes be rough). Move a short distance from the Colva village area and it is still idyllic. **Benaulim** is the more tranquil end of Colva beach. **The nearest town is Margao.** Benaulim runs into **Varca** and **Cavelossim** beaches, still relatively unspoilt though likely to be developed. **Mabor** and **Betul** beaches lie either side of the inlet and are very quiet.

Hotels C *Silver Sands*, Colva Beach, Colva, Salcete. T (08342) 21645-46, Cable: Silversand. 50 a/c rm with balcony. 6 km from Margao Station, 5 km from Margao Bus Interstate Terminal. Restaurant (Continental, Indian, Chinese, Goan), bar, airport transfers, shops, travel, doctor on call, car hire, wind surfing, exchange, indoor games, sightseeing, health club, pool.
D *Whitesands*, near beach. T 3253. 26 rm plus dormitory. Restaurant. **E** *Sea View Cottages*, in front of Silver Sand Hotel. Non a/c rm with bath. **D** *Longuinhos Beach Resorts*, Colva Beach, Salcete. T 22918-19, Telex: 196-242 Inty in. 32 rm. 8 km rly. Boutiques, cultural shows, doctor on call, private taxis. **D** *Prainha Cottages*, Dona Paula. T 4004. 13 cottages by the sea, with shower and balcony. Comfortable and quiet on a secluded black sand beach. Good restaurant. Recommended. **D** *Sukhsagar Beach Resort*, Colva Beach. T (08342) 20224, Cable: Sukhsagar. 19 rm, a/c and non a/c. 6 km rly, 6 km centre. Restaurant (Indian), bar, doctor on call, tours and travel booking, rm service, taxi hire, parking.
E *Garden Cottages*, behind Johnny Cooks restaurant. 4 rm with bath, private balcony, overlooking pleasant surroundings, quiet, clean, friendly, helpful owner, but 5 min walk from beach. Excellent value. **E** *Tourist Cottage*, nr the sea, T 22287. Government rm. Rm and dormitory. **E** *L'Amar*, Benaulim Beach. Cottages and restaurant. **E** *O'Palmar Beach Cottages*, Benaulim Beach. Non a/c with bath. **F** *Brito's Tourist Home*, Benaulim Village. Clean rm with bath. **F** *Tourist Nest*, one road back from the sea: **F** *Lucky Star*, on the beach to the N.

Restaurants *Johnny Cool* and *Connie M's* are recommended. Several others offer cheap western food and beer.

Shopping Small square with usual craft shops and a good bookshop.

Bus To Margao every ½ hr, takes 30 min.

PANAJI TO PONDA AND MARDOL

This round trip gives an attractive view of the embayment in the Western Ghats, intensively cultivated rice fields, coconut trees and some interesting small villages.

From **Panaji** take the ferry across the Mandovi to Betim then drive N. **Mapusa** (13 km) is the main town of Bardez *taluka** and periodic market centre (Friday). Municipal Gardens. **The Church of Our Lady of Miracles** (1594) has been rebuilt twice, in 1719 and in 1838 after it was destroyed by fire. The **Nosa Senhora de Milagres** image is venerated by Hindus and Christians alike.

Leaving Mapusa, take NH17, then after about 3 km turn right for **Bicholim**. The road passes through the villages of **Tivim** and **Assanora** and skirts round the upper waters of the Mapusa River. **Bicholim** is the *taluka* headquarters. **Mayem Lake** is 1 km to the S and is a popular local picnic spot on the road to Piligao.

Carry on for 8 km SE of Dicholim to **Sanguelim**. This is the 'home' area of the **Ranes tribe** who migrated S from Rajasthan in the late 18th century. Originally Rajput, they spent the next century fighting for the Portuguese as mercenaries and then against them for arrears of pay. In 1895 one of their revolts necessitated the despatch of troops from Portugal.

The **Temple of Vitthala**, an aspect of Vishnu, built in the N Indian style of architecture. It has recently been renovated but some of the original carved wooden columns have been retained. Outside there is a temple cart or the kind often seen in S India. This is used to transport a Hanuman image on festive occasions. The Ranes still live in the old family house next to the temple.

Take the road S to **Bambol** (20 km) where you cross the upper waters of the Mandovi and then continue through the village of **Usgao** to **Tisk** (5 km) which is at the intersection with NH 4A. **Bondla Sanctuary** is the smallest of Goa's three nature reserves and is more in the nature of a zoo. It is only 80 sq km in area and is situated in the foothills of the Western Ghats, where you can see sambar and wild boar. The Department of Tourism is promoting it as an educational resource centre. The park has a botanical and rose garden to complement the jungle, a deer park and a group of Tourist Cottages which are comfortable where meals are available. Book in advance.

A further 18 km E along NH4 brings you to **Molem** and the **Bhagwan Mahaveer Sanctuary.** This 240 sq km park is quite different in character containing a magnificent herd of gaur (*Bos gaurus* – often called Indian Bison), leopard, deer, elephants and a rich bird life. The attractive **Dudhsagar waterfalls** (600 m, from hilltop to valley) are located in the SE corner, near the Karnataka border, accessible only by train. Colem Railway Station is 10 km. The 'Devil's Canyon' is also here.

Return to Tisk and proceed along **NH4A** to **Ponda**, an important road junction. It has some of the most important Hindu temples in Goa. Ponda was not officially part of Portuguese Goa until it was ceded to them by the King of Sunda in 1791 but it was one of the first provinces conquered by them. However, it was quickly retaken by the **Adil Shah** dynasty of Bijapur who built the **Safa Mosque** (1560).

It has a simple rectangular chamber on a low plinth, with a pointed pitched roof is very much in the local architectural style but the arches are distinctly Bijapuri. Built of laterite, the lower tier has been quite badly eroded. On the S side is a tank for ablutions with *maharab* designs. The large gardens and fountains here were destroyed during Portuguese rule. Today they are attractively set off by the low rising forest covered hills in the background. During the Inquisition many Hindu devotees were forced to remove images from Portuguese territory to safety. Many were taken only as far as **Ponda** which was just over the border.

The **Shanti Durga Temple** (1738) is located in a picturesque forest clearing and was erected by one of the Maratha rulers of the Western Deccan. The original temple was over 400 years old. In the temple complex there is a tank and a five storeyed bell or lamp tower. These pagoda like structures are peculiar to Goa and suggest the influence of Western Church ideas concerning the place of worship. The domed temple is Neo-Classical in design.

Ponda **fort** was constructed by the Adil Shahi rulers and was destroyed by the Portuguese in 1549. Shivaji conquered the town in 1675 and rebuilt the fort, but was again taken and wrecked by the Portuguese.

Carrying on towards **Panaji**, stop at *Mardol* (7 km) to see two temples. On the left is the **Mahalsa Narayani Temple** (18th century). The original temple was at Verna in Salcete taluka and was the refuge of a group of Portuguese who were under attack from Adil Shah forces. It was re-erected at Mardol in the more European style. The goddess Mahalsa is a form of Lakshmi, Vishnu's consort. Within the temple is a series of carvings of the ten avatars of Vishnu. In front of the temple, alongside the tower, is a brass Garuda pillar which rests on the back of a turtle as in Nepal. Garuda, Vishnu's vehicle sits on top. Main festival in Feb.

1 km road into Panaji on a hillock is the 18th century **Shri Manguesh Temple** at Priol, the principal shrine of Siva in Goa and is being constantly added to. Painted white, it resembles the Jain temples at Palitana – see page 1063.

Return to Panaji via **Banasatri** and **Old Goa** along the S bank of the Mandovi River. Allow a full day for a relaxing trip.

PANAJI TO CHANDOR AND MARGAO

Leave Panaji by **NH4A** which goes through **Old Goa** and **Ponda** and continues on to Molem and the **Bhagwan Mahaveer Sanctuary**. (see Places of Interest and the above excursion itinerary). At **Molem** you can turn right and drive through the forested hills of Sanguem taluka to Colem and Calem railway stations and then **Sanguem**, 20 km from Molem, which is the district headquarters of the largest taluka in Goa and although inland it has the 'backwaters' feel. The 19th century **Jama Masjid** (renovated 1959) has four minarets and two turret.

From here drive to **Chandor** via **Sanvordem**. The enormous *Menezes Braganza House* (part 16th century) is well worth a look. It shows the opulent lifestyle of the old Portuguese families who established great plantation estates, the largest tending to be in the southern provinces.

From **Chandor** drive along the Zuari river by a backroad to *Rachol*. The **fort**, mostly in ruins, was one of the most ancient in Goa. Originally Muslim it was captured by the forces of Vijayanagar in 1520 and then ceded to the Portuguese. During the Maratha Wars of 1737-9 it was heavily armed by the Portuguese with approximately 100 cannons. During the siege that followed it was greatly damaged. The result of the War was that the N provinces were lost and in order to keep the S ones, the Portuguese paid a huge war indemnity.

The fort was repaired by the Marquis of Alorna in 1745 but with the threat of aggression removed most of the buildings gradually disintegrated over the ensuing years. The seminary, transferred to Rachol from Margao in 1580, has enjoyed continuous operation as an educational centre. The **Church of Nossa Senhora das Neves** (1576, subsequently expanded) has five altars and contains a famous library. The vast stone structure of the seminary is built round a large courtyard. The exterior is lime-washed but inside the courtyard the walls are pink. There is an underground cistern.

Carry on to **Margao** (10 km), the largest commercial centre after Panaji. A pleasant provincial town (given the status of town by Royal decree in 1778), headquarters of *Salcete taluka** which is the state's richest and most fertile. The impressive Baroque **Church of the Holy Spirit** with its classic Goan façade dominates a the square surrounded by a number of fine town houses. Originally constructed in 1564 over the ruins of a Hindu temple, it was sacked by Muslims in 1589 and completely rebuilt in 1675. In the square is a monumental cross with a mango tree beside it. The 17th century **da Silva House** (also called Seven Shoulders) is well known for its sumptuous furnishings and the **de Joao Figueiredo House** has a splendid collection of Goan furniture.

From Margao you can either return to Panaji directly on **NH17** or drive out to **Colva beach** (6 km), one of the most attractive in Goa. On the way you pass the large **Church of Our Lady of the Miracles** (1581) which houses an image of Jesus alleged to have been discovered on the African coast. Annual feast in Oct – see Local Festivals. The village has a small fishing fleet and the palm-fringed white sand beach is lovely.

Continuing up the coast past **Majorda beach, Cansaulim** and **Valsao beach** you can rejoin **NH17** at **Cortalim** and the causeway over the Zuari River. The **Pilar Seminary** is in the village of **Velha Goa**, 2 km inland. This ancient institution was founded in 1613 and was sited on the top of a hill over a Siva temple. Relics of a headless Nandi Bull and a rock carving of a Naga serpent were found.

From Velha Goa you go over the bare laterite strewn plateau, past the Goa Medical College and turn left to **Dona Paula**, the headland between the Mandovi River estuary and Marmagao harbour. The point is named after a viceroy's daughter who reputedly fell in love with a fisherman and when permission to marry was refused jumped into the sea from the cliffs. There is a fine view. The return to Panaji is along the Miramar beach, an extension of the Panaji esplanade.

THE COASTAL FORTS

As the Portuguese gradually extended their empire E from Lisbon they built a series of coastal forts to protect their essentially seaboard possessions and to dominate the Arabian sea and East Indies. With their superior naval power, they could blow most 'country boats' out of the water. The purpose of Goa was to supervise the Malabar coast. The forts that you see (listed north to south) are small compared with even the modest Indian forts, due the small number of expatriate Portuguese manning them.

Tiracol is the most northerly of the forts and stands on the N side of the Teracol river estuary. Like all the other forts it is situated on a piece of high ground. Fortified from attacks from the sea, the walls on the land side, rise from a dry moat. The view across the estuary is very picturesque. The church inside the fort has a classic Goan façade and is large enough to have catered for the occupants of the fort and the surrounding settlements.

Chapora (Shapur) fort, now in ruins, stands on the S bank of the Chapora River and dominates the estuary. It was originally built by the Adil Shah. Aurangzeb's son Akbar (not Akbar the Great) used it as his headquarters.

Aguada on the N tip of the Mandovi estuary with the Neerul river to the east, was the strongest of the Portuguese coastal forts, completed in 1612. Open 1600-1730. A channel was excavated to make the headland an island and a large well and a number of springs, provided the fort with drinking water (*agoa*) as well as to passing ships.

The main fortifications are still intact, particularly at the water's edge. Seventy nine guns were placed to give the fort all round defensive fire power and the **Church of St Lawrence** (1630) stood in the centre of the fort. A 13 m high lighthouse with rotating lamp, one of the first in Asia, was added in 1864, the lamp lit on the birthday of Queen Maria Pia of Portugal. During WWII German prisoners of war were interned in the fortress which later served as the Central Jail. The Taj Holiday Village, Fort Aguada and Hermitage now occupy the area and have been constructed with great architectural and environmental sensitivity – see Hotels above.

Reis Magos is 2.5 km E along the north bank of the Mandovi from Fort Aguada and faces Panaji across the river. It is a small town of some charm with a fort that was constructed in 1551 by Don Alfonso de Noronha. It was intended as a second line of defence should an enemy manage to sail past Aguada and Cabo on the headlands. The turreted walls are in almost perfect condition and house a local prison. The Franciscan **Church of Reis Magos** (1550) stands alongside and is one of the first Goan churches. Both stand quite high above water level and are approached by a flight of steep steps.

Cabo de Raj Niwas stands opposite Fort Aguada and was begun as early as 1540. A Franciscan monastery was built alongside. During the Napoleonic Wars British troops were garrisoned at Cabo and built themselves barracks which were subsequently demolished by the Portuguese. Later the Archbishop of Goa was given the monastery as his residence which later became the governor's residence or *Raj Bhawan*. The second line of defence on this side of the estuary was Gaspar Dias near Miramar Beach, 2 km from Cabo de Raj Niwas. It was destroyed during the mutiny of 1835.

Virtually nothing remains of **Marmagao** fort on the S headland of Mormugao Bay. Non-combatants were moved here from Old Goa when it was under threat in 1683 and at one time there was a scheme to shift the capital here. Along with Aguada, Mormugao was the 'throat' through which Goa breathed and is one of the finest natural harbours along the western seaboard of India. Vasco da Gama has been developed into a modern port.

The southernmost fort is *Cabo de Rama,* named after the hero of the *Ramayana* Hindu epic who is said to have lived there with his wife Sita during their period of exile. The site was chosen well as the narrow headland only needed fortification on the landward side. Its origins pre-date the arrival of the Portuguese who acquired it in 1763 and was used as a prison. There are two springs, one of which gives out water through two spouts at different temperatures. Not easily accessible by road, it is best seen by boat.

To complete the list of fortifications in Goa there were inland forts at **Chandor** (see Central Goa Excursion), **Bicholim** (see North Goa Excursion) and **Alorna** in the NE corner of the state. Alorna was acquired by the Portuguese from the Bhonsla in 1746 and lies in a ruined pile on the N bank of the Chapora river.

GUJARAT

Despite its proximity to Rajasthan and Bombay, Gujarat is one of the
least visited states of N India. It lies at the N end of the W coast of
India, and occupies an area of 196,024 sq km, approximately the size
of the United Kingdom. Its name is taken from the Gujara who are
believed to have been a sub-tribe of the Huns who ruled the area
during the 8th and 9th centuries AD. The present state came into
being in 1960 when Bombay state was divided between Maharashtra
and Gujarat on the basis of its language. The new city of Gandhinagar,
20 km N of Ahmadabad, is the state's capital.

For the visitor, Gujarat has much to offer: long stretches of unspoilt
coastline, small villages, attractive villagers dressed in the tight fitting
white kurta waistcoat, baggy jodhpur-like trousers, thick sandals and
loosely tied turbans, the women in a distinctive backless bodice and
skirt.

Trading communities Gujarat has a long history of trading with the Middle East
and its ports have been important sailing points for Muslim pilgrims bound for
Mecca. Most of the European colonial nations established factories and trading
bases around the coast from the late 15th to early 16th century onwards. Gujarat
also has a large emigrant population. In the 19th century many Gujaratis went
to East Africa. They have subsequently become strong in England, Canada and
New Zealand. At home, Gujaratis are prominent in the business community.

Historical sites In **Ahmadabad** there are many fine examples of Muslim
architecture. Gandhi's ashram at **Sabarmati** is just 6 km from the centre of the
city. **Baroda** was the capital of the Gaekwad princely state whilst **Surat** on the
coast was where Parsis settled after being driven from Persia. It was also the site
of the first British factory in India in 1612. Junagadh is notable for its fort and
numerous temples and is a suitable base for visiting the Gir forest, one of the
state's four national parks and last home of the Asian lion. **Porbandar** was
Mahatma Gandhi's birthplace, and **Rajkot** was where he spent his early years
when his father was *diwan* (chief minister) to the Rajah of Saurashtra. The walled
town of **Bhuj** is the major town of Kutch and a delightful haven off the beaten
tourist track. **Palitana** in Saurashtra is an important Jain pilgrimage site.

Social indicators *Area* 196,000 sq km *Population* 42 million Literacy M 54% F 32%
Birth rate Rural 35:1000   Urban 31:1000 *Death rate* Rural 13:1000 Urban 9:1000
Infant mortality Rural 120:1000 Urban 90:1000 *Registered graduate job seekers* 45,000
Average annual income per head : Rs 1830 Inflation 1981-87 81% *Religion* Hindu 89%
Muslim 9% Christian 0.4% Sikh 0.1% Jain 1.4%

INTRODUCTION

The Land
Gujarat lies on the W coast of India and is bounded by Rajasthan to the N, Madhya Pradesh to the E, Maharashtra to the S, the Arabian Sea to the W and Pakistan to the NW. It has nearly 1,600 km of coastline, and no part of the state is more than 160 km from the sea. Physically Gujarat is a land of great contrasts.

Kutch Kutch, the northwesternmost border of the peninsula, has a central ridge of Jurassic sandstones, with underlying basalts penetrating the beds from place to place. It rises to heights of between 275m and 325 m, and like the plains of the Indus into which it drops almost imperceptibly, it is almost desert. To the N of the ridge is the Great Rann of Kutch, a 20,720 sq km salt marsh, which provides a natural boundary with Pakistan. To the S is the Little Rann of Kutch. During the monsoon the Rann floods, virtually making Kutch an island while during the hot dry summer months it is a dusty plain. Some seasonal rivers flow into the Little Rann where they disappear.

The drainage pattern has been strongly affected by earthquakes. A particularly large quake in 1819 formed a new scarp up to 6 m high and 80 km long, diverting the old channel's of the Indus. It has become known as *God's dyke* – Allah's Bund. To the E, the same earthquake caused widespread damage in Ahmadabad.

Saurashtra To the S of the **Gulf of Kutch**, and between it and the **Gulf of Cambay,** is the *Kathiawar* or Saurashtra peninsula. Approximately 432 km long and 320 km wide, broadly comprising a basalt platform, though flanked by sandstones in the north. It rises from the coast to a complex of low scrub-covered hills at the centre, but is rarely more than 180 m high. The two exceptions are to the E of **Rajkot** (335 m) and in the *Gir Range* (640 m). Formed of intruded igneous rocks pushed up into the surrounding Deccan lavas, the resulting plateaus have a completely radial drainage system.

Over most of Kathiawad are great sheets of Deccan lavas, cut across by dykes formed of volcanic lava. Around the ancient and holy city of *Dwarka* in the W and Bhavnagar in the E are limestones and clays, separated by a 50 km belt of alluvium. Some is wind blown, and at Junagarh reaches a depth of over 60 m. Spate points out that its creamy coloured soft stone is widely used as Porbander stone. There are no major rivers and many of the watercourses are seasonal.

NE Gujarat is a continuation of central Kutch and is characterised by small plains and low hills. The railway line from Bombay to Delhi runs through these hills which surround Ahmadabad.

Rivers The river **Narmada** which rises in Central Madhya Pradesh has deposited large quantities of alluvium producing good agricultural land. However, at the coast and in association with the Tapti river to the S there been considerable silting which has contributed to the decline of ports such as Cambay. The Sabarmati and Mahi also flow into the Gulf of Cambay.

To the S of Baroda are the districts of Broach and Surat. The smaller but nevertheless important river **Tapti** rises near Pachmarhi in Madhya Pradesh and flows Surat. These two districts have rich soils and excellent cotton crops. The Western Ghats extend into SE Gujarat. These attract heavy rainfall during the monsoon and are well forested.

Climate
Gujarat lies at the northern edge of the main moisture bearing winds of the SW monsoon. Thus, although temperatures in the state show relatively little contrast, there are great contrasts in rainfall from S to N.

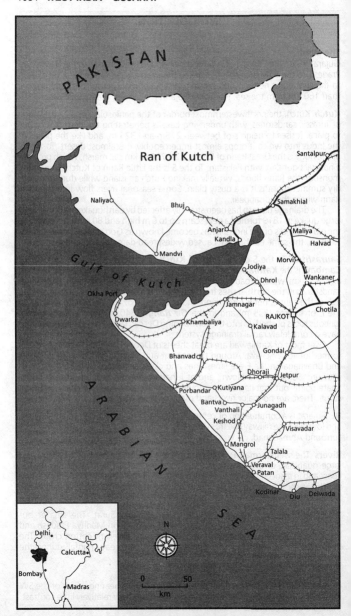

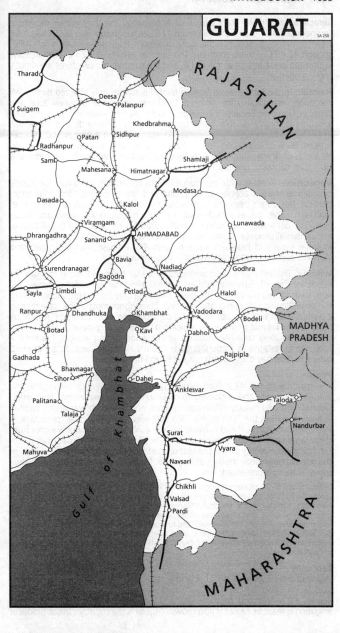

Temperature In the state capital of Ahmadabad the daily winter maximum temperature is 27°C and the minimum 12°C, although sub zero cold spells have been recorded. In summer the daily maximum temperature can reach 48°C, though 42-43°C is more common. The summer minimum is 25°C. Further S the winter temperatures never fall as far, and the summer temperatures are slightly more moderate.

Rainfall In the far S around Daman rainfall is still strongly affected by the SW monsoon, and totals often exceed 1500 mm, nearly all between June and October. However, because it is marginal to the main rain-bearing winds the total amounts are highly variable. These totals fall rapidly northwards, and the rainfall in all the northern regions is meagre. At Ahmadabad it averages 900 mm per annum, 88% of this falling during the monsoon months of June to September. W and N of Ahmadabad rainfall declines still further until Kutch has recorded a minimum rainfall of under 25 mm.

Vegetation In areas with less than 635 mm per annum scrub forest naturally occurs with *babul* acacia, caper, jujube and the toothbrush tree (*Salvadora persica*). Deciduous trees are increasingly common where local rainfall reaches 1000 mm. The species include teak, catechu, bakligum, axlewood and butea gum. The densest concentrations are in Saurashtra and the S and E. Still heavier annual rainfall produces commercially valuable woolly tomentosa, vengai padauk, Malabar simal and heartleaf adina timbers. The E coast produces paper reed (*Cyperus papyrus*), historically useful in paper-making.

Wildlife The last Asiatic lions are found in the Gir National Park; in the Rann of Kutch are the only surviving wild asses in India and the Velavadar conserves the rare, swift footed blackbuck. The Rann is also the only nesting ground in India of the large flamingo (*Phoenicopterus ruber*). Throughout most of the state there is a naturally rich bird life, peacocks and parrots being most common. Migratory birds from N Eurasia find Gujarat a pleasant winter resting ground.

With its long coastline, Gujarat enjoys good fishing waters. Pomfret, a favourite in restaurants throughout the country is caught here, as are prawns, tuna and 'Bombay duck' which is a salted and dried fish .

People
The majority of the 42 million people speak **Gujarati** which belongs to the Indo-Aryan family and is derived from Sanskrit and other ancient languages. Gujarati was also heavily influenced by Apabrahmsa, which was widely spoken in NW India from the 10th to the 14th centuries, while maritime contacts with Persia, Arabia, Portugal and England led to the introduction of many words from these languages. Persian influence was particularly strong in Ahmadabad

The great majority of the population is of Indo-Aryan origin. Nearly 20% of the population is tribal, the Bhil, Bhangi, Koli, Dhubla, Naikda and Macchi-Kharwa tribes all being represented.

Gujarat is one of the modern strongholds of Jainism. Note the "*parabdis**", special feeding places for birds, in the town. Jains specialise in the care of sick animals and birds and run a number of special animal hospitals. Mahatma Gandhi was strongly influenced by Jain principles, including that of *ahimsa*, often translated as non-violence – **see page 70**. He found the deep divisions between high and low caste Hindus deeply repugnant. Re-naming the former untouchables as "Harijans" (God's people), he fought for their recognition as people who should have full rights and dignity. Caste division remains a potent political force in Gujarat today.

Economy
Agriculture Gujarat is an agricultural state with two-thirds of the working population tilling the land. The cultivated area covers about half the state. The staples are wheat and *bajra* (millet), and rice in the wetter parts and where irrigation is feasible. Maize is also grown. Gujarat is the country's major producer

of cotton and groundnuts (peanuts), accounting for one third of India's total. It also produces a sixth of the nation's tobacco. Cotton and groundnut have found good markets and provide a foundation for important textile, edible oil and soap industries. Other important cash crops are cumin, sugar-cane, mangoes and bananas. Cash crops slightly exceed food crops in value and make an important contribution to the regional economy.

Minerals and power The state is rich in limestone, manganese, gypsum, calcite, bauxite, lignite, quartz sand, agate and feldspar. Extensive exploration and production of oil and natural gas at Ankleshwar, Kambhat and Kalol has placed Gujarat at the forefront of the country's major petroleum producing states. Soda ash and salt production account for 90% and 66% respectively of national production. A thermal-power station using coal, natural gas and oil is located at Dhuvaran. Power from the Tarapur nuclear station in Maharashtra supplements the locally generated power.

Industry and resources The most remarkable feature of Gujarat's recent industrial development has been the growth of the dairy industry, much of it conducted on a cooperative basis. There are now 15 milk processing plants with a production capacity of 3.2 million litres per day. Membership of dairying cooperatives exceeds 1 million. Of these the **Kaira District Cooperative Milk Producers' Union** ('Anand' products) is the best known.

The state government plays a significant role in extending financial support and organisational expertise to the establishment of new cooperatives. To support milk production there are over 10 factories processing 1,500-2,000 tonnes of cattlefeed per day. There has been considerable assistance from the European Community's "Operation Flood", using Europe's milk surpluses to guarantee adequate supply of milk while local supply was increased.

The textile industry has traditionally formed the industrial base of Gujarat but in the last two decades manufacturing has been energetically diversified. The oil refinery at Kovali has created a rapidly expanding petrochemical industry. The pharmaceutical industry concentrated at Vadodara, Ahmadabad and Atul (Valsad) produces one-third of the national total. The cement, vegetable oil and industrial machinery and battery industries are all major contributors to the regional economy. An electronics estate has been set up at Gandhinagar to produce components for India's increasingly sophisticated consumer market.

There has also been a steady growth in small scale industry. Handicrafts include, embroidery, leather work, *bandhani* (tie-and-dye), hand-block printing. Surat's 'Tanchoi' and 'Gajee' silks and 'Kinkhab' gold brocades are famous and so is the wood inlay work. Ahmadabad produces fine jewellery and brass and copper ware.

Groundnut oil Gujarati businessmen first started investing in groundnut oil production fifty years ago. Today the three districts of **Rajkot**, **Jamnagar** and **Junagadh** account for nearly one third of India's total production. Used for cooking and in the chemical industry, there are over 600 oil mills and solvent extraction plants in Saurashtra. Press reports suggest that the growth has been accompanied by a considerable amount of graft, as much as half the output being claimed to be sold tax free "out of the back door". The economic power of the groundnut lobby gives them considerable political influence. Today the groundnut oil companies are diversifying into a wide range of other industrial goods.

Communication There is a good road network and Gujarat is also well connected by broad gauge railway with centres in N and W India. The main airport is Ahmadabad and is supported by a network of small regional airports. Kandla is the major international port and is supported by 39 intermediate and minor ports.

History

The earliest settlements Gujarat lies on the margins of the South Asian arid zone. Over the last million years it has experienced successive alternating periods of greater and less rainfall. On these margins some of India's earliest stone age settlements developed, for example at the sites of Rojadi near Rajkot and Adamgarh, north of the Narmada River near the Gujarat-Madhya Pradesh border. Other stone age settlements have been found around the **Sabarmati** and **Mahi** rivers in the S and E of the state.

The Indus Valley Indus Valley civilization and Harappan centres have been discovered at a number of sites, including **Lothal**, Rangpur, Amri, Lakhabaval and Rozdi. Today Lothal is 10 km up the Gulf of Cambay. It was discovered in 1954 by the Indian archaeologist S.R. Rao, and has proved to be one of the most remarkable Indus Valley sites in India, being at the SE edge of Harappan influence. It seems probable that they came by sea, occupying a settlement that was already well-established before they colonised it. Rao has argued that the main Harappan occupation lasted from 2450 BC to 1900 BC, followed by a 300 year period of decline.

In 1988 an exciting new Harappan discovery was made at **Kuntasi** at the head of the Gulf of Kutch, 30 km from **Morvi** in Rajkot district. It has several apparently new features. Like Lothal Kuntasi was a port, but it had a "factory" associated with it. The workers' houses are grouped in one complex of more than 50 rooms, all interlinked and sharing one hearth. Although much work remains to be done, it seems that the site may also hold more clues to the Harappan religious beliefs and practice. The importance of the site as a port for trade is suggested by the discovery of a copper ring with a spiral motif very similar to that found in Crete. The unusual double fortifications seem to date from two separate periods, the first from about 2200 BC and the second from between 1900 and 1700 BC. To date two thirds of the site has been excavated.

Asoka to the Muslims Rock edicts in the Girnar Hills indicate that the Mauryan emperor Asoka extended his domain into Gujarat. The Sakas or Scythians (AD 130-390) controlled it after the fall of the Mauryan Empire and under Rudradaman their empire contained Malwa (in Madhya Pradesh), Saurashtra, Kutch and Rajasthan. During the 4th and 5th centuries it formed part of the Gupta Empire which was succeeded by the Maitraka dynasty.

The **Gurjara-Pratiharas** governed during the 8th and 9th centuries and were replaced by the **Solanki** dynasty, under whom Gujarat attained its greatest territorial extent. The **Vaghela** dynasty followed this before its defeat by the Muslim **Ala-ud-din Khalji**, the King of Delhi. There then followed a long period of Muslim rule. **Ahmad I**, the first independent Muslim ruler of Gujarat founded Ahmadabad in 1411.

Gujarati provincial architecture The period from 1300 to 1550 saw a remarkable flowering of Gujarati provincial architecture. The new Muslim rulers made full use of the already highly-developed skills of Hindu and Jain builders and craftsmen. Percy Brown has shown how the mosques and tombs that resulted reflect the new combination of Muslim political power and architectural requirements with Hindu traditions. Thus, although the mosques obey strict Islamic principles they contain important features that are derived directly from Hindu and Jain precedents.

Mughal power The Mughal Humayun took **Malwa** and **Gujarat** in a brilliant campaign in 1534-5 but soon lost both. His son, **Akbar**, reclaimed both in a similarly daring and inspired military operation, securing the region for the Mughals for the nearly two centuries, terminated by the Marathas in the mid 18th century.

Colonial power In the scramble for trading bases the Dutch, English, French and Portuguese all established bases along the coast in the 17th century. The British East India Company's first headquarters in India was at Surat. It was later moved to Bombay. As British maritime supremacy became established all but the Portuguese at Daman and Diu withdrew. The state came under the control of the East India Company in 1818 and after the 1857 Mutiny was assumed by the Crown. It was then divided into Gujarat province, which had an area of 25,900 square km with the residuary comprising numerous princely states.

Until Independence Kathiawar was one of the most highly fragmented regions of India, having 86 distinct political units in just over 55,000 sq km. The largest, Junagadh, had an area of less than 9000 sq km and a population of under three quarters of a million in 1947.

Recent political history At Independence in 1947, Gujarat prpoper was incorporated into Bombay state. In 1956 Saurashtra and Kutch were added. On 1 May 1960 Bombay state was split into present day Maharashtra and Gujarat states and in 1961 India forcibly annexed Daman and Diu.

After Partition the possession of the **Rann of Kutch** was disputed by India and Pakistan. In 1965 they fought over it, and following the ceasefire on 1 July, division of the area was referred to an international tribunal. In 1968 the tribunal recommended that 90% should remain with India and 10% pass to Pakistan.

Government With the sole exception of 1977 Gujarat remained one of the Congress Party's chief strongholds throughout the period after Independence until 1989. It produced a number of national leaders after Mahatma Gandhi, including the first Prime Minister of the Janata Government in 1977, **Morarji Desai**. In November 1989 the Congress was reduced to holding 3 of the 26 Lok Sabha seats, the BJP taking 12 and the Janata Dal 11. The result showed that the Congress had lost the support of its traditional base, the backward castes and the Muslims. The BJP fought the campaign on a strongly pro-Hindu line, gathering support from the campaign at Ayodhya to build a temple on Ram's supposed birthplace. However, the Janata Dal and BJP did well partly because they did not contest against each other, making it possible for the opposition to the Congress to fight a united battle. In 1991 the Congress made up some of its lost ground.

Cuisine
Whilst Gujarat has a long coastline and an almost endless supply of fish and shellfish, strict Jainism in the past and orthodox Hinduism today have encouraged the widespread adoption of a vegetarian diet. Gujaratis base their diet on rice, wholemeal *chapati,* a wide variety of beans and pulses which are rich in protein, and also coconut and pickles; *thali* would include all these, and the meal end with sweetened yoghurt.

The dishes themselves are not heavily spiced, thoughtsomewhat sweeter than those of neighbouring states. Popular dishes include **kadhi***, a savoury yoghurt curry with chopped vegetables and variety of spices; **Undhyoo** a combination of potatoes, sweet potatoes, aubergines (egg plant) and beans cooked in an earthenware pot in the fire; Surat **Paunk** is made with tender kernels of millet, sugar balls, savoury twists and garlic chutney. Eating freshly prepared vegetable snacks from street vendors is popular. A large variety of farsan or light savoury snacks prepared from chick-pea and wheat flour is a speciality in the state.

The desserts are very sweet. Surat specialises in **gharis** made with butter, dried fruits and thickened milk and rich **halwa***.

AHMADABAD

Situated on the banks of the Sabarmati river, Ahmadabad is the largest city of Gujarat. At the end of the 16th century, 200 years after its foundation, some foreign travellers regarded it as equal to the finest European cities. The Mughal Emperor Jahangir was much less favourably impressed, calling it Gardabad – 'City of Dust'. It is now one of India's foremost industrial centres, the important trades being in cotton manufacture and commerce.

Population 3.5 million (1981) *Area* 104 sq km *Altitude* 53 m. Languages spoken: Gujarati, Hindi, English. Best season Nov-Mar. There are daily Indian Airlines flights connecting Ahmadabad with Bombay (492 km, 55 min) and Delhi (938 km, 1 hr 15 min). The airport is 10 km from the city centre.

	Jan	Feb	Mar	Apr	May	Jun	Jul	Aug	Sep	Oct	Nov	Dec	Av/Tot
Max (°C)	29	31	36	40	41	38	33	32	33	36	33	30	34
Min (°C)	12	15	19	23	26	27	26	25	24	21	16	13	21
Rain (mm)	4	0	1	2	5	100	316	213	163	13	5	1	823

The founding of the city The old city lies on the left (E) bank and has been subject to periods of prosperity and decline. It was founded in 1411 by **Sultan Ahmad I**, then King of Gujarat who made **Asaval**, an old Hindu town in the S his seat of power then expanded the place to become his capital. Almost constantly at war with the neighbouring Rajputs, fortifications were essential.

The city defences The Bhadra towers and the square bastions of the royal citadel were among the first structures to be erected. The city walls contained twelve gates, 139 towers and nearly 6,000 battlements. Most of these have been demolished. However, there are a large number of monuments, many of which are striking examples of Indian Islamic architecture. The provincial Gujarati style flourished from the mid 15th century largely due to the grand designs of its ruler. In addition to the religious buildings, many of the houses have façades beautifully decorated with wood carving.

Ahmadabad's "pols" The old part of the city are divided into unique, self-contained *pols*, or quarters,which are interesting to discover on foot. Huge wooden doors lead off from narrow lanes into a section of houses with decorative wooden screens and brackets where small communities of people practising a craft or skill lived. Merchants, weavers, woodworkers, printers and jewellers – each had their *pol*, their houses along winding alleys met in common courtyards and squares.

The new city The newer part of the city lying on the W bank is the site of Mahatama Gandhi's famous ashram from where he commenced his historic march in protect against the Salt Law in 1915. Modern Ahmadabad has its own share of showpieces designed by famous architects, among them Le Corbusier, Louis Kahn, Doshi and Correa. The *School of Architecture, the National Institute of Design* and the *Indian Institute of Management* are national centres of learning.

Local crafts and industry Ahmadabad has a long tradition in craftsmanship. This is not surprising as the numerous fine buildings indicate. Under Gujarati Sultans and Mughal Viceroys it was one of the most brilliant Indian cities. Its jewellers and goldsmiths are renowned, copper and brassworkers produce very fine screens and *pandans* (betel boxes). The carpenter produce fine *shisham wood* articles.

There are also skilled stonemasons, producers of lacquer boxes, ivory carvers and hand block printers using vegetable dyes and embroiderers producing exquisite pieces with beads and mirrors. These complement the modern industries such as pharmaceuticals and textiles.

Large scale development of cotton mills began later than in Bombay and Ahmadabad had the benefit of Bombay's experience as well as its own natural advantages of cheap land and labour and raw material on the spot.

Local Festivals Mid -Jan *Makar Sankranti* marks the end of winter and the start of the northerly journey of the sun. It is celebrated with kite flying, accompanied by colourful street markets and festivities. People of all ages join in, preparing in detail for the event. The kite strings are prepared with a paste of rice flour and powdered glass. The kites come in all colours, shapes and sizes, the best varieties reputedly being available in Manek Chowk and Tankshala Kalupur. The flying continues after sunset, as the kites are lit with candles. Since 1989 the Government of India has sponsored an international kite flying competition in association with the festival, setting up a special kite town "Patand Nagar" to accommodate it. Sep/Oct *Navaratri* honouring Goddess Amba, has special significance in the city which prepares for it for weeks and celebrates it for 9 days with a great deal of music and dancing, traditionally 'Garba Ras', (sadly often to westernized disco rhythm in some parts of the city). The custom of women balancing clay pots while they dance is still practised.

Places of Interest
Gujarati provincial buildings In the **Jami Masjid**, Ahmadabad contains one of the best examples of the second period of Gujarat's provincial architectural development. **Ahmad Shah I**, the founder of a new dynasty, embarked on an extraordinary building programme. In 1411 he laid the foundations of Ahmadabad, which was to be his new capital. By 1423 the Jami Masjid, regarded by many as one of the finest mosques in India, was completed. He had taken great interest in the whole project himself, and he encouraged others to construct monumental buildings as well. As a result there are over 50 mosques and tombs dating from his period within the city. **Mahmud I Begarha** (r 1459-1511) established the third phase of Gujarati provincial architecture, building some of India's most magnificent Islamic monuments, mainly mausoleums.

The central city

The plan of the city The citadel of the planned city formed a rectangle facing the river. A broad street was designed to run from Ahmad Shah's fortified palace in the citadel to the centre of the city, lying due E.

The citadel The ancient citadel built by Ahmad Shah I in 1411, now known as the **Bhadra**, lies between Nehru and Ellis bridge. It is named after an incarnation of the Hindu goddess Kali. In the E face is the **Palace**, now the Post Office, and other public buildings occupy the site, with the civil court to the S. **Sidi Saiyad's Mosque** (approx 1570) forms part of the wall on the NE corner. Ten windows of very fine stone tracery are patterns of branching tree are famous here. Note particularly those on the W wall.

In the SW corner of the Bhadra is *Ahmad Shah's Mosque* (1414) which was built as a private chapel. This is one of the oldest mosques in Ahmadabad. The façade is plain and the minarets unfinished. The internal pillars and the stone latticed ladies' gallery are thought to be part of a Hindu temple that stood here. By the entrance to the mosque is the **Ganj-i-Shahid**, the place where Muslims killed during the storming of the town, are buried.

The *Jami Masjid* Ideally, Ahmad Shah would have wished the main entrance to the Jami Masjid to face the processional route from the citadel to the centre of the city. Such a plan was impossible because the essential orientation of the Qibla

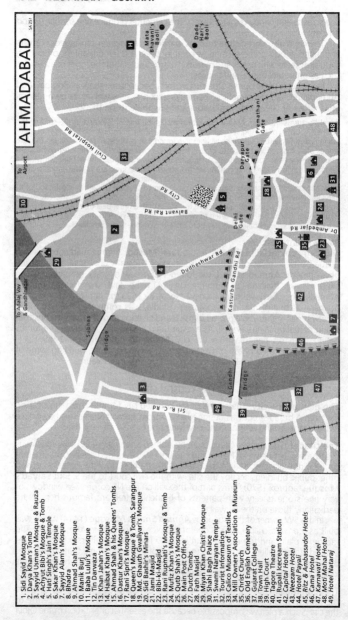

AHMADABAD

1. Sidi Sayid Mosque
2. Darya Khan's Tomb
3. Sayyid Usman's Mosque & Rauza
4. Achyut Bibi's Mosque & Tomb
5. Hari Singh's Temple
6. Sakar Khan's Mosque
7. Sayid Alam's Mosque
8. Bhadra
9. Ahmad Shah's Mosque
10. Manik Burj
11. Baba Lului's Mosque
12. Tin Darwaza
13. Khan Jahan's Mosque
14. Haibat Khan's Mosque
15. Ahmad Shah & his Queens' Tombs
16. Dastur Khan's Mosque
17. Rani Sipri's Mosque
18. Queen's Mosque & Tomb, Sarangpur
19. Md Ghauth Gwaliyari's Mosque
20. Sidi Bashir's Minars
21. Jami Masjid
22. Bibi-ki-Masjid
23. Rani Rupmati's Mosque & Tomb
24. Mufiz Khan's Mosque
25. Qutb Shah's Mosque
26. Main Post Office
27. Dutch Tombs
28. Fath Masjid
29. Miyan Khan Chisti's Mosque
30. Shahi Bagh Palace
31. Swami Narayan Temple
32. Tourist Information
33. Calico Museum of Textiles
34. Mill Owners' Association & Museum
35. Christ Church
36. Old English Cemetery
37. Gujarat College
38. Town Hall
39. High Court
40. Tagore Theatre
41. Rupali Icecream Station
42. Capital Hotel
43. Neezam Hotel
44. Hotel Payali
45. Ritz & Ambassador Hotels
46. Cama Hotel
47. Karnavati Hotel
48. Moti Mahal Hotel
49. Hotel Nataraj

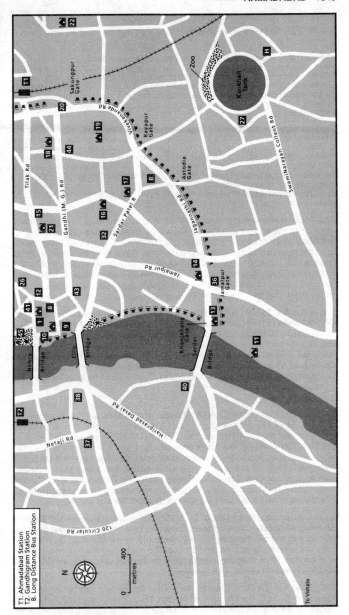

wall to Mecca meant that the main entrance to the mosque itself had to be in its E wall. Thus Ahmad Shah aligned the mosque so that the road would pass its N entrance. This is still the point at which you enter, by a flight of steps.

The sanctuary façade The beauty of the sanctuary is emphasised by the spacious paved courtyard in front, 75 m long by 65 m wide. The façade has a screen of arches flanked by a pillared portico. Brown suggests that "as a composition of solids and voids this façade is superb with its three main openings well balanced and in excellent proportion, the large central archway accentuated and supported by the richly moulded buttresses of the minarets." The two 'shaking minarets', once 26 m high, were destroyed by earthquakes in 1819 and 1957.

The sanctuary The tradition of the Hindu temple mandapa is developed in the Jami Masjid's remarkable sanctuary. Over 300 graceful pillars, set less than 2 metres apart, are organised in 15 square bays, each covered by a dome. The whole rises from a single storey through the two-storeyed side aisles to the three storey central aisle or nave. This comprises two pillared galleries resting on the columns of the lower hall. Such a development was itself an innovation, but the central octagonal lantern, rising through both storeys and covered by a dome, was also strikingly original. The gentle lighting effect is achieved by filtering light through the perforated stone screens which separate the galleries from the verandas outside, preventing any direct light falling in the building.

The Triple Gateway Immediately to the W of the entrance to Ahmad Shah's mosque is the triumphal archway known as **Tin Darwaza** (Three Gates, or **Tripolia**), which once led to the outer court of the royal citadel. At a later period it was surrounded by tamarind and palm trees, but is now crowded by shops, considerably diminishing its effect. Although it is on a comparatively small scale, being only 12 m high, Percy Brown compares it to Roman triple archways built by Constantine in the 4th century. He particularly draws attention to the fineness of the pointed arches, the best in India.

Royal tombs To the E of the Jami Masjid in **Manek Chowk**, is the **Tomb of Ahmad Shah I** (d1442), which was built by his son **Muhammad Shah** (d 1451) in the square Ahmad Shah had designed for the purpose. The central tomb is square with porticos on each side, a central dome, a coloured marble floor and stone *jali* screens. Across the street, in a state of disrepair, are the **Tombs of the Queens of Ahmad Shah**, with a decorative carved façade. There are eight large marble tombs and some smaller ones on a platform inside a rectangular courtyard surrounded by a cloister.

To the E and SE are several buildings from the third Gujarati Muslim period. 0.5 km SE of the Tombs of the Queens is **Dastur Khan's Mosque** (1486) which was built by one of Mahmud Beghara's Chief Ministers. This consists of a cloistered courtyard and the carved stone screens around this are very fine. A few steps to the E of the mosque is **Asa Bhil's** Mound, the site of the fort of the Bhil chief who founded Asaval. To the SE again, towards the Astodiya Gate, is **Rani Sipri's Mosque** (1514). Small but beautifully proportioned, it has two 15 m minarets. Rani Asni, one of Mahmud Beghara's wives, built what has been described as 'the first of a series of buildings more delicately ornate than any that preceded' (Hope). The square tomb (*rauza*) with *jali* screens stands in front of the mosque.

NE of the Astodia Gate and about 1.6 km S of the railway station are **Sidi Bashir's Shaking Minarets**, two tall towers connected by a bridge which was once the entrance to the old mosque. This was destroyed by the Marathas in 1753, and has now been replaced by a modern one. The minarets shake in sympathy with one another since they are cleverly built on flexible sandstone, possibly as a protection against earthquake damage.

SW of the Astodia Gate, towards the **Sardar Bridge** and just before reaching **Jamalpur Gate,** is the **Mosque of Haibat Khan,** one of Ahmad Shah's court nobles. The mosque is quite plain with a triple arched façade and small minarets.

Much of the building material came from Hindu temples as the decoration of the central dome indicates. The **old English Cemetery** is close to Jamalpur Gate.

The north

Sayyid Usman's mausoleum Immediately across the **Gandhi bridge**, on the W side of the Sabarmati River, is the **rauza** (tomb complex) of Sayyid Usman, one of the first examples of the Begarha style. Built about 1460, its pillared sanctuary is the first to have had minarets at each end. The pillars are beautifully made, though Percy Brown suggests that the building lacks a powerful central feature to give it overall unity.

Back on the E side of the Sabarmati River in the NW of the city near **Shahpur Gate** is the **Mosque of Shaikh Hasan Muhammad Chishti**, built in 1565. This has some of the finest tracery work in Ahmadabad.

There are several **Jain temples** in the city, the highly decorated, white marble **Hathi Singh Temple** (1848) just N of the Delhi Gate, dedicated to **Dharamanath**, the 5th Jain Tirthankar, is perhaps the most visited. Along the streets of Ahmadabad, it is quite common to see Jain *parabdis**.

The ***Rani Rupmati Masjid*** (early 16th century), in **Mirzapur district,** SW of Delhi Gate and just S of the Grand Hotel, incorporates Hindu and Islamic design. Rupmati was Princess of Dhar (Madhya Pradesh) and the Sultan's Hindu wife. It has a high central arch and two minarets which were damaged in the 1819 earthquake. The roof carries three domes, each above an entrance. The carvings in the gallery and the *mihrabs* are particularly attractive. Note how the dome is raised to allow light in around its base. **Rupmati's** tomb (mid 15th century) lies to the NE. The tombs themselves are decorated with Hindu motifs.

E of the Rani Masjid is the **Mosque of Muhafiz Khan** (1465), built by the governor of the city. Beautifully proportioned and superbly carved, with a triple-arched façade and corner minarets. To the SE is the **Swami Narayan Temple** (1850) which has an octagonal dome. Close by is the **Pinjrapol,** or Asylum for Animals. This is a simple enclosure surrounded by stalls for the animals.

At **Asarva,** about 1 km NE of **Daryapur Gate** are the **Wells of Dada Hari** (1499) and **Mata Bhavani** (c.1080). These *baolis** (**step wells**) are found in other parts of India, e.g. Mandu in Madhya Pradesh. Those in Gujarat are highly distinctive and often serve a dual purpose of being a cool, secluded sources of water during the summer and a place of religious sanctity. At **Dada Hari** (1499) there is a spiral staircase leading down to three lower platforms and a small octagonal well at the bottom, which has Arabic and Sanskrit letters carved on it. Mid-morning light is best. A short distance to the N is the even older **Mata Bhavani Well** with Hindu carvings, which reputedly dates from the Solanki period (1063-93). Again steps, 52 in all lead down through galleries to the water. The most highly decorated, however, is at **Adalaj Vav,** 19 km away (see under Excursions page 1050).

The British **Cantonment** lies approximately 5 km to the NE of Delhi Gate. Here there is an Anglican Church and a few public buildings. On the W bank of the Sabarmati there is the **Ahmadabad Mill Owner's Association Building** and the **Museum** , both of which were designed by **Le Corbusier** – see also Chandigarh, Haryana (page 421).

Ahmadabad has many other interesting mosques; only the briefest details are given here: **Khan Jahan's Mosque** (early 16th century), Khan Jahan Gate; **Mosque of Sayyid Alam** (1412), nr Nehru Bridge; **Mosque, Tomb and Madrasa of Shujaat Khan** (1695), nr the Lal Gate of the Bhadra; **Mosque of Qutb Shah** (1449), nr Delhi Gate; **Fath Masjid** (c.1450-1500), between Daryapur and Delhi Gates; **Mosque of Dada Hari** (1499), NE of Daryapur Gate; **Sakar Khan's Mosque** (late 15th century), nr Kalupur Gate; **Muhammad Salih Badakhshi's Mosque**; **Mosque of Malik Alam** (reputedly 1422), 1.6 km S of city;

Mosque of Miyan Khan Chishti (1465), S suburbs; **Achyut Bibi's Mosque** (1469), S Ahmadabad; **Bibi-ki-Masjid** (1454), Rajpur; **Queen's Mosque and Tomb** (early 16th century), nr Sarangpur Gate; **Mosque of Muhammad Ghauth Gwaliyari** (c. 1565), Sarangpur quarter; **Rani's Masjid** (c.1500-15), nr village of Kochrab, S of Ahmadabad; **Blessed on All Sides Mosque** (early 16th century), Isanpur, between Vatva and Rasulabad; **Mosque and Rauza of Sayyid Uthman** (1460), Isanpur; **Mosque of Baba Lului** (1560), 2 km SW on banks of Sabarmati. There are also many other tombs in and around the city.

Kankaria Lake, SE of the city is a remarkable artificial lake constructed in 1451 which has 34 sides each 60 m long. It is now a popular local picnic spot. There is a large zoo and children's park – see Parks and Zoos.

Sabarmati Ashram, 6 km W of centre. Open 0830-1200, 1430-1900 (1 Apr – 30 Sep), otherwise 0830-1200, 1430-1830. Last admission, 1 hour before closing. Free. Daily *Son et Lumière* in English at 2030 and Gujarati at 1930. Rs 5.

Gandhi's Ashram was founded in 1917 and disbanded in 1933. It was the starting point for the Mahatma's celebrated 24 day, 385 km march to *Dandi* in March 1930. Gandhi and 81 colleagues, followers and supporters in the Independence Movement began the march, and by the end there were 90,000 protesting against the unpopular British Salt Tax Laws (the manufacture of salt was a government monopoly). The choice of salt was clever in that it was a commodity every peasant used and could understand.

At Dandi beach on 6 April **Gandhi** went down to the sea and made a small amount of salt, for which he was promptly arrested. In the following months, thousands of Indians followed his example and were arrested by the British.
    There is a picture gallery depicting Gandhi's life in photographs and paintings. A 5 min film on his life is shown occasionally from 0800-1900. Gandhi's original room of simple mats, desk, spinning wheel overlooks the central prayer corner and the river and is undisturbed. Next door are some of Gandhi's meagre possessions – *dhoti**, bedsheet etc. The **E** *Gandhi Ashram Guest House*, T 407742, is opp the Ashram and is run by the TCGL (see Hotels).

Calico Museum, Shahibagh, is an attractive old *haveli* in Shahi Bagh gardens, part of the Sarabhai Foundation. Some exhibits date from the 17th century and include a rich displays of heavy brocades, fine embroideries, saris, carpets, turbans, Maharajahs' costumes and royal Mughal tents. Regarded by many as one of the finest museums of its kind in the world and well worth a visit. It also houses an outstanding collection of Jain manuscripts. Open 1030-1230, 1430-1730. Tours 1015-1115, 1430-1530. A 15th century Jain temple is included in the tour. Free. Excellent library of textiles. Museum shop sells cards, reproductions and books.

Utensils Museum, Vishala under Excursions.

Hotels Airport 10 km, most about 3 km from railway and mainly central.
C *Cama*, Khanpur. T 25281, Cable: Hotelcama, Telex: 0121-6377 Cama in. 55 a/c rm, with bath, TV, fridge. Restaurant, bar, exchange, car hire, pool, credit cards. Modern, efficient with good restaurant. Recommended. **C** *Natraj*, nr Income Tax Office, Ashram Rd. T 448747, Cable: Atithi, Telex: 0121-6685 Shiv in. 25 rm. Central a/c. 6 km rly. Restaurant, car hire, credit cards. Comfortable. **C** *Karnavati*, Shri Cinema building, Ashram Rd. T 402161-7, Cable: Shreehotel, Telex: 0121-6519 Cscoin. 48 rm. Central a/c. Restaurant, coffee shop, exchange, Amex, Diners, Visa. **C** *Rivera*, Khanpur Rd. T 24201, Cable: Riverhotel, Telex: 0121-6598 Stay in. 69 rm, central a/c. Restaurant, liquor shop, coffee shop, exchange, car hire, credit cards.
    D *Ambassador*, Khanpur Rd. T 353244, Cable: Hotambass, 31 rm with bath, some a/c. Restaurant, car hire, TV, Amex, Diners. Basic but clean. **D** *Capital*, Behind Gujarat Samachar, Khanpur. T 24633-7, Cable: Hotcap. 35 rm, some a/c. 24 hr restaurant, travel, Diners. **D** *Capri*, Relief Rd (nr cinema). T 24643-6, Cable: Capri. 27 rm, some a/c. Restaurant, 24 hr rm service, exchange,. **D** *City Palace*, opp Calico Dome, Relief Rd. T 386574. 18 rm, some a/c. TV lounge, Visa. **D** *Kingsway*, GPO Rd (nr Relief Cinema). T 26221, Cable: Kingsway. 34 rm with bath and TV, some a/c. Restaurant, car hire. **D** *Meghdoot*, Gupta Chambers, nr New Cloth Market. T 364614-7, Cable: Hotmegh. 27 rm, some a/c. TV, 24 hr rm service, Visa. **D** *Panshikura*, nr Town Hall, Underbridge, Ellisbridge. T 402960, Cable: Hotpan. 24 a/c rm. Restaurant, Amex, Diners. **D** *Prithvi*, nr L.G. Hospital, L.G. Corner, Maninagar. T 366634. 14 rm, some a/c. A/c restaurant, car hire, TV. **D** *Ritz*, Lal Darwaja, nr Nehru Bridge. T 353637-9, Cable: Ritz. 19 rm with bath and TV, some a/c. Restaurant, exchange, Amex, Diners. Old

building, full of character, in peaceful garden on riverside. Helpful staff, but note 9 am checkout. Recommended. **D** *Roopalee*, Lal Darwaja. T 350814. 28 rm, central a/c. Rm service, travel, Diners.

There are a few **cheap** hotels around the city, many in the centre. Near the Kwality restaurant and Capri Hotel is the **E** *Plaza* with non a/c rooms with bath. Somewhat grubby. Close by, just off Relief Rd is the **E** *Metropol*, T 354988 and the **E** Mehul. Both have non a/c rooms with bath, some in the *Mehul* have balconies. **E** *Ashiana*, Murtuza Manzil, opp Soneri Masjid, Salapose Rd, Khas Bazaar, T 351114-5. 13 non a/c rm without bath. Rm service. **E** *Hotel Esquire*, opp Sidi Saiyid Mosque, nr the British Lib, is clean and popular. **E** *Natraj* is next to the Ahmed Khan Mosque while **E** *Relax*, opp Central Telegraph Office, is fairly modern. Rm with bath. **E** *Railway Retiring Rooms* at Ahmadabad Junction station and the **E** Hotel Alankar with 26 rm opp Kalupuir Rly Station in the town centre. The **E** *Gandhi Ashram Guest House*, T 407742, opp Ashram, Sabarmati (TCGL). 10 rm, most non a/c. 7 km. Simple meals available. Out of town but good. Reserve in advance.

Restaurants Indian and Continental *Aab-o-Daana* and *Rangoli*, Hotel Cama, Khanpur, T 25281; *Haveli* and *Jade Room*, Hotel Karnavati, Ashram Rd, T 402161; Opp, the *Saba* does good *thali* meals; *Riwaaz*, Hotel Riviera, Khanpur, T 24201; *Khidmat*, Hotel Panshikura, nr Town Hall, Ashram Rd, T 77100; *Patang*, Chinubhai Centre, Ashram Rd, T 77899. Revolving restaurant with buffet or à la carte. Attractive decor, live classical music at night. 1230-1500, 1900-2300. Reservations essential at night, T 78866. *Kwality*, Relief Rd, T 20309. Also Chinese. A/c. 1200-1600, 1900-2300. Recommended; *Sheeba*, opp Telephone Exchange, Navrangpura, T 440803; *Angithi*, Trade Centre, opp Sardar Patel Stadium; *Side Walk*, Shilp Building, Navrangpura; *Regale*, National Buildings, Ashram Rd. *Volga*, nr Deepali Cinema, Ashram Rd, T 78533. A/c. Also Punjabi food. 1130-1530 and 1900-2300; *Neelam*, Teen Darwaza, T 368814. 1200-1600, 1900-2300; *Paramount*, Khas Bazar, T 390083; *Old Madras Brahmin's Hotel*, opp the Civil Court, T 391005, S Indian, 0830-2200; *Chetna* next to Krishna Cinema, Relief Rd, is open for Indian meals 1100-2300; PD Gati, BG Rly Station is open 24 hr for Indian food.

Gujarati *Vishala Village Hotel*, Sarkhej, Highly recommended, see under excursions; *Chetna*, Relief Rd. A recreation of a traditional village. Veechar Utensil Museum is dedicated to domestic implements. Folk dancers in the evening. Negotiate a return price with the autorickshaw wallah; *Payal*, Khadia Char Rasta, T 362644; *Gaurav Dining Hall*, Shiv cinema compound. Very good *thali*; *Gopi*, NRVS Hospital, nr Town Hall, T 76388; *Saurashtra Dining Hall*, nr Town Hall. *Azad Halwai* sells good sweets. *Havmor*, opp Krishna Cinema has good ice creams.

Chinese Most of the hotel restaurants offer some dishes. Otherwise try *Kwality*.

Bars Prohibition is in force. There are consequently no bars but some of the larger hotels have liquor stores. Liquor permits may be obtained by foreign nationals and for medical reasons. Temporary permits may be issued at the liquor stores.

Clubs Dariapur Gymkhana, Dariapur Dabgharwad. At Ellis Bridge: Gymkhana, opp Nursery, Netaji Rd, T 643676; Law Garden Gymkhana, Old Sharadamandir Char Rasta, T 461548; Orient Club, nr Gujarat College railway crossing, T 76446; Paldi Gymkhana, Pritamnagar Dhal; Rajanagar Club, nr Patmal Garden, T 411993. Gujarat Club, Bhadra, T 393589. Rajpath Club, Thaltej Satellite Rd, T 440499. Reform Club, Nehru Bridge Corner, Ashram Rd, T 77935.

Banks The State Bank of India, Tilak Rd.

Shopping Arts and Crafts The state produces excellent textiles, plus embroidery (bead and mirror work), tie-and-dye, zari on cloth. Also lacquered furniture and wood carvings, jewellery and pottery. Shops are usually open from 0900-1900, most close on Sun. Manek Chowk is the main bazaar. *Garvi* and *Gujari*, on Ashram Rd, nr Times of India office, Ashram (a Govt of Gujarat Undertaking). Three floors of well displayed and carefully selected handicrafts from all over the state. Textiles, rugs, lacquered and inlaid furniture, rosewood beads, wool shawls. Open 1030-1400, 1500-1900, closed Wed. *Sewa* is a Muslim women's cooperative producing very fine shadow embroidery.

Photography: *Ahmadabad Photo Depot*, nr Model Cinema and *New Navrang Studio*, opp Jama Masjid, on Gandhi Rd, T 380675; *Ganesh Colour Lab*, No 14 Spectrum Complex, Salpose Rd, T 25488; *Gujarat Colour Lab*, Ashram Rd, T 78108.

Local Transport Yellow top taxis. Fares negotiable. **City Bus Service**. Available from main bus station, Lal Darwaza, railway station and all major points in the city. Min fare about Re 0.70, max Rs 2.30. **Auto rickshaws**. Min Rs 2, subsequently according to chart (ask to see the revised rate card). Night charges are quite high. **Tourist Taxis** are available for hire from various agencies. The usual tarriff for 3hr/30 km is about Rs 125 (petrol), Rs 100 (diesel). For 5hr /50 km Rs 225 (petrol) Rs 175. For 8hr /80 km Rs 275 and Rs 225. For 12hr/100 km Rs 300 and Rs 275. Basic rate per km Rs 2 (petrol) Re 1.75 (diesel).

Sports Outdoor Sports at the Sardar Patel Stadium. *Boating* at the Kankaria Lake complex. *Swimming* at the Ahmadabad Municipal Corporation's nine swimming pools, the best of which are at Lal Darwaza Bus Terminus, Sardar Patel Stadium and Kankaria Lake.

Sports clubs/associations: Gujarat Cricket Association, Bhadra, T 3950543. Players club, Motera, Sabarmati. Runners Club of Ahmadabad, c/o Dr Mukund Mehta, 8B Nobles, Ashram Rd, T 76543. Sports Club of Gujarat, Sardar Patel Stadium, Navrangpura, T 440371.

Museums Shreyas Folk Museum   Comprehensive collection of folk arts, crafts and costumes from Saurashtra and Kutch. Exhibits include embroideries, utensils, handicrafts, weapons and carts. Also children's section with costumes, puppets, folk art. Open 0900-1100, 1600-1900, closed Wed.

Tribal Research and Training Institute Museum   Gujarat Vidyapith, Ashram Rd, T 79741. Open 1130-1930, closed Sun, Sat early closing at 1430.

N.C. Mehta Collection at Sanskar Kendra, Paldi, T 78369, T75607. Collection of rare Gujarati and Rajasthani miniature paintings in a Le Corbusier designed building. Open 0900-1100, 1600-1900, closed Mon.

Contemporary Art Gallery, nr Orient club, Ellis Bridge. Gujarat Kala Mandir Art Gallery nr Law College Bus Stand, Ellis Bridge. Jyoti Art Gallery, 587 Tilak Rd. T 336996. Hutheesing Visual Art, opp Gujarat University, Navrangpura. Lalit Kala Akademi, nr Ellis Bridge Gymkhana.

Sardar Valabhai Patel National Memorial, Shahibaug. T 65027. Open daily 0930-1730, except Wed.

Parks and Zoos *Large Deer Park* next to Sarita Udyan in Indrada Village, outside the city. *Sundervan Snake Garden*, off M Dayanand Rd with its collection of snakes. Snake handling shows daily.

Useful Addresses Foreigners Regional Registration Office, Police Commissioner's Office, Shahibaug, T 333999. Police T 100; Fire T 101; Ambulance T 102. The British Library is opp the Sidi Saiyid Mosque and is a/c with toilets.

Hospitals and Medical Services Akhand and Ayurvedic Hospital, opp Victoria Garden, T 393576. Ch. Nagri Hospital, Ellis Bridge, T 444724. Civil Hospital, Asarwa, T 66391. ESIC General Hospital, Bapunagar, T 363734/5. Sardar Patel Hospital, Maninagar, T 50573. Sheth Vadilal Sarbhai General Hospital, Ellis Bridge, T 78123. LG Hospital, Maninagar, T 52236-8. Shardaben General Hospital, Nikoli Darwaza, T 370021. Victoria Jubilee Hospital, Panchkuwa Darwaza, T 361080.

Post and Telegraph Central Post Office, Salapose Road, Mirzapur. Also many P.O.s in around the city.

Places of Worship *Hindu*: Bhadra Kali Temple, Gita Mandir, Swaminarayan Temple, Jagannathji Temple at Berhampura. *Muslim*: Jama Masjid, Sidi Saiyad Mosque, Shah Alam Rauza. *Jain*: Hutheesing Jain Temple. *Parsee*: Khamasa Agyari, Kankaria Agyari. *Christian*: St Xavier's Catholic Church, Mirzapur; I.P. Mission, nr Victoria Garden; Methodist Church, Shahpur, Methodist Church, opp Bible House; Marthoma Church, Christian Society, Behrampura; St Mary's Jacobite Church, Christian Society, Behrampura. *Jewish*: Magen Abraham Synagogue, Khamasa, opp Parsee Agyari.

Travel Agents and Tour Operators *Travel Corporation of India* (TCI), nr Natraj Theatre, behind Handloom house, Ashram Rd, T 407061. *Skyjet Aviation Ltd.*, opp Ritz Hotel, Lal Darwaza, T 350747. *Sherry Tours and Travels*, Mirzapur, T 22511. *Sita World Travels*, Suflam Buildings, Mithakhali Underbridge, Ashram Rd. *Good Wind Travels*, No 6 Sahyog Buildings, opp Dinbhai Tower, Lal Darwaza, T 391182. *Ajanta Travels*, 1 Ajanta Commercial Centre, Ashram Rd, T 449037. *Gujarat Tourism*, HK House, Ashram Rd, T 449683.

Tourist Offices and Information Tourism Corporation of Gujarat (TCGL), H.K. House, Ashram Rd, nr Hotel Natraj, T 449172. Director of Tourism, Sachivalaya, Gandhinagar, T 20601. Tourist Office, Ahmadabad Municipal Corporation, nr Khamasa Gate. T 365610-1. Open 1100-1800. Also at airport, T 67568. Open 0600-2200, and Railway station, T 347745. Open 0600-2200. Rajasthan Tourism Development Corporation, Karnavati Society, Usmanpura. T 405289. U.P. Tourism Development Corporation, Smrutikunj Society, opp Asia Engineering School. Jammu & Kashmir Tourism Development Corporation, Indian Airlines Building, Lal Darawaza. T 391043.

Tours Tourist Office, Ahmadabad Municipal Corporation conducts city sightseeing tours. Enquiries and Reservations T 365610-1. Morning tour: Sidi Saiyad, Hutheesing Jain Temple, Sardar Patel Museum, Calico Museum, Dadahari step well, Lake Kankaria, Geeta Mandir, Shah Alam Mosque. Rs 20. Afternoon Tour: Gandhi Ashram, Vechaar Utensils Museum, Snake Farm and Municipal Museum. Rs 20.

TCGL Tours by a/c coach, usually 0800-1430, about Rs 25; Full day Rs 48. Tour 1: Adalaj StepWell, Gandhi Ashram, Hutheesing Temple – Lunch – Badshah No Hajiro, Jama Masjid, Teen Darwaza, Calico Museum, Sarkhej, Vishala. Tour 2: Adalaj, Mohera – Lunch – Sharyas, Sarkhej, Vishala, Vechaar Museum. Tour 3: Hutheesing, Swaminarayan Temple, Ratan Pol, Manek Chowk, Rani No Hajira, Jama Masjid, Badshah No Hajira, Teen Darwaza, Shopping on Ashram Rd – Lunch – NC Mehta Museum, Airport. Children's Special Tour (Bal Yatra) on Sun 0800 for Rs 12.

TCGL also runs two 5-day package tours: Saurashtra Darshan, every Fri, Rs 500; N Gujarat-Rajasthan Tour, first and third Sat in month, Rs 645.

Note Ahmadabad is not an international airport but some airlines are represented.

International Airlines Offices Air India, Premchand House, nr High Court, Ashram Rd, T 448853. Indrama (for British Airways), Sarita Darshan, Ashram Rd, T 78488. Jet Air (Singapore Airlines, Gulf Air, Kuwait Airways), Neptune Tower, Ashram Rd, T 78817-8. Metro Travel Agency (Lufthansa), N.K. House, Ashram Rd, T 77424. Ajanta Tours and Travels, (Kenya Airways), K.B. Commercial Centre, nr Sahayoga Building, Lal Darwaza, T 382527. Samveg Agency (Swissair), N.L. Trust Building, Tilak Rd, T 380401. Sheeba Travels (Ethiopian Airlines), Metro Commercial Centre, Navrangpura, T 445317.

Air Indian airlines have two daily flights from Delhi (1 hr 15 min) and Bombay (55 min) direct and an additional Delhi – Jaipur – Jodhpur – Ahmadabad – Bombay (and v.v) flight. There is also a Madras-Bangalore-Ahmadabad service three times a week. Indian Airlines, City Office and Cargo, Lal Darwaza, nr Roopalee Cinema, T 353333, open 1000-1315 and 1415-1715. Airport, T 67356-8. The airport is 10 km from the city centre. Airport bus leaves from Lal Darwaza at regular intervals to meet flights. Approx Rs10.

Rail Ahmadabad is on a broad gauge line from Bombay and a metre gauge line from Delhi. **Old Delhi:** *Aravalli Exp* 9932. daily, 0545, 23 hr 45 min; *Delhi Mail* 9902. daily, 0825, 23 hr 5 min; *Delhi Exp* 9904. daily, 1800, 25 hr; *Ashram Exp* 2906. daily, 1700, 17 hr. **Bombay Central:** *Bombay Gandhidham Kutch Exp* 9032. daily, 0500, 8 hr 30 min; *Gujarat Exp* 9012. daily, 0715, 9 hr; *Gujarat Mail* 9002. daily, 2200, 8 hr 45 min. **Udaipur City:** *Ahmadabad-Udaipur Exp* 9644. daily, 2315, 9 hr. **Bhopal:** *Rajkot-Bhopal Exp* 1269. daily, 1910, 13 hr 50 min. **Jaipur:** *Delhi Mail* 9902. daily, 0825, 15 hr 35 min; *Delhi Exp* 9904. daily, 1800, 16 hr 20 min; *Ashram Exp*, 2906. daily, 1750, 16 hr 10 min. **Ajmer:** *Aravalli Exp* 9932, daily, 0545, 12 hr 50 min; *Delhi Mail* 9902, daily, 0825, 11 hr 55 min; *Delhi Exp* 9904, daily, 1800, 12 hr 35 min; *Ashram Exp* 2906. daily, 1700, 8 hr 30 min.

Ujjain *Rajkot-Bhopal Exp* 1269, daily, 1910, 9 hr 15 min; *Sabarmati Exp* 9165, daily, 2030, 9 hr 10 min: **Mt. Abu** *Aravalli Exp* 9932, daily, 0545, 5 hr 5 min; *Delhi Mail* 9902, daily, 0825, 4 hr 28 min; *Ashram Exp* 2906, daily, 1700, 3 hr 15 min; *Delhi Exp* 9904, daily, 1800, 4 hr 35 min; *Surya Nagri Exp* 2908, daily, 2115, 3 hr 18 min. **Bhavnagar** *Ahmadabad Bhavnagar Exp* 9810, daily, 1630, 6 hr 5 min; *Girnar Exp* 9846, daily, 2045, 8 hr 15 min. **Junagadh** *Girnar Exp* 9846, daily, 2045, 10 hr 50 min; *Somnath Mail* 9824, daily, 2155, 12 hr 30 min. **Veraval** *Girnar Exp* 9846, daily, 2045, 12 hr 55 min; *Somnath Mail* 9824, daily, 2155, 14 hr 55 min. **Jamnagar** *Saurashtra Exp* 9215, daily, 2100, 6 hr 55 min; *Saurashtra Mail* 9005, daily, 0555, 6 hr 55 min. **Ahmadabad Junction Railway Station** Enquiries T 343535, Reservations T 344657, open for First Class 0730-1530 and Second Class 0700-1430 and 1500-2200.

Road Ahmadabad is situated on **NH8** which is a major route from Delhi to Bombay that passes through Udaipur, Ajmer and Jaipur. **NH8A** branches off from Ahmadabad towards Kandla in Kutch, and **NH8B** towards Porbander. Distances to some destinations are: **Bombay** 492 km, **Vadodara** 113 km, **Surat** 120 km, **Udaipur** 287 km, **Rajkot** 216 km, **Porbander** 394 km, **Palitana** 217 km and **Sasan Gir** 217 km.

Bus Ahmadabad is well connected with other cities and towns in Gujarat and with neighbouring states. The State Transport corporations of Gujarat, Rajasthan, Madhya Pradesh and Maharashtra provide services with Bombay (11 hr), Mt Abu (7 hr), Indore, Ujjain, Bhopal, Pune, Udaipur, Jaipur ad Jodhpur as well as to towns within the state. Central Bus Station, Geeta Mandir, T 344764-6. Reservations open 0700-1900. Advance booking for night services 1500-2300, luxury coach services 1030-1800. Private bus companies also operate services, often at night. *Punjab Travels,* Delhi Darwaza, T 343777. *Sena Travel Agency,* outside

Astodia Darwaza, Bhutni Ambli, T 22799 *J.K. Travels*, Ashram Rd, Dinesh Hall, T 20222 *Pawan Travels*, Pritannagar first Dhal, Ellis Bridge, T 78839.

Excursions *Vishala*, Sarkhej Rd, Vasana. 5 km is a purpose built showpiece of a collection of huts along clay paths which capture the spirit of a traditional Gujarati village. It began as an excellent vegetarian restaurant in 1978 but has grown since to include a museum, live performances of music, dance and puppet shows, as well as craftsmen at work and an excellent shop (open until 2200). You can pick up hand thrown pots, handloom linens, hand crafted shoes, clothes, brassware or embroidery. Good quality but not cheap.

Arrive in good time for lunch (1100-1300) or dinner (1920-2300), when you may receive the traditional greeting of flowers and a *tilak** mark on you forehead. The meal is an experience well worth travelling out for. You sit cross-legged at low tables (chairs available), eat off green leaves and drink from clay tumblers. The portions are generous and there is a large variety of traditional dishes, breads, chutneys, ending with an Indian sweet and nutty ice-cream.

The **Utensils Museum** has an exceptional collection of rare brass and copper utensils, water pots, old betel nut boxes and containers used for temple rituals. Open 1700-2300 weekdays, 1000-1300, 1700-2200 Sun.

Sarkhej, 8 km SW of the city centre is really a suburb of Ahmadabad was once a country retreat of the Muslim rulers. It is noted for its **Rauza** (1445-51), the fine architectural complex of mosque, palace, pavilions and tombs, all grouped around a stepped tank. The style shows distinct Hindu influence. The Dutch established an indigo factory nearby.

Adalaj, 17 km N of Ahmadabad. The *baoli** or step-well at **Adalaj Vav** (1502) is one of the finest in India. A long flight of steps descends to the water. Ornately carved pillars and cross beams create open spaces and four storeys that are quite striking. Queen Rudabai built it to provide the traveller with a cool and pleasant refuge from the summer heat.

Gandhinagar, 23 km N of Ahmadabad. When Bombay state was divided along linguistic lines into Maharashtra and Gujarat in 1960, a new capital city was planned for Gujarat. In the spirit of independence, this new administrative centre was named after the state's most famous modern son, Mahatma Gandhi. As with Chandigarh, Le Corbusier was instrumental in the design. The numbered sectors are similarly impersonal. Construction began in 1965 and the Secretariat was completed in 1970. Regular buses from Ahmadabad.

Hotels C *Express Haveli*, Sector 2, opp Sachivalaya. T 23463, Cable: Express Haveli. 84 rm, some a/c. Restaurant, exchange, shops, travel, TV, credit cards. The **F** *Youth Hostel* in Sector 16 is very good and in Sector 11 is the **F** *Panthik Ashram* which is a government Rest House. There are other *Guest Houses* around Pethapur and Sachivalaya.

AHMADABAD TO UDAIPUR

The main route into Rajasthan from Ahmadabad crosses the short stretch of flat alluvial plains formed by the Sabarmati river before climbing gently from Himatnagar onto the peninsula. The Gujarat-Rajasthan border is approximately half way in the 250 km journey.

From Ahmadabad take the **NH8** NE through **Chamunda Mata** (7 km). After 3 km there is a right turn to **Naroda** (1 km). The road crosses rich canal-irrigated land, using water from the *Hathmati river,* from here well to the NE of Himatnagar. Continue on the **NH8**, crossing the railway after 5 km, and going on through **Parantji** (46 km), which lies on the Tropic of Cancer. The road then passes through **Hajipur** (16 km) to **Himatnagar** (20 km). A left turn in Himatnagar leads to **Khed Brahma** (50 km), **Ambaji** (99 km) and **Mount Abu** (148 km).

Continue on **NH8** out of **Himatnagar** to **Rajgadh** (20 km) and **Shamlapur** (22 km). A road on the left after 2 km leads to the **Sarvodaya ashram**. Continue straight through **Shamlaji** ((2 km) **Ratanpur** (10 km), on the border between Gujarat and Rajasthan. Continue to **Sisod** (28 km), **Kherwara** (9 km), **Parsad** (31 km) and **Barfa** (24 km). The NH 8 then goes straight to **Udaipur** (25 km).

AHMADABAD TO INDORE

The route goes SE to Kheda then E to Nadiad across the flat plain. Politically the region has been an area of fragmentation. Dozens of tiny states and principalities formed, broke up and re-formed over the centuries before the British arrived. The British simply froze the situation by recognising existing Princes. The smallest of the states was 2 sq km and had a population of 96. Much of this area will benefit from the proposed Narmada High level canal which is intended to run all the way from SE of Vadodara to Ahmadabad. The road then runs E through Dohad, climbing onto the plateau and crossing the Gujarat-Madhya Pradesh border at an altitude of about 550 m.

From Ahmadabad take the NH8 SE to **Chandula Lake** (5 km) and **Kaira** (32 km), an ancient settlement, possibly dating from as early as 1400 BC. The first firm evidence of its existence, coming from **Chalukya** inscriptions, can be dated at the 5th century AD. In the 18th century it was acquired by a family named Babi but was taken in 1736 by the Marathas. In 1803 the British took it and developed a military garrison. The **Church** (early 19th century) dates from this time as does the **Town Hall**. An important trading centre on the route from Cambay into N India, it has a Jain temple with superb carving and a church consecrated by Bishop Heber in 1822. Today **Kaira** is one of the major centres of India's *dairy industry*.

Continue 14 km to a road junction where the **NH8** turns S to **Anand** and **Vadodara**. Continue straight on 21 km to **Nadiad** (*Population* 150,000), the largest town in Kaira District. 42 km to its N is the small walled town of **Kapadvanj** which is famous for making glass, leather containers for ghee and soap. Half way between Nadiad and Kapadvanj is the small town of Lasundra, noted for its hot and slightly sulphurous springs, constantly welling up with water at approximately 46°C.

Nearby, **Nalsarovar**, 64 km E of Ahmadabad, is an extensive lake noted for its water-birds. Some indigenous species come here after breeding but it is the migratory ducks, flamingoes and geese that are the main attraction. Season – Nov – Feb. Dec and Jan best. Govt *Holiday Home* near the lake can be booked through the Tourist Office, Ahmadabad.

From **Nadiad** continue through **Dakor** (34 km), where there is a large lake and a temple that is the centre of pilgrimage in October-November. The road runs right alongside the single track broad gauge spur railway line from **Ghodra** to **Cambay**. It passes through **Sevalia** (20 km) and crosses the **River Mahi** (2 km) by a 500 m long bridge to **Tuwa** (10 km), then on to **Godhra** (18 km).

From Godhra the road keeps close to the railway line and climbs steadily onto the plateau. After 15 km it crosses the railway line, passes through **Piplod** (11 km) to **Dohad** (37 km). It then runs through **Katawara** (11 km) to the

Gujarat-Madhya Pradesh border (11 km) and on to **Karawa** (16 km). It then runs across the great expanse of Deccan lava country E through **Jhabua** (6 km) to **Sardarpur** (45 km). Here there is a right turn to the Bagh caves. The main route goes across the watershed between the **Narmada River** catchment area and the **Ganga** catchment, through **Mangode** (17 km), **Dhar** (25 km) and **Jetpura** (4 km) to **Ghat Billod** (23 km), where it crosses the **Chambal River**. A road on the right leads to **Mhow** (29 km; 600 m), an important cantonment town. **Indore** is a further 37 km from **Ghat Billod**.

AHMADABAD TO BOMBAY

The route S from Ahmadabad crosses the fertile alluvial plains of the Sabarmati and Mahi Rivers before entering the Konkan region. In the N the narrow belt of alluvial plains, less than 12 km wide, gradually gives way southwards to broken hills. Inland parallel ridges reach between 500-600 m. Rice dominates agriculture further S, but ragi (finger millet) and pulses are also common. The coastal lowlands are increasingly lush towards the S. On the route to Bombay there are a number of important and interesting places. **Vadodara** (formerly Baroda), was one of the largest Princely States. **Broach** was an important trading centre and **Surat** was the most advanced port and market until superseded by Bombay. **Daman** was one of Portugal's three coastal stations in India.

It should take no more than two hours to reach Vadodara directly. From Ahmadabad take **NH8** S. **Kaira**, centre of the local dairying industry is 32 km. **Nadiad**, **Anand** and **Vasad** are towns in the fertile plain between the **Sabarmati** and **Mahi** rivers. (See above)

In **Kaira** keep on the **NH8**. A road on the right goes to *Khambhat* (Cambay; 61 km).

Cambay 97 km S of Ahmadabad at the mouth of the **Mahi river**. This was Ahmadabad's seaport. At one time Gujarat was known as Cambay. Queen Elizabeth 1st's ambassadors to the Mughal court bore letters for Akbar that were addressed to the King of Cambay. An English factory was established in the **Nawab's Kothi** in 1600 in the wake of Dutch and Portuguese ones. Surat later developed at Cambay's expense and the port declined further when silting presented problems for shipping. It nevertheless bears a rich heritage and was well known to Arab traders. **Ala-ud-din Khalji** sacked it in 1304, and until 1400 it was governed by the Kings of **Anhilwara** (Patan).

   The **Jama Masjid** (1325) is built from materials taken from desecrated Hindu and Jain temples. The enclosed façade to the sanctuary is similar to that of the **Quwwat-ul-Islam** mosque at Delhi – see page 166). The design heavily influenced the Gujarati architectural style.
Return to the **NH8** and continue towards **Nadiad** (14 km). Bypass bears right just before town. **NH8** turns S through Vasad (41 km) to **Vadodara** (21 km).

Vadodara

Population 950,000 *Altitude* 35 m. *Area* 139 sq km. Indian Airlines connects Vadodara with Bombay (425 km) and Delhi (995 km). The airport is 6 km from the city centre.

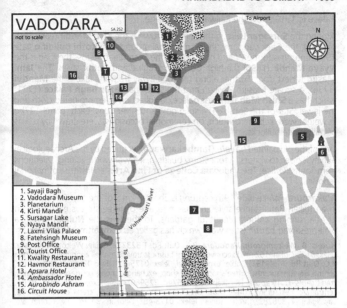

VADODARA SA 252
not to scale

To Airport

N

To Bombay

Vishwamurti River

1. Sayaji Bagh
2. Vadodara Museum
3. Planetarium
4. Kirti Mandir
5. Sursagar Lake
6. Nyaya Mandir
7. Laxmi Vilas Palace
8. Fatehsingh Museum
9. Post Office
10. Tourist Office
11. Kwality Restaurant
12. Havmor Restaurant
13. Apsara Hotel
14. Ambassador Hotel
15. Aurobindo Ashram
16. Circuit House

	Jan	Feb	Mar	Apr	May	Jun	Jul	Aug	Sep	Oct	Nov	Dec	Av/Tot
Max (°C)	30	33	37	40	41	37	32	31	33	35	33	31	34
Min (°C)	13	14	19	23	27	27	26	25	24	21	16	13	21
Rain (mm)	2	0	0	0	5	121	305	283	171	45	3	0	935

Formerly **Baroda**, this was the capital of one of the most powerful princely states, Baroda and covered 21,144 sq km. The family name 'Gaekwad' means 'Protector of Cows'. The Gaekwar stood high in the order of precedence and was only one of five rulers who received a 21 gun salute (Hyderabad, Mysore, Jammu & Kashmir and Gwalior were the others). He was reputedly so rich that he had a carpet woven of diamonds and pearls and cannons cast in gold. Parks, lakes, and palaces dominate the old city. It is now a rapidly expanding industrial centre, yet still a pleasant place to visit.

Places of Interest The *Laxmi Vilas Palace* (1880-90) Built by R.H.Chisholm – see page 700 – after early designs by the military engineer Mant, the façade of this extraordinary building is 150 m wide. You can spend considerable time spotting the number of different Indian and European architectural styles incorporated. The palace is faced in red Agra sandstone with dressings of blue trapstone from Pune and Rajasthani marble. The approach to the palace is very pleasant and the interior spectacular. The Durbar Hall has walls and floor in Venetian mosaic and marble is used extensively throughout, as is stained glass from London.

To the S of the Palace is the **Maharajah Fateh Singh Museum** which contains some fine European paintings. Further S, beyond the railway is the **Pratap Vilas**

Palace (c.1910), now the Railway Staff College.

Around the **Sursagar Lake** in the centre of town is the **Kirti Mandir** (early 20th century), the Gaekwad samadhi, or memorial ground. The **Kothi Building** (late 19th century) is to the W and now houses the Secretariat. Across the road is the **Nyaya Mandir** (1896) the high Court, in Mughal and Gothic styles. The **Jami Masjid** is next door. Further along the road away from the lake is the **Mandvi** (1736), a square Muslim Pavilion and the spacious **Nazar Bagh Palace** (1721) which has a **Shish Mahal** (mirror palace), a collection of embroidered cloth and the jewel 'Star of the South'. The solid gold and silver guns, each barrel 127kg in weight were kept here which, on ceremonial occasions, were drawn by teams of milk-white bullocks.

One of the old painted *havelis* (**Tambekarwada**), acquired by the Archaeological Survey is open to visitors. A four storey building, it is well worth visiting. Directions from Tourist Office. The Vadodara **College of Fine Art** is an institute of national renown.

Makarpura Palace (late 19th century) is about 7 km S of the city. This was built in an Italian Renaissance style and has a façade of three storeys each with an arcade running around. Beautiful gardens. To the N is the **Nulakhi Well**, a well-preserved *baoli** (step well) which has galleried compartments or levels.

Hotels B *Welcomgroup Vadodara*, R.C. Dutt Rd. T 323232, Cable: Welcotel Vadodara, Telex: 0175-Ghl in. 102 rm. Executive Club for business travellers. Well appointed. **C** *Express* R.C. Dutt Rd. T 323131, Cable: Expresshotel, Telex: 0175-311, Fax: 0265-325980. 64 rm, central a/c. Restaurants, coffee shop, pastry shop, exchange, shops, courtesy coach, travel, credit cards. **C** *Alkapuri*, 18 Alkapuri. T 325744, 325960, Cable: Express Alkapuri. 30 rm, central a/c. Restaurant, coffee shop, shops, courtesy coach, travel, credit cards. **C** *Surya*, Sayajiganj. T 328282, Cable: Surya, Telex: 0175-482 Dhpl in. 34 rm, TV, central a/c. Restaurant, courtesy coach, Amex, Diners, Visa.

D *Aditi*, Sardar Patel Statue, Sayajiganj. T 327722. 64 rm, some a/c. Restaurant, rm service, car hire, courtesy coach to airport, TV. **D** *Kaviraj*, R.C. Dutt Rd. T 323401, Cable: Kaviraj. 30 rm, some a/c. nr rly. Restaurant, Amex. **D** *Utsav*, Prof. Manek Rao Rd. T 551415, Cable: Utsav, Telex: 0175-274 Utsa-in. 28 a/c rm. Restaurant, exchange, Amex, Visa. Good value. **E** *Rajdhani*, Dandia Bazar. T 541136. 22 rm. A/c restaurant (Indian, Chinese). **F** *Green*, Race Course Rd. T 323111, Cable: Green hotel. 22 non a/c rm. Nr rly. Car hire.

There are *Railway Retiring Rooms* with the conveniently located **F** *Municipal Corporation Guesthouse* (Pravasi Grih) opposite. There are several cheap hotels nearby. The **E** *Apsara* is small but comfortable with non a/c doubles with bath. The **E** *Laxmi Lodge* is slightly cheaper, while the **E** *Ambassador* is larger.

Restaurants Many of the hotels have good restaurants with extensive menus, with the *Rajdhani* and the *Ambassador* offering good *thalis*.

Outside hotels *Kwality*, Sayajigunj has a good choice incl Italian and Peshwari dishes served indoors or in garden. 0900-2330; *Volga* in Alankar Cinema grounds, Sayaigung does good Mughlai kebabs and Chinese. 1000-2330. **Continental:** *Copper Coin*, World Trade Centre and *Havmor* in Sayajigunj; *Rangoli*, Fatehgunj. **Indian/S Indian:** *Alka* and *Sanman*, Alkapuri. **Gujarati (thali):** *Gokul*, Kothi Char-rasta; *Satya Vijay*, Manjalpur; *Iswar Bhuvan*, Dandia Bazar. Chinese: *Chung Fa*, RC Dutt Rd; *Oriental Spice*, Sayajigung.

Banks Most are in Alkapuri: Bank of Vadodara, Bank of India, Gautam Nagar Society; Bank of Rajasthan; Canara Bank; Dena Bank; Indian Bank, opp Express Hotel; Indian Overseas Bank; Union Bank of India and Vijaya Bank. Allahabad Bank, Girdhar Chamber, R.M. Rd; Central Bank of India, Sayajiganj; New Bank of India, Mahajan Lane, Raopura; State Bank of India, opp Jamunabai Hospital, Mandvi.

Shopping Vadodara is an important centre for silver jewellery. The main shopping areas of the city are Raopura, Mandvi, Teen Darwaza, National Plaza, Leheripura Mandir Bazaar and Alkapuri Arcade. *Khadi Bhandar*, Kothi Rd, is good for handlooms and local handicrafts. *Chimanlal Vrajlal*, M.G. Rd is good for Banarasi silks, cotton saris and Vadodara print saris.

Photography: *Sharp Studio*, Sangeeta Apartments, Alkapuri. *G.N. Hakim & Sons*, Raopura, Fatehgunj. *Ashoka Studio*, Sayajigunj.

Local Transport Yellow top taxis. Min Rs 10. **Auto rickshaws**. Min Rs 2. The **ST bus service** operates all round the city.

Tourist Taxis are available from the following: Gujarat Tourism, Tourist Office (and other recognised travel agents). Non a/c Ambassador (diesel) Rs1.50- 2 per km, Min 200 km per day; Ambassador (petrol) Rs 2-2.50 per km, Min 200 km per day. A.c Ambassador Rs 3-4 per km, min 200 km per day. A/c Datsun 55 km/4hr – Rs 330, 80 km/8hrs – Rs 480. Also available from *Hotel Welcomgroup Vadodara*, T 320891. Non a/c Ambassador Rs 2.75 per km, airport drop Rs 60, airport pick-up Rs 110, 80 km/8hr Rs 275. A/c Ambassador Rs 4 per km, airport drop Rs 120, airport pick-up Rs 220, 80 km/8hr Rs 450. Imported car Rs 9 per km, 80 km/8hr Rs 900 min, out-station trips Re 1.60 per km.

The TCGL also has coaches and mini-buses for hire.

Sports *Boating* at Sursagar Lake provided by Municipal Corporation. *Swimming* Lal Baug Pool; Sardar Baug Pool, Alkapuri; Hotel Welcomgroup Vadodara; Hotel Surya Palace. Polo Club, Polo Ground, T 554903. Gujarat Flying Club, Airport, T 552631.

Museums Maharajah Sayajirao Museum (Vadodara Museum) and Art Gallery, Sayaji Baug. Open daily 0930-1645, Sat 1000-1645. This is contained in the Victoria Diamond Jubilee Institute which was designed by Robert Fellowes Chisholm, who designed several buildings in Madras. Collection incl archaeology, art, ethnology and ancient Jain sculptures. There is a section on Industrial Arts as well as a collection of Mughal miniatures and European paintings.

Maharajah Fateh Singh Museum, Nehru Rd in Palace grounds. Open 0900-1200, 1500-1800 (Jul-Mar), 1600-1900 (Apr-Jun), closed Mon. Royal state collection of European art, including works by Murillo, Titian, Raphael and Chinese, Japanese and Indian artists.

Parks and Zoos *Sayaji Baug* is an extensive park, popular for evening strolls. A Toy Train encircles the park, operating 1500-1700, bookings from 0800-1100 at the Planetarium which has an English language performance each evening. For the children there is a Traffic Park and Elephant Rides from 1700-1800 for Re 1. The Vadodara Museum is also within the park. At the entrance is a large bronze statue of HH Maharajah Sayaji Rao III; inside the park is one of Shivaji.

Useful Services Foreigners' Regional Registration Office, Collector's Office, Kothi Kacheri. Police T 100, Fire T 101, Ambulance T 101.

Hospitals and Medical Services *Aaram Medical Nursing Home*, nr School No.1, Raopura, T 554955. *Sayaji Hospital*, Sayajigunj. *Narhari Arogya Kendra*, Fatehgunj. *Maharani Jamunabai Hospital*, Mandvi.

Post and Telegraph GPO, Raopura. Railway Mail Service, Railway Station.

Places of Worship *Hindu*: Jalaram Temple, Karelibaug; Sidhi Vinayak Temple, Danda Bazaar; EME Temple, Fatehgunj. *Muslim*: Jama Masjid, Mandvi. *Sikh*: Gurudwaras at Chhani Rd and Khanderao Market. *Christian*: Red Church, Fatehgunj; Catholic Church, Fatehgunj.

Travel Agents: *Punit Travels*, Vishwas Colony, T 325959. *Jirawala Travels*, Khanderao Market, T 554495. *Gandhi Travels*, Hathipole Naka, T 554069. *Travel Corporation of India* (TCI), Vishwas Colony, nr Alkapuri Petrol Pump, T 322181-2. *Travel House*, Hotel Welcomgroup Vadodara, R.C. Dutt Rd, T 320891. *Skyjet Aviation*, B.N. Chambers, R.C. Dutt Rd, T 325104, 325149. *Tradewings*, Sayajigunj T 327127-9. *Goodwing Travels*, Raopura, T 550524.

Tourist Offices and Information Gujarat Tourism, Regional Tourist Office, Narmada Bhawan, C-Block, Indira Avenue, T 540797. Open 1030-1810, closed Sun. Instant reservations available from TCGL Tourist Bungalows and selected private hotels all over Gujarat. Tourist Office, Nagar Palika Pravasi Gruh (Municipal Corporation), nr Railway Station, T 329656. Open 0900-1800. Tourist Office (Municipal Corporation), Khanderao Market, Palace Rd, T 551116. Open 1030-1800.

Tours The TCGL: 1. *Saurashtra Darshan* (5 days), every Fri 0630. Rajkot, Jamnagar, Dwarka, Porbander, Somnath, Sasan Gir, Veraval, Junagadh, Virpur, Palitana, Velavadar, Lothal, Ahmadabad. Price includes dormitory accommodation. 2. *N Gujarat and Rajasthan* (5 days), every first and third Sat, 0600. Shamlaji, Udaipur, Chittorgarh, Nathdwara, Charbhuja, Haldighati. 3. *Special tour to Madhya Pradesh* (4 days). Pavagadh, Mandu, Omkareshwar, Ujjain. Further details from Tourism Corporation. 4. *Special Rajasthan Tour* (8 days). Shamlaji, Udaipur, Chittorgarh, Nathdwara, Pushkar, Jaipur, Jodhpur, Mount Abu etc.

Vadodara Municipal Corporation, Tourist Section, Nagar Palika Pravasi Gruh, T 329656: 1. Every Tue, Wed and Fri 1400-1800. Rs 10 (min 10 people). EME Temple, Sayaji Garden,

Kirti Mandir, Geeta Mandir, Vadodara Dairy, Fatehsingh Museum, Aurobindo Society. 2. Every Sat, Sun, Mon between Jul and Sep, 1700-2100. Rs 15(min 10 persons). Numeta (picnic spot), Ajwa (Brindavan pattern garden). 3. Every Sat, Sun, Mon (Oct-Jun) 1400-2100. Rs 25 (min 20 persons). Includes places in Tours 1 and 2.

Air Vadodara is not an international airport but Air India, British Airways and Japan Airlines have offices on R.C. Dutt Rd.

There are daily flights from Delhi via Ahmadabad and non-stop return to Delhi. There are also seven flights a week to and from Bombay (two Mon flights, none Sun). Indian Airlines, City Office, Fatehgunj, T 329178; Airport, T 554433. Open 1000-1330, 1415-1700. The airport is 6 km from the centre of town. Transfers are by taxi or auto rickshaw.

Rail Vadodara is on the main Western Railways' Delhi-Bombay broad gauge line and is well connected with other regional centres. **Bombay Central:** *Bombay Gandhidham Kutch Exp* 9032, daily, 0710, 6 hr 20 min; *Saurashtra Janata Exp* 9018, daily, 2237, 7 hr 28 min; *Vadodara-Bombay Exp* 9028, daily, 2300, 6 hr 30 min. **New Delhi:** *Rajdhani Exp* 2951, daily except Sat, 2131, 11 hr 45 min; *Paschim Exp* 2925, daily, 1726, 17 hr; *Frontier Mail* 2903, daily, 0256, 16 hr. **Vadodara Railway Station**, Sayajigunj. Enquiries, T 557575. Reservations T 65121. Open 0800-2000 (Second class) and 0800-1800 (First Class).

Road Vadodara is situated on **NH 8** (Bombay-Delhi) and is well connected with other parts of the country: **Ahmadabad** (113 km), **Palitana** (325 km), **Sasan Gir** (431 km), **Ujjain** (403 km), **Indore** (348 km), **Junagadh** (372 km), **Delhi** (995 km), **Bombay** (425 km), **Jaipur** (725 km). **Buses** of the State Road Transport Corporations (SRTC) of Gujarat, Rajasthan, Madhya Pradesh and Maharashtra operate between Vadodara and destinations in the region. These include: Ujjain, Bombay, Pune, Udaipur and, Mount Abu. The Gujarat SRTC provides services for Gujarat.\ Central Bus Stand, nr Railway Station. Enquiries, T 327000. Reservations open 0700-2200. Advance booking 0900-1300 and 1330-1700.

Excursions A pleasant day trip by car from Vadodara could include Champaner, Pavagadh and Dabhoi Fort, all listed below, a distance of 146 km via Bodeli.

Champaner, 47 km NE of Vadodara, stands on a 882m high hill in the Girnar Hills. The fortress was the old capital of the local Rajputs who lost it in 1484 to Mahmud Beghara who renamed it Muhammadabad. It is said that it took 23 years to build his new city. In his campaign in Gujarat, the Mughal Emperor Humayun personally led a small team that scaled the walls of the city using iron spikes and then let the rest of the army in through the main gate. With the collapse of the Empire, Champaner passed to the Marathas. In the **Old City**, the remains of many fine mosques and palaces show a blend of Islamic and Jain traditions, a unique style encouraged by Champaner's relative isolation.

The **Jami Masjid** (1523) is intact and is a large, richly ornamented mosque modelled on the Friday Mosque at Ahmadabad. There are interesting Gujarati features such as oriel windows. The government runs *Hotel Champaner*, Pavagadh and **F** *Holiday Home* which has rm and a dormitory.

The **Fort of Pavagadh,** 4 km SW dominates the skyline and is visible for miles around. It occupies a large area and rises in three stages; first the ruined fort, then the palace and middle fort and finally the upper fort with Jain and Hindu temples. Parts of the massive walls still stand. The ascent is steep and passes several ruins including the Buria Darwaza (Gate), the Champavati Mahal, a three storey summer pavilion. The temple at the summit had its spire removed by the Muslims and a shrine of Sadan Shah, a Muslim saint, placed there instead.

The name Pavagadh means 'a quarter of a hill' and was believed to have been part of the Himalaya carried off by the monkey god Hanuman.

Dabhoi Fort 29 km E of Vadodara. The town was fortified by the Solanki Rajputs from 1100 and the fort was built by Jayasimha Siddharaja Chapotkaha, the king of Patan in the 13th century.

Dabhoi is regarded as the birthplace of the Hindu Gujarati architectural style. The fort is a particularly fine example of military architecture with its four gates, a reservoir fed by an aqueduct and farms to provide food at times of siege. The **Vadodara Gate** (NW) is 9 m high with pilasters on each side and carved with images depicting the reincarnation of Vishnu.

The **Nandod Gate** (S) is similarly massive. The **Hira Gate** (E) has a carved relief depicting a man and woman with a tree between them. To the left is a devil and in the centre is an elephant. Local legend has it that the builder is buried beneath this. **Mori Gate** (N) lies next to the old palace and on the left of this is the **Mother Kali Temple** (1225), dedicated to Kali and shaped like a cross with profuse carvings.

Leave Vadodara S on the **NH8**, passing through **Pur** (20 km) and **Karjan** (14 km) to **Baruch** (39 km).

At the mouth of the Narmada River, **Bharuch** (**Broach**) is one of the oldest seaports in Western India and flourished in the 1st century AD. Under the name of Barugaza the town was mentioned by the Romans in c.210 AD. It was ruled by a Gurhara Prince and much later came under the rule of the Solanki Rajputs.

The **Bhrigu Rishi Temple** from which the town got its name (**Bhrigukachba**) is on the bank of the **River Narmada**. It subsequently developed at the lowest crossing of the river, a point of strategic importance. During the rule of Muslims from Sind (1297 to 1772) the British and the Dutch established factories in 1614 and 1617. Aurangzeb ordered the fortifications to be destroyed in 1660 which paved the way for successful attacks by the Marathas in 1675 and 1686 who rebuilt the walls.

The **Fort** overlooks the Narmada and within it are the Collector's Office, Civil Courts, the old Dutch factory, a church, the Victoria Clocktower and other buildings. Below the fort is the **Jama Masjid** (early 14th century) which was built from a demolished Jain temple but in accordance with conventional mosque design. Just over 3 km W of the fort are some early **Dutch tombs,** overlooked by some Parsee **Towers of Silence.**

Today Bharuch is well known for its textile mills and long staple cotton. **Suklatirtha**, about 10 km upstream has a *Holiday Home*.

Continue S. After 48 km the road crosses the second major west-flowing river on the Peninsula after the Narmada, the Tapti (or Tapi). The road then goes through **Kadodra** (14 km). Turn right off the NH8 for **Surat** (16 km). The alternative route to Surat is to go out to the coast from Baruch and then travel via **Hansot** and **Olpud**.

The name **Surat** is associated with the name Saurashtra, 'The Good Land', the regions covering the peninsula of Gujarat. It is situated on the banks of the Tapti river and owes its development to its early and sustained importance as a trading centre. It was large in 1600 and even after a decline in its fortunes the population in 1796 was estimated to be as much as 800,000.

The Parsis, driven from Persia, first arrived in India in the 8th century and many moved from their first settlement on the W coast of the peninsula to Surat in the 12th century. The Mughals, under Akbar, took the town and during their reign, the Portuguese, British, Dutch and French in turn established trading outposts here. The British were the first to establish a factory in their first settlement in India, having arrived in 1608 and Surat remained their headquarters until it moved to Bombay in 1674.

A centre of business During the 17th and 18th centuries, trade flourished and made Surat the mercantile capital of W India. The first dock was built in 1720 and by 1723 there were 2 shipyards. The tide turned, however, in the next century, when a fire destroyed the city centre to be followed by floods when the river Tapti burst its banks. This led many Parsis to move to Bombay to make their fortune.

Places of interest The **Castle** provides a good vantage point for viewing the city and surrounding countryside. It stands right on the banks of the Tapti near the bridge. The **British Factory** House, combined English and Hindu styles and had stained glass windows with carved wooden supports. It is near the Mission

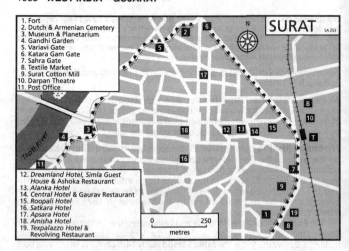

1. Fort
2. Dutch & Armenian Cemetery
3. Museum & Planetarium
4. Gandhi Garden
5. Variavi Gate
6. Katara Gam Gate
7. Sahra Gate
8. Textile Market
9. Surat Cotton Mill
10. Darpan Theatre
11. Post Office

12. Dreamland Hotel, Simla Guest House & Ashoka Restaurant
13. Alanka Hotel
14. Central Hotel & Gaurav Restaurant
15. Roopali Hotel
16. Satkara Hotel
17. Apsara Hotel
18. Amisha Hotel
19. Texpalazzo Hotel & Revolving Restaurant

SURAT SA 253

High School but not much remains. The **Cemetery** is of some interest, and the **Dutch** and **Armenian Cemeteries** are next door, but all are very poorly maintained and unattractive.

The Muslim influence in Surat is strong and there are a number of mosques and tombs. The **Nau Saiyid Mosque** (Mosque of the Nine Saiyids) is on the W bank of the **Gopi Lake**. Others are **Khwaja Diwan Sahib's Mosque** (c.1530), the **Saiyid Idris Mosque** (1639) built by the ruling dynasty of the time. The **Mirza Sami Mosque** (1540) was built by Khudawand Khan who was also responsible for the castle.

There are two **Parsi Fire Temples** (1823) and three Hindu temples. The Swami Narayan Temple with its three white domes is a local landmark.

Today Surat is a busy textile town with several cotton mills. The production of gold and silver thread and *kinkhab* brocades and wood and ivory inlay work are also important. Silk weaving is a cottage industry producing the famous *Tanchoi* and *Gajee* saris and diamond cutting is also a speciality.

Hotels C *Dhawalgiri*, Opposite Collector's Bungalow, Athwa Lines. T 40040, Cable: Dhawalgiri. 10 a/c rm. Restaurant, health club, gym, sauna, pool. D *Oasis*, Vaishali Cinema, Varacha Rd. T 41124-7, Cable: Hoteloasis. 25 rm, some a/c. Restaurants (one in garden), coffee shop, bar, liquor shop, doctor on call, pool, Amex, Diners. D *Sofitel*, Ambika Niketan Bus stop, Patel Point, Athwa Lines. T 45557, Cable: Golwala Surat. 10 a/c rm. Restaurant (inc Mexican), exchange. D *Tex Palazzo*, Ring Rd. T 623018-27, Cable: Texpalazzo, Telex: 0188-376 Tph in. 43 rm, some a/c. Restaurants, coffee shop, credit cards. E *Dreamland*, Sufi Baug, opp railway station. T 39016. 39 rm, some a/c. Snacks only. Near the railway station are F *Subras* and F *Rupali*, both with non a/c rooms without bath and dormitory.

Restaurants There is little choice in Surat, though the hotels offer a varied menu. The *Tex Palazzo* hotel has a ground floor restaurant that serves good thalis. Claims to have the first revolving restaurant in India, but the views are not spectacular. Dwahalgiri's *Health Food Restaurant* is open 1000-2200 has healthy dishes in addition. The *Sahkar*, Ajanta Apartments Corner, Ring Rd is open 1000 until midnight.

Rail Bombay Central *Paschim Exp* 2926, daily, 1053, 4 hr 7 min; *Frontier Mail* 2904, daily, 0250, 4 hr 10 min; *Bombay Gandhidam Kutch Exp* 1032, daily, 0916, 4 hr 14 min; *Gujarat Exp* 9012, daily, 1125, 4 hr 50 min. **Ahmadabad** *Bombay Gandhidharm Kutch Exp* 9031, 2140, 3 hr 30 min; *Gujarat Exp* 9011, daily, 1045, 5 hr 30 min; *Bombay-Ahmadabad Janata*

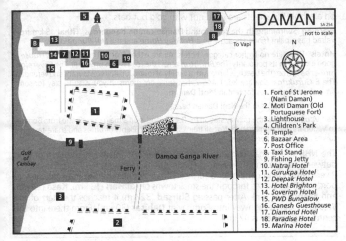

DAMAN SA 254

not to scale

N

1. Fort of St Jerome (Nani Daman)
2. Moti Daman (Old Portuguese Fort)
3. Lighthouse
4. Children's Park
5. Temple
6. Bazaar Area
7. Post Office
8. Taxi Stand
9. Fishing Jetty
10. *Natraj Hotel*
11. *Gurukpa Hotel*
12. *Deepak Hotel*
13. *Hotel Brighton*
14. *Soverign Hotel*
15. *PWD Bungalow*
16. *Ganesh Guesthouse*
17. *Diamond Hotel*
18. *Paradise Hotel*
19. *Marina Hotel*

Exp 9007, daily, 0033, 4 hr; *Saurashtra Exp* 9215, daily, 1410, 5 hr 20 min.

Excursions At *Rander,* 5 km from the city is the site of an ancient Indian city dating to 200 BC. The Muslims sacked it in 1225 and built a **Jami Masjid** on the site of a Jain Temple.

There are a number of **beaches** near Surat: *Dumas,* 16 km is a popular health resort; *Hajira,* 28 km, with Casuarina groves and a *Holiday Home*; *Ubhrat,* 42 km.

Return to NH8 at *Navsari* to travel S. The coastal plain narrows and the road crosses several short rivers that flow W from the crest of the Western Ghats. After 27 km the NH8 passes through **Chikli** and then crosses the **River Auranga** after a further 24 km. The road goes through **Parnera** (6 km) and **Pardi** (15 km) , crossing the railway (6 km) before reaching the turning to the right (10 km) which leads to **Daman** (a further 12 km).

Daman

160 km N of Bombay. The tiny 380 sq km enclave of Daman, along with Diu and Goa, were Portuguese possessions until forcibly taken over by the Indian Government in 1961.

Situated on the S side of the **Gulf of Cambay** (Diu is on the N), Daman developed at the mouth of the Daman Ganga river as a Portuguese trading centre from 1531 onwards. As with other tiny colonial enclaves such as Pondicherry in Tamil Nadu, there is still an atmosphere of its former colonial mother country. Much of its early commerce was with the Portuguese territories in E Africa. Later (1817-1837) it was a link in the opium trade chain until this was broken by the British.

The forts The smaller **Fort of St Jerome** on the N bank encloses a church and cemetery with still a few cannons on the walls. The other **Old Fort** contains the ruins of a monastery, Governor's Palace, barracks, hospital and two churches. The landward (E) side has a moat and drawbridge.

Nani (small) Daman S of the river, which is crossed by a bridge and ferry, are government offices and churches. **Moti (large) Daman** has the hotels and restaurants. Like its sister territory, Daman is exempt from Gujarat's prohibition on alcohol. The streets are lined not with gold but bars.

Warning Swimming in the sea around Daman can be dangerous. **Tithal** , 5 km from Valsad has a palm fringed beach with a *Holiday Home* and the *Hill Bungalow*.

Hotels There are no higher category hotels. All are either **E** or **F**. The *PWD Rest House* is good judging by its popularity. The *Brighton* across the road is also often full. The *Sovereign*, further back from the beach, is large with a variety of rooms, upstairs restaurant and verandah. The **E** *Gurukripa*, Seaface Rd, T 446-7, has some a/c rooms. If you wish to stay for some time, there are houses for rent in **Moti Daman**.

You can rent bicycles in the Nani Daman bazaar.

Rail *Vapi*, 8 km E, is the railway station for Daman and is on a main railway line from Bombay to Vadodara and Ahmadabad. Not all trains stop at Vapi. Plenty of buses and share-taxis into towns (about Rs 6 per person).

The NH8 to Bombay continues S from Daman. At this point the strip of land between the sea and the Western Ghats is at its narrowest. The road crosses the River Damanganga and after a further 14 km reaches the Gujarat-Maharashtra border. It then passes through the small towns of **Talasari** (13 km), **Kasa** (24 km) and **Manor** (23 km). After passing **Shirsad** (32 km) it reaches the start of the Western Express Highway into Bombay at **Dahisar** (30 km). From there into the centre of **Bombay** is 42 km.

AHMADABAD TO BHAVNAGAR, PALITANA AND DIU

This route explores the E coast of the Kathiawar Peninsula. Substantial remains of Harappan culture including the dry dock can be seen at Lothal before the road skirts the marshes to reach the important town of Bhavnagar and the grasslands of the Velavadar National Park. Further on the Jain temple city of Shatrunjaya climbs out of the plain near Palitana. the road returns briefly to the coast at Mahuva before continuing inland along a picturesque road to the old Portuguese island enclave of Diu.

Leave Ahmadabad across the **Ellis Bridge** (narrow and often very congested). The **NH8A** goes through **Sarkhej** (8 km; see above), **Baola** (22 km). 1 km before Baola turn left to **Dholka** (13 km).

Dholka was built as the residence of the Muslim Governor of Delhi. The **Masjid of Hilal Khan Qazi** (1333) has a simple façade with two turrets flanking the central arch. The **Tanka Masjid** (1361) has over 100 Hindu pillars suggesting that a purely Islamic style had not yet developed – see also **Qutb Minar Delhi** (page 165). The other mosque, of **Alif Khan** (1453), is unlike other Gujarati mosques of the period in that it is of brick. Davies suggests that it is S Persian in design and execution, the workers migrating as a result of the coastal shipping trade.

Continue S from Dholka to

Lothal ("Mound of the dead") is sandwiched between the **Sabarmati river** and the **Bhogavo River**, and is now 10 km up from the Gulf of Khambhat (Cambay). 720 km as the crow flies SE of Moenjodaro, it has some of the most substantial remains of the Harappan culture in India, dating from c.2500 BC-1700 BC. Its site and function as a port have led most authorities to argue that it was settled by Harappan trading communities who came by sea from the mouths of the Indus, but some believe that it may have been settled by traders moving across the overland route.

The site is surrounded by a mud-brick embankment 300 m N-S and 400 m E-W. Unlike the defensive walls at Harappa and Moenjodaro, the wall at Lothal enclosed the workers' area as well as the citadel. The presence of a dry dock and a warehouse further distinguish it from other major Harappan sites.

The dry dock This massive excavated structure runs along the E wall of the city and has average dimensions of 214 m by 36 m. A 12 m wide gap in the N side is believed to have been the entrance by which boats came into the dock, while a spillway over the S wall allowed excess water to overflow. The city wall, which is wider at this point than elsewhere, may have been a wharf for unloading.

Excavations of the warehouse has revealed wide evidence of the trade which was clearly the basis of Lothal's existence. The building, at the SW corner of the wharf, had a 4 m high platform made of cubical mud-brick blocks, the gaps between them allowing ventilation.

Over 65 Indus Valley seals have been discovered which show pictures of packing material, bamboo or rope, suggestive of the importance of trade to the community. There have also been many finds of pottery, semi-precious stones, beads and even necklaces made of tiny beads of gold. Rice and millet were clearly in use, and there is some evidence that horses had been domesticated.

The city Excavations show a planned city in a grid pattern, with underground drainage system, wells, brick houses with baths and fireplaces. The raised brick platform to the SE may have been a kiln where seals and plaques were baked. Objects found include painted pottery, ivory, shell, semi-precious stone items, beads and bangles and terracotta toys. The long rectangular tank to the E may have been used as a dock. The discovery of a seal from Bahrain suggests that there was overseas trade. The cemetery to the NW had large funerary vessels indicating pit burials.

The **Archaeological Museum** contains various artefacts including copper and bronze implements from the site. There is a *Toran Holiday Home* here.

Rail Burkhi, on the Ahmadabad-Bhavnagar line is the nearest station, but the trains are slow and inconvenient.

Road Direct buses from Ahmadabad. Allow a full day for a round trip. It is a hard day, with not much to see at the end of it. Comfortably managed by car.

It is possible to take the coast road S from Lothal to Bhavnagar, but this crosses marshes, is poor quality and sometimes is not open. It is necessary to check before travelling. Otherwise return to *Dhingra* (6 km). Turn left and cross the **River Omkar** (11 km). Pass through **Dhandhuka** (24 km) and after crossing the railway twice (after 10 km and 9 km) through **Barvala** (8 km) and **Vala** (30 km). Straight on to **Sihor** (24 km), where there is a left turn to **Bhavnagar** (21 km).

Bhavnagar was founded in 1723 by the Rajput **Bhavsinghji Gohil**, and developed into an important coastal town and seaport, its principal trade being the export of cotton.

The palace-like **Takhtsinghji General Hospital** (1879-83) was designed by William Emerson, President of the Royal Institute of British Architects. He also designed the **Darbargadh (Old Palace** 1894-5) in the centre of town, now used as bank offices.

The **Barton Museum** (1895) has a good collection of arms, armour and coins. In the same building is the more famous **Gandhi Smitri,** a library, memorial and museum dedicated to Mahatma Gandhi.

Gaurishankar Lake is a popular picnic spot and the hilltop **Takhteshwar Temple** has good views.

Hotels C *Nilambag Palace,* (Welcomgroup), T 24340, Cable: Nilambag Palace. 14 a/c rm with bath, many with verandahs. Restaurant, gardens, tennis, pool. Small palace which belonged to Maharajah Krishnakumarsingh, the first Indian Prince to hand over his state to the Govt of India after Independence.
D *Apollo,* opp Central Bus Station. T 25249, Cable: Apollo, Telex: 0182-225 Aplo in. 30 rm, some a/c with TV. 8 km airport, 2 km rly, 2 km centre. Restaurant, fast food counter, exchange, shop, hairdresser,. **D** *Blue Hill,* opp Pill Garden. T 26951-4, Telex: 0182-256 Blue

BHAVNAGAR SA 255

not to scale

To Port

To Rajkot

1. Takteshwar Temple
2. Darbargadh (Old Palace)
3. Post Office
4. Town Hall
5. Municipal Office
6. University Campus

River Gadhechi

N

in. 38 rm, some a/c. 5 km airport. 1 km rly, central. Restaurant, 24 hr coffee shop, exchange, doctor on call, car hire, travel, TV, Visa. **D** *Jubilee*, behind Pil Garden. T 26624, Telex: 0182-204 Jble in. 30 rm, some a/c. 5 km airport, 2 km rly, central. Restaurant, 24 hr rm service, exchange, doctor on call, car hire, travel, TV lounge. **E** *Hotel Mini* Station Rd T 23113 Very close to station. Some a/c rm Clean, excellent value.

Basic **F** hotels include the *Evergreen Guest House*, T 4605, the *Kashmir* and the *Geeta*, T 3985. The Shital Hotel, Amba Chowk, Mali Tekra T 28360 is recommended as clean and good value. Also *Railway Retiring Rooms*.

Restaurants Besides those at the hotels listed which offer a varied menu, there is not much. The *Nataraj* opp Ganga Devi is quite good and does ice-creams. The *Havmor* is on the edge of the shopping area across from the main covered food market. Near the station the *Mahavir Lodge* does good veg *thalis*.

Air Daily Indian Airlines connection with Bombay and a daily Vayudoot connection with Surat.

Rail Ahmadabad: The railway line has to take a circuitous route to skirt the marshes. It is a slow journey. *Girnar Exp* 9845, daily, 2145, 8 hr 25 min; *Bhavnagar Ahmadabad Exp* 9809, daily, 0530, 6 hr 10 min.

Bus There are good bus connections with Ahmadabad and other centres in the state.

Velavadar National Park This compact game reserve with open grassland was created especially for conserving the blackbuck, which is associated with ancient Indian legend. Best time, Oct- early Jun. Jeep on hire. The blackbuck is the second largest of the antelopes and the fastest long-distance runner of all animals. It can keep going at a steady 90 km per hour, described by Krishnan, as though their

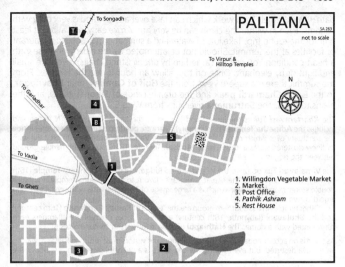

Map legend:
1. Willingdon Vegetable Market
2. Market
3. Post Office
4. *Pathik Ashram*
5. *Rest House*

legs were spring-loaded. It is unfortunately the most hunted animal in India, so consequently is an endangered species.

The nearest accommodation is at Bhavnagar.

Return to **Sihor** (21 km). Turn left to **Songarh** (8 km) and continue to **Palitana** (23 km).

Palitana Population 39,000 *Altitude* 182 m. *Area* 13 sq km. *Climate* Temp. Summer Max 46 C, Min 24 C, Winter Max 38 C, Min 17 C. Annual rainfall 580 mm, mostly Jun-Sep. *Best Season* Nov-Mar. Apr-Jun is extremely hot.

Bhavnagar, 51 km NE is the nearest airport. Indian Airlines has daily flights from Bombay and on to Rajkot. Vayudoot links Bhavnagar with Surat and Bombay.

Palitana is the base for visiting the impressive Jain temple city of Shatrunjaya. It was the capital of a small princely state founded by Shahji, a Gohel Rajput who belonged to the same clan as the Maharajah of Bhavnagar. Besides being a pilgrimage centre, Palitana also has a name for horse-breeding.

Places of Interest The Jain temple city of *Shatrunjaya* is the largest of its kind in India and within its gates are found 863 temples. According to local tradition **Adinatha**, the first Tirthankara, visited the hill several times and the first temple was erected by his son. Thereafter the temple builders could not stop. Jains believe that **Pundarika**, the chief disciple of Adinatha attained *nirvana* (enlightenment) there.

All these monuments are situated on a **Satrunjaya Hill** , a 600 m climb and 3 km SW of Palitana. There are two series of temples strung along the two ridges of the hill with further temples in the hollow between linking them. All are surrounded by a tall battlement, obviously erected for defence. These fortifications are called *tuks* and have created a series of nine enclosures.

Most of the temples are named after their founders, nearly all the structures dating from the 16th century. It would appear that many existed before but were destroyed by the Muslims in the 14th and 15th centuries. Later, Jains obtained religious toleration and began rebuilding.

Temples Open from 0700 to 1900. The climb is around 600 m on a stepped path. It is extremely hard work which can take over an hour and is very busy with pilgrims. Even in winter the climb can be very hot. Arrive early, and allow at least 4 hr for the round trip. Take lots of water and a sun hat or parasol. No restaurant or facilities at the summit. Should not be attempted by the elderly or those with a heart condition. You can be carried up by *dhooli* (string chairs) if you are small and light or by elephant. Once on top, allow an hour to see the temples. From the summit there is a superb view, from the **Gulf of Cambay**, near **Bhavnagar**, to the E, the **Chamardi peak** and the granite range of **Sihor** to the N, and the plains to the S. The **Satrunjaya** river runs from W to E.

The *Khartaravasi Tuk* is the largest and highest of the temples along the **N Ridge** and includes the **Adinatha Temple** (16th century). There are quadruple Tirthankara images inside the sanctuary over which rises a slender tower. The **Vallabhai Temple** (19th century) with its finely clustered spires and the large **Motisah Temple** (1836) occupy the middle ground between the ridges.

The **Vimalavasi Tuk** occupies the W end of the **S Ridge**. In it is the **Adishvara Temple** (16th century) which dominates the site. It is similar in layout to the Adinatha temple and has a double storey mandapa inside which is a large image of Rishabhanatha with crystal eyes and a gold crown of jewels.

Other temples in this southern group are the Temple of **Ramaji Gandharia** (16th century) and the **Bhulavani** (labyrinth, 18th century) which is a series of crypt like chambers each surmounted with a dome. The **Hathiapol** (Elephant Gate, 19th century) faces SE.

As there is no accommodation on the hill, pilgrims and visitors must return to Palitana, leaving Satrunjaya deserted. But even during the day, there is a peaceful serenity in the City of the Gods.

Hotels The *Nilambag Palace* at Bhavnagar is the best deluxe accommodation (see under Bhavnagar, above) **D** *Sumeru* (TCGL), Station Rd, nr Octroi Naka, T 227. A/c and non a/c rm, dormitory. Restaurant. Check out 0900. **D** *Shravak*, opp ST Depot, T 328. 13 rm, some a/c with bath, dormitory. TV lounge, 24 hr rm service. **F** *Pathik Ashram*, nr ST Depot has 9 double rooms. **F** *Mahavir Lodge* is nr the State Bank of Saurashtra. **F** *Readyhuny Guest House*, nr Power House, T 16. Reserve through Executive Engineer, Bhavnagar, T 6951.

There are over 150 *dharamsalas* with modern facilities catering primarily for Jain pilgrims. Non-Jains may be accommodated at the discretion of the management. Some prominent are: *Oswal*, T 140; *Khetlavir*, T 384; *Nanda Bhuvan*, T 285; *Narsinatha*, T 86; *Kuchi Bhavan*, T 37; *Chandra Deepak*, T 135; *Rajendra Vihar Dadavadi*, T 148; *Sona Rupa*, T 276.

Restaurants *Siddh Kshetra Jain Bhojanshala*, nr Sir Mansinhji Hospital. Indian. *Siddhgiri Bhojanalaya*, Taleti Rd. Gujarati thali. *Vaishali*, Main Bazaar, opp State Bank of Saurashtra. Gujarati *thali* and S Indian.

Banks State Bank of Saurashtra, Central Co-operative Bank of Saurashtra, Dena Bank, Indian Overseas Bank, Union Bank of India.

Shopping The local handicrafts are embroidery (saris, dresses, purses, bags, wall hangings etc), metal engraving and diamond cutting. Local industries manufacture harmonium reeds and weighing scales.

Photography *Mahavir Studio*, Main Rd, Danapath, T 118. *Maharajah Studio*, Main Rd, Danapath. *Gyatri Studio*, Main Rd, Kanyahala. There are no processing facilities at Palitana. The nearest are at Bhavnagar.

Local Transport There are taxis and tongas, both rates negotiable. Also available are *dandis** for transport up the hill. Rs 125-150.

Museums Stapitya Kala Sangrah, Taleti. Free. Sri Vishal Jain Kala Sansthan, Taleti Rd. Jain Art. Free.

Useful Services Police T 50. Ambulance T 75.

Hospitals and Medical Services Sir Mansinhji (Govt.) Hospital, Main Rd. T 75. Shatrunjay Hospital, Taleti Rd.

Post and Telegraph PO, Bhairavnath Rd, T 33.

Places of Worship *Hindu*: Bhairav Nath Temple, nr Owen Bridge; Mahalakshmi Mata Mandir. *Jain*: Temples on Shatrujaya Hill. *Muslim*: Jama Masjid, nr Darbar Chowk.

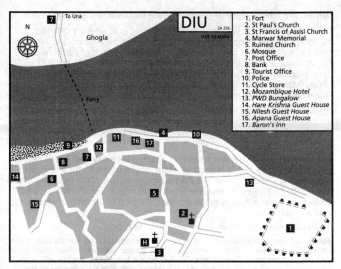

DIU SA 256
not to scale

1. Fort
2. St Paul's Church
3. St Francis of Assisi Church
4. Marwar Memorial
5. Ruined Church
6. Mosque
7. Post Office
8. Bank
9. Tourist Office
10. Police
11. Cycle Store
12. Mozambique Hotel
13. PWD Bungalow
14. Hare Krishna Guest House
15. Nilesh Guest House
16. Apana Guest House
17. Baron's Inn

Tourist Office and Information Manager, *Hotel Sumeru*.

Air Bhavnagar (56 km) is the nearest airport and has daily flights with Bombay. **Vayudoot** links Bombay with Surat and Bombay. **Indian Airlines**, Diwanpura Rd, Bhavnagar, T 27144. Vayudoot Handling Agents, Parag Travels, Vaghawadi Rd, Bhavnagar, T 23752, 20470.

Rail Palitana is on the metre gauge of the Western Railway and has a connection only with Bhavnagar. The nearest railway station connected with all parts of India is Ahmadabad. Railway Enquiries, Palitana, T 8.

Road A State Highway connects Palitana with Bhavnagar. Palitana is connected by good motorable roads with **Bhavnagar** (57 km), **Junagadh** (215 km), **Ahmadabad** (217 km), **Porbander** (294 km), **Dwarka** (400 km), **Gandhidham** (376 km), **Bombay** (768 km), **Delhi** (1,113 km).

Bus Gujarat State Transport service connect Palitana with Bhavnagar, Ahmadabad, Rajkot, Jamnagar, Vadodara and Surat. Gujarat State Transport Depot, T 68. Reservations, 0800-1200, 1400-1800. Private bus companies operate regular deluxe coaches to Palitana from Bombay and Surat via Vadodara. *Paras Travels*, Owen Bridge, T 370. *Khodiar Travels*, opp State Transport depot, T 586 (to Surat only). *Shah Travels*, opp ST depot, T 396.

    Taxis for up to 7 sometimes run between Bhavnagar and Palitana. Rs 10-15 per person.

From Palitana a road runs SW to **Kundla** (69 km). 6 km beyond Kundla a road on the right leads to the hot springs at **Tulshishyam**, then SE to the coastal town of *Mahuva* (60 km). From Mahuva a road runs due W roughly parallel and inland of the coast to **Diu** (110 km). There are no places of great historical importance but it is quite picturesque.

Diu

The 11 km long and 3 km wide island of Diu is situated off the S tip of the Kathiawad peninsula on the N side of the Gulf of Cambay. The island has a fascinating history, excellent cuisine and superb beaches. It is still hardly visited. Like its neighbour Daman across the gulf, it was a Portuguese colony until 1961. In 1987 its administration was separated from Goa, and it remains a Union Territory. With its attractively ornamented buildings with balconies and verandahs, its narrow streets and squares, the town has more of a Portuguese flavour than

Daman. The fishing village of Ghoghla on the mainland was also part of Diu.

The fort, built in 1535, was strategically important as as an easily defended base for controlling the shipping lanes on the NE part of the Arabian Sea. From the 14th to 16th centuries the Sultans of Oman held the reins of maritime power. The Portuguese failed to take Diu at their first attempt in 1531 but succeeded three years later. Like Daman it was once a port for the export of opium from Malwa (Madhya Pradesh). With the decline of Portugal as a naval power it became little more than a backwater.

The N side of the island has been subject to marine deposition and comprises salt pans and marshes. The S coast has some fine limestone cliffs and sandy beaches. The Branching palms were introduced from Africa by the Portuguese. Coconut palms are also very much in evidence.

Diu town is squeezed between **the fort** (E) and a large **city wall** (W). It has two churches, **St Paul's** and **St Francis of Assisi**, one of which is a museum, though there are few Christians now. The *Fort* is considered one of the most important built by the Portuguese in Asia. There were two moats, one of which was tidal. Cannon and cannon balls litter the ramparts and parts of the central keep are still used as a jail.

The buses operate from the main square which is on the N shore.

Hotels Like many other places in Gujarat, what accommodation there is tends to be at the lower end of the scale. **E** *Hotel Mozambique,* off the Bunder. Restaurant. Clean, quiet, good VIP suite, roof terrace. **E** *Baron's Inn*, Old Fort Rd is a fine villa by the sea with a good atmosphere. Non a/c rooms with bath. Meals available. Next door is **E** *Apna Guest House,* Old Fort Rd. Non a/c double rm with bath, best sea view and balcony and dormitory. Rooftop terrace with restaurant and bar.

  F *PWD Rest House,* nr Fort. Best rm with bath and balcony to garden. Good restaurant (Indian). Well run, inexpensive, so very popular. **F** *Nilesh Guest House,* nr Fish Market. Non a/c rm with bath. Restaurant and bar. Spartan but clean. **F** *Hare Krishna Guest House*, between fish market and Tourist Office. Friendly staff, popular restaurant.

Restaurants Only at hotels listed, best at Ahmedpur Mandvi, on mainland. *Deepee* the café, opp Bus Stand, next to Post Office has good snacks and ice-cream. *Saraswati Hotel* opp *Goa Travels* is a tea shop. Good breakfast.

Local Transport You can hire **bicycles** at the *Shilpa Cycle Store*, Main Square or *Kishma Cycle Store* nr the State Bank of Saurashtra. About Rs 10 per day. There are two local bus services from Diu to Nagoa three times daily and Diu to Bucharwada-Vanakbara 16 times per day. The ferry with the mainland runs from Diu Town to Ghoghla.

Hospitals and Medical Services The *Manesh Medical Store* is a pharmacy with a doctor in the same building.

Post and Telegraph Main Post Office is on Main Square, the other at Ghoghla.

Tourist Offices and Information The Tourist Office is on Nagoa Rd to the right as you disembark from the ferry. Open Mon- Fri, 0930-1315, 1400-1745. Has all relevant travel information.

Air Keshod is the nearest airport, 150 km away. The airport at Diu is scheduled to open for Vayudoot flights in 1992.

Rail Delwada, 8 km N is the nearest railhead with trains to and from Junagadh. Shared auto rickshaws available for travel into Diu.

Bus Bus services to Ahmadabad, Bhavnagar, Palitana, Junagadh, Rajkot and Veraval from Una.
  Goa Travels runs a daily bus service with Bombay via Bhavnagar (20 hr). The Agent in Bombay is *Hirup Travel Service*, Prabhakar Sadan, Khetwadi Back Rd, 12th Line, T 358816, 359858. The Daman agent is *Satish General Stores*, Nani Daman.

Excursions In **Fudam**, S side of the island, there is the **Church of Our Lady of the Remedies** which is now rather dilapidated. *Vanakbara* on the W tip of the island has the **Church of Our Lady of Mercy**. There is a ferry service with Kotla.

Nagoa, 7 km from Diu Town on the S side of the island facing the Arabian Sea, has a beautiful palm-fringed beach suitable for swimming. Popular with foreign visitors. The **F** *Ganga Sagar Guest House* on the beach is clean, tidy, basic and well located. Very good meals (order in advance), bar. Plenty of seafood. **Bucharwada** not faraway, does not have attractive beaches but has cheap, spartan rm.

The unspoilt beaches at **Ahmedpur-Mandvi** which looks out to Diu, are also being developed. The bus from Una to Ghoghla may stop if you request, otherwise take a rickshaw from Ghoghla, 3 km or take a shorter path on foot, along the beach. Alternatively, stay in Diu and visit the beaches.

D ITDC *Tourist Bungalow* and TCGL Samundra Beach Resort with good rm in cottages. Restaurant recommended. Surfing, boating, water-skiing and para-sailing.

It is 80 km along the coast to **Somnath** via **Kodinar**. An alternative is to go inland to **Sasan Gir** (40 km) to visit the National Park.

AHMADABAD TO RAJKOT

The road runs across northern Saurashtra, skirting the central hills of the Kathiawar Peninsula. This is one of the major groundnut growing regions of India, but other crops include millets and wheat.

Leave Ahmadabad across the Ellis bridge and follow the **NH8A** through Sarkhej (8 km) and **Baola** (23 km) to **Bagodra**. A road on the left leads to Lothal. Continue through **Mithapur** (10 km) and **Tokrala** (21 km) to **Limdi** (13 km), the capital of a former princely state. The Rajput chief – Thakur Sahib – lived in a very attractive palace, which can still be seen. The town specialised in making ivory bangles and brass ware, especially boxes. Limdi town is 1 km from the main road.

The **NH8A** continues through **Sayla** (35 km) and **Chotila** (31 km). After 12 km the **NH8A** and **NH8B** join. Bear left onto **NH8B** for Rajkot. NH8A, to the right, goes to **Wankaner** (32 km). After 12 km the road crosses the **River Machu**, passes through **Kuvadva** (7 km) and then goes on to **Rajkot** (16 km).

Rajkot *Population* 550,000 *Altitude* 120 m

Although there is an early Palaeolithic site at Rajkot, there is very little evidence of significant settlement before the modern period. The capital of a second ranking Rajput Princely State, the town is best known as the early home of Mohandas Karamchand **Gandhi**. His family home is now a Gandhi museum. Rajkot was the home of the British Resident for the Western Indian States.

Widely regarded as a progressive state, Rajkot still has a number of buildings and institutions which date back to the end of the 19th century – the Rajkumar College (1870), the Alfred High School (1875) and the Kaisar-i-Hind Bridge (1910) are examples. It has become one of India's fast growing middle rank cities, its population nearly doubling in the last twenty years. That growth has been based on a rapid industrialisation, especially the processing of agricultural products such as groundnut.

Places of interest The Rajkumar College Founded in 1870, the College is now one of India's best known public schools. Gandhi was educated at the **Alfred High School,** which has a statue of him outside.

The Jubilee Gardens The Gardens, in the old civil station of the town, house the **Memorial Institute** which has the Lang Library and the Connaught Hall. The Watson Museum is also in the grounds.

Hotels All except Mohit International are central, 2-3 km from rly.

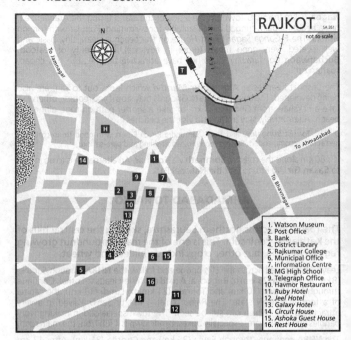

RAJKOT SA 261
not to scale

To Jamnagar
N
River Aji
T
H
14
1
9 7
2
3 8
10
13
4
5
6 15
16
B 11
12
To Ahmadabad
To Bhavnagar

1. Watson Museum
2. Post Office
3. Bank
4. District Library
5. Rajkumar College
6. Municipal Office
7. Information Centre
8. MG High School
9. Telegraph Office
10. Havmor Restaurant
11. *Ruby Hotel*
12. *Jeel Hotel*
13. *Galaxy Hotel*
14. *Circuit House*
15. *Ashoka Guest House*
16. *Rest House*

D *Samrat International,* 37 Karanpura, T 22269. 32 rm, some a/c with TV. Restaurant, exchange, travel, car hire, credit cards. **D** *Galaxy Hotel,* Jawahar Rd, T 31781. 35 rm, most a/c. Restaurant, car hire, credit cards. Clean and good value. **D** *Hotel Tulsi,* Kante Shree Vikas Guru Rd, T 31791. Some a/c rm. Restaurant, exchange, car hire, TV. Clean, modern hotel, excellent restaurant. **D** *Hotel Jayson,* Canal Rd (SVP Rd), T 26170. 18 rm some a/c. Restaurant, exchange, travel, car hire, credit cards. **D** *Hotel Mohit International,* Sir Harilal Gosaliya Marg, T 33338. 36 rm, some a/c. 2 km centre. Restaurant, exchange, credit cards.

F *Babha Guest House,* Panchnath Rd. Excellent vegetarian restaurant. There are several **F** Guest Houses nr the shopping Complex in Lakhajiraj Rd. *Ashok Guest House,* nr Municipal Office; *Himalaya Guest House.* Clean, good value; *Hotel Intimate.*

Restaurants *Kanchan Restaurant* in Hotel Tulsi is the most expensive, but possibly the best. *Rainbow Restaurant* Lakhajiraj Rd Good S Indian food; Varied menu at *Havmmor Restaurant,* nr Galaxy Hotel, also good value.

Shopping Shopping complex in Lakhajiraj Rd, a bazaar to its E and a fruit market just N of Jubilee Gardens.

Museum Watson Museum, Jubilee Gardens. Exhibits from Indus Valley civilisation, medieval sculpture, pottery and crafts, and colonial memorabilia.

Post and Telegraph GPO, MG Rd. The Telegraph Office is just N of MG Rd opp Jubilee Gardens.

Tourist Office and Information In Jubilee Gardens

Air Daily Indian Airlines connections with Bombay. Airlines bus to town.

Rail Bombay (Central) *Saurashtra Exp* 9216, daily 0030, 18 hr 40 min; *Saurashtra Janata Exp* 9018, daily 1430, 15 hr 15 min **Ahmadabad** Same trains as to Bombay; 5 hr 45 min; 5 hr 20 min; **Vadodara** Same as to Bombay, 9 hr 50 min; 8 hr **Porbandar** *Saurashtra Exp*

9215, 0205, 4 hr 40 min.

Road Rajkot is well connected by road to all the towns of the Kathiawar Peninsula, across to Kutch and N to Rajasthan.

Bus Good service to main towns in Gujarat. Private Luxury buses to Ahmadabad and Bombay daily run by Eagle Travels. Junagadh (2 hr), Veraval (5 hr), Jamnagar and Dwarka all served regularly.

RAJKOT TO JUNAGADH, VERAWAL AND SOMNATH

Junagadh is situated on the edge of the Girnar and Datta Hills. Archaeological excavations place the site in the pre-Harappan times. A rock with 14 Asokan edicts (dating from 250 BC) stands on the way to the temple-studded Girnar Hill.

From **Rajkot** take the road S to **Palri** (12 km) and **Ribda** (6 km). Following the railway line it continues S through the small town of **Gondal** (17 km) to **Virpur** (19 km), and then crosses the **River Bhadar** (11 km) by a rail-road bridge just 2 km before entering **Jetpur**.

In Jetpur a road takes a right fork to Porbandar (see below). Take the road straight ahead which goes SW through **Jetalsar** (5 km) and **Vadal** (16 km) to **Junagadh** (11 km).

Junagadh From the 2nd to 4th centuries Junagadh was the capital of Gujarat under the Kshattrapa rulers. It is also associated with the **Chadva Rajputs** who ruled from Junagadh from 875. The fort was expanded in 1472 by Mahmud Beghada, and again in 1683 and 1880. At the time of Partition, the ruler wanted his tiny princely state to join Pakistan. His subjects were predominantly Hindu and their will prevailed. He was exiled.

The town is surrounded by an old wall, large parts of which are now gone, but the narrow winding lanes and colourful bazaars are evocative of earlier centuries. You can often find excellent embroidery work in the shops.

The citadel The old citadel of **Uparkot** lies in the NE of the town and was a stronghold in the Mauryan and Gupta Empires, but was repeatedly under siege. Approached through three ornate gateways, the fort stands on a small plateau and contains the **Jami Masjid**, built from the remains of an Hindu temple, and the **Tomb of Nuri Shah**. The **Adi Chadi Vav** (15th century) is a *baoli** with 172 steps and an impressive spiral staircase. The 52 m deep **Navghan Kuva** is a similar well and has been dated to 1060.

Nearby are some **Buddhist caves** from the time of Asoka. On the W wall are two large guns, The larger is the 5.2 m long 25cm bore **Nilam** which was cast in Egypt in 1531. The smaller, The **Chudanal** is 3.8 m long. Both were left by Sulaiman Pasha, a Turkish Admiral to assist the local ruler repel the Portuguese.

The *Chattris** of the Junagadh rulers are impressive and feature silver doors, intricate and elaborate decoration. The **Maqbara of Baha-ud-din Bhar** almost has a fairground flamboyance.

The **Reay Gate** is a an arcaded two-storey crescent leading to the Clock Tower. The **Nawabs Palace** (c.1870) contains the **Durbar Hall Museum** which houses regal memorabilia incl portraits, palanquins and weapons.

E of the town is the 259 m long, 13.5 m high **Willingdon Dam** (1936).

Also in this direction is the *Girnar Hill*, which rises to 900 m above the surrounding plain and has been an important religious centre for the Jains from the 3rd century

JUNAGADH

SA 257

0   250
metres

N

UPARKOT
CITADEL

1. Adi Chadi Vav
2. Buddhist Caves
3. Navghan Kuva
4. Bapayava Caves
5. Borwad Mosque
6. Durbar Hall & Museum
7. Maqbara
8. Vegetable Market
9. Post Office
10. Library
11. Court
12. Moji Bagh
13. Bank
14. *Lake Guest House*
15. *Muridhar Guest House*
16. *Relief Hotel*
17. *Hotel Vaibhan*
B1. Local Bus Stand
B2. Long Distance Buses

BC. The ascent of this worn volcanic cone by 10,000 stone steps can take about 2 hours in the heat but fortunately there are tea stalls en route. The central peak of the ridges that form the crater is about 650 m. You start just beyond **Damodar Kund** in teak forest. At the foot is the Asoka Edict, carved in the ancient Pali script on a large boulder. Later Sanskrit inscriptions were added in 150 AD and 450 AD by **Sakandagupta**, the last Mauryan Emperor. Open 0900-1200, 1500-1800.

There is a group of 16 Jain temples on the hill. The two near the top are the **Neminatha** (1128), one of the oldest and **Mallinatha Temple** (1231) dedicated to the 19th Tirthankar. The corbelled domes, maidens and flying figures as decoration are typical of the Solanki period. A popular fair is held here during the Kartika Purnima Festival in Nov/Dec. There is also the **Temple of Samprati Raja** (1453), a fine example of the later period and the **Melak Vasahi Temple** (15th century).

You can take an hourly No.3 or 4 bus from the stand opposite the GPO to **Girnar Taleti** at the foot of the hill. It passes the Asoka edicts. About Re 0.50.

Parks and zoos *Sakar Bagh Zoo* Open daily except Wed, second and fourth Sat in the month. Take bus No. 1, 2 or 6. 3.5 km N of the town centre on the Rajkot Rd.

If you are unable to go to Gir, or did not have the good fortune to see the lions there, this small zoo has some. The zoo is well kept and in addition to the lions has tigers, leopards among others. The garden also houses a fine **museum** with local paintings, manuscripts, archaeological finds and natural history.

Hotels E *Vaibhav*, nr S.T. Stand, T 21070-1, Cable: Vaibhav. 48 rm, some a/c. 30 km Keshod airport, nr rly and centre. A/c vegetarian restaurant, 24 hr coffee shop, car hire, 24 hr rm service. The *Railway Retiring Rooms* are clean and well maintained. The **F** *Murlidhar* with restaurant, its annexe, **F** *Jai Shri Guest House* and **F** *Tourist Guest House* are grouped around the Kalwa Chowk, one of the two main squares in Junagadh. The **E** *Relief* on Dhal Rd is regarded as a friendly and reasonable place.

Restaurants The *Vaibhav* has a vegetarian restaurant while the *Relief* Hotel with a reasonable dining hall serves vegetarian and non vegetarian meals. The *Sharda Lodge* nr the railway station does a good *thali*. The *Murlidhar* and *Gita Lodge* also have restaurants.

Banks The *Bank of India* and *Bank of Saurashtra* both change Travellers' Cheques.

Tourist Information Tourism Corporation of Gujarat, Tourist Office, nr Durbar Hall Museum. Open 1130-1700 Mon-Sat. Helpful staff. *Junagadh and Girnar* by S.H. Desai, on sale, is quite useful.

Air Daily flight from Bombay to **Keshod**.

Rail Ahmadabad: *Somnath Mail* 9823, daily, 1706, 12 hr; *Girnar Exp* 9845, daily, 1941, 10 hr 30 min.

Bus Regular bus services to Ahmadabad, Rajkot, Veraval, Porbander and Sasan Gir.

Continue SW to **Vanthli** (15 km). The road goes straight on, a road on the right leading to Porbandar. Continue to **Keshod** (20 km), the nearest point of entry to the **Sasan Gir.**

Sasan Gir National Park

Season Dec-Jun; Best Mar-May, closed during monsoons. Jeeps with guides, camera charges, Rs 30 for movie.

The *Asiatic Lion* *Panthera leo persica*, the Asiatic Lion, once had a wide range in natural territory running from NW India through Persia to Arabia. It is now only found in the Gir forest of Gujarat. Similar to its African cousin, it is a little stockier in build, has a thinner mane and a thicker tuft at the end of its tail. At one time there were only 20 in the park. Gradual conversion of the forest into agricultural land and the activities of the *maldharis* (cattle men) in grazing their livestock in the forest posed problems for the lions' natural habitat.

The conservation programme has been remarkably successful – the 1985 Census put the number of lions at 239, up from 205 in 1980. By 1990 the figure was put at 270, according to a senior research fellow at the Wildlife Institute of India, far too many for the area of the sanctuary. You can be sure of sighting the animal with the help of a tracker and guide.

The savannah environment The National Park covers a total area of 1,412 sq km of which about 10% is forest. The cattle invasion and agricultural colonization are partly responsible for the small proportion but much of the natural vegetation in the region was scrub jungle as opposed to forest. The forest is typically dry deciduous with dry-forest teak dominating stands. Other species include *Terminalia crenulata* (sadad), *Diospyros melanoxylon* (tendu), *Butea monosperma* (palas) and *Wrightia tinctoria* (dudhi). There are extensive clearing covered with savannah-like fodder grasses. In the elevated, E part of the park, tree growth is sparse and stunted.

Wildlife Apart from the lion, Gir has common langur, leopard, hyena, sambar, chital, nilgai, chowsingha, chinkara and wild pig. Lions in Africa do not hunt deer for the simple reason that there aren't any but here the large population of over 8,000 chital should provide suitable prey for the lion in place of cattle. There are over 2,000 **nilgai** and 1,000 **chinkara**. The **chowsingha** is exclusively Indian and is unique in being the only wild animal where in the male there are two pairs of horns. The does are hornless. It is found on flat hilltop where there is short herbage. Like its nearest relative the African **kilpspringer** it can jump high from almost a standing start.

Attacks In 1990 there was a spate of complaints about the rise in attacks on villagers by lions from the parks. In the two years up to May 1990, 15 had been killed and 90 injured.

Lions were reported as wandering as much as 60 km beyond the perimeter of the park itself. Villagers blamed the sanctuary's new policy excluding the cattle herds of *maldharis* (shepherds). They believed that stray cattle from these herds offered ideal prey for the lions, and their removal is now forcing lions to look elsewhere for food.

Hotels There are only two places to stay. The GTDC **D** *Lion Safari Lodge*, Sasan Gir, T 362135. 24 rm with bath, 6 comfortable a/c. Restaurant, tours of sanctuary and folk dances. The **E** *Forest Department Guesthouse*. Small non a/c chalets with bath. Spacious gardens. Book direct two weeks in advance or through Government of Gujarat Office, Dhanraj Mahal, Apollo Bunder, Bombay, T 257039 or the Gujarat Information Centre, Baba Kharak Singh Marg, New Delhi, T 343147.

Also in the park at Tulsishyam there is a scenic hot spring, a temple to Bhim and a TCGL *Toran Holiday Home*. Checkout 0900.

Air The nearest airport is Keshod.

Rail Daily slow train direct from Junagadh to Sasan Gir (2 hr 30 min), continuing on to Delwada near Diu. The station is 10 minutes walk from the forest lodge.

Bus Bus service from **Junagadh** (54 km), 2 hr 30 min, and one from **Veraval** (2 hr).

From Keshod the road goes S to **Galodar** (18 km) and **Gadu** (10 km). A right turn leads to the small seaside town of **Chorvad** (10 km), a popular beach resort where the former summer palace of the Maharajah of Junagadh on the sea shore has been turned into a comfortable resort hotel with a pool.

Continue straight to **Veraval** (20 km), which is 80 km S of Junagadh via **Vanthali** where the road branches. Veraval is to the S and Porbander (71 km) straight on. The local airport of **Keshod** is roughly half way between Junagadh and Veraval.

The town (*Population* 105,000) was the major seaport for pilgrims to Mecca before the rise of Surat. Its importance now is as a fishing port with dhows still being built by the sea. It is a noisy, extremely smelly, and not particularly attractive town, but it is a suitable base for visiting the Hindu pilgrimage centre of Somnath at Prabhas Patan – see **Excursions**.

Hotels The **E** *Toran Tourist Bungalow* (TCGL), nr beach and **E** *Circuit House* nr the lighthouse have pleasant sea views. Others are noisy – The **E** *Satkar*, nr Bus Stand, T 120 is well maintained and clean. Some a/c rooms plus a dormitory. *Railway Retiring Rooms* and **F** *Chandrani Guesthouse* nearby.

Restaurants *Satkar* does good thalis. *La'Bela* is quite good. *Swati* (a/c) and *New Apsara* nr railway station serves vegetarian food.

Air Nearest airport is Keshod. No Indian Airlines office in Veraval but *Somnath Travels*, Satta Bazaar, T 162 will obtain tickets.

Rail Ahmadabad Somnath Mail 9823, daily, 1445, 14 hr 25 min; Girnar Express 9845, daily, 1745, 12 hr 25 min.

Road Buses to **Keshod** (1 hr), Diu via Kodinar, Porbander via Chorvad and Mangrol and also to **Bhavnagar** (9 hr).

Excursions *Somnath*, 6 km E of Veraval. The **Somnath Temple**, a major Hindu pilgrimage centre, is said to have been built out of gold by Somraj, the Moon God (and subsequently in silver, wood and stone). In keeping with the legend the stone façade appears golden at sunset. **Mahmud of Ghazni**, plundered it and removed the gates in 1024. Destroyed by successive Muslim invaders, it was rebuilt each time on the same spot.

The final reconstruction did not take place until 1950 and is still going on. Unfortunately, it lacks character but it has been built to traditional patterns with a soaring 50 m high tower that rises in clusters. Dedicated to Siva, it has one of the 12 sacred *Jyotirlingas** (see page 334).

Krishna was believed to have been hit by an arrow, shot by the Bhil, Jara, when he was mistaken for a deer at Bhalka Teerth, nearby, and was cremated at Triveni Ghat.

Nearby is the ruined **Rudreshvara Temple** which dates from the same time as

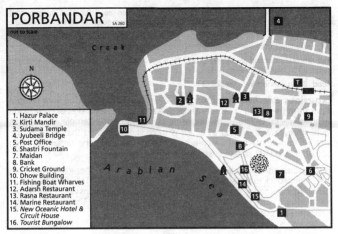

PORBANDAR SA 260
not to scale

1. Hazur Palace
2. Kirti Mandir
3. Sudama Temple
4. Jyubeeli Bridge
5. Post Office
6. Shastri Fountain
7. Maidan
8. Bank
9. Cricket Ground
10. Dhow Building
11. Fishing Boat Wharves
12. Adarsh Restaurant
13. Rasna Restaurant
14. Marine Restaurant
15. *New Oceanic Hotel &
   Circuit House*
16. *Tourist Bungalow*

the Somnath Temple and was laid out in a similar fashion. The sculptures on the walls and doorways give an indication of what the Somnath Temple was like.

Museum There is a small **Archaeological Museum** with pieces from the former temples. Open 0900-1200, 1500-1800, closed Wed and holidays.

Hotels F *Hotel Mayuram*, Triveni Rd. Double rm and restaurant. Good food, clean. F *Shri Somnath Guest House*, nr Temple has 200 very basic rm. Better accommodation at Veraval.

You can reach Somnath from Veraval by auto-rickshaw (Rs 15) or bus (Re 1.50).

RAJKOT TO PORBANDAR

The road runs S past the central hills of Kathiawad Peninsula then W to Porbandar.

Follow the **NH8B** outlined above from **Rajkot** to **Jetpur** (67 km). Turn right in Jetpur and continue W along the **NH8B** through the market town of Dhoraji (16 km) to the bridge over the River Bhadar (6 km). Pass through **Upleta** (13 km) and cross the rivers **Vinu** (9 km) and **Vadal** (7 km) to Chavta (14 km). To the S the rivers run into the marshes behind the coast. The road goes through Kutiyana (4 km), Kandorna (11 km) and Ranawao (13 km) on its way to Porbandar (18 km).

Porbandar is the former capital of the Jethwa Rajput petty princely state (1660 sq km). In ancient times it was known as **Sudamapuri** (after Krishna's comrade) and had a flourishing trade with Africa and Arabia. Today, fine quality silk and cotton are manufactured here. There are also chemical factories and cement works. You can still see dhows being made.

Mahatama Gandhi was born in Porbandar (1869). Next to the house with its carved balconies is **Kirti Mandir**, a small museum that traces his life and contains memorablia and a library. The **Planetarium** here has shows in Gujarati only. The **Bharat Mandir Hall,** situated in a pleasant irrigated garden, has a large relief map of India on the floor and bas reliefs of heroes from Hindu legends on the pillars. The Maharana's deserted **Hazur Palace** is near the sea front.

Warning Swimming is not recommended in the harbour. Down the coast towards **Veraval** is better.

Hotels E *New Tourist Bungalow* (TCGL), Chowpatty, nr sea, T 22745. Good views of harbour and Barda Hills. Checkout 0900. Large, spacious and quiet. The **E** *New Oceanic* is nearby. In town there are a few cheap **F** hotels and *Railway Retiring Rooms*.

Air Daily flight from Bombay via Keshod.

Rail Bombay Central *Saurashtra Exp* 9216, daily, 2000, 23 hr 10 min. Also services with Rajkot and Ahmadabad.

Road Buses connect with Veraval (3 hr.)

Excursions *Bileshwar* approximately 15 km E of Porbander. The **Siva Temple** dates from the early 7th century and is one of the finest examples of early Hindu architecture in Gujarat. The enclosure is later but the temple itself has a multi-storey tower (*shikhara*) which is more like a pyramid than a spire. The exterior is decorated with arch-like motifs but much of the detail has been obscured by a later plaster coating.

In the picturesque wooded valley at *Ghumli* a few km further inland there are ruins dating back to the Solanki period (10th-13th centuries). The **Vikia Vav** (early 12th century) is one of the largest step-wells in Gujarat. Pavilions were constructed over the steps with one at the entrance. All were richly carved. The well also served a religious purpose as a water sanctuary.
   Nearby is a ruined **Naulakha** (900,000) **Temple** (early 13th century).

Gop, approximately 50 km NE of Porbander and midway on the Porbander-Jamnagar road. The 6th century temple dates from the Maitraka period (6th-8th centuries) and is a rare example of an early Hindu temple. The sanctuary is on a raised platform and has a pyramidal roof with an amalaka topping it off. The whole is in a dilapidated state.

RAJKOT TO DWARKA AND OKHA

Millets, sorghum, wheat and cotton dominate the cultivable land between Rajkot and the coast. To the S are large areas of brackish water and saline soils, but where the water is sweet rich crops can be achieved on the alluvial soils. Further W farming becomes progressively more marginal, and towards Dwarka clay soils are occasionally interspersed with higher limestones.

From **Rajkot** take the road NW to **Jamnagar**. Pass through **Paddhari** (24 km) and **Dhrol** (25 km) and then cross the **River Nagmati** (34 km) by a road and rail bridge. **Jamnagar** is a further 3 km.

Jamnagar is a small 16th century pearl fishing town and capital of the Jadeja Rajputs minor princely state of Nawanagar. The famous cricketer Ranjitsinghji was its ruler from 1907-33 and his successor, Jam Sahib, became the President of Saurashtra until it was absorbed into Bombay State in 1956.

The walled city is famous for its *bandhani* (tie-dyed) fabrics, embroidery and silver ware. The **Ayurvedic College and Research Centre** teaches the practice of Indian herbal cures. The old town is built around a lake with the **Lakhota Fort** and **Kotha Bastion** with its arsenal, on the island in it which are reached by a bridge. The fort has a good collection of sculpture and pottery found in ruined medieval villages. Open Th-Tues, 0900-1200, 1500-1800. The bastion has an old well from which water can be drawn by blowing into a small hole in the floor. The **Solarium** uses solar radiation to cure diseases.

Hotels D *President*, Teen Batti. T 70516, 70283, Cable: Sweethome. 27 rm, some a/c with TV. 8 km airport, 3 km rly, central. Restaurant, 24 hr rm service, car hire, Diners. There are a

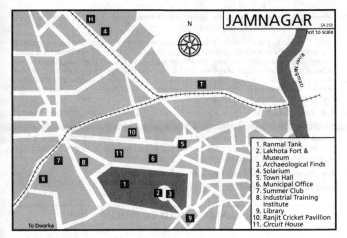

JAMNAGAR SA 259 not to scale

1. Ranmal Tank
2. Lakhota Fort & Museum
3. Archaeological Finds
4. Solarium
5. Town Hall
6. Municipal Office
7. Summer Club
8. Industrial Training Institute
9. Library
10. Ranjit Cricket Pavillion
11. Circuit House

number if **E** and **F** hotels along the Station Rd.

Air There is a daily flight from Bombay that continues on to Bhuj.

Rail Ahmadabad: *Saurashtra Exp* 9216, daily, 2251, 7 hr 25 min; *Saurashtra Mail* 9006, daily, 1435, 7 hr 30 min. **Bombay Central**: *Saurashtra Exp* 9216, daily, 2251, 20 hr 20 min; *Saurashtra Mail* 9006, daily, 1440, 17 hr 25 min.

Road Several buses to **Rajkot** and **Porbandar**.

Continue along the coast through **Vasai** (16 km) to **Khambaliya** (42 km), where you have the choice of going to **Dwarka** and **Okha** (114 km) at the mouth of the Gulf of Kutch or S to **Porbandar** (74 km). The road to Okha continues straight on, a winding road across some rolling countryside. It passes through **Variawader** (34 km), **Bhatia** (11 km) and **Miyani** (14 km) to **Okha Madhi** (8 km). In a further 31 km it reaches **Dwarka**.

Dwarkahas the unique distinction of being one of Hinduism's four Holy Abodes as well as one of its seven Holy Places. It is one of the most sacred sites for Vaishnavite Hindus, celebrated as Krishna's capital.

A small coastal town on the tip of the Kathiawar peninsula it is closely associated with the Krishna legend and it is believed that Krishna set up his capital here after his flight from Mathura. Archaeological excavations indicate that present day Dwarka is built on the sites of four former cities. Work in 1990 by the marine archaeologist SR Rao discovered triangular anchors weighing 250 kg, suggesting that ships of up to 120 tonnes had used the port. The anchors are believed to be identical to those used by ships from Cyprus and Syria during the Bronze Age, going back to the 14th century BC. Much of the town was submerged by rising sea levels. The evidence suggests that in the 15th century BC it was a large trading port, with fortifications and town planning.

It is an important site for the *Janmashtami* festival in Aug/Sep – see Bombay (page 941).

The 12th century **Rukmini Temple** and the 16th century **Dvarkanath Temple** attract thousands of pilgrims each year. The latter was supposedly built in one night where the inner sanctum is thought to be 2,500 years old but non Hindus usually cannot enter. Anyway, the exterior is more interesting. The soaring five storey tower is supported by 60 columns. The BJP started its *'Rath Yatra'* pilgrimage across India to the Babri Masjid mosque in Ayodhya here in 1989, leading to widespread communal rioting.

In the 19th century the Gaekwar rulers developed the town as a popular religious centre. A pilgrimage to Dwarka is not complete until a visit has been made to **Beyt Dwarka**, a Hindu temple on the island off the coast. The temple dates from the 19th century and contains a series of shrines and images of Krishna and his 56 consorts. Archaeological excavations have revealed Harappan artefacts dating from the 2nd millenium BC. Inexpensive **F** category accommodation available. **Toran Tourist Dormitory** nr Govt Guest House. Checkout 0900. *Railway Retiring Room* and a number of small cheap hotels.

Rail Ahmadabad: *Saurashtra Mail* 9006, daily, 1158, 10 hr 7 min. **Bombay Central**: *Saurashtra Mail* 9006, daily, 1203, 20 hr 2 min.

Okha is a small port at the head of the Gulf of Kutch and is about 30 km N of Dwarka. A few **F** category hotels here. The island nearby is connected with the legend of Vishnu slaying the demon.

Rail Ahmadabad: *Saurashtra Mail* 9006, daily, 1115, 10 hr 20 min.

Road Local buses connect Okha with Dwarka.

AHMADABAD TO BHUJ

The route to Kutch follows the NH8 out of Ahmadabad, going towards Rajkot as far as Chotila (see above). It then follows NH8A down the gentle gradient to the waste land of the Little Rann of Kutch, which it crosses at the narrowest point some 25 km inland of the Gulf of Kutch. Once across the mud and salt flats the NH8A curves S to Gandhidham while the road to Bhuj goes straight across the semi desert.

From **Chotila** follow the **NH8A** for 2 km towards **Rajkot**. After 12 km turn right off the Rajkot road towards *Wankaner* (25 km). The Raja of Wankaner came to a political arrangement with the East India Company in 1807. It was then left largely to its own devices through the 19th century. Maharaja Amarsinghji (1881-1948) introduced wide-ranging reforms. He was also responsible for building the *Ranjit Nilas Palace*, visible for miles across the plains. It is built in a variety of European and Indian styles. Today it is run by Maharajah Rajsaheb Pratapsinghji as a guesthouse. Ranjitvilas Palace, T 363621   Cable: Secretary, Palace, Wankaner.

The road continues to the capital of another tiny Princely State, *Morvi* (29 km). Morvi dominated access to the Peninsula. Making use of the trade route, Morvi developed into a modern state under the leadership of Thakur Sahib Waghaji (r1879-1948). There are two palaces of interest. The older is the Dubargadh Waghaji Palace (1880), with a Venetian Gothic exterior and Rajput, Gothic and Indo-Saracenic features inside. It is approached by a suspension bridge. The New Palace (1931-44) contains some late Art Deco features, like the Umaid Bhavan Palace in Jodhpur, and similarly includes some subterranean rooms.

After 33 km there is a road junction, with a left run to Malia (3 km). The **NH8A** continues straight on to the Little Rann of Kutch (13 km). The bridge is 1.2 km long.

Kutch

Kutch is the northwesternmost part of Gujarat, the least appealing climatically, the most sparsely populated and well and truly off the beaten tourist trail. The various communities, such as Rabaris, Ahirs, Meghwals among others, each have a distinct dress and practise a particular craft.

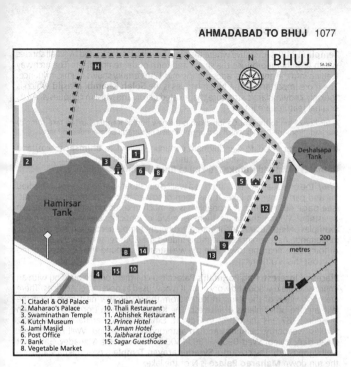

1. Citadel & Old Palace
2. Maharao's Palace
3. Swaminathan Temple
4. Kutch Museum
5. Jami Masjid
6. Post Office
7. Bank
8. Vegetable Market
9. Indian Airlines
10. Thali Restaurant
11. Abhishek Restaurant
12. *Prince Hotel*
13. *Amam Hotel*
14. *Jaibharat Lodge*
15. *Sagar Guesthouse*

The Rann The low lying Rann of Kutch in the N, a part of the Thar desert, is a hard smooth bed of dried mud in the dry season. Some vegetation exists, concentrated on little islands. The herds of the endangered wild ass that roam this barren area feed at night on vegetation at the edge, then retreat inland during the day. A sanctuary has been created for them but there is little point contemplating visiting it because it is a sensitive border area, accommodation is non existent and the beasts themselves are very rarely seen.

The monsoon With the arrival of the SW monsoon in May the saltwater of the Gulf of Kutch invades the Rann and the Rajasthan rivers pour fresh water into it. It then becomes an inland sea and very dangerous for those who get trapped in it. In ancient times armies have perished there. At this time Kutch virtually becomes an island. From Dec to Feb, it becomes the nesting ground of flamingoes. You will also see sand-grouse and Imperial grouse.

Salt An important activity is salt production and railway lines back into the Rann to facilitate the transport of it.

After the bridge the NH8A goes on to **Kataria** (13 km), **Samakhiali** (13 km), and **Bhachau** (16 km), keeping close to the railway. After 18 km there is a left turn to **Gandhidham** (13 km), a new town founded by the Maharaos of Kutch to accommodate refugees from Sind in Pakistan on Partition.

Hotels D *Shiv*, 360 Ward 12-B. T 21630, Telex: 105-237 Siv in. 39 rm with TV, some a/c rm. 9 km airport, 1 km rly, central location. Restaurant, 24 hr rm service, ice cream parlour, car hire, travel, Diners.

Excursions *Bhadreshwar,* 36 km W along the coast from Gandhidam was important as an ancient seaport and has a temple and two mosques. The **Jain**

Temple (1248) is attractive where the main building is surrounded by small shrines which together reproduce the shape and form of the temple itself. The archway leading into the enclosure, added in the mid 12th century.shows Islamic influence. The more important of the two mosques is the **Solah Khambi Masjid** which is the only known Islamic structure that existed before the Muslim conquests. All its original features are intact.

A further 27 km to the S of Gandhidham is the new port of *Kandla*, built to take some of the trade from the Punjab which had been handled by Karachi before Independence.

If you do not divert to Gandhidham continue straight to **Bhimsar** (5 km) and **Anjar** (15 km), where there is a left turn to New Kandla Port. Continue through **Ratnal** (14 km) and **Kumka** (16 km) to **Bhuj** (11 km).

Bhuj, the principal town of Kutch, is a walled city situated at the base of a fortified hill and partly round a lake. It has been described as the 'Jaisalmer of Gujarat' (**see page 400**) though it probably has as much in common with Bundi, also in Rajasthan. Within the walls there is maze of enticing alleyways and many examples of fine Gujarati architecture, exuberant temple decoration and colourful inhabitants. As a reminder that this is indeed the 20th century there is an Indian Airforce Base near the town. The old wall stretches around the hills overlooking Bhuj but this is off limits.

Places of Interest Rag Pagmali's Palace is a charming ornate building with an impressive inlaid wood and ivory door. It is now used as government offices. There are good views of the Rann of Kutch from the clocktower next door. Near the lake are the other places of interest. The **Kutch Museum** (formerly Fergusson Museum, 1877) is the oldest in Gujarat. Exhibits include archaeological finds, textiles, weaponry, paintings and an anthropological section. Well maintained. Open daily except Wed 0900-1130, 1500-1730. Near the Mahadev Gate (not well signposted) the colourful **Swaminarayan Temple** is near the bazaar while the run down **Maharao Palace** is N of the lake.

Hotels D *Park View*, Hospital Rd, T 344. A/c rm with bath and restaurant. **E** *Prince*, Station Rd, T 1095,1370-1. A/c and non a/c rm with bath. Good restaurant. **E** *Anam*, Station Rd, T 1390-3. A/c and non a/c rm and restaurant. **F** *Ratrani*, Station Rd, T 1607. Non a/c rm with bath. **F** *Sagar Guest House* nr Bus Station and **F** *Ambassador*, nr main Post Office are similar. Non a/c rooms with bath and a dormitory. The government Rest House, *Umed Bhavan* has cheap beds.

Restaurants In addition to the hotel restaurants mentioned above, there is the *Grand Punjab Hotel* and the *Omlet Centre* near the bus terminal. The *Abhishek* nr the Prince Hotel serves S Indian snacks.

Banks *State Bank of India*, Station Rd changes money.

Air Indian Airlines have daily flights from Bombay to Bhuj via Jamnagar. Because it is so near the Pakistan border, the security at the airport is tight. Pack cameras away in your checked luggage, along with knives, scissors and batteries. The airport is 4 km from the town centre and taxis and autorickshaws tend to charge about Rs 10.

Rail Daily rail connection with Ahmadabad, but very slow. Also trains between Bhuj and Kandla Port. The most convenient train is the *Bombay-Gandhidham Kutch Exp* 9031, daily, 1715, 14 hr 30 min. The same train departs Ahmadabad 0143, 6 hr.

Road There are buses to Ahmadabad and other centres in Gujarat. It is a two day bus journey from Jaisalmer via Barmer.

AHMADABAD TO MOUNT ABU

The **NH8** runs N across the plains of the Sabarmati, following the railway line all the way to Abu Road. After the fertile irrigated land immediately N of Ahmadabad the countryside becomes increasingly arid northwards towards Rajasthan. It passes nearby some outstanding monuments.

Leave Ahmadabad over the Nehru Bridge. Turn right, and after 6 km turn right again for **Mehsana** on the **NH8** going N. The road goes through Sertha (17 km), by-passes Kalol (6 km) and continues for 43 km, where it crosses the **River Khari**. **Mehsana** is then 4 km. In Mehsana a road on the left leads to the important centre of **Modhera** (26 km).

Today Modhera is a virtually deserted hamlet. However, the partially ruined **Surya (Sun) Temple** (1026), built during the reign of **Bhimdev I**, two centuries before the Sun Temple at Konarak, is one of the finest Hindu temples in Gujarat, a product of the great Solanki period (8th – 13th centuries). Despite its partial destruction by Mahmud of Ghazni and by subsequent earthquakes, it remains an outstanding monument, set against the backdrop of a barren landscape. Superb carvings of goddesses, birds, beasts and blossoms on the pillars decorate the remaining pillars.

The entrance A large rectangular pool (kunda) with flights of steps and subsidiary shrines faced the E front of the temple. On the W side a steep flight of steps leads up to the main entrance of the temple. Unlike the much later Sun Temple at Konarak, with which it is sometimes compared, the main temple stands well above the surrounding land, raised by a high brick terrace faced with stone.

The sabha mandapa Passing through the richly carved archway (torana), the pillared hall is 15 m square. Note the cusped arches which became such a striking feature of Mughal buildings 600 years later. The roof of this entry hall is a low stepped pyramid. Beautiful columns and magnificent carvings decorate the hall.

The raised sanctuary The W part of the temple contains the inner sanctuary within its oblong plan. The upper storeys have been completely destroyed, though it clearly consisted of a low pyramidal roof in front of the tall sikhara (tower) over the sanctuary itself. Surya's image in the sanctuary (now missing) was once illuminated by the first rays of the rising sun at each solar equinox. Archaeologists are slowly restoring the building with sandstone. Unlike the exterior, the interior walls were plain other than for niches to house images of Surya.

Road Far more off the beaten track, and much less well known than the Sun Temple at Konarak, Modhera retains a great deal of its atmosphere and charm. There are direct buses to Modhera from Ahmadabad. Alternatively, you can take the train to **Mehsana** (same as for Patan) and take a bus for the 35 km road trip to the site. The TCGL runs *Toran* which is suitable for a light meal or snack. The **F** *PWD Rest House* has basic accommodation.

Return to **Mehsana** and turn N on the **NH8**. After 15 km cross the **River Pushmawati** and continue through **Unawa** (9 km) to **Unjha** (4 km). After 1 km there is a left turn to **Patan** (28 km).

Patan which in the 8th century under the name of Anahilvada, was the capital of the Hindu kings of Gujarat. **Mahmud of Ghazni** sacked it in 1024, and it was taken by **Ala-ud-din Khalji's** brother Alaf Khan in 1306.

Off the beaten track, Patan has over 100 beautifully carved **Jain temples** and many attractive traditional carved wooden houses. It is a centre for fine textiles, particularly silk *patola* saris produced by the characteristic *ikat** technique. Little remains of the old city except some of the walls, **Rani Vav** (Queen's Well, late 11th century), a step well recently renovated and the **Sahasra Linga** (1,000 Linga) 12th century **Tank**.

Rail Patan is 25 km N of **Mehsana**, the most suitable place for getting off the train.

Return to the main road N, and cross the **River Saraswati**. Pass through **Sidhpur** (2 km), across the **River Amardasi** (17 km) to **Palanpur** (13 km). Continue through **Balaram** (15 km) where the **River Balaram** is crossed to the Gujarat-Rajasthan border at **Amirgarh** (22 km). **Abu Road** is a further 14 km.

PAKISTAN

Official name of the Country Islami Jamhuriya-e-Pakistan (Islamic Republic of Pakistan).

National flag Dark green ground, with white vertical band at the mast. In the centre of the green area is a white crescent and a five-pointed heraldic star.

Official Language Urdu

Official Religion Islam

Basic Indicators *Population* 105m; *Urban* 30%. *Religion Muslim* 97%, *Christian* 1.7%, *Hindu* 1.3%. *Birth rate* 35 per 1000 *Death rate* 10 per 1000 *Infant mortality rate* 105 per 1000 *GNP per capita* US$343.

GENERAL INTRODUCTION

Pakistan lies between 24 °N and 38 °N and 62 °E and 76 °E. It is essentially a borderland and a region of contact. Climatically it is at the northwestern limits of the S Asian monsoon, where the rainbearing monsoon winds reaching it from the south and east have lost most of their moisture. Without irrigation the fertile plains of the Punjab trail into the deserts of Sind and Baluchistan. Physically, the high peaks of the western Himalayas and the Karakoram, which make up Pakistan's northern boundary, decline southwards through the Hindu Kush into Afghanistan and the arid hills of the Afghan border. In the far South these become an extension of the Iranian plateau to the west, forming another area of continuity with the Iranian desert rather than a sharp divide.

A frontier region For centuries Pakistan has been a frontier region. Successive groups have passed from the W through to the new heartland of power in the S Asian subcontinent, the Ganga valley. To find the only exception to this pattern you have to go back nearly 4,000 years, when the Indus valley was a unified political and cultural area. Since the collapse of the Indus Valley civilisation by 1700 BC, much of what is now Pakistan was continuously contested by various warring tribes.

Yet well before the Indus Valley period, the territory of modern Pakistan was another kind of frontier zone, that between settled agriculture and nomadic pastoralism. The evidence of settled agriculture now goes back to more than 10,000 years ago, beginning in the foothills of Baluchistan to the W of the Indus. It spread and developed, using the water from the Indus itself, but nomadic tribes continued to occupy the arid lands of Baluchistan and the NW Frontier, migrating from the mountains where they had their summer pastures down to the valleys and the plains in the winters.

At no time after the Indus Valley civilisation ended was the entire territory of Pakistan under the effective control of one ruler until Pakistan itself was created, for even in the British period there were a number of Princely States, and the Frontier itself was governed in a quite distinct way from elsewhere in British India.

The Islamic Republic of Pakistan became an independent state on 14 Aug 1947. Until 1971 it comprised the 2 wings of East and West Pakistan, but in Dec 1971 East Pakistan seceded to become Bangladesh. Today Pakistan is divided into 4 Provinces. In addition Pakistan controls the northern region. Legally acceded to India soon after Independence by the Maharaja, fighting erupted in Kashmir in 1947, and from early 1949 a cease-fire line has separated Indian held Kashmir to the S from what Pakistan calls "Azad Kashmir" (Free Kashmir) and the Northern Areas of Gilgit, Hunza, Chilas and Skardu. Many maps of S Asia show the *de jure* position of these regions as an integral part of India. The *de facto* line of actual control runs approximately W-E just N of Srinagar, and the area to the N is administered by Pakistan.

The Provinces The 4 Provinces are highly unequal in area and population. The largest, Baluchistan, covers 347,000 sq km (44% of the total land area) but has a population of less than 5 million (under 5% of the total). Punjab, although it has only a quarter of Pakistan's area (205,000 sq km) has over 62 million people (nearly 60%), while Sind covers just under 141,000 square kilometres (18%) and has 25 million people (22%). North West Frontier Province has 75,000 sq km (just over 9% of the total) and 15 million people (13%). To the N is the Agency territory of the Northern Areas, adding a further 72,000 sq km, and Azad Kashmir.

The planned capital Karachi was the first capital of Pakistan, but as Pakistan's only port and major industrial city it grew so rapidly that it threatened to dominate and completely distort the economic and political geography of the country. In 1958 President Ayub Khan decided to build the new capital city of Islamabad next door to the small N Punjab town of Rawalpindi, and the move was confirmed in the Constitution of 1962. Although Islamabad has grown rapidly and now has over 400,000 people it remains less than 1/20th the size of Karachi. Lahore, capital of the Punjab and Pakistan's second largest city, has a far longer urban history than either Karachi or Islamabad, going back over 900 years as the undisputed chief city of Punjab. In 1955 it was chosen as capital of the then Pakistan, but when West Pakistan was divided into 4 Provinces in 1970 it became capital of Punjab.

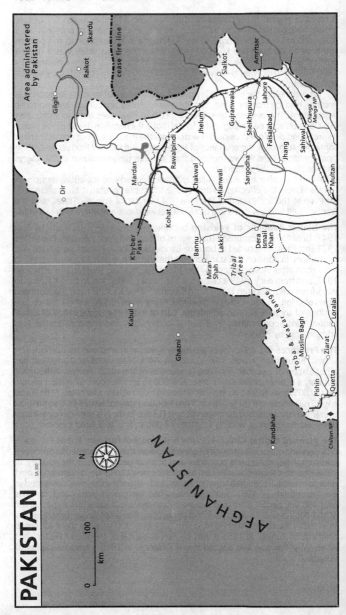

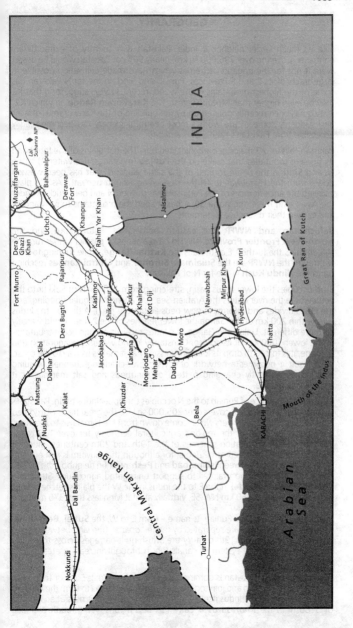

GEOGRAPHY

Like its much larger neighbour India, Pakistan is a country of extraordinary contrasts. Covering over 796,000 sq km, nearly 90% of Pakistan would be desert were it not for the irrigation schemes which have made cultivation possible in large tracts of its E and S Provinces, Punjab and Sind. In the far N Pakistan has some of the highest mountains in the world, recent surveys suggesting that K2 may be even higher than Mount Everest. The **Karakoram Range** in which **K2** stands has been recently opened up by the building of the Karakoram Highway, and suddenly some of the world's most beautiful scenery has become readily accessible from Pakistan's capital of Islamabad.

Pakistan falls into 3 major geographical regions. The flat plains of the Indus and its 5 major tributaries that make up the **Punjab** (meaning "five waters") in the N, and **Sind** in the S, are formed of the same alluvium that has been washed down from the Himalayas to fill the deepening trough beneath. As the plate carrying the ancient rocks of the Peninsula has pushed N and been sucked under the Asian land mass, **see page 30**, it has shaped the mountains to its N and W and caused their distinctive alignments.

Baluchistan and NWFP The eastern borders of **Baluchistan** and the **North-West Frontier Province** (NWFP) have a series of parallel ranges running N-S. In the S the furthest E of these is the **Kirthar Range**, while running to their N through the **NWFP** are the **Sulaiman**, **Surghar** and **Chitral Ranges** reaching up to the **Hindu Kush** in the far N of Pakistan.

Sind occupies the lower Indus basin, stretching from 150 km N of Sukkur to the delta where the river enters the Arabian Sea. It is a land of regular flooding, and the Indus divides and reforms in new beds across the plain. Although the Indus rises within 200 km of the Ganga the lower reaches of the 2 rivers could scarcely be more different. Unlike the Ganga, the Indus receives no significant tributaries in the lower 1000 km of its course. Constantly losing water by evaporation and seepage, it is forced to drop its load progressively as it makes its way to the coast. As a result it becomes a network of myriad ever-changing channels winding through a constantly changing pattern of sandbeds and salt marshes as it approaches the sea.

Punjab The province of Punjab to the N occupies the upper Indus basin. Pakistan's second largest province, it covers over 205,000 sq km. The great tracts of irrigated land between the major rivers which come down from the Himalayas to the Indus have been the heart of the region's agricultural economy for over 100 years. Without the great irrigation schemes of the 19th and 20th centuries, much of Punjab would be deserted semi-jungle, for although the alluvium is rich enough only a narrow band between **Islamabad** and **Peshawar** (in neighbouring NWFP) has anything like enough rainfall to support unirrigated agriculture. Stretching from the **Beas** and **Sutlej** in the E to the Indus in the W the plain stretches about 725 km NE-SW and 550 km NW-SE, virtually all of it lying less than 375 m above sea level.

The 5 rivers that give Punjab its name – from E to W, the **Sutlej**, **Beas**, **Ravi**, **Chenab** and **Jhelum** – are separated by fertile *"doabs"* (the land between "two waters"). From the mid 19th century the British built barrages across the major rivers and a widening system of canals which brought increasing areas under settled agriculture.

Rivers and lakes Pakistan is dominated by the *Indus* and its 5 major tributaries which cross the Punjab and join together 960 km from the sea to form the Panjnad just before joining the Indus itself. Giving its name to India, it rises at an altitude of 5180 m in the *Manasarovar Lake* in Tibet. It runs NW through dramatic mountain passes and gorges before turning sharply S and emerging onto the Punjab plains at Attock, over 1600 km from the sea. Official figures of its length vary, but at approximately 2880 kilometres it is fractionally shorter than the Brahmaputra and just over 300 km longer than the Ganga. To its E rise the 5 major rivers that finally join it in Sind. Of these the waters of the Jhelum, and the Chenab were allocated to Pakistan under the Indus Waters Treaty of 1960, those of the Ravi, Beas and Sutlej being allocated to India.

Huge dams have been built at Mangla on the Jhelum and Tarbela on the Indus to replace irrigation water lost to India under the scheme and to extend the system, as well as to provide new hydro-electricity capacity. Very few rivers join the Indus from the W, the most important being the Kabul River, flowing to the N of Peshawar, and the Gomal River which joins the Indus S of Dera Ismail Khan.

CLIMATE

Rainfall Pakistan is a dry country. Over 75% receives less than 250 mm rainfall a year, while less than 10% receives more than 500 mm. Thus while Pakistan is as affected by the monsoon as most of S Asia, its total rainfall amounts are much lower. Without irrigation, agriculture would be impossible in most of the country.

In the **Indus Plains** of Punjab and Sind over half the rainfall comes in the 3 monsoon months of Jul-Sep. To the N most of the rain comes from depressions travelling eastwards from the Mediterranean. Total rainfall increases N from the deserts of Sind and Baluchistan, where annual totals are less than 150 mm, up to a narrow E-W belt from **Lahore** to **Peshawar**, where totals exceed 800 mm.

To the N the total rainfall again decreases rapidly, to under 100 mm in the high mountains of the **Karakoram**. However, despite the low average totals, extremely heavy rainfall is experienced at places from time to time. This usually occurs because the summer high pressure cell, which stretches from the Sahara across Arabia as far as Pakistan, is sometimes replaced by the great moist monsoon air mass that sweeps across the Arabian Sea. Torrential rainfall and extremely severe flooding can occur throughout the Indus basin.

Temperatures vary sharply both with latitude and altitude. In Jan night frosts are experienced as far S as the plains of Baluchistan, and even day time temperatures can be chill. The air is beautifully sharp and clear, especially as you climb into the hills. Winter min temperatures in the plains as a whole are between 5°C and 10°C, though under clear skies temperatures rise to 15°C and over 20°C in the S.

Further N even day-time temperatures remain lower, and a genuine Mediterranean style spring arrives in Mar. Temperatures rise very rapidly, and by the end of Apr all **Sind** and **Punjab** are in the grip of some of the hottest weather in the sub-continent. Through May temperatures in the plains are often over 40 ˚C, and Sind has some of the highest recorded temperatures in the world. At **Jacobabad** a maximum of 53 ˚C has been reached. From Apr-Sep only the mountains offer any relief from the extreme heat.

Although temperatures drop slightly when the rains start in Jul, the increased humidity makes it an equally uncomfortable period. In the far S there is often high humidity despite the lack of rain. **Las Bela**, inland of Karachi, for example, had one spell of no rain for 4 successive years between **May – Aug**, but average humidities of around 85%.

PEOPLE AND LANGUAGE

Ethnic origins Pakistan's people are almost entirely of Indo-European stock. The exception is the numerically small **Brahui** tribe of Baluchistan, who speak a Dravidian language. **See page 42**. The Brahui may well be a remnant of the Dravidian population which once occupied most of S Asia before being pushed S by successive waves of Indo-European migrants from the NW. The Indo-European groups are themselves however very varied. In the far N tribal peoples include fair-haired and blue-eyed descendants of the Mongols and earlier Aryan groups, originating in the steppes of Russia, as well as clear strands from Anatolian and Arabian ancestors.

Language The linguistic development of Pakistan reflects the isolated and fragmented nature of the tribal populations, and the clearly identifiable regions of settled agriculture on the plains. Apart from the Dravidian Brahui, all Pakistan's languages belong to the **Indo-European** family. **Urdu**, the national language, developed as a synthesis of spoken Hindi and written Persian as the language of the followers of the Mughal court. **See page 43**. However, the heartland of Urdu lay not in modern Pakistan but in N central India. It was the language of the migrants (the 'mohajirs') who came into Pakistan in 1947 at the time of Independence, but the 2 major languages of Pakistan were **Punjabi** and **Sindi**. They remain numerically the most important, although Urdu is the national language. Both are linked to the group known as **Dardic languages** to the N, which include **Kashmiri**, and both also stem from **Prakrit**, and early dialect of Sanskrit.

Migrants and refugees The scale of movement across the borders of India and Pakistan between Independence in Aug 1947, and Apr 1951, when the open border was finally closed, transformed the pre-Independence balance of population. It is estimated that about 15 million people moved. Approximately 7 million non-Muslims moved out of Pakistan to India; perhaps 8 million Muslims moved in the other direction. Most came from E Punjab, Uttar Pradesh, Bihar, Gujurat, Maharashtra and Hyderabad. The 8 million migrants constituted nearly 25% of the then population of Pakistan. Most settled in towns and cities, with **Karachi** growing out of all recognition. Over 600,000 of its 1 million people in 1951 were migrants from India, as were 46% of the total number of people living in Pakistan's towns.

ECONOMY

Agriculture
Wheat dominates the agriculture of the **Punjab** plains but is also important in **Sind** and **NWFP**, accounting for more than half the 12 million ha of cultivated

land. It is the staple crop, vital to a diet based on *chapattis, nan* and *parathas*.

Since independence **rice** has been of increasing significance, especially as an export crop. High quality rice such as *basmati* has become a high value earner of foreign exchange, and rice is particularly well suited to the often salty soils of the lower Indus plains. Both crops have seen new varieties replace traditional ones. **Mexi-Pak wheat** and **IRRI-Pak rice** now account for almost the entire cropped irrigated area. On the unirrigated land of the valleys (known as *baranni** land) in NWFP and Baluchistan local varieties of wheat and hardy crops such as barley, maize, millet and gram predominate.

Cash crops Cotton and sugar cane are by far the most important cash crops. Cotton production is heavily concentrated in Punjab and Sind, while sugar cane is also grown in the Vale of Peshawar. Tobacco is a valuable spring (*Rabi*) crop, especially in the Vale of Peshawar.

Irrigation Pakistan owes its economic livelihood to its irrigation systems. Regular flooding of the lower Indus gave the Indus Valley civilisation the opportunity to develop settled agriculture in the same way as the Egyptians harnessed the Nile delta. In the arid hills of the W farmers used traditional irrigation systems common in Persia, the **karez** system. This makes use of remarkable underground channels, dug to tap springs and lead the water, sometimes many km, with minimum loss through evaporation, onto the fields.

19th century development However, it wasn't until the mid-19th century that large scale engineering works began to control the rivers and to provide the basis for systematic colonisation of land that had previously been jungle. An extraordinary transformation followed, **canal colonies** steadily expanding W and S from the Rivers Beas and Ravi.

Ecological costs Major developments have taken place right up to the present. However, as early as 1859 the benefits of the large scale irrigation development began to be offset by ecological costs. Many of the early schemes suffered from poor drainage. The new canals sometimes cut across natural lines of drainage, damming up the flow of surface water. The irrigation itself was carried out simply by flooding the fields from canals, most of which were unlined. As much as a third of the water that left the barrages and dams was lost by seepage, and a further third by evaporation. During the irrigation of the fields themselves more water also percolated down to the underground water table. In some areas this rose rapidly, causing fields to be waterlogged.

The very high daytime temperatures and low humidity give extremely high evaporation rates through most of the year, and thus the stagnant water in the waterlogged fields was often being dried out, in the process leaving behind the minerals and salts which had been in solution. Huge damage was done to some of the most productive irrigated areas. The Geographer BLC Johnson quotes one engineer as saying that "heroic measures are essential if the Punjab is not to be destroyed".

Remedial measures Before Independence a number of measures were introduced to tackle the problem, including planting deep-rooted species of trees such as Eucalyptus along canal banks to increase the evaporation from the ground, and restricting the use of the canals. However, the scale of the problem was still enormous. In the middle 1970s over a third of Punjab and Sind's irrigated land was moderately to severely affected by waterlogging.

Salinity Control and **Reclamation** After 1947 the Government of Pakistan set up the Water and Power Development Authority (WAPDA), which planned a series of Salinity Control and Reclamation Projects (SCARPS) in the most seriously affected areas. The first of these came into effect in 1959 between the **Ravi** and the **Chenab** rivers in Punjab. Tube wells were sunk at frequent intervals to drain groundwater to the rivers, thereby lowering the watertable. In areas where the groundwater proved 'sweet' it was possible to use it for irrigation. However, much of Sind is underlain be severely saline groundwater, which must simply be drained away, greatly increasing the costs of the programme. The challenge is unending, and of vital significance to Pakistan's economic survival.

Flooding Pakistan's agriculture also has to cope with the natural hazards of flooding. As BLC Johnson has said "Floods in the Punjab represent a hazard to a most complicated man-designed environment". The highly variable flow of the major rivers is still far from being completely controlled. Furthermore, all the rivers carry enormous quantities of silt. It has been estimated that the lower reaches of the **Indus** carry 3 times as much silt as the **Nile**, enough to cover 100 sq km to a depth of 1 m every year. In the lower course of the Indus these deposits of silt have always resulted in flooding and frequent changes in the course of the main stream. Control of the upper tributaries of the Indus and of the Indus itself has still not eliminated the problem, though the effect of building major dams at **Mangla** and **Tarbela** and series of minor dams has yet to be fully analysed.

Resources and industry

One authority has suggested that land, water and a warm climate are Pakistan's main natural resources. To those must be added major reserves of natural gas and some of petroleum, but other mineral resources are limited; limestone is quite widespread and rock salt is common in the Great Salt Range, providing potential for a major chemical industry. There are workable deposits of copper, but there are very poor resources of iron ore and coal.

Natural gas is by far the most important single resource, vital for meeting Pakistan's growing energy needs as well as providing a raw material for the fertiliser industry. Three quarters of the reserves are in the Indus Plains, the major single gas field, and the first to be exploited on a significant scale, being at Sui near Sibi. Gas is piped from here to both Lahore and Karachi. Oil production is still limited, meeting about 20% of the country's needs, and comes mainly from fields in the Potwar Plateau to the S of Islamabad.

Hydro-electricity Pakistan has also been estimated to have about 10,000 MW hydro-electric generating potential. With the completion of the **Tarbela Dam** on the Indus, which has added 2,000 MW capacity, over one third of this is now developed. The **Mangla Dam** on the **Jhelum**, also built as part of the Indus Waters scheme agreed between India and Pakistan in 1960 and financed with large scale help from the World Bank, produces 800 MW. However, all the dams in the Himalayan foothills suffer from the very high levels of erosion in the mountains and are filling rapidly with silt. The life expectancy of the Mangla Dam is now less than 60 years. Furthermore, the area is at constant risk of earthquakes, which adds greatly to the cost and complexity of further development.

Fertilisers Energy resources, especially of gas, have been the basis of some heavy industrial expansion, especially in fertiliser production. Multinational investment in the 1960s from major oil companies has been followed more recently by investment from Saudi Arabia and the Gulf. Pak-Saudi Fertilisers at **Mirpur-Mathelo** in Sind is one example, but there are several other big plants, such as those at **Mianwali**, **Faisalabad**, **Multan** and **Sukkur**. The national oil refinery at **Karachi** has a capacity of nearly 5 million tonnes, and there is a widening range of medium-scale industrial projects.

Imports Pakistan has followed a quite different industrial development path from its neighbour India, with much less emphasis on local production of the full range of industrial products, and a more open door policy to imports, especially of goods such as cars, motorbikes and electrical equipment. There has also been a very large measure of duty free import through the NWFP.

Industries Pakistan had very little industry at Independence in 1947. Lahore and the Punjab had some light industry, including sports goods like cricket bats and hockey sticks, while Montgomery and Lyallpur had some cotton processing. Karachi had light engineering, steel rolling and port industries, but the industrial economy was largely dependent on processing of agricultural products.

Private enterprise In the early years after Independence successive governments tried to encourage private enterprise by protecting "infant" industries and giving considerable help throughout the Pakistan Industrial Development Corporation, which made capital for investment available. Much of the investment that took place remained in the hands of Pakistan's wealthiest 22 families. In the early 1970s Zulfikar Ali Bhutto introduced widespread nationalisation, but this process was reversed once more under the regime of President Zia ul Haq. The policy of the new government under Nawaz Sharif seems set to favour private industrial investment,

Over half a million workers depend on manufacturing industry in Pakistan today. **Karachi** dominates industrial activity in the S, with **Hyderabad** a comparatively minor centre, and **Lahore** the N, **Faisalabad** and **Multan** being important secondary centres. Nearly 40% of industrial jobs are in the **textile industry**, Faisalabad and Multan leading the way. Faisalabad is an important milling centre while Multan specialises in cotton ginning. **Karachi** has a diverse industrial base, food, metal and engineering industries all being important. The recent completion of an integrated iron and steel mill at **Pipri**, 40 km E of Karachi, built with Soviet assistance, adds to Sind's industrial importance. **Lahore** has iron works, textiles, chemicals, printing, food and footwear industries.

Handicrafts Small scale industries and handicrafts depend heavily on the raw materials available locally. By far the most important is cotton, about 60% of the total workforce employed in cottage industries being in handloom cotton textiles. Wool, silk, carpets, leather and footwear, woodwork, cane and bamboo all add variety to the small scale sector. Many are specialist crafts, some producing for local consumption, others for export, notably the metalwork and carpet industries.

HANDICRAFTS

The different regions of the country have developed craft items specific to its artistic traditions and what is locally available by way of raw materials. **Hyderabad** is famous for *Ajrak*, *Soussi* textiles, ceramic tiles, lacquered wooden furniture, gold and silver jewellery (the Sindhi tribal silver jewellery being heavy and chunky), leather shoes and handbags, and glass bangles. The **Azad Kashmir** area excels in fine *Pashmina** woollen shawls with embroidery in silk and gold thread and also wood carving. **Lahore** is known for its woodwork – both carved and inlaid, *bidri ware* (**see page 894**), block printed cloth and enamelled *meena* jewellery.

Multan produces ceramic tiles and vases in handpainted blue and green patterns and textiles, and puts the camels skin and bones to use in their crafts. Rawalpindi uses the local reeds, the Khyber region produces traditional Karakuli caps and copies of guns for decoration. Peshawar makes copper and brass objects, crafts onyx which is plentiful, sometimes with inlaid semiprecious stones and shell, and has a flourishing carpet industry.

Carpets Handwoven, handknotted carpets, both in wool and silk or a mixture, has been produced in the region for centuries. Pakistani weavers adopt designs which are local or closely resemble other designs from neighbouring carpet producing countries, e.g. Iran and Afghanistan. They are often excellent quality and very competitively priced.

Ajrak Hyderabadi handloom fabric which is usually brightly coloured with geometrical patterns, using reds and blues with some white lines. The vegetable dyes traditionally used are obtained from the *neem* fruit, mustard and *thamba* oils, indigo, tamarisk flower and potash. The hand block printed (some with a *batik* look) cotton cloth is used in a variety of ways – a turban, shawl, linen, towel, prayer cloth or to make up into garments.

Jewellery The Indus Valley civilisation developed a unique use of coloured semi-precious stones which adorned ornaments like gold belts, possibly because the precious metal was not easy to get, whereas the agates, jaspers, cornelian, steatite, lapis-lazuli and jade could be found locally or from neighbouring areas, around Afghanistan or Burma. Pakistani designs still bear some resemblance to these ancient finds, and those which evolved later through Hellenic influence in the **Gandhara Period**. Later the Mughals decked themselves with strings of pearls, uncut gem settings and introduced enamelling (**meena** work), synthesizing Persian styles with local craftsmen's skills.

Lahore still remains a centre for enameling and the art is sometimes combined with **kundan** work (setting of uncut stones) which is common in Rajasthani jewellery in India. The pieces of jewellery might have stone setting on one face and enamel on the reverse.

The British period left its influence too on the style of jewellery. The initial decline in interest was replaced with the use of cutting gem stones and setting in gold of lower than 24 carat to make it suitable for claw settings which were popular in the west. Today you will find gem stones which are mined and cut to show off their brilliance (either set in jewellery or loose), heavy tribal siver, copper and brass bangles, necklaces, nose rings and earrings or coloured glass bangles, which Pakistani women, rich or poor, have for everyday wear, renewed at festival time.

RELIGION

Today nearly 97% of Pakistanis are Muslims **see page 62**, the great majority being Sunni Muslims.

The spread of Islam Islam was first introduced into the subcontinent with the Arab conqueror Mohammed bin Qasim in 712 AD and for the following 5 centuries, Sind and much of Punjab remained under Arab influence. However, the Muslim saints, pirs and dervishes from Persia, many of them Sufis, who came here from the 12th century, often travelling vast distances on foot, were really responsible for spreading the faith.

The movement flourished among the common people and the tolerance of Sufism attracted both Muslims and Hindus and is believed to have influenced Guru Nanak, Kabir and the Mughal Emperor Akbar. The movement affected the culture of the region as it has left a lasting influence on the region's literature, poetry and music, interweaving Sufi verses with folk music and folk tales with Sufi sayings. The tradition of music, singing and dancing is very much in evidence when the faithful gather, and you may be able to witness this by visiting a shrine especially during an *Urs* festival.

Sufism Islam lays great stress on the need to develop the soul through prayer and meditation, and Sufism trains a Muslim to do so. **Sufi** originates from *safa* meaning "pure", and the characteristic of the order wass that it combined *'Sharia'* with *'Tareeqat'* (or spirituality) and engaged in missionary activity.

The land occupied by Pakistan gave birth to Brahmanism (later developed to Hinduism), it saw the flourishing of the Buddhists in Gandhara, and later in the post-Mughal period Sikhism flourished. However, the mark left by the *Sufis* distinguishes Pakistan, and you will notice innumerable shrines, large and small, right across the country. These draw the faithful in large numbers, Thursdays being considered particularly holy.

Every saint's death anniversary is celebrated with an *Urs** festival, which reaches enormous proportions in the more important shrines. Thousands of devotees from all sections of society arrive, many in colourful costumes and believers from other religions who hold a saint in reverence, are not uncommon. The Fair with stalls, competitive games of skill, dancing **dervishes**, and folk singers and musicians playing on ancient traditional instruments, make the occasion an essential part of the life of the country. The places with a notable concentration of *Sufi* shrines in Pakistan are Thatta, Sewan Sharif and Sukkur in Sind, and Uchch Sharif, Multan, Lahore, Pak Pattan and Dera Ghazi Khan in the Punjab.

The history of Sufism is traced to the arrival of the followers of the saint **Suhrawardy** as well as the **Qadirya** saints in the 15th century, who spread mysticism across Sind and Punjab. Harzrat Bahauddin Zakaria of Multan, Shaikh Abdul Qadir Jilani, Lal Shahbaz Qalandar, Shah Abdul Latif, Sachal Sarmast and others are revered for their selfless work.

ARCHITECTURE

Some of Pakistan's finest buildings are testimony to the cultural influence and political power of Persian and Afghan sources from the W and the Indianising forces from the E. That power reached its peak under the Mughals. A succession of magnificent tombs, such as those in Multan or Uchch, bear witness to both the political power within the region and the artistic skills developed in successive Muslim courts, but the full flowering of Islamic architecture in Pakistan did not take place until the middle Mughal period, notably the reigns of the Emperors Jahangir, Shah Jahan and Aurangzeb. It was the latter who built the Fort in Lahore, while Aurangzeb added the Badshahi Mosque, the largest mosque in the sub-continent and the second largest in the world.

CUISINE

Pakistani cuisine has much in common with north Indian cuisine. The *kebabs, koftas, tikkas, daals,* milk desserts of *khir, kulfi and firni* and sweet *halwas* and *barfis,* rice and the unleavened 'breads' like *naan, paratha* and *chapati* will all be familiar. However, there is stronger influence from Afghanistan and Persia in the country's favourite dishes and beef preparations, thick 'soups' such as *sajji* and delicacies made from sheep's brains, kidneys and liver are examples where food in Pakistan differs.

Food in Pakistan is close to N Indian food and you will notice particular similarity with Mughlai dishes, (**see page 136**). The country may pose problems for the vegetarian since most Pakistanis take pride in cooking meat dishes. The basic dal (lentils) and chapati or naan bread is available everywhere and *Sabzi* (vegetable curries) and egg dishes' but there the choice will end. Rice is often enriched with spices and meat for special occasions, giving *pulao* and *biryani.*

The principle meat dishes are **Kebabs** which come in various forms. *Shami* – flat patties of mince and dal, *Sheesh* (or *Seekh*) – long skewered rolls of mince cooked on charcoal, *Chapli* – long flat patties of spicy mince and *Botis* made of pieces of beef. Koftas are meat balls served in rich gravy. **Tikkas** (especially chicken) are tender pieces of meat, marinated and barbecued. **Quormas** are rich curries using cubes of meat and spices. **Niharis** prepared from sheep's thigh which is slowly cooked with spices giving a rich thick gravy sprinkled with ginger slices, is eaten with Naan bread. Pakistanis also prepare special delicacies with brain and offal – *Kattakat* made from minced brain, liver and kidney is hot and spicy. There are regional specialities, eg *Sajji* in Hyderabad. The meal includes freshly made chutneys which are delicious. Restrictions on certain weekdays may mean you cannot get beef or lamb every day.

Desserts are similar to some in India – *Kulfi, Halwa, Kheer, Shahi Tukra* and *Firni,* a rice pudding.

Drinks Water accompanies meals and tea (brewed in water with milk and sugar and sometimes with whole spices) is the common drink. In towns you are likely to find bottled water and aerated bottled drinks, familiar in the West. The fruit juice worth sampling is mango juice now available bottled or in cartons (alongside orange and apple juice).

While it is safe to eat and drink at the top class hotels Restaurants, equally safe are *Dhabbas* (Roadside stalls) where you can see food being prepared fresh. Make sure it is served on clean plates.

Warning Be very careful with water, ice in drinks, cut fruit, salads and drinks like cane juice, even when fresh-pressed on the road side. Buffet meals often keep meat dishes warm over heaters which may not be safe.

During **Ramazan**, the month of fasting, only large hotels serve food during daylight hours in their Dining rooms (not poolside) and some Chinese restaurants stay open.

HISTORY

The origins of settlement Pakistan was among the earliest settled regions of S Asia. The **Potwar plateau**, just S of Islamabad, has given abundant evidence of early stone age settlers. By at least 8500 BC agriculturalists had settled on the edge of the Baluchistan Hills and the Indus Plains. From that time on settlement spread across a widening region of what is now Pakistan, flowering into the Indus Valley Civilisation, see page 77. After 1700 BC, successive waves of settlers occupied various parts of the territory. Political power came both from the W and from the E.

The Persian Empire of Darius and his successors rarely penetrated the plains, but **Alexander the Great** reached the Indus in 326 BC. Although his own stay was brief he left Greek governors in Sind and Punjab. By that time Buddhism had been brought from the E, and the Asokan Empire stretched right across N India into Afghanistan. The Buddhist influence is evident in the stupas and monasteries of **Taxila**, and of the stupa which stands on top of the citadel of **Moenjodaro**. Successive waves of tribal settlers also made their presence felt, including the Huns under Kanishka. Much later, the forebears of India's **Rajput** clans moved across the Punjab plains to settle in N India and to dominate the region from Sind to S Rajasthan, and E to central India.

The arrival of the Muslims The Rajputs were in political control of much of present Pakistan when the Muslims came in force from 1000 AD onwards. The first Muslim contact with S Asia had been through Arab traders and then military conquerors in Sind in the 1st century after Muhammad's death. Those attacks gave rise to limited Muslim control in the extreme S. In the 11th century **Mahmud of Ghazni** began a regular series of annual raids down into the Punjab, pillaging the rich agricultural lands, temples and towns of the plains. Those raids were the first extended contact with Islam the Punjab had experienced. In 1192 AD the picture changed permanently. In that year Mu'izzu'd Din defeated the massive Rajput forces at the 2nd Battle of Tarain in 1192. He left his deputy, **Qutb ud Din Aibak**, to hold the territorial gains from his base at **Indraprastha** with his army of occupation. **Mu'izzu'd Din** made further successful raids in the 1190s, inflicting crushing defeats on Hindu opponents from Gwalior to Benaras.

The foundations were then laid for the first extended period of such power, which came under the **Delhi Sultans**. Qutb ud Din Aibak took Lahore in 1206, although it was his lieutenant **Iltutmish** who really established control from Delhi in 1211. However, **Genghis Khan's** raids through central Asia made it impossible to rule India from Afghanistan, and from 1222 Iltutmish ruled from Delhi completely independently. He annexed **Sind** in 1228 and all the territory E to **Bengal** by 1230. Thus the plains of modern Pakistan were incorporated into the region of Muslim power which was to last into the 18th century.

Muslim cultural identity It was among the camp followers of the Mughals that Pakistan's national language developed, a blend of its Persian and Hindi roots, written in a distinctive modification of the Arabic script. Socially, however, the heart of Islamic culture in S Asia lay not in the geographical area of modern Pakistan but in the central plains of India between **Lucknow** and **Aligarh**. It was here that Muslim consciousness was roused, notably in the wake of the 1857 mutiny, a movement particularly associated with Muslim soldiers. Indeed, the British sense that it was essentially a Muslim revolt encouraged the belief that the Muslims constituted a distinct "community", which needed special treatment. A sense of cultural identity grew, epitomised in the work of **Sir Syed Ahmed Khan**, who founded the first

Muslim university at **Aligarh**, in modern India, in 1873.

The demand for Pakistan Pakistan was born out of the partition of the S Asian subcontinent in 1947 when the British transferred power to the newly independent countries of India and Pakistan. The demand for a separate state for S Asia's Muslims had only been articulated clearly 17 years before, when **Dr. Muhammad Iqbal** called for the creation of a separate homeland for those areas where Muslims formed the majority of the population. Nearly twenty years before that, in 1911, he had argued that the Muslims should be regarded as a distinct nation, giving birth to the "two nation theory".

It gained little support until 1937, when it was taken up by Mohammed Ali Jirmah and the **Muslim League** as the political platform on which they campaigned for a separate state. Shape and form were given to the demands by **Chaudhuri Rahmat Ali**, a Punjabi student at Cambridge, who coined the acronym **PAKISTAN**, referring to **P**unjab, **A**fghania, **K**ashmir, **S**ind and "**Ta**n" for Baluchistan, as the provinces which should be the geographical home for independent Muslim territory. By coincidence "Pakistan" also means "land of the pure". Four years later he argued that Muslim Bengal should also be granted independent sovereignty. Even among Muslims, these demands enjoyed relatively little support until 1937, when **Mohammad Ali Jinnah**, widely revered in modern Pakistan as the leader of the nation (the **Quaid i Azam**), swung the Muslim League in India fully behind proposals for the creation of a separate independent Muslim state.

Sind and Punjab Strikingly, there had been little support for the creation of a separate Islamic state among the landlords of Sind or Punjab, while in the NWFP there had been outright opposition to joining Pakistan until the last minute. According to the Pakistani political analyst Javed Burki, in 1947 the 3 Provinces of Sind, Punjab and NWFP were dominated by some 80 landed families. They controlled 10% of the total cultivated land and were responsible for the economic livelihoods of 500,000 households.

The result of the movement of 8 million immigrants into Pakistan's towns and cities was a sharp conflict of interests that has remained a fundamental problem for independent Pakistan. In Javed Burki's words, "it was a trauma because it resulted in a clash between 2 systems based on totally different traditions, beliefs and values. The much older indigenous system was rigidly hierarchical, that imported by the migrants broadly participatory. The first was a tightly organised and stable system with vertical links between different participants; the second was a loosely clustered system of horizontal linkages between members of different social groups who did not owe allegiance to any particular individual." The conflicts of style and interest have dogged Independent Pakistan's political history to the present day.

The Kashmir dispute This state was given concrete form by the Radcliffe Commission which drew the boundary between India and Pakistan according to the distribution of the Muslim and non-Muslim populations. The main variation from that principle was made in the case of Princely States, where the Princes themselves were allowed to choose which country they would accede to, irrespective of the religious composition of their populations. This caused a number of problems, the most difficult being that of Kashmir. On 14th Aug 1947 the Dogra **Maharaja of Kashmir** had not decided whether to accede to India or Pakistan, and still cherished the hope that Kashmir could remain fully independent of both the new states. Within weeks, however, an uprising of Muslim tribes in the NW threatened to move down into the Vale of Kashmir and to capture Srinagar with Pakistan army support.

Under this pressure the Maharaja decided to ask for Indian help, which the Indian Prime Minister, Jawaharlal Nehru refused to give unless Kashmir first acceded to the Indian Union. This was done, and the Indian army moved rapidly N to confront the Pakistan army in a war which dragged on until the cease fire of Jan 1949. From then on the *de facto* border between India and Pakistan has divided Kashmir in two, though legally the whole of the former Princely State is Indian territory. Indian maps continue to show the State in this form, though in practice it has been impossible to go from Srinagar and the Vale of Kashmir into what Pakistan terms *Azad Kashmir* ("Free Kashmir") ever since the cease fire agreement.

The refugees In the words of the Pakistani political analyst Javed Burki "the refugees brought with them a culture and a set of economic and political institutions that were totally alien to the areas of British India that were carved out to form the Muslim state of Pakistan.... Pakistan society was born polarised. On the one side were the rural people, with their own customs and traditions, their own history and institutions. On the other side was an urban population with relatively more modern institutions and with goals and aspirations that were completely different from those of the people who had hitherto dominated the areas that had now become Pakistan. The conflict between these 2 groups determined the course Pakistani society was to take on the road to economic and political development."

Recent political developments

Since Independence Pakistan has experienced a turbulent political history. At Independence 3 key political posts were held by **Muhammad Ali Jinnah** – Governor General of Pakistan, President of the Muslim League and President of the Constituent Assembly. His death in Sep 1948 left a vacuum which was never filled. Pakistan's first Prime Minister, *Liaquat Ali Khan*, was assassinated in 1951, and with his death Pakistan's fragile democratic institutions rapidly underwent radical change. Landlords, excluded from power in the first 5 years after Independence, began to assert their influence, and the refugees who had played a prominent part in government up to 1951 began to lose their power to the landowning elite, especially from Punjab.

From 1953 the bureaucracy played an increasingly important role in economic and social policy, and a growing role for the public sector. In Burki's words "in the 1953-62 period, Pakistan moved from a Parliamentary to a bureaucratic form of government and from an economy dominated by the private sector to an economy guided by the civil service."

Economic crisis The change was partly a result of the economic crisis brought on by the end of the Korean War boom. The War had caused a tremendous increase in prices of cotton and jute, vital to Pakistan's export earnings. The slump produced a major economic crisis, and encouraged the government to take an active hand in industrial policy and management. The **Pakistan Industrial Development Corporation**, which had been set up in 1950, embarked on a number of projects after 1953. It became strongly allied to the landed families of the Indus plains, for while the wealthy refugee families had liquid capital to invest in industry, the landlords of the Punjab and Sind had most of their capital tied up in the land. If they were to share in industrial expansion they therefore needed support from the government to enable them to become industrial entrepreneurs. They played a prominent role in the PIDC, which by 1959 accounted for 16% of Pakistan's industrial wealth.

Landlords and power The economic returns from the public sector, however, were much lower than those from the private sector, but the enormous public sector push was highly successful in bringing in new industrial entrepreneurs from the landed class. This group continued to enjoy control of the major share of agricultural land and, most importantly, control of Pakistan's vital irrigation network. Their developing economic power was matched by a transformation of their political significance. The Muslim League, which had been the vehicle for Pakistan's independence, was converted during the 1950s from a party of the Indian refugees into a party re-organised to take account of the interests of West Pakistan's landlords. Party democracy was replaced by a highly centralised party system.

In doing so it encouraged the creation of break-away factions. The most important was the **National Awami Party**, which itself split into 3 groups: the **Awami League** and the **National Awami Party** in E Pakistan, the **National Awami Party** (Wali Khan group) in W Pakistan. The Awami League became the spearhead for the separation of E Pakistan, which ultimately gave birth to Bangladesh in 1971, while the National Awami Party under **Khan Abdul Ghaffar Khan** and his son **Abdul Wali Khan**, became the focus of a "progressive" movement in the NWFP.

Political instability The political and economic developments of the 1950s were marked by increasing political instability in Pakistan's democratic institutions. None of the institutions created in the early years after Independence took root. As Burki concludes, "Although Jinnah had won the partition of British India on the basis of the two-nation theory, deep social and economic fissures continued to run through the Muslim nation that he created." The institutions of democratic government failed to incorporate the political interests of the powerful groups who had lived for generations in Sind, Punjab and the NW Frontier, and in Oct 1958, after a succession of short-lived governments, **Gen Mohammad Ayub Khan** took power as the President and Chief Martial Law Administrator of Pakistan.

Ayub Khan's basic democracies President Ayub's object was to give Pakistan the stable government it had so evidently lacked in the first 10 years of its existence. The institutional method he chose to create was what he termed "*basic democracies*". He argued that in order to have the privilege of voting, you had also to have responsibilities. He tried to define an electorate which would have a stake in both stability and progress by identifying people who were qualified to vote – by virtue of their literacy, for example. Every village or town area had up to 400 electors whose responsibility was to elect a town or village council. These councillors in turn elected councils at a higher level such as the district. They in turn then elected representatives to Provincial councils. Ayub Khan hoped to ensure both limited political answerability down to the village level and political stability.

Economic growth The 1960s witnessed unprecedented economic growth and a major change in Pakistan's political structure. **Land Reforms** passed in 1959 began to limit the power of the landlords, particularly increasing the power of the middle rank landowners. Ayub Khan also began to curb the bureaucracy, liberalising the economy and dismantling the economic controls that had been imposed through the 1950s. But the rapid economic growth was not without costs. Liberalising the imports of agricultural machinery, for example, has been estimated to have cost 12 jobs for every tractor imported. The cost of 80,000 tractors was thus 1 million rural jobs lost in the course of a decade during which Pakistan's rural population grew by over 10 million.

The landless moved to the towns, and rising urban unemployment found its political outlet in support for Ayub Khan's chief political opponent of the late 1960s, *Zulfikar Ali Bhutto* and his **Pakistan People's Party**. His movement gained added momentum from the low priority General Ayub Khan's regime had given to health and education. Less than 15% of the total population was literate by the end of Ayub Khan's regime, and primary and secondary education remained the privilege of a tiny minority.

The 1965 War These problems were worsened by the economic impact of Pakistan's 1965 war with India. Although Pakistan claimed a victory, in military terms this was at best a stalemate. In economic terms however its impact was entirely negative, and political discontent in the towns and cities escalated. Ayub Khan's system collapsed with the the ending of his own power. He fell seriously ill in Mar 1968. On 25 Mar 1969 he resigned, but by then disillusionment with his political system had already taken deep root. His successor as President and Chief Martial Law Administrator (CMLA), **General Yahya Khan**, survived in power only until the crushing defeat of the Pakistan army in Dec 1971, when Bangladesh completed the secession it had proclaimed on 25 Mar 1971. Already Yahya Khan had promised to restore the democratic institutions which Ayub had demolished. However, he was swept from power by the humiliation of Bangladesh's secession.

A new party By that time the party that was to replace him, the **Pakistan People's Party (PPP)** had been launched in Lahore on 1 Dec 1969. The **PPP** went on to lay out a socialist programme. Iron and steel and the full range of heavy industrial activities were to be nationalised, along with rail, air and road transport. This was to be "**Islamic socialism**", but it didn't offer the sweeping changes in agriculture that were intended for industry.

The 1970 election When the PPP's manifesto for the election was published Bhutto himself emphasised the Islamic nature of the proposed radical programme, but he further diluted programmes for redistribution of land. Alongside the domestic programme Bhutto took a high profile anti-India stance. He argued that President Ayub's agreement signed with India's Prime Minister Shastri in **Tashkent** had been a sell-out, and he promised a 1000 year confrontation with India.

In the elections of Dec 1970 the PPP won over 60% of West Pakistan's seats, though it only received 33% of the votes cast. The triumph of the Awami League in East Pakistan completely overshadowed Bhutto's triumph, however, and the whole of 1971 was taken up with the secessionist struggle. The defeat of the Pakistan army in Dec led General Yahya Khan to hand over the Presidency to Mr. Bhutto. He remained in power – first as President, then as Prime Minister – until 5 Jul 1977, when he was ousted in a military coup led by **General Zia ul Haq**.

Bhutto's fall was precipitated by widespread rioting which followed the elections of 7 Mar 1977. Although his PPP claimed an overwhelming victory, the opposition parties accused the Prime Minister of ballot rigging on a huge scale. They refused to accept the result and increasingly took to the streets.

Although there had been signs of economic recovery and growth after the 1971 war, 1976-77 was a poor year. Despite the growing flow of remittances from Pakistani migrants to the oil rich Gulf countries, which accounted for 30% of Pakistan's US$1,500 m foreign exchange earnings in 1976, the economic problems were mounting sharply as Bhutto went to the elections.

There was a growing sense of crisis, which the Prime Minister tried to counter by strengthening his party's "Islamic" image, and dropping the socialists and their left wing programme from his political platform. However, he also clearly distanced himself from the support of the urban educated population, threatening to limit their freedoms "for the benefit of the masses". To achieve that he tried to strengthen his support among the traditionalists of the landed elite and the poorest sections of the rural population.

Demonstrations and disorder Between the elections in March and 5 July Bhutto was faced with increasingly violent demonstrations against his election victory. He reacted by sending the army onto the streets and imprisoning many opposition leaders. The army became increasingly restless at their role as street fighters on behalf of the government, and when **General Zia ul Haq** took power in a bloodless coup he claimed that the PPP and the 9 Party alliance known as the Pakistan National Alliance (PNA) were unable to reach any compromise, a failure which "would throw the country into chaos."

It was intended to be a short term military government to re-impose order and stability, to be followed in Oct by further elections. Released from "protective custody" by General Zia to campaign for those elections, Bhutto found the Press increasingly claiming to find evidence of corruption and the abuse of power by his previous regime. It was one of these charges, of being responsible for an ambush on one of his political opponents in Nov 1974, that was brought to the Lahore Court. He was found guilty on 19 Mar 1978. On 4 Apr 1979 he was hanged.

Zia's regime Pakistan's politics in the following 10 years were dominated by General Zia ul Haq. His struggle to find political legitimacy at home and abroad was transformed by the decision of **President Brezhnev** of the Soviet Union to send Soviet troops into Afghanistan in Dec 1979.

Suddenly in the eyes of the governments of the United States and the West, Pakistan became a "front-line state", a bulwark against Communist expansion. Aid, particularly military assistance, started flowing again. With increasing revenues from migrants' remittances in the Gulf, Pakistan's economy improved, though the political and economic costs of becoming home to 3 million Afghan refugees became a major burden.

The growth of the armed forces To secure his political base General Zia gradually moved from a purely military position to the political status of President. The armed services grew dramatically in size and political importance, and by 1984 36% of the government's spending went on defence or US$2 bn. By 1987 this had risen to US$2.5 bn, and Pakistan had nearly 500,000 men in its armed services.

Islamic law For much of that period the government seemed comparatively untroubled by political dissent. However, the Soviet withdrawal from Afghanistan was just one signal of major challenges to come. President Zia had tried to build a political base by increasing the government's open commitment to an Islamic legal system and code. "Islamic" punishments such as public beatings were introduced, and the introduction of the "zakat" tax, based on the Koranic system of taxation. While he severely curtailed the power of Pakistan's independent institutions like the judiciary he also promised to return Pakistan to an "Islamic" form of non-Party politics. Elections were held to local bodies, and he called together the *Majlis e Shoura,* which was intended to serve as a national assembly.

Zia's assassination In the event, when he was assassinated in a plane crash at Bahawalpur in Aug 1988 his system proved no more lasting than that of President Ayub Khan before him. But by 1988 there was no obvious political framework from which a successor government could emerge with full authority. The President, **Ghulam Ishaq Khan**, announced that elections would be held as soon as possible. The late President Bhutto's family, and in particular his daughter Benazir, long seen as heir to the Bhutto political legacy, fought a vigorous campaign which ended with the formation of a PPP government. However, it claimed a fragile hold on power. In **Sind** it was dependent on an alliance with the rising power of the political party of the refugees from India, the *MQM*, while it failed to win a majority of seats in the most populous Province of the Punjab, once a PPP stronghold.

Benazir Bhutto's regime Apparently paralysed by the complexity of Pakistan's interlocking domestic and political problems, Benazir Bhutto's government found itself unable to deal with rising factional violence in Sind or the deep political antagonism of its political opponents, the Islamic Democratic Alliance and its leader Nawaz Sharif, in Punjab. After losing a vote of confidence in the Assembly in Sep 1990 Benazir Bhutto's People's Party lost the succeeding elections decisively, to be replaced by a new coalition government under the Prime Ministership of **Nawaz Sharif**. It still seemed to be a coalition fraught with potentially divisive tensions, with the refugee MQM still an unpredictable but powerful force in Sind, increasingly willing to use its capacity for violence to shape the Province's politics to tis own ends.

ISLAMABAD

The Capital, 1098; Rawalpindi, 1102; Excursions from Islamabad-Rawalpindi, 1107; Taxila, 1109.

Population 300,000 *Altitude* 520 m *Best season* Nov-Apr

	Jan	Feb	Mar	Apr	May	Jun	Jul	Aug	Sep	Oct	Nov	Dec	Av/Tot
Max (°C)	17	19	24	31	37	40	37	34	34	32	26	20	29
Min (°C)	3	6	10	15	21	25	25	24	21	15	7	3	15
Rain (mm)	64	63	81	42	23	55	233	158	85	21	12	23	960

THE CAPITAL

Islamabad, was designated as the modern capital of Pakistan by President Ayub Khan in 1958. He envisaged the creation of a completely new city. Located in the far N of Punjab, it was intended to reduce the overwhelming economic importance of the two W Pakistani cities of Karachi and Lahore, as against the much weaker economic role of the E Pakistani capital of Dhaka. At the same time it would keep the country's capital in W Pakistan, rather than transferring it to the eastern wing, which was deemed to be politically unacceptable. The decision was ratified in the Constitution of 1962, by which time progress had already been made on laying out the triangular shaped city and on some of the building.

The new city of Islamabad, N of Rawalpindi, was designed by distinguished architects and planners, among them *Edward Durrell Stone*, Ponti and by the Greek firm of architects Doxiadis Associates. Construction was started in 1961. It was conceived with an attempt to retain the character of the scenic backdrop and divided into sectors for government, commercial, residential, religious, recreational and industrial. Until 1971 the functions of Pakistan's capital were split between **Islamabad** and **Dhaka**, but Islamabad took on the full role after the secession of Bangladesh. Since then it has been growing rapidly, developing as planned into a twin city with **Rawalpindi**.

Major landmarks The site is dominated by the **Margalla Hills** to the N. The base of Islamabad's triangle runs along the foot of the hills in the northern end of the Potwar Plateau and retains an air of spaciousness with parks, gardens, fountains and fine tree-lined avenues. The hills themselves provide opportunities for walking, trekking and jogging. The **State Bank of Pakistan**, a landmark, towers over the city. The **Shah Faisal Masjid, the Presidency**, **Secretariat buildings**, the embassies, the Holiday Inn are all architecturally striking.

Getting around the widely spaced city can be confusing, but the hills serve as a constant point of reference. The city is divided into 9 zones. Theoretically the centre is defined by **Zero Point**, the crossroads from which all distances are measured, but the political commercial and administrative centre of gravity of the city lies clearly to the E and N of Zero Point. At the NE extremity of the city is the **Quaid-i-Azam University**, spread out on a spacious campus. To its SW is the

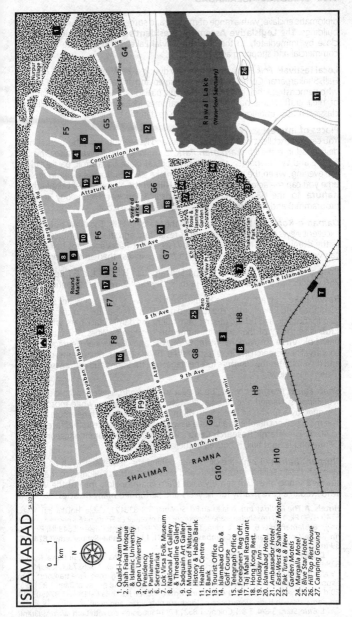

ISLAMABAD

SA 323

N

0 ——— 1
km

1. Quaid-i-Azam Univ.
2. Shah Faisal Mosque
3. Open University
4. Islamic University
5. Presidency
6. Parliament
7. Secretariat
8. Lok Virsa Folk Museum
9. National Art Gallery
   & Threadline Gallery
10. Sadquain Art Gallery
11. Museum of Natural
    History & Habib Bank
    Health Centre
12. Bank
13. Tourist Office
14. Islamabad Club &
    Golf Course
15. Telegraph Office
16. Foreigners' Reg Off.
17. Taj Mahal Restaurant
18. Hong Kong Rest.
19. Holiday Inn
20. Islamabad Hotel
21. Ambassador Hotel
22. East-West & Shahbaz Motels
23. Pak Tures & New
    Garden Motels
24. Margalla Motel
25. Blue Star Hotel
26. Hill Top Rest House
27. Camping Ground

diplomatic enclave, with a range of modern and sometimes adventurous embassy buildings. The **Legislative Assembly**, **President's Palace** and **Secretariat** lie close by, immediately to the N of the Rawal Lake. To their W are a series of commercial and shopping areas.

Local festivals *Folk Festival* held annually during a week in April at the Exhibition Hall, Shakarparian Complex. Master craftsmen and artisans from all over Pakistan who demonstrate their skills in purpose-built pavilions produce excellent examples of their craft. Numerous cultural programmes including concerts of folk and classical music, traditional folk dances are held in the evenings.

Places of interest
You can get excellent views over Islamabad and Rawalpindi from the low hill, now developed into the *Shakarparian Park*, 2 km W of the **Rawal Lake**. This has both E and W viewpoints, and is a very popular place for a stroll, particularly in the evening, when the lights of the cities make a very attractive sight. In the day time you can see across to the **Margalla Hills** in the N, the Rawal Lake in the E, *Kahuta* to the SE (the centre of Pakistan's nuclear technology research programme) and **Rawalpindi** to the S. There is a snack bar.

Daman-e-Koh is the terraced garden in the Margalla Hills. The **view point** offers excellent views over the city, and with its restaurant and snack bar attracts crowds in the evenings. The Mini-zoo is nearby (see under Parks and zoos below). You can walk up to it from the N end of 7th Avenue in less than an hour, or drive.

Rose and Jasmine Gardens behind Shakarparian Hill, off the GT Rd has over 250 varieties of roses and a dozen jasmines. Flower shows in the spring.

Rawal Lake is an artificial lake 8 km from the new city (a major water supply for Islamabad and Rawalpindi). The terraced garden is a favourite for picnics, and the lake for boating and fishing (permit from hut nr the dam). Snack bars. **Islamabad Club** is to the W of the lake with numerous sporting facilities. The city has the only **Lok Virsa,** or *National Institute of Folk and Traditional Heritage,* in the country. The Research Institute (established 1974) collects, documents, preserves and disseminates the country's folk heritage, oral traditions and culture (see under Museums, below).

Shah Faisal Masjid, one of the largest in the world, is said to hold 100,000 worshippers. Named after the Saudi Arabian King, the new white mosque was designed by a Turkish architect with 88 m high minarets which resemble rockets. The main prayer chamber is a unique desert tent-like structure with 8 faces, rising to 40 m. The **Islamic Research Centre** with a library, restaurant, museum, Press Centre and lecture hall, is housed in the courtyard.

Nurpur Shahan (4 km) is the old village behind the Secretariat, with its narrow lanes and stalls selling refreshments and souvenirs, attracts pilgrims to the mirror studded shrine of a 17th century saint (*Barri Imam* or Holy man of the Woods) who lived in a cave nearby for 12 years and performed many miracles.

Hotels A *The Holiday Inn,* Aga Khan Rd, Shalimar 5. T 826121, Cable: Holiday Inn, Telex: 5740 HIISD Pk. 150 rm. *Sheherazade Restaurant* and open-air *La Fontaine Barbecue* (summer only). **B** *Islamabad* G-6, Civic Centre. T 827311, Cable: Islamhotel, Telex: 5643 IHI Pk. 150 rm. Restaurant with barbecue. **C** *Ambassador,* G-6/1, 1 Khayaban-e-Suhrawardy. T 824011. 39 rm, some a/c. Restaurant.
   D *East West Motel,* nr Rawal Dam, T 826143. **D** *Motel Shah Bagh,* nr Rawal Dam, T 828492. **D** *Margalla Motel,*Shahrah-e-Kashmir, nr Sports Complex. T 825273, Cable: Moral. 29 a/c rm, with TV and fridge, a/c restaurant, exchange, travel, garden. Free transport from airport and Secretariat **D** *New Garden Motel,* Islamabad Club Rd nr Rawal Dam. T 821025. 20 d rm, some a/c with bath. **D** *Pak Tours Motel,* Murree Rd nr Rawal Dam. T 824503. 14 rm, some a/c with bath. a/c restaurant. These are nr the dam and quiet.
   E *Blue Star,* G-8/4, T & T Colony. T 852717. 14 rm, some a/c with bath. a/c restaurant.

Modern, pleasant but away from centre. **F** *Tourist Camp* opp Rose and Jasmine Gardens, off Murree Rd behind Shakarparian Hill. Dormitory beds and camping site for foreigners. The *Hill Top Rest House* is S of the Rawal Lake, in an ideal position.

Restaurants Others outside hotels which are a/c, mostly inexpensive, include 2 in Aabpara, *Kamran*, T 820620 and *Danbar*. There are also a few in Blue Area – *Islamabad Banquet Hall*, 38 W Half, nr Presidency, T 827856 and *Four Seasons Restaurant*, also at 38 W Half, T 821271 and the *Usmania Restaurant*, T 812535. In addition there is the *Taj Mahal* on Jinnah Supermarket, F-7 and the *Manno Salva* on School Rd, F-6/1, T 828535. **Chinese a/c** – *Golden Dragon*, F-7/3, Round Market. *Kao Wah*, 1, Shakil Chambers, Suharawardy Rd, T 829898. *Lihua*, Covered Market, G-8/3. *Peking*, Supermarket. **Hong Kong Restaurant**, Khayaban-e-Suhrawardy. *Mei Hua*, Blue Area. **Fast Food** – *Gee Bees*, 3 Saeed Plaza, Blue Area, T 824181. *Mr Chips*, Markaz F-7, T 821922.

Clubs The Islamabad Club, T 825896, Riding Club, T 821044 and the Golf Club, T 812637 are in the Islamabad Park. The Flying Club is at 16, St 31, F-6/1.

Banks Agricultural Dev Bank, Faisal Ave, T 829099. **Allied**, Ghousia Plaza, Blue Area, T 820558. **American Express**, Blue Area. **Bank of America**, T 828801. **Grindlays**, Diplomatic Enclave, PO Box 1004, T 811390. **Habib**, Circle Office, T 826637. **Middle East**, 19, I & T Centre, Aabpara, T 823002. **National Bank of Pakistan**, Civic Centre, PO Box 1201, T 827155. **United**, UBL Building, Main Civic Centre, G-6, T 821541.

Shopping *Aabpara Market*, Ramna 6 is the city's oldest selling household items, where you can pick up fabrics and spices. *Koshar Market*, Shalimar 6, Markaz F-6. *Supermarket*, Markaz Shalimar 6 are good for souvenirs, leather craft (*Ace Leather*), jewellery and garments (particularly *Behbud Boutique*). *Jinnah Supermarket*, Markaz Shalimar 7 has similar goods (*Kraftman* and *Fancy* for handicrafts, *Guys and Dolls*, *Creation* for clothes). The *Covered Market*, Ramna 6 sells green groceries and meat. *Juma* (Friday) *Bazaar*, nr Aabpara, Ramna 6 is busy with shoppers in the wholesale fruit and vegetable market which closes down for prayers at lunchtime. Afghan refugee stalls nearby sell carpets and traditional jewellery. *Itwar* (Sunday) *Bazaar*, G-9/4. *The Civic Centre*, Ramna 6, Markaz G 6. *Duty Free Shop*, Plot 11, Blue Area, T 811021.

Wood carving, silver, brass and copper goods, onyx articles, embroidered linen and clothes, chain-stitched numdah rugs are worth looking for. **Handicrafts** – APWA *Handicraft Shop*, 28 Bazaar Rd, T 27889. Recommended, proceeds to charity. Several others in the *Blue Area* (*Chiltan, Asian Arts and Crafts*) and the *Supermarket* (*Threadlines Gallery*, the govt sponsored shop is recommended , *Afghan, Maharajah*). **Carpets** – In Blue Area, *Baluch, Lahore, Shiraz* and in Melody Market, *Qureshi* and *Pak Persian*. Also try vendors in Friday Market. Books – Supermarket has *Mr Books*, Jinnah Market *Book Fair* and Kosar Market *London Bookshop*.

Local transport Taxis, buses, mini buses and mini wagons. The **Bus Station** is Aabpara, corner of Municipal Rd. **Car Hire** – Avis, 10 Khayaban-e-Suhrawardy, Walji's Building, T 827614. Access, 44E, Blue Area, office Tower Plaza, T 815535.

Entertainment Cinemas – Melody, Civic Centre, Ramna 6. NAFDEC Cinemas, 1 and 2 Nazimuddin Rd.

Sports The large modern Sports Complex on Sharah-e-Kashmir nr the Tourist Camping Site, was built with Chinese assistance. See also sports clubs under Clubs above. Islamabad Club to the W of the Lake has a golf course, tennis, squash and riding (offered to non-members).

Museums Lok Virsa The Complex in the Shakarparian Hills has a museum containing arts and crafts from the whole of Pakistan displayed according area, use and motif. *Lok Virsa Craft Museum*, nr Zero Point on the Rawalpindi-Islamabad Rd.T 826928, also has a sales counter where you can get books, music cassettes and craft items. **Institute of Folk Heritage**, G No 6, St 63, F-7/3. Open 0830-1900. Museum of musical instruments, costumes and jewellery with collections of textiles and other handicrafts. It also has a library of folk music. The Sound Archive has the largest Pakistani collection of recorded songs, ballads, interviews etc while the Audio-visual section produces films of traditions, customs and folk performances for the Video Archive. Open daily except Fri 0730-1400. Another Sales Centre nr the Supermarket.

Museum of Natural History, College Rd, opp Women's College, Commercial Centre F-7/2. Open 0900-1600. Closed Fri. Of particular interest to students and children, the exhibits cover anthropology, geology and wild life. **Contemporary Art Gallery**, 26 Civil Lines.

Parks and zoos The Mini-Zoo is just below the Daman-e-Koh, in the Marghzar. There is a Japanese style children's park which was a gift from the children of Japan. Ayub National

Park, GT Rd, Daman-e-Koh, Margalla Hills and Rose and Jasmine Garden, Garden Ave, nr Aabpara. (see under Places of Interest above). City Park, Shalimar 9. Ratta Hotar Picnic spot nr Nurpur Shahan.

Post and Telegraphs GPO, Civic Centre, Municipal Rd, T 825957. Telephone and Telegraph Office, Shalimar 5, T 829324.

Hospitals Central Govt Poly Clinic. CDA Hospital Pakistan Institute of Medical Sciences National Institute of Health. Islamabad General Hospital Complex. Amaris Clinic Complex (Private), 12-H/1, G/8, Markaz, T 857028. Azmi Hospital, Commercial 31 B, S Town, T 841021. Islamabad Private Hospital, 38 Blue Area, T 811752. Aziz Nursing Home, Saidpura Rd, T 840310.

Useful addresses Foreigners' Registration Office, Zafar Chowk nr Peshawar Mor. For Visa Extension apply with 2 passport photos and fee to Interior Ministry at the Secretariat, Block R, Rm 512, 5th Floor. Open daily 0900-1100, 1200-1600. Closed Fri, Sat. You may be able to get an extension within a day. **Passport Office**, Aabpara Market, nr National Bank, T 826837. The different regions have offices in the federal capital. **Sind House** is in F-6 while Frontier House, **Baluchistan House** and **Punjab House** are in Shalimar 5.

Foreign Missions Australia, Diplomatic Enclave 2, PO Box 1046, T 822111. **Austria**, 13, St 1, F-6/3, T 820137. **Bangladesh**, H 24, St 28, F-6/1, T 826885. **Belgium**, H 39, St 1, F-6/3, T 820131. **Britain**, Ramna 5, PO Box 1122, Diplomatic Enclave, T 822131. **Canada**, Diplomatic Enclave, Plot 5, PO Box 1042, T 821101. **China**, Diplomatic Enclave, Ramna 4, T 826667. **Denmark**, 121. St 90, Ramna 6/3, T 824210. **France**, 11 St 54, F-7/4. PO Box 1068, T 823981. **Germany**, Diplomatic Enclave, Ramna 5, T 822155.
    India, 482-F, G-6/4, T 826718. **Indonesia**, 39, St 1, F-6/3, T 811291. **Iran**, 3 and 5, St 16, Shalimar 6/2, T 822694. **Italy**, 54 Khayaban-e-Margalla, F-6/3, T 825791. **Japan**, 53-70, G-5/4, T 820181. **Kuwait**, Diplomatic Enclave, University Rd, T 822181. **Nepal**, 506, St 84, G-6/4, T 823754. **Netherlands**, 5 St 6, F-6/3, T 922631. **Norway**, 11 St 84, Ramna 6/4, T 822048. **Spain**, 180 G, Attaturk Ave, G-6/3, T 821070. **Sri Lanka**, 2, St 48, F-7/4, T 820754. **Sweden**, Block 6 A, Aga Khan Rd, Markaz Shalimar, T 822557. **Switzerland**, 25, St 19, F-6/2, T 821151. **Thailand**, 23, St 25, F-6/2, T 823974. **USA**, Diplomatic Enclave, T 826161. **USSR**, Ramna 4, Khayaban-e-Suharawardy, Diplomatic Enclave, T 824604.

Cultural Centres National Institute of Historical and Cultural Centre, H 6, St 31, F-8/1, T 851516; Pakistan National Centre, 24 Bazaar Rd, G-6/4, T 27813. Pakistan National Council of Arts, 73, St 22, F-6/2. The Galerie Saequain is nearby at St 25, F-6/2. Permanent exhibitions.

Chambers of Commerce Islamabad Chamber of Commerce and Industry, 38 Khayaban-e-Quaid-e-Azam, Islamabad. T 810490, Telex: 54570 IBCCI PK.

Travel agents PIA, Blue Area, T 825031. **Tour operators** Travel Walji's, Khayaban-e-Suhrawardy, T 823963. Silk Road Tour Services, 37, St 34, F-7/1. T 822495. Karakoram Tours, 1 Baltoro House, St 19, F-7/2.

Tourist offices and information Tourist Information Centre, Islamabad, G-6, Municipal Rd, Civic Centre, T 827311. Also at 6, 13-T/U Commercial Area, College Rd, Markaz F-7, T 816932 and at International Arrival Lounge, Islamabad International Airport. PTDC Head Office, 2, St 61, F-7/4. Ministry of Tourism, College Rd, F-7/2 where you must apply to get a pass for trekking or mountaineering.

Air and **Rail Services** See under Rawalpindi, with which Islamabad shares its travel links. Rly Enquiries, T 62174; Reservation, T 827474. **Road** Buses and mini-buses are more popular than trains as they are more comfortable and faster.

RAWALPINDI

Population 950,000 *Altitude* 515 m. *Climate* See Islamabad (above) *Clothing* Cottons. *Airport* is 6 km away, 15 min from town centre.

The military town President Ayub Khan's decision to move Pakistan's capital to Islamabad has helped to transform its immediate neighbour Rawalpindi from a sleepy cantonment town to one of Pakistan's fastest growing cities. While Islamabad is a planned – and

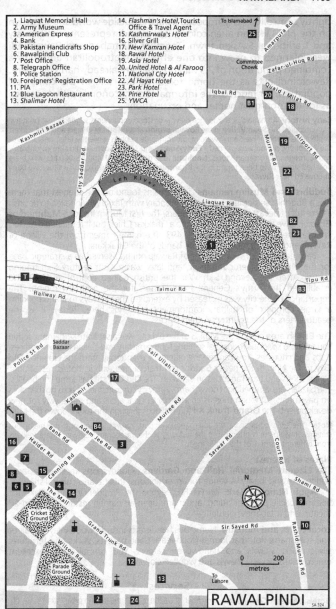

1. Liaquat Memorial Hall
2. Army Museum
3. American Express
4. Bank
5. Pakistan Handicrafts Shop
6. Rawalpindi Club
7. Post Office
8. Telegraph Office
9. Police Station
10. Foreigners' Registration Office
11. PIA
12. Blue Lagoon Restaurant
13. *Shalimar Hotel*
14. *Flashman's Hotel*, Tourist Office & Travel Agent
15. *Kashmirwala's Hotel*
16. Silver Grill
17. *New Kamran Hotel*
18. *Rawal Hotel*
19. *Asia Hotel*
20. *United Hotel & Al Farooq*
21. *National City Hotel*
22. *Al Hayat Hotel*
23. *Park Hotel*
24. *Pine Hotel*
25. YWCA

RAWALPINDI

SA 324

tightly controlled – city, imposed from the outside world and set down on the plain like an alien colony, Rawalpindi represents the homely and traditional S Asian town. Together Islamabad and Rawalpindi were planned to grow into one effective metropolitan unit with a combined population of 2.5 million. They are already half way there. Rawalpindi acts as the home for three quarters of the combined population, for much of the informal sector economic activity as well as for the non-govt homes and occupations.

Early history Archaeological evidence by way of stone implements suggests that primitive man occupied the *Soan Valley* in the **Potwar region** around 300,000 years ago. The earliest implements named "Pre-Soan" were made from large pebbles while the later, finer tools of the Paleolithic period were named "**Early-Soan** "and "**Late-Soan** "which are comparable with European "Cromerian" tools. **Neolithic** tools dating from 10,000-5,000 BC, which are polished stone, have been found in the **Khanpur** area, while Neolithic burial sites have been discovered near **Riwat**.

Buddhist and Muslim remains The remains found on site suggest that there was a Buddhist settlement here, contemporary with Taxila which failed to flourish as a result of devastation by Hun invaders. The first Muslim invader, **Mahmud of Ghazni**, gave the ruined city as a gift to a Ghakkar Chief, but it remained deserted until restored by **Jhanda Khan** in 1493. The name comes from the village of **Rawal**, and the city remained in the hands of the Ghakkars.

Before Islamabad was thought of Rawalpindi had served as a strategic base for the Mughal Emperor **Jahangir**, and later was a 19th century Sikh trading centre. After the Second Sikh War the British gained control in 1849 and established the Army's General Headquarters for the northern region. The importance of the city was increased by extending the railways to it and building a large complex of military cantonment buildings here. Today, it is the headquarters of the country's Armed Forces.

The British area around the **Mall**, S of the old city, was a separate settlement. It had barracks and spacious residential sections for the military and civilians, its own offices, clubs and churches. You can see the difference even today, from the crowded **Old City** to the N, with the newer **Saddar** commercial area with its hotels, restaurants, banks, shops and travel agencies, in between. The **Old City** still has some fine houses. The bazaars are jammed tight down narrow alleys, with craftsmen practising their skills on pavements, although there is an attempt to clear areas and make way for new development. The **Grand Trunk Rd** (GT Rd) goes through the town, down the Mall.

Note The twin cities share the international airport, railway station and the major bus stations. Rawalpindi is often called the gateway to the Karakoram Highway where trekkers from different corners of the world meet.

Places of interest
The **Liaquat Memorial Hall and Gardens** Good sports facilities, a large auditorium and library. A venue for art exhibitions, theatre and cultural shows.

Ayub National Park on GT Rd, beyond the Presidency, with a lake for boating, bridle path for riding, aquarium, open-air garden restaurant, open-air theatre and a Japanese garden.

Local crafts and industry Numerous handicrafts include wood inlay in walnut and sheesham, Potothar *jooties* (footwear), Cane baskets, sticks and furniture; silver work, shawls and handwoven carpets. You can also get excellent embroidered jackets, shawls and woollen clothing.

Services

Hotels A *Pearl Continental*, The Mall. T 62700, Cable: Pearlcont, Telex: 5736 Pearl Pk. 200 rm. Excellent 24 hr *Brasserie* restaurant. Pool open to non-residents for a daily charge of about Rs 80. The best in town with Tourist Information Office. **B** *Shalimar,* off the Mall, GPO Box 93. T 62901, Cable: Cenam, Telex: 5764 Shlmar Pk. 100 rm. Modern hotel with all amenities. *Snahnai Hall, Sandal Corner, Sanobar Room* restaurants recommended. **C** *Flashman's,* 17/22 Shahrah-e-Quaid-e-Azam (PTDC). T 64811, Cable: Flashman's, Telex: 5620 FH Pk. 63 rm (d, suite) some a/c. Restaurant, coffee shop, travel, shop, pool (intermittently full), tennis. Unusual sprawling buildings. Plumbing variable. *Lalarukh* and *Chinar Restaurants* are good. **C** *Kashmirwala's Tourist Inn,* The Mall, T 538186. 24 a/c rm. Central a/c. Restaurant recommended.

D *Silver Grill,* The Mall. T 64729, Cable: Silvergrill. 13 a/c rm (s, d, suite). Central a/c. Restaurant, exchange, car hire. **D** *Rawal,* Committee Chowk, Murree Rd. T 70121, Cable: Rawhot, Telex: 5767 Rawal Pk. 53 a/c rm, some with TV. Central a/c. Restaurant, shops. **D** *United,* Murree Rd. T 70154, Cable: Unihot. 52 a/c rm. Central a/c. Restaurant, car hire. **D** *Potohar,* N 69-76, Murree Rd. T 844303. 36 rm, some a/c. Restaurant. **D** *Gatmell's Motel,* Airport Rd, nr COA House. T 581648. 54 rm, some a/c with TV. Restaurant, exchange. Popular with trekkers and climbers and is recommended. **E** *Marhaba,* 118 Kashmir Rd, T 66021. 29 rm, some a/c with bath. In Liaquat Bagh, Murree Rd there are 2 others – *National City* and *Park,* T 73284 but the location is noisier than Gatmell's. **E** *Asia,* Committee Chowk off Murree Rd. T 70898. 36 rm, with bath. Recommended for large rm, good service and relatively quiet location. **E** *Shama,* opp Motimahal Cinema, Murree Rd, T 70341. 30 rm with bath. Restaurant. Cheaper.

F category hotels without a/c rm in Hathi Chowk, Saddar are *Al-Azam, Al-Hamra, Al-Khali* and *Cantonment View* as well as the *Arosa Guest House* in Commercial Centre, Satellite Town. T 844583. **F** *YWCA* is at 64 Block A, Satellite Town. Women only, very basic. **F** *Railway Retiring Rooms* for passengers only. Bedding not provided.

Youth Hostel is at 25 Gulistan Colony (Bus 10 from GPO) drops on the other side of the park. Inexpensive, in pleasant location but out of town.

Restaurants There are a number of a/c restaurants outside hotels. *Blue Lagoon* on the Mall opp Pearl Continental, T 65377 and *Shexan* on Kashmir Rd, opp Post Office, T 65743. Two on Committee Chowk are *Larosh and Tabbaq,* Taqi Plaza, Murree Rd, T 75808. *Seven Brothers* in Bara Bazaar, Liaqat Rd, T 73132 does Pathan dishes. **Chinese** – *Meikong,* 32 Haider Rd, Saddar, T 66577 is recommended. *Chung Wah,* 69 a Satellite Town, Murree Rd, T 843803. *Peiking,* nr Punjab House, Mayo Rd, T 624535. **Fast Food** – *Kamran,* 64/7 Bank Rd, T 67995, is recommended. Two others on Bank Rd are Seven *Eleven,* at 41 E, T 66464 and *Cook's* at 39. *Burger Express,* London Book Co Building, Kashmir Rd. *Mr. Big,* Ghakar Plaza, Bank Rd, T 66432 *Phoenix Snack Bar,* 125/D 1, Murree Rd, T 68300. *Snack Shack,* Rahim Plaza, nr American Express, Murree Rd, T 64045. The cheaper places are in Saddar Bazaar, Rajah Bazaar and nr the railway station.

Clubs Press Club, Liaquat Garden, T 62994. Golf Club, National Park, T 65732. Dept Club, Bank Rd, T 62351. Alpine Club of Pakistan, Peshawar Rd. Rawalpindi Club, The Mall, T 62209 which has a club ground.

Banks American Express, Rahim Plaza, Murree Rd, T 840851. State Bank of Pakistan, The Mall. Habib, SDV Branch, The Mall.

Shopping Rawalpindi has a series of bazaars with goods ranging from local cloth to illegally imported electrical goods. Take your pick – but perhaps with care! The 2 main shopping streets are Mashmir Rd and Massey Gate. The shopping areas are spread across the city – *Saddar Bazaar, Raja Bazaar, Sarafa Bazaar, Moti Bazaar* and *Marir Hassan Bazaar.* To get to Raja Bazaar, follow the City Saddar Rd N across the river from the station and over the roundabout. The cloth market, Kalan Bazaar is to your right at the main cross roads which leads to the *Sarafa Bazaar,* the jewellery market for beaten gold and silver work including tribal silver jewellery. You will also find brass, copper and tin utensils here. Md Shafi and Sons are recommended. Other jewellery shops are on Murree Rd. *Pakistan Handicrafts Shop,* The Mall. *Camera shops* – Agfa Gevaert, Bank Rd and *Gulf Colour Service* (where you get 45 min service) and *Fuji Colour Service,* Rahim Plaza on Murree Rd.

Maps The Survey of Pakistan Headquarters is near the junction of the Airport Road and Murree Road. You can buy Provincial and National Maps.

Local transport Taxis within city and to Pir Wadhai. **Auto rickshaws** and **tongas** are also available within the city limits. **Mini buses** go to Islamabad and **Miniwagons** to the airport and Pir Wadhai. There is a Super Highway between Rawalpindi and Islamabad. The GTS bus stand is on Kashmir Rd, T 64449. The GTS Pir Wadhai Bus Stand, N of the city, T 860283. Buses and minibuses often wait until they are full before doing the journey. From Pir Wadhai, you can take a wagon to Faizabad and then another to Aabpara, Islamabad.

Entertainment Liquat Memorial Hall, Liaquat Rd, T 70423 for theatre and cultural shows. Cinemas – Gullistan and Shabistan Cinemas, Committee Chowk, Murree Rd. Motimahal, Rialto and Sangeet Cinemas on Murree Rd. Odeon and Plaza cinemas on The Mall and Ciros in Haider Rd.

Sports Liaquat Memorial Hall (see above in Places of interest). **Golf course** adjoins the Ayub Park, the 18 hole course where tournaments are held.

Army Museum, Iftikhar Rd. Collection of military uniforms, weapons and paintings tracing the country's military history. Open Summer (May- mid Sep) 0800-1200, 1730-1900. Winter (mid Sep -April) 0900-1500.

Parks and zoos Ayub National Park, on the GT Rd beyond the Presidency, has boating on the lake, an aquarium, a Japanese garden and restaurant. Children's Park and Mini Sports Complex, Murree Rd.

Post and Telegraphs GPO, Kashmir Rd, T 65691. Central Telegraph Office, The Mall, T 65854.

Hospitals Holy Family, Satellite Town, T 40368. Rawalpindi General, Murree Rd, T 40381. Fauji Foundation Medical Centre, Jhelum Rd.

Places of worship Muslim – Numerous mosques. Christian – Christ Church, behind Pearl Continental, Cantt.

Useful addresses Foreigners' Registration Office, Rashid Minhas Rd, Civil Lines, T 63866. Open 0800-1400 but this office does not deal with visa extension. Passport Office, 6th Rd, Satellite Town, T 840851.

Chambers of commerce Rawalpindi Chamber of Commerce and Industry, Chamber House, 108 Adamjee Rd, T 67598, Telex: 5547 RCCI PK.

Travel agents *Pakistan Tours*, Rm 23-24, *Flashman's*, The Mall, T 581480. *Al-Siddique Corporation*, 2-13, Alflah Askaria, Committee Chowk, Murree Rd, T 71012 who specialize in trekking and mountaineering. *Sitara Travels*, 163 A Bank Rd, T 64750.

Tourist offices and information Tourist Information Centres at Pearl Continental, T 66011 and at Flashman's, The Mall, T 581480, Ext 4. Shangrila Tourist Resort Office (Northern Area), 143-N, Murree Rd, T 73006.

Air PIA's domestic services connect with Karachi, 4 flights daily, Quetta, 3 flights daily, Lahore, 5 flights a week, Peshawar Sat. Also flights to Saidu Sharif, Skardu and Gilgit. PIA, The Mall, T 67011. Flight Enquiry, T 840261.

Rail Trains are slow and tend to get crowded. Rawalpindi City Rly Station, T 72303 Reservations, T 62855, Enquiries, T 65704. There is a city Booking Agency at Lucky Gate and the station has a Left Luggage room. **Lahore** Zulfiqar Exp, 6 a/c, daily, 1015, 6 hr 30 min; Awam Exp, 14, daily, 1315, 5 hr 45 min; **Karachi (Cnt)** Zulfiqar Exp, 6, a/c, daily, 1015, 32 hr; Awam Exp, 14, daily, 1315, 25 hr 30 min; **Peshawar** K273, daily, 0630, 3 hr 40 min; 211, daily, 0830, 5 hr 30 min.

Road Buses are faster and more comfortable than trains. There are State run buses as well as private companies which run services between Rawalpindi and cities in Punjab and the N, to Abbottabad, Ayubia, Faisalabad, Gilgit, Lahore, Murree, Nathia Gali, Peshawar, Sialkot and Swat as well as Bagh, Kotli, Mirpur, Muzaffarabad, Rawalkot in Azad Kashmir. **The Central Bus Station** is at **Pir Wadhai**. Buses to **Gilgit** at 0900, 1300, 1900 and 2300 (about 20 hr) and **Saidu Sharif**. GTS Services for Peshawar, T 74370 **GTS Bus Station**, Saddar Bazaar has buses to many destinations. Mini buses to **Lahore** and **Salt Range** in **Committee Chowk**, Murree Rd. Buses for **Peshawar** and **Lahore** from **Moti Mahal Cinema** off Murree Rd. **Skyways** and **Flying Coach Terminal**, for a/c coaches for Lahore, Sialkot and Peshawar, nr Rawal Hotel and nr Shangrila, Murree Rd. Flying Coach Stop, nr Rawal Hotel, T 70050; National Flying Coach, T 71341; New Flying Coach, T 70136. Pakistan Tours buses for Swat from Flashman's Hotel. Hourly from 0500 in summer and 0600 in winter. **Wagon Stand** for Taxila, Abbottabad and Kaghan is on **Haider Rd**. At Pir Wadhai – Northern Areas Transport Corporation (NATCO), T 860283. Kohistan Bus Service, T 861755. New Khan Road Runner, T 72229. Masherbrum Tours (for northern areas). Blue Lines, T 78229.

EXCURSIONS FROM ISLAMABAD-RAWALPINDI

There are several fascinating and enjoyable excursions that can be made from Islamabad. The Margalla Hills, which dominate the northern skyline from both Islamabad and Rawalpindi, offer some very attractive walks. Within 40 km of the capital is one of the most important archaeological sites in S Asia, Taxila, dating back to the 6th century BC, with its unique blending of the cultures of India and the W. Islamabad and Rawalpindi also serve as the base for longer excursions to the hill stations such as Murree and Thandiani and further afield still to the N and NW.

The _Margalla Hills_ are also known as the **_Islamabad National Park_**.
Formed of limestone, they cover an area of about 12,000 ha. The numerous nature trails which wind around the hills and valleys offer a choice for walkers and riders of distances covering 1.5 km to 15 km (a total length of 110 km), and ranging from heights of 640-1,580 m. Best season Oct – Apr but even in these relatively cooler months, mid day can be very hot. Since about a dozen trails can be managed by all members of a family within a couple of hours, with an early morning start you can enjoy a very pleasant hike. There are also half to full-day hikes listed while the longest hikes can take up to 2 to 3 days: go prepared for these with the best maps and a compass. The easy trails can be undertaken in 'trainers' but several are stony and require strong shoes or walking boots. You can start several treks from Islamabad on foot. See below.

Warning Be prepared for heavy rain in Jan and Feb and chilly nights.

Follow the trails, avoid short cuts, as it is easy to get lost (and the thorn bushes can be painful), and carry drinking water with you. In the dry season there is the added risk of fire. The Asia Study Group's _'Hiking Guide_ (1988 Revised edition) has very good detailed maps and lists the different possibilities in the Margalla hills and a few further N. The Capital Development Authorities _Trekking in the Margalla Hills_ is not accurate enough for the longer trails.

The First and Second Ridge The row of hills facing Islamabad is called the **'First Ridge '** with a number of valleys and ravines with pools, springs and water falls, cutting into them from the plains. Some valleys have descriptive names – _Dara Baliman_ (Quarry Valley), _Santari_ (Banyan Tree Valley), _Nurpur Sara_ (Rock Pools Valley), _Rata Hotter_ (Leopard Valley) among others. The next row, parallel to the first and separated from it by the Nilan Nullah, a deep valley, is known as the **'Second Ridge '**. The only motorable road through the hills is the **Pir Sahawa Rd**, which starts from the **Khayaban-e-Iqbal**, nr the Zoo, and runs up to the 'First Ridge' eastward, with a jeepable track continuing E from Pir Sahawa where there is a _Forest Rest House_. Tracks come down to the **Nilan Nullah** from the Pir Sahawa Rd.

The short walks can either start nr the Zoo (Marghazar), from Daman-e-Koh or from Pir Sahawa. The picnic spots are marked with 'Shades' which can be crowded on Fridays. You can reach the highest point in the hills (1,640 m) from Pir Sahawa. If you are with children keen on bathing, try the Rock Pools Valley which you can get to by driving up N of Nurpur Shahan village, and parking nr the Mandiala water works. **The longer hikes** taking from 4 to 8 hr or 2 to 3 days are described in the booklet. The maps show the locations of tea stalls and _Rest Houses_.

Margalla vegetation The hills have been planted with sub-tropical local as well as non-indigenous ornamental plants with evidence of the primary forest only at the higher levels. The slopes below 1,000 m have dry, semi-evergreen vegetation, with acacia and the

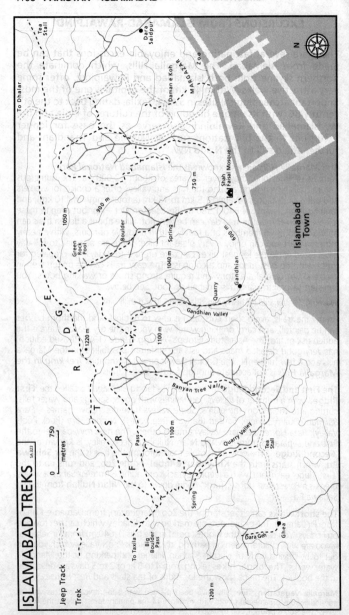

ISLAMABAD TREKS SA 323

0   750
metres

Jeep Track

Trek

N

To Dhalar

Tea
Stall

Dara
Saidpur

Daman e Koh

MARGAZAR
Zoo

Shah
Faisal Mosque

750 m

900 m

1050 m

Green
Rock
Pool

Boulder

Spring

600 m

1040 m

Gandhian

Islamabad
Town

Quarry

Gandhian Valley

1100 m

1220 m

E
G
D
I
R

T
S
R
I
F

Banyan Tree Valley

Pass

1100 m

Quarry Valley

Tea
Stall

Spring

To Taxila

Big
Boulder
Pass

Spring

1200 m

Dara Geh

Ghea

olive predominating and with shrubs to protect against soil erosion. On the higher slopes, taller pines are common, particularly *Pinus roxburghii* and also the white oak (*Quercus incana*) which can be a fire hazard. You will notice numerous other species including *sheesham* and the wild date palm (*Phoenix sylvestris*), the silk cotton tree (*Bombax ceiba*) and the Peepul (*Ficus religiosa*).

Ornamental species which have added to the attraction of the hills include jacaranda, bottle brush, eucalyptus, amalthus, lilies and chir. In the spring, the plants, strikingly similar to European flora, flower in Mar until mid-Apr when they die down. Then with the coming of the monsoon around the beginning of Jul, the barren ground comes to life again with flora of SE Asia. A good guide available in Islamabad is ' *Wild flowers of Rawalpindi-Islamabad Districts* ' by Nasir and others (1987).

Fauna in the Hills The park is becoming the home for a number of animal species and birds since hunting has been banned and afforestation carried out. They include rhesus monkeys, barking deer, jackal, wild boar, porcupines, mongoose, pangolin (scaly ant eater), the rare leopard in the winter as well as black partridges and birds of prey and a large number of butterfly species. Cheer pheasants which had become virtually extinct have been successfully re-introduced into the hills.

Poisonous snakes which have been found in the Hills include cobra, krait, Russell's Viper. Fortunately they hibernate in the winter, but take care when walking off the paths, in the warmer months. The ASG has published a list of birds by Corfield which supplements the handy *Guide to the birds of the sub-continent* published by Collins. If you are keen to identify butterflies, try *Butterflies of India* by Chas and Antram or *Butterflies of the Himalaya* by Mani.

TAXILA

The site at *Taxila* has been occupied from at least the Neolithic period. Excavations at **Sarai Khola**, 3 km SW of Taxila city, have shown a succession of occupations, the earliest has shown several pit dwellings with ground stone axes and burnished pottery. However, until recently it was widely believed that the town first came to prominence when the whole area was incorporated into the Achaemenid Empire of Cyrus the Great (558-530 B.C.).

In an inscription of 519 BC the third Achaemenid Emperor, Darius I, claimed possession of **Gandhara**, and soon after of " Hindush ", a region which may well have covered most of the Punjab. By that time Taxila was already the centre of a major university, which attracted students from as far afield as the eastern Indian kingdom of Magadh, centred on modern Patna. It occupied a strategically important site on one of the ancient world's most important trade routes. If you stand at the monastery of **Jaulian** today you can still gain a sense of the advantage that its site offered, with the hills behind and the broadening lowlands spreading out below.

Recent excavations by the Cambridge-Pakistan team have produced evidence which supports the finds of Sir Mortimer Wheeler at **Charsada** to suggest that Taxila was founded at least 2 centuries earlier than the 6th century date commonly ascribed to it. Allchin and Allchin suggest that discoveries of red burnished pottery and other goods from the **Hathial** area next to the Bhir Mound show strong links with the pottery of Charsada, and even stronger similarities with the pottery of the Swat valley, suggesting that the first city in Taxila may be dated as early as 1000 BC

A centre of learning Taxila probably retained a degree of independence throughout the period of Persian rule. When Alexander the Great arrived it was certainly still a centre of learning and culture, for Alexander himself is recorded as having philosophical discussions with naked ascetics. However, the Greek occupation of Taxila was extraordinarily brief, and their influence at this period slight.

They were succeeded by 310 BC at the latest by **Chandragupta Maurya**. In 305 BC The contacts with the Greeks were maintained through the reign of his son **Bindusara**. He is recorded as having sent a request to the Greek King **Antiochus** for "a present of figs, wine and a sophist". According to Basham, Antiochus responded by sending figs and wine, but sent a message to the effect that "Greek philosophers were not for export". During this period Bindusara's son **Asoka**, who was to become one of India's greatest Kings, became the Mauryan Viceroy in Taxila, and the Mauryan influence remained strong throughout his rule.

In the 4th century BC Taxila was home to a succession of scholars and enjoyed a reputation for learning at least equal to that of Varanasi, with which it was contemporary. However, Taxila was particularly noted for its secular studies. **Caraka**, a master of medicine, **Kautilya**, the Brahman adviser in statecraft to the Emperor Chandragupta and **Panini**, author of the most famous Sanskrit grammar, all worked in Taxila. Throughout this period, the city of Taxila was focused on the area that now is known as the Bhir Mound, immediately to the S of the modern museum.

From the middle of the 3rd century however, Taxila became the scene of a series of invasions from the northwest. Bactrian Greeks under **Euthydemus** gained sufficient independence to break away completely from the Mauryan Empire. They established a bridgehead for the introduction of western ideas into India. Their widespread coinage gives some impression of the extent and length of their rule, and it seems that Western theories of astrology and medicine, as well as Sanskrit drama, entered at this time. However, by the second half of the 2nd century BC Bactria was occupied by Parthians and the Greeks in Taxila and its region were isolated.

Basham suggests that one of the last of these kings, **Gondophernes**, may have been the first Indian to have contact with Christianity. "If we are to believe a very old tradition" he writes "the first Christian converts were made by the disciple Thomas himself, soon after the Crucifixion". Gondophernes sent to Syria for a skilful architect to build him a new city, and the envoy returned with **St Thomas** who told the king of a city not made with hands, and converted him and many members of his court. St Thomas afterwards preached in other parts of India, and died a martyr's death at the hands of a king called in Christian tradition **Misdeos**, who cannot be identified." Many in S India believe that his martyrdom took place at St. Thomas's Mount, just outside Madras. See page 703. At the beginning of the second century BC the Bactrian Greeks built a new and quite different city at Taxila, known as **Sirkap**.

New population movements took place, originating from China, and the Scyths, known in India as the **Sakas** pressed down from the N onto Bactrian lands. By the middle of the 1st century BC the power of the Bactrian Greeks had almost totally disintegrated. It was the Sakas who gave their name to one of the most important systems of dating in India, the "Saka era", and it seems likely that this is associated with the Kushana king **Kanishka**. His dates are still uncertain, though 78 AD seems the most likely.

Kanishka founded the third of Taxila's cities, **Sirsukh**, which was occupied until the middle of the 5th century. The Chinese Buddhist pilgrim described Sirsukh as being extremely flourishing when he visited it in the early 5th century. Shortly afterwards invasion by the Huns then caused widespread destruction, and although the city continued to be occupied for some time it never recovered. Hiuen Tsang, visiting it in the 7th century, described it as very decayed.

Visiting the site Warning Many signs say "photography not allowed". In fact it is perfectly possible to take photographs. Get permission from Director of Archaeological Survey of Punjab at Lahore or in Karachi. Regrettably in practice the signs give the custodians an opportunity to increase their income by "allowing" visitors without permits to take photographs for a fee. Be prepared.

The excavations at Taxila have shown widely scattered settlements. **Jaulian** in the NE is 6 km as the crow flies from Bhir Mound. Buses go to Taxila from Islamabad. Tours are organised by the PTDC. As the site is very spread out, these can be worthwhile. Cars can also be hired in Islamabad – see page 1101. Allow at least half a day yo explore. For a description of the route from Islamabad, see page 1118. The road through the site runs N from **Bhir Mound**, the oldest settlement, past the acropolis and town of **Sirkap** on the right. 2 km from the museum there is a left turn to the Bactrian Greek temple of **Jandial**, and a further 1 km on, another left turn to the third city of **Sirsukh**.

Keeping on the main road a further 3 km brings you to a right turn to the Buddhist monastery of Jaulian, one of the most impressive remaining sets of buildings. To reach the main Buddhist stupa of **Dharmarajika** take the turning to the E just in front of the museum, and follow it to the car park at its end, approximately 2 km. From there follow the clearly marked path down into a

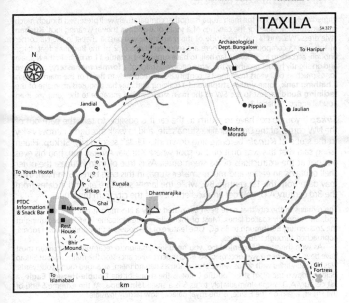

TAXILA
SA 327

ravine, across the stream by stepping stones, and then up the other side.

Note Today very little remains of Sirsukh. If you arrive before the museum opens (for most of the year, early morning is the best time to visit) it may be best to visit Jaulian first, and then return to sites closer to the museum visiting Jandial. However, the tour suggested starts at the museum.

Cross Bhir Mound by the road to the car park and walk to Dharmarajika. **Bhir Mound**, the oldest of the sites, was partially excavated by Sir John Marshall. There is little to see, though the excavations suggest that the settlement was a jumble of unplanned alleys and streets packed tightly together. From the car park at the end of the road walk across the little valley to the great stupa of the **Dharmarajika**. (If you have a driver, the car can be sent round to the entrance to the Sirkap site.)

Dharmarajika The stupa and monastery at the centre of this site possibly date from the time of **Asoka** in the middle of the 3rd century BC The path enters the site from the SW up a steep hill, concealing the stupa and surrounding buildings until you are nearly there. The main stupa, 15 m high, was enlarged after its initial construction and some of the decoration on its E side was added in the 4th century AD.

Originally there was a series of small *votive stupas** (built by wealthy devotees) around the main building, and a series of chapels. If you walk round the stupa to the E side along one of the 2 processional paths that are a feature of Buddhist stupas you will see the great cut where treasure hunters looked for the relics of the Buddha. When the **Emperor Asoka** converted to Buddhism after the great Kalingan War in modern Orissa, by which he established his authority across the whole of northern India, it is said that he disinterred the Buddha's remains from their casket at Sanchi and distributed them to 8 major stupas across his empire, of which the Dharmarajika is one. The best preserved work on this main stupa, the band of **ornamental stone carving** on the E side of the base, dates from the 4th and 5th centuries.

Immediately to the S of the main stupa is another comparatively well preserved though much smaller stupa, notable for the carvings of a series of **Buddhas** shown wearing local **Kushan** style dress. Walking N past the E side of the main stupa you pass a chapel in the NE corner of the stupa's compound where there are representations of 2 of the Buddha's feet, large enough, according to Sir John Marshall, to have supported a statue 11 m high. To the N again and on slightly higher ground is the large enclosed space of a **former monastery**, occupied for as much as 600 years from the 1st century BC. Immediately to the N of the main stupa is a **bathing tank**, some **votive stupas** and a building that may have housed an image of the **reclining Buddha**. Just to the SW of the main stupa, nr the entrance to the complex, is an apsidal ended " chapel ".

Sirkap If you do not have to return to the car it is possible to take the path out of the NW corner of the Dharmarajika stupa's site, and to walk through a narrow valley to the stupa of **Kunala** before going down into Taxila's second city, **Sirkap**. Hiuen Tsang said that this was built on the spot where Kunala, Asoka's son, had his eyes put out at the instructions of his stepmother. As is true of many stupas, the outer shell contains an earlier and much smaller stupa, in this case barely 3 m high. That may date from the 1st century BC, while the larger structure around it dates from the 3rd century A.D. You get an excellent view of the city from the stupa.

The remains of the city that have been excavated show a N-S main street, fortified at the N end, and regularly spaced lanes. Most of the buildings visible come from the beginning of the 2nd century BC through to 85 BC. One feature of the houses is their underground rooms, approached through trap doors.

As with the site of **Moenjodaro**, you need imagination to recapture what Sirkap must have been like when it was occupied. As at its much earlier ancestor, the main street at Sirkap was probably lined with shops with 2 storey houses behind them, arranged round courtyards. Halfway down the main street on the E side is the shrine of the **Double-Headed Eagle**, a 1st century A.D. stupa. Immediately to its S is a small **Jain stupa**. At the extreme S end of the street, again on the E side, is the royal palace, now largely invisible.

Jandial Continue N from Sirkap and take the left turn to the temple, raised above the road. This temple shows obvious signs of its Greek ancestry. It comprised a square inner sanctuary, a meeting hall and a courtyard. Its entrances were flanked by Ionian columns. The existence of a solid tower between the sanctuary and back porch, which would have allowed the rising and setting sun to be observed, have been taken to suggest that this was probably used for **Zoroastrian** worship, see page 76. It dates from the beginning of the Christian era.

Sirsukh Continuing NE up the road, Sirsukh is signposted to the left after about 1 km. Very little has been excavated. Perhaps the most exciting remains visible today are those of the stupa and monastery at **Jaulian**. The site is fully enclosed and there is always a caretaker in attendance. There is a short and fairly steep walk from the car park to the monastery, but you are rewarded with a magnificent view over the plains below.

The entrance is to the lower court leading to the main stupa. This is nothing like the scale of the Dharmarajika, but it is far more fully decorated. Some of the surrounding votive stupas have inscriptions in **Kharaosthi** script. Some of the most important sculptures and relics are in the museum. While several of these stupas date from as late as the 5th century, the main monastery to the W comes from the 2nd century. However, the plaster statues of the Buddha are copies of the originals which are in the museum. Surrounding the monastery courtyard are monks cells, originally with plastered and painted walls, rather than the bare stone which now survives.

Hotels It is quite possible to visit from Islamabad, but accommodation at the 2 *Rest Houses* at the site can be booked through the curator of the Taxila museum or the Director General of Archaeology, Government of Pakistan, Karachi at least 10 days in advance. Caretakers arrange for meals.

Museum At the N end of the Bhir Mound. Open daily 0900-1600 (1 Oct-31 Mar); 0900-1200 and 1400-1800 (1 Apr-30t Sep). Attractively presented collection with some first class examples of Gandharan sculpture and art. Jewellery, coins, relics and gold and silver caskets also on display. open. Please do not eat or drink in public during the day.

PUNJAB

INTRODUCTION

Social indicators *Literacy* M 37% F 17%

Stretching from the foothills of the Himalayas in the N down to well beyond the confluence of the Punjab rivers with the Indus in the S, Punjab covers 205,000 sq km. Its 1972 population of 38 million had grown to 60 million by 1991. Thus although it has only a quarter of Pakistan's area it has nearly 60% of its population. The chief language is Punjabi.

Punjab takes its name from the rivers that brought it into being and which give it its form, the "5 waters" that are tributaries of the great Indus to their W. In the middle 1850s most of the area was scrub jungle, sparsely cultivated and thinly populated. In the course of the following 50 years a massive development of irrigation transformed the land. Today there is no better example in the world of a landscape that is the result of the transformation of a huge area of semi desert that is possible by harnessing major rivers. Although the modern Pakistan province of Punjab is the dominant economic and population centre of Pakistan it is only a part of the pre-Independence region of Punjab, which stretched E across the plains towards Delhi. The border created in 1947 cut through the wider geographical region, leaving the W Punjab rivers in Pakistan and the eastern tributaries of the Indus in India. Under the provisions of the Indus Waters Treaty which was signed between India and Pakistan in 1960 the waters of the Beas, the Sutlej and the Ravi were allocated to India, those of the Chenab, Jhelum and Indus going to Pakistan.

The land
However you enter Punjab you are aware of its physical continuity with the plains of Sind to the S and those of the Indian Punjab to the E. The modern boundary with India is a recent and artificial creation, dividing a region that in terms of its rivers, its economy and its culture had previously been integrated.

The best views of the Punjab are gained from a plane, when you can see the enormous scale of the **Indus** and its tributaries, the broad river beds covered with the silt which has been responsible for the creation of the plains themselves. Geologically they are of very recent origin. In the N of the Province, is the **Potwar Plateau**, a vital source of evidence on early prehistoric settlements. Covering about 13,000 sq km, at altitudes of between 350-580 m, the plateau is frequently characterised by extraordinary landscapes. Formed largely of recent sandstones, with occasional outliers of the Great Salt Range intruding, it is covered by varying depths of loess, wind blown silt. The plateau has been lifted very recently, and the rivers which flow over the plateau have often carved out deep gorges and canyons into the soft rock. Because the rivers are thus cut into deep sided ravines they are generally of little use for irrigation. You can see the dramatic valleys cut through the low hill ranges immediately to the S of Islamabad. Equally you get

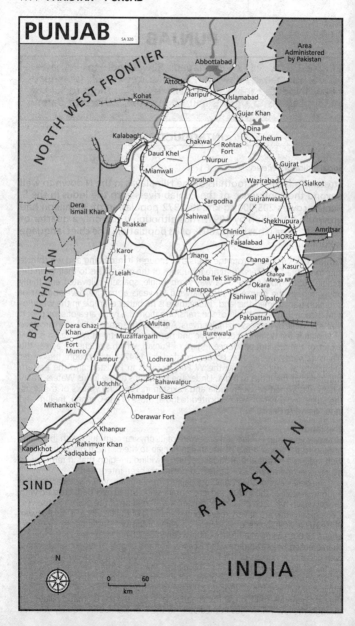

PUNJAB

SA 320

NORTH WEST FRONTIER

Area Administered by Pakistan

Abbottabad

Attock

Kohat

Haripur

Islamabad

Gujar Khan

Kalabagh

Chakwal

Dina

Jhelum

Daud Khel

Rohtas Fort

Nurpur

Mianwali

Khushab

Gujrat

Khushab

Wazirabad

Sialkot

Sargodha

Gujranwala

Sahiwal

Dera Ismail Khan

Bhakkar

Chiniot

Shekhupura

LAHORE

Amritsar

BALUCHISTAN

Karor

Faisalabad

Jhang

Changa

Kasur

Leiah

Toba Tek Singh

Changa Manga NP

Harappa

Okara

Sahiwal Dipalpur

Pakpattan

Dera Ghazi Khan

Multan

Burewala

Fort Munro

Muzaffargarh

Jampur

Lodhran

Uchchh

Bahawalpur

Mithankot

Ahmadpur East

Derawar Fort

Khanpur

Kandhkot

Rahimyar Khan

Sadiqabad

SIND

RAJASTHAN

N

0   60
km

INDIA

magnificent views from the air, of the **Ravi** and the **Chenab**, or further W of the **Jhelum** and the **Indus**.

The flatness of the terrain further S makes long drives rather monotonous, though during the early growing season of the winter wheat crop a delicious light green tinges the landscape, and the freshness of the spring morning air makes early morning travel an enormous pleasure.

Climate

A narrow belt of N Punjab benefits from winter rains as well as the summer monsoon, so the upper plains of the Indus have a quite different climate from the S plains of Sind. Total rainfall increases northwards from 100 mm a year, just to the S of Multan, up to 800 mm a year at **Lahore** and NW towards **Peshawar**. Jul, Aug and Sep are the wettest months in Lahore itself, the traditional S Asian monsoon season. It is also by far the most uncomfortable period, with humidity rates over 90% and temperatures well over 40°C.

Towns and cities

30% of Punjab's population live in towns and cities, a total in 1991 of 17 million people compared with 5 million (25%) in 1972. Although that makes it much less urbanised than Sind, Punjab has Pakistan's largest concentration of cities, as well as Pakistan's second largest city in Lahore and the country's capital, Islamabad.

Migrants and refugees The modern growth of the cities of Punjab owed a great deal to partition in 1947 and the flow of migrants across the Indian border. Between 1951 and 1972 **Lahore** grew from 850,000-2.2 million. The percentage growth figures of several of Punjab's more important towns were remarkable: **Faisalabad** (formerly Lyallpur) 360%, **Rawalpindi** 160%, **Gujranwala** 200%, and **Multan** 185% are just some examples. However, that growth has continued long after the refugee migrants stopped coming, a growth fed by rapid natural increase, often of nearly 3% a year, and by continuing migration from the villages, where increased agricultural activity could not keep pace with the rapid population growth.

Furthermore some technical changes in farming actually displaced labour. One estimate suggests for example that Pakistan's import of tractors in the 2 decades after 1961 cost rural Pakistan 1 million jobs, greatly increasing the pressure to move to towns. Had it not been for increased irrigation and the intensification of agriculture the pressure would have been even greater.

Market centres The pattern of growth of Punjab's towns shows the importance of the main transport route linking Islamabad/Rawalpindi in the N with Lahore and then S through Multan to Karachi. If you drive down this route today you pass through some of the most rapidly growing marketing and industrial centres in the country. The towns "threaded like beads on the string of the main railway line" as Johnson puts it, include five cities with nearly 1 million people each, and towns like **Sahiwal**, **Multan** and **Bahawalpur**. Many of these are the creation of the canal colonies that were developed in the late 19th century. However, Punjab has long urban traditions. **Harappa**, one of the 2 major cities of the Indus Valley civilisation, is just over 150 km SW of Lahore, and there are several other important Indus Valley sites in the Punjab region, testifying to the developed urban civilisation that existed between 2500 BC and 1750 BC.

Early towns It was not until over 1000 years later that new towns developed to replace the lost cities of the Indus Valley. **Multan**, perhaps one of the oldest continually occupied tow~ in the Punjab, may have been the capital of Malli mentioned by **Alexander the Great** i~ BC. In the far N **Taxila** goes back even further to 516 BC, and was a living city unti' Soon after the arrival of the first Muslim conquerors in Sind, Muslim influence Punjab, but it wasn't until the raids of Mahmud of Ghazni after 1000 AD ·' to leave an impression on the towns of the region.

A number of towns have magnificent remains which testify to their e~ **Uchchh Sharif**, S of Multan, for example, has the superb tomb of **Bibi J~** from 1498. The **Mughals** then added their influence, notably through Lahore, capital under the Emperor Jahangir. After the Mughal decline Punjab came unde~

power of the Sikhs, who made Lahore one of their most important cities and added distinctive temples to its architectural traditions.

The British impact The last external influence on Punjab's cities before Independence was that of the British, who added the planned towns of the canal colonies and the military and civil cantonments for their officers, which made the same kind of mark on Punjab's townscapes as they did elsewhere in S Asia. The Mall in Lahore, and the colonial buildings such as Aitchison College reflect this period of Empire city building.

Today however, even that impact has been dwarfed by the scale of modern growth. From the planned and spacious new capital of Islamabad to the new housing estates for returned migrants to the Gulf of the 1970s and 1980s, the formal buildings of Punjab's towns have been transformed. However, like the cities of India, there are also great areas of poverty, informal settlement and "slums", reflecting both the speed of overall population increase and the inability to keep up with the ever increasing demand for housing and services.

People Punjabis are largely descendants of the Indo-Aryans who migrated into S Asia from the 15th century BC, though there are also people of mixed Arab, Persian and Turkish and Mongol stock. Nearly 80% of the population is recorded as having Punjabi as its mother tongue, under 5% speaking Urdu.

Economy

Agriculture Punjab is widely regarded as the heart of Pakistan's agricultural economy. The statistics of production and area show why. It produces over 70% of Pakistan's **wheat** and nearly half its **rice**. Among the cash crops, it produces over 60% of the country's **sugar** and nearly 85% of its **cotton**.

These figures reflect the overwhelming importance of the canal irrigated land which makes up the lion's share of Punjab's agricultural resource. Some new land has been brought into cultivation since Independence, especially through new irrigation schemes to convert the **Thal** desert into agricultural land by using Indus water. In more recent years improvements in production have come through adopting higher quality seeds and increasing the use of fertiliser and pesticide, just as in Indian Punjab. Taken together, the plains of Indian and Pakistani Punjab make up the most rapidly changing agricultural region in S Asia. Today in Pakistan **Mexi-Pak wheat**, cross-bred strains of Mexican and Pakistani wheats, are grown everywhere.

Resources and industry In the 1980s Punjab has become Pakistan's most important oil producer. Although output of **crude petroleum** is still only 10 m barrels, it represents 60% of the country's total, a fourfold increase on production at the start of the 1980s.

The Province is poorly provided with other minerals. **Rock salt** from the Great Salt range provides the basis of a **chemical industry** and about half a million tonnes of **coal** are mined every year.

Not surprisingly, given the poverty of mineral wealth, Punjab's **traditional industries** tend to be small scale and based on processing agricultural raw materials. Today there has been rapid expansion of the **cotton industry** in **Faisalabad** and **Multan**, while **Lahore** has a mix of iron working, engineering, textiles, chemicals, food processing and shoe manufacture. To the N **Sialkot** has a world wide reputation for the production of **sports goods** such as hockey sticks and cricket bats, but it also has an important stainless steel industry specialising in the production of surgical instruments.

History

Earliest settlement Irrigation played a vital role in the wider history of the region for over 4500 years. The N plains were the site of some of man's earliest settlements, and the Harappan civilisation grew on its inundated lands along the banks of rivers like the **Ravi** and the **Indus**. The invading Indo-Aryans came down to India through the Punjab, and it was on the northern borders of the plains the city of **Taxila** grew up in the 6th century BC.

successively that was a centre of Buddhist and Graeco Buddhist influence.

Immediately after **Alexander the Great's** brief visit the Mauryan Empire incorporated the whole of the Punjab and reached across into Afghanistan. Three centuries later invading **Huns**, known in the region as the **Kushan** rulers, plundered the northern plains in the 1st century AD. Their great warrior leader **Kanishka** converted to Buddhism, and the **Gandharan kingdom** centred on what is now the Afghan city of **Kandahar** reached its full artistic flowering during the following century.

Muslim influence Although Punjab did not come fully under Muslim influence until the 11th century, from then until the end of the 18th century a succession of Islamic rulers dominated the politics of the region. Kings of the Delhi sultanate and Arab and Persian rulers succeeded each other for varying periods before the Mughals stamped their controlling influence over the entire Province for over 150 years.

A Sikh kingdom The waning of Mughal power and the bitterness with which the **Emperor Aurangzeb** who put down the rising community of the Sikhs encouraged the tenth Sikh Guru, **Guru Gobind Singh** to introduce the features now universally associated with Sikhism. They had already adopted a more militant stance, and on April 15th 1699, almost at the end of the Mughal Emperor Aurangzeb's reign, Guru Gobind Singh started the new brotherhood called the **Khalsa** (meaning "the pure", from the Persian word *khales*), **see page 72**.
Through the 18th century they became the political force to be reckoned with in the Punjab, coming to fruition under the warrior king *Maharaja Ranjit Singh* (1799-1838). In 1764 the Sikhs fought over the Punjab plains against the Afghans, finally defeating the Afghan **Ahmad Shah Durani** in a battle near **Amritsar**. They then took **Lahore** and made it their capital, developing Amritsar as their main religious centre.
From 1799, when Lahore was formally conceded to Ranjit Singh by the Afghans, until 1820, Ranjit Singh strengthened his grip on the Punjab, which was complete by 1820. Enmity with the Afghans remained an overriding preoccupation, however, and in 1838 Ranjit Singh sided with the British in the **First Afghan War**. In the next decade his successors fought the *First Sikh War* against the British in 1846, concluded by a series of **Treaties in Lahore** (March and Dec 1846) and **Amritsar** (Mar 1846). **See page 71**, Sikhism.

Under the terms of the Treaty the Sikh governors in the provinces agreed to pay a contribution to the maintenance of the newly formed Sikh Council of Regency. However, in 1848 the Governor of Multan refused to pay. British officers were sent to install a new governor in place of the incumbent, Mulraj. However, they were murdered, and **Mulraj** started an open rebellion, to be joined by Sikh forces in Lahore, leading to the **Second Sikh War**. This ended with the storming of Multan Fort on 22 Jan 1849, and the resulting annexation of Punjab to British India.
It was this event that led to the decision to develop canal irrigation on a massive scale, as a way of giving settled and prosperous work to an area of Punjab which was seen at the time as overpopulated and economically backward. The modern history of Punjab can be traced back to the surge of settlement which followed in the wake of this irrigation development. The first Punjab canal was the *Upper Bari Doab* canal, the westernmost branch of which which can still be seen running southwards through **Lahore**. The canals took their names from the rivers between which they flowed – thus Bari was a combination of Beas and Ravi. The Upper Bari Doab Canal was dug mainly for political reasons, to offer agricultural land to Sikh settlers at the end of the Sikh wars as a result of which the British had annexed Punjab in 1849.

River diversion The key to success in Punjab irrigation lay in the building of huge **barrages** across the rivers, diverting water into the canals during the cool dry season as well as during the high flow wet season. As a result irrigation – and intensive cultivation – became possible between Nov and Mar, previously a fallow period. The barrages could also be built high enough upstream to allow land to be irrigated which previously had been too high above the river banks to receive irrigation. Thus huge new areas of what had been unirrigable land came into cultivation.

The schemes gradually moved W. The **Bari Doab** scheme was followed by the much more important **Chenab** canal project in the 1890. Nearly half a million migrants moved from the eastern districts of the Punjab to cultivate this new agricultural land. The **Jhelum Canal** was opened in 1901.

The lie of the land meant that the newly created barrages allowed irrigation of land on the lower E banks of the rivers. Thus the **Ravi** irrigated land to the E of Lahore, while the **Chenab**, for example, irrigated land to its S, around **Gujranwala** and **Faisalabad**.

Between 1905-1915 new schemes were developed to try and overcome the limitations of the individual projects on the E rivers. Although the W rivers, notably the **Indus** and the **Jhelum**, have far more water than the E rivers, they have far smaller command areas. It was proposed to transfer water from the upper reaches of the W rivers to the command areas of the E rivers, giving them far more reliable supplies than they had previously been able to count on. The *Triple Canals Project* achieved this by linking the upper Jhelum with the Chenab. In its turn water was taken from higher up the Chenab to feed eastwards into the Ravi and ultimately into the **Upper Bari Doab Canal**.

The Indus Waters Treaty All of these irrigation projects were carried out without building any storage reservoirs. Further development made dam construction necessary. After the *Indus Waters Treaty* was signed in 1960 work went ahead on building the **Mangla dam** on the Jhelum and the **Tarbela Dam** on the Indus, 2 of the world's largest constructions, both now completed. They have made possible not only the maintenance of existing irrigated agriculture in Punjab but its improvement and extension.

Partition in 1947 resulted in the mass emigration of Sikh's into India, and although some of their **Gurudwaras** (temples) remain, and Lahore is still regarded as one of the Sikhs' most important cities, no Sikhs remain in the city. In their place, and that of the millions of Hindus who also left Punjab, the Province had to absorb several million Muslims from the N regions of India. Although Lahore became the capital of the Punjab, the political and economic dominance of Karachi in the newly Independent state of Pakistan rapidly became apparent, and was widely resented. President Ayub Khan announced the removal of the capital to the new city of Islamabad, on the outskirts of the old Punjab military town of Rawalpindi, in 1958.

ISLAMABAD-RAWALPINDI TO PESHAWAR

After leaving Islamabad the road W to Peshawar joins the Grand Trunk Road 14 km from the centre (**Zero Point**) of Islamabad. Turn right on to the GT road. The road is fast and has recently been widened to carry a lot of heavy traffic from Peshawar and the North West Frontier.

The GT road rises gently just under 30 km from Islamabad to go through the *Margalla Pass*, marked by a distinctive granite obelisk monument to **General John Nicholson**, who died leading an assault on Delhi during the 1857 Mutiny. The inscription states that the monument was "erected by friends, British and Native, to the memory of Brigadier-General John Nicholson CB, who after taking a hero's part in 4 great wars, fell mortally wounded, in leading to victory the main Column of assault at the great siege of Delhi, and died on 22 Sep 1857, age 34". The wars referred to were the 2 Sikh wars, the First Afghan War and the Mutiny.

The cutting through the hills at this point goes back to the Emperor Akbar's period, though the short stretch of cobbled road preserved on the S side of the GT road, behind the various truck driver's tea stalls, was reputedly built by Sher Shah Suri. The route itself can be traced back nearly 2,000 years before that to the campaigns of Chandragupta Maurya in 324 BC which took the Mauryan Empire onto the soil of modern Afghanistan. Immediately after the cutting a right turn leads to **Taxila** (See above – excursions from Islamabad).

Continue W past **Wah** and into **Hasan Abdal** (16 km). There is a small Mughal garden at Wah, signposted to the right off the main road, one of the Mughal Emperors' numerous reported resting places en route to Kashmir. Wah is supposed to have received its name from the exclamation of the Emperor Jahangir when he saw the beauty of the valley -"Wah"! Hasan Abdal has been an important site for Sikhs, Buddhists and Hindus as well as for Muslims. Gandharan Buddhist remains have been found in the centre of the modern settlement.

The early 19th century Sikh **Panja Sahib Gurudwara**, also in the town centre, has a hand cast reputed to be that of **Guru Nanak**, the founder of Sikhism. According to one legend it was through the intervention of the Sikh founder that the temple tank was created. Asking a Muslim saint, **Baba Wali**, for a drink of water, the mystic simply threw down a huge boulder. Guru Nanak placed his hand on it where it fell, leaving his hand impress on the stone and causing a spring to well up from underneath it. **See page 758**.

Near the gurudwara are 2 **Mughal tombs**. The **Maqbara Hakiman** – the tomb of the *hakims*, or doctors – is at the eastern end of a platform nearly 40 m by 20 m. To the W of this platform is a tank, fed by a spring and reputed to remain at a constant level. **Mahseer**, one of the most famous of Indian freshwater fish, a large species of carp, have been kept in the tank for generations. The tomb was built by one of the Mughal building superintendents, Khwaja Shamsuddin Khawafi. Small bricks were used, covered in lime plaster and then decorated with frescoes. The tomb measures 11 m square with a flat outer roof and an inner dome. The plaster has now fallen off in most places.

The second tomb was built for **Khwaja** himself. He died in Lahore in about 1599 and was buried there. Subsequently Akbar ordered that the tomb be used for **Hakim Abdul Gilani** and **Hakim Himan Gilani**. It has been through various uses, serving as the secretariat building for Hari Singh Nalwa in the early 20th century. It was declared a protected monument in 1923.

The Grand Trunk Road passes through **Lawrencepur** (named after the 19th century British resident of Lahore, Sir Henry Lawrence) and Attock. Immediately to the S of the Grand Trunk Road, between **Attock** and Campbellpur the Potwar Plateau is scattered with massive "erratics", boulders washed down from the high Himalayas. Their origin is uncertain. Even today natural temporary dams are created in the high Himalayan valleys by earth and rock slides, impounding huge lakes. When these dams burst enormous floods can result, tumbling down very large rocks.

The most catastrophic recorded flood of this kind took place in 1841, when the Indus Gorge was blocked by a landslide on the Hattu Pir cliff where the **Astor River** flows into the Indus just N of **Nanga Parbat**. When the natural dam burst, the flood washed away the Sikh army which was camped on the Indus bed at Attock 400 km downstream. However, it is also possible that a lake may have occupied the present course of the Indus, and that the rocks could have been brought down by icebergs floating down the lake.

The Tarbela Dam The opportunity provided by the valley of the Indus for creating an artificial lake less than 50 km N of Attock have now been realised in the world's largest earth fill dam at **Tarbela**. The new dam can be visited by driving less than 30 km from the GT road, taking the right turn off it 24 km from **Hasan Abdal**. The dam itself carries 2 new roads, one at the foot and one across the top, which allow you to cross the Indus and continue to Peshawar. The top of the dam is usually closed.

There are scenic drives up the E bank of the lake. From **Ghazi** (24 km from the GT Road) turn right to **Haripur** (26 km), where the road to the left to **Khalbat** runs up the E bank of the lake. There are 2 routes on to **Peshawar**, either down the W bank of the Indus to **Jahangira**, or via the longer but more scenic route via **Swabi**, **Mardan** and **Charsadda**. A guided tour of the dam can be arranged by contacting the Public Relations Office of the Water and Power Development Authority (WAPDA) at Tarbela. T 68941-2.

If you do not take the diversion to Tarbela the Grand Trunk Road to Peshawar crosses the Indus at **Attock** (20 km from the Tarbela turning).

Attock The new bridge across the river gives an excellent view to the N of the confluence of the Kabul River and the Indus. Attock itself (to the S of the main road) has been an important crossing point since **Sher Shah** used it in 1540. The fort, built by **Akbar** in 1586 and occupied by **Ranjit Singh** in 1813, is now a military zone and is closed to the public. Sher Shah's resting place, or *caravanserai*, focused on a large courtyard, gives a commanding view of the river. It can be reached by a short climb of steps from the main road on the E bank, nr the new bridge. The river below passes through a narrow gorge and has been known to rise 30 m in flood. **Hotel** *Indus View* is on GT Rd.

Rail Rawalpindi *Mari-Indus Rawalpindi*, RC133, 2nd only, 0725, 2 hr; *Awam Exp*, 14, 1106, 1 hr 40 min; **Peshawar** *K273*, daily, 0820, 2 hr; 211, daily, 1110, 3 hr; *Awam Exp*, 13, daily, 1247, 2 hr.

Across the Indus the GT road enters the irrigated and fertile Vale of Peshawar on the W bank of the Indus at **Jehangira** and runs along the S side of the Kabul River. The road goes through **Nowshera** (23 km), now an important military base and a growing industrial town. One of Pakistan's largest Afghan refugee settlements lies to the right of the road between Nowshera and **Peshawar** (43 km). See NWFP for details of the last section of this route.

ISLAMABAD-RAWALPINDI TO MURREE

Murree is less than 2 hr by car from Islamabad, in the hills to the NE. The road, which has a small toll charge, takes you through Tret village at nearly 1,000 m, when you will notice the appearance of pines, where there is a Bazaar, a Rest *House* and an *Inspection Bungalow*.

There are TDCP roadside facilities with picnic spots at **Chattar Bagh**, (20 km) with waterfalls, restaurant, nature trails, deer and peacock enclosures and another being developed at **Salgran**, (29 km). Further along you can stop for tea at **Charra Pani**, (38 km) where there are mountain springs and TDCP facilities with a snack bar, or carry on past the Samli TB sanatorium (50 km from Islamabad), and **Ghora gali** at 1,600 m (which gets its name from the days when carriage horses were changed between Rawalpindi and Murree) with a waterfall, bazaar, a forestry school and a good *Rest House*. The Brewery Estate ruins are a reminder of the only attempt at industrializing Murree. You will find a noticeable drop in temperature as you gain height. Next on your route is **Bansragali** where the British built their prestigious **Lawrence College**, then the S shaped turn called *Chitta Morr* and **Sunny Bank**, a military depot, before reaching Murree.

Murree

Developed as a hill station by the British, Murree remained a popular resort until 1876 when Shimla gained prominence as the summer capital. The climate is ideal with cool summers and crisp cold winters. The best season is Apr to Jun. The winters can mean a covering of snow especially in Jan and Feb, and although

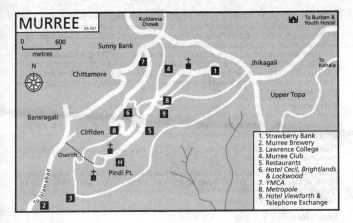

quieter, it can get busy with weekend visitors. You will need light woollens and cottons in summer and heavy woollens in the winter.

	Jan	Feb	Mar	Apr	May	Jun	Jul	Aug	Sep	Oct	Nov	Dec	Av/Tot
Max (°C)	6	8	12	18	23	26	13	22	22	19	15	10	17
Min (°C)	0	1	4	9	13	16	16	16	13	9	6	2	9
Rain (mm)	116	108	155	103	61	106	360	348	138	53	21	54	1623

Murree is the most developed of the hill stations, several of which are in the NW Frontier Province. The British explorer Francis Younghunsband was born here in 1863.

The roads, hotels, restaurants and shopping too are good in Murree and there are attractive parks and gardens. The **Post Office** at the northern end of the Mall is a prominent landmark, from which you can walk down to the colourful bazaars where you will see the local hill people, mostly Kohistani, Gujar and Kashmiri. The Mall itself is a popular meeting point with tea shops with open terraces where you can sit in the summer. During the summer it is closed to motor traffic and you can arrange pony and donkey rides here. There are 2 view points – **Pindi Point** overlooking the twin cities, particularly attractive at night. At the other end, 7 km away, is **Kashmir Point**, the highest spot here, ringed by pines.

The **Government House** at the top, **Bagh-e-Shaheedan** (1965 War Martyrs' garden), and a Forest Dept picnic spot, are all close by. Along the road from the GPO, foreign missions have summer camp offices and residences and the Federal Government offices have *Rest Houses*. By taking the road N, leaving the Post Office to your left, you reach the **Club**, and you will see forest paths down the hill side. The clay hills retain enough moisture to support dense forests. The **Iqbal Municipal Library** built in the early 20th century is in Jinnah Rd. The decorative wooden ceiling is notable. There is a mosque and shrine to Hazrat Rajab Ali Shah, a Hindu Temple and churches.

Though very busy in season, you can escape on long walks N out of town.

Hotels The Foreign Mission and Government *Rest Houses* when not occupied by staff, are sometimes available to those with contacts. It is worth trying for them out of season. **D Cecil's,**

(PTDC) Mount View Rd. T 2247, Cable: Cecil Murree. Restaurant, coffee shop, car hire, tourist information, tennis. Reduced rates off season. **D** *Brightland*, Imtiaz Shaheed Rd, T 2270. 11 rm. Restaurant, car hire. **E** *Blue Pines* and *Murree Inn's*, Cart Rd, T 2233. 60 rm. Restaurant, exchange, travel, shop, indoor games. **E** *Marhaba*, Jinnah Rd, T 2148.

There are many others, in the Post Office area, mainly to its SW. **E** *Al-Subtaini*, Mount View Rd, nr GPO, T 2106. 50 rm, with bath. **E** *Al-Farooq*, Cart Rd, T 2431. 7 d rm with bath. **E** *Chinar*, Jinnah Rd, nr Jinnah Park Dry Fruit Shops, T 2244, Cable: Chinar. 50 rm. Restaurant. There are several others in the **E and F** categories along the Jinnah Rd, Cart Rd, Imtiaz Shaheed and Abid Shaheed Rd.

Restaurants There are some in the better hotels but other eating places are concentrated along the Mall, S of the Post Office. Many serve continental and Pakistani food and some also offer Chinese. Try the *kebabs*, *tikka*, fish and roasted meat. Fruit, both fresh and dried are good – particularly fresh strawberries and apples.

Shopping Look for local handicrafts, cloth, fur coats, caps, woollen shawls and jewellery in the bazaar below the Mall.

Road The 64 km winding road from Islamabad/ Rawalpindi is very good and is easily covered by car or taxi. From Rawalpindi, **Buses** about every 1/2 hr, Flying Coach (Murree Rd) and 'Wagon' (Bank Rd) takes 2 hr. From Murree transport to other hill stations and to Abbottabad, particularly in the tourist season.

Excursions

Bhurban 10 km, at nearly 2,000 m, has a good hotel and a Youth *Hostel* and a Golf Club with a 9 hole golf course which is open from May to Oct (reserved for members only in the high season). It hosts major golf tournaments. The recommended **D** *Golf*, T 2507, has 11 rm.

The Galis The 30 km long hill tract from Murree through Nathiagali to Abbottabad form the *Galis* which are a chain of hill stations in the area. They are excellent for walking and riding. **Barian**, which is the first village on the toll road to Abbottabad, is on the border between Punjab and NWFP. There is a *Forest Lodge* with 3 rm.

Nathiangali (2,500 m), the summer headquarters of the NWFP govt, is the most popular of the minor hill stations particularly for walkers. It retains a colonial air with its church, governor's house and typical bungalows. The *hot spring* in the valley nearby is believed to sooth skin diseases. To the NE rises the 3,000 m high Miran Jani which you can climb in under 3 hr, following the path northwards behind Governor's House. On a clear day you can see Nanga Parbat to the N. By car, Nathiangali is 32 km and about 2 hr by car from Murree.

Hotels **D** *New Green*, T 544. D rm (Child under 5 free). Fine views. **D** *New Nathiangali Trekking Club*. 5 rm. Car hire, indoor games. **D** *Pines*, T 505. 20 rm. Good views, garden. **D** *Valley View*, T 506. 10 rm. **D** *Mukshi Puri*, Dunga Galli, T 567. 18 rm Indoor games. These have attached baths, heating in rm, TV at one point. There are some cheaper **F** category hotels, the *Bismillah*, *Galliat View*, *Karachi*, *Madina*, *New Taj* and *Sultan*. The few *Rest Houses* and privately owned furnished bungalows tend to get fully booked in the summer.

Thandiani, one of the prettiest of the Galis, can be reached on a 2-3 day hike passing through Palakot and Birangali which have Forestry *Rest Houses*.

You can walk to *Ayubia* (8 km) through Dunga Gali which has the **D** *Mukahpuri*, T 567. 15 rm. Ayubia is a cluster of 4 resorts, Khaira and Changla Galis, Khanspur and Gora Dhaka, 28 km and about 1 hr 30 min by car, from Murree. Changla Galli has a *Rest House* and Khanspur, the **F** *Kashmir View*, T 17, with 6 rm with bath. Also **E** *Ayubia Palace* with 7 d rm with bath. They are situated on a spur which juts out towards the Jhelum river with a steep precipice on one side and pine clad hills. Named after the past President it has attractive hiking and riding trails, and the chair lift here has helped in its development.

At the end of the tract, **Abbottabad** takes about 4 hr by car from Murree (64 km). See page 1242.

Kallar Kahar (Salt lake) is 80 km from Islamabad, at an altitude of nearly 1,500 m. Babur, the founder of the Mughal Empire, camped and admired the beauty of the spot, when he led the expedition from Kabul to Delhi. The stone throne is said to be his, and the gardens which he asked to be laid out may have been in the SW of the lake, where you will see orchards, of which there are many in the area on the hillside. It is to the N of the Salt range and when you arrive at the village from the E you will notice marshy and salt encrusted lake. **Peacocks** abound, especially near the shrine on top of the hill, which attracts pilgrims (who believe that harming the birds will lead to blindness), and the spring in the centre of the village provides water.

The **F** *Rest Houses* are on the water's edge which can be booked through the Jhelum District Council Chairman or the Division Forest Officer, Jhelum. A PTDC Tourist Complex is being developed with accommodation in the *Tourist Lodge* with 6 a/c rm and a restaurant. Peacocks in the fruit orchards and provision for angling and boating.

ISLAMABAD-RAWALPINDI TO LAHORE

The route from Islamabad and Rawalpindi to Lahore crosses the undulating terrain of the Potwar Plateau to Jhelum (on the northwest bank of the River Jhelum, and then S over the flat N edge of the Punjab plains, through busy market towns. It crosses the broad bed of the River Ravi just before entering Lahore. This is a historic route, part of the *Grand Trunk Road* first built by the Mauryan Emperor Chandragupta in the 4th century BC and re-built by the Mughals in the 16th and 17th centuries, linking their NW frontiers with Bengal in the E. It is still widely referred to along its entire length across Pakistan and N India as the GT road. It is approximately a 5 hour journey by road along the national highway, some of which is dual carriageway. Much of it is fast when compared with travelling on Indian roads but there is still a huge variety of traffic, from the highly decorated lorries using this as the main road from Peshawar and the NWFP to Lahore, through to local bullock carts, which can be a major hazard after dark.

From **Islamabad** follow the road S to the GT Road. You can pass through Rawalpindi, only 15 km from the centre of Islamabad.

From **Rawalpindi** and **Islamabad** the Grand Trunk Road goes S across the Potwar Plateau (**see page 1113**). The region experiences a very modest rainfall of between 380-635 mm a year, most of it coming not during the monsoon period but in the winter months Jan to Mar. It is cold enough in winter for snow not to be unheard of. It is a hard land to cultivate, and one of Pakistan's poorer regions. Rainfed crops of wheat and barley in winter and millets in summer are supplemented in small patches by a variety of vegetables and fruit.

It is a region rich in the stone tools of S Asia's earliest settlers. Even material that has been deposited recently has been folded by the continuing mountain building process on the edge of the Himalayas. Horizontal layers of silt have been raised, twisted and bent. As a result new layers of sediment have been deposited on top of them. The road from **Islamabad** to *Gujar Khan* passes through the rough terrain associated with this mountain building process, and rivers like the **Soan** have cut their valleys in the resulting beds. There are several **Palaeolithic sites**, the earliest of which were occupied before the most recent folding of the hills took place.

The **Grand Trunk Road** continues S. Just S of the Soan River, it passes through *Riwat* (24 km), where it joins the main road to NWFP. On the banks of the Soan River itself, immediately N of Riwat, is the site of an extraordinary collection of **Middle and Upper Palaeolithic** stone tools, and widespread evidence of settlement by man's earliest ancestors over 100,000 years ago. The 16th century fort of Riwat was built by the **Ghakkars**. Well-preserved remains in the fort include the **mausoleum**, **mosque** and **outside walls**, but the fort was not sufficiently strong to prevent severe treatment at the hands of **Sher Shah**, see page 92.

The GT road keeps close to the railway and after about 8 km passes within 2 km of the *Manikyala Buddhist stupa*, the largest of several stupas in the area, and visible in one of the many clumps of banyan trees. Coins found in the stupa suggest that it dates from the time of **Kanishka's** successor in the 1st century AD, but it may have been rebuilt as late as the 8th century by **Yaso Varma** of **Kanauj**, who replaced the relics and included his own gold coins.

The dome of the stupa is over 30 m high and 40 m in diameter. About 3 km N is another stupa identified by General Cunningham with a stupa referred to by the Chinese traveller Hiuen Tsang as the "stupa of the body-offering", contrasting it with another stupa 300 m to its S named the "stupa of the blood offering". Evidently **Hiuen Tsang** recounted the legend that in a previous life the Buddha had offered his body to ease the hunger of 7 tiger cubs. The stupa of the body offering was opened by General Court (a British officer employed by Ranjit Singh) who found 3 cylindrical caskets made of gold, silver and copper. Four gold coins of the Emperor Kanishka were found in the gold box, 7 silver Roman denarii in the silver box dated no later than 43 BC, and 8 copper coins, again from Kanishka, were in the copper box.

Continue S through the small railway junction town of *Mandra* (10 km) SE to **Gujar Khan** (14 km) and *Dina* (54 km). There are 2 rewarding diversions from Dina. The *Mangla Dam*, one of the largest dams in the world, lies 16 km NE of the GT road at Dina. The dam was completed in 1968 under the provisions of the **Indus Waters Treaty, see page 1118**. It is intended to double its original storage capacity in order to counteract the problem of silting. Originally this was expected to reduce the effective storage capacity of the dam by 30% in the first 50 years. In fact siltation rates have proved much faster than expected, though they are still not nearly as high as at the Tarbela dam on the Indus, where 90% of the storage capacity is expected to be lost in 50 years from its completion. The Mangla dam effectively compensated Pakistan for the diversion of water from the E tributaries to India after Partition. It is placed in an extraordinary setting, with the heavily eroded Potwar Plateau and the old **Mangla Fort** nearby.

Rohtas Fort

Also from Dina you can leave the main road to visit *Rohtas Fort* 7 km away, 16 km NW of **Jhelum** town. (There are no toilet facilities or snacks and drinks available at the fort.) The road is not paved all the way, and can be impassable during the rains. It is another of the outposts of Sher Shah Suri's remarkable kingdom. He began to build the fort in 1543 to keep at bay the Ghakkar tribes, and it commands the gorge of the *Kahan River*, which flows in a broad shallow bed along the N wall of the fort. It becomes an uncrossable raging torrent in the rainy season. To the S of the fort is a long narrow ravine. A wall 4 km in circumference and often up to 15 m thick surrounds the 100 ha of the site. With its 68 towers and 12 gates its defensive capabilities are strengthened by full use of the natural terrain.

One legend suggests that Sher Shah commanded his architect, **Shahu Sultani**, to build a huge and invincible fortress in 3 years. His first effort was so much smaller than Sher Shah had envisaged that he ordered the architect to be beheaded. As an act of clemency however, he agreed to allow him a further 2 years to replace the fort with one closer to his wishes. In the event the fort took 10 years to build, being completed after Sher Shah's death. Within 10 years of its completion Sher Shah's successors deserted it without the fort ever being defended.

Note The visit to the fort involves some stiff walking. The jeepable road from **Dina** enters the fort through the E gate and passes through the village in the middle of the fort before passing out through the **Sohail Gate** in the W wall. There is also a steep footpath entrance by following the footpath along the eastern wall to the **Khawas Khan Gate** in the E wall of the fort. Buses come to the village at the other side of the ford.

The Sohail Gate, built in the Pathan style, is by far the most impressive. Over 20 m high, it has small balconies on the outer walls and is flanked by massive bastions. Immediately to its S is a square water tank, with trees at either end.

To its N is the execution tower, which can be reached by entering the inner fort through the Shah Chand Wali Gate, 200 m E of the Sohail Gate in the wall which divides the outer fort from the inner fort. Shah Chand Wali is revered as a saint who continued to work without wages and right up to his death. He is buried just S of the wall. To the N of the wall is what remains of the Palace of Man Singh, standing on a rocky hillock. Man Singh was one of Akbar's most famous Rajput Generals, who died in 1614. It is one of the fort's most conspicuous buildings, constructed of brick and plaster rather than the stone used elsewhere in the fort. Its domed roof is topped by a lotus emblem, all that remains of its Hindu pinnacle.

Immediately to the W of the palace is the **execution tower** (*burj*). To the N you come first to the **Badshahi Gate**, then the **Shahi** ('royal') **mosque**, a small mosque comprising just a prayer chamber and courtyard. In the NW corner wall is the **Kabuli Gate** (facing Kabul), which has steep steps leading down to the valley floor. A rectangular double gate, its central opening is just over 3 m wide with 2 flanking bastions. From it, about 60 steep steps lead down to the *baoli*, one of the 2 wells dug in the rock to supply the fort with fresh water.

In the centre of the N wall facing the **Kahan** river is the **Shishi Gate**, taking its name from the Persian blue glazed tiles that decorated its outer arch. The NE corner of the walls are pierced by the **Langarkhani Gate** and the **Talaqi** ("divorce") **Gate**. At the foot of the walls is a late 18th century Sikh house. To the SE of the Talaqi Gate are the **Mori** (or Kashmiri) **Gate** and the **Khwas Khani Gate**, the main entrance to the fort and named after Sher Shah's commander. There are few buildings in the fort though there are several inscriptions in the walls in Arabic, Persian and Naksh script.

A further 15 km W of Rohtas fort is the highest peak of the **Great Salt Range**, the 990 metre **Tilla Jogian**, which used to be a summer resort for Government officers. It can be reached by jeep. The road continues SE out of **Dina** to

Jhelum (16 km.) which, with its mid 19th century **gothic church**, stands out strikingly on the N bank of the river when approaching the town from the S. The town marks the E end of the **Salt Range** and was once a recruitment ground for the British Army. The fighting tradition continues today, with many young people joining the country's armed forces. Jhelum is a bare 10 km from the Indian border, the closest point to Indian territory on this N section of the GT Road. Some of the Bactrian Greek pillars and sculptures that have been unearthed at Jhelum are now in the Lahore Museum.

Hotels E *Zelaf*, Rahi Aziz Cantonment, T 3568. 11 rm with bath. **E** *Mehwish*, nr GTS Bus Stand, T 3048. Restaurant. **F** *Paradise*, nr the Bus Stand, T 3533. 16 rm with bath. Dining rm. **F** *Shandar,* Raja Bazaar, T 3333 is the cheapest.

Rail To Lahore *Zulfiqar Exp*, 6, a/c, daily, 1255, 4 hr. **Rawalpindi** *Zulfiqar Exp*, 5, a/c, daily, 1139, 3 hr.

The railway bridge, 1,500 m long, used to carry the GT Rd across the **River Jhelum**, but a new toll bridge has provided an alternative for road traffic. It then goes S through **Kharian** (12 km), where it descends from the broken hills of the Potwar plateau to the plains, and through **Lal Musa** (15 km) to

Gujrat (22 km), the site of the final battle of the **Second Sikh War** on 21 Feb 1849. The town was probably founded by **Sher Shah Sur**, when he extended his rule from Bengal to the Afghan frontier. The Mughals developed the city when they reclaimed power in India, and Akbar built the fort, which is now in its centre. During his reign it was renamed **Gujarat Akbarabad**. In the reign of his grandson **Shah Jahan** the town became home to the saint **Pir Shah**

Daula, some of whose buildings remain.

This was also the site of the battle in the 4th century BC in which **Alexander the Great** defeated the Indian king *Poros*. Alexander had defeated the last of the Persian Achaemenid kings, **Darius III**, in 330 BC. He then set out to conquer the whole empire. He fought a long campaign on the borders of modern Afghanistan and the Soviet Union, Bactria, and then crossed the Hindu Kush to the **Khyber Pass**. He crossed the Indus in the spring of 326 BC. The King of Taxila, **Ambhi** (known to the Greeks as Omphis), surrendered without a fight, happy to join forces with the Greeks against his much feared Indian enemy Poros, who ruled over the plains of the Punjab.

A.L. Basham recounts how "it was only with great difficulty, after a surprise crossing of the Jhelum, that the Macedonians succeeded in defeating the troops of Poros, who was captured. Poros was a very tall handsome man, whose courage and proud bearing made a great impression on the Greeks; when brought before his conqueror he was found to have received 9 wounds, and he could barely stand; but when Alexander asked how he wished to be treated he boldly replied: 'As befits a king!' Alexander was so impressed by his captive that he restored him to his kingdom as a vassal, and on the retreat of the Greek forces, left him in charge of the Punjab."

Hotels On GT Rd: **E** *Grace*, T 4444. 22 rm with bath; *Faisal*, T 3088. On Rly Rd: **E** *Nasheman*, T 3203. 18 rm with bath; **E** *Melody Road*, T 3751.

8 km S of **Gujrat** there is a new bridge and toll road across the **Chenab**, 6 km before Wazirabad. The old **Alexandra bridge**, built in 1876, is now closed.

Wazirabad The town was founded in **Shah Jahan**'s reign in the early 17th century by one of his chief ministers or *Wazirs*, Wazir Khan. A new fortified town was built by the Italian soldier of fortune General Avitabile, who was employed by Ranjit Singh. The rectangular new town is divided by its broad bazaar. Like Gujranwala, Wazirabad specialises in metal work, but is particularly noted for its cutlery. You can divert from the GT road in Wazirabad to **Sialkot**, 30 km to the NE of Gujranwala.

Sialkot

	Jan	Feb	Mar	Apr	May	Jun	Jul	Aug	Sep	Oct	Nov	Dec	Av/Tot
Max (°C)	18	21	27	34	39	41	36	34	35	33	27	20	30
Min (°C)	6	9	13	19	25	27	26	26	24	17	10	6	17
Rain (mm)	47	42	41	20	13	56	269	248	97	21	8	20	883

One of Pakistan's most important industrial centres, located close to the border with India, Sialkot was an important town in the second century BC. Apart from being a centre producing sports goods, it also is well-known for manufacturing surgical instruments. During Mughal times, the *koftars* were known for their fine craftsmanship with daggers and swords. However, the introduction of the rifle in 1857, led to their decline only to be revived when the local American Mission Hospital required some of their equipment to be replaced. Their skills were recognized by not only other mission hospitals in the subcontinent but also by the military hospitals.

Sialkot also produces rubber and plastic goods, ceramics and fine leather saddles and bagpipes! It has an old fort, the tomb of the scholar Mian Abdul Hakim and a much visited shrine to Hazrat Imam Ali-ul-Haq. The church spire is 45 m high, a striking landmark.

Hotels **D** *Meryton*, Wazirabad Rd, T 88989. 25 rm. a/c. **E** *Sarko*, Aziz Shaheed Rd, Cantonment, T 86141. 20 rm. **E** *Al-Shahzad*, Kutchery Rd nr GTS Bus Stand, T 87342. 33 rm, some a/c. Restaurant. If you make a diversion from Wazirabad you can rejoin the road S at Gujranwala.

Rail Wazirabad is an important junction. **Rawalpindi** *Zulfiqar Exp*, 5, daily, a/c, 0950, 4hr

45 min; **Lahore** *Zulfiqar Exp*, 6, daily, a/c, 1446, 2hr 30 min; **Sialkot** *Sialkot-Lahore Express*, 65, daily, 0905, 1 hr.

The road continues S from Wazirabad to **Gujranwala** (32 km). You can leave the main road (which splits into an E and a W by-pass, with little to choose between them) and drive into the town.

Gujranwala *Population* 800,000. The Sikh leader Ranjit Singh was born here in 1780. The town takes its name from the nomadic pastoralist Gujar tribe.

Places of interest On the SE edge of the town is a 25 m high octagonal tower built in memory of **Ranjit Singh**'s father, known as the *Samadh of Mahan Singh*. The rosettes inside mark the place where the ashes are laid and the inscriptions record the names of those commemorated. The rosette nearest the entrance "in in memory of a blue pigeon that fell down into the flames in which Ranjit Singh and his concubines were being consumed at Lahore in 1839." The site is also noteworthy as having one of the comparatively few Hindu works of art in Pakistan. The tall pavilion has numerous murals showing stories from the Mahabharata (**see page 629**). One of these recalls the story of the royal princess of **Draupadi** whom the king had ordered to be stripped of her clothes. However, just as soon as they were torn from her they were mysteriously and supernaturally replaced.

On the NE edge of the town is the fort with a pavilion of the Sikh General Hari Singh Nalwa, killed in battle against the Afghans in 1837. The pavilion in the 15 hectare gardens has niches for lamps, and Hari Singh's memorial 50 m N has a portrait of the General hawking.

Gujranwala is noted for its iron working, especially the manufacture of safes. Local fruit include its famous "Malta" oranges.

Hotels *Rest house* and PWD *bungalow*. Nearby at Aminabad Chowk on GT Rd, *TDCP Motel* and Restaurant with 2 a/c rm with bath in spacious grounds in wildlife park.

Re-join the GT road going S. After 60 km the road crosses the **River Ravi** and enters **Lahore** (67 km).

LAHORE

Population 3,148,000 *Altitude* 213 m *Best Season* Nov – Mar.

	Jan	Feb	Mar	Apr	May	Jun	Jul	Aug	Sep	Oct	Nov	Dec	Av/Tot
Max (°C)	21	22	28	35	40	41	38	36	36	35	28	23	32
Min (°C)	4	7	12	17	22	26	27	26	23	15	8	4	16
Rain (mm)	31	23	24	16	12	38	122	123	80	9	3	11	492

Lahore is Punjab's capital and largest city. Some of the modern visual images contrast sharply with those in Indian cities across the border, modern cars and motorbikes racing down the wide avenues giving it an almost tearaway feel. Yet Lahore, like Delhi, has ancient roots. Like Delhi, it too has been heavily influenced by the Mughal tradition.

Lahore's recorded history goes back to AD 850 when it was a dependency of the Hindu ruler Lalitaditya, although the epic *Ramayana* links it to the city founded by Loh, son of King Rama. The city was conquered by Mahmud of Ghazni in 1021, and later made the capital of the Ghaznavid empire by his son. The Mughal emperor Akbar also made it his capital. **Jahangir**, and his wife **Nur Jahan**, who is believed to have introduced the rose to the city, are buried here. **Shah Jahan**

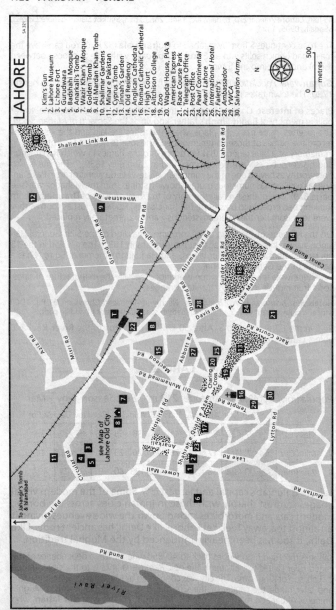

LAHORE

1. Kim's Gun
2. Lahore Museum
3. Lahore Fort
4. Gurdwara
5. Badshahi Mosque
6. Anarkali's Tomb
7. Wazir Khan's Mosque
8. Golden Tomb
9. Ali Mardan Khan Tomb
10. Shalimar Gardens
11. Minar e Pakistan
12. Cyprus Tomb
13. Jinnah's Garden
14. Old Residency
15. Anglican Cathedral
16. Roman Catholic Cathedral
17. High Court
18. Aitchison College
19. Zoo
20. Wapda House, PIA & American Express
21. Race Course Park
22. Telegraph Office
23. Post Office
24. Pearl Continental
25. Avari Lahore
26. International Hotel
27. Faletti's
28. Ambassador
29. YWCA
30. Salvation Army

N

0   500
metres

Shalimar Link Rd
Wheatman Rd
Grand Trunk Rd
Mughalpura Rd
Aziz Rd
Misri Rd
Circular Rd
Ravi Rd
Bund Rd
River Ravi
To Jahangir's Tomb & Islamabad
Lahore Rd
Canal Bund Rd
Sunder Das Rd
Allama Iqbal Rd
Durand Rd
Davis Rd
The Mall
Race Course Rd
Abbot Rd
Macleod Rd
Dil Muhammad Rd
Hospital Rd
Shahrah e Quaid e Azam
Anarkali
Charing Cross
Lake Rd
Temple Rd
Lytton Rd
Multan Rd
Lower Mall
see Map of Lahore Old City

laid out the superb **Shalimar Gardens** and **Aurangzeb** built the **Badshahi Mosque**. With Agra, Fatehpur Sikri, and Delhi it is one of the great centres of Mughal architecture, **see page 267**. Its buildings show elements of early strength and rising greatness in Akbar's fort, the developing styles of Jahangir and Shah Jahan in some of the palace buildings, and signs of decline in Aurangzeb's Badshahi Mosque.

In the late 18th century the Sikhs removed a great deal of the marble and many of the semi-precious inlaid stones, and neglected the fine gardens. **Ranjit Singh**, the Sikh ruler of Lahore, however, has also left his mark in the monuments in the Old City, where there is a small museum and an attempt is being made to restore the havelis or fine merchants' houses.

The British occupied the city between 1849 and 1947, and left some imposing colonial buildings which combined the Gothic and Victorian with the Mughal style – the High Court, Provincial Assembly, Central Museum, Government College, Montgomery Hall, the old University campus and Tollinton Market. Many post-Independence landmarks have made it a modern city, but it is the Mughal past that gives Lahore its character. Culturally and in the field of education, the city leads the country, with the Punjab University considered the premier institution in Pakistan.

Changes in street names The Mall – Shahrah-e-Quaid-e-Azam   Queen Rd – Fatimah Jinnah Rd.

Local Festivals *National Horse and Cattle Show* End Feb – Beginning of Mar. Held at the Fortress Stadium where you will see the finest collection of livestock from all 4 provinces as well as progress made in industry and agriculture. There are displays of horse and camel dancing, tent pegging, and folk dances as well as a military tattoo and music of the brass bands in the evening.

Mela Chirghan (Festival of lights). Last Sun in Mar. Held to honour the mystic and folk poet Shah Hussain who died in 1599, and his friend Madho Lal Hussain who is buried with him, the latter having converted to Islam from Hinduism. Ordinary people from all over Punjab, including peasants and *fakirs* gather near the Shalimar Gardens on the huge esplanade, where the mausoleum is illuminated with lamps on Shah Hussain's death anniversary. This and the arrival of Spring is greeted with music, dancing, sports and magic shows.

Urs of Data Ganj Baksh Second month of *Safar* (Muslim calendar). To celebrate the death anniversary of the patron saint of Lahore, a large number of devotees gather at his tomb. Feasting, dancing and singing marks the occasion which draws famous Qawwali singers.

The Old City

The walled city once had the river **Ravi** flowing along the Fort which is to its N. The 12 original gates in the 9 m high brick wall gave access to the city during the day. They were built in Akbar's time, when he held court in Lahore for 14 years. When Ranjit Singh, the Sikh ruler came to power in the Punjab, he rebuilt the crumbling wall and added a moat which was fed by the river. The British, however, filled the moat and laid out beautiful gardens in its place.

Today, you can still see 6 of the gates. The old city is still alive with busy narrow streets, the old bazaars. In the E is the remarkable **Wazir Khan's Mosque**. The Mosque, built in 1634 by Shah Jahan's governor, given the title Wazir Khan, has superb mosaic tile decoration and paintings, inside and out.

The **Badshahi Mosque**, the largest in the country, was built by Emperor Aurangzeb on the W of the Fort in 1673-4. Modified from its model, the Jama Masjid in Delhi, it has an impressive gateway, 3 large white domes, 8 minarets, and an enormous courtyard where 100,000 worshippers can gather in the open air. Tillotson suggests that "It is distinguished from its predecessor by a certain feebleness of form, typical of the later Mughal period. The mouldings on the façade of the prayer hall are shallow, and the white line markings are a superficial ornament without vigour." It remains a remarkably impressive descendant of the line of magnificent Mughal religious building. You can climb a minaret to get

WILL YOU HELP US?

We do all we can to get our facts right in **THE SOUTH ASIAN HANDBOOK.** Each section is thoroughly revised each year, but the territory covered is vast and our eyes cannot be everywhere.

Your information may be more up to date than ours and if you have enjoyed a tour, trek, train trip, beach, museum, temple, fort or any other activity and would like others to share it, please write with the details. We are always pleased to hear about any restaurants, bars or hotels you have enjoyed.

When writing, it will be very helpful if you can give the year on the cover of your Handbook and the page number referred to.

If your letter reaches us early enough in the year, it will be used in the next annual edition, but write whenever you want to, for all your information will be used.

Thank you very much indeed for your help.

 Write to: The Editor,
South Asian Handbook
Trade & Travel Publications
6 Riverside Court, Lower Bristol Road,
Bath BA2 3DZ. England

excellent views of the town. The small tomb of red sandstone on the outside and marble inside belonging to **Allama Iqbal** the poet and philosopher who died in 1938, stands at the foot of the Big Mosque.

Lahore Fort Open daily Summer 0800-1800, Winter 0800-1630. Closed Fri 1230-1430. Opposite the Badshahi Mosque, Lahore Fort is one of the 3 great forts built by the Mughals (the others being in Agra and Delhi). Built originally by *Malik Ayaz*, it was rebuilt by Akbar in 1566 on a rather smaller scale than the Agra fort. He and his successors rebuilt it like a palace, embellishing it with carved red sandstone, and then marble, *pietra dura* work, glazed coloured tiles and frescoes depicting royal pleasures – horsemen playing polo, elephant fights and musicians.

The special *kashi* tile work, notably on the N wall, was added by Shah Jahan. The colouring and technique show marked Persian influence, but the elephant and hunting motifs are reminders of the pervasive Hindu craftsmanship incorporated in all Mughal architecture. The original features from Akbar's time can be seen in the wall and gate to the NE, the S wall and the N inner wall. Note especially the Hindu style sandstone brackets.

Entering from the **Hathi Pol** (elephant gate) in the W wall, the path leads up a ramp into the main enclosure. The first building passed is Jahangir's white marble **Moti Mahal** (Pearl Mosque, c1615), which has a courtyard in front of it. Much of the cloistered building around the square was destroyed by the Sikh conquerors, who turned the mosque into a treasury. Almost due E of the Moti Masjid is the hall of public audience (the **Diwan i Am**). The chambers at the back were built by Jahangir, the columned hall in front by Shah Jahan (1627). From the Diwan i Am a path leads E to the Masti Darwaza, and the oldest parts of Akbar's fort in the NE. Almost due N of the Diwan i Am, on the N wall of the fort, is Jahangir's **Bari Kwabgah** (large bedroom) in 'Jahangir's Quadrangle'.

Along the wall to its W is a similar but smaller bedroom built by Shah Jahan. To the W again are the finest remaining buildings in the fort. These are the **Sheesh Mahal** (the Palace of Mirrors), which has a semi octagonal plan, and has superb carved marble and *pietra dura* ornamentation, as well as coloured convex "mirrors" (pieces of glass placed over gypsum) in floral and geometric designs on the ceiling and upper part of the main hall.

To its W, the fabulous **Naulakha Pavilion** which has a Bengali *chala* roof, was once studded with *pietra dura* work of semi-precious stones, typical of Shah Jahan's building in Agra and Delhi, *see page 267*. Some believe there were 900,000 pieces of coloured stone and hence its name, while others attribute its name to the cost incurred of Rs 9 lakhs. Finally, Aurangzeb added the huge **Alamgiri Gate** on the W wall.

After the decline of the Mughal Empire, the Sikhs neglected the buildings but later did some restoration noticeable, eg in the wooden mirrored and painted ceiling of the *Naulakha Pavilion*, and the later tile work on the walls of the *Sheesh Mahal*. It was only in 1927 that the Archaeological Dept started restoration work on the Fort and today the **museum** with its collection of costumes and armoury, relates the history of the Sikh period. The buildings and gardens in the Fort are now well maintained.

The **Sikh Gurdwara** is opp Lahore Fort next to the Badshahi Mosque, see page 71. The **Gurdwara of Arjan Singh**, the 5th Guru, who compiled the *Adi Granth* (the Holy book of the Sikhs), has a fluted gilded dome, and is a centre of Sikh pilgrimage. According to legend, Arjun Singh disappeared in the river Ravi which once flowed along the Fort. The gurdwara was built by Raja Ranjit Singh who ruled Lahore for a brief period in the early 19th century, whose own ashes are buried in a *Samadhi* completed in 1848 to the S of the Gurdwara.

The *Minar-e-Pakistan* was built to remember Pakistan Day. It marks the spot where the Muslim League passed the resolution in 1940 to launch the struggle for an independent nation for the Muslims of the subcontinent. The 60 m tower stands in *Iqbal Park* just N of the Fort and has verses from the Q'ran and a history of the Independence struggle engraved on the marble. You can get to the top by lift to get a good view of the city.

The **Golden Mosque** is in a prominent position within the old city walls. It is so named because its 3 domes and minaret tops are covered with gold sheets.

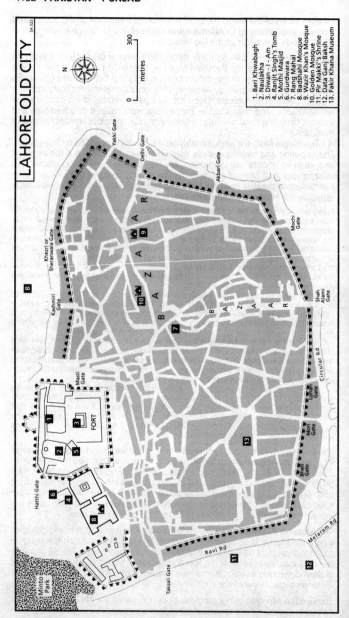

LAHORE OLD CITY

N

0   300
metres

SA 322

Minto Park

Hatthi Gate

Taksali Gate

Ravi Rd

Melaram Rd

Bhati Gate

Mori Gate

Lohari Gate

Circular Rd

Shah Alami Gate

Mochi Gate

Akbari Gate

Delhi Gate

Yakki Gate

Khezri or Sheranwala Gate

Kashmiri Gate

Masti Gate

FORT

1. Bari Khwabagh
2. Naulakha
3. Diwan - I - Am
4. Ranjit Singh's Tomb
5. Moti Masjid
6. Gurdwara
7. Rang Mahal
8. Badshahi Mosque
9. Wazir Khan's Mosque
10. Golden Mosque
11. Pir Makki's Shrine
12. Data Ganj Baksh
13. Fakir Khana Museum

Shrine of Data Ganj Baksh The patron saint of Lahore (also called 'Data ki Nagri'), came here from Ghazni in Afghanistan. He was a scholar, saint and mystic who spread Sufism in Punjab and was the author of the famous 'Kashful Mahjoob'. His generosity earned him the title *data* (one who gives away treasures) since he worked among the poor and needy and helped them. His darbar (shrine) near Bhati Gate in the Old City S of the Fort, is always crowded with devotees. The old tomb which is simple in style on a raised plinth, was built by the Sultans of Ghazni and was extended by subsequent rulers. Today it has several buildings attached to it which serve the public, such as a hospital and dispensary, an organization to help destitute women and a public kitchen where food is distributed to the poor. A new mosque is being built nearby.

Shah Alam Market You can get to the colourful market by entering the Old City through the **Shah Alami Gate** to the S. It includes the Kashmiri Bazaar, Suha Bazaar, Dabbi Bazaar and Chatta Bazaar where craftsmen still work with copper, brass and silver.

Just outside the Old City wall, S of the **Lohari Gate** is the sprawling **Anarkali Bazaar** with its fascinating narrow alleyways with shops selling every traditional craft item produced here, be it textiles in cotton, silk or wool, embroidered and block printed, leather goods, glass bangles or mundane articles for a household. It is named after *Anarkali* (literally Pomegranate Blossom) who was Akbar's favourite in the *harem* and who, it is said, he ordered to be buried alive for having fallen in love with Prince Salim, later Emperor Jahangir. (Her circular tomb is in one corner of the Secretariat Building has a huge dome with 8 arched supports).

Qutbuddin Aibak, who was the subcontinent's first Muslim Emperor was crowned in Lahore in 1206 and died 4 years later. His once magnificent tomb and garden in the bazaar have lost their glory.

The **Shrine of Pir Makki** is on Ravi Rd. Azizuddin, the preacher and saint was given the title because he came from Mecca.

The **Zamzama** or **Kim's Gun** now stands on The Mall in front of the Museum, the original name is supposed to resemble a lion's roar. It was made in Kabul in 1757, brought over by Ahmed Shah Abdali and used in the Battle of Panipat. It is said to have been cast out of brass and copper which was obtained by raising a levy on household utensils. It was then left behind until Ranjit Singh obtained it in 1802 when it became a symbol of the Sikh Empire. After being damaged badly in Multan it was brought to Lahore. Rudyard Kipling who lived and worked in Lahore for a time made it famous in his book 'Kim'.

Wapda House is a modern building which has a glass dome and a roof garden at Charing Cross where 5 roads intersect. In front stands the marble column of the Summit Minaret.

Local industries Lahore produced 10% of Pakistan's industrial output in 1961, but with the growth of a number of other industrial centres has slipped. However, a number of new industries have developed. Textiles, such as hosiery and other clothing, a large number of small scale and craft industries have developed in the N of the city, and there are steel re-rolling mills, light engineering and some modern sector industries.

Services

Hotels AL *Pearl Continental*, Shahrah-e-Quaid-e-Azam. T 67931, 69931, Cable: Pearcont, Telex: 44877 Pearl. 189 rm. All facilities plus golf and tennis. Restaurants recommended. **AL** *Avari Lahore Ramada Renaissance* (previously Hilton International), 87 Shahrah-e-Quaid-e-Azam. 193 rm. All facilities plus golf and jogging track nearby. Good restaurants, excellent buffet, very pleasant service. **B** *International*, Shahrah-e-Quaid-e-Azam. T 870281, Cable: Alcomfort, Telex: 44230 Hintl Pk. 110 rm. All facilities.

C *Faletti's*, Egerton Rd, close to Wapda House. T 303660, Cable: Falettis, Telex: 11469 Flh Pk. 67 rm. Restaurant, coffee shop, travel, shops, TV. **D** *Ambassador,* Davis Rd. T 301861,

Cable: Ambassador, Telex: 44424 Beltx Pk. 53 rm. Restaurant, exchange, travel, shops, pool. Reasonably good value although a little run down. **E YMCA Hostel,** Shahrah-e-Quaid-e-Azam, T 54433. *Salvation Army Hostel,* 35 Fatima Jinnah Rd.

Youth Hostel is nr Firdous Market, 110 B/3, Gulberg III, T 881505. Unfortunately situated away from centre – awkward journey.

Warning Be very careful of cheap hotels in the station area. It is an area known for drugs, and a number of travellers complain of having had drugs planted in their rooms.

Restaurants There is a wide choice of restaurants outside hotels on the Main Boulevard in Gulberg and Shahrah-e-Quaid-e-Azam (the city claiming to offer some of best). Also stalls selling snacks in the Anarkali Bazaar, Mozang Bazaar, Liberty market, along Abbots Rd. On Main Boulevard, Gulberg: *Menage, Rendezvous, Tabaq Cuisine,* 2 K, T 881350. On Shahrah-e-Quaid-e-Azam: *Saloos,* Wapda House, T 325257. *Lords,* T 312235. *Tolenton Kabana.* Also on Davis Rd, T 305489 and Fortress Stadium, Cantonment, T 370550. *Tabaq Restaurant,* 1 Abbot Rd, Laxmi Chowk, T 222137.

    Pakistani On Main Boulevard, Gulberg: *Kabasheesh* at 132 E 1, T 883218. On Shahrah-e-Quaid-e-Azam: *Shezan Oriental.* At the Airport: *Anarkali.* **Chinese** On Main Boulevard, Gulberg: *Tung Fung* at 130 E 1, T 870561, *Tai Wah* at 78 E 1, T 881350. *Cathay Restaurant,* opp American Express, T 302393. *Kim Mun* at 54 (1st Floor), T 301182. Also *Lun Fung,* Kashmir Rd.

    Fast Food and Ice Cream Parlours *Salt and Pepper,* Shahrah-e-Quaid-e-Azam, Liberty Market, Gulberg and Fortress Stadium. *Burger Eleven,* 45 Commercial Zone, Liberty Market, T 883263. *Shezan Snack Bar,* Fortress Stadium, T 372781. *Yammy,* Liberty Market. On Main Boulevard, Gulberg: *Carvel* and *Polka Parlour.*

Banks American Express, 85, Shahrah-e-Qaid-e-Azam, T 306906. **European Asian,** Mall View Plaza, PO Box 1651, T 52917. **Muslim Commercial,** 26 Davis Rd, T 302575. **Hong Kong -Shanghai,** 7-D, Kashmir/Egerton Rd, PO Box 1922, T 306564.

Shopping Most shops are open from Sat to Th 0900-1300 and 1500-1900. The Bazaars – Anarkali spreads N from the Museum up to the walls of the Old City. *Mzang* which stretches S from Charing Cross. *Liberty Market,* Gulberg is to the SE of the city. Shahrah-e-Quaid-e-Azam or The Mall.

    Handicrafts *Apna Shop, Jaanico, Pakistan Handcrafts* on Shahrah-e-Quaid-e-Azam. *China Art Museum,* Rang Mahal; *Sundip Boutique,* Liberty Market, Gulberg. Several good shops in hotels have quality handicrafts but you will pay less in bazaar stalls: *Kashmir Victory House* and *Kimkraft* at the Intercontinental, *Eastern Carpets and Curios* at Faletti's; *Kimkraft* at the Hilton.

    Jewellery *Antique and Fine Art Jewellers,* Liberty Market, Gulberg; *Blue Moon* and *Fahrat Ali* on Shahrah-e-Quaid-e-Azam; *Butt,* Ferozepur Rd, Maclagen Rd and Temple Rd; *Fantasia,* Main Boulevard, Gulberg.

    Carpets *Jamali Traders,* 25 A Nicholson Rd. *Jan Oriental,* and *Prime Carpets* on Empress Rd. *Bokhara Palace* and *Pak Punjab* on Sharah-e-Quaid-e-Azam. *Kashmirian,* 55 B 3 Gulberg III. *Splendour Carpets,* 19/10 Abbot Rd. *Ravi,* Ghore Shah Rd.

Local transport Taxis, Buses, Auto rickshaws, Tongas.

Entertainment The Alhamra Arts Council Hall on Shahrah-e-Quaid-e-Azam, built in 1970 has modern simple lines and is an impressive building using the red brick and lime plaster of the British colonial style in Lahore. It houses 3 auditoria and is a cultural centre offering a varied fare of music and the arts. There is an Open-Air Theatre on Bagh-e-Jinnah and the Wapda Auditorium at Wapda House, Shahrah-e-Quaid-e-Azam.

Sports Lahore Flying Club, Walton Airport, T 850228. **Golf:** Lahore Gymkhana Cricket Ground and Glf Course, Upper Mall; Railway Golf Course, off Shahrah-e-Qaid-e-Azam. **Hockey:** National Hockey Stadium, opp Gaddafi Stadium.

Museums
The **Lahore Central Museum** is the oldest and one of the best in Pakistan. It is superbly housed and excellently maintained. Founded in 1864, it moved to the present building in the Mughal-Gothic style, which was opened to the public in 1894. Some of the collections, notably the Gandharan sculptures, are outstanding.

    Open daily except Sat, the first Wed of month and the following: Eid-ul-Fitr, Eid-ul-Zoha, Eid e Milad-un-Nabi, 9th and 10th Muharram, 1 May, 11 Sep. Winter (1 Oct-15 Apr): 0900-1600. Summer (16 Apr-30 Sep): 0800-1700. These times may be changed without notice. Entry and small camera fee but some exhibits may not be photographed. Free conducted tours and a good printed guide available at the entrance.

The pride of the collection are the **Gandharan** sculptures displayed in Gallery 2. Centred on the present Vale of Peshawar Gandhara played a significant part in the political and cultural life both of W Asia and of the Indian sub-continent. Brought into the Persian Empire as one of its 42 provinces by the Emperor Darius in the 5th century BC. However the most striking remains of the region today come from its Buddhist period. Although western influence, through Greek conquests, is evident stylistically in the art of Gandhara from the reign of the Kushan rulers in the early centuries AD, the subjects are entirely Indian and Buddhist.

The **Coin Collection** is extremely valuable with some from the period of Alexander the Great, the Guptas and the Buddhists.

The **Faqir Khana** in the Old City, approached through the Bhati Gate, is an exceptional private museum belonging to the family of Faqir Azizuddin who was Raja Ranjit Singh's Foreign Minister. It is a treasure house of artistic masterpieces including paintings, sculptures, porcelain, carpets and ancient manuscripts.

Parks and zoos The **Mughal gardens** in the fort and the **Dil Kusha Gardens** around the Mausoleums to Jahangir and Nur Jahan were destroyed but have since been reinstated. Iqbal Park, Azadi Chowk nr Lahore Fort.

Race Course Park, the **Model Town Park** and **Gulshan-e-Iqbal Park**, to the S of the city, are provide recreational facilities for the city's population.

Bagh-e-Jinnah Opp Governor's House was the large Lawrence Garden in British times. It has a small zoo with tigers, elephants, camels, deer, giraffes, ostriches, peacocks.

Zoological Gardens were opened in 1872 in the centre of the city, the main gate is opp Wapda House on Shahrah-e-Quaid-e-Azam. Open daily: Summer 0730-1900; Winter 0800-1700. The management of the Zoo was taken over by the Punjab Wildlife Dept in 1982 and since then a lot of renovation work has been done on the older buildings and some new work undertaken, the latest being the Tiger House with a new Ape House and Cafeteria. Animals include some species peculiar to the region, which will interest a visitor. Well laid out with some of the oldest trees in the city and a children's play area.

Linear Park (Nawaz Sharif Park), Ferozepur Rd. Nasir Bagh, opp Town Hall.

Useful addresses Foreigners' Registration Office, Kutchery Road. Passport Office, Muslim Tower, nr Canal Bank. T 854202. Director of Archaeology, N Circle, Lahore Fort. T 56747. At both Taxila and Harappa it is possible to book quite comfortable *Rest House* accommodation through the Director. Both sites have many signs prohibiting photography, however permits are obtainable from the Director in Lahore. Police station, Montgomery Road.

Foreign representations France, 20 E Gulberg III. Italy, Wapda House. Sweden, Walton Rd, Saddar. USA, 50 Zafar Ali Rd.

Cultural centres American Centre, 77 E 9 Gulberg III, T 873956. Arab Cultural Centre, 5 Gulberg, T 873966. British Council, 32 Mozang Rd, T 52755. French Centre, 20 E/2 Gulberg III. Goethe Institute, 92 E 1 Gulberg III. Iranian Cultural Centre, Main Gulberg Rd, T 873263. Pakistan National Centre, Al Fateh, The Mall, T 301690.

Post and Telegraphs GPO, Shahrah-e-Quaid-e-Azam, T 60821. Central Telegraph Office, Mcleod Rd, T 211021.

Hospitals and medical services Medical Centre Gulberg III, 51-P1-GBG-III T 881906; United Christian Hospital, Gulberg, T 881961

Places of worship Muslim Dai Anga's, nr Rly Station; Golden Mosque, Kashmiri Bazaar; Pearl Mosque, Lahore Fort; Masjid-e-Shuhada, Shahrah-e-Quaid-e-Azam Rd; Muslim Masjid, Lohari Gate. Christian Lahore Cathedral, Shahrah-e-Quaid-e-Azam; Naulakha Church, Nicholson Rd; Sacred Heart, Lawrence Rd; Seventh Day Adventist Church, Mozang Rd; St Andrew's Church and St Anthony's Church, Shahrah-e-Bin Badees; St Joseph's Church, Lahore Cantonment; St Mary's Church, Gulberg; St Mary Magdelene's Church, nr Airport. Others Hindu Mandir, Ravi Rd; Jain Mandir, nr Old Anarkali; Sikh Gurdwara, opp Lahore Fort.

Chambers of Commerce Lahore Chamber of Commerce and Industry, Race Course Rd. Office of Asst Controller of Imports and Exports, Edwards Rd. Export Display Centre, WAPDA House. Export Promotion Bureau, Shadman Market.

Travel agents On Shahrah-e-Quaid-e-Azam: American Express, Global Express, Highland Travels, Tourist Services Corporation. At Wapda House: International Travel Services, Matchless Travels, Skyline. House of Travel, Asif Chambers, Davis Rd. Karvan Travels, Maclaggan Rd. Travel Easy, Egerton Rd. Travel Kings, Hotel Parkway. Waljis Travel Bureau,

Transport House. Tour operators At Faletti's, Din Tours, T 211130 and Pakistan Tours. Montana Travel in Ramada Renaissance.

Tourist offices and information Dept of Tourist Services, Liberty Market, Gulberg III, T 871800. Punjab Tourism Dept, 74 Shadman II. PTDC, Faletti's, Egerton Rd, T 303600. Information Centre at the Airport.

Tours *Tourist Development Corporation of Punjab* (TDCP), 82 Shadman II operates 2 half day tours lasting 3 hr 30 min, which start from the Tourist Information Office, 4 A Lawrence Rd, T 869216 and pick up from Faletti's, Service International, Pearl Continental and Ramada Rennaissance within the next half hour. **Morning Tour**: 0830, Badshahi Mosque, Lahore Fort, Jahangir's Tomb and Lahore Museum. **Afternoon Tour**: 1430 (1530, 1 Apr-30 Sep), Shalimar Gardens, Wazir Khan's Mosque, the Old City and Aibak's Tomb. Special excursions further afield, including Harappa, can be arranged.

Travel To get to Lahore from Karachi, or vice versa it is best to avoid the road journey. Flights are convenient but expensive (lower fares for night flights). Trains (especially Expresses) are best.

Air PIA domestic flights, 4 daily to Karachi (about Rs 1,700), 3 to Quetta, 5 weekly to Rawalpindi, and one weekly to Peshawar. The airport has a foreign currency exchange. Airport to the city centre is 5 km, transfer by minibus, taxi or auto rickshaw.

Rail To Karachi *Zulfiqar Exp*, 6, daily, a/c, 1715, 25hr 15 min; *Awam Exp*, 14, daily, 1935, 19 hr; *Shalimar Exp*, 106, daily, a/c, 0630, 15 hr 35 min. *Khyber Mail*, 2, daily, a/c, 0930, 20 hr. **Multan** *Awam Exp*, 14, daily, 1935, 5 hr 30 min; *Shalimar Exp*, 106, daily, a/c, 0630, 4 hr 35 min **Rawalpindi** *Zulfiqar Exp*, 5, daily, a/c, 0800, 6 hr 35 min; *Awam Exp*, 13, daily, 0445, 6 hr 10 min. **Faisalabad** *83 Exp*, daily, 1035, 2 hr 30 min; *85 Exp*, daily, 1400, 2 hr 30 min; **Sahiwal** (for Harappa) *RC 58*, daily, 0530, 2 hr 30 min; *Khyber Mail*, 2, daily, a/c, 0930, 3 hr Lahore City Station, Enquiries, T 320343; Reservations, T 303472.

Road Buses Punjab Road Transport Corporation (PRTC) runs regular, daily Deluxe coach and bus services on intercity routes, starting from the GTS Stand nr the Rly Station. Students travel on half fare on production of Identity Cards. There are also private companies operating throughout the state. The a/c Flying Coach Service which are more expensive than the 'Wagon' services, start from the Asia Hotel and the GTS Bus Stand nr the Rly Station. The General Bus Stand is in Badami Bagh.

To **Rawalpindi**, a number every hr from 0500, some through the night; **Bahawalpur**, daily at 0900; **Dehra Ismail Khan**, every hr from 0900; **Hyderabad**, daily at 0900; Karachi, daily; **Multan** about 2 every hr from 0830-2400; **Mansehra**, 10 daily, 0500-0100; **Murree**, 4 daily at 0100, 0150, 2330, 0030; **Peshawar**, every hr from 0900; **Saideqabad**, daily at 0900; **Sialkot**, every 30 mins; Sukkur, daily at 0900. The a/c coach companies with offices in Lahore: Blue Lines, T 63184, Farrukh Flying Coach, T 57171, Flying Coach Ltd, T 55156, National Flying Coach, T 57154, New Farrukh Flying Coach, T 250372, New Khan Road Runner, T 60572.

Short excursions

Jahangir's Tomb

7 km NW of the city. Built by **Shah Jahan** in 1637 for his father, **Jahangir**, who died 10 years earlier, the tomb is believed to have been designed by **Jahangir's** wife **Nur Jahan** (see page 274). Sited in the attractive **Dil Kusha Garden**, the flat square tomb in a walled garden has a central dome and 4 tall, 5-storeyed octagonal minarets. The tomb shows similarities with the Itimad ud Daulah, built in Agra by Nur Jahan for her father, the disproportion between the lower and upper storeys and the minarets being even more unfortunately pronounced, **see page 274**. However, the exterior of the tomb is superbly decorated with marble on red sandstone, with perforated marble screens and with beautiful wall paintings inside. Inside the central domed chamber the white marble tomb itself is covered in exquisite *pietra dura* inlay work in black marble, listing the 99 attributes of God.

In the early 19th century, the conquering Sikhs plundered all the tombs here. The mausoleum was used as the private residence of the French General of Ranjit Singh's army. The **Badshahi Mosque**, built by his grandson 37 years later has an interesting alignment with the tomb – from a minaret here, you would only be able to see 3 minarets of the mosque, and vice versa!

The **Akbari Serai,** which you reach before the main tomb, was a Travellers' Rest House, built in the same period. The 180 small restrooms around the square have access to running water channelled through the terraces. To the W is a red sandstone **mosque** beyond which you will see the pointed dome of the **Tomb of Asaf Khan,** Nur Jahan's brother, to whom Shah Jahan, his uncle, built this large memorial. The glazed coloured tilework, which displayed the Persian practice of composite pattern-making with tiles in the way of a mosaic, has largely disappeared, and the dome too has been stripped of its original white marble.

Further W, across the railway line, stands **Nur Jahan's Tomb.** Married to Emperor Jahangir in 1611, she held exceptional power. She died in 1645, 18 years after her husband, and is buried near him. Her own epitaph reads: "Upon my grave when I shall die; No lamp shall burn nor jasmine lie; No candle, with unsteady flame; Serve as a reminder of my fame; No bulbul chanting overhead; Shall tell the world that I am dead." Her own tomb, once richly ornamented with superb floral fresco paintings on lime plaster, retains little of its original decoration. The minarets have gone; the marble platform inside and the decorative sandstone facing are new. Open daily, Summer 0800-1800, Winter 0800-1630.

You can visit the 3 monuments for a small fee and get there easily by car via the Grand Trunk Rd to Rawalpindi, across the Ravi Bridge. The buses (6 and 23) from the Railway Station take about 20 min.

The *Shalimar Gardens*.
8 km E of Lahore. Open daily: Summer 0800-1800, Winter 0800-1630. Chilled drinks are on sale in the Sikh guest house which was added in the 19th century and the toilets are near the Turkish Baths. You can reach the gardens by driving E down Grand Trunk Rd or approach it from Jahangir's Tomb on the Bund Rd. Approx 20 min from the Rly Station on Bus 3, 12 or 17. It is best visited when the flowers are in bloom in Feb and Mar. The shallow niches in the marble wall (a feature of Mughal architecture) were used for hundreds of lamps. The gardens are illuminated on Wed and Sat nights.

The 'Shalimar' ('abode of love') **gardens** were laid out in 1637 on the instructions of Emperor Shah Jahan, 8 km E of the present city. Designed by Ali Mardan Khan, it was a royal pleasure garden – the only one of the Mughal gardens that has survived. Over 450 m long and enclosed within high walls for privacy, with its marble pavilions with carvings, *pietra dura* inlay work and fresco paintings, a marble waterfall, ornamental ponds and over 400 fountains, the gardens provided an alternative residence for the royal family.

Char baghs The gardens were laid out on the principle of 2 "char baghs" (quartered gardens) separated by a terrace in the centre, **see page 278.** Water tanks drawing from the canal supplied water up to height of the highest level, which then cascaded down. The highest 'Farah', reserved for the royal family, is where you will enter the gardens, although when it was laid out the entrance was at the other end, enabling privacy to be maintained at each higher level. This top terrace is divided into quarters, but the original decorations on the once grand buildings have virtually disappeared.

The Emperor's sleeping chamber where you enter, the pavilion to house the *harem* and the ladies in waiting to the W and the *Diwan-e-Khas* (Hall of Private Audience) to the E, were the finest buildings of the garden. Steps lead down to the next terrace, about 4 m lower, and water was channelled down to the water tank and numerous fountains in the centre. The royal entertainers performed for the Emperor who sat on the marble platform here. To the E are the Turkish Baths. The lowest terrace contained the *Diwan-e-Am* (Hall of Public Audience). The garden was stocked with flowering plants and decorative shrubs from all corners of the Mughal empire.

The Mughals chose to be 'formal' in their design rather than 'natural', "the aim being to discipline nature and not to imitate it" as Percy Brown puts it. "A regular arrangement of squares, often subdivided into smaller squares to form the favourite figure *char bagh* or fourfold plot".

Longer excursions

Jallo National Park 27 km. Covering a 200 ha site, the park has amusements for children, a small museum, the Forest Research Centre, a gift shop and a cafeteria. **Shadab Park** next to it has a boating lake. Jallo is on the Grand Trunk Rd and has a rly station. Buses and trains every 30 min from Lahore.

Sheikhpura (Jahangirabad) 34 km, has a fort and a lodge once used by the Emperor for hunting expeditions which was taken over by the Sikh princess Rani Nakayan. Her private apartments still has beautiful fresco paintings preserved. The 32 km road, dual carriageway 2 km from the Ravi Bridge, is fast. You can hire a car or take a bus.

On entering the town, go straight across at the junction with the Gujranwala-Faisalabad Rd, turn left at traffic lights and proceed another 200 m to the Fort where you will see houses with carved wooden doors. You should get authorization from the Dept of Archaeology at Lahore Fort to enter, since the Fort buildings are now occupied by the police. TDCP offers boating facilities and should have a *Rest House* in 1991.

Hiran Minar 6 km. 4 km from Sheikhpura, turn off the Sargodha Rd to the right, along a canal. The deer park is on the other side a couple of km away. Built by Emperor Jahangir in memory of his pet antelope 'Maharaj', the deer park with its square lake with a causeway and arched pavilion in its centre, is an ideal spot to escape to from a busy city. Even in Mughal times, it was a favourite spot for the Emperor. The tall carved stone octagonal memorial tower has 99 steps. **See page 1151**.

Chhanga Manga 68 km. A vast planted forest, a Wildlife Reserve covering nearly 5,000 ha, is now a holiday resort with a lake providing boating facilities and a miniature railway. Attracts large crowds of city dwellers. Forest Dept *Rest Houses* and D PTDC *Motel* which has 5 a/c rm with modern facilities in lovely gardens and a restaurant.

LAHORE TO SUKKUR

The route from Lahore to Sukkur lies runs in a gently curving arc through some of Pakistan's most intensively irrigated and cultivated land. It also crosses a region of enormous historical interest. Harappa, perhaps the joint capital of the Indus Valley civilisation, lies SW of Lahore. Subsequently the plains saw Arab and Persian influence in towns such as Multan and Uchchh Sharif, the rise of Sikhism, which has some of its most revered sites on these plains, and then of Mughal power. In the last phase before Independence the British created irrigation works in the 19th and early 20th centuries which laid the economic foundation for modern Punjab.

Leave Lahore S from the Lahore Museum and the GPO down **Lake Road** and **Multan Road**. The road runs straight across the irrigated plain, after 70 km passing 10 W of **Chhanga Manga**, a wildlife reserve. Planted as a forest reserve in 1890, Changa Manga is a popular tourist outing from Lahore, being only an hour's drive away from the city. Restaurant and Motel with 5 a/c rooms.

The national highway continues SW across classic canal colony irrigation country through **Pattoki** (15 km), **Okara** (47 km) to **Sahiwal** (37 km). Formerly named Montgomery, it is not to be confused with the second Sahiwal in Punjab, 300 km to the northwest. The town took its earlier name from Sir Robert Montgomery, Lieutenant Governor of Punjab between 1859-65. It is difficult to imagine that 100 years ago most of this land was little more than sparsely populated scrub jungle, but the rewards for the extremely hard work necessary to bring the fields under irrigated cultivation lay in the much higher soil fertility than was characteristic of the settlers' homes to the northeast.

Today it lies in the heart of the Punjab's cotton growing belt, and Sahiwal is now a Punjabi market town, with some cotton, dairying and other industries. Sahiwal has its own breed of milk producing cow, and Sahiwal bullocks are fattened for beef. They are widely marketed across Pakistan. **Hotels** *The Five Ways. The Stadium,* nr Sahiwal Stadium.

In Sahiwal the road to **Pakpattan** (45 km) turns due S. Originally there was a Hindu shrine at Pakpattan ("ferry crossing of the pure" – a crossing of the Chenab River), but this was converted to Muslim worship by **Baba Farid-ud-din Ganj Shakkar** (1173-1265), and it is now a major pilgrimage centre every Muharram. The National Highway from Sahiwal to Multan via Harappa continues along the left (S) side of the railway line to **Harappa Road**. Follow this road to visit **Harappa** on the left bank of the River Ravi. At **Harappa Road** (22 km from Sahiwal) there is a sign to Harappa, across the railway line about 7 km. The road crosses the **Lower Bari Doab Canal** before reaching the museum and rest house.

Harappa

The site at Harappa is managed by the Archaeological Survey of Pakistan. **Note** As at Taxila, there are numerous signs suggesting that photography is prohibited. This simply means that theoretically permission to photograph should be obtained from the Director of the Archaeological Survey, either in Lahore or Karachi. This is normally given automatically. The Director of the Archaeological Survey (Northern Circle) can also give you permission to stay in the *Guest House* at Harappa. Contact at Old Fort, Lahore T 56747. Bedding not provided. If you have any difficulty on the site ask to see the curator of the museum. Open: Winter 0900-1600, Summer 0800-1200 and 1400-1800. Closed first Tues of every month.

	Jan	Feb	Mar	Apr	May	Jun	Jul	Aug	Sep	Oct	Nov	Dec	Av/Tot
Max (°C)	20	22	28	35	40	41	38	37	37	35	29	22	32
Min (°C)	5	8	13	19	24	28	28	27	24	18	11	6	18
Rain (mm)	12	12	17	6	7	23	74	75	25	2	2	7	261

The **Archaeological Museum** is just off the highway nr the Rly station, in spacious gardens on the S edge of mounds A and B. It was started in Harappa after the early excavations in 1926. The new museum, with good display cabinets, was completed in 1967 and is housed in 2 wings. Originally the museum restricted itself to exhibits from Harappa alone including terracotta figurines, toys, seals, pots and jewellery, grave furniture from the Cemeteries 37 and H, but has been enlarged to represent the complete pre- and proto-history of Pakistan. Palaeolithic (old stone age) tools from the Soan Valley, Sukkur and Rohri as well as artefacts from Kot Diji and Amri are displayed, **see page 1178**. Comparative material from **Moenjodaro** is also on display.

The model of Harappa gives an impression of its original scale and shape, but the main feature of the museum is its collection of pottery, seals, utensils, beads, necklaces statuary and terracotta figures dating from the 1,000 years following 2500 BC. There is also some material from the post-Harappan period. The museum is very close to the excavations and there are 2 *Rest Houses,* one of which has an air-conditioned room. Cold drinks are available at stalls nr the entrance.

The discovery of the site The existence of the huge mounds, rising nearly 20 m above the plain, which comprise the Harappan site was reported by Masson in 1826 and visited again by Cunningham in 1853 and 1876. When the railway between **Multan** and **Lahore** was being built in the 1870s the railway engineers found their apparently inexhaustible supply of ready-baked bricks invaluable for laying the foundations over a distance of more than 150 km, according to David Ross, writing in 1882.

It wasn't until the Archaeological Survey started full scale excavations under the Indian Archaeologist **Vats** in 1920, which continued until 1934, that the scale and significance of the buried ruins became clear. Further excavations by **Sir Mortimer Wheeler** in 1946 carried the interpretation of vital features of this Indus Valley city still further. Today the site gives the appearance of being rather poorly cared for, and has nothing of the grandeur of Moenjodaro, though the total area of the 2 cities and key features of their basic layout are similar. However, the path across the site is well laid out, and it is possible to walk round the city in about an hour.

The route does not take you past the important sites in chronological order. It starts from the museum at the S edge of the site and passes an area to its left identified as **Cemetery H**, much of which is now grassed over. You get the best view by climbing the path up to the viewing platform and then looking back towards the museum. Cemetery H is a site of vital importance, for although it is one of the last areas of Harappa to be settled it has provided clues to the nature of the last occupants of the town and of the ending of the Indus Valley civilisation. Vats found a range of pottery and other grave goods as well as skeletons, and argued that the "**Cemetery H culture**" was the final stage of the Harappan civilisation.

The cemetery contained graves dug at 2 levels. In the lower (and older) of the 2 bodies were buried intact and the pottery was similar to that in the main part of the Harappan city. However, in the upper level disarticulated bones were buried in large urns. As Allchin and Allchin point out, "the painted urns from this site tell us all that is so far known about the beliefs of their makers."

Peacocks are a common decorative motif, in some cases showing hollow bodies with small horizontal human forms painted inside. Bulls and cows are another common motif, one of which shows a pipal leaf springing from the hump. All these features have elements in common with the beliefs of the Rig Veda. Vats pointed to further similarities, including, in Allchin and Allchin's words, 2 beasts facing each other, held by a man with long wavy hair, while a hound stands menacingly behind one of them; in yet another a little man of similar form stands on the back of a creature which shares the features of a centaur with the Harappan bull-man."

Vats argued that these images bore striking similarities with figures from the Vedas, among them the figure of the hound which he compared with the Vedic God of Death, Yama. Allchin and Allchin suggest that the peacock can be interpreted similarly, "seeing in them the 'One Bird' of the Rg Veda", variously identified with Agni (Fire), Surya (Sun) and Soma.

All these features suggest that there was a continuity in the use of the site between the Indus Valley settlers and the invading Aryans. The pottery of the upper levels shows strong similarities to pottery found in western Iran at a much later period than that of Harappa itself. Although there are as yet no radiocarbon dates available the earliest dates of the Cemetery H culture is put by Allchin and Allchin at around 2000 BC, but the distinctive star and bird motifs on the later pottery is contemporaneous with designs from Iran dating from 1550-1400 BC. They supported the earlier conclusion of Vats that "the Cemetery H culture was the final stage of the Harappan, and continuous with it; but that it must indicate the presence of foreign conquerors or immigrants."

The citadel From the viewing platform the path climbs N up onto the citadel. This has been far less thoroughly excavated than that at Moenjodaro, and far more of the original brickwork has been removed. However, you can see something of the scale of the central city, the outline of some of its roads and its drainage system. The path to the left on top of the citadel leads down to the W edge and overlooks the deep trench cut by Sir Mortimer Wheeler into the fortification wall in 1946. It is possible to scramble down to the bottom and get a good view of the impressive scale of this exterior wall.

The citadel had square towers and bastions, and the widest streets within the citadel ran from N to S, as in Moenjodaro. The path turns right at the top of the citadel mound and descends through the E wall, following this N. It passes a mosque and the 17th or early 18th century shrine to **Baba Nur Shah Wali**. There are several myths surrounding this site and the stones enclosed behind a fence just to its S. The tomb of the saint is exceptionally long – perhaps 5 m. If you ask the woman attendant you will hear that the tomb is as big as that because the saint was indeed that length. The stones in front were reputed once to have been gold pestle, mortar and ring. When a thief tried to steal them they turned to stone. Only 2 are visible today.

Return to the path and continue N. To the right is another mound with a deep excavation made by Sir Mortimer Wheeler, and across in the distance it is just possible to make out the banks of the **Ravi** (flowing from right to left) which once brought boats right up to the N edge of Harappa.

The footpath passes through some low trees, and immediately to its E lies the lower town. Walking across this area you can see the great round brick **working floors**, almost certainly used for grinding grain. Wheat and barley chaff were found in the floors' cracks. Beyond and to the S of the round threshing floors is a group of '**working men's homes**' or single roomed barracks, similar to the small houses in Moenjodaro.

The main path continues N to the remains of what Vats termed the **granary**. It comprises the footings of a series of 2 rows of 6 granaries, each 16 m by 6 m very close to the old river bank. Allchin and Allchin suggest that the combined floor space was over 800 sq m, similar to that at Moenjodaro. Although there is no evidence of the superstructure which once covered the brick plinths their size is still testimony to the sophistication and organisation of an urban civilisation which both needed and could organise grain storage on such a scale.

From **Harappa** rejoin the National Highway to **Multan**. The route goes through Chichawatni, Mian Channun (35 km) and **Khanewal** (45 km, an important railway junction where the main line to **Karachi** cuts S, avoiding Multan) before reaching Multan (45 km), following the Lahore-Multan railway most of the way.

Multan

Population 950,000 *Best season* Nov – Mar. Languages spoken are Punjabi, Urdu, Saraiki and English.

Multan is the most important town of S Punjab, a modern industrial centre grafted onto the ancient cultural capital of the region. The roads into the city are packed with people and traffic, and for much of the year the air seems full of dust.

	Jan	Feb	Mar	Apr	May	Jun	Jul	Aug	Sep	Oct	Nov	Dec	Av/Tot
Max (°C)	21	23	30	37	42	42	40	38	38	36	29	23	33
Min (°C)	6	8	14	20	26	29	29	28	25	18	12	7	19
Rain (mm)	7	10	13	6	8	8	45	33	20	1	2	5	158

Local festivals Religious shrines of famous local saints celebrate the annual death anniversary *Urs* fairs, particularly at the shrines of Shah Rukn-e-Alam, Bahauddin Zakaria, Shah Shams Sabzwari. Shah Jamal among others.

Early history The origin of Multan's name may go back to Hiuen Tsang, who called it **Mulosan Pulu,** and Alberuni, who referred to it as **Multana**. It may well be the city of Malli, the stronghold of Malavas, where Alexander the Great was wounded when he took it around 327 BC. The city's history traces the rule of the Mauryans and Kushans up to about AD 470 when it was taken by the Huns who remained until the middle of the 6th century. The Hindu rulers who followed ruled until the conquering Arabs arrived in 712.

The Arabs This began centuries of predominantly Muslim rule, initially under the Caliph of Baghdad. However, Istakhri, who visited the town in 950, described an idol in a Hindu temple as having human shape with jewels for eyes and a crown of gold. Shortly afterwards the priests were massacred and the idol destroyed by

Jelem, an Iraqi member of the short-lived heretic Qarmatian Islamic sect who captured Multan soon after 950.

His rule was followed by that of **the Afghans** who remained in power until the peaceful transfer of the province in 1528 to the Mughal **Emperor Babur**. However, it suffered numerous incursions and invasions by powerful military forces from Central and Western Asia. Their influence on the architecture of the shrines in Multan is very marked. The Arab conqueror **Mohammed Bin Qasim** is believed to have started the city's first school and library. The Mughals brought over 2 centuries of peace when Multan came to be called *Dar-ul-Aman,* the City of Peace. In 1752 the province came under the rule of the Pathan Governors and the Chiefs of Bahawalpur for a time which was followed by constant wars between the Nawabs of Multan and the Sikhs. Afghans ruled from 1779 until 1818, when the Sikhs held the city until 1845. Multan finally came under nearly a century of British rule from 1849 until independence.

An old Persian couplet suggested that Multan was full of heat, beggars, dust and burial grounds. However, the scene is changing fast, with the transformation of the surrounding district into agriculturally productive land and Multan growing industrially, while retaining its old cultural heritage as a centre of traditional crafts. The new city has grown around the old walled city.

Places of interest
The old walled city has a natural barrier to the N by way of a steep sided valley. The brick wall surrounding the city on the other 3 sides has 6 gates and encloses narrow alleys and colourful bazaars. The **Fort** stands between the city and the dry river bed of the Ravi. It was built on a mound with a very long wall with 46 bastions and 4 gateways each with 2 towers. Much of it was destroyed by the British in 1848 although parts of the wall, the shrine of **Hazarat Bahauddin Zakaria** and **Shah Rukn-e-Alam**, as well as a Hindu temple have survived.

The entrance is from the W, through **Qasim Bagh**. The **Narsingh** or **Prahladpuri Temple**, the first temple, dedicated to the man-lion form of Siva, also known as the Sun Temple, used to be in the middle of the Fort but was destroyed by **Aurangzeb**. The mosque built in its place was blown up in 1848. The highest point of the fort, **Damdama**, gives you excellent views of the city. There is a new stadium for sports where public functions are also held. By the entrance there is a red sandstone obelisk built in memory of Agnew who was murdered in 1848, and also a large domed structure which was supposed to have been the powder magazine of the Sikhs. The old armoury is now a pottery where you can get painted camel skin articles.

Tombs and mosques There are many fascinating tombs and mosques in the city. One houses the remains of the saint *Hazarat Bahauddin Zakaria* who was born in 1182 in **Kot Aror** nr Multan, and educated in Turan, Iran, Baghdad and Medina. In Jerusalem he met important religious leaders and scholars and then travelled to Multan to preach. He was the founder of the **Khanqah** or University in Multan which became a renowned institution in the Islamic world, and also founded the *Suhrawardiya Sufi*.

The mausoleum which is to the NE, inside the fort, is one of 2 examples of this style of architecture (the only other similar structure is in Sonepat in India) was built by the saint himself. It is beautifully decorated with blue tiles and superb frescoes and calligraphy on the walls. The annual *Urs* festival is held on 27th Safar (second month of the Islamic calendar). The graves of several members of the influential Qureshi family, including Nawab Muzaffar Khan, are here.

The *Shah Rukn-e-Alam* which dominates both the fort and the city is the tomb of the saint's grandson, **Shah Rukn-e-Alam** ("pillar of the people"), who died in 1334. His mausoleum is nr the Fort's main gate. The dome over the tomb rises to 30 m and has a diameter of nearly 20 m, making it one of the largest in Asia.

The tomb was originally intended for the **Tughluq** family, having been built in 1320 by Emperor **Ghiyas ud Din Tughluq** whose Delhi fortress remains one of the outstanding ruined monuments of Delhi's 7 cities, **see page 167**. It is a magnificent building, superbly decorated. The octagonal lower chambers support beautifully decorated upper chambers with calligraphy and glazed blue and white mosaic tile work.

It has been brilliantly renovated, winning the Aga Khan's Award for architectural restoration. Its position set on a hill above the town enhances its presence. Seen in the dusk it seems to rise ethereally through the dust laden air hovering over the town below. Often crowded with visitors and pilgrims, it has a commanding view over the old town.

1 km to the northeast of the fort is the tomb of **Sham-i Tabriz**, a Sufi martyr born in Afghanistan in 1165. He moved to Multan in 1202 and was murdered there in 1247. The square tomb, surrounded by a veranda, was rebuilt in 1780, the dome being covered with bright Multani ceramics. The tomb is packed with pilgrims on his festival, 1st Jun. There are numerous other tombs and shrines surrounding the fort area. The shrines not only have the famous *naqqashi* work in glazed tiles but also have decorative pieces of mirror and glass on the walls as well as coloured tiles on the floors.

There are numerous **mosques** and other shrines in the city, of which the **Idgah** (1770) NW of the fort, built by Abdus Samsad Khan, is worth a visit. The older brick **Savi Mosque** off Kotla Tolay Kan Rd was built in 1582 and still has beautiful blue glazed tile work.

Local crafts and industries The tradition of *silk textiles* has ancient origins and existed before the 8th century, when silk from Bokhara was woven into cloth in Multan and then re-exported. Woollen *carpet* weaving is said to have started when families of weavers settled here during the reign of the Ghauris. The carpets are handwoven on looms and occasionally in addition to pure woollen ones, wool/cotton carpets are also produced.

The town in also famous for *painted and glazed pottery*, particularly *naqqashi* designs in the local *Kangri* style. The old blue and white decorative work is seen in the religious monuments, not only in this town but all across the country. The Mughal emperor Shah Jahan is thought to have ordered these tiles specially when the Mosque in Thatta was built and his son Aurangzeb had done likewise for Abu Waraq's shrine. Today you can buy pottery items for every day use, crafted with the same skill.

Multan was once also renowned for metal work especially jewellery making and inlay on gold, silver and copper. Since this was done by the Hindu craftsmen, it has declined since 1947. Multan also produces its particular type of shoes, *khussa*, embroidery work on garments, camel skin articles and lacquered wood.

Hotels D *Sindbad*, Nistar Chowk, T 72294. 40 a/c rm with bath. Restaurant, coffee shop, confectioners. **D** *Silver Sand*, 514 Rly Rd, T 33061. 24 rm with bath. Central a/c. **D** *Hushiana*, Chowk Kurcheri, T 43520. 34 a/c rm, with bath. Restaurant, car hire, shop. **D** *Mangol*, LMQ Rd, T 30164. 29 rm. Central a/c. *Golden Dragon Chinese* Restaurant. **D** *Shezan Residence*, Kutchery Rd, T 30253. 37 rm with bath. Central a/c. Exchange. On Shershah Rd: **E** *United*, close to Rly and Bus Stand, T 44294. 21 rm. Restaurant, book shop. **E** *Al-Sana*, T 42601. 11 rm with bath. Central a/c. Car hire. On Hasan Parwana Rd: **E** *Shabroze*, T 44224. 34 rm. Restaurant; **E** *Mavra*, T 43122. 14 rm with bath. Central a/c. **E** *Aziz* nr Cantt Rly Station and *Plaza* nr GTS Bus Stand are cheaper.

Restaurants *Bamboo Snack Bar* and *Shangrila Snack Bar*, Aziz Shaheed Rd, Saddar. *Bingo Chicken and Burger*, (a/c) 1 Allama Iqbal Shopping Centre and *Cafe Afia*, 4 Shopping Centre in Cantt. *Snack Bar*, Quaid-e-Azam Rd.

Shopping The bazaars below the fort are often packed with people.

Local transport Buses, taxis, auto rickshaws and tongas.

Parks and zoo Company Bagh, Cantt. Stadium and Qasim Bagh, Fort. Number of others including Lange Khan, Aam-Khas and Bohar Gate.

Places of worship Muslim Wali Mohammed Mosque, Godri Bazaar. Mosque Phulhattanwali, Chopar Bazaar. Baqarabadi Mosque and idgah Mosque.

Air Services The airport is 10 km from the centre. **PIA** flights daily between Karachi, Lahore and Islamabad go via Multan.

Rail To Lahore *Khyber Mail*, 1, daily, a/c, 1205, 6 hr; *Shalimar Exp*, 105, daily, a/c, 1725, 4 hr 40 min; *Chiltan Exp*, 21, daily, 0850, 7 hr 20 min; **Karachi** *Khyber Mail*, 2, daily, a/c, 1530, 14 hr; *Shalimar Exp*, 106, daily, a/c, 1105, 11 hr; **Peshawar** *Multan-Peshawar*, 179, daily, 2310, 19 hr 45 min.

Bus connections daily to and from Bahawalpur, Dera Ghazi Khan, Karachi, Lahore, Mianwali and Sukkur among others.

From Multan take the **Hafiz Jamal Road** heading SE out of the eastern gate of Multan. Fork right onto the **Lodhran Road** after 1 km, keeping due S. Cross the railway line and pass the central jail on your right. At the Multan by-pass turn right for **Lodhran** (76 km) and **Bahawalpur** (18 km) across more irrigated fields and the dead flat plains.

Bahawalpur

Population 240,000 *Altitude* 130 m

Bahawalpur was a princely state. On the creation of Pakistan in 1947 it immediately acceded to the new country, but in 1954 it was made an administrative district within the Province of Punjab. Its history dates back to pre-Islamic days which some put as early as the 2nd century although no records exist. After the Arabs conquered the area, the Caliphates in Baghdad and Damascus appointed local rulers who continued to hold power. These 'Amirs' continued to rule their princely state under a special treaty with the British in 1838. The foundations of the town were laid in 1780, the Abbasi family who ruled for 2 centuries are considered to have founded the state, and it retained a distinct character from the rest of Punjab in keeping its Islamic identity.

The Turkish cap was a part of official dress, and **Urdu** was the state language (although **Saraili** is the local language), in contrast with surrounding Punjab, where even today fewer than 5% of the population claim Urdu as their mother tongue. The local dress is colourful and often brightly printed or embroidered, the women either in traditional loose *shalwar* and *kameez* but often in *ghagras*, long full skirts and a *choli* or blouse worn with a scarf. The so called *chalees hath ghagra** is made of 40 "hands" or 20 yards of material. The men too wear colourful and embroidered shirts called *cholas* with loose *shalwars* and the *belaposh* or coat, Turkish cap or turban, and shoes with gold thread *zari* embroidery.

Places of interest The town of Bahawalpur lies E of the dry bed of the Sutlej River and was rebuilt in 1748 after which the *amirs* had some palaces built before moving out to Dera Nawab Sahib at the end of the 19th century. **Bahawalgarh Mahal** was built in 1876 and the **Nur Mahal Palace** to the S, which is Italianate in style, in 1885. The small museum in the Nur Mahal Palace standing in impressive gardens has a collection of fine antiques and art objects. They, and **Gulzar Mahal** (1902) next to Bahawalgarh Mahal, nr Baghdad Railway station to the E of the city, which was once the residence of the rulers of the State, are now occupied by the army. The Daulat Khana was built for the Nawab's mother. There is a beautiful mosque in the gardens within the walls, which is open to the public. The **Jami Masjid** is in the Bazaar.

The **Zoo** has a representative collection of fauna of the region and enjoys the privilege of having bred lions and other animals in captivity and having been able

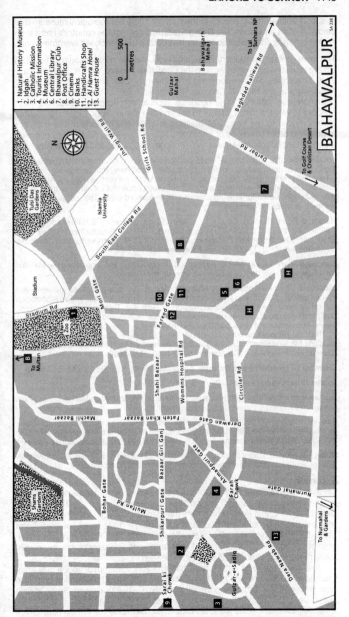

BAHAWALPUR

1. Natural History Museum
2. Idgah
3. Catholic Mission
4. Tourist Information
5. Museum
6. Central Library
7. Bahawalpur Club
8. Post Office
9. Cinema
10. Banks
11. Handicrafts Shop
12. Al Hamra Hotel
13. Guest House

0   500
metres

N

To Lal Sunhara NP

Bahawalgarh Mahal

Gulzar Mahal

Baghdad Railway Rd

Darbar Rd

To Golf Course
& Cholistan Desert

Girls School Rd

Jinnah Wali Rd

Uch Das Gardens

Islamia University

South-East College Rd

Stadium

Stadium Rd

Zoo

To Multan

Mori Gate

Fareed Gate

Shahi Bazaar

Machli Bazaar

Bazaar Giri Ganj

Fateh Khan Bazaar

Womens Hospital Rd

Circular Rd

Derawan Gate

Shams Gardens

Bohar Gate

Multan Rd

Shikarpuri Gate

Ahmadpuri Gate

Farah Chowk

Numahal Gate

Sarai ki Chowk

Gulzar-e-Sidiq

Dea Nawab Rd

To Numahal & Gardens

to supply animals to other zoos in the country. There is a zoological museum (see below) and an aquarium. The **Dring Stadium** is one of the country's finest with cricket grounds, football grounds, tennis courts and an enclosed swimming pool.

The town is expanding with new building work and the introduction of attractions for the tourists who wish to explore the **Cholistan Desert**. Yet it retains a princely air in its avenues, old mansions and as a University town with the famous Islamic University and the Medical College. The Muslim rulers of the 20th century have left impressive Victorian style buildings such as the Hospital (1906), the High School (1911), the fine Library (1924) and the Bahawalpur Club. The Central Library moved to the fine 1924 building in 1947 and has one of the country's largest and best collections of books and rare manuscripts. Today it is becoming an important educational town, with colleges and an expanding university.

Local handicrafts Local *'khussa'* shoes, painted and decorated earthen pottery, embroidery work and reed items such as *morahs* (circular seats). **Cholistan** produces wall hangings and carpets made of camel hair and cotton. *Rilli* or *gindi* which are used as blankets, rugs or bed spreads, are produced with small pieces of coloured cotton cloth. *Changaris* are coloured date leaf baskets used for keeping *chapattis* or unleavened bread. The special embroidery, *aar* work, is typical on garments.

Hotels D *Erum,* The Mall, Circular Rd, T 4291. 32 rm. Central a/c. **E** *Humera,* Multan Rd, T 5959. 19 d rm. Central a/c and in large gardens. **E** *Al-Hamra* outside Fareed Gate, T 4291. 24 rm, with bath. Restaurant. **F** *Abaseen,* Circular Rd, T 2591. 18 rm, with bath. **F** *Shabrose,* nr General Bus Stand, T 4096. 15 rm. **F** *Railway Retiring Rooms.*

Shopping *Shahi Bazaar, Machli Bazaar* and *Gingri Bazaar* and shops along the Mall and Farid Gate which has the Cholistan Craft Development Centre.

Museums The new **Bahawalpur Museum,** next to the library, contains archaeological exhibits including Gandharan sculptures and some sherds from Harappa, and an ethnological section covering the Cholistan desert region in particular. There are examples of dress, ornaments and objects in daily use, wood and stones carvings and paintings on camel skin, as well as collections of coins, paintings and manuscripts.

    Natural History Museum, Zoological Gardens, Stadium Rd. Displays stuffed animals, birds and fish, and objects illustrating local natural history. Miscellaneous arms, toys, stamps. Open daily, Winter 0800-1800, Summer 0700-1400, 1530-1900.

Chamber of commerce and industry is at 40 Multan Rd, New Eid Gah, Model Town B.

Tourist information Centre (PTDC) is at Dring Stadium, T 4657.

Air Services connections with Islamabad and Karachi. PIA, Shah Alam Market, outside Farid Gate, T 3141.

Rail Trains daily to Multan, Lahore, Sukkur, Karachi, Dera Ghazi Khan and other major towns. To Multan *Shalimar Exp,* 105, daily, a/c, 1558, 1 hr 30 min; **Lahore** *Shalimar Exp,* 105, daily, a/c, 1558, 6 hr; **Karachi** *Shalimar Exp,* 106, daily, a/c, 1223, 9 hr 45 min Enquiry, T 3301.

Buses – To **Multan,** Luxury a/c coaches and wagons take about 1 hr 30 min. To **Lahore,** daily 7 buses about every 30 min. Private buses run by New Khan Road Runner, T 2033.

Excursions

Lal Suhanra National Park 36 km to the NE. About 30 min drive, travelling out on the Baghdad Rly Rd. Best season Sep- Apr. Established on the 2 sides of the Desert Branch Canal along which runs the road, the park changes from desert to forest with a large lake and grassland supporting a great variety of animal and particularly rich bird life. Wild cats, black rabbits and black bustards, deer, antelope, Nilgai, fox, porcupine and gazelles as well as peacocks, falcons, quails, owls, parrots and various pheasants can be seen.

    Just inside the main gate is the Children's Park with a mini-zoo, a play area, boating and a 5 a/c rm *Motel* offering accommodation with swimming pool. The *Rest Houses* are in different parts of the park. Camping allowed. Reservations: Forest Dept, Lal Suhanra Park Office, 3A Trust Colony, Bahawalpur, T 3217 or 32 C Jail Rd, Lahore, T 410010. Tours organized daily leave the Bahawalpur Office at 0900. They can also arrange game watching in the park or wild boar hunting in the nearby forests.

The **Cholistan Desert** (56 km), also called **'Rohi'**. This is the largest desert in Pakistan, covering some 25,000 sq km. It runs into the **Thar Desert** in Sind and the **Rajasthan desert** in India. It takes its name from *cholna*, or walking, to describe the semi-nomadic people who inhabit the area and roam in search of water and food and perhaps also the shifting sand dunes. The desert people still keep their old traditions alive and the women wear their brightly coloured distinctive costume of a short blouse, a brightly patterned *ghagra* or full skirt and a printed *chunri*. The red colour and tribal silver jewellery predominate.

Fort Derawar in the centre was the most important fort in the desert as it had a permanent water hole. It is also the best preserved of the series of desert forts here which guarded the trade route through Cholistan.

The **Hakra River** (known in the Vedas as the *River Sarasvati*, and more recently as the **Ghaggar**) once flowed through the region, which was the seat of a civilization which existed at the same time as Harappa and Moenjodaro. It is a region rich in archaeological sites from the Indus Valley civilisation. It has been through a succession of climatic changes during the last 500,000 years.

The presence of a deep layer of red soil below the present sand surface suggests a much moister environment during the Upper and Middle Palaeolithic period , only imaginable now after winter rains have produced a sudden greening of the barren landscape.

This layer has produced evidence of many **stone age settlements**. In historic times the region has been a frontier zone, marked by the building of dozens of forts. It is believed that these once stood in 3 rows, but many have now disappeared. The pastoral nomads find water from underground wells, drawing it up by camels: they also catch precious rainwater by digging troughs and carry it in goat skin water bags.

You can drive to the ruins of **Fort Derawar** from Bahawalpur through Ahmadpur E in 3-4 hr but you need a 4-wheel drive vehicle and a guide to go across the desert road. The fort walls were built of blocks of mud which was plastered for fresco paintings. The subterranean passages leading to vaulted chambers, cellars and dungeons which had air holes, show signs of being used for trolleys. There is a well and 2 water tanks by the tower in the NE, which is topped by a beautifully painted pavilion with a decorated wooden ceiling. The royal cemetery by the fort has tombs decorated with marble and blue tile mosaics.

The personal guards of the 'Amir' of Bahawalpur still stand guard, and you need permission from the senior 'Amir' of Bahawalpur to enter. PTDC, Bahawalpur, or Dy Commissioner, Ahmadpur E, can arrange this. Camel safaris are organized by the **Lal Suhanra National Park** and also by Indus Guides, Lahore, T 304190 and Karakoram Tours, Islamabad, T 829120.

Uchchh Sharif
From Bahawalpur take the **Dera Nawab Road** SW out of the town for **Ahmadpur East** (50 km), a town which has little if anything to recommend it. When you have passed through the town turn right (W) to take the short detour to **Uchchh Sharif** (21 km) now only a small village but with some of the most beautiful ruined tombs in Pakistan. The best time to visit Uchchh is late on a winter or spring afternoon, before the weather has got too hot and when the air is still clear. The single lane but perfectly acceptable country road gives the off the beaten trackfeel of the surrounding rural villages, and the mud walled, flat roofed houses of Uchchh merge with their surroundings. A very attractive book by Dr. Ahmad Nabi Khan is available on the history and architecture of Uchchh, published by the National Institute of Historical and Cultural Research in Islamabad.

Early history The town lies on the S bank of the Sutlej, nr its confluence with the **Chenab** – the *Panjnad*, or junction of the 5 rivers, for this is where all the tributaries of the Indus meet before joining the Indus itself some 50 km downstream. At one time it was a thriving city, capital of an extensive region, and it can trace its origins back to well before Alexander the Great re-named it Alexandria. Some historians believe it pre-dates Buddhist rule over the sub-continent. The region came under the control of the Muslims when Muhammad bin Qasim captured Sind and Multan, but the first record of Uchchh during the Islamic period is in 1005 when Mahmud of Ghazni launched his raids on the Punjab. It was then in the hands of a Rajput prince who was evicted briefly.

Muslim conquest The area was repeatedly contested before finally falling permanently into Islamic hands in the Ghuri invasion of Multan in 1175. Until 1228 it was able to maintain its independence from the newly established Delhi sultanate under **Iltutmish**, becoming an important literary and cultural centre, but on 15 May 1228 Iltutmish was able to take the fort and from then on Uchchh came under the governorship of the Delhi sultans, **see page 89**. However, the Sultans' rule was always contested from several directions and Uchchh was repeatedly subject to chaos and uncertainty. It lost its material prosperity and cultural excellence with the loss of its independence, though it retained and enhanced its reputation as one of the country's most important centres of Islamic piety.

The buildings today There are 2 distinct groups of religious buildings in Uchchh. On the one hand is a group of **square** or **rectangular tombs** with low wood-framed flat roofs and timber columns. The second comprise **domed tombs** built on octagonal plans. Tragically many of the buildings have been seriously damaged or even partially destroyed, mainly by the shifting course of the **Chenab**.

By far the most striking monument still standing is the *Tomb of Bibi Jalwindi*. This is one of 3 such tombs found on the SW edge of the high mound representing the debris of an ancient fortress. Much of the surface comprises a huge graveyard, the earth over the graves standing up sharply from the surrounding baked mud. The earliest of the 3 mausoleums is that of *Baha' al-Din Uchchhi*, also known as *Baha al-Halim*. Bibi Jalwindi's tomb is next to it and is said to date from 1494. The architect-mason who constructed it is buried in the third of the domed tombs.

If you approach these tombs from the narrow lanes of the town you get the impression that they are still intact. The Tomb of Bibi Jalwindi in particular still suggests the magnificence both of form and decoration which was once the hallmark of the completed structures. The structure is essentially brick built, embellished with stunning glazed tile mosaic.

The mausoleum was erected in 3 octagonal storeys. The lower storey was supported by rounded and sloping corner turrets, on which a second storey with a narrow gallery for walking round was supported. A hemispherical dome crowned the building. In the W wall is the beautifully carved wooden **Mihrab**. It is one of the finest achievements of Multani style architecture, for which the Rukn e Alam and the Baha al-Din Zakaria, built 150 years earlier, had served as outstanding examples. Despite their damaged state these tombs are still among the finest of their kind.

The exterior of the tomb of Bibi Jalwindi is almost totally covered with the glazed tile work which is the hall mark of the style. The spandrel of the arches has a variety of floral patterns, the parapet has a frieze of glazed tiles while the turrets are surmounted with a bunch of broad flowering leaves, unique to this tomb. The first storey rises to a height of 9 m, the second storey surmounting it like a drum. The destruction of nearly half of the tomb allows a clear view of the interior decoration, which is equally remarkable. It is well worth scrambling down the slope to the field below to obtain a more distant view, which in the evening light is particularly rewarding.

Next to the Tomb of Bibi Jalwindi is the tomb and mosque of **Jalal al-Din Surkh**. "It was presumed" writes Dr. Ahmad Nabi Khan "that the devoted visitor coming to the tomb to offer *fateha* and to pay homage to the personage lying buried there, might like to pray in a nearby situated mosque attached to it." The mosque of Jalal al-Din Sukh belongs to the flat roofed class of tombs and mosques in Uchchh. It too has suffered damage at various times,; an inscription in Persian on either side of the Mihrab records that it was repaired by Mulla Ahmad under the orders of Sheikh Hamid in 1617. The tomb of Saint Jalaluddin Surkh Bukhari, a 13th century saint, is an oblong room supported by 40 wooden pillars. It is still visited by pious Muslims today.

As Dr. Khan concludes "Today, the dust laden Uchchh Sharif is a small town of little consequence...Its narrow streets and small houses are mostly unsightly. Even its mosques and mausolea have lost their splendid colour. In fact, the most important ones have sacrificed their halves and much of their original revetment to the ravages of time and tide. None the less, the city is still revered by the devotees of those who are lying buried there. They flock to their tombs and their Khanqahs ceaselessly to offer *fateha* and to seek solace from worldly woes. It seems that the practice will continue for ever."

If you are continuing S from Uchchh you can take the road to **Tarind Muhammad Panah** (18 km to the SW) and straight on to **Zahir Pir** (48 km) where you can turn left to rejoin the crowded National Highway at Khanpur (21 km). Zahir Pir is connected with **Mithankot** (25 km) on the W bank of the Indus by a bridge of boats, which is then directly connected with Dera Ghazi Khan (129 km to the N) and Jacobabad (204 km) to the W. 5 km NE of Khanpur is a road which leads S to the Indian border (109 km) and the town of Jaisalmer, a further 87 km across the Thar desert. The border remains closed. The National Highway goes through Khanpur to **Rahim Yar Khan** (47 km) across more richly irrigated land, densely populated and very busy. In Rahim Yar Khan you can turn right to cross the Indus by the **Guddu Barrage** to Kashmor (68 km). The National Highway goes SW through Sadiqabad, crosses the Sind border to Ubauro (68 km) and goes on through Ghotki to **Sukkur** (108 km).

LAHORE TO DERA ISMAIL KHAN

The route goes W across the now-fertile plains of the Punjab irrigation system, passing through Faisalabad, one of Pakistan's most rapidly growing cities

Leave Lahore from the NW and cross the Ravi by the new bridge. Turn left on to the Sheikhupura road and then fork left after 400 m for Jaranwala (100 km) and **Faisalabad** (37 km).

Faisalabad

Population 1.4 million

	Jan	Feb	Mar	Apr	May	Jun	Jul	Aug	Sep	Oct	Nov	Dec	Av/Tot
Max (°C)	19	22	27	34	40	41	38	37	37	34	28	22	32
Min (°C)	5	8	13	18	24	28	28	27	25	18	10	6	17
Rain (mm)	16	18	23	14	9	29	97	97	29	5	2	8	346

Formerly Lyallpur, after Sir James Lyall, Governor of Punjab, re-named Faisalabad on 1 Sep 1977 in honour of King Faisal of Saudi Arabia. The town, founded in 1890, is now Pakistan's third largest city, though it seems destined to be overtaken by the twin city of Islamabad-Rawalpindi by the end of the century.

It has experienced phenomenal growth, rising to its present population from a mere 72,000 in 1947, and is a major industrial town. That industrialisation was based originally on the cotton production made possible by the canal colonies which grew up after the building of the Lower Chenab Canal in the 19th century. Prior to that it had been a waste land known as Sandal Bar which was inhabited by tribal people, mainly from Gujranwala, Jhumra and Rajoa, constantly warring to take possession of the pastures.

Up to the time of the arrival of the British, the old tribal custom of paying *tarni* or grazing tax by the lesser tribes to the chiefs of the dominant tribes continued. The town itself was laid out in the the shape of the Union Jack, with diagonal roads radiating from the central clock tower.

Local industries The centre of the textile industry, Faisalabad is also well known as an agricultural market for cotton and as the region's granary. Several textile mills have their offices on the 4th floor in the MCB Building on Circular Rd.

Places of interest The country's first **Agricultural University** is in Jail Rd. The city's 8 bazaars and mosques centre around the **Clock Tower.**

Hotels A *Serena*, Club Rd. T 32026, Cable: Serena Faisalabad, Telex: 43453 Serena Pk. 148 rm. A modern hotel with all facilities plus golf, squash and tennis. Good, though expensive restaurants – *Jhelum, Bahar Court* and *Basant Court Barbecue*. **D** *Ripple*, 18 A People's Colony, T 40973. 12 rm, some a/c. Restaurant, car hire. **D** *Rays*, Allama Iqbal Rd (Govt College Rd), T 24006. 24 rm. Central a/c. *Babar* and *Al Khayyam* restaurants recommended. Flying Coach stop is nearby. **E** *Al-Khayyam*, Amin Bazaar, Clock Tower, T 30188. 17 rm, with bath. Central a/c. Good restaurant. **E** *Al-Javed*, Kutchery Rd, T 27689. 20 rm, with bath. **F** *Super*, Bhawna Bazaar, nr Clock Tower, T 22726. 22 rm, with bath. A couple of others of similar standard are **F** *Al-Mehr*, Chiniot Bazaar, T 248883 and **F** *Midway*, P35 Midway St, Kutchery Bazaar, T 24595. Restaurant.

Restaurants The best are in the top hotels. Peoples Colony has several – *Deigo* at 241, T 41410, *Four Seasons* at D Ground, T 42872, *Kabana* at 2A, T 40011. Also several fast food places nearby – *Sanza Burger*, 19 D-D, Commercial Area, T 40152, *Spinrose*, 243 B-D, T 42910, *Kabana Snacks* opp Radio Pakistan, T 30188 and *Yummy's 36* Ice cream Parlour at 239 B, D Ground, T 45575.

Sports Faisalabad is one of Pakistan's major **cricket** centres, hosting Test matches.

Chamber of Commerce and Industry, 2nd Floor, National Bank Building, Jail Rd, T 23039.

Travel agents Bluesky, T 23231 and Royal, T 34394 are in Ahmed Mansion, Sargodha Rd. Dreamland, opp District Court, Circular Rd, T 25053. Prince, 9 Jinnah Market, Circular Rd, T 28379. United Air Travels, 160 Kutchery Rd, T 34012.

Air Services PIA Domestic services fly to major towns. PIA, New Civil Lines, T 24001.

Rail To Lahore *78 Exp*, daily, a/c, 0615, 2 hr; *84 Exp*, daily, 0720, 3 hr; *38 Exp*, daily, 1035, 3 hr; *86 Exp*, daily, 1655, 3 hr. Rly Reservations, T 5976, Enquiries, T 23965. **Khanewal** (for Multan) *Multan Exp*, 56, daily, 0455, 4 hr.

Buses Punjab Road Transport Corporation (PRTC) runs deluxe buses between inter-city routes. Daily service to **Chak**, at 1630, to **Chiniot** at 1830, to **Lahore** at 0730 and 0830, to **Peshawar** at 2115. Frequent services to **Lahore** from 0530-2030 Rawalpindi, 7 buses from 0800-2230 and **Sargodha**, every 30 min from 0600-1800. The Bus Stop in the centre is on Shahrah-e-Allama-Iqbal where you get buses to W and S including Multan, Sargodha and Jhang. GTS buses for Lahore (2 hr 30 min) from Central Bus Station, N of the town.

The private companies, Flying Coach T, 24006, which runs faster a/c coaches and New Khan Road Runner , T 23115, have their stops on the same road. Blue Lines, T 23155 and Farrukh Flying Coach, T 31969.

The road W goes through *Jhang* (79 km *Population* 250,000) and then SW to Daraj. If you miss the sign to the Trimmu Barrage and cross the railway line you have gone too far. The main road crosses the Chenab River by the *Trimmu Barrage*. To the S runs the Trimmu -Sidhnai Canal, opened in 1965, part of the great system diverting water from the **Chasma dam** on the Indus through to the Jhelum just S of Sargodha, and finally down to Bahawalpur on the Sutlej. From the barrage it drives straight across the *Thal* desert, which is now been converted into irrigated farm land. The road goes through the tiny settlements of Suro (25 km), Haiderabad (23 km) and Mamkera (25 km) before crossing the main S-N road between Muzzafargarh and Mianwali at **Nageriwala** (23 km). Cross the main road to Bhakkar (21 km) and Darya Khan (18 km), then turn left to cross the Indus into NW Frontier Province and Dera Ismail Khan (15 km).

LAHORE TO BANNU

From Lahore take the road out to the NW across the Ravi. Fork right onto the dual carriageway road and follow the road to

Sheikhupura (39 km). Once known as **Jahangirabad**, Sheikhupura was a favourite hunting place for the Mughal Emperor and later on for Aurangzeb's eldest brother, **Dara Shikoh**. The hunting lodge (1616) and the **Hiran Minar**, built in memory of his pet antelope "Maharaj", and the huge fort, constructed of brick rather than the stone more common in Mughal forts, can still be visited. Follow the main road into town.

Go straight over at the main N-S crossing (Gujranwala-Faisalabad Road) and turn left after 300 m. Most of the buildings in the fort date from the period when it was occupied by Rani Nakayan, wife of Ranjit Singh. Note particularly her **octagonal garden house** in the SW corner, with an inscription and paintings of the 10 gurus over the door. You may be told that you need permission to visit the fort from the Director of Archaeology, Northern Circle, Lahore, but as with other sites in Pakistan, this is unpredictable. Gentle persuasion of the keeper may be necessary if you have not obtained permission in advance, as the Fort buildings are now occupied by the police. To visit the Hiran Minar you could in theory reach it by yet another of S Asia's **'underground tunnels'**, in this case supposed to have been built by Jahangir to link the hunting lodge with the minar.

A quicker route is to continue out of Sheikhupura on the Sargodha road 4 km. Cross the railway and turn right, and after a further 2 km turn left over the canal. There is a square artificial lake and an octagonal tower (99 steps to the top) in a most attractive setting.

Return to the Sargodha road to **Pindi Bhattian** (67 km). From Pindi Bhattian you can make a diversion of just over 30 km to the delightful town of **Chiniot**, crossing the Chenab there to continue to Sargodha via Satiwala and Lalian.

Chiniot (*Population* 135,000), the sub-divisional headquarters for its tehsil, is on the left bank of the **Chenab**. It has been described as "the richest jewel set in one of Pakistan's most picturesque valleys", where the Chenab cuts through a low rocky outcrop and divides around a date palm covered island. Once famous as a centre of boat building, both wood and stone carving survive. Dark *shisham* wood is often used for inlay work with brass. **Craftsmen** from Chiniot are known to have worked on such artistic monuments as the Taj Mahal and Golden Temple in Amritsar as well as recent buildings such as the Minar e Pakistan in Lahore. The skill is passed down through generations and is practised by certain families. Although it is an exceedingly fine art, the artists are often illiterate.

There is plenty of fine wood carving to be seen on houses in the old central part of the town especially on doors, windows and balconies. The **mosque** was built in the 17th century. It is also believed that one of the 3 ancient universities in the Punjab (the other 2 being at Ajodhan and Taxila) was at Ajhan near here. At **Chenab Bridge** nearby there is an a/c *Restaurant* with beautiful lawns on the river bank.

The direct route to Sargodha (63 km) crosses the Chenab due W of Pindi Bhattian. **Sargodha**, established as a colony town in 1903, had ancient origins. Today it is an important route centre and market town for central Punjab, and the railway junction for trains from the NWFP. PIA's feeder service now connects the city with Islamabad. The airport and airlines offices are at **Bhagtanwala**, 20 km away. There is a charge for PIA transport to and from the city for passengers. It is also a centre of the textile industry, sugar production, and is an Air Force base.

At one time the local feudal society was based on agriculture. Some identify the city with skilled young riders in white turbans winning tent-pegging and riding competitions at Gymkhanas on their white chargers. The area is on a plateau of about 200 m, the Salt Range touching just the N of the region.

Continue to **Shahpur** (31 km) and cross the Jhelum River to **Khushab** (14 km). The road then runs due W across the northern stretch of the Thal desert, the Salt Range a wall of hills off to the right of the road less than 20 km away. Its highest peak at its western end reaches 1522 m.

The road passes through **Guniyal Mandi** (41 km), crosses the railway at Wanbhachran (24 km) and then goes on to *Mianwali* (24 km). There are rest houses in Mianwali which provide comfortable accommodation. If you are travelling S from Mianwali you can cross the Indus by the Chasma Barrage and travel down the good but single track road on the W bank to DI Khan.

To continue to Bannu go N, crossing the Indus either on the Jinnah Barrage or the older road and rail bridge just to the N. The *Jinnah Barrage* was built in 1942 but did not provide irrigation to the Thal desert until the full scheme began to be implemented after Independence in 1947. The older bridge gives excellent views of the extraordinary town of *Kalabagh*. The town has been described by Spate and Learmonth as "probably one of the thirstiest places in the world. It is built in close-packed hillside tiers, the roofs of one tier forming the street of the next above; the air is salt impregnated, roads cut through walls of salt, and the town is built on, one might almost say, masses of rock salt." There is a busy bazaar, lined with wood fronted shops, often ornately carved. A track leads NW from Kalabagh to **Kohat**. The only motorable road into the NW Frontier goes SW along the W bank of the Indus flowing the railway line to Isa Khel (45 km), then turns W to **Lakki** (46 km) and finally through Sarai Naurang to **Bannu** (47 km).

SIND

INTRODUCTION

The modern Province of Sind lies between 23°30' and 28°30' North and 66°42' and 71°10' East. The name of Sind is one of S Asia's oldest regional names, coming from the local name for the Indus River and ultimately giving its name to India. Today it is applied to the Province which runs S from the confluence of the five rivers of the Punjab, and across from the margins of the Thar desert in the E to the Kirthar desert ranges in the W. The monotony of the desert relief is broken by the bright green of the irrigated land and the sharp ridge of the Kirthar scarp. It was here that some of the world's earliest civilisations arose, at least contemporary with those of Egypt and possibly earlier. At **Amri** and at **Kot Diji** excavations have revealed evidence of a culture long pre-dating the Indus Valley Civilisation proper.

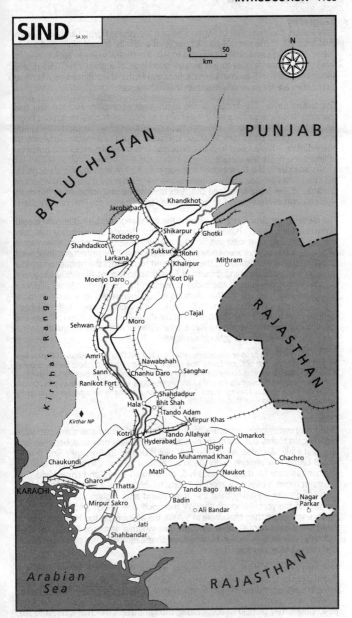

SIND SA 301

0   50
km

N

BALUCHISTAN

PUNJAB

Kirthar Range

Khandkhot

Jacobabad

Rotadero

Shikarpur

Ghotki

Shahdadkot

Larkana

Sukkur   Rohri

Mithram

Moenjo Daro

Khairpur

Kot Diji

RAJASTHAN

Sehwan

Moro

Tajal

Amri

Nawabshah

Sann

Chanhu Daro

Sanghar

Ranikot Fort

Shahdadpur

Hala

Bhit Shah

Tando Adam

Kirthar NP

Mirpur Khas

Kotri

Tando Allahyar

Umarkot

Hyderabad

Digri

Chachro

Chaukundi

Tando Muhammad Khan

Matli

Naukot

Gharo

Thatta

Tando Bago

Mithi

KARACHI

Badin

Nagar Parkar

Mirpur Sakro

Ali Bandar

Jati

Shahbandar

Arabian Sea

RAJASTHAN

Geography

Early visitors drew parallels between Sind and the young Egypt. Lambrick gives a vivid account: "The same 3 parallel tracts, of arid hills, alluvial plain, and sandy desert, lie in the same order from right to left, the central valley in each owing its fertility not to rainfall but to the annual inundation of a great river. Climatically and geologically, in their characteristic flora and fauna, the affinities between the 2 countries are far more obvious than their differences."

The Indus delta The history of the Indus is very complex, and the river has changed its course so frequently that hardly any part of the plains has not been covered by it at some point. The enormous quantitites of silt brought down each year – enough to cover over 1,000 sq km to the depth of a metre, according to one estimate – has caused frequent flooding. Two small but important outcrops of limestone break the surface.

At **Sukkur** in the N limestone hills just over 120 m high are cut through by the Indus. They provide a natural embankment at each end for the massive Sukkur Barrage. To the S the limestone outcrops offer some protection from floods to Hyderabad at its N end, and S to land occupied by a series of the Province's capitals.

The desert margins Certainly without the inundation of the Indus, Sind would almost certainly always have been a barren land, despite the evidence that over the last 5,000 years at least the climate may well have been getting drier than it once was. It has always been known as a difficult region for settlement. In general its boundaries are indistinct. To the E the desert runs across the frontier with India through the gradually rising ground of Rajasthan to Mount Abu, 500 km away. On the W the alluvium of the Indus is overlain by the much coarser alluvium brought down from the *Kirthar Ranges* which themselves form a much more impressive boundary along their N-S extent. This is a distinct region, the Kachho, running from the Suleiman Ranges to S of the Bolan Pass, "a flat desert of clay-like soil, virtually devoid of vegetable life: a natural barrier almost as formidable as the mountains which form its other boundaries."

In the far S, **the Delta proper** merges into the mud and salt flats of the **Rann of Kutch**, see page 932. In the words of Oscar Spate "the coast is fringed with dead creeks and dead ports. When high tides and Indus floods coincide the shoreline is flooded for over 32 km inland. In from the shore mangrove-flats are old sandy beach-ridges succeeded by clayey silts. On the whole the Indus delta is a savage waste." In that sense at least the delta proper could hardly be in greater contrast with that of the Nile.

Climate

Sind experiences great extremes of temperature. In winter the plains can have bitterly cold nights but warm sunny days. The coolness only lasts between late Nov and early Mar, after which the heat builds up rapidly. Physically Sind divides into 3 broad E-W regions, with the Indus at their centre. Climatically, however, the contrasts are far more obvious N-S, or between Upper and Lower Sind. The southern region's climate is modified considerably by the nearness of the coast, with far greater humidity than the areas inland and cooling sea breezes for 4 months of the year. Although the SW monsoon does reach Sind its effects are much less striking than elsewhere in S Asia, the air carrying too little moisture to bring significant rainfall. In N Sind the hot weather lasts for 7 months, with stiflingly hot nights as well as blazing days. Shade temperatures of 47°C-50°C are common in May and Jun.

Not for nothing is there a local proverb, as Spate comments, which says "Oh Allah! Having created Sewistan, why bother to conceive of hell?" Some visitors were equally unimpressed with Sind's climate, which one called "the unhappy valley" and another "the land of uncertainties". In political terms both descriptions may be held to apply today, though there is much of interest to see.

Economy

Agriculture The development of the lower Indus on which Sind's agriculture depends has been comparatively recent. Wheat and rice are the most important cereals, wheat being grown on just over 1 million ha, rice on 720,000 ha, making Sind responsible for the production of around 20% of Pakistan's wheat and nearly 50% of its rice. Cotton is by far the most important cash crop accounting for 25% of Pakistan's area under cotton, though as it is comparatively low yielding it provides less than a sixth of the country's final production.

Resources and industry Natural gas at Sui provides Sind with a vital resource, supplying Karachi with a source of power and a feedstock for fertiliser. 2,500 million cu m of gas came from Sind in the 1980s. The most striking development has been in **oil production**, where output rose from 1.7 m barrels in 1984 to over 8 m barrels in 1990. Sind is also Pakistan's largest single producer of electricity, accounting for 12 Bn KW in 1990.

The limestone outcrops at **Sukkur** and **Hyderabad** have allowed cement industries to be set up, and Sind's suitability for cotton growing has given the Province its most important agricultural raw commodity for the cotton industry. **Cotton spinning** and **weaving** mills have been set up at Khairpur. Industrial activity is completely dominated by Karachi, which has expanded from its traditional port activities and cotton industry. The railway connecting with its hinterland was opened in the mid-1860s, being extended to the Punjab by 1878. Since Independence an enormous surge in industrial activity has taken place, fuelled by the population growth, from under half a million in 1947 to perhaps 10 million today.

History

Sind lies near the cross-roads of S Asian history. To the S of the main lines of communication between the Iranian-Afghan plateaus and the Indian plains, it has often been influenced by events on its borders. In two respects Sind has a unique place in the history of S Asia. In Moenjo Daro it has the site of the major city of S Asia's oldest civilisation. Secondly, it was the region in which Islam arrived and became established 3 centuries before it made an impact elsewhere in the sub-continent. As such it developed a distinct cultural identity which to some extent has survived to this day.

Persians, Buddhists and Hindus Sind's geographical position has exercised a strong influence on its history. King **Darius the Great** sent an army between 515-500 BC to capture and incorporate the region into his Persian Empire, under whose administration it remained until Alexander the Great took the Empire apart between 325-323BC. The region then came under the Buddhist rule of the later **Mauryan** kings, evidenced by the stupa built on the central heights of Moenjo Daro's citadel. 500 year's later Sind was under the political control of a Rajput dynasty, before falling briefly under Persian control again.

In 622 AD a Brahmin, **Chach**, seized the throne, founding a dynasty which survived until it was defeated by the Muslim Arab forces of **Muhammad bin Qasim** in 711-12 AD, and it remained under **Umayyad** rule.

Arab rule brought major cultural developments. **Sindhi** developed as the regional language, and acquired its distinctive **Naksh** script, written like Arabic from right to left. Sindhi scholars became well known across the Muslim world, and the local **Sumra** dynasty of Muslims from Sind, which succeeded the Umayyad in 1058 AD continued the development of an Islamic tradition.

They were succeeded by another Muslim dynasty, the **Sammas**, ruling from **Thatta**. They made Persian the official language again to replace Arabic, coinciding with the development of the mystical *Sufi* movement and the flowering of Sufi poetry. In the 16th century Sind became integrated into the Mughal Empire. **Humayun**, fleeing Delhi with his wife from **Sher Shah**, passed through

Umarkot in 1540, where his son **Akbar** was born. In 1592, long after Akbar had succeeded to the Mughal throne and greatly extended the empire, Sind was brought directly under Mughal rule by his lieutenant **Mirza Abdul Rahim Khan-e-Khanan**. Mughal Governors remained in power in Lower Sind, ruling from Thatta, until 1737.

The British Sind was brought under British rule by Lord Napier as a by-product of the First Afghan Campaign in 1843. Acting against explicit instructions from London not to interfere with Sind he is reported to have telegraphed his announcement of the capture with the Latin word *Peccavi* – I have sinned. Incorporated into the British Indian Presidency of Bombay, this opened the doors to large numbers of Hindu and Parsi merchants to settle in Karachi. Many left at Independence.

Social indicators Literacy M: 40% F: 22% Population Urban: 43% Rural: 57%.

Travel hints
In addition to the safety precautions emphasised throughout this book, travel in Sind and Baluchistan demands special precautions against extreme temperatures and especially the very low humidity. It is often best to be well covered – towelling is very useful, especially if you can wet it from time to time. Skin dries very rapidly, and you need to take plenty of moisturising cream. Also take plenty of bottled water to drink.

Warning It is essential to check before travelling that the routes you intend to follow are safe. Even where it is not compulsory to travel with an armed guard, at the moment it is always best to travel accompanied.

KARACHI

The capital of the Sind Province, the largest city in Pakistan, Karachi has grown from the old fishing village of Kalachi-jo-Goth, at the mouth of the Indus as it enters the Arabian Sea. It is also the country's major commercial and industrial centre with its premier port and an international airport.

Population 6.7 million (1991 est.) *Altitude* Sea Level

	Jan	Feb	Mar	Apr	May	Jun	Jul	Aug	Sep	Oct	Nov	Dec	Av/Tot
Max (°C)	25	26	29	32	34	34	33	31	31	33	31	27	31
Min (°C)	13	14	19	23	26	28	27	26	25	22	18	14	21
Rain (mm)	7	11	6	2	0	7	96	50	15	2	2	6	204

Introduction

Karachi originated from a collection of islands – Baba, Shamspir, Keamari and Manora which supported small fishing villages, as well as the mainland around the bay, which acted as a good natural harbour. The Indus has frequently changed its course and in the early 18th century the port of **Banbhore** declined as the river moved away from it. Gradually Karachi replaced it and became the port where pilgrims to Mecca boarded their boats. The name 'Kalachi' is linked with the legend of a beautiful dancing girl who cast her spell on those she met.

Early history Pliny and Ptolemy writing in the 2nd century, mention a harbour here. Indeed it may be the place from which Alexander the Great's admiral **Nearchus** sailed with the fleet to the Euphrates in 326 BC, as surmised by Alexander Baille in 1885. The city became important in the 19th century when the British took the small fort on Manora in 1839. In 1843, Sir Charles Napier, the Governor of Sind, shifted the capital of the province to Karachi and made efforts to develop the new capital into a planned city and premier harbour. The old walled city still has the two gates from the time of the British occupation, the *Kharadar* (Saltwater Gate) to the sea shore, and the *Mithadar* (Sweetwater Gate) on the **Lyari river** bank.

English institutions of clubs, churches, gardens, zoos, schools and colleges transformed the old town, and it gained a reputation for its tennis, cricket and polo clubs. The earliest buildings include the **Masonic Hall** (1845) and the **Napier Barracks** (1847), which are still in use as Govt offices. In the early 1860s Karachi was linked by rail to the rest of the Province, and the building of the Mereweather Pier at the port was completed by 1882. The Port Trust was established in 1887 and the Municipality, in the following year. By the turn of the century it became the largest port for handling wheat exports from the E.

In 1914 the quaint street lamps which once used coconut oil (later kerosene), were replaced with electric lighting. Tramcars with steam engines joined bullock carts and horse drawn carriages. However, the accidents on the roads led to the withdrawal of the engines, and they were replaced with horses, which were protected from the strong sun by *sola topees**! (**See page 546**.) Links with the outside world improved with the opening of the first air strip at **Drigh Rd** in 1918 and international telephone links, a couple of years later. Karachi was considered the cleanest city of the British India.

Jinnah, the Father of the Nation, was born in Karachi in 1876, and attended the first Sind Madrassa (school) which was established in 1885. Partition from India dramatically transformed the city. Its population more than doubled to over a million by 1951 through the flood of migrants and refugees from India. Some 60% of Karachi's population were immigrants, bringing with them a culture and a society quite distinct from both that of earlier Karachi and of rural Sind. The growth of the city threatened to distort the whole economy of Pakistan, so in 1960 Gen Ayub Khan decided to move the capital away, to the new city of Islamabad.

Karachi's new city, with its high rise buildings, new mosques, housing colonies and sports stadia contrasts strikingly with the old walled town and yet it is not uncommon to see pavement fortune-tellers, hair-dressers and others earning a few rupees by carrying on their age old trades, while camel carts and colourful bazaars alternate with modern limousines and a steel and glass architectural wonder. Yet, while the city gets some of its power from the Nuclear Power Station, as many as 3 million people continue to be very poor.

Warning Since the late 1980s Karachi has become the capital of Pakistan's rival gangs and political factions, notably of the former refugees from India, (Muhajirs), native born Sindhis and Pathans from NWFP. As they contest increasingly violently for supremacy there are frequent assassinations and politically motivated murders. Some quarters of the town are unsafe to travel through, especially after dark, and it is always best to be accompanied by an experienced local person. In common with much of rural Sind the city has also suffered greatly from the activities of drug smugglers and dacoits (bandits). Take real care, especially if you have to travel after dark. Always take local advice before making any journey. Throughout 1990 and early 1991 private journeys out of the city by road were regarded as unsafe except where accompanied by armed guard. It is impossible to predict major improvements for 1992.

Places of interest

The beaches The sea is one of Karachi's attractions. Trips are available in local fishing boats to the **Keamari harbour** by moonlight to catch crabs. You can easily reach *Sandspit*, *Hawkes Bay* and *Paradise Point* (which form a continuous stretch of sand westwards) by car from the town (45 min) or by bus from **Lea Market**, N of the town (1 hr 30 min). Hawkes Bay is 25 km from the centre and buses leave at 0600, 1400, 1700 and return at 0900, 1600, 1800. Travelling W from Hawkes Bay, you will pass *Baleji Beach*, and then the **Karachi Nuclear Power Plant**, when the road turns inland before returning to the sea at Paradise Point. This is particularly good for snorkelling from Dec to Mar.

Warning Periodically there have been attempts by the police and coast guards to stop smugglers from operating from the beaches. You are advised not to go these beaches at night.

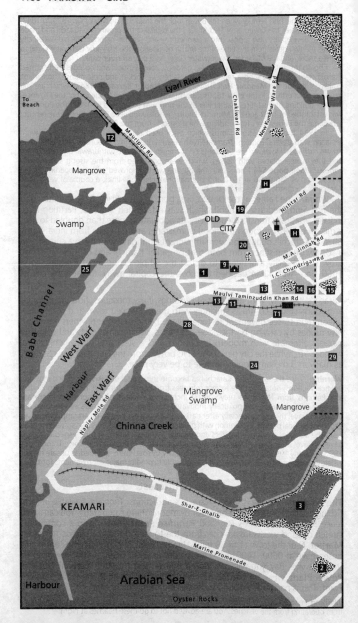

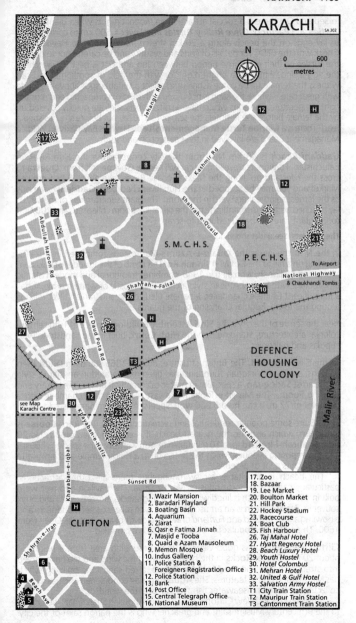

KARACHI
SA 302

N

0 ——— 600
metres

Mangopir Rd

Jehangir Rd

Kashmir Rd

Shahrah-e-Quaid

12

12

H

17

8

18

21

S. M. C. H. S.

P. E. C. H. S.

Abdullah Haroon Rd

33

32

Shahrah-e-Faisal

26

10

To Airport

National Highway
& Chaukhandi Tombs

31

27

22

H

Dr. Daud Pota Rd

DEFENCE
HOUSING
COLONY

Malir River

T3

H

7

see Map
Karachi Centre

30

12

23

Korangi Rd

Khayaban-e-Hafiz

Sunset Rd

H

Khayaban-e-Iqbal

CLIFTON

Shahrah-e-Iran

6

Beach Ave

4

5

1. Wazir Mansion
2. Baradari Playland
3. Boating Basin
4. Aquarium
5. Ziarat
6. Qasr e Fatima Jinnah
7. Masjid e Tooba
8. Quaid e Azam Mausoleum
9. Memon Mosque
10. Indus Gallery
11. Police Station &
    Foreigners Registration Office
12. Police Station
13. Bank
14. Post Office
15. Central Telegraph Office
16. National Museum

17. Zoo
18. Bazaar
19. Lee Market
20. Boulton Market
21. Hill Park
22. Hockey Stadium
23. Racecourse
24. Boat Club
25. Fish Harbour
26. *Taj Mahal Hotel*
27. *Hyatt Regency Hotel*
28. *Beach Luxury Hotel*
29. *Youth Hostel*
30. *Hotel Colombus*
31. *Mehran Hotel*
32. *United & Gulf Hotel*
33. *Salvation Army Hostel*
T1 City Train Station
T2 Mauripur Train Station
T3 Cantonment Train Station

In Sep and Oct there is a special attraction on moonlit nights when giant *Green Turtles* and *Pacific* or *Olive Ridley Turtles* travel over 1,500 km to come ashore to lay eggs on the beach along a 20 km stretch from Sandpit to Hawkes Bay. Check with the PTDC for details of visits and security and be careful not to disturb the turtles or their eggs. The period between Jun and Oct is best for watching the egg-laying, when on a bright night (or with the help of spotlights) you can witness the female turtle come ashore and select a suitable spot above high tide with great care – where the sand is not mixed with mud or compacted and is of the right temperature. The eggs which have a soft, rubbery shell are quickly covered up by the female before she re-enters the sea, but some say not before she has shed a tear! There is a **Marine Turtle Management Site** on Hawkes Bay. Pakistan Wildlife Management Board are involved in their protection and study.

Gaddani Beach is 48 km NW from the city centre across the Hub River, in Baluchistan. Foreigners travelling by car will need a Govt permit from **Quetta** to cross the river and go along the Makran coast. Buses take about 3 hr from Lea Market and you may be stopped at the Hub River checkpost. **Gaddani** is famous as the largest shipbreakers' yard in the world. The giant supertankers of the 1970s lay beached here for dismantling after the oil tanker boom collapsed, and 200,000 tonne giants are still being reduced to scrap.

The markets See under shopping.

In the N of the city is the **Quaid-E-Azam**'s Mausoleum completed in the 70s, standing on a hill to the E of **M A Jinnah Rd**. This tomb of the founder of Pakistan, Mohamad Ali Jinnah, who died in 1948, combines traditional and modern Islamic architecture with high N African style arches. Built mostly of white marble, it has a magnificent Chinese chandelier, Japanese tiled ceiling and Iranian silver railings around the tomb. Regular changing of the guards.

Near the centre of the city is the **Sind Assembly Building,** a piece of 19th century colonial architecture, standing opp the **High Court,** built in red sandstone with cupolas and balconies.

To the E is **Frere Hall.** The British structure, built in 1865 stands in landscaped gardens, and with Victorian fountains, has been redecorated in an Islamic style by the artist **Sadequan**, a specialist in Arabic calligraphy. It houses the Library and Reading Room. The Masjid-e-Tooba has a vast central circular chamber with a diameter of 72 m. It can hold 5,000 worshippers. A single minaret rises to 70 m.

In the S are some popular residential and recreational areas. The **Race Course** is in **Clifton**, which also has the nearest beach. It is easily reached on Bus No 20 from **Shahrah-i-Iraq Rd**, or a 10 min taxi-ride. You will notice the spacious houses and the imposing avenues which the British built, a Hindu temple and a mosque which attracts a lot of pigeons.

The beach is unsuitable for swimming but there are other attractions, particularly camel and horse rides nr Marine Drive. The pavilion and pier were built in 1923. The beach is lined with stalls selling snacks, trinkets, shell and onyx souvenirs. **New Clifton** is an amusement park with roller coasters, dodgems and a bowling alley. *Playland* and *Funland* draw big crowds of local people. Open from 1600. Th and Fri are popular for beach visits, so are crowded.

Clifton Viewpoint has good views of the surrounding area from a height of about 20 m – **Oyster Rocks** in the harbour, which the wind and sea have carved into strange shapes and the **Mohatta Palace**, a red sandstone building which has Mughal and gothic features. The **Aquarium** is air conditioned and has a good collection of fresh and seawater fish from all over the world.

Between Old and New Clifton is the Shrine of Abdullah Shah Ghazi, dedicated to the 9th century Muslim saint and preacher who is the patron saint of the city.

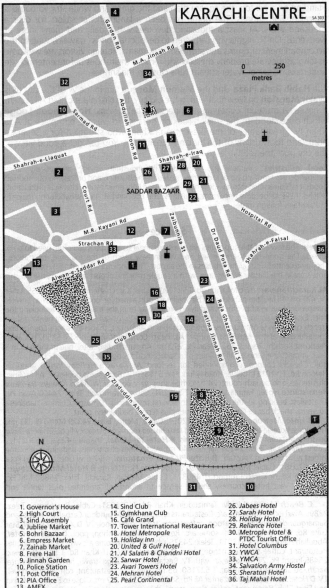

KARACHI CENTRE SA 303

0 250 metres

Garden Rd
M.A. Jinnah Rd
Sarmad Rd
Abdullah Haroon Rd
Shahrah-e-Liaquat
Court Rd
Shahrah-e-Iraq
SADDAR BAZAAR
M.R. Kayani Rd
Zaibunnisa St
Strachan Rd
Hospital Rd
Aiwan-e-Saddar Rd
Dr Daud Pota Rd
Shahrah-e-Faisal
Club Rd
Dr Ziauddin Ahmed Rd
Raja Ghazanfar Ali St
Fatima Jinnah Rd

N

1. Governor's House
2. High Court
3. Sind Assembly
4. Jublaee Market
5. Bohri Bazaar
6. Empress Market
7. Zainab Market
8. Frere Hall
9. Jinnah Garden
10. Police Station
11. Post Office
12. PIA Office
13. AMEX

14. Sind Club
15. Gymkhana Club
16. Café Grand
17. Tower International Restaurant
18. Hotel Metropole
19. Holiday Inn
20. United & Gulf Hotel
21. Al Salatin & Chandni Hotel
22. Sarwar Hotel
23. Avari Towers Hotel
24. Mehran Hotel
25. Pearl Continental

26. Jabees Hotel
27. Sarah Hotel
28. Holiday Hotel
29. Reliance Hotel
30. Metropole Hotel &
    PTDC Tourist Office
31. Hotel Columbus
32. YWCA
33. YMCA
34. Salvation Army Hostel
35. Sheraton Hotel
36. Taj Mahal Hotel

Standing on a hill top, the square plan and the green and white striped dome is typical of Sufi shrines. The dome has been a landmark for sailors for over a thousand years. At least a thousand devotees visit it daily and many more at weekends. On Th nights you can listen to devotional songs (*qawalis*) sung to the accompaniment of drums and stringed instruments. Foreign visitors are welcome as long as they are properly dressed and remove their shoes before entering. An underground sweet water stream runs close to the shrine.

The **Habib Bank Plaza** and the **Memon Mosque** are in the W of the city, as is **Wazir Mansion** on Newnham Rd in the old city, the birthplace of Md Ali Jinnah. It houses a museum containing his personal belongings. **Honeymoon Lodge** which once stood on the small hillock on Korangi Rd was the birthplace of Aga Khan IV, (grandfather of the present Aga Khan) who struggled for a separate homeland for Muslims of the Indian subcontinent. You can get a good view of the city from the spot.

Local industries Karachi has expanded its industrial activity dramatically since Independence. From a base of industries related to shipbuilding and processing of imported goods it has diversified into a wide range – heavy and light engineering, chemical production, textiles, have all become important industries. The city handles the overwhelming majority of Pakistan's foreign trade.

Services

Hotels The few available top hotels are of international standard but you often need to book ahead. The good hotels are central and within easy reach of the museum, rly stations, shopping centres. They all have buses to the airport. The moderately priced, fairly comfortable hotels are in the Saddar Bazaar area, with a couple near the airport and one on the beach.

AL *Karachi Sheraton Hotel*, Club Rd. T 521021, Cable: Karachisheraton, Telex: 25255 Asher Pk. 477 rm. All facilities plus tennis. The Shalimar Court aimed for long-stay guests has private, independent suites of bedroom and living area, away from the main block, overlooking the pool. Excellently equipped. Wide choice of restaurants – *European Express* continental dishes, French cuisine at *Le Marquis*, seafood specialities in *Al-Bustan*, snacks at *Fanoos Lounge* and confectionery at the *Maskada Lounge*. **AL** *Pearl Continental*, Club R. T 515021, Cable: Pearlcont Karachi, Telex: 23617 Pearl Pk. 270 rm. An outstanding hotel, one of the best in S Asia, immaculate service. All facilities plus sports includes pool, tennis, squash, badminton, golf. *Chandni Lounge* recommended for seafood. **AL** *Karachi Holiday Inn*, 9 Abdullah Haroon Rd. T 520111, Cable: Holiday Inn, Fax: 511610. 216 rm, some pool-side. All facilities plus tennis and squash court. 24 hr coffee shop very popular. **A** *Avari Towers Ramada Renaissance Hotel*, Fatima Jinnah Rd. T 525261, Cable: Avaritower, Telex: 24400 Avari Pk. The tallest building in the country, with several restaurants '*Dynasty*' Chinese, Japanese *Fujiyama*, snack bar *Le Cafe*, All amenities plus tennis/ badminton court.

B *Hotel Metropole*, Club Rd. T 512051, Cable: Metro, Telex: 24329 Metro Pk. 93 rm. The oldest hotel in town has modernised refurbished rooms on Regency floor. Chinese '*Four Seasons*' restaurant recommended. Tennis. **B** *Hotel Taj Mahal*, Sharah-e-Faisal. T 520211, , Cable: Mahalkar, Telex: 24257 Taj Pk. 440 rm. All facilities plus tennis, badminton and 'the largest auditorium in Pakistan'. **B** *Hotel Plaza International*, 18/2 Civil Lines, Dr Daud Pota Rd. T 520351, Cable: Marbleking, Telex: 25706 Plaza Pk. 106 rm. **B** *Hotel Midway House*, Star Gate Rd, nr Karachi Airport. T 480371, Cable: Midkap, Karachi, Telex: 25860 Mhl Pk. 2276 rm. Vast hotel, courtesy shuttle service to airport, all amenities plus tennis and badminton.

C *Beach Luxury*, Moulvi Tamizuddin Khan Rd. T 551031, Cable: Beachhotel, Telex: 23899 Avari Pk. 47 rm, some a/c. Restaurants recommended – outdoor *Casbah* for kebabsand *Samarquand* excellent for seafood, coffee shop, travel, shop, pool, TV. **D** *Airport Hotel*, Star Gate Rd, nr airport. 290 rm, some a/c. Restaurant, travel, shop, pool. **D** *Jabees Hotel*, Abdullah Haroon Rd. T 512011, Telex: 24325 Jabis Pk. 95 rm some a/c with bath and phone. Restaurant, coffee shop, exchange, shop. **D** *Imperial Hotel*, MT Khan Rd. T 511046, Telex: 25485 Imdht Pk. 27 rm some a/c with TV. Restaurant, exchange, travel, hairdresser. **D** *Hotel Sarah*, 30 SB 6 Parr St, Saddar. T 527160. 65 rm, some a/c. Restaurant, coffee shop, travel, TV. **D** *Hotel Sarawan*, Raja Gazanfar Ali Rd, Saddar. T 525121. 62 rm. Close to Empress Market and Fleet Club. Restaurant, coffee shop, travel, shop, secretarial service, TV. Courtesy pick up from airport and rly station and very good value. **D** *Hotel Mehran*, Shahrah-e-Faisal. T 515061,

Cable: Hotmehran, Telex: 23616 Mhk Pk. 181 rm, some a/c with TV. Restaurants, coffee shop, travel, secretarial, shop. Courtesy pick up from airport. Modern hotel, good value. **D** *Hostelerie de France*, opp Star Gate, nr airport. T 481101. 52 rm some a/c with bath. Restaurant, exchange, travel, indoor games. **D** *Gulf Hotel*, Saddar,. T 515831. 78 rm, some with TV. Restaurant.

The cheaper hotels, some very good value, are again in the **Saddar Market area** (several on Daud Pota Rd) and also nr the Cantonment Rly Station and in the old city. Some of these don't have a restaurant or western style toilets. **E** *National City Hotel*, Sarmad Rd, Saddar, T 513850. 60 rm, some a/c with bath, phone and TV. **E** *Hotel Savour*, 615/6 CC Area, B 1-2 PECHS, T 431361. Some rm with phone and TV. Restaurant. **E** *Spin Ghar Hotel*, CC Area, PECHS Block, T 448510. 10 d rm, some a/c with TV. **E** *Spring Hotel*, CC Area PECHS Block 2, T 431880. 15 rm some a/c with bath, phone and TV. **E** *Chilton Hotel*, Mir Karam Ali Talpur Rd, Saddar, T 520250. 74 rm some a/c with phone and TV. **F** *YMCA Hostel*, Strachen Rd nr the junction of Alwan-e-Saddar Rd, T 516927. Modern building with some rm with bath. Christians only, temporary membership fee charged and refundable deposit of Rs 100. Women only at the **F** *YWCA* on MA Jinnah Rd, T 711662. Dormitory beds in the **F** *Salvation Army Hostel* 78 NI Lines, Frere St behind Empress Market, T 714260.

Youth Hostel *Amin House Boys Scouts Assoc Youth Hostel*, Moulvi Tamizuddin Khan Rd, nr Cantonment Rly station accepts non-members who are foreign visitors. T 551491. Modern, some rm with bath and dormitory.

Restaurants The top hotels have good restaurants. **Chinese** – *ABC Restaurant*, Zaibunnisa St, T 511442. *Hong Kong*, Abdullah Haroon Rd, T 511971, recommended. In the PECHS area, *Kowloon* , T 435010 and *Tung-Nan*, T 439596 are on Allama Iqbal Rd and *Nanking*, and *Shanghai*, T 432645 are on Tariq Rd.
On Abdullah Haroon Rd there are **Snack bars** and Shezan's *International*, T 526715. Mereweather Rd also has several – *Ampi's*, T 514832, *The Village*, T 512880 and others near the Tower. Also suggested are *Silver Spoon* nr Tariq Rd, PECHS and *Agha's Tavern*, 26 Beaumont Rd, T 510843. Local food is available cheap around the Bus stations and Bazaars. At the Seabreeze Centre at Clifton, there are several places offering barbecues and snacks.

Clubs Boat Club, Moulvi Tamizuddin Rd, T 552057. **Sind Club**, Abdullah Haroon Rd, T 524924. **Karachi Gymkhana**, Club Rd, T 595912. **Yacht Club**, Grindlays Building, I I Chundrigar Rd, T 232127.

Banks Hours of Business: Mon-Th: 0900-1300. Sat, Sun: 0900-1200. Banks in I I Chundrigar Rd: **Allied**, T 227011; **Grindlays**, T228265; **Muslim Commercial**, Adamji House, T 224091; **National**, T 226781. **Chase Manhattan**, T 523070 and **Bank of Tokyo**, T 520171, both in Shaheen Commercial Complex, MR Kayani Rd. Habib Bank, HB Plaza, T 219111. **Exchange** Available in all the major hotels.

Shopping The bazaars in Karachi are a delight to walk through, both for atmosphere and for excellent buys. The **Saddar Bazaar** area is the main shopping centre, between Abdullah Haroon Rd and Zaibun-Nisa St, with the **Zainab Market** just N of Holy Trinity Church. The main roads have impressive large and small shops selling old and new oriental carpets, leather goods, garments etc interspersed with eating places while the bazaar stalls down the narrow alleyways can be the size of a box.
Zainab Market is crowded with tiny shops selling all kinds of craft items – onyx, copper, brass, wood inlay, *zari* (gold) embroidered and hand block-printed cloth and silver tribal jewellery. *Village* and *Marvi Handicrafts* are recommended. **Bohri Bazaar** sells cloth. To its N the **Empress Market**, with its Clock Tower, is a covered market selling groceries, meat, fish, fresh fruit and vegetables, used by local people. There are also sections selling metalware, embroidered cloths and lacquer work. The exotic sights, smells and sounds of an oriental bazaar is best experienced in the area N of the **M A Jinnah Rd** where you will find **Jodia Bazaar**, **Juna Market**, **Khajoor** (date) **Bazaar**. **Sarafa (jewellers) Bazaar** specializes in silver jewellery and also copper and brass articles. The new Sarafa Bazaar is in the **Liaquatabad Shopping Centre** opp the Supermarket.

Other shopping centres are **Jubilee Market**, nr Garden Rd; **Lea Market**, Memon Masjid, Nursery, off Shahrah-e-Faisal; Tariq Rd, PECHS and Clifton.
Karachi Duty Free Shop, Sharah-e-Faisal, T 441360. Imported goods from perfumes to whitegoods such as kitchen appliances are sold here, but to attract tourists, there are also local handicrafts, precious stones and carpets. *Cleandon Enterprises*, 9/10 Dr Ziaduddin Ahmad Rd, T 512561 is recommended for handicrafts. Otherwise for silver jewellery, precious and semi-precious stones, brass and copper ware and other craft items the shops in the top hotels

are worth exploring for good quality goods, although the prices are higher than the markets.

Clothing *Koel*, 36-1 Khayaban-e-Hafiz, DHS V, sells embroidered and printed cloth made up into local garments, as well as household linens. There are a number of boutiques selling good quality garments, both Pakistani and western – *Chaman*, 43 B-4 Block IV. *Cleos*, 4 D-2 Z Gizri Boulevard, DHS IV. *Haveli*, 10 C-1 Gizri Le, DHS IV. *Iridescence*, 10 A-7 Amir Khusro Rd opp American School. *Pashmina Fashions*, 183 C Block 2 PECHS. *Sehr*, 10 Services Club behind Hotel Metropole.

Carpets Pakistan is one of the top producers of hand-knotted wood and silk carpets. They are woven in the traditional style but are less expensive than the Persian originals. Several shops on Zaibunnisa St, Abdullah Haroon Rd, MA Jinnah Rd and numerous others. *Afghan Carpets*, D16 Block 8 Clifton, T 536561 and at Sheraton Hotel, T 527880; *Asian Carpet Palace*, 12 Ekneck Building, Zaibun-nisa St behind General Boot House, T 515864, *Charania Carpet Corporation*, 8th floor, Rimpa Plaza MA Jinnah Rd, T 729405; *Haris Carpets*, A 4/19 Zaibun-nisa St, T 512947; *Iran and Bukhara Palace*, Inverarity Rd, T 513449; *Md Siddiq and Sons*, Abdullah Haroon Rd, T 520841; *Sana Oriental Carpets*, 202 Ground floor, Panorama Centre, T 521052.

Jewellery The major hotels have jewellers in their arcades, including *Believe Star, Goldmine, Jewel Collection, Slavix* at the Sheraton and *Jewels International* and *Maharaja's* at the Holiday Inn. Numerous others on Zaibun-nisa St, Shahrah-e-Iraq and Abdullah Haroon Rd. In Saddar: *Aftab Jewellers,* T 513856 and *AShuja Jewellers*, T T 513197 both in Parr St; *Jewel Paradise*, Paradise Shopping Centre, T 520560 and *Mideast*, Hussain Centre, T 512621, both in Shahrah-e-Iraq; *Star Gold Queen*, Uni Shopping Centre, T 527151;

Leather goods including bags, shoes, jackets, coats are good buys. Some shops will make up articles within 24 hr – *Ace Handicrafts*, Hotel Holiday Inn, T 520111; *Asian Leather Kraft*, *Dice Gifts*, *Mr Leather* and others at the Sheraton Hotel, T 522240; *English Boot House*, Zaibun-nisa St, T 441649; *Khansahib Leather Garments*, A3 Zubaida Gardens, Shahrah-e-Faisal, T 448106; *Maliks International*, 81D Block 6 PECHS, T 447752.

Local transport The main Bus Stations are in Boulton Park, Cantonment Rly Station, Express Market, Saddar, Lea Market and Vegetable Market. **Bus Excursion Tours** during season. KTC from Saddar Terminal, Empress Market on Fri and holidays. To Seaview apartments via Clifton 0800-1900, every 30 min. To Paradise Point via Hawks Bay 0800 -1400, every hr; Return 0930 -1800. To Keenjihar Lake via Makli and Thatta: 0800, 0900 and return 1600, 1700. KTC Manager T 424395, Bus Depots: Korangi, T 311843, Mehran, T 402404, N Karachi, T 651362.

Entertainment Cinemas – On Garden Rd, Bambino, T 529648, Scala, Star, T 528788 and Lyric, T 528334. On MM Jinnah Rd, Capri, T 719904, Prince and Nishat, T 710535. Also Palace on Club Rd and Rio on Zaibun-Nisa St. The 3 Drive-In cinemas are on Rashid Minhas Rd. Auditoria – Adamjee Science College Auditorium, Business Recorder Rd, T 710259. Arts Council Open Air Theatre, MR Kayani Rd. Rex Auditorium, 27 Abdullah Haroon Rd, TR 523726. Rio Auditorium opp Panorama Centre, Fatima Jinnah Rd, T 524592. Rangoonwala Hall, 4/5 KDA Scheme, Block 4, Dhoraji Colony, T 418146.

Sports **Swimming**: Easily accessible beaches for swimming are within a radius of about 20 km of the town.

Warning Avoid the monsoon season from Jun to Aug when the currents can be strong and the sea very rough. Jellyfish can be a nuisance, especially in May and Jun. Sep and Oct are particularly good for surfing. The water is cool in the winter buts warms rapidly in the spring. If you are used to colder seas you will easily brave the water in winter.

You can hire huts which have showering and cooking facilities and this can be arranged beforehand in the city. Joy rides on colourfully bedecked camels and ponies are available. Hawkes Bay and Paradise Point are good for swimming, particularly French Beach at Hawkes Bay (somewhat exclusive since only cars are allowed to it, visitors on foot are turned away).

NB Islamic tradition requires you to dress decently and it is best to wear bikinis on private, hotel beaches only. Village women on the subcontinent usually bathe in the sea fully clothed.

Water sports Yachting, surfing and scuba diving. Diving Season from mid-Oct to mid-Mar when the sea is calm, clear and safe. *Buleji*, about 30 km W of Karachi, has a part submerged reef extending nearly 2 km out to sea, which at low tide is even safe for children wanting to snorkel. The rich variety of fish and the warm water make this an excellent spot for skin diving. The waters 1 km off shore are more challenging and it is best to hire an inflatable dinghy to take you out.

Turtle's Back is a special underwater bank between Gadani and Churna island. Karachi Diving and Salvage Agency, T 224101. Karachi Yachting Club, T 232127. Boating and crab fishing in the harbour and deep sea fishing: boat hire from Boat Basin at Keamari.

Museums

The **National Museum of Pakistan**, Burns Garden. Open 1000-1700, Sat free. The museum started in the **Frere Hall** in 1950 where it remained for 20 years until the impressive new purpose-built museum was ready in 1970. The new building is surrounded by lawns with palm trees and houses a rich archaeological collection from the Indus-Valley civilization and a good Ethnological Gallery. The ground floor has an auditorium, canteen and the reserve collection with galleries of artefacts, pottery, sculpture, art and ethnology on the 1st floor. On the 2nd floor there is a Manuscripts and Numismatics Hall.

The main entrance has been closed for several years as a result of student disturbances from the College opposite. The only entrance, with a sign only in Urdu, is now to the S of the Museum at the corner of M R Kiyani Rd and Dr Zia ud Din Ahmed Rd, about 1 km N of the Sheraton Hotel.

The presentation is disappointing. There is little sense of the dynamism of archaeological research and the significance of recent developments in work on such important themes as the early Indus Valley Civilisation, but there are still remarkable exhibits. The audio-visual aid used in the galleries lend an added dimension for those wishing to hear the stories of the periods told in sound and music.

First Floor Pre and proto-historic gallery. 5,000-1,500 BC, although there are many gaps. Chalcolithic very well represented – village cultures of Baluchistan and Kot Diji and Amri. Diorama of Moenjo Daro depicting life c 3000 BC.

Buddhist gallery Gandhara from sites in Taxila, Peshawar and the N, Swat, Dir, Punjab and parts of Sind dating from 3rd century BC to 6th-7th century AD. A passage, with displays of ornaments and jewellery joins this to the **Hindu Gallery** which has a limited collection of sculptures, mainly from Pakistan and Bangladesh dating from 6th to 11th century.

Muslim gallery (S wing, 1st floor) The exhibits from the 9th-14th century include ceramics, glass, textiles, metalware and scientific instruments including globes and astronomical instruments. The pottery, textiles and a coin excavated in Banbhore from the period dating from the 8th-10th century, are impressive. Arms and armoury from the late Mughal period are displayed on the verandah outside.

The Ethnological Gallery next to the Muslim Gallery and to the W, has representative display of culture of different regions of the country (as well as some tribal hill tracts of Balngladesh) and includes handicrafts, jewellery, fabrics, utensils and furniture.

Second Floor The **Manuscripts Hall** has a collection of documents, illustrated manuscripts, Mughal miniature paintings and interesting examples of calligraphy. A small collection of Coins, some as early as 3rd century BC, is displayed in a part of the Hall. The majority is kept locked and out of view, as a research collection. The Faizi Rehaman Gallery nearby, exhibits the artist's works.

Archaeological Museum, Karachi University, in 2 rooms in Dept of General History, was opened in 1966. Open 0830-1330. Closed Fri and holidays. A small teaching museum with limited scope.

Parks and zoos Bagh-e-Quaid-e- Azam, Polo Ground, Dr Ziauddin Ahmad Rd. Opp Holiday Inn, the park is being improved and has a Japanese Garden. Open 0700-1100, 1500-2300. Nishat Park, Safari Park, Univerisity Rd, T 466080. The plan is to ultimately cover 400 acres with an 'Open Zoo' with 18 separate enclosures, similar in style to safari parks around the world. There is a View Point on a hillock.

There are several other parks, including the Ahmad Ali Park, Aziz Bhatti Park, University Rd. Bagh-e- Jinnah (Frere Hall). Abdullah Haroon Rd. City Park, nr Sohrab Goth. Gabole Park, Hill Park. Jheel Park, KMC Park, Kashmir Rd. Zoological Garden, Garden Rd, T

Business hours Govt offices – Mon to Th: 0830- 1400. Sat, Sun: 0900- 1200, Fri Closed. Private offices – Sat – Thu: 0900- 1700, Fri Closed.

Useful addresses Foreigner's Registration Office, I I Chundrigar Rd. T 233737.

Cultural Centres Alliance Francaise, Plot St, 1 Block 8, Kahkashan, Clifton, T 530547. **Goethe Institute**, 256 Sarawar Shaheed Rd, T 514811. **Japan Cultural Centre**, 233 E I Lines, Somerset St, T 516439. **Pakistan Amercian Cultural Centre**, 11 Fatima Jinnah Rd, T 513836. **Pakistan National Centre**, 191 A, SMHS, T 43133. **Russian Cultural Centre**, Friendship House, 43/4 H, Block 6, PECHS, T 430342.

Foreign Representations Canada, Beach Luxury Hotel, T 551100. **France**, A 12, Md Ali Bogra Rd, Bath Island, T 532048. **Germany**, 90, Clifton, T 531031. **India**, 3 Fatima Jinnah Rd, T 514310. **Italy**, 85 Clifton, T 531006. **Japan**, 233 Raja G Ali Khan Rd, T 532219. **Kuwait**, St 19, Bl IV, Clifton, T 532855. **Nepal**, Textile Plaza, Off I I Chundrigar Rd, T 234458. **Sri**

Lanka, D6, 8B, KDA Scheme 1, T 439990. **Switzerland**, 98 Clifton, T 532038. **UK**, York Pl, Runnymede Le, Clifton, T 532046. **USA**, 8 Abdullah Haroon Rd, T 515081. **USSR**, 8/26 Flench St, T 512852.

Post and telegraphs International Direct Dialling and Telex and Fax facilities available at major hotels and the Central Telegraph Office. General Post Office, I I Chundrigar Rd, T 217328. Central Telegraph Office, I I Chundrigar Rd, T 226100.

Places of worship **Muslim** Defence Society Tooba Mosque; Memon Mosque nr Boulton Market; New Town Mosque; Hussainia Iranian Imambargah; Arambagh Mosque; Jacob Line Mosque; **Christian** Holy Trinity; St Andrews nr Empress Market; St Patricks Roman Catholic Cathedral on Shahrah-e-Iraq.

Hospitals and medical services Good medical facilities are available in govt and private hospitals, fully equipped to deal with emergencies. Aga Khan, Stadium Rd, T 420051. Civil, Baba-e-Urdu Rd, T 729719. Holy Family, Soldier Bazaar, T 718991. Jinnah Post Graduate Medical Centre, Rafiqui Shaheed Rd, T 512551. Karachi Adventist, MA Jinnah Rd, T 718613. Liaquat National, Stadium Rd, T 419612. Mideast Medical Centre, Khayaban-e-Iqbal, Clifton, T 531272. National Institute of Cardiovascular Diseases, Rafiqui Shaheed Rd, T 516716.

Chambers of Commerce American Business Council of Pakistan, 3rd Fl, Shaheen Commercial Complex, MR Keyani Rd, T 526436. Chamber of Commerce and Industry, Aiwan-e-Tijarat Rd, T 226091.

Airlines Foreign At Hotel Metropole, Mereweather Rd: **Air Canada, Alitalia**, T 511097. **Austrian Airlines** No 24, T 510241; **Cathay Pacific**, T 516525; **Continental Airlines**, No 24, T 515633; **Eastern Airlines**, No 143; **Royal Jordanian**, T 512026; **SAS**, T 515893; **Swiss Air**, T 512066; **Thai Airways**, T 515893; **TWA**, No 33, T 511779; **Wardair Canada**, No 14, T 515683.

At Avari Plaza, Avari Towers, 242 Staff Lines, Fatima Jinnah Rd: **American Airlines**, T 526466; **Bangladesh Biman**, T 510069; **Canadian Airlines**, T 526520; **Canadian Pacific**, T 510728; **Egypt Air**, T 528066; **Emirates**, T 527044; **Interflug**, T 512235; **Japan Airlines**, T 510161.

Aeroflot, Taj Mahal Hotel, Sharah-e-Faisal, T 529324. **Air France**, T 520131 and **British Airways**, Hotel Holiday Inn, Abdullah Haroon Rd, T 516076. **Air Lanka**, 8 Services Club, Ext Building, Mereweather Rd, T 514421. **Gulf Air**, Kashif Centre, Shahrah-e-Faisal, T 523737. Iberia, T 529260 and **Indian Airlines**, T 522035, **Lufthansa**, T 515811. Pearl Continental Hotel, Club Rd. **Kuwait Airways**, Hotel Sheraton, Club Rd, T 513272. **Malaysian Airlines**, Sheraton Hotel, T 516491. **Air Portugal**, T 510600 and **Qantas**, T 513636, PIA Building, Strachen Rd. KLM, G6 Haroon Chamber, Main Civic Centre, Garden Rd, T 829685. **Royal Nepal Airlines**, 126-8 Hotel Mehran, Shahrah-e-Faisal, T 525683. **Saudi Arabian Airlines**, Taj Mahal Hotel, Sharah-e-Faisal, T 528241. **Singapore Airlines**, 2 and 3 Services Club, Extension Building, Mereweather Rd, T 521213. **Syrian Arab Airlines**, 6 Club Rd, T 515820.

Travel agents Aly's Travels, 21 Sheraton Hotel, T 521447. Al-Ghazi Travels, 19 Price Complex, Frere Town, Clifton Rd, T 514388.

Tourist offices and information Pakistan Tourism Development Corporation (PTDC), Tourism Information Centre, Shafi Chambers, Club Rd, T 511293 and at the International Arrival Lounge, Terminals 1 and 2, Karachi Airport. Information Cell, Hotel Metropole, T 512811. Keenjihar Lake Booking Office, T 516252 and Ziarat Resort Booking Office, T 510301.

Air Services PIA flies to India, Nepal, Bangladesh, Sri Lanka and Maldives from Karachi. To **Delhi** Wed, Fri, Sat (3 hr); **Bombay** Mon, Tues, Wed, Th, Sat (2 hr 45 min); **Kathmandu** Mon, Th (4 hr 30 min); **Dhaka** Th (5 hr 30 min).

Weekly flights to principal airports in other countries in **Asia**, including Tokyo (10 hr 30 min), Hong Kong (5 hr 30 min), Beijing, Manila, Kuala Lumpur, Singapore, Bangkok. Also weekly flights to several **European** (London, 8hr), **Middle Eastern (Jeddah, 3hr 30 min and Abu Dhabi, 1 hr 45 min) airports and to New York** (19 hr 30 min) and **Toronto**.

Rail Peshawar *Awam Exp*, 13, daily, 0910, 29hr 30min; **Rawalpindi-Islamabad** *Zulfiqar Exp*, 5, daily, AC, 0600, 32hr 35min; *Awam Exp*, 13, daily, 0910, 25hr 20min; **Lahore** *Zulfiqar Exp*, 5, daily, AC, 0600, 26 hr; *Awam Exp*, 13, daily, 0910, 20hr; **Quetta** *Bolan Mail*, 3, daily, AC, 1135, 20hr 20min; *Sind Exp*, 45, daily, 0735, 23hr; **Multan** *Shalimar Exp*,105, daily, AC, 0630, 11hr; *Awam Exp*, 13, daily, 0910, 13hr 35min; **Hyderabad** *Shalimar Exp*,105, daily, AC, 0630, 2hr. *Shah Latif Exp*, 145, daily, 0700, 2hr 35min; **Moenjo Daro** *Moenjo Daro Exp*, 33, daily, AC, 2000, 9hr 25min.

Railway Stations Cantonment Reservations: T 515569, Enquiries: T 510678, 513965. City Reservations: T 226741, 226707. Enquiries: T 232200, 236349.

Road Buses A/c Buses to Lahore, Multan, Peshawar, Sargodha, Bannu and Tank and non a/c to Mingora, Mansehra, Bannu and Chakwal with alternative en route stops.

Deluxe and 'Flying' coaches: **To Badin** via Makli, Thatta and Sajawal, hourly 0800 from Lea Market; **Bannu,** 0730, 0900, 1200, 1600, from Sohrab Goth, via Super Highway or National Highway (20 -22 hr); **Hyderabad,** via Thatta on National Highway (Govt bus), 0600-1500 every hr, from Lea Market (4 hr, 1 hr stop at Thatta); via Super Highway (Private bus), 0600-2400 every 30 min, from Boulton Market (2 hr 30 min); **Kohat,** 0700, 1200, 1600, from Sohrab Goth (22 hr); **Larkana,** 1600, 1700 from Boulton Market. To **Mansehra** 1400, one each from Sabzi Mandi, Cantonment Rly Station, Patel Para (36 hr); **Mingora** 0800 from Lea Market and Pathan Colony (36 hr); **Mirpur Khas** every 30 min from Boulton Market (4 hr); **Quetta,** 0800, 1600, 1700, from Lea Market, Sabzi Mandi, University Rd (12 hr).

Coach Services: Blue Lines, T 511011; Chilton, T 713242; Prince, T 228928; Qadri, T 514546; Super International, T 417873. Sind RTC services from Karachi to Tourist spots at Thatta, Makli and Keenjihar as well as long distance buses to Hyderabad, Badin, Sanghar, Sukkur and Dadu. Enquiries, T 718790.

Excursions **Manghopir** 40 km. Hot sulphur springs which are believed to help sufferers of skin diseases and rheumatism. The shrine to the Muslim saint Mangho is guarded by snub-nosed crocodiles which legend says he brought with him from Arabia in the 13th century. Buses from Lea Market.

KARACHI TO QUETTA

The road from Karachi to Quetta was built as part of the abortive programme of the 1960s for co-operation between Pakistan, Iran and Turkey called Regional Co-operation for Development (RCD). It has recently been resurfaced and is a comparatively fast route, the main road from Karachi to Baluchistan. There are regular buses from Karachi. By car it takes up to 12 hr. The only accommodation en route is in the towns of Kalat, Khuzdar and Las Bela, but the hotels are extremely basic.

The first stage from Karachi to **Las Bela** (160 km; *Population* 35,000) crosses the flat coastal plains to the N of the city. It skirts the S end of the Kirthar range as it dips finally under the coast line. The road passes inland of the coastal town of **Sonmiani** on to **Uthal**, passing through coconut groves. It then climbs from the triangular-shaped alluvial lowlands of the **Purali River** around **Las Bela**, a market town and burial place of Sir Robert Sandeman, due N to the Kalat Plateau, following the river for much of the way. From Las Bela itself it passes through **Wad**, crosses a pass, and down to **Khuzdar**, (227 km; Population 32,000) in the valley of the **River Kolachi** and then climbs through **Surah** up to the Kalat Plateau.

Like the Kirthar range to the E, the Kalat Plateau is part of the great limestone system that dominates SE Baluchistan. The **Kirthar Range** itself is topped by Spitangi limestone, between 25 million and 50 million years old, and raised from the sea bed as the Indian Plate pushed N into the Asian landmass. The Kalat Plateau is formed of the same limestone, and lies at a height of between 2,100 m and 2,440 m.

The whole region is subject to severe earthquakes, and **Kalat**, (160 km; *Population* 29,000) former capital of the Khans of Kalat (all-powerful in the 18th and 19th centuries), was almost totally destroyed by the great Baluchistan earthquake of 31 May 1935. The Khan of Kalat's castle at **Miri**, now a ruin, still dominates the town. Kalat itself has been rebuilt, largely with mud walled houses. This is a region, close to Shi'a Iran, where Shi'a piety has long been prominent, testified by the shrine of the 11th century **Sheikh Abdul Qadir Jalani,** on top of another of Kalat's hills.

Kalat

	Jan	Feb	Mar	Apr	May	Jun	Jul	Aug	Sep	Oct	Nov	Dec	Av/Tot
Max (°C)	9	12	16	22	28	31	32	31	28	23	17	13	22
Min (°C)	-4	-2	2	6	10	13	16	15	9	4	-1	-4	5
Rain (mm)	55	47	37	15	6	3	31	14	2	0	3	19	233

Stretching across to the W and SW of Kalat is one of Pakistan's most difficult environments. In Spate's words, "the landscape of southern **Makran** is bizarre". As Sir Thomas Holditch, Surveyor General of India put it in 1910 "the brazen coast is washed by a molten sea, while inland gigantic cap-crowned pillars and pedestals are balanced in fantastic array about the mountain slopes, with successive strata so well defined that they possess all the appearance of massive masonry construction."

Even high on the plateau there is very little rainfall, but dramatic temperature contrasts. Holditch reported changes of temperature of nearly 45°C in 24 hr as quite common, and you need to be prepared for extreme cold as well as heat. Agriculture is a hazardous business. One district administrator said of Kalat in 1907 that 'dry crop cultivation is like hunting the wild ass', and farmers can expect only one full crop every 5 years.

From Kalat to **Quetta** (145 km) the road runs N down off the Kalat plateau through *Mastung*. It is a barren and uninviting landscape, sparsely populated with only the thinnest of vegetation. The road crosses the railway line to Iran and joins the main road from the Iranian border to Quetta. The *Koh e Mahran* summit on the right is nearly 3,300 m. This part of the journey takes about 3 hr.

KARACHI TO HYDERABAD via National Highway

The main contrasts you see crossing Sind are between the uncultivated desert and the rich, fertile plains of the canal irrigated areas. Apart from the W borders of the Province, the landscape itself is almost dead flat. The Super Highway which crosses the barren desert from Karachi to Hyderabad shows you the bareness of a hot land without water. The National Highway to the S is quite different. It passes through a region which has many old settlements, which you can see if you have some extra time for detours. Some are strongly recommended. The journey is just over 200 km and takes 3.5 hrs.

Warning Check in Karachi that conditions are safe.

This area of Lower Sind has seen a succession of political and cultural influences. In 641 AD it was visited by the Chinese traveller **Yuan Chwang**, a Buddhist monk who was particularly interested in Buddhist sites. Within 70 years the troops of **Mohammad bin Qasim** were taking their heavy artillery up the distributaries of the Indus to launch fierce assaults on Sind's cities. Their 2 year campaign established Islam as a permanent political force in the region. Some of the sites of battle have now been obliterated by the changing course of the Indus, others are speculative, while yet others are clearly identifiable and can be seen on the National Highway and diversions from it. From Karachi travel past the airport E towards **Thatta**.

Chaukandi Tombs (27 km) are on the left of the road. A 13th-16th century site along a low ridge in open ground, the site has superbly carved sandstone tombs. Many are built out of rectangular slabs placed one on top of the other in tall pyramidal fashion, 2- 4 m high, while some are pillared with a flat roof.

You will notice that the women's graves have reproductions of their jewellery – necklaces, bangles, earrings and rings while the men's have horses and riders as well as abstract and floral motifs. Some of the graves belong to Baluchi tribesmen who are said to have come from Syria, while others show Rajput influence. The male graves are symbolically capped by a turban shape, just as the spot on a battlefield would be marked by the sword and turban of a fallen Rajput soldier. **Buses** from Karachi's Lea Market.

The road continues to **Banbhore** (64 km from Karachi), an archaeological site over a wide area of ruins of the periods Scythian – Parthian, Hindu – Buddhist and Islamic (mainly Arab). Banbhore is claimed to be the oldest Muslim site on the subcontinent as tradition now links it with the ancient port of **Debal**, though this remains speculation.

The oldest known Muslim coins, an 8th century mosque (modelled on the one at **Kufa**), and inscriptions have been found. Excavations have also revealed Greek pottery, suggesting that the site may date from the time of Alexander. The pottery is similar to that found in **Taxila** and dates from the 1st century BC, **see page 1109**. Pottery from Syria – thin, white, and unglazed, with raised Kufic inscriptions – and later glazed vessels which show a strong Persian influence, have also been excavated. Superb glass and ceramics from Banbhore are displayed in the National Museum, Karachi.

Debal Up to the 8th century there were periods of Buddhist and Hindu occupation. Debal was the port where the 17 year old Arab conqueror **Mohd Bin Qasim** is believed to have landed in AD 712 in command of the troops of the Baghdad Caliphate. First reports of the region were bleak. "Its water is dark and dirty; its fruit is bitter and poisonous; its land is stony and its earth is saltish." Their opinions were soon to change when they discovered that the parts of the plains that were inundated periodically by the Indus floods could also be extremely fertile and prosperous.

Banbhore Mohd bin Qasim first took the towns on the delta and then proceeded N along the Indus, and within a few months occupied Multan. Remains of the old 8th century city walls at Bhanbore show the S gate opened onto the creek, while the N and E gates opened towards the lake in the N.

A small on-site museum, established in 1960 is open daily, except 1st Mon in month. Summer (Apr-Sep) 0800-1200, 1400-1830. Winter (Oct-Mar) 0900-1600. 2 halls with exhibits of pottery, artefacts, fragments of bones and sculpture, jewellery, coins, inscriptions from 3rd century BC-13th century AD.

Travelling through this part of S Sind today, you can get some impression of its fertility. To catch it at its best you need to leave early in the morning in late autumn or early spring. Then you see the fresh green of young wheat, the gold of harvested millet, and dazzling white open cotton pods. Many of the canals and roads themselves are lined with magnificent *babul* trees. The land throughout this section of the journey is almost dead flat.

To visit ***Haleji Lake Bird Sanctuary***, take turning on left, 82 km from Karachi, just before the village of **Guju**. Haleji lake, which supplies Karachi with water, is one of the most important and largest waterfowl sanctuaries in Asia.

Migratory aquatic birds come from long distances and the 70 varieties include flamingoes, pelicans, herons, partridges, egrets and pheasant-tailed jacanas as well as marsh crocodiles. You can drive around the lake on an 18 km unmetalled road which is on an artificial embankment. Special hides and a Visitors' Centre are provided for birdwatchers. You can reserve simple *Dak Bungalows*. Contact **Chief Engineer**, Karachi Water and Sewerage Board which supplies water to the city from the reservoir. PTDC offers tours.

Makli Hill, just before reaching **Thatta** (nearly 100 km from Karachi). An isolated tract of raised ground surrounded by alluvium, it has been held sacred by the Sindhis for over10 centuries and is considered to be the world's largest necropolis.

The necropolis An area of 15.5 sq km is said to contain 1 million graves, some of kings and queen, saints, scholars and generals, and many of ordinary soldiers. Those dating from the 14th century are sandstone tombs with beautiful carvings, some with perforated work and blue glazed-tile decorations. The majority of the tombs are from the 16th and 17th centuries, the later period including Mughal tombs. The site on the ridge is intersected by the National Highway and you need permission from the Archaelogical Survey Office nr the gate if you wish to drive to the Summa tombs which are about 3 km to the N.

Travelling from S to N you will first pass a well, which has a gallery where guards once stood. The Archeological Dept's *Rest House* is nearby . Reservations, Karachi office, T 431821.

The first group of monuments on the ridge belong to the most recent Mughal period (16th to 18th century), with a number of tombs which have fine carvings in the mosques on their W wall. The tomb of **Mirza Jani Beg** (1599), the last Turkhan ruler is the first one on you right and shows the use of blue and green glazed bricks. The most outstanding blue stone tomb, similar in style to the buildings in Fatehpur Sikri near Agra, is of **Isa Khan Tarkhan** the younger (1644) which stands in a square courtyard surrounded by a high wall. It is finely carved, with a domed square chamber surrounded by a double storey pillared verandah with smaller domes which you can reach by stairs. The tracery in stonework is exceptional.

To the E of this is the low building in the same style with relief carvings on the interior walls, with the tombs of the women in Isa Khan's *zenana**. You get an excellent view towards Thatta, across the lake from the door to the E.

The well-preserved large solid square tomb of **Dewan Shurfa Khan** (1638) a little to the NW has short round towers at each corner. You can see remnants of the blue glazed tiles that once covered the bricks and how strips were used for 'pointing'. It gives an excellent impression of the colourful and ornate decorations used in the tombs of this period. The type of glazed tiles and bricks used in these later tombs are still being made in **Thatta** nearby.

Next are the 16th century tombs of the **Arghun** and **Tarkhan** rulers who came from the N and succeeded the Sammas. The earlier 14th to 16th century tombs belong to the Samma dynasty who came from Lower Sind and rebelled against the authority in Delhi. It includes the one of **Jam Nizamuddin** (Jam Nindo) of the Golden Age of Sind, which has a square plan and is richly decorated with geometric and floral patterns and has an unusual and attractive arched balcony on the W wall. This facade is very much in the Hindu style which suggests that it may have used sections from a Hindu temple. It is possible, however, that the rich decorative style (which contrasts with the austere interior) are a result of employing Hindu craftsmen. They also attempted to use their method to construct the arches to support the vast dome which was never built, so it remains open to the elements.

The power of pietistic Islam in Sind is evidenced in the devotion offered at the modern **Tomb of Abdullah Shah Ash'abi**. Set among the thousands of old tombs on the ridge, it is busy with activity since the revered saint attracts crowds of devotees.

Buses from Karachi's Lea Market.

Thatta
98 km E of Karachi; *Population* 80,000 The new city, opp the Makli Hill, is identified with the site of **Patala**. The ancient link with Alexander the Great suggests that he stopped here with his army in 325 BC after a long dusty march from the N, before launching his attack on Baluchistan. Before that, it is believed to feature in the Hindu epic *Mahabharata*, and was also once the capital of Sind and its artistic centre. The Mughal Empire extended to Thatta in 1592 and it remained an important port, renowned for cotton weaving and wood carving.

The **Shah Jahan Mosque** in Thatta, standing in impressive gardens, is profusely decorated with blue glazed ceramic tiles and sandstone carvings in ornate floral and abstract designs. Shah Jahan was once given refuge in Thatta when he was rebelling against his father Jahangir. He built the mosque between 1644 and 1647 (the same period in which he was building the Taj Mahal), to thank the people of

Thatta for their shelter. In 1742 it was said to be a thriving city with 40,000 weavers and 60,000 dealers. Although undoubtedly a gross overestimate, it was a very busy town, but by the late 18th century the port went into decline as a result of the shifting course of the Indus.

The architecture here shows far stronger **Persian** elements, especially in the decoration, than the Fort in Delhi or the Taj Mahal. This illustrates the importance that local craftsmen retained in the design and building of the Mughals' major works, and is evidenced again in the Lahore Fort, the Persian style decoration of which was also largely the work of Shah Jahan. The decorative tile work in particular shows the strong links betweeen this part of S Sind and Persia to the W. The great mosques of Isfahan or Shiraz the turquoise and white tiling, illustrate today what magnificent tiled decorations were applied to brick built mosques by Persian artists.

The great gateway at the E entrance was added in 1959 when the mosque was refurbished. The rectangular plan differs from the usual, with the main prayer chamber on the W being balanced by a similar one in the E, the 2 being connected by a double arcaded corridor with 93 domes which also serve the acoustic purpose of carrying the words of the Imam to all parts of the mosque.

The mosque, which is on the outskirts of the new town, is surrounded by crowded narrow alleys of the **old town** with lines of mud and brick houses and busy bazaars. It still has the air of living in the past and gives you an insight into village life in the Sind centuries ago. A few old multistoreyed houses still have the carved wooden balconies. The quaint *badgirs* or 'windcatchers' on the roof tops are very effective as they 'catch' the cooler southwesterly breeze during the summer months and circulate it in the rooms below.

Even the 17th century **Khizri Mosque** by the Shahi Bazaar, half a km from the Shah Jahan Mosque has these coolers. They are also found in Hyderabad, as well as further W, notably in Iraq. The **bazaar** sells striped cotton cloth as well as the block-printed *ajrak*, glass bangles and the special Sindhi embroidered cloth with mirror work . The PTDC tours cover Chaukandi, Banbhore, Makli Hill and Thatta (min 5 persons).

Hotels *Aga Mohammed*, Main Rd. Rm with shared bath and **F** *Muzaffarkhanas* are considered unsuitable for foreign visitors. Accommodation is very basic with many to a rm and only rope beds.

Rail Nearest station at **Junvsashi**, 20 km away. **Road** Buses from Karachi's Lea Market.

From **Thatta** the National Highway turns NE to run up the right or W bank of the Indus. After 22 km a road to the left runs to *Kheenjhar (Kalri) Lake*. The richly cultivated fields illustrate the remarkable transformation of the environment that has been produced by controlling the Indus waters.

Keenjihar Lake, which used to supply water to Karachi, was created by linking 2 natural lakes, the **Sunheri** and **Keenjihari**. When full, it extends over 20 km and is 6 km wide. Now it is a PTDC resort offering sailing and fishing. Also good for birdwatching and attracts game including partridges, quails, ducks and snipe.

Hotels The modern a/c **D** *Tourist Resort*, T 510. New resort has 8 deluxe and 16 standard cabanas. Split level a/c cabanas have their own living area dowstairs and d rm (extra bed at small charge) with western toilet upstairs. Excellent facilities include a good a/c restaurant, snack bar, boating, sailing, angling. Restaurant (continental and local cuisine) encourages you to bring your catch back and have the fish cooked to your liking. Prices are higher on holidays than during the week. Also 3 older cottages and a motel block with 2 d rm. Reservations: PTDC Motels (S), Hotel Metropole, Abdullah Haroon Rd, Karachi, T 516252.

Road Pakistan Tours Ltd runs a/c coaches from Karachi (125 km) and Hyderabad (83 km).

From Keenjhar the National Highway continues N through Jerruck to the industrial town of Kotri, the bridging point across the Indus to Hyderabad.

KARACHI TO HYDERABAD via the superhighway

150 km via *Ghulam Mohammad Barrage* (Kotri). Taking the Super Highway out of Karachi, the road to Hyderabad is 164 km and can be covered in about 2 hr 30 min. The Super Highway (Toll road; if driving, keep receipt and hand in at other end) crosses the southernmost ridges of the limestone Kirthar Range up a winding steep escarpment before descending gently to the Indus and the Provincial capital, Hyderabad, on it eastern side. The limestone is used in the building industry. The Govt of Pakistan built a large industrial estate for production of tax free products half way between Karachi and Hyderabad. These include a cement factory and a Ceramics Works, the point where you leave the main road. The twisting road passes through arid desert until you reach the foothills.

When you reach the steep scarp after crossing the flat Indus plain, you will have noticed the dry water courses and stretches of sand. Follow the road to the mosque at the top of the hill, where you can take a track down to the gorge of the *Khadeji Falls*. A further 55 km you reach the 80 km marker stone and turn N, 72 km to the main centre to view the *Kirthar National Park* from *Karchat*. It is also possible to get to the park by taking the road N out of Karachi to the *Hub Dam*.

Kirthar National Park Best season In winter between Nov – Jan. *Area* 3,000 sq km of rolling hills and valleys. Animals include Urial sheep with close set semicircular horns, Sind ibex (wild goat), chinkara, gazelle, black buck, wild cats, as well as pangolins and monitor lizards. The first three have been hunted for their skins and horns but are protected in the park. However, being shy and extremely alert, they are difficult to get close to and photograph successfully, so you need patience and good camera equipment. Occasional sightings of leopard and desert wolf have been reported.

It is best to watch wildlife in the early morning from forest hideouts or make your own blind and wait in silence. The two Visitors' Centres are at Khar nr Hub Dam and Karchat nr Thano Ahmed Khan in the centre of the Park.

Hotels Basic accommodation, though includes running water, flush toilets, and you can hire transport and guides. 5 **E** *Rest Houses*, **F** *Dormitory* or tents for camping. Reservations: Sind Wildlife Management Board, Strachen Rd, Karachi, T 523176. Best to take bedding and all food and drink you need, although the cook on duty will prepare a meal given adequate notice.

On the NE boundary is the Rannikot Fort which is better apprached from the E from the National Highway N of Hyderabad, along the Indus.

HYDERABAD

Population 1 million; *Altitude* 25 m.

	Jan	Feb	Mar	Apr	May	Jun	Jul	Aug	Sep	Oct	Nov	Dec	Av/Tot
Max (°C)	24	27	34	39	42	41	37	36	36	37	32	26	34
Min (°C)	11	13	18	22	26	28	27	26	24	21	15	12	20
Rain (mm)	4	5	1	2	4	6	69	44	15	8	1	3	162

Modern Hyderabad owes its origin in part to the movement in the course of the River Indus in the mid-18th century. In 1758-59 the Indus left its old bed at a point N of the present site of Hyderabad and turned westwards. Over 150 km of the old course was abandoned, though much of it is still traceable. It had been a period of new town building, but Narsapur, one of the intended capitals of Mian Muradyab Khan, was almost immediately washed away in floods. Its successor, Allahabad, never developed, and in 1768 Ghulam Shah Kalhora, who had become ruler of all Sind, founded Hyderabad as his capital, ordering a new fort to be built. His son, Sarfaraz was responsible for the new city.

Early history The group of hills on which Hyderabad stands figured prominently in the region's early history. According to Lambrick, "Mohd bin Qasim, the Arab conqueror of Sind, marched S from **Sehwan**, down the W bank of the Indus and then camped by a fort which was situated on the hills of **Nerun**, clearly identifiable with the site of modern Hyderabad."

From a contemporary account it obviously had its attractions: "there was a pond in its vicinity the water of which was brighter than the eyes of lovers, and its meadow land more pleasant than the garden of Iram." Nerun Kot is where the young Arab General is believed to have built a mosque on an earlier Buddhist site. In the 16th and 17th centuries the Arghun rulers of Thatta made Nerun their district headquarters and the new town took on the name of **Hyder Quli Arghuni**.

The settled rule of the Kalhora period saw the flourishing of poetry, art and architecture although only the fort and the Kalhora tombs remain. It was also a time when the economy expanded with the improvement in irrigation but the period of peace ended with Ghulam Shah's death in 1772. His successors alienated and angered the Baluchis who finally defeated them in 1782. The Baluchi **Talpur Mirs** remained in Hyderabad until the British arrived in 1843.

Today Hyderabad is collection of houses packed together on the higher ground of the hill and spreading onto the lower surrounding land. The distinctive *Badgirs* or windcatchers on the roof tops, trap the cool breezes in the height of summer and channel the cold air down to the interior. See Thatta above.

Places of interest

The Fort (*Qila*). To the S of the city, the irregular outer wall was built on the vertical edge of the plateau. The *Pukka* (brick built) Qila is in a unique strategic position dominating the plain. Built on the order of **Ghulam Shah Kalhora**, the foundation stone, dating from 1768, has an inscription meaning "Oh God, Bring peace to this city".

The Kalhora ruler occupied it during a period of prosperity and peace until his death in 1772 during which time it was also used as a court. The **Talpur Mirs**, who followed in 1782, made it their palace and fort until their defeat by the British in 1843, when it was partly used as a prison. During the siege, a large part of the inner section was destroyed and was replaced by new barracks built for the British troops. Many sections fell into disrepair through neglect, and finally an explosion in 1906 destroyed what was left of the fort.

Only parts of the 15 m high outer wall, a circular tower and the main gate remain intact. The wall, built with special local bricks, is 1.5 m at the base. A room in the *Harem* has some wall painting and lacquer work dating from the Kalhora period. The small **Museum** has interesting historical exhibits of the Mirs, including weapons, clothes and portraits. Open Summer 0700-1400, Winter 0900-1600. Closed Fri and Sat.

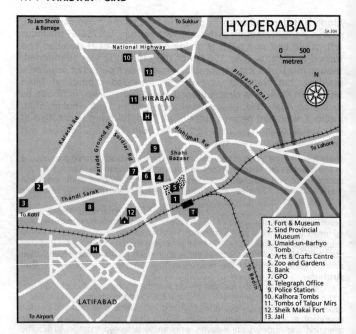

HYDERABAD
SA 304

To Jam Shoro
& Barrage

To Sukkur

National Highway

0   500
metres

N

Pinyari Canal

10

13

11 HIRABAD

H

Karachi Rd

Parade Ground Rd

Soldier Rd

9

Rishighat Rd

Shahi
Bazaar

To Lahore

7   6

Thandi Sarak

4

5

2

3

To Kotri

8

1

12

T

H

To Badin

LATIFABAD

To Airport

1. Fort & Museum
2. Sind Provincial
   Museum
3. Umaid-un-Barhyo
   Tomb
4. Arts & Crafts Centre
5. Zoo and Gardens
6. Bank
7. GPO
8. Telegraph Office
9. Police Station
10. Kalhora Tombs
11. Tombs of Talpur Mirs
12. Sheik Makai Fort
13. Jail

The **Shah Makkai Fort** or *Kucca* (mud built) *Qila* which is close by to the W, was also built by Ghulam Shah Kalhora the year before his death, to protect the tomb of **Sheikh Mohammad Makkai**, a Muslim saint who came there from Mecca (hence the title Makkai) 500 years earlier. His wife, the daughter of a Hindu ruler, was a convert to Islam, and the saint and she are thought to have died together at this same place and so are both buried here. The shrine inside the entrance still attracts devotees from all over Sind, although the fort itself is in ruins.

The 21 **Kalhora Tombs** which stand behind the Central Jail in the N of the city have exceptional craftsmanship, the most remarkable being **Ghulam Shah Kalhora's** (1772). Enter the shady enclosure through a small carved door. The sense of architectural balance achieved is still evident despite the loss of the dome, now replaced by a flat roof. The square tomb with the octagonal chamber still retains some beautiful decoration in blue and white tiles, and parts of carved marble railing that once surrounded the tomb as well as paintings on the walls.

The 4 **Tombs of the Talpur Mirs** and their families, S of the Central Jail, are more mundane than the Kalhora tombs. Built between 1812-1857, they are grouped in 2 enclosures. They show the marble tracery, geometric patterns and coloured tile work typical of the period.

Qadam Gah of Hazrat Ali and Abdul Wahab Jilani shrine In the centre of Hyderabad is the slab of stone with the hand and footprints of the 4th Caliph of Islam, Hazrat Ali. Nearby is the shrine to Abdul Wahab Jilani.

Sind University is NW of the city aross the river and the Super Highway.

Local industries One geography textbook on the Sind lists the industries of Hyderabad as

"Gaiters, scabbards, sword-belts, jesses, jauntlets, calico-printing, embroidery, bracelets, dice, spoons, knives and tiles." That rather curious mixture of antique weaponry and modern kitchen ware catches something of the continuing importance of handicrafts to Hyderabad's industrial activity, but significant modernization has also taken place. Local crafts: Glazed tiles from **Hala** about 60 km away which is famous for its potteries. *Rillis* (patchwork quilts in bright colours), *Ajrak* hand block-printed cloth. Lacquered wood furniture, embroidered cloth, leather and shoes.

Services

Hotels D *Fataz*, Thandi Sarak, T 24425. 26 rm, some a/c. Good *Naushana* and *Zaushan* Restaurants, 24 hr coffee-shop, exchange, travel, shop, pool, TV. **D** *Spinzer*, Gari Khata, T 23537. 10 rm, some a/c. Recommended. *Tung Fung* Chinese Restaurant, travel. **D** *City Gate*, National Highway, opp Central Jail. T 31677, Cable: Citygate. 36 rm, some a/c. *Midway Hill* Restaurant, exchange, car hire, shop, TV. **D** *Faran*, Saddar Bazaar, T 29994, Cable: Hotelfaran. 26 rm, some a/c. Restaurant, exchange, TV. **D** *New Indus*, Thandi Sarak. T 25276. 13 rm, some a/c. **D** *New Sainjees Motel*, Thandi Sarak, T 27275. 23 rm. Restaurant.

E *Ritz*, Cantonment. T 23581. 20 rm, with bath. Restaurant. **E** *Prince*, Market Rd. T 32255. 12 rn, with bath. **E** *Diamond*, Market Rd. T 30255. 20 rm, with bath. Very inexpensive **F** category hotels in the station area include *Palace*, Gari Khata,T 26884 and *Yasrab*, Goods Naka, T 27006. Alternatively stay in Miani *Forest Rest House*, 10 km.

Restaurants Food in first 3 hotels listed recommended. Chinese Restaurants in Station Rd are *Canton* and *Sancha*. *Bombay Bakery* is excellent for bread, biscuits and cakes.

Shopping The main shopping area is nr the Fort, S of town. Shahi Bazaar, over 2 km long and a maze of narrow crowded lanes with small shops, sells a wide variety of goods including jewellery, shoes, lacquerware, handloom textiles, Sindhi embroidery and appliquéd *Rillis*.

Sports Fishing is popular on the lakes nearby. Permits from Asst Director, Fisheries Dept. Duck and partridge shooting is popular. Hog and wild boar hunting is also organized. Permits from Honorary Game Warden and Dy Commissioner (Wildlife).

Museums   **Sind Provincial Museum** Wahdat Colony nr Niaz Stadium and Polytechnic, attached to the Sind Provincial Library. Opened 1971. Well designed, beautifully laid out and clearly labelled. **Section 1**: archaeological display covering the whole span from prehistory to the British period; **2.** Sindhi crafts, **3.** children's section.

   Talpur House Museum A private museum in a house built between 1860-1864 in 19th century European style. The 2 rm of Talpur Harem are furnished with European style period furniture and fittings with original carpets and rugs, European crockery. A particularly good collection of manuscripts, brought out on request. Housed in the Bungalow of *Mir Hasan Ali* in Tando Mir Nur Mohammad Khan, the suburbs of Hyderabad. Open on application to the family.

   Sind University Educational Museum, Inst. of Education, Univ. Sind. Free. Opened in 1959. Sindhi arts and crafts including needlework, carpets, straw and laquer work; local musical instruments, costumes, weapons and jewellery.

Parks The Zoo and gardens are NE of the Fort.

Post and Telegraphs GPO in City centre. Telegraph Office, Thandi Sarak.

Hospitals and medical services Belair Clinic, Cantonment Area, T 23641.

Chambers of Commerce Hyderabad Chamber of Commerce and Industry, Cantonment, opp Ritz Hotel, 526 Quaid-e-Azam Rd, Baitul Inayat, PO Box 99. T 24641, Cable Chambercom.

Travel agents Kashmir Corp, Risala Rd, T 25055. World Express, Gul Centre, T 23078.

Air Services PIA domestic flights from Karachi, 4 times a week, 35 min.

Rail To Karachi *Mehran exp*, 40, daily, 0605, 3hr; *8 Express*, daily, AC, 0635, 2hr 30min; **Multan** *Shalimar Exp*, 105, daily, AC, 0824, 9 hr; **Lahore** *Shalimar Exp*, 105, daily, AC, 0824, 14 hr; Enquiry, T 23156. City Booking Office, 10 Tayak Rd, Gari Khata. Hyderabad Market Talak Chari City Booking Agency. Left Luggage facility.

Road The Sind Road Transport Corporation (SRTC) has frequent services to destinations in all directions. Buses and a/c coaches connect Karachi with **Hyderabad** and proceed to Sukkur, via Kot Diji; **Karachi**, Delux Service via Super Highway, every 30 min from 0530 to 2100. Express, via Thatta is hourly, 0600-1800. Non-stop to Thatta, 0930 (1 hr 45 min); **Kotri**, every 30 min from 0530; **Sanghar**, every 30 min, 0530-2000; **Moro and Dadu**, several daily, some continuing to Larkana. Also to **Kunri** via Mirpurkhas and to **Badin**, the Express runs every 45 min from 0530. In addition there are inter-provincial buses (non a/c) between Karachi and Bannu, Chakwal, Mingora, Manserhra and a/c buses between Karachi and Bannu, Lahore, Multan, Peshawar and Sargodha which pass through Hyderabad.

Excursions

From Hyderabad you can go E through **Mirpur Khas** into the Thar desert, or by train to **Khokhrapar**, nr the border with India. India and Pakistan have signed an agreement to re-open the railway line connecting **Hyderabad** with **Jodhpur**, but it has yet to be implemented.

The potential attractions of this route into Rajasthan for the traveller are enormous, as there are many places of interest on both sides of the border which it would be possible to see in a far more direct way than is possible at the moment. Re-opening does not seem imminent, but enquire locally.

The road to **Mirpur Khas** (65 km); *Population* 200,000. *Altitude* 40 m) crosses the richly irrigated lands of the Sukkur Barrage canals. Between Hyderabad and Mirpur Khas the **Rohri Canal** is the chief feeder of the network of minor canals which have produced a landscape of banana plantations and mango gardens, interspersed with sugar cane, rice and wheat cultivation. The easternmost of the Sukkur Canals, the **Nara Canal**, runs almost due S from Sukkur through Khairpur District and Sanghar, then irrigating the land to the E of Mirpur Khas. The only place of interest, where you will also see old terracotta figures, is the 15 m high *Buddhist stupa*. 2 *Rest Houses* here can be reserved through the Dy Commissioner. **Travel** Several coaches daily from Karachi's **Boulton Market** (4 hr via Super Highway).

Umarkot (74 km) or Amarkot, the desert town, stands on the high road in Sind between **Marwar** and **Indus Valley**. It may have its origins in ancient times, but around the 11th century it became strategically important.

It is remembered today chiefly as the birthplace of the Mughal **Emperor Akbar**, born in 1542 when his father Humayun was fleeing with his young Sindhi wife **Hamida** from the Afghan ruler of N India, **Sher Shah Suri**, see page 92. The Rana of Umarkot vacated the central part of the fort for his royal guests and it was there that the future Emperor was born, who spent his first 5 weeks in the town. He never visited it again, but felt a sentimental attachment for it. The brick-built fort which was constructed 200 years later by the Kalhora ruler **Nur Muhammed** on the site of the earlier Rajput fort, commands the W edge of the desert. Unbaked bricks were used for the walls though the round towers needed baked bricks.

The **Bazaar** is interesting for not only the traditional craft items and handloom cloth but also because you can watch the craftsmen at work. **Hotel** The 19th century *Circuit House* can be reserved through the Dy Commissioner, Mirpur Khas. **Museum** Opened in 1968, in one room. Items from the Mughal period, particularly **Akbar**; fabrics, manuscripts, coins and documents. Open daily except first Mon of each month and annual public holidays. Winter 0900-1600, Summer 0800-1200, 1400-1700.

Despite the intensity of the summer heat, the *Thar desert* has been as much of a route as a barrier to movement and contact. The relatively cool winters and the short distances to trading towns on the Indian side of the desert (less than 200 km to Jodhpur, for example) have given it a much greater importance than its hostile environment might suggest.

Tours Details from the PTDC in **Karachi**, or from **Naukot** itself, where private companies operate local transport.

Warning If you are driving yourself, approach the desert tracks with caution and proper preparation. Shovels, gloves, adequate water supplies, a small cutting tool or axe and a compass are essential. Take a local guide. Tracks often change and you can't trust maps at all.

You can take tours into the desert from a number of points. Tours to the S region are organised from **Naukot**, reached from **Mirpur Khas** via **Digri** (a total of 85 km). Irregular buses run right across the desert to the southeasternmost settlement in Pakistan **Nagar Parkar**, on the edge of the Rann of Kutch.

HYDERABAD TO SUKKUR via the Indus E bank

Leave Hyderabad due N. The national highway, the main route to the N of Pakistan, is extremely busy. Drivers familiar with roads elsewhere in S Asia will find these roads a surprise. The average speed is much higher than in India, and all the vehicles are more modern. Heavy lorries move faster, and in general the quality of the road surface is much better. The E bank route to Sukkur (and beyond) has all these characteristics, though it is still very different from driving in Europe or the United States. If you are driving yourself be prepared for drivers to overtake in unlikely places with extremely limited vision, and to expect you to get out of the way. Do so. The E bank route is far more densely populated and cultivated than the W bank.

The highway crosses an endless succession of former inundation canals taking off from the left bank of the Indus. Slightly lower than the right bank, the rising waters of the Indus were trained through cuts and led away by canals, making this the granary of Sind.

Miani forest, 10 km N of Hyderabad, is where the British, led by Lord Napier, defeated the Talpur Mirs, ending a 60 year rule by the Baluchis. Sind came under British rule, which only ended at Independence in 1947. *Forest Rest House*.

Bhit Shah 50 km after leaving Hyderabad the national highway passes within 4 km of **Bhit Shah** where the Sufi poet *Shah Abdul Latif* selected the "place of the sand dunes", or *bhits,* to pitch his tent . Born in 1690 AD at **Hala**, he studied both Hindu and Muslim ideas, though the latter became dominant. He is regarded as Sind's (and Sindhi's) foremost poet.

The shrine which is said to mark the spot draws thousands of devotees at the annual *Urs* (or festival of his death) anniversary. Pilgrims gather to listen to recitations of his poetry by folksingers, who play their traditional old string instruments like the *dotara* (2 strings), and take part in the ecstatic dancing of the dervishes entering a trance with the beating of drums. Shah Abdul Latif's songs are sung with pride throughout Sind, and are collected in the "*Risalo*".

The mausoleum which has patterned floors, frescoes and beautiful blue and white tile decoration is next to the mirrored mosque. A good example of Sindhi architecture, the limestone is carved in domes and minarets. Behind it is a lake along which pilgrims crowd tented alleyways.

This fusion of Muslim and Hindu ideas is a reflection of the nature of the *Sufi* movement, which stressed devotion to God rather than ideological purity. The Sufis took a liberal attitude to other faiths, contributing to the philosophical base of the Mughal Emperor Akbar's open minded approach to all religions and his attempts to achieve a synthesis of them. (**See page 285**.)

There is a *Rest House,* a new Cultural Centre and **Museum** which has a small collection of local arts and crafts, musical instruments and some modern paintings which are taken out and shown on request.

Hala (26 km N up the National Highway) is a centre of the blue and white ceramics handicraft industry. Recently re-located just off the National Highway after severe Indus flooding, there is a covered bazaar where a wide range of local craft products sre sold. Hala is famous for **Makhdoom Nooh**, who is believed to have prevented a disaster by re-aligning Shah Jahan's Mosque in Thatta so that it faced

Mecca simply by the power of a night in prayer.

Continuing N up the National Highway, it is possible to cross the Indus by a new bridge built at **Moro** (110 km). The bridge crosses to **Dadu** on the W bank, about 130 km S of **Moenjo Daro**. If you carry straight on up the National Highway you reach the important archaeological site of

Kot Diji (116 km). The most visible remains today are those of its impressive 18th century fort, built by the Talpur rulers between 1782 and 1843. Very important remains of a pre-Harappan culture were first discovered in the mid 1950s.

The site of the ancient **Kot Diji** settlement is a low hill by the road side. The first excavations were made by the Pakistan Archaeological Department in 1955-57, and the site is distinctive because it stands on one of the rare outcrops of limestone, part of the **Rohri Hills** further N, which give it a slight elevation above the floodplain. The first settlement was built on the bedrock itself. Above it were discovered houses and a massive defensive wall, preserved to a height of 5 m. in places.

Some of the earliest parts of the site are now underground below the watertable, and there are many unanswered questions about its origins. However, house walls of stone as well as mud-brick in the upper levels are probably similar to those that lie below.

A great deal of wheel thrown pottery has been found, a wide range of stone tools and one terracotta bull. There are clear similarities with the later Harappan period ware, just as at **Amri. See page 1182.** The early period in Kot Diji shows clear evidence of 2 huge fires, after which Harappan elements are dominant. Radiocarbon dating from the Early Indus level suggests a date of 2880 BC, while a date for the upper, or later, fire gives 2520 BC. A comparison of the pottery of Amri and Kot Diji in the period before the Harappan cultures took over suggests that the 2 sites developed quite different traditions.

The **Kot Diji Fort**, built largely out of brick along a natural narrow rise in the ground, commands the ridge on which it stands. It is surrounded by indented walls and rounded bastions, and commands every spur of higher ground. The entrance is at the SE corner, on the opp side from the road, and a steep narrow lane goes up to the flat-topped area inside, with its variety of military and royal buildings. The residence of the royal family is almost centrally placed, half way along the E wall.

About 4 km N of Kot Diji the National Highway crosses the **Kairpur Canal E**, one of the major left bank canals of the **Sukkur Barrage**. Driving N, the road crosses the westernmost parts of the **Thar desert**, transformed now by irrigation.

Khairpur (24 km N of Kot Diji *Population* 260,000 *altitude* 50 m) is bordered on the E by the *pat* desert where impervious clay soils hold up groundwater. Salt lakes are common while the valley bottoms have a natural cover of thick grass. Khairpur is an important regional centre with major weaving and spinning industry. It also has some beautiful tombs of the Talpur princes, perhaps the most striking of which is the tomb of **Mir Karam Ali Khan Talpur**. Until 1947 it was the capital of one of the many small Princely States in India.

It benefitted most from the construction of the Sukkur Barrage, but has also suffered severe environmental damage as a result of the raising of the water table. The waterlogging that followed contributed to a sharp increase in malaria, and the difficulty of eradicating it. The worst effects of waterlogging and salinity are visible around Khairpur, but are particularly striking from the air.

Despite the problems, many of which are being tackled under the Salinity Control and Reclamation Projects (SCARP) of Pakistan's Water and Power Development Authority (WAPDA), Khairpur is still an agriculturally prosperous region. In contrast to the W bank of the Indus, wheat is much more important than rice, it being particularly suited to the *rabi* (winter) cropping season made possible by irrigation from the Sukkur barrage. This has increased the area cultivated during the winter by nearly 500%, though it only had a small effect on cropping during the *kharif* or rainy season.

It is a major wheat exporting region, but a variety of other crops – rice, sugar cane, oil seeds – are also grown. Fruit orchards are common, with dates and mangoes particularly important, and it has also long been famous for its cattle breeding. Although it doesn't have a large cattle population, the **Bhagnari** and **Sahiwal** breeds are famous throughout Pakistan.

Just out of Khairpur the National Highway crosses the railway between Karachi and the N and after a further 10 km crosses the long **Rohri Canal**, another of the Sukkur Barrage canals. From here to Sukkur itself the road continues through the irrigated fields of Upper Sind.

The hills of *Rohri*, on the S or left bank of the Indus, are one of the oldest sites of human habitation in the entire Indian sub-continent, and a stone tool factory (ironically on the flat-topped hill next door to the modern cement factory) occupied the site from the earliest stone age period.

Rohri is an important rail and road junction and contains a mosque built during Akbar's time (1583) which was decorated with coloured tiles. Another 16th century building was said to contain the Prophet's hair.

Rail To Quetta *Quetta Exp*, 24, daily, A/c, 0220, 12hr 15min; *Sind Exp*, 45, daily, 1710, 13hr 15min; **Karachi** *Sind Exp*, 46, daily, 1020, 9hr; *Sukkur Exp*, 70, daily, AC, 2140, 8hr 40min; **Lahore** *Zulfiqar Exp*, 5, daily, A/c, 1805, 13hr 30min; **Rawalpindi-Islamabad** *Zulfiqar Exp*, 5, daily, A/c, 1805, 20hr 30min

Alor (or Aror), the ancient city 8 km E of Rohri, is on the edge of a low range of hills. You can see the dry river bed where the Indus once flowed and the ancient bridge nearby is thought to be one of the country's oldest. The ruins of a fort are at the place where Alexander the Great is believed to have stopped for a time on his march down the Indus. The Chinese traveller Hiuen Tsang also mentioned the city in the 7th century.

To reach *Sukkur* (20 km. *Population* 350,000. *Altitude* 50 m) you have to leave the Highway to Multan and Lahore and cross the *Sukkur Barrage*. The barrage crosses via **Bukkur Island** (300 m wide), which has a ruined fort on its N end and a shrine. Access to the fort at the S end of the island is prohibited because it is a military site.

Sukkur is the most important town in Upper Sind. At a strategic crossing point on the Indus, it developed where the river cut through the last outcrop of solid limestone rock, before continuing to the sea. It has played a vital part in Sind's history for over 2000 years.

Today the barrage diverts the Indus into perennial canals. Planned as far back as 1847, the barrage was finally approved in 1923 and completed (as the Lloyd barrage) in 1932. Up to that point the whole of Sind had depended simply on the floods of the Indus to fill wet season inundation canals. After the Barrage was completed however, Sind was directly affected by the use made in winter of water upstream. The subsequent development of irrigation both in India and Pakistan has had crucial implications for Sindhi's new class of "irrigating farmers", and is a continuing source of political dispute. The desert oasis town has several religious schools in addition to the mosques and shrines and the old sections have the rich merchants' houses, *havelis* which are decorated with colourful patterns.

Places of interest The **Minaret of Masum Shah** (1594-1618). The Mughal Emperor Akbar appointed **Masum Shah** his Nawab of Sukkur. The leaning minaret (25 m tall, 25 m diameter) gives commanding views across the Barrage and the plains. To the E of the new town is the **Mausoleum to Shah Khairuddin Jilani** built in 1760, which has unusual patterns in its tilework and stands out with its blue enamelled dome with a lantern on top. The founder of a spiritual dynasty, Shah Khairuddin, came to Sukkur after years of wandering, and remained in a mountain cave until his death at the reputed age of 116 in 1609.

The **Sadhbella,** on a rocky island here, is the only Hindu monastery of its kind in Pakistan, on the walls of which are scenes from Hindu mythology. Good views.

Hotels D *Inter-Pak Inn*, Barrage Rd, Lab-e-Mehran, T 83051 is on the outskirts and the best hotel in town. 30 rm, some a/c. Restaurant, traveller's cheques. D *Forum Inn*, Workshop Rd, T 83011. 36 a/c rm. *Cherry* Restaurant, traveller's cheques. **D** *Mehran*, Station Rd, T 83792. 43 rm some a/c. Restaurant. **E** *Bolan*, Mission Rd nr Qasim Park, T 84264. 20 rm. Restaurant, traveller's cheques accepted.

On Barrage Rd there are several inexpensive hotels, some of which offer rm with bath. **E** *Al-Habib*, T 84359. 25 rm. Restaurant. **E** *Nusrat*, T 85147. 30 rm. Restaurant. **E** *Shalimar*, T 83177. 12 rm. Restaurant. **E** *Firdous*, T 3404. The Clock Tower area has the **F** *Royal*, T 84371with 27 rm with bath and *Fazal*.

Local transport *Tongas* from Bus Station to town centre where you can get auto rickshaws.

Below the **Ayub Khan arch railway bridge** (S of the Barrage), one the largest in the world, are the *Mohana* boat people (see Manchar Lake below, page 1184), living in their distinctive houseboats, designed to cope with the river in flood. Herons have been tamed and are used to catch fish. Some owners will give rides for a small fee.

HYDERABAD TO SHIKARPUR & QUETTA via Indus Highway W Bank

The E route from Karachi to Quetta takes the Super Highway to Kotri (see page 1172), skirting the S end of the Kirthar Hills, before running N up the W bank of the Indus. The highest and longest range of hills in the Province, the **Kirthar Range** runs almost 240 km from S to N. From the plains the range looks like a fortress wall, with an average height of 1,600 m. It provides a natural frontier, which can usually only be crossed by camels through a dozen or so passes. Today its barrenness makes it seem almost totally inhospitable to human settlement, yet the edge of the hills, northwards to the Bolan Pass and beyond, was one of the most important regions in the early development of settled agriculture in S Asia, going back more than 10,000 years.

Goats and sheep, which provide the livelihood for modern nomadic tribes people, are known to have been domesticated in this region at least 16,000 years ago. Domestic cattle too were increasingly common. These W borderlands were one of perhaps 4 key S Asian regions at the beginning of the Neolithic period, the others being to the N on the Potwar Plateau, the far NE in the Brahmaputra valley and the S central peninsula of India around the Krishna and Tungabhadra Rivers.

Today the route hardly suggests the basis for the flowering of one of the world's great pre-modern cultures. Yet the W highway runs through the heart of the Indus Valley civilisation's centre of power. From 2500 BC to around 1800 BC **Moenjo Daro (Mohenjo Daro)** developed as the southern capital of a civilisation which embraced virtually the entire plains area of the Indus and important regions beyond, especially to the E. (See below). At the same time trade flourished with newly emerging centres to the W in what is now Afghanistan.

Long after the Harappan civilisation had disappeared others followed. The Kushan kings, notably under their great leader **Kanishka**, who was converted to Buddhism in the 1st century AD, spread their power S from the NW passes, building stupas such as that on the citadel at Moenjo Daro between the 1st and 3rd centuries AD. **Yuan Chwang** followed this route between 643-44 AD, as did the Arab armies of Mohammad bin Qasim 70 years later.

The road runs along the dead flat plain of the Indus, often barren desert of dry scrub, but often close to the dramatic mountains on the left. The **Kirthar limestone** is solid and smooth, and has a striking pale grey/beige colour which almost looks chalky in places where the rock is exposed. The dearth of vegetation makes the hill country look particularly desolate.

Although from a distance the rocks look entirely bare, you will notice that the scrub and grass (which dries up very easily) is able to support sheep, goats, wild ibex and urial. The W side of the range also has dwarf palm growing, some wild olive at the higher levels and cactus on the lower sections. A variety of trees grow along the streams, such as tamarisk, *kandi* and pampas grass, where the soil is rich and irrigated a variety of crops are grown. On the W bank of the Indus rice is far more important than wheat. Cotton is common in both the S and the N but almost entirely absent in the central section, where oilseeds become a far more important cash crop. Sugar cane is comparatively rare to the W of the Indus.

The main occupation of the nomadic tribes is breeding and grazing goats and sheep. Some set up their tents where there is a source of water, moving when the grazing land is exhausted. Others live in sheltered valleys in the winter and move to higher levels where they use circular stone-built huts.

From Hyderabad you join the Indus Highway up the W bank of the Indus by crossing the ***Ghulam Mohammad Barrage***, the most recent of the major works on the lower Indus, completed in 1955 and named after the then Governor General of Pakistan. Flooding is a constant problem and many parts of the road suffer damage periodically. Wherever there is a choice of road, keep to the W.

Ranikot Fort Three quarters of the way N (75 km) from the Ghulam Mohammad Barrage to **Amri** is the **Ranikot Fort**, one of the world's largest, with a circumference of 25 km.

Turn left up towards the Kirthar Hills at the crossroads to **Sann**, which is to the right. The remarkable Fort stands above a chasm in the **Lakhi Hills**, about 32 km from the Sann Railway Station. The track runs through a barren, uninhabited area dotted with scrub and stunted trees. It is rough even for a jeep. Camels, available in Sann, are an alternative. As you approach the fort, you will see the high sandstone walls from a distance, with a natural boundary in the form of a cliff to the N where the citadel of ***Shergarh*** stands on high ground.

The fort is first mentioned in 1812 when an older fort on the site was thought to have been refurbished by 2 Talpur Mirs. Some believe that it was built in the 8th century against Arab incursions, others date it back to the Scythians. It stands in isolation, giving no clue as to what it was intended to defend other than the trade route from Central Asia to Thatta through the Kirthar Hills.

The Fort walls are on average 4 m high and 1 m wide, and from a distance gives the impression of the Great Wall of China, especially on the long, unbroken S side. The battlements near the entrance are sandstone, although elsewhere they are shale and limestone. You enter through the **Sann Gate** to the E, where the River Rani used to flow out. Just inside the entrance is a Hindu temple-like structure. The Rani was a fast flowing river once, as can be seen by the broken bridge of which only a stone pillar remains standing. Today you will still come across several pools with fish, waterfalls and a fresh water spring where the river enters the fort at **Mohan Gate** (W). The others are **Amri Gate** (N) and **Shahper Gate** (S). The **Miri Fort,** with its remains of residential buildings and barracks, is on a small hillock in the centre.

The tribal **Gabol** people here are happy to help provide you with food, at an inflated price. Miri appears to have been the seat of the rulers, and is in direct sight of Shergarh Fort and the watch towers on the enclosure wall. **Shergarh** is set on top of a 600 m high hill, protected on 3 sides by sheer rock faces and only entered through the SW. Excellent views on a clear day.

Although it is not impossible to visit Ranikot for a day, if you are really keen to explore properly be prepared to camp. Contact Sind Wildlfe Management Board at Karachi for more information or PTDC Information Centre, Club Rd, Karachi,

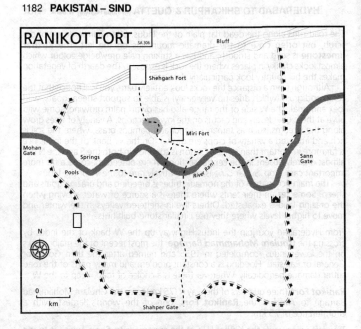

RANIKOT FORT SA 306

Bluff

Shehgarh Fort

Miri Fort

Mohan
Gate

Springs

Pools

River Rani

Sann
Gate

N

0   1
km

Shahper Gate

T 511293 which offers conducted tours.

Warning Take advice on safety of travel before planning a trip.

Amri is about 20 km further N from **Sann**. It takes imagination to visualise the importance of Amri over 5000 years ago, for there is little other than the mound, made of generations of mud houses built on top of each other, to testify to the vitality of this small settlement and its prehistoric importance.

The original inhabitants of Amri were there long before the Harappan people, and represented a quite distinct culture. Excavations on the ancient hilly mounds have found houses and artefacts that clearly predate the Indus Valley sites. The 'strange' pottery found at Amri was at deeper levels, going back perhaps to 5,000 BC, while it appeared mingled with Indus valley pottery at other places nearby.

The Amri people are believed to have disappeared around 2500 BC, when the Harappan Civilization extended its power, French excavations having shown that there were 3 phases of Harappan occupation. They have also found one that was post-Harappan. Copper was used to make jewellery, and stones such as cornelian, agate, chalcedony and steatite were drilled and polished.

The potters produced **Amri ware**, which can be distinguished from the Indus Valley Black-on-Red pottery. The use of fine buff and pale pink paste in bands around the mouth of the vessels, with geometric patterns infilled with checkered work, or diamonds and chevrons, is typical. **Potsherds** dating from 3000 BC and also **Indus bricks** of a millennium later were found. The shallow stone burial chambers of the Amri people also contained pottery and ornaments, but little is known of what they worshipped, and only 'mother goddess' figurines, similar to those in the wider region have been found.

Population pressure The absence of a large settlement has led to the belief that the Amri people lived in scattered villages, possibly using a somewhat better placed, larger and more important village as a centre for trading. The pastoral tribes appear to have preferred the hills, with sheltered valleys and springs. They were slowly forced to move from the W through pressure of population on the land and the changes in climate, and were not attracted by the plains of the Indus. Their settlements appear in the valleys along the Baluchistan- Sind border, forming a pattern similar to that of the Baluchis thousands of years later.

The road N from Amri comes close to the thick forests and the foothills of the Kirthar Hills and next reaches the dusty collection of large houses that once were occupied by residents who reflect the popularity of the Hindu shrine and the sulphurous hotsprings nr **Lakhi** village. The tomb is near the railway line near Lakhi. There are 4 springs at **Lakhi Shah Saddar** near the cave where the Muslim saint Shah Saddar meditated which still draws pilgrims who come in search of a cure for rheumatism and skin ailments. The track to the left off the Indus Highway, is just after the level crossing. The road runs along the foothills until you reach **Sehwan Sharif**, formerly Sewistan.

Sehwan Sharif may be the oldest continuously occupied town in Sind. It's famous **fort**, whose remains lie across the deep and narrow valley to the N of the town, was used by Alexander the Great. You can see part of the wall and battlements. It was also a Buddhist capital when the ascetic brother of **Chandragupta II** ruled in the 4th century. When Mohd bin Qasim marched to Sehwan from Nerun he covered nearly 180 km, probably taking the longer route through the hills for safety.

The river then, as now, probably received its water from the overflowing Manchar Lake. Where the channels of the Indus changed course they left coarse infertile silt with stretches of lowland which support patches of sar grass. However, where the lowlying land remains underwater, the **dhands*** are fringed with a variety of vegetation. The deep basin between the W hills and the Indus in Central Sind forms a vast lake.

An oasis amidst the arid and dusty wasteland on a small hill, **Sehwan** is famous for the shrine of the 13th century Sufi saint **Hazrat Lal Shahbaz Qalander** (Divine Spirit of the Red Falcon). Born in Afghanistan, he came from an order of dervishes from Persia. The **Qalanders** were an 11th century order of wandering sufis, who gave up everything wordly to devote themselves to propagating their religion, which was free from orthodox rituals. The saint was renowned for his scholarship in Persian and Arabic, and for his miracles. He claimed to be the last direct descendant of Mohammad, living in Sehwan for 40 years helping the local people in times of disaster, and amazing them with his miracles.

The original 14th century tomb decorated with tiles and calligraphy, has a dome and a lantern. Another larger **tomb** completed in the 17th century, partly constructed of wood, has beaten silver ornamentation on the railings and spires. You can enter through the new entrance to the S where you will see the gold covered doors given by the Shah of Iran, or from the old E gateway into the courtyard.

The shrine is very popular, both for Muslims and Hindus. The numbers swell on Th, especially just after the new moon, and peaks at the annual Urs festival, which falls on the 18th of Shaban (the month before Ramazan) when thousands of followers arrive from all over the country. During Urs, large numbers of fakirs (spiritual mendicants) congregate, dressed in flowing robes, bracelets and bead necklaces and join in the devotional dance of the dervishes.

In the courtyard there is massed dancing to the accompaniment of large drums and gongs every evening at 1830 for 30 min daily and 1 hr on Th. The disciples express their devotion through rhythmic dancing, music and poetry. The men and women dance separately and reach a trance-like state for up to an hour. The **waterclock** used to keep time is in the form of a pot with a hole which fills and sinks after 15 min.

You can wander around the colourful bazaar with its food and souvenir shops that services the stream of pilgrims. You will find numerous tombs of members of royal families who chose to be buried near the saint's mausoleum as well as a mosque built by **Qutbuddin Aibak**, builder of the Qutb Minar in Delhi.

Hotels *District Council Rest House*, T Sehwan 68. Reservations: Chief Executive Officer, Dadu, T 0229 342. The new Rest House has a/c rm with attached baths. *Irrigation Rest House*, Old Fort. Reservations: Executive Engineer, Irrigation, Dadu, T 0229 404.

To the W, across the road from Sehwan, is the large marshy area covered by

Manchar Lake, caused by the overflowing of the right bank of the Indus river and the drainage of a large area of the Kirthar Hills. The oval shaped lake with clear blue water has a max depth of 5 m.

Many major rivers that flow N-S in the the northern hemisphere, impelled by the force of the earth's rotation, cut into their W banks, and the Indus is no exception. Excess water used to drain off into the Indus through the *Aral river* into the **Manchar Lake**, which acted like a great safety valve. When the Indus was in flood, the waters would flow back into the lake through the Aral. At the peak of the season, between May and Aug, the lake is brimful with fish. In winter the water level is a lot lower and the lake, bedecked with pretty water lilies, attracts game (duck, partridge, quail, snipe) and with them visitors with their guns.

Local people have an ingenious method for catching their prey, by putting an earthen pot with holes (or stuffed egrets), over their heads and swimming towards their catch who remain unaware of the hunter's approach! The tribe of *Mohana* fishermen here also use traditional methods of fishing, frightening the fish into nets, cleverly stretched out on large circular enclosures, supported by poles in the water. By noisy beating of drums and cans from boats, and by disturbing the water with sticks the men scare the fish into the nets and then wade in the water and dive to get them. The old method of spearing has not been totally abandoned though they also catch fish by tying baits on underwater lines.

The community lives in floating villages in groups of big wooden houseboats on the lake or in mud huts along the **Dunister canal.** The large flat bottomed wooden boats have characteristically decorated high prows and usually accommodate a family in 2 rooms. The fish, waterfowl and waterlily stems provide food while the bamboo and long weeds on the lakes' edge provide building material. They also sell the reed mats in neighbouring towns. A section of the lake has been given over to boat building.

You can reach the lake by driving from **Bubak** to the embankment of the canal where you can hire a boat for the day or walk the remaining 3 km along the bank. The *Rest House* at Bubak can be reserved through the PWD at Dadu.

Travelling N from **Sehwan** the road passes through a region of rich rice cultivation. As with rice fields across Asia, they often produce a glorious landscape of varied greens even where the flatness of the terrain would suggest almost unlimited boredom. The National Highway passes through the 18th century capital of Sind, **Khudabad**, so diminished in size now that its two main monuments seem out of place. The Khudabad Jami Mosque is big enough to hold nearly 2000 and has some very attractive tiled decoration. You pass this on the roadside, but have to take a 2 km detour to find the **Tomb of Yar Mohammad Kalhora**. Although this is partially ruined, enough of the beautiful floral tile decoration remains to give an impression of the original.

The road by-passes *Dadu* (*Population* 175,000) and it's possible to cross the Indus on the bridge at **Moro** for the shortest route to Sukkur. If you want to see Moenjo Daro, keep on the W bank Indus highway. Continue through Mehar, where you can stop to sample a local delicacy *Mawar,* a milk dessert enriched with dried fruit and nuts. Continue to Nazipur and turn right off the Indus highway for

Moenjo Daro

Not only one of the most important archaeological sites of S Asia, for its age it is one of the most stunningly restored and preserved pre-historic cities in the world, see page 78.

It is easy to reach from Karachi by air or by train. Allow a full day to walk round. It is one of the most peaceful of famous sites in Pakistan and India, comparatively

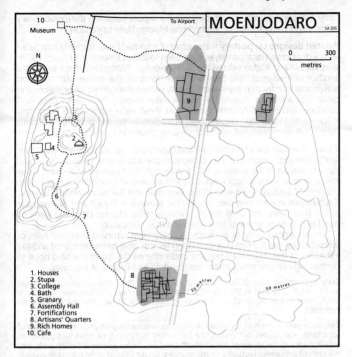

MOENJODARO
SA 305

To Airport

10 Museum

N

0   300
metres

9

1. Houses
2. Stupa
3. College
4. Bath
5. Granary
6. Assembly Hall
7. Fortifications
8. Artisans' Quarters
9. Rich Homes
10. Cafe

52 metres

50 metres

8

little visited, although on special holidays, the grounds of the museum are packed with busloads of cricket-playing Pakistani students, families and elderly people out for the day.

The *Tourist Guest House* behind the museum now serves a limited range of food (a packed lunch is provided by PIA if you are travelling by air), iced drinks and tea, so it is no longer essential to take all these with you, but do carry some water and skin cream. Even by March the temperatures get uncomfortably hot in the middle of the day, and on the site itself there is virtually no shade. The city remains are extensive, and it is at least a 5 km walk to get all round.

	Jan	Feb	Mar	Apr	May	Jun	Jul	Aug	Sep	Oct	Nov	Dec	Av/Tot
Max (°C)	22	26	31	37	42	42	40	39	38	36	30	25	34
Min (°C)	8	11	16	22	26	29	28	27	26	21	15	10	20
Rain (mm)	5	7	6	2	2	3	33	23	4	2	1	1	90

Moenjo Daro represented the culmination of a long period of development within the Indus region. In some places early Indus Valley settlements can be traced back to the Neolithic, and the pottery of the whole Indus system may go back to 4000 BC or even earlier. With the development of the Kot Diji style of pottery came also greater uniformity throughout the region, heralding the extraordinary political and cultural unity of the Harappa-Moenjo Daro city culture..

Painted designs on pottery such as that of a horned head, formerly associated with a distinctive Harappan style, have been found at a number of much earlier sites. Allchin and Allchin call this the "buffalo deity". Alongside it there developed another horned god, this time with the horns of the Indian bull. It seems reasonable to infer that there were already certain associations of buffaloes and cattle with a horned deity of the Mature Indus religion. "It is clearly possible " conclude Allchin and Allchin "to see that these ideas continue to exert their influence on Indian folk religion down to modern times, and that the Early Indus period is in every way part of the continuing growth of Indian civilisation."

If that is the case, then Moenjo Daro and Harappa occupy a position of enormous fascination with respect to the subsequent development of religious ideas and cultural growth in the whole of S Asia. Although the majority of the Indus Valley towns were in what is now Pakistan, there are several important sites in India – the port of **Lothal (see page 1060)**, **Rangpur** and **Rojidi** in modern Gujarat, **Kalibangan** in Rajasthan **(see page 435)**, **Banavli** in Punjab and **Alamgirpur** to the N of Delhi. Yet of all the sites known today Moenjo Daro and Harappa stand out, both by virtue of their scale and their complexity.

An enormous body of evidence has now been retrieved from the ruins of these 2 cities, yet the fact that no written records have been discovered and the remnants of the script itself remains undeciphered still leaves the field open to contrasting interpretations of the rise, function and decline of the cities.

Early excavation Moenjo Daro was first excavated by the Indian Archaeological Survey under Sir John Marshall in 1922 and 1931, and subsequently by Sir Mortimer Wheeler in 1947. Now in the hands of the Pakistan Archaeological Survey, the site is excellently presented.

The main gate is due N of the citadel. It is best to walk up the path and steps to the top of the citadel, now capped by the ruins of a 2nd century Buddhist stupa. From here you get an excellent idea of the layout of the whole city, and can follow a broadly circular path, well marked out with paved footpaths where necessary, to take you round the main built up areas of the city.

The citadel From the top of the mound you get a commanding view of the citadel below and around the central height. The evidence of town planning, an important feature of the major cities, is all around. Moenjo Daro, in common with Harappa and Kalibangan, has its citadel as the westernmost point of the complex, built up on a mound of mud-brick. This would have raised the most important area of the city above the floods of the Indus that regularly inundated the lower town.

The surface level now is more than 10 m higher than it was when Moenjo Daro's first houses were being built and have been submerged under the ever increasing deposits of silt. The 13 m high brick embankment here was probably also a defence against flooding. The long axis in all 3 cities runs N-S. To the E was a lower city – mainly residential houses. The large mural in the museum, suggests that the citadel (probably, also residential areas) was surrounded by massive brick fortifications. Although the layout of the streets is not absolutely precise, the main pattern is of the wider streets running from N to S and a series of narrower E-W streets. The width seems to be deliberately graded, the widest being twice the second and 4 times the width of the lanes.

The civic buildings As you walk down from the top and walk through the citadel area immediately to the W of the stupa, you see other features common to the cities: the presence of civic and administrative buildings, **the great bath** (referred to as the "royal bath", though there is little evidence of the political structure of the society, other than that of its buildings and domestic artefacts) and possibly **a granary**.

Whatever the uncertainties of interpretation the buildings are extraordinarily impressive. The bath is 12 m by 7 m and 3 m deep with flights of steps into it at each end and "changing" cubicles along the side. It may have been used for ritual bathing, still so important in Indian worship today. If you walk down from the edge of the bath to the level immediately below it you can follow the sluice through which the water was drained away – a beautifully made brick-lined drain, about 3 m high. Still further to the W you see what Sir Mortimer Wheeler argued were **granaries**, twenty 7 blocks criss-crossed with ventilation channels.

All around is the **brick work** which was one of the hallmarks of Harappan city building. There is a remarkable standardisation of size. The most common Harappan brick was 28 cm by 14 cm by 7 cm. At Moenjo Daro sun-dried brick was used mainly for filling, burnt brick for facing and structural work. Special bricks were used for particular purposes: sawn bricks for bathrooms and in the residential area to the E, and wedge-shaped bricks for the wells, common in the eastern quarter.

If you walk about 200 m S from the stupa mound and the great bath you cross a shallow valley before climbing to the second main citadel area, with the **Assembly Hall** and **fortifications** at the extreme SE corner. All that remains of this building are 4 rows of 5-brick plinths which Allchin and Allchin suggest must have been the bases of wooden columns.

The artisans' quarter The path goes steeply down past the fortifications and across to the SE to a group of 'artisans houses'. The residential sites in Moenjo Daro show as much evidence of town planning as the citadel. There is a wide range in size, but the archaeologist Sarcina has shown how virtually all the houses in Moenjo Daro, conform to one of 5 basic modules. The main variant is the position of the **courtyard**, and you can still see several of the types in villages in NW India and Pakistan today.

Almost every house had a bathroom (shown by a sawn brick pavement with a surrounding curb). Walking down the narrow streets, drain pipes and vertical chutes for toilet waste disposal, are clearly visible. In the lower city are brick drains, covered over with other bricks or sometimes slabs of stone, and in this S zone there are small, barrack like houses. One of the most remarkable features are the excavated wells which now stand proud of the ground by as much as 4 m. The constant silt deposition was matched by the raising of the brick lining.

The high class residential area Walk N again from the southernmost group of houses in the lower city along the broad main street that links the artisans' area with the main higher-class residential area. The remarkable scale of this road suggests that it may have been used for triumphal processions. At the top of a slight slope look across the low valley between the S and N settlements to the magnificent view of the upper class residential area in front of you. Houses are superbly preserved, and high walls separate both broad streets and narrow lanes. The main street was probably lined with stalls and shops and inside the buildings to the W of this main street is a series of variously labelled rooms. Wheeler suggested that a building where the stone sculpture of a seated figure was found, was a temple.

Jewellery Lambrick surmised that the population of Moenjo Daro may have been about 35,000, but more recent research (taking account of a whole new area of settlement) suggests doubling or even trebling that figure. The city left behind it abundant evidence of its high quality of life. Many **copper and bronze tools** and decorative objects have been found, the ore probably having come from mines in **Rajasthan**. Copper and bronze vessels in the late stages of the city show highly developed form, the work of craft specialists.

Gold objects are quite common – beads, pendants and ornaments. Allchin and Allchin argue that the light quality of the gold point to a source as far afield as **Karnataka** in S India, to the Neolithic settlements that were clustered around the bands of quartz reef gold at **Hatti**. Silver and other metals were also common for works of sculpture, such as the famous figure of the dancing girl.

Dating the city Both the dating of the city and the causes of its decline remain unclear. Early dating relied on the comparison of objects found in Harappan cities with similar objects found in Mesopotamia, and dated the Indus Valley settlements at between 2500 and 1500 BC. Subsequent analysis, aided in places by radiocarbon dating has suggested an earlier rise in some parts of the valley, and a decline by 1750 BC at the latest. But what caused the decline is even more speculative than the dating.

The city's decline As you walk back from the lower city past the citadel towards the museum, the fragile nature of the environmental balance today is obvious. Any one change might well have been enough to tip the balance between success and failure. Probably it was a combination of events. In Lambrick's view, the natural flooding of the Indus may have caused it to move its course massively, resulting in the abandonment of vital agricultural land. Such a change could have been brought about by earthquakes in what is still a highly active earthquake zone, **see page 1033**.

Flooding itself may have wiped out large parts of the city, or encouraged the spread of disease on such a scale as to decimate the population. Short of further evidence the least likely explanation seems to be that of the arrival of the "Indo-Aryan hordes", for there still seems to be a gap of at least 2 centuries between the decline of the Indus Valley civilisation and the first arrivals of the Aryans, but new research may yet change that view.

Hotels D *Shabistan Inn*, T 5. 9 d rm with bath.

Tourist Information Centre at the PTDC Complex.

From the entrance to the site you can drive on to *Larkana* (*Population* 275,000 *Altitude* 50 m), noted today as the home town of former President and Prime Minister Zulfikar Ali Bhutto, deposed in 1977 and hanged in 1978. His daughter Benazir Bhutto was elected as Prime Minister in the election following President Zia ul Haq's assassination in 1988, but she in turn was ousted from power in 1990, to lose the succeeding election in Oct1990. It is an important regional town for the W bank region of Sind.

Hotels D *Gulf*, Bunder Rd, T 22608. a/c rm with bath. **E** *Mehran*, New Station Rd, T 23274. 31 rm with bath. **F** *Faiz*, Old Station Rd, T 60293. 20 rm with bath. **F** *Tourist Inn,* Old Station Rd, T 22482. 15 rm with bath.

For Shikarpur and Sukkur continue NE out of Larkana through *Naudero* (20 km), the Bhutto home village. The Highway bypasses Shikarpur, now greatly reduced from its one-time strategic importance as one of Asia's major trading posts. For Jacobabad and Quetta, take the road N out of Larkana across the railway line to **Rotadero**, Nabi Shah Wagan, Ramazanpur and Jacobabad.

MAKRAN

You sometimes get magnificent views flying to or from Europe of the strange hammerheaded peninsulas and parallel mountain ranges behind that form some of Pakistan's most inhospitable landscapes. This extreme southwestern administrative division of Baluchistan has Iran to its W and the Arabian Sea to the S, along which it has a 400 km coast line.

Hardly visited because of its remoteness, foreigners are rarely given permission to visit the Makran coast. Being close of the straits of Hormuz, it is geostrategically important. The 3 mountain ranges running E to W are the low Coast Range, nearest the sea which rises to about 65 m, then the *Central Makran Range* which varies in height from 165 m to over 3,300 m and finally the *Siahan Range* which is about 1000 m in the E rising to nearly 1,500 m in the NE.

Travelling by road requires a permit and is a long desert drive, only coming down to the coast itself at a few points. At **Hinglaj** on the right bank of the river Hingol there is an ancient Hindu pilgrimage site on the mountain range dividing **Bela** from **Makran**, about 30 km from the sea coast. However, the road from **Karachi** (about 250 km) is very long.

The **temple** is mud-built at the end of a natural cave and contains a stone dedicated to **Hinglaj Devi**, the Goddess of Fate. Muslims consider it holy too and call the stone **Nani**. *Hingula* (cinnabar) was used to cure snake bites; the Goddess, by association, was thought to heal all kinds of diseases. Pilgrims who can swim, brave the deep circular tank nearby by jumping off a cliff and then find the underwater passage to another tank in order to be absolved of their sins. Others throw coconuts into the tank in order to find out what Fate holds for them – the greater the amount of air bubbles, the greater the happiness to be expected!

The pilgrimage is a long journey undertaken through barren, dry desert, and custom requires special observances at various halts. The PTDC's literature describes the practices: The caravans of devotees appoint a leader *Agvo*, who carries a branch of a tree as a 'staff' of authority. At the first halt at **Liary**, every one puts on yellow robes.

Next, at **Chunder Coops**, prayers are recited and coconuts thrown into the "mud volcanoes" (fumeroles) which are a feature here. On reaching the head of the gorge near the shrine, goats are made available for sacrifice and widowers get their heads shaved. *Chunder Coops*, from Chunder Gups or "Moon Volcanoes", which are affected by the tides (the sea being not far away), is considered holy. The deity **Babhaknath** is said to be present.

The road from Bela crosses the S fingers of the heavily folded sandstones and shales of the Kollwar Garr Hills to **Bedi Dat** (161 km). It then runs due W along the S flank of the **Central Makran Rang**e, which rises to heights of between 1,300 m and 1,600 m, to **Hoshab** (167 km), where it enters the long valley of the **Kech River**. The road continues W, flanked on its N side by the great knife-edge walls of the Central Makran range, until it reaches **Turbat** (97 km), the divisional administrative headquarters of the Makran and famous for its 300 varieties of **dates** – but little else.

	Jan	Feb	Mar	Apr	May	Jun	Jul	Aug	Sep	Oct	Nov	Dec	Av/Tot
Max (°C)	17	21	26	31	36	39	39	38	35	31	25	20	30
Min (°C)	4	6	10	15	20	23	24	22	18	13	8	4	14
Rain (mm)	24	19	17	8	3	3	27	8	1	0	1	11	122

Here one road goes straight on to the **Iranian border** (148 km), not open to traffic, while the main road turns S to the coast. The main road runs slightly E of S through **Pidarak** to **Pasni** (115 km) then W along the coast to Pakistan's second port of Gwadur (120 km) the biggest fishing centre on this coast.

Gwadur The town was given by the Khan of Kalat to the Sultan of Oman, becoming a port for Arab trade for 200 years, before being bought back in 1958 by the Pakistan Govt who hope to develop it. It is a Naval Base and imports from the Gulf duty free. The port town has been depopulated in the last two decades with many of the local people leaving to work in the Gulf states.

Air The International airport handles flights to the Gulf States. If you can get a permit there are daily domestic flights from Karachi to Pasni, Gwadur and Jiwani. It is also possible to fly from Quetta.

BALUCHISTAN

Baluchistan, the SW Province which covers nearly 350,000 sq km (44% of Pakistan's area) is made up of a series of arid basins and hills, an extension of the Iranian plateau. Yet the hills which dominate the western borderlands of Pakistan are highly varied. The road from Iran

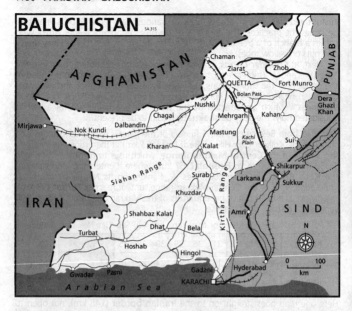

to Baluchistan's capital of Quetta crosses a succession of stone and sand deserts, with magnificent views of the Chagai hills with their remarkable recent volcanoes to the N, but frequent reminders of the harshness of a landscape which claimed the lives of hundreds of Alexander the Great's soldiers on their march back from the Indus through the Makran desert in 324 BC.

INTRODUCTION

The land

The parallel trending ridges which run W to E in W Baluchistan and then turn abruptly N-S closer to the Indus owe their origin and their form to the northwards push of the Indian peninsula. The N of the Province, marked by the **Gomal River**, is made up of the rough terrain of the **Suleiman Ranges**, reaching heights of over 3,000 m in the Takht-e-Sulaiman. At around 30°N the Sulaimans swing W to E, pointing towards Quetta. There is an amazing landscape formed by the succession limestone and sandstone scarps, covered in huge boulders.

To the S of Quetta the same basic pattern is visible, N-S trending hills in the E and close to the Indus, turning to W-E ranges further W. The E limits of these hills is marked by the dramatic **Kirthar Range**, rising to over 2,500 m in the N. Flying across this landscape from Karachi to Moenjo Daro, you get fantastic views of the eroded limestone and sandstone hills.

Baluchis express their feelings in a war song – "the mountains are the Baluchi's forts; the peaks are better than any army; the lofty heights are our comrades; the pathless gorges our friends. Our drink is from the flowing springs; our bed the thorny bush; the ground we make our pillow".

The Makran coast Along the S fringe is one of the world's most arid coastlines, marked by bizarre scenery. Thomas Holditch, the great surveyor of India at the turn of the 20th century, gave a vivid picture of "that brazen coast washed by a molten sea...." Inland he described the "gigantic cap-crowned pillars and pedestals balanced in a fantastic array about the mountain slopes... with successive strata so well defined that they possess all the appearance of massive masonry construction... standing stiff, jagged, naked and uncompromising."

Between the ranges are flat desert depressions, especially of the **Hamun-i-Mashkel**. At a height of between 450-900 m, along the borders of Afghanistan these are lined by the extraordinary recent **volcanoes** of the **Chagai Hills**. At one time there may have been lakes in the basins, as further W in southern Iran where great **salt pans** are temporarily covered in shallow water. As the geographer O.H.K. Spate has written, "small wonder that the local proverb considers Baluchistan as a dump where Allah shot all the rubbish of Creation".

Climate
Rainfall is very low, from as little as 80 mm on the plains to about 300 mm on the hills. Temperatures vary significantly. It can be oppressively hot in the S, temperatures reaching 52°C in the summer. In the hills it remains a very pleasant 27°C at Ziarat.

Altitude has a major effect on temperatures, and the hills and valleys around Quetta and northeastwards are high enough to be well suited to growing temperate fruit. The dry atmosphere makes the climate of the hills particularly attractive after the crushing heat of the plains, but in the winter they get really cold at night, often recording temperatures well below freezing. Even in the hills the max rainfall is under 300 mm per annum, while on the plains it falls to under 50 mm. Most of the rain comes in winter with Mediterranean depressions from the W rather than during the monsoon. Irrigation is therefore as important for successful cultivation as on the dry plains to the E and S.

Settlement
Travelling through Baluchistan today it is difficult to believe that this great region has been the seed bed of S Asian settlement and civilisation. Yet Baluchistan contains some of S Asia's oldest and most important archaeological sites. They give proof of the occupation of the semi-arid hills by early stone age peoples, of the increasing sophistication of stone age technology and then of the first signs of agricultural settlement in the sub-continent, laying the foundations for the ultimate development of the Indus Valley civilisation.

Long before the technology of settled agriculture advanced to a stage at which the Indus Valley itself could be occupied productively, the valleys of Baluchistan had become the home of nomadic hunter gatherers and pastoralists and then of communities who clearly thrived on trade. The transition from the earliest stone age through to the dawn of permanent settlement still has many unanswered questions. However, we can see from centres of stone tool making such as that at **Las Bela** in S Baluchistan the development of small stone tools (microliths) in the Middle Stone Age period. Discoveries at **Mehrgarh** at the foot of the Bolan Pass show the importance of trade through this period.

The People
The population of Baluchistan is just over 5 million, approximately equal to the population of Denmark. The 'Baluchis' include the **Pathans** in the NW, who are the major group, the **Brahui** speakers (of Dravidian origin) who live around Kalat, as well as the **Jattis** of Indo-Aryan origin. Most speak *Pushto* (the language of the Pathans), *Baluchi* or *Brahui*. While Pushto and Baluchi are of Indo-European (Persian) origin, Brahui is Dravidian. **See page 43.**

Nearly half the people of this region live within 80 km of the major city, **Quetta**. Four main groups can be identified. The **Jattis** are cultivators, living mainly around Kalat and Kachhi. The **Pathans** are to the N of Quetta, the **Brahuis** along the mountain border region to the W but separated from the **Bugtis** and **Marri** tribes of the far W and SW.. In Makran there are distinct communities of fishermen (the **Med)** and ancient communities of gypsies, the **Lori.**

The Pakistan Tourism Directory describes the life of some of the **Pathans** in the Zhob Valley. The fair skinned, blue eyed, handsome tribes of *Kakar Pathans* who still lead a nomadic life, leave their homes in Oct in caravans and head for the plains with their sheep, camels and donkeys when you might see "small babies and newly born lambs tied together in nets on camel backs." The turbanned men dress in a *kameez* (shirt), *shalwar* and a long coat while the women wear floor length skirts and waistcoats, often with mirror work, a red shawl and adorn themselves with silver jewellery and tattoos. The custom of wearing red was to make them stand out so as not to be shot at by the men who often took to fighting rivals.

Their food consists of the delicacy, *landhi* (specially fattened sheep, dried and salted), *shorba* (thin meat soup which a group will dunk bread into and eat communally), rice boiled with meat, barbecued lamb, curries and of course their drink of green tea. Tribal customs are kept alive – a bridegroom cannot take the bride away to his house till his party has defeated the bride's party at marksmanship.

Economy

Agriculture Over 100 varieties of *dates* are produced, especially in the Makran District and it is interesting to note that the Baluchi language has about a hundred words for 'dates', just as it has for 'camels'. Wherever there is water available through exploitation of underground and surface water, orchards and fields of wheat have change the landscape dramatically. The local **karez** system uses underground water channels to draw water for irrigation. The **fruit farms** grow a wide variety successfully including apples, grapes, pomegranates, peaches, apricots, cherries, quinces and almonds. Processing plants have emerged so that where certain fresh fruit cannot be easily transported long distances they can still be sent to other parts of the country or exported.

The 750 km coastline from Karachi to the Iranian border lines a sea rich in **fish**. Fishing has been vastly improved and increased through the changeover from small sailing boats to motorised vessels. Projects with assistance from FAO and UNDP have improved techniques, handling and distribution of the catch. **Pasni** and **Turbat** among others have become centres of the industry.

Industry and resources Since Independence a number of small deposits of minerals such as coal and copper have begun to be exploited, but this still stakes place on a very limited scale. Pakistan's total output of **coal** is approximately 2 million tonnes, mostly of mediocre quality, just over half the total coming from mines in Baluchistan. Chromite has been mined at Muslimbagh in Zhob District for decades, but perhaps the best mineral prospect lies in the copper ores that have been discovered in the Saindak deposit near the Iranian border, 650 km W of Quetta. It has been estimated that this contains nearly 350 million tonnes of ore, as well as **gold and molybdenum. Iron** ore is being surveyed near Nok Kundi.

Although it has a disproportionate share of Pakistan's minerals, Baluchistan has a very small industrial output. It has a big **craft industry**, with **reed screen** making for example at Dera Ismail Khan, Kalat and Makran, while some **textile** manufacture has been introduced at Bolan.

History

Baluchistan played a pivotal role in the prehistorical development of S Asia. It was both a route for trade from Mesopotamia and the Iranian plateau into India and the origin of settled agriculture in the sub-continent as far back as 8,000 BC. From the rise of the Indus Valley civilisation however it has always been on the margins of major cultural and political regions, fragmented socially and politically by its diverse, and in places, nomadic tribes.

In the early centuries of Islamic contact it fell under **Arab** rule. In the 17th and 18th century the **Khans** of Kalat united a major part of the modern Province in a Brahui dominated confederacy, sometimes under subject either to **Delhi** or to **Kandahar** but often effectively independent. Between 1840-75 it was brought under **British** rule almost by accident, as a result of British efforts to pacify the NW Frontier and to stabilise its hold of the region bordering Afghanistan. The northern districts were annexed by the British by the Treaty of Gandamak after the Second Afghan War between 1879-81, but it always remained a frontier region. Since 1947 it has been an integral part of Pakistan.

QUETTA

Population 350,000 *Altitude* 1650 m   *Best season* Mar – end May, Sep – Oct.

	Jan	Feb	Mar	Apr	May	Jun	Jul	Aug	Sep	Oct	Nov	Dec	Av/Tot
Max (°C)	10	12	18	23	29	34	35	34	31	25	18	13	24
Min (°C)	-2	-1	3	7	11	15	18	17	10	4	0	-2	7
Rain (mm)	37	43	42	12	7	1	18	4	1	1	6	23	195

Quetta is the State provincial capital and has long been regarded as a hill station for the S. Its main role is strategic. It controls access to the routes from Sibi and the plains across both to Iran and Afghanistan. Originally known as Shal, Quetta played a part in Afghan history, but it enjoyed widely fluctuating fortunes. The Mughals ruled the town until 1556. Akbar then lost it to Persian control but re-took it nearly forty years later. In 1872 it was found in a state of almost total decay, and was taken into British control by Sir Robert Sandeman, the first political agent in Baluchistan, in 1876.

As the capital of Baluchistan it has some administrative and commercial functions. On 31 May 1935 it was almost entirely destroyed by the same catastrophic **earthquake** that destroyed Kalat to the S. Over 40,000 people were killed, and as a result the majority of the new buildings that have been built to replace those destroyed were single storeyed, although you will see double storey buildings now. The new bricks are distinctively yellowish.

The well planned city on a grid pattern is well kept, the streets have tall ashes, cypresses or poplars along them, and the bigger houses have orchards in their compounds. Even modest homes have a garden growing grapes and apricots. **Jinnah Rd** (Bruce Rd) and **Shahrah-e-Zarghoon** (The Mall) are the two main streets, the former for its shops and the latter for the administrative buildings. Three quarters of the area of the city is taken up by the military cantonment, laid out when the town was a vital frontier post for the British and maintained today as an important centre for the Pakistan Army, whose Army Staff College is here.

Places of interest
There are no old buildings in Quetta. The cantonment is an excellent example of British military townships, formally laid out, and the town itself is a planned city.

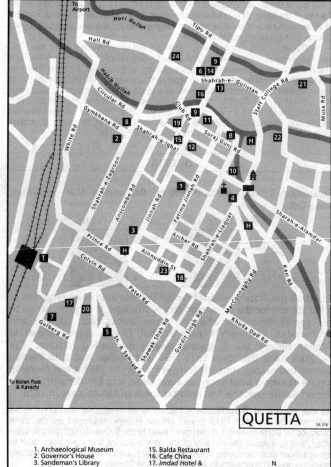

QUETTA

SA 316

1. Archaeological Museum
2. Governor's House
3. Sandeman's Library
4. Police Station
5. Passport Office
6. Iran Consulate
7. Afghan Consulate
8. GPO
9. Bank
10. Market Square
11. Taj Carpets
12. Handicrafts Centre
13. APWA Centre
14. PIA & Tourist Office

15. Balda Restaurant
16. Cafe China
17. *Imdad Hotel & Tourist Information*
18. *Asia Hotel*
19. *Farah Hotel & Restaurant*
20. *Bloom Star Hotel*
21. *Lourde's Hotel*
22. *Bolan Hotel*
23. *Zulfiqar Hotel*
24. *Serena Hotel*

B. Local Bus Station

N

0   250
metres

The main street, Shahara Zarghoon, is the centre of most commercial activity. It runs approximately N-S, is 1.5 km long from the railway station in the S to the Residency in the N. The **Earthquake Recording Office** on **Chiltan Hill** has commanding views over the town (accessible to 4 wheel drive vehicles only).

Local industries Fruit growing is the main activity with the orchards around the city, particularly in Urak, growing a great variety including peaches, cherries, pomegranates, pears, almonds, walnuts and pistachio, and fruit processing has been introduced. Flower growing, especially rose cultivation and production of rose water is also important. Following tradition, there is a factory making medical drugs from herbs (*Artemesia ephedra*). A sulphur refinery was opened in 1956 and there is a small textile industry. The *Small Industries Carpet Centre* is on Shahrah-e-Alamda, T 71137.

Hotels A *Quetta Serena*, Shahrah-e-Zarghoon. T 70070, Cable: Serena Quetta; Telex: 7821 Serena Pk. 142 rm. All amenities plus tennis, squash, golf. Only international class hotel in town. Restaurant recommended. **D** *New Lourdes*, Staff College Rd, T 70168. 31 rm. Restaurant, gardens where you may camp. **D** *Gul's Inn*, Alibhoy Rd behind Jinnah Rd, T 70170. 30 rm. Restaurant.

Several **E** grade hotels on Jinnah Rd offer simple accommodation of rm with fan and attached bath. *Marina*, Quarry Rd corner of Jinnah Rd, T 75109. 26 rm with bath. Restaurant. *Shees*, opp Civil Hospital, T 77876. 28 rm some a/c. Restaurant. *Chilton*, T 75635. 19 rm. *Hotel Nile*, T 70736. 15 rm. Restaurant. *Imdad*, nr Rly Station, T 70166. 74 rm. Restuarant, shop, Tourist Information. Some others are *Bloom Star*, Stewart Rd, T 70177. 46 rm, some a/c. Central. A/c restaurant and coffee shop, lawns. On Prince Rd: *Glacier*, T 75130. 46 rm. Shop. *Zulfiqar*, T 73736. 36 rm. Restaurant, courtyard; *City Baluchistan*, T 70647. *Azeem*, Fatima Jinnah Rd, T 73552. 17 rm, some a/c. A/c restaurant. *Asia*, Fateh Muhammed Rd, T 71681. Shared bath. Clean.

The **F** category hotels on (some on Jinnah Rd, others nr the Taftan Bus Station in the SE of town) usually have shared bath and may not have a restaurant on the premises. Cheap hire of a bed in the courtyard in the summer is allowed by some of these hotels. **F** *Railway Retiring Rooms*, T 71200.

Restaurants Several of the hotels have restaurants, the best at Quetta Serena. Others tend to be nr the Rly Station and on Jinnah Rd. The town offers excellent lamb preparations, steamed *Sajji*, roasted, braised or grilled *kebabs* and many roadside stalls produce very tasty food. On Jinnah Rd: *Data* T 79217; *Rex*, nr Club Rd, T 77210. *Summoon*, opp Civil Hospital, a/c, T 77876. *Lehri Sajji House*. *Cafe Firdousi*, T 71036. *Playland and Jambu Burger*, T 72985 are Snack Bars.

Others are: *Tabbaq*, Circular Rd, T 75196. *Nasheman*, Shahrah-e-Iqbal, T 75937. *Lal Kebab*, Prince Rd. Chinese – *China Cafe*, Jinnah Rd/ Staff College Rd, opp ADBP, a/c, T 74728.

Banks Several on Jinnah Rd, corner of Shahrah-e-Iqbal: **Grindlays**, T 75188, **Habib**, T 75180, **United**, T 71266 and **Muslim Commercial**, T 72064, **National Bank of Pakistan** is on Shahrah-e-Adalat, T 70563.

Shopping Jinnah Rd is lined with shops and the main bazaar is here. Others are Kandahari Bazaar, Sharah-e-Iqbal, Surajgunj Bazaar, Market Square and Liaqat Rd Market. The Baluchi carpets and embroidery work with mirrors, Afghan carpets, fur coats, onyx carvings, semi-precious stones are good buys. The *Carpet Centre* is on Shahrah-e-Alamda to the E of the town, *Mokham Brothers*, *Carpet House* and *Taj Carpet* are on Jinnah Rd, T 75044. For handicrafts on the same Rd, try *Chiltan Government Handicrafts Centre*, T 71139, *Craft Gallery*, T 76705 and *Pakistan Arts and Crafts Centre*, T 75115. Others are *Pak Handicrafts*, T 75359 and *Wata Handicraft*, Art School Rd, T 71213.

Local transport Few taxis. Auto rickshaws and tongas available. **Buses** The New Adda Bus Station is on Sariab Rd and the Local Bus Station on Circular Rd.

Sports Gymkhana Club, Prince Rd, T 77272. Flying Club, Samungali Rd. Also Swimming Club, Golf Club, Riding and Cricket.

Museums Archaeological Museum of Baluchistan, off Jinnah Rd, T 75142. Open 0900-1700, daily except Fri. Opened in 1906 as the MacMahon Museum, it was devasted by the earthquake in 1935. The original collection of exhibits representing not only Baluchistan but also neighbouring countries in the region covering Persia and Arabia which included archeological finds, art and craft items, natural history specimens, was rehoused several times. The present Museum, opened in 1972, has built up its own collection and has galleries for weapons, ceramics, manuscripts, paintings, ethnology and minerals in addition to the archaeolocial section. It has acquired a recent Indus Valley discovery of grave ornaments, thought to date to 2500 BC. You may have to ask to be shown them.

Staff College Museum, Staff College Rd, has a considerable collection of British Army memorabilia. Open 0900-1900, daily except Fri.

National Museum, Tola Ram Rd off Jinnah Rd. Open daily except Fri, 0900-1900. Collection of weapons. **Museum** on Sariah Rd, T 72780.

Libraries The Sandeman Library and the Public Library are on Jinnah Rd.

Useful addresses **Afghan Consulate**, Shahrah-e-Zhargoon, nr the Rly Station, T 74160. **Iranian Consulate**, Hali Rd, T 75054. The *New Lourdes Hotel:* visitors often have information about conditions for travel in Iran. Dy Commissioner, Shahrah-e-Iqbal, T 75070. Police Station. Shahrah-e-Liaqat, T 74147. Passport Office, Sheikh Samad Rd, T 74134. Foreigners Registration Office, Shahrah-e-Iqbal. **Cultural Centres** Iranian Cultural Centre, Shahrah-e-Iqbal, T 75051 and the APWA Centre off Shahrah-e-Gulistan.

Parks and zoo Sadique Park on McConnaughay Rd, Liaqat Park on Shahrah-e-Adalat. The Ayub Stadiaum, off Jail Rd and the Race Course nr Spinny Rd are to the NW of the city.

Post and telegraphs General Post Office and Central Telegraph Office, Shahrah-e-Zhargoon, T 74031.

Hospitals and medical services Civil, Jinnah Rd, corner of Prince Rd, T 70145. Christian, Mission Rd, T 75220. Lady Dufferin, McConaughay Rd, T 75488. Chemists – Quetta Medical Store, T 75126 and Razee Pharmacy on Jinnah Rd, T 71222 and Pak Pharmacy, Prince Rd, T 74353.

Chamber of Commerce and Industry, Jinnah Rd, PO Box 117, T 72642.

Travel agents Quetta Travels, Jinnah Rd, T 72001. Al-Falah Travels, Circular Rd, T 73770.

Tourist offices and information PTDC Tourist Information Centre at the Muslim Hotel, Jinnah Rd, T 79519 and at Hotel Imdad, Jinnah Rd, T 70166. Airport Counter, T 72053.

Air 3 flights weekly to and from Islamabad, 4 for Lahore and Karachi. PIA Office, Jinnah Rd, corner of Hali Rd, T 72011. Airport, T 73757, Enquiry T 71211.

Rail To Karachi *Bolan Mail*, 4, daily, A/c, 1555, 20hr 30min; *Sind Exp*, 46, daily, 2045, 24 hr; **Lahore** *Abbaseen Exp*, 17, daily, A/c,1845, 26 hr 40 min **Islamabad-Rawalpindi** *Abbaseen Exp*, 17, daily, A/c,1845, 33 hr 30 min; *Taftan* *Taftan Exp*, 125, Wed, 1520, 18 hr 45 min; *0485*, Sat, 1520, 21 hr. **Warning** You normally need to book well in advance (about 14 days) for a/c and 1st Class. Station Enquiries and Reservations, T 71200, and Divisional Superintendent of Railway Office, Shahrah-e-Zhargoon, T 70171.

Road The new road to Karachi passes through **Khuzdar**, **Makran** and **Las Bela**. Since several of the major highways are restricted to foreigners travelling by public transport only, enquire before taking a car. For route see Karachi to Quetta.

Buses The Quetta Regional Transport Authority run buses and mini-buses on inter-city routes covering the region and though they may travel through 'controlled' zones, foreigners are permiitted to use the buses. The charges vary according to the road surface, the cheapest routes are on metalled roads, the most expensive on desert roads. Students are charged half fare. Buses for **Ziarat** and **Chaman** are almost hourly from the Local Bus Staion on Circular Rd. Buses for **Karachi** and **Taftan** leave from the New Adda Bus Station on Shariab Rd, W of Rly Station, about every 2 hr.

Excursions

If you visit the staff College it is possible to continue out to *Hanna Lake*, 10 km from the centre of Quetta The lake gives an extraordinary contrast between its own light blue and the surrounding arid brown of the hills. Planted pines provide small patches of contrasting green. From the middle of Quetta go past the Staff College and to a fork in the road. The right fork leads to a 70 km circular drive through some of Baluchistan's most attractive countryside, with orchards, hills and lakes.

The left fork in the road leads to the lake. After 2 km take another left fork for the Hanna Lake which is a popular picnic spot and where you can hire a boat. Daily bus services from Quetta. The right fork goes to *Urak* (a small village surrounded by the mountains, known as "the fruit garden of Quetta") in the Zarghun Hills. Soft drinks are available. The route passes through beautiful scenery, lined with a wide variety of fruit trees.

QUETTA TO SUKKUR via the Bolan Pass

The route from Quetta through the Bolan Pass offers the easiest access from the plains to the Iranian plateau to the S of the Khyber Pass. It is one of the oldest trade routes in the world, followed by prehistoric traders in precious stones, by nomadic hunters and gatherers as well as their settled agricultural successors. Today it is followed by a tarmac road with regular buses and the railway line from Sukkur to Quetta. The journey is 406 km.

The drive is extraordinary. Travel S from Quetta, forking left off the road to Nushki and the Iranian border after 13 km and taking the road to **Spezand** (25 km *Altitude* 1650 m) and the **Bolan Pass**. This is the last settlement of any consequence before Sibi, nearly 5 hr away on the bus, 3 to 4 hr in a car. The 16 km long gorge cuts through the arid conglomerate sandstone rocks, the usually dry bed of the river a jumble of huge boulders, only moved by the periodic floods that sweep down the valley.

In addition to being the route for modern traffic to and from the plains, the Pass continues to be used by nomadic tribes moving from the hills to the plains in winter, and back into the mountains in the summer. The valley is often crowded with their trains of dromedaries during spring and autumn. Beyond the gorge proper, streams begin to appear in the bed of the river, some rising from hot springs along the bank. At the tiny settlement of **Mach** (41 km *Altitude* 990 m), a railway engine changing station, the railway takes a course to the E of the road, while the river becomes progressively more permanent and fuller.

Just S to **Pir Gheib**, 16 km off the main road, is a hot water spring gushing out of the limestone rocks. Isobel Shaw suggests that there is excellent swimming. Turn immediately after sign to Sukkur 316 km. Jeep needed. On the left is a steep cliff, on the right a stony floodplain. A sign in Urdu to the Holy Shrine of Pir Gheib marks the beginning of the rough track across the floodplain. Ask directions or go with a guide.

The main road continues S to Bibi Nani's Bridge and **Gokirat** (20 km), and **Pinjera Pul** (18 km) where the road crosses to the E bank of the Bolan River, the last leg of the Pass. Immediately to the S of the final gorge is **Bolan Weir**. Irrigation Dept *Guest House*. Reservations, Deputy Commissioner, **Dadhar**. The road does a sharp turn N, keeping to the left bank of the **Bolan River**, then due E towards Dadhar. On the right before reaching Dadhar is the ancient site of **Mehrgarh**.

Mehrgarh, is 150 km as the crow flies from the Quetta Valley. Here you are on the borders of quite distinct environments in the heart of a zone of physical and cultural transition. The archaeological site which makes Mehrgarh of such interest and importance was discovered by the French archaeological team under Professor Jean Jarrige which has been working in Pakistan since 1959. Their attention was first drawn to the low mound rising above the plain. Excavations have been extended onto the plains themselves, revealing settlements covering hundreds of acres and going back to Neolithic times.

According to the British archaeologists Bridget and Raymond Allchin the earliest part of the settlement, on the high bank of the Bolan River at the N end of the site, was probably a camp of nomadic pastoralists. The movement and downcutting of the river have exposed over 11 m of levels of occupation.

The topmost layer, which contains mud-brick houses forming an extensive settlement, has been dated with radiocarbon dating to 5100 BC. More recent excavation shows that the date of the site goes back to at least 8500 BC. The settlement not only has distinctive multi-roomed houses and a granary but graves where bodies were found along with beads, baskets lined with bitumen and copper grave goods, suggesting institutionalised burial. The lack of ceramic finds in the lowest levels suggests that Mehrgarh was occupied long before pottery was developed, when stone and bone implements were common.

Turquoise beads found in the burials of the first period suggests that already at this early date these semi-precious stones were being imported from a long distance, possibly Turkmenia. Finds elsewhere support this evidence of extensive trade in luxury goods thousands of years before the Indus Valley Civilisation developed, a trade which Mehrgarh, at the mouth of the Bolan Pass, was well placed to exploit.

Period II Mehrgarh has produced many other important discoveries. From Period II, a direct continuation of the first period, are sherds of **handmade pottery**, increasing towards the end of the period with **wheel thrown pottery** making its first appearance. More evidence of long distance trade comes from the discovery of **conch shell fragments**, which must have come over 500 km from the Arabian Sea, and **lapis lazuli beads** from Badakshan in the far N of modern Afghanistan. The first metal object – tiny **lead pendant** – and an **unbaked figurine** of a male torso have also been discovered, along with more burials. Strikingly in this case the bodies were covered with red ochre "a practice already attested in Middle Palaeolithic burials in Central Asia, and still to be founds among untouchable groups in S India!"

Period III, probably dating from the first half of the 4th millenium BC sees the entry of huge quantities of pottery, with **painted motifs** similar to those found on pottery at **Mundigak** in S Afghanistan. More beads, shells and lapis lazuli are joined at this level by **copper artefacts**. The pottery shows strong similarities with that from Mesopotamia and Iran, and it seems that from an early stage pottery was made using a wheel, probably sunk in a pit, and fired in a kiln with a separate fire-chamber.

Settled agriculture Mehrgarh is the earliest site of settled agriculture yet discovered in S Asia. Dr Richard Meadow, an American archaeologist who has been working with the team, claims that it now possible to say that by 8000 BC there were well developed villages with agriculture, and the beginning of animal domestication. The domestication of sheep, goats and cattle occurred as early in Baluchistan as it did further W. At the same time the hunting of large wild animals continued. Elephants, wild water buffalo and Nilgai deer were among those killed. Cereals were also introduced remarkably early; a local variety of barley and wheat by 8,000 BC, and some evidence of cotton by 5,000 BC.

Much of this astonishing history has still to be imagined by the visitor or passer-by, for there is little on the site itself to illustrate visually the outstanding importance the Mehrgarh holds for the understanding of S Asia's settlement and culture. Despite that, as you come down onto the plains of the Indus across the alluvial fan of the Bolan river there is an unmistakeable sense of being at the point of contact between regions and between cultures.

From Mehrgarh the road crosses the alluvial plains E to Sibi. Where these are now irrigated, as around **Dadhar**, they present a lush green landscape during the winter and spring, giving little hint of the extremes of climate of the natural desert which surrounds it. However, the region of Sewistan and its capital Sibi, is renowned throughout Pakistan for the overwhelming heat of its summers, which run from late Mar until the end of Oct. There is a Persian proverb which runs "Sibi-o-Dhadar Sakhti Dozakh Chira Pardakhti", loosely translated as "Oh Allah, having created hot places like Sibi and Dhadar, why bother to conceive of hell?"

Sibi (59 km *Population* 30,000 *Altitude* 130 m) is an ancient town in its own right. The present town was laid out by the British after they captured it during the Second Afghan Wars in 1878, when it was named **Sandemanabad** after Sir **Robert Sandeman**. Before that it had been part of the 11th century Ghaznavid empire, the Hindu Rai dynasty of Sind, and still earlier kingdoms.

	Jan	Feb	Mar	Apr	May	Jun	Jul	Aug	Sep	Oct	Nov	Dec	Av/Tot
Max (°C)	21	25	31	37	43	45	42	41	40	37	31	24	35
Min (°C)	6	10	15	22	27	31	31	30	27	19	12	7	20
Rain (mm)	17	17	18	6	4	7	38	20	5	1	5	6	143

Today Sibi is known across Pakistan for its *Jirga*, or annual council, and the cattle fair that follows it. Although Jirgas are a traditional tribal council in Afghanistan and the whole of the Frontier region the *Sibi Jirga* was started by Sandeman in 1882 as a means of encouraging the tribes to take responsibility for ensuring stability and peace in a region which had been bitterly fought over in apparently endless feuds.

Initially Sandeman termed the meeting the Shahi Durbar but after Independence it was renamed the Divisional Jirga, and it is attended by tribal Sardars or chiefs. The meet has become part of the annual Sibi week, a national event held in the middle of Feb, which starts with the annual *horse and cattle show* when the town is packed with visitors. Accommodation is very difficult to find. The 19th century guest house with 42 rm *Sohbat Serat* a shaded courtyard and pillared verandah, and a pleasant atmosphere. **Reservations:** District Committee.

One local writer says "There is great hustle and bustle when one could hardly walk in the bazaars and streets due to the surging crowd. The city bazaars, shops, hotels and 'kehwakhanas' (food and tea stalls) are filled to capacity and one comes across a number of familiar faces. You can meet friends living in far flung areas at Sibi on this occasion, whom it becomes very difficult to see for years together otherwise. Kebabs and 'gandaries' are very common but sipping of the specially Green tea at a kehwakhana has its own charm."

Places of interest The **Residency** and the **Victoria Jubilee Memorial Hall** (now the Jirga Hall) remain as testimony to the period of British rule. The latter was built by public subscription in 1903 and is now a **museum**. Sibi has the usual range of public buildings associated with a district headquarters; municipal buildings and a dispensary, a Library and hospitals. There is now a Govt Hospital. On the outskirts of the town towards the airport are the ruins of Mir Chakkand Rind's 15th century **Chakkar Fort** with beehive-shaped store rooms and the round *basti* of the inner fort.

The road to **Bellpat** (60 km) and Jacobabad runs out to the SSE of the town across the **Kacchi Desert**, following the railway line all the way.

Jacobabad (98 km *Population* 175,000)

	Jan	Feb	Mar	Apr	May	Jun	Jul	Aug	Sep	Oct	Nov	Dec	Av/Tot
Max (°C)	23	25	33	39	44	45	43	40	40	37	31	24	35
Min (°C)	7	9	16	22	26	29	30	28	24	19	12	7	19
Rain (mm)	8	8	7	2	4	6	37	22	1	0	1	3	99

It is a barren road taking about 3 hr by bus. Jacobabad was laid out by **General John Jacob**, the remarkable Political Superintendent of the Upper Sind Frontier Region between 1847-1858. His work is still visible in the **Residency** which he built, and he is buried under a massive tomb. Jacob brought the feuding which had reduced upper Sind to anarchy to an end. Although the massive and direct interference with local tribespeople might have been expected to produce strong opposition he is still revered as the man who brought peace to the region, and he is one of the very few Englishmen whose name remains attached to a town in S Asia by popular consent.

Continue SSE out of **Jacobabad** to **Shikarpur** (43 km; *Population* 125,000). This important trading town was founded as a municipal town in 1617, though its trading links with Afghanistan to the W and central Asia to the N go back much further. The town became a trade depot, and traders from Shikarpur themselves travelled very extensively. Before 1949 Shikarpuri traders were influential in Sinkiang, the westernmost province of China, but most were driven out after the Revolution. There is an interesting covered bazaar, and a Church of Pakistan Mission Hospital which specialises in eye diseases named after Sir Henry Holland.

As Murray's guide records drily, the town "has a drainage system, which is unusual".
The road continues through **Lakhi** (15 km) to **Sukkur** (27 km).

QUETTA TO THE IRANIAN BORDER

Quetta has long been the last town of importance on the journey by road or rail from Pakistan directly into Iran. This route is still open for Pakistanis and sometimes for foreigners, and the land crossing into Iran and beyond, which used to be popular until the Iranian Revolution, is still used by some. ***Nok Kundi***, a small desert town, has local style accommodation which is safe but spare. Although there are regular buses every day the road is very little used. Yet in its way the scenery is dramatic. The railway line, which was built for strategic reasons to supply the frontier forces, has a very limited economic role. Trains run once a week, their chief function being to take drinking water to the small settlements en route. The road crosses a series of stone deserts with occasional stretches of dune sand. The air is often startlingly clear and on a cold winter's morning the extreme dryness gives a beautiful freshness despite the lack of surface water or greenery.

Warning If you plan to use this route check with Iranian Consulate in Quetta before you leave. When political conditions allow it is a fascinating, though extremely uncomfortable journey, except in winter. The Iranian border is just over 600 km from Quetta, a full day's journey if you start in the early morning. There is no good accommodation though there are Rest Houses along the way.

Leave Quetta to the S. Just under 1 km S of the station turn right across the railway line, then immediately left. Pass the main Bus Stand and continue S on the road to the Bolan Pass. Take the right fork 30 km from Quetta taking the RCD (Regional Cooperation for Development) road towards Kalat. When you have crossed the **Lak Pass** you reach another fork – left for Kalat and right for Iran. The painted sign used to give the exact distance to London, but that has been obliterated and the sign says Teheran is 2256 km! There is now a customs post here for all traffic.

Nushki (145 km *Altitude* 1020 m) is comparatively new. Tate records that when he was surveying the district in 1899 there was not even one house. By 1902 "what had at that time been a wide and stony plain was now covered with houses". He also illustrates the variability of the desert climate, recording that "on the 20th Jan, heavy rain surprised us. The rain had one advantage, in that it softened the hard soil, which had previously been very trying to both men and animals; but it was followed by storms of wind that raised great clouds of dust, and 2 or 3 days later there was a recurrence of wintry weather, as many as ten degrees of frost being registered on Jan 24th, on which day the maximum temperature never rose above 8°C."

Padag (99 km) and ***Dalbandin*** (84 km; *Altitude* 850 m, but a little way off the road) are small towns with little to stop for, though if you're really stuck you can find accommodation in traveller's bungalows in each. But it's better not to get stuck.

Green onyx is mined near Dalbandin. Immediately to is N is the shallow and seasonal lake, the ***Lora Hamun***, on a traditional trade route from Nushki to the **Helmand River** in Afghanistan. Like many of the shallow depressions in the valley bottoms to the W of Quetta, occasional rains produces temporary lakes which often attract flocks of birds. To the S the arid hills rise to peaks of between 2000 m and 3000 m, the highest being just S of Padag at 3009 m.

To the W of Dalbandin the road runs to the S of the volcanic **Chagai Hills** through **Yakmach**, with local food stalls, to **Nok Kundi** (166 km *Altitude* 680 m) with a *Rest House*. The surfaced road ends here and becomes a graded gravel track across the desert, the quality of which depends on how recently the grader has passed that way. It often gets fiercely corrugated, and is nearly always chokingly dusty. Near the Iranian border, but facing drivers coming from Iran, is a road sign reminding drivers to "Keep Left".

	Jan	Feb	Mar	Apr	May	Jun	Jul	Aug	Sep	Oct	Nov	Dec	Av/Tot
Max (°C)	19	23	28	34	39	42	43	41	38	33	27	21	32
Min (°C)	4	8	12	18	24	27	29	27	22	16	10	6	17
Rain (mm)	15	8	6	4	1	0	1	0	0	0	1	4	39

The road continues to the Pakistani border post at **Taftan** (113 km: Customs and Immigration post). Immediately to the S is the magnificent dormant volcano, the **Koh i Taftan**, rising to a height of almost 4000 m and snow covered in winter. Crossing the border can take some time, and you need to be prepared for an extended wait both on the Pakistan side of the border and at the Iranian customs post of **Mirjawa** (*Altitude* 840 m).

To travel by road across Iran it is of course essential to have the necessary papers. It is also usually required for non-Iranians travelling by car to take an armed escort from the border right across the country, for which a remarkably small fee (about US$40) is charged.

Warning This option is only open to some nationalities. Check in advance at your own embassy or consulate in Pakistan for advice.

QUETTA TO KANDAHAR

You need a permit to take the road to the Afghan border at Chaman. Today there are still many thousands of Afghan refugees on the Pakistan side of the border. **Kuchlagh** (24 km) lies on the N side of the Quetta valley, known particularly for its wide variety of temperate fruit – plums, pears, apples and grapes. From Bostan the railway follows a dramatic and scenic route northeastwards. It skirts the northern slopes of the Takatu Mountain, rising gradually and at one point doing a complete loop to pass over itself before reaching Khanai, where it joins a narrow gauge line to **Muslimbagh** (formerly Hindubagh). The road to the border crosses the Pishin valley, though not actually passing through Pishin.

The **Pishin valley** is one of the major areas of **karez** irrigation and is surrounded by over 5,000 ha of vineyards and orchards. In the early part of this century Murray's Guide commented on the "excellent duck shooting" to be had in Pishin District near Yaru Karez. Its reputation persists, focused on the reservoir at **Bund Khushdil Khan**. 32 km N of **Bostan** the road crosses the **Lora River**, which drains into the central Asian basins rather than flowing into the Arabian Sea.

Qila Abdullah (50 km) is the last settlement before the railway runs through the steep 4 km long **Khojak tunnel**, completed in 1892. Like the Channel Tunnel 100 year later it was begun from both ends at once, but unlike the later feat of engineering, it failed to meet in the middle! Inadequately engineered and ventilated, the air inside is still reputed to be bad at times.

The **Shelabagh** *Rest House* is at the top of the pass. In the present political climate it is still very difficult to get permission to visit and to get the benefit of the views across the plains towards **Kandahar**. This is the modern city which occupies the site of the ancient Gandhara, the centre of Gandharan Buddhist art which, under the 2nd century emperor Kanishka, gave such a distinctive form to the region's artistic development.

The Durand Line Today's frontier with Afghanistan, known as the **Durand Line**, was agreed in 1893 between the governments of Britain and Afghanistan represented by **Sir Mortimer Durand** and **Amir Abdur Rahman**. The S section of this line, some 1300 km, was laid out between Apr 1894 and May 1896 by an extraordinary team, monitored by one of at least equal size from the Afghan side. **G.P. Tate**, the Survey Officer in charge, detailed the forces required: 4 survey officers, a military escort of 150 infantry and 60 cavalry and additional contingents amounting to 1,000. The horse cavalry were augmented by camels.

The work started at **Domandai**, 50 km NE of **Chaman**, and in the first year covered over 600 km to Ghwaza. On the high plateau above the **Lora River,** Tate recorded that the cold was extreme – "Soda water not only froze hard as soon as it left the bottle, but it also froze inside the bottle." The boundary was marked by pillars of stone, and became the frontier of Pakistan and Afghanistan in 1947 when Pakistan became independent, but it has always been a "porous" border across which Afghan tribes have moved to and fro, virtually at will.

QUETTA TO MULTAN via Ziarat and Loralai

The route through the Baluchi hills to Multan travels through wild country, both in the physical and the social sense. The **Zhob Valley** is one of the ancient caravan routes with archaeological interest, and has been described as "a paradise of flowers in the spring and of fruit in the autumn." Peaches, pomegranates, plums, apricots, apples, almonds, grapes, melons and walnuts abound. The wild flower enthusiast will find iris, hyacinths, tulips, poppies, lavender and many more growing wild in great profusion. The spring months of Feb to Apr are exhilarating with a chance to enjoy the snow or see the flowers in bloom in the Zhob Valley. Between Aug and Oct there is a wide range of temperate fruit.

This route too is full of archaeological interest, for increasingly research shows the connections between upland Baluchistan and the very early settlements both to the W in **Afghanistan** at sites like **Mundigak**, and ultimately to the E in the Indus Valley. The "grey ware" pottery bowls link it to sites in Iran.

It is about 560 km or 18 hr driving time. From the railway station leave Quetta along White Rd and travel N to the junction with Baleli Rd. All roads leaving Quetta have checkposts. Turn left across the railway on the road to the **airport**, Zhob and Ziarat.

The road crosses the Quetta plain to **Kuchlagh** (24 km), a busy market town with excellent tea and food stalls. Here the road to **Chaman** and the Afghan border goes straight on through the town, while the road to **Khanai** (25 km; *Altitude* 1670 m), **Zhob** and **Loralai** takes off to the right in the middle of the bazaar. It runs along the edge of an alluvial fan, with streams and *karez* irrigation systems running down it. The narrow gauge railway line from Khanai to Muslimbagh was completed in 1929 as far as **Fort Sandeman**. In the autumn and late spring it is a beautiful drive, but in winter it gets extremely cold and the road to Ziarat is sometimes blocked with snow.

By far the most attractive route to **Loralai** is via Kach and Ziarat. *Kach* (*Altitude* 1,920 m) itself has a small fort and it used to be on the main route up into Baluchistan before the Bolan Pass was leased to the British by the Khan of Kalat.

Ziarat (53 km, *Altitude* 2,500) is famous as a hill station. It was a favourite place of **Mohammad Ali Jinnah**, who died here in 1948. However, its inaccessibility has made it one of the least visited beauty spots in the sub-continent, completely closed in the winter by the snow. Surrounded by juniper forests, *Ziarat* is regarded by Pakistanis as one of their most exhilarating centres for a restful break. There are extensive walks with beautiful views, rock climbing and even mountaineering.

Just over 5 km from the town centre is the much-visited shrine of the **Mullah Tahir Kharwari**, where the saint is buried in the valley. He gave his name to the town – Ziarat means 'pilgrimage' – and it is to his shrine that pilgrims have come ever since his death. During Eid, tribal people gather for competitions of wrestling and marksmanship.

Mohammad Ali Jinnah's Residency is a 2 storey building, now converted into a **National Museum**. Another striking place within 5 km from the town is **Prospect Point**, a gigantic rock jutting out over the valley more than 300 m below. At an altitude of nearly 2,900 m, out of Ziarat on the **Baba Kharwari Rd**, there are beautiful walks around Prospect Point, and the road to it passes magnificent scenery. You can stay in the *Rest House* at the Point. From near there, it is possible to see the peak of Mount Khilafat, 3,485 m high.

Hotels are heavily booked in the summer, closed in winter. **D** PTDC *Tourist Complex*, T Ziarat 15. Neat, comfortable, small stone built 'flats'. Restaurant, Tourist Office. Reservations: PTDC Motels, Hotel Metropole, Abdullah Haroon Rd, Karachi, T 516252, or in Quetta, T 79519. **E** *Ziarat*, New Bus Stand, T Ziarat 68. 11 rm, mostly d with bath. Also cheaper (and less quiet). The smaller **F** *Grand*, T Z 17 has 5 rm. **F** *Sanubar*, T Z 16. 12 rm with bath. Govt *Rest House*.

Bank United, T Z 61, **Muslim Commercial**, T Z 13 and **National Bank of Pakistan**, T Z 32. Ziarat has a small **library** with a collection of English books, the daily newspapers and a table tennis room! **Useful numbers** Police Station, T Z 18. Post Office, T Z 2, Telegraph Office, T Z 5. Hospital, T Z 74.

Road From Quetta there are 3 daily buses and 3 mini-buses to **Ziarat**. Buses can take upto 9 hr for the journey through Chautair Valley, though the slighty more expensive mini-buses are considerably faster. There are regular buses to and from Quetta. Jeep hire possible for Rs 1,200.

The road runs past majestic limestone hills, through stunted juniper forests and fruit orchards. Notice the stone and bark huts on your way, which have no windows. The road through *Chautair* (23 km), goes down to Wani and Raigora and finally to **Loralai** (70 km). The Loralai valley is the site of pre-historic settlement, though the cantonment town doesn't have much to recommend it in itself. The mountains around were long regarded as the N boundary of Sind.

The Arabs reached as far N as these hills after they had conquered the Makran coast, but are reported to have met with fierce resistance from the local inhabitants. One of the the Arab rulers, the **Khalifa Muawiyeh**, was said: " In the country of Sind there is a mountain which is called Kaikanan. There are big and beautiful horses to be found there... the people are very cunning, and in the shelter of those mountains have become refractory and rebellious."

The region still has the reputation of being beyond the limits of effective govt control. Widely regarded as a territory where thieves and brigands have a free hand, you can't travel from **Loralai** to **Fort Munro** (200 km E, on the crest of the **Suleiman Mountains**) without an armed guard. The route passes through **Mekhtar**, **Kingri**, **Rarkan**, and **Rakhni**.

Long before the Arabs came the Loralai Valley was another centre of prehistoric settlement. Bridget and Raymond Allchin write that "At Rana Gundhai in the Loralai Valley the 2nd major period coincides with an important change and the introduction of a new, finely made painted pottery with friezes of hump-backed bulls in black, upon a buff to red surface." The links with Mundigak in Afghanistan and with other Baluchistan settlements are further evidence of the vital importance of Baluchistan in S Asia's agricultural origins.

The road to **Fort Munro** across the border in Punjab, climbs relatively slowly to the town, which is at an altitude of 2000 m. The military name is not justified by the peaceful look of this hill town with gardens and orchards. The new Tourism Development Corporation *Motel and Restaurant* plans to have 5 rm with a garden, and the beautiful **Dane's Lake** proving boating facilities.

From the crest of the Suleimans the road goes down the dramatic slopes of the **Suleiman Range** to the Indus plains and the Punjab town of Dera Ghazi Khan (80 km). 45 km after leaving Fort Munro the road passes the picturesque shrine of **Sakhi Sarwar**, which is now surrounded by a small town bearing the same name.

Dera Ghazi Khan, (*Population* 120,000 *Altitude* 130 m). the District Headquarters, was laid out formally by the British after being destroyed by Indus floods in 1911. The town is an important intersection of roads in several directions: to Multan and Lahore in Punjab, to Karachi in Sind or Laralai and Quetta in Baluchistan or to Peshawar in the NWFP. **Local industries** Famous for making rugs and carpets, wood and lacquer work, leather goods, palm leaf baskets, and rope making.

Hotels E *Shalimar* is the best in town with a/c rm. The cheaper **E** *Parkland*, Faridi Bazaar, T 3022 also has a/c rm. Several others offering basic accommodation include **F** *Victory* on Azmat Rd with the office of the Chamber of Commerce and Industry in Block C, T 3896 and **F** *Al-Fateh*, Faridi Bazaar. Also Govt *Rest Houses*. Reservations: Deputy Commissioner.

Continue E out of Dera Ghazi Khan, crossing the Indus via the Ghazighat Bridge to **Muzaffargarh** (85 km) and then across the Chenab to Multan (10 km). There are several alternative routes N. The most direct route to **Islamabad** goes N from Muzaffargarh through what was the Thal desert to **Mianwali** (282 km). It then turns NE on the N flank of the **Great Salt Range** to **Talagang** (101 km), N to **Dhulian** (35 km) and again NE to **Fatehjang** (51 km). Here it turns right onto the **Kohat-Islamabad** road, Islamabad being a further 45 km. These routes are described under the Punjab section in routes from Lahore and Islamabad.

QUETTA TO PESHAWAR via Zhob, Bannu and Kohat

The road from Quetta through the Zhob Valley N to Bannu and Peshawar runs right along the westernmost border of the S Asian countries. For political reasons access is restricted. Although buses run through the route from Quetta to Dera Ismail Khan (8 hr) via Muslimbagh (formerly Hindubagh) and Zhob, it is usually impossible for foreigners to get permission to travel through the Zhob Valley itself.

The first part of the route from **Quetta** offers an alternative to the S route to Loralai. Leave Quetta for **Kuchlagh** and fork right in the bazaar, taking the road for Muslimbagh. Instead of turning right to Kach continue straight to **Muslimbagh** (*Population Altitude* 1790 m), a centre of chromite mining and an oasis of orchards and wheat fields. There is a *Dak Bungalow*.

From Muslimbagh follow the road to **Quila Saifullah** (64 km *Altitude* 1,550 m), which is renowned for its pistachio nuts, **Shinkai** (70 km Altitude 1500 m) and **Mina Bazar** (38 km *Altitude* 1,455 m) to **Zhob** (40 km. *Population* 33,000 *Altitude* 1,430 m).

	Jan	Feb	Mar	Apr	May	Jun	Jul	Aug	Sep	Oct	Nov	Dec	Av/Tot
Max (°C)	13	17	21	26	31	37	36	36	33	28	21	15	26
Min (°C)	0	3	8	12	17	22	23	23	19	11	5	2	12
Rain (mm)	24	30	41	27	22	13	52	47	4	1	3	15	279

Named originally after Sir Robert Sandeman as **Fort Sandeman**, Zhob still retains the 2 forts that symbolised its strategic role. It is a role that goes back at least as far as 3000 BC. Finds from that period include leaf-shaped arrowheads and female figurines which have been called (without any great evidence) "Zhob Goddesses". Sir Aurel Stein first made excavations in 1924 and was followed by Fairservis in 1950. A particular feature of the finds at Periano Gundhai in the Zhob Valley were the large terracotta figurines of humped bulls.

From Zhob the western route through Wana and Miran Shah is only open to permit holders. The eastern route goes through **Dera Ismail Khan** (180 km) then N through **Bannu**. It then crosses the extraordinary landscape of the Gt Salt Range to **Kohat** and **Peshawar**. 20 km beyond Dera Ismail Khan is the Indus Valley site of **Rehman Deri.**

NORTH WEST FRONTIER PROVINCE

Introduction, 1206; Peshawar, 1212; Peshawar to Dera Ismail Khan, 1217; Peshawar to Islamabad-Rawalpindi, 1221; Peshawar to Swat, 1221; Peshawar to Chitral, 1228.

Even though it is Pakistan's smallest Province, after Northern Areas, North West Frontier Province (NWFP) is a region of great diversity. The semi-deserts of Dera Ismail Khan in the S lead to the lush irrigated farmlands of the Vale of Peshawar. In turn, these give way to the formidable mountain ranges of the Hindu Kush and Shandur, to the N and W. The region has a rich cultural history stretching back to the Indus Valley civilisation. The Gandharan Empire evolved from the 5th century BC, and is much acclaimed for its distinctive art, a fusion of Graeco-Roman and Indian styles, which flourished during the period of Kushan rule in the 2nd century AD.

The North West Frontier Province was created as an administrative unit by the British in 1901. Nearly twice the size of Denmark, or the same area as N Carolina, it covers approximately 75,000 sq km and has a population of over 15 million. The geographical position of the province, between the highland massif of Central Asia and the plains of the Punjab, and its internal features – the passes which dissect the Hindu Kush range, in particular the Khyber pass – have assured a continual cultural flow across its territory.

David Dichter comments that; "Even when populations themselves did not move through the Frontier's passes, armies seeking to conquer Central Asia and N India have been drawn to the area." The turbulent nature of this zone of contact and transition is reflected in the culture of the Pathan tribes which dominate the NWFP- a warlike race who for centuries have exploited the rugged terrain and thrived on banditry and guerilla warfare, eluding the attempts of invading powers to control and pacify them.

During the British Colonial period, the frontier grew in strategic importance and the British established their 'Forward Policy', struggling to gain control of the tribal areas as a buffer zone against Russian expansion. Despite the **Durand Line** of 1893, the British never gained full control of the province. Even today, nearly a third of the region remains tribal territory with internal autonomy from Pakistani state law.

INTRODUCTION

The Land

By far the most important area historically, culturally and economically, is the **Vale of Peshawar**. The city of Peshawar – administrative centre and largest city of the province – is situated at its western edge. The rich alluvial soils of the Vale of Peshawar, watered by the Kabul and Swat rivers, and the extensive irrigation networks that have been developed, make this the most important agricultural area in the province and amongst the most poductive in Pakistan as a whole.

The Vale of Peshawar, along with the **Safed Koh** mountains and **Khyber hills** to the E, can also be thought of as dividing the NWFP into 2 distinctive parts. To the S the land consists almost exclusively of non-metamorphic sedimentary rocks from the Tertiary era. This is part of the Indian Peninsula which broke away from a vast southern landmass of *Gondwanaland* about 100 million years ago, see page 32.

From the N edge of the Vale of Peshawar up to the rugged and partly glaciated Hindu Kush range, is an area dominated by the old resistant metamorphics and igneous rocks of Paleozoic origin. This mountainous area consists of a large part of the geological **"Kohistan Island Arc"**. A mass of magma or liquid rock, which is being squeezed up between the 2 tectonic plates, and tilted up at its N edge by the subduction of the S Asian plate under the C Asian.

Rivers, dams and river basins Five major river valleys dominate the northern regions all running in parallel along a roughly NE-SW alignment. E-W they are the Chitral, Dir, Swat, Indus and Kaghan valleys.

The **Chitral valley** is the most remote, situated in the extreme NW of the province and its river is known as the Yarkhund, Mastuj, Chitral and Kunar at different points along its course. The **Dir valley** is drained by the Panjkora River system which joins the Swat River shortly before it reaches the Vale of Peshawar. It provides a vital access route to Chitral by way of the Lowarai Pass. The **Swat River valley** represents one of the most favourable and extensive areas of valley settlement in the N, and as such is intensively cultivated and densely populated. The Swat River also forms the most important tributary of the Kabul. The **Indus River valley** passes through the NWFP, cutting through the wild and desolate Kohistan mountain region before emerging onto the Punjab plains near Attock. The **Kaghan valley**, situated in the Hazara District, is the only part of the province E of the Indus. It is drained by the Kunhar River and used to provide, by way of the Babusar Pass, the main access route to Gilgit and the Northern Areas before the completion of the Karakoram Highway in 1978.

At **Tarbela**, just N of the Vale of Peshawar, the world's largest earth-filled dam has been constructed in an attempt to harness the waters of the Indus for irrigation and hydro-electric power generation, and as a response to the division of water resources at Partition and the subsequent Indus Waters Treaty of 1960.

The southern half of the NWFP consists of a series of **basins** which proceed in a step-like fashion down to the southern extremities of the region. The most important, and the most northerly, is the **Vale of Peshawar**, separated from the **Kohat** basin to the S by the arid Khattack Hills. Next is the **Bannu** basin and S of

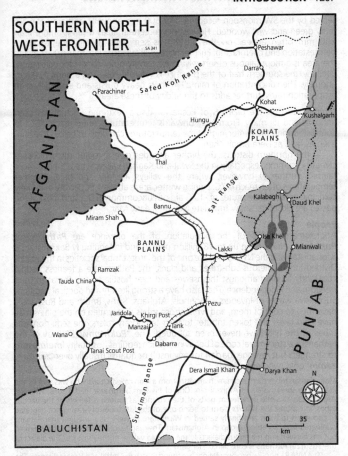

SOUTHERN NORTH-WEST FRONTIER

SA 341

AFGHANISTAN

Parachinar

Safed Koh Range

Peshawar

Darra

Kohat

Hungu

Thal

KOHAT PLAINS

Kushalgarh

Salt Range

Kalabagh

Daud Khel

Bannu

Miram Shah

BANNU PLAINS

Isa Khel

Mianwali

Ramzak

Tauda China

Lakki

Jandola

Khirgi Post

Manzai

Pezu

Tank

PUNJAB

Wana

Tanai Scout Post

Dabarra

Dera Ismail Khan

Darya Khan

Suleiman Range

BALUCHISTAN

0   35
km

N

this, across the Marwat range, is the **Derajat** (or Dera Ismail Khan). Unlike the rivers of the N which follow the major trends of the mountain ranges, the rivers in the S cut across the main grain of the Wazir and Sulaiman ranges to reach the Indus. They are also highly seasonal in character, often only carrying water after severe summer thunderstorms.

Climate

The NWFP is on the margins of the **SW Monsoon** and winter cyclonic depressions making rainfall erratic. Much of the region is arid. The Peshawar basin gets the benefit of rainfall from both climate regimes. In Peshawar itself, the average annual rainfall is 350 mm. Temperatures in the whole region rise rapidly from mid-Mar reaching heights of 45°C by May and Jun. During Oct and Nov, the weather is clear and settled, and the temperatures mild. Until Mar, daytime temperatures average 14°C, dipping to around freezing at night.

The lower sections of the Swat, Indus and Kaghan valleys are relatively well served by the SW monsoon receiving over 600 mm annually, and are generally fairly green and well wooded. However even certain areas receiving more than 800 mm often appear on the ground as semi-arid, usually due to acute deforestation and overgrazing. Further N, rainfall averages less than 100 mm and the area is a mountainous desert relying exclusively on irrigation for cultivation. Similarly, the southern half of the province is very dry, receiving around 150 mm annually. The concentration of rainfall in short heavy bursts and extremely high evaporation rates, further adds to the aridity of these areas.

Temperatures on the plains S of Peshawar display extreme fluctuations both annually and diurnally. From May onwards temperatures often reach 45°C. In contrast, during the winter, night time temperatures can drop to below freezing, even as far S as Dera Ismail Khan.

In the northern districts, the higher altitudes give a cooler, more pleasant climate in summer, especially in the Swat and Kaghan valleys where there is more rainfall. Further N however, where the valleys are dry and bare, summer temperatures often reach 40°C. During winter, areas above 1,500 m are extremely cold. In Chitral, temperatures of -15°C are not uncommon in Dec and most of the passes are closed by snow from late Nov until early Mar.

People

Approximately 90% of the population of the province are **Pathans** (or **Pukhtuns**). Numbering up to 18 million people and inhabiting N Baluchistan, E Afghanistan and the NWFP, they are one of the largest tribal societies in the world. Divided into numerous sub-tribes and clans, the Pathans are a fearless people constantly feuding amongst themselves and ever hostile to any threat to their freedom and independence. They also have a strong literary and poetical tradition. Successive waves of invaders – Moghuls, Afghans, Sikhs, British and Russians – have tried to control them, and while those tribes that settled on the plains may have paid taxes and token tribute to their temporary rulers, the semi-nomadic tribes of the hills have never been subdued. The **"Pukhtunwali"** (way of the Pathans) is a strict moral code of behaviour which requires hospitality (*melmastia*) to strangers but revenge (*badal*) for any insult or quarrel (usually over '*zar, zan, zamin*' gold, women or land).

Many Pathan tribes claim a common ancestry from a man called **Quais** who was sent by the Prophet to spread Islam in Afghanistan. One of his sons, **Afghana**, had 4 sons, who left Afghanistan to settle in different parts of the province as founding fathers of the various tribes. In contrast the **Wazirs** claim to being one of the lost tribes of Israel which migrated E, converted to Islam and finally settled in Waziristan. However it is thought that Pathans originated from an ethnic group in Afghanistan. Their language, **Pushto**, is widely spoken but has evolved into numerous dialects in the isolated valleys of the Province. The dialect of the **Yusufzai Pathans** is considered 'standard'.

The NWFP's non-Pathan populations are found mostly in Chitral and Hazara districts. The **Khowar** language of the **Chitralis**, who call their land *Kho*, relates them closely with various nomadic groups of the Wakhan and Pamir regions. Hazara district consists mainly of non-Pathan **Hindko** speaking tribes whose language and culture is closely related to that of the Punjabis to the S.

The **Kafirs** (non-believers) are a small ethnic group found in the valleys of Humbur, Bumburet and Birir. Their fair complexions led early visitors to liken them to "handsome Europeans, with brown hair and blue eyes" believed to be descendents of Alexander's armies. More probably, they are related to an ancient Indo-Aryan group from Afghanistan who originally fled to escape conversion to Islam.

Economy

Agriculture Agriculture in the NWFP is severely constrained by the harsh physical environment and largely dependant on irrigation. In addition, feudal systems of landownership, the fragmentation of land due to population pressure and the loss of fertile land through soil erosion, waterlogging and salinity, have added further problems. Many of the hill tribes in the region are **semi-nomadic**

pastoralists only partially dependent on cultivation to support their harsh subsistance lifestyle.

The Vale of Peshawar, despite its relatively small area, is highly productive due to its fertile alluvial soils and plentiful supply of irrigation water from the Swat and Kabul rivers. The best land is largely devoted to cash crops, in particular sugar cane and tobacco, as well as to fruit orchards containing oranges, plums, peaches, guavas and pears. On partly irrigated land, the staples wheat and maize are grown as well as some vegetables. Some dairy farming is also practiced. The *barani* (unirrigated) land is generally sown with a single <F85MI*rabi* (winter) crop of wheat.

S of the Vale of Peshawar, the main crops are wheat, barley, maize, the millets *jowra* and *bajra*, and pulses – a major source of protein. Some rice, sugarcane and fruit are also grown particularly around Bannu. However, erratic rainfall and exceptionally high evaporation rates during the summer months greatly inhibit agriculture. In the Dera Ismail Khan district, a form of cultivation known as **rod-kohi** or hill torrent cultivation is practised. The highly seasonal torrents of the Sulaiman and Waziristan hills are blocked by temporary dams and the water carefully fed into selected fields below. This system is highly precarious however and the dams are often swept away and crops ruined.

In the valleys N of Peshawar cultivation is greatly restricted by the lack of suitable land and the dry climate. Agriculture is irrigation based with barley, wheat, millets and pulses, and some rice, vegetables and fruit being grown. The Swat valley however is particularly fertile and intensively cultivated. **Maize,** a relatively recent import from S America, is the most important crop (Swat is the *'maize granary'* of the province), followed by rice and barley. The lower Kaghan valley and parts of Hazara district are similarly fertile, receiving adequate monsoon rainfall.

The Tribal Areas bordering Afghanistan have seen a massive growth over the last 10 years in the illegal cultivation of **opium**. The war in Afghanistan displaced much of the cultivation across the border, and an expanding market in the west and the enormous profit margins have made it an important crop, despite government efforts to eradicate it.

Industry and Resources Industry in the NWFP is extremely limited and mostly related to the processing of tobacco and sugarcane. The re-drying plant at *Akora Khattack* near Nowshera, handles 90% of the province's Virginia tobacco crop, grown mostly for export. Sugar refineries cater for local demand. Cottage industries play an important role locally, especially in the northern districts where handwoven woollen cloth is made into shawls, hats, blankets, rugs etc. Over the last 10 years, the booming gun making industry has been centred in **Darra**, 40 km S of Peshawar.

The only mineral deposits of any significance are found in Kohat district on the edge of the Great Salt Range. Three salt mines, the Bahadur Khel, Jatta and Karak, exist in a 15 km radius around Teri. The industry is an ancient one and the mines are known to have been in operation since recorded history.

There are significant reserves of timber, especially in the Swat and Kaghan valleys, although deforestation is a major problem, and logging needs to be carefully managed. The province also has considerable hydro-electric generating potential. The Tarbela Dam and Warsak Project are the 2 largest in operation although many smaller ones exist. The Tarbela Dam is the world's largest earth-filled dam, generating 2,000 MW of power, **see page 1206**.

Tourism is perhaps the industry with the greatest potential although it is largely undeveloped at present. The picture is changing rapidly, with the spread of international class hotels, and a concerted effort nationally to attract tourists to this fascinating and varied country.

History
The first agricultural communities are thought to have evolved approximately 10,000 years ago on the western flanks of the **Indus Valley** in NWFP and on the borders of the Iranian Plateau in Baluchistan. People began to practice mixed farming cultivating wheat, barley and cotton and keeping cattle and sheep. Archaeological evidence suggests that the climate was much less harsh then. Much of the plains were probably covered in open woodland, and animals such as rhinos and waterbuffalo suited to wetter climates roamed wild. However, irrigation must still have formed the basis for cultivation.

The Indus Valley Civilisation developed out of these early settlements. The number of agricultural villages grew rapidly and substantial walled settlements such as the one found at **Kot Diji** began to show greater cultural uniformity, notably in styles of pottery and the common worship of a buffalo deity. By around 2300 BC, the Indus Valley Civilization began to reach its height, prospering for 600 years until 1700 BC when it is thought to have covered approximately 1.3 million sq km. A total of 70 sites have been excavated in this area so far, the most important being at **Moenjo Daro** in Sind (see page 1184) and **Harappa** in the Punjab (page 1139). The Indus Valley Civilisation is unique in displaying such a strict cultural uniformity over its entire area.

An interesting feature of the civilisation is the complete absence of any evidence of warfare; no weapons have ever been found, nor any evidence of a warrior class. Some scholars feel that the existance of a specifically non violent religion was the unifying force which led the civilisation to evolve and prosper so successfully. Trade was also extensive, both internally and abroad – with S India, Afghanistan and Mesopotamia. However, around 1700 BC the Indus Valley Civilisation came to an abrupt end for reasons which are not entirely clear.

Early Empires From the 5th century BC, the **Gandharan** Empire evolved, incorporating the valleys of Peshawar, lower Swat and Kabul. It was a small semi-independent Empire, and although it remained intact until the 11th century AD, its form and nature were continually and fundementally influenced by waves of invaders who came through the passes of the NWF, and from the Ganga valley in the E.

In the 6th century BC, Gandhara became the easternmost province of the **Archaemenid** Empire under **Darius the Great**. In 327 BC **Alexander the Great** briefly conquered Gandhara. When he withdrew, the **Mauryan** Empire based in the lower Ganga Basin, rapidly expanded gaining control of Gandhara. **Asoka** promoted Buddhism in the region and his famous Rock Edicts can be found throughout N Pakistan. With the decline of the Mauryan Empire shortly after Ashoka's death in 232 BC, Gandhara once again came under the influence of Central Asia. The **Bactrian Greeks** built new cities at Taxila and Pushkalavati (present day Charsadda) only to be displaced by the nomadic tribes of the **Scythians** and **Parthians** in turn.

The **Kushan** Empire brought a period of relative stability and by the 2nd century AD it controlled much of the subcontinent. Peshawar became the imperial winter capital, and under **Kanishka**, the most famous Kushan king (AD 128-151), Buddhism flourished. Monasteries and Stupas were built throughout Gandhara which became something of a religious holy land. In addition, extensive trade with the Roman Empire and China along the Great Silk Route brought widespread prosperity.

By the end of the 3rd century AD, Gandhara had been absorbed by the **Sassanian** Empire. In the 5th century waves of **White Huns** (Hephthalites) invaded from the NW bringing chaos and destruction. Buddhism declined giving way to Hinduism, and only survived in the Upper Swat Valley. A long period of instability followed.

Islam and the Moghul Period The earliest evidence of Islam in the NWFP comes from a stone tablet with Arabic and Sanskrit inscriptions (now in Peshawar Museum) dating from 857 AD which was found in the *Tochi Valley* of Waziristan. However, it was not until the 11th century that **Mahmud of Ghazni** began a series of raids through the province into the Punjab, incorporating the regions into the **Ghaznavid** Empire and initiating conversions to Islam. This was followed by that of the **Ghorids** – the Turkish Muslims of Ghor in present day Afghanistan- which marked the beginnings of the **Dehli Sultanate**.

Islam was spread by *Shahihs* of the Sufi order. These mystics preached amongst the people, especially in the E and W of the subcontinent, where Islam became the religion of the masses, a fact which was later to give distinctive shape to the separate state of Pakistan which emerged at Independence. The greatest challenge to the Sultanate came from the Mongol Hordes of **Ghengis Khan** who swept through the province reaching the Indus in 1221 and later from **Tamerlane** (Timur the Lame) who sacked Delhi in 1399, **see page 147**. However the Sultanate survived under a series of different dynasties until it fell to **Babur**, the displaced descendent of the House of Timur, and first of the great Moghuls at the beginning of the 16th century.

The NWFP was subsequently ruled by the **Moghuls** until the beginning of the 18th century. Peshawar blossomed during this period. The Moghuls planted trees, laid out gardens and built forts and mosques in this regional capital. However, outside of the Vale of Peshawar they exercised minimal control over the Pathan tribes. After the death of *Aurangzeb,* the last of the great Moghul Emperors, in 1707, Peshawar was controlled by the **Durranis** of Afghanistan until 1818 when the **Sikh** *Ranjit Singh,* 'the lion of the Punjab' captured the city. He destroyed Babur's Shalimar Gardens and Bala Hisar fort and razed much of the city.

The British The first British contact with the NWFP came in 1809 when *Mountstuart Elphinstone* led a diplomatic mission to Kabul by way of Kohat and Peshawar. Concerned over potential Russian expansion, the British were anxious to establish a buffer zone in the NW. However, Sikh control of the region was extremely loose and after the **Second Sikh War** of 1849 the British formally annexed the Punjab and NWFP. Initially the whole region was controlled from Lahore, by occupying frontier forts and maintaining military roads between them. Outside the settled areas, agreements were made with the tribes, obliging them to maintain peaceful and friendly relations in return for subsidies and allowances.

In 1893 the **Durand line** was drawn up, dividing British India from Afghanistan. The border cut through the tribal areas of the Pathans, which was to cause great problems after Independence. Indeed the Pathans rose up in series of revolts in 1897, fearing that the British "*Forward Policy*" advocating more direct control of the region would compromise their freedom and independence. 70,000 troops were mobilised in 7 military operations to put down the rebellion which led *Lord Curzon* to establish the NWF as a separate province administered from Peshawar in 1901. The British maintained their tenuous control over the province until Independence in 1947, leaving the tribal areas to govern themselves under the supervision of a political agent. However, force was continually necessary to maintain the status quo. As late as 1937, 40,000 British troops took part in a series of campaigns which ultimately left the tribes of Waziristan masters of their own house.

Developments since Independence Prior to the partition of the subcontinent in 1947, the Pathan tribes were distinctly hostile towards the Pakistan movement though a referendum resulted in an overwhelming vote in favour of joining Pakistan. Immediately after independence, however, the Pathans began agitating for a separate nation of **Pukhtunistan**, led by *Abdul Gaffer Khan* and his son

Abdul Wali Khan. Afghanistan appeared to favour the movement and there were frequent clashes between the Pathans and the Pakistani Frontier Force in the 1950s and '60s.

Successive regimes in Pakistan have made extensive efforts to integrate the Pathans, initiating generous education and agricultural programmes and encouraging permanent settlements, well connected by roads to market outlets. The aim has been to try to persuade the tribesmen to exploit the resources of the frontier rather than its strategic location – to live on the land rather than off it.

The Soviet invasion of **Afghanistan** in Dec 1979 had a major impact on the province. An estimated 3.5 million refugees flooded across the border and the vast majority were settled in some 350 refugee camps. Many have become integrated into the local economy, operating transport services, mainly in and around Peshawar. The capital became the centre for huge relief programmes and by 1988, 79 relief agencies were operating in Peshawar employing thousands of Westerners. Billions of dollars in foreign aid, flooded into Pakistan, suddenly a country of major geopolitical importance to America, the vast majority of which went on military spending. Since the Soviet withdrawal, fighting has so far continued and to date few of the refugees have returned home.

PESHAWAR

Population 750,000. *Altitude* 359 m. *Best season* Nov/Mar.

	Jan	Feb	Mar	Apr	May	Jun	Jul	Aug	Sep	Oct	Nov	Dec	Av/Tot
Max (°C)	29	31	33	35	38	37	35	35	34	32	29	28	33
Min (°C)	20	21	23	23	28	28	26	26	25	24	23	21	24
Rain (mm)	24	7	15	15	52	53	83	124	118	267	309	139	1216

Peshawar, the capital, lies on the W edge of the Vale of Peshawar, just 50 km from the Khyber Pass. Its position and long turbulent history have earned it the reputation of a frontier town and today it is a lively, colourful place full of variety and contrasts. From the narrow bustling streets of the Old City with its densely packed bazaars, through the spacious tree-lined avenues of the British Cantonment area, to the modern university town of the 1950s, Peshawar has been shaped by a succession of conflicting influences.

The city's origins are unclear. The earliest written record was found in a **Kharoshthi** rock inscription at Ara, near Attock dated 119 AD, referred to as *Poshapura* meaning 'City of Flowers'. The city may have first risen to prominence during the reign of the Kushan king *Kanishka* who moved his winter capital from Pushkalavati to Peshawar. The Kushan period saw a great flowering of Buddhist culture in the region and Peshawar became a major pilgrimage centre. The city next acquired importance during the Moghul period, when much building was undertaken. The present form of the city's name is attributed to Akbar who changed it from the Persian *'Parshawar'* to Peshawar, literally meaning 'Frontier Town'.

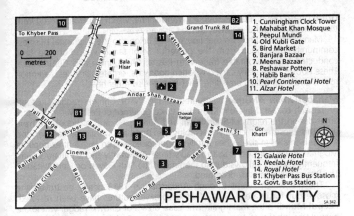

1. Cunningham Clock Tower
2. Mahabat Khan Mosque
3. Peepul Mundi
4. Old Kubli Gate
5. Bird Market
6. Banjara Bazaar
7. Meena Bazaar
8. Peshawar Pottery
9. Habib Bank
10. *Pearl Continental Hotel*
11. *Alzar Hotel*

12. *Galaxie Hotel*
13. *Neelab Hotel*
14. *Royal Hotel*
B1. Khyber Pass Bus Station
B2. Govt. Bus Station

PESHAWAR OLD CITY

SA 342

The Old City

The old city is a distinct unit, formerly completely encircled by a wall and centred on a citadel, in traditional Central Asian style. Today the wall and its 16 gates survive for the most part only in name. The **Bala Hisar** is almost certainly the site of the ancient citadel mentioned by the Chinese pilgrim Hiuen Tsang in 629 AD. This fortified stronghold was the key to control of Peshawar and changed hands many times. When the Moghul Babur arrived in 1509, he occupied and strengthened the existing fort and laid out the **Shalimar Gardens**. After the decline of the Moghuls, the Durranis of Afghanistan controlled it until 1818. The fort at this time was in magnificent condition, as described by Elphinstone when he visited in 1809.

"The throne was covered with a cloth adorned with pearls, on which lay a sword and a small mace set with jewels. The room was open all round. The centre was supported by four high pillars, in the midst of which was a large fountain. The floor was covered with the richest carpets, and round the edges were slips of silk embroidered with gold. The view from the hall was beautiful. Immediately below was an extensive garden, full of cypresses and other trees and beyond was a plain of richest verdure."

The Bala Hisar along with the Shalimar Gardens were destroyed by the Sikh, Ranjit Singh who later rebuilt the Fort of mud. The present fort was built by the British, who replaced the mud walls with 'pucca' brick. Today the Bala Hisar is occupied by the Pakistani military and is closed to the public. **Warning** No photography in the vicinity.

Chowk Yadgar is a good place to start exploring the Old City. Originally, a memorial to Col E. C. Hastings stood at the centre of this large square, which has been replaced by the modern memorial to those who died in the Indo-Pakistani war of 1965. E of Chowk Yadgar along Sethi St, is the **Cunningham Clocktower** built in 1900 by Balmukund to celebrate Queen Victoria's Diamond Jubilee, and in honour of Sir George Cunningham who became Governor of NWFP.

Gor Khatri is an important monument on a mound at the end of Sethi St. It was originally the site of the *'Tower of the Buddha's Bowl'* where the sacred alms bowl was believed to have been housed. Later it became an important place of Hindu pilgrimage, perhaps as a site for funeral sacrifices or for the initiation of *Yogis**. During the reign of Shah Jahan his daughter Jahanara Begum converted the place into a *caravanserai** and built an accompanying Mosque. During the Sikh period the mosque was destroyed and replaced with a temple of

Gorakhnath (Siva) and its subsidiary *Nandi*shrine, which still stand, along with the impressive Moghul gateway to the Caravanserai.

Many of the old houses that line Sethi St belong to the traditional business community, descended from the powerful Sethi family which at one time conducted highly profitable trade with Russia, China, India and Central Asia. These houses have richly carved wooden doorways, ornate balconies, reception rooms and deep cellars providing relief from the summer heat.

Mahabat Khan Mosque is situated to the W of Chowk Yadgar, just off Andarshah bazaar. Mahabat Khan was twice governor of Peshawar in Moghul times during the reigns of Shah Jahan and Aurangzeb, and is thought to have built this mosque. It closely resembles the Badshahi Masjid at Lahore, and although smaller in size, is beautifully proportioned and an excellent example of Moghul architecture from Shah Jahan's time. Apparently the 2 minarets were frequently used as gallows during the time of the Sikh Governor, Gen Avitabile. The Prayer Hall is lavishly decorated.

The fire which swept through Andarshah in 1898 nearly destroyed the mosque but fortunately many of its decorative features have been restored. **Peepul Mundi** is the main grain wholesale area S of Chowk Yadgar where the peepul tree is believed to mark the spot where the Buddha once preached.

The fascinating Bazaars, packed into tiny streets and alleyways, are each given over to a specialised craft or trade. Thus the **Khyber Bazaar** is home to lawyers, doctors and dentists, with boards advertising huge sets of false teeth. Further along, through the Old Kabuli Gate is the *Qissa Khawani Bazaar*, or story-tellers bazaar. Here are the 'Khave Khanas'- the tea shops and eating houses where in the past, travellers and traders congregated to exchange their tales and news of the wider world. Small alleys house shops selling brass and copper, blankets and shawls from Kaghan and Swat, and baskets from Dera Ismail Khan. On the main street, the **Bird Market** sells song birds in cages (a tradition imported from China). The **Banjara bazaar**, just S of Chowk Yadgar, specialises in bells, hair braids, bone and wooden beads and other decorative items.

Andarshah Bazaar (meaning 'inner city') runs W from Chowk Yadgar towards Bala Hisar and houses the silver and goldsmiths, selling a wide range of ethnic, antique and modern jewellry. In an alleyway, to the left, off Sethi St as you approach Gor Khatri is the **Meena Bazaar** (women's bazaar) where *Burqas** and veils for women are sold along with items of embroidery.

The Cantonment

British troops first set up camp in what was to become the cantonment in 1848-49. A barbed wire enclosure with 10 gates was followed by permanent buildings. It was a model piece of England grafted onto the stoney ground W of the Old City. Following the classical colonial style, ubiquitous throughout British India, a wholly independent town was built with long wide tree-lined boulevards designed for horse drawn traffic and spacious bungalows set back from the road, along with all the social infrastructure of Government buildings, schools, churches, clubs etc. The railway line and station which divides the cantonment from the Old City followed. Since Independence, the **Saddar Bazaar** area has grown in size and is now full of hotels, restaurants and shops.

St John's Church on Sir Sayid Rd, the oldest church in Peshawar (1851-1860), was consecrated by Bishop Cotton of Calcutta. **Edwardes College** nr Old Kohati Gate, was founded in 1855 by Sir Herbert Edwardes as a school, and became a mission college in 1901. Formerly the residence of Yor Muhammad Khan in Moghul and Gothic style, its gardens now house the **All Saints Church** (1883) which has a beautifully painted chancel window.

The University Town

7km W of Peshawar on Khyber Rd. The Islamia College and Collegiate School (1913) was built on a "parched, barren and uneven tract interspersed by ancient mounds" in a Moghul/Gothic style and was followed by the University which was founded in 1930. Today a sprawling residential area of red brick buildings and well kept lawns surrounds the University and various Medical, Engineering, Forestry, Science and Industrial Institutes and Research Councils line the main road.

There are a number of other monuments scattered around the outskirts of Peshawar in varying states of repair. **Shah-ji-ki-Dheri** about 3 km S of Gunj Gate, was the site of a magnificent Buddhist stupa and monastery, built by Kanishka and excavated by Spooner in 1907. Today it is the site of a brick factory. Nearby are the tombs of *Arkhund Darweza*, a Sufi saint, and *Rahman Baba*, a famous Pushto poet. The **Old Panch Tirath** was once a centre for Hindu pilgrimage with its 5 water tanks for bathing, but now it is a fisheries centre.

Wazir Bagh, S of the Old City, was first laid between 1802-3 during the Durrani period. Today it does not live up to the Peshawar of the past – a 'city of flowers' scattered with orchards and gardens. To the W of Wazir Bagh is an old **Durrani graveyard,** a brick built walled enclosure with 2 small mosques and some tombs.

Local Festivals End of Apr-Mid Jun Khyber Jashne (Mela/Fair). Jumma Prayer. Fri 1200-1400. Old City.

Note change of street name. The Mall to Shahrah-e-Quaid-e-Azam.

Services

Hotels The best in town is the **AL** *Pearl Continental*, Khyber Rd, PO Box 197. T 76361-9, Telex: 52389 PEARL PK, Cable: PEARLCONT PESHAWAR. 150 rm Central a/c. Golf course. Pool open to non-residents on payment. Good restaurant, excellent buffet, barbecues all with very pleasant service.

The Cantonment area has the better hotels. **C** *Deans* (PTDC), 3 Islamia Rd, T 79781-3, Cable: DEANS. 44 rm with bath. Central a/c. Good restaurant, coffee shop, car hire, Tourist Info. Bungalow style, in well-kept gardens. **C** *Greens*, Saddar Rd, T 76035. 45 rm with bath and phone. Good restaurant (buffet lunches), travel, shop, snooker. Peaceful. **D** *Galaxie*, Khyber Rd, T 72738. 45 rm with bath. Central a /c. Good value, recommended. **D** *Jan's*, Islamia Rd, T 76939. 31 rm with bath. Central a/c. **D** *Habib*, Khyber Rd, T 73061-7. 39 rm with bath, phone and fridge. Indoor games.

There are numerous **E** category hotels, concentrated around Saddar Rd, Cinema Rd, Khyber Rd, Chowk Fawara and the GT Rd. A few are listed. *Neelab*, Khyber Bazaar, T 74255. 28 rm with bath. *Skyline*, Sunchri Masjid Rd, T 74021. 46 rm with bath. *Dubai*, Chowk Qissa Khawani Bazaar, T 62100. 32 rm. Restaurant, exchange, shop. On Saddar Rd: *International (Guls)*, T 72100 has 30 rm with bath. *Shahzad*, T 75741 has 18 rm with bath. Gandhara Travels and Pakistan Express; *Kamran*, T 72701 has rm with bath and dormitories. Also **F** *Rly Retiring Rm*.

Youth Hostel, Peshawar University and also *YMCA* nearby have cheap dormitories but are out-of-town. **Camping** is available 100 m from Jans Hotel.

Restaurants *Salatins*, Cinema Rd, T 73779. Excellent Peshawari / Pakistani cuisine. Two Chinese restaurants on The Mall: *Hong Kong*, T 74504 and *Nan King*, T 72556. There is also excellent street food available from stalls along Khyber Bazaar and Qissa Khawani, and good coffee houses and cheap eating places along Saddar Bazaar and University Rd which has fast food places like *Golden Bite*, *Chief Burgers* and *Kababish*. The Peshwari *Chappli kebab* is spicier than burgers, made with mince, eggs and tomato and comes with Naan instead of the burger roll!

Clubs Peshawar Club, Sayid St, nr the Mall, T 72206. For members and guests only but you can look around the library and buildings. Swimming pool open to the public. Before noon each day, it is partitioned to allow women to swim without offending the rules of Purdah.

Banks Grindlays, Shahrah-e-Quaid-e-Azam, T 72246. Habib, Chowk Yadgar, T 73413. United, Shahrah-e-Pehlavi, T 72994.

Shopping The bazaars of the Old City are worth visiting (see above). **Note** Closed 1200-1400 Fri for Prayers. Engraved wooden furniture of high quality in showroom opp *Jans Hotel* and shops in the Saddar area. *The Afghan metal works* behind the Pearl Continental Hotel is open to visitors and you can see the work in progress. The *Peshawar Pottery* at the end of alley in Quissa Khawani Bazaar offers a wide choice. Comfortable mens' leather sandals called Peshawari chappals are a good buy. Also other leather goods, stone jewellery, printed cottons and woollen shawls.

Local Transport Buses are mostly run by Afghan operators; services and routes change often. Up-to-date information from Tourist Office. Taxis, autorickshaws and tongas are available.

Entertainment Cinemas: Aina and Arshad on Pahalvi Rd.

Sports Arab Niaz Stadium, with Polo Ground nr Shahi Gardens. Peshawar Golf Course, off Shami Rd, T 72205.

Museums Peshawar Museum, City Circular Rd, close to junction with Police Rd. Built in 1905 as the Victoria Memorial Hall, it is an imposing blend of Moghul and European architecture. All the best artefacts from the various stages of Gandharan civilization, not already removed from Pakistan, are here or in Lahore Museum. Well laid out and well worth a visit. Behind it is the Abasin Arts Council, T 73350.

Libraries British Council, The Mall, T 73278. National Central, Saddar Rd, opp GPO. Peshawar Municipal Library, GT Rd, nr Bala Hisar.

Parks and Gardens Khalid-Bin-Walid-Bagh, The Mall, a remnant of Babur's Shalimar Gardens, is still pleasant though it has lost its former splendour. Hayatabad Park, off Jamrud Rd. Jinnah Park, GT Road. Shahi Bagh, Charsadda Rd. Wazir Bagh, nr City Circular Rd.

Useful Addresses Passport and Immigration Office, Gumma Le, Cantt. Foreigners Registration Office, Police Rd, T 75149. Police Stations: E Cantt, T 72119. W Cantt, T 76215.

Post and Telegraphs GPO, Saddar Rd, T 74425. Central Telegraph Office, The Mall, T 74393.

Places of Worship *Muslim* Mahabat Khan Mosque, Andarshah Bazaar. *Christian* St.John's Church, Sir Sayid Rd and All Saint's Church, nr Old Kohati Gate (see in Places of Interest above).

Hospitals and Medical Services Cantonment, Sunehri Masjid Rd, T 76106. Combined Military, The Mall, T 61718. Khyber, Jamrud Rd, T 8112. Lady Reading, off Railway Rd, Khyber Bazaar, T 75281. Mission, T 72771. Medicos Drug Store, The Mall, T 72122.

Foreign Representations USA, Hospital Rd, T 73061. **Aghanistan**, Jamrud Rd, T 73418. Iran, Sir Sayid Rd, T 74643. UK (Courier Office), Khalid Rd, T 72562.

Travel Agents and Tour Operators In Khyber Bazaar: Orakzai, Haroon Mansion; Shirket-e-Maqbool and Suhbat Maqbool Travel. Khyber Tourism, 1 Suddar Rd and others nearby include Sehrai Travels and United Travels.

Tourist Information Centre (PTDC), Deans, 3 Islamia Rd, T 76483-4.

Air PIA connections to Islamabad, Lahore and Karachi, Chitral (3 flights daily), Swat (3 flights weekly). Peshawar Airport, T 72120. PIA Booking Office, The Mall, T 73081.

Rail Cantonment Rly Station. Reservations, T 74436, Enquiries, T 74437.

Road **Bus** Cantt GTS Bus Station, The Mall, T 72360. City GTS Bus Station, Roadway House, GT Road, T 72401. Buses for Darra, Kohat, Bannu and DI Khan. A /c luxury coaches for **Islamabad / Lahore** from GT Rd opp Jinnah Park; **Buses** for **Landi Kotal and Kohat** from Khyber Bazaar; **To Charsadda, Mardan, Dir and Swat** from N of Shahi Bagh on Charsadda Rd; **To Attock, Hasanabad, Taxila and Rawalpindi**, E along the GT Rd.

Excursions

The Khyber Pass The Khyber Pass is currently closed to foreigners but the situation may change. Enquire at the Foreigner's Registration Office and get permit. The road is open as far as **Jamrud**.

Jamrud Fort (18 km) was built by the Sikh General Hari Singh in 1836, which provoked an attack by the Afghans, and cost him his life. It is of rough stonework faced with mud plaster, and in 3 tiers – lower and upper forts and a keep. There is also a stone arched gate on the road, the Bab-i-Khyber, built in 1964. From the fort, the road zigzags up past viewpoints and watchtowers and there are good views back onto the Peshawar plain.

Next is the 1920s British built **Shagai Fort** (30 km). It is now manned by the Frontier Force and closed to the public. In the middle of the pass is **Ali Masjid** (mosque) and high above it the **Ali Masjid Fort** which defends the narrowest point of the gorge, less than 14 m wide at this point.

From here the pass opens out into a wide fertile valley dotted with fortified Pathan villages. Just before Landi Kotal, 15 km from Shagai Fort, there is the **Sphola Stupa**, to the right of the road on a hillock above Zarai. It dates from the 2nd-5th centuries AD and is the last remains (somewhat dilapidated) of an extensive Buddhist monastery. **Landi Kotal** itself is a bustling colourful market town with everything from smuggled electrical goods to drugs. 8 km further on is the border town of **Torkham**.

The Khyber Railway which terminates at Landi Kotal, was built by the British in the 1920's and is a remarkable feat of engineering. It has 34 tunnels and 92 bridges and culverts and at one point climbs 130 m in just over 1 km. The journey takes at least 3 hr.

Warsak Dam, 24 km from Peshawar on the Michni road is a good picnic spot (also accessible from Jamrud). The dam on the Kabul River was completed in 1960 and created a 42 km long lake upstream. It provides irrigation water to the intensively cultivated Peshawar Valley and generates 160,000 kw of electricity.

Afghan Refugee Camps There were originally about 350 refugee camps in the NWFP housing most of the estimated 3.5 million refugees in Pakistan. Since the Soviet withdrawal in 1988, many have stayed due to continued fighting. Most of the camps are on the GT Road between Peshawar and Attock and on the Charsadda Rd. It may be possible to visit these (ask Tourist Information) and buy rugs and handicrafts.

The Vale of Peshawar is rich in historical sites, particularly **Charsadda, Shahbaz Garhi** and **Takht-i-bahi**, which you can visit on day-trips from Peshawar. See Peshawar to Swat, **page 1221**.

PESHAWAR TO DERA ISMAIL KHAN

The road S from Peshawar, through the districts of Kohat, Bannu and DI Khan crosses barren semi-arid countryside with hills and mountains averaging around 1,500 m and occasional fertile oases. To the W, following the border with Afghanistan are the Federally Administered Tribal Areas of Kurram and N and S Waziristan. Note Foreigners need permits to visit these areas. They are not easy to get.

Darra Adam Khel, 42 km S of Peshawar on the Kohat road is the biggest centre of indigenous arms manufacture in the province. Home to the **Adam Afridi tribe**, the town consists almost entirely of gunshops and workshops where working replicas of anything from pen-guns to Kalashnikovs and rocket launchers are meticulously fashioned with only the most primitive of machine tools. Demand, which has always been high, shot up with the Soviet invasion of Afghanistan. In addition, copious quantities of hashish and opium are openly displayed for sale. Permits to visit: may not be issued.

The road continues S over the **Kohat pass** (874 m) to Kohat, 25 km away.

Kohat Today this is a bustling, dusty and untouristed market town serving the surrounding rural areas of Kohat basin. Its primary importance however, is strategic. Centrally located and well connected by road with Peshawar to the N, Afghanistan and the Tribal Areas to the W, Bannu to the S and Islamabad by way of Kushalgarh to the E, Kohat was an important garrison town during the British Era and even today has a well maintained airfield. It centres around the British cantonment area.

The **Residence of the Dy Commissioner**, formerly the home of Louis Cavagnari, once British resident in Kabul, is an elegant and impressive whitewashed house with round-topped french windows. There are also some beautiful gardens remaining from Moghul times, and the British built **Kohat Fort**.

Hotels E *Green Hill*, Hangu Rd, nr Police Line, T 2220. E *Nadria*, outside Tehsil Gates. T 3162. E *Pughman* and *Jan's*.

Air PIA connections with Islamabad twice weekly (Wed, Fri).

Rail A single track narrow gauge rly runs E to **Thal** (foreigners must disembark at previous station), and W to Islamabad.

Road Buses Regular daily services operate in all directions to major urban centres in the region. From **Karachi**, 3 daily (22 hr). Buses leave when full.

Kohat is an important transport centre. Roads leave E to Islamabad and W up into the Tribal Areas. Two routes are briefly described here as diversions from Kohat. The route to Parachinar in the Tribal Areas is beautiful and often exciting, but foreigners need a permit. The route to Islamabad is the quickest way back to the capital.

Kohat to Parachinar

From Kohat there is a good metalled road running W to the to the small town of Parachinar at the head of the **Kurram Valley** (188 km). About 40 km out of Kohat one reaches Hangu. Here one can take a detour up a rough track to the Samana ridge where there is the **Lockhart Fort** built in 1891 and the Saragarhi Obelisk in memory of those who died during one of the many campaigns against the local *Bangash* tribes between 1897-8. There are spectacular views in all directions from here. 98 km from Kohat is *Thal* which evolved as a trading post on the caravan route into Afghanistan.

Parachinar is a further 90 km from Thal, the road following the Kurram River valley which widens as it climbs, giving spectacular views on the snow clad Safed Koh mountains which rise to 5000 m. It has a very distinctive climate, moderated by altitude and much wetter than surrounding arid hills. The town itself is pleasantly green and surrounded by large Chinar trees – hence the name.

	Jan	Feb	Mar	Apr	May	Jun	Jul	Aug	Sep	Oct	Nov	Dec	Av/Tot
Max (°C)	10	12	16	22	27	31	31	29	28	24	19	14	22
Min (°C)	-2	0	4	9	14	18	19	19	15	10	5	1	9
Rain (mm)	82	76	136	104	64	47	122	112	54	18	14	31	858

Kohat to Islamabad

From Kohat a good but narrow metalled road leads E towards Islamabad (175 km). At *Khashalgarh* about 50 km from Kohat, the road crosses the Indus by way of a dual rail and road bridge and enters Punjab Province. From Khashalgarh it is 77 km on to *Fatehjang* and a further 47 km into Islamabad, a journey of about 3-5 hr.

The route SW to Bannu and DI Khan

At Krappa, SW of Kohat, a new road forks S to **Shakadara** on the border with Punjab and then on to **Kalabagh**, where the Indus emerges from its gorge to spread out onto the Indus plain. The road crosses the Indus over the Jinnah Barrage, **See page 1152**. The main road to Bannu crosses the Salt Range passing close to the salt mine at **Jatta**. After about 100 km the road winds down from the Kohat and Wazir hills into the **Bannu Basin**. This is an almost circular alluvial plain shut in on all sides by mountains and drained by 2 rivers, the **Kurram** and the **Tochi** (or Gambila) between which lies a tract of richly irrigated country, thickly populated, well wooded and traversed by numerous streams and water courses. This oasis is the setting for **Bannu** (125 km), refreshingly green and surrounded by palms and shady mango trees.

Bannu

	Jan	Feb	Mar	Apr	May	Jun	Jul	Aug	Sep	Oct	Nov	Dec	Av/Tot
Max (°C)	19	21	25	31	38	41	39	37	36	32	27	21	31
Min (°C)	5	8	13	18	23	27	28	27	24	18	11	6	17
Rain (mm)	22	31	47	32	14	21	70	56	18	3	3	11	327

Early history The District Gazetteer states that Bannu was 'founded' by the British in 1848, but the town, (then called **Pona**) is first mentioned by the Chinese pilgrim Fa-Hien in 404 AD, who describes a Buddhist monastery with 3000 monks. The town grew as a result of its position on the original trading route between Kabul and the Indus, later replaced by the Kurram/Miranzai valley route through Hangu and Kohat.

19th century development The Durranis exercised a precarious hold over the area, followed by the Sikh Ranjit Singh, who built the fort here in 1844. From 1846 the British extended their control over the area through Lieutenant Edwardes who in turn administered through the Sikhs. He named the town Dulipshehr after the young Maharaja. In 1899 it was renamed Edwardesabad and in 1903 Bannu. Edwardes gained the respect of the local tribes and exerted considerable influence, even getting many of the surrounding villagers to pull down their fortifications and accept British protection.

The old town of Bannu is still walled however and the gates shut at night against bandits. As well as the cantonment and fort there is the Pennell **Missionary Hospital** and **school** founded at the turn of the century by the British missionary. 11 km SW of Bannu nr **Barth** are the **Akra Mounds** of uncertain origin – a series of low mounds, much reduced by farmers who have excavated them for use as topsoil.

Hotels F *Government Rest House* (Reservations, Dy Commissioner. Some small basic hotels in the bazaar: *Farid*, Tea Bazaar, with Restaurant and *Rashid*, Tehsil St. The Mission Hospital take in guests.

Air 3 flights a week to both Peshawar and Islamabad.

Rail The narrow gauge railway, daily connects Bannu with Kalabagh through Lakki.

Road Buses Regular daily bus services operate in all directions. From **Karachi**, 4 daily, (20-22 hr). Buses leave when full.

From Bannu one road leads W and then SW into Tribal Territory. It passes **Razmak** (126 km) with its Army Cadet College, **Wana** the administrative capital of S Waziristan and **Tanai Scout Post** (206 km) with its fort, before crossing into Baluchistan and on to **Zhob** (Fort Sandeman 333 km).
    At Taudachina just beyond Ramzak and at Tanai there are turnings heading E which converge at Jandola before going on past **Khirgi Post** with its impressive fort, **Dabarra**, centre for the local falcon trade and arriving at **Tank** (about 110 km from either turning).

Warning   These are dangerous Tribal Areas – kidnapping is described as local sport, ransoms are high and foreigners command a premium. Permits and escorts are essential.

The second road leads S from Bannu following the railway line. After 47 km, a fork leads E to Lakki and Kalabagh while the main road continues S to **Pezu** (82 km) where another fork goes W to Tank (37 km). **Tank** is a large town on the edge of the Tribal Areas and the terminus for another narrow gauge railway which connects with Lakki and Kalabagh by way of Pezu. 6 km W of Tank there is a large mound rich in shards of terracotta pottery and figurines possibly from an *Indus Valley Civilization* settlement.

From Pezu a path leads up to the nearby peak of **Sheikh Budin** (1377 m) named after the Sufi saint *Sheikh-Baha-ud-din* whose shrine is at the top. The mountain owes its height to a cap of imperishable limestone which has prevented erosion. To the SW is the snow-clad **Takht-e-Sulaiman** (*Throne of Solomon*) peak 3,355m, crowning the Sulaiman range. The main road continues S from Pezu crossing the western extremities of the Marwat Range before descending on to the **Derajat Plain** and reaching **Dera Ismail Khan**.

22 km N of DI Khan is **Rahman Dheri**, an Indus Valley Civilization settlement dating from 3200 BC. The basic layout of the city is visible with the ancient brick walls of the houses still surviving. Pottery shards, stone tools and even lapis-lazuli items are in evidence.

Dera Ismail Khan

Lies on the W bank of the Indus by a traditional river crossing, just upstream of the junction of the Gomal River with the Indus. DI Khan's cantonment area consists of a tree-lined promenade following the waterfront. The town is quiet, with only a little light industry and bicycle rickshaws are the main form of local transport. The local brass inlaid woodwork is particularly fine.

The Indus at this point varies from 10-20 km in width according to the season and used to be crossed by a bridge of floating barges during the winter season and by an old ferry in the summer. The ferry, the **SS Jhelum**, (built in Glasgow, 1917), served in World War I in S Iraq. The old river boat is still moored by the promenade and is open to visitors. Today a new bridge spans the river 5 km S of DI Khan. Down on the plains, DI Khan is too far S to benefit significantly from winter rains, receiving most of its very modest total in the monsoon season.

	Jan	Feb	Mar	Apr	May	Jun	Jul	Aug	Sep	Oct	Nov	Dec	Av/Tot
Max (°C)	20	23	27	34	40	42	39	38	38	34	28	22	32
Min (°C)	5	7	13	18	24	27	28	27	24	17	10	5	17
Rain (mm)	15	18	27	20	9	9	65	36	14	2	3	6	223

Hotels   D *Midway*, Indus River Bank, T 2900. **E** *Café Gul Bahar*, Circular Rd, T 3510. **E** *Al Habib*, Topan Wala Rd, T 3106. **E** *New Shahra*, Purani Choungi, T 2705. **E** *Jan's*, N Circular Rd, T 3925. *Govt Rest House*. Reservations, Dy Commissioner.

Air   Daily flights connect DI Khan with Islamabad, Peshawar, Multan and Quetta and also with Kohat, Bannu and Zhob.

Excursions

Chasma Barrage, 90 km up river on the Indus is the starting point for the **Paharpur Canal** which runs along the W bank, irrigating this fertile riverine tract. A single lane metalled road follows the canal up to the Chasma Barrage where there is a *WAPDA Rest House* (T Mianwali 107 to book). On the way you will pass the **Southern Kafir Kot** and **Northern Kafir Kot Forts**, both dating from the time of the Hindu Rajput Kingdom (8th-10th century). You can continue across the Chasma Barrage to reach **Mianwali** in Punjab. Alternatively, you can cross the Indus just S of DI Khan and drive N on a 2 lane metalled road (133 km, 2-3 hr).

From DI Khan a road leads S, crossing into Punjab at **Ramak** and continues along the Indus W bank, arriving at **Karachi** over 1000 km away. Another road leads W and S and W again entering the Tribal Areas and finally reaching **Quetta** 575 km away.

PESHAWAR TO ISLAMABAD-RAWALPINDI

The GT Road leaves Peshawar heading E from the Bala Hisar Fort. The road is a fast, good quality dual-carriageway, but very busy. It passes through the densely populated agricultural land of the fertile Vale of Peshawar with its fields of sugar cane and tobacco, interspersed with orchards, some factories and, more recently, Afghan refugee camps, until it reaches **Nowshera** (44 km).

The town has a large British built cantonment area and today is still an important military centre. A road turns N at the western edge of town, crosses the Kabul River by a new toll bridge and heads up to **Mardan** (22 km).

Jahangira is 23 km further on. A bridge crosses the Kabul River, the start of a road NE up to **Swabi** (26 km). At **Attock**, the GT Road crosses the Indus into Punjab, an important crossing point since the 1540's when *Sher-Shah-Suri* built a caravanserai here. The **Attock Fort**, completed by Akbar in 1586, stands high above the Indus. It is occupied by the military and closed to visitors. The old rail/road bridge was built by the British in 1883. Both are S of the new GT Road Bridge crossing. On the roadside is the courtesan **Randhi ki Muqbara's** tomb.

2.5 km upstream and 10 km downstream of Attock Fort, there are huge boulders with primitive engraved figures of elephants, bulls and men with bows and arrows, and Kharoshthi inscriptions dating from the 1st-2nd century BC. The road to Islamabad (85 km), passes the important sites at **Taxila**. **See page 1109**. If you take the Jahangira to Swabi road, after 16 km, at Amber, the minor road turning E takes you to Hund, 4 km.

Hund, 24 km up river from Attock, on the W bank of the Indus is another ancient crossing place and became the capital of the Hindu Shahi rulers of Gandhara after they defeated the Turki Shahis in Kabul in the 9th century AD. Here Alexander the Great, the Scythians and Kushanas, the Chinese pilgrims, Mahmud of Ghazni, Timurlane, Babur and many others crossed the Indus on their journeys. Today some Buddhist, Hindu and Muslim ruins remain from this ancient capital city, the most recent and prominent being the 16th century **Akbar's Fort**.

The Muslim traveller *Muqaddasi* gave an eyewitness account of the city in the 10th century AD – "It is a capital city of great glory and bigger than Mansura. Situated on a square open plain, it has many gardens, clean and attractive. The fruits of both summer and winter seasons are plentifully available. Around the city are gardens full of walnuts, almonds, banana and date. Prices are low; 3 mounds of honey can be bought for one dirham, bread and milk are very cheap. The houses are built of timber covered with dry grass...it could match with the best cities of Iran."

PESHAWAR TO SWAT

The road towards the Swat Valley leaves Peshawar from the Bala Hisar, heading NE across the Peshawar plain and passes a number of important historical sites before reaching the first hills of lower Swat.

Charsadda, (literally meaning '5 roads') 28 km from Peshawar, is the site of the ancient city of **Pushkalavati**, (the Lotus City), capital of Gandhara from c 6th century BC - 2nd century AD, and embodies the first flowering of this culture. The capital later moved to Peshawar, but Pushkalavati, with its large shrine, remained an important centre of Buddhist pilgrimage. The city, first mentioned in the Hindu Epic the Ramayana, was founded by *Bharata*, *Rama's* brother, as a twin city of Taxila (both, named after his sons).

1 km before Charsadda, where the road turns sharply right before crossing a river, a track leads N to the 2 largest mounds, known as **Bala Hisar**, probably because they were used as a fort in the 18th-19th centuries. The mounds have been twice excavated, by Sir John Marshall in 1902 and by Sir Mortimer Wheeler in 1958. All the important finds have been removed to Peshawar and Lahore Museums, but countless pottery shards still remain.

Across the river are the mounds of the later city **Shaikhan Dheri** excavated by Peshawar University in 1963 and revealing a city founded by the Bactrian Greeks in the 2nd century BC.

Rajur (from "*Rajaghar*" or royal palace) on the E bank of the Jinde River is built on some low mounds, which almost certainly contain the remains of an extensive city. Little has been excavated, although Indo-Greek, Scythian and Kushana coins have been found. Indeed the whole area is surrounded by an ancient graveyard, protecting much of the ground from excavation. Where unprotected, many of the mounds have been dug away by local villagers for use as topsoil and fertilizer. Just N of Rajur are the mounds of Shah-i-Napursan (literally 'Neglected City') and **Mir Ziarat**, perhaps the site of the legendary stupa built by Asoka and said to contain the remains of the Lord Buddha.

Prang, S from the Charsadda crossroads, has more mounds and was probably once the confluence of the Kabul and Swat Rivers. The name is a corruption of *Pravag* or *Prayang* – the sacred town at the confluence of the Jumna and the Ganga Rivers near Allahabad in N India, see page 247.

Throughout its history Charsadda has been subject to continually changing river courses, giving rise to the different sites and finally forcing the move to Peshawar.

From Charsadda the main road contiues E to **Mardan** (31 km). For nearly 200 years it has been a major military base, and was the Headquarters of the elite British *Guides Corps*, formed in 1846 to "guide regular units in the field, collect intelligence and keep the peace on the NW Frontier". In the centre there is an imposing Gothic-Mughal memorial arch to the Guides who died in Kabul in 1879 during the Second Afghan War. From Mardan there are 3 roads leading S to Nowshera (22 km) on the GT Road; E past the Asokan Rock Edicts at **Shahbaz Garhi** and on to **Swabi** (34 km); and N towards **Takht-i-Bahi** and the Swat Valley.

Shahbaz Garhi, 13 km E of Mardan is the site of **Asoka's Rock Edicts**, 2 huge boulders inscribed in the Gandharan Kharoshthi script, with a total of 14 Edicts. See page 83. The rock edicts, scattered throughout India and Pakistan, are most comprehensive here, setting out his Buddhist ideals of moral and social order, promoting the paths of *non-violence, righteousness* and *dhamma*.

Varusha: **Shahbaz Garhi** stands on the site of the ancient city of Varusha, situated at the intersection of 2 ancient trade routes, from China by way of the Indus and Swat Valleys, and from Europe and Afghanistan by way of the old routes through Bajaur and Swat, crossing the Indus at Hund. Today only the barest outlines of the city can be traced, centred on the modern road junction.

Shabaz Garhi is at the SW edge of the **Sudana Plain**, named after Prince Sudana, a previous incarnation of the Buddha. AH Dani writes: "Today the plain is an extensively cultivated area, bereft of its trees and much denuded of the beautiful scenery that commanded admiration from the Chinese travellers. The hills rise free from the traditions of old."

Two Chinese pilgrims, **Sun Yung** and **Xuan Zang** visited the city in 520 and 630 AD. Today the ruins of the **Mekha-Sanda Stupa** and Monastery remain on top of a hill N of the main road, reached by the road up to **Rustam** village. The Chinese pilgrims described a thriving monastic community.

Local legend tells how the *Prince Visvantura*, another incarnation of the Buddha, inherited a holy white elephant which brought rains whenever needed. The Prince, as an example of generosity, gave it to a neighbouring kingdom which was hostile but suffering from a drought. As a result his own people disowned him and he was banished to Mekha-Sanda with his wife and children, and only accepted back years later after giving away his children to be sold in the market – the ultimate act of self denial. On the hill there are 2 rocks resembling water buffalo (with a lot of imagination) and caves where Visvantura and his wife lived as ascetics. **The Chanaka Dheri Stupa** of the legendary white elephant is further N past Rustam to the left of the road, and is also the site of a monastery although there is little to see today.

Back on the main road to Swabi, past the rock edicts, is the site of the *But Sahri*, *'Convent of the gift of the 2 children'* and stupa. The mound is covered by later Muslim graves and unexcavated.

From here it is a further 25 km on to Swabi where the road forks left to Tarbela and right to Attock. It is 137 km by the N route and 119 km via Attock.

Takht-i-Bahi The Buddhist monastery here is 14 km N on the road from Mardan up to the Swat Valley. It is also accessible directly from Charsadda if you go N past Rajur village and then turn E for 22 km before joining the Mardan – Swat road just S of the monastery. The site itself is 3 km W of the main road.

Takht-i-Bahi, literally 'spring on a flat terrace' is the most impressive and best preserved Buddhist monastery in Pakistan. Standing 150 m above the plains, on a rocky ridge reached by a winding path, there are excellent views of the plains of Peshawar and up to the Malakand Pass and the hills of Swat beyond. The monastery's isolation protected it from invaders, but today it has been stripped of its important sculptures and relics, many of them removed to Europe and N America.

Taking the footpath uphill from the E, past some monks' cells on your right, you first enter the **Court of Stupas**, enclosed by 8 m high walls and surrounded by small alcoves, each of which would have contained a plaster Buddha, the largest possibly 10 m high. The remains of some 38 votive stupas are scattered around the centre of the court, built as offerings by pilgrims. The walls were originally lime plastered and decorated with paintings. The statues themselves may have been gilded.

N of the Court of Stupas, up a few steps, is the **Monastery Court** lined on 3 sides by monks' cells which are small and austere. An upper storey once housed more cells. There is a ancient water tank in the SE corner, and remains of the kitchen and refectory to the E, reached through a doorway. The **Court of the Main Stupa** is to the S. It houses the monastery's original stupa, which was about 10 m high. W of the central Court of Stupas, you come to an open court, beneath which are 10 vaulted chambers probably used either for meditation or as granaries. To the N, enclosed by high walls is the **Assembly Court** where the all the monks met; the water tanks here were built during excavation work this century. To the S is a covered area in the **Court of 3 Stupas**, displaying sculptures and fragments from the site. Scattered on the hillside you will see remains of 2 storeyed domestic buildings.

AH Dani suggests 3 stages of development for this monastic community, the earliest settlement occurring around 40 AD, the main peak of activity during the Kushana period of the 1st-4th centuries AD, and the last stage corresponding to the vaulted chambers dating from the 5th and 6th centuries.

From Takht-i-Bahi the road continues N to *Dargia*, a small town at the railhead of the line from Nowshera and Mardan. From here the road climbs up to the *Malakand Pass* (850 m) with good views down into Swat and at the top the **Malakand Fort** where 1000 Sikhs under British command held back 10,000 Yusufzia Pathans in 1897, until reinforcements arrived from Mardan.

Swat Valley

Population 1, 233 000 *Area* 12, 209 Sq km *Climate* Summer (May-Sep) 21°C average (Jul Max 38° C), Winter (Oct-Mar) 7° C average (Jan Min -1° C), Spring (Mar/Apr) 22° C average. Annual Rainfall 810-880 mm. *Best Season* Mar-Oct.

The **Swat Valley** is one of the most fertile and accessible in Pakistan. Rising in the **Shandur Range**, the three principle sources of the Swat River – the Gabral, Bahandra and Ushu – unite at Kalam (2,013 m) into a single hill torrent which then drops 18 m per km in a narrow gorge for 39 km before reaching **Madyan** (1,312 m). Here the river broadens out, liberally fed by both monsoon seasonal rainfall and summer snowmelt. This is the start of the fertile heartland of Swat. Below Mingora the river becomes a huge braided stream up to 5 km wide and rich in silt deposits from the river's massive sediment load.

The broad riverine flats are the richest and most populous areas in Swat. The river is controlled by a complex system of canals and river cuttings, combined with terracing to give some of the most intensively cultivated land in N Pakistan. Known throughout the NWFP as the *'Maize Granary'*, Swat also grows rice, wheat and barley as well as fruits. More recently honey collecting has become popular. Local industries include woollen Swati caps and shawls, blankets, silverware and tribal jewellery. Forestry is also an important source of income with timber being floated down the river to the railhead at Dargai.

The Swat Valley's favourable environment for settlement has been compared with that of the **Zagros Mountains** in present day Iran, the traditional *'Cradle of Civilization'*. The earliest evidence of settlement goes back at least 10,000 years to the early *'Grave Cultures'*, so called because the primary evidence of settlement comes from graves. The first written reference to the valley comes from Vedic literature, of Aryans who called it "*Suvastu*". Later in 327 BC Alexander the Great passed through the valley when he came through Afghanistan, by way of Bajour and Dir. He captured the ancient fort of **Bazira** in present day **Barikot**, and **Ora (Udegram)** before he went on to the plain of Peshawar.

History Fom about the 1st century AD Swat prospered, close to the heart of the Buddhist Gandharan civilization. At its height there were at least 1,400 monasteries in Lower Swat alone. The *Tantric* forms of Buddhism and the *Mahayana* schools were developed here and spread throughout the subcontinent. The valley is still rich in Buddhist monastery ruins, stupas, sculptures and rock reliefs.

From about the 7th century AD Buddhism declined in Gandhara as a whole and the Swat Valley became the refuge for a much reduced Buddhist culture until the 16th century. Meanwhile, Hinduism grew and the *Hindu Shahi* rulers extended their control into the valley during the 8th and 9th centuries AD until they were supplanted by the Muslim, *Mahmud of Ghazni*. Later under the Moghuls, both *Babur* and *Akbar* fought to control the Yusufzai Pathans of Swat, the former marrying into the tribe in 1519.

During the British period, Swat was also the scene for the famous Malakand Campaign of 1897 against the *Sayyid Hajji Shoaib Baba* who preached *jihad* against the British who dubbed him the '*Mad Mullah*', an event covered by the young Winston Churchill for the Daily Telegraph.

Swat Valley was consolidated into an independent state in 1926 by the **Wali** or ruler, *Miangal Gulshehzada Abdul Wadood*, the grandson of the *Akhund* of Swat, a famous Sufi ascetic and religious leader (Akhund meaning teacher). His son *Miangal Jahanzib* took over in 1940 until 1969 when Swat was integrated into NWFP. Between them the two Walis of Swat were competent leaders who achieved internal political integration and promoted the building of roads, hospitals and a free school system.

The people of Swat Valley are mostly **Yusufzai Pathans** who were displaced from the Vale of Peshawar by the related *Mandnar Yusufzais* late in the 16th century. The Yusufzais in turn forced the Dardic speaking *Dilazaks* further up the Swat Valley and into the remoter parts of Kohistan and N Hazara. Today, Upper Swat, or Swat Kohistan, is inhabited by 2 language groups, the *Torwal* and *Gawri*, both Dardic, the former found between Madyan and Kalam, the latter above Kalam up to the Shandur range. In addition there are 2 nomadic groups, the *Gujars* who mainly herd cattle and the *Ajars* who rear sheep and goats. The Ajars practice extreme forms of *transhumance**, involving annual movements of whole village communities between 4,500 and 600 m, accomplished in 4-5 moves to appropriate seasonal altitude belts.

The twin towns of **Mingora** and **Saidu Sharif** have been the centre of extensive development. In 1960 the Queen visited as head of the Commonwealth, and since then tourism has been promoted, culminating in the PDTC's extravagant showpiece; a tourist complex cum ski resort at *Mallam Jabba*, 40 km NE of Saidu Sharif, of dubious local economic benefit and certainly environmentally taxing on the valley's much stretched resources.

The Walis exercised a sustainable forestry programme involving the strict yearly rotation of 20 forest tracts for logging purposes. Nevertheless there is added pressure from nomadic groups and from a poulation which has shot up from about 93,000 people in 1884 to well over 1.2 million in 1981, and on top of that a mushrooming tourist trade. Deforestation is already evident and looking at the landscape of Buner, SE from Barikot across the Karakar Pass, which has gone from full forest cover 100 years ago to a denuded barren landscape with little forest cover today, it is not difficult to see the dangers facing Swat Valley.

From the *Malakand Pass* the road winds down into Swat Valley, passing *Bat Khela* with its good cloth market and the ruins of a Hindu Shahi fort above, and then the headworks of the **Swat Canal** which carries irrigation water by way of a tunnel through the Malakand Pass out on to the plains around Mardan, before reaching Chakdara where the road branches.

Chakdara Situated on the ancient trade route from Afganistan via Bajour and Dir, where it crossed the Swat River, Chakdara was an important centre for thousands of years. The area is dominated by Chakdara **Fort** built in 1896 by the British on the foundations of a 16th century Moghul fort. The fort guards the Chakdara **Bridge**, also British and designed to be strong enough to carry a light railway. Overlooking the fort and bridge is *Churchill's Picket*, perched on a ridge of *Damkot Hill*, which was used as a signalling station back to Malakand and is known locally as *Shiso* (mirror) guard. Excellent views over 7 Passes.

Damkot Hill has been excavated revealing evidence of the first Ayran settlers who developed stone and iron tools and copper and gold jewellry. Later came the Buddhists who left boulders carved with figures of the *Bodhisattva Padmapani*, found at the bottom of the hill. Next came the Hindu Shahis who built a large fort and defensive walls enclosing houses, shops and stables, before it was largely destroyed by Mahmud of Ghazni and then taken over by the Moghuls.

The **Museum** is 2 km N of Chakdara Bridge, on right of the modern village. Small, but some excellent Gandharan sculptures, all well labelled. Also local handicrafts and folk art. Open 0830-1230, 1430-1700 Apr-Oct and 0900-1600 Nov-Mar. Closed Wed.

Chat Pati has ruins of a Buddhist monastery, 1 km W of the road before it enters Chakdara village. This road, N of the Swat river, continues through Dir and up into Chitral, see page 1229.

The main road continues up the Swat Valley on the S side of the river, bypassing **Thana** on the hillside to the right, where a footpath leads to **Mora Pass** and back to the plains of Mardan.

At *Habaitgram*, 8 km from Chakdara Bridge, the ruins of a huge Hindu Shahi **fortress** is perched on the ridge to the right. Below is the *Top Dara Stupa* and monastery ruins nestled in a secluded side valley.

Landakai (12 km) is the start of Swat proper. A rocky spur reaches down to the river forming a natural barrier and checkpost. Beyond, the road climbs gently through terraced fields and orchards. Just before Barikot there is a bridge crossing the Swat River to a track which runs parallel to the main road, N of the river. 4 km W on this track, back along the river, a path leads N up along a secluded valley to the *Nimogram* Monastery and Stupas, 6 km away. The 3 large stupas are devoted to the *Buddha Dharma* and the *Sangha* (Buddhist order). The superb sculptures from this site are found in the Swat Museum at **Saidu Sharif**.

Barikot lies on the ancient trade route S from Bajour and Dir, over the Karakar Pass (1336 m) into Buner and Ambela. Close by is **Birkot Hill,** site of the ancient fort and city of *Bazira*, captured by Alexander in 327 BC. Today only the ruins of the Hindu Shahi fort remain. *Mount Ilam*, (2811m), SE of Barikot, is the largest in Lower Swat and considered sacred. Two large square slabs of rock, perhaps prehistoric altars, crown the top. Buddhists, Hindus and Muslims all consider the mountain holy and until Partition it attracted annual Hindu pilgrimages.

Today there is a metalled road going S from Barikot, over the Karakar Pass into Buner, Ambela and finally back to the Peshawar-Islamabad GT Road. The main road up the Swat Valley continues past Buddhist remains at **Shingerdar**, **Ghalagai** and **Goydara**, before reaching Udegram.

Udegram is an ancient site that has been occupied from at least 1000 BC. It has been identified with **Ora**, captured by Alexander in 327 BC and was also the capital of the Hindu Shahi rulers of Swat from the 8th-10th centuries AD. The remains of their fort, the **Raja Gira**, are scattered up the hillside, while below are the remains of the first mosque in Swat built by Mahmud of Ghazni, and the tree encircled shrine of Pir Khushal Baba, one of his commanders. Much of the hill has been excavated by an Italian team. Nothing is labelled, but there are extensive ruins to explore and excellent views from the top of the hill. From Udegram it is a further 8 km on to the twin towns of Mingora and Saidu Sharif.

Mingora and **Saidu Sharif** The 2 towns are situated 2 km apart (990 m). Mingora is the district headquarters of Swat and the main bazaar area. It has been an important trading post for at least 2000 years and the bazaars are rich in locally made goods and antiques: sandals, woollen waistcoats, caps, blankets and embroidered shawls, silver jewellery, precious and semi-precious stones, old coins and strings of cowrie shells from the Comoro Islands, off E Africa, once used as local currency.

Saidu Sharif Set out in the traditional British colonial style reminiscent of Peshawar cantonment, it is the administrative capital of Swat, 2 km S of Mingora along the Saidu River and contrasts with the busy bazaars of Mingora.

The Saidu Sharif **Museum** is halfway between the two and has many of the Buddhist Gandharan sculptures collected from sites throughout Swat. There are also many reproductions on display and an ethnographic section. Open Apr-Sep 0800-1200, 1500-1800, Oct-Mar 1000-1630.

The Butkara Stupa nr the museum is one of the most important Buddhist shrines in Swat. The stupa, decorated with stone and plaster sculptures, was built around the 2nd century BC and was subsequently enlarged at least 5 times by completely encasing the original. Scattered around are bases of various votive stupas left by pilgrims.

There is also the impressive **Palace of the Walis** of Swat, and nearby the former **British Residency**, now the Swat Serena Hotel. Saidu Sharif is also where the grave of **Habdul Gaffer**, the *Akhund of Swat*, is located. Born in 1784 he lived as a Sufi ascetic, and later united the people of Swat under his rule. He died in 1877. A multicoloured plaster structure has replaced the old carved wooden shrine.

Hotels The best in town is the old Residency, **B** *Swat Serena*. T 4215, Cable: SERENA SWAT. 44 a/c rm. Excellent restaurant, tourist information, TV, squash, badminton, golf course. **C** *Pameer*, GT Rd. Mingora. T 4962, Cable: PAMEER. 60 a /c rm. Restaurant, coffee shop, shops, travel. **E** *Hotel De Shazad*, Shahidra Canal Rd, T 2484. 20 a/c rm. Restaurant, cafeteria, pool, TV. **E** *Abaseen*, New Madyan Rd, T 2122. 27 rm with bath. **E** *Udyana*, GT Rd, Mingora, T 4876. 28 rm with bath. *Zeeshan*, GT Rd. Mingora, T 4010. 10 rm with bath.

Heater on request. **E** *Holiday*, Makan Bagh, Saidu Sharif Rd, T 444. 8 rm with bath. **E** *Malbro*, Kutchery Rd, nr General Bus Stand. 19 rm. Several others on GT Road, Madyan Road and around Green Chowk.

Restaurants There are numerous local restaurants in the bazaar area selling grilled meat and naan dishes as well as international restaurants at the *Swat Serena*, *Pameer* and *De Shazad Hotels*.

Banks Swat Serena will cash Travellers Cheques. Bank Sq. in Mingora.

Sports Golf course on the N side of the Swat River at Kabal, nr airport.

Useful Addresses GPO close to Bank Sq in the centre of Mingora. PIA Domestic Booking Office, Makan Bagh, Grassy Ground, Main Saidu Rd. Mingora T 4624.

Tourist Information Swat Serena, T 5007.

Air Daily flights (except Tue) to Islamabad and 3 flights a week to Peshawar.

Bus and mini-buses daily to Peshawar and Islamabad and long distance to Karachi 1541 km (36 hr). Summer services N to Kalam and also Besham (KKH).

Excursions

S up the Saidu Valley to *Marghazar* 13 km away (1287m), which has the famous **Safed Mahal** (White Palace), summer residence of the Walis of Swat, now converted into the **Marghazar Hotel**, T 5714, with 26 rm. A footpath leads to the top of **Mt Ilam** – the old pilgrimage route – a full day's walk. See under Barikot above.

Jambil Valley SE from Mingora, is dotted with numerous Buddhist monastery and stupa ruins and Ayran graves dating from 1700 BC.

From Mingora take the road N, and turn E of **Manglaur**. A metalled road climbs up past the *Jahanabad Buddha* – a 4 m high seated Buddha, carved into the rock face on the other side of the river. *Malam Jabba* (40 km) is Pakistan's first **ski resort** with 2 chair-lifts, ski equipment and a 52 room luxury **hotel** complex, with summer pony-trekking and mini-golf facilities. Developed with Austrian aid and completed in 1989.

From Mingora, the main route up the Swat Valley continues N past Manglaur to *Khwazakhela* (30 km). Here a road branches E across the **Shangla Pass** to join the KKH at **Besham** (70 km). Khwazakhela used to be an important commercial centre before the opening of the KKH, which diverted traffic away, but still has an interesting bazaar and a bridge across the Swat River here.

Further N at **Fatehpura** the Swat River is again bridged, and the valley begins to narrow to an alpine glen. A few km further, a road branches E up a beautiful secluded valley to the summer resort of *Miandam* (1,800m) which has some lovely walks and pleasant **accommodation**. **C/D** *PTDC Motel*, T 10. 10 rm with bath. Reservations, Direct or PTDC Rawalpindi T 481480). *Miandam*, T 10. 12 rm, with bath. Heater. *Karishma*, T 4. 12 rm. Restaurant, shop. *Pameer Guest House*. Reservations, Mingora, T 4926. **Camping** at PTDC Motel or Miandarn Hotel.

Madyan (1,321m, pronounced Mad-ain), is about 8 km N of Fatehpura on the main road. Surrounded by steeply wooded hills and terraced fields, the Swat River here flows as a torrent through a narrow gorge of bedrock. It is a tourist resort, with hotels, shops and restaurants and even a cinema. The main bazaar has a variety of antique shops but specialises in traditional local embroideries and hand-loom shawls.

Hotels **D** *Madyan*, Bahrain Rd, T 4599. 29 rm with bath. Heater on request, car hire. **D** *Mountain View*, Bahrain Rd, T 7 1 2rm with bath. **E** *Nisar*, T 441. 23 rm with bath. Heater, car hire, tour guide. *Parkway*. 6 rm with bath. *Shalimar*, T 14. 12 with bath. Heater.

Sport Excellent trout fishing (brown and rainbow) throughout the Swat Valley, and especially further N. Permits from Asst Commissioner of Fisheries in Madyan or Kalam.

At Madyan the road crosses the Swat River on to the W bank. 10 km N is *Bahrain* (1,400m), another popular tourist resort with interesting bazaars. The wooden houses are often decorated with intricate carvings and has the last petrol pump in Swat. Above Bahrain the road is only motorable May-Nov, preferably with 4-wheel drive.

Hotels D *Deluxe*, T 15. 26 rm with bath. Heater. *Pakistan*. 10 rm with bath. Heater. **E** *Bahrain*, T 33. 24 rm (1-4 beds) with bath. *Paris*, T 26. 11rm with bath. *Abshar*, T 22.

About 30 km N of Bahrain is *Kalam* (2,100m) where the narrow valley opens out into a small fertile plain, probably once the basin of an ancient lake. There is a Police Station, the first 2 hotels on open ground, with cheaper hotels down by the river along the main road from the bus stop. The **Mosque** has excellent wood carvings.

Hotels D *PTDC Motel*, T 14. Reserve direct or at PTDC Rawalpindi, T 481480. 18 rm, hot water in buckets, western wc. Pleasant garden, Information. camping allowed. *Falaksheer*, T 10. 16 with bath. **E** *Khalid*, T 6. 21 rm with bath. *Heaven Breeze*, T 5. 12 rm with bath. Heater. *Mehran*. 10 rm with bath. Heater. **Camping** at PTDC Motel.

Above Kalam it is possible to walk up to the **Utrot** (or Bahandra) **River** to Utrot (2,200m) 16 km away. NW of Utrot is the *Gabral Valley* and village. Both villages have Rest Houses.

The *Ushu Valley* runs NE from Kalam. **Ushu** village (2300m) 8 km, has a **hotel**. There are excellent views of *Mount Falaksir* (6257m) and numerous picnic spots. 10 km further N is *Lake Mahodand* (Lake of the fishes). All the streams in the area are well stocked with trout.

From Lake Mahodand there are trekking routes NW over the Kachikani Pass (4816m) to Lapsur in Chitral, N over the Dardaril Pass to Handrap in Gilgit or E to the Kandin and Indus valleys. From Utrot a route leads across to Dir.

Warning All these routes are dangerous due to banditry amongst the Kohistani tribal groups. It is essential to take advice and a good local guide.

PESHAWAR TO CHITRAL

The route from Peshawar to Chitral follows the road to Swat, over the Malakand Pass as far as Chakdara. Here the Chitral Road crosses the Swat River and heads N for a short while past the foundations of the *Andan Dheri Stupa* 500 m NE of the road, once 24 m high and the most important on Chakdara plain. Then the road climbs W over a ridge which is guarded by the ruins of a Hindu Shahi fort E of Ziarat.

The fort is identified with the site of *Massaga* where Alexander fought a battle with the *Queen of Gourais* in 327 BC. Beyond is the **Panjkora River** valley. Historically very unstable, this drainage basin (5,000 sq km) is occupied by a number of aggressively lawless tribal groups which were loosely united into **Dir State** under a corrupt *Khan* (or *Nawab*) until 1962 when it became part of Pakistan's 'Tribal Areas'.

The main tribal groups, the *Mohmands, Bajouris, Malazai* and *Kohistani Pathans*, have remained consistently lawless, with the Durand Line of 1893 dividing the *Bar* (Hill) *Mohmands* between Afghanistan and Pakistan. The present road was built in the 1930s close to the ridge to avoid sniping gunfire from *Bajaur* across the river, and as recently as 1977 the Pakistan Air Force was strafing 'Pathan irregulars' over timber rights. Throughout Dir the villages consist of groups of family compounds each with its own watchtower, and beyond the road only 'tribal law' exists.

48 km from Chakdara, is **Timargarha** close to the junction of the Jandul with the Panjkora River. This town lay on one of the ancient trade routes from Bajaur. At Timargarha there is a *Govt Rest House* with 3 rm and basic **hotels** along the GT Road.

There is an excavated site, **Balambut**, on the W bank occupied from at least 1500 BC by Ayrans, Buddhists, Hindus and Muslims and notable for its mud fire altars, still used to burn juniper (a devotional offering common to most of the Tibetan Plateau).

From here the road follows the Panjkora River for 78 km to **Dir**, a rough and lawless town like something straight out of an old western movie. Here the valley narrows and is thickly wooded. There are some basic **hotels** and a *PTDC Rest House* (Reservations *PTDC Peshawar,* T 76428 or Gilgit 683, and a GTS Bus Station.

Beyond Dir the road climbs up to the **Loweri Pass** (3,118 m). This pass is generally closed from late Nov until May and can be treacherous during periods of rain and snowmelt, when avalanches of liquid mud and stone can block the road. On the way up, works can be seen below the road to the W where a tunnel will form a part of the Chitral Diversion and **Panjkora River Steps Irrigation Scheme**. From the top of the pass there are views N on to the Chitral Valley and the Hindu Kush mountains beyond.

Chitral Valley

Population 208,560. *Area* 14,833 sq km. *Climate* Jun Max 35°C, Min 19°C, Sep Max 24°C, Min 8°C, Dec Max 0°C, Min -20°C. Annual Rainfall 330 mm. *Best Season* Jun-Sep.

Chitral is culturally and physically the most isolated region of the NWFP. The **Hindu Kush** range, averaging 4,500 m and dominated by Tirich Mir (7,787 m) and Istora Nal (7,327 m) marks the NW roof of S Asia and the watershed between the valleys draining the Oxus and the Indus Basins. S and E, the **Hindu Raj** mountains (also known as the Shandur or Mashabar) separate Chitral from Gilgit, Swat and Dir.

Only 2 roads connect Chitral with the rest of Pakistan. The main route through Dir and over the **Loweri Pass** (3,118 m) is closed by snow from late Nov until May while the lengthy route from Gilgit on a rough jeep track over the **Shandur Pass** (3,734 m) generally closes earlier and for longer. Before the building of the road from Peshawar to Chitral by the British in 1895, troops leaving Islamabad for Chitral had to travel either via Srinagar and Gilgit, a gruelling 1,000 km journey over 5 passes, or via Abbottabad, Chilas and Gilgit (800 km). The present road route, metalled in the 1930's is 250 km. Historically the Chitral Valley was one of the main arteries of the Silk Road, across the **Boroghil Pass** to Yarkand and Kashgar, but was later replaced by the more southern routes along the Indus and through Kashmir and Ladakh due to persistant banditry and feuding in the region.

The **Chitral River** system known by 4 different names at various stages along its course, rises in the area of the **Chiantar Glacier**, a 40 km sheet of ice which is also the source of the Oxus and Gilgit rivers. Known here as the **Yarkand River**, it flows down from an original height of over 5,000 m to be joined by the **Laspur River** which drains most of the northern slopes of the Shandur range. After this point it becomes the **Mastuj River** until joined by the Lutkoh branch, draining the Tirich Mir region. Here it is called the **Chitral River** for much of its course until, close to Afghanistan, it becomes the **Kunar River**. In total the river valley runs to over 300 km.

Just below **Mastuj** the river plain widens to up to 4 km and follows a broken pattern of cultivated alluvial fans right down to **Nagar**, 10 km S of Drosh.

Cultivation is irrigation based and often complex, involving up to 15 km of gravity flow channels. The main crops are barley, wheat and *jowar* (millet), followed by rice, vegetables and fruit, and pulses on the *barani** land. There is also widespread cultivation of **opium** and **cannabis** along the Afghan border, which aggravates the existing deficit of food grains in the region and depletes soil fertility in the long term.

Due to the low elevation of much of the river plain, double-cropping is extensively practised. However soil erosion is a major problem since most cultivation is on steeply sloping, cleared forest tracts. The Chitrali word for 'level ground' refers to any land at less than a 45° angle! Forest reserves are limited in Chitral to about 120 km of the valley between 1,900 m and 2,300 m. Species include the **Deodar** (Indian Cedar), Blue Pine, Chiligoza Pine and Silver Fir, of which *Deodar* represents 90% of the forest cover and the only viable source of timber, although slow growing (125 years to maturity) and susceptible to cracking.

Cottage industries centre around the production of *Shu*, or *Patti* cloth, a soft handwoven woollen material which is made into intricately embroidered gowns *(chunghas)*, rugs, bags, Chitrali hats etc. Chitral is heavily subsidised by the central government, as a result of the massive influx of Afghan refugees into the valley, and in an effort to integrate it more closely economically and socially with the rest of Pakistan.

The Chitrali people, who call their land *Kho*, are not Pathan, and their language, *Khowar*, although it belongs to the Dardic group, has strong connections with the languages of the Pamir and Wakhan regions to the N, and with Iran. In addition there are 2 minorities. The **Kafir Kalash**, who number about 3,000, inhabit the valleys of **Birir**, **Bumburet** and **Rumbur**, just S of Chitral. The **Wakhi**, a nomadic group, occupy the Pamir (literally meaning upland grazing zone) and the neighbouring Wakhan Corridor, a thin wedge of Afghan territory separating the Soviet Union and Pakistan. The ruling clan, the **Adamzada**, trace their lineage back to *Tamerlane*, **see page 147**, and are known to have ruled from the 1600s.

History In 1889 the **Trans-Caspian Railway** linking the European provinces of Tsarist Russia with Tashkent, was completed. Russian exploration parties visited Hunza in 1889 and Chitral in 1891, and the British became rapidly alarmed at the threat of Russian expansion into S Asia. Thus in 1895 the British forced the *Methar* of Chitral to accept joint British-Kashmiri sovereignty and stationed a garrison of troops there to oppose the "body of around 3,000 Cossacks". This was the beginnings of the British '*Forward Policy*' and there ensued the '*Great Game*' between Britain and Russia, immortalised in Rudyard Kipling's *Kim*. Notwithstanding its strategic significance, the British showed little interest in Chitral and made no effort to develop it.

From the Loweri Pass the road winds down to **Mirkhani** where it joins the Kunar River, following it to **Drosh**, 74 km from Dir. Here the valley has widened, and terraced cultivation is interspersed with forest tracts.

Drosh was the military headquarters of the British from the turn of the century. There is a *Govt Rest House*, bookable through the Dy Commissioner in Chitral, a few basic **hotels** and a GTS **Bus** Stand and petrol.

Beyond Drosh the road passes the **Shishi Valley** to the E, then the valleys of the Kafir Kalash to the W (**see page 1232**) before reaching Chitral Town (42 km).

Chitral Town

Altitude 1,525 m, is on a wide alluvial fan. The valley is at its widest here, about 4 km, and **Tirich Mir** (7,878m) towers to the N. It received large numbers of Afghan refugees during the Soviet occupation, many of them *Mujahedeen* fighters who moved freely back and forth across the border.

The town is centred around the **Main Bazaar** (Shahi Bazaar) which sells locally handwoven wool garments, jewellery, precious and semi-precious stones, Chitrali sitars, drums, oboes and antique/modern weapons. The **Shahi Masjid** and the Chitral **Fort,** on the banks of the **Mastuj River**, stand in a cluster of huge chinar trees. The fort and the old *Methar's* Palace (later occupied by the British) now house the local police headquarters. On a plateau to the NW, at 2,700m, is the **Summer Palace**, a hunting lodge now converted to a *Government Cottage*, with spectacular views N to Tirich Mir and the Hindu Kush, and W to the Shandur range.

At the S end of town, the **Polo Ground** fields tournaments from Jun to Nov. Polo is a popular local sport played throughout the valley and at high altitude grounds on the **Shandur Pass**, **Shah Jinali Pass** and **Lusht Khot** (3050m) to the accompaniment of *Dol** (drums) and *shehnai** (oboe). Horses are a fundamental status symbol to the Chitralis and horsemanship a much admired quality.

Hotels D *PTDC Tourist Complex*, Airport Bazaar, T 683. 14 rm. Car hire, tourist information. Also bookable through PTDC Rawalpindi T 581480. *Mountain Inn*, Ataliq Bazaar, T 581. 12 rm. Pleasant garden. **E** *Dreamland*, Shahi Bazaar, T 615. **E** *Tirich Mir View*, nr Shahi Masjid. Rm with bath. Excellent views. **E** *Fairland*, Ataliq Bazaar. **F** *Shabnam* has dormitory beds.

Restaurants Local and continental food at the *PTDC* and *Mountain Inn Hotels*. Plenty of local meat, potato and naan restaurants and tea shops in the bazaar.

Useful Addresses Habib and National Bank of Pakistan, a Post Office and Telephone Exchange in a lane towards river, in the Main Bazaar. The Dy Commissioner, T 1. Fisheries Dept.

Tourist Office PTDC Tourist Information, T 683. PTDC tours, T 698.

Air 3 daily flights to **Peshawar**, PIA by *Fokker Friendship* (50 min). Subject to weather conditions. PIA Domestic Bookings, Main Bazaar, T 546.

Buses Regular GTS Buses to **Dir** and **Peshawar**. Mini-Buses/Jeeps for private hire from depots at the N and S ends of town. Rates vary according to season/demand. Bargain hard.

Excursions

Biron Shal 3,000 m, can be reached by a footpath leading SW from the District Commissioner's office and is high in a thickly wooded valley, designated the *Chitral Gol National Park*. There are numerous Kashmiri Markhor, which rut in Dec, wolves and reputedly some black bear and snow leopard and also a wide variety of birds. The park extends to the edge of the Kalash Valley.

Garam Chasma 45 km NW of Chitral along the **Lutkho River** are the Hot Springs guarded by a mud walled fort. The hot sulphur springs are reputed to heal ailments and there is a bathhouse and basic *Rest House*. Permits may be needed to stay overnight.

From Garam Chasma, 2 trekking routes approach **Tirich Mir** from the NW along the Arkari River and NE across the S side from Shoghor to Kiyar. From here there is a path across the **Owir Pass** (4,338m) to Barum on the Mastuj River.

The Pamir, upper Chitral

N and E from Chitral is the Pamir region, literally meaning upland grazing zone. Averaging 2,500-4,000 m, this area is characterised by glacial action, with numerous small lakes dammed by old and extensive grass covered moraines and widespread evidence of glacial scouring and morainic debris. The Pamir extends over into Wakhan and the Soviet Union. Generally known as the *Pamir Knot*, it forms the pivotal point from which the Hindu Kush, Karakoram and Shandur ranges originate. As well as the **Wakhi Nomads** the area is home to communities of **Ismaili Muslims**, followers of the *Aga Khan*, settled in the **Lutkoh, Mastuj and Turikho valleys.**

The main jeep track N of Chitral crosses to the E side of the Mastuj (Chitral) River, passing **Koghozi** (19 km). Soon after, the **Golan River** valley joins from the E. Paths lead up the Golan Valley to **Ustor** (14 km). From Ustor there are two full-length treks. Either go S over the **Dok Pass** (4,191m) to the Shishi Valley, or NE across the **Phargram Pass** (5,065m) to Harchin and **Mastuj**.

The main road continues NE towards Parpish (47 km). A turning W leads to Barum. At Kuragh the **Turikho River** valley joins the Mastuj River. The Turikho valley is rich and fertile, running parallel to the main Mastuj River for 70 km. A jeep track reaches up as far as **Sor Rich**. Alternatively, you can trek NW across the **Zani Pass** (3,898 m) into the Tirich Mir River valley, which runs W to **Istora Nal** and **Tirich Mir**, or NE to rejoin the Turikho valley. Connecting the Turikho and Yarkhund (Chitral) River valleys to the N are the Khot Pass 4,320 m and Shah Jinali (King's Polo ground) Pass (4,259 m).

Mastuj, on the main jeep track 107 km from Chitral, is a small busy town with shops and private jeeps and mini-buses. It once lay on the N arm of the Silk Road. There is **tent** accommodation in the **Mastuj Fort**, run by descendents of the ruling family of the old kingdom of Little Bolor, and a polo ground below.

Beyond the town the Yarkhund River valley continues NE up to the **Boroghil Pass** (3,813m) on the Silk Route, an area now closed to visitors. The jeep track meanwhile turns S and climbs up to the **Shandur Pass** (3,734m) and into Gilgit. For details of the valley connecting Gilgit and Chitral, see page 1255.

The *Kafir Kalash*

Permits Foreign tourists require permits to visit, issued by the *Dy Commissioner,* Chitral T 1.

The Kafir Kalash Valleys of **Rumbur**, **Bumburet** and **Birir**, between 1,670 and 2,309m, are about 35 km S of Chitral, each leading off to the E from the main road.

The **Kafir Kalash**, (literally, Black Unbelievers) are an important minority of Chitral, numbering 3 to 4,000. Legends trace their lineage back to soldiers of Alexander the Great's army who are supposed to have settled here. There is certainly historical evidence of contact between the Kafir Kalash and Alexander's army, and the fair complexion and occasional blue eyes and blonde hair of the people suggests intermingling. The distinctive black woollen head-dress of the Kafir women, decked out with *cowrie* shells, buttons and coloured feathers is very similar to ones still worn in Greece and also in Ladakh. However, the Kafir Kalash are probably more closely related to an ancient Indo-Ayran group from Afghanistan, who fled conversion to Islam in the 10th century. Later, at the end of the 19th century there was a second wave of settlers, the **Red Kafirs**, who fled Kafiristan which was annexed by **Abdur Rahman Khan** and renamed **Nuristan** (*Land of the Light*) in 1896.

Religion The **Kalash** people follow their own religion of animism, ancestor and fire worship. *Sarijor* is the overall protector, *Surisan* the god of cattle, *Goshedoi* the god of dairy products, and many others. The Kalash celebrate religious/seasonal festivals; *Chilimjusht* (spring), *Phool* (the walnut and grape harvest) and *Chowas* (winter solstice) when dancing, music, singing, feasting and animal sacrifices take place. Standing effigies marking graves used to dot the hillsides but many have been removed. The wooden houses and temples, often intricately carved, are usually 2 storeys high, due to the steep valley sides.

The Kalash valleys are presented as a prime attraction by the tourist industry and in recent years the number of tourists visiting has been high, especiallly in Bumburet, the largest and most accessible valley.

Note The women do not observe purdah and enjoy relative equality. However this is interpreted as promiscuity by many male Parkistani tourists, and there is considerable animosity in some villages towards outsiders.

Rumbur, the most northerly valley, is jeepable from Ayun, as far as Balanguru, and Bumburet as far as Krakal. The track to Birir is 7 km S of Ayun and goes up as far as Guru. The 3 valleys are also connected by passes running N-S. From Balanguru you can trek across 2 ridge passes to Batrick, in the Bumburet valley, 2 days away, and then up over a ridge and down a narrow wooded valley to Gasguru in Birir.

Hotels F *Kalash Hilton*, Balanguru. F *Rumbur*, Balanguru. **In Bumburet Valley**: F *Peace*, Batrick. F *Benazir*, Anish, camping. E *Ansaf*, Anish. F *Kalash Hilton*, Brun. F *Frontier*, Brun. F *Kalash View*, Brun. F *Govt Rest Houses* are located at Ayun, Bumburet and Birir. They must be booked through the Dy Commissioner, Chitral T 1. **In Birir Valley**: F *Insaf*, Guru.

NORTHERN AREAS

INTRODUCTION

Area: 72,000 sq km *Population* 574,500

The Northern Areas of Pakistan are similar in area to the NWFP, an awesome blend of high mountains, glaciers, plateaus, lakes and river valleys. For centuries the region has provided trade routes between Central Asia and S Asia. The geographical isolation of the river valleys, both from the outside world and internally, has given the small areas of permanent settlement a highly varied and unique cultural history, and a distinctive, vibrant people.

The region, which includes parts of the Hindu Kush, Shandur, Karakoram and Himalayan ranges, has over 100 peaks exceeding 7,000 m and 5 peaks over 8,000 m. The Karakoram range dominates the area with 12 of the 30 highest recorded peaks in the world, and an ice cover estimated at 23-25% (The Alps in comparison have 2.2%). The Indus River cuts a deep gorge through the Northern Areas, entering the region 700 km from its source nr Mt.Kailash and Mansarowar Lake in W Tibet, and trends first E-W then N-S before reaching the wide plains to the S. With the exception of Skardu and Chilas, settlement is largely impractical along the Banks of the Indus, where seasonal discharge varies at a ratio of 20:1 and the gorge itself is often narrow and deeply cut.

The Land
The Northern Areas demonstrate the power generated by movements of the earth's crust, now understood as plate tectonics. The area consists largely of the

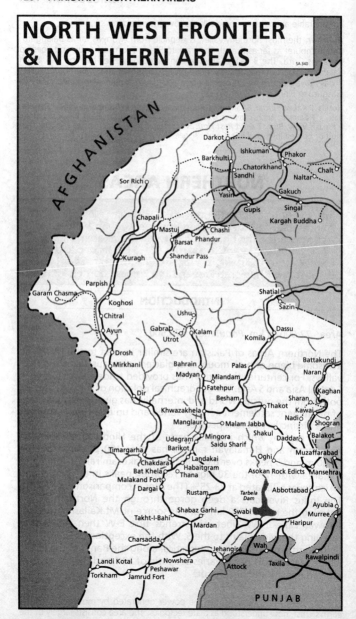

NORTH WEST FRONTIER & NORTHERN AREAS

SA 340

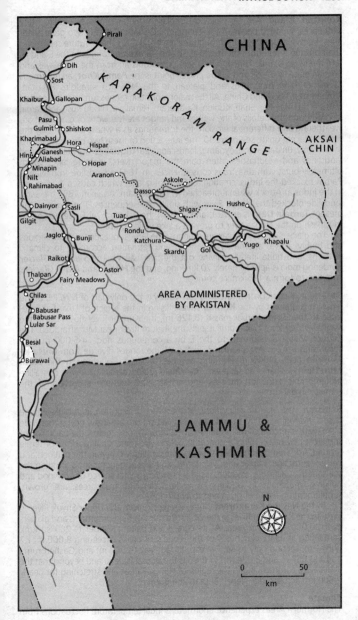

Kohistan Island Arc, a mass of displaced metamorphosed sedimentary sequences, wedged between the Eurasian and S Asian plates. Two great shear lines, known as *sutures*, run through the region; the Northern Suture separating the Kohistan Island from the Hindu Kush and Karakoram ranges to the E and N, and the Main Mantle Thrust, which separates Kohistan from the Himalayas and S Asian plate to the SE and S. The pivotal point is the ***Pamir Knot***, an enormous tangle of high mountains and plateau to the N which straddles Pakistan, Afghanistan, USSR and China. All the major mountain ranges run from this central feature: the Alai, Tian Shan, Kunlun, Karakoram, Himalaya, Hindu Kush and Pamir.

Although the details of the valleys and ranges are the work of glacial action, weathering and differential erosion, the formations as a whole are primarily the result of recent uplift, **see page 30**. The interaction of these two processes results in a highly unstable and dynamic landscape. **Earthquakes** are frequent and landslides and mudflashes often dam the major rivers, creating lakes which ultimately burst with disastrous consequences. In 1841 a landslide from Nanga Parbat blocked the Indus, creating a 55 km long lake, which caused a 24 m rise in the Indus at Attock when it breached its natural dam. Again in 1857 the Sarat landslide blocked the Hunza River with similar consequences. The threat to the present **Tarbela Dam** is evident, and in 1974 the Pakistani Air Force bombed a mudflash on the Hunza river to prevent a lake building up.

The glaciers of the N Areas are amongst the largest outside the Polar regions and highly active, alternately advancing and retreating according to climatic patterns, and quite literally carving out the river valleys. The ***Siachen Glacier*** bordering India is approximately 70 km long, and the ***Hispar*** and ***Biafo Glaciers*** combine to form a 115 km ice corridor.

Situated in Hazara District, the **Kaghan Valley** is the only part of NWFP E of the Indus. It is drained by the **Kunhar River**. Rising in the region of Lular Sar Lake, close to the Nanga Parbat massif (8,126 m), the Kunhar River flows down the Kaghan valley for 177 km until it joins the Jhelum River near Muzaffarabad. The Kaghan Valley is bounded to the E by a continuous ridge 4-5,000 m high separating it from Azad Kashmir. To the W, the ranges diverge from **Musa-ka Musalla** peak (4040 m) sending a series of spurs SW through the **Black Mountains** as far S as Tanawal. The whole region is part of a vast crystalline metamorphic zone of gneisses and schists, the western extension of the Himalayan backbone.

Baltistan The Skardu valley floor, at the heart of Baltistan, is a high-altitude desert, averaging 2,000 m and varying in width from a narrow gorge to a wide plain, with stretches of rolling sand dunes, incongruous against the backdrop of snow-capped peaks. Only around the villages are there small pockets of fertile ground, irrigated by mountain streams and startlingly green in the parched and barren landscape. Poplar and willow trees line the irrigation canals, binding the soil together, acting as windbreaks and providing a vital source of firewood and building materials. In addition a wide variety of fruit trees are grown, supplementing a diet of grain and dairy produce.

To the N is the **Karakoram** range, stretching from the Upper Shyok River in the E to the Kurumbar River in the W; a solid mass of high mountains and glaciers over 20,000 sq km in area. At its core is the Baltoro Glacier (1,200 sq km), containing in its icy clutches 4 of the world's 14 peaks exceeding 8,000 m; K2 (8,611 m, second only to Mt Everest), Broad Peak (8,047 m) and Gasherbrum I and II (8,068 m and 8,034 m). To the S is the Deosai Plateau and beyond that the Himalayas, commencing in the region of Nanga Parbat and stretching for nearly 2,500 km across India, Nepal, Bhutan and Burma.

Climate

The Northern Areas experience enormous annual temperature fluctuations from

-30°C to +48°C in the high altitude areas of exposed rock and glaciers. The Gilgit, Skardu and Hunza valleys have a less extreme regime varying between 0°C and 30°C.

Much of the region is snowbound from Nov to Apr. The N Areas are largely outside the monsoon belt and receive only minimal rainfall of about 100 mm annually, most of which occurs at high altitude feeding snowfields and glaciers. The lower sections of the Kaghan Valley and Hazara lie on the edge of the SW Monsoon and receive upwards of 800 mm of rainfall annually. The tourist season runs from May to Oct and most mountaineering and trekking expeditions are undertaken in Aug. However rivers at this time are swollen with summer snowmelt and difficult to cross. Spring (Apr – May) and Autumn (Sep – Oct) are particularly beautiful seasons although cold at night.

People

A wide variety of different peoples live in the isolated valleys of the N Areas. The people of the Kaghan Valley, the *Swati, Sayyid* and *Gujar* nomads and the *Dilazak* and *Tanaolis* tribes further S are in fact 17th and 18th century refugees from Swat and Buner who fled from the encroaching *Yusufzai Pathans,* who in turn had been displaced from the plains of Peshawar. Baltistan, known as "*Tibet-i-Khurd*", shows strong Tibetan influence, and the language, *Balti,* is an archaic Tibetan dialect very similar to Ladakhi.

Around Gilgit, **Shina**, an Indic language is spoken. Historically a feudal society, the Shins represent the ruling class. Below them are the Yashkuns (landowners), Kamins (craftsmen) and Doms (minstrels). The system of values associated with these classes remained different from the caste stratification of Hinduism, although it was modelled on it. Occupying a central position at the junction of two arteries of the ancient Silk Road, Gilgit has also absorbed Swatis and Chitralis, as well as Kashgaris, Wakhis, Kirghizis and Tshins from Central Asia.

Further N in the Hunza valley, the **Hunzakuts** claim descent from Alexander's armies, but despite their fair complexion, their origins are certainly much older. Their language, **Buruashaski**, is aboriginal, and apparently unrelated to any other. In Upper Hunza, or Gujal, the *Wakhi* speaking people are related to nomadic groups in Sinkiang (Chinese Turkestan) and the Pamir region.

Religion

Before Islam replaced Buddhism and Hinduism in the N Areas, complex indigenous religions were practised. **Ra** or **Aftab**, the solar deity, was an archetypal figure from whom the rulers of **Little Bolor** traced their descent. Spiritual guarantors performed a variety of seasonal religious festivals ensuring the overall fertility of the land and the people. Some of their beliefs are still widely held.

Dani identifies "altitudinal zones of spirituality". All the major peaks, such as Nanga Parbat and Rakaposhi, are considered the abodes of "clean spirits", mostly female, which inhabit fairy castles. Below this is the zone of *Mayaro,* domain of the Markhor and Ibex, both considered sacred and tended by fairies (*Ranchi* or *Peri).* The agricultural zone is considered neutral, man's home. During menstruation and pregnancy women are generally isolated and identified with the demonic sphere, a realm usually reserved for dangerous invisible things; demons lurking near the mouths of glaciers, in dark crevasses or by the raging torrent of a gorge.

Such animistic religious pantheons are common to the whole of N Pakistan and the Greater Himalaya, and in the Northern Areas still survive, deeply rooted in local folklore. First they became adapted to Buddhism, the two becoming inextricably intertwined. Even today, **Shamans*** of an almost Siberian type and closely related to the *Ladakhi* and *Tibetan Oracles,* often act as the voice of public opinion, inhaling the smoke of juniper branches in order to induce a trance. After the arrival of Islam, local religions and folklore existed either secretly, or alongside Islam.

Islam influenced the N Areas in three forms. The initial impetus came from the S, from the *Yusufzai Pathans* of **Sunni** faith who were displaced N by other tribal migrations from the plains of Peshawar. In Gilgit the "six venerable men" arrived in the 12th century during the *Trakhan dynasty*, and **Buddhism** was largely replaced by the Sunni faith. Meanwhile, in Baltistan, the *Makpon* rulers, under *Ali Sher Khan Anchan* developed close ties with Kashmir and adopted the **Shi'ite** faith, thus becoming Islamicised from the E. The Makpon rulers exerted strong influence in the region, and for a while Gilgit also became Shi'ite under *Mirza Khan*. Bloody feuding between the Sunni and Shi'ite factions continues to this day.

The **Ismaili Muslims** arrived from Badakshan in Afghanistan during the 13-14th century. A Mongol prince, in legend *Taj Moghul*, spread the Ismaili faith in Chitral, Punial, Yasin and Hunza. The Ismailis are a reform branch of the Shi'ite (locally called *Maulavi*) which developed in the 9th century in Iraq. They are followers of *Prince Kareem Aga Khan*, a direct descendant of Mohammad, through Mohammad's daughter Fatima, who married the Prophet's cousin Ali.

Economy

Agriculture Situated largely in the rainshadow of the Greater Himalaya, the N Areas are extremely arid and cultivation is mostly irrigation based. Massive annual and diurnal temperature fluctuations and the chronic shortage of cultivable land greatly inhibit agriculture. The traditional crops include wheat, barley, millet, buckwheat and legumes, a mix which was later supplemented and partly replaced by maize and potatoes. In addition apricots form an important part of the local diet and grow very well at higher altitudes. They are supplemented by a variety other fruit lower down. Irrigation is highly developed, involving ambitious and precarious feats of engineering to channel water many miles from springs and streams along steep valley sides to terraced alluvial fans.

The Yusufzai Pathans who migrated into the N Areas brought with them the **wesh** system of landownership whereby plots of land were rotated amongst families of a common descent group, allowing each family access to the best quality land for a given period. The system is still practised in certain areas of Hazara and Indus Kohistan and, although eminently democratic, has been criticised due to the implicit disincentives to carry out any permanent improvements on the land.

Some of the valleys are rich and fertile, especially to the S on the **Pahkli** and **Rash** plains of Mansehra and Abbottabad. The Kaghan Valley is thickly wooded as far up as Naran (2,440 m), and also extensively terraced. Cultivation is primarily a single *kharif* crop of maize, which due to the single cropping and use of manure gives very high yields. Beyond Naran cultivation dwindles. Semi-nomadic tribes of *Gujars, Sayyids* and *Swatis* take advantage of the high summer pastures to graze cattle, sheep and goats, having planted crops of maize in isolated settlements lower down. Throughout the summer, these nomads move gradually, matching their altitude to the changing season.

The thick fir and pine forests of Kaghan and also the **Haripur** and **Gali Hills** to the S have been extensively logged in recent years due to their easy accessibility, and combined with rapid population growth this has greatly increased soil erosion and environmental pressure on the land.

Goats are an integral part of the local economy at higher altitudes, as cattle become more difficult to support. The plentiful supplies of fodder in the altitude zone of the evergreen Holm Oak (Quercus ilex) allows nomadic tribal groups to support large herds at lower altitudes in winter and move up to the higher pastures in summer. In many places the semi nomadic tribes have developed a close interdependence with settled farmers, although the arrival of chemical fertilizers in the region is further lowering the status of the traditionally inferior nomads.

Resources and industry in the N Areas are limited primarily to timber, which is extensively logged in the lower altitude valleys to the S. The *wesh* system of collective ownership applies also to forest tracts ensuring some distribution of profits amongst local populations. However, large scale commercial logging operations often buy off or ignore land rights and have flourished unregulated with the opening of the KKH. Many minerals, including gold, are found in the region but not in commercially significant quantities.

Cottage industries have traditionally centred around the production of handwoven woollen cloth and clothing, and wood carved items. However in the last decade, tourism has expanded rapidly and is now by far the most important and profitable industry in the region. Initially the domain of specialized mountaineering expeditions, the N Areas now also attract large numbers of trekking groups, and since the opening of the Chinese border in May 1986, there has been a steadily increasing flow of tourists along this spectacular route.

The *Karakoram Highway*

The KKH, officially completed in July 1978 after 20 years of planning and construction, is the first metalled road to connect the plains of the Punjab with China and Central Asia beyond the Hindu Kush and Karakoram ranges. The highway runs for approximately 900 km from Islamabad to the Chinese border and a further 400 km on to Kashgar.

Built as a joint Sino-Pak project, the KKH is an ambitious feat of engineering which employed up to 15,000 Pakistanis and 10,000 Chinese at the height of its construction. Nearly 1,000 workers died on the project. In places the highway has been blasted into solid rock faces and is constantly under threat from erosion, mudslides, glaciers and earthquakes. Maintenance, carried out by the **Pakistani Frontier Force**, is continual and often difficult. The building of the KKH has had a major impact on the N Areas, greatly accelerating the rate and pattern of development in the region, and attracting large numbers of trekkers and other visitors.

Recent socio-economic change Greatly improved access, the advent of tourism, and population growth have brought rapid socio-economic change to the N Areas. Cheap subsidised imports have led to increased dependency with the outside world. Thus there has been a shift away from subsistence agriculture to a cash economy, particularly damaging in a region where cultivation is highly labour intensive and agricultural land is quickly eroded and irreversibly destroyed.

Tourism attracts large numbers of the working population who are seasonally employed as porters and guides. In addition, many people move to the plains to supplement their income in winter, or migrate more permanently to work in the oil-rich Gulf states of the Middle East. Various cultural and social habits which were dictated by environmental constraints have also been eroded. Thus the people of Hunza and Baltistan have abandoned their seasonal raw fruit diet and no longer refrain from cooking during the summer to preserve scarce wood-fuel resources. This has led to such acute shortages of firewood that instances of locals cutting down fruit trees for fuel are not uncommon.

On the other hand standards of living have undoubtedly improved, with the spread of schools and hospitals into the remotest areas. It is often the local populations who are most vocal in their demands for new roads and the benefits they bring, while foreign tourists decry the spoiling of a "paradise", which they seem to regard as theirs to enjoy.

Development programmes in the region are relatively enlightened. The *Aga Khan* Rural Support Programme (AKRSP) is particularly successful in Ismaili areas. The project encourages local populations to set up village organizations which identify small income generating projects to be carried out by themselves. In return they receive financial and technical assistance from AKRSP and are encouraged to generate collective village credit reserves for future schemes. Schemes include land reclamation, irrigation, roads and bridges and training selected village representatives to upgrade their skills in various fields. The programme which involves an estimated 800,000 people has been particularly successful in involving women and according to a 1986 World Bank report has "produced outstanding results".

History

Prehistory The prehistory of the Northern Areas can only be interpreted from fragmentary evidence, mostly in the form of rock carvings and inscriptions, and the earliest known inhabitants are commonly referred to as "**Rock Art Peoples**". The carvings they left behind indicate a primitive culture of hunter-gatherers inhabiting rock shelters and worshipping the forces of nature, see page 326.

At some stage there appears to have been an influx of more advanced megalith builders, perhaps from Iran, who practised ritual pit burials and were probably fire worshippers. Carvings suggest the keeping of domesticated horses, cattle, sheep and goats, as well as settled agriculture. In addition iron, bronze, copper, silver and gold appear to have been used in tool-making, weaponry and jewellery.

Early records In the 6th century BC the N Areas became part of the 7th Satrapy of the **Achaemenid** Empire under Darius the Great. Interest was generated by fabulous tales concerning gold in the region. Herodotus recounts how: "Here in this desert (Baltistan /Deosai Plateau) there live amid the sand great ants, in size somewhat less than dogs, but bigger than foxes. These ants make their dwelling underground and throw up sand-heaps as they burrow. Now the sand which they throw up is full of gold...". However exaggerated these tales, gold was certainly present and was used as a form of tribute – a practice which continued into the 20th century.

Alexander the Great barely affected the N Areas, but from 321 BC the Mauryan Empire made significant inroads into the region. *Asoka's* Rock Edicts can be found near Mansehra, and Sanskrit texts relate how he subjugated the *Khasas*, a tribal group based around Chilas. Thus from around this time Buddhism began to penetrate. Between the 1st century BC and 1st century AD, *Kharaoshthi* rock inscriptions from Chilas and Thalpan show definite artistic influence from the cultural centre of Taxila and also further afield from Iran. Bullocks, horses and chariots are depicted and there appears to have been an influx of Buddhist pilgrims.

Kanishka extended Kushan power across the region in the 1st century AD as far as Xinjiang and Tibet. Evidence of rock carvings, such as at Alam Bridge and the Sacred Rock of Hunza, suggest perhaps an earthquake and flooding of the Indus around Chilas. Agriculture was extended and new fruits and crops introduced. Buddhism flourished and the **Silk Road** came into effective use, bringing trade and prosperity to the major river valleys.

Towards the end of the 3rd century the Sassanian Empire of Persia extended into the N Areas from the Trans-Pamir region. The Sogdian and Bactrian cursive scripts were introduced, evidence of both appearing on the Sacred Rock of Hunza and at Shatial.

The White Huns invaded between the 5th and 6th centuries AD, attracted by tales of gold and semi-precious stones, and they appear on numerous rock carvings, always on horseback shooting arrows. They became converted to Hinduism and worshipped Siva. However their control was extremely loose, and numerous semi-independent kingdoms flourished. The most important were those of Great Bolor, based in Baltistan and at times strongly influenced by Tibetan culture, and Little Bolor, centred around Gilgit and Chitral and ruled by the *Patola Shahis*. Both were Buddhist and only minimally influenced by the Huns.

Medieval History Sometime in the 7th century there appears to have been an influx of Turkish peoples into the Gilgit region. These Turks were probably pre-Muslim Zoroastrians and perhaps the founders of the *Trakhan Dynasty* in

Gilgit. Later, in the 8th century there were encroachments into the Northern Areas by both Muslim Arabs who advanced through Central Asia, and Tibetans who moved W through Ladakh and Baltistan. Meanwhile the Chinese T'ang Dynasty, which was anxious to keep open the economically vital Silk Road, forged alliances with the rulers of Gilgit and Kashmir and succeeded in forcing back the Arabs and eventually defeating the Tibetans in 751 AD.

By the 11th century some scholars identify a state of **Dardistan**, which was centred around Gilgit and controlled most of the Northern Areas. However the term is essentially one that has been adapted from Sanskrit by western classical historians and simply refers to peoples related to the Dardic language group. The internal situation was certainly more complex, a region described as "noisy with kingdoms" by Marco Polo in the 13th century. From the 11th century onwards the Northern areas became Islamicised by Sunnis from the S, Shi'ites from Kashmir and Ismailis from Afghanistan (see above). The major river valleys flourished by taxing trade along the Silk Road and slavery was an integral part of the economy.

Historically **Baltistan** was known as **Great Bolor** in Arabic literature and *Po-lu-lo* in Chinese accounts. It remained largely independent due to its isolated position, although at times strongly influenced by Tibet. Internally the region was divided into 8 kingdoms with Skardu forming the most important central power. Next was Khapalu on the Shyok River, Shigar, which included the upper valleys of Braldu and Basna, and Rondu, on the Indus W of Skardu. Finally there were the lesser kingdoms of Kiris, also on the Shyok River and Parkutta, Tolti and Kharmang, each a "fortress principality" guarding the approaches to Ladakh along the Indus. Astor, along with the sparsely populated Deosai Plateau, was at times loosely connected with Baltistan.

The kingdoms of the N Areas prospered due to extensive trade along the **Silk Routes** to China. Gilgit in particular flourished from its central position at the junction of the various routes from the Iranian Plateau through Chitral and Gilgit valleys, and from the plains of the Punjab up the Indus River. Baltistan meanwhile commanded the old trade route along the Indus from Ladakh and Kashmir.

Throughout its history, the N Areas have not only benefited economically from this trade, but have also been fundamentally influenced socially and culturally by it. The Balti people, although now predominantly Shi'ite Muslims, still show a cultural and racial affinity with Tibet, and in places even retain some traces of Buddhism, adopted after the 3rd century and blended with the existing animism and shamanism of the people.

The British Period, Partition and Recent Developments Until the middle of the 19th century the N Areas remained beyond British influence. The various small kingdoms feuded repeatedly among themselves, but periodically succeeded in repelling the Dogras and the Sikhs. In 1846 the British appointed **Gulab Singh** as the first Hindu Maharaja of the Princely State of Jammu and Kashmir, in recognition of his services during the Second Sikh War. The treaty was extremely vague as to the exact geographical extent of Kashmir but it was subsequently understood that Gilgit and Baltistan were to come under his suzerainty. A number of largely unsuccessful campaigns were undertaken in the 1850s and 60s and his control over the N Areas remained entirely nominal.

Towards the end of the 19th century, British interest in the N Areas was heightened due to alarm at Russian expansion into Central Asia. The "Great Game" between the 2 regional powers followed. In 1877 the first **British Agency** was established in Gilgit, but it was abandoned in 1881 after a major revolt of Kohistani tribes. In 1889 a second British Agency was established, this time with improved road and telegraph links as well as a permanent British military presence. Throughout the 1890s, a tenuous control of the region was maintained with various pre-emptive campaigns in Hunza, Chilas and Chitral. Later the **Gilgit Scouts** were established as a well trained and well armed force which could maintain internal order and respond to any external aggression.

Independence and Partition In August 1947 the Muslim majorities in Gilgit and Baltistan revolted against Kashmir, declared independence, and acceded to Pakistan, **see page 471**. The ceasefire line agreed in Jan 1949 between India and Pakistan became the de-facto international boundary, with Gilgit, Baltistan and Azad Kashmir inside Pakistani territory. By 1972 the old autonomous states and political districts had been fully absorbed into Pakistan. Since then the N Areas have been divided into 3 administrative areas; Gilgit, Baltistan and Daimar , each with a Dy Commissioner under an overall Commissioner, answerable to the Ministry of Kashmir Affairs and Northern Areas of Pakistan.

Since Partition the Pakistan government has made concerted efforts to integrate the Northern Areas politically and economically, building hospitals, schools, roads, bridges, irrigation systems etc. The completion of the KKH in 1978 is perhaps the most significant achievement in this respect.

ROUTES VIA THE KARAKORAM HIGHWAY

Access to all the major places of interest in the N Areas is now via the Karakoram Highway. After a brief description of the route from Islamabad-Rawalpindi to Abbottabad, the routes are divided into two main sections: Abbottabad to Muzaffarabad and the Kaghan Valley, and Abbottabad to the Khunjerab Pass. Short excursions from the KKH route are described at appropriate points.

The KKH leaves the Islamabad – Peshawar GT Rd 32 km from Islamabad. 15 km from Zero Point, join the GT Rd heading W towards Peshawar, crossing the **Margalla Pass** and passing the turning N for **Taxila, see page 1109**. Just before **Wah** bear N towards **Haripur** (the turning is signposted). The road passes through an industrial landscape of factories and engineering works, giving way to increasingly eroded countryside.

Haripur (64 km) is situated in the lush, fertile valley of the **Dor River** and today it is a small bustling market town, well stocked with fruit and vegetables. The town was named after *Hari Singh*, one of *Ranjit Singh's* most competent generals and was strategically important until the building of Abbottabad in the 1850s. Haripur is the starting point for a visit to the Tarbela Dam, **see page 1119**.

20 km further on is the town of *Havelian*, terminus for the narrow gauge railway from Taxila and the official starting point of the KKH which runs for 795 km to the Chinese border. The main road passes W of the town, crossing the Dor River and climbs through denuded hills before descending to the town of Abbottabad.

Abbottabad (1,250 m) Founded in 1853, it was named after James Abbott, a British soldier turned administrator who found allies amongst the Mishwani Pathans of Hazara during the Second Sikh War, and played an important part in defeating the Sikhs. He later became the first Dy Commissioner of Hazara.

The town is essentially military, with the Frontier Force HQ, Baluchi Regiments, Medical Corps and Army School of Music. Occasionally there is the incongruous sight of a military band playing bagpipes in full tartan outfit! The Cantonment has tree lined avenues, beautiful parks, bungalows with lush gardens and there is a golf course. The bazaars are crowded, lively and colourful.

Hotels on the Mall: **D** *Spring Field*, T 4770. 26 rm with bath. Restaurant, garden; **D** *Sarban*, T 4876. 31 rm with bath. Central a/c. Restaurant; **E** *Zarbat*, T 5508. 24 rm with bath.

Restaurant, heating. **E** *Orush*, Mandian, T 5565. 14 d rm with bath. **E** *Bolan*, Fawara Chowk, close to GTS Bus Stand, T 4623. 23 rm. Restaurant.

There are a few other **F** category hotels in the town. There are a number of cheaper hotels on Kashmir Rd, Jinnah Rd, The Mall and Eid Gah Rd.

Youth Hostel is 5 km N on KKH. 32 beds.

Restaurants Several of the hotels have their own restaurants. A number of other restaurants, cafés and snackbars, mainly along Jinnah Rd, Manserah Rd and the Mall.

Tourist Information PTDC, Club Annexe, Jinnah Rd. T 2446. Can arrange Jeep hire. There is a **Post Office** with *Modern Bakery* opp.

Buses The GTS Bus Station operates services in all directions, including Peshawar, Lahore and Rawalpindi.

Excursions Nathiangali, see page 1122.

ABBOTTABAD TO MUZAFFARABAD & THE KAGHAN VALLEY

From Abbottabad the KKH continues N through eroded countryside. After 24 km the road forks; the left fork being the KKH route, while the right fork leads to **Mansehra** and continues on to the **Kaghan Valley** and **Muzaffarabad** in Azad Kashmir. If you wish to continue up the KKH, see page 1245. The Kaghan Valley's extremely beautiful alpine forests and lakes provide excellent low altitude walks and fishing. It can be followed as an alternative route, over the **Babusar Pass**, to rejoin the KKH at **Chilas**. Above Naran, the road is unmetalled and suitable only for 4-wheel-drive vehicles. The Babusar Pass is generally closed from Nov-Apr.

The valley covers 2330 sq km (*altitude* 900-4270 m). The climatic table for **Muzaffarabad** shows that in the valley bottoms summer temperatures are very high. Further up the valley maximum temperatures only reach 11°C in May, and the N of the valley receives less than 800 mm of rain.

	Jan	Feb	Mar	Apr	May	Jun	Jul	Aug	Sep	Oct	Nov	Dec	Av/Tot
Max (°C)	15	17	22	27	31	38	35	34	33	30	22	18	27
Min (°C)	4	5	10	14	18	23	24	23	20	15	9	5	14
Rain (mm)	125	104	89	115	80	49	260	325	123	65	73	119	1602

Tourism is fairly well developed as far up as **Naran**, and the Kaghan Valley, along with the **Haripur** and **Gali Hills** are very popular summer hill resorts amongst local Pakistani tourists. Early and late summer are less crowded and the best time for trekking.

From Mansehra the roads climbs NE up to a pine forested ridge, site for the *Batrasi Rest House* (Reservations through PWD Road Division, Mansehra, T 525), before dropping down to the Kunhar river. Here you may cross the river and continue on to Muzaffarabad in Azad Kashmir, or follow the metalled road to

Balakot, the gateway to the Kaghan Valley, and the site of the battle in which the famous Muslim leader **Ahmed Shah Brewli** was killed by Sikh forces attempting to gain control of the region in 1831. The town is essentially a transit point with a GTS Bus Stand and a number of hotels.

Hotels D *PTDC Tourist Lodge*, T 8, (Reservations: PTDC Rawalpindi, T 581480-4 or

Abbottabad, T 2446). 4 d rm. Phone, western WC, hot water in buckets. Pleasant situation, food not very good and over-priced. Booking required at peak periods. Tourist Information Centre. Jeep hire. **D** *Park*, Kaghan Rd. T 23. Pleasantly situated by the river, surrounded by high mountains. There are a number of **F** category hotels nr the bus stand.

Youth Hostel nr PTDC, behind Civil Hospital. 32 beds.

Road Regular bus service to **Naran** (6 hr) and **Kaghan**. Buses to **Mansehra** leave every 30 min. From Mansehra minibus wagons and the Flying Coach goes direct to **Rawalpindi**. You may need to book in advance. (Also regular wagon services to Abbottabad, where you can get a bus to Mansehra and Balakot.) It is possible to do the journey from Rawalpindi to Naran in a day when all the roads are open to traffic in the summer, but be prepared for delays. Carry plenty of water and food.

At Balakot the road crosses to the E bank of the Kunhar river and climbs steeply up the side of the valley giving impressive views. At **Kawai** (24 km), a logging track leads off to the E, climbing up to **Shogran** (2,400 m), where there are 2 recommended *Forestry Dept. Rest Houses*, (book through Conservator of Forests Abbottabad T 2728 or Divisional Forest Officer Balakot T 17) and a branch of the *Park Hotel* (book through *Park Hotel*, Balakot T 23). Shogran is situated on a plateau with lush meadows and colourful flowers in spring and spectacular views of the surrounding mountains.

From Kawai the main road drops down to follow the river closely. At **Paras** a rough jeep track crosses the river and climbs 16 km to **Sharan** (2,400 m), deep in thick forest. Here is another *Forestry Dept. Rest House* and pleasant walks in the surrounding woods.

From Paras the main road passes the villages of **Shinu**, with a trout hatchery, **Jared,** selling woollen garments and carved-wood products, and **Mahandri** (where there is a good Rest House) before arriving at **Kaghan** village (60 km). 22 km further on is **Naran** (2,427 m), the main tourist centre. Here the valley begins to widen and the river is braided.

Naran The main attractions are fishing and walking. The river here is well stocked with brown and rainbow trout. Fishing permits can be obtained from the *Fisheries Dept. PTDC*, and there is some fishing tackle available for hire. The most popular walk is to **Saiful Muluk Lake** (also jeepable).

Hotels C *PTDC Tourist Inn*, 3 VIP cottages, 15 d rm, and 29 tents (absolutely basic). Pleasantly situated by the river at N end of town. Electricity, western toilets, hot water in buckets. Tourist information centre. Often full during the tourist season. **D** *Park* (May also reserve in Balakot T 23). Rates may vary with demand. **F** There are a number of cheaper hotels in the main bazaar, mostly very basic.

Youth Hostel 3 km before Naran, S of road. Very basic. Bring own bedding /food.

Excursions

Saiful Muluk Lake (3,200 m) is 9 km E of Naran, up a small side valley. Travel by jeep, or walk (3 hr), when road is impassable. This high altitude lake ringed by an amphitheatre of mountains, is particularly beautiful in the late spring when the surrounding alpine meadow is in full flower. In early spring the near freezing sapphire waters are afloat with blocks of ice and on a still day reflect the peak of *Malika Parbat*. Local legend relates how the lake was created by a jealous demon who found his fairy lover with the Prince and poet/philosopher *Saiful Muluk*, who had fallen in love with her. A basic *Rest House* is on the lakeside. **Camping** possible.

11 km N of the Lake *Lalazar* has a government *Rest House* with breathtaking views of the mountains. There is a memorable walk down to Naran from the Rest House.

From Naran, the rough jeep track continues E and then N finally climbing to the 4,173 m *Babusar Pass*, 66 km away, a 2 day walk. *Battakundi* (16 km) has a

Youth Hostel, PWD Rest House and some very basic hotels. Above Battakundi, all the settlements are seasonal, being abandoned during the winter months. *Burawai* (30 km) also has a *PWD Rest House* and basic hotels. **Besal**, 48 km away stands at 3,266 m and just beyond the village is *Lular Sar Lake*, larger than Saiful Muluk, completely without tourists, and certainly more beautiful. The water is a deep green in colour and on the opp bank to the track, the sheer mountains rise directly up from the lakeside. Good **camping**.

Gittidas (60 km) is the last village before the Babusar Pass, and stands at 3,600 m on the opp bank of the river. From here the track climbs slowly up to Babusar "Top". The views are spectacular, N towards the distant Karakoram and Hindu Kush, or back down into the Kaghan Valley, where weather systems can often be seen rising up the valley but never crossing over the high ridge.

Beyond the Pass are 13 km of difficult zigzagging track leading down into **Babusar** village where there are basic Rest Houses. You are now in Kohistan, and will see men carrying rifles and bullet belts slung across their shoulders. **Warning** Camping is not advisable. From here it is 37 km through the fertile wooded Babusar Valley to *Chilas*, perched high above the scorched and arid Indus Valley and KKH (see below).

ABBOTTABAD TO THE KHUNJERAB PASS: THE KARAKORAM
HIGHWAY

This route runs through some of the most dramatic scenery in South Asia. In places the road has been carved out of vertical hillsides; rock and mud slides are a daily event on some sections, requiring constant clearing and maintenance by the Pakistan Army. The road is an astonishing feat of engineering, but if you can dare to look the scenery is sometimes even more breathtaking. It is 470 km from Abbottabad to Gilgit, and a further 285 km to the Chinese border.

Leave Abbottabad N on the KKH. After 20 km a right fork goes to Mansehra, the KKH taking the left fork. 4 km further on are 3 big boulders, protected by a modern roof structure, inscribed with more of *Asoka's Rock Edicts*, which date from the 3rd century BC, **see page 83**. However the *Kharaoshthi* script is extremely weathered and barely discernible. Just below is a path leading up to **Bareri Hill** (1,397 km), once a sacred place of Hindu pilgrimage.

5 km past the Rock Edicts a road leads NW from the KKH and follows a slow loop through the **Black Mountains**, passing the village of **Oghi** before rejoining the KKH approximately 30 km further on.

Warning The country here is wild and lawless. Visitors should not explore unaccompanied.

21 km from the Rock Edicts, just before the KKH crosses the **Siran River**, a road leads N up the Siran river valley to *Daddar*. There is a *Forestry Dept Rest House* here (book through Divisional Forest Officer, Abbottabad, T 2433). Beyond Daddar the metalled road gives way to a rough track and climbs to the village of **Nadi** from where you can trek across to *Sharan* in the Kaghan Valley (see above).

The KKH itself continues on through a well wooded valley, alpine in character, crosses a fertile bowl and climbs to a watershed. Here the tiny village of *Shakul* is situated, with a small *PWD Rest House* (book through PWD Mansehra T 525) and lovely views overlooking the plains beyond.

From Shakul the KKH winds gently through emerald green rice paddies, golden wheat fields, orchards and stands of poplar trees before descending slowing to join the scorched, arid canyon of the Indus River at *Thakot*, 237 km from

Islamabad. Here the first of more than 90 Chinese built bridges, gracefully arched and decorated with carved lions, crosses the Indus. Beyond **Thakot Bridge**, the Indus Gorge is extremely narrow, and the KKH follows a natural shelf, or at times is cut into the cliff face, hundreds of metres above the river. Geologically, this is one of the most unstable sections of the route, subject to daily earth tremors and rock slides.

Besham is a small bustling bazaar town 28 km from Thakot Bridge, cut into the hillside high above the Indus. The town is a popular overnight stopping point on the KKH with several restaurants and guest houses. A newly metalled road follows the ancient trade route E from Besham, crossing the **Shangla Pass** and linking it with **Khawazakhela** in the **Swat Valley**, see page 1224.

Hotels D *PTDC Motel* 1 km S of Besham, by the Indus. 17 rm with western toilet, hot water in bucket. T 98. (Reserve direct, or at PTDC Rawalpindi, T 581480-4. There are cheaper hotels; the best is **F** *The Prince* 9 rm with bath, restaurant, shop. Pleasant. T 56 **F** *The International* Gilgit Rd 14 rm T 65; **F** *Besham* 8 rm; **F** *Azam* T 27. All are small, very basic and often full in summer.

Beyond Besham the mountains tower on either side of the Indus, averaging 5000 m, and narrow inaccessible side valleys periodically join the main gorge. The mountainous region between the Swat Valley and Raikot Bridge, on either side of the Indus, is known as *Kohistan*, "Land of Mountains"; some call it **Yagistan**, "Land of the Ungovernable". The people have a harsh semi-nomadic lifestyle. They are invariably armed, and are sometimes hostile towards intruders. Away from the KKH, banditry is commonplace.

Warning Do not explore any of the side valleys unless accompanied by an official guard.

The KKH passes a number of Kohistani villages; **Dobair,** 15 km from Besham, **Jujial** (20 km) and **Pattan** (25 km), situated below the road by the Indus. Here a suspension bridge crosses to the S bank, and a rough track leads up the **Palas Valley.** Further on is **Kayal** (35 km), at the mouth of the **Kayal Valley,** which joins the Indus from the NW, and beyond that the twin towns of **Komila – Dassu** where the KKH crosses to the E side of the Indus.
   This stretch of the highway is geologically fascinating; the contact point between the Indian and Eurasian Tectonic Plates, the latter here exposing layers usually buried 30 m below the earth's surface. This section of the KKH also claimed more lives per km of road built than any other, and in 1974 the area was devastated by an earthquake which killed more than 5,000 people.

Komila is situated on the W bank of the Indus and houses most of the hotels and restaurants along its bazaar, as well as the GTS Bus Stand. Across the bridge, *Dassu* is the administrative centre with the Dy Commissioner's Office, Police Post and petrol pumps. The *Police Guest House* has good accommodation.

Beyond Dassu, the KKH runs due N, blasted into the rock face high above the Indus, deep blue in winter and spring, and muddied brown with silt during the high discharge months of summer and early autumn. Just before the Indus bends slowly round to flow E-W, a new bridge crosses the Indus and a jeep track runs E up the **Kandia Valley** for 35 km. Beyond, pilgrim routes lead over 3 passes to **Kalam** in **Upper Swat**, see page 1228. **Warning**: Do not trek here unaccompanied.

The KKH leads slowly down from its precarious ledge, the valley begins to widen out, and the river slows. This is the start of the Northern Areas proper. The road passes **Sazin**, hidden 3 km to the S, before arriving at **Shatial** 5 km further on. *Shatial* is situated by an irrigated stretch of land between the road and the river, green with fruit trees and corn fields. There is a *Forestry Dept Rest House,* Police post, hospital and petrol pump.

Over the next 70 km there are hundreds of **petroglyphs** – rock carvings and inscriptions concentrated along this stretch of the Indus up to Chilas, dating from Prehistoric to Medieval times. They are the main source of information on the early history of the Northern Areas, left by pilgrims, missionaries, merchants and conquerors, as well as early inhabitants and depict various animals, human figures, Buddhist designs etc. For a full discussion see *Rock Carvings and Inscriptions in the Northern Areas of Pakistan* by Karl Jettmar.

At Shatial a bridge crosses the Indus and jeep tracks lead up the **Tanjir** and **Darel** valleys to the N. Both valleys are green and fertile, with rich forest tracts, although these have been extensively logged. They are inhabited by the typically hostile Kohistanis. Unaccompanied trekking is dangerous. Tanjir and Darel together formed an independent kingdom until 1956. The KKH continues E passing the **Hurban**, **Basha** and **Thor** valleys which all drain into the Indus from the S, before arriving at **Chilas** 68 km from Shatial.

Chilas 3 km S of the KKH, 100 m above the valley floor. There is a petrol pump, police post and a good *Hotel* by the turning off the KKH. Although Chilas is today only a small bazaar town, it is historically important due to its position on the ancient trade routes up the Indus Valley. A rough jeep track follows the route opened up by the British in the 1840s S over the Babusar Pass and down through the Kaghan Valley to Islamabad, **see page 1206**. The road up from the KKH passes a large boulder marking the entrance to Chilas, engraved with a 5th century Gupta inscription referring to the town as *Soma Nagar,* or Moon City. Back on the KKH a bridge crosses the Indus to the **Thalpan Valley**, also rich in rock carvings and inscriptions.

Hotels C *Shangri La Midway House*, on the KKH. T 69 (also bookable in Rawalpindi T 73006). 60 rm. Restaurant, coffee shop, rm service, car hire, shop. A 1990 visitor wrote "Purporting to be an up-market hotel, it was empty and consequently not offering any choice of food or proper air conditioning." There are half a dozen cheaper hotels in Chilas' main bazaar.

From Chilas the KKH continues E following the Indus, which is flanked by wide beaches of sand and shingle. A local tribe, the Soniwal still pan for gold along this stretch. Temperatures exceed 40°C in summer, despite the altitude (1,200 m) of the parched valley, while on either side the mountains tower high above, the **Nanga Parbat** massif exceeding 8,000 m and making this the second deepest gorge on earth (The **Arun Valley** in E Nepal is the deepest, **see page 1318**).

The KKH crosses the **Buner River** draining in from the S, site of the devastating landslide and flood of 1841, before reaching **Raikot** village (64 km). Here the Raikot Valley joins the Indus from the S. From the village a track leads up a short way to another branch of the *Shangri La Hotel* (see Chilas Hotels). Nearby a number of **hot sulphur springs** emerge, used by locals for cooking and also reputed to relieve rheumatic and skin complaints. 19 km further up the valley, a long day's walk, are *Fairy Meadows*, an area of high alpine pasture, ideal for camping and walking, with spectacular views of the snow-clad N face of Nanga Parbat (8,126 m).

Beyond Raikot the KKH crosses to the N bank of the Indus and bears due N, arriving at **Jaglot** 32 km on. This stretch of the valley is green and fertile on both sides of the Indus, irrigated by numerous snow-fed mountain streams. Some 15 km before Jaglot, the **Astor River** can be seen draining from the E and also on the opp bank is the town of **Bunji**. Looking S the snow-clad summits of the **Nanga Parbat** massif are now in full view, while to the N is **Rakaposhi** (7,788 m) and to the E **Haramosh** (7,406 m).

Diversion – The *Astor River Valley*

Just N of Jaglot a bridge crosses the Indus and a jeep track doubles back along the E bank, passing the village of **Bunji**, Headquarters of the **Northern Light Infantry,** and climbs SE up the **Astor** river valley. The lower sections of the valley comprise an extremely narrow gorge, arid and hot, opening out further up to green meadows and patches of forest. **Astor** village is situated on the W side of the valley on a steeply sloping remnant of alluvial plateau, at the junction with a tributary stream from Nanga Parbat. There is a large military presence in the village and little to see apart from the old **fort** and **mosque**.

Beyond Astor, to the W and S, is the wild and desolate *Deosai Plateau*, averaging over 4,000 m, swept by fierce windstorms and snowbound for 9 months. Before Partition, the Astor Valley formed part of the old British supply line connecting Srinagar with Gilgit. There are a number of interesting but difficult walks and treks from here; W up to Rama Meadows, SW over the Deosai Plateau to Skardu, or SW then E to Tarshing, Rupal and Nanga Parbat Base Camp with the possibility of rejoining the KKH where it crosses the Buner River. Only attempt them when accompanied by a local guide.

Back on the KKH, 2 km N of Jaglot, the **Gilgit River** joins the **Indus** from the W. The Indus meanwhile loops sharply and bears SE up through Baltistan, climbing ultimately to its source in the region of Mt. Kailash and **Lake Mansarowar** in W Tibet. Just beyond the confluence, the **Alam Bridge** crosses the Gilgit River and a partly metalled jeep track follows the Indus to **Skardu**. To continue along the KKH see below.

BALTISTAN: JAGLOT TO SKARDU

With the building of an airstrip at Skardu and the improved road link with the KKH, Baltistan has become much more accessible to the outside world. Although no longer self-sufficient in food grains and now heavily dependent on subsidised imports, standards of living here have certainly improved. Tourism has become a major industry and each year Baltistan is the destination for numerous mountaineering expeditions, some of them employing hundreds of porters at a time.

At *Alam Bridge*, where the Baltistan road leaves the KKH, there are more rock carvings and inscriptions (see above). The road first bears NW and then bends sharply SE at **Sasli** (27 km), where there are tea shops and a petrol pump. At the bend in the river, a steep side valley enters from the N, leading up towards the N face Base Camp of **Haramosh.** From here the road enters a narrow gorge and the Indus roars past as a raging torrent.

The gorge begins to widen at **Tuar** (or Thowar) and a little further on is **Rondu**, capital of the former kingdom of that name, perched high up the steep valley side on a flat shelf, across the river. Further E, where the road crosses to the S bank of the Indus, the mountains fall back, and the wide sandy plains of Skardu open out ahead.

On the S side of the river, just W of the bridge, is *Kachura Lake*, surrounded by orchards and good for trout fishing. **A** The *Shangrila Hotel*, T 235. Reservations in Karachi or Rawalpindi. A complex of red pagoda-roofed cottages, pool, and also a curiosity – a double en-suite room in the converted fuselage of a crashed DC-3 plane!

Draining into the Indus from the S is the *Shigarthang Valley*. Trekking routes lead up the valley which divides higher up. The left fork climbs SE over the **Bari La** (pass) and on to the **Deosai Plateau**. From here you can angle sharply NE over the **Burji La** and drop down towards Skardu, or else join the rough Skardu-Astor jeep track to the S (see below). The right fork continues SW up the main stream, crosses the **Alam Pir Pass**, and then follows first the **Bubind** and then the **Das Khirim Valley** down towards Astor.

Warning All these routes are extremely strenuous, reaching high altitudes rapidly. You should carry at least one week's food supply. A guide is recommended as the trails often disappear, especially higher up.

From **Kachura Lake** it is a further 32 km on to Skardu, across the parched and sandy plain. The road first passes **Skardu Airport,** 13 km W of the main town.

Skardu

(*Altitude* 2,269 m) is much smaller than Gilgit, although growing rapidly as the mountaineering and trekking centre of Baltistan. The town itself is dusty and uninteresting, strung out along **Naya Bazaar.** Just S of this, at the W end of town, is the **Purana Bazaar,** with stalls selling handwoven woollen cloth, jewellery and trinkets, as well as basic cooking utensils etc. All around is an awesome scenery of snow-capped peaks and barren hills, with strata of brown, grey, violet and ochre rock rising up from the sandy plains, at once dominating and hostile.

Skardu Rock towers high above the plains between the town and the river. On top is the **Arpochu Fort,** thought to have been built by *Ali Sher Khan Anchan* in the 16th century. The Fort was destroyed by Sikh Forces in 1840 and later rebuilt. There is also the remains of an imposing Sikh fort dating from this time. The climb up onto the rock can be difficult in places but offers spectacular views in all directions. At the base of the E end of the rock, by the Indus, is the small village of Narsok.

Local Festivals *Independence Day* 1 Nov. Polo matches, folk music, dancing. *Nauroze* (spring festival). Polo, music and dancing. *Muharram* This is a Shi'ite Holy Day which involves crowds of men flagellating themselves with chains and flails. The atmosphere becomes very excited and tempers flare easily. Foreigners are advised to keep a low profile.

Hotels C *Karakoram Yurt and Yak Serai*, Link Rd. T 314 (or book through Karakoram Tours, Islamabad, T 829120, Cable BALTORO). *K2 Motel PTDC*, Naya Bazaar, T 104. 10 rm, some with bath. Tourist hotel, car hire. Basic trekkers hotel. **Camping** available in grounds. Superb situation above Indus overlooking Rock and town of Skardu. Good clean food. **D** *Satpura Inn*, Naya Bazaar, T 80. 24 rm, some with bath. **E/F** There are several hotels in this category along the Main (Naya) Bazaar, including; *Karakoram Inn*, T 389; *Kashmir Inn*, T 283. Dining facilities. Good value. *Hunza Inn*, T 124; Siachen Inn, T 205; *Sarhad Inn*, T 25.

Useful addresses Naya Bazaar is the main business and shopping area. It has a number of basic **restaurants/tea shops**; the **Habib Bank** and the **National Bank of Pakistan** (Note: exchange rates are considerably lower than in cities on the plains); and the **GPO** and **Telegraph Office**. The **Dy Commissioner's Office** and Police Station are towards the E end.

Travel Agents *Masherbrum Tours*, T 180; *Karakoram Tours*, T 314; *Waljis*, PIA Reservations Office, T 30.

Tourist Information *PTDC K2 Motel* T 104.

Air 3 flights daily between Islamabad and Skardu, subject to weather conditions. The flights are heavily subsidised and offer spectacular views, but are often fully booked during the tourist season. Book well in advance. If arriving in Skardu with a return ticket, re-confirm the return flight on arrival. 1 flight weekly to **Gilgit**.

Bus NATCO T 84, To *Gilgit*, daily, 0800; intermittent services for *Shigar* and *Khapalu*.

EXCURSIONS AND TREKS FROM SKARDU

Satpara Lake

8 km S of Skardu, but a comfortable walk from the town. The lake is beautiful, and well stocked with trout. There is a *PTDC Rest House* here and a rowing boat across to the island in the middle of the lake. The restaurant at the lakeside is expensive. The **Satpara Buddha** is situated about halfway between Skardu and the lake. The figure of a meditating *Maitreya Buddha* surrounded by *Bodhisattvas* dating from around 900 AD is carved on the N face of a large beige-coloured boulder.

The **Deosai Plateau** is reached by a rough jeep track that continues S up the valley from Satpara Lake, onto the wild and desolate Deosai Plateau and eventually crosses the **Chachor Pass** before descending to **Astor**. See Astor River Valley above.

Note This route passes close to the Line of Control with India and is currently in a restricted zone, closed to tourists. Permit: Enquiry Dy Commissioner's Office in Skardu.

Shigar River Valley

The Shigar River flows into the Indus just N of Skardu. It is formed by the union of the Basna and Braldu Rivers which in turn emanate from the Chogo Lungma, Biafo, Panmah and Baltoro Glaciers to the N. Below this confluence, the valley is wide and fertile, carpeted by gently terraced fields of wheat, barley and maize and rich orchards of apricot, mulberry, peach, plum, apple and pear. Once a powerful independent kingdom, the valley is easily accessible and is the starting point for some of the most spectacular treks in N Pakistan, including the famous **Baltoro Trek** up to **Concordia**.

The road to Shigar bridges the Indus a few km E of Skardu and runs N across a level plain before climbing to a ridge giving excellent views up the valley. **Shigar** village (2,349 m), 32 km from Skardu was the capital of the old kingdom, and a crumbling fort which was also the Raja's palace still stands up on the hillside. Many of the houses in the village are intricately carved of wood and there is an impressive mosque with a 3-tiered roof built by Kashmiri craftsmen. There is a basic *PWD Rest House,* the *Karakoram Hotel* also basic, or camping.

From Shigar a trekking route leads up the **Bauma Lungma**, a narrow sided valley which climbs first NE, then SE up past forests of low cedars and heavily grazed upland pastures to **Thalle La** (4,880 m, pronounced Taalay). From here the trail descends S down the **Thalle Valley** and becomes a jeepable track before joining the **Shyok River** at **Doghani,** where you can continue E towards Khapalu or W back to Skardu. This trek takes about 5 days and is relatively straightforward.

Just N of Shigar a bridge crosses to the W bank of the river and climbs up the **Basna Valley** to the NW, passing several villages and some **hot springs**, to **Arandu** at the snout of the 40 km **Chogo Lungma Glacier**. N of the village the glaciated **Kero Lungma Valley** climbs up to the extremely difficult and deeply crevassed **Nushik La**, which leads over to the **Hispar Glacier**. It was once used as a route connecting Nagar with Baltistan.

The main jeep track continues up the E side of the Shigar Valley to the confluence of the Basna and Braldu Rivers (40 km) and then on to **Dasso**, 11 km up the **Braldu Valley**.

The Baltoro Glacier Trek To *Concordia*

This trek traditionally followed the N bank of the river from **Dasso** for 3 days to **Askole,** the last village in the valley, but today a new jeep track reaches this far, following the flatter S bank. Beyond Askole the trek onto the **Baltoro Glacier** is in a restricted zone and permits are needed. The route is extremely popular and often crowded, and some of the traditional camping sites have become filthy, littered with garbage and faeces. There is also a strong military presence due to the Indian-Pakistani border dispute along the **Siachen Glacier**.

A telegraph line runs from a fuel dump across the river from **Paiju**, right up to **Gasherbrum Base Camp,** and helicopters regularly ply up and down the valley. However, it is also a spectacular trek, traversing the entire length of the Baltoro Glacier, at its junction with **Godwin-Austin Glacier**, descending from K2. This central core of the Karakoram is surrounded by some of the highest peaks in the world, with 7 of them – **K2**, **Broad Peak**, **Gasherbrum**, **Mustagh Tower**, **Golden Throne**, **Chogolisa** and **Masherbrum** – clearly visible. It takes 10 days to reach Concordia (walking from Dasso, and not including rest days), and less to return.

From **Askole** it is possible to attempt to traverse the **Biafo-Hispar Glacier** over to **Nagar**. Although this is in an open zone, it is extremely difficult and technical in parts, involving long stretches of glacier walking along this 115 km ice corridor.

East from Skardu to Khapalu

A road goes E from Skardu, past the bridge-turning up to Shigar. The road bends S across a stony plain to **Gol** (30 km). Just before the village there are several large boulders with weatherbeaten inscriptions in Tibetan and carvings of Buddhist stupas, tridents and other symbols. Immediately S of Gol the **Shyok River** drains into the Indus from the E. 2 roads follow the Shyok River on either bank, the first crossing the Indus at Gol, and the second further S, up river from the confluence.

Note The route along the Indus is currently closed to tourists since it approaches the sensitive Line of Control between Pakistan and India.

The main route E is along the N bank of the Shyok until a bridge crosses to the S bank village of **Yugo**, where there are more Buddhist rock carvings. This first stretch of the river was once the home of the tiny kingdom of **Kiris**. Beyond was the powerful kingdom of **Khapalu**, guarding the old route to Ladakh and second only to Skardu. The road continues past several villages set in isolated patches of cultivation until reaching Khapalu town (2,600 m), 103 km from Skardu.

Khapalu is a dispersed settlement beautifully situated on a wide alluvial fan which slopes steeply down from an amphitheatre of mountains to the S. It is surprisingly green, with numerous irrigation channels feeding terraced fields and orchards, and pleasantly cooler than Skardu in summer. The area provides numerous walks along tree-lined path ways and irrigation channels, and excellent views of **Masherbrum** (7,821 m) above the Hushe Valley to the N.

The people belong to the **Nurbashi** sect of Islam, similar to the Ismailis of Hunza in their more progressive outlook on life. They are warm and friendly and the women go about their business freely, without observing purdah. Dominating the town is the impressive **Palace of the Raja** with a 4-tiered, carved wooden balcony, still occupied by the descendants of the ruling family, but somewhat weatherbeaten today. There are a number of basic *hotels/restaurants* in the town and a *PWD Rest House*.

The *Hushe Valley*

N of Khapalu is the Hushe Valley (pronounced Hooshay) which can be reached by way of a bridge E of Khapalu town, or by continuing along the N bank of the Shyok from the bridge crossing at Yugo. Alternatively rafts buoyed by inflated inner tubes (replacing the goats' skins of the past) still make the river crossing from Khapalu.

The Hushe Valley is gently sloped, climbing only 450 m in the 30 km up to Hushe village. On all sides there are spectacular views of snow-capped peaks with Masherbrum, due N, dominating. Across the valley from **Machilu** the **Saltoro River** enters from the E, and a little further N there is a bridge crossing the Hushe River. The people of Hushe still wear the distinctive woollen peaked hats of Baltistan, black for women and white for men. N of Hushe village 4 glaciers, the **Aling, Masherbrum, Chundurgero** and **Chogolisa** provide the sources of the main river, as well as high summer pastures for the goat herds.

Saltoro Valley

Note The Saltoro River Valley is currently closed to tourists due to the border dispute over the Siachen Glacier.

The valley is particularly stunning in parts with sheer granite pinnacles rising up to nearly 1,000 m above the valley floor. Higher up, the valley divides, the N fork being the *Kondus Valley*, while that to the S keeps the name of Saltoro (*giver of light*). Both valleys offer potentially beautiful trekking and climbing.

GILGIT

The KKH runs 33 km from the Baltistan turnoff at **Alam Bridge** along the Gilgit River to the turn off for Gilgit town. The left fork continues W to **Gilgit** (10 km), while the right fork (the KKH route) crosses a Chinese built bridge over the Gilgit River close to its junction with the Hunza River, and continues N up towards the Chinese border.

Gilgit Since the completion of the KKH, Gilgit, the regional capital and administrative centre of the N Areas, has grown rapidly to a large sprawling bazaar town strung out along the S bank of the Gilgit River. Although not particularly beautiful itself, it is conveniently located and has become the main tourist centre, with all the best hotels and shopping. Historically Gilgit was always an important trading post on the Silk Road. Today the bazaars offer a wide variety of goods from China, Tibet and Central Asia, and well stocked provision stores.

	Jan	Feb	Mar	Apr	May	Jun	Jul	Aug	Sep	Oct	Nov	Dec	Av/Tot
Max (°C)	9	12	18	25	28	35	36	34	31	26	18	11	24
Min (°C)	-1	0	5	10	12	16	19	18	13	5	1	-1	8
Rain (mm)	7	8	13	21	28	7	18	22	8	2	1	2	137

From the airport at the E end of the town, 2 roads run W, one close to the river and the other, known as **Airport Road**, leading through the main Bazaar area before forking S into **Jamaat Khana Bazaar**, or W into **Saddar Bazaar** and **Raja Bazaar**. W and SW of Jamaat Khana Bazaar is the old cantonment and civil area with the Commissioner's Offices, a hospital and a Christian cemetery. E of the airport is **Jutial**, with numerous military compounds and a number of hotels.

Polo is an extremely popular sport throughout the Northern Areas and from Jun to Nov polo tournaments are held in the **Aga Khan Polo Stadium** by the river, to the accompaniment of drums and music. The games are generally fairly wild with few rules, and attract large enthusiastic crowds.

Beside the polo ground is the **Main Mosque** and the **Old Fort**, destroyed by an earthquake in 1871 and with only a lone square tower remaining. Further E, **Chinar Bagh** is a pleasant garden area beside the river with *chinar* and plane trees providing welcome shade during the summer.

Local Festivals: *Independence Day* 1-7 Nov. Sports events and folk dances. *Nauroze* 21 Mar. Polo matches and folk dances.

Hotels B/C *Serena Lodge*, Jutial, outside town S of the main rd. T 3960, Cable: SERENA GLT. 44 rm. Restaurant (very good), coffee shop, rm service, shop, car hire, courtesy van, large grounds, views of Rakaposhi. *Park Hotel*, Airport Rd, T 679. Very good value, with good restaurant. *Chinar Inn*, PTDC, Chinar Bagh, T 2562. 28 rm, car hire. *Gilgit Alpine*, nr Serena Lodge, T 3434. Restaurant.

D-F *Hunza Inn*, Chinar Bagh, T 2814. Restaurant, shop. Popular camping. *Gilgit View*, nr bridge N of airport. T 3508. Pleasant location. *Mountain Movers*, N side of river, T 2967. Car hire, travel, helpful management. *Tourist Cottage*, Jutial. T 2376. Also dorm beds and camping. Restaurant, pleasant garden. *Vershigoom Inn*, Airport Rd. T 2991. Restaurant. Central and popular. *Golden Peak*, Bank Rd, T 3911. Camping, pleasant garden, central and popular. Former palace of Mir of Nagar. There are many more hotels in this category in the main bazaar areas. **Camping** at Hunza Inn, Tourist Cottage, Golden Peak.

Restaurants There are good restaurants serving Pakistani and continental food in the Serena Lodge, Gilgit Alpine, Hunza Inn and other hotels as well as a wide range of local restaurants in the main bazaars and Cinema Rd.

Banks National Bank of Pakistan, Agency Rd. **Allied** and **Habib**, Saddar Bazaar. Co-op, Raja Bazaar. **Note** Exchange Rates are considerably lower than in Islamabad, Peshawar, Lahore or Karachi.

Shopping *GM Baig's Bookshop*, Jamaat Khana Bazaar. Excellent selection of books and maps on the Northern Areas, many of them out of print. *Hunza handicrafts*, Park Hotel, Airport Rd. Handicrafts, trekking gear and other items. The owner is also very knowledgeable and helpful. *The Pak-China Friendship Store*, on the main rd, Jutial. Handicrafts and other items from China. *The Gemstone Corporation*, Cinema Rd. Displays of various semi-precious stones including Lapis lazuli, turquoise, topaz etc. Do not expect any bargains. Shops catering for trekkers and mountaineers sell some equipment and freeze dried food.

Local Transport Small Suzuki vans ply constantly between the airport and bazaars.

Useful Addresses Fisheries Office, National Bank Rd. Commissioner's Office, Hospital Rd. Foreigners Registration Office, Airport Rd.

Travel Agents *Mountain Movers Travel*, Link Rd, off Cinema Bazaar. *Waljis Travel*, Airport Rd, T 3848. *PIA Booking Office*, Link Rd, off Cinema Bazaar. T 433.

Tourist Information *PTDC Chinar Inn*, Chinar Bagh. T 2562.

Air 3 flights daily between Gilgit and Islamabad, subject to weather conditions (cancellations are frequent). Often fully booked during the tourist season, so book well in advance. If arriving in Gilgit with a return ticket, re-confirm the return flight on arrival. Also 1 flight weekly to **Skardu**, weather permitting.

Road NATCO has regular bus, 'wagon' and jeep services in all directions. To **Islamabad** 17 hr **Hunza** 2-3 hr, **Skardu** 7-8 hr, **Gupis** 3-4 hr. Check at NATCO depot on Airport Rd for schedules / road conditions. *Sargin Wagon Service, PTDC, Waljis* and *Mountain Movers* all operate their own services and also hire jeeps. Cargo jeeps operate in all directions but are irregular. Check at the various jeep depots.

EXCURSIONS FROM GILGIT

The *Kargah Buddha* is 10 km W of Gilgit on the old road to Punial. A track leads S from the road up the Kargah valley to the 3 m tall carving of the Buddha situated halfway up the rock face. The carving dates from the 7th century and 400 m upstream are the remains of a monastery and 3 stupas. The site was excavated in 1931, revealing the **Gilgit Manuscripts**, written in Sanskrit and containing Buddhist texts and details of local rulers. With the exception of a few held in Karachi Museum, the manuscripts have been removed to various museums outside Pakistan.

Kargah Valley

The Kargah Valley is now a game sanctuary and provides some pleasant walks. Alternatively one can walk back to Gilgit from here along an irrigation channel which brings you to a point S of the Serena Lodge. The walk gives good views down on to the Gilgit Valley and passes through various villages set in pleasantly green surroundings. The route also passes the mouth of the **Jutial Valley**, marked by a cleft in the cliffs S of Serena Lodge. Although only a narrow gorge to begin with, the valley opens out further up to coniferous forests and meadows ideal for walking.

Naltar Valley

From Gilgit cross to the N side of the river and turn right, following the jeep track N up the W bank of the Hunza River to **Nomal** at the mouth of the Naltar Valley (27 km). Public and cargo jeeps run irregularly as far as here. From Nomal it is 18 km up to **Naltar** (3,000 m), situated in alpine meadows and forests surrounded by spectacular peaks. There is a local hotel and a *PWD Rest House* (book through PWD Gilgit T 2416). Take your own bedding and food. The **camping** is ideal.

Further up is **Naltar Lake** with excellent fishing. 2 treks start from here, over the **Naltar Pass** (4,200 m) to the **Ishkoman Valley**, or over the **Daintar Pass** (4,800 m) to **Chalt**. Both are fairly strenuous and you should take a guide.

Gilgit to Chitral

From Gilgit a jeep track heads W following the Gilgit River Valley and crosses the Shandur Pass (3734 m) to Chitral (350 km). The pass is closed from Nov to May and 4-wheel drive is essential as the jeep track is extremely rough in places. If hiring a jeep, make sure it has been properly serviced; tyres, brakes, steering and suspension all take a hammering. Public and cargo jeeps run irregular services as far as **Phandur**.

During the first week of Aug a polo match takes place on top of the Shandur Pass between the Chitral and Gilgit teams and there are many more jeeps plying this route. The Gilgit River Valley is relatively low in altitude and contrasts with Baltistan, being refreshingly green and fertile in many places.

35 km from Gilgit is **Sher Quila** (*Lions Fort*), on the opp bank of the river, capital of the former **Kingdom of Punial.** The kingdom was a traditional bone of contention between *Shah Rais* and *Trakhan* rulers of Chitral and Gilgit, both of whom struggled to gain control of it. An old carved wooden **mosque** and a **watchtower** crowned with a pair of ibex horns still remain. 16 km further on is **Singal** where there is a guest house. The surrounding countryside is so rich and fertile that the Ismaili people call it "the place where Heaven and Earth meet".

Gakuch (72 km) lies at the mouth of the Ishkoman River Valley which drains in from the N. A bridge crosses the Gilgit River to **Chatorkhand** (24 km) where there is a *PWD Rest House* (book through PWD Gilgit T 2416). From here you can continue up to **Imit** or cross over to the W bank and up to **Ishkoman** village.

Treks Guides are essential for all treks in this area.
2 trekking routes lead W from the Ishkoman Valley across to the Yasin Valley. Both take 3-4 days. The S route climbs W from **Phakor**, 5 km N of Chatorkhand up the Asambar Valley and across the Asambar Pass to Sandhi village in Yasin. The N route climbs W from Ishkoman village across the **Ishkoman Pass** to Darkot village, nr the head of the Yasin Valley. From Chatorkhand and Phakor, 2 trekking routes lead E, converging just before the difficult **Naltar Pass** (4,200 m) which leads over into Naltar. From either starting point this trek takes 4-5 days.

At **Gupis** (108 km), the Yasin and Ghizar Rivers, draining from the N and W respectively, unite to form the Gilgit. Gupis, Yasin and Ghizar were all once semi-independent kingdoms. A jeep track crosses the Gilgit River and follows it N to Yasin village (25 km). From here a trekking route leads W over the **Nazbar Pass** (4,971 m) and then either S down the Bahoushtar Valley to Phandur Lake, or else W over the Zagaro Pass (5,034 m) to **Mastuj**. Both treks are unclear and the passes seldom used.

The jeep track continues up the Yasin Valley to **Sandhi** where you can trek E to the Ishkoman valley, or W up the Thui River and across the **Thui Pass** (4,499 m) to **Gazin** in the Yarkhund River Valley. **Warning** The latter route is in a restricted zone. It follows the difficult **Aghost Bar Glacier** for a while.

Further N up the Yasin Valley the jeep track ends at Barkhulti 45 km from Gupis. A track continues N to Darkot. From Darkot you can trek E into the Ishkoman Valley. A trekking route also leads N over the **Darkot Pass** (4,744 m) towards the upper reaches of the Yarkhund River Valley and Afghanistan beyond. **Warning** This is a restricted zone. There is a checkpost at Darkot; permits are required.

From Gupis the main jeep track continues W, now following the Ghizar River, past **Chashi** and **Shamran**, and on to **Phandur**, 167 km from Gilgit. Phandur is particularly beautiful, a wide fertile bowl with a large lake providing excellent fishing. There is a *PWD Rest House* at the E edge of the bowl on a ridge overlooking the lake and the river. The **Handrap River Valley** joins from the S and is the route to Swat, over the **Dardaril Pass**.

30 km beyond Phandur is Teru village, followed shortly after by Barsat, the last village before the Shandur Pass. From Barsat you can trek due N over **Chumarkhan Pass** to Chapali, 11 km N of Mastuj. The jeep track meanwhile bears S before climbing over the flat-topped **Shandur Pass** (3,734 m), with its polo ground, and looping N again to Mastuj. The remaining 107 km to Chitral are described in the Chitral Section, **see page 1232**.

GILGIT TO THE KHUNJERAB PASS AND THE CHINESE BORDER

After crossing the Gilgit River, the KKH continues N following the E bank of the Hunza River to Dainyor, 3 km from the bridge. There are some rock inscriptions dating from the 8th century in a private garden in the village and a cemetery for the Chinese workers who died building the KKH. A 200 m suspension bridge (one of the longest in Asia) crosses to the W bank, and the jeep track forks, leading back to Gilgit or running N to the village of **Nomal** at the head of the Naltar Valley, see page above. The KKH follows the Hunza River, skirting round the base of Rakaposhi and passing through a deep narrow gorge before arriving at the hamlet of **Rahimabad**, watered by a large spring. From here the KKH continues N for approximately 20 km before bending E.

On the opp bank 2 valleys, the **Chaprot** and **Bar** drain into the Hunza River. At **Nilt,** site of the **Sikanderabad Fort** on the KKH, a bridge provides access to them and there is a *NAWO Rest House* in the village of **Chalt** at the mouth of the Chaprot Valley. Chalt was the scene of a campaign in 1891, against the Hunza and Nagar kingdoms which were threatening the newly re-established Gilgit Agency, then the northernmost outpost of the British Empire. Both valleys are picturesque and offer some beautiful walks. A rough jeep track leads up the W side of the Bar Valley as far as the village of Bar. From Chalt there is a circular trek over the **Daintar Pass** to the **Naltar Valley**.

The KKH continues E and enters **Hunza** proper when it crosses to the N bank of the river and passes the village of **Hini**. From here **Rakaposhi**, previously hidden by the steep valley sides is revealed in all its splendour. Just before the bridge over to Hini a track leads S up to Minapin and beyond is the Minapin Glacier. Further E along the KKH, the valley opens out into the fertile heartland of Hunza; a series of dispersed settlements connected by stretches of lush, irrigated fields, intricately terraced and dotted with plentiful fruit and poplar trees. Hunza is well worth an extended visit, but be prepared for cloud, rain and some cold weather.

Hunza emerged as a powerful separate kingdom from the 11th century onwards and prospered due to its commanding position on the Silk Road, guarding the routes to the N passes which lead into Central Asia. Durand wrote: "The rulers of Hunza were rich compared to those of Nagar, and secure in the fastnesses of their mountains; they snapped their fingers at China and Kashmir, and with fine impartiality plundered caravans to the N and kidnapped slaves to the S."

Before the building of the KKH and the advent of cheap subsidised imports, the **Hunzakuts** were largely self-sufficient, struggling each summer to gather adequate supplies for the long winter months. The diet is still basic, centred around wheat, barley, maize and limited dairy products. In addition fruits, particularly apricots are eaten in large quantities. Nothing is wasted; the seed is broken open and the shell burned, while the kernel is ground into flour, pressed for its oil or eaten as a nut.

Various theories concerning the supposed longevity of the people centre around the importance of this fruit in their diet and are the source of considerable controversy. Hunza's isolation and idyllic setting suggest it as the inspiration for **James Hilton's** fabled Shangri La in the book "Lost Horizon". However the realities of life here are harsh; infant mortality rates are high, disease and malnutrition common, and people age rapidly in this region of climatic extremes.

The Hunzakuts are predominantly Ismaili Muslims and are free from the more rigorous strictures of Islam. The women do not observe purdah and dress colourfully, wearing distinctive embroidered hats draped with light shawls as protection against the sun. Until recently wine was freely available and much enjoyed and had to be officially banned by the Aga Khan. The ancient folklores which centre around demon and fairy worship still have a deep hold on the people here; neither Buddhism in the past, nor Islam today have really succeeded in eroding such beliefs.

Karimabad, the capital of Hunza, is in an outstandingly beautiful situation N of the KKH, up on the hillside. A track leaves the KKH 3 km after the **Hasanabad Bridge** which crosses a deep and narrow gorge running down from the **Hasanabad Glacier**. A shorter but steeper track leads up from *Ganesh* 7 km on. The town has grown considerably in recent years and now has a good selection of hotels and some uninterrupted views of **Rakaposhi** (7,788 m) and **Diran** (7,230 m). To the N up the Ultar Nala (valley) there is **Ultar Peak** (7,388 m) and next to it **Bubelimating** (Bubela's Peak), a towering pinnacle of sheer granite, too steep to hold any snow. Neither peak has yet been climbed.

Hotels C *The Rakaposhi View*, Good value. In theory, hot showers available; in practice often not working. C *Serena Lodge*, Karimabad (opened summer 1991). Reservations: Serena, Karachi. T 537506-9. Cable: SERENA PK. **D-F** *Tourist Park*, T 45. 9 rm some with bath. Restaurant, shop, local guide service, car hire. *Mountain View*. T 17. 16 rm some with bath. Rm service, car hire. *Hilltop*. T 10. 28 rm some with bath. Restaurant, shop. *Silver Jubilee*, T 62. Also dorm beds, magnificent view. *Hunza Inn*. Nice atmosphere, popular. *Karimabad*, excellent views. There are over a dozen more hotels in this category. **Camping** *PTDC* Aliabad (on KKH, 1 km past turnoff for Karimabad). T 60. 20 tents.

Restaurants As well as in the above mentioned hotels, there are a number of small, basic restaurants serving Pakistani, Chinese and European food.

Shopping There are a number of hotel shops and small stores selling local handicrafts. At **Aliabad** the *Pakistan Mineral Development Corporation* sells semi-precious stones.

Road Public buses do not go up to Karimabad. Services heading N or S may be joined at Ganesh on the KKH.

Excursions from Karimabad

Baltit Fort There is a lovely walk to the village of *Baltit*, 1 km to the N, which joins Karimabad, with its polo ground, school and *Jamaat Khana* (Ismaili place of worship and community centre). Perched above all this on a cliff edge is Baltit Fort, the residence of the former Mirs of Hunza, with wonderful views of Hunza Vally and the Karakoram. It is about 400 years old and built by the craftsmen of a Balti Princess who married the Mir of that time. Built of mud plaster, stone and timber beams, the fort is a large affair with 3 storeys and a total of 53 rooms.

It is generally locked and the key held by a *chowkidar* (doorman) who lives nearby. Entering from the ground floor which was used for storage, a wooden ladder leads to a courtyard above. There are some fading photos of former Mirs and important guests in one room and a museum room containing coats of chain mail, weapons and huge drums used to warn of impending attacks. There is also access to the roof which provides fine views over the valley.

Altit Fort is situated 3 km to the E, across the mouth of the Ultar Nala. From Karimabad a rough track passes underneath an arch supporting an irrigation aqueduct and zigzags down across the main stream before climbing to the Fort, perched on a rocky cliff some 300 m directly above the Hunza River.

A *chowkidar* holds the key to Altit Fort, which is older than Baltit's, though very similar in design. The lowest level houses dungeons and a grainstore (a hollow stone pillar in the centre). Above are the royal apartments and stairs leading to the roof. Here there are some later additions and a beautifully carved **mosque** as well as the **watchtower**, with carved doors and windows and a goat's head with ibex horns on top.

Ultar You can walk up the Ultar ravine to an area of high pasture and shepherds' huts. There are spectacular views across the valley to Rakaposhi, Diran and also up the Hispar Valley towards Golden Peak. The lower sections of the gorge are extremely steep and often impassable and an alternative route follows an irrigation channel cut into the rock face high above the stream-torrent. To join it climb up towards the squat building high up on the ridge above Baltit Fort. The path zigzags up the steep rock face and then drops down over the crest of the ridge to join the channel.

There are in fact 2 irrigation channels and on returning be sure to follow the upper one as the lower one becomes impassable, cascading down in a series of steep waterfalls. To visit the shepherd's huts and return to Karimabad is a strenuous full day's walk although the camping up there is ideal. Paths also continue up towards Ultar Glacier and Base Camp. **Warning:** The glaciated upper reaches of the valley can be deceptively treacherous.

Nagar Just after Ganesh, the KKH crosses the Hunza River and a jeep track bears off SE up the **Hispar Valley**. After 6 km the track forks; the left fork continues up the E bank to **Hora,** 10 km on, while the right fork crosses the river and follows the W bank up to the fertile villages of Nagar.

Nagar was formerly a powerful independent kingdom and often locked in conflict with Hunza. It included all the territory on the S side of the Hunza River, as far W as **Chalt**, as well as the **Chaprot** and **Bar** Valleys. Despite being smaller than Hunza, it possessed more fertile land and thus supported a larger population. The region is famous for its apricots, which are dried and exported to the Punjab in considerable quantities and the streams are supposedly rich in gold.

Today the people still differ markedly from the Hunzakuts, being darker in complexion and strict Shi'ite Muslims. Due to the prevailing conservative outlook, tourism remains largely undeveloped.

In **Nagar** village there is the **Mir's Residence,** a private compound complete with polo ground, audience pavilion and a carved wooden mosque. 15 km further on the jeep track ends at **Hopar,** set in an impressive wide, fertile bowl ringed by high peaks. There is a basic *Rest House* and **camping**.

Nearby, below a ridge of moraine, is the ***Bualtar Glacier*** which can be traversed to reach the larger and pristine white ***Barpu Glacier***. Paths follow the W edge of the glacier up to high summer pastures at Hamdar and Miar. Clearly visible up ahead is the towering Golden Peak. Another more difficult route crosses to the E side of Barpu Glacier and climbs up to the higher pastures at **Girgindil**, several days walk away. **Warning:** This route involves some difficult stretches of glacier walking and a guide is essential.

If on ascending the Hispar Valley you continue along the E bank to Hora, where the jeep track ends, you can trek up to Hispar village (20 km) at the snout of the **Hispar Glacier**. The Hispar joins with the **Biafo Glacier** and leads down into the **Braldu Valley** in Baltistan. This trek is extremely demanding and technical in parts, covering some 115 km, often actually on the glacier.

The KKH from Altit

After passing Ganesh and crossing to the S bank of the Hunza River, the KKH continues E. Just past the turning for Nagar, there is the **Sacred Rock of Hunza** known locally as "*Haldikish*" or Place of Rams. Here several large boulders are again carved with numerous inscriptions spanning centuries of passing trade along the Silk Road and the various incursions of neighbouring powers.

For the next 37 km to Gulmit, the Hunza River cuts through a deep narrow gorge and the KKH often climbs high up the steep valley sides. After a while the river valley bends N and the road then crosses to the W bank at Shishkot Bridge. 8 km on is Gulmit, where the valley widens dramatically.

Gulmit is set in a fertile tract of irrigated wheat fields and orchards and marks the start of **Upper Hunza** or Gujal, populated by the semi-nomadic Wakhi people. The village was once the summer residence of the Mir of Hunza. Today there are several basic *Rest Houses*, pleasantly situated, and the Hunza Cultural **Museum**, housing examples of local ethnic dress and displays of traditional living practices, as well as a snow leopard's pelt.

2 glaciers flow down from the W, the Gulmit, and just N of it over a ridge, the *Ghulkin Glacier*, which reaches down almost to the road. There are many possibilities for walks and longer treks from the village, along the various irrigation channels and up the sides of the glaciers. **Warning:** Both glaciers are active and highly unstable, especially in summer.

Pasu is 14 km on. The road first crosses the stream of **Pasu Glacier** which is strikingly white in contrast to the dirty grey morainal glaciers common to this region. The village is situated on a low wide alluvial fan and the houses scattered among irrigated fields and orchards. To the N is a wide stony plain, once the site of the Chinese KKH construction headquarters, and now being developed into farmland by the AKRSP. Also N of the village, the immense **Batura Glacier** flows down from the W. Across the river is a huge and ruggedly beautiful multi-pinnacled ridge of crumbling granite spires. Up river from this, the Shimshal River flows in from the E, finally escaping its narrow gorge.

There are a few basic *Rest Houses* along the road; the *Pasu Inn* and *Batura Inn* at either end of the village are popular and both have maps showing treks in the area, and helpful informative managers. Various treks follow the Batura Glacier up towards summer pastures as high as **Guchashim** (3,550 m). **Warning:** Stretches of glacier walking are involved and a guide is strongly recommended.

Another trek follows the narrow and difficult Shimshal Gorge E, crossing the **Molungutti Glacier** to arrive at Shimshal village (approx 3 days) where there is Camping and a basic *Rest House*. Trails lead up from there to high pastures at the snout of the Shujerab Glacier. An alternative, much shorter and easier walk is up to *Boreet Lake*, between the Pasu and Ghulkin Glaciers. A track leads W from the KKH, just S of the Pasu Glacier, up to the lake where there is a settlement with good **camping** and a basic *Rest House*.

N of Pasu the KKH once again enters a narrow gorge, passing the village of Khaibur high up on an isolated fan, before crossing the Hunza River to the E bank village of Gallapan. Further N, beyond Murkhun , the valley widens as it climbs to **Sost**, 34 km from Pasu, giving spectacular views of the precipitous N slopes of the main Karakoram range.

Sost is the Pakistani Immigration and Customs Post. The offices remain open until 1100 for outgoing traffic and 1600 for incoming traffic. The *Khunjerab Pass* to the N, which marks the actual border, is open from 1 May to 31 Oct for group tours, and from 1 May to 30 Nov for individual travellers. There are a number of basic **Hotels** and guest houses in the **D-F** category, as well as the newly opened **A** *Shangri La Hotel*, which can be booked in Karachi or Rawalpindi. NATCO operates daily bus services from Sost to Pirali.

Across the river from Sost, the **Charpursan Valley** climbs W to the glaciated **Chinjilli Pass** which leads over into the Ishkoman Valley in Gilgit. This route is in a restricted zone. From Sost the KKH climbs up to the Khunjerab Pass (4,733 m) and then drops down to Pirali (120 km), the Chinese Customs and Immigration Post. From Pirali to Tashkurghan is 84 km and then a further 280 km to Kashgar. Chinese bus services operate from **Pirali**. Private vehicles are not allowed into China.

INFORMATION FOR VISITORS

DOCUMENTS

Passports and visas A valid passport is required by all visitors. All nationals of India, Afghanistan, **South Africa**, Bangladesh, Iran, and any country not recognised by Pakistan must have a visa. Israeli passport holders are not permitted entry. Bona fide tourists from most other countries need a visa only if they wish to stay for more than 30 days. Nationals of a few countries may stay up to 90 days without a visa. Check with the Pakistan Embassy or consulate in your own country.

Visas are not issued at entry points. In some circumstances visas can be extended for short periods by applying to Passport Offices in Islamabad, Karachi, Lahore, Peshawar or Quetta. However both the rules and the practice are subject to change without warning.

Restricted areas Some areas of Pakistan such as parts of NWFP, Baluchistan and the Northern Tribal Agencies, are not open to tourists without special permission. Permission is rarely given, and can only be applied for in Pakistan.

The cost of visas is variable according to the nationality of the applicant and the type of visa applied for. Arrangements for visa application and collection vary from office to office, and should be confirmed by phone with the relevant office. Tourists from countries which do not have Pakistani representation may apply to resident British representatives.

Work permits Visitors are not allowed to undertake work without a special permit. Details from Pakistan Embassies and consulates.

Certificates of vaccination and innoculation are no longer required. See Health Section, **page 1271**. **Warning** Visitors arriving from South America and Africa require an inoculation certificate against yellow fever.

TRAVEL

Air PIA and British Airways have direct flights from London to Islamabad. Minimum flying times to Karachi from: New York – 17 hr; Tokyo – 10 hr; Hong Kong – 5 hr; London – 8 hr; Jeddah 4 hr; Abu Dhabi 2 hr. 20 international airlines from over 40 countries, fly to Karachi or Islamabad. A few go to Lahore or Peshawar.

Land Access by land depends largely on political relations with Pakistan's neighbours. It is restricted and unpredictable. The official borders are as follows:

Iran *Taftan*, on the road between Zahedan and Quetta, approx 160 km between the Iranian and Pakistani border checkposts. **Afghanistan** All border posts remain closed. If normal relations resume the border posts may re-open at: *Torkham*, in the Khyber Pass; *Chamman*, in the Khojak Pass. **China** The route to China has been the most reliably open land border of Pakistan in the last decade. It is at *Sost* on the Khunjrab Pass, and is open from May to Nov between 1100 and 1600. **India** *Wagha*, between Lahore and Amritsar. *Ganda Singh Wala*, on the Ferozepur road. These have been open only once or twice a month. Conditions alter unpredictably. Check in Lahore or Amritsar.

CUSTOMS, ARRIVAL AND DEPARTURE REGULATIONS

Arrival The formalities on arrival in Pakistan are straightforward. Immigration forms are handed out on the plane before arrival and these should be given in at the immigration counter. You may also be given a health form, which is normally only relevant if you have been recently in a country where yellow fever is endemic or where cholera is currently prevalent. The customs slip will be returned, for handing over to the customs on leaving the baggage collection hall.

Customs regulations There are no restrictions on the amount of foreign currency or travellers cheques a tourist may bring into Pakistan. However, you are only allowed to take Pakistan **Rs 100** in or out of Pakistan, and you may only exchange **Rs 500** into foreign currency.

If you want cash on arrival it is best to get it at the airport bank where it is generally easier and less time consuming to change money at the airport than at banks in the city.

Duty Free Allowances 200 cigarettes or 50 cigars or 1/2 lb of manufactured tobacco. Perfume and toilet water upto 1/2 pint (225 ml). One camera and 5 rolls of flms. One non-professional (referred to officially as "sub-standard") cine camera, projector with 2 rolls of film. Jewellery up to Rs 1000 in value. Games, sporting requisites (including firearms and cartridges in reasonable quantity) accompanied by an arms licence issued by a competent authority. Gifts and souvenirs of up to Rs 500. Food and confectionery of up to Rs 100. Tourists are allowed to bring in all personal effects "which may reasonably be required" without charge, including equipment such as cameras, film, or lap top computers.

Prohibited and restricted items The import of some items is prohibited or restricted. Importing dangerous drugs, live plants, gold coins, gold and silver bullion and silver coins not in current use is either banned or subject to strict regulation. **Warning** You are not allowed to bring in alcohol. Permits are available for non-Muslims. These may be obtained from some of the larger hotels and from licensed government liquor shops. If liquor is brought in by mistake, you must declare it to the Customs Officer, who will give a receipt and may return it to you on departure from Pakistan. **Departure Tax**   Rs 100 Departure Tax on international departures. An additional foreign travel tax of Rs 250 is levied on those with international tickets bought in Pakistan. Domestic departure tax Rs 10.

INTERNAL TRAVEL

Air PIA has flights to over 30 centres within Pakistan. Flights to some northern areas are heavily subsidised and extremely cheap. All domestic flights depart from Terminal 2 at Karachi. There is a free shuttle service between terminals. There are left luggage halls at the main airports. Rs 15 per piece for 24 hr. Any period over 24 hr is charged at the full day rate. Some routes have tourist and student price concessions. Check with PIA.

Warning Ticket pricing The price of Air travel in Pakistan varies greatly according to the way in which you pay for your ticket. **See page 124.**

Train Over 12,000 km of track. There are 3 classes; Airconditioned, First and Second. Trains are often heavily booked. Bedding available on request. First Class has couchettes, which must be reserved – no bedding supplied. Take food and water. The journeys are generally slow but are good value.

Price Concessions are available for foreign tourists. Students are entitled to a 50% discount in fares in all classes, whether travelling individually or in a group. You need a certificate from the institution or a recognized student card. Two accompanying professors/teachers are also eligible for the discount with each group of 15 students.

Other foreign tourists (except Indians) are entitled to a 25% reduction in all classes except A/c 'sitter' class. Contact the office of the Divisional Superintendent Pakistan Railways in one of the following centres to obtain concessional vouchers, which can be exchanged for tickets when booking your journey: Karachi, Sukkur, Quetta, Multan, Lahore, Rawalpindi, and Peshawar. They can also be obtained from the Chief Marketing Manager, Pakistan Railways, Headquarters Office, Lahore. You must show your passport.

Bus All Pakistan's major routes are served by local and express bus services which may not allow advance reservation. 'Disco' or Mini buses are usually the quickest cheap means of transport. The vans (called 'Wagons') and fast a/c 'Flying Coaches' available on some routes are best booked in advance.

Car It is possible to hire a car with a driver very easily in all the major centres, and tours can be arranged to suit individual requirements. Pakistani driving conditions are often dangerous by European and American standards. Drivers often have only a limited amount of English, though the bigger hire car companies can often supply drivers with some English. The cost of a small car for a week is approximately Rs 6000 (i.e. just over £175). Petrol is extra. It is also possible to hire a/c cars for a comparatively small surcharge. Hertz, Avis and other rental car companies operate in the major cities.

Driving Although self drive cars are available in places, and it is quite possible to drive yourself, special care is needed. Traffic conditions are very different from those in Europe or the United States. There is a wide variety of traffic, from animal drawn vehicles to very large army lorries. Some of the main roads are very busy and cars move fast and unpredictably. Driving after dark is particularly difficult, as many vehicles have no lights and there are very few road markings.

Warning In the uncertain and sometimes violent conditions prevailing in some parts of Pakistan it is essential to confirm the safety of your route in advance. In some places it is also essential to travel with an armed guard. Enquire at the main tourist office in Karachi, Lahore or Islamabad. In 1991 it was unsafe to travel by road outside the main cities in many parts of Sind and Baluchistan. Parts of NWFP and Northern Areas are classified as 'Closed' or 'Restricted'. Permits needed for the latter.

MONEY

Currency Pakistan's currency is the Pakistani **Rupee**. New notes are printed in denominations of Rs 1000, 500, 100, 50, 10, 10, 5, 2, and 1. The Rupee is divided into 100 Paise. Coins are minted in denominations of Rs 1, and 50, 25, 10, 5, 2 and 1 Paise.

Money changing If you are staying in a major hotel you will be able to change money there 24 hours a day. When changing money anywhere in Pakistan it is important to retain the **encashment certificate** as proof of exchange through an authorized dealer. It allows you to change up to the limit of Pakistani Rupees back to your own currency on leaving Pakistan.

Banks often give a substantially better rate of exchange than hotels. On departure you are allowed to reconvert upto Rs 500 of unspent money. For larger amounts it is necessary to apply to an office of the *State Bank of Pakistan* through an authorized exchange bank. There is a currency black market in Pakistan. In 1991 the premiums over the official rate in most places were small. Changing money through unauthorised dealers is illegal and may be risky. In remote areas the rate of exchange may not match that in the larger cities.

Travellers cheques Only foreign banks, the *National Bank of Pakistan* and the *Habib Bank* are allowed to exchange foreign currencies or travellers' cheques. Most travellers cheques are accepted without difficulty, but it is often useful to have cash in the form of dollars. **Warning** In the Northern Areas the National Banks may only accept US$ and £ sterling.

Credit cards Major credit cards are increasingly widely acceptable in the main centres, though in smaller cities and towns and in villages it is still rare to be able to pay by credit card. Payment by credit card can be significantly more expensive than payment by cash. However shopping by credit card for items such as handicrafts, clothing, and carpets from larger dealers, does not mean that you have to accept the first price asked. Bargaining is still expected and essential. American Express cardholders can use their cards to obtain either cash or travellers cheques in the major cities. Diners, Master Card and Visa are widely used.

Cost of Living The cost of living in Pakistan is generally much lower than in Europe or the United States. Food and accommodation in the best hotels is rather more expensive than in India but still considerably less than the equivalent in the West or Japan.

Tipping As in India 10% is regarded as extremely generous. In most places 5% or rounding off with small change is completely acceptable.

Bargaining The same rules apply as elsewhere in South Asia. Outside Government shops and the biggest hotels, expect to bargain hard.

OTHER ESSENTIAL INFORMATION

Official time 5 hr ahead of GMT.

Weights and measures A combination of old local measurements with British units and decimalization are in use and can be confusing particularly when distances are given in either miles or km without being specified. Fruit, vegetables, nuts etc are sold in kilos and grammes. Cloth is sold in yards (called *gaz*) in the markets, rather than metres. Numbers go from 1,000 to 100,000 (*lakh*), 100 *lakhs* making a *crore*.

Postal services Reliable, but in the N Areas there may be delays due to road blocks or flight cancellations. You are advised to have stamps cancelled in a post office to ensure they won't be removed. DHL and similar international services are available in the larger cities. **Poste Restante** facilities are available in the main post offices. American Express offers its usual service to card holders.

Telephone services Direct dialling is available in most parts of the country but public telephones are almost non-existent. Telegraph and telex facilities are offered by Telegraph and larger Post Offices, and shop keepers will often allow you to make calls within Pakistan. International calls can be made from airports and Telegraph Offices in cities. Major hotels also allow international calls but this is often more expensive.

Business hours Shops and offices are closed on **Fridays**. Business hours are from 0730-1430 in the summer and from 0900-1600 in the winter. Government offices are open from 0830-1400 in summer and from 0900-1430 in the winter. **Offices** are usually open Sat to Wed. **Banks** 0900-1300 Mon to Th, 0900-1100 Sat and Sun. **Shops** 0900-1830 Sat to Th. **Central Government Offices** 0900-1300, 1330-1630 Sun-Th. Closed Fri and Sat. Check locally for differences in winter and summer timings. **Note** During the month of Ramazan, business hours are shorter.

Electricity 220-240 volts AC. There may be pronounced variations in the voltage, and power cuts are particularly common in N Pakistan.

Media A number of daily English newspapers are issued from the regional capitals. British and American newspapers and some magazines are available in the major cities. *Dawn, The Muslim,* and *The Independent* are 3 widely read daily newspapers. The *Karachi Herald* is a popular national monthly magazine while the *Weekly Herald, Travelogue* and *Hotel and Travel* carry useful information for visitors.

Maps Good maps are difficult to obtain. Nelles' 1:1.5 million map of Pakistan is extremely clear and probably the most useful map for Pakistan as a whole, though it is not always as accurate as it appears, especially with respect to rivers. The Survey of Pakistan publishes a series of Provincial maps at the somewhat larger scale of 1:1 million. They are available from some bookshops and hotel bookshops in the major cities, and from the Survey of Pakistan Headquarters in Rawalpindi. Bartholomew's 1:4 million Map of South Asia is generally the most reliable small scale map.

Hints on social behaviour Use your right hand for giving, taking, eating or shaking hands as the left is considered to be unclean. Women do not shake hands with men as this form of contact is not traditionally acceptable between acquaintances. Do not photograph women without permission. **Greetings** The common form of greeting is to say *Assalam-o-Alaikum* (Peace be upon you) to which the response is *Walaikum-Assalam* (peace be upon you also). Thank you is *Shukriya*.

Clothing There are sharp contrasts between winter and summer, and with altitude. In the hot periods light cottons are best, with the lightest possible long sleeved cottons for evening. Women should be fully covered. Shorts are unacceptable in most parts of Pakistan.

Liquor Permits Foreign tourists may buy alcoholic drinks from hotels authorised to sell liquor to non-Muslim foreigners after a liquor permit has been signed. Foreign residents can obtain a Liquor Permit from the Excise and Taxation Office.

Visiting Mosques Visitors are welcome, but it is essential to observe customary courtesy. Shoes must always be removed outside. Take thick socks for protection. Women should be covered from head to ankle. Mosques may be closed to non-Muslims shortly before prayers, and occasionally women may not be allowed into some parts.

Warning Photography is not permitted at airports, military installations or of bridges.

Trekking The mountain regions have been divided into 'Open', 'Restricted' and 'Closed' zones. You are allowed to trek without a permit from Kalash valley in Chitral to Hushe valley in E Baltistan and other 'Open' areas (excluding borders, Pathan territories and Kohistan) but only up to 6,000 m (higher altitudes are classified as mountaineering which requires a separate permit). For 'Restricted' area **permits,** contact a recommended trekking company several months ahead. They provide a comprehensive service. **Note** It is often very difficult to get a permit for certain areas.

The Govt owned *Pakistan Tours*, Flashman's Hotel, The Mall, Rawalpindi, T 64811; Travel Walji's *Adventure Pakistan*, 10 Khayaban-e-Suharawardy, Aapara Market, Islamabad, T 28324; *Hunza Treks and Tours*, 253, St 23,E 7, Islamabad, T 28558; *Karakoram Tours*, 1 Baltoro House, St 19, F 7/2, Islamabad, T 29120, specialises in Baltistan; *Nazir Sabir Expeditions*, PO Box 1442, Isalamabad, T 853672, covers treks and mountaineering; *Sitara Travel,* 25-26 Shalimar Plaza, off The Mall, Rawalpindi. All can arrange porters and guides at short notice.

NATIONAL HOLIDAYS AND FESTIVALS

Muslim holidays are based on the lunar calendar and thus change from year to year. (See S. Asia introduction, **page 66**).

Muharram 10th day of the month marks death of Hussain. Special care needed in Peshawar and Skardu, where the period of mourning is marked by large processions with many people in an emotional frenzy.

Ramazan Month of fasting. Food and drink are not sold from dawn to dusk except in large hotels. Transport may be disrupted.

Eid ul Fitr Marks the end of Ramadan and is a public holiday.

Eid ul Zuha commemorates Abraham's offer of blood sacrirfice of his son Ismael. Ritual slaughter of goats (or sheep). Prayers and festivities, and the seasonal greeting of "Eid Mubarak".

Eid ul Azha marks the end of the pilgrimage to Mecca – the 'Haj'. Airlines to the Middle East are often fully booked during this period and airports are particularly busy.

Other Festivals and Public holidays

Feb Lahore and Kasur: *Basant*, festival of kites and mustard flowers. Bahawalpur district: "*Urs*" festival at the shrine of Chanan pir, patron saint of Cholistan Desert.

Mar Lahore: Horse show – festival of regional folklore, tent pegging, horse and camel dances and trick riding. **Shalimar gardens**, Lahore *Mela Chiraghan* – festival of lamps. **Gilgit, Skardu, Hunza** and **Chitral** Nauroze: polo matches and folk dances. **23 Mar** *Pakistan Day*; Celebrates the 1940 decision to press for an independent Muslim state.

Apr Islamabad: *Mela Lok Virsa* – festival of folk heritage.

May 1 May *May Day;* Islamabad "*Urs*" annual festival at the shrine of Bari Imam, patron saint of woods. **Kalash Valleys**, Chitral *Joshi/Chilimjusht*, spring festival of Kafir Kalash. Folk dances and songs.

Jul Chitral *Utchal*, harvest festival of Kafir Kalash. **1 Jul** Bank holiday. Other offices remain open.

Aug Polo matches in **Gilgit and Northern Territories**. **14 Aug** Independence Day celebrated across Pakistan.

Sep *Phool*, grapes and walnut harvest of Kafir Kalash. **Chitral** Folk dances and songs. **6 Sep** *Defence of Pakistan Day*. Commemorates 1965 war with India. **11 Sep** Anniversary of the death of M. A. Jinnah.

Nov *Independence Day* **Gilgit and Skardu, Northern Territories** Polo matches and folk dances. **9 Nov** Allama Iqbal Day.

Dec *Chowas*, winter festival of Kafir Kalash. *Chitral*. **25 Dec** Christmas and Birthday of M.A. Jinnah. **31 Dec** Bank holiday. Other offices remain open.

NEPAL

Official name Nepal Adhirajya (Kingdom of Nepal)

National flag Double pennant of crimson with blue border on peaks; white moon with rays of light in centre of top peak; white quarter sun, recumbent, in centre of bottom peak.

Official language Nepali

Official religion None

Basic indicators *Population* 19 m; *Urban* 7%, *Rural* 93%; *Religion Hindu* 89.5%, *Buddhist* 5.3%, *Muslim* 2.7%; *Birth rate* 41 per 1000 *Death rate* 18.2 per 1000 *Infant mortality rate* 140 per 1000 *GNP per capita* US$160.

GENERAL INTRODUCTION

To the travellers in the early 1950s, Nepal was a country outside time. A medieval society, since the end of the Gurkha Wars with the British in 1815 it had cut itself off from the outside world. The people were charming, naturally friendly and virtually untouched by the social, political and commercial changes taking place beyond its borders. Those early travellers were effusive in their praise of this wonderful but economically backward land.

Much has changed since 1951. In a country with few natural resources, tourism has become one of its biggest foreign exchange earners. Inevitably it has affected the outlook of many thousands of Nepalese. Yet Nepal retains its stunning natural beauty and much of its simple charm.

The Kathmandu Valley is magnificent for its wealth of unique temples. Beyond the Valley are the greatest mountains in the world. Some of the mountain regions, such as the Sola Khumbu(for Everest) and Annapurna, are immensely popular, while others such as West and East Nepal are barely known. Differences in altitude lead to great diversity in vegetation type, from the sub-tropical wet Terai to the

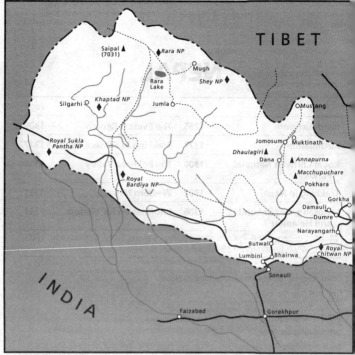

semi-arid mountain wastes of the high altitude West. At the same time, Nepal's position sandwiched between Tibet and India has produced a remarkable mixture of peoples and cultures.

GEOGRAPHY

Nearly twice the size of Portugal, Nepal covers 147,181 sq km and is roughly rectangular in shape. It stretches 800 km from W to E and varies between 150 km – 250 km N to S. Although it a Himalayan state, Nepal has 4 distinct physical regions.

The Terai The N margin of the Gangetic plain runs from UP to West Bengal in India, along the southern edge of Nepal. Formerly a malarial region because of the dense jungle, relatively high rainfall and humidity, it has potentially rich agricultural land and has been used as an overflow area to the congested hills. The southernmost 15 km wide strip contains the best agricultural land, backing onto a marshy region adjoining the hills.

Little of the original Terai forest now remains. The Terai runs the length of the country and apart from the gorge of the Narayani river in the central section, is an unbroken belt, between 20-40 km wide. The hills rise to around 1,300 m and behind them are a number of basins, the Inner Terai, where the Dang and Chitwan are the largest. Malaria is endemic here and the opportunities for agricultural

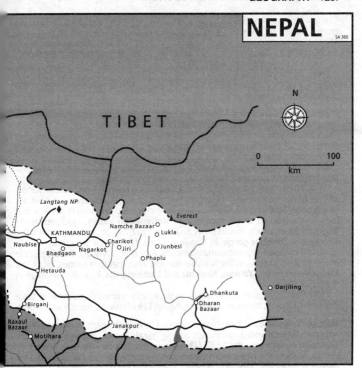

NEPAL
SA 360

TIBET

N

0   100
km

Langtang NP

Everest

Namche Bazaar ○

KATHMANDU □   ○ Lukla

Naubise ○   Charikot ○   Junbesi
     Bhadgaon   Nagarkot ○ Jiri

Hetauda ○   Phaplu ○

            ○ Darjiling

Birganj ○   ○ Dhankuta

Raxaul   ○ Dharan
Bazaar   Bazaar
○ Motihara   ○ Janakpur

colonization not good. The altitude at the lowest points is around 60 m and in places can rise to as much as 300 m. The hills provided an effective barrier to communication and a wall against which potential invaders foundered. The rivers and streams of especially those that are seasonally dry, are polluted and you are ill-advised to drink the water without purifying it first. Local towns as well as areas upstream contribute to the pollution, and around Kathmandu there has been uncontrolled industrial development.

The Siwaliks and Mahabharat Lekh. Immediately N of the Terai are the low lying Siwaliks. Reaching almost 2,000 m in height, and originally well forested, they give way to the higher, barer **Mahabharat Lekh**, ranging from 2,400 m-4,250 m. Some valleys in this belt, which is often referred to as the **Inner Terai**, are fairly broad (up to 35 km wide) and well forested, though many have been cleared to provide grazing and building material.

The Middle Zone. Gradually the elevation of ridges increases across this 80 km wide belt. It includes the Kathmandu and Pokhara Valleys, flat basins, formerly covered with lakes, and formed by the deposition of glacial and fluvial material brought down by rivers. These valleys are fertile and intensively cultivated. They are also densely populated. To reach the high mountains and wilderness areas, many trekking routes cross this band which is mostly open landscape.

The High Himalaya An immense belt of lofty peaks stretching the length of the country and providing the N wall between the Ganga plains of India and the

Tibetan Plateau. A series of massifs are separated from one another by deep gorges, carved by rivers as the mountains were uplifted. The uplift is continuing at a rate of up to 6 cm a year. The 6,000 m deep **Kali Gandaki gorge**, which separates **Dhaulagiri** from the **Annapurnas**, is the deepest gorge in the world.

Eight of the world's fourteen 8,000 m peaks are in Nepal, including, of course, Everest. As they originally lay at the bottom of the the Sea of Tethys and were subject to marine sedimentation, it is not uncommon to find sea fossils on the slopes of these great mountains.

Rivers, glaciers and lakes Nepal's rivers descend further and faster, than any other rivers in the world. As a result many have cut sheer-sided valleys thousands of metres deep, creating enormously unstable hillsides. Any external action – an earthquake, severe rainfall, the building of a road – can trigger catastrophic earth and rock slides in the upper reaches of these rivers. Such slides sometimes create natural dams which may impound huge lakes, only to burst and flood the valleys downstream when the pressure becomes too great for the natural wall to withstand.

The 3 main river systems – the **Kosi, Gandak** and **Karnali** – originate in glaciers and are all part of the massive Gangetic river system. A few actually rise in Tibet but all ultimately flow into the Ganga, and in their lower courses, both in Nepal and in India, are subject to severe flooding. The **Kathmandu Valley** is drained by the **Bagmati River** which rises to the N near Tare Bir (2,732 m) and leaves the valley through the **Chhobar gorge**. By Nepalese standards it is not a great river.

The Himalayan region has many glaciers. As the W is very dry, the biggest are in the E. The largest is in the Mahalangur and Khumbakarna ranges, while the **Kangchendzonga, Yalung, Nupchu** and **Lamtang glaciers** also originate in the E Himalayas.

Most of the lakes owe their origins to glacial activity or earth movements. **Lake Rara**, in W Nepal, is the country's largest, though **Lake Phewa** is equally well known.

Natural Vegetation The natural vegetation follows the pattern of climate and altitude. Tropical moist deciduous in the **Terai** and in patches up to the Mahabharat Lekh includes *khair* (Acacia catechu), a spring flowering tree with yellow flowers, flat pods and a wood that yields commercial catechu used for dyeing and tanning; **sissoo** (Dalbergia sissoo) and **sal** (Shorea robusta). **Sissoo** provides durable timber and sal produces building timber and resin which has a variety of uses. **Sal** is a dipterocarp, a large sub-deciduous tree, seldom completely leafless, with a reddish-brown or grey bark with smooth longitudinal fissures. The timber is used commercially and is a durable building material. Its foliage provides food for lac insects which deposit lac, a resinous substance used for the manufacture of shellac and other varnishes on the tree's twigs. After processing, the seed oil is used as a substitute for cocoa butter in the chocolate industry.

Between 1,000 and 2,000 m of altitude are sparse forests of **Pinus roxburghii** (chir pine of India). There are also oaks, poplars, larches and walnuts. Between 3,050 m and 3,650 m are **rhododendron**, fir and birch.

Forests in the Terai have been devastated by clearing to make way for agriculture. In the densely populated Middle Zone rhododendrons are often restricted to solitary bushes rather than large stands. The best forest exists just below the timber line in the Great Himalaya but that too is rapidly dwindling. Juniper and woody scrub survive immediately above the tree line, with good pasture between the treeline and the snowline.

Wildlife The widest variety of wildlife is found in the Terai, including tigers, leopards, gaur, elephants, buffalo, deer (chital, sambar and swamp). The **Lesser Rapti Valley** in Chitwan district is the last home of the one-horned Great Indian Rhinoceros. Swamp and hog deer are found in the grassland, and crocodiles, Gangetic dolphins and Mahseer in the rivers.

There are few wild animals in the **central zone** because of the lack of forest and other natural vegetation. Higher up, leopards, bears and small carnivores inhabit the forests. Muntjac deer are occasionally found in the woods. Pheasant, including the Impeyan pheasant, the national bird, are common, and *mahseer* are found in the larger rivers. In the evergreen forest are Himalayan bear, barking deer, wild boar and red panda.

Even the alpine zone has been affected by man's activity. **See page 1309**. The musk deer, prized for its musk, has been hunted almost to extinction. Tahr (goats), goral (goat antelopes), wild sheep, are common and snow leopards are still found, along with Himalayan marmots and the mouse hare. The *yeti* continues to be talked of but not seen. Birds include snowcock, snow partridge, choughs, buntings and redstart.

CLIMATE

Climate in Nepal is affected dramatically by height and aspect. Subtropical monsoon conditions prevail in the Terai up to 2,100 m, cool temperate conditions up to 3,350 m, and an alpine climate above that. Above 5,000 m there is invariably snow and the day time temperature range is extreme: it can reach 35°C in the heat of the day and below freezing after sundown.

The **monsoon** lasts across the whole country from Jun to Sep, when over 75% of the annual rainfall occurs, but the amount of rainfall decreases from S to N and from E to W. Pokhara receives 2500 mm on average. The Mahabharat Lekh forces the moist monsoon airstream to rise, causing heavy rain on the hills to the S, especially the Terai. Once beyond, the High Himalaya act as a second, higher and impenetrable wall, causing more rainfall in the central valley. Beyond the Himalayan axis it is arid and similar to the Tibetan plateau, **see page 495**. Thus if you do the classic 3 week Annapurna Circuit Trek you will go from the subtropical lushness S of the mountains to the stark arid beauty to the N.

The **post-monsoon** period of Oct-Nov is characterised by settled weather, clear skies, no rain and moderately high temperatures. As winter approaches it gets cooler, especially at night. This is an ideal time for a visit. The countryside is lush and views are clear.

With winter temperatures drop further. At lower altitudes it is dry and often very dusty. Higher up it is very cold at night. There is extensive trekking over the period from Dec to Feb, but at higher altitudes you need to be well prepared with equipment. Depressions bring some rain to the lower valleys. In Spring from Feb onwards until the beginning of the monsoon, temperatures increase so that at low altitudes by May it gets extremely hot. Feb and Mar is the rhododendron flowering season, bringing vibrant colours. Visibility, however, deteriorates as it becomes increasingly hazy during the day. Dawn tends to be the best time for views.

In **Kathmandu**, the average temperatures range from 10°C in Jan to 26°C in Jul. The extremes are -3°C in Jan and 37°C in Jul. It never snows in Kathmandu. The annual rainfall is 1,500 mm. **Pokhara** is lower and warmer and more pleasant than Kathmandu in winter but hotter, more humid and less comfortable in summer. Rainfall is also higher at 2,500 mm, **see page 1319**.

THE PEOPLE

Nepal's population is 19.5 million (1991 estimate) and increasing at around 2% per annum, resulting in heavy pressure on the land. Today 60% of the farmed land is cultivated twice a year, compared with virtually none at the beginning of the 1970s. Over the last century there has been a drift of population from W to E, and a continuous flow into India. Just over 40% of the population live in the

Terai and a further 56% in the central region, with some 5% in the Kathmandu Valley. The growth rate in the Terai has been 3 times the national average. The Tharus are descended from the original inhabitants of the Terai but there is a strong affinity with the people of Uttar Pradesh and Bihar in India. Hindi and Mailthali are widely spoken in the Terai, in addition to Nepali. There are more than 6 million Nepalis living in the Indian states of Bihar, West Bengal and Assam.

Social origins The tribal groups of Tibetan origin – among the most important being the **Tamang**, **Rai**, **Limbu**, **Bhote** and **Sunwar** – are concentrated in the centre and E, while the Magar and Gurung are in the W. High caste Brahmins, Thakuris and Chettris dominate the Hindu social system. They speak Nepali, an Indo-Aryan language which uses the Devanagari script, and are closely related to the dominant communities of N India. Hindus today make up 90% of Nepal's population. On the trading route between the Gangetic Plains and China, two entirely different ethnic strains have met and mingled in this comparatively small area. Large-scale migrations of Mongoloid peoples from the Tibetan plateau have entered the country from the N, comprising 20% of the modern peoples of Nepal, whilst from the S there has been a similarly large influx of Indo-Aryan people, who make up 80%.

The Newars Of Mongolian origin, the Newars have probably been settled in the Kathmandu Valley for over 2000 years. They have absorbed many Indian characteristics, including Hinduism. Numbering about 700,000, they are concentrated in the Kathmandu Valley. The majority are now Saivite Hindus, but some are still Buddhists. Their language is Newari which although it is commonly placed in the Tibeto-Burman family, was influenced by both Tibeto-Burman and Indo-European languages. Despite losing political power in the mid 18th century, Newaris stubbornly clung to their identity, language and rituals that are an agglomeration of Hinduism, Buddhism and Animism.

Newar beliefs One age-old belief is that the goddess *Kumari* temporarily resides in the bodies of selected Newar Buddhist girls. Nearly a dozen communities have Kumaris, and each is worshipped with offerings of ornaments, food and money. Most give up this holy post on reaching puberty, although comparatively recently the Kumari of Patan retained hers till well past the age of twenty. Since her feet were literally not allowed to touch the ground, a relative carried her around.

Newari tradition holds that the Kathmandu Valley was a deep lake until the Boddhisatva **Manjusri** swung his mighty sword to create a huge cleft in the encircling mountains. See Chobar, **page 1299**, creating **Chhobar gorge**.

The Newars have traditionally been Nepal's leading traders, once organising trains of basket carrying porters over the trans-Himalayan passes to Tibet. The Newars are also remarkable craftsmen. They developed the country's unique building style that successfully blends influences from India, China and Tibet, with carved wood beams and pagoda-like temple roofs. So esteemed was Newar craftsmanship that a Newar was appointed artistic adviser to Kublai Khan. Newar merchants and craftsmen also prospered in Lhasa.

The **Indo-Nepalese** groups comprise 80% of the population and consist of the people of the Terai, the **Paharis** (Hill people) and the **Tharus**. The Indian classics suggest that the central region S of the Himalaya already had close cultural contact with the plains of India at least 2,500 years ago. There was also considerable early Buddhist influence, although the Lamaistic Buddhism that entered Nepal from the N was quite different. The Buddha's birthplace was at Lumbini, just inside Nepal's present border with India. Asoka erected one of his pillars there in the 3rd century BC. The Tharus are believed to be the descendants of some of the original inhabitants of the Terai and are distributed along the length of it. They number around 800,000 are primarily farmers and generally practise a form of Hinduism that is mixed with animist beliefs.

The **Tibeto-Nepalese** groups include the **Gurung, Magar, Rai** and **Tamang** which together have contributed the bulk of the famous **Gurkha** regiments of the British army. The *Gurung* live in the shadow of the great Annapurna Massif, and have a reputation for strength, endurance and fearlessness. As early as the 16th century they were much sought after by Indian princes and in the late 18th century formed the martial stock which created the Gurkha kingdom. Large numbers enlisted in the British army in India in the 19th century. Then the name Gurkha was applied to the people, although it is really a geographical term referring to the Gurung, who came from the fortress town of **Goraknath**. Numbering about 300,000, they have depended strongly on the military as a source of income. Gurkhas have played distinctive and gallant roles in British wars and campaigns since 1815. With 26 Victoria Crosses for gallantry and numerous other battle honours they have come to be regarded as an intrinsic and loyal element in Britain's army. Some villages derive over 75% of their income from military service and have become dependent on it. The *Magars* and *Rais* are numerically large groups, almost indistinguishable from one another and together have also enlisted into the Gurkha regiments. Most are subsistence farmers living in the Middle Zone hill country of Western and Central Nepal from the high mountain down to the Terai.

They all have markedly Mongoloid features. Each group has its own mythology. The *Tamangs* for example believe that the first mother of the Tamangs was a cow who bore 3 sons, the youngest of whom, Tolgu, founded the race. The Tamangs practise a religion which outwardly resembles Tibetan Buddhism blended with Hindu teachings but also incorporate elements of their 'old' religion based on *shamanism**. They live just beyond the Newari-Hindu cultural area of the Kathmandu valley. Whilst most are subsistence farmers, their name apparently is the Tibetan for 'horse trader' which suggests a past somewhat similar to the Sherpas. There are approximately 1 million Tamangs which makes them a sizeable minority group.

The *Thakalis* originate from the Kali Gandaki gorge and like many Nepalese groups have been subject to both Hindu and Buddhist influences. They have cashed in on the trekking boom and have established little hotels all along the Annapurna Circuit and extended their influence as hoteliers to other parts of the country. They are only about 10,000 in number and before Nepal was opened up to tourists were subsistence farmers.

The Bhotiya live in the N part of Bhutan, Sikkim, Nepal and along the Indo-Tibetan border in Garhwal, Kumaon and Himachal Pradesh. They are a Mongoloid people who gradually moved off the Tibetan plateau. They include the world renowned *Sherpas*, who immigrated from Tibet around 600 years ago. Their name tells of their origin: Sha – east, pa – people. Earlier they were traders and porters, carrying butter, meat, rice, sugar, paper and dye from India and salt, wool, jewellery, Chinese silk and porcelain from Tibet and beyond.

Sherpas live in the Solu Khumbu region of glacial valleys at the southern approaches to Everest. Their name is almost synonymous with the great peak that dominates their country. The closure of the border following the 1962 border war between India and China undermined their economy. Fortunately, with the arrival of mountaineering expeditions and trekkers, the Sherpas found their load carrying skills, both on normal treks and at high altitudes, in great demand. However, there are dangers. The Sherpas have received considerable help to st up schools and small hospitals. The Foundation is named after Edmund Hillary, the first European to reach the top of Everest, who felt he had a debt to repay the Sherpas.

The Bhotiya economy Other Bhotiya groups combine the same activities as the Sherpas: subsistence agriculture, animal husbandry and trade, the last two complementing the first which because the altitude at which they live only permits one cropping season per year. The crops grown are wheat, barley, buckwheat and potatoes, all of which are hardy. The livestock includes sheep, goats and yaks (Bos grummans). Like the Sherpas they acted as traders and middlemen. Tibetan Buddhism plays an important role in shaping Bhotiya society. The monastery is the centre of the social environment, and the prayer flags, prayer wheels, and chortens are a vital part of daily life.

The **Dholpos** from N of **Jomosom** and the **Lhopas** of the small kingdom of **Mustang** are also found on the N border. In both cases the population is no more than a few hundred.

In the **Terai** that straddles the border with India are found recent **Indian** arrivals. There are also older established groups who can claim to be Nepalese. These include the Tharus, Danuwars, Majhis and Darais who are found along most of the length of the Terai. Restricted to the E are the Bodos, Dhimals, Rajbansis and Satars. Both groups tend to be non-caste. There are also about 400,000 Muslims.

ECONOMY

The British authority on Asia, B.H. Farmer, has described Nepal's economic position very succinctly: "adherents of the dependency school of underdevelopment see Nepal as the periphery of a periphery, a dependency of India which is in turn a dependency of the world capitalist system; while within the country, the valley around Kathmandu acts as the core within a periphery of a periphery to even more peripheral and remote rural areas."

The statistics of poverty Accurate statistics are hard to come by and should be treated with caution. According to the U.N. Nepal is one of the poorest countries in the world. It is landlocked, which makes trade dependent on the goodwill of India. Soils are generally poor, fields are small, cultivation is labour intensive and the yields are low. 90% of the population is engaged in agriculture, and there is little industry. Per capita income is only US$ 170 per year, and population growth is high. Most villages are dependent on remittances to make up persistent shortfalls in crop production. Furthermore, the highly fragmented nature of the country makes communications very difficult. GDP growth for the year ending Dec 1990 was 2.0%, the foreign debt is US$ 1.4 bn and the current account deficit for the 1990 fiscal year was US$ 275 million. Inflation was 10.1%.

Agriculture The Terai, occupying 23% of the land area and containing 42% of the population, is the most productive region. It accounts for over 80% of Nepal's rice, and 65% of its wheat. Cash crops like sugar cane, jute, tobacco and tea also important. A small surplus of grain and industrial products are exported to India. Land holdings are larger than in the hills and average around 2 hectares.

The Hill region occupies 43% of the area and contains 50% of the population. The fertile Kathmandu Valley which contains 10% of the hill population and is the centre of government. Away from the valley subsistence agriculture is the norm. Elaborate terracing, the careful collection and application of animal manure as fertiliser, and a cropping pattern designed not to overtax the land cannot disguise the fact that soils are low in productivity, the opportunities for irrigation limited, and crop yields stagnant.

The mountain region occupies one third (34%) of Nepal's land, but only 8% of its people. Here pastoral nomads complements agriculture which again is subsistence oriented. Livestock contributes 25% to agricultural GDP but productivity is very low. Most hill and mountain farm households own livestock whose main contribution to human existence is through their provision of manure and draught labour. Dairy yields are very low.

Minerals and energy resources There are known deposits of coal, iron ore, pyrite, limestone and mica but these are considered too small and the investment required too large to be mined commercially. The river systems offer potential for **hydroelectric** development, but the Himalayan valleys offer a costly and dangerous environment for large-scale development.

Most industries are small, localized operations based on processing agricultural products, concentrated in the Terai. The **jute** industry is centred on Biratnagar in the E, **sugar** factories are located at Biratnagar, Birganj, Bhiarawa and Nepalganj, there is a **cigarette factory** at Janakpur, **saw mills** at Hitaura and several small **rice** and **oil mills** throughout the region. Trade with India dominates the pattern of exports. Other activities include brick and tile firing, brewing (beer) and processing forest products.

Tourism An estimated 250,000 foreign tourists visit Nepal each year. Kathmandu boasts a good range of hotels, enterprising villagers have set up **bhattis** (inns) to accommodate trekkers, and brought in Western delicacies like Coca Cola and Mars bars to places like Namche Bazaar that are miles from the nearest roadhead.

RELIGION, ART AND ARCHITECTURE

Day to day life is regulated by the religious calendar and strict codes on ritual observance. Art, architecture, sculpture, literature and drama reflect the vitality of religious belief which combines various strands of Hinduism and Buddhism.

Buddhism Historical and archaeological evidence throws little light on the religion that prevailed before the introduction of Buddhism (**see page 66**). The oldest monuments in Nepal date from the period of the Mauryan Empire in India (4th-3rd centuries BC). Asoka visited Nepal and erected one of his pillars at Lumbini, the Buddha's birthplace, and in the Kathmandu Valley he established one of the country's first stupa temples. His daughter accompanied him, married a Nepalese noble and subsequently founded temples and monasteries.

Mahayana Buddhism Hiuen Tsang testified to the vitality of Buddhism in the 7th century AD, and there were many monasteries of both the Mahayana and Hinayana sects. The pagoda-style temple, first mentioned in the 7th century T'ang Annals, was already a well-established architectural form. Hinayana Buddhism, with its emphasis on asceticism, was gradually usurped by Mahayana doctrine, **see page 76**. The favourite motifs of Mahayan art were the 5 Celestial or **Dhyani Buddhas** and **Bodhisattvas**, whose images became the centres of devotional cults. This can be seen today on a tour of Kathmandu's Durbar Square.

The construction of the 2 great stupas at **Swyambhunath** and **Bodhnath** began during this period. They exhibit features which became typical of Nepalese stupas: the low flat dome, the square top-pieces painted on all sides with the 'all-seeing' eyes of the supreme Buddha, surmounted by a 13 stepped spire symbolizing the steps of knowledge culminating in enlightenment.

Today, Tibetan Lamaistic Buddhism prevails beyond the Himalayan axis of **Dholpo**, **Mustang** and in the valleys of **Khombu** and **Langtang**. The *gompas** and *chortens**, like those in Ladakh, Zanskar, Lahul and Spiti in India, and Sikkim and Bhutan, are modelled on Tibetan institutions. Until the suppression of Buddhism in Tibet by the Chinese there was extensive contact between all these regions and the spiritual homeland. Artisans and craftsmen employed the same styles. Now that the cultural interaction has been severely restricted, the Buddhist population of Nepal must rely on its own resources.

Hinduism During the 5th century the **Licchavi kings** gained the ascendancy and promoted their Vaishnavite Hindu beliefs. Little remains from that period apart from some stone bas-reliefs. The emphasis shifted towards Siva in the 9th century and established Saivite divinities as the most important Hindu deities.

Tantrism This developed further with the absorption of eastern **Tantric** influences. The emphasis on the mystic, esoteric and the erotic as manifested in Shakti, introduced a new class of deities, particularly female, into the pantheon. Ritual blood sacrifice became popular and was incorporated into Tantric Hinduism and Vajrayana Buddhism. In the process the 2 religions, now sharing common beliefs and secret rituals, became inextricably entwined. Followers of the 2 religions worship at each others' shrines and equate their deities with those of the others' pantheon. Nevertheless, Nepal is officially a Hindu Kingdom, and within the country there are important Hindu shrines: Muktinath in the Annapurna region north of Pokhara, Goraknath on the hill above Gorkha between Kathmandu and Pokhara and Sita's supposed birthplace at Janaki in the Terai. Within the valley itself there is **Pashupatinath**, a temple complex to Siva and the reclining Vishnu at **Budhanilkantha**, see page 1292.

Hindu temples Unfortunately, few of the temples and royal palaces in the Kathmandu Valley today predate the 14th century. Most were erected in the Malla era, when 3 separate but related dynasties had capitals in **Kathmandu**, **Bhaktapur** and **Patan**. All 3 towns that lie within 15 km of one another were beautified with numerous temples and palaces in an extraordinary surge of creativity. At the heart of this were the talented Newars.

Newar wood carving The dynasties of the Kiratis and Licchavis (see below) left no great lasting cultural heritage although their religious stone sculptures indicate a strong Indian influence. The Mallas were great patrons of the arts and under them Newar craftsmen constructed many temples. Although stone and metal were commonly used for building and sculpture, it was with outstanding woodcarving that the Newar craftsmen made their most distinctive contribution to art.

Outside influence Nepalese architects and artists were among the builders of S Asia that travelled farthest. They participated in the construction of the great stupa at **Borobodur** in Java around 800 AD, and were also summoned to China as court architects in the 11th century. The towering tiers of pagoda roofs, supported by elaborately carved beams and struts, are characteristic of the cities of the Valley and represent a unique synthesis of exotic building styles.

Medieval development In the late 13th century Kathmandu was a crossroads for Indian and Chinese architectural and artistic styles. **Arniko**, a Newar architect and craftsman, was invited to Tibet as an adviser. From here he joined the court of the Ming Emperor of China before returning to the valley where he introduced the multi-tiered pagoda style which, interestingly, had its origins in the Buddhist stupa. The road to Lhasa is named after him. Other Newari artists travelled abroad, many to Tibet, where there skills were prized. The **Golden Gate of Bhaktapur** (1754), one of Nepal's most astounding pieces of art in the Tibeto-Newari style, is a product of the cultural meld. While **Bhaktapur** artisans tended to concentrate on wood as a building and decorative medium, **Patan** became a centre of metallurgy.

The unique wood carvings in the royal palaces in **Kathmandu**, **Bhaktapur** and **Patan** reveal a mixture of Buddhist, Hindu and early Animist influences. So profuse is the ornamentation of temples and palaces in the Kathmandu Valley that it is said that a true Newar cannot let a piece of wood lie without first decorating it. They developed confidence in a variety of media. The magnificent wood carvings in Bhaktapur show an ability to use highly ornamented dark coloured wood against a base of red brick.

Decline and renewal This age of brilliance passed with the decline of the Mallas in the 18th century. The Rana regime appears to have been little interested in Newari art and even tried to suppress it. The Shah dynasty has encouraged an artistic revival since the 1950s and assistance to restore monuments has been received from Germany and international agencies like UNESCO.

HISTORY

Marginal to the mainstream of South Asian history, Nepal has always been open to profoundly important influences from the S. Successive waves of Indo-Aryan settlers in the Ganga plains ultimately left their mark on later populations of Nepal, and successive political events S of the Terai had implications for the mountain regions to its N. From the birth of the Buddha in the Terai region Nepal's cultural and political history has been interwoven with that of India, and despite over one hundred years of attempted isolation from all outside influence up to the mid 20th century, Nepal has always had to come to terms with its position between the contrasting social and political systems of India and China. Geography has ensured that while it has always been the former that has been the more powerful influence, both China and Tibet have had a role in the country's social and political development. The table below sets out the chief events in Nepal's history.

Date	Kathmandu Valley	Social and economic developments
624 BC	Birth of the **Buddha** at Lumbini.	Rise of regional Kingdoms.
4th C BC	*Gopala dynasty*	
?3rd C BC	*Kirati dynasty*. Claimed Kshatriya status.	Mauryan Empire in India.
c250-880 AD	*Licchavi dynasty*. First dynasty of Indian plains origin.	Hindu Licchavi dynasty tolerant of non-Hindu practices. 462-505.
609	**Amsurvarma** takes throne after marrying king's daughter. Establishes golden period, recorded by Hiuen Tsang.	Re-opens trade routes with Tibet and China, cultural and political relations strengthened.
644 and 647	First Chinese envoy to Nepal and return visit by Nepalese to Peking.	
679	**Narendradeva** – descendant of Lichhavis – regains throne. Strengthens links with Tibet. Amsurvarma's daughter Brikuti marries Tibetan ruler and takes Buddhism to Tibet.	
879-880	**King Raghadeva** inaugurates Nepalese Era. Defeats invading army of **King Jayapita** of Kashmir.	2 centuries of instability; periodic warfare with Tibet and China.
1200	**Ari Malla** founds new dynastic line. Succeeded by 5 **Malla** and 4 **Thakuri** kings.	
1380-1422	**Jayasthiti Malla** – a great reforming king.	Codified Nepali law according to Hindu principles, re-organised caste on the 4-varna principle.
1429-1482	**Yaksa Malla**, grandson of Jayasthita Malla, divided the kingdom between his 3 sons and one daughter, creating independent principalities of **Kathmandu**, **Patan**, **Bhadgaon**, and **Lalitpur**. Subsequently reduced to 3.	Centre of Nepal was dominated by the 3 states, which controlled trade routes between the Terai and Tibet. Many small principalities to E and W, virtually all ruled by high caste Hindu families fleeing from Muslim persecution.

Date	Kathmandu Valley	Social and economic developments
1482-1767	The **second Malla period**. 9 kings in the dynasty.	Great cultural and artistic activity. Large scale irrigation and other building projects, but also intense rivalry.
1559	*Dhruva Shah*	Rajput ruler in W Central Nepal, begins to develop Gurkha power in the W.Mid-18th century.
1757-75	*Prithvi Narayan Shah*, grandson of Dhruva Shah, leads Gurkhas to victory over Mallas. Accepts surrender of Bhadgaon, Lalitpur and Kathmandu, establishing **Shah dynasty** in Nepal, moving his capital to Kathmandu. Regarded as founder of the modern state of Nepal.	Prithvi Nathan launched a series of campaigns to bring all the passes under his control. It heralded a long period of disputes with Tibet over control of the Himalayan trade routes.
1767	**East India Company** recognise Prithvi Narayan Shah.	Uneasy relations between E. India Company and Nepalese Government.
1792-1816	**British** invasions of Nepal following Bhimsen Thapa's claims to the Terai. Treaty in 1816 concluded the Second Nepalese War.	British Resident established in Kathmandu and control of most of Terai under British hands in India. Disputed territory in W returned after the Indian Mutiny in 1857, when Nepalese sided with the British.
1775-1832	Minor kings, regents and nobles competed for power.	
1806-37	**Thapa family** dominant force behind the throne.	A period of extensive feuding and conspiracies.
1846-1951	Rule by the *Rana family* with the Shah in nominal authority. For the British, Nepal (along with Bhutan and Sikkim), formed a strategic buffer between India and the Chinese, who had long claimed suzerainty over Tibet, and the Russians. Thus Curzon's 'string of pearls' became a part of "the Great Game".	Tightly enforced law code, foreigners banned from entry. This prevented surveyors discovering that Everest was the world's highest mountain. All mountaineering expeditions before 1951 approached the mountain from the Tibetan side. **Jang Bahadur** the first Rana "Prime Minister". **Bir Shumshere** founded Bir Library of ancient manuscripts (1885-1901) and several other institutions; **Chandra Shumshere** (1901-29) built the Raxaul-Amlekghanj light railway, a ropeway, a canal and other engineering projects.
1951-1991	Rana rule ended; King **Tribhuvan Bir Bikram Shah** (d 1959) installed, reinstating the line of Prithvi Narayan Shah. Followed by *King Mahendra* (1955-1972), who promulgated a constitutional monarchy in 1959.	The 1962 constitution adopted a partyless panchayat democracy, ended by King Birendra (1972-) in 1990 with a return to party-based elections after extensive rioting and demonstrations.

Political developments since 1979 King Mahendra was succeeded by his western-educated son **Birendra** in 1972. Until 1979 he was able to rule the 'non-party' political system and sought to encourage national economic growth. But, by 1979 a crisis was evident, and King Birendra announced that a referendum would be held to decide between a non-party and multi-party (parliamentary) political system. A general amnesty was extended to all political workers within and outside the country and 160 political prisoners were freed. The result of this was 55% support for the non party system. This relatively small mandate suggested troubles to come.

A period of reform King Birendra introduced 3 important reforms: universal adult franchise to elect the lowest tiers (village and town) of government; the Prime Minister was to be chosen by the elected members of the Rastriya (National) Panchayat, and the government was made more accountable to the public through the national legislature.

Unity among the opposition parties emerged in 1989 when the outlawed National Congress party was joined by other banned organizations to celebrate 'National Awakening Week', to mark the anniversary of the birth of its late leader, **Biseswore Prasad Koirala**. Widespread demonstrations followed as the opposition groups demanded the dissolution of the panchayat system and the restoration of the former short-lived multi-party system. Poor national economic performance, high inflation and unemployment fanned the flames of discontent.

After enormous political pressure, on April 9, 1990, the King announced that he was lifting the ban on political parties. Elections were to be held in the spring of 1991. He also announced his willingness to accept the role of constitutional monarch. The election saw the Nepali Congress win 110 of the 205 seats. The Communist Party of Nepal won 69 seats, mainly in the Kathmandu Valley. G.P. Koirala was elected Prime Minister.

KATHMANDU

Introduction, 1277; **Durbar Square**, 1280; **Makhan Tole**, 1281; **The Taleju Temple and Hanuman Dhoka**, 1282; **Nasal Chowk**, 1282; **NE from Durbar Square**, 1283; **Swayambhunath**, 1284; **Services**, 1286; **Short excursions from Kathmandu**, 1291; **Patan**, 1293; **Bhaktapur**, 1296; **Longer excursions from Kathmandu**, 1299; **Royal Chitwan National Park**, 1300.

INTRODUCTION

Population 250,000 approx. *Altitude* 1,370 m *Best time* mid-Sep to Nov and Feb-Apr.

	Jan	Feb	Mar	Apr	May	Jun	Jul	Aug	Sep	Oct	Nov	Dec	Av/Tot
Max (°C)	15	18	25	28	33	30	30	30	31	25	19	14	23
Min (°C)	6	8	14	17	22	23	23	21	20	14	10	7	13
Rain (mm)	40	41	30	46	106	228	361	356	153	46	41	3	1451

(Unofficial figures)

Occupying only 5% of Nepal's area and with 7% of its population, the Kathmandu Valley is the cultural and political heart of the country. After Nepal's long period of isolation Kathmandu has become the centre of the country's tourist industry, its most important source of foreign exchange. The airport at Kathmandu provides an international link with Bangkok, Calcutta and New Delhi and other foreign cities. The first surfaced road to reach Kathmandu, that from Raxaul Bazar, was only completed in 1956. Now it also has direct connections with E Uttar Pradesh, Lhasa in Tibet and Pokhara to its W.

Early history Kathmandu was founded in 723 AD by the Licchavi king Gunakamadeva at the confluence of the **Bagmati** and **Bishnumati** Rivers. The hub of the city is the area around the oldest building, the **Kastha** ("wood") **mandap** ("temple"), which stood at the crossroads of 2 important trade routes. When the Valley was unified in the 14th century by **Jayasthiti Malla**, Kathmandu became the administrative centre and this sparked off an expansion that was sustained over many years.

European influences In the 19th century as a result of the Ranas' travels overseas, new European styles were introduced. The palaces that Jung Bahadur built from 1850 onwards were European in concept and contrasted sharply with the indigenous Newari style. **Singha Durbar**, a palace of gigantic proportions, was built within a year (1901). It comprised 17 courtyards and over 1,500 rooms. Reputed to have been the largest contemporary building in Asia, it was severely damaged by fire in 1974. Under the Ranas other palaces were built at **Patan** and **Kathmandu** but with the return of the monarchy these became neglected. Many are now used as offices.

There are 2 distinct areas of Kathmandu. The **Old City** is between the **Kantipath** (King's Way), which runs NS, and the **Bishnumati** river. Immediately E of the Kantipath is the **Tundhikhel**, a long parade ground, with the **New City** beyond. At its S end the highway crosses the Bagmati river to Patan. Today, although the river separates the 2 cities they have merged imperceptibly in the urban sprawl.

After the earthquake of 1934 **New Rd**, (**Juddha Sadak**) was constructed from **Tundhikhel** W to **Durbar Sq**. Today New Rd is the city's commercial axis, with shops selling everything from the latest imported Japanese gadgets, to 'antiques'. The old trade route from Tibet cuts diagonally across the northern half of the Old City running in a NE-SW direction through the Durbar Sq.

Local Festivals See Introduction for details. Many are celebrated in the area but some are of particular importance. Feb – *Basanta Panchami* at Hanuman Dhoka Palace. Tibetan New Year at Bodhnath. *Sivaratri* at Pashupatinath. Mar-Apr. *Ghorajatra.* May – *Buddha Jayanti* at Swayambhunath and Bodhnath. Jun-Jul – *Tribhuvan Jayanti* at Tripureswar. Aug – *Gaijatra. Pancha Dan* at Swayambhunath. Sep – *Indrajatra. Teej* at Pashupatinath. Oct -*Bada Dasain.* Govt Offices remain closed for a week. City is very busy and crowded. Accommodation and transport difficult. Nov – *Tihar. Ekadasi* at Budhanilakantha and Pashupatinath. Dec – *Bala Chaturdasi* at Pashupatinath.

PLACES OF INTEREST

Note The description starts at the oldest building in Kathmandu, the Kashtamandap, in the SW corner of the Durbar Square, and moves NE, broadly following the line of the old Tibet trade road. The figures in brackets refer to the numbers on the map.

Durbar Square

The spiritual heart of Kathmandu. The old royal palace was at the centre of the city and was surrounded by temples and other important buildings. Many of the

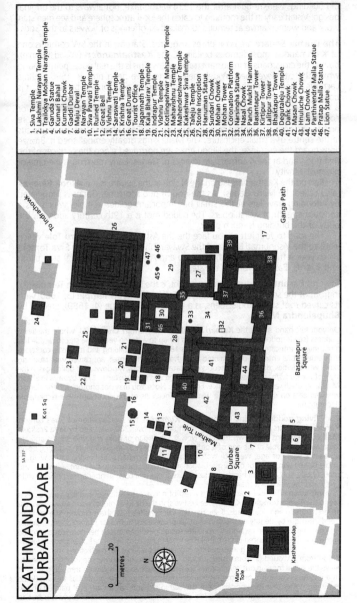

KATHMANDU DURBAR SQUARE

SA 357

1. Siva Temple
2. Lakshmi Narayan Temple
3. Trailokya Mohan Narayan Temple
4. Garuda Statue
5. Kumari Bahal
6. Kumari Chowk
7. Gaddi Durbar
8. Maju Deval
9. Narayan Temple
10. Siva Parvati Temple
11. Ruined Temple
12. Great Bell
13. Vishnu Temple
14. Saraswati Temple
15. Krishna Temple
16. Great Drums
17. Tourist Office
18. Jagannath Temple
19. Kala Bhairav Temple
20. Indrapur Temple
21. Vishnu Temple
22. Kotlingeshwar Mahadev Temple
23. Mahavishnu Temple
24. Mahendreshwar Temple
25. Kakeshwar Siva Temple
26. Taleju Temple
27. Stone Inscription
28. Hanuman Statue
29. Sundari Chowk
30. Mohan Chowk
31. Mohan Tower
32. Coronation Platform
33. Narsingha Statue
34. Nasal Chowk
35. Panch Mukhi Hanuman
36. Basantapur Tower
37. Kirtipur Tower
38. Bhaktapur Tower
39. Degutaleju Temple
40. Dafik Chowk
41. Masan Chowk
42. Hnuluche Chowk
43. Lam Chowk
44. Parthivendra Malla Statue
45. Pratap Malla Statue
46. Lion Statue
47. Lion Statue

old buildings were re-built after the 1934 earthquake, not always to the original design. Visit it early in the morning to catch the local atmosphere and see men start work and women arrive at temples to make their offerings of flowers to the Gods.

The Durbar Square area comprises 3 squares. Starting in the SW corner is one of Kathmandu's most famous buildings, the **Kasthamandap** (Wood temple), built at the crossroads of important trade routes. This is the real nodal point around which the city developed. Widely believed to have been built in 1596 by Raja Lachmina Singh from the wood of one enormous sal (shorea robusta) tree, it is now known to be much earlier, as references to the temple have been found in a manuscript dating from the 11th century. It was originally a rest house or community centre and so has an open ground floor. Later it was made more ornate and converted into a temple dedicated to **Gorakhnath**, whose shrine sits in the centre of a small enclosure. The Malla kings greatly embellished it. Bronze lions guard the entrance, the Hindu epics are portrayed along the cornices of the first floor, and at the 4 corners are images of Ganes. Early morning is the time of greatest activity.

Behind the Kasthamandap on the N side of the square is the **Ashok Binayak** (also called the Maru Ganes). As the god of good fortune, Ganes is propitiated by intending travellers at this small but important golden temple, which has a constant stream of worshippers. The gilded roof is a 19th century addition, the body of the building is much older.

The road to your left as you face the the Ashok Binayak is **Maru Tole** which leads to the Vishnumati River and the Swayambhunath temple. The **Siva Temple** (1) to your left between Kasthamandap and Ashok Binayak has a 9 step plinth and 3 roofs. Barbers work on the steps.

Towards **Basantpur square**, on your right, is the **Lakshmi Narayan Temple** (2). In front of the small 5 tiered **Trailokya Mohan Narayan Temple** (3; 1680) with its carved roof struts and screens, is a fine **Garuda** Statue (4; 1689), erected by **Bhupalendra Malla**.

On your left hand side is the **Kumari Bahal** (5) and **Kumari Chowk** (6), where the living goddess (see Introduction and below) resides for up to a dozen years. The stucco facade has a number of intricately carved windows. This 18th century building and monastic courtyard is guarded at its entrance by 2 painted lions. Note how the lintels are carved with laughing skulls while deities, doves and peacocks decorate the balcony windows. The building is in the style of the Buddhist monasteries of the valley, and was constructed in 1757 by **Jaya Prakash Malla**, reputedly as an act of penance. Entry Re 1. **Note** You may not photograph the Kumari who appears on cue at one of the windows. The walls of the courtyard have remarkable decoration.

The "living goddess" Hindus worship the **Kumari** as the reincarnation of Siva's consort **Parvati**, Buddhists as **Tara**. The cult was instituted just over 200 years ago by **Jaya Prakash Malla**. All Kumaris are drawn from the Newar Sakya clan of gold and silversmiths and are initiated into the role at the age of 4 or 5. They must meet 32 requirements, including being at least 2 years of age, weaned, walking, a virgin, in immaculate health, and having an unblemished skin, black or blue eyes, black hair with curls turning to the right, a flawless and robust body, soft and firm hands, eye lashes like those of a cow, slender arms, brilliant white teeth and the voice of a sparrow.

Initiation The final examination is a test of nerve. A selection of suitable candidates is led to the **Taleju temple** at *Kalratri* (see Festivals) in the dead of night and must walk amidst severed buffalo and goat heads. If she remains calm and fearless, she is chosen. She confirms her divine right by identifying the clothes of her predecessor from a large assortment of similar articles. The installation ceremony is private. Astrologers then match her horoscope with the king's and she is ensconced in the bahal. The royal family consult her before important festive occasions. The bahal is her home until she menstruates or loses her perfection through losing blood from a wound or from losing a tooth. To maintain her purity, she is only allowed to leave the bahal for religious ceremonies (see Festivals) when she is carried through the street in a palanquin or walks on cloth, as her feet must not touch the ground as this would be polluting. Whenever she appears she is dressed in red and has a third eye' painted on her forehead. When her reign ends, she leaves the temple with a handsome dowry, is free to marry and live a normal life. Nowadays she is taught to read and write to prepare her for the ordinary life to come.

To the N of the Kumari Bahal is the **Gaddi Baithak, or Gaddi Darbar** (7), a white neo-classical building built in 1908 by Maharaja Chandra Shumshere. This Rana palace sits uncomfortably with the indigenous Nepalese buildings.

Diagonally across Durbar Sq to your left is *Maju Deval* (8), a 3 storeyed pagoda temple dedicated to Siva, built by the mother of Bhupalendra Malla in 1692. The 9 step plinth is a popular meeting place. The eaves of the 3 roofs are adorned with erotic carvings.

Behind Maju Deval is a small **Narayan Temple** (9) and to its right is the **Siva Parvati Temple** (10). From the centre window of the upper balcony the carved and painted deities look down on the proceeding belows. The platform on which this 18th century temple stands may have been a much older dancing stage.

Makhan Tole

You are now at the SW end of **Makhan Tole** (House St). Opposite is the **Bhagwati Temple** (11), a triple storeyed, triple roofed temple with golden roofs on the top 2 storeys. Built in the first quarter of the 18th century by **Jagat Jaya Malla** this originally had a Narayan image but this was stolen in 1766. When the Gurkha **Prithvi Narayan Shah** conquered the valley in 1767 an image of Bhagwati was installed. Each year it is taken to the village of Nuwakot, 57 km to the N, for a festival.

Proceeding up Makhan Tole on your left is the **Great Bell** (12) which was installed by Bahadur Shah in 1797 and is rung when there is puja (worship) at **Degutaleju Temple**. The **Great Drums** (16) which also mark worship at the temple, are at the top of Makhan Tole where it leads into the northern part of Durbar Sq. Twice a year a goat and buffalo are sacrificed near them. Adjacent is a small **Stone Vishnu Temple** (13) which was badly damaged in the 1934 earthquake and has only recently been restored. Next door is the **Saraswati Temple** (14) which was also affected. The **Krishna Temple** (15; 1648) was built by Pratap Malla, some believe as a reply to the impressive **Krishna Mandir** (temple) in Patan. This is one of the few octagonal temples in Kathmandu.

King **Pratap Malla's column** (17) stands near the corner to the SE on a platform it shares with a number of small temples. The king who was responsible for many of the surrounding structures is joined on his perch by his 2 wives and sons and faces his prayer room on the third floor of the Degutaleju Temple.

The 17th century **Jagannath Temple** (18) behind the column is the oldest structure in this group of buildings and is noted for its erotic carvings at head level. The temple stands on a platform and has doors on each side. Only the centre door is used.

Behind and forming the southern side of the upper square is **Kala Bhairav** (19), a fearsome looking sculpture of Siva the destroyer carved out of a single stone. The 6-armed, black god wears a crown and has a garland of skulls. He carries a sword, a severed head, hatchet, shield and a skull (which has become a bowl for devotees' offerings) and is stamping on a corpse. The image was brought to its present location by Pratap Malla in the second half of the 17th century after being found in a field to the N of the city. Some believe that a lie told before the god is punished with instant death.

The **Indrapur Temple** (20) next to it has a lingam inside suggesting that it is a Siva temple but there is also a Garuda image to the S suggesting that it may be a Vishnu temple. The adjacent **Vishnu Temple** (21) is thought to have been in existence in Pratap Malla's reign (1641-74).

The **Kotlingeshwar Mahadev Temple** (22) differs from the other surrounding temples in that is in the 16th century Gumbhaj style and is a cube with a bulbous dome. There is a certain similarity with the early Muslim tombs in India but the temple is dedicated to Siva and there is a Nandi Bull facing it.

The **Mahavishnu Temple** (23) nearby was built by Jaya Jagat Malla in the early 18th century and was one of the buildings affected by the 1934 earthquake. It is another Siva temple and the shikhara (spire) is topped by a golden umbrella indicating royalty.

Just off the northwestern corner of Durbar Sq is the **Kot Square.** In 1846 Jung Bahadur Rana, the founder of the Rana dynasty, murdered all his potential opponents from the local nobility before seizing power. During the Durga Puja each year, young soldiers attempt to cut off the head of a buffalo with a single stroke of their *kukri*. The 16th century **Mahendreshwar Temple** (24) dedicated to Siva stands just beyond Kot Sq and Durbar Sq.

The Taleju Temple And Hanuman Dhoka

Turning round and looking to the E you will see the **Kakeshwar Siva Temple** (25) and behind it the famous **Taleju Temple** (26) which is in Trisul Chowk (named after the trident of Siva in front of the temple). This magnificent temple is closed to the public except during the Durga Puja festival, when Hindus may enter. Only the Royal family and important priests are allowed regular access. It was built in 1564 by Mahendra Malla. The rulers of Bhaktapur and Patan followed suit and established their own Taleju temples by their palaces. The ornately carved beams and brackets and the decoration around the windows is superb, and the extensive use of gilt makes it an even more attractive sight at sunset. The temple stands on a 12 stage plinth and is 36 m high, soaring above the **Hanuman Dhoka** complex. There are 12 miniature temples outside the wall built on the eighth stage.

Nearby, on the outside of the palace wall is a **Stone Inscription** (27) in 15 languages including French and English, which is in praise of the goddess **Kalika**. It was carved on 14 Jan 1664 during the reign of **Pratap Malla**, a talented poet and linguist.

The Hanuman Dhoka The Royal Palace, takes its name from the **Hanuman Statue** (28; 1672) at the entrance, installed by Pratap Malla. The monkey god is wrapped in a red cloak, his face is smeared with a mixture of red vermilion powder and mustard oil, and has a golden umbrella above. Hanuman is one of the heroes of the Hindu epic the Ramayana and is worshipped to bring success in war. The site apparently dates back to the late Licchavi era. Mahendra Malla started the present buildings in the 16th century, and the 17th century king Pratap Malla added many temples. The S wing was added by Prithvi Narayan Shah in 1771, and the SW wing by King Rithvi Bikram Shah in 1908. Open 1030-1600. Rs 10.

The 'Golden' palace gate is brightly painted in green, blue and gold and is flanked by 2 stone lions, the one on the left carrying Siva, the right bearing his consort Parvati. In the niche above the gate is Krishna in his ferocious Tantric aspect, flanked on one hand by the more gentle, amorous Krishna and his gopis (cowgirls), and on the other by **King Pratap Malla** and his queen. The King was believed to be an incarnation of Vishnu.

In the W wing of Hanuman Dhoka is the **Tribhuvan Museum** (46) dedicated to the king who led a revolt against the Ranas who had built it. The king's bedroom and study have been recreated. See also under Museums.

Nasal Chowk

The entrance is through the Golden Door (*Suvarnaduar*) which leads to the **Nasal Chowk**, the largest of the 10 palace courtyards, where coronations take place. This with the **Sundari Chowk** (29), **Mohan Chowk** (30) and **Mohan Tower** (31) was originally built by Pratap Malla in the 17th century. The **Sundhara,** or golden waterspout, is of special interest. In the 17th century Pratap Malla brought cool clear water from Bodhanikanta, 8 km N and built the elaborately decorated spout 3.5 m below the surface where the king bathed.

The present king Birendra was crowned on the **Coronation Platform** (32) in the centre. Nasal means 'the dancing one' and takes its name from the small figure of a dancing Siva on the eastern side of the square. To the left of the entrance to the square is the silver-inlaid stone **Narsingha Statue** (33; 1673), of Vishnu in his man-lion incarnation, killing the demon Hiranyakashipa. The open verandah houses the throne and portraits of the Shah Kings.

In the NE corner of the square is the **Panch Mukhi Hanuman** (35), a round 5 storeyed building. Only the priests of the temple are allowed in to worship at the Hanuman shrine.

You can climb to the top of the later **Basantapur Tower** (36; 18th century) or Kathmandu Tower, that overlooks the square. It is the 9 storey palace in the SW corner of Basantpur Chowk, with beautiful wooden windows and fine carvings on the roof struts. Prithvi Narayan Shah renovated many of the earlier buildings and from 1768 onwards extended the palace to the E. This work included the smaller towers of **Kirtipur** (37) to the NW with its superb copper roof, **Lalitpur** (38) to the SE and **Bhaktapur** (39) to the NE. It once overlooked beautiful gardens with a clear view of the Taleju Temple, all set round the **Lohan Chowk** (40). The 4 towers represent the 4 ancient cities. He introduced the fortified tower to Durbar Square.

The area W of the Nasal Chowk was constructed in the latter half of the 19th century. This includes the **Dahk Chowk** (41), **Masan Chowk** (42), **Hnuluche Chowk** (43) and **Lam Chowk** (44). The **Degutaleju Temple** (45) dedicated to the Mallas' personal goddess was erected by Siva Singh Malla (r1578-1620).

Running S from Basantapur Chowk, is Jhochne (Freak St) where cheap hotels, restaurants, and hashish shops made it a centre for hippies in the 1960s. It is now just a tourist attraction. Thamel and Chhetrapati have taken over as the centres for backpackers. Chhetrapati is also interesting as the neighbourhood of local brass bandsmen who are in demand during local festivals and Nepalese weddings, especially in Feb.

North East From Durbar Square

If you retrace your steps back to the NE corner of Durbar Square you can walk along the **Makhan Tole** to **Indra Chowk**, **Asan Tole** and the **Rani Pokhari Tank**. The street is the old artery of the city. On your left in the corner of the square is a Garuda Statue. Makhan Tole (*makhan** = butter) was the start of the trade route to Tibet and is lined with interesting temples and shops. After the earthquake, New Rd was diverting much of its traffic. There are medieval houses with colourful facades, overhanging carved wooden balconies and carved windows. Many of the shops sell thangkas, clothes and paintings.

Indra chowk The first square is **Indra Chowk** which is at the intersection of Makhan Tole and **Shukra Path**. In its SW corner is a small brass Ganes shrine. On the W side of the square is the **Akash Bhairab Temple** contains a silver image of the rain god which is displayed outside for a week during *Indra Jatra* – see Festivals. Non-Hindus are not allowed in. The square was a textile market and many shops still specialise in blankets, shawls and cloth.

In the NE corner is a Siva Temple as the street runs towards **Khel Tole**, another market square with Tibetan carpet shops. Off to the W past a small shrine, smeared with fresh blood, is the **Seto Machhendranath**, one of the most venerated shrines in Kathmandu and equally popular with Buddhists and Hindus alike. It has a two-tier bronze roof and 2 brass lions guard the entrance.

The courtyard is filled with small shrines, carved pillars and statues. The image inside the elaborately carved shrine is that of **Padmapani Avalokiteshwara**, a compassionate and benevolent divinity known as Machhendra. There is a colourful procession of the **White** (Seto) god around town during the festival in Mar/Apr. The temple next door on the left is the **Lunchun Lumbun Ajima,** a Shakti Tantric temple with erotic carvings.

Leave **Khel Tole** and continue walking NE until you reach the next square which is Asan Tole. Three temples, to Annapurna, Ganes and Narayan line the square which is regarded as the heart of the Old City. The rice market is here and bicycle and rickshaw repair shops. Continuing you reach Kantipath and the tank of **Rani Pokhari** (1667) built by the wife of Pratap Malla in memory of her son. Except on Diwali the area is locked.

Swayambhunath

The stupa at *Swayambhunath* (Swayambhu), the most important site of Buddhist worship in Nepal, is situated on the top of the Padmachala Hill, 175 m above the valley, 3 km to the W of the city, where the legendary **Manjushri** is believed to have discovered the lotus of the valley.

The shrine was probably established over 2,000 years ago. A pre-Buddhist shrine in the form of a projecting stone was probably used as the central point of the stupa. An inscription dated 450 AD reveals that **King Manadeva I** undertook construction work on the site. By 1234 Swayambhunath was an important centre of Buddhism learning and was closely linked with Lhasa. In the 14th century Muslim troops from Bengal ravaged the shrine but it was rebuilt and subsequently modified and renovated by Pratap Malla in the 17th century. Access from Kathmandu was improved with the construction of a long stairway and a bridge across the Bishnumati River. Pratap Malla also added 2 new temple spires (shikharas) and a large vajra (thunderbolt) in front of the stupa.

The Eastern Stairway Today there is a road to the complex, but a more impressive means of reaching it is by the nearly 400 stone steps built by Pratap Malla. At the bottom are 3 painted images erected by him in 1637 by Pratap Malla and his father – the "three jewel" images. A large footprint in the stone, is said to have been either the Buddha's or Manjushri's. At regular intervals are pairs of eagles, lions, horses and peacocks, the vehicles of the Dhyani Buddhas.

Warning Monkeys that crowd round the temple can attack, given any encouragement: treat with caution.

On entering the compound the first thing you will see is the Great Thunderbolt (*Dorje* in Tibetan, *Vajra* in Sanskrit), symbolizing male strength. It is accompanied by a bell which signifies female wisdom. Around the pedestal are animals from the Tibetan calendar (snake, horse, sheep, monkey, goose, dog, pig, rat, bull, tiger, hare and dragon).

The stupa, 20 m in diameter and 10 m high, was a model for subsequent stupas in the country. Each section has a symbolic meaning. The white hemispherical mound represents the 4 elements **earth, water, wind** and **fire**. Each side of the square stone capital has the eyes of the Buddha, gazing compassionately from beneath heavy black eyebrows, fringed by a curtain of green, gold and red material. The 13 steps of knowledge and enlightenment to Nirvana are symbolised by the crowning umbrella. The all-seeing 'third' eye is the sign of true wisdom, and below it, the nose is in the form of a figure one in Nepali.

The contrast with the Buddhist stupa at Sanchi, **see page 317,** is striking. At the 4 cardinal points of the stupa there are 4 richly decorated niches housing the **Dhyani Buddhas** in different meditational poses. A fifth Dhyani Buddha is in an attached niche facing the stairway and is flanked by 2 monks. Around the stupa prayer wheels are turned by the faithful as they walk clockwise round the shrine.

The thunderbolt at the top of the stairs is flanked by the 2 white shikhara temples Pratap Malla constructed in 1646. On the opposite side of the stupa to the *dorje* is a monastery (Daily service at 1600 hrs). The service is conducted to the sound of trumpets and the long Tibetan horn. Inside the gompa is a huge prayerwheel whilst to the side is the International Buddhist Library. Next to this is a path leading to a guesthouse for pilgrims. This has an open pavilion style ground floor and gompa above it. The temple to the right is to **Harti**, the Hindu goddess of smallpox. On a neighbouring hill is another stupa dedicated to **Sarasvati**, the goddess of wisdom and learning.

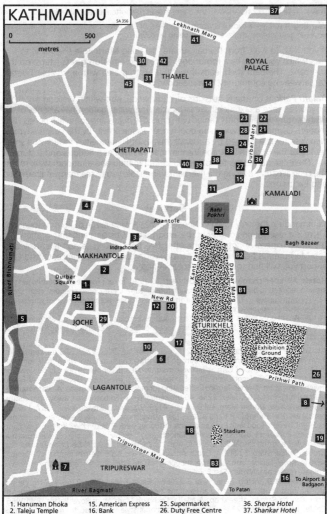

KATHMANDU

SA 356

0 — 500
metres

1. Hanuman Dhoka
2. Taleju Temple
3. Seto Machhendranath
4. Raktakali Temple
5. Bhimsen Temple
6. Bhimsen Tower
7. Siva Temples
8. Singha Durbar
9. British Council
10. Geothe Institute
11. National Theatre
12. American Library
13. French Centre
14. Library

15. American Express
16. Bank
17. GPO
18. Central Telegraph Office
19. National Archives
20. RNAC
21. PIA & Dragonair
22. Indian Airlines
23. Biman Airlines & Singapore Airlines
24. Lufthansa & Thai Airways

25. Supermarket
26. Duty Free Centre
27. Nirula's Restaurant
28. Ghar-e-Kabab & Kushi Fuji Restaurants
29. Jasmine & New Mandarin Restaurants
30. Rumdoodle
31. K.C.'s Restaurant
32. German Bakery
33. *Annapurna Hotel*
34. *Crystal Hotel*
35. *Yak & Yeti*

36. *Sherpa Hotel*
37. *Shankar Hotel*
38. *Yellow Pagoda*
39. *Hotel Nook*
40. *Hotel Siddharth*
41. *Hotel Malla*
42. *Hotel Dreamland*
43. *Kathmandu Guest House*
B1 To Bodhnath, Pashupatinath & Kirtipur
B2 To Bhaktpur
B3 Trolleybus To Bhaktpur

Travel Take a taxi or rickshaw to the S entrance at the bottom of the hill.

Warning If you hire a cycle it is worth paying Re 1 or 2 to have 'minded' by one of the small boys hanging around: this avoids tyres being let down.

If you wish to walk from Durbar Square, go along **Maru Tole** (Pie Alley) to the river which you cross by a footbridge. There are **cremation ghats** (steps) on the riverbank. The path then leads through a built up area with a sizeable Tibetan carpetweaving community, to a meadow.

Balaju Park is on the N outskirts of Kathmandu, also within walking distance, or you can take a taxi, rickshaw or bicycle. The water garden has a series of 22 18th century water spouts carved with crocodile heads and some fish ponds. The modern Olympic size swimming pool is open to the public. By the tank is a typical Nepalese temple flanked by a row of images of Hindu deities including a small replica of the Budhanilakantha Vishnu image as well as a Buddha and a stupa.

There are numerous temples around Kathmandu and a random walk round the central part and along the riverbank will enable you to see many of them. See also Excursions.

Services

Kathmandu is the only town in Nepal that has a wide range of accommodation. There is a reservation counter at the airport, after Customs and Immigration, for the more expensive hotels. Many offer free transfers. In season (Oct-Nov and Feb-Mar) there is heavy demand, so it is worth booking in advance. Outside the airport you will find touts for the cheaper hotels.

Hotels All hotels charge a Govt tax (between 10-15%). Except for the cheapest hotels you are also required to pay your bills either with foreign currency (travellers cheques, cash, credit card) or with Rupees so long as you have an official exchange receipt (given when you change money at any recognised exchange).

All **A** category hotels have restaurants, coffee shop, bar, exchange, travel counter, car hire and most have shops and a swimming pool. Most hotels offer to store baggage for those going on a trek.

AL *Soaltee Oberoi*, Tahachal, T 221211, Cable: Soaltee, Telex: 2203. 300 rm, central a/c. 5 km centre. Country's only Casino, mini golf, courtesy coach to town. *Himalchuli*, for good Indian and Nepalese food with attractive carved wooden decor but service can be slow. For dinner *Gurkha Grill*, French and other European cuisine, live music. Good Italian *Al Fresco* taverna restaurant. *Garden Terrace* Coffee shop for quick Continental meals. **A** *Kathmandu*, Maharajgunj, T 412103, Telex: 2256. 40 rm, central a/c. In Embassy area, away from centre. **A** *Yak and Yeti*, Durbar Marg, Lal Durbar, T 413999, Cable: Yaknyeti, Telex: 2237. 110 rm, central a/c. Part sumptuous Rana palace, fine woodcarving. *Chimney Restaurant* for dinner. Excellent western food with Russian origins, including, paté, Chicken Kiev, Bortsch. Live band at *Sunrise Room* for Indian, Continental, Tandoori, slimmers platter. Nepalese/Indian in palatial *Naachghar* and the casual *Sunrise Café* with superb garden view. **A** *De l'Annapurna*, (Taj Group), Durbar Marg, T 221711, Cable: Annapurna, Telex: 2205. 140 rm, central a/c. Central, next to Royal Palace with exclusive shopping arcade and cultural centre. *Arniko Room*, Chinese restaurant, *Nirula's* Fast Food.

A *Everest Sheraton*, Baneshwor. T 220567, Cable: Malari, Telex: 2260. 162 rm, central a/c. Business centre and Disco. *Far Pavilions* Restaurant has excellent views from seventh floor. *Pancha Ratna* Coffee shop. **A** *Malla*, Lekhnath Marg, W of Royal Palace, T 410966, Cable: Mallotel, Telex: 2238. 75 rm. In traditional style with peaceful garden. Cultural shows. *Mountain City* serves good Szechuan dishes. **A** *Shanker*, Lazimpath, T 410 151, Telex: 2230. 100 rm. 2 km centre. Converted Rana Palace with large garden. *Kailash* offers Indian, Nepalese and Russian dishes. **A** *Shangrila*, Lazimpath, Embassy area, T 410 466, 410 054, Telex: 2276. 50 rm. Tibetan style decor, cultural programmes, interesting library. **A** *Blue Star*, Tripureswar, T 211470, Telex: 2322. 100 rm. Southern edge of city close to Patan bridge. Business centre and Bluebird Dept store next door. **A** *Dwarika's*, Kathmandu Village, Putalisadak. T 412328, Cable: Kathmandap, Telex: 2339. 31 rm. Makes much use of traditional Newar carving. Recently won a Heritage Award from the Pacific Asia Travel Assoc for cultural sensitivity. **A** *Hotel Sherpa*, Durbar Marg, T 222585, Cable: Hotel Sherpa, Telex: 2636 Sherpa, Fax: 977(1)222 026. 96 rm. Some fine traditional brass and woodwork, rooftop terrace garden.

B *Crystal*, 5/694 Shukrapath, corner of New Rd, nr Durbar Sq. T 223397. 55 rm. Car hire, roof garden. Good views of town from roof terrace and convenient for temple visits. *The Other Room* Indian and Continental Restaurant. **B** *Woodlands*, Durbar Marg, T 220123, Cable: Woodlands, Telex: 2282. 71 rm. Restaurant, bar, car hire. **B** *Yellow Pagoda*, Kantipath, T 220392, Telex: 2268. 51 rm. Restaurants, roof garden, central.

C *Ambassador*, Lazimpath, close to Durbar Marg, T 410432. Good restaurant, bar, travel and garden. **C** *Gautam*, Jyatha, Kantipath, T 215014. Excellent *Kabab Corner*, Tandoori dishes recommended. **D** *Nook*, Jyatha. T 213627, Cable: Nook. 24 rm. Restaurant, small garden, central but noisy. **D** *Tushita*, Kantipath. T 216913. Rm with bath. Restaurant, Palpasa Art Gallery, garden. **D** *Manaslu*, Lazimpat, T 413470. Converted Rana palace in quiet area. **D** *Mt Makulu*, 65 Dharmapath. T 214616, Cable: MontMakalu. 30 rm. Breakfast included. Central, clean, top floor rm cheaper. **E** *Kathmandu Lodge*, Pyaphal Tole, off Durbar Sq. T 214893. Some rm with bath.

Cheaper Accommodation There are numerous inexpensive hotels and guesthouses in **Thamel** and **Chhetrapati** in the N part of the city, about 15 min walk from Durbar Square. Along *Jhochne*, made popular by the hippies, there are cheap lodges and guesthouses in **E** and **F** categories with fairly basic rooms and few facilities. Rooms nr the top of the building may have views. Heating is nonexistent or minimal, so a sleeping bag is necessary in winter. Many have rooftop terraces.

The **D** *Kathmandu Guest House*, nr W end of Tridevi Marg, is the point of reference. T 413632, Telex: 2321, Cable: Kathouse, Fax: 977 1-417133. 80 rm. Very popular with overland groups. Restaurant, car park, overseas telephone office, travel, art gallery, pleasant small garden. Smoking prohibited. S/D with bathroom, cheaper with just washbasin. Excellent value. Their Maya card allows discounts at restaurants and hotels elsewhere. Around it are a number of more modest, cheaper establishments: **D** *Hotel Garuda*, T 416340. Good rooms and view. **E** *Shakti* in a garden setting and **E** *Holy Lodge*, are quiet and pleasant; **E** *Earth House Lodge*, T 410500 and **E** *Hotel Asia*, Thamel, T 216541 are in Nepalese homes. Friendly. In Chhhetrapati **E** *Shambala Guest House*, T 212524, 225986. Some rm with bath. Tibetan run, roof garden, attractive views.

In **Bhote Bahal**: **D** *Sayapatri*, T 223398. Breakfast included. Pleasant garden. **D** *Janak*. Large rm. Restaurant, breakfast included, car and bicycle hire. **E** *Hotel Valley View*, Teku, T 216771. Rm with bath. Parking, terrace, clean.

Youth Hostel See under Patan below.

Further away from the centre on the rd from **Thamel** to **Swayambunath** is **C** *Vajra*, Bijeshwari, T 224719, Telex: 2309. Restaurant, bar, library. Looks across river to Kathmandu. Distinctive Newari architecture with own art gallery and theatre for Nepalese dance performances. Recommended as a cultural experience. Sometimes difficult to get taxis. **E** *Catnap*, Chauni, across Bishnumati River, T 272392 and **F** *Peace Lodge* on rd to Swayambhunath are fairly quiet.

Restaurants Kathmandu has a wide range of restaurants, cafés and food shops and a variety of cuisines on offer. At the top restaurants such as the *Chimney* and *Ghare Kabab* a full meal for 2 with drinks will cost Rs 700-800. In Thamel and Chhetrapati areas, a meal without drinks may cost Rs 70. A bottle of beer will cost the same as the food. A Nepalese meal of *Dhal, bhat, tarkari* will often cost as little as Rs 20. **see page 1340**.

On **Durbar Marg** try *Sunkosi*, nr Tiger Tops office, for authentic Nepalese and Tibetan, and *Ghare Kabab* for excellent Indian Tandoori food in attractive surroundings with Indian miniatures on the wall, classical music and *ghazal* singing. Book in advance, T 221711. *Bhanchha Ghar* ('Nepalese Kitchen'), Kamaladi Rd, off Durbar Marg by the clocktower in a 3 storey Newari house, with bar. Beautiful, atmospheric surroundings with music and craft demonstration in the evenings. Try buckwheat *chapatis* and wild mushroom curry. Japanese food at *Sakura-Ya*, Lazimpat in beautiful garden, *Fuji*, Royal Palace end of Kantipath, in old Rana, moated bungalow, and *Kushi Fuji*, above Tiger Tops office, are good but pricey. Counter lunches more affordable.

The Italian restaurants are less expensive: *Mona Lisa* and *La Dolce Vita*, both nr the Kathmandu Guest House in Thamel. *San Francisco Pizza House* and *Le Bistro*, Thamel do cheap pasta and pizzas. *Pizza Maya*, Chhetrapani serves Mexican pasta.

Narayan's, Chhetrapani is a popular moderately priced, Indian restaurant. On Durbar Marg you will find *Bangalore Coffee House* for good S Indian food, *Mike's Breakfast*, Seto Durbar behind Sherpa Hotel in Rana cottage for big breakfasts and lunch, and *Nanglo*, Chinese with dark decor but good food and prices. Also has western snacks in Pub. In Thamel *K.C's Restaurant*, *Coppers* and *Rumdoodle* with bar, offer popular western food. Bar food at *Spam's Spot* and vegetarian *Sanghamitra*. Tibetan restaurants, include *Lhasa*, where you can sample inexpensive *momos* and *thukpa*. *Pumpernickel* nearby, is a popular bakery. Also *Krishna Loaf Store*, Kamal Pokhari. Shops also recommended for cakes, bread and pies are along Pie Alley. The New Rd *Dairy Shop* sells good cheese.

Bars Most hotels and restaurants have bars or sell beer.

Clubs Birdwatchers' Club organises guided tours in Kathmandu and surrounding from Kathmandu Guest House, Thamel. There are Bridge and Chess Clubs and branches of Jaycees, Lions and Rotary. More information from your hotel or travel agent.

Banks Most are open 1000-1400 Sun-Th, 1000-1200 Fri, closed Sat. **Nepal**, Dharmapath, T 221337. **Indo Suez**, Kantipath, T 228229; **Grindlay's**, Kamalpokhari, T 212683. **Citibank**, Hotel Yak and Yeti, T 428884; **Standard Chartered**, Durbar Marg; **Nepal Arab**, Kantipath, T 226585. **Nepal Rashtra**, Baluwater, T 410158. **Rastriya Baniya**, Tangal, T 413884. Open 1000-1700 daily except Sat.

Exchanges Guests can change travellers cheques at most hotels and at the airport. **American Express**, Hotel Mayalu, Jamal Tol, nr Durbar Marg, will make cash advances to card holders. Open 1000-1300. **Grindlay's** will do the same for Visa and Mastercard holders.
   Warning It is illegal to exchange money on the black market.

Shopping Markets around Basantapur Sq, Indra Chowk and Asan Tole offer good opportunities for browsing for bargains.

Handicrafts See Introduction. *Thangkas* are particularly good in the Durbar Square in Bhaktapur, in Thamel, Jhochhe and Hanuman Dhoka in Kathmandu. *Rice paper Prints* are available in Thamel nr the Kathmandu Guest House. Good selection in The Print Shop. Batik, small oil paintings and greeting cards made of pipal leaf, depicting everyday scenes, birds and flowers or the Buddha are becoming popular as souvenirs.
   Tibetan Carpets Jawlakhel, S of Patan and Bodhnath are the carpetweaving centres in the valley where there are numerous shops. Also try Indrachowk and Durbar Marg in Kathmandu and Mangal Bazaar in Patan. *Clothing and Embroidery* In Thamel and Nepalese caps from shops nr Bhairabnath Temple in Bhaktapur and between Indra Chowk and Asan Tole in old Kathmandu. *Terracotta pottery* is particularly good from Thimi and Bhaktapur. The Potters' Sq is worth a visit to see a range lining the square. Thimi specialise in little flowerpots often in animal shapes.
   Papiermâché masks and colourful *puppets* at shops in Kathmandu, Patan, and Bhaktapur. Thimi is the manufacturing centre for masks (Ganes, Bhairab and the Kumari are popular). Some are used in the traditional masked dances in Sep. Puppets made in Bhaktapur often show tribal people with tools of their trade or many-armed deities, clutching little wooden weapons in each hand. Souvenir shops in Makhan Tole, between Hanuman Dhoka and Indrachowk.
   Metalwork is found in Patan, the centre for bronze casting by the *cire perdu* (lost wax) process, **see page 546**, (W Bengal Handicrafts in Kathmandu Valley with a good variety around Patan's Durbar Sq). Metal figures of deities, gameboards and pieces for the traditional Nepalese game *bagh chal* are also available. For *Khukris* try stalls in Basantpur, nr Hanuman Dhoka. *Jewellery* in Kathmandu ranges in both style and quality. Typically, gem stones and turquoise and coral are used in settings. Several good shops in New Rd, Thamel, especially nr Chhetrapati. You can also pick up stamps and coins in New Rd and Basantpur. *Hastakala*, opp Himalaya Hotel for handicrafts by disadvantaged groups, run by UNCF. Reliable antiques from *Tibet Ritual Art Gallery* above Sunkosi Restaurant and *Potala Gallery*, opp Yal and Yeti.

Books Good shops stocking imported books at competitive prices, with good selection of books on Nepal: *Tiwari's Pilgrim Book House*, Thamel, nr Kathmandu Guesthouse. Antiquarian bookshop nearby. Recommended. *Bookland*, Tridevi Marg, opp the Immigration Office. *Himalayan Book Sellers*, Ghantnagar Clock Tower. *Everest Book Service* and *Asia Book House*, off Durbar Marg nr National Theatre in Rani Pakhri. *Ratna Book Distributors* and *Ratna Pustak Bhandar*, Bagh Bazaar nr French Cultural Centre. *Educational Enterprises*, nr Mahakhal Temple, Kantipath opp Hospital. **Maps** see introduction to Nepal.

Photography Kodak and Fuji films are readily available in Kathmandu and processing and printing can now be done with confidence. Send prepaid processing films home.

Local Transport Taxis (metred) easily available and have black registration plates. About Rs 40 for a long trip across town but fares double on rainy evenings and at night. **Autorickshaws** Metered though fares often negotiable, but always agree fare before starting journey. For 2-4 persons pay 10% over meter reading. **Rickshaw** rates negotiable, around Rs 3 per km.

Often cheaper to go by taxi. **Bicycle hire**: Rs 15 for 2 hr, Rs 15-20 per day. Mountain bikes from shops around the Thamel, Thahiti Tole and Chhetrapani Square areas. Hire bikes come with a lock, please use it. **Motorcycle hire**: Rs 55 per hr, Rs 300 per day, T 213569.

Entertainment Everest Cultural Society, Annapurna Hotel, T 220676 has Nepalese folk dances at 1900 (Rs 90). New Himalchuli Cultural Group, Hotel Shanker, offers Nepali cultural programme every evening at 1900 (Rs 60). Hotel Everest International, T 220567, has a programme of Indian classical music most nights. Regular theatre performances at Kanti Path and Rani Pokhari. Details from Rashtriya Naach Ghar, Kanti Path, nr Rani Pokhari, T 211900, Royal Nepal Academy, Kamaldali and the City Hall opp Exhibition Ground. Arniko Cultural Society is in Dilli Bazaar and Chimal Cultural Group in Manaslu Hotel.

    Casino The Soaltee Oberoi Casino is the only official casino in the subcontinent. If you visit within one week of arrival in the the country and show your airline ticket and passport you receive Rs 100 of free chips. Gambling can be with Indian Rupees and US$. Blackjack, poker, roulette and pokies (slot machines). Open round the clock and a free bus service is available from all the major hotels from 2300-0400.

Sports and Recreation Swimming National Stadium, Tripureshwar has a large pool. Open daily except Sun for members and guests and Mon for women only. Large public pool next to Baleju Water Garden, NW Kathmandu. Pools in the Yak and Yeti and Hotel Narayani are open to non-residents on payment of a fee.

    Trekking Excellent opportunities for short or long, easy or difficult. Details and specialist agencies listed in Trekking see below.

    Fishing Mahseer which can grow up to 40 kg, asla, a kind of snow trout and other fish in Terai rivers and valley lakes. For permits, apply to National Parks and Wildlife Conservation Dept, Babar Mahal. For fishing in Karnali, Babai and Narayani rivers, contact Tiger Tops and W Nepal Adventures, Durbar Marg, T 222706. Feb-Mar and Oct-Nov are best for fishing. Bring your own tackle.

    Jungle Safaris Contact Tiger Tops, Durbar Marg, T 222706; Gaida Wildlife Camp, Durbar Marg, T 215840; Gokarna Safari Park, Thapalthali, T 411896. Elephant Camp, Durbar Marg, T 213976; Jungle Safari Camp, Kantipath.

    River Rafting Offered on Trisuli, Narayani, Marsyangdi, Set and Sunkoshi. Inflatable rubber rafts for 5 plus guide, for either scenic or 'white water' trips. Combined with trekking for Chitwan National Park visit. See entry below.

    Golf Two 9 hole golf courses, including the Royal Nepal Golf Club, nr. airport. Temporary members welcome.

Museums National Museum, Chauni, nr Swayambhunath Temple. Open 1030-1630 in summer, 1030-1530 in winter. Closed Tues. Rs 5. Two main buildings in Nepalese style with superb woodcarving. Uniforms, military decorations, portraits. The art gallery contains an interesting collection of sculptures dating from 1st century BC, terracottas, paintings and manuscripts. **Natural History Museum** nearby exhibits flora and fauna of the region. Stuffed animals and large collection of birds. **Tribhuvan Museum**, in Hanuman Dhoka Royal Palace. Open daily, Rs 10. Photos, portraits, memorabilia of the Late King and country's best collection of coins. See above in Places of Interest. **Nepal Assoc of Fine Arts** (NAFA), Sta Bhawan Naxal.

Libraries Indian Cultural Centre and Library, RNAC Building Kantipath. **Keshar Library** in a Rana Palace nr New Royal Palace. Collected by Samsher Jung Bahadur, a Rana noble and scholar. Impressive collection of books and manuscripts on Buddhism. Open during office hr, 1000-1600 or 1700, closed Sat. **Tribhuvan University Library**, Kirtipur. Open 0900-1800 Sun-Fri, closed Sat.

Foreign Cultural Centres and Libraries British Council, Kantipath, T 221305. Open 1100-1800 Sun-Fri, closed Sat. English newspapers and reference material plus books on Nepal. American Library, New Rd, T 221250. Open 1100-1900 Mon-Fri, closed Sat. Goethe Institute, nr Bhimsen Tower and Gen Post Office. T 220528. Library. Film nights (small charge). U.S.S.R. Cultural Centre, Soviet Embassy.

Parks and Zoos Balaju Water Gardens on the outskirts of the city is listed under Places of Interest. Also Ratna Park in the town centre and the quieter Exhibition Ground which occasionally is the venue for fairs.

Useful Services Police: T 216999. Fire: T 221177. Immigration Office (for Visa Renewals and Trekking Permits), Tridevi Marg, nr Thamel. Open Sun-Th 1000- 1300/1400 and Fri 1000-1200, closed Sat. Aim to be there when the office opens as there can be long queues.

Embassies and Consulates Australia, Bhatbheteni, 411578. **Bangladesh**, Naxal, T

414265. **Burma**, Pulchowk, T 521788. **China**, Baluwatar, T 411740. **Denmark**, Meera Home, Kichapokhari, T 215939. **France**, Lazimpat, T 412332. **Germany**, Kantipath, T 221763. **India**, Lainchaur, T 410900. **Italy**, Baluwatar (Lalita Niwas Rd), T 412743. **Japan**, Pani Pokhari, T 414083. **Pakistan**, Pani Pokhari, T 411421. **Sweden**, Meera Home, Kichapokhari, T 215939. **Thailand**, Thapathali, T 213910. *UK*, Lainchaur, T 410583. *USSR*, Baluwatar, T 411063. *USA*, Pani Pokhari, T 411179.

International Agencies Asian Development Bank, Babar Mahal, T 214217. IMF, Rastriya Bank, T 212633. UN, Lainchaur, T 416444. World Bank, Kantipath, T 214792.

Hospitals and Medical Services Bir Hospital, Kantipath, T 221119. Kanti Hospital, Maharajaganj, T 411550. Maternity Hospital, Thapalthani, T 211243. Teaching Hospital, Maharajagani, T 412404.

Post and Telegraphs See Gen Information for details of postal arrangements. For stamps go to the Gen Post Office, Sundhara, open Sun-Fri 1000-1700. **Note** Make sure that cards and letters are franked in your presence. You can also buy stamps and post letters at major hotels. American Express, Yeti Travels, Hotel Mayalu, Jamal Tol, P.O. Box 76, Durbar Marg, Kathmandu, has a 'Poste Restante' service for their cardholders.

Central Telegraph Office, Tripureswar, 200 m S of the GPO has International Telephone Service Counter open 24 hr. Phone calls, telex and fax messages may be sent. For International calls T 186, Domestic information T 197 and Domestic trunk calls T 180. It is more convenient to make calls from hotels, but expect to pay a service charge.

Places of Worship *Hindu* Pashupatinath Temple, Dakshin Kali, Taleju Temple. *Buddhist* Bodhnath, Swayambhunath. *Christian* Protestant Church of Christ, Ram Shah Path; Blue Room, USIS, Rabi Bhawan, Kalimati, T 13966 ; Roman Catholic Jesuit St Xavier College, Jawalkhel, T 221050. *Islam* 2 Mosques nr Clocktower, Central Kathmandu.

Chambers of Commerce Chamber of Commerce, Gangapath, T 212217.

Travel Agents and Tour Operators On Durbar Marg: Annapurna Travels, T 223940; Himalayan Travels, T 223803; Karthak Travels, T 227233; Natraj Tours, T 222014; President Travels, T 220245; Zenith Travels, T 223502. **On Ganga Path**: Everest Travel Service, T 222217 and Kathmandu Travels, T 212511. Marco Polo Travels, Kamalpokhari, T 414192. Namaste Travel, Maitighar, Ramshah Path, T 212918. Nepal Travel Agency, Ramshah Path, T 412899. Shashi's Holidays Ranipokhari, T 216208. Numerous other travel agents on Durbar Marg, Thamel and Kanitpath where you might find very competitive rates.

Trekking agents listed under Trekking offer inclusive packages for rafting as well as trekking.

Tourist Offices and Information Tourist Information Centre, Ganga Path, Basantapur. T 220818. Open Mon to Fri 1000-1600. Tribhuvan International Airport, T 412835. 'Nepal Traveller' is a free magazine and includes practical information and articles of interest. Hotels usually have them. Failing that, contact their offices on Tripureshwar Marg, approx 400 m from Kantipath roundabout.

There are notice boards around town publicising courses and cultural events. Trekkers looking for partners also use these and at Kathmandu Guest House and the Rum Doodle Restaurant.

Tourism Associations Govt Dept of Tourism, Tripureshwar, T 211293. Pacific and Asia Travel Assoc (PATA), Nepal Chapter, RNAC Building, T 214511 Ext. 161. Nepal Assoc of Travel Agents (NATA), Kantipath, T 216976. Trekking Agents Assoc of Nepal (TAAN), c/o NATA, Kantipath, T 216976. Hotel Assoc of Nepal (HAN), nr Yak and Yeti Hotel, T 214638.

Airlines Note It is very important that you re-confirm your tickets on arrival in Nepal and about 72 hr before departure. Flights out of Kathmandu are notoriously overbooked. Arrive early. **Royal Nepal Airlines Corporation** (RNAC), Kanti Path, T 220757, Telex: NP 2212, Airport T 414918. **Indian Airlines**, City Office, Durbar Marg, T 411997. At Tribhuvan Airport, T 411933.

On Kanti Path: **Aeroflot**, T 212397, **Air India**, T 212335; **Cathay Pacific**, T 226765; **TWA**, T 214704. On Durbar Marg: **Air France**, T 223339; **Biman**, T 222544; **British Airways**, T 222266; **Japan Airlines**, T 223871; **KLM**, T 224896; **Lufthansa**, T 223052; **PIA**, T 22202; **Swissair**, T 222452; **Thai International**, T 223565, **Airport** T 413440.

Air Services *Royal Nepal Airlines* (RNAC) links Kathmandu by 28 weekly flights, to Calcutta on Mon, Fri and Delhi daily. RNAC also connects Kathmandu with Rangoon, Dhaka, Bangkok, Karachi, Singapore. *Indian Airlines* has an extensive network linking Kathmandu with Delhi and Varanasi daily, Calcutta on Tue, Wed, Th, Sat and Sun, and Patna on Wed and Sat.

RNAC has an extensive **domestic** service covering Bharatpur, Lukla, Medhauli, Pokhara, Phaplu, Jumla, Simara, Tumlingtar, Jiri, Manang, Nepalganj, Jomosom. **Note** It is advisable to book domestic flights as early as possible and always re-confirm your seat. Flights to trekking destinations are frequent during the season but the timetable is variable. Kathmandu and Jomosom both have winter weather problems, the former with fog, the latter with wind from the Kali Gandaki gorge. Reservations: RNAC, New Rd, Kathmandu, T 214511.

Warning The STOL (Short Take Off and Landing) strip at Lukla for Namche Bazaar and Everest is also subject to closure due to bad weather. If you are trekking there, allow a couple of extra days in case there are flight delays.

Rail The nearest railhead **Amlekhganj** (162 km) in the Terai, is linked with **Raxaul Bazaar** on the Indian border which is connected with Gorakhpur and Patna.

Road There are 12 points of entry for foreign tourists: **Kakarbitta** with connections from Siliguri and Darjiling; from S, **Biratnagar** through **Rani Srikiyahi** (Jogbani) in the Kosi zone; **Jaleswar**; **Birgunj** nr **Raxaul**; **Kodari**, the Tibetan border town on the Chinese border providing access from Lhasa with a special permit (re-opened June 1991); **Sunauli** (Belhaia) nr **Bhairawa** via the road to **Pokhara**; **Kakarbana**; **Nepalgunj**; **Koilabas**; **Dhangadi**; **Mahendranagar**; **Tribhuvan airport**.

5 main highways converge on or in the capital: Tribhuvan Raj Path linking Kathmandu with Raxaul at the Indian border (200 km); Chinese Highway with Kadori at the Tibetan border (114 km); Prithvi Raj Marg linking Kathmandu and Pokhara (200 km); Mahendra Raj Marg or East-West Highway (1,000 km); Ring Rd within Kathmandu (32 km).

Bus Regular bus services from Kathmandu to Pokhara, Sunauli, Birgunj and Kakarbitta. The main Bus Stand is nr City Hall in Durbar Marg. Other starting points are Sundhara and Put Sadak. Approx journey times are in brackets.

Buses for **Pokhara** leave from Sundhara at 0630-0700 and hourly from 0500 from the Bus Stand (6 hr); **Bhairawa** via Pokhara leave from Sundhara and Bus Stand at 0500 (14 hr); **Kakarbitta** from Put Sadak at 0430 and 1740 and Express from Bus Stand at 0500 and 1815 (12-14 hr); **Biratnagar** at 1815 (11 hr); **Birgunj** from Sundhara at 0645 and Bus Stand at 0630, 0800, 1900 and 2000 (10 hr); **Trisuli** from Sorokhuti at 0700 and 1200 (5 hr); **Kodari** from Sundhara at 0600 and Bus Stand from 0500 onwards (6 hr); **Gorkha** from Bus Stand at 0815, 1900 (5 hr); **Janakpur** from Bus Stand at 0600 (9-10 hr); **Narayanghat** from Bus Stand at 0700 and 1330 (5 hr).

SHORT EXCURSIONS FROM KATHMANDU

Bodhnath
8 km NE of Kathmandu's Durbar Square the largest stupa in Nepal, Bodhnath is on an ancient trade route between Kathmandu and Lhasa. It is held sacred by Tibetan Buddhists who believe that it contains the bones of Kashyapa Buddha, one of Gautama's predecessors. The earliest record of the stupa is in the Nepalese Chronicles, assigning it to Manadeva I in 500 AD.

Because of its size, and the fact that it lies on flat land in the centre of a Tibetan settlement, the **Bodhnath** stupa strikes many as being more impressive than that at Swayambhunath. The features are the same: a hemispherical dome topped by a square structure above which rise the steps of enlightenment to the umbrella of Nirvana.

Around the octagonal base of the stupa are 108 images of the Dhyani Buddha Amitabha, whilst surrounding the triple deck of platforms is a brick wall with 147 niches, each holding 4 to 5 prayer wheels. Inside these are hundreds of notes bearing the Buddhist mantra 'Om mani padme hum' so that with each turn of the wheel hundreds of messages are symbolically sent heavenwards. There are small shrines and stupas around the main structure, as well as shops selling handicrafts. To the NE is a Buddhist monastery. The *Tibetan New Year* (usually Feb) is celebrated here with special prayers, processions, masked dances and a feast.

Just over 1 km from Bodnath on the road back to Kathmandu is the smaller but elegant stupa at **Chabahil** with some *chaityas* and old statuary nearby, including a 9th century free standing Boddhisattva. During Licchavi times Chabahil was a village at the crossroads between India and Tibet. Asoka's daughter **Charumati** is said to have lived here and with her husband founded 2 monasteries.

Budhanilkantha

9 km N of Kathmandu, one of the valley's most photographed sights is the 5th century statue of Vishnu reclining on his bed of serpents in the pool, at the village of **Budhanilkantha**. It draws large crowds at *Haribodhini Ekadasi* and *Kartik Poornima*.

The 5 m stone statue is in a small tank at the foot of the Sivapuri Hills and is thought to have come from beyond the valley. In his 4 hands he holds the 4 attributes: a discus (symbol of the mind), mace (primeval knowledge), conch (the 5 elements) and lotus seed (universe). Pilgrims descend to the tank by a stone causeway. A priest washes the god's face each morning at around 0900. Jayasthiti Malla revived the Vishnu cult at the end of the 14th century pronouncing himself to be an incarnation of Vishnu. Successive rulers made the same claim, even down to the present day. Now, there is a Vishnu shrine in front of each former royal palace in the valley. The reigning monarch, however, is not permitted to visit it (following a belief in an ancient curse).

According to legend, Vishnu sleeps for 4 months of the year and the festival of Budhanilkantha (Nov) celebrates the god waking from his monsoon slumber. See Festivals.

Travel To reach Budhanilkantha you can take a bus from nr the National Theatre to Bansbari. From here it is about an hr's walk. Alternatively, you can walk from Kathmandu or cycle.

Pashupatinath

5 km NE of Kathmandu and nr the airport. Nepal's most important Hindu pilgrim site is at **Pashupatinath** on the banks of the Bagmati River, between central Kathmandu and the airport, and may be combined with a visit to Bodhnath.

To reach it, you can follow an ancient road which in medieval times linked the royal palace in Durbar Square and the temple. Cross the Dhobi Khola by a steel bridge. The road then crosses the Pashupatinath plateau which was the probable site of the Licchavi capital of **Deopatan**. After this you reach a crossroads where there is a large dharamshala. Continuing, you pass through a small village. The approach to the temple is on the right hand side of the road.

Pashupatinath belongs to Siva, here in his peaceful form as Mahadev and Pasupati, the shepherd or lord of beasts. The temple is one of the most important to Hindus in the subcontinent and has been closely associated with orthodox S Indian Shaivism since the visit of Shankacharya. Non-Hindus are not allowed into the late 17th century temple, which is a pagoda of brass and gilt with silver plated gateways. You may get a glimpse of the gilt Nandi Bull, Siva's vehicle, said to be around 300 years old. The black, 4-headed image of **Pashupati** inside the temple is older, and replaced one destroyed by Muslim invaders in the 14th century. To the left of the temple is a ramp of steps, taken from former Licchavi buildings. This leads to the small hill of **Mount Kailash**, the mythical centre of the Universe, from which you get a good view of the Pashupatinath site.

There are also good views from the banks of the Bagmati River which is spanned by 2 bridges. To the right of these on the E bank are the **Royal Cremation Ghat** (steps). Especially busy on Sat and at *Ekadashi*, the 11th day after the full moon each month, the scene is like that at Varanasi.

S of the ghats is the 6th century ***Bacchereshwari Temple*** on the W bank. This contains a number of Tantric erotic carvings and it is thought that in the past human sacrifices were made at *Sivaratri*. Nearby is a fine but neglected 7th century Buddha statue whilst a little further down the river is the **Ram Temple** where many congregate during the Sivaratri celebration.

Cross over to the other bank. On the left is a row of 11 **stone chaityas** (chapels). Each contains a stone lingam. View of Pashupatinath temple behind and further N beyond the chaityas, the Hermit's Caves. Climb up to the terrace beyond the ghats. At the top are two temples. The **Goraknath Temple** is a tall brick shikhara structure with a large brass trident in front, surrounded by lingas. A track leads off to the right to the **Vishvarup Temple**. Non-Hindus are not allowed inside.

Beyond the Goraknath Temple and down by the river Bagmati on the other side of its meandering loop is the **Guheshwari Temple** (17th century) dedicated to Kali, Siva's fearsome shakti, the Goddess of Destruction. The arched tubular metal construction covers the main temple. Near the top, 4 gilded snakes support the roof apex illustrating the Tantric *yantra* (geometric triangle). Again, only Hindus are allowed inside to see the gilded shrine room.

The **bus** to Bodhnath passes Pashupatinath. To walk from here to Bodhnath – from Guheshwari walk to your left downstream to the bridge, from Pashupatinath Temple upstream along the W bank. Both paths meet on the N side of the bridge. A footpath leads off to the NE to Bodnath, 1.5 km.

PATAN

Patan is officially the valley's second largest town but in reality it has been absorbed into Kathmandu. Previously known as **Lalitpur**, it has a long history and was important as a Buddhist centre. Asoka is said to have been responsible for the construction of four earth and brick directional stupas at the four corners. Later under the Mallas the city experienced a great flourish of temple building. Its relatively compact scale and the remarkable vivacity of its temple architecture give Patan a unique atmosphere.

With a Durbar Square more densely packed with temples than either Kathmandu or Bhaktapur, and a total of 55 major temples and 136 bahals (monasteries) in the city, Patan claims to be the artistic and architectural centre of the valley.

Local festivals Mar-Apr. *Ghorajatra*. Apr – *Bisket*. Apr/May – *Rato Machhendrath*. The month-long festival when the red faced image of the patron deity of the valley, the God of Rain and Harvest, is taken around the city. His chariot moves by daily stages during Patan's biggest celebration and may not return for some months. The image is prepared for the event in Pulchowk, when it is washed and re-painted awaiting the assembling of the remarkably tall chariot. The procession through the streets is accompanied by musicians and soldiers and the nightly halts are marked by worship and feasting. The arrival in Jawlakhel is witnessed by not only the royal family but also Patan's Kumari, the 'Living Goddess'. Every 12 years, the procession goes to **Bungamati**, 5 km S of Patan where the Red Macchendra is ensconced in his second home for 6 months. The next is in 2003. Jul – *Janai Purnima*. Aug/Sep – *Krishnastami*. (See also Festivals in Introduction.)

Places of interest The palace complex in the centre of the town has changed little in the last century. The main avenue runs from N to S. The **Bhimsen Temple** at the N end has a lion pillar in front of it. Bhimsen in the Mahabharata is the exceptionally strong God of traders. The present 3 storeyed marble and gilt faced building was built in 1682 after an earlier one was destroyed by fire. Next to it is the 2-storey **Vishwanath Temple** (1627) dedicated to Siva with a lingam shrine. Two stone elephants guard the entrance and a Nandi bull the rear. The beams and brackets are profusely decorated with erotic carvings.

The Krishna Mandir Set further back from the main thoroughfare, the wooden **Krishna Mandir** (1637) is unlike the Malla temples in using stone, in a combination of early Mughal and Nagara temple styles. The first 3 floors have *chattri* pavilions and open colonnaded sides reminiscent of Akbar's Panch Mahal at Fatehpur Sikri (**see page 285**). Capping this is a curvilinear Hindu shikhara similar to those in the Kangra Valley in Himachal Pradesh (**see page 462**). A **Garuda pillar** faces the temple. Inside are excellent stone bas relief carvings of scenes from the Hindu epics with fine details, the Mahabharata stories on the first floor and Ramayana on the second. Both are accompanied by Newari explanations. There is a popular festival here on *Krishnastami* in Aug/Sep.

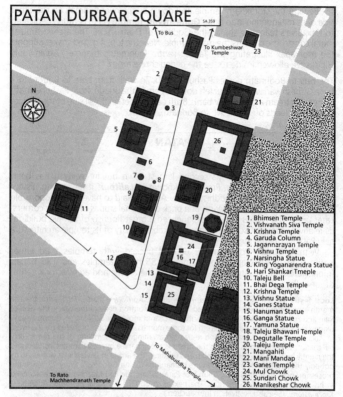

PATAN DURBAR SQUARE

SA 359

↑ To Bus

↑ To Kumbeshwar Temple

N

To Mahabuddha Temple →

To Rato Machhendranath Temple ↓

1. Bhimsen Temple
2. Vishvanath Siva Temple
3. Krishna Temple
4. Garuda Column
5. Jagannarayan Temple
6. Vishnu Temple
7. Narsingha Statue
8. King Yoganarendra Statue
9. Hari Shankar Tmeple
10. Taleju Bell
11. Bhai Dega Temple
12. Krishna Temple
13. Vishnu Statue
14. Ganes Statue
15. Hanuman Statue
16. Ganga Statue
17. Yamuna Statue
18. Taleju Bhawani Temple
19. Degutalle Temple
20. Taleju Temple
21. Mangahiti
22. Mani Mandap
23. Ganes Temple
24. Mul Chowk
25. Sundari Chowk
26. Manikeshar Chowk

The **Jagannarayan Temple** (c1565) dedicated to Vishnu comes next and is held to be the oldest temple in the square. The entrance of the 2-storey sikhara style temple is guarded by 2 stone lions. The carved roof struts depict the avatars (incarnations) of Vishnu.

The **Yoganarendra Malla Statue** sits on top of a pillar facing the palace under the hood of a cobra, on which sits a bird. A local legend suggests that as long as the bird remains, the king may return to his palace. A window is kept open for his return, and a hookah ready for his use! The **Hari Shankar Temple** (1705) is next, was built by Yoganendra's daughter , has 3 storeys and elaborately carved struts and arches. The **Taleju Bell** (1736) was cast by Vishnu Malla and hangs between 2 thick pillars. It is said that by ringing the bell, citizens could draw the king's attention to injustices suffered by them. Beside this is the attractive octagonal Krishna temple of Chyasim Deval (1723). In the lower, SW corner stands the Saivite **Bhai Dega Temple**, a simple cube topped by an onion dome.

Across the street is the **Royal Palace.** The entrance to the **Sundari Chowk** from the main street is guarded by stone statues of Ganes, Hanuman and Vishnu. The **Palace** is a fine 3 storey structure with carved roof struts and the gilded metal window over the entrance is flanked by carved ivory windows. In the centre is the

Tushahiti tank, a sunken royal bath decorated with fine stone and bronze carvings. There is an incomplete set of *Ashta* (8) *Matrikas*, divine mother goddesses who attend Siva and the god of war Skanda, the 8 Bhairavs and the 8 Nagas.

To your left (N) is the central **Mul Chowk** (1668), the core of the complex built for Srinivasa Malla with the small gilded Bidya Mandir temple shrine at the centre. The cloister is a 2 storey building and was the residence of the Patan Royal family. There are also 3 Taleju temples around the court. Two brass images of the goddess Ganga on a tortoise and Yamuna on the mythical makara sea monster flank the doorway of the Bhutanese style **Taleju Bhawani** shrine on the S side of the square. In the NE corner is the **Degutalle Temple** (1640) to the personal deity of the Mallas. Destroyed by fire, it was rebuilt in 1662.

Move through to the most N and recent courtyard, the **Mani Keshar Chowk** (1734) which took 60 years to complete. The entrance from the street is through a splendid gilded door topped by a golden *torana*. Beyond the Mani Keshar Chowk is the **Mangahiti**, another tank in a lotus pattern and with 3 carved crocodile stone waterspouts with the **Mani Mandap** (1700; Royal Pavilion adjacent to it).

Other sites in Patan Some of the many other temples and bahals in Patan can be visited on a tour of the city starting at Durbar Square and finishing at the zoo and Tibetan refugee camp at Jawlakhel.

Going NW from the Square, a few mins' walk brings you to the **Hiranya Varna Mahivihar** or Golden Temple. The monastery is a triple-roofed pagoda, (the gold plating dedicated by a rich merchant) and has a richly embossed facade. The entrance is guarded by decorative lions. Though first documented in 1409, it is attributed to King Bhaskar Varma in the 12th century. Shoes must be removed at the door. Inside, the shrine has a frieze depicting the life of the Buddha where the strong Hindu component of some images indicate the extent of religious cross-fertilization in the valley. You will also see a rack of prayer wheels and a large suspended bell.

Another 300 m along the road, N of Durbar Square, stands the imposing 5 storey **Kumbeshwar Temple** (1392), dedicated to Siva, the oldest existing temple here. It is finely proportioned with numerous carvings including figures of Ganes, Narayan and other deities. There are small Bhairab and Baglamukhi temples around the main structure. The natural spring which feeds the tank in the courtyard is said to have the glacial lake Gosainkund as its source. A bath here is considered as holy as the long pilgrimage to the High Himalayan lake. At *Janai Poornima* in Jul/Aug, large crowds of pilgrims come to worship a silver and gold lingam that is placed in the tank and take a ritual bath. Brahmins and Chettris replace their sacred threads at the festival, amidst frenetic dancing by strikingly dressed *jhankris* (witch doctors). Further N is the northern Asoka Stupa, the best preserved of the 4 accredited to Emperor Ashoka in the 3rd century BC.

Walking S, along the road parallel to Durbar Square and on its E, you reach the 16th century Shikhara style **Mahaboudha Temple**, 'Temple of the Thousand Buddhas'. Tightly hemmed in by surrounding buildings the terracotta and tile temple is a little difficult to locate. It bears some resemblance to the Mahabodhi temple at Bodhgaya in Bihar, India. Each of the 9,000 or so bricks is said to carry an image of the Buddha and though completely destroyed after the 1934 earthquake it was rebuilt like the original.

Rato Machendranath Temple Returning to the area just S of Durbar Square, you will come to the **Rato** (Red) **Machendranath Temple.** This is venerated by Buddhists as the home of the god **Avalokiteshwara** in his Tantric form. The present 3 storey temple dates from 1673 and stands in a courtyard filled with sculptures of animals including horses, lions and bulls, symbols of the Tibetan calender. 4 richly adorned entrances lead into the shrine which houses the large-eyed clay image, decorated with jewellery and garlands. See above, under Local festivals.

Walk S a short distance and turn right. You pass **Patan Hospital** and after about 1 km you reach the **Tibetan Refugee Camp** at *Jawlakhel*. Following the flight of the Dalai Lama and many Tibetans in 1959, refugees were accommodated in a camp here. Now it is a permanent settlement and centre of typical Tibetan industry. You can watch carpets, blankets, jackets and pullovers being made and can buy them at a competitive price. Closed Sat. Nearby is the rather disappointing **Zoo** (see below under Parks and Zoos).

The road N takes you past the **W Asoka stupa** (Pulchowk) and joins **Kopundol** which crosses the Bagmati. From here is it a short distance to the centre of Kathmandu.

Hotels A *Himalaya Hotel*, Pulchowk, T 521887, Cable: Flora. 100 rm. Good views of Himalaya. Pleasant and cool *Base Camp* Coffee Shop. **B** *Summit*, Kopundol Height, Lalitpur, nr UN Office, T 521894. Traditional style architecture, good restaurant, pool, gardens. Sometimes difficult to get taxis. **B** *Narayani*, T 525015, Cable: Honarayani. Telex: 2262. 90 rm. Restaurant, café, bar, car hire, pool, travel, pleasant garden. Facilities of **D** *Oasis* available including squash and tennis. 22 rm with bath. Restaurant, bar, exchange, travel.

Youth Hostel F *Mahendra Yuvalaya*, Jawlakhel, about 15 min walk from Patan Bus Stop. T 521003. Rm and dormitory. Quiet.

Restaurants There are comparatively few places to eat in Patan. One of the best is *Café de Patan* in the SW corner of Durbar Square. *The German Bakery* is good for bread, pastries, cakes and cold drinks.

Shopping Patan is regarded as the best place for handicrafts in the valley (See under Kathmandu). It has a long metal working tradition and produces fine statues of the Buddha, the Taras and other Tantric Buddhist deities. Prices for gold plated bronze figurines range from Rs 2,000 to over Rs 10,000. Go to *Patan Industrial Centre* to see craftsmen at work.

S Asian music is available on cassette at the shop adjacent to the Café de Patan. *Arjun* and *Madhu Chandra Art Gallery* are in Durbar Square. In Jawlakhel you will find Tibetan handicrafts, crafts from all over Nepal at *Cheez Beez, Mahaguthi* and the *BB Thapa Gallery*. Carpets are good in Mangal Bazaar and you can watch weavers (and buy) in the *Tibetan Refugee Centre*.

Local Transport Regular bus service from Ratna Park, Bus Stop No.4, to Patan Gate from which it is a very short walk to Durbar Square. Fare Rs 1.50. A **taxi** will cost around Rs 30 one way. You can also take a **tempo**, **rickshaw**, **cycle** or walk the 5 km or so.

Museum National Bronze Museum contains a good collection of ancient statues, paintings and thangkas. Also the **Picture Gallery** in Durbar Square.

Library Rastriya Pustakalaya (Nepal National Library), Pulchowk, Patan. Books in English, Nepali and Indian languages.

Zoo At Jawlakhel, a small zoo has animals, birds and reptiles including lions, leopards, tigers, elephants and rhinos. Re 0.50. Not recommended as a special trip.

Hospital Patan Hospital, Lagankhel, T 521333.

BHAKTAPUR

Also known as **Bhadgaon**, this is the valley's third major city, about 14 km E of Kathmandu. **Bhaktapur** has preserved its medieval character better than Patan and Kathmandu and developed independently until Gurkha unification in 1768. After this its growth stopped as Kathmandu became more cosmopolitan and merged with Patan. In the 1970s it benefited from a W German funded restoration project. The town is known for its pottery, weaving and Nepali caps.

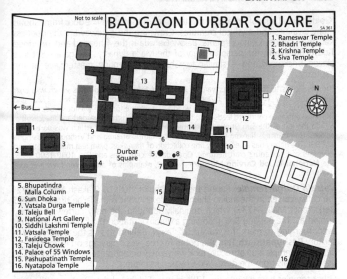

Not to scale · **BADGAON DURBAR SQUARE** · SA 361

1. Rameswar Temple
2. Bhadri Temple
3. Krishna Temple
4. Siva Temple

5. Bhupatindra Malla Column
6. Sun Dhoka
7. Vatsala Durga Temple
8. Taleju Bell
9. National Art Gallery
10. Siddhi Lakshmi Temple
11. Vatsala Temple
12. Fasidega Temple
13. Taleju Chowk
14. Palace of 55 Windows
15. Pashupatinath Temple
16. Nyatapola Temple

On the N bank of the **Hanumante River**, Bhaktapur was capital of the whole valley from the 14th to 16th century and was fortified in the 15th century. The original centre of the city was the E square (around the 15th century), the **Dattatraya Temple** and the **Pujahari Math,** but later shifted to Durbar Square. The temple to Vishnu with a Garuda pillar is one of the oldest here and was said to have been built out of a single tree.

As you approach Bhaktapur from the W, you pass through a grove of pine trees on a low hill, by 2 tanks which supplied the population with drinking water. The bus stop is near the walled **Siddha Pokhari**, considered holy by Hindus and Buddhists. Beyond this the road divides, the left fork running into Durbar Square.

Local festivals Apr – *Bisket*. (Snake slaughter) Special celebrations to commemorate the great battle in the Hindu epic Mahabharata. Chariots carrying Bhariab and Bhadrakali are drawn through the narrow streets. A tug-of-war between upper and lower parts of the town decides who will be fortunate for the coming year. A tall wooden pole (sometimes 20 m high) is erected near the river side with cross beam from which 2 banners, signifying snake demons are hung. On the following day (New Year), it is brought crashing down after another tug-of-war. There is much dancing and singing in the street over 4 days.

Places of interest *Durbar Square* The 1934 earthquake caused considerable damage to buildings in the square which consequently appears more spacious than its 2 namesakes. It is still an architectural showpiece with numerous superb examples of the skills of Nepali artists and craftsmen over several centuries.

As you enter the outer square from the W end, in front of you is a Siva/Parvati Temple. To the right are 2 smaller temples to Siva/Parvati and Siva. Walking past the house of a Malla Prince on your right you come to 2 large stone lions and a small gateway on your left where there are 2 fine stone statues representing the 18-armed Ugrachandi Durga and 12-armed Bhairav. To the left, on the N side of the square is the ruined palace. Opposite this are a number of minor temples which from your right are to Rameshwar, Bhadri, Krishna and Siva.

Here in the centre of Durbar Sq, the most striking feature is a life size gilded **Statue of Bhupatindra Malla**, seated on a tall stone pillar facing the **Sun Dhoka**

(Golden Gate), one of the artistic masterpieces of the valley. The door frame shows many divinities and mythical creatures. Crowning the gateway are the goddess Kali and Garuda, killing serpents. Below Garuda is the 4 headed and 16 armed **Taleju Bhawani**, the personal deity of the Malla dynasty. The gate is set into glazed brickwork and is similar to Ghiberti's Florentine masterpiece at the Baptistry.

The gate leads to the main courtyard of *Palace of Fifty-five Windows* which was built during the early 15th century but remodelled by Bhupatindra Malla (r1696-1722) and completed in 1754. The balcony with 55 windows is unique for its marvellous woodcarving. The small entrance courtyard leads onto the **Mul Chowk** which is guarded and inaccessible.

To the left of the Sun Dhoka stands the **National Art Gallery** which was part of the palace. Its entrance is flanked by Hanuman as the Tantric Bhairab and Vishnu as Narsingha (c1698). The gallery has an especially fine collection of *thangkas*, palm leaf manuscripts, and examples of Bhaktapur's craft heritage. Open daily except Tues and Sat, 1030-1600. Rs 5. The **National Wood Carving Museum** has fine examples of arched windows and roof struts.

Vatsala Durga Temple Facing the Sun Dhoka, built by Prakash Malla, 1672, intricately carved in the Indian shikhara style. In front is the large bronze **Taleju Bell** (Ranjit Malla, 1737) which originally sounded the daily curfew. Popularly known as 'The Barking Bell' following a dream visitation the king had, it is rung every morning to mark the worship of Taleju. Behind this is the 2 storey, 17th century **Pashupatinath Temple,** noted for the erotic carvings on its roof struts. Beside the temple is an attractive tank with a new octagonal temple behind, which used materials from the destroyed Chyaslin Mandapa.

Other temples here include the 17th century Siddhi Lakshmi Temple with stone attendants lining the steps. By this temple are stone lions and a second **Vatsala Temple.** The **Fasidega Temple** in the NE corner sits on a 6 level platform with an attractive flight of steps flanked by decorative elephants.

Nyatapola Temple S of the Square, at the N end of **Taumadhi Tole,** is Nepal's tallest temple (30 m). It is one of the few five-storey temples in the country. Built by Bhupatindra Malla in 1702 and only mildly damaged in the 1934 earthquake, the successive tiled roofs are supported by extravagantly carved and painted beams and struts. 5 pairs of stone carved figures line the steps of the 5 terraces, each thought to be 10 times stronger than the one below. The legendary wrestlers of enormous strength, Jaya Malla and Phatta Malla, elephants, lions, griffins, Baghini and Singhini, the tiger and lion goddesses. The interior is Chinese and Thai in character and accessible only to priests. It has the shrine of the Tantric Goddess **Siddhi Lakshmi** who is also carved into the 108 roof struts.

S of the Nyatapola Temple is the **Bhairabnath Temple** (1717) with a dance platform in front and Siva and Narayan Shrines behind. Leaving the square by the SW exit, marked by a Jagannath Temple is the route to the Potter's Square and Bus Stop.

There are **Restaurants** nr the Dattatreya and Nyatapola Temples and also nr the Bus Stop. The Bhaktapur speciality is *Jujudhau* a sweet curd.

Shopping Particularly good for thangkas, caps, masks and puppets (See under Kathmandu). *The Handicrafts Centre* is nr the Dattatreya Temple. *Himalaya Book Store*, Bagh Bazaar nr the Bus Stand.

French **Cultural Centre**, Bagh Bazaar, Bhaktapur, T 224326. Regular French film nights (small charge).

Changu Narayan Temple is 12 km E of Kathmandu and approx 5 km N of Bhaktapur. The temple is 125 m above the Kathmandu valley and dates from the 4th century AD. It can be reached on foot from Bhaktapur, or even Kathmandu if you are feeling energetic, and may be combined with a visit to the Tibetan shrine at Bodhnath. The walk through cultivated fields of rice up to the low hill is most attractive, especially if you descend at sundown.

The old temple destroyed by fire in 1702 was completely rebuilt. Stone elephants guard the entrance to the 2 tiered temple dedicated to Narayana or Vishnu. It is possibly the oldest in the valley in the pagoda style. In front is Garuda (c 5th century) with an important Licchavi inscription in Gupta script nearby. There are 4 pillars capped by a conch and lotus, Vishnu's traditional weapons. For Bodhnath there is a steep descent to the N to the Manohara River which you cross by a temporary dry season bridge you reach the road. Bodhnath is 6 km to the W. Less than an hour's walk along the ridge to the E brings you to

Nagarkot (1,985 m), 30 km E of Kathmandu. Set on a ridge on the NW rim of the valley, it has the best vantage point for a view of the Himalaya from the Kathmandu Valley – a panorama stretching from Annapurna (8,090 m) and Machhapuchhare (7,059 m) in the W, to Everest (8,848 m) and Kangchendzonga (8,597 m) in the E.

An hour's walk above the village will give you a better view from a lookout tower (2,195 m) especially at sunrise. Visibility is good from Oct to Apr but cloud cover interferes with the vista over the monsoon. In Apr and May it can be quite hazy. The spring flowers and unusual rock formations make short, undemanding treks from Nagarkot particularly attractive. Nagarkot is only a small village with an army camp, a temple and market place and a number of hotels of varying standards.

Hotels Many visitors come for an overnight stay, take in the view then return to Kathmandu. The comparatively luxurious **C** *Flora* and the Govt run **D** *Taragaon Village Resort*, nr Army Camp have electricity. T 410409, Telex: 2214. Bungalows only. Good for long stays. Good value. The rest are basic **E** and **F** category with no electricity .

Travel A **taxi** from Kathmandu costs approximately Rs 400 for the return trip. **Tours** leaving Kathmandu well before dawn cost around Rs 150. **Buses** leave Bhaktapur every few hr, cost Rs 6 and takes about an hr.

Chhobar Gorge 6 km SW of Kathmandu. The origins of this striking gorge have been given various explanations. One suggests that the legendary Bodhisattva **Manjushri**, wishing to worship the sacred flame of Buddhism burning on a lotus flower, slashed the valley wall with his flaming sword of wisdom to drain off the lake that covered the whole valley. Chhobar Gorge was caused by his powerful blow. Another belief is that Krishna hurled a thunderbolt at the valley walls.

Scientists provide a much more prosaic explanation, but what is certain is that the Kathmandu valley was drained and now the muddy waters of the Bagmati River flow through it. Below the gorge is the **Jal Binayak Temple** (1602). The shrine of Siva and Parvati is believed to be 11th century. A huge rock has a Ganes carved into it though this is now indistinct and does not resemble the usual image of the elephant-headed god. A bronze shrew, Ganes's vehicle in Nepali Hinduism (as distinct from a rat more comon in India), faces the shrine.

Above the gorge is Chhobar village which has a Buddhist temple of **Adinath Lokeshwar** (15th century, rebuilt 1640). This triple-roofed temple has numerous vessels for containing water nailed to its walls. The inner sanctum contains an image of the Red Macchendra and facing the shrine is a stone shikhara.

Walks around the Kathmandu Valley There are a number of attractive walks in the valley which visit some interesting sites, provide a good appreciation of the countryside and offer good mountain vistas. You may need a taxi or hire car to drop you at the starting point. Nagarkot is a popular area for pleasant walks.

LONGER EXCURSIONS FROM KATHMANDU

Lumbini, the birthplace of the Buddha, S of the foothills of the Churia Range, is marked by an Ashoka Pillar which was erected in 250 BC, in the 20th year of the Buddhist Emperor's reign. The inscription in Brahmi declares, he made "the village free of taxes and a recipient of wealth". The Chinese traveller Fa-Hien, described the ruins at Lumbini in the 4th century AD but the ancient pillar was only discovered by a German archaeologist in 1895. The Lumbini Development Trust was set up in 1970 which has opened a **Museum** and library.

Places of interest The **Maya Devi temple** (19th century) which is sacred to both Hindus and Buddhists has a stone bas-relief of the Buddha's birth scene and is thought to have been built over an earlier 5th century temple which itself may have replaced an Asokan temple. The sacred pool **Puskarani** to its S with its 3 terraces, is where the Buddha's mother Queen Maya Devi is believed to have bathed before giving birth and where Gautama was given his ritual purification bath. The **Tibetan style monastery** (1975) has old murals and a large bronze image of the Buddha. The other Buddhist Monastery is also modern and contains a large thangka and carved wooden gate. In addition to ruins of ancient walls, a pond and mounds, excavations have shows evidence of stupas and a monastery.

Hotels *Lumbini Garden Guest House*, in pleasant gardens. In the border town of **Bhairawa C** *Himalayan Inn* and *Hotel Lumbini* are the best. Cheaper **E** *Kailash, Shambala Guest House* and *Pashupati Lodge*.

Air Services Lumbini is close to Siddharthanagar which has regular flights from Kathmandu. **Road** A 22 km road connects it to Bhairawa (about 1 hr) with a regular bus and it is possible to do a round trip. Also roads from Pokhara and Kathmandu via Narayanghat. From Tiger Tops 3 hr by road.

ROYAL CHITWAN NATIONAL PARK

Those stretches of the the Terai not already cultivated have been secured by Nepal's Parks Department and converted into National Parks. Scattered along the length of this narrow strip are wildlife reserves: *Kosi Tappu* in the Kosi flood plain of the eastern Terai, home to a rare herd of wild buffaloes and numerous migratory birds; the *Royal Suklaphanta Reserve* the Mahakali River, a grassland reserve for over 1,000 swamp deer; *The Karnali Reserve* on the Karnali river in the W covers 368 sq km and contains 32 species of mammals, Nepal's second largest tiger population (after Chitwan) and 250 species of birds. However, the oldest, best known, most developed and frequently visited is the **Royal Chitwan Park**.

Chitwan lies 120 km SW of Kathmandu in the valley of the **Rapti** and **Narayani rivers**. It is 932 sq km in extent and consists of swamp, tall elephant grass and thick forest.

Park entrance fee Rs 250 . *Best Season* Oct-Mar (grass is shorter in Feb, Mar). *Clothing* Summer – Cool cottons, preferably with long sleeves for evenings, Winter – woollens. Sunhat and sunblock. Swimming costume for river bathing. Also take insect repellent and binoculars.

Chitwan is a 3,800 sq km basin surrounded by hills, the Siwaliks to the S, and the Mahabharat Lekh to the N and the rivers Narayani and Rapti flowing from E to W. Before 1950 the Tharus lived here in small numbers, apparently immune to malaria. The National Park now occupies the area between the Rapti and its tributary the Reu, with the centre rising to 738 m. **Mt Manaslu** and **Himalchuli** can be seen on clear days. There is an airstrip at **Meghauli** on the N bank of the Rapti.

The Rana Prime Ministers held Chitwan as their private hunting preserve. Massive *shikars** were organised for visiting dignitaries such as European royalty and Viceroys of India. They were aided by a continuous line of beaters driving the game towards the guns and there was wholesale slaughter. The Maharajah of Nepal and his guests shot 433 tigers and 53 rhino in the period 1933-40.

The natural habitat of the tiger, great one-horned Indian rhinoceros, leopard, gaur, sloth and wild bear, sambar, hog and barking deer, civet, mongoose and otter, was reduced to its present extent by land clearance for farming. The malaria eradication programme encouraged settlement and land-hungry peasant farmers reduced the area under natural vegetation cover.

In 1973 the park became a national sanctuary and strict measures against poaching and unauthorised conversion of forest to farmland saved the dwindling wildlife, with an estimated 100 rhino and only 20 tigers left. Hunting and poaching have been banned though the latter continues as there is a high demand for fur and powdered rhino horn (regarded by some E Asians as an aphrodisiac). Conservation measures have increased the rhino and tiger population to about 400 and 80. In addition there are 50 other species of mammals, 400 species of birds, the marsh mugger crocodile, the gharial, the Gangetic dolphin while several varieties of fish that constitute the food web. The long snouted fish-eating gharial is an endangered species and a breeding farm has been established at Kasara. Elephants, though not native, are used for taking visitors through the park.

Warning In the monsoons, beware of **leeches**, see page 1341.

Hotels There is a choice of accommodation inside and outside the park. That in the park is more atmospheric, more expensive and more exclusive. The tariff is usually all-inclusive.

Inside Park The facilities offered include accommodation and meals plus camp activities such as elephant rides. With the exception of bar bills and gratuities, the price tends to be all-inclusive and often there is a min 2 nights' stay. Some firms offer round trip packages from Kathmandu, with a couple of nights at Chitwan. Most hotels offer elephant rides, canoe trips on the river, landrover drives into the park, nature walks often accompanied by a local naturalist, fishing (in season), and bird watching. **A** *Tiger Tops Jungle Lodge*, on the Rapti River. Bookings Durbar Marg, nr Hotel de l'Annapurna, Kathmandu, PO Box 242, T 212706, Telex: NP 216 Tigtop, Cable: Tigertops. Internationally known and listed among the world's best 300 hotels. The accommodation is in large tree houses. 20 rooms with solar heated showers. The dining and lounge area and bar has a thatched roof, hardwood and rattan decor. Continental and Nepali cuisine. **A** *Tiger Tops Tented Camp*, on Bandarjhola Island in the Narayani River. More modest, in African-style Safari tents. **A** *Tiger Tops* Tharu Village, just outside the park. Traditional Tharu longhouse. Tharu cultural evening of song and dance. Nepali and Continental cuisine.

A *Gaida Wildlife Camp*, Dubarmarg, T Kathmandu 410786. Just outside the park nr the village of Sauraha. Rms have park views. Central lodge in Nepali style with a central hearth, is dining hall with bar, Nepali and Continental cuisine. Raised twin bedded wooden huts with toilet and shower facilities. Also **A** *Gaida Wildlife Jungle Camp* inside the park, at the foot of the Churia hills. Good site for viewing gaur. **A** *Temple Tiger*, T Kathmandu 221585. Tents. **A** *Island Jungle Resort*. Tented camp on island in the Narayani River. **A** *Chitwan Jungle Lodge*, Dubarmarg, E end of park, Kathmandu 222679. Traditional mud and thatch huts, no electricity. Restaurant and open-air bar. **A** *Machan Wildlife Resort*, W end of park, T Kathmandu 222823. Wooden bungalows or tents, restaurant and pool. Packages for 2 night stay with river raft option.

Outside Park Accommodation is much cheaper at Sauraha, a typical Terai village. There is no electricity (hence no a/c) so summers can be very hot. An exception is **A** *Elephant Camp*, Dubarmarg, T 213976. Comfortable rm with electricity. Restaurant (Nepali & Continental), cultural shows.

The bewildering choice of lodges, hotels and camps reflects the growing popularity of Chitwan. They are all basically similar, with simple rooms, usually with insect screens and mosquito nets, and shared bathrooms. Most have their own restaurants. **E** category – *Rhino Lodge* and *Jungle Express Camp* used by budget packages. Among many others are *Jungle Safari Camp*, Dubarmarg, T 213533, *Chitwan Jungle Lodge* and *Crocodile Safari Camp* has a pleasant garden.

Restaurants and Bars *Tiger, Paradise* and *Cake & Pie Restaurants* all in Sauraha. Most lodges have bars where you can buy beer and some spirits.

Local Transport You can hire **bicycles** at **Tapi Bazaar** if you are travelling to Chitwan by bus from Pokhara or Kathmandu. Also available in Sauraha.

Museums Small displays at Visitors Centre, Sauraha. Open 0800-1700. Park Headquarters, Kasara, has a small museum and a crocodile breeding farm.

Tourist Offices & Information Park Visitor Centre, Sauraha. Open 0800-1700. Information about the park, its creation and management.

Tours from Kathmandu and Pokhara to Chitwan and back. Usually 2 nights min in park, 5 days if river rafting is included.

Air Services RNAC daily flights to Meghauli, nr Tiger Tops. Also 3 flights a week to Bharatpur (Narayanghat), approx 30 km from Meghauli and Tiger Tops and 20 km from Sauraha.

Road Bus Regular buses from **Pokhara** and **Kathmandu** to Tadi Bazaar (7hr), 8 km N of **Sauraha**. Fare about Rs 45 from both places. You can rent bicycles or hire Ox-carts at **Tadi Bazaar**. There are shops at the road junction. The **Rapti** river is crossed at **Chitrasali** (Gauthali) and when the river is high you must cross by dugout canoe.

Car Lodges with offices in Kathmandu arrange the round trip on a 2-3 day package. The driver waits with the vehicle to return passengers to Kathmandu or Pokhara at the end of their jungle stay. The journey from Kathmandu takes around 5 hr and the road via **Hitaura** is worth taking in preference to the Mahendra and Prithvi Highways as it is more scenic and the road is well engineered and tar sealed all the way. At the park, lodges inside pick you up and take you to the accommodation. This can either be by 4WD vehicle or elephant (definitely the latter when the river is swollen after the monsoon).

River It is possible to raft down the Narayani from Mugling on the Kathmandu-Pokhara Highway. There are a large number of operators in Kathmandu offering this trip. The Chitwan Lodges also arrange their own combination package tours. 5 day 4 night (2 in Chitwan). Establish what you are getting for your money before parting with it.

Warning In the monsoon, beware of **leeches**. See page 1341.

TREKKING IN NEPAL

ORGANISING A TREK

For ease of organization and the requirements of the different types of trek, Nepal is matchless.

Warning Treks described are only for guidance. Independent trekkers should get a specialist publication with detailed route description and a good map.

The escorted trek from overseas A company or individual with local knowledge and expertise organises a trip and sells it. Some or all camp equipment, food, cooking, planning the stages, decision-making based on progress and weather conditions, liaison with porters, shopkeepers etc are all taken care of.

This has the advantage of being a good, safe introduction to the country. You will be able to travel with limited knowledge of the region and its culture and get to places more easily which as an individual you might not reach, without the expense of completely kitting yourself out. You should read and follow any advice in the preparatory material you are sent, as your enjoyment greatly depends on it. This applies particularly to recommendations concerning physical fitness.

An escorted trek involves going with a group. If you are willing to trade some of your independence for careful, efficient organisation and make the effort to ensure the group works well together, the experience can be very rewarding.

Ideally there should be no more than 20 trekkers (preferably around 12). Check the itinerary (is it too demanding for you, or is it not adventurous enough?) and what exactly is provided by way of equipment, before booking.

The Backpacking Camping Approach Hundreds of people arrive in Nepal each year with a pack and some personal equipment, buy some food and set off trekking, carrying their own gear and choosing their own campsites or places to stay. Of all the regions in the Himalayas, Nepal caters for this group best. There are some outstandingly beautiful treks, though these are often not through the "wilderness" that is conjured up by some outdated literature.

Note Many areas outside the Kathmandu Valley are quite densely populated. Supplies of fuel wood are scarce and flat ground suitable for camping rare. It is not always easy to find isolated and "private" campsites.

Independent trekking without a tent: teahouse trekking This demands less equipment and uses the local inns. It is comparatively cheap, and requires little equipment, but facilities are basic. Probably most suited to those who have trekked in Nepal before and have a good idea of what to expect.

You carry clothes and bedding, as with youth hostelling, and for food and shelter you rely on *bhattis**, **see page 1305**. These are inns or teahouses, homes along the trekking route where for a few rupees a night you get a space on the floor, a wooden pallet or a camp bed, or in the more luxurious inns, a room and shower. The food is simple, usually vegetable curry, rice and *dal* which although repetitive, is healthy and can be tasty. You may be pleasantly surprised by finding banana cake and Coke in a remote village! On the popular treks to Everest and in the Annapurna region such delicacies as apple pie, carrot cake and pancakes are often available, and can be washed down with soft drinks or beer (at a premium).

This approach brings you into more contact with the local population, the limiting factor being the routes where accommodation is available. **Note** Bed bugs are common (carry a thin plastic sheet) and kitchen hygiene may be poor. With an organised group, companies have reputations to maintain and try to comply with Western concepts of hygiene.

The Locally Organised Trek with guide and/or porters There are trekking companies based in Kathmandu who will organise treks for a fee and provide all sherpas, porters, cooks, food and equipment but it requires effort and careful consideration on your part. This is the recommended method for a group that wants to follow a specific itinerary and demands greater control than would be offered on escorted group treks.

You can make arrangements in advance, which can be a protracted business as the postal service can be slow. Alternatively, wait until you get to Nepal, but allow at least a week to make arrangements.

Note You have to follow a pre-arranged itinerary as porters expect to arrive at certain points on schedule. Although many sherpas speak some English you may find yourself up against problems with communication and misunderstandings may result. If you go through a reputable agency you will be in very good hands and the sherpas will make every reasonable effort to accommodate you. Many sherpas are highly skilled professionals. The agency will probably insist that you take one with you as leader who will act in your interest and on your instructions.

Agencies The following agencies based in Kathmandu make arrangements for many foreign companies and also offer the 'Instant trek' service. They offer relatively expensive trips to include mess tents, dining tables, chairs, food, porters, cooks, sirdar (guide/ head sherpa), toilet tent.

Ama Dablam Trekking, Lazimpat, T 410219. *Mountain Travel Nepal*, Naxal, T 414508. *Malla Treks*, Malla Hotel, T 418389. *Sherpa Co-operative Trekking*, PO Box 1338, Durbar Marg, T 224068. *Tiger Mountain*, PO Box 170, Durbar Marg, T 414508.

In addition smaller companies can organise less lavish, cheaper treks. Camping equipment may be taken or as with Sherpa Co-operative treks, you can stay in village lodges.

Above the Clouds Trekking, Thamel, T 412921. *Adventure Jungle Camp*, Thamel, T 417184. *Asian Trekking*, Thamel, T 412821. *Glacier Safari Trekking*, Thamel, T 412116. *Himalayan Journeys*, Kantipath, T 215885. *Kangchendzonga Trekking*, T 214139. *Machhapuchhare Trekking*, Thamel, T 214873. *Nepal Tashi Trekking*, Thamel, T 415920. *Sherpa Co-operative Trekking*, PO Box 1338, Durbar Marg, T 224068. *Sherpa Trekking Services*, Kamaldi, T 220243. *Wilderness Experience*, Kantipath, T 227152. *Yangrima Tours and Travels*, Tripureswar, T 220334.

There are dozens of other small companies in Kathmandu, especially in Thamel and Durbar Marg, but take care to specify exactly what you require and ascertain what is being offered.

Warning Make sure that both you and the trekking company understand exactly who is expected to provide what equipment. For high altitude treks, porters may expect warm clothing. A sherpa guide will cost more and although he may be prepared to carry a load, his principal function will be as a guide and overseer for the porters.

Trekking Seasons Oct and Nov are the best months. The air is clear, the vegetation still lush after the monsoon, and both day and night temperatures are pleasant. **Dec and Jan** are colder (especially at higher altitudes) and generally dustier. High passes, like Thorong La on the Annapurna Circuit, can be closed and you need more equipment. Everest looks bare as it has very little snow cover. **Mar and Apr** are hazy, though in Mar, rhododendrons are particularly attractive. **May** is very hot and quite dusty and streams do not carry much water.

The monsoons (**Jun-mid Sep**) are wet, though you may get breaks of 3 or 4 days in the rain. Clouds can lift to give you some good mountain views. Equipment may feel a little damp. Weather in late Sep is unpredictable, but the trails are much less crowded, and hence, more pleasant. **Warning** Leeches can be unpleasant in damper places, **see page 1341**.

The daily routine The Nepalese eat very little breakfast, have a large but early lunch at around 1000 then a second meal later in the day around sundown. On an organised trek you will probably be woken at around 0600, have a light breakfast, start walking at around 0730, stop for a cooked midday meal at about 1100, start again a couple of hours later and arrive in camp at 1500-1600. This routine differs from other regions in the Himalaya so don't be surprised if the porters stop mid-morning for their big meal.

PRACTICAL INFORMATION

The Sierra Club motto is worth remembering 'Leave only footprints, take only photographs'. Please burn or bury all rubbish, including toilet paper. Carry a pocket lighter if you prefer to burn.

Footpaths Away from roads the footpath is the principal line of communication between villages. Tracks tend to be very good, well graded and in good condition but without many flat stretches.

Accommodation The popular treks such as the Annapurna Circuit and Everest Base Camp have quite good hotels with private rooms, occasionally showers and reasonable menus. On less popular routes there are teahouses and simple *bhattis**.

Security There are still only a few reported cases of thefts and muggings each year but it is on the increase. Keep your valuables with you at all times, make sure the tent 'doors' are closed when you are going for meals etc, and lock you room door in lodges.

Warning Be very wary of porters hired in the bazaar who may be cheaper to hire but may be unreliable. You can trust porters hired through an agency.

Travelling Alone This is not recommended as you may fall and break a limb, be severely incapacitated and not have help at hand. Injury through misadventure is more likely to occur than through robbery. The Himalayan Rescue Association notice board in the Kathmandu Guest House carries notices of individuals looking for trekking partners.

Acclimatisation and Mountain Sickness You will probably experience Mountain Sickness in its mildest form. It occurs when a too rapid ascent above approximately 3,500 m. is attempted. The body tries to adapt to the considerably reduced concentration of oxygen in the atmosphere at higher altitudes. Mild symptoms are a slight shortness of breath, a mild headache and increased urine output. If the trekker remains at the altitude where these symptoms first appeared, they will gradually disappear as the body becomes acclimatised. These mild symptoms are nothing to worry about. Most poeple are affected, regardless of age, sex or physical fitness.

The maxim 'walking high, sleeping low' is worth remembering. You can go quite high and manage for short periods and all will be well if you camp much lower. The *Himalayan Rescue Association* has a good pamphlet on Mountain Sickness.

Warning A continued rapid ascent beyond the body's ability to adjust may ultimately induce a total breakdown in the acclimatisation process. This condition is potentially fatal. It can be prevented by understanding the causes and taking the necessary precautions. **It is essential to read 'Mountain Sickness' in the Health Section page 24.**

Other Health Hints Take extra care to avoid sun burn and snow blindness. Take great care of your feet. Dehydration is a constant threat at altitude due to the cold dry air. Thirst is not a reliable indicator of your body's needs. Drink as much as possible during the day, preferably 3-4 litre.

Women Carry extra tampons or sanitary napkins which are not easily available. High altitude can affect the menstrual cycle and cause irregular periods. It is advisable not to take oral contraceptives if spending any time above 4,000 m (13,000 ft). Because of potential blood clotting problems associated with the pill, it is best to discontinue taking it for several weeks before going to altitude.

Trekking Permits and currency formalities Your visa only allows you to travel around the Kathmandu and Pokhara Valleys, to Chitwan National Park and along the few main roads in the country. For all other places, away from main roads, you need a trekking permit which is stamped in your passport.

Organised trekking agencies take care of this, but If you are arranging your own trek, go to the Immigration Office on Tridevi Marg nr Thamel, Kathmandu 1000-1300 Sun to Thr, and 1000-1200 Fri with your fee (about Rs 100 per wk for the first month and a little higher thereafter) and 2 passport photographs. In **Pokhara**, the office is between the airport and the lake.

You need to specify the route, including any side trips or variations likely. The office will also handle visa extensions, although a trekking permit automatically extends your visa. Go early as there can be long queues. In an emergency, you can extend a permit at the local Police Station for a max of a week at a time. You must change US$ 10 per day for the duration of your trek and keep a receipt to prove it was done on the official market. Thamel Passport Office has a bank counter. There are also entrance fees for the various National Parks and conservation areas: about Rs 250 for Sagarmatha (Everest) and Langtang area, Rs 200 for Annapurna region.

Warning Always carry your passport. There are regular trekking permit inspection points along most trails. Without one you can be turned back or, if in a restricted area, be deported.

EQUIPMENT AND CLOTHING

If you have good equipment, it is worth taking it even though good quality equipment can be bought or hired from a variety of trekking shops in Kathmandu or in Namche Bazaar. The daily hire charges are usually quite small but a large deposit is required, e.g. US$ 100. Running shoes are adequate for low level treks.

Down jackets are optional and are often available through trekking companies or can be hired. For rental of trekking clothing, or for purchasing ex-climbing expedition gear you will find a large number of shops in Thamel, Kathmandu. Down jackets and pants can be hired for high altitude trips like the Everest Base Camp trek. Sleeping bags can be dry cleaned at *Himal Hiking Home* in Yethka nr Durbar Square and also at *Annapurna Mountaineering* in Thamel.

Note You are strongly advised to bring your own boots and these should be comfortable, especially in hot weather and well worn in. Blisters can ruin a trek.

Clothes *Waterproof jacket* with hood and overtrousers (Gore-tex and similar makes that are windproof, waterproof and 'breather' are particularly good); *Warm sweater*; *Woollen shirt* or fibre-pile jacket.; Good lightweight *walking boots* (light yet durable boots have replaced old-style heavy ones); *Good running shoes* (suitable for many treks except in snow and off the trails); *Track suit* or woollen lightweight trousers; *Shorts*; *Skirt*; Cotton *T shirts*; *Gloves*; *Socks*; *Cotton underwear*; *Warm underwear*. (Vests, longjohns, gloves, balaclavas in Polypropylene light, warm with 'wicking' properties are best); *Woollen hat*; *Sun hat*; *Swimming costume*; *Umbrella*.

Note See S Asia Introduction and Health for further advice to all travellers.

TREKS ROUND LANGTANG, GOSAINKUND AND HELAMBU

This region north of Kathmandu, until comparatively recently, did not receive many foreign visitors. Although accessible, it lacks the 8,000 m plus giants, and so is not as popular as the Everest and Annapurna regions. The entrance to the Langtang Valley is only 30 km from the capital and the modern route through the **Trisuli River Gorge** follows an ancient trade route to Tibet. Up a side valley is *Gosainkund*. According to legend, it was formed by Siva thrusting his *trisul* (trident) into the mountain, creating the three springs. It attracts numerous Saivite pilgrims to the *Janai Poornima* full-moon festival in Jul/Aug who bathe in the holy waters.

The *Helambu* area is about 75 km NE of Kathmandu and may be reached on foot from Langtang via Gosainkund or by a circuitous route via Panchkhal and Mahakal. It consists of a number of valleys of which the Malemchi is the most important. The people are Sherpas but different from those in Sola Khumbu.

Langtang Lirung (7,245 m) dominates the valley. The technically difficult **Ganja La** (5,122 m) connects the upper valley with that of the Ripal Khola and Malemchi Khola in Helambu. The inhabitants are of Tibetan stock who intermarried with Tamangs from Helambu.

Langtang National Park, Nepal's second largest, opened in 1976. Its vegetation ranges from alpine to sub-tropical. Within its area of 1,710 sq km are 45 villages, plus a rich flora of over 1,000 plant species, 30 animal and 160 bird species. The forests of fir, pine, birch and rhododendron harbour leopard, Himalayan black bear, musk deer, red panda and monkeys. The migratory birds use the Bhote-Kosi-Trisuli river to travel between Tibet and India.

Langtang – Gosainkund – Helambu Circuit

It is possible to trek in Langtang all year round providing you stay below 3,500 m and do not make crossings out of the valley. It is best to visit Langtang first because if you cannot cross into Helambu you can at least reach Gosainkund or go some way towards it.

Day 1 Kathmandu-Dhunche Dhunche is the roadhead, about 4 hr drive from Kathmandu. From nr **Rani Pauwa** (29 km) there are good views of **Annapurna II**, **Ganes Himal** and **Manaslu**. You can depend on buses reaching *Trisuli Bazaar* (541 m), but the remaining unpaved 42 km may prove a problem. You may have to walk, adding 2 days to the trip.

Up to about 1,500 m the valley is inhabited by Brahmins and Chhetris. Tamangs live at the higher altitudes. *Dhunche* is a compact village with a few hotels, a police checkpost, where you must show your trekking permit, and a Park Office where you pay your entrance fee of about Rs 250, and where you can get an insight into the park's ecology. Keep your ticket as you will need to show it later.

Day 2 Dhunche to Syabru. A short distance from Dhunche the trail crosses the **Trisuli Khola**. This is followed by a short stiff climb to the intersection of the **Langtang Valley** and **Gosainkund** trails. Take the left hand trail which leads to **Bharku** (1,860 m). From here there is a fairly new trail which climbs over the ridge to **Syabru**. The other is longer and passes through **Syabrubesi** (1,463 m) and **Sherpagaon**. The former saves a day and climbs steeply above **Bharku** to a 2,300 m pass from which you can see **Langtang Lirung**, **Ganes Himal** and mountains in Tibet. *Syabru* (2,130 m) is situated on a spur, a few hundred metres below the pass, and has a few hotels.

Day 3 Syabru to Chomgong. Walk through forest to the **Langtang Khola** (1,860 m) then follow it upstream gaining height rapidly. After some distance you cross the river by a bridge to the N bank and the thinner, drier forest. *Chomgong* (2,380 m) is a small hamlet with a hotel and camping ground.

Day 4 Chomgong to Langtang Village. Climb above the village then follow the trail around the cliffs. **Ghora Tabela** (3,000 m) has a police checkpost where you will have to show your permit and entrance fee receipt. The valley becomes wider and you pass some Tamang villages. *Langtang* (3,500 m) has Tibetan style houses and walled fields. The airstrip nearby is for charter flights.

Day 5 Langtang to *Kyanjin Gompa*. The valley continues to become wider. Kyanjin Gompa (3,800 m) has a monastery and a yak cheese factory established by the Swiss in 1955. It only takes half a day to reach the village but it is wise not to continue higher in order to acclimatise.

Day 6 Use Kyanjin Gompa as a base and make a day trip to the glacial moraine to get a good view of **Langtang Lirung** (7,245 m) the highest peak in the area.

Tarke Gyang Via Ganja La

This is a difficult trek. From Langtang it is possible for groups with sufficient skill to cross the Chimse Danda ridge to the South using the Ganja La pass (5,122 m). The pass is generally open from May until Nov. There are stone shepherds' huts but some of these are not particularly comfortable so a tent is necessary. Allow 4 days for the trip.

Warning Single trekkers should not attempt it without a local guide.

Day 1 You make relatively short but steep ascent to **Ngegang** (4,000 m), a seasonal (monsoon) yak pasture. Much of this is through rhododendron and juniper forest.

Day 2 You climb steeply towards the pass and will probably encounter snow fairly early on. The last few hundred metres is precarious so the utmost care is needed. From the pass there are spectacular views of **Langtang Lirung** and the Tibetan peaks beyond. The descent is on a steep and dangerous scree slope for over 1 km. Again care is needed. After some distance you reach the basin of **Ganja La Chuli** (5,846 m). Further down you reach the **Yangri Khola** which you follow until you reach the stone shepherd's huts at **Keldang** (4,270 m). Again, a tent is necessary.

Day 3 It is a long, undulating grind along the ridge to **Phedi**. Apart from the post monsoon months of Oct and Nov and during the monsoon itself there is no water.

Day 4 You first have to cross a 4,020 m pass which offers good views before descending through rhododendron to pine forest. Some stretches are quite steep. **Gekye Gompa** (3,020 m) is above the Sherpa village of **Tarke Gyang** (2,560 m).

To Gosainkund and Tarke Gyang

A moderately difficult trek. To avoid confusion, the numbering of days is continued from Day 6 at Kyanjin Gompa (see first route).

Day 7 and 8 Retrace your steps to **Syabru**.

Day 9 From Syabru there is a confusing trail that involves a lot of climbing. You have to stay to the right of the spur and travel in a S direction. Stay high and cross the ridge into the **Trisuli Khola** Valley. About 1 hr's walk from the ridge you reach **Sing Gompa** and **Chandan Bari** (3,350 m) where there is a small cheese factory. A local guide is recommended for the stretch to **Tharepati** (Day 12).

Day 10 Sing Gompa to Gosainkund. The trail continues upwards through forest. There are no villages, only a few shepherd's huts. There are magnificent views of *Himal Chuli* (6,893 m) and *Manaslu* (8,156 m) to the W and **Langtang Lirung** to the N. The trail tends to follow the ridge and descends to the first lake, **Saraswati Kund** (4,100 m). A few stone shelters are situated round the lake. You will have to carry your own food. **Gosainkund** (4,380 m) is the third lake with **Bhairav Kund** in between.

Day 11 Gosainkund to Gopte. Either return down the valley to **Dhunche** or cross over into the **Helambu** region. The latter climbs though rugged country, passing 4 more small lakes and ascending the **Lauribina Pass** (4,610 m). Good views from here. You then descend along a stream and ascend a forested ridge. **Gopte** (3,260 m) has a cave shelter.

Day 12 Gopte to Tharepati and Tarke Gyang From the ridge you descend towards the valley, mostly through forest, passing the occasional shepherd's hut. After crossing a stream at 3,310 m you climb to **Tharepati** (3,490 m). You can continue along the ridge to Khulumsang, Gul Bhaniyang and Pati Baniyang to Borlang Bhaniyang and Sundarijal, where you can get a bus back to **Kathmandu**. Alternatively go down into the valley to **Tarke Gyanga** and walk out by the easier valley route. The ridge walk is tiring as there are constant ups and downs, and the path may be indistinct in places. To reach Tarke Gyang, you drop down to cross the **Malemchi Khola** at **Malemchigaon** (1,890 m) and then climb steadily.

Tarke Gyang is the main village in Helambu and has a number of hotels. The renovated gompa is quite impressive. The Helambu Sherpas are a trading community. **Warning** The 'antique' items here, are more likely to be new manufactures bought in from Kathmandu and Patan and rapidly aged.

Day 13 Tarke Gyang to Kiul The easiest way is to take the path to **Timbu** and then follow the river to **Kiul**. Descend through rhododendron forest, passing several *chortens** and *mani** walls, to **Kakani** (2,070 m) and **Timbu** (1,870 m) where the countryside is more extensively cultivated. This also marks the boundary between Sherpa country to the N and the Newar and Brahmin /Chhetri Hindu dominated area to the S. The trail now descends steeply to **Kiul** (1,280 m). A longer walk follows the ridge running down the E side of the valley to Malemchi.

Day 14 Kiul to Pati Bhaniyang. Follow the river downstream and cross by the suspension bridge to **Mahenkhal** (1,130 m) with a road. *Taramarang* (940 m) is a roadhead village. Cross the **Taramarang Khola** and follow it up towards its source, first walking through terraced fields and then into the boulder strewn valley. Above this is **Batache** village, below the 1,900 m ridge. Go over the ridge and descend to **Pati Bhaniyang** (1,770 m), a large Tamang village with hotels, shops and a police checkpost.

Day 15 Pati Bhaniyang to Sundarijal and Kathmandu. Follow the ridge along to **Borlang Bhaniyang** just below the ridge and pass over to *Mulkharka* (1,895 m) with its fine views of the Kathmandu Valley. The forest of rhododendron, pine and oak around here is the source of much of Kathmandu's wood fuel and in the mornings hundreds of villagers can be seen going to cut it. Drop down from the **Seopuri** ridge to a dam and then continue through forest to *Sundarijal* (1,285 m) where you can easily get transport back to Kathmandu.

THE EVEREST REGION

George Mallory, the British mountaineer, when asked why he wanted to climb **Mount Everest**, replied 'Because, it is there'. Everest is the magnet of Nepal. Many are attracted by the mountain itself, others by the **Sola Khumbu** region, the home of the Sherpas, and some by both. The Everest Base Camp trek is the second most popular in Nepal and the longest established.

Everest (8,848 m) – *Sagarmatha* in Nepali ("Mother of the Sea") and *Chomolungma* (Tibetan). It is part of the 3,104 sq km **Sagarmatha National Park**, established in 1976 with help from the New Zealand government . The Sherpas live within its boundaries. Visitors must abide by a few simple rules, the most important being that they must carry in fuel and dispose their rubbish carefully. In 1979 Sagarmatha was declared a World Heritage Site.

The park has only been a partial success. Deforestation continues, although alternative energy sources such as small-scale hydro-electricty schemes are being developed to meet the needs of the growing Sherpa population and up to 10,000 trekkers a year. *Sir Edmund Hillary* had noted on the 1953 British Expedition a forest of junipers around Pangboche which, thirty years later had practically disappeared. He felt a sense of responsibility, knowing that the expedition had paved the way for others who recruited small armies of porters who attacked the forests. To rectify the destruction, he set up the Himalayan Trust which, as an independent non-governmental organisation, has undertaken extensive building works in the region. The Trust has been careful to provide the services that the Sherpas themselves have asked for, namely schools and hospitals. By 1973 Hillary realised that some sort of control was needed if the Khumbu region was not to become a treeless desert. Responding to his overtures the New Zealand government assisted with the creation and management of the park.

Tenzing The Khumbu region has provided a valuable contingent of able-bodied, hardy and seemingly fearless Sherpa porters and guides. Over 80 years they have built up a mountaineering reputation as the elite of Himalayan porters. Early expeditions took Sherpas from Darjiling to climb in far flung places in the Himalayas, who were often referred to as 'Tigers', but they were rarely accorded the recognition of their full worth. **Tenzing Norkay** (1912-1986), the quintessential Himalayan mountain guide, had to make do with a George Medal, the British civilian award for bravery, whilst Hunt was elevated to the peerage and Hillary was knighted. Hillary said years later that in his view, Tenzing should also have been knighted. He would have handled it with great dignity.

Tenzing began his career as the companion and guide of the Tibetologist Guiseppe Tucci. After being a member of 5 unsuccessful British expeditions to Everest from 1921-38 and the Swiss Expedition of 1952 which very nearly made it, he and Hillary finally succeeded and stood on top of the mountain at 1130 on 29 May 1953. Unable to write, he dictated his biography to Malcolm Barnes, became a household name, an honorary Indian and Director of the Himalayan Mountaineering Institute at Darjiling. Without Tenzing and his Sherpas it is doubtful that the 1953 Expedition, or many others afterwards for that matter, would have been successful.

Travel You can either walk to the Park or take a 40 min flight from Kathmandu (RNAC into *Lukla* airstrip, 2,850 m) and then walk several km up the Dudh Kosi Valley to the entrance. Lukla is a STOL (short take-off and landing) airstrip and touching down can be unnerving for some! The first alternative is preferable as it allows the body to acclimatise gradually and it a very scenic route. **Warning** If you fly, allow time for acclimatisation at Lukla, Namche Bazaar or Thyangboche before proceeeding higher.

The classic trek to **Everest Base Camp** from **Jiri** takes around 3 weeks. You move from the predominantly Hindu Middle Hills to the Tibetan Buddhist High Himalaya. Mountaineering expeditions enjoyed it as a means of getting fit as well as acclimatising. Some trekkers fly both ways, but most walk in and fly out. Delays at Lukla are common so allow a few days for flexibility.

Because of its popularity, the trail and Sagarmatha region is well served with guesthouses and inns, though less luxurious than in the Annapurna region.

Health Because of its status and popularity and the unstinting efforts of Hillary's Himalayan Trust, there is a hospital at **Khumjung**. The Himalayan Rescue Association has a medical facility at **Pheriche** and there are small hospitals at Jiri, Phaphlu and Khunde. In the case of an extreme necessity, e.g. cardiac arrest, there is a helicopter evacuation service.

Rescue The **Himalayan Rescue Association** maintains a **Trekkers' Aid Post** at *Pheriche*. This is staffed by a physician and trained Sherpa assistants during the 2 trekking seasons whose job is to advise people about the problems of altitude and when necessary, arrange rescues and treat victims. If a person is having problems above Pheriche, come down, carrying or assisting the affected person. Always accompany anyone with severe symptoms of mountain sickness. Descent invariably brings about a marked improvement.

Khunde also has a hospital which is staffed by a doctor and Sherpa assistants. If a member of a group is severely affected, one or 2 others should go on ahead to the Trekkers' Aid Post where staff may decide to evacuate the victim by helicopter. On no account leave an affected person on his/her own. Helicopter evacuation is the last resort though it may take up to 24 hr to arrive and then, only if some guarantee of payment is made. Trekking agencies often arrange for this contingency for their clients.

The Base Camp trail involves many ascents and descents as you move from one N-S valley to the next. A high degree of fitness is essential to fully enjoy the trek. Many trekking companies worldwide offer the Base Camp trek in their programme so you will pass numerous trekking parties of all nationalities. Popular campsites can be congested and water sources polluted, so infection is a hazard.

Note Out of courtesy to sherpas do not attempt to climb *Khumbi-yul-lha*, the mountain directly behind Khunde and Khumjung, as this is the sacred abode of the deity that protects the Khumbu region. Please read important sections on Health in S Asia Introduction **page 22** and Hints on Social behaviour in Information for Visitors **page 1339**).

Climate Weather conditions can change very rapidly at high altitude, particularly as a result of unforeseeable changes in the W jet stream, **see page 36**. The Khumbu climate is dominated by the mountains that enclose the valleys. They deflect much of the wind coming off the Tibetan Plateau and act as a wall for the rain-bearing monsoon clouds brought in from the Bay of Bengal.

The trekking season Heavy frosts are common in Namche Bazaar from late Oct onwards and gradually the ground freezes to a depth of around 500 mm. There is light snow in autumn. Dec, Jan and Feb are the coldest months and heavy falls of snow occur after Dec. From Jan. to Mar. the weather is fairly settled with periods of clear weather lasting for up to 3 weeks at a time. These are broken by short stormy periods lasting a few days.

Between Nov and Mar the average daily temperature is only a few degrees above freezing. At night it can fall to minus 15°C at **Namche Bazaar** and below 20°C beyond **Lobuche**. These temperatures rise steadily from March onwards until the onset of the monsoon. This is a period of little rain and increasing heat and haziness.

The monsoon 'arrives' in mid-June. Rapidly forming rain clouds cover the peaks and fill the valleys by midday. Light mist turns into heavy rainfall by nightfall. At higher altitudes this turns to snow. Visibility is poor and clinging mists can hang around in valleys for weeks. From mid-Sep the clouds and rain withdraw. 75% of the annual rainfall of 1,000 mm comes during the monsoon. The peaks receive most of their snow at this time and the snowline comes down to 5,500 m.

Everest Base Camp Trek

Day 1 Kathmandu to Jiri via Lamosanga. Buses leave Kathmandu throughout the day for Jiri. It takes 12 hr by public bus, much less by private. The route passes through **Bhaktapur**, **Banepa** and **Dhulikhel**. Trekkers going into the **Helambu** region get down at **Panchkal**. Others continue to **Lamosangu**, a market town approximately 50 km from the Tibetan border and 78 km from Kathmandu. **Jiri** (1,800 m), 110 km from **Lamosangu**, has a STOL airstrip so you can fly in, though it is much more expensive. There are several hotels.

Day 2 Jiri to Bhandar The **Solu Khumbu** trail starts at the head of the road behind the hospital and climbs through forest and the occasional hamlet to cross an open ridge at **Chitre** (2,400 m). You then descend into the **Khimti Khola Valley** and **Shivalaya** (1,800 m), a large village with a market.

From **Shivalaya** you ascend to a 2,705 m pass passing through **Sangbadanda** (2,150 m) and **Kosaribas** (2,500 m). You will notice the first *mani* walls of the trip which marks your moving from a predominantly Hindu region into regions inhabited by the Tibetan Buddhist Tamangs and Sherpas. Walk to the left of mani walls and chortens.

The pass is approached through forest. There is an impressive mani wall and a good view of the **Likhu Khola** and **Bhandar**. A short distance below the pass, the path forks. The right goes to the **Solu region** via Roshi. Take the left hand trail for **Bhandar** which you reach after crossing pasture and the cultivated area. **Bhandar** has a gompa and 2 striking *chortens*. The village has a number of hotels and a good camping ground about 15 min walk beyond the settlement.

Day 3 Bhandar to Sagar The trail descends to **Baranda** and the **Likhu Khola** (1,580 m) which you cross by suspension bridge. Following the river upstream to **Kenja** 1,630 m) you may see grey langur monkey troops in the forest. From **Kenja**, home of the Newars, Sherpas and Magars, where there are shops, restaurants and hotels, you climb up to the **Lamjura ridge**, first steeply then more gradually. At the trail junction the left fork leads up to the Sherpa village of **Sagar** (2,440 m). There is a Himalayan Trust School here and some small hotels. People often camp in the schoolyard. If you take the right hand fork you reach **Sete** (2,575 m) which is difficult for camping but has a number of hotels. You are now in Sherpa country. All the remaining villages on the trek are Sherpa.

Day 4 Sagar/Sete to Junbesi Start with a long, mostly steady climb through forest of rhododendron, magnolia, maple and birch to **Lamjura Pass** (3,530 m). The trails from Sagar and Sete merge before the pass. **Goyem** (3,300 m) is a good rest stop, Tragboduk being at least 3 hr away. On the pass is a cairn topped with prayer flags marking the highest point between Jiri and Namche Bazaar. On the far side you descend gradually, first through forest, then through meadows and fields to **Tragboduk** (2,860) which has a few hotels.

Climb again to a huge rock at the head of the valley, then go over the ridge to **Junbesi** (2,675 m, Jun in Sherpa dialect) in the Solu region. The village has a monastery and several large hotels. Camping is below the village on the river bank. Around the village are a few sights worth seeing. To the N, 2 hr walk away, is the large monastery of **Thubten Chhuling** (**Mopung** on Schneider map), and there is a Sherpa art centre at **Phugmoche**. The monastery situated at 3,000 m, with about 200 Tibetan refugee monks, was founded in 1960.

Day 5 Junbesi to Nuntala The trail drops to **Phaphlu**, where there is an airstrip and Himalayan Trust Hospital, then climbs to cross the ridge at 3,080 m, giving the first view of Everest (7,317 m) and **Makalu** (8,463 m). Descend through **Salung** (2,980 m) to the **Ringmo Khola** (2,650 m), a good place for washing – the next river, the **Dudh Kosi**, is much colder. Climb to Ringmo village, where you join the improved trail to Namche Bazaar, and then to the **Trakshindo Pass** (3,070 m; hotels). Drop down past the impressive **Trakshindo monastery** and through rhododendron forest to **Nuntala** (Manidingma, 2320 m), which has reasonable accommodation.

Day 6 Nuntala to Khari Khola Descend to the **Dudh Kosi**. Cross and turn N to follow the river to **Namche Bazaar**. The trail climbs to **Jubing** (Dorakbuk, 1,680 m),inhabited by the **Rais** (a group recruited into the Gurkha regiments), who have adopted both Hinduism and Buddhism. It continues up to **Khari Kholi** (Khat Thenga, 2,070 m) Good hotel accommodation. The campsite is beyond the village across the bridge. It is possible to reach **Bupsa** (see Day 7) from **Nuntala**. However, it may be difficult to persuade hired porters to go further. Independent walkers have no problem.

Day 7 Khari Khola to Puiyan Drop to cross the **Khari Khola** at 2,100 m where there are some mills, then climb up to **Bupsa** (*Bumshing*) where there is a white chorten and some hotels. Continuing, you climb steadily to the ridge. The **Dudh Kosi Canyon** is very precipitous here. From the 2,900 m pass you descend along an impressive, scary for some, section of the trail into the side canyon of the **Puiyan Khola**. The village is situated at 2,730 m and has hotels.

Day 8 Puiyan to Phakding You climb for about 1 hr to the 2,800 m ridge above Puiyan, from where you can see Lukla airstrip, recognised by the roof of the Sherpa Co-operative Hotel, and possibly still some wrecked planes. The trail descends to just above **Surkhe** (Buwa, 2,293 m) which is situated on a tributary of the Dudh Kosi. From Surkhe you climb for about 15 min to a trail junction. **Lukla** airstrip is about 1 hr's steep climb, up a stone staircase to the right. The **Khumbu** trail continues N to **Mushe** (Nangbug)which merges with Chaunrikarka (Dungde, 2,680 m). There are hotels here, but you can carry on through terraced fields to **Chablung** (Lomdza) where the track is joined by that from Lukla.

Ghat (*Lhawa*, 2,550 m) is the next village, followed after an undulating section of the trail, by **Phakding** (2,800 m), situated on both sides of the river. From here the trail climbs up the **Dudh Kosi** canyon, crossing from side to side through forests of blue pine, fir and juniper.

Between 3,600 m and 4,200 m birch and rhododendron predominate. Solid villages with long dry stone walls of the type so common in the English Yorkshire dales and the Lake District can be seen running down from the high meadows. Many of the huge boulders are carved with the now familiar Buddhist mantra *'Om mani padme hum'*. The highest village in this region is *Jorsale*, the entrance to the **Sagarmatha National Park**. All trekkers must register here. You may pay for the entry ticket here, which you show again at the Namche checkpost. Accommodation is not a problem with over 100 inns and hotels in the Khumbu region.

Note Do not remove anything from the park, e.g. rock samples, flora and fauna specimens. Do not disturb wildlife or carry arms or explosives.

Day 9 Phakding to Namche Bazaar The trail from Phakding follows the Dudh Kosi about 100 m above the river, crosses over to **Benkar**, crosses back some distance afterwards, then climbs to the village of **Chomoa**. Descend to cross a stream, then climb again to **Monjo** on the very edge of the park. A short distance up the W bank of the river through forest is **Jorsale** (*Thumbug*, 2,850 m). Numerous hotels; a good lunch stop as it is a further 3 hr to Namche Bazaar. The entrance to the park is just beyond the village (Rs.250 entry fee).

Warning You are also forbidden to scale any mountain without permission or any sacred peak of any elevation. You are requested to keep to the main trails and carry sufficient fuel for your stay. Buying firewood from the local population is forbidden, which applies to porters as well. Park personnel are entitled to arrest anyone suspected of infringing these regulations and may search a trekkers' and porters' belongings. Kerosene is often available at Namche Bazaar's Sat market. As with most S Asian kerosene, a filter is usually required to sift out pieces of dirt which if left can clog up a stove and render it inoperable.

Beyond **Jorsale** the trail undulates up the W side of the valley up to the confluence of the **Bhote Kosi** and **Dudh Kosi**. This part of the trail is sunless and notoriously cold and windy, the wind funnelling down the gorges of both rivers. Camping in this inhospitable spot may however be rewarded with sighting a Red Panda.

In terms of animal conservation Sagarmatha has proved to be an outstanding success. Within its sheltered environment many creatures are on the increase. The sure-footed Himalayan *tahr*, the size of an American mountain goat, can be seen on seemingly unscalable hillsides. Nepal's national bird, the Impeyan pheasant (the male, beautifully coloured) is also fairly common, although farmers regard it as a pest. Sagarmatha is one of the few places where the prized musk deer is safe from poachers. Only the males, which have two fang-like canine teeth, produce the musk, secreted from a small orifice near the urethra. The Chinese value it as a folk medicine and aphrodisiac, and about 30 g can fetch what an average Nepalese would earn in a year.

From here you begin the final steep climb to **Namche Bazaar**. From 2 places along the trail you can see Everest, **Nuptse** and **Lhotse,** but by the afternoon these are usually covered in cloud.

  Namche Bazaar (*Nauche*, 3,440 m) is situated in a a sheltered horse-shoe shaped basin high above the **Bhote Kosi Gorge**. Terraced houses cling to the hillside. There are numerous hotels here and many have hot showers, a great luxury when trekking in the Himalaya. There is also a bank, police checkpost, restaurants, a bakery and the park office. Exotic delicacies such as banana cake, cinnamon roll, apple pie and Mars bars are available.

Day 10 A rest day should be spent relaxing in Namche Bazaar for acclimatisation. Another should be built into your programme if you are going to the Base Camp. It is important that you allow 2 nights at the same place twice between Lukla and Lobuche.
  The Sat market is usually colourful and noisy. Traders from lower altitudes, mostly Tamangs and Rais, carry in baskets of rice, millet and other produce, often having been on the road for up to a week. Sherpas from surrounding villages converge to make their purchases and socialise in the tea and *chang** shops.
  You must present your trekking permit and park entrance ticket at the police checkpost. Above it is the Sagarmatha National Park Headquarters with a **Visitors' Centre** for information and a good presentation on the park's ecosystem and the impact of tourism.

Day 11 Namche Bazaar to Thyangboche. There are 2 routes to Thyangboche, the direct one from Chhorkung and a slightly longer but more interesting one via Khumjung and Khunde which is described here.

There are 3 other trails splaying out from **Namche**, and all 4 follow the major valleys in the Park: the **Bhote Kosi**, the traditional trading route to Tibet; the **Dudh Kosi**, leading to the Ngozumpa Glacier, Gokyo Lake and Mt Cho Oyu; the **Imja Valley** running up under Nuptse and Lhotse, Baruntse and the back of Ama Dablam; the main **Khumbu Valley** leading up to Everest Base Camp. The other 3 routes are described later.

From **Namche Bazaar** it is 1 hr long steep climb to *Shyangboche* (3,720 m), where there is an airstrip which was built to service the problem ridden Everest View Hotel. Closed since 1983, it expects to reopen by 1991 with plans to build a pressurised room to enable guests to acclimatize. There are good views of **Ama Dablam** and **Everest** from here.

The trail then descends from the hotel to the village of **Khumjung** (3,790 m). The *gompa* claims to possess the skull of a yeti though scientific examination suggests that it is probably a *serow,* an antelope. The mixed forest of rhododendron, birch and silver fir is quite a contrast to the bare slopes of the gorge and you may see musk deer and Impeyan pheasant.

The village of ***Khunde*** with its Himalayan Trust school and hospital is a short distance away. Across the canyon from Khunde and opp the confluence of the Imja Khola and Dudh Kosi rivers is *Thyangboche* (3,870 m) with its famous monastery. The trail to it from **Khumjung** goes down the valley, past chortens and mani walls and soon meets the direct Namche Bazaar-Thyangboche trail. Just beyond is **Kenjoma** with its few hotels. Further on you descend to Teshinga and lower still to *Phunki Tenga* (3,250 m), noted for its water driven prayer wheels.

Climb steeply at first through forest, and then more gradually to the Thyangboche saddle. At dawn the view is magnificent: **Kwangde** (6,187 m), **Tawachee** (6,542 m), **Everest** (8,848 m), **Nuptse** (7,855 m), **Lhotse** (8,616 m), **Ama Dablam** (6,856 m), **Kangtega** (6,779 m) and **Thamserku** (6,608 m), arrayed in a stunning panorama. National Park Lodge and a number of hotels. Certain campsites are reserved for individual companies. The monastery was burnt down by fire in 1988 and should have been rebuilt by the end of 1991. The monastery expects a donation of around Rs 10 per tent (receipted by a monk) for camping in the grounds.

At the Nov/Dec full moon the *Mani Rimdu* festival takes place. The colourful masked dances depict the triumph of Buddhism over the old Bon faith of Tibet. Entry charge and additional movie camera surcharge. The festival is also held at **Thami** monastery in May – see Bhote Kosi section later.

Day 12 Thyangboche to Pheriche Descend through the forest to *Devuche* where there are a few travellers' lodges and a nunnery. After crossing the **Imja Khola** on a steel suspension bridge climb up past some mani stones to *Pangboche* (3,860 m), the highest all-year settlement in the valley. The gompa claims to have a yeti scalp and hand, visible for a small fee. Himalayan Rescue Association Trekkers' First Aid Post and a number of hotels. There are 2 parts to the village. The lower can be visited on the way to Everest Base Camp, the upper on the return.

From Pangboche the trail initially remains fairly steady above the Imja Khola then climbs through a small group of houses called **Shomare**. Continue along a broad terrace to the confluence of the **Imja Khola** and **Lobuche Khola**. The track diverges, the right hand one running up to **Dingboche**, the highest permanently settled area and a producer of high quality barley for *tsampa**.

Take the left hand trail which passes above some houses, mounts a shoulder then descends and crosses the **Khumbu Khola**. This valley is wide and flat until it reaches the terminal moraine of the Khumbu Glacier. Pheriche (4,240 m) is at the lower end and consists mainly of hotels and teashops plus a shop selling expedition leftovers.

Day 13 Spend a **rest day** here even if you are feeling in good condition. A side trip can be made up to **Nangkartshang Gompa** (approx 4,600 m) which offers a good view of Makalu. There is another, more strenuous side trip to **Chhukung** (4,700 m) a small summer settlement where you get excellent views of **Island Peak**, **Lhotse** and **Ama Dablam**. Climb the hill to Dingboche, then follow the Imja Khola to **Chhukung**.

Day 14 Pheriche to Lobuje The first part of the route passes up the long scrubby flat bottom of the valley to **Phulong Karpo**. It rises steadily then drops down, crosses the river and enters **Duglha** (4,620 m) with its teashops. From here the trail climbs higher and onto the moraine. A row of chortens in memory of the Sherpas who have died on Everest marks the top of the climb. Follow the small valley and stream bed on the left hand side of the moraine. **Lobuje** (4,930) has several hotels including the National Park Lodge. Everything in Lobuje is expensive, hardly surprising considering its location. The views of **Tawache** and **Nuptse** are very spectacular.

Day 15 Lobuje to Gorak Shep Continue up the grassy valley beside the Khumbu Glacier moraine until the terminal moraine of the **Changri Nup** and **Changri Shar** glaciers is reached. It then becomes steeper and rougher as you climb to the top of the moraine. As it crosses an unconsolidated slope, the route changes from season to season. Usually there are small stone cairns and tell-tale signs of yak droppings to indicate the way. Then it is a short descent to the dry sandy area of Gorak Shep which has a small lake beyond. **Pumori** (7,161 m) is easily seen and if you follow the S ridge down you can see **Kala Pattar** (5,545 m), the common vantage point for viewing Everest.

You can reach Gorak Shep by lunchtime. There is little in the way of hotel accommodation. If you leave Lobuje early, you can climb **Kala Pattar** (Black Rock) and then return to Lobuje at the end of a tiring but immensely satisfying day. If you are in a party, you do not need to strike camp and can travel fairly light. However, be sure to take plenty of clothing for bitterly cold mornings, and some emergency rations. It is tiring because of the altitude, the grass slope and the steepness of the ascent, but from the top you can see the S face of **Everest** off to the E (in winter you may be surprised at how little snow there is on Everest's S Face), the W Ridge running down to the **Lho La** (6,026 m). To the SW is **Nuptse** (7,861 m).

Everest For 13 years after it was found to be the highest mountain in the world, **Peak XV** had no European name. In 1865 the then Surveyor Gen of India suggested that it be named it after his predecessor, Sir George Everest, the man responsible for the remarkable Great Trigonometrical Survey which ultimately determined its height. Everest himself, while honoured, was privately unhappy, as it was official policy that mountains be given their local vernacular name. However, an exception was made and the name stuck.

Everest has now been climbed many times and by many routes since 1953. The route taken by Hunt's expedition is the 'Ordinary Route', disparagingly called the 'Yak' route by Sherpas. Following his achievement on Annapurna's S Face, Chris Bonington led 2 expeditions to tackle Everest's SW Face and succeeded in 1975. The Americans traversed it in 1963. In 1970 Yuichiro Muira tried to ski down the Lhotse Face from the S Col, spent most of it airborne and out of control and ended up unconscious on the edge of a crevasse! Rheinhold Messner climbed it without oxygen and then solo. Ang Pertember has been there twice as well. Peter Hillary followed in his father's footsteps and stood on the summit in 1990. In April 1988 2 teams of Japanese climbers met on top, having scaled the N and S Faces. There to record the event was a television crew!

Day 16 Gorak Shep to Base Camp To do this trip you need to stay at Gorak Shep and make a day trip. Most prefer not to, being quite content with the view from Kala Pattar. Everest Base Camp is to the E of the Khumbu Glacier. After leaving the head of the lake at Gorak Shep you climb through a boulder strewn area, some of the rocks having inscriptions to the many climbers and Sherpas who have died in the pursuit of the summit. The trail then crosses the moraine wall and descends to the **Khumbu Glacier** which you cross. Cairns mark the route which changes constantly. Take great care.

The Base Camp area is at 5,400 m and if there are expeditions in residence you may not be welcome. Some put signs up to dissuade calls. The round trip from Gorak Shep takes over 6 hr and is not as rewarding as the Kala Pattar walk, as Everest is not in view from the camp. Beyond the Base Camp requires mountaineering skills.

The return to Namche Bazaar and Lukla 3 to 4 days should be allowed for the return. You will probably be pleasantly surprised that as you descend you feel great rushes of energy. Going down can be done at any speed, but care is needed and on long descents it can be quite tiring on the knees and calves.

An interesting variation is to visit **Dingboche** (4,360 m) at the mouth of the **Imja Khola Valley**. Take the uphill route to **Dugha** on the opp side of the valley, past yak pastures to a chorten and Dingboche, a typical summer village with a few hotels. The view of **Island Peak** (6,189 m) at the head of the valley, and Ama Dablam and Makalu in the distance, is impressive. To reach the main route back to Namche you can either cross to **Pheriche** on the W side, or follow the Imja Khola down to its confluence with the Khumbu Khola.

From Namche Bazaar to **Lukla** you retrace your steps as far **Chablung** then turn off above **Chaunrikarka** towards Lukla. There are some good hotels, including the *Sherpa Co-Operative*. The RNAC office in Lukla is usually open 1700-1800, sometimes 1 hr later, for you to re-confirm your flight. Failure to do this may mean loss of your seat. Check-in begins early in the morning and can be chaotic, especially if there is a backlog of passengers. Your hotelier will have all the relevant information.

Gokyo Lakes

Dudh Kosi Valley does not receive as many visitors as the Khombu Khola to Kala Pattar, but this does not mean that it is less spectacular. If anything, it is more so. There is a **Kala Pattar** (5,483 m) here as well, from which you can see 4 of the world's eight highest mountains: Everest (1), Lhotse (4), Makalu (5), Cho Oyu (8), as well as Gyachung Kang, Cholatse, Tawachee and many others. The ridge between Cho Oyu (8,021 m) and Gyachung Kang (7,952 m) is stunning. It is also possible, given good weather, the proper equipment and basic mountaineering skills to traverse the **Chola Lha** (5,420 m) into the Khumbu Valley.

Days 1-2 The same requirements for acclimatisation apply, so you should allow at least 2 days before you actually enter the valley at Phortse. A rest day at **Namche Bazaar** followed by the walk to **Phortse** then possibly another rest day is recommended.

From Namche, follow the main route up the Dudh Kosi to some teashops at **Sarnasa** where there is a junction with the Phortse trail, above which the trail divides. You can take either way – the right is wider and suitable for livestock, the left climbs the bluffs on a staircase, through a cleft. Near the top of the ridge the 2 trails rejoin and continue towards a chorten. This ridge runs down from **Khumbi-yul-lha**, the Sherpa's guardian mountain. **Warning** You should not climb this on any account.

Beyond Phortse village, the track on the W side of the valley offers a good choice of campsites. It then climbs steeply through rhododendron forest and past the Sherpa summer settlements of **Tongba** (3,950 m), **Gyele** (3,960 m), **Dole** and **Lhabarma** (4,220 m). **Luza** (4,360 m) is situated in another side valley by a perennial water source. There are good views of **Tawachee** and **Khumbila**.

Day 3 From **Luza** a gentle climb high above the river brings you to the wide **Machhermo Valley**. Cross the stream and veer back towards the Dudh Kosi. Opp **Pangkha** village is the terminal moraine of the **Ngozumpa glacier**, the longest in Nepal. You climb the moraine to the first lake at 4,650 m and the trail levels off. The second lake is at 4,750 m and **Gokyo Lake** (4,750 m). The fourth and fifth lakes are beyond Gokyo.

Day 4 Many of the who have been to both **Kala Pattars** reckon that from Gokyo, which takes 2 hr, it offers the better views.

Days 5-6 The return to **Namche Bazaar** should take only 2 days. It is possible to go over the **Chola La** (5,420 m) to **Pheriche**. Whilst not technically difficult, you should have basic mountaineering equipment in case conditions become difficult, e.g. ice-axe, rope and preferably crampons. Yaks and heavily laden porters cannot negotiate the terrain but can take the main Khumbu trail and meet up after 2-3 days.

Imja Khola and Island Peak

See above (Everest Base Camp Trek) for route to **Pheriche**, where the track divides. The right hand trail leads up the **Imja Khola Valley** to **Island Peak** (6,189 m), the most popular trekking peak in Nepal. You need a permit, and a guide if you are not very experienced. You climb above the river to some terraces and a low ridge. **Dingboche** (4,360 m) is on a wide alluvial terrace and near the stream is a chorten and hotels. Bibre is the next village and the next night halt is **Chhukong**, a summer grazing village. Food and accommodation in season.

From Chukong the route ascends and follows a moraine ridge before descending to a wide, open area between the Imja and Lhotse moraines. Beyond is the terminal moraine of the **Imja Glacier** and near its base is an old lake bed, a suitable place for a base camp.

The Bhote Kosi and Thami Valleys

Running NW from Namche Bazaar is the Bhote Kosi Valley which has some facilities for trekkers. The Thami gompa is the site of the other *Mani Rimdu Festival* – see Thyangboche.

Leaving **Namche Bazaar** the trail climbs through forest to **Thamo**. You pass through open country with fine mani walls and descend to the river. The trail then climbs the W bank and through a rhododendron forest, into the side valley of **Thengpo Khola** and the fields of **Lower Thami**. Here the trail divides, the left going into the village, the other up a low ridge dividing the **Thengpo** from the **Bhote Kosi**. Good views up both valleys.

Upper Thami is up the Bhote Kosi on its W bank. The monastery clinging to the mountainside, an important Buddhist centre in the Park, is still relatively unspoilt. The National Park Guard Post and Police checkpost are in the village. Because it is a sensitive border area, you are not allowed to go further, towards the **Nangpa La** pass.

The Return to Kathmandu
Warning It is essential to be prepared for delays getting back to Kathmandu from Lukla. If you are really desperate for an alternative, with a 5 day trek you can reach *Lamidanda*, the air traffic control point for this region, with flights to Kathmandu and Biratnagar.

Day 1 Lukla to Bupsa The trail begins at the end of Lukla airstrip and descends to join the main trail to Kathmandu. At Surkhe you begin to climb across the pass at Puiyan and descend to Bupsa (2,300 m) which has Hotels.

Day 2 Bupsa to Wobsa Khani A short steep descent brings you to the important market village of **Khari Khola** (2,070 m) where you can stock up with provisions. The trail climbs above it and after nearly 30 min, you cross the ridge to **Jube** (2,100 m) Descend and cross the **Thana Khola** and ascend a side valley. After about 2 hr you reach **Wobsa Khani** (1,800 m), a Rai village below which there is a copper mine and smelter.

Day 3 From Wobsa descend through Waku (1,500 m) and Suntale (1,100 m) to the **Hinku Khola river** (980 m). Cross, and climb over the 1,290 m ridge to **Khorde**, descending again to cross the same river at 900 m. Climb to the ridge (1,590 m) passing **Utha**. There are stone huts here or you can camp. **Lokhim** (1,800 m),is about 1½hr further.

Day 4 The trail contours round the **Dudu Kosi Valley** before climbing steeply to **Deorali**. Go over the pass, descend to the Sherpa village of Harise (2,300 m) then drop down to Aiselukharka (2,100 m). From here a wide track leads to Ilim (1,450 m).

Day 5 The trail descends through sub-tropical vegetation to the **Ra Khola** river then ascends to **Pipal Danda**, afterwards following the hillside round to **Lamidanda**.

TREKKING IN EASTERN NEPAL

This region of Nepal has been opened comparatively recently to trekking and a number of long treks are available, e.g. up the long Arun River towards Everest, Makalu Base Camp and Kangchendzonga.

These 3 treks begin from the roadhead at Hille. **Dharan Bazaar** (365 m) is the nearest large centre on the edge of the hills and Terai. From Kathmandu buses take 11 hr. You can also start from **Tumlingtar,** connected by air to Kathmandu and Biratnagar, which cuts the round trip by around 10 days.

Makalu base camp/Arun valley

The trek to the Base Camp of Makalu (8,481 m), the world's fifth highest mountain, is not particularly hard, but is quite long, taking around 25 days, starting and finishing at **Hille**. At its lowest altitude the vegetation is sub-tropical whilst at the source of the Arun, it is Alpine and frozen, so the trek upstream along one of the great rivers of Nepal provides plenty of contrasts.

Everest via the Arun Valley

This trek also starts at Hille and reaches its high point at **Kala Pattar** in Khumbu, so anyone wishing to do a long trek could go from Jiri at the beginning of the classic Everest Base Camp trek to Khumbu via Namche Bazaar and then trek out down the Arun Valley to Hille. This is more arduous than the Makalu Base Camp Trek as it is against the grain, running from E to W, traversing some roughly longitudinal (N-S) valleys with numerous ascents and descents.

Many commercial operators are offering Everest via the Arun Valley as an alternative route. These are well-provisioned and porters carry much of the gear. A suitably equipped independent party could undertake it, but although there are villages all the way, there are no luxurious inns and hotels found on the long established routes. Allow around 12 days to trek from Hille to Lukla. For Lukla to Kala Pattar, follow the route for Everest Base Camp Trek and remember the need to acclimatise.

Kangchendzonga Trek

The far eastern region bordering Sikkim, the circuit for **Kangchendzonga** ('The 5 Treasures of the Snows'), has only recently been opened for trekking. Like the other 2 treks, it requires careful organisation and professional guidance.

THE POKHARA VALLEY

The Pokhara Valley is situated in the geographical centre of Nepal. 400 m lower than Kathmandu, the valley is hemmed in far more closely by the giant peaks of the Himalaya. Dominated by the Annapurna Massif to the N, the valley is dotted with lakes, of which the Phewa Tal is the largest. Its stunningly beautiful setting has helped to make it Nepal's most popular tourist destination after Kathmandu. The town of Pokhara itself, at an altitude of just under 900 m on the Seti Khola river is overshadowed by the towering *Macchapuchare* (6,999 m), the Fishtail Mountain. Reflected in the still waters of the Phewa Lake it is one of the most beautiful mountains in the world from Pokhara Macchapuchare appearing only as an almost perfect pyramid. The twin peak which gives it its name only appears after travelling some days to the W. Annapurna is a bare 30 km to the N, towering more than 7,000 m above the valley, and flanked by a range of superb and sometimes daunting mountains. The vegetation is sub tropical with banana palms, citrus trees, rice paddies and mustard fields.

About 40,000 people live in the valley around Pokhara, while the mountains are left to snow leopards and blue sheep. From the snow covered peaks, vegetation grows ever more luxurious with the drop in height, passing through one of the largest rhododendron forests in the world to the humid lowlands, where many of Nepal's native plants thrive, including over 100 varieties of orchids.

Annapurna Conservation Area Park Headquarters is at Ghandruk, Kaski District and an Annapurna Information Centre, Prithvi Narayan, Campus Museum, Pokhara. The **King Mahendra Trust for Nature Conservation** is a non-profit, non-governmental organisation dedicated to conserving natural resources in Nepal. The Trust supports the Project for conservation, education and participation to revitalize villagers' independent initiatives.

Getting To Pokhara From Kathmandu

Pokhara is 206 km due W of Kathmandu along the **Prithvi Highway**, built from Kathmandu to Dumre with Indian Government help and from Dumre to Pokhara with Chinese assistance. It is a much slower journey than the distance suggests.

Once out of the Kathmandu Valley the road follows the Trisuli River to *Mugling* (110 km). This is the confluence of the **Trisuli** and **Marsyandi Rivers**, which together form the *Narayani* or **Sapt Gandaki**, which flows S to the plains. If you turn left at Mugling the road brings you to **Narayangarh** and the **Chitwan National Park** (See above). It then skirts along the edge of the Siwaliks to **Butawal**, where it joins the Siddhartha Highway from Pokhara.

However, you carry straight on and follow the **Marsyandi River** to Damauli (42 km), which is where the Madi Khola and Seti Khola join. Roughly mid-way is *Dumre*, which marks the beginning of the Annapurna circuit trek. Dumre is 70 km from Pokhara and Damauil 54 km. The Pokhara valley is entered just beyond and below Khairani. At the E end are the **Rupkot** and **Begnas Tals** (lakes).

Note If you sit on the driver's side of the bus or other vehicle you get glimpses at various stages of the mountains to the N.

Hotels en route Mugling is the natural stopping place as it is at the junction of the road from Chitwan. Rafting trips down to Chitwan begin here. **C** *Motel du Mugling*, Mugling T 2-25242 **E** *Laxmi Nauli*, Mugling. European style. Double rooms.

Dumre has a few cheap hotels for travellers finishing the Annapurna circuit or doing it in reverse. None are very good, all are basic. **F** *Mustang, Chandrag* and *Ravi Hotel & Lodge*.

Gurkha (1,145 m) or **Gorkha**, 18 km N of Siling on the Prithvi Highway, 136 km W of Kathmandu and 106 km E of Pokhara. This was the ancestral home of the Shah dynasty and is connected with the Prithvi highway by a good all-weather road. The Thakuri, Tamang and Magar soldiers under the command of the greatest Shah king, Prithvi Narayan, were the Gurkhas. It is at the heart of the recruiting area for current Gurkha regiments.

To celebrate his conquest of the Kathmandu Valley, Pritvi Narayan Shah built an impressive fort/temple/palace complex on the hill overlooking the town. The **Gorkha Durbar** is about 1 km from the bus stand. Surrounding a tank in the square 100 m N of the bus stand are a number of locally important buildings. The temples are to Vishnu, Krishna and and Ganes. There is also a column with a statue of the great king. Veering right, you pass the Tallo Durbar on your right. This pre-dates the conquest of Kathmandu and was the royal palace. 100 m further on, steps lead off to your left. Gradual at first but steeper towards the end, these bring you to the fort. **Note** Photography is not allowed in the complex.

Pokhara

Population 50,000 approx. *Altitude* 884 m. *Climate* Daytime temp never falls below 10°C and reaches 20°C plus. Summer temp can rise to 36°C when it is hot and humid. The monsoon lasts from mid-Jun to mid-Sep. *Best time* for a visit Oct to Apr.

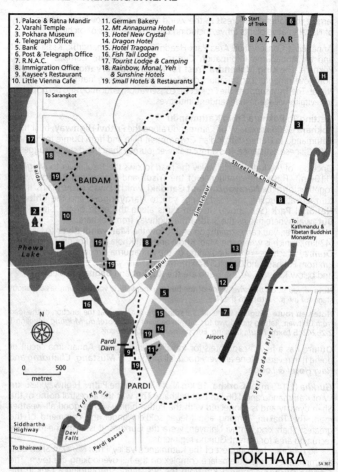

1. Palace & Ratna Mandir
2. Varahi Temple
3. Pokhara Museum
4. Telegraph Office
5. Bank
6. Post & Telegraph Office
7. R.N.A.C.
8. Immigration Office
9. Kaysee's Restaurant
10. Little Vienna Cafe
11. German Bakery
12. *Mt Annapurna Hotel*
13. *Hotel New Crystal*
14. *Dragon Hotel*
15. *Hotel Tragopan*
16. *Fish Tail Lodge*
17. *Tourist Lodge & Camping*
18. *Rainbow, Monal, Yeh*
    & Sunshine Hotels
19. *Small Hotels & Restaurants*

POKHARA

SA 367

Pokhara's splendid natural setting, and the fact that it is suitable base for treks in the Annapurna region, have given the town its raison d'être. It was a seasonal market town for the Gurungs and Newaris, where traders from Mustang on the Tibetan border and merchants from Butwal on the Terai exchanged goods. Pokhara is in the region of the Gurungs but the majority of the inhabitants of the valley are Brahmins and Chettris from Kathmandu and Tibetan settlers.

Health Warning Hepatitis is common. It is particularly important to be extremely careful with drinking water.

The town really came into existence after the malaria eradication programme of the early 1950s. A hydro-electric dam was constructed with Indian aid in 1968, an airstrip laid, and the connecting road with Kathmandu built to link the village with the capital, and provide part of the infrastructure required for developing it into a tourist centre. It stretches almost 5 km from N to S. The older part, including the bazaar, is in the N. The airport is in the S. The major hotel areas are around the lake, 'Lakeside' being the most popular, with an eccentric looking Royal Villa, built in the late 1950s. You can see the Annapurnas from the Phewa Tal, the second largest lake in Nepal.

Places of Interest In the centre of *Phewa lake* is an island with a temple dedicated to **Varaha** the boar, the Hindu god Vishnu's third incarnation. A Newari style temple to **Bhimsen** is situated in the bazaar whilst further N on a shady platform is the **Bidhyavasini Temple** dedicated to Durga in her Bhagwati manifestation. The shrine is a *shaligram** (marine fossil) of black ammonite.

The *Devi Falls*, 2 km SW of the airport on Siddhartha Highway to Kathmandu is a sink hole, where the **Pardi Khola** from the lake disappears and emerges some 200 m away.

Tashling Tibetan Village, just beyond Devi Falls, is a 30 min walk from the airport. Along with the community of Tashi Palikhel at Hyangia on the Seti Gandaki about 5 km from the lake, this is a bustling centre for the manufacture of carpets for export. The Tibetan Monastery is comparatively new, situated on a hill beyond **Mahendrapul Bridge**.

Hotels These are concentrated in 4 localities: **Pardi Dam** area, at the E end of the Phewa Tal; **Airport** for Annapurna and New Crystal; **Lakeside** with the greatest concentration and the widest range of hotels, and the real tourist centre of the town; the noisy **Bazaar** area for cheaper hotels.

Pardi Dam C *Dragon*, PO Box 15, Pardi Lake, T 20052. Half way between the airport and lake. 20 rm with bath, some a/c. Restaurant, bar, daily performance by Mandala Folk Troupe. **C** *Tragopan*, between Lake and Dam. **D** *Garden*, T 20870, and *Peaceful*, T 20861. Rm, some with bath and mountain views. **D** *Mount View*, T 20860. Rm, some with bath. Pleasant garden. Recommended. **D** A *shoka Guest House*. Fairly new with garden. **E** *Green View*. Restaurant. **E** *Yak & Yuppie Guest House*. In addition to these are a large number of *Thakali Guest Houses*, nearly all in a triangle extending E from the dam.

Airport C *New Crystal*, facing the airport. T 20036, Cable: New hotel. 70 rm, some a/c. Restaurant, bar. **C** *Mount Annapurna*, facing the airport, T 20037, Cable: Mountanna. 64 rm. Good restaurant (Nepali, Tibetan and Continental) and bar, both with fine Tibetan murals. Pleasant gardens and rooftop view of Annapurna.

Lakeside The most popular area. **B** *Fishtail Lodge*, T 20071, Cable: Fishtail. 29 rm. Stands on a rocky promontory at the E end of the lake accessible only by wooden raft. Spectacular views of Macchapuchare. A series of charming thatched bungalows with an attractive lawn with restaurant and bar. Bookings from Kathmandu at Hotel De l'Annapurna, Durbar Marg. **C** *Kantipur Resort*, T 20886. Rm with bath. Recommended. Also **D** *Kantipur Hotel* Older and cheaper. **D** *Gurkha Lodge* 3 rm. Run by an ex-Gurkha soldier and English wife. Pleasant garden. Popular.

There are numerous **E** category hotels, each offering basically the same as the rest: *Baba's Lodge and Restaurant*. Good value; *Green Lake*, Lakeside; *New Solitary Guest House, Gauri Shanker; Lonely Guest House; New Tourist Guest House; Travellers Guest House* has camping; *Snowlands*, W end of lake road, T 20384. 18 rm. Kantipur restaurant serves good food. Quiet, secluded and popular; *Alka; Puspa; Fewa; Yeti Guest House*, Monal;

Bazaar Some distance from the Lake, and noisy, but there are some cheap guesthouses. **E** *New Hotel Asia* and *Mandar Hotel* are Tibetan.

Restaurants The restaurants in Fishtail Lodge, New Crystal, Mount Annapurna and Dragon hotels are very good. The *New Kantipur* in Baidam and the *Himalayan Tibetan Hotel* near the airport serve excellent and inexpensive Tibetan and Nepali meals; the former, also has good French cuisine. Try the *Baba Lodge*; for breakfast and their Malaya Steak, good Tibetan and Chinese dishes. *Nawoste* on the edge of the lake is run by a Swiss classical music fan. Good for breakfast, as is *Welcome. Hungry Eyes* for excellent pies. There are many other **Lakeside** restaurants.

Bars The larger hotels have bars.

Banks Off Ratnapuri nr Immigration Office at the Lakeside end of town.

Shopping The Tibetan community produce a number of attractive knick-knacks and carpets mostly in a traditional style. Marine fossils, evidence that the area was once at the bottom of the sea of Tethys, are also for sale. There are a number of reasonable **bookshops**, some doing exchanges. In Lakeside E there is *Pokhara Bookshop, As You Like It, Holy Bookshop, Kiwi Bookshop, Collector's Bookshop*.

Local Transport Walking around is certainly good exercise for trekking as Pokhara is a sprawling town on a slight incline from N to S. **Taxis** are available at the bus station, airport and lakeside. From Lakeside to airport about Rs 3, to Bazaar Rs 6. **Bicycles** (for adults and children) can be rented and there are many places along the lakeside, at the dam and the airport. About Rs 15-20 per day.

Entertainment The Fishtail Lodge has nightly show of Nepalese dancing by the Danfe Dance Club. 1800-1900 (Winter), 1830-1930 (Summer). Rs 50. The Dragon Hotel near Phewa Dam has a nightly performance of folk dance and song by the Mandala Folk Troupe. Daily at 1830. T 52 for booking. Dinner and transportation can be arranged.

Museums Pokhara Museum, Nadipur Nadi Pode Tole, just N of Bus Station. Open daily except Tue. Local historical and cultural exhibits. **Natural History Museum** (Annapurna Regional Museum), N end of Nadipur Patan Pode Tole near Bhim Bazaar. Open daily except Tue. Collection of Nepalese moths and butterflies.

Useful Addresses Immigration Office for visa renewals and trekking permits is just off Ratnapuri, nr the Bank. See Trekking section.

Hospitals and Medical Services Nr Bog Bazaar at the N end of town.

Post and Telegraph GPO, Nadipur Patan Rd, approx 2 km from airport at S end of bazaar. Overseas telephone calls can be made from the Telecommunications Building which is E of the PO and by the bridge.

Tourist Offices & Information Tourist Office, opp the airport terminal. Open Winter (Feb-Nov) 1000-1700, Summer 0900-1600, closes 1500 Friday. Closed Sat and public holidays.

Air Daily Royal Nepal Airlines service from Kathmandu (206 km, 30 min).

Bus Daily buses to Kathmandu leave early in the morning. **Public buses** from Bhimsen Tower nr Post Office in Pokhara and from the Central Bus Station in Kathmandu take 7-8 hr. Rs 45. **Tourist buses**, at 0700, cost about 3 times as much. They are quicker (stopping only at Mugling) and more comfortable. Book in advance. Tickets available around lakeside. Daily buses leave for **Tadi Bazaar** (for Chitwan, about Rs 35) and Bhairawa/ Lumbini on the border (Rs 55, from main Pokhara Bus Stand at 0630).

Trekking From Pokhara

Trekking routes Trekking from Pokhara tends to be in a northwesterly direction to the Annapurna Conservation Area. There are 3 classic treks with variations to each. The *Annapurna Circuit* is considered by many to be the best trek in Nepal, surpassing the Everest Trek in terms of scenic and cultural variety, and is the most popular, attracting 10,000 trekkers in a season. It is also quite arduous, requiring 3 weeks. The **Annapurna Base Camp Trek** enables you to get right into the massif and be surrounded with peaks, whilst the **Jomosom** (Apple Pie) **Trek** is ideal for those who wish to travel light and stay in inns. It is, in fact half of the Annapurna Circuit and can be undertaken when the *Thorong La* into the *Manang Valley* is closed preventing completion of the circuit. Many foreign trekking companies offer all 3 and attract large numbers of 'freedom' walkers.

The effect of the massive tourist influx on the local people has been dramatic. Living and educational standards have improved, life expectancy increased, and many now speak some English, but traditional cultural values are rapidly being discarded.

Annapurna was the first peak over 8,000 m to be climbed. The successful assault is a reminder that the mountains are both awe-inspiring and dangerous. The French expedition, led by Maurice Herzog, arrived in Nepal in April 1950. Nothing was known by Europeans of either Dhaulagiri or Annapurna. The French spent the better part of a month reconnoitering the Dhaulagiri massif before giving up. "Dhaulagiri isn't just difficult, it is impossible. I never want to set foot on the mountain again", one of the team wrote later. Although Herzog and his companion Lachenal suffered appalling frostbite injuries on their attempt to climb Annapurna and had a succession of miraculous escapes, they reached the summit and, with the help of their sherpa porters and team, returned. Both lost fingers and toes, and took nearly a year to regain their health. It was just one of the tales of heroism and endurance which the mountains have continued to witness to the present.

The Annapurna Circuit Trek

There are 18 to 20 days trekking involved. You can trek to Manang at any time of year but October and November provide the best mountain views.

The circuit is best done anti-clockwise to be in a good position for a crossing of the 5,410 m **Thorang La**, which is snowbound from mid-Dec to mid-Apr. Snow and altitude sickness can make a W-E crossing a nightmare. Also, approaching it from the **Manang Valley** ensures that you become acclimatised. From the Muktinath side you are forced to make a 1,300 m ascent and 900 m descent in one day, which is hard going.

Warning A high level of fitness is needed for this trek. A good regime of exercise beforehand, will see you through when the going gets rough or you have a stomach upset. If you are hiring your own porters, ensure that they have sufficient warm clothing and sunglasses. Snowblindness is not uncommon.

Day 1-2 Most treks start from the village of **Dumre** (440 m), 70 km E of Pokhara on the Prithvi Highway, between **Kathmandu** and **Pokhara**. It can be reached quite easily, and has a few basic hotels (see Kathmandu to Pokhara sections). Some now start from **Pokhara** by walking to **Begnas Tal** and **Rupa Tal**, then through **Karputar** to **Besi Sahar** (790 m) which is 41 km from Dumre. A road is being constructed and jeeps and 4WD vehicles run a taxi service to **Bhote Odar**, a 3 hr walk from Besi Sahar (hot and dusty but good exercise). There is a police checkpost, shops and trekkers' hotels. Above the village to the W is the ruined fortress of **Gaonsahar** (1,370 m).

Day 3 The first half of the trek follows the **Marsyandi Khola** which divides the Annapurna and Manaslu massifs. Keep on the W bank of the river and cross the 150 m gorge. You then walk through terraced fields and forest to reach **Khudi**, the first Gurung village of the trek. You continue to **Bhulbule** (825 m) where you cross the river to the E bank. Further on you cross the **Nagdi Khola**, just beyond the village of Nagdi at its mouth.

The trail up the **Marsyandi Valley** gives excellent views of the Himalayan peaks. Dominating the E skyline is **Manaslu** (8,156 m), **Himalchuli** (7,893 m), **Peak 29** /Manaslu II /Ngadi Chuli (7,835 m) and **Baudha Himal** (6,672 m).

Above Ngadi is **Usta**, and then a steady climb to **Lampata** (1,135 m) and Bahundanda, 1 km further on, both Manangi villages. *Lampata* has better hotels. **Bahundanda** (1,310 m) is the most northerly Brahmin village and has reasonably good camping.

Day 4 From Bahundanda the path drops steeply to **Syange** (1,100 m). Cross the **Marsyandi** by a suspension bridge. **Syange** has a number of hotels. The track then climbs high above the river along steep hillsides of rhododendron and pine forest to **Jagat** (1,070). **Chyamje** (1,300 m) after 1 km, has a hotel and shops.

Day 5 This walk is to Bagarchap where the **Marsyandi Khola** curves W and enters the **Manang Valley**. The climate and cultural landscape both change. A long uphill climb brings you to **Tal** (1,675 m), a pretty village at the foot of a picturesque waterfall, the southernmost village in Manang district.

Cross the broad flat valley, once a lake bed, through fields of corn, barley and potatoes then climb steeply up a stone stairway to 1,860 m. The staircase then descends to Orad where the vegetation consists of blue pine and fir. Drop down to **Dharapani** (1.890 m) a Tibetan Buddhist village with chorten entrances at each end.

Over a spur is **Bagarchhap** (2,160 m), a bazaar town of closely packed, wooden roofed Tibetan style houses. Timber for building is comparatively abundant in this region which marks the transition between the monsoonal region S of the main Himalayan axis and the more arid rainshadow area to the N. Further on, wood is replaced by slate as a roofing material.

Day 6 *Chame*, the district headquarters, is today's destination. You walk a rough and rocky trail through forest to **Danejung** (2,290 m) and **Tyanja** (2,360 m). **Kopar** (2,590 m) lies in a meadow between **Tyanja** and **Chame** (2,685 m) which has a post office, hotels and a bank. There are fine views of **Annapurna II** (7,937 m) as you approach the town.

Day 7 Between **Chame** and **Pisang** the effects of rainshadowing can be seen as the forests become sparser and the density of juniper increases. The valley is steep and narrow and the path crosses the river twice. By the second bridge at 3,040 m is the **Paungda Danda rock face** that arches upwards for more than 1,500 m. The trail climbs further into the upper **Marsyandi valley** and Pisang (3,200 m), a large sprawling village with numerous hotels, good camping grounds and a mani wall.

Day 8 The Manang region was only opened for trekking in 1977 so generally the facilities are not as good as on the Pokhara-Jomosom sector of the circuit. The inhabitants of Manang village though, are amongst the most sophisticated in Nepal. The region receives relatively sparse rainfall, reflected in the crops – barley, buckwheat and potatoes. The semi-arid conditions and altitude allows only one cropping season a year.

By Himalayan standards this should be a poor village. However, In 1784 King Rana Bahadur Shah granted the *Manangbhot* (people of Manang) special trading rights which they have enjoyed ever since. Today they trade local gold, silver, turquoise and other gems for cameras, watches and electronic goods from other parts of Asia. Affluent, westernised in dress and with many speaking English, they have also been quick to seize the opportunities presented by mass trekking. The village has a number of popular hotels and also sells Tibetan sweaters, hats and gloves but prices are high.

A short distance beyond Pisang is a trail leading to the ridge the cuts across the valley. From the top you get a good view of the valley and **Tilicho Peak** (7,132 m). Descending into the upper valley the track bifurcates, the N one taking a route via **Ghyaru**. It rejoins the southern trail at Mungji. This route involves less climbing. It runs past *Ongre* (3,325 m), with an airstrip that caters exclusively to the Manang trading community. The village has a police checkpost and a number of small hotels. 30 min walk beyond Ongre on the left, is the valley leading up to **Annapurna III** (7,555 m) and **Annapurna IV** (7,525 m). Close by is the Nepal Mountaineering Association's mountaineering school. The Himalayan Rescue Association has a clinic here.

At **Mungji** (3,360 m) the path crosses the Marsyandi again to reach *Braga* (3,475 m) which has hotels and a camping ground below. The gompa is believed to be around 500 years old and belongs to the **Kagyu-pa** Tibetan Lamaist Buddhist sect. A climb up **Braga Hill** offers a stunning panorama of the Annapurna group. **Manang** (3,535 m) is 30 min further on.

Day 9 You have now travelled from 440 m at **Dumre**, to 3,585 m at **Manang**, an altitude gain of over 3,000 m although in real terms you have climbed double that. However, because of this gradual ascent you should be well acclimatised having made a daily height gain of around 500 m. **Note** This is the altitude to which people can travel fairly rapidly and feel little or no ill effect from it. From now on you have to be much more careful. It is 2 days' walk to **Muktinath** with a crossing of the **Thorung La** (5,416 m) en route. This means that you will be gaining nearly 2,000 m in less than 2 days.

Warning This can, and often does, induce Mountain Sickness. Spend a day in and around Manang becoming acclimatised and relaxing rather than charging on. There is a comfortable side trip to the glacial lake fed by the icefall on *Gangapurna* (around 4,000 m).

Day 10 **Tengi** (3,805 m) is the next village beyond Manang. Just beyond it the path veers right. To the left is a track leading up a side valley to **Tilicho Lake**. Above **Gunsang** (3,960 m) village there is juniper forest, the source of firewood for the nearby villages. Further on is **Ledar** which has a shop – not cheap, but there's not much choice. You are now in the *Jarsang Khola* valley, one of the source streams of the **Marsyandi**. The track continues upwards along the E bank of the stream, crosses it at 4,310 m, traverses a scree slope, then descends to **Phedi** (4,420 m) which has hotels and a campsite below, and 2 others within 30 min. **Note** Snow (and blocked passes) can mean overcrowded hotels and campsites leading to unsanitary toilet facilities.

Day 11 It is not necessary to start for the Pass too early (0300 as some do) as it can be extremely cold. A 0500-0600 start gives you only an hr at most in the bitter cold before it is light. The trail is well defined and has been used for centuries by traders though it seems to go on forever and has a number of dispiriting false summits. It takes around 4 hr from Phedi. In Dec and Jan a crossing of the pass is well nigh impossible, and at all times care is needed. There is a chorten and prayer flags to mark the pass and the views are magnificent. You can see the N faces of the **Annapurnas**, the Kali Gandaki Valley and **Thorungtse** (6,482 m). Some well-equipped parties camp on the pass and climb higher on the peaks around it.

Warning Great care is needed for the descent (1600 m), which is far more tiring than the ascent.

As the trail descends through snow, moraines and grassy slopes into **Muktinath**, the symmetrical summit of *Dhaulagiri* (8,167 m) appears on the southern horizon. The final part of the day's walk is along the upper part of the **Jhong Khola** valley, past a few bhattis which sell drinks and have beds, to **Muktinath** (3,800 m). The hotels are in *Ranipowa*, about 10 min from the temple.

This completes the northern half of the Annapurna circuit. The remaining part of the journey to Pokhara is along the **Pokhara-Jomosom** trail which is described next, but taken in reverse order.

Pokhara to Jomosom and Muktinath

The route from Pokhara to Jomosom follows an ancient trade route up the Kali Gandaki valley and has a busy traffic of local people and porters, mules and yaks. It passes through the largest gorge in the world, a deep slit between Dhaulagiri and Annapurna, two of the world's highest mountains, whose summits are only 30 km apart. The trek is also one of contrasts.

When you go through the gorge, you pass from the rain sodden, well vegetated and lush southern slopes of the great Himalaya, to the arid, rainshadowed zone where only the hardiest crops survive. You also move from a predominantly Hindu area to one steeped in the culture of Tibetan Buddhism.

In the first few days out of Pokhara, there are one or 2 variations. From Deorali, just beyond Poon Hill, it is one trail. There are some interesting side trips, so allow a few extra days for flexibility. You will not regret it.

You can undertake the trek with little difficulty from Oct to May but it is best from Oct – Dec, post monsoon but pre-winter with wonderfully clear skies and pleasantly hot days. In Jan it snows, ruling out some of the side trips. **Mar** and **Apr** are good for the rhododendrons around **Ghorapani** though the skies are somewhat hazy. May is very hot and to be avoided if possible.

Duration The trip can be done in a week though longer is more enjoyable.

Day 1 Take a bus, taxi or walk to the Shining Hospital. Here a Jeep track follows the **Seti Khola** to its confluence with the **Yangdi Khola**. The road then climbs up to the Tibetan Camp and the large village of **Hyangja** (1,070 m). Beyond these the road leaves the Seti Khola and ascends the spur that separates the 2 rivers. The wide grassy track then follows an irrigation ditch to **Suikhet** (1,125 m). Alternative trails make short cuts across the terraced fields during the dry season. Suikhet has a number of bhattis on the far side of the village.

You continue along the riverside for 30 min then cross to the S side of the valley. From here you climb the ridge between the **Yangdo Khola** and the **Harpan Khola**. The 370 m climb rewards you with a view of the Pokhara valley and Phewa Tal. *Naudanda* (1,430 m) lies along this ridge and has a police checkpost and several hotels varying from simple bhattis to well maintained western style establishments. Allow about 5 hr for the journey. Make sure that you have your trekking permit as the police are conscientious in the execution of their responsibilities. Another point worth mentioning, particularly on the first night of a trek is the noise. If you intend sleeping near, or in villages you will have to get used to the dogs barking all night, an unavoidable recreational hazard.

Day 2 At the far end of Naudanda you have a choice of tracks. Both converge again but the right hand track is shorter. The trail climbs to Khare (1,710 m), a dispersed village at the head of the **Yamdi Khola** Valley. Proceed down the stone steps below the British agricultural research station and rehabilitation centre for retiring Gurkha soldiers. One hr beyond **Khare** you reach **Lumle** (1,585 m). Keep to the main street which is paved with flagstones and continue along the side of the ridge. The track then descends to **Chandrakot** (1,550 m) where you get excellent views of Annapurna and Machhapuchhare. From here you have to descend to and cross the **Modi Khola**. On the far side is **Birethanti** which has some excellent hotels. It is a good stopping place if you are coming the other way on the Annapurna circuit.

The trail follows the bank of the **Bhurungdi Khola** past some pleasant waterfalls. Do not cross the suspension bridge. It climbs steadily up the side of the valley to **Hille** (1,495 m) and **Tirkedhunga** (1,525 m). Both villages have hotels and are good halting places for the night after 6 hr plus on the road.

Day 3 The track descends from Tirkedhunga to cross the river, then steeply ascends some stone steps for 600 m to **Ulleri** (2,070 m), a large Magar village. Continuing above the village you pass through the cultivated area and some pastures to a dense forest of rhododendron, daphne and azalea mixed with giant conifers. 3 hr beyond Ulleri and after crossing 3 streams by bridge **Thante** (2,460 m) is reached. This stands in a small clearing. The track gets pretty muddy after snow melt and during the monsoon necessitating numerous detours. A good campsite is located on the hill behind the first group of huts. **Ghorapani** ('Horse water' in Hindi and Nepali, 2,775 m) is 1 hr further, and 15 min beyond that is the pass at **Deorali** (2,834).

Of the 2 places it is worth staying at Deorali for the spectacular panorama of Dhaulagiri, Tukche, Nilgiri, Annapurna I and Annapurna S. The view of these is gained by climbing to **Poon Hill** (3,030 m), 1 hr's walk away. On the hill is a wooden tower. Dawn is the best time. Allow around 7 hr for the day's walk (this does not include the Poon Hill excursion).

Day 4 From **Ghorapani** the trail descends through forest to **Chitre** (2,390 m) then enters an extensively cultivated region of Magar villages. **Sikha** (1,890 m), 3 hr from Deorali, has many shops, hotels, a post office and an army training centre. Beyond Sikha, the descent becomes stonier but is quite gentle to Ghare (1,705 m). There is a further drop to the suspension bridge over the **Ghar Khola**. The trail turns N and crosses the **Kali Gandaki** on a steel suspension bridge to the W bank. **Tatopani** ('Hot water', 1,189 m) is a short distance upstream. As its name suggests there are hot springs below the village near the river. The choice of places is wide and includes a municipal bath. The village is well-provided with hotels, many using generators for cooking and lighting. The shops are well stocked and sell beer; accommodation and food are good. It is understandably popular with trekkers. Allow about 7 hr for the day's walk.

Day 5 You are now in the **Kali Gandaki Gorge** and under the steep walls the pine forest of higher elevations is replaced with low vegetation suited to semi-arid areas. The presence of such a deep, boldly carved gorge is evidence that the great rivers of the Himalaya, many of which have their source not on the watershed of the Himalayan axis but further N, were there before the mountains. As these rose the rivers maintained their courses by inexorably eroding a passage through them. The Kali Gandaki's headwaters are beyond the small kingdom of Mustang (see later). The gorge is the deepest in the world.

30 min beyond Tatopani is the confluence of the **Kali Gandaki** and the **Miritsi Khola**. The French base camp was located at its source.

Rukse Chhara (1,550 m) is the next small hamlet and a very short distance beyond is a spectacular waterfall as a tributary stream tumbles into the Kali Gandaki. You cross this on a wooden bridge to the E bank and continue to **Kopchepani** where there is a 'Welcome to Mustang' signboard. You are now in the southernmost part of the district of **Mustang**. The old kingdom is still a long distance off. At the fork in the trail you have a choice of 2 routes, both of which will bring you to **Ghasa** after about a 3 hr walk.

The left hand trail climbs abruptly then continues N along the western wall of the canyon. This is an older track, and in many places is carved out of the overhanging rock. Several precarious looking, rickety but safe bridges span gaps between ledges. It is best avoided during the rainy season as there is some risk of being hit by falling debris. First you climb steeply up the hillside and remain high, passing the village of **Kabre** after ½hr. This is below the steepest part of the gorge and the track has been hewn out of the walls. Frequently there are roaring winds and this can be tiring. After 2 hr the gorge widens and the trail descends to a gravel bar and a bridge to the other side. Ghasa is ½hr further on.

The E bank trail takes a little less time to cover and at first stays reasonably level. After you pass a small village it begins to climb through forest. This high route then traverses the steepest section of the gorge before descending to the gravel bar and bridge.

Ghasa (2,000 m) is a long strung out Thakali village, and marks the southernmost limit of Lamaistic Buddhism. The Kali Gandaki gorge is thus a tunnel through to another world. On the N side not only does the vegetation and the culture change but also the name of river, becoming the **Thak Khola**. The middle part of Ghasa has the best guesthouses and hotels. Upper Ghasa has fine chortens (kanis).

The trail ascends steadily but not steeply through forests to the Lete Khola. After about 1 hr the canyon widens further and the trail turns a corner to reveal a magnificent view of **Dhaulagiri** and its ice fall. Across the river is an impressive cliff. This can be quite a noisy place as dislodged rocks from the cliff crash down into the canyon and the icefall shifts.

You then descend into the ravine of the **Lete Khola** which enters the Kali Gandaki nearly 1 kilometre to the right. You cross the stream on a wooden bridge, although there is also usually a log laid across as well. The trail then climbs up to *Lete* (2,470 m), another village strung out along a river terrace. Lete coalesces with *Kalopani*, about 20 min further on. In Kalopani there are guesthouses and restaurants, a camping ground and an air of prosperity. You are encircled by peaks. Allow 9 hr for the walk, a full but varied and enjoyable day.

Day 6   There are 2 trails to **Tukche** which is 3 hr away. On the E bank of the river you take a trail that rises above the gravel bar that stretches up to Jomsom. You pass through *Dhumpu* after 15-20 min and another settlement after 45 min. The trail then leaves the valley floor to cross a wooded ridge above some cliffs, before descending to the gravel bar again. Here you have a further choice of either remaining on the bank at the edge of the valley floor or of walking up the riverbed. In dry weather the latter is more direct. The views of **Dhaulagiri** and **Annapurna** are wonderful. After 30 min you reach a bridge. On the W bank is the village of **Larjung** (2,560 m) which has a number of hotels. If you stay on the E bank you have to cross the river on a series of temporary bridges just before **Tukche**.

The W bank trail climbs to **Sukung** then descends through forest to **Larjung**. A little farther on is **Kanti** (also known as **Khopang**) (2,560 m) and between are some of the best views of the mountains in this stretch of the **Thak Khola**. Above Kanti are a row of caves housing Buddhist shrines and relics. You also pass the old monastery of **Rani Gomba**.

Tukche (2,590 m) was an important place on the trade route. Caravans from Tibet bartered their goods of salt and wool for grain and other goods carried up from the S. It was once the most important **Thakali** village. With the drying up of trade many families moved out. Tourism has been a welcome substitute.

The Thakalis had a virtual monopoly on the lucrative trade and developed a keen business sense. This has enabled them to invest in and manage enterprises throughout Nepal. The secret of Thakali success is a system of communal investment. The **dighur system** is where a family or friends pool a fixed amount of money per person and give the total to one among them. The recipient can use it at his own discretion and his only obligation is to contribute to the *dighur*. When everyone has received their lump sum, the group is dissolved. The system is based on trust and encourages individualism.

Their religion is a mixture of Hinduism, Buddhism, shamanism and animism, and they are related the Magars, Tamangs and Gurungs. In this they differ from the Tibetan related neighbours at Mustang. The Thakalis cultivate barley and potatoes, an indication of the severity of the climate, and their flat roofs are useful for drying grain. Yaks are good grazing livestock and the females' (naks) milk is drunk and made into cheese. The hides and coarse wool are also used. Juniper is often used for tea.

Beyond Tukche the going is made difficult by the wind, which is funnelled down between the mountains. Junipers and small pines begin to dominate the increasingly arid land. An hr further on is the government experimental farm at *Marpha* (2,665 m) which also has an important monastery at the S end. There are guesthouses in the village, generally regarded as some of the best in Nepal, with their private rooms, menus, indoor toilets and often room service. Across the river is a Tibetan carpet factory

N of Marpha the trail is wide and easy to follow. The **Longpoghyun Khola** flows down from the **Meso Kanto Pass** (5,099 m) to the E. This is a difficult but immensely rewarding side trip to the famous lake at the foot of **Tilicho Peak**. **Syang** is just beyond and staying on the trail you pass the **Jomosom** airstrip. Allow 8 hr from Lete/Kalopani to Jomosom.

Jomosom (from *Dzongsam*, 'New fort', 2713 m) is the major centre of the region now and has an airlink with Kathmandu and Pokhara. There are a number of hot springs located on the hillside to the W of the town. On the river valley floor there are shaligrams (ammonite fossils) to be found if you look hard enough.

Warning Flights are often delayed in winter because of fog in the Kathmandu Valley, which usually does not lift until 1000 hrs, and wind around Jomsom which usually starts at the same time! When a number of flights have been delayed there is serious backlog of anxious, often frenzied travellers. One recommendation is to allow sufficient time so that if necessary you can trek back to Pokhara. This can be done in 4 days. The flights from Pokhara arrive earlier and therefore are more reliable. There is a hospital and a police checkpoint. Trekkers on the Annapurna Circuit and coming from the Manang Valley must have their passes stamped here.

Day 7 The trail follows the river then crosses it and continues up the valley to *Chhancha Lhumba* (2,370 m). From here the direct route to Muktinath climbs a plateau above the village then turns E up the **Jhong Khola** valley. The landscape is quite arid and bare here but the views are excellent. From **Khingar** (3,200 m) the walk is across meadows and groves of poplar and fruit trees. The trail climbs above the river to **Jharkot** (3,500 m), a Tibetan style village with some hotels. Some use solar heating. From here the trails climbs further to **Muktinath** (3,710 m), the end of this S section of the **Annapurna Circuit**.

There is an interesting detour to Kangbeni on this walk. At **Chhancha Lhumba** a trail follows the river to *Kangbeni* (2,810 m), the furthest N that tourists can travel. The village has a hotel with dormitory accommodation so it is possible to stay. It gives a taste of what Mustang is like although contact with visitors has already made some impact. The houses are mud and stone, tightly packed. There are striking chortens and a large gompa.

From Kangbeni the trail makes a steep ascent up the Jhong Khola Valley and joins the Muktinath route below Khingar.

The first part of *Muktinath* is called **Ranipowa**. Most of the hotels are here and it is busy not only with trekkers but also with pilgrims. Tibetan traders tend to spoil the atmosphere with their persistent attempts to make a sale. The object of the pilgrimage is the Hindu Vaishnavite **Jiwali Mayi** temple and the **Buddhist gompa**. Inside the temple is an eternal flame and a spring. This combination of earth, water and fire is considered particularly holy and attracts devotees of both faiths. The main religious festival at the time of the full moon in Aug/Sep attracts thousands of pilgrims.

Mustang To the N of Muktinath and at present not accessible to trekkers, is the remote and small kingdom of Mustang, described in the French anthropologist Michel Peissel's vivid book *Mustang: The Lost Kingdom*. The territory occupies just over 3,000 sq km and has an average altitude of 4,000 m, just below the **Photu La** pass (4,600 m), itself only 75 m above the Tsangpo plain of Tibet. In all respects, geographically, climatically and culturally it belongs to Tibet. Today it is a Nepalese district with a certain degree of autonomy. The **Thak Khola/Kali Gandaki** originates here and flows out of the Mustang valley in a series of deep gorges.

Also called the **Kingdom of Lo**, it is said to have existed as an independent state as early as the 5th century AD, but was absorbed into Tibet under **Songtsenampo** in the 7th century. Later it achieved a degree of independence, becoming an important centre of the **Lamaistic Sakyapa** sect. After the disintegration of Gumthang in the early 15th century, **Gayalpo Ame Pal** founded a dynasty that has survived to the present day.

The Mongols overran it in the 17th century, and in 1760 the Rajah of Jumla conquered it. It passed to the Gurkhas thirty years later who also appreciated its strategic and commercial significance on the Salt Straight from the middle hills to Tibet. The Thakalis gradually wrested control of the salt-grain trade from Mustang and when Indian salt replaced Tibetan salt in Nepalese markets, its fortunes declined further. The drying up of most of the trade saw Mustang retreat into its own remote shell. Now, the principal economic activity is subsistence barley farming in small irrigated tracts near the rivers. This is complemented by yak, horse, mule and goat breeding and rearing. There is a significant nomadic pastoralist element in the lifestyle which has been dictated by the climate and arid environment.

The inhabitants of Mustang are **Bhotiyas**, or pure Tibetans, and both follow Lamaistic Buddhism. In the S of what is now Mustang district are the Thakalis who belong more to the middle hill group of Gurungs, Magars and Tamangs and who provide a bridge between the 2 largely geographically determined cultures.

The Annapurna Sanctuary Trek

Access to this spectacular amphitheatre is more restricted because of its location and altitude. Heavy winter snows obliterate tracks so this trek should not be attempted later than Nov and earlier than April. The pre-monsoon season of April and May is very good as the winter snows have melted and attractive meadows bedecked with alpine flowers can be camped on. Care is needed at all times as there is an avalanche risk and the attendant risk of being stranded.

Duration The round trip trek from Pokhara may be completed in 10 days. It is wise to allow 2 weeks.

The entrance to the sanctuary is 2 day's walk from the nearest occupied settlement. Therefore food, fuel, shelter in the form of tents, cooking equipment and warm clothing must be carried in. This is for porters as well as trekkers. The trek then becomes an expedition and an important exercise in planning and logistics. Whilst it is feasible to arrange your own trip, it is far easier to either book on a commercially organised trip in your home country or approach one of the reputable agencies in Kathmandu. The simplest trek is a trip from **Hinko Cave** to the base camp and back, and can be attempted with only 4 days supply of food and without a stove. Foodstuffs, such as tinned cheese, sardines, milk and fruit can be purchased at Birethanti and usually at Ghadrung.

Days 1 and 2 There are 3 approaches from **Pokhara** to **Ghandrung** where a single track enters the sanctuary. All take 2 days (3 at the very most) and 12-14 hr walking.

Chandrakot and Sholebhati Chandrakot is reached using the same stages as on the Jomosom trek. Overnight here. From here, instead of descending into the **Modi Khola** Valley, turn N on the W side of the village. The trail descends gradually but remains high for about 1 hr. At **Phatlikhet** it descends to the valley floor. An hr beyond you cross the river to a Sholebhati hamlet. This has some guesthouses and teahouses. Enquire before leaving Chandrakot whether the bridge at Sholebhati is there as it tends to get washed away after the winter snow melt. From Sholebhati follow the river upstream through **Kimche** to **Ghandrung** (2,000 m).

Chandrakot and Birethanti When the bridge at Sholebhati has gone, use this route. Of the 3 this offers the best accommodation. Use the Jomosom trail as far as Birethanti where the new trail leaves the village between the bridge and Gauchan Lodge. At first it picks its way through terraced fields, then becomes a well-defined track higher up. It does not climb much and after nearly 2 hr join the route from **Sholebhati** described above.

Dhampus and Landrung This route is the most direct. From **Pokhara** walk to **Suikhet,** described in the Jomosom trek. Here, follow the trail which ascends the

N wall of the **Yangdi Khola** canyon. An hr out of Suikhet you reach **Astam**. Stay on the track near to the ridge line to **Hyengjakot,** which offers good views down both sides. Another hr of walking and you reach *Dhampus* (1,700 m).

Warning Make particularly sure that you do not to leave any valuables unattended. Theft has become common here.

3 hr beyond Dhampus you go over a 2,165 m pass with good views of **Annapurna S.** Descend through attractive open glades to **Landrung** (1,650 m), a Gurung village. Below the village through terraced fields is a suspension bridge (1,370 m). On the other side it ascends to Ghandrung on an enormously long flight of stone steps. En route it joins the trail from **Birethanti**.

Ghandrung (2,000 m) is the second largest Gurung village in Nepal, and is a labyrinth of narrow alleys between tightly packed houses. On the left hand side of the trail is an information board describing Ghandrung's many and varied attractions. Ask for directions to wherever takes your fancy.

Of the 3 routes, the first is more direct than the second and the third involves the most climbing but does have some wonderful stretches, particularly between **Dhampus** and **Landrung.**

Day 3 The trail climbs through the village and crosses a small stream. It is then a gradual 1 ½hr climb up a boulder strewn hillside to a saddle at 2,220 m. There are a number of teahouses on the pass but no hotels. Descend steeply to the **Khummu Khola**, cross the stream, then ascend stone steps to the hamlet of **Khummu** on the N side of the valley. Continue to climb steeply, joining a trail from **Landrung** at 2,220 m. Follow the hillside E and turn N up the **Modi Khola** Valley and descend through thick forest to **Chhomro** (1,950 m).
This Gurung village is the highest permanent settlement in the Modi Khola Valley, with a marvellous view up the valley to **Macchapuchhare**. From here you can see the fish tail profile that has given the mountain its name. The largest hotel is by the school and there are a number of inns. The shops are well stocked with provisions. Allow about 5 hr for the day's walk.

Day 4 Descend through the village and cross the river below on a suspension bridge. The trail climbs out of the **Chhomro** valley and into mixed forest of oak and rhododendron. There is a seasonal hamlet at **Sinwa** with a couple of hotels. **Khuldi** is a short distance from here, below the trail which works its way upwards along the W wall of the canyon. There is a lodge in the village. **Kuldi Ghar** is a single stone hut situated in a clearing and lies beyond a piece of exposed bedrock into which footholds have been hacked. This is a suitable place to camp, especially if you reach Kuldi Ghar in the late afternoon. It is 30 min down a muddy trail to the Bamboo Hotel. During the monsoon leeches are common along stretches of bamboo forest like this. Allow 4 hr to reach Kuldi Ghar.

Day 5 From Kuldi Ghar descend to a flat patch of land from which there is a path leading to the British Experimental Sheep Breeding Farm. Beyond, the trail drops steeply into a ravine with a creek, then ascends the other side more or less continuously through bamboo forest. This can be quite hazardous and tiring as it is often muddy. 2½hr out from Kuldi Ghar the trail passes across **Tomo** grazing ground, a convenient campsite. ½hr further on the trail descends to the river where there are some waterfalls. **Hinko Cave** (3,020 m) is nearly 3 hr walking from here and 900 m higher. The track can get very boggy and this will be tiring. Nearly all of it is through forest. Hinko Cave is a large rock overhang with a small camping area beneath. Allow 6-7 hr to reach Hinko Cave.

Day 6 A short distance beyond the cave the trail continues along the river bed and is marked with cairns which get washed away every year. It then climbs through boulders towards the entrance to the Sanctuary. Near the entrance are suitable looking camping grounds. These are prone to avalanches from the unseen faces of **Hiunchuli** and **Annapurna S**, particularly in winter and spring, so at these times they should be avoided.
Around 3½hr from Hinko a moraine divides the valley into two. This is *Macchapuchhare Base Camp*. If you stay under the ridge and keep to your left it bends round into the Sanctuary, climbing as it goes. After 1 ½hr you arrive at the confluence of 2 moraines. By climbing to your right you will get magnificent views of the S Face of Annapurna.
The best campsites are on the meadows near to Machhapuchhare Base Camp and from here you can make a number of day trips higher up. There are a number of stone huts in the Sanctuary that call themselves inns. They are very basic and really only a roof above your

head. The food served is basic and they are operated in season by the denizens of Chhomro.

There are a number of climable peaks if you are suitably equipped. **Tent Peak** (5,500 m), and **Fluted Peak** (6,390 m) are open to trekking parties, but Fluted Peak involves mountaineering. **Hiunchuli** (6,441 m) is open to parties who applied to the Nepal Mountaineering Association and paid the appropriate fee. **Machhapuchhare** is forbidden and has not been climbed because Wilf Noyce and David Cox, members of Jimmy Roberts' 1957 expedition, deferred to local religious feelings and stopped 50 m below the summit.

The awesome and seemingly impregnable S Face of **Annapurna** was climbed by Chris Bonington's expedition in 1970, including Dougal Haston and Don Whillans. Technically the effort broke new ground in that this was the first time the face of an 8,000 m peak had been climbed.

The Ghorapani-Ghandrung Link
This short section enables trekkers doing the **Annapurna Circuit** in the recommended anti-clockwise fashion to combine that with the Annapurna Sanctuary trek. This can be accomplished in a long tiring day. 2 days are recommended. From Ghorapani the trail climbs directly E up a broad watershed between the **Modi Khola** and **Kali Gandaki** valleys. After 2 hr you reach a grassy knoll where you get a good view of the mountains, including Machhapuchhare which is not visible from the Ghorapani Pass.

The trail makes a steep descent into a canyon and follows the stream. **Bahunthanti** has a number of newish hotels. Between here and the next village of **Tada Pani** (2,530 m) is a climb through forest to an open patch, often under bamboo, then a descent to a stream followed by another climb. There are hotels here too. From **Tada Pani** the track drops through forests and cultivated areas to the **Khummu Khola** and **Ghandrung**.

Other Treks From Pokhara

The *Dhaulagiri Circuit* is a strenuous 3 week trek from Pokhara around the massif to the W of Annapurna. At present the area around Dhaulagiri (8,167 m), the seventh highest mountain in the world, is restricted, though some trekking companies offer the trek on a clockwise route that often takes in the Base Camp.

TREKKING IN WESTERN NEPAL

The Western region of Nepal is rarely visited by westerners. W Nepal is as densely populated as the other regions. Its historic and scenic grandeur approaches that of Kathmandu and Pokhara. It is remote in that it is not easy to reach. There is no sealed road and airstrips and flights are few. This, more than anything else explains why it is little visited. At present, only a few companies offer treks in the region, and conditions are basic. It is difficult to get on the flights into Jumla, the regional centre, and these are often delayed or cancelled due to bad weather. Large areas are off-limits to foreign visitors.

Dholpo And Jumla

Overlooked for centuries because of its bleak geography, *Dholpo* became part of what is now Nepal 200 years ago when the Gurkhas gained control over the region. Ties of blood and religion made the district a natural refuge for Tibetans who fled the communist Chinese takeover of their homeland in 1959. Within Dholpo's ring of massive mountains live a people economically and culturally disrupted by their estrangement from Tibet. Dholpo lies between the Great Himalaya range and the Tibetan border.

Climatically and biogeographically it has much in common with Ladakh, Zanskar, Lahul and Spiti in India and Mustang, its Nepalese neighbour. Thousand year-old Buddhist monasteries dot the Shey and Ban Tshang valleys. The religion practiced is Tibetan Buddhism, heavily influenced by shamanism. Dholpo's subsistence economy, based on livestock and barley cultivation wrested from the steep mountainsides as high as 4,000 m.

2 groups of ethnic Tibetans make up Dolpo's sparse population: the **Rungba** or valley farmers, and the **Drok**, nomadic yak herders. Peter Matthiessen has described how each year, in the seventh lunar month and before the barley harvest, villagers and nomads assemble to make the **kora**, a 16 km walk around the mountain. Cairns, sometimes piled high with bleached yak skulls, mark the route, which passes through a canyon marked with images of gods and goddesses. Here the pilgrims scrape rock dust from the boulders and swallow it with water from sacred springs.

According to legend, a thousand years ago a Tibetan ascetic called Drutob Senge Yeshe flying on a magic snow lion, conquered the mountain god and the rock metamorphosed into crystal. The mountain, is in fact, layered with marine fossils indicating its seabed position in former geological times.

Two National Parks have been created in Dolpo. **Shey-Phuksundo** covers 2,500 sq km and includes **Shey**, the spectacular **Phuksundo lake** and **Crystal Mountain**. The ecosystem is that of the arid high altitude desert that covers much of Tibet. The comparatively sparse vegetation supports a varied wildlife which includes the rare snow leopard, blue sheep, Tibetan sheep, musk deer, Tibetan hares and small rodents.

Khaptad National Park covers only 190 sq km and is a forest reserve lying between 2,200 m and 3,200 m. The vegetation includes oak, rhododendron and high altitude conifers. Both parks were created for conservation rather than recreation purposes and at present it is not possible to visit them.

Jumla (Altitude 2,240 m) 360 km W of Kathmandu and 150 km N of **Nepalganj**, boasts a rich past. It was the 14th century capital of the Khasa Mallas whose kingdom extended from the Kali Gandaki near Pokhara to the Kumaon region of India in the W, and from Taklakhar in Western Tibet to the Terai. There are a number of finely carved temples in the town attesting to its period of greatness. It is now a market town for the region and depends on imports of basic foodstuffs from Nepalganj, hence the difficulties trekkers experience in obtaining provisions. The local population is Thakuri which practises Hinduism. Porters can be obtained with difficulty and once hired your troubles are not likely to ease as English is not spoken. Accommodation is basic.

Jumla is the focal centre of W Nepal, and is serviced by a 2 hr Royal Nepalese Airlines flight from Kathmandu. Seats on the flight are not easy to obtain and there is a weight restriction. This makes planning a trek difficult as both porters and food are not easy to come by. A further problem for the independent trekker in the region is the shortgae of inns or teahouses. However, from here you can reach **Rara Lake** (2,980 m), Nepal's largest lake.

Jumla To Rara Lake Trek

Duration Around 10 days for the round trip, allowing for a rest day at the lake.

Day 1 From Jumla you trek W along the N bank of the **Tila river** down an old trade route, so it is not uncommon to see baggage trains of goats and horses plying the route. After some distance the track turns N up the **Chaudhaise River**. **Uthagaon** (2,530 m) is the first village. It is possible to camp here.

Day 2 From **Uthagaon** climb through the gorge of the **Ghurseni Khola** through pine forest to the town of **Padmora**. Water beyond here can be a problem, the limiting factor in deciding where to camp. There is a climb through rhododendron and birch forest to the 3,400 pass leading to the Sinj Khola valley. From here there are views of **Patrasi Himal** (6,860 m) and **Jagdula Himal** (5,785 m). There is a shepherd's hut near the pass close to a small waterfall.

Day 3 From the pass you descend to the **Sinj Khola** and along the populated valley. The village of **Bumra** (2,580 m) is on the N side of the valley. You then climb quite steeply to the tributary valley of the **Chautha Khola** and the village of Chautha which has a small hotel. You can stay here or push on a further hr or so in order to make the 4th day's walk easier.

Day 4 The upper **Chautha Khola** valley is also well wooded. The **Ghurchi Lagna Pass** (3,450 m) offers good views of the **Mugu Karnali river** and the peaks on the Tibetan border. From the pass you have a choice. You can either go left and follow the ridge and descend to **Rara Lake** from the S, or descend to the village of **Pina** (2,400 m) in the **Mandu Khola** valley, then turn NW, cross the intervening 3,000 m ridge and approach the lake from the SE. The latter is the easier even though you have to first descend then ascend to reach the lake. You can break the journey at Pina. The former ridge walk is steeper and reaches 4,000 m, offers magnificent views but is not easy to pick out without a local guide.

Day 5 *Rara Lake* is 10 sq km in area and has a circumference of around 13 km. This 170 m deep crystal blue expanse of water is surrounded by pine forest and the area was designated a National Park in 1975. Migratory birds from the N include mallards, teals, grebes and pochards. There are numerous places to camp around the lake and you may see some of the parks mammals which include the Himalayan black bear, thar, serow, musk deer, goral, the small red panda and Rhesus and Langur monkeys. In spring the area is carpeted with flowers. There are fish and otters in the lake.

Day 6 Rest day. The **National Park Office** is on the N side of the lake nr the deserted village of Rara. Entrance Rs 100.

Day 7 To return to Jumla you can go by the same route or take the route which leaves the lake at its W end. Follow the **Khatyar Khola** a couple of kilometres to the village of **Murma**, cross the river and walk S climbing to a 3,300 m pass. Views from here are good. You cross into the **Ghatta Khola** valley descending to *Gossain* (3,100 m) There are several good camping sites here.

Day 8 A short and easy walk. Follow the **Ghatta Khola** down to its confluence with the **Sinja Khola** (which you crossed upstream on the third day). The village of **Botan** is near the confluence. Turn right and go along the N bank of the Sinja through the village of Ganj to Sinja (2,400 m). There is a 14th century ruined Malla Palace across the river.

Day 9 From **Sinja** the track follows the **Jal Jala Khola** to its source below a 3,500 m pass. A meadow just below the pass makes a good campsite if you wish to break this long march into 2 more relaxing days. From the pass you descend through birch and pine forest to Jumla.

Longer treks from Jumla head NW into the Kanjiroba Himal. The highest peak here is Kanjiroba S (6,883 m). The treks are isolated and tough, and you need to be even better prepared, as it is more sparsely populated than around Jumla and Rara Lake.

INFORMATION FOR VISITORS

DOCUMENTS

Visas Visas are required by most nationalities. They are available from Nepalese embassies or consulates, and at the Indian border and Kathmandu airport. The cost of a visa varies according to your country of origin, (£20 from UK) and is valid for 30 days. A visa issued on arrival is only valid for 15 days. It can be extended for another 15 days at no extra cost, but you must provide proof that you have officially exchanged US$15 for each day of the extension.

Warning Visa extensions are very time consuming so it is best to get a 30 day visa in advance. From outside your home country it is easiest in Bangkok,

Calcutta, and New Delhi.

Extensions Beyond 1 month, costs Rs 80 per week for the second month, and more for the third month, with additional proof of exchanging US$15 per day. Visas cannot be extended further than 3 months. After a 3 months, at least 1 month must be spent outside Nepal before re-entry is permitted, India being the usual choice. Studying, teaching, research (University or Govt Institute) may provide grounds for exemption. The Kathmandu Immigration Office (T 412337) is only a short stroll from Thamel, on Tridevi Marg. In **Pokhara** the Immigration office is near the lake. In an emergency local police stations can extend visas or trekking permits for up to 7 days.

Validity A visa is officially only valid for the Kathmandu and Pokhara valleys, and the Royal Chitwan National Park, although in practice this includes all major roads through the country.

Trekking Permits See page 1302. **Note** You must apply for a trekking permit to use trekking routes. This automatically extends your visa.

Work Permits Work permits are required in Nepal which should normally be obtained before entering the country. Your employer applies for the permit, which can take months. If you arrange to work after arriving in Nepal, you should leave the country while the paperwork is negotiated. It is almost impossible to change a tourist visa into a work permit.

Nepalese Embassies Overseas *Australia*, 3rd Level, 377 Sussex St, Sydney, NSW 2000 (T (02) 264 7197): 66 High St, Toowong, Queensland 4006 (T (07) 378 0124): Suite 23, 18-20 Bank Place, Melbourne, Vic 3000 (T (03) 602 1271): 4th Floor, Airways House, 195 Adelaide Tce, Perth, WA 6000 (T (09) 221 1207). *Bangladesh*, Lake Rd, Road No 2, Baridhara Diplomatic Enclave, Dhaka. *Belgium*, M25 Ballegeer, RNCG Office, 20/8 Antwerp. *Burma*, 16 Natmauk Yeiktha (Park Ave), PO Box 84, Rangoon. *Denmark*, 36 Kronprinsessegade, DK 1006, Copenhagen K (T (01) 143175). *France*, 7 Rue de Washington, Paris 75008. *Germany*, Im Hag 15, 5300 Bonn, Bad Godesberg 2 (T 34 3097). Flinschtrasse 63, 6000 Frankfurt am Main (T 06 114 0871): Landsbergertrasse 191, 8000 Munchen 21 (T 089 570 4406): Handwerkstrasse 5-7, 7000 Stuttgart 80 (T 0711 7864 614 617). *India*, 1 Barakhamba Rd, New Delhi 110001 (T 38 1484); 19 Woodlands, Sterndale Rd, Alipore, Calcutta 700027 (T 45 2024). *Italy*, Piassa Medaglie d'Orro 20, Rome (T 348 176).

Japan, 16-23 Highashi-Gotanda, 3 chome, Shinagawa-ku, Tokyo 141. *Netherlands*, Prinsengracht 687, Gelderland Bdg, NI 1017 J V Amsterdam (T 020 25 0388). *Norway*, Haakon, VIIs gt-5, 0116 Oslo (T 2 414743). *Pakistan*, 506 84th St, Ataturk Ave, Ramna 6/4, Islamabad 23. Karachi, Memon Cooperative Housing Society, Block 7-8 Modem Club Rd, Karachi 29 (T 201908). *Sri Lanka*, 290 R A de Mel Mawatha, Colombo 7. *Sweden*, Birger Jarlsgatan 64, Karlavagen 97 S-115 22, Stockholm. *Switzerland*, Schanzeigasse 22, CH-8044 Zurich (T 816023). *UK*, 12A Kensington Palace Gardens, London W8 4QU (T 229 6231). *USA*, 1500 Lake Shore Dr, Chicago, IL 60610. Heidelberg College, Tiffin, OH 44883 (T (419) 448 2202); 473 Jackson St, San Francisco, CA 94111 (T (415) 434 1111): 16250 Dallas Parkway, Suite 110, Dallas, TX 75248 (T (214) 931 1212); 212 15th St NE, Atlanta, GA 30309 (T (404) 892 8152): 2131 Leroy Place NW, Washington, DC 20008 (T (202) 667 4550).

Driving If you are considering driving a car or motorcycle in Nepal you should have an International Drivers Permit.

Student cards An International Student Identity Card (ISIC) can be help to get travel discounts.

Onward Travel The visa section of the **Chinese Embassy** in Kathmandu is open 1000-1200 Mon and Wed. It takes 4 to 5 days to issue a visa which costs about US$20, although that cost can increased by another US$20 if the embassy decides they have to telex Beijing. Visas for **India** are required of every nationality. It is best to obtain them in your country of origin where possible. Visas for **Burma** are currently only being issued for group tourists, although they do claim to issue visas for longer than the old 7 days maximum. Visas for **Thailand** are issued without complication, they can be issued at Bangkok Airport for stays of 14 days or less.

TRAVEL

By air From Europe, N America and Australasia a change of plane and/or airline en route is usually necessary.

From Europe Lufthansa fly Frankfurt to Kathmandu. RNAC fly London, Frankfurt, Dubai, Kathmandu (about £580 return).

From N America Flights from the US E coast usually require transferring in New Delhi to RNAC or Indian Airlines. From the W coast transfers are usually required in Hong Kong or Singapore. (about US$1500 return for both). Fares from Canada are similar to the USA, westbound from Vancouver or eastbound from Toronto or Montreal. Bangladesh Biman and PIA offer discounted fairs through small agents.

From Australasia Thai International and Royal Nepal Airlines connect Bangkok with Kathmandu. Bangkok is the most popular transit point although you can also fly directly from Singapore or Hong Kong to Kathmandu.

From Asia India New Delhi is the main departure point (1 hr). Calcutta, Patna and Varanasi have direct connections with Kathmandu.

Other departure points for Kathmandu include: **Colombo**, Sri Lanka; **Dhaka**, Bangladesh; **Dubai**, UAE; **Karachi**, Pakistan; **Lhasa**, Tibet; **Paro**, Bhutan.

Note Discounts If you are under 26 years of age and hold and ISIC card you are eligible for 25% reduction on Royal Nepal Airlines (RNAC) on both domestic and international flights. Simply being under 30 years of ages makes you eligible for a similar discount on certain RNAC and Indian Airlines routes.

Airport Taxes At the time of going to press departure tax for international flights is Rs 300, for domestic flights Rs 30. You should confirm this on arrival. On departure, it is possible to re-exchange up to 15% of the Nepalese rupees you have officially changed, but you must show bank receipts.

By land There are 21 recognised border crossing points. 12 are normally open, but only three are used by foreign travellers.

Both the **Sunauli/Bhairawa** and **Raxaul Bazaar/Birganj** border posts can be reached from **Varanasi** and **Patna** respectively by train or bus. Bus travel is much quicker. In Nepal the blue government-owned **Saja Sewa** are less crowded and quicker – good value.

Varanasi to Kathmandu and Pokhara
From New Delhi and Varanasi the most popular route is through **Sunauli/Bhairawa**. This is the shortest route to Pokhara or Kathmandu. The

Royal Chitwan National Park can be reached via the Mahendra Highway. There are Deluxe buses from Varanasi. The price includes a basic breakfast in Varanasi, transportation and very basic overnight accommodation at the border. An alternative is to get a bus to **Gorakhpur** (5 hr) where you change buses for **Sunauli** (3 hr). Frequent buses from Sunauli to Kathmandu. There are also direct buses from Varanasi to Sunauli.

A through ticket from Varanasi is the easiest method, but it is much cheaper to take each leg separately and organise your own accommodation at Sunauli. Once in Nepal you have a good choice of buses to Kathmandu, Pokhara or points between. Buses to Kathmandu follow the the **Siddhartha Highway** to **Butwal**, then turn right along the **Mahendra Highway** via **Narayanghat** (for Chitwan) and take around 9 hr.

The route to **Pokhara** follows the **Siddhartha Highway** and the journey takes around 9 hr. At **Butwal** (24 km) you leave the Terai and enter the hills following the **Tinau River** along its gorge to Tansen beyond which you cross the **Kali Gandaki River** and climb over the hills to **Pokhara**. Descending into the valley there are fine views of the **Annapurna Massif** and **Machhapuchhare**.

Patna to Kathmandu

This route uses the Raxaul Bazaar/Birganj border crossing. The railhead is at Raxaul Bazaar. It is quicker to take a bus from Patna – 3 hr. **Raxaul Bazaar** and **Birganj** are only a few kilometres apart, and from either the bus stand or the railway station you can get a cycle rickshaw to the border post (open 24 hr) and Birganj. There are cheap hotels in both towns.

It is an 11 hr bus journey from Birganj to Kathmandu. The most direct route to the capital is along the Tribhuvan Highway which runs N to **Daman** and **Naubise**. Most buses use the longer, though easier route W along the Mahendra Highway to Narayanghat and then north to Mugling where the road meets the Prithvi Narayan Highway between Pokhara and Kathmandu.

The journey to **Pokhara** takes about 10 hr and follows the same route to **Mugling** where instead of turning right for Kathmandu you turn left. From the border the route crosses the Terai to its N edge. From **Hetauda** the road runs along the E-W flowing Rapti River.

Tadi Bazaar is the 'jumping off point' for the Royal Chitwan National Park and a convenient place to halt if you wish to break your journey into two stages. The "Inner Terai" is heavily populated and intensively cultivated.

Darjiling to Kathmandu

The **Kakarbhitta** crossing gives access from Darjiling to Kathmandu along the Mahendra Highway. It is a long, tiring and slightly complicated journey if you are travelling independently. "All inclusive" trips available from Darjiling, but all require a change of bus at the border and entail travelling overnight. The trip lasts 17 hours and the distance is over 600 km. It is cheaper to make your own arrangements, but this involves three changes; at **Siliguri** (bus), a rickshaw ride across the border, and at **Kakaphitta**. There is a choice of buses and you have the option of not travelling at night.

During the monsoon, some of the route may be blocked by flooding or landslides. If the Kakarbhitta route is blocked by floods, travel by train from Siliguri to Patna before entering Nepal by the route described above.

From Tibet The route from Tibet across the Kodari/Khasa border point was opened in 1986 allowing access to Lhasa along the Friendship Highway. However in 1989 this crossing was closed again to individual travellers due to political troubles within Tibet. In June 1991 this road route was re-opened to tourists. From the Friendship Bridge on the Nepal side of the border buses run twice a day to Kathmandu and taxis are also available. Depending upon the season the road may be blocked by either landslides and snow.

MONEY

Currency The Nepalese Rupee (Rs) is divided into 100 paisa (p). Major international currencies are readily accepted. The Indian Rupee is also like hard currency, but Indian Rupees are traded 1 for 1 with Nepali Rupees, so it is better value to change foreign excahge into Nepali Rupees. Coins are 5, 10, 25 and 50 paisa and 1 rupee. Notes are 1, 2, 5, 10, 20, 50, 100, 500 and 1000 Rupees. The last two are often difficult to change outside major towns, so carry smaller notes.

Travellers' cheques Most travellers cheques are accepted at banks and major hotels. If travelling or trekking individually you will need cash.

Credit cards Most credit cards are widely accepted in main centres, but not outside.

Bank hours are 1000-1400, Sun to Th, and 1000-1200 Fri. Larger hotels will exchange travellers cheques at bank rates, but usually only for guests. Visitors to Nepal are issued currency exchange forms on arrival on which official exchanges should be entered. You need this form if you wish to extend your visa and need to offer proof of exchange os US$15 per day of extension. You also require the form if you wish to exchange your rupees to other currency on departure – only 10% of the total or the last amount exchanged, which ever greater, will be exchanged. Trekkers should carry cash, as it is impossible to exchange foreign currency or traveller cheques.

Cost of Living Cost of living in Nepal is generally low by western standards. The top of the range hotels and the best restaurants are considerably cheaper than their equivalent in the West or Japan.

Tipping and bargaining Try to get an idea of the prices being charged for goods before you start bargaining. Tipping is becoming more prevalent in Kathmandu. In expensive establishments tip up to 10%, in smaller places the loose change or Rs 10 will be appreciated. **Note** Taxi drivers do not expect a tip.

Shopping and best buys Nepal is a shopper's paradise whether you are looking for a cheap souvenir or a work of art. Remember to bargain except in a 'Fixed price' shop.

Thangkas (*paubha* in Newari) are the traditional Tibetan paintings of religious and ceremonial subjects, often of gods, deities, mandalas and the wheel of life. The central figure of a deity is usually surrounded by lesser gods. The paintings are on cloth (often silk) and were a convenient way of carrying and storing a religious icon. They are believed to have been originated by Napalese artists who took them to Tibet along with illuminated manuscripts and metal sculptures, as early as the 10th century. The professional thangka painters live in Bhaktapur.

Rice Paper Prints produced by wooden blocks on locally produced paper of Nepalese, Tibetan and Chinese deities make good gifts. You can buy these (sometimes along with an old block) from Basantpur in Kathmandu or a handicrafts shop.

Tibetan Carpets are handwoven and nowadays use chemical dyes in addition to the traditional vegetable dyes. You will be able to see weavers at work in Bodhnath and Jawalkhel. The traditional designs include dragons, geometric and floral patterns and you can get one small enough to pack easily into a suitcase.

Clothing, both Nepalese and Tibetan, is a popular buy, including Tibet jackets and machine embroidered cloth. Nepalese caps are traditionally made in Bhaktapur.

Tea is grown in E Nepal. *Ilam* and *Mai Valley* are recommended brands.

Other Nepalese **crafts** include the *khukri*, the traditional Gurkha knife. The genuine ones come with two extra smaller knives for skinning, and the main blade has a notch to stop blood reaching the handle. Woodcarving is centred in Bhaktapur and can be found around Tachupal Tole. The Crafts Centre is in Dattatraya. Tibetan crafts include prayer wheels and other religious items. Check inside the wheel to see if it contains the printed prayer on a roll.

Crafts sold around Bodhnath and Swayambhunath are often highly priced. Trinkets and jewellery with turquoise setting are good value while stamps and coins attract collectors. Gold and silver jewellery should only be bought from reputable shops.

Warning The bronze and metal statues, sold as antiques are mostly mass produced and 'aged' which will be obvious from the price. Antiques cannot be taken out of the country, and Nepalese Customs is strict **on departure**. You need a permit from the **Department of Archaeology** if you want to take out any article which looks older than 100 years. The office (T 215358) is in the National Archives bldg, Ram Shah Path. If you go between 1000-1300 you should be able to pick up the permit by 1700 the same day. The Customs Office, Tripureshwar, T 215525 provides information.

Sending Purchases Home If you cannot carry your goods with you you can ship them, though it can be risky and expensive. The Foreign Post Office requires inspection by officials before you wrap your purchases for mailing. Reliable packing companies in Kathmandu include *Sharma and Sons Packers & Movers* (T 411474) and *Atlas Packers & Movers* (T 221402). *DHL international couriers* has an office in Durbar Marg.

OTHER ESSENTIAL INFORMATION

Official time Nepal is 10 min ahead of Indian Standard Time, and 5 hours 40 min ahead of Greenwich Mean Time. 12 noon in Kathmandu is: New Delhi 1150 today; London 0620, today; San Francisco 2220, yesterday; New York 0120 today; Tokyo 1520 today.

Weights and measures Nepal uses the decimal system, but people often use traditional measures for some purposes, counting in **lakhs** (100,000) and **crores** (10 million). **For rice, cereals, milk and sugar**: 1 *mana* equals about 1/2 a litre; 1 *paathi* equals 3.75 litres, which contains 8 mana; 1 *muri* equals 20 paathi (75 litres). **For vegetables and fruit**: 1 *pau* equals 250 grams; 1 *ser* equals 1 kg (4 pau); 1 *dharmi* equals 3 kg (3 ser). The term *mutthara* means 'a handful', for vegetables or firewood. **For all metals** 1 *tola* equals 11.5 grams. **For precious stones** 1 *carat* equals 0.2 grams.

Postal services The Central Post Office in Kathmandu has three sections. They are located close together at the junction of **Kanti Path** and **Kicha-Pokhari Rd**. For stamps and Poste Restante go to the General Post Office, Sundhara,1000-1700, Sun-Fri. Make sure that the stamps on your letters and postcards are cancelled in front of you. The **Poste Restante** section is to the left of the main entrance and is efficiently run. You must show your passport for collecting mail. Ask correspondents to underline your surname or print it in bold block capitals and only your initials. Open Sun to Th 1015-1700 (1015-1600 from mid-Nov to mid-Feb), 1015-1400 Fri, closed Sat. Hotels will also receive and hold mail if you are a guest. The **Foreign Post Office**, N of the GPO, deals only with parcels sent or received from outside Nepal. Open 1000-1700 Sun-Th, 1000-1200 Fri, closed Sat. Sending a parcel is time consuming and, if possible, should be avoided. They have to be examined and sealed by a Customs officer then sealed in an approved manner. **Note** Main hotels will handle mail, which is more convenient.

Telephone services The Telecommunication Office, Tripureshwar deals with telephone calls, cables and telexs. The international telephone office is open 1000-1700, Sun-Fri. International telephone connections are almost impossible.

Business hours Government Offices 1000-1700, Sun to Fri. Winter 1000-1600. Note Saturday in Nepal is a rest day and Sunday is a full working day for offices and banks. Embassies and international organisations take a two-day weekend but are generally open 0900 or 0930 to 1700 or 1730 during the week. Shops are open on Sat and holidays from 1000-1900 or 2000.

Electricity Major towns in Nepal have electricity, 220 volt AC; fluctuations in current are common. A few major hotels have their own generators, as there are frequent power cuts.

Media Nepal's daily English-language paper the Rising Nepal, is often difficult to find. The International Herald Tribune, Time, Newsweek, Statesman, and Times of India, can all be easily found in Kathmandu. Nepal Traveller, is a free monthly tourist magazine distributed at many hotels. It includes articles on sightseeing, festivals, trekking and other activities in Nepal. Himal, is a six-times-yearly magazine published in Nepal and devoted to development and environment issues throughout the Himalaya.

Maps Asian Highway Route Map, India-Nepal-Bangladesh 1981 United Nations, ESCAP, Transport, Communications and Tourism Division, Asian Highway Project. 3 maps 1:1,250,000. Bridgestone Tire Co. Includes information on these areas as well as geography, places of interest, advice to motorists, road conditions and traffic regulations.

A Nepal Map Series produced by Arbeitsgemeinscaft fur Vergleichende Hochgebirgsforschung (Association for Comparative Alpine Research) and published by Kartographische Anstalt Freytag-Berndt und Artaria, Vienna – "Schneider Maps". Used by mountaineers and trekkers.

9 general topographical maps produced in accordance with the results of the Survey of India include: Everest 1957 1:25,000. Khumbu Himal 1967 1:50,000. Tamba Kosi-Likhu Khola 1969 1:50,000. Rolwaling Himal 1974 1:50,000. Shorong/Hinku 1974 1:50,000. Dudh Kosi 1974 1:50,000. Lapchi Kang 1974 1:50,000. Kathmandu Valley 1977 1:50,000, including a basic map series of 16 sheets at 1:10,000. Useful tourist maps include a city plan of Kathmandu at 1:10,000, and Patan 1:7,500. Helambu-Langtang 1987 1:100,000.

Mount Everest Region 1961 Royal Geographic Society, London. 1:100,000 topographical map. Mount Everest 1988 National Geographic Society, Washington D.C. 1:50,000 topographical map. Nepal Natraj Tours and Travels, Kathmandu. 1:506,880 Country map including roads, villages, rivers and mountains. Lamosangu to Mt Everest 1977 International Book House, Kamalokashi, Kathmandu. 1:126,720 topographical map including trek route, villages and tea houses. The 1983/84 version of this map includes sketches of the mountains, Namche Bazaar, Everest Base Camp course and Gokyo course.

Hints on social behaviour (See also eating and drinking customs above). When trekking, do not give money, cigarettes, sweets or other items indiscriminately, but do give to pilgrims and holy men who live on alms. Do not swim or bathe nude in rivers or hot springs. Help Nepal retain its beauty and its forests. **Burn or bury litter.** Do not use firewood or encourage its use.

Photography Many Nepalese like being photographed, particularly if you have a Polaroid and can give them a copy. If in any doubt, ask, but you are encouraged not to pay. Most festivals allow photography. Participants sometimes go into a trance and may act unpredictably. It is safest to avoid taking photographs under such circumstances.

Out of courtesy to sherpas The name of a dead person should not be mentioned to his close relatives or in his old house as this may attract his reincarnated spirit. Many Sherpas do not allow whistling in their homes for the same reason. Do not write a Sherpa's name in red ink, as this symbolises death and is used for inscriptions at funeral services. Do not ask a Sherpa to kill a wild animal for you. If you offer food or drink to a Sherpa and it is politely refused, you should offer it twice more. Traditional Sherpa hospitality requires that you offer something three times. The Sherpa word for 'thank you' is *tuche*.

Visiting temples or monasteries Some Hindu temples are open to non-Hindus, most are not. Look for signs or ask. Remove shoes and any leather items before entering. Walk on the left of shrines and stupas. Also walk on the left hand side inside monasteries. Buddhist monasteries are open to all. You may even visit the resident lama (priest), offering him a khada (white ceremonial scarf of silk or cotton – available in Asan, Kathmandu). If you wish to make a contribution, put money in the donation box. It will be used for the upkeep of the temple or monastery.

Accommodation Accommodation has been graded from **AL** down to **F**. The price for each category is a guide to what you would pay for the best room (double) remembering that taxes vary widely from state to state and can sometimes add considerably to the basic price.

AL Rs 1,750+. **A** Rs 1,200+ International class. Central a/c, rooms with attached baths, telephone and TV with video channel, a business centre, multicuisine restaurants, bar, and all the usual facilities including 24 service, shopping arcade, exchange, laundry, travel counter, swimming pool and often other sports such as tennis and squash, accept credit cards. They often have hairdresser, beauty parlour and a health club. **B** Rs 800-1,200 Most of the facilities of **A** but perhaps not business centre and swimming pool and sports and lacking the feeling of luxury. **C** Rs 400-800. A/c rooms. Restaurant, , rooms with attached baths and TV, and most have a shopping arcade, exchange, travel counter and accept credit cards. If a hotel has central a/c or do not accept credit cards this is mentioned. **D** Rs 200-400. Reasonably comfortable, probably with some a/c rooms, attached baths and a restaurant. **E** Rs 75-200. Simple. Usually shared bath. may have a dining room. **F** Less than Rs 75. Very basic.

Clothing The weather ranges from sticky heat in the Terai to freezing in Himalaya. Therefore you should have clothing that will suit your travels. If you intend to trek you should have the correct clothing. See list in S Asia Introduction and Trekking, **page 1306**.

Food Real Nepalese food consists of *dhal* (lentils), *bhat* (rice) and *tarkari* (vegetable curry). It can get monotonous. However, Kathmandu has a genuinely cosmopolitan cuisine.

Other popular local food includes: **Water buffalo**, is the usual substitute for beef since cows are sacred and cannot be eaten. You will come across 'buff' curry and even 'buff' burgers or steaks. **Dahi** – yoghurt or curd. The rich buffalo milk curd can be very good. **Sikarni** – a sweet curd dessert. **Gundruk** – a traditional Nepalese soup made from dried vegetables. **Gurr** – made from raw potatoes ground and mixed with spices and then grilled like a large pancake and eaten with cheese. **Potatoes** are the staple food of the Sherpa although they are relatively recent introduction. **Momo** or **Kothe** – Tibetan dish made by steaming or frying meat or vegetables wrapped in dough similar to the Chinese 'dim sum' or Italian ravioli. **Tama** – a traditional Nepalese soup made from dried bamboo shoots. **Thukpa** – a traditional Tibetan pasta, meat and vegetable soup. **Tsampa** – the staple dish in the hill country of ground grain usually mixed with tea, water or milk.

Drink   Chiya is local tea prepared with milk and sugar. **Coke** as well as orange and lemon bottled drinks, are available in the main towns. **Lassi** – a refreshing drink made of curd mixed with water, but make sure the water is safe. The locally produced **beer** is generally good. Beer can sometimes be found in the hills which is refreshing after a day trekking. 'Iceberg' is regarded as the best but is the most expensive. 'Leo and Star' beers are good. **Chang** – the home brew made from barley, rye or maize, is the popular alcoholic drink. **Arak** is from potato and rakshi from wheat or rice. **Tongba** is the Tibetan drink.

Warning See health section in introduction for detailed health advice.

Eating and Drinking Customs You must not touch somebody else's food. You will notice that the Nepalese, when drinking water from a bottle or tumbler, may pour the liquid into their mouth without their mouth touching the container. In this way they avoid caste rules on ritual pollution. You should only use your right hand for eating or passing food. The left is considered unclean as it is associated with washing after defecating.

A cup of tea usually starts the morning, followed by a substantial 'brunch' late morning. If you are invited for a meal, socializing takes place before dinner (which may be served late by Western standards), and guests often leave soon after finishing the meal.

The kitchen in a Hindu home is sacred so non-Hindus should ask before entering.

Health See section on health in introduction, **page 24**.

Warning When trekking in the monsoon, beware of **leeches**. They sway on the ground waiting for a passer by and get in boots when you are walking. When they are gorged with blood they drop off. Don't try pulling one off as the head will be left behind and cause infection. Put some salt, or hold a lighted cigarette to it, which will make it quickly fall off. Before starting off in the morning it helps to spray socks and bootlaces with an insect repellent.

Vaccinations In Kathmandu you can get certain vaccinations free of charge from the **Infectious Diseases Clinic** (T 215550) in **Teku** or from the **CIWEC Clinic** (T 410983) and **Kalimati Clinic** (T 214743) for a charge.

Health Insurance Many travel insurances include cover for theft, loss and medical problems. There is a large variety of different insurance covers, so it is recommended that careful consideration is made of all the options. Read the fine print carefully. Many policies exclude dangerous activities which can include trekking.

NATIONAL HOLIDAYS, FAIRS AND FESTIVALS

Public holidays National hoildays 1991-92 **Jan 11** Unity Day (King Prithvi Narayan Shah's death anniversary). **Feb 9** Martyrs Day. **Feb 18** National Democracy Day. **Feb/Mar** Siva Ratri **Mar 8** Nepalese Women's Day. **Mar 18** Holi **Apr 10** Teachers' Day **Sep/Oct** Dasain **Oct 25-27** Deepavali **Nov 7** Queen Aishworya's Birthday **Dec 17** Constitution and King Mahendra Day **Dec 28** King Birendra's birthday.

Festivals The 2 solar calendars, the Nepalese and Gregorian are in common use, but there are 3 lunar calendars, Nepalese, Newari and Tibetan! The latter depending on the waxing and waning of the moon affects the festival dates, the full moon considered particularly auspicious, eclipses often thought to be a bad omen.

Exact dates of festivals change annually, calculated by astrologers. The Dept of Tourism in Kathmandu publishes an annual brochure so please check. The Nepalese New Year is in mid-April and the two most important festivals are Dasain and Tihar in Sep/Oct. (Nepalese months are in brackets).

Jan-Feb (*Magha*) *Magha Sankranti*, marks the transition from winter to spring. *Tribeni Mela*, on the new moon, is held on the banks of the Narayani River. *Basanta Panchami* (9 Feb 1992), celebrates the start of the spring season. Ceremonies at Kathmandu's Hanuman Dhoka Palace, street parades by children, and dedications at temples and sanctuaries characterise this festival. *Magha Purnima*, on the last day of Magha, bathers walk from the Bagmati River ghats to various temples and take a ritual bath in the Salindi River.

Feb-Mar (*Falgun*) *Rashtriya Prajatantra Divas or Democracy Day*, includes parades and procession to celebrate the 1951 overthrow of the autocratic Rana regime. *Holi* (18 Mar 1992), a colourful festival to mark the beginning of Spring. People put on new clothes and go round throwing coloured powder and water at each other. The same as in India. *Tibetan New Year*. *Maha Sivaratri* (Siva's Night) Special celebrations at Pashupatinath, with a big *mela* (fair). All night vigil, music, while many pilgrims take holy baths every 3 hr. Gun Salute at Tundhikhel, Kathmandu and thousands of oil lamps and bonfires at night, brighten the festivities.

Mar-Apr (*Chaitra*) *Ghorajatra*, in Patan, includes horse races and displays of gymnastics and horsemanship. Sacrifices are made to temples of the Ashta Matrikas, or mother goddess. *Pasa Chare*, a Newar festival, is a time of hospitality among the Newar. On the same day as the horse show of the Ghorajatra festival the demon Gurumpa is carried to the Tundhikhel in a midnight procession. *Chaitra Dasain* (10 Apr 1992) and Seto Machhendranath, occur simultaneously in Kathmandu. *Ram Navami*, at the Janaki Mandir in Janakpur in the eastern Terai, celebrates the birthday of Rama.

Apr-May (*Baisakh*) *New Year* celebrations of *Bisket* (13 Apr 1992) in Bhaktapur, (**see page 1296**), *Balkumari Jatra* in Thimi, and *Rato Machhendranath* Jatra in Patan (**see page 1293**). *Matatritha Snan* in late Apr is highlighted by ritual baths at Matatirtha, near Thankot, for people whose mothers have died during the past year. *Astami* in Naxal, is highlighted by ritual sacrifices to insure a prosperous summer. *Buddha Jayanti* (14 August 1992) throughout Nepal, celebrates the birthday of Gautama Buddha. Pilgrimages to Buddhist shrines, especially Swayambhunath and Bodhnath Stupas in the Kathmandu Valley.

May-Jun (*Jesth*) *Sithinakha*, throughout the Kathmandu Valley, celebrates the 'divine warrior' by giving domestic offerings. *Mani Rimdu*, the Sherpa religious festival at Thame monastery Namche Bazaar, lasting three days. Monks seek to gain merit by performing masked dramas and dances. The festival is repeated six months later at Thyangboche monastery.

Jun-Jul (*Asadh*) *Tribhuvan Jayanti*, is the national holiday honouring the late King Tribhuvan. The ceremony is at Tripureshwar, at the statue of the late King.

Jul-Aug (*Srawan*) *Ghanta Karna*, held in all Newar settlements, marks the completion of the paddy planting season in the Kathmandu Valley. The festival is a remnant of demon worship and the decorations are intended to ward off evil spirits. *Naga Panchhami*, in the Kathmandu Valley, honours nagas, the divine serpents. Celebrations include the pinning of paintings depicting nagas to doors and being blessed by priests. *Lakhe*, mask dancing, also starts in Kathmandu. *Janai Purnima* or *Rakshya Vandhana*, at the Kumbeshwar temple in Patan and Gosainkund Lake in the foothills north of the Valley, is in honour of Siva Mahadev. Brahmins and Chhetris renew their *munja* (sacred thread), while priests distribute yellow threads (*rikhi doro*), to other castes.

Aug-Sep (*Bhadra*) *Gaijatra*, Indrajatra and Dasain all fall within 30 days of each other. *Indrajatra* starts with the erection of a wooden pole to honour the God of Rain. *Krishnastami*, in 11 sanctuaries and temples dedicated to Krishna especially the Krishna Mandir in Patan's Durbar Sq, commemorates Krishna's birth with offerings of tulsi plants.

Pancha Dan or *Banda Yatra*, the festival of the five summer gifts, in Swayambhunath stupa and Kathmandu Valley. Women give gifts of rice and grains to priests as the march through the streets chanting hymns. *Gokarna Aunshi*, Father's Day, is highlighted by ritual bathing in the Bagmati River at Gokarna for those whose fathers have died during the last year. *Teej Brata* (11 Sep 1991, 30 Aug 1992) throughout the Kathmandu Valley, to pray to Siva and Parvati for a long happy married life. Married women wear scarlet and gold wedding saris. Ceremonial baths at Bagmati are taken to honour husbands.

Sep-Oct (*Ashwin*) *Ganes Festival*, at the Sep full moon, honours Ganes, without whose blessing no religious ceremony begins. *Dasain* (Durga Puja). First of the ten day Puja is marked in homes, by planting and nurturing barley seeds in sand and water from the holy river. The devout bathe in holy places during the next 9 days. On *Fulpati*, the 7th day, sacred flowers and leaves from the Gorkha Palace reach Kathmandu where they are received by crowds accompanied by brass bands at Hanuman Dhoka gate and firing of guns in Tundikhel. *Mahasthami*, the 8th, the devout fast and by sacrifices of animals including buffaloes, sheep and goats at *Kalratri* (Black night) followed on the 9th day with the elaborate mass sacrifices at Kathmandu's Taleju Temple (which is open to Hindus on this single day each year) and the sprinkling of the blood blessed by the goddess on all vehicles and instruments in the hope of preventing accidents. The climax, on the 10th (Day of Victory), *Vijaya Dashami* marks Rama and Durga's triumph over evil. Hindus receive a Tikka of vermilion, curd and rice on the forehead from elders, to ensure health and happiness. The fortnight of festivities ends with the full moon night when many women start a month long fast. Throughout the Puja period you are likely to see 8 days of masked dances in Patan's Durbar Sq, kite flying and erection of bamboo swings.

Oct-Nov (*Kartik*) *Tihar* Festival of lights – **see page 155** Diwali. (*Deepavali* 5 Nov 1991, 25 Oct 1992, Bhai Tika 8 Nov 1991, 27 October 1992). The 1st, when small lamps are lit and the first portion of the family meal is given to the crows. The 2nd, when dogs are decked with garlands and a tikka is marked on their foreheads. Both the crow and dog are associated with the *Yama*, God of Death who is given offerings and thanks. The 3rd, is marked with worshipping cows and is also Lakshmi Puja when towns and villages are lit with thousands of tiny wick lamps and candles, as on Diwali in India, to invite the goddess of good fortune to enter the home, and fireworks are set off. The 4th day is Newari New Year and set aside for the worship of the divine in one's Self when families get together. The last day is Bhai Tika when sisters place multicoloured Tikas on their brothers' foreheads to protect them from evil and brothers make generous gifts in return. The five days marks the end of harvest, the beginning of a year and the worship of animals and *Haribodhani Ekadasi* (1 Nov 1992), is a pilgrimage in honour of Vishnu to Budhanilkantha.

Nov-Dec (*Marga*) *Bala Chaturdasi* (6 Dec 1991, 19 Nov 1992), pilgrimage to Pashupatinath, includes offerings to Lord Pashupati. Lighting of oil lamps the 1st night of celebrations is followed by a morning bath in the Bagmati River. Pilgrims follow the traditional route through the Mrigasthali Forest offering seeds and sweets so that dead relations can benefit in the next world. *Vivaha Panchami*, in Janakpur in the eastern Terai, recalls Sita's marriage to Rama, **see page 47**.

Dec-Jan (*Poush* **Constitution Day**, celebrated in every town in Nepal, commemorates the 1962 Constitution Act in tribute to the late King Mahendra. *Birthday of His Majesty the King*, celebrated throughout Nepal, included ceremonies, processions and military parades. King Birendra Bir Bikram Shah Dev was born 28 Dec 1945.

BHUTAN

Official name Druk-yul

National flag Saffron and orange red, divided diagonally, with a dragon in the centre.

Official language Dzongkha **Medium of instruction in schools** English

Basic indicators *Population* 1.5 m *Density* 35.4 per sq km. Urban 4%, Rural 96%; 1990 1,628,000. Bhutia 61%, Gurung 16%, Assamese 14% and others. *Religion*: Buddhist 70%, Hindu 25%, Muslim 5%. *Birth rate* 39%; Infant mortality 143 per 1,000. Life expectancy Male 46, Female 44.5 years. *Land use* (1981) 70% forested, pasture 5%, agriculture 2%, other 23%. *Literacy* (1977) 18% Male 31%, Female 9%.

Bhutan, dwarfed by its great neighbours India and China, and only one third the size of Nepal, is none the less slightly larger than Switzerland. Its official name, Druk Yul, means 'Land of the Thunder Dragon', portrayed on the flag. It is also the most mysterious and the least modernised country in South Asia. It has an agreement under which it accepts Indian guidance in foreign relations, but in all other respects retains its independence. It has been consistently cautious with respect to contact with the outside world. The flow of foreign tourists is tightly controlled, and it has tried to control the speed of its own social and economic change. The government is making considerable efforts to uphold traditional values and beliefs, and strongly guards the country's religious and cultural tradition.

GEOGRAPHY

Location Bhutan lies between 89° and 92°E and 27° and 28°N. India lies along the entire length of its S border with Tibet to its N, from which it is separated by the relatively narrow part of the High Himalaya.

The Land In the high Himalayan region of Bhutan there are several peaks over 7,000 m. The highest is *Gangri* (7,540 m) and the most famous and picturesque is *Chomo Lhari* (7,313 m). In the W the watershed of the Tibetan Chumbi valley forms the border. The alignment of this border has been repeatedly disputed by China.

The border with India was established by the British in the 18th and 19th centuries. In the S it generally runs along the base of the abruptly rising Himalayan foothills and in some areas it includes the N rim of the Brahmaputra river lowlands called the *Duars*. These are doors or *dwars** (Hindi – gates) and there are 18 of

them. At each the Himalayan rivers have cut through. All the motor roads from the S pass through the Duars. In the W the boundary with Sikkim was again established by the British and accepted by India.

The largest part of the country is part of the middle Himalayan range with altitudes ranging from 1,600 to 5,000 m. The rivers tend to run N-S and the Black Mountain Range forms a divide between the W & E parts of the country and is crossed by the **Pele Pass** (3,369 m).

Vegetation The wetness of the Duars allows a lush forest vegetation to flourish with bamboos, ferns, hanging plants and giant orchids on banyan, giant sal and teak trees. As you move higher the forest thins out but there is still a wide range of trees: poplar, ash, aspen, magnolia, oak, conifers and beautiful rhododendron.

Above 3,000 m bamboo and conifer forests take over, with fir, larch, cypress and pine. At 4,000 m birch, pine and rhododendron dominate and then give way to juniper and other bushes. Mosses and lichens can occasionally be found at high altitude and it is only in E Bhutan that the forest reaches the otherwise bleak N side of the main Himalaya range.

Wildlife A large number of animals are found in the forests – monkeys, deer and buffalo, leopards, tigers and rhino. There are also many birds, many kinds of butterflies, and various reptiles.

CLIMATE

The climate and vegetation are largely influenced by the monsoon which begins in Jun and lasts until mid Oct when 85% of the annual rainfall is received. The windward S facing mountain slopes consistently receive heavier precipitation.

Temperature Min temperatures range from -10°C (Paro, Thimphu) to 15°C (Southern Foothills); Max from 30°C (Southern Foothills) to 35°C (Paro, Thimphu).

Rainfall In the Duars Plain and at heights of up to 1,500 m, the climate is sub tropical with high humidity and heavy rainfall (2,000-5,000 mm per year). From 3,000 – 4,500 m the climate is temperate with cold winters and cool summers. Here the rainfall averages 1000 mm -1,500 mm per year. In the winter snowfall can close many passes. Above 4,500 m an alpine/arctic climate prevails with most areas permanently covered with snow and ice.

The climate within the mountains varies greatly according to sunshine, precipitation and wind conditions yet is basically similar to the middle European climate. The daily air mass exchange between highland and lowlands often causes stormy winds and these often have the effect of preventing rain in the middle portions of cross valleys so that between 900 to 1800 m it is quite dry, requiring irrigation for farming while higher up it is often wet.

PEOPLE AND LANGUAGES

Over 50% of the population are **Bhotiyas**, of Tibetan origin, **see page 1271**. The majority belong to the Tibeto-Burmese language group. There are a large number of Nepalese, belonging largely to tribes such as the Rai, Gurung and Limbu. Since 1959 the immigration of Nepalese has been banned, and Nepalese are not allowed to move into the central plain. There are also other tribal groups such as the Lepcha, an indigenous people – **see Sikkim page 1408**, and the Santal who migrated from N Bihar.

Bhutan also has the lowest population density in S Asia. The total of approximately 1.5 million is rural and concentrated mainly along the S border and in the high valleys to the N, particularly along the E-W trade route that passes through Thimphu and Punakha. In the mountain region the Bhotias are predominant, ('Bhutan' means land of the Bhotias), whilst in the S, the ethnic mix is dominated by the Nepalese settlers.

The Bhotias share a common Tibetan heritage of culture, language and religion. The teaching of the national language, *Dzongkha* (a Tibeto-Burmese language) is compulsory at all levels of education, although English and Hindi are also taught. Primary education has been encouraged since the 1960s with the opening of state funded schools throughout the country.

The people take pride in their national dress which is influenced by the harsh climate. The men wear a long *ko* or *baku* (robe), hitched up to the knees with a tight belt, and long boots, while women wear an *onju* or *gyenja* (blouse), a *kira* (ankle-lenth loose garment, wrapped around from under the arm, held by silver brooches), a belt, and a *togo* (short jacket). Traditionally special ceremonial scarves are worn – the king wears yellow, the ministers orange, senior officials red and the ordinary subjects white, while the women wear red flowery printed scarves.

ECONOMY

Agriculture Over 93% of the population depends on agriculture and livestock rearing. The most important area is in the Duars and the middle sections of the large river valleys. Maize is the most important crop, total output being about 90,000 tonnes, with rice second at 70,000 tonnes. Rice is cultivated on the valley floors and on more level slopes up to 2,400 m with the slopes are terraced and irrigated wherever possible. Farming in Bhutan is at the subsistence level although in some years a rice surplus has been exported. At lower altitudes bananas and oranges are grown, oranges being a particularly important cash crop. Above the rice area the land is sown with corn, millet, wheat, red pepper and potatoes.

The extensive forests (covering about 70% of the total area) are managed within the framework of a modern forestry law, but are nonetheless damaged by shifting cultivation and forest poaching for *agar**, which is used in *agarbati* (joss) sticks. The alpine pastures above the tree line are used as pasture for herds of yak and sheep. They also carry large herds of wild Blue Sheep which are rare elsewhere in the Himalaya. They have a split lip, enabling them to pull grass straight out of the ground rather than crop it, so they pose conservation problems. The New Zealand govt is advising on forest management, while the Swiss are assisting with the establishment of a **dairying** industry.

Because of the cessation of **trade** with Tibet in 1959 two patterns have emerged: economic dependence on India and smuggling. In formal trade, Bhutan has come to depend on the exchange of goods with India which is contributing to Bhutan's economic development; road building, small industries (fruit processing) development and hydro-electric power plant construction. These all benefit India as well. Smuggling over the Tibetan border has increased. Grain and sugar are carried on yak trains into Tibet and watches, Thermos flasks and plimsolls/sneakers from China are brought into the country.

Industry and resources Bhutan has no oil or natural gas. It is mining its reserves of minerals such as dolomite and limestone for export to India, along with gypsum and slate. It also mines 30,000 tonnes of coal a year. The main industries are cement and distillery products, but Bhutan is also producing veneer woods and plywood, gypsum, and high density polythene pipe. Its main exports, all to India, are cement, timber, block boards, cardomom, fruit and alcoholic drinks.

Tourism is deliberately kept on a small scale with an annual average of under 2,500, though intended to rise to 3,000 in 1992. Tourists are only allowed in minimum groups of 6, so independent travelling is discouraged. As late as the early 1960's the only way to Thimphu was either on foot or by pack animal. The building of roads had been forbidden until 1959 and began in 1960 on the issue of a royal decree. By 1964 the first all-weather road was completed – from the capital to **Paro Dzong** and then on to the new capital of Thimphu.

Each tourist must spend US$ 160 per day in the off-season, and US$ 360 per day in the high season. By S Asian standards this is a lot. Consequently it is only the affluent tourists from Western countries, virtually all in tour groups, that see this marvellous, peaceful country, with its charming and friendly people.

Philately Bhutan has made a specialty of exporting stamps, now a significant source of foreign exchange.

Handicrafts Traditional handicrafts include handloom textiles, metal and wood work, paper manufacture, baskets and embroidery. Mining of slate has gained importance. The handloom cloth using raw silk, cotton, wool or yak hair, in traditional patterns and weaves, is very striking. The jewellery, mainly in silver sometimes set with turquoise, coral and pearl is very distinctive.

RELIGION

Religion plays a crucial role in the social affairs of Bhutan with a form of Lamaist Buddhism upheld as the state religion. There are said to be 8 major monasteries (which are also *dzong* – fortresses) and nearly 200 small shrines (*gompa*) scattered throughout the country.

Lamaism (Tantric Buddhism) is practised, but in contrast to the predominating Gelugpa sects in Tibet, the Bhutanese belong to the **Drukpa** school, a 12th century splinter movement from the **Kagyupa** (one of the Red Hat sects). The religious goal of the Drukpa is redemption from the cycle of rebirth, entering into Nirvana. With Lamaism this is believed to be achieved by castigation and magic deeds and formulas. The highly colourful ceremonies in Bhutan have a strong element of wizardry.

There are an estimated 4,000-5,000 monks in Bhutan and the larger monasteries or lamaseries, (eg Tashi Chho Dzong at Thimphu) house several hundred monks. The popular attitude towards the clergy is one of respect and contributions toward their support are freely given. Giving acquires merit and the services of lamas are essential in important life-cycle ceremonies such as weddings and funerals.

Traditionally the **dzong*** have been the centres of artistic and intellectual life and their construction, ornamentation and maintenance have absorbed much of the nation's wealth. The high whitewashed walls are made of earth and stone, the windows are deep and richly ornamented. The interior walls are usually covered with murals depicting episodes in Buddhist mythology.

The villagers congregate at the *dzong* for the major festivals and for seasonal agricultural feasts providing an opportunity to wear their finest clothes and for merrymaking after the religious ceremony. In the non-religious festivals, the participating monks do so as cultivators or archers (archery being a highly popular sport closely associated with all celebrations). *Cham* dances can be very colourful and spectacular, performed in special costumes and masks to the accompaniment of drums and cymbals and may conclude with the display of a prized *thankha*.

HISTORY

Two Tibetan style Buddhist temples, dating from the 7th century AD, the **Kyichu lhakang** and the **Jampe lhakang**, are the earliest evidence of Bhutan's historical origins. Little is known of its early history. It is widely held that after the country had come under the influence of the Tibetan kingdom of Songtsengampo, a wave of immigration began at the start of the 9th century. **Shabdung Ngawang Namgyal** is considered the founder of unified Bhutan and was a lama of the Drukpa sect. He ruled the country as spiritual and secular leader in the 17th century and succesfully repelled Tibetan and Mongolian attacks. His successors were believed to be reincarnations of his person. Spiritual and secular power were divided however between the Dharma Rajah (spiritual) and Deb Rajah (secular). The various valley districts were ruled over by governors (*Penlops*) who resided in the fortified monasteries called *dzongs*.

The 2 rajah system existed for 300 years and was only discontinued in the 20th century when no successor could be found for the Dharma Rajah. The Deb Rajah temporarily took on both responsibilites until with British support, Ugyen Wangchuk, the *penlop* of Tongsa province, was elected hereditary Maharajah of the country in 1907. Secular and religious rule was vested in his family.

In the 18th century Bhutan became a tributary of Tibet but at the same time expanded E and W. When its armies attacked Cooch Behar in N Bengal in 1772, its Rajah called on the East India Company to assist. Bhutan's relations with the British began with the peace treaty of 1774. Disputes along the S border continued into the 19th century with the result that in 1841 the British annexed the Duars plain and created the present boundary, agreeing to pay a small annual subsidy as long as the Bhutanese remained peaceful.

However, Bhutanese raiders continued to make forays across the border, carrying off Indian subjects of the British as slaves. In 1863 a representative was sent to complain but was kidnapped and forced to sign an agreement returning the Duars plain to Bhutan. This was promptly repudiated and followed by a British show of strength which forced Bhutan to sue for peace. The Duars and Kalimpong were reained by the British and their annual subsidy greatly increased.

In 1910, in return for an increase in its annual subsidy, Bhutan agreed to accept British guidance in its external affairs. Bhutan, however, did not receive help in building roads, expanding communications and developing the economy as did Sikkim which was a British protectorate. The pace of development was therefore much slower.

Observing the changes that were set in motion in Sikkim by the continuing arrival of immigrants from Nepal, a process which was actively encouraged by the British, the rulers of Bhutan chose as far as possible to insulate the country against exposure to the outside world. However, it has joined several international organizations since 1970, including the United Nations in 1971.

After independence, India took over the responsibilities of Bhutan's foreign affairs. With Indian support and the guidance of a forward-looking King, the country has made a cautious and measured, but nevertheless optimistic entry into the modern world. King Jigme Dorje Wangchuk (1952-1972) brought in changes to allow for a National Assembly, the Tshogdu, to assume some representative power with 110 out of 150 members being elected by a limited electorate (village elders and heads of households). Although the present King Jigme Singye Wangchuk wields considerable power, the 15 districts into which the country is divided have been given increasingly more administrative power and a greater say in economic policy.

Recent developments The end of the 1980s was marked by major unrest in the neighbouring Indian states of Assam and West Bengal. The response of the Bhutan government was to strengthen its programme of self-reliance and to underline its commitment to maintaining traditional Bhutanese values. The King toured extensively at the end of the decade, and renewed support for the wearing of national dress came from many parts of the country, especially in the S, bordering India.

Language posed a particular problem, as English was increasingly becoming the lingua franca of the educated. While promoting the use of Dzongka, the King also took steps to encourage the Hindu population of the S to feel integrated with the Buddhist population, himself taking part in one of the major Hindu festivals. Considerable discussion took place in late 1988 over the question of citizenship rights. Bhutan has played an active part in the SAARC meetings, and has increasingly welcomed contacts with the outside world, establishing diplomatic relations with Pakistan at the end of 1988, exchanging ambassadors with Austria and welcoming a visit from the UN Secretary General in 1989.

THIMPU

Altitude 2,285 m, *Population* 25,000 approx

Thimpu is a relatively new town, having been built by the late King Dorje Wangchuk to replace the former capital of Punakha. The 400 year old Tashichho Dzong orginally occupied the site although the building itself is also recent, having been faithfully modelled on the original. It stands on the outskirts of the town, next to a nine-hole golf course, the only one in the country.

The Dzong houses the Central Secretariat, the summer headquarters of the Central Monk Authority and is where the 150 member National Assembly meets. The present King's (Jigme Sigye Wangchuk) father who died in 1972 initiated popular rule by voluntarily giving up his absolute powers. The gilded throne room and the King's Headquarters are also here. Half of the Tashichho Dzong is an active monastery to which non-Buddhists are not allowed: as is true of all active monasteries in Bhutan.

A short distance away is a chorten to the late king. Across the Thimphu river and up the valley is the Dechenchholing Palace while 5 km downstream is *Simtoka*, Bhutan's oldest dzong. This now houses the university.

Hotels The Tourism Corporation's *Motithang* in the outskirts, in a park, is the best. *Bhutan* (BTC) has rm with terraces. Good views. *Homolhari* and *Druk* are privately owned and efficiently run.

Restaurants All hotels have restaurants, most offering Indian, Chinese, Continental and sometimes local dishes. Non-residents need to give notice to eat at the *Motithang*.

Shopping Thimphu is a sprawling capital with rows of neat, traditionally painted shops in the Bazaar. The *Bhutanese Handicrafts Emporium* has the most extensive range including textiles, masks and paintings. Shops are usually open from 0800-2000.

Pel Jorkhang, Crossroads, specializes in local textiles. Tshering Dolkar and Ethometho, Tourism Building by Cinema, offer a wide range of handicrafts and cloth. Ethometho stocks books, postcards and stamps. There is also a Sunday Market.

Warning Do not bargain. Foreigners are not allowed to buy antiques (See Practical information below).

Excursions

Punakha Valley is just close enough to Thimphu to make a long day trip feasible. You take the new road over the spectacular *Dochu-La Pass* (2,743 m) with excellent views of the northern peaks. The valley is situated in a rainshadow area and is lower than most midland valleys. Its climate is mild and a wide range of crops are grown.

Punakha Dzong, built in 1637, stands at the the confluence of the Pho Chu (Father) and Mo Chu (Mother) rivers. Built in 1637, it was subsequently damaged by floodwaters. It was the winter capital of Bhutan and is still the winter headquarters of the Head Abbot.

Paro Most foreign visitors arrive by air at Paro which has the only airstrip. It is a 90 minute drive to Thimpu. The Paro Valley with its forests of blue pine is considered the most beautiful of Bhutan's main valleys. The vast white **Paro Dzong** dominates the skyline and life of Paro, with its small bazaar and a farming population living in groups of shingle roofed houses surrounded by paddy fields. Set above the glacial Paro Chu river, it is built on the site of a temple constructed by Guru Padma Sambhava himself in the early 9th century.

The imposing 5 storeyed dzong was constructed by Ngawang Namgyal in 1646. For the next 250 years it served as a bastion against invasions from the N. The dzong burnt down in 1907 and all the treasures except the enormous Thongdel thankha (30 m by 45 m) were destroyed. The thankha depicts Padma Sambhava (Guru Rimpoche) flanked by 2 escorts bringing Buddhism to Bhutan. On the Tibetan New Year's Day, it is unfurled for a few hours. Hero dances are performed before it is carefully rolled up again.

The present monastery was built immediately after the fire and now houses a collection of ancient and modern Bhutanese dress. Above the dzong is the largest of the orginal watchtowers which houses the **National Museum of Bhutan** with a varied collection of paintings, sculptures and traditional articles in daily use. You should carry a flashlight because of erratic electric supply! Across the river lies the **Ugyen Pelri Palace** the former seat of the National Assembly.

A few km to the N is the **Kyichu Lakhang**, said to be the oldest temple in Bhutan, built by a 7th century king, which is surrounded by prayer flags. The courtyard and decoration are particularly attractive. A few km further, at the end of the valley stands the 17th century **Drukgyel Dzong** (Victorious Dragon Dzong) built to commemorate victory over the Tibetans but ruined by fire in 1954. Situated on a hill with views away to Chomolhari, it is protected by 3 towers and can only be approached from one direction.

The **Takstang Monastery** (Tiger's Nest) is one of the popular tourist attractions in Bhutan. As its name suggests it is almost inaccessible. Built on the almost sheer 1,000 m rock face and approached by a narrow path, it dates from the 8th century when Padma Sambhava is said to have meditated here. The monastery is where he is believed to have landed on the back of a flying tiger. Because of its supposed origin it is a popular pilgrimage place.

Non-Bhutanese visitors are now only allowed to within about 100 m of the

Takstang monastery, usually reached by horseback and a short walk or a 3 hr strenuous walk. Much of the time a wall of trees conceals the sheer cliff from the walkers' view. Higher still, though not in such a spectacular setting, is the **Sangtog Monastery**.

Hotel *Olahtang* run by the Tourism Corpn is 3 km from the bazaar. The restaurant may need advance notice.

Phuntsholing is the border town and 13 km N of Hasimara, the last town on the Indian side of the border. The road from here to Thimphu crosses Eastern and Central Bhutan and reaches altitudes of 3,000 m. Because of its location on the road and border, Phuntsholing has become commercially and industrially important. With Swedish assistance, cement and match factories have been set up. The town is not particularly attractive, and is more Indian than Bhutanese in character. Travellers by road are usually obliged to spend a night here. The new monastery with 8 *chortens* nearby at Kharbanadi is on a hilltop with fine views of the Bengal plains and the Torsa river.

Hotels The 2 hotels are comfortable. *Druk*, built and run by India's Welcomgroup is the best. *Kharbandi*, 5 km out of town nr the monastery, has a good restaurant.

Bumthang is the most popular and important of the eastern towns. **Padma Sambhava** (Guru Rinpoche) is associated with the 8th century **Jampa lhakhang** temple and is said to have left his body print on a rock wall while restoring the life force of Sindhu Raja, then ruler of this region. The 17th century **Kurje lhakhang** was built alongside this print. Kings in the past were cremated nearby.

There is a samll *Tourist Lodge* next to the Wangdichholing palace, a fine wooden structure formerly used by the king's aunt.

Manas Wildlife Sanctuary is in the SE lowlands, adjacent to Assam. Comparable physically with **Chitwan** in Nepal (**see page 1300**) it is richer in species and less disturbed. See Manas Sanctuary, Assam (**see page 590**).

TREKKING IN BHUTAN

Trekkking in Bhutan offers not only spectacular scenery but also a chance to see the people in their villages carrying out ancient skills and crafts. The advantages here include the relatively clear paths and the ease and accessibility of good fishing.

There are a limited number of trekking routes in Bhutan but as few use them at any one time, this is not a problem. It is virtually impossible to trek unless you are part of a group.

The King would like to restrict the number of trekkers each year to 600. At present there are around 1,500 compared with over 30,000 in Nepal. It is his desire that there is only one trekking group at any one time on the 8-9 day Chomolhari trek.

Ponies and yaks to transport trekking loads and a guide, cook and helper are assigned to each group by the Trekking Manager, Bhutan Tourism Corpn, PO Box 159, Thimphu, who needs advance notice of a trip. You will be provided with food, tents and mattresses but must bring your own sleeping bags. In the monsoons some paths can be very muddy and below 2,000 m, leeches can be a problem. See Trekking in Nepal section for detailed advice, **page 1302**.

Paro to Ha via the Chili La

From Paro, most of the early part is through dense forest. As you reach Chili La Pass, broad panoramas of the mountains around Chomolhari open out. Above the forest, the trekking is across yak pastures. There are two important passes, the Kalai La and Sage La, both important burial areas. Towards the finish, you will descend into deciduous forest and the Paro Valley.

Although comparatively short, taking no more than 7 days, the variation in altitude and vegetation plus the rich flora and fauna and stunnng views make it an exceptionally good trek.

Bumthang Trek

The easy 5-6 day trek remains below 3,500 m and gives you a chance to see a number of typical villages of Central Bhutan with traditional craftsmen at work producing baskets, weaving on tradition1al looms or making hand-made paper from bark. The trek also allows you to visit interesting monasteries including Thamshing, Tharpaling and Bumthang itself (see above).

Paro-Thimphu Trek

Although most people use motor transport from Paro to Thimphu, it is possible to do a 3-day easy trek along a path instead of the road, going through a 3,900 m pass. It gives the not-so-energetic a wonderful, relaxed insight into Bhutanese life. There are also some fine ridge views of the mountains and pleasant stretches through lush forest.

Chomolhari Base Camp

This is the hardest of the 4, and takes around 8 days. There are 4 high passes to traverse on the way from Thimphu to the Base Camp of the Indo-Bhutanese expedition which climbed to within a few metres of the summit of **Chomolhari** (7,313 m) in 1970. The trek gives excellent views of the mountains and passes the **Lingshi Dzong** which once guarded the frontier.

You can drive to Dodina from Thimphu (1 hr). You reach the Base camp in 4-5 days and return to Paro via the Drugkel Dzong. You will see the yak herdsmen with their black tents and in the higher reaches, large flocks of blue sheep, which are rare in most other parts of the Himalaya and only seen as solitaries or in small groups. Bears are relatively common, and the guides often make a lot of noise so as not to take them by surprise.

Note The Bhutanese believe that the spirit of the mountain is offended by fire. Consequently, you are not allowed to light an open fire within sight of it.

INFORMATION FOR VISITORS

Documents

Valid passports and entry visa are essential. As there is a fixed government quota on the number of tourists visiting Bhutan and as the tour companies have taken up most of this, the only way to see Bhutan is as a member of a commercially organised tour group.

Visas are obtained through Bhutanese missions and Embassies. The tour company usually arranges this and the cost is around US$20. Theoretically, foreign visitors can also enter the country as guests of well-connected Bhutanese. Each Embassy, Mission and development agency has a quota of entry permits. Apply several weeks in advance (the Tourism Corporation needs 15 days officially) and pay on arrival at Phuntsholing or Paro. **Note** Special permission is needed to visit monasteries and temples.

Travel

By air The airport is at Paro and Druk air, the national carrier, has connections with Delhi and Calcutta (90 min) on Fri, and Dhaka, Bangladesh, Fri and Sun. An 80 seater jet flies from New Delhi and carries most of the limited tourist traffic in and out of the country. It is a 90 min drive to Thimphu. Druk Air, 48 Tivoli Court, Ballygunge Circular Rd, Calcutta. **Note** Bad weather can delay flights during monsoons.

By road The road from Bagdogra enters Bhutan at Phuntsholing.

Customs 8 mm cameras are allowed. No 16 mm cameras. Permits (available for a fee) are needed for filming. Contact Gen. Manager, B.T.C., Box 159, Thimpu. You are not permitted to take antiquities out of the country – all old items must have a certificate clearing them from the Dept of Antiquities.

Internal Travel

Local road transport The road network is not extensive and the principal means of road transport is by public bus. 4-wheel drive and Japanese cars are available for hire. Phuntsholing is the border town and is a 3-4 hr drive from Bagdogra airport (**see page 564**) which can be reached by plane from Calcutta and Delhi. It takes about 6 hr to negotiate the winding 179 km road from Phuntsoling through to Thimphu (2,316 m).

Travel agent Bhutan Tourism Corporation, Box 159, Thimphu, T 2647.

Tours start in Calcutta: Fri (6 days) and Wed (8 days) to Paro, Thimphu and Punakha. Bhutan Travel Service: c/o Royal Bhutan Embassy, Chandra Gupta Marg, Chanakyapuri, T 604076, New Delhi 11021; 48 Tivoli Court, 1A Ballygunge Circular Rd, Calcutta; Royal Bhutanese Embassy, 58, Rd No 3A, Dhanmondi RA, Dhaka, Bangladesh, T 545018 and in the USA 120 E 56th St, New York, NY 10022.

Money

Currency The national currency is the Ngultrum (Nu). 100 Chetrum = 1 Nu. Exchange rate is approx. US $1 = Nu 16.50. Indian Rupees circulate at par.

Money changing Bank of Bhutan in Thimphu and Phuntsholing will change travellers cheques and hard currency. The Bank of Bhutan has 26 branches across the country. Head Office is at Phuntsoling T 300. Moneychangers prefer travellers cheques to currency notes.

Tipping Tipping is forbidden by law.

Shopping and best buys Traditional handicrafts, jewellery, baskets, masks, textiles. Paintings and woodcarving make good buys. See Thimphu Shopping below. Get a receipt and do not attempt to bargain.

Other Essential Information

Official time Bhutanese time is 30 min ahead of Indian National Time or GMT +6 hrs.

Weights and measures Metric – the same as in India.

Postal services A postal service was introduced in 1962 and now this covers most of the country. Allow at least 14 days for delivery to Australia and Europe and longer for the Americas. Attractive country stamps are sold at the GPO, Thimphu and Philatelic Bureau, Phuntsholing.

Telephone services Bhutan is not on the International Direct Dialling system and the country has few phones. Give the operator the full telephone number including code.

Electricity 230-240 volts 50 cycles A.C. The current is variable.

Hints on social behaviour Useful words include – Kadrinche (thank you), Kousousangpo (good morning) and Lass (when leavetaking). The interiors of monasteries were closed last year because the tourists were disturbing the lamas and stealing mementoes.

Security The crime rate in this unspoilt country is very low.

Accommodation Bhutan has only been accepting foreign visitors for the last 15 years and limited the numbers to 2,000-3,000 so there is neither a well developed hotel industry nor category **A-C** hotels. See India Information for Visitors, **see page 134**. The best are at Phontsholing, Thimphu and Paro which are comfortable with Bhutanese decor and offer modern facilities. Elsewhere Guest Houses are very basic.

Clothing A combination of clothing from cottons to light woollens in summer to heavy woollens in winter. Take a raincoat and an umbrella (obtained cheaply in India) for the monsoons.

Food and drink Rice is the staple, eaten with spicy and hot vegetable curry. Alternatively, buckwheat, barley or wheat is used. Pork, yak meat (dried and cooked), and less frequently, chicken and beef are available. Chillies and cheese are particular favourites of the Bhutanese. Sweet or buttered tea and fruit juices are drunk. Low alcohol *chang* and *temka* are brewed from cereals while the distilled *arak* is stronger. For ceremonies *chang* is mixed with eggs and butter. Bhutan produces spirits, including whisky, gin and rum.

Photography There is some spectacular scenery, but if you go during the wet season make sure to protect film against humidity. Carry plenty of film and batteries with you.

Best time for a visit Mar-May and Sep-Nov, either side of the rainy season.

Health Protection is *recommended* against cholera, typhoid, tetanus, polio, hepatitis, malaria and rabies, and *optional* for meningitis. See Health in S Asia Introduction, **page 22**. **Leeches** can be a hazard in the wet season, below 2,000 m. They can be a nuisance as a bite can become septic. To remove do not pull away but use a spray (eg Waspeeze), some salt, a lighted cigarette or match or, as a last resort, a sharp knife to encourage it to drop off.

Warning Thimphu Valley has been experiencing increased incidence of rabies because of the growing number of stray dogs. 52 people had to be treated for dog bites in the first 2 months of 1991.

National holidays and festivals

Jan 1 Guen Nyidnok/Winter Solstice. **3** Meeting of Nine Evils. **27** Traditional day of offering. **Feb 7,8** Losar. **May 2** Birth anniversary of Jigme Dorji Wangchuk. **20** The Buddha's Parinirvana. **June 2** Anniversary of Coronation of King Druk Gyalpo. **13** Birth anniversary of Guru Rinpoche. **July 21** Anniversary of the death of Drukgyal Sumpa. **Aug 5** First Sermon of the Buddha. **Sep 22** Blessed Rainy Day. **Oct 6** Thimphu Dubchen. **10-12** Thimphu Tsechhu/Dusehra. **Nov 11** Descending day of Guru Rinpoche from heaven. **11-13** Birth anniversary of the King. **Dec 17** National Day.

The dates of the religious festivals vary since they are dictated by a lunar calendar (contact the Tourism Corpn), most taking place in the spring and autumn with the *tschechu* on the 10th day of a month. The Paro Dzong *cham* is a major event.

BANGLADESH

Official name Ghana Praja Tantri Bangladesh – People's Republic of Bangladesh, Independence 26 Mar 1971. (Unitary and Sovereign republic).

National flag Bottle green background with a solid circle of red in it.

Emblem *Shapla* flower (nymphoea nouchali) on water, with an ear of paddy, and 3 leaves of jute with 2 stars on each side.

Official Language Bangla (English is spoken in cities and to a limited extent in large towns).

Official Religion Islam

National anthem First 10 lines of Rabindranath Tagore's *Amar Sonar Bangla*.

Basic indicators *Population* 1991 114 million Annual growth rate 2.2% Birth rate 33 per 1000 Death rate 12 per 1000 Life expectancy 55 Urban population 15% Infant mortality 110 per 1000 *Area* 144,000 sq km *Population density* 790 per sq km *Religion*, Muslim 86%, Hindu 12.7%, Buddhist 0.6% *GNP per capita 1990* Tk 5527. Average Annual growth rate of Net National Income 1984-89 1.5% per capita per annum. External resources (aid) 52% of total resources 1987-88.
  Literacy (1981) Total for 5+ years 23.8% (Male 31% Female 16%) *Labour force* Civilian 10+ years (1986) 44% (Male 79.9% Female 9.4%) Major towns Dhaka 4.6 m Chittagong 2.03 m Khulna 900,000 Rajshahi 320,000 Mymensingh 210,000 Comilla 205,000 Sylhet 190,000.

To many who have never visited it, Bangladesh is a country that seems locked in endless and desperate poverty. Yet it is a country of paradoxes. Despite being subject to the repeated devastation of natural events on a scale unheard of in the rest of the world, the population continues not only to survive but to multiply. Although today the majority of its people are among the poorest in the world, it is the world's most densely populated country because generations have found the deltaic lowlands of the Ganga-Brahmaputra one of the richest environments known to traditional agriculture. Again, lacking even the basic elements of modern technology, with over 75% of the population illiterate and 50% of the population without land, Bangladeshi farmers have shown extraordinary skill in adapting to an

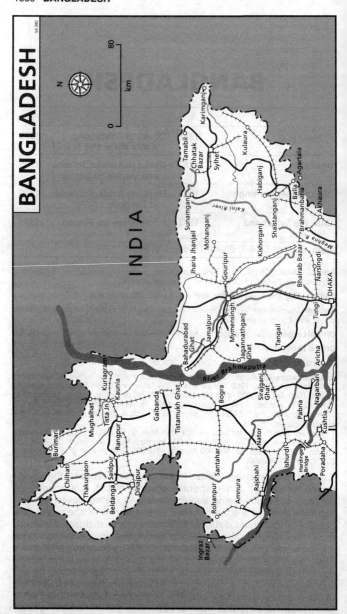

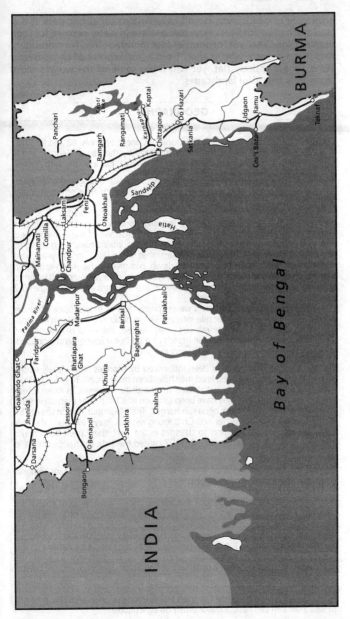

environment which most would have written off as hopeless. It is a land much of which lives under half a metre of water or more for four months of the year, yet for another four months suffers from drought. And it is a country which, apart from a small corner of the extreme SE, is almost entirely flat, yet which has some of the world's most stunningly beautiful landscapes.

GEOGRAPHY

Location Bangladesh lies astride the Tropic of Cancer, between 88 and 9230′ E, and 2150′ and 2630′ N. To the S it is bordered by the Bay of Bengal, and is surrounded by India except in the extreme SE, where it has a border with Burma.

The land Covering an area of 144,000 sq km, the size of England and Wales, Bangladesh is for the most part a flat deltaic plain. The chief exception is found in the low hills around Chittagong in the SE.

The geography of Bangladesh has been dictated by its rivers. It has been created and constantly re-shaped by the endless deposition of silt from the **Ganga**, the **Brahmaputra** and the **Meghna**. The first two of these major rivers and their tributaries rise in the Himalayas. The mountains have been rising so rapidly, and the rivers cutting down so fast, that in the last 1 million years, vast quantities of debris have been washed down into them. It has been estimated that the Ganga alone carries over 1.4 billion tonnes of silt a year – nearly five times as much as the Amazon. On top of that the Brahmaputra carries a further 0.7 billion tonnes.

The seasonal flow of the rivers varies greatly, and as they subside after the annual high flow period, great quantities of silt are deposited freshly on the land. From that silt most of Bangladesh has been created. The delta has progressed steadily out into the Bay of Bengal, islands of mud being formed and extended. Wherever the silt is deposited, fertile ground is left.

The form of the land has also been influenced by changes in sea level. At the height of the last Ice Age, sea level may have been more than 130 m lower than today. As a result the rivers cut down into the delta. However, in more recent warmer periods sea level may have been as much as 30 m higher than at present. Most of the land would have been submerged. The Madhupur Tract in the centre of the country, and the Sylhet and Chittagong regions, may have been the only areas above water. In addition to changes in sea level, there have been major earth movements. An earthquake in 1897 caused the Tista to change course in the N.

Despite the fact that much of it is so flat, Bangladesh has important regional contrasts. There are 6 major regions.

The North In the N, the plains at the foot of the Himalayas, lying between the Ganga and the Brahmaputra – the **Barind** tract – is made up of coarse old alluvium. This was deposited by the River Tista as it came down onto the plains, following an earlier course. It is the driest region of Bangladesh, and has relatively poor soils. Recently there has been development of its groundwater resources.

The floodplain To the S, the main course of the Ganga, or *Padma* as it is known in Bangladesh, which has been moving progressively E, joins the Brahmaputra and Meghna in a broad active floodplain. Rivers flowing over deltas run on beds raised above the general level of the land, known as alluvial ridges. Between the rivers lie alternating patches of low lying sand and clay. The rivers have frequently changed their channels across the delta, and variations in height of less than 2 m can have a major effect on agriculture.

The SW In the SW lies the 'moribund delta'. Old courses of the Ganga and its distributaries have been abandoned. Some sections of the old river bed have become ox-bow lakes, known as *bhils*. They are clearly visible from the air. On the ground they often have very heavy soils, difficult to work, and sometimes are permanent lakes.

The *Sylhet basin* NE of Dhaka, in the valleys of the Meghna and Surma Rivers, earth movements have caused great depressions, known as *haors**. The area may still be subsiding. Some of the lakes in the depression, over 320 km from the coast, are only 3 m above sea level. These are flooded every year to depths of 5 to 7 m. For 6 months of the years it is a vast lake, and is also highly subject to cyclone damage.

The tidal coast Along the S edge of the country the land is steadily being built up on the saline fringes. In the W the *Sundarbans* are dense forests on tidal land at sea level. Some parts of the coast experience large tidal contrasts. The island of Sandwip, for example, has a difference of 4 m between high and low tide. Spring tides during the dry season, when the flow of the rivers is very low, push salt water far inland, sometimes over 100 km.

The SE hill tracts In the SE of the country, the Chittagong Hill Tracts offer the only area of high relief. The highest point, near the Burmese border, is 1,003 m. Parallel ridges of recent sedimentary rocks run N-S, comprising sandstones, shales and sandy clays.

Rivers and lakes The *Padma*, the *Brahmaputra* (known as the *Jamuna*) and the *Meghna*, are the 3 major rivers. However, Bangladesh is criss-crossed by the *distributaries** that take off from these. 90% of the catchment area of these great rivers lies outside Bangladesh. In flood they are an awesome sight, often over 20 km wide, and surging with powerful currents down to the coast. However, in the dry season they shrink to a fraction of their earlier width. The flow of the Padma varies from a maximum in September of over 55,000 cubic m per second down to as little as 2,500 cubic m per second between Feb-May. The Jamuna experiences similar variations.

In addition to the natural lakes of the **haor** depressions and the smaller **bhils**, of the N and W, Bangladesh has the large artificial lake created by the Kaptai Dam in the Chittagong Hill Tracts. It is also estimated that there are over half a million small tanks and village ponds (*dighis**), which play an essential part in village life, notably as a source of fish.

Vegetation Little of Bangladesh's original vegetation cover remains. The chief exceptions are the Sundarban forest of the SW, mangrove swamps of the extreme SE, and small patches of forest in the Chittagong Hill Tracts. Less than 15% of the total area remains under forest. However, settlements are often surrounded by clumps of trees – especially various fruiting species such as mango, plaintains, jackfruit, papaya and date palm.

There are four major regional types of vegetation. Bamboo and rattan, a species of climbing palm, are common in the NE. Bamboo is the main raw material for Bangladesh's paper industry. In the central region of the Madhupur Jungle Tract sal forest is common, while in the W babul (*Acacia arabica*) is common. In the S the mangrove swamps of the Sundarbans have a number of economically important species, including a softwood used for paper making, *Exocoecaria agallocha*. Marigolds, roses and waterlilies are common, and water hyacinth has become an almost universal river plant. This is now widely harvested for converting into compost.

Wildlife With a great variety of wildlife in its forests, jungles, swamps and rivers, Bangladesh claims to have about 200 species of mammals and fish, 750 of birds and over 150 of reptiles including some poisonous snakes, python, lizards (including large monitors), turtles and marsh crocodiles.

The most majestic of all is the Bengal tiger which inhabits the Sundarbans to the south. Leopards, clouded leopards, civet and other wild cats are other carnivores found in the jungles. The Chittagong Hill Tracts are the home of herds of Indian elephants while deer vary from the small spotted, barking and hog deer to the larger *Sambar* in the eastern forests and *Barasingha* in the swamplands to the south.

Other common mammals include wild buffalo, rhesus monkeys, whitebrowed gibbon, lemur and long-tailed langur, a variety of mongooses (including the grey-brown and the crab mongoose, often mistaken for a badger), wild dogs and jackals which often come close to villages to carry away a lamb or chicken. There are also Himalayan black bear, Malayan bear and the sloth which harmlessly feeds at night on fruit and insects and is partial to honey.

Fly catchers, mynahs, barbets, hornbills, woodpeckers, kingfishers, hoopoes, warblers, *bulbuls,* cuckoos, parrots, game birds and birds of prey, vultures and the everpresent crow, are common. There are also a large variety of waterfowl – snipes, herons, cranes, coots, several kinds of ducks, many of which come as winter migrants.

CLIMATE

Seasons Winter (Nov-Feb) Ave Max 29°C Min 11°C Summer (Mar-Jun) Ave Max 34°C Min 21°C Monsoon (Jul-Oct)

Temperature Bangladesh never experiences really cold weather. However, minimum night temperatures across the plains fall to as low as 8°C, slightly lower in the N, and the early morning can often be chilly and misty. These low minimum temperatures act as a brake on the growth of rice. Day time maximum temperatures rise sharply, so that in January they are in the mid- 20's. Summer temperatures are not as high as further W, average maxima being generally 34°C or occasionally 35°C. However, humidity levels are high, and the atmosphere can be very uncomfortable. Apr and May are generally the hottest months.

Rainfall The main features of Bangladesh's climate are dictated by seasonal patterns of rainfall rather than temperature. There are 3 main seasons. The dry season lasts from the end of November to March, many areas have virtually no rain during this period, and nowhere receives more than 10% of its annual total during these 5 months. April and May is the period known as the 'little rains' – the *chota barsat*. Up to 20% of the total rain falls now, a prelude to the main rainy season from June-Oct, which accounts for the remaining 70%.

Rainfall totals are high, in most regions being over 1500 mm. The total diminishes generally from SE to NW, Cox's Bazar in the extreme SE receiving over 3,500 mm while Jessore in the W receives less than half that. Although generally Bangladesh is calm, periodically it is hit by tremendous storms. They generally come in 2 seasons, Apr-May and Oct-Dec.

In Apr-May they are usually severe local storms, known as **nor-westers**. Hail is a particular hazard, especially in Sylhet and the NE, sometimes of ferocious intensity. However, this season is also sometimes affected by **tropical cyclones**. Sweeping up the Bay of Bengal, such cyclones may hit any part of the coastal districts. The devastating cyclone of 29-30 April 1991, which probably killed over 200,000 people, hit the SE coastal towns of **Cox's Bazar** and **Chittagong** and a number of islands including **Hatia**. Winds of over 240 kph and a 7-8 m high storm surge from the Bay of Bengal devastated hundreds of square km.

Such severity is unusual in the Apr-May period, but is not uncommon between Oct-Dec. Since 1960 there have been 6 cyclones with winds of around 200 kph. The worst was on November 12 1970, when as many as 500,000 people may have been killed.

Major Storms in Bangladesh

Year	Date	Area affected	Nature of storm	Loss
1795	June 3	Chittagong town and district	Severe cyclonic storm from evening to midnight	Only 5 brick built houses survived
1797	May	Chittagong	Severe cyclone	Every house destroyed. 2 ships sunk in harbour
1822	May	Barisal	Very severe cyclone	All houses destroyed. 40,000 people and 100,000 cattle dead.
1831	October	Barisal	Storm surge	No figures.
1872	October	Cox's Bazar	Severe cyclonic storm	"Many deaths".
1876	October	Hatiya, Noakhali, Patuakhali, Chittagong	Most severe storm wave: 14 m high	Enormous loss of life. All property destroyed in path of tidal bore
1895	October	Sandwip	Cyclone	Loss unknown
1897	Oct 24	Chittagong	Hurricane and storm waves	Kutubdia Island and coastal villages swept away. 32,000 dead.
1901-1960	20 major storms reported	South East region	Cyclones and storm waves	No estimates available.
1960	Oct 10	Meghna estuary	Severe cyclone – 200 kph	3,000 dead, islands inundated
1960	Oct 30	Chittagong	Severe cyclone – 210 kph	70% buildings on Hatiya destroyed, 2 ocean liners washed ashore, 7 capsized in port
1961	May 9 & May 30	Comilla	Chittagong	Cyclonic storms
1962	October	Feni	Severe cyclone	Heavy loss of life
1963	May 28-29, June 5	Oct 25	Chittagong, Cox's Bazar and islands	Jessore
1965	Dec 14-15	Cox's Bazar	Severe cyclonic storm 220 kph	Great loss of life
1966-1970	6 storms	SE coastal region	Cyclones	Severe damage, no accurate loss estimates
1970	Nov 12-13	Megha estuary: Khulna to Chittagong	Most severe storm on record to date 220 kph. Storm surge.	Between 200,000-500,000 dead, enormous loss of property

Year	Date	Area affected	Nature of storm	Loss
1974	Nov 24-28	Cox's Bazar-Chittagong	Severe cyclonic storm, storm surge of 6 m	Some loss of life, major damage to property.
1983	Oct 15 & Nov 9th	Chittagong and islands	Severe cyclonic storm	Storm surge.
1987	Oct	Chittagong and SE	Severe cyclone,	
1991	April 30	Chittagong and islands	Severe cyclone; 220 kph	Islands of Sandwip and Hatia devastated, Chittagong port damaged, ships washed ashore. Estimates of 200,000 dead.

PEOPLE AND LANGUAGE

Bangladesh today is the most densely populated country in the world. In 1872, the year of the first census, the population of the current area of Bangladesh was 22 m. In 1961 its population was 51 m. In 1991 it has grown to 114 m. Although towns have been growing fast in the last decade, it is one of the most rural countries in S. Asia, 85% of the population living in scattered hamlets across the country. As much of the land is flooded every wet season, village houses are often built on slightly raised mud mounds. During the monsoon homesteads are dotted just above the flood level in an astonishingly dense network of isolated houses.

Cities The capital, **Dhaka**, had a population of 3.4 m in 1981, and is estimated to have grown by up to 2 m since. Other major cities have also been growing fast. **Chittagong**, the major port, is approaching 2 m, and **Khulna**, the only other city with over 1 m, has also more than doubled in 20 years.

Ethnic origins The overwhelming majority of Bangladeshis are of Indo-Aryan origin. They came to the region as part of the great wave of immigrants from the NW in the 2nd millennium BC. Before them the earliest inhabitants had been small numbers of aboriginal peoples, Veddas, who in turn had been followed by Caucasoid people of Mediterranean origin. Today some of the tribal people in Bangladesh are their direct descendants, such as the **Santals** (who live in the N and NW) and the **Khasis** (in the Khasi Hills on the borders with Assam).

Other tribes, such as the Garo, the Hajang, the Kacharis, and the Chakmas of the SE, are of Mongoloid origin. The most recent additions to the ethnic diversity of Bangladesh have come from the Arab and Turkish settlers who came with the spreading wave of Islam from the 13th century onwards.

Language The national language is *Bangla* (known in India as Bengali), spoken by 98% of the people. Modern Bangla traces its origins to a branch of Prakrit, known as Gaudiya Prakrit, which developed under the Buddhist Pala rulers of Bengal. The basis of the language began to emerge by the 2nd century BC, but it did not develop its modern form as a distinct language until after the 12th century AD. English is the most important foreign language among the educated, and is widely understood in the towns. There are also several tribal languages spoken by very small numbers, see page 43.

Levels of literacy remain very low. 26% of children 5 years old and above were classified as literate in 1991, 34% of men and 17% of women. In many rural areas female literacy rates were under 10%.

ECONOMY

Agriculture The silt of the Ganga, the Brahmaputra and the Meghna have been estimated to have a higher concentration of plant nutrients than an equivalent weight of farmyard manure. This has provided the basis for one of the most productive regions in the world in terms of traditional agriculture. It has also contributed to the fact that Bangladesh is the world's most densely populated country. For many observers the high density of population is itself an insoluble problem. Over 100 years ago Sir William Hunter wrote that Bangladesh would never be able to feed itself. Then the population was around 20 m. Yet today, when the population is rising towards six times that figure, Bangladesh is moving closer towards the ever shifting target of agricultural self-sufficiency.

Over 75% of Bangladesh's 14 million ha is cultivated at least once a year. Double cropping is common, and in some areas 3 crops are grown in a year. Thus the total cultivated area in any year is greater than the gross surface area of the country – about 160%. The main factor limiting further cultivation is the extended dry season, when irrigation is essential. About 2 m ha are currently irrigated.

In detail the cropping pattern of Bangladesh is immensely complex. Farmers have adapted different varieties of the major crops, especially rice, to even the most minor contrasts of soil and relative relief, as well as to the major seasons. There are local names for both the seasons and for the crops associated with them. Jute, Bangladesh's most important cash crop, and the first rice crop (*aus**) are grown in the period of the early rains (*Bhadoi season**). The Aus rice crop, which accounts for about 3.5 m ha, is sown between Mar-May and harvested in Jul-Aug. Jute is sown on just under 1 m ha, and is concentrated on the freshly deposited silt near the main river banks in the N central part of the country. The main rice crop is sown during the wet season itself (*Aghani**) in June and July, and harvested in November. This is the transplanted *aman** crop (over 4 m ha) and the broadcast *aman* crop (1.7 m ha).

Some of the adaptations to wet season crops are remarkable. Variations in the level of flooding of a few centimetres can be crucial, and a wide range of different rice varieties is grown. In the *haors* of the NE, where flood waters rise up to 6 m every year, a variety of 'floating rice' is grown with stalks up to 6 m long, and which draws its nutrition from the flood waters themselves. Even transplanted *aman* crops can keep pace with flood waters rising at 2.5 cm per day. The transplanted varieties yield nearly half as much again as broadcast sown rice, and are harvested in Nov-Dec. The coastal fringe of the delta, and the N tract of the Barind, have over 80% of the land under transplanted *aman* crops.

The most striking recent changes in Bangladesh agriculture have taken place in the dry season (*rabi*). The increase in irrigation has allowed a rapid expansion of the *boro* crop – particularly significant in the haors of the Meghna depression. Wheat, pulses and oilseeds have become important crops during this period, and because cultivation conditions are often much more controllable than during the wet season, productivity per ha is comparatively high.

Production of rice stood at 7 m tonnes in 1961. It had risen to 13.4 m tonnes in 1981 and was over 16 m tonnes in 1990. Wheat production more than doubled in the 1980s, as did the output of *gram** and some other minor crops.

In addition to its cereal and jute production, Bangladesh is an important producer of tea. 96% of production comes from Sylhet district where over 40,000 ha are planted. Unlike the high grown tea of Sri Lanka or S India, Bangladeshi tea is 'lowland tea'. Harvested for 9 months of the year, there is a 3 month shutdown.

In the Chittagong Hills of the SE the tribal population still practices shifting cultivation. However, population increase, and programmes of Bangladeshi peasant settlement in the tribal areas, have greatly restricted the amount of land available.

Fishing Possibly 6 m Bangladeshis make their living from fishing. The majority of the fishermen are very poor, often Hindu, and depend on inland freshwater fish. About 3.5 m ha of paddy land is flooded every year, which with the major rivers makes a rich source of fish. On top of this an estimated 1.5 m ponds are in use, giving up to half a million tonnes of fish a year. Some attempts have been made to introduce freezing facilities for the export of prawns. Fish and fish products, including prawns and frogs legs, accounted for 12% of Bangladesh's total exports in 1990.

Resources There are very limited resources of raw material and minerals. Natural gas has been exploited for over 30 years, and now contributes over 40% of the energy for electricity production. Proven reserves are over 110 bn cu m, about 100 years at current rates of use. Production has risen threefold since 1981 to the equivalent of 30 m barrels of crude oil a year. Natural gas provides the basis for an important fertilizer industry, which accounts for nearly half the total gas production.

There are deposits of coal near Bogra, though there will be major operational difficulties extracting it. Lignite, limestone, ceramic clay and glass sand are also found. The country's deltaic location has meant that even basic resources such as building stone are almost totally absent from many regions.

Hydroelectricity, generated from the Kaptai Dam in the Chittagong Hills, contributes over 25% of Bangladesh's demand for electricity.

Industries At Independence in 1947 East Pakistan had no industries to talk of, and was almost entirely the rural hinterland of industrial Calcutta. Processing of raw jute became the first priority. Today there are 70 jute mills. Although the number of full time workers in the jute industry rose from 105,000 in 1981 to over 180,000 in 1990, output has declined slightly over the period. There are now over 60 cotton mills, but output was static through the 1980s.

By 1991 readymade garments had become Bangladesh most important export, valued at over 35% of the total. Jute (raw and manufactured) accounted for a further 30% and leather and leather goods 11%. Tea, newsprint, fish and a variety of other products made up the remainder.

HANDICRAFTS

Dhaka built its reputation for the fineness of its muslin – 'woven wind' was known round the world, and captured the 17th century fashion markets of Paris and London. Carpets, ceramics and furniture, especially of cane, are important cottage industries. Fabrics, printed saris, dolls and coconut carving are widely produced, as are terracotta figures, and jute carpets. Metalwork, including silver and other jewellery, and brassware make attractive gifts. Coconut fibre is used for various products, including string and rope.

RELIGION

Over 85% of the population is **Muslim**, the great majority being Sunni's. Until the beginning of the 20th century **Hindus** were in a majority in Bengal as a whole, and even in East Bengal there was an even balance between Hindu and Muslim. Conversions from low caste Hindu communities, and the migration of Muslims from N India, contributed to the changing balance. Today 12% of the population is Hindu. There are over 600,000 **Buddhists** and 300,000 **Christians**, and nearly 1 million people are classified as adhering to tribal religions.

ARCHITECTURE

The architecture of Bangladesh owes its most formative influences to the Muslim rulers of the Bengal sultans, and subsequently of the Mughals. Pandua and Gaur (now in India; **see page 558**) were spectacular capitals in their time, going back to well before the Muslim conquest. Bengal added two distinctive features to the emerging Muslim tradition, the widespread (though not exclusive) use of brick, and the curved Bengali roof, which came to play such a prominent and distinctive part in Muslim and Rajput design in NW India.

The first phase lasted from 1201-1576, when Bengal became a province under the Mughal control of Emperor Akbar. The results of the first phase are largely to be found in West Bengal. However, the earliest Muslim monument in Bangladesh, the tomb of Sultan Ghiyasuddin Azam Shah, on the site of the former capital **Sonargaon**, dates from this period.

Bangladesh's largest pre-modern mosque, the **Shait Gumbad**, dates from the mid-15th century, and is built in the style associated with **Khan Jahan Ali**, whose tile-inlaid tomb (1459) also serves as a reminder of the distinctive architectural development of the dynasty. In a cluster of buildings around Bagerghat, they testify to the presence of an 15th century independent power.

There are only limited remains of the powers that controlled Bengal before the arrival of the Mughals. The **Sura** mosque in Dinajpur, the **Shankarpasha** mosque in Sylhet and the **Goaldi** mosque in Sonargaon are examples. All the buildings are comparatively small. The last surviving pre-Mughal mosque is the early 16th century **Qutb** mosque at Ashtagram in Mymensingh.

The Mughals spread their uniform imperial style of architecture right across N India, although by the time it was given expression in Bengal it was on a miniature scale compared to the masterpieces of N and NW India. The Mughal governor of Bengal, Islam Khan, established Dhaka as his provincial capital in 1610. It was set up to make possible the defeat of the Afghans in lower Bengal. Once its purpose had been achieved, great building work took place. By 1640, Manrique commented that Dhaka had risen ' to an eminence of wealth which is actually stupefying.'

Only a few buildings survive from the Dhaka of this period. The Bara Katra, a caravanserai in the Chowk area, was built in 1644, and Muhammad Azam, third son of Aurangzeb, started Lalbagh Fort in 1678. It was never completed, but it houses the tomb of Bibi Pari, unique in Dhaka for its use of black basalt from the Rajmahal Hills. Although there are numerous other Mughal remains, many only show glimpses of their former splendour, and there is little hint in the surviving architecture of a city which, at its Mughal peak, is claimed to have housed 900,000 people.

HISTORY

When India and Pakistan gained Independence in 1947 East Bengal successfully pressed its claim to be regarded as the home for Muslims in East Bengal, and became the country's eastern Province. Tensions between East Pakistan and West Pakistan rapidly came to the surface, however. Roughly equal in population to West Pakistan, Bangalis began to fear that they could not begin to pull either political or economic weight to match their Western counterparts. By 1970 it was clear that key areas of Pakistan's political life remained firmly in the hands of a

Punjabi elite. Only 3 Bangalis had reached the rank of Assistant Secretary in the government, for example out of a total of 20. Out of 35 Generals, only 1 was a Bangali.

More serious was the belief that East Pakistan's economy, especially its earnings from jute, were being systematically channelled into development in West Pakistan, rather than back into the East. On top of this sense of grievance was the perception among Bangalis that their cultural heritage was being sacrificed to the Urdu language and West Pakistani cultural values.

After the collapse of Ayub Khan's government in 1968, military rule continued under General Yahya Khan who promised elections for a new democratic assembly. In East Pakistan they were fought by the Awami League under its leader, **Sheikh Mujibur Rahman**, on a six point platform which barely stopped short of demanding full autonomy for the East. The elections on 7 December 1970 saw the **Awami League** win 160 out of 162 seats. The army command then made it clear that they would not allow the Awami League to form a government, although they would have had a clear majority in the new Assembly, had it been convened. When Mujib declared a full scale movement of non-cooperation with the government, the Pakistan Army arrested political leaders and banned political activity on 25 March 1971.

A nine month struggle followed, during which up to 10 million refugees fled into India. Sheikh Mujib himself was imprisoned in West Pakistan, and a Bangladesh Government in exile was established. In December 1971 the Indian Army launched a massive offensive, in response to a Pakistan army strike, and in 10 days forced the Pakistan army in the East to capitulate.

Born out of this fierce struggle, Bangladesh rapidly went through a succession of crises. Sheikh Mujib was released from prison in Pakistan and immediately formed a new Awami League government. Fresh elections were held on 7 March 1972, the Awami League winning 292 seats out of 300. However, nominally socialist policies failed to deliver improved economic well-being or social reform. Millions were threatened with starvation, while on the political front the Awami League's friendship with India was rapidly turned against it as a sign of political subservience.

In August 1975 Sheikh Mujib and many of his family were assassinated by middle ranking officers in the army, who claimed that the freedom struggle had been betrayed. There were also sharp divisions within the army between those who had taken an active part in the freedom struggle and those who had remained, either voluntarily or by force, in the Pakistan army.

A short period of political chaos followed the revolution. Coups and counter coups succeeded each other in increasing violence. On 6 November **General Ziaur Rahman** was installed as Chief Martial Law Administrator. Over the next 2 years he put down all signs of rebellion within the army, while gradually trying to develop a political system which would move the country away from permanent military rule. Forming a new political party, the **Bangladesh National Party (BNP)**, he called and won the Presidential elections on 3 June 1978. In the succeeding Parliamentary election in February 1979 the BNP won 44% of the vote, but gained 207 of the 300 seats. In contrast the Awami League won only 39 of the 300 seats, though it gained 25% of the popular vote.

Ziaur Rahman's success was shortlived, for he in turn was assassinated by a group of army officers on 31 May 1981. The Vice President, Abdus Sattar, took over as President, but he was never seen as more than a stop gap successor. On 24 March 1982 **Lieutenant General H.M. Ershad** took over in a bloodless coup, and proceeded to establish his power through massive new support for the army. He sustained comparatively high levels of pay and perks for military personnel, but at the same time gradually tried to ease away from military rule. Following the precedent of President Ziaur Rahman, he established his own political party, the Jatiya Party.

However, both general Zia's old party, the BNP, and the Awami League persistently demanded his resignation. After Ziaur Rahman's assassination the BNP had been led by Zia's widow, **Begum Khaleda Zia**, while the Awami League was led by Sheikh Mujibur Rahman's daughter, **Sheikh Hasina**.The May 1986 elections, in which the Awami League took part, failed to provide convincing evidence that President Ershad had succeeded in gaining popular support for his new government, but the opposition parties showed little sign that they could provide a sufficiently united force to evict him.

The situation changed dramatically in late 1990. Strikes and fierce demonstrations on the streets forced President Ershad to resign and hand over to a caretaker President, Chief Justice Shahabuddin Ahmed. Elections were held under his supervision on 27 February 1991 in which Begum Khaleda's BNP won 138 of the 300 seats, enough to form the government, but without a clear majority. The former President Ershad won an overwhelming victory in his home constituency of Rangpur, though he continued to be held under house arrest and was subsequently jailed in June 1991. Within weeks Begum Khaleda's new government faced the devastation of Bangladesh's worst cyclone for 20 years.

DHAKA

816 sq km *Population* 3.4 million (1981) *Altitude* 8 m.
Founded in 1608, the city rose to prominence under the Mughals. It lies on the N bank of the Burhi Ganga, protected from normal flooding by being raised on a low spur of slightly higher ground trailing S from the Madhupur Jungle Tract, which lies about 10 m above the surrounding plain. The old part of the town still hugs the banks of the river, a *distributary** of the Padma, but the city has grown dramatically in the last 20 years. From the airport to the commercial centre has been laid out with wide roads, parks and gardens, and has the appearance of a most attractive modern city. However, at least half the population live in extreme poverty, crowded in huts on any available open and public land.

	Jan	Feb	Mar	Apr	May	Jun	Jul	Aug	Sep	Oct	Nov	Dec	Av/Tot
Max (°C)	26	28	32	35	34	32	31	31	31	31	29	26	31
Min (°C)	12	13	19	24	25	26	26	26	26	24	17	13	21
Rain (mm)	3	0	33	230	109	316	526	462	363	104	7	33	2186

Local festivals All the national festivals are celebrated in the capital (**see page 1398**). 21 Feb *Shadid Dibosh* Service of mourning beginning at midnight terminates at the Shahid Minar. 26 Mar *Independence Day* Laying of wreaths ceremony at Martyrs' Memorial at Savar. Children's rally at the Stadium and sensational boat races on the Burhiganga river. 14 Apr *Pahela Baishakh* Spring gathering in Ramna Park with tournaments, boat races etc. 8 May *Rabindra Jayanti* Birth anniversary of the Bengali poet Rabindranath Tagore, when all educational institutions are closed and there are performances of Tagore songs and dances and discussions on his works. 26 May *Nazrul Jayanti* celebrates the birth anniversary on of the 'rebel poet' with functions at the mausoleum next to the Dhaka University mosque.
Large congregational prayers are held for *Eid-ul-Fitr* and *Eid-ul-Azha* and for *Muharram*, when there is a special procession of the Shia community from the Hussaini Dalan Imambara.

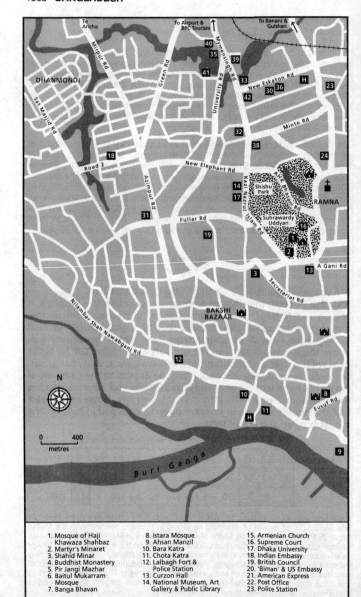

1. Mosque of Haji
   Khawaza Shahbaz
2. Martyr's Minaret
3. Shahid Minar
4. Buddhist Monastery
5. Pir Jangi Mazhar
6. Baitul Mukarram
   Mosque
7. Banga Bhavan

8. Istara Mosque
9. Ahsan Manzil
10. Bara Katra
11. Chota Katra
12. Lalbagh Fort &
    Police Station
13. Curzon Hall
14. National Museum, Art
    Gallery & Public Library

15. Armenian Church
16. Supreme Court
17. Dhaka University
18. Indian Embassy
19. British Council
20. 'Biman' & US Embassy
21. American Express
22. Post Office
23. Police Station

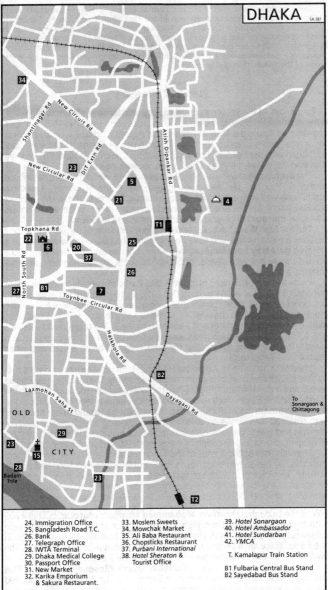

DHAKA SA 381

34

Shantinagar Rd
New Circuit Rd
DIT Extn Rd
Atish Dipankar Rd

New Circular Rd

23

5

21

4

Topkhana Rd

T1

22

6

20

37

25

26

North South Rd

27

B1

7

Toynbee Circular Rd

Hatkhola Rd

B2

Laxmohan Saha St

Dayaganj Rd

To
Sonargaon &
Chittagong

OLD

29

23

15

CITY

28
Badam
Tole

23

T2

24. Immigration Office
25. Bangladesh Road T.C.
26. Bank
27. Telegraph Office
28. IWTA Terminal
29. Dhaka Medical College
30. Passport Office
31. New Market
32. Karika Emporium
    & Sakura Restaurant.

33. Moslem Sweets
34. Mowchak Market
35. Ali Baba Restaurant
36. Chopsticks Restaurant
37. *Purbani International*
38. *Hotel Sheraton &*
    Tourist Office

39. *Hotel Sonargaon*
40. *Hotel Ambassador*
41. *Hotel Sundarban*
42. *YMCA*

T. Kamalapur Train Station

B1 Fulbaria Central Bus Stand
B2 Sayedabad Bus Stand

Dec *Christmas* Services at St Mary's Cathedral, Ramna, Portuguese Church, Tejgaon, Church of Bangladesh (Protestant), Johnson Rd and Bangladesh Baptist Sangha, Sadarghat.

Hindus celebrate *Durga Puja* and *Siva Ratri*. Langlaband, a sacred pilgrimage place 12 km SE of Dhaka where Hindus take a ritual bath in the sacred water of the River Brahmaputra in Apr-May. *Dhamrai Fair* held at a village 40 km NW of the city. The 10 day fair attracts thousands – devotees draw the wooden *Rath* (ceremonial temple car) which is kept in the centre of the market, through the streets.

Places of Interest

Lalbagh Fort At the SW corner of the Old city, with its maze of narrow alleyways, is the incomplete Fort (also known as Aurangabad Fort), started in 1678 by Prince Mohammed Azam, the Mughal Emperor Aurangzeb's 3rd son, who was Viceroy for a year. His successor, the Mughal governor of Bengal, Shayesta Khan, continued with the building, but the death of his favourite daughter, nicknamed **Bibi Pari** (fairy), was taken as a bad omen, so work was stopped.

The **Burhiganga** river which once ran along the S wall of the fort, has moved further S. You can see the imposing gateway in the SE corner, a western fortification wall with a 3 domed mosque nearby, 2 gates to the N, the shrine of Bibi Pari, a tank and the Audience Hall and Hammam in the centre, which houses a Mughal **museum** displaying armour, costumes and jewellery.

The 8 m high **Walls** have plaster decorations and some of the semi-octagonal bastions are earth-filled, and have underground chambers. The unfinished SE 3 storeyed **gateway** has a large archway which opened onto the river front and a domed square hall with slender octagonal minarets, guard chambers on either side and a staircase.

Inside the fort on a raised platform is **Bibi Pari's shrine** which follows a plan not dissimilar to Humayun's tomb in Delhi: it is an 18 m square mausoleum with octagonal turrets in the 4 corners. The once gilt-covered dome now has copper. Inside, the central tomb chamber is covered in white marble with an inlaid floor, marble *jali* screens on 3 sides and a doorway to the S. The *takhti* marks a female grave. The 8 other chambers that surround are decorated with coloured tiles and marble. It is interesting to note that the black Rajmahal basalt is used with white marble from Rajasthan.

Shayesta Khan built his **Audience Hall** and Hamman which has a central hall, flanked by 2 square chambers and a similar upper storey. The walls have decorative panels and arched niches. You enter the hall with a sunken fountain through the 3 arches on the E side which overlook the tank. A large arched door leads to the square **Hammam** (bath) chamber which has a dome above and a floor decorated with coloured tiles, similar to those in the surrounding antechambers used for dressing and toilet. The tank here was fed by warm water. The complex system of heating, piping and disposing of water for the bath is particularly interesting.

The staircases at the 2 ends of the building lead to the upper storey where the main hall has arched openings to the E and W which may have had marble screens. The exceptional architectural feature is its *dochala* Bangla roof, an imitation of the thatched hut in masonry which found an expression blending with Mughal imperial architecture in Delhi, Agra, Rajasthan and Lahore.

NW of the Lalbagh is the *Khan Mohammed Mirdha's Mosque*, built in 1706 with its unusual raised platform with a vaulted living chamber below. The mosque occupies the upper floor with an arcaded hall to the N and is reached by steps on the E side. There are 4 tall corner minarets and 3 domes over the prayer hall. The walls have decorative plaster panels and each of the 3 bays has a *mihrab*.

One built in a similar style is **Kartalab Khan's Mosque** (or Murshid Quli Khan's), built around 1700 in the Begum Bazaar area. The 2 storeyed mosque has 5 domes and a small minaret, and in addition a *dochala* Bengali roof to the N. It stands by a *Baoli* or stepped well which, though common in W India, is the only one that exists in Bangladesh.

Returning to the centre of Old Dhaka in Chowk Bazaar you will find the fruit and vegetable market, on the N bank of Burhiganga.

Near the Chowk in the Armanitola on Mohantole Rd is the **Istara Mosque** (Star Mosque or Mirza Ghulam Pir's mosque) which is decorated with coloured mosaics in geometric patterns, including stars on the domes. Originally built in the 18th century it has seen more recent redecoration.

Nearby, the **Bara Katra** is one of the city's earliest and most important Mughal ruins. Built by Abul Qasim, Dewan of Shah Shuja in 1644 as a caravanserai in the Central Asian tradition (initially possibly as a royal residence), it had an enclosed quadrangle in the style of a *Katra* with a large 70 m frontage on the Burhiganga river. Each side of the central courtyard once had 22 cells for travellers but little remains. You can still some of the grandeur in the southern arched gateway and the octagonal corner towers of the dilapidated E and W walls. The 3 storeyed gateway has elaborate plasterwork under the archway. The much smaller **Chota Katra** built in a similar style by Shaista Khan in 1663, is 200 m E.

Hussaini Dalan on Urdu Rd, nr the Central Jail, was originally built as an Imambara for the Shia Muslims towards the end of Mughal rule in Dhaka where Muharram is celebrated annually. The earthquake of 1897 destroyed the original roof which has been replaced by a flat roof. The central part contains 2 large halls with additions of 2 storeyed chambers. There is an arched entrance gateway to the N from which you see the wide frontage of the Dalan broken by 4 columns and a tank at the back. The 4 corner turrets topped by kiosks are original as is much of the building, a silver model of which you can see in the Dacca Museum.

Going E from the Chowk, along the Bund on the bank of the river between the 2 ghats, Badam Tole and Saddarghat is the **Ashan Manzil**. It was once the impressive Palace of the last Nawab, with a grand staircase and large halls, built in 1872 on the site of a French trading post. Today it is neglected and in sad disrepair, threatened with encroaching slum dwellings.

Nearby is the somewhat crumbling **Armenian Church** off the Nawabpur Rd within high walls in an area where the Armenian community once had flourishing businesses. On Hindu St here you will come across *sankharis* (shell craftsmen) making bangles and rings as they do across the border in W Bengal.

Moving N from the Old City you come to the **Shahid Minar** off Secretariat Rd. The monument commemorating the martyrs of the Language Movement of 1952, started as a struggle to get recognition of Bangla as one of the state languages of Pakistan (of which Bangladesh formed the eastern wing, E Pakistan). However, the movement grew into the struggle for independence of the nation. The minar resembles a scaffold for hanging.

The European quarter was originally established by the Mughals, where the rulers wanted to keep the foreign traders (Portuguese, Dutch and French) separate. The British continued to build their administrative offices in the same area – the Governor's House (c1905) now the Supreme Court, the Secretariat and the Dacca College. You will see one of the earliest examples of the style of this period in the impressive **Curzon Hall** in Ramna. Built in 1904 as a town hall by Lord Curzon it is now a part of the University. It combines Victorian with Mughal architecture – note the cusped arches, kiosks and perforated screens.

The old Race Course is the site of the popular park **Suhrawardy Uddyan**, close to the Sheraton Hotel. The oath of Independence was taken here on 7th Mar 1971 and coincidentally, later that year, the occupation forces surrendered here on 16 Dec. At the N end is Shishu Park, an amusement ground and the Ramna Park across the road has a boating lake.

To the W of the Uddyan are the **Museum**, Public Library and the **National**

Art Gallery, at the Shilpakala Academy which houses folk art and works of Bangladeshi artists.

To the SE of the Uddyab are the GPO, the Stadium and the Baitul Moharram Mosque, the largest in the city. The design is based on the Kaaba in Mecca – the large hall has a verandah which allows vast crowds to be accommodated at festivals, as during Eid. **Banga Bhavan,** nr the Stadium is the President's residence which can only be seen from outside. **Motijheel** Commercial Area (CA) with its high rise modern buildings shows a different face of the capital and is the heart of the city with hotels, restaurants, business houses, shops and travel agents.

To the E is the Central **Kamalpur Railway Station** and not far away the Dharmarajikha Buddhist Monastery.

To the NW Sher e Bangla with its architectural showpiece designed by the American architect Louis Kahn is the **Parliament Building.** It combines traditional brick with natural coloured concrete and uses some of the vernacular forms with modern design – the stretches of water are used to reflect the vast building to effect. Further N is **Sat Gumbad** (Mosque of Seven domes) in Jafarabad. Probably built by Shaysta Khan in the 17th century, it stands in a commanding position overlooking the flood plain of the Burhiganga. The Mosque itself has 3 domes, while each of the 4 corner octagonal towers has one.

N of the town is the diplomatic enclave, **Banani** and **Gulshan CA**, the Garden Suburb of the affluent.

National Memorial at Savar commemorates martyrs of the war of Independence. The Jahangir Nagar University campus is nearby. The weekly *hat* (fair) at **Savar** attracts large crowds of villages and you will see a colourful sight of stalls selling sweetmeats, fruits, vegetables, fish and handicrafts.

Dhakeswari Temple on Dhakeswari Rd N of the city.

Services

Hotels AL *Sonargaon*, 107 Kazi Nazrul Islam Av, Kawran Bazaar. T 315071, Fax: 008802 411324. 10 min business district and 20 min drive from international airport. 350 rm. Impressive public areas, interior fountains, superb restaurants. 270 refurbished rm. 4 speciality restaurants including *Vintage Room*, in large grounds, overlooking Ramna gardens. Japanese interpreter available. Floodlit tennis, transport to 18 hole golf 5 km. 11 storey building and interior showing Mughal influence. **AL** *Sheraton*, 1 Minto Rd. T 505061,Telex: 642401 SHER BJ. 20 min international airport, 3 km business district. Parjatan Tourist Office, *Gourmet* patisserie. **B** *Purbani International*, 1 Dilkusha CA. T 254081, Telex: 642460 BHL BJ. 175 a/c rm. Excellent Bengali Restaurant. **B** *Abakash*, Mohakhali CA, T 605398. **B** *Sundarbans*, Sonargaon Rd T 505055. 125 rm, some a/c. **C** *Parjatan Tourist Hotel*, Mohakhali CA, T 607085. A/c rm. **C** *Zakaria International*, 35 Gulshan Rd, Mohakhali CA, T 608188. Some a/c rm. **C** *Golden Gate*, 28 Mirpur Rd, nr New Market, T 505111. Some a/c rm. **C** *Park International*, 45 Kakrail, T 405191. Some a/c rm. Restaurant, travel.

D *Blue Nile*, 36 New Elephant Rd, T 501440. Some a/c rm. Restaurant. **D** *Metropolitan*, 44 Ropkhana Rd, R 257367. Rm with bath. **D** *City*, 21 Bangabandhu Av, T 257905. Some a/c rm. **E** *Rajdoot*, 24 Outer Circular Rd, T 405030. Restaurant. **E** *Al-Helal*, Arambagh, Motijheel CA. T 406533. Restaurant. **E** *YMCA Hostel*, 96/97 New Eskaton Rd. Rm and dorm in annexe. Restaurant open for breakfast and simple meals.

Restaurants Continental *Diplomat*, Gulshan, T 602282; *Golfer's Inn*, Kurmitola, T 604592; *Red Button*, Farm Gate, T 317717. Bengali: *Ali Baba*, Mymensingh Rd. Rec but expensive; *Ruchira*, Bangabandhu Av, T 254081. Chinese: *Chop Stick*, New Eskaton Rd, rec; *Hwang Ho*, Banani; *Chung Wahk*, N-S Rd, T 251044; *Shanghai*, 16 DRA, T 314375; *Panda Garden*, nr Mahakhali Rail Gate, T 608469; *Sakura*, above Karika Handicrafts, nr Sheraton Hotel, T 509296. Japanese plus continental and Chinese; Thai and Korean restaurants at W end of Gulshan Av. Good **patisserie** at the *Sonargaon Hotel* and snacks at *Eva* in Dilkusha CA nr Purbani International. There are cheap eating places around New Eskaton Rd. You can also get *kebab* and *nan* in the evenings in the Farm Gate area.

Banks Nationalised: **Sonali**, Motijheel CA, T 252990; **Janata**, 1 Dilkusha CA, T 236215; **Agrani**, 9D Dilkusha CA, T 232982; **Rupali**, 34 Dilkusha CA, T 251827. Foreign: **American Express**, 18-20 Motijheel CA, T 238350; **Chartered**, 18-20 Motijheel CA, T 236372; **Grindlays**, 2 Dilkusha CA, T 230225; **Habib**, 53 Motijheel CA, T 235091; **State Bank of India**, 24-25 Dilkusha CA, R 253914.

Shopping Best buys are textiles, ready made clothing, jewellery, and articles made of brass, leather, jute and terracotta. Bangladeshi pink pearls and the fine "Dacca muslin" are expensive but unique. **Note** Antiques (over 100 years old) must have clearance from the Dept of Archaeology, before being taken out of the country, which is not always obtained. If in doubt it is best to get an article checked and get a certificate for a genuine object to be sure that it does qualify as an antique.

Arcade shops at Sonargaon and Sheraton Hotels have a good selection of quality goods although you are likely to pay more than in the markets. The **Karika** Emporium, opp Dacca Sheraton has a good selection of handicrafts.

For **Handicrafts**: **Bangladesh Handicrafts**, 68 Outer Circular Rd, Mogh Bazaar; **Charuta** (Rd 5, Dhanmondi RA); **Aarong** opp Sobhanbagh Colony; **Shade**, 1 Outer Circular Rd; **Karunapannya**, Airport Rd. Brassware: **Upahar**, **Otobi**, New Elephant Rd; **East-West** handicrafts, 17, Rd 6, Dhanmondi RA.

Chandan (DIT Super Market) has good jewellery. **Pearl Paradise** is at 20 Baitul Moharram. Silks from **Sericulture Display Centre**, 140 Jakanara Garden, Green Rd.

Duty free shops (All purchases to be paid for in foreign currency). At the International Airport and a city sales centre **Mahakali** which claim to be well marked down. The **Export Promotion Bureau** sales room, Mymensingh Rd, opp Dhaka Sheraton, has good handicrafts. **Moloo's**, **Kanika**, **Chandan**, DIT Supermarket, Mymensingh Rd. **Charula**, Rd 5, Dhanmond. **Aarong**, opp Sobhanbag Colony, Mirpur Rd. **Shade**, 1 Outer Circle Rd. **Otobi** and **Upahar** (New Elephant Rd) **Karupanaya**, 112 Airport Rd.

Other shopping centres are Baitul Mukaram, Stadium Market, Bangabandhu Av, DMC Supermarket, Gulshan Markets, New Market, Green Supermarket.

Photography Colour films from Sonargaon Hotel shop. Quick processing in various photo shops in the city.

Local transport **Taxis** usually around the commercial area and large hotels, particularly Sonangaon Hotel. **'Baby taxis'** (3 wheelers) are more common. Negotiate prices as for **cycle rickshaws** which are only convenient for short journeys. Make sure your destination is clearly understood. **Car hire** – From Parjatan Tourist Information Centres and from the larger hotels.

Buses and **mini-buses** on main routes. Central Bus Station, Fulbaria serves the city and suburban routes including Sonargaon, Savar and Narayanganj. Bus Nos and destinations are in Bangla – No 6 calls at the main bus stops en route from the airport to the Central Rly Station in Kamalpur. No 2, 9, 22 covers Farm Gate to Mirpur. No 5 connects the affluent suburb and diplomatic enclave Banani and Gulshan CA with Fulbaria.

Entertainment Art Galleries – Bangladesh Shilpakala Academy, Segunbagicha. Contemporary Art Ensemble, 1 Commercial Building, S Av, Gulshan. At the DIT Supermarket: Jiraj Art Gallery, F33 Gulshan 2; Hoque Handicrafts, F 43 Gulshan 2; Saju Arts and Crafts, F 18-38 Gulshan.

Sports Swimming – Pools at the Sonargaon and Dhaka Sheraton Hotels are open to the public.

Dhaka Club, T 502165. Accommodation, restaurant, bar, pool and sports; **Golf Club**, Kurmitola, T 604592. Well landscaped with good facilities. Restaurant and bar – temporary membership for tourists. **Tennis** and **squash** at the big hotels.

The following for swimming, tennis and squash, are open to nationals of certain countries: Australian Club, 83, Gulshan, T 600091 (also New Zealanders); American Club, Gulshan, T 602111. Restaurant; Swedish Club, 47 Gulshan, T 601043 (also guests). Netherlands Recreation Centre, 71 Gulshan, T 602039. Restaurant. Automobile Assoc, 3/B Outer Circular Rd, Moghbazaar, T 402241.

Museums **Bangladesh Museum**, New Elephant Rd, opp Shishu Park. Open 1000-1600 Sat-Wed, 1500-1900 Fri, closed Th. Collection of paintings and sculptures from the Hindu, Buddhist and Muslim periods and Arabic inscriptions of the Quran, Persian and Bengali manuscripts. Also coins, silver filigree and ivory carvings. **Institute of Art and Crafts** pleasantly situated in Shahbagh has a collection of folk art and works of Bangladeshi artists.

Libraries British Council Library nr Univ of Dhaka; American Centre, 9 Dhanmondi RA, Rd 8; Dhaka Public Library, Mymensingh Rd.

Parks and Gardens Baldha Gardens has a good collection of botanical plants. Ramna Park, Suhrawardy Uddyan and Shishu Park (see above under places of interest).

The **Zoo** is at **Mirpur**, 16 km NW of Dhaka and covers about 100 ha. To the E is the **Botanical Garden**, over 75 ha, which in addition carries out research, preservation and botanical education.

Important services Police, Shahbagh, nr Shishu Park, T 509922. **Foreigners' Registration Office**, Malibag crossing nr Petrol pump, T 403217. **Passport and Immigration**, 30 New Circuit House Rd, T 403217. **Dept of Archaeology Office**, 22/1 Babur Rd, Mohammedpur.

Foreign Representations Australia, 184 Gulshan Av, T 600091. **Bhutan**, 58, Rd 3A, Dhanmondi RA, T 505418. **Canada**, 16A, Rd 48, Gulshan, T 607071. **France**, 18, Rd 108, Gulshan, T 607083. **Germany**, 178 Gulshan, T 600166. **India**, 120, Rd 2, Dhanmondi RA, T 503606. **Indonesia**, 75 Gulshan Av, T 600131. **Italy**, NWD 4, Rd 58/62, Gulshan, T 603161. **Japan**, 110, Rd 27, Block A Banani, T 608191. **Malaysia**, 4, Rd 118, Gulshan, T 600291. **Nepal**, UN Rd, 2, Baridhara Diplomatic Enclave, T 602091. **Netherlands**, 49, Rd 90, Gulshan, T 608185. **Pakistan**, NE(C) 2, Rd 71, Gulshan, T 600276. **Philippines**, NE(L) 5, Rd 83, Gulshan, T 600077. **Saudi Arabia**, 12 NE(N), Rd 92, Gulshan, T 600221. **Sri Lanka**, 22, Rd 65, Gulshan, T 601057. **Switzerland**, 5, Rd 104, Gulshan, T 600181. **Thailand**, 21 Block B, Rd 16, Banani, T 601475. **UK**, Abu Baker House, Plot 7, Rd 84, Gulshan, T 600133. **USA**, Baridhara Diplomatic Enclave, T 608170. **USSR**, NE(J) 9, Rd 79, Gulshan, T 601050.

Hospitals IPGMR, T 505194; Dhaka Medical College, T 505025; Holy Family, T 400011; Metropolitan Medical Centre, opp Mahakali Bus Station, T 606364; Adventist Dental Clinic, 20, Rd 99, Gulshan, T 602845.

Post and Telegraphs GPO, Abdul Gani Rd, nr the Stadium. For **Poste Restante**, turn right from the main hall. CTO is on N-S Rd, close to the Fulbaria Bus Stand.

Places of worship Muslim – Several mosques in the city including Istara Mosque, nr Lalbagh; Hussain Dolan, Urdu Rd; Kashaituli Mosque, Old City; Kartalab Khan Mosque, Begum Bazaar; Haji Khwaza Mosque, nr High Court. Hindu – Dhakeswari Temple nr Engineering Univ. **Christian** – St Mary's Cathedral, Ramna; Portuguese Church, Tejgaon; Church of Bangladesh (Protestant), Johnson Rd and Bangladesh Baptist Sangha, Sadarghat; Armenian Church. **Buddhist** – Dharmarajika Buddhist Monastery, nr Rly station.

Tourist Information Centre The Parjatan Office is at the Dacca Sheraton Hotel, 1 Minto Rd. Also counter at Zia International Airport. Parjatan offers a number of tours round the city and further afield. **Note** Parjatan advise that on some of their longer tours overnight accommodation will be very simple, but the best available. You need to be prepared, so ask for details at the office.

Tour 1 Dhaka city tour. 3 hr morning tour, Fri and Sat, Apr-Sep. **2** Old Dhaka tour. 3hr 30 min afternoon tour of old city and bazaar. Every Fri and Sat, Apr-Sep. Includes boat trip on Burhiganga to watch sunset. **3** All day Dhaka tour. Every Fri and Sat, Oct- Mar, other days on request. Includes short boat cruise. **4** Day tour, boat trip on Sitalakhya. Fri- Sat, Oct-Mar, other days on request. **5** Morning tour to sites outside Dhaka – Savar, Narayanganj, Sonargaon. Japanese, German and French speaking guides available on request. **6** Day trip to village. 45 min car or bus ride from Dhaka, 3 km rickshaw. Overnight accommodation can be arranged. **7** 4 day tour. River cruise by 'Rocket' paddle steamer Dhaka to Khulna, sightseeing around Khulna, flight from Jessore to Dhaka. **8** Sundarbans. Air to Jessore, boat to Daingmari forest station. Walk through Sundarbans to Kotka. Return via Mongla port to Jessore and Dhaka. (A variant on this arrangement is possible). **9** Chittagong, Cox's Bazar and the Hill Tracts. St. Martin's island coral reef. 4 day tour to Cox's Bazar, bus to Teknaf (85 km) boat to St. Martin's (23 km). Return via Chittagong. **10** Extended version of the former, with return by bus from Chittagong to Dhaka. **11** 4 day trip to Hill tracts – Rangamati. **12** 3 day trip to Cox's Bazar. **13** 4 day trip to Sylhet and Mainamati. **14** Buddhist sites of Bangladesh. 7 day trip, including Bogra (Mahasthan and Paharpur), Dinajpur, Comilla and Mainamati, Kaptai and Cox's Bazar. Japanese speaking guides provided on request.

Prices range from US$20 to US$2,000 per person if undertaken on an individual basis. Prices per person are much less when 2 or more people travel. Price per person for groups (min of 16) range from US$5 to US$580.

Note Passengers in transit at Zia International Airport are now offered Dhaka City sight seeing tours lasting 2 or 3 hr for US$10. Enquire at Parjatan desk.

Travel agents *Aeropath*, 11/2 Toynbee Circular Rd, T 255056. *Asia Travels and Tours*, 99 Motijheel CA, T 230236. *Beacon*, 115/116 Motijheel CA, T 232942. *Ganges*, Hotel Purbani,

T 233049. *Karnaphuli*, 60/1 Purana Paltan, T 231813. *Olympic*, 49 Motijheel CA, T 280463. *Seasons*, 56 Dilkusha, T 244457. *Travel Services*, 188 Motijheel Circular Rd, T 414891. *United*, 63 Purana Paltan, T 230828.

Airlines At Hotel Dhaka Sheraton, Minto Rd: Aeroflot, T 506636; Air India, T500071; Lufthansa, T 502856; PIA, T 501112; Swiss Air and Thai Airways, T 500079. Air France, T 251900; Qantas, T 259594; Royal Nepal Airlines, T 239353; Alitalia, QC Shipping, BCIC Bldg, Gr Floor, 30-31 Dilkusha CA, T 238144. Biman, Biman Bhavan, Motijheel, T 255911. British Airways, Sadharan Bima Shadan, 33 Dilkusha CA, T 231156. Druk Air c/o Biman. Emirates, ABC Air, 64 Motijheel CA, T 239303. Gulf Air, Capital Travels, 55-56 Motijheel CA, T 236262. Indian Airlines, Sharif Mansions, Motijheel CA, T 231687. Japan Airlines, Travelways, 21 Motijheel CA, T 258390. KLM, Travel Scene, HR Bhaban, Kakrail, T 413254.

Air services Daily flights to Chittagong, Jessore, Sylhet, and also to Ishurdi (Tues, Th, Fri, Sun), Saidpur (Mon, Wed, Fri) and Cox's Bazar (Fri). You can get a taxi, minibus or a bus between the airport and the city (Farm Gate is the most convenient Bus stop to get off). Zia International Airport, T 609416.

Rail To Chittagong *Mohangar Probhati*, 702, daily except Wed, 0800, 5 hr 40 min; *Mohangar Purabi*, 702, daily except Wed, 1600, 5 hr 40 min; *Urmi Exp*, 728, daily, 1500, 6 hr 15 min. **Sylhet** *Parabat Exp*, 709, daily except Th, 0720, 6 hr 30 min; *Joyontika*, 717 daily except Sat, 1430, 8 hr 40 min; *Upaban*, 739, daily, 2200, 7 hr 30 min. **Noakhali** *Upakul*, daily except Sat, 0840, 5 hr 15 min; *Noakhali Exp*, 12, daily, 2030, 8 hr 50 min. **Rajshahi** *Padma Exp*, 705, daily except Sun, 0820, 12 hr 20 min; *Jamun Exp*, 745, daily except Wed, 1620, 13 hr 10 min. **Dinajpur** *Tista Exp*, 707, daily except Mon, 0700, 15 hr 20 min; *Ekota Exp*, daily except Wed, 1700, 15 hr 40 min. **Mymensingh** *Tista*, 707, daily except Mon, 0700, 2 hr 40 min; *Balaka Exp*, 89, daily, 0930, 3 hr 35 min; *Ekota Exp*, 743, daily, 1700, 3 hr 15 min. Rly Station booking office and City Booking Office, Fulbaria, opp Govt Hospital.

Road The Bangladesh Road Transport Corp has a wide network over the whole country. It is the cheapest mode of transport, but can also be very uncomfortable. You will often find no information or signs in English but will have no difficulty if you ask for directions. The Central Bus Station in **Fulbaria** on Station Rd handles city and suburban services. The other terminals in the city serve different regions – **Mirpur BT**, to N Dhaka and NW and SW Bangladesh (Rajshahi, 11 hr and Khulna, 10 hr); **Gabtole BT** (also NW Bangladesh) – Rangpur, 10 hr; Saidpur, and Dinajpur, 1800, 12 hr; **Moakhali BT** – for the N (Mymensingh and Tangail); **Jatrabari BT**, Narayanganj Rd – Chittagong, 7 hr ; Sylhet, 9 hr; Comilla, Cox's Bazar. Enquire at the Parjatan Office for up to date information on timetables.

    Paribahan Bus Agency runs deluxe overnight services to Chittagong (7 hr) from their stop nr the Immigration Office in Motijheel.

River Bangladesh Inland Water Transport Corp (BIWTC) Services operate between Dhaka and Khulna via Chandpur, Barisal, Hjalkati, Hulerhat, Charkhali, Morolganj and Mongla. From Dhaka To **Khulna** BIWTC 'Rocket' ferry, daily 1745. **Barisal** *Express Service*, Mon, Wed, Th, Sat, 1745, arr Barisal 0500, dep 0600, arr **Khulna** 2100. BIWTC 'Rocket' ferry ghat is **Badam Tole**, Saddarghat for launches to Khulna and Barisal. Reservations: First Cl, T 239779, 2nd Cl, T 251706.

Excursions

Rajendrapur 40 km N on the Dhaka-Trishal-Mymensingh Highway, has the **National Recreational Park,** over 500 ha.

Sonargaon 29 km is one of the oldest capitals. The Deva Dynasty ruled from here in the 13th century after which the Sultanate of Bengal had it as a capital until the arrival of the Mughals in the early 17th century. They moved the capital to Dacca, fearing that the location of Sonargaon too vulnerable for attack from the Portuguese. It was once the 'Golden village/city' of riches, but today there are only the ruins of buildings, bridges and moats nr Painam Village. The tomb of Ghiasuddin (r1399-1409), shrines of Panjpirs and Shah Abdul Alla are in a courtyard within walls.

    There is a **National Folk Art and Craft Museum** which is housed in a *haveli* (former merchant's mansion) at Sardar Bari on the way to the **Goaldi Mosque** (1519) which is 8 km N of Sonargaon. There are several other interesting and ornate *havelis** here down the narrow lanes.

DHAKA TO MYMENSINGH

The road due N from Dhaka runs past the international airport along a ridge of slightly higher ground to the industrial settlement of Tungi. The metre gauge railway line forks NE to Mymensingh and SE to Chittagong. The road is an attractive and often shaded drive across the higher ground of the Madhupur Jungle tract, up to 10 m above the floodplain to the W. On the higher ridges there are extensive stands of sal forest, with farming on the lower land between. It has been one of the areas most quick to take up high yield variety seeds.

From Dhaka drive N through the industrial township of **Tungi** (19 km) to **Chourasta** (13 km). **Joydevpur** is off to the right (3 km), while the main road turns NW to **Chandra** (19 km). It continues through **Mirzapur** (15 km) to

Tangail (29 km), a district headquarters town and the centre of one of the most rapidly improving agricultural areas in Bangladesh. Many of the fields grow 3 crops in the year.

Places of interest

The **Atia Jami mosque** (1609) is the best example of the period, with a single dome over a square hall with a verandah to the E which has 3 domes. The cornice has a pronounced curve and is beautifully decorated with terracotta panels.

The square single-domed **Sadi mosque** at **Egara Sindur**, a village on the Brahmaputra river, en route to Mymensingh, was built in 1652 in the early Mughal style. The facade has decorative panels and there are 2 smaller domes and short corner towers. The similar smaller brick-built **Shah Muhammad Mosque** (1680) is nearby, which stands on a platform with a single dome with a lotus finial and 4 octagonal towers, topped by kiosks. Inside there are 3 *mihrabs* on the W wall, while the E wall has terracotta panel decorations. The Gate house is particularly interesting since it has the form of a local bamboo *dochala* hut built in masonry.

Continue to **Madhupur** (32 km). The road goes straight on to **Jamalpur** (48 km), which lies on an old near-abandoned course of the Brahmaputra. This used to flow to the N and E of the Madhupur tract until it took its present course in 1787, when the Tista was diverted by an earthquake into the Brahmaputra. Together they established the new and present main channel to the W of the Madhupur tract. The road to Mymensingh goes to the right through **Rasulpur** (32 km) and **Muktaganj** (19 km) to

Mymensingh (13 km) population 110,000. The centre of one of the most important jute growing districts in Bangladesh, Mymensingh is a district headquarters and an agricultural university. Like Jamalpur, the town lies on the former main course of the Brahmaputra, now reduced to a fraction of its former flow. The district is home to a large tribal population.

	Jan	Feb	Mar	Apr	May	Jun	Jul	Aug	Sep	Oct	Nov	Dec	Av/Tot
Max (°C)	25	27	32	34	32	31	31	31	32	31	29	27	30
Min (°C)	11	14	18	22	23	25	26	26	25	23	18	13	20
Rain (mm)	11	18	42	135	313	453	376	406	341	198	17	3	2313

Rail To Dhaka *Ekota Exp,* 744, daily except Wed, 0625, 2 hr 50 min; *Tista Exp,* 708, daily except Mon, 1850, 2 hr 40 min. Haluaghat (40 km).

It is impossible to travel much further E of Mymensingh by land during the wet season as the Meghna-Surma valley is flooded. Even during the dry season E-W communication to Sylhet is virtually impossible, the route going back through Dhaka.

DHAKA TO SYLHET AND JAFFLONG

The route from Dhaka to Sylhet runs E across the upper delta of the Padma-Meghna to Comilla, then N, close to the Indian border of Tripura State. It passes through some of Bangladesh's most important natural gas fields, and across the low, tea-covered hills, on the way up to Sylhet. The road itself is generally narrow, in the early part on a raised embankment above flood level, then keeping close to the edge of the hills. The lack of material for road building across the delta is evident, brick often being used to provide the hard base.

The road leaves Dhaka to the E and runs along the N embankment of the 6000 ha Dhaka-Demra flood protection scheme. Designed to keep out the waters of the **Lakhya River** to the N and E, and the **Burhiganga River** to the SW, a pumping station at **Demra** removes surplus monsoon water, but reverses the flow in the winter by pumping water from the Lakhya to irrigate winter crops. About 5,000 ha are irrigated, making possible heavy winter cropping. In 10 years the total output from this area increased more than five times.

There is a bridge and a ferry across the **Lakhya River** at **Katchpur** (4 km), and another ferry across the **Meghna River** (13 km). The ferry crossing is only about 15 minutes, but cars and buses may have to wait up to an hour. The road passes through **Daudkandi** (18 km), where there is a *BPC Motel*, to **Chandina** (35 km) and the site of the old Buddhist monastery at

Mainamati (13 km). It is possible to go N to Sylhet from either Chandina or Mainamati. A very small town, Mainamati has an impressive ruined site. The 18 km long range of low hills known as the Lalmai-Mainamati range are the first sign of raised ground at the edge of the delta. They contain the remains of over 50 Buddhist settlements dating from the 8th-12th century. Uncrowded by visitors, they have a distinctive aura of quiet. Sadly, there is little information in the site to explain the ruined remains of monasteries that were active until their final destruction by the Turkish Muslim invasions at the end of the 12th century.

Lalmai (Red Hills) derives its name from the colour of the soil, while the place itself is named after the Queen Mother during Govinda Chandra's reign. **Salban Vihara**, nr the middle of the row of hills, has 115 cells around a courtyard with a temple, with a cruciform plan in the centre. The original brick-built vihara is ascribed to the 4th Deva ruler in the 8th century AD, though archaeologists have discovered that subsequent rebuilding took place at different periods. Terracotta plaques found along the *pradakshina* (ambulatory path) are displayed in the museum.

5 km N of this is the **Kotila Mura** where 3 brick stupas were found, some believe representing the *Tripitaka* ('3 jewels': the Buddha, Dharma, and the Sangha, or community). 2.5 km NW is the rectangular **Charpatra Mura** discovered by the army who now occupy part of the area. The long hall which you enter from the E leads to shrine chamber. The site yielded some interesting royal copper-plate grants.

The Mainamati Archaeological Museum is where many of the finds are exhibited including statues, terracotta plaques, coins, jewellery, pottery and inscriptions.

The road N goes through **Companyganj** (10 km) to **Brahmanbaria** (42 km), a small district headquarters town and market. N to Sarail (7 km), the road then turns E back towards the Indian border to the small centre of *Itakhola* (38 km), and the first tea estates. The town is only a few km from the Indian border, the road S running to the capital of Tripura, Agartala, 45 km away.

Shaistaganj (34 km) is a minor railway junction on the metre gauge line, the main line from the N being joined by short branches from **Habiganj** to the N (where there is an important agricultural research centre) and the Indian border town of **Khowai** to the SE. Shaistaganj was founded by Syed Shaista of Taraf, but became the home of the exiled Maharaja of Tripura in 1809 who took refuge in Bishgaon. There is a 3 rm **F** *Rest House* just over 400 m from the railway station.

The road continues E, running parallel with the railway line, to *Srimongol* (30 km), one of the most important service towns for the tea estates. The headquarters of the Bangladesh Tea Research Institute is 3 km outside the town, and there is a weather forecasting station, and several banks. Accommodation is available in a four berth **F** *Dak Bungalow*. Just beyond Srimongol the road turns N. It passes through *Akbarpur* (13 km) where there is an **F** *BPC Rest House,* to

Maulvi Bazaar (10 km), situated on the left bank of the Manu River in a very attractive setting on the N slopes of the Balisira Hills. A park has been made around the horseshoe shaped Berry Lake, covering some 10 ha, and there is a **F** *Circuit House* and a **F** *Tourist Lodge*. The area is noted for its hunting. The road then crosses the Bibiyana River at **Bakshpur** before entering

Sylhet (69 km). *Population* 180,000.

	Jan	Feb	Mar	Apr	May	Jun	Jul	Aug	Sep	Oct	Nov	Dec	Av/Tot
Max (°C)	25	27	31	33	31	31	31	32	31	30	29	26	30
Min (°C)	13	14	17	22	23	25	25	25	25	22	17	14	20
Rain (mm)	2	29	351	394	217	971	1272	581	901	157	53	13	4941

Formerly in Assam, Sylhet is the District Headquarters. Located on the N bank of the Surma River, it was the one of the earliest Muslim settlements in East Bengal, being founded in 1303 by Shah Jalal. Under the Mughals it became one of the region's largest market towns, but when Cachar was opened up trade was diverted. The bed of the Surma River, on which it stands, silted up, and tea estates stimulated growth elsewhere.

At the beginning of the 19th century it was a small but still important market centre, with a population of 30,000. It already had many mosques. Through the 19th century it stagnated and then declined, its population falling to around 17,000 in the first Census of 1872 and 13,000 in 1901. Thereafter, the linking of the town with Chittagong by rail gave it a new importance, especially for the tea industry. However, its trade was disrupted at Independence, for it had previously acted as a main market for the Khasi and the Jaintia Hills. After Partition, and the closing of the border with India, that trade came to a halt. The metre gauge railway line, however, was extended up to Chatak after Independence to service the cement and fertilizer factories.

Places of interest There are many small mosques and tombs. The two main bazaars – the **Kazi** and the **Bunder** bazaars – are separated by the open space and administrative area in the centre of the town. Among the most important shrines are those of *Hazrat Shahjalal*, who came from Delhi to preach Islam in the region in 1303. It contains some relics of the saint and is an important pilgrimage Dargah 3 km from the town railway station. The Dargah to Farhand Khan, built between 1670-88 is also much visited. The Surma bridge, known as the Keane Bridge after Sir Michael Keane, the British Governor, was built in 1937.

Emperor Aurangazeb's fort-like 17th century **Shahi Idgah** built for Eid celebrations is 3 km NE of the Circuit House. You may be able to visit the Lakootola or Malinisora Tea Garden about 6 km out to the SW. The **Madhabkunda Waterfall,** a unique phenomenon in Bangladesh, is 3 km away

Local festivals *Rash Leela* The night of the full moon in Feb is marked by tribal dances. Manipuri tribal performances are given in the town and region.

Hotels C *Hilltown*, Telehaor, T 8262. 56 rm, some a/c. Restaurant, bar. **D** *Anurag*, Duphadighi N Rd, T 6718. 51 rm, some a/c with bath. **D** *Shahban*, Talatola Rd, T 7459. Some a/c rm. Restaurant. **D** *BPC Rest Houses*, Aximganj in tea garden. 2 rm and kitchen. **E** *Gulshan Boarding*, Taltala, T 6437. 45 rm Rs 45.

Bank *Sonali*, Zinda Bazaar for foreign exchange. **Bangladesh Bank** nr Hilltown Hotel.

Handicrafts Sylhet is a centre of tribal handicrafts. Cane furniture, tea trays and vases, and a distinctive Sital Pati mats are all widely available.

Travel agents *Musa*, Darga Gate, T 7917. *Latif*, Station Rd, T 7437. *Taher*, Jallarpar Rd, T 4802. *Surma*, 19 Surma Mansions, T 7232. *United*, Zinda Bazaar, T 7138.

Air services Biman has 3 daily flights. Office on Shah Jallal Rd, Zinda Bazaar.

Rail To Dhaka *Joyontika*, 718, daily except Sun, 0555, 7 hr; *Parabat*, 710, daily except Tue, 1410, 6 hr 40 min; *Upaban*, 740, daily except Th, 2130, 8 hr. The Rly Station is to the SE of town.

Buses for **Dhaka** (10 hr) and **Comilla** (8 hr) are frequent and leave from the Bus station nr the Rly station. Express buses have a separate stop nr the Dhaka Bus Stop.

From Sylhet there is a very attractive drive N to Jafflong. The route runs N towards the Khasi Hills and the Indian border. It passes through **Haipur** (23 km), a natural gas field, on its way to **Jaintiapur** (43 km). Jaintiapur was the capital of an independent kingdom until the British took it over in 1835, pensioning off Rajendra Singh, the last king, who ruled from 1832-35. The family line finally died out in 1911. Despite the closing of the border with India and the cutting off of links with the Khasi and Jaintia Hills it remains an important market town.

Just before Jaintiapur a road turns left to the small market of **Jafflong** (5 km). The scenery is some of the most attractive in Bangladesh. If you go through the small centre – no more than the bus stand and a few shops – you can ford the river to the tea estate on the other side. There are wonderful views of the Khasi Hills of the Shillong Plateau (in India), the wettest slopes in the world. Morning light is best, with the broad sandy bed of the river and the crystal water a really beautiful sight.

35 km NW of Sylhet town are the orange gardens of **Chhatak**, now also important for its cement factory.

DHAKA TO CHITTAGONG, COX'S BAZAR AND TEKNAF

The route crosses the Sita Lakhya, the Meghna and the Gomti on the way E to Comilla. From Comilla the road runs S to Feni, clinging to the foothills of Tripura and the Indian border close by on the E to keep above flood level. It continues ESE through the small town of Dhoom to Chittagong. This is Bangladesh's busiest road artery, linking the country's major port with the capital, but it remains a relatively quiet road. Although it is flat nearly all the way to Chittagong, there are some beautiful land and water scapes. Although the ferry crossings can take time, they also give a superb view of the boat traffic. Dhaka to Chittagong is 264 km, Chittagong to Cox's Bazar another 154 km.

Route as above to Mainamati. The road then goes straight on to **Comilla** (8 km)

	Jan	Feb	Mar	Apr	May	Jun	Jul	Aug	Sep	Oct	Nov	Dec	Av/Tot
Max (°C)	26	28	32	33	33	31	31	31	32	31	29	27	30
Min (°C)	12	15	20	23	25	25	25	25	24	24	18	14	21
Rain (mm)	10	44	53	158	316	479	404	417	337	226	45	3	2492

Very close to the international border with India, Comilla lies on the highway from Chittagong to Sylhet. The whole area is crowded with fish ponds (*dighis**). The region is known for its traditional pottery and handloom weaving, and the manufacture of pharmaceuticals. In the 1959 the Pakistan Academy for Rural Development was established here by Dr Akhteer Hameed Khan. He developed a programme for integrated rural development, in which co-operatives played a prominent part. This was spread through Pakistan as the 'Comilla model'. Today the centre is known as the Bangladesh Academy for Rural Development, and is still a centre of research and development work.

Local festivals In Nov a large fair is held for 10 days, in conjunction with a Hindu and Buddhist festival.

From Comilla the road runs SSE parallel to the Indian border, to **Feni** (50 km. Population 15,000). Headquarters of its district, Feni has a number of schools, a hospital and a **F** *Rest House*. A road to the W from Feni runs to Begumganj and **Noakhali** (40 km). Noakhali ("new channel") lies on the edge of the delta. The old town was washed away in the 1930s and the new town was built a few km away. Most of the houses are corrugated iron sheeting and bamboo. "Even considered generously" says the gazetteer "the town does not have the look of a modern urban area". A delicate understatement.

To the S is an expanding area of new *char land*, being added to by the Meghna every year. Offshore to the S are the islands of Sandwip and Hatia. Cruelly exposed to the risk of cyclone damage (see above), **Hatiya** is an attractive island. Lying in the Meghna estuary, it has constantly been changing its shape, growing significantly since it was first surveyed by Rennell in 1770. It is now over 43 km long and 13 km wide. There is an ever-changing number of temporary islands, or *char* lands, between the mainland and Hatia, all occupied and cultivated at some periods of the year. The estuary experiences remarkable tides, increasing dramatically in height from W to E. The normal rise of the tide at Hatiya is less than 5 m, but at the mouth of the Feni River it increases to over 12 m. At every full and new moon a tidal bore, up to 6 m high and moving at 25 kph, rushes up the channel between Hatiya and the mainland. The township, near the N tip of the island, is headquarters of the Thana, with a High School and a number of Government agency offices. It has a rich vegetation, with coconuts and date palms dominating.

E and SE of Hatia is **Sandwip** Island, the largest of Bangladesh's offshore islands. **Harishpur**, or Sandwip township, is approximately halfway down the W shore. This has all the major government departments, an important bazaar, and schools. There are daily ferry services by streamer to Chittagong and Barisal, and the island exports coconuts, betel and paddy.

5 km to the E of Feni, very close to the border with India, is an extraordinary group of Hindu shrines by the tank at **Chaggalnaya**, distinguished by their very tall and slender sikharas. **F** *Rest House* There are beautiful views of the Tripura Hills to the E and NE. The road continues S from Feni to the railway town of **Dhoom** (49 km). The shrine of a Muslim saint, *Chin-Ki Astana*, is near the station on the Grand Trunk Road, and is a popular place of pilgrimage. **Sitakunda** (27 km) is famous

for its hill top Hindu temple nearby. In Feb thousands of Hindu pilgrims visit it to celebrate *Siva Chaturdasi*. There are also hot springs nearby and a salt water spring, Labanakhya, 5 km N. Continue S to **Chittagong** 37 km (*Population 2,050,000*).

Chittagong

	Jan	Feb	Mar	Apr	May	Jun	Jul	Aug	Sep	Oct	Nov	Dec	Av/Tot
Max (°C)	26	28	31	32	32	31	30	30	31	31	29	26	30
Min (°C)	13	15	19	23	24	25	25	24	24	23	19	14	21
Rain (mm)	3	20	80	297	63	394	1267	673	411	36	49	17	3310

The country's main port and its second largest city was described by 7th century Chinese traveller Hiuen Tsang as "a sleeping beauty emerging from mists and water". In the 16th century Portuguese seamen called it the 'Porte Grande', and it reputedly had trading links with China, Arabia and Persia before the Europeans arrived.

Situated near the mouth of the Karnaphuli river, Chittagong has a recorded history from the 9th century. The district was called Islamabad by the Mughals when they captured it in 1666 from the Arakanese. The District Gazetteer of Chittagong suggests that several derivations for the name of Chittagong have been put forward. *Chaityagram*, or 'land of the Chaityas is suggested by Buddhist sources. The Burmese suggest that an Arakan king erected a pillar after a victorious campaign in the 9th century, on which was inscribed the words *Tsi-ta-gung*, meaning 'to make war is improper'. The great oriental scholar Sir William Jones gives a third derivation, saying that he believed the name to be taken from the 'chatag' bird "the most beautiful little bird I ever saw". However, a later British resident, the author of the 1908 Gazetteer, argued that the true derivation was from a version of the Sanskrit 'Chaturgrama' – four villages.

The town was first brought under Muslim control in 1340 by King Kakhruddin Mubarak Shah of Sonargaon. The District Gazetteer records that it was a Muslim *pir* or saint, who gave it the name by which it is still known in the region, *Chatigaon*. It is believed that the saint Hazrat Badar Aulia set out to remove the evil spirits from the land with which it was infested. The region was so densely forested that there was no room even to sit to pray, so he negotiated an agreement with the spirits that he should be allowed space to put an earthen lamp, a *chati*. As soon as he had placed the lamp on the ground he bellowed out "azan', and the spirits fled in terror, as far as the light of the lamp and the sound of the azan reached. The area that was reclaimed then became known as Chatigaon, the land of the lamp.

The town is built on several low hillocks scattered round the town. The court, government offices and European houses were all on hilltops, while the bazaars and local housing were on the flat plain. There are excellent views of the Karnaphuli from the High Court building.

Because of sandbars, large ships can only be brought in to the port with the help of river pilots. The building of the Kaptai Dam in the Chittagong Hill Tracts has stabilised the flow of the Karnaphuli River, considerably improving the port. Several heavy and light industries have been located in the suburbs, including those producing plywood, safety matches, paper and rayon. It also has the country's only steel mill and oil refinery.

Warning The town is one of the areas most affected by cyclones in Bangladesh, usually in

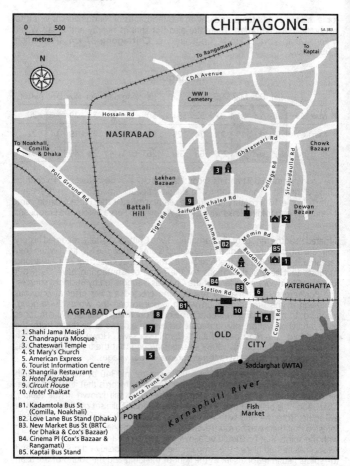

CHITTAGONG SA 383

0 500
metres

N

To Rangamati
To Kaptai

CDA Avenue

WW II
Cemetery

Hossain Rd

NASIRABAD

Ghateswari Rd

Chowk
Bazaar

To Noakhali,
Comilla
& Dhaka

Polo Ground Rd

Lakhan
Bazaar

College Rd

Sirajudaulla Rd

3

9

Saifuddin Khaled Rd

Nur Ahmed R

Dewan
Bazaar

Battali
Hill

Tiger Rd

2

Momin Rd

B2

Buddhist Rd

B5

1

Jubilee Rd

B4

B3

6

PATERGHATTA

Station Rd

B1

T **10**

4

Court Rd

AGRABAD C.A.

8

OLD

7

CITY

5

Saddarghat (IWTA)

To Airport
Dacca Trunk Le

Karnaphuli River

PORT

Fish
Market

1. Shahi Jama Masjid
2. Chandrapura Mosque
3. Chateswari Temple
4. St Mary's Church
5. American Express
6. Tourist Information Centre
7. Shangrila Restaurant
8. Hotel Agrabad
9. Circuit House
10. Hotel Shaikat

B1. Kadamtola Bus St
(Comilla, Noakhali)
B2. Love Lane Bus Stand (Dhaka)
B3. New Market Bus St (BRTC
for Dhaka & Cox's Bazaar)
B4. Cinema Pl (Cox's Bazaar &
Rangamati)
B5. Kaptai Bus Stand

Oct-Nov but occasionally in Apr-May. It was severely damaged in the cyclone of 30 April 1991. Repair to the facilities is expected to take many months.

Places of interest The old part of the city, which has now changed, is by the river where BIWTC services leave from Saddarghat. However, you can still attend services at the 17th century Portuguese Church of Our Lady of the Rosary, though it too has been rebuilt. The British occupied a slightly higher area (Fairy Hills) to the N of Sadarghat, where they built their administrative offices, the Secretariat, High Court, a hospital and churches. The Circuit House on S Saifuddin Khaled Rd remains as a good example.

The 17th century **Jama Masjid**, on a hillock in Anderkilla, resembles a fort, while the **Qadam Mubarak** in Rahmatganj has a stone slab with the 'footprint' of the Prophet. **Hazrat Bayezid Bostani,** 6 km away in **Nasirabad**, is a pilgrim centre. It has a large tank with hundreds of tortoises.

The **Ethnological Museum** at Agrabad has a representative collection of the area's tribal heritage.

Hotels A *Agrabad*, Agrabad CA, T 500111. 101 a/c rm. 3 restaurants, bar, exchange, travel, shops, roof top garden, disco, open-air pool. **C** *Shahjahan*, Sadarghat Rd, T 203446. Restaurant, bar, exchange. **C** *Shaikat*, Station Rd, T 209845. 28 rm, some a/c. Govt run. Restaurant, Tourist Office. **D** *Hawaii*, 39 Agrabad CA, T 500071. Restaurant, bar, exchange. **D** *Miska*, Station Rd, T opp Shaikat, T 203623. Restaurant. **E** *Manila*, Station Rd has rm with bath and a dining hall. **E** *YMCA*, 150 Jubilee Rd which provides lodging for students has a rm for travellers.

Restaurants There are a large number of Chinese Restaurants in town. Best is *Chunking*, Sh Mujib Rahman Rd, Agrabad CA. *Shangrila*, 39 Agrabad is reasonable. A number of inexpensive eating places in Jubilee Rd.

Banks American Express, off Muji Rahman Rd, Agrabad CA.; **Chartered**, Suhrawardi Rd; **Grindlay's**, Saddarghat Rd.

Shopping *Biponi Bitan*, Karnafull Market.

Travel agents *Balaka*, Hotel Shahjahan, T 207795. *Globe Express*, 54/3 Chatteshwari Rd, T 221978. *United Travels*, 39 Agrabad, T 502843.

Air services Direct Biman connection with Dhaka and Calcutta.

Rail To **Dhaka** *Mohangar Probhati*, 701, daily except Tues, 0640, 5 hr 40 min; *Mohangar Purabi*, 703, daily except Wed, 1440, 5 hr 40 min; *Turna Nishitha*, 741, daily except Sun, 2330, 6 hr 30 min. **Sylhet** *Jalalabad Exp*, 13, daily, 2030, 13 hr; *Paharika Exp*, 719, daily, 1030, 8 hr 55 min.

Road BRTC buses leave for **Dhaka** early morning (7 hr). Buses to **Comilla** take 3 hr 30 min.

River To **Barisal** Coastal service, via Sandwip, Hatiya, Ramgati and Daulatkhan, Mon-Th, 0900, 20 hr. To **Hatiya** via Sandwip, Express Service, Sat, 0900, 9 hr.

Excursions The 425 sq km *Kaptai Lake* (58 km) was created by the damming of the Karnaphuli river for the country's only hydroelectric project. The good road runs E along the Karnaphuli valley through intensively cultivated rice fields. It passes through Rangunia and Chandraghona, small settlements on the N bank of the river. At *Chandraghona* the Government has built what is claimed to be the largest paper-making factory in Asia, built with Japanese assistance in the 1960s and using Karnaphuli power. There is also a well known Baptist Mission hospital with a specialist leprosy unit, village medical programme and agricultural development work.

The drive up to Kaptai leads into the low hills of the Chittagong Hill Tracts, suddenly giving a completely different feel to the landscape. The hills are now covered in scrub jungle, with occasional pineapple and other plantations. Until recently the hills were densely forested. They contain a number of valuable species, including Indian mahogany. There are still wild elephants in the hills, and a range of other wild animals. The great reptiles are also found, including pythons and hamadryads, though cobras are uncommon.

The lake is very attractive, surrounded by tropical forest. You can get a permit to take a motor launch trip on the lake lasting about 90 min, starting from the ghat, and visit Rangamati. There is a remarkable boat lift to raise river boats from the Karnaphuli onto the lake itself and a Parjatan Hanging Bridge.

Warning There is heavy security in Kaptai and you are not allowed to take photographs. The flooding of the valley led to great protests from the Chakma, Magh tribes. Many lost their valley-bottom land, crucial to their system of shifting cultivation. Increasing population pressure has led the Government to sponsor the settlement of Bangali cultivators in the Hill Tracts, and the competition for land has encouraged the development of a fierce resistance movement by the Tribals. Many thousands are living in refugee camps on the Indian side of the border, and foreigners are not allowed to travel in some parts of the district.

Chit Morong Buddhist Temple with several statues of the Buddha (3 km on the Chittagong road), celebrates the last day of the Bengali year, 12/13 April followed by the *Water Festival* lasting several days.

Rangamati, an attractive little town on an isthmus on the W bank of the lake, is more tourist-oriented with swimming, boating and various water sports including water skiing on offer. It is surrounded by attractive wooded hills which were once the home of wild elephants, tigers and leopards. The tribal groups still live in small settlements of bamboo huts built on raised platforms in the thick forests. The Buddhist *khyaungs* (temples) nearby are also built of bamboo, thatched with grass and have rustic tree trunks with notches as a staircase up to the platform. You can visit the Tabalchhari Tribal Handicraft Centre to see Chakma, Tanchangya, Marma and Tripura handicrafts, especially the handwoven fabrics with unique patterns.

Note You have to register at the Foreigners Registration Office.

Hotels C *BPC Motel*, Deer Hill, T 3126. 18 rm, 3 a/c. Restaurant, speed boat hire, cultural programmes, Tourist information. **D** *BPC Cottages*, at the foot of Deer Hill, T 3126. 3 sleeping 4, 2 sleeping 8, each with a kitchen. Some **E/F** category hotels and boarding houses in town.

Shopping There is a *Tribal handicrafts Centre* making home-spun, handwoven tribal textiles, silver jewellery, bamboo bags, souvenirs of cane, leather and straw. Other shops in New Market.

Buses to and from **Chittagong** (70 km) takes 2 hr 30 min and can be crowded. From Kaptai Lake to Chittagong takes 1 hr 30 min.

The road from Chittagong to Cox's Bazar and Teknaf continues to hug the edge of the hills. It crosses beautifully contrasting wooded ridges and rice-cultivated valleys.

Leave Chittagong E through ***Kalurghat*** (13 km). Now incorporated into the suburbs NE of Chittagong, Kalurghat has grown from an insignificant village in 1947 to one of Bangladesh's most important industrial areas. Today it has Bangladesh's biggest jute mill, tanneries, match factories and glass works. It also has a modern dry dock, and has become a regular stopping point for all passenger boats going up the Karnaphuli to Chandraghona.

Follow the road E and then SE to ***Patiya*** (16 km), a settlement which dates from before the Mughals on the **Chandkhali River**. Immediately to the S is *Dohazari* (19 km). The town was named after 2 divisions of soldiers (each 1,000 strong: *do* – two, *hazari* – thousand), one under a Khatriya and the other under a Pathan commander, who were left on either bank of **River Sangu** to guard the route of the fugitive son of Shah Jahan, Shah Shuja, who was fleeing to Arakan.

The road continues S to ***Harbang*** (37 km), which has the remnants of a Portuguese fort. It then goes on to ***Dulahazara*** (27 km) *Population* 6,000. Prince Shah Shuja, having failed to free his imprisoned father Shah Jahan, who was kept imprisoned in Agra by his younger brother Aurangzeb, returned to the safety of Bengal. Meeting with little support in Dacca he travelled towards the Arakan Hills and passed through this village on his way, reputedly "with 1,000 palanquins" – hence the name. There is a very good forest bungalow on a small hillock on Arakan Rd. Wildlife on surrounding hills.

Continue through **Idgaon** (13 km) and **Joarianala** (11 km). ***Ramu*** (3 km, just off the main road) is an important market, which was mentioned by the Elizabethan traveller Ralph Fitch as being in the country of the Maghs. It had an Arakan fort which was stormed by Mughals in 1660. The Raja of Arakan tried but failed to recapture it. This marked the southern limit of Mughal power. In the **Alamgiranama**, it appears this is explained: "as the space between Chatgaon and Ramu is very hard to cover, full of hills and jungles and intersected by one or two streams, which cannot be crossed without boats, and as in the rainy season the whole path is flooded,...therefore the sending of a Mughal army into Arakan was put off."

The area has numerous white Buddhist pagodas and Burmese *khyangs* or monasteries built by refugees from the Arakan. The latter are built of wood with pitched roofs in several tiers, with intricate fretwork.

The interesting Burmese Bara Khyang at *Lama Bazar* has the country's largest bronze statue of the Buddha, and in its 3 buildings houses a number of relics, precious Buddhist images in silver and gold, set with gems.

From Ramu the road to the coast turns due W, across the narrow coastal strip and estuarine lowland to Cox's Bazar (16 km).

Cox's Bazar

	Jan	Feb	Mar	Apr	May	Jun	Jul	Aug	Sep	Oct	Nov	Dec	Av/Tot
Max (°C)	26	28	30	32	32	30	30	30	31	30	30	30
Min (°C)	13	10	20	23	25	25	25	25	25	24	20	16	21
Rain (mm)	11	12	32	80	293	771	993	780	443	275	63	33	3786

Founded in 1798, Cox's Bazar was named after Lieutenant Hiram Cox, who was sent by the British East India Company to settle the area with Magh refugees from the Arakan Hills when they were captured by the Burmese. The town is the administrative centre of the district, but it is primarily visited as a holiday resort with an excellent surfing beach, backed by hills. The 120 km stretch at *Inani* is claimed to be the world's longest sandy beach. The town is frequently hit by cyclones, and was devastated by the cyclone of April 30 1991.

The town has retained the Burmese *Mogh* inheritance in its people (up to two thirds of the population) who have kept their religion and culture alive. You can visit the Buddhist monastery, the *Aggameda Khyang* which is in active use by the community and has monks in residence. Many of the houses are built in Burmese style on stilts. The shops nearby sell typical Burmese handicrafts, handwoven cloth, shell crafts and jewellery. The tribal people still continue make *cheroots*! Buddhists here celebrate their annual *Water Festival* from 13-18 April as in other parts of SE Asia.

The *Karpupannya Emporium* on Motel Rd has a good selection of handicrafts. There is a busy fish market – the local catch is excellent.

Hotels Most are on Motel Rd. The BPC Holiday Complex has a variety of accommodation to offer. **B** *Hotel Shaibal*, T 202. 22 a/c rm in a modern 3 storey building. Rec. **B** *Honeymoon Cottages*, T 274. 5 a/c cottages. **C** *Motel Upal*, T 258. 19 a/c and 19 non a/c rm. **D** *Probal*, T 211. 36 rm. **D** *5 cottages* with 2 twin rm each.T 274. The shared facilities include 3 restaurants, *Sagarika* being the best, tourist office and travel at the Shaibal, indoor pool, tennis, squash, indoor games, walk-ways to the beach. **D** *Hotel Sayeman*, Forest Colony Rd, T 231. Restaurant, pool, exchange, Biman office. Central. **E** *Youth Inn*, T 274. Dormitory accom for 94 with shared bath, at the end of Motel Rd nr the beach. Reservations also at BPC Head Office, Dhaka, T 325155.

Air services 4 weekly flights to and from Dhaka, via Chittagong.

Road Direct BRTC buses from Fulbaria Bus Stand, Dhaka. Several from Chittagong, 0500, returning from Cox's Bazar, 1500.

You can get to the *Himachari Beach* nr Cox's Bazar with buses which go most of the way, the road passing through low hills. The road S to the Burmese border at *Teknaf* is often closed to foreigners.

DHAKA TO KHULNA, JESSORE AND THE INDIAN BORDER

The route from Dhaka to Khulna runs W along embankments raised above the surrounding plain. Rice and occasional fields of jute dominate the view, interspersed with hamlets raised above the normal flood level, while the channels still have water fishermen who perch precariously on bamboo poles, from which nets are draped for the catch. Aricha Ghat, the busiest of Bangladesh's ferry crossings, serves the route both to Goalundo Ghat for the SW and Nagarbari for the NW.

At this point where the Ganga and the Jamuna join to become the Padma the river stretches almost as far as the eye can see during the wet season. The ferry terminus at Goalundo is moved up to 25 km as the flood waters recede. The totally flat terrain of the moribund delta is marked by endless scattered hamlets, with coconut groves and ponds, occasional large lakes or sometimes dried out by the start of summer, but which are a haven for wildlife when full, especially birds. The Indian border at Benapol, 37 km from Jessore, is only 64 km from Calcutta.

The road goes NW out of Dhaka to **Savar** (21 km), with a noted health clinic and a **National Martyrs' Memorial**, which commemorates martyrs of the war of Independence. On 26 Mar, *Independence Day,* there is a laying of wreaths ceremony at the Memorial. The weekly *hat* (fair) attracts large crowds of villagers and you will see a colourful sight of stalls selling sweetmeats, fruits, vegetables, fish and handicrafts. The Jahangir Nagar University campus is nearby.

Continue through **Nayarhat** (21 km) and **Manikganj** (22 km) to **Aricha** (26 km). This is the terminus of Bangladesh's busiest ferry crossing, linking the main road to Dhaka with Khulna and Jessore in the SW and Rajshahi, Dinajpur and Rangpur in the NW. There can be long queues to get on to the ferry, lorries sometimes having to wait for days. Cars and buses have priority. There is no real town, but there are tea and refreshment stalls by the ferry ghat. The ferry to the SW goes downstream across the Padma to **Goalundo Ghat**. The actual terminus is shifted from season to season by as much as 20 km, temporary roads being extended to the ferry terminal in use at the time.

From the ferry ghat follow the road to **Faridpur** (26 km) a small town with the Orankandi Hindu Temple in the town centre and several others. It is the birthplace of Sheikh Mujibur Rahman, the Father of the Nation. The *Hotel Luxury,* Goal Chamot, does not live up to its name but has rm with bath and a restaurant. The road passes through the very small towns of **Kumarkalighat** (28 km) and **Magura** (10 km) to **Jhenida** (29 km), then turns S to

Jessore (47 km).

	Jan	Feb	Mar	Apr	May	Jun	Jul	Aug	Sep	Oct	Nov	Dec	Av/Tot
Max (°C)	25	28	33	36	35	33	31	31	32	32	29	26	31
Min (°C)	10	13	18	23	24	25	25	25	25	23	16	11	20
Rain (mm)	14	22	35	88	189	275	314	307	188	136	22	2	1592

Jessore is an important junction for road routes. It has some medieval mosques, particularly the 6 domed Jama Masjid in Sailkupa, and is a market town for local produce. The road to Khulna runs SE out of the town, while the road to the Indian border at **Benapol** (37 km) follows the broad gauge railway line which originally went to Calcutta. The Benapol border is the main land crossing to India. Buses and minibuses go to the bus station at Benapol, still on the Bangladesh side of the border. Rickshaws are available for the 1 km distance to the border itself, and on the Indian side to go on to the railway station. Buses also run to Calcutta. **Warning** Regulations about the land crossing are subject to change. It is essential to enquire in Dhaka before making the land crossing. Arrive at the border before 1500, as crossing often takes time.

From Jessore the road goes SE, following the railway all the way to **Khulna**, 56 km (*Population* 950,000), the administrative centre for the SW district, bordering India and covered by dense jungle and marshland over ⅔rds of its area. The Sundarbans to the S are famous for their wildlife. The difficult access to the region, and its inhospitable topography, resulted in it remaining largely uninhabited until Hindu settlers were forced to leave their homes in the N with the arrival of Muslim invaders. To the S of Khulna it is impossible to travel without a boat. Considerable development work has taken place in the intensively cultivated land immediately N of the Sundarbans. The journey down any of the S flowing distributaries of the Ganga such as the **Betna**, the **Sibsa**, the **Pusur** or the **Bhadra** Rivers gives a view of the river-based way of life, coupled with the cultivation of land often now protected from salt water incursions at high tide by a series of embankment projects.

	Jan	Feb	Mar	Apr	May	Jun	Jul	Aug	Sep	Oct	Nov	Dec	Av/tot
Max (°C)	26	29	33	35	34	32	31	31	32	31	29	27	31
Min (°C)	14	16	21	24	25	26	26	26	26	24	19	15	22
Rain(mm)	2	3	55	134	113	315	518	497	189	41	48	7	1922

The river port in Khulna, the District Headquarters, and the development of **Mongla** (formerly Chalna) as a sea port have encouraged the location of small industries, making it the 3rd largest industrial city in Bangladesh. It remains a town without a distinguishable form or character, but is one of the termini for the Rocket steamship journey from Dhaka. The Sundarbans to the S are a tourist attraction, while Khulna is a centre for the jute industry, fish and shrimp processing and the manufacture of newsprint, cable and matches.

Hotels **D** *Hotel Holiday*, N Jessore Rd. a/c rm. Restaurant, bar, pool. **D** *Rupsa International*, Jessore Rd, T 61563. 30 rm, some a/c. **D** *Selim*, 33 Shamshur Rahman Rd, T 20109. 11 rm with bath, a/c suite. Restaurant, bar. **E** *Park*, Khulna Bazaar Rd. T 20990. Rm with bath. Restaurant. **E** *Hotel Royal*, T 21638.

Restaurants Outside hotels, are several Chinese Restaurants, mostly on Lower Jessore Rd.

The Hotel Selim has **Tourist Information**. There is a branch of the Sonali **Bank,** and the New Market on N Jessore Rd has handicrafts shops.

Important services Police, T 20220. Sadar **Hospital**, T 20133. Divisional Forest Officer, T 20665.

Air services Biman flights twice a day between Dhaka via Jessore, and once a week between Chittagong via Jessore. Biman office, N Jessore Rd, T 61020.

Rail To Rajshahi *Kopotakkho Exp,* 715, daily except Fri, 0830, 6 hr; *Mahanando Exp,* 15, daily, 1400, 8 hr.

Road **Buses** to Dhaka via Jessore, and to Bogra and Rajshahi via Ishurdi. To Mongla, (if you are visiting the Sundarbans) buses from W bank of Rupsa River, which you cross from the ghat at the end of Khan Jahan Ali Rd. Across the river you can pick up a **taxi** or baby taxi (**autorickshaw**) but ask for the boat ghat on the opp bank which is closer to the Rly if you are catching a minibus. **Note** Make sure you have a **permit** before leaving Khulna (see below).

River Daily 'Rocket Ferry' service to **Dhaka**, 0600, 22 hr approx. Daily to **Mongla**, 2 hr. The BIWTC ferry is nr the Rly Station to the NE of the town. 'Rocket' Booking Office, T 21532.

Excursions

Bagerghat (40 km SE of Khulna, its name suggesting tiger territory), on the N edge of the Sudarbans, was once the prosperous mint town of

Khalifatabad, founded by the Sufi saint/Chief, Khan Jalan Ali, who brought Islam to the inhospitable S of the country in the mid-15th century. He is believed to have built about 360 impressive mosques, brick paved roads radiating to neighbouring towns, tanks (with stepped *ghats* provide salt-free water), bridges, palaces and mausolea. You can still see the ruins of several of these, including the **Shait Gumbad Mosque** (misleadingly named, '60 dome mosque') nearby. In fact it has 77 small domes and 4 corner turrets. It is the country's largest standing brick mosque and the best example of the Khanjehani style of architecture, which combined the imperial style of Delhi with the indigenous style of Bengal.

Built in 1459, the simplicity and starkness of this large, fortress-like mosque, with 2 m thick walls and almost separate corner turrets with rounded domes, are reminders of the Tughlaq style of architecture. The vast hall with its 7 aisles with 11 bays with impressive arches, the numerous domes supported by stone colonnades are best seen with the sun filtering through in the morning. The central line of 7 Bengali *'chala'* domes and terracotta decorations around the *mihrab* to the W and on the plain facade, and the curved battlements give away the influence of local architecture. There is a large freshwater tank behind, called **Ghora Dighi**, with coconut palms on 3 banks.

Three other single domed mosques- the **Bibi Begni** and the **Sringar** and **Chunakhola** mosques, built in the same style, with thick walls and corner turrets, are nearby.

Along the narrow road from the group, is the **mausoleum** of Khan Jahan Ali. A 14 m square plain structure with a single hemispherical dome, it has 4 circular, faceted corner towers with a large tank, **Thakur Dighi**, to the S. The stone and brick steps lead up to the stone sarcophagus which is engraved with verses from the Quran, while the stepped terraces are decorated with coloured tiles with religious calligraphy, dating the death of the saint in 1459. The shrine and attached mosque attract large numbers of pilgrims. They stand on the area raised by the excavated earth from the building of the vast tank which has several, apparently harmless, marsh mugger crocodiles.

The other ruins, some with 9 or 10 domes, here show the same characteristic architectural style and include the remains of the single domed **Ranvijoypur Mosque** which has the country's largest dome measuring 11 m.

Rail Several slow trains, approx every 90 min, from Khulna from about 0730, stop at Shait Gombad (2 hr 30 min) before Bagerhat. Rickshaws to mausoleum and other mosques, but fix rate first allowing for waiting time. **Minibuses** are faster and more frequent (15 min), but very crowded, and for return journey you should board at Bagerghat to be sure of a seat (instead of attempting to board at Shait Gombad).

Mongla, 38 km S of Khulna is the country's 2nd sea-port and the point you board motor launches to visit the forests. You can either take the 2 hr river boat from Khulna or cover the distance by road on the Khulna-Mongla Highway by first crossing the Rupsa river from the ghat at the end of Khan Jahan Ali Rd (see above).

The Sundarbans

To visit the *Sundarbans National Park*, you can hire a private motor launch, speed boat, a country boat or a Mongla Port Authority boat. Alternatively travel on a package tour (see below).

Literally meaning the 'beautiful forest', the Sundarbans are in the SW of Khulna district. They cover nearly 3,600 sq km. The vegetation is dominated by the *Sundari* tree (Heriteria fomes) which grows well in marshland, reaching a height of 25 m and is a rich source of timber for export. Its straight strong trunk makes it suitable for the building industry as well as for shipbuilding while the wood of *gewa* (Excoecaria agallocha) is used for newsprint. You will also see the *goran* (Ceriops roxburghiana) **mangroves**. Going down the rivers you will see boats carrying huge loads of timber being rowed slowly up to the port by teams of 4 or more men.

The Sundarbans form the **largest block** of littoral forest, across islands intersected by hundreds of shifting creeks. The tidal forest is spread across nearly 300 km of coastline which penetrates over 100 km inland in places and is bounded by Bagerhat, Khulna and Satkhira Dt in the N; Bay of Bengal in the S; Baleswar river, Perojpur, Barisal Dt in the E; Raimangal and Hariahnanga rivers (border) in the W.

Best season – Nov-Mar (Monsoons Jun-Sep). Average annual rainfall is 1700 mm so it always feels humid. When the tide is out the land is about 2 m above water, but at high tide, which comes in at 50 kph, the forest floats on water.

National Park has a fascinating environment of mangrove swamps, harbouring the world famous **Royal Bengal Tiger**, herds of spotted deer, crocodiles, wild boar, rhesus monkeys, lizards and pythons. The very rich birdlife includes a variety of snipes, heron, cranes, coots, yellow-lags, wood cocks, sandpipers and migratory water fowl from great distances. There are excellent opportunities for viewing the wildlife, and for photography, wild call recording, boating and also for watching the local fishermen, woodcutters and honey-collectors. It is also of particular interest to the botanist and the painter.

The principal means of transport is the boat – there are few forest paths or trails – and you will have the chance to watch the local people earning their livelihood in the forest. You will pass local boats carrying daily necessities like fresh water in large earthen vessels, *gol* leaves and bamboo reeds. In Apr and May, you can watch honey collectors working in groups to locate hives. The forest produces good timber – woodcutters either live on boats or make temporary dwellings about 3 m off the ground, or suspend shelters from branches, to protect themselves from wildlife on land and water.

In the **Chandpai** district the fishermen who live in large boats with thatched roofs have trained *otters* to catch fish which are driven into nets placed at the mouth of a stream. In **Dublar Char**, with its herds of spotted deer, fishermen from Chittagong arrive from mid-Oct and stay until mid-Feb. They fish day and night for 3 months when the harvest from the sea is rich with shrimps, which they can sell at points with cold stores. They also catch fish which they then dry.

Permits You must apply in writing in advance to the Divisional Forest Office, Circuit Rd, Khulna, T 20665. Entry fees, boat tickets are payable to the relevant range offices. Shooting of certain bird species is permitted with permits from the Divisional Forest Officer. **Warning** Hunting of animals is prohibited. **Note** For commercial photography, fees vary for Movie (Tk 5,000), Video (Tk 4,000) and Still (Tk 1,000).

Advice You should be vaccinated against cholera, take anti-malarial and carry anti-diarrhoeal medication. In addition take plenty of insect repellent cream, **drinking water**, green coconuts (nutritious, thirst quenching and safe) and thick rubber soled boots. If you are travelling independently, you would do well to take a guide.

Tours *Bangladesh Parjatan* offers inclusive packages from Dhaka from Oct-Mar, min 10 persons (US$180 for 3-day tour). Enquiries to Manager (Tours), BPC, 233 Airport Rd, Tejgaon, Dhaka 1215, T 325155. Private tour companies also operate eg *Intraco*, Red Cross Building, 2nd Fl, 114 Motijheel CA, T 250075 (US$30-110 per day. 6-day tour); *The Guide*, 47 New Eskaton Rd, Gr Fl, T 400511.

River From Dhaka, the Rocket Steamer takes about 22 hr to **Mongla** and **Khulna**. Reservations: Dhaka T239779; Khulna T 21532. Journey time varies with the tides but usually motor launches take 6-10 hr from Mongla to **Hiron Point**

or **Katka**. The 'Rockets' are old British paddle steamers with a choice of fares for the different classes! The First Class ticket offers one of the most relaxing and attractive journeys in Bangladesh, with beautiful river scenes. Dolphins are common, and there are interesting ports of call such as Barisal, where something of town and river life can be seen from the boat.

Hiron Point (Nilkamal) formerly Heron Point, is where river pilots are picked up by large ocean going vessels who need to be guided up the Pusur channel. You will see deer, monkeys and crocodiles and it offers good bird watching. **Hotels** 3 storey Port Authority *Rest House*. A/c rm, restaurant, bar. Book in advance.

Other islands include *Katka*, where grassy meadows stretch from Kachi-Khali (Tiger Point). Deer, tiger, crocodiles, monkeys and birds are found. Forest Dept *Rest House*. Book in advance. *Kolna Island* also has deer and tiger.

DHAKA TO PABNA, RAJSHAHI, AND RANGPUR

From Dhaka take the road to Aricha (90 km: see above). Take the ferry crossing to *Nagarbari Ghat*. Current timings are listed as follows, but check locally: Dep Aricha **to Nagarbari**: 0600, 0830,1000,1300,1500,1700. Dep Nagarbari **to Aricha**: 0600,1000,1200,1400,1700,1900

From the ferry terminal the road runs through the small town of **Kashinatpur** (10 km). The direct road to **Bogra** via **Siraijgonj** goes off to the N – see below. To its E is the great Brahmaputra Right Bank embankment scheme, which runs N for over 220 km, a colossal scheme designed to protect the lowlying land to the W of the river from annual flooding.

The road to *Pabna* (40 km) goes due W. The town stands on the N bank of the Ganga. It has a population of 105,000, but still gives the impression of a small town with few facilities. It has some medieval Mosques and temples, but there is little to see. **Shahzadpur Mosque** (1528) has a single dome.

Continue to **Dissuria** (22 km). *Ishurdi airport* is 8 km to the N. The road runs N to *Natore* (45 km) then W to Rajshahi (44 km) The Rajshahi division shares a border with India, partly demarcated by the wide Ganga river, and partly through jungle. To the N it reaches the foothills of the Himalayas. The district town of *Rajshahi*, 36 km (*Population* 300,000) is situated on the Ganga – the threat from flooding has been met by a dyke. The Farakka Barrage nr the border with India, controls the flow of the river, and has been the source of continuing disagreements between the Indian and Bangladeshi governments.

Rajshahi literally 'Royal territory', flourished during the Buddhist Pala period (8th century) and has in nearby Paharpur the famous ancient centre of Buddhist learning. It was also the regional capital of the Khilji dynasty and the Afghans who followed. However, the Mughals neglected the town, and it was not until the 19th century that the British regenerated it, for its economic potential, developing its sugarcane and cotton production.

The archaeological finds nearby, bear witness to the glorious reign of the Pala kings who until the 11th century kept Buddhism alive, long after it had waned in the rest of the subcontinent. Silk production here has a long history, and the flourishing silk trade with China is linked with the spread of Buddhism to the Far East. Today, it remains the centre of the country's silk industry. The **Sericulture Research Institute** (10 min walk from the Parjatan Motel) is on the outskirts of the city, and there are jute mills, a university, and medical, agricultural and engineering colleges. It was once the centre of the indigo trade. The area produces excellent mangoes and lichees, with sugarcane an important cash crop.

The **Varendra Research Museum** housed in an interesting building combining Hindu and Buddhist architectural styles, within a pleasant garden, displays archaeological exhibits dating from 3,000 BC. The **Sericulture Display Centre** is nr the station and has a good selection of silk articles.

Hotels *Parjatan Motel*, Abdul Majid Rd, T 2393. 49 rm, 8 a/c with bath. Restaurant, bar, Tourist Office. The *Rajmahal Hotel*, Shaheb Bazaar Rd, close to the Bus Stations, is cheaper but has rm with bath. Other simple hotels near the bus station.

Air services Biman flights to **Dhaka** (Tues, Th, Sun). Town office, Sagarpara, Ghoramora. Airport at Noahatai, 8 km from Rajshahi.

Rail To Dhaka *Jamuna Exp*, 746, 2050, 13 hr 45 min; *Padma Exp*, 706, daily except Sun, 0615, 13 hr 10 min. **Chittagong** *Rajshahi Exp*, 9, daily except Wed, 1215, 21 hr 20 min.

Bus Station is on the Natore Rd, not far from the river. Buses for **Bogra** leave from the stop on Shaheb Bazaar Rd and for **Kusumba Mosque** from the stop nr the station.

Excursions from Rajshahi The *Kusumba Mosque* (46 km) was built during the reign of Ghiasuddin Shah I in 1558. It is rectangular mosque built of Rajmahal blackstone with 6 domes over the six sections of the prayer hall which has slender pillars and 3 mihrabs on the W wall with very elaborate decoration in front with pilasters and cusped arches. The Ladies Gallery on the upper floor has some fine decoration. Buses from Rajshahi, nr Rly Station.

From Rajshahi the road, returns E to Natore (44 km) then goes NE to *Bogra* (54 km), the most convenient base from which to visit the important archaeological sites at **Sherpur**, **Mahastanagar** and **Paharpur**. The small district itself has large deposits of coal and lime and in addition sugar, textile and chemical industries are well established. It also produces good handloom cloth and rice and the local sweetmeats and yoghurt.

Hotels D *Parjatan Hotel*, Sherpur Rd, 6 km S of town, T 6753. If travelling by bus ask to be dropped off at the motel. 17 rm, 7 a/c. Restaurant. BPC's simple **E** *Drivers' Inn*, has 8 units. Few others in centre of town.

Excursions from Bogra *Mahastanagar*, (17 km N or Bogra) is on W bank of the Karatoa river. It is considered to be the oldest capital of the region having been identified with the 3rd century BC Mauryan capital Pundra Nagara, which remained the administrative centre until the 15th century, and hence is of great historical interest. The archaeological site, dating from the 8th century, raised about 5 m above the surrounding plain, covers an area of 1,700 m by nearly 1,500 m which is fortified by ramparts and a moat on 3 sides and protected by the river to the E. Isolated mounds with ancient ruins have been discovered within a few km of the fortifications, among them are Govinda Bhita Temple, Khodai Pathar Mound and 2 *kundas* or *tankas*.

The brick built **Govinda Bhita Temple,** 1.5 km from the main site, is a pilgrimage centre for Hindus who come to take a holy bath in the nearby river, every Apr and once in 12 years in Dec. The site museum displays finds here and at nearby Sherpur and includes terracotta objects, toys, gold ornaments and coins (some ancient square ones). The ornamental arch in the museum garden comes from Sherpur. The simple Archaeological *Rest House* is across the road.

Sherpur has an example of the Early Mughal period in the 3-domed **Kherua** mosque (1582) built in outlying areas which show the transitional phase when the imperial style combined with the local.

From the small market town of *Jaipurhat* (which has a railway station on the line from Ishurdi to Saidpur or Rangpur), you can reach Parharpur (5 km) during the dry season on a rough track. A private vehicle is very helpful. The bus journey is over 2 hr, with a 45 min walk at the end. Enquire in Bogra for details.

Paharpur 56 km W of Bogra, 5 km from Paharpur, where the largest Buddhist monastery S of the Himalayas has been excavated. It first attracted attention in the early 19th century. The 7th century site is spread over 11 ha, and the monastery complex consists of a square courtyard enclosed in 5 m thick walls rising to over 4 m in height. The elaborate entrance gateway is on the N wall with 45 monks' cells with 44 cells on each of the other sides, several of which have decorated pedestals while there are scenes of contemporary life recorded on terracotta tiles. A system of drainage with stone water spouts discharging water into the courtyard can be seen. The kitchen and refectory appears to have been housed in a separate building to the W. The rectangular building to the S, joined by a causeway, may have been for washing and toilet.

The 20 m high brick built **Somapur Vihara** temple at the centre of the courtyard follows the pattern of the pyramidal cruciform structures of Burma or Java. It dominates the surrounding countryside, measuring 280 m on each side and has *pradakshina paths* (circumambulatories) on 2 levels. To the E there appears to have been a small model of it. From the finds at the site, it is obvious that after the Buddhists, Jains and finally Hindus occupied the vihara and left their mark in decorations and deities. The excavations unearthed a rich collection of pottery, mostly dating from the 10-12th centuries, sandstone and basalt carvings, images of the Buddha (including a large bronze from the Gupta period, cast by the *cire perdu* or 'lost wax' process), clay seals and stupas, statues of Hindu deities, terracotta plaques typical of the area depicting human figures, birds and animals, coins, copper plate inscriptions and ornamental bricks. Also of great interest are the everyday objects found, including cooking pots, grinding stones, toys, seals, and beads.

A selection is displayed in the small **museum** here with the rest is in the Varendra Research Museum in Rajshahi.' The site museum is open daily from 0900-1200, 1400-1700 and 1000-1700 on Fri. There is a basic *Rest House* nearby, with a cook who will prepare a meal if you bring some food.

400 m E of the Vihara are the ruins **Satyapir Bhita** another Buddhist temple complex. The main rectangular temple has a large pillared hall and a stupa which contained votive offerings.

The road N from Bogra goes across the dead flat land of the Brahmaputra Right Bank Irrigation and flood protection scheme through **Rahbal** (34 km) and **Palashbari** (28 km) to

Rangpur (53 km).

	Jan	Feb	Mar	Apr	May	Jun	Jul	Aug	Sep	Oct	Nov	Dec	Av/Tot
Max (°C)	24	27	31	35	34	32	32	32	32	31	29	25	30
Min (°C)	11	13	17	22	24	24	26	26	26	22	16	13	20
Rain (mm)	2	3	55	134	113	315	518	497	189	41	48	7	1922

The town stands on an abandoned course of the Tista River, the **Ghaghat River**. In the distance the snow clad Himalayan peaks, including Kangchendzonga, are frequently visible. The town was established by the Mughals, but they thought it so unhealthy that they always abandoned it for Murshidabad during the rainy season. It was notorious for its bad drainage, and consequently for its damp, malaria and rheumatic diseases. The 1897 earthquake seemed to change all that. Although it demolished most of the buildings, it also brought some benefits. The natural drainage improved dramatically as the Tista changed its course, and as two *bhils* (lakes) silted up, the whole area became much drier.

Today the town is a collection of villages, grouped together for administrative purposes. It has a heliport, radio station, cigar factory and medical college. It is also the home town of the former President Ershad.

To the W is the town of **Dinajpur** (63 km), near the Indian border and the Headquarters of Dinajpur district. It has a number of educational institutions, and a much above average literacy rate.

	Jan	Feb	Mar	Apr	May	Jun	Jul	Aug	Sep	Oct	Nov	Dec	Av/Tot
Max (˚C)	24	26	32	34	33	32	32	32	32	31	28	24	30
Min (˚C)	9	12	16	21	23	25	26	26	26	22	16	11	19
Rain (mm)	10	13	16	47	187	346	390	354	300	137	11	1	1812

At its centre is the large maidan, with the Magistrate's Courts, and Government offices. The new Circuit House is opposite. The Station Club, also in the Maidan, probably dates from about 1820. The **Khwaja Nazimuddin Muslim Hall and Library**, set up in 1932, has an interesting collection. There are several small bazaars and markets. The town has Hindu shrines to Ganesh (in **Ganeshtala**) and Kali (in **Kalitala**), both thought to be quite old.

From Dinajpur the road goes N to *Thakurgaon* (50 km). A district headquarters, Thakurgaon is an educational centre, with an attractive high school built in 1904. There is an old Vishnu temple at Govindanagar on the opposite bank of the River Tangan from the town.

INFORMATION FOR VISITORS

Documents

Passports and visas A valid passport is needed by all foreign nationals. **Visas** are also need by nationals of most countries – except those from many countries of Africa (not S Africa), the Caribbean and S Pacific islands, and in addition from Bhutan, Cyprus, Fiji, Malta and the Vatican. Contact the nearest Bangladesh Diplomatic mission for details.

No visa is required for up to 15 days' stay for nationals of Australia, Austria, Belgium, Canada, Denmark, Finland, France, Germany, Greece, Indonesia, Italy, Luxembourg, Maldives, Norway, The Netherlands, Nepal, The Philippines, Portugal, Sweden, Spain, Switzerland, Thailand, USA, provided they hold return or onward tickets. If the stay exceeds 15 days, visas are obtainable from the Director Gen of Immigration and Passport or the nearest Regional Passport Office. Visas are issued by Bangladesh diplomatic missions abroad, or trade commissions. All foreigners must fill up a disembarkation card at the entry point. Registration and an exit permit is only required for Pakistani nationals.

The cost of visas varies according to the nationality of the applicant and the type of visa applied for. Arrangements for visa application and collection vary from office to office, and should be checked by phone with the relevant office. Tourists from countries which do not have Bangladeshi representatives may apply to resident British representatives. Theoretically it is possible for tourists who are in India to obtain visas in Delhi or Calcutta. In practice visas are often refused by the Calcutta Deputy High Commission on apparently arbitrary grounds. It is very strongly recommended to obtain visas in your home country whenever possible.

Work permits No visitor is allowed to work without a permit. This should be applied for in your country of origin.

Bangladesh representations overseas Australia 11 Moineaux Pl, Farrer ACT 2607, T 062 861200. **Belgium** 29-31 Rue Jacques, Jordaens, 1050 Brussels, T 6405500. **Bhutan** PO Box 178, Thimphu, T 2539. **Canada** 85 Range Rd, Suite 402, Ottawa, Ontario, T 613 236 0138. **China** 42 Guang Hua Lu, Beijing, T 522521. **France** 5 Square Petrarque, 75016

Paris, T 47049435. **Germany** Bonner Str 48, 5300 Bonn 2, T 0228 352525. **Hong Kong** Rm 3807 China Resources Bldg, 26 Harbour Rd, T 5728278. **India** 56 Ring Rd, Lajpat Nagar 111, New Delhi 110024, T 615668. **Italy** Via Antonio Bertoloni 14, Rome 00197. **Japan** 7-45 Shirogane, 2 chome, Minato-ku, Tokyo 108, T 03 442 1501. **Kenya**, 35A Riverside Drive, Nairobi, 43687. **Malaysia** 204-1, Jalan Ampang 50450, Kuala Lumpur, T 242371. **Nepal** Bhagabati Bahal, GPO 789, Kathmandu, T 414943. **Pakistan** House 24, St 28, F-6/1 Islamabad, T 826885. **Philippines** 150 Legaspi St, 5th Fl, JEC Bldg, Legaspi Vill, Makati Metro, Manila, T 815 5010. **Saudi Arabia** Mr Abdur Rahman Al-Zaban's house, N of Arabia St, Sualimaniya, Riyadh, T 4465 5300. **Singapore** 101 Thomson Rd, 0607 Goldhill Sq, Singapore 1130, T 2550075. **Sri Lanka** 207/1 Dharmapala Mawatha, Colombo 7, T 595963. **Sweden** Grev Turegaten 7,S-11446, Stockholm, T 08 109555. **Switzerland** 65 Rue de Laussane, 1202 Geneva, T 325940. **Thailand** 8 Charoenmitr Sukhumvit 63, Bangkok, T 391 8069 70. **UK** 128 Queens Gate, London SW7 5JA, T 918016. **USA** 2001 Wisconsin Av, NW Suite 300, Washington DC 20007, T 202 342 8372 76. **USSR** 6 Semledelehski Pereulok, Moscow, T 246 76 00.

Heath regulations You are advised to get inoculated against cholera for your own safety. Yellow Fever vaccination is required for those coming from or passing through infected areas.

Travel

By air Bangladesh is connected by air with major cities in Europe, the United States and Australasia, as well as with several important cities in Asia. The national Biman Bangladesh Airlines connects Dhaka with most Middle Eastern capitals and in addition with Amsterdam, Athens, Bangkok, Bombay, Calcutta, Karachi, Kathmandu, Kuala Lumpur, London, Rangoon, Rome and Singapore. They often are able to offer non-stop flights and the cheapest fares.

Customs regulations The formalities on arrival in Bangladesh are straightforward. Disembarkation cards are handed out to passengers during the inward flight. The immigration form should be handed in at the immigration counter on arrival. The customs slip will be returned, for handing over to the customs on leaving the baggage collection hall. As is true throughout South Asia, you may need to be patient while clearing immigration. Facilities at Dhaka airport have been improved since the separate Tourists' Reporting Centre was opened, which in theory attempts to take care of Health, Immigration and Customs formalities swiftly.

Duty free allowances All reasonable items for personal use are allowed. One portable camera for still photography (value not exceeding Tk 6,000) and 5 rolls or 12 plates of film. Foreigners may bring in 200 cigarettes, 50 cigars or 250 gm of tobacco (or in combination). Foodstuffs, value not exceeding Tk 500. For non-Muslim foreigners, one bottle or 1/6 gal of alcoholic beverage (spirits, wines, beer).

Prohibited and restricted items Foreign visitors may take out souvenirs and handicrafts up to the value of Tk 3,000 free of tax. Importing dangerous drugs, live plants, gold coins, gold and silver bullion, and silver coins not in current use, is either banned or subject to strict regulation.

Arrival There are separate queues for foreigners at Dhaka International Airport, though the distinction is not always obvious, as some immigration officers seem to be willing to process anyone. If the foreigners queue is long and slow moving it is worth trying your luck on shorter queues. The procedure conforms to a normal international pattern, with immigration first, followed by luggage collection and customs. For currency exchange there are branches of several **banks** in the ground floor lounge area.

Note that baggage trolleys are available free and in theory porters should only carry bags when asked. They are not allowed to ask for tips, though they are very pressing if given half a chance. You are well advised to use a trolley and choose your own travel arrangements into the city rather than have the question decided by a porter.

Departure Tax Tk 200 for international and Tk 20 for domestic departures.

Connections to the city The main hotels have a counter just outside the customs gate before passing through into the lounge. They will make travel arrangements into town for their guests and will take reservations. It is possible to hire a limousine taxi (book in the lounge), or to take a taxi, a baby taxi or a bus from outside.

Internal Travel

Air services Biman Bangladesh has flights connecting Dhaka with Chittagong, Cox's Bazar, Sylhet, Jessore, Rajshahi and Saidpur. Fares are very reasonable and flights usually get fully booked, so if you intend flying within the county book in advance.

Train Bangladesh's rail network is divided between the broad gauge system, which used to connect W Bangladesh with Calcutta, and the metre gauge system, built to provide a route for tea exports from the NE through Chittagong. The routes are often very roundabout, and train journeys are slow and crowded. They still have their devotees. Rail timetables and signs at stations are usually in Bengali but you will be directed if you ask in English in towns. '*Express*' trains are not necessarily the fastest available. In recent years Bangladesh Railways has been receiving support from the Canadian Government, including the purchase of General Motors locomotives.

Concessions are available to students (50%), tourists and tour groups (25%) when travelling by 1st Class a/c or 1st Class. Enquiries: Commercial Manager or Divisional Rly Officer in Dhaka and Chittagong Rly stations.

Road Considerable efforts are being made to improve Bangladesh's rudimentary road network. New bridges have been opened between Dhaka and Comilla on the main route to the eastern part of the country. The journey time for the 150 km between the 2 cities can be expected to come down to under 3 hours when the bridges are completed, and Sylhet in the NE will also become more accessible. The main road to Mymensingh in the N is fair and does not include any ferry crossings. However, road routes to the W all involve crossing the Padma (Ganga) and/or Jamuna (Brahmaputra) which can be very time consuming.

Buses Bangladesh Road Transport Corporation and private companies link the major towns in the country. Inter-city services tend to run from early morning to late afternoon and then resume for a few hours in the late evening. Mini-buses, ordinary and video coaches often stop frequently to pick up passengers en-route. Buses can get crowded and uncomfortable.

Car Hire cars (only with driver) are obtainable through the Bangladesh Tourist Development Board. Cars can be imported provided you have a Carnet de Passage, have it registered in your home country and re-export it within the specified time.

Taxi Bangladesh Parjatan Taxis have fixed rates: Tk 65 per hr, Tk 7 per km plus 10% service. Private taxi rates are negotiable. **Baby taxis** in the towns (the equivalent of autorickshaws in India) are the most economical way of getting about quickly. Rates have to be negotiated.

River Transport The vast network of inland waterways has made this a popular mode of transport and a particular attraction for the visitor wanting to explore the S. Bangladesh Inland Water Transport Corpn (BIWTC) and private ferry companies operate scheduled services on the main routes. The BIWTC 'Rocket' Service runs on selected routes using old paddle steamers on which you book tickets for different classes! The service between Dhaka and Khulna (to visit the Sundarbans) is popular with tourists. Motor launches are often large, having 2 or even 3 decks. In addition, ordinary river boats are available in the countryside.

The flat bottomed, diesel powered ferries transporting passengers across rivers are sometimes laden with 50 buses, lorries and cars – the passenger ferries are usually equally crowded. The country boats, by contrast are either single or double sailed (triple for cargo boats). The sails are usually a patchwork of cloth stitched together, often picturesquely colourful. The boats are dependent on oars lashed to the sides, when the wind drops.

Travel tips Travelling is slower and more unpredictable in Bangladesh than in most other parts of S. Asia. Although the country is compact and flat, the huge and often unbridged rivers interrupt the road and rail networks. In the dry season a network of informal dust roads appears out of the mud of the wet season, but boats remain the only way of getting about in some areas of S Bangladesh throughout the year. Allow time for travelling by land or boat, and where possible book well in advance. Internal flights are often extremely heavily booked. Again, book well in advance. Although travel by train or boat is slow, it can also be very rewarding. Longer rail journeys in 1st class often have food and drink provided, but it always a good rule to travel with plenty of your own supplies.

Money

Currency Bangladesh's currency is the Taka. New notes are printed in denominations of Tk 500, 100, 50, 20, 10, 5, 2 though some Tk 1 notes are still in circulation (Tk 1000 notes are very unusual). The Taka is divided into 100 paise. Coins are minted in denominations of 100, 50, 25, 10, 5 and 1 Paise. It can be useful to keep a supply of change.

Money changing If you are staying in a major hotel you will be able to change money there 24 hours a day. However, if you want cash on arrival it is best to get it at the airport bank. Banks often give a substantially better rate of exchange than hotels.

When changing money anywhere in Bangladesh it is important to retain the **encashment certificate**. This gives proof of exchange through an authorized dealer. It allows you to change Bangladesh Taka back to your own currency on leaving the country (you are not allowed to take any Taka out of Bangladesh). It also enables you to use Taka to pay hotel and other bills for which payment in foreign exchange is compulsory. Airport tax on exit is Tk 200. Theoretically it is possible to change Taka back into dollars at the airport but the banks do not always have adequate change in dollars. It is best to have as few taka as possible to change at the airport itself.

Black market The laws prohibiting the export of Taka create a demand for exchangeable foreign currency. As in India, from time to time a premium may be offered for hard currencies by street corner dealers. In 1990 such premiums in most places were small. Changing money through unauthorised dealers is illegal and may be risky.

Travellers cheques Most travellers cheques are accepted without difficulty, but some organisations only accept travellers cheques from the biggest companies. They nearly always have to be exchanged in banks or hotels, and can only very rarely be used directly for payment. Identification documents, usually a passport, need to be shown. Except in hotels and at the airport, encashing travellers cheques nearly always takes up to half an hour and may take longer, so it is worth taking larger denomination travellers cheques and changing enough money to last for some days. Hotels will normally only cash travellers cheques for resident guests.

Credit cards Major credit cards are increasingly widely acceptable in the major centres, though in smaller cities, towns and villages it is still rare to be able to pay by credit card. Payment by credit card can be significantly more expensive than payment by cash. However shopping by credit card for items such as handicrafts, clothing, and carpets from larger dealers, does not mean that you have to accept the first price asked. Bargaining is still expected and essential. American Express cardholders can use their cards to obtain either cash or travellers cheques in Dhaka. Diners, Master Card and Visa are widely used.

Cost of Living In general the cost of living is comparable with that in India. The largest hotels are more expensive than in India but still cheaper than their equivalent in the West.

Tipping and bargaining When negotiating a fare for travelling by unmetered 'baby taxis' (3 wheelers) or cycle rickshaws, you will invariably be asked initially to pay more than is reasonable, so do bargain. If unsure, ask at the hotel desk for the fair rate.

In Govt Handicrafts Emporia and some 'Fixed price' shops you will not be expected to bargain but elsewhere, especially in bazaars, when buying souvenirs it is worth offering less than the asking price and reaching an agreed figure. As in the rest of S Asia, this is common practice.

Taxi drivers do not expect a tip but they will appreciate a small extra if it rounds off the fare. In larger restaurants pay about 10% of the bill as a tip, if service is not included. If it is already included, and you want to show your appreciation personally, you may wish leave a small amount for the waiter.

Shopping and best buys Handloom fabrics (silk and cotton), Dhakai Jamdani and printed saris, pink pearls, jute products, wood, brass, bamboo, cane, conch-shell and horn crafts, coconut masks, jewellery and dolls.

Other Essential Information

Official time Bangladesh Standard Time +6 hr GMT

Weights and measures Bangladesh uses Imperial measures.

Postal services The GPO in Dhaka operates a Poste Restante service, **see page 1374**. The YMCA also runs a similar service in Dhaka.

Telephone and telegraph services International Direct Dialling is available from Dhaka and the major cities. Approx charges for foreign calls per min: Tk 65 to UK, Tk 80 to USA, Tk 60 to Japan; NWD Tk 18; STD Tk 12. Local Tk 1.30 per call. In Chittagong local calls are Tk 15 per min and in Khulna Tk 11.

Business hours Govt Offices 0730-1400, Sat-Th. Closed Fri. Banks 0900-1300, Sat-Wed, 0930-1100 Th. Closed Fri. Shops 1000-2000.

Electricity 220 AC volts, 50 cycles.

Media Bangladesh Times and Bangladesh Observer are English language dailies and The Holiday a weekly. There are daily English broadcasts on radio and television.

Maps In addition to the Bartholomew 1:4 million map of South Asia, the Survey of Bangladesh publishes a 1:1m map and a four sheet 1:500,000 map of the country. Both are rather crude and unreliable. The Tourist Office map of the country is also not very accurate. The city map of Dhaka on their information sheet is of some help.

Hints on social behaviour Both men and women should dress modestly. Even in the towns it is unusual for men and women to meet socially outside the family. Bangladeshi Muslims use the same Urdu greeting as in Pakistan *Assalam alaikum* (peace be upon you), the response being *Walaikum salam* (Upon you also peace). These are appreciated as much as *Khudahafiz* at parting and *Dhonyobad* (thank you).

Accommodation The capital has two excellent International class hotels. Reasonably priced comfortable hotels are also available in Dhaka and some large towns; elsewhere, especially in places of tourist interest, the Bangladesh Parjatan Corporation (BPC) run a range of hotels, motels and cottages which vary from comfortable to basic. It is also possible to book in at government *Rest Houses*, which are often basic, when rooms are available.

The pricing categories used in this Handbook are as follows: **Note** Some international class hotels quote rates in US $ and some have deluxe suites and rm which are 2 or 3 times the price of the 'standard'. In addition 21% Excise Duty and 12.5% Service Charge is added. **AL** Double rm US$80 + **A** US$50-80 **B** US$25-50 **C** Tk 450-750 **D** Tk 200-450 **E** Tk 75-200 **F** Less than Tk 75.

Clothing Cottons in summer and cottons and light woollens in winter. Umbrella essential (and a raincoat preferably) during the monsoons: also useful against the strong sun.

Food and drink Bangladeshi food includes a variety of curried dishes. Fish – both fresh water and sea fish – are excellent. **Hilsa** is the most popular variety, which can be obtained smoked. Lobsters and prawns are common. Rice forms the staple food, during the winter supplemented by a range of vegetables. Pulao (rice and vegetables) and biriyani (normally rice and meat) are the favourite dishes, and various kebabs are also popular. Wheat has become increasingly widely available, and chapatis and puris can be excellent.

Bangalis make some very sweet sweets. One of the most delicious is *mishti doi*, a sweet yoghurt. If you like that kind of sweet, it is unbeatable. Bangladesh also has many varieties of tropical fruit. Apart from bananas most are seasonal – mangos, guavas, pineapples, jack fruit, litchis, pomelos.

Alcoholic drinks are sold in hotels to foreigners. Bottled soft drinks are widely available, and you can get tender coconut virtually anywhere – safe, clean and healthy. In the bigger hotels fresh lime soda – either sweet or salt – is very refreshing.

National holidays, fairs and festivals

The Bengali Era began when the Mughal emperor Akbar changed the Hijri calendar from a lunar to a solar one from the day he ascended the throne in 1556.

Feb 21 *Shahid Dibosh* Commemorates those who died on 21 Feb 1952 (including many students) in an effort to establish Bangla as the state language in place of Urdu. **March** 26 *Independence Day* Floral wreaths placed at martyrs' Monument at Savar. Colourful children's rally, tournaments, boat races throughout the country. Public buildings are illuminated. **April** 14 *Bengali New Year's Day* Many fairs in Dhaka and villages Cultural shows, music, dancing, tournaments, boat races. **May** May Day observed by business, labour and social organisations. Offices, factories and educational institutions close.

The **Muslim festivals** follow a lunar calendar. Dates of these public holidays are available from the Tourist Office each year. *Eid-e-Miladunnabi* Birth and death anniversary of the Prophet Mohammed celebrated on 12th Rabiul Awal. Public buildings are illuminated. The life and teachings of the Prophet are discussed at *milad mahfils*. *Shab-e-Barat* Special prayers are offered for mercy and grace by Muslims *Eid-ul-Fitr* Special day of rejoicing, marking the end of the month of fasting, Ramadan. Public prayers are held in large grounds before 9 in the morning. Marked by wearing festive clothes, visiting friends and relations and feasting. *Eid-ul-Azha* Marks the Hajj in Mecca. Public prayers held in the morning. Goats and other animals are sacrificed in remembrance of Ibrahim's preparedness to make the supreme sacrifice. *Muharram* 10th day of Muharram in memory of the martyrdom of Hussain at Karbala. *Biswa Istima*, a world Islamic congregation is held annually in Tungi Industrial Town, 19 km N of Dhaka. Special train and bus services for the 3 day 'conference' in Jan-Feb.

In addition to the Muslim Festivals **Hindus** celebrate *Durga Puja* and *Siva Ratri* **(see page 521)**, **Christians**, *Christmas* and **national celebrations** are held in memory of great Bengali poets, **Nazrul Islam** and **Rabindranath Tagore**.

Photography Many areas, even within towns and cities are 'military zones' where photography is not permitted. Take special care and check before taking photos near borders or any sensitive area, such as the Chittagong Hill Tracts.

Best time for a visit Dec to Mar is a beautiful season, with warm days but chilly nights. From Mar to May the temperatures rise sharply, and there is an increasing risk of storms towards the middle and end of May. June to Sep is wet across the whole country, and is the main flood season. Movement around the country is often disrupted. Although the floods recede through Oct-Nov, there is a risk of cyclones, especially in the S.

SRI LANKA

Official name *Sri Lanka Prajatantrika Samajawadi Janarajaya* (Democratic Socialist Republic of Sri Lanka)

National flag On a dark red field, within a golden border, a golden lion passant holding a sword in its right paw, and a representation of a bo-leaf coming from each corner; to its right, 2 vertical saffron and green stripes (representing Hindu and Muslim minorities), also within a golden border.

National Anthem *Namo Namo Matha* (We all stand together).

Basic indicators *Population* 1990 17 m Annual growth rate 1.6% Crude birth rate 2.4% Crude death rate 0.6% Urban population 21% Infant mortality 2.9% of live births *Area* 66,000 sq km *Population density* 256 per sq km *GNP per capita* US$400 *Average Annual growth rate* 1965-86 2.9% Long term debt 1970 US$317 m 1986 US$3,448 m.

GEOGRAPHY

Location Situated between 5°55'-9°51'N, Sri Lanka is at the heart of the Indian Ocean trading routes. After the opening of the route round the Cape of Good Hope by Vasco da Gama in 1498 the island was brought into direct contact with Western Europe. The opening of the Suez Canal in 1869 further strengthened the trading links with the West.

The land Geologically Sri Lanka is a continuation of the Indian Peninsula, from which it was separated less than 10,000 years ago by the 10 m deep and 35 km wide *Palk Straits*. Its area of 65,610 sq km makes Sri Lanka approximately the same size as W Virginia or a little smaller than Belgium and the Netherlands combined. It is 435 km long and at its broadest 225 km wide. One of its greatest assets is its 1,600 km of coastline, lined with fine sandy beaches, coral reefs and lagoons.

Virtually the whole of Sri Lanka is underlain by crystalline Pre-Cambrian rocks dating from between 570 m and 4,500 m years ago. Part of the old Gondwanaland block that originated in the S hemisphere as part of the great S

SRI LANKA

SA 400

African landmass, the island was carried across the Arabian Sea on the Indian Plate during the last 50 m years. Today these rocks form a highland massif with its centre of gravity somewhat to the SW of the geographical centre of the pear-shaped island.

From *Piduratalaga* (Sri Lanka's highest mountain at 2,524 m) and sacred *Adam's Peak*, the hills descend in 3 great steps of varying widths to the coastal lowlands. Formerly it was believed that these steps were the result of massive faulting, but recent evidence suggests that the very early folding of the ancient rocks, followed by erosion at different speeds, have formed the scarps and plateaus, often deeply cut by the rivers which radiate out from the centre of the island. In the central highlands the Khondalite series of metamorphosed sandstones, similar to the rocks of Orissa and Tamil Nadu, are widespread. The limestones of the Jaffna Peninsula in the N, cover most of the area. Underlain by a coral reef, Jaffna's limestone was laid down in shallow seas between 7 m and 26 m years ago. They provide the chief exception to the Pre-Cambrian rocks, some containing important gemstones.

Rivers and lakes Most of Sri Lanka's rivers are short, radiating out from the central highlands. The only river of any length is the Mahaweli Ganga which rises about 50 km S of Kandy and flows N then NE to the sea at Trincomalee, covering a distance of 320 km. The course of many of the rivers is adjusted to the strike of the rocks, the most notable being the N-S valley cut in the middle course of the Mahaweli Ganga. A number of the rivers have now been developed both for irrigation and power, the Victoria project of development on the Mahaweli Ganga being one of the biggest in Asia – and one of the most controversial. It has created Sri Lanka's largest lake.

Wildlife Sri Lanka's 24 wildlife sanctuaries are home to a wide range of native species eg elephants, leopard, sloth bear, the unique loris, a variety of deer and monkeys (particularly the purple-faced langur), the endangered wild boar, porcupines and ant-eaters in addition to reptiles including the marsh crocodile. The 3 largest sanctuaries are the National Parks at **Ruhuna**, **Wilpattu** and **Gal Oya**.

Among the 16 amphibians unique to the island are the ***Nanophrys frogs*** in the hills. Most of the fish are river or marsh dwelling – the trout, introduced by the British, being found in the cool streams of the Horton Plains.

The indigenous 240 (of the total of 440) species of butterflies are seen below 1,000 m and Mar/Apr is the period of seasonal migration. Sri Lanka is also the ornithologist's paradise with over 250 resident species, mostly found in the Wet Zone, including the Grackle, whistling thrush, yellow-eared Bulbul, Malkoha and brown-capped Babbler. The **Sinharaja Reserve** and the highland **Peak Wilderness Sanctuary** are famous. The winter migrants come from distant Siberia and W Europe, the reservoirs attracting vast numbers of waterbirds (stilts, sandpipers, terns and plover, as well as herons, egrets and storks). The forests attract species of warblers, thrushes, cuckoo and many others. The **Kumana** in the E, and **Bundala** (famed for flamingoes), **Kalametiya** and **Wirawila** in the S, all with lagoons, are the principal Bird Sanctuaries. The Wildlife Conservation programme is undertaken by the government with an office in Colombo.

CLIMATE

Rainfall Sri Lanka is divided into 2 unequal climatic regions. About three quarters of the island – the entire N and E region – comprises the "dry zone". In the rainshadow of the central highlands during the SW monsoon, this area only receives most of its rain during the Oct-Dec period of the retreating monsoon. Despite the term 'dry zone', during this period it can be very wet indeed, some areas receiving over 1,000 mm. The SW quarter of the island receives rain both from the NE and from the SW monsoon. The wet SW lowlands around Colombo receive over 2,250 mm a year, while in the wetter highlands the total rises to over 5,500 mm. Although the timing of the monsoons is very irregular, the wetter times of year are also extremely humid, producing a very sticky atmosphere.

Temperatures Apart from the contrast between wet and dry zones the major climatic differences reflect contrasts in altitude. Nuwara Eliya, at over 2,200 m, experiences night frost. On the plains temperature reflects the degree of cloud cover, but maximum temperatures are rarely as high as in India. Because it lies so close to the Equator there is little variation in temperature from month to month. Colombo, virtually at sea level, has minimum of 25°C in Dec and a maximum of 28°C in May. At Nuwara Eliya, the average daytime temperatures hover around 16°C, but you need to be prepared for the chill in the evenings. Only the NE occasionally experiences temperatures of up to 38°C.

PEOPLE AND LANGUAGES

People As in most parts of S Asia, *homo sapiens* appeared in Sri Lanka around 500,000 B.C. Later Stone Age cultures are traceable to approximately 10,000 BC. The earliest occupants were aboriginal tribes of Australoid, Negrito and Mediterranean stock, now almost entirely absorbed in the settled populations. Evidence for their origins is limited, but megalithic burial sites suggest that there may well have been migrations from S India from before the major migrations that brought Buddhism and Hinduism into the island up until about 100 B.C. The earliest named culture is that of *Balangoda*, distributed across the whole island between 5,000 and 500 B.C. The *Veddas* are the only inhabitants today whose ancestors were in Sri Lanka before the Aryan migrations. Related to the Dravidian jungle peoples in S India, they dwelt in caves and rock shelters, and lived by hunting and gathering. They practised a cult of the dead, communicating with ancestors through reincarnated spirits. Today the Veddas have been largely absorbed into the Sinhalese community and have virtually ceased to have a separate existence. In the mid 1960s their numbers had shrunk to under 800, from over 5,000 at the beginning of the century.

Migration from India The overwhelming majority of the present population of Sri Lanka owes its origins to successive waves of migration from 2 different regions of India. Most people are of Indo-Aryan origin and came from N India. *Sinhala*, the language of the Sinhalese, is an Indo-European language, unlike the Dravidian language Tamil. The earliest migrations from N India may have taken place as early as the 5th century BC. Although these migrants brought with them their N Indian language, they were not yet Buddhists, for Buddhism did not arrive in Sri Lanka until the 3rd century BC. The origins of Tamil settlement are unclear, but are thought to go back at least to the 3rd century BC, when there is clear evidence of trade between Sri Lanka and S India.

Today the *Sinhalese* make up 74% of the total population. Sri Lanka's *Tamil* population comprises the long settled Tamils of the N and E (12.6%) and the migrant workers on the tea plantations in the central highlands (5.5%) who settled in Sri Lanka from the late 19th century onwards. By 1985 over 335,000 adults from this Tamil community had been repatriated to India, though there has been virtually no increase since then. The so-called '*Moors*', Tamil speaking Muslims of Indian-Arab descent, were traders on the E coast and now number over 1.1 m (7.7%). A much smaller but highly distinct community is that of the *Burghers*, numbering about 50,000. The Dutch (mainly members of the Dutch Reformed Church), and the Portuguese intermarried with local people, and their descendants were urban and ultimately English speaking. There are similar numbers of Malays and smaller groups of Kaffirs. The Malays are Muslims who were brought by the Dutch from Java. The Kaffirs were brought by the Portuguese from Mozambique and other parts of E Africa as mercenaries.

ECONOMY

Agriculture and fishing   About a quarter of Sri Lanka's area is cultivated by sedentary farmers or under cultivated forests, a further 15% being under shifting cultivation. About half is under forest, grassland, swamp and waste land. In the wet zone virtually all the cultivable land is now taken up.

It is striking that Sri Lanka has not produced enough food to meet the needs of its population since the 18th century, yet in many respects it has been the most obviously prosperous state in S Asia. After Independence the growing food deficit was an enormous economic problem. In the 1970s more than half the money earned from the export of tea, rubber and coconuts was spent on importing foodgrains, leaving little surplus for investment. Attempts to increase rice production have ranged from land reform to the introduction of high yielding varieties (hyv) of seed.

Sri Lanka has 2 main rice growing seasons. The *Maha** crop is harvested between Jan and Mar, the *Yala** crop between Aug-Sep. By 1970 75% of all rice sown was high yielding, and by the early 1980s there was virtually a 100% takeup of new varieties. Yields have increased to over 3.5 tonnes per ha, and production has showed a marked increase, rising towards 80% of domestic needs despite the speed of population growth. In addition to the intensification programme based on hyv's and high fertiliser use, the Government has also carried out major colonisation schemes, bringing new land under rice cultivation. This has been expensive and certainly not always cost effective, but in part has been a response to political pressures to reclaim land for Sinhalese cultivators.

The cash crops of tea, rubber and coconuts continue to contribute the lion's share of Sri Lanka's foreign exchange earnings. In 1950 this stood at 96%. In 1991 over 50% of foreign exchange earnings still came from these 3 products alone. **Tea** has suffered from inadequate investment and fierce competition from expanding production in other countries of cheaper, lower quality tea. The area cropped under tea fell steadily, but production nearly doubled between 1948 and 1965. It declined to around 180 m kg in 1983. Since then it has risen again to over 210 m kg in 1991. Tea alone still accounts for Rs 10.6 bn of exports, 33% of the total value of exports, followed by rubber (Rs 3 bn) and coconuts (Rs 1.4 bn).

Potentially rich fishery resources have yet to be fully developed. Fresh water stocking programmes have increased the yield of rivers and lakes, and brackish water fishing is becoming increasingly commercialised. However, nearly 40% of households which depend on fishing have no boats or equipment, and despite the potential of the export market production does not meet domestic demand.

Resources and industry   Sri Lanka has few fossil fuels and limited metallic minerals. Gemstones, graphite (crystalline carbon) and heavy mineral sands are the most valuable resources, though clays, sands and limestones are abundant. Gemstones include sapphires, rubies, topaz, zircon, tourmaline and many others. Gem bearing gravels are common, especially in the SW around the appropriately named Ratnapura (*city of gems*). Other minerals are also concentrated in the SW. Heavy mineral sands – ilmenite, rutile and monazite – are found in beach sands, the greatest concentration being N of Trincomalee, where deposits are 95% pure. Monazite is found on the W coast. There are scattered deposits of iron ore, largely limonite and haematite in the SW, and some veins of magnetite in the NW interior. High evaporation rates make shallow lagoons, as in the NE, suitable for salt manufacture. The most important salterns are at Puttalam, Elephant Pass and

Hambantota in the S

Due to the lack of fossil fuel resources, 95% of the island's electricity is now generated by hydro power. In the mid 1960s estimates suggested that Sri Lanka had about 800 mw Hydro potential. This was then projected to be adequate until 1990. The first HEP project was opened in the 1930s, but firewood still accounts for 60% of all energy used. Supplies are under increasing pressure, and the Mahaveli Project undertaking has meant that most of the HEP is now developed.

Sri Lanka had very little industry at Independence, manufacturing accounting for less than 5% of the GDP. By 1990 a number of new industries had been developed – cement, mineral sands, ceramics, cloth. These were all planned originally in the state controlled sector. The socialist government under Mrs Bandaranaike envisaged public ownership of all major industries, but the United National Party government elected under President Jayawardene's leadership in 1977 reversed this policy, moving towards a free trade economy.

Among the leading sectors of the new policy was tourism, with particular efforts to exploit the superb beaches and equable climate. This programme has been severely hit by the political troubles which have dogged the island since 1983, and in 1989 tourism ceased almost completely before picking up again in 1990. In 1991 the total value of industrial production was just under Rs 50 bn, the food and beverages industry, textiles and leather, and chemicals each contributing about Rs 14 bn.

The present government is pushing still harder towards ending all public subsidies and state involvement in economic activity.

HANDICRAFTS

Traditional crafts are being revived through Government programmes, while indigenous craft skills are still practised widely in households across the country. Pottery, coir fibre, carpentry, handloom weaving and metalwork all receive government assistance. Some of the crafts are concentrated in just a few villages. Brasswork, for example, is restricted to a few villages around Kandy, where there is also a 'city of arts', Kalapura where over 70 families of craftsmen make superb brass, wood, silver and gold items. Fine gold and silver chain work is done both in the Pettah area of Colombo and in Jaffna. Batiks, from wall hangings to sarongs, and a wide range of handloom household linen are widely available. Silver jewellery, trays, ornaments and inlay work is a further specialisation. Masks are also a popular product in the SW of the island, based on traditional masks used in dance dramas.

RELIGION

Sri Lankan Buddhism Sri Lankan Buddhism survived in the Hinayana form which became extinct in mainland India, **See S. Asia introduction, page 66**. King **Devanampiya Tissa** (d 207 BC), converted by Asoka's son Mahinda, established the Mahavihara monastery, and successors repeatedly struggled to preserve its distinct identity from that of neighbouring Hinduism and Tantrism. It was also constantly struggling with Mahayana Buddhism, which gained the periodic support of successive royal patrons. King Mahasena (AD 276-303) and his son Sri Meghavarna, who brought the famous "tooth of the Buddha" to the island, both advocated Mahayana forms of the faith.

Despite the fact that Sri Lankan Buddhism is of the Hinayana school, it is not strictly orthodox. The personal character of the Buddha is emphasised, as was the virtue of being a disciple of the Buddha. *Maitreya*, the 'future' Buddha, is recognised as the only Bodhisattva, and it has been a feature of Buddhism in the island for kings to identify themselves with this incarnation of the Buddha.

The Sinhalese see themselves as guardians of the original Buddhist faith. They believe that Pali scripture was first written down by King **Vattagamani Abhaya** in the 1st century BC. The *Pali canon* of scripture are referred to as 3 'baskets', because the palm leaf texts on which they were written were stored in baskets. They are '**conduct**' (*vinaya*), or rules; '**sermon**' (*sutta*), the largest and most important of the three; and '**metaphysics**' (*Abhidhamma*). There are also several works that lack the full authority of the canon but are none the less important. Basham suggests that the main propositions of the literature are psychological rather than metaphysical. Suffering, sorrow and dissatisfaction are the nature of ordinary life, and can only be eliminated by giving up desire. In turn, desire is a result of the misplaced belief in the reality of individual existence. In its Theravada form, Hinanaya Buddhism taught that there is no soul and ultimately no god. Nirvana was a state of rest beyond the universe, once found never lost.

The cosmology Basham states that, despite the Buddha's discouragement of developing cosmologies, the Hinayana Buddhists produced a cyclical view of the universe, evolving through 4 time periods. **Period 1** Man slowly declines until everything is destroyed except the highest heaven. The good go to this heaven, the remainder to various hells. **Period 2** A quiescent phase. **Period 3** Evolution begins again. However, 'the good *karma** of beings in the highest heaven' (**see page 51**) now begins to fail, and a lower heaven evolves, a *world of form*. Basham suggests that during this period a great being in the higher heaven dies, and is re-born in the world of form as Brahma. Feeling lonely, he wishes that others were with him. Soon other beings from the higher heaven die and are reborn in this world. Brahma interprets these people as his own creation, and himself as The Creator. **Period 4** The first men, who initially had supernatural qualities, deteriorate and become earthbound, and the period fluctuates between advance and deterioration.

The four-period cycles continue for eternity, alternating between 'Buddha cycles' – one of which we live in today – and 'empty cycles'. It is believed that in the present cycle 4 Buddhas – *Krakucchanda*, *Kanakamuni*, *Kasyapa*, and *Sakyamuni* – have already taught and one, *Maitreya*, is still to come.

In Sri Lanka the scriptures came to be attributed with almost magical powers. Close ties developed between Buddhist belief and **Sinhalese nationalism**. The Sinhalese scholar *Buddhaghosa* translated Sinhalese texts into Pali in the 5th century AD. At the beginning of the 11th century Sri Lanka sent Buddhist missionaries to SE Asia, who were responsible for the conversion of Thailand, Burma, Cambodia and Laos to Theravadin Buddhism. In the face of continued threats to their continued survival, Sri Lanka's Buddhist monks had to be re-ordained into the valid line of Theravadin lineage by monks from SE Asia. Links with Buddhism in Thailand remain close.

Buddhist practice The Sri Lankan historian Rahula has suggested that several features became characteristic of Sri Lankan Buddhism in its first 13 centuries on the island. By the time Buddhism was brought to the Island there was a well developed religious organisation which had made strong links with secular authorities. There had also been significant developments in Buddhist thought and belief, which made it possible for peasants and lay people to share in the religious beliefs of the faith. As it developed in Sri Lanka the main outlines of practice became clearly defined. The king and the orders of monks became interdependent; a monastic hierarchy was established; most monks were learning and teaching, rather than practising asceticism and complete withdrawal from the world. Most important, Buddhism accepted a much wider range of goals for living than simply the release from permanent rebirth.

The historian Malagoda suggests that the most important of these was 'good rebirth' within the cycle of rebirths (*samsara*), the prevention of misfortune and the increase in good fortune during the present life. These additions to original Buddhist thought led to a number of contradictions and tensions, summarised by Tambiah as: the Buddha as a unique individual, or as one of a type of person (*Bodhisattva*) coming into the world periodically to help achieve release from *samsara* (rebirth), or rebirth into a better life; Buddhism as a path to salvation for all, or as a particular, nationalist religion; Buddhism as renunciation of the world and all its obligations, in contrast with playing a positive social role; and finally, whether monasteries should be run by the monks themselves, or with the support and involvement of secular authorities. These tensions are reflected in many aspects of Buddhism in Sri Lanka today, as in debates between monks who argue for political action as against withdrawal from the world.

Until the 16th century Buddhism in Sri Lanka enjoyed the active support of the state. Gradually that support was withdrawn, largely under colonial influence. It remained longest in Kandy, but was withdrawn steadily after the British took control in 1815. The 18th century revival of Buddhism in the wet zone was sponsored by the landowning village headmen, not by royalty, and castes such as the Goyigama and Salagama played a prominent role. Through the 19th century they became the dominant influence on Buddhist thought, while the remaining traditional Buddhist authority in Kandy, the Siyam Nikaya, suffered permanent loss of influence. This growth of a new, independent, Buddhism, became active and militant. It entered into direct competition with Christians in proselytising, and in setting up schools, special associations and social work.
    After Independence political forces converged to encourage State support for Buddhism. Malagoda suggests that the lay leadership wanted government action to protect Buddhists from competition with other religious groups, but all Buddhist groups, including the Sinhalese political parties, saw benefits in emphasising the role of Buddhism in society.

Hinduism Hindu beliefs are outlined in the introduction to S. Asia, **see page 49**. Hinduism in N Sri Lanka was brought over by successive Tamil kings and their followers. Most Hindus in Sri Lanka are Saivite, and the summit of Adam's Peak is held to be sacred to Siva.
    Jaffna was subject to Christian missionary work, especially through education, from the early 19th century. It produced a Hindu response, and a Hindu renaissance took place in the late 19th century under the leadership of *Arumuga Navalar*. Setting up an extensive network of schools, he was anxious to strengthen orthodox Saivism, on the one hand through restoring temples and on the other by publishing religious texts.

Virtually all Hindu temples in Sri Lanka were destroyed by the Portuguese and the Dutch. Those that have been rebuilt never had the resources available to compare with those in India, not having had their lands restored in the post colonial period, so they are generally small. However, they play a prominent part in Hindu life. De Silva suggests that Navalar's failure to argue for social reform meant that caste was virtually untouched, and with it untouchability remained a fundamental characteristic. The high caste **Vellalas**, a small minority of the total Hindu population, maintained their status and their power unchallenged until after Independence. Removal of caste disabilities started in the 1950s: however, the struggle by Tamils for Independence may well have transformed the whole basis of caste discrimination far more thoroughly than any programme of social reform.

Islam Islam was brought to Sri Lanka by Arab traders. However, numbers were swelled by conversion from both Buddhists and Hindus, and by immigrant

Muslims from S India who fled the Portuguese along the W coast of India. There are also Muslims of Malay origin. Both in Kandy and the coastal districts Muslims have generally lived side by side with Buddhists, often sharing common interests against the colonial powers. However, one of the means by which Muslims maintained their identity was to refuse to be drawn into the education provided by the colonial powers. As a result, by the end of the 19th century the Muslims were among the least educated groups, few Muslims holding any positions of economic or political power. A Muslim lawyer, *Siddi Lebbe*, helped to change attitudes and encourage participation by Muslims.

In 1915 there were major Sinhalese-Muslim riots, and Muslims began a period of active collaboration with the British colonial power, joining other minorities led by the Tamils in the search for security and protection of their rights against the perceived threat of majority Sinhalese Buddhism. The Muslims have been particularly anxious to maintain Muslim family law, and to gain concessions on education. One of the chief of these is the teaching of Arabic in government schools to Muslim children. Until 1974 Muslims were unique among minorities in having the right to chose which of 3 languages – Sinhala, Tamil or English – would be their medium of instruction. Since then a new category of Muslim schools has been set up, allowing them to distance themselves from the Tamil Hindu community, whose language most of them speak.

Christianity Christianity was introduced by the Portuguese, who actively encouraged proselytisation. Unlike India, where Christian missionary work in from the late 18th century was often carried out in spite of colonial government rather than with its active support, in Sri Lanka missionary activity enjoyed various forms of state backing. One Sinhalese king, Dharmapala, was converted, endowing the church, and even some high caste families became Christian. When the Dutch evicted the Portuguese they tried to suppress Roman Catholicism, and the Dutch Reformed Church found some converts. Other Protestant denominations followed the arrival of the British, though not always with official support or encouragement. Many of the missionary societies, and the churches that grew from their work, remained dependent on outside support. Between the 2 World Wars Christian influence in government was radically reduced. Denominational schools lost their protection and special status, of particular significance for the Roman Catholics, and since the 1960s have had to come to terms with a completely different role in Sri Lankan society.

Caste The elements of the emerging caste system were probably present in pre-Buddhist Sri Lanka. There were certainly both the priestly caste of Brahmins and a range of low caste groups such as scavengers. Although Buddhism encouraged its followers to eradicate distinction based on caste, the system clearly survived. There are 25 castes among the contemporary Sinhalese, some dominant in the Highlands and others in the lowlands. The highest is the *goyigama* caste of cultivators.

Unlike India, where fishing is a low caste occupation, the *Karava* caste of fishermen among the Sinhalese is high caste. Service castes are at the bottom of the hierarchy. The Tamil Hindus have evolved a distinct caste hierarchy from their Indian neighbours, having no significant Brahmin community. The *Vellalas*, who control land rights, carried out priestly functions, and are top of the hierarchy in N Sri Lanka. At the bottom of the scale were the landless labourers such as the Pallas and Nallavas. The tea plantation workers are all regarded as low caste.

ART AND ARCHITECTURE

Sri Lankan architecture has many features in common with Buddhist and Hindu Indian traditions, but the long period of relative isolation, and the determined preservation of Buddhism long after its demise in India, have contributed to some very distinctive features.

Buddhist architecture   Stupas were the most striking feature of Buddhist architecture in India. S Asia Intro. Originally they were funeral mounds, built to house the remains of the Buddha and his disciples. The tradition was developed by Sri Lanka's Sinhalese kings, notably in golden age of the 4th and 5th centuries AD, and the revival during the 11th-12th centuries AD. Some of the stupas, known in Sri Lanka as *Dagobas*, are huge structures, and even those such as the 4th century *Jetavana* at Anuradhapura, now simply a grassed-over brick mound, is impressively large.

Few of the older Buddhist monuments are in their original form, either having become ruins or been renovated. Hemispherical mounds built of brick and filled with brick and rubble, they stand on a square terrace, surmounted by 3 concentric platforms. In its original or its restored form, the brick mound is covered with plaster and painted white. Surrounding it on a low platform (*vahalakadas*) is the ambulatory, or circular path, reached from the cardinal directions by stone stairways. Around some of the dagobas there are fine sculptures on these circular paths at the head of each stairway.

The domes themselves are classified by the Sinhalese into six different types, such as bell-shaped, or bubble-shaped. On top of the dome is a small square enclosure (*hataraes kotuwa*), which contained valuable offerings, surrounded by a railed pavilion. Above it is the ceremonial umbrella (*chatta*). However, unlike the parasol-like umbrellas on other stupas, the Sri Lankan parasols are furled into a staff-like shape (**see page 1284**). Percy Brown suggests that they are more reminiscent of the totem poles of the Veddas, and may be derived from aboriginal symbols. Originally the cubical box housed the sacred relics themselves. However, Percy Brown suggests that the post left little room for the relics and offerings. A compartment was then hollowed out of the brickwork immediately below the staff. Into it was lowered the 'mystic stone', a granite block carved with 9 recesses to contain the relics and offerings. The finial staff then sealed and surmounted the relic stone and the whole dagoba.

The scale of many of these buildings is immense, and enormous effort and skill went into ensuring that they would last. The Mahavansa records how King Dutthagamani prepared the foundations for his great dagobas. The base was laid of round stones, crushed by pounding and then trampled by huge elephants with leather shoes to protect their feet. Clay was then spread over the hard core, followed by a layer of iron, another layer of stones and then a layer of ordinary stone.

As in other Buddhist stupas, the design is filled with symbolic meaning. The hemisphere is the dome of heaven, the axis of the cosmos being represented by the central finial on top, while the umbrella-like tiers are the rising heavens of the gods. Worshippers walk round the stupa on the raised platform in a clockwise direction (*pradakshina*), in doing so following the rotational movement of the celestial bodies.

Many smaller stupas were built within circular buildings. These were covered with a metal and timber roof resting on concentric rows of stone pillars. Today the roofs have disappeared, but examples such as the *Vatadage* at Polonnaruwa can still be seen. King Parakramabahu I also built another feature of Sri Lankan architecture at Polonnaruwa, a large rectangular hall in which was placed an image of the Buddha.

Most of Sri Lanka's early secular architecture has disappeared. Made of wood, there are remnants of what must have been magnificent royal palaces at both Anuradhapura and Sigiriya.

Moonstones   Sri Lanka's moonstones are among the world's finest artistic achievements in miniature. Polished semi-circular granite, they are carved in concentric rings portraying various animals, flowers and birds, and normally placed at the foot of flights of steps or entrances to important buildings. There are particularly fine examples in Anuradhapura and Polonnaruwa.

Hindu architecture   Sri Lankan Hindu architecture bears close resemblances with the Dravida styles of neighbouring Tamil Nadu, **see page 681**.

Sculpture   Early Sri Lankan sculpture shows close links with Indian Buddhist sculpture. The first images of the Buddha, some of which are still in Anuradhapura, are similar to 2nd-3rd century AD images from Andhra Pradesh. The middle period of the 5th to 11th centuries AD contains some magnificent sculptures on rocks, but there is a range of other sculpture, notably moonstones. These are decorated bands of flower motifs, geese and a variety of animals, both Anuradhapura and Polonnaruwa having outstanding examples. While the moonstones are brilliant works in miniature, Sri Lankan sculptors also produced outstanding colossal works, such as the 13 m high Buddha at Avukana or the reclining Buddha at Polonnaruwa.

Painting Perhaps Sri Lanka's most famous art forms are its rock paintings from Sigiriya, dating from the 6th century AD. The heavenly nymphs (*apsaras*), scattering flowers from the clouds, are shown with extraordinary grace and beauty. Polonnaruwa saw a later flowering of the painting tradition in the 12th and 13th centuries, but thereafter Sri Lankan art declined.

HISTORY

Prehistory Stone tools from the Middle Palaeolithic have been found in several places, evidence of settlement in Sri Lanka perhaps as much as 500,000 years ago. However, there is a complete absence of Neolithic tools, and the Copper Age which is so well represented in peninsular India from the 2nd millennium BC also appears to be absent. The picture changes with the arrival of the Iron Age, for the megalithic graves, associated with black and red pottery, which have been found at a number of sites, suggest that Sri Lanka had direct contact with S India well before the Aryans immigrated from N. India from around 500 BC. However, in comparison with India, Sri Lanka's archaeological record is comparatively sparse, with barely any evidence with which to date the development of Stone Age cultures or the later spread of domesticated animals and cultivation.

Early history Sri Lanka has a written political history possibly dating from the 6th century AD, and a conception of that history traced back to the origins of Buddhism itself, nearly 1,000 years before. Myth and legend are bound up with specific historical events, but the Sri Lankan historian K M de Silva has noted that the historical mythology of the Sinhalese "is the basis of their conception of themselves as the chosen guardians of Buddhism."

Sri Lanka is seen as the island home and the last bastion of Buddhist sanctity against the advancing tide of Hinduism. The basic text through which this view of the island's history has been passed on by successive generations of Buddhist monks is the **Mahavansa** (the *Great Chronicle*), which de Silva suggests possibly goes back to the 6th century AD, but is probably much more recent. It was continued in the 13th century text the **Culavamsa**, which gives a very full account of the medieval history of the island. These works were compiled by *bhikkus* (Buddhist monks) and inevitably they have the marks of both their religious and sectarian origins. However, they remain invaluable sources concerning Sri Lanka's history.

Proximity to India has played a permanent part in Sri Lanka's developing history. Separated by less than 30 km of shallow water, not only have the peoples of the island themselves originated from the mainland, but through more than 2,000 years political contacts have been an essential element in all Sri Lanka's political equations.

According to the Mahavansa the Buddha commanded the king of the gods, **Sakra**, to protect Lanka as the home in which Buddhism would flourish. In recent years much has been read into both the text and to more recent history to suggest that Sinhalese have always been at war with the Tamils. The truth is far more complicated. The earliest settlement of the island took place in the NE, the region now known as the dry zone. Until the 13th century AD this was the region of political and cultural development for Sinhalese and Tamil alike.

The economy and the culture developed around the creation of an extraordinarily sophisticated irrigation system, taking advantage of the rivers flowing from the central highlands across the much drier N and E plains. As in Tamil Nadu, traditional agriculture depended entirely on the rainfall brought by the retreating monsoon between Oct-Dec. Also as in Tamil Nadu the developing kingdoms of N Sri Lanka realised the need to control water to improve the reliability of agriculture, and a system of tank irrigation was already well advanced by the 1st century BC. This developed into possibly the most advanced system of hydraulic engineering in the world at that time by the end of the 5th century AD. **Rajarata** in the N central part of the island's plains grew into one of the major core regions of developing Sinhalese culture. To its N was **Uttaradesa** ('northern country'), while in the S E region of the island **Rohana** developed as the third political centre.

The rise of Buddhism Periodically these centres of Sinhalese power came into conflict with each other, and with Tamil kings from across the Palk Straits. The Mahavansa records how the Ruhana Sinhalese King Dutthagamani defeated the Chola Tamil King Elara, who had ruled N Sri Lanka from Anuradhapura, in 140 BC. Dutthagamani's victory was claimed by the chroniclers as a historic assertion of Buddhism's inalienable hold on Sri Lanka. In fact it is clear that at the time this was not a Tamil-Sinhalese conflict, for the armies and leadership of both sides contained Tamils and Sinhalese. By that time Buddhism had already been a power in the island for 2 centuries, when the king **Devanampiya Tissa** (307-267 BC) converted to Buddhism, probably under the influence of missionaries sent by the Mauryan Emperor Asoka led by Mahinda, who was either Asoka's son or brother.

From then on Buddhism became the state religion, identified with the growth of Sinhalese culture and political power. In fact, as de Silva has shown, the power of the central kingdom based at *Anuradhapura* was rarely unchallenged or complete. Political power was highly decentralised, with a large measure of local autonomy. Furthermore, provincial centres periodically established their independence. However, Anuradhapura became one of Asia's pre-eminent cities. From the 11th century AD *Polonnaruva* took over as capital, but although it developed in a more compact form it too had the stupas, tanks, palaces and parks which had become characteristic features of the earlier Buddhist capital.

The Tamil involvement Although Buddhist power was predominant in Sri Lanka from the 1st century BC, India and its Hindu Tamil population were never far below the horizon. Often Sri Lankan kings deliberately sought Tamil support in their own internecine disputes. As a result Sri Lanka was affected by political developments in S India, and the rise of the expansionist Tamil kingdoms of the Pandiyas, Pallavas and Cholas from the 5th century AD increased the scope for interaction with the mainland. In de Silva's words, "S Indian auxiliaries became in time a vitally important, if not the most powerful element in the armies of the Sinhalese rulers, and an unpredictable, turbulent group who were often a threat to political stability. They were also the nucleus of a powerful Tamil influence in the court."

It was not a one way flow. Occasionally the Sinhalese were themselves drawn in to attack Tamil kings in India, as in the 9th century when they attacked the Cholas. The Chola Emperor **Rajaraja I** responded by invading N Sri Lanka and adding Jaffna and the N plains, including Anuradhapura, to his empire. **See pages 688** and **745**. The Cholas ruled from Polonnaruva for 75 years, finally being driven out by the Rohana king **Vijayabahu I** in 1070 AD. He established peace and a return to some prosperity in the N before civil war broke out and disrupted the civil administration again. Only the 33 year rule of **Parakramabahu I** (1153-1186) interrupted the decline. Some of Sri Lanka's most remarkable monuments date from his reign, including the massive irrigation embankment 12 m high and 15 km long which enclosed the *Parakrama Samudra* (*Sea of Parakrama*) at Polonnaruwa. However, it was the collapse of this kingdom and its ultimate annihilation by the Tamils in the 13th century that left not only its physical imprint on the N Sri Lankan landscape but also an indelible psychological mark on the Sri Lankan perception of neighbouring Tamil Hindus.

The Sinhalese move South It is still not clear whether it was the Tamil invasions themselves or other factors, such as the spread of malaria which occurred with the deterioration in maintenance of the irrigation system, that led to the progressive desertion of the N and E plains and the movement S of the centre of gravity of the Island's population. Between the 12th and 17th centuries Sinhalese moved from the dry to the wet zone. This required a change in agriculture from irrigated to rainfed crops. It was also accompanied by a growth in the importance of trade, especially in cinnamon, an activity controlled by the rising population of Muslim seafarers. A Tamil kingdom was set up in Jaffna for the first time, briefly coming back under Sinhalese power (under the Sinhalese king *Parakramabahu VI*, 1412-67, based in his capital at *Kotte*, but generally remaining independent, and a frequent threat to the power of the Sinhalese kingdoms to the S. Other threats came from overseas. As early as the 13th century a Buddhist king from Malaya invaded Sri Lanka twice to try and capture the tooth relic and the Buddha's alms bowl. De Silva records how in the early 15th century the Island was even invaded by a fleet of Chinese junks sent by the Ming Emperors.

The Kandyan kingdom Between the S and N kingdoms, Kandy became the capital of a new kingdom around 1480. Establishing its base in the central highlands, it became a powerful independent kingdom by the end of the 15th century. By the early 16th century the Sinhalese kingdom of Kotte in the S was hopelessly fragmented, giving impetus to Kandy's rise to independent power. It's remote and inaccessible position gave it added protection from the early colonial invasions. Using both force and diplomacy to capitalise on its geographical advantages, it survived as the last independent Sinhalese kingdom until 1815. It had played the game of seeking alliances with one colonial power against another with considerable success, first seeking the help of the Dutch against the Portuguese, then of the British against the Dutch. However, this policy ran out of potential allies when the British established their supremacy over the Island in 1796, and by 1815 the last Kandyan King , a Tamil Hindu converted to Buddhism, was deposed by his Sinhalese chiefs, who sought an accord with the new British rulers in exchange for retaining a large measure of their own power.

Colonial power The succession of 3 colonial powers, the Portuguese, Dutch and finally the British, finally ended the independent Sinhalese and Tamil rule. There also lay the threat of expanding Islam, evidenced in the conversion of the inhabitants of islands on the Arab trading routes such as the Maldives and the Laccadives as well as significant numbers on the SW coast of India. The Portuguese arrived in Sri Lanka 1605 and established control over some of the island's narrow coastal plains around Colombo. They were responsible for large-scale conversions to Roman Catholicism which today accounts for 90% of the island's Christians (under 7% of the population). As in Goa, the Portuguese left both a linguistic legacy and an imprint on the population, evidenced today in many names of Portuguese origin.

During this period the rest of the island was dominated by the rulers of Sitavaka, who overpowered the Kotte kingdom in 1565 and dominated the whole of the SW apart from Colombo. For 10 years they occupied Kandy itself, nearly evicted the Portuguese and came close to reasserting Sinhalese power in the far N.

By 1619 the **Portuguese** had annexed Jaffna, which thereafter was treated by the **Dutch**, and more importantly the British, as simply part of the Island state. They were less successful in subjugating Kandy, and in 1650 they were ousted by the *Dutch*, who extended colonial control from Negombo (40 km N of Colombo), S right round the coast to Trincomalee, as well as the entire N peninsula, leaving the Kandyan kingdom in charge of the remainder. Because the Portuguese and Dutch were interested in little other than the spice trade, they bent most of their efforts to producing the goods necessary for their trade. The British replaced the Dutch in 1795-6 when British power was being consolidated in S India at the expense of the French and the Mysore Muslim Raja, Tipu Sultan, **see page 843**. Their original purpose was simply to secure the important Indian Ocean port of Trincomalee. B.H. Farmer, a leading authority on Sri Lanka, points out that by 1802 "it was apparent that Madras-trained officials were, apart from other disabilities, quite unable to understand the language and customs of the Sinhalese, and Ceylon became a Crown Colony."

When the British came to control the whole island after 1815 they established a quite distinctive imprint on the island's society and economy. This was most obvious in the introduction of plantation agriculture. During the British period coffee took over from cinnamon, but by the beginning of the 20th century, even though coffee had largely been wiped out by disease, plantation agriculture was the dominant pillar of the cash economy. The subsistence economy of rice production stagnated and then declined, and Sri Lanka became dependent on the export of cash crops and the import of food, so that by the early years of Independence it was only producing about 35% of its rice needs. While the economy was being transformed, so society too underwent radical changes, with the widespread adoption of English education among the urban middle class.

The moves to Independence Unlike India, the Independence movement in Ceylon took a largely religious and communal tone, being Buddhist and Sinhalese dominated in its early stages during the last quarter of the 19th century. However, as K.M. de Silva has suggested, no one in public life at the turn of the century would have believed that British rule would end within 50 years – nor would many have wanted it to. The **Ceylon National Congress**, formed in 1919 some 40 years after its Indian equivalent, was conservative and pragmatic, but the pressures of imminent democratic self-rule made themselves felt throughout the 1930s, as minority groups pressed to protect their position. Universal suffrage came in 1931, along with the promise of self rule from the British Government. It had the positive benefit of encouraging the development of welfare policies such as health care, nutrition and and public education. However, it also had the immediate impact on the electorate of encouraging a resurgence of nationalism linked with Buddhist revivalism and its associated cultural heritage.

Independence came with scarcely a murmur on 4 February 1948, 6 months after that of India and Pakistan. Ceylon's first Prime Minister, **Dudley Senanayake**, was identified with a pragmatic nationalism. The heart of his programme was the recolonisation of the deserted Sinhalese heartlands of the dry zone, a programme which still continues.

Recent developments In its first 30 years of Independence Sri Lanka held 8 general elections, sometimes accompanied by radical changes in political direction. Between 1956 and 1977 the governing party always lost. Unlike India, power alternated between 2 major political parties, the socialist **Sri Lanka Freedom Party** (SLFP), and the **United National Party** (UNP), which had formed the first government after Independence. One strand of political development has related to the contrast between the socialist policies of the Sri Lanka Freedom Party and the free market policies of the UNP. Neither has succeeded in achieving the economic success which could keep pace with the growing demands of an increasingly young and literate population, struggling for jobs.

At the same time a second major element in political debate has been the series of moves to turn from British institutions and styles of government to ones that are closer to Sri Lanka's traditional culture. Both parties have competed in the search for more and more potent symbols of national identity. The preponderance of Buddhist Sinhalese in the population of Sri Lanka has ensured that these symbols have themselves reflected that demographic and historical situation. The 1980s have seen the divisions worked out in ethnic conflict of these 2 fundamental aspects of political development.

Since July 1983, when an anti-Tamil pogrom devastated many Tamil areas of Colombo and led to the loss of hundreds of Tamil lives, Sri Lanka has been locked in a bitter conflict between the government forces and Tamil guerrillas. Over 150,000 Tamils fled as refugees to India. In the N and E, Tamil militancy rapidly gained ground, and between 1983 and 1987 the **Liberation Tigers of Tamil Eelam** (LTTE or just 'the Tigers') waged an increasingly successful battle for control of what they regarded as the Tamil homeland, both against rival Tamil groups and against the Sri Lankan armed forces. In response the Government mounted increasingly strong attacks into the N, and in summer 1987 launched what was hailed as a final offensive.

The conflict had been watched with growing concern by the Indian government, which strongly opposed the creation of a separate Tamil State in Sri Lanka while fearing the domestic political consequences of failing to support Sri Lankan Tamils in the face of what were increasingly seen as genocidal attacks. In July 1987 Rajiv Gandhi forced President Jayawardene and the Sri Lankan Government to accept a peace accord, under which the Indian army would enter Sri Lanka to restore law and order and elections would be held to elect new Provincial Councils.

It soon became clear that the objective of disarming the Tigers would not be achieved, and the Indian army became bogged down in a conflict with the Tigers themselves. At the same time the presence of the Indian forces roused fierce opposition from the Sinhalese, and the angry upsurge of support among young people for the fiercely anti-Tamil **JVP party** in the S of the island was accompanied by escalating violence and disruption.

In November 1989 the 2 key leaders of the JVP were killed, and the new Sri Lankan Government of President Premadasa claimed its first major success. Soon it was able to claim another, for it appeared to have succeeded in reaching an agreement with the Tigers on a withdrawal of the Indian Peace Keeping Force, which was finally completed in March 1990. However, that accord soon broke down. Although the S was now quiet, in mid 1991 civil war was raging across the N of the Island again, with no sign of the Tigers being forced to give up their struggle for independence.

COLOMBO

Altitude Sea level *Population* 1.9 m

Sheltered from the SW Monsoon by a barely perceptible promontory jutting out into the sea, Colombo's bay was an important site for Muslim traders before the colonial period. However, it is essentially a colonial city, whose rise to pre-eminence did not start until the 19th century and the establishment of British power. Before that it was a much less important town than Galle, but when the British took control of Kandy and encouraged the development of commercial estates, the Island's economic centre of gravity moved N. Colombo offered two easy routes into the Kandyan highlands.

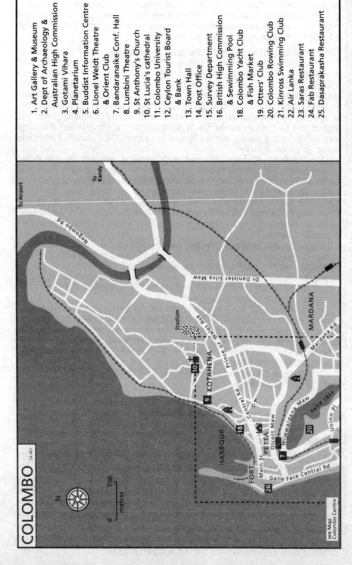

COLOMBO

N

0   700
metres

To Airport

To Kandy

Negombo Rd

Dr Danister Silva Maw

MARDANA

Mardana Rd

MARDANA

Stadium

Prince of Water Ave

KOTAHENA

Central Rd

10

9

18

HARBOUR

PETTA

Main St

Olcott Maw

Wijewardana Maw

Beira Lake

Union Pl

FORT

Galle Face Central Rd

26

20

see Map
Colombo Centre

1. Art Gallery & Museum
2. Dept of Archaeology &
   Australian High Commission
3. Gotami Vihara
4. Planetarium
5. Buddist Information Centre
6. Lionel Weldt Theatre
   & Orient Club
7. Bandaranaike Conf. Hall
8. Lumbini Theatre
9. St Anthony's Church
10. St Lucia's cathedral
11. Colombo University
12. Ceylon Tourist Board
    & Bank
13. Town Hall
14. Post Office
15. Survey Department
16. British High Commission
    & Swimming Pool
17. Colombo Yacht Club
    & Fish Market
18. Otters' Club
19.
20. Colombo Rowing Club
21. Kinross Swimming Club
22. Air Lanka
23. Saras Restaurant
24. Fab Restaurant
25. Dasaprakasha Restaurant

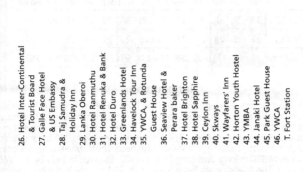

26. Hotel Inter-Continental & Tourist Board
27. Galle Face Hotel & US Embassy
28. Taj Samudra & Holiday Inn
29. Lanka Oberoi
30. Hotel Ranmuthu
31. Hotel Renuka & Bank
32. Hotel Duro
33. Greenlands Hotel
34. Havelock Tour Inn
35. YWCA, & Rotunda Guest House
36. Seaview Hotel & Perara baker
37. Hotel Brighton
38. Hotel Sapphire
39. Ceylon Inn
40. Skways
41. Wayfarers' Inn
42. Horton Youth Hostel
43. YMBA
44. Janaki Hotel
45. Park Guest House
46. YWCA
T. Fort Station

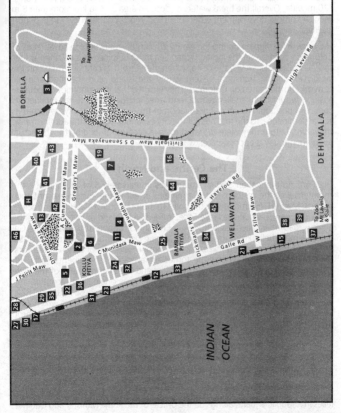

Main languages: Sinhala, Tamil, English

	Jan	Feb	Mar	Apr	May	Jun	Jul	Aug	Sep	Oct	Nov	Dec	Av/Tot
Max (°C)	32	32	32	33	32	31	30	30	30	31	31	30	31
Min (°C)	22	23	24	26	26	26	25	26	24	24	23	23	24
Rain (mm)	70	88	121	286	388	186	154	99	216	396	329	193	2526

Introduction

The key to the city's development lay in the building of the harbour. The small promontory offered little protection for larger ships, and in the late 19th century the British started work on a series of breakwaters which were to provide an effective harbour round the year. The SW breakwater, over 1000 m long, was completed in 1885. It has the pilot station at its head. The NE breakwater, a rubble embankment 350 m long, was completed in 1902, followed in 1907 by the NW breakwater. This 'island' work has a S entrance 250 m wide and a N entrance 220 m wide. Overall the breakwaters enclose an area of 3 sq km more than 8 m deep. A harbour development scheme in 1954 improved the whole range of port facilities.

The growth in shipping during the early 20th century reflected the advantages of Colombo's position on the Indian Ocean Sea route between Europe, the Far East and Australasia. However, the city also benefitted from its central position on the rapidly expanding transport system within the Island, and the road and rail networks both focused on Colombo. They ensured that its economic and political position would be unchallengeable, and after Independence it has retained its dominant position. The official population of the city has not always reflected its actual dominance, as the true area of the city expanded beyond the administrative limits long before they were redrawn to take account of its growth. The actual population today is approximately 1.9 m.

The Centre and North

The Fort, no more than 500 m square, lies immediately S of the harbour, the commercial centre of the city. Little remains of either the Portuguese or Dutch periods. Marine Drive runs down the coast to the Intercontinental Hotel and across the wide open space of the Galle Face. Immediately inland of its N section is the narrow road now called Galle Buck, an English corruption of the old name Gal Bokka – rocky belly. From the N end of Marine Drive, Church St runs E, past **St. Peter's Church** on the right. Part of the former residence of Dutch Governors, the Church cemetery contains the tombs of several British residents, including William Tolfrey (1778-1817), an army officer and the first translator of the Bible into Pali and Sinhalese. The nave of the church was originally a reception and banqueting hall, first converted into a church in 1804 and consecrated in 1821.

To the E is the Hotel Taprobane, formerly the Grand Oriental, from which **York St**, one of the main shopping areas, runs due S. Half way down it is Sir Baron Jayatilleke Mawatha, the main banking street. Nearly all the buildings are in red brick. Hospital St, running W at the S end of York St, is a lively centre of low cost restaurants, fruit sellers, and pavement merchants.

Running S from Church St to the W of St Peter's Church is **Janadhipathi Mawatha** (formerly Queen St). At the N end are Gordon Gardens, with a statue of Queen Victoria and a stone bearing the Portuguese Coat of Arms. Threats of terrorist violence have led to entrance to the Gordon Gardens being restricted, as it lies in Republic Square, alongside the offices of the Prime Minister and Cabinet.

The N end of **Janadhipathi Mawatha** is now normally closed to the public. Colombo is not graced with many fine buildings, but the GPO, which stands on the E side of Janadhipathi Mawatha is a good example of Victorian colonial building. Opposite it is the President's House, *Janadhipathi Medura*. The Chartered Bank building is another imposing commercial structure, decorated with reliefs of domesticated elephants.

The statue in front of the President's House is of the 19th century British Governor Edward Barnes. An adjutant of the Duke of Wellington during the Battle of Waterloo, Barnes is better known in Sri Lanka as the Governor who built the Colombo-Kandy road. His statue is the point from which the distances of all towns in Sri Lanka from Colombo are measured. Just to the S again is the Lighthouse Clock Tower, built in 1837. Its function as a lighthouse has been taken over by the new tower on Marine Drive.

Sir Baron Jayatilleka Mawatha runs E, immediately N of the GPO, with a number of impressive commercial buildings, including a good example of inter-war architecture in the Bank of India.

E of the Taprobane Hotel is the Central YMCA, next to the Moors Islamic Cultural Home in Bristol St. Across Duke St. is the Young Mens Buddhist Association, where the shrine houses a noted modern image of the Buddha. The Fort Mosque, housed in a building of the Dutch period, is to the S on Chatham St.

The Pettah While the Fort is the centre of Colombo's modern commercial activity, the Pettah (Tamil: *'pettai'* – 'suburb'; Sinhalese: *'pitakotuwa'* – outer fort) is the hub of its traditional markets. The small shops and narrow streets are covered in advertising hoardings. Specialist streets house such craftsmen and traders as goldsmiths (**Sea St**), fruit and vegetable dealers (the end of **Main St**) and ayurvedic herbs and medicines (**Gabo's Lane**).

At the SE edge of the Pettah is the Fort Railway Station. In the market area to the N, Arabs, Portuguese, Dutch and British traded. Half way along Main St on the left hand side after 2nd Cross St is the **Jami ul Alfar** mosque. Entry permitted on removing shoes. At the end of Main St, Central Road goes E from a large roundabout, just N of the Market. A left turn off Central Rd immediately after the roundabout, Brass Founder St, leads to a right fork, Ratnajothi Saravana Mawatha, formerly Wolfendahl St. At the end is the **Wolfendahl Church**, the most remarkable Dutch Church in Sri Lanka. Built in 1749 on the site of an earlier Portuguese church, it is prominently placed on a hill, where its massive cruciform shape stands out, commanding a view over the harbour. It's doric style facade is solid and heavy, and inside it has many tombstones and memorial tablets to Dutch officials. It is the most interesting surviving Dutch monument in Sri Lanka.

To its NE is perhaps the most remarkable Roman Catholic cathedral in the island, **Santa Lucia**. With a classical façade, inside are the tombs of 3 French bishops. Begun in 1876 it was completed in 1910, but there is little of interest inside. To the S in New Moor St is the Grand Mosque, a modern building in the style, as one critic puts it, of a modern international airport covered in metallic paint.

Also in the Pettah are 3 modest Hindu temples, of little intrinsic architectural interest in comparison with those in S India, but giving an insight into Hindu building style and worship. Of all Saivite temples, perhaps the most striking is that of **Sri Ponnambula Vanesvara** at 38 Sri Ramanathan Rd. The gopuram (entrance gateway) has typical sculptures of gods from the Hindu pantheon. A Siva lingam is in the innermost shrine, with a Nandi in front and a dancing Siva (*Nataraja*) to one side, see page 57.

Further NE across the Kelaniya River is the **Raja Maha Vihara**, 13 km from the centre of the city and, after the temple of the tooth in Kandy, the most visited Buddhist temple in Sri Lanka. In the 13th century *Kelaniya* was an impressive city, but its chief attraction today is the legendary visit of the Buddha to the site. The

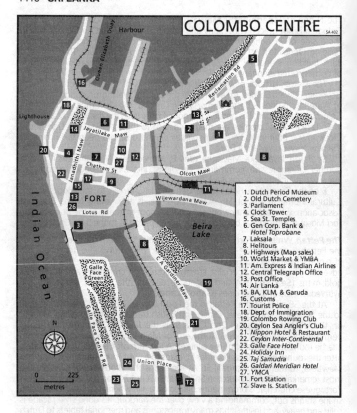

COLOMBO CENTRE SA 402

1. Dutch Period Museum
2. Old Dutch Cemetery
3. Parliament
4. Clock Tower
5. Sea St. Temples
6. Gen Corp. Bank & Hotel Toprobane
7. Laksala
8. Helitours
9. Highways (Map sales)
10. World Market & YMBA
11. Am. Express & Indian Airlines
12. Central Telegraph Office
13. Post Office
14. Air Lanka
15. BA, KLM, & Garuda
16. Customs
17. Tourist Police
18. Dept. of Immigration
19. Colombo Rowing Club
20. Ceylon Sea Angler's Club
21. Nippon Hotel & Restaurant
22. Ceylon Inter-Continental
23. Galle Face Hotel
24. Holiday Inn
25. Taj Samudra
26. Galdari Meridian Hotel
27. YMCA
T1. Fort Station
T2. Slave Is. Station

Mahavansa recorded that the original stupa enshrined a gem-studded throne on which the Buddha sat when he supposedly visited Sri Lanka. Ultimately destroyed by the Portuguese, the present dagoba is in the shape of a heap of paddy. There is a famous image of the reclining Buddha, but there are also many images of Hindu deities. The temple is the meeting place for the **Duruthu Perahera** in January every year, which draws thousands of pilgrims from all over the Island.

The South

There are some attractive walks and drives to the S of the Fort area and Beira Lake. On the sea front itself is the wide and windswept open space of the Galle Face. Galle Rd runs almost due S, from the sea's edge itself in the N but gradually moving away from it southwards, and separated from it by the railway. Inland and parallel with it runs R.A. de Mel Mawatha, built up all the way S. Inland again lies the most prestigious residential area of Colombo, Cinnamon Gardens – widely referred to by its postal code, Colombo 7. Wide roads and shaded avenues make it a very attractive area. The Town Hall was completed in 1927, and there is a range of parks, the national museum and conference facilities.

Services

Hotels Colombo now has several world class hotels, but the city is poorly provided with good cheap accommodation. The best area for moderately priced guesthouses is Mount Lavinia, close enough to the city and with a wide range of choice.

AL *Ceylon Intercontinental*, 48 Jandhipathi Mawatha, Fort, T 21221. 250 rm, all with superb sea-view. 9 storey seafront hotel, roof-top *Cats Eye* restaurant (good buffet lunches), *Pearl* for seafood and bar with panoramic views. Snackbar serves Sinhalese specialities. Open-air dining with live music, in season. Well located good bookshop. **AL** *La Galdari Meriden*, 64 Lotus Rd, corner of Janadhipathi Mawatha, T 544544. 500 rm. In the business centre, overlooking the Indian Ocean, one of the newer hotels with a French restaurant, *Café Fleuri* and *Colombo 2000* nightclub. **AL** *Pegasus Reef*, Santa Maria Mawatha, Hendala, Wattala. 11 km from city centre, 18 km airport, T 530 205. 150 attractively decorated rm. 500 m of superb, coconut-fringed beach, good restaurants, huge open-air swimming pool. **AL** *Ramada Renaissance*, 115 C Gardiner Mawatha, T 544200. One of the city's newest, overlooking the sea with Renaissance Club on 6th and 7th floors and 4 speciality restaurants.

A *Taj Samudra*, 25 Galle Face Rd, overlooking the sea and Green, T 546622. 400 rm. Well designed, ideally situated in large well kept gardens. **A** *Lanka Oberoi*, 56/2 Galle Rd, Steuart Pl, opp Galle Face Hotel, T 20001. 525 rm, some with sea-view, many recently refurbished. Unimpressive exterior but atrium and Batik hangings very attractive in public area. Roof-top night club. Excellent restaurants include oriental cuisine in *Ran Malu* and western in *London Grill*. **A** *Holiday Inn*, 30 Sir M Markar Mawatha, S of the Green nr Taj Samudra, T 422001. 100 rm in attractive Moghul style building. Open-air pool and specialist *Alhambra* Restaurant for Muslim cuisine, *Golden Seer* for fish. **A** *Galle Face*, Fort, 2 Kollupitiya Rd, S of the Green, bordering the sea, T 541010. 54 rm, many refurbished, some especially large. Rm on Galle Rd can be noisy, best with sea-view. Raj-style, with character in 1894 building which is worth visiting. Good restaurant, Superb terrace overlooking Green, indoor garden for breakfasts, *Seaspray* fish restaurant and sea-water pool.

Most in the next category are comfortable with a/c, restaurant, exchange, shop and pool. **B** *Havelock Tour Inn*, 20 Dickman's Rd, Bambalapitya, T 85251. Charming, in quiet residential area, with a tropical garden and excellent restaurant. Recommended. **B** *Taprobane*, 2 York St, Fort, overlooking the harbour, T 20391. The old *Grand Orient* which once catered for travellers arriving by sea, has 60 rm. *Harbour Room* restaurant on the top floor with excellent views. **B** *Ceylinco*, 69 Janadhipathi Mawatha, Fort, T 20431. Small establishment with 15 rm in a modern building with the *Akasa kade* restaurant below, with superb views. **B** *Renuka*, 328 Galle Rd, Colombo 3, towards Mt Lavinia, T 573598. 44 rm with TV. Central a/c. Basement *Palmyrah* restaurant serves good curries. Bar, exchange, shops, pool.

C *Lanka Orchard*, 6 Galle Rd, Colombo 6, T 580809. Modern, central. Further S, along Galle Rd, which is busy and noisy, are several moderately priced hotels which vary: price is not always the best guide so you would do well to visit before booking. **C** *Ranmuthu*, 112 Galle Rd, Colombo 3, T 433968. 54 rm. Central a/c. Restaurant, bar, exchange, car hire, pool. **C** *Brighton*, 57 Ramakrishna Rd, Wellawatte, T 585211. 62 rm in a modern hotel on seafront close to rly line but away from busy rd. **C** *Empress*, 383 de Mel Mawatha, Colombo 3, T 27205. 33 rm. **C** *Galaxy*, Union Place, Col 2, T 696372. 52 a/c rm. Restaurant, 24 hr coffee shop, bar, business centre, travel, pool. **C** *Sapphire*, 371 Galle Rd, Wellawatte, T 583306. 40 rm, 20 a/c. Good beach nearby. Restaurant, exchange, car hire. **C** *Ceylon Inns*, 501 Galle Rd, Wellawatte, T 580474. 74 rm some a/c. Popular with tour groups. Restaurant, bar, exchange, pool. Nearby **C** *Silver Bird*, 382 Galle Rd, Wellawatte, T 83143. 50 rm. **C** *Duro*, 429 Kollupitiya Rd, T 85338. 27 rm. **C** *Skyways Tourist Inn*, 28 Cross Rd, off Ward Pl, Col 8, T 698313. Some a/c rm. Restaurant, exchange, car hire, tours, pool.

D *Wayfarer's Inn*, 77 Rosmead Pl, Col 7, nr Town Hall, T 93936. Some a/c rm. Restaurant, car hire, tours, pool, garden. **D** *Sea View*, 15 Sea View Av, Colombo 3. Central but quiet. **D** *Orchid Inn*, 571/6 Galle Rd, Colombo 6, T 83916. **D** *YWCA International*, 393 Union Place, Colombo 2. 20 rm with bath (for women and couples). Well located, in residential area. Good restaurant and spice shop. **E** *YWCA Rotunda Guest House*, 7 Rotunda Gardens, Col 3 nr Lanka Oberoi. Rm with bath and dorms.

E *Lank Inns*, 239 Galle Rd, Colombo 4, T 84220. **F** *YMCA*, 39 Bristol St, Fort, T 25252. 58 dorm beds. Inexpensive, self-service cafeteria.

Youth Hostel at 35/1 Horton Pl, Colombo 7, E of Viharamanadevi Park. Affiliated to international YHA. Some rm and dorm. Restaurant and cooking facilities.

Restaurants Some of the best restaurants are in hotels, but there is a wide range of restaurants outside. Chinese, Indian and continental specialties are all available. However, quality has sometimes changed rapidly in the late 1980s. The list below contains some suggestions, but enquire locally for completely up to date advice.

Sri Lankan – *Fountain Café*, Bridge St, Col 2 Local and European food, excellent. **Chinese** – *Peking Palace*, 3 Sellamuttu Ave, Col 3; *Nanking*, 33 Chatham St, Col 1; *Park View Lodge*, 70, Park St. Col 2; *Lotus Motel*, 265 Galle Rd, Col 3; *Jade Garden*, 126 Havelock Rd, Col 5. **Japanese** – *Kyoto*, 19 De Vos Ave, Col 4; *Nippon*, 123, Kumaran Ratnam Rd, Col 2; *Sakura*, 14 Rhineland Place, Kollupitya, Col 3. **Indian** – *Kohinoor*, 49 Dharmapala Mawatha, Col 3; *Saras Indian Restaurant*, 25 Charles Drive, Col 3. For good vegetarian try *Dasaprakash*, 237 Galle Rd, Col 4. **Western and Seafood** – *Seafish*, 5 Sir Chittampalam Gardiner Mawatha, Col 2. Worth trying for excellent fish at very reasonable prices, though lacking in atmosphere; *Alt Heidelberg*, 11 Galle Court 2, Col 3. German; *The Fab*, Kolpiti, 474 Galle Rd. Western food and excellent patisseries; **Italian** *Da Guido*, 47/4 Dharmapala Mawatha, Col 7. Excellent, recommended; *Ginza Araliya*, 286 Galle Rd. Col 3. **Fast foods** – *Nectar*, Mudalige Mawatha, corner of York St, Fort for snacks, ice reams. *Fountain Café*, 199 Union Pl in a garden is open all day for cold drinks, ice creams. Good value. *Peera*, 217 Galle Rd, Col 3, for cakes, snacks, breads, mainly take-away.

Bars All the main hotels have bars.

Banks Bank of Ceylon, Bureau de Change, Ground Fl, York St, T 22730. 0900-1800; weekends and holidays 0900-1600. Also at New HQ Bldg, 1st Fl, Janadhipathi Mawatha. 0900-1300 Mon, 0900-1330 Tue-Fri. Airport counter, T 030 2424, Open 24 hr. Airlanka Office, GCEC Bldg, Sir Baron Jayatilleke Mawatha. Issues Traveller's cheques, daily 0900-1530. People's Bank Foreign Branch, 27 MICH Bldg, Bristol St, T 20651. 0900-1330 Mon-Fri. Night Service at HQ Branch, Sir Chittampalam A Gardier Mawatha, T 36948. Card Centre, 1st Fl, 20 CA Gardiner Mawatha, Col 2, T 434147.

Shopping Gemstones, Batik, handlooms, silver jewellery, crafts (lac, reed, wood, brass, Demon dance masks, betel-nut boxes etc), spices and tea are best buys. You can shop with confidence at govt run shops although it may be interesting to wander in the bazaars and look for good bargains – *Sunday Bazaar* on Main St, Pettah and Duke St, Fort. The top hotels have good shopping arcades but prices are often higher than elsewhere. The shops in the Fort tend to be good but more expensive than equally good quality items in Kollupitiya. The boutiques in Pettah are worth a visit too.

The *Duty Free Complex* at the Katunayake International Airport stocks the usual articles, to be paid for in foreign currency and noted in your passport. The city shop is on Galle Rd, Kollupitiya. **State Gem Corpn**, 24 York St, Col 1, T 23377, has a showroom, guarantees all it sells and will test purchases from the dozens of jewellers in the capital, free at their laboratory. Branches at Hotel Intercontinental and at the Airport. The *Travel Information Centre*, 78 Steuart Pl, Col 3 has cassettes on pilgrim sites of words and music, booklets on the ancient cities, posters and picture post cards. *The Philatelic Bureau*, 4th Fl, Ceylinco House, Janadhipathi Mawatha, Fort has a good stock of stamps.

Gemstones, silver and gold articles, however, should only be bought at reputable shops – Arcades in the top hotels; *Premadas*, 17 Sir Baron Jayatilleke Mawatha, Col 1; *Zam Gems*, 81 Galle Rd, Col 4 with a few branches; *Janab*, 9 Temple Le, Col 3. Sea St in Pettah has a number of private Jewellers; *Hemchandra*, 229 Galle Rd, Col 3.

The govt also has outlets for handloom weaving and crafts, including *Laksala*, Australia House, York St, Col 1 which has a wide range of arts and crafts items. Other branches in Galle Face and Bambalapitiya. Open 0900-1700, except Sat and Sun, Apr-Oct. *Viskam Niwasa* (Dept of Industries), Bauddhaloka Mawatha, Col 7 also has high quality craft goods. *Handloom Shop*, 71 Galle Rd, Col 4. *Ceylon Ceramics Corpn* showroom in Bambalapitiya also has terracotta ware. *Lakmedura*, 113 Dharmapala Mawatha, Col 7.

For good batiks try *Serendib*, 100 Galle Rd, Col 4, *Fantasy Lanka*, 302 (1st Fl), Unity Plaza, 2 Galle Rd, Col 4, *Barbara Sansoni*, Galle Rd, Bambalipitiya and *Ena de Silva*, Duplication Rd, Kollupitiya.

Supermarkets in the centre include *Cornell's* nr the Duty Free Centre. Also *YWCA Spice Shop*, Union Pl. *Sri Lanka Tea Board*, 574 Galle Rd, Col 3, T 582121. *Mlesna Tea Centre*, Libery Plaza, Gr Fl.

Maps *Survey Dept, Map Sales Branch*, Kirula Rd, Narahenpita, T 585111, and *Map Sales Centre*, York St, Col 1 T 35328.

Books Good shops in the Inter-Continental and Taprobane Hotels. *Lakehouse*, 100 Sir C Gardiner Mawatha. *KVG de Silva*, 415 Galle Rd, Col 4; *MD Gunasena*, Olcott Mawatha, Col 11; others on Sir Baron Jayatilleka Mawatha, Fort. Second hand books from *Ashok Trading*, 183 Galle Rd, Col 4. *Children's Bookshop*, 20 Bogala Bldg, Janadhipathi Mawatha, nr Fort clocktower for Sri Lankan music cassettes. Books on Buddhism from *Buddhist Information Centre*, 50 Ananda Coomaraswamy Mawatha, Col 7

Photography Numerous in town. *Hayleys*, 303 Galle Rd, Col 3 offers special 1 hr service.

Local Transport Taxis – Metred taxis have yellow tops and red-on-white number plates. Make certain that the driver has understood where you wish to go and fix a rate for long-distance travel. 'Radio Cabs' are recommended (available at airport and in town) which have a higher min charge (Rs 28) but the meters are more dependable. Quick Radio Cabs, 911/1 Galle Rd, Col 4, T 502888 offers 24 hr service, no extra for 15 km of city, sp rates for return trips of 60+ km.

    Car Hire – Avis, Hertz and Europcar are represented. Self drive cars are available, though it is easier (and safer!) to have a chauffeur-driven car charged at a similar rate. Mackinnons, 4 Leyden Bastian Rd, Col 1, T 29881; Quickshaw's, 3 Kalinga Place, Col 5, T 583133; Mercantile Tours, 586 Galle Rd, Col 3, T 501946; Aban Tours, 498 Galle Rd, Col 3, T 574160. Sudans, 18-1/2 Mudalige Mawatha, T 431 865 or at Airport.

    Scooter-rickshaws (3-wheelers) for 2 passengers, are metred, but you can negotiate a price.

    Bus Good network of buses and mini-buses. Ceylon Transport Board (CTB), private and mini-buses compete on popular routes. Local CTB buses have white signs, yellow for long-distance. Central Bus Stand, Olcott Mawatha, SE corner of Pettah. Enquiries. T 28081.

    Trains Suburban services to Bambalapitya, Kollupitiya, Dehiwala and Mt Lavinia all along the Galle Rd. The Fort Station, SW corner of Pettah.

    Warning Beware of pickpockets on public transport.

Entertainment Cultural shows, performances of Sinhala dance and music can be seen at the YMBA Hall, Borella, Navarangahala, Cumaratunga Munidasa Mawatha, and at Lionel Wendt Hall, 19 Guildford Crescent both at Col 7. Lumbini Hall, Havelock Town specialises in Sinhalese theatre. Some of the top hotels put on regular folk dance shows and also have western floor shows and live music for dancing, open to non-residents.

    The larger a/c cinemas along Galle Rd sometimes have English language films.

Cultural Centres Buddhist Information Centre, 50 Ananda Coomaraswamy Mawatha, T 573285. Alliance Française 54 Ward Place, Col 7.

Sports Visitors may take out temporary membership at the various local clubs. Swimming, Cricket, Otters Aquatic, Rowing, C Gardiner Mawatha. *Bridge* The Contract Bridge Association of Sri Lanka, 532/3 Galle Rd, Col 3.

National Museum, Albert Crescent. 0900-1700, Sun-Th. Closed on public holidays. Rs 40. (Bus 114, 138). Opened in 1877 – collection of paintings, sculptures, furniture and porcelain. Also masks and the library houses a unique collection of over 4,000 *Ola* (palm manuscripts). An extremely rich archaeological and artistic collection. Very well labelled and organised, a visit is an excellent introduction to a tour of Sri Lanka. Exhibits include an outstanding collection of bronzes from Polonnaruwa between the 10th and 12th centuries, and the lion throne of *King Nissanka Mala*, which has become the symbol of Sri Lanka. On the ground floor is a collection of Buddhist sculpture, including a striking 1500 year old stone statue of the Buddha from Toluvila. Dance masks line the stairs to the 1st floor, where there are superbly executed scale reproductions of the wall paintings at Sigiriya and Polonnaruwa. There are also very good natural history and geological galleries.

Dutch Period Museum, *Prince St, Pettah. 0900-1700, Mon-Fri. The fine old Dutch town hall, which has been used as a hospital, police station and a post office before being renovated to house the museum.*

Bandaranaike Museum, Bauddhaloka Mawatha. 0900-1600 except Mon and Poya holidays. Devoted to the life and times of the late prime minister.

Libraries See the National Museum above.

Parks and Zoos Dehiwala Zoo, Allan Avenue, 10 km SW from centre. 0800-1800. Entry Rs 30, plus charge for photography. One of the most attractive in Asia. 15 ha undulating ground, beautifully laid out with shrubs, flowering trees and plants, orchids, lakes and fountains. Over 2,000 animals include sloth bear, leopard, civets and other small cats, many kinds of lizard, crocodiles and snakes. Lions, tigers, jaguars, black panthers, and many exotic species such as hippopotami, rhinos, giraffes and kangaroos. The zoo also has an aquarium with over 500 species of fish, and is particularly noted for its collection of birds. There is a troupe of trained elephants which are shown every afternoon. **Bus** no 132 or 176, also train to Dehiwala Station.

   Vihara Mahadevi Park (formerly Victoria Park), on the site of the old Cinnamon Gardens. Now re-named after the mother of the Sinhalese King Dutthagamani. A botanical garden, including named species ranging from a bo tree to an enormous profusion of climbing plants, parasites and rare orchids.

Clubs Orient Club; Rotary and Lions Clubs.

Post Office GPO, Janadhipathi Mawatha, Col 1. Telegraph Office, Lower Chatham St, Col 1, T 31967.

Places of Worship Buddhist – Vajiraramaya, Bambalapitiya; Gotami Vihara, Borella; Dipaduttaramaya, Kotahena; Gangaramaya Bhikku Training Centre and Sima Malaka, 61 Sri Jinaratana Rd, Col 2; Mettaramaya, Lauries Rd, Col 4. **Hindu** – Temples at Bambalapitiya, Kochchikade, Kotahena, Pettah and Siva Subramaniam Kovil, Gintupitiya reached from Sea St, Pettah. **Mosques** – Devatagaha, CWW Kannangara Mawatha, Union Pl; Afar Jummah Masjid, Pettah. **Christian** – St Peter's, Fort; St Lucia's Cathedral, Kotahena; St Andrew's Scots Church, Col 3; Methodist, Col 3.

Hospitals and Medical Services General Hospital, Regent St, T 91111 (24 hr Accident and Emergency). Cardiology Unit, T 91111. Lady Ridgeway (Children's), T 593711. 0700-1600. **Chemists** A number on Galle Rd, Union Place, Pettah and Fort.

Useful Addresses/ Emergency Numbers Fire, T 22222, Police, T 33333. Police Station, S of Maradana Rly Station, Kollupitiya, Bambalapitya and Wellawatte. Dept of Immigration and Emigration, Chaitya Rd, T 29851. Tourist Police, 12, Hospital St, New Secretariat Bldg, Fort, T 26941. Automobile Association of Ceylon, 40 Sir Mohammad Macan Marker Mawatha, Galle Face, Col 3. T 21528
   For visiting ancient sites: Ministry of Cultural Affairs, Maly St, Col 2, T 587912. Open 0830-1615, Dept of Archaeology, Marcus Fernando Mawatha, Col 7 and Cultural Triangle Office, 212 Bauddalaka Mawatha, Col 7

Foreign Representations Australia, 3 Cambridge Pl, T 59876. **Austria**, Col 2, T 91613. **Bangladesh**, Col 7, T 502397. **Canada**, 6 Gregory's Rd, T 595841. **France**, Col 5, T 583621. **Germany**, 40 Alfred House Av, T 580531. **India**, 18-3/1 Sir Baron Jayatilleka Mawatha, T 21604. **Indonesia**, 1 Police Park Terrace, T 580113. **Italy**, Col 5, T 588622. **Japan**, Col 7, T 93831. **Malaysia**, 63A Ward Pl, T 94837. **Maldives**, 25 Melbourne Av, T 586762. **Nepal**, Col 4, T 586762. **Netherlands**, 25 Torrington Av, T 589626. **Pakistan**, 211 De Saram Pl, T 596301. **Sweden**, 315 Vauxhall St, T 20201. **Thailand**, 26 Gregory's Rd, T 597406. **UK**, 190 Galle Rd, Col 3, T 27611. **USA**, Col 3, T 548007. **USSR**, Col 3, T 573555.

Chambers of Commerce Dept of Small Industries, 71 Galle Rd, Col 4. T 501209, Telex: 21713 BSDS CE. Trade enquiries for Sir Lanka Handicrafts Board, Laksala, York St, Col 1. T 29247, Telex: 22773 LAKSAL CE; Investment Promotion Dept, Greater Colombo Economic Commission, PO Box 1768, 14 Sir Baron Jayatileke Mawatha, Col 1. T 22447, Fax: 547995.

Travel Agents and Tour Operators The are numerous travel agents. Among them are: *Aitken Spence*, 13 Sir Baron Jayatilleke Mawatha, Col 1; *Ceylon Tours*, Col 2, T 21722; *Thomas Cook*, 15 Sir Baron Jayatilleka Mawatha, T 54597; *Cox & Kings*, Col 2, T 34295; *Paradise Holidays*, 5 Palmyra Ave, Col 3, T 380106; *Gemini Tours*, 40 Wijerama Mawatha, Col 7, T 598 446.

Tourist Information Centre TIC, Ceylon Tourist Board, 78 Steuart Pl, Galle Rd, T 437059. Open 0830-1615, Mon-Fri, 0800-1230, weekends and public holidays. Free literature in English, German, French, Italian, Swedish and Japanese to personal callers. Guide service arranged (see under General Information). Tickets and permits for ancient archaeological sites, contact offices listed above in Useful addresses.
   Tours City Tours by car with a chauffeur/Guide for 3 – Half day: 40 km, Buddhist Temple, Hindu Temple, Zoo and residential area. About Rs 225. Full Day: also includes Kelaniya Temple. About Rs 350. For nature safaris, hiking and birdwatching contact Wildlife and Nature Protection Soc, Chaitiya Rd, Marine Drive, Fort, T 25248.

Airlines Airlanka, 14 Sir Baron Jayatilleke Mawatha, T 21291. **Aeroflot**, 79/81 Hemas Bldg, York St, T 25580. **Air France**, Mack Air, 4 Leyden Bastion Rd, T 35333. **British Airways**, Airline Services, Ramada Renaissance Hotel, 115 C Gardiner Mawatha, T 20231. **Gulf Air**, 11 York St, T 547627. **Indian Airlines and Maldives International**, 95 Sir Baron Jayatilleke Mawatha, T 26844. **Japan Airlines**, Delmege Air Services, Meridien Hotel, 64 Lotus Rd, T 545480. KLM, 61 Janadhipathi Mawatha, T 545531. **Lufthansa**, Freudenberg Air Services, 8 Galle Face Rd, Col 3, T 35536. **PIA**, 432 Galle Rd, Col 3, T 573475. **Qantas**, A Baur, 5 Upper Chatham St, T 20551. **Royal Nepal Airlines**, 434 Galle Rd, Col 3, T 24045. **Singapore**

Airlines, 15A Jayatilleke Mawatha, T 22711. **SAS** and **Thai International**, c/o Browns Tours, 16 Janadhipathi Mawatha, T 36201. **TWA**, Mercantile Tours, 51 Janadhipathi Mawatha, T 26611.

Air Services International Airport, Katunayake, T 030 2911. TIC, 030 2411 (Flight times, day and night). Ratmalana Airport, T 716261. Upali Travels charter helicopter services to places of interest and resort hotels and charter aircraft for domestic airports. Air Taxi Ltd flies 5 passengers on Cessna aircraft and helicopters with landing facilities at Batticaloa, Hingurakgoda, Vavuniya, Anuradhapura, Kankesanthurai, Koggala, Sigiriya, Amparai, Puttalam, Katunayake and Trincomalee. Contact Thomas Cook, 15 Sir Baron Jayatilleke Mawatha, Col 1, T 545971.

Rail Trains to all important places of interest. **Anuradhapura** *Yal Devi*, 77, daily, 0545, 4 hr; *Rajarata Rajini*, 85, daily, 1405, 4 hr 45; **Polonnaruwa** *Udaya Devi*, 79, daily, 0605, 6 hr 20; *Mail*, 93, daily, 2000, 7 hr 30. **Kandy** *Podi Menike*, 5, daily, 0555, 2 hr 50; *Intercity Express*, 9, daily, 0655, 2 hr 35; *Intercity Express*, 29, daily, 1535, 2 hr 30; **Galle** (No 1st class on this service) 50, daily, 0730, 2 hr 45; 52, daily, 0845, 2 hr 45; *Galu Kumari*, 56, daily, 1335, 2 hr 45; 775, daily, 1915, 3 hr 15; **Matara**, (No 1st class on this service) 50, daily, 0730, 4 hr 30; 52, daily, 0845,4 hr 30; *Galu Kumari*, 56, daily, 1335, 4 hr 30; **Nanu-Oye, (Nuwara Eliya)**, *Podi Menike*, 5, daily, 0555, 7hr 35; 123 Express, daily, 0945, 6 hr; *Colombo-Kandy Mail*, 45, daily, 2015, 8 hr; **Bandarawela**, *Podi Menike*, 5, daily, 0555, 7hr 35; 123 Express, daily, 0945, 8 hr; *Colombo-Kandy Mail*, 45, daily, 2015, 8 hr 15.

Special a/c Hitachi trains for day tours to Kandy and Hikkaduwa. Inter-city Expresses to Kandy and Bandarawela. Occasional tours on vintage steam trains – details from the Railway Tourist Office, Fort Station, T 35838.

Road Bus The Sri Lanka Transport Board has a good island-wide network and travel is cheap. Principal towns have an Express Service every 1/2 hr; Regular buses leave every 15 from Pettah and a fast Inter-city service operates to Kandy. Central Bus Stand, Olcott Mawatha, Pettah. Enquiries. T 28081. Frequent services to Kandy, Galle, Ratnapura, Anuradhapura, Kurunegala, Matara. 8 buses daily to Kataragama, 2 to Medawachchiya. Minibuses also leave from the bus stop and from the Rly station.

Excursions

Mt Lavinia Galle Rd continues S to *Mt Lavinia*, one of the most popular excursions just 13 km from Colombo, and 3 km beyond the Dehiwala zoo. It takes its name from a corruption of the Sinhalese 'Lihinia Kanda' – *gull rock*. An attractive picnic spot, the original Mt Lavinia Hotel was Governor Edward Barnes' weekend retreat. He was forced to sell the house by the Government in England who approved neither the expenditure nor the luxurious style.

Hotels A *Mount Lavinia Hotel* T 715 221. 275 a/c 80 rm. For 50 years it was a centre for well-to-do tourists and visitors from the city, but it gradually fell into disrepair. It has now been radically renovated and extended. Excellent buffet meals. **C** *Mount Royal Beach*, 36 College Av, T 714001. 90 rm. Central a/c. Restaurants, bar, exchange, pool/Hydrospa, nightclub, beach huts. **C** *Riviras*, 50/2 De Saram Rd, T 717786. 16 rm, some a/c. Villa style. **C** *Palm Beach*, 52 De Saram Rd T 712713. 30 rm, 10 a/c. Restaurant, bar, exchange, pool, indoor games. **C** *Sea Breeze Tour Inn*, De Saram Rd, T 714017. 23 rm. **C** *Saltaire*, 50/5 De Saram Rd, T 717731. Wooden cabanas, in a large garden nr the sea. Breakfast available. **D** *Sunray Beach Villas*, 3 De Saram Rd, T 716272. A guest house with 3 rm in a comfortable house with garden. **D** *Estoril Beach Resort*, 30 Sri Dharmapala Rd. 25 rm.

On the seaward side of Galle Rd, S of St. Mary's Church, there is a wide range of basic **E** and **F** category accommodation.

Jawardenepura – Kotte The Gramodaya Folk Arts Centre (11 ha) has craftsmen working with brass, silver, leather, coir and producing jewellery, pottery, natural silk, lace and reed baskets. There is a shop, a herbal health drink counter, an aquarium and a restaurant serving Sri Lankan specialities.

COLOMBO TO NEGOMBO, PUTTALAM AND ANURADHAPURA

The coastal route to Puttalam (NH 3) runs due N through apparently endless groves of coconut palms. It passes the International Airport about 4 km S of Negombo, then runs close to the coast and coastal lagoons all the way to Puttalam. The road from Puttalam to Anuradhapura crosses much more open terrain, the dryness leading to much less dense forest and sparser cultivation.

The NH 1 crosses the **Kelaniya River** and runs N, 3 or 4 km inland of the coast. At **Dalugama** a left turn leads to the minor road which runs along the coast itself. At *Wattala* (11 km from the city centre) it passes the *Pegasus Reef Hotel* (see above). It is difficult to tell where Colombo begins and ends. The main road passes through some built up areas and an industrial estate, and is very densely populated. Half way to Negombo it passes through **Ja-ela**, at the heart of what used to be one of Sri Lanka's main cinnamon producing areas. Now the road runs through coconut groves, following the line of a Dutch canal up to the *Negombo* lagoon and beyond to Chilaw.

Negombo (*Population* 55,000, *Altitude* Sea level). Just 6 km from the international airport, it is Sri Lanka's biggest tourist resort complex, with some pollution problems to match. The Dutch had captured it from the Portuguese in 1644, and made it an important centre. It has a high reputation for its brasswork, and today the Negombo Lagoon has become the country's main fishing port, and a centre of prawn and shrimp fishing and research.

Tourists come here for the exciting diving it offers and for other water sports. Scuba diving allows you get excellent views of corals within 10-20 m and the marine life includes barracuda, blue ringed angels and unusual star fish. The reef is 3 km W of the beach hotel area.

Local festivals 24 July *Fishermen's festival*. St Mary's Church. Pilgrims flock to the church for what is one of the major festivals of the region.

Places of interest The town still has a few remains from its period as a Dutch settlement, notably the residence of the District Judge, the Dutch church, and the impressive gateway to the Fort (1672). **St Mary's Church** is one of many that bears witness to the extent of Portuguese conversions to Roman Catholicism, especially among the fishermen in Negombo District. The fishermen go out in old fashioned catamarans and outrigger canoes and bring up their catch onto the beach every day. Seer, skipjack, herring, mullet, pomfret, amber-jack, and sometimes sharks, are usually landed in the afternoon. Prawns and lobster are caught in the lagoon.

Warning It is often dangerous to swim, particularly during the SW monsoon, May-Oct. Warning notices are now posted on the beach.

Hotels Many hotels and guest houses have been built, most along Lewis Place, which is the beach road, due N of the lagoon. Some are a few km out of Negombo. The **B** category do not have the same facilities as comparable city hotels (*Dolphin, Goldi Sands* and *Royal Oceanic* offer conference facilities) but all have swimming pools, watersports and often tennis and squash. Meals normally included in price, especially in season. **B** *Dolphin*, Waikkal, T 031 3129. **B** *Browns Beach Hotel* 175 Lewis Place, T 031 20 31 130 a/c rm, 10 bungalows. **B** *Royal Oceanic*, Ethukala, T 031 2377. 85 large a/c rm with sea view. **C** *Goldi Sands*, Ethukala, T 031 2021. 75 rm with balcony and sea view. Restaurants, bar, exchange, shops, pool, squash, tennis, night club. **C** *Blue Lagoon*, Talahena, T 031 3004. 28 rm with garden or lagoon view. Restaurant, bar, pool, some water sports, large garden. **C** *Catamaran Beach* 89 Lewis Place, T 031 2342 48 rm. **C** *Don's Beach* 75 Lewis Place, T 031 2342. 60 rm. **E** *The Rainbow Guest House* 3, Carron Place, T 031 2082. Excellent food, recommended. **E** *Beach View Guest House* Lewis Place (next to Blue Oceanic Hotel). Clean, well recommended. **F** There are lots of cheap guest houses along Lewis Place. Among the best value for money is *Seaforth*, 31 Customs House Rd.

Restaurants Sea food is the speciality of many hotels and restaurants. Lobsters, crabs and prawns are all excellent. In the very difficult political circumstances of the last 5 years many restaurants have come and gone with the seasons. Experiment.

Cycle hire Easy to arrange – the flat roads make a short trip out of Negombo an attractive option.

Travel Regular bus and train services to Colombo.

From Negombo follow the NH 3 N. To the left just after passing *Kochchikade* is the hotel **A** *The Dolphin* Kammala South, Waikkal T 031 31 29. 125 rm. A beautiful hotel, probably the best in the Negombo region. Surrounded by a garden of palm trees, superb swimming pool. **B** *Ranweli Holiday Village*, T 031 2136 84 rm.

NH 3 goes on to **Marawila** (20 km), one of many villages with large Roman Catholic churches. One of the regions most influenced by the Portuguese, the coastal strip has a high proportion of Catholics. In 1991 23% of the population of Gampaha District, inland from Negombo, was Christian, increasing northwards to 38% in Puttalam District. Crossing the estuary just after passing through **Mahawewa** (6 km) the road passes through **Madampe** (7 km), known for its Coconut Research Institute. Running between the coastal lagoon and the railway, the road then enters *Chilaw* (12 km). A small village, but an important Roman Catholic centre, with another very large church, there is also an interesting Saivite Temple at Munneswaram. Contains Tamil inscriptions, and is an important pilgrimage centre.

Crossing the *Deduru Oya* 7 km N of Chilaw, the road then runs due N. A left turn at **Battuluoya** leads to *Udappawa*, 12 km N of Chilaw. A tiny Tamil Hindu village, it is noted for its firewalking ceremonies which take place in Jul-Aug every year. Experiments conducted in 1935-36 showed that the coals were heated to about 500C during the ceremony.

Marshes and lagoons lie between the road and the sea for much of the route N to Puttalam, which crosses a series of minor rivers and a few major ones such as the **Battulu Oya**, 17 km N of Chilaw. At **Palavi**, 3 km S of Puttalam, a left turn goes up the W side of the Puttalam lagoon to *Kalpitya* (25 km), with an excellent road. The town has an old Dutch Fort and an attractive 18th century church. Continuing up the main road to Puttalam is the Lake View Restaurant, 139 Colombo Road. Clean and good food. You can cross the Puttalam Lagoon by ferry to Kavaitia, travelling S to complete a round trip to Puttalam.

From Puttalam the NH 12 goes NE to Anuradhapura, fringing the **Wilpattu National Park**, particularly famous for its leopards and sloth bears. The largest reserve in Sri Lanka, this is best seen by staying at **Kal Oya** (30 km) and taking advantage of the government organised tours. Private cars are not allowed into the reserve, which unlike some of the island's other parks has some dense jungle, interspersed with savannah and sand dunes. A number of *villus* * – the small lakes which attract animals to drink, have crocodiles and a large variety of water birds, especially winter migrants from Nov-Jan. Some Sinhalese ruins have been discovered in the forested areas to the E.

30 km before Anuradhapura, turn off the NH and go another 7 km to reach the entrance to the park which covers 1,900 sq km. About 300 km of jeep track cover the area. In addition to paying an entrance fee, if you have not come on a tour from Kal Oya, you will have to choose between hiring a jeep with driver/guide (min charge is high) or taking a seat in a mini-bus. Although a jeep is more expensive, unless you can share with others, it is by far the best way to get a glimpse of a leopard and see the wildlife which includes a variety of deer, mongoose,wild buffaloes and wild boar.

Early morning or late afternoon are the best times for a visit, to avoid the heat of the day and also to see the animals. If you wish to visit the Park from Anuradhapura there are **Buses**, twice daily, or taxis.

Hotels Several very basic *Park Bungalows* are located within the perimeter, which can be reserved through Wildlife Dept, Transwork House, Col 1, T 33787. You need to bring your bedding and food (cook provided). The *Nature and Wildlife Conservation Soc* can sleep up to 10. Reservations: Soc Offices, Chaitiya Rd, Marine Drive, Fort, Col, T 25248. At **Kal Oya, C** *The Wilpattu Hotel*, T 29 752, 41 rm with fan, shower and mosquito nets. Dining room overlooks Kal Oya river. Excellent bungalows. Recommended. Alternatively there is the *Pershamel Safari Hotel*, Pahamaragahawewa has 12 rm.

From Kal Oya it is 44 km to Anuradhapura along the rather poor quality NH 12. See below for description.

COLOMBO TO ANURADHAPURA AND JAFFNA

The route runs NE from Colombo across the coastal plain. Once outside Colombo, the first few km are through a patchwork of paddy fields fringed with coconut trees. This lush and beautiful scenery continues 65 km, through fields interspersed with clumps of tall areca nut palms, endless bananas and then climbing gently over attractive rolling low hills, the site of *chena* (shifting) cultivation for generations. Leaving the wet zone just N of Colombo, rainfall declines steadily NW.

Leave Colombo on NH 1 through *Peligayoda* (8 km), now virtually a suburb of Colombo, and pass through **Mahara**, where there is an excellent *Rest House*, and **Kadawata** (7 km) to Pasyala *(for Cadjugama*, 30 km). 5 km off the National Highway to the left after a further 14 km are the Botanical Gardens of **Heneratgoda** near *Gampaha*, a beautiful garden town. These are particularly famous as the nursery of Asia's first rubber trees, introduced from the Amazon basin over a century ago. Several of the early imports are now magnificent specimens, the first tree planted carrying the No 2. It is over 100 years old. The trees include *Hevea brasiliensis*, *Uncaria gambier*, rubber producing lianas (*Landolphia*), and the drug *ipecacuanha*. A female of the Coco de Mer was imported from the Seychelles and bore fruit in 1915. The garden has a portion of original jungle preserved.

The road passes by the former estate of Sir Solomon Dias Bandaranaike, who was aide de camp to the British Governor at the time of the First World War. His son, **Solomon Western Ridgway Dias Bandaranaike**, became Prime Minister of independent Ceylon in 1956, but was assassinated in 1959. His tombstone is by the side of the road 38 km out of Colombo. His widow succeeded him as Prime Minister, and remains an active force in Sri Lankan politics. The family home, where visitors such as King George V and Jawaharlal Nehru stayed, can be seen nearby. After a further 7 km *Pasyala* is on the W edge of the central highland massif. The area is noted for its graphite (*plumbago*) mines and betel nuts.

The road passes through a series of small villages and towns, including *Warakapola* (10 km). After 2 km the main road to Kandy goes off to the right, via **Kegalla** (see below). For Anuradhapura the road goes straight on, through **Polgahawela** (literally 'the field of the coconut') 17 km, and **Pottuhera** (10 km) to reach **Kurunegala** (10 km). *Rest house* overlooking the lake. Clean and pleasant. The town is surrounded by a chain of bare rocks which look like animals – elephant rock, tortoise rock etc. They radiate tremendous heat, often making the town intensely uncomfortable. The town is at the foot of the 325 m rock **Etagala**. Excellent views from top. There is an attractive artificial lake at foot of the hills. 18 km NE of Kurunegala is an ancient Buddhist temple, some of the doors being carved and inlaid with ivory.

From Kurunegala 2 routes go N to Anuradhapura. The W route is 106 km via

Padeniya. It passes 3 small sites but only goes through small villages on the way. The E route is the road to Trincomalee. It goes up to Dambulla, where there are famous rock caves and temples. Dambulla is also only 15 km from the magnificent and dramatic site of Sigiriya. 5 km after Dambulla the road is joined from the S by the road from Kandy, then after a further 1 km the Trincomalee road turns right while the Anuradhapura road goes straight on. The E route from Kurunegala to Anuradhapura is 116 km. The railway line follows a route between the 2 major roads in the S section, joining the W route just N of **Uduweriya** and then keeping close to the road all the way to Anuradhapura.

The W route turns right for Anuradhapura at *Pandeniya* (26 km). The NH10 road goes straight on to *Puttalam* (60 km) see above. The road goes N from Pandeniya to *Balalla* (17 km), then 1 km and turns right to *Maho* (2 km), the base from which to see the 13th century capital of *Yapahuwa* (4 km). To see Yapahuwa, take the road to the left, which leads to the foot of the rock on which the fortress stands. The tooth relic now enshrined at Kandy was carried from the temple here to India, then recovered in 1288 by **Parakrama Bahu III**. It was built as the fortress capital of the Sinhalese kings in 1301 and when abandoned was inhabited by Buddhist monks and religious ascetics.

Somewhat similar to Sigiriya in its setting, it is set on a vast granite rock rising 100 m abruptly from the surrounding plain, with a 1 km long encircling path rising to the top. The fort is encircled by a moat and ramparts, and there are signs of other ancient means of defence. The impressive ornamental staircase is still well preserved, and the ruins at the head of the remarkable flight of granite steps are unique. One of the two window frames is now exhibited in the Colombo Museum.

Return to the main road and turn N through **Uduweriya** (2 km) to **Galgamuwa** (17 km), **Mahagalkadawala** (5 km; turn left in town to see *Rajagane* 1 km), and *Anuradhapura* (37 km). The road into Anuradhapura enters past the lake, *Tissa Wewa*, on the right, and passes some of the main dagobas before reaching the new town.

Anuradhapura

	Jan	Feb	Mar	Apr	May	Jun	Jul	Aug	Sep	Oct	Nov	Dec	Av/Tot
Max (°C)	31	35	37	38	35	34	35	35	33	34	31	30	34
Min (°C)	21	22	24	25	25	26	25	26	25	24	23	23	24
Rain (mm)	94	47	71	178	89	10	34	40	67	263	244	223	1360

Anuradhapura is Sri Lanka's most sacred town. At its height it was said to have stretched 25 km in each direction. Its ruins and monuments today are widely scattered, which makes a thorough tour time consuming, but it more than repays the effort. From origins as a settlement in the 6th century BC, it was made capital in 377 BC by King *Pandukhabhaya*, and named after the constellation Anuradha. Pandukhabhaya started the great irrigation works on which it depended.

The first era of religious building followed the conversion of King *Devanampiyatissa*. In the 40 years of his reign these included the Thuparama Dagoba and Vihara, and the Maha Vihara. Also during his reign a branch of the Bo tree under which the Buddha was believed to have gained his enlightenment was brought from India and successfully transplanted. It is one of the holiest Buddhist sites in the world.

Anuradhapura remained a capital city until the 9th century AD, when it reached its peak of power and vigour. After the 13th century it almost entirely disappeared, the irrigation works on which it had depended falling into total disuse, and its political functions taken over first by Polonnaruwa, and then by

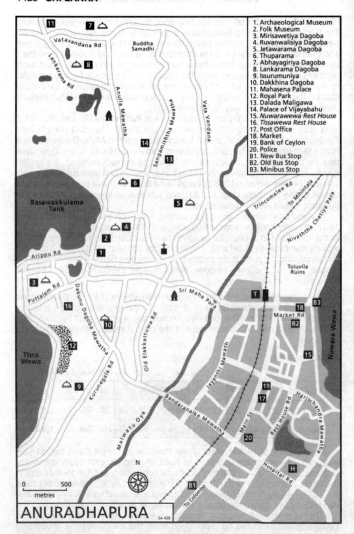

1. Archaeological Museum
2. Folk Museum
3. Mirisawetiya Dagoba
4. Ruvanwalisiya Dagoba
5. Jetawarama Dagoba
6. Thuparama
7. Abhayagiriya Dagoba
8. Lankarama Dagoba
9. Issurumuniya
10. Dakkhina Dagoba
11. Mahasena Palace
12. Royal Park
13. Dalada Maligawa
14. Palace of Vijayabahu
15. *Nuwarawewa Rest House*
16. *Tissawewa Rest House*
17. Post Office
18. Market
19. Bank of Ceylon
20. Police
B1. New Bus Stop
B2. Old Bus Stop
B3. Minibus Stop

ANURADHAPURA

SA 409

capitals to the S. The earliest restoration work began in 1872, and has continued ever since. The town is now the headquarters of the Ceylon Archaeological Survey.

Entry Individual entry to the Anuradhapura sites is US$4. Combined tickets for the triangle of ancient sites can be obtained from Colombo. **See page 1461.**

Photography Permits are essential, obtainable from the Office of Antiquities, next door to the Archaeological Museum.

Local festivals June At the full moon in the season of *Poson* is the festival celebrating the introduction of Buddhism to Sri Lanka. There are huge processions and many pilgrims visit the town.

Places of interest

Note The sites of interest are scattered, and the most enjoyable way of seeing them is by bicycle. Some guest houses can provide cycles or arrange hire. Cars may also be hired.

The **Archaeological Museum** is central to the site and makes a good starting point for a tour. Immediately to its W is the Basawakkulama Tank, the oldest artificial lake in the city, built by King Pandukabhaya in the 4th century BC.

Opposite the museum is the *Ruvanwelisiya Dagoba*. The renovation has flattened the shape of the dome, and some of the painting is of questionable style, but it remains a remarkably striking monument. The dome is 80 m in diameter at its base and 55 m high. It was begun by King Dutthagamani (*Dutugemunu*) to house relics, and priests from all over India were recorded as being present at the enshrinement of the relics in 140 BC. A small passage leads to the relic chamber. At the cardinal points are four 'chapels' which were reconstructed in 1873, when renovation started.

About 1 km to the SW, near the Tissawewa *Rest House*, is the *Mirisawetiya Dagoba*. Dating originally from the 2nd century BC, it was completely rebuilt during the reign of King Kasyapa V in 930 AD. Surrounded by the ruins of monasteries on 3 sides, there are some superb sculptures of Dhayani Buddhas in the shrines of its chapels. Completely ruined, renovation work on the dagoba started in 1979 with support from Unesco.

To the S is the *Tissa Wewa* lake, covering 150 ha and built by King Devanampiyatissa. You can either go S along the tank *bund* or round by the road to the **Royal Park** and *Issurumuniyagala*. This small group of black rocks, standing out from the green fields and trees, is one of the most attractive and peaceful places in the town. It also has some outstanding sculpture. The rock temple, itself carved out of solid rock, houses a large statue of the seated Buddha. On the terraces outside is a small square pool, and behind the pool some of the best sculptures in Anuradhapura. One shows a horse's head on the shoulders of a man, the superbly executed 'Kapila'. There are also some beautifully carved elephants, showing great individual character. Perhaps the most famous of the sculptures is that known as 'the lovers', carved on a small panel to the left of the front terrace.

From Issurumuniyagala return E to the road and follow it back towards the centre, passing after 1 km *King Elara's* tomb, also known as *Dakkhina dagoba* (Southern dagoba). The Chola Tamil king had captured Anuradhapura in 205 BC, setting up a Tamil kingdom which lasted over 40 years. Sinhalese kingdoms in the S eventually rose against him, and he was killed in a single-handed duel by King Dutthagamani, who gave him full battle honours. A.L. Basham gives a flavour of the Mahavansa's account of the battle between Dutthagamani's and Elara's forces:

> The city had three moats, And was guarded by a high wall.
> > Its gate was covered with iron, Hard for foes to shatter.
> The elephant knelt on his knees, and battering with his tusks
> > stone and mortar and brick, he attacked the iron gate.
> The Tamils from the watch-tower, threw missiles of every kind,
> > balls of red hot iron and vessels of molten pitch.
> Down fell the molten pitch upon Kandula's back.
> > In anguish of pain he fled and plunged in a pool of water.
> "This is no drinking bout!" cried Gothaimbara.
> > "Go, batter the iron gate! Batter down the gate!!"
> In his pride the best of tuskers took heart and trumpeted loud.
> He reared up out of the water and stood on the bank defiant.
> The elephant-doctor washed away the pitch, and put on balm.
> > The King mounted the elephant and rubbed his brow with his hand.
> 'Dear Kandula, I'll make you the lord of all Ceylon!' he said,

> *and the beast was cheered, and was fed with the best fodder.*
> *He was covered with a cloth, and he was armoured well*
>   *with armour for his back of seven-fold buffalo hide.*
> *On the armour was placed a skin soaked in oil.*
>   *Then, trumpeting like thunder, he came on, fearless of danger.*
> *He pierced the door with his tusks. With his feet he trampled the threshold.*
>   *And the gate and the lintel crashed loudly to earth.*

800 m to the N is one of Sri Lanka's most sacred sites, the **Bo tree** (Pipal, or *Ficus religiosa*). This magnificent tree was planted as a cutting brought from India by Mahinda's sister, the **Princess Sanghamitta**, at some point after 236 BC. A succession of guardians has kept uninterrupted watch over the tree ever since. Immediately opposite is the **Brazen Palace**, so called after its now-disappeared roof, reputedly made of bronze. It is the most remarkable of many monastic buildings scattered across the site. Described in the Mahavansa as having 9 storeys, there are 600 pillars laid out over an area 70 m square. The pillars, just under 4 m high, supported the first floor. You need imagination to visualise the scale of the building as it may have been, for there is no hint of the structural style or decoration that may have characterised it. The walls between the pillars were made of brick, while the upper floors were wooden. Both have long since disappeared. Built in 161 BC by Dutthagamani, it was the heart of the monastic life of the city, the *Mahavihara*.

The road E between the Brazen Palace and the Bo tree goes to the new town, the railway station and the Nuwarawewa, the largest of Anuradhapura's artificial lakes, covering over 1000 ha and completed about 20 BC. Going E from the Brazen Palace (along the Trincomalee and Mihintale Rd), a left fork after 800 m goes N to the ruined **Jetawarama Dagoba** (after the first Buddhist monastery). **Note** The names of the Jetawarama and Abhayagiriya dagobas are sometimes reversed, which can still be confusing. Now covered in vegetation, this is the largest dagoba in Anuradhapura. It is also being renovated with help from Unesco. Started by King Mahasena (AD 275-292), the paved platform on which it stands covers more than 3 ha and it has a diameter of over 100 m. It has been calculated to have enough bricks to build a 3 m high brick wall from the S tip of Sri Lanka to Jaffna and back down the coast to Trincomalee. Near the dagoba are 3 great seated Buddhas and the **Kuttan-Pokuna** – recently restored 8th and 9th century ritual baths. You can see the underground water supply channel at one end of the second bath.

Continuing N from the Jetawarama Dagoba, turn left at the crossroads to the oldest dagoba, the **Thuparama**. Built by Devanampitiya in 307 BC, the 19 m high dagoba has retained its beautiful bell shape, despite restoration work. It is surrounded by concentric circles of graceful granite monolithic pillars, possibly originally designed to support an over-arching thatched cover. However, it is also a centre of active pilgrimage, and is highly decorated with flags and lights. Immediately to its NE was the original **Dalada Maligawa**, where the Tooth Relic was first enshrined when it was brought to Ceylon in AD 313. Fa Hien, who visited the site when the relic was still in place in Anuradhapura, gave a vivid description of its exhibition.

The road N (Sanghamitta Mawatha) goes 1.5 km through the site of the 11th century palace of Vijayabahu I to the **Abhayagiriya dagoba**. 400 m round and supposedly 135 m high in its original form, part of the pinnacle has disappeared. It is now about 110 m high. Built in 88 BC by *Valagam Bahu*, the temple and its associated monastery were built in an attempt to weaken the political hold of the Hinayana Buddhists, and to give shelter to monks of the Mahayana school. There are 2 splendid sculpted guardians at the threshold. Immediately to the E is the superb statue of the Buddha in meditation (**Samadhi Buddha**). Roofed to protect it from the weather, it probably dates from the 4th century AD. To the W of the

Abhayagiri dagoba are the ruins of the *Mahasena Palace*, where there is a particularly fine carved stone tablet and one of the most beautifully carved moonstones, **see page 1408**.

Hotels There are many small guesthouses and hotels, mainly in the new town. Although there are no luxury hotels, some of the rest houses are excellent value. Most will arrange car/cycle hire.

C *Nuwarawewa Rest House*, T 025 2565. Nr New Town. 60 rm, 35 a/c. Restaurant, bar, exchange, shop, entertainment, pool. Restaurant serves excellent mild curries (ask for a selection). Evening meals European but curries to order. On the edge of the lake in attractive garden, friendly and helpful staff. Good value and recommended. **C** *Tissawewa Rest House*, T 025 2299. 25 rm, 2 a/c. Near Tissawewa tank. Formerly the Grand Hotel, the charming colonial house is beautifully situated in a secluded parkland with lots of monkeys. Within the religious area hence no alcohol served. Excellent and very good value, but often heavily booked. Good restaurant, exchange. **D** *Miridya Hotel*, Rowing Club Rd, T 025 2519. 40 a/c rm. View over Lake Nuwara Wewa. Restaurant, bar, exchange, entertainment, shop, lake fishing. **D** *Rajarata Hotel*, Rowing Club Rd, T 025 2578. 100 rm, 70 a/c. Restaurant, exchange, pool. **D** *Ashok Hotel*, Rowing Club Rd, T 025 2753. 26 rm. **D** *Monara House* 63 Freeman Mawatha, T 025 2110. 8 rm. Basic. **E** *Sevana Tourist Rest*, 394/8 Harishchandra Mawatha, next door to the Miridya Hotel. Simple, but clean and good value.

Museums The Archaeological Museum. 0800-1600 (Closed Tue). An excellent small museum, with some beautiful pieces of sculpture.

Rail Colombo, *Rajarata Rajini*, 86, daily, 0505, 4 hr 35; *78 Express*, daily, 1428, 4 hr 17; 868, daily, 1540, 5 hr. **Jaffna** *Yal Devi*, 77, daily, 0945, 5 hr; 91 Mail, daily, 0045, 6 hr. **Talaimannar** 463, daily, 1335, 5 hr 15; 97 Mail, daily , 0112, 4 hr. **Note** Services to Jaffna and Talaimannar may be disrupted. In mid-1991 the ferry service to India was not operating; enquire locally.

Bus Frequent bus service to Colombo (6 hr 30) and Kandy (5 hr). In normal times the journey to Jaffna is 6 hr, but the service is currently completely unreliable.

Excursions

Mihintale 16 km E of Anuradhapura, and just S of the Anuradhapura-Trincomalee road, Mihintale is revered as the place where Mahinda converted King Devanampiya Tissa to Buddhism in 243 BC, thereby enabling Buddhism to spread to the whole island. It is a beautiful site, worth spending time over. The legend tells how King Tissa was chasing a stag during a hunting expedition. The stag reached Mahintale and fled up the hill side, followed by the King, until he reached a place surrounded by hills, where he was astonished to find a man. It was Mahinda, Asoka's son, who had come to preach the Buddha's teachings.

The top of the hill became a monastery, reached by a flight of 1,840 broad but shallow granite steps, lined with frangipani. The climb starts gently, rising in a broad stairway of 350 steps. This is followed by a flat platform, then a steep flight of steps up to the dagoba of **Kantaka Cetiya**, built before 60 BC. Unearthed in 1932-35, it had been severely damaged. Over 130 m round, today it is only about 12 m high, compared with its original height of perhaps 30 m. At the four cardinal points it has some beautiful sculptures – geese, dwarves, and a variety of animals – and several rock cells around it. Return to the main path.

The climb continues up a second and then a third flight of steps. Half way up on the left is a path to a stone aqueduct and a stone bathing trough beyond. Further up is a ruined shrine, at the entrance of which are slabs covered in 10th century inscriptions. These give detailed rules about access to the hill and the sacred site.

Return to the third flight of steps and continue to the top, where there is a refectory for the priests, the *Bhojana Salava*. (It is also possible to travel this far by road if you want to avoid the first climb). The last flight of steps leads up to the *Ambasthala* ('mango tree') dagoba, with a diversion to the right about half way up, which leads to the *Naga Pokuna*, a 40 m bathing pool carved out of solid rock.

Shoes must be removed before climbing to the *Ambasthala dagoba*, the holiest part of the site. Walking on to the NE of the dagoba, built on the traditional site of the meeting between King Tissa and Mahinda, is the stone couch of Mahinda, carved out of bare rock. A short path to the SW leads to the summit (310 m) and the *Maha Sewa dagoba*. This was supposedly built on the orders of King Tissa as a reliquary for a lock of the Buddha's hair, or relics of Mahinda. The views across Anuradhapura are magnificent.

Warning The civil war continues to claim many lives in N and E Sri Lanka in mid 1991. It is impossible to travel to Jaffna or to Trincomalee at the time of writing without Government approval, and even when it is allowed it is dangerous to do so. The civil war has made it impossible to make recommendations about accommodation in the N and E for 1992. Below is a brief summary of the route to Jaffna.

From Anuradhapura take the Trincomalee road for 1 km then fork left to Rambewa (15 km) where you join the road from the S and turn N to **Medawachchiya** (10 km). Through the town the road forks left to *Mannar* and the ferry to India from Talaimannar (114 km; ferry service not operating). The main road to Jaffna goes due N to *Vavuniya* (26 km), then follows close by the railway nearly the whole route N through small towns to *Kilinochchi* (77 km), across the Jaffna lagoon (15 km) through the *Elephant Pass* onto the Jaffna Peninsula. The road then runs westwards into *Jaffna* (49 km). The change in scenery is dramatic, palmyra palms suddenly replacing coconuts at the Elephant Pass, reflecting the much greater aridity of the N peninsula.

Jaffna *Population* 120,000 *Altitude* Sea level

	Jan	Feb	Mar	Apr	May	Jun	Jul	Aug	Sep	Oct	Nov	Dec	Av/Tot
Max (°C)	29	32	33	34	33	31	31	31	30	31	30	28	31
Min (°C)	23	25	26	27	29	28	29	27	27	26	25	24	26
Rain (mm)	59	28	25	57	50	20	20	32	41	258	337	257	1184

COLOMBO TO SIGIRIYA AND TRINCOMALEE

The route as far as Kurunegala is described above. From Kurunegala the NH6 continues NE, skirting the N fringe of the Central Highlands to Dambulla, Sigiriya being a few km to the E of the main road. From Sigiriya rejoin the main road at Habarane, then follow the straight road NE across the gently sloping plain to **Trincomalee** (85 km).

Dambulla a gigantic granite outcrop, towers more than 160 m above the surrounding land. The rock is more than 1.5 km around its base and the summit is at an altitude of 550 m.

The caves Open 0600-1100; 1400-1900. Entry US$3. The caves were the refuge of *King Valagam Bahu* when he was in exile for 14 years. When he returned to the throne at Anuradhapura in the 1st century BC, he had a magnificent rock temple built at Dambulla. From the road it is a hot and tiring climb in the daytime up bare rock. The caves have a mixture of Buddhist and Hindu painting and sculpture. In one is the 15 m high sculpture of the reclining Buddha, with other Buddhist figures. The frescoes on the walls and ceilings date from the 15th-18th centuries. The second is the largest and most impressive, containing over 150 statues of deities and also of the Buddha. The ceiling frescoes show scenes from the Buddha's life and Sinhalese history. The rock is best visited in the early morning to avoid the heat. Panoramic views from the top of surrounding jungle and lakes, and of Sigiriya, 19 km away.

F *Dambulla Rest House*, T 066 8299. Close to caves, pleasant. Recommended.

Excursion *Aukana* Direct buses run from Dambulla to the remarkable 13 m high statue of the standing Buddha, carved out of the rock. Dating from the 5th century, it is near the Kalawewa Tank.

From Dambulla, take the main road NE to Trincomalee. After about 9 km, turn right at Inamaluwa to see the rock fort at *Sigiriya*, 11 km. Frequent buses from Dambulla, fewer in the afternoon. From Kandy, there is a direct bus daily to Sigiriya.

Sigiriya Entry US$4. **See page 1408.** Allow half a day for a visit. The rewards of the site justify the difficult climb up sometimes up precarious steps. An early morning start is best for the climb, but the frescoes are best seen in the late afternoon light as the best are on a vertical rock gallery on the W side of the hill. In addition to the rock fortress, there are extensive grounds at the foot of the hill. Refreshments at the Rest House nr the entrance. Carry your drink if you want to avoid paying an excessive price at the kiosk half way up. **Note** Since the number climbing is controlled owing to the nature of the path and stairways, it is best to avoid public holidays when there can be long queues. **Warning** Visitors suffering from vertigo are advised not to attempt it. Not suitable for the frail or unfit.

The vast flat-topped 200 m high **Lion Rock** (*Siha-Giri*) stands starkly above the surrounding countryside of the central forest, and was an exceptional natural site for a fortress. It takes its name because lions were believed to occupy the caves. The remains of a gigantic brick lion can still be seen guarding the entrance to the citadel. Hieroglyphs here suggest that it was occupied by humans from very early times, long before the fortress was built. The royal citadel dates from 477-495 AD, and it was much more than simply a rock-fort, as is suggested by its impressive wall and surrounding moat. The city had the Palace and quarters for the ordinary people who built the royal pavilions, pools and fortifications.

When the citadel ceased to be a palace, it was inhabited by monks until 1155, and then abandoned. It was only rediscovered by archaeologists in 1828. The Mahavansa records that it was built out of fear. **King Kasyapa**, having killed his father in order to gain the throne, lived in terror that his half-brother, who had taken refuge in India, would return to kill him. He did come back, after 18 years, to find that Kasyapa had built a combination of pleasure palace and massive fortress. However, Kasyapa came down from the hill to face his half brother's army on elephant back. Mistakenly thinking he had been abandoned, he killed himself with his dagger.

At Sigiriya, Kasyapa intended to reproduce on earth the legendary palace of *Kubera*, the God of wealth, and so had it decorated lavishly with impressive gardens, cisterns and ponds. For the famous frescoes he gathered together the best artists of his day. Excavations have also revealed surface and underground drainage systems. The top of the rock has a surface area of 1.5 ha, to the NW of which was the palace, the main building, built on the precipitous edge. Excellent views.

Of the 500 or so frescoes, which vie with those in the Ajanta Caves in W India (**see page 1461**), only 21 remain. They are remarkably well preserved, as they are sheltered from the elements in a niche, about half way up the path to the top. In the style of Ajanta, the first drawing was done on wet plaster and then painted with red, yellow, green and black. The figures are 'portraits' of celestial nymphs and attendants above clouds - offering flowers, scattering petals or bathing-beauties, which prompted the 'graffiti' (sometimes in verse) on the Mirror Wall.

To see the frescoes you climb a spiral staircase up the W face of Sigiriya rock. Further along, the path is protected on the outer side by a 3 m high, highly polished plaster wall believed to have been coated with egg white and wild honey. This is the famous **Mirror Wall**, which after 15 centuries still produces a reflection. Visitors and pilgrims have left their mark on the surface, in tiny Sinhalese script- 'graffiti' of their impressions on seeing the frescoes.

The main path takes you to the top of the rock up the steep W and N sides. The original staircase that led up to the top is in ruins, so it is a rough climb up steps roughly cut on the rock. The path reaches the Lion Terrace on the N ledge where it leads through the giant rock paws of the lion – steep steps and rickety railings help you to get to the top. To reach the palace there were 25 flights of steps. On the top the Summer Palace had bathing pools for the royal family. You can see the granite throne, audience hall, niches to hold oil lamps, and precariously positioned platforms for guards at the top. 2nd century inscriptions were found in the 'Cobra Hood Cave', which you can see from a distance.

At the western approach to the rock are the 5th century water gardens, restored by the Central Cultural Fund sponsored by Unesco, with walks, pavilions, ponds and fountains which are gravity fed from the moats as they were 1,500 years ago.

The small **Museum** is at the beginning of the path up, and there is a dagoba and other ruins on the roadside just over a km away.

Hotels The best two are 1 km away. They are comfortable with restaurants, games, shops and pools. **D** *Sigiriya*, T 066 8311. 50 rm in bungalows with terrace in a picturesque location set against the rock in a large garden. **D** *Sigiriya Village*, 066 8216. 105 rm in 60 bungalows with terraces. Both pools are open to non-residents for a fee. The moderately priced **D** *Rest House*, T 066 8324 is conveniently close to the entrance. 15 rm, 2 a/c. Very good restaurant, comfortable. Recommended. Some smaller *Guest Houses* nr the rock including the *Ajantha* which provides good food.

Bus Buses hourly to Dambulla. Daily bus to Kandy and Colombo.

From Sigiriya rejoin the main NH 6 at *Habarane* (24 km), an important crossroads. **Note** The quality of the accommodation and the central location make this an excellent place to stay if you are travelling by car. There is an attractive Buddhist temple, with excellent paintings. Behind the tank next to the temple is a rock, with superb views from the top over the forest to Sigiriya.

Hotel A *The Lodge*, T 066 8321. 150 rm, in bungalows. Very good value in every respect. **B** *The Village*, T 066 8316. 106 rm. Enormous gardens, excellent food, warm welcome. Highly recommended. **F** *Habarana Rest House* 4 rm.

Take the NH 11 E from Habarane through the **Minneriya-Giritale sanctuary** to *Polonnaruwa* (30 km) 216 km from Colombo, SE of Anuradhapura. **Polonnaruwa** was first used as a residence by the Sinhalese kings of Anuradhapura in 369 AD, but did not rank as a capital until the 8th century. The Cholas destroyed the Sinhalese kingdom at the beginning of the 11th century, and taking control of most of the island, they established their capital at Polonnaruwa. In 1056 King Vijayabahu I defeated the Cholas, and set up his own capital in the city. It remained a vibrant centre of Sinhalese culture under his successors, notably **Parakrama Bahu I** (1153-1186) and **Nissanka Malla** (1187-1196), when the kingdom went into terminal decline. Many of the remains are in an excellent state of repair, and illustrate the close ties with India that Parakrama Bahu I maintained, importing architects and engineers. The city was abandoned in 1288, after the tank embankment was breached.

Allow a day to get some impression of this ancient site. You can cover part of the tour by taxi and part on foot. Guides are available although at the monuments, officials are happy to answer questions or explain details (with expectations of a tip!). Entry US$4. **See page 1461.**

It owes its much of its glory to the artistic conception of King *Parakramabahu I* who built a magnificent palace with walls over 3 m thick, and to king *Nissanka Malla* who built a temple for the Buddha's tooth. In its imperial intentions, and the brevity of its existence, Polonnaruwa has been likened by Percy Brown to the great Mughal emperor Akbar's city building at Fatehpur Sikri, **see page 283.** The whole was planned as an expression and statement of imperial power. Its great artificial lake, covering over 2,500 ha, provided defence along its entire W flank, cooling breezes through the city, and water for irrigation. It was named after its imperial designer, the **Sea of Parakrama**. Today it attracts numerous water birds, including cormorants and pelicans. The rectangular shaped city was enclosed by 3 concentric walls, and was made attractive with parks and gardens.

Places of interest

If you are staying at the lakeside *Rest House*, or one of the hotels nearby you can

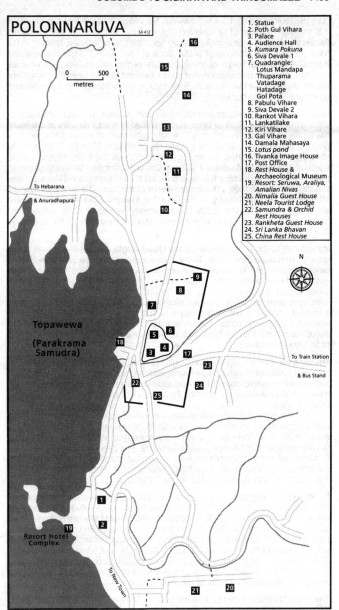

POLONNARUVA

SA 412

0   500
metres

To Hebarana
& Anuradhapura

Topawewa

(Parakrama Samudra)

To Train Station

& Bus Stand

Resort Hotel
Complex

To New Town

N

1. Statue
2. Poth Gul Vihara
3. Palace
4. Audience Hall
5. *Kumara Pokuna*
6. Siva Devale 1
7. Quadrangle:
   Lotus Mandapa
   Thuparama
   Vatadage
   Hatadage
   Gol Pota
8. Pabulu Vihare
9. Siva Devale 2
10. Rankot Vihara
11. Lankatilake
12. Kiri Vihare
13. Gal Vihara
14. Damala Mahasaya
15. *Lotus pond*
16. Tivanka Image House
17. Post Office
18. *Rest House &
    Archaeological Museum*
19. *Resort: Seruwa, Araliya,
    Amalian Nivas*
20. *Nimalia Guest House*
21. *Neela Tourist Lodge*
22. *Samundra & Orchid
    Rest Houses*
23. *Rankheta Guest House*
24. *Sri Lanka Bhavan*
25. *China Rest House*

start the tour by going 1.5 km S towards the village. You will first see the giant 3.5 m high **statue** of a bearded figure, now believed to be the **King Parakramabahu** himself, looking away from the city he restored, holding in his hand the palm leaf manuscript of the 'Book of Law'. To its S is the now restored **Poth Gul Vihara** (or library dagoba), a circular *gedige* type building, with 4 small dagobas. It has been renovated, and is now believed to have been the monastery library. Inside, a circular rm with 5 m thick walls is thought to have housed numerous Sinhalese books.

Returning to the Rest House and taking the path to the E, you cross the road, to arrive at the **Palace.** Built of brick, it is described in the Chronicles as originally having had 3 storeys, though only 2 remain, after most of it was destroyed by a fire. The large central hall on the ground floor measures 31 m by 13 m, with 30 columns which supported the roof. It has porticos on the E and W and a wide stairway. The **Hall of Audience** and the **Council Chamber** are immediately to the E. The Council Chamber has superb friezes of elephants (each different), lions and dwarves, which follow the entire exterior of the base. The hall has 4 rows of 10 sculpted columns. Nearby, to the SE, is the **Kumara Pokuna** (Prince's Bath) which was restored in the 1930s. It was formerly flanked by 2 lion statues. You can still see one of the spouts where the water channelled through the open jaws of a crocodile.

Immediately to the N of the Palace is the **Quadrangle**, a series of ruins on raised ground, surrounded by a wall. To the E of the entrance is the **Siva Devale I**, a Hindu Temple (one of several Siva and Vishnu temples here) built in 1200, revealing the influence of the Indian architectural style, so obvious at the site. It shows exceptional stone carving, and the fine bronze statues discovered in the ruins have been transferred to the Colombo Museum. King Nissana Malla built a small dagoba, the **Lotus Mandapa** with a stone fence imitating a latticed wooden railing with posts. The ornamental stone pillars which surround the dagoba are in the form of lotus buds on stalks, a design which has become one of Sri Lanka's emblems.

Thuparama, to the S of the Quadrangle is a small gedige which was developed here as a fusion of Indian and Sinhalese Buddhist architecture. This one has the only surviving vaulted dome of its type and houses a number of Buddha statues. It has very thick walls with a staircase embedded in it which leads you to the roof. Excellent views.

Near the entrance is the **Vatadage**, the 'hall of the relic', a circular building with a dagoba on concentric terraces with sculptured railings, the largest with a diameter of 18 m. There are guardstones at the entrances of the second terrace, the *moonstone* to the N being particularly fine. The dagoba at the centre has 4 Buddhas with a later stone screen. A superbly planned and executed 12th century masterpiece, the Vatadage has modest proportions but remarkably graceful lines. It was almost certainly intended to house the tooth relic.

Opposite is the **Hatadage** "built in 60 Sinhalese hours" which made up a day. With extraordinary *moonstones* at its entrance (**see page 1408**), the sanctuary to house the tooth of the Buddha was built by **Nissanka Malla** and is also referred to as the *Temple of the Tooth*, since the relic may have been placed here for a time. To the E of the Hatadage (sometimes known as the Atadaga – 'house of 8 relics') is the **Gol Pota** ('Book of Stone'). According to the inscription it weighs 25 tons, and has been brought over 90 km from Mihintale. It is in the form of a palm leaf measuring over 9 m by 1.2 m, over 60 cm thick in places, with Sinhalese inscriptions praising the works of the King Nissanka Malla.

The Hindu temples belong to different periods, The earliest is the **Siva Devala 2**, which was built by the Indian Cholas in a style similar to that they were developing in neighbouring Tamil Nadu, as at Thanjavur **see page 745**, except that they used brick rather than stone. Another group of scattered monuments are further N and you can reach this either by taxi or cycle rickshaw. You will pass the **Rankot Vihara** to the left of the path, the 4th largest dagoba on the island with a height of 55 m, built by Nissanka Malla in the 12th century. Note the perfection of the spire and the clarity of the statues round the drum.

The next group are in the royal cremation ground (*Alahana Parivena*) set aside by Parakramabahu. The large *gedige* **Jetawanarama** (See Anuradhapura above) or **Lankatilaka** ('ornament of Lanka') has walls which are 4 m thick and still stand 17 m high, although the roof has crumbled. The design illustrates the development in thinking which underlay the massive building, for it marks a turning away from the abstract form of the dagoba to a much more personalised faith in the Buddha in human form. The building is essentially a shrine, built to focus the attention of worshippers on the 18 m high statue of the Buddha at the end of the nave. Like the building itself, the statue was built of brick and covered in stucco, but the overall design of the building shows strong Tamil influences.

The King's wife Subhadra is believed to have built the 'milk white' **Kiri Vihara,** so named because of the unspoilt white plasterwork when it was first discovered. It remains the best preserved of the island's unrestored dagobas. In addition this separate group also has the *mandapa* with carved columns and a Hall, just S of the Jetawanarama.

N again from the **Kiri Vihara** you arrive at the principle attraction of Polonnaruwa, the **Gal Vihara**, (Cave of the Spirits of Knowledge) forming a part of Parakramabahu's monastery where a gigantic Buddha seated on a pedestal under a canopy, was carved out of an 8 m high rock. On either side of the rock shrine are further vast carvings of a seated and a 14 m recumbent Buddha. The grain of the rock is beautiful as is the expression. Near the head of the reclining figure of the Parinirvana Buddha, the 7 m standing image with folded arms, was believed to be his grieving disciple Ananda but is now thought to be of the Buddha himself.

You can rejoin the road by taking a path to the N. On the other side of the road a path leads to the **Lotus Pond** a little further along. The bathing pool has 5 concentric circles of eight petals which form the steps down which bathers stepped down into the water. The road ends at the **Tivanka Image House** where the Buddha image is in the unusual 'thrice bent' posture associated with a female figure. This is the largest brick-built shrine here and there are excellent frescoes inside depicting scenes from the *Jatakas* and carvings of dwarves on the outside. The restoration at the site is by the UNESCO sponsored Central Cultural Fund. The **Archaeological Museum** nr the Rest House is small but interesting.

Hotels **C** *Rest House*, T 027 2411. 15 rm, 5 a/c. Built on the occasion of Queen Elizabeth II's visit, pleasant though now a little old-fashioned. Well located for visiting the site with superb views over lake and popular so advance reservations advisable. Restaurant, bar, exchange, boating, fishing. The National Holiday Complex nr the Poth Gul Vihara, has the best accommodation in a group of 3 comfortable hotels by the Lakeside further S, but 3 km from old town so you will need transport to visit the site. All have exchange, boating, pool. **D** *Seruwa*, T 027 2411. 40 a/c rm, some with bath. Restaurant, bar. Comfortable. **D** *Araliya*, T 027 2421. 30 a/c rm. **D** *Amalian Nivas*, T 027 2405. 36 a/c rm. Bar, rm service.

The best of the less expensive hotels in the **E** category are also nr the New Town some distance from the site, so you need transport. Alternatively, you can get a bus from the rly station or the Old Town bus stop to the New Town and take the path signposted beyond the Statue, for a km to the E. *Nimalia Guest House*, No 2 Channel. Good restaurant. *Sri Lankan Lodge*, T 027 2403, nearby has 17 rm with baths. The small *Neela Tourist Lodge* only has a few rm.

The Old Town nr the site offers a choice of inexpensive hotels. Towards the Rly Station and Bus Stop, on the Batticaloa Rd, are a couple of simple hotels which have rm with baths. The *Ranketha Guest House*, T 027 2080 with a good restaurant and *Sri Lanka Bhavan*, off the road. Nearer the centre of the Old town are cheaper hotels with rm with or without bath. The *Samudra* and *Free Tourist Resort* are simple, clean and have reasonable restaurants. Three others are *Wijaya*, *Orchid* and *China Rest Houses*.

Restaurants Mainly in the hotels. If you are in the Old Town, the *Rest House* and the *Ranketha* offer the best food.

Rail The Rly Station is a few km W of the Old Town on the Batticaloa Rd. **Colombo** *Udaya Devi*, 80, daily, 1225, 6 hr; *Mail*, 94, daily, 2147, 8 hr.

Bus The out-of-town Bus Stop is nr the Rly station. Several buses daily to **Colombo** (6 hr), via **Dambulla**. Minibuses from Anuradhapura, Kandy and Batticaloa.

From Habarana take the NH 6 NE direct to **Trincomalee**.

	Jan	Feb	Mar	Apr	May	Jun	Jul	Aug	Sep	Oct	Nov	Dec	Av/Tot
Max (°C)	28	31	33	34	36	36	35	35	35	33	29	28	33
Min (°C)	25	24	25	27	28	27	26	26	26	25	22	24	25
Rain (mm)	169	89	48	59	52	25	63	92	97	235	344	345	1618

Known above all for its excellent natural harbour, the best in S Asia. In the 1770s Lord Nelson described it as 'the best in the world', and even with the changes in sea transport since then it remains an outstandingly well-sheltered deep port with an area of more than 80 sq km.

The harbour has often been fiercely contested, and it was a crucial naval base for the British during the Second World War. Given that fact, it may seem surprising that the town itself has never been very important, but that reflects its location in Sri Lanka's dry NE region, where the interior has been difficult to cultivate and malaria-infested for centuries. Only today, with the completion of the Victoria Dam and the re-settlement scheme of colonisers using irrigation from the Mahaweli Ganga Project, is the region inland developing into an important agricultural region. However, it is also torn by political strife, and in mid 1991 there is little sign that the civil war which continues to take a sporadic toll of life is coming to a close.

Hotels A *Hotel Club Oceanic*, T 026 2307. 83 rm. Superb facilities in delightful palm tree garden setting right on the beach. **B** *Seven Islands*, Orrs Hill Rd, T 026 2373. 25 rm, each with individual terrace. An old hotel, fully renovated, it dominates the promontory and has magnificent views. The old Naval Officers' Club now has most of the surrounding land taken over by the Naval Base.
  F There are several small guesthouses, both in Trincomalee and in beach resorts along the coast. *Rest House*, corner of Dockyard Rd and Kachcheri Rd. Good restaurant. *Rainbow Beach*, 322 Dyke St, T 026 2365. Nr waterfront. Some rm with bath. Good open-air restaurant. *Newland*, 87 Raja Varothayam Rd, nr the Clock Tower, T 026 2668. Some rm with bath. Clean, friendly, good sea-food. Also a modest *Chinese Guest House*, Duke St, backing onto beach, T 026 2455. Basic. *Votre Maison*, 45 Green Rd, backing onto Nelson Cinema. Simple, but good food.

Restaurants Some of the hotels serve good sea food specialities. Chinese along Ehamparam Rd, best being *Chinese Eastern* nr the clock Tower. Fast food, ice creams and cold drinks along Dockyard Rd – *Flora Fountain* recommended. Cheap local food nr the Bus Station.

The **Post Office** is on the corner of Power House Rd and Kachcheri Rd.

Bank Bank of Ceylon on Inner Harbour Rd, nr Customs Rd.

Rail Colombo (Change at Gal Oya), 883, daily, 0745, 10 hr 40.

Bus 3 buses a day to Colombo. 8 hr. Frequent buses to Anuradhapura. Daily bus to Polonnaruwa.

COLOMBO TO KANDY AND BATTICALOA

The trunk road from Colombo to Kandy was the first modern road to be opened. Taking 11 years to complete, it was opened to traffic in 1832, when the first mail service ran between the two cities. Although the road route is quicker the train often gives better views. The first part of the route follows the NH1 to Warakapola (see above). Just after Warakapola a right turn climbs into the hills to Kegalla. Some beautiful hill scenery lies between Kegalla and Mawanella.

19 km E of Warakapola is **Kegalla**, a long straggling town in beautiful scenery. The road begins to climb at *Rambukkana* (11 km) *Altitude* 100 m. On either side the vegetation is stunningly rich. **Mawanella** Rest House is in a superb location between Kegalle and *Kadugannawa* (17 km). At the top of the *Balana* pass is a precipice called Sensation Point. The railway goes through 2 tunnels to Peradeniya (10 km), where the road crosses the Mahaweli Ganga, Sri Lanka's longest river.

Peradeniya *Altitude* 500 m. Famous for its magnificent Royal Botanic Gardens, Peradeniya is also the home of the Sri Lanka University.

Places of interest The Botanic Gardens Entry Rs 15. Conceived originally in 1371 as a royal garden, Peradeniya became the residence of a Kandyan Prince between 1741-1782. It was converted into a botanic garden in 1821, six years after the fall of the last Kandyan King. The gardens cover 60 ha.

Giant bamboo, extensive well-kept lawns, magnificent trees, especially palms (palmyra, talipot, royal palm, cabbage palm), and *Ficus elastica* (rubber with buttressed roots) are just a few of the superb specimens. There is also a line of double coconut (Coco de Mer), unique in their native habitat to the island of *Praslin* in the Seychelles. There is an outstanding orchid collection, and research into various important spices, as well as into tea, coffee, rubber, coconuts and rice. Best to visit in early morning or late afternoon.

Peradeniya is now almost a suburb of *Kandy* (5 km).

Kandy

Altitude 488 m *Population* 50,000

	Jan	Feb	Mar	Apr	May	Jun	Jul	Aug	Sep	Oct	Nov	Dec	Av/Tot
Max (°C)	29	33	34	35	31	29	29	28	28	30	29	28	30
Min (°C)	18	18	20	22	22	21	21	22	20	20	19	19	20
Rain (mm)	90	82	83	207	154	150	129	113	140	298	296	203	1945

Kandy is one of the most important symbols of Sinhalese national identity. The last bastion of Buddhist political power against colonial forces, the home of the Temple of the Buddha's tooth relic, and the site of one of the world's most impressive annual festivals, the city is the gateway to the higher hills and the tea plantations. Its architectural monuments date mainly from a final surge of grandiose building by King Sri Vikrama Raja Sinha in the early 19th century, so extravagant, and achieved only with such enormous costs for the people of Kandy, that his nobles betrayed him to the British rather than continue enduring his excesses. The result is some extraordinary buildings, none of great architectural merit, but sustaining a genuinely Kandyan style going back to the 16th century, and rich in symbolic significance of the nature of the king's view of his world.

History Although the city of Kandy (originally *Senkadagala*) is commonly held to have been founded by a general named *Vikramabahu* in 1472, there was a settlement on the site for at least 150 years before that. On asserting his independence from the reigning monarch, Vikramabahu made Kandy his capital. He built a palace for his mother and a shrine on pillars. In 1542 the **Tooth Relic** was brought to the city, stimulating a flurry of new religious building – a 2 storey house for the relic itself, and 86 houses for the monks. As in Anuradhapura and

Polonnaruwa, the Tooth temple was built next to the Palace.

The American Geographer James Duncan suggests that defensive fortifications only came with the attacks of the Portuguese. Forced to withdraw from the town during an attack in 1594, **King Vimala Dharma Suriya** set half the city on fire, a tactic that was repeated by several successors in the face of expulsion by foreign armies. However, he won it back, and promptly set about building a massive wall, interspersed with huge towers. Inside, a new palace replaced the one destroyed by fire, and the city rapidly gained a reputation as a cosmopolitan centre of splendour and wealth. As early as 1597 some Portuguese showed scepticism about the claims that the enshrined tooth was the Buddha's. De Quezroy, writing in 1597, described the seven golden caskets in which the tooth was kept, but added the disclaimer that it was the tooth of a buffalo. By then the Portuguese were already claiming that they had captured the original, exported it to Goa and incinerated it.

By 1602 the city had probably taken the form (though not the actual buildings) which would survive to the beginning of the 19th century, and the major temples were also already in place. Kandy was repeatedly attacked by the Portuguese, and in the 17th century the Tooth relic was removed for a time by the retreating King Senarat. In 1611 the city was captured and largely destroyed, and again in 1629 and 1638. A new earth rampart was built between the hills in the S of the city. In 1681 there is evidence of a moat being built using forced labour, and possibly the first creation of the **Bogambara Lake** to the SW, as a symbol of the cosmic ocean.

Vimala Dharma Suriya I had a practical use for the symbolic lake, for he is reputed to have kept some of his treasure sunk in the middle, guarded by crocodiles in the water. Duncan suggests that there was also the symbolic link with Kubera, the god of wealth, who was believed to have kept his wealth at the bottom of the cosmic ocean. Crocodiles are often shown on the dragon gateways (*makara torana*) of temples.

A new Temple of the Tooth was built by Vimala Dharma Suriya II between 1687-1707, on the old site. 3 storeys high, it contained a reliquary of gold encrusted with jewels. Between 1707-1739 Narendra Sinha added a new palace 7 km SE of Kandy, though the old palace in the town was still used. He also undertook new building in the city itself, renovating the **Temple of the Tooth** and enclosing the **Temple of Natha** and the sacred **Bo tree**. He established the validity of his royal line by importing princesses from Madurai, and set aside a separate street for them in the town.

Major new building awaited **King Kirti Sri** (1747-1782). He added a temple to Vishnu NW of the palace, but at the same time he asserted his support for Buddhism, twice bringing monks from Thailand to re-validate the Sinhalese order of monks. Yet his works too suffered from attack, this time from the Dutch, who captured the city in 1765, plundering the temples and palaces. The Palace and the Temple of the Tooth were destroyed and many other buildings were seriously damaged.

Kirti Sri started building all over again, more opulently than ever, but it was the last king of Kandy, **Sri Vikrama Raja Sinha** (1798-1815) who gave Kandy many of its present buildings. More interested in palaces and parks than temples, he set about demonstrating his kingly power with an exhibition of massive building works. Once again he had started almost from scratch, for in 1803 the city was taken by the British, but in order to avoid its desecration was once again burned to the ground. The British were thrown out, and between 1809-1812 there was massive re-building. The palace was fully renovated by 1810 and a new octagonal structure added to the palace, the **pattiripuwa**. Two years later the royal complex was surrounded by a moat and a single massive stone gateway replaced the earlier entrances.

In the W new shops and houses were built, at the same time building more houses in the E for his Tamil relatives. But by far the greatest work was the construction of the lake. Previously the low lying marshy land in front of the palace had been drained for paddy fields. Duncan records that between 1810-1812 up to 3,000 men were forced to work on building the dam at the W end of the low ground, creating an artificial lake given the cosmically symbolic name of the Ocean of Milk. A pleasure house was built in the middle of the lake, connected by drawbridge to the palace. At last the city had taken virtually its present form.

Local festivals *Esala Perahera*, held in Jul-Aug, is Sri Lanka's greatest festival. It is of special significance; the lunar month in which the Buddha was conceived and in which he left his father's home, it had also long been associated with rituals to ensure renewed fertility for the year ahead. The last Kandy kings turned the Perahera into a mechanism for reinforcing their own power, trying to bring identify themselves with the gods who needed to be appeased. By focusing on the Tooth relic, the Tamil kings hoped to establish their own authority and their divine legitimacy within the Buddhist community. The Sri Lankan historian Seneviratne has suggested that fear both of the king and of divine retribution encouraged nobles and peasants alike to come to the Perahera, and witnessing the scale of the spectacle reinforced their loyalty.

The entire organisation of the Perahera was designed to symbolise and enable the flow of cosmic power to be renewed through the god-chosen king to the people for the following year. It was rich with potent symbolism. Seneviratne shows how the ritual pole used in the processions represents the cosmic axis. Cut specially each year from a male tree with milk-like sap, symbolising fertility, milk and semen, the chosen tree was encircled with a magic symbol to transform it into the axis of the world. An E facing branch (the auspicious direction) would be cut and divided into 4 sections, one for each of the four temples: each piece (*kapa*) would then be taken to its respective temple, linking the temple with the cosmic axis and thereby renewing its access to the source of all power. Further rituals at each of the temples, in which the kapa were taken round the temple three times, linked the temple directly with the three worlds. The planting of the kapa then inaugurated the Perahera.

In the second stage of the Perahera, the *Kumbal Perahera*, the symbols of the four gods were joined with the Tooth Relic and processed for the first time with elephants. Duncan suggests that at this stage there were in fact five processions joined in one; that of the Tooth Relic, which was started by King Kirti Sri in 1747; of *Natha*, the next Buddha; of Visnu, due to be Buddha after Natha; of Katagarama, the general; and of the goddess Pattini. This procession marched round the sacred Bo tree in the centre of the square for several nights in succession, drawing on the strength which flowed through the Bo tree as another representation of the central axis of the city and of the world.

The third and last stage of the Perahera, *Randoli Perahera*, saw the procession move out to encompass the whole city, at which point the king made his first entry. He would be seen first at the windows of the *Pattirippuwa*, and then went to the Temple of the Tooth, raised the relic and placed it on the elephant. Duncan points out that the eight sided building symbolically controlled the eight directions, and that it was built specifically for this ritual purpose. The procession then moved off clockwise round the city, the king and the representatives of the 21 Kandyan provinces, in a parade that was itself intended to secure fertility. The 21 days of the festival may themselves have been symbolic of the 21 provinces. Seneviratne has suggested that the Perahera was believed to be capable of producing light rains, symbolised by the flowers strewed in front of the elephant carrying the Tooth Relic. Elephants themselves were seen as able to bring rain, for grey and massive, like rain clouds themselves, they could attract the clouds of heaven.

Today the festival is a magnificent 15 day spectacle of elephants, musicians, dancers and tens of thousands of pilgrims in procession, Buddhists drawn to the temple by the power of the Tooth Relic rather than by that of the King's authority. The power of the Relic certainly long preceded that of the Kandyan dynasty. Fa Hien described the annual festival in Anuradhapura in 399 AD, which even then was a lavish procession in which roads were vividly decorated, elephants covered in jewels and flowers, and models of figures such as Bodhisattvas were paraded. When the tooth was moved to Kandy, the Perahera moved with it. However, today the tooth relic itself is no longer taken out.

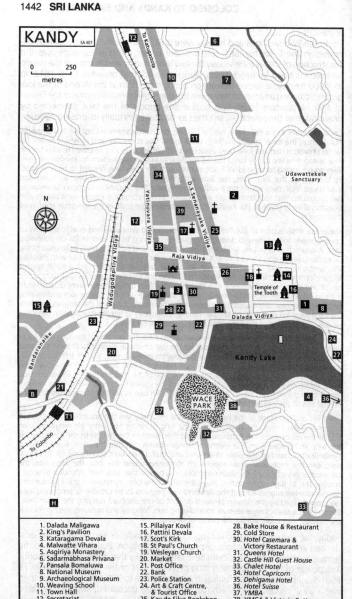

KANDY SA 407

0   250
metres

To Katugastota

Udawattekele Sanctuary

Temple of the Tooth

Kandy Lake

WACE PARK

To Colombo

1. Dalada Maligawa
2. King's Pavilion
3. Kataragama Devala
4. Malwatte Vihara
5. Asgiriya Monastery
6. Sadarmabhasa Privana
7. Pansala Bomaluwa
8. National Museum
9. Archaeological Museum
10. Weaving School
11. Town Hall
12. Secretariat
13. Maha Vishnu Devala
14. Nathe Devala

15. Pillaiyar Kovil
16. Pattini Devala
17. Scot's Kirk
18. St Paul's Church
19. Wesleyan Church
20. Market
21. Post Office
22. Bank
23. Police Station
24. Art & Craft Centre, & Tourist Office
25. Kav de Silva Bookshop
26. Laksala
27. Lakeside Cafe

28. Bake House & Restaurant
29. Cold Store
30. *Hotel Casemara & Victory Restaurant*
31. *Queens Hotel*
32. *Castle Hill Guest House*
33. *Chalet Hotel*
34. *Hotel Capricorn*
35. *Dehigama Hotel*
36. *Hotel Suisse*
37. *YMBA*
38. *YMCA & Victoria Cottage*
39. *YMCA*

The first five days of the festival are celebrated only within the grounds of the four Hindu *devalas* (temples). On the sixth night the torchlight processions set off from the temples for the Temple of the Tooth. Every night the procession grows, moving from the *Dalada Maligawa* along Dalada Vidiya and Trincomalee St to the Adahanamaluwa, where the relic casket is left in the keeping of the temple trustees. The separate temple processions go back to their temples, coming out in the early morning for the water cutting ceremony. Originally, the temple guardians went to the lake with golden water pots to empty water collected the previous year. They would then be refilled and taken back to the temple for the following year, symbolising the fertility protected by the gods. On the last day of the festival a daylight procession accompanies the return of the Relic to the Temple of the Tooth.

Places of interest The chief focus of interest is the Palace area, with the Temple of the Tooth and associated buildings. The entrance is in Palace Square opposite the Natha Devala. Entry US$3. **See page 1461.**

The original **Temple of the Tooth** (*Dalada Maligawa*) dated from the 16th century, though most of the present building and the *Pathiruppuwa*, or Octagon, were built in the early 19th century. The gilded roof over the relic chamber is a recent addition. The oldest part is the inner shrine, built by Kirti Sri after 1765. The drawbridge, moat and gateway were the work of Sri Wickrama Raja Sinha. There is a moonstone step at the entrance to the archway, and a stone depicting Lakshmi against the wall facing the entrance. The main door to the temple is in the wall of the upper veranda, covered in restored frescoes depicting Buddhist conceptions of hell. The doorway is a typical *makrana torana* showing mythical beasts. A second Kandyan style door leads into the courtyard, across which is the building housing the Tooth Relic. The door has ivory, inlay work, with copper and gold handles. The **Udmale** – upper storey – houses the Relic.

Caged behind gilded iron bars, you can see the large outer casket (*karanduwa*), made of silver. Inside it are seven smaller caskets, each made of gold studded with jewels. Today the temple is controlled by a layman (the *Diyawadne*) elected by the high priests of the monasteries in Kandy and Asgiria. The administrator holds the key to the iron cage, but there are 3 different keys to the caskets themselves, one held by the administrator, one each by the high priests of Malwatte and Asgiriya, so that the caskets can only be opened when all three are present.

The sanctuary is opened at dawn. Ceremonies start at 0530, 0930 and 1830. These are moments when the temple comes to life with pilgrims, making offerings of flowers amidst clouds of incense and the beating of drums. You are very unlikely to be allowed to see the relic itself, which for many years has only been displayed to the most important of visitors. The eyewitness account of Bella Sidney Woolf in 1914 captures something of the atmosphere.

She wrote that "the relic is only shown to royal visitors, or on certain occasions to Burmese and other pilgrims. If the passenger happens to be in Kandy at such a time he should try to see the Tooth, even though it may mean many hours of waiting. It is an amazing sight. The courtyard is crammed with worshippers of all ages, bearing offerings in their hands, leaves of young coconut, scent, flowers, fruit. As the door opens, they surge up the dark and narrow stairway to the silver and ivory doors behind which lies the Tooth.

The doors are opened and a flood of hot heavy scented air pours out. The golden 'Karandua' or outer casket of the tooth stands revealed dimly behind gilded bars. In the weird uncertain light of candles in golden candelabra the yellow-robed priests move to and fro.

The Tooth is enclosed in five Karanduas and slowly and solemnly each is removed in turn; some of them are encrusted with rubies, emeralds and diamonds.

At last the great moment approaches. The last Karandua is removed – in folds of red silk lies the wondrous relic – the centre point of the faith of millions. It is a shock to see a tooth of discoloured ivory at least 3 inches long – unlike any human tooth ever known. The priest sets it in a golden lotus – the Temple Korala gives a sharp cry – the tom-toms and conches and pipes blare out – the kneeling worshippers, some with tears streaming down their faces, stretch out their hands in adoration."

The **Audience Hall** was rebuilt in the Kandyan style with a wooden pillared hall (1784). The historic document ending the Kandyan kingdom was signed, and the territory was handed over to the British. Today it is the High Court.

On the lakeside is the 18th century **Malwatte** (Flower Garden) **Monastery**, decorated with ornate wood and metal work where important ordinations take place. This and the **Asigiriya** are particularly important monasteries because of the senior position of their incumbents. There is a large recumbent Buddha statue at the latter, and the mound of the old Royal Burial Ground nearby.

The lake walk An attractive 4 km walk round the lake, named by its creator King Vikrama the 'ocean of milk' after its cosmic parallel. Some beautiful views, especially of the island pavilion in the lake. The Royal Palace Park (*Wace Park*), next to the Hotel Suisse, overlooks the lake and also has superb views.

The **Elephant bath** at **Katugastota** (4 km) on the Mahaveli Ganga. Elephants are brought for their daily 'bath' in the afternoon and their mahouts brush, sponge and splash them with water (essential for the animals' health). A trip out makes a pleasant diversion, but you may have to pay to take photographs. Rides available. Bus 625 from Kandy.

The **Royal Botanical Gardens**, Peradeniya, is 6 km away on the Colombo road, in a 60 ha site in a 'bow' of the river Mahaveli, the longest in the island. Allow 2-3 hr, though those with a special interest would prefer to spend longer. There is a central drive, with paths and avenues branching away. It is best to walk around the garden, but if short of time you are allowed to take a car in or find a bicycle for private hire at the entrance. There are buses from Kandy.
    Once the Queen's pleasure garden in the 14th century then turned into a princely residence for royal visitors, the park was turned into a Botanical Garden and is still beautifully maintained. There are pavilions, an excellent Orchid House, Octagon Conservatory, Fernery, Great Palm Avenue and numerous flower borders with cannas, hibiscus, chrysanthemums, croton and colourful bougainvilleas. You will see magnificent old specimen trees, unusual exotic species, banks of bamboo, rubber trees, medicinal herbs and collections of spice plants. The central tank has water plants including the giant water lily and papyrus reeds. The economic **Museum** has botanical and agricultural exhibits.
    A bridge across the river, takes you to the **School of Tropical Agriculture** at Gannoruwa, where research and trials into growing coffee, tea, cocoa, coconut as well as varieties of rice, cash crops etc are carried out. There is a restaurant at the *Rest House* nr the entrance. The **University** (1942) is nearby, built in the old Kandyan style in an impressive setting of a large park with the river Mahaveli Ganga and the surrounding hillocks.

The Western Shrines, on the Kadugannawa-Peradeniya Rd, 16 km away, is a group of 14th century temples. The ***Gadaladeniya Temple*** is in a beautiful setting, built on a rock, about a km from the main road. The stone temple, influenced by Indian temple architecture has lacquered doors, carvings and frescoes and a moonstone at the entrance of the shrine. 3 km away along the road is the second of the group. You climb up a rock cut stairway to the **Lankatilleke Temple**, with a large Buddha, with 6 other divinities, carved wooden doors and well preserved frescoes. It is one of oldest and best examples of the Kandyan temple style. A path, leads to the ***Embekke Temple*** (dedicated to God *Kataragama* or *Skanda*) 1.5 km away. It is famous for its carved wooden pillars (which may have once adorned the Audience Hall in Kandy) with vibrant figures of soldiers, wrestlers, dancers, musicians, mythical animals and birds. You can see similar carved pillars at the remains of the old **Pilgrim's Rest** nearby. The village has craftsmen working on silver, brass and copper. Buses from Kandy will drop you close to the temples and also take you on to the Botanical Gardens.

Others

The unusual incomplete 14th **Galmaduwa Temple**, 6 km SE on the Kundasala road, was an attempt to combine the features of Sinhalese, Indian, Islamic and Christian architectural styles. Bus 655 from the Market Bus Stop drops you at the bridge, across the river from the temple.

The **Medawela Temple**, 10 km NE, though built in the 18th century is on an ancient site. The interesting features include the shrine room built in wood and wattle and daub similar to the old Kandyan grain stores and the wall paintings. Bus 603 from Market Bus Stop.

Note Change in street names: Gregory Rd to *Rajapihilla Mawatha*; Lady Horton's Drive to *Vihara Mahadevi Mawatha*; Lady McCallum Drive to *Srimath Kuda Ratwatte Mawatha*; Lady Blacke's Drive to *Devani Rajasinghe Mawatha* etc.

Hotels Owing to its elevation, a/c is not necessary. **Note** Prices during Perahera are highly inflated and accommodation difficult to find. **Warning** Hotel touts are extremely persistent (sometimes boarding trains before they arrive at Kandy) and should be avoided at all costs. Insist on choosing your own hotel as otherwise prices for you will be raised by small hotels and guest houses to pay off the tout. You can telephone a hotel and reserve a rm and may then be sent transport or have the taxi fare paid.

The best are in 2 interesting buildings but since rm vary, it is advisable to see before booking in. **AL** *Queens* (Oberoi), Dalada Vidiya, T 08 22121. 120 rm. Good restaurant, bar, beer garden, by Lake side. The oldest in the country, it has been a hotel since the 1860s, refurbished after the takeover by the Indian chain. The advantage of its position opp the Temple of the Tooth, allows most guests excellent vantage point for seeing the procession from their balcony.

C *Suisse*, 130 Sangaraja Mawatha, T 08 22637. 100 rm, 15 a/c, best with balcony on lakeside. Restaurant, beer garden, travel, shops, tennis, billiards, night club. A colonial style hotel in quiet location on the lake, in parkland, 15 min walk from the Temple. Now govt run. **C** *The Citadel*, 124 Srimanth Kuda, Ratwatte Mawatha, T 08 25314. 93 rm on 3 flower-filled terraces. Good restaurant, pool, billiards. Modern but in local architectural style, located by the River Mahaveli, 5 km out of town. **C** *Tourmaline*, Anniewatte, 1.6 km from town, T 08 32326. 25 a/c rm with TV. Restaurant, bar, exchange, travel, shops, pool, tennis. **C** *Hill Top*, 200 Bahirawakanda, on rd to Peradeniya, T 08 24162. 57 rm, 15 a/c. Attractive and comfortable hotel with a restaurant, bar, shops and pool. **C** *Hantana*, Hantana Rd, T 08 23155. 100 rm in a pleasant hotel on high ground. **C** *Mahaweli Reach*, 35 Siyambalagastenna Rd, by Katugastota Bridge, T 08 32062. 50 rm. Restaurant, pool. **C** *Topaz*, T 08 32073. 75 rm, 7 a/c. Restaurant, bar, exchange, shops, travel, pool. Well kept, quiet.

There are numerous **D** category hotels and guest houses which are good value. *The Chalet*, 32 Gregory Rd, T 08 24353. 31 rm. Good restaurant, pool. Beautifully located among wooded hills, by the lake. Recommended. *Castle Hill Guest House*, 22 Gregory Rd, T 08 24376. 4 rm. Small comfortable guest house with good views over lake. Large rm and garden. There are several small, family guest houses by the lake with meals available and within easy reach of the Hotel Suisse swimming pool – *Lake Inn*, 43 Sarananjara Rd, T 08 22208 has 6 rm; *Lake Cottage*, 28 Sangaraja Mawatha, T 08 23234; *Lake View Rest*, 71 Gregory's Rd, T 08 32034 and *Hilway Tour Inn*, 90A/1 Gregory Rd, T 08 25430 with 2 rm. Most will send a car to the station to pick you up.

Guest Houses: *Thilanka*, 3 Sangamitta Mawatha, behind the Temple of the Tooth. 65 rm. Good restaurant, pool. The advantage is in its location. A second *Chalet*, 20 Gregory Rd, T 08 23608. 3 rm with bath. Recommended. *Blue Star*, 30 Hewatha Rd, T 08 24392. Cabanas. Good restaurant. Recommended. *Gem Inn* out of town to the W, taking the Anagarika Dharmapala Mawatha, is pleasantly located on a ridge with good views. Good rm with bath. The Tourist Office has a list of other small guest houses.

Inexpensive accommodation **E** Category includes *Lakshmi* uphill nr the Suisse, has clean rm; *Victoria Cottage*, 6 Victoria Drive, next to YMCA on the lake which has rm with bath; *City Mission*, 125 Trincomalee St. Good rm and restaurant recommended as good value for snacks. Clean, comfortable, home made bread and cheese. *YMCA* in town centre is at Kotugodella Vidya. Rm, some with bath, dorm. The cheaper **F** *YMCA* is at 4 Sangaraja Mawatha, on lakeside. 10 rm. Basic. *YMBA* (Young Men's Buddhist Assoc), 5 Gregory Rd, nr

Royal Palace, overlooking lake. *Rly Retiring Rm* at Kandy station.

Youth Hostel *Travellers Halt*, 53/4 Siyambalagastenna. 25 beds. 4 km from centre. Bus from opp Police Station to Katugastota, Rly Crossing Bus Stop where you cross the bridge.

27 km out of town in **Elkaduwa**, higher in the hills, is the modern hotel, **B** *Hunas Falls*, T 08 76402. The most up-to-date in the area, it has a/c rm, restaurant, bar, exchange, pool, boating, fishing, tennis. Beautifully located in a tea garden, by a waterfall with excellent walks. Visits to tea estate, factory and spice gardens

Restaurants The hotels in the town are good but can be expensive and have slow service. The *Royal Park Cafeteria* is worth trying at lunchtime if you are visiting. In town, try *Bake House*, 36 Dalada Vidiya, the *Cold Store* and *Devon* opp and *Lyon's* on *Pera*deniya Rd, nr main roundabout, which are inexpensive and good value.

Shopping Numerous shops sell handicrafts, batik and jewellery. *Laksala* and *Kandyan Art Association* (Tourist Office) are govt sales outlets. At the latter you can watch weavers and craftsmen working on wood, silver, copper and brass, and buy lacquer ware and batik. *Dalada Vidya* nr the Temple of the Tooth. Several antique shops, many along the lake. Good batiks from *Fresco*, 901 Peradeniya Rd, *Presar* and *Kjreil*. Books from *KVJ de Silva*, 86 DS Senanayake Veediya.

The crafts village set up with govt help is at *Kalapuraya Nattaropotha*, 7 km away in the beautiful Dumbara Valley where craft skills have been handed down from father to son.

A visit to the *Municipal Market*, W of the lake is worthwhile even if you are not planning to bargain for superb Sri Lankan fruit. The *Wheel* by the Lake sells Buddhist literature.

Entertainment Daily performances of highland Kandyan dancing in different parts of the town. At Amungama, 10 km away is the Kandyan Dance Academy where the art and skill is handed down from father to son. Keppetipola Hall and the Lake Club performances are recommended. The show usually lasts about 90 mins, ending with the fire dance.

Museums

The **Archaeological Museum**, Palace Square. Open 0900-1700, closed Tues. Superb sculptures, wood and stone housed in what remains of the old Palace. Some architectural pieces, notably columns and capitals from the Kandyan kingdom. The **Kandy National Museum** In the Queen's Palace, behind the Temple of the Tooth. Open 0900-1700, closed Fri. A vivid history of the development and culture of the Kandyan kingdom. Jewels, armaments, ritual objects, sculptures, clothes, games, medical instruments – an enormous range of everyday and exceptional objects.

Libraries The British Council is opp the Clock Tower, the USIS on Kotugodalle Vidya and United Services Library by the Lake, opp the Temple of the Tooth.

Useful addresses Alliance Française, 492/2A Riachand Garden St. **Tourist Office** Kandy Art Assoc Bldg, Sangaraja Mawatha. There is a Market **Bus Stop** and one further S nr the Station. **Post Offices** are opp the Rly Station and on Senanayaje Vidiya (crossing with Kande Vidiya). **Bank** of Ceylon on Dalada Vidya.

Rail Colombo *Intercity Express*, 30, daily, 0630, 2 hr 30; *24 Express*, daily, 1000, 3 hr; *Intercity Express*, 10, daily, 1500, 2 hr 30. **Nanu Oya** (for Nuwara Eliya) *Podi Menike*, 5, daily, 0906, 4 hr 20. **Badulla** *Podi Menike*, 5, daily, 0906, 7 hr 50; *Mail*, 45, daily, 2355, 7 hr 50.

Bus Local buses use the Torrington Bus stand near the market. Frequent service. Long distance buses leave from the Goodshed Bus Stand. CTB buses leave from the Central Bus Stand, in front of the market. Frequent buses to Colombo, and all major cities on the island.

The route from Kandy to Batticaloa by road now goes via the tea country surrounding Nuwara Eliya and Badulla. These are described in the next route. It is then possible to go due E to the coast at Arugam Bay, driving up all along the coast to Batticaloa. The coastal road was devastated by a cyclone in 1978, and the damage to housing is still visible. It is a desolate journey. Alternatively you can follow the NH 5 due N from Passala to Kehelulla, leaving the hills, and turning NE to Eravur. Here a road turns SE to Batticaloa. The old direct route from Kandy due E has now been flooded by the Victoria Dam project.

Warning Batticaloa has been the centre of repeated violent fighting in the first half of 1991 between the Tamil Tigers and the Army. Check locally whether it is possible and safe to go.

Batticaloa is an old Dutch town, called the town of Tamarinds by its predominantly Tamil population. The Dutch fortified the town in 1602, the remains of which can be seen near the present day *Rest House*, but today it is famous for its singing fish, heard in the middle of the lagoon on still nights. The centre of the lagoon bridge is reputed to be the best place for listening to the extraordinary resonating sounds.

Hotels Only simple accommodation is available. Near the Dutch Fort on Arugam Bay side is the rebuilt **Rest House**. *Sunshine Inn*, 118 Bar Rd, on the other side of the rly track from the station. Clean, in a pleasant garden. *Rly Retiring Rm*, T 065 2271. 8 rm.

5 km from town, at the end of the bus route are two – *Beach House Guest House*, Bar Rd, nr Lighthouse. Quiet, good food; *East Winds*, next door.

Rly Retiring Rm, T 065 2271. 8 rm.

COLOMBO TO NUWARA ELIYA, BADULLA AND ARUGAM BAY

The shortest and most attractive route runs W from the Colombo Fort and the Pettah, along the S bank of the Kelaniya River. It is a scenically beautiful route up into the hills, past Adam's Peak, the third highest mountain in Sri Lanka, and through the great tea estates of the Hatton-Dikoya region to the most popular holiday resort for Sri Lankans at Nuwara Eliya.

The NH 4 now runs SE out of Colombo through Nugegoda. The slower but more attractive route follows the left (S) bank of the Kelaniya River. **Kaduwela** (16 km) has a *Rest House* in beautiful position overlooking the river with a constant succession of varied river traffic. There is a fairly large Buddhist temple and irrigation tank of *Mulleriyawa*. Continuing along the Kelaniya River the road passes through **Hanwella** (33 km), where there is another excellent *Rest House*, again with a beautiful view up and down the river. On site of Portuguese fort, Hanwella is noted as the place where the last king of Kandy, **Sri Vikrama Raja Sinha**, was defeated.

At Hanwella the road joins the NH 4 and turns left towards *Avisawella* (18 km). The centre of rubber industry, Avisawella is in beautiful wooded surroundings. The ruins of a royal palace and temple destroyed by Portuguese on opposite bank of the river. The *Rest House* is recommended. The NH 4 to **Ratnapura** (43 km) goes off to the right (see below). Continue on the NH 7 E and then N to **Karawanella** (13 km), then turning right to **Yatiyantota** (7 km). After a further 18 km the road climbs steeply up the **Ginigathena Pass**, to magnificent views at the top. The left hand road in the small town goes to Kandy, the right continues to Hatton.

From here on the road runs through tea country. *Ginighathena* is a small bazaar for the tea estates and their workers. The road winds up through a beautiful valley, surrounded by green, evenly picked tea bushes to Watawala (10 km). The air becomes noticeably cooler, and from occasional twists in the road you get views right across the plains to Colombo and the Kelani Valley. At *Watawala* the Carolina Falls are spectacular in the wet season. Follow the lower road to

Hatton (12 km), is one of the major centres of Sri Lanka's tea industry. It is the base from which most pilgrims and tourists make the trek to the top of Adam's Peak. Hotels will arrange tours. Buses run the tortuously winding route from Hatton to *Maskeliya* (20 km; *Altitude* 1,280 m) and on to Dalhousie. By car it takes about an hour, going through some of the most productive tea growing areas towards Norwood. Keep to the Maskeliya road up the Pass before Norwood. The air is already strikingly fresh, and the higher road is lined with tropical ferns.

The bus journey takes about 2 hr to Dalhousie, where the climb itself starts. There are tea shops in **Dalhousie**, but nowhere good to stay. A steep footpath leads to **Adam's Peak** (2,250 m), sacred to Buddhists, Hindus and Muslims, one of Sri Lanka's main centres of pilgrimage. The climb to the top from Maskeliya takes about 3 hours. The path is clearly marked throughout, beginning fairly easily but rapidly become steeper. Most people do the walk by moonlight, arriving in time to see the dawn. It is completely safe, even the steepest parts being protected, and steps and chains provided where necessary. The route is ancient – Marco Polo commented on the chains provided for pilgrims in the 13th century. However, it is very cold on top of the peak until well after sunrise. It is essential to take warm clothing, as well as some food and drink. The object of pilgrimage on the summit is the giant footprint – of the Buddha, of Adam, of Siva? – covered by a huge stone slab, in which has been carved another print. An alternative route, much steeper and more difficult, comes up from the Ratnapura side. Local Buddhist tradition promises any woman who succeeds in climbing by this route that she will be re-born in the next life as a man. At dawn the conical peak, only 50 m square, forms an extraordinary shadow across the plains to the W.

From Hatton the road crosses the railway line and winds up through the tea estates of *Dimbula* to **Talawakele** (10 km). Sri Lanka's Tea Research Institute (sometimes open to visitors) has played a major role in improving Sri Lanka's tea production. A right turn after Talawakele leads up a beautiful mountain road to Agrapatana, but the main road continues through Nanuoya, and finally down into

Nuwara Eliya (*Altitude* 1,990 m)

	Jan	Feb	Mar	Apr	May	Jun	Jul	Aug	Sep	Oct	Nov	Dec	Av/Tot
Max (°C)	20	24	25	25	23	20	20	19	19	21	20	20	21
Min (°C)	9	9	9	11	13	14	13	14	14	12	11	12	12
Rain (mm)	116	87	69	170	185	215	185	161	177	245	222	213	2045

Nuwara Eliya ('New – rail – eeya') is the highest town in Sri Lanka and a major hill resort. 'The City of Light' (*Altitude* 1,990 m) was a favourite hill station of the British and has retained all the paraphernalia of one, with its colonial houses, parks, the Hill Club, an 18 hole golf course, and trout streams. It offers a cool escape from the plains and is particularly popular during the New Year holidays in April when hotels tend to raise their prices and are still full. The Golf Course is thought to exceptionally good and for added entertainment there are horse races during the 3 week holiday.

Places of interest In 1914 Bella Sidney Woolf wrote that "when the visitor looks out of his window in the early morning and sees the whole world glistening under hoar frost and the garden brimming with geraniums, pansies, sweet peas, and every English flower, with never a palm in sight, he wonders if he is really in the Tropics after all. He does not doubt it when the sun rises higher and melts the hoar frost away." Part of the charm of the town certainly lies in its fresh and distinctive feel.

Some of the buildings are of Georgian and Queen Anne periods, and there are attractive walks round the small town, which has lawns, parks, and Anglican church and the Hill Club. The **Horton Plains** nearby, the island's highest and most isolated plateau, harbours many wild animals and is rich in bird life. A bridle paths lead to the **World's End** which has a spectacular precipice with a 1050 m drop.

Excursions

Pidurutalagala (Mt Pedro) is the island's highest peak (2,524 m) and is a 2 hr climb up the track from nr the RC Church, N of the town, in places still through dense forest. It is a steep but quite manageable climb.

The **Hakgala Gardens** (10 km) was once a Cinchona Plantation and then a Botanical Garden, but now is famous for its roses. The name Hakgala or 'Jaw Rock' comes from the story in the epic *Ramayana* where the Monkey god, takes back a part of the mountainside in his jaw, when asked by Rama to seek out a special herb! The *Humbugs* restaurant and bar is beautifully located and does good meals and snacks. You will pass the temple to Rama's wife **Sita Eliya** a short distance before you reach the gardens which is thought to mark the spot where she was kept a prisoner by King Ravana. There are buses from Nuwara Eliya.

Hotels Warning Beware of hotel touts – see note under Kandy.
The 2 best are by the Golf Course are in the Raj style. Well kept, good restaurants, with plenty of atmosphere. **C** *The Grand*, Grand Hotel Rd, T 052 2881. 114 rm. Pleasant restaurant, bar, coffee shop, travel, shops, golf, tennis, cultural shows. **C** *Hill Club*, up a path from the Grand Hotel Rd. *22 rm. Formal restaurant (you are expected to be properly dressed* for dinner – tie essential for men). **C** *St Andrews*, 10 St Andrews Drive, overlooking Golf Course, T 052 2445. 55 rm. Restaurant, bar, exchange, tours.
    D The *Rest*, off the Hakgala Rd, T 0522 436 is less expensive and has a restaurant. Govt run. *Tourinn*, Park Rd, T 052 2410. 7 rm. **D** *The Grosvenor*, 4 Haddon Hill Rd, T 052 2307. 19 rm. In charming old Colonial house. **D** *Oatlands*, St Andrews Drive, T 052 2572. 5 rm. Small, family run guest house serving good food. Several others along Upper Lake Drive. **D** *Collingwood*, Badulla Rd. In old Planter's house, retaining its old-world British character. Only 1 guest rm. **D** *Alpen Guest House*, nr the Grosvenor. Comfortable and friendly. **D** *Princess Guest House*, 12 Wedderburn Rd, 052 2462. 7 rm. Rm service.

Rail The nearest station is *Nanu Oya*, a short bus ride away. **Colombo** *Uda Rakamenike*, 16, daily, 0936, 6 hr; *Podi Menike Exp*, 6, daily, 1244, 7 hr 15; *Mail*, 46, daily, 2206, 7 hr 30. **Kandy** *Podi Menike Exp*, 6, daily, 1244, 4 hr 20.

Bus Frequent buses to Badulla and Kandy. 2 CTB buses a day to Colombo (6 hr 30).

From Nuwara Eliya the NH 5 continues E to Badulla. Just past the **Hakgala Gardens** (10 km) is a superb view SE across the hills of Bandarawela and over the baked plains of the E coastlands. The road drops rapidly through to **Welimada**, where a right turn leads to Bandarawela (See below), past terraced fields of paddy and across occasional streams. This area is already in the rainshadow of the hills to the W, sheltered from the SW monsoon and much drier than Nuwara Eliya. Rubber plantations cover some of the slopes before

Badulla (*Altitude* 675 m, 45 km) the capital of Uva district and one of the oldest towns in Sri Lanka. In a hollow, and surrounded by paddy fields along the banks of a river, it has a backcloth of mountains. It once had a race course, long since out of use, and there are no traces of the earlier settlement. There are two large temples, the Buddhist Mutiyangane Vihare and the Hindu Kataragama Devale. Both are on sites of earlier temples, and there is also a revered Bo tree. The park was once a small botanic garden.

From Badulla, take NH 22 E to Hulandawa (53 km) and continue towards Arugam Bay. As a detour, or to travel to Batticaloa from here, at Siyambalamduwa (36 km) turn left taking the NH 25 northwards. At Wadingala (25 km), there is a road to the left to **Inginiyagala** where you can stay to visit the **Gal Oya National Park** early in the morning.

The Park, inland from the E Coast, covers 540 sq km, and is famous for its elephants and the large number of water birds which are attracted by the huge lake, Senanayaka Samudra. Best visited in the early morning for watching elephants and white buffaloes which come down to the lake, the crocodiles in the water and the birds rising from the lake to perch on the dead trees around the lake. You can take motor boat tours on the lake, lasting 2-3 hr.

Hotel B *Inginiyagala Safari Inn*, superbly situated, booked through Mercantile Tours, T 063 2499 or in Colombo, T 91805. 22 comfortable rm, restaurant. A 10 min walk brings you to the lake, picturesque at sunset. The hotel will organise tours into the Park and also a Vedda village. **D** *Duhinda Falls Inn*, 35/11 -1/1 Bandaranayake Mawatha, T 055 2406. 12 rm. Restaurant, bar, exchange, car/cycle hire, visits to tea gardens.

If you do not wish to visit the National Park continue on NH 22 towards Arugam

Bay. At **Lahugala Sanctuary** (20 km) by a large tank, you can stop to see the numerous species of birds and the large elephant herds that come down to the water in the dry season (Aug-Oct). A few km on, to the S of the main rd is **Magul Maha Vihara** – ruins in a jungle setting of a Vatadage and a dagoba with impressive *moonstones* and guardstones.

Arugam Bay is 15 km from here, passing through Pottuvil. The Bay with its good beach is particularly interesting for not only those keen on water sports (it has excellent surf), and underwater photography but also offers exciting possibilities for divers keen to explore wrecked ships. The lagoon here attracts water birds.

Hotels Large number of moderately priced simple hotels, cabanas and beach cottages to choose from, the cheaper places S of the bridge. *Rest House*, on the beach. 3 rm. Restaurant. Pleasant and comfortable.

The coastal road S of Arugam Bay takes you to **Kumana Bird Sanctuary** (40 km). Kumana, to the E of the larger Yala National Park, is visited for its resident and migratory aquatic birds including flamingoes, ibis, herons, pheasants, particularly impressive in May and June. There are 2 simple *Bungalows* with warden/cook. Bring your bedding and food. *Reservations*: Wildlife Dept, Transwork House, Col 1, T 33787.

COLOMBO TO RATNAPURA, BANDARAWELA AND BADULLA

The most attractive route to Ratnapura takes the road E along the Kelani river to Avissawella (described above), then turns SE to Ratnapura. It runs through the heart of the wet zone, densely forested land interspersed with pockets of rice cultivation, before reaching the centre of Sri Lanka's gem producing region. It is a gentle drive to the foot of the hills, but there are superb views of Adam's Peak and the hills. From Ratnapura the NH 4 circles to the S of Adam's Peak, climbing into the hills through Balangoda to Bandarawela. The NH 8, offers an alternative route to Ratnapura, which can be taken on the way back if the previous route is used to climb into the hills. It also runs through attractive countryside.

Note the option of high level road from Colombo through the suburb of **Nugegoda** and the new capital of **Jayawardenepuram-Kotte** to **Homagama**, Ingiriya and **Ratnapura**. This avoids the danger of floods in the wet season.

The S route to Ratnapura, the NH 8, goes S to **Panadura** (27 km) then turns left to *Horana (16 km)*. The *Rest House* (good value) is built in the remains of an ancient Buddhist monastery. On the opposite side of road is a large Buddhist temple with a particularly noteworthy bronze candlestick, over 2 m tall. From Nambapane *(29 km)* the road keeps quite close to the Kalu Ganga River, staying in its valley to

Ratnapura (21 km).

	Jan	Feb	Mar	Apr	May	Jun	Jul	Aug	Sep	Oct	Nov	Dec	Av/Tot
Max (°C)	34	36	36	36	34	31	31	31	30	33	32	31	33
Min (°C)	22	23	24	24	25	25	24	24	23	23	23	23	24
Rain (mm)	120	52	215	359	479	420	305	270	388	453	355	221	3637

The climate of Ratnapura has been likened to a Turkish bath. The vegetation is correspondingly luxuriant, but the city is best known for its gem stones, washed down the river bed. The 'City of Gems', Ratnapura is thus aptly named. A number of precious stones are found nearby including sapphire, ruby, topaz, amethyst, cat's eye, alexandrite, aquamarine, tourmaline, garnet and zircon. It is surrounded by rubber and tea estates in a lush and beautiful setting, and gives better views of Adam's Peak than almost anywhere else on the island. The quality of Ratnapura's gems is legendary. In the 7th century Hiuen Tsang claimed that there was a ruby on the spire of the temple at Anuradhapura whose magnificence illuminated the sky. Today sapphires are much more important. Advice given to travellers at the beginning of the century still holds: "As regards buying stones, it is a risky business unless the passenger has expert knowledge or advice. It is absolute folly to buy stones from itinerant vendors. It is far better to go to one of the large Colombo jewellers and take the chance of paying more and obtaining a genuine stone." It is still difficult for the untrained eye to tell the difference between glass and stone.

It is well worth going to the top of the fort for the views. Driving up to Gilimale from the bridge gives you a chance to see the massive curtain wall of the central highlands to the N. Sapphires, rubies, topaz, cat's eyes are mined from pits dug into a special form of gravel. Genuine stones common, valuable stones by definition rarer. 3 km W of Ratnapura is Maha Saman Dewale, the richest Buddhist temple in Sri Lanka.

Hotels B *Ratnaloka Tour Inns* Kosgala Kahangama, T 045 2455. 53 rm. Pool. Central a/c. Good food, open to non-residents. **E** *Rest House* T 045 2299. 11 rm. Above the town, outstanding views and delightful site. Food also excellent value. **F** Some basic hotels nr bus stand. **F** *Traveller's Rest*, 66 Inner Circular Rd. Basic.

Museums Ratnapura National Museum Small exhibition of pre-historic fossil skeletons from the region, such as elephants and rhinoceros. **The Gem Museum** Getangama Gems from different parts of Sri Lanka and an exhibition of gem polishing.

Excursions Travel agents can organise visits to gem mines.

Adam's Peak This is the base from which the much steeper and more strenuous route leads to Adam's Peak. Route: Malwala (8 km) on River Kalu Ganga, Gilimale (3 km), Palabadalla (8 km; 375 m). Then very steep path to Heramitipana (13 km 1100 m) and the summit (5 km, 2260 m). An imprint of the Buddha's footmark is on the summit.

The road between Ratnapura and *Pelmadulla* (18 km) continues across the fertile and undulating low country, with paddy fields and palm trees. A diversion is possible from Pelmadulla, where the NH 17 and NH 18 go SE together to **Madampe** (13 km) before parting. NH 17 then goes S through *Rakwana*, the chief village of a tea-growing district. Good *Rest House*, with views that are some of the most beautiful in Sri Lanka. Beautiful flowering trees in season, notably *Dendrodium maccarthii*. It continues S to Galle or Matara. The NH 18 goes SE from Madampe to *Maduwanwela* (35 km) to one of best known *walauwas* of the Kandyan chiefs. Small inward-looking courtyards were built on the "Pompeiian plan". The road continues SE to Hambantota and Tissa Maharama (See below).

The NH 4 continues to **Balangoda** (24 km) through superb scenery all the way, rubber estates being important. Adam's Peak and the Maskeliya Range rise magnificently to the N, although during the SW monsoon they are almost permanently covered in cloud. The densely forested land to the E has now largely been cleared, and the road goes on through *Belihuloya* (19 km) with tea estates, the road rising to *Haldummulla* (15 km) *Altitude* 1020 m. There are excellent views across to the sea. The NH 16 goes NE shortly after Haldummulla, a short but steep climb to *Haputale* (*Altitude* 1,400 m). Magnificent views of the dawn over the Low Country to the E -'almost worth staying a night at the Rest House to see'. On a clear day you can see the salt pans at Hambantota to the S, and the horizon is the sea. To the N in magnificent contrast are the peaks.

Diversion The NH 4 turns right after Haldummulla to *Koslande*, past the *Diyaluma* waterfall (170 m) to *Wellawaya* (good Rest House). It then continues E across the plains to Arugam Bay (105 km).

Bandarawela (*Altitude* 1,230 m) Benefitting from the rain shadow of the Central Highlands, which gives it a drier SW monsoon than the hills immediately to the W, Bandarawela has possibly the best climate in Sri Lanka, and the most renowned tea. A small and straggling town, Bandarawela is a good base for pleasant walks.

	Jan	Feb	Mar	Apr	May	Jun	Jul	Aug	Sep	Oct	Nov	Dec	Av/Tot
Max (°C)	23	28	28	29	27	28	27	27	26	26	24	23	26
Min (°C)	14	13	14	15	17	17	18	18	17	16	15	16	16
Rain (mm)	125	98	108	193	121	45	58	77	115	262	256	203	1661

Hotels D *Orient Hotel* Centre of town, T 407. 35 rm. Huge concrete barracks like building. **E** *Bandarawela Hotel*, T 501. 36 rm. Renovated in 1983, but still not very exciting. **F** *Rest House* Nr the Orient Hotel. Good location and value.

It is probably best to stay at *Ella* (13 km), where there is an excellent **F** *Rest House*. T 806. 6 rm, so necessary if possible to book in advance. Superb views from its position high above the plains. To reach Ella from Bandarawela keep on the NH 16. After 7 km turn right. At this junction the road to **Badulla** goes straight on (20 km).

Rail Colombo *Uda Rakamenike*, 16, daily, 0726, 8 hr 10; *Podi Menike Exp*, 6, daily, 1244, 7 hr 15; *Mail*, 46, daily, 2206, 7 hr 30. **Kandy** *Podi Menike Exp*, 6, daily, 1022, 6 hr 20.

Bus Frequent buses to Haputale, Badulla and Ella.

Badulla More open than Kandy, it lies in the middle of rice fields, surrounded by the high hills. There is a small lake, and some large Buddhist temples. At one time it was an extremely active social centre for planters, with a race course, golf, tennis and cricket club. These have long since fallen into disuse. For details today see above.

Rail Colombo *Uda Rakamenike*, 16, daily, 0555, 9 hr 40; *Podi Menike Express*, 6, daily, 0850, 11hr 50; *Mail*, 46, daily,1745, 12 hr. **Kandy** *Podi Menike Express*, 6, daily, 0850, 8 hr.

Bus Frequent buses to Nuwara Eliya, Bandarawela. Occasional buses to E coast.

COLOMBO TO GALLE, HAMBANTOTA & TISSAMAHARAMA

For most of the journey this follows close to the coast, with its magnificent bays and sandy beaches. It is a wholly distinctive drive, contrasting sharply with the routes into and through the hills or across the dry zone of the N and E. Some of the beaches are now developed, but even so they retain their largely rural settings. The political crises of the late 1980s left many of the beaches deserted by tourists. In 1991 the situation was much more peaceful, and it was becoming possible again to consider travelling down the W coast. The road

follows immediately by the railway line all the way to Matara. From there the road continues, completing the 264 km between Colombo and Tissamaharama.

Take the NH 2 S of Colombo, through *Mount Lavinia* (11 km). See excursions from Colombo for details of hotels. The small town of *Moratuwa* (17 km) is noted for its furniture making and its college. 8 km S the road goes through *Panadura*, then on to *Kalutara* (16 km). Cross over River Kalu Ganga ('Black River'). The river is over 300 m wide.

Kalutara The Portuguese built a fort on the site of a Buddhist temple, the Dutch took it over and the British Agent converted it to his residence. It now has a Buddhist shrine again. Wild hog deer, introduced by Dutch from Ganga Delta, are reputedly still found. The centre of the arrack industry, Kalutara is known for its basket making. Leaves of the wild date are dyed red, orange, green and black, and woven into hats and baskets. The area is also famous for its mangosteen fruit, and graphite is mined in district.

Kalutara has a huge stretch of fine sand. S is one of the most densely populated parts of the Island. Many people depend on fishing, and every day fishermen bring in their catch at numerous points along the coast. The coconut palms that also line the shore all the way down to Galle and beyond provide fibre for local use as well as for export.

Hotels AL *Tangerine Hotel* T 042 2640. 94 rm. Enormous lawn stretches beneath the coconut trees to the sea. **A** *Ocean View*, Wadduwa (8 km), T 046 2463. 78 rm, non a/c. **E** *Rest House*. Excellent value.

The road continues S to *Beluwera* (16 km; derived from the Sinhalese word Baeruala – the place where the sail is lowered), the spot where the first Muslim settlers are believed to have landed. The Kitchimalai mosque, on a headland, is worth seeing. It is a major pilgrimage centre at the end of Ramazan. You can also go out to the lighthouse raised on a small island offshore. There is an excellent view of the coastline from the top. Most of the hotels cater for package tours.

Hotels AL *Neptune*, T 048 5218. 104 rm. Full board. Beach and shady trees in front and woods behind. **A** *Wornels Reef*, Moragella, T 048 5430. 99 rm. Very well situated. **C** *Berberyn Reef* T 048 5220 84 rm (some a/c), cottage style. Full board.

Road and rail continue S to *Alutgama* (5 km), the main bus and railway station for the beaches to both N and S. Very good *Rest House*, the town is famous for its oysters, and as a weekend resort from Colombo. Immediately to the S is the famous beach resort of *Bentota* (3 km), built entirely for foreign tourists as a specially designed beach complex with **B** category and less hotels. A sand spit separates the river from the sea, giving excellent calm waters for wind surfing and sailing. A full range of watersports is available plus tennis, mini golf, pool etc. From here to Galle the road is nearly always in sight of the sea.

Ambalangoda (18 km), is the home of Devil Dancing and mask making. Good *Rest House* next to the sea and good swimming. Originally the Rest House was a Dutch warehouse for cinnamon and coconuts. Meetiyagoda (6 km) is a moonstone quarry.

Hikkaduwa 13 km This has become the most popular and developed beach on the West Coast. Excellent swimming and a wide range of facilities for snorkelling and scuba diving. Famous for its 'Coral Gardens' – you can hire a glass-bottomed boat to view the splendid underwater collection. In the 1980s it was being heavily developed, and its long seaside road was packed with tourists, hotels, and guest houses. Some of the development was ugly.

The road continues S. Off the road is *Baddegama* (11 km) The Anglican church is the first in Sri Lanka, built in 1818 and consecrated by Bishop Heber in 1825.

It has noteworthy ironwood pillars.

Dodanduwa (6 km), further to the S, has a beautiful lake and a fine Buddhist temple approached by a long steep and narrow flight of stone stairs. The road crosses the Dutch Canal to enter

Galle (15 km).

It is the most important town in the S and has retained much of its colonial atmosphere. The Portuguese, Dutch and British used the natural harbour as their main port until 1875, when reconstruction of breakwaters and the enlarged harbour made Colombo the island's major port. Its origins as a port go back well before the Portuguese. Ibn Battuta, the great Moroccan traveller, visited it in 1344. The historian of Ceylon Sir Emerson Tennant claimed that Galle was the ancient city of Tarshish, which had traded not only with Persians and Egyptians, but with King Solomon.

The Portuguese Lorenzo de Almeida drifted into Galle by accident in 1505. It was a further 82 years before the Portuguese captured it from the Sinhala Kings, and they controlled the port until the Dutch laid siege in 1640. The old Portuguese Fort on a promontory was strengthened by the Dutch.

Places of interest The Dutch left their mark on the town. The Dutch Reformed Church (1754), built as a result of a vow taken by the Dutch Governor of Galle, Casparaous de Jong, contains a number of interesting memorials, and in the quiet backstreets of the fort there are still some fine houses, now often mildewed and fading. Over the gateway of the citadel which leads to the port are the monogrammed arms of the Dutch East India Company, V.O.C. – *Vereenigde Oost Indische Campagnie* – dated 1699, the year when the fortifications were completed. The Government offices on Hospital St were once the Dutch warehouse ('factory').

The ramparts of the fort are over 2.5 km long. Surrounded on 3 sides by the sea, they make a very pleasant walk. They are marked by a series of bastions covering the promontory. Nearest to the harbour were two bastions – The sun and Zwart bastions – which controlled the traffic into the harbour. They were followed by the *Aurora* and *Point Utrecht* bastions before the lighthouse, then *Triton*, *Neptune*, *Clippenburg*, *Aeolus*, *Star* and *Moon*.

The crescent-shaped shoreline was dotted with islands, though some have now been joined up or altered by the harbour developments. Galle is famous for its lace-making, gem polishing and ebony carving, all of which make a good souvenirs. The lighthouse is nearly 20 m high.

Hotels **C** *New Oriental*, 10 Church St, Fort, T 09 2059. 36 rm. Restaurant, bar, pool. Well maintained old hotel, good atmosphere, very good food, excellent value. **C** *Closenberg*, 11 Closenberg Rd, Magalle, overlooking Harbour, *T 092* 3073. 20 rm. Restaurant, bar, boating, sea fishing. On the promontory overlooking the bay 3 km E of Galle. Colonial house built in 1858, with character and attractive atmosphere. Out of town but recommended. **D** *Beach Haven Guest House*, 65 Lighthouse St, T 09 2663. 25 rm. Restaurant, exchange, shops, pool. Pleasant with good restaurant. **E** *Rly Retiring Rm.*

Restaurants Best at the New Oriental, which has a bakery next door. *Chinese Golden Restaurant* opp Rly station and *Snack Bar* nearby.

Shopping There are some interesting shops near the lighthouse. *Universal Gems*, 42 A Jiffriya St (Cripps Rd).

Post office Church St GPO (on the site of the old Dutch burial ground).

Train Colombo *Samudra Devi*, 327, daily, 0500, 3 hr 10; *Ruhunu Kumari Express*, 57, daily, 0825, 2 hr 30; 51, daily, 1456, 2 hr 45; 53, daily, 1700, 2 hr 36. **Matara** 50, daily, 1022, 1 hr 18; 52, daily, 1123, 52; *Ruhunu Kumari*, daily, 1815, 55.

The NH 2 continues E along the coast. 1 km before ***Weligama*** (28 km) there is

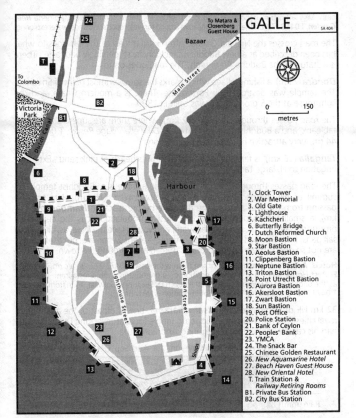

GALLE

SA 404

N

0   150
metres

1. Clock Tower
2. War Memorial
3. Old Gate
4. Lighthouse
5. Kachcheri
6. Butterfly Bridge
7. Dutch Reformed Church
8. Moon Bastion
9. Star Bastion
10. Aeolus Bastion
11. Clippenberg Bastion
12. Neptune Bastion
13. Triton Bastion
14. Point Utrecht Bastion
15. Aurora Bastion
16. Akersloot Bastion
17. Zwart Bastion
18. Sun Bastion
19. Post Office
20. Police Station
21. Bank of Ceylon
22. Peoples' Bank
23. YMCA
24. The Snack Bar
25. Chinese Golden Restaurant
26. New Aquamarine Hotel
27. Beach Haven Guest House
28. New Oriental Hotel
T. Train Station &
    Railway Retiring Rooms
B1. Private Bus Station
B2. City Bus Station

a huge stone statue of Kushta Raja. Various legends surround him, and he is sometimes known as the 'Leper King'. There is a lovely bay, and the tiny island opposite the *Rest House* was once owned by the French Count de Maunay, who built the house on the island. The bay is best known for its remarkable fishermen who perch silently for hours on stilts out in the bay and also for locally made lace. *Bay Beach Hotel*, T 0415 201 en route from Galle. 56 rm. Restaurant, pool.

From Weligama to Tangalla is an outstandingly beautiful stretch from road. There seems to be an endless succession of bays, the road often running right by the startling blue sea and palm fringed rocky headlands. The district is famous for the manufacture and export of citronella perfume.

Matara (15 km) A lively little town, Matara has 2 Dutch forts, and the gateway (1770) to the Coral Star Fort (which houses the library) is particularly picturesque. The fort itself is private property. The Buddhist hermitage, *Chula Lanka*, on a tiny island joined by causeway to the mainland, was founded by a Thai Prince priest. As with several of the coastal towns, a local delicacy is the fine curd.

Hotels D *Rest House* in main Fort, close to Clock Tower and Bus Stop. Better rm in new part with bath. Very attractive, good food and good value. The more comfortable **C** *Polhena Reef Garden*, T 041 2478, off the main rd to Matara is good for water sports and underwater exploring.

The road crosses the Nilwala Ganga. After 5 km a road to the left goes to what has been described as a new Buddhist sanctuary in 'stupefyingly bad taste'. There is a statue of the Buddha 40 m high. The road goes on to

Dondra (7 km), a fishing village which marks the southernmost point of Sri Lanka. The temple was destroyed by Portuguese. There is a modern vihara, and the lighthouse at the S promontory was built in 1899.

The road passes through *Dikwella* (12 km) where there are superb statues and tableaux, and a Buddhist temple. **Hotel A** *Dikwella Village Resort*, T 041 2961. 44 rm. Very attractive hotel on the promontory.

Tangalla (16 km), is famous for its turtles and its beach of pink sand . Extensive irrigation to N, large tank.

The road passes through *Ranna* (12 km) where there is a Buddhist temple on summit of hill approaching Ranna, and *Ambalantota* (16 km). Here you are passing from the wet zone to the dry zone before reaching **Hambantota** (14 km), a small fishing port with a big Muslim population. It is the centre for producing salt from evaporated sea water and you will see the *lewayas*, or shallow salt pans, from the road. The small bay offers excellent swimming, but the beaches are not so good. There are sand dunes immediately around the town.

Hotels A *Peacock Beach Hotel*, nr the town is the best. T 0472 277. 80 a/c rm. There is a **E** *Rest House* situated in a superb position on a promontory, with a restaurant. Described as 'the bright spot of Hambantota'. On the beach **D** *Seaspray*, Galwala, 1 km from Bus stop. T 0472 212. Some a/c rm. Other accommodation is fairly basic.

32 km NE of Hambantota is **Tissamaharama**, one of oldest of the abandoned royal cities. The ruins had been hidden in jungle for centuries. King Dutthagamani had his capital here before recapturing Anuradhapura.

	Jan	Feb	Mar	Apr	May	Jun	Jul	Aug	Sep	Oct	Nov	Dec	Av/Tot
Max (°C)	31	31	31	32	31	31	31	31	30	30	30	30	31
Min (°C)	23	23	24	26	26	26	26	25	24	24	24	24	25
Rain (mm)	81	56	57	98	91	58	55	49	67	141	193	127	1073

The tank at Tissawewa, thought to have been created at the end of the 3rd century BC, was restored with two others and attracts a lot of water birds. Numerous dagobas, including one 50 m high, which too had been lost under the sand having been destroyed by the invading Dravidians, have been restored entirely by local Buddhists. Other buildings resemble a palace and a multistoreyed monastery.

Hotel The **B** *Tissamaharama Rest House*, in gardens on the lakeside is very comfortable. 43 rm. Restaurant and open-air bar. Recommended. Other nearby are simpler guest houses which are less expensive. Toward Kataragama, there are a couple, the *Hatari* and the *Travelogue Inn*.

Excursions
Kataragama, 16 km from Tissamaharama, is a tiny village which comes vividly to life at the the Esala (Jul-Aug) festival. Pilgrims flock to the temple, and which ends with fire walking and 'water cutting' ceremonies. The pilgrims come to perform penance for sins they have committed, and some of the scenes of self-mutilation, performed in a trance, are horrific.

Hotels The *Rest House* has 45 rm. Enquire in Colombo about rm at the attractive *Bank of Ceylon* guest house.

Kirinda, on the coast, is 10 km SE of Tissamaharama, and has a good beach and some Buddhist ruins on the rocks. It is historically linked to the King Dutthagamani. His mother, having been banished by her father, landed at the village and married the local king. Although popular with scuba divers who are attracted by the reefs at Great and Little Basses off the coast, the currents can be treacherous.

Hotel *Brown's Safari Beach Hotel*, has 8 rm.

Yala in the dry zone, also known as *Ruhuna National Park*, is 20 km from Tissamaharama. **Kumana** *(see above)* to the E is a Bird Sanctuary, reached from Pottuvil and Arugam Bay. You need to spend a day at the 1260 sq km park which varies from open parkland, scrub, to dense jungle on the plains, rocky outcrops and streams, small lakes and lagoons and has a picturesque ocean frontage. With the Lahugala Sanctuary bordering it, the elephants are the main attraction, with deer, wild boar, buffaloes and numerous species of birds. Best time to visit is Oct-Dec, early morning or late afternoon. Buses or jeep tours within the Park. Safari tours, last 3 hr.

Hotels 6 *Park Bungalows*, have a cook. Bring your own bedding and food. Reservations: Wildlife Dept, Transwork House, Col 1, T 33787. *Yala Safari Beach Hotel*, Amaduwa.

INFORMATION FOR VISITORS

Documents

Passports and visas Nationals of the following countries as tourists do not need a visa for a period of 30 days: Australia, Austria, Bahrain, Bangladesh, Belgium, Britain, Canada, Denmark, Eire, Germany, Finland, France, Indonesia, Israel, Italy, Japan, Kuwait, Luxembourg, Malaysia, the Maldives, Nepal, Netherlands, New Zealand, Norway, Oman, Pakistan, Philippines, Qatar, Saudi Arabia, Singapore, South Korea, Spain, Sweden, Switzerland, Thailand, UAE, USA and Yugoslavia. **Note** All tourists should have a valid visa for the country that is their next destination if that country requires a visa. Nationals of all other countries require a visa. Check with your nearest Sri Lankan representative.

    Extensions Extensions beyond one month may be permitted on condition that the tourist has US$30 per day, a valid passport and an onward or return ticket. You may also be required to prove that you have spent $30 a day during the first month of your stay. Apply to: The Dept Immigration and Emigration, Chaitiya Rd, Colombo 1, Unit 06, T 21509.

    Registration Tourists from non-Commonwealth countries granted an extension of their tourist visa must register at the Aliens Bureau, Ground Floor, New Secretariat Bldg, Colombo 1.

Work permits All foreigners require work permits. Apply to the Sri Lankan Representative in your country of origin.

Representation overseas
Australia 35 Empire Circuit, Forrest, Canberra ACT 2603. **Belgium** 21-22 Ave des Arts (4e étage), 1040 Brussels, T 513 98 92. **Canada** 102-104, 85 Range Rd, Ottawa, Ontario K1M 8J6. **France** 15 Rue d'Astorg, 75008 Paris. T 266-35-01. 0900-1200, 1400-1700, Mon-Fri. **Germany** Rolandstrasse 52, 5300 Bonn 2. **India** 27 Kautilya Marg, Chanakyapuri, New Delhi 110021. **Indonesia** 70 Jalan Diponegoro, Jakarta. **Singapore** 1207-1212 Goldhill Plaza, Singapore 11. **Thailand** Lailart Bldg, 87 Sukhumvit Rd, Bangkok. **Switzerland** 56 Rue de Moillebeau, 1211, Geneva 19. **UK** 13 Hyde Park Gardens, London W2 2LU. **USA** 2148 Wyoming Av, NW, Washington DC 20008. T 483 4025, Fax: 282 7181.

Ceylon Tourist Board offices overseas
Australia 241 Abercrombie St, Chippendale NSW 2008, T 02 698 5226. **Canada** 2 Carlton St, Toronto, Ontario M5B 1K2. **Thailand** 1/8 Soi 10, Sukhumvit Rd, Bangkok, T 251 8062, Fax: 662 2544820. **France** 19, Rue du Quatre Septembre, 75002 Paris. T 42 60 49 99, Telex:

210577 OFTCF. **Japan** Dowa Bldg 7-2-22, Ginza Chuo-Ku. T (03) 289 0771, Fax: (03)289 0772. **Germany** Allerheukugebtir 2-4, D 6000 Frankfurt/Main 1. T 287734, Fax: (069) 288371. **UK** 13 Hyde Park Gardens, London W2 2LU. T 071 262 5009, Fax: 01 262 7970. **USA** 609 Fifth Av, New York, T (212) 935 0369;

Travel

By air Air Lanka, the National airline and several international carriers (principally KLM, Gulf Air, Emirates, UTA, Aeroflot and PIA) link airports around the world with Colombo. The following tour companies (among others) operate from the UK – Thomsons, Kuoni, Speedbird, Hayes and Jarvis, Sovereign, Paradise Sri Lanka, Cosmos, Sri Lanka Tours, JBS Study Tours, Explore Worldwide, Annis Travels and Eleanor Travels.

Sri Lanka's modern International Airport at **Katunayake**, 35 km N of the capital, has several facilities, including a duty-free shop, bank and an expensive restaurant. The Bank of Ceylon exchange counter, airport restaurant, day rooms and the tobacco counter are open 24 hr. The Tourist Information Centre and the Tea Centre (behind Customs area) are open for flight arrivals and departures. Porter, left luggage and bond baggage service are available, as well as assistance with meeting passengers. **Note** Passengers must go through customs at both arrival and departure.

Customs regulations You are permitted to bring in items for 'personal use' provided they are not intended for sale. You must declare all currency including travellers cheques, drafts etc, precious metals and gem stones, firearms, weapons, drugs, narcotics and any goods in commercial quantities (see Prohibited and restricted items below). In addition to completing Part II of the Immigration Landing Card, a tourist may be asked by the Customs Officer to complete a Baggage Declaration Form.

Duty Free Allowances 200 cigarettes or 50 cigars or.375 g of tobacco (or in combination). 2 bottles of wine and 1.5 litres of spirits. A small quantity of perfume and 250 ml of toilet water. Travel souvenirs up to a max value of Rs 1,000.

Prohibited and restricted items Export of the following without a permit is forbidden: precious metals (gold, platinum and silver), antiques (rare books, palm leaf manuscripts, rare anthropological material etc), ivory, precious and semi-precious stones (even when set in jewellery), narcotics, firearms, explosives, dangerous weapons, and fauna and flora. A max of Rs 250 in local currency, 3 kg of tea and goods purchased for personal use, using foreign currency can be exported. See 'Money changing' below for regulations on reconverting unspent rupees.

Import of all the items listed above and in addition, Indian and Pakistani currency, obscene and seditious literature or pictures is prohibited.

Warning It is illegal to purchase items made from wild animals and reptiles.

Arrival Tourists must hand in completed, Part I of the Immigration Landing Card and present Part II for certification by the Customs officer. This should be retained and produced at the time of departure from the country.

Departure Tax Embarkation Tax of Rs 350.

Connections to the city It is worth buying the monthly guide *This month in Sri Lanka* at the airport bookshop before leaving. Airport Taxis (up to 3 passengers), a/c coaches, minibuses and local buses are available for transfer to Colombo and Negombo. Tickets are for ale in the airport arrivals hall. Local bus Nos. 187, 300 and 875 -often crowded, but the cheapest way. Tickets on the bus. In addition there are train services to the city at 0746, 0820, 1632 and 1720.

Internal travel

Warning Travel in Sri Lanka has been seriously disrupted by civil war in the N and E of the island and by political uprisings in the S. 30,000 people were reported killed in the S in 1989-90. In 1991 the S became much more peaceful, and travelling was beginning to open up again. However, routes to the N and E remained dangerous, with frequent acts of violence. Official reports in Apr 1991 claimed that over 1,000 Tamil Tigers had been killed in fighting in the NW. Between June 1990 and April 1991 over 1,200 Sri Lankan soldiers had been killed.

Routes and schedules have often been completely disrupted, and in mid-1991 it is still impossible to advise accurately on detailed travel arrangements in Sri Lanka. It is essential to seek advice in Colombo before travelling any distance beyond the city.

The political upheavals of the last 3 years have also had a major effect on many hotels and guest houses. Some have closed, others have changed hands. In some areas it is still too soon to offer reliable advice as to individual hotels, particularly the cheapest ones. For places along the SW coast, the N and E, this Handbook gives only an abbreviated list of accommodation because it has been impossible to verify conditions and changes which have taken place in 1990-91. Government Rest Houses often offer the safest, and often the best accommodation in the lower price range, though in Sri Lanka these are not as cheap as in India. However, some are outstanding value, in beautiful settings. The difficult circumstances have encouraged many of the larger hotels to offer big discounts throughout the year. Check when you arrive.

Air All internal air services are unscheduled. Upali Travels and Air Taxi Ltd operate charter helicopter and fixed winged aircraft to destinations of tourist interest and to domestic airports from the Ratmalana Airport, Colombo. Details under Colombo. Also from Government Tourist Offices and Thomas Cook, 15 Sir Baron Jayatilleka Mawatha, Col 1, T 545971-4.

Rail Although the network is restricted there are train services to a number of major destinations, and journeys are comparatively short. Special a/c trains operate to Kandy and Hikkaduwa, and there is an inter-city express service (one class) Colombo-Kandy and Colombo-Bandarawela.

Road Bus The nationalised bus service (CTB) has competition from a range of private operators, especially minibuses. CTB buses carry white signs for local routes and yellow signs for long distance routes.

Car There are several self drive car hire firms based in Colombo including some of the main international operators. International driving permit needed to obtain temporary local licence. Contact Automobile Association of Sri Lanka. However, it may actually be cheaper to hire a car with driver, available through travel agents and tour operators.

Taxis Taxis have yellow tops with red numbers on white plates. Available in most towns. Negotiation needed on price for long journeys, otherwise metred.

Travel Tips No distances are great, and roads are generally good, though they are slow. If travelling by train hang on to your baggage at the station. Beware: porters will take charge of you unless you negotiate firmly first.

Money

Currency The Sri Lanka rupee is made up of 100 cents. Notes in denominations of Rs 1000, 500, 100, 50, 20, 10, 5, 2; coins of Rs 5, 2, and 1, and of 50, 25, 10, 5, 2, and 1c. Keep plenty of small change and low denomination notes as they can be difficult to find, and changing a large note can also be difficult.

Money changing Banking Hours: 0900-1300 Mon and 0900-1330 Tue-Fri. The

Bank of Ceylon in York St, Fort, is open 0800-2000 every day, including holidays. It is easier to get cash using a Visa card in Sri Lanka than elsewhere in South Asia. The Bank of Ceylon may accept UK cheques backed by Visa cards, and the Bank of America head branch will give cash on a Visa card. **Note** All foreign exchange transactions must be made through authorised banks and exchanges and entered on the Customs and Immigration form. Unspent rupees may be reconverted at time of departure at a commercial bank. Govt approved hotels and shops are allowed to deal in foreign currency. Keep the receipts when you change money. If you want to extend your visa you may have to prove that you have spent US$15 a day during the first month.

Travellers cheques Travellers cheques are widely acceptable by commercial banks and authorised dealers, and get a better rate of exchange than other forms of currency.

Credit cards Shops accept all major credit cards although some may try to add a surcharge which is not authorised. The Hong Kong Bank, 24 Sir Baron Jayatilleke Mawatha, Colombo allows Visa and Master Card holders to obtain cash and travellers cheques. See note above on exchange transactions.

Cost of Living Both the standard and the cost of living are higher than in India, but much less than in Europe of the United States.

Tipping and bargaining The same principles apply as in India – **see page 131**.

Other essential information

Official time 5 hr 30 ahead of GMT.

Weights and measures Sri Lanka now uses metric weights and measures. Officially distances are given in kilometres, though English miles are sometimes still in use (1 mile = 1.609 km).

Postal services Details of postal rates to other countries can be obtained from major hotels, or from the Inquiries Counter of the GPO in Janadhipathi Mawatha, Colombo 1. A Poste Restante service is available. Information in Colombo T 26203. The GPO is open 24 hr for the sale of stamps and for local telephone calls.

Telephone and telegraph services International phone calls can be made from the GPO between 0700 and 2100. Foreign cables also accepted at GPO. Directory Enquiries, T 161, International Calls, T 100, Trunk Calls, T 101.

Business hours Banks are open Mon 0900-1300, Tue-Fri 0900-1330. Business hours: 0830-1630 Mon-Fri. Some open on Sat 0830-1300. Shops often close for lunch from 1300-1400 on weekdays, most close on Sun. Sunday street bazaars in some areas. **Note** *Poya* (Full moon) days are holidays.

Electricity 230-240 volts 50 cycles A.C. The current is variable.

Media Newspapers *The Sun, The Daily News* and *The Island* are national daily newspapers published in English. In Colombo and some other hotels a wide range of international daily and periodical newspapers and magazines is available.

Radio and Television Sri Lanka Broadcasting Corporation operates in 9 languages, between 0530 and 2300. 2 TV channels. *ITN* from 1830. News in English at 2200. *Rupavahini* – English newscast at 2130.

Maps Large scale maps available at the Survey Dept, Map Sales Branch, Kirula Rd, Narahenpita, T 585111 and Map Sales Centre, York St, Colombo 1 T 35328.

Accommodation The Tourist Board issues lists at the International Airport and at their office at 78 Steuart Pl, Galle Rd, Colombo. From international class hotels in the capital with a full range of facilities, the choice ranges from moderately priced comfortable accommodation in the city to *Rest Houses* in converted colonial houses, often in superb locations and very simple Wildlife Conservation Dept bungalows in the parks. It is also possible to book rooms in plantation estate bungalows or in family guest houses.

Many higher range hotels quote their prices in US dollars. The **price categories** for Sri Lanka used in the Handbook are: **AL** US$90+ **A** US$60-90 **B** US$30-60 **C** Rs 450-900 **D**

Rs 200-450 **E** Rs 100-200 **F** Rs 100 or less.

Clothing Light and loose cottons throughout the year. Some warmer clothes for the hills, especially in the evenings. Topless bathing is prohibited and heavy fines can be imposed.

Food and drink Rice and curry are the staple main course food of Sri Lanka, but that term conceals an enormous variety of subtle flavours. Coriander, chillies, mustard, cumin, pepper, cinnamon and garlic are just some of the common ingredients which add flavour to both sea food and meat curries. Fresh sea food – crab, lobster and prawn, as well as fish – is excellent, and meat is cheap. Rice forms the basis of many Sri Lankan sweet dishes, palm treacle being used as the main traditional sweetener. This is also served on curd as a delicious dessert.

Sri Lanka has a wide variety of tropical fruit throughout the year, pineapple, papaya and banana being particularly good. The extraordinarily rich jack fruit are also available all year. Seasonal fruit include mangosteen (no relation of mangos), passion fruit, custard apples, avocado pears, durian and rambutan from July-Oct. In addition to ordinary green coconuts, Sri Lanka is also home to the distinctive King Coconut (*thambili*). The milk is particularly sweet and nutritious.

Many spices are grown in the island and are widely available in the markets and shops. Cinnamon, nutmeg, cloves, cardomom and pepper are all grown, the Kandy region being a major centre of spice production. Many private spice gardens are open to the public.

All big hotels will serve filtered water and mineral water, and there is a wide range of bottled soft drinks. Always take great care with water. Alcoholic drinks are widely available, though imported drinks are very expensive. Local beer (*Lion* and *Three Coins*) is acceptable. The local spirit *arrack*, is distilled from coconut toddy.

Visiting religious sites Visitors to Buddhist temples are welcome everywhere. Parts of Hindu temples are sometimes closed to non-Hindus. Visitors to both Buddhist and Hindu temples should be properly dressed – swim wear is not suitable. Shoes should be left at the entrance and any head covering taken off. (Best to visit early in the day during hot months to avoid walking on very hot surfaces)

Do not attempt to shake hands or be photographed with Buddhist *bhikkus* (monks) or to pose for photos with statues of the Buddha or other deities and paintings. Remember that monks are not permitted to touch money so donations should be put in temple offering boxes. Monks renounce all material possessions and so live on offerings. (However, you are advised not to give to ordinary beggars.)

Tourist Information Centres will help with providing trained English speaking guides (and occasionally speaking a European language, Malay or Japanese). Fees are specified. Alternatively ask at hotel.

Note Entry fees to ancient archaeological sites, museums etc are much higher for foreign visitors than for Sri Lankans. Inclusive tickets are sold in Colombo. See Colombo section and below under Photography.

Photography Permits are needed to photograph at certain archaeological sites (Anuradhapura, Kandy, Sigiriya, Polonnaruwa etc) obtainable from Ministry of Cultural Affairs, Maly St, Col 2, T 587912 who will issue inclusive tickets covering entry to sites and museums from 0830-1615. **Tickets** Inclusive for all sites – US$12; Anuradhapura, Sigiriya, Polonnoruwa – US$4 each; Dambulla, Kandy, Nalanda – US$3 each. Children under 12 – half price.

For photography of museum exhibits at the ancient sites you need a permit from the Dept of Archaeology, Marcus Fernando Mawatha, Col 7. Filming permits are obtainable from Cultural Triangle Office, 212 Bauddalaka Mawatha, Col 7. Individual site offices also issue permits with tickets from 0600-1800. Please ask before taking photographs of local people.

National holidays and festivals
Sat and Sun are always holidays. Poya (full moon) days, are also holidays. No liquor is sold (you can order drinks at your hotel, the day before) and all places of entertainment are closed. Some other festivals and public holidays in Sri Lanka are determined by the lunar calendar and therefore change from year to year. Below is the list for Sep-Dec 1991. Dates for 1992 will be notified at the end of 1991. Unless specified they are public and bank holidays.

1991
Sep 23 *Binara* Poya Day.
Oct 22 *Wap* Poya Day; *Milad-un-Nabi* Prophet Mohammed's birthday; *Deepavali* Festival.
Nov 21 *Il* Poya Day.
Dec 20 *Unduwap* Poya Day; **25** Christmas Day; **31** Special Bank Holiday.

1992

Jan *Duruthu* Poya day. Sri Lankan Buddhists believe that the Buddha visited the island and celebrate with Colombo's biggest annual festival. **14** *Tamil Thai Pongal* day.

Feb 4 National Day. Processions, dances, parades. *Navam* Poya Day. A large celebration with elephant processions in Colombo. **23** *Maha Sivarathri* Day.

Mar *Medin* Poya Day.

Apr *Bak* Poya Day. Good Friday **13-14** Sinhala and Tamil New Year Day. The celebrations are accompanied by closure of many shops and restaurants. *Eid ul Fitr* (Ramazan).

May 1 May Day; *Wesak* Poya Day and day following. The major Poya holiday, celebrating the key events in the Buddha's life: his birth, enlightenment and death. Lamps are light across the island. **22** National Heroes Day.

Jun *Poson* Poya Day, celebrating Mahinda's arrival in Sri Lanka as the first Buddhist missionary. **30** Bank Holiday.

Jul *Esala* Poya Day. This is the most important Sri Lankan festival with a great procession honouring the Sacred Tooth of the Buddha in Kandy. It lasts 10 days.

Aug *Nikini* Poya Day.

WILL YOU HELP US?

We do all we can to get our facts right in **THE SOUTH ASIAN HANDBOOK.** Each section is thoroughly revised each year, but the territory covered is vast and our eyes cannot be everywhere.

Your information may be more up to date than ours and if you have enjoyed a tour, trek, train trip, beach, museum, temple, fort or any other activity and would like others to share it, please write with the details. We are always pleased to hear about any restaurants, bars or hotels you have enjoyed.

When writing, it will be very helpful if you can give the year on the cover of your Handbook and the page number referred to.

If your letter reaches us early enough in the year, it will be used in the next annual edition, but write whenever you want to, for all your information will be used.

Thank you very much indeed for your help.

Write to: The Editor,
South Asian Handbook
Trade & Travel Publications
6 Riverside Court, Lower Bristol Road,
Bath BA2 3DZ. England

MALDIVES

Official name Divehi Jumhuriya (Republic of Maldives)

Official language Divehi

Official religion Islam

Basic indicators *Population* 165,000, Male 58,000; *Urban* 22%, *Rural* 78%; *Religion*, *Muslim* 100%; *Birth rate* 44 per 1000 *Death rate* 13 per 1000 *Infant mortality rate* 76 per 1000 *GNP per capita* US$440.

INTRODUCTION

Divehi Jumhuriyya, or the Republic of the Maldives, comprises a group of islands that stretch over 750 km N to S and nearly 120 km from E to W in the Indian Ocean. They lie approximately 650 km southwest of the southern tip of India. Of the 1190 coral islands only 200 are inhabited. It is the smallest member State of the UNited Nations. The tiny islands are grouped around the fringes of shallow lagoons and are collectively known by the Maldivian word which has entered the English language, **atoll**. There are 19 administrative groups of atolls each named after a letter of the **Divehi** alphabet, the Maldivian language, which belongs to the Indo-Aryan group.

The Maldivian people are of a mixed race descended from Aryan, Dravidian, Arab and Negro ancestors. There is some sensitivity on the islands to the nature of pre-Islamic settlement, but the first settlers were probably Buddhists from Ceylon (Sri Lanka) who sailed there around 500 AD, though in the 12th century Islam became the dominant religion. It remained an independent country with a sultanate for many centuries until the Portuguese arrived in Male and ruled for a brief 15 years from 1558 to 1573. In the 17th century the Dutch considered the islands a protectorate while they ruled over Ceylon, to be followed by the British. The country remained a sultanate although with British defence protection until 1965, when it became totally independent. Three years later a new republic was proclaimed, abolishing the sultanate.

The approach by air is dramatic. A line of white waves indicates the reefs nearing but often not breaking the surface. Inside, are the aquamarine and turquoise shallows, with the coral clearly visible beneath, and then tiny patches of islands.

The vegetation consists of tall coconut palms and salt resistant bushy plants. Coconut and breadfruit grow in profusion while others such as mangoes, pawpaws, sweet potatoes, pumpkins and plantains are found on some of the inhabited islands.

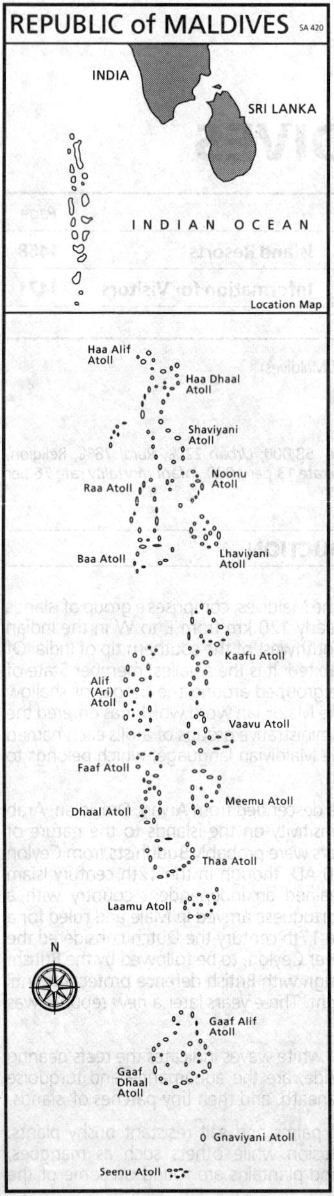

REPUBLIC of MALDIVES SA 420

INDIA

SRI LANKA

INDIAN OCEAN

Location Map

Haa Alif Atoll

Haa Dhaal Atoll

Shaviyani Atoll

Noonu Atoll

Raa Atoll

Baa Atoll

Lhaviyani Atoll

Kaafu Atoll

Alif (Ari) Atoll

Vaavu Atoll

Faaf Atoll

Meemu Atoll

Dhaal Atoll

Thaa Atoll

Laamu Atoll

N

Gaaf Alif Atoll

Gaaf Dhaal Atoll

0 Gnaviyani Atoll

Seenu Atoll

MALE

The capital, Male, has a population of 58,000. The altitude is sea level. It is just over 3 sq km in area and can be driven round on a motor bike in under 5 min. It is easy to walk from one end of the island to the other in twenty minutes, and to find all the major streets and restaurants.

Places of interest

Grand Friday Mosque, Masjid-al-Sultan Mohamed Thakurufaan Al-A'z'am is the largest in the country and is also the Islamic Centre with a library and conference hall. It is named after the great national hero who defeated the Portuguese occupying forces in 1573. It has a large gold coloured dome and can accommodate about 5,000 worshippers. If you are interested in visiting it, please dress suitably. Non-Muslim visitors are welcome from 0900-1700 except at prayer times. Late morning and mid-afternoon are suitable times. You will be expected to remove shoes and wash your feet before entering.

The old **Friday Mosque**, Hukuru Miskiiy on Meduziyaraiy Magu, had the foundation stone laid in 1656 during the reign of Sultan Ibrahim Iskandhar and is built of stone with verses of the Koran carved on the walls. It has the tombs of Sultan Ibrahim Iskandhar and the royal family who reigned after him as well as other famous Maldivians. The white minaret at its gate was built ten years later and was inspired by those in Mecca after the King visited the holy city.

Mulee-Aage The official residence of the President is close to the Friday Mosque.

Markets There are vegetable and fruit markets and a firewood market on Marine Drive which are worth visitng by those travelling to the E for the first time. The Fish Market is particularly busy in the early evening.

Local industries Boat building and fishing are by far the most important traditional industries; on the outlying islands they continue to be the most important means of gaining a livelihood while coir production continues to provide some employment.

Attempts are being made to diversify. There is some textile printing and lace making on a small scale for the tourist market, and the collection of shells and the making of simple jewellery is also carried out on a very limited scale. Tourism has become the Maldives overwhelmingly most important industry, accounting for the transformation of the economy since the early 1970s.

Hotels All the accommodation on Male is simple. It is the only island on which it is possible to stay quite cheaply, but it is not a place for a long visit. There are no beaches, the island is now almost completely built up, and in one day's visit it is easily possible to see the sights of interest. There are hotels with airconditioning, but there are also several guest houses simply with fan and attached shower which are often relatively inexpensive rooms in private homes and usually don't provide meals. There are several that are 'government registered' and charge between US$15-20 per night. Most are small (less than ten rooms), and have a very limited range of services, but those listed here are clean and are good value.

Sosunge Hotel on Sosun Magu a few blocks from Marine Drive. T 323025, Telex: 66019 TOURISM MF. 4 rm. Former government guest house, now the most expensive small hotel in town. Fresh water. *Nasandhura Palace Hotel*, Marine Drive at the eastern end. T 322360, Telex: 66091 POLYCOM MF, Fax: 323380. 31 rm. Restaurant, bar, fresh water. *Hotel Alia*, 32 Marine Drive at the western end. T 322080, Telex: 77032 TAJ MF. 18 rm. Restaurant, bar, fresh water. Guest houses with attached baths *Nivikoa*, Chandanee Magu. T 322942. 7 rm. Recommended. *Mermaid Inn*, Marine Drive at the western end. T 323329. *Sony*, Janavaree Magu. T 323249. 6 rm. *Araarootuge*, Madhoshi Goalhi. Bed and breakfast. *Gadhoo*, Marine Drive, eastern end. T 323222. 3 rm, bed and breakfast.

The following **guest houses** are conveniently situated fairly close to the shops, sights and restaurants. *Male Tour Inn*. T 326220 Prop. Shaheed Ali Hingun. *Sakeena Manzil*, Meduziyaraiy Magu, T 323281. Dining hall, but crowded rm. Being near the mosque you may be woken early by the call to prayer. *Greenlin*. T 322279. *Andaapoolge*. T 322173. *Thaalin*. T 324036. *Kosheege*. T 323585. *Ever Pink*. T 324751. *Maafaru*. T 322220. *Kaimoo Stop Over Inn*. T 323241. *Dheraha*. T 323018.

Restaurants The range of options on Male is limited, as is the menu. Most are on Majeedee Magu. *Downtown* is the most popular. *Quench*, across the road gives you the option of choosing tables outside, under a thatch and has a variety of Indian, continental and American fast food style menu. The *Eagle Restaurant* is conveniently close to the Male Tour Inn guest house and there is also a specialist *Indian Restaurant* here. *Gelato Italiano* is open during the day for coffee, ice creams and soft drinks, and is more upmarket than the cafes listed below. The *Canteen* is opp the Indoor Sports Centre. The *New Pot* on Marine Drive is recommended.

The **cafés** open early and close late. You will often have a plate of savoury and sweet snacks on the table which you can select from and have with a drink of tea of sweetened milk. *Seagull Cafe House*, Majeedee Uafa and *Junction Hotel* are at the crossing of Chandanee Magu and Faridee Magu close to the Museum.

Soft Drinks There are shops clustered just behind Marine Drive where the boats from the airport and other islands berth. Soft drinks are twice as expensive immediately around the jettys as they are in the small local stores just a little further inland.

Bars Tourist hotels serve a full range of alcoholic drinks, so principle (in the form of making it illegal for tourists to import alcohol) is not put before profit.

Banks Open 0900-1300, Sun-Th, 0900-1100, Sat. Closed Fri. They are the only authorised money changers. *Bank of Ceylon*, Alia Building, Ground Floor, Orchid Magu. T 323046. *Bank of Credit and Commerce*, Chandanee Magu. T 323605/6. *Bank of Maldives Ltd*, Marine Drive. T 323095. *Habib Bank*, 23 Chandanee Magu. T 323052. *Maldives Monetary Authority*, Majeedee Building, Marine Drive. T 322291. *State Bank of India*, Marine Drive. T 323052.

Shopping In Male there is a duty free shopping complex in *Umar Shopping Arcade* on Chandanee Magu, T 325539 which has a range of electrical goods, hi-fi and stereo equipment, watches and cosmetics. The *Lemon Souvenir Shop*, T 323776 on the same road sells jewellery made from tortoise shell, mother of pearl, and red and black coral, colourful T-shirts and books and postcards. The *Crafts Market* is worth visiting. The *Asrafee*, Orchid Magu, *Cyprea* and *Novelty Bookshop*, Faridee Magu, sell a limited range of books and a selection of postcards. The *airport duty free* shop is small but claims to be very competitively priced.

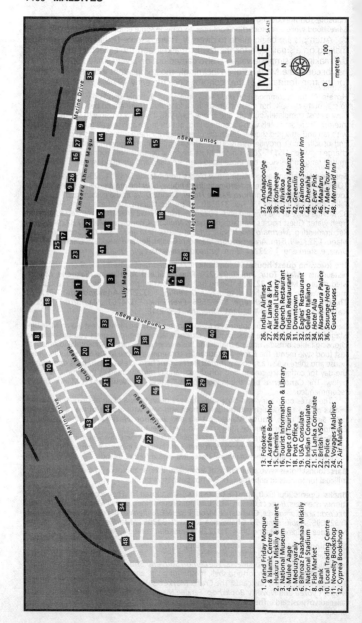

MALE

N

0   100
metres

1. Grand Friday Mosque
   & Islamic Centre
2. Hukuru Miskiiy & Minaret
3. National Museum
4. Mulee Aage
5. Meduziyaraiy
6. Bihroaz Faashanaa Miskiiy
7. National Stadium
8. Fish Market
9. Bank
10. Local Trading Centre
11. Novelty Bookshop
12. Cyprea Bookshop

13. Fotokenik
14. Asrafee Bookshop
15. Chemist
16. Tourist Information & Library
17. Dept of Tourism
18. Post Office
19. USA Consulate
20. Indian Consulate
21. Sri Lanka Consulate
22. British VSO
23. Police
24. Voyages Maldives
25. Air Maldives

26. Indian Airlines
27. Air Lanka & PIA
28. National Library
29. Quench Restaurant
30. Indian Restaurant
31. Downtown
32. Eagles Restaurant
33. Gelato Italiano
34. Dheraha
35. Nasandhura Palace
36. Sosunge Hotel
   Guest Houses

37. Andaapoolge
38. Thaalin
39. Kosheege
40. Nivikoa
41. Sakeena Manzil
42. Greeniln
43. Kaimoo Stopover Inn
44. Dheraha
45. Evafaru
46. Maafaru
47. Male Tour Inn
48. Mermaid Inn

Camera shops For films and processing, *Fototeknik, Fotogenic* and *Centofoto* are on Majeedee Magu.

Local transport The usual mode of transport on Male is **bicycles**. However, all sightseeing and shopping areas are within walking distance and although taxis are available, you are not likely to need one. Should you wish to hire a **taxi** it is best to agree the fare in advance which should be between Rf 10 and Rf 15. *Dialcab Transport Services*. T 323132.

Entertainment and **Sports.** See under 'Island Resorts' below.

Museums The **National Museum** is in the grounds of the Park behind the Islamic Centre. A visit takes between 30 min and an hr. Open 0900-1140, 1500-1740. Entry Rf 5, children under twelve Rf 2. Attractively housed in one of Male's older wooden two storey houses, it includes collections of early sculptures, mainly in coral, some in wood, probably of the pre-Islamic Buddhist period in the Maldives. There are some wooden boards with examples of early Divehi script. Dates of most of the early artefacts are uncertain, and are broadly listed as 11th century A.D. More recent exhibits include royal memorabilia (furniture, clothes, transport such as palanquins, and arms); coins from the time of the first Sultan (Mohamad Imaadudin) in 1620, up to recent and contemporary items such as two motorbikes hit by bullets during the November 1988 coup attempt.

The **Library** is on Majeedee Magu, open daily, 0900-1200, 1400-1700. Closed Fri. The private library on Amir Ahmed Magu, belonging to the Didi family which has some good reference books and books about the islands. Open daily 1400-2200, 1730-2000 during Ramazan. Monthly subscription and deposit.

Post and telegraph The Post Office (with poste restante) is at the corner of Marine Drive and Changdani Magu. Open daily 0730-1245, 1600-1745 (even though official times of opening are advertised otherwise). Closed Fri.

Parks and zoos Male has a small park behind the Islamic Centre, within which stands the National Museum.

Useful addresses Embassies and Consulates in the Maldives.
  Most European countries have their embassy and consular staff based in Sri Lanka. Their telephone numbers are given in the Sri Lanka section (**see page 1422**). In emergency they should be contacted by telephone, which can be done readily from Male and from some other islands.
  India, High Commission Orchid Magu. T 323015. *Pakistan*, High Commission, Noomaraage Lily Magu. T 323005. *Sri Lanka*, High Commission, Orchid Magu. T 323046 *Denmark/Sweden*, Abdulla Saeed, CYPREA, 25 Marine Drive. T 322452/325367. *USA*, Rasheeda Mohamed Didi, Mandhu-edhuruge, Violet-Magu. T 322581.
  Ministry of Foreign Affairs, Ibrahim Shaheed Zaki, Assistant to the Minister, Maldives. T 323408, Res 322578.

Hospitals and medical services *Central Hospital*, Sosun Magu, Henveira. T 322400. *Flying Swiss Ambulance Clinic*, Huvadhoo, Marine Drive. T 324508/324509. Emergency Number 324500 (24 hr). This is a small private health clinic service. It has its own speedboat to reach outlying islands and has European medical staff. To insure yourself or your family with the company before departing for the Maldives, contact the head office in Switzerland at Postfach 259, FL-9495, Triesen. The Inter-Atoll flying boat service helps to transport emergency cases.

Chambers of Commerce Ministry of Trade and Industries, F/1 Ghazee Building, Ameeru Ahmed Magu. T 323668.

Travel agents and Tour operators Internal travel and accommodation on the islands can be arranged for by the following: *Voyages Maldives* (Pvt) Ltd, PO Box 2019, 2 Faridee Magu, Male. T 322017, Fax: 960-325336. They offer special 'Divers' Dream' (VMDD) US$85 per day, min. 8 days, 'Sailing Safaris' (VMSS) US$50 per day, min 8 days, 'Adventure Sailing' (VMAS) or simply a 'Beach Holiday' (VMBH). *ZSS Hotels and Travel Service*, 5, Fiyaathoshi Goalhi, Henveiru, Male. They also offer similar special packages – 'Maldives Intimate', 'Dream Holidays' and 'Safari Tour'. *Treasure Island Enterprises* Pvt. Ltd. (Manager Mohamed Haleem). Agents for American Express, 8 Marine Drive, Male, PO Box 2009. T 930-322165, Fax: 960 322798. They organise diving holidays on three island resorts which have special diving bases – Furana, Maayafushi and Bathala, as well as a few other island resorts. *Jetan Travel Service*, 55 Marine Drive, Male. T 323323, Telex: 66086; Fax: 960 324628, offer holidays on Rannali.

Tourist offices and information Ministry of Tourism, F/2 Ghazee Building, Ameeru Ahmed Magu. T 323224.

ISLAND RESORTS

The resort islands are scattered around three atolls – N and S Male (*Kaafu atoll*) where only 9 out of the 81 islands are inhabited and *Ari* or Alif atoll where 18 of the 76 islands are inhabited. Travel agents and tour operators offer packages to the Maldives either flying direct to the islands for 2 to 4 weeks or as an extension to a holiday in India or Sri Lanka. It is possible to choose a holiday that will allow you to visit two or more islands. The resorts listed below all offer a good selection of water sports and many are good value. The high season rates apply from November to April and also in August and there is an extra 15% surcharge over the Christmas/New Year period. The transfer cost (payable in US$) is for return travel between the airport and the resort. Travel between islands can be fairly expensive.

Entertainment Some islands have some form of entertainment provided in the resort hotels such as live bands and/or discos. However, it is government policy to keep tourists apart from the local population as far as reasonably possible. This means that all the holiday islands are separate from the settled islands, and there are no indigenous cultural activities or entertainments accessible to outsiders.

Sports All the sports reflect the Maldives' equatorial maritime location. Scuba diving, snorkelling, fishing, windsurfing, waterskiing, parasailing are all available on various islands. Diving in certain waters will reward you with close encounters with tunas, mantas, sharks, barracudas, bonitos and a rich variety of coral fish while catches of groupers and red snappers when you go fishing are fairly common. It is essential to choose islands you wish to visit in relation to the available activities. Facilities for other sports are available on some islands; lawn tennis, football, volleyball, billiards, table tennis, chess or darts.

Dhoni Safaris A few wooden sailing boats have been refurbished and fitted with diesel engines. Others are purpose built 12 to 15 m long 'Dhoni Yachts' with lateen rig, diesel engines and radio. They can take groups of 8 with a crew of 3 or 4 on trips around the islands. The sleeping accommodation for the tourists is separate but very basic, usually on bunks in a saloon. Meals are provided and windsurfing, snorkelling and diving equipment is usually taken. *Scuba diving* is safe provided you make sure you have taken professional advice and have all the necessary equipment. **NB** Scuba diving is not covered by most holiday insurance policies so extra cover should be taken out. The resorts specializing in diving which are recommended are Bandos, Furana, Helengeli, Kanifinolhu, Villivaru.

A *Nika Island* on the northern end of the Ari atoll, 70 km and 2 hr by speed boat from the airport, is one of the most exclusive in the Maldives (US$200). 25 thatched bungalows of unusual design, built partly out of coral and wood, are spacious and surrounded by a garden. Each has a solarium on the private beach side and the showers with hot/cold fresh water. Restaurant serves a variety of Italian food in addition to continental and eastern dishes available elsewhere, with barbecue and a Maldivian supper twice a week. All the usual watersports available and the diving school is very well equipped. Volleyball, badminton and tennis with equipment free for residents. Italian character of this resort is quite obvious. In Italy, contact Nika Hotel, 5 Via Albricci, 20122, Milan, Italy. T 02/8077983.

A *Cocoa Island* or Makunufushi on the eastern side of the S Male atoll is 29 km from the airport. T 343713, Telex: 77037 COCOA MF. One of the more expensive destinations and designed to catch the eye, the 8 resort's cottages are built of striking white coral with high thatched roofs lined with palm leaves. Raised sleeping area within is reached by stairs. Restaurant and bar have a good reputation. Windsurfing, catamaran, fishing and waterskiing. Diving on a neighbouring island.

A *Rhiveli* **Beach Resort** is on the southern side of the S Male atoll about 40 km from Male (US$110). T 343731, Telex: 66072 PITTMAT MF, Fax: 344775. 42 rm. From this silver sand resort you can make your own way across to the neighbouring Island of Birds and Rising Sun Island. French owned with a particularly good restaurant and bar. Free watersports includes windsurfing, sailing, waterskiing and tennis. Also included in package is a two-day cruise around the nearby islands.

A *Kurumba* was Maldive's first resort island which has been recently modernised. Only 3 km from airport which takes less than 1/2 hr to cover (US$10). T342324, Telex: 77083 KURUMBA MF, Fax: 3438085. 160 comfortable rooms in single/double storey bungalows or deluxe cottages, set apart from the main reception area. All have a/c and hot and cold fresh water to bathrooms. Restaurant (with à la carte), bar, coffee shop. Regular entertainment. Full range of water sports are on offer.

A *Bathala* is a small island on the NE edge of the Ari atoll about 60 km and just over 3 hr by boat from the airport (US$65). T 350504, Fax: 350504. The island can be traversed in 10 min. and is completely encircled by the reef, the inner reef being only 30 m from the waters' edge. 36 small round bungalows have pointed palm thatch roofs. Simply furnished with outdoor showers in private walled gardens. Restaurant and bar are open-sided. Expert diving instruction, catamaran, waterskiing and windsurfing (for the experienced since currents can be strong). A 'Treasure Island Enterprise' resort popular with Germans and the young.

A *Nakatchafushi* is on the western side of the N Male atoll, 24 km from the airport and about 2 1/2 hr boat ride (US$25). T 343846, Fax: 343848. This pretty island has retained the Maldivian character by building rondavels, some with thatch, to accommodate guests. 52 simply furnished a/c rooms with fresh water for bath rooms. Open-air restaurant, bar and a pleasant terrace bar overhanging the water. Dance floor for parties. All kinds of water sports, the hiring charges of equipment more expensive than at cheaper resorts. German diving school.

A *Farukolufushi* in the N Male atoll, just N of the airport so a quick transfer. It is a French run, Club Med resort which is one of the largest and only takes guests staying a min of a week, T 343021. No day trippers are allowed. The large thatched restaurant serves good food. Usual water sports but no water skiing.

B *Biyadoo* is a new resort run by the Taj group of hotels. T 343516, Telex: 77003 TAJ MF, Fax: 343742. It is 29 km from the airport in the S Male atoll, close to Cocoa Island (US$30) and has 96 comfortable a/c rooms on two storeys with heated freshwater for showers. The island offers virtually every kind of water sport including parasailing with the additional provision of a decompression chamber. A/c restaurant and bar, weekly barbecue and disco.

B *Villivaru*, close to Biyadoo is another Taj resort 29 km from Male (US$30). T 343598, Telex: 77003 TAJ MF, Fax: 343742. It is smaller than Biyadoo, and slightly less expensive. 60 mostly non-a/c rooms with fresh hot and cold water for showers and each with a private verandah open to the beach. A/c restaurant and bar with weekly barbecue and disco. Snorkelling and diving. The coral reef harbouring a large variety of fish is approximately 25 m offshore and excellent for experienced divers. A daily ferry service is available to Biyadoo.

B *Vabinfaru* 17 km NW of the airport in the N Male atoll is about 1 hr 30 min by boat. T 343147. It is a small French run resort with accommodation in 25 thatched rondavels. The attractions are good food and a variety of water sports (some of which are free). Popular with Australian and Italian tourists.

B *Baros* the oval shaped island 16 km from the airport on the N Male atoll is over an hr by boat (US$20). T 342672, Fax: 343497. 50 simply furnished bungalows, half with a/c. One of the oldest and popular with British tourists. The water is usually desalinated. Restaurant, bar, gift shop and dive shop. The coral, just offshore on one side of the island makes diving and snorkelling particularly interesting for beginners. The other side is suitable for windsurfing and waterskiing.

B *Bandos* conveniently situated to the S of the N Male atoll, 9 km from the airport and less than an hr for the transfer (US$20). T 343310, Telex: 66050 BANDOS MF, Fax: 343877. One of the larger tourist islands from which you can cross to uninhabited and attractive Kuda Bandos nearby. 180 comfortable rooms, half a/c, with terraces and unheated spring water showers. A/c restaurant, bar, 24 hr open-air coffee shop and aquarium. Excellent watersports and diving school with a decompression chamber.

C *Maayafushi* is on NE fringe of the Ari atoll about 65 km W of Male, the transfer taking 4 hr (US$65). T 350529, Fax: 350529. The accommodation is in 60 small thatched units in rows with terraces. Restaurant serving hot and cold buffets and bar. Expert diving instruction for beginners (the house reef is only 70 m away) and the more experienced can venture further afield. For non-divers there is a large lagoon for snorkelling, windsurfing, waterskiing, parasailing and sailing. Also volleyball and table-tennis. A 'Treasure Island Enterprise' resort popular with under 35s.

C Furana is just N of Male, close to the airport and reached in 20 min (US$25). T 343878, Telex: 66012 FUR MF, Fax: 343879. The 80 beach bungalows and terraces, some luxury with a/c and some with 'garden showers' for honeymooners! Desalinated water. Two restaurants (one Chinese à la carte), barbecues, bar and coffee shop next to the diving base. Expert diving instruction for beginners and shallow water training for those with some experience. Located on the eastern outer reef, diving waters are 15 min away. The large lagoon offers plenty of scope for windsurfing, sailing and waterskiing. Volleyball and tennis. Free transfer from Male on Mon, Wed and Sat at 1630 and from Furana at 1400. A 'Treasure Island Enterprise' resort popular with Germans.

C Kanifinolhu is on the eastern edge of the N Male atoll, 12 km from the airport, the transfer taking nearly 90 min (US$20). T 343152, Telex: 77096 EUROKAN MF, Fax: 344859. It is a smallish semicircular island with a sheltered lagoon. It offers 106 rooms, ranging from non-a/c to comfortable luxury a/c suites with verandahs. All accommodation is on the beach side, with a fresh water supply to showers while the amenities are in the centre of the island. Restaurant (with à la carte), bar, coffee shop, gift shop. Weekly disco and occasional live band. Most kinds of watersports available including good diving, good snorkelling to the S, and also tennis, volleyball, table tennis and billiards. Popular with under 35s.

C Kurumathi is situated on the northern fringe of the Ari atoll 60 km W of Male with a transfer time of about 2 hr by speed boat (US$60). T 350556. It is one of the larger islands with the coral reef within easy reach on one side making it attractive for diving and snorkelling. The northern tip of the island is occupied by the **B Blue Lagoon Club** with its own private pier. The 50 units are all comfortable with hot/cold desalinated water. The 20 thatched cottages on the eastern side are built on stilts in the water and are reached by walkways. They have their own terrace which enables you to step straight into the water. The *Lagoon* restaurant has an option à la carte and the *Laguna* bar has a terrace. At low tide it is possible to walk a long distance out beyond the norther tip but take care not to get stranded! The **Kurumathi Village** is less expensive and is in the SE corner of the island with its 122 units, some of which are thatched round houses. The *Haruge* restaurant and *Fung* bar and *Atoll* coffee shop are all open-sided. Live entertainment weekly and discos on other evenings. The **Cottage Club** is the third centre on the island run by Universal Enterprises Ltd.

Water sports include snorkelling, diving (with a dive shop) and windsurfing school and night fishing. There is also tennis and archery.

C Bodufinholhu, also called **Fun Island** is on the eastern reef of the S Male atoll, 40 km from the airport which takes about 3 hr by boat (US$30). T 344706, Telex: 77099 FUNISLE MF, FAX: 343958. A very small island which may feel a little over crowded but has the advantage of a shallow lagoon making it possible to walk across to two tiny neighbouring uninhabited islands at low tide. 88 comfortable rooms, all a/c, with verandah and baths with hot and cold desalinated water. Comfortable open-sided restaurant, bar and coffee shop with an attractive terrace overhanging the lagoon. Disco and weekly cultural shows. Diving, windsurfing, snorkelling, fishing and waterskiing.

D Lhohifushi is a smaller quieter island with pretty, lush vegetation, to the N of Kanifinolhu, 18 km from Hulule with a transfer time of over 90 min (US$18). T 343451, Fax: 343451. The resort is unsophisticated and has attempted to retain the Maldivian character in its buildings. 65 mostly non-a/c simply furnished rooms with small verandahs have island water to showers. Open-sided restaurant and bar/lounge, open-air coffee shop with balcony overhanging the sea. Water sports are limited to diving, windsurfing and sailing.

D Hudhuveli is a very small island on the N Male atoll 10 km from the airport and about 45 min journey (US$20). T 343396, Telex: 77035 HUDVELI MF, Fax: 343849. The 44 units, some rondavels and some terraced bungalows, are all thatched and painted white. Restaurant, bar and open-air coffee shop. The island claims to be the cleanest in the Maldives, with the best water in the whole atoll and no mosquitos! Diving (either in the inner coral reef or in the outer reef close to huge fish), snorkelling, windsurfing, fishing and waterskiing. Also volleyball, badminton and table tennis.

D Ranaalhi on the western fringe of the S Male atoll is 38 km away from the airport about 3 hr 30 min by boat (US$40). T 342688, Fax: 342688. There are 54 beach front bungalows, 5 a/c. Cold water showers. Restaurant serving continental and Eastern cuisine, bar, coffee shop. Beach barbecues, music and dancing and cultural shows. Most water sports available incuding parasailing.

D Meerufenfushi or 'sweet water island' is to the E of the N Male atoll. T 343157, Telex:

77002 CHAMPA MF, Fax: 343157. It is 40 km from the airport which takes about 3 hr by boat (US$25). One of the larger island resorts (28 ha) with a large lagoon. 174 non-a/c simply furnished rooms in single storey bungalows built close to the beach with unheated island water showers. Restaurant, open-sided bar, gift shop. Diving, windsurfing, snorkelling, night fishing, volleyball and table tennis. Sailboarding popular on the lagoon.

D *Eriyadu* is 29 km NW of Male and 3 hr by boat (US$30). T 4487, Telex: 66031, Fax: 344487. One of the cheaper resort islands with 46 rooms in white-washed bungalows with fresh water. Wide stretch of beach, shaded. Restaurant and bar. Diving (Swiss sub-aqua), snorkelling, windsurfing, fishing and volleyball.

D *Velassaru* is on the northern tip of the S Male atoll, only 10 km from the airport (US$20). T 343041, Fax: 343041. The accommodation, fairly inexpensive, is in 67 rooms in well-appointed bungalows. Restaurant and lively bar. There is a diving school. An upmarket resort when opened in1974, it suffered from neglect. Walls of coral between cottages!

D *Helengeli* in the far N of the N Male atoll, is about 50 km from the airport. T 344615. Small resort with 30 rm with salt water showers. Good coral reef so convenient for unlimited diving for which charges are reasonable.

INFORMATION FOR VISITORS

Documents

Visas All tourists, except those from Sri Lanka, are permitted to enter the Maldives for 30 days; those from India, Pakistan, Bangladesh and Italy are permitted to stay for 90 days. The stay can be extended for a nominal fee. Sri Lankans must obtain a visa before entering the country and Israeli passport holders are not allowed to enter. A valid passport is necessary as well as a certificate of innoculation against yellow fever for those arriving from countries where yellow fever is found. Vaccination against cholera is required for those arriving from or through the other S. Asian countries. Tourists must carry US$10 minimum per day except those travelling with a tour company or coming on recruitment to an Agency.

Travel

Most tourists arrive by air. The airport tax to be paid on departure is Rs 50.
From Asia and Europe, the following scheduled airlines, with their addresses in Male, fly directly to the Maldives. *From Colombo*: **Air Lanka**, 17 Marine Drive. T 322532. *From Colombo, Dubai*: **Emirates Airways**, Marine Drive. T 325491. *From Colombo, Karachi*: **Pakistan International Airlines**, Luxwood, 1 Marine Drive. T 323532. *From Trivandrum*: **Indian Airlines**, Sifaa, Marine Drive. T 323003. *From Kathmandu*: **Royal Nepal Airlines**, c/o Air Maldives, Marine Drive. T 322436. *From Rome*: **Alitalia**, c/o Air Maldives. T 322436. *From Singapore, Zurich, Vienna, Brussels, Amsterdam*: **Singapore Airlines**, Sisil Corner, 3/5 Faamadheyri, Magu, PO Box 2046. T 324252.

Charter Airlines flying direct to the Maldives are as follows: *From London*: **Monarch**, c/o Voyages Maldives, 2 Faridee Magu. T 322019. *From Dusseldorf, Munich*: LTU/LTS, c/o Faihu Agency, Maaleythila. T 322032. *From Frankfurt, Dusseldorf, Munich*: Condor, c/o Universal Travel Dept., 18 Marine Drive. T 323116. *From Vienna*: **Lauda Air**, c/o Fantasy Trade & Travels, Faridee Magu. T 324668. *From Stockholm, Copenhagen*: **Sterling Airways**, c/o Voyages Maldives, 2 Faridee Magu. T 322019. *From Zurich, Rome*: **Balair**, c/o Voyages Maldives, 2 Faridee Magu. T 322019.

From Sri Lanka This is still the simplest connection, as it is made by several airlines and there is at least one flight *from Colombo* to Male every day.

From India Flights *from Trivandrum* are extremely heavily booked. It is often necessary to make a reservation four weeks in advance to obtain an OK ticket. Waiting lists are long, but it is sometimes possible to fly even if well down the waiting list. The only travel agent who has direct links with the Maldives in Trivandrum is *Aries Travels*, Ayswarya Building, Press Road, Trivandrum 695001. T 65417, 64881, Telex: 0435 – 444 ARIS IN, Gram: Airtour. A new direct service *from Bombay* to Male was opened by Indian Airlines in mid 1990. They operate an Airbus flight twice weekly. Although this costs twice the Trivandrum – Male airfare it has relieved some of the pressure from the Trivandrum link.

The airport has been built on Hulule island fifteen minutes' boat ride to the N of Male itself. There is a **bank** at the airport; it is well worthwhile changing money immediately, as banks on Male are only open in the mornings. Hotels and some shops will accept payment in travellers' cheques or in foreign currency, and will give change in dollars. A **travel agent** is available at the airport on arrival. A boat jetty lies directly outside the airport exit and help is available to carry bags if required. The boat fare to Male from the airport is US$5, and taxi fares on Male itself are up to US$2.50. Fares to other islands depend on distance, but some of the most developed islands are within an hour's boat journey by *dhoni*. See map for details

Customs regulations

The entry and customs formalities are simple and straightforward. **NB Prohibited items** You are not allowed to import alcohol. Alcohol is available in most hotels, but any carried by passengers will be kept at the airport. It can be reclaimed on departure. You are also not allowed to bring in drugs, pork products, pornographic magazines or videos. Landing cards have to be completed on board the plane before arrival, and it is necessary to state where you will be staying.

Internal Travel

There is no centralised transport between the islands. Local boats (**dhonis**) are the commonest form of transport which average about 13 km per hour. Dhonis and speedboats are available for hire. Tourist resorts have their own boats and the transfer charges are listed below. *Hummingbird Helicopters* Ltd, Luxwood, 2 Marine Drive, Male. T 325708, offers 'flips' which are 15 min flights from the airport which capture the magic of the local reefs. Away-day excursions take you to distant atolls and include lunch or beach barbecue, diving and snorkelling. They provide a transfer service between the airport and your resort island and are at the airport Main Arrivals behind the Tourist Information desk.

Money

Currency The unit of currency is the Ruffiyaa divided into 100 Laari. Notes are in denominations of 100, 50, 20, 10, 5 and 2 Rufiyaa. Coins are in denominations of 1 Rufiya, 50, 20, 10 and 5 Laari.

Money Changing The law requires all transactions to be conducted in Maldivian currency. Most banks, shops and tourist resorts will convert to local currency, American dollars being the commonest foreign currency.

Travellers cheques and credit cards Hotels accept foreign curency, travellers cheques and credit cards, most commonly are American Express, Visa, Master Card, Diners Card and Euro Card.

Unauthorized dealing Don't convert your currency with an unauthorised dealer and keep your exchange receipts as you will need them when you re-convert any Maldivian currency when you depart. Exchange rate is US$1= 7 Ruffiya.

Other Essential Information

Official time 5 hr. ahead of GMT.

Weights and measures Metric.

Postal Services Post Offices are open 0745-1245, 1600-1750, Sat-Thurs.

Telephone services International telephone, Telefax, Telex and Telegraph services are available 24 hrs. International calls are handled by operator at 190. Phonecards may be bought from post offices. Some shops permit you to use their telephones for a small charge.

Hours of business Most offices are open from Sat to Thurs although banks are also open on Sun. Banks: 0900-1300; Government offices: 0730-1330; Shops are open daily 0600-2300, some remaining closed on Fri morning. During the day shops and restaurants close their doors for 15 min a few times a day when there are calls to prayer. If you are in a cafe or restaurant, you are not expected to leave but can carry on eating.

Electricity Islands generate their own electricity at 240 volts.

Media The one Male daily, the 'Haveeru' which carries a section in English. Entertainments are also advertised in English. Fortnightly English 'News Bulletin' published locally. Some weekly international news magazines are also available at the Male bookshops. English TV news nightly at 2100 for about 20 min can only be received by nearby island resorts. Don't expect daily newspapers in every hotel bedroom.

Accommodation, food and drink If you do not have accommodation fixed, you can ask for assistance at the Airport Tourist Information Unit and you are allowed to find accommodation through the tourist agent in the airport on arrival before completing customs formalities.

Hotel and guest house accommodation is limited, and during the season it is advisable to book well in advance. There is some hotel and guest room space on Male itself, but most is spread over about 60 outlying resort islands which can cater for about 7,500 visitors. The government has followed a deliberate policy to develop the uninhabited islands as tourist resorts thus keeping the local Maldivians undisturbed. They are all small with self contained communities and it will take you between 15 to 30 minutes to walk around each. The accommodation is mainly in bungalow style rooms or in 'rondavels', round thatched houses, with modern conveniences. Some offer air-conditioned rooms, many have open-air restaurants and bars and a few have discos and other entertainment. The attraction of the islands is in the beautiful, pollution free beaches and the wealth of water sports on offer.

The hotel categories are based on price in US$ per person per day. **A** US$100; **B** US$80-100; **C** US$60-80; **D** US$60 . In comfort, facilities and sophistication, however, they don't compare with what is expected in similarly priced hotels in Western seaside resorts and you may be surprised by the sand floors in some of the hotels' public areas. Rates quoted by hotels often include full board.

Clothing Light cottons are best. Nudity is forbidden and it is advisable for tourists visiting inhabited islands to be clothed modestly. The Department of Tourism advises "Minimum dress – Men: T-shirts and shorts, but jeans or long trousers are preferable. Women: T-shirts, blouses or shirts and skirts or adequate shorts which cover the thighs, made of non seethrough or diaphanous material; a piece of cloth simply wrapped around the torso is not acceptable or indeed permitted". Two laundries in Majeedee Magu in Male.

Food and Drink Local and continental cuisine is available, often heavily dependent on freshly caught fish (*mas*) and a variety of sea food with occasional buffets and barbecues organized for guests. Unlike some other tropical resorts, the islands produce very little by way of fruit and vegetables, although the coconut (*kurumba*) palm thrives and there are some bananas (*donkeo*), mangoes (*don ambu*), breadfruit (*bambukeyo*) and pawpaws (*falor*). The Maldivians usually eat rice (*bai*), sometimes unleavened bread similar to a *roti* or *chapati* (*roshi*) with a fish dish, curried (*mas riha*), fried (*teluli mas*), smoked (*valo mas*) or as a soup (*garudia*) accompanied by pickles. Meat and chicken are only eaten on special occasions. To drink the alternatives are tea, which is invariably with milk and sugar already added (*sa*) and milk (*kiru*) which too is often served sweetened. If you prefer your tea unsweetened ask for *hakuru naala sa* and for black tea *kiri naala sa.*

Alcohol is readily available for visitors on tourist islands. You may not import it or offer it to Maldivian nationals. The local toddy *raa,* can be an acquired taste, which is drunk after the juice from the palm has been left to ferment, but freshly tapped is considered delicious by those who don't wish to take alcohol.

NB Water supply can be erratic and different from what you are accustomed to. 'Island water' is sea water pumped and filtered and remains slightly salty. It is adequate for showers and washing but you will find it quite hard. Some resorts have desalination plants or rain water reservoirs while a few provide fresh water. Most resorts only supply unheated water although this does not create a problem as it is usually luke-warm. During the peak season and dry periods the supply of fresh water and rain water may be restricted.

Shopping. Opportunities for shopping are extremely limited. Local sea shells and some coral are available, but most other goods for sale have been imported, largely from India, Sri Lanka and SE Asia. The range is generally narrow, the quality rather mediocre and the price comparatively high, but it is possible to find attractive items reasonably priced.

Climate Situated almost on the equator the islands have no winter season. The average temperature ranges from a minimum of 25°C to a maximum of 31°C. The monsoons are not as pronounced as in the rest of S Asia. The two periods are: SW monsoon from May to October which brings rain and the NE Monsoon from November to April which is marked by strong winds. End of May-June and Nov-Dec are likely to be most showery although these are not persistent.

Security Crime is virtually unknown on the islands.

Health Health care is far from comprehensive in the Maldives and facilities are basic. Maldivians themselves have to go abroad for any specialist treatment. Come prepared with reasonable precautions. Know your blood group if possible, and be properly insured, as good health care is not cheap. Take a high protection factor suntan lotion, wear a straw hat and a T-shirt for the first few days to avoid over-exposure.

Best time for a visit There is no really unsuitable time to visit, but the best time is Nov to Apr. May to Sep is wetter.

Public holidays Fri. National Day July 26th.

Tourist Information Ministry of Tourism, f/2 Ghazee Building, Ameeru Ahmed Magu. T 323224, 323228. Tourist Information Unit at the airport.

Glossary of architectural terms

A

abacus	square or rectangular table resting on top of a pillar (phalaka/ palagai)
Acanthus	thick-leaved plant, common decoration on pillars, esp. Greek.
alinda	verandah.
amalaka	circular ribbed pattern (based on a gourd) at the top of a temple tower.
ambulatory	processional path.
anda	lit. 'egg,' spherical part of the stupa.
antarala	vestibule, chamber in front of shrine or cella.
antechamber	chamber in front of the sanctuary.
apsara	heavenly nymph.
apse	semi-circular plan, as in apse of a church.
arabesque	ornamental decoration with intertwining lines.
architrave	horizontal beam across posts or gateways.
ardha mandapam	chamber in front of main hall of temple.
asana	a seat or throne.
astanah	threshold.
atrium	court open to the sky in the centre. In modern architecture, enclosed in glass.

B

bada	cubical portion of a temple up to the roof or spire.
badgir	rooftop structure to channel cool breeze into the house (mainly Pakistan and N and W India).
bagh	garden.
baluster	(balustrade) a small pillar or column supporting a handrail.
Bangla	(Bangaldar) curved roof, based on thatched roofs in Bengal; imitated in brick temples.
baoli or wav	rectangular well surrounded by steps; esp. in Gujarat and W India.
baradari	lit. 'twelve pillared,' a portico or pavilion with columns.
barrel-vault	semi-cylindrical shaped roof or ceiling.
basement	lower part of walls, usually adorned with decorated mouldings.
basti	Jain temple.
bas-relief	carving of low projection.
batter	slope of a wall, esp in a fort.
bedi	platform for reading the holy books or vedas.
beki	the cylindrical stone below the amala in the finial of a building.
belvedere	summer house; small room on a house roof.
bhadra	flat face of the sikhara (tower).
bhavan	building or house.
bhoga-mandapa	the refectory hall of a temple, particularly in Orissa.
bhumi	'earth'; refers to a horizontal moulding of a shikhara.
bo-tree	*Ficus religiosa*, large spreading tree
brahma-kanda	column with a rectangular section.
burj	tower or bastion.

C

capital	upper part of a column or pilaster.
caryatid	sculptured human female figure used as a support for columns.
cave temple	rock-cut shrine or monastery.
cella	small chamber, compartment for the image of a deity.
cenotaph	commemorative monument, usually an open domed pavilion
chajja	overhanging cornice or eaves.

chakra	sacred Buddhist wheel of the law; also Vishnu's discus.
chala	Bengali curved roof.
chamfer	bevelled surface, obtained by cutting away a corner.
chandra	moon.
chankrama	place of the promenade of the Buddha at Bodh Gaya.
char bangla	(char-chala) four temples in Bengal, built like huts.
char bagh	formal Mughal garden, divided into quarters.
chatta	ceremonial umbrella on stupa (Buddhist).
chauki	recessed space between pillars: also entrance to a porch.
chaultri	travellers' rest house; pillared hall adjoining Dravidian temple.
chaumukha	Jain sanctuary with a quadruple image, approached through four doorways.
chauri	fly-whisk, symbol for royalty.
chhatra	honorific umbrella; a pavilion (Buddhist).
chhatri	umbrella shaped dome or paviliion. See also cenotaph.
chillah khanah	room to which Muslim hermits retreat for 40 days.
chlorite	soft greenish stone that hardens on exposure, permitting intricate carving.
chokhang	Tibetan Buddhist prayer hall.
chowk	open space or court yard.
chunam	lime plaster or stucco made from burnt seashells which can be polished to shine like marble.
circumambulation	clockwise movement around a stupa or shrine while worshiping.
clerestory	upper section of the walls of a building which allowed light in.
cloister	passage usually around an open square.
corbel	horizontal block supporting a vertical structure or covering an opening.
cornice	horizontal band at the top of a wall.
crenellated	having battlements.
cupola	small dome.
curvilinear	gently curving shape, generally of a tower.
cusp, cusped	projecting point between small sections of an arch.
cutcherry	(kutchery) a court; an office where any public business is conducted.

D

dado	part of a pedestal between its base and cornice; also the lower section of walls.
dagoba	stupa (Sinhalese).
dais	raised platform.
dargah	a Muslim tomb complex.
darwaza	gateway, door.
daulat khana	treasury.
dentil	small block used as part of a cornice.
deul	in Bengal and Orissa, generic name for temple; also used to signify the sanctuary only.
deval	memorial pavilion built to mark royal funeral pyre.
devala	temple or shrine, (Buddhist or Hindu).
dharmachakra	wheel of the law (Buddhist).
dhvajastambham	tall pillar in front of temple.
dikka	raised platform around ablution tank.
dikpala	guardian of one of the cardinal directions (N,S,E or W).
dipdan	lamp pillar.
divan (diwan)	smoking-room; also a chief minister.
diwan-i-am	hall of public audience.
diwan-i-khas	hall of private audience.
do-chala	rectangular Bengali style roof.
double dome	composed of an inner and outer shell of masonry.
drum	circular wall on which the dome rests.
dry masonry	stones laid without mortar.
dvarpala	doorkeeper.
dvipa	lamp-column, generally of stone or brass-covered wood.
dzong	Tibetan lamasery or monastery.

E

eave	overhang that shelters a porch or verandah.
epigraph	carved inscription.

F

faience	coloured tilework, earthenware or porcelain.
fan-light	fan-shaped window over door.
fenestration	with windows or openings.
filigree	ornamental work or delicate tracery.
finial	emblem at the summit of a stupa, tower, dome, or at the end of a parapet; generally in the form of a tier of umbrella-like motifs, or a pot.
foliation	ornamental design derived from foliage.
frieze	horizontal band of figures or decorative designs.

G

gable	end of an angled roof.
gaddi	throne.
gana	child figures in art.
gandharvas	celestial musicians of Indra.
garbhagriha	Lit. 'womb-chamber'; a temple sanctuary.
Garuda	vehicle (riding bird) of Vishnu.
gedige	ancient Sinhalese architectural style, extremely thick walls and a corbelled roof.
ghanta	bell.
godown	warehouse.
gola	conical-shaped storehouse.
gompa	Tibetan Buddhist monastery.
gopura	towered gateway in S Indian temples.
gudi	temple (Karnataka).
gumbaz	(gumbad) dome.
gumpha	monastery, cave temple.
gurudwara	Sikh religious complex, usually with a temple and rest-house.

H

hammam	Turkish bath.
harem	women's quarters (Muslim), from 'haram', Arabic for 'forbidden by law'.
harmika	the finial of a stupa in the form of a pedestal where the shaft of the honorific umbrella was set.
hathi pol	elephant gate.
haveli	usually a merchant's house in rajasthan, particularly finely decorated.
hawa mahal	palace of the winds.
hippogryph	fabulous griffin-like creature with body of a horse.
hiti	a water channel; a bath or tank with water spouts.
huzra	a Muslim tomb chamber.
hypostyle	hall with pillars.

I

icon	statue or image of worship in a temple.
imambara	tomb of a Shiite Muslim holy man; focus of Muharram procession.
iwan	main arch in mosque.

J

jaga mohan	audience hall or ante-chamber of an Orissan temple in front of the sanctuary.

jagati	railed parapet.
jala durga	water fort.
jali	lit. 'net,'; any lattice or perforated pattern.
jamb	vertical side slab of doorway.
Jami masjid	(Jama, Jumma) Friday mosque, used for congregational worship.
jangha	broad band of sculpture on the outside of the temple wall.
jarokha	balcony.
jawab	lit. 'answer,' a building which duplicates another to provide symmetry.
jaya stambha	victory tower.
jhilmil	projecting canopy over a window or door opening.
jorbangla	double hut-like temple in Bengal.
Jyotirlinga	Luminous energy of Siva manifested at 12 holy places (including Kedarnath, Prabhas Patan, Srisailam, Ujjain, Varanasi), miraculously formed lingams having special significance.

K

kailasa	Siva's heaven.
kalasha	pot-like finial of a tower.
kalyan mandapa	hall with columns, used for the symbolic marriage ceremony of the temple deity.
kashi-work	special kind of glazed tiling, probably derived from Kashan in Persia.
keep	tower of a fort, stronghold.
keystone	central wedge-shaped block in a masonry arch.
khondalite	crudely grained basalt.
kirti-stambha	'pillar of fame,' free standing pillar in front of temple.
kos minars	Mughal mile stones, common along Grand Trunk Road.
kothi	house.
kotla	citadel.
kovil	temple in Tamil Nadu.
kumbha	a vase-like motif.
kund	well or pool.
kutcha	mud built with sun-dried bricks.
kwabgah	bedroom; lit. 'palace of dreams'.

L

lat	pillar, column (also stambha).
lattice	screen of cross laths: perforated.
lena	cave, usually a rock-cut sanctuary.
lingam	(linga) Siva as the phallic emblem.
lintel	horizontal beam over doorway.
liwan	cloisters of a mosque.
lunette	semicircular window opening.

M

madrassa	Islamic theological school or college.
mahal	palace, grand building.
maha-mandapam	large enclosed hall in front of main shrine.
makara	crocodile-shaped mythical creature symbolizing the river Ganga.
manastambha	free-standing pillar in front of temple.
mandala	geometric diagram symbolizing the structure of the Universe, the basis of a temple plan; orders deities into pantheons.
mandapa	columned hall preceding the sanctuary in a Jain or Hindu temple
mandir	temple.
mani	(mani wall) stones with sacred inscriptions at Buddhist sites.
maqbara	chamber of a Muslim tomb.
maqsura	screen or arched facade of a mosque.
masjid	lit. 'place of prostration'; mosque.
math	Hindu or Jain monastery.

mausoleum	large tomb building.
medallion	circle or part-circle framing a figure or decorative motif.
mihrab	niche or arched recess in the western wall of a mosque towards which worshippers turn for prayer.
mimbar	pulpit in mosque.
minar	(minaret) slender tower of a mosque from which the muezzin calls the faithful to prayer.
mithuna	couple in sexual embrace.
monolith	single block of stone shaped into a pillar or monument.
moonstone	the semi-circular stone step before a shrine (also chandrasila).
mukha mandapa	hall for shrine.
muqarna	Muslim stalactite design.
mural	wall decoration.

N

nakkar khana	drum house; arched structure or gateway for musicians (also naubat khana).
nal	staircase.
nal mandapa	porch over a staircase.
nandi mandapa	portico or pavilion erected over the sacred bull (nandi).
nata mandapa	(nat-mandir; nritya sala) dancing hall in a temple (usually the middle structure in Orissa).
navagraha	nine planets, represented usually on the lintel or architrave of the front door of a temple.
navaranga	central hall of temple.
niche	wall recess containing a sculpted image or emblem, mostly framed by a pair of pilasters.
nirvana	enlightenment; (lit. 'extinguished').
niwas	small palace.

O

obelisk	tapering and usually monolithic shaft of stone with pyramidal apex.
ogee	form of moulding or arch comprising a double curved line made up of a concave and convex part.
oriel	projecting window.

P

pada	foot or base.
padma	lotus, moulding having the curves of the lotus petal. (padmasana, lotus throne).
paga	projecting pilaster-like surface of an Orissan temple (exterior).
pagoda	tall structure in several stories.
parapet	wall extending above the roof.
parterre	level space in a garden occupied by flower-beds.
patina	green film that covers materials exposed to the air.
pediment	mouldings, often in a triangular formation above an opening or niche.
pendant	hanging, generally refers to a motif depicted upside down.
peristyle	range of columns surrounding a court or temple.
pida	(pitha) basement.
pida deul	hall with a pyramidal roof in an orissan temple.
pietra dura	inlaid mosaic of hard and expensive stones.
pilaster	ornamental small column, with capital and bracket, usually forming part of the wall construction.
pinjra	lattice work.
pitha	base, pedestal.
podium	stone bench; low pedestal wall.
pokana	bathing tank (Sri Lanka).
pol	fortified gateway.

porch	covered entrance to a shrine or hall, generally open and with columns.
portico	space enclosed between columns.
potgul	library.
pradakshina patha	processional passage or ambulatory, also vedika.
prakaram	open courtyard.
pukka	solidly built, reliable; lit. 'ripe' or 'finished'.
pushkarani	sacred pool or tank.

Q

qabr	Muslim grave
qibla	direction for Muslim prayer.
qila	fort.
qutb	axis or pivot.

R

ranga mandapa	painted hall or theatre.
ratha	temple chariot; sometimes also refers to a temple model.
rekha	curvilinear portion of a spire or sikhara. (rekha deul, sanctuary, curved tower of an Orissan temple).
reredos	screen behind an altar.

S

sabha	columned hall (sabha mandapa, assembly hall).
sahn	open courtyard of a mosque.
sal	hall.
samadhi	funerary memorial, like a temple but enshrining an image of the deceased.
samudra	large tank or inland sea.
sangarama	monastery.
sankha	a shell, emblem of the god Vishnu.
sangrahalaya	rest-house for Jain pilgrims.
sarai	caravansarai, halting place.
sati stone/pillar	stone commemorating self-immolation of a widow.
schist	grey or green finely grained stone in North-Western Pakistan.
shala	barrel-vaulted roof .
sheesh mahal	palace apartment enriched with mirror work.
shikhara	curved temple tower or spire.
sileh khana	armoury.
sinha stambha	lion pillar.
soma sutra	spout to carry away oblations in the shrine of a temple.
spandrel	triangular space between the curve of an arch and the square enclosing it.
squinch	arch across an interior angle.
sridhara	pillar with octagonal shaft and square base.
stalactite	system of vaulting remotely resembling stalactite formations in a cave.
stambha	free-standing column or pillar, often with lamps or banners.
steatite	finely grained grey mineral.
stele	upright inscribed slab or pillar used as a gravestone.
stellate	arranged like a star, radiating.
stucco	plasterwork.
stupa	hemispheric funerary mound; principal votive monument in a Buddhist religious complex.
stylobate	base or sub-structure on which a colonnade is placed.
sun window	chaitya window, large arched opening in the facade of a chaitya hall or Buddhist temple.
superstructure	tower rising over a sanctuary or gateway, roof above a hall.

suraj-mukh	'sun-face,' a symbolic decorative element.
surya	the sun god.
sutradhara	chief architect.

T

taikhana	underground apartments, cool retreats from the fierce summer heat.
talar	tank.
tandava	dance of Siva.
tank	reservoir; in temple architecture a masonry-lined body of water, often with stepped sides.
tatties	cane or grass screens used for shade.
tempera	distemper; method of mural painting by means of a 'body,' such as white pigment.
terracotta	burnt clay used as building material.
thakur bari	sanctuary (Bengal).
thangka	(thankha) cloth painted with a Tibetan Buddhist deity.
torana	gateway with two posts linked by architraves.
trisula	trident, emblem of Siva.
tuk	fortified enclosure containing Jain shrines.
tykhana	an underground room in a house in Upper India for use in hot weather.
tympanum	triangular space within the cornices of a pediment.

V

vahana mandapa	(Chalukyan) hall in which the vahanas or temple vehicles are stored.
vatadage	ancient Sinhalese architectural style; 'circular relic house'.
vedi	altar, also a wall or screen.
verandah	enlarged porch in front of a hall.
vihara	Buddhist or Jain monastery with cells opening off a central court.
vilas	house or pleasure palace.
vimana	towered sanctuary containing the cell in which the deity is enshrined.
vyala	leogryph, lion like sculpture.

W

Wav	step-well, pariticularly in Gujarat and W India (baoli)

Y

yagasala	hall where the sacred fire is maintained and worshipped; place of sacrifice.
yaksha	semi-divine being.
yali	hippopotamus-like creature in the ornamentation of Chalukyan temples.
yashti	stick, pole or shaft, (Buddhist).
yoni	a hole in a stone, symbolising the vagina or female sexuality.

Z

zarih	cenotaph in a Muslim tomb.
zenana	segregated women's apartments.
ziarat	holy Muslim tomb.

Glossary of Names

A

Adinatha	First of the 24 Tirthankaras, distinguished by his bull mount.
Agastya	Legendary sage who brought the Vedas to S India.
Agni	Vedic fire divinity, intermediary between gods and men; guardian of the SE.
Ananda	The Buddha's chief disciple.
Ananta	A huge snake on whose coils Vishnu rests.
Andhaka	Demon killed by Siva.
Annapurna	Goddess of abundance; one aspect of Devi.
Ardhanarisvara	Siva represented as half-male and half-female.
Arjuna	Hero of the Mahabharata, to whom Krishna delivered the Bhagavad Gita.
Aruna	Charioteer of Surya, the Sun God; Red.
Ashta Matrikas	The 8 mother goddesses who attended on Siva or Skanda.
Avalokiteshwara	Lord Who Looks Down; Bodhisattva, the Compassionate.

B

Balabhadra	Balarama, elder brother of Krishna, also an incarnation of Vishnu.
Bhadrakali	Tantric goddess and consort of Bhairav.
Bhagavad-Gita	Song of the Lord; section of the Mahabharata in which Krishna preaches a sermon to Arjuna explaining the Hindu ways of knowledge, duty and devotion.
Bhagiratha	The king who prayed to Ganga to descend to earth.
Bhairava	Siva, the Fearful.
Bharata	Half-brother of Rama.
Bhima	Pandava hero of the Mahabharata, famous for his strength.
Bhimsen	Deity worshipped for his strength and courage.
Bodhisattva	Enlightened One, destined to become Buddha.
Bon	Pre-Buddhist religion of Tibet, incorporating animism and sorcery.
Brahma	Universal self-existing power; Creator in the Hindu Triad. Often represented in art, with four heads.
Brahmanism	Ancient Indian religion, precursor of modern Hinduism and Buddhism.
Buddha	The enlightened One; founder of Buddhism who is worshipped as god by certain sects.

C

Chamunda	Terrifying form of the goddess Durga.
Chandra	Moon; a planetary deity.

D

Dakshineshvara	Lord of the South; name of Siva.
Dasaratha	King of Ayodhya and father of Rama in the Ramayana.
Dattatraya	Syncretistic deity; an incarnation of Vishnu, a teacher of Siva, or a cousin of the Buddha.
Devi	Goddess; later, the Supreme Goddess; Siva's consort, Parvati.
Dikpala	Guardian of the directions; mostly appear in a group of eight.
Draupadi	Wife in common of the five Pandava brothers in the Mahabharata.
Durga	Principal goddess of the Shakti cult; riding on a tiger and armed with the weapons of all the gods, she slays the demon (Mahisha).

G

Ganes	(Ganesh/Ganapati) Lord of the Ganas; popular elephant-headed son of Siva and Parvati. The god of good fortune and remover of obstacles.
Gandharva	Semi-divine flying figure; celestial musician.
Ganga	Goddess personifying the Ganga river.
Garuda	Mythical eagle, half-human. Vishnu's vehicle.
Gauri	'Fair One'; Parvati; Gaurishankara, Siva with Parvati.
Gita Govinda	Jayadeva's poem of the Krishnalila.
Gopala	(Govinda) Cowherd; a name of Krishna.
Gopis	Cowherd girls; milk maids who played with Krishna.
Gorakhnath	Historically, an 11th-century yogi who founded a Saivite cult; an incarnation of Siva.

H

Hanuman	Monkey hero of the Ramayana; devotee of Rama; bringer of success to armies.
Hara	(Hara Siddhi) Siva.
Hari	Vishnu. Harihara, Vishnu-Siva as a single divinity.
Hariti	Goddess of prosperity and patroness of children, consort of Kubera.
Hasan	The murdered eldest son of Ali, commemorated at Muharram.
Hidimba Devi	Durga worshipped at Manali, India, as an angry goddess.
Hiranyakashipu	Demon king killed by Narasimha.
Hussain	The second murdered son of Ali, commemorated at Muharram.

I

Indra	King of the gods; God of rain; guardian of the East.
Ishana	Guardian of the North East.
Ishvara	Lord; Siva.

J

Jagadambi	lit. Mother of the World; Parvati.
Jagannath	lit. Lord of the World; particularly, Krishna worshipped at Puri (Orissa, India).
Jambudvipa	Continent of the Rose-Apple Tree; the earth.
Jamuna	Hindu goddess who rides a tortoise.
Janaka	Father of Sita in the Ramayana.
Jina	lit. 'victor'; spiritual conqueror or Tirthankara, after whom Jainism is named.
Jogini	Mystical goddess.

K

Kailasa	Mountain home of Siva.
Kali	lit. 'black'; terrifying form of the goddess Durga, wearing a necklace of skulls/heads.
Kalki	Future incarnation of Vishnu on horseback.
Kartikkeyea/ Kartik	Son of Siva, God of war. Also known as Skanda or Subrahmanyam.
Krishna	8th incarnation of Vishnu; the mischievous child, the cowherd (Gopala, Govinda) playing with gopis; the charioteer of Arjuna in the Mahabharata epic (see above).
Kubera	Chief of the yakshas; keeper of the treasures of the earth, Guardian of the North.
Kumari	Virgin; Durga.

L

Lakshmana	Younger brother of Rama in the Ramayana.

Lakshmi	Goddess of wealth and good fortune, associated with the lotus; consort of Vishnu.
Lakulisha	Founder of the Pashupata sect, believed to be an incarnation of Siva, seen holding a club.
Lingaraja	Siva worshipped at Bhubaneshwar.
Lokeshwar	'Lord of the World', Avalokiteshwara to Buddhists and of Siva to Hindus.

M

Machhendra	The guardian deity of the Kathmandu Valley, guarantor of rain and plenty; worshipped as the *Rato* (Red) machhendra in Patan and the *Seto* (White) Machhendra in Kathmandu.
Mahabharata	Story of the Great Bharatas; ancient Sanskrit epic about the battle between the Pandavas and Kauravas.
Mahabodhi	Great Enlightenment of Buddha.
Mahadeva	lit. 'Great Lord'; Siva.
Mahavira	lit. 'Great Hero'; last of the 24 Tirthankaras, teacher contemporary with Buddha, founder of Jainism.
Mahesha	(Maheshvara) Great Lord; Siva.
Mahisha	Buffalo demon killed by Durga.
Maitreya	The future Buddha.
Manjushri	Legendary Buddhist patron of the Kathmandu Valley; God of learning, destroyer of falsehood/ ignorance.
Makara	Mythical aquatic creature.
Manasa	Snake goddess; form of Sakti.
Mara	Tempter, who with sent his daughters (and soldiers) to disturb the Buddha's meditation.
Meru	Axial mountain supporting the heavens.
Minakshi	lit. 'fish-eyed'; Parvati worshipped at Madurai, India.
Mohammad	'the praised'; The Prophet; founder of Islam.

N

Naga	(nagi/nagini) Snake deity; associated with fertility and protection.
Nandi	A bull, Siva's vehicle and a symbol of fertility.
Narayana	Vishnu as the creator of life.
Nataraja	Siva, Lord of the cosmic dance.
Nihang	Lit. 'crocodile': followers of Guru Gobind Singh (Sikh).

P

Parvati	Daughter of the Mountain; Siva's consort, sometimes serene, sometimes fearful.
Pashupati	lit. Lord of the Beasts; Siva.

R

Radha	Krishna's favourite consort.
Rama	Seventh incarnation of Vishnu; hero of the Ramayana epic.
Ravana	Demon king of Lanka; kidnapper of Sita, killed by Rama in the battle of the Ramayana.

S

Saiva	(Shaiva) the cult of Siva.
Saraswati	Wife of Brahma and goddess of knowledge; usually seated on a swan, holding a veena.
Sati	Wife of Siva who destroyed herself by fire.
Shakti	Energy; female divinity often associated with Siva; also a name of the cult.

Shankara	Siva.
Shesha	(Sesha) serpent who supports Vishnu.
Shitala Mai	A former ogress who became a protector of children, worshipped at Swayambhunath.
Siva	The Destroyer among Hindu gods; often worshipped as a lingam or phallic symbol.
Sivaratri	Lit. 'Siva's night'; festival (Feb-Mar) dedicated to Siva.
Sita	Rama's wife, heroine of the Ramayana epic. Worshipped in Janakpur, India, her legendary birthplace.
Skanda	The Hindu god of war.
Subrahmanya	Skanda, one of Siva's sons; Kartikkeya in S India.
Surya	Sun; the Sun God who rides in a seven-horse chariot.

T

Tara	Historically a Nepalese princess, now worshipped by Buddhists and Hindus, particularly in Nepal.
Tirthankara	lit.'ford-maker'; title given to twenty-four saviours or teachers, worshipped by Jains.
Trimurti	Triad of Hindu divinities, Brahma, Vishnu and Siva.

U

Uma	Siva's consort in one of her many forms.
Upanishads	Ancient Sanskrit philosophical texts, part of the Vedas.

V

Valmiki	Sage, author of the Ramayana epic.
Vamana	Dwarf incarnation of Vishnu.
Varaha	Boar incarnation of Vishnu.
Varuna	Guardian of the West, accompanied by Makara (see above).
Vayu	Guardian of the North-West; wind.
Veda	(Vedic) Oldest known religious texts; include hymns to Agni, Indra and Varuna, adopted as Hindu deities.
Vishnu	A principal Hindu deity; creator and preserver of universal order; appears in 10 incarnations (Dashavatara).

Y

Yaksha	(Yakshi) a demi-god, associated with nature in folk religion.
Yama	God of death, judge of the living; guardian of the south.

Glossary of terms

**Words in *italics* are common elements of words, often
making up part of a place name**

A

aarti	(arati) Hindu worship with lamps
abad	peopled
achalam	hill (Tamil)
acharya	religious teacher
Adi Granth	Holy book of the Sikhs
agarbathi	incense
aghani	wet season (Bengal)
ahimsa	non-harming, non-violence
ajrak	Hyderabadi handloom fabric (Pakistan)
akhand path	unbroken reading of the Guru Granth Sahib
aman	wet season rice crop (Jul-Dec) Bengal
amrita	ambrosia; drink of immortality
ananda	joy
anicut	irrigation channel (Tamil)
anna	(ana) one sixteenth of a rupee (still occasionally referred to)
apsara	celestial nymph
aram	pleasure garden
aru	river (Tamil)
arrack	whisky fermented from potatoes or grain
Aryans	lit. 'noble' (Sanskrit); prehistoric peoples who settled in Persia and N India
asram	hermitage or retreat
atman	philosophical concept of universal soul or spirit
aus	summer rice crop (Apr-Aug) Bengal
avatara	'descent'; incarnation of a divinity, usually Vishnu's incarnations
ayacut	irrigation command area (Tamil)
ayah	children's nurse or nanny

B

baba	old man
babu	clerk
badlands	eroded landscape with deforestation and gullying
baghara baigan	mutton and wheat preparation
bahadur	title, meaning 'the brave'
baksheesh	tip, bribe, or simply donation to a beggar
bandh	strike
bandhani	tie dyeing (W India, Rajasthan)
bania	merchant caste
baranni	rainfed agricultural land (Pakistan)
barkandaz	guard watchman; doorkeeper
basti	temple (Kanarese)
bazaar	market
begum	Muslim princess; Muslim woman's courtesy title
bhaati	An inn or tea shop in Nepal especially those of the Thakali people
bhaat	cooked rice also refers to a meal (of rice)
bhabar	coarse alluvium at foot of Himalayas
bhadoi	season of early rain (Bengal)
bhai	brother
bhakti	adoration of a particular god or goddess
bhang	Indian hemp
bharal	Bhutanese blue sheep

bhavan	house, home
bhikku	Buddhist monk
bhisti	A water-carrier
bhit	sand dune (Pakistan)
bidi	(beedi) small hand-rolled tobacco leaf
bigha	measure of land - normally about one-third of an acre
bodi	tuft of hair on back of the shaven head (also Tikki)
Bon	an animist religion
Brahmachari	religious student, accepting rigorous discipline imposed for a set period, including absolute chastity
Brahman	(Brahmin) highest Hindu (and Jain) caste of priests
bund	An embankment; a causeway
burqa	An over-dress worn by Muslim women observing purdah (see below)
bustee	urban huts, slum (Bengal)

C

cantonment	large planned military or civil area in town
catamaran	log raft, logs (*maram*) tied (*kattu*) together(Tamil)
chaam	Himalayan Buddhist masked dance
chadar	sheet worn as clothing by men and women
chai	tea
chakra	wheel, the Buddhist wheel of the law
chapatti	unleavened Indian bread cooked on a griddle
chaprassi	messenger or often orderly usually wearing a badge
char	sand-bank or island in the bed of a river
charka	spinning wheel
charpoi	Indian rope bed
chaukidar	night-watchman; guard
charan	foot print
chauth	25% tax raised for revenue by Marathas
chena	shifting cultivation (Sri Lanka)
cheri	outcaste settlement; urban huts, slum (Tamil Nadu)
cheruva	tank (Telugu)
chhetri	Hindu warrior caste second in status only to brahmins
chhang	strong mountain beer of fermented barley maize rye or millet
chikan	shadow embroidery on fine cotton (especially in Lucknow)
chikki	a fruit
chiya	Nepalese tea brewed together with milk sugar and spices
chitrakar	picture maker
chit sabha	hall of wisdom (Tamil)
chogyal	heavenly king
choli	blouse
chorten	Himalayan Buddhist relic shrine or memorial stupa
choultry	travellers' rest house (from Telugu)
chowk	(chauk) a block; open place in a city where the market is held; a square
chowkidar	watchman
crewel work	chain stitching
crore	10 million

D

dabba	meals: stainless steel meal containers (Pakistan and West India)
dacoit	bandit
dada	grandfather; elder brother
dahi	yoghurt
Dak	post
dak bungalow	rest house for official travellers
dakini	sorceress
dan	gift
dandi	wooden palanquin carried by bearers

darbar	(durbar) a royal gathering
dargah	Muslim tomb complex
darshan	(darshana) viewing of a deity
Dasain	principal Nepalese festival, Sep/Oct
Dasara	(dassara/dussehra/dassehra) 10 day festival (Sep-Oct)
deodar	Himalayan cedar; from *deva-daru*, the 'wood of the gods'
dervish	member of Muslim brotherhood, committed to poverty
devasthanam	temple trust
dhaba	hole-in-the-wall restaurant or snack bar particularly in N India and Pakistan
dhal	(daal) lentil 'soup'
dhansak	special Parsi dish made with lentils
dharma	moral and religious duty
dharamshala	(dharamsala) pilgrims' rest-house
dharo	river (Sindi)
dhobi	washerman
dhol	drums
dholi	swinging chair on a pole, carried by bearers
dhoti	loose loincloth worn by Indian men
dhyana	meditation
digambara	lit.'sky-clad'; one of the two main Jain sects in which the monks go naked
dighi	village pond (Bengal)
dikshitar	person who makes oblations or offerings
distributary	river that flows away from main channel, usually in deltas
Divali	festival of lights (Sep-Oct) usually marks the end of the rainy season
diwan	chief financial minister
dokra	tribal name for lost wax metal casting (cire perdu)
doab	interfluve, land between two rivers
dosai	thin pancake
drug	(*durg*)fort (Tamil, Telugu)
duar	(dwar)door, gateway
dun	valley
dupatta	scarf (usually very thin) worn by Punjabi women
durrie	(dhurrie) rug
durwan	watchman
dzong	Tibetan lamasery, monastery

E

ek	the number 1, a symbol of unity
ekka	one horse carriage
eri	tank (Tamil)

F

fakir	one who has taken a vow of poverty (usually Muslim); sometimes a Hindu ascetic
firman	a royal order or grant

G

gadba	woollen blanket (Kashmir)
gadi	bullock cart (Rajasthan)
gali	(galli) lane; an alley
ganj	market
ganja	Indian hemp
gaon	village
garh	fort
Gelugpa	Tibetan sect
ghagra	(ghongra) long flared skirt with many gathers
ghat	landing place; steps on the river bank; range of hills in S India

ghazal	Urdu songs from poems with sad love themes
ghee	clarified butter for cooking
gherao	industrial action, surrounding home or office of politician or industrial manager
giri	hill
godown	warehouse
goncha	loose woollen robe, tied at waist with wide coloured band (Leh)
gosain	monk or devotee (Hindi)
gram	chick pea, pulse
gram	village; gramadan, gift of village
gur	palm sugar
gur gur	salted butter tea (Leh)
guru	teacher; spiritual leader, Sikh religious leader

H

Haj	(Hajj) annual Muslim pilgrimage to Mecca (Haji, One who has performed the Haj)
hakim	judge; a physician(usually Muslim)
halwa	sweet meat
handi	Punjabi dish cooked in a pot
haor	tectonic depression, flooded during rainy season (Bengal)
hartal	general strike
hat	market
hathi	(hati) elephant
hauz	tank or reservoir
havildar	army sergeant
hindola	swing
Holi	spring festival (Feb-Mar) associated with Krishna
hookah	water pipe through which tobacco is smoked
horst	block mountain
howdah	seat on elephant's back, sometimes canopied
hundi	temple offering
hypothecated	mortgaged

I

Id	principal Muslim festivals
Idgah	open space for the Id prayers, on the W of town
idli	steamed rice cake (Tamil)
ikat	'resist-dyed' woven fabric
imam	Muslim religious leader in a mosque
Impeyan	Nepal's national bird; a species of the pheasant
Isvara	Lord (Sanskrit)

J

jadu	magic
jaggery	brown sugar, usually made from palm sap
jahaz	ship:building constructed in form of ship
jataka stories	Buddhist accounts of the previous lives of the Buddha
jatra	Bengali folk theatre
jawan	army recruit, soldier
jelebi	sweet snack prepared by frying circles of batter and soaking in syrup
jhankri	shaman or sorcerer (Nepal)
jheel	(jhil) lake; a marsh; a swamp
-ji	honorific suffix added to names out of reverence and/or politeness; also abbreviated 'yes' (Hindi/Urdu)
jihad	striving in the way of god; holy war by Muslims against non-believers
johar	(jauhar) mass suicide by fire of women, particularly in Rajasthan, to avoid capture

K

kabalai	(kavalai) well irrigation using bullock power (Tamil Nadu)
kabigan	folk debate in verse
kadal	wooden bridge (Kashmir)
kadhi	savoury yoghurt curry (Gujarat)
kadu	forest (Tamil)
kalamkari	special painted cotton hanging from Andhra
kameez	shirt
kanga	comb
kankar	limestone nodules, used for road making
kantha	Bengali quilting
kapok	the silk cotton tree
kara	steel bracelet
karma	present consequences of past lives; impurity resulting from past misdeeds
kata	ceremonial scarf presented to high Tibetan Buddhist figures
katchari	(cutchery) public office or court
kati-roll	Muslim snack of meat rolled in a 'paratha' bread
kattakat	mixed brain, liver and kidney (Gujarat)
kebab	variety of meat dishes
kere	tank (Kanarese)
khadi	homespun cloth encouraged by Mahatma Gandhi
khal	creek; a canal
khave khana	tea shop
khana	suffix for room/office/place; also food or meal
kharif	monsoon season crop
kheda	enclosure in which wild elephants are caught; elephant depot
khet	field
khola	river or stream in Nepal
khukri	traditional curved knife best known as the weapon of Gurkha soldiers
khutba	Muslim Friday sermon
khyaung	Buddhist temple (Chittagong Hill tracts)
kikar	gum arabic
kirpan	sabre, dagger
kofta	meat balls
kohl	antimony, used as eye shadow
konda	hill (Telugu)
korma	rich curry using cubes of meat
kot	(kota/kottai//kotte) fort
kothi	house
kovil	temple (Tamil)
kritis	S Indian devotional music
kulam	tank or pond (Tamil)
kumari	young girl; young virgin regarded as a living goddess in Kathmandu Valley towns
kumar	potter (Bengal)
kumbha	pot
Kumbhayog	auspicious time for bathing to wash away sins
kund	lake
kundan	jewellery setting of uncut gems (Pakistan and Rajasthan)
kuppam	hamlet
kurta	Punjabi shirt
kurti-kanchali	small blouse
kutcha	(cutcha/kachcha) raw; crude; unpaved

L

la	Himalayan mountain pass
laddu	sweet snack
lakh	100,000
lama	Buddhist priest in Tibet

lassi	refreshing yoghurt and iced-water drink
lath	monolithic pillar
lathi	bamboo stick with metal bindings, used by police
lingam	phallus, Siva's symbol
lungi	wrapped around loin cloth, normally checked

M

madrassa	school usually attached to a mosque
maha	great
maha	the winter rice crop (Sri Lanka)
mahalla	(mohulla)division of a town; a quarter; a ward
mahant	head of a monastery
maharaja	king; maharajkumar, crown prince
maharani	queen
maharishi	(Maharshi) lit'great teacher'
mahout	elephant rider/keeper
Mahayana	The Greater Vehicle; form of Buddhism practised in East Asia, Tibet and Nepal
mahseer	large freshwater fish found especially in Himalayan rivers
maidan	large open grassy area in a city or town
makhan	butter
malai	hill (Tamil)
mali	gardener
mandalam	region, tract of country (Tamil)
mandi	market
mantra	sacred chant for meditation by Hindus and Buddhists
marg	wide road way
mata	mother
maulana	scholar (Muslim)
maulvi	religious teacher (Muslim)
maund	measure of weight about 20 kilos
maya	illusion
meena	enamel work
mela	festival or fair, usually Hindu
memsahib	married European lady
mithai	Indian sweets
mofussil	the country or hinterland, as distinct from the town
mohalla	quarter of a town inhabited by members of one caste or religion
momos	Tibetan stuffed pastas somewhat like ravioli
moksha	salvation, enlightenment; lit.'release'
mouza	(mowza) village; a parcel of lands having a separate name in the revenue records
mridangam	barrel-shaped drum
muballigh	second prayer leader
mudra	symbolic hand gesture
muezzin	mosque official who calls the faithful to prayer
Muharram	Period of mourning in remembrance of Hasan and Hussain, two murdered sons of Ali
mullah	religious teacher (Muslim)
mund	Toda village
muri	a dry measure equal to about 75 litres It contains 30 'paathis' or 160 'manas' (Nepal)
musalla	prayer mat
muta	limited duration marriage (Leh)
muthi	measure equal to 'a handful'
muzzaffarkhana	traditional dormitory accommodation for travellers (Pakistan)

N

naan	unleavened bread cooked in a special clay oven, tandoor

nadi	river
nadu	region, country (Tamil)
nagara	city, sometimes capital
nallah	(nullah) ditch, channel
namaste	common Hindu greeting (with joined palms) translated as: 'I salute all divine qualities in you'
namaaz	Muslim prayers, worship
namda	rug
namkeen	(nimkee) savory snacks
nara durg	type of large fort built on a flat plain
nath	lit.'place' e.g. Amarnath
natya	the art of dance
nautch	display by dancing girls
navaratri	lit.'9 nights'; name of the Dasara festival
nawab	prince, wealthy Muslim, sometimes used as a title
nihari	sheep's thigh cooked in spices (Pakistan)
nirvana	enlightenment; lit.'extinguished'
nritta	'pure' dance

O

ola	palm manuscripts (Sri Lanka)

P

padam	dance which tells a story
padma	lotus flowerPadmasana, lotus seat; posture of meditating figures
pahar	hill
paisa	(poisha) one hundredth of a rupee or taka (currency in India, Nepal, Pakistan and Bengal)
palanquin	covered litter for one carried by four or six men
palayam	minor kingdom (Tamil)
pali	the original language of Buddhist scriptures
palli	village
pan	leaf of the betel vinesliced areca nut and chewing additives are wrapped in the leaf
panchayat	A 'council of five'; a government system of elected councils at local and regional levels
pandal	marquee made of bamboo and cloth
pandas	temple priests
pandit	teacher or wise man sometimes used as a title; a Sanskrit scholar
parabdis	special feeding place for birds (Jain)
paratha	unleavened bread prepared with flour and fat
pargana	sub-division of a district usually comprising many villages; a fiscal unit
Parinirvana	the Buddha's state prior to nirvana, shown usually as a reclining figure
parishads	political division of group of villages
Parsi	(Parsee) Zoroastrians who fled from Iran to W India in the 9th century to avoid persecution
pashmina	a fine mountain goat's wool found mainly in Kashmir and Ladakh (pashm, goat's wool)
pata	painted hanging scroll
patan	town or city (Sanskrit)
patel	village headman
pattachitra	specially painted cloth (especially Orissan)
pau	measure for vegetables and fruit equal to 250 grams
paya	soup
payasam	sweet rice or vermicelli pudding
peon	servant, messenger (rom Portuguese *peao*)
perak	black hat, studded with turquoise and lapis lazuli (Ladakh)
Persian wheel	well irrigation system using bucket lift and bullock power
pettah	suburbs, outskirts of town (Tamil:*pettai*); the market outside the Fort in Colombo

pice	1/100th of a rupee
picottah	water lift using horizontal pole pivoted on vertical pole (Tamil Nadu)
pinjrapol	animal hospital (Jain)
pipal	Ficus religiosa, the Bodhi tree
pir	Muslim holy man
pithasthana	place of pilgrimage
pralaya	the end of the world
prasadam	consecrated temple food
prayag	confluence considered sacred by Hindus
puja	ritual offerings to the gods; worship (Hindu)
pujari	worshipper one who performs puja (Hindu)
punkah	(punkha) fan swung by pulling a cord
punya	merit earned through actions and religious devotion (Buddhist)
Puranas	Sanskrit sacred poems, lit. 'the old'
purdah	seclusion of Muslim women from public view (lit.curtains)
puri	fried Indian 'bread'

Q

qila	fort
Quran	holy Muslim scriptures

R

rabi	winter/spring season crop in northern areas of S Asia
raj	rule or government
raja	king, ruler (variations include rao rawal); prefix 'maha' means great
rajbari	palaces of a small kingdom
Rajput	dynasties of western and central India
Rakshakas	Earth spirits
Ramayana	Ancient Sanskrit epic - the story of Rama
Ramazan	(Ramadan) Muslim month of fasting
rana	warrior (Nepal)
rani	queen
rath	chariot or temple car
rawal	head priest
rasam	clear pepper soup (Tamil)
rickshaw	3-wheeled bicycle-powered (or 2-wheeled hand-powered) vehicle to transport passengers
Rig Veda	(Rg) Oldest and most sacred of the Vedas
Rimpoche	blessed incarnation; abbot of a Tibetan Buddhist monastery (gompa)
rishi	great sage, now any distinguished poet philosopher or spiritual personality
rumal	handkerchief, specially painted in Chamba (Himachal Pradesh)
rupee	Unit of currency in India, Pakistan, Nepal, and Sri Lanka
ryot	(rayat/raiyat) a subject; a cultivator; a farmer

S

sabzi	vegetables, vegetable curry
sadhu	ascetic; religious mendicant, holy man
sadar	(sadr/saddar) chief, main
safa	turban (Rajasthan)
sagar	lake; reservoir
sahib	title of address, like 'sir'
sal	hardwood tree of the lower slopes of Himalayan foothills
salaam	greeting (Muslim); lit. 'peace'
salwar	(shalwar) loose trousers (Punjab)
samadh	(samadhi) Hindu memorial
sambar	lentil and vegetable soup dish, accompanying main meal (Tamil)
samsara	eternal transmigration of the soul

sangam	junction of rivers
sangha	ascetic order founded by Buddha
sankha	(shankha) the conch shell (symbolically held by Vishnu); the shell bangle worn by Bengali women
sannyasin	wandering ascetic; final stage in the ideal life of a man
saranghi	small four-stringed viola shaped from a single piece of wood and played with a horsehair bow
sarkar	the government; the state; a writer; an accountant
sarod	Indian stringed musical instrument
sarvodaya	uplift, improvement of all
sati	(suttee) a virtuous woman; later applied to the act of self-immolation on a husband's funeral pyre
satyagraha	'truth force'; passive resistance
sayid	title (Muslim)
seer	(ser) unit of weight equal to about 1 kg
sepoy	(sepai) private in the infantry, sentry
serow	a wild Himalayan antelope
seth	merchant, businessman
seva	voluntary service
shahtush	very fine wool from the Tibetan antelope
shalagrama	stone containing fossils worshipped as a form of Vishnu
shaman	doctor/priest, using magic
shamiana	cloth canopy
sharia	corpus of Muslim theological law
shastras	Ancient texts setting norms of conduct for temple architecture, use of images and worship
shastri	religious title (Hindu)
shehnai	(shahnai) Indian wind instrument similar to an oboe
sherwani	knee-length coat for men
shikar	hunting expedition now virtually extinct
shikhara	boat (Kashmir)
shisham	a valuable building timber
shloka	Sanskrit sacred verse
shola	patch of forest or wood (Tamil)
sindur	vermilion powder often combined with mustard oil used in temple ritual; applied in the parting of the hair by women as a sign of marriage in parts of E India
singh	(sinha) lion; also Rajput caste name adopted by Sikhs
sirdar	a guide, usually a Sherpa, who leads trekking groups
sitar	classical Indian stringed musical instrument with a gourd for soundbox
soma	sacred drink mentioned in the Vedas
sri	(shri) honorific title, often used for 'Mr.'; repeated as sign of great respect
sthan	place
subahdar	the governor of a province; a viceroy under the Mughal government
sudra	lowest of the Hindu castes
sufis	Muslim mystics; sufism, Muslim mystic worship
sultan	Muslim prince (sultana, wife of sultan)
svami	(swami) holy man; also used as a suffix for temple deities
svastika	(swastika) auspicious Hindu/ Buddhist emblem
swadeshi	home made goods
swaraj	home rule
swatantra	freedom
syce	groom

T

tabla	a pair of hand drums which are played with the fingers
tahr	wild Himalayan goat
tahsildar	tax-collector; a collector of revenue
taka	unit of currency in Bangladesh
takht	throne

tale	tank (Sinhalese)
taluk	administrative subdivision of a district; talukdar petty proprietor
tamasha	spectacle, festive celebration
tapas	(tapasya) ascetic meditative self-denial
tareeqat	'spirituality' (Islamic)
tari	fermented palm wine drunk by hill tribes from the Chittagong Hill Tracts
tarkashi	Orissan silver filigree
Teej	Hindu festival
tehsil	administrative subdivision of a district (N India)
tempo	3 wheeler public transport vehicle
terai	narrow strip of land along Himalayan foothills
teri	soil formed from wind blown sand (Tamil nadu)
thali	S Indian vegetarian meal - the name derives from the 'thali' plate the food is served on
thana	village; a police jurisdiction; police station
thangka	(thankha) cloth (often silk) painted with a Tibetan Mahayana deity
thakur	high Hindu caste
thug	Follower of 'thuggee' religious-inspired ritual murderers in the last century
thukba	thick Tibetan soup
tiffin	snack, light meal
tika	vermilion powder applied by Hindus to the forehead as a symbol of the presence of the divine
tikka	tender pieces of meat, marinated and barbecued
tilak	auspicious mark on forehead
tillana	abstract dance
tirtha	ford, bathing place, holy spot (Sanskrit)
tole	street (Nepal)
tonga	2 wheeled horse or pony carriage
topi	(topee) pith helmet, formerly believed to prevent sunstroke
tottam	garden (Tamil)
tribhanga	favourite triple-bended posture for standing figures of deities
tripolia	triple gateway
trisul	the trident chief symbol of the god Siva
triveni	triple-braided
tsampa	ground and roasted barley, sometimes eaten dry. Often mixed with milk, tea or water (Himalayan)
tulsi	sacred basil plant

U

untouchable	lowest caste for whom the most menial tasks were reserved
ur	village (Tamil)
usta	painted camel leather goods
ustad	master
uttarayana	northwards

V

vaisya	the 'middle-class' caste of merchants and farmers
vana	grove, forest
varam	village (Tamil)
varna	'colour'; social division of Hindus into Brahmin, Kshatriya, Vaishya and Sudra
varnam	S Indian musical etude, conforming to a raga
vina	plucked stringed instrument, relative of sitar
villu	small lake (Sri Lanka)

W

-wallah	suffix often used with a occupational name, e.g. rickshaw-wallah
wazir	prime minister
wazwan	ceremonial meal (Kashmir)
wewa	tank or lake (Sinhalese)

Y

yagya	(yajna) major ceremonial sacrifice
yala	summer rice crop (Sri Lanka)
yantra	magical diagram used in meditation; machine
yatra	pilgrimage
yeti	mythical Himalayan animal often referred to as 'the abominable snowman'
yoga	school of philosophy concentrating on different mental and physical disciplines (yogi, a practitioner)
yura	water channel (Ladakh)

Z

zamindar	landlord granted a right to land (zamin) and income by Moghul rulers
zeenat	decoration
zilla	(zillah) district

TEMPERATURE CONVERSION TABLE

°C	°F	°C	°F	°C	°F	°C	°F	°C	°F
1	34	11	52	21	70	31	88	41	106
2	36	12	54	22	72	32	90	42	108
3	38	13	56	23	74	33	92	43	109
4	39	14	57	24	75	34	93	44	111
5	41	15	59	25	77	35	95	45	113
6	43	16	61	26	79	36	97	46	115
7	45	17	63	27	81	37	99	47	117
8	46	18	64	28	82	38	100	48	118
9	48	19	66	29	84	39	102	49	120
10	50	20	68	30	86	40	104	50	122

The formula for converting °C to °F is: $°C \times 9 \div 5 + 32 = °F$

WEIGHTS AND MEASURES

Metric	**British and U.S.**

Weight:
1 kilogram (kg.) = 2,205 pounds
1 metric ton = 1.102 short tons
= 0.984 long ton

1 pound (lb.) = 454 grams
1 short ton (2,000 lb.) = 0.907 metric ton
1 long ton (2,240 lb.) = 1.016 metric tons

Length:
1 millimetre (mm.) = 0.03937 inch
1 metre = 3.281 feet
1 kilometre (km.) = 0.621 mile

1 inch = 25.417 millimetres
1 foot (ft.) = 0.305 metre
1 mile = 1.609 kilometres

Area:
1 hectare = 2.471 acres
1 square km. (km²) = 0.386 sq. mile

1 acre = 0.405 hectare
1 square mile (sq. mile) = 2,590 km²

Capacity:
1 litre = 0.220 Imperial gallon
= 0.264 U.S. gallon

1 Imperial gallon = 4.546 litres
1 U.S. gallon = 3.785 litres
(5 Imperial gallons are approximately equal to 6 U.S. gallons)

Volume:
1 cubic metre (m³) = 35.31 cubic feet
= 1.31 cubic yards

1 cubic foot (cu. ft) = 0.028 m³
1 cubic yard (cu. yd.) = 0.765 m³

N.B. The *manzana,* used in Central America, is about 0.7 hectare (1.73 acres).

ECONOMIC INDICATORS

+ Source: World Bank
* 1990 latest month in brackets except Pakistan, 1991

Exchange rates at 12 July 1991, which take account of the devaluation of the Indian Rupee in July 1991.

Sterling, French franc and Deutsch Mark rates are cross rates using the US dollar as a base.

COUNTRY	CURRENCY	US$ GNP per head (1989)+	%change (1980-89)+	annual inflation*+	Exchange rate US$	£	FFr	DM
BANGLADESH	Taka	180	0.7%	12.0%(11)	37.2	60.0	6.0	20.4
BHUTAN	Ngultrum	205	7.8%	10.9%(6)	25.9	41.8	4.2	14.2
INDIA	Rupee	350	3.2%	12.5%(11)	25.9	41.8	4.2	14.2
MALDIVES	Rufiyaa	420	5.9%	n.a	10.0	16.1	1.6	5.5
NEPAL	Rupee	170	2.1%	7.1%(10)	42.7	68.9	6.9	23.4
PAKISTAN	Rupee	370	2.9%	14.1%(1)	24.6	39.8	4.0	13.5
SRI LANKA	Rupee	430	2.4%	19.6%(12)	41.2	66.5	6.7	22.6

NUMBERS IN SOUTH ASIA'S MOST COMMON LANGUAGES

	ONE	TWO	THREE	FOUR	FIVE	SIX	SEVEN	EIGHT	NINE	TEN	ELEVEN	TWELVE
Devanagari/Urdu	ek	do	tin	chaar	paanch	chhey	saat	aat	nau	duss	gyara	bara
Bengali	ak	dui	tin	chaar	paanch	chhoy	shaat	aat	noy	dosh	egaro	baro
Sinhala	eka	deka	tuna	hatara	paha	haya	hata	ata	namaya	dahaya		
Divehi	eke	da	tine	hatare	fahe	haie	hate	ashe	nue	diha	egaara	baara

INDEX OF CULTURE AND SOCIETY

INDEX OF NATURAL FEATURES

INDEX OF PERSONALITIES

INDEX OF PLACES OF INTEREST

INDEX OF PLACES

TREKKING IN THE HIMALAYAS

The Himalayas have some of the best trekking routes available anywhere in the world. The Handbook has extensive sections on trekking in the regional sections, which are summarised here in the following quick reference listing.

A wide selection of walks and full scale treks is given, as well as trips and side excursions from mountain routes like the Karakoram Highway.

Nepal has the longest tradition of trekking and mountaineering expeditions and in this section you will find useful notes on **Organising a Trek** (page 1302), **Practical Information** (page 1303) and **Equipment and Clothing** (page 1306), which also apply to the other trekking areas.

In addition you should read the **Health Information** (page 22) especially the notes on Altitude, which covers mountain sickness and other problems encountered in the high Himalayas.

It is also essential to check with the appropriate authorities before travelling, to ensure you can gain access to the places you want to visit. Many trekking routes pass through sensitive 'Inner Line' border areas like Kashmir. Permits are often required and some areas may be closed to visitors altogether.

THOMAS COOK MASTERCARD TRAVELLERS CHEQUES
REFUND ASSISTANCE POINTS

Visitors to the South Asia area should telephone Thomas Cook, Peterborough, Great Britain (44) 733-502995 (collect)—24 hour service—or contact one of the following Thomas Cook MasterCard Refund Agents:-

Bangladesh

Chittagong	Grindlays Bank	Sheikh Mujib Road	500677/9
Dhaka	Grindlays Bank	No.2 Dilkusha Commercial Road	412226

India

Bangalore	Thomas Cook India	70 Mahatma Gandhi Road	(812) 571.066/7
Bombay	Thomas Cook India	Dadabhai Naoroji Road	(22) 204. 8556
Calcutta	Thomas Cook India	C/O Mirta Lina Private Ltd Mezzanine Fl. 12-B/1 Park St	(33) 298862
Hyderabad	Thomas Cook India	Nasir Arcade, 6-1-57 Saifabad	(842) 231988
Madras	Thomas Cook India	El Dorado Building 112 Nungambakkam High Rd	(44) 473092
Madras	Thomas Cook India	20 Rajaji Road	(44) 58994
New Delhi	Thomas Cook India	Rishya Mook Building 85a Panchkuin Road	(11) 350404
Pune	Thomas Cook India	13 Thackers House 2418 Gen. Thimmaya Road	(212) 667188

Maldives

Male	Bank of Ceylon	Orchid Magu 2	3045/6

Nepal

Kathmandu	Yeti Travels	Durbar Marg	2-21754

Pakistan

Islamabad	Travel Walji's	10 Khyaban e Suhrawardy	(51) 828324/6
Karachi	Travel Walji's	14 Services Club Mereweather Road	(21) 516698
Lahore	Travel Walji's	122A Tufail Road	(42) 374429
Peshawar	Travel Walji's	Doctor's Plaza 12 Saddar Road	(521) 72093

Sri Lanka

Colombo	Thomas Cook Overseas Lloyds Building, 15 Sir Baron Jayatilake Mawatha		(1) 545971/3
Colombo	Thomas Cook Overseas 245C Galle Road, Bambalapitiya		(1) 580141

Generally visitors should take Thomas Cook US Dollar travellers cheques to South Asia, although other major currencies may be acceptable in the Maldives, Nepal and Pakistan. However you should shop around for rates since they may vary considerably and while Hotel exchange rates may be better than the official rates, they are rarely the best.

In some countries only specific bank branches may deal in foreign exchange and you may have difficulty obtaining local currency when far from capital cities so do ensure you always have a small supply of local currency with you.

SOAS
School of Oriental and African Studies

University of London

The School of Oriental and African Studies, situated in the heart of London, is the largest centre in Europe and has one of the finest libraries in the world for the study of Asia and Africa. Those interested in South Asia may find some of the following study opportunities at SOAS attractive.

MA in Area Studies (South Asia)

The School of Oriental and African Studies offers a course leading to the award of a University of London Master of Arts degree in Area Studies (South Asia).

The course is designed for graduates and those with equivalent qualifications and provides a wide ranging interdisciplinary analysis of the countries that make up South Asia - India, Bangladesh, Pakistan, Nepal and Sri Lanka. Students normally choose one major and two minor subjects from a list which includes anthropology, art, architecture, economics, geography, history, languages, law, music, politics and religious studies and they can concentrate on pre-modern or modern South Asia.

It may be followed for one year full-time or two years part-time.

Other Courses

The School also offers a wide range of other courses concerned with aspects of South Asia at both undergraduate and postgraduate level leading to Bachelor degrees, Certificates in South Asian Studies and in South Asian Language and Culture, a Diploma in Asian Arts and MPhil and PhD degrees.

Further Information

Further information about the School and its courses is available from the Registrar (Ref TT), School of Oriental and African Studies, University of London, Thornhaugh Street, Russell Square, London WC1H 0XG. Tel: 071-637 2388 Fax: 071-436 4211